TheStreet Ratings' Guide to Exchange-Traded Funds

TheStreet Ratings' Guide to Exchange-Traded Funds

A Quarterly Compilation of Investment Ratings and Analyses Covering ETFs and Other Closed-End Mutual Funds

Winter 2015-16

GREY HOUSE PUBLISHING

TheStreet, Inc.
14 Wall Street, 15th Floor
New York, NY 10005
800-706-2501

TheStreet Ratings

Published by Grey House Publishing, Inc. located at 4919 Route 22, Amenia, NY, 12501; telephone 518-789-8700. Grey House Publishing neither guarantees the accuracy of the data contained herein nor assumes any responsibility for errors, omissions or discrepancies. Grey House Publishing accepts no payment for listing; inclusion in the publication of any organization agency, institution, publication, service or individual does not imply endorsement of the publisher.

Edition No. 51, Winter 2015-16

ISBN: 978-1-61925-981-2
ISSN: 2158-6101

Contents

Introduction

Welcome 3

How to Use This Guide 5

About TheStreet Investment Ratings 7

Important Warnings and Cautions 11

Section I. Index of ETFs and Other Closed-End Funds 13

Section II. Analysis of ETFs and Other Closed-End Funds 109

Section III. Top ETFs and Other Closed-End Funds 799

Section IV. Bottom ETFs and Other Closed-End Funds 807

Section V. Performance: Best and Worst ETFs * 815

Section VI. Top-Rated ETFs by Fund Type * 825

Appendix

What is a Mutual Fund? 853

How Do Open-End Funds, ETFs and other Closed-End Funds Differ? 855

Performance Benchmarks 858

Exchange-Traded Funds Summary Data 859

Fund Type Descriptions 861

* Includes other Closed-End Funds

Terms and Conditions

This Document is prepared strictly for the confidential use of our customer(s). It has been provided to you at your specific request. It is not directed to, or intended for distribution to or use by, any person or entity who is a citizen or resident of or located in any locality, state, country or other jurisdiction where such distribution, publication, availability or use would be contrary to law or regulation or which would subject TheStreet or its affiliates to any registration or licensing requirement within such jurisdiction.

No part of the analysts' compensation was, is, or will be, directly or indirectly, related to the specific recommendations or views expressed in this research report.

This Document is not intended for the direct or indirect solicitation of business. TheStreet, Inc. and its affiliates disclaims any and all liability to any person or entity for any loss or damage caused, in whole or in part, by any error (negligent or otherwise) or other circumstances involved in, resulting from or relating to the procurement, compilation, analysis, interpretation, editing, transcribing, publishing and/or dissemination or transmittal of any information contained herein.

TheStreet has not taken any steps to ensure that the securities or investment vehicle referred to in this report are suitable for any particular investor. The investment or services contained or referred to in this report may not be suitable for you and it is recommended that you consult an independent investment advisor if you are in doubt about such investments or investment services. Nothing in this report constitutes investment, legal, accounting or tax advice or a representation that any investment or strategy is suitable or appropriate to your individual circumstances or otherwise constitutes a personal recommendation to you.

The ratings and other opinions contained in this Document must be construed solely as statements of opinion from TheStreet, Inc., and not statements of fact. Each rating or opinion must be weighed solely as a factor in your choice of an institution and should not be construed as a recommendation to buy, sell or otherwise act with respect to the particular product or company involved.

Past performance should not be taken as an indication or guarantee of future performance, and no representation or warranty, expressed or implied, is made regarding future performance. Information, opinions and estimates contained in this report reflect a judgment at its original date of publication and are subject to change without notice. TheStreet offers a notification service for rating changes on companies you specify. For more information call 1-800-706-2501 or visit www.thestreet.com/ratings. The price, value and income from any of the securities or financial instruments mentioned in this report can fall as well as rise.

Welcome to TheStreet Ratings
Guide to Exchange-Traded Funds

With the growing popularity of mutual fund investing, consumers need a reliable source to help them track and evaluate the performance of their mutual fund holdings. Plus, they need a way of identifying and monitoring other funds as potential new investments. Unfortunately, the hundreds of performance and risk measures available – multiplied by the vast number of mutual fund investments on the market today – can make this a daunting task for even the most sophisticated investor.

TheStreet Investment Ratings simplify the evaluation process. We condense all of the available mutual fund data into a single composite opinion of each fund's risk-adjusted performance. This allows you to instantly identify those funds that have historically done well and those that have underperformed the market. While there is no guarantee of future performance, TheStreet Investment Ratings provide a solid framework for making informed investment decisions.

TheStreet Ratings' Mission Statement

TheStreet Ratings' mission is to empower consumers, professionals, and institutions with high quality advisory information for selecting or monitoring financial investments.

In doing so, TheStreet Ratings will adhere to the highest ethical standards by maintaining our independent, unbiased outlook and approach to advising our customers.

Why rely on TheStreet Ratings?

Our goal is to provide fair, objective information to help professionals and consumers alike make educated purchasing decisions.

At TheStreet Ratings, objectivity and total independence are never compromised. We never take a penny from rated companies for issuing our ratings, and we publish them without regard for the companies' preferences. TheStreet's ratings are more frequently reviewed and updated than any other ratings, so you can be sure that the information you receive is accurate and current.

Our rating scale, from A to E, is easy to understand as follows:

	Rating	Description
Top 10% of funds	A	Excellent
Next 20% of funds	B	Good
Middle 40% of funds	C	Fair
Next 20% of funds	D	Weak
Bottom 10% of funds	E	Very Weak

In addition, a plus or minus sign designates that a fund is in the top third or bottom third of funds with the same letter grade.

Thank you for your trust and purchase of this Guide. If you have any comments, or wish to review other products from TheStreet Ratings, please call 1-800-706-2501 or visit www.thestreetratings.com. We look forward to hearing from you.

How to Use This Guide

The purpose of the *Guide to Exchange-Traded Funds* is to provide investors with a reliable source of investment ratings and analyses on a timely basis. We realize that past performance is an important factor to consider when making the decision to purchase shares in a mutual fund. The ratings and analyses in this Guide can make that evaluation easier when you are considering ETF and other closed-end:

- growth funds
- sector or international funds
- municipal bond funds
- corporate bond funds
- or other ETFs and closed-end funds

However, this Guide does not include open-end mutual funds since they represent a whole separate class of investments with unique risk profiles and performance expectations. For information on open-end equity funds, refer to *TheStreet Ratings' Guide to Stock Mutual Funds.* And if you are interested in open-end bond or money market funds, refer to *TheStreet Ratings' Guide to Bond and Money Market Mutual Funds*.

The rating for a particular fund indicates our opinion regarding that fund's past risk-adjusted performance. When evaluating a specific mutual fund, we recommend you follow these steps:

Step 1 **Confirm the fund name and ticker symbol.** To ensure you evaluate the correct mutual fund, verify the fund's exact name and ticker symbol as it was given to you in its prospectus or appears on your account statement. Many funds have similar names, so you want to make sure the fund you look up is really the one you are interested in evaluating.

Step 2 **Check the fund's Investment Rating.** Turn to Section I, the Index of Exchange-Traded Funds, and locate the fund you are evaluating. This section contains all ETFs and other closed-end mutual funds analyzed by TheStreet Ratings, including those that did not receive a Investment Rating. All funds are listed in alphabetical order by the name of the fund with the ticker symbol following the name for additional verification. Once you have located your specific fund, the first column after the ticker symbol shows its Investment Rating. Turn to *About TheStreet Investment Ratings* on page 7 for information about what this rating means.

Step 3 **Analyze the supporting data.** Following TheStreet Investment Rating are some of the various measures we have used in rating the fund. Refer to the Section I introduction (beginning on page 15) to see what each of these factors measures. In most cases, lower rated funds will have a low performance rating and/or a low risk rating (i.e., high volatility). Bear in mind, however, that TheStreet Investment Rating is the result of a complex computer-generated analysis which cannot be reproduced using only the data provided here.

When looking to identify a mutual fund that achieves your specific investing goals, we recommend the following:

Step 4 **View the top-performing funds.** If your priority is to achieve the highest return, regardless of the amount of risk, turn to Section V which lists the ETFs and other closed-end mutual funds with the best financial performance. Keep in mind that past performance alone is not always a true indicator of the future since these funds have already experienced a run up in price and could be due for a correction.

Step 5 **View the top-rated funds by fund type.** If you are looking to invest in a particular type of mutual fund (e.g., corporate high-yield bond or emerging market), turn to Section VI, Top-Rated ETFs and Other Closed-End Mutual Funds by Fund Type. There you will find the ETFs and other closed-end mutual funds with the highest performance rating in each category. Please be careful to also consider the risk component when selecting a fund from one of these lists.

Step 6 **Refer back to Section I.** Once you have identified a particular fund that interests you, refer back to Section I, the Index of ETFs and Other Closed-End Mutual Funds, for a more thorough analysis.

Always remember:

Step 7 **Read our warnings and cautions.** In order to use TheStreet Investment Ratings most effectively, we strongly recommend you consult the Important Warnings and Cautions listed on page 11. These are more than just "standard disclaimers." They are very important factors you should be aware of before using this Guide.

Step 8 **Stay up to date.** Periodically review the latest TheStreet Investment Ratings for the funds that you own to make sure they are still in line with your investment goals and level of risk tolerance. For information on how to acquire follow-up reports on a particular mutual fund, call 1-800-706-2501 or visit www.thestreetratings.com.

Data Source: Thomson Wealth Management
1455 Research Boulevard
Rockville, MD 20850

Date of data analyzed: Dec. 31, 2015

About TheStreet Investment Ratings

TheStreet Investment Ratings represent a completely independent, unbiased opinion of a mutual fund's historical risk-adjusted performance. Each fund's rating is based on two primary components:

Primary Component #1

A fund's **Performance Rating** is based on its total return to shareholders over a period of up to three years, including share price appreciation and distributions to shareholders. This total return figure is stated net of the expenses and fees charged by the fund.

This adjusted return is then weighted to give more recent performance a slightly greater emphasis. Thus, two mutual funds may have provided identical returns to their shareholders over the last three years, but the one with the better performance in the last 12 months will receive a slightly higher performance rating.

Primary Component #2

The **Risk Rating** is based on the level of volatility in the fund's monthly returns, also over a period of up to three years. We use several statistical measures – standard deviation, semi-deviation and a drawdown factor – as our barometer of volatility. Funds with more volatility relative to other mutual funds are considered riskier, and thus receive a lower risk rating. By contrast, funds with very stable returns are considered less risky and receive a higher risk rating. In addition to considering the fund's volatility, the risk rating also considers the fund's discount/premium as compared to its historical average, as well as an assessment of the valuation and quality of the fund's holdings.

Note that none of the mutual funds listed in this publication have received a risk rating in the A (Excellent) range. This is because all closed-end mutual fund investments, by their very nature, involve at least some degree of risk.

Rarely will you ever find a mutual fund that has both a very high Performance Rating plus, at the same time, a very high Risk Rating. Therefore, the funds that receive the highest overall Investment Ratings are those that attain the ideal combination of both primary components. There is always a tradeoff between risk and reward.

The two ratings have totally independent meanings. Based on these measures, funds are divided into percentiles, and an individual performance rating and a risk rating are assigned to each fund. Then these measures are combined to derive a fund's composite percentile ranking. Finally, TheStreet Investment Ratings are assigned to their corresponding percentile rankings as shown on page 3.

How Our Ratings Differ From Those of Other Services

Balanced approach: TheStreet Investment Ratings are designed to meet the needs of aggressive *as well as* conservative investors. We realize that your investment goals can be different from those of other investors based upon your age, income, and tolerance for risk. Therefore, our ratings balance a fund's performance against the amount of risk it poses to identify those funds that have achieved the optimum mix of both factors. Some of these top funds have achieved excellent returns with only average risk. Others have achieved average returns with only moderate risk. Whatever your personal preferences, we can help you identify a top notch fund that meets your investing style.

Other investment rating firms give a far greater weight to performance and insufficient consideration to risk. In effect, they bet too heavily on a rising market and do not give enough consideration to the risk of a decline. While performance is obviously a very important factor to consider, we believe that the riskiness of a fund is also very important. Therefore, we weigh these two components more equally when assigning TheStreet Investment Ratings.

But we don't stop there. We also assign a separate performance rating and risk rating to each fund so you can focus on the component that is most important to you.

Easy to use: Unlike those of other services, TheStreet Investment Ratings are extremely intuitive and easy to use. Our rating scale (A to E) is easily understood by members of the general public based on their familiarity with school grades. So, there are no stars to count and no numbering systems to interpret.

More funds: *TheStreet Ratings Guide to Exchange-Traded Funds* tracks more closed-end mutual funds than any other publication – with updates that come out more frequently than those of other rating agencies. We've included more than 1,500 funds in this edition, all of which are updated every three months.

Recency: Recognizing that every fund's performance is going to have its peaks and valleys, superior long-term performance is a major consideration in TheStreet Investment Ratings. Even so, we do not give a fund a top rating solely because it did well 10 or 15 years ago. Times change and the top performing funds in the current economic environment are often very different from those of a decade ago. Thus, our ratings are designed to keep you abreast of the best funds available *today* and in the *near future,* not the distant past.

Thoroughness: One of the unique characteristics of closed-end funds is that they often trade either above (premium) or below (discount) their net asset value (NAV). Our ratings not only consider performance and risk factors of each fund, but we also evaluate the current premium or discount of each fund as compared to its historical average. This evaluation is factored into the overall rating and can help investors identify funds that may be overvalued or undervalued.

What Our Ratings Mean

A — **Excellent**. The mutual fund has an excellent track record for maximizing performance while minimizing risk, thus delivering the best possible combination of total return on investment and reduced volatility. It has made the most of the recent economic environment to maximize risk-adjusted returns compared to other mutual funds. While past performance is just an indication – not a guarantee – we believe this fund is among the most likely to deliver superior performance relative to risk in the future.

B — **Good.** The mutual fund has a good track record for balancing performance with risk. Compared to other mutual funds, it has achieved above-average returns given the level of risk in its underlying investments. While the risk-adjusted performance of any mutual fund is subject to change, we believe that this fund has proven to be a good investment in the recent past.

C — **Fair.** In the trade-off between performance and risk, the mutual fund has a track record which is about average. It is neither significantly better nor significantly worse than most other mutual funds. With some funds in this category, the total return may be better than average, but this can be misleading since the higher return was achieved with higher than average risk. With other funds, the risk may be lower than average, but the returns are also lower. In short, based on recent history, there is no particular advantage to investing in this fund.

D — **Weak.** The mutual fund has underperformed the universe of other funds given the level of risk in its underlying investments, resulting in a weak risk-adjusted performance. Thus, its investment strategy and/or management has not been attuned to capitalize on the recent economic environment. While the risk-adjusted performance of any mutual fund is subject to change, we believe that this fund has proven to be a bad investment over the recent past.

E — **Very Weak.** The mutual fund has significantly underperformed most other funds given the level of risk in its underlying investments, resulting in a very weak risk-adjusted performance. Thus, its investment strategy and/or management has done just the opposite of what was needed to maximize returns in the recent economic environment. While the risk-adjusted performance of any mutual fund is subject to change, we believe this fund has proven to be a very bad investment in the recent past.

+ — **The plus sign** is an indication that the fund is in the top third of its letter grade.

- — **The minus sign** is an indication that the fund is in the bottom third of its letter grade.

U — **Unrated.** The mutual fund is unrated because it is too new to make a reliable assessment of its risk-adjusted performance.

Important Warnings and Cautions

1. **A rating alone cannot tell the whole story.** Please read the explanatory information contained here, in the section introductions and in the appendix. It is provided in order to give you an understanding of our rating methodology as well as to paint a more complete picture of a mutual fund's strengths and weaknesses.

2. **Investment ratings shown in this Guide were current as of the publication date.** In the meantime, the rating may have been updated based on more recent data. TheStreet Ratings offers a notification service for ratings changes on companies that you specify. For more information call 1-800-706-2501 or visit www.thestreet.com/ratings.

3. **When deciding to buy or sell shares in a specific mutual fund, your decision must be based on a wide variety of factors in addition to TheStreet Investment Rating**. These include any charges you may incur from switching funds, to what degree it meets your long-term planning needs, and what other choices are available to you.

4. **TheStreet Investment Ratings represent our opinion of a mutual fund's past risk-adjusted performance.** As such, a high rating means we feel that the mutual fund has performed very well for its shareholders compared to other closed-end mutual funds. A high rating is not a guarantee that a fund will continue to perform well, nor is a low rating a prediction of continued weak performance. TheStreet Investment Ratings are not deemed to be a recommendation concerning the purchase or sale of any mutual fund.

5. **A mutual fund's individual performance is not the only factor in determining its rating.** Since TheStreet Investment Ratings are based on performance relative to other funds, it is possible for a fund's rating to be upgraded or downgraded based strictly on the improved or deteriorated performance of other funds.

6. **All funds that have the same TheStreet Investment Rating should be considered to be essentially equal from a risk/reward perspective.** This is true regardless of any differences in the underlying numbers which might appear to indicate greater strengths.

7. **Our rating standards are more consumer-oriented than those used by other rating agencies.** We make more conservative assumptions as we attempt to identify those funds that have historically provided superior returns with only little or moderate risk.

8. **We are an independent rating agency and do not depend on the cooperation of the managers operating the mutual funds we rate**. Our data are derived, for the most part, from price quotes obtained and documented on the open market. This is supplemented by information collected from the mutual fund prospectuses and regulatory filings. Although we seek to maintain an open line of communication with the mutual fund managers, we do not grant them the right to stop or influence publication of the ratings. This policy stems from the fact that this Guide is designed for the information of the consumer.

9. **This Guide does not cover open-end funds.** Because open-end funds represent a whole separate class of investments with unique risk profiles and performance expectations, they are available in separate publications. Please see our *Guide to Stock Mutual Funds* and our *Guide to Bond and Money Market Mutual Funds* for our analyses of open-end mutual funds.

Section I

Index of ETFs and Other Closed-End Funds

An analysis of all rated and unrated

Exchange-Traded Funds and

Other Closed-End Mutual Funds.

Funds are listed in alphabetical order.

Section I Contents

Left Pages

1. Fund Type

The mutual fund's peer category based on an analysis of its investment portfolio.

COH	Corporate – High Yield	HL	Health
COI	Corporate – Inv. Grade	IN	Income
EM	Emerging Market	LP	Loan Participation
EN	Energy/Natural Resources	MTG	Mortgage
FS	Financial Services	MUH	Municipal – High Yield
FO	Foreign	MUN	Municipal – National
GEI	General – Inv. Grade	MUS	Municipal – Single State
GEN	General Bond	PM	Precious Metals
GL	Global	USA	U.S. Gov. – Agency
GR	Growth	UT	Utilities
GI	Growth and Income		

A blank fund type means that the mutual fund has not yet been categorized.

2. Fund Name

The name of the mutual fund as stated in its prospectus, which can sometimes differ slightly from the name that the company uses for advertising. If you cannot find the particular mutual fund you are interested in, or if you have any doubts regarding the precise name, verify the information with your broker or on your account statement. Also, use the fund's ticker symbol for confirmation. (See column 3.)

3. Ticker Symbol

The unique alphabetic symbol used for identifying and trading a specific mutual fund. No two funds can have the same ticker symbol.

4. Overall Investment Rating

Our overall rating is measured on a scale from A to E based on each fund's risk-adjusted performance. Please see page 10 for specific descriptions of each letter grade. Also, refer to page 7 for information on how our ratings are derived. Most important, when using this rating, please be sure to consider the warnings beginning on page 11 regarding the ratings' limitations and the underlying assumptions.

5.	**Price**	Closing price of the fund on the date shown.
6.	**52-Week High**	Highest price at which the fund has traded in the last 52 weeks.
7.	**52-Week Low**	Lowest price at which the fund has traded in the last 52 weeks.
8.	**Performance Rating/Points**	A letter grade rating based solely on the mutual fund's financial performance over the trailing three years, without any consideration for the amount of risk the fund poses. Like the overall Investment Rating, the Performance Rating is measured on a scale from A to E for ease of interpretation. The points score indicates where the Performance Rating falls on a scale of 0 to 10.
9.	**3-Month Total Return**	The total return the fund has provided to investors over the preceding 13 weeks. This total return figure is computed based on the fund's dividend distributions and share price appreciation/depreciation during the period, net of the expenses and fees it imposes on its shareholders. The 3-Month Total Return shown here is not annualized.
10.	**6-Month Total Return**	The total return the fund has provided investors over the preceding 26 weeks, not annualized.
11.	**1-Year Total Return**	The total return the fund has provided investors over the preceding 52 weeks.
12.	**1-Year Total Return Percentile**	The fund's percentile rank based on its one-year performance compared to that of all other closed-end funds in existence for at least one year. A score of 99 is the best possible, indicating that the fund outperformed 99% of the closed-end mutual funds. Zero is the worst possible percentile score.
13.	**3-Year Total Return**	The total annual return the fund has provided investors over the preceding 156 weeks.
14.	**3-Year Total Return Percentile**	The fund's percentile rank based on its three-year performance compared to that of all other closed-end funds in existence for at least three years. A score of 99 is the best possible, indicating that the fund outperformed 99% of the closed-end mutual funds. Zero is the worst possible percentile score.
15.	**5-Year Total Return**	The total annual return the fund has provided investors over the preceding 260 weeks.
16.	**5-Year Total Return Percentile**	The fund's percentile rank based on its five-year performance compared to that of all other closed-end funds in existence for at least five years. A score of 99 is the best possible, indicating that the fund outperformed 99% of the closed-end mutual funds. Zero is the worst possible percentile score.

Right Pages

1. Dividend Yield

Most recent quarterly dividend to fund investors annualized, expressed as a percent of the fund's current share price. The dividend yield of a fund can have little correlation to the amount of dividends the fund has received from its underlying investments. Rather, dividend distributions are based on a fund's need to pass earnings from both dividends and gains on the sale of investments along to shareholders. Thus, these dividend distributions are included as a part of the fund's total return.

Keep in mind that dividend income may be taxed at a different rate than capital gains depending on your income tax bracket.

2. Expense Ratio

The expense ratio is taken directly from each fund's annual report with no further calculation. It indicates the percentage of the fund's assets that are deducted each fiscal year to cover its expenses, although for practical purposes, it is actually accrued daily. Typical fund expenses include management fees and other costs incurred by the fund. Brokerage costs incurred by the fund to buy or sell shares of the underlying securities are not included in the expense ratio.

If a mutual fund's net assets are small, its expense ratio can be quite high because the fund must cover its expenses from a smaller asset base. Conversely, as the net assets of the fund grow, the expense percentage should ideally diminish since the expenses are being spread across a larger asset base.

Funds with higher expense ratios are generally less attractive since the expense ratio represents a hurdle that must be met before the investment becomes profitable to its shareholders. Since a fund's expenses affect its total return though, they are already factored into its TheStreet Investment Rating.

3. Risk Rating/Points

A letter grade rating based solely on the mutual fund's risk as determined by its monthly performance volatility over the trailing three years. The risk rating does not take into consideration the overall financial performance the fund has achieved or the total return it has provided to its shareholders. Like the overall Investment Rating, the Risk Rating is measured on a scale from A to E for ease of interpretation. The points score indicates where the Risk Rating falls on a scale of 0 to 10.

4. Standard Deviation

A statistical measure of the amount of volatility in a fund's monthly performance over the last trailing 36 months. In absolute terms, standard deviation provides a historical measure of a fund's deviation from its mean, or average, monthly total return over the period.

A high standard deviation indicates a high degree of volatility in the past, which usually means you should expect to see a high degree of volatility in the future as well. This translates into higher risk since a large negative swing could easily become a sizable loss in the event you need to liquidate your shares.

5. Beta

The level of correlation between the fund's monthly performance over the last trailing 36 months and the performance of its investment category as a whole.

A beta of 1.00 means that the fund's returns have matched those of the index one for one during the stock market's ups and downs. A beta of 1.10 means that on average the fund has outperformed the index by 10% during rising markets and underperformed it by 10% during falling markets. Conversely, a beta of 0.85 means that the fund has typically performed 15% worse than the overall market during up markets and 15% better during down markets.

6. Average Duration

Expressed in years, duration is a measure of a bond fund's sensitivity to interest rate fluctuations, or its level of interest rate risk.

The longer a fund's duration, the more sensitive the fund is to shifts in interest rates. For example, a fund with a duration of eight years is twice as sensitive to a change in rates as a fund with a four year duration.

7. NAV

The fund's net asset value (NAV) as of the date indicated. A fund's NAV is computed by dividing the value of the fund's asset holdings, less accrued fees and expenses, by the number of its shares outstanding.

Because a closed-end fund's shares trade on an exchange and the price is based on investor demand, the fund may trade at a price higher or lower than its NAV.

8. Net Assets

The total value (stated in millions of dollars) of all of the fund's asset holdings including stocks, bonds, cash, and other financial instruments, less accrued expenses and fees.

Larger funds have the advantage of being able to spread their expenses over a greater asset base so that the effect per share is lessened. On the other hand, if a fund becomes too large, it can be more difficult for the fund manager to buy and sell investments for the benefit of shareholders.

9. Premium/

A comparison of the fund's price to its NAV as of the date indicated.

Discount

The premium (+) or discount (-) indicates the percentage the shares are trading above or below the fund's NAV per share.

If the price is above the fund's NAV, the fund is said to be trading at a premium. If the price is lower than the fund's NAV, the fund is trading at a discount.

10. 1-Year Average Premium/ Discount

The average of the fund's premium/discount over the preceding year.

It can be useful to compare the fund's current premium/discount to its one-year average. If the fund is currently trading at a premium/discount that is lower/higher than its one-year average, then there has been less demand for the fund in more recent times than over the past year. Conversely, if the fund is currently trading at a premium/discount that is higher/lower than its one-year average, this indicates that there has been greater demand for the fund in more recent times than over the past year.

11. Weighted Average Price-to-Earnings

The average of the price-to-earnings (P/E) ratios for the equity securities of the fund, where larger holdings are weighted more heavily than smaller holdings. A high P/E multiple indicates that investors have high expectations for future growth of the securities of that fund.

Compare this number to that of funds of the same type to get a feel for whether the equity securities of the fund might be overvalued or undervalued.

12. Cash %

The percentage of the fund's assets held in cash or money market funds as of the last reporting period. Investments in this area will tend to hamper the fund's returns while adding to its stability during market swings.

13. Stocks %

The percentage of the fund's assets held in common or preferred stocks as of the last reporting period. Since stocks are inherently riskier investments than the other categories, it is common for funds invested primarily or exclusively in stocks to receive a lower risk rating.

14. Bonds %

The percentage of the fund's assets held in bonds as of the last reporting period. This category includes corporate bonds, municipal bonds, and government bonds such as T-bills and T-bonds.

15. Other %

The percentage of the fund's assets invested as of the last reporting period in other types of financial instruments such as convertible securities, options, and warrants.

16. Portfolio Turnover Ratio

The average annual portion of the fund's holdings that have been moved from one specific investment to another over the past three years. This indicates the amount of buying and selling the fund manager engages in. A portfolio turnover ratio of 100% signifies that on average, the entire value of the fund's assets is turned over once during the course of a year.

A high portfolio turnover ratio has implications for shareholders since the fund is required to pass all realized earnings along to shareholders each year. Thus a high portfolio turnover ratio will result in higher annual distributions for shareholders, effectively increasing their annual taxable income. In contrast, a low turnover ratio means a higher level of unrealized gains that will not be taxable until you sell your shares in the fund.

17. Manager Quality Percentile

The manager quality percentile is based on a ranking of the fund's alpha, a statistical measure representing the difference between a fund's actual returns and its expected performance given its level of risk. Fund managers who have been able to exceed the fund's statistically expected performance receive a high percentile rank with 99 representing the highest possible score. At the other end of the spectrum, fund managers who have actually detracted from the fund's expected performance receive a low percentile rank with 0 representing the lowest possible score.

18. Manager Tenure

The number of years the current manager has been managing the fund. Since fund managers who deliver substandard returns are usually replaced, a long tenure is usually a good sign that shareholders are satisfied that the fund is achieving its stated objectives.

Fund Type	Fund Name (99 Pct = Best, 0 Pct = Worst)	Ticker Symbol	Overall Investment Rating	PRICE: Price As of 12/31/15	52 Week High	52 Week Low	PERFORMANCE: Performance Rating/Pts	% Total Return Through 12/31/15: 3 Mo	6 Mo	1Yr/Pct	Annualized 3Yr/Pct	Annualized 5Yr/Pct
GI	*AdvisorShares EquityPro ETF	EPRO	C	27.82	32.00	27.65	C / 5.5	-2.10	-5.73	-3.34 / 45	4.19 / 58	--
FO	*AdvisorShares Gartman Gold Euro	GEUR	C-	11.24	14.90	11.10	D+ / 2.4	-4.27	-7.38	-3.63 / 44	--	--
FO	*AdvisorShares Gartman Gold Yen E	GYEN	D+	11.14	14.72	10.58	D- / 1.2	-6.77	-12.15	-12.68 / 21	--	--
LP	*AdvisorShares Pac Asset Enh FR E	FLRT	U	47.18	N/A	N/A	U /	-2.26	-4.06	--	--	--
GEI	*AdvisorShares Sage Core Rsvs ETF	HOLD	B-	98.90	99.70	98.86	C- / 4.2	-0.18	-0.19	0.10 / 61	--	--
FS	*AdvisorShares YieldPro	YPRO	C+	22.94	24.10	21.80	C- / 3.7	-0.35	0.13	-1.99 / 50	--	--
GI	*AlphaClone Alternative Alpha ETF	ALFA	C	37.49	47.66	33.00	C+ / 6.1	-8.05	-17.19	-11.33 / 23	9.45 / 74	--
GR	*AlphaMark Actively Managed Sm Ca	SMCP	U	21.95	N/A	N/A	U /	3.66	-11.48	--	--	--
EN	*ALPS Alerian Energy Infra ETF	ENFR	E+	17.44	28.58	15.57	E- / 0.1	-13.74	-29.99	-37.63 / 4	--	--
EN	*Alps Alerian MLP ETF	AMLP	D	12.05	17.59	9.55	D / 2.2	-8.11	-19.27	-26.24 / 9	-3.87 / 27	0.72 / 30
GR	*ALPS Barrons 400 ETF	BFOR	C-	30.22	34.30	28.05	D+ / 2.8	1.67	-8.22	-2.71 / 48	--	--
GL	*Alps Emerg Sector Dividend Dogs	EDOG	D	19.37	26.17	18.05	E+ / 0.8	-5.20	-17.01	-16.87 / 16	--	--
GR	*ALPS Enhanced Put Write Strategy	PUTX	U	24.62	N/A	N/A	U /	3.61	--	--	--	--
IN	*Alps Equal Sector Weight ETF	EQL	B	54.76	58.49	38.44	B / 8.0	4.61	-2.35	-1.65 / 52	11.85 / 81	10.98 / 72
GL	*Alps Global Commodity Equity	CRBQ	D	29.08	41.65	28.41	D- / 1.4	-4.14	-21.37	-22.41 / 12	-12.00 / 15	-8.33 / 15
GR	*Alps Intll Sec Div Dogs ETF	IDOG	D+	23.48	28.84	22.57	D / 2.1	-1.00	-9.57	-6.57 / 35	--	--
GR	*Alps Janus Vel Vol Hdg LC	SPXH	C-	28.84	31.73	26.18	C- / 3.4	2.45	-4.03	-2.27 / 49	--	--
GEN	*ALPS RiverFront Strategic Income	RIGS	C	24.19	25.51	23.65	C / 4.4	0.87	-1.47	0.63 / 65	--	--
IN	*Alps Sector Dividend Dogs ETF	SDOG	B	35.55	39.05	19.11	B / 8.2	4.55	-2.65	-4.17 / 42	12.70 / 83	--
PM	*ALPS Sprott Gold Miners ETF	SGDM	E	12.73	22.00	11.61	E / 0.5	-3.24	-18.56	-28.16 / 8	--	--
PM	*ALPS Sprott Junior Gold Miners	SGDJ	U	19.25	N/A	N/A	U /	-6.94	-22.14	--	--	--
FO	*Alps STOXX Europe 600	STXX	C-	24.14	27.71	21.65	C- / 3.5	4.24	-6.13	-1.33 / 53	--	--
GR	*Alps US Equity High Vol Put Writ	HVPW	C	20.91	24.19	13.51	C- / 3.4	1.62	-5.01	-1.52 / 52	--	--
GR	*Alps VelShTail Risk Hdgd Lg Cp E	TRSK	C-	27.26	29.02	26.57	C- / 3.3	1.51	-2.55	-3.71 / 43	--	--
GL	*ARK Genomic Revolution Multi-Sec	ARKG	C-	20.97	24.94	18.20	C- / 4.0	10.11	-7.81	-1.57 / 52	--	--
GL	*ARK Industrial Innovation	ARKQ	C	19.18	20.78	16.38	C / 5.4	11.44	-2.82	-1.38 / 53	--	--
GR	*ARK Innovation	ARKK	C+	20.46	22.24	17.51	C+ / 6.5	9.67	-1.52	3.75 / 76	--	--
GR	*ARK Web x.0	ARKW	A-	23.17	24.47	19.69	A / 9.4	9.58	3.24	16.65 / 96	--	--
GI	*Arrow Dow Jones Global Yield ETF	GYLD	D	17.16	26.15	16.87	D / 1.7	-10.37	-22.65	-23.68 / 11	-7.36 / 21	--
GI	*Arrow DWA Tactical	DWAT	C+	9.90	10.97	8.66	C+ / 6.0	8.78	0.81	0.05 / 61	--	--
GR	*Arrow QVM Equity Factor ETF	QVM	U	22.93	N/A	N/A	U /	0.65	-6.79	--	--	--
GL	*Athena High Dividend ETF	DIVI	D-	14.89	21.92	14.22	E / 0.5	-6.29	-20.54	-25.65 / 10	--	--
FO	*Barclays ETN + FI Enh Eur 50	FEEU	D-	93.80	126.48	87.68	D- / 1.3	-1.92	-17.27	-8.80 / 29	--	--
GR	*Barclays ETN + FI Enh Gl Hi Yld	FIGY	D-	111.89	131.14	93.01	C- / 3.2	6.62	-5.84	-4.54 / 41	--	--
EN	*Barclays ETN + OFI SteelPath MLP	OSMS	E	16.98	26.07	14.14	E / 0.5	-2.40	-21.43	-29.74 / 8	--	--
EN	*Barclays ETN + Select MLP ETN	ATMP	E-	18.61	31.00	15.09	E- / 0.1	-14.68	-29.56	-36.80 / 5	--	--
IN	*Barclays ETN + Shiller CAPE ETN	CAPE	C+	81.30	82.33	53.72	A- / 9.2	10.16	2.91	4.73 / 78	16.09 / 91	--
GR	*Barclays ETN + VEQTOR ETN	VQT	D	138.33	155.62	131.78	C / 4.5	3.23	-3.51	-9.54 / 27	1.92 / 48	4.92 / 47
GL	*Barclays Inverse US Treasury Com	TAPR	D-	32.99	41.92	24.57	C- / 3.0	14.75	-15.86	-3.67 / 43	--	--
GL	*Barclays Women in Leadership	WIL	D	51.71	55.81	49.13	C- / 3.9	4.51	-2.25	-2.36 / 49	--	--
FO	*BLDRS Asia 50 ADR Index	ADRA	C+	27.00	32.75	22.78	C / 5.1	4.39	-8.31	-2.38 / 49	2.52 / 51	1.49 / 32
FO	*BLDRS Developed Mkts 100 ADR Ind	ADRD	C	20.94	25.00	20.19	C / 5.1	-0.59	-9.37	-2.94 / 47	3.01 / 53	3.44 / 4
EM	*BLDRS Emerging Market 50 ADR Ind	ADRE	D	29.07	38.97	19.55	D / 2.0	1.64	-15.25	-15.25 / 17	-8.83 / 19	-6.97 / 17
FO	*BLDRS Europe Select ADR Index	ADRU	C-	20.49	24.55	19.74	C / 4.8	-0.33	-9.30	-4.73 / 40	2.75 / 52	3.70 / 4
GR	*Brclys ETN+ Inv S&P500 VIX STF E	XXV	D+	38.12	40.75	38.05	C / 4.4	-0.03	-0.47	-0.50 / 57	0.26 / 38	2.77 / 37
IN	*C-Tracks ETN Citi Volatility Idx	CVOL	E-	0.43	1.33	0.39	E- / 0.0	-39.89	-25.17	-60.11 / 1	-73.97 / 0	-76.75 /
GR	*C-Tracks ETN MillerHoward MLP FI	MLPC	E-	15.46	26.00	13.37	E- / 0.2	-8.26	-29.63	-37.82 / 4	--	--
IN	*C-Tracks ETN MillerHoward Str Di	DIVC	D	24.97	33.65	21.91	C- / 3.6	4.87	-6.58	-1.15 / 54	--	--
GR	*Calamos Focus Growth	CFGE	C-	10.57	11.50	9.60	C- / 3.6	-1.28	-4.24	0.76 / 65	--	--
GL	*Cambria Foreign Shareholder Yiel	FYLD	D+	20.04	24.50	18.43	D / 2.2	1.03	-9.18	-7.47 / 32	--	--
GI	*Cambria Global Asset Allocation	GAA	D+	23.09	25.72	21.61	D+ / 2.8	-0.24	-5.09	-4.09 / 42	--	--
FO	*Cambria Global Momentum ETF	GMOM	D-	22.58	26.39	19.25	D / 2.0	-2.35	-6.99	-8.94 / 28	--	--

* Denotes ETF Fund, N/A denotes number is not availabl

Incl. in Returns		RISK				NET ASSETS		VALUATION			ASSET					FUND MANAGER	
			3 Year					Premium / Discount									
Dividend Yield %	Expense Ratio	Risk Rating/ Pts	Standard Deviation	Beta	Avg Dura-tion	NAV as of 12/31/15	Total $(Mil)	As of 12/31/15	1 Year Average	Wtd Avg P/E	Cash %	Stocks %	Bonds %	Other %	Portfolio Turnover Ratio	Manager Quality Pct	Manager Tenure (Years)
1.09	1.25	**C+ / 6.8**	8.8	0.71	N/A	27.37	21	1.64	-0.02	N/A	0	0	0	100	349	32	N/A
7.94	0.65	**B- / 7.4**	N/A	N/A	N/A	11.32	2	-0.71	-0.02	N/A	0	0	0	100	N/A	48	2
3.68	0.65	**B- / 7.7**	N/A	N/A	N/A	11.22	4	-0.71	0.11	N/A	0	0	0	100	N/A	14	2
4.27	N/A	**U /**	N/A	N/A	N/A	47.45	N/A	-0.57	N/A	N/A	0	0	0	100	N/A	N/A	1
0.59	0.35	**B+ / 9.9**	N/A	N/A	N/A	99.02	37	-0.12	0.03	N/A	0	0	0	100	59	68	N/A
3.31	1.05	**B+ / 9.1**	N/A	N/A	N/A	22.99	68	-0.22	-0.13	N/A	0	0	0	100	128	54	1
0.00	0.95	**C+ / 6.6**	13.3	0.80	N/A	37.47	78	0.05	0.03	N/A	0	0	0	100	78	59	N/A
0.00	N/A	**U /**	N/A	N/A	N/A	21.89	N/A	0.27	N/A	N/A	0	0	0	100	N/A	N/A	1
1.43	0.65	**C- / 3.9**	N/A	N/A	N/A	17.42	17	0.11	-0.10	N/A	0	0	0	100	27	5	3
9.93	0.85	**C / 4.7**	14.9	0.51	N/A	11.99	9,617	0.50	0.04	N/A	0	100	0	0	29	61	5
0.86	0.65	**C+ / 6.9**	N/A	N/A	N/A	30.07	231	0.50	0.02	N/A	0	0	0	100	55	34	3
1.82	0.60	**C+ / 6.6**	N/A	N/A	N/A	19.60	8	-1.17	-0.02	N/A	0	0	0	100	19	9	2
1.15	N/A	**U /**	N/A	N/A	N/A	24.66	N/A	-0.16	N/A	N/A	0	0	0	100	N/A	N/A	N/A
1.97	0.34	**B- / 7.2**	10.2	0.96	N/A	54.65	134	0.20	0.01	N/A	0	100	0	0	3	57	7
2.65	0.65	**C+ / 6.3**	15.3	0.94	N/A	29.27	61	-0.65	-0.26	N/A	0	100	0	0	12	10	5
1.80	0.50	**B- / 7.3**	N/A	N/A	N/A	23.67	153	-0.80	0.08	N/A	0	0	0	100	19	20	3
1.66	0.65	**B- / 7.2**	N/A	N/A	N/A	28.71	52	0.45	0.04	N/A	0	0	0	100	1	35	3
3.70	0.22	**B- / 7.6**	N/A	N/A	N/A	24.16	369	0.12	0.15	N/A	0	0	0	100	27	75	N/A
2.63	0.40	**B- / 7.0**	11.0	0.93	N/A	35.54	852	0.03	0.02	N/A	0	0	0	100	12	67	4
1.47	N/A	**D+ / 2.4**	N/A	N/A	N/A	12.72	41	0.08	0.01	N/A	0	0	0	100	N/A	83	2
1.13	N/A	**U /**	N/A	N/A	N/A	19.37	N/A	-0.62	N/A	N/A	0	0	0	100	N/A	N/A	1
0.99	N/A	**C+ / 6.3**	N/A	N/A	N/A	23.83	N/A	1.30	0.34	N/A	0	0	0	100	N/A	60	2
9.10	0.95	**B / 8.1**	N/A	N/A	N/A	20.96	56	-0.24	-0.09	N/A	0	0	0	100	N/A	51	N/A
1.57	0.65	**B- / 7.5**	N/A	N/A	N/A	27.10	32	0.59	-0.01	N/A	0	0	0	100	2	31	3
0.00	0.95	**C+ / 5.7**	N/A	N/A	N/A	20.81	N/A	0.77	0.07	N/A	0	0	0	100	65	60	2
0.98	0.95	**C+ / 6.5**	N/A	N/A	N/A	19.09	N/A	0.47	0.12	N/A	0	0	0	100	86	50	2
2.27	0.95	**C+ / 6.5**	N/A	N/A	N/A	20.43	N/A	0.15	0.13	N/A	0	0	0	100	108	83	2
2.29	0.95	**C+ / 6.9**	N/A	N/A	N/A	23.05	N/A	0.52	0.07	N/A	0	0	0	100	103	97	N/A
8.88	0.75	**C+ / 6.2**	14.5	0.87	N/A	17.46	191	-1.72	-0.06	N/A	0	0	0	100	87	8	4
0.00	1.40	**B- / 7.0**	N/A	N/A	N/A	9.88	N/A	0.20	-0.02	N/A	0	0	0	100	111	64	2
1.59	N/A	**U /**	N/A	N/A	N/A	22.88	N/A	0.22	N/A	N/A	0	0	0	100	N/A	N/A	N/A
2.78	0.99	**C / 4.3**	N/A	N/A	N/A	14.85	N/A	0.27	0.14	N/A	0	0	0	100	193	4	N/A
0.00	N/A	**C / 4.4**	N/A	N/A	N/A	94.92	N/A	-1.18	-0.13	N/A	0	0	0	100	N/A	18	N/A
0.00	N/A	**C- / 3.0**	N/A	N/A	N/A	111.38	1,502	0.46	-0.07	N/A	0	0	0	100	N/A	21	N/A
6.17	N/A	**D- / 1.5**	N/A	N/A	N/A	16.63	68	2.10	0.87	N/A	0	0	0	100	N/A	34	N/A
6.88	N/A	**D- / 1.5**	N/A	N/A	N/A	18.56	403	0.27	0.08	N/A	0	0	0	100	N/A	6	3
0.00	N/A	**C- / 3.9**	11.2	1.02	N/A	80.97	22	0.41	0.01	N/A	0	0	0	100	N/A	79	4
0.00	N/A	**C- / 3.2**	7.3	0.58	N/A	137.98	642	0.25	-0.01	N/A	0	0	0	100	N/A	26	6
0.00	N/A	**D+ / 2.9**	N/A	N/A	N/A	32.93	N/A	0.18	-0.10	N/A	0	0	0	100	N/A	55	N/A
0.00	N/A	**C- / 3.6**	N/A	N/A	N/A	51.36	N/A	0.68	0.26	N/A	0	0	0	100	N/A	48	N/A
2.86	0.30	**B- / 7.8**	14.4	1.02	N/A	27.04	26	-0.15	-0.34	N/A	0	99	0	1	3	50	N/A
4.46	0.30	**C+ / 6.3**	13.0	1.01	N/A	20.89	57	0.24	0.06	N/A	0	99	0	1	7	53	N/A
3.13	0.30	**C+ / 6.2**	18.3	1.19	N/A	29.13	214	-0.21	-0.19	N/A	0	99	0	1	8	63	N/A
5.10	0.30	**C+ / 6.0**	13.6	1.03	N/A	20.45	20	0.20	-0.05	N/A	0	99	0	1	8	49	N/A
0.00	N/A	**C- / 4.2**	0.8	0.05	N/A	38.11	4	0.03	N/A	N/A	0	0	0	100	N/A	64	N/A
0.00	N/A	**E- / 0.1**	93.5	-7.27	N/A	0.41	N/A	4.88	1.13	N/A	0	0	0	100	N/A	2	N/A
6.34	N/A	**D- / 1.1**	N/A	N/A	N/A	15.44	N/A	0.13	0.13	N/A	0	0	0	100	N/A	1	N/A
0.00	N/A	**C- / 3.3**	N/A	N/A	N/A	23.86	N/A	4.65	-0.01	N/A	0	0	0	100	N/A	38	N/A
0.00	0.90	**B- / 7.0**	N/A	N/A	N/A	10.48	N/A	0.86	0.48	N/A	0	0	0	100	147	56	2
2.09	0.59	**B- / 7.1**	N/A	N/A	N/A	20.36	78	-1.57	-0.24	N/A	0	0	0	100	48	23	3
2.85	N/A	**C / 5.5**	N/A	N/A	N/A	23.11	N/A	-0.09	0.02	N/A	0	0	0	100	N/A	32	N/A
2.91	N/A	**C- / 3.3**	N/A	N/A	N/A	22.56	N/A	0.09	-0.03	N/A	0	0	0	100	N/A	19	2

* Denotes ETF Fund, N/A denotes number is not available

99 Pct = Best
0 Pct = Worst

Fund Type	Fund Name	Ticker Symbol	Overall Investment Rating	PRICE: Price As of 12/31/15	52 Week High	52 Week Low	PERFORMANCE: Performance Rating/Pts	% Total Return Through 12/31/15: 3 Mo	6 Mo	1Yr/Pct	Annualized: 3Yr/Pct	5Yr/Pct
GL	*Cambria Global Value ETF	GVAL	**D**	17.72	22.64	17.60	**D / 1.6**	-3.96	-12.11	-8.33 / 30	--	--
IN	*Cambria Shareholder Yield ETF	SYLD	**D+**	28.90	32.59	15.26	**D+ / 2.4**	-1.14	-7.37	-5.35 / 38	--	--
GI	*Cambria Value and Momentum	VAMO	**U**	23.08	N/A	N/A	**U /**	-6.53	--	--	--	--
GI	*Cohen & Steers Global Realty Maj	GRI	**C+**	42.53	46.98	32.56	**C+ / 6.1**	2.57	1.51	0.61 / 65	4.74 / 60	7.46 / 56
GEI	*Columbia Core Bond ETF	GMTB	**C+**	51.22	53.00	50.78	**C / 5.0**	-0.28	1.14	0.55 / 64	1.41 / 44	--
MUN	*Columbia Intermediate Muni Bd ET	GMMB	**C+**	53.51	54.12	52.38	**C+ / 6.0**	2.31	3.74	3.74 / 81	2.18 / 54	4.85 / 56
GR	*Columbia Large Cap Growth ETF	RPX	**A-**	46.63	48.96	39.01	**A / 9.5**	11.30	1.25	10.30 / 89	18.56 / 94	14.10 / 88
GR	*Columbia Select Large Cap Gro ET	RWG	**A-**	46.51	50.20	41.89	**A / 9.5**	10.44	-0.25	10.01 / 88	20.13 / 95	12.67 / 83
IN	*Columbia Select Large Cap Value	GVT	**B**	42.60	46.64	39.66	**B / 8.1**	6.04	-4.48	-4.31 / 41	12.51 / 83	10.42 / 68
GR	*Consumer Discretionary Sel Sec S	XLY	**A+**	78.16	81.90	66.00	**A / 9.4**	3.85	2.48	11.18 / 90	18.85 / 94	17.52 / 95
GR	*Consumer Staples Select Sector S	XLP	**A+**	50.49	51.37	43.72	**A- / 9.2**	7.06	7.03	7.95 / 85	15.31 / 90	14.94 / 91
EN	*Credit Suisse Cushing 30 MLP ETN	MLPN	**E+**	18.61	32.58	15.72	**D- / 1.5**	-12.77	-32.56	-40.02 / 4	-6.34 / 22	-1.66 / 24
GR	*Credit Suisse FI Enh Big Cap Gr	FIBG	**C**	58.55	63.25	50.92	**B+ / 8.5**	11.69	2.19	8.15 / 85	--	--
FO	*Credit Suisse FI Enhanced Europe	FIEU	**D-**	98.13	129.89	90.83	**D- / 1.5**	-1.52	-16.06	-7.82 / 31	--	--
GR	*Credit Suisse FI Large Cap Growt	FLGE	**C**	124.46	133.16	98.96	**B+ / 8.8**	12.52	1.15	10.00 / 88	--	--
PM	*Credit Suisse Gold Shs Covered C	GLDI	**E+**	10.26	12.60	10.20	**D- / 1.1**	-7.90	-10.68	-14.71 / 18	--	--
GR	*Credit Suisse L/S Liq Idx ETN	CSLS	**C**	27.76	27.91	25.25	**B / 7.6**	4.20	6.73	8.14 / 85	7.50 / 68	4.78 / 47
GR	*Credit Suisse Merger Arb Lq Id E	CSMA	**D+**	19.34	20.53	18.64	**C- / 4.0**	--	-1.88	-0.71 / 56	-0.58 / 35	-0.77 / 26
FO	*CSOP China CSI 300 A H Dynamic	HAHA	**U**	29.95	N/A	N/A	**U /**	--	--	--	--	--
FO	*CSOP FTSE China A50	AFTY	**U**	14.23	N/A	N/A	**U /**	23.45	-3.90	--	--	--
FO	*CSOP MSCI China A Intl Hedged	CNHX	**U**	31.32	N/A	N/A	**U /**	--	--	--	--	--
GL	*DB 3x Inverse Jpn Gvt Bond Fut E	JGBD	**D**	14.52	18.10	14.04	**D+ / 2.3**	-0.62	-6.47	-6.05 / 36	-8.38 / 19	--
GL	*DB 3x Japanese Govt Bd Futures E	JGBT	**C-**	27.02	27.48	24.22	**B- / 7.0**	2.82	7.77	4.65 / 78	6.74 / 66	--
USA	*DB 3x Long 25+ Year Treasury ETN	LBND	**D**	49.50	79.07	41.61	**C / 5.4**	-4.70	14.72	-14.29 / 19	3.85 / 57	19.19 / 97
USA	*DB 3x Short 25+ Year Treasury ET	SBND	**E**	4.80	5.79	3.69	**D / 1.6**	7.49	-13.63	0.21 / 62	-15.01 / 12	-28.96 / 3
GR	*DB Agriculture Double Long ETN	DAG	**E-**	3.27	5.87	3.05	**E / 0.3**	-4.98	-29.13	-37.07 / 4	-33.49 / 3	-25.00 / 4
GR	*DB Agriculture Double Short ETN	AGA	**C+**	30.15	36.02	23.24	**A+ / 9.8**	0.48	19.68	23.65 / 99	28.69 / 98	10.27 / 67
GR	*DB Agriculture Long ETN	AGF	**E**	11.00	13.88	8.80	**D- / 1.3**	-3.31	17.86	-19.37 / 14	-17.61 / 10	-12.49 / 11
GR	*DB Agriculture Short ETN	ADZ	**C+**	35.98	43.50	24.32	**A+ / 9.6**	10.03	35.52	24.07 / 99	18.21 / 94	8.53 / 59
PM	*DB Base Metals Double Long ETN	BDD	**E-**	4.10	8.30	3.71	**E / 0.5**	-8.32	-31.42	-43.40 / 3	-26.66 / 5	-25.75 / 4
PM	*DB Base Metals Double Short ETN	BOM	**C+**	25.40	27.98	13.17	**A+ / 9.9**	11.50	51.58	60.65 / 99	26.44 / 98	17.83 / 96
PM	*DB Base Metals Short ETN	BOS	**C**	29.00	31.68	21.30	**A / 9.5**	9.97	19.17	26.51 / 99	12.61 / 83	9.03 / 61
GR	*DB Commodity Double Long ETN	DYY	**E-**	3.17	6.50	3.00	**E / 0.4**	-12.54	-27.71	-22.08 / 12	-30.41 / 4	-20.81 / 5
GR	*DB Commodity Double Short ETN	DEE	**C+**	96.14	103.16	50.97	**A+ / 9.9**	33.89	65.40	59.04 / 99	49.77 / 99	20.47 / 98
GR	*DB Commodity Long ETN	DPU	**E**	8.54	12.07	6.60	**E+ / 0.6**	-14.99	-29.28	-33.56 / 6	-23.16 / 7	-14.53 / 9
GR	*DB Commodity Short ETN	DDP	**C**	57.98	59.30	36.01	**A+ / 9.8**	16.64	32.59	30.96 / 99	23.75 / 97	11.42 / 75
GR	*DB Crude Oil Double Short ETN	DTO	**C+**	158.12	169.32	56.36	**A+ / 9.9**	59.93	124.31	92.54 / 99	54.95 / 99	23.30 / 99
GR	*DB Crude Oil Long ETN	OLO	**E-**	4.63	7.98	4.45	**E / 0.4**	-21.46	-35.73	-43.16 / 3	-28.98 / 4	-19.36 / 6
GR	*DB Crude Oil Short ETN	SZO	**C+**	91.70	95.94	53.15	**A+ / 9.9**	26.73	57.32	50.63 / 99	29.87 / 98	15.26 / 92
GL	*DB FI Enhanced Global Hi Yld ETN	FIEG	**D**	111.37	131.61	92.13	**C- / 3.5**	7.22	-5.14	-3.82 / 43	--	--
GL	*DB German Bond Futures ETN	BUNL	**C-**	27.57	28.53	26.09	**C+ / 6.2**	1.44	3.96	0.80 / 66	5.17 / 62	--
PM	*DB Gold Double Long ETN	DGP	**E**	18.14	28.45	17.81	**E / 0.5**	-13.93	-19.00	-23.27 / 11	-29.09 / 4	-14.46 / 9
PM	*DB Gold Double Short ETN	DZZ	**C+**	8.87	9.08	5.97	**A+ / 9.7**	13.72	17.17	17.95 / 97	24.78 / 97	0.64 / 30
PM	*DB Gold Short ETN	DGZ	**C+**	17.10	17.26	12.40	**B+ / 8.9**	6.75	8.64	9.34 / 87	12.73 / 84	1.69 / 33
GL	*DB Inverse Japanese Govt Bd Fut	JGBS	**D**	17.50	18.67	17.10	**D+ / 2.9**	-0.97	-4.82	-4.46 / 41	-3.99 / 27	--
GR	*Deep Value ETF	DVP	**D+**	21.83	26.81	14.02	**D+ / 2.3**	3.55	-6.68	-9.50 / 27	--	--
FO	*Deutsche X-trackers CSI300 ChA H	ASHX	**U**	25.43	N/A	N/A	**U /**	--	--	--	--	--
GI	*Deutsche X-trackers DJ Hdg Intl	DBRE	**U**	22.86	N/A	N/A	**U /**	3.31	-2.00	--	--	--
EM	*Deutsche X-trackers EM Bd IR Hdg	EMIH	**U**	23.75	N/A	N/A	**U /**	2.07	-1.58	--	--	--
FO	*Deutsche X-trackers Hvst CSI300	ASHR	**D-**	27.98	55.19	27.95	**D+ / 2.9**	8.90	-14.26	-2.43 / 48	--	--
FO	*Deutsche X-trackers Hvst CSI500	ASHS	**B-**	41.46	76.61	32.27	**A+ / 9.6**	19.19	-10.99	27.16 / 99	--	--
COH	*Deutsche X-trackers HY CrpBd IR	HYIH	**U**	21.52	N/A	N/A	**U /**	-0.02	-8.71	--	--	--

* Denotes ETF Fund, N/A denotes number is not available

Incl. in Returns		RISK				NET ASSETS		VALUATION			ASSET					FUND MANAGER	
		Risk	3 Year					Premium / Discount									
Dividend Yield %	Expense Ratio	Rating/ Pts	Standard Deviation	Beta	Avg Dura-tion	NAV as of 12/31/15	Total $(Mil)	As of 12/31/15	1 Year Average	Wtd Avg P/E	Cash %	Stocks %	Bonds %	Other %	Portfolio Turnover Ratio	Manager Quality Pct	Manager Tenure (Years)
1.54	0.69	C+ / 6.6	N/A	N/A	N/A	17.92	60	-1.12	0.07	N/A	0	0	0	100	25	20	2
1.90	0.59	C+ / 6.8	N/A	N/A	N/A	28.82	213	0.28	-0.02	N/A	0	0	0	100	41	23	3
0.80	N/A	U /	N/A	N/A	N/A	23.20	N/A	-0.52	N/A	N/A	0	0	0	100	N/A	N/A	1
1.98	0.55	B- / 7.8	13.3	0.56	N/A	42.68	94	-0.35	0.14	100.3	0	100	0	0	11	45	5
2.09	0.57	B- / 7.8	3.2	0.84	N/A	50.44	5	1.55	0.12	N/A	9	0	90	1	197	69	5
2.28	0.45	B- / 7.5	5.5	1.32	N/A	53.47	5	0.07	-0.39	N/A	0	0	100	0	9	54	N/A
0.23	0.83	B- / 7.0	12.4	1.04	N/A	46.20	4	0.93	0.07	N/A	0	100	0	0	87	86	5
0.00	0.82	C+ / 6.6	14.4	1.06	N/A	45.76	11	1.64	0.02	N/A	0	99	0	1	84	86	5
2.11	0.75	C+ / 6.7	12.4	1.10	N/A	42.19	9	0.97	-0.02	N/A	0	99	0	1	36	47	12
3.33	0.15	B / 8.0	12.8	1.12	N/A	78.20	6,713	-0.05	N/A	153.7	0	100	0	0	7	82	18
5.86	0.15	B / 8.3	11.4	0.86	N/A	50.49	7,576	0.00	N/A	36.1	0	100	0	0	3	84	18
6.39	N/A	D+ / 2.5	20.2	0.80	N/A	18.63	949	-0.11	-0.07	N/A	0	0	0	100	N/A	53	6
0.00	N/A	C- / 3.4	N/A	N/A	N/A	58.29	30	0.45	-0.02	N/A	0	0	0	100	N/A	86	N/A
0.00	N/A	C- / 3.3	N/A	N/A	N/A	98.26	197	-0.13	0.18	N/A	0	0	0	100	N/A	32	3
0.00	N/A	C- / 3.2	N/A	N/A	N/A	123.56	527	0.73	-0.09	N/A	0	0	0	100	N/A	91	N/A
0.00	N/A	D+ / 2.9	N/A	N/A	N/A	10.29	29	-0.29	-0.02	N/A	0	0	0	100	N/A	42	3
0.00	N/A	C- / 4.0	7.6	0.43	N/A	27.40	13	1.31	0.09	N/A	0	0	0	100	N/A	77	6
0.00	N/A	C / 5.3	4.3	0.19	N/A	19.67	16	-1.68	-0.33	N/A	0	0	0	100	N/A	41	N/A
0.00	N/A	U /	N/A	N/A	N/A	29.86	N/A	0.30	N/A	N/A	0	0	0	100	N/A	N/A	N/A
4.69	0.99	U /	N/A	N/A	N/A	14.38	N/A	-1.04	N/A	N/A	0	0	0	100	266	N/A	N/A
0.00	N/A	U /	N/A	N/A	N/A	30.71	N/A	1.99	N/A	N/A	0	0	0	100	N/A	N/A	1
0.00	N/A	C / 4.4	5.9	-0.40	N/A	17.89	47	-18.84	-17.32	N/A	0	0	0	100	N/A	17	5
0.00	N/A	C- / 3.8	5.5	0.34	N/A	26.68	5	1.27	0.06	N/A	0	0	0	100	N/A	93	5
0.00	N/A	D+ / 2.7	33.1	2.98	N/A	49.91	32	-0.82	-0.34	N/A	0	0	0	100	N/A	27	6
0.00	N/A	E+ / 0.9	35.5	-3.29	N/A	4.80	54	0.00	0.01	N/A	0	0	0	100	N/A	25	6
0.00	0.75	D- / 1.1	35.0	0.73	N/A	3.28	87	-0.30	8.00	N/A	0	0	0	100	N/A	1	8
0.00	0.75	C- / 3.5	35.4	-0.44	N/A	30.32	4	-0.56	-0.14	N/A	0	0	0	100	N/A	99	8
0.00	0.75	D / 2.0	31.8	-0.09	N/A	11.10	5	-0.90	-0.40	N/A	0	0	0	100	N/A	9	8
0.00	0.75	C- / 3.3	24.3	0.31	N/A	33.62	3	7.02	1.05	N/A	0	0	0	100	N/A	97	8
0.00	0.75	D- / 1.0	26.4	0.45	N/A	4.09	23	0.24	0.64	N/A	0	0	0	100	N/A	6	8
0.00	0.75	C- / 3.4	26.9	-0.42	N/A	24.27	2	4.66	-0.19	N/A	0	0	0	100	N/A	98	8
0.00	0.75	C- / 3.0	31.3	0.40	N/A	29.37	3	-1.26	-0.93	N/A	0	0	0	100	N/A	98	8
0.00	0.75	E- / 0.1	35.8	0.68	N/A	1.83	43	73.22	32.99	N/A	0	0	0	100	N/A	1	8
0.00	0.75	C- / 3.9	32.1	-0.85	N/A	97.81	6	-1.71	-0.44	N/A	0	0	0	100	N/A	99	8
0.00	0.75	D / 1.6	27.8	0.52	N/A	8.19	7	4.27	-0.52	N/A	0	0	0	100	N/A	4	8
.00	0.75	D+ / 2.9	27.3	-0.64	N/A	57.87	10	0.19	-0.99	N/A	0	0	0	100	N/A	99	8
.00	0.75	C- / 3.1	64.0	-1.12	N/A	159.60	97	-0.93	0.05	N/A	0	0	0	100	N/A	99	8
.00	0.75	E+ / 0.8	27.2	0.82	N/A	4.62	15	0.22	0.28	N/A	0	0	0	100	N/A	1	8
.00	0.75	C- / 3.9	31.6	-0.70	N/A	92.83	14	-1.22	-0.51	N/A	0	0	0	100	N/A	99	8
.00	N/A	C / 4.5	N/A	N/A	N/A	111.73	178	-0.32	0.21	N/A	0	0	0	100	N/A	29	N/A
.00	N/A	C- / 3.9	5.2	0.03	N/A	27.38	9	0.69	0.01	N/A	0	0	0	100	N/A	89	5
.00	N/A	D- / 1.5	33.8	1.88	N/A	18.18	165	-0.22	0.10	N/A	0	0	0	100	N/A	23	8
.00	N/A	C- / 3.2	32.7	-1.79	N/A	8.86	60	0.11	-0.07	N/A	0	0	0	100	N/A	37	8
.00	N/A	C- / 4.0	15.9	-0.89	N/A	17.09	18	0.06	-0.05	N/A	0	0	0	100	N/A	59	8
.00	N/A	C- / 3.6	3.2	-0.17	N/A	14.53	39	20.44	19.07	N/A	0	0	0	100	N/A	34	5
.06	0.80	C+ / 6.8	N/A	N/A	N/A	21.83	N/A	0.00	0.07	N/A	0	0	0	100	62	14	N/A
.47	N/A	U /	N/A	N/A	N/A	25.30	N/A	0.51	N/A	N/A	0	0	0	100	N/A	N/A	1
.45	N/A	U /	N/A	N/A	N/A	22.85	N/A	0.04	N/A	N/A	0	0	0	100	N/A	N/A	1
.59	N/A	U /	N/A	N/A	N/A	23.58	N/A	0.72	N/A	N/A	0	0	0	100	N/A	N/A	N/A
.13	0.80	C- / 3.1	N/A	N/A	N/A	28.09	N/A	-0.39	-0.41	N/A	0	0	0	100	58	54	N/A
.41	0.80	C / 4.7	N/A	N/A	N/A	41.99	12	-1.26	-0.14	N/A	0	0	0	100	131	99	N/A
.78	N/A	U /	N/A	N/A	N/A	21.66	N/A	-0.65	N/A	N/A	0	0	0	100	N/A	N/A	N/A

Denotes ETF Fund, N/A denotes number is not available

99 Pct = Best
0 Pct = Worst

Fund Type	Fund Name	Ticker Symbol	Overall Investment Rating	PRICE: Price As of 12/31/15	PRICE: 52 Week High	PRICE: 52 Week Low	PERFORMANCE: Performance Rating/Pts	% Total Return Through 12/31/15: 3 Mo	6 Mo	1Yr/Pct	Annualized: 3Yr/Pct	Annualized: 5Yr/Pct
COI	*Deutsche X-trackers Iv GrdBd IR	IGIH	**U**	23.93	N/A	N/A	**U** /	2.35	-0.85	--	--	--
FO	*Deutsche X-trackers Jp JPX-N 400	JPN	**U**	23.65	N/A	N/A	**U** /	7.20	-4.67	--	--	--
FO	*Deutsche X-trackers Jp JPX-N400	JPNH	**U**	23.40	N/A	N/A	**U** /	9.14	--	--	--	--
FO	*Deutsche X-trackers MSCI All Ch	CN	**C-**	31.01	50.88	28.93	**C-** / **4.1**	10.79	-11.94	1.29 / 69	--	--
FO	*Deutsche X-trackers MSCI AP xJp	DBAP	**D+**	22.01	32.10	20.00	**D** / **1.9**	1.45	-11.67	-8.38 / 30	--	--
FO	*Deutsche X-trackers MSCI Aus Hdg	DBAU	**U**	24.43	N/A	N/A	**U** /	6.39	--	--	--	--
FO	*Deutsche X-trackers MSCI AW xUS	HDAW	**U**	22.67	N/A	N/A	**U** /	-0.49	--	--	--	--
FO	*Deutsche X-trackers MSCI AW xUS	DBAW	**C-**	23.13	27.70	21.62	**C-** / **3.4**	2.47	-7.22	-0.06 / 60	--	--
FO	*Deutsche X-trackers MSCI Br Hdg	DBBR	**D-**	8.04	14.43	8.03	**D-** / **1.0**	-12.80	-24.86	-21.88 / 12	-16.51 / 11	--
FO	*Deutsche X-trackers MSCI EAFE Hd	DBEF	**B+**	27.16	31.36	24.64	**B-** / **7.4**	3.09	-5.58	3.73 / 76	9.41 / 73	--
FO	*Deutsche X-trackers MSCI EAFE HD	HDEF	**U**	22.98	N/A	N/A	**U** /	2.34	--	--	--	--
FO	*Deutsche X-trackers MSCI EAFE SC	DBES	**U**	25.34	N/A	N/A	**U** /	3.23	--	--	--	--
EM	*Deutsche X-trackers MSCI EM Hdg	DBEM	**C-**	18.28	23.70	16.63	**D** / **2.2**	-2.62	-13.17	-13.09 / 20	-6.72 / 22	--
FO	*Deutsche X-trackers MSCI Eu Hdg	DBEU	**C+**	25.85	30.42	21.05	**C** / **5.2**	2.57	-4.29	3.80 / 76	--	--
FO	*Deutsche X-trackers MSCI Eur Hdg	DBEZ	**C**	26.16	30.84	23.42	**C+** / **6.9**	4.50	-3.66	9.93 / 88	--	--
FO	*Deutsche X-trackers MSCI Eur HDY	HDEZ	**U**	24.38	N/A	N/A	**U** /	7.20	--	--	--	--
FO	*Deutsche X-trackers MSCI Ger Hdg	DBGR	**B**	24.01	29.80	21.03	**B-** / **7.4**	8.53	-5.04	6.72 / 83	8.23 / 70	--
FO	*Deutsche X-trackers MSCI Jp Hdg	DBJP	**A**	38.09	44.82	33.72	**A-** / **9.2**	4.77	-7.84	4.69 / 78	17.62 / 93	--
EM	*Deutsche X-trackers MSCI Mx Hdg	DBMX	**C-**	20.22	26.20	20.14	**C-** / **3.2**	-0.47	-5.51	-0.87 / 55	--	--
FO	*Deutsche X-trackers MSCI SKor Hd	DBKO	**C-**	22.41	25.60	19.57	**C-** / **3.0**	1.72	-5.40	-3.32 / 45	--	--
FO	*Deutsche X-trackers MSCI Sth Eu	DBSE	**U**	22.27	N/A	N/A	**U** /	--	--	--	--	--
FO	*Deutsche X-trackers MSCI UK Hdg	DBUK	**D+**	22.05	26.43	20.49	**C-** / **3.3**	3.90	-5.22	-3.33 / 45	--	--
MUN	*Deutsche X-trackers Muni Inf Rev	RVNU	**B+**	26.29	27.05	24.90	**B+** / **8.3**	3.93	5.29	4.19 / 82	--	--
GL	*Deutsche X-trackers S&P Hdg Gl I	DBIF	**U**	21.47	N/A	N/A	**U** /	-1.45	-8.53	--	--	--
GR	*Diamond Hill Valuation Weighted	DHVW	**U**	23.51	N/A	N/A	**U** /	5.19	-1.04	--	--	--
GI	*Direxion All Cap Insider Sentime	KNOW	**A-**	71.15	73.34	44.13	**A-** / **9.2**	5.56	0.16	3.83 / 76	16.98 / 92	--
FO	*Direxion Brazil Bull 3X	BRZU	**E-**	11.63	98.20	11.50	**E-** / **0.0**	-32.38	-80.11	-85.43 / 0	--	--
GL	*Direxion Daily 20+ Yr Treas Bear	TYBS	**D+**	22.61	24.48	21.08	**D+** / **2.7**	2.06	-6.59	-1.97 / 50	-6.32 / 22	--
USA	*Direxion Daily 20+ Yr Treas Bear	TMV	**E**	27.98	36.74	23.42	**E+** / **0.9**	4.83	-20.35	-8.92 / 29	-21.58 / 7	-34.26 / 2
USA	*Direxion Daily 20+ Yr Treas Bull	TMF	**C-**	74.23	113.35	64.26	**C** / **5.0**	-9.45	11.62	-16.30 / 16	3.75 / 56	18.46 / 96
USA	*Direxion Daily 7-10 Yr Trs Bear	TYO	**D+**	16.66	19.00	15.73	**D** / **1.9**	3.80	-9.16	-10.04 / 25	-10.92 / 16	-18.34 / 6
USA	*Direxion Daily 7-10 Yr Trs Bull	TYD	**D+**	44.21	51.96	40.19	**C** / **5.2**	-7.28	3.48	-0.44 / 58	2.48 / 51	11.78 / 77
FO	*Direxion Daily CSI300 Ch A Shs B	CHAU	**U**	23.22	N/A	N/A	**U** /	21.67	-31.70	--	--	--
FO	*Direxion Daily CSI300 Ch A Shs B	CHAD	**U**	42.14	N/A	N/A	**U** /	-14.02	-11.19	--	--	--
GR	*Direxion Daily Cyber Security Bl	HAKK	**U**	36.65	N/A	N/A	**U** /	1.66	--	--	--	--
GR	*Direxion Daily Cyber Security Br	HAKD	**U**	43.71	N/A	N/A	**U** /	-9.61	--	--	--	--
FO	*Direxion Daily FTSE Ch Bear 3x E	YANG	**E**	99.11	152.53	48.80	**E** / **0.4**	-0.24	45.36	-12.53 / 21	-40.49 / 2	-35.03 / 2
FO	*Direxion Daily FTSE Ch Bull 3x E	YINN	**E-**	17.74	68.50	14.80	**D-** / **1.3**	-11.26	-59.25	-50.58 / 1	-4.76 / 25	-17.54 / 6
GL	*Direxion Daily FTSE Em Mkt Bl 1.	LLEM	**U**	19.35	N/A	N/A	**U** /	1.60	-21.70	--	--	--
FO	*Direxion Daily FTSE Europe Bull	EURL	**D-**	24.30	39.52	21.88	**E+** / **0.7**	-2.13	-25.32	-15.01 / 18	--	--
PM	*Direxion Daily Gold Mnrs Id Bear	DUST	**E**	16.52	39.99	11.07	**D+** / **2.3**	-40.02	-9.33	-40.66 / 3	0.82 / 40	-3.88 / 21
PM	*Direxion Daily Gold Mnrs Id Bull	NUGT	**E-**	24.26	214.00	21.70	**E-** / **0.0**	-27.41	-69.22	-79.91 / 0	-83.17 / 0	-72.68 / 0
HL	*Direxion Daily Healthcare Bull 3	CURE	**C-**	33.40	43.77	16.14	**A+** / **9.9**	15.53	-16.14	6.24 / 82	67.86 / 99	--
GR	*Direxion Daily Hmbldrs and Sup B	CLAW	**U**	43.11	N/A	N/A	**U** /	-18.57	--	--	--	--
GR	*Direxion Daily Hmbldrs and Sup B	NAIL	**U**	28.91	N/A	N/A	**U** /	5.21	--	--	--	--
EM	*Direxion Daily India Bull 3X	INDL	**E-**	13.47	27.35	10.70	**D-** / **1.0**	-9.90	-35.46	-36.19 / 5	-13.70 / 13	-21.70 / 5
FO	*Direxion Daily Japan Bull 3X	JPNL	**D+**	45.47	64.75	35.50	**C+** / **6.0**	12.49	-21.81	13.76 / 94	--	--
FO	*Direxion Daily Latin Amer Bull 3	LBJ	**E-**	12.00	51.12	11.95	**E-** / **0.0**	-24.48	-67.04	-72.65 / 0	-58.11 / 1	-49.03 / 0
GR	*Direxion Daily Mid Cap Bear 3X	MIDZ	**E+**	45.09	62.51	37.67	**E** / **0.4**	-7.52	10.10	-8.51 / 30	-36.58 / 2	-39.37 / 1
GR	*Direxion Daily Mid Cap Bull 3X	MIDU	**C**	20.81	29.53	12.98	**A+** / **9.6**	1.41	-22.67	-14.79 / 18	27.36 / 98	20.73 / 98
GR	*Direxion Daily MSCI Eu Cu Hdg Bl	HEGE	**U**	33.00	N/A	N/A	**U** /	0.99	-14.81	--	--	--
GR	*Direxion Daily MSCI Jp Cu Hdg Bl	HEGJ	**U**	31.60	N/A	N/A	**U** /	8.11	-18.33	--	--	--

* Denotes ETF Fund, N/A denotes number is not available

Incl. in Returns		RISK	3 Year			NET ASSETS		VALUATION			ASSET					FUND MANAGER	
								Premium / Discount									
ividend Yield %	Expense Ratio	Risk Rating/ Pts	Standard Deviation	Beta	Avg Dura- tion	NAV as of 12/31/15	Total $(Mil)	As of 12/31/15	1 Year Average	Wtd Avg P/E	Cash %	Stocks %	Bonds %	Other %	Portfolio Turnover Ratio	Manager Quality Pct	Manager Tenure (Years)
3.76	N/A	U /	N/A	N/A	N/A	23.61	N/A	1.36	N/A	N/A	0	0	0	100	N/A	N/A	N/A
0.97	N/A	U /	N/A	N/A	N/A	23.84	N/A	-0.80	N/A	N/A	0	0	0	100	N/A	N/A	1
2.20	N/A	U /	N/A	N/A	N/A	23.20	N/A	0.86	N/A	N/A	0	0	0	100	N/A	N/A	1
4.00	0.26	C+ / 5.9	N/A	N/A	N/A	31.11	6	-0.32	-0.11	N/A	0	0	0	100	20	80	2
2.26	0.60	B- / 7.4	N/A	N/A	N/A	22.28	7	-1.21	0.19	N/A	0	0	0	100	19	22	3
0.41	N/A	U /	N/A	N/A	N/A	24.26	N/A	0.70	N/A	N/A	0	0	0	100	N/A	N/A	1
6.33	N/A	U /	N/A	N/A	N/A	22.76	N/A	-0.40	N/A	N/A	0	0	0	100	N/A	N/A	1
5.25	0.40	C+ / 6.2	N/A	N/A	N/A	23.03	5	0.43	0.62	N/A	0	0	0	100	24	69	2
8.73	0.60	C- / 4.0	18.4	0.80	N/A	8.28	4	-2.90	-0.08	N/A	1	97	0	2	141	7	5
1.63	0.35	B / 8.1	11.6	0.82	N/A	27.38	661	-0.80	0.17	N/A	0	95	0	5	12	91	5
9.97	N/A	U /	N/A	N/A	N/A	22.92	N/A	0.26	N/A	N/A	0	0	0	100	N/A	N/A	1
3.05	N/A	U /	N/A	N/A	N/A	24.50	N/A	3.43	N/A	N/A	0	0	0	100	N/A	N/A	1
1.71	0.65	B- / 7.6	11.3	0.72	N/A	18.44	30	-0.87	0.02	N/A	0	93	0	7	58	62	5
1.49	0.45	B- / 7.9	N/A	N/A	N/A	25.97	320	-0.46	0.23	N/A	0	0	0	100	13	89	3
1.23	N/A	C / 4.9	N/A	N/A	N/A	26.28	N/A	-0.46	0.41	N/A	0	0	0	100	N/A	95	2
3.42	N/A	U /	N/A	N/A	N/A	24.36	N/A	0.08	N/A	N/A	0	0	0	100	N/A	N/A	1
0.45	0.45	B- / 7.3	16.6	0.64	N/A	24.35	42	-1.40	0.09	N/A	0	97	0	3	20	88	5
2.36	0.45	B- / 7.6	17.9	0.94	N/A	38.60	568	-1.32	0.05	N/A	0	96	0	4	14	96	5
5.63	0.50	B- / 7.1	N/A	N/A	N/A	20.42	5	-0.98	0.16	N/A	0	0	0	100	22	82	2
0.13	0.58	B / 8.2	N/A	N/A	N/A	22.66	5	-1.10	-0.10	N/A	0	0	0	100	287	43	2
7.80	N/A	U /	N/A	N/A	N/A	21.97	N/A	1.37	N/A	N/A	0	0	0	100	N/A	N/A	1
1.44	0.45	C+ / 5.9	N/A	N/A	N/A	21.89	5	0.73	0.56	N/A	0	0	0	100	19	52	3
2.85	0.30	B- / 7.6	N/A	N/A	N/A	26.26	19	0.11	0.24	N/A	0	0	0	100	4	48	3
2.90	N/A	U /	N/A	N/A	N/A	21.39	N/A	0.37	N/A	N/A	0	0	0	100	N/A	N/A	1
1.67	N/A	U /	N/A	N/A	N/A	23.46	N/A	0.21	N/A	N/A	0	0	0	100	N/A	N/A	1
.33	0.66	B- / 7.2	10.2	0.88	N/A	70.92	23	0.32	0.06	N/A	0	100	0	0	835	89	5
.00	0.95	E- / 0.1	N/A	N/A	N/A	11.56	19	0.61	0.08	N/A	0	0	0	100	229	N/A	3
.00	0.65	C+ / 5.6	11.8	0.12	N/A	22.58	9	0.13	0.05	N/A	100	0	0	0	N/A	27	5
.00	0.90	D- / 1.5	36.2	-3.37	N/A	27.88	593	0.36	0.02	N/A	100	0	0	0	N/A	12	N/A
.00	0.95	C / 5.1	36.8	3.42	N/A	75.11	47	-1.17	-0.03	N/A	24	0	75	1	741	22	N/A
.00	0.95	C+ / 6.3	16.5	-1.48	N/A	16.71	57	-0.30	0.01	N/A	100	0	0	0	N/A	23	N/A
.00	0.95	C- / 3.1	19.9	1.46	N/A	44.74	4	-1.18	-0.21	N/A	15	0	84	1	N/A	50	N/A
.00	N/A	U /	N/A	N/A	N/A	23.15	N/A	0.30	N/A	N/A	0	0	0	100	N/A	N/A	1
.00	N/A	U /	N/A	N/A	N/A	42.21	N/A	-0.17	N/A	N/A	0	0	0	100	N/A	N/A	1
.00	N/A	U /	N/A	N/A	N/A	35.62	N/A	2.89	N/A	N/A	0	0	0	100	N/A	N/A	1
.00	N/A	U /	N/A	N/A	N/A	41.97	N/A	4.15	N/A	N/A	0	0	0	100	N/A	N/A	1
.00	0.95	D- / 1.5	64.5	-2.64	N/A	99.13	19	-0.02	N/A	N/A	100	0	0	0	N/A	2	7
.00	0.95	E- / 0.2	69.1	2.84	N/A	17.73	95	0.06	0.02	N/A	0	100	0	0	103	10	7
.64	N/A	U /	N/A	N/A	N/A	20.27	N/A	-4.54	N/A	N/A	0	0	0	100	N/A	N/A	1
.00	0.95	C / 4.3	N/A	N/A	N/A	24.31	9	-0.04	0.01	N/A	0	0	0	100	N/A	10	2
.00	0.95	E- / 0.1	N/A	-5.76	N/A	16.26	184	1.60	-0.25	N/A	100	0	0	0	N/A	N/A	6
.00	0.95	D / 1.8	N/A	5.58	N/A	24.36	698	-0.41	0.09	N/A	0	100	0	0	435	N/A	6
.00	0.95	E- / 0.2	39.5	3.03	N/A	33.39	129	0.03	0.01	N/A	75	24	0	1	46	96	5
.00	N/A	U /	N/A	N/A	N/A	44.34	N/A	-2.77	N/A	N/A	0	0	0	100	N/A	N/A	1
.00	N/A	U /	N/A	N/A	N/A	28.10	N/A	2.88	N/A	N/A	0	0	0	100	N/A	N/A	1
.00	0.95	E- / 0.2	63.4	2.13	N/A	13.38	75	0.67	0.01	N/A	67	32	0	1	195	75	6
.00	0.95	C- / 3.4	N/A	N/A	N/A	45.34	7	0.29	0.05	N/A	0	0	0	100	N/A	97	8
.00	0.95	E- / 0.1	70.9	3.50	N/A	11.94	18	0.50	0.22	N/A	60	39	0	1	64	N/A	7
.00	0.95	C- / 3.0	36.0	-2.89	N/A	45.19	11	-0.22	N/A	N/A	100	0	0	0	N/A	20	7
.00	0.95	D / 1.7	37.6	3.04	N/A	20.89	63	-0.38	-0.03	N/A	73	26	0	1	100	11	7
.22	N/A	U /	N/A	N/A	N/A	34.18	N/A	-3.45	N/A	N/A	0	0	0	100	N/A	N/A	1
04	N/A	U /	N/A	N/A	N/A	31.77	N/A	-0.54	N/A	N/A	0	0	0	100	N/A	N/A	1

Denotes ETF Fund, N/A denotes number is not available

Fund Type	Fund Name (99 Pct = Best, 0 Pct = Worst)	Ticker Symbol	Overall Investment Rating	PRICE: Price As of 12/31/15	52 Week High	52 Week Low	PERFORMANCE: Performance Rating/Pts	% Total Return Through 12/31/15: 3 Mo	6 Mo	1Yr/Pct	Annualized 3Yr/Pct	Annualized 5Yr/Pct
GR	*Direxion Daily Nat Gas Rel Bull	GASL	E-	6.14	247.00	4.81	E- / 0.0	-71.36	-92.86	-97.14 / 0	-82.35 / 0	-70.79 / 0
GR	*Direxion Daily Pharma and Med Bl	PILL	U	35.88	N/A	N/A	U /	11.43	--	--	--	--
GR	*Direxion Daily Pharma and Med Br	PILS	U	38.13	N/A	N/A	U /	-20.01	--	--	--	--
GR	*Direxion Daily Real Estate Bear	DRV	E	19.54	30.76	18.78	E / 0.3	-19.49	-27.69	-21.47 / 12	-37.14 / 2	-44.37 / 1
GR	*Direxion Daily Real Estate Bull	DRN	C-	75.55	105.07	52.90	A+ / 9.6	15.03	15.95	-8.26 / 30	22.83 / 96	23.17 / 98
GR	*Direxion Daily Regional Banks Bl	DPST	U	32.80	N/A	N/A	U /	17.90	--	--	--	--
GR	*Direxion Daily Regional Banks Br	WDRW	U	35.94	N/A	N/A	U /	-18.22	--	--	--	--
GR	*Direxion Daily Retail Bull 3X	RETL	C-	37.64	40.48	15.18	A+ / 9.9	16.24	21.97	47.33 / 99	62.27 / 99	55.49 / 99
GI	*Direxion Daily Russia Bear 3x	RUSS	E-	37.52	126.32	24.08	D- / 1.1	-9.52	10.29	-65.78 / 1	-12.20 / 15	--
FO	*Direxion Daily Russia Bull 3x	RUSL	E	11.17	37.59	10.29	E- / 0.0	-15.64	-51.58	-34.29 / 6	-63.71 / 0	--
GL	*Direxion Daily S&P Biotech Bear	LABD	U	31.09	N/A	N/A	U /	-35.20	-7.14	--	--	--
GL	*Direxion Daily S&P Biotech Bull	LABU	U	21.10	N/A	N/A	U /	11.58	-52.58	--	--	--
GR	*Direxion Daily S&P O&G E&P Bear	DRIP	U	83.57	N/A	N/A	U /	13.75	62.43	--	--	--
GR	*Direxion Daily S&P O&G E&P Bull	GUSH	U	6.63	N/A	N/A	U /	-44.93	-77.68	--	--	--
IN	*Direxion Daily Semiconductor Bea	SOXS	E-	40.17	87.25	35.84	E- / 0.1	-29.25	-12.92	-25.17 / 10	-55.92 / 1	-48.55 / 1
IN	*Direxion Daily Semiconductor Bul	SOXL	C-	26.77	42.43	15.06	A+ / 9.9	26.27	-16.45	-20.58 / 13	53.39 / 99	14.25 / 89
GR	*Direxion Daily Small Cap Bear 3x	TZA	E-	45.00	56.44	35.24	E / 0.4	-11.73	14.93	-7.72 / 32	-38.57 / 2	-42.82 / 1
GR	*Direxion Daily Small Cap Bull 1.	LLSC	U	24.99	N/A	N/A	U /	-5.29	-8.33	--	--	--
GR	*Direxion Daily Small Cap Bull 2x	SMLL	E-	29.37	37.85	26.71	D / 1.6	7.70	-16.91	-11.17 / 23	--	--
GR	*Direxion Daily Small Cap Bull 3x	TNA	C	63.53	99.00	55.56	A- / 9.1	3.76	-27.92	-20.16 / 13	22.60 / 96	12.16 / 80
GR	*Direxion Daily Technology Bear 3	TECS	E-	31.10	54.90	28.37	E- / 0.1	-23.32	-21.81	-31.49 / 7	-43.75 / 1	-41.21 / 1
GR	*Direxion Daily Technology Bull 3	TECL	C-	36.43	41.03	22.00	A+ / 9.9	21.35	3.49	4.98 / 79	41.48 / 99	24.86 / 99
GR	*Direxion Daily Tot Bond Mkt Bear	SAGG	C-	32.99	33.51	32.50	C- / 3.5	1.17	-1.20	-1.23 / 54	-2.46 / 29	--
GR	*Direxion Daily Total Market Bear	TOTS	D	18.92	21.25	18.57	D- / 1.5	-6.43	-0.58	-4.54 / 40	-14.24 / 13	--
GL	*Direxion Developed Markets Bear	DPK	D-	30.91	40.68	23.94	D- / 1.0	-7.04	13.06	-15.20 / 18	-21.93 / 7	-29.06 / 3
GL	*Direxion Developed Markets Bull	DZK	D	49.92	79.02	43.03	C- / 3.8	2.11	-25.50	-11.86 / 22	2.43 / 50	-2.71 / 22
GL	*Direxion Emerging Markets Bear 3	EDZ	C-	46.98	72.94	24.49	B / 7.8	3.46	47.55	20.96 / 98	3.04 / 53	-14.66 / 9
GL	*Direxion Emerging Markets Bull 3	EDC	E-	11.51	31.41	9.47	E- / 0.2	-13.13	-50.22	-47.92 / 2	-32.88 / 3	-29.57 / 3
EN	*Direxion Energy Bear 3x Shares	ERY	D-	29.31	40.52	15.75	C- / 3.7	2.34	36.70	41.46 / 99	-11.55 / 15	-26.23 / 4
EN	*Direxion Energy Bull 3x Shares	ERX	E	23.43	68.79	21.28	E / 0.4	-19.10	-52.09	-61.81 / 1	-24.07 / 6	-16.82 / 7
FS	*Direxion Financial Bear 3x Share	FAZ	E-	41.18	60.00	38.00	E- / 0.2	-18.71	-8.73	-18.62 / 15	-42.30 / 1	-43.57 / 1
FS	*Direxion Financial Bull 3x Share	FAS	C-	29.07	35.73	23.25	A+ / 9.8	14.00	-9.78	-8.83 / 29	37.58 / 99	19.19 / 97
GR	*Direxion iBillionaire Index ETF	IBLN	C-	24.34	26.74	20.20	C- / 3.4	6.15	-3.35	-5.24 / 38	--	--
GR	*Direxion Jr Gold Miners Idx Bear	JDST	E-	29.74	73.00	20.08	E- / 0.2	-9.16	-15.99	-45.81 / 2	--	--
GR	*Direxion Jr Gold Miners Idx Bull	JNUG	E-	31.05	242.50	27.58	E- / 0.0	-26.38	-65.07	-77.20 / 0	--	--
IN	*Direxion NASDAQ-100 Eq Weighted	QQQE	A-	64.92	68.02	32.84	A / 9.3	6.41	-0.70	2.61 / 73	18.55 / 94	--
GR	*Direxion S&P 500 Bear 3X Shares	SPXS	E-	16.92	25.25	15.80	E / 0.3	-17.38	-8.79	-18.14 / 15	-39.75 / 2	-39.73 / 1
GR	*Direxion S&P 500 Bull 1.25X Shar	LLSP	U	26.12	N/A	N/A	U /	9.79	-0.65	--	--	--
GR	*Direxion S&P 500 Bull 3X Shares	SPXL	C	82.88	97.55	64.00	A+ / 9.8	14.13	-7.47	-5.43 / 37	37.78 / 99	27.58 / 99
GI	*Direxion S&P 500 Vol Response Sh	VSPY	B	54.60	60.95	49.39	C+ / 6.8	1.74	-6.67	-6.95 / 33	9.33 / 73	--
FO	*Direxion South Korea Bull 3X	KORU	E-	22.74	48.05	14.33	E / 0.4	2.77	-30.54	-29.48 / 8	--	--
GL	*Direxion Value Line Conservative	VLLV	U	25.95	N/A	N/A	U /	8.53	2.07	--	--	--
GR	*Direxion Value Line Mid & Lg Cap	VLML	U	22.98	N/A	N/A	U /	3.69	-5.68	--	--	--
GR	*Direxion Value Line Sm & MdCp HD	VLSM	U	22.66	N/A	N/A	U /	1.56	-8.16	--	--	--
EN	*Direxion Zacks MLP High Inc Shar	ZMLP	E+	17.39	34.82	15.24	E- / 0.1	-20.63	-34.43	-43.51 / 3	--	--
FO	*EGShares Beyond BRICs ETF	BBRC	D	14.50	20.96	14.42	D- / 1.5	-6.33	-21.02	-22.60 / 11	-10.84 / 16	--
EM	*EGShares EM Core ex China	XCEM	U	18.50	N/A	N/A	U /	1.47	--	--	--	--
GI	*EGShares EM Quality Dividend	HILO	D	11.47	15.57	11.33	D- / 1.2	-4.81	-20.19	-18.52 / 15	-14.59 / 12	--
FO	*EGShares Emer Mrkts Dom Demand E	EMDD	D+	17.73	24.83	17.47	D / 2.1	-6.41	-20.63	-17.76 / 15	-5.69 / 24	--
EM	*EGShares Emerging Markets Cons E	ECON	D+	21.26	28.43	20.00	D / 2.1	-4.02	-17.85	-13.80 / 19	-6.69 / 22	-0.64 / 26
EM	*EGShares Emerging Markets Core E	EMCR	D+	16.20	22.74	15.62	D / 1.9	-5.26	-19.60	-19.52 / 14	-7.80 / 20	--
GI	*EGShares India Consumer ETF	INCO	C+	32.11	37.74	27.37	C+ / 6.9	0.97	-7.84	-1.95 / 51	9.08 / 72	--

* Denotes ETF Fund, N/A denotes number is not availabl

		RISK				NET ASSETS		VALUATION			ASSET					FUND MANAGER	
Incl. in Returns		Risk Rating/ Pts	3 Year		Avg Dura- tion	NAV as of 12/31/15	Total $(Mil)	Premium / Discount		Wtd Avg P/E	Cash %	Stocks %	Bonds %	Other %	Portfolio Turnover Ratio	Manager Quality Pct	Manager Tenure (Years)
Dividend Yield %	Expense Ratio		Standard Deviation	Beta				As of 12/31/15	1 Year Average								
0.00	0.95	**D / 1.8**	N/A	4.56	N/A	6.19	21	-0.81	0.16	N/A	42	57	0	1	133	N/A	6
0.00	N/A	**U /**	N/A	N/A	N/A	35.95	N/A	-0.19	N/A	N/A	0	0	0	100	N/A	N/A	1
0.00	N/A	**U /**	N/A	N/A	N/A	38.22	N/A	-0.24	N/A	N/A	0	0	0	100	N/A	N/A	1
0.00	0.95	**D+ / 2.4**	45.5	-1.27	N/A	19.58	16	-0.20	N/A	N/A	100	0	0	0	N/A	4	7
0.00	0.95	**D- / 1.4**	47.0	1.43	N/A	75.54	78	0.01	-0.03	N/A	72	27	0	1	167	81	7
0.00	N/A	**U /**	N/A	N/A	N/A	32.14	N/A	2.05	N/A	N/A	0	0	0	100	N/A	N/A	1
0.00	N/A	**U /**	N/A	N/A	N/A	37.48	N/A	-4.11	N/A	N/A	0	0	0	100	N/A	N/A	1
0.00	0.95	**E- / 0.1**	40.5	2.96	N/A	37.53	15	0.29	0.14	N/A	65	34	0	1	2	94	6
0.00	0.95	**E- / 0.2**	85.9	-2.73	N/A	37.43	24	0.24	-0.04	N/A	100	0	0	0	N/A	99	5
0.00	0.95	**D / 1.8**	N/A	4.03	N/A	11.20	145	-0.27	0.05	N/A	54	45	0	1	72	N/A	5
0.00	N/A	**U /**	N/A	N/A	N/A	31.11	N/A	-0.06	N/A	N/A	0	0	0	100	N/A	N/A	1
0.00	N/A	**U /**	N/A	N/A	N/A	21.15	N/A	-0.24	N/A	N/A	0	0	0	100	N/A	N/A	1
0.00	N/A	**U /**	N/A	N/A	N/A	83.97	N/A	-0.48	N/A	N/A	0	0	0	100	N/A	N/A	1
0.00	N/A	**U /**	N/A	N/A	N/A	6.63	N/A	0.00	N/A	N/A	0	0	0	100	N/A	N/A	1
0.00	0.95	**D / 1.7**	50.1	-3.43	N/A	40.21	27	-0.10	-0.04	N/A	100	0	0	0	N/A	2	6
0.00	0.95	**E- / 0.2**	52.9	3.66	N/A	26.75	114	0.07	0.01	N/A	59	40	0	1	8	29	6
0.00	0.95	**E+ / 0.9**	43.5	-3.12	N/A	44.80	814	0.45	0.01	N/A	100	0	0	0	N/A	20	8
0.43	N/A	**U /**	N/A	N/A	N/A	24.41	N/A	2.38	N/A	N/A	0	0	0	100	N/A	N/A	N/A
1.36	N/A	**E- / 0.1**	N/A	N/A	N/A	29.14	2	0.79	-1.16	N/A	0	0	0	100	N/A	13	N/A
0.00	0.95	**D+ / 2.7**	44.8	3.23	N/A	63.83	990	-0.47	-0.10	N/A	90	9	0	1	N/A	7	8
0.00	0.95	**D- / 1.1**	34.2	-2.84	N/A	31.09	15	0.03	0.01	N/A	100	0	0	0	N/A	8	8
0.00	0.95	**D- / 1.0**	36.3	3.02	N/A	36.43	164	0.00	0.01	N/A	71	28	0	1	21	26	7
0.00	0.65	**B- / 7.5**	3.3	0.03	N/A	32.91	3	0.24	-0.18	N/A	100	0	0	0	N/A	44	5
0.00	0.65	**C+ / 6.5**	11.1	-1.02	N/A	19.06	2	-0.73	0.25	N/A	100	0	0	0	N/A	47	5
0.00	0.95	**C- / 4.0**	38.0	-2.85	N/A	30.97	6	-0.19	0.03	N/A	100	0	0	0	N/A	16	8
0.00	0.95	**C- / 3.3**	39.8	3.00	N/A	49.89	47	0.06	0.02	N/A	54	46	0	0	32	14	8
0.00	0.95	**D / 1.8**	45.2	-2.63	N/A	46.94	119	0.09	-0.02	N/A	100	0	0	0	N/A	97	8
0.00	0.95	**D- / 1.0**	47.2	2.77	N/A	11.51	284	0.00	0.02	N/A	82	17	0	1	116	1	11
0.00	0.95	**D+ / 2.7**	55.2	-2.82	N/A	29.34	47	-0.10	N/A	N/A	100	0	0	0	N/A	5	8
0.00	0.95	**D / 1.8**	59.6	3.04	N/A	23.48	187	-0.21	0.01	N/A	60	39	0	1	196	14	8
0.00	0.95	**D- / 1.4**	33.7	-2.90	N/A	41.16	345	0.05	-0.05	N/A	100	0	0	0	N/A	10	8
0.00	0.95	**D- / 1.0**	35.9	3.08	N/A	29.07	1,241	0.00	0.02	N/A	84	15	0	1	118	19	8
1.50	N/A	**C+ / 6.4**	N/A	N/A	N/A	24.21	37	0.54	0.03	N/A	0	0	0	100	N/A	23	2
0.00	0.95	**E- / 0.2**	N/A	N/A	N/A	29.72	48	0.07	-0.18	N/A	0	0	0	100	N/A	N/A	3
0.00	0.95	**D / 1.8**	N/A	N/A	N/A	31.13	240	-0.26	0.19	N/A	0	0	0	100	168	N/A	3
0.11	0.35	**B- / 7.1**	13.0	1.13	N/A	64.90	27	0.03	0.01	N/A	0	0	0	100	80	83	4
0.00	0.95	**D- / 1.4**	31.8	-2.93	N/A	16.91	250	0.06	N/A	N/A	100	0	0	0	N/A	14	8
0.00	N/A	**U /**	N/A	N/A	N/A	25.98	N/A	0.54	N/A	N/A	0	0	0	100	N/A	N/A	1
0.00	0.95	**D / 1.8**	33.7	3.10	N/A	82.97	419	-0.11	-0.04	N/A	87	12	0	1	110	19	8
1.42	0.47	**B / 8.3**	10.3	0.90	N/A	54.63	39	-0.05	0.04	N/A	0	0	0	100	145	39	4
0.00	0.95	**E / 0.4**	N/A	N/A	N/A	22.46	2	1.25	-0.01	N/A	0	0	0	100	N/A	3	3
2.44	N/A	**U /**	N/A	N/A	N/A	25.69	N/A	1.01	N/A	N/A	0	0	0	100	N/A	N/A	1
2.90	N/A	**U /**	N/A	N/A	N/A	22.83	N/A	0.66	N/A	N/A	0	0	0	100	N/A	N/A	1
3.87	N/A	**U /**	N/A	N/A	N/A	22.51	N/A	0.67	N/A	N/A	0	0	0	100	N/A	N/A	1
9.20	0.65	**C- / 3.6**	N/A	N/A	N/A	17.45	48	-0.34	0.13	N/A	0	0	0	100	92	4	2
4.60	0.58	**C+ / 6.4**	13.6	0.76	N/A	14.70	286	-1.36	-0.32	N/A	0	0	0	100	33	11	2
1.10	N/A	**U /**	N/A	N/A	N/A	19.12	N/A	-3.24	N/A	N/A	0	0	0	100	N/A	N/A	N/A
3.54	0.89	**C+ / 5.8**	15.3	1.01	N/A	11.61	46	-1.21	-0.51	N/A	0	0	0	100	168	4	2
3.22	0.85	**C+ / 6.8**	16.0	0.95	N/A	17.93	28	-1.12	0.01	N/A	0	0	0	100	8	16	2
1.10	0.83	**B- / 7.1**	15.4	0.92	N/A	21.42	1,267	-0.75	-0.09	N/A	0	99	0	1	12	64	2
1.60	0.71	**B- / 7.0**	14.2	0.90	N/A	16.41	4	-1.28	0.20	N/A	0	0	0	100	20	60	4
0.00	0.90	**C+ / 6.8**	24.4	0.96	N/A	32.46	9	-1.08	0.19	N/A	0	100	0	0	82	36	2

* Denotes ETF Fund, N/A denotes number is not available

	99 Pct = Best *0 Pct = Worst*			PRICE			PERFORMANCE					
					52 Week			% Total Return Through 12/31/15			Annualized	
Fund Type	Fund Name	Ticker Symbol	Overall Investment Rating	Price As of 12/31/15	High	Low	Performance Rating/Pts	3 Mo	6 Mo	1Yr/Pct	3Yr/Pct	5Yr/Pct
FO	*EGShares India Infrastructure ET	INXX	D	10.56	13.99	9.58	D / 2.1	-2.64	-16.20	-17.50 / 15	-6.91 / 21	-9.00 / 14
FO	*EGShares India Small Cap ETF	SCIN	C-	15.69	18.87	12.60	C / 4.7	4.75	-0.22	-9.23 / 28	1.73 / 47	-4.51 / 20
EN	*ELEMENTS MLCX Biofuels Tot Ret	FUE	E+	7.50	9.84	6.72	D / 1.6	1.63	-6.95	-14.48 / 18	-12.33 / 15	-7.90 / 16
EN	*ELEMENTS MLCX Grains Idx Tot Ret	GRU	E	4.10	5.33	3.99	D- / 1.1	-10.98	-21.53	-20.16 / 13	-16.14 / 11	-10.23 / 13
EN	*ELEMENTS RIC Energy Total Return	RJN	E-	2.33	4.41	2.20	E / 0.3	-22.59	-39.64	-40.41 / 3	-29.18 / 4	-18.22 / 6
EN	*ELEMENTS RIC Index Agri Total Re	RJA	E+	6.25	7.46	6.18	D / 1.6	-2.33	-13.78	-14.25 / 19	-11.21 / 16	-9.78 / 13
EN	*ELEMENTS RIC Index Total Return	RJI	E	4.63	6.40	4.48	E+ / 0.8	-11.30	-24.72	-26.04 / 9	-18.68 / 9	-12.54 / 11
EN	*ELEMENTS RIC Metals Total Return	RJZ	E+	6.49	8.31	6.20	D- / 1.2	-5.31	-12.71	-18.81 / 14	-15.47 / 11	-11.59 / 12
GR	*Elkhorn S&P 500 Capital Expendit	CAPX	U	22.75	N/A	N/A	U /	5.96	-6.38	--	--	--
EM	*EMQQ The EM Intrt Ecom ETF	EMQQ	C	23.78	27.00	13.85	C+ / 6.6	16.21	-5.47	2.94 / 74	--	--
EN	*Energy Select Sector SPDR	XLE	D+	60.32	83.66	58.21	D+ / 2.4	-3.85	-16.90	-21.14 / 12	-4.03 / 27	-0.24 / 27
HL	*ETFis BioShares Biotech Clinical	BBC	D-	29.05	50.00	24.95	D+ / 2.8	4.38	-18.51	2.29 / 72	--	--
HL	*ETFis BioShares Biotech Products	BBP	C-	30.82	38.63	25.74	B- / 7.5	5.84	-11.36	16.39 / 96	--	--
EN	*ETFis InfraCap MLP	AMZA	E	11.15	22.97	8.75	E- / 0.0	-21.59	-39.32	-47.04 / 2	--	--
UT	*ETFis Reaves Utilities ETF	UTES	U	26.40	N/A	N/A	U /	3.08	--	--	--	--
GI	*ETFis Tuttle Tactical Mgmt MS In	TUTI	U	23.23	N/A	N/A	U /	-2.02	-4.70	--	--	--
GR	*ETFis Tuttle Tactical Mgmt US Co	TUTT	U	22.50	N/A	N/A	U /	-0.19	-6.10	--	--	--
GL	*ETFis Virtus Newfleet MS Uncon B	NFLT	U	24.76	N/A	N/A	U /	-0.09	--	--	--	--
FO	*ETFS Diversified-Factor Dev Euro	SBEU	U	24.59	N/A	N/A	U /	1.19	-2.68	--	--	--
GR	*ETFS Diversified-Factor US LC Id	SBUS	U	24.46	N/A	N/A	U /	5.90	-0.01	--	--	--
PM	*ETFS Physical Palladium Shares	PALL	D-	54.17	80.75	50.44	D / 1.6	-19.70	-19.21	-29.85 / 7	-7.08 / 21	-6.20 / 17
PM	*ETFS Physical Platinum Shares	PPLT	E+	85.83	124.95	80.10	D- / 1.0	-2.40	-18.12	-26.37 / 9	-17.61 / 10	-13.10 / 11
PM	*ETFS Physical PM Basket Shares	GLTR	D-	52.29	67.51	51.72	D- / 1.1	-8.30	-11.34	-14.40 / 18	-17.18 / 10	-9.05 / 14
GL	*ETFS Physical Silver Shares	SIVR	E+	13.56	18.16	13.44	E+ / 0.8	-9.48	-11.83	-12.69 / 21	-23.19 / 7	-14.04 / 10
PM	*ETFS Physical Swiss Gold Shares	SGOL	D	103.50	127.85	102.29	D- / 1.4	-6.91	-9.15	-11.02 / 24	-14.15 / 13	-5.34 / 18
PM	*ETFS Physical WM Basket Shares	WITE	E+	26.41	36.60	25.71	E+ / 0.9	-9.01	-15.29	-20.66 / 13	-19.56 / 8	-12.81 / 11
GR	*ETFS Zacks Earnings Lg Cap US Id	ZLRG	U	22.99	N/A	N/A	U /	0.09	-7.88	--	--	--
GR	*ETFS Zacks Earnings Sm Cap US Id	ZSML	U	21.75	N/A	N/A	U /	-3.50	-18.14	--	--	--
GR	*Falah Russell-IdealRatings US LC	FIA	C+	25.66	27.66	23.23	C+ / 6.3	10.80	1.41	0.31 / 62	--	--
COI	*Fidelity Corporate Bond ETF	FCOR	C-	47.33	51.54	47.08	C- / 3.2	-1.20	-2.13	-2.53 / 48	--	--
COI	*Fidelity Limited Term Bond ETF	FLTB	C+	49.69	52.47	49.59	C- / 4.2	-1.15	-0.40	0.71 / 65	--	--
GL	*Fidelity MSCI Cons Staples Idx E	FSTA	B+	30.28	30.88	24.66	B / 8.2	6.67	5.89	7.01 / 83	--	--
GL	*Fidelity MSCI Consmr Discr Idx E	FDIS	C+	30.68	32.22	23.50	C+ / 6.7	2.97	-0.45	7.75 / 84	--	--
EN	*Fidelity MSCI Energy Index ETF	FENY	D-	17.09	24.99	16.54	E+ / 0.6	-4.39	-18.20	-22.86 / 11	--	--
FS	*Fidelity MSCI Financials Index E	FNCL	C+	28.30	30.33	19.82	C / 5.1	5.72	-1.71	-0.19 / 59	--	--
HL	*Fidelity MSCI Health Care Index	FHLC	C+	34.53	37.70	24.08	C+ / 6.4	6.07	-3.90	7.16 / 83	--	--
GL	*Fidelity MSCI Industrials Index	FIDU	C-	27.21	29.73	20.14	C- / 4.1	6.41	-2.06	-2.82 / 47	--	--
GR	*Fidelity MSCI Info Tech Idx ETF	FTEC	B	32.84	34.33	25.00	B- / 7.5	7.36	2.99	5.79 / 81	--	--
GL	*Fidelity MSCI Materials Index ET	FMAT	D	24.28	29.25	21.82	D / 2.2	5.87	-9.68	-9.61 / 27	--	--
GI	*Fidelity MSCI Real Estate Index	FREL	U	22.63	N/A	N/A	U /	7.38	6.50	--	--	--
GR	*Fidelity MSCI Telecom Svcs Idx E	FCOM	C+	26.72	28.55	24.24	C+ / 6.6	8.47	0.44	3.49 / 75	--	--
UT	*Fidelity MSCI Utilities Index ET	FUTY	C	27.89	32.14	26.04	C / 4.8	2.77	5.68	-4.13 / 42	--	--
GR	*Fidelity Nasdaq Comp Tracker Sto	ONEQ	B+	196.79	205.63	141.00	A / 9.4	7.38	1.08	7.90 / 85	18.80 / 94	14.43 / 89
COI	*Fidelity Total Bond ETF	FBND	C	48.00	51.20	47.63	C- / 3.6	-0.65	-2.00	-1.16 / 54	--	--
FS	*Financial Select Sector SPDR	XLF	A+	23.83	25.62	18.52	B+ / 8.7	6.28	-1.59	-1.14 / 54	14.01 / 88	10.04 / 65
FS	*Financial Services Select Sect S	XLFS	U	30.88	N/A	N/A	U /	--	--	--	--	--
HL	*First Trust AMEX Biotechnology	FBT	A	113.02	132.21	64.08	A+ / 9.8	7.59	-7.99	10.42 / 89	33.01 / 99	23.53 / 99
FO	*First Trust AsiaPac Ex-Jpn Alpha	FPA	C	27.45	33.55	24.87	C / 4.7	0.22	-10.09	0.40 / 63	1.82 / 47	--
FO	*First Trust Australia AlphaDEX	FAUS	D+	28.12	32.39	25.51	C / 4.3	10.27	-3.00	-0.24 / 59	-0.69 / 35	--
FO	*First Trust BICK Index	BICK	D	18.99	26.22	17.84	D / 1.9	-0.98	-19.65	-18.13 / 15	-8.50 / 19	-8.85 / 15
FO	*First Trust Brazil AlphaDEX	FBZ	E+	8.86	15.35	8.34	E+ / 0.6	-0.62	-31.04	-36.49 / 5	-25.12 / 5	--
IN	*First Trust Capital Strength ETF	FTCS	A	38.20	39.52	23.24	A- / 9.1	6.54	1.50	1.99 / 71	15.73 / 91	12.45 / 82

* Denotes ETF Fund, N/A denotes number is not available

Incl. in Returns		RISK				NET ASSETS		VALUATION			ASSET					FUND MANAGER	
			3 Year					Premium / Discount									
Dividend Yield %	Expense Ratio	Risk Rating/ Pts	Standard Deviation	Beta	Avg Dura-tion	NAV as of 12/31/15	Total $(Mil)	As of 12/31/15	1 Year Average	Wtd Avg P/E	Cash %	Stocks %	Bonds %	Other %	Portfolio Turnover Ratio	Manager Quality Pct	Manager Tenure (Years)
0.91	0.88	**C / 5.5**	29.7	1.18	N/A	10.69	50	-1.22	-0.08	N/A	0	100	0	0	75	14	2
0.60	0.92	**C / 5.2**	31.3	1.15	N/A	15.72	27	-0.19	-0.14	N/A	0	99	0	1	117	42	2
0.00	0.75	**D+ / 2.4**	23.8	-0.02	N/A	7.50	2	0.00	0.89	N/A	0	0	0	100	N/A	13	8
0.00	0.75	**D / 2.2**	25.0	0.24	N/A	4.10	16	0.00	0.06	N/A	0	0	0	100	N/A	10	8
0.00	0.75	**E+ / 0.9**	27.9	0.92	N/A	2.33	53	0.00	0.02	N/A	0	0	0	100	N/A	4	9
0.00	0.75	**C- / 3.0**	14.7	0.25	N/A	6.25	303	0.00	-0.05	N/A	0	0	0	100	N/A	15	9
0.00	0.75	**D / 2.1**	14.9	0.54	N/A	4.63	511	0.00	-0.01	N/A	0	0	0	100	N/A	9	9
0.00	0.75	**D+ / 2.4**	13.1	0.31	N/A	6.49	58	0.00	-0.10	N/A	0	0	0	100	N/A	11	9
0.00	N/A	**U /**	N/A	N/A	N/A	22.66	N/A	0.40	N/A	N/A	0	0	0	100	N/A	N/A	1
0.08	0.86	**C / 5.3**	N/A	N/A	N/A	23.82	N/A	-0.17	0.27	N/A	0	0	0	100	28	99	N/A
7.19	0.15	**C+ / 6.0**	18.0	0.97	N/A	60.32	10,242	0.00	N/A	15.7	0	100	0	0	6	74	18
0.00	N/A	**D+ / 2.6**	N/A	N/A	N/A	29.03	N/A	0.07	-0.01	N/A	0	0	0	100	N/A	84	2
0.00	N/A	**D+ / 2.8**	N/A	N/A	N/A	30.78	N/A	0.13	0.06	N/A	0	0	0	100	N/A	97	2
18.48	N/A	**D+ / 2.8**	N/A	N/A	N/A	11.15	N/A	0.00	0.25	N/A	0	0	0	100	N/A	3	2
0.00	N/A	**U /**	N/A	N/A	N/A	26.36	N/A	0.15	N/A	N/A	0	0	0	100	N/A	N/A	N/A
0.94	N/A	**U /**	N/A	N/A	N/A	23.16	N/A	0.30	N/A	N/A	0	0	0	100	N/A	N/A	1
0.20	N/A	**U /**	N/A	N/A	N/A	22.47	N/A	0.13	N/A	N/A	0	0	0	100	N/A	N/A	1
3.02	N/A	**U /**	N/A	N/A	N/A	24.73	N/A	0.12	N/A	N/A	0	0	0	100	N/A	N/A	1
1.13	N/A	**U /**	N/A	N/A	N/A	24.52	N/A	0.29	N/A	N/A	0	0	0	100	N/A	N/A	1
9.85	N/A	**U /**	N/A	N/A	N/A	24.48	N/A	-0.08	N/A	N/A	0	0	0	100	N/A	N/A	N/A
0.00	0.60	**C- / 3.7**	26.0	0.76	N/A	52.77	444	2.65	0.26	N/A	0	0	0	100	N/A	85	N/A
0.00	0.60	**C- / 3.4**	20.0	0.85	N/A	84.12	695	2.03	0.33	N/A	0	0	0	100	N/A	26	N/A
0.00	0.60	**C- / 4.0**	18.2	0.99	N/A	52.18	159	0.21	0.21	N/A	0	0	0	100	N/A	35	N/A
0.00	0.45	**C- / 3.6**	24.9	0.33	N/A	13.56	320	0.00	0.35	N/A	0	0	0	100	N/A	5	N/A
0.00	0.39	**C+ / 6.2**	16.2	0.92	N/A	103.64	1,020	-0.14	0.12	N/A	0	0	0	100	N/A	53	N/A
0.00	0.60	**C- / 3.3**	20.2	1.00	N/A	26.11	23	1.15	0.25	N/A	0	0	0	100	N/A	24	N/A
2.84	N/A	**U /**	N/A	N/A	N/A	23.42	N/A	-1.84	N/A	N/A	0	0	0	100	N/A	N/A	N/A
0.11	N/A	**U /**	N/A	N/A	N/A	22.38	N/A	-2.82	N/A	N/A	0	0	0	100	N/A	N/A	N/A
1.24	0.70	**C+ / 6.7**	N/A	N/A	N/A	25.58	N/A	0.31	-0.74	N/A	0	0	0	100	20	60	N/A
4.37	0.45	**B- / 7.5**	N/A	N/A	N/A	47.26	N/A	0.15	0.07	N/A	0	0	0	100	28	55	2
1.59	0.45	**B+ / 9.6**	N/A	N/A	N/A	49.72	N/A	-0.06	0.21	N/A	0	0	0	100	312	76	2
5.07	0.12	**B- / 7.2**	N/A	N/A	N/A	30.21	120	0.23	0.02	N/A	0	0	0	100	10	92	3
2.76	0.12	**B- / 7.2**	N/A	N/A	N/A	30.67	151	0.03	0.02	N/A	0	0	0	100	8	92	3
5.38	0.12	**C+ / 5.6**	N/A	N/A	N/A	17.10	144	-0.06	0.02	N/A	0	0	0	100	8	64	3
3.48	0.12	**B- / 7.8**	N/A	N/A	N/A	28.30	148	0.00	0.03	N/A	0	0	0	100	7	64	3
2.43	0.12	**C+ / 6.5**	N/A	N/A	N/A	34.50	237	0.09	0.03	N/A	0	0	0	100	10	91	3
0.17	0.12	**C+ / 6.7**	N/A	N/A	N/A	27.18	161	0.11	N/A	N/A	0	0	0	100	6	44	3
2.39	0.12	**B- / 7.2**	N/A	N/A	N/A	32.81	224	0.09	0.03	N/A	0	0	0	100	6	86	3
0.12	0.12	**C+ / 5.8**	N/A	N/A	N/A	24.21	113	0.29	0.02	N/A	0	0	0	100	7	18	3
0.34	N/A	**U /**	N/A	N/A	N/A	22.55	N/A	0.35	N/A	N/A	0	0	0	100	N/A	N/A	1
1.65	0.12	**B- / 7.0**	N/A	N/A	N/A	26.68	74	0.15	N/A	N/A	0	0	0	100	23	82	3
7.26	0.12	**C+ / 6.5**	N/A	N/A	N/A	27.83	73	0.22	0.01	N/A	0	0	0	100	7	60	3
0.13	0.21	**C+ / 6.5**	12.1	1.08	N/A	196.50	405	0.15	0.06	131.9	0	100	0	0	7	85	12
3.90	0.45	**B- / 7.7**	N/A	N/A	N/A	47.67	N/A	0.69	0.24	N/A	0	0	0	100	276	63	2
.03	0.15	**B / 8.8**	12.1	1.07	N/A	23.84	18,665	-0.04	-0.01	31.9	0	100	0	0	4	60	18
.45	N/A	**U /**	N/A	N/A	N/A	30.76	N/A	0.39	N/A	N/A	0	0	0	100	N/A	N/A	N/A
.05	0.58	**C+ / 6.7**	20.7	0.99	N/A	113.06	1,550	-0.04	0.03	194.9	0	99	0	1	58	98	10
.63	0.80	**B- / 7.8**	14.6	0.90	N/A	27.72	145	-0.97	-0.07	N/A	0	100	0	0	186	46	5
.02	0.80	**C / 5.2**	19.0	1.00	N/A	27.10	2	3.76	0.42	N/A	0	90	0	10	99	29	4
.07	0.64	**C+ / 6.3**	19.8	1.21	N/A	19.09	18	-0.52	-0.76	N/A	0	98	0	2	70	12	6
.00	0.80	**C- / 3.4**	27.7	1.46	N/A	8.87	5	-0.11	-0.60	N/A	0	99	0	1	104	3	5
.50	0.65	**B- / 7.5**	12.0	1.04	N/A	38.12	78	0.21	0.03	41.2	0	99	0	1	89	78	10

Denotes ETF Fund, N/A denotes number is not available

99 Pct = Best
0 Pct = Worst

Fund Type	Fund Name	Ticker Symbol	Overall Investment Rating	PRICE: Price As of 12/31/15	PRICE: 52 Week High	PRICE: 52 Week Low	PERFORMANCE: Performance Rating/Pts	% Total Return Through 12/31/15: 3 Mo	6 Mo	1Yr/Pct	Annualized: 3Yr/Pct	Annualized: 5Yr/Pct
IN	*First Trust CBOE S&P500 VIXTail	VIXH	C+	24.24	30.85	23.10	C+ / 6.9	4.88	-3.09	-5.13 / 38	8.65 / 71	--
FO	*First Trust China AlphaDEX	FCA	D+	20.51	38.13	15.90	D+ / 2.6	-1.56	-17.85	-7.72 / 32	-4.48 / 26	--
IN	*First Trust Consumer Dis AlphaDE	FXD	A	34.10	37.92	19.08	B+ / 8.4	-1.50	-6.73	-3.08 / 46	14.30 / 89	12.51 / 82
IN	*First Trust Consumer Stap AlphaD	FXG	A	44.45	46.24	27.63	A / 9.5	4.60	0.75	6.91 / 83	21.12 / 95	17.82 / 96
FO	*First Trust Dev Mkt Ex-US AlphaD	FDT	C	46.64	53.76	42.08	C / 5.4	2.58	-8.03	0.37 / 63	3.32 / 54	--
GL	*First Trust DJ Glb Sel Div Idx F	FGD	C	21.76	27.07	19.96	C- / 3.8	0.32	-9.88	-10.11 / 25	0.94 / 41	3.60 / 41
GL	*First Trust Dorsey Wright Focus	FV	C	23.49	25.59	11.70	C+ / 6.2	4.68	-3.83	7.02 / 83	--	--
GL	*First Trust Dorsey Wright Intl F	IFV	C	17.89	21.01	15.84	C- / 3.6	3.09	-7.28	0.44 / 63	--	--
GR	*First Trust Dow Jones Internet I	FDN	B+	74.61	78.09	35.34	A+ / 9.7	9.74	10.57	21.81 / 98	22.75 / 96	16.23 / 93
GR	*First Trust Dow Jones Sel Micro	FDM	A+	32.90	35.53	22.32	B+ / 8.4	4.33	-4.25	1.81 / 71	12.95 / 84	9.41 / 63
EM	*First Trust Emerg Mkt AlphaDEX	FEM	D	17.97	25.68	17.03	D / 1.7	-3.08	-20.05	-13.48 / 20	-10.25 / 17	--
EM	*First Trust Emerg Mkts Local Cur	FEMB	U	39.58	49.25	39.58	U /	-2.61	-7.33	--	--	--
EN	*First Trust Energy AlphaDEX	FXN	D	13.85	23.82	13.30	D- / 1.2	-8.79	-28.09	-32.89 / 6	-11.05 / 16	-7.05 / 17
COI	*First Trust Enhanced Short Matur	FTSM	C+	59.82	61.00	59.78	C / 4.4	0.06	0.08	0.22 / 62	--	--
FO	*First Trust Europe AlphaDEX	FEP	B-	29.52	33.39	27.76	C+ / 6.3	2.41	-4.76	2.88 / 74	6.12 / 65	--
FO	*First Trust Eurozone AlphaDEX	FEUZ	C-	31.44	35.22	28.90	C / 5.5	5.53	-4.28	3.33 / 75	--	--
FS	*First Trust Financial AlphaDEX	FXO	A+	23.18	24.63	12.50	B+ / 8.7	3.34	-2.47	1.30 / 69	13.99 / 88	11.42 / 75
GI	*First Trust FTSE EPRA/NAREIT Glb	FFR	C	42.68	47.14	30.55	C+ / 6.2	3.55	3.03	-0.65 / 56	5.23 / 62	7.20 / 55
GL	*First Trust Gl Tct Cmdty Strateg	FTGC	D	20.31	27.14	19.53	E+ / 0.6	-8.85	-17.34	-22.33 / 12	--	--
HL	*First Trust Health Care AlphaDEX	FXH	B+	60.45	70.72	44.41	A / 9.4	1.36	-12.10	-0.05 / 60	21.79 / 96	18.42 / 96
IN	*First Trust High Income	FTHI	C+	20.07	21.69	18.61	C+ / 6.2	5.83	0.79	2.86 / 74	--	--
IN	*First Trust Industrials AlphaDEX	FXR	C+	26.10	31.80	17.97	C+ / 6.4	0.45	-11.93	-13.19 / 20	9.69 / 74	8.16 / 58
GL	*First Trust International IPO ET	FPXI	D-	27.14	32.74	24.89	D+ / 2.5	5.85	-11.84	-5.13 / 38	--	--
FO	*First Trust Intl MA Dvsfd Inc In	YDIV	D+	16.61	19.75	15.54	D+ / 2.6	5.68	-5.19	-8.80 / 29	--	--
IN	*First Trust ISE Chindia Index	FNI	B	28.36	32.70	18.48	B / 7.6	7.12	-6.27	-1.76 / 51	10.56 / 77	3.63 / 41
GL	*First Trust ISE Cloud Computing	SKYY	B+	30.04	31.71	26.01	B+ / 8.9	4.85	1.86	5.66 / 80	13.84 / 87	--
GL	*First Trust ISE Glb Eng & Constr	FLM	C	44.24	50.70	42.50	C / 5.1	0.95	-7.89	-0.88 / 55	2.45 / 50	1.80 / 33
EN	*First Trust ISE Glb Wind Energy	FAN	A+	11.36	12.35	9.89	A / 9.5	8.41	-0.44	10.80 / 89	18.89 / 94	4.31 / 45
IN	*First Trust ISE Water Index	FIW	C+	30.11	33.27	24.87	C+ / 5.7	7.86	-3.40	-9.41 / 27	4.82 / 61	7.38 / 56
IN	*First Trust ISE-Revere Natural G	FCG	E	4.46	12.43	4.05	E- / 0.2	-26.04	-48.93	-59.17 / 1	-34.11 / 3	-24.92 / 4
FO	*First Trust Japan AlphaDEX	FJP	A-	47.09	54.38	43.48	B / 7.7	3.77	-6.66	5.25 / 80	10.21 / 76	--
GR	*First Trust Large Cap Gro AlphaD	FTC	A+	48.21	50.47	28.02	A- / 9.2	3.91	-1.12	4.45 / 78	16.98 / 92	11.90 / 77
IN	*First Trust Large Cap Val AlphaD	FTA	B-	38.45	45.58	21.20	C+ / 6.4	1.10	-8.76	-10.33 / 25	8.81 / 72	9.32 / 62
FO	*First Trust Latin America AlphaD	FLN	D-	13.21	19.77	12.69	E+ / 0.8	0.15	-24.40	-27.31 / 9	-19.81 / 8	--
GL	*First Trust Long/Short Equity	FTLS	B-	32.73	33.42	29.93	C+ / 6.5	3.84	1.49	5.39 / 80	--	--
IN	*First Trust Low Beta Income	FTLB	B-	19.75	21.21	18.63	C / 5.4	4.94	-0.82	0.85 / 66	--	--
MTG	*First Trust Low Dur Mtge Oppty E	LMBS	C-	50.43	51.26	49.69	C+ / 5.7	1.38	1.75	2.83 / 74	--	--
GI	*First Trust Lrg Cap Core AlphaDE	FEX	B+	43.26	47.64	20.11	B / 8.0	2.30	-5.40	-3.91 / 43	12.43 / 83	10.64 / 69
MUN	*First Trust Managed Municipal	FMB	B+	52.01	54.22	50.76	B / 7.6	2.25	3.48	4.50 / 83	--	--
IN	*First Trust Materials AlphaDEX	FXZ	C-	28.10	33.61	26.33	C / 4.6	1.57	-10.56	-9.91 / 26	3.01 / 53	4.95 / 47
GR	*First Trust Mega Cap AlphaDEX	FMK	B	26.40	27.73	24.16	B / 8.2	5.58	-1.12	0.24 / 62	11.74 / 81	--
GR	*First Trust Mid Cap Core AlphaDE	FNX	C+	48.06	55.95	31.06	C+ / 6.4	-1.05	-10.20	-7.68 / 32	8.77 / 72	8.82 / 60
GR	*First Trust Mid Cap Growth Alpha	FNY	A-	28.84	31.70	21.04	B / 7.6	1.53	-6.33	-0.73 / 56	10.94 / 78	--
GR	*First Trust Mid Cap Val AlphaDEX	FNK	C+	26.45	32.50	25.95	C+ / 5.6	-3.39	-13.07	-12.73 / 21	6.96 / 67	--
IN	*First Trust Morningstar Div Lead	FDL	B+	23.70	24.53	12.31	B+ / 8.4	7.19	5.06	2.56 / 73	11.50 / 80	12.06 / 79
IN	*First Trust Morningstar Mgd Fut	FMF	C	49.24	57.22	46.00	C- / 3.9	0.33	-1.70	-0.46 / 57	--	--
GR	*First Trust Multi Cap Grth Alpha	FAD	B+	49.72	52.73	23.64	B+ / 8.8	3.86	-2.73	2.91 / 74	14.28 / 88	11.08 / 73
IN	*First Trust Multi Cap Val AlphaD	FAB	C+	40.74	49.45	33.22	C+ / 5.9	-0.55	-11.31	-12.02 / 22	7.68 / 69	8.58 / 59
IN	*First Trust MultiAsst Dvsfd Inc	MDIV	C	18.34	21.68	13.00	C / 4.5	0.13	-5.29	-8.73 / 29	2.32 / 50	--
GR	*First Trust NASD Cln Edge Smt Gd	GRID	C	33.39	38.00	27.71	C+ / 5.7	4.63	-6.07	-4.86 / 39	4.56 / 59	2.20 / 34
IN	*First Trust NASDAQ ABA Community	QABA	B+	38.98	43.75	32.84	A- / 9.0	3.97	-0.92	9.03 / 86	14.83 / 90	11.02 / 72
IN	*First Trust NASDAQ Cln Edg US Li	QCLN	B-	16.05	19.93	13.31	A- / 9.0	11.57	-11.88	-6.52 / 35	17.53 / 93	-0.10 / 27

* Denotes ETF Fund, N/A denotes number is not available

Incl. in Returns		RISK				NET ASSETS		VALUATION			ASSET					FUND MANAGER	
			3 Year					Premium / Discount									
Dividend Yield %	Expense Ratio	Risk Rating/ Pts	Standard Deviation	Beta	Avg Duration	NAV as of 12/31/15	Total $(Mil)	As of 12/31/15	1 Year Average	Wtd Avg P/E	Cash %	Stocks %	Bonds %	Other %	Portfolio Turnover Ratio	Manager Quality Pct	Manager Tenure (Years)
1.87	0.60	**B- / 7.1**	9.9	0.74	N/A	24.07	5	0.71	0.10	N/A	0	0	0	100	7	54	4
2.38	0.80	**C+ / 5.9**	25.1	0.98	N/A	20.78	7	-1.30	-0.04	N/A	0	99	0	1	79	19	5
0.92	0.63	**B / 8.3**	13.0	1.06	N/A	34.11	1,385	-0.03	0.02	87.5	0	100	0	0	131	62	9
1.35	0.62	**B- / 7.3**	12.8	1.00	N/A	44.43	1,472	0.05	0.02	48.2	0	99	0	1	87	91	9
2.93	0.80	**C+ / 6.9**	11.9	0.87	N/A	46.63	125	0.02	0.28	N/A	0	100	0	0	115	59	5
4.40	0.60	**B- / 7.7**	13.0	0.94	N/A	21.84	562	-0.37	-0.10	17.9	0	100	0	0	34	38	9
0.28	0.30	**C+ / 6.5**	N/A	N/A	N/A	23.47	567	0.09	0.07	N/A	0	0	0	100	N/A	92	2
2.00	0.30	**B / 8.0**	N/A	N/A	N/A	17.93	N/A	-0.22	0.11	N/A	0	0	0	100	7	69	N/A
0.00	0.54	**C+ / 6.1**	16.4	1.15	N/A	74.63	1,757	-0.03	0.01	323.6	0	100	0	0	27	90	10
2.59	0.60	**B / 8.5**	14.6	0.98	N/A	32.92	51	-0.06	-0.01	29.1	0	99	0	1	49	63	11
0.63	0.80	**C+ / 6.4**	17.4	1.15	N/A	18.10	425	-0.72	-0.37	N/A	0	100	0	0	116	48	5
4.73	N/A	**U /**	N/A	N/A	N/A	39.21	N/A	0.94	0.96	N/A	0	0	0	100	N/A	11	N/A
1.98	0.64	**C / 5.5**	25.7	1.33	N/A	13.87	424	-0.14	-0.02	17.4	0	99	0	1	97	28	9
0.80	N/A	**B+ / 9.4**	N/A	N/A	N/A	59.86	N/A	-0.07	-0.05	N/A	0	0	0	100	N/A	71	2
0.48	0.80	**B- / 7.8**	14.2	1.01	N/A	29.61	693	-0.30	0.32	N/A	0	100	0	0	106	74	5
0.16	N/A	**C / 5.0**	N/A	N/A	N/A	31.65	N/A	-0.66	-0.16	N/A	0	0	0	100	N/A	87	N/A
2.68	0.64	**B / 8.9**	11.4	0.98	N/A	23.19	919	-0.04	0.01	50.4	0	99	0	1	80	72	9
1.18	0.60	**C+ / 6.5**	12.8	0.55	N/A	42.45	109	0.54	-0.16	93.9	0	99	0	1	10	48	9
0.00	0.95	**C+ / 6.3**	N/A	N/A	N/A	20.32	183	-0.05	-0.01	N/A	0	0	0	100	N/A	6	3
0.00	0.62	**C+ / 6.4**	14.1	0.88	N/A	60.43	2,405	0.03	0.02	113.0	0	99	0	1	125	94	9
4.78	0.85	**B- / 7.1**	N/A	N/A	N/A	19.92	3	0.75	0.27	N/A	0	0	0	100	191	79	2
1.22	0.63	**C+ / 6.7**	14.4	1.23	N/A	26.09	1,220	0.04	N/A	32.5	0	99	0	1	105	24	9
1.50	0.70	**C- / 3.0**	N/A	N/A	N/A	27.09	N/A	0.18	0.29	N/A	0	0	0	100	98	32	N/A
3.19	0.70	**C+ / 5.7**	N/A	N/A	N/A	15.99	13	3.88	0.55	N/A	0	0	0	100	132	17	3
.53	0.60	**B- / 7.0**	18.9	1.17	N/A	28.36	68	0.00	N/A	64.7	0	99	0	1	40	28	9
.18	0.60	**B- / 7.2**	14.0	0.83	N/A	29.98	342	0.20	0.09	N/A	0	0	0	100	25	95	5
.88	0.70	**B- / 7.1**	14.3	0.87	N/A	44.24	17	0.00	-0.03	N/A	0	99	0	1	46	55	8
2.35	0.60	**B- / 7.9**	17.9	0.57	N/A	11.37	87	-0.09	-0.17	27.2	0	99	0	1	25	98	8
.79	0.59	**B- / 7.8**	16.0	1.23	N/A	30.13	184	-0.07	-0.02	50.6	0	99	0	1	24	15	9
3.27	0.60	**C- / 3.0**	39.1	1.40	N/A	4.46	407	0.00	0.04	11.9	0	100	0	0	42	N/A	9
.67	0.80	**B / 8.4**	14.2	0.75	N/A	47.18	40	-0.19	0.04	N/A	0	100	0	0	148	90	5
.97	0.63	**B- / 7.9**	11.2	0.97	N/A	48.21	418	0.00	0.04	78.7	0	99	0	1	143	84	9
.63	0.62	**B- / 7.8**	11.9	1.04	N/A	38.45	1,150	0.00	0.01	22.9	0	99	0	1	78	31	9
.23	0.80	**C / 4.7**	21.6	1.17	N/A	13.28	7	-0.53	-0.25	N/A	0	100	0	0	103	5	5
.74	N/A	**B- / 7.6**	N/A	N/A	N/A	32.68	N/A	0.15	0.10	N/A	0	0	0	100	N/A	89	2
.34	0.85	**B / 8.7**	N/A	N/A	N/A	19.79	3	-0.20	0.14	N/A	0	0	0	100	205	61	2
.07	N/A	**C- / 4.1**	N/A	N/A	N/A	50.22	N/A	0.42	0.20	N/A	0	0	0	100	N/A	84	N/A
.92	0.61	**B / 8.0**	11.0	1.01	N/A	43.26	1,309	0.00	0.02	48.8	0	99	0	1	91	56	9
.65	N/A	**B / 8.1**	N/A	N/A	N/A	51.75	20	0.50	0.28	N/A	0	0	0	100	N/A	76	N/A
.09	0.64	**C+ / 6.4**	14.9	1.21	N/A	28.09	667	0.04	0.01	38.5	0	99	0	1	104	13	9
.01	0.70	**B- / 7.0**	11.6	1.06	N/A	26.31	15	0.34	0.06	N/A	0	99	0	1	134	47	5
.34	0.62	**B- / 7.0**	13.0	1.05	N/A	48.03	891	0.06	0.01	73.8	0	99	0	1	102	30	9
.50	0.70	**B / 8.5**	12.7	0.99	N/A	28.87	46	-0.10	0.03	N/A	0	99	0	1	159	47	5
.94	0.70	**B / 8.0**	14.2	1.09	N/A	26.49	68	-0.15	0.02	N/A	0	99	0	1	88	22	5
.15	0.45	**B- / 7.4**	9.7	0.74	N/A	23.69	791	0.04	0.02	23.6	0	99	0	1	40	78	19
.00	0.95	**B- / 7.6**	N/A	N/A	N/A	49.21	13	0.06	0.17	N/A	0	0	0	100	N/A	61	3
.70	0.70	**C+ / 6.8**	11.7	0.97	N/A	49.48	68	0.49	0.07	101.4	0	99	0	1	135	73	9
.00	0.70	**B- / 7.0**	13.1	1.08	N/A	40.71	174	0.07	0.02	26.8	0	99	0	1	82	25	9
50	0.50	**B / 8.2**	8.7	0.61	N/A	18.36	784	-0.11	0.02	N/A	0	0	0	100	116	30	4
94	0.70	**C+ / 6.3**	12.6	0.83	N/A	32.61	14	2.39	0.23	N/A	0	100	0	0	18	27	7
36	0.60	**C+ / 6.7**	16.5	0.89	N/A	38.94	88	0.10	0.04	N/A	0	99	0	1	26	84	7
94	0.60	**C / 5.5**	25.1	1.47	N/A	16.01	122	0.25	-0.02	47.1	0	100	0	0	37	53	9

■ Denotes ETF Fund, N/A denotes number is not available

99 Pct = Best
0 Pct = Worst

Fund Type	Fund Name	Ticker Symbol	Overall Investment Rating	PRICE: Price As of 12/31/15	PRICE: 52 Week High	PRICE: 52 Week Low	PERFORMANCE: Performance Rating/Pts	% Total Return Through 12/31/15: 3 Mo	6 Mo	1Yr/Pct	Annualized: 3Yr/Pct	Annualized: 5Yr/Pct
GL	*First Trust NASDAQ Global Auto	CARZ	B	36.22	42.44	20.01	C+ / 6.9	5.90	-7.25	-0.30 / 58	8.18 / 70	--
IN	*First Trust NASDAQ Rising Div Ac	RDVY	C-	20.73	22.98	16.04	C- / 3.2	2.95	-5.28	-2.99 / 46	--	--
GL	*First Trust NASDAQ Smartphone In	FONE	B+	36.36	43.00	32.63	B+ / 8.3	4.17	-6.14	-3.52 / 44	13.18 / 85	--
IN	*First Trust NASDAQ Tech Div Idx	TDIV	B+	25.27	28.62	15.40	B / 7.7	4.11	-3.19	-6.32 / 35	11.48 / 80	--
GR	*First Trust NASDAQ-100 Equal Wei	QQEW	A	43.48	45.70	32.40	A / 9.3	6.43	-0.91	2.37 / 72	18.22 / 94	13.34 / 86
IN	*First Trust NASDAQ-100 Ex-Tech S	QQXT	B+	41.47	44.64	35.00	A / 9.3	5.88	-1.71	4.97 / 79	18.23 / 94	15.06 / 91
GR	*First Trust NASDAQ-100-Technolog	QTEC	A	42.65	45.59	33.85	A / 9.3	7.35	0.54	-1.31 / 53	18.21 / 93	10.95 / 72
EN	*First Trust North Am Energy Infr	EMLP	D+	20.18	28.60	14.01	D+ / 2.9	-9.92	-18.76	-25.83 / 9	1.42 / 44	--
GEN	*First Trust Pref Sec and Inc	FPE	C+	18.95	19.48	18.61	C+ / 6.8	2.43	3.08	6.07 / 82	--	--
IN	*First Trust RBA Amer Indus Rens	AIRR	D+	16.51	19.52	14.92	D+ / 2.5	7.99	-9.08	-8.81 / 29	--	--
IN	*First Trust RBA Quality Income	QINC	C-	20.08	22.15	19.55	D+ / 2.7	2.19	-4.77	-6.13 / 35	--	--
IN	*First Trust S&P REIT Index	FRI	B-	22.08	24.46	19.73	B / 7.8	5.57	7.04	0.48 / 64	9.79 / 75	11.44 / 75
LP	*First Trust Senior Loan	FTSL	C+	46.87	49.90	46.71	C- / 3.7	-1.57	-2.50	0.17 / 61	--	--
GR	*First Trust Small Cap Core Alpha	FYX	B-	44.18	51.93	32.38	C+ / 6.3	0.70	-10.39	-8.41 / 30	8.42 / 71	8.64 / 59
GR	*First Trust Small Cap Gro AlphaD	FYC	B	30.51	32.81	21.89	B / 8.1	3.97	-3.52	2.64 / 73	11.58 / 80	--
GR	*First Trust Small Cap Val AlphaD	FYT	C+	27.08	34.81	23.94	C / 5.2	-1.59	-15.05	-16.21 / 16	5.90 / 64	--
FO	*First Trust South Korea AlphaDEX	FKO	C-	22.72	34.78	19.50	D+ / 2.7	1.88	-12.28	-4.23 / 42	-4.99 / 25	--
FO	*First Trust STOXX European Sel D	FDD	C	12.18	14.06	11.62	C / 5.5	0.70	-4.87	-2.02 / 50	3.84 / 56	2.24 / 35
GL	*First Trust Strategic Income	FDIV	C-	46.49	53.02	44.20	C- / 3.0	1.09	-2.63	-4.99 / 39	--	--
COH	*First Trust Tactical High Yield	HYLS	C-	46.97	51.95	46.13	C- / 3.6	-0.54	-3.75	0.06 / 61	--	--
GR	*First Trust Technology AlphaDEX	FXL	B	33.24	37.51	28.70	B+ / 8.6	3.62	-5.92	-3.02 / 46	14.78 / 90	7.76 / 57
GI	*First Trust Total US Mkt AlphaDE	TUSA	B-	24.55	27.18	23.60	B- / 7.2	2.47	-6.53	-5.05 / 38	10.18 / 75	5.05 / 48
GR	*First Trust US IPO Index	FPX	B+	51.13	56.71	31.85	A- / 9.2	3.00	-6.48	1.99 / 71	17.95 / 93	17.55 / 95
UT	*First Trust Utilities AlphaDEX	FXU	A-	22.39	25.83	21.23	B- / 7.4	-0.38	2.25	-6.88 / 34	10.36 / 76	9.18 / 61
GR	*First Trust Value Line 100	FVL	B	19.80	21.83	18.50	B+ / 8.3	2.48	-5.61	-2.59 / 48	13.56 / 86	8.21 / 59
GI	*First Trust Value Line Dividend	FVD	A-	23.88	24.63	14.85	B+ / 8.6	4.63	2.39	1.30 / 69	13.17 / 85	12.51 / 82
GI	*FlexShares Global Quality RE Ind	GQRE	C+	56.85	59.61	44.18	C+ / 6.0	3.47	1.54	2.79 / 73	--	--
FO	*FlexShares Int Qual Div Def Idx	IQDE	D+	21.09	26.04	20.56	D / 1.8	-0.50	-10.10	-8.93 / 28	--	--
FO	*FlexShares Int Qual Div Dyn Idx	IQDY	D	22.45	27.77	21.39	D / 2.1	2.30	-11.02	-7.16 / 33	--	--
FO	*FlexShares Intl Qual Div Idx	IQDF	D+	21.52	26.97	20.83	D / 1.7	-0.70	-11.65	-9.42 / 27	--	--
EM	*FlexShares MS EM Fact Tilt Idx	TLTE	D+	41.72	55.52	39.73	D / 2.0	-2.98	-18.52	-14.14 / 19	-7.96 / 20	--
IN	*FlexShares Quality Div Defens In	QDEF	C-	34.62	37.27	31.30	C- / 4.0	2.75	-2.47	-0.88 / 55	--	--
IN	*FlexShares Quality Div Dynamic I	QDYN	C-	33.50	37.46	31.17	D+ / 2.8	2.97	-5.55	-5.08 / 38	--	--
IN	*FlexShares Quality Dividend Inde	QDF	C-	34.82	37.63	29.23	C- / 3.8	3.14	-2.81	-1.72 / 51	--	--
GL	*FlexShares Ready Access Var Inc	RAVI	B-	75.10	75.99	74.42	C / 4.6	-0.25	0.12	0.15 / 61	0.59 / 39	--
GL	*FlexShares STOXX Gl Broad Infra	NFRA	D+	41.13	47.35	39.98	D / 2.2	-1.11	-7.61	-7.17 / 33	--	--
COI	*FlexShs Crdt-Scrd US Lng Crp Bd	LKOR	U	49.49	N/A	N/A	U /	-2.15	--	--	--	--
COI	*FlexShs Credit-Scored US Crp Bd	SKOR	D+	50.00	51.97	49.86	C / 4.7	-1.50	0.63	1.42 / 70	--	--
MTG	*FlexShs Dscpld Duration MBS Inde	MBSD	C+	24.73	29.08	24.58	C / 5.3	0.18	1.35	1.77 / 71	--	--
USA	*FlexShs iB 3Y Tgt Dur TIPS Idx	TDTT	C+	24.18	24.69	24.01	C- / 3.7	-1.27	-1.75	-0.62 / 57	-1.33 / 32	--
USA	*FlexShs iB 5Y Tgt Dur TIPS Idx	TDTF	C+	24.32	25.22	24.23	C- / 3.6	-1.94	-2.01	-0.97 / 55	-1.78 / 32	--
EN	*FlexShs Morningstar Gl Upstream	GUNR	D	22.25	32.81	21.98	D- / 1.3	-3.99	-21.92	-24.51 / 10	-12.34 / 15	--
IN	*FlexShs Morningstar US Mkt Fac T	TILT	B	83.73	91.25	77.74	B / 8.1	4.02	-3.67	-1.71 / 51	12.27 / 82	--
FO	*FlexShs MS Dev Mkts exUS Fctrs T	TLTD	C+	55.18	64.44	53.59	C / 5.4	1.69	-7.31	-1.08 / 54	3.37 / 54	--
GR	*FlexShs US Quality Large Cap Ind	QLC	U	25.95	N/A	N/A	U /	4.30	--	--	--	--
USA	*Franklin Short Duration US Govt	FTSD	C	98.27	99.60	97.74	C / 4.4	-0.03	0.08	0.30 / 62	--	--
EM	*Gavekal Knowledge Leaders Dev Wo	KLDW	U	24.83	N/A	N/A	U /	6.79	--	--	--	--
EM	*Gavekal Knowledge Leaders Em Mkt	KLEM	U	22.61	N/A	N/A	U /	3.93	--	--	--	--
FO	*Glo X Scientific Beta Asia ex-Ja	SCIX	U	21.24	N/A	N/A	U /	6.81	--	--	--	--
GL	*Global Echo ETF	GIVE	C+	60.45	68.25	52.00	C+ / 6.0	2.25	-3.01	-2.97 / 46	5.47 / 63	--
FO	*Global X Brazil Consumer ETF	BRAQ	E	8.00	14.21	7.31	E / 0.5	-0.42	-33.69	-40.02 / 4	-25.53 / 5	-15.53 / 8
FO	*Global X Brazil Mid Cap ETF	BRAZ	E+	6.03	10.22	5.91	E+ / 0.6	-3.44	-31.38	-36.93 / 5	-24.75 / 6	-17.01 / 7

* Denotes ETF Fund, N/A denotes number is not availabl

Incl. in Returns		RISK				NET ASSETS		VALUATION			ASSET					FUND MANAGER	
			3 Year					Premium / Discount									
Dividend Yield %	Expense Ratio	Risk Rating/ Pts	Standard Deviation	Beta	Avg Duration	NAV as of 12/31/15	Total $(Mil)	As of 12/31/15	1 Year Average	Wtd Avg P/E	Cash %	Stocks %	Bonds %	Other %	Portfolio Turnover Ratio	Manager Quality Pct	Manager Tenure (Years)
2.09	0.70	**B- / 7.9**	15.4	0.94	N/A	36.43	65	-0.58	0.01	N/A	0	99	0	1	18	87	5
2.24	0.50	**B- / 7.8**	N/A	N/A	N/A	20.73	7	0.00	0.06	N/A	0	0	0	100	71	34	2
1.15	0.70	**B- / 7.3**	12.9	0.82	N/A	36.36	11	0.00	-0.05	N/A	0	99	0	1	28	95	5
2.25	0.50	**B / 8.2**	12.8	1.08	N/A	25.35	684	-0.32	-0.01	N/A	0	0	0	100	27	42	4
0.83	0.60	**B- / 7.5**	12.8	1.12	N/A	43.48	460	0.00	0.01	99.8	0	99	0	1	27	80	10
0.64	0.60	**C+ / 6.2**	12.9	1.10	N/A	41.45	92	0.05	0.04	142.7	0	99	0	1	23	82	10
1.12	0.60	**B- / 7.3**	13.8	1.13	N/A	42.64	271	0.02	0.03	57.1	0	99	0	1	20	80	10
5.31	0.95	**C+ / 6.3**	13.5	0.46	N/A	20.18	863	0.00	0.03	N/A	0	0	0	100	7	88	4
5.21	0.85	**B- / 7.1**	N/A	N/A	N/A	18.89	81	0.32	0.19	N/A	0	0	0	100	91	90	3
0.82	0.70	**C+ / 6.3**	N/A	N/A	N/A	16.51	80	0.00	-0.06	N/A	0	0	0	100	66	15	2
2.87	0.70	**B- / 7.9**	N/A	N/A	N/A	20.08	5	0.00	0.02	N/A	0	0	0	100	163	23	N/A
4.31	0.50	**C+ / 6.4**	14.8	0.47	N/A	22.07	204	0.05	N/A	88.9	0	99	0	1	11	85	9
4.10	0.85	**B+ / 9.4**	N/A	N/A	N/A	46.95	200	-0.17	0.15	N/A	0	0	0	100	97	80	3
1.24	0.63	**B / 8.2**	14.7	1.07	N/A	44.24	513	-0.14	0.01	59.8	0	99	0	1	97	27	9
0.61	0.70	**C+ / 6.9**	14.7	1.05	N/A	30.47	37	0.13	0.04	N/A	0	99	0	1	153	45	5
1.04	0.70	**B- / 7.9**	15.8	1.09	N/A	27.09	60	-0.04	N/A	N/A	0	99	0	1	96	20	5
0.23	0.80	**B- / 7.2**	17.8	0.89	N/A	22.89	4	-0.74	-0.81	N/A	0	100	0	0	97	18	5
1.79	0.60	**C+ / 6.0**	12.9	0.91	N/A	12.17	168	0.08	0.18	N/A	0	96	0	4	33	58	N/A
4.13	N/A	**B- / 7.4**	N/A	N/A	N/A	46.46	N/A	0.06	-0.14	N/A	0	0	0	100	N/A	28	2
5.88	0.95	**B- / 7.1**	N/A	N/A	N/A	46.95	185	0.04	0.10	N/A	0	0	0	100	54	87	3
0.45	0.63	**C+ / 6.6**	13.4	1.09	N/A	33.23	847	0.03	0.02	111.3	0	99	0	1	91	62	9
1.27	0.70	**B- / 7.1**	11.0	0.93	N/A	24.34	5	0.86	0.04	63.4	0	99	0	1	183	39	10
0.81	0.60	**C+ / 6.6**	13.4	1.11	N/A	51.11	534	0.04	0.02	N/A	0	99	0	1	46	80	10
4.53	0.69	**B / 8.8**	11.8	0.75	N/A	22.40	205	-0.04	-0.01	21.4	0	99	0	1	94	80	9
0.41	0.70	**C+ / 6.9**	13.4	1.12	N/A	19.71	61	0.46	-0.04	88.0	0	99	0	1	325	51	13
2.74	0.70	**B- / 7.6**	9.8	0.83	N/A	23.86	921	0.08	0.03	34.9	0	99	0	1	63	79	13
3.52	0.45	**B- / 7.3**	N/A	N/A	N/A	56.55	36	0.53	0.37	N/A	0	0	0	100	44	83	3
4.40	0.47	**B- / 7.4**	N/A	N/A	N/A	21.33	57	-1.13	-0.11	N/A	0	0	0	100	69	18	3
4.32	0.47	**C / 5.3**	N/A	N/A	N/A	22.44	59	0.04	0.14	N/A	0	0	0	100	45	27	3
2.90	0.47	**B- / 7.3**	N/A	N/A	N/A	21.72	268	-0.92	0.16	N/A	0	0	0	100	61	18	3
2.00	0.65	**B- / 7.2**	14.4	0.96	N/A	41.83	257	-0.26	-0.07	N/A	0	0	0	100	19	63	3
3.79	0.37	**B- / 7.3**	N/A	N/A	N/A	34.61	85	0.03	0.03	N/A	0	0	0	100	73	54	3
6.86	0.37	**C+ / 6.8**	N/A	N/A	N/A	33.32	91	0.54	-0.05	N/A	0	0	0	100	75	26	3
3.61	0.37	**B- / 7.1**	N/A	N/A	N/A	34.81	511	0.03	0.02	N/A	0	0	0	100	67	50	3
0.64	0.25	**B+ / 9.8**	0.5	0.02	N/A	75.16	72	-0.08	-0.04	N/A	0	0	0	100	135	74	4
2.71	0.47	**B- / 7.0**	N/A	N/A	N/A	41.10	223	0.07	0.26	N/A	0	0	0	100	17	24	3
0.00	N/A	**U /**	N/A	N/A	N/A	48.76	N/A	1.50	N/A	N/A	0	0	0	100	N/A	N/A	1
2.02	N/A	**C- / 4.1**	N/A	N/A	N/A	49.79	N/A	0.42	0.45	N/A	0	0	0	100	N/A	81	2
2.45	N/A	**B / 8.1**	N/A	N/A	N/A	24.53	N/A	0.82	0.27	N/A	0	0	0	100	N/A	77	2
0.00	0.20	**B+ / 9.5**	2.0	0.06	N/A	24.25	2,237	-0.29	0.01	N/A	0	0	0	100	179	54	5
0.21	0.20	**B+ / 9.3**	3.8	0.21	N/A	24.34	307	-0.08	0.07	N/A	0	0	0	100	150	46	5
4.50	0.48	**C+ / 6.0**	15.5	0.70	N/A	22.38	2,965	-0.58	0.06	N/A	0	0	0	100	11	17	3
1.98	0.27	**B- / 7.0**	11.5	1.04	N/A	83.63	708	0.12	0.01	N/A	0	0	0	100	25	51	N/A
2.56	0.42	**B- / 7.7**	11.8	0.91	N/A	55.19	656	-0.02	0.03	N/A	0	0	0	100	16	59	3
0.00	N/A	**U /**	N/A	N/A	N/A	25.93	N/A	0.08	N/A	N/A	0	0	0	100	N/A	N/A	1
1.85	0.30	**B / 8.0**	N/A	N/A	N/A	98.01	28	0.27	0.03	N/A	0	0	0	100	198	70	3
0.57	N/A	**U /**	N/A	N/A	N/A	24.76	N/A	0.28	N/A	N/A	0	0	0	100	N/A	N/A	1
2.09	N/A	**U /**	N/A	N/A	N/A	22.58	N/A	0.13	N/A	N/A	0	0	0	100	N/A	N/A	1
5.04	N/A	**U /**	N/A	N/A	N/A	21.13	N/A	0.52	N/A	N/A	0	0	0	100	N/A	N/A	1
2.36	1.50	**B- / 7.5**	5.9	0.33	N/A	60.17	6	0.47	0.13	N/A	0	0	0	100	68	87	4
1.48	0.78	**D / 1.8**	29.2	1.53	N/A	7.98	10	0.25	-0.51	N/A	0	100	0	0	19	3	6
2.96	0.69	**C- / 3.6**	26.4	1.48	N/A	6.12	8	-1.47	-0.57	N/A	0	100	0	0	18	3	6

* Denotes ETF Fund, N/A denotes number is not available

				PRICE			PERFORMANCE					
99 Pct = Best *0 Pct = Worst*					52 Week			% Total Return Through 12/31/15			Annualized	
Fund Type	Fund Name	Ticker Symbol	Overall Investment Rating	Price As of 12/31/15	High	Low	Performance Rating/Pts	3 Mo	6 Mo	1Yr/Pct	3Yr/Pct	5Yr/Pct
FO	*Global X China Consumer ETF	CHIQ	D+	12.16	16.46	10.40	D+ / 2.8	-0.05	-11.50	1.62 / 70	-5.03 / 25	-6.32 / 17
EN	*Global X China Energy ETF	CHIE	D	10.10	16.00	9.78	D- / 1.5	-2.08	-23.83	-22.18 / 12	-10.74 / 16	-6.82 / 17
FS	*Global X China Financials ETF	CHIX	C-	13.69	20.24	11.54	C- / 3.6	1.90	-18.96	-9.84 / 26	0.73 / 40	1.53 / 32
FO	*Global X China Industrials ETF	CHII	D+	12.65	20.63	12.13	C- / 3.2	-8.80	-20.76	-11.41 / 23	0.37 / 39	-4.61 / 19
FO	*Global X China Materials ETF	CHIM	D	12.04	21.37	11.44	D- / 1.5	-0.94	-28.43	-13.52 / 20	-11.30 / 16	-14.99 / 9
PM	*Global X Copper Miners ETF	COPX	E	11.81	24.78	11.01	E / 0.3	-9.98	-40.74	-45.70 / 2	-32.70 / 3	-24.94 / 4
GL	*Global X Fertilizers/Potash ETF	SOIL	D	9.02	12.08	9.02	D- / 1.5	-2.39	-18.98	-10.61 / 24	-12.24 / 15	--
FO	*Global X FTSE Andean 40 ETF	AND	D-	6.22	9.61	5.98	E+ / 0.6	-6.95	-22.08	-29.21 / 8	-23.64 / 7	--
FO	*Global X FTSE Greece 20 ETF	GREK	E	7.96	14.59	7.95	E+ / 0.6	-15.22	-25.53	-41.19 / 3	-24.16 / 6	--
GL	*Global X FTSE Nordic Region ETF	GXF	B-	21.43	25.08	21.11	C+ / 6.0	0.08	-5.60	0.12 / 61	5.73 / 63	4.91 / 47
FO	*Global X FTSE Portugal 20 ETF	PGAL	D+	10.11	12.95	9.78	C- / 3.2	-0.25	-7.01	0.04 / 60	--	--
FO	*Global X GF China Bond ETF	CHNB	D-	35.85	38.33	18.63	C- / 3.8	-0.44	-2.78	0.13 / 61	--	--
GL	*Global X Gold Explorers ETF	GLDX	E-	16.43	25.60	15.40	E / 0.5	-1.81	-8.76	-12.92 / 20	-32.05 / 3	-32.25 / 2
GL	*Global X Guru Activist Index	ACTX	U	12.78	N/A	N/A	U /	3.33	-10.51	--	--	--
GI	*Global X Guru Index ETF	GURU	B	23.22	27.40	12.60	C+ / 6.3	-1.77	-11.80	-10.89 / 24	9.02 / 72	--
FO	*Global X Guru International Idx	GURI	D+	12.46	15.57	11.61	D / 1.9	9.16	-13.38	-12.24 / 22	--	--
EN	*Global X Junior MLP ETF	MLPJ	E+	7.87	14.95	6.86	E- / 0.1	-14.09	-35.27	-39.37 / 4	--	--
GR	*Global X Lithium ETF	LIT	D	20.09	25.86	14.64	D / 1.9	8.46	-10.73	-8.99 / 28	-11.09 / 16	-13.78 / 10
EN	*Global X MLP & Energy Infra	MLPX	D-	11.61	19.67	10.35	E- / 0.1	-18.88	-33.61	-36.17 / 5	--	--
EN	*Global X MLP ETF	MLPA	D-	10.39	16.10	8.52	D / 1.8	-8.83	-23.83	-30.78 / 7	-6.10 / 23	--
FO	*Global X MSCI Argentina ETF	ARGT	C-	18.08	22.66	15.62	C / 4.9	13.11	-7.88	-1.88 / 51	1.09 / 42	--
FO	*Global X MSCI Colombia	GXG	E+	7.46	12.88	6.61	E / 0.4	-10.00	-28.17	-40.52 / 3	-28.55 / 4	-16.42 / 7
EM	*Global X MSCI Nigeria ETF	NGE	E+	7.06	11.22	6.63	E / 0.3	-14.62	-23.24	-29.34 / 8	--	--
FO	*Global X MSCI Norway ETF	NORW	D	9.69	13.93	9.67	D / 1.6	-5.32	-17.17	-15.64 / 17	-10.53 / 17	-5.41 / 18
EM	*Global X MSCI Pakistan ETF	PAK	U	13.02	N/A	N/A	U /	-1.23	-15.30	--	--	--
FO	*Global X NASDAQ China Tech ETF	QQQC	B+	22.97	29.00	16.73	A / 9.3	23.34	-10.41	9.60 / 87	16.66 / 92	6.68 / 53
EM	*Global X Next Emerg and Front ET	EMFM	D	17.24	23.97	16.76	E+ / 0.6	-3.87	-19.49	-23.09 / 11	--	--
GI	*Global X Permanent ETF	PERM	C-	23.10	25.51	23.01	C- / 3.5	-0.37	-2.41	-4.95 / 39	-1.79 / 31	--
FO	*Global X Scientific Beta Europe	SCID	U	23.64	N/A	N/A	U /	-1.86	--	--	--	--
FO	*Global X Scientific Beta Japan	SCIJ	U	25.33	N/A	N/A	U /	7.21	--	--	--	--
GR	*Global X Scientific Beta US	SCIU	U	24.28	N/A	N/A	U /	4.87	-0.48	--	--	--
PM	*Global X Silver Miners ETF	SIL	E	18.51	33.57	17.86	E / 0.3	-9.90	-27.15	-34.30 / 6	-34.91 / 3	-23.62 / 5
GL	*Global X Social Media Index ETF	SOCL	A-	19.87	21.21	15.20	A- / 9.0	10.89	-0.19	9.54 / 87	13.91 / 87	--
GL	*Global X Southeast Asia ETF	ASEA	D+	12.13	16.44	11.02	D / 2.0	3.86	-16.66	-19.65 / 14	-8.01 / 20	--
GL	*Global X SuperDividend Alternati	ALTY	U	13.85	N/A	N/A	U /	2.27	--	--	--	--
EM	*Global X SuperDividend Em Mkts	SDEM	U	12.28	N/A	N/A	U /	-2.81	-23.97	--	--	--
GL	*Global X SuperDividend ETF	SDIV	C	19.72	24.34	18.55	C / 4.4	0.97	-7.74	-9.20 / 28	2.27 / 50	--
GI	*Global X SuperDividend REIT	SRET	U	12.64	N/A	N/A	U /	0.62	-5.10	--	--	--
IN	*Global X SuperDividend US ETF	DIV	D+	23.94	29.57	16.00	D / 2.0	1.31	-5.82	-11.84 / 22	--	--
GL	*Global X SuperIncome Preferred E	SPFF	C+	13.15	14.76	11.32	C / 5.0	0.03	-3.22	-3.90 / 43	2.32 / 50	--
GL	*Global X Uranium ETF	URA	E+	13.99	24.42	12.72	E / 0.5	0.63	-22.28	-37.58 / 4	-28.02 / 4	-33.37 / 2
FS	*Global X Yieldco Index	YLCO	U	10.72	N/A	N/A	U /	8.06	-22.94	--	--	--
GR	*Goldman Sachs ActiveBeta US LC E	GSLC	U	41.51	N/A	N/A	U /	5.92	--	--	--	--
GI	*GreenHaven Continuous Commodity	GCC	D	18.52	22.94	17.96	D- / 1.3	-5.71	-15.66	-18.66 / 15	-13.59 / 13	-10.53 / 13
GR	*GS Cnct S&P GSCI Enh Cmd TR Str	GSC	E+	20.08	31.61	19.51	E / 0.5	-15.06	-31.35	-32.98 / 6	-25.19 / 5	-15.96 / 8
FO	*Guggenheim Australian Dollar Tr	FXA	D	72.97	82.47	69.11	D / 2.1	3.76	-3.83	-8.61 / 29	-9.80 / 18	-3.80 / 21
COI	*Guggenheim BltShs 2016 Corp Bond	BSCG	B	22.08	22.29	22.02	C / 4.9	-0.18	0.07	0.99 / 67	1.20 / 43	3.08 / 38
COH	*Guggenheim BltShs 2016 Hi Yld Co	BSJG	B	25.87	26.46	25.58	C+ / 5.6	0.73	-0.20	2.56 / 73	3.15 / 54	--
COI	*Guggenheim BltShs 2017 Corp Bond	BSCH	B	22.52	22.91	21.65	C / 4.9	-0.27	-0.14	0.81 / 66	1.26 / 43	3.72 / 42
COH	*Guggenheim BltShs 2017 Hi Yld Co	BSJH	B-	24.96	26.75	24.73	C / 5.1	-0.54	-3.88	-0.55 / 57	2.13 / 49	--
COI	*Guggenheim BltShs 2018 Corp Bond	BSCI	C+	21.02	21.40	20.77	C / 5.1	-0.45	-0.18	1.40 / 69	1.61 / 46	--
COH	*Guggenheim BltShs 2018 Hi Yld Co	BSJI	C+	23.66	26.35	23.50	C- / 4.1	-2.45	-6.61	-4.16 / 42	1.19 / 43	--

* Denotes ETF Fund, N/A denotes number is not available

Incl. in Returns		RISK				NET ASSETS		VALUATION			ASSET					FUND MANAGER	
		Risk Rating/ Pts	3 Year		Avg Dura-tion	NAV as of 12/31/15	Total $(Mil)	Premium / Discount		Wtd Avg P/E					Portfolio Turnover Ratio	Manager Quality Pct	Manager Tenure (Years)
Dividend Yield %	Expense Ratio		Standard Deviation	Beta				As of 12/31/15	1 Year Average		Cash %	Stocks %	Bonds %	Other %			
4.86	0.65	**C+ / 6.6**	19.7	1.00	N/A	12.22	139	-0.49	-0.47	N/A	0	99	0	1	19	18	7
3.26	0.65	**C+ / 6.0**	20.6	0.86	N/A	10.12	5	-0.20	-0.22	N/A	0	99	0	1	13	25	7
5.33	0.65	**C+ / 6.4**	25.4	0.71	N/A	13.87	46	-1.30	-0.32	N/A	0	99	0	1	7	21	7
2.72	0.65	**C+ / 5.9**	27.2	0.86	N/A	12.71	3	-0.47	0.02	N/A	0	99	0	1	11	47	7
5.88	0.65	**C / 5.4**	27.6	0.94	N/A	12.22	3	-1.47	0.39	N/A	0	99	0	1	14	12	6
1.20	0.65	**D+ / 2.4**	34.9	0.67	N/A	11.81	31	0.00	0.28	N/A	0	100	0	0	16	5	6
3.66	0.69	**C+ / 6.1**	16.7	0.81	N/A	9.05	18	-0.33	-0.41	N/A	0	100	0	0	19	10	5
2.75	0.72	**C / 4.4**	19.5	1.00	N/A	6.30	9	-1.27	0.25	N/A	0	99	0	1	20	3	5
1.52	0.62	**D+ / 2.7**	42.1	2.04	N/A	8.11	188	-1.85	0.97	N/A	0	99	0	1	64	3	5
2.95	0.50	**B / 8.0**	13.4	0.95	N/A	21.55	63	-0.56	-0.09	N/A	0	99	0	1	6	76	7
4.53	0.61	**C / 5.4**	N/A	N/A	N/A	10.15	44	-0.39	-0.04	N/A	0	0	0	100	54	84	3
4.52	N/A	**D+ / 2.6**	N/A	N/A	N/A	36.67	N/A	-2.24	-0.34	N/A	0	0	0	100	N/A	61	2
1.70	0.65	**D- / 1.3**	51.8	0.16	N/A	16.35	37	0.49	-0.03	N/A	0	100	0	0	30	2	6
1.36	N/A	**U /**	N/A	N/A	N/A	12.79	N/A	-0.08	N/A	N/A	0	0	0	100	N/A	N/A	1
0.47	0.75	**B / 8.4**	13.0	1.10	N/A	23.23	491	-0.04	-0.04	N/A	0	0	0	100	128	29	4
1.74	0.75	**B- / 7.0**	N/A	N/A	N/A	12.48	2	-0.16	-0.19	N/A	0	0	0	100	63	14	2
3.72	0.75	**C / 4.5**	N/A	N/A	N/A	7.90	18	-0.38	-0.05	N/A	0	0	0	100	70	12	3
0.24	0.75	**C+ / 6.1**	22.2	1.16	N/A	20.24	54	-0.74	-0.20	N/A	0	100	0	0	43	5	6
5.50	0.45	**C+ / 5.7**	N/A	N/A	N/A	11.62	183	-0.09	0.01	N/A	0	0	0	100	29	8	3
8.66	0.47	**C / 4.4**	15.2	0.52	N/A	10.36	139	0.29	N/A	N/A	0	0	0	100	31	42	4
0.89	0.74	**C / 4.8**	26.8	1.37	N/A	18.00	24	0.44	0.07	N/A	0	99	0	1	95	32	5
1.58	0.66	**C- / 3.4**	27.8	1.05	N/A	7.47	109	-0.13	0.23	N/A	1	98	0	1	48	2	7
4.30	0.68	**C- / 4.2**	N/A	N/A	N/A	7.23	20	-2.35	0.32	N/A	0	0	0	100	55	3	3
3.84	0.50	**C / 5.4**	19.2	1.18	N/A	9.73	209	-0.41	0.13	N/A	0	99	0	1	27	10	6
4.21	N/A	**U /**	N/A	N/A	N/A	13.07	N/A	-0.38	N/A	N/A	0	0	0	100	N/A	N/A	1
0.63	0.65	**C+ / 6.5**	26.5	0.98	N/A	22.99	22	-0.09	-0.58	N/A	1	98	0	1	65	96	7
2.69	0.58	**C+ / 6.4**	N/A	N/A	N/A	17.39	157	-0.86	-0.35	N/A	0	0	0	100	24	11	3
1.10	0.48	**B- / 7.2**	6.5	0.12	N/A	23.05	11	0.22	0.26	N/A	0	0	0	100	25	37	4
2.49	N/A	**U /**	N/A	N/A	N/A	23.51	N/A	0.55	N/A	N/A	0	0	0	100	N/A	N/A	1
1.40	N/A	**U /**	N/A	N/A	N/A	25.34	N/A	-0.04	N/A	N/A	0	0	0	100	N/A	N/A	1
2.05	N/A	**U /**	N/A	N/A	N/A	24.08	N/A	0.83	N/A	N/A	0	0	0	100	N/A	N/A	1
0.38	0.65	**D+ / 2.8**	40.5	1.95	N/A	18.56	200	-0.27	0.06	N/A	0	99	0	1	24	12	6
0.01	0.65	**B- / 7.3**	21.1	0.94	N/A	19.97	136	-0.50	-0.14	N/A	0	0	0	100	27	95	5
3.64	0.65	**C+ / 6.4**	15.9	0.94	N/A	12.29	30	-1.30	-0.37	N/A	0	99	0	1	8	13	5
5.59	N/A	**U /**	N/A	N/A	N/A	13.77	N/A	0.58	N/A	N/A	0	0	0	100	N/A	N/A	1
1.01	N/A	**U /**	N/A	N/A	N/A	12.28	N/A	0.00	N/A	N/A	0	0	0	100	N/A	N/A	N/A
.72	0.58	**B- / 7.3**	13.6	1.34	N/A	19.84	1,071	-0.60	-0.02	N/A	0	100	0	0	34	94	5
.22	N/A	**U /**	N/A	N/A	N/A	12.55	N/A	0.72	N/A	N/A	0	0	0	100	N/A	N/A	N/A
.14	0.45	**C+ / 6.3**	N/A	N/A	N/A	23.92	211	0.08	0.01	N/A	0	0	0	100	40	14	3
.57	0.58	**B / 8.8**	3.6	0.19	N/A	13.19	145	-0.30	0.03	N/A	0	0	0	100	85	86	4
.96	0.69	**C- / 3.5**	30.9	1.03	N/A	14.09	239	-0.71	-0.19	N/A	0	99	0	1	21	2	6
.48	N/A	**U /**	N/A	N/A	N/A	10.68	N/A	0.37	N/A	N/A	0	0	0	100	N/A	N/A	1
.46	N/A	**U /**	N/A	N/A	N/A	41.50	N/A	0.02	N/A	N/A	0	0	0	100	N/A	N/A	1
.00	1.05	**C+ / 6.6**	11.4	0.30	N/A	18.56	321	-0.22	-0.02	N/A	100	0	0	0	N/A	9	N/A
.00	N/A	**C- / 3.4**	21.6	0.64	N/A	20.08	N/A	0.00	-0.05	N/A	0	0	0	100	N/A	2	9
.40	0.40	**C / 5.3**	10.1	0.39	N/A	72.84	259	0.18	0.02	N/A	100	0	0	0	N/A	14	10
.02	0.24	**B+ / 9.9**	1.1	0.14	N/A	22.09	658	-0.05	0.02	N/A	0	0	100	0	17	76	3
.82	0.43	**B+ / 9.5**	3.7	0.56	N/A	25.88	617	-0.04	-0.04	N/A	0	0	0	100	40	82	3
.49	0.24	**B+ / 9.8**	1.9	0.39	N/A	22.54	688	-0.09	0.14	N/A	0	0	100	0	8	74	3
.99	0.43	**B+ / 9.2**	4.1	0.73	N/A	24.97	363	-0.04	0.16	N/A	0	0	0	100	20	77	3
.81	0.24	**B- / 7.9**	2.4	0.50	N/A	20.96	411	0.29	0.26	N/A	0	0	0	100	5	75	3
.33	0.43	**B / 8.8**	4.5	0.80	N/A	23.75	272	-0.38	0.18	N/A	0	0	0	100	28	70	4

Denotes ETF Fund, N/A denotes number is not available

Fund Type	Fund Name (99 Pct = Best, 0 Pct = Worst)	Ticker Symbol	Overall Investment Rating	PRICE: Price As of 12/31/15	PRICE: 52 Week High	PRICE: 52 Week Low	PERFORMANCE: Performance Rating/Pts	% Total Return Through 12/31/15: 3 Mo	6 Mo	1Yr/Pct	Annualized 3Yr/Pct	Annualized 5Yr/Pct
COI	*Guggenheim BltShs 2019 Corp Bond	BSCJ	C+	20.86	21.45	20.80	C / 5.2	-0.73	0.15	1.46 / 70	1.77 / 47	--
COH	*Guggenheim BltShs 2019 Hi Yld Co	BSJJ	C-	22.73	25.55	22.56	D+ / 2.4	-1.96	-7.47	-4.80 / 40	--	--
COI	*Guggenheim BltShs 2020 Corp Bond	BSCK	C+	20.89	22.22	20.83	C / 5.2	-1.49	-0.43	1.39 / 69	2.14 / 49	--
COH	*Guggenheim BltShs 2020 Hi Yld Co	BSJK	C-	22.52	26.41	22.28	D / 2.1	-2.81	-8.88	-6.03 / 36	--	--
COI	*Guggenheim BltShs 2021 Corp Bond	BSCL	C	20.52	21.46	20.43	C- / 4.2	-1.26	-0.02	0.47 / 64	--	--
COH	*Guggenheim BltShs 2021 Hi Yld Co	BSJL	C-	22.84	26.05	22.58	D+ / 2.8	-1.32	-5.74	-2.46 / 48	--	--
COI	*Guggenheim BltShs 2022 Corp Bond	BSCM	C	20.29	21.43	20.19	C- / 4.0	-1.30	-0.03	0.01 / 60	--	--
COH	*Guggenheim BltShs 2022 Hi Yld Co	BSJM	C	22.57	25.66	21.99	D+ / 2.6	-1.94	-6.87	-3.38 / 45	--	--
COI	*Guggenheim BltShs 2023 Corp Bond	BSCN	C	19.93	22.00	19.83	C- / 3.9	-1.01	0.05	-0.62 / 57	--	--
COH	*Guggenheim BltShs 2023 Hi Yld Co	BSJN	U	24.15	N/A	N/A	U /	--	--	--	--	--
COI	*Guggenheim BltShs 2024 Corp Bond	BSCO	C	19.77	22.01	19.40	C- / 3.8	-1.01	0.32	-1.24 / 54	--	--
COI	*Guggenheim BltShs 2025 Corp Bond	BSCP	U	19.64	N/A	N/A	U /	--	--	--	--	--
IN	*Guggenheim BRIC ETF	EEB	D	24.34	32.93	19.08	D / 1.8	1.86	-16.36	-12.73 / 21	-10.58 / 17	-9.22 / 14
FO	*Guggenheim British Pound Sterlin	FXB	C-	144.32	156.04	143.59	C- / 3.1	-3.07	-5.70	-4.18 / 42	-3.18 / 28	-1.36 / 24
FO	*Guggenheim Canadian Dollar Tr	FXC	D	71.67	84.63	70.90	D / 1.7	-4.98	-9.55	-15.21 / 18	-10.59 / 16	-6.36 / 17
EN	*Guggenheim Canadian Energy Inc E	ENY	E+	6.77	12.03	6.45	E+ / 0.6	-10.37	-31.30	-40.25 / 3	-22.19 / 7	-16.97 / 7
FO	*Guggenheim China All-Cap ETF	YAO	C-	24.95	34.56	19.90	C- / 3.8	4.13	-16.48	-7.01 / 33	0.66 / 40	0.21 / 28
GI	*Guggenheim China Real Estate ETF	TAO	C-	19.80	26.47	16.88	C- / 3.4	3.23	-10.24	-2.49 / 48	-2.23 / 30	1.45 / 32
FO	*Guggenheim China Small Cap ETF	HAO	C-	24.18	36.40	20.26	C- / 4.0	1.94	-18.05	-3.61 / 44	1.43 / 44	-2.35 / 23
FO	*Guggenheim China Technology ETF	CQQQ	B+	36.01	45.64	26.00	A / 9.3	17.57	-6.66	6.28 / 82	17.07 / 92	6.30 / 52
GI	*Guggenheim Chinese Renminbi Tr	FXCH	C-	76.47	80.96	74.05	C- / 3.5	-1.41	-4.59	-2.92 / 47	-1.50 / 32	--
IN	*Guggenheim Defensive Equity ETF	DEF	B	34.83	39.89	30.34	C+ / 6.8	1.55	-3.87	-4.73 / 40	8.74 / 72	9.93 / 65
GI	*Guggenheim Em Mkt RE ETF	EMRE	D+	21.08	28.12	19.00	D / 1.7	2.67	-12.38	-10.42 / 25	--	--
GR	*Guggenheim Enhanced Short Dur	GSY	C+	49.86	50.21	49.76	C / 4.8	-0.08	0.04	0.83 / 66	0.98 / 42	0.93 / 30
FO	*Guggenheim Euro	FXE	D+	106.40	117.73	102.92	D+ / 2.5	-3.14	-2.21	-9.98 / 26	-6.41 / 22	-3.68 / 21
GL	*Guggenheim Frontier Markets ETF	FRN	D	10.70	14.26	10.45	D- / 1.1	-0.79	-17.71	-20.99 / 12	-17.02 / 10	-12.11 / 12
IN	*Guggenheim Insider Sentiment ETF	NFO	B-	46.54	51.86	32.80	B- / 7.3	4.69	-6.25	-3.59 / 44	9.98 / 75	8.76 / 60
FO	*Guggenheim Intl Multi-Asset Inc	HGI	C-	14.26	18.50	13.91	D+ / 2.9	-1.32	-14.42	-12.40 / 21	-2.20 / 30	-1.54 / 24
FO	*Guggenheim Japanese Yen Trust	FXY	D	80.63	83.66	77.19	D+ / 2.3	-0.16	2.18	-0.11 / 59	-10.17 / 17	-7.49 / 16
GR	*Guggenheim Mid-Cap Core ETF	CZA	B+	47.93	52.36	36.11	B / 8.0	1.47	-5.13	-1.73 / 51	12.39 / 83	11.67 / 76
EM	*Guggenheim MSCI EM Eq Cntry Weig	EWEM	D	25.89	34.70	24.41	D / 1.8	-2.71	-18.19	-17.50 / 15	-8.99 / 18	-7.09 / 17
IN	*Guggenheim Multi-Asset Income ET	CVY	C-	18.18	23.10	17.50	C- / 3.0	-2.28	-11.39	-14.32 / 19	-1.71 / 32	3.61 / 41
IN	*Guggenheim Raymond James SB1 Eq	RYJ	C+	32.57	38.07	24.78	B- / 7.2	0.65	-10.19	-5.92 / 36	10.74 / 78	9.46 / 63
IN	*Guggenheim Russ Top 50 Mega Cap	XLG	A+	144.58	149.09	68.05	B+ / 8.9	7.68	2.56	4.42 / 78	13.38 / 85	12.21 / 80
GR	*Guggenheim Russell 1000 Eq Wght	EWRI	B	48.03	53.53	45.42	B / 7.7	2.87	-6.02	-3.95 / 43	11.47 / 79	10.70 / 70
GR	*Guggenheim Russell 2000 Eq Wght	EWRS	C+	40.23	47.99	38.50	C+ / 5.9	1.68	-10.74	-9.67 / 26	6.98 / 67	6.22 / 52
GR	*Guggenheim Russell MC Eq Wght ET	EWRM	B+	47.39	53.59	31.61	B- / 7.4	1.01	-6.89	-5.27 / 38	10.85 / 78	10.41 / 68
GR	*Guggenheim S&P 500 Eq WgCon Dsc	RCD	A+	84.69	93.31	71.00	B+ / 8.5	-1.00	-6.49	-2.36 / 49	14.70 / 89	14.51 / 90
GR	*Guggenheim S&P 500 Eq WgCon St E	RHS	A+	116.02	117.82	69.51	A+ / 9.6	8.10	9.74	13.70 / 94	19.81 / 95	17.90 / 96
EN	*Guggenheim S&P 500 Eq Wght Engy	RYE	D	47.09	74.09	44.33	D- / 1.5	-8.64	-25.07	-28.92 / 8	-9.51 / 18	-4.27 / 20
FS	*Guggenheim S&P 500 Eq Wght Finl	RYF	A+	43.20	45.80	30.83	B+ / 8.8	5.41	-1.85	-1.46 / 52	14.35 / 89	11.32 / 74
GR	*Guggenheim S&P 500 Eq Wght HC ET	RYH	A+	153.49	165.20	116.04	A+ / 9.6	6.44	-4.17	7.93 / 85	24.52 / 97	20.15 / 98
GR	*Guggenheim S&P 500 Eq Wght Ind E	RGI	B	82.96	92.55	48.13	B / 7.8	4.57	-3.74	-6.76 / 34	12.09 / 82	10.50 / 68
GR	*Guggenheim S&P 500 Eq Wght Mat E	RTM	C	76.43	91.46	70.10	C+ / 5.9	4.00	-10.42	-7.48 / 32	6.35 / 65	5.64 / 50
GR	*Guggenheim S&P 500 Eq Wght Tech	RYT	A+	92.27	95.91	75.85	A / 9.4	7.15	2.42	2.90 / 74	18.67 / 94	12.00 / 78
UT	*Guggenheim S&P 500 Eq Wght Util	RYU	A-	72.35	81.93	68.03	B / 7.8	2.88	4.84	-4.64 / 40	10.72 / 77	11.31 / 74
GI	*Guggenheim S&P 500 Equal Weight	EWRE	U	26.10	N/A	N/A	U /	11.91	--	--	--	--
IN	*Guggenheim S&P 500 Equal Wght	RSP	A+	76.64	83.15	43.77	B+ / 8.4	3.16	-3.68	-2.62 / 48	13.42 / 86	11.77 / 77
GR	*Guggenheim S&P 500 Pure Growth	RPG	A+	80.70	85.30	39.80	A- / 9.2	2.41	-0.90	2.25 / 72	17.47 / 93	13.80 / 87
IN	*Guggenheim S&P 500 Pure Value	RPV	A	49.20	56.22	41.06	B / 8.0	1.82	-7.67	-8.26 / 30	13.58 / 86	13.00 / 84
IN	*Guggenheim S&P Gl Div Opps Idx E	LVL	D+	8.73	12.44	8.41	D / 1.9	-2.00	-18.72	-19.50 / 14	-8.17 / 20	-3.83 / 21
EN	*Guggenheim S&P Global Water Idx	CGW	B	27.14	30.14	24.50	C+ / 6.8	2.58	-3.89	-1.31 / 54	8.07 / 70	7.72 / 57

* Denotes ETF Fund, N/A denotes number is not available

Incl. in Returns		RISK				NET ASSETS		VALUATION			ASSET					FUND MANAGER	
			3 Year					Premium / Discount									
Dividend Yield %	Expense Ratio	Risk Rating/ Pts	Standard Deviation	Beta	Avg Dura-tion	NAV as of 12/31/15	Total $(Mil)	As of 12/31/15	1 Year Average	Wtd Avg P/E	Cash %	Stocks %	Bonds %	Other %	Portfolio Turnover Ratio	Manager Quality Pct	Manager Tenure (Years)
2.12	0.24	**B- / 7.8**	3.1	0.67	N/A	20.83	201	0.14	0.27	N/A	0	0	0	100	5	75	4
5.23	0.43	**B / 8.6**	N/A	N/A	N/A	22.79	72	-0.26	0.20	N/A	0	0	0	100	30	68	3
3.00	0.24	**B- / 7.7**	3.7	0.84	N/A	20.84	176	0.24	0.29	N/A	0	0	0	100	4	74	3
5.98	0.43	**B / 8.5**	N/A	N/A	N/A	22.58	34	-0.27	0.25	N/A	0	0	0	100	22	67	3
2.83	0.24	**B- / 7.9**	N/A	N/A	N/A	20.44	68	0.39	0.28	N/A	0	0	0	100	3	79	3
5.03	0.43	**B / 8.0**	N/A	N/A	N/A	22.84	N/A	0.00	0.23	N/A	0	0	0	100	3	84	N/A
3.05	0.24	**B- / 7.8**	N/A	N/A	N/A	20.24	56	0.25	0.18	N/A	0	0	0	100	2	76	3
5.38	0.43	**B / 8.7**	N/A	N/A	N/A	22.67	N/A	-0.44	0.22	N/A	0	0	0	100	6	81	N/A
4.37	0.24	**B- / 7.8**	N/A	N/A	N/A	19.86	N/A	0.35	0.47	N/A	0	0	0	100	1	79	2
8.88	N/A	**U /**	N/A	N/A	N/A	24.57	N/A	-1.71	N/A	N/A	0	0	0	100	N/A	N/A	1
4.72	0.24	**B / 8.4**	N/A	N/A	N/A	19.77	N/A	0.00	0.24	N/A	0	0	0	100	8	75	2
5.65	N/A	**U /**	N/A	N/A	N/A	19.68	N/A	-0.20	N/A	N/A	0	0	0	100	N/A	N/A	1
1.99	0.64	**C+ / 6.0**	20.6	1.23	N/A	24.36	162	-0.08	-0.23	N/A	0	100	0	0	24	5	3
0.00	0.40	**B- / 7.7**	7.5	0.29	N/A	144.31	88	0.01	0.01	N/A	100	0	0	0	N/A	30	10
0.00	0.40	**C+ / 5.7**	8.8	0.35	N/A	71.42	258	0.35	-0.01	N/A	100	0	0	0	N/A	13	10
4.18	0.70	**C- / 3.5**	25.4	1.23	N/A	6.75	41	0.30	-0.08	9.2	0	99	0	1	28	8	6
3.50	0.70	**C+ / 6.7**	20.6	1.00	N/A	25.06	51	-0.44	-0.17	N/A	0	99	0	1	17	39	3
4.90	0.70	**B- / 7.1**	18.6	0.68	N/A	20.10	38	-1.49	-0.38	N/A	0	100	0	0	16	16	6
3.88	0.75	**C+ / 6.3**	23.7	0.92	N/A	24.42	213	-0.98	-0.36	N/A	0	100	0	0	31	52	6
1.77	0.70	**C+ / 6.3**	26.0	1.17	N/A	36.21	76	-0.55	-0.33	N/A	0	99	0	1	32	96	3
0.00	0.40	**B- / 7.3**	5.2	0.06	N/A	75.16	8	1.74	0.07	N/A	0	0	0	100	N/A	48	5
3.31	0.65	**B / 8.1**	9.6	0.70	N/A	34.83	201	0.00	-0.01	39.4	0	82	0	18	96	62	3
1.65	0.65	**B- / 7.0**	N/A	N/A	N/A	21.25	N/A	-0.80	-0.04	N/A	0	0	0	100	25	14	N/A
2.07	0.25	**B / 8.4**	0.3	0.01	N/A	49.85	717	0.02	-0.01	N/A	1	29	44	26	44	75	5
0.00	0.40	**C+ / 6.2**	8.4	0.23	N/A	106.34	218	0.06	-0.04	N/A	100	0	0	0	N/A	20	11
1.90	0.70	**C / 5.5**	15.8	0.87	N/A	10.78	95	-0.74	-0.50	N/A	0	100	0	0	94	7	6
1.54	0.65	**C+ / 6.9**	13.5	1.17	N/A	46.45	166	0.19	-0.02	70.9	0	100	0	0	112	28	3
3.65	0.70	**B- / 7.6**	13.4	0.96	N/A	14.36	33	-0.70	-0.24	9.6	0	100	0	0	108	24	6
0.00	0.40	**C+ / 5.8**	7.7	-0.11	N/A	80.55	67	0.10	-0.01	N/A	100	0	0	0	N/A	16	8
1.37	0.65	**B- / 7.3**	10.6	0.94	N/A	47.87	142	0.13	0.10	42.6	0	86	0	14	164	64	3
0.76	0.60	**C / 5.1**	15.1	0.98	N/A	25.49	14	1.57	-0.12	N/A	3	96	0	1	25	47	6
5.51	0.65	**B- / 7.4**	11.6	0.95	N/A	18.21	1,300	-0.16	-0.10	23.5	0	95	0	5	213	12	3
.93	0.75	**C+ / 6.9**	13.0	1.03	N/A	32.56	255	0.03	-0.07	84.7	0	94	0	6	95	43	3
.89	0.20	**B / 8.5**	11.2	1.03	N/A	144.63	532	-0.03	0.02	68.6	0	99	0	1	6	59	11
.35	0.41	**B- / 7.0**	11.5	1.02	N/A	47.88	118	0.31	-0.01	N/A	0	99	0	1	27	51	N/A
.97	0.42	**B- / 7.6**	15.5	1.12	N/A	40.24	38	-0.02	-0.03	N/A	0	99	0	1	43	23	N/A
.31	0.41	**B / 8.2**	11.6	1.01	N/A	47.40	143	-0.02	-0.03	N/A	0	99	0	1	29	45	N/A
.62	0.40	**B / 8.7**	13.5	1.15	N/A	84.73	108	-0.05	0.01	66.6	0	99	0	1	22	56	N/A
.77	0.40	**B- / 7.7**	10.8	0.81	N/A	115.93	146	0.08	0.04	39.1	0	99	0	1	20	93	N/A
.54	0.40	**C / 5.2**	21.8	1.14	N/A	47.09	212	0.00	N/A	14.6	0	99	0	1	25	36	N/A
.61	0.40	**B / 8.9**	11.6	1.02	N/A	43.22	133	-0.05	0.01	36.1	0	99	0	1	19	71	N/A
.56	0.40	**B- / 7.5**	12.3	0.92	N/A	153.51	335	-0.01	0.04	81.6	0	99	0	1	23	95	N/A
.75	0.40	**B- / 7.1**	12.4	1.09	N/A	82.75	106	0.25	-0.01	39.8	0	99	0	1	15	45	N/A
.72	0.40	**C+ / 6.6**	15.2	1.20	N/A	76.11	79	0.42	0.04	39.2	0	99	0	1	22	17	N/A
.69	0.40	**B / 8.3**	13.0	1.12	N/A	92.33	620	-0.06	0.01	70.0	0	99	0	1	22	82	N/A
.56	0.40	**B / 8.4**	12.8	0.86	N/A	72.37	82	-0.03	-0.01	22.3	0	99	0	1	31	77	N/A
.26	N/A	**U /**	N/A	N/A	N/A	25.81	N/A	1.12	N/A	N/A	0	0	0	100	N/A	N/A	N/A
.76	0.40	**B / 8.6**	10.9	1.01	N/A	76.69	8,677	-0.07	-0.01	48.4	0	99	0	1	18	62	N/A
.05	0.35	**B / 8.3**	11.8	1.01	N/A	80.75	1,754	-0.06	0.02	86.8	0	99	0	1	46	84	N/A
13	0.35	**B / 8.6**	13.5	1.18	N/A	49.24	1,326	-0.08	-0.01	20.6	0	99	0	1	25	45	N/A
12	0.65	**C+ / 6.8**	15.9	1.06	N/A	8.80	94	-0.80	-0.22	18.0	0	100	0	0	74	7	6
67	0.64	**B- / 7.8**	12.4	0.48	N/A	27.14	350	0.00	0.08	41.4	0	100	0	0	9	95	3

Denotes ETF Fund, N/A denotes number is not available

99 Pct = Best
0 Pct = Worst

Fund Type	Fund Name	Ticker Symbol	Overall Investment Rating	PRICE: Price As of 12/31/15	PRICE: 52 Week High	PRICE: 52 Week Low	PERFORMANCE: Performance Rating/Pts	% Total Return Through 12/31/15: 3 Mo	6 Mo	1Yr/Pct	Annualized: 3Yr/Pct	Annualized: 5Yr/Pct
GL	*Guggenheim S&P High Income Infr	GHII	U	21.41	N/A	N/A	U /	-1.66	-9.51	--	--	--
GR	*Guggenheim S&P Mid Cap 400 Pure	RFV	C+	47.65	57.07	31.47	C+ / 6.2	-0.85	-11.47	-10.58 / 25	8.72 / 72	8.34 / 59
GR	*Guggenheim S&P Mid Cap 400 Pure	RFG	B-	124.69	139.53	93.68	B / 7.6	0.29	-5.69	2.95 / 74	10.50 / 76	10.37 / 67
GR	*Guggenheim S&P Sm Cap 600 Pure G	RZG	B-	80.86	93.18	58.03	B / 8.0	-0.69	-9.30	1.65 / 70	12.39 / 82	11.51 / 75
GR	*Guggenheim S&P Sm Cap 600 Pure V	RZV	C+	54.82	66.52	47.48	C+ / 5.9	1.52	-12.74	-12.11 / 22	7.65 / 69	7.89 / 57
GL	*Guggenheim Shipping ETF	SEA	D-	12.67	20.43	12.12	D / 2.0	-13.16	-26.45	-25.32 / 10	-4.61 / 25	-11.34 / 12
GL	*Guggenheim Singapore Dollar Tr	FXSG	C-	69.13	77.33	66.48	D / 2.2	0.19	-7.46	-7.77 / 31	--	--
EN	*Guggenheim Solar ETF	TAN	C	30.64	50.00	25.25	A / 9.3	8.62	-19.25	-8.39 / 30	20.70 / 95	-12.59 / 11
IN	*Guggenheim Spin-Off ETF	CSD	C+	38.44	49.27	33.50	C+ / 6.4	1.31	-13.96	-12.00 / 22	9.40 / 73	12.39 / 81
FO	*Guggenheim Swedish Krona	FXS	C-	116.47	125.60	111.90	D+ / 2.3	-1.20	-0.91	-7.38 / 32	-8.46 / 19	-3.66 / 21
FO	*Guggenheim Swiss Franc	FXF	C	96.37	115.42	93.75	C- / 3.1	-3.26	-6.39	-1.07 / 54	-3.26 / 28	-1.24 / 25
GL	*Guggenheim Timber ETF	CUT	B-	23.57	27.16	20.00	C+ / 6.1	5.18	-6.81	-0.71 / 56	5.83 / 64	4.32 / 45
IN	*Guggenheim Wilshire MicroCap ETF	WMCR	B	25.51	29.30	24.39	B / 7.9	3.06	-8.53	-3.53 / 44	12.33 / 82	8.16 / 58
GI	*Guggenheim Wilshire US REIT ETF	WREI	B	45.82	49.99	40.92	B+ / 8.4	7.40	8.86	2.66 / 73	11.16 / 79	12.29 / 81
HL	*Health Care Select Sector SPDR	XLV	A+	72.03	77.40	56.63	A+ / 9.6	6.35	-2.60	6.93 / 83	22.80 / 96	19.73 / 97
LP	*Highland/iBoxx Senior Loan ETF	SNLN	C	18.05	19.49	17.62	C / 4.3	-1.30	-4.02	-2.09 / 50	0.88 / 41	--
FO	*Horizons Korea KOSPI 200 ETF	HKOR	C-	28.17	36.70	26.44	D+ / 2.6	3.64	-8.60	-5.25 / 38	--	--
GR	*Horizons S&P 500 Covered Call	HSPX	C	43.77	48.35	39.88	C+ / 5.8	6.49	0.48	1.29 / 69	--	--
GR	*Hull Tactical US	HTUS	U	25.05	N/A	N/A	U /	2.08	1.32	--	--	--
GL	*Huntington EcoLogical Strategy E	HECO	B+	35.65	47.08	34.72	B / 8.2	7.01	-1.30	1.93 / 71	11.47 / 79	--
IN	*Huntington US Eq Rotation Strat	HUSE	A-	37.89	39.34	22.41	A- / 9.0	9.27	2.42	4.40 / 78	14.95 / 90	--
GR	*Industrial Select Sector SPDR	XLI	A+	53.01	58.23	47.60	B+ / 8.4	6.40	-0.52	-3.60 / 44	13.10 / 85	10.92 / 71
FS	*Innovator IBD 50	FFTY	U	22.17	N/A	N/A	U /	-0.27	-11.64	--	--	--
EN	*iPath Bloomberg Agri SI TR A	JJA	E+	34.35	42.77	31.85	D- / 1.3	-3.24	-15.33	-16.26 / 16	-13.92 / 13	-10.86 / 13
EN	*iPath Bloomberg Almin SI TR A	JJU	E	13.59	19.13	13.02	D- / 1.0	-4.80	-14.34	-25.88 / 9	-17.32 / 10	-16.42 / 7
EN	*iPath Bloomberg Cocoa SI TR A	NIB	C	41.32	44.28	34.59	B / 8.2	3.46	-3.66	7.60 / 84	11.05 / 79	0.52 / 29
EN	*iPath Bloomberg Coffee SI TR A	JO	E+	19.70	33.79	17.98	D- / 1.1	-2.43	-7.73	-32.28 / 7	-15.92 / 11	-20.47 / 6
GR	*iPath Bloomberg Commodity Index	DJP	D-	21.47	30.98	20.72	E+ / 0.8	-12.37	-25.58	-27.59 / 8	-19.36 / 9	-14.80 / 9
EN	*iPath Bloomberg Copper SI TR A	JJC	E	24.64	35.60	22.95	E+ / 0.8	-10.17	-21.43	-27.21 / 9	-19.19 / 9	-15.41 / 8
EN	*iPath Bloomberg Cotton SI TR A	BAL	D-	42.04	46.30	38.80	C- / 3.1	4.73	-6.72	3.65 / 76	-4.98 / 25	-10.03 / 13
EN	*iPath Bloomberg Energy SI TR A	JJE	E-	5.66	11.21	5.13	E / 0.3	-26.10	-43.67	-44.34 / 3	-30.74 / 4	-24.20 / 4
EN	*iPath Bloomberg Grains SI TR A	JJG	E+	30.35	40.00	30.30	D- / 1.1	-8.09	-21.60	-20.51 / 13	-16.13 / 11	-9.90 / 13
EN	*iPath Bloomberg Ind Me SI TR A	JJM	E+	19.10	28.28	18.08	E+ / 0.9	-8.50	-21.24	-29.18 / 8	-18.32 / 9	-16.05 / 7
EN	*iPath Bloomberg Lead SI TR A	LD	E+	35.59	47.65	34.57	D- / 1.4	-0.34	-6.54	-13.78 / 19	-14.38 / 12	-11.71 / 12
EN	*iPath Bloomberg Live Stk SI TR A	COW	D-	23.93	30.61	21.46	D / 2.2	-3.70	-12.18	-21.64 / 12	-5.94 / 23	-4.59 / 20
EN	*iPath Bloomberg Nkl SI TR A	JJN	E-	10.81	20.99	9.80	E / 0.5	-13.10	-31.15	-44.59 / 2	-23.93 / 6	-21.17 / 5
EN	*iPath Bloomberg Ntrl Gas SI TR A	GAZ	E-	0.72	2.09	0.30	E- / 0.2	-17.81	-43.31	-64.18 / 1	-35.40 / 3	-38.43 / 2
EN	*iPath Bloomberg Platinum SI TR A	PGM	E	18.57	27.91	16.93	E+ / 0.9	-2.87	-18.22	-28.29 / 8	-19.25 / 9	-14.54 / 9
EN	*iPath Bloomberg Prec Mtls SI TR	JJP	E+	48.47	62.75	46.86	D- / 1.1	-8.11	-10.90	-13.87 / 19	-17.91 / 10	-8.98 / 14
EN	*iPath Bloomberg Softs SI TR A	JJS	E	34.15	40.32	28.40	D / 1.8	8.97	4.24	-11.51 / 23	-13.48 / 13	-15.46 / 8
EN	*iPath Bloomberg Sugar SI TR A	SGG	E	34.69	41.46	24.16	D- / 1.3	13.81	15.06	-4.12 / 42	-20.07 / 8	-17.70 / 6
EN	*iPath Bloomberg Tin SI TR A	JJT	E	31.82	44.69	28.23	D- / 1.2	-5.66	2.12	-24.76 / 10	-16.64 / 11	-12.60 / 11
GR	*iPath CBOE S&P 500 BuyWrite Idx	BWV	B	65.38	66.51	45.68	B- / 7.0	5.30	1.21	4.28 / 77	7.24 / 68	6.33 / 52
EN	*iPath Cptl Glbl Carbon Tot Ret E	GRN	C-	10.21	13.75	8.23	B / 7.7	-4.77	4.71	8.38 / 85	9.29 / 73	-16.78 / 7
USA	*iPath ETN US Treasury 5Yr Bear E	DFVS	D-	31.91	37.58	27.20	D+ / 2.8	14.66	-1.42	-8.96 / 28	-6.30 / 22	--
USA	*iPath ETN US Treasury 5Yr Bull E	DFVL	D+	64.42	68.04	60.52	C / 5.3	-3.81	1.10	6.44 / 82	1.86 / 48	--
FO	*iPath EUR/USD Exch Rate ETN	ERO	D+	41.35	45.65	39.87	D+ / 2.4	-1.87	-0.46	-9.75 / 26	-7.34 / 21	-3.75 / 21
GR	*iPath GBP/USD Exchange Rate ETN	GBB	C-	38.78	42.64	39.12	C- / 3.2	-2.16	-2.51	-3.50 / 44	-3.02 / 28	-1.15 / 25
FO	*iPath GEMS Asia 8 ETN	AYT	D	40.24	44.56	39.87	C- / 3.0	1.26	-5.65	-4.64 / 40	-3.87 / 27	-2.23 / 23
GI	*iPath GEMS Index ETN	JEM	D-	29.25	34.05	28.17	D+ / 2.5	2.77	-4.49	-8.97 / 28	-6.52 / 22	-4.11 / 20
FO	*iPath JPY/USD Exchange Rate ETN	JYN	D+	47.06	48.55	45.13	D / 1.9	2.86	4.28	-0.17 / 59	-13.19 / 14	-7.97 / 16
IN	*iPath Long Ext S&P 500 TR Idx ET	SFLA	C+	181.63	183.00	159.00	A+ / 9.7	4.81	14.23	1.47 / 70	25.80 / 97	24.48 / 99

* Denotes ETF Fund, N/A denotes number is not available

Incl. in Returns		RISK				NET ASSETS		VALUATION			ASSET					FUND MANAGER	
		Risk Rating/ Pts	3 Year		Avg Duration	NAV as of 12/31/15	Total $(Mil)	Premium / Discount		Wtd Avg P/E	Cash %	Stocks %	Bonds %	Other %	Portfolio Turnover Ratio	Manager Quality Pct	Manager Tenure (Years)
Dividend Yield %	Expense Ratio		Standard Deviation	Beta				As of 12/31/15	1 Year Average								
4.79	0.45	U /	N/A	N/A	N/A	21.43	N/A	-0.09	N/A	N/A	0	0	0	100	13	N/A	1
1.61	0.35	B- / 7.2	14.6	1.13	N/A	47.64	115	0.02	-0.03	27.5	0	99	0	1	40	26	N/A
0.58	0.35	C+ / 6.5	13.6	1.05	N/A	124.11	777	0.47	N/A	117.5	0	99	0	1	75	38	N/A
0.84	0.35	C+ / 6.2	14.8	1.05	N/A	80.82	98	0.05	0.04	126.7	0	99	0	1	78	51	N/A
0.68	0.35	B / 8.0	17.5	1.25	N/A	54.95	170	-0.24	-0.03	26.8	0	99	0	1	51	19	N/A
13.46	0.65	C- / 3.9	18.2	0.96	N/A	12.65	95	0.16	-0.11	N/A	0	100	0	0	27	20	8
0.00	0.40	B / 8.6	N/A	N/A	N/A	69.72	8	-0.85	-0.18	N/A	0	0	0	100	N/A	29	N/A
1.60	0.70	C- / 3.5	42.7	0.92	N/A	30.61	395	0.10	0.04	N/A	0	100	0	0	51	99	3
2.61	0.65	B- / 7.5	16.6	1.31	N/A	38.46	580	-0.05	-0.02	N/A	0	100	0	0	56	20	3
0.00	0.40	B- / 7.5	8.4	0.20	N/A	116.56	35	-0.08	-0.06	N/A	100	0	0	0	N/A	17	10
0.00	0.40	B / 8.3	8.7	0.22	N/A	96.47	205	-0.10	-0.05	N/A	100	0	0	0	N/A	32	10
1.52	0.70	B / 8.4	14.4	0.86	N/A	23.69	224	-0.51	-0.10	24.7	0	100	0	0	29	81	6
1.68	0.50	B- / 7.0	13.8	0.89	N/A	25.42	16	0.35	0.01	57.1	0	100	0	0	30	71	3
3.32	0.32	C+ / 6.5	13.6	0.42	N/A	45.68	18	0.31	-0.04	N/A	0	100	0	0	11	90	3
3.36	0.15	B / 8.1	12.1	0.96	N/A	72.05	11,127	-0.03	-0.01	89.1	0	100	0	0	3	93	18
4.39	0.55	B / 8.2	2.9	34.40	N/A	18.05	216	0.00	-0.15	N/A	0	0	0	100	9	79	N/A
1.82	0.38	B- / 7.0	N/A	N/A	N/A	29.60	5	-4.83	-0.33	N/A	0	0	0	100	46	15	2
20.05	0.65	C+ / 6.9	N/A	N/A	N/A	43.55	32	0.51	-0.06	N/A	0	0	0	100	12	68	3
0.00	N/A	U /	N/A	N/A	N/A	25.04	N/A	0.04	N/A	N/A	0	0	0	100	N/A	N/A	1
0.09	0.95	B- / 7.0	11.3	0.69	N/A	35.48	11	0.48	-0.02	N/A	0	0	0	100	54	94	1
1.10	0.95	B- / 7.2	10.8	0.98	N/A	37.35	11	1.45	-0.10	N/A	0	0	0	100	16	78	4
4.81	0.15	B / 8.7	12.0	1.06	N/A	53.03	8,693	-0.04	-0.01	36.5	0	100	0	0	6	54	18
0.00	N/A	U /	N/A	N/A	N/A	22.17	N/A	0.00	N/A	N/A	0	0	0	100	N/A	N/A	N/A
0.00	0.75	C- / 3.4	19.4	0.26	N/A	34.45	68	-0.29	0.01	N/A	0	0	0	100	N/A	12	9
0.00	0.75	D- / 1.4	17.4	0.23	N/A	13.47	7	0.89	0.11	N/A	0	0	0	100	N/A	9	8
0.00	0.75	C- / 4.2	20.1	0.30	N/A	41.39	28	-0.17	-0.14	N/A	0	0	0	100	N/A	96	8
0.00	0.75	D+ / 2.5	33.2	0.13	N/A	19.91	8	-1.05	0.23	N/A	0	0	0	100	N/A	10	8
0.00	0.75	C+ / 5.7	14.4	0.34	N/A	21.48	1,897	-0.05	-3.35	N/A	0	100	0	0	N/A	5	10
0.00	0.75	D- / 1.4	18.7	0.41	N/A	24.61	130	0.12	0.04	N/A	0	0	0	100	N/A	8	9
0.00	0.75	C- / 3.3	22.8	0.43	N/A	42.05	23	-0.02	0.03	N/A	0	0	0	100	N/A	39	8
0.00	0.75	E- / 0.1	28.9	0.77	N/A	5.60	11	1.07	0.32	N/A	0	0	0	100	N/A	3	9
0.00	0.75	D+ / 2.4	25.1	0.22	N/A	30.38	57	-0.10	-0.03	N/A	0	0	0	100	N/A	9	9
0.00	0.75	D+ / 2.8	15.8	0.31	N/A	19.15	50	-0.26	-0.13	N/A	0	0	0	100	N/A	9	9
0.00	0.75	C- / 3.3	23.1	0.41	N/A	38.83	14	-8.34	-0.77	N/A	0	0	0	100	N/A	12	8
0.00	0.75	C- / 3.6	14.2	0.06	N/A	23.99	110	-0.25	N/A	N/A	0	0	0	100	N/A	28	9
0.00	0.75	E+ / 0.6	30.1	0.65	N/A	10.68	15	1.22	0.50	N/A	0	0	0	100	N/A	6	9
0.00	0.75	E- / 0.1	48.4	-0.23	N/A	0.54	208	33.33	7.13	N/A	0	0	0	100	N/A	2	9
0.00	0.75	D / 2.0	22.0	0.28	N/A	18.61	103	-0.21	-0.89	N/A	0	0	0	100	N/A	8	8
0.00	0.75	D+ / 2.8	20.7	0.20	N/A	48.55	8	-0.16	-0.09	N/A	0	0	0	100	N/A	8	8
0.00	0.75	D- / 1.4	20.4	0.31	N/A	34.03	5	0.35	-0.10	N/A	0	0	0	100	N/A	13	8
0.00	0.75	D / 1.7	24.0	0.41	N/A	34.77	27	-0.23	0.14	N/A	0	0	0	100	N/A	7	8
0.00	0.75	D- / 1.1	24.8	0.08	N/A	31.77	2	0.16	-0.61	N/A	0	0	0	100	N/A	10	8
0.00	0.75	B- / 7.6	7.1	0.52	N/A	65.24	10	0.21	-0.11	N/A	0	0	0	100	N/A	72	9
0.00	0.75	D / 2.0	61.4	-0.01	N/A	10.31	4	-0.97	0.66	N/A	0	0	0	100	N/A	94	8
0.00	N/A	C- / 3.3	18.9	-1.43	N/A	32.05	6	-0.44	0.04	N/A	0	0	0	100	N/A	47	5
0.00	N/A	C- / 3.5	9.5	0.53	N/A	64.35	1	0.11	-0.07	N/A	0	0	0	100	N/A	73	5
0.00	0.40	C+ / 5.9	9.7	0.19	N/A	41.00	8	0.85	-0.21	N/A	0	0	0	100	N/A	19	9
0.00	0.40	B / 8.0	10.9	-0.11	N/A	39.12	2	-0.87	-0.32	N/A	0	0	0	100	N/A	51	9
3.07	N/A	C / 4.4	5.7	0.28	N/A	40.47	4	-0.57	-0.36	N/A	0	0	0	100	N/A	28	8
7.16	N/A	C- / 3.1	7.0	0.42	N/A	29.28	1	-0.10	-0.34	N/A	0	0	0	100	N/A	14	8
0.00	0.40	C+ / 6.8	10.4	0.10	N/A	47.16	11	-0.21	-0.33	N/A	0	0	0	100	N/A	12	9
0.00	N/A	C- / 4.0	18.0	0.57	N/A	180.52	7	0.61	-4.87	N/A	0	0	0	100	N/A	98	N/A

* Denotes ETF Fund, N/A denotes number is not available

Fund Type	Fund Name (99 Pct = Best, 0 Pct = Worst)	Ticker Symbol	Overall Investment Rating	PRICE: Price As of 12/31/15	PRICE: 52 Week High	PRICE: 52 Week Low	PERFORMANCE: Performance Rating/Pts	% Total Return Through 12/31/15: 3 Mo	6 Mo	1Yr/Pct	Annualized 3Yr/Pct	Annualized 5Yr/Pct
EM	*iPath MSCI India Index ETN	INP	C-	63.91	78.32	59.32	C- / 3.9	-4.61	-10.77	-9.40 / 27	1.86 / 47	-2.71 / 22
IN	*iPath Pure Beta Agriculture ETN	DIRT	E+	31.16	40.60	31.03	D- / 1.5	-3.47	-16.03	-16.62 / 16	-12.49 / 14	--
IN	*iPath Pure Beta Aluminum ETN	FOIL	E	21.69	28.92	20.56	D- / 1.2	-4.04	-12.19	-20.83 / 13	-14.87 / 12	--
IN	*iPath Pure Beta Broad Commodity	BCM	E	23.69	33.07	23.52	E+ / 0.9	-11.58	-24.31	-25.92 / 9	-18.44 / 9	--
IN	*iPath Pure Beta Cocoa ETN	CHOC	C	47.69	50.56	37.80	B+ / 8.7	3.79	-0.85	12.58 / 92	12.55 / 83	--
IN	*iPath Pure Beta Coffee ETN	CAFE	E+	13.71	22.33	12.60	D- / 1.2	-1.82	-6.26	-29.53 / 8	-14.31 / 12	--
IN	*iPath Pure Beta Crude Oil ETN	OLEM	E-	14.90	27.99	14.32	E / 0.4	-20.92	-38.56	-39.90 / 4	-27.39 / 5	--
EN	*iPath Pure Beta Energy ETN	ONG	E-	15.45	26.64	15.14	E / 0.4	-20.06	-40.71	-40.85 / 3	-27.38 / 5	--
IN	*iPath Pure Beta Grains ETN	WEET	E+	32.91	41.30	32.91	D- / 1.4	-5.97	-18.84	-18.03 / 15	-12.34 / 14	--
IN	*iPath Pure Beta Lead ETN	LEDD	D-	29.22	36.02	26.99	D / 1.7	-0.98	-4.29	-8.89 / 29	-12.74 / 14	--
IN	*iPath Pure Beta Livestock ETN	LSTK	D	42.80	54.57	40.47	D+ / 2.9	-2.64	-11.51	-21.23 / 12	-0.88 / 34	--
PM	*iPath Pure Beta S&P GW ETN	SBV	E	19.38	30.27	19.38	E+ / 0.6	-15.06	-31.92	-35.97 / 5	-22.55 / 7	--
IN	*iPath Pure Beta Softs ETN	GRWN	E+	21.24	26.47	18.77	D / 1.7	13.16	3.71	-17.96 / 15	-13.63 / 13	--
GI	*iPath Pure Beta Sugar ETN	SGAR	E	23.30	29.29	16.18	D- / 1.3	15.28	12.55	-11.58 / 23	-18.91 / 9	--
GL	*IPath S&P 500 Dynamic VIX ETN	XVZ	E+	25.79	33.01	25.69	D- / 1.2	-9.83	-7.66	-9.83 / 26	-16.12 / 11	--
IN	*IPath S&P 500 VIX Mid-Trm Futr E	VXZ	E-	11.14	14.54	10.08	E+ / 0.7	-11.66	0.72	-14.50 / 18	-24.46 / 6	-29.52 / 3
IN	*IPath S&P 500 VIX Sm-Trm Futr ET	VXX	E-	20.10	37.35	15.48	E- / 0.2	-16.35	0.64	-35.14 / 6	-43.29 / 1	-48.90 / 1
EN	*iPath S&P GSCI Crude Oil TotRet	OIL	E-	6.23	13.17	6.01	E- / 0.2	-26.71	-45.40	-48.98 / 2	-34.48 / 3	-24.12 / 5
GR	*iPath S&P GSCI Total Return ETN	GSP	E+	13.01	21.86	12.24	E / 0.4	-19.49	-35.63	-37.03 / 4	-26.89 / 5	-17.20 / 6
EN	*iPath S&P MLP ETN	IMLP	E-	18.35	30.83	15.47	E- / 0.1	-12.68	-28.83	-36.11 / 5	--	--
EN	*iPath Seasonal Natural Gas ETN	DCNG	E-	15.90	21.70	15.24	E+ / 0.8	-20.51	-20.10	-28.57 / 8	-18.65 / 9	--
USA	*iPath US Treas 10Yr Bear ETN	DTYS	D-	20.27	23.75	16.04	D+ / 2.3	20.37	-8.16	-9.14 / 28	-9.98 / 17	-17.38 / 6
USA	*iPath US Treas 10Yr Bull ETN	DTYL	C-	74.81	78.67	73.60	C / 5.2	-4.43	1.15	1.64 / 70	2.13 / 49	9.71 / 64
USA	*iPath US Treas 2Yr Bear ETN	DTUS	D	33.17	35.98	29.01	D+ / 2.8	12.82	5.37	-8.37 / 30	-6.48 / 22	-7.65 / 16
USA	*iPath US Treas 2Yr Bull ETN	DTUL	D+	63.37	66.22	61.40	C / 5.4	-1.98	-3.22	5.06 / 79	2.90 / 52	4.49 / 45
USA	*iPath US Treas Flattener ETN	FLAT	D+	60.04	64.46	57.00	C- / 4.0	-0.31	4.79	-2.70 / 48	-0.86 / 34	5.25 / 49
USA	*iPath US Treas Lng Bd Bear ETN	DLBS	E	21.62	25.89	17.04	D / 2.2	8.92	-13.86	3.25 / 75	-10.28 / 17	-16.67 / 7
USA	*iPath US Treas Lng Bd Bull ETN	DLBL	D+	75.04	78.69	71.53	C / 5.5	-1.74	3.94	0.42 / 63	2.99 / 53	10.16 / 66
USA	*iPath US Treas Steepen ETN	STPP	D-	34.91	38.98	32.07	C- / 3.7	-0.14	-8.34	2.04 / 72	-1.21 / 33	-8.04 / 16
FO	*IQ 50 Percent Hedged FTSE Europe	HFXE	U	17.94	N/A	N/A	U /	0.11	--	--	--	--
FO	*IQ 50 Percent Hedged FTSE Intern	HFXI	U	18.18	N/A	N/A	U /	1.68	--	--	--	--
FO	*IQ 50 Percent Hedged FTSE Japan	HFXJ	U	18.67	N/A	N/A	U /	6.12	--	--	--	--
FO	*IQ Australia Small Cap ETF	KROO	D	13.39	16.98	12.03	D / 2.1	8.86	-4.68	-9.52 / 27	-11.10 / 16	-9.23 / 14
FO	*IQ Canada Small Cap ETF	CNDA	E+	11.90	19.11	11.77	E+ / 0.7	-9.39	-29.94	-35.83 / 5	-19.56 / 8	-17.06 / 7
GL	*IQ Global Agribusiness SmCp ETF	CROP	B+	27.85	30.28	23.91	C+ / 6.9	9.91	0.37	13.66 / 93	3.87 / 57	--
GL	*IQ Global Oil Small Cap ETF	IOIL	D-	9.96	17.58	5.06	D- / 1.0	-11.45	-31.91	-33.29 / 6	-14.85 / 12	--
EN	*IQ Global Resources ETF	GRES	D+	20.84	27.49	20.78	D / 1.6	-0.14	-16.17	-19.66 / 14	-10.37 / 17	-6.06 / 18
FS	*IQ Hedge Event-Driven Tracker ET	QED	U	18.94	N/A	N/A	U /	-1.35	-4.15	--	--	--
GL	*IQ Hedge Macro Tracker ETF	MCRO	C-	24.35	26.29	24.25	C- / 3.1	-1.08	-3.70	-4.79 / 40	-3.24 / 28	-1.55 / 24
PM	*IQ Hedge Market Neutral Tracker	QMN	C	24.93	26.47	24.58	C- / 4.2	-1.49	-1.46	-1.46 / 53	0.34 / 38	--
GL	*IQ Hedge Multi-Strategy Tracker	QAI	C+	28.46	31.00	28.12	C / 4.7	-1.32	-3.39	-2.46 / 48	1.66 / 46	1.88 / 33
GI	*IQ Leaders GTAA Tracker ETF	QGTA	U	20.73	N/A	N/A	U /	2.32	--	--	--	--
GL	*IQ Merger Arbitrage ETF	MNA	C+	28.07	29.15	26.62	C+ / 5.7	0.68	-2.67	0.57 / 64	4.20 / 58	2.50 / 36
IN	*IQ Real Return ETF	CPI	C	26.53	27.90	25.27	C / 4.5	0.95	-0.36	0.38 / 63	0.38 / 39	1.02 / 30
GI	*IQ US Real Estate SmCp ETF	ROOF	C+	24.22	29.00	23.30	C+ / 5.9	2.37	-4.95	-11.21 / 23	6.49 / 66	--
COH	*iShares 0-5 Yr Hi Yld Corp Bd ET	SHYG	C-	44.53	49.86	43.80	D+ / 2.9	-0.28	-5.54	-3.02 / 46	--	--
COI	*iShares 0-5 Yr Invest Grde Corp	SLQD	C+	50.24	51.53	49.97	C / 5.1	0.39	0.71	1.25 / 68	--	--
USA	*iShares 0-5 Yr TIPS Bond ETF	STIP	C	98.92	100.19	98.54	C- / 3.9	-0.66	-1.11	-0.19 / 59	-1.00 / 33	0.56 / 29
GL	*iShares 1-3 Year Intl Treas Bd E	ISHG	D+	77.92	83.73	76.32	D+ / 2.6	-2.24	-1.55	-6.94 / 34	-6.47 / 22	-3.94 / 21
COI	*iShares 1-3 Yr Credit Bd ETF	CSJ	C+	104.60	105.76	104.36	C / 4.7	-0.09	0.09	0.68 / 65	0.81 / 40	1.39 / 31
USA	*iShares 1-3 Yr Treasury Bd ETF	SHY	B-	84.36	85.12	84.31	C / 4.4	-0.64	-0.28	0.33 / 62	0.37 / 38	0.56 / 29
GL	*iShares 10+ Year Credit Bond	CLY	C-	55.68	64.80	55.36	C / 4.3	-0.96	0.64	-6.07 / 36	0.87 / 41	5.84 / 50

* Denotes ETF Fund, N/A denotes number is not available

Incl. in Returns		RISK	3 Year			NET ASSETS		VALUATION Premium / Discount			ASSET					FUND MANAGER	
Dividend Yield %	Expense Ratio	Risk Rating/ Pts	Standard Deviation	Beta	Avg Dura-tion	NAV as of 12/31/15	Total $(Mil)	As of 12/31/15	1 Year Average	Wtd Avg P/E	Cash %	Stocks %	Bonds %	Other %	Portfolio Turnover Ratio	Manager Quality Pct	Manager Tenure (Years)
0.00	0.89	C+ / 6.9	20.3	0.69	N/A	64.58	1,059	-1.04	0.20	N/A	0	0	0	100	N/A	93	10
0.00	N/A	C- / 3.2	17.6	0.30	N/A	31.18	1	-0.06	-0.17	N/A	0	0	0	100	N/A	9	5
0.00	N/A	D / 1.9	14.0	0.20	N/A	21.54	3	0.70	-0.04	N/A	0	0	0	100	N/A	9	5
0.00	N/A	D- / 1.3	14.0	0.39	N/A	23.65	18	0.17	0.06	N/A	0	0	0	100	N/A	5	5
0.00	N/A	C- / 3.3	17.1	0.37	N/A	47.52	10	0.36	-0.16	N/A	0	0	0	100	N/A	92	5
0.00	N/A	D+ / 2.8	31.0	0.05	N/A	13.81	8	-0.72	0.08	N/A	0	0	0	100	N/A	11	5
0.00	N/A	D- / 1.1	27.8	0.59	N/A	14.92	3	-0.13	0.02	N/A	0	0	0	100	N/A	2	5
0.00	N/A	E- / 0.2	28.0	0.97	N/A	15.24	2	1.38	0.92	N/A	0	0	0	100	N/A	4	5
0.00	N/A	D+ / 2.7	19.8	0.29	N/A	32.93	1	-0.06	-0.05	N/A	0	0	0	100	N/A	9	5
0.00	N/A	C- / 3.5	23.1	0.38	N/A	30.50	2	-4.20	0.07	N/A	0	0	0	100	N/A	9	5
0.00	N/A	C- / 4.0	11.6	0.18	N/A	43.33	1	-1.22	-0.09	N/A	0	0	0	100	N/A	42	5
0.00	N/A	D+ / 2.3	18.3	0.14	N/A	19.50	1	-0.62	-0.09	N/A	0	0	0	100	N/A	6	5
0.00	N/A	D+ / 2.3	18.5	0.70	N/A	21.85	1	-2.79	0.13	N/A	0	0	0	100	N/A	6	5
0.00	N/A	D / 1.7	20.3	0.45	N/A	23.38	3	-0.34	-0.05	N/A	0	0	0	100	N/A	5	5
0.00	N/A	D+ / 2.4	14.7	-0.76	N/A	25.80	23	-0.04	-0.08	N/A	0	0	0	100	N/A	11	5
0.00	0.89	E+ / 0.8	28.8	-2.21	N/A	11.10	29	0.36	0.03	N/A	0	0	0	100	N/A	72	7
0.00	0.89	E+ / 0.6	60.7	-4.69	N/A	19.95	665	0.75	0.22	N/A	0	0	0	100	N/A	88	7
0.00	0.75	D- / 1.2	35.7	1.20	N/A	5.73	564	8.73	2.21	N/A	0	0	0	100	N/A	3	10
0.00	0.75	C- / 3.1	22.6	0.61	N/A	13.01	79	0.00	-0.04	N/A	0	0	0	100	N/A	2	10
8.01	N/A	D- / 1.2	N/A	N/A	N/A	17.95	795	2.23	0.01	N/A	0	0	0	100	N/A	7	3
0.00	N/A	D- / 1.0	21.4	-0.03	N/A	15.84	1	0.38	0.42	N/A	0	0	0	100	N/A	8	5
0.00	N/A	D+ / 2.9	31.5	-2.63	N/A	20.46	101	-0.93	N/A	N/A	0	0	0	100	N/A	45	6
0.00	N/A	C / 5.1	10.5	0.80	N/A	75.21	3	-0.53	0.06	N/A	0	0	0	100	N/A	62	6
0.00	N/A	C- / 4.0	9.7	-0.49	N/A	33.25	21	-0.24	0.19	N/A	0	0	0	100	N/A	29	6
0.00	N/A	C- / 4.0	5.4	0.17	N/A	62.43	2	1.51	-0.48	N/A	0	0	0	100	N/A	84	6
0.00	N/A	C / 5.0	7.9	0.66	N/A	60.30	5	-0.43	-0.07	N/A	0	0	0	100	N/A	43	6
0.00	N/A	E+ / 0.8	28.7	-2.67	N/A	21.52	44	0.46	-0.09	N/A	0	0	0	100	N/A	46	6
0.00	N/A	C- / 3.3	10.4	0.87	N/A	74.16	2	1.19	0.07	N/A	0	0	0	100	N/A	67	6
0.00	N/A	D+ / 2.8	13.8	-1.17	N/A	34.72	11	0.55	-0.09	N/A	0	0	0	100	N/A	83	6
2.30	N/A	U /	N/A	N/A	N/A	17.96	N/A	-0.11	N/A	N/A	0	0	0	100	N/A	N/A	1
1.86	N/A	U /	N/A	N/A	N/A	18.21	N/A	-0.16	N/A	N/A	0	0	0	100	N/A	N/A	1
0.00	N/A	U /	N/A	N/A	N/A	18.87	N/A	-1.06	N/A	N/A	0	0	0	100	N/A	N/A	1
5.23	0.70	C / 5.4	21.3	1.18	N/A	13.55	7	-1.18	-0.65	N/A	0	100	0	0	36	10	5
2.95	0.69	C- / 3.8	23.1	1.04	N/A	11.90	16	0.00	-0.04	N/A	0	100	0	0	33	6	5
1.69	0.76	B / 8.6	10.6	0.61	N/A	28.27	18	-1.49	-0.29	N/A	0	100	0	0	33	77	5
2.90	0.76	C- / 4.1	26.3	1.45	N/A	10.07	2	-1.09	-0.02	N/A	0	100	0	0	58	7	5
2.70	0.75	B- / 7.2	14.1	0.51	N/A	21.00	91	-0.76	-0.26	25.0	0	100	0	0	182	19	5
2.48	N/A	U /	N/A	N/A	N/A	19.08	N/A	-0.73	N/A	N/A	0	0	0	100	N/A	N/A	1
1.10	0.75	B- / 7.3	4.1	0.23	N/A	24.29	24	0.25	-0.02	N/A	1	98	0	1	101	35	7
.00	0.76	B- / 7.7	2.7	0.05	N/A	24.92	17	0.04	-0.04	N/A	0	0	0	100	101	77	4
.48	0.76	B / 8.5	4.6	0.29	N/A	28.46	856	0.00	0.01	N/A	0	81	0	19	81	70	8
2.66	N/A	U /	N/A	N/A	N/A	20.59	N/A	0.68	N/A	N/A	0	0	0	100	N/A	N/A	1
.87	0.76	B- / 7.9	3.8	0.08	N/A	28.01	62	0.21	0.11	N/A	0	100	0	0	447	87	5
.01	0.48	B- / 7.9	2.9	0.17	N/A	26.48	25	0.19	-0.01	N/A	0	100	0	0	91	50	5
.88	0.69	B / 8.1	14.1	0.82	N/A	24.23	65	-0.04	-0.01	N/A	1	98	0	1	17	40	5
.78	0.38	B- / 7.1	N/A	N/A	N/A	44.33	84	0.45	0.36	N/A	0	0	0	100	22	65	3
.89	0.15	B / 8.1	N/A	N/A	N/A	49.95	23	0.58	0.32	N/A	0	0	0	100	15	79	3
.00	0.16	B / 8.1	1.7	0.04	N/A	98.83	518	0.09	0.07	N/A	0	0	100	0	25	58	6
.09	0.35	C+ / 6.4	6.2	0.88	N/A	77.86	179	0.08	-0.06	N/A	2	0	95	3	51	41	6
.67	0.20	B / 8.1	0.6	0.09	N/A	104.45	11,355	0.14	0.08	N/A	0	0	98	2	17	74	6
.12	0.15	B+ / 9.9	0.6	0.04	N/A	84.40	8,221	-0.05	0.02	N/A	0	0	100	0	122	70	6
.80	0.20	C+ / 6.6	8.7	0.65	N/A	55.66	548	0.04	0.25	N/A	1	0	96	3	23	86	6

Denotes ETF Fund, N/A denotes number is not available

	99 Pct = Best 0 Pct = Worst			PRICE			PERFORMANCE					
					52 Week			% Total Return Through 12/31/15				
											Annualized	
Fund Type	Fund Name	Ticker Symbol	Overall Investment Rating	Price As of 12/31/15	High	Low	Performance Rating/Pts	3 Mo	6 Mo	1Yr/Pct	3Yr/Pct	5Yr/Pct
USA	*iShares 10-20 Yr Treasury Bd ETF	TLH	B-	134.21	157.26	131.19	C / 5.4	-2.04	2.79	0.60 / 65	2.50 / 51	6.18 / 51
USA	*iShares 20+ Yr Treasury Bd ETF	TLT	C+	120.58	138.50	114.88	C+ / 5.6	-2.36	5.45	-2.84 / 47	3.51 / 55	8.78 / 60
USA	*iShares 3-7 Yr Treasury Bd ETF	IEI	C+	122.61	125.34	121.90	C / 4.8	-1.42	0.63	1.43 / 70	1.07 / 42	2.52 / 36
USA	*iShares 7-10 Yr Treasury Bd ETF	IEF	B-	105.59	110.59	103.76	C / 5.1	-1.91	1.98	1.01 / 67	1.63 / 46	4.51 / 45
COI	*iShares Aaa - A Rated Corporate	QLTA	B	50.52	53.33	50.23	C / 5.2	0.31	2.36	0.38 / 63	1.55 / 45	--
USA	*iShares Agency Bond ETF	AGZ	C+	113.15	115.85	112.41	C / 5.0	-0.35	0.97	1.09 / 67	1.29 / 44	2.00 / 34
FO	*iShares Asia 50	AIA	C-	42.27	55.10	38.01	C- / 3.4	3.17	-12.83	-5.08 / 38	-1.54 / 32	0.59 / 29
FO	*iShares Asia/Pacific Dividend ET	DVYA	D+	39.25	52.42	36.60	D+ / 2.5	5.29	-14.77	-16.49 / 16	-5.46 / 24	--
COI	*iShares B - Ca Rated Corp Bond E	QLTC	C-	41.35	51.26	39.58	C- / 3.2	-3.76	-11.70	-9.96 / 26	-1.29 / 32	--
COI	*iShares Baa - Ba Rated Corp Bd E	QLTB	C+	48.63	54.10	48.46	C / 4.5	-0.93	-2.62	-4.22 / 42	1.39 / 44	--
MUS	*iShares California AMT Free Muni	CMF	B-	118.15	121.39	115.12	C+ / 6.6	1.46	3.87	2.98 / 78	3.78 / 64	6.65 / 66
FO	*iShares China Large-Cap ETF	FXI	D+	35.29	52.85	32.80	D+ / 2.9	-0.53	-19.64	-11.20 / 23	-1.99 / 31	-1.22 / 25
COI	*iShares CMBS ETF	CMBS	C+	50.66	52.61	50.48	C / 5.0	-0.95	0.23	0.68 / 65	1.40 / 44	--
IN	*iShares Cohen and Steers REIT ET	ICF	B	99.24	107.41	64.00	B+ / 8.7	8.06	11.79	5.50 / 80	11.60 / 80	12.48 / 82
GL	*iShares Commodities Select Strat	COMT	D-	28.44	42.00	27.49	E / 0.3	-12.07	-26.19	-30.13 / 7	--	--
GL	*iShares Commodity Optimized	CMDT	D	32.03	44.00	31.53	E / 0.5	-8.95	-21.62	-24.33 / 10	--	--
GI	*iShares Convertible Bond	ICVT	U	45.74	N/A	N/A	U /	4.72	-3.97	--	--	--
USA	*iShares Core 1-5 Year USD Bond	ISTB	C+	99.27	101.42	98.99	C / 4.7	-0.38	-0.17	0.56 / 64	0.84 / 41	--
GL	*iShares Core 10+ Year USD Bond	ILTB	C+	58.45	67.38	58.20	C / 5.0	-1.67	2.00	-4.88 / 39	2.03 / 48	6.80 / 54
GI	*iShares Core Aggressive Allocati	AOA	B+	44.84	49.94	30.89	C+ / 6.7	2.09	-4.22	-0.96 / 55	7.96 / 70	7.73 / 57
GI	*iShares Core Conservative Alloc	AOK	C+	31.64	33.84	15.00	C / 5.4	0.49	-1.20	-1.07 / 54	2.98 / 53	4.09 / 44
IN	*iShares Core Dividend Growth ETF	DGRO	C	25.69	27.04	22.75	C / 5.4	5.41	0.22	-0.08 / 60	--	--
GEI	*iShares Core GNMA Bond ETF	GNMA	C	50.11	51.66	49.60	C / 5.0	-0.39	1.26	0.75 / 65	1.27 / 44	--
GI	*iShares Core Growth Allocation	AOR	C+	38.88	42.54	26.70	C+ / 6.2	1.53	-2.90	-1.02 / 55	6.31 / 65	6.56 / 53
GL	*iShares Core High Dividend	HDV	B+	73.41	78.27	40.32	B / 8.0	6.31	2.00	0.60 / 65	10.93 / 78	--
GI	*iShares Core Moderate Allocation	AOM	C+	34.05	36.89	21.50	C+ / 5.7	0.52	-2.05	-1.18 / 54	4.14 / 58	4.78 / 46
EM	*iShares Core MSCI EAFE	IEFA	B-	54.38	62.59	51.55	C+ / 5.9	2.57	-5.95	1.75 / 71	4.74 / 60	--
EM	*iShares Core MSCI Emerging Marke	IEMG	D+	39.39	53.17	36.51	D / 2.2	-1.44	-16.22	-12.33 / 21	-7.04 / 21	--
FO	*iShares Core MSCI Europe ETF	IEUR	C	42.24	49.11	40.59	C- / 3.4	0.75	-6.09	0.32 / 62	--	--
FO	*iShares Core MSCI Pacific ETF	IPAC	C+	47.72	54.68	41.99	C+ / 5.9	6.86	-5.20	5.10 / 79	--	--
EM	*iShares Core MSCI Total Intl Sto	IXUS	C	49.48	59.33	47.00	C / 4.3	1.81	-8.69	-3.08 / 46	1.16 / 43	--
GR	*iShares Core S&P 500 ETF	IVV	A+	204.87	215.23	128.74	B+ / 8.9	5.80	--	1.97 / 71	14.20 / 88	12.36 / 81
GR	*iShares Core S&P Mid-Cap ETF	IJH	A-	139.32	155.13	109.03	B / 7.8	1.76	-5.97	-1.69 / 51	11.52 / 80	10.58 / 69
GR	*iShares Core S&P Small-Cap ETF	IJR	A-	110.11	122.10	77.53	B / 8.2	3.49	-5.27	-0.88 / 55	12.47 / 83	11.56 / 75
IN	*iShares Core S&P Tot US Stk Mkt	ITOT	A-	92.86	97.87	76.41	B+ / 8.8	5.51	-0.63	1.56 / 70	13.93 / 87	12.18 / 80
GL	*iShares Core Total USD Bond Mark	IUSB	C	99.18	113.59	98.98	C- / 4.2	-1.00	0.41	-0.03 / 60	--	--
GEI	*iShares Core US Aggregate Bond E	AGG	C+	108.01	112.52	107.60	C / 5.1	-0.68	1.15	0.21 / 62	1.55 / 45	3.18 / 39
COI	*iShares Core US Credit Bond	CRED	C	106.71	114.89	106.33	C / 4.9	-0.70	0.63	-1.69 / 51	1.43 / 44	4.08 / 44
GR	*iShares Core US Growth	IUSG	B+	81.18	84.80	43.45	A- / 9.1	5.55	0.40	5.72 / 81	15.60 / 91	12.98 / 84
USA	*iShares Core US Treasury Bond	GOVT	C	25.06	26.00	24.83	C / 4.8	-1.35	1.00	0.22 / 62	1.10 / 42	--
IN	*iShares Core US Value	IUSV	A	127.39	139.04	84.01	B / 7.9	4.49	-3.50	-3.34 / 45	11.67 / 80	10.69 / 69
GL	*iShares Cur Hdg Intl Hi Yld Bd E	HHYX	U	24.00	N/A	N/A	U /	0.17	--	--	--	--
GL	*iShares Curr Hedged MSCI EAFE ET	HEFA	C	25.40	29.14	19.12	C+ / 5.7	4.16	-4.34	4.96 / 79	--	--
EM	*iShares Curr Hedged MSCI Em Mkts	HEEM	D	20.00	26.37	19.23	D+ / 2.4	1.52	-9.22	-5.68 / 37	--	--
FO	*iShares Curr Hedged MSCI Germany	HEWG	C+	24.37	31.93	15.47	C+ / 6.8	9.28	-4.34	6.93 / 83	--	--
FO	*iShares Curr Hedged MSCI Japan E	HEWJ	C	28.67	32.97	25.00	C+ / 6.0	5.02	-7.81	8.36 / 85	--	--
IN	*iShares DJ US Index ETF	IYY	A-	101.97	108.00	53.68	B+ / 8.7	5.21	-1.22	1.13 / 68	13.66 / 86	11.90 / 77
COI	*iShares Emerging Markets Corp B	CEMB	C	46.06	51.50	45.97	C- / 3.7	-0.37	-4.38	-1.65 / 52	-0.96 / 34	--
EM	*iShares Emerging Markets Dividen	DVYE	D	30.11	46.73	29.16	D- / 1.1	-4.31	-24.22	-22.90 / 11	-15.23 / 12	--
EM	*iShares Emerging Markets HY Bd E	EMHY	C-	45.05	49.86	43.41	C- / 3.9	1.78	-2.07	1.93 / 71	-1.21 / 33	--
GL	*iShares Emerging Markets Infr ET	EMIF	D+	27.26	37.57	25.34	D+ / 2.4	-2.08	-16.84	-12.81 / 21	-5.39 / 24	-1.80 / 23
GL	*iShares Emerging Mkts Loc Cur Bo	LEMB	D	40.32	47.08	39.04	D+ / 2.3	0.09	-7.56	-11.30 / 23	-7.25 / 21	--

* Denotes ETF Fund, N/A denotes number is not available

		RISK				NET ASSETS		VALUATION			ASSET					FUND MANAGER	
cl. in Returns			3 Year					Premium / Discount									
dend eld %	Expense Ratio	Risk Rating/ Pts	Standard Deviation	Beta	Avg Dura- tion	NAV as of 12/31/15	Total $(Mil)	As of 12/31/15	1 Year Average	Wtd Avg P/E	Cash %	Stocks %	Bonds %	Other %	Portfolio Turnover Ratio	Manager Quality Pct	Manager Tenure (Years)
.08	0.15	**B / 8.9**	6.8	0.64	N/A	134.37	313	-0.12	0.05	N/A	0	0	100	0	9	72	6
.63	0.15	**B / 8.2**	11.8	1.13	N/A	120.73	4,010	-0.12	0.04	N/A	0	0	100	0	32	66	6
.65	0.15	**B / 8.8**	2.8	0.23	N/A	122.63	3,407	-0.02	0.03	N/A	0	0	100	0	58	71	6
.41	0.15	**B+ / 9.2**	5.5	0.49	N/A	105.68	4,898	-0.09	0.03	N/A	0	0	100	0	142	68	6
.13	0.15	**B+ / 9.4**	4.0	0.95	N/A	50.58	419	-0.12	-0.09	N/A	0	0	0	100	18	67	4
.94	0.20	**B / 8.0**	2.0	0.16	N/A	112.78	365	0.33	0.11	N/A	0	0	100	0	68	75	6
.08	0.50	**B- / 7.4**	15.1	0.84	N/A	42.72	313	-1.05	-0.05	N/A	0	99	0	1	12	27	8
.96	0.49	**C+ / 6.0**	17.1	1.01	N/A	39.49	47	-0.61	-0.28	N/A	0	0	0	100	40	16	4
.32	0.55	**B- / 7.8**	7.3	0.48	N/A	42.27	21	-2.18	-0.19	N/A	0	0	0	100	26	54	4
.16	0.30	**B / 8.9**	5.6	1.11	N/A	48.85	26	-0.45	0.22	N/A	0	0	0	100	15	65	4
.22	0.25	**B- / 7.8**	4.8	1.32	10.0	117.88	303	0.23	0.24	N/A	0	0	100	0	6	64	6
.78	0.73	**C+ / 6.4**	21.1	0.92	N/A	35.52	5,505	-0.65	-0.10	N/A	0	99	0	1	36	26	8
.60	0.25	**B- / 7.9**	2.7	0.47	N/A	50.57	120	0.18	0.22	N/A	0	0	0	100	45	74	4
.66	0.35	**C+ / 6.4**	15.2	0.34	N/A	99.21	2,862	0.03	N/A	95.6	0	99	0	1	8	92	8
.44	N/A	**C / 4.8**	N/A	N/A	N/A	28.44	N/A	0.00	-0.09	N/A	0	0	0	100	N/A	3	2
.00	0.83	**B- / 7.1**	N/A	N/A	N/A	32.11	N/A	-0.25	-0.06	N/A	0	0	0	100	N/A	4	N/A
.77	N/A	**U /**	N/A	N/A	N/A	45.29	N/A	0.99	N/A	N/A	0	0	0	100	N/A	N/A	1
.44	0.12	**B / 8.2**	1.2	0.07	N/A	98.96	190	0.31	0.29	N/A	0	0	0	100	116	73	4
.96	0.12	**B / 8.3**	9.5	0.62	N/A	58.49	109	-0.07	0.33	N/A	1	0	98	1	15	87	6
.56	0.11	**B+ / 9.0**	9.0	0.82	N/A	44.86	273	-0.04	0.06	N/A	0	99	0	1	58	42	8
.05	0.11	**B- / 7.6**	4.1	0.33	N/A	31.59	187	0.16	0.01	N/A	0	21	78	1	83	54	8
.22	0.05	**C+ / 6.9**	N/A	N/A	N/A	25.67	71	0.08	0.07	N/A	0	0	0	100	47	56	2
.85	0.15	**B- / 7.8**	2.8	0.79	N/A	50.03	40	0.16	0.12	N/A	0	0	0	100	1,242	68	4
.13	0.11	**B- / 7.5**	7.0	0.63	N/A	38.81	318	0.18	0.04	N/A	0	57	42	1	75	48	8
.80	0.14	**B- / 7.9**	10.2	0.52	N/A	73.41	4,433	0.00	N/A	N/A	0	99	0	1	63	97	5
.17	0.11	**B- / 7.7**	5.2	0.44	N/A	34.04	255	0.03	0.06	N/A	0	32	67	1	83	51	8
.17	0.12	**B / 8.2**	12.2	0.64	N/A	54.67	2,586	-0.53	0.18	N/A	0	0	0	100	5	95	4
55	0.18	**B- / 7.1**	14.4	0.98	N/A	39.62	5,706	-0.58	0.11	N/A	0	0	0	100	7	64	4
66	0.05	**B / 8.0**	N/A	N/A	N/A	42.27	166	-0.07	0.31	N/A	0	0	0	100	1	68	2
27	0.05	**B / 8.1**	N/A	N/A	N/A	48.11	187	-0.81	0.04	N/A	0	0	0	100	4	90	2
64	0.14	**B / 8.0**	11.9	0.70	N/A	49.59	814	-0.22	0.27	N/A	0	0	0	100	4	91	4
46	0.07	**B / 8.6**	10.6	1.00	N/A	205.02	61,119	-0.07	N/A	60.6	0	99	0	1	4	68	8
97	0.13	**B / 8.5**	11.9	0.99	N/A	139.44	23,368	-0.09	-0.01	78.3	0	99	0	1	15	52	8
62	0.13	**B / 8.2**	13.2	1.00	N/A	110.14	12,716	-0.03	N/A	90.0	0	99	0	1	14	58	8
45	0.07	**B- / 7.5**	10.6	1.00	N/A	92.84	1,380	0.02	0.03	62.7	0	99	0	1	4	66	8
03	N/A	**B / 8.0**	N/A	N/A	N/A	99.08	25	0.10	0.38	N/A	0	0	0	100	N/A	62	2
53	0.07	**B- / 7.8**	3.0	1.03	N/A	107.82	18,853	0.18	0.06	N/A	0	0	99	1	318	67	6
22	0.16	**B- / 7.5**	4.3	1.04	N/A	106.52	729	0.18	0.16	N/A	0	0	98	2	10	66	6
33	0.12	**C+ / 6.8**	11.0	1.02	N/A	81.14	493	0.05	0.01	98.0	0	99	0	1	13	76	8
22	0.15	**B- / 7.7**	3.1	0.28	N/A	25.05	213	0.04	0.06	N/A	0	0	0	100	38	70	4
35	0.11	**B / 8.7**	10.8	1.00	N/A	127.43	716	-0.03	0.01	28.4	0	99	0	1	13	51	8
94	N/A	**U /**	N/A	N/A	N/A	23.95	N/A	0.21	N/A	N/A	0	0	0	100	N/A	N/A	1
37	0.05	**C+ / 6.4**	N/A	N/A	N/A	25.35	3	0.20	0.05	N/A	0	0	0	100	16	90	2
50	0.02	**C+ / 5.7**	N/A	N/A	N/A	19.95	N/A	0.25	0.19	N/A	0	0	0	100	7	87	2
76	0.05	**C+ / 6.6**	N/A	N/A	N/A	24.37	74	0.00	0.03	N/A	0	0	0	100	21	93	2
28	0.01	**C+ / 6.4**	N/A	N/A	N/A	28.66	43	0.03	0.02	N/A	0	0	0	100	12	94	2
53	0.20	**B- / 7.5**	10.6	1.00	N/A	101.95	941	0.02	-0.01	62.9	0	99	0	1	4	64	8
08	0.60	**B / 8.5**	7.3	1.05	N/A	46.33	25	-0.58	0.21	N/A	0	0	0	100	20	47	4
71	0.49	**C / 5.4**	17.2	1.14	N/A	30.43	282	-1.05	-0.09	N/A	0	0	0	100	59	19	4
21	0.65	**C+ / 6.3**	8.7	0.59	N/A	44.98	202	0.16	0.21	N/A	0	0	0	100	24	80	4
79	0.75	**B- / 7.0**	15.9	0.99	N/A	27.45	101	-0.69	-0.34	N/A	0	98	0	2	14	17	7
27	0.59	**C+ / 5.8**	9.1	0.98	N/A	40.06	584	0.65	-0.03	N/A	0	0	0	100	43	41	5

Denotes ETF Fund, N/A denotes number is not available

Fund Type	Fund Name (99 Pct = Best, 0 Pct = Worst)	Ticker Symbol	Overall Investment Rating	PRICE: Price As of 12/31/15	PRICE: 52 Week High	PRICE: 52 Week Low	PERFORMANCE: Performance Rating/Pts	% Total Return Through 12/31/15: 3 Mo	6 Mo	1Yr/Pct	Annualized 3Yr/Pct	Annualized 5Yr/Pct
FO	*iShares Enhanced Intl Large Cap	IEIL	C+	22.90	25.78	21.54	C / 5.5	3.42	-3.49	3.95 / 76	--	--
FO	*iShares Enhanced Intl Small Cap	IEIS	C+	22.77	24.99	21.06	C+ / 6.8	5.72	-2.15	7.42 / 84	--	--
GR	*iShares Enhanced US Large Cap ET	IELG	C	31.53	33.40	30.10	C / 5.1	2.21	-0.58	1.09 / 67	--	--
GR	*iShares Enhanced US Small Cap ET	IESM	C-	29.62	33.45	28.68	D+ / 2.8	1.86	-6.96	-3.52 / 44	--	--
FO	*iShares Europe	IEV	C+	40.11	47.64	38.81	C / 5.3	-0.10	-7.74	-2.19 / 50	3.55 / 55	4.02 / 43
GI	*iShares Europe Developed RE ETF	IFEU	B	37.59	41.30	35.70	B / 8.1	0.03	4.12	8.46 / 86	10.40 / 76	9.58 / 63
GR	*iShares FactorSelect MSCI USA	LRGF	U	24.05	N/A	N/A	U /	4.55	-3.12	--	--	--
GR	*iShares FactorSelect MSCI USA Sm	SMLF	U	29.61	N/A	N/A	U /	5.74	-1.69	--	--	--
COI	*iShares Floating Rate Bond ETF	FLOT	C	50.44	50.72	50.34	C / 4.5	0.38	-0.06	0.44 / 63	0.38 / 39	--
GL	*iShares Glbl High Yield Corp Bd	GHYG	C	44.62	52.22	43.54	C- / 3.6	-2.29	-7.01	-6.20 / 35	-0.57 / 35	--
GR	*iShares Global 100	IOO	C+	72.83	80.83	65.18	C+ / 6.7	5.67	-1.68	-0.46 / 57	7.25 / 68	6.73 / 54
EN	*iShares Global Clean Energy ETF	ICLN	B-	9.84	13.05	8.35	B / 8.2	5.29	-9.90	3.92 / 76	12.02 / 82	-6.15 / 17
GL	*iShares Global Consumer Discr	RXI	A	89.02	94.68	78.21	B+ / 8.9	3.24	-2.17	6.74 / 83	13.94 / 88	12.51 / 82
GL	*iShares Global Consumer Staples	KXI	A+	93.03	95.91	81.11	B / 8.2	5.09	4.66	7.74 / 84	10.26 / 76	11.55 / 75
EN	*iShares Global Energy	IXC	D	28.03	39.42	27.11	D / 2.0	-2.80	-16.51	-20.67 / 13	-7.52 / 21	-3.48 / 22
FS	*iShares Global Financials	IXG	C+	52.99	60.34	38.96	C+ / 6.4	4.13	-5.94	-2.34 / 49	7.15 / 67	5.81 / 50
HL	*iShares Global Healthcare	IXJ	A+	102.62	113.95	58.64	A / 9.4	5.77	-2.48	7.57 / 84	18.92 / 94	17.33 / 95
GL	*iShares Global Industrials	EXI	B+	67.62	74.81	62.26	B- / 7.0	5.74	-2.43	-1.44 / 53	8.46 / 71	6.97 / 55
GL	*iShares Global Inflation-Linked	GTIP	D+	46.02	50.46	45.87	D+ / 2.9	-2.09	-5.37	-7.15 / 33	-3.76 / 27	--
GL	*iShares Global Infrastructure	IGF	C+	35.94	44.31	35.04	C / 4.7	-3.47	-9.33	-10.73 / 24	3.60 / 55	4.79 / 47
GL	*iShares Global Materials	MXI	D+	45.01	61.12	43.28	D / 2.1	0.81	-16.47	-15.56 / 17	-8.10 / 20	-6.33 / 17
GI	*iShares Global REIT ETF	REET	C+	25.25	28.08	21.08	C+ / 6.3	4.98	5.17	1.09 / 67	--	--
GL	*iShares Global Tech	IXN	A+	97.52	102.17	79.96	B+ / 8.9	7.64	2.28	4.87 / 79	14.00 / 88	10.67 / 69
GL	*iShares Global Telecom	IXP	B	57.85	65.59	47.55	C+ / 6.6	5.98	-3.81	2.01 / 71	6.81 / 66	6.16 / 51
GL	*iShares Global Timber&Forestry E	WOOD	C+	48.03	56.69	44.10	C / 5.2	7.82	-7.46	-6.74 / 34	3.08 / 53	2.83 / 37
UT	*iShares Global Utilities	JXI	B	44.02	50.81	42.35	C+ / 6.2	1.45	0.90	-5.78 / 36	6.33 / 65	4.10 / 44
PM	*iShares Gold Trust	IAU	D	10.23	12.65	10.12	D- / 1.4	-7.00	-9.23	-11.04 / 24	-14.05 / 13	-5.23 / 19
USA	*iShares Govt/Credit Bond ETF	GBF	C	111.70	117.07	111.23	C / 4.9	-0.76	0.86	-0.24 / 59	1.25 / 43	3.29 / 39
COI	*iShares iBonds Dec 2016 Corporat	IBDF	D-	25.17	26.44	24.92	C / 5.0	0.30	0.45	1.24 / 68	--	--
COI	*iShares iBonds Dec 2017 Corporat	IBDJ	U	24.78	N/A	N/A	U /	-0.23	-0.03	--	--	--
COI	*iShares iBonds Dec 2018 Corporat	IBDH	D-	24.98	25.65	24.69	C / 4.7	-0.49	-0.03	1.36 / 69	--	--
COI	*iShares iBonds Dec 2019 Corporat	IBDK	U	24.65	N/A	N/A	U /	-0.66	0.24	--	--	--
COI	*iShares iBonds Dec 2020 Corporat	IBDL	D-	24.95	26.42	24.72	C / 4.8	-1.08	0.19	1.89 / 71	--	--
MUN	*iShares iBonds Dec 2021 AMT-Fr M	IBMJ	U	25.56	N/A	N/A	U /	1.04	--	--	--	--
COI	*iShares iBonds Dec 2021 Corporat	IBDM	U	24.31	N/A	N/A	U /	-0.91	0.02	--	--	--
MUN	*iShares iBonds Dec 2022 AMT-Fr M	IBMK	U	25.70	N/A	N/A	U /	1.16	--	--	--	--
COI	*iShares iBonds Dec 2022 Corporat	IBDN	U	24.33	N/A	N/A	U /	-0.18	1.06	--	--	--
COI	*iShares iBonds Dec 2023 Corporat	IBDO	U	24.17	N/A	N/A	U /	-0.14	1.43	--	--	--
COI	*iShares iBonds Dec 2024 Corporat	IBDP	U	24.00	N/A	N/A	U /	-0.25	1.30	--	--	--
COI	*iShares iBonds Dec 2025 Corporat	IBDQ	U	23.97	N/A	N/A	U /	0.10	1.96	--	--	--
COI	*iShares iBonds Mar 2016 Corp ex-	IBCB	B-	99.35	100.18	98.94	C / 4.4	0.11	0.22	0.04 / 60	--	--
COI	*iShares iBonds Mar 2016 Corporat	IBDA	C	100.90	101.48	98.57	C / 4.5	-0.05	0.35	0.35 / 63	--	--
COI	*iShares iBonds Mar 2018 Corp ex-	IBCC	C+	98.99	101.21	98.26	C / 4.8	0.41	0.01	1.11 / 67	--	--
COI	*iShares iBonds Mar 2018 Corporat	IBDB	C+	102.26	105.06	101.86	C / 5.0	0.69	0.15	1.38 / 69	--	--
COI	*iShares iBonds Mar 2020 Corp ex-	IBCD	C	97.42	101.43	96.92	C / 4.6	-0.46	0.33	0.88 / 66	--	--
COI	*iShares iBonds Mar 2020 Corporat	IBDC	C	103.40	107.74	102.95	C- / 4.2	-1.33	0.31	0.36 / 63	--	--
COI	*iShares iBonds Mar 2023 Corp ex-	IBCE	C	94.80	100.44	94.40	C / 4.8	-0.49	0.42	1.28 / 68	--	--
COI	*iShares iBonds Mar 2023 Corporat	IBDD	C+	103.87	110.76	102.10	C / 5.1	0.11	2.24	0.48 / 64	--	--
GEI	*iShares iBonds Sep 2016 AMT-Fr M	IBME	D+	26.52	27.45	26.42	C / 4.6	0.20	0.21	0.11 / 61	0.63 / 40	2.47 / 35
GEI	*iShares iBonds Sep 2017 AMT-Fr M	IBMF	D	27.35	27.64	27.30	C / 4.7	-0.21	0.30	0.56 / 64	0.75 / 40	2.87 / 37
MUN	*iShares iBonds Sep 2018 AMT-Fr M	IBMG	C	25.52	26.29	25.26	C / 4.6	-0.16	0.46	0.36 / 64	--	--
MUN	*iShares iBonds Sep 2019 AMT-Fr M	IBMH	C+	25.62	25.85	24.14	C+ / 5.9	0.62	1.78	2.09 / 75	--	--

* Denotes ETF Fund, N/A denotes number is not availabl

Incl. in Returns		RISK				NET ASSETS		VALUATION			ASSET					FUND MANAGER	
			3 Year					Premium / Discount									
Dividend Yield %	Expense Ratio	Risk Rating/ Pts	Standard Deviation	Beta	Avg Dura- tion	NAV as of 12/31/15	Total $(Mil)	As of 12/31/15	1 Year Average	Wtd Avg P/E	Cash %	Stocks %	Bonds %	Other %	Portfolio Turnover Ratio	Manager Quality Pct	Manager Tenure (Years)
3.16	0.35	**B / 8.1**	N/A	N/A	N/A	22.98	63	-0.35	0.26	N/A	0	0	0	100	41	88	N/A
3.14	0.49	**C+ / 6.7**	N/A	N/A	N/A	22.72	9	0.22	0.54	N/A	0	0	0	100	61	93	2
4.34	0.18	**B- / 7.4**	N/A	N/A	N/A	31.43	64	0.32	0.04	N/A	0	0	0	100	44	65	3
4.30	0.35	**C+ / 6.9**	N/A	N/A	N/A	29.49	16	0.44	0.09	N/A	0	0	0	100	53	26	3
2.27	0.60	**B- / 7.7**	13.7	1.04	N/A	40.37	3,124	-0.64	0.06	72.8	0	99	0	1	4	53	8
9.76	0.48	**C+ / 6.8**	14.1	0.73	N/A	37.33	41	0.70	0.23	N/A	0	99	0	1	15	67	8
0.19	N/A	**U /**	N/A	N/A	N/A	23.95	N/A	0.42	N/A	N/A	0	0	0	100	N/A	N/A	1
3.45	N/A	**U /**	N/A	N/A	N/A	29.19	N/A	1.44	N/A	N/A	0	0	0	100	N/A	N/A	1
1.17	0.20	**B / 8.0**	0.4	-0.01	N/A	50.38	4,053	0.12	0.01	N/A	0	0	0	100	13	71	5
13.11	0.40	**B / 8.3**	6.4	0.44	N/A	44.96	98	-0.76	0.49	N/A	0	0	0	100	21	79	4
4.42	0.40	**B- / 7.2**	11.7	1.05	N/A	72.81	1,746	0.03	-0.01	34.0	0	99	0	1	12	23	8
3.10	0.47	**C+ / 6.1**	21.5	0.57	N/A	9.78	66	0.61	0.28	21.2	0	99	0	1	32	98	8
1.93	0.47	**B- / 7.8**	12.7	0.88	N/A	89.32	158	-0.34	0.02	149.2	0	99	0	1	6	94	8
3.86	0.47	**B / 8.8**	11.4	0.72	N/A	93.22	601	-0.20	0.01	34.8	0	99	0	1	5	92	8
7.57	0.47	**C / 5.0**	17.9	0.94	N/A	28.02	1,001	0.04	0.06	14.3	0	99	0	1	6	41	8
5.05	0.47	**B- / 7.1**	12.1	0.93	N/A	52.81	313	0.34	-0.03	29.1	0	99	0	1	5	28	8
0.60	0.47	**B / 8.2**	11.6	0.88	N/A	102.93	1,265	-0.30	0.04	88.4	0	99	0	1	3	90	8
3.28	0.47	**B / 8.5**	11.9	0.84	N/A	67.98	281	-0.53	-0.12	35.3	0	99	0	1	5	89	8
0.13	0.40	**C+ / 6.6**	7.1	0.72	N/A	45.95	25	0.15	0.03	N/A	0	0	0	100	19	58	5
7.10	0.47	**B / 8.2**	11.2	0.71	N/A	36.10	977	-0.44	0.05	20.2	0	99	0	1	14	69	8
5.56	0.47	**B- / 7.1**	15.5	1.03	N/A	45.28	357	-0.60	-0.09	43.5	0	99	0	1	4	13	8
6.95	0.14	**C+ / 6.6**	N/A	N/A	N/A	25.01	N/A	0.96	0.51	N/A	0	0	0	100	12	76	2
2.29	0.47	**B / 8.6**	11.6	0.73	N/A	97.85	750	-0.34	-0.01	60.9	0	99	0	1	7	95	8
0.29	0.47	**B / 8.0**	12.4	0.83	N/A	58.05	469	-0.34	-0.08	22.2	0	99	0	1	8	84	8
3.68	0.47	**B / 8.0**	14.8	0.79	N/A	48.23	282	-0.41	-0.14	21.9	0	99	0	1	12	67	8
6.03	0.47	**B / 8.5**	11.8	0.71	N/A	44.23	232	-0.47	-0.08	21.4	0	99	0	1	4	52	8
0.00	0.25	**C+ / 6.3**	16.2	0.92	N/A	10.25	6,352	-0.20	0.11	N/A	0	0	0	100	N/A	53	11
4.70	0.20	**B- / 7.8**	3.3	0.29	N/A	111.47	124	0.21	0.19	N/A	0	0	98	2	15	72	6
0.97	N/A	**E- / 0.1**	N/A	N/A	N/A	25.00	10	0.68	0.53	N/A	0	0	0	100	N/A	79	N/A
1.63	N/A	**U /**	N/A	N/A	N/A	24.67	N/A	0.45	N/A	N/A	0	0	0	100	N/A	N/A	1
2.19	N/A	**E- / 0.1**	N/A	N/A	N/A	24.85	10	0.52	0.64	N/A	0	0	0	100	N/A	80	2
2.54	N/A	**U /**	N/A	N/A	N/A	24.51	N/A	0.57	N/A	N/A	0	0	0	100	N/A	N/A	1
2.85	N/A	**E- / 0.2**	N/A	N/A	N/A	24.81	N/A	0.56	0.69	N/A	0	0	0	100	N/A	83	2
1.31	N/A	**U /**	N/A	N/A	N/A	25.51	N/A	0.20	N/A	N/A	0	0	0	100	N/A	N/A	1
3.28	N/A	**U /**	N/A	N/A	N/A	24.13	N/A	0.75	N/A	N/A	0	0	0	100	N/A	N/A	1
1.49	N/A	**U /**	N/A	N/A	N/A	25.62	N/A	0.31	N/A	N/A	0	0	0	100	N/A	N/A	1
3.49	N/A	**U /**	N/A	N/A	N/A	24.02	N/A	1.29	N/A	N/A	0	0	0	100	N/A	N/A	1
4.40	N/A	**U /**	N/A	N/A	N/A	23.93	N/A	1.00	N/A	N/A	0	0	0	100	N/A	N/A	1
4.68	N/A	**U /**	N/A	N/A	N/A	23.77	N/A	0.97	N/A	N/A	0	0	0	100	N/A	N/A	1
4.20	N/A	**U /**	N/A	N/A	N/A	23.76	N/A	0.88	N/A	N/A	0	0	0	100	N/A	N/A	1
0.67	0.10	**B+ / 9.9**	N/A	N/A	N/A	99.47	35	-0.12	N/A	N/A	0	0	0	100	16	70	3
0.32	0.07	**B / 8.2**	N/A	N/A	N/A	100.77	40	0.13	0.06	N/A	0	0	0	100	2	71	3
1.20	0.10	**B / 8.0**	N/A	N/A	N/A	98.07	163	0.94	0.66	N/A	0	0	0	100	15	79	3
2.53	0.08	**B / 8.1**	N/A	N/A	N/A	101.80	67	0.45	0.35	N/A	0	0	0	100	3	77	3
4.12	0.10	**B- / 7.9**	N/A	N/A	N/A	96.99	54	0.44	0.49	N/A	0	0	0	100	43	78	3
3.99	0.08	**B / 8.0**	N/A	N/A	N/A	102.87	26	0.52	0.59	N/A	0	0	0	100	9	75	3
5.86	0.10	**B- / 7.5**	N/A	N/A	N/A	94.55	48	0.26	0.57	N/A	0	0	0	100	8	81	3
5.52	0.08	**B- / 7.7**	N/A	N/A	N/A	101.89	26	1.94	0.93	N/A	0	0	0	100	3	81	3
0.67	0.20	**C- / 3.9**	2.1	-0.03	N/A	26.53	128	-0.04	-0.08	N/A	0	0	100	0	2	73	6
1.52	0.20	**D / 2.2**	2.3	0.39	N/A	27.33	146	0.07	0.09	N/A	0	0	100	0	1	69	6
1.64	0.19	**B- / 7.9**	N/A	N/A	N/A	25.43	66	0.35	0.23	N/A	0	0	0	100	1	63	3
1.91	0.19	**B / 8.1**	N/A	N/A	N/A	25.44	28	0.71	0.25	N/A	0	0	0	100	N/A	59	2

* Denotes ETF Fund, N/A denotes number is not available

	99 Pct = Best 0 Pct = Worst			PRICE			PERFORMANCE					
					52 Week			% Total Return Through 12/31/15			Annualized	
Fund Type	Fund Name	Ticker Symbol	Overall Investment Rating	Price As of 12/31/15	High	Low	Performance Rating/Pts	3 Mo	6 Mo	1Yr/Pct	3Yr/Pct	5Yr/Pct
MUN	*iShares iBonds Sep 2020 AMT-Fr M	IBMI	C+	25.53	25.76	24.88	C+ / 5.8	0.37	1.75	2.07 / 75	--	--
COH	*iShares iBoxx $ Hi Yld Corp Bd E	HYG	C-	80.58	91.97	78.21	C- / 4.0	-0.28	-6.08	-4.93 / 39	0.59 / 39	4.00 / 43
COI	*iShares iBoxx $ Inv Grade Cor B	LQD	C+	114.01	123.90	113.70	C / 5.0	-0.80	0.74	-1.59 / 52	1.69 / 46	4.83 / 47
EM	*iShares India 50 ETF	INDY	C-	27.20	33.45	25.16	C / 4.4	-3.37	-10.38	-9.85 / 26	3.06 / 53	-1.16 / 25
COH	*iShares Interest Rate Hgd HY Bon	HYGH	C-	83.05	96.50	79.17	D+ / 2.4	0.48	-7.09	-6.62 / 34	--	--
GL	*iShares Internat Infl-Link Bd ET	ITIP	C-	39.01	44.54	38.95	D+ / 2.3	-1.74	-6.65	-11.50 / 23	-7.13 / 21	--
GL	*iShares International High Yield	HYXU	C-	44.37	50.32	44.02	C- / 3.0	-3.46	-4.00	-9.60 / 27	-2.75 / 29	--
COI	*iShares International Preferred	IPFF	D	16.08	22.44	15.14	D- / 1.5	3.26	-14.25	-22.81 / 11	-11.26 / 16	--
GL	*iShares International Treas Bd E	IGOV	C-	89.67	96.44	87.30	C- / 3.1	-2.36	0.60	-7.03 / 33	-3.22 / 28	-0.22 / 27
GI	*iShares Interntl Developed RE ET	IFGL	C-	27.89	32.64	27.09	C- / 4.1	-0.83	-4.56	-3.51 / 44	0.47 / 39	3.50 / 40
FO	*iShares Intl Developed Property	WPS	C	35.13	40.16	31.77	C / 5.4	1.28	-3.33	0.66 / 65	2.91 / 52	5.04 / 48
FO	*iShares Intl Select Dividend ETF	IDV	C-	28.71	36.00	27.57	C- / 3.7	2.74	-8.49	-9.19 / 28	-0.10 / 37	2.68 / 36
COI	*iShares Intrm Credit Bond ETF	CIU	C+	107.28	111.27	107.00	C / 5.0	-0.48	0.18	0.45 / 63	1.47 / 45	3.34 / 40
GEI	*iShares Intrm Govt/Crdt Bond ETF	GVI	C	109.61	112.71	109.32	C / 4.8	-0.94	0.37	0.53 / 64	0.98 / 42	2.36 / 35
EM	*iShares JPMorgan USD Emg Mkts B	EMB	C-	105.78	114.31	105.03	C / 4.3	0.85	-0.79	1.54 / 70	-0.30 / 36	4.52 / 46
FO	*iShares Latin America 40	ILF	D-	21.19	33.26	21.16	E+ / 0.7	-6.71	-27.16	-28.89 / 8	-19.92 / 8	-14.23 / 9
MTG	*iShares MBS ETF	MBB	B	107.70	110.57	107.44	C / 5.2	-0.31	1.59	1.33 / 69	1.82 / 47	2.69 / 36
GR	*iShares Micro Cap	IWC	B	72.10	84.28	68.48	B / 7.6	3.47	-9.24	-4.23 / 41	11.56 / 80	8.97 / 61
GR	*iShares Morningstar Large-Cp ETF	JKD	A+	119.07	125.91	62.55	B+ / 8.9	6.55	0.26	-0.37 / 58	14.86 / 90	13.39 / 86
GR	*iShares Morningstar Large-Cp Gr	JKE	B+	120.29	125.95	84.47	A / 9.3	5.42	1.27	7.91 / 85	16.64 / 92	13.85 / 88
IN	*iShares Morningstar Large-Cp V E	JKF	A	81.76	87.35	57.37	B / 7.8	6.46	-0.92	-1.00 / 55	10.42 / 76	9.34 / 62
GR	*iShares Morningstar Mid-Cp ETF	JKG	B+	143.06	156.97	58.52	B+ / 8.5	3.55	-4.41	-0.85 / 56	13.75 / 87	12.65 / 83
GR	*iShares Morningstar Mid-Cp Gr ET	JKH	B	154.55	170.62	138.23	B / 8.2	1.41	-5.98	0.49 / 64	12.58 / 83	10.40 / 67
GR	*iShares Morningstar Mid-Cp Val E	JKI	A-	118.84	128.82	69.94	B+ / 8.7	4.36	-2.63	-1.72 / 51	14.33 / 89	11.86 / 77
GI	*iShares Morningstar MltAsst Inc	IYLD	C	23.27	26.69	17.69	C / 4.6	0.66	-2.69	-4.94 / 39	1.63 / 46	--
GR	*iShares Morningstar Sm-Cp ETF	JKJ	B+	128.49	148.19	91.99	B- / 7.2	1.23	-9.08	-4.95 / 39	10.59 / 77	9.09 / 61
GR	*iShares Morningstar Sm-Cp Gr ETF	JKK	B-	134.68	150.36	126.05	B / 8.2	3.43	-5.83	1.21 / 68	12.44 / 83	10.30 / 67
GR	*iShares Morningstar Sm-Cp Val ET	JKL	B-	114.77	133.18	82.94	C+ / 6.9	3.36	-6.88	-7.67 / 32	9.52 / 74	9.38 / 63
IN	*iShares Mortgage Real Estate Cp	REM	C-	9.56	12.14	9.17	C- / 3.9	0.68	-3.06	-8.15 / 31	0.23 / 38	3.15 / 39
GL	*iShares MSCI ACW Minimum Vol	ACWV	B+	69.27	74.41	58.12	B / 7.8	4.45	0.89	4.44 / 78	9.88 / 75	--
GL	*iShares MSCI ACWI ETF	ACWI	B	55.82	63.08	50.37	C+ / 6.5	4.01	-4.43	-0.82 / 56	7.18 / 67	6.29 / 52
FO	*iShares MSCI ACWI ex US ETF	ACWX	C	39.61	47.89	37.95	C- / 4.0	0.78	-9.74	-4.49 / 41	0.61 / 40	1.03 / 31
EN	*iShares MSCI ACWI Low Carbon Tar	CRBN	D+	93.03	102.82	86.67	C / 5.3	5.90	-2.90	1.25 / 68	--	--
FO	*iShares MSCI All Ctry Asia xJap	AAXJ	C-	53.41	69.94	47.61	C- / 3.1	1.64	-13.06	-8.39 / 30	-2.06 / 31	-1.30 / 25
FO	*iShares MSCI All Peru Capped ETF	EPU	D-	20.18	32.09	20.00	E+ / 0.6	-9.29	-30.65	-35.81 / 5	-23.29 / 7	-14.18 / 9
FO	*iShares MSCI Asia ex-Japan Min V	AXJV	C-	45.91	57.01	45.21	D+ / 2.4	0.76	-10.89	-4.12 / 42	--	--
FO	*iShares MSCI Australia	EWA	D+	18.96	24.43	17.20	C- / 3.0	9.55	-6.53	-7.28 / 33	-4.04 / 27	0.47 / 29
FO	*iShares MSCI Austria Capped	EWO	C-	15.65	18.05	14.38	C- / 3.7	3.21	-1.56	3.75 / 76	-2.76 / 29	-3.53 / 22
FO	*iShares MSCI Belgium Capped	EWK	A+	18.06	18.49	15.60	A- / 9.0	8.35	4.20	14.21 / 94	12.85 / 84	11.04 / 72
FO	*iShares MSCI Brazil Capped	EWZ	E+	20.68	38.20	20.06	E / 0.5	-8.21	-35.93	-39.11 / 4	-26.23 / 5	-20.47 / 5
FO	*iShares MSCI Brazil Small-Cap ET	EWZS	E+	6.88	13.85	6.53	E- / 0.2	-3.75	-37.31	-48.26 / 2	-35.49 / 2	-23.45 / 5
FO	*iShares MSCI BRIC	BKF	D+	29.27	41.70	27.28	D / 2.1	-1.43	-18.81	-12.23 / 22	-8.31 / 19	-7.23 / 16
FO	*iShares MSCI Canada	EWC	D	21.50	29.58	21.21	D / 2.0	-5.46	-17.32	-22.44 / 11	-6.82 / 22	-4.68 / 19
FO	*iShares MSCI Chile Capped	ECH	D-	31.92	44.80	29.50	D- / 1.0	-4.52	-15.09	-17.20 / 16	-19.66 / 8	-13.94 / 10
FO	*iShares MSCI China ETF	MCHI	C-	44.62	64.56	39.88	C- / 3.3	0.03	-17.61	-7.76 / 31	-0.63 / 35	--
FO	*iShares MSCI China Small-Cap ETF	ECNS	C	44.55	70.48	34.81	C+ / 5.9	8.03	-16.54	4.18 / 77	4.83 / 61	-1.51 / 24
GEI	*iShares MSCI Colombia Capped	ICOL	E	10.57	18.32	9.08	E- / 0.1	-8.80	-27.58	-39.81 / 4	--	--
FO	*iShares MSCI Denmark Capped ETF	EDEN	A+	55.85	57.16	45.75	A+ / 9.6	4.22	3.01	19.14 / 98	21.52 / 96	--
FO	*iShares MSCI EAFE ETF	EFA	C+	58.72	68.52	55.88	C+ / 5.6	2.13	-6.65	0.31 / 62	3.98 / 57	3.76 / 42
FO	*iShares MSCI EAFE Growth ETF	EFG	B-	67.14	74.62	61.73	C+ / 6.3	4.10	-3.84	4.36 / 77	5.67 / 63	4.52 / 45
FO	*iShares MSCI EAFE Minimum Vol ET	EFAV	A	64.87	69.57	60.00	B / 7.8	4.59	0.68	9.53 / 87	9.10 / 73	--
FO	*iShares MSCI EAFE Small-Cap ETF	SCZ	A	49.95	53.99	45.40	B / 7.9	4.73	-1.22	10.09 / 88	9.55 / 74	6.71 / 54

* Denotes ETF Fund, N/A denotes number is not available

Incl. in Returns		RISK				NET ASSETS		VALUATION			ASSET					FUND MANAGER	
			3 Year					Premium / Discount									
Dividend Yield %	Expense Ratio	Risk Rating/ Pts	Standard Deviation	Beta	Avg Dura- tion	NAV as of 12/31/15	Total $(Mil)	As of 12/31/15	1 Year Average	Wtd Avg P/E	Cash %	Stocks %	Bonds %	Other %	Portfolio Turnover Ratio	Manager Quality Pct	Manager Tenure (Years)
1.71	0.18	**B / 8.0**	N/A	N/A	N/A	25.48	N/A	0.20	0.23	N/A	0	0	0	100	N/A	64	2
11.57	0.50	**C+ / 6.8**	5.8	1.02	N/A	79.97	12,412	0.76	0.27	N/A	1	0	97	2	11	61	6
6.22	0.15	**B / 8.3**	5.1	1.24	N/A	114.01	17,377	0.00	0.07	N/A	0	0	97	3	9	65	6
0.69	0.93	**C+ / 6.8**	21.1	0.76	N/A	27.46	672	-0.95	0.08	N/A	0	99	0	1	5	94	7
7.26	N/A	**B / 8.3**	N/A	N/A	N/A	83.19	44	-0.17	0.02	N/A	0	0	0	100	N/A	55	2
0.15	0.40	**B- / 7.5**	8.7	1.02	N/A	39.02	125	-0.03	-0.14	N/A	0	0	0	100	20	42	5
2.29	0.40	**B- / 7.6**	9.5	1.05	N/A	44.59	134	-0.49	0.27	N/A	0	0	0	100	25	81	4
32.93	0.55	**C+ / 6.1**	13.5	0.21	N/A	16.26	39	-1.11	-0.56	N/A	0	0	0	100	47	14	5
0.43	0.35	**C+ / 6.8**	6.2	0.98	N/A	89.54	541	0.15	-0.01	N/A	1	0	96	3	28	73	6
4.87	0.48	**C+ / 6.2**	13.6	0.65	N/A	28.03	792	-0.50	-0.04	215.6	0	99	0	1	11	19	8
8.03	0.48	**C+ / 6.8**	13.9	0.79	N/A	35.32	168	-0.54	-0.22	205.3	0	99	0	1	8	57	8
1.25	0.50	**B- / 7.4**	14.6	1.06	N/A	28.92	4,360	-0.73	-0.08	13.4	0	99	0	1	53	28	8
5.27	0.20	**B / 8.0**	2.6	0.61	N/A	107.18	6,213	0.09	0.09	N/A	1	0	97	2	7	72	6
3.33	0.20	**B- / 7.8**	2.1	0.71	N/A	109.57	1,427	0.04	0.07	N/A	2	0	96	2	22	66	6
1.40	0.59	**C+ / 6.3**	7.3	0.59	7.9	105.44	4,422	0.32	0.40	N/A	2	0	96	2	52	82	6
2.03	0.49	**C / 4.7**	22.0	1.16	N/A	21.33	1,165	-0.66	-0.13	N/A	0	99	0	1	11	5	8
7.89	0.25	**B+ / 9.4**	2.6	1.08	14.2	107.77	6,288	-0.06	0.03	N/A	0	0	97	3	936	65	6
4.24	0.60	**B- / 7.5**	15.0	0.97	N/A	72.10	813	0.00	-0.03	43.6	0	99	0	1	26	56	8
2.29	0.20	**B / 8.7**	11.0	1.01	N/A	119.15	490	-0.07	N/A	38.1	0	99	0	1	27	73	8
2.16	0.25	**C+ / 6.6**	11.5	1.02	N/A	120.19	571	0.08	0.04	132.0	0	99	0	1	21	80	8
6.36	0.25	**B / 8.9**	10.7	0.96	N/A	81.79	312	-0.04	-0.03	22.2	0	99	0	1	14	46	8
4.23	0.25	**B- / 7.3**	11.4	1.01	N/A	143.01	299	0.03	0.04	50.9	0	99	0	1	55	66	8
1.56	0.30	**C+ / 6.8**	11.5	0.95	N/A	153.20	199	0.88	-0.02	105.6	0	99	0	1	50	63	8
5.74	0.30	**B- / 7.4**	11.2	0.99	N/A	118.41	216	0.36	-0.01	30.7	0	99	0	1	33	73	8
8.89	0.24	**C+ / 6.7**	7.3	0.39	N/A	23.21	186	0.26	0.03	N/A	0	0	0	100	47	39	4
4.08	0.25	**B / 8.1**	13.2	1.06	N/A	128.72	206	-0.18	-0.02	90.2	0	99	0	1	61	39	8
1.46	0.30	**C+ / 6.3**	13.9	1.01	N/A	133.95	120	0.54	-0.07	137.6	0	99	0	1	61	55	8
6.01	0.30	**B- / 7.1**	13.2	1.08	N/A	114.73	375	0.03	-0.02	24.6	0	99	0	1	40	32	8
2.51	0.48	**C+ / 6.1**	14.5	0.49	N/A	9.56	1,215	0.00	-0.02	8.2	0	97	0	3	42	31	8
4.90	0.20	**B / 8.1**	9.3	0.59	N/A	69.28	1,253	-0.01	0.12	N/A	0	0	0	100	22	92	5
0.19	0.33	**B / 8.4**	10.9	0.82	N/A	55.96	6,422	-0.25	N/A	58.0	0	99	0	1	6	85	8
3.11	0.33	**B / 8.2**	12.3	0.95	N/A	39.82	1,702	-0.53	0.06	18.6	0	99	0	1	6	37	8
4.01	0.20	**C- / 3.4**	N/A	N/A	N/A	91.94	N/A	1.19	0.19	N/A	0	0	0	100	4	96	2
.74	0.69	**B- / 7.4**	13.8	0.83	N/A	53.77	2,731	-0.67	-0.10	N/A	0	99	0	1	13	26	8
2.57	0.61	**C / 5.4**	19.2	0.58	N/A	20.38	288	-0.98	-0.40	29.6	0	99	0	1	21	4	7
.44	0.35	**B- / 7.5**	N/A	N/A	N/A	46.41	5	-1.08	-0.08	N/A	0	0	0	100	44	33	2
.75	0.48	**C+ / 6.1**	19.4	1.07	N/A	19.09	1,813	-0.68	-0.11	N/A	0	94	0	6	9	18	8
.42	0.48	**C+ / 6.9**	16.9	1.10	N/A	15.80	58	-0.95	-0.06	N/A	1	98	0	1	18	20	8
.84	0.48	**B / 8.7**	12.1	0.86	N/A	18.13	147	-0.39	0.05	N/A	0	99	0	1	7	93	8
.50	0.62	**C- / 3.4**	29.7	1.49	N/A	20.95	5,099	-1.29	-0.17	N/A	0	98	0	2	63	2	8
.25	0.62	**C- / 3.2**	27.8	1.44	N/A	7.06	34	-2.55	0.35	N/A	0	91	0	9	172	1	6
.45	0.69	**C+ / 6.6**	18.0	1.03	N/A	29.54	364	-0.91	-0.42	N/A	0	99	0	1	9	13	8
.39	0.48	**C+ / 5.8**	13.8	0.77	N/A	21.42	3,501	0.37	-0.03	18.2	0	99	0	1	5	16	8
.44	0.62	**C / 5.1**	17.9	0.81	N/A	32.40	319	-1.48	-0.14	N/A	0	99	0	1	71	6	8
.66	0.62	**C+ / 6.6**	19.4	0.90	N/A	44.73	1,164	-0.25	0.01	N/A	0	99	0	1	14	33	5
.13	0.62	**C+ / 6.1**	26.2	0.95	N/A	45.71	33	-2.54	-0.66	54.3	0	99	0	1	35	77	6
.21	0.61	**D / 1.8**	N/A	N/A	N/A	10.54	23	0.28	0.94	N/A	0	0	0	100	86	1	22
.07	0.53	**B / 8.7**	13.4	0.81	N/A	56.40	57	-0.98	-0.03	N/A	0	99	0	1	9	98	4
.46	0.33	**B- / 7.9**	12.6	0.98	N/A	59.18	53,613	-0.78	0.08	81.1	0	99	0	1	2	60	8
.57	0.40	**B / 8.1**	11.9	0.92	N/A	67.54	1,639	-0.59	0.09	86.1	0	99	0	1	25	76	8
.13	0.20	**B / 8.8**	10.6	0.69	N/A	65.16	1,135	-0.45	0.17	N/A	0	0	0	100	23	90	5
.41	0.40	**B / 8.8**	11.7	0.84	N/A	50.21	3,672	-0.52	0.25	0.2	0	99	0	1	13	89	8

Denotes ETF Fund, N/A denotes number is not available

Fund Type	Fund Name (99 Pct = Best, 0 Pct = Worst)	Ticker Symbol	Overall Investment Rating	PRICE: Price As of 12/31/15	52 Week High	52 Week Low	PERFORMANCE: Performance Rating/Pts	% Total Return Through 12/31/15: 3 Mo	6 Mo	1Yr/Pct	Annualized 3Yr/Pct	Annualized 5Yr/Pct
FO	*iShares MSCI EAFE Value ETF	EFV	C	46.52	56.93	45.19	C / 4.5	0.45	-9.97	-4.57 / 40	2.11 / 49	2.56 / 36
EM	*iShares MSCI EM Asia ETF	EEMA	C-	50.40	67.15	44.04	C- / 3.0	1.28	-14.25	-9.05 / 28	-2.50 / 29	--
FO	*iShares MSCI Em Mkts Lat Amer ET	EEML	D-	24.39	37.62	24.22	E+ / 0.7	-4.34	-25.42	-27.86 / 8	-20.71 / 8	--
EM	*iShares MSCI Emerging Markets	EEM	D+	32.19	44.19	30.00	D / 2.1	-1.97	-16.61	-13.78 / 19	-8.12 / 20	-5.17 / 19
EM	*iShares MSCI Emerging Mkts Min V	EEMV	C-	48.66	63.71	45.27	D+ / 2.6	-1.72	-13.98	-10.15 / 25	-4.49 / 26	--
EM	*iShares MSCI Emerging Mkts Sm-Ca	EEMS	D+	40.95	51.93	36.96	C- / 3.1	2.94	-13.38	-5.04 / 39	-2.76 / 29	--
EM	*iShares MSCI Emg Mkts Horizon ET	EMHZ	D	17.47	23.85	16.56	E+ / 0.8	-1.23	-15.67	-21.22 / 12	--	--
FS	*iShares MSCI Europ Financials ET	EUFN	C	20.30	24.80	19.88	C / 5.0	-1.81	-10.15	-4.00 / 42	3.33 / 54	2.38 / 35
FO	*iShares MSCI Europe Minimum Vol	EUMV	B	23.56	25.72	22.33	C+ / 6.1	2.49	-0.13	5.30 / 80	--	--
FO	*iShares MSCI Europe Small-Cap	IEUS	A	45.28	49.77	40.23	B / 7.9	2.47	-1.24	12.01 / 92	9.91 / 75	6.63 / 53
FO	*iShares MSCI Eurozone	EZU	C+	35.04	40.73	33.52	C / 5.5	0.95	-6.58	-1.48 / 52	4.04 / 57	3.47 / 40
FO	*iShares MSCI Finland Capped ETF	EFNL	B+	32.61	35.46	29.68	B / 7.6	5.09	0.87	2.45 / 73	9.29 / 73	--
FO	*iShares MSCI France	EWQ	C+	24.21	27.90	23.30	C+ / 5.6	-0.50	-5.51	1.13 / 68	3.77 / 56	3.22 / 39
FO	*iShares MSCI Frontier 100 ETF	FM	C-	24.89	31.55	24.27	C- / 3.5	-0.96	-14.13	-16.01 / 17	1.09 / 42	--
FO	*iShares MSCI Germany	EWG	C+	26.19	30.84	24.17	C+ / 5.6	5.35	-6.56	-2.27 / 49	3.81 / 56	4.64 / 46
FO	*iShares MSCI Germany Small-Cap	EWGS	A	41.35	43.15	36.60	B+ / 8.6	2.79	4.17	11.27 / 90	11.67 / 80	--
PM	*iShares MSCI Gl Met&MP	PICK	E	8.42	16.63	8.00	E+ / 0.6	-9.80	-33.13	-38.37 / 4	-24.11 / 6	--
GL	*iShares MSCI Glbl Agri Prod	VEGI	D+	22.44	28.47	21.31	D+ / 2.7	5.84	-14.96	-12.05 / 22	-4.38 / 26	--
EN	*iShares MSCI Global Engy Prod	FILL	D	16.34	22.95	15.94	D / 1.7	-4.01	-16.53	-20.51 / 13	-9.21 / 18	--
PM	*iShares MSCI Global Gold Miners	RING	E-	5.48	9.47	4.99	E / 0.4	-2.07	-22.10	-27.29 / 9	-33.25 / 3	--
PM	*iShares MSCI Global Silver Miner	SLVP	E	5.62	10.25	5.52	E / 0.3	-8.22	-30.11	-36.28 / 5	-35.11 / 3	--
FO	*iShares MSCI Hong Kong	EWH	C+	19.82	24.65	17.57	C / 5.4	2.42	-11.66	0.01 / 60	3.59 / 55	3.17 / 39
FO	*iShares MSCI India ETF	INDA	C	27.50	33.64	25.29	C / 4.3	-3.28	-9.44	-7.80 / 31	2.33 / 50	--
FO	*iShares MSCI India Small-Cap	SMIN	C	33.28	37.95	28.60	B- / 7.1	0.22	-1.44	-0.66 / 56	9.08 / 72	--
FO	*iShares MSCI Indonesia ETF	EIDO	D	20.87	28.32	16.52	D / 1.8	16.97	-11.72	-20.74 / 13	-10.79 / 16	-4.55 / 20
GR	*iShares MSCI Intl Dev Mom Factor	IMTM	U	25.37	N/A	N/A	U /	3.79	-5.67	--	--	--
FO	*iShares MSCI Intl Dev Qual Facto	IQLT	U	25.24	N/A	N/A	U /	3.12	-4.05	--	--	--
FO	*iShares MSCI Ireland ETF	EIRL	A-	41.56	42.08	33.23	A+ / 9.6	7.60	6.89	22.97 / 98	20.77 / 95	18.28 / 96
FO	*iShares MSCI Israel Capped	EIS	B+	49.19	56.02	45.21	B- / 7.2	3.85	-3.04	9.63 / 88	7.80 / 69	-1.55 / 24
FO	*iShares MSCI Italy Capped	EWI	C	13.74	16.23	12.71	C / 4.5	-5.78	-7.73	3.26 / 75	2.57 / 51	-0.47 / 26
FO	*iShares MSCI Japan	EWJ	B+	12.12	13.35	10.89	B- / 7.5	5.54	-4.69	9.76 / 88	8.68 / 71	3.71 / 42
FO	*iShares MSCI Japan Minimum Vol E	JPMV	A+	57.00	59.75	48.52	A / 9.3	7.47	2.29	17.01 / 97	--	--
FO	*iShares MSCI Japan Small Cap	SCJ	A+	58.45	60.60	50.49	B+ / 8.8	6.55	-0.43	15.85 / 96	11.73 / 81	7.08 / 55
IN	*iShares MSCI KLD 400 Social ETF	DSI	A	75.71	79.11	50.44	B+ / 8.8	5.83	0.02	0.83 / 66	14.22 / 88	11.58 / 76
GL	*iShares MSCI Kokusai ETF	TOK	B+	51.76	57.50	38.04	B- / 7.5	5.44	-2.73	-0.02 / 60	9.73 / 74	8.48 / 59
FO	*iShares MSCI Malaysia	EWM	C-	7.74	14.23	7.46	C / 5.3	32.95	7.71	2.56 / 73	-1.78 / 31	0.75 / 30
FO	*iShares MSCI Mexico Capped	EWW	D+	49.83	61.62	46.34	D / 1.9	-2.08	-11.59	-11.28 / 23	-9.81 / 18	-2.79 / 22
FO	*iShares MSCI Netherlands	EWN	B	23.84	27.45	22.67	C+ / 6.6	1.62	-6.20	2.59 / 73	7.23 / 68	5.85 / 51
FO	*iShares MSCI Norway Capped ETF	ENOR	D	18.91	27.05	18.43	D / 1.6	-4.15	-16.21	-15.03 / 18	-11.09 / 16	--
FO	*iShares MSCI NZ Capped ETF	ENZL	B	37.48	41.65	31.13	B / 7.9	20.50	11.32	0.69 / 65	8.01 / 70	11.29 / 74
FO	*iShares MSCI Pacific ex Japan	EPP	C-	38.39	48.77	35.05	C- / 3.4	7.56	-8.50	-6.17 / 35	-2.18 / 30	1.11 / 31
FO	*iShares MSCI Philippines ETF	EPHE	C-	33.74	43.09	31.03	C- / 3.2	-2.71	-13.20	-10.32 / 25	-0.70 / 35	7.57 / 56
FO	*iShares MSCI Poland Capped ETF	EPOL	D-	18.08	26.54	17.19	D- / 1.4	-11.74	-17.91	-20.87 / 13	-11.63 / 15	-7.46 / 16
EM	*iShares MSCI Qatar Capped ETF	QAT	D-	19.28	25.04	17.92	E+ / 0.8	-11.42	-15.24	-14.64 / 18	--	--
FO	*iShares MSCI Russia Capped ETF	ERUS	D-	11.13	16.12	10.35	D- / 1.2	-0.35	-14.35	4.15 / 77	-18.86 / 9	--
EM	*iShares MSCI Saudi Arabia Capped	KSA	U	24.22	N/A	N/A	U /	-4.35	--	--	--	--
FO	*iShares MSCI Singapore	EWS	D+	10.28	13.80	9.83	D+ / 2.5	6.41	-14.65	-15.70 / 17	-5.16 / 25	-1.75 / 23
FO	*iShares MSCI South Africa	EZA	D	46.71	73.08	42.45	D- / 1.3	-14.63	-26.38	-23.24 / 11	-10.46 / 17	-5.31 / 19
FO	*iShares MSCI South Korea Capped	EWY	C-	49.67	63.13	42.94	D+ / 2.7	3.92	-6.70	-4.90 / 39	-5.66 / 24	-2.54 / 23
FO	*iShares MSCI Spain Capped	EWP	C-	28.27	36.95	28.04	C- / 3.6	-3.61	-12.63	-14.84 / 18	1.65 / 46	1.42 / 31
FO	*iShares MSCI Sweden	EWD	C	29.18	35.18	27.89	C / 4.7	-0.64	-7.76	-3.72 / 43	2.20 / 49	3.06 / 38
FO	*iShares MSCI Switzerland Capped	EWL	B	31.04	36.18	29.80	C+ / 6.4	0.16	-6.39	0.84 / 66	6.85 / 67	7.57 / 56

* Denotes ETF Fund, N/A denotes number is not availabl

cl. in Returns		RISK				NET ASSETS		VALUATION			ASSET					FUND MANAGER	
			3 Year					Premium / Discount									
dend eld %	Expense Ratio	Risk Rating/ Pts	Standard Deviation	Beta	Avg Dura- tion	NAV as of 12/31/15	Total $(Mil)	As of 12/31/15	1 Year Average	Wtd Avg P/E	Cash %	Stocks %	Bonds %	Other %	Portfolio Turnover Ratio	Manager Quality Pct	Manager Tenure (Years)
.19	0.40	**B- / 7.6**	13.5	1.05	N/A	46.75	2,605	-0.49	0.17	N/A	0	99	0	1	25	43	8
.74	0.49	**B- / 7.4**	14.4	0.95	N/A	50.95	88	-1.08	0.05	N/A	0	0	0	100	16	88	4
.83	0.49	**C / 4.6**	21.3	1.13	N/A	24.41	13	-0.08	-0.06	N/A	0	0	0	100	7	4	4
.22	0.69	**B- / 7.3**	14.7	0.99	N/A	32.46	39,253	-0.83	-0.14	37.3	0	99	0	1	10	56	8
.27	0.25	**B- / 7.5**	12.5	0.81	N/A	48.85	1,991	-0.39	0.19	N/A	0	0	0	100	28	76	5
.71	0.69	**C+ / 5.7**	15.3	0.96	N/A	40.83	42	0.29	0.34	N/A	0	0	0	100	23	88	5
.07	0.50	**C+ / 6.9**	N/A	N/A	N/A	17.77	N/A	-1.69	-0.62	N/A	0	0	0	100	28	13	2
.21	0.48	**B- / 7.5**	16.0	0.91	N/A	20.44	456	-0.68	0.03	N/A	0	99	0	1	6	18	6
.39	0.25	**B / 8.6**	N/A	N/A	N/A	23.71	5	-0.63	0.19	N/A	0	0	0	100	25	89	2
.65	0.41	**B / 8.8**	12.3	0.89	N/A	45.64	37	-0.79	0.51	0.2	0	99	0	1	65	90	8
.88	0.48	**B- / 7.6**	15.1	1.10	N/A	35.35	8,485	-0.88	0.11	72.8	0	99	0	1	5	53	8
.57	0.53	**B / 8.0**	14.4	1.01	N/A	33.03	36	-1.27	-0.10	N/A	0	99	0	1	12	89	4
.20	0.48	**B- / 7.6**	15.2	1.10	N/A	24.27	251	-0.25	0.13	N/A	0	99	0	1	6	49	8
.34	0.79	**C+ / 6.5**	14.0	0.61	N/A	25.18	811	-1.15	0.12	N/A	0	0	0	100	47	55	4
.93	0.48	**B- / 7.5**	15.5	1.07	N/A	26.58	4,819	-1.47	0.01	72.8	0	99	0	1	3	52	8
.02	0.59	**B / 8.1**	13.0	0.74	N/A	41.68	35	-0.79	-0.02	N/A	0	99	0	1	18	93	4
.02	0.39	**D / 2.1**	24.2	0.46	N/A	8.38	173	0.48	0.45	N/A	0	0	0	100	17	8	4
.07	0.38	**C+ / 5.7**	13.8	0.81	N/A	22.32	45	0.54	-0.22	N/A	0	0	0	100	10	20	4
.79	0.39	**C+ / 5.7**	18.8	0.98	N/A	16.47	8	-0.79	0.68	N/A	0	0	0	100	4	30	4
.58	0.39	**E+ / 0.9**	40.9	1.85	N/A	5.43	56	0.92	0.34	N/A	0	0	0	100	20	13	4
.23	0.39	**D / 1.8**	39.5	1.86	N/A	5.62	12	0.00	0.50	N/A	0	0	0	100	31	11	4
.32	0.48	**B- / 7.6**	16.2	0.97	N/A	19.90	3,010	-0.40	-0.03	N/A	0	96	0	4	7	58	8
.91	0.68	**B- / 7.0**	19.5	0.74	N/A	27.72	1,479	-0.79	0.22	N/A	0	99	0	1	30	57	4
.46	0.74	**C+ / 5.6**	27.8	0.87	N/A	33.79	14	-1.51	0.17	N/A	0	99	0	1	73	89	4
.76	0.62	**C / 4.7**	26.1	0.82	N/A	21.04	540	-0.81	-0.27	N/A	0	100	0	0	4	11	6
64	0.30	**U /**	N/A	N/A	N/A	25.32	N/A	0.20	N/A	N/A	0	0	0	100	55	N/A	1
69	0.30	**U /**	N/A	N/A	N/A	25.08	N/A	0.64	N/A	N/A	0	0	0	100	16	N/A	1
44	0.48	**C+ / 6.5**	14.8	0.72	N/A	41.04	119	1.27	0.80	N/A	0	96	0	4	26	97	6
20	0.62	**B / 8.3**	12.8	0.67	N/A	49.31	125	-0.24	0.02	N/A	0	99	0	1	14	88	8
21	0.48	**B- / 7.0**	19.9	1.12	N/A	13.92	1,389	-1.29	0.06	N/A	0	99	0	1	22	44	8
89	0.48	**B / 8.3**	14.4	0.80	N/A	12.28	14,397	-1.30	-0.01	N/A	0	99	0	1	2	88	8
94	0.30	**B / 8.8**	N/A	N/A	N/A	57.51	10	-0.89	-0.03	N/A	0	0	0	100	18	98	2
36	0.48	**B / 8.6**	13.8	0.58	N/A	59.08	159	-1.07	0.09	N/A	0	99	0	1	10	94	8
57	0.50	**B- / 7.9**	10.7	1.01	N/A	75.72	385	-0.01	0.05	66.5	0	99	0	1	14	68	8
69	0.25	**B- / 7.7**	11.3	0.81	N/A	51.76	486	0.00	0.12	59.5	0	99	0	1	5	90	8
92	0.48	**C / 4.6**	21.2	0.72	N/A	7.76	742	-0.26	-0.13	N/A	0	99	0	1	24	29	8
99	0.48	**C+ / 6.6**	15.0	0.72	N/A	50.05	3,048	-0.44	-0.12	N/A	0	99	0	1	13	13	8
42	0.48	**B / 8.2**	14.8	1.01	N/A	23.95	160	-0.46	0.02	N/A	0	100	0	0	6	80	8
23	0.53	**C+ / 5.6**	19.0	1.16	N/A	19.11	27	-1.05	0.03	N/A	0	100	0	0	14	10	4
40	0.48	**B- / 7.1**	19.2	1.04	N/A	37.87	139	-1.03	-0.11	N/A	0	99	0	1	14	82	6
66	0.49	**C+ / 6.8**	17.0	1.04	N/A	38.64	3,141	-0.65	-0.18	N/A	0	99	0	1	7	22	8
45	0.62	**B- / 7.0**	18.4	0.82	N/A	34.22	364	-1.40	-0.45	N/A	0	100	0	0	12	36	6
53	0.62	**C / 4.3**	17.3	0.76	N/A	18.07	287	0.06	N/A	N/A	2	97	0	1	17	10	6
25	0.62	**C / 4.3**	N/A	N/A	N/A	19.25	37	0.16	0.46	N/A	0	0	0	100	85	17	2
56	0.62	**C / 4.4**	27.5	1.18	N/A	11.14	276	-0.09	-0.04	N/A	0	99	0	1	19	6	6
30	N/A	**U /**	N/A	N/A	N/A	23.63	N/A	2.50	N/A	N/A	0	0	0	100	N/A	N/A	1
79	0.48	**C+ / 6.8**	16.2	0.95	N/A	10.33	936	-0.48	-0.07	N/A	0	97	0	3	10	17	8
22	0.62	**C+ / 6.2**	19.0	0.87	N/A	47.02	463	-0.66	0.01	N/A	0	98	0	2	9	11	8
84	0.62	**B- / 7.0**	16.5	0.76	N/A	50.43	4,725	-1.51	-0.38	N/A	0	99	0	1	24	18	8
40	0.48	**C+ / 6.5**	19.4	1.31	N/A	28.45	2,350	-0.63	0.06	N/A	0	99	0	1	15	31	8
35	0.92	**B- / 7.6**	13.8	0.94	N/A	29.58	394	-1.35	0.01	N/A	0	100	0	0	4	47	8
58	0.48	**B / 8.3**	12.3	0.89	N/A	31.24	1,237	-0.64	0.04	N/A	0	99	0	1	7	82	8

Denotes ETF Fund, N/A denotes number is not available

Fund Type	Fund Name (99 Pct = Best, 0 Pct = Worst)	Ticker Symbol	Overall Investment Rating	PRICE: Price As of 12/31/15	PRICE: 52 Week High	PRICE: 52 Week Low	PERFORMANCE: Performance Rating/Pts	% Total Return Through 12/31/15: 3 Mo	6 Mo	1Yr/Pct	Annualized: 3Yr/Pct	Annualized: 5Yr/Pct
FO	*iShares MSCI Taiwan	EWT	C-	12.77	17.09	11.43	C- / 3.7	-0.26	-15.23	-9.27 / 28	1.07 / 42	-0.19 / 27
FO	*iShares MSCI Thailand Capped	THD	D	58.64	84.47	57.37	D / 1.8	-5.25	-19.39	-20.37 / 13	-8.36 / 19	0.91 / 30
FO	*iShares MSCI Turkey	TUR	D-	36.36	59.16	34.19	D- / 1.0	-3.86	-18.97	-30.75 / 7	-17.07 / 10	-9.66 / 14
EM	*iShares MSCI UAE Capped ETF	UAE	E+	15.81	21.60	14.43	E+ / 0.7	-10.83	-21.11	-13.34 / 20	--	--
FO	*iShares MSCI UK Small-Cap ETF	EWUS	A	39.54	44.20	35.86	B+ / 8.4	3.03	-4.07	11.54 / 91	11.63 / 80	--
FO	*iShares MSCI United Kingdom	EWU	C	16.14	19.93	15.73	C- / 4.1	-0.74	-8.78	-4.35 / 41	1.00 / 42	3.12 / 38
IN	*iShares MSCI USA Equal Weighted	EUSA	B+	42.20	45.94	38.99	B+ / 8.3	3.66	-3.63	-1.46 / 53	12.90 / 84	11.50 / 75
GR	*iShares MSCI USA ESG Select ETF	KLD	B+	83.38	88.48	69.77	B+ / 8.3	5.13	-1.39	-1.32 / 53	12.44 / 83	10.24 / 66
IN	*iShares MSCI USA Minimum Vol ETF	USMV	A+	41.82	42.72	26.41	A- / 9.0	5.50	4.24	6.05 / 81	14.54 / 89	--
GR	*iShares MSCI USA Momentum Factor	MTUM	B+	73.29	76.30	55.00	B / 8.1	5.59	2.69	9.41 / 87	--	--
GR	*iShares MSCI USA Quality Factor	QUAL	B+	64.57	66.82	41.10	B- / 7.3	6.32	2.77	5.93 / 81	--	--
GR	*iShares MSCI USA Size Factor ETF	SIZE	C+	65.29	68.10	60.51	C+ / 6.1	5.62	0.81	2.54 / 73	--	--
GR	*iShares MSCI USA Value Factor ET	VLUE	C-	62.24	67.97	51.72	C- / 3.8	4.37	-3.58	-1.87 / 51	--	--
GL	*iShares MSCI World	URTH	B-	69.60	77.35	60.01	B- / 7.4	5.53	-2.53	0.43 / 63	9.41 / 73	--
HL	*iShares Nasdaq Biotechnology	IBB	B+	338.33	400.79	284.16	A+ / 9.8	7.25	-8.63	10.48 / 89	33.48 / 99	29.10 / 99
MUN	*iShares National AMT Free Muni B	MUB	C+	110.71	112.20	107.58	C+ / 6.1	1.77	3.85	3.16 / 79	2.52 / 57	5.25 / 58
MUS	*iShares New York AMT Free Muni B	NYF	B-	111.93	113.64	109.14	C+ / 6.3	2.06	3.96	3.19 / 79	2.91 / 59	5.29 / 58
IN	*iShares North Amer Tech Software	IGV	B+	103.81	107.02	86.66	A / 9.4	7.21	4.39	12.78 / 92	17.57 / 93	12.09 / 79
GR	*iShares North Amer Tech-Mmedia N	IGN	B-	37.08	40.59	30.13	B- / 7.3	2.03	-1.99	1.13 / 68	9.20 / 73	1.96 / 33
EN	*iShares North American Natural R	IGE	D	28.14	40.88	27.55	D / 1.7	-4.97	-19.36	-23.95 / 11	-8.31 / 19	-5.46 / 18
GR	*iShares North American Tech	IGM	A-	110.69	114.96	78.05	A / 9.4	8.85	6.82	9.98 / 88	18.09 / 93	13.24 / 85
IN	*iShares PHLX Semiconductor ETF	SOXX	B+	89.79	101.78	73.39	A / 9.4	9.69	-2.29	-1.75 / 51	20.34 / 95	10.75 / 70
IN	*iShares Real Estate 50 ETF	FTY	B-	47.33	51.33	42.10	B / 8.1	8.43	10.44	4.35 / 77	9.60 / 74	11.41 / 74
IN	*iShares Residential Rl Est Cap E	REZ	B+	63.45	65.80	55.02	A- / 9.0	7.64	13.36	10.32 / 89	12.97 / 84	14.18 / 88
GR	*iShares Russell 1000 ETF	IWB	A+	113.31	119.74	93.25	B+ / 8.8	5.24	-0.97	1.39 / 69	13.94 / 87	12.16 / 79
GR	*iShares Russell 1000 Growth ETF	IWF	A	99.48	103.50	84.82	A- / 9.1	5.75	1.19	6.01 / 81	15.76 / 91	13.18 / 85
IN	*iShares Russell 1000 Value ETF	IWD	B+	97.86	106.49	89.69	B / 8.0	4.69	-3.12	-3.33 / 45	11.93 / 81	10.95 / 71
GR	*iShares Russell 2000 ETF	IWM	B+	112.62	129.10	106.99	B- / 7.4	2.70	-7.96	-3.48 / 44	10.56 / 77	9.21 / 62
GR	*iShares Russell 2000 Growth ETF	IWO	B+	139.28	159.71	123.85	B+ / 8.3	2.76	-8.49	-0.35 / 58	13.23 / 85	10.71 / 70
GR	*iShares Russell 2000 Value ETF	IWN	B	91.94	105.42	85.43	C+ / 6.4	2.67	-7.37	-6.59 / 34	7.91 / 69	7.61 / 56
IN	*iShares Russell 3000	IWV	A	120.31	127.97	100.00	B+ / 8.6	5.10	-1.48	0.97 / 67	13.63 / 86	11.86 / 77
GR	*iShares Russell Mid Cap	IWR	A	160.18	176.48	138.61	B+ / 8.3	2.47	-4.72	-2.08 / 50	13.00 / 84	11.25 / 73
GR	*iShares Russell Mid Cap Growth	IWP	A+	91.92	100.53	83.28	B+ / 8.5	2.63	-4.39	--	13.60 / 86	11.22 / 73
GR	*iShares Russell Mid Cap Value	IWS	A	68.66	76.89	41.61	B / 7.9	2.34	-5.14	-4.39 / 41	12.20 / 82	11.08 / 73
IN	*iShares Russell Top 200	IWL	A-	46.99	48.65	39.39	A- / 9.0	7.01	1.16	3.34 / 75	14.49 / 89	12.67 / 83
GR	*iShares Russell Top 200 Growth	IWY	A+	53.54	55.10	33.15	A / 9.3	7.17	3.57	8.51 / 86	16.64 / 92	14.03 / 88
IN	*iShares Russell Top 200 Value	IWX	B	41.72	44.92	35.28	B / 8.1	6.46	-1.94	-2.72 / 47	11.93 / 81	10.87 / 71
GR	*iShares S&P 100	OEF	A+	91.17	94.97	71.52	B+ / 8.8	6.74	1.31	3.11 / 74	13.62 / 86	12.14 / 79
GR	*iShares S&P 500 Growth	IVW	A+	115.80	119.85	85.21	A- / 9.2	6.22	2.28	5.93 / 81	16.16 / 92	13.77 / 87
IN	*iShares S&P 500 Value	IVE	A	88.53	95.92	72.55	B / 8.0	5.32	-2.64	-2.59 / 48	11.75 / 81	10.60 / 69
IN	*iShares S&P GSCI Commodity-Index	GSG	E	14.23	22.34	13.84	E+ / 0.6	-16.54	-31.42	-32.94 / 6	-24.19 / 6	-15.66 / 8
GR	*iShares S&P Mid Cap 400 Grow	IJK	A-	160.96	174.83	126.00	B / 8.1	2.08	-4.48	2.15 / 72	12.03 / 82	10.92 / 71
GR	*iShares S&P Mid Cap 400 Value	IJJ	B-	117.20	134.01	85.09	B- / 7.3	1.49	-7.64	-6.00 / 36	10.71 / 77	10.02 / 65
GR	*iShares S&P Small Cap 600 Growth	IJT	B+	124.31	135.45	82.07	B+ / 8.7	3.40	-4.05	3.77 / 76	13.89 / 87	12.46 / 82
GR	*iShares S&P Small Cap 600 Value	IJS	B	108.16	122.03	78.41	B- / 7.3	3.63	-6.79	-5.79 / 36	10.66 / 77	10.34 / 67
IN	*iShares Select Dividend ETF	DVY	A	75.15	81.01	48.00	B+ / 8.3	4.47	1.86	-1.20 / 54	12.46 / 83	12.63 / 83
MUN	*iShares Sh-Term Natl AMT-Fr Muni	SUB	C+	105.95	106.48	105.20	C / 4.9	0.17	0.62	0.65 / 67	0.62 / 41	1.29 / 34
GEI	*iShares Short Maturity Bond	NEAR	C	50.02	50.18	49.91	C / 4.8	0.19	0.39	0.84 / 66	--	--
MUN	*iShares Short Maturity Municipal	MEAR	U	50.01	N/A	N/A	U /	0.15	0.93	--	--	--
USA	*iShares Short Treasury Bond ETF	SHV	C	110.22	110.34	110.16	C / 4.3	-0.06	-0.02	0.03 / 60	0.01 / 37	0.02 / 28
PM	*iShares Silver Trust	SLV	E+	13.19	17.69	13.04	E+ / 0.8	-9.35	-11.77	-12.71 / 21	-23.31 / 7	-14.04 / 10
USA	*iShares TIPS Bond ETF	TIP	C	109.68	115.76	108.98	C- / 3.5	-1.78	-1.86	-2.38 / 49	-2.08 / 31	2.33 / 35

* Denotes ETF Fund, N/A denotes number is not available

Incl. in Returns		RISK				NET ASSETS		VALUATION			ASSET					FUND MANAGER	
Dividend Yield %	Expense Ratio	Risk Rating/ Pts	3 Year Standard Deviation	3 Year Beta	Avg Dura-tion	NAV as of 12/31/15	Total $(Mil)	Premium / Discount As of 12/31/15	Premium / Discount 1 Year Average	Wtd Avg P/E	Cash %	Stocks %	Bonds %	Other %	Portfolio Turnover Ratio	Manager Quality Pct	Manager Tenure (Years)
6.25	0.62	**B- / 7.5**	13.3	0.75	N/A	12.95	3,070	-1.39	-0.05	N/A	0	99	0	1	14	44	8
3.72	0.62	**C+ / 6.0**	19.4	0.85	N/A	59.14	565	-0.85	-0.03	N/A	0	99	0	1	13	13	8
0.12	0.62	**C / 4.5**	28.1	1.08	N/A	36.42	442	-0.16	-0.03	N/A	0	99	0	1	6	6	8
1.58	0.62	**C- / 3.7**	N/A	N/A	N/A	15.76	59	0.32	-0.15	N/A	0	0	0	100	72	40	2
6.17	0.59	**B / 8.1**	14.4	0.75	N/A	39.69	29	-0.38	-0.03	N/A	0	99	0	1	17	93	4
7.83	0.48	**B- / 7.4**	13.8	1.01	N/A	16.16	4,069	-0.12	0.04	N/A	0	99	0	1	4	37	8
0.66	0.15	**B- / 7.4**	10.7	1.00	N/A	42.16	46	0.09	0.06	51.4	0	99	0	1	39	59	6
3.53	0.50	**B- / 7.2**	10.6	0.99	N/A	83.25	275	0.16	0.03	58.9	0	99	0	1	19	59	8
5.04	0.15	**B / 8.4**	9.1	0.76	N/A	41.82	2,853	0.00	0.02	N/A	0	99	0	1	23	87	5
2.21	0.15	**B- / 7.4**	N/A	N/A	N/A	73.27	363	0.03	0.03	N/A	0	0	0	100	106	93	3
3.35	0.15	**B / 8.2**	N/A	N/A	N/A	64.56	562	0.02	0.05	N/A	0	0	0	100	26	88	3
4.77	0.15	**B- / 7.3**	N/A	N/A	N/A	64.48	163	1.26	0.06	N/A	0	0	0	100	22	76	3
0.29	0.15	**B- / 7.0**	N/A	N/A	N/A	62.03	333	0.34	0.07	N/A	0	0	0	100	15	36	3
4.30	0.24	**C+ / 6.9**	11.3	0.81	N/A	69.34	186	0.37	0.15	N/A	0	0	0	100	5	90	4
0.06	0.48	**C+ / 5.6**	21.0	1.11	N/A	338.42	5,424	-0.03	0.02	335.4	0	99	0	1	33	97	8
4.29	0.25	**B- / 7.8**	4.3	1.21	9.6	110.34	3,659	0.34	0.08	N/A	0	0	98	2	5	60	6
4.58	0.25	**B- / 7.8**	4.8	1.32	10.0	111.69	155	0.21	0.16	N/A	0	0	98	2	8	58	6
0.43	0.47	**C+ / 6.2**	13.3	1.03	N/A	103.70	1,050	0.11	0.01	174.4	0	99	0	1	15	82	8
1.74	0.47	**B- / 7.2**	13.5	0.94	N/A	36.85	278	0.62	-0.01	43.7	0	99	0	1	23	40	8
9.70	0.47	**C+ / 5.7**	18.7	0.99	N/A	28.14	2,214	0.00	-0.01	17.1	0	99	0	1	9	36	8
1.88	0.47	**C+ / 6.8**	12.2	1.06	N/A	110.57	743	0.11	0.02	125.3	0	99	0	1	6	83	8
1.72	0.47	**C+ / 6.6**	16.3	1.19	N/A	89.76	543	0.03	0.01	56.7	0	99	0	1	21	84	8
9.11	0.48	**C+ / 6.4**	14.4	0.46	N/A	46.98	76	0.75	N/A	88.9	0	99	0	1	10	86	8
6.05	0.48	**C+ / 6.3**	16.1	0.16	N/A	63.39	225	0.09	N/A	108.5	0	99	0	1	21	95	8
0.36	0.15	**B / 8.8**	10.4	0.98	N/A	113.35	9,852	-0.04	N/A	62.2	0	99	0	1	5	69	8
3.08	0.20	**B- / 7.7**	10.8	1.00	N/A	99.49	24,930	-0.01	N/A	96.4	0	99	0	1	13	78	8
5.46	0.20	**B / 8.0**	10.7	1.00	N/A	97.87	23,463	-0.01	-0.01	28.1	0	99	0	1	13	54	8
3.52	0.20	**B / 8.2**	14.2	1.06	N/A	112.76	23,993	-0.12	-0.02	75.2	0	99	0	1	19	38	8
2.41	0.25	**B- / 7.5**	15.2	1.10	N/A	139.51	5,646	-0.16	-0.02	135.1	0	99	0	1	30	51	8
5.68	0.25	**B / 8.5**	13.6	1.02	N/A	92.12	5,474	-0.20	-0.02	33.5	0	99	0	1	26	28	8
0.51	0.20	**B- / 7.9**	10.6	1.00	N/A	120.32	5,659	-0.01	N/A	62.9	0	99	0	1	5	65	8
4.39	0.20	**B / 8.6**	10.9	0.97	N/A	160.27	10,232	-0.06	-0.01	55.8	0	99	0	1	10	65	8
2.54	0.25	**B / 8.6**	11.4	1.01	N/A	91.96	4,911	-0.04	N/A	82.2	0	99	0	1	20	64	8
5.83	0.25	**B / 8.7**	10.8	0.94	N/A	68.70	6,555	-0.06	N/A	33.3	0	99	0	1	22	62	8
4.59	0.15	**B- / 7.1**	10.9	1.02	N/A	46.75	90	0.51	0.04	N/A	0	99	0	1	5	68	7
3.29	0.20	**B- / 7.6**	10.9	1.00	N/A	53.53	502	0.02	0.03	N/A	0	99	0	1	10	81	7
5.51	0.20	**C+ / 6.9**	11.0	1.00	N/A	41.58	151	0.34	0.02	N/A	0	99	0	1	13	53	7
4.27	0.20	**B / 8.5**	10.9	1.02	N/A	91.20	4,493	-0.03	N/A	63.4	0	99	0	1	6	61	8
3.46	0.18	**B- / 7.8**	10.9	1.01	N/A	115.80	10,573	0.00	N/A	90.0	0	99	0	1	26	79	8
5.33	0.18	**B / 8.7**	10.7	0.99	N/A	88.56	8,086	-0.03	-0.01	28.1	0	99	0	1	25	52	8
0.00	0.82	**D+ / 2.8**	20.0	0.57	N/A	14.21	979	0.14	0.06	N/A	0	100	0	0	N/A	3	N/A
2.90	0.25	**B / 8.3**	11.9	0.96	N/A	161.03	4,488	-0.04	N/A	110.8	0	99	0	1	50	59	8
4.76	0.25	**B- / 7.0**	12.4	1.02	N/A	117.15	4,070	0.04	N/A	40.8	0	99	0	1	42	44	8
3.14	0.25	**B- / 7.0**	13.3	0.97	N/A	124.30	2,566	0.01	N/A	148.0	0	99	0	1	50	71	8
3.43	0.25	**B- / 7.8**	13.6	1.04	N/A	108.16	2,864	0.00	N/A	42.3	0	99	0	1	41	40	8
7.38	0.39	**B / 8.3**	10.0	0.77	N/A	75.16	13,926	-0.01	N/A	27.2	0	99	0	1	20	80	8
0.74	0.25	**B / 8.1**	0.9	0.14	N/A	105.68	908	0.26	-0.01	N/A	2	0	96	2	23	69	6
1.28	0.25	**B / 8.0**	N/A	N/A	N/A	49.96	361	0.12	0.04	N/A	0	0	0	100	35	75	3
1.95	N/A	**U /**	N/A	N/A	N/A	49.91	N/A	0.20	N/A	N/A	0	0	0	100	N/A	N/A	1
.10	0.08	**B / 8.2**	0.1	N/A	N/A	110.19	2,349	0.03	0.02	N/A	6	0	92	2	1	67	6
.00	0.50	**D+ / 2.7**	24.9	1.17	N/A	13.17	5,987	0.15	0.33	N/A	0	0	0	100	N/A	18	10
.11	0.20	**B+ / 9.0**	5.2	0.37	N/A	109.77	12,439	-0.08	0.07	N/A	0	0	99	1	47	41	6

* Denotes ETF Fund, N/A denotes number is not available

Fund Type	Fund Name (99 Pct = Best, 0 Pct = Worst)	Ticker Symbol	Overall Investment Rating	PRICE: Price As of 12/31/15	PRICE: 52 Week High	PRICE: 52 Week Low	PERFORMANCE: Performance Rating/Pts	% Total Return Through 12/31/15: 3 Mo	6 Mo	1Yr/Pct	Annualized 3Yr/Pct	Annualized 5Yr/Pct
IN	*iShares Transportation Average E	IYT	**B**	134.73	165.69	128.26	**B- / 7.1**	-4.13	-6.55	-16.24 / 16	12.20 / 82	8.87 / 60
LP	*iShares Treasury Floatg Rate Bd	TFLO	**C+**	50.34	51.50	49.95	**C / 4.8**	0.64	0.49	0.69 / 65	--	--
COI	*iShares Ultra Short-Term Bond	ICSH	**B-**	49.73	50.08	49.73	**C / 4.3**	-0.16	-0.17	0.26 / 62	--	--
IN	*iShares US Aerospace & Def ETF	ITA	**A-**	118.22	125.85	85.34	**A / 9.5**	8.38	-0.19	4.54 / 78	20.29 / 95	15.80 / 93
IN	*iShares US Basic Material ETF	IYM	**C-**	70.53	87.28	62.98	**C- / 4.1**	6.88	-10.66	-12.27 / 22	1.67 / 46	0.32 / 28
FS	*iShares US Broker-Dealers ETF	IAI	**A-**	41.52	45.60	28.77	**A / 9.4**	9.94	-4.47	-0.37 / 58	20.43 / 95	9.02 / 61
IN	*iShares US Consumer Goods ETF	IYK	**A**	108.43	111.35	84.48	**A- / 9.0**	5.72	4.14	7.05 / 83	14.50 / 89	13.48 / 86
IN	*iShares US Consumer Services ETF	IYC	**A+**	144.65	151.16	99.84	**A / 9.4**	3.63	1.17	7.18 / 84	18.65 / 94	17.64 / 95
EN	*iShares US Energy ETF	IYE	**D**	33.86	47.19	32.76	**D+ / 2.3**	-4.00	-17.26	-21.92 / 12	-4.86 / 25	-0.81 / 26
FS	*iShares US Financial Services ET	IYG	**A**	89.98	98.50	79.01	**B+ / 8.8**	6.09	-3.78	-0.15 / 59	14.75 / 89	10.36 / 67
FS	*iShares US Financials ETF	IYF	**A+**	88.38	94.18	74.32	**B+ / 8.6**	5.88	-1.06	0.05 / 60	13.68 / 86	10.55 / 68
HL	*iShares US Healthcare ETF	IYH	**A+**	150.01	164.98	108.00	**A+ / 9.6**	5.56	-4.12	6.08 / 82	22.48 / 96	19.59 / 97
HL	*iShares US Healthcare Providers	IHF	**A+**	124.35	146.77	96.02	**A / 9.5**	-0.79	-12.47	5.55 / 80	22.17 / 96	17.83 / 96
IN	*iShares US Home Construction ETF	ITB	**B**	27.10	29.86	23.50	**B- / 7.1**	2.12	-1.40	6.04 / 81	7.66 / 69	15.07 / 92
IN	*iShares US Industrials ETF	IYJ	**B+**	102.92	111.20	75.85	**B+ / 8.3**	6.21	-1.46	-1.38 / 53	12.56 / 83	11.02 / 72
IN	*iShares US Insurance ETF	IAK	**A**	51.15	53.70	29.11	**A- / 9.1**	6.27	0.59	4.82 / 79	16.08 / 91	11.95 / 78
HL	*iShares US Medical Devices ETF	IHI	**A+**	122.48	127.82	100.01	**A+ / 9.6**	8.78	4.28	10.75 / 89	22.31 / 96	16.83 / 95
EN	*iShares US Oil & Gas Exp & Pro E	IEO	**D**	52.95	79.85	50.66	**D / 2.0**	-9.19	-23.05	-24.70 / 10	-5.65 / 24	-2.65 / 23
EN	*iShares US Oil Equip & Svcs ETF	IEZ	**D-**	35.78	54.93	34.41	**D- / 1.3**	-4.41	-22.07	-26.87 / 9	-11.34 / 15	-7.15 / 16
HL	*iShares US Pharmaceuticals ETF	IHE	**B-**	161.69	184.64	113.55	**A+ / 9.6**	6.48	-6.48	8.46 / 86	24.27 / 97	21.88 / 98
IN	*iShares US Preferred Stock	PFF	**B+**	38.85	40.17	32.32	**C+ / 6.5**	3.54	3.18	4.67 / 78	5.54 / 63	6.65 / 53
IN	*iShares US Real Estate ETF	IYR	**B-**	75.08	83.54	68.28	**B / 7.7**	7.09	7.02	1.67 / 70	8.85 / 72	10.55 / 68
FS	*iShares US Regional Banks ETF	IAT	**A**	34.96	37.99	26.89	**B+ / 8.5**	5.83	-3.27	2.98 / 74	13.09 / 84	9.42 / 63
GR	*iShares US Technology ETF	IYW	**A+**	107.03	112.08	73.71	**A- / 9.1**	7.13	2.66	4.38 / 77	15.66 / 91	11.33 / 74
IN	*iShares US Telecommunications ET	IYZ	**B+**	28.79	31.80	24.54	**C+ / 6.9**	7.27	-0.58	0.18 / 61	7.48 / 68	6.95 / 54
UT	*iShares US Utilities ETF	IDU	**B**	107.92	124.63	101.68	**B / 8.0**	2.98	6.36	-3.99 / 43	11.28 / 79	10.92 / 71
GEN	*iShares Yield Optimized Bond ETF	BYLD	**C+**	24.01	25.75	23.98	**C- / 3.5**	-0.99	-1.51	-1.37 / 53	--	--
GR	*Janus Eq Risk Weighted LC	ERW	**C**	50.04	55.19	48.86	**C- / 3.1**	0.02	-6.06	-1.59 / 52	--	--
EN	*JPMorgan Alerian MLP Idx ETN	AMJ	**E+**	28.97	46.56	24.05	**D / 1.8**	-9.27	-24.07	-34.10 / 6	-5.57 / 24	0.50 / 29
EM	*JPMorgan Diversified Ret Em Mkts	JPEM	**U**	40.79	N/A	N/A	**U /**	-2.50	-19.99	--	--	--
GL	*JPMorgan Diversified Ret Glbl Eq	JPGE	**C+**	49.31	53.29	45.72	**C+ / 6.0**	5.03	-1.53	4.03 / 77	--	--
GL	*JPMorgan Diversified Ret Intl Eq	JPIN	**D+**	49.30	57.53	37.65	**C / 4.9**	2.40	-3.59	2.60 / 73	--	--
GR	*JPMorgan Diversified Return US E	JPUS	**U**	53.70	N/A	N/A	**U /**	6.38	--	--	--	--
FO	*KraneShares Bosera MSCI China A	KBA	**D**	34.85	72.13	34.83	**D+ / 2.3**	5.63	-15.96	-4.85 / 39	--	--
FO	*KraneShares E Fd China Comm Pape	KCNY	**D**	33.96	35.76	26.69	**C- / 3.4**	-0.77	-3.22	-1.12 / 54	--	--
EM	*KraneShares FTSE Emerging Market	KEMP	**U**	21.70	N/A	N/A	**U /**	6.27	-14.93	--	--	--
FO	*KraneShares New China	KFYP	**B-**	63.40	83.10	46.97	**A / 9.5**	31.76	3.12	6.65 / 82	--	--
FO	*Lattice Developed Markets xUS St	RODM	**U**	23.74	N/A	N/A	**U /**	6.75	-4.51	--	--	--
EM	*Lattice Emerging Markets Strateg	ROAM	**U**	19.08	N/A	N/A	**U /**	-1.64	-18.81	--	--	--
GL	*Lattice Global Small Cap Strateg	ROGS	**U**	23.06	N/A	N/A	**U /**	3.91	-7.97	--	--	--
GI	*Lattice US Equity Strategy	ROUS	**U**	23.77	N/A	N/A	**U /**	4.49	-2.46	--	--	--
HL	*Loncar Cancer Immunotherapy	CNCR	**U**	28.56	N/A	N/A	**U /**	--	--	--	--	--
GR	*Madrona Domestic ETF	FWDD	**B**	41.28	47.20	35.18	**B / 8.2**	4.72	-6.03	-4.22 / 42	13.13 / 85	--
GL	*Madrona Global Bond ETF	FWDB	**C**	24.47	26.50	23.02	**C- / 4.1**	-0.76	-1.26	-2.34 / 49	0.17 / 38	--
FO	*Madrona International ETF	FWDI	**C-**	23.93	29.95	22.29	**C- / 3.8**	2.53	-13.73	-7.75 / 32	0.65 / 40	--
FO	*Market Vectors Africa Index ETF	AFK	**D**	17.79	27.25	17.37	**D- / 1.0**	-10.53	-25.59	-30.25 / 7	-15.35 / 12	-10.13 / 13
GL	*Market Vectors Agribusiness ETF	MOO	**C-**	46.49	58.08	44.76	**C- / 3.0**	2.29	-14.10	-8.88 / 29	-2.51 / 29	-1.07 / 25
GR	*Market Vectors BDC Income ETF	BIZD	**D+**	15.77	19.00	14.05	**D+ / 2.8**	3.27	-5.44	-5.33 / 38	--	--
IN	*Market Vectors Biotech ETF	BBH	**B+**	126.95	145.52	95.76	**A+ / 9.8**	7.34	-5.78	9.32 / 87	31.90 / 98	--
FO	*Market Vectors Brazil Small-Cap	BRF	**E**	10.38	20.54	9.92	**E- / 0.2**	-3.37	-35.31	-47.30 / 2	-35.60 / 2	-25.29 / 4
MUN	*Market Vectors CEF Muni Inc ETF	XMPT	**C+**	26.86	27.54	24.85	**C+ / 6.9**	6.19	9.99	7.32 / 90	2.53 / 57	--
FO	*Market Vectors ChinaAMC A-Share	PEK	**C**	44.08	70.26	35.78	**C+ / 6.6**	8.47	-14.19	-1.41 / 53	8.02 / 70	0.43 / 29

* Denotes ETF Fund, N/A denotes number is not available

	RISK					NET ASSETS		VALUATION			ASSET					FUND MANAGER	
ncl. in Returns			3 Year					Premium / Discount									
idend ield %	Expense Ratio	Risk Rating/ Pts	Standard Deviation	Beta	Avg Dura- tion	NAV as of 12/31/15	Total $(Mil)	As of 12/31/15	1 Year Average	Wtd Avg P/E	Cash %	Stocks %	Bonds %	Other %	Portfolio Turnover Ratio	Manager Quality Pct	Manager Tenure (Years)
2.68	0.43	B- / 7.5	13.3	1.01	N/A	134.74	1,471	-0.01	-0.01	39.0	0	99	0	1	22	57	8
1.27	N/A	B / 8.1	N/A	N/A	N/A	50.06	10	0.56	0.05	N/A	0	0	0	100	57	68	2
2.01	0.18	B+ / 9.8	N/A	N/A	N/A	49.80	20	-0.14	-0.04	N/A	0	0	0	100	71	70	N/A
1.52	0.43	B- / 7.0	12.2	0.92	N/A	118.16	339	0.05	0.01	64.3	0	99	0	1	15	92	8
5.29	0.43	C+ / 6.7	15.8	1.23	N/A	70.53	921	0.00	-0.01	47.8	0	99	0	1	7	12	8
4.68	0.43	B- / 7.0	16.4	1.23	N/A	41.38	239	0.34	N/A	49.0	2	97	0	1	19	83	8
5.04	0.43	B- / 7.6	10.7	0.92	N/A	108.30	474	0.12	N/A	33.7	0	99	0	1	4	79	8
2.10	0.43	B- / 7.7	12.3	1.07	N/A	144.68	504	-0.02	0.01	143.5	0	99	0	1	8	85	8
3.24	0.43	C / 5.3	18.5	0.99	N/A	33.85	1,191	0.03	-0.01	15.2	0	99	0	1	7	67	8
3.36	0.43	B- / 7.9	14.3	1.19	N/A	89.97	572	0.01	0.02	22.9	0	99	0	1	3	52	8
1.58	0.43	B / 8.7	11.4	1.01	N/A	88.41	1,293	-0.03	N/A	35.3	0	99	0	1	6	65	8
1.28	0.43	B / 8.1	12.4	0.95	N/A	150.07	2,658	-0.04	0.01	104.3	0	99	0	1	8	93	8
).85	0.43	B / 8.2	12.6	0.64	N/A	124.38	614	-0.02	0.01	48.8	0	100	0	0	12	96	8
).81	0.43	B- / 7.9	20.3	1.15	N/A	27.12	1,446	-0.07	-0.01	18.0	0	100	0	0	13	21	8
3.44	0.43	B- / 7.3	12.3	1.10	N/A	102.82	1,749	0.10	N/A	39.4	0	99	0	1	6	46	8
3.98	0.43	B- / 7.4	14.1	1.18	N/A	51.10	123	0.10	-0.02	22.6	2	97	0	1	12	65	8
'.02	0.43	B- / 7.5	12.9	0.92	N/A	122.47	736	0.01	0.01	96.1	0	99	0	1	19	93	8
.80	0.43	C / 4.7	22.4	1.17	N/A	52.91	535	0.08	0.01	13.6	0	99	0	1	7	65	8
.06	0.43	C / 4.7	26.2	1.32	N/A	35.78	531	0.00	N/A	20.3	0	99	0	1	14	30	8
.10	0.43	C / 4.7	15.3	1.02	N/A	161.48	738	0.13	0.01	287.8	0	99	0	1	37	94	8
.63	0.47	B+ / 9.1	4.1	0.16	N/A	38.88	10,398	-0.08	0.04	N/A	2	0	0	98	13	86	8
.23	0.43	C+ / 6.7	13.7	0.50	N/A	75.04	4,679	0.05	-0.01	83.8	0	100	0	0	21	81	8
.32	0.43	B / 8.1	13.8	1.03	N/A	34.96	472	0.00	0.01	15.3	0	99	0	1	5	60	8
.59	0.43	B- / 7.8	12.1	1.03	N/A	107.02	4,115	0.01	N/A	67.3	0	99	0	1	8	73	8
.07	0.43	B / 8.6	14.0	0.89	N/A	28.84	575	-0.17	-0.02	26.2	1	98	0	1	49	34	8
.85	0.43	C+ / 6.8	14.1	0.97	N/A	107.87	653	0.05	N/A	23.6	0	99	0	1	3	67	8
.48	0.01	B+ / 9.4	N/A	N/A	N/A	24.10	9	-0.37	0.04	N/A	0	0	0	100	47	54	2
.81	0.65	B / 8.5	N/A	N/A	N/A	50.11	8	-0.14	0.45	N/A	0	0	0	100	45	53	1
.93	N/A	D / 1.9	18.9	0.70	N/A	28.96	6,716	0.03	-0.04	N/A	0	0	0	100	N/A	57	7
.51	N/A	U /	N/A	N/A	N/A	41.18	N/A	-0.95	N/A	N/A	0	0	0	100	N/A	N/A	1
.95	0.38	B- / 7.1	N/A	N/A	N/A	49.03	N/A	0.57	0.22	N/A	0	0	0	100	14	86	2
.18	N/A	C- / 3.6	N/A	N/A	N/A	49.17	N/A	0.26	0.35	N/A	0	0	0	100	N/A	84	N/A
.94	N/A	U /	N/A	N/A	N/A	53.18	N/A	0.98	N/A	N/A	0	0	0	100	N/A	N/A	1
.19	1.31	C / 4.5	N/A	N/A	N/A	35.31	4	-1.30	-0.92	N/A	0	0	0	100	110	38	2
.53	N/A	C- / 3.9	N/A	N/A	N/A	33.87	N/A	0.27	-0.19	N/A	0	0	0	100	N/A	58	2
.07	N/A	U /	N/A	N/A	N/A	21.19	N/A	2.41	N/A	N/A	0	0	0	100	N/A	N/A	1
.82	0.71	C / 4.9	N/A	N/A	N/A	58.30	3	8.75	-1.33	N/A	0	0	0	100	36	92	1
.64	0.50	U /	N/A	N/A	N/A	23.69	N/A	0.21	N/A	N/A	0	0	0	100	42	N/A	1
.75	0.65	U /	N/A	N/A	N/A	19.26	N/A	-0.93	N/A	N/A	0	0	0	100	17	N/A	1
.21	0.60	U /	N/A	N/A	N/A	23.06	N/A	0.00	N/A	N/A	0	0	0	100	44	N/A	1
.39	0.35	U /	N/A	N/A	N/A	23.68	N/A	0.38	N/A	N/A	0	0	0	100	38	N/A	1
.22	N/A	U /	N/A	N/A	N/A	28.52	N/A	0.14	N/A	N/A	0	0	0	100	N/A	N/A	1
.37	1.25	C+ / 6.9	12.6	1.15	N/A	41.00	29	0.68	-0.01	N/A	1	97	0	2	15	46	5
.71	0.95	B- / 7.5	4.2	0.43	N/A	24.40	26	0.29	-0.10	N/A	6	0	89	5	34	81	N/A
.40	1.25	C+ / 5.9	14.7	1.08	N/A	23.65	18	1.18	0.21	N/A	1	98	0	1	85	35	5
.16	0.78	C+ / 6.3	16.0	0.87	N/A	18.11	120	-1.77	-0.14	7.0	0	99	0	1	30	8	8
.89	0.56	B- / 7.8	12.7	0.76	N/A	46.55	1,576	-0.13	-0.11	53.5	0	99	0	1	14	28	9
.10	0.40	C / 5.5	N/A	N/A	N/A	15.73	46	0.25	0.06	N/A	0	0	0	100	20	30	3
27	0.35	C+ / 6.1	20.8	1.06	N/A	126.82	539	0.10	0.01	N/A	0	0	0	100	12	97	5
84	0.59	C- / 3.2	27.9	1.49	N/A	10.44	130	-0.57	0.37	N/A	0	92	0	8	64	1	7
80	0.40	C+ / 6.2	10.0	2.22	N/A	26.73	35	0.49	0.09	N/A	0	0	0	100	6	44	5
18	0.72	C+ / 5.9	29.6	0.57	N/A	44.76	29	-1.52	-0.54	N/A	100	0	0	0	59	89	6

Denotes ETF Fund, N/A denotes number is not available

99 Pct = Best
0 Pct = Worst

Fund Type	Fund Name	Ticker Symbol	Overall Investment Rating	PRICE: Price As of 12/31/15	PRICE: 52 Week High	PRICE: 52 Week Low	PERFORMANCE: Performance Rating/Pts	% Total Return Through 12/31/15: 3 Mo	6 Mo	1Yr/Pct	Annualized: 3Yr/Pct	Annualized: 5Yr/Pct
FO	*Market Vectors ChinaAMC China Bo	CBON	D+	24.18	25.32	23.41	C- / 3.9	-0.50	-2.21	0.60 / 65	--	--
FO	*Market Vectors ChinaAMC SME-ChiN	CNXT	B-	41.29	66.04	28.96	A+ / 9.8	17.36	-6.27	42.39 / 99	--	--
FO	*Market Vectors Chinese RMB USD E	CNY	C+	41.22	43.81	31.41	C- / 3.9	-1.39	-4.74	-2.32 / 49	-0.27 / 36	0.42 / 28
EN	*Market Vectors Coal ETF	KOL	E+	6.25	14.66	6.14	E- / 0.2	-19.71	-41.85	-55.17 / 1	-36.11 / 2	-31.88 / 2
FO	*Market Vectors Double Long Euro	URR	D	17.00	21.65	15.11	D- / 1.4	-5.97	-7.66	-22.52 / 11	-12.85 / 14	-8.90 / 14
FO	*Market Vectors Double Shrt Euro	DRR	A	59.70	66.84	49.11	B+ / 8.8	6.13	2.40	17.82 / 97	10.83 / 78	4.15 / 44
EM	*Market Vectors Egypt Index ETF	EGPT	D-	38.21	63.00	34.66	D / 1.6	-2.34	-18.57	-33.79 / 6	-8.02 / 20	-10.93 / 13
GEI	*Market Vectors EM Aggregate Bd E	EMAG	C-	19.81	22.64	19.81	D+ / 2.7	-1.39	-6.17	-7.79 / 31	-4.96 / 25	--
EM	*Market Vectors Emg Mkts Hi Yld B	HYEM	C	22.12	24.80	22.00	C- / 4.0	-0.46	-5.20	2.84 / 74	-0.70 / 35	--
IN	*Market Vectors Environment Svc E	EVX	C	58.67	66.35	56.86	C+ / 5.6	1.79	-5.85	-9.50 / 27	5.24 / 62	4.60 / 46
GEI	*Market Vectors FA Hi Yld Bd ETF	ANGL	C+	24.33	29.14	24.03	C / 4.9	-3.13	-7.42	-1.16 / 54	2.54 / 51	--
GL	*Market Vectors Gaming ETF	BJK	D	31.73	40.54	29.16	C- / 3.1	5.37	-9.44	-12.46 / 21	-2.15 / 30	2.71 / 37
EN	*Market Vectors Global Alt Enrgy	GEX	B	54.81	64.75	45.60	A- / 9.1	7.56	-10.23	1.42 / 69	17.30 / 92	-0.44 / 27
FS	*Market Vectors Global Spin-Off	SPUN	U	17.68	N/A	N/A	U /	3.26	-9.96	--	--	--
PM	*Market Vectors Gold Miners ETF	GDX	E+	13.72	23.22	12.62	E / 0.4	-4.52	-21.52	-26.95 / 9	-32.31 / 3	-24.16 / 5
FO	*Market Vectors Gulf States Idx E	MES	C	22.10	29.49	20.96	C / 5.2	-7.66	-14.50	-11.92 / 22	5.91 / 64	1.67 / 32
MUH	*Market Vectors Hi-Yld Mun Idx ET	HYD	C+	30.88	31.67	29.48	C+ / 6.5	1.61	5.89	4.48 / 83	3.15 / 61	7.25 / 73
FO	*Market Vectors India Small-Cap E	SCIF	C-	43.27	50.94	36.00	C- / 4.0	4.91	1.17	-2.60 / 48	-0.88 / 34	-9.49 / 14
FO	*Market Vectors Indian Rupee USD	INR	C+	36.87	40.00	35.47	C / 4.8	-0.14	0.19	4.74 / 78	0.11 / 38	-1.70 / 24
FO	*Market Vectors Indonesia Idx ETF	IDX	D-	18.41	25.20	15.11	D / 1.7	15.81	-12.67	-21.01 / 12	-11.80 / 15	-6.10 / 17
FO	*Market Vectors Indonesia SC ETF	IDXJ	E+	7.90	14.49	7.07	E+ / 0.8	6.28	-27.50	-42.19 / 3	-18.14 / 9	--
MUN	*Market Vectors Interm Muni Idx E	ITM	B-	23.97	24.43	22.98	C+ / 6.3	1.74	4.46	3.45 / 80	2.99 / 60	5.50 / 59
GL	*Market Vectors Intl Hi Yld Bond	IHY	C	22.50	25.49	22.38	C- / 3.5	-2.03	-6.17	-4.93 / 39	-0.93 / 34	--
COI	*Market Vectors Invest Grade FR E	FLTR	B-	24.67	25.04	24.60	C / 4.5	0.09	-0.37	-0.45 / 58	0.57 / 39	--
FO	*Market Vectors Israel ETF	ISRA	C-	28.76	34.47	28.25	D+ / 2.6	-1.06	-11.06	-0.45 / 58	--	--
GL	*Market Vectors JP Morgan EM LC B	EMLC	D	17.00	21.54	16.74	D / 1.8	-1.48	-10.84	-14.85 / 18	-10.13 / 17	-3.72 / 21
PM	*Market Vectors Junior Gold Mnrs	GDXJ	E	19.21	30.72	17.92	E / 0.3	-5.44	-18.84	-22.49 / 11	-37.65 / 2	-31.67 / 2
MUN	*Market Vectors Long Muni Index E	MLN	C+	19.92	20.40	19.08	C+ / 6.6	2.51	5.41	3.58 / 80	3.47 / 62	7.41 / 74
FO	*Market Vectors Morningstar Itl M	MOTI	U	26.92	N/A	N/A	U /	2.62	--	--	--	--
IN	*Market Vectors MS Wide Moat ETF	MOAT	B+	28.91	31.99	26.58	B- / 7.1	4.56	-4.16	-4.97 / 39	9.35 / 73	--
MTG	*Market Vectors Mtge REIT Income	MORT	D+	19.53	24.46	18.66	C- / 3.3	-3.73	-7.89	-13.29 / 20	-0.22 / 36	--
GL	*Market Vectors Natural Resources	HAP	D+	26.34	36.16	25.69	D / 1.9	-2.20	-18.77	-19.93 / 13	-8.13 / 20	-5.32 / 18
EN	*Market Vectors Oil Refiners	CRAK	U	19.74	N/A	N/A	U /	6.12	--	--	--	--
IN	*Market Vectors Oil Services ETF	OIH	D-	26.45	39.80	25.40	D- / 1.4	-4.92	-20.05	-24.70 / 10	-11.65 / 15	--
IN	*Market Vectors Pharmaceutical ET	PPH	B+	65.31	74.97	45.23	A / 9.3	1.30	-8.27	3.20 / 75	19.13 / 94	--
EM	*Market Vectors Poland ETF	PLND	D-	13.30	20.20	12.95	D- / 1.2	-13.43	-21.46	-23.48 / 11	-12.71 / 14	-9.37 / 14
MUN	*Market Vectors Pre-Refnded Muni	PRB	C+	24.55	24.67	24.21	C / 4.5	-0.09	1.25	1.52 / 72	-0.07 / 37	1.01 / 32
COI	*Market Vectors Prfrd Secs ex Fin	PFXF	B-	19.15	21.48	17.48	C / 5.3	0.06	-2.49	-2.86 / 47	3.20 / 54	--
IN	*Market Vectors Retail ETF	RTH	A+	77.72	80.10	66.66	A+ / 9.6	5.68	5.66	11.37 / 91	21.88 / 96	--
FO	*Market Vectors Russia ETF	RSX	D-	14.65	20.84	14.00	D- / 1.2	-2.47	-15.69	2.60 / 73	-18.95 / 9	-14.84 / 9
FO	*Market Vectors Russia SmallCap E	RSXJ	D-	19.10	26.14	17.40	E+ / 0.9	3.30	-13.37	-3.02 / 46	-23.69 / 6	--
IN	*Market Vectors Semiconductor ETF	SMH	A+	53.28	60.13	43.53	A / 9.4	8.10	-1.30	-0.16 / 59	18.91 / 94	--
MUH	*Market Vectors Short HY Muni Ind	SHYD	C+	24.53	26.05	24.44	C- / 3.9	-0.47	-0.60	-0.57 / 57	--	--
MUN	*Market Vectors Short Muni Index	SMB	B	17.53	17.72	17.31	C / 5.1	0.02	1.45	1.10 / 71	0.81 / 43	1.95 / 38
EN	*Market Vectors Solar Energy ETF	KWT	C+	61.38	90.47	48.40	B+ / 8.3	11.85	-16.39	-7.78 / 31	14.20 / 88	-16.20 / 7
IN	*Market Vectors Steel Index ETF	SLX	D-	19.50	37.09	18.80	E / 0.5	-8.96	-31.82	-41.43 / 3	-24.49 / 6	-20.79 / 5
COH	*Market Vectors Trs Hdg Hi Yld Bd	THHY	C-	21.85	26.49	21.49	D+ / 2.4	1.26	-6.65	-7.74 / 32	--	--
GL	*Market Vectors Uranium+Nuc Engy	NLR	C+	45.07	52.70	44.36	C / 5.4	-0.49	-3.84	-9.10 / 28	4.40 / 59	-5.29 / 19
FO	*Market Vectors Vietnam ETF	VNM	D	14.79	19.93	12.34	D / 2.2	-3.32	-20.04	-19.46 / 14	-5.38 / 24	-8.52 / 15
IN	*Master Income	HIPS	U	15.88	N/A	N/A	U /	-2.84	-12.30	--	--	--
GR	*Materials Select Sector SPDR	XLB	C+	43.42	52.22	38.83	C+ / 6.0	6.51	-8.64	-8.12 / 31	6.45 / 66	4.94 / 47
GI	*Meidell Tactical Advantage ETF	MATH	C	28.07	32.08	27.41	C / 4.4	-2.18	-9.12	-6.52 / 35	2.28 / 50	--

* Denotes ETF Fund, N/A denotes number is not available

cl. in Returns		RISK				NET ASSETS		VALUATION			ASSET					FUND MANAGER	
dend eld %	Expense Ratio	Risk Rating/ Pts	3 Year Standard Deviation	3 Year Beta	Avg Dura- tion	NAV as of 12/31/15	Total $(Mil)	Premium / Discount As of 12/31/15	Premium / Discount 1 Year Average	Wtd Avg P/E	Cash %	Stocks %	Bonds %	Other %	Portfolio Turnover Ratio	Manager Quality Pct	Manager Tenure (Years)
.98	N/A	**C+ / 5.6**	N/A	N/A	N/A	24.47	N/A	-1.19	-0.76	N/A	0	0	0	100	N/A	74	2
.00	N/A	**C / 4.6**	N/A	N/A	N/A	41.74	N/A	-1.08	-0.45	N/A	0	0	0	100	N/A	99	2
.00	0.55	**B+ / 9.4**	3.8	0.07	N/A	41.66	27	-1.06	-0.77	N/A	0	0	0	100	N/A	61	8
.62	0.59	**C / 4.5**	21.9	0.87	N/A	6.28	158	-0.48	-0.35	4.2	0	100	0	0	27	2	8
.00	0.65	**C+ / 5.6**	18.0	0.33	N/A	17.06	5	-0.35	-0.24	N/A	0	0	0	100	N/A	10	8
.00	0.65	**B / 8.0**	17.4	-0.50	N/A	59.93	28	-0.38	-0.08	N/A	0	0	0	100	N/A	97	8
.59	0.92	**C / 4.8**	26.7	0.66	N/A	39.01	98	-2.05	-0.31	N/A	0	100	0	0	69	40	6
.97	0.49	**B- / 7.7**	7.9	1.53	N/A	20.23	18	-2.08	-0.57	N/A	0	0	0	100	24	23	4
.09	0.40	**B / 8.1**	7.5	0.26	N/A	22.27	433	-0.67	-0.57	N/A	0	0	0	100	35	76	4
.16	0.55	**C+ / 6.9**	11.2	0.88	N/A	58.42	16	0.43	-0.02	48.3	0	99	0	1	19	25	10
.26	0.40	**B / 8.6**	6.4	0.88	N/A	24.36	17	-0.12	-0.05	N/A	0	0	0	100	50	79	4
.09	0.65	**C / 4.6**	21.2	1.37	N/A	31.59	43	0.44	-0.08	55.7	0	99	0	1	27	21	8
.56	0.62	**C+ / 6.0**	21.3	0.65	N/A	54.57	100	0.44	0.06	56.9	0	99	0	1	31	98	9
.26	N/A	**U /**	N/A	N/A	N/A	17.37	N/A	1.78	N/A	N/A	0	0	0	100	N/A	N/A	1
85	0.53	**C- / 3.1**	40.3	1.84	N/A	13.72	6,704	0.00	-0.01	31.3	0	100	0	0	18	14	10
24	0.98	**C+ / 6.1**	20.6	0.55	N/A	22.19	27	-0.41	-1.25	N/A	0	100	0	0	77	86	8
50	0.35	**C+ / 6.8**	7.3	1.89	N/A	30.78	1,231	0.32	-0.17	N/A	1	0	98	1	9	46	8
11	0.85	**C+ / 6.3**	33.2	1.17	N/A	43.66	295	-0.89	-0.21	N/A	0	100	0	0	120	28	6
00	0.55	**B / 8.1**	12.2	0.05	N/A	37.16	7	-0.78	-0.86	N/A	0	0	0	100	N/A	66	8
43	0.57	**C- / 3.2**	24.3	0.89	N/A	18.36	214	0.27	-0.26	N/A	0	100	0	0	12	10	7
03	0.61	**C- / 3.4**	33.2	1.24	N/A	7.93	8	-0.38	1.31	N/A	0	94	0	6	46	6	4
26	0.24	**B- / 7.8**	5.1	1.42	7.0	23.88	736	0.38	0.11	N/A	1	0	98	1	3	56	9
81	0.40	**B / 8.1**	7.3	0.61	N/A	22.73	206	-1.01	-0.16	N/A	0	0	0	100	37	81	4
80	0.17	**B+ / 9.7**	0.9	0.02	N/A	24.73	90	-0.24	-0.10	N/A	0	0	0	100	33	73	4
31	0.59	**B / 8.2**	N/A	N/A	N/A	28.81	51	-0.17	0.02	N/A	0	0	0	100	17	58	3
89	0.47	**C+ / 5.7**	10.0	0.87	N/A	17.00	891	0.00	-0.06	N/A	0	0	0	100	36	24	4
72	0.54	**D / 2.1**	48.4	2.31	N/A	19.22	2,331	-0.05	0.05	N/A	0	99	0	1	65	14	7
24	0.24	**C+ / 6.8**	8.0	2.26	N/A	19.90	87	0.10	-0.11	N/A	1	0	98	1	4	40	8
01	N/A	**U /**	N/A	N/A	N/A	26.86	N/A	0.22	N/A	N/A	0	0	0	100	N/A	N/A	N/A
13	0.49	**B / 8.3**	12.5	1.06	N/A	28.92	854	-0.03	-0.03	N/A	0	0	0	100	14	33	4
24	0.40	**C / 4.9**	15.0	3.69	N/A	19.44	118	0.46	N/A	N/A	0	0	0	100	29	32	5
00	0.49	**B- / 7.0**	15.0	0.96	N/A	26.38	97	-0.15	0.05	35.2	0	99	0	1	13	13	8
40	N/A	**U /**	N/A	N/A	N/A	19.69	N/A	0.25	N/A	N/A	0	0	0	100	N/A	N/A	1
39	0.35	**C- / 3.7**	26.2	1.19	N/A	26.45	1,171	0.00	-0.02	N/A	0	0	0	100	15	5	5
25	0.35	**C+ / 6.6**	13.1	0.91	N/A	65.24	406	0.11	0.01	N/A	0	0	0	100	12	90	5
27	0.60	**C- / 3.8**	18.2	0.76	N/A	13.28	26	0.15	0.01	N/A	0	99	0	1	19	19	7
89	0.24	**B+ / 9.4**	2.8	0.48	N/A	24.60	30	-0.20	-0.69	N/A	1	0	98	1	51	55	8
15	0.40	**B+ / 9.0**	5.6	0.94	N/A	19.27	176	-0.62	-0.02	N/A	0	0	0	100	16	82	4
25	0.35	**B / 8.1**	12.5	0.94	N/A	77.71	67	0.01	0.02	N/A	0	0	0	100	5	92	5
54	0.61	**C / 4.3**	28.5	1.27	N/A	14.69	1,907	-0.27	-0.02	N/A	0	100	0	0	23	5	9
00	0.67	**C- / 4.0**	30.9	1.53	N/A	19.31	74	-1.09	-0.24	N/A	0	99	0	1	32	3	5
14	0.35	**B / 8.1**	15.2	1.08	N/A	53.36	415	-0.15	0.01	N/A	0	0	0	100	18	85	5
13	0.35	**B+ / 9.5**	N/A	N/A	N/A	24.96	71	-1.72	-0.30	N/A	0	0	0	100	26	49	2
16	0.20	**B+ / 9.6**	1.9	0.37	N/A	17.54	258	-0.06	-0.26	N/A	0	0	100	0	2	65	8
97	0.65	**C / 5.2**	36.9	1.02	N/A	61.64	23	-0.42	-0.50	N/A	0	99	0	1	50	99	8
35	0.55	**C / 4.9**	24.3	1.35	N/A	19.52	103	-0.10	N/A	7.0	0	100	0	0	11	1	10
44	0.50	**B / 8.2**	N/A	N/A	N/A	21.99	10	-0.64	0.14	N/A	0	0	0	100	35	39	3
30	0.60	**B / 8.5**	11.6	0.54	N/A	45.25	69	-0.40	-0.29	21.6	0	99	0	1	31	81	9
34	0.65	**C / 5.1**	25.2	0.92	N/A	14.79	602	0.00	0.18	N/A	3	96	0	1	67	20	7
12	N/A	**U /**	N/A	N/A	N/A	15.91	N/A	-0.19	N/A	N/A	0	0	0	100	N/A	N/A	1
91	0.15	**B- / 7.7**	14.9	1.19	N/A	43.46	5,108	-0.09	-0.01	46.8	0	100	0	0	9	18	18
37	1.35	**B- / 7.2**	7.1	0.52	N/A	27.79	15	1.01	0.27	N/A	14	85	0	1	434	34	5

Denotes ETF Fund, N/A denotes number is not available

Fund Type	Fund Name (99 Pct = Best, 0 Pct = Worst)	Ticker Symbol	Overall Investment Rating	PRICE: Price As of 12/31/15	PRICE: 52 Week High	PRICE: 52 Week Low	PERFORMANCE: Performance Rating/Pts	% Total Return Through 12/31/15: 3 Mo	6 Mo	1Yr/Pct	Annualized 3Yr/Pct	Annualized 5Yr/Pct
GL	*Merk Gold	OUNZ	**D+**	10.52	13.02	10.43	**D-** / **1.4**	-6.98	-9.29	-11.15 / 24	--	--
EN	*Mk Vectors Unconv O&G ETF	FRAK	**E**	13.28	24.69	12.47	**E+** / **0.8**	-14.95	-32.82	-38.69 / 4	-15.93 / 11	--
GI	*Morgan Creek Global Tact ETF Fun	GTAA	**C-**	22.49	26.20	21.28	**C-** / **3.3**	0.89	-7.19	-9.00 / 28	-1.75 / 32	-0.97 / 25
GR	*Morgan Stanley Technology ETF	MTK	**C**	54.08	56.36	42.50	**A** / **9.4**	7.73	7.77	8.76 / 86	16.83 / 92	10.94 / 71
GR	*Mrkt Vectors Rare Earth/Str Met	REMX	**E+**	13.41	28.30	12.35	**E-** / **0.2**	-8.15	-36.41	-44.57 / 2	-35.94 / 2	-30.13 / 3
GR	*Nashville Area ETF	NASH	**D**	25.94	35.00	25.79	**D-** / **1.1**	-0.83	-17.91	-13.08 / 20	--	--
GEN	*Newfleet Multi-Sector Income ETF	MINC	**C**	48.37	59.20	46.75	**C** / **4.5**	-0.55	-0.14	0.96 / 67	--	--
GR	*Nuveen Diversified Commodity	CFD	**D-**	9.02	13.00	8.44	**D-** / **1.1**	-10.62	-22.62	-21.90 / 12	-15.71 / 11	-11.21 / 12
GL	*Nuveen Long/Short Commodity Tot	CTF	**C-**	15.54	17.06	15.27	**C-** / **3.2**	-1.01	-1.26	0.90 / 66	-4.18 / 26	--
FO	*O'Shares FTSE Asia Pac Qty Div H	OAPH	**U**	25.44	N/A	N/A	**U** /	5.79	--	--	--	--
FO	*O'Shares FTSE Asia Pacific Qty D	OASI	**U**	24.18	N/A	N/A	**U** /	6.88	--	--	--	--
FO	*O'Shares FTSE Europe Qlty Div He	OEUH	**U**	25.20	N/A	N/A	**U** /	4.88	--	--	--	--
FO	*O'Shares FTSE Europe Quality Div	OEUR	**U**	22.98	N/A	N/A	**U** /	2.06	--	--	--	--
IN	*O'Shares FTSE US Quality Dividen	OUSA	**U**	25.06	N/A	N/A	**U** /	6.91	--	--	--	--
IN	*Oppenheimer ADR Revenue ETF	RTR	**D+**	29.48	39.89	28.81	**D+** / **2.5**	-4.60	-18.67	-15.55 / 17	-3.72 / 27	-1.99 / 23
FS	*Oppenheimer Financials Sector Re	RWW	**B+**	48.09	52.27	42.33	**B+** / **8.5**	5.24	-4.13	-3.31 / 45	13.83 / 87	9.13 / 61
GL	*Oppenheimer Global Growth Revenu	RGRO	**U**	40.54	N/A	N/A	**U** /	-0.20	-13.07	--	--	--
GR	*Oppenheimer Large Cap Revenue	RWL	**A+**	39.44	42.32	21.75	**B+** / **8.6**	3.37	-3.31	-1.93 / 51	14.15 / 88	12.31 / 81
GR	*Oppenheimer Mid Cap Revenue	RWK	**B**	45.29	51.42	29.36	**B** / **7.6**	0.10	-8.21	-5.44 / 37	11.74 / 81	10.49 / 68
IN	*Oppenheimer Navellier Overall A1	RWV	**C+**	46.77	52.93	44.31	**B** / **7.9**	-2.29	-8.85	-2.08 / 50	12.58 / 83	9.18 / 62
GR	*Oppenheimer Small Cap Revenue	RWJ	**B+**	51.70	60.40	34.71	**B-** / **7.1**	1.31	-10.26	-8.12 / 31	10.90 / 78	10.71 / 70
IN	*Oppenheimer Ultra Dividend Reven	RDIV	**C-**	27.63	31.38	26.90	**D+** / **2.9**	0.49	-2.02	-5.51 / 37	--	--
GL	*Pacer Trendpilot 100 ETF	PTNQ	**U**	23.92	N/A	N/A	**U** /	2.13	-3.18	--	--	--
GR	*Pacer Trendpilot 450 ETF	PTMC	**U**	23.17	N/A	N/A	**U** /	-0.17	-5.67	--	--	--
GR	*Pacer Trendpilot 750 ETF	PTLC	**U**	23.06	N/A	N/A	**U** /	-1.96	-6.06	--	--	--
COH	*Peritus High Yield ETF	HYLD	**D+**	32.64	42.72	31.65	**D** / **2.2**	-7.33	-16.09	-14.14 / 19	-6.28 / 23	-1.12 / 25
COI	*PIMCO 0-5 Year Hi Yield Corp Bd	HYS	**C**	91.62	102.51	90.01	**C-** / **4.0**	-1.50	-6.18	-5.22 / 38	0.70 / 40	--
USA	*PIMCO 1-3 Year US Treasury Idx E	TUZ	**B-**	50.66	52.53	50.61	**C** / **4.4**	-0.68	-0.29	0.18 / 61	0.33 / 38	0.57 / 29
USA	*PIMCO 1-5 Year US TIPS Index ETF	STPZ	**C**	51.33	52.44	51.08	**C-** / **3.8**	-0.81	-1.19	-0.45 / 57	-1.22 / 33	0.60 / 30
USA	*PIMCO 15 Plus Year US TIPS Idx E	LTPZ	**D+**	60.86	72.00	59.30	**D+** / **2.9**	-2.34	-2.15	-10.16 / 25	-3.52 / 28	4.47 / 45
USA	*PIMCO 25+ Year Zero Coupon US Tr	ZROZ	**C**	109.31	138.99	102.33	**C+** / **5.6**	-4.07	7.51	-8.14 / 31	4.48 / 59	13.48 / 86
USA	*PIMCO Broad US TIPS Index ETF	TIPZ	**C**	55.25	58.99	55.10	**C-** / **3.4**	-2.10	-2.06	-3.22 / 45	-2.27 / 30	2.39 / 35
GEN	*PIMCO Dvsfd Inc Active Exch Trad	DI	**C**	45.83	53.00	45.75	**C-** / **3.6**	-1.02	-1.97	-0.97 / 55	--	--
COI	*PIMCO Enhanced Sht Maturity Act	MINT	**B-**	100.61	101.35	100.61	**C** / **4.6**	0.15	-0.07	0.35 / 63	0.58 / 39	0.92 / 30
GL	*PIMCO Global Adv Infl-Link Bond	ILB	**C-**	40.05	46.58	39.12	**D+** / **2.3**	0.13	-6.86	-10.01 / 25	-7.70 / 20	--
MUN	*PIMCO Intermediate Muni Bd Act E	MUNI	**C+**	53.97	54.60	51.43	**C+** / **5.8**	1.99	3.45	2.48 / 76	1.89 / 53	3.71 / 50
COI	*PIMCO Investment Grade Crp Bond	CORP	**C+**	98.98	105.98	98.75	**C** / **4.8**	-1.01	0.36	-1.62 / 52	1.29 / 44	4.36 / 45
COI	*PIMCO Low Duration Active Exch T	LDUR	**C+**	99.67	104.49	98.14	**C** / **5.3**	0.81	0.33	2.16 / 72	--	--
MUN	*PIMCO Short Term Muni Bd Act ETF	SMMU	**B**	50.27	50.58	50.06	**C** / **4.9**	-0.11	0.45	0.89 / 69	0.62 / 41	0.97 / 32
COI	*PIMCO Total Return Active Exch T	BOND	**C+**	104.22	110.68	103.83	**C** / **5.3**	-0.14	0.69	0.36 / 63	2.21 / 49	--
USA	*PowerShares 1-30 Laddered Treasu	PLW	**C**	32.28	34.64	31.38	**C** / **5.3**	-1.93	3.01	-0.75 / 56	2.37 / 50	5.73 / 50
GI	*PowerShares Act US Real Estate	PSR	**B-**	72.75	79.54	65.99	**B** / **8.0**	6.53	7.81	1.26 / 68	10.19 / 76	11.85 / 77
IN	*PowerShares Aerospace & Defense	PPA	**A+**	35.64	37.86	15.30	**A** / **9.5**	8.24	1.62	4.24 / 77	19.67 / 95	14.73 / 90
USA	*PowerShares Build America Bond	BAB	**B-**	28.99	31.43	28.40	**C+** / **5.7**	-0.38	3.42	-0.62 / 57	3.74 / 56	8.30 / 59
IN	*PowerShares Buyback Achievers	PKW	**B+**	45.46	50.26	28.50	**B+** / **8.7**	2.60	-6.49	-4.07 / 42	15.23 / 90	14.49 / 89
MUN	*PowerShares CA AMT-Free Muni Bon	PWZ	**B**	25.88	26.20	24.98	**B-** / **7.1**	2.56	4.88	3.23 / 79	4.59 / 67	7.06 / 71
IN	*PowerShares CEF Inc Composite Po	PCEF	**C**	21.34	24.18	16.15	**C** / **5.1**	3.66	-2.59	-1.68 / 52	1.88 / 48	4.73 / 46
FO	*PowerShares China A Shares Port	CHNA	**C-**	28.03	52.87	24.93	**C+** / **6.2**	12.90	-1.43	0.50 / 64	--	--
GL	*PowerShares Chinese YDS Bd	DSUM	**C**	22.71	25.24	21.96	**C-** / **3.8**	-2.80	-7.10	-3.91 / 43	0.17 / 38	--
IN	*PowerShares Cleantech Portfolio	PZD	**C+**	29.40	32.00	25.85	**B-** / **7.3**	9.78	-3.02	2.71 / 73	8.41 / 71	3.32 / 39
GL	*PowerShares Contrarian Opptys	CNTR	**D+**	24.44	27.39	22.40	**D** / **2.2**	3.61	-8.52	-9.32 / 27	--	--
IN	*PowerShares DB Agriculture Fund	DBA	**D+**	20.61	25.21	19.94	**D** / **1.9**	-1.53	-11.43	-16.36 / 16	-9.32 / 18	-8.21 / 15

* Denotes ETF Fund, N/A denotes number is not available

ncl. in Returns		RISK				NET ASSETS		VALUATION			ASSET					FUND MANAGER	
			3 Year					Premium / Discount									
vidend ield %	Expense Ratio	Risk Rating/ Pts	Standard Deviation	Beta	Avg Dura-tion	NAV as of 12/31/15	Total $(Mil)	As of 12/31/15	1 Year Average	Wtd Avg P/E	Cash %	Stocks %	Bonds %	Other %	Portfolio Turnover Ratio	Manager Quality Pct	Manager Tenure (Years)
0.00	0.40	**B- / 7.7**	N/A	N/A	N/A	10.55	N/A	-0.28	0.14	N/A	0	0	0	100	N/A	15	N/A
2.58	0.54	**D / 2.1**	27.8	1.40	N/A	13.24	90	0.30	-0.01	N/A	0	0	0	100	11	16	4
1.48	1.25	**C+ / 6.9**	7.6	0.54	N/A	22.46	20	0.13	-0.09	N/A	33	56	11	0	244	19	N/A
2.12	0.42	**D / 2.2**	12.9	1.06	N/A	53.88	228	0.37	0.06	176.8	0	100	0	0	9	78	16
4.77	0.57	**C- / 3.4**	24.8	1.13	N/A	13.68	75	-1.97	-0.50	N/A	0	97	0	3	37	N/A	6
1.08	0.49	**C+ / 6.0**	N/A	N/A	N/A	25.81	9	0.50	0.30	N/A	0	0	0	100	38	11	3
3.34	0.75	**B- / 7.8**	N/A	N/A	N/A	48.35	173	0.04	0.03	N/A	0	0	0	100	49	74	N/A
7.72	1.81	**C- / 3.9**	15.3	0.35	N/A	9.47	148	-4.75	-4.93	N/A	0	0	0	100	N/A	7	N/A
6.95	1.73	**C+ / 6.7**	16.5	-0.19	N/A	16.45	321	-5.53	-5.02	N/A	0	0	0	100	N/A	57	N/A
3.64	N/A	**U /**	N/A	N/A	N/A	25.40	N/A	0.16	N/A	N/A	0	0	0	100	N/A	N/A	1
2.13	N/A	**U /**	N/A	N/A	N/A	24.01	N/A	0.71	N/A	N/A	0	0	0	100	N/A	N/A	1
6.71	N/A	**U /**	N/A	N/A	N/A	25.35	N/A	-0.59	N/A	N/A	0	0	0	100	N/A	N/A	1
5.52	N/A	**U /**	N/A	N/A	N/A	23.06	N/A	-0.35	N/A	N/A	0	0	0	100	N/A	N/A	1
4.37	N/A	**U /**	N/A	N/A	N/A	25.03	N/A	0.12	N/A	N/A	0	0	0	100	N/A	N/A	N/A
1.70	0.49	**B- / 7.0**	15.8	1.17	N/A	29.58	22	-0.34	0.01	N/A	1	98	0	1	26	8	N/A
1.38	0.49	**C+ / 6.8**	13.7	1.17	N/A	47.87	33	0.46	0.02	N/A	0	99	0	1	13	50	2
0.59	N/A	**U /**	N/A	N/A	N/A	40.73	N/A	-0.47	N/A	N/A	0	0	0	100	N/A	N/A	1
2.32	0.49	**B / 8.7**	10.8	1.01	N/A	39.45	259	-0.03	0.01	44.0	0	99	0	1	19	70	2
0.92	0.54	**B- / 7.2**	13.4	1.12	N/A	45.13	209	0.35	0.04	46.6	0	99	0	1	14	42	2
0.63	0.60	**C+ / 5.9**	13.0	0.98	N/A	46.73	8	0.09	0.21	N/A	0	100	0	0	200	67	N/A
0.75	0.54	**B / 8.3**	15.7	1.21	N/A	51.80	275	-0.19	0.02	46.6	0	99	0	1	21	29	2
5.33	0.49	**B- / 7.1**	N/A	N/A	N/A	27.55	27	0.29	0.02	N/A	0	0	0	100	52	27	2
0.48	N/A	**U /**	N/A	N/A	N/A	23.90	N/A	0.08	N/A	N/A	0	0	0	100	N/A	N/A	1
0.14	N/A	**U /**	N/A	N/A	N/A	23.18	N/A	-0.04	N/A	N/A	0	0	0	100	N/A	N/A	1
1.02	N/A	**U /**	N/A	N/A	N/A	23.04	N/A	0.09	N/A	N/A	0	0	0	100	N/A	N/A	1
2.84	1.23	**C+ / 6.5**	9.3	1.36	N/A	33.08	749	-1.33	-0.63	N/A	9	0	90	1	88	20	N/A
4.92	0.55	**B / 8.7**	4.4	0.45	N/A	92.02	3,868	-0.43	-0.21	N/A	0	0	0	100	28	69	1
0.61	0.14	**B+ / 9.9**	0.5	0.03	N/A	50.74	127	-0.16	-0.01	N/A	5	0	95	0	60	70	1
0.58	0.20	**B- / 7.8**	2.1	0.07	N/A	51.23	1,407	0.20	0.01	N/A	25	0	75	0	31	56	1
0.34	0.21	**C+ / 6.1**	12.0	0.99	N/A	60.65	77	0.35	N/A	N/A	1	0	99	0	14	24	1
2.55	0.16	**B- / 7.2**	19.2	1.81	N/A	110.24	65	-0.84	0.03	N/A	0	0	100	0	18	56	1
0.65	0.21	**B / 8.8**	5.7	0.40	N/A	55.36	124	-0.20	-0.01	N/A	10	0	90	0	23	38	1
7.20	0.85	**B / 8.7**	N/A	N/A	N/A	46.03	43	-0.43	0.75	N/A	0	0	0	100	44	51	2
1.01	0.35	**B+ / 9.7**	0.3	0.04	N/A	100.67	3,723	-0.06	-0.03	N/A	6	0	94	0	193	72	7
0.97	0.61	**B- / 7.4**	10.0	0.99	N/A	40.24	123	-0.47	-0.74	N/A	0	0	0	100	114	36	4
2.14	0.35	**B- / 7.7**	3.4	0.95	N/A	53.77	217	0.37	-0.03	N/A	2	0	98	0	13	59	5
2.89	0.20	**B / 8.9**	4.6	1.04	N/A	99.11	238	-0.13	-0.02	N/A	0	0	0	100	12	65	1
5.73	0.50	**B / 8.0**	N/A	N/A	N/A	99.33	145	0.34	0.04	N/A	0	0	0	100	1,591	82	2
0.85	0.35	**B+ / 9.9**	0.8	0.13	N/A	50.33	76	-0.12	-0.09	N/A	0	0	100	0	20	69	2
2.03	0.55	**B- / 7.7**	3.7	0.82	N/A	103.95	3,010	0.26	-0.03	N/A	0	0	0	100	180	75	N/A
2.14	0.25	**B- / 7.3**	7.0	0.67	N/A	32.25	269	0.09	0.02	N/A	4	0	95	1	5	70	9
4.64	0.80	**C+ / 6.5**	13.3	0.49	N/A	72.43	39	0.44	0.03	107.9	0	100	0	0	169	86	8
2.97	0.66	**B / 8.7**	11.8	0.93	N/A	35.66	152	-0.06	-0.02	46.9	0	100	0	0	13	91	9
4.71	0.27	**B / 8.7**	6.6	0.54	N/A	29.13	683	-0.48	-0.33	N/A	3	0	96	1	7	80	7
.45	0.63	**B- / 7.0**	12.2	1.11	N/A	45.44	2,739	0.04	-0.03	48.1	0	99	0	1	68	63	9
3.19	0.26	**B- / 7.8**	4.7	1.31	14.4	25.80	60	0.31	0.24	N/A	2	0	97	1	28	72	9
3.54	0.50	**C+ / 6.4**	7.5	0.52	N/A	21.31	619	0.14	0.01	N/A	0	100	0	0	19	32	6
0.00	0.43	**C- / 3.5**	N/A	N/A	N/A	27.87	2	0.57	0.09	N/A	0	0	0	100	N/A	77	3
3.25	0.45	**B / 8.8**	6.2	-0.10	N/A	22.98	186	-1.17	-0.45	N/A	0	0	0	100	34	66	5
0.21	0.67	**C+ / 6.6**	15.5	1.28	N/A	29.37	75	0.10	-0.16	49.8	0	99	0	1	22	19	9
.18	0.50	**C+ / 6.6**	N/A	N/A	N/A	23.96	4	2.00	-0.16	N/A	0	0	0	100	2	18	2
0.00	0.93	**B- / 7.1**	12.4	0.18	N/A	20.67	1,165	-0.29	-0.05	N/A	0	0	0	100	N/A	14	9

Denotes ETF Fund, N/A denotes number is not available

99 Pct = Best 0 Pct = Worst				PRICE			PERFORMANCE					
					52 Week			% Total Return Through 12/31/15				
											Annualized	
Fund Type	Fund Name	Ticker Symbol	Overall Investment Rating	Price As of 12/31/15	High	Low	Performance Rating/Pts	3 Mo	6 Mo	1Yr/Pct	3Yr/Pct	5Yr/Pct
IN	*PowerShares DB Base Metals Fund	DBB	**D-**	11.88	16.78	11.29	**D- / 1.1**	-6.68	-18.35	-25.38 / 10	-14.67 / 12	-13.21 / 11
GR	*PowerShares DB Commodity Idx Tra	DBC	**E+**	13.36	18.68	13.13	**E+ / 0.7**	-11.82	-24.73	-26.71 / 9	-21.42 / 7	-13.20 / 11
EN	*PowerShares DB Energy Fund	DBE	**E**	11.20	18.71	10.75	**E / 0.5**	-17.30	-33.39	-33.86 / 6	-26.29 / 5	-15.87 / 8
IN	*PowerShares DB G10 Currency Harv	DBV	**C-**	23.34	25.66	21.68	**C- / 3.0**	4.76	-0.81	-7.71 / 32	-4.08 / 26	-0.22 / 27
PM	*PowerShares DB Gold Fund	DGL	**D**	34.66	43.38	34.26	**D- / 1.3**	-7.05	-9.65	-11.60 / 23	-15.15 / 12	-6.44 / 17
EN	*PowerShares DB Oil Fund	DBO	**E+**	9.05	15.70	8.68	**E / 0.3**	-20.75	-35.72	-40.77 / 3	-29.81 / 4	-20.04 / 6
GL	*PowerShares DB Opt Yld Dvsd Comd	PDBC	**E**	15.61	31.05	15.26	**E / 0.4**	-9.93	-23.65	-26.23 / 9	--	--
PM	*PowerShares DB Precious Metals F	DBP	**D**	32.22	41.06	31.93	**D- / 1.1**	-7.68	-10.23	-12.35 / 21	-17.11 / 10	-8.25 / 15
PM	*PowerShares DB Silver Fund	DBS	**E+**	21.87	30.04	21.65	**E+ / 0.7**	-9.93	-12.27	-13.93 / 19	-25.09 / 5	-15.49 / 8
GR	*PowerShares DB US Dollar Bearish	UDN	**D+**	21.42	23.53	20.99	**D+ / 2.4**	-2.36	-2.18	-8.62 / 29	-7.23 / 21	-3.96 / 21
GR	*PowerShares DB US Dollar Bullish	UUP	**B**	25.65	26.50	24.19	**C+ / 6.3**	1.96	1.39	5.45 / 80	5.09 / 62	1.78 / 33
IN	*PowerShares Div Achievers	PFM	**B**	20.55	21.98	6.58	**B / 7.6**	4.85	-0.06	-3.12 / 46	10.11 / 75	10.69 / 70
IN	*PowerShares DWA Basic Materials	PYZ	**C**	48.83	56.10	35.23	**C+ / 6.1**	6.20	-6.81	-5.83 / 36	6.34 / 65	7.94 / 58
IN	*PowerShares DWA Con Cyc Mom	PEZ	**B+**	44.04	49.23	24.89	**B+ / 8.3**	-3.96	-6.55	-0.05 / 60	13.65 / 86	12.40 / 82
IN	*PowerShares DWA Cons Staples Mom	PSL	**A-**	56.79	59.43	37.83	**A+ / 9.6**	4.10	5.93	14.58 / 94	20.12 / 95	16.64 / 94
FO	*PowerShares DWA Dev Mkt Momentum	PIZ	**B**	23.70	26.75	20.93	**C+ / 6.8**	4.02	-0.84	-0.10 / 59	7.48 / 68	3.92 / 43
EM	*PowerShares DWA Emg Mkts Momentu	PIE	**D+**	14.95	19.57	14.10	**D / 2.2**	-4.65	-17.55	-13.21 / 20	-6.43 / 22	-3.18 / 22
EN	*PowerShares DWA Energy Momentum	PXI	**D-**	33.57	50.46	32.18	**D / 1.7**	-10.70	-24.50	-24.29 / 11	-7.75 / 20	-0.89 / 25
FS	*PowerShares DWA Financial Moment	PFI	**B+**	30.69	32.75	17.75	**B+ / 8.7**	4.43	0.73	1.37 / 69	13.51 / 86	11.62 / 76
HL	*PowerShares DWA Healthcare Momen	PTH	**A+**	55.11	67.32	20.91	**A- / 9.1**	-1.20	-12.59	2.06 / 72	17.83 / 93	15.74 / 93
IN	*PowerShares DWA Industrials Mome	PRN	**B-**	44.58	49.78	19.63	**B / 7.6**	5.85	-3.69	-5.09 / 38	10.74 / 78	9.58 / 63
IN	*PowerShares DWA Momentum	PDP	**A**	41.37	44.61	26.59	**B+ / 8.5**	1.39	-4.23	1.56 / 70	13.39 / 85	12.16 / 80
GR	*PowerShares DWA NASDAQ Momentum	DWAQ	**B**	74.53	84.86	68.48	**B+ / 8.9**	0.89	-7.07	6.02 / 81	14.69 / 89	9.10 / 61
IN	*PowerShares DWA SmallCap Momentu	DWAS	**B+**	37.60	43.33	22.18	**B- / 7.5**	0.44	-8.76	-2.33 / 49	11.04 / 78	--
GR	*PowerShares DWA Technology Momen	PTF	**B-**	39.69	44.48	19.66	**B+ / 8.6**	1.41	-6.83	5.08 / 79	13.66 / 86	9.13 / 61
UT	*PowerShares DWA Utilities Moment	PUI	**B**	22.41	24.73	20.54	**B / 8.1**	4.96	8.62	-2.76 / 47	11.05 / 79	10.34 / 67
HL	*PowerShares Dynamic Biotech&Geno	PBE	**B+**	50.52	63.21	32.92	**A+ / 9.7**	5.21	-11.57	1.40 / 69	29.56 / 98	19.01 / 97
IN	*PowerShares Dynamic Bldg & Cons	PKB	**B**	23.80	25.59	20.19	**B / 8.1**	3.63	0.40	11.08 / 90	10.12 / 75	12.87 / 84
EN	*PowerShares Dynamic Enrg Exp & P	PXE	**D**	21.91	32.40	20.50	**D / 2.1**	-9.72	-22.69	-19.91 / 14	-5.71 / 24	1.02 / 30
IN	*PowerShares Dynamic Food & Bever	PBJ	**A+**	32.20	34.38	16.16	**A / 9.3**	1.34	-0.31	7.18 / 84	17.75 / 93	13.71 / 87
GR	*PowerShares Dynamic Large Cap Gr	PWB	**A+**	31.29	32.20	16.98	**A / 9.4**	5.18	1.63	7.97 / 85	17.87 / 93	14.77 / 90
IN	*PowerShares Dynamic Large Cap Va	PWV	**B+**	29.09	32.00	19.55	**B / 7.7**	3.29	-4.46	-4.82 / 39	11.60 / 80	11.73 / 76
IN	*PowerShares Dynamic Leisure&Ente	PEJ	**A+**	36.76	39.36	23.77	**A- / 9.1**	1.96	1.04	4.11 / 77	15.86 / 91	15.06 / 91
GR	*PowerShares Dynamic Market	PWC	**A-**	73.22	77.92	39.41	**B+ / 8.8**	3.41	-3.34	0.77 / 66	14.50 / 89	11.96 / 78
IN	*PowerShares Dynamic Media	PBS	**B+**	25.14	27.96	19.22	**B+ / 8.7**	3.55	-6.18	0.53 / 64	14.52 / 89	12.96 / 84
GR	*PowerShares Dynamic Networking	PXQ	**B**	34.62	39.75	26.35	**B / 7.7**	4.38	-6.42	0.56 / 64	10.53 / 76	5.24 / 49
EN	*PowerShares Dynamic Oil & Gas Sv	PXJ	**E+**	11.83	19.25	10.82	**E+ / 0.9**	-6.88	-24.61	-31.06 / 7	-17.09 / 10	-10.34 / 13
HL	*PowerShares Dynamic Pharmaceutic	PJP	**B**	69.97	83.97	44.22	**A+ / 9.8**	10.13	-2.99	14.64 / 95	30.56 / 98	28.09 / 99
IN	*PowerShares Dynamic Retail	PMR	**B+**	37.21	41.91	35.71	**B+ / 8.6**	1.47	-4.72	-2.77 / 47	14.68 / 89	15.95 / 93
IN	*PowerShares Dynamic Semiconducto	PSI	**B+**	25.23	29.15	20.28	**A / 9.4**	6.34	-5.70	-0.43 / 58	20.48 / 95	9.51 / 63
GR	*PowerShares Dynamic Software	PSJ	**A**	42.27	45.16	25.82	**A- / 9.0**	3.73	-1.45	7.85 / 85	15.14 / 90	11.01 / 72
EM	*PowerShares Emg Mkts Infrastruct	PXR	**D**	27.35	41.72	26.11	**D- / 1.2**	-7.43	-22.56	-22.40 / 12	-13.39 / 14	-11.08 / 12
EM	*PowerShares Emrg Mkt Sovereign D	PCY	**C-**	27.31	29.09	26.73	**C / 4.5**	-0.14	0.58	2.67 / 73	-0.02 / 37	5.55 / 49
GL	*PowerShares Europe Curr Hdg LV P	FXEU	**U**	24.66	N/A	N/A	**U /**	5.52	3.38	--	--	--
FS	*PowerShares Financial Preferred	PGF	**B**	18.83	18.85	12.24	**B- / 7.5**	5.01	6.34	8.51 / 86	6.85 / 67	7.87 / 57
FO	*PowerShares FTSE RAFI Asia Pac E	PAF	**D+**	43.07	56.05	39.56	**D+ / 2.5**	4.55	-11.92	-11.08 / 24	-5.86 / 23	-1.53 / 24
FO	*PowerShares FTSE RAFI DM exUS Sm	PDN	**C+**	25.92	29.56	24.76	**C+ / 5.9**	1.73	-6.97	2.02 / 72	4.89 / 61	3.52 / 41
FO	*PowerShares FTSE RAFI Dvlp Mkt e	PXF	**C**	36.20	43.82	33.80	**C / 4.7**	0.30	-10.78	-5.36 / 37	2.64 / 51	1.54 / 32
EM	*PowerShares FTSE RAFI Emg Mkts	PXH	**D**	13.94	21.29	13.70	**D- / 1.3**	-5.17	-25.38	-21.85 / 12	-12.80 / 14	-8.98 / 14
IN	*PowerShares FTSE RAFI US 1000	PRF	**A-**	86.83	94.40	76.76	**B / 8.2**	3.98	-3.39	-2.81 / 47	12.77 / 84	11.21 / 73
IN	*PowerShares FTSE RAFI US 1500 Sm	PRFZ	**B-**	93.89	107.25	76.00	**B- / 7.2**	2.27	-8.40	-5.02 / 39	10.50 / 76	9.04 / 61
COH	*PowerShares Fundamental High Yie	PHB	**C+**	17.44	19.20	17.18	**C- / 4.2**	-0.91	-4.42	-2.99 / 46	0.82 / 40	4.00 / 43

* Denotes ETF Fund, N/A denotes number is not available

Incl. in Returns		RISK				NET ASSETS		VALUATION			ASSET					FUND MANAGER	
		Risk	3 Year		Avg			Premium / Discount		Wtd					Portfolio		
ividend Yield %	Expense Ratio	Rating/ Pts	Standard Deviation	Beta	Dura- tion	NAV as of 12/31/15	Total $(Mil)	As of 12/31/15	1 Year Average	Avg P/E	Cash %	Stocks %	Bonds %	Other %	Turnover Ratio	Manager Quality Pct	Manager Tenure (Years)
0.00	0.78	C / 4.5	13.9	0.28	N/A	11.87	329	0.08	0.01	N/A	0	0	0	100	N/A	8	N/A
0.00	0.88	C- / 3.5	15.5	0.44	N/A	13.35	4,997	0.07	-0.08	N/A	0	0	0	100	N/A	4	N/A
0.00	0.78	D / 2.1	24.5	0.91	N/A	11.15	279	0.45	-0.09	N/A	0	0	0	100	N/A	5	N/A
0.00	0.81	C+ / 6.5	8.2	0.55	N/A	23.29	98	0.21	-0.05	N/A	65	0	0	35	N/A	15	N/A
0.00	0.80	C+ / 6.2	16.7	0.95	N/A	34.69	145	-0.09	0.04	N/A	0	0	0	100	N/A	45	N/A
0.00	0.78	C- / 3.3	29.0	1.04	N/A	9.07	243	-0.22	-0.14	N/A	0	0	0	100	N/A	4	N/A
0.00	N/A	D+ / 2.9	N/A	N/A	N/A	15.50	N/A	0.71	0.05	N/A	0	0	0	100	N/A	4	2
0.00	0.79	C+ / 5.7	17.9	1.00	N/A	32.28	168	-0.19	-0.01	N/A	0	0	0	100	N/A	36	N/A
0.00	0.76	C- / 4.1	26.5	1.25	N/A	21.90	22	-0.14	-0.04	N/A	0	0	0	100	N/A	17	N/A
0.00	0.81	B- / 7.1	7.2	0.14	N/A	21.42	45	0.00	-0.02	N/A	100	0	0	0	N/A	17	N/A
0.00	0.81	B / 8.4	6.7	-0.13	N/A	25.65	713	0.00	0.02	N/A	1	0	0	99	N/A	93	N/A
2.85	0.55	B- / 7.3	10.2	0.93	N/A	20.52	354	0.15	-0.06	34.2	0	99	0	1	20	47	9
1.76	0.60	C+ / 6.4	14.7	1.19	N/A	48.64	119	0.39	-0.08	55.3	0	100	0	0	80	18	9
0.38	0.60	B- / 7.0	13.0	0.93	N/A	44.02	49	0.05	0.05	63.1	0	100	0	0	114	72	9
1.09	0.60	C+ / 6.9	12.3	0.90	N/A	56.77	40	0.04	0.02	98.4	0	100	0	0	83	92	9
0.67	0.80	B / 8.0	13.6	0.93	N/A	23.87	501	-0.71	-0.13	71.6	0	100	0	0	99	82	9
1.92	0.90	C+ / 6.8	16.3	0.92	N/A	15.13	407	-1.19	-0.31	N/A	0	100	0	0	147	65	9
1.69	0.60	C / 4.4	24.2	1.23	N/A	33.53	246	0.12	-0.04	18.1	0	100	0	0	109	50	9
1.80	0.60	B- / 7.2	12.7	0.96	N/A	30.61	33	0.26	-0.10	59.7	0	99	0	1	115	69	9
0.00	0.60	B- / 7.9	17.4	0.95	N/A	55.15	79	-0.07	0.03	50.3	0	100	0	0	151	87	9
0.24	0.60	C+ / 6.7	15.2	1.26	N/A	44.46	131	0.27	0.01	69.5	0	100	0	0	121	26	9
0.25	0.63	B / 8.2	10.8	0.92	N/A	41.40	1,313	-0.07	N/A	110.9	0	100	0	0	73	72	9
0.07	0.60	C+ / 6.2	15.2	1.10	N/A	74.06	27	0.63	0.06	134.4	0	100	0	0	154	62	9
0.25	0.60	B / 8.2	17.4	1.12	N/A	37.66	359	-0.16	0.01	N/A	0	0	0	100	168	37	9
0.00	0.60	C+ / 5.6	15.3	1.15	N/A	39.69	59	0.00	-0.04	337.2	0	100	0	0	157	51	9
4.80	0.60	B- / 7.1	12.5	0.80	N/A	22.25	40	0.72	-0.07	25.2	0	100	0	0	47	80	9
1.83	0.57	C / 5.5	22.7	1.10	N/A	50.56	395	-0.08	-0.02	322.6	0	99	0	1	95	96	9
0.12	0.63	B- / 7.0	16.3	1.15	N/A	23.77	109	0.13	-0.02	36.6	0	100	0	0	96	27	9
3.90	0.64	C / 4.6	25.2	1.26	N/A	21.90	128	0.05	-0.06	10.8	0	100	0	0	140	96	9
2.09	0.58	B- / 7.7	12.2	0.93	N/A	32.19	246	0.03	-0.01	35.8	0	100	0	0	124	88	9
0.81	0.58	B- / 7.5	10.3	0.89	N/A	31.28	275	0.03	0.01	53.3	0	99	0	1	143	89	9
2.92	0.57	B / 8.0	10.9	0.98	N/A	29.09	908	0.00	-0.02	26.1	0	99	0	1	82	51	9
.21	0.63	B / 8.5	13.6	1.00	N/A	36.77	148	-0.03	0.05	66.8	0	100	0	0	187	81	9
.11	0.59	B- / 7.4	12.4	1.06	N/A	72.65	187	0.78	-0.04	46.6	0	100	0	0	237	64	9
2.00	0.59	C+ / 6.9	15.9	1.27	N/A	25.03	151	0.44	-0.01	55.8	0	100	0	0	131	39	9
.00	0.63	B- / 7.0	15.8	1.09	N/A	34.46	28	0.46	-0.04	49.1	0	99	0	1	74	33	9
.54	0.63	C- / 3.4	28.8	1.42	N/A	11.82	102	0.08	-0.10	18.2	0	100	0	0	79	15	9
.87	0.56	C / 5.2	16.6	1.08	N/A	69.98	1,263	-0.01	N/A	523.5	0	100	0	0	47	96	9
.94	0.63	C+ / 6.9	15.5	1.04	N/A	36.96	21	0.68	-0.04	58.1	0	99	0	1	111	61	9
.04	0.63	C+ / 6.4	17.3	1.16	N/A	25.18	29	0.20	0.01	74.5	0	100	0	0	103	86	9
.15	0.63	B- / 7.6	13.4	1.02	N/A	42.27	48	0.00	-0.03	86.4	0	99	0	1	132	72	9
.97	0.76	C+ / 6.8	15.6	0.94	N/A	27.55	38	-0.73	-0.45	18.1	0	99	0	1	20	22	8
.47	0.50	C+ / 6.7	8.9	0.80	8.5	27.31	2,329	0.00	-0.09	N/A	1	0	98	1	14	86	9
.41	N/A	U /	N/A	N/A	N/A	24.71	N/A	-0.20	N/A	N/A	0	0	0	100	N/A	N/A	1
.89	0.63	B- / 7.7	4.0	0.05	N/A	18.82	1,395	0.05	N/A	N/A	0	0	0	100	9	91	9
.97	0.49	C+ / 6.6	16.2	1.03	N/A	43.27	44	-0.46	-0.25	N/A	0	99	0	1	16	16	N/A
.27	0.49	B / 8.1	11.6	0.81	N/A	26.11	109	-0.73	0.53	96.3	0	99	0	1	24	77	9
.84	0.45	B / 8.0	13.3	1.04	N/A	36.50	831	-0.82	0.04	14.3	0	99	0	1	16	48	9
.66	0.49	C+ / 5.9	18.9	1.25	N/A	14.06	382	-0.85	-0.14	N/A	0	99	0	1	22	31	9
.40	0.39	B / 8.0	10.9	1.01	N/A	86.84	3,817	-0.01	-0.03	36.8	0	99	0	1	10	58	9
.13	0.39	B- / 7.1	13.6	1.05	N/A	93.84	959	0.05	-0.02	69.1	0	99	0	1	26	38	9
.80	0.50	B / 8.9	5.0	0.90	N/A	17.46	610	-0.11	-0.04	N/A	1	0	98	1	20	65	9

Denotes ETF Fund, N/A denotes number is not available

Fund Type	Fund Name (99 Pct = Best, 0 Pct = Worst)	Ticker Symbol	Overall Investment Rating	PRICE: Price As of 12/31/15	PRICE: 52 Week High	PRICE: 52 Week Low	PERFORMANCE: Performance Rating/Pts	% Total Return Through 12/31/15: 3 Mo	6 Mo	1Yr/Pct	Annualized 3Yr/Pct	Annualized 5Yr/Pct
EM	*PowerShares Fundmntl Em Loc Dbt	PFEM	D	16.54	20.46	16.18	D / 1.6	2.14	-8.47	-13.66 / 19	--	--
COI	*PowerShares Fundmntl Inv Gr Corp	PFIG	C+	25.02	25.96	24.83	C / 5.1	-0.54	-0.35	0.91 / 66	1.53 / 45	--
PM	*PowerShares Glb Gold & Precious	PSAU	E+	11.75	19.60	11.08	E / 0.4	-5.25	-21.59	-27.45 / 8	-31.07 / 4	-23.54 / 5
GL	*PowerShares Glbl Sh Tm Hi Yld	PGHY	C+	22.92	24.00	22.11	C / 5.5	0.94	-0.11	3.41 / 75	--	--
GL	*PowerShares Global Agriculture P	PAGG	D	23.18	31.23	22.53	D / 2.0	-1.99	-20.97	-17.95 / 15	-7.51 / 21	-4.91 / 19
EN	*PowerShares Global Clean Energy	PBD	B+	11.42	13.75	9.64	B / 8.2	5.84	-9.58	-0.09 / 59	12.59 / 83	-2.58 / 23
IN	*PowerShares Global Listed Priv E	PSP	B+	10.52	12.41	9.01	B- / 7.3	-1.72	-8.92	1.67 / 70	10.12 / 75	6.96 / 54
EN	*PowerShares Global Water Portfol	PIO	C+	20.93	25.25	11.72	C+ / 5.8	1.77	-11.24	-7.15 / 33	6.38 / 66	2.86 / 37
GL	*PowerShares Golden Dragon China	PGJ	B+	32.90	36.36	23.00	A+ / 9.6	21.36	0.39	17.00 / 96	19.56 / 95	5.31 / 49
IN	*PowerShares High Yld Eq Div Ach	PEY	A	13.35	13.81	9.20	A- / 9.0	5.15	2.49	3.12 / 74	14.96 / 90	12.73 / 83
FO	*PowerShares India Portfolio	PIN	C-	19.52	23.69	17.85	C- / 4.2	-2.29	-11.05	-8.18 / 30	2.40 / 50	-3.51 / 22
GL	*PowerShares International Corp B	PICB	C-	25.23	28.18	25.04	C- / 3.2	-2.11	-2.57	-8.37 / 30	-2.40 / 30	2.14 / 34
FO	*PowerShares Intl BuyBack Achieve	IPKW	B-	26.01	29.08	23.12	C+ / 5.8	1.92	-4.65	7.30 / 84	--	--
FO	*PowerShares Intl Dividend Ach	PID	C-	13.58	18.72	13.09	D+ / 2.6	-6.88	-18.50	-18.95 / 14	-2.09 / 31	1.04 / 31
IN	*PowerShares KBW Bank	KBWB	B	37.59	41.60	33.98	B+ / 8.4	5.80	-4.74	0.34 / 63	12.86 / 84	--
IN	*PowerShares KBW Capital Markets	KBWC	B+	52.75	58.72	47.82	A / 9.3	7.16	-6.75	-2.39 / 49	19.31 / 95	--
GI	*PowerShares KBW High Div Yield F	KBWD	C	20.99	25.75	2.41	C / 4.4	-2.99	-10.40	-10.89 / 24	3.12 / 53	6.03 / 51
IN	*PowerShares KBW Insurance	KBWI	A-	69.14	74.41	45.22	A / 9.3	4.34	-2.42	0.77 / 66	18.04 / 93	--
IN	*PowerShares KBW Premium Yld Eq R	KBWY	C	30.45	38.11	27.67	C+ / 6.2	3.48	-0.28	-9.36 / 27	6.85 / 67	9.28 / 62
GR	*PowerShares KBW Prop & Casualty	KBWP	A	48.06	49.98	36.07	A / 9.5	6.66	6.07	16.26 / 96	19.06 / 94	16.59 / 94
IN	*PowerShares KBW Regional Banking	KBWR	A-	41.11	45.77	35.01	B+ / 8.9	4.53	-5.01	6.66 / 82	14.44 / 89	--
GI	*PowerShares Multi-Strategy Alt	LALT	C-	22.24	25.06	21.76	D+ / 2.3	-2.46	-3.64	-8.10 / 31	--	--
IN	*PowerShares NASDAQ Internet Port	PNQI	B-	80.23	83.50	55.56	A+ / 9.7	12.45	9.69	19.71 / 98	23.22 / 97	17.59 / 95
MUN	*PowerShares Natl AMT-Free Muni B	PZA	B-	25.47	25.94	24.67	C+ / 6.7	2.26	4.70	3.65 / 80	3.70 / 63	6.93 / 69
MUN	*PowerShares NY AMT-Free Muni Bon	PZT	B+	24.31	24.88	23.60	C+ / 6.5	1.49	3.56	2.74 / 77	3.48 / 62	6.01 / 62
GEI	*PowerShares Preferred Port	PGX	B-	14.95	14.95	11.16	B- / 7.3	4.24	5.81	7.53 / 84	6.65 / 66	7.72 / 57
GR	*PowerShares QQQ	QQQ	A	111.86	115.75	84.74	A / 9.5	7.88	3.94	9.50 / 87	20.21 / 95	16.24 / 93
GR	*PowerShares Rus 1000 Equal Weigh	EQAL	D-	23.66	26.41	22.40	D+ / 2.9	1.88	-5.72	-3.66 / 44	--	--
GR	*PowerShares Russell 2000 Equal W	EQWS	C+	31.89	37.73	30.47	C+ / 6.7	2.89	-10.71	-7.60 / 32	9.43 / 74	8.77 / 60
GR	*PowerShares Russell 2000 Pure Gr	PXSG	C+	24.51	27.02	18.08	B / 7.8	3.76	-5.02	1.03 / 67	10.77 / 78	9.23 / 62
GR	*PowerShares Russell 2000 Pure Va	PXSV	B	22.93	26.91	20.47	C+ / 6.9	1.62	-9.19	-8.33 / 30	10.19 / 76	10.54 / 68
GR	*PowerShares Russell Midcap Equal	EQWM	B-	36.55	41.51	33.06	B- / 7.4	2.43	-7.16	-6.51 / 35	11.10 / 79	9.61 / 63
GR	*PowerShares Russell Midcap Pure	PXMG	C	30.08	33.00	28.22	B- / 7.0	1.94	-6.33	-3.74 / 43	9.40 / 73	7.92 / 58
GR	*PowerShares Russell Midcap Pure	PXMV	A	24.78	28.43	17.67	B / 7.7	1.34	-6.59	-7.21 / 33	12.35 / 82	11.49 / 75
GR	*PowerShares Russell Top 200 Eq W	EQWL	B+	38.91	41.45	35.91	B+ / 8.7	6.33	-1.97	-1.54 / 52	14.14 / 88	12.08 / 79
GR	*PowerShares Russell Top 200 Pure	PXLG	A-	34.30	35.48	27.00	A- / 9.1	6.16	1.04	6.63 / 82	15.76 / 91	--
GR	*PowerShares Russell Top200 Pure	PXLV	B-	28.66	31.21	26.75	B- / 7.5	4.19	-4.66	-4.76 / 40	10.69 / 77	--
IN	*PowerShares S&P 500 BuyWrite Por	PBP	C+	20.51	21.84	12.71	C+ / 6.8	2.60	0.40	4.53 / 78	6.74 / 66	6.01 / 51
GI	*PowerShares S&P 500 Downside Hed	PHDG	C	24.68	28.21	23.66	C / 4.5	2.84	-3.67	-9.87 / 26	2.05 / 48	--
COH	*PowerShares S&P 500 Hi Div Low V	SPHD	A	33.34	34.21	19.83	A- / 9.0	6.23	6.29	4.86 / 79	13.96 / 88	--
IN	*Powershares S&P 500 High Beta Po	SPHB	B-	29.28	35.92	27.05	C+ / 6.5	0.44	-11.57	-12.66 / 21	9.86 / 75	--
IN	*PowerShares S&P 500 High Quality	SPHQ	A-	23.13	23.94	18.67	A- / 9.0	4.79	0.92	1.80 / 71	15.06 / 90	13.82 / 87
GR	*Powershares S&P 500 Low Vol Port	SPLV	A-	38.57	39.24	20.14	B+ / 8.9	6.88	5.04	3.90 / 76	13.50 / 86	--
EM	*PowerShares S&P EM High Beta	EEHB	D	14.21	23.60	12.74	D- / 1.1	-2.32	-28.68	-28.89 / 8	-15.05 / 12	--
EM	*PowerShares S&P EM Low Vol	EELV	D+	20.29	27.54	19.02	D / 1.8	-4.23	-17.48	-17.65 / 15	-8.81 / 19	--
FO	*PowerShares S&P Intl Dev Hi Beta	IDHB	D+	23.37	34.38	22.69	C- / 3.1	0.40	-19.79	-11.57 / 23	-0.76 / 34	--
FO	*PowerShares S&P Intl Dev High Qu	IDHQ	B	20.15	21.60	17.58	B- / 7.0	4.17	-2.09	8.51 / 86	7.12 / 67	4.71 / 46
FO	*PowerShares S&P Intl Dev Low Vol	IDLV	C+	28.60	32.95	19.07	C / 5.5	1.69	-5.31	-3.48 / 44	3.99 / 57	--
GR	*PowerShares S&P MidCap Low Vol	XMLV	B-	34.01	35.35	18.02	C+ / 6.9	4.74	2.61	5.17 / 79	--	--
GR	*PowerShares S&P SC Cnsmr Discr	PSCD	C+	45.92	59.99	45.08	C+ / 6.8	-4.37	-15.49	-7.96 / 31	10.98 / 78	11.62 / 76
GR	*PowerShares S&P SC Cnsmr Staples	PSCC	A-	54.90	62.76	43.61	A- / 9.1	0.43	-1.89	3.33 / 75	16.75 / 92	15.17 / 92
GR	*PowerShares S&P SC Energy	PSCE	E	15.37	32.81	14.35	E / 0.5	-10.66	-38.13	-48.26 / 2	-23.73 / 6	-13.61 / 10

* Denotes ETF Fund, N/A denotes number is not availabl

Incl. in Returns		RISK				NET ASSETS		VALUATION			ASSET					FUND MANAGER	
vidend Yield %	Expense Ratio	Risk Rating/ Pts	3 Year Standard Deviation	3 Year Beta	Avg Dura- tion	NAV as of 12/31/15	Total $(Mil)	Premium / Discount As of 12/31/15	Premium / Discount 1 Year Average	Wtd Avg P/E	Cash %	Stocks %	Bonds %	Other %	Portfolio Turnover Ratio	Manager Quality Pct	Manager Tenure (Years)
5.26	0.50	**C+ / 5.6**	N/A	N/A	N/A	16.36	5	1.10	-0.12	N/A	0	0	0	100	23	14	3
2.70	0.22	**B- / 7.8**	3.5	0.76	N/A	24.94	28	0.32	0.11	N/A	0	0	0	100	9	71	5
0.51	0.75	**C- / 4.0**	36.9	1.74	N/A	11.85	22	-0.84	-0.12	26.7	0	99	0	1	18	15	8
4.76	0.35	**B- / 7.5**	N/A	N/A	N/A	22.87	37	0.22	-0.22	N/A	0	0	0	100	29	86	3
2.52	0.75	**C+ / 5.9**	14.0	0.80	N/A	23.10	60	0.35	-0.16	58.9	0	99	0	1	22	15	8
1.94	0.76	**B- / 7.1**	19.9	0.64	N/A	11.46	82	-0.35	N/A	106.9	0	100	0	0	53	98	9
1.29	0.64	**B / 8.2**	13.2	1.03	N/A	10.53	552	-0.09	-0.06	15.7	0	100	0	0	30	36	9
1.67	0.76	**B- / 7.7**	14.1	0.55	N/A	20.99	281	-0.29	-0.21	90.1	0	99	0	1	28	94	9
0.18	0.70	**C+ / 5.8**	25.2	1.19	N/A	32.85	290	0.15	-0.14	58.2	0	99	0	1	25	97	9
4.72	0.54	**B- / 7.8**	10.5	0.84	N/A	13.34	432	0.07	-0.01	21.6	0	99	0	1	45	85	9
0.03	0.85	**B- / 7.0**	19.9	0.79	N/A	19.73	547	-1.06	0.04	N/A	0	100	0	0	49	57	8
2.28	0.50	**C+ / 6.7**	7.0	0.93	N/A	25.17	245	0.24	-0.04	N/A	0	0	100	0	17	77	6
1.40	0.55	**B / 8.4**	N/A	N/A	N/A	26.13	17	-0.46	0.24	N/A	0	0	0	100	130	92	2
5.68	0.55	**B- / 7.3**	13.5	0.92	N/A	13.62	1,348	-0.29	-0.09	39.6	0	99	0	1	66	25	9
2.50	0.35	**C+ / 6.8**	14.3	0.99	N/A	37.58	234	0.03	-0.01	N/A	0	0	0	100	5	65	5
2.51	0.35	**C+ / 6.6**	16.1	1.23	N/A	52.58	5	0.32	-0.03	N/A	0	0	0	100	16	71	5
7.42	0.35	**B- / 7.0**	11.3	0.77	N/A	20.99	260	0.00	-0.01	N/A	0	100	0	0	30	26	6
2.48	0.35	**B- / 7.0**	14.3	1.20	N/A	69.00	7	0.20	-0.05	N/A	0	100	0	0	14	76	5
6.02	0.35	**C+ / 6.0**	16.0	0.70	N/A	30.41	90	0.13	-0.03	N/A	0	99	0	1	27	49	6
2.73	0.35	**B- / 7.2**	11.8	0.83	N/A	47.76	10	0.63	0.04	N/A	0	99	0	1	4	92	6
2.99	0.35	**B- / 7.4**	17.7	1.02	N/A	41.11	33	0.00	-0.03	N/A	0	0	0	100	13	77	5
.00	N/A	**B / 8.9**	N/A	N/A	N/A	22.34	22	-0.45	-0.06	N/A	0	0	0	100	N/A	20	2
.00	0.60	**C / 4.8**	17.2	1.15	N/A	80.12	314	0.14	-0.01	328.7	0	99	0	1	31	91	8
3.70	0.28	**B- / 7.6**	5.5	1.51	14.1	25.40	706	0.28	0.14	N/A	2	0	97	1	15	59	9
.58	0.26	**B / 8.9**	5.3	1.41	14.2	24.46	47	-0.61	0.03	N/A	3	0	96	1	18	60	9
.79	0.50	**B- / 7.3**	4.5	1.08	N/A	14.91	2,258	0.27	0.10	N/A	0	0	0	100	13	90	8
.92	0.20	**B- / 7.3**	12.4	1.08	N/A	111.87	42,596	-0.01	-0.01	140.8	0	100	0	0	5	87	N/A
.85	N/A	**C- / 3.5**	N/A	N/A	N/A	23.54	N/A	0.51	-0.05	N/A	0	0	0	100	N/A	25	2
.75	0.39	**B- / 7.0**	13.5	1.06	N/A	31.87	15	0.06	0.07	51.1	0	99	0	1	7	34	9
.12	0.39	**C+ / 6.2**	12.3	0.92	N/A	24.37	29	0.57	-0.03	151.2	0	99	0	1	6	55	9
.51	0.39	**B- / 7.7**	14.9	1.09	N/A	22.93	63	0.00	-0.02	27.0	0	99	0	1	5	35	9
.49	0.39	**B- / 7.0**	11.2	1.02	N/A	36.41	32	0.38	0.01	62.6	0	99	0	1	5	45	9
.05	0.39	**C / 5.5**	11.0	0.97	N/A	29.85	89	0.77	-0.02	230.0	0	99	0	1	3	39	9
.18	0.39	**B / 8.8**	12.5	1.08	N/A	24.79	48	-0.04	-0.02	21.6	0	99	0	1	4	49	9
.54	0.39	**B- / 7.1**	11.6	1.06	N/A	38.81	42	0.26	-0.05	59.5	0	99	0	1	3	65	9
.98	0.39	**B- / 7.2**	10.5	0.95	N/A	34.11	124	0.56	-0.04	N/A	0	99	0	1	2	82	5
.31	0.39	**C+ / 6.9**	11.2	1.00	N/A	28.58	35	0.28	0.01	N/A	0	100	0	0	2	44	5
.36	0.75	**B- / 7.2**	6.9	0.55	N/A	20.50	378	0.05	0.04	60.7	0	100	0	0	50	61	9
.37	0.36	**B / 8.1**	7.3	0.57	N/A	24.70	422	-0.08	0.01	N/A	0	0	0	100	58	28	4
.58	0.30	**B- / 7.7**	9.5	1.10	N/A	33.32	177	0.06	-0.01	N/A	0	0	0	100	53	97	4
.30	0.25	**B- / 7.8**	15.2	1.27	N/A	29.29	290	-0.03	-0.05	N/A	0	99	0	1	78	23	5
.92	0.29	**B- / 7.4**	10.0	0.92	N/A	23.12	399	0.04	N/A	43.7	0	99	0	1	18	81	9
.13	0.25	**B- / 7.5**	10.2	0.77	N/A	38.56	4,547	0.03	-0.04	N/A	0	100	0	0	51	83	5
.52	0.29	**C / 5.5**	21.6	1.19	N/A	14.27	6	-0.42	-0.47	N/A	0	0	0	100	127	24	4
19	0.29	**C+ / 6.8**	13.0	0.84	N/A	20.56	233	-1.31	-0.17	N/A	0	0	0	100	82	41	4
.23	0.26	**C / 5.2**	20.2	1.36	N/A	23.30	4	0.30	0.96	N/A	0	0	0	100	109	22	4
.90	0.47	**B- / 7.6**	9.5	0.68	N/A	20.12	17	0.15	0.45	13.7	0	100	0	0	57	86	9
.06	0.25	**B / 8.1**	11.8	0.78	N/A	28.67	254	-0.24	0.06	N/A	0	0	0	100	61	66	4
.97	0.25	**B- / 7.4**	N/A	N/A	N/A	33.99	39	0.06	0.01	N/A	0	0	0	100	58	88	3
29	0.29	**C+ / 6.3**	15.7	1.09	N/A	45.80	104	0.26	0.03	N/A	0	99	0	1	13	39	6
30	0.29	**B- / 7.2**	13.0	0.87	N/A	54.56	18	0.62	-0.03	N/A	0	100	0	0	33	89	6
24	0.29	**D+ / 2.9**	36.1	1.55	N/A	15.38	35	-0.07	-0.03	N/A	0	100	0	0	27	1	6

Denotes ETF Fund, N/A denotes number is not available

99 Pct = Best
0 Pct = Worst

Fund Type	Fund Name	Ticker Symbol	Overall Investment Rating	PRICE: Price As of 12/31/15	52 Week High	52 Week Low	PERFORMANCE: Performance Rating/Pts	% Total Return Through 12/31/15: 3 Mo	6 Mo	1Yr/Pct	Annualized 3Yr/Pct	Annualized 5Yr/Pct
GR	*PowerShares S&P SC Financials	PSCF	**B**	40.78	44.37	35.95	**B / 7.9**	3.45	-2.47	0.46 / 64	11.28 / 79	11.31 / 74
GR	*PowerShares S&P SC Health Care	PSCH	**A**	71.87	75.50	43.25	**A+ / 9.7**	9.09	1.47	21.58 / 98	26.28 / 98	21.49 / 98
GR	*PowerShares S&P SC Industrials	PSCI	**C+**	43.23	48.64	40.86	**B- / 7.1**	4.08	-7.65	-3.36 / 45	9.70 / 74	9.42 / 63
GR	*PowerShares S&P SC Information T	PSCT	**A**	52.32	55.17	39.41	**A / 9.4**	7.83	0.51	5.74 / 81	18.25 / 94	12.54 / 82
GR	*PowerShares S&P SC Materials	PSCM	**D**	31.32	42.47	30.69	**D+ / 2.6**	-1.13	-19.94	-25.54 / 10	-1.47 / 32	3.18 / 39
GR	*PowerShares S&P SC Utilities	PSCU	**A-**	41.17	50.59	34.80	**A- / 9.1**	10.12	13.93	8.09 / 85	13.70 / 86	11.36 / 74
GR	*PowerShares S&P SmallCap Low Vol	XSLV	**C+**	33.75	36.42	16.15	**C+ / 6.4**	5.64	2.10	3.05 / 74	--	--
LP	*PowerShares Senior Loan	BKLN	**C+**	22.40	24.28	22.04	**C- / 4.0**	-1.77	-4.03	-2.89 / 47	0.37 / 39	--
GL	*PowerShares Variable Rate Prefer	VRP	**C+**	24.26	29.30	23.70	**C / 5.5**	1.35	0.70	2.65 / 73	--	--
MUH	*PowerShares VRDO Tax-Free Weekly	PVI	**B-**	24.91	24.96	24.83	**C- / 4.2**	-0.04	-0.20	-0.18 / 59	-0.08 / 37	0.07 / 28
IN	*PowerShares Water Resources	PHO	**C-**	21.67	26.33	20.16	**C- / 3.7**	3.14	-12.72	-15.21 / 17	1.45 / 45	3.67 / 41
EN	*PowerShares Wilder Clean Energy	PBW	**C**	4.74	6.00	3.65	**C+ / 5.7**	11.36	-9.96	-8.54 / 30	5.00 / 61	-12.65 / 11
EN	*PowerShares WilderHill Progr Ene	PUW	**D**	19.46	29.01	17.31	**D / 1.6**	-3.28	-26.41	-25.08 / 10	-8.27 / 19	-5.82 / 18
GR	*PowerShares Zacks Micro Cap	PZI	**B-**	15.48	16.69	14.26	**B- / 7.2**	6.20	-4.19	-2.80 / 47	9.36 / 73	6.77 / 54
GL	*Precidian Maxis Nikkei 225 Index	NKY	**B+**	18.48	20.07	16.59	**B / 7.7**	4.17	-6.38	8.42 / 85	9.42 / 74	--
GI	*Principal EDGE Active Income	YLD	**U**	36.82	N/A	N/A	**U /**	-0.02	--	--	--	--
GEI	*ProShares 30 Year TIPS TSY Sprea	RINF	**D+**	28.24	32.68	27.51	**D / 2.0**	1.10	-10.28	-8.77 / 29	-10.23 / 17	--
COH	*ProShares CDS N Amer HY Credit	TYTE	**C**	39.05	40.45	38.07	**C- / 3.8**	1.67	-0.89	-2.15 / 50	--	--
GL	*ProShares CDS Short NA HY Credit	WYDE	**C**	38.09	48.25	37.70	**C- / 3.1**	-3.00	-1.58	-2.81 / 47	--	--
GL	*ProShares DJ Brookfield Global I	TOLZ	**D+**	35.95	45.40	24.42	**D- / 1.2**	-5.17	-10.56	-14.12 / 19	--	--
GL	*ProShares German Sovereign Sub S	GGOV	**D+**	35.51	39.60	34.72	**D+ / 2.8**	-3.41	-3.99	-8.65 / 29	-4.22 / 26	--
GL	*ProShares Glb Lstd Priv Eqty	PEX	**C**	36.73	43.99	36.01	**C / 5.4**	3.51	-2.36	3.04 / 74	--	--
GL	*ProShares Hedge Replication ETF	HDG	**C+**	42.09	43.69	37.17	**C / 5.0**	1.11	-1.87	-0.05 / 60	1.47 / 45	--
FO	*ProShares Hedged FTSE Europe ETF	HGEU	**U**	37.09	N/A	N/A	**U /**	1.77	-3.30	--	--	--
FO	*ProShares Hedged FTSE Japan ETF	HGJP	**U**	35.80	N/A	N/A	**U /**	8.23	-6.33	--	--	--
COH	*ProShares Hi Yld-Int Rte Hdgd	HYHG	**C-**	62.57	76.38	60.93	**D / 1.7**	-1.27	-11.22	-9.65 / 26	--	--
GEI	*ProShares Investment Grd-Int Rte	IGHG	**C-**	73.21	79.20	71.80	**C- / 3.7**	1.27	-2.63	-1.45 / 53	--	--
IN	*ProShares Large Cap Core Plus	CSM	**C-**	49.36	51.92	27.33	**B+ / 8.9**	5.45	-0.69	-1.03 / 55	14.92 / 90	12.47 / 82
IN	*ProShares Managed Futures Strate	FUTS	**D**	20.76	22.22	16.20	**C- / 3.4**	-0.62	-1.00	-2.63 / 48	--	--
GL	*ProShares Merger ETF	MRGR	**C-**	36.40	38.83	34.52	**C- / 3.6**	0.14	0.28	-0.69 / 56	-2.28 / 30	--
GL	*ProShares Mornstr Alt Solutiion	ALTS	**C-**	38.47	41.98	30.42	**D+ / 2.7**	-0.03	-3.26	-5.73 / 36	--	--
FO	*ProShares MSCI EAFE Div Grower	EFAD	**C-**	36.24	40.89	34.47	**C- / 4.0**	0.92	-3.84	1.08 / 67	--	--
FO	*ProShares MSCI Europe Div Grower	EUDV	**U**	39.62	N/A	N/A	**U /**	2.34	--	--	--	--
IN	*ProShares RAFI Long/Short	RALS	**C**	38.91	42.32	38.64	**C / 4.5**	0.36	-3.02	-6.40 / 35	1.75 / 47	-0.38 / 27
IN	*ProShares Russell 2000 Dividend	SMDV	**U**	40.21	N/A	N/A	**U /**	6.07	0.56	--	--	--
GR	*ProShares S&P 500 Div Aristocrat	NOBL	**C**	49.33	51.35	36.98	**C / 5.5**	5.18	0.01	0.51 / 64	--	--
GR	*ProShares S&P 500 Ex-Energy ETF	SPXE	**U**	42.45	N/A	N/A	**U /**	7.21	--	--	--	--
GR	*ProShares S&P 500 Ex-Financials	SPXN	**U**	43.13	N/A	N/A	**U /**	9.03	--	--	--	--
GR	*ProShares S&P 500 Ex-Health Care	SPXV	**U**	42.78	N/A	N/A	**U /**	7.71	--	--	--	--
GR	*ProShares S&P MC 400 Div Aristoc	REGL	**U**	39.32	N/A	N/A	**U /**	3.56	-1.34	--	--	--
EM	*ProShares Sh Trm USD Em Mkts Bd	EMSH	**A**	75.60	78.00	70.34	**B- / 7.5**	0.19	2.57	10.19 / 88	--	--
USA	*ProShares Short 20+ Year Treas	TBF	**D**	24.73	26.85	22.87	**D+ / 2.7**	1.90	-6.61	-0.72 / 56	-6.29 / 23	-11.22 / 12
GEI	*ProShares Short 7-10 Year Treasu	TBX	**C-**	29.52	31.90	25.01	**C- / 3.2**	1.60	-2.53	-2.91 / 47	-3.33 / 28	--
GR	*ProShares Short Dow30	DOG	**D**	22.60	27.35	22.07	**D / 1.8**	-6.65	-1.27	-2.92 / 47	-12.36 / 14	-12.45 / 12
GI	*ProShares Short Euro	EUFX	**B+**	43.74	46.16	40.26	**C+ / 6.4**	2.68	1.28	8.45 / 86	4.76 / 60	--
FS	*ProShares Short Financials	SEF	**D**	16.87	19.05	16.28	**D- / 1.5**	-6.64	-1.29	-3.65 / 44	-14.84 / 12	-14.13 / 10
FO	*ProShares Short FTSE China 50	YXI	**D+**	29.13	33.41	21.59	**C- / 3.4**	0.73	18.41	3.96 / 76	-5.36 / 24	-7.39 / 16
GEI	*ProShares Short High Yield	SJB	**C-**	28.65	29.76	26.20	**C- / 3.5**	0.03	5.41	2.36 / 72	-3.55 / 28	--
COI	*ProShares Short Inv Grade Corp	IGS	**C**	28.34	29.25	27.47	**C- / 3.1**	0.15	-2.61	-0.45 / 57	-4.20 / 26	--
GR	*ProShares Short Midcap 400	MYY	**D**	16.26	18.18	15.10	**D / 1.9**	-2.34	4.84	-0.85 / 56	-12.69 / 14	-13.24 / 11
FO	*ProShares Short MSCI EAFE	EFZ	**C-**	33.47	37.09	30.30	**D+ / 2.7**	-2.28	5.42	-3.43 / 45	-6.64 / 22	-8.01 / 16
EM	*ProShares Short MSCI Emg Mkts	EUM	**C+**	29.46	32.92	23.06	**C+ / 6.6**	1.76	16.72	10.67 / 89	3.87 / 57	-0.96 / 25

* Denotes ETF Fund, N/A denotes number is not availabl

ncl. in Returns		RISK				NET ASSETS		VALUATION			ASSET					FUND MANAGER	
vidend Yield %	Expense Ratio	Risk Rating/ Pts	3 Year Standard Deviation	3 Year Beta	Avg Dura-tion	NAV as of 12/31/15	Total $(Mil)	Premium / Discount As of 12/31/15	Premium / Discount 1 Year Average	Wtd Avg P/E	Cash %	Stocks %	Bonds %	Other %	Portfolio Turnover Ratio	Manager Quality Pct	Manager Tenure (Years)
4.52	0.29	B- / 7.2	12.5	0.87	N/A	40.74	104	0.10	-0.08	N/A	0	99	0	1	16	63	6
0.00	0.29	C+ / 6.9	14.8	0.78	N/A	71.79	151	0.11	0.05	N/A	0	100	0	0	27	97	6
1.39	0.29	C+ / 6.6	17.2	1.28	N/A	43.20	104	0.07	-0.09	N/A	0	100	0	0	15	23	6
0.15	0.29	B- / 7.2	14.4	0.99	N/A	52.27	215	0.10	0.02	N/A	0	99	0	1	10	87	6
2.16	0.29	C / 4.7	19.4	1.46	N/A	31.27	58	0.16	-0.15	N/A	0	99	0	1	12	8	6
2.93	0.29	B- / 7.1	15.0	0.85	N/A	41.14	35	0.07	-0.08	N/A	0	100	0	0	34	81	6
3.85	0.25	B- / 7.1	N/A	N/A	N/A	33.72	55	0.09	0.05	N/A	0	0	0	100	68	80	3
4.42	0.64	B+ / 9.0	2.6	1.95	N/A	22.43	6,475	-0.13	-0.13	N/A	0	0	0	100	61	72	5
4.95	0.50	B- / 7.8	N/A	N/A	N/A	24.16	80	0.41	0.27	N/A	0	0	0	100	6	86	2
0.00	0.25	B+ / 9.9	0.3	-0.02	12.1	24.92	124	-0.04	-0.02	N/A	6	0	93	1	34	67	9
0.85	0.61	B- / 7.3	15.6	1.27	N/A	21.69	919	-0.09	-0.08	78.8	0	99	0	1	25	11	9
0.51	0.70	C+ / 6.0	26.1	0.74	N/A	4.75	174	-0.21	-0.10	55.7	0	99	0	1	48	95	9
1.21	0.70	C+ / 6.1	20.4	0.96	N/A	19.48	37	-0.10	-0.06	41.7	0	99	0	1	41	37	9
0.68	0.70	C+ / 6.9	14.8	1.05	N/A	15.43	33	0.32	-0.18	23.6	0	99	0	1	115	35	9
1.12	0.50	B / 8.4	14.1	0.10	N/A	18.79	120	-1.65	-0.10	N/A	0	0	0	100	3	95	5
6.08	N/A	U /	N/A	N/A	N/A	36.35	N/A	1.29	N/A	N/A	0	0	0	100	N/A	N/A	1
1.63	0.75	B- / 7.1	8.9	-0.71	N/A	28.29	5	-0.18	0.14	N/A	0	0	0	100	110	17	4
0.00	0.50	B- / 7.6	N/A	N/A	N/A	38.55	N/A	1.30	0.19	N/A	0	0	0	100	N/A	77	2
0.00	0.50	B+ / 9.4	N/A	N/A	N/A	38.27	N/A	-0.47	-0.08	N/A	0	0	0	100	N/A	40	2
6.92	0.45	B- / 7.7	N/A	N/A	N/A	36.06	20	-0.31	0.05	N/A	0	0	0	100	11	11	2
0.29	0.45	C+ / 6.4	7.0	0.68	N/A	35.39	6	0.34	0.80	N/A	0	0	0	100	45	57	4
5.66	0.60	C+ / 6.1	N/A	N/A	N/A	36.59	10	0.38	0.12	N/A	0	0	0	100	18	80	3
0.00	0.95	B- / 7.9	4.0	0.28	N/A	42.02	34	0.17	0.01	N/A	0	0	0	100	164	70	3
4.11	N/A	U /	N/A	N/A	N/A	36.93	N/A	0.43	N/A	N/A	0	0	0	100	N/A	N/A	1
0.07	N/A	U /	N/A	N/A	N/A	35.97	N/A	-0.47	N/A	N/A	0	0	0	100	N/A	N/A	1
6.00	0.50	B- / 7.9	N/A	N/A	N/A	63.00	173	-0.68	0.06	N/A	0	0	0	100	82	38	3
3.35	0.30	B- / 7.3	N/A	N/A	N/A	72.99	124	0.30	0.16	N/A	0	0	0	100	43	54	3
1.21	0.45	D / 1.9	11.0	1.04	N/A	49.31	379	0.10	-0.01	N/A	0	97	0	3	49	69	3
0.00	N/A	C / 4.3	N/A	N/A	N/A	20.53	N/A	1.12	0.85	N/A	0	0	0	100	N/A	51	2
0.12	0.75	B- / 7.5	4.2	-0.06	N/A	36.26	2	0.39	0.47	N/A	0	0	0	100	332	50	3
0.40	0.16	B- / 7.6	N/A	N/A	N/A	38.16	N/A	0.81	0.31	N/A	0	0	0	100	34	27	N/A
1.78	0.50	C+ / 6.6	N/A	N/A	N/A	36.04	N/A	0.55	0.50	N/A	0	0	0	100	24	75	2
1.48	N/A	U /	N/A	N/A	N/A	38.96	N/A	1.69	N/A	N/A	0	0	0	100	N/A	N/A	1
2.14	0.95	B- / 7.3	5.4	0.08	N/A	38.78	63	0.34	0.01	N/A	0	0	0	100	65	71	3
1.64	N/A	U /	N/A	N/A	N/A	40.24	N/A	-0.07	N/A	N/A	0	0	0	100	N/A	N/A	1
2.36	0.35	B- / 7.3	N/A	N/A	N/A	49.28	259	0.10	0.02	N/A	0	0	0	100	18	61	3
2.06	N/A	U /	N/A	N/A	N/A	42.29	N/A	0.38	N/A	N/A	0	0	0	100	N/A	N/A	1
2.09	N/A	U /	N/A	N/A	N/A	42.04	N/A	2.59	N/A	N/A	0	0	0	100	N/A	N/A	1
2.22	N/A	U /	N/A	N/A	N/A	42.18	N/A	1.42	N/A	N/A	0	0	0	100	N/A	N/A	1
1.35	N/A	U /	N/A	N/A	N/A	39.20	N/A	0.31	N/A	N/A	0	0	0	100	N/A	N/A	N/A
5.60	0.50	B+ / 9.1	N/A	N/A	N/A	75.71	8	-0.15	-0.46	N/A	0	0	0	100	106	92	N/A
0.00	0.95	C / 5.3	11.7	-1.13	N/A	24.72	1,514	0.04	-0.03	N/A	9	0	0	91	N/A	44	7
0.00	0.95	B- / 7.8	5.6	-1.86	N/A	29.52	71	0.00	-0.06	N/A	0	0	0	100	N/A	63	5
0.00	0.95	C / 5.0	10.8	-0.99	N/A	22.59	285	0.04	N/A	N/A	8	0	0	92	N/A	67	3
0.00	0.96	B / 8.8	8.4	-0.15	N/A	43.78	17	-0.09	N/A	N/A	0	0	0	100	N/A	93	4
0.00	0.95	C+ / 6.4	11.1	-0.98	N/A	16.94	20	-0.41	-0.01	N/A	20	0	0	80	N/A	41	3
0.00	0.95	C+ / 5.6	21.2	-0.91	N/A	29.18	5	-0.17	0.19	N/A	23	0	0	77	N/A	53	6
0.00	0.95	B- / 7.7	6.0	-0.81	N/A	28.65	80	0.00	-0.01	N/A	0	0	0	100	N/A	45	5
0.00	0.95	B / 8.5	5.5	-1.15	N/A	28.38	3	-0.14	0.21	N/A	0	0	0	100	N/A	48	5
0.00	0.95	C+ / 5.7	11.9	-0.99	N/A	16.26	134	0.00	N/A	N/A	0	0	0	100	N/A	60	3
0.00	0.95	B- / 7.4	12.6	-0.98	N/A	33.55	228	-0.24	-0.02	N/A	11	0	0	89	N/A	50	7
0.00	0.95	C+ / 6.9	14.6	-0.98	N/A	29.46	234	0.00	-0.03	N/A	14	0	0	86	N/A	41	7

Denotes ETF Fund, N/A denotes number is not available

Fund Type	Fund Name (99 Pct = Best, 0 Pct = Worst)	Ticker Symbol	Overall Investment Rating	PRICE: Price As of 12/31/15	PRICE: 52 Week High	PRICE: 52 Week Low	PERFORMANCE: Performance Rating/Pts	% Total Return Through 12/31/15: 3 Mo	6 Mo	1Yr/Pct	Annualized: 3Yr/Pct	Annualized: 5Yr/Pct
IN	*ProShares Short Oil and Gas	DDG	C+	31.03	34.83	24.16	C+ / 6.6	2.58	16.13	19.35 / 98	0.14 / 38	-5.16 / 19
GR	*ProShares Short QQQ	PSQ	D	52.20	64.45	50.81	D- / 1.0	-8.13	-6.49	-12.46 / 21	-19.43 / 8	-17.33 / 6
GI	*ProShares Short Real Estate	REK	D+	19.28	23.11	18.77	D / 1.9	-6.63	-7.70	-4.73 / 40	-11.00 / 16	-13.62 / 10
GR	*ProShares Short Russell 2000	RWM	D	62.11	66.43	56.20	D / 1.9	-3.36	6.57	0.05 / 61	-12.90 / 14	-13.49 / 11
GR	*ProShares Short S&P500	SH	D+	20.87	23.90	20.33	D / 1.6	-5.73	-1.51	-4.31 / 41	-14.21 / 13	-13.61 / 10
GR	*ProShares Short Small Cap 600	SBB	D	51.77	85.82	48.07	D / 1.7	-3.99	3.97	-2.41 / 49	-13.92 / 13	-14.75 / 9
GI	*ProShares Short VIX Sh-Tm Fut ET	SVXY	D	50.45	98.12	41.64	C+ / 5.8	-0.59	-36.52	-18.98 / 14	10.72 / 77	--
GL	*ProShares Ult Hmbldrs and Suppli	HBU	U	18.89	N/A	N/A	U /	6.12	-5.46	--	--	--
EN	*ProShares Ult Oil and Gas Ex and	UOP	U	21.51	N/A	N/A	U /	-26.55	-62.53	--	--	--
IN	*ProShares Ult Telecommunications	LTL	B	83.01	102.17	55.08	B / 7.9	16.07	-9.35	-5.87 / 36	11.58 / 80	9.76 / 64
HL	*ProShares UltPro Sht Nasdaq Biot	ZBIO	U	20.51	N/A	N/A	U /	-28.19	-6.52	--	--	--
USA	*ProShares Ultra 20+ Year Treasur	UBT	C	73.26	97.00	66.60	C / 5.5	-6.35	8.31	-9.46 / 27	4.43 / 59	14.83 / 91
USA	*ProShares Ultra 7-10 Year Treasu	UST	C+	56.13	60.35	53.60	C / 5.3	-4.21	3.14	0.96 / 67	2.22 / 50	8.03 / 58
IN	*ProShares Ultra Basic Materials	UYM	D	36.18	55.50	28.36	D+ / 2.8	11.98	-23.47	-27.32 / 8	-0.84 / 34	-5.26 / 19
IN	*ProShares Ultra Bloomberg Commod	UCD	E+	28.07	52.84	13.04	E / 0.3	-20.94	-41.75	-45.56 / 2	-33.10 / 3	-27.26 / 3
EN	*ProShares Ultra Bloomberg Crude	UCO	E-	12.54	53.60	11.56	E- / 0.0	-45.24	-69.49	-74.69 / 0	-56.35 / 1	-44.40 / 1
EN	*ProShares Ultra Bloomberg Nat Ga	BOIL	E-	18.48	78.48	12.42	E- / 0.0	-38.69	-59.27	-71.16 / 1	-50.14 / 1	--
IN	*ProShares Ultra Consumer Goods	UGE	C+	105.50	109.53	53.41	A+ / 9.8	14.16	6.78	11.83 / 91	28.20 / 98	25.68 / 99
IN	*ProShares Ultra Consumer Service	UCC	C	106.68	118.79	36.07	A+ / 9.8	11.18	0.01	9.62 / 87	37.33 / 99	34.11 / 99
GR	*ProShares Ultra Dow30	DDM	C	64.30	71.69	48.50	A / 9.5	12.25	-3.10	-3.48 / 44	21.17 / 96	19.16 / 97
FO	*ProShares Ultra Euro	ULE	D-	15.51	19.39	14.67	D- / 1.3	-6.62	-5.43	-20.91 / 13	-13.69 / 13	-8.39 / 15
FS	*ProShares Ultra Financials	UYG	C+	71.00	80.95	57.21	A+ / 9.6	9.96	-5.32	-4.45 / 41	25.43 / 97	16.49 / 94
FO	*ProShares Ultra FTSE China 50	XPP	E	48.35	109.51	40.80	D- / 1.3	-6.10	-41.11	-30.36 / 7	-9.84 / 18	-8.41 / 15
FO	*ProShares Ultra FTSR Europe	UPV	C-	39.96	54.00	35.00	C / 5.4	0.40	-15.59	-5.87 / 36	5.16 / 62	3.79 / 42
PM	*ProShares Ultra Gold	UGL	E	29.73	46.80	29.25	E / 0.5	-13.93	-18.81	-23.18 / 11	-29.12 / 4	-14.63 / 9
PM	*ProShares Ultra Gold Miners	GDXX	U	20.75	N/A	N/A	U /	-14.74	-47.50	--	--	--
HL	*ProShares Ultra Health Care	RXL	C	65.98	80.30	31.00	A+ / 9.9	9.67	-11.53	7.32 / 84	44.94 / 99	38.24 / 99
COH	*ProShares Ultra High Yield	UJB	C-	47.78	63.34	46.00	C- / 3.0	-4.25	-14.99	-13.40 / 20	-1.20 / 33	--
IN	*ProShares Ultra Industrials	UXI	B+	106.85	125.13	85.59	A / 9.5	12.41	-5.66	-6.70 / 34	22.78 / 96	18.07 / 96
COI	*ProShares Ultra Invest Grade Cor	IGU	C	57.38	64.63	56.63	C / 5.1	1.10	0.76	-2.07 / 50	1.86 / 48	--
GL	*ProShares Ultra Junior Miners	GDJJ	U	25.50	N/A	N/A	U /	-15.59	-43.56	--	--	--
GR	*ProShares Ultra MidCap 400	MVV	C	67.86	84.00	60.06	A- / 9.1	1.92	-13.95	-7.38 / 32	19.69 / 95	16.35 / 94
FO	*ProShares Ultra MSCI Brazil Capp	UBR	E-	25.45	92.64	24.54	E- / 0.0	-20.19	-62.79	-68.36 / 1	-51.29 / 1	-43.04 / 1
IN	*ProShares Ultra MSCI EAFE	EFO	C-	90.02	122.45	81.84	C / 5.1	4.33	-15.31	-6.37 / 35	3.70 / 56	1.68 / 32
EM	*ProShares Ultra MSCI Emerging Mk	EET	E+	44.98	84.40	33.00	E+ / 0.7	-7.39	-34.57	-31.27 / 7	-20.07 / 8	-16.04 / 8
FO	*ProShares Ultra MSCI Japan	EZJ	C+	88.18	107.44	72.14	B+ / 8.5	9.66	-12.55	13.77 / 94	12.54 / 83	2.19 / 34
FO	*ProShares Ultra MSCI Mex Cap IMI	UMX	E	24.12	35.67	21.64	E+ / 0.7	-2.93	-22.02	-27.79 / 8	-22.43 / 7	-10.72 / 13
FO	*ProShares Ultra MSCI Pacific ex-	UXJ	D-	27.43	44.09	24.00	D / 1.8	6.00	-22.06	-20.32 / 13	-9.21 / 18	-4.15 / 20
HL	*ProShares Ultra Nasdaq Biotech	BIB	C-	71.49	106.10	51.95	A+ / 9.9	12.94	-21.34	11.86 / 91	65.97 / 99	56.19 / 99
EN	*ProShares Ultra Oil and Gas	DIG	D-	29.93	59.26	28.31	E+ / 0.9	-11.23	-36.20	-44.45 / 2	-14.45 / 12	-7.78 / 16
GR	*ProShares Ultra QQQ	QLD	C	78.36	83.77	55.00	A+ / 9.9	15.39	5.50	15.22 / 95	40.03 / 99	29.80 / 99
IN	*ProShares Ultra Real Estate	URE	C+	104.54	124.58	84.17	A- / 9.0	10.97	9.65	-2.74 / 47	14.50 / 89	17.17 / 95
GR	*ProShares Ultra Russell2000	UWM	B+	79.14	104.39	71.78	B+ / 8.8	3.43	-18.03	-11.30 / 23	17.65 / 93	13.05 / 85
FS	*ProShares Ultra S&P Regional Ban	KRU	B	98.88	118.30	73.89	A+ / 9.7	11.53	-8.08	13.18 / 93	26.05 / 97	16.69 / 94
GR	*ProShares Ultra S&P500	SSO	C+	63.00	69.13	50.00	A+ / 9.7	9.75	-3.36	-1.06 / 55	26.17 / 97	21.38 / 98
IN	*ProShares Ultra Semiconductors	USD	B-	86.62	104.99	52.00	A+ / 9.8	27.13	0.01	-7.94 / 31	40.06 / 99	16.64 / 94
EN	*ProShares Ultra Silver	AGQ	E-	27.08	52.29	26.55	E- / 0.1	-19.04	-25.36	-29.52 / 8	-46.21 / 1	-37.05 / 2
GR	*ProShares Ultra SmallCap 600	SAA	C	53.85	65.30	30.50	A / 9.5	9.26	-11.29	-3.21 / 46	22.56 / 96	18.45 / 96
GR	*ProShares Ultra Technology	ROM	C	78.74	85.68	29.01	A+ / 9.8	14.13	2.88	4.04 / 77	29.47 / 98	18.85 / 97
UT	*ProShares Ultra Utilities	UPW	B	92.00	118.50	78.40	A / 9.3	6.83	9.19	-13.27 / 20	19.65 / 95	19.01 / 97
GI	*ProShares Ultra VIX Sh-Tm Fut ET	UVXY	E-	28.35	170.05	23.83	E- / 0.0	-42.14	-33.42	-76.70 / 0	-79.00 / 0	--
FO	*ProShares Ultra Yen	YCL	D-	54.70	59.88	50.86	D- / 1.2	-0.98	3.46	-2.39 / 49	-20.53 / 8	-15.64 / 8

* Denotes ETF Fund, N/A denotes number is not available

ncl. in Returns		RISK				NET ASSETS		VALUATION			ASSET					FUND MANAGER	
			3 Year					Premium / Discount									
idend ield %	Expense Ratio	Risk Rating/ Pts	Standard Deviation	Beta	Avg Dura-tion	NAV as of 12/31/15	Total $(Mil)	As of 12/31/15	1 Year Average	Wtd Avg P/E	Cash %	Stocks %	Bonds %	Other %	Portfolio Turnover Ratio	Manager Quality Pct	Manager Tenure (Years)
.00	0.95	C+ / 6.5	19.3	-1.18	N/A	31.06	2	-0.10	0.01	N/A	13	0	0	87	N/A	98	3
.00	0.95	C+ / 6.4	12.1	-1.05	N/A	52.22	257	-0.04	N/A	N/A	10	0	0	90	N/A	21	3
.00	0.95	C+ / 6.9	13.5	-0.45	N/A	19.37	39	-0.46	-0.03	N/A	0	0	0	100	N/A	26	3
.00	0.95	C / 4.8	14.2	-1.06	N/A	62.05	946	0.10	0.02	N/A	7	0	0	93	N/A	66	3
.00	0.90	C+ / 6.7	10.5	-0.99	N/A	20.88	1,642	-0.05	-0.01	N/A	3	0	0	97	N/A	48	3
.00	0.95	C / 5.3	12.7	-1.02	N/A	51.74	10	0.06	-0.24	N/A	2	0	0	98	N/A	52	3
.00	1.49	D / 1.8	66.9	5.02	N/A	50.82	277	-0.73	-0.20	N/A	0	0	0	100	N/A	1	N/A
.00	N/A	U /	N/A	N/A	N/A	18.66	N/A	1.23	N/A	N/A	0	0	0	100	N/A	N/A	1
.01	N/A	U /	N/A	N/A	N/A	21.56	N/A	-0.23	N/A	N/A	0	0	0	100	N/A	N/A	1
.38	0.95	C+ / 6.9	32.6	1.46	N/A	84.35	7	-1.59	-0.73	26.2	22	45	0	33	158	21	3
.00	N/A	U /	N/A	N/A	N/A	20.45	N/A	0.29	N/A	N/A	0	0	0	100	N/A	N/A	3
.75	0.95	C+ / 6.6	24.2	2.29	N/A	74.08	34	-1.11	-0.02	N/A	1	63	0	36	48	44	6
.90	0.95	B / 8.4	10.9	0.98	N/A	56.20	21	-0.12	0.01	N/A	14	0	9	77	349	60	6
.56	0.95	C / 4.3	32.7	2.49	N/A	36.04	102	0.39	-0.03	48.5	10	41	0	49	9	3	3
.00	0.95	C- / 4.0	28.3	0.89	N/A	28.43	3	-1.27	0.28	N/A	0	100	0	0	N/A	1	N/A
.00	0.99	D / 1.8	67.5	2.20	N/A	12.58	184	-0.32	-0.17	N/A	0	100	0	0	N/A	N/A	N/A
.00	1.13	D / 1.8	68.9	-0.07	N/A	18.57	71	-0.48	-0.05	N/A	0	0	0	100	N/A	N/A	N/A
.61	0.95	C- / 3.1	23.2	1.98	N/A	104.33	26	1.12	-0.07	33.6	18	57	0	25	34	65	3
.15	0.95	D+ / 2.9	25.4	2.19	N/A	106.64	24	0.04	-0.04	145.2	34	25	0	41	54	83	3
.08	0.95	D+ / 2.9	22.7	2.06	N/A	64.32	286	-0.03	N/A	N/A	41	48	0	11	9	21	9
.00	0.95	C / 4.9	17.1	0.48	N/A	15.51	2	0.00	0.03	N/A	0	0	100	0	N/A	10	N/A
.36	0.95	C- / 3.5	23.2	2.03	N/A	71.01	787	-0.01	-0.02	35.3	0	99	0	1	7	37	3
.00	0.95	D / 1.7	44.1	1.89	N/A	48.33	49	0.04	0.04	N/A	80	0	0	20	N/A	9	7
.00	0.95	C / 4.6	28.2	2.11	N/A	39.79	21	0.43	0.02	N/A	47	0	0	53	N/A	30	7
.00	0.95	D+ / 2.3	33.3	1.85	N/A	29.73	113	0.00	0.20	N/A	0	0	0	100	N/A	22	N/A
.00	N/A	U /	N/A	N/A	N/A	21.00	N/A	-1.19	N/A	N/A	0	0	0	100	N/A	N/A	1
.26	0.95	D / 2.1	26.2	1.97	N/A	65.99	121	-0.02	-0.01	104.3	0	99	0	1	22	96	3
.85	0.95	B- / 7.5	13.0	2.23	N/A	49.02	3	-2.53	-0.35	N/A	34	0	0	66	387	36	5
.49	0.95	C+ / 5.9	26.5	2.30	N/A	106.74	31	0.10	0.03	39.4	0	99	0	1	23	18	3
.34	0.95	C+ / 6.8	10.6	2.39	N/A	57.07	3	0.54	-0.37	N/A	15	0	0	85	N/A	52	5
.00	N/A	U /	N/A	N/A	N/A	25.69	N/A	-0.74	N/A	N/A	0	0	0	100	N/A	N/A	1
.17	0.95	D+ / 2.6	24.2	1.99	N/A	67.72	774	0.21	-0.02	78.7	0	100	0	0	56	21	3
.00	0.95	D / 1.8	61.3	2.98	N/A	26.17	13	-2.75	0.07	N/A	23	0	0	77	N/A	N/A	6
.00	0.95	C / 4.6	28.7	2.21	N/A	89.66	47	0.40	0.78	N/A	51	0	0	49	N/A	5	7
.00	0.95	D+ / 2.8	31.0	2.06	N/A	44.88	45	0.22	0.05	N/A	39	14	0	47	N/A	21	7
.00	0.95	C / 5.0	29.4	1.61	N/A	87.57	25	0.70	-0.01	N/A	12	0	0	88	N/A	87	7
.00	0.95	D / 2.2	33.0	1.61	N/A	23.86	7	1.09	-0.12	N/A	36	0	0	64	N/A	3	6
.00	0.95	C / 4.3	35.6	1.97	N/A	28.57	2	-3.99	0.61	N/A	50	0	0	50	N/A	7	6
.00	0.95	E- / 0.2	44.7	2.31	N/A	71.43	327	0.08	0.02	N/A	21	59	0	20	41	98	3
.11	0.95	C- / 4.1	39.0	2.04	N/A	29.94	137	-0.03	-0.01	15.2	0	99	0	1	15	28	3
.12	0.95	D / 2.1	25.6	2.19	N/A	78.33	904	0.04	0.01	140.0	0	100	0	0	8	88	3
.70	0.95	C / 5.0	27.9	1.03	N/A	104.45	257	0.09	-0.01	83.8	0	99	0	1	14	72	3
.50	0.95	C+ / 6.9	29.3	2.15	N/A	79.34	524	-0.25	-0.04	75.2	0	99	0	1	179	15	3
.75	0.95	C / 5.0	34.5	2.35	N/A	96.52	8	2.45	-0.13	N/A	0	63	22	15	77	23	3
.92	0.89	C- / 3.3	21.8	2.03	N/A	63.03	2,127	-0.05	-0.02	N/A	0	99	0	1	31	38	3
.48	0.95	C / 4.5	33.0	2.13	N/A	86.17	44	0.52	-0.09	N/A	0	99	0	1	50	91	3
.00	0.95	E / 0.3	52.4	0.62	N/A	27.06	357	0.07	0.60	N/A	0	0	0	100	N/A	N/A	N/A
00	0.95	D / 2.2	27.4	2.10	N/A	52.96	22	1.68	-0.08	89.9	0	99	0	1	17	24	3
14	0.95	D+ / 2.5	25.1	2.09	N/A	78.26	171	0.61	-0.06	67.3	0	99	0	1	14	48	3
39	0.95	C / 5.5	29.3	1.96	N/A	91.00	25	1.10	-0.04	23.6	0	99	0	1	7	42	3
00	1.80	E- / 0.1	N/A	-9.17	N/A	28.09	284	0.93	0.36	N/A	0	0	0	100	N/A	2	N/A
00	0.95	C / 5.3	15.8	-0.25	N/A	54.75	2	-0.09	-0.03	N/A	0	0	0	100	N/A	7	N/A

Denotes ETF Fund, N/A denotes number is not available

Fund Type	Fund Name (99 Pct = Best, 0 Pct = Worst)	Ticker Symbol	Overall Investment Rating	PRICE: Price As of 12/31/15	PRICE: 52 Week High	PRICE: 52 Week Low	PERFORMANCE: Performance Rating/Pts	% Total Return Through 12/31/15: 3 Mo	6 Mo	1Yr/Pct	Annualized: 3Yr/Pct	Annualized: 5Yr/Pct
GR	*ProShares UltraPro Dow30	UDOW	C+	64.54	77.06	44.50	A+ / 9.7	18.28	-6.84	-8.48 / 30	30.37 / 98	26.18 / 99
GI	*ProShares UltraPro Finl Sel Sect	FINU	C-	80.27	97.36	47.99	A+ / 9.8	17.74	-9.51	-8.19 / 30	37.28 / 99	--
GR	*ProShares UltraPro MidCap400	UMDD	C-	50.01	69.20	37.72	A+ / 9.6	3.71	-21.15	-12.65 / 21	28.74 / 98	20.48 / 98
HL	*ProShares UltraPro Nasdaq Biotec	UBIO	U	57.85	N/A	N/A	U /	18.61	-34.34	--	--	--
GR	*ProShares UltraPro QQQ	TQQQ	C	114.14	128.65	65.40	A+ / 9.9	22.63	4.88	17.94 / 97	60.47 / 99	41.79 / 99
GR	*ProShares UltraPro Russell2000	URTY	C	74.12	115.00	64.73	A- / 9.2	3.97	-27.68	-19.62 / 14	23.43 / 97	13.14 / 85
IN	*ProShares UltraPro S&P500	UPRO	C	62.56	73.65	43.50	A+ / 9.8	14.23	-7.36	-5.08 / 38	38.19 / 99	29.06 / 99
GR	*ProShares UltraPro Short Dow30	SDOW	E+	17.72	29.46	16.66	E / 0.4	-19.78	-7.76	-13.85 / 19	-34.65 / 3	-35.92 / 2
GR	*ProShares UltraPro Short MidCap4	SMDD	E+	34.28	42.82	28.62	E / 0.5	-7.65	10.76	-7.80 / 31	-36.22 / 2	-39.84 / 1
GR	*ProShares UltraPro Short QQQ	SQQQ	E-	18.72	44.86	17.37	E- / 0.1	-23.59	-22.64	-37.77 / 4	-50.09 / 1	-47.31 / 1
GR	*ProShares UltraPro Short S&P500	SPXU	E-	31.71	48.00	29.51	E / 0.3	-17.01	-8.03	-16.75 / 16	-38.84 / 2	-39.02 / 2
GR	*ProShares UltraPro Shrt Russell2	SRTY	E-	29.32	36.64	22.80	E / 0.4	-11.58	15.61	-6.42 / 35	-37.67 / 2	-42.13 / 1
USA	*ProShares UltraPro Sht 20+ Yr Tr	TTT	E	37.65	49.39	31.31	D- / 1.0	4.96	-20.42	-7.63 / 32	-20.22 / 8	--
GI	*ProShares UltraPro Sht Finl Sel	FINZ	E-	20.08	27.00	11.38	E- / 0.2	-24.70	-6.12	-16.02 / 17	-41.46 / 1	--
IN	*ProShares UltraShort 20+ Year Tr	TBT	D-	44.07	52.25	38.15	D / 1.7	3.65	-13.21	-3.08 / 46	-12.74 / 14	-22.07 / 5
GEI	*ProShares UltraShort 3-7 Yr Trea	TBZ	C-	28.54	29.89	27.22	C- / 3.1	3.67	-2.06	-4.89 / 39	-3.78 / 27	--
IN	*ProShares UltraShort 7-10 Year T	PST	C-	23.24	25.11	15.71	D+ / 2.6	3.15	-5.30	-5.33 / 38	-6.12 / 23	-11.28 / 12
IN	*ProShares UltraShort Basic Mater	SMN	D	34.32	47.28	25.91	D+ / 2.4	-14.71	16.03	16.14 / 96	-11.95 / 15	-15.06 / 8
IN	*ProShares UltraShort Blmbrg Nat	KOLD	C-	139.66	221.70	61.76	A+ / 9.8	36.39	86.86	75.01 / 99	9.64 / 74	--
IN	*ProShares UltraShort Bloomberg C	CMD	A+	140.41	183.29	72.42	A+ / 9.9	23.96	57.83	59.72 / 99	38.75 / 99	22.43 / 98
EN	*ProShares UltraShort Bloomberg C	SCO	C	133.64	147.69	50.90	A+ / 9.9	56.85	114.00	67.26 / 99	50.45 / 99	20.05 / 97
IN	*ProShares UltraShort Consumer Go	SZK	E+	21.51	29.99	21.51	E / 0.5	-17.11	-10.41	-22.68 / 11	-28.75 / 4	-27.92 / 3
IN	*ProShares UltraShort Consumer Se	SCC	E	42.66	61.19	40.31	E / 0.4	-8.22	-7.22	-20.40 / 13	-33.78 / 3	-34.17 / 2
GR	*ProShares UltraShort Dow30	DXD	D-	20.16	27.96	19.29	E+ / 0.8	-13.14	-3.72	-7.27 / 33	-23.74 / 6	-24.36 / 4
FO	*ProShares UltraShort Euro	EUO	A	25.53	28.58	22.11	B+ / 8.4	5.28	2.08	16.31 / 96	9.72 / 74	3.28 / 39
FS	*ProShares UltraShort Financials	SKF	D-	45.87	57.15	43.34	E+ / 0.6	-12.46	-3.32	-8.42 / 30	-28.12 / 4	-28.40 / 3
FO	*ProShares UltraShort FTSE China	FXP	D-	41.94	56.27	24.54	D / 2.2	0.79	34.81	-0.52 / 57	-14.10 / 13	-18.50 / 6
FO	*ProShares UltraShort FTSE Europe	EPV	D	58.54	69.53	48.17	D- / 1.4	-1.99	9.46	-8.57 / 29	-17.07 / 10	-24.55 / 4
EN	*ProShares UltraShort Gold	GLL	A-	115.83	118.85	81.59	A+ / 9.7	13.15	16.06	16.22 / 96	22.06 / 96	-0.66 / 26
GL	*ProShares UltraShort Gold Miners	GDXS	U	27.10	N/A	N/A	U /	-7.57	6.44	--	--	--
HL	*ProShares UltraShort Health Care	RXD	E+	47.39	63.10	44.73	E / 0.3	-13.44	-0.38	-21.23 / 12	-39.10 / 2	-36.37 / 2
IN	*ProShares UltraShort Industrials	SIJ	D-	40.27	62.00	37.46	E+ / 0.7	-13.35	-2.38	-4.71 / 40	-26.95 / 5	-27.79 / 3
GL	*ProShares UltraShort Junior Mine	GDJS	U	20.47	N/A	N/A	U /	-6.53	-2.15	--	--	--
GR	*ProShares UltraShort MidCap 400	MZZ	D-	40.53	46.00	35.26	E+ / 0.9	-4.75	8.48	-3.34 / 45	-24.56 / 6	-26.50 / 4
FO	*ProShares UltraShort MSCI Br Cap	BZQ	C	81.13	115.84	34.72	A+ / 9.9	8.38	94.53	85.40 / 99	38.82 / 99	21.19 / 98
FO	*ProShares UltraShort MSCI EAFE	EFU	D	41.11	48.37	34.35	D / 1.7	-4.73	9.51	-8.40 / 30	-13.95 / 13	-17.86 / 6
EM	*ProShares UltraShort MSCI Emg Mk	EEV	C+	23.85	30.16	15.04	B / 7.8	2.72	32.88	17.85 / 97	5.08 / 61	-5.83 / 18
FO	*ProShares UltraShort MSCI Japan	EWV	D-	48.79	69.50	45.11	E+ / 0.7	-11.16	3.35	-24.88 / 10	-24.47 / 6	-18.35 / 6
FO	*ProShares UltraShort MSCI PXJ	JPX	D	26.11	47.34	19.97	D+ / 2.7	-17.80	6.00	1.04 / 67	-5.54 / 24	-15.41 / 8
HL	*ProShares UltraShort Nasdaq Biot	BIS	E	28.71	47.66	24.12	E- / 0.1	-18.81	0.56	-36.47 / 5	-54.53 / 1	-50.68 / 0
EN	*ProShares UltraShort Oil & Gas	DUG	D+	71.87	86.53	45.07	C+ / 6.2	3.54	29.24	35.94 / 99	-2.86 / 29	-13.54 / 10
GR	*ProShares UltraShort QQQ	QID	E+	29.71	44.00	28.20	E / 0.3	-16.08	-14.11	-25.09 / 10	-35.91 / 2	-33.03 / 2
IN	*ProShares UltraShort Real Estate	SRS	D-	44.81	58.29	42.92	E+ / 0.8	-12.66	-15.10	-9.59 / 27	-21.62 / 7	-27.18 / 4
GR	*ProShares UltraShort Russell2000	TWM	E+	39.29	45.24	32.65	E+ / 0.9	-7.14	12.00	-1.85 / 51	-25.32 / 5	-27.70 / 3
GR	*ProShares UltraShort S&P500	SDS	E+	19.93	25.60	18.95	E+ / 0.6	-11.30	-4.04	-9.61 / 27	-26.97 / 5	-26.52 / 4
IN	*ProShares UltraShort Semiconduct	SSG	E	39.50	73.35	39.47	E- / 0.2	-28.39	-16.83	-19.03 / 14	-41.22 / 2	-31.89 / 2
EN	*ProShares UltraShort Silver	ZSL	C+	64.55	66.70	42.25	A+ / 9.9	17.56	17.68	9.61 / 87	37.39 / 99	-10.45 / 13
GR	*ProShares UltraShort SmallCap 60	SDD	D-	37.17	42.89	32.98	E+ / 0.7	-9.34	5.45	-7.54 / 32	-27.32 / 5	-29.72 / 3
GR	*ProShares UltraShort Technology	REW	E+	45.91	96.94	42.72	E / 0.5	-14.98	-11.30	-18.25 / 15	-31.39 / 3	-27.85 / 3
GR	*ProShares UltraShort TIPS	TPS	C	28.18	28.90	26.25	C+ / 5.6	3.53	2.96	2.10 / 72	2.47 / 51	--
UT	*ProShares UltraShort Utilities	SDP	D-	47.72	58.09	43.55	E+ / 0.8	-7.63	-13.70	0.90 / 66	-24.56 / 6	-24.40 / 4
FO	*ProShares UltraShort Yen	YCS	A+	87.89	97.60	83.73	A- / 9.2	-0.18	-5.67	-2.78 / 47	18.84 / 94	12.33 / 81

* Denotes ETF Fund, N/A denotes number is not available

Incl. in Returns		RISK				NET ASSETS		VALUATION			ASSET					FUND MANAGER	
		Risk Rating/ Pts	3 Year		Avg Dura- tion	NAV as of 12/31/15	Total $(Mil)	Premium / Discount		Wtd Avg P/E					Portfolio Turnover Ratio	Manager Quality Pct	Manager Tenure (Years)
vidend Yield %	Expense Ratio		Standard Deviation	Beta				As of 12/31/15	1 Year Average		Cash %	Stocks %	Bonds %	Other %			
0.21	0.95	C- / 3.5	34.5	3.09	N/A	64.56	112	-0.03	N/A	35.6	0	100	0	0	24	12	3
0.62	0.95	D- / 1.0	35.9	3.04	N/A	78.30	11	2.52	0.12	N/A	0	0	0	100	18	24	3
0.07	0.95	E- / 0.1	37.1	3.00	N/A	49.24	44	1.56	0.01	N/A	1	98	0	1	17	13	6
0.00	N/A	U /	N/A	N/A	N/A	57.76	N/A	0.16	N/A	N/A	0	0	0	100	N/A	N/A	1
0.00	0.95	D+ / 2.9	39.4	3.31	N/A	114.17	834	-0.03	0.01	N/A	0	100	0	0	9	85	3
0.00	0.95	D+ / 2.6	45.1	3.25	N/A	74.39	175	-0.36	-0.05	N/A	20	64	0	16	38	7	3
0.63	0.95	D / 1.9	33.6	3.09	N/A	62.70	768	-0.22	-0.03	N/A	1	99	0	0	6	20	3
0.00	0.95	C- / 3.1	32.7	-2.92	N/A	17.73	133	-0.06	-0.03	N/A	0	0	0	100	N/A	36	3
0.00	0.95	C- / 3.0	36.5	-2.91	N/A	34.34	8	-0.17	0.04	N/A	4	0	0	96	N/A	21	3
.00	0.95	E+ / 0.6	36.8	-3.07	N/A	18.70	329	0.11	-0.01	N/A	0	0	0	100	N/A	4	7
0.00	0.93	D / 1.6	31.8	-2.92	N/A	31.66	515	0.16	0.01	N/A	0	0	0	100	N/A	16	3
.00	0.95	E+ / 0.8	43.5	-3.09	N/A	29.21	124	0.38	0.08	N/A	0	0	0	100	N/A	22	3
.00	0.95	D- / 1.5	36.2	-3.36	N/A	37.50	120	0.40	-0.08	N/A	0	0	0	100	N/A	15	4
.00	0.95	D- / 1.5	34.3	-2.64	N/A	18.76	4	7.04	0.26	N/A	0	0	0	100	N/A	9	3
.00	0.93	C- / 3.2	23.7	0.50	N/A	43.96	4,257	0.25	-0.06	N/A	8	0	0	92	N/A	8	8
.00	0.95	C+ / 6.9	5.5	-1.56	N/A	28.33	4	0.74	0.14	N/A	0	0	0	100	N/A	55	5
.00	0.95	B- / 7.6	10.9	0.17	N/A	23.31	299	-0.30	-0.08	N/A	15	0	0	85	N/A	20	8
.00	0.95	C / 4.5	32.1	-2.45	N/A	34.37	14	-0.15	-0.02	N/A	2	0	0	98	N/A	98	3
.00	1.18	E / 0.5	68.5	0.06	N/A	139.60	20	0.04	0.05	N/A	0	0	0	100	N/A	95	N/A
.00	0.95	B- / 7.3	30.4	-0.77	N/A	141.90	4	-1.05	-0.42	N/A	0	0	0	100	N/A	99	N/A
.00	0.98	D+ / 2.8	64.7	-2.03	N/A	133.21	196	0.32	0.18	N/A	0	0	0	100	N/A	99	N/A
.00	0.95	C- / 4.0	20.8	-1.60	N/A	22.00	4	-2.23	0.43	N/A	0	0	0	100	N/A	13	3
.00	0.95	D / 1.9	24.4	-2.07	N/A	42.24	7	0.99	0.26	N/A	0	0	0	100	N/A	12	3
.00	0.95	C / 4.6	21.7	-1.96	N/A	20.17	218	-0.05	-0.01	N/A	22	0	0	78	N/A	58	3
.00	0.95	B / 8.2	17.0	-0.46	N/A	25.54	478	-0.04	N/A	N/A	0	0	0	100	N/A	97	N/A
.00	0.95	C / 4.4	22.4	-1.96	N/A	45.96	72	-0.20	N/A	N/A	55	0	0	45	N/A	21	3
.00	0.95	D+ / 2.9	42.6	-1.79	N/A	42.01	82	-0.17	-0.01	N/A	9	0	0	91	N/A	21	7
.00	0.95	C / 5.4	27.1	-2.02	N/A	58.59	40	-0.09	-0.03	N/A	0	0	0	100	N/A	19	7
.00	0.95	C+ / 6.7	32.7	-0.28	N/A	115.88	82	-0.04	-0.21	N/A	0	0	0	100	N/A	98	N/A
.00	N/A	U /	N/A	N/A	N/A	27.02	N/A	0.30	N/A	N/A	0	0	0	100	N/A	N/A	1
.00	0.95	C- / 3.6	24.6	-1.76	N/A	47.79	2	-0.84	0.05	N/A	12	0	0	88	N/A	5	3
.00	0.95	C / 4.5	24.8	-2.11	N/A	40.42	3	-0.37	0.26	N/A	0	0	0	100	N/A	36	3
.00	N/A	U /	N/A	N/A	N/A	21.25	N/A	-3.67	N/A	N/A	0	0	0	100	N/A	N/A	1
.00	0.95	C / 5.2	23.6	-1.93	N/A	40.55	15	-0.05	0.04	N/A	0	0	0	100	N/A	39	9
.00	0.95	D+ / 2.3	60.5	-2.84	N/A	81.43	19	-0.37	-0.02	N/A	8	0	0	92	N/A	99	7
.00	0.95	C+ / 5.7	25.1	-1.92	N/A	41.13	8	-0.05	0.05	N/A	25	0	0	75	N/A	28	7
00	0.95	C+ / 5.8	29.7	-1.95	N/A	23.88	42	-0.13	-0.04	N/A	0	0	0	100	N/A	19	7
00	0.95	C / 4.7	29.2	-1.54	N/A	48.86	9	-0.14	0.09	N/A	6	0	0	94	N/A	8	7
.00	0.95	C- / 3.8	32.9	-1.92	N/A	25.03	2	4.31	-0.48	N/A	18	0	0	82	N/A	90	7
.00	0.95	D / 2.0	41.2	-2.15	N/A	28.75	75	-0.14	N/A	N/A	0	0	0	100	N/A	1	3
00	0.95	C- / 3.4	37.0	-1.94	N/A	71.85	49	0.03	N/A	N/A	7	0	0	93	N/A	14	3
00	0.95	C- / 4.1	24.3	-2.07	N/A	29.73	383	-0.07	-0.01	N/A	22	0	0	78	N/A	10	9
00	0.95	C / 4.5	27.1	-0.98	N/A	44.86	49	-0.11	0.01	N/A	4	0	0	96	N/A	15	3
00	0.95	D+ / 2.7	28.6	-2.09	N/A	39.22	342	0.18	0.03	N/A	14	0	0	86	N/A	49	3
00	0.91	C- / 3.2	20.9	-1.96	N/A	19.93	1,548	0.00	N/A	N/A	0	0	0	100	N/A	27	3
00	0.95	C- / 3.1	32.0	-2.01	N/A	41.56	4	-4.96	0.03	N/A	7	0	0	93	N/A	5	3
00	0.95	C- / 3.2	51.5	-0.63	N/A	64.58	60	-0.05	-0.62	N/A	0	0	0	100	N/A	99	N/A
00	0.95	C / 4.3	26.2	-1.95	N/A	37.30	8	-0.35	0.11	N/A	18	0	0	82	N/A	24	3
00	0.95	C- / 3.7	24.8	-2.01	N/A	45.92	4	-0.02	0.02	N/A	6	0	0	94	N/A	16	3
00	0.95	B- / 7.0	9.7	-0.09	N/A	28.02	13	0.57	-0.12	N/A	0	0	0	100	N/A	88	5
00	0.95	C / 4.4	28.7	-1.91	N/A	47.83	6	-0.23	0.02	N/A	3	0	0	97	N/A	21	3
00	0.95	B / 8.7	15.6	0.24	N/A	87.95	424	-0.07	-0.01	N/A	0	0	0	100	N/A	98	N/A

Denotes ETF Fund, N/A denotes number is not available

Fund Type	Fund Name (99 Pct = Best, 0 Pct = Worst)	Ticker Symbol	Overall Investment Rating	PRICE: Price As of 12/31/15	PRICE: 52 Week High	PRICE: 52 Week Low	PERFORMANCE: Performance Rating/Pts	% Total Return Through 12/31/15: 3 Mo	6 Mo	1Yr/Pct	Annualized 3Yr/Pct	Annualized 5Yr/Pct
GI	*ProShares UltraSht Australian Dl	CROC	A+	58.15	66.91	49.70	A- / 9.1	-9.03	4.16	11.33 / 91	16.14 / 91	--
FO	*ProShares UltraSht MSCI Mex Cap	SMK	C	26.90	34.31	22.49	C+ / 6.5	-5.55	16.30	10.36 / 89	4.58 / 60	-12.27 / 12
GL	*ProShares USD Covered Bond	COBO	C+	98.52	102.15	89.81	C / 4.3	-0.86	0.54	-0.40 / 58	-0.01 / 37	--
GEI	*ProShares VIX Mid-Term Futures E	VIXM	E+	54.04	70.77	49.11	E+ / 0.7	-11.70	0.60	-14.72 / 18	-24.76 / 5	--
GEI	*ProShares VIX Short-Term Futures	VIXY	E-	13.33	24.83	10.33	E- / 0.2	-16.79	0.30	-35.32 / 5	-43.47 / 1	--
GR	*PureFunds ISE Cyber Security ETF	HACK	D	25.90	33.91	18.29	D / 2.2	-0.08	-17.01	-1.07 / 54	--	--
GL	*PureFunds ISE Jr Silver SCM/E ET	SILJ	E-	5.07	10.05	5.02	E- / 0.2	-7.90	-27.89	-38.70 / 4	-36.99 / 2	--
GL	*QAM Equity Hedge ETF	QEH	C	27.32	29.24	26.34	C / 5.2	2.51	-6.21	-2.57 / 48	2.54 / 51	--
GR	*QuantShares Hedged Dividend Inco	DIVA	U	23.17	N/A	N/A	U /	4.75	1.40	--	--	--
GR	*QuantShares US Market Neutral Si	SIZ	C-	21.35	24.67	21.26	D+ / 2.5	-7.05	-12.75	-11.12 / 24	-5.38 / 24	--
IN	*QuantShares US Market Neutral Va	CHEP	C	24.18	27.30	23.55	C- / 3.3	-3.87	-6.75	-10.44 / 25	-1.00 / 33	--
GR	*QuantShares US Mkt Neut Anti-Bet	BTAL	C	20.68	21.52	17.76	C / 4.3	-1.90	6.93	4.33 / 77	-1.21 / 33	--
GR	*QuantShares US Mkt Neutral Momen	MOM	B+	27.62	34.99	23.26	B- / 7.0	-0.63	11.18	15.07 / 95	4.19 / 58	--
GR	*Ranger Equity Bear ETF	HDGE	D-	10.76	12.49	10.20	D- / 1.5	-4.78	-1.37	-6.27 / 35	-15.40 / 11	--
GI	*Real Estate Select Sector SPDR	XLRE	U	31.18	N/A	N/A	U /	--	--	--	--	--
GL	*Reality Shares DIVS ETF	DIVY	C-	23.32	28.57	21.01	C / 4.7	0.56	0.86	0.14 / 61	--	--
GR	*Recon Cap NASDAQ 100 Cov Call	QYLD	C-	23.41	24.91	17.96	C / 4.4	3.54	-0.18	-1.69 / 51	--	--
FO	*Recon Capital DAX Germany	DAX	C-	24.89	29.20	22.77	C- / 3.1	6.23	-6.39	-4.87 / 39	--	--
FO	*Recon Capital FTSE 100	UK	U	21.39	N/A	N/A	U /	-5.81	-13.96	--	--	--
FO	*Renaissance International IPO ET	IPOS	C-	19.48	28.36	18.66	D+ / 2.6	1.49	-11.18	-2.82 / 47	--	--
GR	*Renaissance IPO ETF	IPO	D	20.89	25.37	11.85	D / 1.9	2.08	-13.03	-7.90 / 31	--	--
GL	*Restaurant ETF	BITE	U	24.51	N/A	N/A	U /	--	--	--	--	--
GR	*ROBO Glbl Robots and Auto Index	ROBO	C-	24.20	27.50	12.83	C- / 3.0	7.72	-7.62	-5.24 / 38	--	--
FO	*Schwab Emerging Markets Equity E	SCHE	D+	19.51	26.85	18.40	D / 2.0	-3.79	-18.90	-15.72 / 17	-7.62 / 20	-4.61 / 20
EM	*Schwab Fndmtl EM Lrg Compny Idx	FNDE	D	18.33	26.76	17.92	E+ / 0.6	-4.18	-22.07	-19.32 / 14	--	--
FO	*Schwab Fndmtl Intl Lrg Co Idx ET	FNDF	C-	23.82	28.52	23.20	D+ / 2.3	0.17	-9.79	-5.14 / 38	--	--
FO	*Schwab Fndmtl Intl Sm Co Idx ETF	FNDC	C	26.61	29.14	24.78	C+ / 5.7	3.65	-3.96	5.24 / 80	--	--
GI	*Schwab Fndmtl US Broad Mkt Idx E	FNDB	C-	28.54	30.91	24.00	C- / 3.6	4.01	-3.30	-2.95 / 46	--	--
GI	*Schwab Fndmtl US Lrg Compny Idx	FNDX	C-	28.64	30.93	25.43	C- / 3.6	4.01	-3.09	-2.99 / 46	--	--
GI	*Schwab Fndmtl US Sm Compny Idx E	FNDA	D+	27.97	31.55	24.95	D+ / 2.7	2.08	-7.33	-4.70 / 40	--	--
FO	*Schwab International Equity ETF	SCHF	C+	27.57	32.23	26.61	C / 5.1	1.07	-8.09	-2.12 / 50	2.70 / 52	3.55 / 41
FO	*Schwab Intl Small-Cap Equity ETF	SCHC	C	28.87	32.97	27.42	C+ / 5.8	1.92	-6.20	2.17 / 72	4.28 / 58	3.60 / 41
USA	*Schwab Intmdt-Term US Treasury E	SCHR	C+	53.60	54.96	53.11	C / 4.8	-1.60	1.02	1.28 / 68	1.17 / 43	2.99 / 38
USA	*Schwab Short-Term US Treas ETF	SCHO	C+	50.44	51.32	50.37	C / 4.5	-0.59	-0.16	0.38 / 63	0.42 / 39	0.59 / 29
GEN	*Schwab US Aggregate Bond ETF	SCHZ	C	51.49	53.39	51.28	C / 5.1	-0.81	1.04	0.08 / 61	1.54 / 45	--
IN	*Schwab US Broad Market ETF	SCHB	A+	49.04	52.03	39.50	B+ / 8.6	4.53	-1.96	0.51 / 64	13.57 / 86	12.24 / 80
GI	*Schwab US Dividend Equity ETF	SCHD	A+	38.56	40.83	31.75	B+ / 8.5	6.41	1.59	-0.19 / 59	12.98 / 84	--
IN	*Schwab US Large-Cap ETF	SCHX	A	48.57	51.17	41.50	B+ / 8.7	4.92	-1.13	1.03 / 67	13.81 / 87	12.36 / 81
GR	*Schwab US Large-Cap Growth ETF	SCHG	A	52.83	55.93	40.11	A- / 9.0	3.82	-1.58	3.41 / 75	15.94 / 91	13.17 / 85
IN	*Schwab US Large-Cap Value ETF	SCHV	B+	42.44	44.93	36.57	B / 8.1	5.93	-0.69	-1.23 / 54	11.70 / 81	11.44 / 75
GR	*Schwab US Mid-Cap ETF	SCHM	B+	40.07	44.10	28.67	B+ / 8.4	1.93	-5.66	0.02 / 60	13.28 / 85	--
GI	*Schwab US REIT ETF	SCHH	B	39.64	42.97	30.00	B+ / 8.3	5.97	8.65	1.90 / 71	11.10 / 79	--
GR	*Schwab US Small-Cap ETF	SCHA	B	52.08	59.44	48.04	B- / 7.5	1.63	-8.47	-3.91 / 43	11.22 / 79	10.49 / 68
GEI	*Schwab US TIPS ETF	SCHP	C	53.13	55.96	52.85	C- / 3.5	-1.78	-1.70	-2.26 / 50	-2.08 / 31	2.36 / 35
FO	*Shares JPX-Nikkei 400	JPXN	B+	52.54	59.04	40.60	B- / 7.5	6.15	-4.00	11.25 / 90	8.26 / 70	3.82 / 42
USA	*Sit Rising Rate	RISE	U	24.23	N/A	N/A	U /	3.01	-0.84	--	--	--
FS	*SP Bank ETF	KBE	A+	33.82	37.28	29.92	B+ / 8.4	3.74	-5.32	3.82 / 76	12.53 / 83	7.18 / 55
FS	*SP Capital Markets ETF	KCE	C+	43.60	52.59	36.68	C+ / 6.5	6.97	-12.72	-11.01 / 24	9.24 / 73	5.20 / 48
IN	*SP Insurance ETF	KIE	A+	69.50	73.16	62.54	A / 9.3	4.08	1.87	7.22 / 84	17.07 / 92	11.85 / 77
FS	*SP Regional Banking ETF	KRE	A+	41.92	46.33	35.01	B+ / 8.9	4.70	-3.13	6.67 / 82	14.50 / 89	12.31 / 81
GEI	*SPDR Barclays 0-5 Year TIPS ETF	SIPE	C	19.35	19.60	19.20	C- / 4.2	0.32	-1.05	0.18 / 61	--	--
GEI	*SPDR Barclays 1-10 Year TIPS ETF	TIPX	C	19.18	19.64	18.86	C- / 4.1	-0.35	-0.51	-0.07 / 60	--	--

* Denotes ETF Fund, N/A denotes number is not availab

Incl. in Returns		RISK				NET ASSETS		VALUATION			ASSET					FUND MANAGER	
Dividend Yield %	Expense Ratio	Risk Rating/ Pts	3 Year Standard Deviation	3 Year Beta	Avg Duration	NAV as of 12/31/15	Total $(Mil)	Premium / Discount As of 12/31/15	Premium / Discount 1 Year Average	Wtd Avg P/E	Cash %	Stocks %	Bonds %	Other %	Portfolio Turnover Ratio	Manager Quality Pct	Manager Tenure (Years)
0.00	1.01	B- / 7.9	20.3	-0.63	N/A	58.54	21	-0.67	-0.01	N/A	0	0	0	100	N/A	99	N/A
0.00	0.95	C+ / 5.8	28.7	-1.20	N/A	28.74	1	-6.40	-0.03	N/A	0	0	0	100	N/A	94	7
2.03	0.35	B+ / 9.3	4.4	0.16	N/A	100.29	7	-1.76	-1.68	N/A	0	0	0	100	153	73	3
0.00	0.87	D+ / 2.7	28.4	-0.44	N/A	53.96	46	0.15	-0.10	N/A	0	0	0	100	N/A	4	N/A
0.00	0.92	E- / 0.1	60.8	-0.80	N/A	13.24	138	0.68	0.21	N/A	0	0	0	100	N/A	N/A	N/A
0.00	0.75	C / 5.1	N/A	N/A	N/A	25.98	N/A	-0.31	0.03	N/A	0	0	0	100	31	35	2
2.46	0.69	E+ / 0.6	47.9	0.68	N/A	5.05	7	0.40	0.71	N/A	0	0	0	100	55	1	4
0.00	1.50	B- / 7.3	7.0	0.44	N/A	26.77	7	2.05	-0.27	N/A	0	0	0	100	131	77	N/A
4.79	N/A	U /	N/A	N/A	N/A	22.81	N/A	1.58	N/A	N/A	0	0	0	100	N/A	N/A	1
0.00	1.49	B / 8.3	6.7	-0.02	N/A	21.41	1	-0.28	-0.05	N/A	0	0	0	100	108	30	5
0.00	1.49	B / 8.4	8.5	0.31	N/A	24.23	3	-0.21	-0.08	N/A	0	0	0	100	351	31	5
0.00	0.99	B / 8.3	10.0	-0.50	N/A	20.71	3	-0.14	0.07	N/A	0	0	0	100	577	89	5
0.00	1.49	B / 8.7	11.2	-0.26	N/A	27.75	1	-0.47	0.64	N/A	0	0	0	100	398	93	5
0.00	1.65	C / 4.6	13.0	-1.03	N/A	10.75	182	0.09	N/A	N/A	12	88	0	0	419	42	N/A
3.08	N/A	U /	N/A	N/A	N/A	31.04	N/A	0.45	N/A	N/A	0	0	0	100	N/A	N/A	1
0.00	N/A	C+ / 5.7	N/A	N/A	N/A	23.35	N/A	-0.13	0.42	N/A	0	0	0	100	N/A	71	2
0.00	0.60	C+ / 6.8	N/A	N/A	N/A	23.23	12	0.77	0.17	N/A	0	0	0	100	18	39	3
0.00	N/A	B- / 7.8	N/A	N/A	N/A	25.07	N/A	-0.72	0.01	N/A	0	0	0	100	N/A	33	N/A
0.00	N/A	U /	N/A	N/A	N/A	21.23	N/A	0.75	N/A	N/A	0	0	0	100	N/A	N/A	1
0.13	0.80	B- / 7.9	N/A	N/A	N/A	19.66	N/A	-0.92	0.67	N/A	0	0	0	100	101	52	N/A
0.23	0.60	C+ / 6.0	N/A	N/A	N/A	20.84	33	0.24	-0.09	N/A	0	0	0	100	86	17	3
0.00	N/A	U /	N/A	N/A	N/A	24.48	N/A	0.12	N/A	N/A	0	0	0	100	N/A	N/A	1
0.28	0.95	B- / 7.8	N/A	N/A	N/A	24.35	102	-0.62	-0.06	N/A	0	0	0	100	23	23	1
2.50	0.14	C+ / 6.9	15.4	0.92	N/A	19.59	1,212	-0.41	0.34	N/A	0	97	0	3	8	14	6
0.07	0.46	C+ / 6.2	N/A	N/A	N/A	18.41	42	-0.43	0.28	N/A	0	0	0	100	13	36	3
2.08	0.32	B- / 7.8	N/A	N/A	N/A	23.90	138	-0.33	0.39	N/A	0	0	0	100	11	30	3
1.30	0.46	C+ / 6.8	N/A	N/A	N/A	26.60	38	0.04	0.53	N/A	0	0	0	100	21	90	3
2.35	0.32	B- / 7.0	N/A	N/A	N/A	28.46	140	0.28	0.03	N/A	0	0	0	100	10	34	3
2.40	0.32	B- / 7.1	N/A	N/A	N/A	28.62	176	0.07	0.03	N/A	0	0	0	100	10	35	3
1.47	0.32	C+ / 6.7	N/A	N/A	N/A	27.94	94	0.11	0.03	N/A	0	0	0	100	22	25	3
2.26	0.08	B / 8.3	12.0	0.93	N/A	27.67	2,660	-0.36	0.25	16.1	0	97	0	3	4	51	7
2.33	0.18	C+ / 6.8	11.8	0.84	N/A	28.81	384	0.21	0.49	74.2	0	93	0	7	23	70	6
1.42	0.10	B / 8.0	3.3	0.27	N/A	53.55	230	0.09	0.02	N/A	0	0	100	0	49	71	6
0.68	0.08	B / 8.4	0.5	0.03	N/A	50.43	617	0.02	0.01	N/A	1	0	98	1	109	71	6
1.98	0.05	B- / 7.7	3.0	1.00	N/A	51.41	899	0.16	0.09	N/A	0	0	100	0	74	67	5
2.04	0.04	B / 8.5	10.6	1.00	N/A	49.05	3,615	-0.02	0.01	N/A	0	99	0	1	3	64	7
2.82	0.07	B / 8.8	10.6	0.97	N/A	38.58	2,135	-0.05	0.02	N/A	0	99	0	1	19	62	5
2.08	0.04	B / 8.0	10.5	0.99	N/A	48.57	3,209	0.00	0.02	N/A	1	99	0	0	4	66	7
1.15	0.07	B- / 7.5	10.8	1.00	N/A	52.82	1,496	0.02	0.02	N/A	0	99	0	1	10	79	7
2.87	0.07	B- / 7.9	10.8	1.01	N/A	42.44	1,156	0.00	0.03	N/A	0	99	0	1	15	50	7
1.73	0.07	B- / 7.4	11.8	1.00	N/A	40.06	1,170	0.02	0.03	N/A	0	99	0	1	12	63	5
0.16	0.07	C+ / 6.3	14.8	0.45	N/A	39.62	968	0.05	0.03	N/A	0	99	0	1	15	89	5
1.78	0.08	B- / 7.1	13.3	1.05	N/A	52.07	1,996	0.02	0.02	N/A	1	98	0	1	9	43	7
0.28	0.07	B+ / 9.1	5.3	1.61	N/A	53.15	490	-0.04	0.05	N/A	0	0	99	1	20	33	6
3.02	0.50	B / 8.3	14.0	0.77	N/A	53.16	76	-1.17	0.34	N/A	0	99	0	1	2	88	8
0.00	N/A	U /	N/A	N/A	N/A	24.21	N/A	0.08	N/A	N/A	0	0	0	100	N/A	N/A	1
4.13	0.35	B / 8.7	15.4	1.14	N/A	33.85	2,570	-0.09	N/A	15.4	0	100	0	0	18	44	11
5.46	0.35	C+ / 6.5	17.8	1.44	N/A	43.32	187	0.65	-0.05	29.6	0	100	0	0	28	17	11
4.65	0.35	B / 8.1	12.8	1.05	N/A	69.50	299	0.00	N/A	39.9	0	100	0	0	17	82	11
4.43	0.35	B / 8.6	16.9	1.18	N/A	41.94	2,197	-0.05	-0.01	17.2	0	100	0	0	27	55	10
0.00	0.15	B / 8.0	N/A	N/A	N/A	19.31	6	0.21	N/A	N/A	0	0	0	100	26	67	2
0.06	0.15	B- / 7.7	N/A	N/A	N/A	18.97	10	1.11	0.09	N/A	0	0	0	100	28	70	3

* Denotes ETF Fund, N/A denotes number is not available

				PRICE			PERFORMANCE					
99 Pct = Best 0 Pct = Worst					52 Week			% Total Return Through 12/31/15			Annualized	
Fund Type	Fund Name	Ticker Symbol	Overall Investment Rating	Price As of 12/31/15	High	Low	Performance Rating/Pts	3 Mo	6 Mo	1Yr/Pct	3Yr/Pct	5Yr/Pct
USA	*SPDR Barclays 1-3 Month T-Bill E	BIL	**C+**	45.68	45.74	45.67	**C-** / **4.2**	-0.04	-0.07	-0.11 / 59	-0.10 / 37	-0.07 / 28
GI	*SPDR Barclays Conv Sec ETF	CWB	**C+**	43.28	49.52	31.04	**C+** / **6.9**	1.15	-3.01	-0.86 / 55	8.31 / 71	6.56 / 53
GI	*SPDR Barclays Em Mkt Local Bond	EBND	**C-**	24.76	29.47	24.06	**D** / **2.2**	-0.36	-8.57	-12.32 / 22	-7.56 / 21	--
COH	*SPDR Barclays High Yield Bond ET	JNK	**C-**	33.91	39.79	33.22	**C-** / **3.6**	-2.46	-8.89	-6.91 / 34	-0.23 / 36	3.70 / 42
GEI	*SPDR Barclays Int Term Crp Bond	ITR	**C+**	33.43	34.81	33.34	**C** / **5.0**	-0.94	-0.17	0.17 / 61	1.58 / 46	3.67 / 41
USA	*SPDR Barclays Int Tr Treas ETF	ITE	**C+**	60.19	64.83	58.36	**C** / **4.9**	-0.61	1.05	1.54 / 70	1.03 / 42	2.19 / 34
COI	*SPDR Barclays Intl Corporate Bd	IBND	**C-**	30.80	34.65	29.90	**C-** / **3.0**	-2.12	-1.37	-9.99 / 25	-3.13 / 28	0.27 / 28
GL	*SPDR Barclays Intl High Yld Bd E	IJNK	**C-**	21.63	26.42	21.39	**C-** / **3.1**	1.63	-2.92	-4.47 / 41	--	--
GL	*SPDR Barclays Intl Treasury Bd E	BWX	**C-**	51.63	55.66	50.66	**C-** / **3.0**	-1.56	-0.14	-6.28 / 35	-3.74 / 27	-0.03 / 28
COI	*SPDR Barclays Invest Grade FlRt	FLRN	**C**	30.42	30.77	30.20	**C** / **4.4**	0.07	-0.28	0.47 / 64	0.34 / 38	--
COI	*SPDR Barclays Iss Sco Corp Bond	CBND	**C**	30.99	33.44	23.16	**C** / **4.9**	-0.83	0.06	-1.58 / 52	1.59 / 46	--
USA	*SPDR Barclays LongTerm Treasury	TLO	**C+**	69.88	79.37	66.79	**C+** / **5.6**	-2.53	4.83	-2.24 / 50	3.43 / 55	8.14 / 58
GEI	*SPDR Barclays LongTrm Corp Bond	LWC	**C**	37.58	44.23	36.77	**C** / **4.8**	-0.98	0.95	-5.87 / 36	1.86 / 47	6.49 / 53
MTG	*SPDR Barclays Mortg Backed Bond	MBG	**C+**	26.82	28.00	26.63	**C** / **5.3**	-0.51	1.39	2.05 / 72	2.01 / 48	2.97 / 38
COH	*SPDR Barclays Short Term HiYld B	SJNK	**C-**	25.69	29.53	25.40	**C-** / **3.5**	-2.35	-8.32	-6.61 / 34	-0.42 / 36	--
COI	*SPDR Barclays Sht Trm Corp Bond	SCPB	**C+**	30.40	30.79	30.35	**C** / **4.9**	-0.08	0.22	0.87 / 66	1.05 / 42	1.65 / 32
USA	*SPDR Barclays Sht Trm Treasury E	SST	**C**	30.10	31.96	28.79	**C** / **4.6**	-0.76	0.05	0.83 / 66	0.62 / 40	--
GL	*SPDR Barclays ST Intl Treas Bd E	BWZ	**C-**	29.75	32.23	29.25	**D+** / **2.6**	-1.30	-2.31	-6.54 / 35	-6.43 / 22	-3.21 / 22
USA	*SPDR Barclays TIPS ETF	IPE	**C**	54.63	58.53	54.36	**C-** / **3.4**	-1.97	-1.84	-3.18 / 46	-2.22 / 30	2.67 / 36
LP	*SPDR Blackstone/GSO Senior Loan	SRLN	**C**	46.13	49.70	45.00	**C-** / **3.2**	-1.84	-3.79	-1.15 / 54	--	--
EM	*SPDR BofA Merrill Lynch Em Mkt C	EMCD	**C-**	26.99	30.50	26.32	**C-** / **3.9**	-1.04	-3.96	-0.45 / 58	-0.58 / 35	--
GL	*SPDR DB Intl Gvt Inflation Pt Bo	WIP	**C-**	50.36	57.46	50.25	**D+** / **2.6**	-3.08	-6.66	-9.68 / 26	-5.15 / 25	0.34 / 28
IN	*SPDR DJ REIT ETF	RWR	**B**	91.63	100.11	81.32	**B+** / **8.5**	7.01	9.71	3.72 / 76	11.24 / 79	12.43 / 82
GI	*SPDR DJ Wilshire Glb Real Est ET	RWO	**C+**	46.80	51.79	32.28	**C+** / **6.9**	3.98	3.59	1.32 / 69	7.03 / 67	8.83 / 60
FO	*SPDR DJ Wilshire Intl Real Estat	RWX	**C+**	39.12	45.40	37.48	**C** / **4.9**	-0.64	-4.87	-2.44 / 48	2.08 / 49	4.95 / 47
GEN	*SPDR DoubleLine Tot Rtn Tact ETF	TOTL	**U**	48.60	N/A	N/A	**U** /	-0.97	0.05	--	--	--
GR	*SPDR Dow Jones Industrial Averag	DIA	**A-**	173.99	183.35	150.57	**B** / **8.2**	6.62	-0.28	0.40 / 63	11.72 / 81	11.02 / 72
GL	*SPDR EURO STOXX 50 Currency Hedg	HFEZ	**U**	35.00	N/A	N/A	**U** /	8.01	-2.79	--	--	--
FO	*SPDR Euro STOXX 50 ETF	FEZ	**C**	34.43	40.81	33.02	**C** / **5.2**	1.23	-7.25	-3.44 / 44	2.98 / 53	3.06 / 38
FO	*SPDR EURO STOXX Small Cap ETF	SMEZ	**C**	48.38	56.49	46.07	**C-** / **3.9**	1.08	-4.97	1.58 / 70	--	--
GL	*SPDR Global Dow ETF	DGT	**B-**	64.67	75.87	58.57	**C+** / **6.3**	3.90	-5.93	-3.31 / 45	6.81 / 66	4.59 / 46
PM	*SPDR Gold Shares	GLD	**D**	101.46	125.58	100.23	**D-** / **1.4**	-6.91	-9.22	-11.06 / 24	-14.17 / 13	-5.35 / 18
GR	*SPDR MFS Systematic Core Equity	SYE	**B**	58.95	61.25	53.68	**B** / **7.8**	7.12	1.94	7.68 / 84	--	--
GR	*SPDR MFS Systematic Gro Equity E	SYG	**B**	60.34	63.59	52.10	**B** / **7.8**	6.39	1.66	8.54 / 86	--	--
GR	*SPDR MFS Systematic Value Eqty E	SYV	**C-**	52.64	60.88	51.11	**C-** / **4.1**	5.34	-3.54	-1.37 / 53	--	--
GL	*SPDR MSCI ACWI ex-US ETF	CWI	**C**	30.80	37.22	29.54	**C** / **4.3**	1.87	-8.83	-3.72 / 43	1.30 / 44	1.41 / 31
GL	*SPDR MSCI ACWI IMI ETF	ACIM	**B-**	61.50	77.10	53.16	**B-** / **7.4**	5.54	-2.26	-0.23 / 59	9.44 / 74	--
EN	*SPDR MSCI ACWI Low Carbon Target	LOWC	**D+**	70.36	78.90	67.02	**C-** / **4.1**	6.69	-4.89	-1.04 / 55	--	--
FO	*SPDR MSCI Australia Quality Mix	QAUS	**D**	45.04	56.57	41.26	**C-** / **3.5**	12.01	-4.88	-6.93 / 34	--	--
FO	*SPDR MSCI Canada Quality Mix ETF	QCAN	**D-**	44.42	58.60	43.91	**E+** / **0.9**	-2.61	-13.56	-19.18 / 14	--	--
FO	*SPDR MSCI China A Shares IMI ETF	XINA	**U**	26.23	N/A	N/A	**U** /	--	--	--	--	--
FO	*SPDR MSCI EAFE Quality Mix ETF	QEFA	**C**	54.96	62.00	52.25	**C+** / **5.8**	4.50	-2.86	4.30 / 77	--	--
EM	*SPDR MSCI EM 50 ETF	EMFT	**D+**	37.25	52.54	36.64	**D** / **2.2**	2.33	-19.52	-15.28 / 17	-6.77 / 22	--
EM	*SPDR MSCI EM Beyond BRIC ETF	EMBB	**D**	46.20	60.63	45.04	**D-** / **1.0**	-0.10	-16.04	-16.47 / 16	--	--
EM	*SPDR MSCI Emerg Markets Ql Mix E	QEMM	**D**	47.43	62.77	45.88	**D-** / **1.3**	-1.21	-13.82	-12.05 / 22	--	--
FO	*SPDR MSCI Germany Quality Mix ET	QDEU	**C**	51.62	59.33	47.49	**C** / **4.4**	6.22	-4.40	-0.42 / 58	--	--
GI	*SPDR MSCI Intl Real Estate Curr	HREX	**U**	39.90	N/A	N/A	**U** /	5.75	--	--	--	--
FO	*SPDR MSCI Japan Quality Mix ETF	QJPN	**A**	64.48	69.19	56.43	**B+** / **8.4**	9.41	-1.33	11.23 / 90	--	--
FO	*SPDR MSCI Mexico Quality Mix ETF	QMEX	**D**	22.15	26.33	21.72	**D** / **1.9**	-1.65	-7.29	-9.62 / 27	--	--
FO	*SPDR MSCI South Korea Quality Mi	QKOR	**D+**	25.01	29.68	22.16	**D+** / **2.8**	4.56	-4.10	-7.47 / 32	--	--
FO	*SPDR MSCI Spain Quality Mix ETF	QESP	**D**	42.98	53.61	42.98	**D** / **2.0**	-1.19	-7.75	-9.06 / 28	--	--
FO	*SPDR MSCI United Kingdom Qual Mi	QGBR	**C-**	49.65	59.63	40.17	**C-** / **3.1**	4.65	-7.05	-3.59 / 44	--	--

* Denotes ETF Fund, N/A denotes number is not available

		RISK				NET ASSETS		VALUATION			ASSET					FUND MANAGER	
cl. in Returns			3 Year					Premium / Discount									
dend eld %	Expense Ratio	Risk Rating/ Pts	Standard Deviation	Beta	Avg Dura- tion	NAV as of 12/31/15	Total $(Mil)	As of 12/31/15	1 Year Average	Wtd Avg P/E	Cash %	Stocks %	Bonds %	Other %	Portfolio Turnover Ratio	Manager Quality Pct	Manager Tenure (Years)
.00	0.14	B / 8.9	0.1	N/A	N/A	45.68	947	0.00	N/A	N/A	0	0	99	1	620	66	N/A
.76	0.40	C+ / 6.7	7.7	0.61	N/A	43.16	2,940	0.28	0.07	N/A	0	0	0	100	38	66	N/A
.00	0.50	B- / 7.5	9.4	0.50	N/A	24.83	113	-0.28	-0.37	N/A	2	0	97	1	35	11	5
.70	0.40	C+ / 6.6	6.3	1.14	N/A	33.75	8,897	0.47	0.25	N/A	0	0	99	1	34	52	N/A
.75	0.14	B / 8.7	2.9	0.94	N/A	33.43	466	0.00	0.21	N/A	0	0	99	1	13	69	4
.26	0.12	B / 8.0	2.0	0.17	N/A	59.83	173	0.60	0.03	N/A	0	0	99	1	27	73	2
.01	0.54	C+ / 6.7	7.3	0.18	N/A	30.78	312	0.06	-0.05	N/A	0	0	99	1	28	37	4
.57	0.40	C+ / 6.8	N/A	N/A	N/A	21.24	34	1.84	-0.55	N/A	0	0	0	100	50	45	2
.00	0.50	B- / 7.3	6.2	1.00	7.9	51.39	2,222	0.47	-0.03	N/A	0	0	99	1	19	67	4
.73	0.15	B / 8.2	0.9	N/A	N/A	30.40	395	0.07	0.03	N/A	0	0	100	0	21	71	5
.18	0.16	B- / 7.6	4.6	1.00	N/A	30.86	13	0.42	0.39	N/A	0	0	99	1	8	70	5
.63	0.11	B / 8.4	10.8	1.04	N/A	69.94	108	-0.09	-0.01	N/A	0	0	99	1	18	68	6
.68	0.14	C+ / 6.8	8.7	2.67	N/A	37.44	212	0.37	0.25	N/A	0	0	99	1	10	50	N/A
.13	0.20	B- / 7.9	2.6	1.07	N/A	26.73	123	0.34	0.18	N/A	0	0	99	1	221	66	N/A
.94	0.40	C+ / 6.8	4.3	0.78	N/A	25.62	3,936	0.27	0.21	N/A	0	0	0	100	39	55	N/A
.52	0.12	B / 8.0	0.8	0.15	N/A	30.34	3,686	0.20	0.08	N/A	0	0	99	1	46	75	6
.99	0.11	B- / 7.8	4.9	0.18	N/A	30.07	12	0.10	0.02	N/A	0	0	0	100	35	68	5
.00	0.35	B / 8.2	5.7	0.83	N/A	29.76	266	-0.03	-0.12	N/A	1	0	98	1	83	42	6
.23	0.17	B / 8.8	5.5	0.41	N/A	54.73	596	-0.18	-0.01	N/A	0	0	99	1	18	39	8
.02	0.71	B+ / 9.4	N/A	N/A	N/A	46.20	N/A	-0.15	-0.02	N/A	0	0	0	100	65	67	3
.93	0.50	C+ / 6.7	8.1	0.43	N/A	26.91	24	0.30	-0.48	N/A	0	0	0	100	11	78	N/A
.09	0.50	B / 8.3	8.0	1.02	10.5	50.64	892	-0.55	-0.16	N/A	0	0	99	1	36	57	4
.33	0.25	C+ / 6.4	14.8	0.42	N/A	91.59	2,620	0.04	N/A	91.5	0	100	0	0	5	90	2
.63	0.50	C+ / 6.8	13.4	0.55	N/A	46.79	1,464	0.02	0.09	N/A	0	100	0	0	6	62	8
.92	0.60	B / 8.0	14.2	0.82	N/A	39.34	4,902	-0.56	0.04	58.2	0	100	0	0	8	47	N/A
.89	N/A	U /	N/A	N/A	N/A	48.59	N/A	0.02	N/A	N/A	0	0	0	100	N/A	N/A	1
.62	0.17	B / 8.1	10.9	1.01	N/A	174.00	11,861	-0.01	N/A	35.6	0	100	0	0	18	49	N/A
.48	N/A	U /	N/A	N/A	N/A	34.88	N/A	0.34	N/A	N/A	0	0	0	100	N/A	N/A	1
.42	0.29	B- / 7.3	16.2	1.16	N/A	34.58	4,977	-0.43	0.05	N/A	0	100	0	0	6	43	14
.43	0.46	B / 8.0	N/A	N/A	N/A	48.66	8	-0.58	0.18	N/A	0	0	0	100	46	82	N/A
.37	0.50	B / 8.3	12.0	0.90	N/A	64.69	112	-0.03	-0.05	53.0	0	99	0	1	13	83	16
.00	0.40	C+ / 6.2	16.3	0.93	N/A	101.63	30,097	-0.17	0.10	N/A	0	0	0	100	N/A	53	N/A
.26	0.60	B- / 7.2	N/A	N/A	N/A	57.97	3	1.69	N/A	N/A	0	0	0	100	54	91	2
.74	0.60	B- / 7.2	N/A	N/A	N/A	60.13	3	0.35	0.11	N/A	0	0	0	100	67	91	2
.39	0.60	C+ / 6.7	N/A	N/A	N/A	52.56	3	0.15	0.12	N/A	0	0	0	100	61	45	2
.31	0.32	B / 8.2	12.2	0.94	N/A	30.92	576	-0.39	0.07	16.5	0	100	0	0	8	41	N/A
.86	0.25	B- / 7.1	9.3	0.65	N/A	60.80	57	1.15	1.14	N/A	0	99	0	1	3	92	4
.59	0.20	C / 5.0	N/A	N/A	N/A	70.56	N/A	-0.28	0.22	N/A	0	0	0	100	4	96	2
.82	0.30	C / 4.7	N/A	N/A	N/A	44.92	6	0.27	-0.07	N/A	0	0	0	100	12	24	N/A
.36	0.30	C / 5.1	N/A	N/A	N/A	44.23	3	0.43	0.18	N/A	0	0	0	100	15	7	N/A
.14	N/A	U /	N/A	N/A	N/A	26.11	N/A	0.46	N/A	N/A	0	0	0	100	N/A	N/A	1
.18	0.30	C+ / 6.7	N/A	N/A	N/A	54.60	6	0.66	0.37	N/A	0	0	0	100	14	85	N/A
.46	0.50	C+ / 6.5	19.3	1.17	N/A	37.96	2	-1.87	0.68	N/A	0	100	0	0	9	74	4
.44	0.52	C+ / 6.7	N/A	N/A	N/A	46.57	3	-0.79	-0.25	N/A	0	0	0	100	9	37	3
.72	0.30	C / 5.4	N/A	N/A	N/A	46.96	6	1.00	0.66	N/A	0	0	0	100	23	68	N/A
.17	0.30	B / 8.0	N/A	N/A	N/A	52.08	5	-0.88	0.05	N/A	0	0	0	100	18	49	N/A
.92	N/A	U /	N/A	N/A	N/A	40.17	N/A	-0.67	N/A	N/A	0	0	0	100	N/A	N/A	1
.16	0.30	B / 8.5	N/A	N/A	N/A	65.28	6	-1.23	-0.23	N/A	0	0	0	100	23	96	N/A
.12	0.40	C+ / 6.2	N/A	N/A	N/A	22.05	N/A	0.45	0.41	N/A	0	0	0	100	7	17	2
.00	0.40	C+ / 5.7	N/A	N/A	N/A	24.77	N/A	0.97	0.47	N/A	0	0	0	100	16	22	2
.78	0.30	C / 5.4	N/A	N/A	N/A	42.86	8	0.28	N/A	N/A	0	0	0	100	12	19	N/A
.15	0.30	B- / 7.6	N/A	N/A	N/A	49.74	6	-0.18	0.43	N/A	0	0	0	100	31	41	N/A

Denotes ETF Fund, N/A denotes number is not available

Fund Type	Fund Name (99 Pct = Best, 0 Pct = Worst)	Ticker Symbol	Overall Investment Rating	PRICE: Price As of 12/31/15	PRICE: 52 Week High	PRICE: 52 Week Low	PERFORMANCE: Performance Rating/Pts	% Total Return Through 12/31/15: 3 Mo	6 Mo	1Yr/Pct	Annualized: 3Yr/Pct	Annualized: 5Yr/Pct
GR	*SPDR MSCI USA Quality Mix ETF	QUS	**U**	60.32	N/A	N/A	**U** /	8.81	3.11	--	--	--
GL	*SPDR MSCI World Quality Mix ETF	QWLD	**B+**	60.16	64.82	57.21	**B** / **8.2**	12.24	2.00	6.49 / 82	--	--
MUN	*SPDR Nuveen Barclays Bld Amr Bd	BABS	**B**	59.62	66.33	56.70	**C+** / **6.3**	-0.12	5.38	-2.30 / 49	3.84 / 64	9.52 / 90
MUN	*SPDR Nuveen Barclays CA Muni Bd	CXA	**B-**	24.26	24.62	23.34	**C+** / **6.7**	1.58	4.44	4.12 / 82	3.71 / 63	7.48 / 75
MUN	*SPDR Nuveen Barclays Muni Bond E	TFI	**B-**	24.38	24.68	23.53	**C+** / **6.3**	1.63	4.38	3.31 / 79	3.03 / 60	5.73 / 60
MUN	*SPDR Nuveen Barclays NY Muni Bd	INY	**B-**	23.77	24.41	22.69	**C+** / **6.7**	3.53	5.55	2.97 / 78	3.55 / 63	6.25 / 64
MUN	*SPDR Nuveen Barclays ST Muni Bd	SHM	**C+**	24.36	24.52	24.12	**C** / **5.3**	0.19	0.96	1.13 / 71	1.16 / 47	1.80 / 37
COH	*SPDR Nuveen S&P Hi Yld Muni Bd E	HYMB	**C**	57.05	59.01	54.68	**C+** / **6.1**	2.21	5.64	3.74 / 76	4.14 / 58	--
GR	*SPDR Russell 1000 ETF	ONEK	**A-**	96.05	100.84	87.28	**B+** / **8.9**	7.05	-0.22	1.98 / 71	14.27 / 88	12.23 / 80
GR	*SPDR Russell 1000 Low Volatility	LGLV	**B+**	73.99	76.50	65.00	**B** / **8.2**	10.54	5.21	5.30 / 80	--	--
GR	*SPDR Russell 2000 ETF	TWOK	**C-**	67.42	76.48	63.81	**C-** / **4.1**	5.86	-5.21	-0.57 / 57	--	--
GR	*SPDR Russell 2000 Low Volatility	SMLV	**C**	74.67	80.03	54.66	**C+** / **5.6**	6.80	-0.28	0.19 / 62	--	--
GR	*SPDR Russell 3000 ETF	THRK	**B+**	152.18	160.31	101.78	**B+** / **8.8**	6.27	-0.53	1.57 / 70	14.00 / 88	12.06 / 79
GR	*SPDR Russell Small Cap Completen	RSCO	**B**	76.78	89.81	75.23	**B+** / **8.5**	5.84	-3.51	1.11 / 67	13.00 / 84	11.51 / 75
FO	*SPDR Russell/Nomura PRIME Japan	JPP	**A-**	46.16	50.65	32.50	**B** / **7.8**	6.45	-2.55	11.24 / 90	8.97 / 72	4.44 / 45
FO	*SPDR Russell/Nomura Small Cap Ja	JSC	**A+**	54.28	55.66	46.67	**B+** / **8.5**	7.28	0.39	16.01 / 96	10.32 / 76	6.49 / 53
IN	*SPDR S&P 1500 Momentum TILT ETF	MMTM	**A-**	90.07	94.50	80.75	**A-** / **9.2**	10.81	2.87	6.02 / 81	15.42 / 90	--
IN	*SPDR S&P 1500 Value TILT ETF	VLU	**B+**	78.24	86.44	74.47	**A-** / **9.2**	11.95	2.56	3.56 / 76	15.86 / 91	--
GR	*SPDR S&P 400 Mid Cap Growth ETF	MDYG	**A-**	117.45	129.03	72.72	**B+** / **8.8**	5.77	-0.80	5.79 / 81	13.40 / 85	11.73 / 76
GR	*SPDR S&P 400 Mid Cap Value ETF	MDYV	**B**	76.12	88.99	40.79	**B** / **7.8**	3.66	-5.59	-3.89 / 43	11.54 / 80	10.52 / 68
GR	*SPDR S&P 500 Buyback ETF	SPYB	**U**	46.18	N/A	N/A	**U** /	5.92	-5.29	--	--	--
GR	*SPDR S&P 500 ETF	SPY	**A+**	203.87	213.78	182.40	**B+** / **8.9**	5.82	0.02	1.89 / 71	14.16 / 88	12.32 / 81
GR	*SPDR S&P 500 Growth ETF	SPYG	**A+**	100.09	103.97	68.60	**A-** / **9.2**	6.17	2.15	5.79 / 81	16.15 / 91	13.78 / 87
IN	*SPDR S&P 500 High Dividend ETF	SPYD	**U**	29.26	N/A	N/A	**U** /	--	--	--	--	--
IN	*SPDR S&P 500 Value ETF	SPYV	**B**	95.94	103.87	59.45	**B** / **8.0**	5.98	-2.59	-2.30 / 49	11.81 / 81	10.68 / 69
GR	*SPDR S&P 600 Small Cap ETF	SLY	**B+**	98.88	111.66	61.53	**B** / **7.9**	2.95	-5.86	-1.42 / 53	12.04 / 82	11.30 / 74
GR	*SPDR S&P 600 Small Cap Growth ET	SLYG	**B**	172.78	196.03	129.25	**B+** / **8.6**	2.85	-4.42	3.66 / 76	13.65 / 86	12.34 / 81
GR	*SPDR S&P 600 Small Cap Value ETF	SLYV	**B**	92.97	109.51	59.00	**B+** / **8.3**	8.09	-2.64	-1.56 / 52	12.28 / 82	11.30 / 74
IN	*SPDR S&P Aerospace & Defense ETF	XAR	**C-**	52.88	60.00	34.82	**A** / **9.5**	11.30	-1.63	4.14 / 77	20.75 / 95	--
HL	*SPDR S&P Biotech ETF	XBI	**C-**	70.20	91.11	59.16	**A+** / **9.8**	7.65	-14.29	12.66 / 92	32.53 / 99	27.63 / 99
FO	*SPDR S&P BRIC 40 ETF	BIK	**D+**	18.61	25.65	17.07	**D+** / **2.4**	1.05	-17.06	-10.29 / 25	-6.09 / 23	-4.42 / 20
FO	*SPDR S&P China ETF	GXC	**C**	73.49	100.10	63.41	**C** / **4.6**	5.88	-13.18	-3.37 / 45	1.99 / 48	1.49 / 32
IN	*SPDR S&P Dividend ETF	SDY	**A-**	73.57	79.91	46.22	**A-** / **9.0**	9.50	4.32	3.22 / 75	14.00 / 88	12.90 / 84
EM	*SPDR S&P Emerg Middle East&Afric	GAF	**D**	49.79	74.03	45.78	**D** / **1.6**	-10.73	-22.02	-20.76 / 13	-9.19 / 18	-4.98 / 19
EM	*SPDR S&P Emerging Asia Pacific E	GMF	**C**	73.60	96.20	64.45	**C-** / **4.2**	4.99	-11.01	-5.63 / 37	1.25 / 43	0.56 / 29
EM	*SPDR S&P Emerging Europe ETF	GUR	**D**	22.48	33.07	20.31	**D-** / **1.1**	-3.14	-15.67	-13.60 / 20	-16.86 / 11	-11.44 / 12
EM	*SPDR S&P Emerging Latin America	GML	**D-**	35.16	53.41	34.00	**E+** / **0.7**	-4.47	-25.16	-28.72 / 8	-20.33 / 8	-14.55 / 9
EM	*SPDR S&P Emerging Markets ETF	GMM	**C-**	52.08	70.41	48.33	**D+** / **2.3**	-0.57	-16.73	-13.40 / 20	-6.22 / 23	-4.19 / 20
GI	*SPDR S&P Emg Markets Dividend ET	EDIV	**D-**	23.72	36.74	23.30	**D-** / **1.0**	-6.72	-25.22	-26.50 / 9	-16.85 / 11	--
GL	*SPDR S&P Emg Markets Sm Cap ETF	EWX	**C-**	37.71	48.44	32.42	**D+** / **2.7**	3.64	-12.58	-9.75 / 26	-4.33 / 26	-4.41 / 20
EN	*SPDR S&P Glbl Natural Resources	GNR	**D-**	32.10	47.39	31.06	**D-** / **1.4**	-0.84	-20.79	-22.50 / 11	-12.09 / 15	-8.82 / 15
GL	*SPDR S&P Global Dividend ETF	WDIV	**D+**	56.96	69.48	56.09	**D+** / **2.5**	-0.18	-7.72	-4.94 / 39	--	--
GL	*SPDR S&P Global Infrastructure	GII	**C**	41.54	51.16	40.22	**C** / **5.4**	-1.03	-7.91	-9.65 / 26	4.92 / 61	4.52 / 45
HL	*SPDR S&P Health Care Equipment E	XHE	**C-**	44.57	55.40	42.46	**A+** / **9.7**	14.68	8.80	17.93 / 97	21.90 / 96	--
HL	*SPDR S&P Health Care Services ET	XHS	**C-**	57.38	68.06	53.25	**A** / **9.5**	3.42	-9.58	6.19 / 82	21.19 / 96	--
IN	*SPDR S&P Homebuilders ETF	XHB	**C+**	34.18	39.22	31.70	**C+** / **6.7**	-1.39	-6.45	1.75 / 71	7.93 / 70	14.80 / 91
EM	*SPDR S&P International Div ETF	DWX	**D+**	33.36	46.55	32.43	**D+** / **2.3**	-1.24	-15.99	-14.92 / 18	-6.16 / 23	-3.33 / 22
GL	*SPDR S&P International Mid Cap E	MDD	**C+**	29.79	33.50	27.28	**B-** / **7.2**	6.74	-4.06	8.62 / 86	7.46 / 68	5.21 / 48
FO	*SPDR S&P International Small Cap	GWX	**B-**	28.23	31.60	25.81	**C+** / **6.3**	3.60	-5.49	6.36 / 82	5.73 / 63	3.45 / 40
FO	*SPDR S&P Intl Div Curr Hdgd	HDWX	**U**	37.89	N/A	N/A	**U** /	5.19	--	--	--	--
IN	*SPDR S&P Metals & Mining ETF	XME	**E+**	14.95	30.80	14.35	**E** / **0.3**	-12.06	-35.77	-50.06 / 2	-30.05 / 4	-25.03 / 4
GR	*SPDR S&P MidCap 400 ETF	MDY	**B+**	254.04	282.41	216.91	**B** / **7.7**	1.57	-6.14	-1.95 / 51	11.26 / 79	10.35 / 67

* Denotes ETF Fund, N/A denotes number is not availabl

Incl. in Returns		RISK				NET ASSETS		VALUATION			ASSET					FUND MANAGER	
		Risk Rating/ Pts	3 Year		Avg Dura- tion	NAV as of 12/31/15	Total $(Mil)	Premium / Discount		Wtd Avg P/E	Cash %	Stocks %	Bonds %	Other %	Portfolio Turnover Ratio	Manager Quality Pct	Manager Tenure (Years)
Dividend Yield %	Expense Ratio		Standard Deviation	Beta				As of 12/31/15	1 Year Average								
5.35	N/A	U /	N/A	N/A	N/A	59.18	N/A	1.93	N/A	N/A	0	0	0	100	N/A	N/A	N/A
8.87	0.30	B- / 7.2	N/A	N/A	N/A	59.97	6	0.32	-0.22	N/A	0	0	0	100	13	92	N/A
4.00	0.35	B / 8.3	9.4	2.34	N/A	60.33	73	-1.18	-1.15	N/A	0	0	99	1	59	37	N/A
2.52	0.20	B- / 7.6	6.2	1.72	8.6	24.24	79	0.08	N/A	N/A	1	0	98	1	13	54	N/A
2.24	0.23	B- / 7.9	4.3	1.22	8.0	24.33	1,079	0.21	-0.07	N/A	0	0	99	1	20	61	N/A
2.74	0.20	B- / 7.7	5.3	1.33	8.6	23.53	26	1.02	-0.28	N/A	0	0	99	1	23	63	N/A
0.90	0.20	B / 8.4	1.7	0.32	3.7	24.29	2,351	0.29	-0.02	N/A	0	0	100	0	23	67	N/A
4.50	0.45	C+ / 6.7	7.6	0.37	N/A	56.96	296	0.16	-0.33	N/A	0	0	88	12	38	87	N/A
4.68	0.11	B- / 7.2	10.8	1.01	N/A	95.55	51	0.52	0.07	62.2	0	100	0	0	3	70	11
0.54	0.15	B- / 7.1	N/A	N/A	N/A	73.84	11	0.20	0.04	N/A	0	0	0	100	75	86	3
8.46	0.12	C+ / 6.6	N/A	N/A	N/A	66.64	59	1.17	0.05	N/A	0	0	0	100	17	47	3
9.10	0.18	B- / 7.0	N/A	N/A	N/A	73.99	14	0.92	0.06	N/A	0	0	0	100	38	55	3
3.95	0.11	B- / 7.2	10.6	1.00	N/A	151.21	199	0.64	0.08	62.6	0	100	0	0	3	68	16
7.14	0.10	C+ / 6.7	12.3	1.02	N/A	76.67	74	0.14	-0.14	79.8	0	100	0	0	17	59	11
4.26	0.37	B / 8.3	14.9	0.75	N/A	46.73	27	-1.22	0.12	N/A	0	100	0	0	2	90	N/A
3.04	0.45	B / 8.5	13.7	0.59	N/A	54.72	73	-0.80	-0.30	N/A	0	100	0	0	19	92	N/A
3.99	0.25	B- / 7.3	9.9	0.88	N/A	88.17	17	2.15	0.22	N/A	0	0	0	100	70	84	4
8.48	0.24	C+ / 6.7	11.9	0.93	N/A	76.77	8	1.91	-0.52	N/A	0	0	0	100	12	79	4
3.14	0.21	B- / 7.4	11.4	0.91	N/A	117.43	175	0.02	0.07	110.8	0	100	0	0	53	75	11
5.05	0.21	B- / 7.0	12.1	1.00	N/A	75.95	106	0.22	0.08	40.9	0	100	0	0	44	51	11
3.95	N/A	U /	N/A	N/A	N/A	46.01	N/A	0.37	N/A	N/A	0	0	0	100	N/A	N/A	N/A
4.75	0.09	B / 8.6	10.6	1.00	N/A	204.02	180,378	-0.07	0.01	60.6	0	100	0	0	4	68	N/A
3.80	0.18	B / 8.4	10.9	1.02	N/A	100.15	425	-0.06	0.04	90.0	0	100	0	0	22	78	16
3.58	N/A	U /	N/A	N/A	N/A	29.19	N/A	0.24	N/A	N/A	0	0	0	100	N/A	N/A	1
5.72	0.18	B- / 7.2	11.1	1.03	N/A	95.90	220	0.04	N/A	28.1	0	100	0	0	24	49	16
.77	0.18	B / 8.1	13.4	1.03	N/A	98.91	314	-0.03	0.08	90.0	0	100	0	0	16	51	11
.80	0.20	C+ / 6.3	13.4	0.97	N/A	172.55	372	0.13	0.07	147.7	0	100	0	0	49	70	16
.00	0.21	C+ / 6.9	13.4	1.03	N/A	92.91	287	0.06	0.06	42.1	0	100	0	0	42	55	16
2.36	0.35	D- / 1.4	13.3	1.00	N/A	52.84	60	0.08	0.04	N/A	0	100	0	0	42	92	5
.70	0.35	E+ / 0.9	30.8	1.20	N/A	70.20	1,192	0.00	-0.06	272.5	0	100	0	0	78	97	10
.94	0.50	C+ / 6.8	18.4	1.08	N/A	18.75	156	-0.75	-0.25	N/A	0	100	0	0	12	16	N/A
.21	0.59	B- / 7.0	19.7	0.97	N/A	73.79	948	-0.41	-0.14	63.1	0	100	0	0	14	49	N/A
.11	0.35	B- / 7.4	10.6	0.91	N/A	73.55	12,668	0.03	-0.01	32.6	0	100	0	0	28	77	11
.47	0.53	C+ / 6.4	17.6	0.99	N/A	50.14	63	-0.70	-0.85	N/A	0	100	0	0	4	44	N/A
.21	0.53	B- / 7.6	14.1	0.92	N/A	74.29	688	-0.93	-0.18	60.9	0	100	0	0	28	94	N/A
.32	0.53	C+ / 5.9	20.0	1.09	N/A	22.63	67	-0.66	-0.13	1.3	0	100	0	0	7	16	N/A
.20	0.53	C- / 4.1	21.5	1.32	N/A	35.15	49	0.03	-0.11	32.2	0	100	0	0	6	13	N/A
.06	0.59	B- / 7.4	15.0	1.01	N/A	52.45	285	-0.71	-0.10	35.3	0	99	0	1	18	75	N/A
.76	0.53	C / 5.2	16.9	0.97	N/A	23.98	491	-1.08	-0.14	N/A	0	100	0	0	78	3	N/A
.48	0.65	B- / 7.5	14.7	0.90	N/A	37.90	609	-0.50	-0.26	19.2	0	99	0	1	12	20	N/A
.82	0.40	C / 4.6	16.2	0.73	N/A	32.08	574	0.06	0.09	N/A	2	97	0	1	21	18	N/A
.08	0.40	C+ / 6.1	N/A	N/A	N/A	56.94	29	0.04	0.24	N/A	0	0	0	100	31	28	N/A
.77	0.40	C+ / 6.8	11.7	0.73	N/A	41.46	112	0.19	-0.05	20.2	0	99	0	1	7	78	N/A
.14	0.35	D- / 1.4	13.9	0.67	N/A	44.28	34	0.65	0.10	N/A	0	100	0	0	40	96	5
.93	0.35	D- / 1.5	12.5	0.69	N/A	57.34	118	0.07	0.03	N/A	0	100	0	0	37	95	5
.39	0.35	C+ / 6.9	17.4	1.12	N/A	34.17	1,453	0.03	-0.01	30.5	0	100	0	0	25	23	10
.77	0.46	B- / 7.0	15.5	0.95	N/A	33.62	1,450	-0.77	-0.10	9.7	0	100	0	0	76	73	N/A
.19	0.45	C+ / 6.6	12.4	0.89	N/A	29.35	70	1.50	0.42	37.0	0	100	0	0	29	85	N/A
87	0.47	B- / 7.8	11.9	0.81	N/A	28.36	793	-0.46	0.03	28.9	0	100	0	0	17	79	N/A
95	N/A	U /	N/A	N/A	N/A	38.04	N/A	-0.39	N/A	N/A	0	0	0	100	N/A	N/A	1
97	0.35	C- / 3.8	26.6	1.25	N/A	14.95	500	0.00	-0.02	14.8	0	100	0	0	38	1	10
16	0.25	B / 8.2	11.9	0.99	N/A	254.27	14,017	-0.09	-0.02	78.6	0	100	0	0	17	49	N/A

Denotes ETF Fund, N/A denotes number is not available

99 Pct = Best
0 Pct = Worst

Fund Type	Fund Name	Ticker Symbol	Overall Investment Rating	PRICE: Price As of 12/31/15	PRICE: 52 Week High	PRICE: 52 Week Low	PERFORMANCE: Performance Rating/Pts	% Total Return Through 12/31/15: 3 Mo	6 Mo	1Yr/Pct	Annualized 3Yr/Pct	Annualized 5Yr/Pct
EN	*SPDR S&P Oil & Gas Equip & Serv	XES	D-	17.54	30.80	16.58	E+ / 0.7	-5.46	-29.28	-36.75 / 5	-20.51 / 8	-12.46 / 11
IN	*SPDR S&P Oil & Gas Expl & Prod	XOP	D-	30.22	56.18	28.30	E+ / 0.8	-13.46	-31.82	-36.09 / 5	-17.44 / 10	-9.45 / 14
HL	*SPDR S&P Pharmaceuticals ETF	XPH	C-	51.20	67.25	38.28	A+ / 9.8	16.79	-7.40	7.81 / 85	29.49 / 98	22.57 / 98
IN	*SPDR S&P Retail ETF	XRT	C-	43.24	51.25	41.63	B- / 7.2	-3.13	-11.66	-7.90 / 31	11.71 / 81	14.28 / 89
EM	*SPDR S&P Russia	RBL	D-	13.85	20.13	13.27	D- / 1.3	2.92	-11.98	5.37 / 80	-17.84 / 10	-13.69 / 10
IN	*SPDR S&P Semiconductor ETF	XSD	C+	43.68	46.49	33.28	A+ / 9.7	14.81	2.16	10.31 / 89	23.86 / 97	9.35 / 62
GR	*SPDR S&P Software & Services ETF	XSW	C-	50.72	53.16	35.25	A / 9.4	7.17	0.39	10.39 / 89	17.77 / 93	--
GR	*SPDR S&P Telecom ETF	XTL	C+	56.22	61.34	51.85	C+ / 6.8	5.97	-0.52	-1.02 / 55	7.32 / 68	--
UT	*SPDR S&P Transportation ETF	XTN	C-	42.85	55.68	39.95	B+ / 8.3	-1.31	-9.03	-18.64 / 15	16.25 / 92	--
GL	*SPDR S&P WORLD EX-US ETF	GWL	C+	25.75	30.13	24.68	C+ / 5.6	2.53	-6.38	0.37 / 63	3.60 / 55	3.20 / 39
GL	*SPDR SP Intl Con Disc Sect ETF	IPD	B+	36.80	42.50	32.66	B- / 7.0	1.41	-5.58	2.27 / 72	8.37 / 71	7.04 / 55
GL	*SPDR SP Intl Con Stap Sect ETF	IPS	B	41.47	52.00	36.49	B / 7.7	5.90	3.15	12.75 / 92	7.38 / 68	9.23 / 62
EN	*SPDR SP Intl Energy Sector ETF	IPW	D-	15.32	21.90	14.65	D- / 1.4	-2.99	-18.02	-21.17 / 12	-11.96 / 15	-7.42 / 16
FS	*SPDR SP Intl Finl Sector ETF	IPF	C+	19.82	26.90	18.75	C+ / 6.0	6.88	-5.25	0.87 / 66	4.51 / 59	4.29 / 44
HL	*SPDR SP Intl Health Care ETF	IRY	A	50.37	55.62	45.75	B+ / 8.9	4.34	-2.28	10.22 / 89	13.76 / 87	13.35 / 86
GL	*SPDR SP Intl Industrial ETF	IPN	C+	27.75	32.12	25.51	C / 5.5	3.59	-6.40	-0.85 / 56	3.45 / 55	2.18 / 34
GL	*SPDR SP Intl Materials Sec ETF	IRV	D	16.93	22.71	16.10	D / 1.7	0.91	-16.90	-12.82 / 20	-10.51 / 17	-8.65 / 15
GL	*SPDR SP Intl Tech Sector ETF	IPK	B-	31.20	35.16	25.04	C+ / 6.6	8.38	-0.54	1.43 / 70	6.25 / 65	4.15 / 44
GL	*SPDR SP Intl Telecom Sect ETF	IST	B+	25.08	27.95	23.24	B / 8.2	6.36	-3.25	4.66 / 78	11.45 / 79	7.26 / 55
UT	*SPDR SP Intl Utils Sector ETF	IPU	C+	16.08	18.49	14.98	C / 4.9	0.69	-3.53	-5.05 / 38	2.27 / 50	-0.57 / 26
GI	*SPDR SSgA Global Allocation ETF	GAL	C+	32.87	36.50	32.27	C+ / 5.7	1.55	-3.91	-3.22 / 46	4.37 / 59	--
GI	*SPDR SSgA Income Allocation ETF	INKM	C	29.58	34.09	28.07	C / 4.5	0.58	-3.42	-5.74 / 36	1.55 / 46	--
GI	*SPDR SSgA Multi Asset Real Retur	RLY	D	22.25	27.52	17.22	D / 1.9	-2.65	-13.17	-15.75 / 17	-8.89 / 19	--
GEI	*SPDR SSgA Ultra Short Term Bond	ULST	B-	39.90	41.00	39.63	C- / 4.2	-0.22	-0.24	0.14 / 61	--	--
FO	*SPDR STOXX Europe 50 ETF	FEU	C	31.82	37.85	30.85	C / 4.7	-0.23	-7.86	-3.03 / 46	2.03 / 48	3.22 / 39
IN	*SPDR Wells Fargo Preferred Stk E	PSK	B-	44.69	45.50	31.26	B / 7.6	6.11	7.82	9.28 / 87	6.48 / 66	6.84 / 54
GI	*Star Global Buy Write ETF	VEGA	C+	25.88	27.83	24.55	C / 4.8	2.01	-3.00	-1.86 / 51	1.44 / 45	--
FS	*Stock Split Index	TOFR	C-	15.01	17.00	14.86	C- / 4.1	2.29	-4.38	1.13 / 68	--	--
GR	*Technology Select Sector SPDR	XLK	A+	42.83	44.65	31.32	A- / 9.2	7.91	4.11	6.23 / 82	15.54 / 90	12.79 / 83
GL	*Teucrium Agricultural Fund	TAGS	D-	26.47	33.05	25.16	D- / 1.0	-0.86	-13.75	-19.91 / 14	-18.25 / 9	--
GR	*Teucrium Corn	CORN	D-	21.22	27.32	21.20	E+ / 0.8	-9.85	-19.04	-19.86 / 14	-20.83 / 8	-10.73 / 13
GL	*Teucrium Soybean	SOYB	D+	17.33	21.42	17.13	D / 1.8	-2.37	-15.59	-15.26 / 17	-9.59 / 18	--
GL	*Teucrium Sugar	CANE	D-	10.06	12.95	7.89	D- / 1.5	11.26	6.79	-13.20 / 20	-16.63 / 11	--
GL	*Teucrium Wheat	WEAT	E+	9.14	12.93	9.09	E+ / 0.6	-8.94	-21.95	-27.11 / 9	-23.51 / 7	--
IN	*TrimTabs Float Shrink ETF	TTFS	A+	54.09	58.90	46.50	B+ / 8.9	1.70	-4.94	-1.31 / 54	15.98 / 91	--
GL	*TrimTabs Intl Free-Cash-Flow ETF	FCFI	U	21.52	N/A	N/A	U /	1.61	-13.02	--	--	--
IN	*UBS AG FI Enhanced BC Growth ETN	FBG	C+	59.39	65.67	45.00	A+ / 9.7	9.37	1.35	8.10 / 85	26.20 / 98	--
GR	*UBS AG FI Enhanced Large Cap Gro	FBGX	C	124.19	133.00	97.36	B+ / 8.6	11.17	0.71	9.83 / 88	--	--
IN	*UBS E Tracs Alerian MLP Infrast	MLPI	E+	26.19	41.12	21.02	D / 2.0	-8.39	-23.16	-33.00 / 6	-4.28 / 26	1.92 / 33
GR	*UBS E Tracs CMCI Agriculture TR	UAG	D-	18.08	22.16	17.60	D- / 1.4	-0.93	-12.60	-15.52 / 17	-13.53 / 13	-9.45 / 14
GR	*UBS E Tracs CMCI Energy TR	UBN	E	6.00	12.99	6.00	E / 0.4	-22.28	-39.82	-41.63 / 3	-26.68 / 5	-17.08 / 7
GR	*UBS E Tracs CMCI Food Tr	FUD	D-	18.57	22.97	18.00	D- / 1.5	1.17	-11.60	-16.82 / 16	-12.49 / 14	-8.34 / 15
GR	*UBS E Tracs CMCI Gold TR	UBG	E+	27.15	34.50	26.01	D- / 1.3	-5.18	-10.32	-12.18 / 22	-14.77 / 12	-6.00 / 18
GR	*UBS E Tracs CMCI Industrial Meta	UBM	E	11.68	16.48	11.18	D- / 1.1	-4.76	-19.34	-25.94 / 9	-16.09 / 11	-13.66 / 10
GR	*UBS E Tracs CMCI Livestock Tr	UBC	D	18.73	23.83	17.23	D+ / 2.7	-3.39	-11.51	-21.40 / 12	-1.98 / 31	-2.31 / 23
GR	*UBS E Tracs CMCI Silver TR	USV	E-	18.71	25.14	17.17	E+ / 0.8	-6.96	-9.74	-11.62 / 23	-23.78 / 6	-14.48 / 9
GR	*UBS E Tracs CMCI Total Return	UCI	E+	12.07	20.04	11.51	E+ / 0.9	-10.11	-23.30	-25.67 / 10	-18.06 / 9	-12.05 / 12
IN	*UBS E Tracs DJ-UBS Comm Idx Tot	DJCI	E	14.22	19.42	13.85	E+ / 0.9	-11.13	-23.84	-25.59 / 10	-17.98 / 9	-13.77 / 10
GR	*UBS E Tracs Long Platinum ETN	PTM	E	9.44	14.24	8.62	E+ / 0.9	-2.87	-19.45	-27.60 / 8	-19.11 / 9	-14.28 / 9
GR	*UBS E-TRACS 1xMo Sht Alerian MLP	MLPS	C-	15.30	20.63	10.48	B- / 7.0	10.93	27.16	42.19 / 99	-1.44 / 32	-7.39 / 16
EN	*UBS E-TRACS 2x Levd Lng Alerian	MLPL	E	22.16	59.55	14.85	E+ / 0.9	-17.25	-43.67	-57.47 / 1	-10.22 / 17	1.72 / 33
GR	*UBS E-TRACS 2x Levd Long WF BDC	BDCL	E+	15.98	22.72	14.00	D+ / 2.8	2.70	-13.15	-11.76 / 23	-3.57 / 28	--

* Denotes ETF Fund, N/A denotes number is not availabl[e]

Incl. in Returns		RISK				NET ASSETS		VALUATION			ASSET					FUND MANAGER	
		Risk Rating/ Pts	3 Year		Avg Dura- tion			Premium / Discount		Wtd Avg P/E					Portfolio Turnover Ratio		
Dividend Yield %	Expense Ratio		Standard Deviation	Beta		NAV as of 12/31/15	Total $(Mil)	As of 12/31/15	1 Year Average		Cash %	Stocks %	Bonds %	Other %		Manager Quality Pct	Manager Tenure (Years)
4.10	0.35	**C / 4.3**	31.6	1.55	N/A	17.55	251	-0.06	N/A	18.5	0	100	0	0	36	11	10
3.81	0.35	**C / 4.5**	30.5	1.32	N/A	30.23	1,384	-0.03	-0.02	15.2	0	100	0	0	44	3	10
1.11	0.35	**D- / 1.5**	22.7	1.19	N/A	51.21	975	-0.02	0.01	852.4	0	100	0	0	65	95	10
2.77	0.35	**C- / 3.8**	14.9	1.11	N/A	43.28	646	-0.09	N/A	64.7	0	100	0	0	45	38	10
18.47	0.59	**C- / 4.1**	28.2	1.18	N/A	13.86	23	-0.07	0.03	N/A	0	100	0	0	7	16	N/A
1.34	0.35	**C- / 3.8**	19.1	1.21	N/A	43.71	176	-0.07	N/A	58.4	0	100	0	0	42	90	10
2.96	0.35	**D / 1.7**	14.6	1.05	N/A	50.26	26	0.92	-0.05	N/A	0	0	0	100	36	83	5
3.28	0.35	**C+ / 6.9**	11.5	0.89	N/A	55.95	25	0.48	0.07	N/A	0	100	0	0	47	35	5
5.16	0.35	**D- / 1.5**	16.5	0.19	N/A	42.84	274	0.02	-0.03	N/A	0	100	0	0	26	97	5
5.42	0.34	**B / 8.3**	11.9	0.93	N/A	25.86	825	-0.43	0.15	19.5	0	100	0	0	8	59	N/A
4.36	0.44	**B / 8.6**	12.3	0.88	N/A	37.14	18	-0.92	-0.07	18.5	0	100	0	0	9	87	N/A
1.76	0.43	**B- / 7.4**	12.1	0.82	N/A	41.38	43	0.22	0.01	18.4	0	100	0	0	5	84	8
10.81	0.43	**C / 4.7**	19.4	0.92	N/A	15.17	19	0.99	0.31	10.1	0	100	0	0	5	19	N/A
16.92	0.44	**C+ / 6.9**	14.3	0.71	N/A	19.33	11	2.53	0.25	12.1	0	100	0	0	12	29	N/A
2.60	0.44	**B- / 7.9**	11.5	0.69	N/A	50.57	66	-0.40	0.01	124.3	1	98	0	1	11	87	N/A
6.20	0.45	**B / 8.3**	12.0	0.90	N/A	27.99	24	-0.86	-0.08	24.2	1	98	0	1	12	60	N/A
1.96	0.45	**C+ / 5.6**	16.2	1.01	N/A	16.79	8	0.83	-0.02	24.8	0	100	0	0	2	11	N/A
6.46	0.45	**B- / 7.9**	13.0	0.83	N/A	31.48	13	-0.89	-0.06	100.1	0	99	0	1	5	80	N/A
10.00	0.44	**B- / 7.4**	14.5	1.02	N/A	25.08	44	0.00	-0.11	11.2	0	100	0	0	21	91	N/A
5.39	0.45	**B / 8.0**	13.7	0.42	N/A	16.22	70	-0.86	-0.20	34.9	0	100	0	0	6	48	N/A
3.90	0.05	**B- / 7.2**	8.0	0.67	N/A	32.80	112	0.21	0.04	N/A	0	0	0	100	98	32	N/A
4.19	0.35	**B- / 7.9**	7.8	0.52	N/A	29.58	106	0.00	N/A	N/A	0	0	0	100	64	28	N/A
1.95	0.23	**C / 5.5**	10.1	0.65	N/A	22.23	168	0.09	-0.02	N/A	0	0	0	100	33	9	N/A
0.45	0.20	**B+ / 9.9**	N/A	N/A	N/A	39.92	18	-0.05	0.01	N/A	0	0	0	100	79	68	N/A
3.91	0.29	**B- / 7.6**	13.3	1.02	N/A	31.93	262	-0.34	0.11	N/A	0	100	0	0	9	43	14
4.82	0.45	**C+ / 6.9**	5.3	0.06	N/A	44.61	252	0.18	0.04	N/A	3	0	0	97	48	90	7
0.00	1.85	**B+ / 9.1**	6.8	0.57	N/A	25.95	26	-0.27	-0.10	N/A	0	0	0	100	45	25	4
1.33	0.55	**C+ / 6.9**	N/A	N/A	N/A	14.91	N/A	0.67	0.14	N/A	0	0	0	100	57	71	2
4.03	0.15	**B / 8.6**	11.5	0.99	N/A	42.86	13,858	-0.07	N/A	56.2	0	100	0	0	5	78	18
0.00	0.50	**C / 5.3**	20.9	0.20	N/A	26.59	2	-0.45	-1.87	N/A	0	0	0	100	N/A	7	N/A
0.00	3.57	**C / 4.6**	22.0	0.09	N/A	21.24	104	-0.09	-0.04	N/A	0	0	0	100	N/A	6	N/A
0.00	3.87	**C+ / 6.4**	18.5	0.14	N/A	17.34	4	-0.06	-0.06	N/A	0	0	0	100	N/A	15	N/A
0.00	1.88	**C- / 3.3**	18.7	0.50	N/A	10.02	3	0.40	0.16	N/A	0	0	0	100	N/A	7	N/A
0.00	3.74	**C- / 4.0**	29.7	0.23	N/A	9.15	27	-0.11	-0.02	N/A	0	0	0	100	N/A	4	N/A
0.77	0.99	**B / 8.0**	11.5	1.04	N/A	54.09	147	0.00	0.03	N/A	0	0	0	100	52	79	1
2.23	N/A	**U /**	N/A	N/A	N/A	21.38	N/A	0.65	N/A	N/A	0	0	0	100	N/A	N/A	1
0.00	N/A	**C- / 3.7**	16.6	1.53	N/A	59.24	130	0.25	-0.03	N/A	0	0	0	100	N/A	86	4
0.00	N/A	**C- / 3.2**	N/A	N/A	N/A	123.44	571	0.61	-0.01	N/A	0	0	0	100	N/A	91	N/A
7.60	N/A	**D- / 1.4**	18.9	1.08	N/A	26.13	2,328	0.23	0.03	N/A	0	0	0	100	N/A	9	6
0.00	0.65	**C- / 3.3**	17.9	0.42	N/A	18.38	3	-1.63	0.17	N/A	0	0	0	100	N/A	7	8
0.00	0.65	**D / 1.8**	26.2	0.43	N/A	6.14	4	-2.28	-0.25	N/A	0	0	0	100	N/A	3	8
0.00	0.65	**C- / 3.5**	14.8	0.29	N/A	18.63	6	-0.32	0.07	N/A	0	0	0	100	N/A	9	8
0.00	0.30	**D+ / 2.9**	17.8	0.02	N/A	27.21	5	-0.22	-0.04	N/A	0	0	0	100	N/A	10	8
0.00	0.65	**D / 1.6**	13.4	0.43	N/A	11.62	4	0.52	-0.15	N/A	0	0	0	100	N/A	7	8
0.00	0.65	**C- / 4.0**	12.8	0.23	N/A	18.85	8	-0.64	0.09	N/A	0	0	0	100	N/A	31	8
0.00	0.40	**E / 0.5**	27.2	0.03	N/A	18.08	4	3.48	0.10	N/A	0	0	0	100	N/A	5	8
0.00	0.65	**D+ / 2.9**	14.0	0.46	N/A	12.10	12	-0.25	N/A	N/A	0	0	0	100	N/A	5	8
0.00	N/A	**D / 1.7**	12.9	0.33	N/A	14.21	119	0.07	0.01	N/A	0	0	0	100	N/A	6	7
0.00	0.65	**D+ / 2.5**	21.6	0.40	N/A	9.49	66	-0.53	0.07	N/A	0	0	0	100	N/A	5	8
0.00	N/A	**C- / 3.6**	20.0	-1.21	N/A	14.70	4	4.08	0.41	N/A	0	0	0	100	N/A	97	N/A
2.59	N/A	**D- / 1.1**	38.5	1.33	N/A	22.16	312	0.00	0.42	N/A	0	0	0	100	N/A	47	6
9.48	N/A	**D- / 1.1**	25.5	1.38	N/A	15.84	222	0.88	-0.01	N/A	0	0	0	100	N/A	8	5

* Denotes ETF Fund, N/A denotes number is not available

99 Pct = Best
0 Pct = Worst

Fund Type	Fund Name	Ticker Symbol	Overall Investment Rating	PRICE: Price As of 12/31/15	PRICE: 52 Week High	PRICE: 52 Week Low	PERFORMANCE: Performance Rating/Pts	% Total Return Through 12/31/15: 3 Mo	6 Mo	1Yr/Pct	Annualized: 3Yr/Pct	Annualized: 5Yr/Pct
EN	*UBS E-TRACS Alerian MLP Index ET	AMU	**E+**	18.22	29.48	14.56	**D / 1.7**	-9.48	-24.14	-34.27 / 6	-5.59 / 24	--
EN	*UBS E-TRACS Alerian Nat Gas MLP	MLPG	**E+**	22.96	36.71	18.34	**D / 2.1**	-1.57	-20.31	-32.59 / 7	-4.06 / 26	0.54 / 29
GR	*UBS E-TRACS Daily Long-Sht VIX E	XVIX	**D-**	15.95	17.62	15.77	**D+ / 2.7**	-3.04	-3.86	-0.83 / 56	-6.03 / 23	-8.77 / 15
IN	*UBS E-TRACS Diversified Hi Inc E	DVHI	**D-**	20.73	25.15	19.75	**D- / 1.5**	-0.33	-8.01	-15.08 / 18	--	--
IN	*UBS E-TRACS Mnth Pay 2xL DJ SDI	DVYL	**C**	44.78	53.94	22.93	**A+ / 9.6**	7.47	1.52	-3.65 / 44	24.00 / 97	--
GR	*UBS E-TRACS Mnth Pay 2xLev CE	CEFL	**E+**	15.35	23.13	14.06	**D- / 1.2**	4.00	-15.85	-16.24 / 16	--	--
GL	*UBS E-TRACS Mnth Pay 2xLev Dvs H	DVHL	**E**	16.91	24.87	14.97	**D- / 1.0**	-2.15	-13.45	-16.87 / 16	--	--
IN	*UBS E-TRACS MnthPay 2xL S&P Div	SDYL	**C**	52.45	56.56	43.00	**A+ / 9.7**	14.54	2.80	0.04 / 60	26.09 / 97	--
GR	*UBS E-TRACS Mo Pay 2xLevd US SCH	SMHD	**U**	14.54	N/A	N/A	**U /**	-0.74	-21.83	--	--	--
GR	*UBS E-TRACS Mo Pay 2xLevd WF MLP	LMLP	**E**	12.67	27.00	11.43	**E- / 0.1**	-13.64	-42.31	-33.93 / 6	--	--
FO	*UBS E-TRACS Mo Py 2x Levd DJ Int	RWXL	**D**	29.52	41.22	27.71	**C / 4.5**	1.88	-3.59	-7.68 / 32	1.81 / 47	--
GL	*UBS E-TRACS Mo Py 2x Levd Mort R	MORL	**E**	13.28	21.62	11.45	**D+ / 2.5**	-3.50	-12.35	-22.81 / 11	-3.01 / 29	--
GR	*UBS E-TRACS Mo Rst 2xLevd SP500	SPLX	**C-**	31.11	36.96	26.15	**B- / 7.1**	16.82	-0.80	1.15 / 68	--	--
PM	*UBS E-TRACS S&P 500 Gold Hedged	SPGH	**D-**	48.74	80.17	47.21	**C- / 3.1**	-1.09	-8.86	-9.95 / 26	-2.26 / 30	5.67 / 50
GR	*UBS E-TRACS Wells Fargo BDC Inde	BDCS	**D-**	20.19	23.79	18.16	**C- / 3.6**	0.93	-4.26	-5.01 / 39	-1.24 / 33	--
GL	*UBS E-TRACS Wells Fargo MLP ex-E	FMLP	**E**	18.25	26.59	17.52	**E+ / 0.6**	-11.61	-23.02	-17.57 / 15	--	--
EN	*UBS E-TRACS Wells Fargo MLP Inde	MLPW	**E+**	21.56	35.83	18.06	**D / 1.7**	-8.40	-29.52	-35.69 / 5	-5.30 / 24	1.16 / 31
EN	*United States 12 Month Oil Fund	USL	**E**	17.02	28.84	16.31	**E / 0.5**	-17.34	-33.82	-35.41 / 5	-24.84 / 5	-16.53 / 7
GL	*United States Agriculture Index	USAG	**D+**	19.39	22.52	18.60	**D / 2.1**	-2.51	-9.81	-14.09 / 19	-8.84 / 19	--
EN	*United States Brent Oil Fund	BNO	**E-**	12.24	25.29	11.82	**E- / 0.2**	-25.77	-44.36	-44.41 / 2	-33.19 / 3	-17.03 / 7
IN	*United States Commodity Index	USCI	**D+**	40.47	48.52	38.38	**D / 1.6**	-3.27	-14.28	-15.90 / 17	-11.32 / 15	-8.55 / 15
IN	*United States Copper Index	CPER	**D-**	14.27	19.85	13.00	**D- / 1.0**	-8.78	-20.06	-24.97 / 10	-17.87 / 10	--
EN	*United States Diesel-Heating Oil	UHN	**E+**	12.45	25.10	12.30	**E / 0.3**	-31.25	-44.76	-41.36 / 3	-28.15 / 4	-15.75 / 8
EN	*United States Gasoline Fund LP	UGA	**D-**	29.26	42.95	27.28	**E+ / 0.9**	-6.01	-28.49	-11.92 / 22	-20.58 / 8	-7.00 / 17
EN	*United States Natural Gas Fund	UNG	**E+**	8.67	16.93	6.91	**E+ / 0.6**	-23.13	-36.06	-42.04 / 3	-22.21 / 7	-29.05 / 3
EN	*United States Oil Fund	USO	**E**	11.00	21.50	10.52	**E / 0.3**	-25.52	-41.89	-44.70 / 2	-31.27 / 3	-21.82 / 5
EN	*United States Short Oil Fund	DNO	**B+**	81.43	85.49	47.43	**A+ / 9.9**	29.05	53.76	44.68 / 99	29.62 / 98	14.22 / 89
EN	*US 12 Month Natural Gas Fund	UNL	**D-**	9.70	14.80	8.53	**E+ / 0.9**	-12.78	-24.77	-29.99 / 7	-17.03 / 10	-22.64 / 5
GL	*US Global Jets ETF	JETS	**U**	24.92	N/A	N/A	**U /**	7.08	12.95	--	--	--
UT	*Utilities Select Sector SPDR	XLU	**B+**	43.28	49.78	40.80	**B / 7.8**	1.87	5.56	-4.40 / 41	10.92 / 78	10.86 / 71
GR	*Validea Market Legends	VALX	**D-**	23.06	27.25	22.43	**D / 1.8**	-0.76	-12.36	-7.97 / 31	--	--
FO	*ValueShares Intl Quantitative Va	IVAL	**D**	23.95	28.63	22.01	**D+ / 2.9**	3.94	-8.59	-2.94 / 47	--	--
GR	*ValueShares US Quantitative Valu	QVAL	**D**	22.20	28.88	21.93	**D- / 1.1**	-3.93	-15.11	-12.67 / 21	--	--
IN	*Vanguard 500 Index ETF	VOO	**A+**	186.93	195.94	168.10	**B+ / 8.9**	5.79	-0.01	1.92 / 71	14.22 / 88	12.37 / 81
IN	*Vanguard Consumer Discret ETF	VCR	**A-**	122.55	129.65	100.00	**A / 9.3**	2.41	-0.83	7.19 / 84	17.54 / 93	16.52 / 94
IN	*Vanguard Consumer Staples ETF	VDC	**A+**	129.07	133.00	84.62	**A- / 9.1**	5.75	4.99	6.49 / 82	15.19 / 90	14.88 / 91
GR	*Vanguard Div Appreciation ETF	VIG	**A-**	77.76	83.28	47.70	**B / 7.7**	4.69	-0.73	-1.75 / 51	10.63 / 77	10.58 / 69
EM	*Vanguard Em Mkt Govt Bd Idx ETF	VWOB	**C**	73.96	79.45	73.50	**C / 4.6**	0.33	-1.41	1.61 / 70	--	--
EN	*Vanguard Energy ETF	VDE	**D+**	83.12	118.46	81.05	**D / 2.1**	-5.29	-18.87	-23.55 / 11	-5.61 / 24	-1.62 / 24
GR	*Vanguard Extended Market Index E	VXF	**B+**	83.80	95.03	74.41	**B / 7.7**	1.65	-7.80	-3.03 / 46	11.62 / 80	10.27 / 66
USA	*Vanguard Extnd Durtn Trea Idx ET	EDV	**C**	113.20	141.91	106.44	**C+ / 5.8**	-4.05	7.62	-6.52 / 35	4.71 / 60	13.01 / 84
FS	*Vanguard Financials ETF	VFH	**A+**	48.45	51.96	31.35	**B+ / 8.5**	5.18	-2.04	-0.59 / 57	13.20 / 85	10.08 / 66
FO	*Vanguard FTSE All-Wld ex-US S/C	VSS	**C**	92.87	108.24	85.00	**C / 5.5**	3.06	-6.00	1.28 / 68	3.37 / 54	2.07 / 34
FO	*Vanguard FTSE All-World ex-US ET	VEU	**C**	43.41	52.13	41.51	**C- / 4.2**	1.28	-9.29	-3.67 / 43	1.10 / 42	1.61 / 32
FO	*Vanguard FTSE Developed Markets	VEA	**C+**	36.72	42.51	34.71	**C+ / 5.7**	2.28	-6.72	0.75 / 65	4.29 / 58	3.88 / 43
EM	*Vanguard FTSE Emerging Markets E	VWO	**D+**	32.71	45.08	30.90	**D / 2.1**	-3.07	-18.50	-14.45 / 18	-7.56 / 20	-4.73 / 19
FO	*Vanguard FTSE Europe ETF	VGK	**C+**	49.88	58.51	47.95	**C+ / 5.6**	0.36	-6.93	-0.98 / 55	4.10 / 58	4.63 / 46
FO	*Vanguard FTSE Pacific Fund ETF	VPL	**C+**	56.67	65.52	51.20	**C+ / 6.0**	5.85	-5.73	3.40 / 75	4.50 / 59	2.99 / 38
GL	*Vanguard Global ex-US RE ETF	VNQI	**C**	51.11	59.96	47.26	**C- / 4.2**	0.07	-6.11	-2.31 / 49	0.69 / 40	4.08 / 44
GR	*Vanguard Growth ETF	VUG	**A-**	106.39	111.92	93.61	**A- / 9.0**	4.41	-0.60	3.40 / 75	14.82 / 90	12.89 / 84
HL	*Vanguard HealthCare Index ETF	VHT	**A+**	132.88	146.00	91.31	**A+ / 9.6**	5.64	-4.11	6.95 / 83	23.17 / 97	19.97 / 97
IN	*Vanguard High Dividend Yield ETF	VYM	**A+**	66.75	70.66	48.05	**B+ / 8.7**	7.06	1.08	1.21 / 68	13.34 / 85	13.09 / 85

* Denotes ETF Fund, N/A denotes number is not available

Incl. in Returns		RISK	3 Year			NET ASSETS		VALUATION			ASSET					FUND MANAGER	
ividend Yield %	Expense Ratio	Risk Rating/ Pts	Standard Deviation	Beta	Avg Dura- tion	NAV as of 12/31/15	Total $(Mil)	Premium / Discount As of 12/31/15	Premium / Discount 1 Year Average	Wtd Avg P/E	Cash %	Stocks %	Bonds %	Other %	Portfolio Turnover Ratio	Manager Quality Pct	Manager Tenure (Years)
7.99	N/A	**D+ / 2.8**	18.9	0.70	N/A	18.24	354	-0.11	N/A	N/A	0	0	0	100	N/A	56	4
7.69	N/A	**D- / 1.3**	21.1	0.71	N/A	22.85	38	0.48	-0.05	N/A	0	0	0	100	N/A	71	6
0.00	N/A	**C- / 3.7**	12.2	0.20	N/A	15.68	N/A	1.72	-0.20	N/A	0	0	0	100	N/A	18	N/A
6.11	N/A	**C / 4.5**	N/A	N/A	N/A	20.86	26	-0.62	0.05	N/A	0	0	0	100	N/A	17	N/A
10.57	N/A	**C- / 3.1**	20.4	1.58	N/A	44.66	18	0.27	-0.09	N/A	0	0	0	100	N/A	77	4
21.25	N/A	**D+ / 2.9**	N/A	N/A	N/A	15.56	184	-1.35	0.05	N/A	0	0	0	100	N/A	7	N/A
14.62	N/A	**D / 2.2**	N/A	N/A	N/A	16.86	N/A	0.30	0.06	N/A	0	0	0	100	N/A	8	N/A
7.21	N/A	**C- / 3.0**	21.6	1.84	N/A	50.80	19	3.25	-0.01	N/A	0	0	0	100	N/A	61	4
16.43	N/A	**U /**	N/A	N/A	N/A	14.50	N/A	0.28	N/A	N/A	0	0	0	100	N/A	N/A	N/A
36.19	N/A	**D+ / 2.7**	N/A	N/A	N/A	12.69	23	-0.16	0.01	N/A	0	0	0	100	N/A	2	N/A
4.81	N/A	**D+ / 2.9**	30.2	1.73	N/A	29.42	13	0.34	0.23	N/A	0	0	0	100	N/A	23	4
3.85	N/A	**E / 0.5**	30.0	1.13	N/A	13.25	266	0.23	0.12	N/A	0	0	0	100	N/A	27	4
0.00	N/A	**C- / 3.0**	N/A	N/A	N/A	30.80	28	1.01	-0.15	N/A	0	0	0	100	N/A	33	N/A
0.00	N/A	**D+ / 2.7**	22.7	1.13	N/A	48.10	19	1.33	0.36	N/A	0	0	0	100	N/A	98	6
8.74	N/A	**D+ / 2.5**	12.4	0.68	N/A	20.10	68	0.45	0.01	N/A	0	0	0	100	N/A	17	5
1.26	N/A	**D+ / 2.4**	N/A	N/A	N/A	18.21	N/A	0.22	0.48	N/A	0	0	0	100	N/A	9	N/A
8.59	N/A	**D+ / 2.5**	19.3	0.74	N/A	21.58	16	-0.09	-0.13	N/A	0	0	0	100	N/A	49	N/A
0.00	0.93	**D / 1.9**	26.4	0.98	N/A	17.00	48	0.12	-0.14	N/A	91	0	0	9	N/A	6	N/A
0.00	0.88	**C+ / 6.5**	23.5	0.50	N/A	19.79	2	-2.02	-2.76	N/A	0	0	0	100	N/A	15	N/A
0.00	0.92	**E / 0.3**	32.3	1.21	N/A	12.22	40	0.16	-0.12	N/A	0	0	0	100	N/A	3	N/A
0.00	1.04	**B- / 7.0**	10.8	0.29	N/A	40.52	835	-0.12	0.01	N/A	0	0	0	100	N/A	10	N/A
0.00	0.82	**C- / 3.8**	17.7	0.45	N/A	14.24	3	0.21	0.03	N/A	0	0	0	100	N/A	6	N/A
0.00	0.85	**C- / 3.4**	28.1	0.92	N/A	12.48	3	-0.24	0.09	N/A	100	0	0	0	N/A	4	N/A
0.00	0.82	**C / 4.3**	28.5	0.88	N/A	29.30	52	-0.14	-0.03	N/A	91	0	0	9	N/A	8	N/A
0.00	1.14	**C- / 3.2**	34.2	-0.03	N/A	8.69	722	-0.23	-0.01	N/A	100	0	0	0	N/A	6	N/A
0.00	0.72	**C- / 3.1**	32.1	1.06	N/A	11.02	652	-0.18	-0.09	N/A	64	0	0	36	N/A	3	N/A
0.00	0.80	**C / 5.5**	31.4	-1.01	N/A	81.24	10	0.23	0.12	N/A	0	0	0	100	N/A	98	N/A
0.00	0.93	**C / 4.7**	22.2	0.07	N/A	9.72	16	-0.21	-0.10	N/A	0	0	0	100	N/A	9	N/A
0.26	N/A	**U /**	N/A	N/A	N/A	24.86	N/A	0.24	N/A	N/A	0	0	0	100	N/A	N/A	1
8.23	0.15	**B / 8.1**	14.3	0.98	N/A	43.29	5,487	-0.02	-0.01	21.5	0	100	0	0	4	63	18
0.28	N/A	**C- / 3.6**	N/A	N/A	N/A	23.04	N/A	0.09	0.09	N/A	0	0	0	100	N/A	17	N/A
1.66	N/A	**C / 4.8**	N/A	N/A	N/A	24.11	N/A	-0.66	N/A	N/A	0	0	0	100	N/A	43	N/A
1.76	N/A	**C+ / 6.1**	N/A	N/A	N/A	22.16	N/A	0.18	0.04	N/A	0	0	0	100	N/A	11	2
4.67	0.05	**B / 8.6**	10.4	0.98	N/A	187.05	21,814	-0.06	-0.01	60.6	0	0	0	100	3	71	25
0.77	0.10	**B- / 7.2**	12.7	1.11	N/A	122.54	1,260	0.01	0.02	144.1	0	100	0	0	6	79	6
1.39	0.10	**B / 8.2**	11.0	0.88	N/A	129.05	1,976	0.02	0.01	36.9	0	100	0	0	6	83	6
2.44	0.10	**B / 8.6**	10.9	1.01	N/A	77.78	19,921	-0.03	N/A	39.2	0	100	0	0	20	42	10
5.92	0.34	**B- / 7.4**	N/A	N/A	N/A	73.69	236	0.37	0.46	N/A	0	0	0	100	27	76	3
.64	0.10	**C+ / 6.6**	18.9	1.02	N/A	83.16	3,181	-0.05	0.01	15.2	0	100	0	0	4	61	6
.42	0.10	**B- / 7.6**	12.6	1.03	N/A	83.80	3,412	0.00	0.01	77.9	0	100	0	0	9	48	19
3.60	0.10	**C+ / 5.6**	17.7	1.68	N/A	113.04	256	0.14	0.45	N/A	0	0	100	0	16	60	3
.03	0.10	**B / 8.5**	11.1	0.99	N/A	48.46	2,227	-0.02	0.02	35.0	0	99	0	1	4	63	6
.75	0.19	**C+ / 6.7**	11.8	0.83	1.0	92.75	2,015	0.13	0.20	75.4	0	99	0	1	13	62	1
.17	0.14	**B- / 7.7**	12.5	0.96	N/A	43.45	12,524	-0.09	0.08	N/A	0	99	0	1	4	39	8
.81	0.09	**B / 8.1**	12.4	0.97	N/A	36.75	23,072	-0.08	0.12	67.9	0	99	0	1	4	63	3
.89	0.15	**B- / 7.1**	15.2	1.02	1.0	32.86	46,907	-0.46	-0.09	59.3	0	99	0	1	9	63	8
.24	0.12	**B- / 7.7**	13.6	1.03	1.0	49.98	14,084	-0.20	0.10	72.8	0	100	0	0	7	58	8
.79	0.12	**B- / 7.8**	13.4	0.87	1.0	56.68	2,704	-0.02	0.04	N/A	0	99	0	1	5	69	19
.28	0.24	**B / 8.0**	13.7	0.82	N/A	51.41	2,099	-0.58	0.19	N/A	0	99	0	1	8	39	1
.55	0.09	**B- / 7.5**	11.6	1.06	N/A	106.40	15,547	-0.01	0.01	104.8	0	100	0	0	9	65	22
.72	0.09	**B- / 7.7**	12.5	0.95	N/A	132.91	3,453	-0.02	0.02	104.7	0	98	0	2	4	94	12
.18	0.10	**B / 8.7**	10.3	0.95	N/A	66.77	9,132	-0.03	0.01	28.4	0	99	0	1	12	68	10

Denotes ETF Fund, N/A denotes number is not available

99 Pct = Best
0 Pct = Worst

Fund Type	Fund Name	Ticker Symbol	Overall Investment Rating	PRICE: Price As of 12/31/15	PRICE: 52 Week High	PRICE: 52 Week Low	PERFORMANCE: Performance Rating/Pts	% Total Return Through 12/31/15: 3 Mo	6 Mo	1Yr/Pct	Annualized: 3Yr/Pct	Annualized: 5Yr/Pct
IN	*Vanguard Industrials Index ETF	VIS	B+	101.03	110.27	83.92	B+ / 8.3	5.88	-1.64	-3.30 / 45	12.88 / 84	10.97 / 72
GR	*Vanguard Info Tech Ind ETF	VGT	A	108.29	113.32	77.11	A / 9.3	7.01	2.71	5.32 / 80	16.74 / 92	12.63 / 83
GEI	*Vanguard Intermediate Term Bond	BIV	C	83.06	87.33	82.75	C / 5.1	-1.44	0.85	0.83 / 66	1.66 / 46	4.35 / 45
COI	*Vanguard Intm-Term Corp Bd Idx E	VCIT	C+	84.10	88.70	83.77	C / 5.3	-0.60	0.65	0.62 / 65	2.09 / 49	5.10 / 48
USA	*Vanguard Intm-Term Govt Bd Idx E	VGIT	C	64.44	66.12	63.88	C / 4.9	-1.42	0.98	1.34 / 69	1.27 / 43	3.01 / 38
GR	*Vanguard Large Cap ETF	VV	A+	93.50	98.32	58.50	B+ / 8.7	5.11	-1.04	1.10 / 67	13.87 / 87	12.11 / 79
GEI	*Vanguard Long Term Bd Idx ETF	BLV	C	86.81	100.49	86.30	C / 5.0	-2.08	1.96	-4.67 / 40	2.22 / 49	7.07 / 55
COI	*Vanguard Long-Term Corp Bd Idx E	VCLT	C	84.19	97.64	83.67	C / 4.9	-1.27	1.34	-5.23 / 38	2.09 / 49	6.71 / 54
USA	*Vanguard Long-Term Govt Bd Idx E	VGLT	C	74.62	84.70	71.50	C / 5.5	-2.46	4.85	-2.17 / 50	3.33 / 54	7.91 / 57
IN	*Vanguard Materials ETF	VAW	C+	94.19	114.13	85.05	C / 5.4	4.93	-10.35	-10.42 / 25	4.79 / 60	4.83 / 47
IN	*Vanguard Mega Cap ETF	MGC	A	69.76	72.93	55.00	B+ / 8.8	5.76	-0.34	1.57 / 70	13.89 / 87	12.25 / 80
GR	*Vanguard Mega Cap Growth ETF	MGK	A+	83.04	87.26	54.15	A- / 9.0	5.09	0.11	3.91 / 76	15.03 / 90	13.27 / 85
IN	*Vanguard Mega Cap Value ETF	MGV	A	59.03	62.22	43.12	B+ / 8.5	6.38	-0.49	-0.15 / 59	13.05 / 84	11.34 / 74
GR	*Vanguard Mid Cap ETF	VO	B+	120.11	132.70	111.00	B+ / 8.4	1.77	-4.71	-1.33 / 53	13.75 / 87	11.40 / 74
GR	*Vanguard Mid Cap Growth ETF	VOT	A	99.71	110.11	84.46	B / 8.2	0.95	-5.94	-1.03 / 55	12.90 / 84	10.53 / 68
GR	*Vanguard Mid Cap Value Index ETF	VOE	A+	85.95	94.02	65.78	B+ / 8.6	2.38	-3.81	-1.85 / 51	14.30 / 89	12.10 / 79
MTG	*Vanguard Mort-Backed Secs Idx ET	VMBS	C+	52.72	53.60	52.53	C / 5.3	-0.45	1.14	1.30 / 69	1.93 / 48	2.79 / 37
IN	*Vanguard REIT ETF	VNQ	B	79.73	89.27	71.67	B / 8.0	5.72	7.28	0.91 / 66	10.32 / 76	11.90 / 77
GR	*Vanguard Russell 1000 Gro Idx ET	VONG	A-	102.00	106.12	89.24	A- / 9.1	5.55	0.76	5.58 / 80	15.67 / 91	13.05 / 85
GR	*Vanguard Russell 1000 Index ETF	VONE	A	93.63	98.76	85.07	B+ / 8.6	4.88	-1.42	0.75 / 65	13.75 / 87	12.00 / 78
GR	*Vanguard Russell 1000 Val Index	VONV	B	85.66	93.09	74.50	B / 7.9	4.23	-3.74	-4.04 / 42	11.77 / 81	10.89 / 71
GR	*Vanguard Russell 2000 Gro Idx ET	VTWG	B	102.06	116.09	92.80	B+ / 8.4	3.46	-8.08	0.19 / 62	13.34 / 85	10.88 / 71
GR	*Vanguard Russell 2000 Idx ETF	VTWO	B+	90.14	103.40	85.29	B- / 7.2	2.22	-8.41	-4.00 / 42	10.34 / 76	9.03 / 61
GR	*Vanguard Russell 2000 Val Index	VTWV	C+	79.76	91.50	72.78	C+ / 6.2	2.89	-8.04	-7.09 / 33	7.60 / 69	7.49 / 56
GR	*Vanguard Russell 3000 Index ETF	VTHR	B-	93.59	98.91	86.55	B+ / 8.6	4.95	-1.54	-0.48 / 57	13.61 / 86	11.85 / 77
GR	*Vanguard S&P 500 G Indx ETF	VOOG	A	103.80	107.53	84.18	A- / 9.2	5.75	1.73	5.39 / 80	16.06 / 91	13.79 / 87
GR	*Vanguard S&P 500 Val Indx ETF	VOOV	B+	85.25	92.26	73.02	B / 7.8	4.69	-3.32	-3.27 / 45	11.52 / 80	10.59 / 69
GR	*Vanguard S&P Mid-Cap 400 Gro ETF	IVOG	B	98.97	107.68	75.06	B / 8.0	1.80	-4.76	1.83 / 71	11.90 / 81	10.99 / 72
GR	*Vanguard S&P Mid-Cap 400 Index E	IVOO	B	93.84	104.68	82.33	B / 7.7	1.34	-6.31	-2.11 / 50	11.30 / 79	10.48 / 68
GR	*Vanguard S&P Mid-Cap 400 Value E	IVOV	B	88.41	101.43	54.23	B- / 7.1	0.80	-8.29	-6.63 / 34	10.43 / 76	9.88 / 65
GR	*Vanguard S&P SC 600 G Indx ETF	VIOG	B+	106.86	116.09	96.60	B+ / 8.7	3.41	-3.93	3.81 / 76	13.83 / 87	12.52 / 82
GR	*Vanguard S&P SC 600 Indx ETF	VIOO	A-	99.15	110.23	94.41	B / 8.0	2.90	-5.84	-1.47 / 52	12.12 / 82	11.26 / 73
GR	*Vanguard S&P SC 600 Val Indx ETF	VIOV	B+	93.09	105.29	55.54	B- / 7.3	3.10	-7.20	-6.04 / 36	10.45 / 76	10.26 / 66
GEI	*Vanguard Short-Term Bd Idx ETF	BSV	C+	79.57	80.71	79.42	C / 4.6	-0.75	0.07	0.92 / 67	0.83 / 41	1.46 / 32
COI	*Vanguard Short-Term Crp Bd Idx E	VCSH	C+	78.98	80.44	78.79	C / 5.1	-0.32	0.47	1.36 / 69	1.59 / 46	2.58 / 36
USA	*Vanguard Short-Term Gvt Bd Idx E	VGSH	C	60.76	68.51	60.68	C / 4.5	-0.53	-0.17	0.46 / 64	0.46 / 39	0.61 / 30
GR	*Vanguard Small Cap ETF	VB	B+	110.64	125.51	90.03	B / 7.6	1.58	-7.52	-3.43 / 44	11.26 / 79	10.27 / 66
GR	*Vanguard Small Cap Growth ETF	VBK	B	121.44	138.60	92.99	B- / 7.4	1.61	-8.39	-2.38 / 49	10.69 / 77	9.95 / 65
GR	*Vanguard Small Cap Value ETF	VBR	A-	98.77	111.60	94.00	B / 7.6	1.55	-6.78	-4.42 / 41	11.48 / 79	10.33 / 67
GEI	*Vanguard ST Inf Prot Sec Idx ETF	VTIP	C	48.35	48.85	48.05	C- / 4.0	-0.41	-0.76	0.04 / 60	-0.84 / 34	--
MUN	*Vanguard Tax Exempt Bond Index E	VTEB	U	50.99	N/A	N/A	U /	1.82	--	--	--	--
IN	*Vanguard Telecom Serv ETF	VOX	A-	83.91	91.45	76.21	B / 7.6	7.91	0.21	2.62 / 73	8.92 / 72	8.48 / 59
GI	*Vanguard Tot Stk Mkt Idx ETF	VTI	A+	104.30	110.90	93.00	B+ / 8.7	5.08	-1.47	0.99 / 67	13.76 / 87	12.03 / 78
GEI	*Vanguard Total Bond Market ETF	BND	C	80.76	84.35	80.47	C / 5.0	-0.96	0.90	0.23 / 62	1.48 / 45	3.17 / 39
GL	*Vanguard Total Internatl Bd Idx	BNDX	C+	52.88	54.25	51.97	C / 5.2	0.22	2.55	0.74 / 65	--	--
GL	*Vanguard Total Intl Stock Index	VXUS	C-	45.12	53.92	43.06	C- / 4.1	0.43	-9.85	-3.89 / 43	1.16 / 42	--
EM	*Vanguard Total World Stock ETF	VT	C+	57.62	64.59	53.10	C+ / 6.5	3.33	-5.20	-0.97 / 55	7.22 / 68	6.46 / 52
UT	*Vanguard Utilities Index ETF	VPU	B+	93.93	107.79	87.84	B / 7.7	1.61	4.52	-5.35 / 37	10.64 / 77	10.71 / 70
IN	*Vanguard Value ETF	VTV	A+	81.52	86.80	72.25	B+ / 8.6	6.23	-0.77	-0.30 / 58	13.37 / 85	11.54 / 75
GL	*VelocityShares 3x Inv Nat Gas ET	DGAZ	D	12.52	29.44	4.45	B- / 7.0	46.78	120.81	62.60 / 99	-17.09 / 10	--
GL	*VelocityShares 3x Inverse Crude	DWTI	C-	199.79	236.65	56.32	A+ / 9.9	90.84	165.61	59.26 / 99	62.92 / 99	--
GL	*VelocityShares 3x Inverse Gold E	DGLD	C	94.84	98.60	56.60	A+ / 9.8	19.96	24.90	23.84 / 99	30.74 / 98	--

* Denotes ETF Fund, N/A denotes number is not available

ncl. in Returns		RISK				NET ASSETS		VALUATION			ASSET					FUND MANAGER	
			3 Year					Premium / Discount									
vidend ield %	Expense Ratio	Risk Rating/ Pts	Standard Deviation	Beta	Avg Dura- tion	NAV as of 12/31/15	Total $(Mil)	As of 12/31/15	1 Year Average	Wtd Avg P/E	Cash %	Stocks %	Bonds %	Other %	Portfolio Turnover Ratio	Manager Quality Pct	Manager Tenure (Years)
1.08	0.10	**B- / 7.1**	12.5	1.10	N/A	100.94	1,857	0.09	0.01	38.4	0	100	0	0	4	48	6
0.74	0.10	**B- / 7.5**	12.0	1.04	N/A	108.27	5,948	0.02	0.01	65.2	0	99	0	1	3	78	6
2.71	0.10	**B- / 7.6**	4.4	1.49	N/A	82.95	4,183	0.13	0.15	N/A	0	0	99	1	60	62	8
3.85	0.10	**B- / 7.6**	4.5	1.07	N/A	83.74	4,032	0.43	0.19	N/A	0	0	0	100	56	73	7
2.03	0.10	**B- / 7.8**	3.3	0.28	N/A	64.29	172	0.23	0.07	N/A	1	0	98	1	35	72	3
2.17	0.09	**B / 8.4**	10.6	1.00	1.0	93.52	5,195	-0.02	N/A	61.0	0	100	0	0	3	66	12
4.21	0.10	**B- / 7.6**	9.3	3.01	N/A	86.80	873	0.01	0.19	N/A	1	0	98	1	39	46	3
5.26	0.10	**C+ / 6.8**	8.9	2.04	N/A	83.65	896	0.65	0.20	N/A	0	0	0	100	64	57	7
3.23	0.10	**C+ / 6.7**	10.6	1.03	N/A	74.52	127	0.13	0.10	N/A	0	0	0	100	24	67	3
1.27	0.10	**B- / 7.9**	14.9	1.21	N/A	94.23	1,371	-0.04	N/A	48.0	0	100	0	0	4	15	1
2.45	0.09	**B- / 7.9**	10.8	1.02	N/A	69.77	824	-0.01	0.02	62.5	0	100	0	0	8	63	9
1.68	0.09	**B / 8.3**	11.5	1.05	N/A	83.07	1,516	-0.04	0.02	110.5	0	100	0	0	9	81	1
2.92	0.09	**B / 8.1**	10.5	0.97	N/A	59.02	868	0.02	0.03	26.9	0	99	0	1	5	64	1
1.52	0.09	**B- / 7.3**	11.2	0.95	N/A	120.07	8,569	0.03	0.02	52.5	0	99	0	1	11	73	18
1.07	0.09	**B / 8.6**	11.4	0.97	N/A	99.75	2,276	-0.04	0.01	77.0	0	100	0	0	17	64	3
1.88	0.09	**B+ / 9.0**	10.8	0.98	N/A	85.99	3,033	-0.05	0.01	33.0	0	100	0	0	14	74	10
2.37	0.10	**B / 8.0**	2.3	0.95	N/A	52.68	542	0.08	0.07	N/A	0	0	0	100	713	68	7
5.51	0.12	**B- / 7.2**	14.9	0.46	N/A	79.72	22,958	0.01	N/A	89.0	0	99	0	1	8	87	20
.74	0.12	**B- / 7.3**	10.8	1.00	N/A	101.97	299	0.03	N/A	N/A	0	99	0	1	20	78	6
2.29	0.12	**B / 8.0**	11.3	1.04	N/A	93.62	386	0.01	-0.01	N/A	0	99	0	1	4	61	6
2.99	0.12	**B- / 7.3**	11.0	1.02	N/A	85.64	298	0.02	0.02	N/A	0	100	0	0	18	50	6
.51	0.20	**C+ / 6.6**	15.3	1.11	N/A	101.26	95	0.79	0.05	N/A	0	100	0	0	34	51	1
.06	0.15	**B / 8.2**	14.2	1.06	N/A	90.23	352	-0.10	N/A	N/A	0	100	0	0	17	37	1
.46	0.20	**C+ / 6.6**	13.7	1.04	N/A	79.67	66	0.11	-0.01	N/A	0	100	0	0	28	27	1
.40	0.15	**C+ / 5.7**	10.6	0.97	N/A	93.33	109	0.28	0.06	N/A	0	100	0	0	4	69	6
.72	0.15	**B- / 7.6**	10.8	1.00	N/A	103.78	335	0.02	0.07	N/A	0	100	0	0	21	79	3
.69	0.15	**B- / 7.8**	10.8	1.00	N/A	85.24	208	0.01	0.05	N/A	0	100	0	0	23	50	3
.04	0.20	**C+ / 6.9**	12.2	0.98	N/A	98.92	281	0.05	0.04	N/A	0	100	0	0	47	56	3
.95	0.15	**B- / 7.3**	12.0	1.00	N/A	93.82	329	0.02	N/A	N/A	0	99	0	1	12	49	3
.66	0.20	**B- / 7.7**	12.4	1.01	N/A	88.40	87	0.01	0.04	N/A	0	99	0	1	47	43	3
.76	0.20	**C+ / 6.9**	13.3	0.97	N/A	106.31	58	0.52	0.01	N/A	0	100	0	0	63	72	3
.26	0.15	**B / 8.5**	13.5	1.03	N/A	99.25	151	-0.10	0.03	N/A	0	100	0	0	11	52	3
.84	0.20	**B / 8.1**	13.6	1.03	N/A	93.11	84	-0.02	0.01	N/A	0	100	0	0	43	40	3
.37	0.10	**B / 8.2**	1.2	0.36	N/A	79.49	14,944	0.10	0.06	N/A	0	0	99	1	45	70	3
.54	0.10	**B / 8.1**	1.4	0.31	N/A	78.76	8,660	0.28	0.12	N/A	0	0	0	100	62	76	7
.11	0.10	**B- / 7.9**	0.5	0.03	N/A	60.73	512	0.05	0.03	N/A	0	0	0	100	64	71	3
.70	0.09	**B / 8.3**	12.7	1.03	N/A	110.71	8,745	-0.06	N/A	N/A	0	99	0	1	10	46	25
.14	0.09	**B- / 7.4**	12.9	1.00	N/A	121.53	3,642	-0.07	0.01	155.3	0	99	0	1	26	44	12
.26	0.09	**B / 8.7**	12.8	1.07	1.0	98.81	4,257	-0.04	0.01	39.0	0	100	0	0	12	44	18
.00	0.08	**B- / 7.9**	1.8	0.34	N/A	48.18	1,336	0.35	0.10	N/A	0	0	0	100	26	56	4
03	N/A	**U /**	N/A	N/A	N/A	50.81	N/A	0.35	N/A	N/A	0	0	0	100	N/A	N/A	1
.52	0.10	**B / 8.8**	12.0	0.75	N/A	83.94	749	-0.04	0.01	23.2	0	100	0	0	18	58	12
47	0.05	**B / 8.7**	10.7	1.01	N/A	104.34	45,764	-0.04	N/A	62.8	0	99	0	1	3	64	22
63	0.07	**B- / 7.8**	3.1	1.08	N/A	80.58	22,814	0.22	0.07	N/A	0	0	99	1	72	66	24
06	0.19	**B / 8.0**	N/A	N/A	N/A	52.69	2,022	0.36	0.20	N/A	0	0	0	100	16	73	3
08	0.14	**C+ / 6.7**	12.2	0.93	N/A	45.08	3,160	0.09	0.23	23.1	0	99	0	1	3	40	8
11	0.17	**B- / 7.0**	11.0	0.60	1.0	57.54	3,604	0.14	0.13	59.9	0	100	0	0	7	96	3
74	0.10	**B- / 7.7**	14.1	0.97	N/A	93.93	1,605	0.00	N/A	23.6	0	97	0	3	7	63	1
77	0.09	**B+ / 9.0**	10.5	0.98	1.0	81.56	15,471	-0.05	N/A	27.5	0	100	0	0	6	65	22
00	N/A	**E- / 0.1**	N/A	-0.80	N/A	12.40	228	0.97	N/A	N/A	0	0	0	100	N/A	14	4
00	N/A	**E+ / 0.9**	N/A	-1.78	N/A	198.77	3	0.51	0.28	N/A	0	0	0	100	N/A	99	4
00	N/A	**D+ / 2.9**	49.8	-0.41	N/A	94.71	10	0.14	-0.21	N/A	0	0	0	100	N/A	99	5

Denotes ETF Fund, N/A denotes number is not available

Fund Type	Fund Name (99 Pct = Best, 0 Pct = Worst)	Ticker Symbol	Overall Investment Rating	PRICE: Price As of 12/31/15	PRICE: 52 Week High	PRICE: 52 Week Low	PERFORMANCE: Performance Rating/Pts	% Total Return Through 12/31/15: 3 Mo	6 Mo	1Yr/Pct	Annualized: 3Yr/Pct	Annualized: 5Yr/Pct
GL	*VelocityShares 3x Inverse Silver	DSLV	C	71.69	79.01	41.84	A+ / 9.9	24.05	19.30	-0.26 / 58	38.29 / 99	--
GL	*VelocityShares 3x Long Crude ETN	UWTI	E-	3.95	43.20	3.51	E- / 0.0	-63.25	-85.89	-91.38 / 0	-76.34 / 0	--
GL	*VelocityShares 3x Long Gold ETN	UGLD	E-	7.37	15.09	7.10	E- / 0.1	-20.67	-28.10	-35.12 / 6	-43.36 / 1	--
GL	*VelocityShares 3x Long Nat Gas E	UGAZ	E-	2.44	27.15	1.29	E- / 0.0	-57.71	-77.20	-88.07 / 0	-71.05 / 0	--
GL	*VelocityShares 3x Long Silver ET	USLV	E-	9.81	30.53	9.55	E- / 0.0	-29.17	-39.03	-49.12 / 2	-66.28 / 0	--
IN	*VelocityShares Daily 2x VIX S-T	TVIX	E-	6.27	37.39	5.31	E- / 0.0	-41.51	-32.53	-76.44 / 0	-79.26 / 0	-83.97 / 0
IN	*VelocityShares Dly 2x VIX Med-T	TVIZ	E-	13.32	24.99	12.69	E- / 0.1	-29.26	-10.72	-38.59 / 4	-48.83 / 1	-55.60 / 0
GEI	*VelocityShares Dly Invs VIX M-T	ZIV	C	41.49	50.86	34.38	A- / 9.1	6.88	-11.48	-1.03 / 55	17.62 / 93	24.36 / 99
GI	*VelocityShares Dly Invs VIX ST E	XIV	D+	25.78	50.10	21.31	C+ / 5.9	-0.54	-36.53	-18.73 / 15	11.04 / 78	15.56 / 92
GI	*VelocityShares VIX Medium-Term E	VIIZ	E-	15.44	19.92	14.11	E+ / 0.7	-11.82	-2.40	-14.55 / 18	-24.51 / 6	-29.49 / 3
GI	*VelocityShares VIX Short-Term ET	VIIX	E-	27.12	50.25	20.95	E- / 0.2	-16.50	0.63	-35.14 / 6	-43.29 / 1	-48.92 / 1
FO	*Victory CEMP Develop Enh Vol Wtd	CIZ	C-	31.35	42.79	30.71	D / 1.8	-2.01	-11.34	-7.91 / 31	--	--
FO	*Victory CEMP International Vol W	CIL	U	33.71	N/A	N/A	U /	2.26	--	--	--	--
FO	*Victory CEMP Intl Hi Div Vol Wtd	CID	U	32.25	N/A	N/A	U /	-0.63	--	--	--	--
GR	*Victory CEMP US 500 Enh Vol Wtd	CFO	C-	35.76	37.96	32.79	C- / 4.1	3.26	-2.64	-0.69 / 56	--	--
GR	*Victory CEMP US 500 Volatility W	CFA	C	35.80	37.99	34.04	C / 4.4	3.46	-2.55	0.12 / 61	--	--
GEI	*Victory CEMP US Discovery Enh Vo	CSF	D+	34.55	40.43	34.13	D / 1.8	-2.13	-11.24	-7.42 / 32	--	--
GR	*Victory CEMP US EQ Inc Enh Vol W	CDC	C	35.51	37.61	32.29	C / 5.2	3.42	1.07	-0.32 / 58	--	--
IN	*Victory CEMP US LC Hi Div Vol Wt	CDL	U	34.42	N/A	N/A	U /	3.94	--	--	--	--
IN	*Victory CEMP US SC Hi Div Vol Wt	CSB	U	32.91	N/A	N/A	U /	3.86	--	--	--	--
GR	*Victory CEMP US Small Cap Vol Wt	CSA	U	32.94	N/A	N/A	U /	3.72	--	--	--	--
COI	*Vident Core US Bond Strategy	VBND	C+	49.11	53.29	48.93	C- / 4.0	-1.05	0.21	-0.26 / 58	--	--
GR	*Vident Core US Equity	VUSE	D+	24.81	28.05	23.70	D+ / 2.6	2.52	-7.57	-5.69 / 37	--	--
FO	*Vident International Equity	VIDI	D+	20.08	25.15	15.82	D- / 1.5	0.24	-12.71	-10.91 / 24	--	--
GI	*WBI Tactical High Income	WBIH	C-	23.32	26.09	22.98	D+ / 2.8	-1.23	-3.90	-4.17 / 42	--	--
GI	*WBI Tactical Income	WBII	C+	24.51	26.41	24.49	C- / 3.4	-1.59	-2.76	-0.78 / 56	--	--
GL	*WBI Tactical LCG	WBIE	D+	23.11	26.61	22.43	D+ / 2.5	1.67	-5.67	-7.00 / 33	--	--
GL	*WBI Tactical LCS	WBIL	D+	22.48	24.78	22.15	D+ / 2.4	0.30	-6.55	-6.91 / 34	--	--
GL	*WBI Tactical LCV	WBIF	C-	22.84	25.35	22.45	D+ / 2.8	1.13	-5.36	-4.12 / 42	--	--
GL	*WBI Tactical LCY	WBIG	D+	21.67	25.30	21.46	D / 1.8	-0.97	-8.34	-10.25 / 25	--	--
GL	*WBI Tactical SMG	WBIA	C-	22.60	26.47	21.13	D / 2.2	5.96	-10.38	-8.93 / 29	--	--
GL	*WBI Tactical SMS	WBID	D+	21.30	25.15	21.02	D / 1.7	-1.63	-9.20	-10.68 / 24	--	--
GL	*WBI Tactical SMV	WBIB	D+	22.89	25.56	22.35	D+ / 2.5	-0.70	-7.45	-4.28 / 41	--	--
GL	*WBI Tactical SMY	WBIC	D+	21.64	25.22	21.28	D / 1.6	-3.14	-9.68	-10.34 / 25	--	--
GL	*WCM/BNY Mellon Focused Gro ADR E	AADR	C+	38.53	40.84	34.01	B- / 7.1	6.22	-1.72	5.72 / 81	7.39 / 68	5.88 / 51
GL	*WisdomTree Asia Local Debt	ALD	C-	42.98	47.63	41.89	D+ / 2.9	1.41	-3.95	-5.84 / 36	-4.56 / 25	--
FO	*WisdomTree Asia Pacific ex-Japan	AXJL	C-	54.59	73.00	51.48	D+ / 2.5	-0.51	-15.97	-12.83 / 20	-4.47 / 26	0.22 / 28
FO	*WisdomTree Australia and NZ Debt	AUNZ	C-	16.94	19.39	16.01	D+ / 2.5	3.99	-1.41	-7.13 / 33	-7.22 / 21	-3.83 / 21
FO	*WisdomTree Australia Divide	AUSE	D+	44.61	57.36	40.71	D+ / 2.6	5.45	-12.04	-10.82 / 24	-5.12 / 25	-0.44 / 27
COI	*WisdomTree Barclays US AB Enh Yi	AGGY	U	49.00	N/A	N/A	U /	-0.59	--	--	--	--
COI	*WisdomTree Barclays US AB Neg Du	AGND	C	44.17	45.98	43.20	C- / 3.7	-0.49	-2.38	-0.31 / 58	--	--
COI	*WisdomTree Barclays US AB Zero D	AGZD	C	48.10	49.44	47.51	C- / 4.1	1.02	-0.65	-0.79 / 56	--	--
LP	*WisdomTree Bloomberg Float Rt Tr	USFR	C+	24.85	25.09	24.34	C- / 4.1	-0.52	-0.20	-0.12 / 59	--	--
GEI	*WisdomTree Bloomberg US Dollar B	USDU	A+	27.36	29.40	27.06	A+ / 9.8	13.97	15.91	19.69 / 98	--	--
COH	*WisdomTree BofA ML HY Bd Neg Dur	HYND	C-	19.39	23.01	18.86	D / 2.1	-0.96	-11.25	-5.42 / 37	--	--
COH	*WisdomTree BofA ML HY Bd Zero Du	HYZD	C-	21.92	24.99	21.33	C- / 3.0	-0.68	-6.51	-1.05 / 55	--	--
FO	*WisdomTree Brazilian Real Strate	BZF	D	12.60	17.70	11.55	D- / 1.3	1.69	-18.23	-24.53 / 10	-12.80 / 14	-9.02 / 14
FO	*WisdomTree China ex-State-Owned	CXSE	C-	49.04	66.03	37.00	C- / 3.5	11.66	-9.89	-3.26 / 45	-2.40 / 30	--
FO	*WisdomTree Chinese Yuan Strategy	CYB	C+	24.31	26.42	7.42	C / 4.3	-2.68	-5.26	-3.34 / 45	1.35 / 44	2.03 / 3[illegible]
FO	*WisdomTree Commodity Country Equ	CCXE	D	19.62	27.56	18.78	D- / 1.5	-2.93	-17.90	-18.53 / 15	-11.60 / 15	-4.78 / 1[illegible]
GL	*WisdomTree Commodity Curr Str	CCX	D	15.26	17.95	15.00	D / 1.8	0.07	-9.48	-12.15 / 22	-10.59 / 17	-5.78 / 18
IN	*WisdomTree Dividend Ex-Financial	DTN	B	70.29	77.91	49.46	B / 7.6	3.94	-3.28	-5.35 / 37	10.91 / 78	12.04 / 78

* Denotes ETF Fund, N/A denotes number is not availab

		RISK				NET ASSETS		VALUATION			ASSET					FUND MANAGER	
Incl. in Returns			3 Year					Premium / Discount									
Dividend Yield %	Expense Ratio	Risk Rating/ Pts	Standard Deviation	Beta	Avg Dura-tion	NAV as of 12/31/15	Total $(Mil)	As of 12/31/15	1 Year Average	Wtd Avg P/E	Cash %	Stocks %	Bonds %	Other %	Portfolio Turnover Ratio	Manager Quality Pct	Manager Tenure (Years)
0.00	N/A	**D / 1.9**	82.4	-1.09	N/A	71.91	16	-0.31	-0.12	N/A	0	0	0	100	N/A	99	5
0.00	N/A	**D / 1.7**	N/A	2.23	N/A	3.99	7	-1.00	-0.36	N/A	0	0	0	100	N/A	N/A	4
0.00	N/A	**E+ / 0.9**	52.1	0.25	N/A	7.37	46	0.00	0.21	N/A	0	0	0	100	N/A	N/A	5
0.00	N/A	**D / 1.8**	N/A	1.15	N/A	2.47	234	-1.21	-0.02	N/A	0	0	0	100	N/A	N/A	4
0.00	N/A	**E+ / 0.8**	82.8	0.77	N/A	9.77	134	0.41	0.09	N/A	0	0	0	100	N/A	N/A	5
0.00	N/A	**E+ / 0.6**	N/A	-8.71	N/A	6.16	264	1.79	1.80	N/A	0	0	0	100	N/A	2	6
0.00	N/A	**D / 1.7**	60.6	-4.45	N/A	13.60	1	-2.06	-0.32	N/A	0	0	0	100	N/A	18	6
0.00	N/A	**C- / 3.7**	29.4	0.17	N/A	41.58	139	-0.22	0.04	N/A	0	0	0	100	N/A	98	6
0.00	N/A	**D+ / 2.4**	66.8	5.01	N/A	25.99	591	-0.81	-0.20	N/A	0	0	0	100	N/A	1	6
0.00	N/A	**E+ / 0.7**	29.2	-2.26	N/A	15.39	2	0.32	-0.11	N/A	0	0	0	100	N/A	77	6
0.00	N/A	**E+ / 0.6**	60.6	-4.68	N/A	26.96	8	0.59	0.18	N/A	0	0	0	100	N/A	88	6
1.21	0.63	**B / 8.1**	N/A	N/A	N/A	31.42	N/A	-0.22	0.61	N/A	0	0	0	100	31	24	N/A
1.72	N/A	**U /**	N/A	N/A	N/A	33.68	N/A	0.09	N/A	N/A	0	0	0	100	N/A	N/A	1
5.29	N/A	**U /**	N/A	N/A	N/A	32.27	N/A	-0.06	N/A	N/A	0	0	0	100	N/A	N/A	1
1.85	0.59	**B- / 7.2**	N/A	N/A	N/A	35.75	N/A	0.03	0.04	N/A	0	0	0	100	13	47	N/A
1.33	0.54	**B- / 7.3**	N/A	N/A	N/A	35.78	N/A	0.06	0.07	N/A	0	0	0	100	23	55	N/A
1.46	0.59	**C+ / 6.7**	N/A	N/A	N/A	34.49	N/A	0.17	0.06	N/A	0	0	0	100	10	20	N/A
6.11	0.59	**B- / 7.3**	N/A	N/A	N/A	35.37	24	0.40	0.05	N/A	0	0	0	100	17	55	N/A
4.97	N/A	**U /**	N/A	N/A	N/A	34.43	N/A	-0.03	N/A	N/A	0	0	0	100	N/A	N/A	N/A
8.35	N/A	**U /**	N/A	N/A	N/A	32.84	N/A	0.21	N/A	N/A	0	0	0	100	N/A	N/A	N/A
1.38	N/A	**U /**	N/A	N/A	N/A	32.87	N/A	0.21	N/A	N/A	0	0	0	100	N/A	N/A	N/A
2.90	0.45	**B+ / 9.3**	N/A	N/A	N/A	49.12	N/A	-0.02	N/A	N/A	0	0	0	100	409	73	2
3.19	0.55	**C+ / 6.7**	N/A	N/A	N/A	24.78	175	0.12	0.03	N/A	0	0	0	100	90	22	2
3.42	0.71	**B- / 7.5**	N/A	N/A	N/A	20.36	717	-1.38	-0.16	N/A	0	0	0	100	43	15	1
3.63	0.98	**B- / 7.5**	N/A	N/A	N/A	23.29	N/A	0.13	0.08	N/A	0	0	0	100	293	33	2
4.00	0.99	**B+ / 9.5**	N/A	N/A	N/A	24.53	N/A	-0.08	0.06	N/A	0	0	0	100	308	59	2
0.75	1.02	**C+ / 6.7**	N/A	N/A	N/A	23.04	N/A	0.30	0.05	N/A	0	0	0	100	240	22	2
0.07	1.02	**B- / 7.1**	N/A	N/A	N/A	22.42	N/A	0.27	0.08	N/A	0	0	0	100	296	22	2
0.46	1.04	**C+ / 6.9**	N/A	N/A	N/A	22.78	N/A	0.26	0.10	N/A	0	0	0	100	294	32	2
0.17	1.02	**C+ / 6.7**	N/A	N/A	N/A	21.61	N/A	0.28	0.09	N/A	0	0	0	100	277	16	2
0.68	1.03	**B / 8.0**	N/A	N/A	N/A	22.61	N/A	-0.04	0.03	N/A	0	0	0	100	255	17	2
0.69	1.06	**C+ / 6.6**	N/A	N/A	N/A	21.23	N/A	0.33	0.06	N/A	0	0	0	100	311	15	2
1.90	1.07	**B- / 7.0**	N/A	N/A	N/A	22.80	N/A	0.39	0.07	N/A	0	0	0	100	278	29	2
2.44	1.03	**C+ / 6.7**	N/A	N/A	N/A	21.56	N/A	0.37	0.07	N/A	0	0	0	100	264	15	2
0.05	1.25	**C+ / 6.9**	12.9	0.97	N/A	38.41	14	0.31	0.11	N/A	3	96	0	1	27	84	N/A
2.51	0.55	**B / 8.2**	6.4	0.59	N/A	43.20	319	-0.51	-0.44	N/A	0	0	0	100	10	50	5
1.31	0.49	**B- / 7.2**	14.3	0.91	N/A	55.20	47	-1.11	-0.20	N/A	0	100	0	0	17	18	8
1.77	0.45	**B- / 7.2**	10.8	0.46	6.1	17.06	32	-0.70	-0.89	N/A	100	0	0	0	9	17	1
2.67	0.59	**C+ / 6.1**	19.9	1.17	N/A	45.22	48	-1.35	-0.25	N/A	0	100	0	0	26	16	8
2.55	N/A	**U /**	N/A	N/A	N/A	49.08	N/A	-0.16	N/A	N/A	0	0	0	100	N/A	N/A	1
1.90	0.28	**B+ / 9.0**	N/A	N/A	N/A	44.27	24	-0.23	-0.10	N/A	0	0	0	100	424	59	3
1.75	0.23	**B / 8.0**	N/A	N/A	N/A	48.00	60	0.21	-0.16	N/A	0	0	0	100	359	59	3
0.00	0.15	**B+ / 9.8**	N/A	N/A	N/A	24.96	3	-0.44	-0.20	N/A	0	0	0	100	118	68	1
6.48	0.50	**B+ / 9.0**	N/A	N/A	N/A	27.39	57	-0.11	0.04	N/A	0	0	0	100	N/A	98	1
4.95	0.48	**B / 8.0**	N/A	N/A	N/A	19.72	11	-1.67	0.41	N/A	0	0	0	100	34	60	1
4.65	0.43	**C+ / 6.8**	N/A	N/A	N/A	21.91	22	0.05	-0.35	N/A	0	0	0	100	55	84	1
0.00	0.45	**C+ / 6.3**	14.7	0.60	N/A	12.77	29	-1.33	-0.22	N/A	0	0	75	25	N/A	10	2
0.66	0.64	**C+ / 6.4**	20.5	0.95	N/A	50.08	18	-2.08	-0.82	N/A	0	0	0	100	30	24	2
0.00	0.45	**B+ / 9.1**	4.4	0.12	N/A	24.35	152	-0.16	-0.15	N/A	0	0	72	28	N/A	75	1
5.11	0.59	**C+ / 6.6**	17.2	1.13	N/A	19.86	16	-1.21	-0.79	12.7	0	100	0	0	20	9	8
0.00	0.55	**C+ / 5.6**	9.5	0.48	N/A	15.09	12	1.13	-0.20	N/A	0	0	0	100	N/A	12	1
3.58	0.39	**B- / 7.2**	10.4	0.93	N/A	70.26	1,187	0.04	-0.01	27.3	0	100	0	0	32	52	8

* Denotes ETF Fund, N/A denotes number is not available

	99 Pct = Best 0 Pct = Worst			PRICE			PERFORMANCE					
					52 Week			% Total Return Through 12/31/15			Annualized	
Fund Type	Fund Name	Ticker Symbol	Overall Investment Rating	Price As of 12/31/15	High	Low	Performance Rating/Pts	3 Mo	6 Mo	1Yr/Pct	3Yr/Pct	5Yr/Pct
IN	*WisdomTree Earnings 500 Fund	EPS	B+	69.36	74.03	44.78	B+ / 8.4	4.96	-2.27	-1.35 / 53	13.09 / 84	12.04 / 78
EM	*WisdomTree EM Corporate Bond	EMCB	C	65.58	74.46	64.99	C- / 3.3	-0.91	-7.08	-3.66 / 44	-2.10 / 30	--
EM	*WisdomTree EM ex-State-Owned Ent	XSOE	D-	20.43	27.14	18.51	D / 1.6	5.08	-14.87	-11.81 / 22	--	--
EM	*WisdomTree Em Mkts Cons Gro	EMCG	D	19.33	26.87	17.00	E+ / 0.7	-2.72	-19.51	-19.63 / 14	--	--
EM	*WisdomTree Em Mkts Qual Div Gro	DGRE	D	19.36	25.83	18.02	E+ / 0.9	-2.41	-17.43	-16.47 / 16	--	--
FO	*WisdomTree Emerging Currency Str	CEW	D+	16.80	18.95	15.57	D+ / 2.3	-0.53	-8.05	-9.43 / 27	-7.37 / 21	-3.47 / 22
EM	*WisdomTree Emg Mkts High Dividen	DEM	D	31.64	48.56	30.98	D- / 1.2	-6.32	-24.13	-20.81 / 13	-14.39 / 12	-7.88 / 16
EM	*WisdomTree Emg Mkts Local Debt F	ELD	D	34.28	42.31	33.73	D / 1.9	-0.81	-9.48	-12.80 / 21	-9.81 / 18	-3.82 / 21
EM	*WisdomTree Emg Mkts SmCap Div Fd	DGS	D+	35.06	47.83	32.41	D / 1.9	-3.99	-17.90	-15.55 / 17	-8.16 / 20	-5.17 / 19
FO	*WisdomTree Europe Hedged Equity	HEDJ	B	53.81	68.72	52.50	B- / 7.5	4.30	-6.73	5.05 / 79	9.47 / 74	7.53 / 56
FO	*WisdomTree Europe Hedged SmCp Eq	EUSC	U	24.56	N/A	N/A	U /	4.91	-0.39	--	--	--
FO	*WisdomTree Europe LR	EZR	U	23.98	N/A	N/A	U /	--	--	--	--	--
FO	*WisdomTree Europe Quality Div Gr	EUDG	C+	22.50	24.85	20.97	C+ / 5.8	3.69	-1.89	4.19 / 77	--	--
FO	*WisdomTree Europe Small Cap Div	DFE	A+	56.00	61.92	50.22	B+ / 8.9	2.36	-1.26	11.27 / 90	13.77 / 87	10.13 / 66
FO	*WisdomTree Germany Hedged Equity	DXGE	B-	26.62	32.56	24.03	C+ / 6.6	8.60	-4.39	6.87 / 83	--	--
FO	*WisdomTree Global ex US Hedged D	DXUS	U	22.38	N/A	N/A	U /	3.44	-7.19	--	--	--
GI	*WisdomTree Global ex-US Hedged R	HDRW	U	24.47	N/A	N/A	U /	--	--	--	--	--
GL	*WisdomTree Global ex-US Qual Div	DNL	C-	45.27	54.51	42.14	C- / 3.0	1.65	-10.96	-5.70 / 37	-3.19 / 28	-0.74 / 26
FO	*WisdomTree Global ex-US Real Est	DRW	C-	26.12	31.65	24.54	C- / 3.9	1.75	-6.26	-2.80 / 47	-0.14 / 36	3.80 / 42
UT	*WisdomTree Global ex-US Utilitie	DBU	C-	15.25	19.35	14.92	D+ / 2.9	-4.65	-12.05	-12.32 / 21	-2.28 / 30	-0.63 / 26
GL	*WisdomTree Global High Dividend	DEW	C	39.37	47.40	37.19	C- / 4.0	1.73	-7.72	-6.28 / 35	0.63 / 40	3.48 / 40
EN	*WisdomTree Global Natural Resour	GNAT	D-	11.01	17.72	10.63	E+ / 0.7	-8.74	-26.74	-30.01 / 7	-20.69 / 8	-12.77 / 11
GI	*WisdomTree Global Real Return Fu	RRF	C-	38.48	44.11	38.48	C- / 3.2	-0.31	-3.42	-3.07 / 46	-3.41 / 28	--
GI	*WisdomTree High Dividend	DHS	B+	59.09	62.67	36.96	B / 8.2	6.04	0.74	-0.84 / 56	11.73 / 81	12.82 / 84
FO	*WisdomTree India Earnings Fund	EPI	C-	19.86	24.37	17.76	C- / 3.8	-1.03	-9.49	-10.02 / 25	1.11 / 42	-3.61 / 21
FO	*WisdomTree Indian Rupee Strategy	ICN	C	20.97	21.55	15.50	C / 4.4	-0.02	-1.87	1.28 / 68	0.48 / 39	-1.41 / 24
FO	*WisdomTree International Equity	DWM	C+	46.59	55.19	44.48	C / 5.3	1.01	-8.25	-2.73 / 47	3.68 / 56	4.26 / 44
FO	*WisdomTree International Hdg Eqt	HDWM	U	24.05	N/A	N/A	U /	3.92	--	--	--	--
FO	*WisdomTree International Hi Div	DTH	C	37.74	46.25	36.68	C / 4.3	-0.49	-9.71	-6.78 / 34	2.04 / 48	3.73 / 42
FO	*WisdomTree Intl Div Ex-Financial	DOO	C-	38.04	47.18	37.18	C- / 3.8	-1.42	-9.72	-7.71 / 32	0.85 / 41	2.26 / 35
FO	*WisdomTree Intl Hdgd Qual Div Gr	IHDG	A	26.43	28.54	23.43	B+ / 8.4	5.83	1.45	11.70 / 91	--	--
FO	*WisdomTree Intl Hdgd SmCp Div	HDLS	U	23.12	N/A	N/A	U /	5.50	-1.21	--	--	--
FO	*WisdomTree Intl LargeCap Dividen	DOL	C	43.16	51.81	41.44	C / 4.7	0.13	-9.34	-4.14 / 42	2.35 / 50	3.58 / 41
FO	*WisdomTree Intl MidCap Dividend	DIM	B	55.50	63.23	51.97	C+ / 6.3	3.14	-5.51	2.73 / 73	6.16 / 65	5.28 / 49
FO	*WisdomTree Intl Small Cap Divide	DLS	B	58.10	64.67	54.36	C+ / 6.9	4.21	-3.15	7.26 / 84	7.22 / 67	6.77 / 54
FO	*WisdomTree Japan Dividend Growth	JDG	U	23.53	N/A	N/A	U /	9.40	-3.02	--	--	--
FO	*WisdomTree Japan Hedged Cap Good	DXJC	C-	24.70	30.74	22.48	C- / 4.2	11.15	-10.65	0.34 / 63	--	--
FO	*WisdomTree Japan Hedged Equity	DXJ	A	50.08	60.59	45.68	A- / 9.2	6.04	-8.79	6.83 / 83	17.61 / 93	10.69 / 70
FO	*WisdomTree Japan Hedged Financia	DXJF	C	26.01	31.37	22.19	C / 4.3	0.57	-13.55	8.96 / 86	--	--
FO	*WisdomTree Japan Hedged Health C	DXJH	A+	34.70	36.43	25.04	A+ / 9.9	18.52	7.77	35.61 / 99	--	--
FO	*WisdomTree Japan Hedged Qual Div	JHDG	U	24.54	N/A	N/A	U /	8.33	-5.64	--	--	--
FO	*WisdomTree Japan Hedged Real Est	DXJR	C+	26.13	29.60	24.63	C / 4.8	0.94	-3.23	2.88 / 74	--	--
FO	*WisdomTree Japan Hedged SmallCap	DXJS	A+	34.02	37.70	29.09	B+ / 8.5	5.33	-3.80	15.70 / 96	--	--
FO	*WisdomTree Japan Hedged TM & Tel	DXJT	C	26.40	31.62	24.51	C+ / 6.7	9.33	-6.28	7.88 / 85	--	--
GL	*WisdomTree Japan Interest Rate S	JGBB	C+	48.53	51.00	47.88	C+ / 5.6	3.42	0.25	2.03 / 72	--	--
FO	*WisdomTree Japan SmallCap Div Fd	DFJ	A+	56.56	58.22	47.53	B+ / 8.8	5.92	-0.36	18.01 / 98	11.06 / 79	7.41 / 56
FO	*WisdomTree Korea Hedged Equity	DXKW	C-	19.94	23.35	14.41	C- / 3.3	1.98	-4.64	-2.55 / 48	--	--
GI	*WisdomTree LargeCap Dividend Fun	DLN	A	71.14	75.68	45.10	B / 8.1	5.12	-1.07	-1.36 / 53	11.94 / 82	12.29 / 80
IN	*WisdomTree LargeCap Value Fund	EZY	B+	63.70	71.94	60.40	B+ / 8.4	3.06	-3.51	-0.28 / 58	13.25 / 85	11.74 / 76
GR	*WisdomTree Mgd Futures Strategy	WDTI	C	42.07	46.13	39.36	C / 4.6	1.62	-0.94	-3.51 / 44	1.17 / 43	--
GR	*WisdomTree MidCap Dividend Fund	DON	A	80.51	87.34	58.53	B+ / 8.5	3.56	-1.43	-1.15 / 54	13.77 / 87	12.94 / 84
GR	*WisdomTree MidCap Earnings Fund	EZM	A-	87.14	98.26	64.35	B / 7.7	0.66	-7.76	-4.54 / 40	11.91 / 81	11.56 / 75

* Denotes ETF Fund, N/A denotes number is not available

Incl. in Returns		RISK				NET ASSETS		VALUATION			ASSET					FUND MANAGER	
			3 Year					Premium / Discount									
Dividend Yield %	Expense Ratio	Risk Rating/ Pts	Standard Deviation	Beta	Avg Duration	NAV as of 12/31/15	Total $(Mil)	As of 12/31/15	1 Year Average	Wtd Avg P/E	Cash %	Stocks %	Bonds %	Other %	Portfolio Turnover Ratio	Manager Quality Pct	Manager Tenure (Years)
2.65	0.29	**B- / 7.3**	11.0	1.04	N/A	69.23	114	0.19	N/A	39.4	0	100	0	0	16	58	8
4.85	0.60	**B / 8.1**	7.2	0.48	N/A	65.95	114	-0.56	-0.70	N/A	0	0	0	100	25	69	4
1.23	N/A	**C- / 4.1**	N/A	N/A	N/A	20.67	N/A	-1.16	-0.11	N/A	0	0	0	100	N/A	82	2
1.60	0.64	**C+ / 6.9**	N/A	N/A	N/A	19.36	20	-0.15	-0.26	N/A	0	0	0	100	41	22	3
5.06	0.64	**C+ / 6.8**	N/A	N/A	N/A	19.66	31	-1.53	0.23	N/A	0	0	0	100	47	22	3
0.00	0.55	**C+ / 6.5**	6.5	0.38	N/A	16.76	87	0.24	-0.19	N/A	100	0	0	0	N/A	18	1
2.67	0.64	**C+ / 5.6**	17.1	1.12	N/A	31.90	3,437	-0.82	-0.26	N/A	0	100	0	0	39	21	8
5.08	0.55	**C+ / 5.9**	9.5	0.85	N/A	34.28	779	0.00	-0.20	N/A	5	0	94	1	22	24	6
0.96	0.64	**C+ / 6.6**	14.0	0.90	N/A	35.56	1,939	-1.41	-0.50	N/A	0	100	0	0	42	49	8
1.53	0.59	**B- / 7.5**	15.8	0.90	N/A	54.25	2,933	-0.81	0.13	N/A	0	100	0	0	12	89	7
7.89	N/A	**U /**	N/A	N/A	N/A	24.69	N/A	-0.53	N/A	N/A	0	0	0	100	N/A	N/A	1
0.41	N/A	**U /**	N/A	N/A	N/A	24.58	N/A	-2.44	N/A	N/A	0	0	0	100	N/A	N/A	1
0.86	0.58	**B / 8.1**	N/A	N/A	N/A	22.53	14	-0.13	0.35	N/A	0	0	0	100	21	86	2
1.23	0.59	**B / 8.1**	14.0	0.92	N/A	56.29	1,009	-0.52	0.12	N/A	0	100	0	0	42	94	8
1.65	0.49	**B- / 7.5**	N/A	N/A	N/A	27.03	15	-1.52	0.09	N/A	0	0	0	100	11	93	3
4.68	N/A	**U /**	N/A	N/A	N/A	22.41	N/A	-0.13	N/A	N/A	0	0	0	100	N/A	N/A	1
3.78	N/A	**U /**	N/A	N/A	N/A	24.23	N/A	0.99	N/A	N/A	0	0	0	100	N/A	N/A	1
0.24	0.59	**B / 8.0**	12.1	0.85	N/A	45.30	66	-0.07	-0.03	28.1	0	100	0	0	64	22	8
7.63	0.59	**B- / 7.1**	14.3	0.88	N/A	26.35	118	-0.87	-0.21	130.5	0	100	0	0	26	34	8
2.66	0.59	**B- / 7.8**	13.3	0.40	N/A	15.42	24	-1.10	-0.20	12.4	0	100	0	0	36	24	8
3.37	0.59	**B- / 7.8**	12.7	0.96	N/A	39.41	116	-0.10	-0.06	24.3	0	100	0	0	30	38	8
4.39	0.59	**C / 5.4**	19.8	0.90	N/A	11.04	21	-0.27	0.10	17.8	0	100	0	0	34	8	8
4.61	0.60	**C+ / 6.4**	7.6	0.33	N/A	38.19	5	0.76	-0.90	N/A	0	0	0	100	8	19	3
4.64	0.39	**B- / 7.6**	9.8	0.83	N/A	59.05	912	0.07	0.01	29.1	0	100	0	0	27	71	8
.47	0.84	**C+ / 6.5**	22.1	0.88	N/A	20.07	1,992	-1.05	0.06	N/A	0	100	0	0	26	44	8
.00	0.45	**B / 8.3**	8.5	0.31	N/A	21.04	25	-0.33	-0.32	N/A	20	0	79	1	N/A	52	1
2.69	0.49	**B- / 7.8**	13.1	1.02	N/A	46.95	579	-0.77	0.20	N/A	0	100	0	0	19	57	8
1.72	N/A	**U /**	N/A	N/A	N/A	24.19	N/A	-0.58	N/A	N/A	0	0	0	100	N/A	N/A	1
2.90	0.59	**B- / 7.4**	13.8	1.06	N/A	38.07	327	-0.87	0.10	N/A	0	100	0	0	20	42	8
2.98	0.59	**B- / 7.4**	13.4	1.02	N/A	38.38	393	-0.89	-0.03	N/A	0	100	0	0	44	35	8
1.33	0.58	**B / 8.4**	N/A	N/A	N/A	26.51	8	-0.30	0.36	N/A	0	0	0	100	14	96	N/A
2.48	N/A	**U /**	N/A	N/A	N/A	23.12	N/A	0.00	N/A	N/A	0	0	0	100	N/A	N/A	1
2.58	0.49	**B- / 7.7**	13.3	1.03	N/A	43.44	339	-0.64	0.23	N/A	0	100	0	0	12	45	8
2.10	0.59	**B / 8.3**	12.2	0.94	N/A	55.85	145	-0.63	0.23	N/A	0	100	0	0	29	79	8
2.43	0.59	**B / 8.2**	12.1	0.87	N/A	58.39	931	-0.50	0.14	N/A	0	100	0	0	25	83	8
2.87	N/A	**U /**	N/A	N/A	N/A	23.79	N/A	-1.09	N/A	N/A	0	0	0	100	N/A	N/A	1
.35	0.43	**C+ / 6.8**	N/A	N/A	N/A	24.89	3	-0.76	0.01	N/A	0	0	0	100	35	75	2
.37	0.49	**B- / 7.6**	17.0	0.96	N/A	50.80	10,863	-1.42	N/A	N/A	0	100	0	0	31	96	8
.73	0.43	**B- / 7.3**	N/A	N/A	N/A	26.40	8	-1.48	0.10	N/A	0	0	0	100	29	95	2
.58	0.43	**B- / 7.9**	N/A	N/A	N/A	35.05	1	-1.00	N/A	N/A	0	0	0	100	29	99	N/A
.87	N/A	**U /**	N/A	N/A	N/A	24.83	N/A	-1.17	N/A	N/A	0	0	0	100	N/A	N/A	1
.80	0.43	**B / 8.1**	N/A	N/A	N/A	26.51	20	-1.43	-0.01	N/A	0	0	0	100	20	86	2
.28	0.59	**B / 8.6**	N/A	N/A	N/A	34.60	88	-1.68	0.07	N/A	0	0	0	100	41	97	3
.59	0.43	**C / 5.5**	N/A	N/A	N/A	26.39	3	0.04	0.14	N/A	0	0	0	100	28	94	2
.00	0.50	**B- / 7.6**	N/A	N/A	N/A	47.48	5	2.21	-0.33	N/A	0	0	0	100	N/A	65	3
.24	0.59	**B / 8.5**	13.0	0.53	N/A	56.99	301	-0.75	0.09	N/A	0	100	0	0	36	93	8
.26	0.59	**B- / 7.7**	N/A	N/A	N/A	20.21	9	-1.34	-0.23	N/A	0	0	0	100	84	48	3
.23	0.29	**B / 8.7**	10.2	0.95	N/A	71.16	1,836	-0.03	-0.01	34.2	0	100	0	0	12	58	8
.87	0.39	**B- / 7.3**	11.5	1.05	N/A	63.35	28	0.55	0.06	45.0	0	100	0	0	63	56	8
.00	0.95	**B- / 7.6**	5.1	-0.05	N/A	41.80	178	0.65	0.02	N/A	0	0	0	100	N/A	81	5
.35	0.39	**B / 8.1**	10.8	0.93	N/A	80.52	1,126	-0.01	0.03	37.4	0	100	0	0	30	76	8
67	0.39	**B / 8.4**	13.0	1.10	N/A	87.20	591	-0.07	0.03	55.4	0	100	0	0	36	43	8

Denotes ETF Fund, N/A denotes number is not available

	99 Pct = Best 0 Pct = Worst			PRICE			PERFORMANCE					
					52 Week			% Total Return Through 12/31/15			Annualized	
Fund Type	Fund Name	Ticker Symbol	Overall Investment Rating	Price As of 12/31/15	High	Low	Performance Rating/Pts	3 Mo	6 Mo	1Yr/Pct	3Yr/Pct	5Yr/Pct
FO	*WisdomTree Middle East Dividend	GULF	C	16.65	21.37	15.72	C / 5.5	-8.33	-15.35	-14.54 / 18	7.52 / 69	3.58 / 41
GR	*WisdomTree SmallCap Dividend Fd	DES	B+	64.93	72.99	37.40	B- / 7.3	2.86	-6.07	-5.30 / 38	10.57 / 77	10.37 / 67
GR	*WisdomTree SmallCap Earnings Fun	EES	C+	75.80	100.28	69.69	B- / 7.0	2.61	-9.06	-6.18 / 35	10.01 / 75	9.36 / 63
GL	*WisdomTree Strategic Corporate B	CRDT	C+	71.54	76.45	71.46	C- / 4.0	-0.55	-0.20	-0.31 / 58	--	--
EM	*WisdomTree Strong Dollar EM Equi	EMSD	U	23.62	N/A	N/A	U /	--	--	--	--	--
GR	*WisdomTree Strong Dollar US Equi	USSD	U	24.35	N/A	N/A	U /	8.90	--	--	--	--
IN	*WisdomTree Total Dividend	DTD	B+	71.66	76.31	52.04	B / 8.2	5.05	-1.06	-1.39 / 53	12.08 / 82	12.25 / 80
IN	*WisdomTree Total Earnings Fund	EXT	B+	71.09	76.53	29.04	B+ / 8.5	5.63	-2.64	-1.40 / 53	13.21 / 85	12.04 / 78
FO	*WisdomTree United Kingdom Hedged	DXPS	C-	23.06	28.06	20.94	D+ / 2.6	-0.47	-6.39	-3.97 / 43	--	--
IN	*WisdomTree US Dividend Growth	DGRW	C	30.35	32.28	25.50	C / 5.0	4.91	-1.71	0.16 / 61	--	--
IN	*WisdomTree US SmCp Qual Dividend	DGRS	C-	26.53	30.52	24.82	D+ / 2.4	1.79	-8.51	-6.31 / 35	--	--
GR	*WisdomTree Weak Dollar US Equity	USWD	U	23.36	N/A	N/A	U /	6.72	--	--	--	--
FS	*WisdomTree Western Asset Uncons	UBND	U	47.01	N/A	N/A	U /	-1.22	-4.29	--	--	--
GL	*YieldShares High Income ETF	YYY	C	17.82	21.67	13.82	C- / 4.0	2.36	-7.92	-7.93 / 31	0.88 / 41	--
EN	*Yorkville High Income Infras MLP	YMLI	E+	12.62	21.40	10.31	E- / 0.1	-11.55	-29.76	-36.61 / 5	--	--
GL	*Yorkville High Income MLP ETF	YMLP	E	4.68	13.33	4.09	E- / 0.2	-31.78	-50.66	-58.52 / 1	-29.51 / 4	--
GL	Aberdeen Asia-Pacific Income Fund	FAX	D+	4.57	5.72	4.35	D / 2.1	3.27	-3.15	-10.73 / 24	-10.34 / 17	-0.72 / 26
FO	Aberdeen Australia Equity Fund	IAF	D	5.45	7.50	5.07	D / 2.0	4.28	-9.71	-9.28 / 28	-10.22 / 17	-3.48 / 22
FO	Aberdeen Chile Fund	CH	E+	5.58	7.93	5.42	E+ / 0.9	-4.80	-14.92	-16.07 / 17	-20.34 / 8	-12.84 / 11
EM	Aberdeen Emerging Mkt Sm Co Opptys	ETF	D-	10.86	13.73	10.15	D / 2.0	-0.96	-15.66	-16.76 / 16	-8.37 / 19	-1.88 / 23
GL	Aberdeen Global Income Fund	FCO	D	7.69	9.84	7.39	D / 1.9	4.07	-5.80	-11.87 / 22	-11.23 / 16	-0.95 / 25
FO	Aberdeen Greater China	GCH	D+	8.56	11.20	7.70	D+ / 2.4	4.07	-10.79	-9.36 / 27	-7.01 / 21	-4.23 / 20
EM	Aberdeen Indonesia Fund	IF	D-	5.52	8.61	5.14	D- / 1.1	7.09	-18.78	-32.92 / 6	-16.33 / 11	-6.38 / 17
FO	Aberdeen Israel Fund	ISL	B+	17.26	20.59	14.03	B / 7.7	0.94	-7.25	5.24 / 80	10.54 / 77	2.85 / 37
FO	Aberdeen Japan Equity	JEQ	A-	7.70	8.57	6.64	A- / 9.1	15.56	-3.75	17.25 / 97	12.60 / 83	6.55 / 53
FO	Aberdeen Latin America Equity Fund	LAQ	E+	15.25	23.12	15.10	E+ / 0.7	-3.98	-24.96	-29.29 / 8	-21.34 / 7	-12.07 / 12
FO	Aberdeen Singapore	SGF	D	8.56	12.07	8.44	D+ / 2.3	6.17	-15.37	-17.48 / 16	-6.38 / 22	-4.01 / 20
IN	Adams Diversified Equity	ADX	A-	12.83	14.36	12.33	B+ / 8.6	6.58	-2.89	0.65 / 65	13.38 / 85	10.70 / 70
EN	Adams Natural Resources	PEO	D+	17.74	25.25	17.00	D+ / 2.5	-1.42	-14.83	-19.75 / 14	-4.06 / 26	-1.51 / 24
GI	Advent Claymore Cnv Sec & Inc	AVK	C-	13.52	17.52	12.78	C- / 3.4	5.32	-14.22	-10.94 / 24	-0.46 / 36	1.04 / 31
GL	Advent Claymore Enhanced Gr & Inc	LCM	C	8.27	9.80	7.34	C+ / 5.7	2.49	-4.84	1.77 / 71	3.61 / 55	1.25 / 31
GI	Advent/Claymore Con Sec & Inc	AGC	C-	5.55	7.00	5.02	C / 4.7	5.23	-9.34	-3.30 / 45	1.73 / 47	-1.96 / 23
MUS	Alliance CA Municipal Income Fund	AKP	B+	14.09	14.30	13.16	B / 7.7	2.78	7.95	9.55 / 95	3.51 / 62	8.05 / 81
GL	AllianceBernstein Global High Inc	AWF	C-	10.78	12.79	10.43	C- / 3.3	1.77	-4.78	-4.80 / 40	-2.70 / 29	4.85 / 47
GL	AllianceBernstein Income Fund	ACG	C+	7.67	8.05	7.41	C+ / 6.5	0.33	7.11	9.42 / 87	4.35 / 58	7.45 / 56
MUN	AllianceBernstein Nat Muni Inc Fun	AFB	C+	13.81	14.54	12.97	C+ / 5.9	4.86	7.64	6.57 / 88	0.84 / 44	8.48 / 84
GI	AllianzGI Convertible & Income II	NCZ	D-	5.05	8.80	4.74	D / 1.6	-4.14	-33.89	-37.87 / 4	-6.10 / 23	-1.72 / 23
GI	AllianzGI Convertible and Income	NCV	D	5.54	9.32	5.32	D / 2.1	-2.01	-29.16	-32.44 / 7	-4.30 / 26	-0.57 / 26
GI	AllianzGI Diversified Inc and Conv		U	18.16	N/A	N/A	U /	4.18	-20.02	--	--	--
IN	AllianzGI Equity and Conv Inc	NIE	B-	17.96	20.69	15.68	B- / 7.0	5.26	-3.04	-5.40 / 37	8.98 / 72	6.49 / 53
GI	AllianzGI NFJ Div Int and Prem Str	NFJ	C-	12.39	16.75	11.01	C- / 3.7	-0.69	-12.93	-14.31 / 19	1.72 / 47	3.40 / 40
GL	Alpine Global Dynamic Div Fd	AGD	C	8.85	10.67	8.22	C / 4.4	4.43	-7.44	-2.50 / 48	0.98 / 42	-1.60 / 24
GI	Alpine Global Premier Properties F	AWP	C-	5.77	7.05	5.44	C- / 3.7	4.55	-6.76	-11.03 / 24	-0.05 / 37	4.68 / 46
GL	Alpine Total Dynamic Dividend Fund	AOD	C+	7.68	9.16	7.35	C+ / 5.9	2.48	-7.61	-3.30 / 45	5.64 / 63	1.36 / 31
LP	Apollo Senior Floating Rate Fd Inc	AFT	C-	15.15	18.70	14.57	C- / 3.6	-0.31	-13.42	-2.63 / 48	-0.48 / 36	--
GEI	Apollo Tactical Income Fund Inc	AIF	C-	13.89	16.65	11.56	D+ / 2.5	0.08	-7.76	-4.55 / 40	--	--
COH	Ares Dynamic Credit Allocation Fun	ARDC	D+	13.36	16.77	12.90	D+ / 2.5	-2.18	-9.68	-8.63 / 29	-5.73 / 24	--
PM	ASA Gold & Precious Metals Ltd	ASA	E+	7.17	12.31	6.73	E / 0.4	-12.10	-24.87	-30.86 / 7	-30.34 / 4	-24.08 / 5
FO	Asia Pacific Fund	APB	C-	10.07	13.36	9.62	C- / 3.2	2.74	-17.38	-5.00 / 39	-1.64 / 32	-2.53 / 23
FO	Asia Tigers Fund	GRR	D+	9.06	12.31	8.83	D / 2.0	0.45	-17.91	-17.10 / 16	-7.90 / 20	-5.79 / 18
LP	Avenue Income Credit Strategies	ACP	D	11.35	15.58	10.60	D / 2.1	-7.49	-16.99	-16.71 / 16	-6.04 / 23	--
GEI	Babson Capital Corporate Investors	MCI	A+	17.25	17.89	15.27	A+ / 9.6	9.81	13.49	17.03 / 97	--	--

* Denotes ETF Fund, N/A denotes number is not availabl

Incl. in Returns		RISK				NET ASSETS		VALUATION			ASSET					FUND MANAGER	
Dividend Yield %	Expense Ratio	Risk Rating/ Pts	3 Year Standard Deviation	3 Year Beta	Avg Dura- tion	NAV as of 12/31/15	Total $(Mil)	Premium / Discount As of 12/31/15	Premium / Discount 1 Year Average	Wtd Avg P/E	Cash %	Stocks %	Bonds %	Other %	Portfolio Turnover Ratio	Manager Quality Pct	Manager Tenure (Years)
0.61	0.89	C+ / 6.8	16.4	0.47	N/A	16.94	58	-1.71	-1.13	N/A	0	100	0	0	89	89	N/A
0.75	0.39	B / 8.6	13.2	1.03	N/A	65.01	981	-0.12	0.04	33.2	0	100	0	0	33	40	8
1.74	0.39	C+ / 6.9	14.9	1.09	N/A	75.75	396	0.07	-0.02	52.2	0	100	0	0	43	33	8
3.35	0.45	B+ / 9.3	N/A	N/A	N/A	71.91	8	-0.51	-0.40	N/A	0	0	0	100	15	60	3
0.53	N/A	U /	N/A	N/A	N/A	23.63	N/A	-0.04	N/A	N/A	0	0	0	100	N/A	N/A	1
4.27	N/A	U /	N/A	N/A	N/A	24.18	N/A	0.70	N/A	N/A	0	0	0	100	N/A	N/A	1
4.33	0.29	B- / 7.3	10.3	0.95	N/A	71.63	516	0.04	N/A	34.4	0	100	0	0	13	59	8
2.48	0.29	B- / 7.3	11.2	1.04	N/A	70.91	95	0.25	-0.02	41.5	0	100	0	0	16	58	8
2.10	0.49	B- / 7.9	N/A	N/A	N/A	23.21	22	-0.65	0.47	N/A	0	0	0	100	20	39	3
3.89	0.29	B- / 7.1	N/A	N/A	N/A	30.34	133	0.03	0.05	N/A	0	0	0	100	35	54	3
6.82	0.39	B- / 7.4	N/A	N/A	N/A	26.53	24	0.00	0.01	N/A	0	0	0	100	53	20	3
3.52	N/A	U /	N/A	N/A	N/A	23.64	N/A	-1.18	N/A	N/A	0	0	0	100	N/A	N/A	1
4.08	N/A	U /	N/A	N/A	N/A	47.26	N/A	-0.53	N/A	N/A	0	0	0	100	N/A	N/A	1
0.77	0.50	B- / 7.3	11.4	0.65	N/A	17.84	72	-0.11	-0.01	N/A	0	0	0	100	111	46	4
9.51	0.84	C- / 3.8	N/A	N/A	N/A	12.60	46	0.16	-0.04	N/A	0	0	0	100	47	5	1
5.21	0.83	C- / 3.0	29.6	1.24	N/A	4.70	331	-0.43	-0.01	N/A	0	0	0	100	44	2	1
4.70	1.97	C+ / 6.2	13.6	1.32	6.9	5.49	1,719	-16.76	-14.10	N/A	0	0	99	1	49	34	N/A
1.76	1.48	C / 4.9	17.9	0.63	N/A	6.16	190	-11.53	-9.15	N/A	0	92	0	8	13	12	N/A
0.75	2.58	C- / 3.7	19.3	0.19	N/A	6.45	77	-13.49	-10.36	N/A	0	100	0	0	6	7	7
.00	1.61	C- / 4.0	17.2	1.01	N/A	12.66	153	-14.22	-12.37	N/A	2	97	0	1	10	53	N/A
.92	2.18	C+ / 5.9	14.7	1.63	8.3	8.98	106	-14.37	-13.63	N/A	0	0	99	1	59	32	N/A
4.17	1.99	C+ / 6.3	16.1	0.93	N/A	10.07	104	-15.00	-13.88	26.6	5	94	0	1	11	15	N/A
.01	1.53	C- / 3.8	20.0	0.87	N/A	6.50	88	-15.08	-12.13	N/A	0	100	0	0	5	16	7
.00	1.55	B / 8.1	11.8	0.43	N/A	20.64	79	-16.38	-14.31	60.5	3	94	0	3	16	94	7
.63	1.04	B- / 7.4	14.9	0.75	N/A	8.48	114	-9.20	-11.47	N/A	0	99	0	1	98	95	N/A
.06	1.26	C- / 3.7	21.7	1.20	N/A	17.26	229	-11.65	-10.42	N/A	1	98	0	1	14	4	7
.25	1.47	C+ / 5.6	14.9	0.87	N/A	10.01	107	-14.49	-13.05	N/A	0	95	0	5	11	16	5
.17	0.58	B- / 7.8	11.4	1.06	N/A	15.04	1,528	-14.69	-14.43	80.2	4	95	0	1	27	57	6
.69	0.63	C+ / 5.9	17.9	0.92	N/A	20.74	755	-14.46	-13.88	22.8	3	97	0	0	20	74	3
.33	2.32	C+ / 6.7	14.2	1.02	N/A	16.25	448	-16.80	-12.95	N/A	8	1	23	68	264	12	N/A
.16	2.10	C+ / 6.8	12.3	0.73	3.6	9.58	148	-13.67	-13.47	78.8	1	17	18	64	344	75	9
.16	3.06	C+ / 6.3	14.2	1.02	3.8	6.71	246	-17.29	-15.34	89.3	1	0	14	85	249	15	9
.97	1.44	B- / 7.6	10.5	2.02	10.1	15.43	128	-8.68	-8.16	N/A	1	0	98	1	32	52	N/A
.23	1.01	C+ / 6.4	9.1	0.53	N/A	12.30	1,208	-12.36	-12.32	N/A	0	0	98	2	48	69	24
.24	0.67	B- / 7.3	8.3	0.44	N/A	7.86	2	-2.42	-7.03	N/A	1	0	98	1	32	91	29
.42	1.17	B- / 7.6	11.5	2.65	9.8	15.15	425	-8.84	-8.23	N/A	0	0	100	0	26	27	N/A
.66	1.19	C / 4.8	18.8	0.92	N/A	5.55	559	-9.01	2.03	N/A	3	0	46	51	57	10	13
.08	1.23	C / 5.2	18.3	1.05	N/A	6.24	740	-11.22	0.08	N/A	3	0	46	51	56	9	13
.46	N/A	U /	N/A	N/A	N/A	20.72	N/A	-12.36	N/A	N/A	0	0	0	100	N/A	N/A	N/A
.46	1.13	B- / 7.5	11.2	1.00	N/A	20.90	613	-14.07	-12.83	N/A	3	69	0	28	63	35	N/A
.69	0.96	C+ / 6.8	11.2	0.61	N/A	14.29	1,607	-13.30	-9.81	N/A	4	71	0	25	47	27	N/A
81	1.42	B- / 7.8	12.4	0.73	4.0	10.42	141	-15.07	-13.64	45.4	0	100	0	0	110	55	N/A
.40	1.29	C+ / 6.3	16.7	1.14	N/A	6.99	672	-17.45	-14.78	91.3	0	100	0	0	58	11	9
98	1.14	B- / 7.8	11.2	0.77	N/A	9.21	1,077	-16.61	-14.86	45.4	0	100	0	0	99	83	N/A
.74	3.07	B- / 7.2	8.5	-126.88	N/A	16.93	285	-10.51	-7.15	N/A	0	0	0	100	80	43	N/A
16	2.90	B- / 7.2	N/A	N/A	N/A	16.10	263	-13.73	-13.26	N/A	0	0	0	100	79	37	N/A
51	2.58	B- / 7.0	8.4	1.11	N/A	15.67	321	-14.74	-13.78	N/A	0	0	0	100	96	22	1
56	1.37	C- / 3.7	32.4	1.48	N/A	8.33	222	-13.93	-10.75	29.3	0	99	0	1	7	12	N/A
06	2.05	C+ / 6.8	17.1	0.80	N/A	11.77	135	-14.44	-12.61	N/A	0	99	0	1	76	31	2
81	2.33	B- / 7.0	13.8	0.83	N/A	10.62	48	-14.69	-12.77	26.6	1	94	0	5	10	14	N/A
69	2.89	C+ / 5.8	11.6	N/A	N/A	12.80	236	-11.33	-10.75	N/A	0	0	81	19	48	39	N/A
96	2.22	B- / 7.3	N/A	N/A	N/A	14.70	280	17.35	9.68	N/A	3	20	56	21	38	98	N/A

Denotes ETF Fund, N/A denotes number is not available

Fund Type	Fund Name	Ticker Symbol	Overall Investment Rating	PRICE: Price As of 12/31/15	52 Week High	52 Week Low	PERFORMANCE: Performance Rating/Pts	% Total Return Through 12/31/15: 3 Mo	6 Mo	1Yr/Pct	Annualized 3Yr/Pct	Annualized 5Yr/Pct
	99 Pct = Best 0 Pct = Worst											
GL	Babson Capital Glb Sht Dur Hi Yiel	BGH	C-	16.49	21.54	15.59	C- / 3.0	-0.90	-13.10	-9.82 / 26	-1.94 / 31	--
GEI	Babson Capital Participation Inv	MPV	A-	13.75	14.54	12.07	A+ / 9.6	8.30	18.15	12.54 / 92	--	--
GI	Bancroft Fund Ltd.	BCV	B-	18.20	21.91	17.52	C+ / 6.6	3.08	-8.29	-0.21 / 59	7.90 / 69	5.79 / 50
MUS	BlackRock CA Muni 2018 Income Trus	BJZ	C+	15.04	15.70	14.75	C / 5.2	1.70	2.48	0.43 / 65	0.89 / 44	4.13 / 52
MUS	BlackRock CA Municipal Income Trus	BFZ	B+	15.95	16.00	14.40	B+ / 8.6	6.38	12.37	12.49 / 98	3.78 / 63	11.52 / 96
GEI	BlackRock Core Bond Trust	BHK	C	12.64	14.03	12.37	C / 4.8	-0.29	3.33	2.01 / 71	0.58 / 39	7.49 / 56
COH	BlackRock Corporate High Yield	HYT	C-	9.78	11.54	9.16	C- / 4.1	4.37	-3.87	-4.99 / 39	0.25 / 38	5.70 / 50
IN	BlackRock Credit Alloc Inc Tr	BTZ	C+	12.34	13.65	11.67	C+ / 5.8	4.16	1.86	2.10 / 72	3.34 / 54	8.16 / 58
COH	BlackRock Debt Strategies Fund Inc	DSU	C-	3.37	3.83	3.17	C- / 4.0	3.63	-2.96	-1.16 / 54	-0.61 / 35	5.43 / 49
LP	BlackRock Defined Opp Credit Trust	BHL	C+	13.02	13.58	12.56	C+ / 6.0	3.48	-0.12	6.03 / 81	3.47 / 55	5.01 / 48
EN	BlackRock Energy & Resources	BGR	D-	12.53	22.80	12.17	D- / 1.3	-9.82	-25.17	-32.98 / 6	-9.61 / 18	-6.51 / 17
GI	BlackRock Enhanced Capital and Inc	CII	A	14.14	15.67	12.52	B+ / 8.8	7.59	-0.66	8.19 / 85	12.57 / 83	8.71 / 60
IN	BlackRock Enhanced Equity Div	BDJ	B+	7.61	8.38	6.71	B- / 7.4	7.91	-0.28	1.29 / 68	8.71 / 72	5.39 / 49
USA	BlackRock Enhanced Government	EGF	C	13.65	14.37	12.99	C / 4.5	0.56	3.53	0.13 / 61	0.11 / 37	2.50 / 36
MUS	BlackRock FL Muni 2020 Term Tr	BFO	B-	14.94	15.66	14.70	C / 5.5	0.89	2.50	1.97 / 74	1.29 / 48	5.98 / 62
LP	BlackRock Floating Rate Inc Strat	FRA	C	12.90	14.15	11.84	C / 4.6	2.72	-1.53	2.34 / 72	0.13 / 38	3.69 / 41
LP	BlackRock Floating Rt Income	BGT	C	12.50	13.73	11.90	C / 4.3	3.02	-1.14	2.39 / 73	-0.56 / 35	1.91 / 33
GL	BlackRock Global Opportunities Eq	BOE	C+	12.76	14.20	11.95	C+ / 6.5	6.88	-2.92	5.71 / 81	5.88 / 64	2.89 / 38
HL	BlackRock Health Sciences Trust	BME	B+	39.35	49.94	36.45	A+ / 9.7	11.43	4.69	10.11 / 88	25.19 / 97	20.16 / 98
MTG	BlackRock Income Trust	BKT	C+	6.38	6.52	6.02	C+ / 5.6	1.80	3.95	5.23 / 79	1.55 / 45	5.05 / 48
FO	BlackRock Intl Grth and Inc Tr	BGY	C	6.24	7.60	5.79	C / 5.2	4.52	-10.27	1.23 / 68	2.24 / 50	-0.05 / 28
MUN	BlackRock Investment Qual Muni Tr	BKN	C+	15.39	16.84	14.44	C+ / 6.2	4.14	8.51	-0.50 / 57	2.73 / 58	10.12 / 92
GEN	BlackRock Limited Duration Income	BLW	C	14.58	16.26	13.53	C / 4.6	5.28	-0.26	0.62 / 65	0.04 / 37	5.72 / 50
MUN	BlackRock Long Term Muni Adv	BTA	C+	11.50	11.77	10.67	C+ / 6.8	5.78	10.57	8.26 / 92	2.15 / 54	10.03 / 92
MUS	BlackRock Massachusetts Tax-Exempt	MHE	C	13.38	15.19	12.84	C / 5.0	3.54	2.78	-1.56 / 52	0.60 / 41	6.53 / 65
MUS	BlackRock MD Muni Bond Trust	BZM	C	14.95	15.72	14.25	C+ / 6.2	4.29	4.39	7.42 / 91	0.84 / 44	5.29 / 58
GEI	BlackRock Multi-Sector Income Trus	BIT	C+	15.81	17.81	14.91	C+ / 6.0	4.26	0.72	2.87 / 74	--	--
MUN	BlackRock Muni 2020 Term Trust	BKK	B-	15.86	16.74	15.25	C+ / 5.8	2.20	3.94	0.62 / 67	2.05 / 53	6.26 / 64
MUS	BlackRock Muni Bond Invt Trust	BIE	C+	14.97	15.70	13.93	C+ / 5.9	6.10	10.19	7.65 / 91	0.34 / 39	8.78 / 86
MUN	BlackRock Muni Interm Duration	MUI	C	14.17	15.08	13.48	C / 5.2	4.56	8.31	4.96 / 84	-0.74 / 35	7.07 / 71
MUS	BlackRock Muni NY Interm Duration	MNE	A-	15.18	15.34	13.67	B+ / 8.6	9.72	9.43	13.89 / 98	3.37 / 62	8.75 / 86
MUN	BlackRock MuniAssets Fund	MUA	B+	14.27	14.47	13.22	B+ / 8.7	7.45	7.97	9.14 / 94	5.27 / 70	10.34 / 93
MUN	BlackRock Municipal 2018 Income Tr	BPK	C+	15.50	16.28	15.13	C / 5.3	0.92	2.84	0.10 / 61	1.18 / 47	4.66 / 55
MUN	BlackRock Municipal Bond Trust	BBK	B-	16.14	16.93	14.80	B- / 7.2	5.23	9.73	7.76 / 92	3.28 / 61	10.61 / 94
MUS	BlackRock Municipal Income Inv Qly	BAF	C+	14.78	15.29	13.70	C+ / 6.8	6.76	7.71	8.33 / 93	0.95 / 45	8.52 / 85
MUS	BlackRock Municipal Income Invt Tr	BBF	B-	14.60	14.88	13.19	B- / 7.4	8.93	13.62	10.98 / 96	2.54 / 57	10.08 / 92
MUN	BlackRock Municipal Income Quality	BYM	C+	14.88	15.33	13.28	C+ / 6.9	9.21	12.79	10.15 / 96	1.55 / 50	9.51 / 90
MUN	BlackRock Municipal Income Trust	BFK	B-	14.75	14.99	13.28	B / 7.6	6.69	12.69	10.49 / 96	3.31 / 62	11.10 / 95
MUN	BlackRock Municipal Income Trust I	BLE	C+	15.31	16.67	13.82	C+ / 6.7	6.52	12.37	2.16 / 75	2.76 / 58	10.83 / 94
MUN	BlackRock Municipal Target Term	BTT	C+	21.57	21.75	19.49	B- / 7.2	6.21	9.00	11.81 / 98	0.99 / 45	--
MUN	BlackRock MuniEnhanced Fund	MEN	B+	11.85	12.14	10.87	B / 7.8	5.28	10.56	10.38 / 96	4.15 / 65	9.40 / 89
MUS	BlackRock MuniHoldings CA Qly	MUC	C+	14.85	15.15	13.10	C+ / 6.3	4.55	8.83	8.33 / 92	1.43 / 49	9.15 / 88
MUN	BlackRock MuniHoldings Fund	MHD	C+	17.11	17.99	15.75	C+ / 6.8	3.56	9.34	5.96 / 87	2.99 / 60	10.07 / 92
MUN	BlackRock MuniHoldings Fund II	MUH	C+	15.35	16.37	14.03	C+ / 6.5	3.88	10.54	4.21 / 82	2.39 / 56	9.78 / 91
MUS	BlackRock MuniHoldings Inv Quality	MFL	C+	14.53	15.15	13.19	C+ / 6.3	4.29	8.41	7.20 / 90	1.81 / 52	9.56 / 90
MUS	BlackRock MuniHoldings New York Ql	MHN	B-	14.56	14.63	13.32	B- / 7.5	6.92	9.20	9.35 / 94	1.82 / 52	8.04 / 81
MUS	BlackRock MuniHoldings NJ Qly	MUJ	C+	14.43	15.33	13.14	C+ / 6.1	8.22	12.67	5.66 / 86	0.76 / 43	7.83 / 79
MUN	BlackRock MuniHoldings Quality	MUS	B	13.73	13.97	12.58	B- / 7.5	7.70	9.24	9.73 / 95	1.68 / 51	9.38 / 89
MUN	BlackRock MuniHoldings Quality II	MUE	C+	13.61	14.31	12.67	C+ / 6.2	4.28	9.63	6.85 / 89	1.35 / 49	9.23 / 88
MUN	BlackRock MuniVest Fund	MVF	B-	10.25	10.59	9.20	B- / 7.1	7.81	10.77	9.63 / 95	2.38 / 56	9.22 / 88
MUN	BlackRock MuniVest Fund II	MVT	B	16.41	16.65	14.53	B / 7.8	7.08	14.50	12.38 / 98	3.35 / 62	10.92 / 95
MUS	BlackRock MuniYield AZ Fund	MZA	B	16.86	17.76	15.56	B+ / 8.5	0.88	2.92	8.24 / 92	7.49 / 80	11.99 / 96

* Denotes ETF Fund, N/A denotes number is not availabl

Incl. in Returns		RISK	3 Year			NET ASSETS		VALUATION			ASSET					FUND MANAGER	
Dividend Yield %	Expense Ratio	Risk Rating/ Pts	Standard Deviation	Beta	Avg Dura-tion	NAV as of 12/31/15	Total $(Mil)	Premium / Discount As of 12/31/15	Premium / Discount 1 Year Average	Wtd Avg P/E	Cash %	Stocks %	Bonds %	Other %	Portfolio Turnover Ratio	Manager Quality Pct	Manager Tenure (Years)
11.75	2.20	**C+ / 6.5**	9.4	0.45	N/A	18.46	441	-10.67	-9.51	N/A	0	0	0	100	64	74	4
7.86	1.94	**C+ / 6.8**	N/A	N/A	N/A	13.64	138	0.81	-5.61	N/A	0	0	0	100	32	96	N/A
5.08	1.10	**B- / 7.7**	8.6	0.66	N/A	21.71	124	-16.17	-15.18	N/A	2	0	0	98	43	60	20
3.41	0.57	**B / 8.6**	5.1	0.27	5.3	15.15	98	-0.73	-1.22	N/A	0	0	100	0	12	66	10
5.43	1.53	**C+ / 6.7**	11.9	2.31	13.1	15.99	505	-0.25	-4.39	N/A	1	0	98	1	37	50	10
6.74	0.95	**B- / 7.4**	9.2	2.28	N/A	13.88	771	-8.93	-9.98	N/A	2	0	95	3	55	55	9
27.01	1.37	**B- / 7.1**	10.1	1.29	N/A	10.84	1,527	-9.78	-12.43	N/A	1	5	86	8	57	59	10
7.83	1.16	**B- / 7.7**	9.2	0.29	N/A	13.75	1,549	-10.25	-12.94	N/A	0	0	80	20	19	64	5
7.12	1.24	**B- / 7.0**	8.9	1.10	N/A	3.85	802	-12.47	-13.59	N/A	0	2	95	3	54	50	7
6.74	2.01	**B- / 7.5**	6.5	-2.52	N/A	13.22	125	-1.51	-4.73	N/A	0	1	98	1	42	85	N/A
10.53	1.26	**C / 5.1**	22.3	1.01	N/A	14.05	741	-10.82	-3.29	14.9	0	100	0	0	85	31	4
8.49	0.93	**B- / 7.8**	12.6	1.03	N/A	15.11	682	-6.42	-6.46	42.2	0	100	0	0	80	54	4
7.36	0.86	**B / 8.1**	10.4	0.86	N/A	8.70	1,649	-12.53	-11.41	28.6	0	100	0	0	63	43	6
4.31	1.20	**B- / 7.9**	5.4	0.23	N/A	14.29	120	-4.48	-5.93	N/A	6	0	90	4	86	64	N/A
2.49	0.68	**B / 8.9**	3.1	0.23	5.4	15.28	86	-2.23	-2.68	N/A	0	0	99	1	14	78	10
6.87	1.56	**B- / 7.6**	6.4	-59.03	N/A	14.26	555	-9.54	-10.55	N/A	0	0	98	2	43	62	7
5.60	1.55	**B- / 7.5**	7.2	-23.07	N/A	13.77	335	-9.22	-9.40	N/A	0	1	98	1	42	62	7
9.12	1.08	**B- / 7.3**	12.8	0.89	N/A	14.25	1,080	-10.46	-11.57	67.3	0	100	0	0	150	81	7
44.84	1.11	**C+ / 6.2**	20.4	0.97	N/A	36.17	314	8.79	3.01	98.8	0	100	0	0	74	95	11
5.83	0.99	**B- / 7.6**	6.1	1.79	14.6	6.94	453	-8.07	-9.86	N/A	1	0	99	0	191	52	28
9.42	1.05	**B- / 7.0**	14.7	1.03	N/A	6.94	868	-10.09	-8.67	31.6	0	100	0	0	195	48	9
5.77	1.45	**B- / 7.2**	12.8	2.03	12.5	16.33	276	-5.76	-4.84	N/A	2	0	97	1	37	50	10
2.16	1.15	**B- / 7.4**	7.5	0.59	N/A	16.16	630	-9.78	-11.24	N/A	2	1	95	2	47	63	9
6.05	1.47	**B- / 7.1**	10.6	2.35	14.8	12.58	168	-8.59	-10.32	N/A	0	0	99	1	8	37	10
5.36	1.71	**B- / 7.6**	11.9	2.21	14.2	14.15	33	-5.44	-1.91	N/A	1	0	98	1	8	31	11
4.38	1.88	**C+ / 5.8**	15.9	2.86	12.5	15.26	31	-2.03	-2.00	N/A	11	0	88	1	18	24	10
5.38	2.09	**B- / 7.7**	N/A	N/A	N/A	18.23	726	-13.27	-13.24	N/A	0	0	0	100	21	83	N/A
3.39	0.72	**B / 8.7**	6.0	0.75	6.2	16.16	330	-1.86	-1.76	N/A	0	0	100	0	11	73	10
6.09	1.84	**B- / 7.4**	11.0	2.19	13.9	16.15	53	-7.31	-9.61	N/A	0	0	100	0	17	29	N/A
5.55	1.52	**B- / 7.3**	9.8	1.77	8.7	15.83	607	-10.49	-10.82	N/A	2	0	97	1	18	33	10
4.55	1.74	**B- / 7.5**	10.0	1.86	9.0	15.77	65	-3.74	-8.82	N/A	2	0	97	1	15	57	12
5.56	0.82	**B- / 7.1**	10.4	2.30	14.6	14.19	505	0.56	-2.12	N/A	2	0	97	1	22	61	10
5.19	0.64	**B / 8.0**	5.9	0.49	5.3	15.34	251	1.04	0.40	N/A	1	0	98	1	14	72	10
5.58	1.73	**C+ / 6.9**	11.8	2.56	12.9	16.89	173	-4.44	-4.93	N/A	1	0	98	1	34	40	10
5.56	1.50	**C+ / 6.9**	10.9	2.24	13.4	16.13	138	-8.37	-9.95	N/A	1	0	98	1	13	32	10
5.95	1.76	**C+ / 6.7**	11.6	2.42	14.1	15.26	102	-4.33	-9.16	N/A	2	0	97	1	11	36	10
5.77	1.47	**C+ / 6.8**	12.0	2.69	12.4	15.60	402	-4.62	-8.93	N/A	1	0	98	1	12	31	10
6.11	1.60	**C+ / 6.6**	12.0	2.57	14.6	14.93	667	-1.21	-4.65	N/A	1	0	98	1	10	41	10
6.19	1.55	**C+ / 6.7**	13.4	3.17	14.5	15.57	358	-1.67	-3.85	N/A	2	0	97	1	10	30	10
4.53	1.06	**C+ / 6.5**	13.5	3.32	N/A	23.77	1,602	-9.26	-10.02	N/A	0	0	0	100	12	21	4
6.13	1.43	**B- / 7.6**	9.8	2.13	12.3	12.32	363	-3.81	-6.15	N/A	1	0	98	1	12	54	27
5.48	1.45	**B- / 7.0**	10.5	2.19	12.7	16.03	647	-7.36	-8.57	N/A	2	0	97	1	25	35	18
7.10	1.50	**B- / 7.1**	12.4	2.33	14.3	17.66	249	-3.11	-3.94	N/A	1	0	98	1	11	42	10
6.57	1.48	**B- / 7.3**	12.5	2.75	13.9	16.28	183	-5.71	-6.84	N/A	1	0	98	1	11	33	10
5.91	1.49	**C+ / 6.6**	12.3	2.27	N/A	15.49	574	-6.20	-7.60	N/A	5	0	94	1	13	34	N/A
5.58	1.52	**B- / 7.0**	9.6	1.87	13.2	15.14	461	-3.83	-6.21	N/A	2	0	97	1	19	41	N/A
6.19	1.57	**B- / 7.5**	10.0	1.91	12.0	15.92	471	-9.36	-11.01	N/A	1	0	98	1	10	33	10
5.90	1.57	**B- / 7.2**	12.0	3.00	13.3	14.64	190	-6.22	-9.18	N/A	4	0	95	1	11	25	10
6.00	1.49	**B- / 7.4**	11.7	2.38	13.4	14.71	326	-7.48	-8.52	N/A	5	0	94	1	13	33	10
6.38	1.43	**B- / 7.1**	11.9	2.42	14.0	10.17	643	0.79	-2.28	N/A	0	0	100	0	18	41	10
6.37	1.50	**C+ / 6.8**	12.6	2.82	14.2	16.01	336	2.50	-1.43	N/A	0	0	100	0	10	35	10
4.95	1.63	**C+ / 6.6**	13.7	2.08	11.6	14.93	68	12.93	13.49	N/A	3	0	96	1	16	81	23

Denotes ETF Fund, N/A denotes number is not available

				PRICE			PERFORMANCE					
99 Pct = Best *0 Pct = Worst*					52 Week			% Total Return Through 12/31/15			Annualized	
Fund Type	Fund Name	Ticker Symbol	Overall Investment Rating	Price As of 12/31/15	High	Low	Performance Rating/Pts	3 Mo	6 Mo	1Yr/Pct	3Yr/Pct	5Yr/Pct
MUS	BlackRock MuniYield CA Fund	MYC	B-	15.82	16.56	14.94	B- / 7.1	0.29	8.22	8.74 / 93	2.93 / 59	10.51 / 93
MUS	BlackRock MuniYield California Qly	MCA	B-	15.60	15.94	14.25	B- / 7.3	4.73	10.52	8.49 / 93	3.38 / 62	10.65 / 94
MUN	BlackRock MuniYield Fund	MYD	C+	14.87	15.45	13.74	C+ / 6.5	5.75	10.27	7.36 / 90	1.86 / 52	9.58 / 90
MUS	BlackRock MuniYield Inv Quality	MFT	C+	14.10	14.50	12.88	C+ / 6.2	5.27	10.53	8.39 / 93	1.06 / 46	9.53 / 90
MUS	BlackRock MuniYield Invt Fund	MYF	C+	15.65	16.39	14.23	C+ / 6.9	6.05	12.71	8.05 / 92	2.36 / 55	11.23 / 95
MUS	BlackRock MuniYield Michigan Qly	MIY	C+	13.96	14.67	12.95	C+ / 6.2	6.76	8.81	6.67 / 89	1.19 / 47	7.74 / 77
MUS	BlackRock MuniYield New York Qly	MYN	B-	13.52	13.86	12.76	C+ / 6.9	4.50	6.81	9.35 / 94	1.67 / 51	8.21 / 83
MUS	BlackRock MuniYield NJ Fund	MYJ	B	15.47	15.80	7.98	B- / 7.3	6.78	11.85	9.90 / 95	2.84 / 59	8.92 / 87
MUS	BlackRock MuniYield PA Qly	MPA	C+	14.54	15.31	13.33	C+ / 6.4	7.82	11.24	7.66 / 91	1.27 / 48	7.57 / 76
MUN	BlackRock MuniYield Quality Fund	MQY	C+	15.83	16.20	14.38	B- / 7.1	4.78	8.40	9.13 / 94	1.72 / 51	10.19 / 93
MUN	BlackRock MuniYield Quality Fund I	MQT	B-	13.28	14.18	12.26	C+ / 6.9	5.82	9.67	7.04 / 90	2.65 / 57	10.44 / 93
MUN	BlackRock MuniYield Quality III	MYI	B	14.73	14.90	13.62	B / 8.1	6.07	9.46	9.99 / 95	3.40 / 62	10.17 / 92
MUS	BlackRock New York Muni Inc Qly	BSE	C	13.72	13.85	12.74	C / 5.5	6.78	7.68	9.12 / 94	-0.80 / 34	6.92 / 69
MUS	BlackRock NJ Muni Bond Trust	BLJ	C	14.74	16.54	13.65	C / 5.3	5.09	10.03	4.70 / 84	-0.45 / 36	8.33 / 84
MUS	BlackRock NJ Municipal Income Trus	BNJ	C	15.19	17.49	13.79	C+ / 6.3	7.85	11.58	7.22 / 90	1.14 / 47	9.29 / 89
MUS	BlackRock NY Muni 2018 Income Trus	BLH	C	14.94	15.19	14.65	C / 4.3	0.51	2.15	2.03 / 74	-0.54 / 35	2.47 / 42
MUS	BlackRock NY Muni Bond Trust	BQH	C+	14.85	14.99	13.46	C+ / 6.5	7.86	10.07	9.93 / 95	1.40 / 49	7.30 / 73
MUS	BlackRock NY Municipal Income Tr I	BFY	C+	14.98	15.50	13.91	B- / 7.1	5.56	3.76	9.12 / 94	2.36 / 56	7.78 / 78
MUS	BlackRock NY Municipal Income Trus	BNY	B	15.58	15.70	13.80	B+ / 8.7	7.59	13.53	14.40 / 98	3.08 / 60	9.18 / 88
IN	BlackRock Res & Commdty Strat Trus	BCX	D-	7.13	10.17	6.59	D- / 1.5	1.86	-17.44	-19.98 / 13	-11.32 / 16	--
GL	BlackRock Sci and Tech Trust	XBSTX	C	17.31	18.57	14.03	B- / 7.5	10.30	1.54	4.87 / 79	--	--
MUN	BlackRock Strategic Municipal Tr	BSD	C+	13.85	14.64	12.95	C+ / 6.7	3.20	9.35	5.06 / 85	2.89 / 59	9.44 / 90
MUN	BlackRock Taxable Municipal Bond T	BBN	B	20.98	23.48	19.60	B / 7.9	6.01	10.66	2.25 / 75	5.33 / 70	11.28 / 95
GL	BlackRock Utility & Infrastructure	BUI	C	16.78	21.00	15.89	C / 5.2	3.76	-4.37	-11.81 / 22	3.93 / 57	--
MUS	BlackRock VA Muni Bond Trust	BHV	B-	19.75	20.50	15.90	A+ / 9.7	20.70	20.07	29.42 / 99	5.38 / 70	8.45 / 84
LP	Blackstone / GSO Lng-Sht Credit In	BGX	C-	13.48	16.39	12.84	D+ / 2.8	-1.77	-9.53	-6.01 / 36	-3.74 / 27	--
COH	Blackstone / GSO Strategic Credit	BGB	D+	13.37	16.44	12.90	D+ / 2.7	-2.18	-11.40	-9.73 / 26	-4.05 / 27	--
LP	Blackstone/GSO Sr Floating Rate Tr	BSL	D+	14.85	17.84	14.38	D+ / 2.9	-3.72	-10.40	-5.58 / 37	-3.27 / 28	1.02 / 31
GI	Boulder Growth&Income Fund	BIF	B-	7.74	9.01	7.01	C+ / 6.7	5.70	-6.45	-12.56 / 21	9.41 / 73	7.78 / 57
GL	Brookfield Gl Lstd Infr Inc Fd	INF	D-	11.75	22.48	10.82	D- / 1.5	-8.12	-24.53	-37.95 / 4	-8.23 / 19	--
COH	Brookfield High Income Fund	HHY	D+	6.88	9.09	6.42	D+ / 2.7	--	-11.78	-13.42 / 20	-3.62 / 27	4.74 / 46
MTG	Brookfield Mortgage Opportunity In	BOI	C	14.75	16.66	13.93	C- / 4.2	4.32	-1.81	-1.60 / 52	--	--
MTG	Brookfield Total Return	HTR	C	21.95	25.15	20.46	C+ / 6.8	5.66	2.31	-0.33 / 58	7.22 / 67	9.49 / 63
GI	Calamos Convertible Opport&Income	CHI	C-	9.91	13.53	9.37	C- / 3.8	5.34	-13.56	-15.59 / 17	1.65 / 46	3.88 / 43
GI	Calamos Convertible&High Income	CHY	C-	10.51	14.90	9.79	C- / 3.9	2.42	-16.48	-16.66 / 16	2.71 / 52	5.09 / 48
GI	Calamos Dynamic Convertible And In		U	18.05	N/A	N/A	U /	1.67	-13.82	--	--	--
GL	Calamos Global Dynamic Income Fd	CHW	C	7.16	9.16	6.70	C / 4.6	5.81	-12.51	-11.35 / 23	2.96 / 53	5.71 / 50
GI	Calamos Global Total Return Fund	CGO	C	11.42	14.10	10.87	C / 4.6	4.90	-10.76	-4.44 / 41	1.88 / 48	3.39 / 40
GI	Calamos Strategic Total Return Fun	CSQ	C+	9.90	11.59	8.80	C+ / 6.7	8.90	-4.81	-4.78 / 40	7.84 / 69	9.70 / 64
FO	Canadian General Investments Ltd	T.CGI	C	18.75	22.00	17.08	B- / 7.4	4.61	-8.40	-1.47 / 52	10.17 / 75	4.16 / 44
GL	Canadian World Fund Limited	T.CWF	B	4.96	5.25	4.00	B+ / 8.8	3.33	-1.78	19.81 / 98	12.00 / 82	3.73 / 42
GI	CBRE Clarion Global Real Estate In	IGR	C	7.64	9.47	7.11	C / 4.4	4.69	-0.85	-9.29 / 27	1.17 / 43	6.71 / 53
EN	Center Coast MLP & Infrastructure	CEN	E+	10.12	19.89	8.17	E- / 0.1	-16.50	-29.77	-38.22 / 4	--	--
FO	Central Europe Russia and Turkey	CEE	D-	16.63	24.12	16.37	D- / 1.1	-2.79	-18.39	-13.67 / 19	-17.36 / 10	-10.54 / 13
PM	Central Fund of Canada	CEF	D-	9.99	13.73	9.84	E+ / 0.8	-8.85	-13.80	-14.31 / 19	-22.08 / 7	-12.11 / 12
PM	Central Gold-Trust	GTU	D	37.70	46.73	37.25	D- / 1.3	-6.57	-7.53	-7.33 / 33	-15.78 / 11	-5.96 / 18
GR	Central Securities	CET	B-	19.02	22.60	17.08	B- / 7.3	4.32	-2.20	-4.45 / 41	9.79 / 74	5.85 / 50
FO	China Fund	CHN	C-	15.52	22.24	14.25	C / 4.6	5.30	-14.73	-7.86 / 31	2.80 / 52	-0.91 / 25
GL	ClearBridge American Energy MLP In	CBA	E+	8.19	16.96	6.51	E- / 0.1	-20.75	-37.72	-45.00 / 2	--	--
EN	ClearBridge Energy MLP Fund Inc	CEM	D-	15.18	27.34	12.56	D- / 1.2	-13.64	-31.52	-40.79 / 3	-9.26 / 18	-0.98 / 25
EN	ClearBridge Energy MLP Oppty Fd In	EMO	D-	12.74	23.55	10.41	D- / 1.1	-15.25	-28.23	-41.79 / 3	-11.24 / 16	--
IN	ClearBridge Engy MLP To Rtn Fd Inc	CTR	D-	12.31	21.52	9.87	D- / 1.2	-14.30	-28.30	-38.57 / 4	-9.80 / 18	--

* Denotes ETF Fund, N/A denotes number is not available

Incl. in Returns		RISK				NET ASSETS		VALUATION			ASSET					FUND MANAGER	
Incl. in Returns		Risk Rating/ Pts	3 Year		Avg Duration	NAV as of 12/31/15	Total $(Mil)	Premium / Discount		Wtd Avg P/E	Cash %	Stocks %	Bonds %	Other %	Portfolio Turnover Ratio	Manager Quality Pct	Manager Tenure (Years)
Dividend Yield %	Expense Ratio		Standard Deviation	Beta				As of 12/31/15	1 Year Average								
5.63	1.37	B- / 7.3	12.3	2.54	14.0	16.50	349	-4.12	-4.95	N/A	2	0	97	1	32	37	24
5.62	1.32	B- / 7.2	9.8	2.02	11.9	16.31	554	-4.35	-6.33	N/A	2	0	97	1	36	50	24
6.85	1.36	C+ / 6.7	12.1	2.60	14.2	15.35	713	-3.13	-4.58	N/A	1	0	98	1	11	32	10
6.04	1.56	B- / 7.3	11.1	2.52	12.9	15.19	127	-7.18	-9.50	N/A	5	0	94	1	13	29	14
6.25	1.46	B- / 7.0	12.6	2.55	13.8	15.74	213	-0.57	-3.22	N/A	1	0	98	1	13	36	14
5.93	1.48	B- / 7.3	11.8	2.58	12.5	15.76	283	-11.42	-12.40	N/A	0	0	99	1	19	29	10
5.60	1.44	B- / 7.2	9.7	1.81	13.4	14.50	560	-6.76	-7.30	N/A	2	0	97	1	20	40	24
6.39	1.50	B- / 7.3	11.4	2.25	13.6	16.28	229	-4.98	-7.19	N/A	4	0	95	1	11	41	N/A
5.90	1.45	B- / 7.5	10.5	2.10	12.6	16.10	211	-9.69	-11.55	N/A	2	0	97	1	21	34	10
6.06	1.46	C+ / 6.7	11.1	2.31	12.4	16.22	494	-2.40	-4.05	N/A	1	0	98	1	14	33	24
6.05	1.47	B- / 7.5	11.6	2.52	12.7	14.22	320	-6.61	-7.52	N/A	1	0	98	1	13	35	16
6.04	1.39	C+ / 6.8	11.4	2.13	11.8	15.00	1,004	-1.80	-4.93	N/A	1	0	98	1	11	53	24
5.03	1.70	B- / 7.2	10.6	2.35	13.0	15.21	97	-9.80	-11.30	N/A	0	0	99	1	20	23	10
5.66	1.98	C+ / 6.6	14.2	2.42	12.1	16.09	36	-8.39	-7.22	N/A	5	0	94	1	13	25	10
6.31	1.79	C+ / 6.4	13.7	2.87	12.8	15.79	119	-3.80	-4.08	N/A	3	0	96	1	12	24	10
3.66	0.79	B / 8.3	5.2	0.63	4.6	15.08	55	-0.93	-1.45	N/A	2	0	97	1	4	54	10
5.01	2.07	C+ / 6.6	12.3	3.07	14.4	16.23	44	-8.50	-11.05	N/A	1	0	98	1	22	22	10
5.61	1.83	C+ / 6.8	11.3	2.27	14.0	15.97	78	-6.20	-7.33	N/A	1	0	98	1	20	40	10
5.31	1.73	C+ / 6.3	11.6	2.40	13.5	15.34	193	1.56	-3.12	N/A	1	0	98	1	11	39	10
1.02	1.06	C / 4.8	16.0	0.88	N/A	8.35	582	-14.61	-14.92	N/A	22	78	0	0	62	7	N/A
3.86	N/A	C / 5.1	N/A	N/A	N/A	19.71	N/A	-12.18	-10.92	N/A	0	0	0	100	N/A	91	N/A
6.31	1.72	C+ / 6.9	10.9	2.16	14.6	14.78	108	-6.29	-7.29	N/A	3	0	96	1	10	46	10
7.54	1.18	B- / 7.1	12.0	1.80	N/A	22.36	1,284	-6.17	-8.05	N/A	0	0	100	0	5	60	6
8.65	1.10	B- / 7.2	13.0	0.69	N/A	19.50	379	-13.95	-11.65	N/A	0	0	0	100	41	77	5
4.22	1.77	C / 4.7	18.6	3.37	13.6	16.12	25	22.52	7.13	N/A	1	0	98	1	9	33	10
9.45	1.86	C+ / 6.8	7.8	24.15	N/A	15.36	226	-12.24	-13.35	N/A	0	0	99	1	66	44	5
9.42	2.32	C+ / 6.6	8.4	0.99	N/A	15.20	803	-12.04	-12.68	N/A	0	0	0	100	76	32	4
7.27	3.02	C+ / 6.6	9.5	N/A	N/A	15.95	275	-6.90	-6.95	N/A	6	0	0	94	66	53	N/A
1.22	1.72	B- / 7.8	12.6	0.98	N/A	9.71	289	-20.29	-20.54	30.4	7	88	1	4	4	38	N/A
1.92	2.03	C / 4.5	21.6	1.15	N/A	14.20	237	-17.25	-12.85	N/A	0	0	0	100	19	12	5
3.08	1.92	C+ / 6.6	10.7	1.44	N/A	7.68	211	-10.42	-10.14	N/A	1	1	98	0	27	31	7
).34	2.32	B / 8.0	N/A	N/A	N/A	17.06	413	-13.54	-13.41	N/A	0	0	0	100	32	52	N/A
).39	1.55	C / 5.6	10.7	2.04	16.2	21.95	353	0.00	-11.02	N/A	0	0	100	0	28	84	N/A
1.50	1.47	B- / 7.3	11.5	0.78	N/A	10.91	932	-9.17	-5.34	N/A	4	1	58	37	40	20	14
.42	1.47	B- / 7.1	13.7	0.96	N/A	11.56	1,030	-9.08	-2.72	N/A	5	1	64	30	35	18	13
3.64	N/A	U /	N/A	N/A	N/A	20.52	N/A	-12.04	N/A	N/A	0	0	0	100	N/A	N/A	1
.73	1.79	C+ / 6.9	15.0	0.98	4.0	8.40	582	-14.76	-11.39	59.9	4	59	19	18	32	58	9
.51	1.92	B- / 7.4	13.8	1.09	3.6	12.63	120	-9.58	-5.97	44.2	3	44	21	32	95	13	11
.00	1.72	B- / 7.2	12.9	1.10	3.1	11.11	1,932	-10.89	-10.03	59.0	1	54	21	24	20	24	12
.24	3.57	C / 5.3	12.6	0.41	N/A	24.37	288	-23.06	-26.85	45.8	1	98	0	1	27	93	28
).00	3.04	C+ / 5.8	10.5	0.47	N/A	7.54	20	-34.22	-34.56	33.1	4	95	0	1	19	95	N/A
.85	1.14	B- / 7.1	14.4	0.68	N/A	9.04	1,185	-15.49	-14.67	72.3	0	74	0	26	21	21	10
.36	2.26	C- / 3.8	N/A	N/A	N/A	10.53	298	-3.89	-4.58	N/A	0	0	0	100	105	4	N/A
.92	1.31	C / 4.3	19.8	1.25	N/A	19.01	257	-12.52	-10.78	N/A	0	100	0	0	93	6	2
.10	0.32	C- / 4.1	24.5	1.30	N/A	11.26	3,238	-11.28	-8.56	N/A	1	0	0	99	N/A	29	10
.00	0.36	C+ / 5.8	19.2	1.04	N/A	38.66	855	-2.48	-4.90	N/A	1	0	0	99	N/A	56	13
.95	0.67	B- / 7.3	10.3	0.81	N/A	23.53	650	-19.17	-17.61	57.2	0	99	0	1	13	51	43
.37	1.31	C / 5.5	17.7	0.85	N/A	17.76	380	-12.61	-13.08	N/A	7	92	0	1	67	59	4
.90	2.65	C- / 3.9	N/A	N/A	N/A	9.05	1,096	-9.50	-7.77	N/A	0	0	0	100	21	N/A	N/A
.59	2.19	C / 4.4	24.3	0.95	N/A	15.99	2,033	-5.07	-4.50	N/A	0	99	0	1	14	35	N/A
.40	2.20	C / 4.3	22.4	0.90	N/A	13.84	798	-7.95	-9.21	N/A	0	0	0	100	10	25	N/A
.70	2.26	C / 4.6	21.5	1.25	N/A	13.49	935	-8.75	-9.39	N/A	0	0	0	100	13	6	N/A

Denotes ETF Fund, N/A denotes number is not available

Fund Type	Fund Name (99 Pct = Best, 0 Pct = Worst)	Ticker Symbol	Overall Investment Rating	PRICE: Price As of 12/31/15	PRICE: 52 Week High	PRICE: 52 Week Low	PERFORMANCE: Performance Rating/Pts	% Total Return Through 12/31/15: 3 Mo	6 Mo	1Yr/Pct	Annualized 3Yr/Pct	Annualized 5Yr/Pct
GI	Clough Global Allocation Fund	GLV	**B**	13.47	15.69	12.18	**B-** / **7.1**	5.29	-4.21	0.86 / 66	8.61 / 71	5.86 / 51
GL	Clough Global Equity Fund	GLQ	**C+**	12.53	15.72	11.37	**C+** / **6.1**	0.82	-12.04	-5.41 / 37	7.48 / 68	5.25 / 49
GL	Clough Global Opportunities Fund	GLO	**C**	10.44	12.86	10.20	**C** / **5.4**	-0.54	-10.06	-9.34 / 27	5.16 / 62	4.25 / 44
GL	Cohen & Steers Closed-End Opp Fd	FOF	**C**	10.96	13.38	10.48	**C** / **4.9**	0.99	-5.35	-9.01 / 28	2.98 / 53	4.19 / 44
GL	Cohen & Steers Global Inc Builder	INB	**C+**	9.46	12.23	8.41	**C+** / **5.7**	0.21	-12.66	-9.27 / 28	6.61 / 66	7.01 / 55
GL	Cohen Steers Ltd Dur Pref and Inc	LDP	**C+**	22.52	24.48	21.31	**C+** / **6.1**	2.08	-0.53	6.02 / 81	4.35 / 58	--
UT	Cohen&Steers Infrastructure Fund	UTF	**C+**	19.08	23.58	17.50	**C+** / **6.1**	2.10	-5.74	-9.74 / 26	7.18 / 67	11.19 / 73
IN	Cohen&Steers MLP Inc and Energy Op	MIE	**D-**	10.46	20.38	7.89	**E-** / **0.1**	-13.47	-35.76	-42.76 / 3	--	--
GI	Cohen&Steers Quality Income Realty	RQI	**B+**	12.22	12.97	10.32	**A-** / **9.1**	11.75	16.21	7.82 / 85	13.33 / 85	14.70 / 90
IN	Cohen&Steers REIT& Preferred Incom	RNP	**B+**	18.44	20.03	16.52	**B** / **8.1**	8.92	9.59	4.39 / 78	9.68 / 74	13.37 / 86
IN	Cohen&Steers Sel Preferred & Incom	PSF	**B-**	24.90	27.09	23.07	**B-** / **7.1**	9.65	7.74	5.03 / 79	6.20 / 65	9.26 / 62
GI	Cohen&Steers Total Return Realty	RFI	**C**	12.60	13.91	9.09	**C+** / **5.7**	4.55	5.99	3.19 / 75	2.27 / 50	6.82 / 54
GR	Columbia Seligman Prem Tech Gro	STK	**A-**	17.93	20.12	12.56	**A** / **9.4**	8.37	1.30	4.43 / 78	18.87 / 94	9.84 / 65
IN	Cornerstone Strategic Value Fund	CLM	**C**	15.66	23.03	12.75	**C** / **5.5**	5.63	-16.37	-0.65 / 56	4.26 / 58	3.35 / 40
IN	Cornerstone Total Return Fund	CRF	**C+**	16.89	27.18	14.23	**B-** / **7.5**	7.61	-20.15	7.45 / 84	9.95 / 75	5.94 / 51
COH	Credit Suisse Asset Mgmt Income	CIK	**D+**	2.78	3.32	2.67	**D+** / **2.8**	1.99	-7.64	-7.30 / 33	-4.41 / 26	3.75 / 42
COH	Credit Suisse High Yield Bond Fund	DHY	**C-**	2.28	2.86	2.00	**C-** / **3.5**	4.98	-6.76	-8.81 / 29	-1.23 / 33	5.50 / 49
USA	Cushing Energy Income	SRF	**E-**	8.42	40.15	7.33	**E-** / **0.1**	-37.04	-56.86	-75.37 / 0	-45.48 / 1	--
IN	Cushing Renaissance	SZC	**D**	14.27	22.90	12.95	**D** / **1.6**	-1.71	-21.27	-27.13 / 9	-8.97 / 19	--
COI	Cutwater Select Income	CSI	**C+**	18.26	20.21	17.88	**C** / **5.3**	-2.74	2.18	0.21 / 62	2.43 / 50	6.52 / 53
GL	Delaware Enhanced Glb Div & Inc Fd	DEX	**C-**	9.35	11.87	8.89	**C-** / **3.7**	3.55	-9.57	-9.38 / 27	0.05 / 37	2.49 / 35
MUS	Delaware Inv CO Muni Inc	VCF	**B**	14.59	15.28	13.35	**B** / **7.6**	5.51	7.90	8.83 / 93	2.75 / 58	7.80 / 78
GI	Delaware Inv Div & Inc	DDF	**B-**	8.82	10.44	8.11	**B-** / **7.0**	6.98	-7.92	-4.53 / 41	9.37 / 73	10.48 / 68
MUS	Delaware Inv MN Muni Inc Fund II	VMM	**C**	13.33	14.18	12.69	**C** / **5.0**	2.50	2.71	4.45 / 83	-0.24 / 36	6.44 / 65
MUN	Delaware Inv Nat Muni Inc	VFL	**C+**	12.99	13.67	12.50	**C+** / **6.3**	3.07	6.48	6.07 / 87	2.28 / 55	7.11 / 71
GL	Deutsche Global High Income	LBF	**C**	7.55	8.51	7.14	**C** / **4.7**	1.93	-4.01	2.56 / 73	0.84 / 41	5.90 / 51
COH	Deutsche High Income	KHI	**C-**	7.95	9.15	7.59	**C-** / **3.8**	2.94	-1.01	-1.90 / 51	-1.13 / 33	4.46 / 45
GL	Deutsche High Income Opportunities	DHG	**C**	13.06	14.94	12.43	**C** / **4.7**	0.50	-6.66	0.34 / 62	1.39 / 44	6.37 / 52
GL	Deutsche Multi-Market Income	KMM	**D+**	7.64	8.66	7.05	**C-** / **3.3**	5.97	-2.59	-3.02 / 46	-3.22 / 28	2.63 / 36
MUN	Deutsche Municipal Income	KTF	**C+**	13.48	14.29	12.51	**C+** / **6.6**	3.72	10.53	6.84 / 89	2.36 / 55	10.92 / 95
GL	Deutsche Strategic Income	KST	**C-**	10.51	11.94	9.50	**C-** / **3.4**	4.22	-2.95	-1.39 / 53	-2.83 / 29	4.40 / 45
MUN	Deutsche Strategic Municipal Incom	KSM	**C+**	13.20	14.78	12.36	**C+** / **6.1**	4.89	4.73	2.75 / 77	2.11 / 54	9.54 / 90
GL	Diversified Real Asset Income Fund	XDRAX	**D**	15.51	18.40	15.14	**D+** / **2.8**	-0.91	-7.17	-1.67 / 52	--	--
GI	Dividend and Income Fund	DNI	**C-**	11.01	15.75	10.14	**C** / **4.3**	4.55	-16.33	-16.31 / 16	3.45 / 55	2.40 / 35
UT	DNP Select Income Fund Inc	DNP	**C**	8.96	11.00	8.12	**C+** / **5.7**	2.94	-7.84	-6.23 / 35	5.46 / 63	7.31 / 55
COH	DoubleLine Income Solutions	DSL	**D+**	16.22	20.66	15.51	**D-** / **1.4**	-3.10	-13.32	-10.00 / 25	--	--
GEI	DoubleLine Opportunistic Credit Fd	DBL	**B-**	25.31	26.51	22.61	**B** / **8.0**	6.40	14.64	14.11 / 94	7.55 / 69	--
COH	Dreyfus High Yield Strategies Fund	DHF	**C-**	3.08	3.75	2.75	**C-** / **3.9**	5.68	-2.98	-5.96 / 36	-0.55 / 35	2.82 / 37
MUN	Dreyfus Municipal Bond Infra	DMB	**A+**	12.38	13.14	11.45	**A** / **9.5**	6.25	9.44	8.15 / 92	--	--
MUN	Dreyfus Municipal Income	DMF	**C+**	9.44	10.10	8.63	**C+** / **6.2**	1.16	9.52	4.94 / 84	1.88 / 52	8.86 / 87
MUN	Dreyfus Strategic Muni Bond Fund	DSM	**C+**	8.07	8.34	7.58	**C+** / **5.8**	4.81	8.45	7.25 / 90	0.59 / 41	8.57 / 85
MUN	Dreyfus Strategic Municipals	LEO	**C+**	8.54	8.65	7.77	**C+** / **6.7**	4.98	12.38	10.98 / 96	1.52 / 50	9.29 / 89
MUN	DTF Tax Free Income	DTF	**C+**	15.11	15.88	14.25	**C+** / **5.7**	4.78	8.66	4.43 / 83	0.40 / 40	6.29 / 64
UT	Duff & Phelps Global Utility Incom	DPG	**D+**	14.73	21.36	13.39	**C-** / **3.2**	-1.57	-11.23	-25.14 / 10	1.08 / 42	--
EN	Duff & Phelps Select Energy MLP	DSE	**E-**	5.98	16.50	4.91	**E-** / **0.0**	-22.58	-47.64	-53.71 / 1	--	--
GEI	Duff & Phelps Utilities & Crp Bd T	DUC	**C-**	9.19	9.92	9.06	**C-** / **3.4**	-2.00	0.74	-0.12 / 59	-2.95 / 29	3.07 / 38
GR	Eagle Capital Growth Fund	GRF	**B+**	7.59	8.64	6.78	**B-** / **7.5**	4.93	3.19	-7.13 / 33	10.08 / 75	10.96 / 72
IN	Eagle Growth and Income Opps		**U**	15.16	N/A	N/A	**U** /	-7.58	-25.81	--	--	--
MUS	Eaton Vance CA Muni Bond	EVM	**B+**	12.15	12.41	11.12	**B** / **8.2**	4.26	10.29	9.82 / 95	5.17 / 70	8.53 / 85
MUS	Eaton Vance CA Muni Bond II	EIA	**C+**	12.81	13.69	11.74	**C+** / **6.1**	2.65	9.81	7.50 / 91	1.09 / 46	10.13 / 92
MUS	Eaton Vance CA Muni Inc Tr	CEV	**B-**	13.33	13.83	12.34	**B-** / **7.1**	3.70	9.76	7.76 / 91	3.25 / 61	10.32 / 93
IN	Eaton Vance Enhanced Eqty Inc	EOI	**A**	13.42	14.10	8.90	**A-** / **9.2**	14.36	5.86	5.57 / 80	15.55 / 90	10.20 / 66

* Denotes ETF Fund, N/A denotes number is not available

ncl. in Returns		RISK				NET ASSETS		VALUATION			ASSET					FUND MANAGER	
			3 Year					Premium / Discount									
/idend 'ield %	Expense Ratio	Risk Rating/ Pts	Standard Deviation	Beta	Avg Duration	NAV as of 12/31/15	Total $(Mil)	As of 12/31/15	1 Year Average	Wtd Avg P/E	Cash %	Stocks %	Bonds %	Other %	Portfolio Turnover Ratio	Manager Quality Pct	Manager Tenure (Years)
0.69	3.25	B- / 7.6	11.0	0.82	12.6	15.07	177	-10.62	-13.45	62.5	5	77	17	1	110	45	12
1.01	3.68	B- / 7.2	12.8	0.74	6.7	14.51	294	-13.65	-12.19	63.3	8	74	15	3	102	88	11
1.49	3.86	B- / 7.2	13.1	0.70	12.9	12.43	730	-16.01	-13.68	75.5	8	66	23	3	111	82	10
9.49	0.95	B- / 7.3	9.5	0.50	N/A	12.34	392	-11.18	-10.61	17.2	0	45	43	12	33	78	N/A
1.84	1.72	B- / 7.4	12.6	0.73	15.6	10.32	269	-8.33	-3.99	57.8	0	95	0	5	77	85	N/A
8.31	1.57	B- / 7.5	10.2	0.24	N/A	25.27	741	-10.88	-9.29	N/A	0	0	0	100	47	91	N/A
8.39	2.01	B- / 7.0	14.4	0.66	N/A	22.22	2,210	-14.13	-14.42	N/A	0	77	0	23	33	66	12
9.46	2.26	C / 4.7	N/A	N/A	N/A	10.87	604	-3.77	-10.11	N/A	0	0	0	100	28	1	3
3.93	1.89	C+ / 6.8	17.3	0.32	15.6	13.46	1,485	-9.21	-12.74	101.6	0	81	0	19	48	94	N/A
8.03	1.71	B- / 7.2	13.9	0.42	N/A	21.63	1,033	-14.75	-15.25	N/A	0	46	0	54	54	88	13
8.29	1.57	B- / 7.5	10.3	0.41	N/A	26.74	326	-6.88	-7.56	N/A	1	0	6	93	28	76	N/A
1.07	0.94	B- / 7.1	13.3	0.42	15.6	13.60	370	-7.35	-8.45	95.3	0	82	0	18	41	51	N/A
0.50	1.17	C+ / 6.9	14.2	0.74	N/A	17.29	271	3.70	2.80	N/A	0	100	0	0	60	93	N/A
3.20	1.33	C+ / 6.2	19.2	0.99	N/A	15.11	168	3.64	8.18	45.7	0	99	0	1	51	22	15
3.58	1.44	C+ / 5.6	24.0	0.78	N/A	15.05	84	12.23	19.83	69.6	0	99	0	1	32	74	N/A
9.50	0.71	C+ / 6.7	8.8	1.26	N/A	3.21	189	-13.40	-13.33	N/A	0	0	96	4	67	25	N/A
2.63	1.82	B- / 7.0	11.2	1.71	N/A	2.41	303	-5.39	-7.27	N/A	0	0	99	1	59	37	N/A
7.38	2.39	D / 1.8	50.5	-0.99	N/A	9.39	151	-10.33	-8.48	N/A	0	0	0	100	93	1	N/A
.49	1.96	C / 5.1	19.8	1.26	N/A	17.01	156	-16.11	-15.72	N/A	0	0	0	100	26	6	4
.48	0.74	B- / 7.8	9.2	1.45	N/A	19.67	230	-7.17	-7.59	N/A	0	0	99	1	31	75	11
.63	1.88	B- / 7.1	13.2	0.94	10.3	11.14	209	-16.07	-14.22	38.4	6	46	44	4	56	34	9
.93	1.43	B- / 7.6	9.5	1.88	13.4	15.51	75	-5.93	-7.74	N/A	0	0	100	0	14	53	12
.14	1.55	B- / 7.4	12.7	1.02	4.7	9.94	100	-11.27	-10.74	32.4	1	53	32	14	48	35	10
.73	1.40	B- / 7.6	10.8	1.93	11.4	14.92	172	-10.66	-9.29	N/A	0	0	100	0	10	30	13
.54	1.60	B- / 7.6	10.0	2.45	12.6	14.86	68	-12.58	-12.27	N/A	0	0	100	0	38	35	13
.15	2.29	B- / 7.4	9.7	0.51	N/A	8.18	61	-7.70	-8.95	N/A	4	0	96	0	37	87	10
.70	1.57	B- / 7.0	8.9	1.31	N/A	8.78	156	-9.45	-10.52	N/A	2	0	98	0	48	45	18
.51	2.04	B- / 7.6	8.4	0.52	N/A	14.26	221	-8.42	-9.37	N/A	0	0	100	0	46	64	6
.68	1.52	C+ / 6.0	14.3	0.81	N/A	8.66	238	-11.78	-13.67	N/A	1	0	99	0	82	75	N/A
.23	1.45	B- / 7.2	11.3	2.49	12.7	13.48	544	0.00	-2.11	N/A	0	0	100	0	18	40	6
.28	1.83	C+ / 6.4	11.0	0.83	N/A	12.07	61	-12.92	-14.14	N/A	1	0	99	0	70	78	N/A
.36	1.73	C+ / 6.9	12.2	2.79	13.2	12.96	148	1.85	2.02	N/A	0	0	100	0	19	31	17
.53	1.40	C / 4.9	N/A	N/A	N/A	17.92	410	-13.45	-11.13	N/A	0	0	0	100	104	56	N/A
.82	1.55	C+ / 6.1	15.6	1.14	N/A	13.11	144	-16.02	-12.82	33.1	6	40	51	3	52	15	5
.71	1.60	C+ / 6.9	11.6	0.42	13.8	8.20	2,821	9.27	10.91	25.6	0	71	25	4	10	78	20
.53	2.27	B- / 7.1	N/A	N/A	N/A	18.09	2,007	-10.34	-10.04	N/A	0	0	0	100	51	42	N/A
.00	1.65	C+ / 6.4	11.2	2.27	N/A	22.73	357	11.35	3.60	N/A	0	0	0	100	4	87	N/A
.30	1.74	C+ / 6.4	14.0	1.94	N/A	3.22	279	-4.35	-7.90	N/A	0	0	99	1	48	43	N/A
06	1.67	B- / 7.8	N/A	N/A	N/A	13.92	255	-11.06	-11.00	N/A	0	0	0	100	13	43	N/A
72	1.25	B- / 7.2	12.6	2.92	9.5	9.64	198	-2.07	-2.25	N/A	0	0	100	0	11	28	5
17	1.09	B- / 7.5	11.2	2.60	10.3	8.64	420	-6.60	-7.55	N/A	0	0	100	0	7	26	N/A
04	1.13	B- / 7.3	11.5	2.52	10.0	8.88	541	-3.83	-6.49	N/A	0	0	100	0	10	32	5
56	1.89	B- / 7.7	11.1	2.40	12.4	16.48	142	-8.31	-8.73	N/A	2	0	97	1	9	28	N/A
50	1.55	C+ / 6.2	14.7	0.55	N/A	17.25	924	-14.61	-13.96	N/A	0	0	0	100	29	38	N/A
07	N/A	D / 1.7	N/A	N/A	N/A	6.53	N/A	-8.42	-2.23	N/A	0	0	0	100	N/A	2	2
53	1.48	B- / 7.1	8.6	2.10	N/A	10.05	297	-8.56	-9.23	N/A	0	0	100	0	8	28	20
36	1.40	B- / 7.8	14.1	0.47	N/A	8.52	27	-10.92	-12.42	30.3	5	94	0	1	6	85	N/A
19	N/A	U /	N/A	N/A	N/A	17.77	N/A	-14.69	N/A	N/A	0	0	0	100	N/A	N/A	1
63	1.51	B- / 7.5	10.6	2.29	10.0	12.93	272	-6.03	-7.55	N/A	0	0	100	0	7	57	2
70	1.38	B- / 7.0	13.7	2.77	10.8	13.47	51	-4.90	-3.81	N/A	0	0	100	0	5	27	2
29	1.69	B- / 7.1	12.4	2.69	10.5	14.14	102	-5.73	-6.72	N/A	0	0	100	0	11	34	2
73	1.11	B- / 7.5	11.7	1.00	N/A	13.98	525	-4.01	-8.76	80.3	0	96	0	4	72	78	8

Denotes ETF Fund, N/A denotes number is not available

Fund Type	Fund Name (99 Pct = Best, 0 Pct = Worst)	Ticker Symbol	Overall Investment Rating	PRICE: Price As of 12/31/15	52 Week High	52 Week Low	PERFORMANCE: Performance Rating/Pts	% Total Return Through 12/31/15: 3 Mo	6 Mo	1Yr/Pct	Annualized 3Yr/Pct	Annualized 5Yr/Pct
IN	Eaton Vance Enhanced Eqty Inc II	EOS	**A**	13.64	14.48	11.13	**A / 9.3**	9.15	1.58	6.44 / 82	16.82 / 92	11.37 / 74
LP	Eaton Vance Floating Rate Income T	EFT	**C-**	12.64	14.94	12.06	**D+ / 2.9**	-1.72	-5.93	-2.48 / 48	-4.06 / 26	1.00 / 30
LP	Eaton Vance Floating-Rate Inc Plus	EFF	**C-**	14.15	17.42	13.45	**D+ / 2.3**	-0.21	-8.67	-5.98 / 36	--	--
GEN	Eaton Vance Limited Duration Incom	EVV	**C-**	12.76	14.69	11.00	**C- / 3.8**	4.36	-2.93	-0.90 / 55	-1.29 / 32	3.77 / 42
MUS	Eaton Vance MA Muni Bond	MAB	**B-**	14.83	15.09	13.40	**B- / 7.3**	8.88	12.37	10.09 / 96	2.47 / 56	9.02 / 88
MUS	Eaton Vance MA Muni Inc Tr	MMV	**B-**	14.03	14.86	13.19	**B- / 7.0**	6.21	7.44	8.38 / 93	1.60 / 51	6.53 / 66
MUS	Eaton Vance MI Muni Bond	MIW	**B+**	13.85	14.33	13.00	**B / 8.0**	7.26	6.74	10.26 / 96	3.55 / 63	8.87 / 87
MUS	Eaton Vance MI Muni Inc Tr	EMI	**B**	13.13	13.25	12.26	**B- / 7.3**	6.85	9.49	9.22 / 94	3.09 / 60	9.05 / 88
MUN	Eaton Vance Muni Bond Fund	EIM	**B-**	12.98	13.35	11.93	**C+ / 6.7**	4.48	9.94	7.21 / 90	2.45 / 56	9.46 / 90
MUN	Eaton Vance Muni Bond II	EIV	**B**	13.18	13.39	11.92	**B / 7.9**	6.54	12.51	9.78 / 95	4.04 / 65	9.06 / 88
MUN	Eaton Vance Municipal Inc 2028 Ter	ETX	**A+**	18.49	18.65	16.69	**A+ / 9.7**	7.40	12.07	10.24 / 96	--	--
MUN	Eaton Vance Municipal Inc Tr	EVN	**B**	13.73	14.25	12.14	**B+ / 8.8**	9.03	13.28	9.79 / 95	5.84 / 72	12.18 / 97
MUN	Eaton Vance National Municipal Opp	EOT	**B-**	21.43	21.78	19.94	**B- / 7.0**	4.55	8.27	7.25 / 90	3.10 / 60	8.12 / 82
MUS	Eaton Vance NJ Muni Bond	EMJ	**C+**	13.81	14.93	12.31	**C+ / 6.4**	7.77	13.02	15.01 / 98	-0.07 / 37	7.96 / 80
MUS	Eaton Vance NJ Muni Inc Tr	EVJ	**C**	12.69	13.29	11.60	**C+ / 5.6**	7.41	12.42	9.82 / 95	-1.18 / 33	5.92 / 61
MUS	Eaton Vance NY Muni Bond	ENX	**B**	13.13	13.17	12.22	**B / 7.8**	5.66	8.47	11.11 / 97	2.65 / 58	7.94 / 80
MUS	Eaton Vance NY Muni Bond II	NYH	**B-**	12.47	12.70	11.48	**C+ / 6.8**	1.80	8.19	9.21 / 94	1.68 / 51	6.80 / 68
MUS	Eaton Vance NY Muni Inc Tr	EVY	**B**	14.15	14.19	13.09	**B- / 7.3**	7.57	6.87	8.91 / 94	1.80 / 52	9.51 / 90
MUS	Eaton Vance OH Muni Bond	EIO	**B+**	13.42	14.40	12.08	**B+ / 8.5**	7.50	12.41	12.64 / 98	2.92 / 59	8.78 / 87
MUS	Eaton Vance OH Muni Inc Tr	EVO	**C**	14.02	14.83	13.09	**C / 5.2**	6.19	8.76	7.80 / 92	-1.28 / 33	8.49 / 85
MUS	Eaton Vance PA Muni Bond	EIP	**C+**	13.22	13.43	11.87	**C+ / 6.0**	9.16	10.30	9.81 / 95	-0.17 / 36	8.89 / 87
MUS	Eaton Vance PA Muni Inc Tr	EVP	**C**	12.08	12.73	11.51	**C / 5.3**	3.23	6.54	4.73 / 84	-0.11 / 36	6.18 / 63
IN	Eaton Vance Risk Mgd Div Eq Inc	ETJ	**B**	10.16	11.15	9.48	**B- / 7.4**	5.71	0.11	4.23 / 77	8.52 / 71	4.74 / 46
LP	Eaton Vance Senior Floating Rate	EFR	**C-**	12.41	14.89	11.87	**C- / 3.3**	-2.63	-6.38	-2.38 / 49	-2.46 / 29	0.78 / 30
LP	Eaton Vance Senior Income Trust	EVF	**C-**	5.77	6.61	5.46	**C- / 3.3**	0.68	-3.54	-0.78 / 56	-2.95 / 29	1.96 / 33
GL	Eaton Vance Sh Dur Diversified Inc	EVG	**C**	13.41	15.10	12.79	**C- / 3.9**	5.42	-0.02	1.46 / 70	-1.85 / 31	2.04 / 34
GL	Eaton Vance Tax Adv Glob Div Inc	ETG	**B+**	15.52	18.03	11.68	**B / 7.9**	6.02	-4.29	3.41 / 75	10.70 / 77	10.18 / 66
GL	Eaton Vance Tax Adv Global Div Opp	ETO	**B**	21.32	25.72	18.00	**B / 7.9**	5.24	-4.12	-2.24 / 50	11.58 / 80	9.84 / 65
IN	Eaton Vance Tax Advantage Div Inc	EVT	**A-**	19.34	21.05	15.24	**B+ / 8.3**	7.26	1.76	2.01 / 72	11.54 / 80	10.90 / 71
IN	Eaton Vance Tax Mgd Buy Write Opp	ETV	**A-**	15.30	15.50	12.18	**A / 9.5**	10.81	7.72	17.56 / 97	16.13 / 91	13.45 / 86
IN	Eaton Vance Tax Mgd Div Eqty Inc	ETY	**A**	11.20	11.96	9.64	**A- / 9.1**	6.54	2.73	9.21 / 87	14.49 / 89	9.92 / 65
IN	Eaton Vance Tax-Managed Buy-Write	ETB	**A**	16.69	16.97	14.07	**A / 9.3**	11.70	10.98	14.03 / 94	13.64 / 86	12.03 / 78
GL	Eaton Vance Tax-Mgd Gbl Div Eq Inc	EXG	**B**	8.85	10.15	7.62	**B- / 7.5**	6.84	-4.21	3.03 / 74	9.25 / 73	7.10 / 55
MUN	Eaton Vance Tx Adv Bd&Option Str	EXD	**C-**	12.57	14.00	9.83	**C- / 4.1**	3.22	3.02	7.39 / 91	-2.11 / 30	3.36 / 48
GL	Eaton Vance Tx Mgd Glb Buy Wrt Opp	ETW	**B+**	11.23	12.25	10.36	**B+ / 8.3**	6.05	0.40	11.13 / 90	10.60 / 77	8.68 / 60
GI	Ellsworth Growth and Income Fd Ltd	ECF	**C+**	7.75	9.29	7.34	**C+ / 6.6**	4.26	-8.19	-1.58 / 52	7.93 / 69	5.93 / 51
MUN	Federated Prem Intermediate Muni	FPT	**B-**	13.46	13.54	12.16	**B- / 7.0**	3.10	6.03	11.01 / 96	1.81 / 52	7.24 / 73
MUN	Federated Premier Muni Income	FMN	**B**	14.91	15.13	13.75	**B- / 7.3**	4.65	9.85	8.90 / 94	3.45 / 62	9.14 / 88
EN	Fiduciary/Claymore MLP Opp	FMO	**D-**	12.98	26.84	10.48	**D- / 1.0**	-17.82	-38.98	-46.51 / 2	-11.38 / 15	-3.04 / 22
LP	First Tr Senior Floating Rte Inc I	FCT	**C-**	12.35	14.02	11.71	**C- / 3.7**	0.02	-3.41	1.14 / 68	-1.67 / 32	3.99 / 43
FS	First Tr Specialty Finance &Fin Op	FGB	**D+**	5.57	8.09	5.25	**D+ / 2.4**	-5.52	-9.47	-20.47 / 13	-4.70 / 25	1.52 / 32
GL	First Trust Dividend and Income	FAV	**A-**	8.46	9.10	6.90	**B+ / 8.4**	8.60	4.01	0.44 / 63	11.71 / 81	2.67 / 36
FO	First Trust Dynamic Europe Eqty In	XFDEX	**U**	17.16	N/A	N/A	**U /**	-13.75	--	--	--	--
EN	First Trust Energy Income and Gro	FEN	**D**	23.00	36.76	18.56	**D / 2.0**	-12.37	-22.80	-33.06 / 6	-3.85 / 27	3.67 / 41
EN	First Trust Energy Infrastructure	FIF	**D**	14.59	24.16	12.44	**D+ / 2.3**	-8.98	-22.14	-32.73 / 7	-2.22 / 30	--
IN	First Trust Enhanced Equity Income	FFA	**B**	13.20	15.57	10.27	**B- / 7.5**	4.39	-4.87	-1.19 / 54	10.01 / 75	8.67 / 59
GL	First Trust High Income Long/Short	FSD	**C-**	14.08	16.73	13.29	**C- / 3.4**	3.86	-6.68	-5.39 / 37	-1.88 / 31	2.50 / 36
IN	First Trust Inter Dur Pref & Inc	FPF	**B-**	21.27	23.05	20.68	**C+ / 6.1**	1.94	3.26	3.23 / 75	--	--
IN	First Trust MLP and Energy Income	FEI	**D**	13.22	21.58	10.75	**D- / 1.5**	-19.00	-24.42	-33.70 / 6	-6.86 / 22	--
MTG	First Trust Mortgage Income Fund	FMY	**C**	14.54	15.24	13.70	**C / 4.5**	2.31	5.97	4.39 / 78	-0.95 / 34	2.85 / 37
EN	First Trust New Opptys MLP & Energ	FPL	**D-**	10.77	18.63	8.82	**E- / 0.1**	-18.15	-28.28	-35.73 / 5	--	--
GEN	First Trust Strategic High Inc II	FHY	**D+**	11.13	14.59	10.55	**D+ / 2.5**	0.05	-11.81	-15.92 / 17	-4.70 / 25	4.90 / 4

* Denotes ETF Fund, N/A denotes number is not availab

		RISK				NET ASSETS		VALUATION			ASSET					FUND MANAGER	
Incl. in Returns		Risk Rating/ Pts	3 Year		Avg Duration	NAV as of 12/31/15	Total $(Mil)	Premium / Discount		Wtd Avg P/E	Cash %	Stocks %	Bonds %	Other %	Portfolio Turnover Ratio	Manager Quality Pct	Manager Tenure (Years)
Dividend Yield %	Expense Ratio		Standard Deviation	Beta				As of 12/31/15	1 Year Average								
7.70	1.11	B- / 7.3	11.0	0.97	N/A	14.41	693	-5.34	-6.06	135.9	0	96	0	4	77	85	8
7.22	2.17	B- / 7.1	7.0	-22.32	N/A	13.99	623	-9.65	-8.97	N/A	0	0	0	100	32	35	12
7.97	2.39	B- / 7.5	N/A	N/A	N/A	15.79	140	-10.39	-10.32	N/A	0	0	0	100	28	25	3
9.56	1.89	B- / 7.0	9.3	1.09	N/A	14.38	1,882	-11.27	-12.21	N/A	1	0	66	33	35	48	13
5.12	1.49	B- / 7.2	12.3	1.82	12.6	15.70	27	-5.54	-6.32	N/A	0	0	100	0	7	46	6
4.89	1.73	B- / 7.5	9.8	2.17	11.9	15.32	42	-8.42	-9.66	N/A	0	0	100	0	2	36	6
5.69	1.48	B- / 7.2	12.5	2.51	12.3	15.49	22	-10.59	-9.41	N/A	0	0	100	0	3	41	1
5.40	1.87	B- / 7.4	10.5	2.27	12.7	14.88	30	-11.76	-13.37	N/A	0	0	100	0	26	44	1
5.90	1.43	B- / 7.4	11.4	2.80	10.5	14.12	945	-8.07	-9.52	N/A	0	0	100	0	5	30	2
5.60	1.30	B- / 7.3	12.2	2.54	11.7	14.02	137	-5.99	-8.03	N/A	0	0	100	0	6	49	2
4.59	1.46	B- / 7.8	N/A	N/A	N/A	20.48	224	-9.72	-11.09	N/A	0	0	0	100	43	67	1
6.19	1.85	C+ / 6.4	14.0	3.39	11.2	13.22	307	3.86	1.70	N/A	0	0	100	0	36	42	1
4.80	0.86	B- / 7.3	8.9	2.04	N/A	22.74	351	-5.76	-7.83	N/A	0	0	100	0	13	49	7
5.43	1.29	C+ / 6.8	15.8	2.08	9.6	14.85	37	-7.00	-7.28	N/A	0	0	100	0	5	25	6
5.74	1.68	B- / 7.2	12.2	2.11	11.9	13.93	66	-8.90	-11.09	N/A	0	0	100	0	6	25	6
5.47	1.57	B- / 7.3	11.1	2.15	8.7	14.14	218	-7.14	-9.38	N/A	0	0	100	0	5	42	11
5.51	1.53	B- / 7.5	11.0	2.37	9.9	13.75	34	-9.31	-8.74	N/A	0	0	100	0	1	36	11
5.66	1.75	B- / 7.3	11.4	2.05	12.4	14.69	80	-3.68	-6.32	N/A	0	0	100	0	4	40	17
5.23	1.28	B- / 7.1	14.0	3.21	11.3	14.36	35	-6.55	-7.68	N/A	0	0	100	0	4	26	1
5.21	1.70	B- / 7.1	11.6	2.65	11.8	15.33	43	-8.55	-10.01	N/A	0	0	100	0	9	20	1
5.85	1.33	B- / 7.0	13.3	2.46	11.8	14.63	42	-9.64	-10.37	N/A	0	0	100	0	4	24	9
6.02	1.83	B- / 7.2	10.4	2.24	12.5	13.98	38	-13.59	-13.03	N/A	0	0	100	0	4	24	9
10.98	1.10	B- / 7.5	9.8	0.60	N/A	11.15	769	-8.88	-10.10	80.3	0	100	0	0	66	73	9
7.64	1.76	B- / 7.0	8.5	-188.95	N/A	13.59	565	-8.68	-7.72	N/A	0	0	0	100	35	26	13
7.89	2.27	B- / 7.2	6.9	N/A	N/A	6.38	266	-9.56	-10.04	N/A	3	1	7	89	33	75	18
8.05	1.89	B- / 7.5	7.4	0.52	12.9	15.00	306	-10.60	-12.11	N/A	0	0	73	27	41	74	11
7.93	1.42	B- / 7.7	15.8	1.05	N/A	17.03	1,383	-8.87	-7.29	49.9	1	80	0	19	122	91	6
0.13	1.50	B- / 7.3	13.6	0.87	N/A	22.99	380	-7.26	-3.51	N/A	1	77	0	22	89	93	6
8.25	1.35	B- / 7.9	11.5	0.96	N/A	21.31	1,545	-9.24	-9.81	N/A	1	68	0	31	99	56	6
8.69	1.09	B- / 7.0	10.0	0.68	N/A	14.56	945	5.08	0.07	99.2	0	100	0	0	2	91	11
9.03	1.08	B- / 7.7	12.0	1.00	N/A	11.86	1,844	-5.56	-7.54	80.4	0	100	0	0	83	74	10
7.77	1.13	B- / 7.3	11.0	0.72	N/A	15.51	402	7.61	0.12	53.6	0	100	0	0	2	87	11
1.02	1.07	B- / 7.4	13.4	0.94	N/A	9.71	3,198	-8.86	-6.90	81.4	0	100	0	0	210	89	9
9.23	1.42	C+ / 6.6	12.1	1.95	N/A	14.32	148	-12.22	-11.60	N/A	21	0	78	1	52	22	6
0.40	1.10	B- / 7.2	12.6	0.84	N/A	11.56	1,308	-2.85	-4.37	87.1	0	100	0	0	2	92	11
0.41	1.10	B- / 7.0	10.3	0.86	5.5	9.19	121	-15.67	-15.39	30.6	2	6	0	92	45	38	30
4.95	1.51	B- / 7.5	9.7	1.79	8.1	14.57	101	-7.62	-9.76	N/A	0	0	100	0	19	45	14
5.92	1.43	B- / 7.4	11.2	2.11	12.7	15.42	95	-3.31	-4.58	N/A	0	0	100	0	19	47	14
3.28	1.79	C / 5.3	24.2	0.69	N/A	14.43	892	-10.05	-2.10	35.8	0	100	0	0	8	21	12
7.29	1.69	B- / 7.3	8.4	-195.68	N/A	13.55	393	-8.86	-8.60	N/A	0	0	0	100	63	32	N/A
2.57	1.71	C+ / 6.5	17.7	0.42	N/A	6.07	110	-8.24	-2.37	29.1	0	100	0	0	14	19	N/A
8.04	1.91	B- / 7.8	11.6	0.66	N/A	9.12	84	-7.24	-12.25	27.5	0	100	0	0	112	94	N/A
2.82	N/A	U /	N/A	N/A	N/A	19.07	N/A	-10.02	N/A	N/A	0	0	0	100	N/A	N/A	N/A
0.09	2.04	C+ / 5.9	18.6	0.58	N/A	23.55	737	-2.34	-5.34	23.1	0	100	0	0	21	64	N/A
9.05	1.80	C / 5.1	20.9	0.74	N/A	16.54	456	-11.79	-10.91	N/A	0	0	0	100	42	81	N/A
3.07	1.18	B- / 7.7	11.3	0.96	N/A	14.99	319	-11.94	-10.06	50.3	0	100	0	0	44	42	N/A
8.52	1.75	B- / 7.0	9.3	0.55	N/A	16.41	702	-14.20	-14.10	N/A	0	1	95	4	28	37	N/A
8.40	1.69	B / 8.1	N/A	N/A	N/A	23.48	1,482	-9.41	-8.13	N/A	0	0	0	100	62	77	N/A
0.74	1.79	C+ / 5.9	16.5	0.77	N/A	14.40	1,057	-8.19	-7.59	N/A	0	0	0	100	34	9	N/A
3.43	1.78	B- / 7.1	6.4	1.74	14.6	15.88	72	-8.44	-10.75	N/A	0	0	100	0	54	43	N/A
.70	1.94	C / 5.1	N/A	N/A	N/A	11.64	485	-7.47	-8.90	N/A	0	0	0	100	23	7	N/A
.86	2.34	C+ / 6.5	10.7	1.14	N/A	13.00	141	-14.38	-13.09	N/A	0	0	99	1	28	28	N/A

Denotes ETF Fund, N/A denotes number is not available

Fund Type	Fund Name (99 Pct = Best, 0 Pct = Worst)	Ticker Symbol	Overall Investment Rating	PRICE: Price As of 12/31/15	PRICE: 52 Week High	PRICE: 52 Week Low	PERFORMANCE: Performance Rating/Pts	% Total Return Through 12/31/15: 3 Mo	6 Mo	1Yr/Pct	Annualized: 3Yr/Pct	Annualized: 5Yr/Pct
GL	First Trust/Aberdeen Emerg Opp Fd	FEO	**D**	13.06	17.31	12.10	**D / 1.9**	1.13	-13.58	-13.09 / 20	-10.04 / 17	-2.96 / 22
GL	First Trust/Aberdeen Glob Opp Inc	FAM	**D**	10.13	12.09	9.27	**D+ / 2.4**	6.98	-1.94	-7.01 / 33	-8.93 / 19	-0.38 / 27
GL	Flaherty & Crumrine Dyn Pfd and In	DFP	**A**	22.90	24.08	19.87	**B+ / 8.9**	6.04	8.20	9.75 / 88	--	--
IN	Flaherty & Crumrine Pref Sec Inc	FFC	**B**	20.05	20.99	16.75	**B+ / 8.7**	9.59	9.28	10.95 / 90	9.81 / 75	14.50 / 89
IN	Flaherty & Crumrine Total Return	FLC	**C+**	19.17	21.37	13.79	**C+ / 6.6**	5.78	0.90	3.89 / 76	6.04 / 64	11.63 / 76
IN	Flaherty&Crumrine Preferred Inc Op	PFO	**C+**	10.67	12.76	8.32	**C+ / 6.5**	5.92	2.97	0.01 / 60	6.08 / 64	11.23 / 73
IN	Flaherty&Crumrine Preferred Income	PFD	**C+**	12.92	15.78	9.36	**C+ / 5.9**	4.91	-1.77	-0.84 / 56	4.53 / 59	11.08 / 73
GEI	Fort Dearborn Inc. Secs.	FDI	**C+**	14.51	14.80	13.50	**C+ / 5.6**	3.99	7.39	6.76 / 83	1.44 / 45	8.23 / 59
IN	Foxby Corp	FXBY	**C**	1.59	1.90	1.50	**C / 4.4**	1.26	-13.44	-13.90 / 19	3.60 / 55	7.57 / 56
GEN	Franklin Limited Duration Income	FTF	**C-**	10.72	12.42	10.18	**C- / 3.0**	0.99	-5.87	-5.58 / 37	-3.67 / 27	2.92 / 38
GI	Franklin Universal Trust	FT	**C-**	5.73	7.31	5.46	**C- / 3.3**	1.45	-7.30	-12.35 / 21	-0.94 / 34	4.94 / 47
GI	Gabelli Convertible&Income Sec Fun	GCV	**C**	4.78	6.71	4.36	**C / 4.8**	0.09	-14.29	-12.33 / 21	4.30 / 58	3.60 / 41
IN	Gabelli Dividend & Income Trust	GDV	**B**	18.46	21.87	16.47	**B- / 7.2**	4.37	-8.07	-8.51 / 30	10.72 / 77	10.85 / 70
IN	Gabelli Equity Trust	GAB	**C**	5.31	6.71	4.96	**C+ / 6.3**	3.28	-10.04	-8.75 / 29	8.16 / 70	9.35 / 62
GL	Gabelli Gl Sm & Mid Cap Value Tr	XGGZX	**C-**	10.40	10.95	9.40	**C / 4.9**	4.94	-2.16	0.10 / 61	--	--
UT	Gabelli Global Utility&Income Trus	GLU	**C-**	16.62	19.78	15.55	**C- / 4.2**	4.19	-5.56	-8.17 / 31	1.22 / 43	4.59 / 46
HL	Gabelli Healthcare & WellnessRx Tr	GRX	**A+**	10.25	11.67	9.47	**A- / 9.2**	5.84	-7.20	3.05 / 74	17.21 / 92	18.66 / 97
GL	Gabelli Multimedia Trust	GGT	**C**	7.50	10.15	7.01	**C+ / 6.1**	2.29	-13.43	-15.77 / 17	8.89 / 72	10.61 / 69
UT	Gabelli Utility Trust	GUT	**C**	5.70	7.44	5.55	**C+ / 5.7**	4.59	-3.04	-14.15 / 19	5.84 / 64	7.80 / 57
PM	GAMCO Global Gold Nat ResandIncome	GGN	**D-**	4.75	7.85	4.46	**E+ / 0.9**	-2.62	-20.76	-21.50 / 12	-19.14 / 9	-13.92 / 10
EN	GAMCO Nat Res Gold & Income Trust	GNT	**D-**	5.73	8.85	5.37	**D- / 1.1**	1.13	-18.62	-19.50 / 14	-16.26 / 11	--
GL	GDL Fund	GDL	**C+**	10.01	10.54	9.69	**C+ / 6.0**	4.30	0.24	4.38 / 77	3.69 / 56	3.34 / 40
GR	General American Investors	GAM	**B**	31.94	36.11	29.90	**B- / 7.3**	5.64	-4.76	-4.32 / 41	10.05 / 75	10.02 / 65
EM	Global High Income Fund	GHI	**D+**	8.50	9.03	7.52	**C- / 3.2**	11.70	4.15	5.79 / 81	-6.19 / 23	-0.13 / 27
EN	Goldman Sachs MLP and Energy Ren	XGERX	**E-**	5.48	16.20	4.70	**E- / 0.0**	-33.97	-53.00	-57.97 / 1	--	--
EN	Goldman Sachs MLP Income Oppty	XGMZX	**E**	8.23	18.72	7.06	**E- / 0.0**	-21.46	-41.43	-49.36 / 2	--	--
GEI	Guggenheim Build America Bd Mgd Du	GBAB	**C+**	21.38	23.90	20.21	**C+ / 6.4**	1.29	9.06	4.33 / 77	4.99 / 61	10.97 / 72
GEI	Guggenheim Credit Allocation	GGM	**C-**	19.49	23.95	17.15	**C- / 3.0**	1.45	-9.81	-0.01 / 60	--	--
IN	Guggenheim Enhanced Equity Income	GPM	**B-**	7.68	8.84	6.75	**B- / 7.0**	9.09	-3.26	1.41 / 69	7.55 / 69	6.90 / 54
IN	Guggenheim Enhanced Equity Strateg	GGE	**C+**	15.81	18.16	14.01	**C+ / 6.6**	7.45	-1.94	0.56 / 64	6.58 / 66	9.82 / 64
IN	Guggenheim Equal Weight Enh Eq Inc	GEQ	**C+**	16.34	20.79	13.01	**C+ / 6.0**	3.17	-5.60	-9.19 / 28	6.37 / 65	--
GI	Guggenheim Strategic Opportunities	GOF	**C-**	16.83	21.63	16.02	**C- / 3.9**	-2.75	-10.75	-10.51 / 25	1.87 / 48	6.69 / 53
FO	Herzfeld Caribbean Basin Fund	CUBA	**D**	6.62	11.99	6.27	**C- / 3.0**	-1.86	-31.23	-24.83 / 10	1.85 / 47	4.09 / 44
FO	India Fund	IFN	**C+**	22.74	30.16	20.00	**C+ / 6.5**	-1.92	-8.14	-6.64 / 34	8.86 / 72	-0.77 / 26
MUN	Invesco Adv Muni Inc II	VKI	**B-**	11.78	12.20	10.78	**C+ / 6.9**	4.99	10.92	8.51 / 93	2.47 / 56	8.51 / 85
GEI	Invesco Bond	VBF	**C**	17.57	19.00	16.50	**C / 4.4**	0.26	3.76	0.31 / 62	-0.28 / 36	5.80 / 50
MUS	Invesco CA Value Municipal Income	VCV	**B+**	13.25	13.70	12.13	**B / 8.0**	5.87	10.31	9.38 / 94	4.69 / 67	10.64 / 94
LP	Invesco Dynamic Credit Opps	VTA	**C**	10.55	12.26	10.02	**C- / 4.2**	1.92	-6.51	-3.76 / 43	0.70 / 40	4.16 / 44
COH	Invesco High Income Tr II	VLT	**C-**	12.85	15.35	12.04	**C- / 3.3**	2.69	-6.20	-6.81 / 34	-2.35 / 30	4.08 / 43
MUN	Invesco Municipal Income Opp Tr	OIA	**B+**	7.29	7.45	6.48	**B+ / 8.4**	8.38	12.79	11.18 / 97	4.72 / 68	10.17 / 92
MUN	Invesco Municipal Opportunity	VMO	**B-**	13.17	13.43	11.95	**C+ / 6.9**	6.44	11.36	9.77 / 95	2.04 / 53	7.94 / 80
MUN	Invesco Municipal Trust	VKQ	**C+**	12.77	13.36	11.85	**C+ / 6.4**	5.76	10.33	7.94 / 92	1.64 / 51	7.83 / 79
MUS	Invesco Pennsylvania Val Muni Inc	VPV	**C**	12.82	14.03	11.97	**C / 4.9**	5.43	8.90	-0.63 / 57	-0.47 / 36	7.53 / 76
MUN	Invesco Quality Municipal Income T	IQI	**B**	12.69	13.18	11.57	**B- / 7.2**	5.79	10.85	8.59 / 93	2.95 / 59	8.27 / 83
LP	Invesco Senior Income Trust	VVR	**C-**	4.04	5.20	3.84	**C- / 3.3**	-0.56	-7.25	-4.51 / 41	-1.88 / 31	3.25 / 39
MUN	Invesco Tr Fr Inv Gr Mun	VGM	**C+**	13.33	13.97	12.49	**C+ / 6.2**	4.81	9.15	7.24 / 90	1.40 / 49	7.62 / 76
MUS	Invesco Tr Fr Inv NY Mun	VTN	**B+**	14.61	14.67	13.18	**B / 8.0**	7.51	12.82	13.73 / 98	1.42 / 49	8.20 / 83
MUN	Invesco Value Municipal Income Tr	IIM	**B**	16.25	17.31	14.02	**B / 7.9**	6.16	14.64	5.27 / 85	4.57 / 67	10.24 / 93
COH	Ivy High Income Opportunities Fund	IVH	**D**	12.38	16.76	11.01	**D- / 1.4**	-0.36	-12.35	-12.95 / 20	--	--
GI	J Hancock Hedged Eqty & Inc Fd	HEQ	**C+**	14.46	16.95	14.02	**C+ / 6.1**	3.68	-4.49	-2.15 / 50	5.83 / 64	--
GEI	J Hancock Income Securities Tr	JHS	**C**	13.43	14.49	12.99	**C- / 3.9**	-1.88	-0.34	-0.52 / 57	-0.73 / 35	5.75 / 50
GEI	J Hancock Investors Trust	JHI	**D+**	14.38	18.53	13.29	**D+ / 2.4**	2.38	-6.74	-10.75 / 24	-7.21 / 21	2.22 / 34

* Denotes ETF Fund, N/A denotes number is not available

cl. in Returns		RISK				NET ASSETS		VALUATION			ASSET					FUND MANAGER	
			3 Year					Premium / Discount									
dend eld %	Expense Ratio	Risk Rating/ Pts	Standard Deviation	Beta	Avg Dura- tion	NAV as of 12/31/15	Total $(Mil)	As of 12/31/15	1 Year Average	Wtd Avg P/E	Cash %	Stocks %	Bonds %	Other %	Portfolio Turnover Ratio	Manager Quality Pct	Manager Tenure (Years)
.72	1.71	C+ / 5.7	15.1	0.95	6.8	15.34	99	-14.86	-13.48	26.6	0	43	56	1	48	12	N/A
.66	2.16	C+ / 5.8	12.1	0.88	8.5	11.66	240	-13.12	-14.64	N/A	0	0	100	0	61	30	N/A
.38	1.67	B- / 7.8	N/A	N/A	N/A	24.20	475	-5.37	-7.23	N/A	0	0	0	100	31	96	N/A
.14	1.39	C+ / 6.2	14.6	0.23	N/A	18.84	865	6.42	2.33	N/A	1	0	4	95	29	91	13
.51	1.77	B- / 7.3	12.7	0.36	N/A	20.16	209	-4.91	-4.10	N/A	1	0	6	93	29	79	13
.21	1.85	B- / 7.1	14.6	0.44	N/A	11.06	143	-3.53	-0.52	N/A	1	0	3	96	28	72	N/A
.36	1.82	B- / 7.1	16.0	0.50	N/A	13.28	154	-2.71	2.51	N/A	1	0	3	96	28	62	N/A
.48	0.75	B- / 7.3	7.4	1.65	N/A	14.68	131	-1.16	-7.82	N/A	0	0	95	5	26	57	N/A
.26	1.92	B- / 7.8	13.4	0.52	N/A	2.44	7	-34.84	-31.90	32.7	2	97	0	1	53	43	11
.94	1.14	B- / 7.5	7.8	0.70	N/A	12.38	372	-13.41	-13.32	N/A	1	0	98	1	290	36	N/A
.27	1.97	C+ / 6.9	11.1	0.64	N/A	6.67	179	-14.09	-12.60	N/A	0	28	71	1	20	18	25
.04	1.62	B- / 7.5	12.5	0.69	N/A	5.30	85	-9.81	-3.30	30.7	19	54	0	27	22	30	27
.15	1.36	B- / 7.5	15.4	1.38	N/A	21.07	1,951	-12.39	-11.54	31.1	4	94	0	2	18	21	N/A
.31	1.33	C+ / 6.5	17.4	1.38	N/A	5.70	1,486	-6.84	-5.52	41.3	0	99	0	1	11	16	30
.00	1.58	C / 5.4	N/A	N/A	N/A	12.20	98	-14.75	-13.92	N/A	0	0	0	100	20	66	N/A
.22	1.39	C+ / 6.7	15.1	0.56	N/A	19.57	90	-15.07	-14.40	24.1	3	95	0	2	27	34	12
.07	1.63	B- / 7.8	12.1	0.92	N/A	11.79	235	-13.06	-12.32	45.6	6	94	0	0	44	85	N/A
.93	1.50	C+ / 6.3	21.6	0.98	N/A	8.36	239	-10.29	-6.52	43.4	6	93	0	1	16	89	22
.53	1.59	C+ / 6.8	15.8	0.65	N/A	5.13	260	11.11	17.93	27.5	0	98	0	2	17	62	17
.68	1.24	C / 4.5	28.2	1.18	N/A	5.34	828	-11.05	-7.30	22.8	2	90	4	4	87	46	11
.66	1.25	C- / 3.7	25.2	0.80	N/A	6.47	184	-11.44	-11.05	N/A	0	0	0	100	102	12	N/A
.39	3.07	B / 8.0	4.7	0.23	N/A	11.94	245	-16.16	-16.18	47.6	56	42	0	2	315	83	9
.06	1.10	B- / 7.6	12.0	1.09	N/A	37.72	1,228	-15.32	-15.40	50.1	0	100	0	0	15	34	N/A
.60	1.31	C+ / 5.7	15.3	0.95	7.1	8.81	241	-3.52	-11.38	N/A	8	0	90	2	45	53	N/A
.45	N/A	D / 1.8	N/A	N/A	N/A	5.87	N/A	-6.64	4.53	N/A	0	0	0	100	N/A	2	N/A
.77	1.75	D / 1.9	N/A	N/A	N/A	8.80	847	-6.48	0.11	N/A	0	0	0	100	54	3	3
76	1.32	B- / 7.3	11.0	2.46	N/A	22.60	407	-5.40	-5.97	N/A	0	0	97	3	11	80	N/A
16	2.04	B- / 7.4	N/A	N/A	N/A	19.98	155	-2.45	-3.03	N/A	0	0	0	100	55	60	N/A
50	1.69	B- / 7.1	13.2	1.01	N/A	8.37	175	-8.24	-8.36	N/A	0	100	0	0	664	29	N/A
27	1.81	B- / 7.3	13.8	1.00	N/A	17.73	98	-10.83	-9.97	N/A	0	100	0	0	566	26	5
39	1.71	B- / 7.4	10.8	0.83	N/A	17.98	183	-9.12	-6.36	N/A	0	0	0	100	59	36	5
98	2.16	B- / 7.1	9.0	0.34	11.9	17.64	343	-4.59	3.44	N/A	7	10	73	10	86	49	9
42	2.97	C / 4.9	31.3	1.01	N/A	6.36	42	4.09	21.40	23.7	1	98	0	1	14	56	22
59	1.47	C+ / 6.4	22.8	0.83	N/A	25.95	848	-12.37	-9.82	N/A	2	97	0	1	3	89	N/A
62	1.69	B- / 7.3	10.8	2.23	10.3	12.63	567	-6.73	-9.00	N/A	0	0	98	2	9	39	11
26	0.55	B- / 7.3	8.6	2.12	N/A	18.91	233	-7.09	-8.60	N/A	1	0	98	1	218	43	6
98	1.05	B- / 7.3	11.5	2.10	10.0	13.83	662	-4.19	-5.82	N/A	0	0	97	3	8	58	7
53	2.52	B- / 7.6	8.0	N/A	4.0	12.11	984	-12.88	-12.07	N/A	0	0	0	100	103	85	9
67	1.49	C+ / 6.9	10.5	1.67	N/A	14.81	139	-13.23	-13.07	N/A	0	0	99	1	99	36	N/A
40	0.79	B- / 7.2	9.5	1.78	12.6	7.63	360	-4.46	-8.11	N/A	0	0	100	0	11	72	7
68	1.57	B- / 7.3	10.8	2.10	11.0	14.11	960	-6.66	-9.16	N/A	0	0	97	3	10	42	7
39	1.64	B- / 7.3	10.9	2.35	10.5	14.05	783	-9.11	-10.42	N/A	0	0	97	3	10	34	7
20	1.61	B- / 7.6	11.0	2.17	11.5	14.47	348	-11.40	-11.94	N/A	0	0	98	2	12	26	7
00	1.07	B- / 7.5	10.3	2.54	9.3	13.93	738	-8.90	-10.77	N/A	0	0	100	0	10	38	7
72	2.20	B- / 7.0	8.2	-2.67	N/A	4.49	909	-10.02	-9.16	N/A	1	0	3	96	63	56	9
57	1.64	B- / 7.4	10.1	2.04	10.7	14.55	799	-8.38	-9.48	N/A	0	0	99	1	10	38	7
82	1.35	B- / 7.4	10.3	2.28	10.9	15.21	296	-3.94	-8.46	N/A	0	0	100	0	12	32	9
17	0.91	B- / 7.3	12.7	2.69	9.1	16.57	779	-1.93	-4.16	N/A	0	0	100	0	11	40	7
00	1.98	C+ / 6.5	N/A	N/A	N/A	14.32	258	-13.55	-12.63	N/A	0	0	0	100	47	41	2
40	1.17	B- / 7.5	9.3	0.65	N/A	16.78	248	-13.83	-11.98	N/A	7	92	0	1	42	49	5
53	1.43	B- / 7.4	8.4	1.33	13.3	14.63	176	-8.20	-9.36	29.2	1	2	94	3	51	51	10
39	1.53	C+ / 6.2	12.2	1.88	N/A	16.04	151	-10.35	-9.24	N/A	5	1	89	5	74	19	10

Denotes ETF Fund, N/A denotes number is not available

Fund Type	Fund Name (99 Pct = Best, 0 Pct = Worst)	Ticker Symbol	Overall Investment Rating	PRICE: Price As of 12/31/15	PRICE: 52 Week High	PRICE: 52 Week Low	PERFORMANCE: Performance Rating/Pts	% Total Return Through 12/31/15: 3 Mo	6 Mo	1Yr/Pct	Annualized: 3Yr/Pct	Annualized: 5Yr/Pct
IN	J Hancock Preferred Inc	HPI	**C+**	20.02	21.38	17.47	**C+ / 6.1**	6.18	7.15	5.07 / 79	3.44 / 55	9.92 / 65
IN	J Hancock Preferred Income II	HPF	**C+**	19.61	21.45	16.00	**C+ / 5.9**	5.62	5.23	3.43 / 75	3.18 / 54	9.63 / 64
IN	J Hancock Preferred Income III	HPS	**B-**	17.86	18.77	14.28	**C+ / 6.8**	9.57	10.52	6.26 / 82	5.03 / 61	10.73 / 70
GL	J Hancock Tax Adv Glb Shlr Yield	HTY	**C+**	10.23	12.88	8.38	**B- / 7.1**	13.62	8.66	3.90 / 76	6.00 / 64	6.18 / 51
IN	J Hancock Tax Advantage Div Income	HTD	**A-**	20.57	23.27	18.88	**B+ / 8.3**	7.27	8.08	0.21 / 62	10.99 / 78	14.08 / 88
FO	Japan Smaller Cap Fund Inc.	JOF	**A+**	10.23	11.03	8.75	**A / 9.5**	10.04	1.68	24.45 / 99	16.38 / 92	4.95 / 47
FS	John Hancock Financial Opptys	BTO	**A+**	28.03	29.44	21.23	**A+ / 9.7**	15.34	3.77	25.29 / 99	21.19 / 96	16.40 / 94
IN	John Hancock Premium Dividend	PDT	**B+**	13.71	14.47	12.45	**B / 8.1**	9.86	10.34	8.44 / 86	8.82 / 72	12.42 / 82
FO	JPMorgan China Region	JFC	**C**	15.32	21.21	12.55	**C+ / 5.8**	11.50	-13.12	-3.83 / 43	4.93 / 61	0.98 / 30
EN	Kayne Anderson Energy Tot Ret	KYE	**E+**	8.47	27.95	6.71	**E / 0.3**	-33.07	-55.90	-66.00 / 1	-23.87 / 6	-15.16 / 8
EN	Kayne Anderson Engy Development Co	KED	**D-**	17.56	36.20	12.62	**D- / 1.4**	-17.91	-24.68	-48.92 / 2	-5.77 / 24	5.38 / 49
IN	Kayne Anderson Midstream/Energy	KMF	**E**	12.37	35.15	9.99	**E / 0.5**	-34.43	-52.19	-57.65 / 1	-17.86 / 10	-5.85 / 18
EN	Kayne Anderson MLP Inv Co	KYN	**D-**	17.29	37.85	12.62	**D- / 1.0**	-25.09	-40.69	-50.61 / 1	-10.32 / 17	-4.05 / 20
GEI	KKR Income Opportunities Fund	KIO	**D+**	13.86	16.92	13.24	**D / 2.2**	-1.96	-8.06	-5.82 / 36	--	--
FO	Korea Equity Fund	KEF	**C-**	6.97	8.61	6.74	**C- / 3.1**	1.11	-9.35	-4.34 / 41	-2.87 / 29	-0.05 / 28
FO	Korea Fund	KF	**D+**	31.85	43.56	31.68	**D+ / 2.8**	0.81	-13.40	-2.36 / 49	-4.69 / 25	-1.84 / 23
FO	Latin American Discovery Fund	LDF	**D-**	7.43	11.64	7.07	**E+ / 0.7**	-6.97	-27.84	-31.42 / 7	-21.36 / 7	-15.30 / 8
GL	Lazard Global Total Return&Income	LGI	**C-**	13.08	16.75	12.23	**C- / 3.9**	5.65	-11.49	-10.62 / 24	0.95 / 41	4.31 / 45
GL	Lazard World Div&Inc Fd	LOR	**D+**	9.11	13.20	8.58	**D+ / 2.3**	1.07	-18.96	-24.41 / 10	-4.27 / 26	0.53 / 29
GL	Legg Mason BW Global Income Opps	BWG	**D**	11.58	17.49	10.97	**D / 2.0**	2.20	-13.49	-20.92 / 12	-8.29 / 19	--
IN	Liberty All-Star Equity Fund	USA	**B+**	5.35	6.04	4.43	**B / 7.7**	8.06	-2.33	-1.84 / 51	10.34 / 76	8.83 / 60
IN	Liberty All-Star Growth Fund	ASG	**B+**	4.58	5.41	4.20	**A / 9.4**	16.89	7.45	11.67 / 91	15.51 / 90	11.69 / 76
GI	LMP Capital and Income Fund Inc	SCD	**C-**	12.37	17.35	11.00	**C- / 3.7**	3.16	-14.26	-20.46 / 13	2.36 / 50	7.62 / 57
LP	LMP Corporate Loan Fund Inc	TLI	**C-**	9.88	11.75	9.43	**C- / 3.3**	-0.72	-6.99	-3.04 / 46	-2.23 / 30	3.51 / 40
GI	LMP Real Estate Income Fund Inc	RIT	**B**	13.04	13.61	11.13	**B+ / 8.6**	6.12	12.88	9.91 / 88	10.81 / 78	12.29 / 80
GL	Macquarie Global Infr Total Return	MGU	**C**	19.05	26.73	17.20	**C / 4.6**	-1.37	-15.23	-17.58 / 15	4.90 / 61	8.17 / 58
GL	Macquarie/FTG Infr/ Util Div&Inc	MFD	**D+**	11.62	17.52	11.05	**D+ / 2.7**	-5.77	-19.15	-19.49 / 14	-1.18 / 33	4.39 / 45
IN	Madison Covered Call & Equity Stra	MCN	**B-**	7.38	8.49	6.30	**C+ / 6.7**	4.85	-2.74	-0.61 / 57	7.30 / 68	4.99 / 47
IN	Madison Strategic Sector Premium	MSP	**B-**	10.77	12.36	10.17	**C+ / 6.6**	3.46	-3.52	-0.52 / 57	7.26 / 68	5.23 / 49
GEI	MainStay DefinedTerm Muncipal Opp	MMD	**C+**	18.83	19.26	17.06	**C+ / 6.7**	7.73	12.39	9.33 / 87	4.09 / 58	--
MUN	Managed Duration Investment Grd Mu	MZF	**C+**	13.76	14.32	12.71	**C+ / 6.6**	4.41	6.01	7.10 / 90	1.62 / 51	7.81 / 78
GL	Managed High Yield Plus Fund	HYF	**C**	1.76	1.97	1.57	**C+ / 5.7**	13.07	2.23	1.10 / 67	2.00 / 48	4.74 / 46
FO	Mexico Equity & Income Fund	MXE	**D+**	10.76	12.93	9.99	**C- / 3.5**	3.38	-8.34	-8.41 / 30	-0.67 / 35	5.00 / 48
FO	Mexico Fund	MXF	**D**	16.62	22.80	15.20	**D / 1.8**	-1.61	-17.35	-11.91 / 22	-9.82 / 18	-0.64 / 26
MUS	MFS CA Muni	CCA	**A-**	11.84	12.10	10.65	**A- / 9.0**	8.08	12.55	15.02 / 99	4.50 / 67	9.48 / 90
GEI	MFS Charter Income Trust	MCR	**C-**	7.62	9.10	6.91	**C- / 3.1**	0.79	-6.65	-8.75 / 29	-2.60 / 29	3.33 / 39
GL	MFS Government Markets Income Trus	MGF	**C**	5.30	5.91	5.04	**C- / 4.0**	0.73	1.14	-0.38 / 58	-0.97 / 34	2.61 / 36
MUH	MFS High Inc Muni Tr	CXE	**C+**	4.91	5.07	4.51	**C+ / 6.5**	5.38	10.67	8.37 / 93	1.75 / 52	8.02 / 81
MUH	MFS High Yield Muni Trust	CMU	**B-**	4.51	4.72	4.06	**C+ / 6.9**	3.90	12.79	8.49 / 93	2.51 / 57	8.32 / 83
COH	MFS Interm High Inc	CIF	**C-**	2.32	2.85	2.11	**C- / 3.4**	5.08	-8.37	-3.29 / 45	-1.98 / 31	3.82 / 42
GL	MFS Intermediate Income Trust	MIN	**C-**	4.57	5.01	4.23	**C- / 3.8**	2.61	2.62	3.23 / 75	-2.58 / 29	2.35 / 35
MUN	MFS Invst Gr Muni Tr	CXH	**B**	9.94	10.07	8.85	**B / 7.8**	2.65	9.97	11.40 / 97	3.02 / 60	8.76 / 86
GEN	MFS Multimarket Income Trust	MMT	**C-**	5.51	6.50	5.35	**C- / 3.4**	1.28	-6.80	-7.75 / 32	-1.13 / 33	3.68 / 41
MUN	MFS Municipal Income Trust	MFM	**C+**	6.80	7.01	6.17	**C+ / 6.3**	8.47	9.31	8.67 / 93	0.98 / 45	7.74 / 77
GI	MFS Special Value Trust	MFV	**D+**	5.31	7.50	4.92	**C- / 3.5**	4.87	-7.87	-18.23 / 15	0.38 / 39	2.73 / 37
GL	Miller/Howard High Income Equity	XHIEX	**E+**	11.46	20.35	10.00	**E- / 0.2**	-4.61	-29.27	-36.85 / 5	--	--
FO	Morgan Stanley Asia Pacific Fund	APF	**C-**	13.83	16.77	11.92	**C- / 3.8**	7.19	-11.92	-5.37 / 37	-0.32 / 36	-0.68 / 26
FO	Morgan Stanley China A Share Fund	CAF	**C**	19.91	38.08	19.44	**B / 8.1**	11.28	-4.65	2.43 / 73	11.03 / 78	6.25 / 52
EM	Morgan Stanley Emerging Markets	MSF	**C-**	12.85	15.97	11.65	**D+ / 2.4**	-0.51	-14.01	-10.20 / 25	-6.46 / 22	-4.09 / 20
EM	Morgan Stanley Emerging Mkts Debt	MSD	**C-**	8.57	9.78	8.16	**C- / 3.2**	5.49	-1.47	1.15 / 68	-4.44 / 26	2.52 / 36
EM	Morgan Stanley Emg Mkts Dom Debt	EDD	**D-**	6.80	10.69	6.58	**E+ / 0.9**	0.15	-16.37	-27.28 / 9	-19.03 / 9	-8.34 / 15
GEN	Morgan Stanley Income Sec	ICB	**C+**	16.87	18.49	16.64	**C / 5.1**	0.28	2.53	-0.58 / 57	1.45 / 45	5.07 / 48

* Denotes ETF Fund, N/A denotes number is not available

cl. in Returns dend eld %	Expense Ratio	RISK Risk Rating/ Pts	3 Year Standard Deviation	3 Year Beta	Avg Dura- tion	NET ASSETS NAV as of 12/31/15	NET ASSETS Total $(Mil)	VALUATION Premium / Discount As of 12/31/15	VALUATION Premium / Discount 1 Year Average	Wtd Avg P/E	ASSET Cash %	ASSET Stocks %	ASSET Bonds %	ASSET Other %	Portfolio Turnover Ratio	FUND MANAGER Manager Quality Pct	FUND MANAGER Manager Tenure (Years)
.69	1.68	B- / 7.6	10.6	0.31	N/A	21.79	565	-8.12	-7.53	18.6	3	1	1	95	11	72	14
.85	1.69	B- / 7.8	10.2	0.25	N/A	21.57	459	-9.09	-7.64	18.6	3	2	3	92	13	76	14
.53	1.67	B- / 7.6	10.4	0.27	N/A	19.13	601	-6.64	-8.30	18.6	4	0	3	93	13	82	13
.51	1.26	C+ / 6.1	16.6	0.55	N/A	9.36	106	9.29	2.69	25.1	2	96	0	2	261	86	9
.06	1.63	B- / 7.9	13.0	0.64	N/A	22.94	836	-10.33	-10.35	24.0	0	61	0	39	11	82	N/A
.63	1.13	B / 8.1	13.6	0.62	N/A	11.63	311	-12.04	-12.44	N/A	0	79	0	21	41	97	N/A
.28	1.80	B- / 7.3	16.4	1.14	N/A	26.17	482	7.11	-1.29	19.6	1	96	0	3	18	88	10
.88	1.85	B- / 7.5	13.2	0.60	N/A	14.96	733	-8.36	-10.13	28.0	2	33	0	65	15	71	11
.54	2.14	C+ / 6.2	19.5	0.93	N/A	17.49	125	-12.41	-14.83	N/A	0	99	0	1	87	74	11
.58	3.60	C- / 3.6	35.7	1.44	4.0	9.54	1,050	-11.22	-8.03	25.1	0	87	13	0	38	7	11
.05	3.40	C / 4.5	27.9	0.66	N/A	23.44	348	-25.09	-4.98	N/A	0	82	18	0	31	45	N/A
.55	3.60	D / 2.1	35.2	2.22	N/A	12.60	854	-1.83	-7.82	N/A	0	84	16	0	45	1	N/A
21	2.40	C / 4.5	26.7	0.68	N/A	17.72	4,027	-2.43	6.99	22.2	0	100	0	0	18	20	12
82	2.29	B- / 7.2	N/A	N/A	N/A	15.88	289	-12.72	-11.56	N/A	0	0	0	100	65	27	N/A
76	1.49	C+ / 6.6	14.4	0.66	N/A	8.01	87	-12.98	-11.46	N/A	1	92	0	7	19	26	11
00	1.13	C+ / 6.3	15.1	0.64	N/A	35.45	329	-10.16	-9.89	N/A	0	97	0	3	51	21	N/A
44	1.40	C / 4.8	21.0	1.17	N/A	8.41	84	-11.65	-10.21	59.3	0	100	0	0	21	4	14
51	1.51	C+ / 6.9	15.7	1.15	6.0	15.26	171	-14.29	-13.23	28.9	0	67	32	1	10	37	N/A
08	1.75	C+ / 6.2	18.9	1.25	5.8	10.59	97	-13.98	-12.25	21.9	1	71	27	1	71	17	N/A
47	1.74	C / 5.1	17.2	1.17	N/A	13.70	420	-15.47	-14.87	N/A	0	0	0	100	62	41	4
72	1.03	B- / 7.6	13.1	1.17	N/A	6.18	1,225	-13.43	-13.80	72.9	2	97	0	1	36	29	14
12	1.34	C+ / 6.7	14.8	1.12	N/A	4.99	138	-8.22	-10.00	149.9	3	96	0	1	63	67	30
02	1.44	C+ / 6.7	15.0	1.07	N/A	14.77	348	-16.25	-13.68	39.3	12	75	12	1	27	16	5
81	1.88	B- / 7.1	6.7	0.01	N/A	11.02	117	-10.34	-10.46	N/A	0	0	0	100	45	54	N/A
52	1.48	C+ / 6.4	17.9	0.55	N/A	13.57	164	-3.91	-9.16	81.4	0	61	0	39	11	88	N/A
77	2.20	B- / 7.0	17.1	1.12	N/A	22.78	356	-16.37	-14.10	22.9	0	100	0	0	61	69	4
05	1.95	C+ / 6.8	15.9	0.97	N/A	13.17	151	-11.77	-6.04	23.9	0	76	0	24	158	26	N/A
76	1.06	B- / 7.6	9.6	0.79	N/A	8.48	179	-12.97	-12.06	63.2	0	100	0	0	131	41	N/A
66	0.98	B- / 7.8	8.4	0.63	N/A	12.55	79	-14.18	-13.20	63.6	0	100	0	0	139	59	11
25	1.56	C+ / 6.9	10.8	2.28	N/A	19.60	524	-3.93	-5.62	N/A	0	0	0	100	27	77	4
37	1.35	B- / 7.3	11.9	2.57	11.8	14.99	101	-8.21	-10.39	N/A	0	0	100	0	12	28	13
86	1.46	C+ / 6.5	14.8	0.65	N/A	1.85	135	-4.86	-11.88	N/A	1	0	98	1	35	90	7
00	1.76	C / 5.5	16.6	0.85	5.6	12.52	102	-14.06	-12.13	N/A	1	97	1	1	175	39	26
00	1.57	C / 4.8	21.2	0.94	N/A	18.87	403	-11.92	-6.51	N/A	1	98	0	1	39	13	25
17	2.38	B- / 7.4	11.1	2.16	11.3	12.76	35	-7.21	-10.24	N/A	3	0	97	0	17	52	9
75	0.87	B- / 7.0	10.0	0.86	N/A	8.97	549	-15.05	-12.44	N/A	0	0	99	1	44	42	12
77	0.75	B- / 7.5	7.5	0.58	13.3	5.61	198	-5.53	-6.33	N/A	10	0	90	0	62	78	N/A
11	2.19	B- / 7.2	11.2	2.42	12.8	5.43	170	-9.58	-11.07	N/A	0	0	100	0	11	33	9
25	2.01	B- / 7.1	13.0	2.86	12.8	4.87	137	-7.39	-9.52	N/A	1	0	99	0	12	31	9
28	1.61	C+ / 6.5	12.1	1.64	N/A	2.59	65	-10.42	-12.26	N/A	0	1	98	1	48	41	9
35	0.65	C+ / 6.6	10.0	0.61	N/A	4.95	642	-7.68	-9.25	N/A	0	0	100	0	25	70	14
13	1.74	B- / 7.4	9.5	1.85	11.7	10.68	123	-6.93	-9.94	N/A	0	0	100	0	15	53	9
69	0.98	C+ / 6.8	10.8	0.94	N/A	6.46	570	-14.71	-12.60	N/A	0	0	100	0	46	47	N/A
65	1.73	B- / 7.2	10.2	1.99	12.5	7.42	302	-8.36	-10.90	N/A	1	0	99	0	14	38	23
30	1.35	C+ / 5.6	10.2	0.60	6.0	5.74	48	-7.49	-4.20	46.4	2	25	73	0	39	22	N/A
15	N/A	C- / 3.4	N/A	N/A	N/A	12.89	N/A	-11.09	-4.87	N/A	0	0	0	100	N/A	1	2
04	1.32	C+ / 6.7	14.2	0.86	N/A	15.53	230	-10.95	-11.64	N/A	5	94	0	1	79	37	4
32	1.80	C / 4.5	28.9	0.53	N/A	23.47	759	-15.17	-19.00	N/A	0	99	0	1	98	94	N/A
21	1.55	B- / 7.2	13.8	0.90	N/A	14.29	234	-10.08	-10.71	45.6	3	96	0	1	41	69	25
52	1.14	C+ / 6.4	10.5	0.71	6.4	10.08	243	-14.98	-15.71	N/A	0	0	99	1	80	62	14
76	2.20	C / 4.8	17.7	1.32	7.4	8.20	954	-17.07	-14.71	N/A	0	0	100	0	107	12	9
20	0.72	B- / 7.9	6.8	1.71	N/A	18.24	171	-7.51	-9.82	N/A	1	0	98	1	44	60	8

Denotes ETF Fund, N/A denotes number is not available

Fund Type	Fund Name (99 Pct = Best, 0 Pct = Worst)	Ticker Symbol	Overall Investment Rating	PRICE: Price As of 12/31/15	PRICE: 52 Week High	PRICE: 52 Week Low	PERFORMANCE: Performance Rating/Pts	% Total Return Through 12/31/15: 3 Mo	6 Mo	1Yr/Pct	Annualized: 3Yr/Pct	Annualized: 5Yr/Pct
FO	Morgan Stanley India Inv Fund	IIF	**C+**	25.47	29.99	19.34	**B- / 7.1**	-4.09	-9.63	-6.26 / 35	10.87 / 78	1.33 / 31
MUS	Neuberger Berman CA Inter Muni Fun	NBW	**B+**	15.75	17.29	13.88	**B / 8.1**	9.03	10.79	4.34 / 83	5.32 / 70	7.90 / 79
COH	Neuberger Berman High Yield Strat	NHS	**C-**	10.09	12.82	9.31	**D+ / 2.9**	2.36	-10.11	-10.88 / 24	-3.20 / 28	1.84 / 33
MUN	Neuberger Berman Intermediate Muni	NBH	**B**	15.72	16.29	14.52	**B- / 7.2**	2.57	8.61	7.34 / 90	3.71 / 63	8.73 / 86
GL	Neuberger Berman MLP Income	NML	**E+**	8.16	19.65	6.10	**E- / 0.0**	-33.38	-47.58	-50.28 / 2	--	--
MUS	Neuberger Berman NY Int Muni	NBO	**B-**	14.10	14.76	13.34	**C+ / 6.6**	3.29	1.42	8.37 / 93	2.52 / 57	6.68 / 67
GI	Neuberger Berman Real Est Secs Inc	NRO	**B**	5.01	5.67	4.12	**B- / 7.5**	9.69	8.31	1.35 / 69	7.94 / 70	10.82 / 70
COH	New America High Income Fund	HYB	**C-**	7.66	9.30	7.27	**C- / 3.2**	0.53	-8.63	-7.21 / 33	-1.92 / 31	4.61 / 46
FO	New Germany Fund	GF	**B**	14.70	16.27	13.27	**A / 9.4**	7.39	2.44	14.57 / 94	17.51 / 93	13.76 / 87
GEN	NexPoint Credit Strategies Fund	HCF	**C-**	20.44	49.44	19.21	**C+ / 6.7**	-7.35	-25.33	-23.11 / 11	14.02 / 88	8.52 / 59
EN	Nuveen All Cap Energy MLP Opps	JML	**E-**	6.97	17.39	5.49	**E- / 0.0**	-27.44	-47.45	-50.36 / 1	--	--
MUN	Nuveen AMT-Fr Muni Income	NEA	**B-**	13.85	14.36	12.61	**C+ / 6.7**	7.61	11.69	6.15 / 87	2.13 / 54	7.18 / 72
MUN	Nuveen AMT-Free Municipal Value	NUW	**B-**	17.86	18.76	16.03	**B / 7.7**	5.32	13.02	6.60 / 88	4.02 / 65	8.26 / 83
MUS	Nuveen AZ Prem Inc Muni	NAZ	**B**	15.19	15.25	13.94	**B / 8.1**	3.26	5.81	11.36 / 97	4.40 / 66	9.69 / 91
MUN	Nuveen Build America Bond Fund	NBB	**B**	20.09	21.94	19.01	**B- / 7.4**	3.86	7.50	1.42 / 72	5.04 / 69	8.63 / 86
GEI	Nuveen Build America Bond Oppty Fd	NBD	**C+**	20.29	22.57	19.28	**C+ / 6.0**	5.21	6.79	-1.40 / 53	4.06 / 57	8.36 / 59
MUS	Nuveen CA AMT-Free Municipal Incom	NKX	**A-**	15.36	15.45	13.90	**A- / 9.0**	5.48	10.38	11.47 / 97	6.28 / 74	11.45 / 95
MUS	Nuveen CA Div Adv Muni	NAC	**B**	15.48	15.87	14.14	**B / 7.6**	3.47	10.54	9.35 / 94	3.95 / 64	11.82 / 96
MUS	Nuveen CA Div Adv Muni 2	NVX	**B+**	15.31	15.43	13.46	**B+ / 8.3**	3.61	16.02	13.68 / 98	4.42 / 66	10.16 / 92
MUS	Nuveen CA Div Adv Muni 3	NZH	**B+**	14.15	14.28	12.61	**B+ / 8.4**	5.97	14.07	11.06 / 97	4.97 / 69	10.42 / 93
MUS	Nuveen CA Muni Value	NCA	**A-**	10.88	10.98	10.12	**B+ / 8.8**	3.25	7.44	8.09 / 92	6.64 / 76	10.04 / 92
MUS	Nuveen CA Select Tax-Free Inc Port	NXC	**B+**	15.63	16.13	14.12	**B / 8.0**	3.41	9.18	5.96 / 87	5.61 / 71	9.29 / 89
MUN	Nuveen California Municipal Value	NCB	**B+**	17.02	17.65	15.84	**B+ / 8.6**	7.18	8.52	8.26 / 92	6.42 / 75	8.94 / 87
IN	Nuveen Core Equity Alpha Fund	JCE	**A-**	14.27	17.88	13.13	**A- / 9.2**	4.24	3.38	0.43 / 63	16.95 / 92	14.46 / 89
GI	Nuveen Credit Strategies Income	JQC	**C-**	7.84	9.18	7.34	**C- / 3.7**	1.28	-5.82	-3.42 / 45	-0.97 / 34	5.61 / 49
MUS	Nuveen CT Prem Inc Muni	NTC	**B-**	12.76	13.19	12.14	**C+ / 6.2**	4.47	4.91	6.73 / 89	0.79 / 43	4.99 / 57
MUN	Nuveen Div Adv Muni	NAD	**B**	14.55	14.80	13.31	**B- / 7.2**	7.02	11.03	7.74 / 91	2.98 / 59	9.21 / 88
MUN	Nuveen Div Adv Muni 3	NZF	**B**	14.36	14.64	13.24	**B- / 7.4**	7.19	10.73	9.61 / 95	3.08 / 60	7.83 / 79
MUN	Nuveen Div Adv Muni Income	NVG	**B**	14.48	14.83	13.50	**B- / 7.0**	5.21	9.76	7.94 / 92	2.96 / 59	7.69 / 77
GI	Nuveen Diversified Dividend&Income	JDD	**C+**	10.83	12.92	9.69	**C+ / 6.4**	6.73	-2.23	1.23 / 68	5.91 / 64	9.08 / 61
MUN	Nuveen Dividend Advantage Muni 2	NXZ	**B-**	14.16	14.76	13.22	**C+ / 6.7**	5.94	8.56	6.27 / 88	2.49 / 56	8.18 / 82
IN	Nuveen Dow 30 Dynamic Overwrite	DPD	**B+**	14.36	15.78	11.53	**B- / 7.3**	7.70	-0.44	-5.03 / 39	9.36 / 73	7.07 / 55
GI	Nuveen Energy MLP Total Return Fun	JMF	**D-**	11.10	20.26	8.85	**D- / 1.2**	-16.67	-29.27	-41.12 / 3	-9.78 / 18	--
GEI	Nuveen EnhancedMunicipal Value	NEV	**C+**	15.71	16.04	14.31	**C+ / 6.6**	6.36	11.22	10.19 / 88	4.05 / 57	11.27 / 74
IN	Nuveen Flexible Investment Income	JPW	**C-**	14.67	18.48	14.05	**D+ / 2.9**	1.52	-7.76	-1.92 / 51	--	--
LP	Nuveen Floating Rate Income Fund	JFR	**C**	10.24	11.52	9.33	**C / 4.4**	4.95	-1.79	-0.23 / 59	-0.01 / 37	3.95 / 43
LP	Nuveen Floating Rate Income Opp	JRO	**C-**	9.80	11.85	7.96	**C- / 3.5**	1.43	-7.25	-6.83 / 34	-1.11 / 33	2.37 / 35
MUS	Nuveen GA Div Adv Muni Fund 2	NKG	**B**	13.50	13.55	12.54	**B- / 7.3**	6.25	8.01	12.46 / 98	1.19 / 47	6.48 / 65
GL	Nuveen Global Equity Income	JGV	**D+**	10.92	13.85	9.96	**C- / 3.3**	8.29	-7.30	-6.90 / 34	-2.75 / 29	-3.45 / 22
GL	Nuveen Global High Income	XJGHX	**D-**	13.74	17.98	13.01	**D- / 1.3**	-0.91	-13.10	-12.87 / 20	--	--
COH	Nuveen High Income 2020 Target Ter	XJHYX	**U**	9.95	N/A	N/A	**U /**	0.62	--	--	--	--
MUN	Nuveen Intermdt Dur Qlty Mun Term	NIQ	**A**	12.88	13.43	12.13	**A- / 9.2**	5.21	7.33	6.37 / 88	--	--
MUN	Nuveen Intermediate Dur Mun Term	NID	**C**	12.86	13.19	12.06	**C+ / 5.7**	5.37	7.97	7.85 / 92	0.01 / 37	--
MUN	Nuveen Investment Quality Muni Fun	NQM	**B**	15.42	16.04	14.41	**B- / 7.4**	5.14	9.36	7.64 / 91	3.71 / 63	9.75 / 91
MUS	Nuveen MA Prem Inc Muni	NMT	**C+**	13.73	14.17	12.70	**C+ / 6.4**	1.66	5.46	8.83 / 93	1.43 / 49	6.12 / 63
MUS	Nuveen MD Prem Inc Muni Fund	NMY	**C**	12.69	13.06	12.15	**C / 4.3**	3.87	5.36	5.56 / 86	-1.64 / 32	4.25 / 53
MUS	Nuveen MI Quality Inc Muni	NUM	**C+**	13.69	14.48	13.05	**C+ / 5.9**	5.00	6.70	5.76 / 86	1.11 / 47	7.29 / 73
MUS	Nuveen Minnesota Municipal Income	MXA	**C**	14.60	15.58	14.08	**C / 4.6**	1.21	5.39	6.23 / 87	-1.11 / 33	6.52 / 65
MUS	Nuveen MO Prem Inc Muni	NOM	**C**	15.38	17.07	14.12	**C+ / 5.8**	6.12	10.37	7.18 / 90	0.20 / 38	6.68 / 67
MTG	Nuveen Mortgage Opportunity Term	JLS	**C**	22.71	23.62	22.11	**C / 5.4**	3.04	3.37	4.91 / 79	0.62 / 40	6.35 / 5
MTG	Nuveen Mortgage Opportunity Term 2	JMT	**C**	22.29	23.22	21.15	**C+ / 5.6**	4.12	3.26	4.69 / 78	1.49 / 45	7.48 / 5
MTG	Nuveen Multi-Market Income	MRF	**C**	7.10	8.03	6.67	**C / 4.3**	3.59	2.54	-3.75 / 43	--	3.33 / 4

* Denotes ETF Fund, N/A denotes number is not availab

Incl. in Returns		RISK				NET ASSETS		VALUATION			ASSET					FUND MANAGER	
Dividend Yield %	Expense Ratio	Risk Rating/ Pts	3 Year Standard Deviation	3 Year Beta	Avg Dura- tion	NAV as of 12/31/15	Total $(Mil)	Premium / Discount As of 12/31/15	Premium / Discount 1 Year Average	Wtd Avg P/E	Cash %	Stocks %	Bonds %	Other %	Portfolio Turnover Ratio	Manager Quality Pct	Manager Tenure (Years)
0.00	1.44	C+ / 6.8	21.2	0.73	N/A	29.07	450	-12.38	-11.37	57.7	3	96	0	1	16	92	22
5.18	1.70	B- / 7.4	11.8	1.70	7.7	15.48	86	1.74	-0.75	N/A	2	0	97	1	24	74	N/A
9.51	1.89	C+ / 6.8	11.2	1.78	N/A	11.62	282	-13.17	-13.61	N/A	0	0	100	0	60	27	13
5.73	1.41	B- / 7.5	10.1	2.14	8.5	15.98	302	-1.63	-3.71	N/A	2	0	97	1	24	52	N/A
15.44	1.77	C- / 3.6	N/A	N/A	N/A	8.20	1	-0.49	-4.07	N/A	0	0	0	100	10	N/A	N/A
4.85	1.71	B- / 7.4	12.1	2.17	7.2	14.41	74	-2.15	-2.71	N/A	4	0	95	1	32	38	N/A
7.19	2.09	B- / 7.2	15.5	0.63	N/A	5.69	340	-11.95	-15.34	81.7	0	58	0	42	21	64	N/A
14.49	1.54	C+ / 6.7	10.3	1.16	N/A	8.84	236	-13.35	-13.65	N/A	0	0	96	4	48	39	N/A
0.54	1.14	C+ / 5.7	15.1	0.92	N/A	16.19	228	-9.20	-9.38	72.8	0	100	0	0	55	96	N/A
15.26	2.48	C- / 3.2	17.2	1.01	4.6	23.67	861	-13.65	-13.07	72.5	0	10	28	62	59	96	N/A
19.63	1.77	D / 1.8	N/A	N/A	N/A	7.50	236	-7.07	-0.77	N/A	0	0	0	100	25	2	2
5.42	1.60	B- / 7.5	10.8	2.27	13.0	15.13	1,193	-8.46	-10.32	N/A	11	0	89	0	13	40	10
4.37	0.75	C+ / 6.7	9.8	2.10	N/A	17.23	227	3.66	-0.88	N/A	2	0	92	6	10	57	7
5.25	1.56	C+ / 6.8	11.8	2.22	11.7	14.88	174	2.08	-0.49	N/A	3	0	96	1	13	54	5
6.69	1.07	B- / 7.5	9.0	1.86	N/A	21.40	612	-6.12	-8.17	N/A	8	0	91	1	13	61	N/A
6.42	1.02	B- / 7.4	9.2	2.22	N/A	21.86	172	-7.18	-9.36	N/A	18	0	81	1	6	76	N/A
6.09	1.63	B- / 7.4	11.0	2.16	13.7	16.07	761	-4.42	-6.58	N/A	4	0	90	6	13	74	14
6.38	1.53	B- / 7.1	12.0	2.49	12.8	15.97	1,714	-3.07	-4.30	N/A	9	0	90	1	9	45	14
5.73	1.50	B- / 7.1	11.4	2.46	13.3	15.95	233	-4.01	-6.87	N/A	9	0	90	1	14	48	14
6.16	1.56	B- / 7.3	10.3	2.11	13.4	14.82	355	-4.52	-7.22	N/A	8	0	91	1	15	60	14
4.66	0.64	B- / 7.6	7.1	1.29	11.8	10.53	268	3.32	0.83	N/A	2	0	97	1	13	85	14
4.03	0.37	B- / 7.6	9.9	1.93	10.2	15.50	97	0.84	0.09	N/A	3	0	96	1	7	70	24
4.96	0.75	B- / 7.3	9.5	2.04	N/A	17.21	58	-1.10	-3.80	N/A	5	0	94	1	7	73	N/A
8.49	1.03	B- / 7.2	11.9	0.97	N/A	14.93	280	-4.42	-4.82	49.2	0	95	0	5	111	85	N/A
7.88	1.95	B- / 7.1	8.1	0.43	N/A	8.93	1,345	-12.21	-12.80	N/A	5	36	0	59	61	25	13
5.36	1.68	B- / 7.9	7.7	1.84	11.8	14.63	209	-12.78	-13.12	N/A	3	0	93	4	15	35	N/A
5.86	1.73	B- / 7.5	10.0	2.19	10.5	15.66	614	-7.09	-9.45	N/A	3	0	91	6	9	45	14
5.77	1.73	B- / 7.6	9.9	2.23	13.6	16.03	575	-10.42	-12.35	N/A	1	0	91	8	14	41	10
5.35	1.75	B- / 7.6	9.6	2.37	13.0	16.34	433	-11.38	-12.55	N/A	1	0	93	6	13	38	10
9.97	1.84	C+ / 6.9	13.7	0.85	9.2	12.53	270	-13.57	-12.83	77.4	3	0	0	97	50	29	13
5.17	1.60	B- / 7.7	9.8	2.30	11.2	16.00	466	-11.50	-12.41	N/A	3	0	93	4	12	37	N/A
7.41	1.12	B / 8.1	11.0	0.87	N/A	15.78	607	-9.00	-9.58	35.6	0	100	0	0	6	46	5
2.14	1.84	C / 4.7	23.4	1.20	N/A	12.57	872	-11.69	-9.29	N/A	0	99	0	1	6	6	N/A
6.11	1.08	C+ / 6.6	12.1	2.87	N/A	15.62	331	0.58	-2.23	N/A	0	0	84	16	5	78	6
9.65	1.82	B- / 7.0	N/A	N/A	N/A	17.18	69	-14.61	-11.46	N/A	0	0	0	100	122	45	3
7.03	2.29	B- / 7.2	7.5	-253.44	N/A	10.86	663	-5.71	-10.41	N/A	5	2	6	87	33	31	N/A
0.40	2.31	B- / 7.2	8.8	-62.23	N/A	10.81	464	-9.34	-9.61	N/A	3	1	8	88	34	50	9
4.76	1.62	B- / 7.4	9.2	2.14	12.5	14.17	147	-4.73	-7.95	N/A	1	0	96	3	7	31	9
8.57	1.11	C+ / 6.2	13.3	0.77	17.0	12.29	278	-11.15	-13.27	201.6	24	53	11	12	128	25	3
1.53	N/A	C / 4.5	N/A	N/A	N/A	16.04	N/A	-14.34	-14.50	N/A	0	0	0	100	N/A	13	2
6.87	N/A	U /	N/A	N/A	N/A	8.73	N/A	13.97	N/A	N/A	0	0	0	100	N/A	N/A	N/A
4.43	1.16	B- / 7.5	N/A	N/A	N/A	13.99	179	-7.93	-8.59	N/A	0	0	0	100	15	46	3
5.32	1.23	C+ / 6.9	9.9	1.42	N/A	13.78	643	-6.68	-8.52	N/A	0	0	0	100	18	34	4
6.03	1.67	B- / 7.4	10.9	2.31	12.0	16.19	673	-4.76	-5.70	N/A	2	0	89	9	9	50	N/A
4.85	1.96	B- / 7.6	9.8	1.38	13.2	14.98	137	-8.34	-9.42	N/A	3	0	94	3	14	52	5
5.25	1.55	B- / 7.6	7.5	1.71	12.2	14.81	344	-14.31	-14.73	N/A	2	0	94	4	23	26	5
5.89	1.57	B- / 7.7	10.3	2.28	11.4	15.82	329	-13.46	-13.60	N/A	1	0	96	3	15	32	9
5.47	1.64	B- / 7.6	13.7	2.38	10.7	15.61	64	-6.47	-5.02	N/A	0	0	100	0	8	23	N/A
4.76	2.80	C+ / 6.7	12.7	2.07	11.7	14.15	32	8.69	7.30	N/A	1	0	97	2	8	45	N/A
3.68	2.20	B- / 7.0	9.3	1.69	N/A	25.09	416	-9.49	-11.45	N/A	7	0	93	0	17	56	N/A
3.81	2.42	C+ / 6.9	9.6	1.41	N/A	24.28	124	-8.20	-11.09	N/A	17	0	82	1	16	66	N/A
3.76	1.26	B- / 7.0	9.3	2.17	15.3	8.00	79	-11.25	-12.06	N/A	0	0	100	0	143	40	N/A

Denotes ETF Fund, N/A denotes number is not available

				PRICE			PERFORMANCE					
99 Pct = Best 0 Pct = Worst					52 Week			% Total Return Through 12/31/15				
											Annualized	
Fund Type	Fund Name	Ticker Symbol	Overall Investment Rating	Price As of 12/31/15	High	Low	Performance Rating/Pts	3 Mo	6 Mo	1Yr/Pct	3Yr/Pct	5Yr/Pct
MUN	Nuveen Muni Advantage	NMA	C+	13.85	14.41	12.68	C+ / 6.4	5.58	9.47	7.43 / 91	1.82 / 52	7.95 / 80
MUH	Nuveen Muni High Income Opport	NMZ	B+	13.82	14.19	12.87	B+ / 8.8	4.78	9.51	9.86 / 95	5.66 / 72	11.69 / 96
MUN	Nuveen Muni Income	NMI	B-	11.98	12.39	10.46	B / 7.8	12.88	10.60	5.65 / 86	3.98 / 64	8.28 / 83
MUN	Nuveen Muni Market Opportunity	NMO	B	13.79	14.23	12.71	B- / 7.0	6.18	10.25	6.89 / 89	2.92 / 59	8.01 / 81
MUN	Nuveen Muni Opportunity	NIO	B-	14.33	15.10	13.31	C+ / 6.4	3.05	7.79	3.92 / 81	2.51 / 57	8.46 / 84
MUN	Nuveen Muni Value	NUV	B+	10.18	10.27	9.28	B / 7.9	4.46	7.81	9.84 / 95	3.60 / 63	6.95 / 69
IN	Nuveen Nasdaq 100 Dynamic Overwrit	QQQX	A	19.37	19.96	14.92	A / 9.4	13.21	9.69	9.21 / 87	16.03 / 91	14.83 / 91
MUS	Nuveen NC Prem Inc Muni	NNC	C	13.10	13.52	12.25	C / 4.8	3.61	5.05	5.40 / 85	-0.98 / 34	4.02 / 51
MUN	Nuveen New Jersey Municipal Value	NJV	C	14.49	15.85	13.70	C / 5.2	6.44	9.12	4.17 / 82	-0.85 / 34	6.15 / 63
MUN	Nuveen New York Municipal Value 2	NYV	C+	15.30	15.62	14.17	C+ / 6.4	3.21	6.09	5.81 / 86	2.48 / 56	6.76 / 67
MUS	Nuveen NJ Div Adv Muni	NXJ	C+	13.50	14.16	12.53	C / 5.5	6.26	8.04	5.92 / 86	-0.27 / 36	6.66 / 66
MUS	Nuveen NY AMT/Fr Muni Income	NRK	C+	13.13	13.62	12.40	C+ / 5.6	5.13	6.76	6.90 / 89	-0.03 / 37	5.21 / 58
MUS	Nuveen NY Div Adv Muni	NAN	B	14.23	14.25	13.10	B- / 7.4	5.99	6.48	11.33 / 97	2.00 / 53	7.84 / 79
MUS	Nuveen NY Muni Value	NNY	B-	10.04	10.18	9.47	C+ / 6.8	4.42	5.90	6.70 / 89	2.21 / 54	6.31 / 64
MUS	Nuveen NY Select Tax-Free Inc Port	NXN	C+	13.70	14.38	12.90	C / 5.3	3.75	5.16	4.34 / 83	0.20 / 38	5.29 / 58
MUS	Nuveen OH Quality Inc Muni	NUO	C	15.26	16.05	14.12	C / 4.6	7.05	9.81	4.89 / 84	-1.97 / 31	7.17 / 72
MUS	Nuveen PA Investment Quality Muni	NQP	C+	13.70	14.79	12.90	C+ / 5.7	5.53	7.36	5.94 / 87	0.34 / 39	6.66 / 66
MUN	Nuveen Pennsylvania Municipal Valu	NPN	C+	15.03	16.81	14.51	C+ / 5.8	1.95	1.44	2.96 / 78	1.91 / 53	6.03 / 62
MUN	Nuveen Performance Plus Muni	NPP	B-	14.96	15.55	13.87	C+ / 6.8	6.76	10.36	7.38 / 91	2.34 / 55	8.90 / 87
GL	Nuveen Preferred and Income Term	JPI	B+	22.76	23.90	20.95	B / 7.6	7.10	7.49	10.60 / 89	6.24 / 65	--
GI	Nuveen Preferref Income Opps	JPC	B-	9.16	9.78	6.90	C+ / 6.5	4.12	3.22	5.69 / 80	4.90 / 61	10.73 / 70
MUN	Nuveen Prem Inc Muni	NPI	B	14.10	14.49	12.97	B- / 7.2	6.00	10.93	7.78 / 92	3.08 / 60	8.33 / 84
MUN	Nuveen Prem Inc Muni 4	NPT	B	13.38	14.03	12.57	B- / 7.2	4.19	6.16	6.41 / 88	3.00 / 60	9.34 / 89
MUN	Nuveen Premier Muni Inc	NPF	C+	13.66	14.49	12.72	C+ / 6.2	5.78	8.67	3.64 / 80	1.95 / 53	7.63 / 76
MUN	Nuveen Premium Income Muni 2	NPM	B	14.46	14.69	13.15	B- / 7.5	7.88	12.34	8.28 / 92	3.35 / 62	8.57 / 85
MUN	Nuveen Quality Inc Muni	NQU	B-	14.18	14.75	13.21	C+ / 6.7	6.04	10.01	7.64 / 91	2.10 / 54	7.26 / 73
MUN	Nuveen Quality Municipal	NQI	C+	13.64	13.83	12.58	C+ / 6.3	5.96	10.59	8.59 / 93	1.27 / 48	7.74 / 77
IN	Nuveen Quality Preferred Income	JTP	B	8.28	8.76	7.67	B- / 7.5	6.63	8.00	9.69 / 88	6.01 / 64	10.68 / 69
IN	Nuveen Quality Preferred Income 2	JPS	B	9.11	9.48	8.10	B- / 7.2	4.66	10.68	9.85 / 88	6.22 / 65	11.07 / 72
IN	Nuveen Quality Preferred Income 3	JHP	B	8.49	8.78	7.72	B / 7.6	8.02	7.82	9.71 / 88	6.00 / 64	9.82 / 64
GL	Nuveen Real Asset Income and Growt	JRI	C	15.24	20.26	14.15	C+ / 5.9	6.08	-8.47	-12.28 / 22	6.70 / 66	--
GI	Nuveen Real Estate Inc Fund	JRS	C+	10.62	12.30	9.82	B- / 7.1	7.85	8.51	-1.33 / 53	7.41 / 68	9.75 / 64
IN	Nuveen S&P 500 Buy Write Income	JPZ	A+	13.43	13.64	10.80	A- / 9.2	12.88	8.98	15.26 / 95	11.85 / 81	10.14 / 66
IN	Nuveen S&P 500 Dynamic Overwrite	JPG	B+	13.47	14.63	11.87	B- / 7.4	7.27	2.07	2.44 / 73	8.32 / 71	8.14 / 58
MUN	Nuveen Select Maturities Muni	NIM	B-	10.24	11.07	9.90	C+ / 5.6	2.99	2.08	-0.20 / 59	1.77 / 52	4.40 / 54
MUN	Nuveen Select Quality Muni	NQS	C+	14.05	14.65	13.12	C+ / 6.0	6.15	9.34	5.58 / 86	0.86 / 44	7.62 / 76
MUN	Nuveen Select T-F Inc Portf	NXP	C+	14.29	14.96	13.25	C+ / 6.1	6.18	7.60	4.03 / 82	1.68 / 51	5.82 / 61
MUN	Nuveen Select T-F Inc Portf 2	NXQ	B-	13.68	14.29	12.85	C+ / 6.4	4.90	6.87	4.38 / 83	2.49 / 56	6.08 / 62
MUN	Nuveen Select Tax-Free Inc 3	NXR	B	14.54	14.93	13.47	C+ / 6.9	6.61	6.92	5.81 / 86	3.13 / 61	6.87 / 69
GI	Nuveen Short Duration Credit Oppty	JSD	C-	14.83	17.57	13.93	C- / 3.3	0.60	-7.09	-4.72 / 40	-2.12 / 30	--
LP	Nuveen Sr Inc	NSL	C-	5.77	6.84	5.37	C- / 3.3	1.11	-7.89	-7.08 / 33	-2.00 / 31	2.30 / 35
IN	Nuveen Tax-Advant Tot Ret Strat Fd	JTA	B	11.67	14.05	10.97	B- / 7.2	4.85	-6.21	-3.66 / 43	9.77 / 74	8.88 / 60
GI	Nuveen Tax-Advantaged Dividend Grt	JTD	C+	13.91	16.57	13.00	C+ / 5.8	3.14	-7.25	-4.69 / 40	5.43 / 62	9.75 / 64
MUS	Nuveen TX Quality Inc Muni	NTX	C+	14.43	14.91	13.25	C+ / 5.8	6.55	8.15	3.89 / 81	0.90 / 44	3.99 / 51
MUS	Nuveen VA Premium Income Municipal	NPV	C+	13.60	14.25	13.12	C+ / 5.9	1.92	4.27	9.22 / 94	0.08 / 38	4.16 / 52
COH	Pacholder High Yield Fund	PHF	D+	6.07	7.89	5.83	D+ / 2.7	-1.67	-8.91	-9.85 / 26	-3.95 / 27	2.95 / 38
MTG	PCM Fund	PCM	C-	9.24	11.10	8.00	C- / 4.0	-0.89	-3.45	-5.72 / 37	0.33 / 38	6.78 / 54
MUS	PIMCO CA Municipal Income Fund	PCQ	B	15.70	16.57	14.04	B+ / 8.3	4.61	14.02	7.48 / 91	5.43 / 71	12.92 / 97
MUS	PIMCO CA Municipal Income Fund II	PCK	B+	9.94	10.39	9.32	B+ / 8.6	4.23	10.10	13.01 / 98	4.42 / 66	11.00 / 95
MUS	PIMCO CA Municipal Income Fund III	PZC	A-	11.92	11.97	10.23	A / 9.5	9.28	20.50	20.31 / 99	8.42 / 84	13.94 / 98
COH	PIMCO Corporate and Income Oppty	PTY	C-	13.34	16.97	12.03	C / 4.3	3.69	-2.57	-8.78 / 29	1.18 / 43	8.99 / 61
COH	PIMCO Corporate and ncome Strategy	PCN	C-	13.40	15.75	11.93	C / 4.6	2.97	-1.62	-4.21 / 42	1.21 / 43	8.31 / 59

* Denotes ETF Fund, N/A denotes number is not available

Incl. in Returns		RISK				NET ASSETS		VALUATION			ASSET					FUND MANAGER	
			3 Year					Premium / Discount									
Dividend Yield %	Expense Ratio	Risk Rating/ Pts	Standard Deviation	Beta	Avg Duration	NAV as of 12/31/15	Total $(Mil)	As of 12/31/15	1 Year Average	Wtd Avg P/E	Cash %	Stocks %	Bonds %	Other %	Portfolio Turnover Ratio	Manager Quality Pct	Manager Tenure (Years)
5.72	1.71	**B- / 7.6**	10.0	2.35	11.9	15.52	606	-10.76	-12.09	N/A	3	0	91	6	8	33	14
6.60	1.28	**C+ / 6.9**	10.5	1.95	11.9	13.69	686	0.95	-0.93	N/A	2	0	88	10	13	69	13
4.16	0.76	**C+ / 6.8**	14.1	2.46	10.9	11.55	95	3.72	-0.39	N/A	3	0	92	5	15	40	N/A
5.53	1.76	**B- / 7.7**	9.5	2.14	11.7	15.45	699	-10.74	-12.01	N/A	2	0	94	4	10	44	14
6.11	1.49	**B- / 7.8**	9.6	1.78	13.5	15.79	1,506	-9.25	-9.33	N/A	1	0	92	7	15	53	10
3.83	0.56	**B- / 7.7**	8.3	1.89	11.1	10.28	2,099	-0.97	-3.41	N/A	2	0	94	4	17	53	29
7.23	1.00	**B- / 7.2**	13.2	1.07	N/A	19.98	726	-3.05	-6.18	119.9	0	100	0	0	17	72	5
4.49	1.54	**B- / 7.8**	7.9	1.98	12.4	15.24	246	-14.04	-14.23	N/A	1	0	96	3	12	26	9
4.06	0.87	**B- / 7.4**	8.3	1.36	N/A	16.14	25	-10.22	-11.67	N/A	1	0	96	3	13	34	N/A
4.12	0.75	**B- / 7.5**	8.8	1.53	N/A	16.00	37	-4.38	-6.66	N/A	1	0	92	7	11	58	N/A
4.36	1.71	**B- / 7.7**	9.0	2.01	10.3	15.69	669	-13.96	-14.35	N/A	1	0	97	2	14	29	5
5.35	1.43	**B- / 7.6**	9.2	1.96	14.2	14.58	1,258	-9.95	-10.67	N/A	1	0	96	3	18	30	N/A
5.61	1.70	**B- / 7.6**	8.5	1.80	13.0	15.46	475	-7.96	-10.42	N/A	4	0	88	8	17	47	N/A
3.88	0.60	**B- / 7.7**	7.8	1.59	13.6	10.10	152	-0.59	-2.40	N/A	1	0	97	2	31	52	N/A
4.03	0.43	**B / 8.0**	8.2	1.15	13.1	14.44	57	-5.12	-5.85	N/A	1	0	96	3	16	44	N/A
5.71	1.62	**B- / 7.4**	9.8	2.01	11.9	17.01	315	-10.29	-11.65	N/A	2	0	97	1	15	21	N/A
5.91	1.60	**B- / 7.6**	10.2	2.15	11.8	15.76	593	-13.07	-13.49	N/A	7	0	92	1	9	30	5
4.15	0.85	**B- / 7.7**	7.9	1.37	N/A	16.38	20	-8.24	-7.30	N/A	5	0	94	1	5	55	N/A
5.86	1.76	**B- / 7.5**	10.0	1.98	10.9	16.32	980	-8.33	-10.13	N/A	4	0	95	1	10	46	14
0.15	1.66	**B- / 7.8**	8.3	0.36	N/A	24.38	566	-6.64	-7.78	N/A	0	0	0	100	26	94	N/A
8.78	1.63	**B- / 7.6**	9.0	0.38	N/A	10.22	1,013	-10.37	-10.24	N/A	6	36	57	1	44	73	N/A
5.83	1.58	**B- / 7.6**	10.0	2.30	13.5	15.61	990	-9.67	-11.52	N/A	9	0	90	1	17	43	10
6.10	1.64	**B- / 7.5**	10.6	2.15	12.5	14.51	625	-7.79	-8.30	N/A	7	0	92	1	13	48	N/A
5.71	1.66	**B- / 7.6**	10.8	2.37	10.4	15.28	305	-10.60	-11.20	N/A	9	0	90	1	11	35	N/A
5.98	1.58	**B- / 7.6**	10.4	2.26	12.9	15.65	1,106	-7.60	-10.67	N/A	7	0	92	1	15	46	19
5.80	1.87	**B- / 7.4**	10.6	2.38	12.5	15.89	768	-10.76	-12.24	N/A	5	0	94	1	9	37	14
5.23	1.54	**B- / 7.4**	9.9	2.33	11.8	15.28	580	-10.73	-12.81	N/A	2	0	91	7	14	31	N/A
7.97	1.69	**B- / 7.4**	10.6	0.27	N/A	9.01	590	-8.10	-9.38	N/A	8	0	0	92	9	83	N/A
7.64	1.64	**B- / 7.4**	10.8	0.24	N/A	9.60	1,174	-5.10	-7.18	N/A	11	0	0	89	8	84	N/A
4.21	1.74	**B- / 7.6**	9.6	0.38	N/A	9.39	226	-9.58	-11.11	N/A	13	0	0	87	10	76	N/A
9.80	1.91	**C+ / 6.4**	18.5	0.98	N/A	17.27	194	-11.75	-6.56	N/A	0	0	0	100	139	80	N/A
9.04	1.75	**C+ / 6.8**	20.7	0.70	N/A	11.71	349	-9.31	-6.79	93.6	0	66	0	34	61	61	N/A
7.42	1.02	**B- / 7.8**	7.8	0.47	N/A	13.34	1,414	0.67	-5.89	62.6	3	96	0	1	14	90	N/A
.75	0.96	**B / 8.0**	7.9	0.62	N/A	14.72	252	-8.49	-9.15	52.3	0	99	0	1	8	70	2
3.05	0.58	**B / 8.5**	7.1	1.33	9.0	10.55	132	-2.94	-1.87	N/A	1	0	98	1	16	57	N/A
.42	1.67	**B- / 7.5**	9.7	2.06	11.7	15.78	552	-10.96	-12.22	N/A	7	0	92	1	14	32	14
.82	0.32	**B- / 7.7**	8.6	1.79	9.4	15.17	251	-5.80	-7.01	N/A	1	0	98	1	28	45	17
.90	0.37	**B- / 7.9**	8.9	2.08	10.1	14.67	259	-6.75	-6.93	N/A	2	0	97	1	19	43	17
.76	0.38	**B- / 7.7**	9.4	2.11	8.8	15.44	200	-5.83	-6.69	N/A	1	0	98	1	21	47	17
.85	1.78	**B- / 7.0**	7.3	0.38	N/A	16.77	188	-11.57	-11.52	N/A	0	0	0	100	31	22	5
.28	2.37	**B- / 7.0**	8.8	-154.05	N/A	6.47	277	-10.82	-11.18	N/A	2	1	7	90	34	31	17
.32	1.85	**B- / 7.6**	14.6	1.17	N/A	13.10	199	-10.92	-9.56	36.8	7	68	0	25	34	30	12
.29	1.95	**B- / 7.7**	11.3	0.93	N/A	15.67	251	-11.23	-9.62	43.7	4	72	1	23	32	25	9
.53	2.33	**B- / 7.8**	8.5	1.87	11.6	15.69	158	-8.03	-9.73	N/A	2	0	97	1	12	35	N/A
.81	1.67	**B- / 7.2**	10.6	2.12	11.1	14.65	260	-7.17	-7.27	N/A	5	0	94	1	17	27	N/A
.88	2.04	**C+ / 6.3**	13.8	1.86	N/A	6.98	106	-13.04	-12.78	N/A	0	0	100	0	43	23	N/A
.39	1.89	**C+ / 6.7**	11.4	2.34	15.8	9.82	124	-5.91	-3.89	N/A	1	0	97	2	11	36	15
.89	1.32	**C+ / 6.7**	11.6	2.40	14.4	14.61	68	7.46	6.46	N/A	0	0	100	0	11	56	5
49	1.32	**B- / 7.2**	10.7	1.97	13.0	8.95	273	11.06	10.63	N/A	1	0	98	1	12	62	5
04	1.30	**C+ / 6.8**	11.1	2.21	14.6	10.31	223	15.62	8.13	N/A	0	0	100	0	24	81	5
92	0.91	**C / 5.3**	19.7	1.39	12.0	13.10	1,082	1.83	5.15	N/A	0	0	94	6	44	62	N/A
94	1.09	**C+ / 6.3**	14.1	1.21	13.1	14.01	114	-4.35	-2.05	N/A	11	0	84	5	48	68	N/A

Denotes ETF Fund, N/A denotes number is not available

Fund Type	Fund Name (99 Pct = Best, 0 Pct = Worst)	Ticker Symbol	Overall Investment Rating	PRICE: Price As of 12/31/15	PRICE: 52 Week High	PRICE: 52 Week Low	PERFORMANCE: Performance Rating/Pts	% Total Return Through 12/31/15: 3 Mo	6 Mo	1Yr/Pct	Annualized: 3Yr/Pct	Annualized: 5Yr/Pct
GL	PIMCO Dynamic Credit Income	PCI	C-	18.03	21.40	17.17	C- / 3.3	2.03	-4.66	-2.57 / 48	--	--
GL	PIMCO Dynamic Income	PDI	B+	27.36	30.73	23.60	B+ / 8.7	5.42	6.88	7.30 / 84	12.01 / 82	--
GL	PIMCO Global StocksPLUS&Inc	PGP	C	18.12	23.65	13.62	B / 8.1	23.51	8.96	4.57 / 78	8.30 / 71	6.39 / 52
COH	PIMCO High Income Fund	PHK	D+	8.18	12.73	6.87	C- / 3.7	11.88	-13.42	-17.99 / 15	0.87 / 41	3.38 / 40
GL	Pimco Income Opportunity Fund	PKO	C-	21.17	26.98	19.98	C- / 3.9	-2.94	-7.18	-5.70 / 37	0.70 / 40	7.83 / 57
LP	PIMCO Income Strategy Fund	PFL	C-	9.74	12.02	9.04	C- / 3.8	3.13	-5.81	-9.14 / 28	-0.03 / 37	6.48 / 52
LP	PIMCO Income Strategy Fund II	PFN	C	8.77	10.38	8.28	C / 4.7	3.12	-5.70	-2.72 / 47	1.58 / 46	7.70 / 57
MUN	PIMCO Municipal Income Fund	PMF	B+	15.45	16.06	13.61	A- / 9.0	8.07	16.35	15.69 / 99	6.11 / 73	12.07 / 97
MUN	PIMCO Municipal Income Fund II	PML	B	12.51	12.85	11.46	B / 7.9	5.04	11.66	11.13 / 97	4.19 / 66	11.89 / 96
MUN	PIMCO Municipal Income Fund III	PMX	B+	11.51	11.74	10.53	B+ / 8.4	6.32	10.27	11.27 / 97	3.73 / 63	9.61 / 91
MUS	PIMCO NY Muni Income Fund	PNF	B+	11.90	12.10	10.92	B / 8.0	3.82	8.06	10.02 / 95	4.08 / 65	9.62 / 91
MUS	PIMCO NY Municipal Income Fund II	PNI	B	12.35	12.98	10.94	B / 7.9	4.69	8.76	8.71 / 93	4.70 / 68	10.68 / 94
MUS	PIMCO NY Municipal Income Fund III	PYN	B+	10.27	10.63	9.16	B+ / 8.5	5.45	14.11	11.21 / 97	5.19 / 70	10.86 / 94
MTG	PIMCO Strategic Income	RCS	C	8.95	9.90	6.01	C+ / 5.9	8.18	8.67	4.72 / 78	2.21 / 49	8.76 / 60
GL	Pioneer Diversified High Income Tr	HNW	C-	14.59	17.66	13.31	C- / 3.6	2.66	-6.10	-8.46 / 30	-0.78 / 34	4.06 / 43
LP	Pioneer Floating Rate Trust	PHD	C	10.85	11.80	9.36	C- / 4.1	-0.51	-1.58	1.31 / 69	-0.41 / 36	3.27 / 39
GL	Pioneer High Income Trust	PHT	D-	9.50	17.39	8.90	D / 1.7	-1.17	-12.15	-38.01 / 4	-7.73 / 20	0.74 / 30
MUH	Pioneer Municipal High Income Adv	MAV	C	13.35	15.70	12.21	C+ / 6.0	4.64	11.42	-3.89 / 43	2.16 / 54	10.52 / 93
MUH	Pioneer Municipal High Income Trus	MHI	C	13.06	14.89	11.95	C / 5.4	3.51	12.10	-0.47 / 57	0.30 / 39	7.80 / 78
GI	Principal Real Estate Income	PGZ	C-	16.68	20.00	15.62	C- / 3.0	-0.28	-4.79	-2.54 / 48	--	--
GL	Prudential Glb Sht Dur Hi Yield In	GHY	C-	14.15	16.77	13.21	C- / 3.8	7.40	-1.39	-2.02 / 50	-1.67 / 32	--
COH	Prudential Sht Dur Hi Yield Fd Inc	ISD	C-	14.60	16.77	13.53	C- / 4.1	3.89	-0.48	-2.07 / 50	-0.58 / 35	--
GEN	Putnam High Income Securities	PCF	C	7.31	8.35	6.83	C / 4.7	4.70	-4.26	-5.20 / 38	1.56 / 46	2.84 / 37
MUN	Putnam Managed Muni Inc Tr	PMM	B-	7.36	7.47	6.86	B- / 7.2	4.19	8.22	8.40 / 93	2.27 / 55	8.32 / 83
GEN	Putnam Master Intermediate Inc Tr	PIM	C+	4.55	5.00	4.30	C / 5.4	3.54	-0.48	-0.99 / 55	2.55 / 51	1.57 / 32
MUN	Putnam Muni Opp Tr	PMO	B	12.28	12.62	11.47	B- / 7.1	4.72	8.68	8.39 / 93	3.19 / 61	9.26 / 89
GEN	Putnam Premier Income Trust	PPT	C	4.95	5.36	4.60	C / 5.5	3.67	0.52	-0.16 / 59	2.79 / 52	1.94 / 33
UT	Reaves Utility Income Trust	UTG	C+	25.97	33.90	24.11	C+ / 5.8	-6.81	-7.37	-15.60 / 17	8.15 / 70	10.48 / 68
GI	RENN Fund	RCG	D-	0.90	1.39	0.74	D- / 1.0	-12.62	-26.83	-30.23 / 7	-14.30 / 13	-13.88 / 10
GI	RMR Real Estate Income	RIF	B-	19.28	22.69	17.44	B- / 7.4	8.64	5.93	-2.26 / 50	8.41 / 71	7.39 / 56
GL	Royce Global Value Trust	RGT	C-	7.45	8.80	6.84	D+ / 2.6	5.77	-9.28	-6.30 / 35	--	--
GR	Royce Micro-Cap Trust	RMT	C	7.26	10.14	6.95	C+ / 6.1	2.34	-12.12	-14.20 / 19	8.40 / 71	7.21 / 55
GR	Royce Value Trust	RVT	C	11.77	14.82	10.83	C+ / 5.8	5.93	-9.48	-9.44 / 27	6.11 / 64	5.26 / 49
IN	Salient Midstream and MLP Fund	SMM	E+	9.53	23.97	8.07	E+ / 0.6	-33.38	-50.36	-57.26 / 1	-14.79 / 12	--
GL	Self Storage Group	SELF	B-	3.75	3.98	3.28	C+ / 6.8	-4.34	7.69	8.94 / 86	6.32 / 65	6.43 / 52
IN	Source Capital	SOR	B+	66.26	76.43	62.85	B / 8.0	-0.57	-6.84	0.25 / 62	12.33 / 82	10.30 / 67
MUN	Special Opportunities Fund	SPE	C	13.22	15.66	12.62	C / 4.8	-6.24	-13.59	-15.20 / 18	4.90 / 69	6.28 / 64
GR	Sprott Focus Trust	FUND	C-	5.81	7.63	5.30	C- / 3.6	0.82	-13.64	-13.34 / 20	0.91 / 41	1.11 / 31
EM	Stone Harbor Emg Markets Income	EDF	D-	12.05	17.51	11.41	D / 1.7	1.43	-14.40	-9.79 / 26	-11.51 / 15	-3.66 / 21
GL	Stone Harbor Emg Markets Total Inc	EDI	D-	11.37	15.34	10.91	D- / 1.4	3.46	-13.30	-14.47 / 18	-14.61 / 12	--
GL	Strategic Global Income Fund	SGL	C	8.76	9.13	7.73	C / 5.5	13.23	11.10	11.86 / 91	-0.94 / 34	3.36 / 40
FO	Swiss Helvetia Fund	SWZ	C+	10.56	12.63	10.31	B- / 7.0	2.00	-5.21	0.88 / 66	8.51 / 71	6.15 / 51
FO	Taiwan Fund	TWN	C-	14.63	18.45	12.95	C- / 3.6	-1.48	-18.45	-8.90 / 29	1.09 / 42	-1.71 / 24
GI	TCW Strategic Income Fund	TSI	C+	5.27	5.50	5.00	C+ / 5.7	0.96	3.52	1.06 / 67	3.32 / 54	8.88 / 60
HL	Tekla Healthcare Investors	HQH	B	29.66	39.17	25.00	A+ / 9.7	4.67	-10.66	4.01 / 77	28.75 / 98	26.73 / 99
GL	Tekla Healthcare Opportunities	THQ	C-	17.39	21.50	15.54	D+ / 2.7	7.71	-8.39	-7.01 / 33	--	--
HL	Tekla Life Sciences Investors	HQL	B-	23.64	31.21	21.13	A+ / 9.7	4.25	-10.88	5.44 / 80	26.19 / 97	27.27 / 99
GL	Tekla World Healthcare		U	15.83	N/A	N/A	U /	9.15	-17.86	--	--	--
FO	Templeton Dragon Fund	TDF	D+	17.81	28.06	16.85	C- / 3.2	1.95	-10.94	-10.21 / 25	-1.82 / 31	0.18 / 28
EM	Templeton Emerging Markets Fd	EMF	D-	9.97	16.52	9.45	D- / 1.2	0.60	-22.86	-26.92 / 9	-13.38 / 14	-10.28 / 13
EM	Templeton Emerging Markets Income	TEI	D	9.97	11.30	9.10	D+ / 2.3	6.28	-3.10	-4.44 / 41	-9.64 / 18	-0.63 / 26
GL	Templeton Global Income	GIM	D+	6.35	7.51	5.93	D+ / 2.6	5.15	-7.67	-8.97 / 28	-6.22 / 23	-1.27 / 25

* Denotes ETF Fund, N/A denotes number is not availabl

ncl. in Returns		RISK				NET ASSETS		VALUATION			ASSET					FUND MANAGER	
			3 Year					Premium / Discount									
'idend 'ield %	Expense Ratio	Risk Rating/ Pts	Standard Deviation	Beta	Avg Dura- tion	NAV as of 12/31/15	Total $(Mil)	As of 12/31/15	1 Year Average	Wtd Avg P/E	Cash %	Stocks %	Bonds %	Other %	Portfolio Turnover Ratio	Manaaer Quality Pct	Manager Tenure (Years)
6.58	2.36	**B- / 7.3**	N/A	N/A	N/A	20.42	3,132	-11.70	-11.99	N/A	0	0	0	100	35	63	3
6.97	3.12	**C+ / 6.7**	11.6	0.79	N/A	27.17	1,398	0.70	-4.25	N/A	0	0	0	100	10	97	N/A
2.15	2.30	**C / 4.3**	29.3	1.41	15.0	10.88	135	66.54	54.44	N/A	1	0	98	1	92	87	11
5.18	1.18	**C / 4.7**	25.2	2.95	11.9	6.76	950	21.01	38.41	N/A	3	0	95	2	58	66	N/A
0.77	2.01	**C+ / 5.8**	12.1	0.70	13.7	22.68	425	-6.66	-4.18	N/A	0	0	94	6	175	88	9
1.09	1.30	**C+ / 6.7**	10.8	-106.50	13.4	10.34	166	-5.80	-4.49	N/A	28	0	72	0	67	53	N/A
0.38	1.16	**B- / 7.1**	10.6	-82.23	13.6	9.26	607	-5.29	-4.87	N/A	35	0	65	0	63	71	N/A
6.31	1.25	**C+ / 6.3**	15.9	3.92	14.6	13.26	69	16.52	12.42	N/A	4	0	96	0	9	29	5
6.24	1.16	**B- / 7.1**	11.8	2.60	14.8	12.39	742	0.97	-0.54	N/A	8	0	92	0	10	41	5
6.50	1.23	**B- / 7.1**	10.8	2.58	15.4	11.13	355	3.41	2.01	N/A	8	0	92	0	5	43	5
5.75	1.39	**B- / 7.4**	11.7	2.79	13.4	12.10	74	-1.65	-3.41	N/A	7	0	93	0	1	38	5
3.44	1.40	**C+ / 6.8**	12.5	2.74	14.3	11.41	124	8.24	7.62	N/A	9	0	91	0	7	47	5
3.13	1.55	**B- / 7.0**	10.4	1.76	14.4	9.55	53	7.54	4.90	N/A	0	0	100	0	13	69	5
5.81	1.18	**C+ / 6.0**	12.5	2.75	15.3	8.03	356	11.46	6.44	N/A	2	0	97	1	90	46	11
3.46	1.85	**C+ / 6.7**	12.4	0.78	N/A	16.00	153	-8.81	-8.87	N/A	3	0	96	1	48	84	N/A
3.64	1.80	**B- / 7.6**	6.7	-46.88	N/A	12.04	317	-9.88	-10.40	N/A	0	5	8	87	61	58	N/A
.53	1.33	**C / 4.7**	16.5	1.11	N/A	9.42	344	0.85	6.31	N/A	0	0	93	7	37	55	N/A
.19	1.22	**C+ / 6.8**	15.1	2.75	13.2	12.47	300	7.06	11.24	N/A	2	0	97	1	20	29	N/A
.43	1.03	**C+ / 6.9**	14.1	2.52	12.3	13.38	303	-2.39	-0.17	N/A	2	0	97	1	14	25	N/A
.43	2.59	**B- / 7.9**	N/A	N/A	N/A	19.31	145	-13.62	-10.42	N/A	0	0	0	100	18	49	3
.33	1.61	**C+ / 6.9**	10.6	0.97	N/A	16.04	699	-11.78	-10.94	N/A	0	0	0	100	62	83	N/A
.04	1.58	**C+ / 6.9**	9.1	0.65	N/A	16.37	593	-10.81	-11.16	N/A	0	0	0	100	58	63	4
.07	0.90	**B- / 7.6**	8.8	0.88	N/A	8.24	127	-11.29	-12.89	N/A	2	2	40	56	35	75	N/A
.92	0.91	**B- / 7.3**	10.1	2.03	12.3	8.01	446	-8.11	-9.68	N/A	1	0	98	1	14	44	27
.86	0.96	**B / 8.0**	6.0	0.13	N/A	4.99	278	-8.82	-10.04	N/A	0	0	100	0	724	83	22
.81	0.96	**B- / 7.8**	8.5	2.03	11.8	13.42	522	-8.49	-9.87	N/A	1	0	98	1	12	50	17
.30	0.87	**C+ / 6.1**	5.5	-0.04	14.7	5.49	670	-9.84	-10.77	N/A	0	0	100	0	654	84	22
.99	1.71	**B- / 7.5**	15.6	0.89	N/A	28.21	949	-7.94	-4.29	28.3	1	97	0	2	26	54	12
.00	4.86	**C / 4.7**	23.9	0.04	N/A	1.54	10	-41.56	-39.44	N/A	1	87	0	12	43	11	22
.85	2.12	**C+ / 6.9**	16.6	0.61	N/A	23.53	193	-18.06	-19.07	N/A	3	97	0	0	15	69	N/A
.34	1.49	**B- / 7.1**	N/A	N/A	N/A	8.81	95	-15.44	-15.41	N/A	0	0	0	100	43	27	N/A
61	1.18	**C+ / 5.9**	14.3	1.02	N/A	8.59	387	-15.48	-13.63	55.4	11	88	0	1	41	30	23
57	0.61	**B- / 7.0**	13.2	1.01	N/A	13.56	1,232	-13.20	-13.34	41.2	6	93	0	1	40	23	30
49	2.44	**C- / 3.4**	31.4	1.70	N/A	10.94	493	-12.89	-11.88	N/A	0	0	0	100	46	2	N/A
93	3.71	**B- / 7.3**	16.1	-0.32	N/A	5.70	38	-34.21	-31.75	N/A	0	56	41	3	1	92	N/A
75	0.80	**B / 8.1**	13.4	0.98	N/A	73.07	696	-9.32	-9.47	32.2	4	89	4	3	6	61	20
65	1.40	**C+ / 6.7**	10.9	-0.36	N/A	15.11	172	-12.51	-11.55	10.8	10	0	89	1	59	95	N/A
26	1.15	**C+ / 6.9**	13.4	0.90	N/A	6.87	188	-15.43	-14.63	56.4	13	86	0	1	29	17	14
93	2.07	**C / 4.7**	20.2	1.02	N/A	13.51	N/A	-10.81	-7.63	N/A	0	0	0	100	97	30	N/A
95	2.13	**C / 4.6**	19.2	0.87	N/A	13.39	161	-15.09	-13.32	N/A	0	0	0	100	79	16	N/A
48	1.16	**C+ / 6.9**	10.9	0.66	8.7	9.11	186	-3.84	-12.05	N/A	3	0	96	1	46	83	N/A
63	1.41	**C+ / 6.4**	11.7	0.73	N/A	12.33	340	-14.36	-13.74	N/A	0	96	0	4	48	89	N/A
00	1.86	**C+ / 6.4**	13.7	0.70	N/A	16.74	138	-12.60	-10.40	N/A	0	95	0	5	92	49	5
64	0.87	**B / 8.1**	8.4	0.23	N/A	5.83	284	-9.61	-10.40	N/A	0	0	89	11	12	78	N/A
59	1.00	**C / 5.1**	23.8	1.48	N/A	30.72	1,104	-3.45	1.10	310.3	7	82	0	11	37	91	12
33	1.60	**B- / 7.3**	N/A	N/A	N/A	19.49	824	-10.77	-9.13	N/A	0	0	0	100	93	31	N/A
36	1.17	**C / 4.9**	24.6	1.47	N/A	24.18	463	-2.23	0.33	359.1	5	84	0	11	46	88	24
37	N/A	**U /**	N/A	N/A	N/A	18.40	N/A	-13.97	N/A	N/A	0	0	0	100	N/A	N/A	N/A
73	1.35	**C+ / 5.7**	21.3	0.71	N/A	20.51	925	-13.16	-13.12	75.3	0	99	0	1	22	77	22
13	1.37	**C / 4.3**	18.3	1.20	N/A	11.13	240	-10.42	-10.85	N/A	0	80	0	20	19	27	29
92	1.09	**C / 5.3**	11.4	0.97	7.2	11.56	576	-13.75	-13.49	N/A	4	0	95	1	24	30	N/A
72	0.73	**C+ / 6.5**	10.9	0.35	6.0	7.25	990	-12.41	-10.91	N/A	5	0	94	1	36	33	28

)enotes ETF Fund, N/A denotes number is not available

Fund Type	Fund Name (99 Pct = Best, 0 Pct = Worst)	Ticker Symbol	Overall Investment Rating	PRICE: Price As of 12/31/15	PRICE: 52 Week High	PRICE: 52 Week Low	PERFORMANCE: Performance Rating/Pts	% Total Return Through 12/31/15: 3 Mo	6 Mo	1Yr/Pct	Annualized: 3Yr/Pct	Annualized: 5Yr/Pct
FO	Thai Fund	TTF	D-	6.86	11.98	6.51	C- / 3.5	-2.36	-15.38	-10.43 / 25	0.86 / 41	12.00 / 78
GI	The Cushing MLP Total Return Fund	SRV	E+	10.67	32.45	8.82	E / 0.3	-11.85	-41.83	-63.06 / 1	-28.40 / 4	-17.14 / 6
FO	The European Equity Fund	EEA	C+	8.06	9.02	7.71	C+ / 6.0	2.54	-4.56	-0.06 / 60	5.02 / 61	3.96 / 43
FO	The New Ireland Fund	IRL	A+	13.93	15.14	12.11	A+ / 9.8	22.23	20.51	36.24 / 99	25.10 / 97	21.61 / 98
LP	THL Credit Senior Loan	TSL	D+	15.86	19.49	14.32	C / 5.3	6.75	-2.20	0.58 / 64	--	--
GL	Tortoise Energy Independence Fund	NDP	D-	11.28	21.99	9.95	D- / 1.0	-11.71	-34.63	-35.47 / 5	-13.85 / 13	--
EN	Tortoise Energy Infrastr Corp	TYG	D	27.82	45.86	21.31	D / 1.8	-2.31	-21.37	-33.14 / 6	-6.01 / 23	--
GR	Tortoise MLP Fund Inc	NTG	D	17.34	27.40	13.25	D / 2.0	-1.04	-14.45	-32.74 / 7	-5.82 / 23	-0.20 / 27
EN	Tortoise Pipeline & Enrgy Fund Inc	TTP	E+	14.51	30.94	12.16	E+ / 0.8	-23.95	-42.11	-50.96 / 1	-12.38 / 14	--
EN	Tortoise Power and Energy Inf Fund	TPZ	D	16.78	28.78	14.88	D / 1.6	-12.15	-25.40	-30.30 / 7	-6.94 / 21	-0.45 / 27
IN	Tri-Continental Corporation	TY	B+	20.02	22.20	18.01	B / 7.6	3.91	-3.84	-2.04 / 50	10.60 / 77	11.53 / 75
FO	Turkish Investment Fund	TKF	E+	7.78	11.90	7.31	D- / 1.4	-3.42	-19.75	-26.92 / 9	-11.00 / 16	-5.89 / 18
GL	Virtus Global Multi-Sector Income	VGI	C-	14.13	17.49	13.08	C- / 4.2	3.60	-5.16	0.40 / 63	-0.06 / 37	--
GI	Virtus Total Return	DCA	C+	3.81	4.90	3.60	C+ / 5.9	1.94	-10.43	-6.71 / 34	6.48 / 66	8.82 / 60
GL	Voya Asia Pacific High Div Eq Inc	IAE	D	9.03	12.50	8.02	D / 2.1	8.22	-18.00	-11.49 / 23	-8.73 / 19	-4.93 / 19
EM	Voya Emerging Markets High Div Eqt	IHD	D-	7.40	10.86	7.00	D- / 1.4	0.41	-18.44	-19.05 / 14	-12.70 / 14	--
GL	Voya Glbl Eqty Div & Prem Oppty	IGD	C	7.00	8.62	5.54	C / 5.0	3.75	-8.05	-5.56 / 37	2.80 / 52	2.73 / 37
GL	Voya Global Advantage and Prem Opp	IGA	C+	10.45	12.81	10.18	C+ / 6.1	2.75	-10.39	0.22 / 62	6.21 / 65	5.04 / 48
GR	Voya Infrastructure Indus & Mtrls	IDE	C-	12.26	15.95	11.13	C- / 3.5	6.04	-8.41	-11.78 / 23	-0.70 / 35	0.56 / 29
GL	Voya International High Div Eq Inc	IID	D+	6.36	8.49	6.12	D+ / 2.6	3.36	-16.55	-11.11 / 24	-4.59 / 25	-1.62 / 24
EN	Voya Natural Resources Equity Inc	IRR	D	5.46	9.50	5.36	D- / 1.5	-4.86	-21.12	-25.34 / 10	-10.40 / 17	-8.87 / 15
LP	Voya Prime Rate Trust	PPR	C	5.06	5.69	4.62	C- / 4.2	3.59	-1.41	1.51 / 70	-0.60 / 35	3.94 / 43
GL	Wells Fargo Global Div Oppty	EOD	C-	5.92	7.80	5.51	C- / 3.8	2.32	-10.10	-11.39 / 23	1.22 / 43	1.34 / 3
COH	Wells Fargo Income Oppty	EAD	C-	7.45	9.09	6.95	C- / 3.4	2.03	-7.71	-7.05 / 33	-1.62 / 32	4.21 / 4
GL	Wells Fargo Multi-Sector Inc	ERC	D+	11.32	13.80	10.53	D+ / 2.9	2.26	-7.45	-9.69 / 26	-3.75 / 27	2.15 / 3
UT	Wells Fargo Utilities&High Inc	ERH	C+	11.20	14.00	10.30	C+ / 6.5	7.60	1.58	-7.57 / 32	6.97 / 67	6.88 / 5
EM	Western Asset Emerging Market Debt	ESD	D+	13.73	16.40	13.00	D+ / 2.5	5.46	-3.56	-4.18 / 42	-7.58 / 20	1.92 / 3
EM	Western Asset Emerging Mkts Inc	EMD	D+	9.73	11.52	9.36	D+ / 2.6	5.93	-2.90	-1.62 / 52	-7.22 / 21	2.24 / 3
GL	Western Asset Global Corp Def Oppt	GDO	C-	15.80	18.34	15.50	C- / 3.6	2.72	-3.70	-5.86 / 36	-1.27 / 33	5.15 / 4
GL	Western Asset Global High Income	EHI	D+	8.72	11.35	8.34	D+ / 2.6	1.11	-10.46	-11.48 / 23	-5.22 / 24	1.94 / 3
GL	Western Asset Global Partners Inc	GDF	D	7.73	9.86	7.21	D / 2.2	-0.02	-11.92	-12.30 / 22	-7.76 / 20	0.38 / 2
GL	Western Asset High Inc Fd II	HIX	D+	6.31	8.29	6.09	D+ / 2.5	0.91	-11.37	-14.78 / 18	-4.99 / 25	2.10 / 3
COH	Western Asset High Income Opp Inc.	HIO	C-	4.69	5.43	4.35	C- / 3.1	3.11	-5.87	-5.49 / 37	-3.53 / 28	2.71 / 3
COH	Western Asset High Yld Def Opp	HYI	C-	14.10	16.75	13.41	C- / 3.7	4.86	-5.14	-2.30 / 49	-1.37 / 32	3.10 / 3
GEI	Western Asset Income Fund	PAI	C	13.02	14.14	12.84	C / 4.7	-0.31	2.00	2.13 / 72	0.28 / 38	5.54 / 4
MUN	Western Asset Intermediate Muni	SBI	B+	10.21	10.71	9.52	B- / 7.4	3.63	6.73	11.02 / 96	2.53 / 57	6.99 / 7
COH	Western Asset Managed High Income	MHY	C-	4.52	5.28	4.11	C- / 3.2	3.22	-4.86	-4.42 / 41	-3.07 / 28	1.81 / 3
MUN	Western Asset Managed Municipals	MMU	B	14.18	14.44	13.09	B / 7.9	3.21	8.15	10.30 / 96	3.70 / 63	9.75 / 9
MTG	Western Asset Mtge Defined Oppty	DMO	B+	23.55	25.25	22.41	B+ / 8.9	0.96	6.76	13.42 / 93	12.84 / 84	15.19 / 9
MUN	Western Asset Municipal Defined Op	MTT	B	24.24	24.71	22.16	B / 8.1	4.68	11.21	8.02 / 92	5.01 / 69	8.72 / 8
MUH	Western Asset Municipal High Inc	MHF	B	7.80	7.93	7.00	B- / 7.3	9.49	10.89	6.76 / 89	3.00 / 60	7.04 / 7
MUN	Western Asset Municipal Partners	MNP	B-	15.61	16.12	14.64	B- / 7.0	6.31	6.93	11.23 / 97	0.95 / 45	9.69 / 9
GEI	Western Asset Premier Bond Fund	WEA	C-	12.16	15.21	11.82	C- / 3.6	0.50	-4.41	-4.12 / 42	-1.31 / 32	5.03 / 4
GL	Western Asset Var Rt Strat Fd	GFY	C	15.83	17.08	15.01	C / 4.9	4.77	-1.30	0.65 / 65	0.85 / 41	4.07 / 4
EM	Western Asset Worldwide Inc Fd	SBW	D+	10.08	11.78	9.51	D+ / 2.8	5.85	-2.96	-2.42 / 49	-5.80 / 23	1.97 / 3
USA	Western Asset/Claymore Inf-Link O&	WIW	C-	10.29	11.58	10.16	D+ / 2.7	0.39	-7.10	-6.72 / 34	-4.85 / 25	-0.19 / 2
USA	Western Asset/Claymore Inf-Link S&	WIA	C-	10.57	11.97	10.39	D+ / 2.9	1.10	-4.35	-6.67 / 34	-3.87 / 27	-0.31 / 2
COI	Western Asst Invst Grade Define Op	IGI	C	20.17	21.88	19.70	C / 5.0	-2.15	1.35	2.91 / 74	1.14 / 42	6.51 / 5
IN	Zweig Fund	ZF	B-	13.14	15.84	12.33	C+ / 6.5	3.56	-7.67	-8.92 / 29	8.67 / 71	7.32 / 5
GI	Zweig Total Return Fund	ZTR	B-	12.18	14.07	11.00	C+ / 6.8	8.73	-2.03	-4.55 / 40	7.84 / 69	6.44 / 5

* Denotes ETF Fund, N/A denotes number is not availab

Incl. in Returns		RISK				NET ASSETS		VALUATION			ASSET					FUND MANAGER	
			3 Year					Premium / Discount									
Dividend Yield %	Expense Ratio	Risk Rating/ Pts	Standard Deviation	Beta	Avg Dura- tion	NAV as of 12/31/15	Total $(Mil)	As of 12/31/15	1 Year Average	Wtd Avg P/E	Cash %	Stocks %	Bonds %	Other %	Portfolio Turnover Ratio	Manager Quality Pct	Manager Tenure (Years)
3.58	1.01	**D+ / 2.3**	21.5	0.81	N/A	8.07	161	-14.99	-12.55	N/A	5	94	0	1	13	46	8
9.28	2.93	**C- / 3.8**	36.8	1.80	N/A	12.03	200	-11.31	-13.23	35.6	0	90	9	1	137	1	9
1.74	1.59	**B- / 7.7**	12.4	0.85	N/A	8.98	86	-10.24	-10.47	N/A	0	100	0	0	107	76	7
1.17	1.68	**B- / 7.9**	14.7	0.48	N/A	15.90	71	-12.39	-14.28	N/A	0	94	0	6	29	98	5
16.65	2.38	**C- / 4.1**	N/A	N/A	N/A	17.27	139	-8.16	-8.21	N/A	0	0	0	100	93	37	N/A
15.51	1.38	**C- / 4.0**	25.9	1.41	N/A	13.14	330	-14.16	-9.95	N/A	0	0	0	100	43	8	N/A
9.42	3.16	**C / 5.0**	28.3	0.82	N/A	28.79	2,369	-3.37	-6.21	29.9	0	100	0	0	15	57	12
9.75	2.51	**C+ / 5.6**	17.8	0.73	N/A	18.60	1,402	-6.77	-9.98	N/A	0	100	0	0	18	11	N/A
12.41	2.11	**C- / 3.6**	24.8	1.12	N/A	16.64	351	-12.80	-12.28	N/A	0	0	0	100	18	24	5
9.83	1.50	**C / 5.2**	18.9	0.72	N/A	19.37	216	-13.37	-10.52	N/A	2	97	0	1	18	43	N/A
4.18	0.49	**B / 8.2**	9.5	0.87	6.0	23.49	1,511	-14.77	-14.86	49.2	0	99	0	1	76	58	6
1.92	1.31	**C- / 3.2**	23.4	0.85	N/A	9.02	65	-13.75	-12.33	N/A	5	94	0	1	8	11	19
13.25	2.13	**C+ / 6.9**	10.3	0.51	N/A	16.30	204	-13.31	-11.69	N/A	0	0	0	100	45	84	N/A
10.50	1.93	**B- / 7.5**	15.1	0.95	12.7	4.47	140	-14.77	-12.67	26.1	6	70	7	17	33	25	N/A
11.30	1.40	**C / 5.1**	18.0	0.92	N/A	10.23	166	-11.73	-10.73	N/A	0	99	0	1	28	13	9
12.43	1.42	**C / 4.8**	18.1	1.11	N/A	8.43	226	-12.22	-11.27	N/A	0	100	0	0	40	32	5
13.03	1.20	**B- / 7.3**	13.6	0.82	N/A	8.05	909	-13.04	-10.79	32.8	4	95	0	1	31	61	11
10.72	0.97	**B- / 7.5**	11.4	0.66	N/A	11.42	237	-8.49	-6.97	32.4	0	99	0	1	17	85	4
11.91	1.19	**C+ / 6.6**	13.3	0.97	N/A	14.26	340	-14.03	-12.05	N/A	0	98	0	2	62	13	6
13.02	1.25	**C+ / 6.8**	14.6	0.90	N/A	7.08	72	-10.17	-6.96	27.7	1	98	0	1	37	19	9
14.80	1.19	**C / 5.4**	17.5	0.81	N/A	6.36	212	-14.15	-9.11	19.0	0	100	0	0	96	23	10
6.28	2.09	**B- / 7.2**	7.9	-115.16	N/A	5.48	876	-7.66	-9.02	N/A	0	0	0	100	68	47	N/A
2.16	1.07	**B- / 7.3**	11.4	0.66	N/A	6.82	419	-13.20	-11.80	23.0	4	60	0	36	76	55	3
0.95	0.96	**C+ / 6.9**	9.7	1.24	N/A	8.29	692	-10.13	-10.83	N/A	5	0	94	1	33	44	N/A
0.25	1.21	**C+ / 6.5**	10.2	0.92	N/A	13.20	677	-14.24	-14.33	N/A	1	0	98	1	41	73	N/A
8.04	1.19	**B- / 7.5**	12.3	0.37	4.1	12.02	115	-6.82	-7.15	21.9	9	52	28	11	61	85	12
8.35	1.25	**C+ / 5.8**	14.8	1.08	N/A	16.37	559	-16.13	-14.65	N/A	0	0	99	1	35	47	3
7.27	1.33	**C+ / 5.6**	12.0	0.94	N/A	11.67	375	-16.62	-15.74	N/A	0	0	99	1	40	48	3
8.62	1.28	**B- / 7.3**	9.1	0.55	N/A	17.96	308	-12.03	-11.38	N/A	3	0	96	1	22	74	N/A
3.25	1.48	**C+ / 6.3**	11.4	0.85	N/A	10.22	383	-14.68	-12.78	N/A	3	0	96	1	40	56	N/A
1.25	1.65	**C+ / 6.0**	12.4	0.94	N/A	9.25	157	-16.43	-13.74	N/A	4	0	95	1	45	40	N/A
3.12	1.45	**C+ / 6.7**	11.9	0.74	N/A	6.94	738	-9.08	-7.81	N/A	3	0	96	1	41	58	N/A
9.08	0.89	**C+ / 6.7**	9.1	1.13	N/A	5.17	457	-9.28	-12.68	N/A	3	0	96	1	59	33	10
9.36	0.88	**C+ / 6.8**	9.1	1.27	N/A	15.44	386	-8.68	-11.98	N/A	0	0	99	1	42	46	6
0.60	0.71	**B- / 7.5**	8.0	1.79	N/A	13.84	140	-5.92	-8.03	N/A	0	0	99	1	38	54	6
4.70	0.94	**B- / 7.9**	7.9	1.36	8.0	10.52	N/A	-2.95	-5.42	N/A	4	0	95	1	11	62	4
9.16	0.92	**C+ / 6.5**	10.3	1.05	N/A	4.99	277	-9.42	-12.84	N/A	4	0	96	0	48	34	N/A
5.50	0.99	**C+ / 6.8**	12.2	2.13	N/A	14.34	617	-1.12	-2.40	N/A	3	0	97	0	4	57	24
0.70	2.36	**C+ / 6.7**	11.4	1.08	N/A	22.77	258	3.43	-1.51	N/A	1	0	98	1	35	95	N/A
2.04	0.70	**C+ / 6.7**	9.4	1.38	N/A	22.56	276	7.45	3.22	N/A	0	0	99	1	6	80	7
4.31	0.71	**B- / 7.4**	9.6	1.66	13.7	8.00	175	-2.50	-6.51	N/A	0	0	100	0	16	61	N/A
5.57	1.20	**B- / 7.5**	11.1	2.41	11.5	16.91	159	-7.69	-8.72	N/A	0	0	99	1	10	30	N/A
7.76	1.47	**C+ / 6.8**	14.3	3.02	N/A	13.09	176	-7.10	-6.19	N/A	4	0	95	1	32	33	N/A
5.87	1.12	**B- / 7.7**	7.2	0.16	N/A	17.35	117	-8.76	-9.28	N/A	1	0	98	1	30	80	6
.26	1.38	**C+ / 6.1**	12.3	0.94	N/A	11.85	171	-14.94	-15.30	N/A	0	0	99	1	38	57	N/A
3.58	0.95	**B- / 7.4**	7.4	0.39	N/A	12.16	793	-15.38	-14.20	N/A	0	0	91	9	49	26	N/A
3.33	0.89	**B- / 7.4**	7.6	0.38	N/A	12.47	385	-15.24	-14.13	N/A	0	0	92	8	30	31	N/A
5.95	0.80	**B- / 7.2**	8.4	1.21	N/A	19.88	233	1.46	-0.84	N/A	0	0	99	1	38	66	7
.33	1.26	**B- / 7.6**	11.5	1.03	N/A	14.78	359	-11.10	-12.45	61.3	14	81	3	2	57	33	13
3.05	1.03	**B- / 7.5**	8.7	0.74	N/A	13.56	501	-10.18	-12.21	52.8	24	44	30	2	38	49	13

Denotes ETF Fund, N/A denotes number is not available

Section II

Analysis of ETFs and Other Closed-End Funds

A summary analysis of all

Exchange-Traded Funds and

Other Closed-End Mutual Funds

receiving a TheStreet Investment Rating.

Funds are listed in alphabetical order.

Section II Contents

1. Fund Name

The name of the mutual fund as stated in its prospectus, which can sometimes differ slightly from the name that the company uses for advertising. If you cannot find the paritcular mutual fund you are interested in, or if you have any doubts regarding the precise name, verify the information with your broker or on your account statement. Also, use the fund's ticker symbol for confirmation.

2. Ticker Symbol

The unique alphabetic symbol used for identifying and trading a specific mutual fund. No two funds can have the same ticker symbol.

3. Investment Rating

Our overall rating is measured on a scale from A to E based on each fund's risk-adjusted performance. Please see page 10 for specific descriptions of each letter grade. Also refer to page 7 for information on how our ratings are derived. Most important, when using this rating, please be sure to consider the warnings beginning on page 11 regarding the ratings' limitations and the underlying assumptions.

4. Fund Family

The umbrella group of mutual funds to which the fund belongs.

5. Fund Type

The mutual fund's peer category based on an analysis of its investment portfolio.

COH	Corporate – High Yield	HL	Health
COI	Corporate – Inv. Grade	IN	Income
EM	Emerging Market	LP	Loan Participation
EN	Energy/Natural Resources	MTG	Mortgage
FS	Financial Services	MUH	Municipal – High Yield
FO	Foreign	MUN	Municipal – National
GEI	General – Inv. Grade	MUS	Municipal – Single State
GEN	General Bond	PM	Precious Metals
GL	Global	USA	U.S. Gov. – Agency
GR	Growth	UT	Utilities
GI	Growth and Income		

A blank fund type means that the mutual fund has not yet been categorized.

6. Inception Date

The date on which the fund began.

7. Major Rating Factors

A synopsis of the key ratios and sub-factors that have most influenced the rating of a particular mutual fund, including an examination of the fund's performance, risk, and managerial performance. There may be additional factors which have influenced the rating but do not appear due to space limitations.

How to Read the Annualized Total Return Graph

The annualized total return graph provides a clearer picture of a fund's yearly financial performance. In addition to the solid line denoting the fund's calendar year returns for the last six years, the graph also shows the yearly return for a benchmark index for easy comparison using a dotted line. The S&P 500 Composite Index is used for ETFs and other closed-end mutual funds that are primarily invested in stocks. One of two indexes is shown for funds with the majority of their assets held in bonds. Municipal bond funds display the Lehman Brothers Municipals Index, and other bond funds will show the Lehman Brothers Aggregate Bond Index.

The top of the shaded area of the graph denotes the average returns for all funds within the same fund type. If the solid line falls into the shaded area, that means that the fund has performed below the average for its type.

How to Read the Historical Data Table

Data Date:
The quarter-end or year-end as of date used for evaluating the mutual fund.

Price:
The fund's share price as of the date indicated. A fund's price is determined by investor demand. The fund may trade at a price higher or lower than its net asset value (NAV).

Risk Rating/Pts:
A letter grade rating based solely on the mutual fund's risk as determined by its monthly performance volatility over the trailing three years. Pts are rating points where 0=worst and 10=best.

Data Date	Investment Rating	Net Assets ($Mil)	Price	Performance Rating/Pts	Total Return Y-T-D	Risk Rating/Pts
12-15	B+	126.6	8.91	A- / 9.2	52.38%	C+ / 6.0
2014	C+	178.56	7.43	C+ / 5.7	2.57%	C+ / 6.1
2013	B+	86.42	19.76	B / 7.8	8.78%	C+ / 6.8
2012	B	87.35	14.30	C / 5.4	4.71%	B / 8.3
2010	D+	284.1	6.90	C- / 3.2	5.19%	C / 4.6

Investment Rating:
Our overall opinion of the fund's risk-adjusted performance at the specified time period.

Net Assets $(Mil):
The total value of all of the fund's asset holdings (in millions) including stocks, bonds, cash, and other financial instruments, less accrued expenses and fees.

Performance Rating/Pts:
A letter grade rating based solely on the mutual fund's return to shareholders over the trailing three years, without any consideration for the amount of risk the fund poses.
Pts are rating points where
0=worst and 10=best

Total Return Y-T-D:
The fund's total return to shareholders since the beginning of the calendar year specified.

*AdvisorShares EquityPro ETF (EPRO) C Fair

Fund Family: AdvisorShares Investments LLC
Fund Type: Growth and Income
Inception Date: July 10, 2012

Data Date	Investment Rating	Net Assets ($Mil)	Price	Performance Rating/Pts	Total Return Y-T-D	Risk Rating/Pts
12-15	C	21.10	27.82	C / 5.5	-3.34%	C+ / 6.8
2014	C-	21.10	30.29	C- / 3.0	3.97%	B- / 7.5
2013	A+	17.40	30.10	B / 7.7	14.28%	B+ / 9.7

Major Rating Factors: Middle of the road best describes *AdvisorShares EquityPro ETF whose TheStreet.com Investment Rating is currently a C (Fair). The fund currently has a performance rating of C (Fair) based on an annualized return of 4.19% over the last three years and a total return of -3.34% year to date 2015. Factored into the performance evaluation is an expense ratio of 1.25% (average).

The fund's risk rating is currently C+ (Fair). It carries a beta of 0.71, meaning the fund's expected move will be 7.1% for every 10% move in the market. Volatility, as measured by both the semi-deviation and a drawdown factor, is considered low. As of December 31, 2015, *AdvisorShares EquityPro ETF traded at a premium of 1.64% above its net asset value, which is worse than its one-year historical average discount of .02%.

Joseph Lu currently receives a manager quality ranking of 32 (0=worst, 99=best). If you desire an average level of risk, then this fund may be an option.

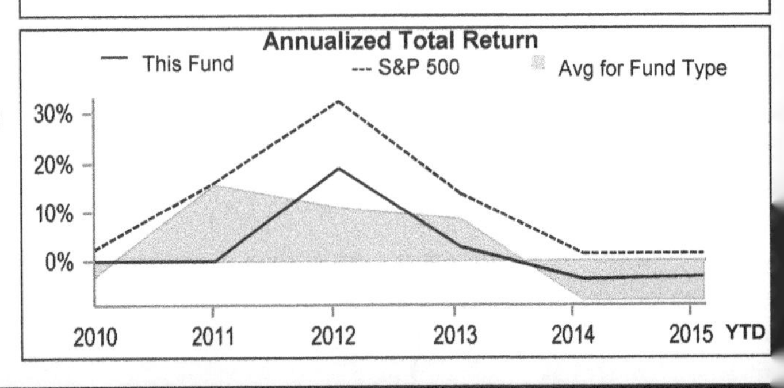

*AdvisorShares Gartman Gold Euro (GEUR) C- Fair

Fund Family: AdvisorShares Investments LLC
Fund Type: Foreign
Inception Date: February 12, 2014

Data Date	Investment Rating	Net Assets ($Mil)	Price	Performance Rating/Pts	Total Return Y-T-D	Risk Rating/Pts
12-15	C-	1.60	11.24	D+ / 2.4	-3.63%	B- / 7.4

Major Rating Factors:
Disappointing performance is the major factor driving the C- (Fair) TheStreet.com Investment Rating for *AdvisorShares Gartman Gold Euro. The fund currently has a performance rating of D+ (Weak) based on an annualized return of 0.00% over the last three years and a total return of -3.63% year to date 2015. Factored into the performance evaluation is an expense ratio of 0.65% (very low).

The fund's risk rating is currently B- (Good). It carries a beta of 0.00, meaning the fund's expected move will be 0.0% for every 10% move in the market. Volatility, as measured by both the semi-deviation and a drawdown factor, is considered low. As of December 31, 2015, *AdvisorShares Gartman Gold Euro traded at a discount of .71% below its net asset value, which is better than its one-year historical average discount of .02%.

Ade Odunsi has been running the fund for 2 years and currently receives a manager quality ranking of 48 (0=worst, 99=best). This fund offers only a moderate level of risk but investors looking for strong performance are still waiting.

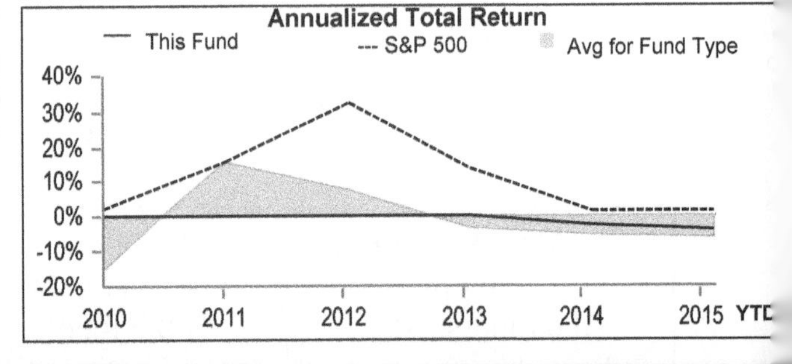

*AdvisorShares Gartman Gold Yen E (GYEN) D+ Weak

Fund Family: AdvisorShares Investments LLC
Fund Type: Foreign
Inception Date: February 12, 2014

Data Date	Investment Rating	Net Assets ($Mil)	Price	Performance Rating/Pts	Total Return Y-T-D	Risk Rating/Pts
12-15	D+	3.80	11.14	D- / 1.2	-12.68%	B- / 7.7

Major Rating Factors:
Disappointing performance is the major factor driving the D+ (Weak) TheStreet.com Investment Rating for *AdvisorShares Gartman Gold Yen E. The fund currently has a performance rating of D- (Weak) based on an annualized return of 0.00% over the last three years and a total return of -12.68% year to date 2015. Factored into the performance evaluation is an expense ratio of 0.65% (very low).

The fund's risk rating is currently B- (Good). It carries a beta of 0.00, meaning the fund's expected move will be 0.0% for every 10% move in the market. Volatility, as measured by both the semi-deviation and a drawdown factor, is considered low. As of December 31, 2015, *AdvisorShares Gartman Gold Yen E traded at a discount of .71% below its net asset value, which is better than its one-year historical average premium of .11%.

Ade Odunsi has been running the fund for 2 years and currently receives a manager quality ranking of 14 (0=worst, 99=best). This fund offers only a moderate level of risk but investors looking for strong performance are still waiting.

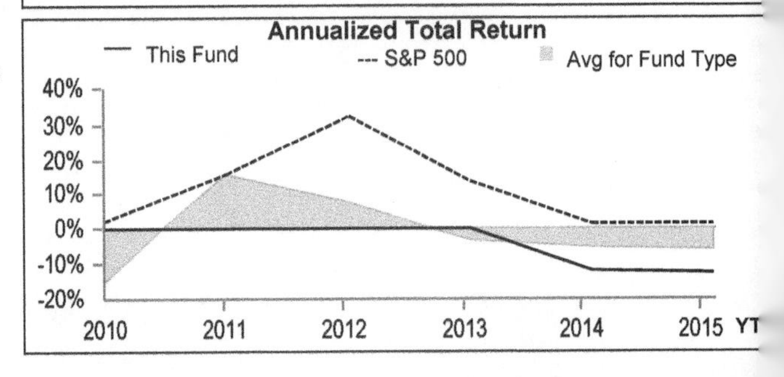

*AdvisorShares Sage Core Rsvs ETF (HOLD) B- Good

Fund Family: AdvisorShares Investments LLC
Fund Type: General - Investment Grade
Inception Date: January 14, 2014

Major Rating Factors: *AdvisorShares Sage Core Rsvs ETF receives a TheStreet.com Investment Rating of B- (Good). The fund currently has a performance rating of C- (Fair) based on an annualized return of 0.00% over the last three years and a total return of 0.10% year to date 2015. Factored into the performance evaluation is an expense ratio of 0.35% (very low).

The fund's risk rating is currently B+ (Good). It carries a beta of 0.00, meaning the fund's expected move will be 0.0% for every 10% move in the market. Volatility, as measured by both the semi-deviation and a drawdown factor, is considered very low. As of December 31, 2015, *AdvisorShares Sage Core Rsvs ETF traded at a discount of .12% below its net asset value, which is better than its one-year historical average premium of .03%.

Thomas H. Urano currently receives a manager quality ranking of 68 (0=worst, 99=best). If you desire an average level of risk, then this fund may be an option.

Data Date	Investment Rating	Net Assets ($Mil)	Price	Performance Rating/Pts	Total Return Y-T-D	Risk Rating/Pts
12-15	B-	37.40	98.90	C- / 4.2	0.10%	B+ / 9.9

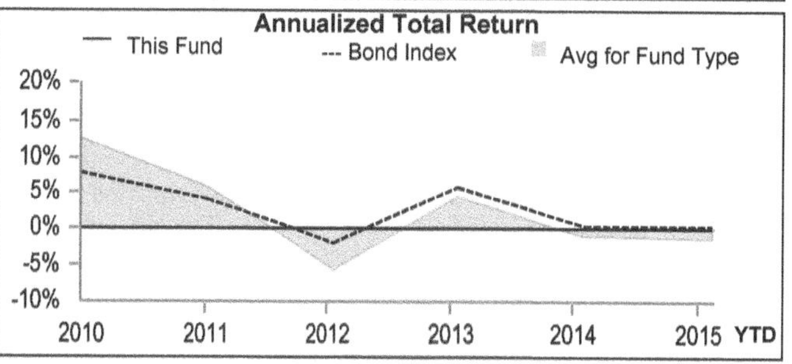

*AdvisorShares YieldPro (YPRO) C+ Fair

Fund Family: AdvisorShares Investments LLC
Fund Type: Financial Services
Inception Date: March 4, 2014

Major Rating Factors: Middle of the road best describes *AdvisorShares YieldPro whose TheStreet.com Investment Rating is currently a C+ (Fair). The fund currently has a performance rating of C- (Fair) based on an annualized return of 0.00% over the last three years and a total return of -1.99% year to date 2015. Factored into the performance evaluation is an expense ratio of 1.05% (low).

The fund's risk rating is currently B+ (Good). It carries a beta of 0.00, meaning the fund's expected move will be 0.0% for every 10% move in the market. Volatility, as measured by both the semi-deviation and a drawdown factor, is considered very low. As of December 31, 2015, *AdvisorShares YieldPro traded at a discount of .22% below its net asset value, which is better than its one-year historical average discount of .13%.

Philip A. Voelker has been running the fund for 1 year and currently receives a manager quality ranking of 54 (0=worst, 99=best). If you desire an average level of risk, then this fund may be an option.

Data Date	Investment Rating	Net Assets ($Mil)	Price	Performance Rating/Pts	Total Return Y-T-D	Risk Rating/Pts
12-15	C+	68.40	22.94	C- / 3.7	-1.99%	B+ / 9.1

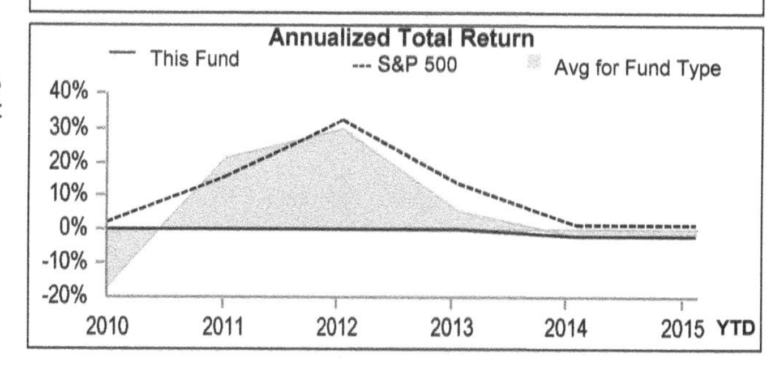

*AlphaClone Alternative Alpha ETF (ALFA) C Fair

Fund Family: Exchange Traded Concepts LLC
Fund Type: Growth and Income
Inception Date: May 31, 2012

Major Rating Factors: Middle of the road best describes *AlphaClone Alternative Alpha ETF whose TheStreet.com Investment Rating is currently a C (Fair). The fund currently has a performance rating of C+ (Fair) based on an annualized return of 45% over the last three years and a total return of -11.33% year to date 2015. Factored into the performance evaluation is an expense ratio of 0.95% (low).

The fund's risk rating is currently C+ (Fair). It carries a beta of 0.80, meaning the fund's expected move will be 8.0% for every 10% move in the market. Volatility, as measured by both the semi-deviation and a drawdown factor, is considered low. As of December 31, 2015, *AlphaClone Alternative Alpha ETF traded at a premium of .05% above its net asset value, which is worse than its one-year historical average premium of .03%.

Michael J. Gompers currently receives a manager quality ranking of 59 (0=worst, 99=best). If you desire an average level of risk, then this fund may be an option.

Data Date	Investment Rating	Net Assets ($Mil)	Price	Performance Rating/Pts	Total Return Y-T-D	Risk Rating/Pts
12-15	C	77.80	37.49	C+ / 6.1	-11.33%	C+ / 6.6
2014	B-	77.80	42.36	B- / 7.1	13.15%	B- / 7.5
2013	A+	33.90	37.64	A / 9.5	30.94%	B+ / 9.7

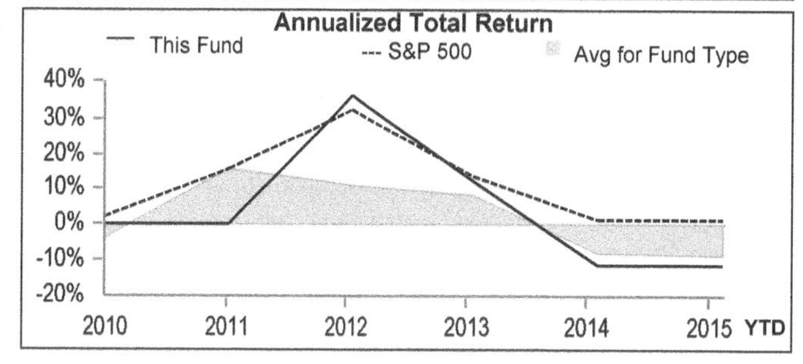

*ALPS Alerian Energy Infra ETF (ENFR) E+ Very Weak

Fund Family: ALPS Advisors Inc
Fund Type: Energy/Natural Resources
Inception Date: November 1, 2013

Data Date	Investment Rating	Net Assets ($Mil)	Price	Performance Rating/Pts	Total Return Y-T-D	Risk Rating/Pt
12-15	E+	16.50	17.44	E- / 0.1	-37.63%	C- / 3.
2014	D+	16.50	28.40	C / 4.8	14.72%	C / 4.

Major Rating Factors:
Very poor performance is the major factor driving the E+ (Very Weak) TheStreet.com Investment Rating for *ALPS Alerian Energy Infra ETF. The fund currently has a performance rating of E- (Very Weak) based on an annualized return of 0.00% over the last three years and a total return of -37.63% year to date 2015. Factored into the performance evaluation is an expense ratio of 0.65% (very low).

The fund's risk rating is currently C- (Fair). It carries a beta of 0.00, meaning the fund's expected move will be 0.0% for every 10% move in the market. Volatility, as measured by both the semi-deviation and a drawdown factor, is considered average. As of December 31, 2015, *ALPS Alerian Energy Infra ETF traded at a premium of .11% above its net asset value, which is worse than its one-year historical average discount of .10%.

Michael Akins has been running the fund for 3 years and currently receives a manager quality ranking of 5 (0=worst, 99=best). This fund offers an average level of risk but investors looking for strong performance will be frustrated.

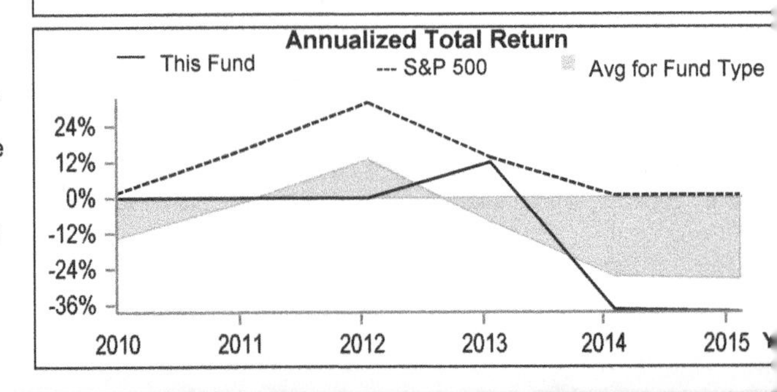

*Alps Alerian MLP ETF (AMLP) D Weak

Fund Family: ALPS Advisors Inc
Fund Type: Energy/Natural Resources
Inception Date: August 25, 2010

Data Date	Investment Rating	Net Assets ($Mil)	Price	Performance Rating/Pts	Total Return Y-T-D	Risk Rating/P
12-15	D	9,617.10	12.05	D / 2.2	-26.24%	C / 4.
2014	C+	9,617.10	17.52	C / 4.7	6.59%	B / 8.
2013	B-	7,553.60	17.79	C+ / 6.1	12.78%	B+ / 9.
2012	C	4,449.10	15.95	C- / 3.3	7.44%	B+ / 9.
2011	B-	1,989.90	16.62	C+ / 6.0	10.77%	B+ / 9.

Major Rating Factors:
Disappointing performance is the major factor driving the D (Weak) TheStreet.com Investment Rating for *Alps Alerian MLP ETF. The fund currently has a performance rating of D (Weak) based on an annualized return of -3.87% over the last three years and a total return of -26.24% year to date 2015. Factored into the performance evaluation is an expense ratio of 0.85% (very low).

The fund's risk rating is currently C (Fair). It carries a beta of 0.51, meaning the fund's expected move will be 5.1% for every 10% move in the market. Volatility, as measured by both the semi-deviation and a drawdown factor, is considered average. As of December 31, 2015, *Alps Alerian MLP ETF traded at a premium of .50% above its net asset value, which is worse than its one-year historical average premium of .04%.

Michael Akins has been running the fund for 5 years and currently receives a manager quality ranking of 61 (0=worst, 99=best). This fund offers an average level of risk but investors looking for strong performance will be frustrated.

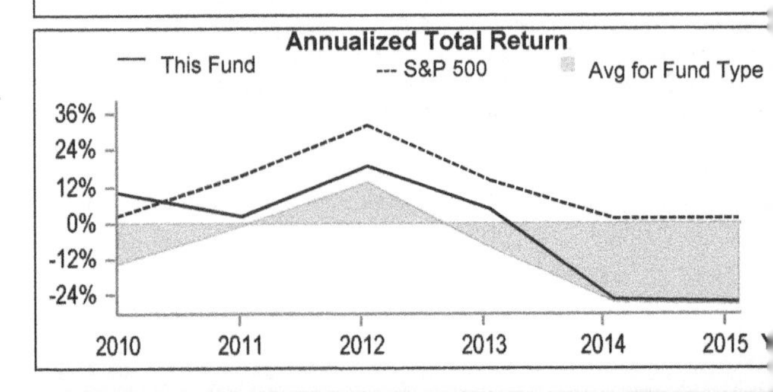

*ALPS Barrons 400 ETF (BFOR) C- Fai

Fund Family: ALPS Advisors Inc
Fund Type: Growth
Inception Date: June 4, 2013

Data Date	Investment Rating	Net Assets ($Mil)	Price	Performance Rating/Pts	Total Return Y-T-D	Risk Rating/P
12-15	C-	231.10	30.22	D+ / 2.8	-2.71%	C+ / 6
2014	C	231.10	31.52	C / 5.1	7.89%	B- / 7

Major Rating Factors:
Disappointing performance is the major factor driving the C- (Fair) TheStreet.com Investment Rating for *ALPS Barrons 400 ETF. The fund currently has a performance rating of D+ (Weak) based on an annualized return of 0.00% over the last three years and a total return of -2.71% year to date 2015. Factored into the performance evaluation is an expense ratio of 0.65% (very low).

The fund's risk rating is currently C+ (Fair). It carries a beta of 0.00, meaning the fund's expected move will be 0.0% for every 10% move in the market. Volatility, as measured by both the semi-deviation and a drawdown factor, is considered low. As of December 31, 2015, *ALPS Barrons 400 ETF traded at a premium of .50% above its net asset value, which is worse than its one-year historical average premium of .02%.

Michael Akins has been running the fund for 3 years and currently receives a manager quality ranking of 34 (0=worst, 99=best). This fund offers only a moderate level of risk but investors looking for strong performance are still waiting.

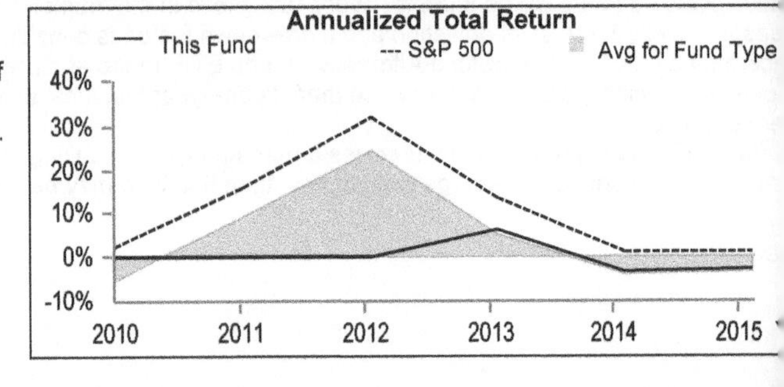

*Alps Emerg Sector Dividend Dogs (EDOG) D Weak

Fund Family: ALPS Advisors Inc
Fund Type: Global
Inception Date: March 28, 2014

Data Date	Investment Rating	Net Assets ($Mil)	Price	Performance Rating/Pts	Total Return Y-T-D	Risk Rating/Pts
12-15	D	7.90	19.37	E+ / 0.8	-16.87%	C+ / 6.6

Major Rating Factors:
Very poor performance is the major factor driving the D (Weak) TheStreet.com Investment Rating for *Alps Emerg Sector Dividend Dogs. The fund currently has a performance rating of E+ (Very Weak) based on an annualized return of 0.00% over the last three years and a total return of -16.87% year to date 2015. Factored into the performance evaluation is an expense ratio of 0.60% (very low).

The fund's risk rating is currently C+ (Fair). It carries a beta of 0.00, meaning the fund's expected move will be 0.0% for every 10% move in the market. Volatility, as measured by both the semi-deviation and a drawdown factor, is considered low. As of December 31, 2015, *Alps Emerg Sector Dividend Dogs traded at a discount of 1.17% below its net asset value, which is better than its one-year historical average discount of .02%.

Michael Akins has been running the fund for 2 years and currently receives a manager quality ranking of 9 (0=worst, 99=best). This fund offers only a moderate level of risk but investors looking for strong performance are still waiting.

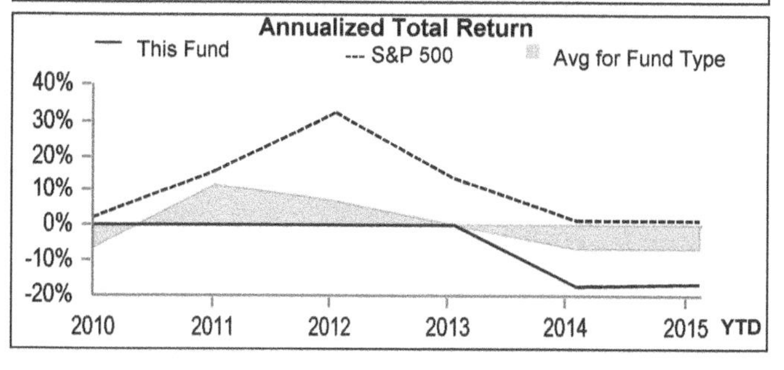

*Alps Equal Sector Weight ETF (EQL) B Good

Fund Family: ALPS Advisors Inc
Fund Type: Income
Inception Date: July 7, 2009

Data Date	Investment Rating	Net Assets ($Mil)	Price	Performance Rating/Pts	Total Return Y-T-D	Risk Rating/Pts
12-15	B	133.60	54.76	B / 8.0	-1.65%	B- / 7.2
2014	A-	133.60	56.73	B / 8.1	15.56%	B / 8.3
2013	B+	114.90	51.05	B / 7.8	25.00%	B / 8.5
2012	C	77.80	39.89	C / 5.0	15.06%	B / 8.3
2011	C-	62.30	35.60	D+ / 2.9	3.50%	B / 8.4
2010	A+	53.00	35.36	A- / 9.1	14.85%	B- / 7.9

Major Rating Factors: Strong performance is the major factor driving the B (Good) TheStreet.com Investment Rating for *Alps Equal Sector Weight ETF. The fund currently has a performance rating of B (Good) based on an annualized return of 11.85% over the last three years and a total return of -1.65% year to date 2015. Factored into the performance evaluation is an expense ratio of 0.34% (very low).

The fund's risk rating is currently B- (Good). It carries a beta of 0.96, meaning that its performance tracks fairly well with that of the overall stock market. Volatility, as measured by both the semi-deviation and a drawdown factor, is considered low. As of December 31, 2015, *Alps Equal Sector Weight ETF traded at a premium of .20% above its net asset value, which is worse than its one-year historical average premium of .01%.

Daniel Franciscus has been running the fund for 7 years and currently receives a manager quality ranking of 57 (0=worst, 99=best). If you desire only a moderate level of risk and strong performance, then this fund is an excellent option.

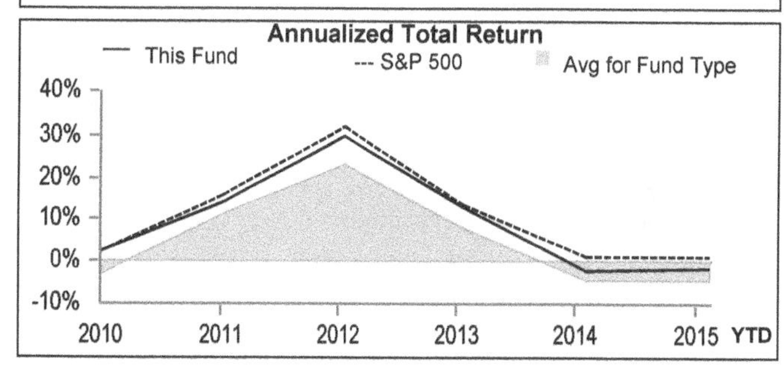

*Alps Global Commodity Equity (CRBQ) D Weak

Fund Family: ALPS Advisors Inc
Fund Type: Global
Inception Date: September 21, 2009

Data Date	Investment Rating	Net Assets ($Mil)	Price	Performance Rating/Pts	Total Return Y-T-D	Risk Rating/Pts
12-15	D	61.20	29.08	D- / 1.4	-22.41%	C+ / 6.3
2014	D+	61.20	38.70	D / 2.1	-8.68%	B- / 7.7
2013	D	67.90	43.89	D+ / 2.3	-2.73%	B- / 7.0
2012	D	73.90	44.72	D+ / 2.3	5.35%	C+ / 6.9
2011	D	83.50	42.54	D- / 1.3	-10.30%	B- / 7.1
2010	A+	111.00	49.58	A / 9.5	16.98%	B- / 7.3

Major Rating Factors:
Disappointing performance is the major factor driving the D (Weak) TheStreet.com Investment Rating for *Alps Global Commodity Equity. The fund currently has a performance rating of D- (Weak) based on an annualized return of -12.00% over the last three years and a total return of -22.41% year to date 2015. Factored into the performance evaluation is an expense ratio of 0.65% (very low).

The fund's risk rating is currently C+ (Fair). It carries a beta of 0.94, meaning that its performance tracks fairly well with that of the overall stock market. Volatility, as measured by both the semi-deviation and a drawdown factor, is considered low. As of December 31, 2015, *Alps Global Commodity Equity traded at a discount of .65% below its net asset value, which is better than its one-year historical average discount of .26%.

Michael Akins has been running the fund for 5 years and currently receives a manager quality ranking of 10 (0=worst, 99=best). This fund offers only a moderate level of risk but investors looking for strong performance are still waiting.

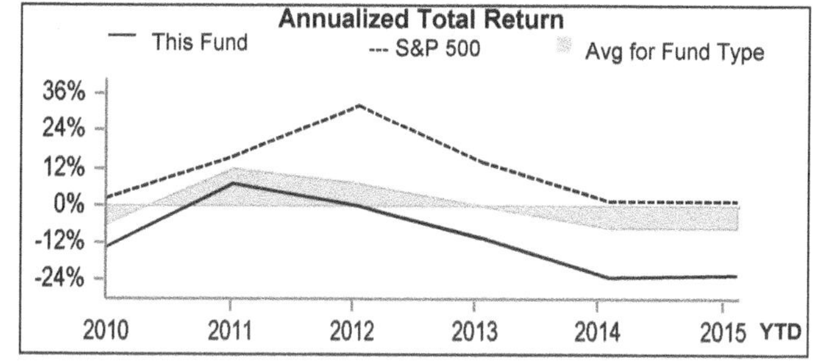

*Alps Intll Sec Div Dogs ETF (IDOG) D+ Weak

Fund Family: ALPS Advisors Inc
Fund Type: Growth
Inception Date: June 28, 2013

Major Rating Factors:
Disappointing performance is the major factor driving the D+ (Weak) TheStreet.com Investment Rating for *Alps Intll Sec Div Dogs ETF. The fund currently has a performance rating of D (Weak) based on an annualized return of 0.00% over the last three years and a total return of -6.57% year to date 2015. Factored into the performance evaluation is an expense ratio of 0.50% (very low).

The fund's risk rating is currently B- (Good). It carries a beta of 0.00, meaning the fund's expected move will be 0.0% for every 10% move in the market. Volatility, as measured by both the semi-deviation and a drawdown factor, is considered low. As of December 31, 2015, *Alps Intll Sec Div Dogs ETF traded at a discount of .80% below its net asset value, which is better than its one-year historical average premium of .08%.

Michael Atkins has been running the fund for 3 years and currently receives a manager quality ranking of 20 (0=worst, 99=best). This fund offers only a moderate level of risk but investors looking for strong performance are still waiting.

Data Date	Investment Rating	Net Assets ($Mil)	Price	Performance Rating/Pts	Total Return Y-T-D	Risk Rating/Pts
12-15	D+	153.10	23.48	D / 2.1	-6.57%	B- / 7.3
2014	D	153.10	26.01	D- / 1.1	-5.41%	C+ / 6.4

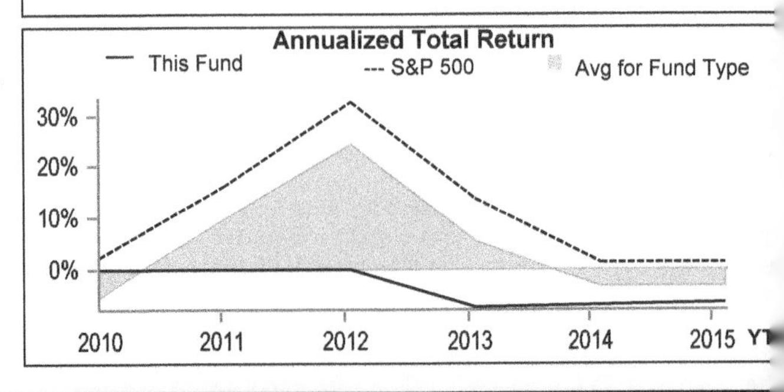

*Alps Janus Vel Vol Hdg LC (SPXH) C- Fair

Fund Family: ALPS Advisors Inc
Fund Type: Growth
Inception Date: June 21, 2013

Major Rating Factors: Middle of the road best describes *Alps Janus Vel Vol Hdg LC whose TheStreet.com Investment Rating is currently a C- (Fair). The fund currently has a performance rating of C- (Fair) based on an annualized return of 0.00% over the last three years and a total return of -2.27% year to date 2015. Factored into the performance evaluation is an expense ratio of 0.65% (very low).

The fund's risk rating is currently B- (Good). It carries a beta of 0.00, meaning the fund's expected move will be 0.0% for every 10% move in the market. Volatility, as measured by both the semi-deviation and a drawdown factor, is considered low. As of December 31, 2015, *Alps Janus Vel Vol Hdg LC traded at a premium of .45% above its net asset value, which is worse than its one-year historical average premium of .04%.

Michael Akins has been running the fund for 3 years and currently receives a manager quality ranking of 35 (0=worst, 99=best). If you desire an average level of risk, then this fund may be an option.

Data Date	Investment Rating	Net Assets ($Mil)	Price	Performance Rating/Pts	Total Return Y-T-D	Risk Rating/Pts
12-15	C-	52.00	28.84	C- / 3.4	-2.27%	B- / 7.2
2014	C	52.00	30.29	C / 4.7	8.43%	B / 8.0

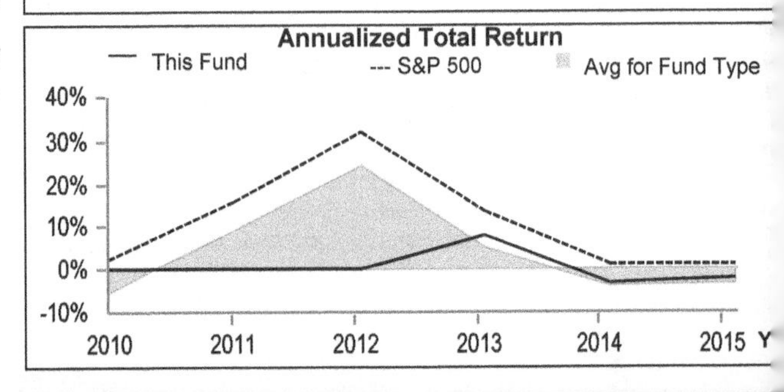

*ALPS RiverFront Strategic Income (RIGS) C Fair

Fund Family: ALPS Advisors Inc
Fund Type: General Bond
Inception Date: October 8, 2013

Major Rating Factors: Middle of the road best describes *ALPS RiverFront Strategic Income whose TheStreet.com Investment Rating is currently a C (Fair). The fund currently has a performance rating of C (Fair) based on an annualized return of 0.00% over the last three years and a total return of 0.63% year to date 2015. Factored into the performance evaluation is an expense ratio of 0.22% (very low).

The fund's risk rating is currently B- (Good). It carries a beta of 0.00, meaning the fund's expected move will be 0.0% for every 10% move in the market. Volatility, as measured by both the semi-deviation and a drawdown factor, is considered low. As of December 31, 2015, *ALPS RiverFront Strategic Income traded at a premium of .12% above its net asset value, which is better than its one-year historical average premium of .15%.

Paul M. Jones currently receives a manager quality ranking of 75 (0=worst, 99=best). If you desire an average level of risk, then this fund may be an option.

Data Date	Investment Rating	Net Assets ($Mil)	Price	Performance Rating/Pts	Total Return Y-T-D	Risk Rating/Pts
12-15	C	368.90	24.19	C / 4.4	0.63%	B- / 7.
2014	D	368.90	24.84	C- / 3.1	2.25%	C / 5.

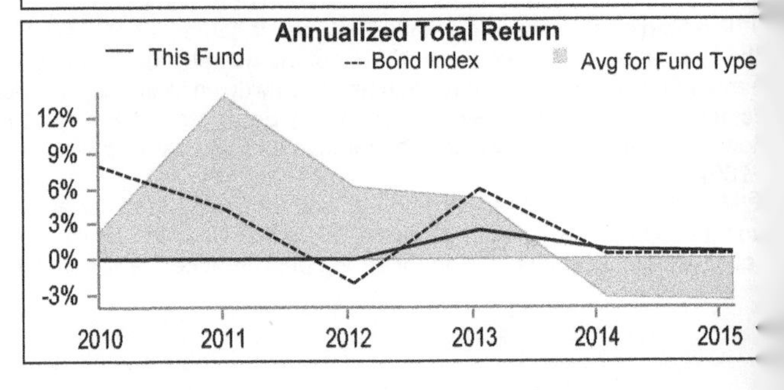

*Alps Sector Dividend Dogs ETF (SDOG) B Good

Fund Family: ALPS Advisors Inc
Fund Type: Income
Inception Date: June 29, 2012

Major Rating Factors: Strong performance is the major factor driving the B (Good) TheStreet.com Investment Rating for *Alps Sector Dividend Dogs ETF. The fund currently has a performance rating of B (Good) based on an annualized return of 12.70% over the last three years and a total return of -4.17% year to date 2015. Factored into the performance evaluation is an expense ratio of 0.40% (very low).

The fund's risk rating is currently B- (Good). It carries a beta of 0.93, meaning that its performance tracks fairly well with that of the overall stock market. Volatility, as measured by both the semi-deviation and a drawdown factor, is considered low.

As of December 31, 2015, *Alps Sector Dividend Dogs ETF traded at a premium of .03% above its net asset value, which is worse than its one-year historical average premium of .02%.

Michael Akins has been running the fund for 4 years and currently receives a manager quality ranking of 67 (0=worst, 99=best). If you desire only a moderate level of risk and strong performance, then this fund is an excellent option.

Data Date	Investment Rating	Net Assets ($Mil)	Price	Performance Rating/Pts	Total Return Y-T-D	Risk Rating/Pts
12-15	B	852.40	35.55	B / 8.2	-4.17%	B- / 7.0
2014	A	852.40	38.04	B- / 7.3	17.64%	B+ / 9.5
2013	A+	501.80	34.24	A / 9.3	28.37%	B+ / 9.8

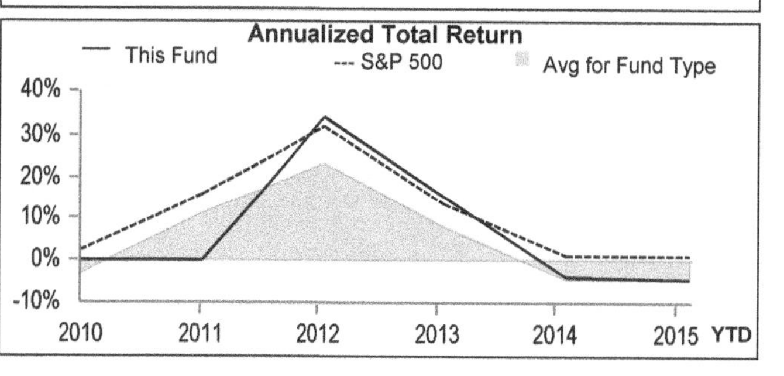

*ALPS Sprott Gold Miners ETF (SGDM) E Very Weak

Fund Family: ALPS Advisors Inc
Fund Type: Precious Metals
Inception Date: July 15, 2014

Major Rating Factors: *ALPS Sprott Gold Miners ETF has adopted a risky asset allocation strategy and currently receives an overall TheStreet.com Investment Rating of E (Very Weak). The fund has an above average level of volatility, as measured by both semi-deviation and drawdown factors. It carries a beta of 0.00, meaning the fund's expected move will be 0.0% for every 10% move in the market. As of December 31, 2015, *ALPS Sprott Gold Miners ETF traded at a premium of .08% above its net asset value, which is worse than its one-year historical average premium of .01%. Unfortunately, the high level of risk (D+, Weak) failed to pay off as investors endured very poor performance.

The fund's performance rating is currently E (Very Weak). It has registered an annualized return of 0.00% over the last three years but is down -28.16% year to date 2015.

Michael Akins has been running the fund for 2 years and currently receives a manager quality ranking of 83 (0=worst, 99=best). If you can tolerate high levels of risk in the hope of improved future returns, holding this fund may be an option.

Data Date	Investment Rating	Net Assets ($Mil)	Price	Performance Rating/Pts	Total Return Y-T-D	Risk Rating/Pts
12-15	E	41.40	12.73	E / 0.5	-28.16%	D+ / 2.4

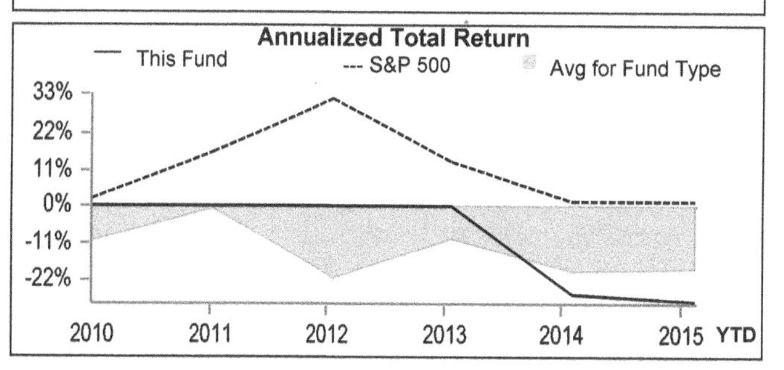

*Alps STOXX Europe 600 (STXX) C- Fair

Fund Family: ALPS Advisors Inc
Fund Type: Foreign
Inception Date: October 31, 2014

Major Rating Factors: Middle of the road best describes *Alps STOXX Europe 600 whose TheStreet.com Investment Rating is currently a C- (Fair). The fund currently has a performance rating of C- (Fair) based on an annualized return of 0.00% over the last three years and a total return of -1.33% year to date 2015.

The fund's risk rating is currently C+ (Fair). It carries a beta of 0.00, meaning the fund's expected move will be 0.0% for every 10% move in the market. Volatility, as measured by both the semi-deviation and a drawdown factor, is considered low. As of December 31, 2015, *Alps STOXX Europe 600 traded at a premium of 1.30% above its net asset value, which is worse than its one-year historical average premium of .34%.

Michael Akins has been running the fund for 2 years and currently receives a manager quality ranking of 60 (0=worst, 99=best). If you desire an average level of risk, then this fund may be an option.

Data Date	Investment Rating	Net Assets ($Mil)	Price	Performance Rating/Pts	Total Return Y-T-D	Risk Rating/Pts
12-15	C-	0.00	24.14	C- / 3.5	-1.33%	C+ / 6.3

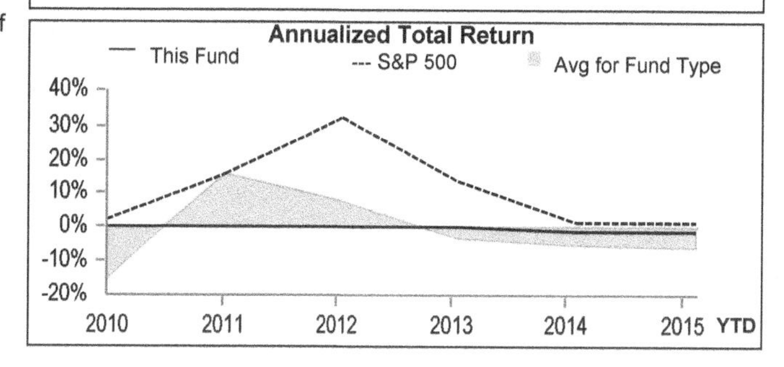

* Denotes ETF Fund

*Alps US Equity High Vol Put Writ (HVPW) C Fair

Fund Family: ALPS Advisors Inc
Fund Type: Growth
Inception Date: February 28, 2013

Data Date	Investment Rating	Net Assets ($Mil)	Price	Performance Rating/Pts	Total Return Y-T-D	Risk Rating/Pts
12-15	C	55.80	20.91	C- / 3.4	-1.52%	B / 8.1
2014	C-	55.80	23.25	D+ / 2.5	-0.27%	B- / 7.9

Major Rating Factors: Middle of the road best describes *Alps US Equity High Vol Put Writ whose TheStreet.com Investment Rating is currently a C (Fair). The fund currently has a performance rating of C- (Fair) based on an annualized return of 0.00% over the last three years and a total return of -1.52% year to date 2015. Factored into the performance evaluation is an expense ratio of 0.95% (low).

The fund's risk rating is currently B (Good). It carries a beta of 0.00, meaning the fund's expected move will be 0.0% for every 10% move in the market. Volatility, as measured by both the semi-deviation and a drawdown factor, is considered low. As of December 31, 2015, *Alps US Equity High Vol Put Writ traded at a discount of .24% below its net asset value, which is better than its one-year historical average discount of .09%.

William R. Parmentier, Jr. currently receives a manager quality ranking of 51 (0=worst, 99=best). If you desire an average level of risk, then this fund may be an option.

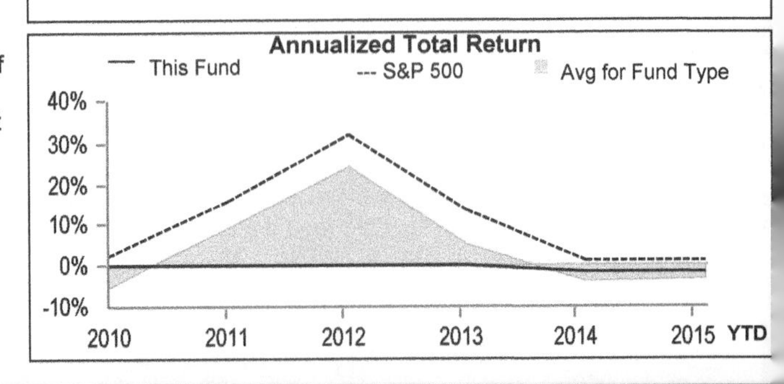

*Alps VelShTail Risk Hdgd Lg Cp E (TRSK) C- Fair

Fund Family: ALPS Advisors Inc
Fund Type: Growth
Inception Date: June 20, 2013

Data Date	Investment Rating	Net Assets ($Mil)	Price	Performance Rating/Pts	Total Return Y-T-D	Risk Rating/Pts
12-15	C-	32.40	27.26	C- / 3.3	-3.71%	B- / 7.5
2014	C	32.40	28.70	C / 4.9	7.61%	B / 8.0

Major Rating Factors: Middle of the road best describes *Alps VelShTail Risk Hdgd Lg Cp E whose TheStreet.com Investment Rating is currently a C- (Fair). The fund currently has a performance rating of C- (Fair) based on an annualized return of 0.00% over the last three years and a total return of -3.71% year to date 2015. Factored into the performance evaluation is an expense ratio of 0.65% (very low).

The fund's risk rating is currently B- (Good). It carries a beta of 0.00, meaning the fund's expected move will be 0.0% for every 10% move in the market. Volatility, as measured by both the semi-deviation and a drawdown factor, is considered low. As of December 31, 2015, *Alps VelShTail Risk Hdgd Lg Cp E traded at a premium of .59% above its net asset value, which is worse than its one-year historical average discount of .01%.

Michael Akins has been running the fund for 3 years and currently receives a manager quality ranking of 31 (0=worst, 99=best). If you desire an average level of risk, then this fund may be an option.

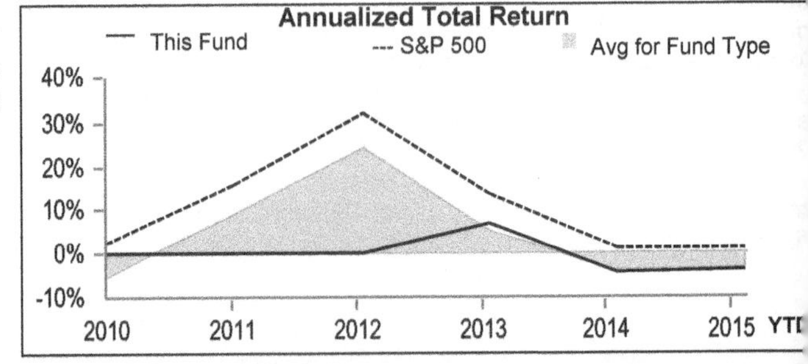

*ARK Genomic Revolution Multi-Sec (ARKG) C- Fair

Fund Family: ARK Investment Management LLC
Fund Type: Global
Inception Date: October 31, 2014

Data Date	Investment Rating	Net Assets ($Mil)	Price	Performance Rating/Pts	Total Return Y-T-D	Risk Rating/Pts
12-15	C-	0.00	20.97	C- / 4.0	-1.57%	C+ / 5.7

Major Rating Factors: Middle of the road best describes *ARK Genomic Revolution Multi-Sec whose TheStreet.com Investment Rating is currently a C- (Fair). The fund currently has a performance rating of C- (Fair) based on an annualized return of 0.00% over the last three years and a total return of -1.57% year to date 2015. Factored into the performance evaluation is an expense ratio of 0.95% (low).

The fund's risk rating is currently C+ (Fair). It carries a beta of 0.00, meaning the fund's expected move will be 0.0% for every 10% move in the market. Volatility, as measured by both the semi-deviation and a drawdown factor, is considered low. As of December 31, 2015, *ARK Genomic Revolution Multi-Sec traded at a premium of .77% above its net asset value, which is worse than its one-year historical average premium of .07%.

Catherine D. Wood has been running the fund for 2 years and currently receives a manager quality ranking of 60 (0=worst, 99=best). If you desire an average level of risk, then this fund may be an option.

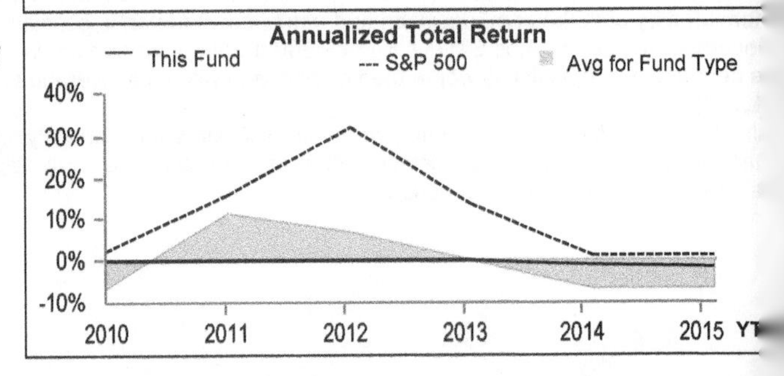

*ARK Industrial Innovation (ARKQ) C Fair

Fund Family: ARK Investment Management LLC
Fund Type: Global
Inception Date: September 30, 2014

Data Date	Investment Rating	Net Assets ($Mil)	Price	Performance Rating/Pts	Total Return Y-T-D	Risk Rating/Pts
12-15	C	0.00	19.18	C / 5.4	-1.38%	C+ / 6.5

Major Rating Factors: Middle of the road best describes *ARK Industrial Innovation whose TheStreet.com Investment Rating is currently a C (Fair). The fund currently has a performance rating of C (Fair) based on an annualized return of 0.00% over the last three years and a total return of -1.38% year to date 2015. Factored into the performance evaluation is an expense ratio of 0.95% (low).

The fund's risk rating is currently C+ (Fair). It carries a beta of 0.00, meaning the fund's expected move will be 0.0% for every 10% move in the market. Volatility, as measured by both the semi-deviation and a drawdown factor, is considered low. As of December 31, 2015, *ARK Industrial Innovation traded at a premium of .47% above its net asset value, which is worse than its one-year historical average premium of .12%.

Catherine D. Wood has been running the fund for 2 years and currently receives a manager quality ranking of 50 (0=worst, 99=best). If you desire an average level of risk, then this fund may be an option.

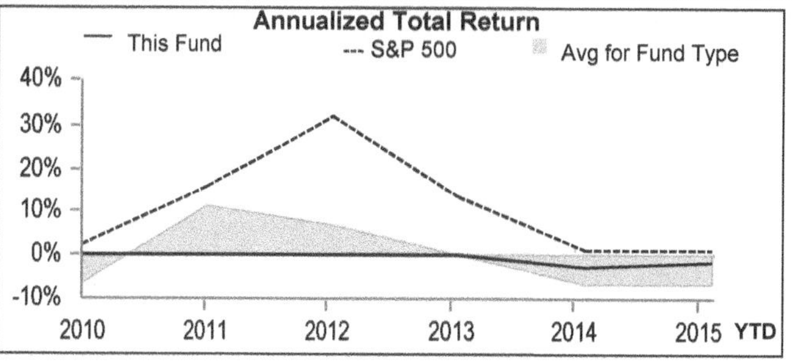

*ARK Innovation (ARKK) C+ Fair

Fund Family: ARK Investment Management LLC
Fund Type: Growth
Inception Date: October 31, 2014

Data Date	Investment Rating	Net Assets ($Mil)	Price	Performance Rating/Pts	Total Return Y-T-D	Risk Rating/Pts
12-15	C+	0.00	20.46	C+ / 6.5	3.75%	C+ / 6.5

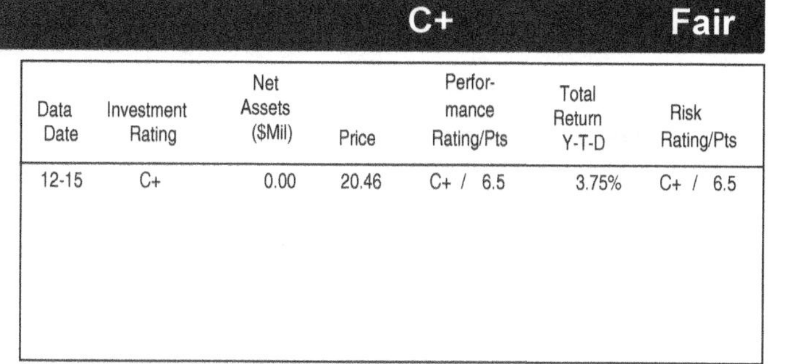

Major Rating Factors: Middle of the road best describes *ARK Innovation whose TheStreet.com Investment Rating is currently a C+ (Fair). The fund currently has a performance rating of C+ (Fair) based on an annualized return of 0.00% over the last three years and a total return of 3.75% year to date 2015. Factored into the performance evaluation is an expense ratio of 0.95% (low).

The fund's risk rating is currently C+ (Fair). It carries a beta of 0.00, meaning the fund's expected move will be 0.0% for every 10% move in the market. Volatility, as measured by both the semi-deviation and a drawdown factor, is considered low. As of December 31, 2015, *ARK Innovation traded at a premium of .15% above its net asset value, which is worse than its one-year historical average premium of .13%.

Catherine D. Wood has been running the fund for 2 years and currently receives a manager quality ranking of 83 (0=worst, 99=best). If you desire an average level of risk, then this fund may be an option.

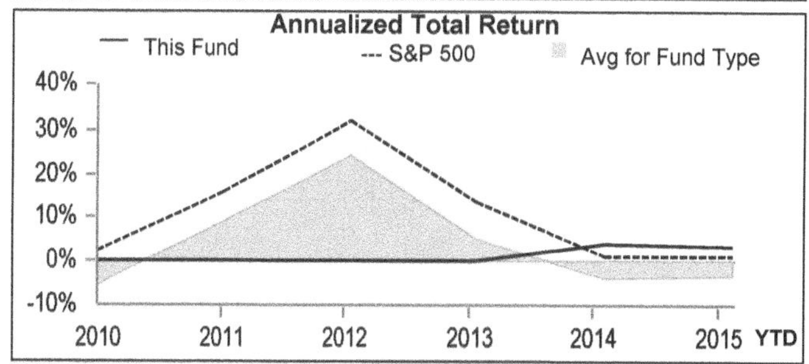

*ARK Web x.0 (ARKW) A- Excellent

Fund Family: ARK Investment Management LLC
Fund Type: Growth
Inception Date: September 30, 2014

Data Date	Investment Rating	Net Assets ($Mil)	Price	Performance Rating/Pts	Total Return Y-T-D	Risk Rating/Pts
12-15	A-	0.00	23.17	A / 9.4	16.65%	C+ / 6.9

Major Rating Factors:
Exceptional performance is the major factor driving the A- (Excellent) TheStreet.com Investment Rating for *ARK Web x.0. The fund currently has a performance rating of A (Excellent) based on an annualized return of 0.00% over the last three years and a total return of 16.65% year to date 2015. Factored into the performance evaluation is an expense ratio of 0.95% (low).

The fund's risk rating is currently C+ (Fair). It carries a beta of 0.00, meaning the fund's expected move will be 0.0% for every 10% move in the market. Volatility, as measured by both the semi-deviation and a drawdown factor, is considered low. As of December 31, 2015, *ARK Web x.0 traded at a premium of .52% above its net asset value, which is worse than its one-year historical average premium of .07%.

Catherine D. Wood currently receives a manager quality ranking of 97 (0=worst, 99=best). If you desire only a moderate level of risk and strong performance, then this fund is an excellent option.

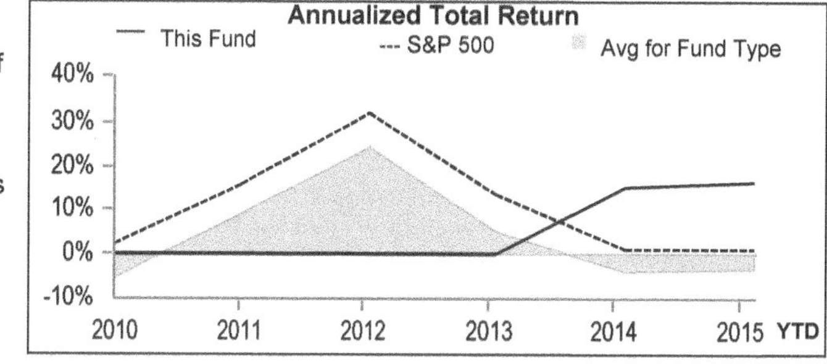

* Denotes ETF Fund

*Arrow Dow Jones Global Yield ETF (GYLD) D Weak

Fund Family: Arrow Investment Advisors LLC
Fund Type: Growth and Income
Inception Date: May 8, 2012

Data Date	Investment Rating	Net Assets ($Mil)	Price	Perfor-mance Rating/Pts	Total Return Y-T-D	Risk Rating/Pts
12-15	D	191.00	17.16	D / 1.7	-23.68%	C+ / 6.2
2014	D+	191.00	23.87	D / 1.6	-1.03%	B / 8.0
2013	C+	90.10	26.55	C / 5.2	4.32%	B / 8.7

Major Rating Factors:
Disappointing performance is the major factor driving the D (Weak) TheStreet.com Investment Rating for *Arrow Dow Jones Global Yield ETF. The fund currently has a performance rating of D (Weak) based on an annualized return of -7.36% over the last three years and a total return of -23.68% year to date 2015. Factored into the performance evaluation is an expense ratio of 0.75% (very low).

The fund's risk rating is currently C+ (Fair). It carries a beta of 0.87, meaning the fund's expected move will be 8.7% for every 10% move in the market. Volatility, as measured by both the semi-deviation and a drawdown factor, is considered low. As of December 31, 2015, *Arrow Dow Jones Global Yield ETF traded at a discount of 1.72% below its net asset value, which is better than its one-year historical average discount of .06%.

William E. Flaig, Jr. has been running the fund for 4 years and currently receives a manager quality ranking of 8 (0=worst, 99=best). This fund offers only a moderate level of risk but investors looking for strong performance are still waiting.

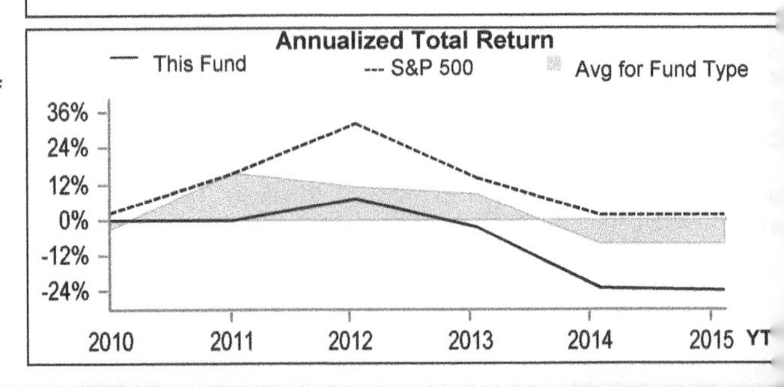

*Arrow DWA Tactical (DWAT) C+ Fair

Fund Family: Arrow Investment Advisors LLC
Fund Type: Growth and Income
Inception Date: September 30, 2014

Data Date	Investment Rating	Net Assets ($Mil)	Price	Perfor-mance Rating/Pts	Total Return Y-T-D	Risk Rating/Pts
12-15	C+	0.00	9.90	C+ / 6.0	0.05%	B- / 7.0

Major Rating Factors: Middle of the road best describes *Arrow DWA Tactical whose TheStreet.com Investment Rating is currently a C+ (Fair). The fund currently has a performance rating of C+ (Fair) based on an annualized return of 0.00% over the last three years and a total return of 0.05% year to date 2015. Factored into the performance evaluation is an expense ratio of 1.40% (average).

The fund's risk rating is currently B- (Good). It carries a beta of 0.00, meaning the fund's expected move will be 0.0% for every 10% move in the market. Volatility, as measured by both the semi-deviation and a drawdown factor, is considered low. As of December 31, 2015, *Arrow DWA Tactical traded at a premium of .20% above its net asset value, which is worse than its one-year historical average discount of .02%.

Jon Guyer has been running the fund for 2 years and currently receives a manager quality ranking of 64 (0=worst, 99=best). If you desire an average level of risk, then this fund may be an option.

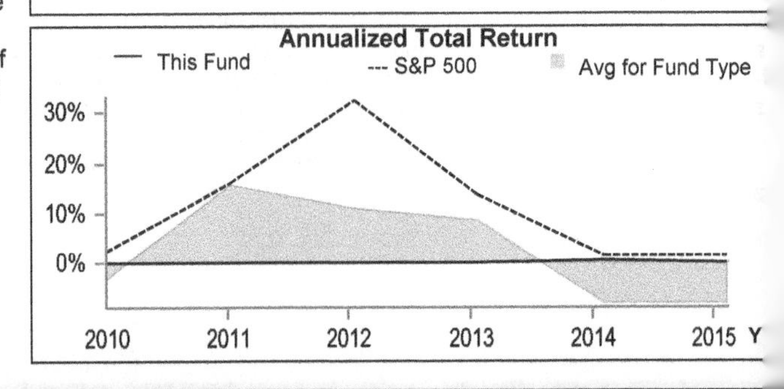

*Athena High Dividend ETF (DIVI) D- Weak

Fund Family: AdvisorShares Investments LLC
Fund Type: Global
Inception Date: July 30, 2014

Data Date	Investment Rating	Net Assets ($Mil)	Price	Perfor-mance Rating/Pts	Total Return Y-T-D	Risk Rating/Pts
12-15	D-	0.00	14.89	E / 0.5	-25.65%	C / 4.

Major Rating Factors:
Very poor performance is the major factor driving the D- (Weak) TheStreet.com Investment Rating for *Athena High Dividend ETF. The fund currently has a performance rating of E (Very Weak) based on an annualized return of 0.00% over the last three years and a total return of -25.65% year to date 2015. Factored into the performance evaluation is an expense ratio of 0.99% (low).

The fund's risk rating is currently C (Fair). It carries a beta of 0.00, meaning the fund's expected move will be 0.0% for every 10% move in the market. Volatility, as measured by both the semi-deviation and a drawdown factor, is considered average. As of December 31, 2015, *Athena High Dividend ETF traded at a premium of .27% above its net asset value, which is worse than its one-year historical average premium of .14%.

C. Thomas Howard currently receives a manager quality ranking of 4 (0=worst, 99=best). This fund offers an average level of risk but investors looking for strong performance will be frustrated.

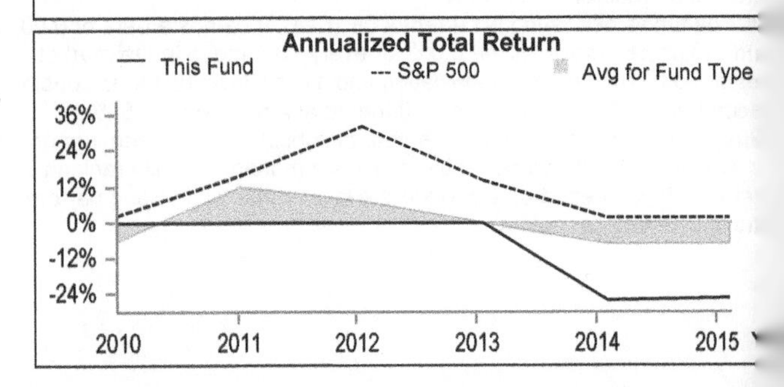

*Barclays ETN + FI Enh Eur 50 (FEEU) D- Weak

Fund Family: Barclays Bank PLC
Fund Type: Foreign
Inception Date: May 22, 2013

Data Date	Investment Rating	Net Assets ($Mil)	Price	Perfor-mance Rating/Pts	Total Return Y-T-D	Risk Rating/Pts
12-15	D-	0.00	93.80	D- / 1.3	-8.80%	C / 4.4

Major Rating Factors:
Disappointing performance is the major factor driving the D- (Weak) TheStreet.com Investment Rating for *Barclays ETN + FI Enh Eur 50. The fund currently has a performance rating of D- (Weak) based on an annualized return of 0.00% over the last three years and a total return of -8.80% year to date 2015.

The fund's risk rating is currently C (Fair). It carries a beta of 0.00, meaning the fund's expected move will be 0.0% for every 10% move in the market. Volatility, as measured by both the semi-deviation and a drawdown factor, is considered average. As of December 31, 2015, *Barclays ETN + FI Enh Eur 50 traded at a discount of 1.18% below its net asset value, which is better than its one-year historical average discount of .13%.

This is team managed and currently receives a manager quality ranking of 18 (0=worst, 99=best). This fund offers an average level of risk but investors looking for strong performance will be frustrated.

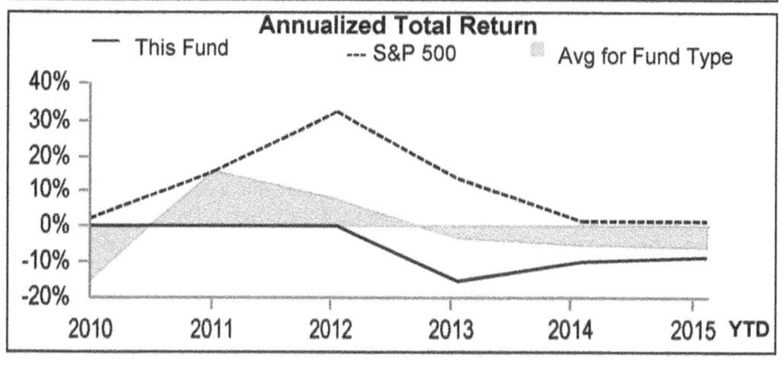

*Barclays ETN + FI Enh Gl Hi Yld (FIGY) D- Weak

Fund Family: Barclays Bank PLC
Fund Type: Growth
Inception Date: May 21, 2013

Data Date	Investment Rating	Net Assets ($Mil)	Price	Perfor-mance Rating/Pts	Total Return Y-T-D	Risk Rating/Pts
12-15	D-	1,501.50	111.89	C- / 3.2	-4.54%	C- / 3.0
2014	D+	1,501.50	118.10	D+ / 2.8	7.37%	C+ / 6.8

Major Rating Factors: *Barclays ETN + FI Enh Gl Hi Yld receives a TheStreet.com Investment Rating of D- (Weak). The fund currently has a performance rating of C- (Fair) based on an annualized return of 0.00% over the last three years and a total return of -4.54% year to date 2015.

The fund's risk rating is currently C- (Fair). It carries a beta of 0.00, meaning the fund's expected move will be 0.0% for every 10% move in the market. Volatility, as measured by both the semi-deviation and a drawdown factor, is considered average. As of December 31, 2015, *Barclays ETN + FI Enh Gl Hi Yld traded at a premium of .46% above its net asset value, which is worse than its one-year historical average discount of .07%.

If you desire an average level of risk, then this fund may be an option.

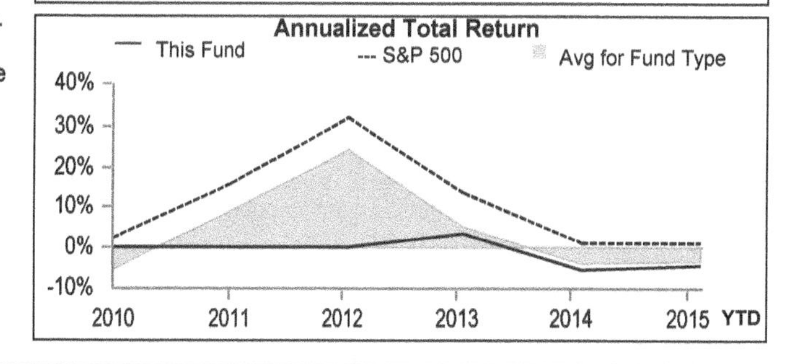

*Barclays ETN + OFI SteelPath MLP (OSMS) E Very Weak

Fund Family: Barclays Bank PLC
Fund Type: Energy/Natural Resources
Inception Date: April 23, 2014

Data Date	Investment Rating	Net Assets ($Mil)	Price	Perfor-mance Rating/Pts	Total Return Y-T-D	Risk Rating/Pts
12-15	E	68.30	16.98	E / 0.5	-29.74%	D- / 1.5

Major Rating Factors: *Barclays ETN + OFI SteelPath MLP has adopted a very risky asset allocation strategy and currently receives an overall TheStreet.com Investment Rating of E (Very Weak). The fund has a high level of volatility, as measured by both semi-deviation and drawdown factors. It carries a beta of 0.00, meaning the fund's expected move will be 0.0% for every 10% move in the market. As of December 31, 2015, *Barclays ETN + OFI SteelPath MLP traded at a premium of 2.10% above its net asset value, which is worse than its one-year historical average premium of .87%. Unfortunately, the high level of risk (D-, Weak) failed to pay off as investors endured very poor performance.

The fund's performance rating is currently E (Very Weak). It has registered an annualized return of 0.00% over the last three years but is down -29.74% year to date 2015.

If you can tolerate very high levels of risk in the hope of improved future returns, holding this fund may be an option.

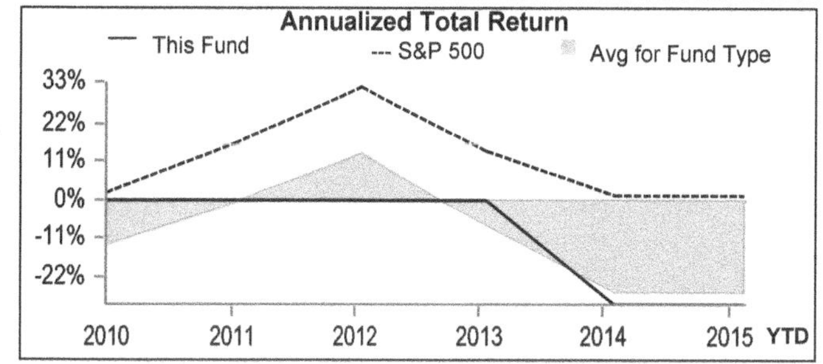

*Barclays ETN + Select MLP ETN (ATMP) — E- Very Weak

Fund Family: Barclays Bank PLC
Fund Type: Energy/Natural Resources
Inception Date: March 12, 2013

Major Rating Factors: *Barclays ETN + Select MLP ETN has adopted a very risky asset allocation strategy and currently receives an overall TheStreet.com Investment Rating of E- (Very Weak). The fund has a high level of volatility, as measured by both semi-deviation and drawdown factors. It carries a beta of 0.00, meaning the fund's expected move will be 0.0% for every 10% move in the market. As of December 31, 2015, *Barclays ETN + Select MLP ETN traded at a premium of .27% above its net asset value, which is worse than its one-year historical average premium of .08%. Unfortunately, the high level of risk (D-, Weak) failed to pay off as investors endured very poor performance.

The fund's performance rating is currently E- (Very Weak). It has registered an annualized return of 0.00% over the last three years but is down -36.80% year to date 2015.

This fund has been team managed for 3 years and currently receives a manager quality ranking of 6 (0=worst, 99=best). If you can tolerate very high levels of risk in the hope of improved future returns, holding this fund may be an option.

Data Date	Investment Rating	Net Assets ($Mil)	Price	Performance Rating/Pts	Total Return Y-T-D	Risk Rating/Pts
12-15	E-	402.70	18.61	E- / 0.1	-36.80%	D- / 1.5
2014	B-	402.70	30.59	C+ / 5.8	17.07%	B / 8.9

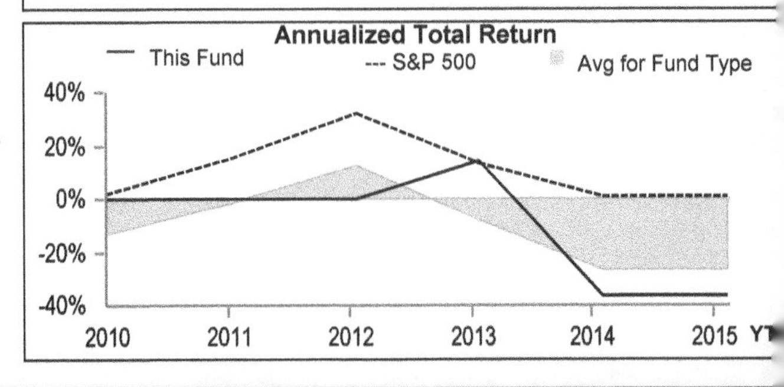

*Barclays ETN + Shiller CAPE ETN (CAPE) — C+ Fair

Fund Family: Barclays Bank PLC
Fund Type: Income
Inception Date: October 10, 2012

Major Rating Factors:
Exceptional performance is the major factor driving the C+ (Fair) TheStreet.com Investment Rating for *Barclays ETN + Shiller CAPE ETN. The fund currently has a performance rating of A- (Excellent) based on an annualized return of 16.09% over the last three years and a total return of 4.73% year to date 2015.

The fund's risk rating is currently C- (Fair). It carries a beta of 1.02, meaning that its performance tracks fairly well with that of the overall stock market. Volatility, as measured by both the semi-deviation and a drawdown factor, is considered average. As of December 31, 2015, *Barclays ETN + Shiller CAPE ETN traded at a premium of .41% above its net asset value, which is worse than its one-year historical average premium of .01%.

This fund has been team managed for 4 years and currently receives a manager quality ranking of 79 (0=worst, 99=best). If you desire an average level of risk and strong performance, then this fund is a good option.

Data Date	Investment Rating	Net Assets ($Mil)	Price	Performance Rating/Pts	Total Return Y-T-D	Risk Rating/Pts
12-15	C+	22.30	81.30	A- / 9.2	4.73%	C- / 3.9
2014	B+	22.30	77.75	B / 7.9	17.62%	B- / 7.7
2013	B	16.50	67.16	A / 9.3	28.09%	C+ / 5.9

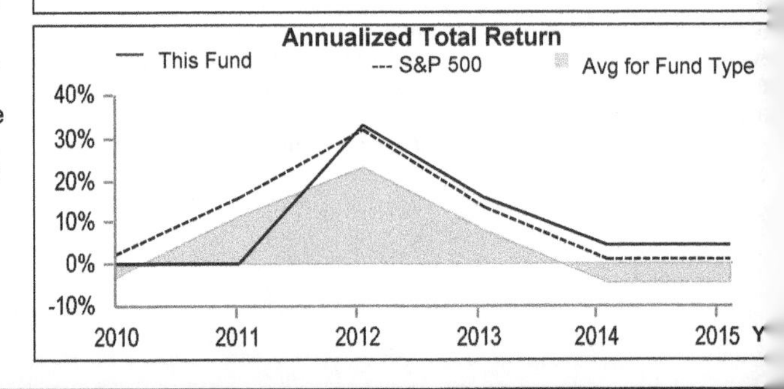

*Barclays ETN + VEQTOR ETN (VQT) — D Weak

Fund Family: Barclays Bank PLC
Fund Type: Growth
Inception Date: August 31, 2010

Major Rating Factors: *Barclays ETN + VEQTOR ETN receives a TheStreet.com Investment Rating of D (Weak). The fund currently has a performance rating of C (Fair) based on an annualized return of 1.92% over the last three years and a total return of -9.54% year to date 2015.

The fund's risk rating is currently C- (Fair). It carries a beta of 0.58, meaning the fund's expected move will be 5.8% for every 10% move in the market. Volatility, as measured by both the semi-deviation and a drawdown factor, is considered average. As of December 31, 2015, *Barclays ETN + VEQTOR ETN traded at a premium of .25% above its net asset value, which is worse than its one-year historical average discount of .01%.

This fund has been team managed for 6 years and currently receives a manager quality ranking of 26 (0=worst, 99=best). If you desire an average level of risk, then this fund may be an option.

Data Date	Investment Rating	Net Assets ($Mil)	Price	Performance Rating/Pts	Total Return Y-T-D	Risk Rating/Pts
12-15	D	641.60	138.33	C / 4.5	-9.54%	C- / 3
2014	C	641.60	153.71	C / 4.6	5.81%	B- / 7.
2013	C-	654.70	146.12	C+ / 6.3	10.88%	C+ / 5.
2012	D-	364.20	129.27	D / 2.0	2.25%	C+ / 5
2011	C	192.50	125.97	C+ / 6.8	16.64%	C+ / 5

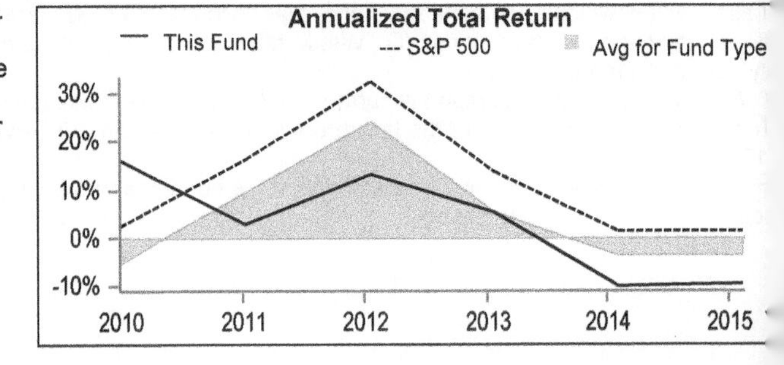

*Barclays Inverse US Treasury Com (TAPR) D- Weak

Fund Family: Barclays Bank PLC
Fund Type: Global
Inception Date: July 14, 2014

Major Rating Factors: *Barclays Inverse US Treasury Com has adopted a risky asset allocation strategy and currently receives an overall TheStreet.com Investment Rating of D- (Weak). The fund has an above average level of volatility, as measured by both semi-deviation and drawdown factors. It carries a beta of 0.00, meaning the fund's expected move will be 0.0% for every 10% move in the market. As of December 31, 2015, *Barclays Inverse US Treasury Com traded at a premium of .18% above its net asset value, which is worse than its one-year historical average discount of .10%. Unfortunately, the high level of risk (D+, Weak) has only provided investors with average performance.

The fund's performance rating is currently C- (Fair). It has registered an annualized return of 0.00% over the last three years but is down -3.67% year to date 2015.

If you are comfortable owning a high risk investment, then this fund may be an option.

Data Date	Investment Rating	Net Assets ($Mil)	Price	Performance Rating/Pts	Total Return Y-T-D	Risk Rating/Pts
12-15	D-	0.00	32.99	C- / 3.0	-3.67%	D+ / 2.9

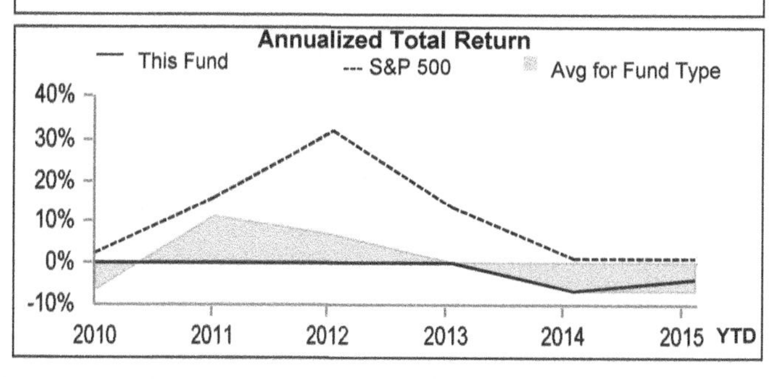

*Barclays Women in Leadership (WIL) D Weak

Fund Family: Barclays Bank PLC
Fund Type: Global
Inception Date: July 9, 2014

Major Rating Factors: *Barclays Women in Leadership receives a TheStreet.com Investment Rating of D (Weak). The fund currently has a performance rating of C- (Fair) based on an annualized return of 0.00% over the last three years and a total return of -2.36% year to date 2015.

The fund's risk rating is currently C- (Fair). It carries a beta of 0.00, meaning the fund's expected move will be 0.0% for every 10% move in the market. Volatility, as measured by both the semi-deviation and a drawdown factor, is considered average. As of December 31, 2015, *Barclays Women in Leadership traded at a premium of .68% above its net asset value, which is worse than its one-year historical average premium of .26%.

If you desire an average level of risk, then this fund may be an option.

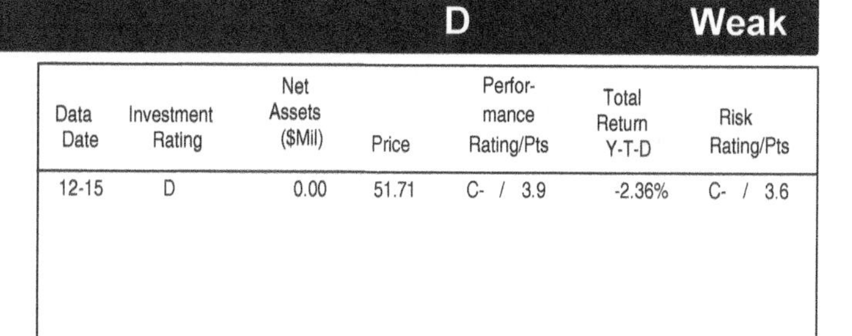

Data Date	Investment Rating	Net Assets ($Mil)	Price	Performance Rating/Pts	Total Return Y-T-D	Risk Rating/Pts
12-15	D	0.00	51.71	C- / 3.9	-2.36%	C- / 3.6

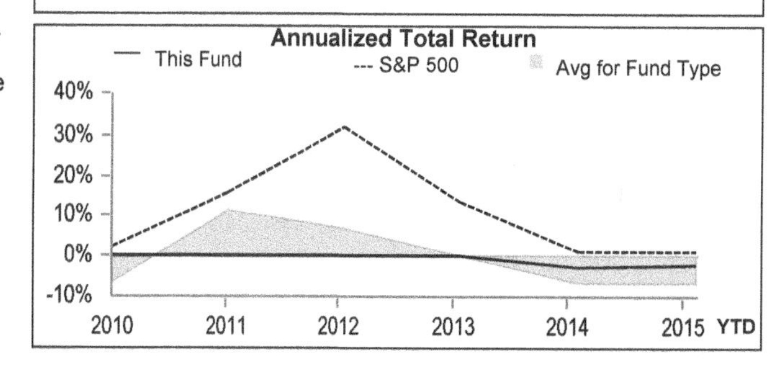

*BLDRS Asia 50 ADR Index (ADRA) C+ Fair

Fund Family: Bank of New York Mellon
Fund Type: Foreign
nception Date: November 13, 2002

lajor Rating Factors: Middle of the road best describes *BLDRS Asia 50 ADR ndex whose TheStreet.com Investment Rating is currently a C+ (Fair). The fund urrently has a performance rating of C (Fair) based on an annualized return of .52% over the last three years and a total return of -2.38% year to date 2015. actored into the performance evaluation is an expense ratio of 0.30% (very low).

The fund's risk rating is currently B- (Good). It carries a beta of 1.02, meaning hat its performance tracks fairly well with that of the overall stock market. Volatility, s measured by both the semi-deviation and a drawdown factor, is considered low. s of December 31, 2015, *BLDRS Asia 50 ADR Index traded at a discount of .15% elow its net asset value, which is worse than its one-year historical average discount f .34%.

Andrew Nicholas currently receives a manager quality ranking of 50 (0=worst, 9=best). If you desire an average level of risk, then this fund may be an option.

Data Date	Investment Rating	Net Assets ($Mil)	Price	Performance Rating/Pts	Total Return Y-T-D	Risk Rating/Pts
12-15	C+	26.20	27.00	C / 5.1	-2.38%	B- / 7.8
2014	C-	26.20	28.48	C / 4.9	-0.67%	C+ / 6.3
2013	C	34.00	29.31	C / 4.8	10.97%	B- / 7.4
2012	D+	29.10	26.18	D+ / 2.8	15.88%	B- / 7.4
2011	D+	29.40	22.43	D+ / 2.7	-16.46%	B- / 7.6
2010	C-	50.10	28.66	C- / 3.9	14.13%	C / 5.1

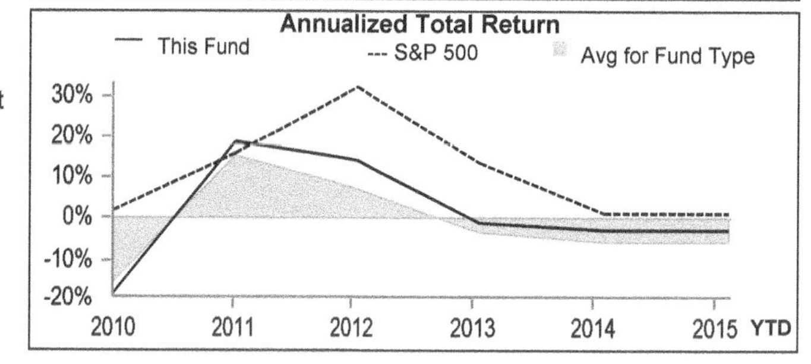

*BLDRS Developed Mkts 100 ADR Ind (ADRD) C Fair

Fund Family: Bank of New York Mellon
Fund Type: Foreign
Inception Date: November 13, 2002

Major Rating Factors: Middle of the road best describes *BLDRS Developed Mkts 100 ADR Ind whose TheStreet.com Investment Rating is currently a C (Fair). The fund currently has a performance rating of C (Fair) based on an annualized return of 3.01% over the last three years and a total return of -2.94% year to date 2015. Factored into the performance evaluation is an expense ratio of 0.30% (very low).

The fund's risk rating is currently C+ (Fair). It carries a beta of 1.01, meaning that its performance tracks fairly well with that of the overall stock market. Volatility, as measured by both the semi-deviation and a drawdown factor, is considered low. As of December 31, 2015, *BLDRS Developed Mkts 100 ADR Ind traded at a premium of .24% above its net asset value, which is worse than its one-year historical average premium of .06%.

Andrew Nicholas currently receives a manager quality ranking of 53 (0=worst, 99=best). If you desire an average level of risk, then this fund may be an option.

Data Date	Investment Rating	Net Assets ($Mil)	Price	Performance Rating/Pts	Total Return Y-T-D	Risk Rating/Pts
12-15	C	56.90	20.94	C / 5.1	-2.94%	C+ / 6.3
2014	C-	56.90	22.41	C / 4.8	-4.00%	C+ / 6.4
2013	C+	52.60	25.06	C+ / 6.9	18.58%	B- / 7.4
2012	C-	46.60	21.03	C- / 4.1	20.69%	B- / 7.2
2011	D+	55.10	18.69	D+ / 2.4	-10.11%	B- / 7.4
2010	D-	76.20	21.45	D- / 1.4	3.96%	C / 4.8

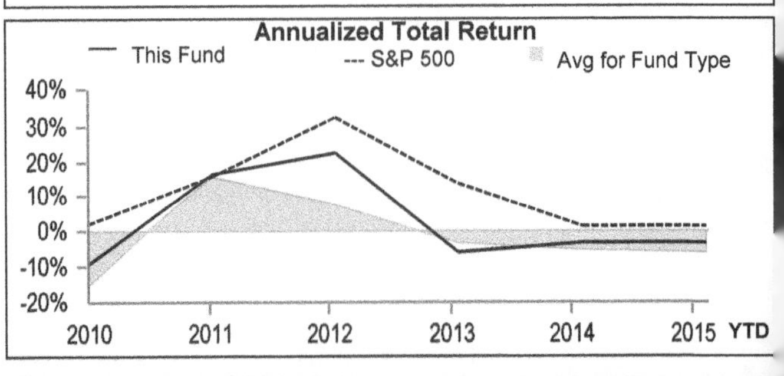

*BLDRS Emerging Market 50 ADR Ind (ADRE) D Weak

Fund Family: Bank of New York Mellon
Fund Type: Emerging Market
Inception Date: November 13, 2002

Major Rating Factors:
Disappointing performance is the major factor driving the D (Weak) TheStreet.com Investment Rating for *BLDRS Emerging Market 50 ADR Ind. The fund currently has a performance rating of D (Weak) based on an annualized return of -8.83% over the last three years and a total return of -15.25% year to date 2015. Factored into the performance evaluation is an expense ratio of 0.30% (very low).

The fund's risk rating is currently C+ (Fair). It carries a beta of 1.19, meaning it is expected to move 11.9% for every 10% move in the market. Volatility, as measured by both the semi-deviation and a drawdown factor, is considered low. As of December 31, 2015, *BLDRS Emerging Market 50 ADR Ind traded at a discount of .21% below its net asset value, which is better than its one-year historical average discount of .19%.

Andrew Nicholas currently receives a manager quality ranking of 63 (0=worst, 99=best). This fund offers only a moderate level of risk but investors looking for strong performance are still waiting.

Data Date	Investment Rating	Net Assets ($Mil)	Price	Performance Rating/Pts	Total Return Y-T-D	Risk Rating/Pts
12-15	D	213.70	29.07	D / 2.0	-15.25%	C+ / 6.2
2014	D	213.70	35.52	D+ / 2.4	1.04%	C / 5.2
2013	D	230.60	37.14	D- / 1.5	-10.54%	C+ / 6.8
2012	D	323.70	40.22	D / 1.8	4.38%	B- / 7.1
2011	C-	405.80	38.07	C- / 4.0	-16.05%	B- / 7.3
2010	D+	674.10	48.15	C- / 3.8	11.58%	C / 4.5

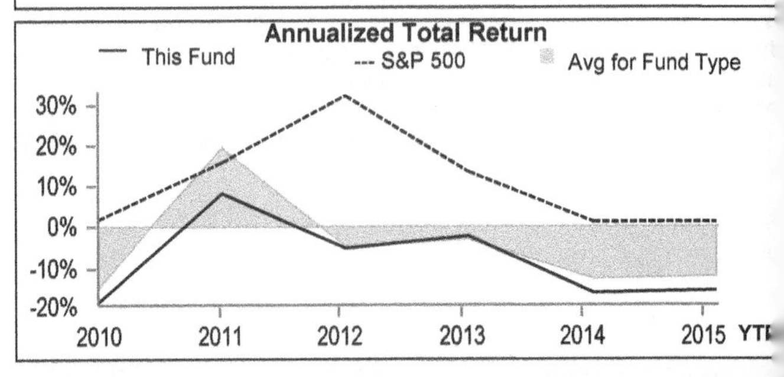

*BLDRS Europe Select ADR Index (ADRU) C- Fair

Fund Family: Bank of New York Mellon
Fund Type: Foreign
Inception Date: November 13, 2002

Major Rating Factors: Middle of the road best describes *BLDRS Europe Select ADR Index whose TheStreet.com Investment Rating is currently a C- (Fair). The fund currently has a performance rating of C (Fair) based on an annualized return of 2.75% over the last three years and a total return of -4.73% year to date 2015. Factored into the performance evaluation is an expense ratio of 0.30% (very low).

The fund's risk rating is currently C+ (Fair). It carries a beta of 1.03, meaning that its performance tracks fairly well with that of the overall stock market. Volatility, as measured by both the semi-deviation and a drawdown factor, is considered low. As of December 31, 2015, *BLDRS Europe Select ADR Index traded at a premium of .20% above its net asset value, which is worse than its one-year historical average discount of .05%.

Andrew Nicholas currently receives a manager quality ranking of 49 (0=worst, 99=best). If you desire an average level of risk, then this fund may be an option.

Data Date	Investment Rating	Net Assets ($Mil)	Price	Performance Rating/Pts	Total Return Y-T-D	Risk Rating/Pts
12-15	C-	19.50	20.49	C / 4.8	-4.73%	C+ / 6.0
2014	C-	19.50	22.33	C / 5.0	-3.29%	C+ / 6.3
2013	C+	17.30	24.81	C+ / 6.8	18.79%	B- / 7.3
2012	D+	13.60	20.83	C- / 3.4	21.85%	B- / 7.1
2011	D+	14.80	18.63	D+ / 2.6	-8.19%	B- / 7.0
2010	D-	22.90	20.82	D- / 1.0	1.77%	C / 5.0

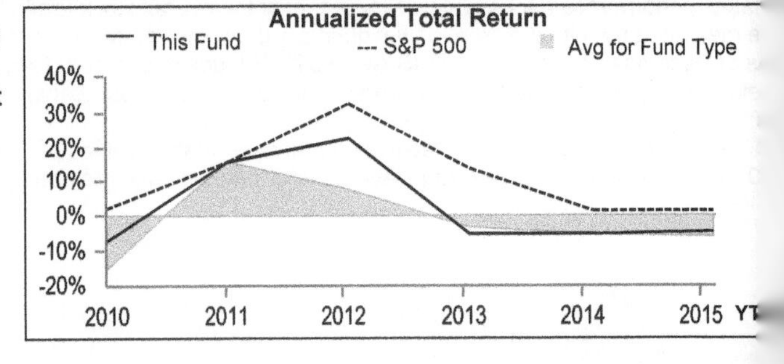

*Brclys ETN+ Inv S&P500 VIX STF E (XXV) D+ Weak

Fund Family: Barclays Bank PLC
Fund Type: Growth
Inception Date: July 20, 2010

Data Date	Investment Rating	Net Assets ($Mil)	Price	Performance Rating/Pts	Total Return Y-T-D	Risk Rating/Pts
12-15	D+	3.80	38.12	C / 4.4	-0.50%	C- / 4.2
2014	C	3.80	38.31	C- / 3.7	-0.47%	B / 8.9
2013	D	3.70	38.49	C / 4.3	1.77%	C / 4.9
2012	D	4.60	37.82	C- / 4.0	12.74%	C / 4.9
2011	D-	14.70	33.00	D+ / 2.3	1.02%	C / 5.0

Major Rating Factors: *Brclys ETN+ Inv S&P500 VIX STF E receives a TheStreet.com Investment Rating of D+ (Weak). The fund currently has a performance rating of C (Fair) based on an annualized return of 0.26% over the last three years and a total return of -0.50% year to date 2015.

The fund's risk rating is currently C- (Fair). It carries a beta of 0.05, meaning the fund's expected move will be 0.5% for every 10% move in the market. Volatility, as measured by both the semi-deviation and a drawdown factor, is considered average. As of December 31, 2015, *Brclys ETN+ Inv S&P500 VIX STF E traded at a premium of .03% above its net asset value.

This is team managed and currently receives a manager quality ranking of 64 (0=worst, 99=best). If you desire an average level of risk, then this fund may be an option.

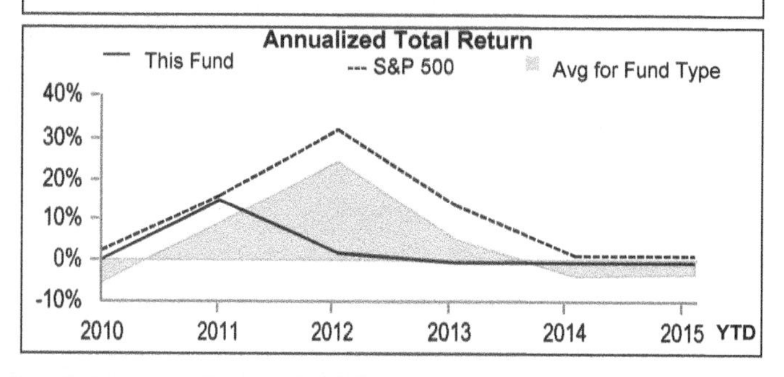

*C-Tracks ETN Citi Volatility Idx (CVOL) E- Very Weak

Fund Family: Citi Fund Management Inc
Fund Type: Income
Inception Date: November 15, 2010

Data Date	Investment Rating	Net Assets ($Mil)	Price	Performance Rating/Pts	Total Return Y-T-D	Risk Rating/Pts
12-15	E-	0.00	0.43	E- / 0	-60.11%	E- / 0.1
2014	E-	0.00	1.09	E- / 0	-73.31%	E- / 0
2013	E-	0.00	3.40	E- / 0	-85.05%	D / 1.9
2012	E-	0.00	29.70	E- / 0	-90.16%	D / 1.9
2011	E-	0.00	28.41	E- / 0	-60.94%	D / 2.1

Major Rating Factors: *C-Tracks ETN Citi Volatility Idx has adopted a very risky asset allocation strategy and currently receives an overall TheStreet.com Investment Rating of E- (Very Weak). The fund has a high level of volatility, as measured by both semi-deviation and drawdown factors. It carries a beta of -7.27, meaning the fund's expected move will be -72.7% for every 10% move in the market. As of December 31, 2015, *C-Tracks ETN Citi Volatility Idx traded at a premium of 4.88% above its net asset value, which is worse than its one-year historical average premium of 1.13%. Unfortunately, the high level of risk (E-, Very Weak) failed to pay off as investors endured very poor performance.

The fund's performance rating is currently E- (Very Weak). It has registered an annualized return of -73.97% over the last three years and is down -60.11% year to date 2015.

This is team managed and currently receives a manager quality ranking of 2 (0=worst, 99=best). If you can tolerate very high levels of risk in the hope of improved future returns, holding this fund may be an option.

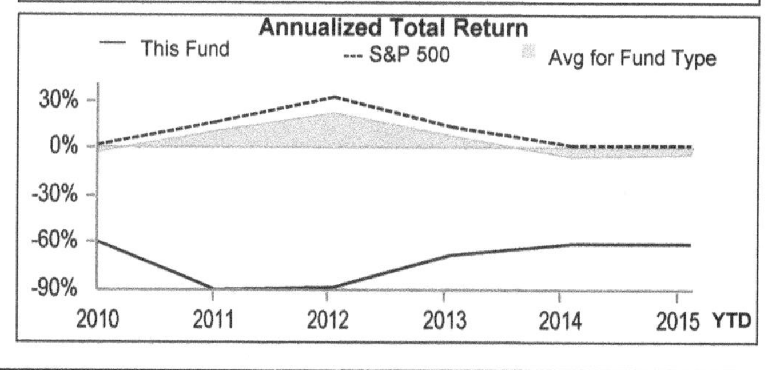

*C-Tracks ETN MillerHoward MLP FI (MLPC) E- Very Weak

Fund Family: Citi Fund Management Inc
Fund Type: Growth
Inception Date: September 25, 2013

Data Date	Investment Rating	Net Assets ($Mil)	Price	Performance Rating/Pts	Total Return Y-T-D	Risk Rating/Pts
12-15	E-	0.00	15.46	E- / 0.2	-37.82%	D- / 1.1
2014	D-	0.00	25.50	D / 1.6	3.37%	C- / 4.1

Major Rating Factors: *C-Tracks ETN MillerHoward MLP FI has adopted a very risky asset allocation strategy and currently receives an overall TheStreet.com Investment Rating of E- (Very Weak). The fund has a high level of volatility, as measured by both semi-deviation and drawdown factors. It carries a beta of 0.00, meaning the fund's expected move will be 0.0% for every 10% move in the market. As of December 31, 2015, *C-Tracks ETN MillerHoward MLP FI traded at a premium of .13% above its net asset value, which is in line with its one-year historical average premium of .13%. Unfortunately, the high level of risk (D-, Weak) failed to pay off as investors endured very poor performance.

The fund's performance rating is currently E- (Very Weak). It has registered an annualized return of 0.00% over the last three years but is down -37.82% year to date 2015.

If you can tolerate very high levels of risk in the hope of improved future returns, holding this fund may be an option.

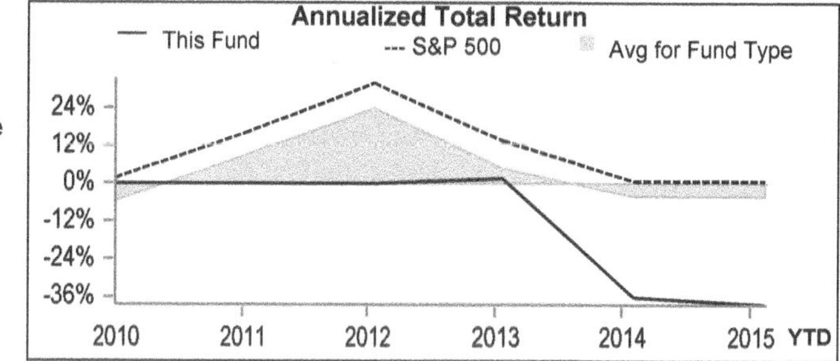

*C-Tracks ETN MillerHoward Str Di (DIVC) D Weak

Fund Family: Citi Fund Management Inc
Fund Type: Income
Inception Date: September 16, 2014

Major Rating Factors: *C-Tracks ETN MillerHoward Str Di receives a TheStreet.com Investment Rating of D (Weak). The fund currently has a performance rating of C- (Fair) based on an annualized return of 0.00% over the last three years and a total return of -1.15% year to date 2015.

The fund's risk rating is currently C- (Fair). It carries a beta of 0.00, meaning the fund's expected move will be 0.0% for every 10% move in the market. Volatility, as measured by both the semi-deviation and a drawdown factor, is considered average. As of December 31, 2015, *C-Tracks ETN MillerHoward Str Di traded at a premium of 4.65% above its net asset value, which is worse than its one-year historical average discount of .01%.

If you desire an average level of risk, then this fund may be an option.

Data Date	Investment Rating	Net Assets ($Mil)	Price	Performance Rating/Pts	Total Return Y-T-D	Risk Rating/Pts
12-15	D	0.00	24.97	C- / 3.6	-1.15%	C- / 3.

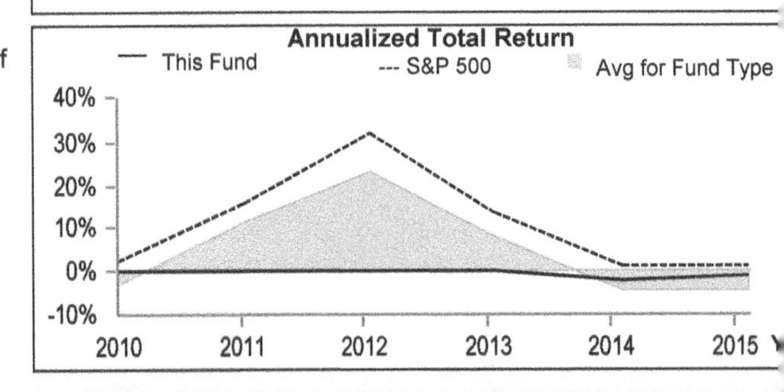

*Calamos Focus Growth (CFGE) C- Fair

Fund Family: Calamos Advisors LLC
Fund Type: Growth
Inception Date: July 14, 2014

Major Rating Factors: Middle of the road best describes *Calamos Focus Growth whose TheStreet.com Investment Rating is currently a C- (Fair). The fund currently has a performance rating of C- (Fair) based on an annualized return of 0.00% over the last three years and a total return of 0.76% year to date 2015. Factored into the performance evaluation is an expense ratio of 0.90% (low).

The fund's risk rating is currently B- (Good). It carries a beta of 0.00, meaning the fund's expected move will be 0.0% for every 10% move in the market. Volatility, as measured by both the semi-deviation and a drawdown factor, is considered low. As of December 31, 2015, *Calamos Focus Growth traded at a premium of .86% above its net asset value, which is worse than its one-year historical average premium of .48%.

John P. Calamos, Sr. has been running the fund for 2 years and currently receives a manager quality ranking of 56 (0=worst, 99=best). If you desire an average level of risk, then this fund may be an option.

Data Date	Investment Rating	Net Assets ($Mil)	Price	Performance Rating/Pts	Total Return Y-T-D	Risk Rating/Pts
12-15	C-	0.00	10.57	C- / 3.6	0.76%	B- / 7.

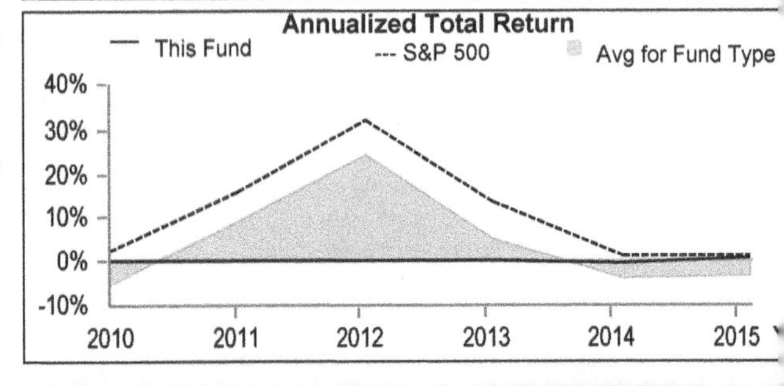

*Cambria Foreign Shareholder Yiel (FYLD) D+ Weak

Fund Family: Cambria Investment Management LP
Fund Type: Global
Inception Date: December 2, 2013

Major Rating Factors:
Disappointing performance is the major factor driving the D+ (Weak) TheStreet.com Investment Rating for *Cambria Foreign Shareholder Yiel. The fund currently has a performance rating of D (Weak) based on an annualized return of 0.00% over the last three years and a total return of -7.47% year to date 2015. Factored into the performance evaluation is an expense ratio of 0.59% (very low).

The fund's risk rating is currently B- (Good). It carries a beta of 0.00, meaning the fund's expected move will be 0.0% for every 10% move in the market. Volatility, as measured by both the semi-deviation and a drawdown factor, is considered low. As of December 31, 2015, *Cambria Foreign Shareholder Yiel traded at a discount of 1.57% below its net asset value, which is better than its one-year historical average discount of .24%.

Eric W. Richardson has been running the fund for 3 years and currently receives a manager quality ranking of 23 (0=worst, 99=best). This fund offers only a moderate level of risk but investors looking for strong performance are still waiting.

Data Date	Investment Rating	Net Assets ($Mil)	Price	Performance Rating/Pts	Total Return Y-T-D	Risk Rating/Pts
12-15	D+	78.30	20.04	D / 2.2	-7.47%	B- / 7
2014	E+	78.30	22.40	E+ / 0.9	-8.88%	C / 4

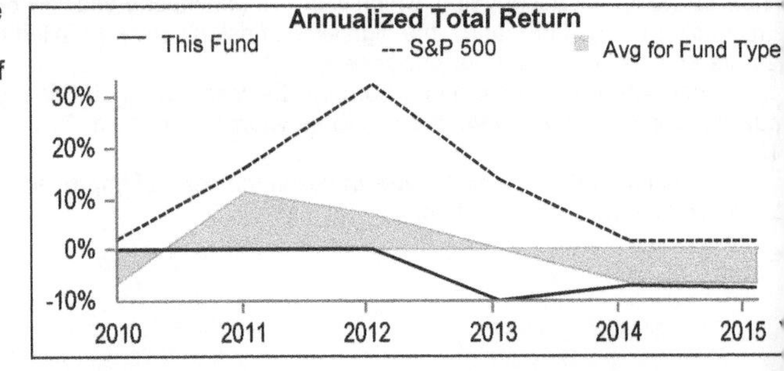

*Cambria Global Asset Allocation (GAA) D+ Weak

Fund Family: Cambria Investment Management LP
Fund Type: Growth and Income
Inception Date: December 9, 2014

Data Date	Investment Rating	Net Assets ($Mil)	Price	Performance Rating/Pts	Total Return Y-T-D	Risk Rating/Pts
12-15	D+	0.00	23.09	D+ / 2.8	-4.09%	C / 5.5

Major Rating Factors:
Disappointing performance is the major factor driving the D+ (Weak) TheStreet.com Investment Rating for *Cambria Global Asset Allocation. The fund currently has a performance rating of D+ (Weak) based on an annualized return of 0.00% over the last three years and a total return of -4.09% year to date 2015.

The fund's risk rating is currently C (Fair). It carries a beta of 0.00, meaning the fund's expected move will be 0.0% for every 10% move in the market. Volatility, as measured by both the semi-deviation and a drawdown factor, is considered average. As of December 31, 2015, *Cambria Global Asset Allocation traded at a discount of .09% below its net asset value, which is better than its one-year historical average premium of .02%.

Eric W. Richardson currently receives a manager quality ranking of 32 (0=worst, 99=best). This fund offers an average level of risk but investors looking for strong performance will be frustrated.

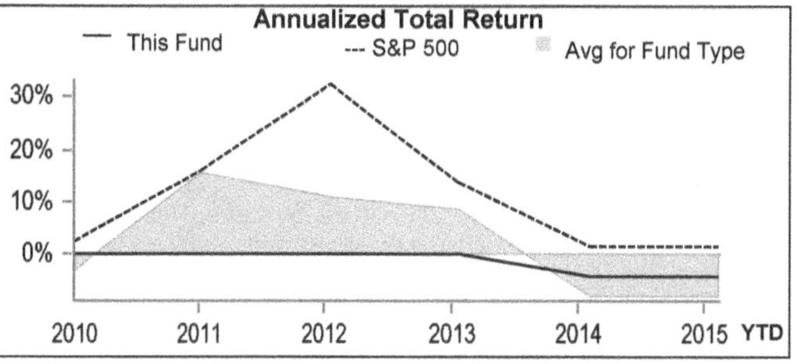

*Cambria Global Momentum ETF (GMOM) D- Weak

Fund Family: Cambria Investment Management LP
Fund Type: Foreign
Inception Date: November 3, 2014

Data Date	Investment Rating	Net Assets ($Mil)	Price	Performance Rating/Pts	Total Return Y-T-D	Risk Rating/Pts
12-15	D-	0.00	22.58	D / 2.0	-8.94%	C- / 3.3

Major Rating Factors:
Disappointing performance is the major factor driving the D- (Weak) TheStreet.com Investment Rating for *Cambria Global Momentum ETF. The fund currently has a performance rating of D (Weak) based on an annualized return of 0.00% over the last three years and a total return of -8.94% year to date 2015.

The fund's risk rating is currently C- (Fair). It carries a beta of 0.00, meaning the fund's expected move will be 0.0% for every 10% move in the market. Volatility, as measured by both the semi-deviation and a drawdown factor, is considered average. As of December 31, 2015, *Cambria Global Momentum ETF traded at a premium of .09% above its net asset value, which is worse than its one-year historical average discount of .03%.

Eric W. Richardson has been running the fund for 2 years and currently receives a manager quality ranking of 19 (0=worst, 99=best). This fund offers an average level of risk but investors looking for strong performance will be frustrated.

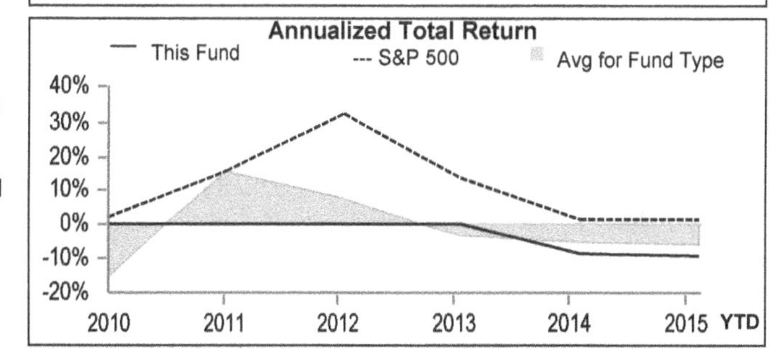

*Cambria Global Value ETF (GVAL) D Weak

Fund Family: Cambria Investment Management LP
Fund Type: Global
Inception Date: March 11, 2014

Data Date	Investment Rating	Net Assets ($Mil)	Price	Performance Rating/Pts	Total Return Y-T-D	Risk Rating/Pts
12-15	D	60.30	17.72	D / 1.6	-8.33%	C+ / 6.6

Major Rating Factors:
Disappointing performance is the major factor driving the D (Weak) TheStreet.com Investment Rating for *Cambria Global Value ETF. The fund currently has a performance rating of D (Weak) based on an annualized return of 0.00% over the last three years and a total return of -8.33% year to date 2015. Factored into the performance evaluation is an expense ratio of 0.69% (very low).

The fund's risk rating is currently C+ (Fair). It carries a beta of 0.00, meaning the fund's expected move will be 0.0% for every 10% move in the market. Volatility, as measured by both the semi-deviation and a drawdown factor, is considered low. As of December 31, 2015, *Cambria Global Value ETF traded at a discount of 1.12% below its net asset value, which is better than its one-year historical average premium of .07%.

Eric W. Richardson has been running the fund for 2 years and currently receives a manager quality ranking of 20 (0=worst, 99=best). This fund offers only a moderate level of risk but investors looking for strong performance are still waiting.

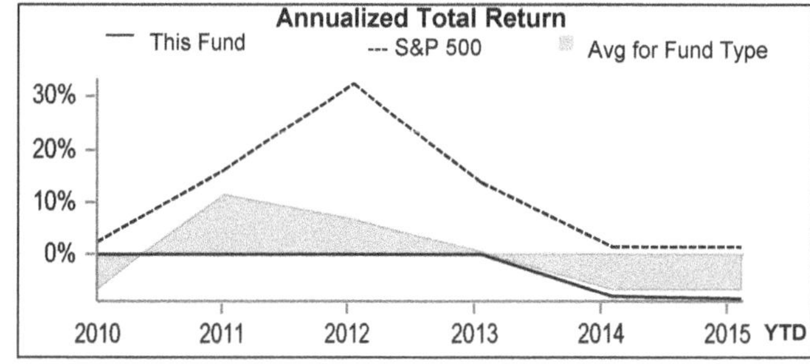

*Cambria Shareholder Yield ETF (SYLD) D+ Weak

Fund Family: Cambria Investment Management LP
Fund Type: Income
Inception Date: May 13, 2013

Major Rating Factors:
Disappointing performance is the major factor driving the D+ (Weak) TheStreet.com Investment Rating for *Cambria Shareholder Yield ETF. The fund currently has a performance rating of D+ (Weak) based on an annualized return of 0.00% over the last three years and a total return of -5.35% year to date 2015. Factored into the performance evaluation is an expense ratio of 0.59% (very low).

The fund's risk rating is currently C+ (Fair). It carries a beta of 0.00, meaning the fund's expected move will be 0.0% for every 10% move in the market. Volatility, as measured by both the semi-deviation and a drawdown factor, is considered low. As of December 31, 2015, *Cambria Shareholder Yield ETF traded at a premium of .28% above its net asset value, which is worse than its one-year historical average discount of .02%.

Eric W. Richardson has been running the fund for 3 years and currently receives a manager quality ranking of 23 (0=worst, 99=best). This fund offers only a moderate level of risk but investors looking for strong performance are still waiting.

Data Date	Investment Rating	Net Assets ($Mil)	Price	Perfor-mance Rating/Pts	Total Return Y-T-D	Risk Rating/Pts
12-15	D+	213.40	28.90	D+ / 2.4	-5.35%	C+ / 6.8
2014	C+	213.40	31.18	C+ / 6.4	11.70%	B- / 7.6

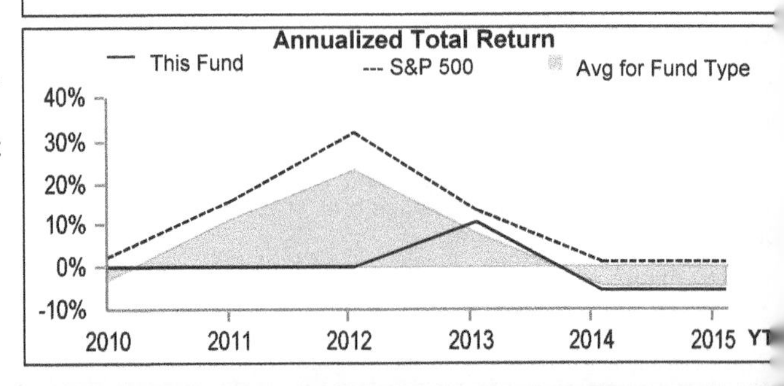

*Cohen & Steers Global Realty Maj (GRI) C+ Fair

Fund Family: ALPS Advisors Inc
Fund Type: Growth and Income
Inception Date: May 7, 2008

Major Rating Factors: Middle of the road best describes *Cohen & Steers Global Realty Maj whose TheStreet.com Investment Rating is currently a C+ (Fair). The fund currently has a performance rating of C+ (Fair) based on an annualized return of 4.74% over the last three years and a total return of 0.61% year to date 2015. Factored into the performance evaluation is an expense ratio of 0.55% (very low).

The fund's risk rating is currently B- (Good). It carries a beta of 0.56, meaning the fund's expected move will be 5.6% for every 10% move in the market. Volatility, as measured by both the semi-deviation and a drawdown factor, is considered low. As of December 31, 2015, *Cohen & Steers Global Realty Maj traded at a discount of .35% below its net asset value, which is better than its one-year historical average premium of .14%.

Michael Akins has been running the fund for 5 years and currently receives a manager quality ranking of 45 (0=worst, 99=best). If you desire an average level of risk, then this fund may be an option.

Data Date	Investment Rating	Net Assets ($Mil)	Price	Perfor-mance Rating/Pts	Total Return Y-T-D	Risk Rating/Pts
12-15	C+	93.90	42.53	C+ / 6.1	0.61%	B- / 7.8
2014	B	93.90	43.48	B- / 7.3	15.78%	B- / 7.8
2013	C	105.80	39.16	C / 4.9	-0.77%	B- / 7.5
2012	B-	70.30	39.25	B / 7.6	29.99%	C+ / 6.9
2011	C-	50.50	32.59	C / 4.6	-5.32%	C+ / 6.3
2010	B+	40.90	35.86	A- / 9.2	20.75%	C / 4.5

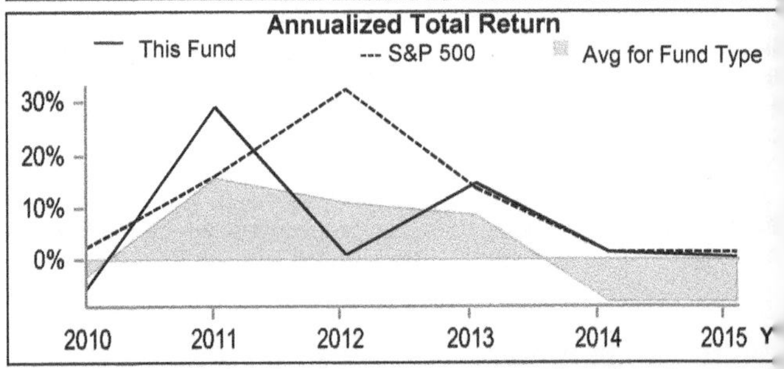

*Columbia Core Bond ETF (GMTB) C+ Fair

Fund Family: Columbia Management Inv Advisers LL
Fund Type: General - Investment Grade
Inception Date: January 29, 2010

Major Rating Factors: Middle of the road best describes *Columbia Core Bond ETF whose TheStreet.com Investment Rating is currently a C+ (Fair). The fund currently has a performance rating of C (Fair) based on an annualized return of 1.41% over the last three years and a total return of 0.55% year to date 2015. Factored into the performance evaluation is an expense ratio of 0.57% (very low).

The fund's risk rating is currently B- (Good). It carries a beta of 0.84, meaning the fund's expected move will be 8.4% for every 10% move in the market. Volatility, as measured by both the semi-deviation and a drawdown factor, is considered low. As of December 31, 2015, *Columbia Core Bond ETF traded at a premium of 1.55% above its net asset value, which is worse than its one-year historical average premium of .12%.

Orhan Imer has been running the fund for 5 years and currently receives a manager quality ranking of 69 (0=worst, 99=best). If you desire an average level of risk, then this fund may be an option.

Data Date	Investment Rating	Net Assets ($Mil)	Price	Perfor-mance Rating/Pts	Total Return Y-T-D	Risk Rating/Pt
12-15	C+	5.20	51.22	C / 5.0	0.55%	B- / 7.
2014	C	5.20	51.93	C- / 3.6	5.63%	B+ / 9.
2013	C-	5.10	50.28	D+ / 2.4	-2.41%	B+ / 9.
2012	C-	5.30	52.90	D / 1.8	4.41%	B+ / 9

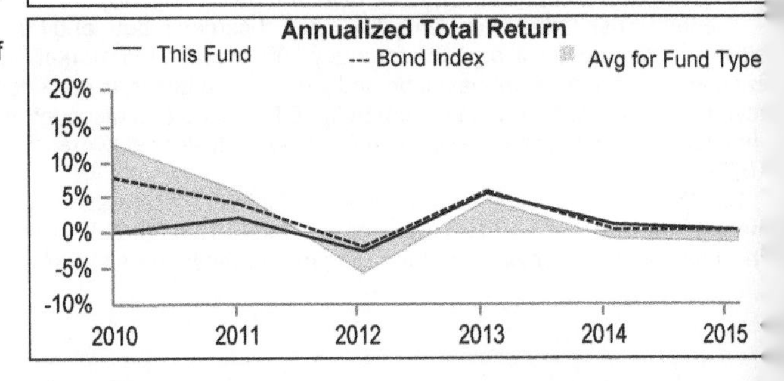

*Columbia Intermediate Muni Bd ET (GMMB) C+ Fair

Fund Family: Columbia Management Inv Advisers LL
Fund Type: Municipal - National
Inception Date: January 29, 2010

Major Rating Factors: Middle of the road best describes *Columbia Intermediate Muni Bd ET whose TheStreet.com Investment Rating is currently a C+ (Fair). The fund currently has a performance rating of C+ (Fair) based on an annualized return of 2.18% over the last three years and a total return of 3.74% year to date 2015. Factored into the performance evaluation is an expense ratio of 0.45% (very low).

The fund's risk rating is currently B- (Good). It carries a beta of 1.32, meaning it is expected to move 13.2% for every 10% move in the market. Volatility, as measured by both the semi-deviation and a drawdown factor, is considered low. As of December 31, 2015, *Columbia Intermediate Muni Bd ET traded at a premium of .07% above its net asset value, which is worse than its one-year historical average discount of .39%.

Brian M. McGreevy currently receives a manager quality ranking of 54 (0=worst, 99=best). If you desire an average level of risk, then this fund may be an option.

Data Date	Investment Rating	Net Assets ($Mil)	Price	Performance Rating/Pts	Total Return Y-T-D	Risk Rating/Pts
12-15	C+	5.40	53.51	C+ / 6.0	3.74%	B- / 7.5
2014	C	5.40	53.22	C- / 4.1	5.47%	B / 8.2
2013	C+	5.20	51.90	C / 5.2	-2.50%	B / 8.5
2012	C-	8.20	54.40	D+ / 2.6	4.02%	B / 8.9
2011	B	5.30	53.03	C+ / 6.8	11.80%	B+ / 9.3

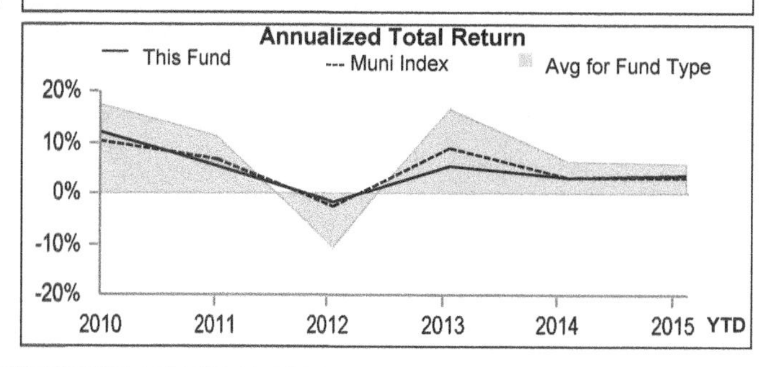

*Columbia Large Cap Growth ETF (RPX) A- Excellent

Fund Family: Columbia Management Inv Advisers LL
Fund Type: Growth
Inception Date: October 2, 2009

Major Rating Factors:
Exceptional performance is the major factor driving the A- (Excellent) TheStreet.com Investment Rating for *Columbia Large Cap Growth ETF. The fund currently has a performance rating of A (Excellent) based on an annualized return of 18.56% over the last three years and a total return of 10.30% year to date 2015. Factored into the performance evaluation is an expense ratio of 0.83% (very low).

The fund's risk rating is currently B- (Good). It carries a beta of 1.04, meaning that its performance tracks fairly well with that of the overall stock market. Volatility, as measured by both the semi-deviation and a drawdown factor, is considered low. As of December 31, 2015, *Columbia Large Cap Growth ETF traded at a premium of .93% above its net asset value, which is worse than its one-year historical average premium of .07%.

John T. Wilson has been running the fund for 5 years and currently receives a manager quality ranking of 86 (0=worst, 99=best). If you desire only a moderate level of risk and strong performance, then this fund is an excellent option.

Data Date	Investment Rating	Net Assets ($Mil)	Price	Performance Rating/Pts	Total Return Y-T-D	Risk Rating/Pts
12-15	A-	4.20	46.63	A / 9.5	10.30%	B- / 7.0
2014	B+	4.20	42.89	A- / 9.0	16.35%	C+ / 6.9
2013	B	2.00	38.88	B / 7.7	29.95%	B- / 7.6
2012	C-	1.50	30.46	C- / 4.2	17.75%	B- / 7.6
2011	D+	1.30	28.00	D / 1.7	-2.99%	B- / 7.7
2010	A+	4.70	31.22	B+ / 8.8	12.99%	B / 8.1

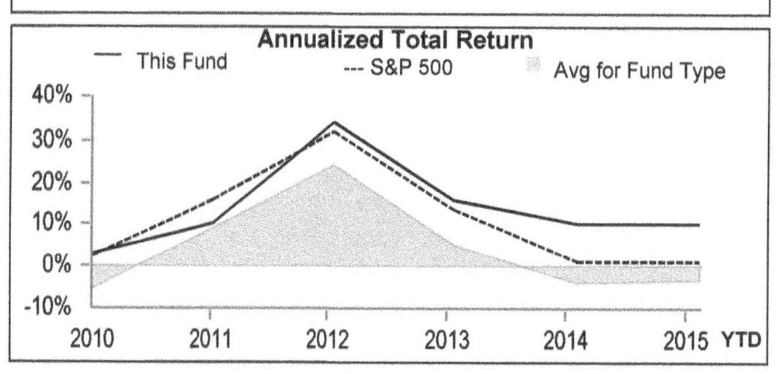

*Columbia Select Large Cap Gro ET (RWG) A- Excellent

Fund Family: Columbia Management Inv Advisers LL
Fund Type: Growth
Inception Date: October 2, 2009

Major Rating Factors:
Exceptional performance is the major factor driving the A- (Excellent) TheStreet.com Investment Rating for *Columbia Select Large Cap Gro ET. The fund currently has a performance rating of A (Excellent) based on an annualized return of 20.13% over the last three years and a total return of 10.01% year to date 2015. Factored into the performance evaluation is an expense ratio of 0.82% (very low).

The fund's risk rating is currently C+ (Fair). It carries a beta of 1.06, meaning that its performance tracks fairly well with that of the overall stock market. Volatility, as measured by both the semi-deviation and a drawdown factor, is considered low. As of December 31, 2015, *Columbia Select Large Cap Gro ET traded at a premium of .64% above its net asset value, which is worse than its one-year historical average premium of .02%.

Richard A. Carter has been running the fund for 5 years and currently receives a manager quality ranking of 86 (0=worst, 99=best). If you desire only a moderate level of risk and strong performance, then this fund is an excellent option.

Data Date	Investment Rating	Net Assets ($Mil)	Price	Performance Rating/Pts	Total Return Y-T-D	Risk Rating/Pts
12-15	A-	11.30	46.51	A / 9.5	10.01%	C+ / 6.6
2014	B	11.30	43.94	B+ / 8.8	10.91%	C+ / 6.1
2013	B+	13.00	43.18	B+ / 8.9	43.43%	B- / 7.5
2012	C	7.60	29.85	C / 4.7	16.92%	B- / 7.5
2011	D	8.00	26.26	D- / 1.2	-7.98%	B- / 7.8
2010	A+	9.30	30.90	A- / 9.0	14.11%	B / 8.2

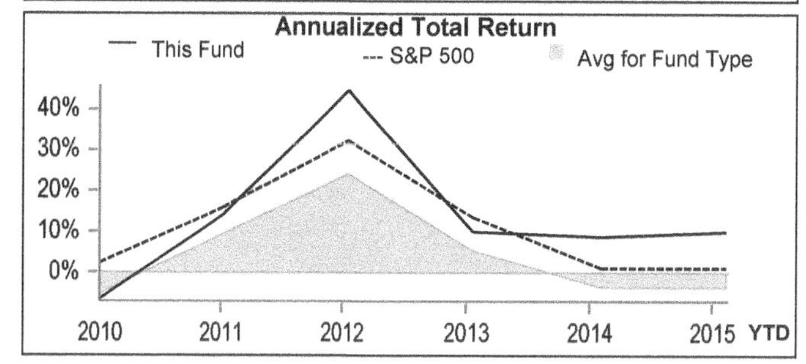

*Columbia Select Large Cap Value (GVT) B Good

Fund Family: Columbia Management Inv Advisers LL
Fund Type: Income
Inception Date: May 1, 2009

Major Rating Factors: Strong performance is the major factor driving the B (Good) TheStreet.com Investment Rating for *Columbia Select Large Cap Value. The fund currently has a performance rating of B (Good) based on an annualized return of 12.51% over the last three years and a total return of -4.31% year to date 2015. Factored into the performance evaluation is an expense ratio of 0.75% (very low).

The fund's risk rating is currently C+ (Fair). It carries a beta of 1.10, meaning it is expected to move 11.0% for every 10% move in the market. Volatility, as measured by both the semi-deviation and a drawdown factor, is considered low. As of December 31, 2015, *Columbia Select Large Cap Value traded at a premium of .97% above its net asset value, which is worse than its one-year historical average discount of .02%.

Keith Quinton has been running the fund for 12 years and currently receives a manager quality ranking of 47 (0=worst, 99=best). If you desire only a moderate level of risk and strong performance, then this fund is an excellent option.

Data Date	Investment Rating	Net Assets ($Mil)	Price	Performance Rating/Pts	Total Return Y-T-D	Risk Rating/Pts
12-15	B	9.10	42.60	B / 8.1	-4.31%	C+ / 6.7
2014	B	9.10	45.52	B+ / 8.5	12.88%	B- / 7.0
2013	B	4.20	41.55	B+ / 8.4	31.87%	B- / 7.5
2011	D+	2.70	27.20	D+ / 2.5	-2.65%	B- / 7.6
2010	A+	1.60	31.75	A- / 9.1	15.99%	B- / 7.9

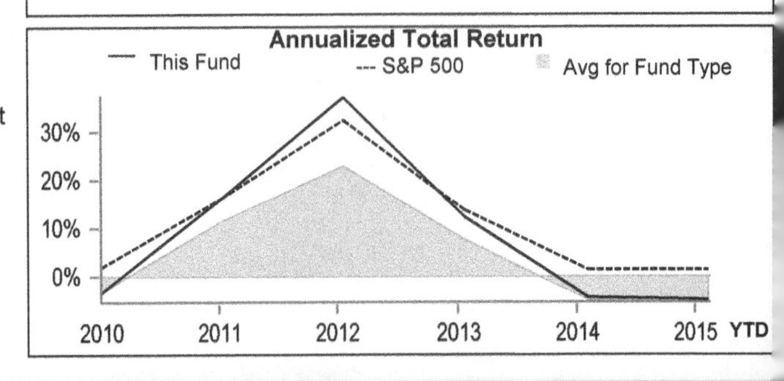

*Consumer Discretionary Sel Sec S (XLY) A+ Excellent

Fund Family: SSgA Funds Management Inc
Fund Type: Growth
Inception Date: December 16, 1998

Major Rating Factors:
Exceptional performance is the major factor driving the A+ (Excellent) TheStreet.com Investment Rating for *Consumer Discretionary Sel Sec S. The fund currently has a performance rating of A (Excellent) based on an annualized return of 18.85% over the last three years and a total return of 11.18% year to date 2015. Factored into the performance evaluation is an expense ratio of 0.15% (very low).

The fund's risk rating is currently B (Good). It carries a beta of 1.12, meaning it is expected to move 11.2% for every 10% move in the market. Volatility, as measured by both the semi-deviation and a drawdown factor, is considered low. As of December 31, 2015, *Consumer Discretionary Sel Sec S traded at a discount of .05% below its net asset value.

John A. Tucker has been running the fund for 18 years and currently receives a manager quality ranking of 82 (0=worst, 99=best). If you desire only a moderate level of risk and strong performance, then this fund is an excellent option.

Data Date	Investment Rating	Net Assets ($Mil)	Price	Performance Rating/Pts	Total Return Y-T-D	Risk Rating/Pts
12-15	A+	6,712.80	78.16	A / 9.4	11.18%	B / 8.0
2014	B+	6,712.80	72.15	A- / 9.1	10.27%	C+ / 6.9
2013	A	7,562.70	66.83	A- / 9.2	37.92%	B- / 7.9
2012	B+	3,743.20	47.44	B+ / 8.4	23.04%	B- / 7.9
2011	B	2,487.80	39.02	B / 7.7	7.93%	B- / 7.8
2010	B+	2,478.90	37.41	B / 8.0	27.50%	C+ / 5.9

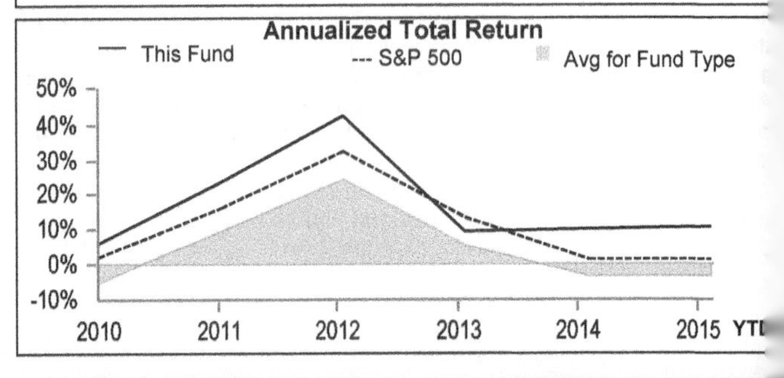

*Consumer Staples Select Sector S (XLP) A+ Excellent

Fund Family: SSgA Funds Management Inc
Fund Type: Growth
Inception Date: December 16, 1998

Major Rating Factors:
Exceptional performance is the major factor driving the A+ (Excellent) TheStreet.com Investment Rating for *Consumer Staples Select Sector S. The fund currently has a performance rating of A- (Excellent) based on an annualized return of 15.31% over the last three years and a total return of 7.95% year to date 2015. Factored into the performance evaluation is an expense ratio of 0.15% (very low).

The fund's risk rating is currently B (Good). It carries a beta of 0.86, meaning the fund's expected move will be 8.6% for every 10% move in the market. Volatility, as measured by both the semi-deviation and a drawdown factor, is considered low. As of December 31, 2015, *Consumer Staples Select Sector S traded at a price exactly equal to its net asset value.

John A. Tucker has been running the fund for 18 years and currently receives a manager quality ranking of 84 (0=worst, 99=best). If you desire only a moderate level of risk and strong performance, then this fund is an excellent option.

Data Date	Investment Rating	Net Assets ($Mil)	Price	Performance Rating/Pts	Total Return Y-T-D	Risk Rating/Pts
12-15	A+	7,575.80	50.49	A- / 9.2	7.95%	B / 8.3
2014	B+	7,575.80	48.49	B / 8.0	17.39%	B- / 7.6
2013	A	6,734.80	42.98	B / 7.8	21.35%	B+ / 9.2
2012	C+	5,530.70	34.90	C / 5.3	15.23%	B+ / 9.0
2011	B-	5,836.70	32.49	C+ / 5.9	13.98%	B / 8.6
2010	B-	3,104.00	29.31	C+ / 5.9	13.81%	B- / 7.3

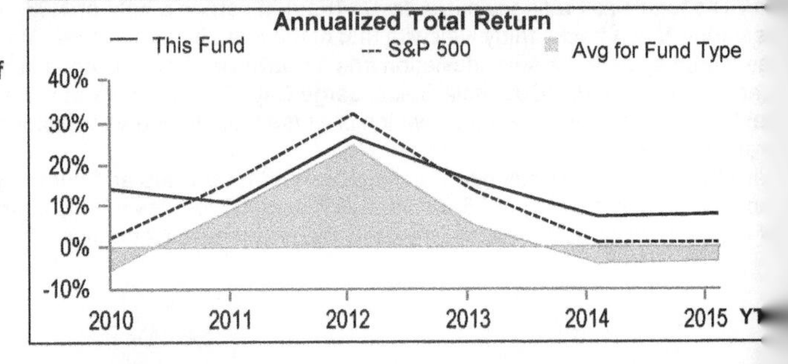

* Denotes ETF Fund

*Credit Suisse Cushing 30 MLP ETN (MLPN) E+ Very Weak

Fund Family: Credit Suisse Asset Management LLC
Fund Type: Energy/Natural Resources
Inception Date: April 13, 2010

Major Rating Factors: *Credit Suisse Cushing 30 MLP ETN has adopted a risky asset allocation strategy and currently receives an overall TheStreet.com Investment Rating of E+ (Very Weak). The fund has an above average level of volatility, as measured by both semi-deviation and drawdown factors. It carries a beta of 0.80, meaning the fund's expected move will be 8.0% for every 10% move in the market. As of December 31, 2015, *Credit Suisse Cushing 30 MLP ETN traded at a discount of .11% below its net asset value, which is better than its one-year historical average discount of .07%. Unfortunately, the high level of risk (D+, Weak) failed to pay off as investors endured poor performance.

The fund's performance rating is currently D- (Weak). It has registered an annualized return of -6.34% over the last three years and is down -40.02% year to date 2015.

This fund has been team managed for 6 years and currently receives a manager quality ranking of 53 (0=worst, 99=best). If you can tolerate high levels of risk in the hope of improved future returns, holding this fund may be an option.

Data Date	Investment Rating	Net Assets ($Mil)	Price	Performance Rating/Pts	Total Return Y-T-D	Risk Rating/Pts
12-15	E+	949.20	18.61	D- / 1.5	-40.02%	D+ / 2.5
2014	C+	949.20	31.93	C+ / 5.6	6.66%	B / 8.4
2013	C	689.10	31.41	B- / 7.4	27.26%	C / 5.1
2012	D	303.10	24.10	C- / 4.1	8.36%	C / 5.0
2011	C-	0.00	24.95	C / 5.4	7.80%	C / 5.1

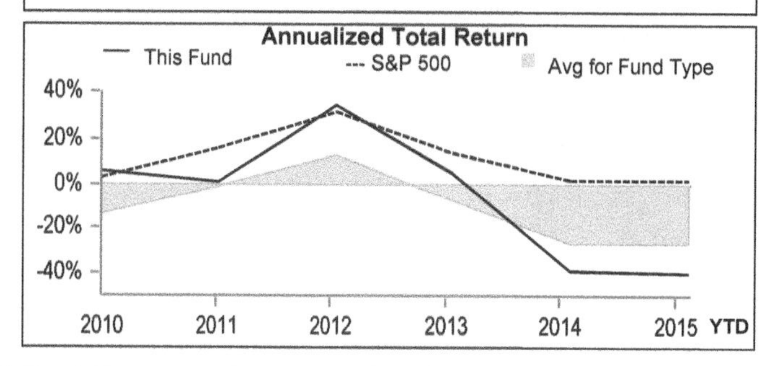

*Credit Suisse FI Enh Big Cap Gr (FIBG) C Fair

Fund Family: Credit Suisse Asset Management LLC
Fund Type: Growth
Inception Date: October 17, 2013

Major Rating Factors: Strong performance is the major factor driving the C (Fair) TheStreet.com Investment Rating for *Credit Suisse FI Enh Big Cap Gr. The fund currently has a performance rating of B+ (Good) based on an annualized return of 0.00% over the last three years and a total return of 8.15% year to date 2015.

The fund's risk rating is currently C- (Fair). It carries a beta of 0.00, meaning the fund's expected move will be 0.0% for every 10% move in the market. Volatility, as measured by both the semi-deviation and a drawdown factor, is considered average. As of December 31, 2015, *Credit Suisse FI Enh Big Cap Gr traded at a premium of .45% above its net asset value, which is worse than its one-year historical average discount of .02%.

If you desire an average level of risk and strong performance, then this fund is a good option.

Data Date	Investment Rating	Net Assets ($Mil)	Price	Performance Rating/Pts	Total Return Y-T-D	Risk Rating/Pts
12-15	C	30.10	58.55	B+ / 8.5	8.15%	C- / 3.4
2014	C+	30.10	55.40	A- / 9.2	22.48%	C / 4.6

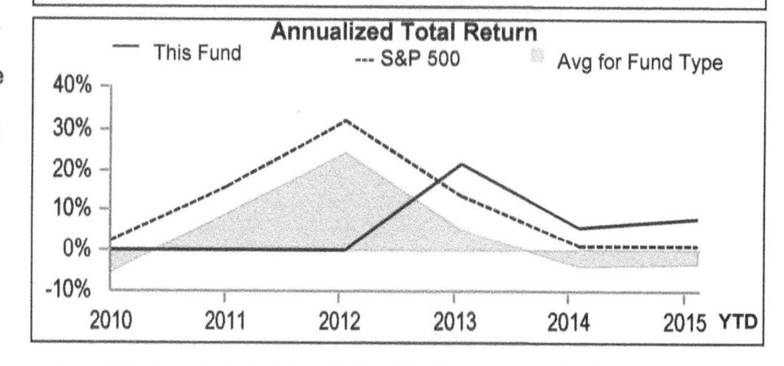

*Credit Suisse FI Enhanced Europe (FIEU) D- Weak

Fund Family: Credit Suisse Asset Management LLC
Fund Type: Foreign
Inception Date: September 5, 2013

Major Rating Factors:
Disappointing performance is the major factor driving the D- (Weak) TheStreet.com Investment Rating for *Credit Suisse FI Enhanced Europe. The fund currently has a performance rating of D- (Weak) based on an annualized return of 0.00% over the last three years and a total return of -7.82% year to date 2015.

The fund's risk rating is currently C- (Fair). It carries a beta of 0.00, meaning the fund's expected move will be 0.0% for every 10% move in the market. Volatility, as measured by both the semi-deviation and a drawdown factor, is considered average. As of December 31, 2015, *Credit Suisse FI Enhanced Europe traded at a discount of .13% below its net asset value, which is better than its one-year historical average premium of .18%.

Not Managed has been running the fund for 3 years and currently receives a manager quality ranking of 32 (0=worst, 99=best). This fund offers an average level of risk but investors looking for strong performance will be frustrated.

Data Date	Investment Rating	Net Assets ($Mil)	Price	Performance Rating/Pts	Total Return Y-T-D	Risk Rating/Pts
12-15	D-	196.60	98.13	D- / 1.5	-7.82%	C- / 3.3
2014	D-	196.60	103.70	E+ / 0.7	-10.43%	C+ / 6.0

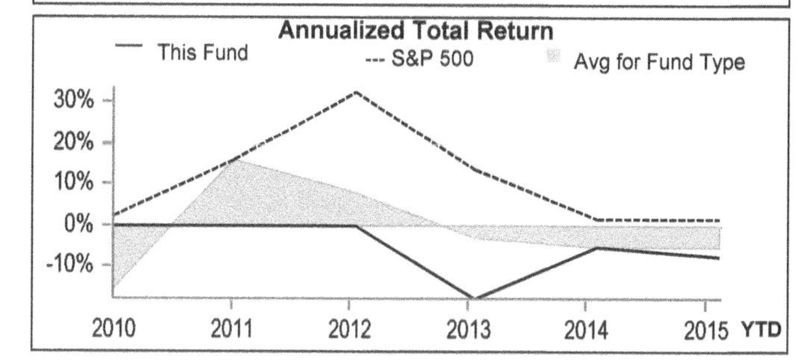

* Denotes ETF Fund

*Credit Suisse FI Large Cap Growt (FLGE) C Fair

Fund Family: Credit Suisse Asset Management LLC
Fund Type: Growth
Inception Date: June 10, 2014

Data Date	Investment Rating	Net Assets ($Mil)	Price	Performance Rating/Pts	Total Return Y-T-D	Risk Rating/Pts
12-15	C	526.60	124.46	B+ / 8.8	10.00%	C- / 3.2

Major Rating Factors: Strong performance is the major factor driving the C (Fair) TheStreet.com Investment Rating for *Credit Suisse FI Large Cap Growt. The fund currently has a performance rating of B+ (Good) based on an annualized return of 0.00% over the last three years and a total return of 10.00% year to date 2015.

The fund's risk rating is currently C- (Fair). It carries a beta of 0.00, meaning the fund's expected move will be 0.0% for every 10% move in the market. Volatility, as measured by both the semi-deviation and a drawdown factor, is considered average. As of December 31, 2015, *Credit Suisse FI Large Cap Growt traded at a premium of .73% above its net asset value, which is worse than its one-year historical average discount of .09%.

If you desire an average level of risk and strong performance, then this fund is a good option.

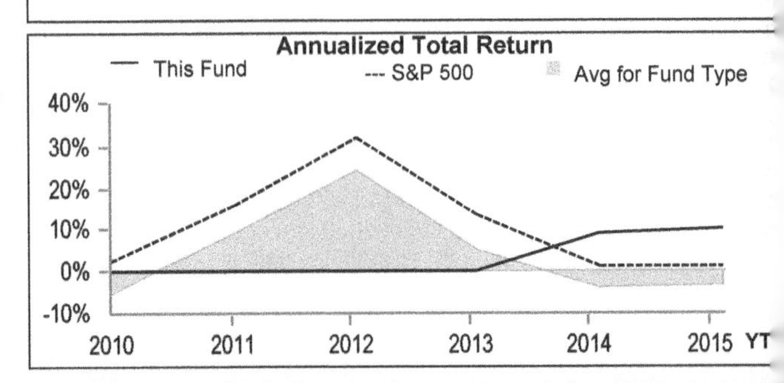

*Credit Suisse Gold Shs Covered C (GLDI) E+ Very Weak

Fund Family: Credit Suisse Asset Management LLC
Fund Type: Precious Metals
Inception Date: January 28, 2013

Data Date	Investment Rating	Net Assets ($Mil)	Price	Performance Rating/Pts	Total Return Y-T-D	Risk Rating/Pts
12-15	E+	29.00	10.26	D- / 1.1	-14.71%	D+ / 2.9
2014	D-	29.00	11.97	E+ / 0.9	-14.46%	C+ / 5.8

Major Rating Factors: *Credit Suisse Gold Shs Covered C has adopted a risky asset allocation strategy and currently receives an overall TheStreet.com Investment Rating of E+ (Very Weak). The fund has an above average level of volatility, as measured by both semi-deviation and drawdown factors. It carries a beta of 0.00, meaning the fund's expected move will be 0.0% for every 10% move in the market. As of December 31, 2015, *Credit Suisse Gold Shs Covered C traded at a discount of .29% below its net asset value, which is better than its one-year historical average discount of .02%. Unfortunately, the high level of risk (D+, Weak) failed to pay off as investors endured poor performance.

The fund's performance rating is currently D- (Weak). It has registered an annualized return of 0.00% over the last three years but is down -14.71% year to date 2015.

This fund has been team managed for 3 years and currently receives a manager quality ranking of 42 (0=worst, 99=best). If you can tolerate high levels of risk in the hope of improved future returns, holding this fund may be an option.

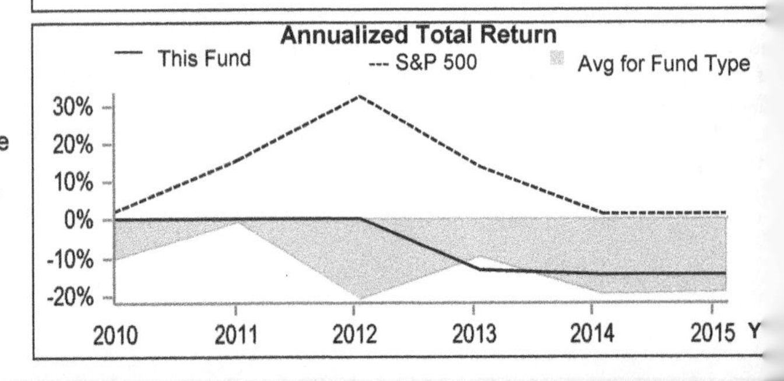

*Credit Suisse L/S Liq Idx ETN (CSLS) C Fair

Fund Family: Credit Suisse Asset Management LLC
Fund Type: Growth
Inception Date: February 19, 2010

Data Date	Investment Rating	Net Assets ($Mil)	Price	Performance Rating/Pts	Total Return Y-T-D	Risk Rating/Pts
12-15	C	13.40	27.76	B / 7.6	8.14%	C- / 4.
2014	C	13.40	26.04	C / 5.1	12.00%	B- / 7.
2013	D	13.10	23.92	C- / 3.3	3.54%	C / 5.
2012	D-	21.10	22.36	D / 1.9	2.06%	C / 5.
2011	D-	32.30	21.65	D / 1.7	-1.36%	C / 5.

Major Rating Factors: Strong performance is the major factor driving the C (Fair) TheStreet.com Investment Rating for *Credit Suisse L/S Liq Idx ETN. The fund currently has a performance rating of B (Good) based on an annualized return of 7.50% over the last three years and a total return of 8.14% year to date 2015.

The fund's risk rating is currently C- (Fair). It carries a beta of 0.43, meaning the fund's expected move will be 4.3% for every 10% move in the market. Volatility, as measured by both the semi-deviation and a drawdown factor, is considered average. As of December 31, 2015, *Credit Suisse L/S Liq Idx ETN traded at a premium of 1.31% above its net asset value, which is worse than its one-year historical average premium of .09%.

This fund has been team managed for 6 years and currently receives a manager quality ranking of 77 (0=worst, 99=best). If you desire an average level of risk and strong performance, then this fund is a good option.

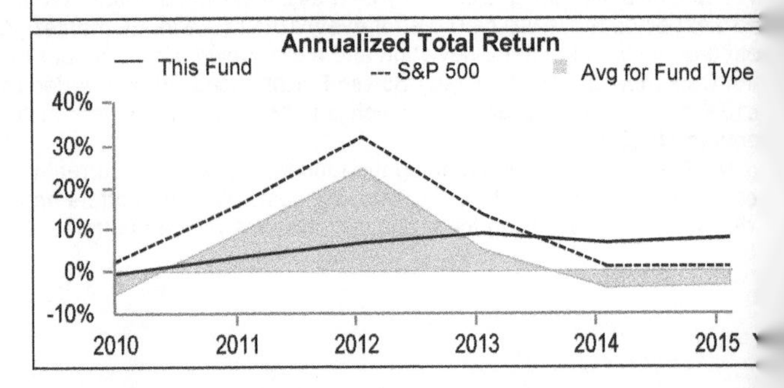

*Credit Suisse Merger Arb Lq Id E (CSMA) D+ Weak

Fund Family: Credit Suisse Asset Management LLC
Fund Type: Growth
Inception Date: October 1, 2010

Data Date	Investment Rating	Net Assets ($Mil)	Price	Performance Rating/Pts	Total Return Y-T-D	Risk Rating/Pts
12-15	D+	16.00	19.34	C- / 4.0	-0.71%	C / 5.3
2014	C-	16.00	19.48	D / 2.2	-7.51%	B+ / 9.2
2013	D	52.70	21.10	C- / 3.6	7.01%	C / 5.5
2012	D-	74.60	19.65	D- / 1.1	-3.72%	C / 5.5
2011	D	94.40	21.00	D / 2.1	1.84%	C+ / 5.8

Major Rating Factors: *Credit Suisse Merger Arb Lq Id E receives a TheStreet.com Investment Rating of D+ (Weak). The fund currently has a performance rating of C- (Fair) based on an annualized return of -0.58% over the last three years and a total return of -0.71% year to date 2015.

The fund's risk rating is currently C (Fair). It carries a beta of 0.19, meaning the fund's expected move will be 1.9% for every 10% move in the market. Volatility, as measured by both the semi-deviation and a drawdown factor, is considered average. As of December 31, 2015, *Credit Suisse Merger Arb Lq Id E traded at a discount of 1.68% below its net asset value, which is better than its one-year historical average discount of .33%.

This is team managed and currently receives a manager quality ranking of 41 (0=worst, 99=best). If you desire an average level of risk, then this fund may be an option.

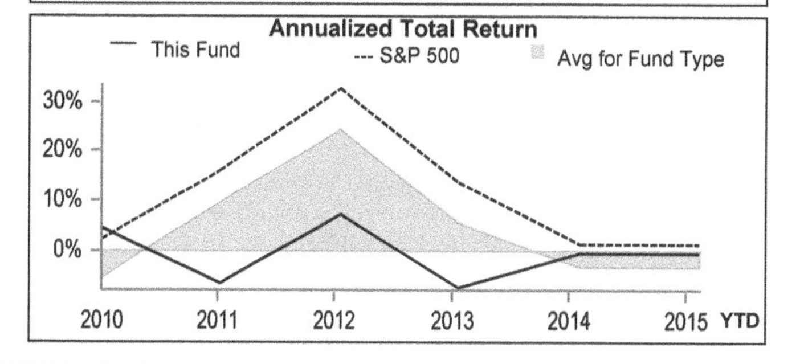

*DB 3x Inverse Jpn Gvt Bond Fut E (JGBD) D Weak

Fund Family: DB Commodity Services LLC
Fund Type: Global
Inception Date: November 8, 2011

Data Date	Investment Rating	Net Assets ($Mil)	Price	Performance Rating/Pts	Total Return Y-T-D	Risk Rating/Pts
12-15	D	47.00	14.52	D+ / 2.3	-6.05%	C / 4.4
2014	D+	47.00	15.37	D- / 1.4	-12.40%	B / 8.0
2013	D-	53.00	17.60	D- / 1.3	-6.87%	C / 5.2
2012	D-	0.00	18.63	D- / 1.0	-5.74%	C / 5.5

Major Rating Factors:
Disappointing performance is the major factor driving the D (Weak) TheStreet.com Investment Rating for *DB 3x Inverse Jpn Gvt Bond Fut E. The fund currently has a performance rating of D+ (Weak) based on an annualized return of -8.38% over the last three years and a total return of -6.05% year to date 2015.

The fund's risk rating is currently C (Fair). It carries a beta of -0.40, meaning the fund's expected move will be -4.0% for every 10% move in the market. Volatility, as measured by both the semi-deviation and a drawdown factor, is considered average. As of December 31, 2015, *DB 3x Inverse Jpn Gvt Bond Fut E traded at a discount of 8.84% below its net asset value, which is better than its one-year historical average discount of 17.32%.

This fund has been team managed for 5 years and currently receives a manager quality ranking of 17 (0=worst, 99=best). This fund offers an average level of risk but investors looking for strong performance will be frustrated.

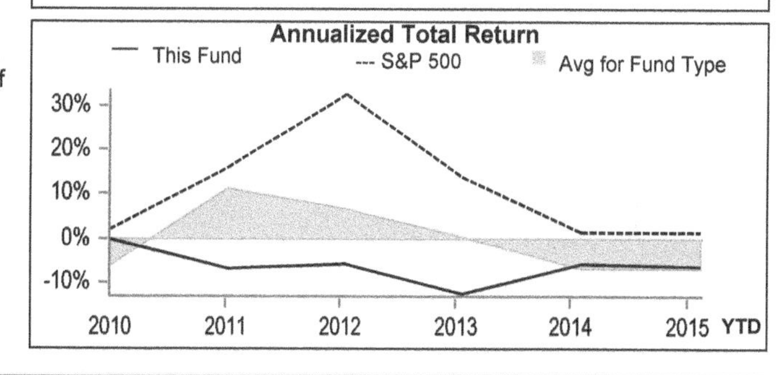

*DB 3x Japanese Govt Bd Futures E (JGBT) C- Fair

Fund Family: DB Commodity Services LLC
Fund Type: Global
Inception Date: March 22, 2011

Data Date	Investment Rating	Net Assets ($Mil)	Price	Performance Rating/Pts	Total Return Y-T-D	Risk Rating/Pts
12-15	C-	5.00	27.02	B- / 7.0	4.65%	C- / 3.8
2014	C+	5.00	25.83	C / 5.1	11.04%	B / 8.3
2013	D+	4.50	23.55	C / 4.8	4.73%	C+ / 5.6

Major Rating Factors: Strong performance is the major factor driving the C- (Fair) TheStreet.com Investment Rating for *DB 3x Japanese Govt Bd Futures E. The fund currently has a performance rating of B- (Good) based on an annualized return of 6.74% over the last three years and a total return of 4.65% year to date 2015.

The fund's risk rating is currently C- (Fair). It carries a beta of 0.34, meaning the fund's expected move will be 3.4% for every 10% move in the market. Volatility, as measured by both the semi-deviation and a drawdown factor, is considered average. As of December 31, 2015, *DB 3x Japanese Govt Bd Futures E traded at a premium of 1.27% above its net asset value, which is worse than its one-year historical average premium of .06%.

This fund has been team managed for 5 years and currently receives a manager quality ranking of 93 (0=worst, 99=best). If you desire an average level of risk and strong performance, then this fund is a good option.

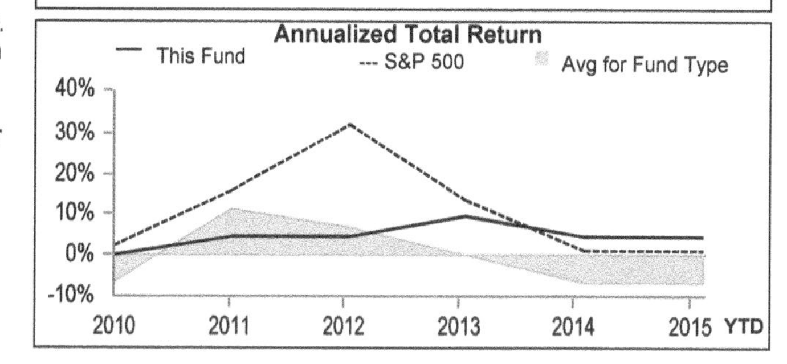

* Denotes ETF Fund

*DB 3x Long 25+ Year Treasury ETN (LBND) — D — Weak

Fund Family: DB Commodity Services LLC
Fund Type: US Government/Agency
Inception Date: June 28, 2010

Major Rating Factors: *DB 3x Long 25+ Year Treasury ETN has adopted a risky asset allocation strategy and currently receives an overall TheStreet.com Investment Rating of D (Weak). The fund has an above average level of volatility, as measured by both semi-deviation and drawdown factors. It carries a beta of 2.98, meaning it is expected to move 29.8% for every 10% move in the market. As of December 31, 2015, *DB 3x Long 25+ Year Treasury ETN traded at a discount of .82% below its net asset value, which is better than its one-year historical average discount of .34%. Unfortunately, the high level of risk (D+, Weak) has only provided investors with average performance.

The fund's performance rating is currently C (Fair). It has registered an annualized return of 3.85% over the last three years but is down -14.29% year to date 2015.

This fund has been team managed for 6 years and currently receives a manager quality ranking of 27 (0=worst, 99=best). If you are comfortable owning a high risk investment, then this fund may be an option.

Data Date	Investment Rating	Net Assets ($Mil)	Price	Performance Rating/Pts	Total Return Y-T-D	Risk Rating/P
12-15	D	32.40	49.50	C / 5.4	-14.29%	D+ / 2
2014	C	32.40	57.75	A / 9.5	81.85%	D+ / 2
2013	D	23.20	30.02	C / 4.9	-31.92%	C- / 3
2012	E+	0.00	47.22	E+ / 0.7	0.62%	C / 4
2011	B	0.00	45.77	A+ / 9.9	105.10%	C / 5

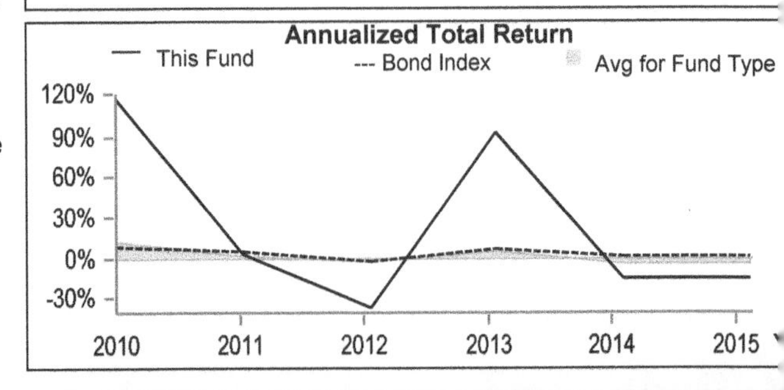

*DB 3x Short 25+ Year Treasury ET (SBND) — E — Very Weak

Fund Family: DB Commodity Services LLC
Fund Type: US Government/Agency
Inception Date: June 28, 2010

Major Rating Factors: *DB 3x Short 25+ Year Treasury ET has adopted a very risky asset allocation strategy and currently receives an overall TheStreet.com Investment Rating of E (Very Weak). The fund has a high level of volatility, as measured by both semi-deviation and drawdown factors. It carries a beta of -3.29, meaning the fund's expected move will be -32.9% for every 10% move in the market. As of December 31, 2015, *DB 3x Short 25+ Year Treasury ET traded at a price exactly equal to its net asset value, which is better than its one-year historical average premium of .01%. Unfortunately, the high level of risk (E+, Very Weak) failed to pay off as investors endured poor performance.

The fund's performance rating is currently D (Weak). It has registered an annualized return of -15.01% over the last three years and is up 0.21% year to date 2015.

This fund has been team managed for 6 years and currently receives a manager quality ranking of 25 (0=worst, 99=best). If you can tolerate very high levels of risk in the hope of improved future returns, holding this fund may be an option.

Data Date	Investment Rating	Net Assets ($Mil)	Price	Performance Rating/Pts	Total Return Y-T-D	Risk Rating/P
12-15	E	53.90	4.80	D / 1.6	0.21%	E+ / 0
2014	E-	53.90	5.01	E / 0.5	-51.89%	D / 1
2013	E-	0.10	10.54	E+ / 0.6	33.08%	D / 1
2012	E	0.10	7.47	D / 1.7	-14.24%	D / 1
2011	E-	0.00	8.97	E- / 0	-64.15%	D / 1

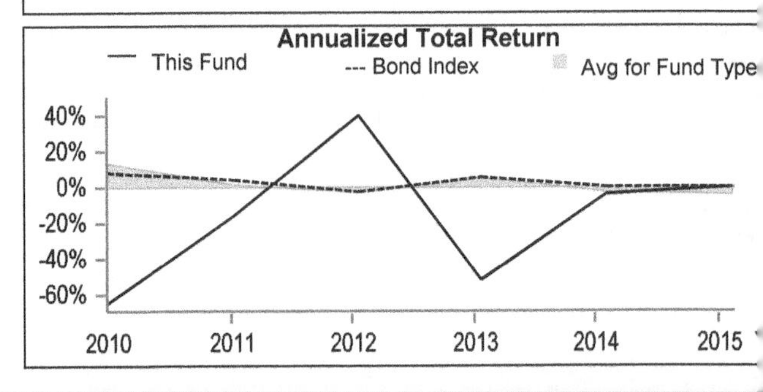

*DB Agriculture Double Long ETN (DAG) — E- — Very Weak

Fund Family: Deutsche Bank AG (London)
Fund Type: Growth
Inception Date: April 15, 2008

Major Rating Factors: *DB Agriculture Double Long ETN has adopted a very risky asset allocation strategy and currently receives an overall TheStreet.com Investment Rating of E- (Very Weak). The fund has a high level of volatility, as measured by both semi-deviation and drawdown factors. It carries a beta of 0.73, meaning the fund's expected move will be 7.3% for every 10% move in the market. As of December 31, 2015, *DB Agriculture Double Long ETN traded at a discount of .30% below its net asset value, which is better than its one-year historical average premium of 8.00%. Unfortunately, the high level of risk (D-, Weak) failed to pay off as investors endured very poor performance.

The fund's performance rating is currently E (Very Weak). It has registered an annualized return of -33.49% over the last three years and is down -37.07% year to date 2015. Factored into the performance evaluation is an expense ratio of 0.75% (very low).

This fund has been team managed for 8 years and currently receives a manager quality ranking of 1 (0=worst, 99=best). If you can tolerate very high levels of risk in the hope of improved future returns, holding this fund may be an option.

Data Date	Investment Rating	Net Assets ($Mil)	Price	Performance Rating/Pts	Total Return Y-T-D	Risk Rating/P
12-15	E-	87.09	3.27	E / 0.3	-37.07%	D- / 1
2014	E-	14.00	5.20	E+ / 0.6	-27.20%	D / 1
2013	E-	87.09	7.26	E / 0.5	-34.30%	D+ / 2
2012	E	87.09	11.79	D- / 1.5	9.55%	C- / 3
2011	E+	87.09	10.79	D- / 1.5	-22.13%	C- / 3
2010	C	87.09	14.07	A+ / 9.9	30.88%	D- / 1

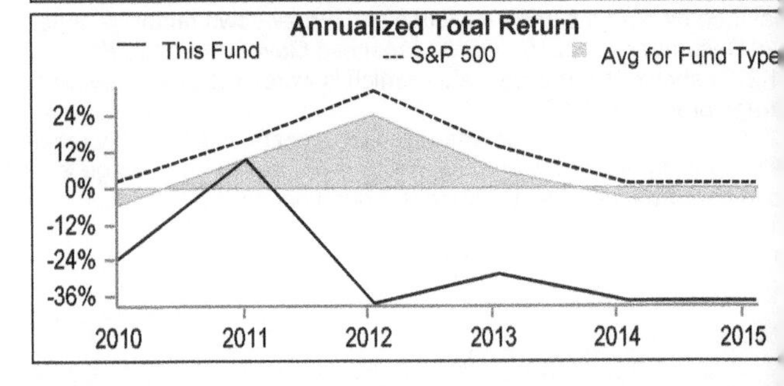

*DB Agriculture Double Short ETN (AGA) C+ Fair

Fund Family: Deutsche Bank AG (London)
Fund Type: Growth
Inception Date: April 15, 2008

Major Rating Factors:
Exceptional performance is the major factor driving the C+ (Fair) TheStreet.com Investment Rating for *DB Agriculture Double Short ETN. The fund currently has a performance rating of A+ (Excellent) based on an annualized return of 28.69% over the last three years and a total return of 23.65% year to date 2015. Factored into the performance evaluation is an expense ratio of 0.75% (very low).

The fund's risk rating is currently C- (Fair). It carries a beta of -0.44, meaning the fund's expected move will be -4.4% for every 10% move in the market. Volatility, as measured by both the semi-deviation and a drawdown factor, is considered average. As of December 31, 2015, *DB Agriculture Double Short ETN traded at a discount of .56% below its net asset value, which is better than its one-year historical average discount of .14%.

This fund has been team managed for 8 years and currently receives a manager quality ranking of 99 (0=worst, 99=best). If you desire an average level of risk and strong performance, then this fund is a good option.

Data Date	Investment Rating	Net Assets ($Mil)	Price	Performance Rating/Pts	Total Return Y-T-D	Risk Rating/Pts
12-15	C+	3.98	30.15	A+ / 9.8	23.65%	C- / 3.5
2014	C	2.30	24.13	C+ / 6.8	55.87%	C / 5.2
2013	E+	3.98	14.21	D- / 1.5	1.74%	C- / 3.6
2012	E-	3.98	13.03	E / 0.4	-26.22%	D / 1.9
2011	E-	3.98	17.79	E+ / 0.9	-0.49%	D / 1.9
2010	E-	3.98	18.00	E- / 0	-47.14%	D / 1.7

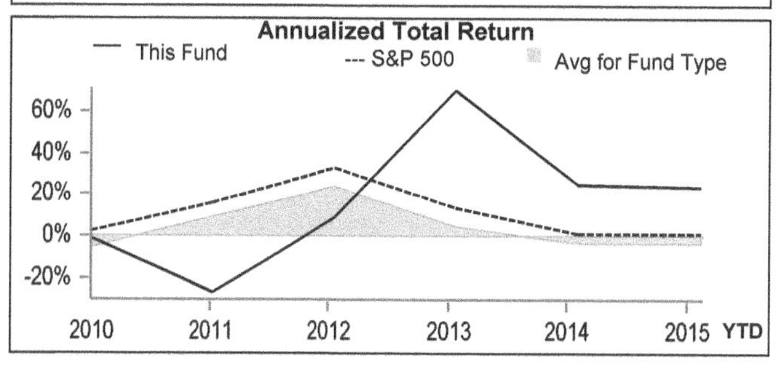

*DB Agriculture Long ETN (AGF) E Very Weak

Fund Family: Deutsche Bank AG (London)
Fund Type: Growth
Inception Date: April 15, 2008

Major Rating Factors: *DB Agriculture Long ETN has adopted a very risky asset allocation strategy and currently receives an overall TheStreet.com Investment Rating of E (Very Weak). The fund has a high level of volatility, as measured by both semi-deviation and drawdown factors. It carries a beta of -0.09, meaning the fund's expected move will be -0.9% for every 10% move in the market. As of December 31, 2015, *DB Agriculture Long ETN traded at a discount of .90% below its net asset value, which is better than its one-year historical average discount of .40%. Unfortunately, the high level of risk (D, Weak) failed to pay off as investors endured poor performance.

The fund's performance rating is currently D- (Weak). It has registered an annualized return of -17.61% over the last three years and is down -19.37% year to date 2015. Factored into the performance evaluation is an expense ratio of 0.75% (very low).

This fund has been team managed for 8 years and currently receives a manager quality ranking of 9 (0=worst, 99=best). If you can tolerate very high levels of risk in the hope of improved future returns, holding this fund may be an option.

Data Date	Investment Rating	Net Assets ($Mil)	Price	Performance Rating/Pts	Total Return Y-T-D	Risk Rating/Pts
12-15	E	4.96	11.00	D- / 1.3	-19.37%	D / 2.0
2014	E+	3.00	13.98	D / 1.8	10.60%	C- / 3.1
2013	E	4.96	12.64	E / 0.5	-34.68%	C- / 3.1
2012	D-	4.96	20.00	D / 2.1	9.20%	C / 4.6
2011	E+	4.96	18.71	D / 1.9	-12.95%	C- / 4.1
2010	C+	4.96	20.96	A+ / 9.6	19.57%	D+ / 2.5

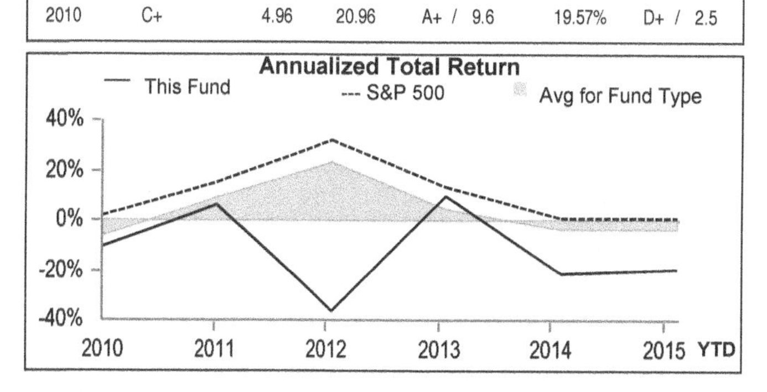

*DB Agriculture Short ETN (ADZ) C+ Fair

Fund Family: Deutsche Bank AG (London)
Fund Type: Growth
Inception Date: April 15, 2008

Major Rating Factors:
Exceptional performance is the major factor driving the C+ (Fair) TheStreet.com Investment Rating for *DB Agriculture Short ETN. The fund currently has a performance rating of A+ (Excellent) based on an annualized return of 18.21% over the last three years and a total return of 24.07% year to date 2015. Factored into the performance evaluation is an expense ratio of 0.75% (very low).

The fund's risk rating is currently C- (Fair). It carries a beta of 0.31, meaning the fund's expected move will be 3.1% for every 10% move in the market. Volatility, as measured by both the semi-deviation and a drawdown factor, is considered average. As of December 31, 2015, *DB Agriculture Short ETN traded at a premium of 7.02% above its net asset value, which is worse than its one-year historical average premium of 1.05%.

This fund has been team managed for 8 years and currently receives a manager quality ranking of 97 (0=worst, 99=best). If you desire an average level of risk and strong performance, then this fund is a good option.

Data Date	Investment Rating	Net Assets ($Mil)	Price	Performance Rating/Pts	Total Return Y-T-D	Risk Rating/Pts
12-15	C+	3.34	35.98	A+ / 9.6	24.07%	C- / 3.3
2014	C	0.90	29.00	C / 5.3	23.14%	B- / 7.3
2013	D	3.34	23.55	C- / 3.1	8.13%	C / 4.6
2012	E	3.34	21.34	E+ / 0.7	-13.23%	D+ / 2.7
2011	E+	3.34	24.38	D- / 1.4	3.64%	C- / 3.1
2010	E	3.34	23.93	E- / 0.2	-23.05%	C- / 3.1

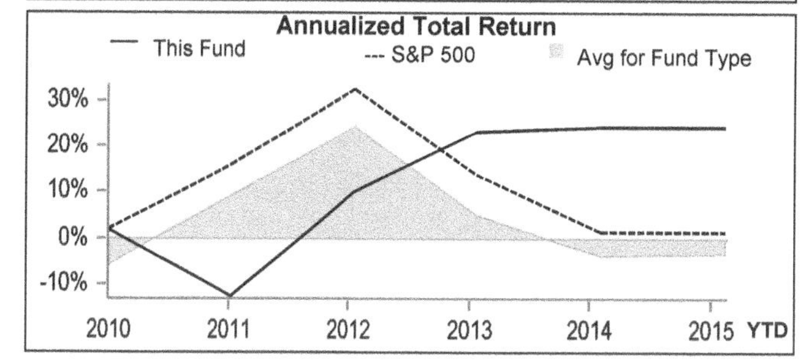

*DB Base Metals Double Long ETN (BDD) E- Very Weak

Fund Family: Deutsche Bank AG (London)
Fund Type: Precious Metals
Inception Date: June 16, 2008

Major Rating Factors: *DB Base Metals Double Long ETN has adopted a very risky asset allocation strategy and currently receives an overall TheStreet.com Investment Rating of E- (Very Weak). The fund has a high level of volatility, as measured by both semi-deviation and drawdown factors. It carries a beta of 0.45, meaning the fund's expected move will be 4.5% for every 10% move in the market. As of December 31, 2015, *DB Base Metals Double Long ETN traded at a premium of .24% above its net asset value, which is better than its one-year historical average premium of .64%. Unfortunately, the high level of risk (D-, Weak) failed to pay off as investors endured very poor performance.

The fund's performance rating is currently E (Very Weak). It has registered an annualized return of -26.66% over the last three years and is down -43.40% year to date 2015. Factored into the performance evaluation is an expense ratio of 0.75% (very low).

This fund has been team managed for 8 years and currently receives a manager quality ranking of 6 (0=worst, 99=best). If you can tolerate very high levels of risk in the hope of improved future returns, holding this fund may be an option.

Data Date	Investment Rating	Net Assets ($Mil)	Price	Performance Rating/Pts	Total Return Y-T-D	Risk Rating/Pts
12-15	E-	22.78	4.10	E / 0.5	-43.40%	D- / 1.0
2014	E	0.10	7.52	D- / 1.2	-9.28%	D+ / 2.5
2013	E-	22.78	8.40	E / 0.5	-22.86%	D / 1.9
2012	E-	22.78	10.82	E+ / 0.7	-10.92%	D+ / 2.4
2011	E+	22.78	10.47	C- / 3.1	-43.75%	D+ / 2.9
2010	C	22.78	19.27	A+ / 9.7	9.12%	D- / 1.0

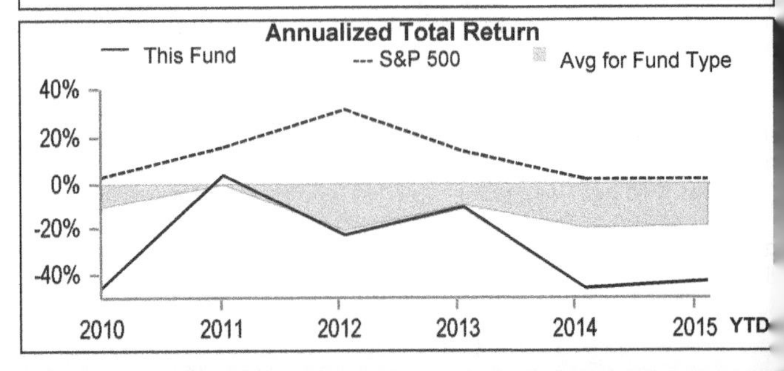

*DB Base Metals Double Short ETN (BOM) C+ Fair

Fund Family: Deutsche Bank AG (London)
Fund Type: Precious Metals
Inception Date: June 16, 2008

Major Rating Factors:
Exceptional performance is the major factor driving the C+ (Fair) TheStreet.com Investment Rating for *DB Base Metals Double Short ETN. The fund currently has a performance rating of A+ (Excellent) based on an annualized return of 26.44% over the last three years and a total return of 60.65% year to date 2015. Factored into the performance evaluation is an expense ratio of 0.75% (very low).

The fund's risk rating is currently C- (Fair). It carries a beta of -0.42, meaning the fund's expected move will be -4.2% for every 10% move in the market. Volatility, as measured by both the semi-deviation and a drawdown factor, is considered average. As of December 31, 2015, *DB Base Metals Double Short ETN traded at a premium of 4.66% above its net asset value, which is worse than its one-year historical average discount of .19%.

This fund has been team managed for 8 years and currently receives a manager quality ranking of 98 (0=worst, 99=best). If you desire an average level of risk and strong performance, then this fund is a good option.

Data Date	Investment Rating	Net Assets ($Mil)	Price	Performance Rating/Pts	Total Return Y-T-D	Risk Rating/Pts
12-15	C+	2.20	25.40	A+ / 9.9	60.65%	C- / 3.4
2014	D	0.10	15.15	C- / 4.0	10.69%	C / 4.6
2013	D	2.20	13.47	C- / 4.1	11.51%	C- / 4.2
2012	E-	2.20	11.87	E+ / 0.7	-7.88%	D / 2.2
2011	E-	2.20	14.95	E+ / 0.8	38.60%	D / 1.9
2010	E-	2.20	10.54	E- / 0.1	-33.71%	D- / 1.0

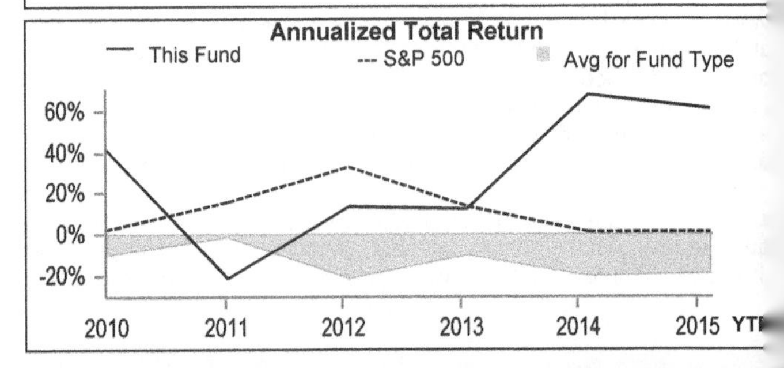

*DB Base Metals Short ETN (BOS) C Fair

Fund Family: Deutsche Bank AG (London)
Fund Type: Precious Metals
Inception Date: June 16, 2008

Major Rating Factors:
Exceptional performance is the major factor driving the C (Fair) TheStreet.com Investment Rating for *DB Base Metals Short ETN. The fund currently has a performance rating of A (Excellent) based on an annualized return of 12.61% over the last three years and a total return of 26.51% year to date 2015. Factored into the performance evaluation is an expense ratio of 0.75% (very low).

The fund's risk rating is currently C- (Fair). It carries a beta of 0.40, meaning the fund's expected move will be 4.0% for every 10% move in the market. Volatility, as measured by both the semi-deviation and a drawdown factor, is considered average. As of December 31, 2015, *DB Base Metals Short ETN traded at a discount of 1.26% below its net asset value, which is better than its one-year historical average discount of .93%.

This fund has been team managed for 8 years and currently receives a manager quality ranking of 98 (0=worst, 99=best). If you desire an average level of risk and strong performance, then this fund is a good option.

Data Date	Investment Rating	Net Assets ($Mil)	Price	Performance Rating/Pts	Total Return Y-T-D	Risk Rating/Pts
12-15	C	2.52	29.00	A / 9.5	26.51%	C- / 3.0
2014	C-	0.10	22.60	C+ / 5.7	47.62%	C+ / 5.8
2013	E+	2.52	15.20	D- / 1.1	-23.53%	C- / 3.9
2012	E+	2.52	20.34	D- / 1.0	-2.92%	C- / 3.9
2011	E	2.52	22.14	D- / 1.2	19.63%	D / 2.0
2010	E-	2.52	18.49	E / 0.4	-13.44%	D / 2.0

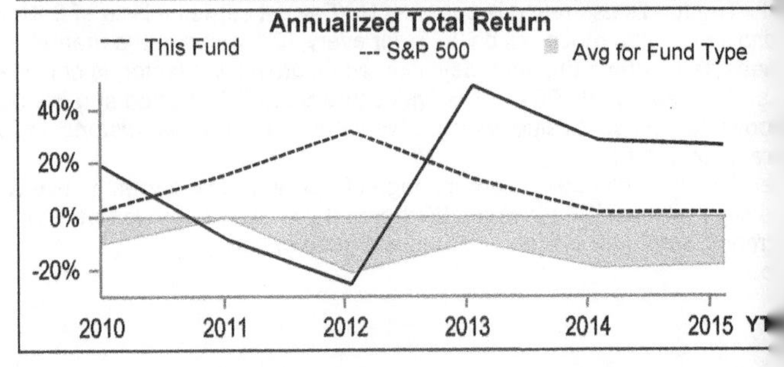

*DB Commodity Double Long ETN (DYY) E- Very Weak

und Family: Deutsche Bank AG (London)
und Type: Growth
ception Date: April 28, 2008

ajor Rating Factors: *DB Commodity Double Long ETN has adopted a very risky set allocation strategy and currently receives an overall TheStreet.com Investment ating of E- (Very Weak). The fund has a high level of volatility, as measured by both mi-deviation and drawdown factors. It carries a beta of 0.68, meaning the fund's pected move will be 6.8% for every 10% move in the market. As of December 31, 15, *DB Commodity Double Long ETN traded at a premium of 73.22% above its t asset value, which is worse than its one-year historical average premium of .99%. Unfortunately, the high level of risk (E-, Very Weak) failed to pay off as vestors endured very poor performance.

The fund's performance rating is currently E (Very Weak). It has registered an nualized return of -30.41% over the last three years and is down -22.08% year to te 2015. Factored into the performance evaluation is an expense ratio of 0.75% ery low).

This fund has been team managed for 8 years and currently receives a manager ality ranking of 1 (0=worst, 99=best). If you can tolerate very high levels of risk in e hope of improved future returns, holding this fund may be an option.

Data Date	Investment Rating	Net Assets ($Mil)	Price	Perfor-mance Rating/Pts	Total Return Y-T-D	Risk Rating/Pts
12-15	E-	43.11	3.17	E / 0.4	-22.08%	E- / 0.1
2014	E-	0.10	3.87	E / 0.4	-38.85%	D- / 1.0
2013	E	43.11	6.71	E+ / 0.8	-25.06%	D+ / 2.7
2012	E+	43.11	9.21	D / 2.1	-3.30%	C- / 3.1
2011	D	43.11	9.18	C / 4.6	-0.88%	C- / 3.7
2010	C	43.11	10.00	A+ / 9.7	19.62%	D- / 1.0

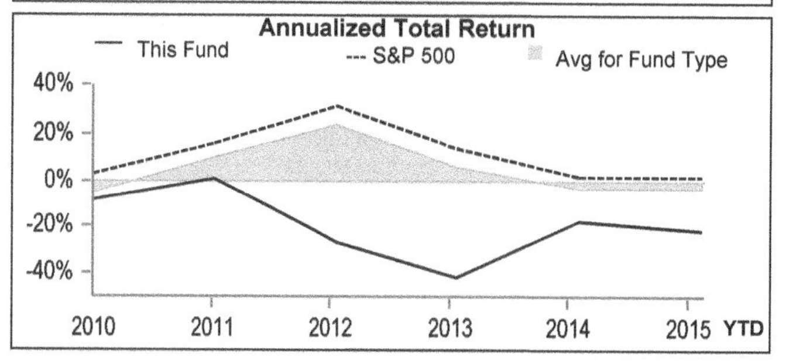

*DB Commodity Double Short ETN (DEE) C+ Fair

und Family: Deutsche Bank AG (London)
und Type: Growth
ception Date: April 28, 2008

ajor Rating Factors:
ceptional performance is the major factor driving the C+ (Fair) TheStreet.com vestment Rating for *DB Commodity Double Short ETN. The fund currently has a rformance rating of A+ (Excellent) based on an annualized return of 49.77% over e last three years and a total return of 59.04% year to date 2015. Factored into the rformance evaluation is an expense ratio of 0.75% (very low).

The fund's risk rating is currently C- (Fair). It carries a beta of -0.85, meaning the nd's expected move will be -8.5% for every 10% move in the market. Volatility, as easured by both the semi-deviation and a drawdown factor, is considered average. of December 31, 2015, *DB Commodity Double Short ETN traded at a discount of 71% below its net asset value, which is better than its one-year historical average scount of .44%.

This fund has been team managed for 8 years and currently receives a manager ality ranking of 99 (0=worst, 99=best). If you desire an average level of risk and ong performance, then this fund is a good option.

Data Date	Investment Rating	Net Assets ($Mil)	Price	Perfor-mance Rating/Pts	Total Return Y-T-D	Risk Rating/Pts
12-15	C+	5.65	96.14	A+ / 9.9	59.04%	C- / 3.9
2014	A-	0.10	53.60	A+ / 9.8	92.11%	C+ / 6.4
2013	E+	5.65	27.90	D- / 1.3	0.79%	C- / 4.0
2012	E-	5.65	26.50	E / 0.5	-2.42%	D / 2.1
2011	E-	5.65	30.65	E+ / 0.6	-21.64%	D / 1.9
2010	E-	5.65	35.00	E- / 0.1	-30.83%	D / 1.9

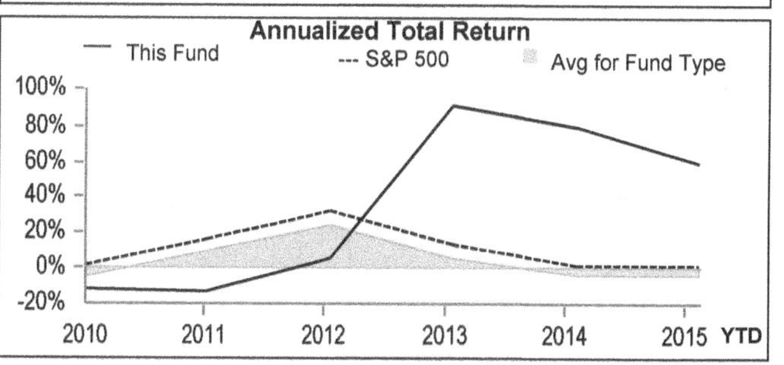

*DB Commodity Long ETN (DPU) E Very Weak

nd Family: Deutsche Bank AG (London)
nd Type: Growth
ception Date: April 28, 2008

ajor Rating Factors: *DB Commodity Long ETN has adopted a very risky asset ocation strategy and currently receives an overall TheStreet.com Investment Rating E (Very Weak). The fund has a high level of volatility, as measured by both semi-viation and drawdown factors. It carries a beta of 0.52, meaning the fund's pected move will be 5.2% for every 10% move in the market. As of December 31, 15, *DB Commodity Long ETN traded at a premium of 4.27% above its net asset ue, which is worse than its one-year historical average discount of .52%. fortunately, the high level of risk (D, Weak) failed to pay off as investors endured y poor performance.

The fund's performance rating is currently E+ (Very Weak). It has registered an nualized return of -23.16% over the last three years and is down -33.56% year to te 2015. Factored into the performance evaluation is an expense ratio of 0.75% ry low).

This fund has been team managed for 8 years and currently receives a manager ality ranking of 4 (0=worst, 99=best). If you can tolerate very high levels of risk in hope of improved future returns, holding this fund may be an option.

Data Date	Investment Rating	Net Assets ($Mil)	Price	Perfor-mance Rating/Pts	Total Return Y-T-D	Risk Rating/Pts
12-15	E	6.87	8.54	E+ / 0.6	-33.56%	D / 1.6
2014	E+	0.10	11.85	D- / 1.0	3.63%	C- / 3.4
2013	E	6.87	12.65	E / 0.5	-35.43%	C- / 3.0
2011	D	6.87	17.40	C- / 3.6	2.70%	C / 4.7
2010	C	6.87	18.00	A- / 9.1	9.89%	D / 2.1

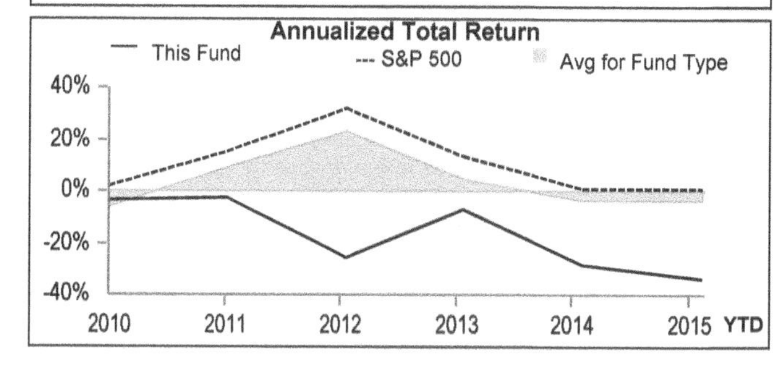

*DB Commodity Short ETN (DDP) C Fair

Fund Family: Deutsche Bank AG (London)
Fund Type: Growth
Inception Date: April 28, 2008

Data Date	Investment Rating	Net Assets ($Mil)	Price	Performance Rating/Pts	Total Return Y-T-D	Risk Rating/Pts
12-15	C	10.11	57.98	A+ / 9.8	30.96%	D+ / 2.9
2014	C	0.10	43.39	A+ / 9.7	105.35%	D+ / 2.3
2013	E-	10.11	20.85	E+ / 0.6	-30.26%	D+ / 2.6
2012	E+	10.11	30.70	E+ / 0.8	-0.83%	C- / 3.7
2011	E	10.11	31.38	D- / 1.2	-7.33%	C- / 3.1
2010	E+	10.11	32.50	E / 0.4	-14.16%	C- / 3.2

Major Rating Factors: *DB Commodity Short ETN has adopted a risky asset allocation strategy and currently receives an overall TheStreet.com Investment Rating of C (Fair). The fund has shown an above average level of volatility, as measured by both semi-deviation and drawdown factors. It carries a beta of -0.64, meaning the fund's expected move will be -6.4% for every 10% move in the market. As of December 31, 2015, *DB Commodity Short ETN traded at a premium of .19% above its net asset value, which is worse than its one-year historical average discount of .99%. The high level of risk (D+, Weak) did however, reward investors with excellent performance.

The fund's performance rating is currently A+ (Excellent). It has registered an annualized return of 23.75% over the last three years and is up 30.96% year to date 2015. Factored into the performance evaluation is an expense ratio of 0.75% (very low).

This fund has been team managed for 8 years and currently receives a manager quality ranking of 99 (0=worst, 99=best). If you are comfortable owning a high risk investment, this fund may be an option.

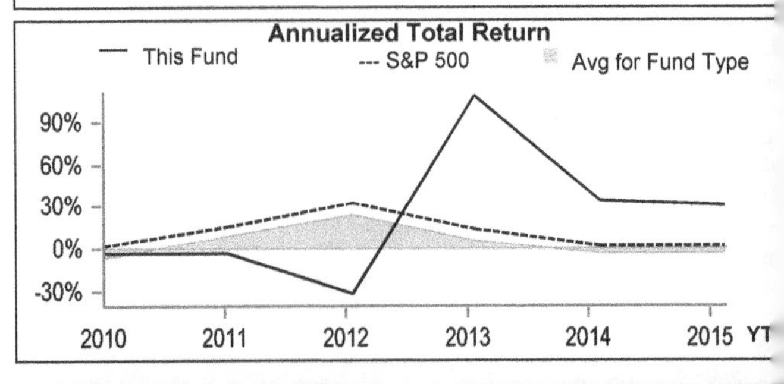

*DB Crude Oil Double Short ETN (DTO) C+ Fair

Fund Family: Deutsche Bank AG (London)
Fund Type: Growth
Inception Date: June 16, 2008

Data Date	Investment Rating	Net Assets ($Mil)	Price	Performance Rating/Pts	Total Return Y-T-D	Risk Rating/Pts
12-15	C+	97.05	158.12	A+ / 9.9	92.54%	C- / 3.1
2014	C+	0.10	80.51	A+ / 9.9	110.45%	C- / 4.2
2013	E	97.05	35.47	D- / 1.2	-10.97%	D / 2.2
2012	E-	97.05	44.69	E+ / 0.6	3.62%	D / 2.1
2011	E-	97.05	41.42	E / 0.4	-30.97%	D / 1.9
2010	E-	97.05	53.35	E / 0.3	-20.25%	D- / 1.3

Major Rating Factors:
Exceptional performance is the major factor driving the C+ (Fair) TheStreet.com Investment Rating for *DB Crude Oil Double Short ETN. The fund currently has a performance rating of A+ (Excellent) based on an annualized return of 54.95% over the last three years and a total return of 92.54% year to date 2015. Factored into the performance evaluation is an expense ratio of 0.75% (very low).

The fund's risk rating is currently C- (Fair). It carries a beta of -1.12, meaning the fund's expected move will be -11.2% for every 10% move in the market. Volatility, as measured by both the semi-deviation and a drawdown factor, is considered average. As of December 31, 2015, *DB Crude Oil Double Short ETN traded at a discount of .93% below its net asset value, which is better than its one-year historical average premium of .05%.

This fund has been team managed for 8 years and currently receives a manager quality ranking of 99 (0=worst, 99=best). If you desire an average level of risk and strong performance, then this fund is a good option.

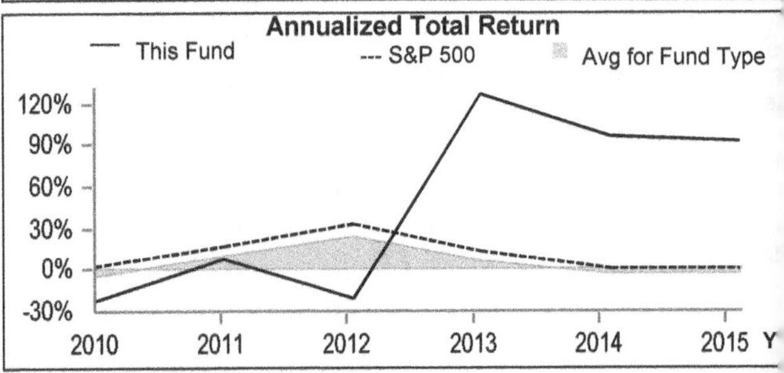

*DB Crude Oil Long ETN (OLO) E- Very Weak

Fund Family: Deutsche Bank AG (London)
Fund Type: Growth
Inception Date: June 16, 2008

Data Date	Investment Rating	Net Assets ($Mil)	Price	Performance Rating/Pts	Total Return Y-T-D	Risk Rating/Pt
12-15	E-	14.59	4.63	E / 0.4	-43.16%	E+ / 0.
2014	E	0.10	8.30	E / 0.5	-36.39%	C- / 3.
2013	D-	14.59	13.73	D / 2.2	0.79%	C- / 4.
2012	E+	14.59	12.72	D- / 1.2	-8.37%	C- / 3.
2011	D+	14.59	14.02	C / 5.4	6.90%	C- / 4.
2010	C	14.59	14.00	B+ / 8.5	3.09%	D / 2.

Major Rating Factors: *DB Crude Oil Long ETN has adopted a very risky asset allocation strategy and currently receives an overall TheStreet.com Investment Rating of E- (Very Weak). The fund has a high level of volatility, as measured by both semi-deviation and drawdown factors. It carries a beta of 0.82, meaning the fund's expected move will be 8.2% for every 10% move in the market. As of December 31, 2015, *DB Crude Oil Long ETN traded at a premium of .22% above its net asset value, which is better than its one-year historical average premium of .28%. Unfortunately, the high level of risk (E+, Very Weak) failed to pay off as investors endured very poor performance.

The fund's performance rating is currently E (Very Weak). It has registered an annualized return of -28.98% over the last three years and is down -43.16% year to date 2015. Factored into the performance evaluation is an expense ratio of 0.75% (very low).

This fund has been team managed for 8 years and currently receives a manager quality ranking of 1 (0=worst, 99=best). If you can tolerate very high levels of risk in the hope of improved future returns, holding this fund may be an option.

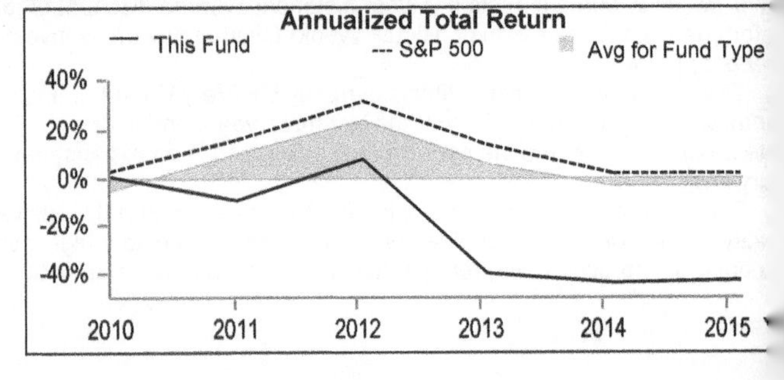

*DB Crude Oil Short ETN (SZO) C+ Fair

Fund Family: Deutsche Bank AG (London)
Fund Type: Growth
Inception Date: June 16, 2008

Major Rating Factors:
Exceptional performance is the major factor driving the C+ (Fair) TheStreet.com Investment Rating for *DB Crude Oil Short ETN. The fund currently has a performance rating of A+ (Excellent) based on an annualized return of 29.87% over the last three years and a total return of 50.63% year to date 2015. Factored into the performance evaluation is an expense ratio of 0.75% (very low).

The fund's risk rating is currently C- (Fair). It carries a beta of -0.70, meaning the fund's expected move will be -7.0% for every 10% move in the market. Volatility, as measured by both the semi-deviation and a drawdown factor, is considered average. As of December 31, 2015, *DB Crude Oil Short ETN traded at a discount of 1.22% below its net asset value, which is better than its one-year historical average discount of .51%.

This fund has been team managed for 8 years and currently receives a manager quality ranking of 99 (0=worst, 99=best). If you desire an average level of risk and strong performance, then this fund is a good option.

Data Date	Investment Rating	Net Assets ($Mil)	Price	Performance Rating/Pts	Total Return Y-T-D	Risk Rating/Pts
12-15	C+	14.43	91.70	A+ / 9.9	50.63%	C- / 3.9
2014	A	0.10	62.12	A+ / 9.6	49.90%	B- / 7.0
2013	D-	14.43	38.99	D / 2.0	-4.79%	C- / 4.0
2012	E+	14.43	43.41	D- / 1.0	4.67%	C- / 3.9
2011	E	14.43	40.74	D- / 1.0	-14.17%	D+ / 2.7
2010	E	14.43	44.31	E+ / 0.6	-7.69%	D+ / 2.9

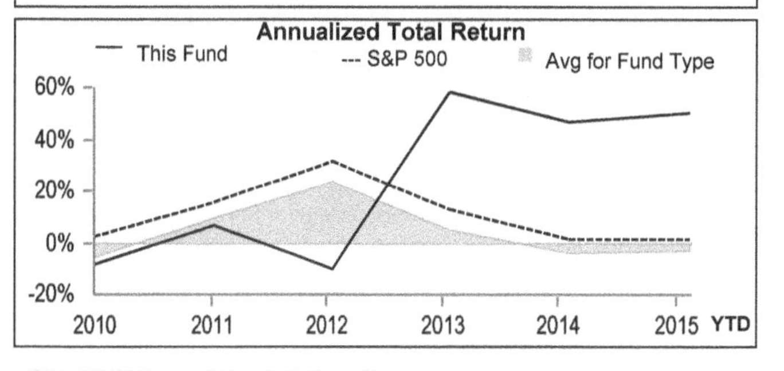

*DB FI Enhanced Global Hi Yld ETN (FIEG) D Weak

Fund Family: Deutsche Bank AG (London)
Fund Type: Global
Inception Date: October 8, 2013

Major Rating Factors: *DB FI Enhanced Global Hi Yld ETN receives a TheStreet.com Investment Rating of D (Weak). The fund currently has a performance rating of C- (Fair) based on an annualized return of 0.00% over the last three years and a total return of -3.82% year to date 2015.

The fund's risk rating is currently C (Fair). It carries a beta of 0.00, meaning the fund's expected move will be 0.0% for every 10% move in the market. Volatility, as measured by both the semi-deviation and a drawdown factor, is considered average. As of December 31, 2015, *DB FI Enhanced Global Hi Yld ETN traded at a discount of .32% below its net asset value, which is better than its one-year historical average premium of .21%.

If you desire an average level of risk, then this fund may be an option.

Data Date	Investment Rating	Net Assets ($Mil)	Price	Performance Rating/Pts	Total Return Y-T-D	Risk Rating/Pts
12-15	D	177.80	111.37	C- / 3.5	-3.82%	C / 4.5
2014	D-	177.80	118.18	D+ / 2.8	7.37%	C- / 4.1

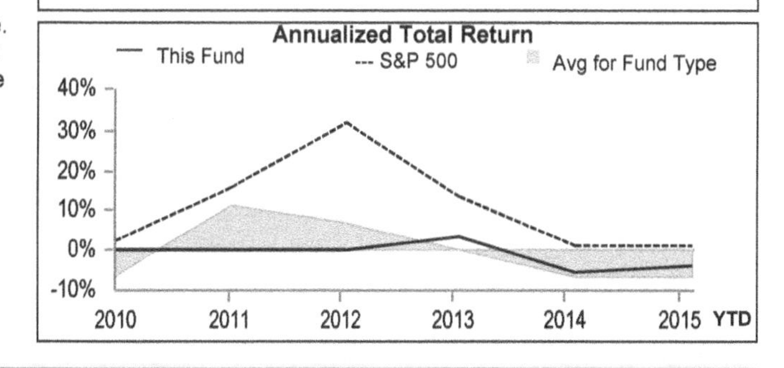

*DB German Bond Futures ETN (BUNL) C- Fair

Fund Family: DB Commodity Services LLC
Fund Type: Global
Inception Date: March 22, 2011

Major Rating Factors: Middle of the road best describes *DB German Bond Futures ETN whose TheStreet.com Investment Rating is currently a C- (Fair). The fund currently has a performance rating of C+ (Fair) based on an annualized return of 17% over the last three years and a total return of 0.80% year to date 2015.

The fund's risk rating is currently C- (Fair). It carries a beta of 0.03, meaning the fund's expected move will be 0.3% for every 10% move in the market. Volatility, as measured by both the semi-deviation and a drawdown factor, is considered average. As of December 31, 2015, *DB German Bond Futures ETN traded at a premium .69% above its net asset value, which is worse than its one-year historical average premium of .01%.

This fund has been team managed for 5 years and currently receives a manager quality ranking of 89 (0=worst, 99=best). If you desire an average level of risk, then this fund may be an option.

Data Date	Investment Rating	Net Assets ($Mil)	Price	Performance Rating/Pts	Total Return Y-T-D	Risk Rating/Pts
12-15	C-	9.20	27.57	C+ / 6.2	0.80%	C- / 3.9
2014	C+	9.20	27.37	C / 5.4	15.73%	B- / 7.7
2013	D	8.40	23.65	D+ / 2.4	-0.30%	C+ / 5.8
2012	D-	0.00	23.93	D / 1.9	3.55%	C+ / 5.8

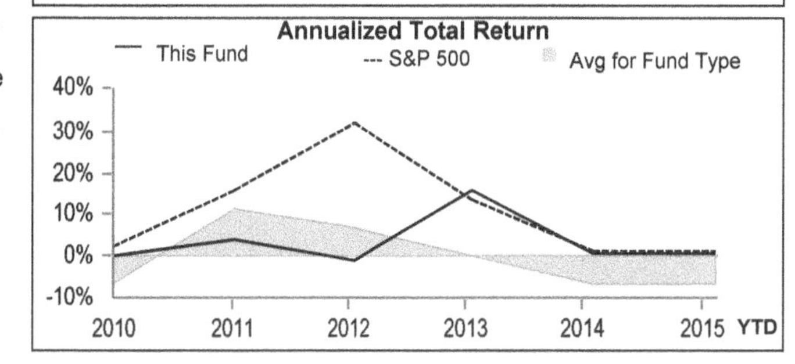

*DB Gold Double Long ETN (DGP) E Very Weak

Fund Family: Deutsche Bank AG (London)
Fund Type: Precious Metals
Inception Date: February 28, 2008

Data Date	Investment Rating	Net Assets ($Mil)	Price	Perfor-mance Rating/Pts	Total Return Y-T-D	Risk Rating/P
12-15	E	165.00	18.14	E / 0.5	-23.27%	D- / 1.
2014	E	165.00	23.50	E+ / 0.7	-8.83%	C- / 3.
2013	E-	0.10	25.10	E+ / 0.6	-48.00%	D / 1.
2012	C-	0.10	52.03	B- / 7.5	-1.29%	C- / 3.
2011	C+	0.00	47.61	A+ / 9.8	28.98%	C- / 4
2010	B-	0.10	42.93	A+ / 9.8	62.37%	D+ / 2

Major Rating Factors: *DB Gold Double Long ETN has adopted a very risky asset allocation strategy and currently receives an overall TheStreet.com Investment Rating of E (Very Weak). The fund has a high level of volatility, as measured by both semi-deviation and drawdown factors. It carries a beta of 1.88, meaning it is expected to move 18.8% for every 10% move in the market. As of December 31, 2015, *DB Gold Double Long ETN traded at a discount of .22% below its net asset value, which is better than its one-year historical average premium of .10%. Unfortunately, the high level of risk (D-, Weak) failed to pay off as investors endured very poor performance.

The fund's performance rating is currently E (Very Weak). It has registered an annualized return of -29.09% over the last three years and is down -23.27% year to date 2015.

This fund has been team managed for 8 years and currently receives a manager quality ranking of 23 (0=worst, 99=best). If you can tolerate very high levels of risk in the hope of improved future returns, holding this fund may be an option.

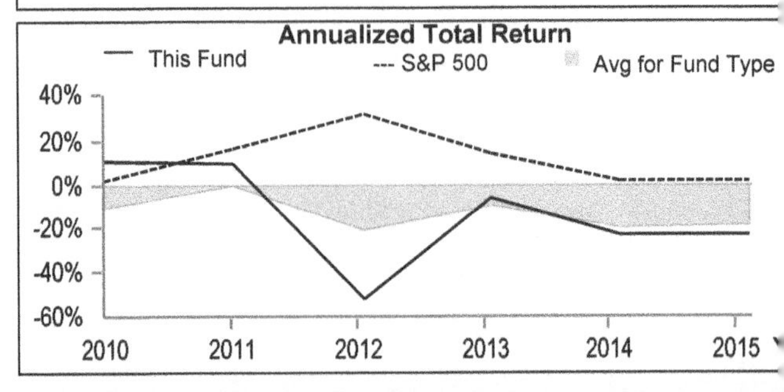

*DB Gold Double Short ETN (DZZ) C+ Fair

Fund Family: Deutsche Bank AG (London)
Fund Type: Precious Metals
Inception Date: February 28, 2008

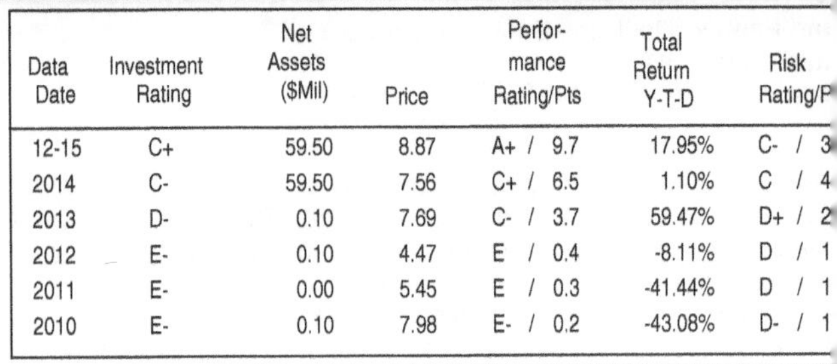

Data Date	Investment Rating	Net Assets ($Mil)	Price	Perfor-mance Rating/Pts	Total Return Y-T-D	Risk Rating/P
12-15	C+	59.50	8.87	A+ / 9.7	17.95%	C- / 3
2014	C-	59.50	7.56	C+ / 6.5	1.10%	C / 4
2013	D-	0.10	7.69	C- / 3.7	59.47%	D+ / 2
2012	E-	0.10	4.47	E / 0.4	-8.11%	D / 1
2011	E-	0.00	5.45	E / 0.3	-41.44%	D / 1
2010	E-	0.10	7.98	E- / 0.2	-43.08%	D- / 1

Major Rating Factors:
Exceptional performance is the major factor driving the C+ (Fair) TheStreet.com Investment Rating for *DB Gold Double Short ETN. The fund currently has a performance rating of A+ (Excellent) based on an annualized return of 24.78% over the last three years and a total return of 17.95% year to date 2015.

The fund's risk rating is currently C- (Fair). It carries a beta of -1.79, meaning the fund's expected move will be -17.9% for every 10% move in the market. Volatility, as measured by both the semi-deviation and a drawdown factor, is considered average. As of December 31, 2015, *DB Gold Double Short ETN traded at a premium of .11% above its net asset value, which is worse than its one-year historical average discount of .07%.

This fund has been team managed for 8 years and currently receives a manager quality ranking of 37 (0=worst, 99=best). If you desire an average level of risk and strong performance, then this fund is a good option.

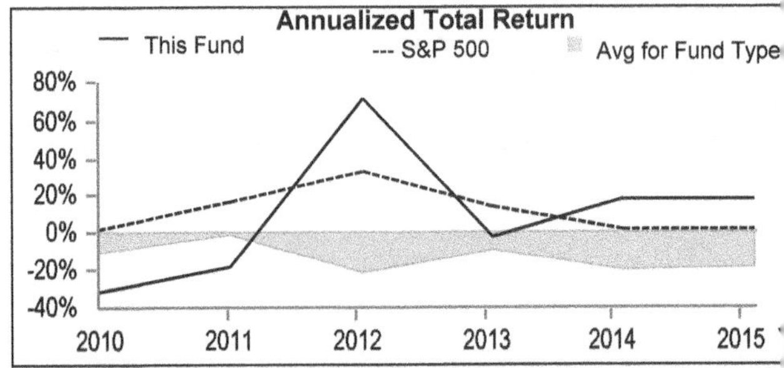

*DB Gold Short ETN (DGZ) C+ Fair

Fund Family: Deutsche Bank AG (London)
Fund Type: Precious Metals
Inception Date: February 29, 2008

Data Date	Investment Rating	Net Assets ($Mil)	Price	Perfor-mance Rating/Pts	Total Return Y-T-D	Risk Rating/P
12-15	C+	18.00	17.10	B+ / 8.9	9.34%	C- / 4
2014	C-	18.00	15.67	C / 4.8	1.05%	C+ / 6
2013	D	0.10	15.73	C- / 3.6	28.25%	C- / 4
2012	E	0.10	11.81	E+ / 0.6	-3.34%	C- / 3
2011	E	0.00	12.89	E+ / 0.8	-21.06%	D+ / 2
2010	E	0.10	15.16	E / 0.4	-24.05%	D+ / 2

Major Rating Factors: Strong performance is the major factor driving the C+ (Fair) TheStreet.com Investment Rating for *DB Gold Short ETN. The fund currently has a performance rating of B+ (Good) based on an annualized return of 12.73% over the last three years and a total return of 9.34% year to date 2015.

The fund's risk rating is currently C- (Fair). It carries a beta of -0.89, meaning the fund's expected move will be -8.9% for every 10% move in the market. Volatility, as measured by both the semi-deviation and a drawdown factor, is considered average. As of December 31, 2015, *DB Gold Short ETN traded at a premium of .06% above its net asset value, which is worse than its one-year historical average discount of .05%.

This fund has been team managed for 8 years and currently receives a manager quality ranking of 59 (0=worst, 99=best). If you desire an average level of risk and strong performance, then this fund is a good option.

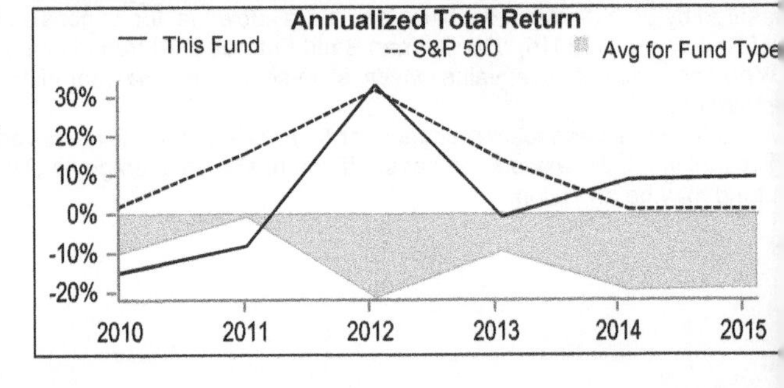

*DB Inverse Japanese Govt Bd Fut (JGBS) D Weak

Fund Family: DB Commodity Services LLC
Fund Type: Global
Inception Date: November 8, 2011

Data Date	Investment Rating	Net Assets ($Mil)	Price	Performance Rating/Pts	Total Return Y-T-D	Risk Rating/Pts
12-15	D	38.50	17.50	D+ / 2.9	-4.46%	C- / 3.6
2014	D+	38.50	18.20	D / 2.1	-5.77%	B- / 7.5
2013	D	40.20	19.37	D / 2.2	-1.96%	C+ / 5.7
2012	D-	0.00	19.54	D- / 1.2	-1.95%	C+ / 5.8

Major Rating Factors:
Disappointing performance is the major factor driving the D (Weak) TheStreet.com Investment Rating for *DB Inverse Japanese Govt Bd Fut. The fund currently has a performance rating of D+ (Weak) based on an annualized return of -3.99% over the last three years and a total return of -4.46% year to date 2015.

The fund's risk rating is currently C- (Fair). It carries a beta of -0.17, meaning the fund's expected move will be -1.7% for every 10% move in the market. Volatility, as measured by both the semi-deviation and a drawdown factor, is considered average. As of December 31, 2015, *DB Inverse Japanese Govt Bd Fut traded at a premium of 20.44% above its net asset value, which is worse than its one-year historical average premium of 19.07%.

This fund has been team managed for 5 years and currently receives a manager quality ranking of 34 (0=worst, 99=best). This fund offers an average level of risk but investors looking for strong performance will be frustrated.

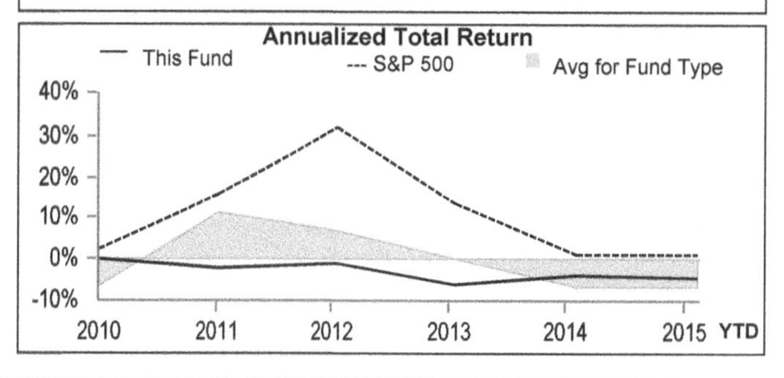

*Deep Value ETF (DVP) D+ Weak

Fund Family: Exchange Traded Concepts LLC
Fund Type: Growth
Inception Date: September 22, 2014

Data Date	Investment Rating	Net Assets ($Mil)	Price	Performance Rating/Pts	Total Return Y-T-D	Risk Rating/Pts
12-15	D+	0.00	21.83	D+ / 2.3	-9.50%	C+ / 6.8

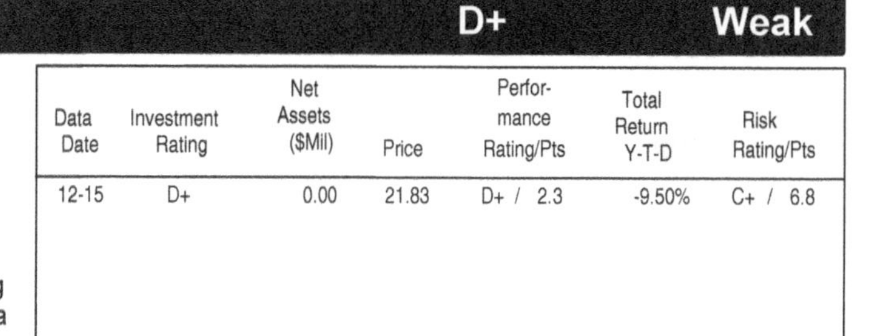

Major Rating Factors:
Disappointing performance is the major factor driving the D+ (Weak) TheStreet.com Investment Rating for *Deep Value ETF. The fund currently has a performance rating of D+ (Weak) based on an annualized return of 0.00% over the last three years and a total return of -9.50% year to date 2015. Factored into the performance evaluation is an expense ratio of 0.80% (very low).

The fund's risk rating is currently C+ (Fair). It carries a beta of 0.00, meaning the fund's expected move will be 0.0% for every 10% move in the market. Volatility, as measured by both the semi-deviation and a drawdown factor, is considered low. As of December 31, 2015, *Deep Value ETF traded at a price exactly equal to its net asset value, which is better than its one-year historical average premium of .07%.

James G. Stevens currently receives a manager quality ranking of 14 (0=worst, 99=best). This fund offers only a moderate level of risk but investors looking for strong performance are still waiting.

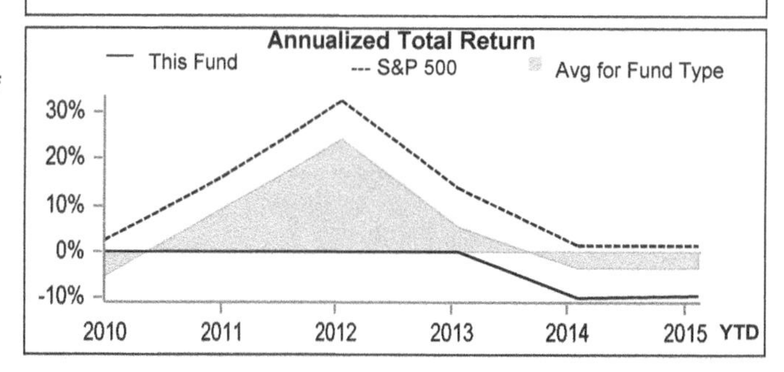

*Deutsche X-trackers Hvst CSI300 (ASHR) D- Weak

Fund Family: DBX Advisors LLC
Fund Type: Foreign
Inception Date: November 6, 2013

Data Date	Investment Rating	Net Assets ($Mil)	Price	Performance Rating/Pts	Total Return Y-T-D	Risk Rating/Pts
12-15	D-	0.00	27.98	D+ / 2.9	-2.43%	C- / 3.1

Major Rating Factors:
Disappointing performance is the major factor driving the D- (Weak) TheStreet.com Investment Rating for *Deutsche X-trackers Hvst CSI300. The fund currently has a performance rating of D+ (Weak) based on an annualized return of 0.00% over the last three years and a total return of -2.43% year to date 2015. Factored into the performance evaluation is an expense ratio of 0.80% (very low).

The fund's risk rating is currently C- (Fair). It carries a beta of 0.00, meaning the fund's expected move will be 0.0% for every 10% move in the market. Volatility, as measured by both the semi-deviation and a drawdown factor, is considered average. As of December 31, 2015, *Deutsche X-trackers Hvst CSI300 traded at a discount of .39% below its net asset value, which is worse than its one-year historical average discount of .41%.

Zhixi Guo currently receives a manager quality ranking of 54 (0=worst, 99=best). This fund offers an average level of risk but investors looking for strong performance will be frustrated.

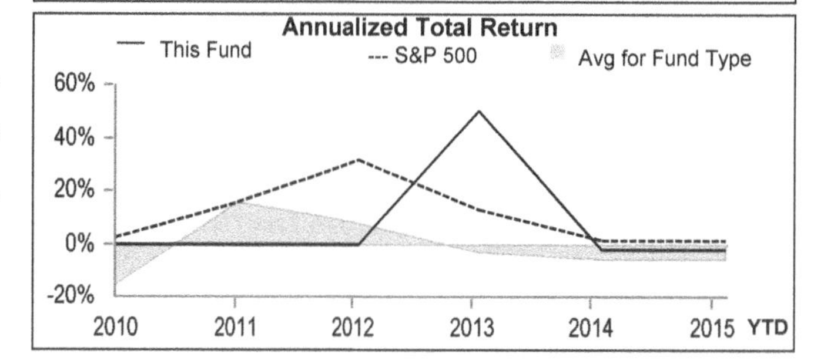

*Deutsche X-trackers Hvst CSI500 (ASHS) B- Good

Fund Family: DBX Advisors LLC
Fund Type: Foreign
Inception Date: May 21, 2014

Data Date	Investment Rating	Net Assets ($Mil)	Price	Performance Rating/Pts	Total Return Y-T-D	Risk Rating/Pts
12-15	B-	11.70	41.46	A+ / 9.6	27.16%	C / 4.7

Major Rating Factors:
Exceptional performance is the major factor driving the B- (Good) TheStreet.com Investment Rating for *Deutsche X-trackers Hvst CSI500. The fund currently has a performance rating of A+ (Excellent) based on an annualized return of 0.00% over the last three years and a total return of 27.16% year to date 2015. Factored into the performance evaluation is an expense ratio of 0.80% (very low).

The fund's risk rating is currently C (Fair). It carries a beta of 0.00, meaning the fund's expected move will be 0.0% for every 10% move in the market. Volatility, as measured by both the semi-deviation and a drawdown factor, is considered average. As of December 31, 2015, *Deutsche X-trackers Hvst CSI500 traded at a discount of 1.26% below its net asset value, which is better than its one-year historical average discount of .14%.

Janice Dai currently receives a manager quality ranking of 99 (0=worst, 99=best). If you desire an average level of risk and strong performance, then this fund is a good option.

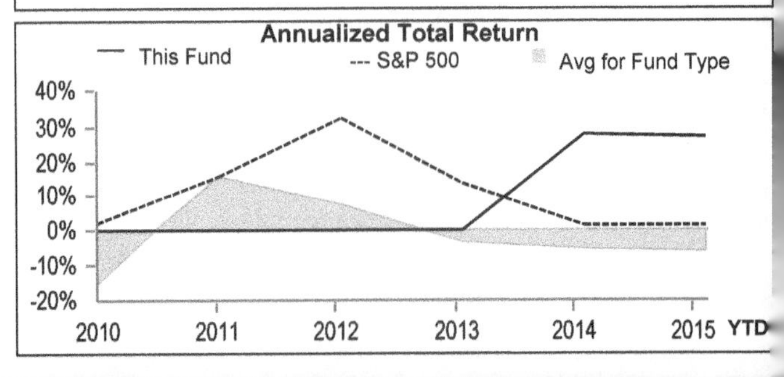

*Deutsche X-trackers MSCI All Ch (CN) C- Fair

Fund Family: DBX Advisors LLC
Fund Type: Foreign
Inception Date: April 30, 2014

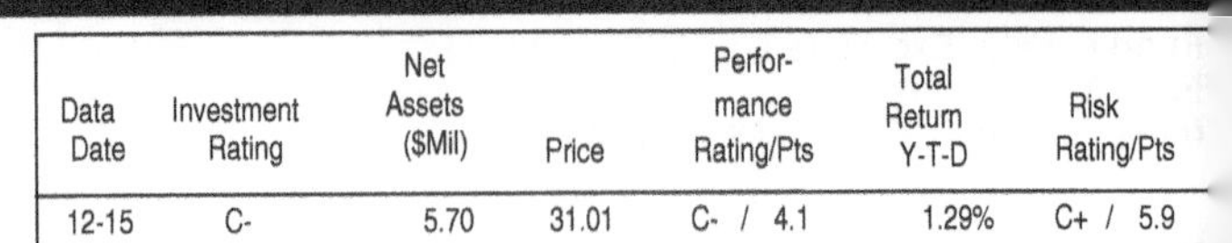

Data Date	Investment Rating	Net Assets ($Mil)	Price	Performance Rating/Pts	Total Return Y-T-D	Risk Rating/Pts
12-15	C-	5.70	31.01	C- / 4.1	1.29%	C+ / 5.9

Major Rating Factors: Middle of the road best describes *Deutsche X-trackers MSCI All Ch whose TheStreet.com Investment Rating is currently a C- (Fair). The fund currently has a performance rating of C- (Fair) based on an annualized return of 0.00% over the last three years and a total return of 1.29% year to date 2015. Factored into the performance evaluation is an expense ratio of 0.26% (very low).

The fund's risk rating is currently C+ (Fair). It carries a beta of 0.00, meaning the fund's expected move will be 0.0% for every 10% move in the market. Volatility, as measured by both the semi-deviation and a drawdown factor, is considered low. As of December 31, 2015, *Deutsche X-trackers MSCI All Ch traded at a discount of .32% below its net asset value, which is better than its one-year historical average discount of .11%.

Lance McGray has been running the fund for 2 years and currently receives a manager quality ranking of 80 (0=worst, 99=best). If you desire an average level of risk, then this fund may be an option.

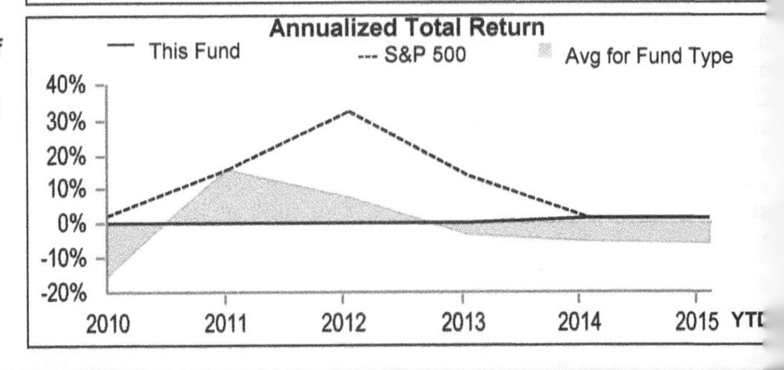

*Deutsche X-trackers MSCI AP xJp (DBAP) D+ Weak

Fund Family: DBX Advisors LLC
Fund Type: Foreign
Inception Date: October 1, 2013

Data Date	Investment Rating	Net Assets ($Mil)	Price	Performance Rating/Pts	Total Return Y-T-D	Risk Rating/Pts
12-15	D+	6.70	22.01	D / 1.9	-8.38%	B- / 7.4
2014	D+	6.70	25.96	C / 5.1	6.65%	C- / 4.0

Major Rating Factors:
Disappointing performance is the major factor driving the D+ (Weak) TheStreet.com Investment Rating for *Deutsche X-trackers MSCI AP xJp. The fund currently has a performance rating of D (Weak) based on an annualized return of 0.00% over the last three years and a total return of -8.38% year to date 2015. Factored into the performance evaluation is an expense ratio of 0.60% (very low).

The fund's risk rating is currently B- (Good). It carries a beta of 0.00, meaning the fund's expected move will be 0.0% for every 10% move in the market. Volatility, as measured by both the semi-deviation and a drawdown factor, is considered low. As of December 31, 2015, *Deutsche X-trackers MSCI AP xJp traded at a discount of 1.21% below its net asset value, which is better than its one-year historical average premium of .19%.

Dino Bourdos has been running the fund for 3 years and currently receives a manager quality ranking of 22 (0=worst, 99=best). This fund offers only a moderate level of risk but investors looking for strong performance are still waiting.

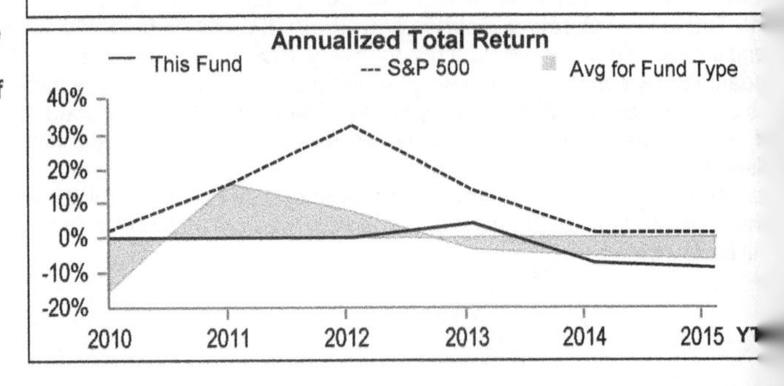

* Denotes ETF Fund

*Deutsche X-trackers MSCI AW xUS (DBAW) C- Fair

Fund Family: DBX Advisors LLC
Fund Type: Foreign
Inception Date: January 23, 2014

Major Rating Factors: Middle of the road best describes *Deutsche X-trackers MSCI AW xUS whose TheStreet.com Investment Rating is currently a C- (Fair). The fund currently has a performance rating of C- (Fair) based on an annualized return of 0.00% over the last three years and a total return of -0.06% year to date 2015. Factored into the performance evaluation is an expense ratio of 0.40% (very low).

The fund's risk rating is currently C+ (Fair). It carries a beta of 0.00, meaning the fund's expected move will be 0.0% for every 10% move in the market. Volatility, as measured by both the semi-deviation and a drawdown factor, is considered low. As of December 31, 2015, *Deutsche X-trackers MSCI AW xUS traded at a premium of .43% above its net asset value, which is better than its one-year historical average premium of .62%.

Dino Bourdos has been running the fund for 2 years and currently receives a manager quality ranking of 69 (0=worst, 99=best). If you desire an average level of risk, then this fund may be an option.

Data Date	Investment Rating	Net Assets ($Mil)	Price	Performance Rating/Pts	Total Return Y-T-D	Risk Rating/Pts
12-15	C-	5.20	23.13	C- / 3.4	-0.06%	C+ / 6.2

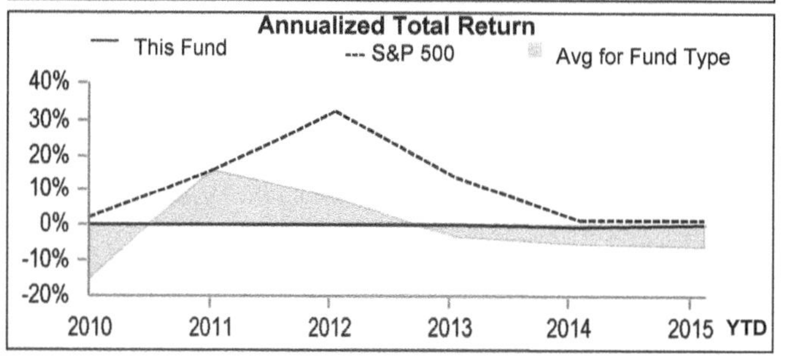

*Deutsche X-trackers MSCI Br Hdg (DBBR) D- Weak

Fund Family: DBX Advisors LLC
Fund Type: Foreign
Inception Date: June 9, 2011

Major Rating Factors:
Disappointing performance is the major factor driving the D- (Weak) TheStreet.com Investment Rating for *Deutsche X-trackers MSCI Br Hdg. The fund currently has a performance rating of D- (Weak) based on an annualized return of -16.51% over the last three years and a total return of -21.88% year to date 2015. Factored into the performance evaluation is an expense ratio of 0.60% (very low).

The fund's risk rating is currently C- (Fair). It carries a beta of 0.80, meaning the fund's expected move will be 8.0% for every 10% move in the market. Volatility, as measured by both the semi-deviation and a drawdown factor, is considered average. As of December 31, 2015, *Deutsche X-trackers MSCI Br Hdg traded at a discount of .90% below its net asset value, which is better than its one-year historical average discount of .08%.

Dino Bourdos has been running the fund for 5 years and currently receives a manager quality ranking of 7 (0=worst, 99=best). This fund offers an average level of risk but investors looking for strong performance will be frustrated.

Data Date	Investment Rating	Net Assets ($Mil)	Price	Performance Rating/Pts	Total Return Y-T-D	Risk Rating/Pts
12-15	D-	4.40	8.04	D- / 1.0	-21.88%	C- / 4.0
2014	E+	4.40	12.85	D- / 1.5	-12.18%	C- / 3.1
2013	D	3.80	15.56	D- / 1.4	-12.65%	C+ / 6.2
2012	B-	4.20	20.12	B- / 7.2	4.78%	B- / 7.8

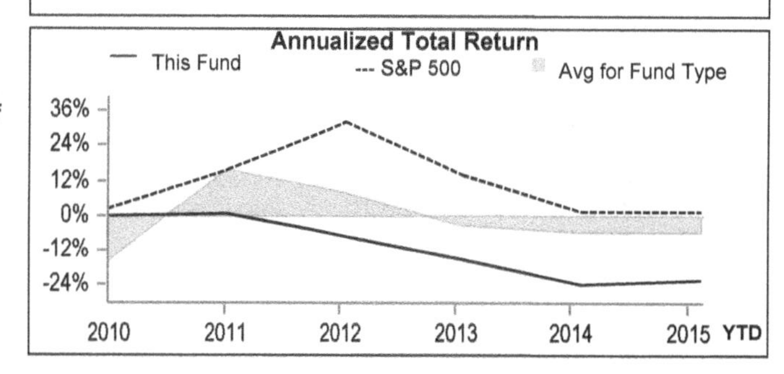

*Deutsche X-trackers MSCI EAFE Hd (DBEF) B+ Good

Fund Family: DBX Advisors LLC
Fund Type: Foreign
Inception Date: June 9, 2011

Major Rating Factors: Strong performance is the major factor driving the B+ (Good) TheStreet.com Investment Rating for *Deutsche X-trackers MSCI EAFE Hd. The fund currently has a performance rating of B- (Good) based on an annualized return of .41% over the last three years and a total return of 3.73% year to date 2015. Factored into the performance evaluation is an expense ratio of 0.35% (very low).

The fund's risk rating is currently B (Good). It carries a beta of 0.82, meaning the fund's expected move will be 8.2% for every 10% move in the market. Volatility, as measured by both the semi-deviation and a drawdown factor, is considered low. As of December 31, 2015, *Deutsche X-trackers MSCI EAFE Hd traded at a discount .80% below its net asset value, which is better than its one-year historical average premium of .17%.

Vishal Bhatia has been running the fund for 5 years and currently receives a manager quality ranking of 91 (0=worst, 99=best). If you desire only a moderate level risk and strong performance, then this fund is an excellent option.

Data Date	Investment Rating	Net Assets ($Mil)	Price	Performance Rating/Pts	Total Return Y-T-D	Risk Rating/Pts
12-15	B+	660.70	27.16	B- / 7.4	3.73%	B / 8.1
2014	B	660.70	27.00	C+ / 6.8	5.08%	B / 8.4
2013	A-	257.20	27.42	B+ / 8.6	19.64%	B / 8.2
2012	A+	14.30	22.06	A / 9.5	19.21%	B / 8.0

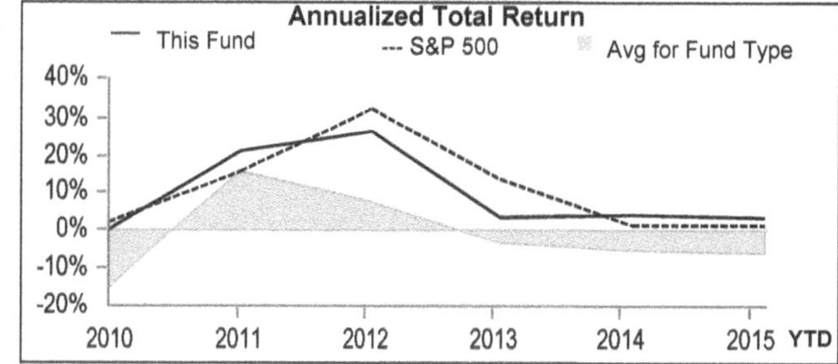

*Deutsche X-trackers MSCI EM Hdg (DBEM) C- Fair

Fund Family: DBX Advisors LLC
Fund Type: Emerging Market
Inception Date: June 9, 2011

Major Rating Factors:
Disappointing performance is the major factor driving the C- (Fair) TheStreet.com Investment Rating for *Deutsche X-trackers MSCI EM Hdg. The fund currently has a performance rating of D (Weak) based on an annualized return of -6.72% over the last three years and a total return of -13.09% year to date 2015. Factored into the performance evaluation is an expense ratio of 0.65% (very low).

The fund's risk rating is currently B- (Good). It carries a beta of 0.72, meaning the fund's expected move will be 7.2% for every 10% move in the market. Volatility, as measured by both the semi-deviation and a drawdown factor, is considered low. As of December 31, 2015, *Deutsche X-trackers MSCI EM Hdg traded at a discount of .87% below its net asset value, which is better than its one-year historical average premium of .02%.

Vishal Bhatia has been running the fund for 5 years and currently receives a manager quality ranking of 62 (0=worst, 99=best). This fund offers only a moderate level of risk but investors looking for strong performance are still waiting.

Data Date	Investment Rating	Net Assets ($Mil)	Price	Performance Rating/Pts	Total Return Y-T-D	Risk Rating/Pts
12-15	C-	29.90	18.28	D / 2.2	-13.09%	B- / 7.6
2014	D-	29.90	21.44	C- / 3.3	3.81%	C- / 3.8
2013	D-	22.50	21.68	D / 1.6	-9.83%	C / 5.4
2012	C+	4.50	22.84	B / 7.9	13.10%	C / 5.5

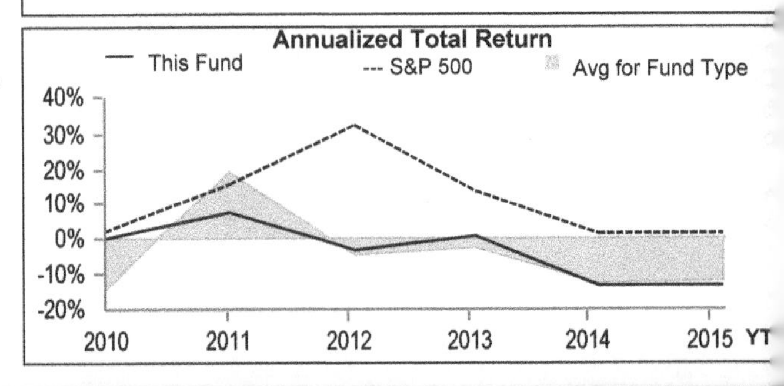

*Deutsche X-trackers MSCI Eu Hdg (DBEU) C+ Fair

Fund Family: DBX Advisors LLC
Fund Type: Foreign
Inception Date: October 1, 2013

Major Rating Factors: Middle of the road best describes *Deutsche X-trackers MSCI Eu Hdg whose TheStreet.com Investment Rating is currently a C+ (Fair). The fund currently has a performance rating of C (Fair) based on an annualized return of 0.00% over the last three years and a total return of 3.80% year to date 2015. Factored into the performance evaluation is an expense ratio of 0.45% (very low).

The fund's risk rating is currently B- (Good). It carries a beta of 0.00, meaning the fund's expected move will be 0.0% for every 10% move in the market. Volatility, as measured by both the semi-deviation and a drawdown factor, is considered low. As of December 31, 2015, *Deutsche X-trackers MSCI Eu Hdg traded at a discount of .46% below its net asset value, which is better than its one-year historical average premium of .23%.

Dino Bourdos has been running the fund for 3 years and currently receives a manager quality ranking of 89 (0=worst, 99=best). If you desire an average level of risk, then this fund may be an option.

Data Date	Investment Rating	Net Assets ($Mil)	Price	Performance Rating/Pts	Total Return Y-T-D	Risk Rating/Pts
12-15	C+	319.90	25.85	C / 5.2	3.80%	B- / 7.9
2014	D	319.90	26.05	C- / 3.1	3.20%	C / 5.1

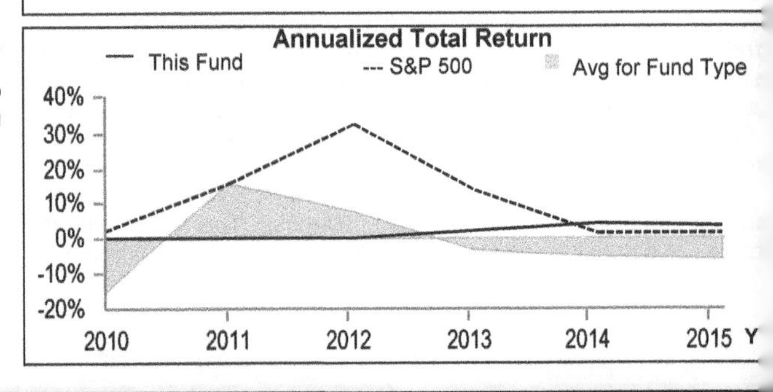

*Deutsche X-trackers MSCI Eur Hdg (DBEZ) C Fair

Fund Family: DBX Advisors LLC
Fund Type: Foreign
Inception Date: December 10, 2014

Major Rating Factors: Middle of the road best describes *Deutsche X-trackers MSCI Eur Hdg whose TheStreet.com Investment Rating is currently a C (Fair). The fund currently has a performance rating of C+ (Fair) based on an annualized return of 0.00% over the last three years and a total return of 9.93% year to date 2015.

The fund's risk rating is currently C (Fair). It carries a beta of 0.00, meaning the fund's expected move will be 0.0% for every 10% move in the market. Volatility, as measured by both the semi-deviation and a drawdown factor, is considered average. As of December 31, 2015, *Deutsche X-trackers MSCI Eur Hdg traded at a discount of .46% below its net asset value, which is better than its one-year historical average premium of .41%.

Vishal Bhatia has been running the fund for 2 years and currently receives a manager quality ranking of 95 (0=worst, 99=best). If you desire an average level of risk, then this fund may be an option.

Data Date	Investment Rating	Net Assets ($Mil)	Price	Performance Rating/Pts	Total Return Y-T-D	Risk Rating/Pts
12-15	C	0.00	26.16	C+ / 6.9	9.93%	C / 4.

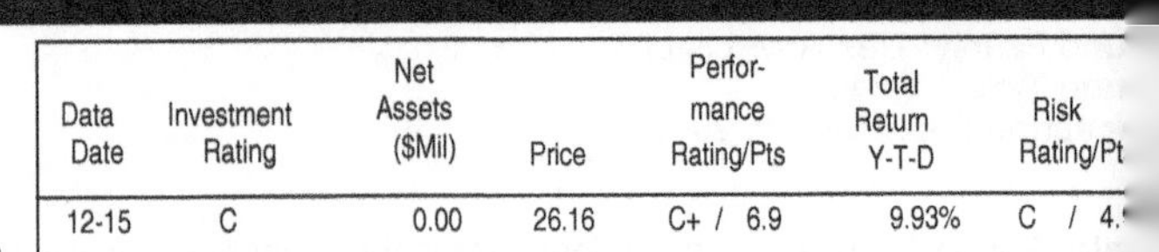

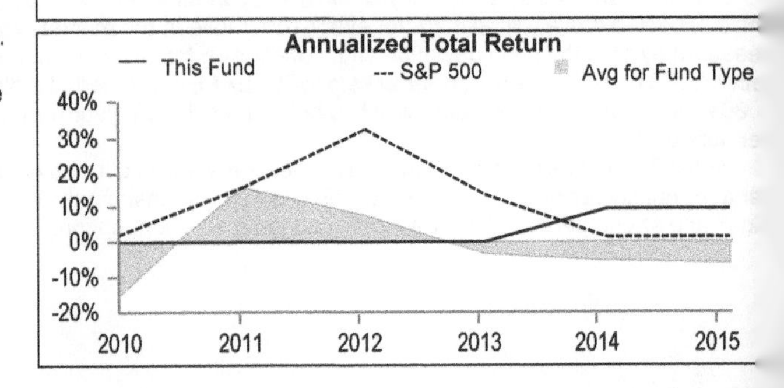

*Deutsche X-trackers MSCI Ger Hdg (DBGR) B Good

.und Family: DBX Advisors LLC
.und Type: Foreign
ception Date: June 9, 2011

ajor Rating Factors: Strong performance is the major factor driving the B (Good) eStreet.com Investment Rating for *Deutsche X-trackers MSCI Ger Hdg. The fund rrently has a performance rating of B- (Good) based on an annualized return of 23% over the last three years and a total return of 6.72% year to date 2015. ctored into the performance evaluation is an expense ratio of 0.45% (very low).

The fund's risk rating is currently B- (Good). It carries a beta of 0.64, meaning the nd's expected move will be 6.4% for every 10% move in the market. Volatility, as easured by both the semi-deviation and a drawdown factor, is considered low. As of ecember 31, 2015, *Deutsche X-trackers MSCI Ger Hdg traded at a discount of 40% below its net asset value, which is better than its one-year historical average emium of .09%.

Vishal Bhatia has been running the fund for 5 years and currently receives a anager quality ranking of 88 (0=worst, 99=best). If you desire only a moderate level risk and strong performance, then this fund is an excellent option.

Data Date	Investment Rating	Net Assets ($Mil)	Price	Performance Rating/Pts	Total Return Y-T-D	Risk Rating/Pts
12-15	B	42.40	24.01	B- / 7.4	6.72%	B- / 7.3
2014	C	42.40	23.48	C / 4.7	1.38%	B / 8.2
2013	B	4.60	26.14	B- / 7.2	16.03%	B / 8.3

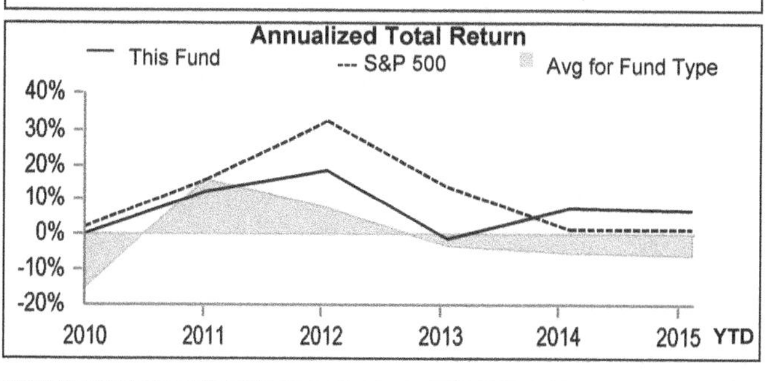

*Deutsche X-trackers MSCI Jp Hdg (DBJP) A Excellent

.und Family: DBX Advisors LLC
.und Type: Foreign
ception Date: June 9, 2011

ajor Rating Factors:
ceptional performance is the major factor driving the A (Excellent) TheStreet.com estment Rating for *Deutsche X-trackers MSCI Jp Hdg. The fund currently has a rformance rating of A- (Excellent) based on an annualized return of 17.62% over last three years and a total return of 4.69% year to date 2015. Factored into the rformance evaluation is an expense ratio of 0.45% (very low).

The fund's risk rating is currently B- (Good). It carries a beta of 0.94, meaning at its performance tracks fairly well with that of the overall stock market. Volatility, measured by both the semi-deviation and a drawdown factor, is considered low. of December 31, 2015, *Deutsche X-trackers MSCI Jp Hdg traded at a discount of 32% below its net asset value, which is better than its one-year historical average emium of .05%.

Vishal Bhatia has been running the fund for 5 years and currently receives a anager quality ranking of 96 (0=worst, 99=best). If you desire only a moderate level risk and strong performance, then this fund is an excellent option.

Data Date	Investment Rating	Net Assets ($Mil)	Price	Performance Rating/Pts	Total Return Y-T-D	Risk Rating/Pts
12-15	A	568.30	38.09	A- / 9.2	4.69%	B- / 7.6
2014	A	568.30	37.03	A- / 9.2	7.38%	B- / 7.5
2013	A+	354.50	38.74	A+ / 9.7	43.94%	B- / 7.8

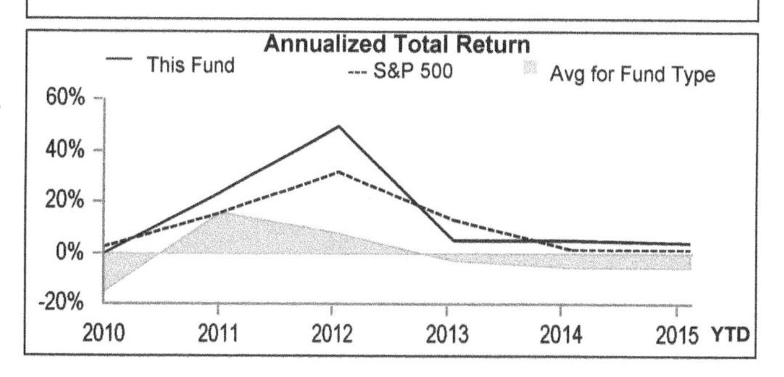

Deutsche X-trackers MSCI Mx Hdg (DBMX) C- Fair

.nd Family: DBX Advisors LLC
.nd Type: Emerging Market
ception Date: January 23, 2014

ajor Rating Factors: Middle of the road best describes *Deutsche X-trackers MSCI Hdg whose TheStreet.com Investment Rating is currently a C- (Fair). The fund rently has a performance rating of C- (Fair) based on an annualized return of 0% over the last three years and a total return of -0.87% year to date 2015. ctored into the performance evaluation is an expense ratio of 0.50% (very low).

The fund's risk rating is currently B- (Good). It carries a beta of 0.00, meaning the d's expected move will be 0.0% for every 10% move in the market. Volatility, as asured by both the semi-deviation and a drawdown factor, is considered low. As of cember 31, 2015, *Deutsche X-trackers MSCI Mx Hdg traded at a discount 98% below its net asset value, which is better than its one-year historical average mium of .16%.

Vishal Bhatia has been running the fund for 2 years and currently receives a nager quality ranking of 82 (0=worst, 99=best). If you desire an average level of , then this fund may be an option.

Data Date	Investment Rating	Net Assets ($Mil)	Price	Performance Rating/Pts	Total Return Y-T-D	Risk Rating/Pts
12-15	C-	5.20	20.22	C- / 3.2	-0.87%	B- / 7.1

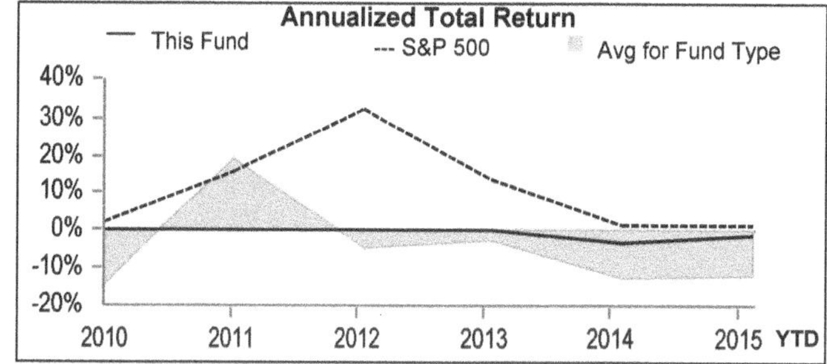

* Denotes ETF Fund

*Deutsche X-trackers MSCI SKor Hd (DBKO) C- Fair

Fund Family: DBX Advisors LLC
Fund Type: Foreign
Inception Date: January 23, 2014

Major Rating Factors: Middle of the road best describes *Deutsche X-trackers MSCI SKor Hd whose TheStreet.com Investment Rating is currently a C- (Fair). The fund currently has a performance rating of C- (Fair) based on an annualized return of 0.00% over the last three years and a total return of -3.32% year to date 2015. Factored into the performance evaluation is an expense ratio of 0.58% (very low).

The fund's risk rating is currently B (Good). It carries a beta of 0.00, meaning the fund's expected move will be 0.0% for every 10% move in the market. Volatility, as measured by both the semi-deviation and a drawdown factor, is considered low. As of December 31, 2015, *Deutsche X-trackers MSCI SKor Hd traded at a discount of 1.10% below its net asset value, which is better than its one-year historical average discount of .10%.

Dino Bourdos has been running the fund for 2 years and currently receives a manager quality ranking of 43 (0=worst, 99=best). If you desire an average level of risk, then this fund may be an option.

Data Date	Investment Rating	Net Assets ($Mil)	Price	Performance Rating/Pts	Total Return Y-T-D	Risk Rating/Pts
12-15	C-	4.90	22.41	C- / 3.0	-3.32%	B / 8.2

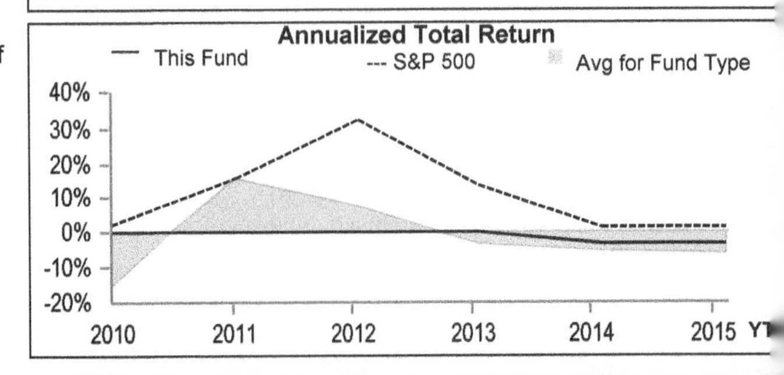

*Deutsche X-trackers MSCI UK Hdg (DBUK) D+ Weak

Fund Family: DBX Advisors LLC
Fund Type: Foreign
Inception Date: October 1, 2013

Major Rating Factors: *Deutsche X-trackers MSCI UK Hdg receives a TheStreet.com Investment Rating of D+ (Weak). The fund currently has a performance rating of C- (Fair) based on an annualized return of 0.00% over the last three years and a total return of -3.33% year to date 2015. Factored into the performance evaluation is an expense ratio of 0.45% (very low).

The fund's risk rating is currently C+ (Fair). It carries a beta of 0.00, meaning the fund's expected move will be 0.0% for every 10% move in the market. Volatility, as measured by both the semi-deviation and a drawdown factor, is considered low. As of December 31, 2015, *Deutsche X-trackers MSCI UK Hdg traded at a premium of .73% above its net asset value, which is worse than its one-year historical average premium of .56%.

Dino Bourdos has been running the fund for 3 years and currently receives a manager quality ranking of 52 (0=worst, 99=best). If you desire an average level of risk, then this fund may be an option.

Data Date	Investment Rating	Net Assets ($Mil)	Price	Performance Rating/Pts	Total Return Y-T-D	Risk Rating/Pts
12-15	D+	5.20	22.05	C- / 3.3	-3.33%	C+ / 5.9
2014	D-	5.20	24.16	D+ / 2.3	-1.03%	C- / 3.9

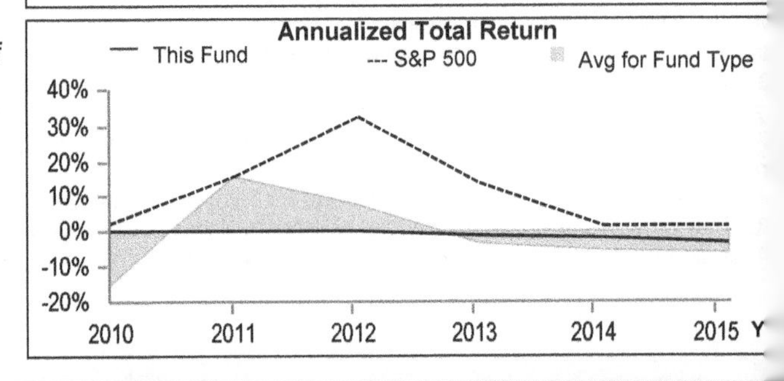

*Deutsche X-trackers Muni Inf Rev (RVNU) B+ Good

Fund Family: DBX Advisors LLC
Fund Type: Municipal - National
Inception Date: June 4, 2013

Major Rating Factors: Strong performance is the major factor driving the B+ (Good) TheStreet.com Investment Rating for *Deutsche X-trackers Muni Inf Rev. The fund currently has a performance rating of B+ (Good) based on an annualized return of 0.00% over the last three years and a total return of 4.19% year to date 2015. Factored into the performance evaluation is an expense ratio of 0.30% (very low).

The fund's risk rating is currently B- (Good). It carries a beta of 0.00, meaning the fund's expected move will be 0.0% for every 10% move in the market. Volatility, as measured by both the semi-deviation and a drawdown factor, is considered low. As of December 31, 2015, *Deutsche X-trackers Muni Inf Rev traded at a premium of .11% above its net asset value, which is better than its one-year historical average premium of .24%.

Blair Ridley has been running the fund for 3 years and currently receives a manager quality ranking of 48 (0=worst, 99=best). If you desire only a moderate level of risk and strong performance, then this fund is an excellent option.

Data Date	Investment Rating	Net Assets ($Mil)	Price	Performance Rating/Pts	Total Return Y-T-D	Risk Rating/Pts
12-15	B+	19.10	26.29	B+ / 8.3	4.19%	B- / 7.
2014	B+	19.10	25.95	B / 7.9	13.85%	B- / 7.

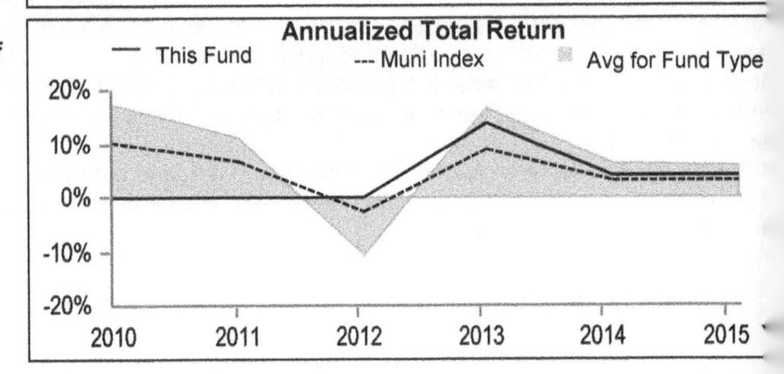

*Direxion All Cap Insider Sentime (KNOW) A- Excellent

Fund Family: Rafferty Asset Management LLC
Fund Type: Growth and Income
Inception Date: December 8, 2011

Major Rating Factors:
Exceptional performance is the major factor driving the A- (Excellent) TheStreet.com Investment Rating for *Direxion All Cap Insider Sentime. The fund currently has a performance rating of A- (Excellent) based on an annualized return of 16.98% over the last three years and a total return of 3.83% year to date 2015. Factored into the performance evaluation is an expense ratio of 0.66% (very low).

The fund's risk rating is currently B- (Good). It carries a beta of 0.88, meaning the fund's expected move will be 8.8% for every 10% move in the market. Volatility, as measured by both the semi-deviation and a drawdown factor, is considered low. As of December 31, 2015, *Direxion All Cap Insider Sentime traded at a premium of .32% above its net asset value, which is worse than its one-year historical average premium of .06%.

Paul Brigandi has been running the fund for 5 years and currently receives a manager quality ranking of 89 (0=worst, 99=best). If you desire only a moderate level of risk and strong performance, then this fund is an excellent option.

Data Date	Investment Rating	Net Assets ($Mil)	Price	Performance Rating/Pts	Total Return Y-T-D	Risk Rating/Pts
12-15	A-	22.60	71.15	A- / 9.2	3.83%	B- / 7.2
2014	B+	22.60	69.11	A- / 9.1	19.25%	C+ / 6.5
2013	A+	23.70	58.78	A / 9.5	29.44%	B / 8.2
2012	B+	4.40	43.64	B / 8.0	13.71%	B / 8.0

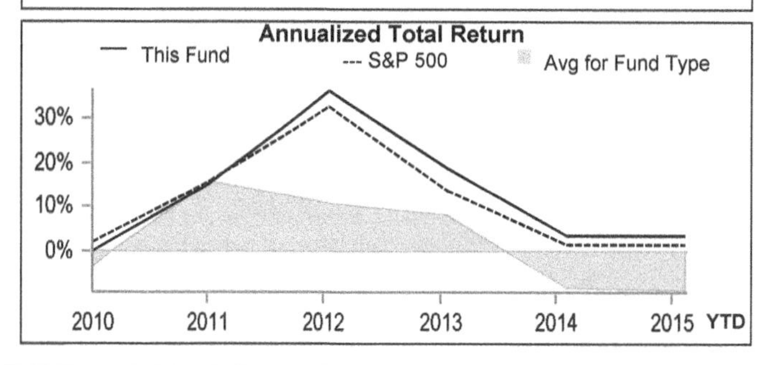

*Direxion Brazil Bull 3X (BRZU) E- Very Weak

Fund Family: Rafferty Asset Management LLC
Fund Type: Foreign
Inception Date: April 10, 2013

Major Rating Factors: *Direxion Brazil Bull 3X has adopted a very risky asset allocation strategy and currently receives an overall TheStreet.com Investment Rating of E- (Very Weak). The fund has a high level of volatility, as measured by both semi-deviation and drawdown factors. It carries a beta of 0.00, meaning the fund's expected move will be 0.0% for every 10% move in the market. As of December 31, 2015, *Direxion Brazil Bull 3X traded at a premium of .61% above its net asset value, which is worse than its one-year historical average premium of .08%. Unfortunately, the high level of risk (E-, Very Weak) failed to pay off as investors endured very poor performance.

The fund's performance rating is currently E- (Very Weak). It has registered an annualized return of 0.00% over the last three years but is down -85.43% year to date 2015. Factored into the performance evaluation is an expense ratio of 0.95% (low).

Paul Brigandi has been running the fund for 3 years and currently receives a manager quality ranking of 0 (0=worst, 99=best). If you can tolerate very high levels of risk in the hope of improved future returns, holding this fund may be an option.

Data Date	Investment Rating	Net Assets ($Mil)	Price	Performance Rating/Pts	Total Return Y-T-D	Risk Rating/Pts
12-15	E-	18.50	11.63	E- / 0	-85.43%	E- / 0.1
2014	E-	18.50	8.81	E- / 0	-52.58%	E / 0.3

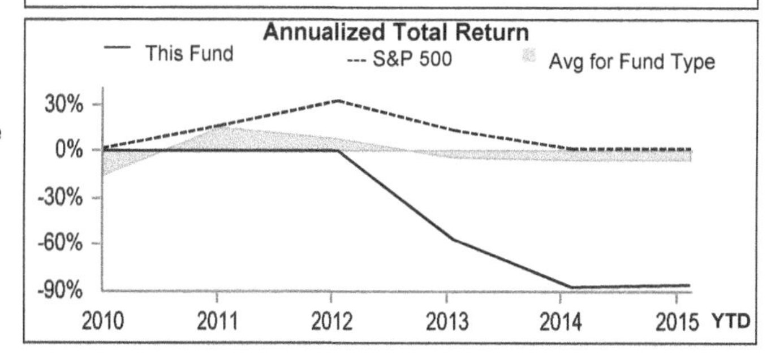

*Direxion Daily 20+ Yr Treas Bear (TYBS) D+ Weak

Fund Family: Rafferty Asset Management LLC
Fund Type: Global
Inception Date: March 23, 2011

Major Rating Factors:
Disappointing performance is the major factor driving the D+ (Weak) TheStreet.com Investment Rating for *Direxion Daily 20+ Yr Treas Bear. The fund currently has a performance rating of D+ (Weak) based on an annualized return of -6.32% over the last three years and a total return of -1.97% year to date 2015. Factored into the performance evaluation is an expense ratio of 0.65% (very low).

The fund's risk rating is currently C+ (Fair). It carries a beta of 0.12, meaning the fund's expected move will be 1.2% for every 10% move in the market. Volatility, as measured by both the semi-deviation and a drawdown factor, is considered low. As of December 31, 2015, *Direxion Daily 20+ Yr Treas Bear traded at a premium of .13% above its net asset value, which is worse than its one-year historical average premium of .05%.

Paul Brigandi has been running the fund for 5 years and currently receives a manager quality ranking of 27 (0=worst, 99=best). This fund offers only a moderate level of risk but investors looking for strong performance are still waiting.

Data Date	Investment Rating	Net Assets ($Mil)	Price	Performance Rating/Pts	Total Return Y-T-D	Risk Rating/Pts
12-15	D+	8.90	22.61	D+ / 2.7	-1.97%	C+ / 5.6
2014	D-	8.90	23.06	D- / 1.3	-23.13%	C / 5.5
2013	C	9.10	30.15	C+ / 5.6	9.09%	C+ / 6.6
2012	D-	2.70	26.45	D- / 1.2	-6.44%	C+ / 6.4

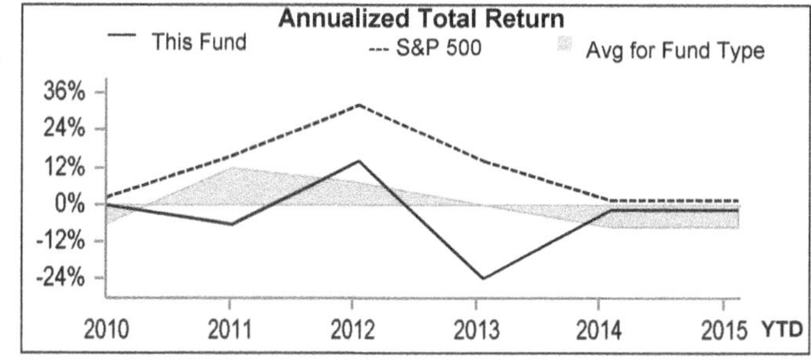

*Direxion Daily 20+ Yr Treas Bear (TMV) E Very Weak

Fund Family: Rafferty Asset Management LLC
Fund Type: US Government/Agency
Inception Date: April 16, 2009

Data Date	Investment Rating	Net Assets ($Mil)	Price	Performance Rating/Pts	Total Return Y-T-D	Risk Rating/Pts
12-15	E	592.70	27.98	E+ / 0.9	-8.92%	D- / 1.5
2014	E-	592.70	31.73	E / 0.4	-55.92%	D- / 1.3
2013	E-	656.40	72.76	E / 0.5	24.10%	D+ / 2.4
2012	E-	299.50	54.24	E- / 0.2	-18.14%	D+ / 2.4
2011	E-	258.60	67.96	E- / 0	-68.34%	D+ / 2.6
2010	E+	303.90	43.21	E+ / 0.7	-36.69%	C- / 3.5

Major Rating Factors: *Direxion Daily 20+ Yr Treas Bear has adopted a very risky asset allocation strategy and currently receives an overall TheStreet.com Investment Rating of E (Very Weak). The fund has a high level of volatility, as measured by both semi-deviation and drawdown factors. It carries a beta of -3.37, meaning the fund's expected move will be -33.7% for every 10% move in the market. As of December 31, 2015, *Direxion Daily 20+ Yr Treas Bear traded at a premium of .36% above its net asset value, which is worse than its one-year historical average premium of .02%. Unfortunately, the high level of risk (D-, Weak) failed to pay off as investors endured very poor performance.

The fund's performance rating is currently E+ (Very Weak). It has registered an annualized return of -21.58% over the last three years and is down -8.92% year to date 2015. Factored into the performance evaluation is an expense ratio of 0.90% (low).

Paul Brigandi currently receives a manager quality ranking of 12 (0=worst, 99=best). If you can tolerate very high levels of risk in the hope of improved future returns, holding this fund may be an option.

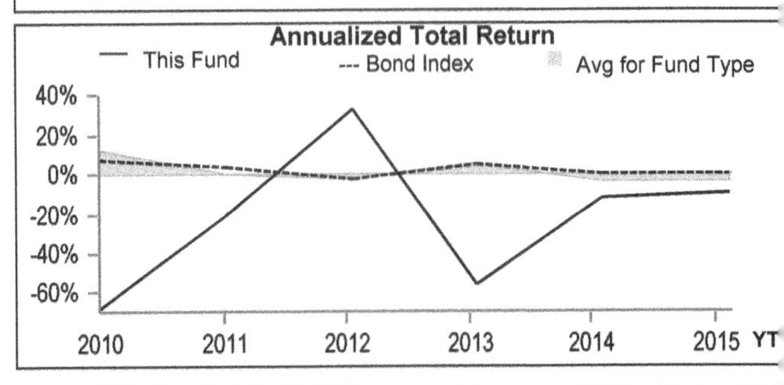

*Direxion Daily 20+ Yr Treas Bull (TMF) C- Fair

Fund Family: Rafferty Asset Management LLC
Fund Type: US Government/Agency
Inception Date: April 16, 2009

Data Date	Investment Rating	Net Assets ($Mil)	Price	Performance Rating/Pts	Total Return Y-T-D	Risk Rating/Pts
12-15	C-	46.70	74.23	C / 5.0	-16.30%	C / 5.1
2014	C+	46.70	86.04	A+ / 9.6	95.28%	C / 4.4
2013	D	19.30	43.60	C- / 4.1	-33.72%	C / 4.6
2012	C+	25.30	71.81	A- / 9.2	-1.79%	C / 5.3
2011	B-	42.90	71.52	A+ / 9.9	109.46%	C / 5.2
2010	D-	19.30	34.45	D- / 1.1	19.49%	C / 5.0

Major Rating Factors: Middle of the road best describes *Direxion Daily 20+ Yr Treas Bull whose TheStreet.com Investment Rating is currently a C- (Fair). The fund currently has a performance rating of C (Fair) based on an annualized return of 3.75% over the last three years and a total return of -16.30% year to date 2015. Factored into the performance evaluation is an expense ratio of 0.95% (low).

The fund's risk rating is currently C (Fair). It carries a beta of 3.42, meaning it is expected to move 34.2% for every 10% move in the market. Volatility, as measured by both the semi-deviation and a drawdown factor, is considered average. As of December 31, 2015, *Direxion Daily 20+ Yr Treas Bull traded at a discount of 1.17% below its net asset value, which is better than its one-year historical average discount of .03%.

Paul Brigandi currently receives a manager quality ranking of 22 (0=worst, 99=best). If you desire an average level of risk, then this fund may be an option.

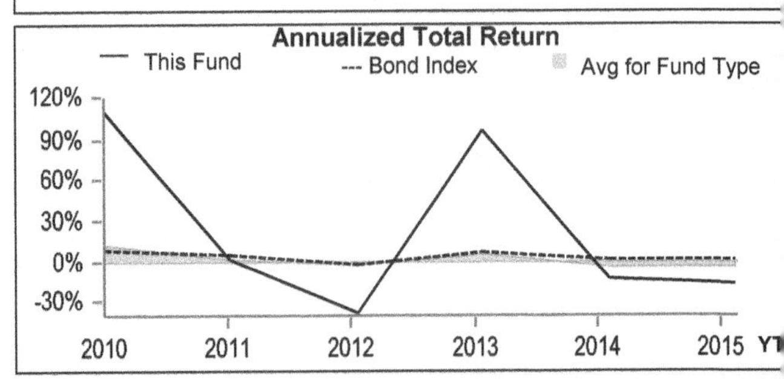

*Direxion Daily 7-10 Yr Trs Bear (TYO) D+ Weak

Fund Family: Rafferty Asset Management LLC
Fund Type: US Government/Agency
Inception Date: April 16, 2009

Data Date	Investment Rating	Net Assets ($Mil)	Price	Performance Rating/Pts	Total Return Y-T-D	Risk Rating/Pts
12-15	D+	56.50	16.66	D / 1.9	-10.04%	C+ / 6.3
2014	D-	56.50	18.84	D- / 1.0	-26.55%	C / 4.6
2013	E+	63.40	25.91	E+ / 0.8	8.82%	C / 5.1
2012	E+	49.20	22.98	E / 0.4	-13.93%	C / 4.4
2011	E+	57.30	27.38	E- / 0.2	-39.53%	C / 4.5
2010	D-	68.40	45.84	E+ / 0.6	-28.62%	C+ / 5.6

Major Rating Factors:
Disappointing performance is the major factor driving the D+ (Weak) TheStreet.com Investment Rating for *Direxion Daily 7-10 Yr Trs Bear. The fund currently has a performance rating of D (Weak) based on an annualized return of -10.92% over the last three years and a total return of -10.04% year to date 2015. Factored into the performance evaluation is an expense ratio of 0.95% (low).

The fund's risk rating is currently C+ (Fair). It carries a beta of -1.48, meaning the fund's expected move will be -14.8% for every 10% move in the market. Volatility, as measured by both the semi-deviation and a drawdown factor, is considered low. As of December 31, 2015, *Direxion Daily 7-10 Yr Trs Bear traded at a discount of .30% below its net asset value, which is better than its one-year historical average premium of .01%.

Paul Brigandi currently receives a manager quality ranking of 23 (0=worst, 99=best). This fund offers only a moderate level of risk but investors looking for strong performance are still waiting.

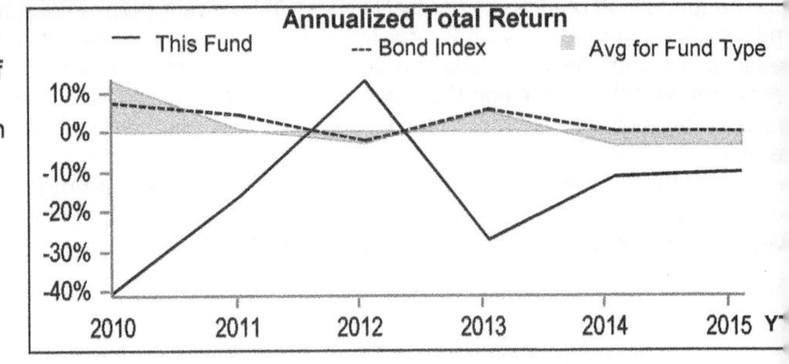

*Direxion Daily 7-10 Yr Trs Bull (TYD) D+ Weak

Fund Family: Rafferty Asset Management LLC
Fund Type: US Government/Agency
Inception Date: April 16, 2009

Major Rating Factors: *Direxion Daily 7-10 Yr Trs Bull receives a TheStreet.com Investment Rating of D+ (Weak). The fund currently has a performance rating of C (Fair) based on an annualized return of 2.48% over the last three years and a total return of -0.44% year to date 2015. Factored into the performance evaluation is an expense ratio of 0.95% (low).

The fund's risk rating is currently C- (Fair). It carries a beta of 1.46, meaning it is expected to move 14.6% for every 10% move in the market. Volatility, as measured by both the semi-deviation and a drawdown factor, is considered average. As of December 31, 2015, *Direxion Daily 7-10 Yr Trs Bull traded at a discount of 1.18% below its net asset value, which is better than its one-year historical average discount of .21%.

Andrey A. Belov currently receives a manager quality ranking of 50 (0=worst, 99=best). If you desire an average level of risk, then this fund may be an option.

Data Date	Investment Rating	Net Assets ($Mil)	Price	Performance Rating/Pts	Total Return Y-T-D	Risk Rating/Pts
12-15	D+	4.10	44.21	C / 5.2	-0.44%	C- / 3.1
2014	D	4.10	43.96	C+ / 5.8	24.43%	D+ / 2.7
2013	D	3.50	35.00	C / 5.3	-15.36%	C- / 3.1
2012	B+	4.30	85.82	B+ / 8.7	6.67%	B- / 7.8
2011	A-	3.90	77.87	A+ / 9.9	51.89%	B- / 7.6
2010	A	10.90	54.11	B+ / 8.5	28.71%	C+ / 6.9

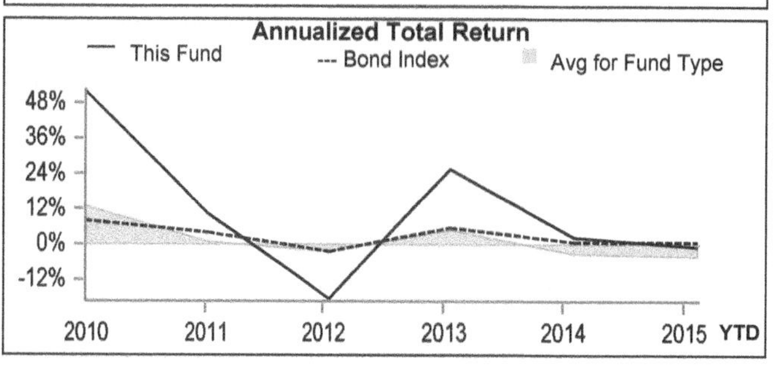

*Direxion Daily FTSE Ch Bear 3x E (YANG) E Very Weak

Fund Family: Rafferty Asset Management LLC
Fund Type: Foreign
Inception Date: December 3, 2009

Major Rating Factors: *Direxion Daily FTSE Ch Bear 3x E has adopted a very risky asset allocation strategy and currently receives an overall TheStreet.com Investment Rating of E (Very Weak). The fund has a high level of volatility, as measured by both semi-deviation and drawdown factors. It carries a beta of -2.64, meaning the fund's expected move will be -26.4% for every 10% move in the market. As of December 31, 2015, *Direxion Daily FTSE Ch Bear 3x E traded at a discount of .02% below its net asset value. Unfortunately, the high level of risk (D-, Weak) failed to pay off as investors endured very poor performance.

The fund's performance rating is currently E (Very Weak). It has registered an annualized return of -40.49% over the last three years and is down -12.53% year to date 2015. Factored into the performance evaluation is an expense ratio of 0.95% (low).

Paul Brigandi has been running the fund for 7 years and currently receives a manager quality ranking of 2 (0=worst, 99=best). If you can tolerate very high levels of risk in the hope of improved future returns, holding this fund may be an option.

Data Date	Investment Rating	Net Assets ($Mil)	Price	Performance Rating/Pts	Total Return Y-T-D	Risk Rating/Pts
12-15	E	18.80	99.11	E / 0.4	-12.53%	D- / 1.5
2014	E-	18.80	11.39	E- / 0.1	-52.24%	E- / 0.1
2013	E-	9.90	20.99	E- / 0.2	-49.29%	D / 1.9
2012	E-	7.80	10.45	E- / 0.1	-40.43%	D / 1.9
2011	E+	12.40	19.01	D+ / 2.4	1.17%	D / 2.1
2010	E-	11.90	18.41	E- / 0.1	-56.32%	D / 1.9

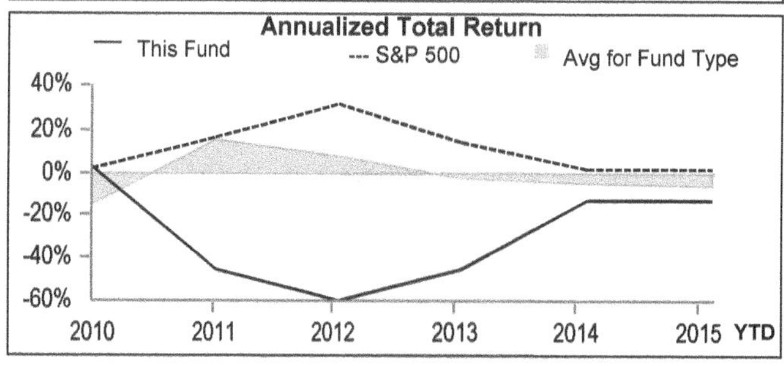

*Direxion Daily FTSE Ch Bull 3x E (YINN) E- Very Weak

Fund Family: Rafferty Asset Management LLC
Fund Type: Foreign
Inception Date: December 3, 2009

Major Rating Factors: *Direxion Daily FTSE Ch Bull 3x E has adopted a very risky asset allocation strategy and currently receives an overall TheStreet.com Investment Rating of E- (Very Weak). The fund has a high level of volatility, as measured by both semi-deviation and drawdown factors. It carries a beta of 2.84, meaning it is expected to move 28.4% for every 10% move in the market. As of December 31, 2015, *Direxion Daily FTSE Ch Bull 3x E traded at a premium of .06% above its net asset value, which is worse than its one-year historical average premium of .02%. Unfortunately, the high level of risk (E-, Very Weak) failed to pay off as investors endured poor performance.

The fund's performance rating is currently D- (Weak). It has registered an annualized return of -4.76% over the last three years and is down -50.58% year to date 2015. Factored into the performance evaluation is an expense ratio of 0.95% (low).

Paul Brigandi has been running the fund for 7 years and currently receives a manager quality ranking of 10 (0=worst, 99=best). If you can tolerate very high levels of risk in the hope of improved future returns, holding this fund may be an option.

Data Date	Investment Rating	Net Assets ($Mil)	Price	Performance Rating/Pts	Total Return Y-T-D	Risk Rating/Pts
12-15	E-	94.70	17.74	D- / 1.3	-50.58%	E- / 0.2
2014	C+	94.70	35.76	A+ / 9.6	37.15%	C- / 3.5
2013	E	76.90	30.10	D- / 1.3	26.97%	D / 1.9
2012	E-	76.90	18.70	E+ / 0.8	7.58%	D / 1.9
2011	E-	35.90	16.37	E- / 0	-62.69%	D / 1.9
2010	A-	65.50	43.51	A+ / 9.6	25.05%	C / 4.9

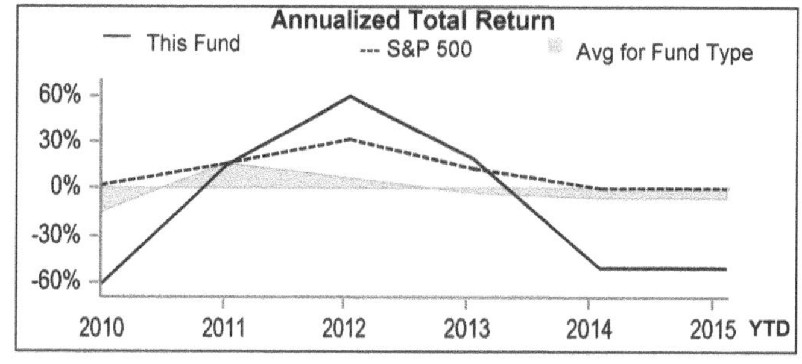

*Direxion Daily FTSE Europe Bull (EURL) D- Weak

Fund Family: Rafferty Asset Management LLC
Fund Type: Foreign
Inception Date: January 22, 2014

Major Rating Factors:
Very poor performance is the major factor driving the D- (Weak) TheStreet.com Investment Rating for *Direxion Daily FTSE Europe Bull. The fund currently has a performance rating of E+ (Very Weak) based on an annualized return of 0.00% over the last three years and a total return of -15.01% year to date 2015. Factored into the performance evaluation is an expense ratio of 0.95% (low).

The fund's risk rating is currently C (Fair). It carries a beta of 0.00, meaning the fund's expected move will be 0.0% for every 10% move in the market. Volatility, as measured by both the semi-deviation and a drawdown factor, is considered average. As of December 31, 2015, *Direxion Daily FTSE Europe Bull traded at a discount of .04% below its net asset value, which is better than its one-year historical average premium of .01%.

Paul Brigandi has been running the fund for 2 years and currently receives a manager quality ranking of 10 (0=worst, 99=best). This fund offers an average level of risk but investors looking for strong performance will be frustrated.

Data Date	Investment Rating	Net Assets ($Mil)	Price	Performance Rating/Pts	Total Return Y-T-D	Risk Rating/Pts
12-15	D-	8.60	24.30	E+ / 0.7	-15.01%	C / 4.3

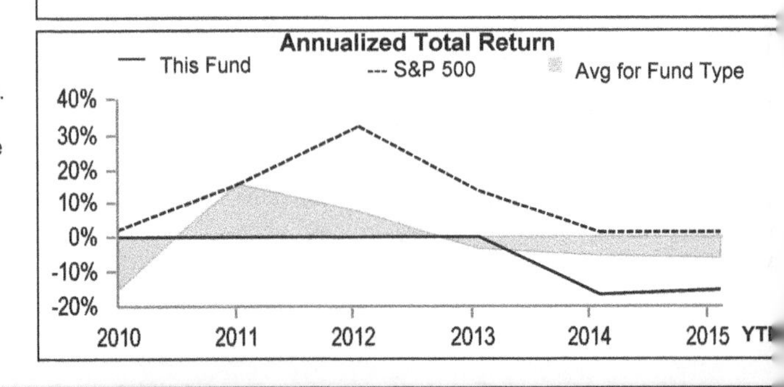

*Direxion Daily Gold Mnrs Id Bear (DUST) E Very Weak

Fund Family: Rafferty Asset Management LLC
Fund Type: Precious Metals
Inception Date: December 8, 2010

Major Rating Factors: *Direxion Daily Gold Mnrs Id Bear has adopted a very risky asset allocation strategy and currently receives an overall TheStreet.com Investment Rating of E (Very Weak). The fund has a high level of volatility, as measured by both semi-deviation and drawdown factors. It carries a beta of -5.76, meaning the fund's expected move will be -57.6% for every 10% move in the market. As of December 31, 2015, *Direxion Daily Gold Mnrs Id Bear traded at a premium of 1.60% above its net asset value, which is worse than its one-year historical average discount of .25%. Unfortunately, the high level of risk (E-, Very Weak) failed to pay off as investors endured poor performance.

The fund's performance rating is currently D+ (Weak). It has registered an annualized return of 0.82% over the last three years but is down -40.66% year to date 2015. Factored into the performance evaluation is an expense ratio of 0.95% (low).

Paul Brigandi has been running the fund for 6 years and currently receives a manager quality ranking of 0 (0=worst, 99=best). If you can tolerate very high levels of risk in the hope of improved future returns, holding this fund may be an option.

Data Date	Investment Rating	Net Assets ($Mil)	Price	Performance Rating/Pts	Total Return Y-T-D	Risk Rating/Pts
12-15	E	184.40	16.52	D+ / 2.3	-40.66%	E- / 0.1
2014	D	184.40	24.77	C+ / 6.2	-42.37%	D / 1.9
2013	C-	32.90	44.05	A+ / 9.9	199.68%	D / 1.9
2012	E	32.90	31.50	D / 1.8	-5.88%	D / 2.2
2011	E+	6.40	42.60	D- / 1.2	-6.52%	C / 4.3

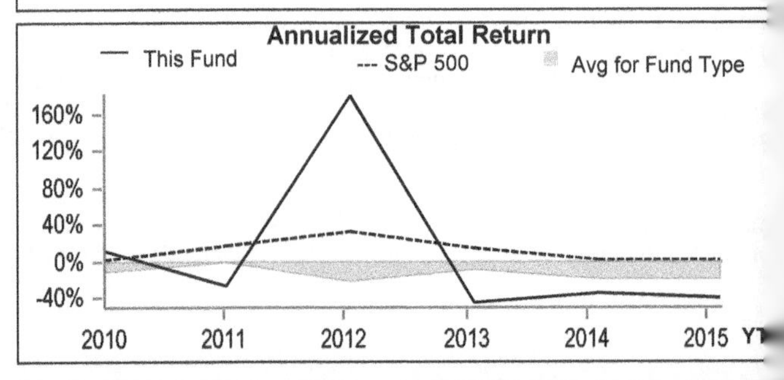

*Direxion Daily Gold Mnrs Id Bull (NUGT) E- Very Weak

Fund Family: Rafferty Asset Management LLC
Fund Type: Precious Metals
Inception Date: December 8, 2010

Major Rating Factors: *Direxion Daily Gold Mnrs Id Bull has adopted a very risky asset allocation strategy and currently receives an overall TheStreet.com Investment Rating of E- (Very Weak). The fund has a high level of volatility, as measured by both semi-deviation and drawdown factors. It carries a beta of 5.58, meaning it is expected to move 55.8% for every 10% move in the market. As of December 31, 2015, *Direxion Daily Gold Mnrs Id Bull traded at a discount of .41% below its net asset value, which is better than its one-year historical average premium of .09%. Unfortunately, the high level of risk (D, Weak) failed to pay off as investors endured very poor performance.

The fund's performance rating is currently E- (Very Weak). It has registered an annualized return of -83.17% over the last three years and is down -79.91% year to date 2015. Factored into the performance evaluation is an expense ratio of 0.95% (low).

Paul Brigandi has been running the fund for 6 years and currently receives a manager quality ranking of 0 (0=worst, 99=best). If you can tolerate very high levels of risk in the hope of improved future returns, holding this fund may be an option.

Data Date	Investment Rating	Net Assets ($Mil)	Price	Performance Rating/Pts	Total Return Y-T-D	Risk Rating/Pts
12-15	E-	697.80	24.26	E- / 0	-79.91%	D / 1.8
2014	E-	697.80	11.16	E- / 0	-62.95%	D / 1.9
2013	E-	642.40	27.41	E- / 0	-94.08%	D / 1.9
2012	E-	464.20	11.00	E- / 0.1	-54.60%	D / 1.9
2011	E	90.60	19.57	E- / 0.2	-32.16%	D+ / 2.9

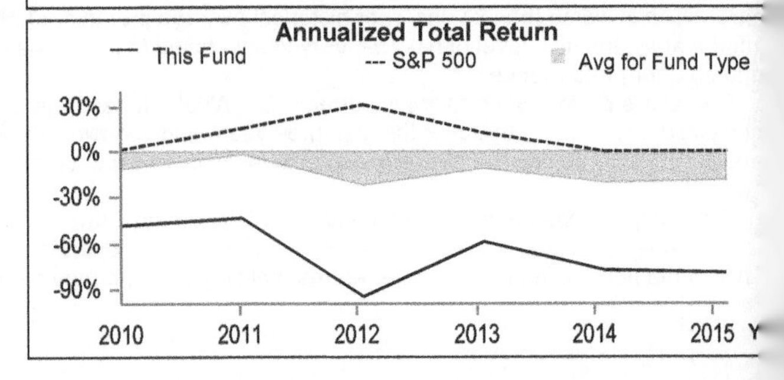

*Direxion Daily Healthcare Bull 3 (CURE) C- Fair

Fund Family: Rafferty Asset Management LLC
Fund Type: Health
Inception Date: June 15, 2011

Data Date	Investment Rating	Net Assets ($Mil)	Price	Performance Rating/Pts	Total Return Y-T-D	Risk Rating/Pts
12-15	C-	129.20	33.40	A+ / 9.9	6.24%	E- / 0.2
2014	C	129.20	124.43	A+ / 9.9	82.00%	D+ / 2.6
2013	C	72.40	69.11	A+ / 9.9	142.04%	D+ / 2.7
2012	A-	5.30	52.92	A+ / 9.9	66.44%	C+ / 6.9

Major Rating Factors: *Direxion Daily Healthcare Bull 3 has adopted a very risky asset allocation strategy and currently receives an overall TheStreet.com Investment Rating of C- (Fair). The fund has shown a high level of volatility, as measured by both semi-deviation and drawdown factors. It carries a beta of 3.03, meaning it is expected to move 30.3% for every 10% move in the market. As of December 31, 2015, *Direxion Daily Healthcare Bull 3 traded at a premium of .03% above its net asset value, which is worse than its one-year historical average premium of .01%. The high level of risk (E-, Very Weak) did however, reward investors with excellent performance.

The fund's performance rating is currently A+ (Excellent). It has registered an annualized return of 67.86% over the last three years and is up 6.24% year to date 2015. Factored into the performance evaluation is an expense ratio of 0.95% (low).

Paul Brigandi has been running the fund for 5 years and currently receives a manager quality ranking of 96 (0=worst, 99=best). If you are comfortable owning a very high risk investment, this fund may be an option.

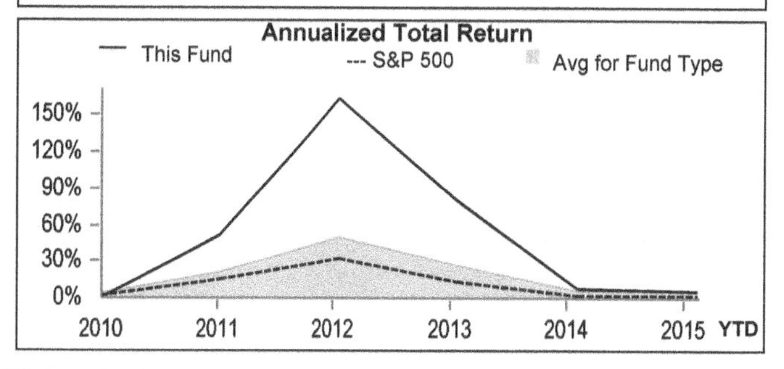

*Direxion Daily India Bull 3X (INDL) E- Very Weak

Fund Family: Rafferty Asset Management LLC
Fund Type: Emerging Market
Inception Date: March 11, 2010

Data Date	Investment Rating	Net Assets ($Mil)	Price	Performance Rating/Pts	Total Return Y-T-D	Risk Rating/Pts
12-15	E-	75.40	13.47	D- / 1.0	-36.19%	E- / 0.2
2014	D-	75.40	80.47	C / 5.1	60.46%	D / 2.1
2013	E-	37.10	54.98	E / 0.3	-40.18%	D / 1.9
2012	D	28.20	20.14	C+ / 6.0	2.97%	D / 2.1
2011	E-	10.70	16.52	E- / 0	-60.26%	D+ / 2.4

Major Rating Factors: *Direxion Daily India Bull 3X has adopted a very risky asset allocation strategy and currently receives an overall TheStreet.com Investment Rating of E- (Very Weak). The fund has a high level of volatility, as measured by both semi-deviation and drawdown factors. It carries a beta of 2.13, meaning it is expected to move 21.3% for every 10% move in the market. As of December 31, 2015, *Direxion Daily India Bull 3X traded at a premium of .67% above its net asset value, which is worse than its one-year historical average premium of .01%. Unfortunately, the high level of risk (E-, Very Weak) failed to pay off as investors endured poor performance.

The fund's performance rating is currently D- (Weak). It has registered an annualized return of -13.70% over the last three years and is down -36.19% year to date 2015. Factored into the performance evaluation is an expense ratio of 0.95% (low).

Paul Brigandi has been running the fund for 6 years and currently receives a manager quality ranking of 75 (0=worst, 99=best). If you can tolerate very high levels of risk in the hope of improved future returns, holding this fund may be an option.

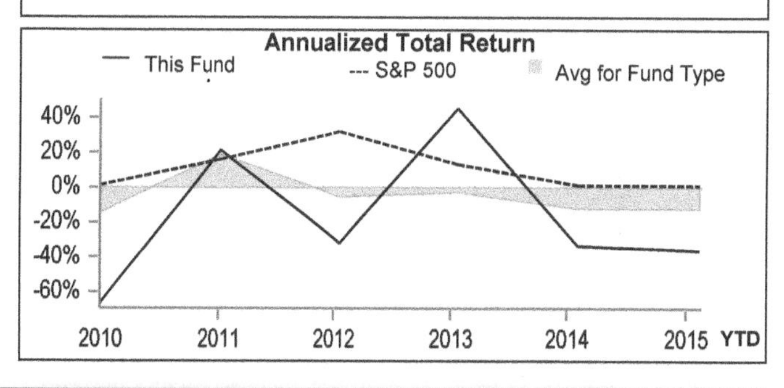

*Direxion Daily Japan Bull 3X (JPNL) D+ Weak

Fund Family: Rafferty Asset Management LLC
Fund Type: Foreign
Inception Date: June 26, 2013

Data Date	Investment Rating	Net Assets ($Mil)	Price	Performance Rating/Pts	Total Return Y-T-D	Risk Rating/Pts
12-15	D+	6.90	45.47	C+ / 6.0	13.76%	C- / 3.4
2014	D-	6.90	39.73	E / 0.4	-22.33%	C / 5.3

Major Rating Factors: *Direxion Daily Japan Bull 3X receives a TheStreet.com Investment Rating of D+ (Weak). The fund currently has a performance rating of C+ (Fair) based on an annualized return of 0.00% over the last three years and a total return of 13.76% year to date 2015. Factored into the performance evaluation is an expense ratio of 0.95% (low).

The fund's risk rating is currently C- (Fair). It carries a beta of 0.00, meaning the fund's expected move will be 0.0% for every 10% move in the market. Volatility, as measured by both the semi-deviation and a drawdown factor, is considered average. As of December 31, 2015, *Direxion Daily Japan Bull 3X traded at a premium of .29% above its net asset value, which is worse than its one-year historical average premium of .05%.

Paul Brigandi has been running the fund for 8 years and currently receives a manager quality ranking of 97 (0=worst, 99=best). If you desire an average level of risk, then this fund may be an option.

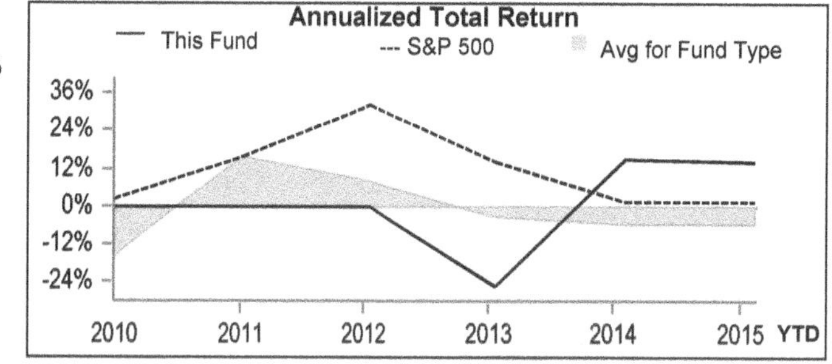

*Direxion Daily Latin Amer Bull 3 (LBJ) E- Very Weak

Fund Family: Rafferty Asset Management LLC
Fund Type: Foreign
Inception Date: December 3, 2009

Major Rating Factors: *Direxion Daily Latin Amer Bull 3 has adopted a very risky asset allocation strategy and currently receives an overall TheStreet.com Investment Rating of E- (Very Weak). The fund has a high level of volatility, as measured by both semi-deviation and drawdown factors. It carries a beta of 3.50, meaning it is expected to move 35.0% for every 10% move in the market. As of December 31, 2015, *Direxion Daily Latin Amer Bull 3 traded at a premium of .50% above its net asset value, which is worse than its one-year historical average premium of .22%. Unfortunately, the high level of risk (E-, Very Weak) failed to pay off as investors endured very poor performance.

The fund's performance rating is currently E- (Very Weak). It has registered an annualized return of -58.11% over the last three years and is down -72.65% year to date 2015. Factored into the performance evaluation is an expense ratio of 0.95% (low).

Paul Brigandi has been running the fund for 7 years and currently receives a manager quality ranking of 0 (0=worst, 99=best). If you can tolerate very high levels of risk in the hope of improved future returns, holding this fund may be an option.

Data Date	Investment Rating	Net Assets ($Mil)	Price	Performance Rating/Pts	Total Return Y-T-D	Risk Rating/Pts
12-15	E-	18.30	12.00	E- / 0	-72.65%	E- / 0.1
2014	E-	18.30	11.97	E- / 0.2	-39.09%	E- / 0
2013	E-	20.10	21.61	E- / 0.1	-51.86%	D / 1.9
2012	E-	32.80	74.14	E+ / 0.7	1.19%	D / 1.9
2011	E-	43.00	72.83	E- / 0.1	-57.35%	D / 1.9
2010	B	44.80	40.60	A+ / 9.8	25.82%	C- / 3.4

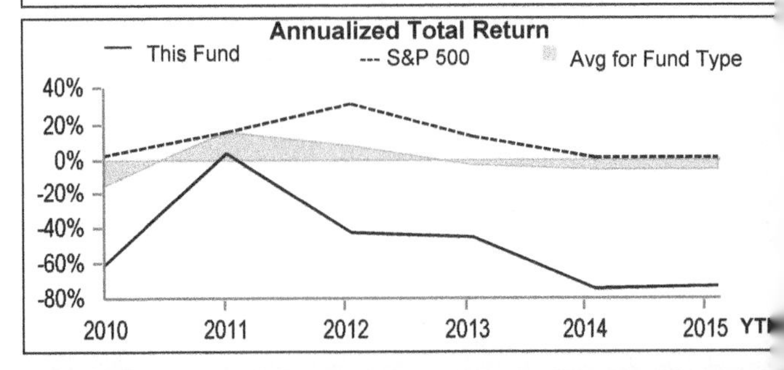

*Direxion Daily Mid Cap Bear 3X (MIDZ) E+ Very Weak

Fund Family: Rafferty Asset Management LLC
Fund Type: Growth
Inception Date: January 8, 2009

Major Rating Factors:
Very poor performance is the major factor driving the E+ (Very Weak) TheStreet.com Investment Rating for *Direxion Daily Mid Cap Bear 3X. The fund currently has a performance rating of E (Very Weak) based on an annualized return of -36.58% over the last three years and a total return of -8.51% year to date 2015. Factored into the performance evaluation is an expense ratio of 0.95% (low).

The fund's risk rating is currently C- (Fair). It carries a beta of -2.89, meaning the fund's expected move will be -28.9% for every 10% move in the market. Volatility, as measured by both the semi-deviation and a drawdown factor, is considered average. As of December 31, 2015, *Direxion Daily Mid Cap Bear 3X traded at a discount of .22% below its net asset value.

Paul Brigandi has been running the fund for 7 years and currently receives a manager quality ranking of 20 (0=worst, 99=best). This fund offers an average level of risk but investors looking for strong performance will be frustrated.

Data Date	Investment Rating	Net Assets ($Mil)	Price	Performance Rating/Pts	Total Return Y-T-D	Risk Rating/Pts
12-15	E+	10.90	45.09	E / 0.4	-8.51%	C- / 3.0
2014	E-	10.90	12.29	E- / 0.1	-34.03%	D+ / 2.6
2013	E-	8.40	18.29	E- / 0	-57.84%	D+ / 2.4
2012	E-	13.60	16.41	E- / 0	-48.52%	D+ / 2.4
2011	E-	16.40	31.13	E / 0.3	-34.74%	D / 1.9
2010	E-	12.40	9.36	E- / 0	-62.04%	D- / 1.0

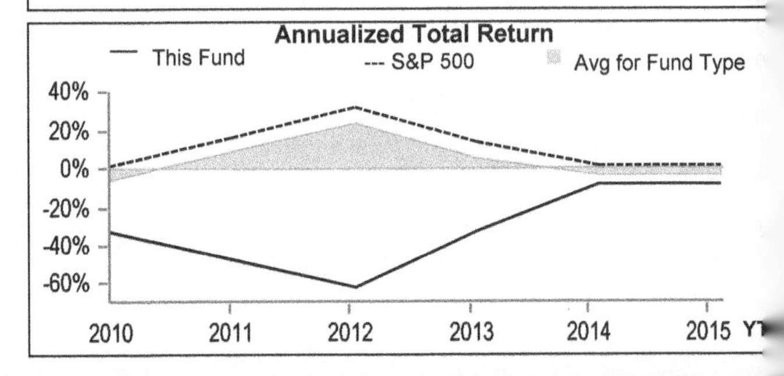

*Direxion Daily Mid Cap Bull 3X (MIDU) C Fair

Fund Family: Rafferty Asset Management LLC
Fund Type: Growth
Inception Date: January 8, 2009

Major Rating Factors: *Direxion Daily Mid Cap Bull 3X has adopted a very risky asset allocation strategy and currently receives an overall TheStreet.com Investment Rating of C (Fair). The fund has shown a high level of volatility, as measured by both semi-deviation and drawdown factors. It carries a beta of 3.04, meaning it is expected to move 30.4% for every 10% move in the market. As of December 31, 2015, *Direxion Daily Mid Cap Bull 3X traded at a discount of .38% below its net asset value, which is better than its one-year historical average discount of .03%. The high level of risk (D, Weak) did however, reward investors with excellent performance.

The fund's performance rating is currently A+ (Excellent). It has registered an annualized return of 27.36% over the last three years but is down -14.79% year to date 2015. Factored into the performance evaluation is an expense ratio of 0.95% (low).

Paul Brigandi has been running the fund for 7 years and currently receives a manager quality ranking of 11 (0=worst, 99=best). If you are comfortable owning a very high risk investment, this fund may be an option.

Data Date	Investment Rating	Net Assets ($Mil)	Price	Performance Rating/Pts	Total Return Y-T-D	Risk Rating/Pts
12-15	C	62.60	20.81	A+ / 9.6	-14.79%	D / 1.7
2014	B-	62.60	98.01	A+ / 9.9	25.33%	C / 4.6
2013	C	59.90	79.93	A+ / 9.8	94.06%	C- / 3.4
2012	C-	37.90	37.66	A+ / 9.7	54.09%	D / 1.9
2011	E-	56.70	31.44	E+ / 0.8	-22.90%	D / 1.9
2010	C	52.20	47.61	A+ / 9.9	75.27%	D- / 1.1

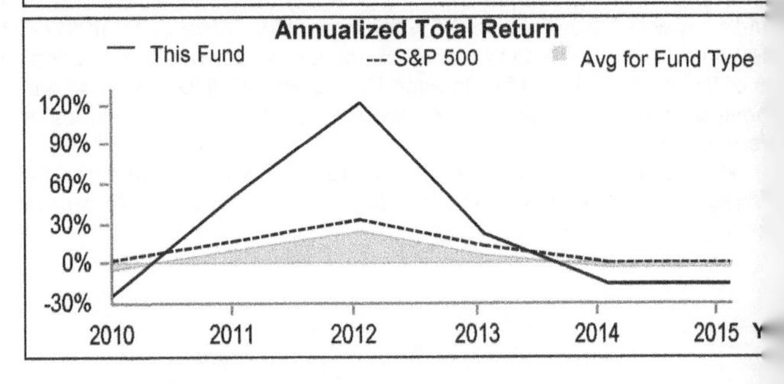

*Direxion Daily Nat Gas Rel Bull (GASL) E- Very Weak

Fund Family: Rafferty Asset Management LLC
Fund Type: Growth
Inception Date: July 14, 2010

Major Rating Factors: *Direxion Daily Nat Gas Rel Bull has adopted a very risky asset allocation strategy and currently receives an overall TheStreet.com Investment Rating of E- (Very Weak). The fund has a high level of volatility, as measured by both semi-deviation and drawdown factors. It carries a beta of 4.56, meaning it is expected to move 45.6% for every 10% move in the market. As of December 31, 2015, *Direxion Daily Nat Gas Rel Bull traded at a discount of .81% below its net asset value, which is better than its one-year historical average premium of .16%. Unfortunately, the high level of risk (D, Weak) failed to pay off as investors endured very poor performance.

The fund's performance rating is currently E- (Very Weak). It has registered an annualized return of -82.35% over the last three years and is down -97.14% year to date 2015. Factored into the performance evaluation is an expense ratio of 0.95% (low).

Paul Brigandi has been running the fund for 6 years and currently receives a manager quality ranking of 0 (0=worst, 99=best). If you can tolerate very high levels of risk in the hope of improved future returns, holding this fund may be an option.

Data Date	Investment Rating	Net Assets ($Mil)	Price	Performance Rating/Pts	Total Return Y-T-D	Risk Rating/Pts
12-15	E-	21.40	6.14	E- / 0	-97.14%	D / 1.8
2014	E-	21.40	4.27	E- / 0	-86.69%	D / 1.8
2013	E	16.90	33.80	D / 1.6	43.73%	D / 1.9
2012	E-	29.00	19.98	E- / 0.1	-36.84%	D / 1.9
2011	E	9.90	39.53	E+ / 0.6	-26.46%	D+ / 2.7

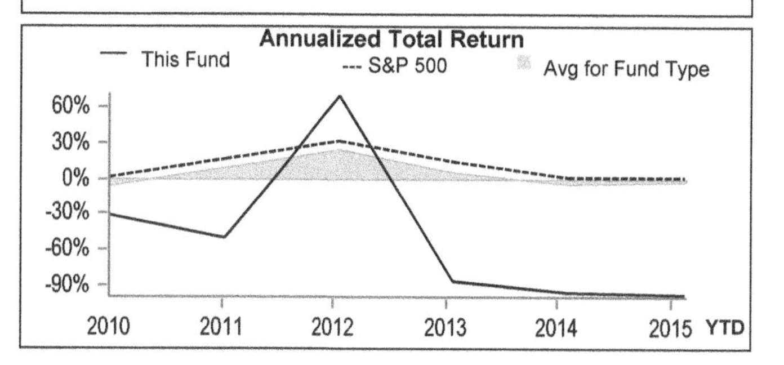

*Direxion Daily Real Estate Bear (DRV) E Very Weak

Fund Family: Rafferty Asset Management LLC
Fund Type: Growth
Inception Date: July 16, 2009

Major Rating Factors: *Direxion Daily Real Estate Bear has adopted a risky asset allocation strategy and currently receives an overall TheStreet.com Investment Rating of E (Very Weak). The fund has an above average level of volatility, as measured by both semi-deviation and drawdown factors. It carries a beta of -1.27, meaning the fund's expected move will be -12.7% for every 10% move in the market. As of December 31, 2015, *Direxion Daily Real Estate Bear traded at a discount of .20% below its net asset value. Unfortunately, the high level of risk (D+, Weak) failed to pay off as investors endured very poor performance.

The fund's performance rating is currently E (Very Weak). It has registered an annualized return of -37.14% over the last three years and is down -21.47% year to date 2015. Factored into the performance evaluation is an expense ratio of 0.95% (low).

Paul Brigandi has been running the fund for 7 years and currently receives a manager quality ranking of 4 (0=worst, 99=best). If you can tolerate high levels of risk in the hope of improved future returns, holding this fund may be an option.

Data Date	Investment Rating	Net Assets ($Mil)	Price	Performance Rating/Pts	Total Return Y-T-D	Risk Rating/Pts
12-15	E	16.40	19.54	E / 0.3	-21.47%	D+ / 2.4
2014	E-	16.40	26.01	E- / 0.1	-58.95%	E+ / 0.6
2013	E-	13.40	64.36	E- / 0.2	-19.49%	D / 2.0
2012	E-	19.30	20.70	E- / 0	-48.85%	D / 1.9
2011	E-	26.70	38.86	E- / 0	-57.32%	D / 1.9
2010	E-	55.50	18.01	E- / 0	-71.73%	D- / 1.3

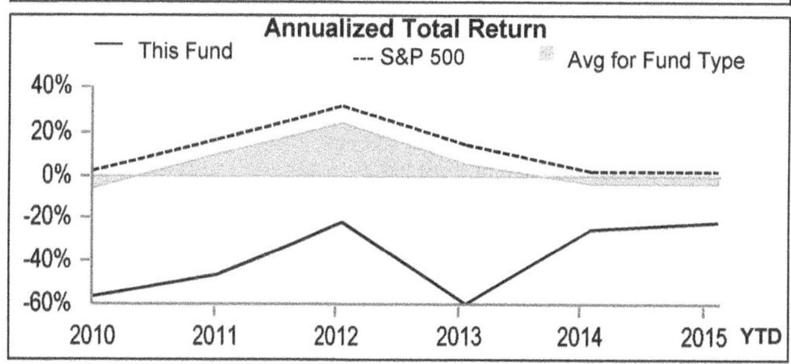

*Direxion Daily Real Estate Bull (DRN) C- Fair

Fund Family: Rafferty Asset Management LLC
Fund Type: Growth
Inception Date: July 16, 2009

Major Rating Factors: *Direxion Daily Real Estate Bull has adopted a very risky asset allocation strategy and currently receives an overall TheStreet.com Investment Rating of C- (Fair). The fund has shown a high level of volatility, as measured by both semi-deviation and drawdown factors. It carries a beta of 1.43, meaning it is expected to move 14.3% for every 10% move in the market. As of December 31, 2015, *Direxion Daily Real Estate Bull traded at a premium of .01% above its net asset value, which is worse than its one-year historical average discount of .03%. The high level of risk (D-, Weak) did however, reward investors with excellent performance.

The fund's performance rating is currently A+ (Excellent). It has registered an annualized return of 22.83% over the last three years but is down -8.26% year to date 2015. Factored into the performance evaluation is an expense ratio of 0.95% (low).

Paul Brigandi has been running the fund for 7 years and currently receives a manager quality ranking of 81 (0=worst, 99=best). If you are comfortable owning a very high risk investment, this fund may be an option.

Data Date	Investment Rating	Net Assets ($Mil)	Price	Performance Rating/Pts	Total Return Y-T-D	Risk Rating/Pts
12-15	C-	78.00	75.55	A+ / 9.6	-8.26%	D- / 1.4
2014	C	78.00	78.87	A+ / 9.9	105.12%	D+ / 2.4
2013	D	126.90	37.88	C+ / 5.9	-5.68%	D / 2.0
2012	C-	108.70	77.50	A+ / 9.8	57.28%	D / 1.9
2011	D-	118.50	51.57	C / 5.2	3.97%	D / 1.9
2010	C	170.20	56.82	A+ / 9.9	63.42%	D- / 1.0

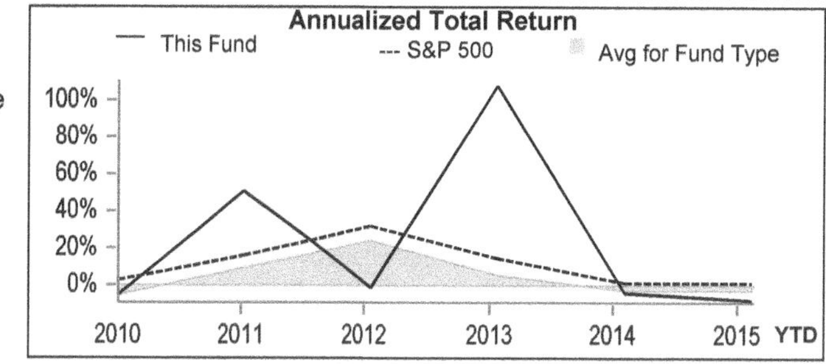

*Direxion Daily Retail Bull 3X (RETL) C- Fair

Fund Family: Rafferty Asset Management LLC
Fund Type: Growth
Inception Date: July 14, 2010

Major Rating Factors: *Direxion Daily Retail Bull 3X has adopted a very risky asset allocation strategy and currently receives an overall TheStreet.com Investment Rating of C- (Fair). The fund has shown a high level of volatility, as measured by both semi-deviation and drawdown factors. It carries a beta of 2.96, meaning it is expected to move 29.6% for every 10% move in the market. As of December 31, 2015, *Direxion Daily Retail Bull 3X traded at a premium of .29% above its net asset value, which is worse than its one-year historical average premium of .14%. The high level of risk (E -, Very Weak) did however, reward investors with excellent performance.

The fund's performance rating is currently A+ (Excellent). It has registered an annualized return of 62.27% over the last three years and is up 47.33% year to date 2015. Factored into the performance evaluation is an expense ratio of 0.95% (low).

Paul Brigandi has been running the fund for 6 years and currently receives a manager quality ranking of 94 (0=worst, 99=best). If you are comfortable owning a very high risk investment, this fund may be an option.

Data Date	Investment Rating	Net Assets ($Mil)	Price	Performance Rating/Pts	Total Return Y-T-D	Risk Rating/Pts
12-15	C-	14.80	37.64	A+ / 9.9	47.33%	E- / 0.1
2014	D+	14.80	104.35	A+ / 9.9	32.24%	E- / 0.1
2013	C-	27.90	78.62	A+ / 9.9	123.94%	D / 1.9
2012	A+	10.00	99.26	A+ / 9.9	84.71%	B- / 7.9
2011	C+	5.90	59.11	C+ / 5.9	15.19%	B / 8.4

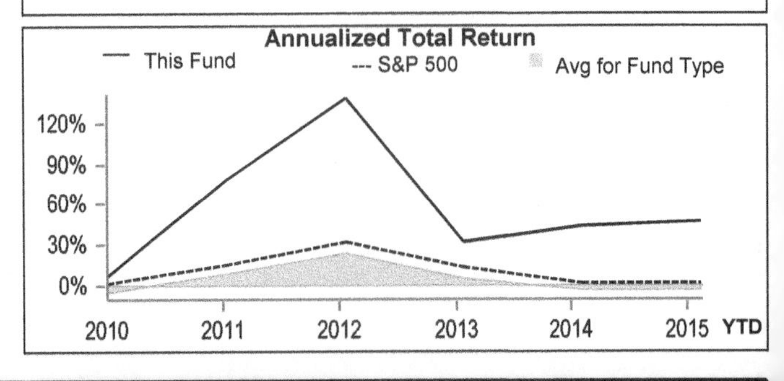

*Direxion Daily Russia Bear 3x (RUSS) E- Very Weak

Fund Family: Rafferty Asset Management LLC
Fund Type: Growth and Income
Inception Date: May 25, 2011

Major Rating Factors: *Direxion Daily Russia Bear 3x has adopted a very risky asset allocation strategy and currently receives an overall TheStreet.com Investment Rating of E- (Very Weak). The fund has a high level of volatility, as measured by both semi-deviation and drawdown factors. It carries a beta of -2.73, meaning the fund's expected move will be -27.3% for every 10% move in the market. As of December 31, 2015, *Direxion Daily Russia Bear 3x traded at a premium of .24% above its net asset value, which is worse than its one-year historical average discount of .04%. Unfortunately, the high level of risk (E-, Very Weak) failed to pay off as investors endured poor performance.

The fund's performance rating is currently D- (Weak). It has registered an annualized return of -12.20% over the last three years and is down -65.78% year to date 2015. Factored into the performance evaluation is an expense ratio of 0.95% (low).

Paul Brigandi has been running the fund for 5 years and currently receives a manager quality ranking of 99 (0=worst, 99=best). If you can tolerate very high levels of risk in the hope of improved future returns, holding this fund may be an option.

Data Date	Investment Rating	Net Assets ($Mil)	Price	Performance Rating/Pts	Total Return Y-T-D	Risk Rating/Pts
12-15	E-	24.20	37.52	D- / 1.1	-65.78%	E- / 0.2
2014	D+	24.20	28.10	A+ / 9.6	125.52%	E- / 0
2013	E-	5.60	11.21	E / 0.4	-10.10%	D / 1.9
2012	E-	5.90	14.85	E- / 0	-54.83%	D / 1.9

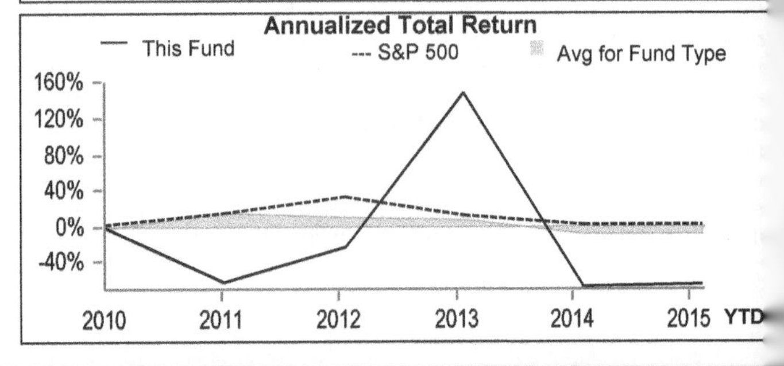

*Direxion Daily Russia Bull 3x (RUSL) E Very Weak

Fund Family: Rafferty Asset Management LLC
Fund Type: Foreign
Inception Date: May 25, 2011

Major Rating Factors: *Direxion Daily Russia Bull 3x has adopted a very risky asset allocation strategy and currently receives an overall TheStreet.com Investment Rating of E (Very Weak). The fund has a high level of volatility, as measured by both semi-deviation and drawdown factors. It carries a beta of 4.03, meaning it is expected to move 40.3% for every 10% move in the market. As of December 31, 2015, *Direxion Daily Russia Bull 3x traded at a discount of .27% below its net asset value, which is better than its one-year historical average premium of .05%. Unfortunately, the high level of risk (D, Weak) failed to pay off as investors endured very poor performance.

The fund's performance rating is currently E- (Very Weak). It has registered an annualized return of -63.71% over the last three years and is down -34.29% year to date 2015. Factored into the performance evaluation is an expense ratio of 0.95% (low).

Paul Brigandi has been running the fund for 5 years and currently receives a manager quality ranking of 0 (0=worst, 99=best). If you can tolerate very high levels of risk in the hope of improved future returns, holding this fund may be an option.

Data Date	Investment Rating	Net Assets ($Mil)	Price	Performance Rating/Pts	Total Return Y-T-D	Risk Rating/Pts
12-15	E	145.10	11.17	E- / 0	-34.29%	D / 1.8
2014	E-	145.10	16.54	E- / 0	-89.98%	D / 1.9
2013	E	21.70	31.00	D / 1.6	-29.34%	D / 1.9
2012	C-	25.90	36.77	A / 9.5	2.68%	D / 1.9

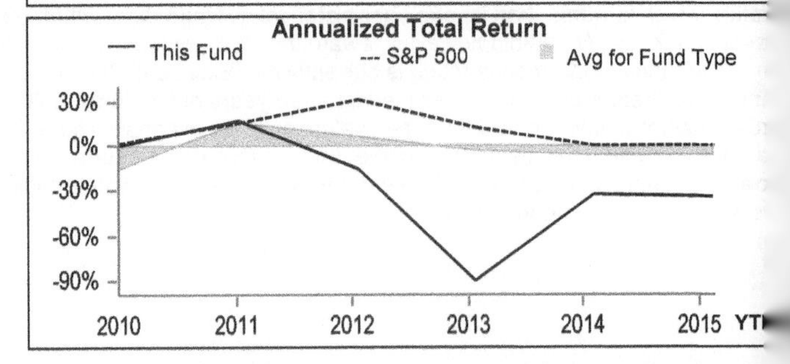

*Direxion Daily Semiconductor Bea (SOXS) E- Very Weak

'und Family: Rafferty Asset Management LLC
'und Type: Income
nception Date: March 11, 2010

Data Date	Investment Rating	Net Assets ($Mil)	Price	Performance Rating/Pts	Total Return Y-T-D	Risk Rating/Pts
12-15	E-	27.20	40.17	E- / 0.1	-25.17%	D / 1.7
2014	E-	27.20	13.39	E- / 0	-65.97%	D / 1.8
2013	E-	24.50	37.52	E- / 0	-66.44%	D / 1.9
2012	E-	26.40	32.84	E- / 0	-41.32%	D / 1.9
2011	E-	17.00	56.94	E / 0.4	-25.48%	D / 1.9

lajor Rating Factors: *Direxion Daily Semiconductor Bea has adopted a very risky sset allocation strategy and currently receives an overall TheStreet.com Investment ating of E- (Very Weak). The fund has a high level of volatility, as measured by both emi-deviation and drawdown factors. It carries a beta of -3.43, meaning the fund's xpected move will be -34.3% for every 10% move in the market. As of December 31, 015, *Direxion Daily Semiconductor Bea traded at a discount of .10% below its net sset value, which is better than its one-year historical average discount of .04%. nfortunately, the high level of risk (D, Weak) failed to pay off as investors endured ery poor performance.

The fund's performance rating is currently E- (Very Weak). It has registered an nnualized return of -55.92% over the last three years and is down -25.17% year to ate 2015. Factored into the performance evaluation is an expense ratio of 0.95% ow).

Paul Brigandi has been running the fund for 6 years and currently receives a anager quality ranking of 2 (0=worst, 99=best). If you can tolerate very high levels f risk in the hope of improved future returns, holding this fund may be an option.

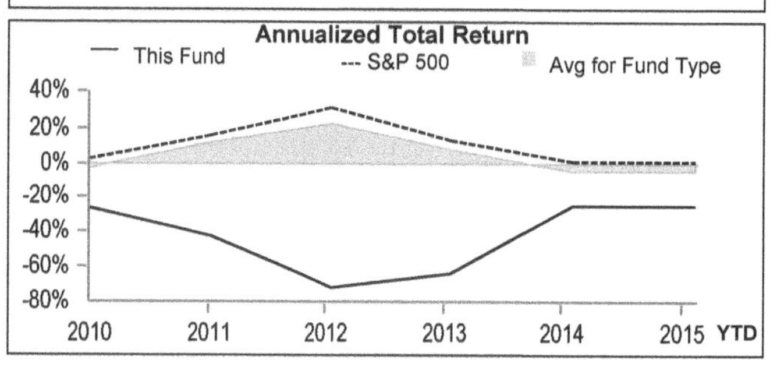

*Direxion Daily Semiconductor Bul (SOXL) C- Fair

und Family: Rafferty Asset Management LLC
und Type: Income
nception Date: March 11, 2010

Data Date	Investment Rating	Net Assets ($Mil)	Price	Performance Rating/Pts	Total Return Y-T-D	Risk Rating/Pts
12-15	C-	113.50	26.77	A+ / 9.9	-20.58%	E- / 0.2
2014	C	113.50	135.17	A+ / 9.9	105.81%	D / 2.2
2013	C-	58.50	69.02	A / 9.5	121.37%	D+ / 2.3
2012	C-	97.10	26.89	A+ / 9.6	2.76%	D / 1.9
2011	E-	109.20	25.96	E- / 0.1	-48.55%	D / 1.9

lajor Rating Factors: *Direxion Daily Semiconductor Bul has adopted a very risky sset allocation strategy and currently receives an overall TheStreet.com Investment ating of C- (Fair). The fund has shown a high level of volatility, as measured by both emi-deviation and drawdown factors. It carries a beta of 3.66, meaning it is expected move 36.6% for every 10% move in the market. As of December 31, 2015, Direxion Daily Semiconductor Bul traded at a premium of .07% above its net asset alue, which is worse than its one-year historical average premium of .01%. The high vel of risk (E-, Very Weak) did however, reward investors with excellent erformance.

The fund's performance rating is currently A+ (Excellent). It has registered an nnualized return of 53.39% over the last three years but is down -20.58% year to ate 2015. Factored into the performance evaluation is an expense ratio of 0.95% ow).

Paul Brigandi has been running the fund for 6 years and currently receives a anager quality ranking of 29 (0=worst, 99=best). If you are comfortable owning a ery high risk investment, this fund may be an option.

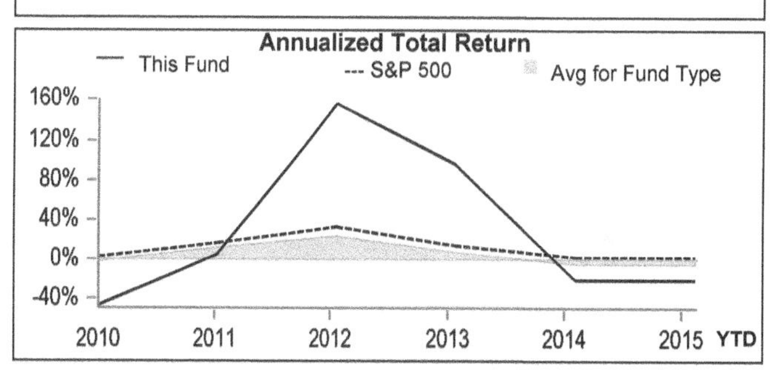

*Direxion Daily Small Cap Bear 3x (TZA) E- Very Weak

und Family: Rafferty Asset Management LLC
und Type: Growth
nception Date: November 5, 2008

Data Date	Investment Rating	Net Assets ($Mil)	Price	Performance Rating/Pts	Total Return Y-T-D	Risk Rating/Pts
12-15	E-	814.10	45.00	E / 0.4	-7.72%	E+ / 0.9
2014	E-	814.10	12.00	E- / 0.1	-30.52%	D / 2.1
2013	E-	559.70	16.97	E- / 0	-64.41%	D / 1.9
2012	E-	681.70	13.50	E- / 0	-49.42%	D / 1.9
2011	E-	741.80	26.48	E- / 0	-44.70%	D / 1.9
2010	E-	635.20	15.61	E- / 0	-68.34%	D- / 1.0

ajor Rating Factors: *Direxion Daily Small Cap Bear 3x has adopted a very risky sset allocation strategy and currently receives an overall TheStreet.com Investment ating of E- (Very Weak). The fund has a high level of volatility, as measured by both emi-deviation and drawdown factors. It carries a beta of -3.12, meaning the fund's xpected move will be -31.2% for every 10% move in the market. As of December 31,)15, *Direxion Daily Small Cap Bear 3x traded at a premium of .45% above its net sset value, which is worse than its one-year historical average premium of .01%. nfortunately, the high level of risk (E+, Very Weak) failed to pay off as investors ndured very poor performance.

The fund's performance rating is currently E (Very Weak). It has registered an nnualized return of -38.57% over the last three years and is down -7.72% year to ate 2015. Factored into the performance evaluation is an expense ratio of 0.95% ow).

Paul Brigandi has been running the fund for 8 years and currently receives a anager quality ranking of 20 (0=worst, 99=best). If you can tolerate very high levels risk in the hope of improved future returns, holding this fund may be an option.

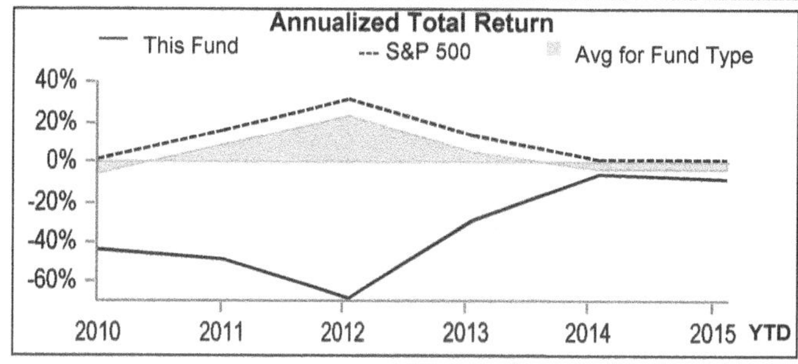

*Direxion Daily Small Cap Bull 2x (SMLL) E- Very Weak

Fund Family: Rafferty Asset Management LLC
Fund Type: Growth
Inception Date: July 29, 2014

Major Rating Factors: *Direxion Daily Small Cap Bull 2x has adopted a very risky asset allocation strategy and currently receives an overall TheStreet.com Investment Rating of E- (Very Weak). The fund has a high level of volatility, as measured by both semi-deviation and drawdown factors. It carries a beta of 0.00, meaning the fund's expected move will be 0.0% for every 10% move in the market. As of December 31, 2015, *Direxion Daily Small Cap Bull 2x traded at a premium of .79% above its net asset value, which is worse than its one-year historical average discount of 1.16%. Unfortunately, the high level of risk (E-, Very Weak) failed to pay off as investors endured poor performance.

The fund's performance rating is currently D (Weak). It has registered an annualized return of 0.00% over the last three years but is down -11.17% year to date 2015.

Paul Brigandi currently receives a manager quality ranking of 13 (0=worst, 99=best). If you can tolerate very high levels of risk in the hope of improved future returns, holding this fund may be an option.

Data Date	Investment Rating	Net Assets ($Mil)	Price	Performance Rating/Pts	Total Return Y-T-D	Risk Rating/Pts
12-15	E-	1.90	29.37	D / 1.6	-11.17%	E- / 0.1

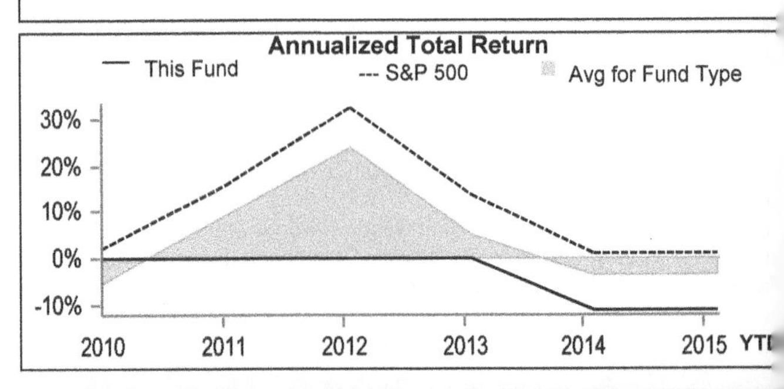

*Direxion Daily Small Cap Bull 3x (TNA) C Fair

Fund Family: Rafferty Asset Management LLC
Fund Type: Growth
Inception Date: November 5, 2008

Major Rating Factors: *Direxion Daily Small Cap Bull 3x has adopted a risky asset allocation strategy and currently receives an overall TheStreet.com Investment Rating of C (Fair). The fund has shown an above average level of volatility, as measured by both semi-deviation and drawdown factors. It carries a beta of 3.23, meaning it is expected to move 32.3% for every 10% move in the market. As of December 31, 2015, *Direxion Daily Small Cap Bull 3x traded at a discount of .47% below its net asset value, which is better than its one-year historical average discount of .10%. The high level of risk (D+, Weak) did however, reward investors with excellent performance.

The fund's performance rating is currently A- (Excellent). It has registered an annualized return of 22.60% over the last three years but is down -20.16% year to date 2015. Factored into the performance evaluation is an expense ratio of 0.95% (low).

Paul Brigandi has been running the fund for 8 years and currently receives a manager quality ranking of 7 (0=worst, 99=best). If you are comfortable owning a high risk investment, this fund may be an option.

Data Date	Investment Rating	Net Assets ($Mil)	Price	Performance Rating/Pts	Total Return Y-T-D	Risk Rating/Pts
12-15	C	990.40	63.53	A- / 9.1	-20.16%	D+ / 2.7
2014	C-	990.40	80.93	A+ / 9.8	7.32%	E+ / 0.6
2013	C-	895.30	77.43	A+ / 9.8	118.72%	D / 1.9
2012	C-	732.10	63.96	A / 9.4	43.44%	D+ / 2.4
2011	D-	1,027.30	44.84	C / 4.3	-36.44%	D / 2.2
2010	B+	565.00	72.43	A+ / 9.9	69.80%	C- / 3.7

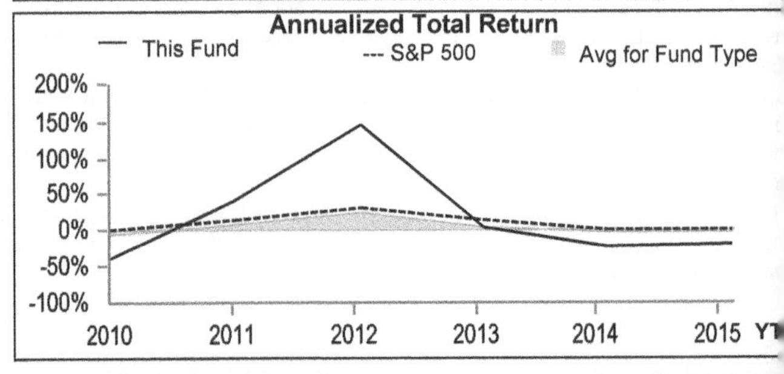

*Direxion Daily Technology Bear 3 (TECS) E- Very Weak

Fund Family: Rafferty Asset Management LLC
Fund Type: Growth
Inception Date: December 17, 2008

Major Rating Factors: *Direxion Daily Technology Bear 3 has adopted a very risky asset allocation strategy and currently receives an overall TheStreet.com Investment Rating of E- (Very Weak). The fund has a high level of volatility, as measured by both semi-deviation and drawdown factors. It carries a beta of -2.84, meaning the fund's expected move will be -28.4% for every 10% move in the market. As of December 31, 2015, *Direxion Daily Technology Bear 3 traded at a premium of .03% above its net asset value, which is worse than its one-year historical average premium of .01%. Unfortunately, the high level of risk (D-, Weak) failed to pay off as investors endured very poor performance.

The fund's performance rating is currently E- (Very Weak). It has registered an annualized return of -43.75% over the last three years and is down -31.49% year to date 2015. Factored into the performance evaluation is an expense ratio of 0.95% (low).

Paul Brigandi has been running the fund for 8 years and currently receives a manager quality ranking of 8 (0=worst, 99=best). If you can tolerate very high levels of risk in the hope of improved future returns, holding this fund may be an option.

Data Date	Investment Rating	Net Assets ($Mil)	Price	Performance Rating/Pts	Total Return Y-T-D	Risk Rating/Pts
12-15	E-	15.00	31.10	E- / 0.1	-31.49%	D- / 1.1
2014	E	15.00	11.29	E- / 0.1	-48.40%	D+ / 2.9
2013	E-	17.20	20.95	E- / 0.1	-49.93%	D+ / 2.6
2012	E-	26.70	9.36	E- / 0.1	-41.82%	D+ / 2.3
2011	E-	32.00	16.30	E- / 0	-32.43%	D / 1.9
2010	E-	44.50	23.91	E- / 0	-45.29%	D- / 1.0

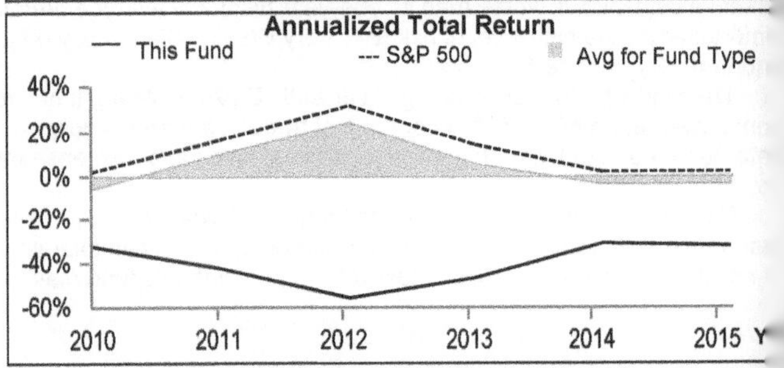

*Direxion Daily Technology Bull 3 (TECL) C- Fair

Fund Family: Rafferty Asset Management LLC
Fund Type: Growth
Inception Date: December 17, 2008

Major Rating Factors: *Direxion Daily Technology Bull 3 has adopted a very risky asset allocation strategy and currently receives an overall TheStreet.com Investment Rating of C- (Fair). The fund has shown a high level of volatility, as measured by both semi-deviation and drawdown factors. It carries a beta of 3.02, meaning it is expected to move 30.2% for every 10% move in the market. As of December 31, 2015, *Direxion Daily Technology Bull 3 traded at a price exactly equal to its net asset value, which is better than its one-year historical average premium of .01%. The high level of risk (D-, Weak) did however, reward investors with excellent performance.

The fund's performance rating is currently A+ (Excellent). It has registered an annualized return of 41.48% over the last three years and is up 4.98% year to date 2015. Factored into the performance evaluation is an expense ratio of 0.95% (low).

Paul Brigandi has been running the fund for 7 years and currently receives a manager quality ranking of 26 (0=worst, 99=best). If you are comfortable owning a very high risk investment, this fund may be an option.

Data Date	Investment Rating	Net Assets ($Mil)	Price	Performance Rating/Pts	Total Return Y-T-D	Risk Rating/Pts
12-15	C-	164.00	36.43	A+ / 9.9	4.98%	D- / 1.0
2014	C+	164.00	139.20	A+ / 9.9	59.25%	C- / 4.2
2013	C+	137.10	91.30	A+ / 9.7	69.86%	C / 4.7
2012	D	138.60	48.73	C+ / 6.3	30.36%	D / 1.9
2011	C-	178.80	36.45	A+ / 9.9	-17.63%	D / 1.9
2010	C	208.60	45.50	A+ / 9.8	21.21%	D- / 1.0

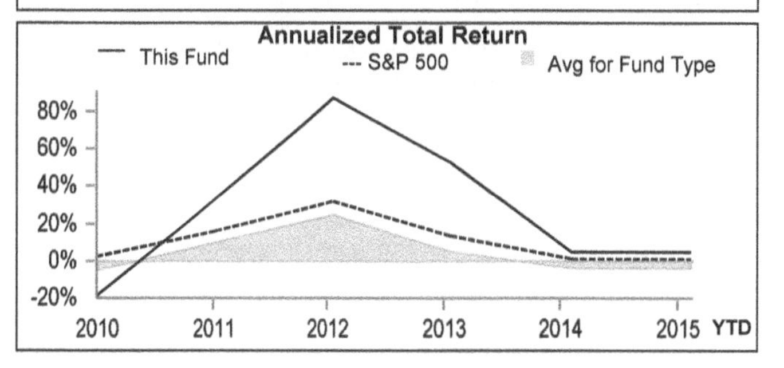

*Direxion Daily Tot Bond Mkt Bear (SAGG) C- Fair

Fund Family: Rafferty Asset Management LLC
Fund Type: Growth
Inception Date: March 23, 2011

Major Rating Factors: Middle of the road best describes *Direxion Daily Tot Bond Mkt Bear whose TheStreet.com Investment Rating is currently a C- (Fair). The fund currently has a performance rating of C- (Fair) based on an annualized return of -2.46% over the last three years and a total return of -1.23% year to date 2015. Factored into the performance evaluation is an expense ratio of 0.65% (very low).

The fund's risk rating is currently B- (Good). It carries a beta of 0.03, meaning the fund's expected move will be 0.3% for every 10% move in the market. Volatility, as measured by both the semi-deviation and a drawdown factor, is considered low. As of December 31, 2015, *Direxion Daily Tot Bond Mkt Bear traded at a premium of .24% above its net asset value, which is worse than its one-year historical average discount of .18%.

Paul Brigandi has been running the fund for 5 years and currently receives a manager quality ranking of 44 (0=worst, 99=best). If you desire an average level of risk, then this fund may be an option.

Data Date	Investment Rating	Net Assets ($Mil)	Price	Performance Rating/Pts	Total Return Y-T-D	Risk Rating/Pts
12-15	C-	3.40	32.99	C- / 3.5	-1.23%	B- / 7.5
2014	C-	3.40	33.40	D / 2.1	-6.42%	B / 8.3
2013	C-	8.90	35.73	D+ / 2.3	0.39%	B+ / 9.2

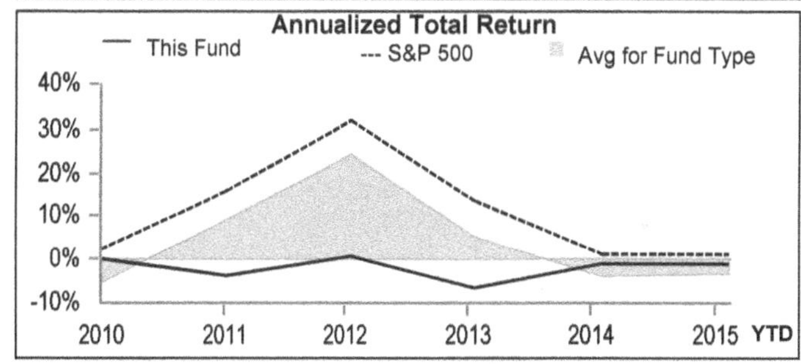

*Direxion Daily Total Market Bear (TOTS) D Weak

Fund Family: Rafferty Asset Management LLC
Fund Type: Growth
Inception Date: June 15, 2011

Major Rating Factors:
Disappointing performance is the major factor driving the D (Weak) TheStreet.com Investment Rating for *Direxion Daily Total Market Bear. The fund currently has a performance rating of D- (Weak) based on an annualized return of -14.24% over the last three years and a total return of -4.54% year to date 2015. Factored into the performance evaluation is an expense ratio of 0.65% (very low).

The fund's risk rating is currently C+ (Fair). It carries a beta of -1.02, meaning the fund's expected move will be -10.2% for every 10% move in the market. Volatility, as measured by both the semi-deviation and a drawdown factor, is considered low. As of December 31, 2015, *Direxion Daily Total Market Bear traded at a discount of .73% below its net asset value, which is better than its one-year historical average premium of .25%.

Paul Brigandi has been running the fund for 5 years and currently receives a manager quality ranking of 47 (0=worst, 99=best). This fund offers only a moderate level of risk but investors looking for strong performance are still waiting.

Data Date	Investment Rating	Net Assets ($Mil)	Price	Performance Rating/Pts	Total Return Y-T-D	Risk Rating/Pts
12-15	D	2.10	18.92	D- / 1.5	-4.54%	C+ / 6.5
2014	D-	2.10	19.71	D- / 1.0	-13.85%	C+ / 5.8
2013	D-	1.10	22.68	E / 0.4	-23.73%	C+ / 5.8

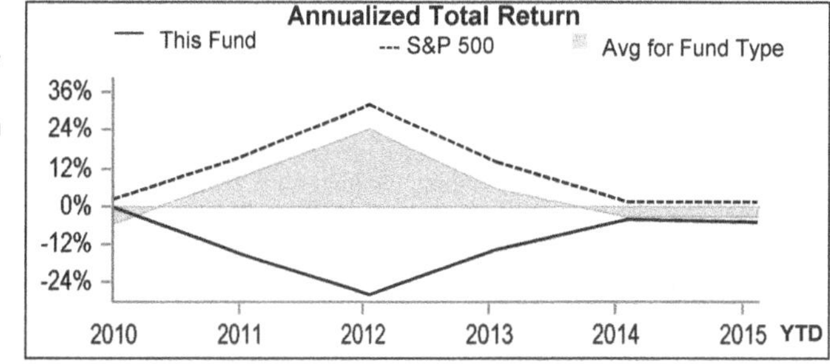

*Direxion Developed Markets Bear (DPK) D- Weak

Fund Family: Rafferty Asset Management LLC
Fund Type: Global
Inception Date: December 17, 2008

Data Date	Investment Rating	Net Assets ($Mil)	Price	Performance Rating/Pts	Total Return Y-T-D	Risk Rating/Pts
12-15	D-	6.10	30.91	D- / 1.0	-15.20%	C- / 4.0
2014	E	6.10	35.94	E / 0.5	3.42%	D+ / 2.7
2013	E-	7.80	33.07	E- / 0.1	-46.51%	D+ / 2.4
2012	E-	10.80	16.82	E- / 0.1	-53.99%	D / 2.2
2011	E-	17.00	34.75	E- / 0.2	-18.16%	D / 1.9
2010	E-	15.20	8.22	E- / 0.1	-46.41%	D- / 1.0

Major Rating Factors:
Disappointing performance is the major factor driving the D- (Weak) TheStreet.com Investment Rating for *Direxion Developed Markets Bear. The fund currently has a performance rating of D- (Weak) based on an annualized return of -21.93% over the last three years and a total return of -15.20% year to date 2015. Factored into the performance evaluation is an expense ratio of 0.95% (low).

The fund's risk rating is currently C- (Fair). It carries a beta of -2.85, meaning the fund's expected move will be -28.5% for every 10% move in the market. Volatility, as measured by both the semi-deviation and a drawdown factor, is considered average. As of December 31, 2015, *Direxion Developed Markets Bear traded at a discount of .19% below its net asset value, which is better than its one-year historical average premium of .03%.

Paul Brigandi has been running the fund for 8 years and currently receives a manager quality ranking of 16 (0=worst, 99=best). This fund offers an average level of risk but investors looking for strong performance will be frustrated.

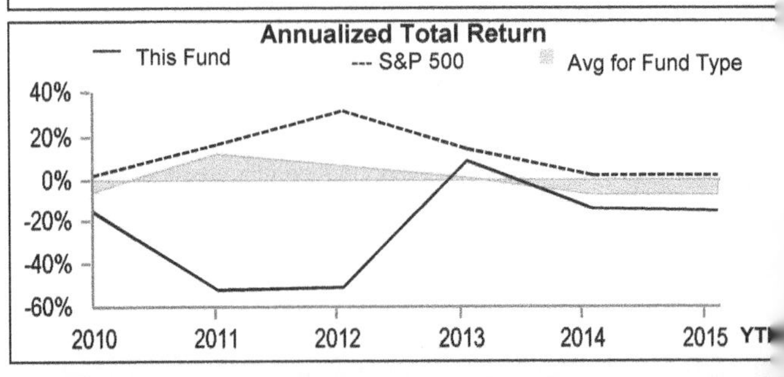

*Direxion Developed Markets Bull (DZK) D Weak

Fund Family: Rafferty Asset Management LLC
Fund Type: Global
Inception Date: December 17, 2008

Data Date	Investment Rating	Net Assets ($Mil)	Price	Performance Rating/Pts	Total Return Y-T-D	Risk Rating/Pts
12-15	D	46.70	49.92	C- / 3.8	-11.86%	C- / 3.3
2014	D+	46.70	57.17	B- / 7.2	-19.25%	C- / 3.0
2013	C-	44.60	74.49	B+ / 8.9	52.42%	D+ / 2.3
2012	E+	27.00	44.95	C- / 3.5	59.68%	D / 2.1
2011	E	19.70	30.35	D- / 1.1	-48.82%	D+ / 2.3
2010	C+	23.50	67.07	A+ / 9.8	11.84%	D+ / 2.5

Major Rating Factors: *Direxion Developed Markets Bull receives a TheStreet.com Investment Rating of D (Weak). The fund currently has a performance rating of C- (Fair) based on an annualized return of 2.43% over the last three years and a total return of -11.86% year to date 2015. Factored into the performance evaluation is an expense ratio of 0.95% (low).

The fund's risk rating is currently C- (Fair). It carries a beta of 3.00, meaning it is expected to move 30.0% for every 10% move in the market. Volatility, as measured by both the semi-deviation and a drawdown factor, is considered average. As of December 31, 2015, *Direxion Developed Markets Bull traded at a premium of .06% above its net asset value, which is worse than its one-year historical average premium of .02%.

Adam Gould has been running the fund for 8 years and currently receives a manager quality ranking of 14 (0=worst, 99=best). If you desire an average level of risk, then this fund may be an option.

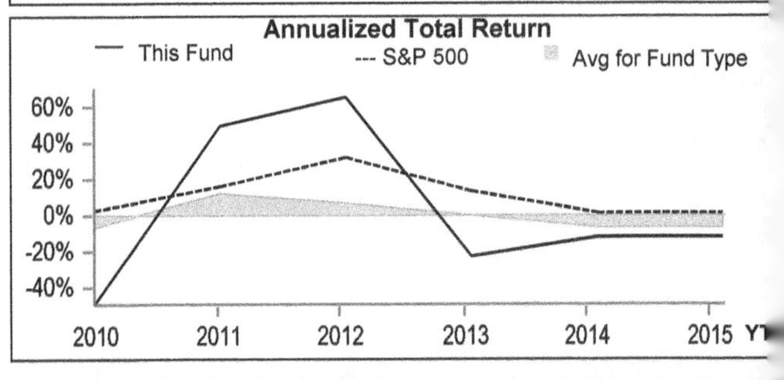

*Direxion Emerging Markets Bear 3 (EDZ) C- Fair

Fund Family: Rafferty Asset Management LLC
Fund Type: Global
Inception Date: December 17, 2008

Data Date	Investment Rating	Net Assets ($Mil)	Price	Performance Rating/Pts	Total Return Y-T-D	Risk Rating/Pts
12-15	C-	119.40	46.98	B / 7.8	20.96%	D / 1.8
2014	E	119.40	37.51	E+ / 0.6	-16.14%	C- / 3.2
2013	E-	89.00	39.83	E / 0.5	4.15%	D / 1.9
2012	E-	88.20	9.02	E- / 0.1	-49.14%	D / 1.9
2011	E-	125.90	19.69	E- / 0	-8.00%	D / 1.9
2010	E-	87.20	20.29	E- / 0	-59.34%	D- / 1.0

Major Rating Factors: *Direxion Emerging Markets Bear 3 has adopted a very risky asset allocation strategy and currently receives an overall TheStreet.com Investment Rating of C- (Fair). The fund has shown a high level of volatility, as measured by both semi-deviation and drawdown factors. It carries a beta of -2.63, meaning the fund's expected move will be -26.3% for every 10% move in the market. As of December 31, 2015, *Direxion Emerging Markets Bear 3 traded at a premium of .09% above its net asset value, which is worse than its one-year historical average discount of .02%. The high level of risk (D, Weak) did however, reward investors with excellent performance.

The fund's performance rating is currently B (Good). It has registered an annualized return of 3.04% over the last three years and is up 20.96% year to date 2015. Factored into the performance evaluation is an expense ratio of 0.95% (low).

Paul Brigandi has been running the fund for 8 years and currently receives a manager quality ranking of 97 (0=worst, 99=best). If you are comfortable owning a very high risk investment, this fund may be an option.

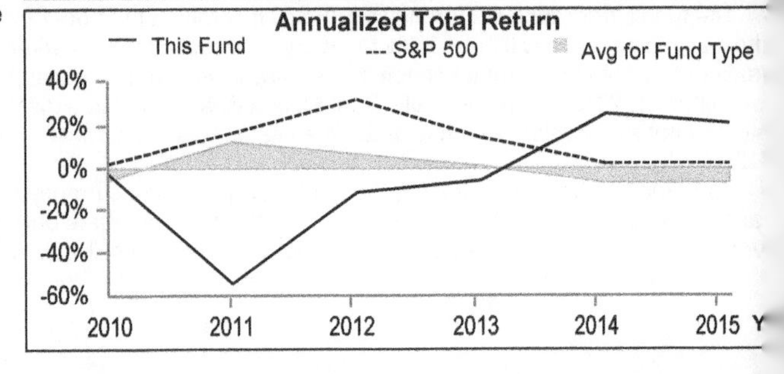

*Direxion Emerging Markets Bull 3 (EDC) E- Very Weak

Fund Family: Rafferty Asset Management LLC
Fund Type: Global
Inception Date: December 17, 2008

Data Date	Investment Rating	Net Assets ($Mil)	Price	Performance Rating/Pts	Total Return Y-T-D	Risk Rating/Pts
12-15	E-	284.10	11.51	E- / 0.2	-47.92%	D- / 1.0
2014	E-	284.10	22.94	D / 1.7	-9.22%	E- / 0.1
2013	E-	346.00	28.70	E / 0.4	-33.60%	D / 1.9
2012	E-	351.40	109.28	D- / 1.2	33.47%	D / 1.9
2011	E	369.70	74.61	D / 1.9	-60.88%	D / 1.9
2010	C	426.80	41.31	A+ / 9.8	24.29%	D- / 1.0

Major Rating Factors: *Direxion Emerging Markets Bull 3 has adopted a very risky asset allocation strategy and currently receives an overall TheStreet.com Investment Rating of E- (Very Weak). The fund has a high level of volatility, as measured by both semi-deviation and drawdown factors. It carries a beta of 2.77, meaning it is expected to move 27.7% for every 10% move in the market. As of December 31, 2015, *Direxion Emerging Markets Bull 3 traded at a price exactly equal to its net asset value, which is better than its one-year historical average premium of .02%. Unfortunately, the high level of risk (D-, Weak) failed to pay off as investors endured very poor performance.

The fund's performance rating is currently E- (Very Weak). It has registered an annualized return of -32.88% over the last three years and is down -47.92% year to date 2015. Factored into the performance evaluation is an expense ratio of 0.95% (low).

Paul Brigandi has been running the fund for 11 years and currently receives a manager quality ranking of 1 (0=worst, 99=best). If you can tolerate very high levels of risk in the hope of improved future returns, holding this fund may be an option.

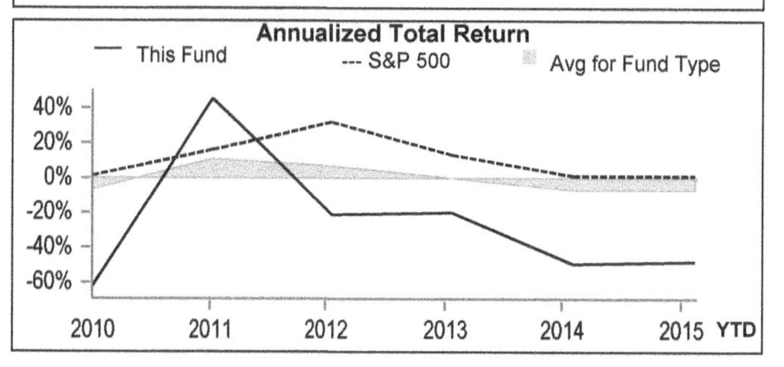

*Direxion Energy Bear 3x Shares (ERY) D- Weak

Fund Family: Rafferty Asset Management LLC
Fund Type: Energy/Natural Resources
Inception Date: November 6, 2008

Data Date	Investment Rating	Net Assets ($Mil)	Price	Performance Rating/Pts	Total Return Y-T-D	Risk Rating/Pts
12-15	D-	47.10	29.31	C- / 3.7	41.46%	D+ / 2.7
2014	E-	47.10	21.00	E+ / 0.8	-0.66%	E+ / 0.6
2013	E-	60.10	20.12	E- / 0.1	-50.09%	D / 1.9
2012	E-	73.70	7.82	E- / 0.1	-36.27%	D / 1.9
2011	E-	94.90	11.31	E- / 0	-52.28%	D / 1.9
2010	E-	50.60	22.55	E- / 0	-60.02%	D- / 1.1

Major Rating Factors: *Direxion Energy Bear 3x Shares has adopted a risky asset allocation strategy and currently receives an overall TheStreet.com Investment Rating of D- (Weak). The fund has an above average level of volatility, as measured by both semi-deviation and drawdown factors. It carries a beta of -2.82, meaning the fund's expected move will be -28.2% for every 10% move in the market. As of December 31, 2015, *Direxion Energy Bear 3x Shares traded at a discount of .10% below its net asset value. Unfortunately, the high level of risk (D+, Weak) has only provided investors with average performance.

The fund's performance rating is currently C- (Fair). It has registered an annualized return of -11.55% over the last three years and is up 41.46% year to date 2015. Factored into the performance evaluation is an expense ratio of 0.95% (low).

Paul Brigandi has been running the fund for 8 years and currently receives a manager quality ranking of 5 (0=worst, 99=best). If you are comfortable owning a high risk investment, then this fund may be an option.

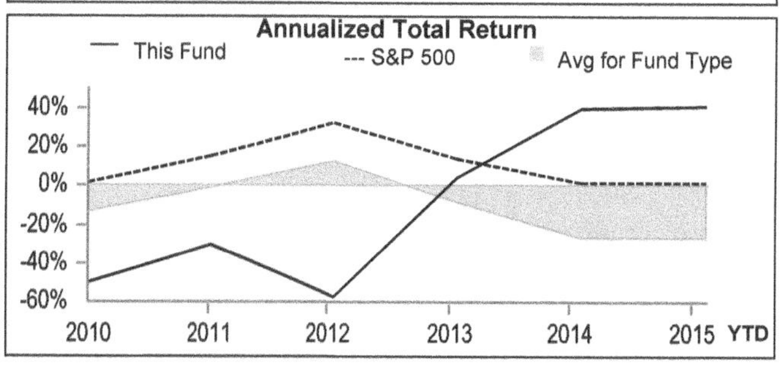

*Direxion Energy Bull 3x Shares (ERX) E Very Weak

Fund Family: Rafferty Asset Management LLC
Fund Type: Energy/Natural Resources
Inception Date: November 6, 2008

Data Date	Investment Rating	Net Assets ($Mil)	Price	Performance Rating/Pts	Total Return Y-T-D	Risk Rating/Pts
12-15	E	186.90	23.43	E / 0.4	-61.81%	D / 1.8
2014	E+	186.90	60.47	D / 2.0	-29.17%	D+ / 2.9
2013	C-	161.70	89.88	A- / 9.1	59.51%	D+ / 2.3
2012	E+	264.80	48.48	C- / 3.9	12.68%	D / 2.1
2011	E+	384.20	46.85	C- / 3.9	-16.40%	D / 2.1
2010	B	241.40	58.45	A+ / 9.9	48.98%	C- / 3.3

Major Rating Factors: *Direxion Energy Bull 3x Shares has adopted a very risky asset allocation strategy and currently receives an overall TheStreet.com Investment Rating of E (Very Weak). The fund has a high level of volatility, as measured by both semi-deviation and drawdown factors. It carries a beta of 3.04, meaning it is expected to move 30.4% for every 10% move in the market. As of December 31, 2015, *Direxion Energy Bull 3x Shares traded at a discount of .21% below its net asset value, which is better than its one-year historical average premium of .01%. Unfortunately, the high level of risk (D, Weak) failed to pay off as investors endured very poor performance.

The fund's performance rating is currently E (Very Weak). It has registered an annualized return of -24.07% over the last three years and is down -61.81% year to date 2015. Factored into the performance evaluation is an expense ratio of 0.95% (low).

Paul Brigandi has been running the fund for 8 years and currently receives a manager quality ranking of 14 (0=worst, 99=best). If you can tolerate very high levels of risk in the hope of improved future returns, holding this fund may be an option.

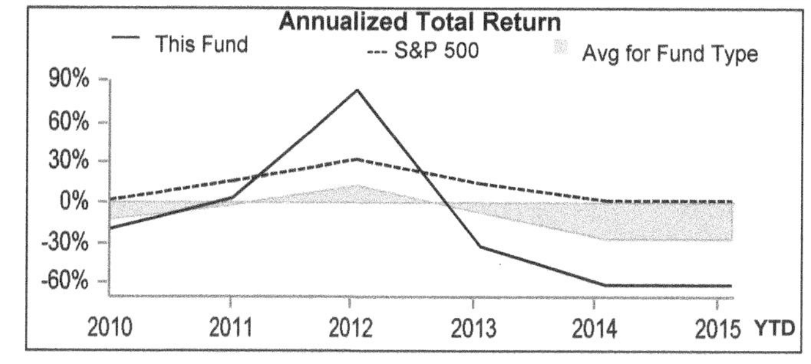

*Direxion Financial Bear 3x Share (FAZ) E- Very Weak

Fund Family: Rafferty Asset Management LLC
Fund Type: Financial Services
Inception Date: November 6, 2008

Major Rating Factors: *Direxion Financial Bear 3x Share has adopted a very risky asset allocation strategy and currently receives an overall TheStreet.com Investment Rating of E- (Very Weak). The fund has a high level of volatility, as measured by both semi-deviation and drawdown factors. It carries a beta of -2.90, meaning the fund's expected move will be -29.0% for every 10% move in the market. As of December 31, 2015, *Direxion Financial Bear 3x Share traded at a premium of .05% above its net asset value, which is worse than its one-year historical average discount of .05%. Unfortunately, the high level of risk (D-, Weak) failed to pay off as investors endured very poor performance.

The fund's performance rating is currently E- (Very Weak). It has registered an annualized return of -42.30% over the last three years and is down -18.62% year to date 2015. Factored into the performance evaluation is an expense ratio of 0.95% (low).

Paul Brigandi has been running the fund for 8 years and currently receives a manager quality ranking of 10 (0=worst, 99=best). If you can tolerate very high levels of risk in the hope of improved future returns, holding this fund may be an option.

Data Date	Investment Rating	Net Assets ($Mil)	Price	Performance Rating/Pts	Total Return Y-T-D	Risk Rating/Pts
12-15	E-	345.20	41.18	E- / 0.2	-18.62%	D- / 1.4
2014	E-	345.20	12.67	E- / 0	-41.06%	E+ / 0.7
2013	E-	406.70	21.50	E- / 0	-59.90%	D / 2.0
2012	E-	574.80	15.11	E- / 0.1	-58.56%	D / 2.0
2011	E-	823.80	37.35	E- / 0	-23.05%	D / 1.9
2010	E-	971.50	9.45	E- / 0	-51.36%	D- / 1.0

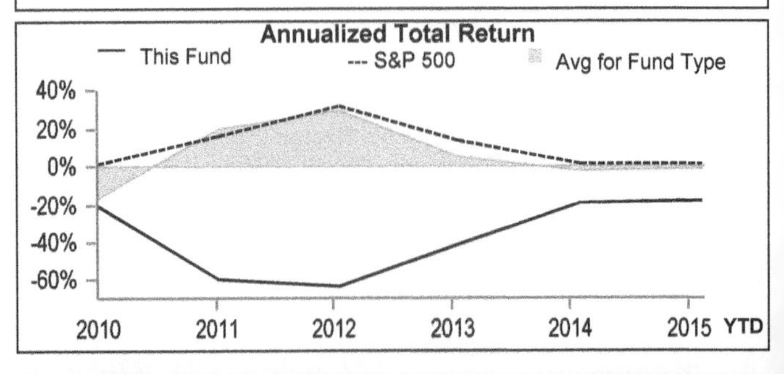

*Direxion Financial Bull 3x Share (FAS) C- Fair

Fund Family: Rafferty Asset Management LLC
Fund Type: Financial Services
Inception Date: November 6, 2008

Major Rating Factors: *Direxion Financial Bull 3x Share has adopted a very risky asset allocation strategy and currently receives an overall TheStreet.com Investment Rating of C- (Fair). The fund has shown a high level of volatility, as measured by both semi-deviation and drawdown factors. It carries a beta of 3.08, meaning it is expected to move 30.8% for every 10% move in the market. As of December 31, 2015, *Direxion Financial Bull 3x Share traded at a price exactly equal to its net asset value, which is better than its one-year historical average premium of .02%. The high level of risk (D-, Weak) did however, reward investors with excellent performance.

The fund's performance rating is currently A+ (Excellent). It has registered an annualized return of 37.58% over the last three years but is down -8.83% year to date 2015. Factored into the performance evaluation is an expense ratio of 0.95% (low).

Paul Brigandi has been running the fund for 8 years and currently receives a manager quality ranking of 19 (0=worst, 99=best). If you are comfortable owning a very high risk investment, this fund may be an option.

Data Date	Investment Rating	Net Assets ($Mil)	Price	Performance Rating/Pts	Total Return Y-T-D	Risk Rating/Pts
12-15	C-	1,240.60	29.07	A+ / 9.8	-8.83%	D- / 1.0
2014	C-	1,240.60	127.15	A+ / 9.9	40.96%	D / 1.9
2013	C-	1,227.00	90.30	A+ / 9.7	102.02%	D / 1.9
2012	C-	1,135.20	119.92	A- / 9.0	80.74%	D / 1.9
2011	E-	1,391.00	64.87	E+ / 0.6	-52.08%	D / 1.9
2010	C	1,921.20	27.84	A+ / 9.6	12.75%	D- / 1.0

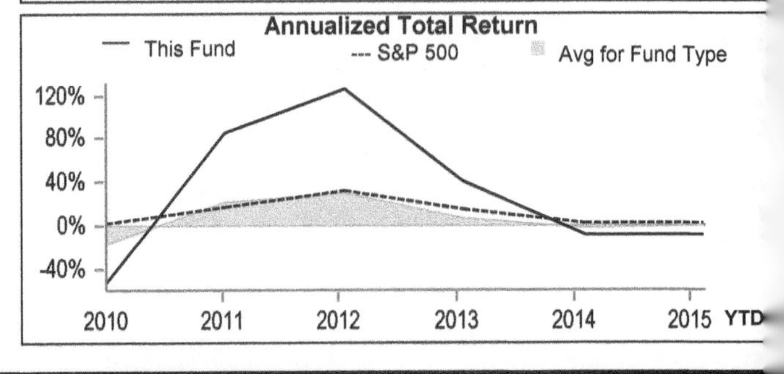

*Direxion iBillionaire Index ETF (IBLN) C- Fair

Fund Family: Rafferty Asset Management LLC
Fund Type: Growth
Inception Date: August 1, 2014

Major Rating Factors: Middle of the road best describes *Direxion iBillionaire Index ETF whose TheStreet.com Investment Rating is currently a C- (Fair). The fund currently has a performance rating of C- (Fair) based on an annualized return of 0.00% over the last three years and a total return of -5.24% year to date 2015.

The fund's risk rating is currently C+ (Fair). It carries a beta of 0.00, meaning the fund's expected move will be 0.0% for every 10% move in the market. Volatility, as measured by both the semi-deviation and a drawdown factor, is considered low. As of December 31, 2015, *Direxion iBillionaire Index ETF traded at a premium of .54% above its net asset value, which is worse than its one-year historical average premium of .03%.

Paul Brigandi has been running the fund for 2 years and currently receives a manager quality ranking of 23 (0=worst, 99=best). If you desire an average level of risk, then this fund may be an option.

Data Date	Investment Rating	Net Assets ($Mil)	Price	Performance Rating/Pts	Total Return Y-T-D	Risk Rating/Pts
12-15	C-	36.70	24.34	C- / 3.4	-5.24%	C+ / 6.4

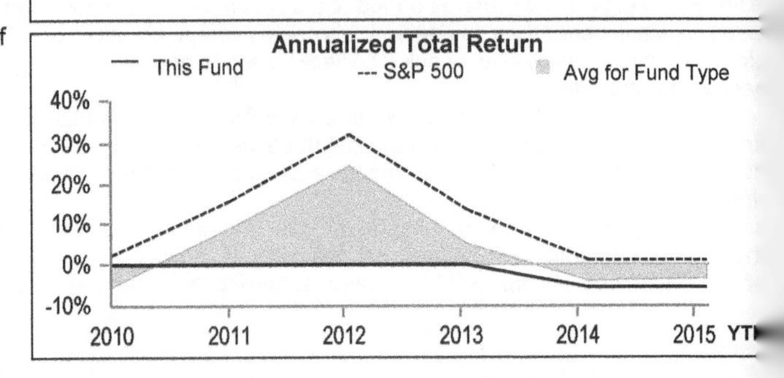

* Denotes ETF Fund

*Direxion Jr Gold Miners Idx Bear (JDST) E- Very Weak

und Family: Rafferty Asset Management LLC
und Type: Growth
nception Date: October 3, 2013

Data Date	Investment Rating	Net Assets ($Mil)	Price	Performance Rating/Pts	Total Return Y-T-D	Risk Rating/Pts
12-15	E-	48.40	29.74	E- / 0.2	-45.81%	E- / 0.2
2014	E-	48.40	15.70	E / 0.3	-69.27%	E / 0.4

ajor Rating Factors: *Direxion Jr Gold Miners Idx Bear has adopted a very risky sset allocation strategy and currently receives an overall TheStreet.com Investment ating of E- (Very Weak). The fund has a high level of volatility, as measured by both emi-deviation and drawdown factors. It carries a beta of 0.00, meaning the fund's xpected move will be 0.0% for every 10% move in the market. As of December 31, 015, *Direxion Jr Gold Miners Idx Bear traded at a premium of .07% above its net sset value, which is worse than its one-year historical average discount of .18%. nfortunately, the high level of risk (E-, Very Weak) failed to pay off as investors ndured very poor performance.

The fund's performance rating is currently E- (Very Weak). It has registered an nnualized return of 0.00% over the last three years but is down -45.81% year to date 015. Factored into the performance evaluation is an expense ratio of 0.95% (low).

Paul Brigandi has been running the fund for 3 years and currently receives a anager quality ranking of 0 (0=worst, 99=best). If you can tolerate very high levels f risk in the hope of improved future returns, holding this fund may be an option.

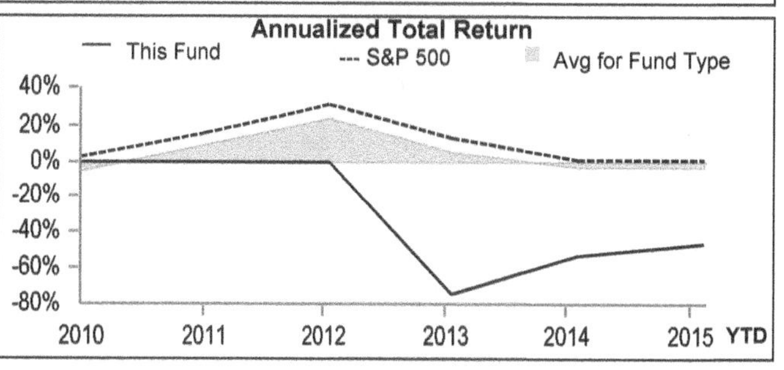

*Direxion Jr Gold Miners Idx Bull (JNUG) E- Very Weak

und Family: Rafferty Asset Management LLC
und Type: Growth
nception Date: October 3, 2013

Data Date	Investment Rating	Net Assets ($Mil)	Price	Performance Rating/Pts	Total Return Y-T-D	Risk Rating/Pts
12-15	E-	239.70	31.05	E- / 0	-77.20%	D / 1.8
2014	E-	239.70	24.34	E- / 0	-86.09%	D- / 1.5

ajor Rating Factors: *Direxion Jr Gold Miners Idx Bull has adopted a very risky sset allocation strategy and currently receives an overall TheStreet.com Investment ating of E- (Very Weak). The fund has a high level of volatility, as measured by both emi-deviation and drawdown factors. It carries a beta of 0.00, meaning the fund's xpected move will be 0.0% for every 10% move in the market. As of December 31, 015, *Direxion Jr Gold Miners Idx Bull traded at a discount of .26% below its net sset value, which is better than its one-year historical average premium of .19%. nfortunately, the high level of risk (D, Weak) failed to pay off as investors endured ery poor performance.

The fund's performance rating is currently E- (Very Weak). It has registered an nnualized return of 0.00% over the last three years but is down -77.20% year to date 015. Factored into the performance evaluation is an expense ratio of 0.95% (low).

Paul Brigandi has been running the fund for 3 years and currently receives a anager quality ranking of 0 (0=worst, 99=best). If you can tolerate very high levels f risk in the hope of improved future returns, holding this fund may be an option.

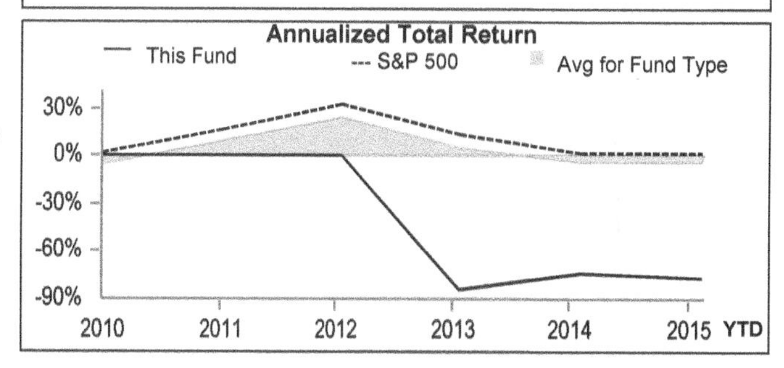

*Direxion NASDAQ-100 Eq Weighted (QQQE) A- Excellent

und Family: Rafferty Asset Management LLC
und Type: Income
nception Date: March 21, 2012

Data Date	Investment Rating	Net Assets ($Mil)	Price	Performance Rating/Pts	Total Return Y-T-D	Risk Rating/Pts
12-15	A-	26.80	64.92	A / 9.3	2.61%	B- / 7.1
2014	B+	26.80	63.68	A- / 9.0	20.84%	B- / 7.0
2013	A+	24.40	54.12	A+ / 9.6	34.56%	B+ / 9.0

ajor Rating Factors:
xceptional performance is the major factor driving the A- (Excellent) TheStreet.com vestment Rating for *Direxion NASDAQ-100 Eq Weighted. The fund currently has a erformance rating of A (Excellent) based on an annualized return of 18.55% over the st three years and a total return of 2.61% year to date 2015. Factored into the erformance evaluation is an expense ratio of 0.35% (very low).

The fund's risk rating is currently B- (Good). It carries a beta of 1.13, meaning it is xpected to move 11.3% for every 10% move in the market. Volatility, as measured both the semi-deviation and a drawdown factor, is considered low. As of ecember 31, 2015, *Direxion NASDAQ-100 Eq Weighted traded at a premium .03% above its net asset value, which is worse than its one-year historical average emium of .01%.

Paul Brigandi has been running the fund for 4 years and currently receives a anager quality ranking of 83 (0=worst, 99=best). If you desire only a moderate level risk and strong performance, then this fund is an excellent option.

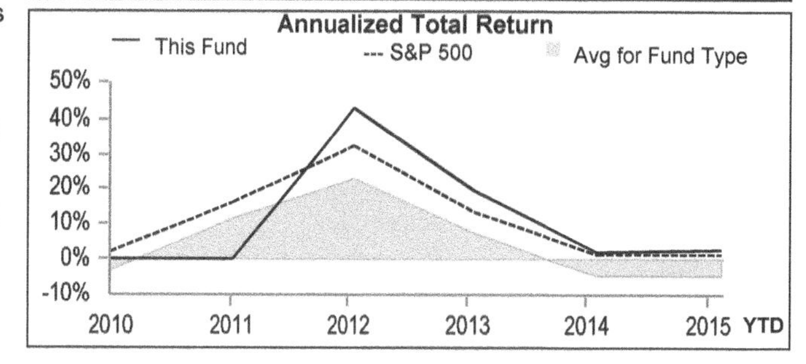

*Direxion S&P 500 Bear 3X Shares (SPXS) E- Very Weak

Fund Family: Rafferty Asset Management LLC
Fund Type: Growth
Inception Date: November 5, 2008

Major Rating Factors: *Direxion S&P 500 Bear 3X Shares has adopted a very risky asset allocation strategy and currently receives an overall TheStreet.com Investment Rating of E- (Very Weak). The fund has a high level of volatility, as measured by both semi-deviation and drawdown factors. It carries a beta of -2.93, meaning the fund's expected move will be -29.3% for every 10% move in the market. As of December 31, 2015, *Direxion S&P 500 Bear 3X Shares traded at a premium of .06% above its net asset value. Unfortunately, the high level of risk (D-, Weak) failed to pay off as investors endured very poor performance.

The fund's performance rating is currently E (Very Weak). It has registered an annualized return of -39.75% over the last three years and is down -18.14% year to date 2015. Factored into the performance evaluation is an expense ratio of 0.95% (low).

Paul Brigandi has been running the fund for 8 years and currently receives a manager quality ranking of 14 (0=worst, 99=best). If you can tolerate very high levels of risk in the hope of improved future returns, holding this fund may be an option.

Data Date	Investment Rating	Net Assets ($Mil)	Price	Performance Rating/Pts	Total Return Y-T-D	Risk Rating/Pts
12-15	E-	250.00	16.92	E / 0.3	-18.14%	D- / 1.4
2014	E	250.00	20.60	E- / 0.1	-39.71%	C- / 3.0
2013	E-	172.30	33.22	E- / 0.1	-55.83%	D+ / 2.8
2012	E-	167.90	16.91	E- / 0.1	-43.62%	D+ / 2.7
2011	E-	155.90	29.53	E- / 0.1	-34.24%	D / 2.1
2010	E-	194.00	8.77	E- / 0	-48.74%	D- / 1.0

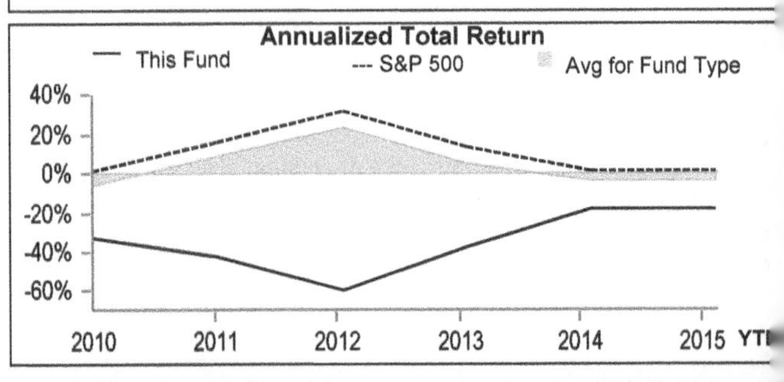

*Direxion S&P 500 Bull 3X Shares (SPXL) C Fair

Fund Family: Rafferty Asset Management LLC
Fund Type: Growth
Inception Date: November 5, 2008

Major Rating Factors: *Direxion S&P 500 Bull 3X Shares has adopted a very risky asset allocation strategy and currently receives an overall TheStreet.com Investment Rating of C (Fair). The fund has shown a high level of volatility, as measured by both semi-deviation and drawdown factors. It carries a beta of 3.10, meaning it is expected to move 31.0% for every 10% move in the market. As of December 31, 2015, *Direxion S&P 500 Bull 3X Shares traded at a discount of .11% below its net asset value, which is better than its one-year historical average discount of .04%. The high level of risk (D, Weak) did however, reward investors with excellent performance.

The fund's performance rating is currently A+ (Excellent). It has registered an annualized return of 37.78% over the last three years but is down -5.43% year to date 2015. Factored into the performance evaluation is an expense ratio of 0.95% (low).

Paul Brigandi has been running the fund for 8 years and currently receives a manager quality ranking of 19 (0=worst, 99=best). If you are comfortable owning a very high risk investment, this fund may be an option.

Data Date	Investment Rating	Net Assets ($Mil)	Price	Performance Rating/Pts	Total Return Y-T-D	Risk Rating/Pts
12-15	C	419.40	82.88	A+ / 9.8	-5.43%	D / 1.8
2014	C-	419.40	87.72	A+ / 9.9	41.78%	D- / 1.0
2013	C-	391.80	63.80	A+ / 9.9	95.24%	D / 1.9
2012	C+	219.20	87.65	A / 9.5	46.04%	C- / 4.1
2011	C-	307.50	60.84	B / 7.7	-13.05%	C- / 4.1
2010	A-	235.20	71.50	A+ / 9.9	39.78%	C / 4.6

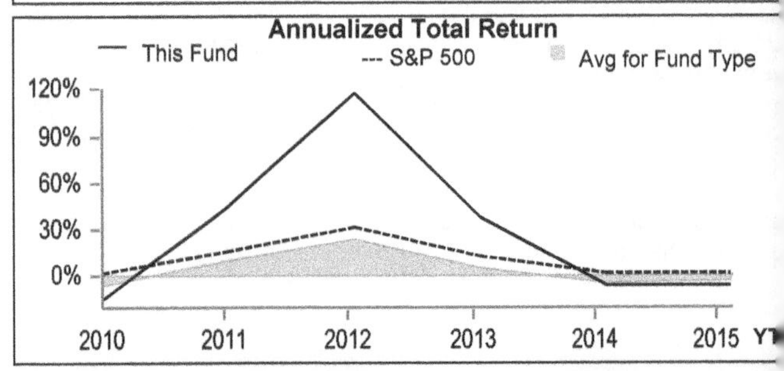

*Direxion S&P 500 Vol Response Sh (VSPY) B Good

Fund Family: Rafferty Asset Management LLC
Fund Type: Growth and Income
Inception Date: January 11, 2012

Major Rating Factors: *Direxion S&P 500 Vol Response Sh receives a TheStreet.com Investment Rating of B (Good). The fund currently has a performance rating of C+ (Fair) based on an annualized return of 9.33% over the last three years and a total return of -6.95% year to date 2015. Factored into the performance evaluation is an expense ratio of 0.47% (very low).

The fund's risk rating is currently B (Good). It carries a beta of 0.90, meaning that its performance tracks fairly well with that of the overall stock market. Volatility, as measured by both the semi-deviation and a drawdown factor, is considered low. As of December 31, 2015, *Direxion S&P 500 Vol Response Sh traded at a discount of .05% below its net asset value, which is better than its one-year historical average premium of .04%.

Paul Brigandi has been running the fund for 4 years and currently receives a manager quality ranking of 39 (0=worst, 99=best). If you desire an average level of risk, then this fund may be an option.

Data Date	Investment Rating	Net Assets ($Mil)	Price	Performance Rating/Pts	Total Return Y-T-D	Risk Rating/Pts
12-15	B	38.60	54.60	C+ / 6.8	-6.95%	B / 8.3
2014	C	38.60	59.46	C / 5.4	10.92%	B- / 7.3
2013	A+	5.30	55.85	A / 9.3	26.60%	B+ / 9.1

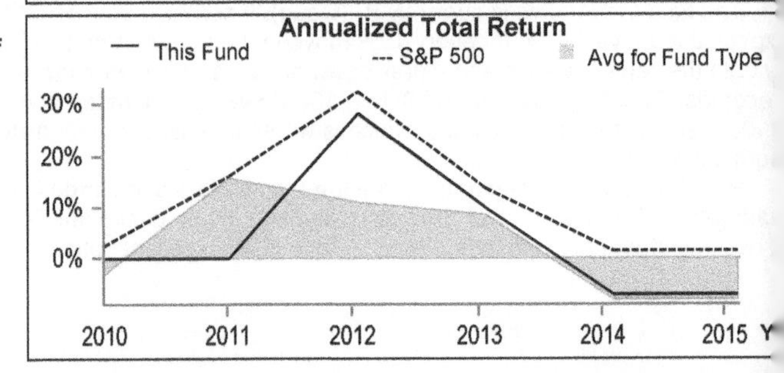

*Direxion South Korea Bull 3X (KORU) E- Very Weak

und Family: Rafferty Asset Management LLC
und Type: Foreign
ıception Date: April 10, 2013

ajor Rating Factors: *Direxion South Korea Bull 3X has adopted a very risky asset location strategy and currently receives an overall TheStreet.com Investment Rating E- (Very Weak). The fund has a high level of volatility, as measured by both semi-eviation and drawdown factors. It carries a beta of 0.00, meaning the fund's xpected move will be 0.0% for every 10% move in the market. As of December 31,)15, *Direxion South Korea Bull 3X traded at a premium of 1.25% above its net sset value, which is worse than its one-year historical average discount of .01%. nfortunately, the high level of risk (E, Very Weak) failed to pay off as investors ndured very poor performance.
The fund's performance rating is currently E (Very Weak). It has registered an nnualized return of 0.00% over the last three years but is down -29.48% year to date)15. Factored into the performance evaluation is an expense ratio of 0.95% (low).
Paul Brigandi has been running the fund for 3 years and currently receives a anager quality ranking of 3 (0=worst, 99=best). If you can tolerate very high levels risk in the hope of improved future returns, holding this fund may be an option.

Data Date	Investment Rating	Net Assets ($Mil)	Price	Performance Rating/Pts	Total Return Y-T-D	Risk Rating/Pts
12-15	E-	2.20	22.74	E / 0.4	-29.48%	E / 0.4
2014	E-	2.20	33.30	E- / 0.1	-30.22%	D- / 1.4

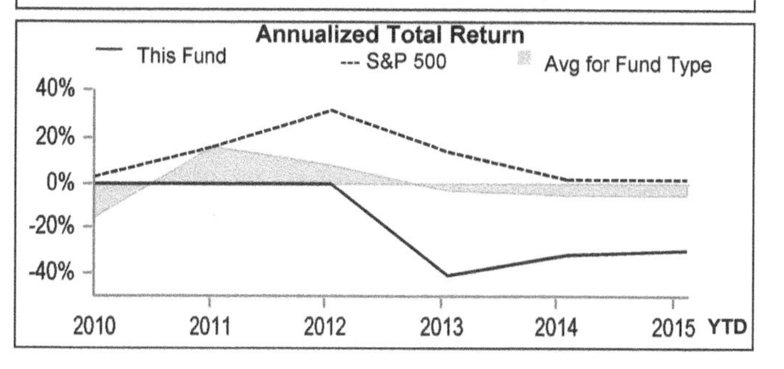

*Direxion Zacks MLP High Inc Shar (ZMLP) E+ Very Weak

und Family: Rafferty Asset Management LLC
und Type: Energy/Natural Resources
ıception Date: January 23, 2014

ajor Rating Factors:
ery poor performance is the major factor driving the E+ (Very Weak) TheStreet.com vestment Rating for *Direxion Zacks MLP High Inc Shar. The fund currently has a erformance rating of E- (Very Weak) based on an annualized return of 0.00% over e last three years and a total return of -43.51% year to date 2015. Factored into the erformance evaluation is an expense ratio of 0.65% (very low).
The fund's risk rating is currently C- (Fair). It carries a beta of 0.00, meaning the nd's expected move will be 0.0% for every 10% move in the market. Volatility, as easured by both the semi-deviation and a drawdown factor, is considered average. s of December 31, 2015, *Direxion Zacks MLP High Inc Shar traded at a discount .34% below its net asset value, which is better than its one-year historical average emium of .13%.
Paul Brigandi has been running the fund for 2 years and currently receives a anager quality ranking of 4 (0=worst, 99=best). This fund offers an average level of sk but investors looking for strong performance will be frustrated.

Data Date	Investment Rating	Net Assets ($Mil)	Price	Performance Rating/Pts	Total Return Y-T-D	Risk Rating/Pts
12-15	E+	48.00	17.39	E- / 0.1	-43.51%	C- / 3.6

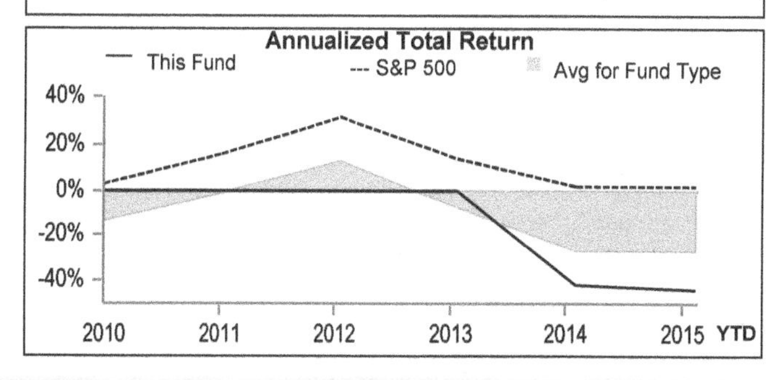

*EGShares Beyond BRICs ETF (BBRC) D Weak

und Family: Emerging Global Advisors LLC
und Type: Foreign
ıception Date: August 15, 2012

ajor Rating Factors:
sappointing performance is the major factor driving the D (Weak) TheStreet.com vestment Rating for *EGShares Beyond BRICs ETF. The fund currently has a erformance rating of D- (Weak) based on an annualized return of -10.84% over the st three years and a total return of -22.60% year to date 2015. Factored into the erformance evaluation is an expense ratio of 0.58% (very low).
The fund's risk rating is currently C+ (Fair). It carries a beta of 0.76, meaning the nd's expected move will be 7.6% for every 10% move in the market. Volatility, as easured by both the semi-deviation and a drawdown factor, is considered low. As of ecember 31, 2015, *EGShares Beyond BRICs ETF traded at a discount of 1.36% low its net asset value, which is better than its one-year historical average discount .32%.
Robert C. Holderith has been running the fund for 2 years and currently receives manager quality ranking of 11 (0=worst, 99=best). This fund offers only a moderate vel of risk but investors looking for strong performance are still waiting.

Data Date	Investment Rating	Net Assets ($Mil)	Price	Performance Rating/Pts	Total Return Y-T-D	Risk Rating/Pts
12-15	D	286.30	14.50	D- / 1.5	-22.60%	C+ / 6.4
2014	D	286.30	19.77	D- / 1.5	-0.52%	C+ / 6.2
2013	D+	22.40	20.57	D / 1.7	-7.12%	B / 8.2

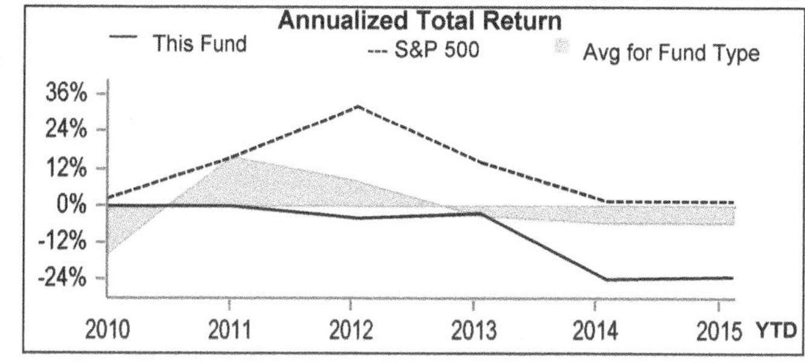

*EGShares EM Quality Dividend (HILO) D Weak

Fund Family: Emerging Global Advisors LLC
Fund Type: Growth and Income
Inception Date: August 4, 2011

Major Rating Factors:
Disappointing performance is the major factor driving the D (Weak) TheStreet.com Investment Rating for *EGShares EM Quality Dividend. The fund currently has a performance rating of D- (Weak) based on an annualized return of -14.59% over the last three years and a total return of -18.52% year to date 2015. Factored into the performance evaluation is an expense ratio of 0.89% (low).

The fund's risk rating is currently C+ (Fair). It carries a beta of 1.01, meaning that its performance tracks fairly well with that of the overall stock market. Volatility, as measured by both the semi-deviation and a drawdown factor, is considered low. As of December 31, 2015, *EGShares EM Quality Dividend traded at a discount of 1.21% below its net asset value, which is better than its one-year historical average discount of .51%.

Robert C. Holderith has been running the fund for 2 years and currently receives a manager quality ranking of 4 (0=worst, 99=best). This fund offers only a moderate level of risk but investors looking for strong performance are still waiting.

Data Date	Investment Rating	Net Assets ($Mil)	Price	Performance Rating/Pts	Total Return Y-T-D	Risk Rating/Pts
12-15	D	45.50	11.47	D- / 1.2	-18.52%	C+ / 5.8
2014	D	45.50	14.46	D / 1.8	-10.49%	C+ / 6.5
2013	D	85.80	17.45	E+ / 0.8	-14.05%	B- / 7.5
2012	B+	81.90	20.29	B / 8.2	13.68%	B- / 7.8

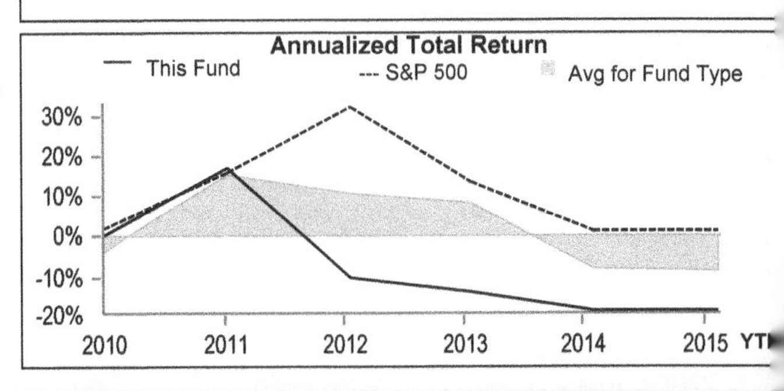

*EGShares Emer Mrkts Dom Demand E (EMDD) D+ Weak

Fund Family: Emerging Global Advisors LLC
Fund Type: Foreign
Inception Date: August 15, 2012

Major Rating Factors:
Disappointing performance is the major factor driving the D+ (Weak) TheStreet.com Investment Rating for *EGShares Emer Mrkts Dom Demand E. The fund currently has a performance rating of D (Weak) based on an annualized return of -5.69% over the last three years and a total return of -17.76% year to date 2015. Factored into the performance evaluation is an expense ratio of 0.85% (very low).

The fund's risk rating is currently C+ (Fair). It carries a beta of 0.95, meaning that its performance tracks fairly well with that of the overall stock market. Volatility, as measured by both the semi-deviation and a drawdown factor, is considered low. As of December 31, 2015, *EGShares Emer Mrkts Dom Demand E traded at a discount of 1.12% below its net asset value, which is better than its one-year historical average premium of .01%.

Robert C. Holderith has been running the fund for 2 years and currently receives a manager quality ranking of 16 (0=worst, 99=best). This fund offers only a moderate level of risk but investors looking for strong performance are still waiting.

Data Date	Investment Rating	Net Assets ($Mil)	Price	Performance Rating/Pts	Total Return Y-T-D	Risk Rating/Pts
12-15	D+	27.50	17.73	D / 2.1	-17.76%	C+ / 6.8
2014	D+	27.50	22.60	D+ / 2.6	3.76%	C+ / 6.4
2013	C-	2.10	22.44	D+ / 2.7	-0.12%	B / 8.6

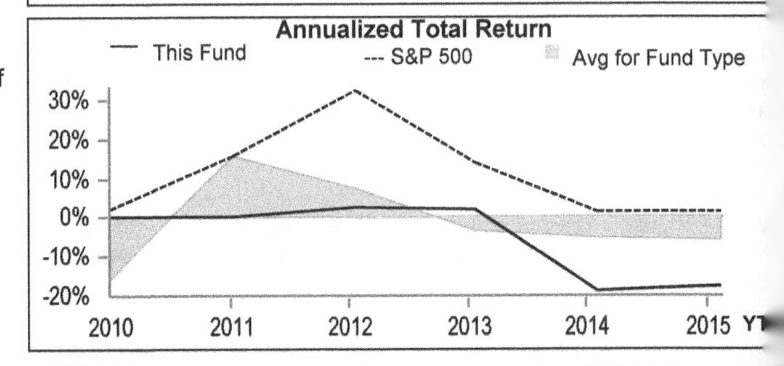

*EGShares Emerging Markets Cons E (ECON) D+ Weak

Fund Family: Emerging Global Advisors LLC
Fund Type: Emerging Market
Inception Date: September 14, 2010

Major Rating Factors:
Disappointing performance is the major factor driving the D+ (Weak) TheStreet.com Investment Rating for *EGShares Emerging Markets Cons E. The fund currently has a performance rating of D (Weak) based on an annualized return of -6.69% over the last three years and a total return of -13.80% year to date 2015. Factored into the performance evaluation is an expense ratio of 0.83% (very low).

The fund's risk rating is currently B- (Good). It carries a beta of 0.92, meaning that its performance tracks fairly well with that of the overall stock market. Volatility, as measured by both the semi-deviation and a drawdown factor, is considered low. As of December 31, 2015, *EGShares Emerging Markets Cons E traded at a discount of .75% below its net asset value, which is better than its one-year historical average discount of .09%.

Robert C. Holderith has been running the fund for 2 years and currently receives a manager quality ranking of 64 (0=worst, 99=best). This fund offers only a moderate level of risk but investors looking for strong performance are still waiting.

Data Date	Investment Rating	Net Assets ($Mil)	Price	Performance Rating/Pts	Total Return Y-T-D	Risk Rating/Pts
12-15	D+	1,266.80	21.26	D / 2.1	-13.80%	B- / 7.1
2014	D+	1,266.80	25.34	C- / 3.8	-0.91%	C+ / 6.3
2013	C-	1,292.50	26.88	C- / 3.8	-3.33%	B- / 7.8
2012	B+	476.60	26.64	A- / 9.0	19.39%	B- / 7.6
2011	D	293.90	21.98	D- / 1.5	-3.23%	B- / 7.7

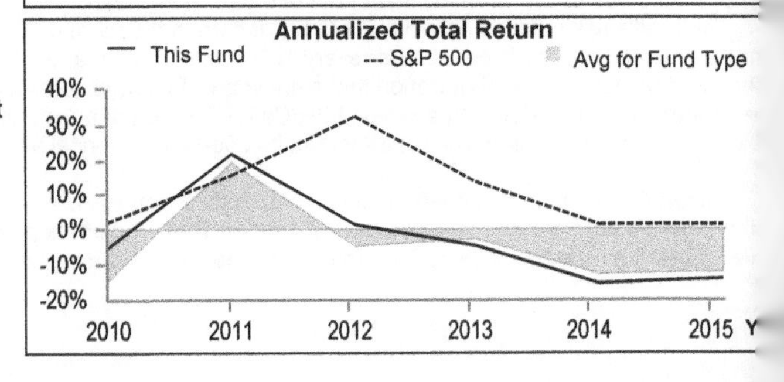

*EGShares Emerging Markets Core E (EMCR) D+ Weak

Fund Family: Emerging Global Advisors LLC
Fund Type: Emerging Market
Inception Date: October 16, 2012

Major Rating Factors:
Disappointing performance is the major factor driving the D+ (Weak) TheStreet.com Investment Rating for *EGShares Emerging Markets Core E. The fund currently has a performance rating of D (Weak) based on an annualized return of -7.80% over the last three years and a total return of -19.52% year to date 2015. Factored into the performance evaluation is an expense ratio of 0.71% (very low).

The fund's risk rating is currently B- (Good). It carries a beta of 0.90, meaning that its performance tracks fairly well with that of the overall stock market. Volatility, as measured by both the semi-deviation and a drawdown factor, is considered low. As of December 31, 2015, *EGShares Emerging Markets Core E traded at a discount of 1.28% below its net asset value, which is better than its one-year historical average premium of .20%.

Richard C. Kang has been running the fund for 4 years and currently receives a manager quality ranking of 60 (0=worst, 99=best). This fund offers only a moderate level of risk but investors looking for strong performance are still waiting.

Data Date	Investment Rating	Net Assets ($Mil)	Price	Performance Rating/Pts	Total Return Y-T-D	Risk Rating/Pts
12-15	D+	4.30	16.20	D / 1.9	-19.52%	B- / 7.0
2014	D	4.30	20.13	D+ / 2.3	2.58%	C+ / 6.5
2013	D+	4.10	20.56	D / 2.0	-5.09%	B / 8.6

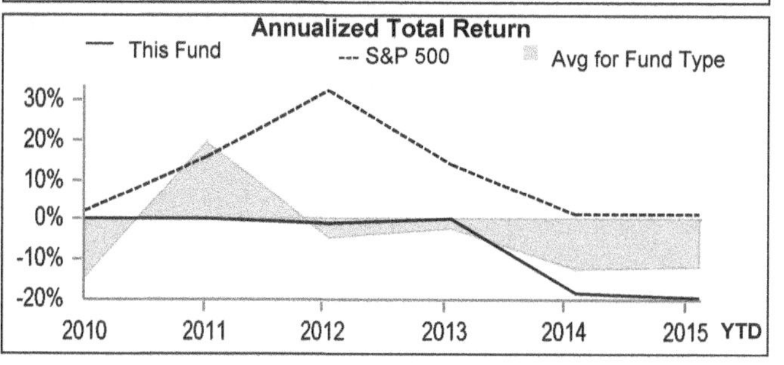

*EGShares India Consumer ETF (INCO) C+ Fair

Fund Family: Emerging Global Advisors LLC
Fund Type: Growth and Income
Inception Date: August 10, 2011

Major Rating Factors: Middle of the road best describes *EGShares India Consumer ETF whose TheStreet.com Investment Rating is currently a C+ (Fair). The fund currently has a performance rating of C+ (Fair) based on an annualized return of 9.08% over the last three years and a total return of -1.95% year to date 2015. Factored into the performance evaluation is an expense ratio of 0.90% (low).

The fund's risk rating is currently C+ (Fair). It carries a beta of 0.96, meaning that its performance tracks fairly well with that of the overall stock market. Volatility, as measured by both the semi-deviation and a drawdown factor, is considered low. As of December 31, 2015, *EGShares India Consumer ETF traded at a discount of 1.08% below its net asset value, which is better than its one-year historical average premium of .19%.

Robert C. Holderith has been running the fund for 2 years and currently receives a manager quality ranking of 36 (0=worst, 99=best). If you desire an average level of risk, then this fund may be an option.

Data Date	Investment Rating	Net Assets ($Mil)	Price	Performance Rating/Pts	Total Return Y-T-D	Risk Rating/Pts
12-15	C+	9.20	32.11	C+ / 6.9	-1.95%	C+ / 6.8
2014	A-	9.20	32.30	A / 9.5	47.14%	C+ / 6.7
2013	D	4.50	22.33	D- / 1.5	-11.27%	C+ / 6.3
2012	B+	2.40	24.32	A+ / 9.9	44.13%	C+ / 6.7

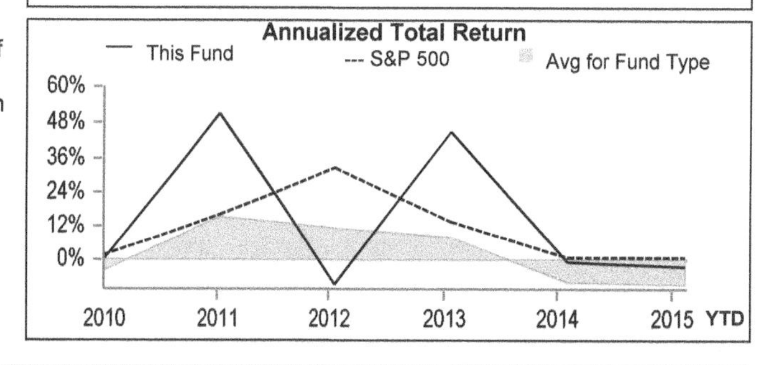

*EGShares India Infrastructure ET (INXX) D Weak

Fund Family: Emerging Global Advisors LLC
Fund Type: Foreign
Inception Date: August 11, 2010

Major Rating Factors:
Disappointing performance is the major factor driving the D (Weak) TheStreet.com Investment Rating for *EGShares India Infrastructure ET. The fund currently has a performance rating of D (Weak) based on an annualized return of -6.91% over the last three years and a total return of -17.50% year to date 2015. Factored into the performance evaluation is an expense ratio of 0.88% (low).

The fund's risk rating is currently C (Fair). It carries a beta of 1.18, meaning it is expected to move 11.8% for every 10% move in the market. Volatility, as measured by both the semi-deviation and a drawdown factor, is considered average. As of December 31, 2015, *EGShares India Infrastructure ET traded at a discount of 1.22% below its net asset value, which is better than its one-year historical average discount of .08%.

Robert C. Holderith has been running the fund for 2 years and currently receives a manager quality ranking of 14 (0=worst, 99=best). This fund offers an average level of risk but investors looking for strong performance will be frustrated.

Data Date	Investment Rating	Net Assets ($Mil)	Price	Performance Rating/Pts	Total Return Y-T-D	Risk Rating/Pts
12-15	D	50.00	10.56	D / 2.1	-17.50%	C / 5.5
2014	D+	50.00	12.66	C / 4.5	24.61%	C / 4.8
2013	E+	16.50	10.64	E+ / 0.7	-23.64%	C- / 4.2
2012	C-	58.00	14.57	C+ / 6.4	12.92%	C / 4.7
2011	E+	48.60	11.60	E- / 0.1	-39.11%	C / 4.8

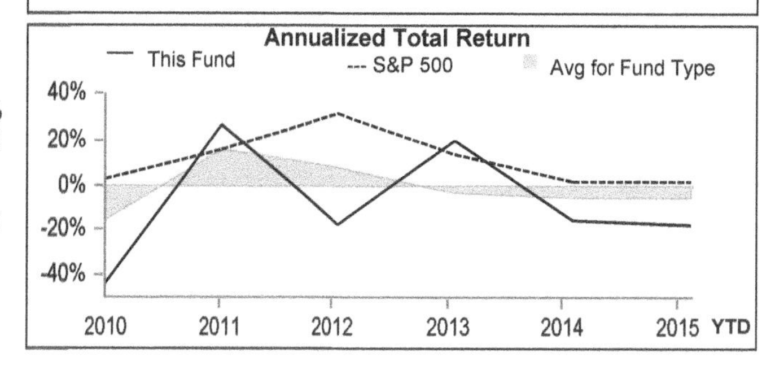

*EGShares India Small Cap ETF (SCIN) C- Fair

Fund Family: Emerging Global Advisors LLC
Fund Type: Foreign
Inception Date: July 7, 2010

Major Rating Factors: Middle of the road best describes *EGShares India Small Cap ETF whose TheStreet.com Investment Rating is currently a C- (Fair). The fund currently has a performance rating of C (Fair) based on an annualized return of 1.73% over the last three years and a total return of -9.23% year to date 2015. Factored into the performance evaluation is an expense ratio of 0.92% (low).

The fund's risk rating is currently C (Fair). It carries a beta of 1.15, meaning it is expected to move 11.5% for every 10% move in the market. Volatility, as measured by both the semi-deviation and a drawdown factor, is considered average. As of December 31, 2015, *EGShares India Small Cap ETF traded at a discount of .19% below its net asset value, which is better than its one-year historical average discount of .14%.

Robert C. Holderith has been running the fund for 2 years and currently receives a manager quality ranking of 42 (0=worst, 99=best). If you desire an average level of risk, then this fund may be an option.

Data Date	Investment Rating	Net Assets ($Mil)	Price	Performance Rating/Pts	Total Return Y-T-D	Risk Rating/Pts
12-15	C-	27.10	15.69	C / 4.7	-9.23%	C / 5.2
2014	C+	27.10	17.00	B+ / 8.7	50.99%	C / 4.7
2013	E+	20.40	11.65	E+ / 0.7	-24.93%	C- / 3.7
2012	C-	24.90	14.84	B / 7.8	16.78%	C- / 4.1
2011	E	17.00	11.18	E- / 0	-43.15%	C- / 4.1

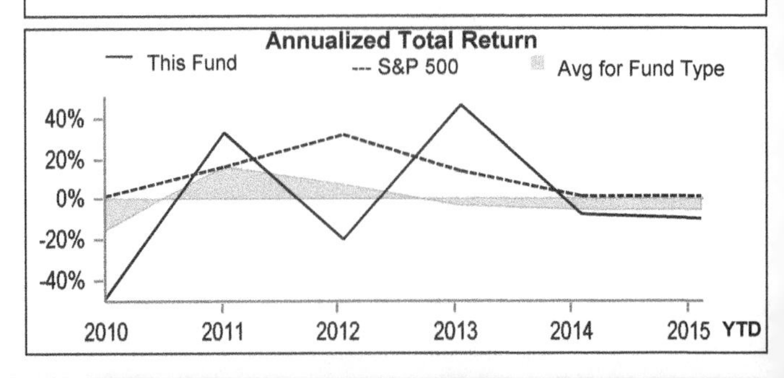

*ELEMENTS MLCX Biofuels Tot Ret (FUE) E+ Very Weak

Fund Family: Swedish Export Credit Corporation
Fund Type: Energy/Natural Resources
Inception Date: February 5, 2008

Major Rating Factors: *ELEMENTS MLCX Biofuels Tot Ret has adopted a risky asset allocation strategy and currently receives an overall TheStreet.com Investment Rating of E+ (Very Weak). The fund has an above average level of volatility, as measured by both semi-deviation and drawdown factors. It carries a beta of -0.02, meaning the fund's expected move will be -0.2% for every 10% move in the market. As of December 31, 2015, *ELEMENTS MLCX Biofuels Tot Ret traded at a price exactly equal to its net asset value, which is better than its one-year historical average premium of .89%. Unfortunately, the high level of risk (D+, Weak) failed to pay off as investors endured poor performance.

The fund's performance rating is currently D (Weak). It has registered an annualized return of -12.33% over the last three years and is down -14.48% year to date 2015. Factored into the performance evaluation is an expense ratio of 0.75% (very low).

This fund has been team managed for 8 years and currently receives a manager quality ranking of 13 (0=worst, 99=best). If you can tolerate high levels of risk in the hope of improved future returns, holding this fund may be an option.

Data Date	Investment Rating	Net Assets ($Mil)	Price	Performance Rating/Pts	Total Return Y-T-D	Risk Rating/Pts
12-15	E+	1.86	7.50	D / 1.6	-14.48%	D+ / 2.4
2014	D-	0.90	8.77	D / 1.8	-12.48%	C- / 3.8
2013	E+	1.86	9.69	D / 1.7	-9.97%	C- / 4.1
2012	D-	1.86	11.20	C- / 3.0	6.15%	C / 4.5
2011	D	2.40	10.80	C- / 3.9	-7.24%	C / 4.6
2010	C+	2.50	11.35	A+ / 9.7	27.82%	D+ / 2.6

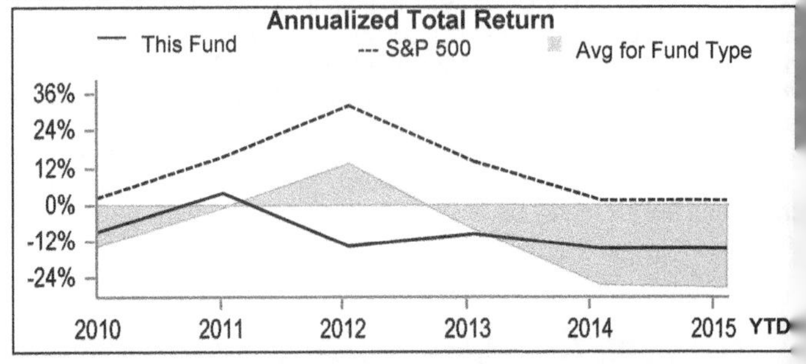

*ELEMENTS MLCX Grains Idx Tot Ret (GRU) E Very Weak

Fund Family: Swedish Export Credit Corporation
Fund Type: Energy/Natural Resources
Inception Date: February 5, 2008

Major Rating Factors: *ELEMENTS MLCX Grains Idx Tot Ret has adopted a very risky asset allocation strategy and currently receives an overall TheStreet.com Investment Rating of E (Very Weak). The fund has a high level of volatility, as measured by both semi-deviation and drawdown factors. It carries a beta of 0.24, meaning the fund's expected move will be 2.4% for every 10% move in the market. As of December 31, 2015, *ELEMENTS MLCX Grains Idx Tot Ret traded at a price exactly equal to its net asset value, which is better than its one-year historical average premium of .06%. Unfortunately, the high level of risk (D, Weak) failed to pay off as investors endured poor performance.

The fund's performance rating is currently D- (Weak). It has registered an annualized return of -16.14% over the last three years and is down -20.16% year to date 2015. Factored into the performance evaluation is an expense ratio of 0.75% (very low).

This fund has been team managed for 8 years and currently receives a manager quality ranking of 10 (0=worst, 99=best). If you can tolerate very high levels of risk in the hope of improved future returns, holding this fund may be an option.

Data Date	Investment Rating	Net Assets ($Mil)	Price	Performance Rating/Pts	Total Return Y-T-D	Risk Rating/Pts
12-15	E	15.58	4.10	D- / 1.1	-20.16%	D / 2.2
2014	E+	7.30	5.20	D / 2.0	-9.86%	C- / 3.2
2013	E+	15.58	5.78	D- / 1.2	-17.10%	C- / 4.0
2012	D-	15.58	7.17	C- / 3.2	20.82%	C / 4.5
2011	E+	17.90	6.25	D / 1.6	-12.86%	C- / 4.0
2010	C+	18.50	7.24	A+ / 9.7	27.24%	D / 2.2

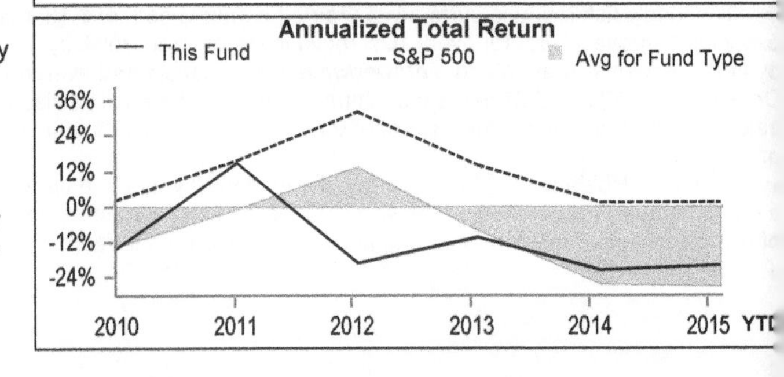

* Denotes ETF Fund

*ELEMENTS RIC Energy Total Return (RJN) E- Very Weak

Fund Family: Swedish Export Credit Corporation
Fund Type: Energy/Natural Resources
Inception Date: October 17, 2007

Major Rating Factors: *ELEMENTS RIC Energy Total Return has adopted a very risky asset allocation strategy and currently receives an overall TheStreet.com Investment Rating of E- (Very Weak). The fund has a high level of volatility, as measured by both semi-deviation and drawdown factors. It carries a beta of 0.92, meaning that its performance tracks fairly well with that of the overall stock market. As of December 31, 2015, *ELEMENTS RIC Energy Total Return traded at a price exactly equal to its net asset value, which is better than its one-year historical average premium of .02%. Unfortunately, the high level of risk (E+, Very Weak) failed to pay off as investors endured very poor performance.

The fund's performance rating is currently E (Very Weak). It has registered an annualized return of -29.18% over the last three years and is down -40.41% year to date 2015. Factored into the performance evaluation is an expense ratio of 0.75% (very low).

This fund has been team managed for 9 years and currently receives a manager quality ranking of 4 (0=worst, 99=best). If you can tolerate very high levels of risk in the hope of improved future returns, holding this fund may be an option.

Data Date	Investment Rating	Net Assets ($Mil)	Price	Performance Rating/Pts	Total Return Y-T-D	Risk Rating/Pts
12-15	E-	53.46	2.33	E / 0.3	-40.41%	E+ / 0.9
2014	E	33.70	3.99	E / 0.5	-40.36%	D+ / 2.9
2013	D-	53.46	6.95	D+ / 2.7	1.98%	C / 4.3
2012	E+	53.46	6.54	D / 1.7	-2.80%	C / 4.3
2011	D	75.90	6.72	C / 4.5	9.42%	C / 4.4
2010	E-	56.60	6.38	E+ / 0.7	0.00%	D- / 1.3

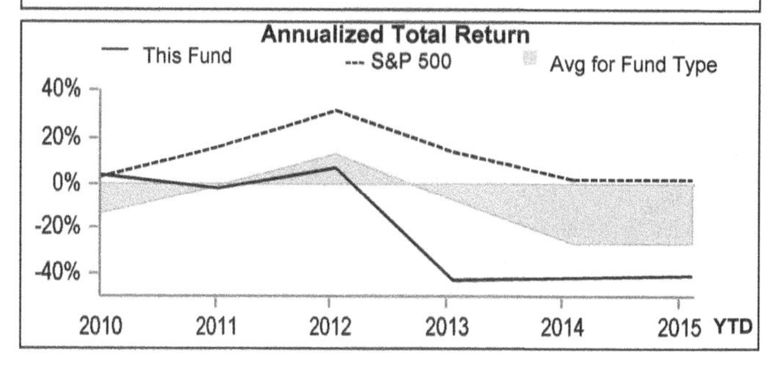

*ELEMENTS RIC Index Agri Total Re (RJA) E+ Very Weak

Fund Family: Swedish Export Credit Corporation
Fund Type: Energy/Natural Resources
Inception Date: October 17, 2007

Major Rating Factors:
Disappointing performance is the major factor driving the E+ (Very Weak) TheStreet.com Investment Rating for *ELEMENTS RIC Index Agri Total Re. The fund currently has a performance rating of D (Weak) based on an annualized return of -11.21% over the last three years and a total return of -14.25% year to date 2015. Factored into the performance evaluation is an expense ratio of 0.75% (very low).

The fund's risk rating is currently C- (Fair). It carries a beta of 0.25, meaning the fund's expected move will be 2.5% for every 10% move in the market. Volatility, as measured by both the semi-deviation and a drawdown factor, is considered average. As of December 31, 2015, *ELEMENTS RIC Index Agri Total Re traded at a price exactly equal to its net asset value, which is worse than its one-year historical average discount of .05%.

This fund has been team managed for 9 years and currently receives a manager quality ranking of 15 (0=worst, 99=best). This fund offers an average level of risk but investors looking for strong performance will be frustrated.

Data Date	Investment Rating	Net Assets ($Mil)	Price	Performance Rating/Pts	Total Return Y-T-D	Risk Rating/Pts
12-15	E+	302.91	6.25	D / 1.6	-14.25%	C- / 3.0
2014	D-	178.20	7.37	D / 1.8	-7.06%	C / 5.0
2013	E+	302.91	7.97	D- / 1.2	-11.20%	C- / 4.0
2012	D-	302.91	9.06	D+ / 2.3	2.84%	C- / 4.1
2011	D-	420.40	8.95	D / 2.1	-14.91%	C / 4.5
2010	C-	408.50	10.67	C+ / 6.8	34.05%	D+ / 2.6

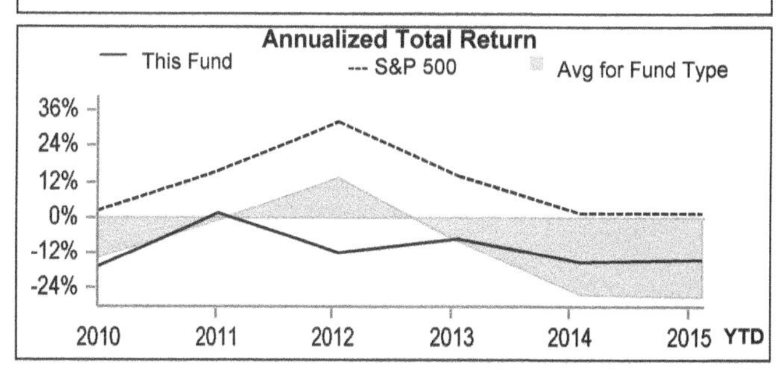

*ELEMENTS RIC Index Total Return (RJI) E Very Weak

Fund Family: Swedish Export Credit Corporation
Fund Type: Energy/Natural Resources
Inception Date: October 17, 2007

Major Rating Factors: *ELEMENTS RIC Index Total Return has adopted a very risky asset allocation strategy and currently receives an overall TheStreet.com Investment Rating of E (Very Weak). The fund has a high level of volatility, as measured by both semi-deviation and drawdown factors. It carries a beta of 0.54, meaning the fund's expected move will be 5.4% for every 10% move in the market. As of December 31, 2015, *ELEMENTS RIC Index Total Return traded at a price exactly equal to its net asset value, which is worse than its one-year historical average discount of .01%. Unfortunately, the high level of risk (D, Weak) failed to pay off as investors endured very poor performance.

The fund's performance rating is currently E+ (Very Weak). It has registered an annualized return of -18.68% over the last three years and is down -26.04% year to date 2015. Factored into the performance evaluation is an expense ratio of 0.75% (very low).

This fund has been team managed for 9 years and currently receives a manager quality ranking of 9 (0=worst, 99=best). If you can tolerate very high levels of risk in the hope of improved future returns, holding this fund may be an option.

Data Date	Investment Rating	Net Assets ($Mil)	Price	Performance Rating/Pts	Total Return Y-T-D	Risk Rating/Pts
12-15	E	510.91	4.63	E+ / 0.8	-26.04%	D / 2.1
2014	D-	836.60	6.31	D- / 1.0	-21.32%	C / 4.7
2013	D-	510.91	8.17	D / 1.7	-6.85%	C / 4.4
2012	D-	510.91	8.62	D / 2.1	0.81%	C / 4.4
2011	D	666.30	8.51	C- / 3.8	-4.20%	C / 4.6
2010	E+	566.30	9.16	D+ / 2.5	16.24%	D / 2.1

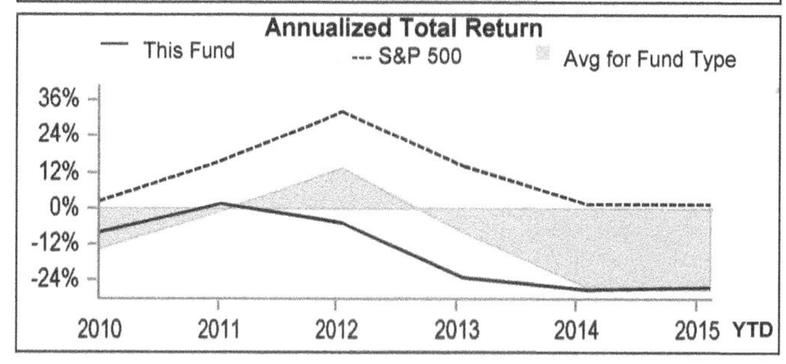

*ELEMENTS RIC Metals Total Return (RJZ) E+ Very Weak

Fund Family: Swedish Export Credit Corporation
Fund Type: Energy/Natural Resources
Inception Date: October 17, 2007

Data Date	Investment Rating	Net Assets ($Mil)	Price	Perfor-mance Rating/Pts	Total Return Y-T-D	Risk Rating/Pts
12-15	E+	57.91	6.49	D- / 1.2	-18.81%	D+ / 2.4
2014	D	16.10	7.95	D- / 1.4	-10.02%	C+ / 6.6
2013	E+	57.91	8.83	D- / 1.1	-17.74%	C- / 3.8
2012	D-	57.91	10.73	D / 1.9	0.84%	C / 4.3
2011	D+	46.30	10.15	C / 4.8	-14.65%	C / 4.6
2010	C	57.20	12.25	B / 8.1	23.36%	D+ / 2.5

Major Rating Factors: *ELEMENTS RIC Metals Total Return has adopted a risky asset allocation strategy and currently receives an overall TheStreet.com Investment Rating of E+ (Very Weak). The fund has an above average level of volatility, as measured by both semi-deviation and drawdown factors. It carries a beta of 0.31, meaning the fund's expected move will be 3.1% for every 10% move in the market. As of December 31, 2015, *ELEMENTS RIC Metals Total Return traded at a price exactly equal to its net asset value, which is worse than its one-year historical average discount of .10%. Unfortunately, the high level of risk (D+, Weak) failed to pay off as investors endured poor performance.

The fund's performance rating is currently D- (Weak). It has registered an annualized return of -15.47% over the last three years and is down -18.81% year to date 2015. Factored into the performance evaluation is an expense ratio of 0.75% (very low).

This fund has been team managed for 9 years and currently receives a manager quality ranking of 11 (0=worst, 99=best). If you can tolerate high levels of risk in the hope of improved future returns, holding this fund may be an option.

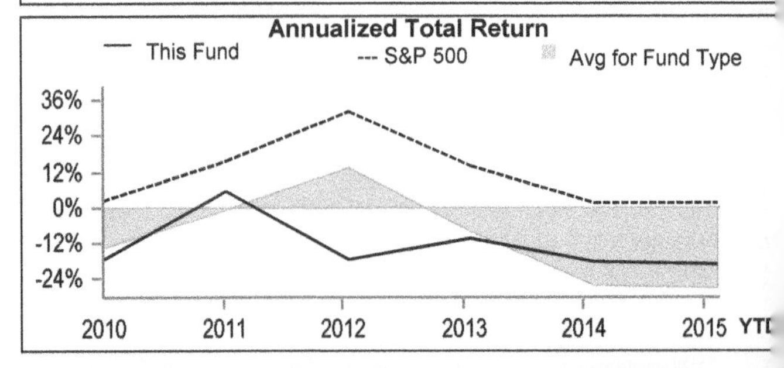

*EMQQ The EM Intrt Ecom ETF (EMQQ) C Fair

Fund Family: Exchange Traded Concepts LLC
Fund Type: Emerging Market
Inception Date: November 12, 2014

Data Date	Investment Rating	Net Assets ($Mil)	Price	Perfor-mance Rating/Pts	Total Return Y-T-D	Risk Rating/Pts
12-15	C	0.00	23.78	C+ / 6.6	2.94%	C / 5.3

Major Rating Factors: Middle of the road best describes *EMQQ The EM Intrt Ecom ETF whose TheStreet.com Investment Rating is currently a C (Fair). The fund currently has a performance rating of C+ (Fair) based on an annualized return of 0.00% over the last three years and a total return of 2.94% year to date 2015. Factored into the performance evaluation is an expense ratio of 0.86% (very low).

The fund's risk rating is currently C (Fair). It carries a beta of 0.00, meaning the fund's expected move will be 0.0% for every 10% move in the market. Volatility, as measured by both the semi-deviation and a drawdown factor, is considered average. As of December 31, 2015, *EMQQ The EM Intrt Ecom ETF traded at a discount of .17% below its net asset value, which is better than its one-year historical average premium of .27%.

James G. Stevens currently receives a manager quality ranking of 99 (0=worst, 99=best). If you desire an average level of risk, then this fund may be an option.

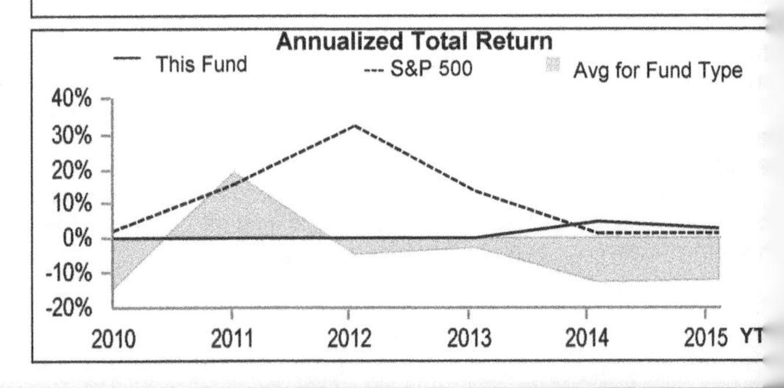

*Energy Select Sector SPDR (XLE) D+ Weak

Fund Family: SSgA Funds Management Inc
Fund Type: Energy/Natural Resources
Inception Date: December 16, 1998

Data Date	Investment Rating	Net Assets ($Mil)	Price	Perfor-mance Rating/Pts	Total Return Y-T-D	Risk Rating/Pts
12-15	D+	10,242.10	60.32	D+ / 2.4	-21.14%	C+ / 6.0
2014	C-	10,242.10	79.16	C- / 3.2	-7.03%	B- / 7.8
2013	C+	8,004.10	88.51	B- / 7.0	20.01%	B- / 7.5
2012	C-	6,770.20	71.42	C- / 3.8	7.99%	B- / 7.3
2011	C	6,717.60	69.13	C / 5.3	4.75%	B- / 7.1
2010	C	8,385.10	68.25	C / 5.1	21.81%	C+ / 5.6

Major Rating Factors:
Disappointing performance is the major factor driving the D+ (Weak) TheStreet.com Investment Rating for *Energy Select Sector SPDR. The fund currently has a performance rating of D+ (Weak) based on an annualized return of -4.03% over the last three years and a total return of -21.14% year to date 2015. Factored into the performance evaluation is an expense ratio of 0.15% (very low).

The fund's risk rating is currently C+ (Fair). It carries a beta of 0.97, meaning that its performance tracks fairly well with that of the overall stock market. Volatility, as measured by both the semi-deviation and a drawdown factor, is considered low. As of December 31, 2015, *Energy Select Sector SPDR traded at a price exactly equal to its net asset value.

John A. Tucker has been running the fund for 18 years and currently receives a manager quality ranking of 74 (0=worst, 99=best). This fund offers only a moderate level of risk but investors looking for strong performance are still waiting.

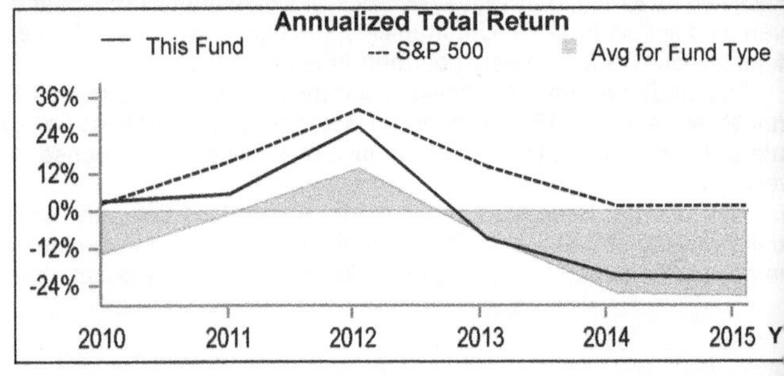

*ETFis BioShares Biotech Clinical (BBC) D- Weak

Fund Family: Etfis Capital LLC
Fund Type: Health
Inception Date: December 17, 2014

Data Date	Investment Rating	Net Assets ($Mil)	Price	Performance Rating/Pts	Total Return Y-T-D	Risk Rating/Pts
12-15	D-	0.00	29.05	D+ / 2.8	2.29%	D+ / 2.6

Major Rating Factors: *ETFis BioShares Biotech Clinical has adopted a risky asset allocation strategy and currently receives an overall TheStreet.com Investment Rating of D- (Weak). The fund has an above average level of volatility, as measured by both semi-deviation and drawdown factors. It carries a beta of 0.00, meaning the fund's expected move will be 0.0% for every 10% move in the market. As of December 31, 2015, *ETFis BioShares Biotech Clinical traded at a premium of .07% above its net asset value, which is worse than its one-year historical average discount of .01%. Unfortunately, the high level of risk (D+, Weak) failed to pay off as investors endured poor performance.

The fund's performance rating is currently D+ (Weak). It has registered an annualized return of 0.00% over the last three years and is up 2.29% year to date 2015.

Andrew McDonald has been running the fund for 2 years and currently receives a manager quality ranking of 84 (0=worst, 99=best). If you can tolerate high levels of risk in the hope of improved future returns, holding this fund may be an option.

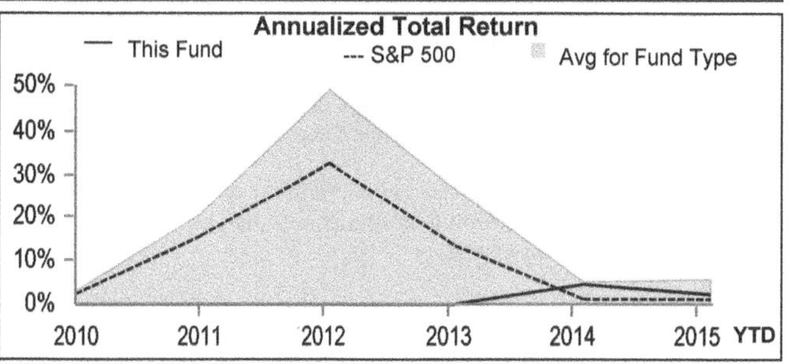

*ETFis BioShares Biotech Products (BBP) C- Fair

Fund Family: Etfis Capital LLC
Fund Type: Health
Inception Date: December 17, 2014

Data Date	Investment Rating	Net Assets ($Mil)	Price	Performance Rating/Pts	Total Return Y-T-D	Risk Rating/Pts
12-15	C-	0.00	30.82	B- / 7.5	16.39%	D+ / 2.8

Major Rating Factors: *ETFis BioShares Biotech Products has adopted a risky asset allocation strategy and currently receives an overall TheStreet.com Investment Rating of C- (Fair). The fund has shown an above average level of volatility, as measured by both semi-deviation and drawdown factors. It carries a beta of 0.00, meaning the fund's expected move will be 0.0% for every 10% move in the market. As of December 31, 2015, *ETFis BioShares Biotech Products traded at a premium of .13% above its net asset value, which is worse than its one-year historical average premium of .06%. The high level of risk (D+, Weak) did however, reward investors with excellent performance.

The fund's performance rating is currently B- (Good). It has registered an annualized return of 0.00% over the last three years and is up 16.39% year to date 2015.

Andrew McDonald has been running the fund for 2 years and currently receives a manager quality ranking of 97 (0=worst, 99=best). If you are comfortable owning a high risk investment, this fund may be an option.

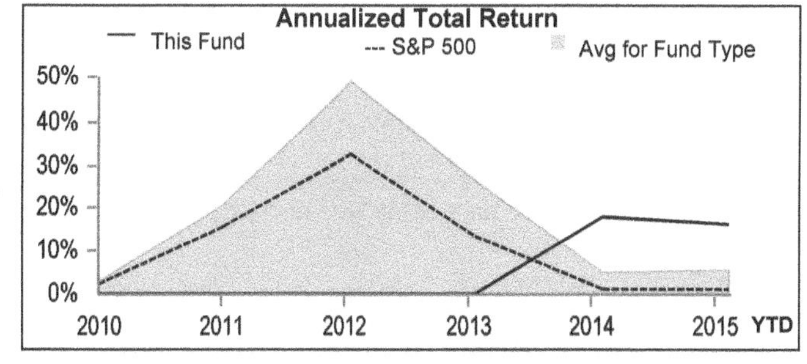

*ETFis InfraCap MLP (AMZA) E Very Weak

Fund Family: Etfis Capital LLC
Fund Type: Energy/Natural Resources
Inception Date: October 1, 2014

Data Date	Investment Rating	Net Assets ($Mil)	Price	Performance Rating/Pts	Total Return Y-T-D	Risk Rating/Pts
12-15	E	0.00	11.15	E- / 0	-47.04%	D+ / 2.8

Major Rating Factors: *ETFis InfraCap MLP has adopted a risky asset allocation strategy and currently receives an overall TheStreet.com Investment Rating of E (Very Weak). The fund has an above average level of volatility, as measured by both semi-deviation and drawdown factors. It carries a beta of 0.00, meaning the fund's expected move will be 0.0% for every 10% move in the market. As of December 31, 2015, *ETFis InfraCap MLP traded at a price exactly equal to its net asset value, which is better than its one-year historical average premium of .25%. Unfortunately, the high level of risk (D+, Weak) failed to pay off as investors endured very poor performance.

The fund's performance rating is currently E- (Very Weak). It has registered an annualized return of 0.00% over the last three years but is down -47.04% year to date 2015.

Jay D. Hatfield has been running the fund for 2 years and currently receives a manager quality ranking of 3 (0=worst, 99=best). If you can tolerate high levels of risk in the hope of improved future returns, holding this fund may be an option.

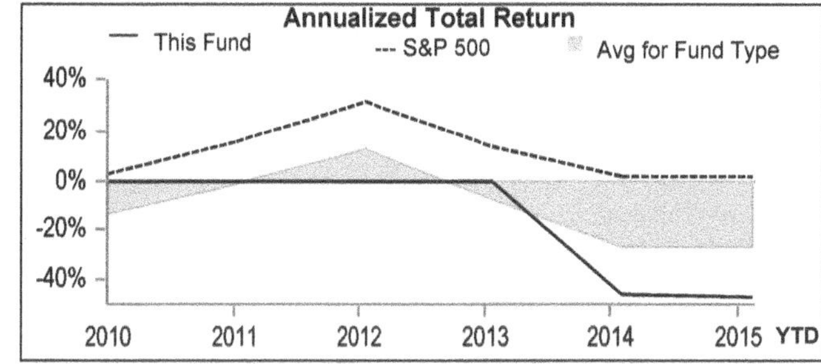

*ETFS Physical Palladium Shares (PALL)   D-   Weak

Fund Family: ETF Securities USA LLC
Fund Type: Precious Metals
Inception Date: January 7, 2010

Data Date	Investment Rating	Net Assets ($Mil)	Price	Performance Rating/Pts	Total Return Y-T-D	Risk Rating/Pts
12-15	D-	444.40	54.17	D / 1.6	-29.85%	C- / 3.7
2014	C-	444.40	77.49	C / 5.0	8.96%	C / 5.4
2013	D	510.20	69.81	D+ / 2.6	5.35%	C+ / 6.3
2012	C+	497.80	69.22	B / 8.1	9.27%	C+ / 6.4
2011	D-	373.90	64.57	E+ / 0.8	-18.39%	C+ / 6.6

Major Rating Factors:
Disappointing performance is the major factor driving the D- (Weak) TheStreet.com Investment Rating for *ETFS Physical Palladium Shares. The fund currently has a performance rating of D (Weak) based on an annualized return of -7.08% over the last three years and a total return of -29.85% year to date 2015. Factored into the performance evaluation is an expense ratio of 0.60% (very low).

The fund's risk rating is currently C- (Fair). It carries a beta of 0.76, meaning the fund's expected move will be 7.6% for every 10% move in the market. Volatility, as measured by both the semi-deviation and a drawdown factor, is considered average. As of December 31, 2015, *ETFS Physical Palladium Shares traded at a premium of 2.65% above its net asset value, which is worse than its one-year historical average premium of .26%.

Benoit Autier currently receives a manager quality ranking of 85 (0=worst, 99=best). This fund offers an average level of risk but investors looking for strong performance will be frustrated.

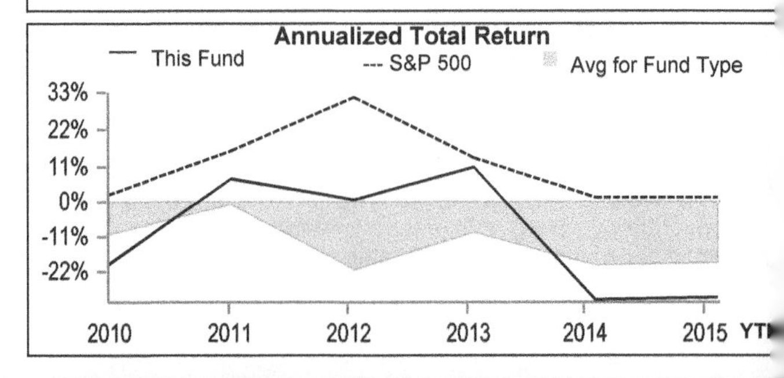

*ETFS Physical Platinum Shares (PPLT)   E+   Very Weak

Fund Family: ETF Securities USA LLC
Fund Type: Precious Metals
Inception Date: January 7, 2010

Data Date	Investment Rating	Net Assets ($Mil)	Price	Performance Rating/Pts	Total Return Y-T-D	Risk Rating/Pts
12-15	E+	694.90	85.83	D- / 1.0	-26.37%	C- / 3.4
2014	D-	694.90	117.05	D / 1.6	-15.22%	C / 4.8
2013	D	716.00	133.89	D- / 1.4	-10.05%	C+ / 6.5
2012	C-	770.40	151.36	C / 4.6	8.82%	C+ / 6.9
2011	D-	607.30	137.82	E+ / 0.7	-19.98%	B- / 7.0

Major Rating Factors:
Disappointing performance is the major factor driving the E+ (Very Weak) TheStreet.com Investment Rating for *ETFS Physical Platinum Shares. The fund currently has a performance rating of D- (Weak) based on an annualized return of -17.61% over the last three years and a total return of -26.37% year to date 2015. Factored into the performance evaluation is an expense ratio of 0.60% (very low).

The fund's risk rating is currently C- (Fair). It carries a beta of 0.85, meaning the fund's expected move will be 8.5% for every 10% move in the market. Volatility, as measured by both the semi-deviation and a drawdown factor, is considered average. As of December 31, 2015, *ETFS Physical Platinum Shares traded at a premium of 2.03% above its net asset value, which is worse than its one-year historical average premium of .33%.

Benoit Autier currently receives a manager quality ranking of 26 (0=worst, 99=best). This fund offers an average level of risk but investors looking for strong performance will be frustrated.

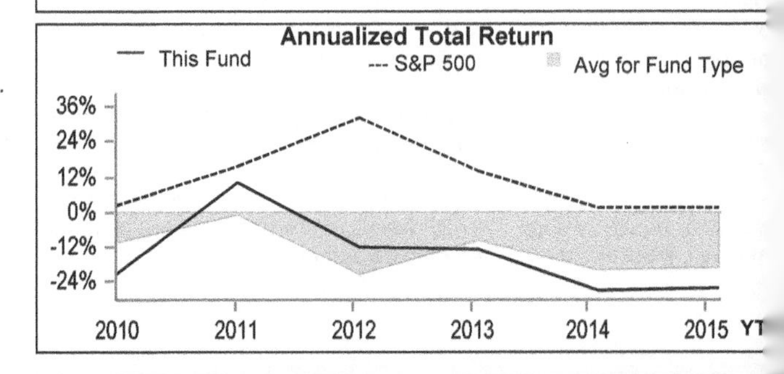

*ETFS Physical PM Basket Shares (GLTR)   D-   Weak

Fund Family: ETF Securities USA LLC
Fund Type: Precious Metals
Inception Date: October 21, 2010

Data Date	Investment Rating	Net Assets ($Mil)	Price	Performance Rating/Pts	Total Return Y-T-D	Risk Rating/Pts
12-15	D-	159.10	52.29	D- / 1.1	-14.40%	C- / 4.0
2014	E+	159.10	60.86	D- / 1.1	-10.57%	C- / 3.8
2013	D-	202.20	66.05	D- / 1.2	-26.06%	C / 5.4
2012	D	202.20	92.81	D / 2.0	2.22%	C+ / 6.8
2011	D	0.00	86.25	D / 1.9	6.54%	C+ / 6.6

Major Rating Factors:
Disappointing performance is the major factor driving the D- (Weak) TheStreet.com Investment Rating for *ETFS Physical PM Basket Shares. The fund currently has a performance rating of D- (Weak) based on an annualized return of -17.18% over the last three years and a total return of -14.40% year to date 2015. Factored into the performance evaluation is an expense ratio of 0.60% (very low).

The fund's risk rating is currently C- (Fair). It carries a beta of 0.99, meaning that its performance tracks fairly well with that of the overall stock market. Volatility, as measured by both the semi-deviation and a drawdown factor, is considered average. As of December 31, 2015, *ETFS Physical PM Basket Shares traded at a premium of .21% above its net asset value, which is in line with its one-year historical average premium of .21%.

Benoit Autier currently receives a manager quality ranking of 35 (0=worst, 99=best). This fund offers an average level of risk but investors looking for strong performance will be frustrated.

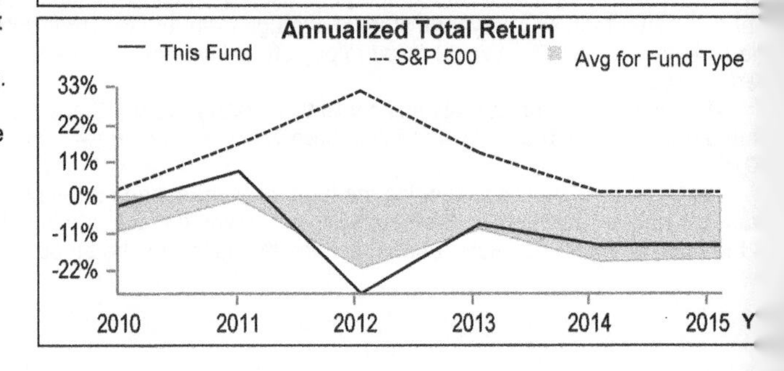

*ETFS Physical Silver Shares (SIVR) E+ Very Weak

Fund Family: ETF Securities USA LLC
Fund Type: Global
Inception Date: July 20, 2009

Major Rating Factors:
Very poor performance is the major factor driving the E+ (Very Weak) TheStreet.com Investment Rating for *ETFS Physical Silver Shares. The fund currently has a performance rating of E+ (Very Weak) based on an annualized return of -23.19% over the last three years and a total return of -12.69% year to date 2015. Factored into the performance evaluation is an expense ratio of 0.45% (very low).

The fund's risk rating is currently C- (Fair). It carries a beta of 0.33, meaning the fund's expected move will be 3.3% for every 10% move in the market. Volatility, as measured by both the semi-deviation and a drawdown factor, is considered average. As of December 31, 2015, *ETFS Physical Silver Shares traded at a price exactly equal to its net asset value, which is better than its one-year historical average premium of .35%.

Benoit Autier currently receives a manager quality ranking of 5 (0=worst, 99=best). This fund offers an average level of risk but investors looking for strong performance will be frustrated.

Data Date	Investment Rating	Net Assets ($Mil)	Price	Performance Rating/Pts	Total Return Y-T-D	Risk Rating/Pts
12-15	E+	320.10	13.56	E+ / 0.8	-12.69%	C- / 3.6
2014	E+	320.10	15.43	E+ / 0.7	-22.62%	C- / 4.0
2013	E	346.30	19.20	E+ / 0.8	-33.36%	C- / 3.2
2012	C-	551.30	30.06	C+ / 6.3	2.52%	C / 4.9
2011	D-	534.30	27.52	D- / 1.1	-1.38%	C / 5.2
2010	A+	391.80	30.73	A+ / 9.9	82.16%	B / 8.4

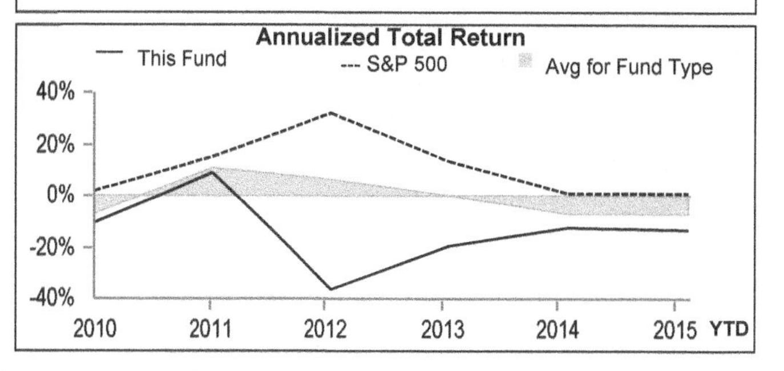

*ETFS Physical Swiss Gold Shares (SGOL) D Weak

Fund Family: ETF Securities USA LLC
Fund Type: Precious Metals
Inception Date: September 8, 2009

Major Rating Factors:
Disappointing performance is the major factor driving the D (Weak) TheStreet.com Investment Rating for *ETFS Physical Swiss Gold Shares. The fund currently has a performance rating of D- (Weak) based on an annualized return of -14.15% over the last three years and a total return of -11.02% year to date 2015. Factored into the performance evaluation is an expense ratio of 0.39% (very low).

The fund's risk rating is currently C+ (Fair). It carries a beta of 0.92, meaning that its performance tracks fairly well with that of the overall stock market. Volatility, as measured by both the semi-deviation and a drawdown factor, is considered low. As of December 31, 2015, *ETFS Physical Swiss Gold Shares traded at a discount of .14% below its net asset value, which is better than its one-year historical average premium of .12%.

Benoit Autier currently receives a manager quality ranking of 53 (0=worst, 99=best). This fund offers only a moderate level of risk but investors looking for strong performance are still waiting.

Data Date	Investment Rating	Net Assets ($Mil)	Price	Performance Rating/Pts	Total Return Y-T-D	Risk Rating/Pts
12-15	D	1,019.70	103.50	D- / 1.4	-11.02%	C+ / 6.2
2014	D-	1,019.70	115.85	D- / 1.3	-4.82%	C / 4.5
2013	D	1,033.70	118.36	D- / 1.5	-25.59%	C+ / 6.4
2012	C	1,930.10	165.16	C / 4.3	1.10%	B / 8.1
2011	C+	1,677.40	154.93	C / 5.3	17.62%	B / 8.2
2010	A+	1,087.70	141.39	A / 9.3	29.23%	B / 8.4

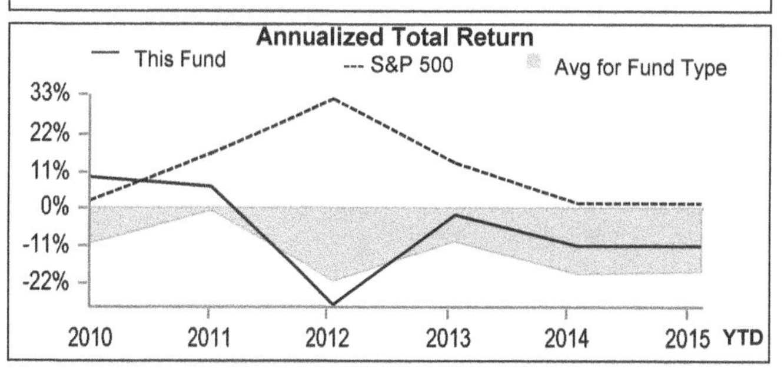

*ETFS Physical WM Basket Shares (WITE) E+ Very Weak

Fund Family: ETF Securities USA LLC
Fund Type: Precious Metals
Inception Date: December 2, 2010

Major Rating Factors:
Very poor performance is the major factor driving the E+ (Very Weak) TheStreet.com Investment Rating for *ETFS Physical WM Basket Shares. The fund currently has a performance rating of E+ (Very Weak) based on an annualized return of -19.56% over the last three years and a total return of -20.66% year to date 2015. Factored into the performance evaluation is an expense ratio of 0.60% (very low).

The fund's risk rating is currently C- (Fair). It carries a beta of 1.00, meaning that its performance tracks fairly well with that of the overall stock market. Volatility, as measured by both the semi-deviation and a drawdown factor, is considered average. As of December 31, 2015, *ETFS Physical WM Basket Shares traded at a premium of 1.15% above its net asset value, which is worse than its one-year historical average premium of .25%.

Benoit Autier currently receives a manager quality ranking of 24 (0=worst, 99=best). This fund offers an average level of risk but investors looking for strong performance will be frustrated.

Data Date	Investment Rating	Net Assets ($Mil)	Price	Performance Rating/Pts	Total Return Y-T-D	Risk Rating/Pts
12-15	E+	23.10	26.41	E+ / 0.9	-20.66%	C- / 3.3
2014	E+	23.10	33.30	D- / 1.1	-15.37%	C- / 3.6
2013	E+	26.60	38.10	D- / 1.1	-22.46%	C / 4.6
2012	D	37.60	50.76	C- / 3.0	4.99%	C / 5.4
2011	E+	39.80	46.69	E+ / 0.9	-9.49%	C / 5.1

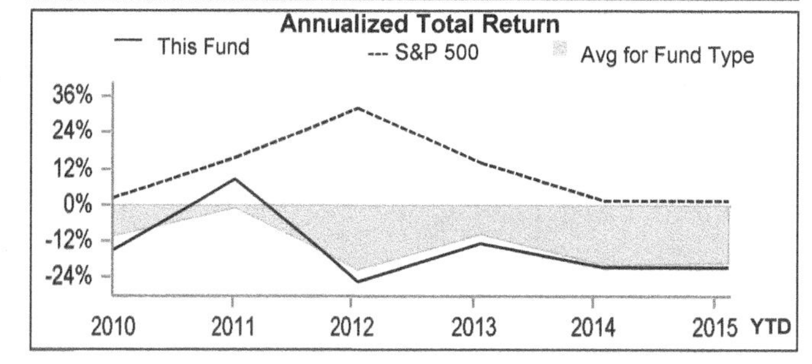

*Falah Russell-IdealRatings US LC (FIA) C+ Fair

Fund Family: Exchange Traded Concepts LLC
Fund Type: Growth
Inception Date: October 1, 2014

Major Rating Factors: Middle of the road best describes *Falah Russell-IdealRatings US LC whose TheStreet.com Investment Rating is currently a C+ (Fair). The fund currently has a performance rating of C+ (Fair) based on an annualized return of 0.00% over the last three years and a total return of 0.31% year to date 2015. Factored into the performance evaluation is an expense ratio of 0.70% (very low).

The fund's risk rating is currently C+ (Fair). It carries a beta of 0.00, meaning the fund's expected move will be 0.0% for every 10% move in the market. Volatility, as measured by both the semi-deviation and a drawdown factor, is considered low. As of December 31, 2015, *Falah Russell-IdealRatings US LC traded at a premium of .31% above its net asset value, which is worse than its one-year historical average discount of .74%.

James G. Stevens currently receives a manager quality ranking of 60 (0=worst, 99=best). If you desire an average level of risk, then this fund may be an option.

Data Date	Investment Rating	Net Assets ($Mil)	Price	Perfor-mance Rating/Pts	Total Return Y-T-D	Risk Rating/Pts
12-15	C+	0.00	25.66	C+ / 6.3	0.31%	C+ / 6.7

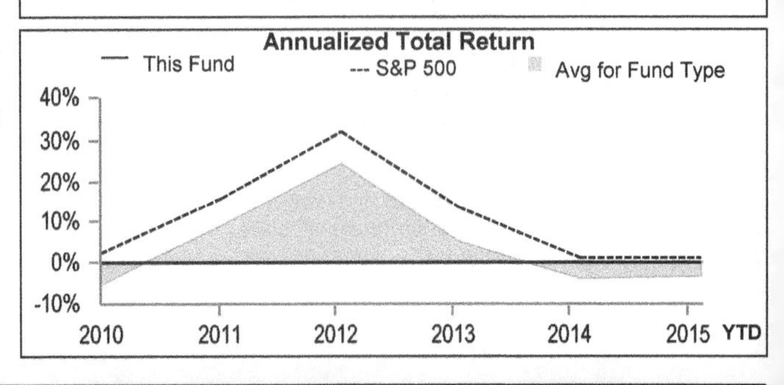

*Fidelity Corporate Bond ETF (FCOR) C- Fair

Fund Family: Fidelity Management & Research Comp
Fund Type: Corporate - Investment Grade
Inception Date: October 6, 2014

Major Rating Factors: Middle of the road best describes *Fidelity Corporate Bond ETF whose TheStreet.com Investment Rating is currently a C- (Fair). The fund currently has a performance rating of C- (Fair) based on an annualized return of 0.00% over the last three years and a total return of -2.53% year to date 2015. Factored into the performance evaluation is an expense ratio of 0.45% (very low).

The fund's risk rating is currently B- (Good). It carries a beta of 0.00, meaning the fund's expected move will be 0.0% for every 10% move in the market. Volatility, as measured by both the semi-deviation and a drawdown factor, is considered low. As of December 31, 2015, *Fidelity Corporate Bond ETF traded at a premium of .15% above its net asset value, which is worse than its one-year historical average premium of .07%.

David Prothro has been running the fund for 2 years and currently receives a manager quality ranking of 55 (0=worst, 99=best). If you desire an average level of risk, then this fund may be an option.

Data Date	Investment Rating	Net Assets ($Mil)	Price	Perfor-mance Rating/Pts	Total Return Y-T-D	Risk Rating/Pts
12-15	C-	0.00	47.33	C- / 3.2	-2.53%	B- / 7.5

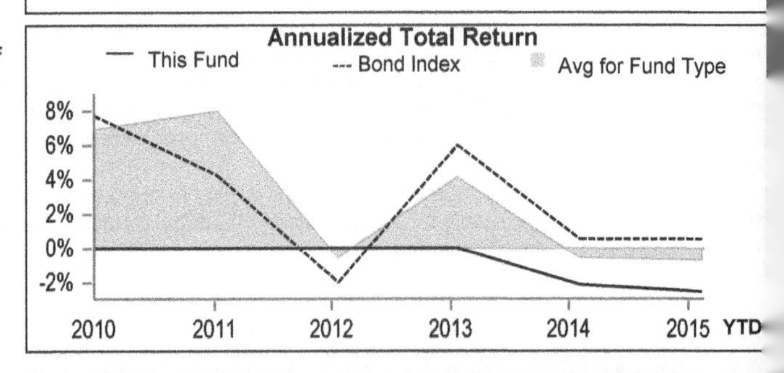

*Fidelity Limited Term Bond ETF (FLTB) C+ Fair

Fund Family: Fidelity Management & Research Comp
Fund Type: Corporate - Investment Grade
Inception Date: October 6, 2014

Major Rating Factors: Middle of the road best describes *Fidelity Limited Term Bond ETF whose TheStreet.com Investment Rating is currently a C+ (Fair). The fund currently has a performance rating of C- (Fair) based on an annualized return of 0.00% over the last three years and a total return of 0.71% year to date 2015. Factored into the performance evaluation is an expense ratio of 0.45% (very low).

The fund's risk rating is currently B+ (Good). It carries a beta of 0.00, meaning the fund's expected move will be 0.0% for every 10% move in the market. Volatility, as measured by both the semi-deviation and a drawdown factor, is considered very low. As of December 31, 2015, *Fidelity Limited Term Bond ETF traded at a discount of .06% below its net asset value, which is better than its one-year historical average premium of .21%.

David Prothro has been running the fund for 2 years and currently receives a manager quality ranking of 76 (0=worst, 99=best). If you desire an average level of risk, then this fund may be an option.

Data Date	Investment Rating	Net Assets ($Mil)	Price	Perfor-mance Rating/Pts	Total Return Y-T-D	Risk Rating/Pts
12-15	C+	0.00	49.69	C- / 4.2	0.71%	B+ / 9.6

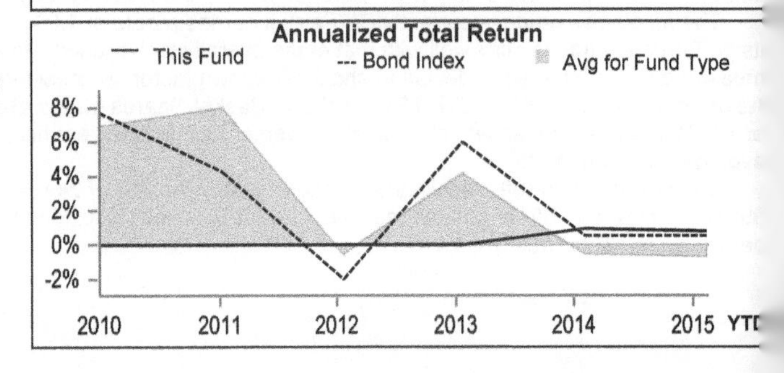

*Fidelity MSCI Cons Staples Idx E (FSTA) B+ Good

Fund Family: Fidelity SelectCo LLC
Fund Type: Global
Inception Date: October 21, 2013

Major Rating Factors: Strong performance is the major factor driving the B+ (Good) TheStreet.com Investment Rating for *Fidelity MSCI Cons Staples Idx E. The fund currently has a performance rating of B (Good) based on an annualized return of 0.00% over the last three years and a total return of 7.01% year to date 2015. Factored into the performance evaluation is an expense ratio of 0.12% (very low).

The fund's risk rating is currently B- (Good). It carries a beta of 0.00, meaning the fund's expected move will be 0.0% for every 10% move in the market. Volatility, as measured by both the semi-deviation and a drawdown factor, is considered low. As of December 31, 2015, *Fidelity MSCI Cons Staples Idx E traded at a premium of .23% above its net asset value, which is worse than its one-year historical average premium of .02%.

Jennifer F.Y. Hsui has been running the fund for 3 years and currently receives a manager quality ranking of 92 (0=worst, 99=best). If you desire only a moderate level of risk and strong performance, then this fund is an excellent option.

Data Date	Investment Rating	Net Assets ($Mil)	Price	Performance Rating/Pts	Total Return Y-T-D	Risk Rating/Pts
12-15	B+	120.30	30.28	B / 8.2	7.01%	B- / 7.2
2014	C	120.30	29.46	B+ / 8.3	17.18%	C / 4.3

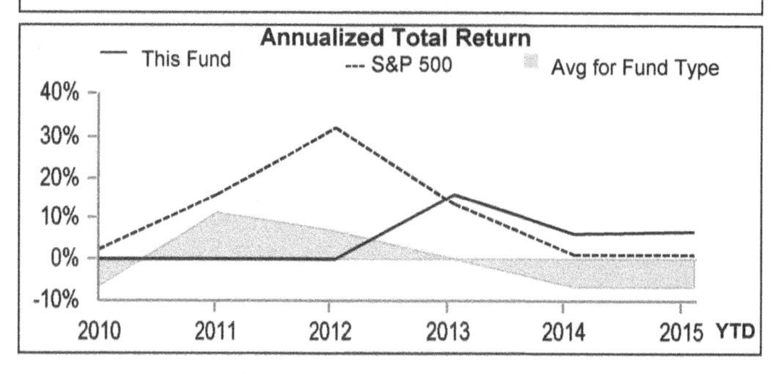

*Fidelity MSCI Consmr Discr Idx E (FDIS) C+ Fair

Fund Family: Fidelity SelectCo LLC
Fund Type: Global
Inception Date: October 21, 2013

Major Rating Factors: Middle of the road best describes *Fidelity MSCI Consmr Discr Idx E whose TheStreet.com Investment Rating is currently a C+ (Fair). The fund currently has a performance rating of C+ (Fair) based on an annualized return of 0.00% over the last three years and a total return of 7.75% year to date 2015. Factored into the performance evaluation is an expense ratio of 0.12% (very low).

The fund's risk rating is currently B- (Good). It carries a beta of 0.00, meaning the fund's expected move will be 0.0% for every 10% move in the market. Volatility, as measured by both the semi-deviation and a drawdown factor, is considered low. As of December 31, 2015, *Fidelity MSCI Consmr Discr Idx E traded at a premium of .03% above its net asset value, which is worse than its one-year historical average premium of .02%.

Jennifer F.Y. Hsui has been running the fund for 3 years and currently receives a manager quality ranking of 92 (0=worst, 99=best). If you desire an average level of risk, then this fund may be an option.

Data Date	Investment Rating	Net Assets ($Mil)	Price	Performance Rating/Pts	Total Return Y-T-D	Risk Rating/Pts
12-15	C+	150.50	30.68	C+ / 6.7	7.75%	B- / 7.2
2014	C-	150.50	29.22	C+ / 6.8	10.13%	C- / 4.2

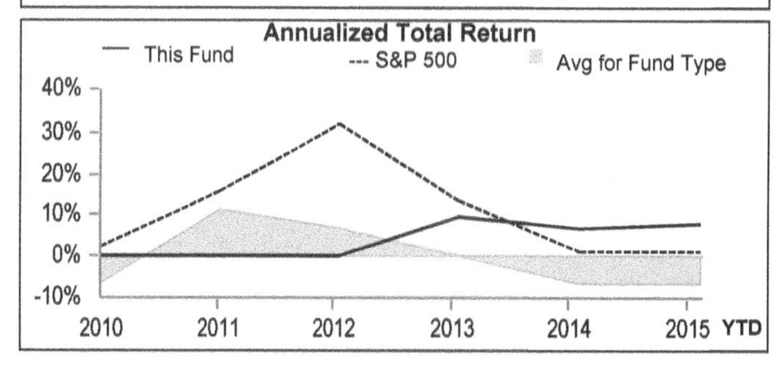

*Fidelity MSCI Energy Index ETF (FENY) D- Weak

Fund Family: Fidelity SelectCo LLC
Fund Type: Energy/Natural Resources
Inception Date: October 21, 2013

Major Rating Factors:
Very poor performance is the major factor driving the D- (Weak) TheStreet.com Investment Rating for *Fidelity MSCI Energy Index ETF. The fund currently has a performance rating of E+ (Very Weak) based on an annualized return of 0.00% over the last three years and a total return of -22.86% year to date 2015. Factored into the performance evaluation is an expense ratio of 0.12% (very low).

The fund's risk rating is currently C+ (Fair). It carries a beta of 0.00, meaning the fund's expected move will be 0.0% for every 10% move in the market. Volatility, as measured by both the semi-deviation and a drawdown factor, is considered low. As of December 31, 2015, *Fidelity MSCI Energy Index ETF traded at a discount of .06% below its net asset value, which is better than its one-year historical average premium of .02%.

Jennifer F.Y. Hsui has been running the fund for 3 years and currently receives a manager quality ranking of 64 (0=worst, 99=best). This fund offers only a moderate level of risk but investors looking for strong performance are still waiting.

Data Date	Investment Rating	Net Assets ($Mil)	Price	Performance Rating/Pts	Total Return Y-T-D	Risk Rating/Pts
12-15	D-	143.50	17.09	E+ / 0.6	-22.86%	C+ / 5.6
2014	E+	143.50	22.83	E+ / 0.7	-8.59%	C- / 4.1

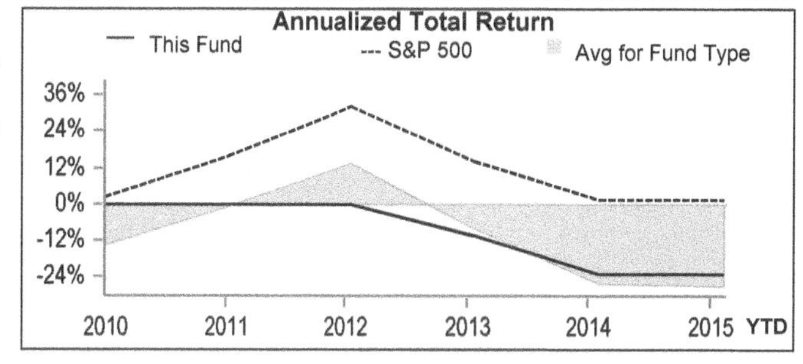

* Denotes ETF Fund

*Fidelity MSCI Financials Index E (FNCL) C+ Fair

Fund Family: Fidelity SelectCo LLC
Fund Type: Financial Services
Inception Date: October 21, 2013

Major Rating Factors: Middle of the road best describes *Fidelity MSCI Financials Index E whose TheStreet.com Investment Rating is currently a C+ (Fair). The fund currently has a performance rating of C (Fair) based on an annualized return of 0.00% over the last three years and a total return of -0.19% year to date 2015. Factored into the performance evaluation is an expense ratio of 0.12% (very low).

The fund's risk rating is currently B- (Good). It carries a beta of 0.00, meaning the fund's expected move will be 0.0% for every 10% move in the market. Volatility, as measured by both the semi-deviation and a drawdown factor, is considered low. As of December 31, 2015, *Fidelity MSCI Financials Index E traded at a price exactly equal to its net asset value, which is better than its one-year historical average premium of .03%.

Jennifer F.Y. Hsui has been running the fund for 3 years and currently receives a manager quality ranking of 64 (0=worst, 99=best). If you desire an average level of risk, then this fund may be an option.

Data Date	Investment Rating	Net Assets ($Mil)	Price	Performance Rating/Pts	Total Return Y-T-D	Risk Rating/Pts
12-15	C+	147.90	28.30	C / 5.1	-0.19%	B- / 7.8
2014	C	147.90	29.13	B- / 7.3	13.37%	C / 5.4

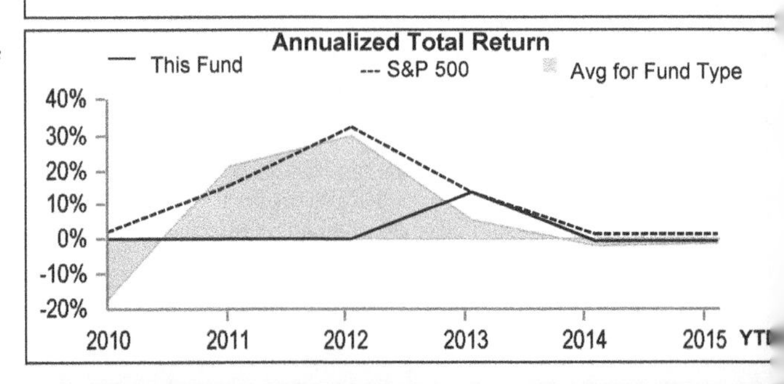

*Fidelity MSCI Health Care Index (FHLC) C+ Fair

Fund Family: Fidelity SelectCo LLC
Fund Type: Health
Inception Date: October 21, 2013

Major Rating Factors: Middle of the road best describes *Fidelity MSCI Health Care Index whose TheStreet.com Investment Rating is currently a C+ (Fair). The fund currently has a performance rating of C+ (Fair) based on an annualized return of 0.00% over the last three years and a total return of 7.16% year to date 2015. Factored into the performance evaluation is an expense ratio of 0.12% (very low).

The fund's risk rating is currently C+ (Fair). It carries a beta of 0.00, meaning the fund's expected move will be 0.0% for every 10% move in the market. Volatility, as measured by both the semi-deviation and a drawdown factor, is considered low. As of December 31, 2015, *Fidelity MSCI Health Care Index traded at a premium of .09% above its net asset value, which is worse than its one-year historical average premium of .03%.

Jennifer F.Y. Hsui has been running the fund for 3 years and currently receives a manager quality ranking of 91 (0=worst, 99=best). If you desire an average level of risk, then this fund may be an option.

Data Date	Investment Rating	Net Assets ($Mil)	Price	Performance Rating/Pts	Total Return Y-T-D	Risk Rating/Pts
12-15	C+	237.20	34.53	C+ / 6.4	7.16%	C+ / 6.5
2014	B-	237.20	32.90	A / 9.4	25.65%	C / 5.3

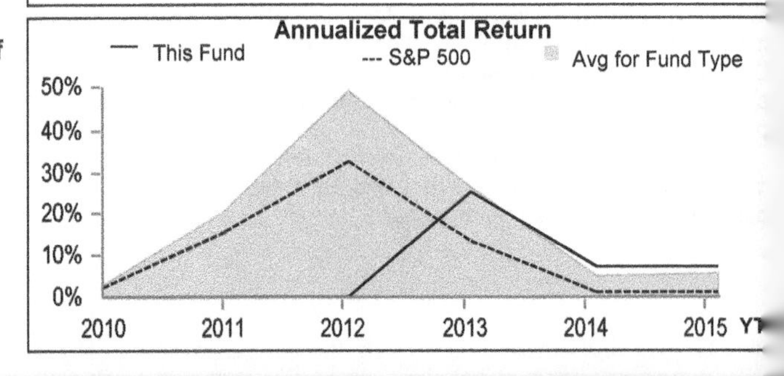

*Fidelity MSCI Industrials Index (FIDU) C- Fair

Fund Family: Fidelity SelectCo LLC
Fund Type: Global
Inception Date: October 21, 2013

Major Rating Factors: Middle of the road best describes *Fidelity MSCI Industrials Index whose TheStreet.com Investment Rating is currently a C- (Fair). The fund currently has a performance rating of C- (Fair) based on an annualized return of 0.00% over the last three years and a total return of -2.82% year to date 2015. Factored into the performance evaluation is an expense ratio of 0.12% (very low).

The fund's risk rating is currently C+ (Fair). It carries a beta of 0.00, meaning the fund's expected move will be 0.0% for every 10% move in the market. Volatility, as measured by both the semi-deviation and a drawdown factor, is considered low. As of December 31, 2015, *Fidelity MSCI Industrials Index traded at a premium of .11% above its net asset value.

Jennifer F.Y. Hsui has been running the fund for 3 years and currently receives a manager quality ranking of 44 (0=worst, 99=best). If you desire an average level of risk, then this fund may be an option.

Data Date	Investment Rating	Net Assets ($Mil)	Price	Performance Rating/Pts	Total Return Y-T-D	Risk Rating/Pts
12-15	C-	161.00	27.21	C- / 4.1	-2.82%	C+ / 6.7
2014	D+	161.00	28.79	C / 5.3	7.21%	C- / 4.2

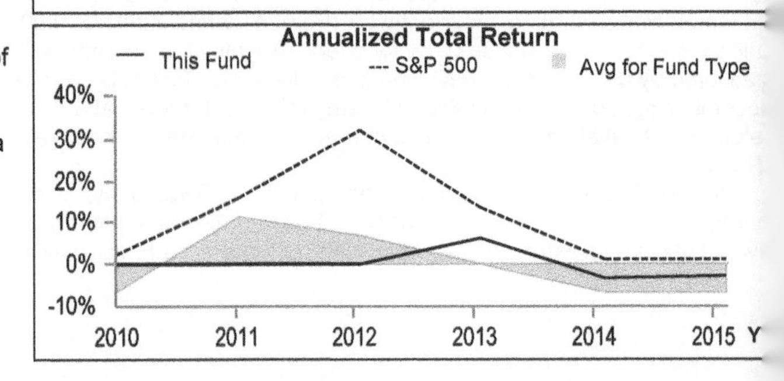

*Fidelity MSCI Info Tech Idx ETF (FTEC) — B — Good

Fund Family: Fidelity SelectCo LLC
Fund Type: Growth
Inception Date: October 21, 2013

Major Rating Factors: Strong performance is the major factor driving the B (Good) TheStreet.com Investment Rating for *Fidelity MSCI Info Tech Idx ETF. The fund currently has a performance rating of B- (Good) based on an annualized return of 0.00% over the last three years and a total return of 5.79% year to date 2015. Factored into the performance evaluation is an expense ratio of 0.12% (very low).

The fund's risk rating is currently B- (Good). It carries a beta of 0.00, meaning the fund's expected move will be 0.0% for every 10% move in the market. Volatility, as measured by both the semi-deviation and a drawdown factor, is considered low. As of December 31, 2015, *Fidelity MSCI Info Tech Idx ETF traded at a premium of .09% above its net asset value, which is worse than its one-year historical average premium of .03%.

Jennifer F.Y. Hsui has been running the fund for 3 years and currently receives a manager quality ranking of 86 (0=worst, 99=best). If you desire only a moderate level of risk and strong performance, then this fund is an excellent option.

Data Date	Investment Rating	Net Assets ($Mil)	Price	Performance Rating/Pts	Total Return Y-T-D	Risk Rating/Pts
12-15	B	223.90	32.84	B- / 7.5	5.79%	B- / 7.2
2014	C+	223.90	31.69	B+ / 8.6	19.81%	C / 4.4

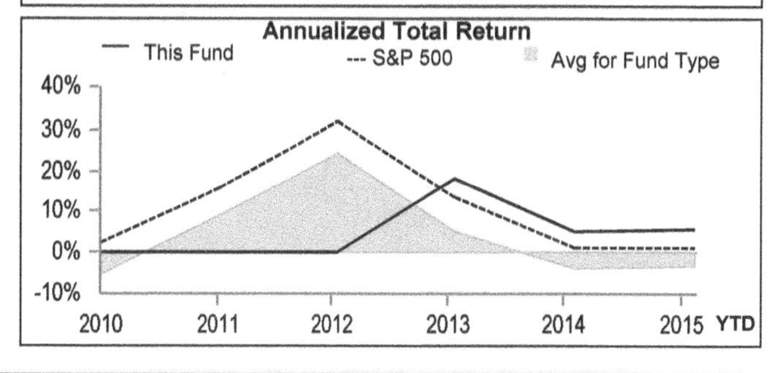

*Fidelity MSCI Materials Index ET (FMAT) — D — Weak

Fund Family: Fidelity SelectCo LLC
Fund Type: Global
Inception Date: October 21, 2013

Major Rating Factors:
Disappointing performance is the major factor driving the D (Weak) TheStreet.com Investment Rating for *Fidelity MSCI Materials Index ET. The fund currently has a performance rating of D (Weak) based on an annualized return of 0.00% over the last three years and a total return of -9.61% year to date 2015. Factored into the performance evaluation is an expense ratio of 0.12% (very low).

The fund's risk rating is currently C+ (Fair). It carries a beta of 0.00, meaning the fund's expected move will be 0.0% for every 10% move in the market. Volatility, as measured by both the semi-deviation and a drawdown factor, is considered low. As of December 31, 2015, *Fidelity MSCI Materials Index ET traded at a premium of .29% above its net asset value, which is worse than its one-year historical average premium of .02%.

Jennifer F.Y. Hsui has been running the fund for 3 years and currently receives a manager quality ranking of 18 (0=worst, 99=best). This fund offers only a moderate level of risk but investors looking for strong performance are still waiting.

Data Date	Investment Rating	Net Assets ($Mil)	Price	Performance Rating/Pts	Total Return Y-T-D	Risk Rating/Pts
12-15	D	112.80	24.28	D / 2.2	-9.61%	C+ / 5.8
2014	D+	112.80	27.52	C- / 3.7	6.64%	C / 5.2

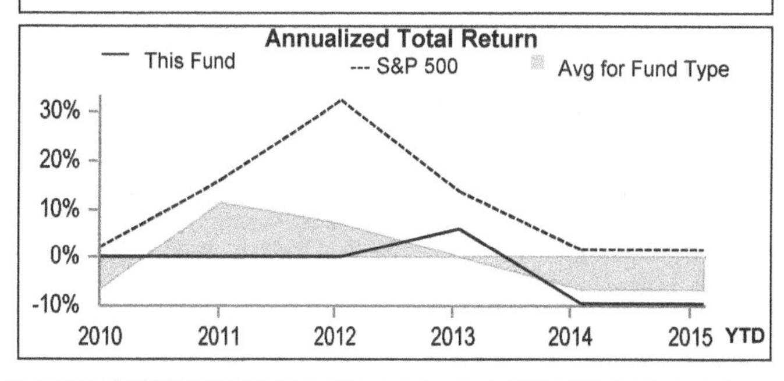

*Fidelity MSCI Telecom Svcs Idx E (FCOM) — C+ — Fair

Fund Family: Fidelity SelectCo LLC
Fund Type: Growth
Inception Date: October 21, 2013

Major Rating Factors: Middle of the road best describes *Fidelity MSCI Telecom Svcs Idx E whose TheStreet.com Investment Rating is currently a C+ (Fair). The fund currently has a performance rating of C+ (Fair) based on an annualized return of 0.00% over the last three years and a total return of 3.49% year to date 2015. Factored into the performance evaluation is an expense ratio of 0.12% (very low).

The fund's risk rating is currently B- (Good). It carries a beta of 0.00, meaning the fund's expected move will be 0.0% for every 10% move in the market. Volatility, as measured by both the semi-deviation and a drawdown factor, is considered low. As of December 31, 2015, *Fidelity MSCI Telecom Svcs Idx E traded at a premium of .15% above its net asset value.

Jennifer F.Y. Hsui has been running the fund for 3 years and currently receives a manager quality ranking of 82 (0=worst, 99=best). If you desire an average level of risk, then this fund may be an option.

Data Date	Investment Rating	Net Assets ($Mil)	Price	Performance Rating/Pts	Total Return Y-T-D	Risk Rating/Pts
12-15	C+	74.20	26.72	C+ / 6.6	3.49%	B- / 7.0
2014	D+	74.20	26.63	C / 4.3	7.73%	C / 5.3

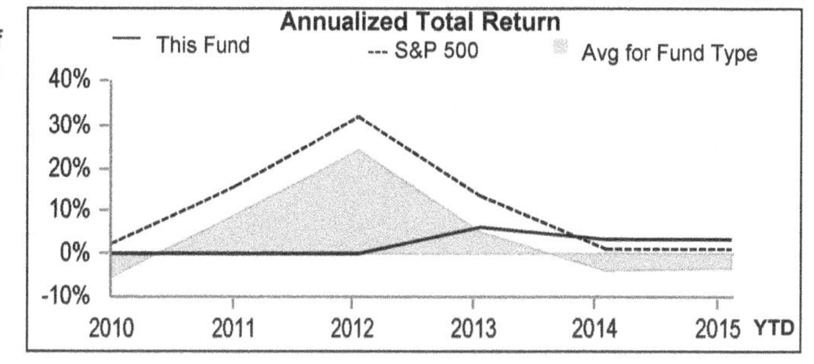

*Fidelity MSCI Utilities Index ET (FUTY) C Fair

Fund Family: Fidelity SelectCo LLC
Fund Type: Utilities
Inception Date: October 21, 2013

Major Rating Factors: Middle of the road best describes *Fidelity MSCI Utilities Index ET whose TheStreet.com Investment Rating is currently a C (Fair). The fund currently has a performance rating of C (Fair) based on an annualized return of 0.00% over the last three years and a total return of -4.13% year to date 2015. Factored into the performance evaluation is an expense ratio of 0.12% (very low).

The fund's risk rating is currently C+ (Fair). It carries a beta of 0.00, meaning the fund's expected move will be 0.0% for every 10% move in the market. Volatility, as measured by both the semi-deviation and a drawdown factor, is considered low. As of December 31, 2015, *Fidelity MSCI Utilities Index ET traded at a premium of .22% above its net asset value, which is worse than its one-year historical average premium of .01%.

Diane Hsiung has been running the fund for 3 years and currently receives a manager quality ranking of 60 (0=worst, 99=best). If you desire an average level of risk, then this fund may be an option.

Data Date	Investment Rating	Net Assets ($Mil)	Price	Performance Rating/Pts	Total Return Y-T-D	Risk Rating/Pts
12-15	C	73.40	27.89	C / 4.8	-4.13%	C+ / 6.5
2014	B-	73.40	30.56	A+ / 9.6	29.27%	C / 5.0

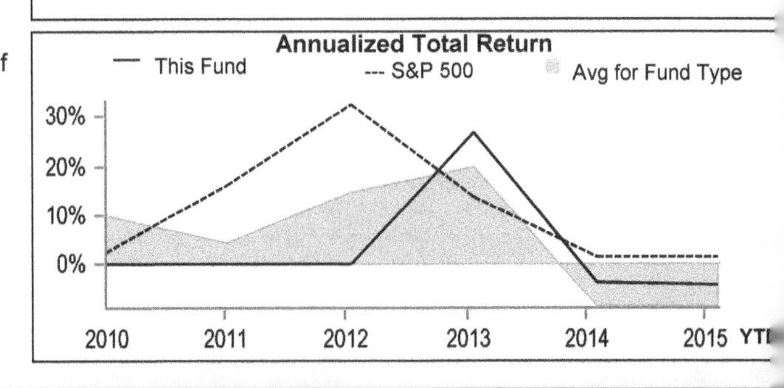

*Fidelity Nasdaq Comp Tracker Sto (ONEQ) B+ Good

Fund Family: Fidelity Management & Research Comp
Fund Type: Growth
Inception Date: September 25, 2003

Major Rating Factors:
Exceptional performance is the major factor driving the B+ (Good) TheStreet.com Investment Rating for *Fidelity Nasdaq Comp Tracker Sto. The fund currently has a performance rating of A (Excellent) based on an annualized return of 18.80% over the last three years and a total return of 7.90% year to date 2015. Factored into the performance evaluation is an expense ratio of 0.21% (very low).

The fund's risk rating is currently C+ (Fair). It carries a beta of 1.08, meaning that its performance tracks fairly well with that of the overall stock market. Volatility, as measured by both the semi-deviation and a drawdown factor, is considered low. As of December 31, 2015, *Fidelity Nasdaq Comp Tracker Sto traded at a premium of .15% above its net asset value, which is worse than its one-year historical average premium of .06%.

Patrick J. Waddell has been running the fund for 12 years and currently receives a manager quality ranking of 85 (0=worst, 99=best). If you desire only a moderate level of risk and strong performance, then this fund is an excellent option.

Data Date	Investment Rating	Net Assets ($Mil)	Price	Performance Rating/Pts	Total Return Y-T-D	Risk Rating/Pts
12-15	B+	405.40	196.79	A / 9.4	7.90%	C+ / 6.5
2014	B+	405.40	185.78	A- / 9.0	15.77%	C+ / 6.7
2013	B+	312.00	164.07	B+ / 8.8	34.86%	B- / 7.3
2012	C	178.40	118.41	C / 5.3	16.58%	B- / 7.1
2011	C+	154.00	103.02	C+ / 6.4	-0.23%	B- / 7.2
2010	C+	156.80	104.77	C+ / 6.3	17.79%	C / 5.5

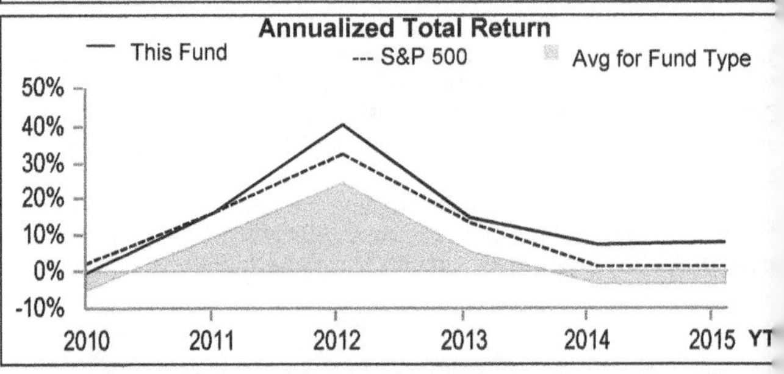

*Fidelity Total Bond ETF (FBND) C Fair

Fund Family: Fidelity Management & Research Comp
Fund Type: Corporate - Investment Grade
Inception Date: October 6, 2014

Major Rating Factors: Middle of the road best describes *Fidelity Total Bond ETF whose TheStreet.com Investment Rating is currently a C (Fair). The fund currently has a performance rating of C- (Fair) based on an annualized return of 0.00% over the last three years and a total return of -1.16% year to date 2015. Factored into the performance evaluation is an expense ratio of 0.45% (very low).

The fund's risk rating is currently B- (Good). It carries a beta of 0.00, meaning the fund's expected move will be 0.0% for every 10% move in the market. Volatility, as measured by both the semi-deviation and a drawdown factor, is considered low. As of December 31, 2015, *Fidelity Total Bond ETF traded at a premium of .69% above its net asset value, which is worse than its one-year historical average premium of .24%.

Ford O'Neil has been running the fund for 2 years and currently receives a manager quality ranking of 63 (0=worst, 99=best). If you desire an average level of risk, then this fund may be an option.

Data Date	Investment Rating	Net Assets ($Mil)	Price	Performance Rating/Pts	Total Return Y-T-D	Risk Rating/Pts
12-15	C	0.00	48.00	C- / 3.6	-1.16%	B- / 7.7

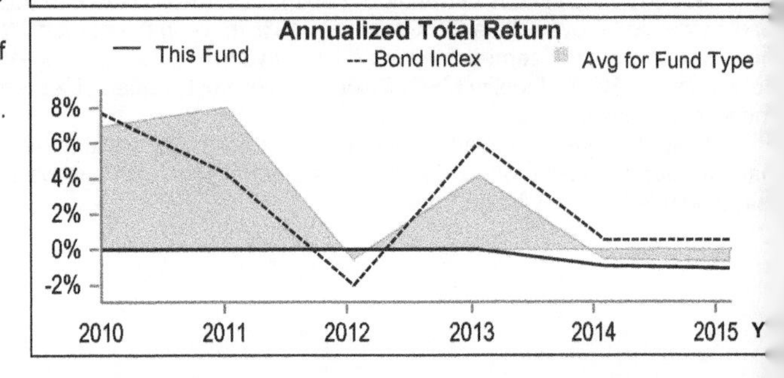

*Financial Select Sector SPDR (XLF) A+ Excellent

Fund Family: SSgA Funds Management Inc
Fund Type: Financial Services
Inception Date: December 16, 1998

Major Rating Factors:
Strong performance is the major factor driving the A+ (Excellent) TheStreet.com Investment Rating for *Financial Select Sector SPDR. The fund currently has a performance rating of B+ (Good) based on an annualized return of 14.01% over the last three years and a total return of -1.14% year to date 2015. Factored into the performance evaluation is an expense ratio of 0.15% (very low).

The fund's risk rating is currently B (Good). It carries a beta of 1.07, meaning that its performance tracks fairly well with that of the overall stock market. Volatility, as measured by both the semi-deviation and a drawdown factor, is considered low. As of December 31, 2015, *Financial Select Sector SPDR traded at a discount of .04% below its net asset value, which is better than its one-year historical average discount of .01%.

John A. Tucker has been running the fund for 18 years and currently receives a manager quality ranking of 60 (0=worst, 99=best). If you desire only a moderate level of risk and strong performance, then this fund is an excellent option.

Data Date	Investment Rating	Net Assets ($Mil)	Price	Perfor-mance Rating/Pts	Total Return Y-T-D	Risk Rating/Pts
12-15	A+	18,665.20	23.83	B+ / 8.7	-1.14%	B / 8.8
2014	A+	18,665.20	24.73	A / 9.3	14.90%	B- / 7.9
2013	B-	17,091.00	21.86	B / 7.7	30.45%	B- / 7.4
2012	C	9,237.20	16.39	C / 5.1	26.16%	B- / 7.2
2011	D	5,373.30	13.00	D+ / 2.7	-16.02%	C+ / 6.6
2010	D-	7,470.50	15.95	E+ / 0.8	11.91%	C- / 4.1

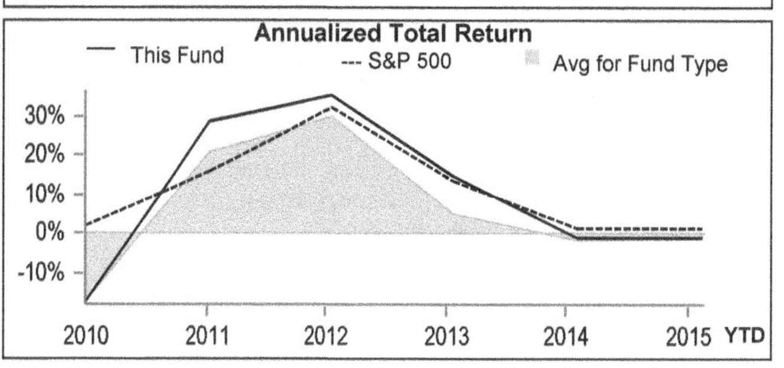

*First Trust AMEX Biotechnology (FBT) A Excellent

Fund Family: First Trust Advisors LP
Fund Type: Health
Inception Date: June 19, 2006

Major Rating Factors:
Exceptional performance is the major factor driving the A (Excellent) TheStreet.com Investment Rating for *First Trust AMEX Biotechnology. The fund currently has a performance rating of A+ (Excellent) based on an annualized return of 33.01% over the last three years and a total return of 10.42% year to date 2015. Factored into the performance evaluation is an expense ratio of 0.58% (very low).

The fund's risk rating is currently C+ (Fair). It carries a beta of 0.99, meaning that its performance tracks fairly well with that of the overall stock market. Volatility, as measured by both the semi-deviation and a drawdown factor, is considered low. As of December 31, 2015, *First Trust AMEX Biotechnology traded at a discount of .04% below its net asset value, which is better than its one-year historical average premium of .03%.

Stan Ueland has been running the fund for 10 years and currently receives a manager quality ranking of 98 (0=worst, 99=best). If you desire only a moderate level of risk and strong performance, then this fund is an excellent option.

Data Date	Investment Rating	Net Assets ($Mil)	Price	Perfor-mance Rating/Pts	Total Return Y-T-D	Risk Rating/Pts
12-15	A	1,549.80	113.02	A+ / 9.8	10.42%	C+ / 6.7
2014	A	1,549.80	102.02	A+ / 9.8	48.35%	B- / 7.0
2013	B-	953.90	69.18	A- / 9.1	44.42%	C+ / 5.9
2012	B-	239.40	45.95	B+ / 8.3	31.41%	C+ / 6.3
2011	C	183.00	32.66	C+ / 5.8	-11.61%	C+ / 6.2
2010	A	201.20	39.11	A- / 9.1	36.94%	C+ / 6.0

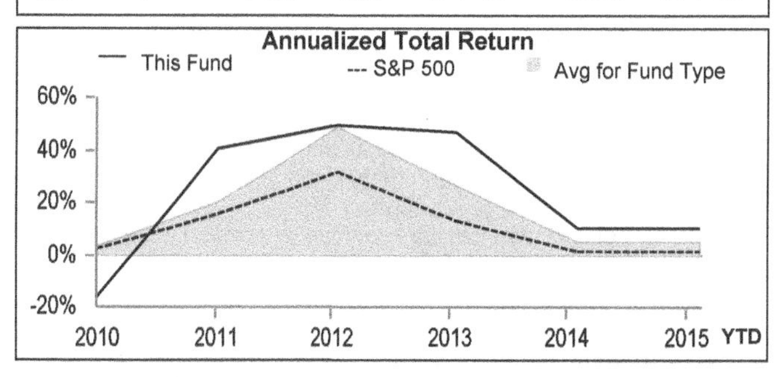

*First Trust AsiaPac Ex-Jpn Alpha (FPA) C Fair

Fund Family: First Trust Advisors LP
Fund Type: Foreign
Inception Date: April 18, 2011

Major Rating Factors: Middle of the road best describes *First Trust AsiaPac Ex-Jpn Alpha whose TheStreet.com Investment Rating is currently a C (Fair). The fund currently has a performance rating of C (Fair) based on an annualized return of 1.82% over the last three years and a total return of 0.40% year to date 2015. Factored into the performance evaluation is an expense ratio of 0.80% (very low).

The fund's risk rating is currently B- (Good). It carries a beta of 0.90, meaning that its performance tracks fairly well with that of the overall stock market. Volatility, as measured by both the semi-deviation and a drawdown factor, is considered low. As of December 31, 2015, *First Trust AsiaPac Ex-Jpn Alpha traded at a discount of .97% below its net asset value, which is better than its one-year historical average discount of .07%.

Daniel J. Lindquist has been running the fund for 5 years and currently receives a manager quality ranking of 46 (0=worst, 99=best). If you desire an average level of risk, then this fund may be an option.

Data Date	Investment Rating	Net Assets ($Mil)	Price	Perfor-mance Rating/Pts	Total Return Y-T-D	Risk Rating/Pts
12-15	C	144.70	27.45	C / 4.7	0.40%	B- / 7.8
2014	C	144.70	27.89	C / 4.9	5.45%	B- / 7.8
2013	C-	57.20	28.25	C / 5.0	-0.49%	B- / 7.0
2012	B+	13.80	27.94	A / 9.5	22.14%	C+ / 6.8

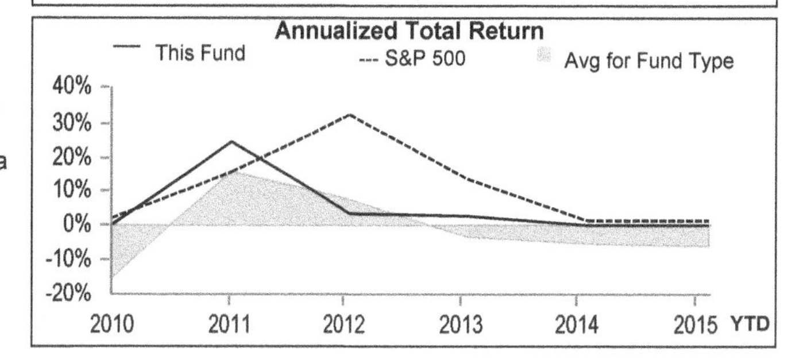

*First Trust Australia AlphaDEX (FAUS) D+ Weak

Fund Family: First Trust Advisors LP
Fund Type: Foreign
Inception Date: February 14, 2012

Major Rating Factors: *First Trust Australia AlphaDEX receives a TheStreet.com Investment Rating of D+ (Weak). The fund currently has a performance rating of C (Fair) based on an annualized return of -0.69% over the last three years and a total return of -0.24% year to date 2015. Factored into the performance evaluation is an expense ratio of 0.80% (very low).

The fund's risk rating is currently C (Fair). It carries a beta of 1.00, meaning that its performance tracks fairly well with that of the overall stock market. Volatility, as measured by both the semi-deviation and a drawdown factor, is considered average. As of December 31, 2015, *First Trust Australia AlphaDEX traded at a premium of 3.76% above its net asset value, which is worse than its one-year historical average premium of .42%.

Daniel J. Lindquist has been running the fund for 4 years and currently receives a manager quality ranking of 29 (0=worst, 99=best). If you desire an average level of risk, then this fund may be an option.

Data Date	Investment Rating	Net Assets ($Mil)	Price	Performance Rating/Pts	Total Return Y-T-D	Risk Rating/Pts
12-15	D+	1.50	28.12	C / 4.3	-0.24%	C / 5.2
2014	D+	1.50	29.14	D / 2.1	2.51%	B- / 7.3
2013	D	1.50	29.83	D / 1.8	-3.84%	B- / 7.5

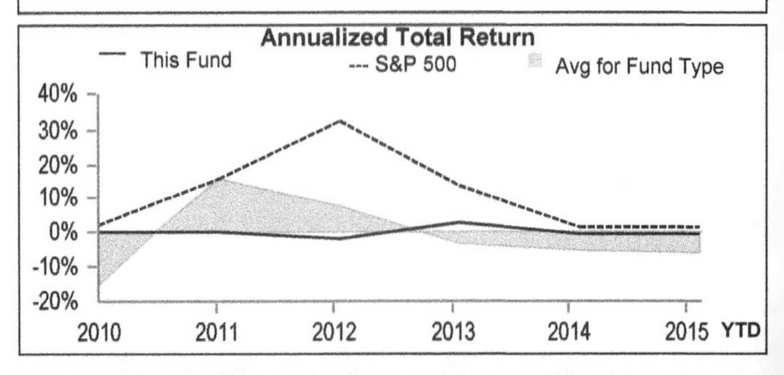

*First Trust BICK Index (BICK) D Weak

Fund Family: First Trust Advisors LP
Fund Type: Foreign
Inception Date: April 12, 2010

Major Rating Factors:
Disappointing performance is the major factor driving the D (Weak) TheStreet.com Investment Rating for *First Trust BICK Index. The fund currently has a performance rating of D (Weak) based on an annualized return of -8.50% over the last three years and a total return of -18.13% year to date 2015. Factored into the performance evaluation is an expense ratio of 0.64% (very low).

The fund's risk rating is currently C+ (Fair). It carries a beta of 1.21, meaning it is expected to move 12.1% for every 10% move in the market. Volatility, as measured by both the semi-deviation and a drawdown factor, is considered low. As of December 31, 2015, *First Trust BICK Index traded at a discount of .52% below its net asset value, which is worse than its one-year historical average discount of .76%.

Daniel J. Lindquist has been running the fund for 6 years and currently receives a manager quality ranking of 12 (0=worst, 99=best). This fund offers only a moderate level of risk but investors looking for strong performance are still waiting.

Data Date	Investment Rating	Net Assets ($Mil)	Price	Performance Rating/Pts	Total Return Y-T-D	Risk Rating/Pts
12-15	D	17.60	18.99	D / 1.9	-18.13%	C+ / 6.3
2014	D+	17.60	23.54	D+ / 2.8	-0.93%	C+ / 6.9
2013	D-	19.90	24.82	D / 1.6	-5.26%	C+ / 5.7
2012	C	48.20	25.33	B- / 7.3	7.65%	C+ / 5.9
2011	D-	43.30	22.68	E / 0.5	-29.46%	C+ / 6.0

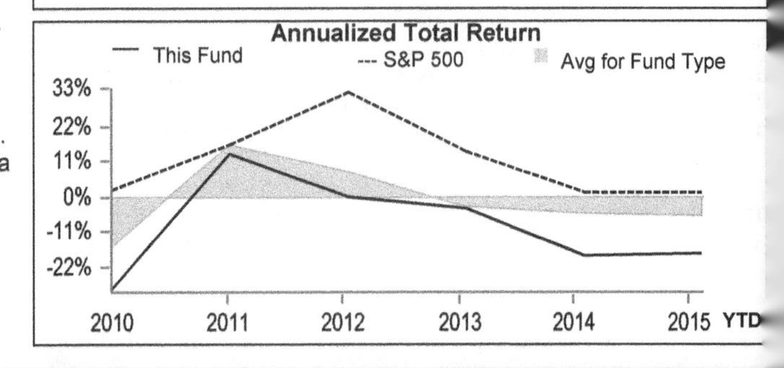

*First Trust Brazil AlphaDEX (FBZ) E+ Very Weak

Fund Family: First Trust Advisors LP
Fund Type: Foreign
Inception Date: April 18, 2011

Major Rating Factors:
Very poor performance is the major factor driving the E+ (Very Weak) TheStreet.com Investment Rating for *First Trust Brazil AlphaDEX. The fund currently has a performance rating of E+ (Very Weak) based on an annualized return of -25.12% over the last three years and a total return of -36.49% year to date 2015. Factored into the performance evaluation is an expense ratio of 0.80% (very low).

The fund's risk rating is currently C- (Fair). It carries a beta of 1.46, meaning it is expected to move 14.6% for every 10% move in the market. Volatility, as measured by both the semi-deviation and a drawdown factor, is considered average. As of December 31, 2015, *First Trust Brazil AlphaDEX traded at a discount of .11% below its net asset value, which is worse than its one-year historical average discount of .60%.

Daniel J. Lindquist has been running the fund for 5 years and currently receives a manager quality ranking of 3 (0=worst, 99=best). This fund offers an average level of risk but investors looking for strong performance will be frustrated.

Data Date	Investment Rating	Net Assets ($Mil)	Price	Performance Rating/Pts	Total Return Y-T-D	Risk Rating/Pts
12-15	E+	4.50	8.86	E+ / 0.6	-36.49%	C- / 3.4
2014	E+	4.50	15.65	D- / 1.1	-15.82%	C- / 3.1
2013	D-	5.80	19.55	D- / 1.0	-17.37%	C+ / 5.7
2012	D	5.90	23.83	D+ / 2.4	-0.58%	C+ / 6.4

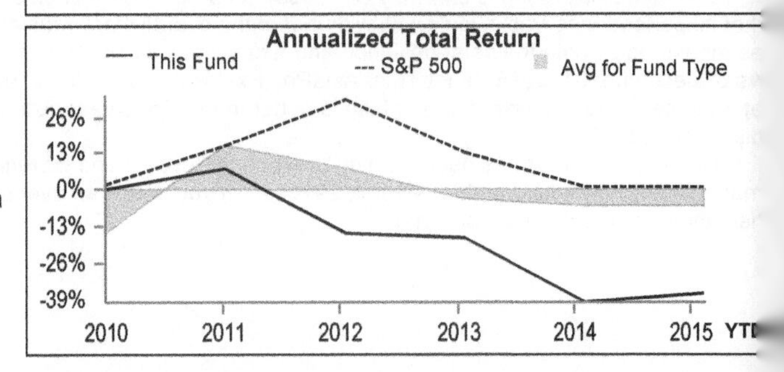

*First Trust Capital Strength ETF (FTCS) A Excellent

'und Family: First Trust Advisors LP
'und Type: Income
nception Date: July 6, 2006

lajor Rating Factors:
xceptional performance is the major factor driving the A (Excellent) TheStreet.com ivestment Rating for *First Trust Capital Strength ETF. The fund currently has a erformance rating of A- (Excellent) based on an annualized return of 15.73% over le last three years and a total return of 1.99% year to date 2015. Factored into the erformance evaluation is an expense ratio of 0.65% (very low).

The fund's risk rating is currently B- (Good). It carries a beta of 1.04, meaning lat its performance tracks fairly well with that of the overall stock market. Volatility, s measured by both the semi-deviation and a drawdown factor, is considered low. s of December 31, 2015, *First Trust Capital Strength ETF traded at a premium f .21% above its net asset value, which is worse than its one-year historical average remium of .03%.

Daniel J. Lindquist has been running the fund for 10 years and currently receives manager quality ranking of 78 (0=worst, 99=best). If you desire only a moderate vel of risk and strong performance, then this fund is an excellent option.

Data Date	Investment Rating	Net Assets ($Mil)	Price	Performance Rating/Pts	Total Return Y-T-D	Risk Rating/Pts
12-15	A	78.10	38.20	A- / 9.1	1.99%	B- / 7.5
2014	B+	78.10	38.26	A- / 9.0	17.63%	B- / 7.0
2013	B+	65.70	33.73	B+ / 8.3	30.68%	B- / 7.9
2012	C	32.70	24.88	C / 5.0	16.05%	B- / 7.8
2011	C	31.60	21.85	C / 5.3	-1.20%	B- / 7.9
2010	C	36.60	22.91	C / 5.1	13.81%	C+ / 6.1

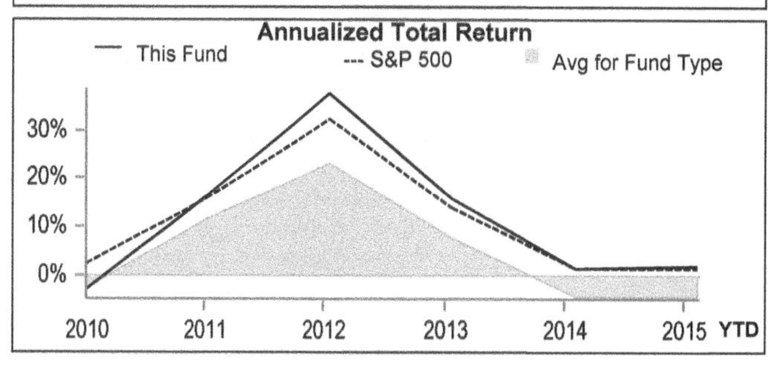

*First Trust CBOE S&P500 VIXTail (VIXH) C+ Fair

'und Family: First Trust Advisors LP
'und Type: Income
nception Date: August 29, 2012

lajor Rating Factors: Middle of the road best describes *First Trust CBOE S&P500 'IXTail whose TheStreet.com Investment Rating is currently a C+ (Fair). The fund urrently has a performance rating of C+ (Fair) based on an annualized return of .65% over the last three years and a total return of -5.13% year to date 2015. actored into the performance evaluation is an expense ratio of 0.60% (very low).

The fund's risk rating is currently B- (Good). It carries a beta of 0.74, meaning the ınd's expected move will be 7.4% for every 10% move in the market. Volatility, as easured by both the semi-deviation and a drawdown factor, is considered low. As of ecember 31, 2015, *First Trust CBOE S&P500 VIXTail traded at a premium of .71% bove its net asset value, which is worse than its one-year historical average remium of .10%.

John Gambla has been running the fund for 4 years and currently receives a lanager quality ranking of 54 (0=worst, 99=best). If you desire an average level of sk, then this fund may be an option.

Data Date	Investment Rating	Net Assets ($Mil)	Price	Performance Rating/Pts	Total Return Y-T-D	Risk Rating/Pts
12-15	C+	4.80	24.24	C+ / 6.9	-5.13%	B- / 7.1
2014	A	4.80	26.05	B+ / 8.9	17.58%	B- / 7.6
2013	A+	5.70	22.83	B / 8.1	17.26%	B+ / 9.5

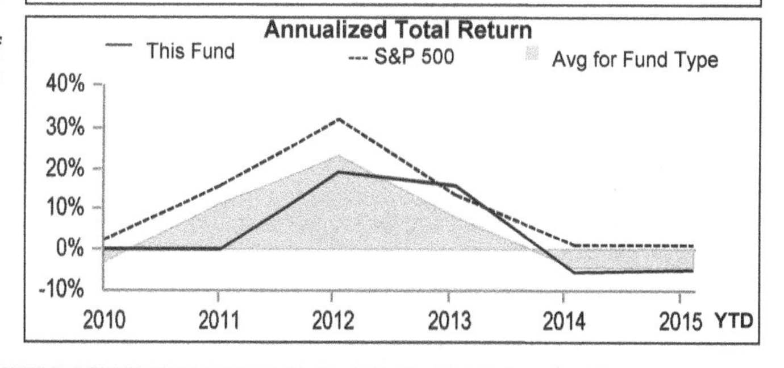

*First Trust China AlphaDEX (FCA) D+ Weak

'und Family: First Trust Advisors LP
'und Type: Foreign
nception Date: April 18, 2011

lajor Rating Factors:
isappointing performance is the major factor driving the D+ (Weak) TheStreet.com ivestment Rating for *First Trust China AlphaDEX. The fund currently has a erformance rating of D+ (Weak) based on an annualized return of -4.48% over the st three years and a total return of -7.72% year to date 2015. Factored into the erformance evaluation is an expense ratio of 0.80% (very low).

The fund's risk rating is currently C+ (Fair). It carries a beta of 0.98, meaning that s performance tracks fairly well with that of the overall stock market. Volatility, as easured by both the semi-deviation and a drawdown factor, is considered low. As of ecember 31, 2015, *First Trust China AlphaDEX traded at a discount of 1.30% elow its net asset value, which is better than its one-year historical average discount f .04%.

Daniel J. Lindquist has been running the fund for 5 years and currently receives a lanager quality ranking of 19 (0=worst, 99=best). This fund offers only a moderate vel of risk but investors looking for strong performance are still waiting.

Data Date	Investment Rating	Net Assets ($Mil)	Price	Performance Rating/Pts	Total Return Y-T-D	Risk Rating/Pts
12-15	D+	6.60	20.51	D+ / 2.6	-7.72%	C+ / 5.9
2014	C-	6.60	22.67	C / 5.0	0.21%	C+ / 6.9
2013	C-	4.70	23.42	C / 5.4	-7.49%	C+ / 6.0
2012	B	2.30	25.13	A+ / 9.8	29.58%	C+ / 5.8

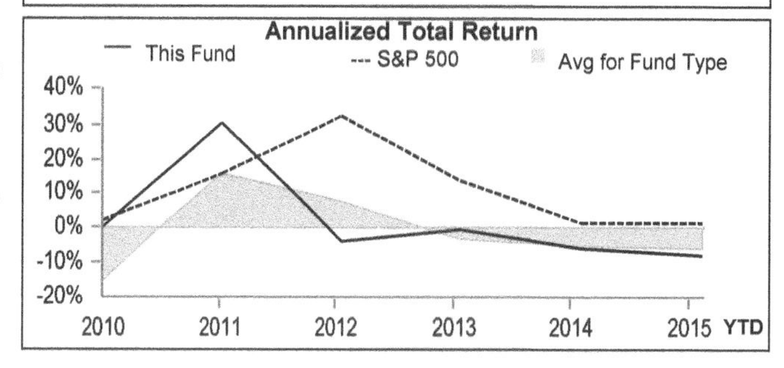

*First Trust Consumer Dis AlphaDE (FXD) A Excellent

Fund Family: First Trust Advisors LP
Fund Type: Income
Inception Date: May 8, 2007

Data Date	Investment Rating	Net Assets ($Mil)	Price	Performance Rating/Pts	Total Return Y-T-D	Risk Rating/Pts
12-15	A	1,384.50	34.10	B+ / 8.4	-3.08%	B / 8.3
2014	B+	1,384.50	35.80	A- / 9.0	12.68%	C+ / 6.9
2013	A-	1,035.90	32.25	A- / 9.0	38.52%	B- / 7.6
2012	B-	493.20	22.60	B- / 7.1	15.72%	B- / 7.8
2011	B	461.80	19.84	B / 7.9	2.77%	B- / 7.8
2010	B	401.00	19.78	B / 8.2	32.01%	C / 5.1

Major Rating Factors:
Strong performance is the major factor driving the A (Excellent) TheStreet.com Investment Rating for *First Trust Consumer Dis AlphaDE. The fund currently has a performance rating of B+ (Good) based on an annualized return of 14.30% over the last three years and a total return of -3.08% year to date 2015. Factored into the performance evaluation is an expense ratio of 0.63% (very low).

The fund's risk rating is currently B (Good). It carries a beta of 1.06, meaning that its performance tracks fairly well with that of the overall stock market. Volatility, as measured by both the semi-deviation and a drawdown factor, is considered low. As of December 31, 2015, *First Trust Consumer Dis AlphaDE traded at a discount of .03% below its net asset value, which is better than its one-year historical average premium of .02%.

Daniel J. Lindquist has been running the fund for 9 years and currently receives a manager quality ranking of 62 (0=worst, 99=best). If you desire only a moderate level of risk and strong performance, then this fund is an excellent option.

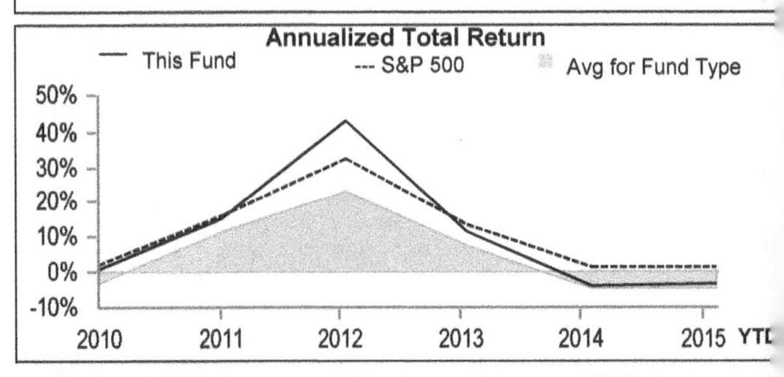

*First Trust Consumer Stap AlphaD (FXG) A Excellent

Fund Family: First Trust Advisors LP
Fund Type: Income
Inception Date: May 8, 2007

Data Date	Investment Rating	Net Assets ($Mil)	Price	Performance Rating/Pts	Total Return Y-T-D	Risk Rating/Pts
12-15	A	1,471.70	44.45	A / 9.5	6.91%	B- / 7.3
2014	A	1,471.70	42.57	A / 9.3	23.81%	B- / 7.5
2013	A+	956.80	35.66	A- / 9.1	36.85%	B / 8.6
2012	B-	398.30	25.33	C+ / 6.2	12.81%	B / 8.8
2011	B-	206.70	23.65	C+ / 6.7	13.12%	B / 8.4
2010	B+	33.70	21.10	B- / 7.0	19.75%	C+ / 6.9

Major Rating Factors:
Exceptional performance is the major factor driving the A (Excellent) TheStreet.com Investment Rating for *First Trust Consumer Stap AlphaD. The fund currently has a performance rating of A (Excellent) based on an annualized return of 21.12% over the last three years and a total return of 6.91% year to date 2015. Factored into the performance evaluation is an expense ratio of 0.62% (very low).

The fund's risk rating is currently B- (Good). It carries a beta of 1.00, meaning that its performance tracks fairly well with that of the overall stock market. Volatility, as measured by both the semi-deviation and a drawdown factor, is considered low. As of December 31, 2015, *First Trust Consumer Stap AlphaD traded at a premium of .05% above its net asset value, which is worse than its one-year historical average premium of .02%.

Daniel J. Lindquist has been running the fund for 9 years and currently receives a manager quality ranking of 91 (0=worst, 99=best). If you desire only a moderate level of risk and strong performance, then this fund is an excellent option.

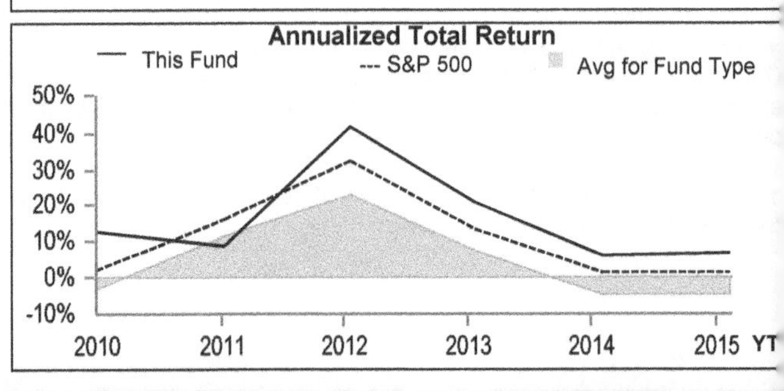

*First Trust Dev Mkt Ex-US AlphaD (FDT) C Fair

Fund Family: First Trust Advisors LP
Fund Type: Foreign
Inception Date: April 18, 2011

Data Date	Investment Rating	Net Assets ($Mil)	Price	Performance Rating/Pts	Total Return Y-T-D	Risk Rating/Pts
12-15	C	124.60	46.64	C / 5.4	0.37%	C+ / 6.9
2014	C-	124.60	47.33	C / 4.3	-4.91%	C+ / 6.4
2013	B	147.90	51.44	B / 7.8	15.66%	B- / 7.7
2012	B+	92.30	44.27	A- / 9.0	16.75%	B- / 7.5

Major Rating Factors: Middle of the road best describes *First Trust Dev Mkt Ex-US AlphaD whose TheStreet.com Investment Rating is currently a C (Fair). The fund currently has a performance rating of C (Fair) based on an annualized return of 3.32% over the last three years and a total return of 0.37% year to date 2015. Factored into the performance evaluation is an expense ratio of 0.80% (very low).

The fund's risk rating is currently C+ (Fair). It carries a beta of 0.87, meaning the fund's expected move will be 8.7% for every 10% move in the market. Volatility, as measured by both the semi-deviation and a drawdown factor, is considered low. As of December 31, 2015, *First Trust Dev Mkt Ex-US AlphaD traded at a premium of .02% above its net asset value, which is better than its one-year historical average premium of .28%.

Daniel J. Lindquist has been running the fund for 5 years and currently receives a manager quality ranking of 59 (0=worst, 99=best). If you desire an average level of risk, then this fund may be an option.

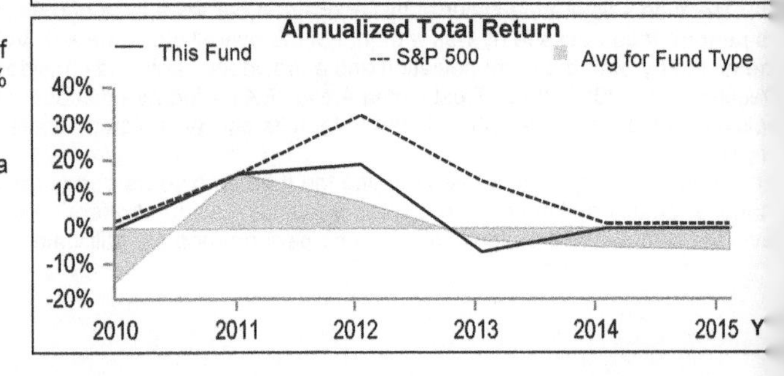

*First Trust DJ Glb Sel Div Idx F (FGD) C Fair

Fund Family: First Trust Advisors LP
Fund Type: Global
Inception Date: November 21, 2007

Major Rating Factors: Middle of the road best describes *First Trust DJ Glb Sel Div Idx F whose TheStreet.com Investment Rating is currently a C (Fair). The fund currently has a performance rating of C- (Fair) based on an annualized return of 0.94% over the last three years and a total return of -10.11% year to date 2015. Factored into the performance evaluation is an expense ratio of 0.60% (very low).

The fund's risk rating is currently B- (Good). It carries a beta of 0.94, meaning that its performance tracks fairly well with that of the overall stock market. Volatility, as measured by both the semi-deviation and a drawdown factor, is considered low. As of December 31, 2015, *First Trust DJ Glb Sel Div Idx F traded at a discount of .37% below its net asset value, which is better than its one-year historical average discount of .10%.

Daniel J. Lindquist has been running the fund for 9 years and currently receives a manager quality ranking of 38 (0=worst, 99=best). If you desire an average level of risk, then this fund may be an option.

Data Date	Investment Rating	Net Assets ($Mil)	Price	Performance Rating/Pts	Total Return Y-T-D	Risk Rating/Pts
12-15	C	562.20	21.76	C- / 3.8	-10.11%	B- / 7.7
2014	C+	562.20	25.37	C / 5.3	1.04%	B / 8.4
2013	B-	434.60	27.09	C+ / 6.7	14.34%	B / 8.2
2012	C	231.40	24.22	C / 4.9	19.30%	B / 8.1
2011	C+	124.60	21.97	C+ / 6.3	-2.09%	B- / 7.9
2010	D	59.80	23.67	D+ / 2.9	12.56%	C / 5.0

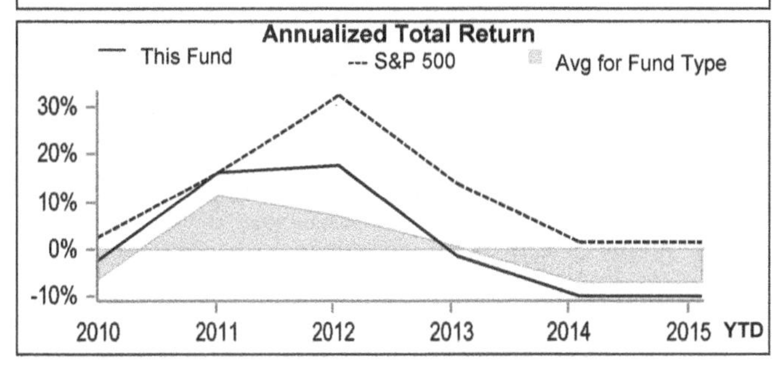

*First Trust Dorsey Wright Focus (FV) C Fair

Fund Family: First Trust Advisors LP
Fund Type: Global
Inception Date: March 5, 2014

Major Rating Factors: Middle of the road best describes *First Trust Dorsey Wright Focus whose TheStreet.com Investment Rating is currently a C (Fair). The fund currently has a performance rating of C+ (Fair) based on an annualized return of 0.00% over the last three years and a total return of 7.02% year to date 2015. Factored into the performance evaluation is an expense ratio of 0.30% (very low).

The fund's risk rating is currently C+ (Fair). It carries a beta of 0.00, meaning the fund's expected move will be 0.0% for every 10% move in the market. Volatility, as measured by both the semi-deviation and a drawdown factor, is considered low. As of December 31, 2015, *First Trust Dorsey Wright Focus traded at a premium of .09% above its net asset value, which is worse than its one-year historical average premium of .07%.

Daniel J. Lindquist has been running the fund for 2 years and currently receives a manager quality ranking of 92 (0=worst, 99=best). If you desire an average level of risk, then this fund may be an option.

Data Date	Investment Rating	Net Assets ($Mil)	Price	Performance Rating/Pts	Total Return Y-T-D	Risk Rating/Pts
12-15	C	567.10	23.49	C+ / 6.2	7.02%	C+ / 6.5

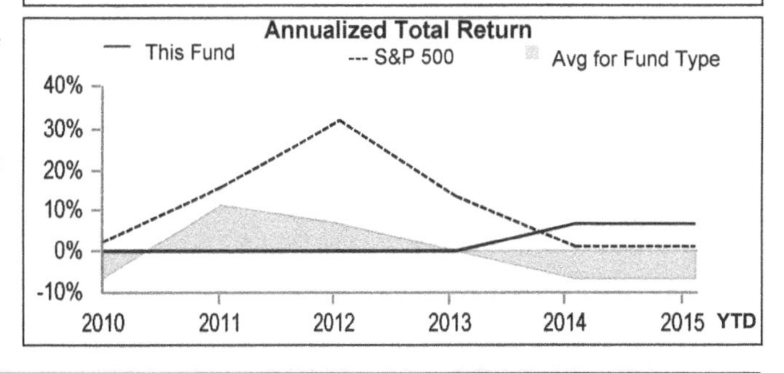

*First Trust Dorsey Wright Intl F (IFV) C Fair

Fund Family: First Trust Advisors LP
Fund Type: Global
Inception Date: July 22, 2014

Major Rating Factors: Middle of the road best describes *First Trust Dorsey Wright Intl F whose TheStreet.com Investment Rating is currently a C (Fair). The fund currently has a performance rating of C- (Fair) based on an annualized return of 0.00% over the last three years and a total return of 0.44% year to date 2015. Factored into the performance evaluation is an expense ratio of 0.30% (very low).

The fund's risk rating is currently B (Good). It carries a beta of 0.00, meaning the fund's expected move will be 0.0% for every 10% move in the market. Volatility, as measured by both the semi-deviation and a drawdown factor, is considered low. As of December 31, 2015, *First Trust Dorsey Wright Intl F traded at a discount of .22% below its net asset value, which is better than its one-year historical average premium of .11%.

Robert F. Carey currently receives a manager quality ranking of 69 (0=worst, 99=best). If you desire an average level of risk, then this fund may be an option.

Data Date	Investment Rating	Net Assets ($Mil)	Price	Performance Rating/Pts	Total Return Y-T-D	Risk Rating/Pts
12-15	C	0.00	17.89	C- / 3.6	0.44%	B / 8.0

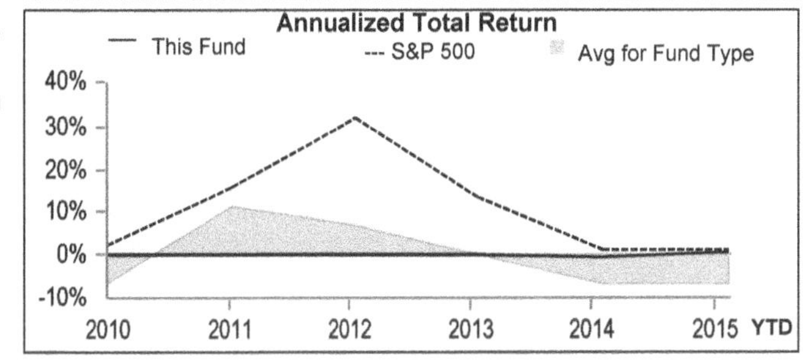

*First Trust Dow Jones Internet I (FDN) B+ Good

Fund Family: First Trust Advisors LP
Fund Type: Growth
Inception Date: June 19, 2006

Major Rating Factors:
Exceptional performance is the major factor driving the B+ (Good) TheStreet.com Investment Rating for *First Trust Dow Jones Internet I. The fund currently has a performance rating of A+ (Excellent) based on an annualized return of 22.75% over the last three years and a total return of 21.81% year to date 2015. Factored into the performance evaluation is an expense ratio of 0.54% (very low).

The fund's risk rating is currently C+ (Fair). It carries a beta of 1.15, meaning it is expected to move 11.5% for every 10% move in the market. Volatility, as measured by both the semi-deviation and a drawdown factor, is considered low. As of December 31, 2015, *First Trust Dow Jones Internet I traded at a discount of .03% below its net asset value, which is better than its one-year historical average premium of .01%.

Stan Ueland has been running the fund for 10 years and currently receives a manager quality ranking of 90 (0=worst, 99=best). If you desire only a moderate level of risk and strong performance, then this fund is an excellent option.

Data Date	Investment Rating	Net Assets ($Mil)	Price	Performance Rating/Pts	Total Return Y-T-D	Risk Rating/Pts
12-15	B+	1,756.80	74.61	A+ / 9.7	21.81%	C+ / 6.1
2014	C+	1,756.80	61.32	B+ / 8.8	4.03%	C / 5.0
2013	B-	1,929.80	59.86	A / 9.3	47.00%	C+ / 5.9
2012	C+	557.90	38.97	B+ / 8.6	25.60%	C+ / 5.8
2011	C+	519.70	32.30	B / 8.1	-7.15%	C+ / 6.2
2010	B-	589.50	34.32	B+ / 8.7	36.72%	C- / 4.0

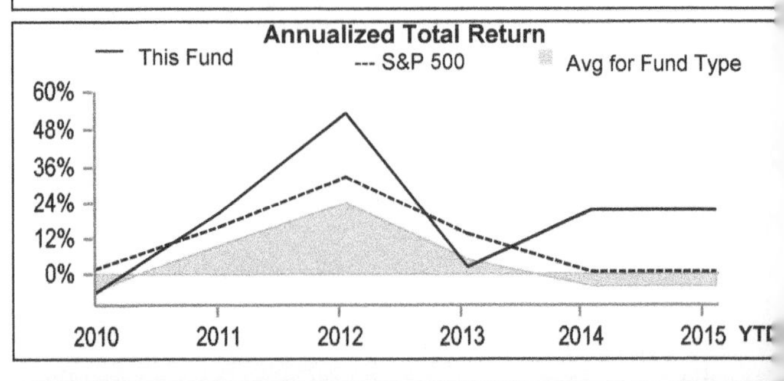

*First Trust Dow Jones Sel Micro (FDM) A+ Excellent

Fund Family: First Trust Advisors LP
Fund Type: Growth
Inception Date: September 27, 2005

Major Rating Factors:
Strong performance is the major factor driving the A+ (Excellent) TheStreet.com Investment Rating for *First Trust Dow Jones Sel Micro. The fund currently has a performance rating of B+ (Good) based on an annualized return of 12.95% over the last three years and a total return of 1.81% year to date 2015. Factored into the performance evaluation is an expense ratio of 0.60% (very low).

The fund's risk rating is currently B (Good). It carries a beta of 0.98, meaning that its performance tracks fairly well with that of the overall stock market. Volatility, as measured by both the semi-deviation and a drawdown factor, is considered low. As of December 31, 2015, *First Trust Dow Jones Sel Micro traded at a discount of .06% below its net asset value, which is better than its one-year historical average discount of .01%.

Daniel J. Lindquist has been running the fund for 11 years and currently receives a manager quality ranking of 63 (0=worst, 99=best). If you desire only a moderate level of risk and strong performance, then this fund is an excellent option.

Data Date	Investment Rating	Net Assets ($Mil)	Price	Performance Rating/Pts	Total Return Y-T-D	Risk Rating/Pts
12-15	A+	50.70	32.90	B+ / 8.4	1.81%	B / 8.5
2014	B	50.70	33.39	B / 7.8	4.83%	B- / 7.0
2013	B	91.10	32.59	B+ / 8.6	36.68%	B- / 7.2
2012	C	41.30	22.83	C / 4.9	15.05%	B- / 7.2
2011	C-	52.30	20.08	C / 4.5	-7.22%	B- / 7.0
2010	C+	153.00	22.15	C+ / 6.9	25.58%	C+ / 5.7

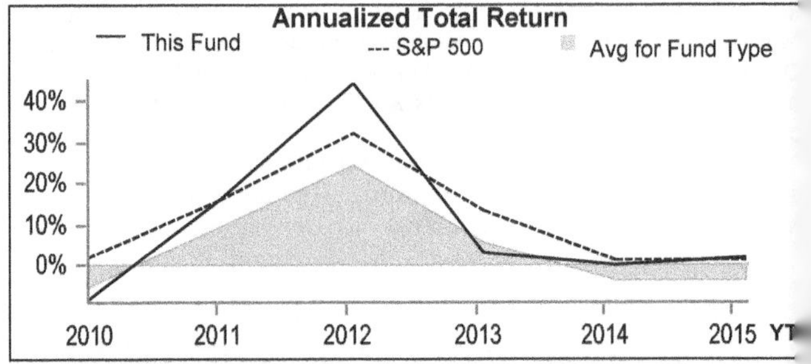

*First Trust Emerg Mkt AlphaDEX (FEM) D Weak

Fund Family: First Trust Advisors LP
Fund Type: Emerging Market
Inception Date: April 18, 2011

Major Rating Factors:
Disappointing performance is the major factor driving the D (Weak) TheStreet.com Investment Rating for *First Trust Emerg Mkt AlphaDEX. The fund currently has a performance rating of D (Weak) based on an annualized return of -10.25% over the last three years and a total return of -13.48% year to date 2015. Factored into the performance evaluation is an expense ratio of 0.80% (very low).

The fund's risk rating is currently C+ (Fair). It carries a beta of 1.15, meaning it is expected to move 11.5% for every 10% move in the market. Volatility, as measured by both the semi-deviation and a drawdown factor, is considered low. As of December 31, 2015, *First Trust Emerg Mkt AlphaDEX traded at a discount of .72% below its net asset value, which is better than its one-year historical average discount of .37%.

Daniel J. Lindquist has been running the fund for 5 years and currently receives a manager quality ranking of 48 (0=worst, 99=best). This fund offers only a moderate level of risk but investors looking for strong performance are still waiting.

Data Date	Investment Rating	Net Assets ($Mil)	Price	Performance Rating/Pts	Total Return Y-T-D	Risk Rating/Pts
12-15	D	424.70	17.97	D / 1.7	-13.48%	C+ / 6.4
2014	D+	424.70	21.56	D+ / 2.3	-8.27%	B- / 7.2
2013	D	330.10	24.83	D / 1.8	-8.74%	B- / 7.2
2012	B+	129.20	26.39	A / 9.4	19.13%	B- / 7.1

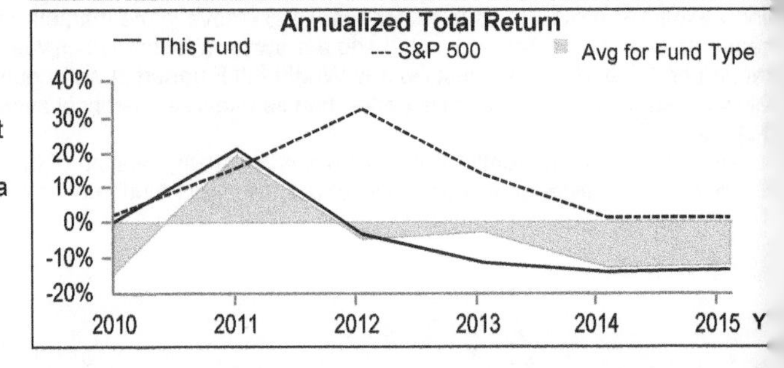

*First Trust Energy AlphaDEX (FXN) D Weak

Fund Family: First Trust Advisors LP
Fund Type: Energy/Natural Resources
Inception Date: May 8, 2007

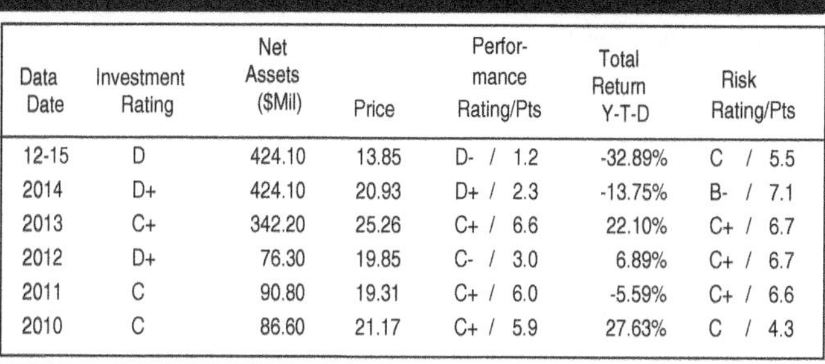

Data Date	Investment Rating	Net Assets ($Mil)	Price	Performance Rating/Pts	Total Return Y-T-D	Risk Rating/Pts
12-15	D	424.10	13.85	D- / 1.2	-32.89%	C / 5.5
2014	D+	424.10	20.93	D+ / 2.3	-13.75%	B- / 7.1
2013	C+	342.20	25.26	C+ / 6.6	22.10%	C+ / 6.7
2012	D+	76.30	19.85	C- / 3.0	6.89%	C+ / 6.7
2011	C	90.80	19.31	C+ / 6.0	-5.59%	C+ / 6.6
2010	C	86.60	21.17	C+ / 5.9	27.63%	C / 4.3

Major Rating Factors:
Disappointing performance is the major factor driving the D (Weak) TheStreet.com Investment Rating for *First Trust Energy AlphaDEX. The fund currently has a performance rating of D- (Weak) based on an annualized return of -11.05% over the last three years and a total return of -32.89% year to date 2015. Factored into the performance evaluation is an expense ratio of 0.64% (very low).

The fund's risk rating is currently C (Fair). It carries a beta of 1.33, meaning it is expected to move 13.3% for every 10% move in the market. Volatility, as measured by both the semi-deviation and a drawdown factor, is considered average. As of December 31, 2015, *First Trust Energy AlphaDEX traded at a discount of .14% below its net asset value, which is better than its one-year historical average discount of .02%.

Daniel J. Lindquist has been running the fund for 9 years and currently receives a manager quality ranking of 28 (0=worst, 99=best). This fund offers an average level of risk but investors looking for strong performance will be frustrated.

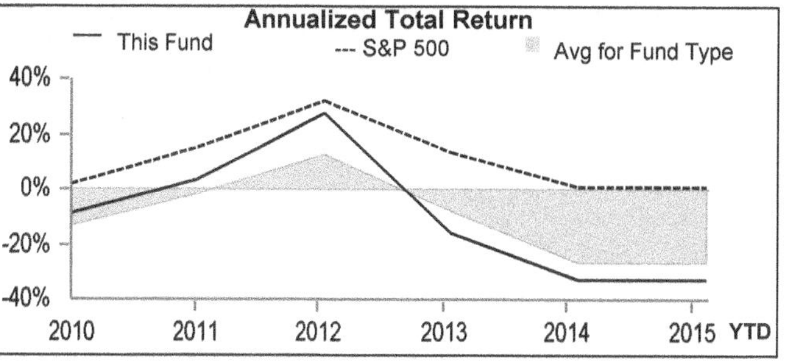

*First Trust Enhanced Short Matur (FTSM) C+ Fair

Fund Family: First Trust Advisors LP
Fund Type: Corporate - Investment Grade
Inception Date: August 5, 2014

Data Date	Investment Rating	Net Assets ($Mil)	Price	Performance Rating/Pts	Total Return Y-T-D	Risk Rating/Pts
12-15	C+	0.00	59.82	C / 4.4	0.22%	B+ / 9.4

Major Rating Factors: Middle of the road best describes *First Trust Enhanced Short Matur whose TheStreet.com Investment Rating is currently a C+ (Fair). The fund currently has a performance rating of C (Fair) based on an annualized return of 0.00% over the last three years and a total return of 0.22% year to date 2015.

The fund's risk rating is currently B+ (Good). It carries a beta of 0.00, meaning the fund's expected move will be 0.0% for every 10% move in the market. Volatility, as measured by both the semi-deviation and a drawdown factor, is considered very low. As of December 31, 2015, *First Trust Enhanced Short Matur traded at a discount of .07% below its net asset value, which is better than its one-year historical average discount of .05%.

Todd Larson has been running the fund for 2 years and currently receives a manager quality ranking of 71 (0=worst, 99=best). If you desire an average level of risk, then this fund may be an option.

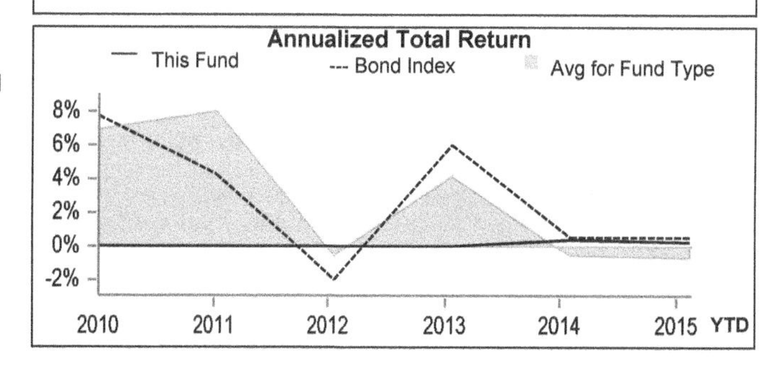

*First Trust Europe AlphaDEX (FEP) B- Good

Fund Family: First Trust Advisors LP
Fund Type: Foreign
Inception Date: April 18, 2011

Data Date	Investment Rating	Net Assets ($Mil)	Price	Performance Rating/Pts	Total Return Y-T-D	Risk Rating/Pts
12-15	B-	693.30	29.52	C+ / 6.3	2.88%	B- / 7.8
2014	C-	693.30	29.41	C / 5.3	-8.87%	C+ / 5.8
2013	A	405.50	33.44	A / 9.5	27.41%	B- / 7.4
2012	A-	30.80	26.20	A+ / 9.7	24.40%	B- / 7.2

Major Rating Factors: *First Trust Europe AlphaDEX receives a TheStreet.com Investment Rating of B- (Good). The fund currently has a performance rating of C+ (Fair) based on an annualized return of 6.12% over the last three years and a total return of 2.88% year to date 2015. Factored into the performance evaluation is an expense ratio of 0.80% (very low).

The fund's risk rating is currently B- (Good). It carries a beta of 1.01, meaning that its performance tracks fairly well with that of the overall stock market. Volatility, as measured by both the semi-deviation and a drawdown factor, is considered low. As of December 31, 2015, *First Trust Europe AlphaDEX traded at a discount of .30% below its net asset value, which is better than its one-year historical average premium of .32%.

Daniel J. Lindquist has been running the fund for 5 years and currently receives a manager quality ranking of 74 (0=worst, 99=best). If you desire an average level of risk, then this fund may be an option.

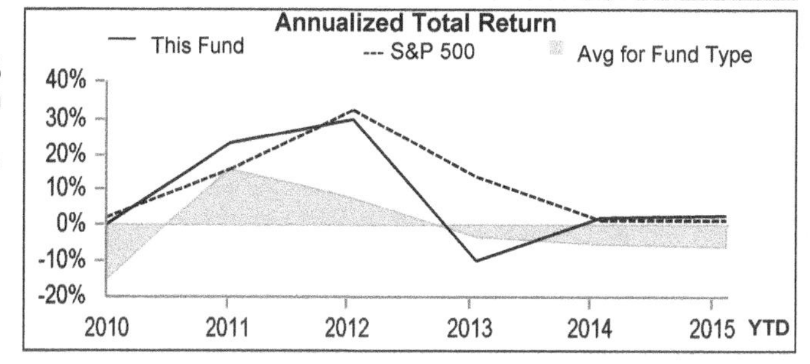

*First Trust Eurozone AlphaDEX (FEUZ) C- Fair

Fund Family: First Trust Advisors LP
Fund Type: Foreign
Inception Date: October 21, 2014

Major Rating Factors: Middle of the road best describes *First Trust Eurozone AlphaDEX whose TheStreet.com Investment Rating is currently a C- (Fair). The fund currently has a performance rating of C (Fair) based on an annualized return of 0.00% over the last three years and a total return of 3.33% year to date 2015.

The fund's risk rating is currently C (Fair). It carries a beta of 0.00, meaning the fund's expected move will be 0.0% for every 10% move in the market. Volatility, as measured by both the semi-deviation and a drawdown factor, is considered average. As of December 31, 2015, *First Trust Eurozone AlphaDEX traded at a discount of .66% below its net asset value, which is better than its one-year historical average discount of .16%.

Timothy S. Henry currently receives a manager quality ranking of 87 (0=worst, 99=best). If you desire an average level of risk, then this fund may be an option.

Data Date	Investment Rating	Net Assets ($Mil)	Price	Performance Rating/Pts	Total Return Y-T-D	Risk Rating/Pts
12-15	C-	0.00	31.44	C / 5.5	3.33%	C / 5.0

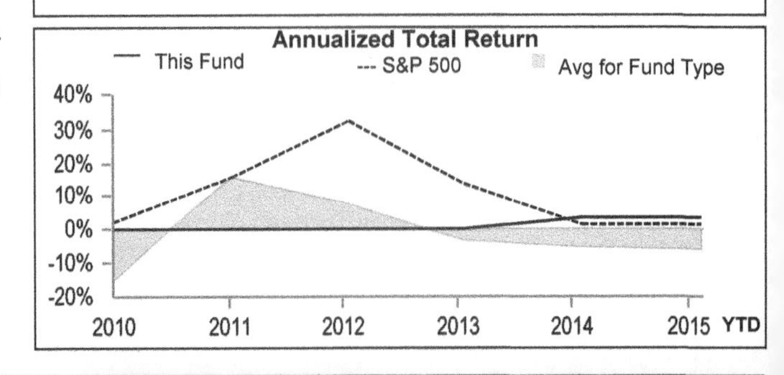

*First Trust Financial AlphaDEX (FXO) A+ Excellent

Fund Family: First Trust Advisors LP
Fund Type: Financial Services
Inception Date: May 8, 2007

Major Rating Factors:
Strong performance is the major factor driving the A+ (Excellent) TheStreet.com Investment Rating for *First Trust Financial AlphaDEX. The fund currently has a performance rating of B+ (Good) based on an annualized return of 13.99% over the last three years and a total return of 1.30% year to date 2015. Factored into the performance evaluation is an expense ratio of 0.64% (very low).

The fund's risk rating is currently B (Good). It carries a beta of 0.98, meaning that its performance tracks fairly well with that of the overall stock market. Volatility, as measured by both the semi-deviation and a drawdown factor, is considered low. As of December 31, 2015, *First Trust Financial AlphaDEX traded at a discount of .04% below its net asset value, which is better than its one-year historical average premium of .01%.

Daniel J. Lindquist has been running the fund for 9 years and currently receives a manager quality ranking of 72 (0=worst, 99=best). If you desire only a moderate level of risk and strong performance, then this fund is an excellent option.

Data Date	Investment Rating	Net Assets ($Mil)	Price	Performance Rating/Pts	Total Return Y-T-D	Risk Rating/Pts
12-15	A+	919.40	23.18	B+ / 8.7	1.30%	B / 8.9
2014	A-	919.40	23.27	B+ / 8.9	10.79%	B- / 7.4
2013	B+	637.10	21.74	B+ / 8.5	32.90%	B- / 7.8
2012	C+	196.90	15.67	C+ / 6.0	21.27%	B- / 7.7
2011	C	77.80	13.19	C / 4.9	-6.76%	B- / 7.3
2010	C-	330.00	14.61	C / 4.9	19.25%	C / 5.1

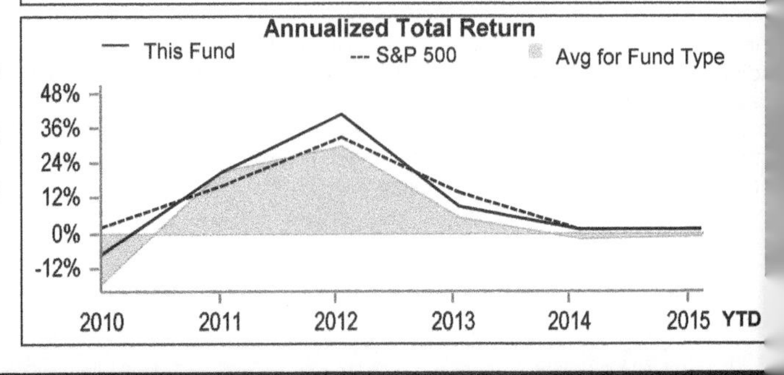

*First Trust FTSE EPRA/NAREIT Glb (FFR) C Fair

Fund Family: First Trust Advisors LP
Fund Type: Growth and Income
Inception Date: August 27, 2007

Major Rating Factors: Middle of the road best describes *First Trust FTSE EPRA/NAREIT Glb whose TheStreet.com Investment Rating is currently a C (Fair). The fund currently has a performance rating of C+ (Fair) based on an annualized return of 5.23% over the last three years and a total return of -0.65% year to date 2015. Factored into the performance evaluation is an expense ratio of 0.60% (very low).

The fund's risk rating is currently C+ (Fair). It carries a beta of 0.55, meaning the fund's expected move will be 5.5% for every 10% move in the market. Volatility, as measured by both the semi-deviation and a drawdown factor, is considered low. As of December 31, 2015, *First Trust FTSE EPRA/NAREIT Glb traded at a premium of .54% above its net asset value, which is worse than its one-year historical average discount of .16%.

Daniel J. Lindquist has been running the fund for 9 years and currently receives a manager quality ranking of 48 (0=worst, 99=best). If you desire an average level of risk, then this fund may be an option.

Data Date	Investment Rating	Net Assets ($Mil)	Price	Performance Rating/Pts	Total Return Y-T-D	Risk Rating/Pts
12-15	C	108.90	42.68	C+ / 6.2	-0.65%	C+ / 6.5
2014	B	108.90	43.73	B- / 7.5	16.59%	B- / 7.9
2013	C	98.00	39.21	C / 4.9	1.00%	B- / 7.5
2012	C+	101.80	39.37	B- / 7.2	28.61%	B- / 7.0
2011	C-	71.70	32.00	C / 4.6	-6.48%	C+ / 6.1
2010	D	59.20	34.93	C- / 3.1	19.23%	C- / 4.2

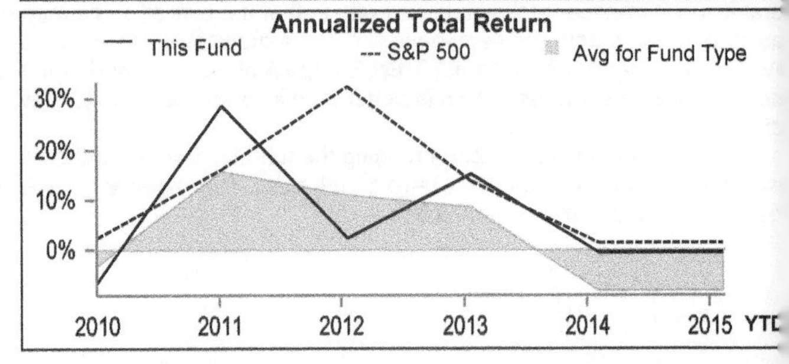

*First Trust Gl Tct Cmdty Strateg (FTGC) D Weak

Fund Family: First Trust Advisors LP
Fund Type: Global
Inception Date: October 22, 2013

Major Rating Factors:
Very poor performance is the major factor driving the D (Weak) TheStreet.com Investment Rating for *First Trust Gl Tct Cmdty Strateg. The fund currently has a performance rating of E+ (Very Weak) based on an annualized return of 0.00% over the last three years and a total return of -22.33% year to date 2015. Factored into the performance evaluation is an expense ratio of 0.95% (low).

The fund's risk rating is currently C+ (Fair). It carries a beta of 0.00, meaning the fund's expected move will be 0.0% for every 10% move in the market. Volatility, as measured by both the semi-deviation and a drawdown factor, is considered low. As of December 31, 2015, *First Trust Gl Tct Cmdty Strateg traded at a discount of .05% below its net asset value, which is better than its one-year historical average discount of .01%.

Daniel J. Lindquist has been running the fund for 3 years and currently receives a manager quality ranking of 6 (0=worst, 99=best). This fund offers only a moderate level of risk but investors looking for strong performance are still waiting.

Data Date	Investment Rating	Net Assets ($Mil)	Price	Performance Rating/Pts	Total Return Y-T-D	Risk Rating/Pts
12-15	D	182.90	20.31	E+ / 0.6	-22.33%	C+ / 6.3
2014	E	182.90	26.29	E+ / 0.6	-11.71%	D+ / 2.8

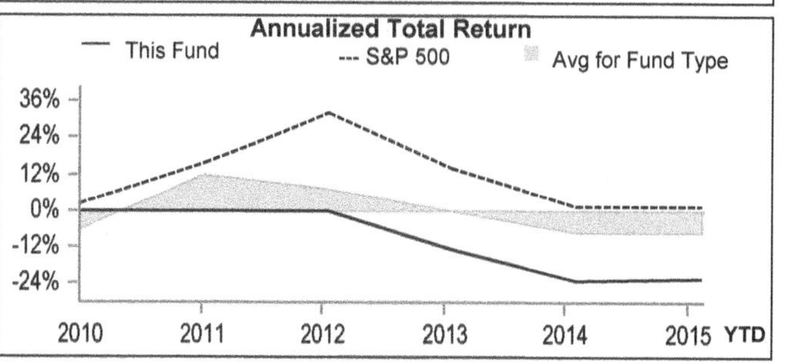

*First Trust Health Care AlphaDEX (FXH) B+ Good

Fund Family: First Trust Advisors LP
Fund Type: Health
Inception Date: May 8, 2007

Major Rating Factors:
Exceptional performance is the major factor driving the B+ (Good) TheStreet.com Investment Rating for *First Trust Health Care AlphaDEX. The fund currently has a performance rating of A (Excellent) based on an annualized return of 21.79% over the last three years and a total return of -0.05% year to date 2015. Factored into the performance evaluation is an expense ratio of 0.62% (very low).

The fund's risk rating is currently C+ (Fair). It carries a beta of 0.88, meaning the fund's expected move will be 8.8% for every 10% move in the market. Volatility, as measured by both the semi-deviation and a drawdown factor, is considered low. As of December 31, 2015, *First Trust Health Care AlphaDEX traded at a premium of .03% above its net asset value, which is worse than its one-year historical average premium of .02%.

Daniel J. Lindquist has been running the fund for 9 years and currently receives a manager quality ranking of 94 (0=worst, 99=best). If you desire only a moderate level of risk and strong performance, then this fund is an excellent option.

Data Date	Investment Rating	Net Assets ($Mil)	Price	Performance Rating/Pts	Total Return Y-T-D	Risk Rating/Pts
12-15	B+	2,404.80	60.45	A / 9.4	-0.05%	C+ / 6.4
2014	A+	2,404.80	60.29	A+ / 9.6	27.11%	B / 8.7
2013	A	1,464.00	48.07	A / 9.3	42.98%	B- / 7.7
2012	B	644.00	32.57	B- / 7.2	22.85%	B / 8.3
2011	B	401.20	27.12	B- / 7.5	5.78%	B- / 7.8
2010	A-	59.00	25.69	B / 7.6	19.02%	C+ / 6.8

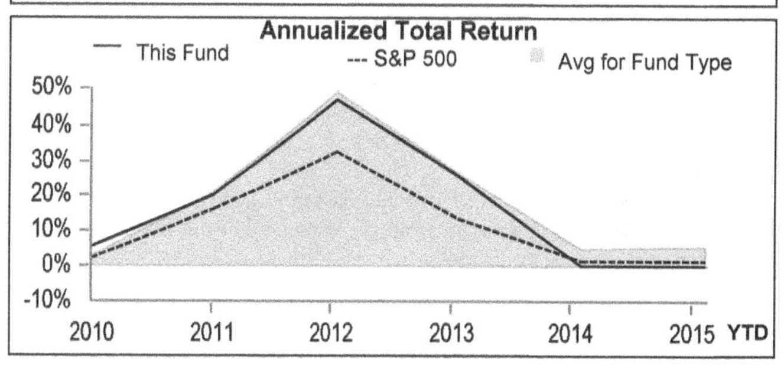

*First Trust High Income (FTHI) C+ Fair

Fund Family: First Trust Advisors LP
Fund Type: Income
Inception Date: January 6, 2014

Major Rating Factors: Middle of the road best describes *First Trust High Income whose TheStreet.com Investment Rating is currently a C+ (Fair). The fund currently has a performance rating of C+ (Fair) based on an annualized return of 0.00% over the last three years and a total return of 2.86% year to date 2015. Factored into the performance evaluation is an expense ratio of 0.85% (very low).

The fund's risk rating is currently B- (Good). It carries a beta of 0.00, meaning the fund's expected move will be 0.0% for every 10% move in the market. Volatility, as measured by both the semi-deviation and a drawdown factor, is considered low. As of December 31, 2015, *First Trust High Income traded at a premium of .75% above its net asset value, which is worse than its one-year historical average premium of .27%.

Daniel J. Lindquist has been running the fund for 2 years and currently receives a manager quality ranking of 79 (0=worst, 99=best). If you desire an average level of risk, then this fund may be an option.

Data Date	Investment Rating	Net Assets ($Mil)	Price	Performance Rating/Pts	Total Return Y-T-D	Risk Rating/Pts
12-15	C+	3.00	20.07	C+ / 6.2	2.86%	B- / 7.1

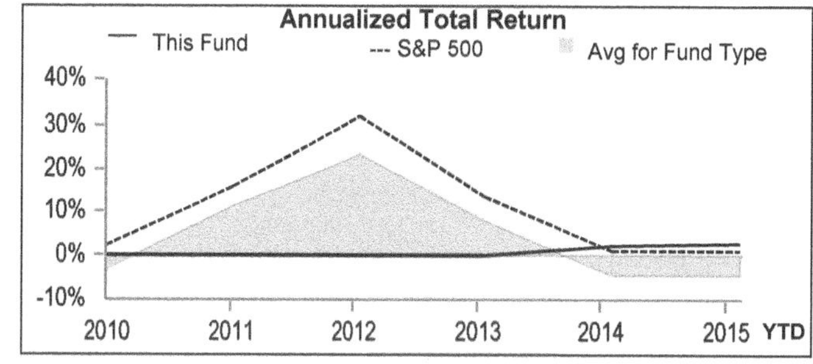

*First Trust Industrials AlphaDEX (FXR) C+ Fair

Fund Family: First Trust Advisors LP
Fund Type: Income
Inception Date: May 8, 2007

Major Rating Factors: Middle of the road best describes *First Trust Industrials AlphaDEX whose TheStreet.com Investment Rating is currently a C+ (Fair). The fund currently has a performance rating of C+ (Fair) based on an annualized return of 9.69% over the last three years and a total return of -13.19% year to date 2015. Factored into the performance evaluation is an expense ratio of 0.63% (very low).

The fund's risk rating is currently C+ (Fair). It carries a beta of 1.23, meaning it is expected to move 12.3% for every 10% move in the market. Volatility, as measured by both the semi-deviation and a drawdown factor, is considered low. As of December 31, 2015, *First Trust Industrials AlphaDEX traded at a premium of .04% above its net asset value.

Daniel J. Lindquist has been running the fund for 9 years and currently receives a manager quality ranking of 24 (0=worst, 99=best). If you desire an average level of risk, then this fund may be an option.

Data Date	Investment Rating	Net Assets ($Mil)	Price	Performance Rating/Pts	Total Return Y-T-D	Risk Rating/Pts
12-15	C+	1,219.60	26.10	C+ / 6.4	-13.19%	C+ / 6.7
2014	B+	1,219.60	30.33	B+ / 8.6	9.78%	B- / 7.3
2013	A-	727.60	28.39	A- / 9.0	38.91%	B- / 7.6
2012	C	132.30	19.43	C / 5.1	13.70%	B- / 7.4
2011	C	54.20	17.17	C+ / 5.8	-4.75%	B- / 7.2
2010	C	43.20	18.48	C+ / 6.2	26.08%	C / 4.3

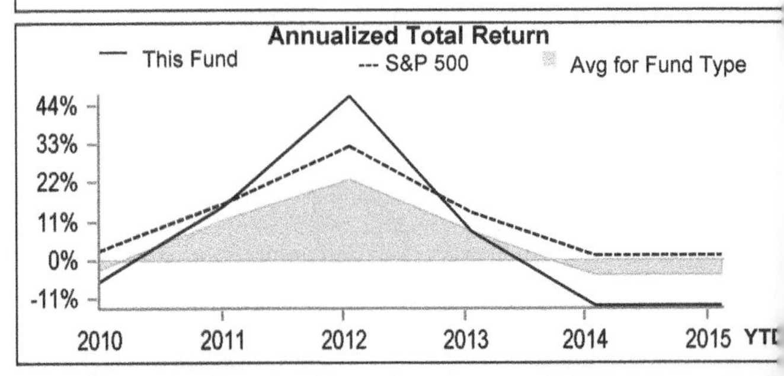

*First Trust International IPO ET (FPXI) D- Weak

Fund Family: First Trust Advisors LP
Fund Type: Global
Inception Date: November 4, 2014

Major Rating Factors:
Disappointing performance is the major factor driving the D- (Weak) TheStreet.com Investment Rating for *First Trust International IPO ET. The fund currently has a performance rating of D+ (Weak) based on an annualized return of 0.00% over the last three years and a total return of -5.13% year to date 2015. Factored into the performance evaluation is an expense ratio of 0.70% (very low).

The fund's risk rating is currently C- (Fair). It carries a beta of 0.00, meaning the fund's expected move will be 0.0% for every 10% move in the market. Volatility, as measured by both the semi-deviation and a drawdown factor, is considered average. As of December 31, 2015, *First Trust International IPO ET traded at a premium of .18% above its net asset value, which is better than its one-year historical average premium of .29%.

Robert F. Carey currently receives a manager quality ranking of 32 (0=worst, 99=best). This fund offers an average level of risk but investors looking for strong performance will be frustrated.

Data Date	Investment Rating	Net Assets ($Mil)	Price	Performance Rating/Pts	Total Return Y-T-D	Risk Rating/Pts
12-15	D-	0.00	27.14	D+ / 2.5	-5.13%	C- / 3.0

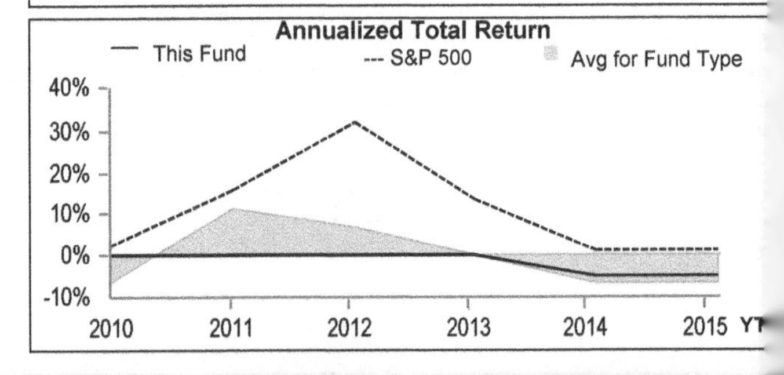

*First Trust Intl MA Dvsfd Inc In (YDIV) D+ Weak

Fund Family: First Trust Advisors LP
Fund Type: Foreign
Inception Date: August 22, 2013

Major Rating Factors:
Disappointing performance is the major factor driving the D+ (Weak) TheStreet.com Investment Rating for *First Trust Intl MA Dvsfd Inc In. The fund currently has a performance rating of D+ (Weak) based on an annualized return of 0.00% over the last three years and a total return of -8.80% year to date 2015. Factored into the performance evaluation is an expense ratio of 0.70% (very low).

The fund's risk rating is currently C+ (Fair). It carries a beta of 0.00, meaning the fund's expected move will be 0.0% for every 10% move in the market. Volatility, as measured by both the semi-deviation and a drawdown factor, is considered low. As of December 31, 2015, *First Trust Intl MA Dvsfd Inc In traded at a premium of 3.88% above its net asset value, which is worse than its one-year historical average premium of .55%.

Daniel J. Lindquist has been running the fund for 3 years and currently receives a manager quality ranking of 17 (0=worst, 99=best). This fund offers only a moderate level of risk but investors looking for strong performance are still waiting.

Data Date	Investment Rating	Net Assets ($Mil)	Price	Performance Rating/Pts	Total Return Y-T-D	Risk Rating/Pts
12-15	D+	13.10	16.61	D+ / 2.6	-8.80%	C+ / 5.7
2014	D	13.10	19.32	D / 2.0	0.74%	C+ / 6.9

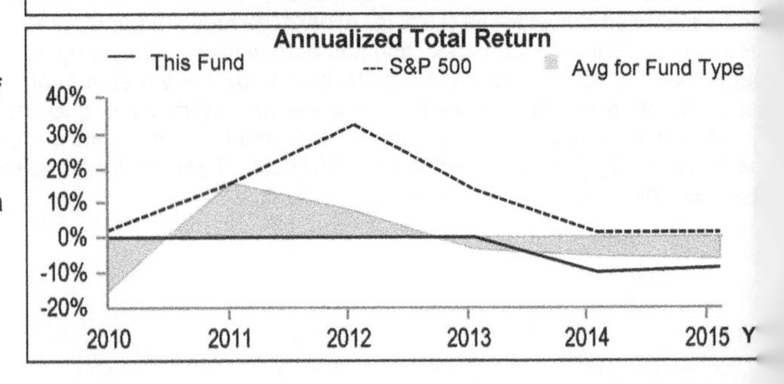

* Denotes ETF Fund

*First Trust ISE Chindia Index (FNI) B Good

und Family: First Trust Advisors LP
und Type: Income
nception Date: May 8, 2007

ajor Rating Factors: Strong performance is the major factor driving the B (Good) heStreet.com Investment Rating for *First Trust ISE Chindia Index. The fund urrently has a performance rating of B (Good) based on an annualized return of 0.56% over the last three years and a total return of -1.76% year to date 2015. actored into the performance evaluation is an expense ratio of 0.60% (very low).

The fund's risk rating is currently B- (Good). It carries a beta of 1.17, meaning it is xpected to move 11.7% for every 10% move in the market. Volatility, as measured y both the semi-deviation and a drawdown factor, is considered low. As of ecember 31, 2015, *First Trust ISE Chindia Index traded at a price exactly equal to s net asset value.

Daniel J. Lindquist has been running the fund for 9 years and currently receives a anager quality ranking of 28 (0=worst, 99=best). If you desire only a moderate level f risk and strong performance, then this fund is an excellent option.

Data Date	Investment Rating	Net Assets ($Mil)	Price	Performance Rating/Pts	Total Return Y-T-D	Risk Rating/Pts
12-15	B	67.90	28.36	B / 7.6	-1.76%	B- / 7.0
2014	B-	67.90	28.60	C+ / 6.8	3.01%	B- / 7.6
2013	C	72.00	28.24	C+ / 6.6	32.15%	C+ / 6.1
2012	D	66.10	20.95	D+ / 2.6	14.51%	C+ / 6.1
2011	D+	79.30	18.15	C / 4.3	-24.45%	C+ / 5.9
2010	D	176.30	25.02	C- / 3.7	18.17%	C- / 4.1

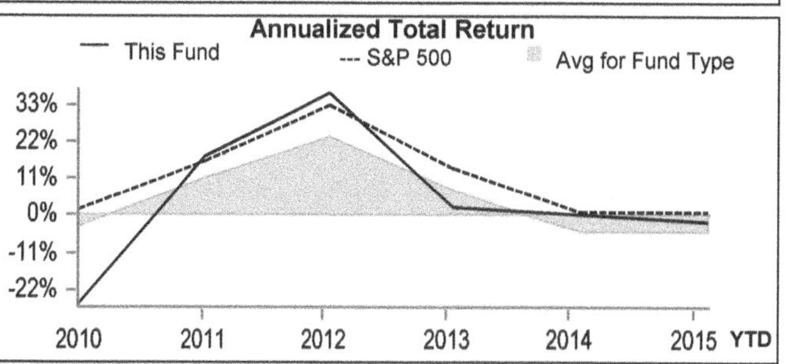

*First Trust ISE Cloud Computing (SKYY) B+ Good

und Family: First Trust Advisors LP
und Type: Global
nception Date: July 5, 2011

ajor Rating Factors: Strong performance is the major factor driving the B+ (Good) heStreet.com Investment Rating for *First Trust ISE Cloud Computing. The fund urrently has a performance rating of B+ (Good) based on an annualized return of 3.84% over the last three years and a total return of 5.66% year to date 2015. actored into the performance evaluation is an expense ratio of 0.60% (very low).

The fund's risk rating is currently B- (Good). It carries a beta of 0.83, meaning the ind's expected move will be 8.3% for every 10% move in the market. Volatility, as easured by both the semi-deviation and a drawdown factor, is considered low. As of ecember 31, 2015, *First Trust ISE Cloud Computing traded at a premium of .20% bove its net asset value, which is worse than its one-year historical average remium of .09%.

Daniel J. Lindquist has been running the fund for 5 years and currently receives a anager quality ranking of 95 (0=worst, 99=best). If you desire only a moderate level risk and strong performance, then this fund is an excellent option.

Data Date	Investment Rating	Net Assets ($Mil)	Price	Performance Rating/Pts	Total Return Y-T-D	Risk Rating/Pts
12-15	B+	341.80	30.04	B+ / 8.9	5.66%	B- / 7.2
2014	C+	341.80	28.45	B / 7.6	8.74%	C+ / 6.4
2013	A	168.40	26.55	A / 9.5	28.67%	B- / 7.8
2012	B+	77.50	19.87	A- / 9.1	18.50%	B- / 7.6

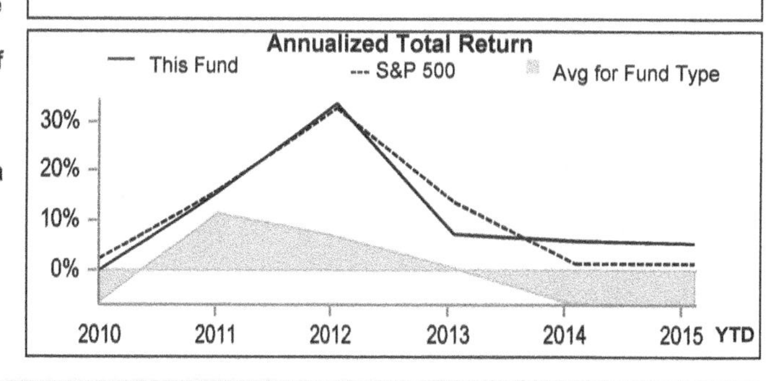

*First Trust ISE Glb Eng & Constr (FLM) C Fair

und Family: First Trust Advisors LP
und Type: Global
nception Date: October 13, 2008

ajor Rating Factors: Middle of the road best describes *First Trust ISE Glb Eng & onstr whose TheStreet.com Investment Rating is currently a C (Fair). The fund urrently has a performance rating of C (Fair) based on an annualized return of 45% over the last three years and a total return of -0.88% year to date 2015. actored into the performance evaluation is an expense ratio of 0.70% (very low).

The fund's risk rating is currently B- (Good). It carries a beta of 0.87, meaning the nd's expected move will be 8.7% for every 10% move in the market. Volatility, as easured by both the semi-deviation and a drawdown factor, is considered low. As of ecember 31, 2015, *First Trust ISE Glb Eng & Constr traded at a price exactly equal its net asset value, which is worse than its one-year historical average discount .03%.

Daniel J. Lindquist has been running the fund for 8 years and currently receives a anager quality ranking of 55 (0=worst, 99=best). If you desire an average level of sk, then this fund may be an option.

Data Date	Investment Rating	Net Assets ($Mil)	Price	Performance Rating/Pts	Total Return Y-T-D	Risk Rating/Pts
12-15	C	16.80	44.24	C / 5.1	-0.88%	B- / 7.1
2014	C	16.80	45.18	C / 4.3	-8.47%	B- / 7.7
2013	C	25.60	51.46	C+ / 6.2	19.22%	C+ / 6.7
2012	D+	19.10	42.28	C- / 3.4	18.58%	C+ / 6.5
2011	D	25.30	36.03	D+ / 2.3	-15.96%	C+ / 6.7
2010	A	37.90	44.71	A / 9.4	17.63%	C+ / 6.6

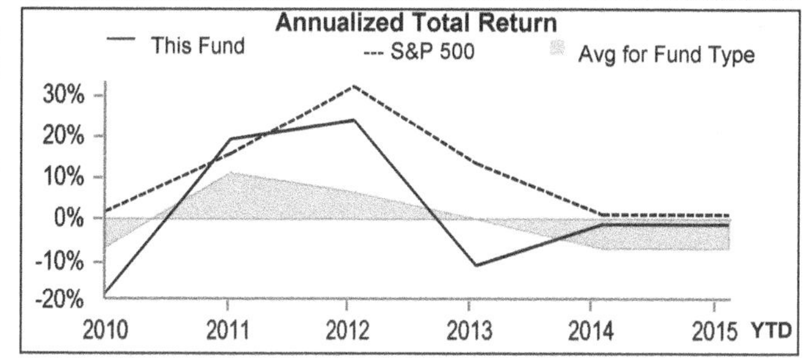

*First Trust ISE Glb Wind Energy (FAN)   A+   Excellent

Fund Family: First Trust Advisors LP
Fund Type: Energy/Natural Resources
Inception Date: June 16, 2008

Major Rating Factors:
Exceptional performance is the major factor driving the A+ (Excellent) TheStreet.com Investment Rating for *First Trust ISE Glb Wind Energy. The fund currently has a performance rating of A (Excellent) based on an annualized return of 18.89% over the last three years and a total return of 10.80% year to date 2015. Factored into the performance evaluation is an expense ratio of 0.60% (very low).

The fund's risk rating is currently B- (Good). It carries a beta of 0.57, meaning the fund's expected move will be 5.7% for every 10% move in the market. Volatility, as measured by both the semi-deviation and a drawdown factor, is considered low. As of December 31, 2015, *First Trust ISE Glb Wind Energy traded at a discount of .09% below its net asset value, which is worse than its one-year historical average discount of .17%.

Daniel J. Lindquist has been running the fund for 8 years and currently receives a manager quality ranking of 98 (0=worst, 99=best). If you desire only a moderate level of risk and strong performance, then this fund is an excellent option.

Data Date	Investment Rating	Net Assets ($Mil)	Price	Perfor-mance Rating/Pts	Total Return Y-T-D	Risk Rating/Pts
12-15	A+	86.70	11.36	A / 9.5	10.80%	B- / 7.9
2014	C-	86.70	10.17	C / 4.5	-7.65%	C+ / 6.9
2013	C+	76.70	11.35	B / 8.2	58.86%	C+ / 5.6
2012	E+	19.40	6.94	E+ / 0.6	-1.56%	C / 4.9
2011	D-	29.20	7.92	D- / 1.0	-21.27%	C / 5.5
2010	E+	51.80	10.25	E / 0.5	-31.11%	C- / 3.8

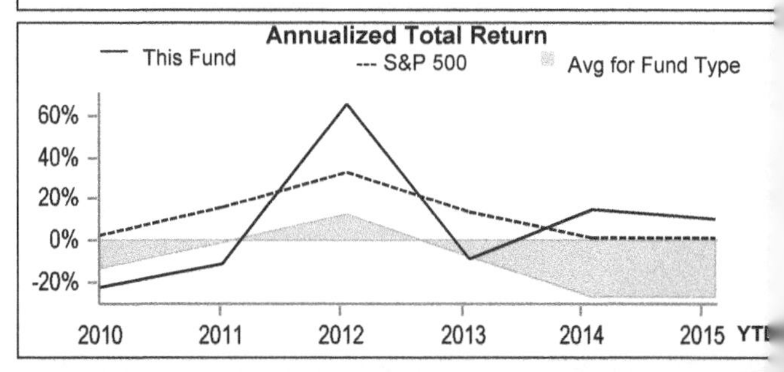

*First Trust ISE Water Index (FIW)   C+   Fair

Fund Family: First Trust Advisors LP
Fund Type: Income
Inception Date: May 8, 2007

Major Rating Factors: Middle of the road best describes *First Trust ISE Water Index whose TheStreet.com Investment Rating is currently a C+ (Fair). The fund currently has a performance rating of C+ (Fair) based on an annualized return of 4.82% over the last three years and a total return of -9.41% year to date 2015. Factored into the performance evaluation is an expense ratio of 0.59% (very low).

The fund's risk rating is currently B- (Good). It carries a beta of 1.23, meaning it is expected to move 12.3% for every 10% move in the market. Volatility, as measured by both the semi-deviation and a drawdown factor, is considered low. As of December 31, 2015, *First Trust ISE Water Index traded at a discount of .07% below its net asset value, which is better than its one-year historical average discount of .02%.

Daniel J. Lindquist has been running the fund for 9 years and currently receives a manager quality ranking of 15 (0=worst, 99=best). If you desire an average level of risk, then this fund may be an option.

Data Date	Investment Rating	Net Assets ($Mil)	Price	Perfor-mance Rating/Pts	Total Return Y-T-D	Risk Rating/Pts
12-15	C+	183.80	30.11	C+ / 5.7	-9.41%	B- / 7.8
2014	B-	183.80	33.71	B- / 7.4	2.62%	B- / 7.0
2013	B+	197.60	33.84	B+ / 8.3	25.42%	B / 8.0
2012	B	72.80	26.02	B / 7.6	25.92%	B- / 7.6
2011	C-	58.00	20.77	C- / 4.2	-3.05%	C+ / 6.7
2010	C+	53.10	22.17	C+ / 6.2	19.90%	C / 5.4

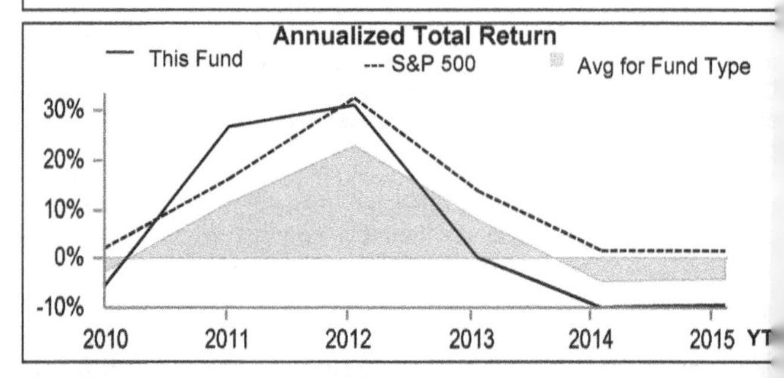

*First Trust ISE-Revere Natural G (FCG)   E   Very Weak

Fund Family: First Trust Advisors LP
Fund Type: Income
Inception Date: May 8, 2007

Major Rating Factors: Very poor performance is the major factor driving the E (Very Weak) TheStreet.com Investment Rating for *First Trust ISE-Revere Natural G. The fund currently has a performance rating of E- (Very Weak) based on an annualized return of -34.11% over the last three years and a total return of -59.17% year to date 2015. Factored into the performance evaluation is an expense ratio of 0.60% (very low).

The fund's risk rating is currently C- (Fair). It carries a beta of 1.40, meaning it is expected to move 14.0% for every 10% move in the market. Volatility, as measured by both the semi-deviation and a drawdown factor, is considered average. As of December 31, 2015, *First Trust ISE-Revere Natural G traded at a price exactly equal to its net asset value, which is better than its one-year historical average premium of .04%.

Daniel J. Lindquist has been running the fund for 9 years and currently receives a manager quality ranking of 0 (0=worst, 99=best). This fund offers an average level of risk but investors looking for strong performance will be frustrated.

Data Date	Investment Rating	Net Assets ($Mil)	Price	Perfor-mance Rating/Pts	Total Return Y-T-D	Risk Rating/Pts
12-15	E	407.40	4.46	E- / 0.2	-59.17%	C- / 3.0
2014	D-	407.40	11.21	E / 0.5	-40.71%	C / 5.0
2013	D+	464.80	19.50	C- / 3.8	18.84%	C+ / 6.6
2012	D-	387.90	15.68	E+ / 0.9	-7.33%	C+ / 6.6
2011	C-	346.50	18.19	C / 4.5	-4.73%	C+ / 6.7
2010	D	396.90	19.68	C- / 3.4	12.23%	C / 4.5

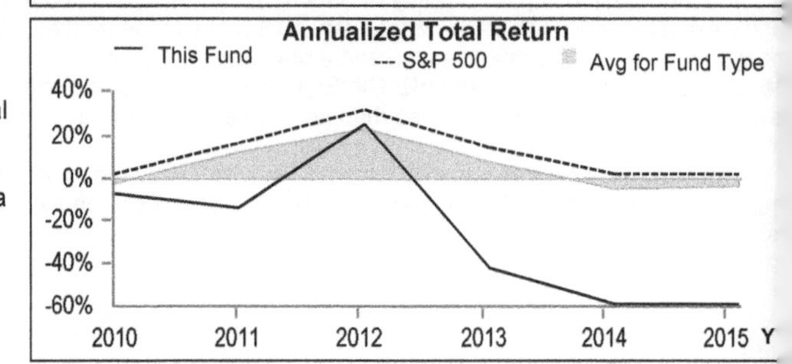

*First Trust Japan AlphaDEX (FJP) A- Excellent

Fund Family: First Trust Advisors LP
Fund Type: Foreign
Inception Date: April 18, 2011

Major Rating Factors:
Strong performance is the major factor driving the A- (Excellent) TheStreet.com nvestment Rating for *First Trust Japan AlphaDEX. The fund currently has a performance rating of B (Good) based on an annualized return of 10.21% over the ast three years and a total return of 5.25% year to date 2015. Factored into the performance evaluation is an expense ratio of 0.80% (very low).

The fund's risk rating is currently B (Good). It carries a beta of 0.75, meaning the und's expected move will be 7.5% for every 10% move in the market. Volatility, as measured by both the semi-deviation and a drawdown factor, is considered low. As of December 31, 2015, *First Trust Japan AlphaDEX traded at a discount of .19% below ts net asset value, which is better than its one-year historical average premium of .04%.

Daniel J. Lindquist has been running the fund for 5 years and currently receives a manager quality ranking of 90 (0=worst, 99=best). If you desire only a moderate level of risk and strong performance, then this fund is an excellent option.

Data Date	Investment Rating	Net Assets ($Mil)	Price	Performance Rating/Pts	Total Return Y-T-D	Risk Rating/Pts
12-15	A-	39.70	47.09	B / 7.7	5.25%	B / 8.4
2014	C	39.70	45.13	C / 4.3	-0.88%	B / 8.4
2013	A	103.60	46.66	B+ / 8.8	28.39%	B / 8.2
2012	D	1.80	36.33	D- / 1.5	-0.97%	B / 8.0

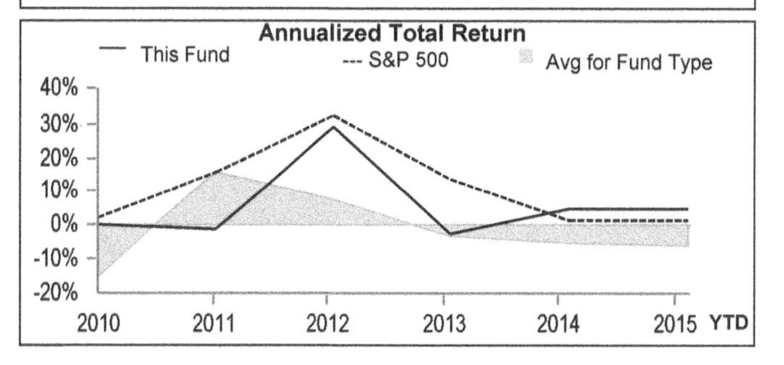

*First Trust Large Cap Gro AlphaD (FTC) A+ Excellent

Fund Family: First Trust Advisors LP
Fund Type: Growth
Inception Date: May 8, 2007

Major Rating Factors:
Exceptional performance is the major factor driving the A+ (Excellent) TheStreet.com nvestment Rating for *First Trust Large Cap Gro AlphaD. The fund currently has a performance rating of A- (Excellent) based on an annualized return of 16.98% over he last three years and a total return of 4.45% year to date 2015. Factored into the performance evaluation is an expense ratio of 0.63% (very low).

The fund's risk rating is currently B- (Good). It carries a beta of 0.97, meaning hat its performance tracks fairly well with that of the overall stock market. Volatility, as measured by both the semi-deviation and a drawdown factor, is considered low. As of December 31, 2015, *First Trust Large Cap Gro AlphaD traded at a price exactly equal to its net asset value, which is better than its one-year historical average premium of .04%.

Daniel J. Lindquist has been running the fund for 9 years and currently receives a manager quality ranking of 84 (0=worst, 99=best). If you desire only a moderate level of risk and strong performance, then this fund is an excellent option.

Data Date	Investment Rating	Net Assets ($Mil)	Price	Performance Rating/Pts	Total Return Y-T-D	Risk Rating/Pts
12-15	A+	417.50	48.21	A- / 9.2	4.45%	B- / 7.9
2014	B+	417.50	46.46	B+ / 8.7	16.56%	B- / 7.3
2013	B	237.40	40.96	B / 8.0	32.67%	B- / 7.6
2012	C	116.50	29.88	C / 4.7	11.76%	B- / 7.7
2011	C	125.10	27.48	C / 5.1	-1.98%	B- / 7.6
2010	C	82.50	28.48	C / 5.1	23.63%	C+ / 5.7

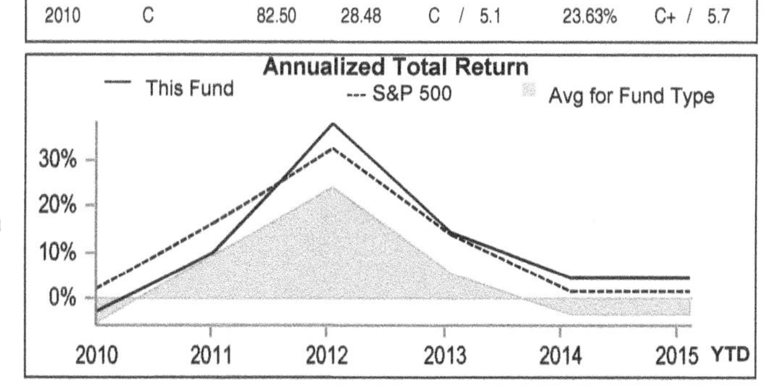

*First Trust Large Cap Val AlphaD (FTA) B- Good

Fund Family: First Trust Advisors LP
Fund Type: Income
Inception Date: May 8, 2007

Major Rating Factors: *First Trust Large Cap Val AlphaD receives a TheStreet.com nvestment Rating of B- (Good). The fund currently has a performance rating of C+ Fair) based on an annualized return of 8.81% over the last three years and a total eturn of -10.33% year to date 2015. Factored into the performance evaluation is an expense ratio of 0.62% (very low).

The fund's risk rating is currently B- (Good). It carries a beta of 1.04, meaning hat its performance tracks fairly well with that of the overall stock market. Volatility, as measured by both the semi-deviation and a drawdown factor, is considered low. As of December 31, 2015, *First Trust Large Cap Val AlphaD traded at a price exactly equal to its net asset value, which is better than its one-year historical average premium of .01%.

Daniel J. Lindquist has been running the fund for 9 years and currently receives a manager quality ranking of 31 (0=worst, 99=best). If you desire an average level of isk, then this fund may be an option.

Data Date	Investment Rating	Net Assets ($Mil)	Price	Performance Rating/Pts	Total Return Y-T-D	Risk Rating/Pts
12-15	B-	1,149.60	38.45	C+ / 6.4	-10.33%	B- / 7.8
2014	A-	1,149.60	43.73	B / 8.2	13.32%	B / 8.1
2013	A-	624.20	40.21	B / 8.2	27.80%	B / 8.3
2012	C+	278.90	30.48	C+ / 6.2	16.64%	B / 8.2
2011	C+	184.90	26.45	C+ / 6.4	1.96%	B- / 7.8
2010	C+	92.50	26.45	C+ / 6.5	18.69%	C+ / 5.7

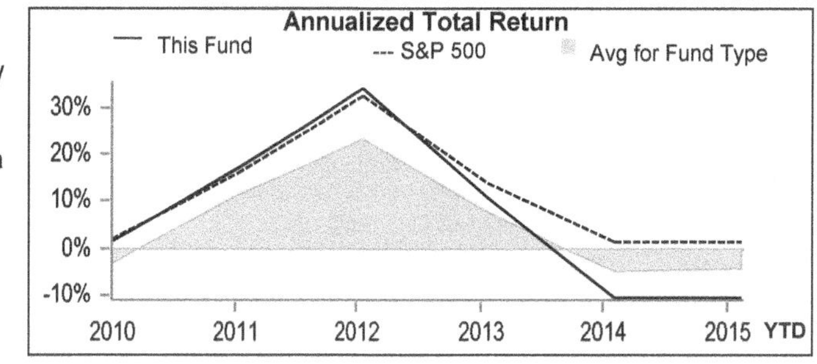

*First Trust Latin America AlphaD (FLN) D- Weak

Fund Family: First Trust Advisors LP
Fund Type: Foreign
Inception Date: April 18, 2011

Data Date	Investment Rating	Net Assets ($Mil)	Price	Performance Rating/Pts	Total Return Y-T-D	Risk Rating/Pts
12-15	D-	6.60	13.21	E+ / 0.8	-27.31%	C / 4.7
2014	E+	6.60	19.02	D- / 1.4	-15.06%	C- / 4.0
2013	D	8.20	23.56	D- / 1.0	-14.24%	C+ / 6.7
2012	C+	9.30	27.16	B / 7.6	11.18%	C+ / 6.8

Major Rating Factors:
Very poor performance is the major factor driving the D- (Weak) TheStreet.com Investment Rating for *First Trust Latin America AlphaD. The fund currently has a performance rating of E+ (Very Weak) based on an annualized return of -19.81% over the last three years and a total return of -27.31% year to date 2015. Factored into the performance evaluation is an expense ratio of 0.80% (very low).

The fund's risk rating is currently C (Fair). It carries a beta of 1.17, meaning it is expected to move 11.7% for every 10% move in the market. Volatility, as measured by both the semi-deviation and a drawdown factor, is considered average. As of December 31, 2015, *First Trust Latin America AlphaD traded at a discount of .53% below its net asset value, which is better than its one-year historical average discount of .25%.

Daniel J. Lindquist has been running the fund for 5 years and currently receives a manager quality ranking of 5 (0=worst, 99=best). This fund offers an average level of risk but investors looking for strong performance will be frustrated.

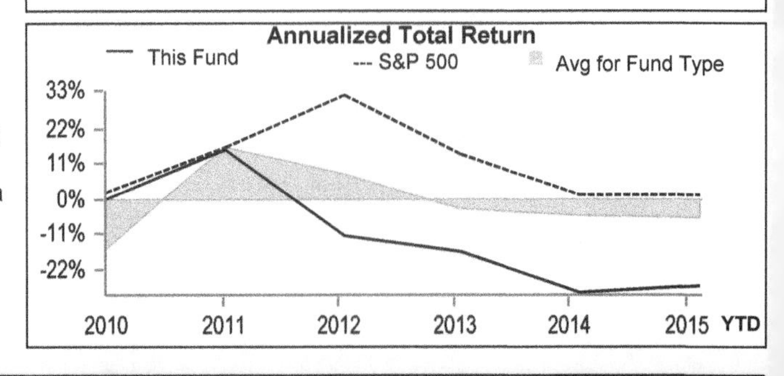

*First Trust Long/Short Equity (FTLS) B- Good

Fund Family: First Trust Advisors LP
Fund Type: Global
Inception Date: September 8, 2014

Data Date	Investment Rating	Net Assets ($Mil)	Price	Performance Rating/Pts	Total Return Y-T-D	Risk Rating/Pts
12-15	B-	0.00	32.73	C+ / 6.5	5.39%	B- / 7.6

Major Rating Factors: *First Trust Long/Short Equity receives a TheStreet.com Investment Rating of B- (Good). The fund currently has a performance rating of C+ (Fair) based on an annualized return of 0.00% over the last three years and a total return of 5.39% year to date 2015.

The fund's risk rating is currently B- (Good). It carries a beta of 0.00, meaning the fund's expected move will be 0.0% for every 10% move in the market. Volatility, as measured by both the semi-deviation and a drawdown factor, is considered low. As of December 31, 2015, *First Trust Long/Short Equity traded at a premium of .15% above its net asset value, which is worse than its one-year historical average premium of .10%.

John W. Gambla has been running the fund for 2 years and currently receives a manager quality ranking of 89 (0=worst, 99=best). If you desire an average level of risk, then this fund may be an option.

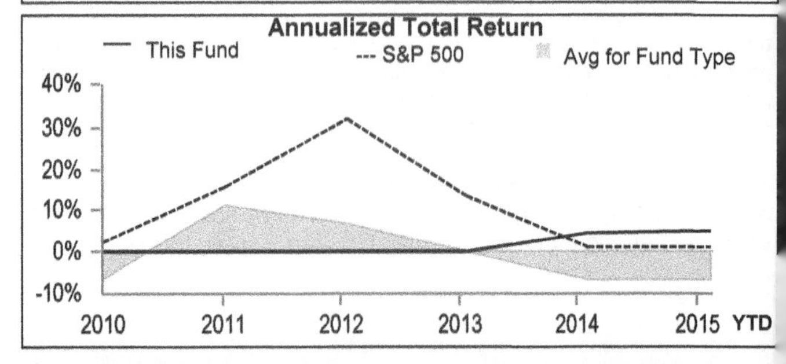

*First Trust Low Beta Income (FTLB) B- Good

Fund Family: First Trust Advisors LP
Fund Type: Income
Inception Date: January 6, 2014

Data Date	Investment Rating	Net Assets ($Mil)	Price	Performance Rating/Pts	Total Return Y-T-D	Risk Rating/Pts
12-15	B-	3.00	19.75	C / 5.4	0.85%	B / 8.7

Major Rating Factors: *First Trust Low Beta Income receives a TheStreet.com Investment Rating of B- (Good). The fund currently has a performance rating of C (Fair) based on an annualized return of 0.00% over the last three years and a total return of 0.85% year to date 2015. Factored into the performance evaluation is an expense ratio of 0.85% (very low).

The fund's risk rating is currently B (Good). It carries a beta of 0.00, meaning the fund's expected move will be 0.0% for every 10% move in the market. Volatility, as measured by both the semi-deviation and a drawdown factor, is considered low. As of December 31, 2015, *First Trust Low Beta Income traded at a discount of .20% below its net asset value, which is better than its one-year historical average premium of .14%.

Jonathan C. Erickson has been running the fund for 2 years and currently receives a manager quality ranking of 61 (0=worst, 99=best). If you desire an average level of risk, then this fund may be an option.

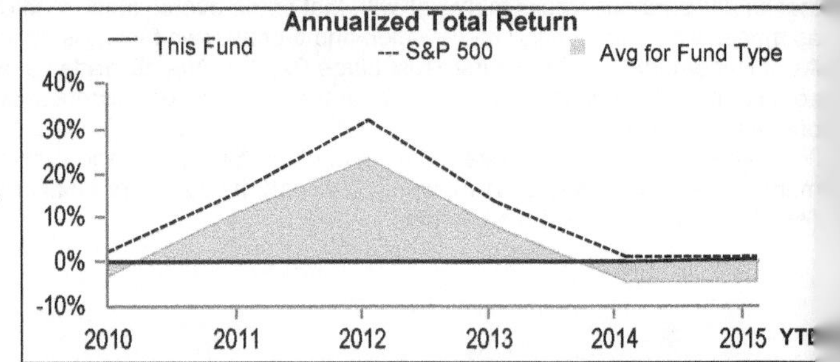

* Denotes ETF Fund

*First Trust Low Dur Mtge Oppty E (LMBS) C- Fair

Fund Family: First Trust Advisors LP
Fund Type: Mortgage
Inception Date: November 4, 2014

Data Date	Investment Rating	Net Assets ($Mil)	Price	Perfor-mance Rating/Pts	Total Return Y-T-D	Risk Rating/Pts
12-15	C-	0.00	50.43	C+ / 5.7	2.83%	C- / 4.1

Major Rating Factors: Middle of the road best describes *First Trust Low Dur Mtge Oppty E whose TheStreet.com Investment Rating is currently a C- (Fair). The fund currently has a performance rating of C+ (Fair) based on an annualized return of 0.00% over the last three years and a total return of 2.83% year to date 2015.

The fund's risk rating is currently C- (Fair). It carries a beta of 0.00, meaning the fund's expected move will be 0.0% for every 10% move in the market. Volatility, as measured by both the semi-deviation and a drawdown factor, is considered average. As of December 31, 2015, *First Trust Low Dur Mtge Oppty E traded at a premium of .42% above its net asset value, which is worse than its one-year historical average premium of .20%.

Robert F. Carey currently receives a manager quality ranking of 84 (0=worst, 99=best). If you desire an average level of risk, then this fund may be an option.

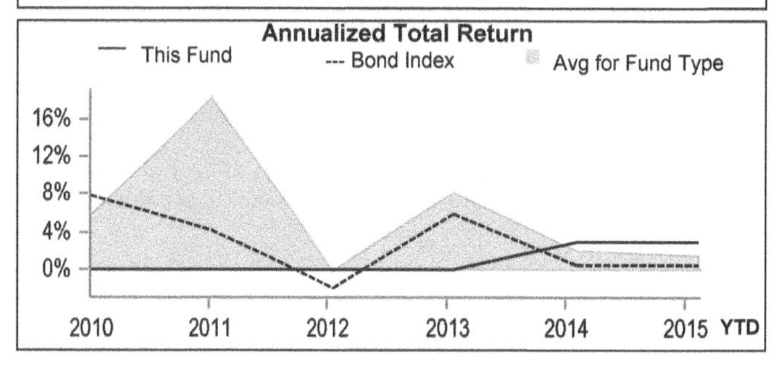

*First Trust Lrg Cap Core AlphaDE (FEX) B+ Good

Fund Family: First Trust Advisors LP
Fund Type: Growth and Income
Inception Date: May 8, 2007

Data Date	Investment Rating	Net Assets ($Mil)	Price	Perfor-mance Rating/Pts	Total Return Y-T-D	Risk Rating/Pts
12-15	B+	1,308.60	43.26	B / 8.0	-3.91%	B / 8.0
2014	B+	1,308.60	45.63	B+ / 8.6	14.57%	B- / 7.2
2013	B+	730.00	41.20	B / 8.2	30.12%	B / 8.1
2012	C+	344.70	30.65	C+ / 5.6	14.61%	B / 8.0
2011	C+	267.70	27.17	C+ / 6.1	0.34%	B- / 7.9
2010	C+	128.00	27.58	C+ / 5.9	20.67%	C+ / 5.8

Major Rating Factors: Strong performance is the major factor driving the B+ (Good) TheStreet.com Investment Rating for *First Trust Lrg Cap Core AlphaDE. The fund currently has a performance rating of B (Good) based on an annualized return of 12.43% over the last three years and a total return of -3.91% year to date 2015. Factored into the performance evaluation is an expense ratio of 0.61% (very low).

The fund's risk rating is currently B (Good). It carries a beta of 1.01, meaning that its performance tracks fairly well with that of the overall stock market. Volatility, as measured by both the semi-deviation and a drawdown factor, is considered low. As of December 31, 2015, *First Trust Lrg Cap Core AlphaDE traded at a price exactly equal to its net asset value, which is better than its one-year historical average premium of .02%.

Daniel J. Lindquist has been running the fund for 9 years and currently receives a manager quality ranking of 56 (0=worst, 99=best). If you desire only a moderate level of risk and strong performance, then this fund is an excellent option.

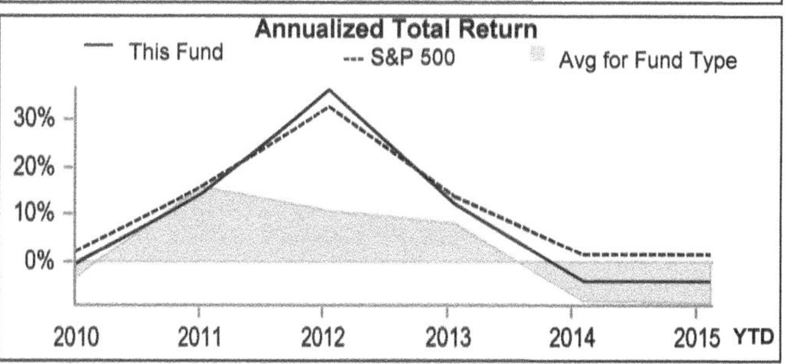

*First Trust Managed Municipal (FMB) B+ Good

Fund Family: First Trust Advisors LP
Fund Type: Municipal - National
Inception Date: May 13, 2014

Data Date	Investment Rating	Net Assets ($Mil)	Price	Perfor-mance Rating/Pts	Total Return Y-T-D	Risk Rating/Pts
12-15	B+	20.30	52.01	B / 7.6	4.50%	B / 8.1

Major Rating Factors: Strong performance is the major factor driving the B+ (Good) TheStreet.com Investment Rating for *First Trust Managed Municipal. The fund currently has a performance rating of B (Good) based on an annualized return of 0.00% over the last three years and a total return of 4.50% year to date 2015.

The fund's risk rating is currently B (Good). It carries a beta of 0.00, meaning the fund's expected move will be 0.0% for every 10% move in the market. Volatility, as measured by both the semi-deviation and a drawdown factor, is considered low. As of December 31, 2015, *First Trust Managed Municipal traded at a premium of .50% above its net asset value, which is worse than its one-year historical average premium of .28%.

Johnathan N. Wilhelm currently receives a manager quality ranking of 76 (0=worst, 99=best). If you desire only a moderate level of risk and strong performance, then this fund is an excellent option.

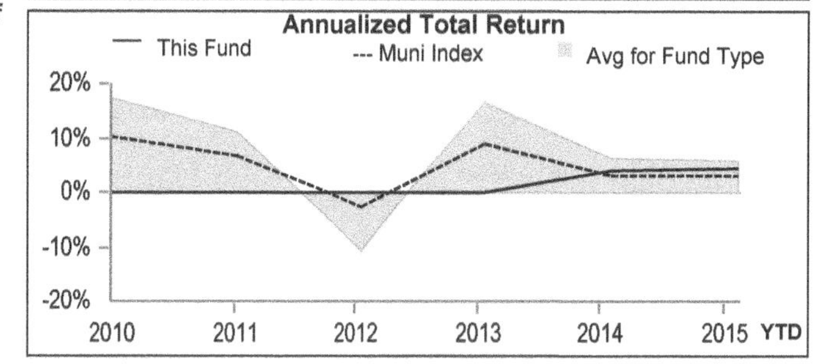

*First Trust Materials AlphaDEX (FXZ) C- Fair

Fund Family: First Trust Advisors LP
Fund Type: Income
Inception Date: May 8, 2007

Major Rating Factors: Middle of the road best describes *First Trust Materials AlphaDEX whose TheStreet.com Investment Rating is currently a C- (Fair). The fund currently has a performance rating of C (Fair) based on an annualized return of 3.01% over the last three years and a total return of -9.91% year to date 2015. Factored into the performance evaluation is an expense ratio of 0.64% (very low).

The fund's risk rating is currently C+ (Fair). It carries a beta of 1.21, meaning it is expected to move 12.1% for every 10% move in the market. Volatility, as measured by both the semi-deviation and a drawdown factor, is considered low. As of December 31, 2015, *First Trust Materials AlphaDEX traded at a premium of .04% above its net asset value, which is worse than its one-year historical average premium of .01%.

Daniel J. Lindquist has been running the fund for 9 years and currently receives a manager quality ranking of 13 (0=worst, 99=best). If you desire an average level of risk, then this fund may be an option.

Data Date	Investment Rating	Net Assets ($Mil)	Price	Performance Rating/Pts	Total Return Y-T-D	Risk Rating/Pts
12-15	C-	667.10	28.10	C / 4.6	-9.91%	C+ / 6.4
2014	B-	667.10	31.55	C+ / 6.4	0.77%	B- / 7.8
2013	B-	466.40	32.42	B / 7.6	21.33%	B- / 7.2
2012	C+	203.90	25.80	C+ / 6.7	20.07%	B- / 7.0
2011	C+	121.10	21.23	B- / 7.0	-6.63%	B- / 7.1
2010	C+	417.20	23.76	B / 7.6	28.28%	C / 4.7

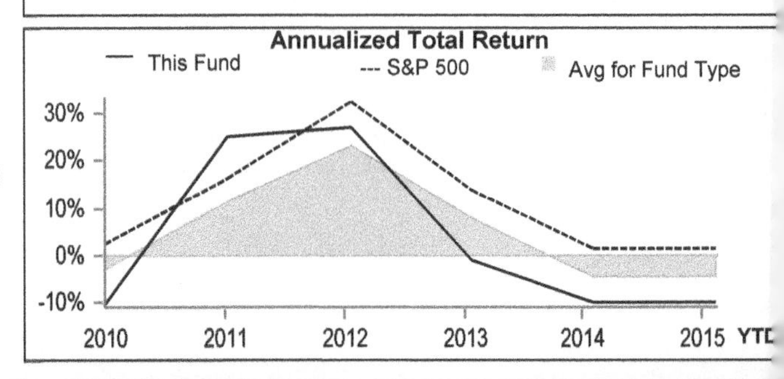

*First Trust Mega Cap AlphaDEX (FMK) B Good

Fund Family: First Trust Advisors LP
Fund Type: Growth
Inception Date: May 11, 2011

Major Rating Factors: Strong performance is the major factor driving the B (Good) TheStreet.com Investment Rating for *First Trust Mega Cap AlphaDEX. The fund currently has a performance rating of B (Good) based on an annualized return of 11.74% over the last three years and a total return of 0.24% year to date 2015. Factored into the performance evaluation is an expense ratio of 0.70% (very low).

The fund's risk rating is currently B- (Good). It carries a beta of 1.06, meaning that its performance tracks fairly well with that of the overall stock market. Volatility, as measured by both the semi-deviation and a drawdown factor, is considered low. As of December 31, 2015, *First Trust Mega Cap AlphaDEX traded at a premium of .34% above its net asset value, which is worse than its one-year historical average premium of .06%.

Daniel J. Lindquist has been running the fund for 5 years and currently receives a manager quality ranking of 47 (0=worst, 99=best). If you desire only a moderate level of risk and strong performance, then this fund is an excellent option.

Data Date	Investment Rating	Net Assets ($Mil)	Price	Performance Rating/Pts	Total Return Y-T-D	Risk Rating/Pts
12-15	B	14.50	26.40	B / 8.2	0.24%	B- / 7.0
2014	C+	14.50	26.93	B- / 7.1	10.96%	C+ / 6.8
2013	A+	12.50	24.94	A / 9.3	26.29%	B / 8.3
2012	C+	9.50	18.93	C+ / 6.2	10.13%	B / 8.2

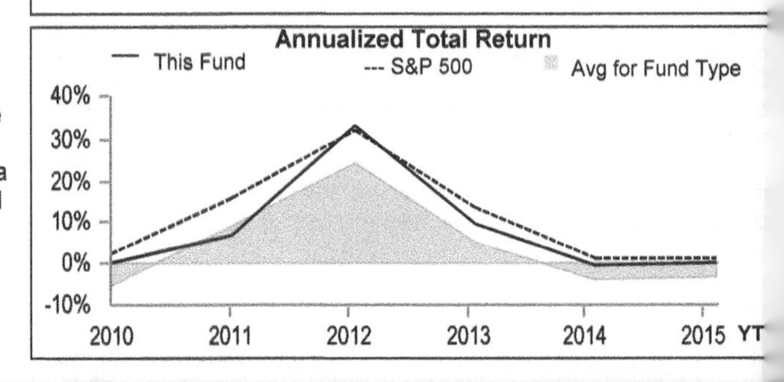

*First Trust Mid Cap Core AlphaDE (FNX) C+ Fair

Fund Family: First Trust Advisors LP
Fund Type: Growth
Inception Date: May 8, 2007

Major Rating Factors: Middle of the road best describes *First Trust Mid Cap Core AlphaDE whose TheStreet.com Investment Rating is currently a C+ (Fair). The fund currently has a performance rating of C+ (Fair) based on an annualized return of 8.77% over the last three years and a total return of -7.68% year to date 2015. Factored into the performance evaluation is an expense ratio of 0.62% (very low).

The fund's risk rating is currently B- (Good). It carries a beta of 1.05, meaning that its performance tracks fairly well with that of the overall stock market. Volatility, as measured by both the semi-deviation and a drawdown factor, is considered low. As of December 31, 2015, *First Trust Mid Cap Core AlphaDE traded at a premium of .06% above its net asset value, which is worse than its one-year historical average premium of .01%.

Daniel J. Lindquist has been running the fund for 9 years and currently receives a manager quality ranking of 30 (0=worst, 99=best). If you desire an average level of risk, then this fund may be an option.

Data Date	Investment Rating	Net Assets ($Mil)	Price	Performance Rating/Pts	Total Return Y-T-D	Risk Rating/Pts
12-15	C+	891.30	48.06	C+ / 6.4	-7.68%	B- / 7.0
2014	B-	891.30	52.83	B / 7.6	7.63%	B- / 7.0
2013	B+	637.60	50.46	B+ / 8.5	30.95%	B- / 7.9
2012	C+	301.10	36.88	C+ / 6.5	14.87%	B- / 7.7
2011	B-	244.70	32.62	B- / 7.3	1.54%	B- / 7.8
2010	B+	151.20	32.51	B / 7.8	26.64%	C+ / 5.7

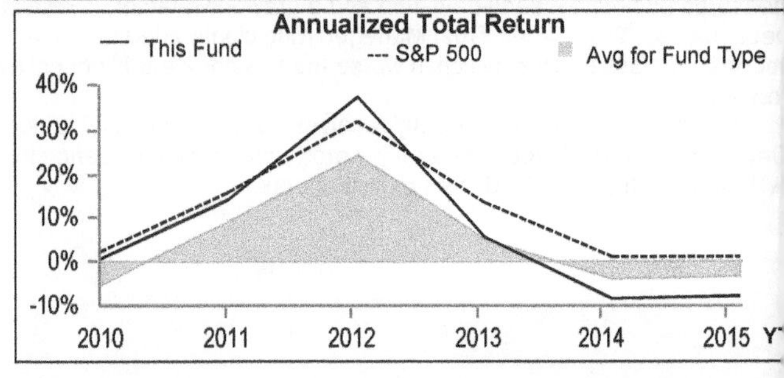

*First Trust Mid Cap Growth Alpha (FNY) — A- Excellent

Fund Family: First Trust Advisors LP
Fund Type: Growth
Inception Date: April 19, 2011

Data Date	Investment Rating	Net Assets ($Mil)	Price	Performance Rating/Pts	Total Return Y-T-D	Risk Rating/Pts
12-15	A-	45.60	28.84	B / 7.6	-0.73%	B / 8.5
2014	B-	45.60	29.36	B- / 7.2	6.66%	B- / 7.0
2013	A+	40.60	28.07	A / 9.4	29.94%	B / 8.7
2012	B-	16.50	20.63	C+ / 6.2	11.40%	B / 8.6

Major Rating Factors:
Strong performance is the major factor driving the A- (Excellent) TheStreet.com Investment Rating for *First Trust Mid Cap Growth Alpha. The fund currently has a performance rating of B (Good) based on an annualized return of 10.94% over the last three years and a total return of -0.73% year to date 2015. Factored into the performance evaluation is an expense ratio of 0.70% (very low).

The fund's risk rating is currently B (Good). It carries a beta of 0.99, meaning that its performance tracks fairly well with that of the overall stock market. Volatility, as measured by both the semi-deviation and a drawdown factor, is considered low. As of December 31, 2015, *First Trust Mid Cap Growth Alpha traded at a discount of .10% below its net asset value, which is better than its one-year historical average premium of .03%.

Daniel J. Lindquist has been running the fund for 5 years and currently receives a manager quality ranking of 47 (0=worst, 99=best). If you desire only a moderate level of risk and strong performance, then this fund is an excellent option.

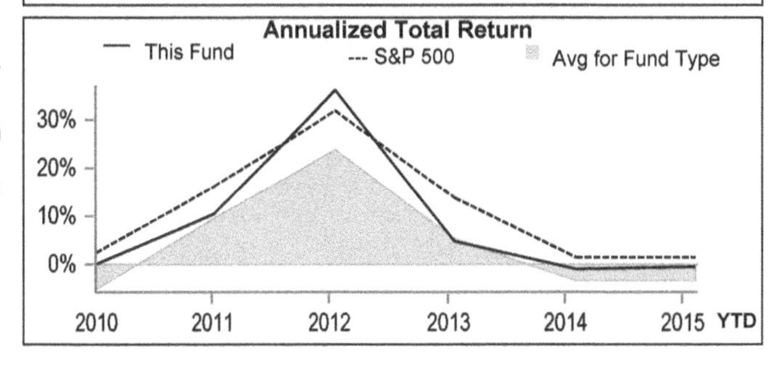

*First Trust Mid Cap Val AlphaDEX (FNK) — C+ Fair

Fund Family: First Trust Advisors LP
Fund Type: Growth
Inception Date: April 19, 2011

Data Date	Investment Rating	Net Assets ($Mil)	Price	Performance Rating/Pts	Total Return Y-T-D	Risk Rating/Pts
12-15	C+	68.20	26.45	C+ / 5.6	-12.73%	B / 8.0
2014	B-	68.20	30.98	B / 7.7	7.99%	C+ / 6.8
2013	A+	28.10	29.64	A / 9.4	31.68%	B / 8.6
2012	A-	9.70	21.58	B+ / 8.5	17.45%	B / 8.4

Major Rating Factors: Middle of the road best describes *First Trust Mid Cap Val AlphaDEX whose TheStreet.com Investment Rating is currently a C+ (Fair). The fund currently has a performance rating of C+ (Fair) based on an annualized return of 6.96% over the last three years and a total return of -12.73% year to date 2015. Factored into the performance evaluation is an expense ratio of 0.70% (very low).

The fund's risk rating is currently B (Good). It carries a beta of 1.09, meaning that its performance tracks fairly well with that of the overall stock market. Volatility, as measured by both the semi-deviation and a drawdown factor, is considered low. As of December 31, 2015, *First Trust Mid Cap Val AlphaDEX traded at a discount of .15% below its net asset value, which is better than its one-year historical average premium of .02%.

Daniel J. Lindquist has been running the fund for 5 years and currently receives a manager quality ranking of 22 (0=worst, 99=best). If you desire an average level of risk, then this fund may be an option.

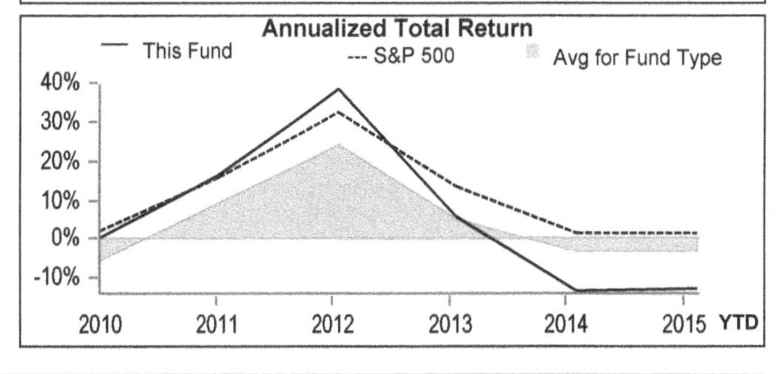

*First Trust Morningstar Div Lead (FDL) — B+ Good

Fund Family: First Trust Advisors LP
Fund Type: Income
Inception Date: March 9, 2006

Data Date	Investment Rating	Net Assets ($Mil)	Price	Performance Rating/Pts	Total Return Y-T-D	Risk Rating/Pts
12-15	B+	791.00	23.70	B+ / 8.4	2.56%	B- / 7.4
2014	A	791.00	23.97	B- / 7.3	15.84%	B+ / 9.4
2013	A-	687.40	21.91	B- / 7.4	18.11%	B+ / 9.4
2012	B-	545.50	18.46	C / 5.4	12.90%	B+ / 9.2
2011	C+	447.00	17.58	C+ / 6.2	12.42%	B- / 7.4
2010	C-	143.30	15.94	C- / 3.5	16.19%	C / 5.4

Major Rating Factors: Strong performance is the major factor driving the B+ (Good) TheStreet.com Investment Rating for *First Trust Morningstar Div Lead. The fund currently has a performance rating of B+ (Good) based on an annualized return of 1.50% over the last three years and a total return of 2.56% year to date 2015. Factored into the performance evaluation is an expense ratio of 0.45% (very low).

The fund's risk rating is currently B- (Good). It carries a beta of 0.74, meaning the fund's expected move will be 7.4% for every 10% move in the market. Volatility, as measured by both the semi-deviation and a drawdown factor, is considered low. As of December 31, 2015, *First Trust Morningstar Div Lead traded at a premium of .04% above its net asset value, which is worse than its one-year historical average premium of .02%.

Daniel J. Lindquist has been running the fund for 19 years and currently receives a manager quality ranking of 78 (0=worst, 99=best). If you desire only a moderate level of risk and strong performance, then this fund is an excellent option.

Annualized Total Return
This Fund
--- S&P 500
Avg for Fund Type
40%
30%
20%
10%
0%
-10%
2010
2011
2012
2013
2014
2015 YTD

* Denotes ETF Fund

*First Trust Morningstar Mgd Fut (FMF) C Fair

Fund Family: First Trust Advisors LP
Fund Type: Income
Inception Date: August 2, 2013

Data Date	Investment Rating	Net Assets ($Mil)	Price	Performance Rating/Pts	Total Return Y-T-D	Risk Rating/Pts
12-15	C	12.50	49.24	C- / 3.9	-0.46%	B- / 7.6
2014	C-	12.50	49.59	D+ / 2.4	-0.56%	B / 8.7

Major Rating Factors: Middle of the road best describes *First Trust Morningstar Mgd Fut whose TheStreet.com Investment Rating is currently a C (Fair). The fund currently has a performance rating of C- (Fair) based on an annualized return of 0.00% over the last three years and a total return of -0.46% year to date 2015. Factored into the performance evaluation is an expense ratio of 0.95% (low).

The fund's risk rating is currently B- (Good). It carries a beta of 0.00, meaning the fund's expected move will be 0.0% for every 10% move in the market. Volatility, as measured by both the semi-deviation and a drawdown factor, is considered low. As of December 31, 2015, *First Trust Morningstar Mgd Fut traded at a premium of .06% above its net asset value, which is better than its one-year historical average premium of .17%.

Daniel J. Lindquist has been running the fund for 3 years and currently receives a manager quality ranking of 61 (0=worst, 99=best). If you desire an average level of risk, then this fund may be an option.

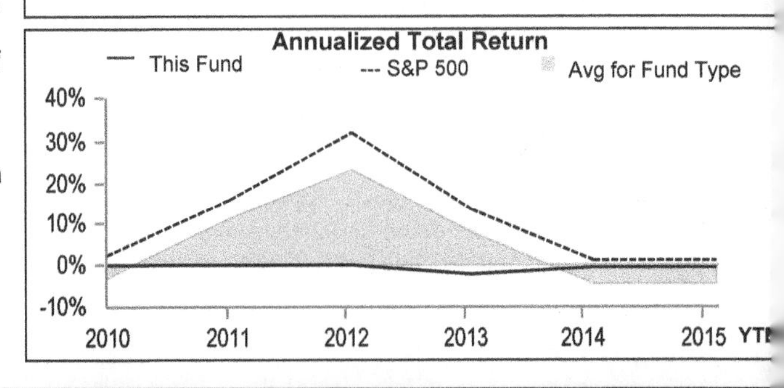

*First Trust Multi Cap Grth Alpha (FAD) B+ Good

Fund Family: First Trust Advisors LP
Fund Type: Growth
Inception Date: May 8, 2007

Data Date	Investment Rating	Net Assets ($Mil)	Price	Performance Rating/Pts	Total Return Y-T-D	Risk Rating/Pts
12-15	B+	68.20	49.72	B+ / 8.8	2.91%	C+ / 6.8
2014	B-	68.20	48.84	B / 7.7	10.05%	B- / 7.0
2013	B+	51.90	45.15	B+ / 8.5	33.31%	B- / 7.6
2012	C	31.10	32.73	C / 5.1	12.03%	B- / 7.5
2011	C+	25.40	29.94	C+ / 6.0	0.45%	B- / 7.5
2010	C+	18.10	30.27	C+ / 6.4	25.14%	C+ / 5.6

Major Rating Factors: Strong performance is the major factor driving the B+ (Good) TheStreet.com Investment Rating for *First Trust Multi Cap Grth Alpha. The fund currently has a performance rating of B+ (Good) based on an annualized return of 14.28% over the last three years and a total return of 2.91% year to date 2015. Factored into the performance evaluation is an expense ratio of 0.70% (very low).

The fund's risk rating is currently C+ (Fair). It carries a beta of 0.97, meaning that its performance tracks fairly well with that of the overall stock market. Volatility, as measured by both the semi-deviation and a drawdown factor, is considered low. As of December 31, 2015, *First Trust Multi Cap Grth Alpha traded at a premium of .49% above its net asset value, which is worse than its one-year historical average premium of .07%.

Daniel J. Lindquist has been running the fund for 9 years and currently receives a manager quality ranking of 73 (0=worst, 99=best). If you desire only a moderate level of risk and strong performance, then this fund is an excellent option.

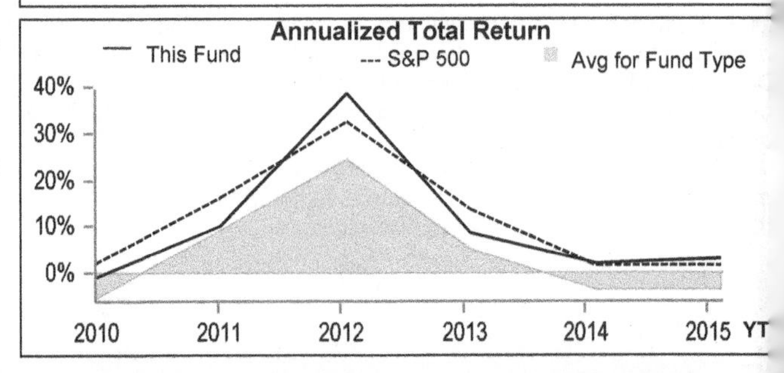

*First Trust Multi Cap Val AlphaD (FAB) C+ Fair

Fund Family: First Trust Advisors LP
Fund Type: Income
Inception Date: May 8, 2007

Data Date	Investment Rating	Net Assets ($Mil)	Price	Performance Rating/Pts	Total Return Y-T-D	Risk Rating/Pts
12-15	C+	173.50	40.74	C+ / 5.9	-12.02%	B- / 7.0
2014	B	173.50	47.26	B / 8.0	9.97%	B- / 7.3
2013	A	117.70	44.48	B+ / 8.6	30.91%	B / 8.2
2012	B-	55.70	32.78	C+ / 6.5	16.63%	B / 8.1
2011	B-	39.70	28.48	B- / 7.1	1.12%	B- / 7.8
2010	B	25.70	28.69	B- / 7.3	22.42%	C+ / 5.7

Major Rating Factors: Middle of the road best describes *First Trust Multi Cap Val AlphaD whose TheStreet.com Investment Rating is currently a C+ (Fair). The fund currently has a performance rating of C+ (Fair) based on an annualized return of 7.68% over the last three years and a total return of -12.02% year to date 2015. Factored into the performance evaluation is an expense ratio of 0.70% (very low).

The fund's risk rating is currently B- (Good). It carries a beta of 1.08, meaning that its performance tracks fairly well with that of the overall stock market. Volatility, as measured by both the semi-deviation and a drawdown factor, is considered low. As of December 31, 2015, *First Trust Multi Cap Val AlphaD traded at a premium of .07% above its net asset value, which is worse than its one-year historical average premium of .02%.

Daniel J. Lindquist has been running the fund for 9 years and currently receives a manager quality ranking of 25 (0=worst, 99=best). If you desire an average level of risk, then this fund may be an option.

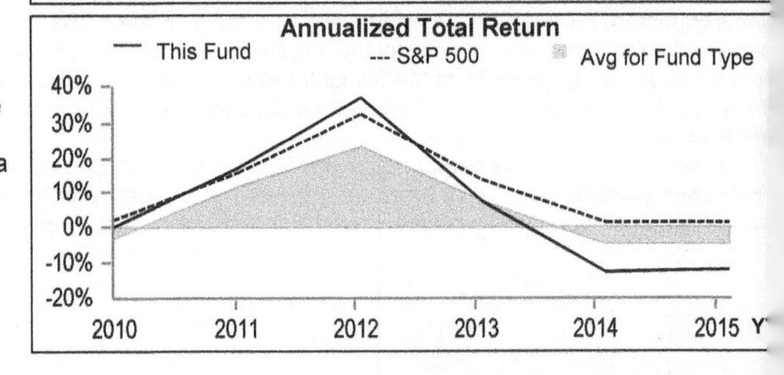

* Denotes ETF Fund

*First Trust MultiAsst Dvsfd Inc (MDIV) C Fair

Fund Family: First Trust Advisors LP
Fund Type: Income
Inception Date: August 13, 2012

Major Rating Factors: Middle of the road best describes *First Trust MultiAsst Dvsfd Inc whose TheStreet.com Investment Rating is currently a C (Fair). The fund currently has a performance rating of C (Fair) based on an annualized return of 2.32% over the last three years and a total return of -8.73% year to date 2015. Factored into the performance evaluation is an expense ratio of 0.50% (very low).

The fund's risk rating is currently B (Good). It carries a beta of 0.61, meaning the fund's expected move will be 6.1% for every 10% move in the market. Volatility, as measured by both the semi-deviation and a drawdown factor, is considered low. As of December 31, 2015, *First Trust MultiAsst Dvsfd Inc traded at a discount of .11% below its net asset value, which is better than its one-year historical average premium of .02%.

This fund has been team managed for 4 years and currently receives a manager quality ranking of 30 (0=worst, 99=best). If you desire an average level of risk, then this fund may be an option.

Data Date	Investment Rating	Net Assets ($Mil)	Price	Performance Rating/Pts	Total Return Y-T-D	Risk Rating/Pts
12-15	C	783.90	18.34	C / 4.5	-8.73%	B / 8.2
2014	C	783.90	21.27	C- / 4.1	8.17%	B / 8.8
2013	B-	526.60	20.82	C / 5.4	7.30%	B+ / 9.1

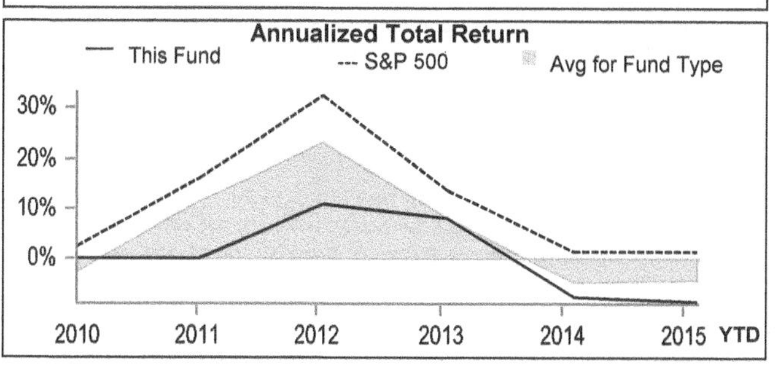

*First Trust NASD Cln Edge Smt Gd (GRID) C Fair

Fund Family: First Trust Advisors LP
Fund Type: Growth
Inception Date: November 16, 2009

Major Rating Factors: Middle of the road best describes *First Trust NASD Cln Edge Smt Gd whose TheStreet.com Investment Rating is currently a C (Fair). The fund currently has a performance rating of C+ (Fair) based on an annualized return of 4.56% over the last three years and a total return of -4.86% year to date 2015. Factored into the performance evaluation is an expense ratio of 0.70% (very low).

The fund's risk rating is currently C+ (Fair). It carries a beta of 0.83, meaning the fund's expected move will be 8.3% for every 10% move in the market. Volatility, as measured by both the semi-deviation and a drawdown factor, is considered low. As of December 31, 2015, *First Trust NASD Cln Edge Smt Gd traded at a premium of 2.39% above its net asset value, which is worse than its one-year historical average premium of .23%.

Daniel J. Lindquist has been running the fund for 7 years and currently receives a manager quality ranking of 27 (0=worst, 99=best). If you desire an average level of risk, then this fund may be an option.

Data Date	Investment Rating	Net Assets ($Mil)	Price	Performance Rating/Pts	Total Return Y-T-D	Risk Rating/Pts
12-15	C	14.20	33.39	C+ / 5.7	-4.86%	C+ / 6.3
2014	C	14.20	35.75	C+ / 6.2	1.14%	C+ / 6.6
2013	C	12.70	36.06	C+ / 6.3	20.32%	C+ / 6.9
2012	D	13.30	29.23	D / 2.1	19.52%	C+ / 6.7
2011	D-	14.90	24.93	E+ / 0.7	-21.25%	C+ / 6.7
2010	B-	28.60	31.77	C+ / 6.5	-1.06%	B- / 7.2

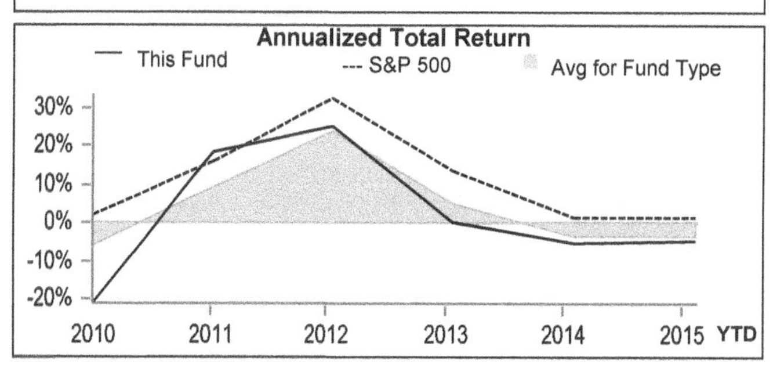

*First Trust NASDAQ ABA Community (QABA) B+ Good

Fund Family: First Trust Advisors LP
Fund Type: Income
Inception Date: June 29, 2009

Major Rating Factors:
Exceptional performance is the major factor driving the B+ (Good) TheStreet.com Investment Rating for *First Trust NASDAQ ABA Community. The fund currently has a performance rating of A- (Excellent) based on an annualized return of 14.83% over the last three years and a total return of 9.03% year to date 2015. Factored into the performance evaluation is an expense ratio of 0.60% (very low).

The fund's risk rating is currently C+ (Fair). It carries a beta of 0.89, meaning the fund's expected move will be 8.9% for every 10% move in the market. Volatility, as measured by both the semi-deviation and a drawdown factor, is considered low. As of December 31, 2015, *First Trust NASDAQ ABA Community traded at a premium of .10% above its net asset value, which is worse than its one-year historical average premium of .04%.

Daniel J. Lindquist has been running the fund for 7 years and currently receives a manager quality ranking of 84 (0=worst, 99=best). If you desire only a moderate level of risk and strong performance, then this fund is an excellent option.

Data Date	Investment Rating	Net Assets ($Mil)	Price	Performance Rating/Pts	Total Return Y-T-D	Risk Rating/Pts
12-15	B+	87.80	38.98	A- / 9.0	9.03%	C+ / 6.7
2014	C+	87.80	36.75	B- / 7.3	5.03%	C+ / 6.9
2013	B+	52.40	36.22	B+ / 8.5	34.91%	B- / 7.6
2012	D+	8.90	25.54	D+ / 2.7	8.78%	B- / 7.0
2011	D+	12.60	22.96	D+ / 2.7	-3.98%	B- / 7.1
2010	A	10.00	25.05	B+ / 8.7	11.73%	C+ / 6.9

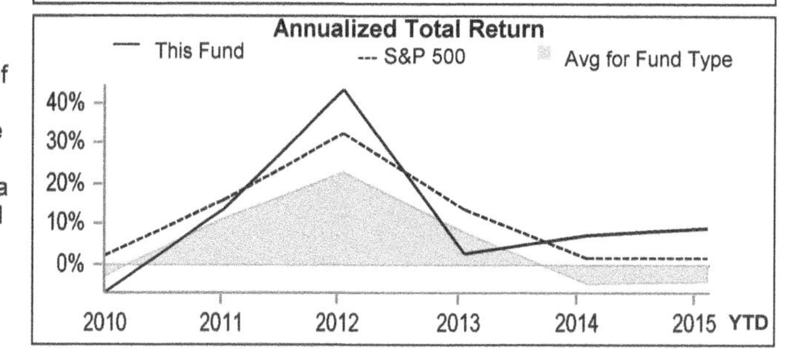

*First Trust NASDAQ Cln Edg US Li (QCLN) B- Good

Fund Family: First Trust Advisors LP
Fund Type: Income
Inception Date: February 8, 2007

Major Rating Factors:
Exceptional performance is the major factor driving the B- (Good) TheStreet.com Investment Rating for *First Trust NASDAQ Cln Edg US Li. The fund currently has a performance rating of A- (Excellent) based on an annualized return of 17.53% over the last three years and a total return of -6.52% year to date 2015. Factored into the performance evaluation is an expense ratio of 0.60% (very low).

The fund's risk rating is currently C (Fair). It carries a beta of 1.47, meaning it is expected to move 14.7% for every 10% move in the market. Volatility, as measured by both the semi-deviation and a drawdown factor, is considered average. As of December 31, 2015, *First Trust NASDAQ Cln Edg US Li traded at a premium of .25% above its net asset value, which is worse than its one-year historical average discount of .02%.

Daniel J. Lindquist has been running the fund for 9 years and currently receives a manager quality ranking of 53 (0=worst, 99=best). If you desire an average level of risk and strong performance, then this fund is a good option.

Data Date	Investment Rating	Net Assets ($Mil)	Price	Performance Rating/Pts	Total Return Y-T-D	Risk Rating/Pts
12-15	B-	122.10	16.05	A- / 9.0	-6.52%	C / 5.5
2014	B-	122.10	17.23	B- / 7.3	-4.93%	B- / 7.3
2013	C+	97.60	17.92	B+ / 8.6	81.92%	C / 5.5
2012	D-	13.70	9.29	E+ / 0.7	-2.08%	C / 5.4
2011	D-	20.70	9.59	D- / 1.1	-41.33%	C+ / 5.7
2010	E+	36.10	16.42	E+ / 0.7	2.18%	C- / 4.0

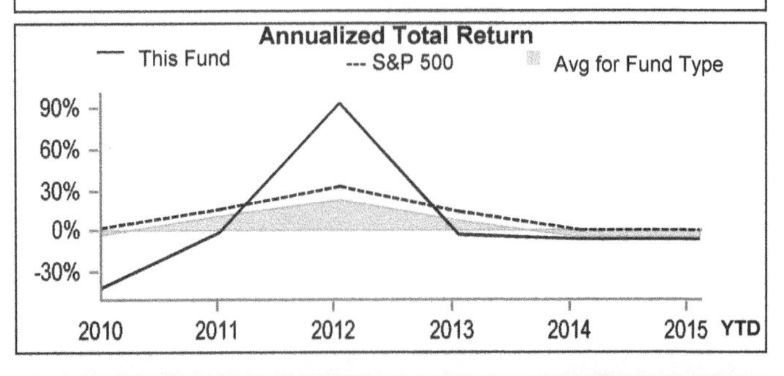

*First Trust NASDAQ Global Auto (CARZ) B Good

Fund Family: First Trust Advisors LP
Fund Type: Global
Inception Date: May 9, 2011

Major Rating Factors: *First Trust NASDAQ Global Auto receives a TheStreet.com Investment Rating of B (Good). The fund currently has a performance rating of C+ (Fair) based on an annualized return of 8.18% over the last three years and a total return of -0.30% year to date 2015. Factored into the performance evaluation is an expense ratio of 0.70% (very low).

The fund's risk rating is currently B- (Good). It carries a beta of 0.94, meaning that its performance tracks fairly well with that of the overall stock market. Volatility, as measured by both the semi-deviation and a drawdown factor, is considered low. As of December 31, 2015, *First Trust NASDAQ Global Auto traded at a discount of .58% below its net asset value, which is better than its one-year historical average premium of .01%.

Daniel J. Lindquist has been running the fund for 5 years and currently receives a manager quality ranking of 87 (0=worst, 99=best). If you desire an average level of risk, then this fund may be an option.

Data Date	Investment Rating	Net Assets ($Mil)	Price	Performance Rating/Pts	Total Return Y-T-D	Risk Rating/Pts
12-15	B	64.50	36.22	C+ / 6.9	-0.30%	B- / 7.9
2014	C	64.50	37.30	C+ / 6.8	-3.00%	C+ / 6.2
2013	B+	53.30	39.70	A / 9.3	31.75%	C+ / 6.9
2012	B+	7.30	29.12	A+ / 9.8	26.04%	C+ / 6.6

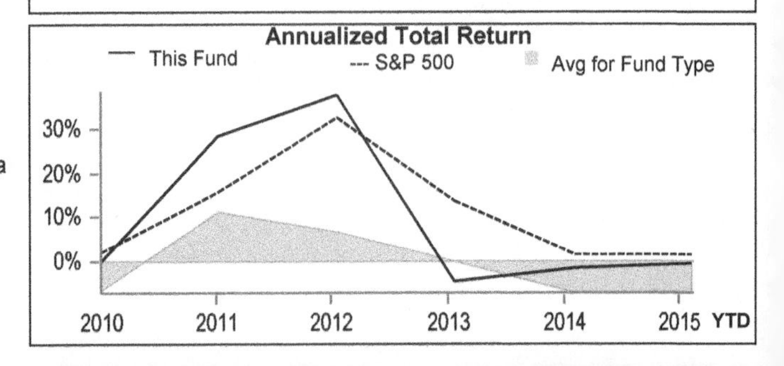

*First Trust NASDAQ Rising Div Ac (RDVY) C- Fair

Fund Family: First Trust Advisors LP
Fund Type: Income
Inception Date: January 6, 2014

Major Rating Factors: Middle of the road best describes *First Trust NASDAQ Rising Div Ac whose TheStreet.com Investment Rating is currently a C- (Fair). The fund currently has a performance rating of C- (Fair) based on an annualized return of 0.00% over the last three years and a total return of -2.99% year to date 2015. Factored into the performance evaluation is an expense ratio of 0.50% (very low).

The fund's risk rating is currently B- (Good). It carries a beta of 0.00, meaning the fund's expected move will be 0.0% for every 10% move in the market. Volatility, as measured by both the semi-deviation and a drawdown factor, is considered low. As of December 31, 2015, *First Trust NASDAQ Rising Div Ac traded at a price exactly equal to its net asset value, which is better than its one-year historical average premium of .06%.

Daniel J. Lindquist has been running the fund for 2 years and currently receives a manager quality ranking of 34 (0=worst, 99=best). If you desire an average level of risk, then this fund may be an option.

Data Date	Investment Rating	Net Assets ($Mil)	Price	Performance Rating/Pts	Total Return Y-T-D	Risk Rating/Pts
12-15	C-	7.40	20.73	C- / 3.2	-2.99%	B- / 7.8

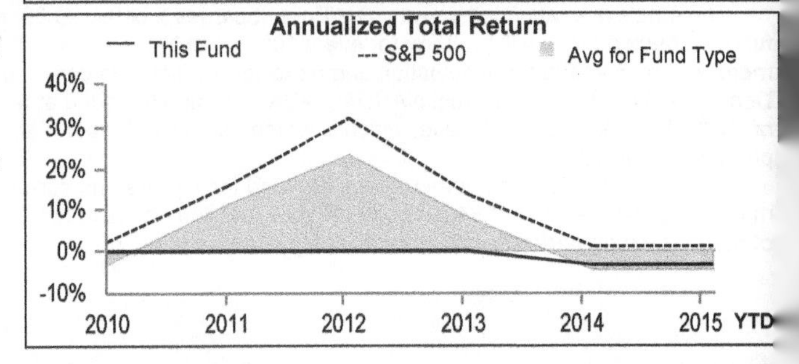

*First Trust NASDAQ Smartphone In (FONE) B+ Good

Fund Family: First Trust Advisors LP
Fund Type: Global
nception Date: February 17, 2011

Data Date	Investment Rating	Net Assets ($Mil)	Price	Performance Rating/Pts	Total Return Y-T-D	Risk Rating/Pts
12-15	B+	11.10	36.36	B+ / 8.3	-3.52%	B- / 7.3
2014	C+	11.10	38.20	B / 7.7	16.99%	C+ / 5.9
2013	A-	10.00	33.40	A / 9.3	28.47%	B- / 7.4
2012	B	11.40	25.10	B+ / 8.7	7.56%	B- / 7.2

lajor Rating Factors: Strong performance is the major factor driving the B+ (Good) heStreet.com Investment Rating for *First Trust NASDAQ Smartphone In. The fund urrently has a performance rating of B+ (Good) based on an annualized return of 3.18% over the last three years and a total return of -3.52% year to date 2015. actored into the performance evaluation is an expense ratio of 0.70% (very low).

The fund's risk rating is currently B- (Good). It carries a beta of 0.82, meaning the ınd's expected move will be 8.2% for every 10% move in the market. Volatility, as ıeasured by both the semi-deviation and a drawdown factor, is considered low. As of ecember 31, 2015, *First Trust NASDAQ Smartphone In traded at a price exactly qual to its net asset value, which is worse than its one-year historical average iscount of .05%.

Daniel J. Lindquist has been running the fund for 5 years and currently receives a ıanager quality ranking of 95 (0=worst, 99=best). If you desire only a moderate level f risk and strong performance, then this fund is an excellent option.

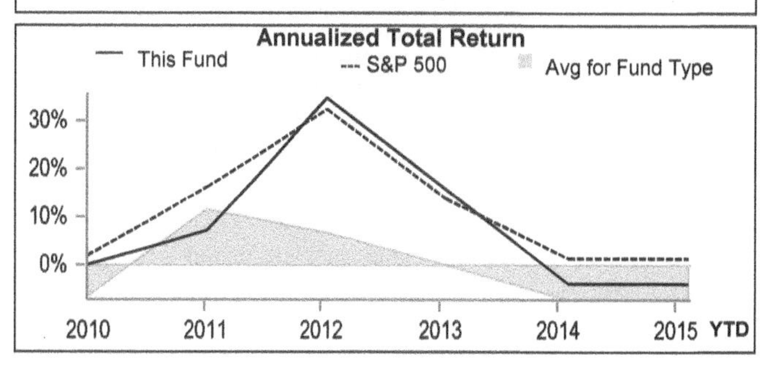

*First Trust NASDAQ Tech Div Idx (TDIV) B+ Good

Fund Family: First Trust Advisors LP
Fund Type: Income
nception Date: August 13, 2012

Data Date	Investment Rating	Net Assets ($Mil)	Price	Performance Rating/Pts	Total Return Y-T-D	Risk Rating/Pts
12-15	B+	684.30	25.27	B / 7.7	-6.32%	B / 8.2
2014	B	684.30	27.68	B- / 7.5	18.49%	B- / 7.4
2013	A+	283.30	24.67	A- / 9.1	24.90%	B+ / 9.4

lajor Rating Factors: Strong performance is the major factor driving the B+ (Good) heStreet.com Investment Rating for *First Trust NASDAQ Tech Div Idx. The fund urrently has a performance rating of B (Good) based on an annualized return of 1.48% over the last three years and a total return of -6.32% year to date 2015. actored into the performance evaluation is an expense ratio of 0.50% (very low).

The fund's risk rating is currently B (Good). It carries a beta of 1.08, meaning that s performance tracks fairly well with that of the overall stock market. Volatility, as ıeasured by both the semi-deviation and a drawdown factor, is considered low. As of ecember 31, 2015, *First Trust NASDAQ Tech Div Idx traded at a discount of .32% elow its net asset value, which is better than its one-year historical average discount f .01%.

Daniel J. Lindquist has been running the fund for 4 years and currently receives a ıanager quality ranking of 42 (0=worst, 99=best). If you desire only a moderate level f risk and strong performance, then this fund is an excellent option.

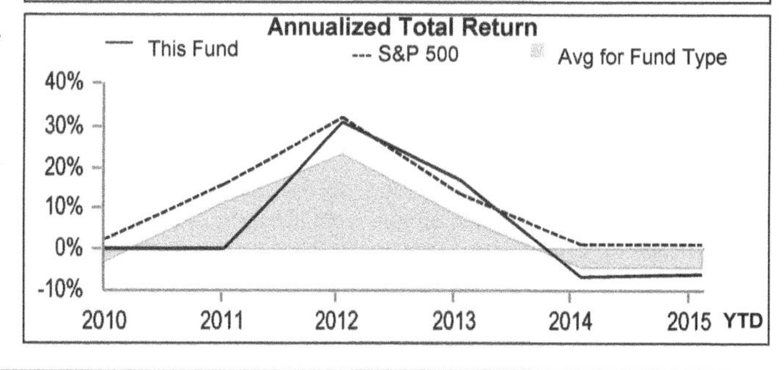

*First Trust NASDAQ-100 Equal Wei (QQEW) A Excellent

Fund Family: First Trust Advisors LP
Fund Type: Growth
nception Date: April 19, 2006

Data Date	Investment Rating	Net Assets ($Mil)	Price	Performance Rating/Pts	Total Return Y-T-D	Risk Rating/Pts
12-15	A	459.90	43.48	A / 9.3	2.37%	B- / 7.5
2014	B+	459.90	42.83	A / 9.3	21.51%	C+ / 6.7
2013	B+	288.90	36.37	B+ / 8.5	34.24%	B- / 7.5
2012	C+	84.80	26.13	C+ / 5.7	14.59%	B- / 7.6
2011	B-	73.50	22.95	C+ / 6.9	-2.25%	B- / 7.7
2010	C+	76.00	23.72	C+ / 6.9	20.10%	C / 5.5

lajor Rating Factors:
xceptional performance is the major factor driving the A (Excellent) TheStreet.com ıvestment Rating for *First Trust NASDAQ-100 Equal Wei. The fund currently has a erformance rating of A (Excellent) based on an annualized return of 18.22% over the ıst three years and a total return of 2.37% year to date 2015. Factored into the erformance evaluation is an expense ratio of 0.60% (very low).

The fund's risk rating is currently B- (Good). It carries a beta of 1.12, meaning it is xpected to move 11.2% for every 10% move in the market. Volatility, as measured y both the semi-deviation and a drawdown factor, is considered low. As of ecember 31, 2015, *First Trust NASDAQ-100 Equal Wei traded at a price exactly qual to its net asset value, which is better than its one-year historical average remium of .01%.

Daniel J. Lindquist has been running the fund for 10 years and currently receives manager quality ranking of 80 (0=worst, 99=best). If you desire only a moderate vel of risk and strong performance, then this fund is an excellent option.

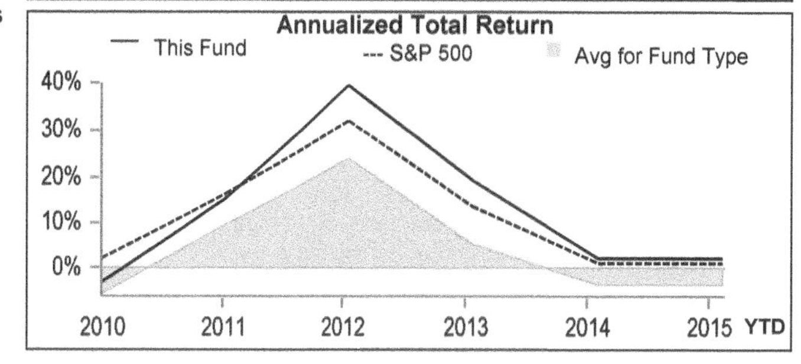

*First Trust NASDAQ-100 Ex-Tech S (QQXT) B+ Good

Fund Family: First Trust Advisors LP
Fund Type: Income
Inception Date: February 8, 2007

Major Rating Factors:
Exceptional performance is the major factor driving the B+ (Good) TheStreet.com Investment Rating for *First Trust NASDAQ-100 Ex-Tech S. The fund currently has a performance rating of A (Excellent) based on an annualized return of 18.23% over the last three years and a total return of 4.97% year to date 2015. Factored into the performance evaluation is an expense ratio of 0.60% (very low).

The fund's risk rating is currently C+ (Fair). It carries a beta of 1.10, meaning it is expected to move 11.0% for every 10% move in the market. Volatility, as measured by both the semi-deviation and a drawdown factor, is considered low. As of December 31, 2015, *First Trust NASDAQ-100 Ex-Tech S traded at a premium of .05% above its net asset value, which is worse than its one-year historical average premium of .04%.

Daniel J. Lindquist has been running the fund for 10 years and currently receives a manager quality ranking of 82 (0=worst, 99=best). If you desire only a moderate level of risk and strong performance, then this fund is an excellent option.

Data Date	Investment Rating	Net Assets ($Mil)	Price	Performance Rating/Pts	Total Return Y-T-D	Risk Rating/Pts
12-15	B+	92.40	41.47	A / 9.3	4.97%	C+ / 6.2
2014	B+	92.40	40.00	A / 9.3	17.00%	C+ / 6.4
2013	B+	90.40	34.79	B+ / 8.9	35.74%	B- / 7.1
2012	C+	42.00	24.65	C+ / 6.5	18.85%	B- / 7.5
2011	C+	30.20	20.78	C+ / 6.3	0.62%	B- / 7.7
2010	C+	22.20	21.10	C+ / 5.7	19.48%	C+ / 5.7

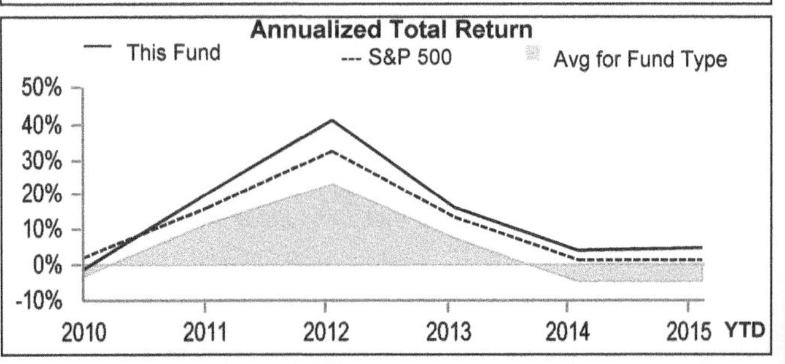

*First Trust NASDAQ-100-Technolog (QTEC) A Excellent

Fund Family: First Trust Advisors LP
Fund Type: Growth
Inception Date: April 19, 2006

Major Rating Factors:
Exceptional performance is the major factor driving the A (Excellent) TheStreet.com Investment Rating for *First Trust NASDAQ-100-Technolog. The fund currently has a performance rating of A (Excellent) based on an annualized return of 18.21% over the last three years and a total return of -1.31% year to date 2015. Factored into the performance evaluation is an expense ratio of 0.60% (very low).

The fund's risk rating is currently B- (Good). It carries a beta of 1.13, meaning it is expected to move 11.3% for every 10% move in the market. Volatility, as measured by both the semi-deviation and a drawdown factor, is considered low. As of December 31, 2015, *First Trust NASDAQ-100-Technolog traded at a premium of .02% above its net asset value, which is better than its one-year historical average premium of .03%.

Daniel J. Lindquist has been running the fund for 10 years and currently receives a manager quality ranking of 80 (0=worst, 99=best). If you desire only a moderate level of risk and strong performance, then this fund is an excellent option.

Data Date	Investment Rating	Net Assets ($Mil)	Price	Performance Rating/Pts	Total Return Y-T-D	Risk Rating/Pts
12-15	A	271.40	42.65	A / 9.3	-1.31%	B- / 7.3
2014	B+	271.40	43.75	A / 9.3	27.54%	C+ / 6.7
2013	B	177.20	35.42	B / 7.7	32.54%	B- / 7.7
2012	C-	106.00	25.85	C- / 4.0	8.66%	B- / 7.6
2011	B-	149.70	24.12	B / 7.6	-6.43%	B- / 7.6
2010	B+	453.40	25.71	B / 8.0	21.22%	C / 5.5

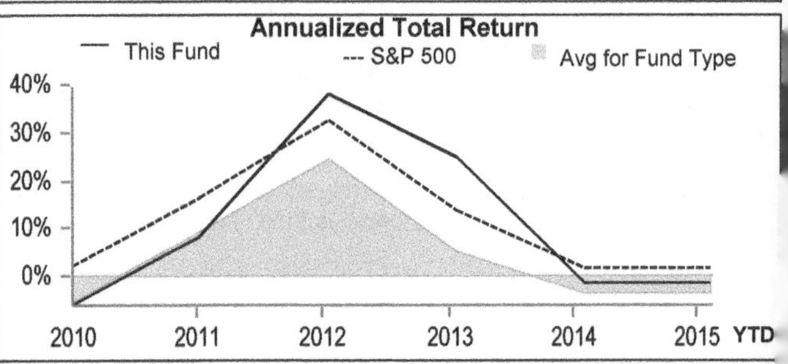

*First Trust North Am Energy Infr (EMLP) D+ Weak

Fund Family: First Trust Advisors LP
Fund Type: Energy/Natural Resources
Inception Date: June 20, 2012

Major Rating Factors:
Disappointing performance is the major factor driving the D+ (Weak) TheStreet.com Investment Rating for *First Trust North Am Energy Infr. The fund currently has a performance rating of D+ (Weak) based on an annualized return of 1.42% over the last three years and a total return of -25.83% year to date 2015. Factored into the performance evaluation is an expense ratio of 0.95% (low).

The fund's risk rating is currently C+ (Fair). It carries a beta of 0.46, meaning the fund's expected move will be 4.6% for every 10% move in the market. Volatility, as measured by both the semi-deviation and a drawdown factor, is considered low. As of December 31, 2015, *First Trust North Am Energy Infr traded at a price exactly equal to its net asset value, which is better than its one-year historical average premium of .03%.

Eva Pao has been running the fund for 4 years and currently receives a manager quality ranking of 88 (0=worst, 99=best). This fund offers only a moderate level of risk but investors looking for strong performance are still waiting.

Data Date	Investment Rating	Net Assets ($Mil)	Price	Performance Rating/Pts	Total Return Y-T-D	Risk Rating/Pts
12-15	D+	862.50	20.18	D+ / 2.9	-25.83%	C+ / 6.3
2014	A+	862.50	28.15	A / 9.3	26.61%	B+ / 9.0
2013	B	443.80	23.49	C+ / 6.1	10.70%	B+ / 9.3

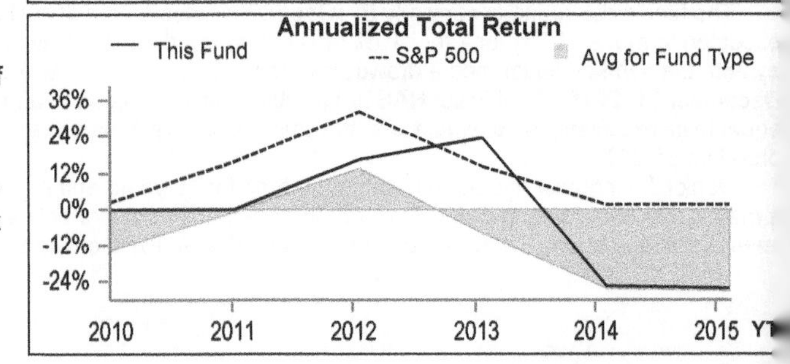

*First Trust Pref Sec and Inc (FPE) C+ Fair

Fund Family: First Trust Advisors LP
Fund Type: General Bond
Inception Date: February 11, 2013

Major Rating Factors: Middle of the road best describes *First Trust Pref Sec and Inc whose TheStreet.com Investment Rating is currently a C+ (Fair). The fund currently has a performance rating of C+ (Fair) based on an annualized return of 0.00% over the last three years and a total return of 6.07% year to date 2015. Factored into the performance evaluation is an expense ratio of 0.85% (very low).

The fund's risk rating is currently B- (Good). It carries a beta of 0.00, meaning the fund's expected move will be 0.0% for every 10% move in the market. Volatility, as measured by both the semi-deviation and a drawdown factor, is considered low. As of December 31, 2015, *First Trust Pref Sec and Inc traded at a premium of .32% above its net asset value, which is worse than its one-year historical average premium of .19%.

Robert Wolf has been running the fund for 3 years and currently receives a manager quality ranking of 90 (0=worst, 99=best). If you desire an average level of risk, then this fund may be an option.

Data Date	Investment Rating	Net Assets ($Mil)	Price	Performance Rating/Pts	Total Return Y-T-D	Risk Rating/Pts
12-15	C+	80.60	18.95	C+ / 6.8	6.07%	B- / 7.1
2014	C	80.60	18.86	C / 5.3	10.67%	C+ / 6.9

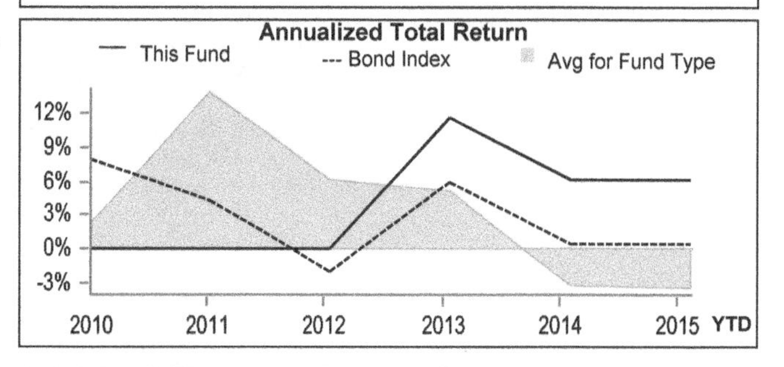

*First Trust RBA Amer Indus Rens (AIRR) D+ Weak

Fund Family: First Trust Advisors LP
Fund Type: Income
Inception Date: March 10, 2014

Major Rating Factors:
Disappointing performance is the major factor driving the D+ (Weak) TheStreet.com Investment Rating for *First Trust RBA Amer Indus Rens. The fund currently has a performance rating of D+ (Weak) based on an annualized return of 0.00% over the last three years and a total return of -8.81% year to date 2015. Factored into the performance evaluation is an expense ratio of 0.70% (very low).

The fund's risk rating is currently C+ (Fair). It carries a beta of 0.00, meaning the fund's expected move will be 0.0% for every 10% move in the market. Volatility, as measured by both the semi-deviation and a drawdown factor, is considered low. As of December 31, 2015, *First Trust RBA Amer Indus Rens traded at a price exactly equal to its net asset value, which is worse than its one-year historical average discount of .06%.

Jonathan C. Erickson has been running the fund for 2 years and currently receives a manager quality ranking of 15 (0=worst, 99=best). This fund offers only a moderate level of risk but investors looking for strong performance are still waiting.

Data Date	Investment Rating	Net Assets ($Mil)	Price	Performance Rating/Pts	Total Return Y-T-D	Risk Rating/Pts
12-15	D+	79.50	16.51	D+ / 2.5	-8.81%	C+ / 6.3

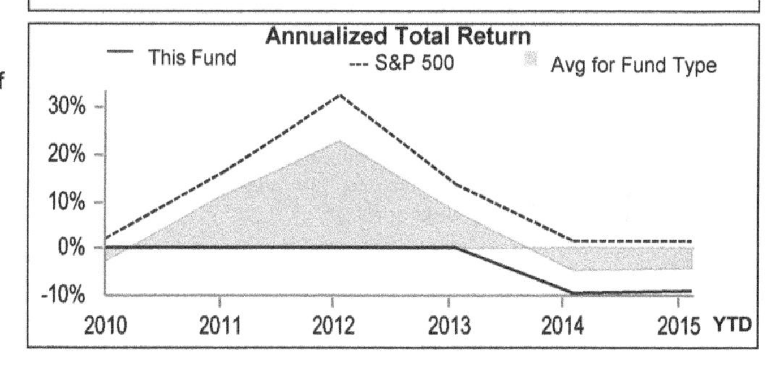

*First Trust RBA Quality Income (QINC) C- Fair

Fund Family: First Trust Advisors LP
Fund Type: Income
Inception Date: March 10, 2014

Major Rating Factors:
Disappointing performance is the major factor driving the C- (Fair) TheStreet.com Investment Rating for *First Trust RBA Quality Income. The fund currently has a performance rating of D+ (Weak) based on an annualized return of 0.00% over the last three years and a total return of -6.13% year to date 2015. Factored into the performance evaluation is an expense ratio of 0.70% (very low).

The fund's risk rating is currently B- (Good). It carries a beta of 0.00, meaning the fund's expected move will be 0.0% for every 10% move in the market. Volatility, as measured by both the semi-deviation and a drawdown factor, is considered low. As of December 31, 2015, *First Trust RBA Quality Income traded at a price exactly equal to its net asset value, which is better than its one-year historical average premium of .02%.

Daniel J. Lindquist currently receives a manager quality ranking of 23 (0=worst, 99=best). This fund offers only a moderate level of risk but investors looking for strong performance are still waiting.

Data Date	Investment Rating	Net Assets ($Mil)	Price	Performance Rating/Pts	Total Return Y-T-D	Risk Rating/Pts
12-15	C-	5.00	20.08	D+ / 2.7	-6.13%	B- / 7.9

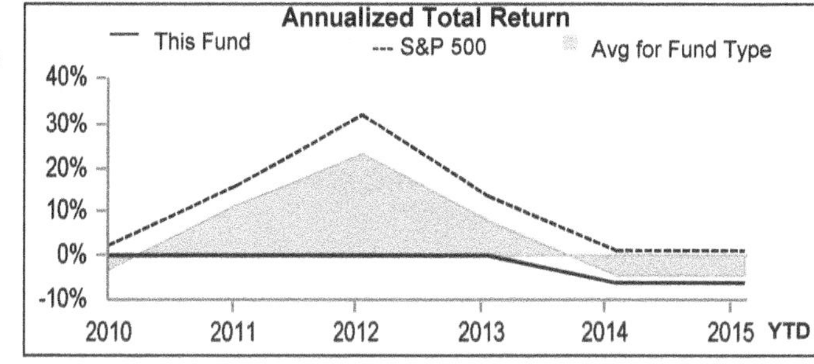

*First Trust S&P REIT Index (FRI) B- Good

Fund Family: First Trust Advisors LP
Fund Type: Income
Inception Date: May 8, 2007

Major Rating Factors: Strong performance is the major factor driving the B- (Good) TheStreet.com Investment Rating for *First Trust S&P REIT Index. The fund currently has a performance rating of B (Good) based on an annualized return of 9.79% over the last three years and a total return of 0.48% year to date 2015. Factored into the performance evaluation is an expense ratio of 0.50% (very low).

The fund's risk rating is currently C+ (Fair). It carries a beta of 0.47, meaning the fund's expected move will be 4.7% for every 10% move in the market. Volatility, as measured by both the semi-deviation and a drawdown factor, is considered low. As of December 31, 2015, *First Trust S&P REIT Index traded at a premium of .05% above its net asset value.

Daniel J. Lindquist has been running the fund for 9 years and currently receives a manager quality ranking of 85 (0=worst, 99=best). If you desire only a moderate level of risk and strong performance, then this fund is an excellent option.

Data Date	Investment Rating	Net Assets ($Mil)	Price	Perfor-mance Rating/Pts	Total Return Y-T-D	Risk Rating/Pts
12-15	B-	203.60	22.08	B / 7.8	0.48%	C+ / 6.4
2014	A+	203.60	22.27	A- / 9.0	31.08%	B / 8.0
2013	C	148.20	17.54	C / 5.3	-0.47%	B- / 7.8
2012	B-	402.90	17.75	B- / 7.3	18.74%	B- / 7.6
2011	C+	325.00	15.49	B / 7.7	8.36%	C+ / 6.4
2010	C	71.10	14.65	B- / 7.0	27.73%	C- / 4.2

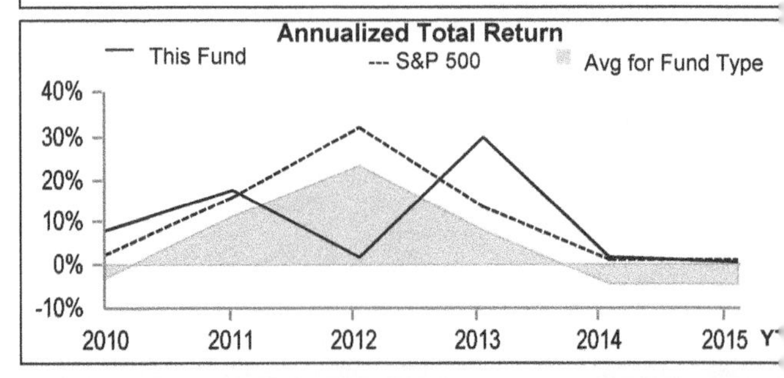

*First Trust Senior Loan (FTSL) C+ Fair

Fund Family: First Trust Advisors LP
Fund Type: Loan Participation
Inception Date: May 1, 2013

Major Rating Factors: Middle of the road best describes *First Trust Senior Loan whose TheStreet.com Investment Rating is currently a C+ (Fair). The fund currently has a performance rating of C- (Fair) based on an annualized return of 0.00% over the last three years and a total return of 0.17% year to date 2015. Factored into the performance evaluation is an expense ratio of 0.85% (very low).

The fund's risk rating is currently B+ (Good). It carries a beta of 0.00, meaning the fund's expected move will be 0.0% for every 10% move in the market. Volatility, as measured by both the semi-deviation and a drawdown factor, is considered very low. As of December 31, 2015, *First Trust Senior Loan traded at a discount of .17% below its net asset value, which is better than its one-year historical average premium of .15%.

Scott D. Fries has been running the fund for 3 years and currently receives a manager quality ranking of 80 (0=worst, 99=best). If you desire an average level of risk, then this fund may be an option.

Data Date	Investment Rating	Net Assets ($Mil)	Price	Perfor-mance Rating/Pts	Total Return Y-T-D	Risk Rating/Pts
12-15	C+	200.40	46.87	C- / 3.7	0.17%	B+ / 9.4
2014	C	200.40	48.49	D+ / 2.9	1.26%	B+ / 9.5

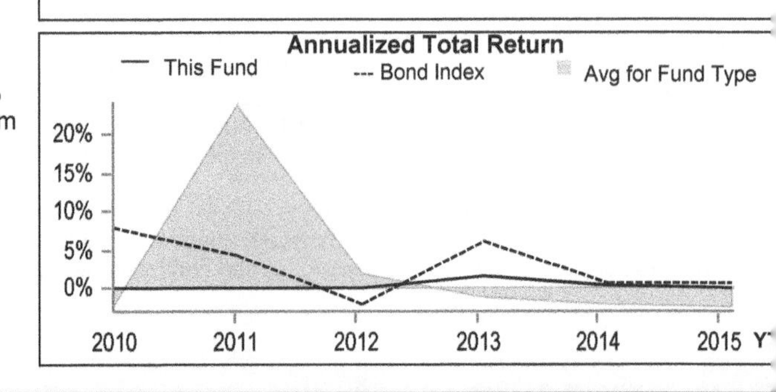

*First Trust Small Cap Core Alpha (FYX) B- Good

Fund Family: First Trust Advisors LP
Fund Type: Growth
Inception Date: May 8, 2007

Major Rating Factors: *First Trust Small Cap Core Alpha receives a TheStreet.com Investment Rating of B- (Good). The fund currently has a performance rating of C+ (Fair) based on an annualized return of 8.42% over the last three years and a total return of -8.41% year to date 2015. Factored into the performance evaluation is an expense ratio of 0.63% (very low).

The fund's risk rating is currently B (Good). It carries a beta of 1.07, meaning that its performance tracks fairly well with that of the overall stock market. Volatility, as measured by both the semi-deviation and a drawdown factor, is considered low. As of December 31, 2015, *First Trust Small Cap Core Alpha traded at a discount of .14% below its net asset value, which is better than its one-year historical average premium of .01%.

Daniel J. Lindquist has been running the fund for 9 years and currently receives a manager quality ranking of 27 (0=worst, 99=best). If you desire an average level of risk, then this fund may be an option.

Data Date	Investment Rating	Net Assets ($Mil)	Price	Perfor-mance Rating/Pts	Total Return Y-T-D	Risk Rating/Pts
12-15	B-	512.60	44.18	C+ / 6.3	-8.41%	B / 8.2
2014	B-	512.60	49.00	B- / 7.5	3.23%	B- / 7.0
2013	A-	488.60	48.66	B+ / 8.9	36.49%	B- / 7.8
2012	C+	163.70	34.12	C+ / 6.5	15.20%	B- / 7.6
2011	B-	125.60	29.91	C+ / 6.9	0.90%	B- / 7.5
2010	B	82.50	30.08	B / 7.8	27.35%	C / 5.5

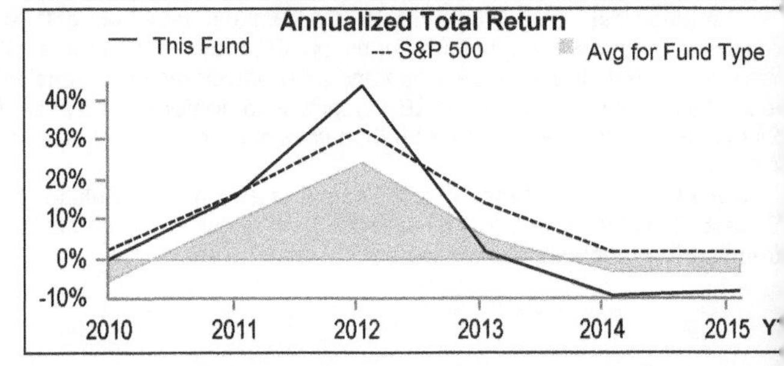

*First Trust Small Cap Gro AlphaD (FYC) B Good

Fund Family: First Trust Advisors LP
Fund Type: Growth
Inception Date: April 19, 2011

Major Rating Factors: Strong performance is the major factor driving the B (Good) TheStreet.com Investment Rating for *First Trust Small Cap Gro AlphaD. The fund currently has a performance rating of B (Good) based on an annualized return of 11.58% over the last three years and a total return of 2.64% year to date 2015. Factored into the performance evaluation is an expense ratio of 0.70% (very low).

The fund's risk rating is currently C+ (Fair). It carries a beta of 1.05, meaning that its performance tracks fairly well with that of the overall stock market. Volatility, as measured by both the semi-deviation and a drawdown factor, is considered low. As of December 31, 2015, *First Trust Small Cap Gro AlphaD traded at a premium of .13% above its net asset value, which is worse than its one-year historical average premium of .04%.

Daniel J. Lindquist has been running the fund for 5 years and currently receives a manager quality ranking of 45 (0=worst, 99=best). If you desire only a moderate level of risk and strong performance, then this fund is an excellent option.

Data Date	Investment Rating	Net Assets ($Mil)	Price	Performance Rating/Pts	Total Return Y-T-D	Risk Rating/Pts
12-15	B	37.30	30.51	B / 8.1	2.64%	C+ / 6.9
2014	C+	37.30	30.02	B- / 7.0	-0.24%	C+ / 6.8
2013	A+	25.90	30.52	A+ / 9.7	36.63%	B / 8.7
2012	B	9.60	21.30	B- / 7.1	15.12%	B / 8.5

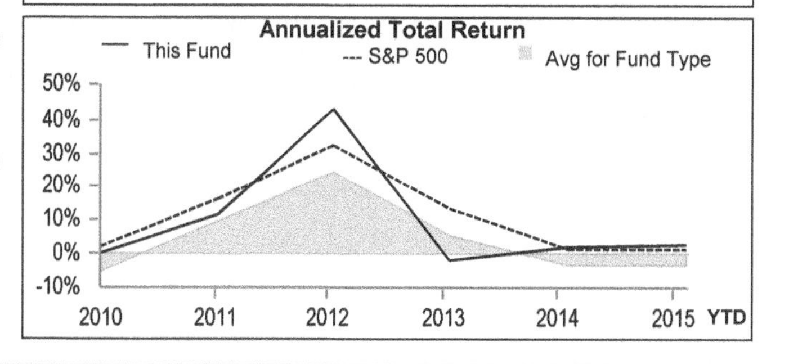

*First Trust Small Cap Val AlphaD (FYT) C+ Fair

Fund Family: First Trust Advisors LP
Fund Type: Growth
Inception Date: April 19, 2011

Major Rating Factors: Middle of the road best describes *First Trust Small Cap Val AlphaD whose TheStreet.com Investment Rating is currently a C+ (Fair). The fund currently has a performance rating of C (Fair) based on an annualized return of 5.90% over the last three years and a total return of -16.21% year to date 2015. Factored into the performance evaluation is an expense ratio of 0.70% (very low).

The fund's risk rating is currently B- (Good). It carries a beta of 1.09, meaning that its performance tracks fairly well with that of the overall stock market. Volatility, as measured by both the semi-deviation and a drawdown factor, is considered low. As of December 31, 2015, *First Trust Small Cap Val AlphaD traded at a discount of .04% below its net asset value.

Daniel J. Lindquist has been running the fund for 5 years and currently receives a manager quality ranking of 20 (0=worst, 99=best). If you desire an average level of risk, then this fund may be an option.

Data Date	Investment Rating	Net Assets ($Mil)	Price	Performance Rating/Pts	Total Return Y-T-D	Risk Rating/Pts
12-15	C+	59.50	27.08	C / 5.2	-16.21%	B- / 7.9
2014	B-	59.50	32.86	B / 7.8	5.11%	C+ / 6.5
2013	A+	78.10	31.91	A+ / 9.6	35.76%	B / 8.5
2012	A-	24.60	22.38	B+ / 8.4	15.26%	B / 8.3

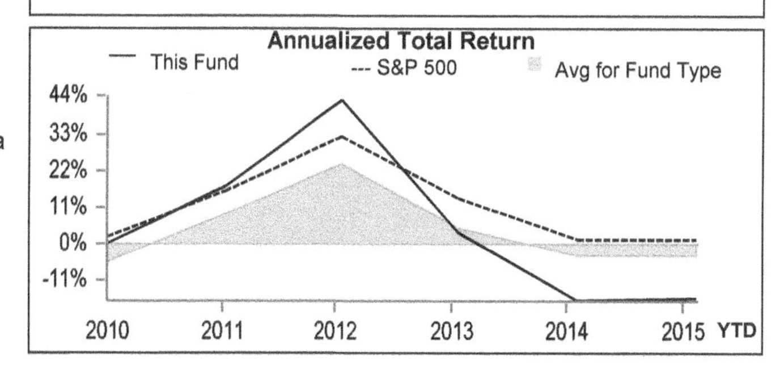

*First Trust South Korea AlphaDEX (FKO) C- Fair

Fund Family: First Trust Advisors LP
Fund Type: Foreign
Inception Date: April 18, 2011

Major Rating Factors:
Disappointing performance is the major factor driving the C- (Fair) TheStreet.com Investment Rating for *First Trust South Korea AlphaDEX. The fund currently has a performance rating of D+ (Weak) based on an annualized return of -4.99% over the last three years and a total return of -4.23% year to date 2015. Factored into the performance evaluation is an expense ratio of 0.80% (very low).

The fund's risk rating is currently B- (Good). It carries a beta of 0.89, meaning the fund's expected move will be 8.9% for every 10% move in the market. Volatility, as measured by both the semi-deviation and a drawdown factor, is considered low. As of December 31, 2015, *First Trust South Korea AlphaDEX traded at a discount of .74% below its net asset value, which is worse than its one-year historical average discount of .81%.

Daniel J. Lindquist has been running the fund for 5 years and currently receives a manager quality ranking of 18 (0=worst, 99=best). This fund offers only a moderate level of risk but investors looking for strong performance are still waiting.

Data Date	Investment Rating	Net Assets ($Mil)	Price	Performance Rating/Pts	Total Return Y-T-D	Risk Rating/Pts
12-15	C-	4.20	22.72	D+ / 2.7	-4.23%	B- / 7.2
2014	D	4.20	24.27	D+ / 2.6	-9.27%	C+ / 5.6
2013	C+	5.60	28.20	C+ / 6.3	0.03%	B- / 7.0
2012	B+	2.60	26.83	A- / 9.2	18.28%	C+ / 6.8

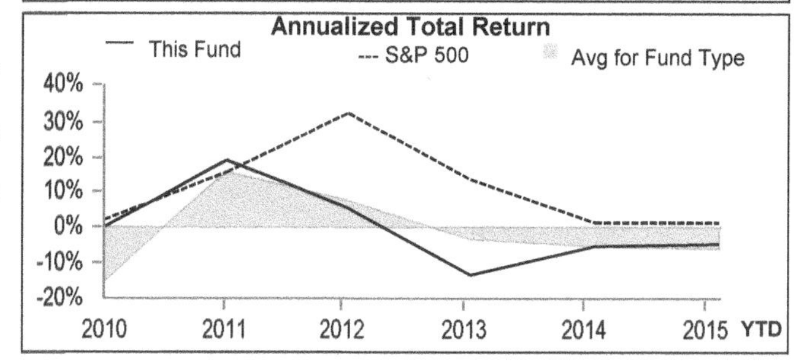

* Denotes ETF Fund

*First Trust STOXX European Sel D (FDD) C Fair

Fund Family: First Trust Advisors LP
Fund Type: Foreign
Inception Date: August 27, 2007

Major Rating Factors: Middle of the road best describes *First Trust STOXX European Sel D whose TheStreet.com Investment Rating is currently a C (Fair). The fund currently has a performance rating of C (Fair) based on an annualized return of 3.84% over the last three years and a total return of -2.02% year to date 2015. Factored into the performance evaluation is an expense ratio of 0.60% (very low).

The fund's risk rating is currently C+ (Fair). It carries a beta of 0.91, meaning that its performance tracks fairly well with that of the overall stock market. Volatility, as measured by both the semi-deviation and a drawdown factor, is considered low. As of December 31, 2015, *First Trust STOXX European Sel D traded at a premium of .08% above its net asset value, which is better than its one-year historical average premium of .18%.

Daniel J. Lindquist currently receives a manager quality ranking of 58 (0=worst, 99=best). If you desire an average level of risk, then this fund may be an option.

Data Date	Investment Rating	Net Assets ($Mil)	Price	Perfor-mance Rating/Pts	Total Return Y-T-D	Risk Rating/Pts
12-15	C	167.50	12.18	C / 5.5	-2.02%	C+ / 6.0
2014	C-	167.50	13.05	C / 4.9	1.54%	C+ / 6.3
2013	C	80.50	13.82	C+ / 5.6	15.37%	B- / 7.0
2012	D	18.20	12.31	D+ / 2.5	15.79%	C+ / 6.8
2011	D+	9.90	11.86	D / 2.2	-12.17%	B- / 7.4
2010	E+	9.60	13.69	E+ / 0.6	1.93%	C- / 3.7

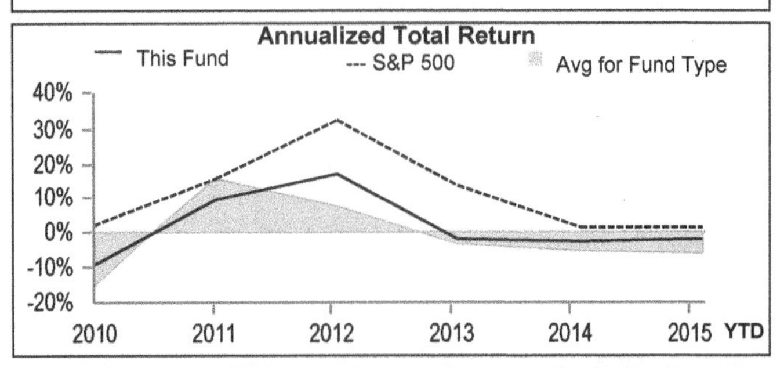

*First Trust Strategic Income (FDIV) C- Fair

Fund Family: First Trust Advisors LP
Fund Type: Global
Inception Date: August 13, 2014

Major Rating Factors: Middle of the road best describes *First Trust Strategic Income whose TheStreet.com Investment Rating is currently a C- (Fair). The fund currently has a performance rating of C- (Fair) based on an annualized return of 0.00% over the last three years and a total return of -4.99% year to date 2015.

The fund's risk rating is currently B- (Good). It carries a beta of 0.00, meaning the fund's expected move will be 0.0% for every 10% move in the market. Volatility, as measured by both the semi-deviation and a drawdown factor, is considered low. As of December 31, 2015, *First Trust Strategic Income traded at a premium of .06% above its net asset value, which is worse than its one-year historical average discount of .14%.

Richard Bernstein has been running the fund for 2 years and currently receives a manager quality ranking of 28 (0=worst, 99=best). If you desire an average level of risk, then this fund may be an option.

Data Date	Investment Rating	Net Assets ($Mil)	Price	Perfor-mance Rating/Pts	Total Return Y-T-D	Risk Rating/Pts
12-15	C-	0.00	46.49	C- / 3.0	-4.99%	B- / 7.4

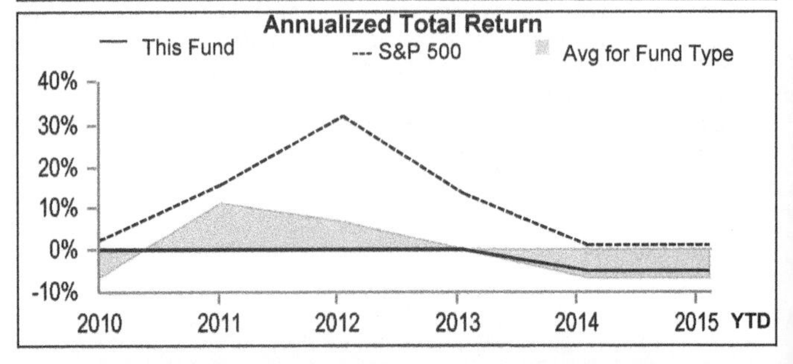

*First Trust Tactical High Yield (HYLS) C- Fair

Fund Family: First Trust Advisors LP
Fund Type: Corporate - High Yield
Inception Date: February 25, 2013

Major Rating Factors: Middle of the road best describes *First Trust Tactical High Yield whose TheStreet.com Investment Rating is currently a C- (Fair). The fund currently has a performance rating of C- (Fair) based on an annualized return of 0.00% over the last three years and a total return of 0.06% year to date 2015. Factored into the performance evaluation is an expense ratio of 0.95% (low).

The fund's risk rating is currently B- (Good). It carries a beta of 0.00, meaning the fund's expected move will be 0.0% for every 10% move in the market. Volatility, as measured by both the semi-deviation and a drawdown factor, is considered low. As of December 31, 2015, *First Trust Tactical High Yield traded at a premium of .04% above its net asset value, which is better than its one-year historical average premium of .10%.

Peter J. Fasone has been running the fund for 3 years and currently receives a manager quality ranking of 87 (0=worst, 99=best). If you desire an average level of risk, then this fund may be an option.

Data Date	Investment Rating	Net Assets ($Mil)	Price	Perfor-mance Rating/Pts	Total Return Y-T-D	Risk Rating/Pts
12-15	C-	185.00	46.97	C- / 3.6	0.06%	B- / 7.1
2014	C-	185.00	49.66	D+ / 2.7	1.66%	B+ / 9.1

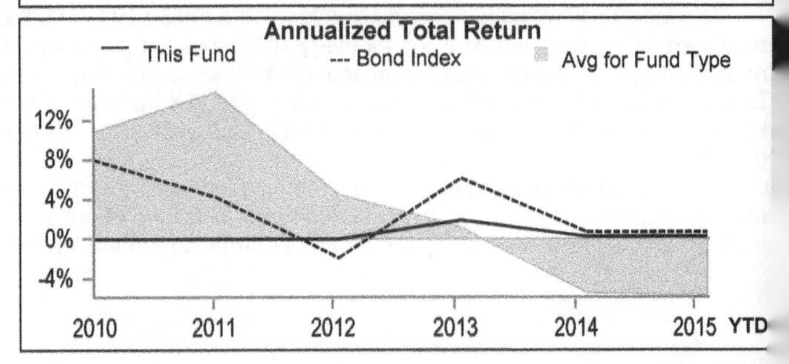

*First Trust Technology AlphaDEX (FXL) B Good

Fund Family: First Trust Advisors LP
Fund Type: Growth
Inception Date: May 8, 2007

Major Rating Factors: Strong performance is the major factor driving the B (Good) TheStreet.com Investment Rating for *First Trust Technology AlphaDEX. The fund currently has a performance rating of B+ (Good) based on an annualized return of 14.78% over the last three years and a total return of -3.02% year to date 2015. Factored into the performance evaluation is an expense ratio of 0.63% (very low).

The fund's risk rating is currently C+ (Fair). It carries a beta of 1.09, meaning that its performance tracks fairly well with that of the overall stock market. Volatility, as measured by both the semi-deviation and a drawdown factor, is considered low. As of December 31, 2015, *First Trust Technology AlphaDEX traded at a premium of .03% above its net asset value, which is worse than its one-year historical average premium of .02%.

Daniel J. Lindquist has been running the fund for 9 years and currently receives a manager quality ranking of 62 (0=worst, 99=best). If you desire only a moderate level of risk and strong performance, then this fund is an excellent option.

Data Date	Investment Rating	Net Assets ($Mil)	Price	Performance Rating/Pts	Total Return Y-T-D	Risk Rating/Pts
12-15	B	847.30	33.24	B+ / 8.6	-3.02%	C+ / 6.6
2014	B	847.30	34.51	B+ / 8.6	18.07%	C+ / 6.5
2013	C+	489.30	29.85	B- / 7.4	33.06%	B- / 7.1
2012	D+	138.10	21.68	C- / 3.7	7.83%	C+ / 6.9
2011	C+	188.30	20.04	C+ / 6.5	-11.07%	B- / 7.2
2010	C+	119.10	22.70	B- / 7.2	26.64%	C / 4.8

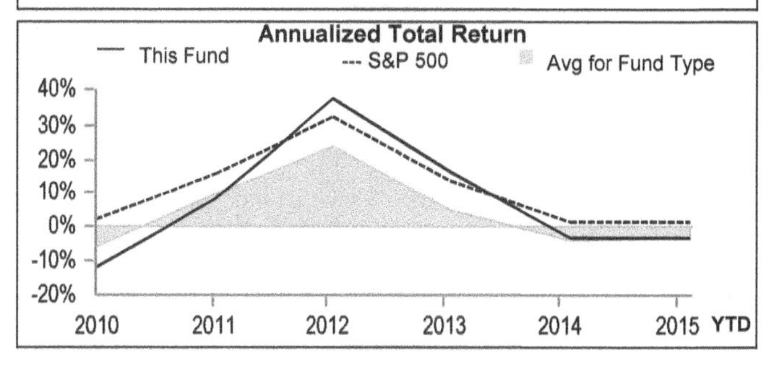

*First Trust Total US Mkt AlphaDE (TUSA) B- Good

Fund Family: First Trust Advisors LP
Fund Type: Growth and Income
Inception Date: December 5, 2006

Major Rating Factors: Strong performance is the major factor driving the B- (Good) TheStreet.com Investment Rating for *First Trust Total US Mkt AlphaDE. The fund currently has a performance rating of B- (Good) based on an annualized return of 10.18% over the last three years and a total return of -5.05% year to date 2015. Factored into the performance evaluation is an expense ratio of 0.70% (very low).

The fund's risk rating is currently B- (Good). It carries a beta of 0.93, meaning that its performance tracks fairly well with that of the overall stock market. Volatility, as measured by both the semi-deviation and a drawdown factor, is considered low. As of December 31, 2015, *First Trust Total US Mkt AlphaDE traded at a premium of .86% above its net asset value, which is worse than its one-year historical average premium of .04%.

Daniel J. Lindquist has been running the fund for 10 years and currently receives a manager quality ranking of 39 (0=worst, 99=best). If you desire only a moderate level of risk and strong performance, then this fund is an excellent option.

Data Date	Investment Rating	Net Assets ($Mil)	Price	Performance Rating/Pts	Total Return Y-T-D	Risk Rating/Pts
12-15	B-	5.20	24.55	B- / 7.2	-5.05%	B- / 7.1
2014	B-	5.20	26.09	C+ / 6.4	4.32%	B / 8.3
2013	B	5.20	25.71	B- / 7.4	35.90%	B- / 7.8
2012	D+	3.90	18.90	C- / 3.0	9.90%	B- / 7.7
2011	C	6.40	18.23	C / 4.3	-9.21%	B- / 7.7
2010	C+	7.10	20.35	C+ / 6.0	19.25%	C+ / 6.0

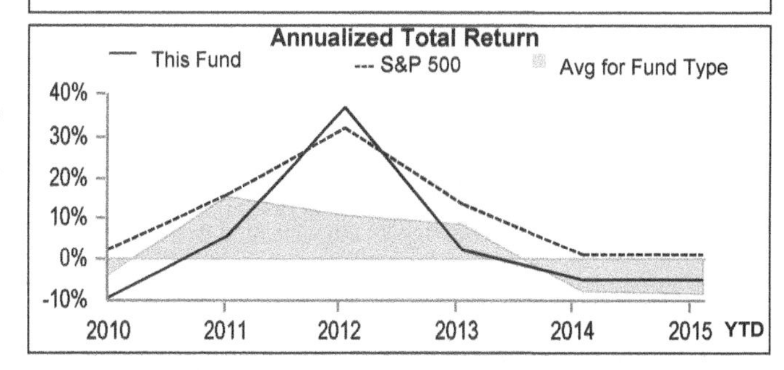

*First Trust US IPO Index (FPX) B+ Good

Fund Family: First Trust Advisors LP
Fund Type: Growth
Inception Date: April 12, 2006

Major Rating Factors:
Exceptional performance is the major factor driving the B+ (Good) TheStreet.com Investment Rating for *First Trust US IPO Index. The fund currently has a performance rating of A- (Excellent) based on an annualized return of 17.95% over the last three years and a total return of 1.99% year to date 2015. Factored into the performance evaluation is an expense ratio of 0.60% (very low).

The fund's risk rating is currently C+ (Fair). It carries a beta of 1.11, meaning it is expected to move 11.1% for every 10% move in the market. Volatility, as measured by both the semi-deviation and a drawdown factor, is considered low. As of December 31, 2015, *First Trust US IPO Index traded at a premium of .04% above its net asset value, which is worse than its one-year historical average premium of .02%.

Daniel J. Lindquist has been running the fund for 10 years and currently receives a manager quality ranking of 80 (0=worst, 99=best). If you desire only a moderate level of risk and strong performance, then this fund is an excellent option.

Data Date	Investment Rating	Net Assets ($Mil)	Price	Performance Rating/Pts	Total Return Y-T-D	Risk Rating/Pts
12-15	B+	533.50	51.13	A- / 9.2	1.99%	C+ / 6.6
2014	A+	533.50	50.29	A / 9.5	13.95%	B / 8.9
2013	A+	351.40	45.39	A / 9.4	42.30%	B / 8.2
2012	A-	21.30	30.90	B+ / 8.8	31.61%	B / 8.0
2011	B-	15.60	23.97	C+ / 6.6	3.29%	B / 8.2
2010	C	15.30	23.51	C / 5.2	18.17%	C / 5.1

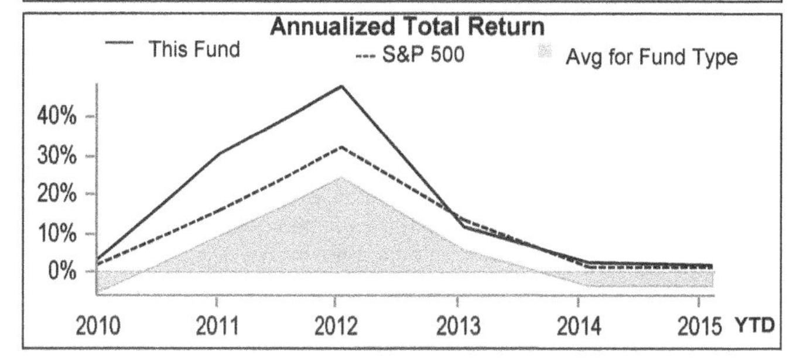

*First Trust Utilities AlphaDEX (FXU) A- Excellent

Fund Family: First Trust Advisors LP
Fund Type: Utilities
Inception Date: May 8, 2007

Major Rating Factors:
Strong performance is the major factor driving the A- (Excellent) TheStreet.com Investment Rating for *First Trust Utilities AlphaDEX. The fund currently has a performance rating of B- (Good) based on an annualized return of 10.36% over the last three years and a total return of -6.88% year to date 2015. Factored into the performance evaluation is an expense ratio of 0.69% (very low).

The fund's risk rating is currently B (Good). It carries a beta of 0.75, meaning the fund's expected move will be 7.5% for every 10% move in the market. Volatility, as measured by both the semi-deviation and a drawdown factor, is considered low. As of December 31, 2015, *First Trust Utilities AlphaDEX traded at a discount of .04% below its net asset value, which is better than its one-year historical average discount of .01%.

Daniel J. Lindquist has been running the fund for 9 years and currently receives a manager quality ranking of 80 (0=worst, 99=best). If you desire only a moderate level of risk and strong performance, then this fund is an excellent option.

Data Date	Investment Rating	Net Assets ($Mil)	Price	Performance Rating/Pts	Total Return Y-T-D	Risk Rating/Pts
12-15	A-	204.60	22.39	B- / 7.4	-6.88%	B / 8.8
2014	A+	204.60	24.88	B+ / 8.9	29.72%	B+ / 9.1
2013	B	107.40	20.28	C+ / 6.2	12.29%	B+ / 9.0
2012	C	140.30	17.98	C- / 3.1	5.84%	B+ / 9.0
2011	C+	331.30	17.93	C / 4.9	6.98%	B / 8.4
2010	C	39.70	16.53	C- / 3.6	10.47%	C+ / 6.8

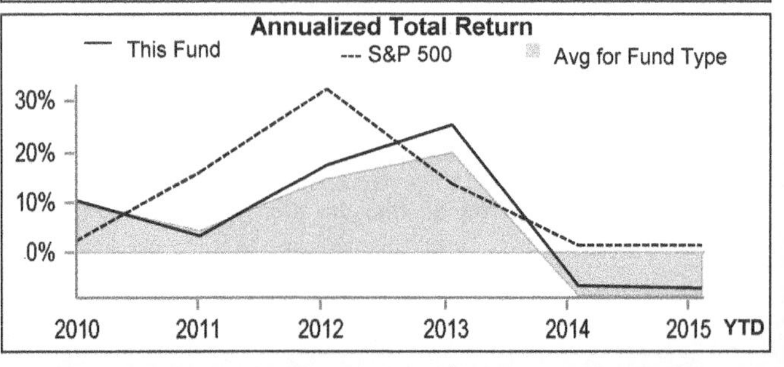

*First Trust Value Line 100 (FVL) B Good

Fund Family: First Trust Advisors LP
Fund Type: Growth
Inception Date: June 12, 2003

Major Rating Factors: Strong performance is the major factor driving the B (Good) TheStreet.com Investment Rating for *First Trust Value Line 100. The fund currently has a performance rating of B+ (Good) based on an annualized return of 13.56% over the last three years and a total return of -2.59% year to date 2015. Factored into the performance evaluation is an expense ratio of 0.70% (very low).

The fund's risk rating is currently C+ (Fair). It carries a beta of 1.12, meaning it is expected to move 11.2% for every 10% move in the market. Volatility, as measured by both the semi-deviation and a drawdown factor, is considered low. As of December 31, 2015, *First Trust Value Line 100 traded at a premium of .46% above its net asset value, which is worse than its one-year historical average discount of .04%.

David G. McGarel has been running the fund for 13 years and currently receives a manager quality ranking of 51 (0=worst, 99=best). If you desire only a moderate level of risk and strong performance, then this fund is an excellent option.

Data Date	Investment Rating	Net Assets ($Mil)	Price	Performance Rating/Pts	Total Return Y-T-D	Risk Rating/Pts
12-15	B	60.50	19.80	B+ / 8.3	-2.59%	C+ / 6.9
2014	B-	60.50	20.43	B / 7.7	12.52%	C+ / 6.9
2013	B-	56.10	18.45	B / 7.7	34.47%	B- / 7.3
2012	C-	45.60	13.26	C- / 4.1	8.12%	B- / 7.1
2011	C-	55.50	12.39	C- / 4.1	-6.65%	B- / 7.2
2010	D	88.40	13.52	D+ / 2.6	28.27%	C / 5.2

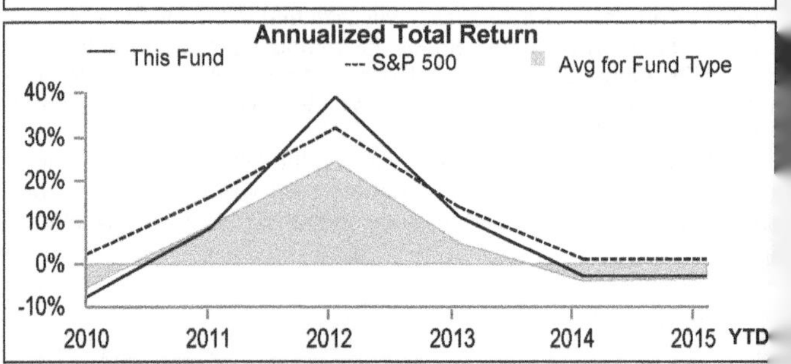

*First Trust Value Line Dividend (FVD) A- Excellent

Fund Family: First Trust Advisors LP
Fund Type: Growth and Income
Inception Date: August 19, 2003

Major Rating Factors:
Strong performance is the major factor driving the A- (Excellent) TheStreet.com Investment Rating for *First Trust Value Line Dividend. The fund currently has a performance rating of B+ (Good) based on an annualized return of 13.17% over the last three years and a total return of 1.30% year to date 2015. Factored into the performance evaluation is an expense ratio of 0.70% (very low).

The fund's risk rating is currently B- (Good). It carries a beta of 0.83, meaning the fund's expected move will be 8.3% for every 10% move in the market. Volatility, as measured by both the semi-deviation and a drawdown factor, is considered low. As of December 31, 2015, *First Trust Value Line Dividend traded at a premium of .08% above its net asset value, which is worse than its one-year historical average premium of .03%.

Daniel J. Lindquist has been running the fund for 13 years and currently receives a manager quality ranking of 79 (0=worst, 99=best). If you desire only a moderate level of risk and strong performance, then this fund is an excellent option.

Data Date	Investment Rating	Net Assets ($Mil)	Price	Performance Rating/Pts	Total Return Y-T-D	Risk Rating/Pts
12-15	A-	920.90	23.88	B+ / 8.6	1.30%	B- / 7.6
2014	A-	920.90	24.16	B+ / 8.5	18.86%	B- / 7.7
2013	A-	796.30	21.40	B / 7.6	21.91%	B / 8.9
2012	C+	508.10	17.30	C / 5.2	13.66%	B / 8.8
2011	C+	366.40	16.01	C / 5.4	8.76%	B / 8.1
2010	C+	218.50	15.09	C+ / 5.7	16.07%	C+ / 6.5

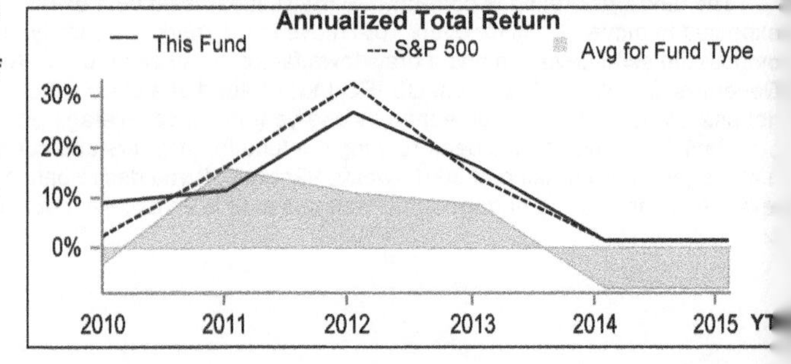

*FlexShares Global Quality RE Ind (GQRE) C+ Fair

Fund Family: Northern Trust Investments Inc
Fund Type: Growth and Income
Inception Date: November 5, 2013

Major Rating Factors: Middle of the road best describes *FlexShares Global Quality RE Ind whose TheStreet.com Investment Rating is currently a C+ (Fair). The fund currently has a performance rating of C+ (Fair) based on an annualized return of 0.00% over the last three years and a total return of 2.79% year to date 2015. Factored into the performance evaluation is an expense ratio of 0.45% (very low).

The fund's risk rating is currently B- (Good). It carries a beta of 0.00, meaning the fund's expected move will be 0.0% for every 10% move in the market. Volatility, as measured by both the semi-deviation and a drawdown factor, is considered low. As of December 31, 2015, *FlexShares Global Quality RE Ind traded at a premium of .53% above its net asset value, which is worse than its one-year historical average premium of .37%.

Robert Anstine has been running the fund for 3 years and currently receives a manager quality ranking of 83 (0=worst, 99=best). If you desire an average level of risk, then this fund may be an option.

Data Date	Investment Rating	Net Assets ($Mil)	Price	Performance Rating/Pts	Total Return Y-T-D	Risk Rating/Pts
12-15	C+	36.20	56.85	C+ / 6.0	2.79%	B- / 7.3
2014	C	36.20	56.32	B / 8.0	17.74%	C- / 4.1

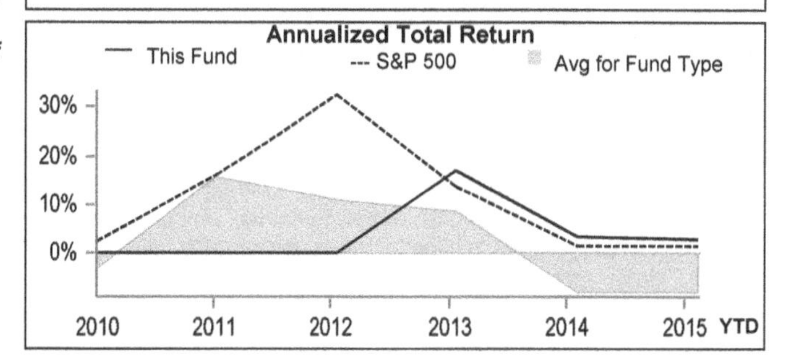

*FlexShares Int Qual Div Def Idx (IQDE) D+ Weak

Fund Family: Northern Trust Investments Inc
Fund Type: Foreign
Inception Date: April 12, 2013

Major Rating Factors:
Disappointing performance is the major factor driving the D+ (Weak) TheStreet.com Investment Rating for *FlexShares Int Qual Div Def Idx. The fund currently has a performance rating of D (Weak) based on an annualized return of 0.00% over the last three years and a total return of -8.93% year to date 2015. Factored into the performance evaluation is an expense ratio of 0.47% (very low).

The fund's risk rating is currently B- (Good). It carries a beta of 0.00, meaning the fund's expected move will be 0.0% for every 10% move in the market. Volatility, as measured by both the semi-deviation and a drawdown factor, is considered low. As of December 31, 2015, *FlexShares Int Qual Div Def Idx traded at a discount of 1.13% below its net asset value, which is better than its one-year historical average discount of .11%.

Chad M. Rakvin has been running the fund for 3 years and currently receives a manager quality ranking of 18 (0=worst, 99=best). This fund offers only a moderate level of risk but investors looking for strong performance are still waiting.

Data Date	Investment Rating	Net Assets ($Mil)	Price	Performance Rating/Pts	Total Return Y-T-D	Risk Rating/Pts
12-15	D+	57.00	21.09	D / 1.8	-8.93%	B- / 7.4
2014	D	57.00	24.41	D- / 1.4	-3.29%	C+ / 6.7

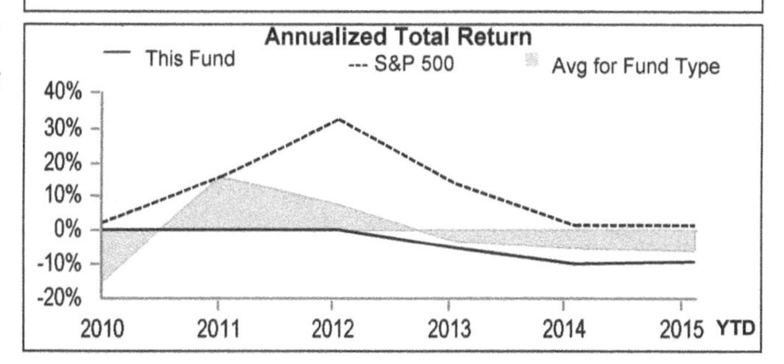

*FlexShares Int Qual Div Dyn Idx (IQDY) D Weak

Fund Family: Northern Trust Investments Inc
Fund Type: Foreign
Inception Date: April 12, 2013

Major Rating Factors:
Disappointing performance is the major factor driving the D (Weak) TheStreet.com Investment Rating for *FlexShares Int Qual Div Dyn Idx. The fund currently has a performance rating of D (Weak) based on an annualized return of 0.00% over the last three years and a total return of -7.16% year to date 2015. Factored into the performance evaluation is an expense ratio of 0.47% (very low).

The fund's risk rating is currently C (Fair). It carries a beta of 0.00, meaning the fund's expected move will be 0.0% for every 10% move in the market. Volatility, as measured by both the semi-deviation and a drawdown factor, is considered average. As of December 31, 2015, *FlexShares Int Qual Div Dyn Idx traded at a premium of .04% above its net asset value, which is better than its one-year historical average premium of .14%.

Chad M. Rakvin has been running the fund for 3 years and currently receives a manager quality ranking of 27 (0=worst, 99=best). This fund offers an average level of risk but investors looking for strong performance will be frustrated.

Data Date	Investment Rating	Net Assets ($Mil)	Price	Performance Rating/Pts	Total Return Y-T-D	Risk Rating/Pts
12-15	D	59.40	22.45	D / 2.1	-7.16%	C / 5.3
2014	D	59.40	24.85	D- / 1.1	-5.78%	B- / 7.5

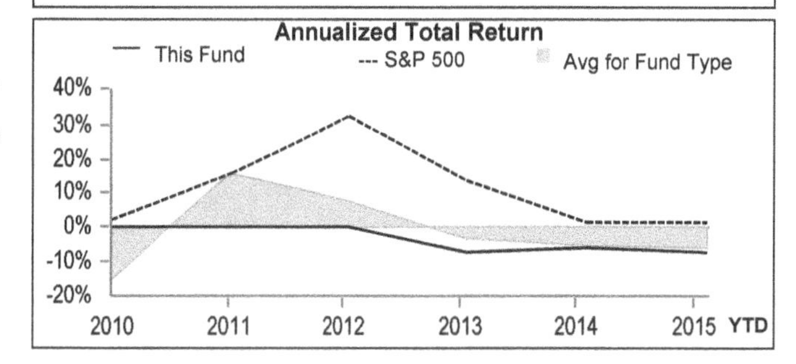

*FlexShares Intl Qual Div Idx (IQDF) D+ Weak

Fund Family: Northern Trust Investments Inc
Fund Type: Foreign
Inception Date: April 12, 2013

Major Rating Factors:
Disappointing performance is the major factor driving the D+ (Weak) TheStreet.com Investment Rating for *FlexShares Intl Qual Div Idx. The fund currently has a performance rating of D (Weak) based on an annualized return of 0.00% over the last three years and a total return of -9.42% year to date 2015. Factored into the performance evaluation is an expense ratio of 0.47% (very low).

The fund's risk rating is currently B- (Good). It carries a beta of 0.00, meaning the fund's expected move will be 0.0% for every 10% move in the market. Volatility, as measured by both the semi-deviation and a drawdown factor, is considered low. As of December 31, 2015, *FlexShares Intl Qual Div Idx traded at a discount of .92% below its net asset value, which is better than its one-year historical average premium of .16%.

Jordan Dekhayser has been running the fund for 3 years and currently receives a manager quality ranking of 18 (0=worst, 99=best). This fund offers only a moderate level of risk but investors looking for strong performance are still waiting.

Data Date	Investment Rating	Net Assets ($Mil)	Price	Performance Rating/Pts	Total Return Y-T-D	Risk Rating/Pts
12-15	D+	267.50	21.52	D / 1.7	-9.42%	B- / 7.3
2014	D+	267.50	24.66	D- / 1.2	-3.88%	B- / 7.8

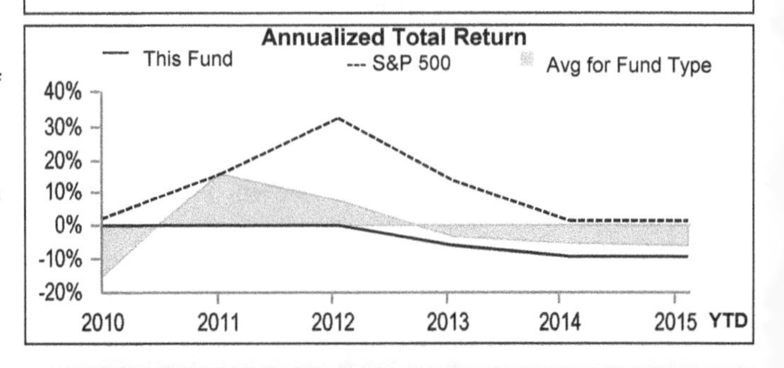

*FlexShares MS EM Fact Tilt Idx (TLTE) D+ Weak

Fund Family: Northern Trust Investments Inc
Fund Type: Emerging Market
Inception Date: September 25, 2012

Major Rating Factors:
Disappointing performance is the major factor driving the D+ (Weak) TheStreet.com Investment Rating for *FlexShares MS EM Fact Tilt Idx. The fund currently has a performance rating of D (Weak) based on an annualized return of -7.96% over the last three years and a total return of -14.14% year to date 2015. Factored into the performance evaluation is an expense ratio of 0.65% (very low).

The fund's risk rating is currently B- (Good). It carries a beta of 0.96, meaning that its performance tracks fairly well with that of the overall stock market. Volatility, as measured by both the semi-deviation and a drawdown factor, is considered low. As of December 31, 2015, *FlexShares MS EM Fact Tilt Idx traded at a discount of .26% below its net asset value, which is better than its one-year historical average discount of .07%.

Robert Anstine has been running the fund for 3 years and currently receives a manager quality ranking of 63 (0=worst, 99=best). This fund offers only a moderate level of risk but investors looking for strong performance are still waiting.

Data Date	Investment Rating	Net Assets ($Mil)	Price	Performance Rating/Pts	Total Return Y-T-D	Risk Rating/Pts
12-15	D+	256.70	41.72	D / 2.0	-14.14%	B- / 7.2
2014	D+	256.70	48.49	D / 1.6	-2.08%	B- / 7.9
2013	C-	199.30	52.11	D / 2.2	-7.49%	B / 8.7

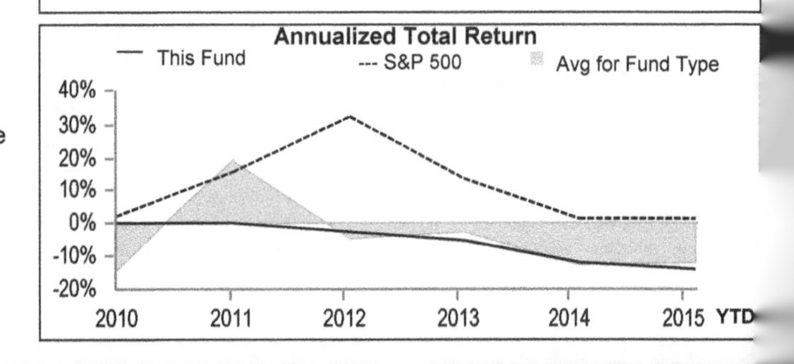

*FlexShares Quality Div Defens In (QDEF) C- Fair

Fund Family: Northern Trust Investments Inc
Fund Type: Income
Inception Date: December 14, 2012

Major Rating Factors: Middle of the road best describes *FlexShares Quality Div Defens In whose TheStreet.com Investment Rating is currently a C- (Fair). The fund currently has a performance rating of C- (Fair) based on an annualized return of 0.00% over the last three years and a total return of -0.88% year to date 2015. Factored into the performance evaluation is an expense ratio of 0.37% (very low).

The fund's risk rating is currently B- (Good). It carries a beta of 0.00, meaning the fund's expected move will be 0.0% for every 10% move in the market. Volatility, as measured by both the semi-deviation and a drawdown factor, is considered low. As of December 31, 2015, *FlexShares Quality Div Defens In traded at a premium of .03% above its net asset value, which is in line with its one-year historical average premium of .03%.

Robert Anstine has been running the fund for 3 years and currently receives a manager quality ranking of 54 (0=worst, 99=best). If you desire an average level of risk, then this fund may be an option.

Data Date	Investment Rating	Net Assets ($Mil)	Price	Performance Rating/Pts	Total Return Y-T-D	Risk Rating/Pts
12-15	C-	84.50	34.62	C- / 4.0	-0.88%	B- / 7.3
2014	B	84.50	35.88	B- / 7.3	14.69%	B- / 7.7

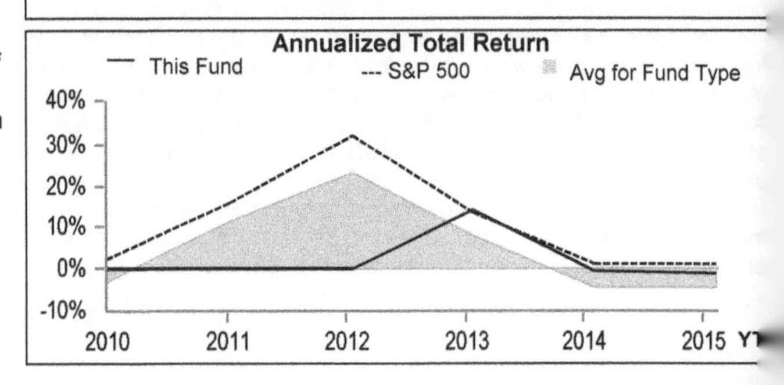

* Denotes ETF Fund

*FlexShares Quality Div Dynamic I (QDYN) C- Fair

Fund Family: Northern Trust Investments Inc
Fund Type: Income
Inception Date: December 14, 2012

Data Date	Investment Rating	Net Assets ($Mil)	Price	Performance Rating/Pts	Total Return Y-T-D	Risk Rating/Pts
12-15	C-	91.10	33.50	D+ / 2.8	-5.08%	C+ / 6.8
2014	C+	91.10	36.49	C+ / 6.4	12.59%	B- / 7.8

Major Rating Factors:
Disappointing performance is the major factor driving the C- (Fair) TheStreet.com Investment Rating for *FlexShares Quality Div Dynamic I. The fund currently has a performance rating of D+ (Weak) based on an annualized return of 0.00% over the last three years and a total return of -5.08% year to date 2015. Factored into the performance evaluation is an expense ratio of 0.37% (very low).

The fund's risk rating is currently C+ (Fair). It carries a beta of 0.00, meaning the fund's expected move will be 0.0% for every 10% move in the market. Volatility, as measured by both the semi-deviation and a drawdown factor, is considered low. As of December 31, 2015, *FlexShares Quality Div Dynamic I traded at a premium of .54% above its net asset value, which is worse than its one-year historical average discount of .05%.

Robert Anstine has been running the fund for 3 years and currently receives a manager quality ranking of 26 (0=worst, 99=best). This fund offers only a moderate level of risk but investors looking for strong performance are still waiting.

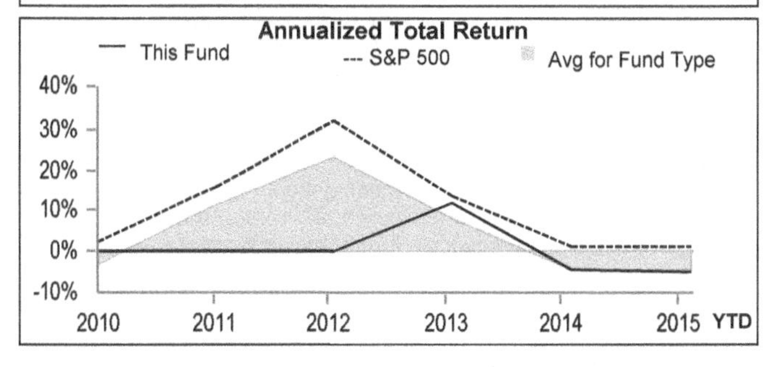

*FlexShares Quality Dividend Inde (QDF) C- Fair

Fund Family: Northern Trust Investments Inc
Fund Type: Income
Inception Date: December 14, 2012

Data Date	Investment Rating	Net Assets ($Mil)	Price	Performance Rating/Pts	Total Return Y-T-D	Risk Rating/Pts
12-15	C-	511.00	34.82	C- / 3.8	-1.72%	B- / 7.1
2014	B-	511.00	36.20	C+ / 6.5	13.00%	B- / 7.8

Major Rating Factors: Middle of the road best describes *FlexShares Quality Dividend Inde whose TheStreet.com Investment Rating is currently a C- (Fair). The fund currently has a performance rating of C- (Fair) based on an annualized return of 0.00% over the last three years and a total return of -1.72% year to date 2015. Factored into the performance evaluation is an expense ratio of 0.37% (very low).

The fund's risk rating is currently B- (Good). It carries a beta of 0.00, meaning the fund's expected move will be 0.0% for every 10% move in the market. Volatility, as measured by both the semi-deviation and a drawdown factor, is considered low. As of December 31, 2015, *FlexShares Quality Dividend Inde traded at a premium of .03% above its net asset value, which is worse than its one-year historical average premium of .02%.

Robert Anstine has been running the fund for 3 years and currently receives a manager quality ranking of 50 (0=worst, 99=best). If you desire an average level of risk, then this fund may be an option.

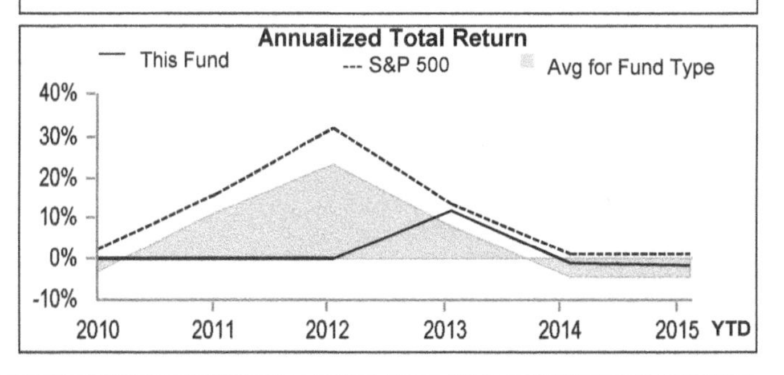

*FlexShares Ready Access Var Inc (RAVI) B- Good

Fund Family: Northern Trust Investments Inc
Fund Type: Global
Inception Date: October 9, 2012

Data Date	Investment Rating	Net Assets ($Mil)	Price	Performance Rating/Pts	Total Return Y-T-D	Risk Rating/Pts
12-15	B-	71.80	75.10	C / 4.6	0.15%	B+ / 9.8
2014	C	71.80	75.34	D+ / 2.8	0.61%	B+ / 9.4
2013	C	49.00	75.38	D+ / 2.9	1.01%	B+ / 9.9

Major Rating Factors: *FlexShares Ready Access Var Inc receives a TheStreet.com Investment Rating of B- (Good). The fund currently has a performance rating of C (Fair) based on an annualized return of 0.59% over the last three years and a total return of 0.15% year to date 2015. Factored into the performance evaluation is an expense ratio of 0.25% (very low).

The fund's risk rating is currently B+ (Good). It carries a beta of 0.02, meaning the fund's expected move will be 0.2% for every 10% move in the market. Volatility, as measured by both the semi-deviation and a drawdown factor, is considered very low. As of December 31, 2015, *FlexShares Ready Access Var Inc traded at a discount of .08% below its net asset value, which is better than its one-year historical average discount of .04%.

Bilal Memon has been running the fund for 4 years and currently receives a manager quality ranking of 74 (0=worst, 99=best). If you desire an average level of risk, then this fund may be an option.

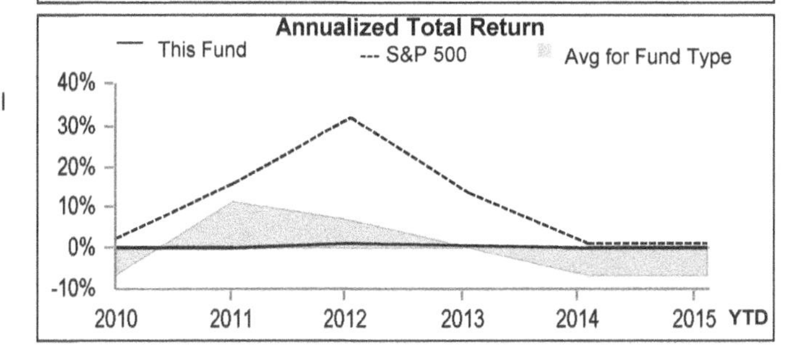

* Denotes ETF Fund

*FlexShares STOXX Gl Broad Infra (NFRA) D+ Weak

Fund Family: Northern Trust Investments Inc
Fund Type: Global
Inception Date: October 8, 2013

Data Date	Investment Rating	Net Assets ($Mil)	Price	Performance Rating/Pts	Total Return Y-T-D	Risk Rating/Pts
12-15	D+	222.80	41.13	D / 2.2	-7.17%	B- / 7.0
2014	D+	222.80	45.15	C / 5.1	11.29%	C / 4.3

Major Rating Factors:
Disappointing performance is the major factor driving the D+ (Weak) TheStreet.com Investment Rating for *FlexShares STOXX Gl Broad Infra. The fund currently has a performance rating of D (Weak) based on an annualized return of 0.00% over the last three years and a total return of -7.17% year to date 2015. Factored into the performance evaluation is an expense ratio of 0.47% (very low).

The fund's risk rating is currently B- (Good). It carries a beta of 0.00, meaning the fund's expected move will be 0.0% for every 10% move in the market. Volatility, as measured by both the semi-deviation and a drawdown factor, is considered low. As of December 31, 2015, *FlexShares STOXX Gl Broad Infra traded at a premium of .07% above its net asset value, which is better than its one-year historical average premium of .26%.

Jordan Dekhayser has been running the fund for 3 years and currently receives a manager quality ranking of 24 (0=worst, 99=best). This fund offers only a moderate level of risk but investors looking for strong performance are still waiting.

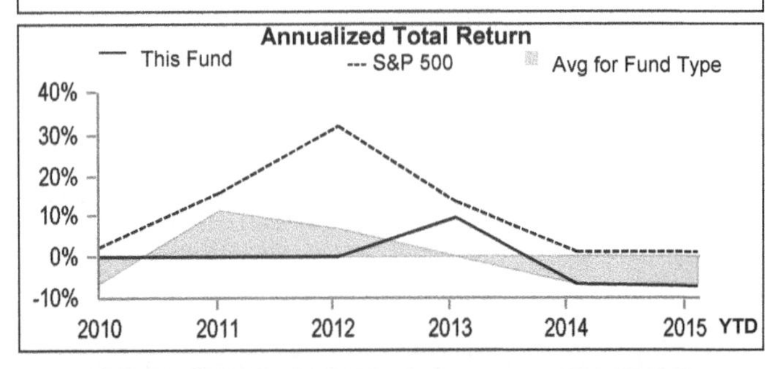

*FlexShs Credit-Scored US Crp Bd (SKOR) D+ Weak

Fund Family: Northern Trust Investments Inc
Fund Type: Corporate - Investment Grade
Inception Date: November 12, 2014

Data Date	Investment Rating	Net Assets ($Mil)	Price	Performance Rating/Pts	Total Return Y-T-D	Risk Rating/Pts
12-15	D+	0.00	50.00	C / 4.7	1.42%	C- / 4.1

Major Rating Factors: *FlexShs Credit-Scored US Crp Bd receives a TheStreet.com Investment Rating of D+ (Weak). The fund currently has a performance rating of C (Fair) based on an annualized return of 0.00% over the last three years and a total return of 1.42% year to date 2015.

The fund's risk rating is currently C- (Fair). It carries a beta of 0.00, meaning the fund's expected move will be 0.0% for every 10% move in the market. Volatility, as measured by both the semi-deviation and a drawdown factor, is considered average. As of December 31, 2015, *FlexShs Credit-Scored US Crp Bd traded at a premium of .42% above its net asset value, which is better than its one-year historical average premium of .45%.

Bradley Camden has been running the fund for 2 years and currently receives a manager quality ranking of 81 (0=worst, 99=best). If you desire an average level of risk, then this fund may be an option.

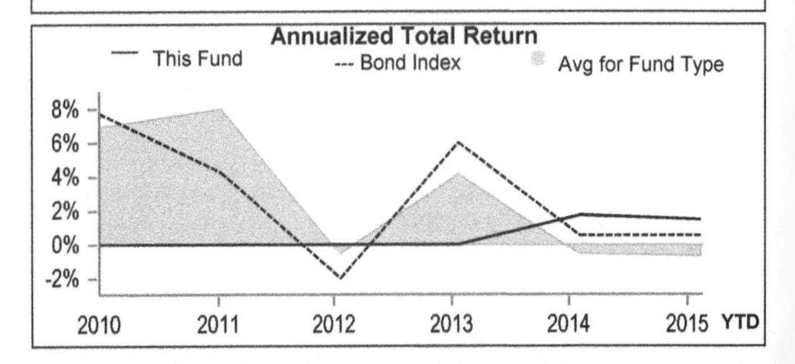

*FlexShs Dscpld Duration MBS Inde (MBSD) C+ Fair

Fund Family: Northern Trust Investments Inc
Fund Type: Mortgage
Inception Date: September 3, 2014

Data Date	Investment Rating	Net Assets ($Mil)	Price	Performance Rating/Pts	Total Return Y-T-D	Risk Rating/Pts
12-15	C+	0.00	24.73	C / 5.3	1.77%	B / 8.1

Major Rating Factors: Middle of the road best describes *FlexShs Dscpld Duration MBS Inde whose TheStreet.com Investment Rating is currently a C+ (Fair). The fund currently has a performance rating of C (Fair) based on an annualized return of 0.00% over the last three years and a total return of 1.77% year to date 2015.

The fund's risk rating is currently B (Good). It carries a beta of 0.00, meaning the fund's expected move will be 0.0% for every 10% move in the market. Volatility, as measured by both the semi-deviation and a drawdown factor, is considered low. As of December 31, 2015, *FlexShs Dscpld Duration MBS Inde traded at a premium of .82% above its net asset value, which is worse than its one-year historical average premium of .27%.

Bradley Camden has been running the fund for 2 years and currently receives a manager quality ranking of 77 (0=worst, 99=best). If you desire an average level of risk, then this fund may be an option.

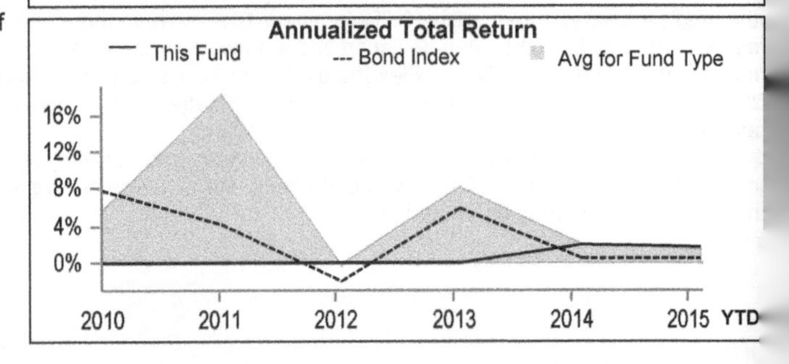

*FlexShs iB 3Y Tgt Dur TIPS Idx (TDTT) C+ Fair

Fund Family: Northern Trust Investments Inc
Fund Type: US Government/Agency
Inception Date: September 19, 2011

Major Rating Factors: Middle of the road best describes *FlexShs iB 3Y Tgt Dur TIPS Idx whose TheStreet.com Investment Rating is currently a C+ (Fair). The fund currently has a performance rating of C- (Fair) based on an annualized return of -1.33% over the last three years and a total return of -0.62% year to date 2015. Factored into the performance evaluation is an expense ratio of 0.20% (very low).

The fund's risk rating is currently B+ (Good). It carries a beta of 0.06, meaning the fund's expected move will be 0.6% for every 10% move in the market. Volatility, as measured by both the semi-deviation and a drawdown factor, is considered very low. As of December 31, 2015, *FlexShs iB 3Y Tgt Dur TIPS Idx traded at a discount of .29% below its net asset value, which is better than its one-year historical average premium of .01%.

Brandon P. Ferguson has been running the fund for 5 years and currently receives a manager quality ranking of 54 (0=worst, 99=best). If you desire an average level of risk, then this fund may be an option.

Data Date	Investment Rating	Net Assets ($Mil)	Price	Performance Rating/Pts	Total Return Y-T-D	Risk Rating/Pts
12-15	C+	2,236.50	24.18	C- / 3.7	-0.62%	B+ / 9.5
2014	C	2,236.50	24.29	D+ / 2.5	-1.80%	B+ / 9.6
2013	C-	2,012.60	24.92	D+ / 2.3	-1.74%	B+ / 9.9
2012	C-	719.80	25.52	D / 1.9	2.94%	B+ / 9.9

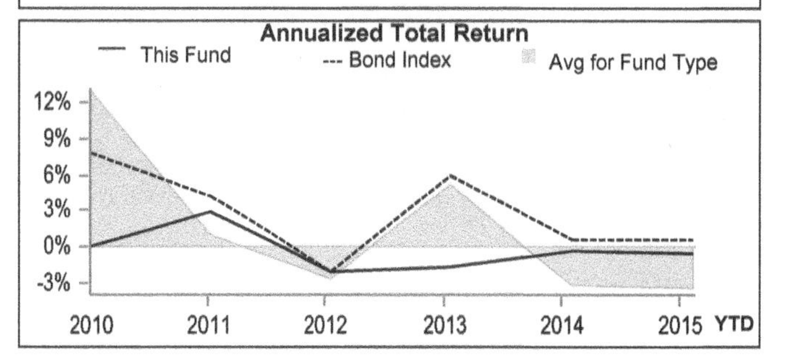

*FlexShs iB 5Y Tgt Dur TIPS Idx (TDTF) C+ Fair

Fund Family: Northern Trust Investments Inc
Fund Type: US Government/Agency
Inception Date: September 19, 2011

Major Rating Factors: Middle of the road best describes *FlexShs iB 5Y Tgt Dur TIPS Idx whose TheStreet.com Investment Rating is currently a C+ (Fair). The fund currently has a performance rating of C- (Fair) based on an annualized return of -1.78% over the last three years and a total return of -0.97% year to date 2015. Factored into the performance evaluation is an expense ratio of 0.20% (very low).

The fund's risk rating is currently B+ (Good). It carries a beta of 0.21, meaning the fund's expected move will be 2.1% for every 10% move in the market. Volatility, as measured by both the semi-deviation and a drawdown factor, is considered very low. As of December 31, 2015, *FlexShs iB 5Y Tgt Dur TIPS Idx traded at a discount of .08% below its net asset value, which is better than its one-year historical average premium of .07%.

Brandon P. Ferguson has been running the fund for 5 years and currently receives a manager quality ranking of 46 (0=worst, 99=best). If you desire an average level of risk, then this fund may be an option.

Data Date	Investment Rating	Net Assets ($Mil)	Price	Performance Rating/Pts	Total Return Y-T-D	Risk Rating/Pts
12-15	C+	307.20	24.32	C- / 3.6	-0.97%	B+ / 9.3
2014	C	307.20	24.45	D+ / 2.6	-0.68%	B+ / 9.3
2013	C-	339.10	24.87	D / 1.9	-4.29%	B+ / 9.5
2012	C	384.80	26.30	D+ / 2.3	5.31%	B+ / 9.9

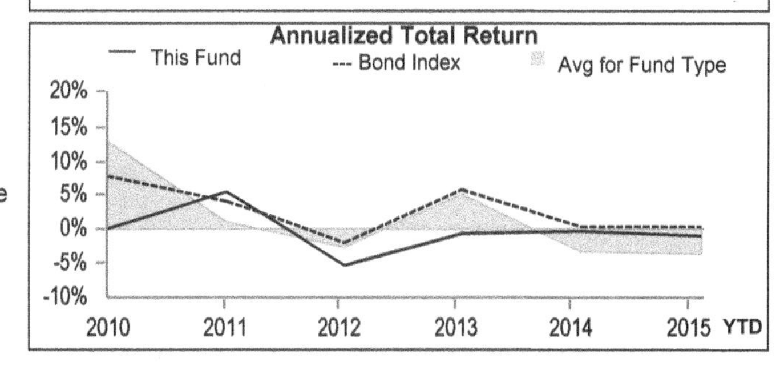

*FlexShs Morningstar Gl Upstream (GUNR) D Weak

Fund Family: Northern Trust Investments Inc
Fund Type: Energy/Natural Resources
Inception Date: September 16, 2011

Major Rating Factors:
Disappointing performance is the major factor driving the D (Weak) TheStreet.com Investment Rating for *FlexShs Morningstar Gl Upstream. The fund currently has a performance rating of D- (Weak) based on an annualized return of -12.34% over the last three years and a total return of -24.51% year to date 2015. Factored into the performance evaluation is an expense ratio of 0.48% (very low).

The fund's risk rating is currently C+ (Fair). It carries a beta of 0.70, meaning the fund's expected move will be 7.0% for every 10% move in the market. Volatility, as measured by both the semi-deviation and a drawdown factor, is considered low. As of December 31, 2015, *FlexShs Morningstar Gl Upstream traded at a discount of .58% below its net asset value, which is better than its one-year historical average premium of .06%.

Robert Anstine has been running the fund for 3 years and currently receives a manager quality ranking of 17 (0=worst, 99=best). This fund offers only a moderate level of risk but investors looking for strong performance are still waiting.

Data Date	Investment Rating	Net Assets ($Mil)	Price	Performance Rating/Pts	Total Return Y-T-D	Risk Rating/Pts
12-15	D	2,964.70	22.25	D- / 1.3	-24.51%	C+ / 6.0
2014	D+	2,964.70	30.62	D / 2.1	-7.45%	B- / 7.7
2013	C-	2,690.00	34.31	C- / 3.7	-4.21%	B / 8.2
2012	C	604.20	35.62	C / 4.9	7.60%	B / 8.1

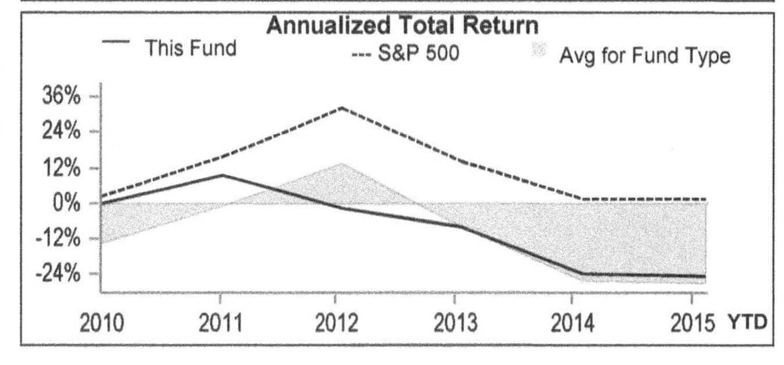

*FlexShs Morningstar US Mkt Fac T (TILT) B Good

Fund Family: Northern Trust Investments Inc
Fund Type: Income
Inception Date: September 16, 2011

Major Rating Factors: Strong performance is the major factor driving the B (Good) TheStreet.com Investment Rating for *FlexShs Morningstar US Mkt Fac T. The fund currently has a performance rating of B (Good) based on an annualized return of 12.27% over the last three years and a total return of -1.71% year to date 2015. Factored into the performance evaluation is an expense ratio of 0.27% (very low).

The fund's risk rating is currently B- (Good). It carries a beta of 1.04, meaning that its performance tracks fairly well with that of the overall stock market. Volatility, as measured by both the semi-deviation and a drawdown factor, is considered low. As of December 31, 2015, *FlexShs Morningstar US Mkt Fac T traded at a premium of .12% above its net asset value, which is worse than its one-year historical average premium of .01%.

Robert P. Browne currently receives a manager quality ranking of 51 (0=worst, 99=best). If you desire only a moderate level of risk and strong performance, then this fund is an excellent option.

Data Date	Investment Rating	Net Assets ($Mil)	Price	Performance Rating/Pts	Total Return Y-T-D	Risk Rating/Pts
12-15	B	707.60	83.73	B / 8.1	-1.71%	B- / 7.0
2014	B	707.60	87.58	B / 8.1	11.34%	B- / 7.2
2013	A+	521.80	80.29	A / 9.4	30.33%	B+ / 9.2
2012	A-	153.90	59.72	B / 7.9	16.96%	B+ / 9.1

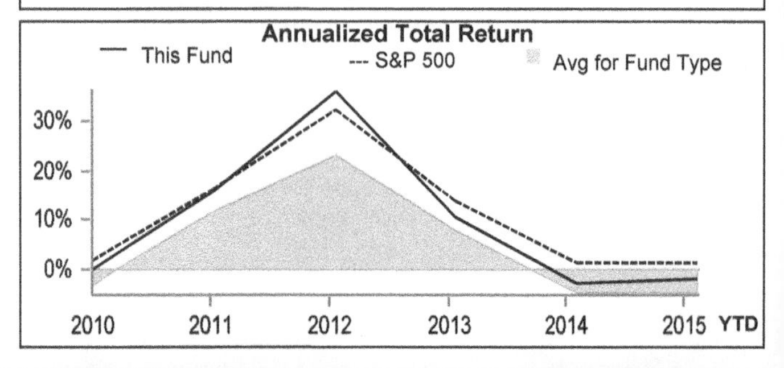

*FlexShs MS Dev Mkts exUS Fctrs T (TLTD) C+ Fair

Fund Family: Northern Trust Investments Inc
Fund Type: Foreign
Inception Date: September 25, 2012

Major Rating Factors: Middle of the road best describes *FlexShs MS Dev Mkts exUS Fctrs T whose TheStreet.com Investment Rating is currently a C+ (Fair). The fund currently has a performance rating of C (Fair) based on an annualized return of 3.37% over the last three years and a total return of -1.08% year to date 2015. Factored into the performance evaluation is an expense ratio of 0.42% (very low).

The fund's risk rating is currently B- (Good). It carries a beta of 0.91, meaning that its performance tracks fairly well with that of the overall stock market. Volatility, as measured by both the semi-deviation and a drawdown factor, is considered low. As of December 31, 2015, *FlexShs MS Dev Mkts exUS Fctrs T traded at a discount of .02% below its net asset value, which is better than its one-year historical average premium of .03%.

Robert Anstine has been running the fund for 3 years and currently receives a manager quality ranking of 59 (0=worst, 99=best). If you desire an average level of risk, then this fund may be an option.

Data Date	Investment Rating	Net Assets ($Mil)	Price	Performance Rating/Pts	Total Return Y-T-D	Risk Rating/Pts
12-15	C+	655.70	55.18	C / 5.4	-1.08%	B- / 7.7
2014	D+	655.70	57.26	D- / 1.3	-5.17%	B / 8.2
2013	A+	374.70	63.11	B+ / 8.7	17.76%	B+ / 9.5

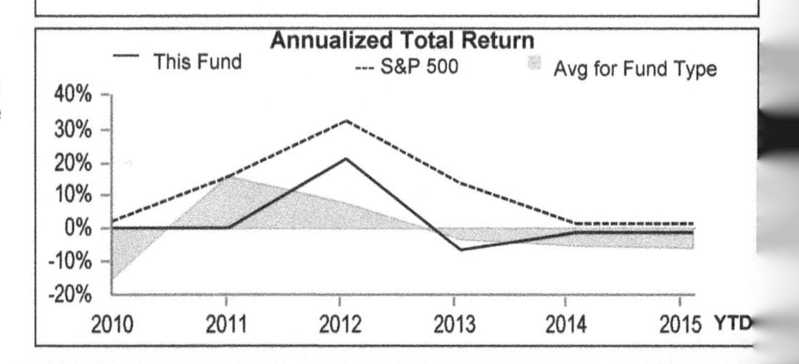

*Franklin Short Duration US Govt (FTSD) C Fair

Fund Family: Franklin Advisers Inc
Fund Type: US Government/Agency
Inception Date: November 4, 2013

Major Rating Factors: Middle of the road best describes *Franklin Short Duration US Govt whose TheStreet.com Investment Rating is currently a C (Fair). The fund currently has a performance rating of C (Fair) based on an annualized return of 0.00% over the last three years and a total return of 0.30% year to date 2015. Factored into the performance evaluation is an expense ratio of 0.30% (very low).

The fund's risk rating is currently B (Good). It carries a beta of 0.00, meaning the fund's expected move will be 0.0% for every 10% move in the market. Volatility, as measured by both the semi-deviation and a drawdown factor, is considered low. As of December 31, 2015, *Franklin Short Duration US Govt traded at a premium of .27% above its net asset value, which is worse than its one-year historical average premium of .03%.

Patrick Klein has been running the fund for 3 years and currently receives a manager quality ranking of 70 (0=worst, 99=best). If you desire an average level of risk, then this fund may be an option.

Data Date	Investment Rating	Net Assets ($Mil)	Price	Performance Rating/Pts	Total Return Y-T-D	Risk Rating/Pts
12-15	C	27.50	98.27	C / 4.4	0.30%	B / 8.0
2014	D	27.50	99.25	D+ / 2.9	0.72%	C / 4.5

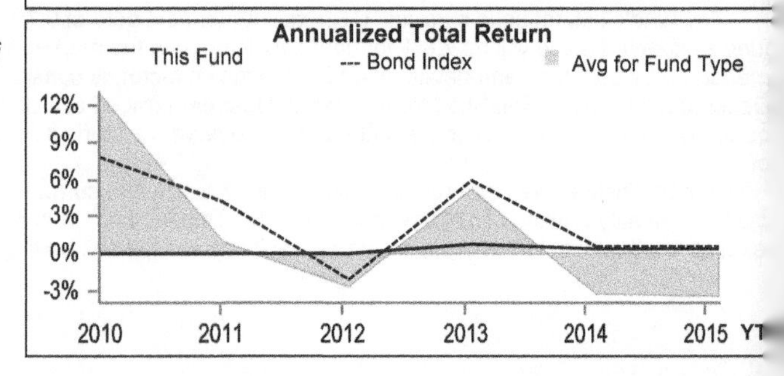

*Global Echo ETF (GIVE) C+ Fair

Fund Family: AdvisorShares Investments LLC
Fund Type: Global
Inception Date: May 23, 2012

Major Rating Factors: Middle of the road best describes *Global Echo ETF whose TheStreet.com Investment Rating is currently a C+ (Fair). The fund currently has a performance rating of C+ (Fair) based on an annualized return of 5.47% over the last three years and a total return of -2.97% year to date 2015. Factored into the performance evaluation is an expense ratio of 1.50% (average).

The fund's risk rating is currently B- (Good). It carries a beta of 0.33, meaning the fund's expected move will be 3.3% for every 10% move in the market. Volatility, as measured by both the semi-deviation and a drawdown factor, is considered low. As of December 31, 2015, *Global Echo ETF traded at a premium of .47% above its net asset value, which is worse than its one-year historical average premium of .13%.

Patrick J. McVeigh has been running the fund for 4 years and currently receives a manager quality ranking of 87 (0=worst, 99=best). If you desire an average level of risk, then this fund may be an option.

Data Date	Investment Rating	Net Assets ($Mil)	Price	Performance Rating/Pts	Total Return Y-T-D	Risk Rating/Pts
12-15	C+	6.00	60.45	C+ / 6.0	-2.97%	B- / 7.5
2014	C	6.00	63.73	C / 4.7	4.19%	B- / 7.9
2013	A+	6.10	60.72	B+ / 8.5	17.57%	B+ / 9.9

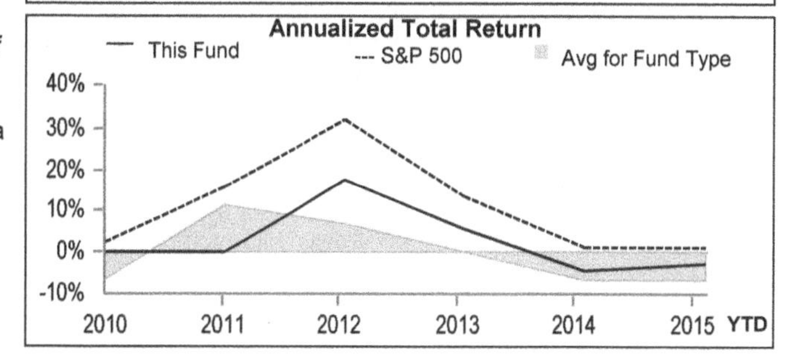

*Global X Brazil Consumer ETF (BRAQ) E Very Weak

Fund Family: Global X Management Company LLC
Fund Type: Foreign
Inception Date: July 7, 2010

Major Rating Factors: *Global X Brazil Consumer ETF has adopted a very risky asset allocation strategy and currently receives an overall TheStreet.com Investment Rating of E (Very Weak). The fund has a high level of volatility, as measured by both semi-deviation and drawdown factors. It carries a beta of 1.53, meaning it is expected to move 15.3% for every 10% move in the market. As of December 31, 2015, *Global X Brazil Consumer ETF traded at a premium of .25% above its net asset value, which is worse than its one-year historical average discount of .51%. Unfortunately, the high level of risk (D, Weak) failed to pay off as investors endured very poor performance.

The fund's performance rating is currently E (Very Weak). It has registered an annualized return of -25.53% over the last three years and is down -40.02% year to date 2015. Factored into the performance evaluation is an expense ratio of 0.78% (very low).

Bruno Del Ama has been running the fund for 6 years and currently receives a manager quality ranking of 3 (0=worst, 99=best). If you can tolerate very high levels of risk in the hope of improved future returns, holding this fund may be an option.

Data Date	Investment Rating	Net Assets ($Mil)	Price	Performance Rating/Pts	Total Return Y-T-D	Risk Rating/Pts
12-15	E	9.70	8.00	E / 0.5	-40.02%	D / 1.8
2014	D-	9.70	13.91	D / 2.0	-8.79%	C- / 3.6
2013	D-	14.50	16.03	D- / 1.1	-22.48%	C+ / 6.1
2012	B	24.20	20.27	A+ / 9.7	26.72%	C+ / 6.1
2011	D-	27.00	15.08	E+ / 0.8	-22.79%	C+ / 6.1

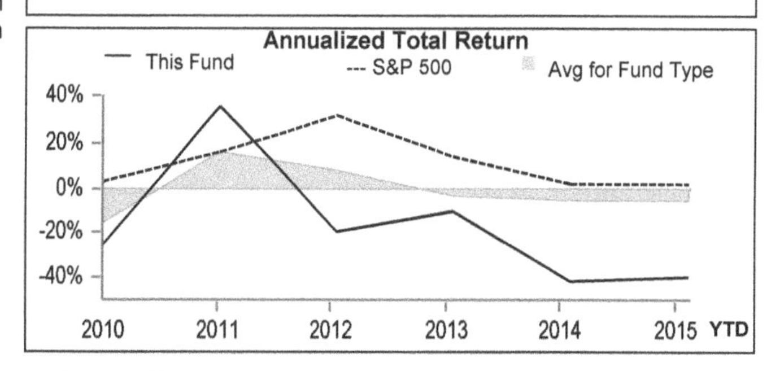

*Global X Brazil Mid Cap ETF (BRAZ) E+ Very Weak

Fund Family: Global X Management Company LLC
Fund Type: Foreign
Inception Date: June 21, 2010

Major Rating Factors:
Very poor performance is the major factor driving the E+ (Very Weak) TheStreet.com Investment Rating for *Global X Brazil Mid Cap ETF. The fund currently has a performance rating of E+ (Very Weak) based on an annualized return of -24.75% over the last three years and a total return of -36.93% year to date 2015. Factored into the performance evaluation is an expense ratio of 0.69% (very low).

The fund's risk rating is currently C- (Fair). It carries a beta of 1.48, meaning it is expected to move 14.8% for every 10% move in the market. Volatility, as measured by both the semi-deviation and a drawdown factor, is considered average. As of December 31, 2015, *Global X Brazil Mid Cap ETF traded at a discount of 1.47% below its net asset value, which is better than its one-year historical average discount of .57%.

Bruno Del Ama has been running the fund for 6 years and currently receives a manager quality ranking of 3 (0=worst, 99=best). This fund offers an average level of risk but investors looking for strong performance will be frustrated.

Data Date	Investment Rating	Net Assets ($Mil)	Price	Performance Rating/Pts	Total Return Y-T-D	Risk Rating/Pts
12-15	E+	7.90	6.03	E+ / 0.6	-36.93%	C- / 3.6
2014	E+	7.90	10.17	D- / 1.3	-15.73%	C- / 3.2
2013	D-	9.60	12.78	D- / 1.2	-17.11%	C+ / 5.9
2012	C-	18.80	15.61	C / 4.9	8.42%	C+ / 6.4
2011	D-	20.70	14.23	D- / 1.0	-17.89%	C+ / 6.4

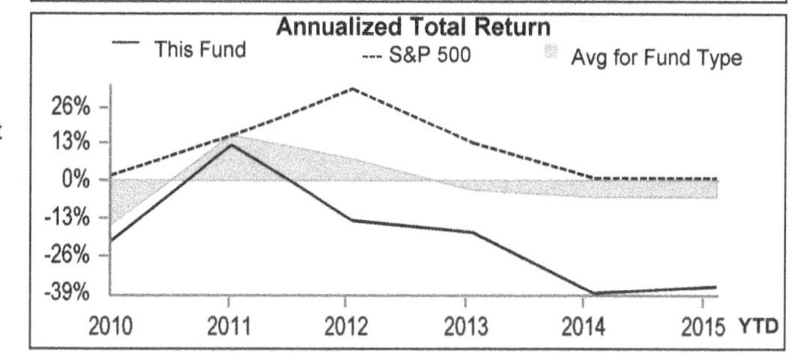

*Global X China Consumer ETF (CHIQ) D+ Weak

Fund Family: Global X Management Company LLC
Fund Type: Foreign
Inception Date: November 30, 2009

Major Rating Factors:
Disappointing performance is the major factor driving the D+ (Weak) TheStreet.com Investment Rating for *Global X China Consumer ETF. The fund currently has a performance rating of D+ (Weak) based on an annualized return of -5.03% over the last three years and a total return of 1.62% year to date 2015. Factored into the performance evaluation is an expense ratio of 0.65% (very low).

The fund's risk rating is currently C+ (Fair). It carries a beta of 1.00, meaning that its performance tracks fairly well with that of the overall stock market. Volatility, as measured by both the semi-deviation and a drawdown factor, is considered low. As of December 31, 2015, *Global X China Consumer ETF traded at a discount of .49% below its net asset value, which is better than its one-year historical average discount of .47%.

Bruno Del Ama has been running the fund for 7 years and currently receives a manager quality ranking of 18 (0=worst, 99=best). This fund offers only a moderate level of risk but investors looking for strong performance are still waiting.

Data Date	Investment Rating	Net Assets ($Mil)	Price	Performance Rating/Pts	Total Return Y-T-D	Risk Rating/Pts
12-15	D+	138.50	12.16	D+ / 2.8	1.62%	C+ / 6.6
2014	D+	138.50	12.62	D / 2.0	-16.88%	B- / 7.1
2013	D	208.70	15.79	D / 2.1	2.07%	C+ / 6.1
2012	D-	186.30	14.87	D / 1.7	8.63%	C+ / 5.7
2011	D-	119.20	13.71	E+ / 0.6	-25.85%	C+ / 5.8
2010	B-	165.00	18.09	C+ / 6.0	9.64%	B- / 7.5

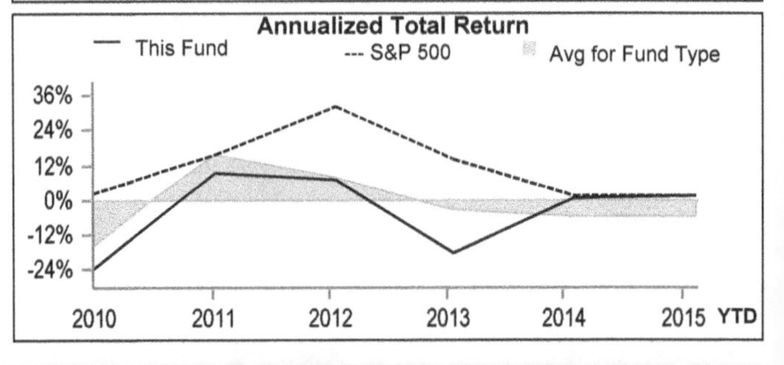

*Global X China Energy ETF (CHIE) D Weak

Fund Family: Global X Management Company LLC
Fund Type: Energy/Natural Resources
Inception Date: December 15, 2009

Major Rating Factors:
Disappointing performance is the major factor driving the D (Weak) TheStreet.com Investment Rating for *Global X China Energy ETF. The fund currently has a performance rating of D- (Weak) based on an annualized return of -10.74% over the last three years and a total return of -22.18% year to date 2015. Factored into the performance evaluation is an expense ratio of 0.65% (very low).

The fund's risk rating is currently C+ (Fair). It carries a beta of 0.86, meaning the fund's expected move will be 8.6% for every 10% move in the market. Volatility, as measured by both the semi-deviation and a drawdown factor, is considered low. As of December 31, 2015, *Global X China Energy ETF traded at a discount of .20% below its net asset value, which is worse than its one-year historical average discount of .22%.

Bruno Del Ama has been running the fund for 7 years and currently receives a manager quality ranking of 25 (0=worst, 99=best). This fund offers only a moderate level of risk but investors looking for strong performance are still waiting.

Data Date	Investment Rating	Net Assets ($Mil)	Price	Performance Rating/Pts	Total Return Y-T-D	Risk Rating/Pts
12-15	D	5.30	10.10	D- / 1.5	-22.18%	C+ / 6.0
2014	D+	5.30	13.40	D+ / 2.6	-7.94%	C+ / 6.5
2013	D	4.60	15.17	D+ / 2.9	-0.71%	C+ / 6.3
2012	D	5.10	14.50	D+ / 2.7	11.42%	C+ / 6.4
2011	D-	3.90	13.01	D- / 1.1	-15.80%	C+ / 6.4
2010	A	7.10	15.75	B / 8.1	5.07%	B- / 7.5

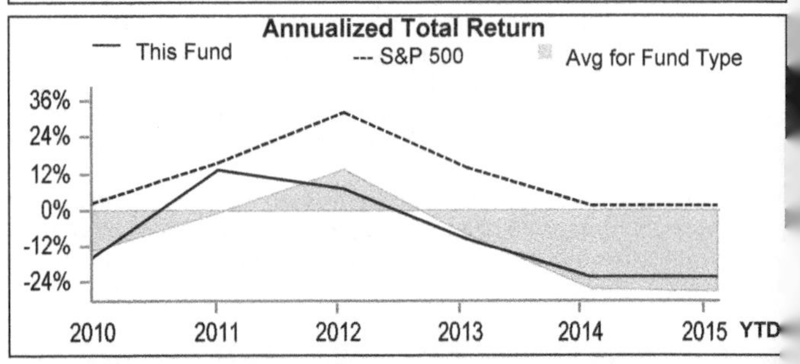

*Global X China Financials ETF (CHIX) C- Fair

Fund Family: Global X Management Company LLC
Fund Type: Financial Services
Inception Date: December 10, 2009

Major Rating Factors: Middle of the road best describes *Global X China Financials ETF whose TheStreet.com Investment Rating is currently a C- (Fair). The fund currently has a performance rating of C- (Fair) based on an annualized return of 0.73% over the last three years and a total return of -9.84% year to date 2015. Factored into the performance evaluation is an expense ratio of 0.65% (very low).

The fund's risk rating is currently C+ (Fair). It carries a beta of 0.71, meaning the fund's expected move will be 7.1% for every 10% move in the market. Volatility, as measured by both the semi-deviation and a drawdown factor, is considered low. As of December 31, 2015, *Global X China Financials ETF traded at a discount of 1.30% below its net asset value, which is better than its one-year historical average discount of .32%.

Bruno Del Ama has been running the fund for 7 years and currently receives a manager quality ranking of 21 (0=worst, 99=best). If you desire an average level of risk, then this fund may be an option.

Data Date	Investment Rating	Net Assets ($Mil)	Price	Performance Rating/Pts	Total Return Y-T-D	Risk Rating/Pts
12-15	C-	45.50	13.69	C- / 3.6	-9.84%	C+ / 6.4
2014	B+	45.50	15.68	B+ / 8.9	24.04%	B- / 7.0
2013	D-	48.90	13.34	D / 2.2	-10.33%	C / 5.3
2012	D	6.70	13.66	C- / 4.1	32.91%	C / 5.2
2011	E+	14.00	10.39	E+ / 0.8	-27.08%	C / 5.2
2010	D+	67.40	13.35	D- / 1.2	-6.58%	B- / 7.4

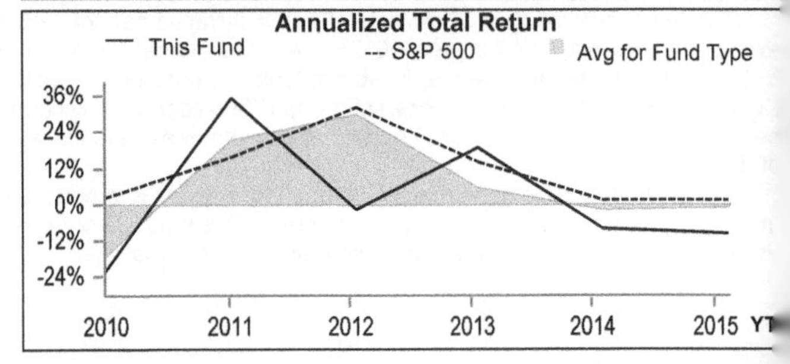

*Global X China Industrials ETF (CHII) D+ Weak

Fund Family: Global X Management Company LLC
Fund Type: Foreign
Inception Date: November 30, 2009

Major Rating Factors: *Global X China Industrials ETF receives a TheStreet.com Investment Rating of D+ (Weak). The fund currently has a performance rating of C- (Fair) based on an annualized return of 0.37% over the last three years and a total return of -11.41% year to date 2015. Factored into the performance evaluation is an expense ratio of 0.65% (very low).

The fund's risk rating is currently C+ (Fair). It carries a beta of 0.86, meaning the fund's expected move will be 8.6% for every 10% move in the market. Volatility, as measured by both the semi-deviation and a drawdown factor, is considered low. As of December 31, 2015, *Global X China Industrials ETF traded at a discount of .47% below its net asset value, which is better than its one-year historical average premium of .02%.

Bruno Del Ama has been running the fund for 7 years and currently receives a manager quality ranking of 47 (0=worst, 99=best). If you desire an average level of risk, then this fund may be an option.

Data Date	Investment Rating	Net Assets ($Mil)	Price	Performance Rating/Pts	Total Return Y-T-D	Risk Rating/Pts
12-15	D+	3.10	12.65	C- / 3.2	-11.41%	C+ / 5.9
2014	C+	3.10	14.07	B- / 7.5	17.93%	C+ / 6.5
2013	D-	4.30	12.26	D- / 1.4	-7.08%	C / 4.6
2012	D-	4.90	12.45	D / 2.1	25.46%	C / 4.8
2011	E+	4.10	10.28	E / 0.4	-41.10%	C / 4.8
2010	A	10.70	16.40	B / 8.0	6.01%	B- / 7.6

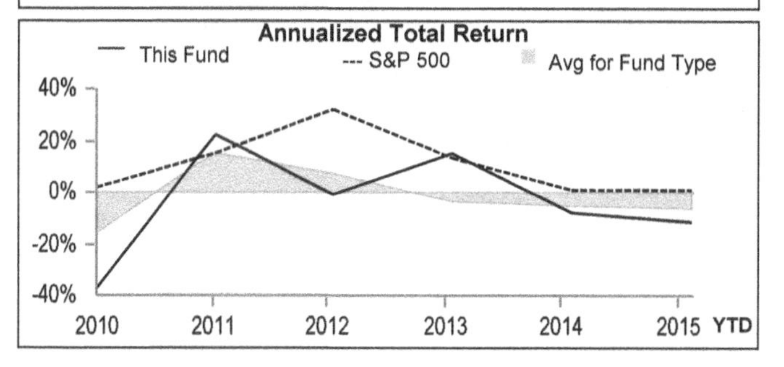

*Global X China Materials ETF (CHIM) D Weak

Fund Family: Global X Management Company LLC
Fund Type: Foreign
Inception Date: January 12, 2010

Major Rating Factors:
Disappointing performance is the major factor driving the D (Weak) TheStreet.com Investment Rating for *Global X China Materials ETF. The fund currently has a performance rating of D- (Weak) based on an annualized return of -11.30% over the last three years and a total return of -13.52% year to date 2015. Factored into the performance evaluation is an expense ratio of 0.65% (very low).

The fund's risk rating is currently C (Fair). It carries a beta of 0.94, meaning that its performance tracks fairly well with that of the overall stock market. Volatility, as measured by both the semi-deviation and a drawdown factor, is considered average. As of December 31, 2015, *Global X China Materials ETF traded at a discount of 1.47% below its net asset value, which is better than its one-year historical average premium of .39%.

Bruno Del Ama has been running the fund for 6 years and currently receives a manager quality ranking of 12 (0=worst, 99=best). This fund offers an average level of risk but investors looking for strong performance will be frustrated.

Data Date	Investment Rating	Net Assets ($Mil)	Price	Performance Rating/Pts	Total Return Y-T-D	Risk Rating/Pts
12-15	D	3.00	12.04	D- / 1.5	-13.52%	C / 5.4
2014	D	3.00	14.93	D+ / 2.4	4.05%	C+ / 6.3
2013	E+	2.20	14.91	E+ / 0.6	-21.41%	C / 4.3
2012	C+	2.70	8.77	A / 9.5	8.46%	C / 4.5
2011	E+	2.20	8.71	E- / 0.2	-43.14%	C / 5.0

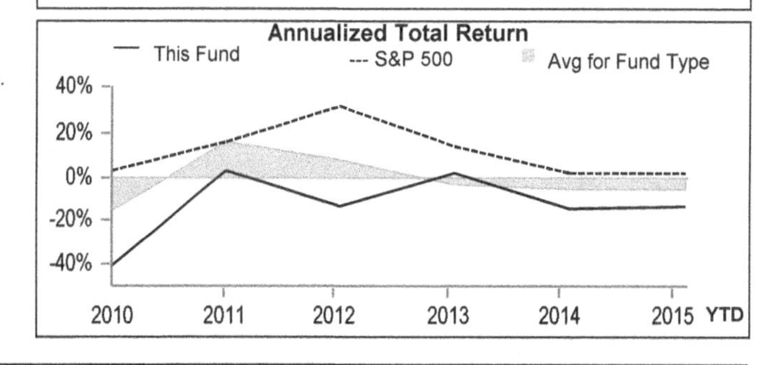

*Global X Copper Miners ETF (COPX) E Very Weak

Fund Family: Global X Management Company LLC
Fund Type: Precious Metals
Inception Date: April 19, 2010

Major Rating Factors: *Global X Copper Miners ETF has adopted a risky asset allocation strategy and currently receives an overall TheStreet.com Investment Rating of E (Very Weak). The fund has an above average level of volatility, as measured by both semi-deviation and drawdown factors. It carries a beta of 0.67, meaning the fund's expected move will be 6.7% for every 10% move in the market. As of December 31, 2015, *Global X Copper Miners ETF traded at a price exactly equal to its net asset value, which is better than its one-year historical average premium of .28%. Unfortunately, the high level of risk (D+, Weak) failed to pay off as investors endured very poor performance.

The fund's performance rating is currently E (Very Weak). It has registered an annualized return of -32.70% over the last three years and is down -45.70% year to date 2015. Factored into the performance evaluation is an expense ratio of 0.65% (very low).

Bruno Del Ama has been running the fund for 6 years and currently receives a manager quality ranking of 5 (0=worst, 99=best). If you can tolerate high levels of risk in the hope of improved future returns, holding this fund may be an option.

Data Date	Investment Rating	Net Assets ($Mil)	Price	Performance Rating/Pts	Total Return Y-T-D	Risk Rating/Pts
12-15	E	30.70	11.81	E / 0.3	-45.70%	D+ / 2.4
2014	E+	30.70	7.36	E+ / 0.8	-18.57%	C- / 4.2
2013	E	31.70	9.37	E+ / 0.6	-31.54%	C- / 3.5
2012	C	31.20	13.02	B+ / 8.3	2.17%	C / 4.4
2011	E+	38.00	12.84	E+ / 0.7	-25.53%	C / 4.7

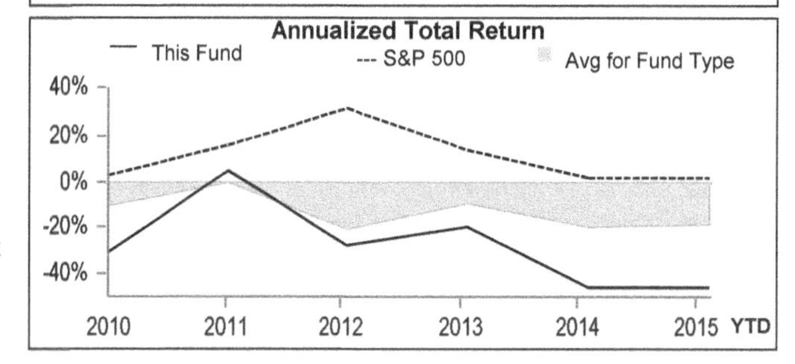

*Global X Fertilizers/Potash ETF (SOIL) D Weak

Fund Family: Global X Management Company LLC
Fund Type: Global
Inception Date: May 25, 2011

Data Date	Investment Rating	Net Assets ($Mil)	Price	Performance Rating/Pts	Total Return Y-T-D	Risk Rating/Pts
12-15	D	17.60	9.02	D- / 1.5	-10.61%	C+ / 6.1
2014	D	17.60	10.43	D / 2.0	-5.08%	C+ / 6.7
2013	D-	22.20	11.41	E+ / 0.6	-20.46%	C+ / 6.1
2012	B-	28.70	14.04	B+ / 8.3	15.92%	C+ / 6.5

Major Rating Factors:
Disappointing performance is the major factor driving the D (Weak) TheStreet.com Investment Rating for *Global X Fertilizers/Potash ETF. The fund currently has a performance rating of D- (Weak) based on an annualized return of -12.24% over the last three years and a total return of -10.61% year to date 2015. Factored into the performance evaluation is an expense ratio of 0.69% (very low).

The fund's risk rating is currently C+ (Fair). It carries a beta of 0.81, meaning the fund's expected move will be 8.1% for every 10% move in the market. Volatility, as measured by both the semi-deviation and a drawdown factor, is considered low. As of December 31, 2015, *Global X Fertilizers/Potash ETF traded at a discount of .33% below its net asset value, which is worse than its one-year historical average discount of .41%.

Bruno Del Ama has been running the fund for 5 years and currently receives a manager quality ranking of 10 (0=worst, 99=best). This fund offers only a moderate level of risk but investors looking for strong performance are still waiting.

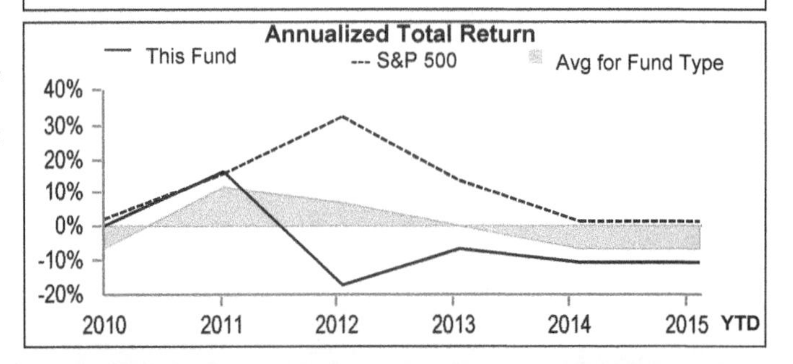

*Global X FTSE Andean 40 ETF (AND) D- Weak

Fund Family: Global X Management Company LLC
Fund Type: Foreign
Inception Date: February 2, 2011

Data Date	Investment Rating	Net Assets ($Mil)	Price	Performance Rating/Pts	Total Return Y-T-D	Risk Rating/Pts
12-15	D-	9.20	6.22	E+ / 0.6	-29.21%	C / 4.4
2014	E+	9.20	9.12	D- / 1.2	-16.68%	C- / 3.9
2013	D-	9.90	11.17	E / 0.5	-23.85%	C+ / 6.7
2012	C+	8.70	14.58	B- / 7.4	15.73%	B- / 7.1

Major Rating Factors:
Very poor performance is the major factor driving the D- (Weak) TheStreet.com Investment Rating for *Global X FTSE Andean 40 ETF. The fund currently has a performance rating of E+ (Very Weak) based on an annualized return of -23.64% over the last three years and a total return of -29.21% year to date 2015. Factored into the performance evaluation is an expense ratio of 0.72% (very low).

The fund's risk rating is currently C (Fair). It carries a beta of 1.00, meaning that its performance tracks fairly well with that of the overall stock market. Volatility, as measured by both the semi-deviation and a drawdown factor, is considered average. As of December 31, 2015, *Global X FTSE Andean 40 ETF traded at a discount of 1.27% below its net asset value, which is better than its one-year historical average premium of .25%.

Bruno Del Ama has been running the fund for 5 years and currently receives a manager quality ranking of 3 (0=worst, 99=best). This fund offers an average level of risk but investors looking for strong performance will be frustrated.

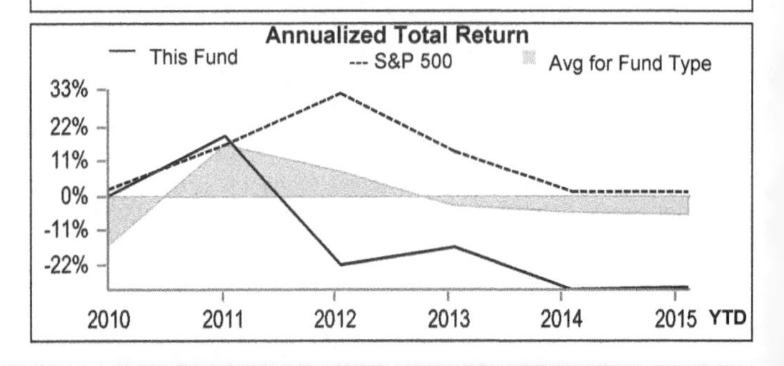

*Global X FTSE Greece 20 ETF (GREK) E Very Weak

Fund Family: Global X Management Company LLC
Fund Type: Foreign
Inception Date: December 7, 2011

Data Date	Investment Rating	Net Assets ($Mil)	Price	Performance Rating/Pts	Total Return Y-T-D	Risk Rating/Pts
12-15	E	187.50	7.96	E+ / 0.6	-41.19%	D+ / 2.7
2014	E+	187.50	13.40	D- / 1.3	-39.88%	C- / 3.5
2013	C+	129.70	22.53	A+ / 9.7	20.21%	C / 4.7
2012	C+	22.70	18.06	A+ / 9.9	48.10%	C / 4.4

Major Rating Factors: *Global X FTSE Greece 20 ETF has adopted a risky asset allocation strategy and currently receives an overall TheStreet.com Investment Rating of E (Very Weak). The fund has an above average level of volatility, as measured by both semi-deviation and drawdown factors. It carries a beta of 2.04, meaning it is expected to move 20.4% for every 10% move in the market. As of December 31, 2015, *Global X FTSE Greece 20 ETF traded at a discount of 1.85% below its net asset value, which is better than its one-year historical average premium of .97%. Unfortunately, the high level of risk (D+, Weak) failed to pay off as investors endured very poor performance.

The fund's performance rating is currently E+ (Very Weak). It has registered an annualized return of -24.16% over the last three years and is down -41.19% year to date 2015. Factored into the performance evaluation is an expense ratio of 0.62% (very low).

Bruno Del Ama has been running the fund for 5 years and currently receives a manager quality ranking of 3 (0=worst, 99=best). If you can tolerate high levels of risk in the hope of improved future returns, holding this fund may be an option.

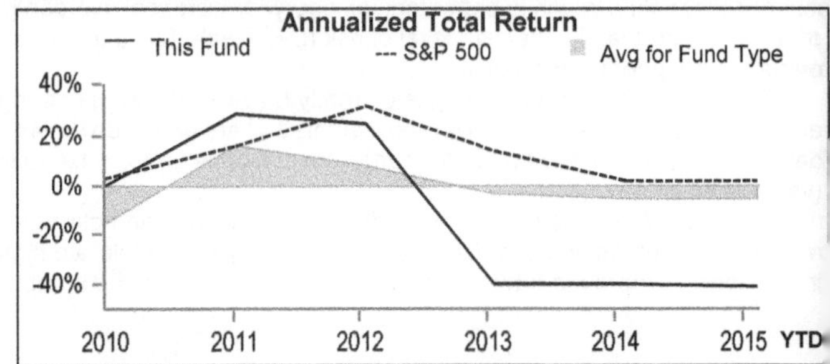

*Global X FTSE Nordic Region ETF (GXF) B- Good

Fund Family: Global X Management Company LLC
Fund Type: Global
Inception Date: August 19, 2009

Major Rating Factors: *Global X FTSE Nordic Region ETF receives a TheStreet.com Investment Rating of B- (Good). The fund currently has a performance rating of C+ (Fair) based on an annualized return of 5.73% over the last three years and a total return of 0.12% year to date 2015. Factored into the performance evaluation is an expense ratio of 0.50% (very low).

The fund's risk rating is currently B (Good). It carries a beta of 0.95, meaning that its performance tracks fairly well with that of the overall stock market. Volatility, as measured by both the semi-deviation and a drawdown factor, is considered low. As of December 31, 2015, *Global X FTSE Nordic Region ETF traded at a discount of .56% below its net asset value, which is better than its one-year historical average discount of .09%.

Bruno Del Ama has been running the fund for 7 years and currently receives a manager quality ranking of 76 (0=worst, 99=best). If you desire an average level of risk, then this fund may be an option.

Data Date	Investment Rating	Net Assets ($Mil)	Price	Performance Rating/Pts	Total Return Y-T-D	Risk Rating/Pts
12-15	B-	62.60	21.43	C+ / 6.0	0.12%	B / 8.0
2014	C+	62.60	22.05	C+ / 5.9	-4.02%	B- / 7.8
2013	C+	57.00	24.30	B- / 7.3	23.00%	C+ / 6.5
2012	C+	27.30	19.54	B- / 7.1	32.53%	C+ / 6.4
2011	D-	22.20	15.64	E+ / 0.9	-16.80%	C+ / 6.7
2010	A+	18.20	20.08	A / 9.4	25.42%	B- / 7.5

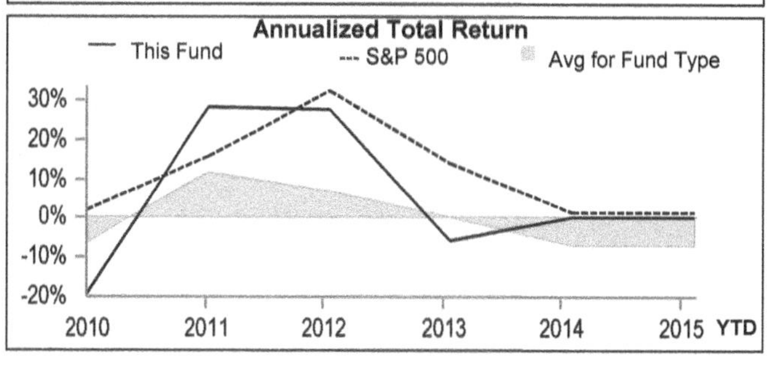

*Global X FTSE Portugal 20 ETF (PGAL) D+ Weak

Fund Family: Global X Management Company LLC
Fund Type: Foreign
Inception Date: November 12, 2013

Major Rating Factors: *Global X FTSE Portugal 20 ETF receives a TheStreet.com Investment Rating of D+ (Weak). The fund currently has a performance rating of C- (Fair) based on an annualized return of 0.00% over the last three years and a total return of 0.04% year to date 2015. Factored into the performance evaluation is an expense ratio of 0.61% (very low).

The fund's risk rating is currently C (Fair). It carries a beta of 0.00, meaning the fund's expected move will be 0.0% for every 10% move in the market. Volatility, as measured by both the semi-deviation and a drawdown factor, is considered average. As of December 31, 2015, *Global X FTSE Portugal 20 ETF traded at a discount of .39% below its net asset value, which is better than its one-year historical average discount of .04%.

Bruno del Ama has been running the fund for 3 years and currently receives a manager quality ranking of 84 (0=worst, 99=best). If you desire an average level of risk, then this fund may be an option.

Data Date	Investment Rating	Net Assets ($Mil)	Price	Performance Rating/Pts	Total Return Y-T-D	Risk Rating/Pts
12-15	D+	43.80	10.11	C- / 3.2	0.04%	C / 5.4
2014	E-	43.80	10.32	E- / 0.1	-34.28%	D+ / 2.5

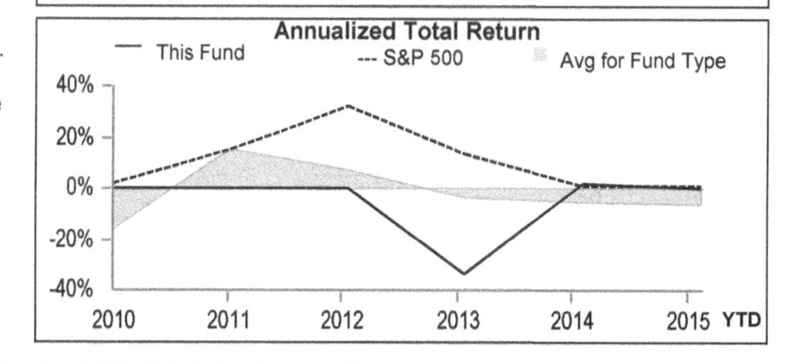

*Global X GF China Bond ETF (CHNB) D- Weak

Fund Family: Global X Management Company LLC
Fund Type: Foreign
Inception Date: November 18, 2014

Major Rating Factors: *Global X GF China Bond ETF has adopted a risky asset allocation strategy and currently receives an overall TheStreet.com Investment Rating of D- (Weak). The fund has an above average level of volatility, as measured by both semi-deviation and drawdown factors. It carries a beta of 0.00, meaning the fund's expected move will be 0.0% for every 10% move in the market. As of December 31, 2015, *Global X GF China Bond ETF traded at a discount of 2.24% below its net asset value, which is better than its one-year historical average discount of .34%. Unfortunately, the high level of risk (D+, Weak) has only provided investors with average performance.

The fund's performance rating is currently C- (Fair). It has registered an annualized return of 0.00% over the last three years and is up 0.13% year to date 2015.

Chang Kim has been running the fund for 2 years and currently receives a manager quality ranking of 61 (0=worst, 99=best). If you are comfortable owning a high risk investment, then this fund may be an option.

Data Date	Investment Rating	Net Assets ($Mil)	Price	Performance Rating/Pts	Total Return Y-T-D	Risk Rating/Pts
12-15	D-	0.00	35.85	C- / 3.8	0.13%	D+ / 2.6

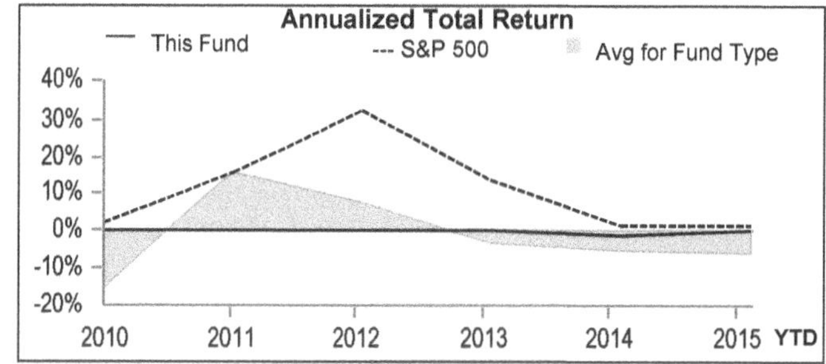

* Denotes ETF Fund

*Global X Gold Explorers ETF (GLDX) E- Very Weak

Fund Family: Global X Management Company LLC
Fund Type: Global
Inception Date: November 3, 2010

Major Rating Factors: *Global X Gold Explorers ETF has adopted a very risky asset allocation strategy and currently receives an overall TheStreet.com Investment Rating of E- (Very Weak). The fund has a high level of volatility, as measured by both semi-deviation and drawdown factors. It carries a beta of 0.16, meaning the fund's expected move will be 1.6% for every 10% move in the market. As of December 31, 2015, *Global X Gold Explorers ETF traded at a premium of .49% above its net asset value, which is worse than its one-year historical average discount of .03%. Unfortunately, the high level of risk (D-, Weak) failed to pay off as investors endured very poor performance.

The fund's performance rating is currently E (Very Weak). It has registered an annualized return of -32.05% over the last three years and is down -12.92% year to date 2015. Factored into the performance evaluation is an expense ratio of 0.65% (very low).

Bruno Del Ama has been running the fund for 6 years and currently receives a manager quality ranking of 2 (0=worst, 99=best). If you can tolerate very high levels of risk in the hope of improved future returns, holding this fund may be an option.

Data Date	Investment Rating	Net Assets ($Mil)	Price	Performance Rating/Pts	Total Return Y-T-D	Risk Rating/Pts
12-15	E-	36.50	16.43	E / 0.5	-12.92%	D- / 1.3
2014	E-	36.50	10.25	E- / 0.2	-13.23%	D / 1.9
2013	E-	28.30	11.00	E- / 0.1	-59.54%	D / 2.1
2012	E	39.30	7.32	E / 0.4	-30.83%	C- / 3.1
2011	E+	24.00	10.75	E / 0.4	-34.86%	C / 4.3

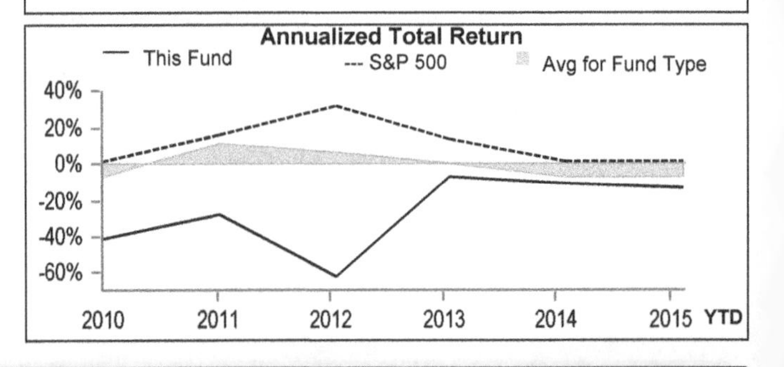

*Global X Guru Index ETF (GURU) B Good

Fund Family: Global X Management Company LLC
Fund Type: Growth and Income
Inception Date: June 4, 2012

Major Rating Factors: *Global X Guru Index ETF receives a TheStreet.com Investment Rating of B (Good). The fund currently has a performance rating of C+ (Fair) based on an annualized return of 9.02% over the last three years and a total return of -10.89% year to date 2015. Factored into the performance evaluation is an expense ratio of 0.75% (very low).

The fund's risk rating is currently B (Good). It carries a beta of 1.10, meaning it is expected to move 11.0% for every 10% move in the market. Volatility, as measured by both the semi-deviation and a drawdown factor, is considered low. As of December 31, 2015, *Global X Guru Index ETF traded at a discount of .04% below its net asset value, which is in line with its one-year historical average discount of .04%.

Bruno Del Ama has been running the fund for 4 years and currently receives a manager quality ranking of 29 (0=worst, 99=best). If you desire an average level of risk, then this fund may be an option.

Data Date	Investment Rating	Net Assets ($Mil)	Price	Performance Rating/Pts	Total Return Y-T-D	Risk Rating/Pts
12-15	B	491.30	23.22	C+ / 6.3	-10.89%	B / 8.4
2014	C	491.30	26.15	C- / 3.5	4.53%	B+ / 9.3
2013	A+	406.90	25.61	A+ / 9.7	38.91%	B+ / 9.9

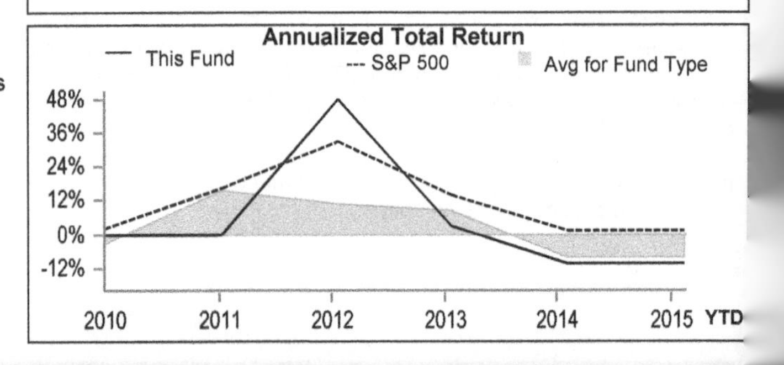

*Global X Guru International Idx (GURI) D+ Weak

Fund Family: Global X Management Company LLC
Fund Type: Foreign
Inception Date: March 10, 2014

Major Rating Factors:
Disappointing performance is the major factor driving the D+ (Weak) TheStreet.com Investment Rating for *Global X Guru International Idx. The fund currently has a performance rating of D (Weak) based on an annualized return of 0.00% over the last three years and a total return of -12.24% year to date 2015. Factored into the performance evaluation is an expense ratio of 0.75% (very low).

The fund's risk rating is currently B- (Good). It carries a beta of 0.00, meaning the fund's expected move will be 0.0% for every 10% move in the market. Volatility, as measured by both the semi-deviation and a drawdown factor, is considered low. As of December 31, 2015, *Global X Guru International Idx traded at a discount of .16% below its net asset value, which is worse than its one-year historical average discount of .19%.

Bruno Del Ama has been running the fund for 2 years and currently receives a manager quality ranking of 14 (0=worst, 99=best). This fund offers only a moderate level of risk but investors looking for strong performance are still waiting.

Data Date	Investment Rating	Net Assets ($Mil)	Price	Performance Rating/Pts	Total Return Y-T-D	Risk Rating/Pts
12-15	D+	2.30	12.46	D / 1.9	-12.24%	B- / 7.0

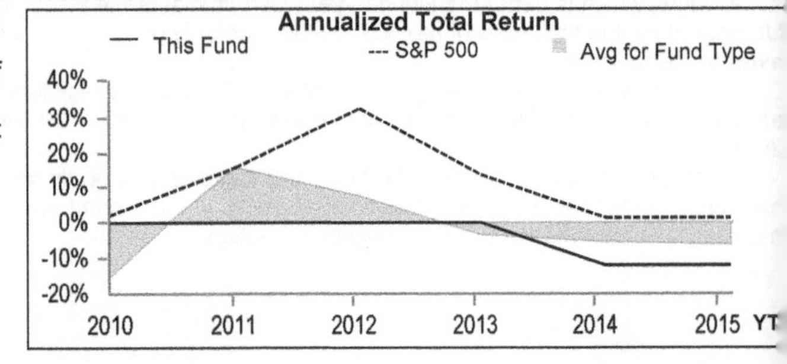

*Global X Junior MLP ETF (MLPJ) E+ Very Weak

Fund Family: Global X Management Company LLC
Fund Type: Energy/Natural Resources
Inception Date: January 14, 2013

Major Rating Factors:
Very poor performance is the major factor driving the E+ (Very Weak) TheStreet.com Investment Rating for *Global X Junior MLP ETF. The fund currently has a performance rating of E- (Very Weak) based on an annualized return of 0.00% over the last three years and a total return of -39.37% year to date 2015. Factored into the performance evaluation is an expense ratio of 0.75% (very low).

The fund's risk rating is currently C (Fair). It carries a beta of 0.00, meaning the fund's expected move will be 0.0% for every 10% move in the market. Volatility, as measured by both the semi-deviation and a drawdown factor, is considered average. As of December 31, 2015, *Global X Junior MLP ETF traded at a discount of .38% below its net asset value, which is better than its one-year historical average discount of .05%.

Bruno Del Ama has been running the fund for 3 years and currently receives a manager quality ranking of 12 (0=worst, 99=best). This fund offers an average level of risk but investors looking for strong performance will be frustrated.

Data Date	Investment Rating	Net Assets ($Mil)	Price	Performance Rating/Pts	Total Return Y-T-D	Risk Rating/Pts
12-15	E+	18.00	7.87	E- / 0.1	-39.37%	C / 4.5
2014	D	18.00	13.91	E+ / 0.7	-7.98%	B- / 7.2

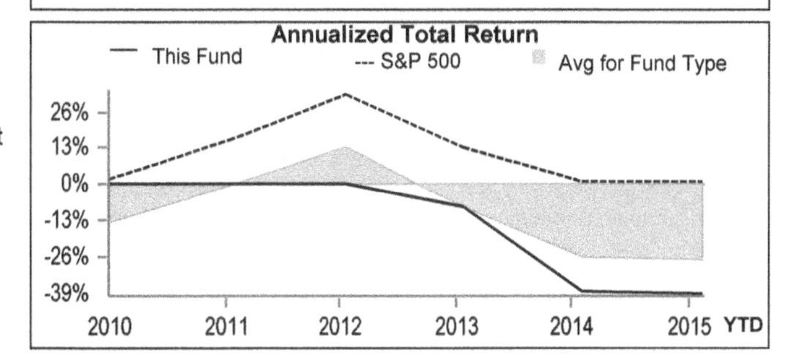

*Global X Lithium ETF (LIT) D Weak

Fund Family: Global X Management Company LLC
Fund Type: Growth
Inception Date: July 22, 2010

Major Rating Factors:
Disappointing performance is the major factor driving the D (Weak) TheStreet.com Investment Rating for *Global X Lithium ETF. The fund currently has a performance rating of D (Weak) based on an annualized return of -11.09% over the last three years and a total return of -8.99% year to date 2015. Factored into the performance evaluation is an expense ratio of 0.75% (very low).

The fund's risk rating is currently C+ (Fair). It carries a beta of 1.16, meaning it is expected to move 11.6% for every 10% move in the market. Volatility, as measured by both the semi-deviation and a drawdown factor, is considered low. As of December 31, 2015, *Global X Lithium ETF traded at a discount of .74% below its net asset value, which is better than its one-year historical average discount of .20%.

Bruno Del Ama has been running the fund for 6 years and currently receives a manager quality ranking of 5 (0=worst, 99=best). This fund offers only a moderate level of risk but investors looking for strong performance are still waiting.

Data Date	Investment Rating	Net Assets ($Mil)	Price	Performance Rating/Pts	Total Return Y-T-D	Risk Rating/Pts
12-15	D	54.00	20.09	D / 1.9	-8.99%	C+ / 6.1
2014	D	54.00	11.13	D- / 1.3	-12.40%	C+ / 6.1
2013	E+	49.70	13.01	E+ / 0.8	-12.79%	C / 4.7
2012	D-	66.40	14.36	D / 1.9	-1.17%	C / 5.3
2011	E+	86.70	14.33	E / 0.5	-33.13%	C / 5.4

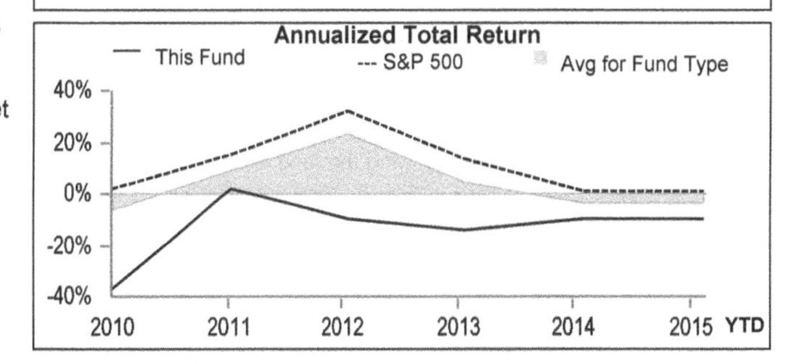

*Global X MLP & Energy Infra (MLPX) D- Weak

Fund Family: Global X Management Company LLC
Fund Type: Energy/Natural Resources
Inception Date: August 7, 2013

Major Rating Factors:
Very poor performance is the major factor driving the D- (Weak) TheStreet.com Investment Rating for *Global X MLP & Energy Infra. The fund currently has a performance rating of E- (Very Weak) based on an annualized return of 0.00% over the last three years and a total return of -36.17% year to date 2015. Factored into the performance evaluation is an expense ratio of 0.45% (very low).

The fund's risk rating is currently C+ (Fair). It carries a beta of 0.00, meaning the fund's expected move will be 0.0% for every 10% move in the market. Volatility, as measured by both the semi-deviation and a drawdown factor, is considered low. As of December 31, 2015, *Global X MLP & Energy Infra traded at a discount of .09% below its net asset value, which is better than its one-year historical average premium of .01%.

Bruno Del Ama has been running the fund for 3 years and currently receives a manager quality ranking of 8 (0=worst, 99=best). This fund offers only a moderate level of risk but investors looking for strong performance are still waiting.

Data Date	Investment Rating	Net Assets ($Mil)	Price	Performance Rating/Pts	Total Return Y-T-D	Risk Rating/Pts
12-15	D-	183.00	11.61	E- / 0.1	-36.17%	C+ / 5.7
2014	C+	183.00	18.55	C / 5.0	17.86%	B / 8.4

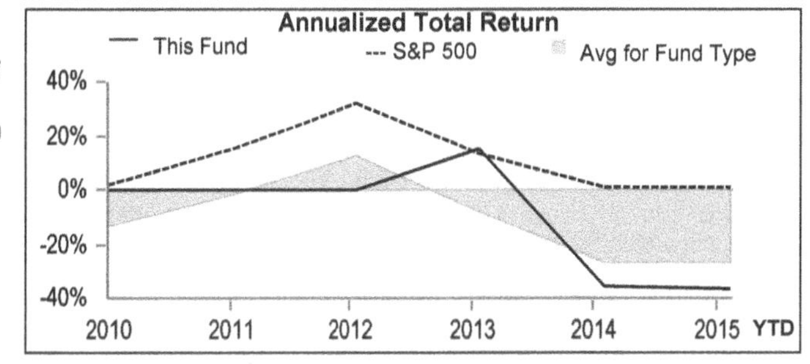

*Global X MLP ETF (MLPA) D- Weak

Fund Family: Global X Management Company LLC
Fund Type: Energy/Natural Resources
Inception Date: April 18, 2012

Major Rating Factors:
Disappointing performance is the major factor driving the D- (Weak) TheStreet.com Investment Rating for *Global X MLP ETF. The fund currently has a performance rating of D (Weak) based on an annualized return of -6.10% over the last three years and a total return of -30.78% year to date 2015. Factored into the performance evaluation is an expense ratio of 0.47% (very low).

The fund's risk rating is currently C (Fair). It carries a beta of 0.52, meaning the fund's expected move will be 5.2% for every 10% move in the market. Volatility, as measured by both the semi-deviation and a drawdown factor, is considered average. As of December 31, 2015, *Global X MLP ETF traded at a premium of .29% above its net asset value.

Bruno del Ama has been running the fund for 4 years and currently receives a manager quality ranking of 42 (0=worst, 99=best). This fund offers an average level of risk but investors looking for strong performance will be frustrated.

Data Date	Investment Rating	Net Assets ($Mil)	Price	Performance Rating/Pts	Total Return Y-T-D	Risk Rating/Pts
12-15	D-	138.80	10.39	D / 1.8	-30.78%	C / 4.4
2014	C-	138.80	15.94	D+ / 2.5	5.07%	B / 8.9
2013	B	69.50	16.18	C+ / 6.2	12.69%	B+ / 9.2

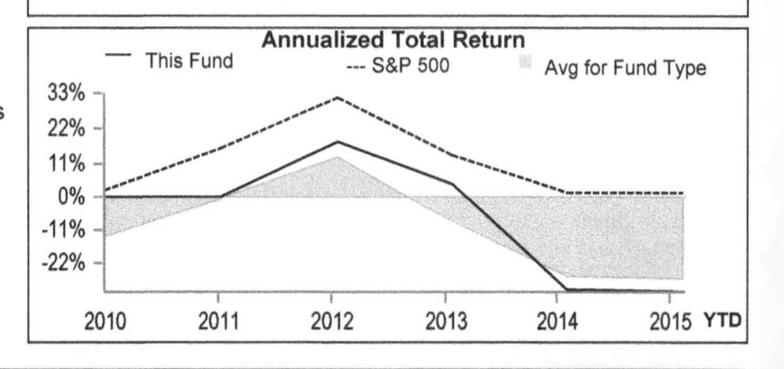

*Global X MSCI Argentina ETF (ARGT) C- Fair

Fund Family: Global X Management Company LLC
Fund Type: Foreign
Inception Date: March 3, 2011

Major Rating Factors: Middle of the road best describes *Global X MSCI Argentina ETF whose TheStreet.com Investment Rating is currently a C- (Fair). The fund currently has a performance rating of C (Fair) based on an annualized return of 1.09% over the last three years and a total return of -1.88% year to date 2015. Factored into the performance evaluation is an expense ratio of 0.74% (very low).

The fund's risk rating is currently C (Fair). It carries a beta of 1.37, meaning it is expected to move 13.7% for every 10% move in the market. Volatility, as measured by both the semi-deviation and a drawdown factor, is considered average. As of December 31, 2015, *Global X MSCI Argentina ETF traded at a premium of .44% above its net asset value, which is worse than its one-year historical average premium of .07%.

Bruno Del Ama has been running the fund for 5 years and currently receives a manager quality ranking of 32 (0=worst, 99=best). If you desire an average level of risk, then this fund may be an option.

Data Date	Investment Rating	Net Assets ($Mil)	Price	Performance Rating/Pts	Total Return Y-T-D	Risk Rating/Pts
12-15	C-	23.80	18.08	C / 4.9	-1.88%	C / 4.8
2014	D-	23.80	18.76	D / 1.8	-2.29%	C- / 3.8
2013	C-	7.30	19.56	B- / 7.1	8.67%	C / 4.6
2012	E+	3.00	8.55	D- / 1.0	-18.48%	C / 4.4

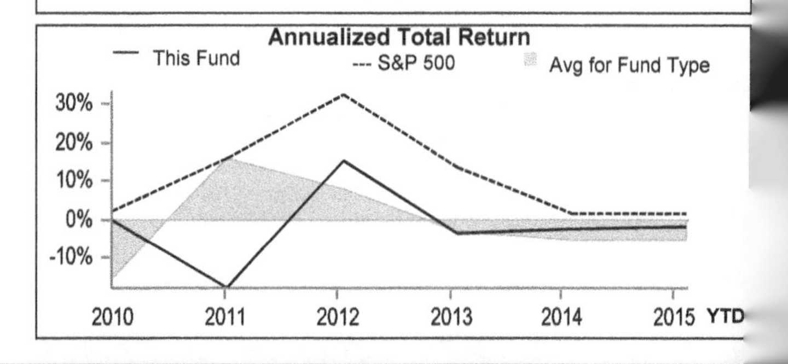

*Global X MSCI Colombia (GXG) E+ Very Weak

Fund Family: Global X Management Company LLC
Fund Type: Foreign
Inception Date: February 5, 2009

Major Rating Factors:
Very poor performance is the major factor driving the E+ (Very Weak) TheStreet.com Investment Rating for *Global X MSCI Colombia. The fund currently has a performance rating of E (Very Weak) based on an annualized return of -28.55% over the last three years and a total return of -40.52% year to date 2015. Factored into the performance evaluation is an expense ratio of 0.66% (very low).

The fund's risk rating is currently C- (Fair). It carries a beta of 1.05, meaning that its performance tracks fairly well with that of the overall stock market. Volatility, as measured by both the semi-deviation and a drawdown factor, is considered average. As of December 31, 2015, *Global X MSCI Colombia traded at a discount of .13% below its net asset value, which is better than its one-year historical average premium of .23%.

Bruno Del Ama has been running the fund for 7 years and currently receives a manager quality ranking of 2 (0=worst, 99=best). This fund offers an average level of risk but investors looking for strong performance will be frustrated.

Data Date	Investment Rating	Net Assets ($Mil)	Price	Performance Rating/Pts	Total Return Y-T-D	Risk Rating/Pts
12-15	E+	109.20	7.46	E / 0.4	-40.52%	C- / 3.4
2014	E+	109.20	12.86	E+ / 0.9	-26.39%	C- / 3.2
2013	E+	111.10	18.15	D / 1.8	-16.07%	C- / 3.3
2012	C-	179.30	22.24	B / 7.6	20.96%	C- / 3.3
2011	E+	121.60	17.82	D- / 1.2	-9.61%	C- / 3.6
2010	A+	170.40	42.53	A+ / 9.6	50.18%	B- / 7.9

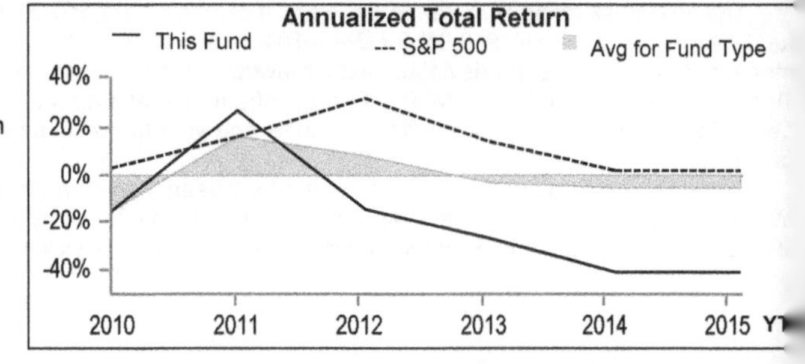

*Global X MSCI Nigeria ETF (NGE) E+ Very Weak

Fund Family: Global X Management Company LLC
Fund Type: Emerging Market
Inception Date: April 2, 2013

Data Date	Investment Rating	Net Assets ($Mil)	Price	Performance Rating/Pts	Total Return Y-T-D	Risk Rating/Pts
12-15	E+	20.30	7.06	E / 0.3	-29.34%	C- / 4.2
2014	E	20.30	10.57	E- / 0.1	-32.66%	C- / 3.9

Major Rating Factors:
Very poor performance is the major factor driving the E+ (Very Weak) TheStreet.com Investment Rating for *Global X MSCI Nigeria ETF. The fund currently has a performance rating of E (Very Weak) based on an annualized return of 0.00% over the last three years and a total return of -29.34% year to date 2015. Factored into the performance evaluation is an expense ratio of 0.68% (very low).

The fund's risk rating is currently C- (Fair). It carries a beta of 0.00, meaning the fund's expected move will be 0.0% for every 10% move in the market. Volatility, as measured by both the semi-deviation and a drawdown factor, is considered average. As of December 31, 2015, *Global X MSCI Nigeria ETF traded at a discount of 2.35% below its net asset value, which is better than its one-year historical average premium of .32%.

Bruno Del Ama has been running the fund for 3 years and currently receives a manager quality ranking of 3 (0=worst, 99=best). This fund offers an average level of risk but investors looking for strong performance will be frustrated.

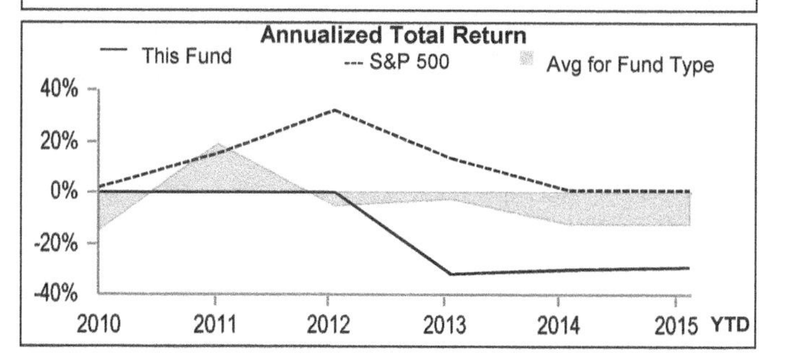

*Global X MSCI Norway ETF (NORW) D Weak

Fund Family: Global X Management Company LLC
Fund Type: Foreign
Inception Date: November 9, 2010

Data Date	Investment Rating	Net Assets ($Mil)	Price	Performance Rating/Pts	Total Return Y-T-D	Risk Rating/Pts
12-15	D	208.70	9.69	D / 1.6	-15.64%	C / 5.4
2014	D	208.70	11.93	D / 2.0	-21.80%	C+ / 6.1
2013	C-	85.40	16.67	C / 5.1	8.44%	C+ / 6.3
2012	B	55.70	15.25	A+ / 9.6	26.06%	C+ / 6.2
2011	D-	44.00	12.54	D- / 1.0	-15.80%	C+ / 6.2

Major Rating Factors:
Disappointing performance is the major factor driving the D (Weak) TheStreet.com Investment Rating for *Global X MSCI Norway ETF. The fund currently has a performance rating of D (Weak) based on an annualized return of -10.53% over the last three years and a total return of -15.64% year to date 2015. Factored into the performance evaluation is an expense ratio of 0.50% (very low).

The fund's risk rating is currently C (Fair). It carries a beta of 1.18, meaning it is expected to move 11.8% for every 10% move in the market. Volatility, as measured by both the semi-deviation and a drawdown factor, is considered average. As of December 31, 2015, *Global X MSCI Norway ETF traded at a discount of .41% below its net asset value, which is better than its one-year historical average premium of .13%.

Bruno Del Ama has been running the fund for 6 years and currently receives a manager quality ranking of 10 (0=worst, 99=best). This fund offers an average level of risk but investors looking for strong performance will be frustrated.

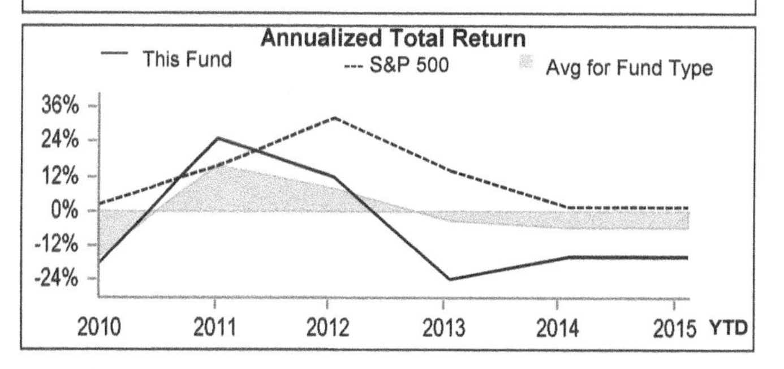

*Global X NASDAQ China Tech ETF (QQQC) B+ Good

Fund Family: Global X Management Company LLC
Fund Type: Foreign
Inception Date: December 8, 2009

Data Date	Investment Rating	Net Assets ($Mil)	Price	Performance Rating/Pts	Total Return Y-T-D	Risk Rating/Pts
12-15	B+	22.40	22.97	A / 9.3	9.60%	C+ / 6.5
2014	C+	22.40	21.11	C+ / 6.3	-3.32%	B- / 7.3
2013	B-	13.00	21.80	B+ / 8.7	49.98%	C+ / 6.2
2012	D	2.80	14.23	D / 1.6	7.99%	C+ / 6.2
2010	A	4.90	16.50	B+ / 8.3	8.34%	B- / 7.7

Major Rating Factors:
Exceptional performance is the major factor driving the B+ (Good) TheStreet.com Investment Rating for *Global X NASDAQ China Tech ETF. The fund currently has a performance rating of A (Excellent) based on an annualized return of 16.66% over the last three years and a total return of 9.60% year to date 2015. Factored into the performance evaluation is an expense ratio of 0.65% (very low).

The fund's risk rating is currently C+ (Fair). It carries a beta of 0.98, meaning that its performance tracks fairly well with that of the overall stock market. Volatility, as measured by both the semi-deviation and a drawdown factor, is considered low. As of December 31, 2015, *Global X NASDAQ China Tech ETF traded at a discount of .09% below its net asset value, which is worse than its one-year historical average discount of .58%.

Bruno Del Ama has been running the fund for 7 years and currently receives a manager quality ranking of 96 (0=worst, 99=best). If you desire only a moderate level of risk and strong performance, then this fund is an excellent option.

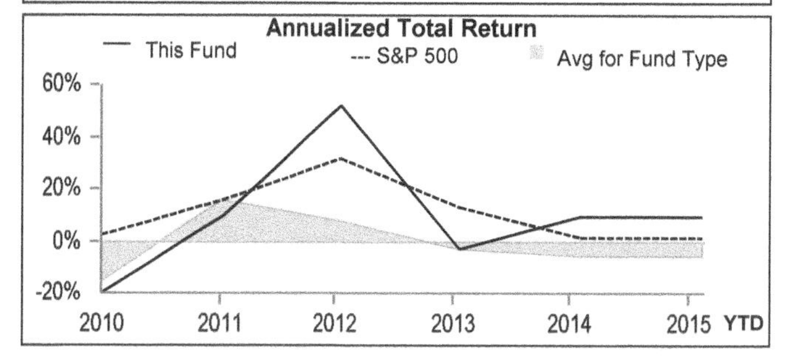

*Global X Next Emerg and Front ET (EMFM) D Weak

Fund Family: Global X Management Company LLC
Fund Type: Emerging Market
Inception Date: November 7, 2013

Major Rating Factors:
Very poor performance is the major factor driving the D (Weak) TheStreet.com Investment Rating for *Global X Next Emerg and Front ET. The fund currently has a performance rating of E+ (Very Weak) based on an annualized return of 0.00% over the last three years and a total return of -23.09% year to date 2015. Factored into the performance evaluation is an expense ratio of 0.58% (very low).

The fund's risk rating is currently C+ (Fair). It carries a beta of 0.00, meaning the fund's expected move will be 0.0% for every 10% move in the market. Volatility, as measured by both the semi-deviation and a drawdown factor, is considered low. As of December 31, 2015, *Global X Next Emerg and Front ET traded at a discount of .86% below its net asset value, which is better than its one-year historical average discount of .35%.

Bruno Del Ama has been running the fund for 3 years and currently receives a manager quality ranking of 11 (0=worst, 99=best). This fund offers only a moderate level of risk but investors looking for strong performance are still waiting.

Data Date	Investment Rating	Net Assets ($Mil)	Price	Performance Rating/Pts	Total Return Y-T-D	Risk Rating/Pts
12-15	D	156.80	17.24	E+ / 0.6	-23.09%	C+ / 6.4
2014	E+	156.80	23.35	D- / 1.5	-1.05%	C- / 3.6

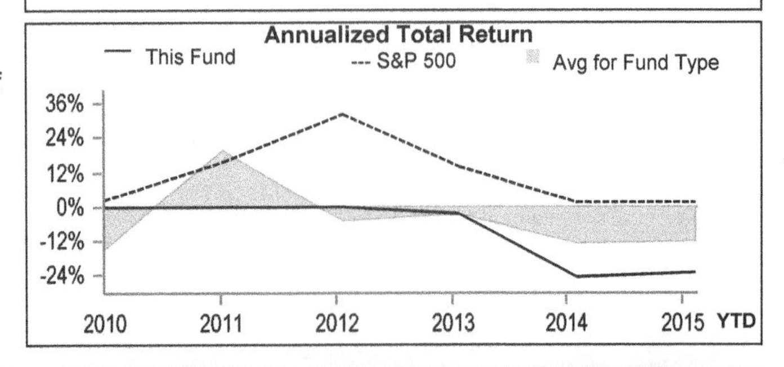

*Global X Permanent ETF (PERM) C- Fair

Fund Family: Global X Management Company LLC
Fund Type: Growth and Income
Inception Date: February 7, 2012

Major Rating Factors: Middle of the road best describes *Global X Permanent ETF whose TheStreet.com Investment Rating is currently a C- (Fair). The fund currently has a performance rating of C- (Fair) based on an annualized return of -1.79% over the last three years and a total return of -4.95% year to date 2015. Factored into the performance evaluation is an expense ratio of 0.48% (very low).

The fund's risk rating is currently B- (Good). It carries a beta of 0.12, meaning the fund's expected move will be 1.2% for every 10% move in the market. Volatility, as measured by both the semi-deviation and a drawdown factor, is considered low. As of December 31, 2015, *Global X Permanent ETF traded at a premium of .22% above its net asset value, which is better than its one-year historical average premium of .26%.

Bruno del Ama has been running the fund for 4 years and currently receives a manager quality ranking of 37 (0=worst, 99=best). If you desire an average level of risk, then this fund may be an option.

Data Date	Investment Rating	Net Assets ($Mil)	Price	Performance Rating/Pts	Total Return Y-T-D	Risk Rating/Pts
12-15	C-	11.10	23.10	C- / 3.5	-4.95%	B- / 7.2
2014	C	11.10	24.63	C / 4.9	7.51%	B- / 7.1
2013	C-	13.80	23.20	D / 1.9	-7.08%	B+ / 9.0

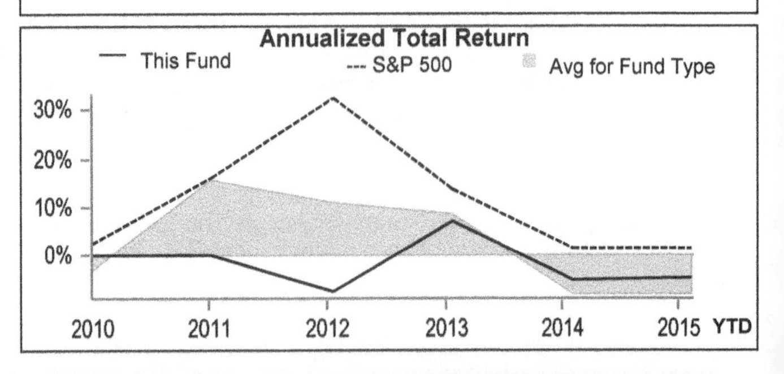

*Global X Silver Miners ETF (SIL) E Very Weak

Fund Family: Global X Management Company LLC
Fund Type: Precious Metals
Inception Date: April 19, 2010

Major Rating Factors: *Global X Silver Miners ETF has adopted a risky asset allocation strategy and currently receives an overall TheStreet.com Investment Rating of E (Very Weak). The fund has an above average level of volatility, as measured by both semi-deviation and drawdown factors. It carries a beta of 1.95, meaning it is expected to move 19.5% for every 10% move in the market. As of December 31, 2015, *Global X Silver Miners ETF traded at a discount of .27% below its net asset value, which is better than its one-year historical average premium of .06%. Unfortunately, the high level of risk (D+, Weak) failed to pay off as investors endured very poor performance.

The fund's performance rating is currently E (Very Weak). It has registered an annualized return of -34.91% over the last three years and is down -34.30% year to date 2015. Factored into the performance evaluation is an expense ratio of 0.65% (very low).

Bruno Del Ama has been running the fund for 6 years and currently receives a manager quality ranking of 12 (0=worst, 99=best). If you can tolerate high levels of risk in the hope of improved future returns, holding this fund may be an option.

Data Date	Investment Rating	Net Assets ($Mil)	Price	Performance Rating/Pts	Total Return Y-T-D	Risk Rating/Pts
12-15	E	200.00	18.51	E / 0.3	-34.30%	D+ / 2.8
2014	E	200.00	9.26	E / 0.5	-20.18%	D+ / 2.7
2013	E	192.30	11.20	E / 0.4	-48.08%	C- / 3.1
2012	D+	349.90	22.65	C / 4.4	2.33%	C / 5.2
2011	D-	314.10	21.12	D- / 1.2	-8.95%	C+ / 6.1

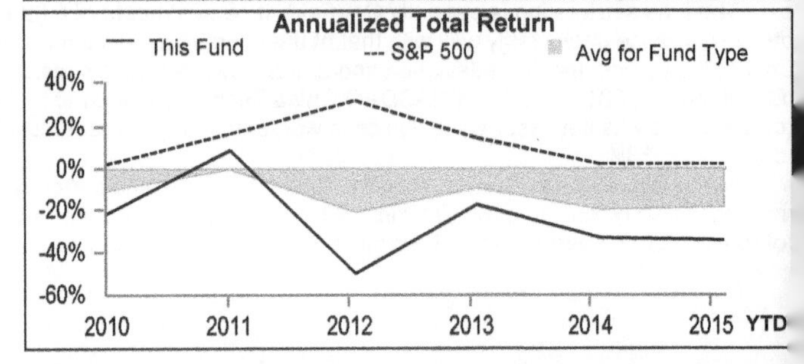

*Global X Social Media Index ETF (SOCL) A- Excellent

Fund Family: Global X Management Company LLC
Fund Type: Global
Inception Date: November 14, 2011

Data Date	Investment Rating	Net Assets ($Mil)	Price	Performance Rating/Pts	Total Return Y-T-D	Risk Rating/Pts
12-15	A-	136.10	19.87	A- / 9.0	9.54%	B- / 7.3
2014	C-	136.10	18.02	C / 4.9	-15.04%	C+ / 6.7
2013	A	125.00	21.22	A+ / 9.9	57.77%	B- / 7.4
2012	D+	11.60	12.94	C- / 3.5	6.67%	B- / 7.0

Major Rating Factors:
Exceptional performance is the major factor driving the A- (Excellent) TheStreet.com Investment Rating for *Global X Social Media Index ETF. The fund currently has a performance rating of A- (Excellent) based on an annualized return of 13.91% over the last three years and a total return of 9.54% year to date 2015. Factored into the performance evaluation is an expense ratio of 0.65% (very low).

The fund's risk rating is currently B- (Good). It carries a beta of 0.94, meaning that its performance tracks fairly well with that of the overall stock market. Volatility, as measured by both the semi-deviation and a drawdown factor, is considered low. As of December 31, 2015, *Global X Social Media Index ETF traded at a discount of .50% below its net asset value, which is better than its one-year historical average discount of .14%.

Bruno Del Ama has been running the fund for 5 years and currently receives a manager quality ranking of 95 (0=worst, 99=best). If you desire only a moderate level of risk and strong performance, then this fund is an excellent option.

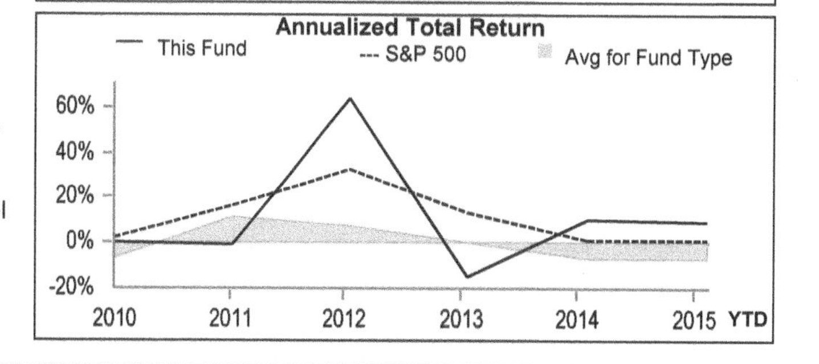

*Global X Southeast Asia ETF (ASEA) D+ Weak

Fund Family: Global X Management Company LLC
Fund Type: Global
Inception Date: February 16, 2011

Data Date	Investment Rating	Net Assets ($Mil)	Price	Performance Rating/Pts	Total Return Y-T-D	Risk Rating/Pts
12-15	D+	29.50	12.13	D / 2.0	-19.65%	C+ / 6.4
2014	C-	29.50	15.79	C- / 4.0	8.16%	C+ / 6.6
2013	D	37.20	15.50	E+ / 0.9	-9.62%	B- / 7.3
2012	C+	37.70	17.04	B- / 7.1	16.74%	B- / 7.3

Major Rating Factors:
Disappointing performance is the major factor driving the D+ (Weak) TheStreet.com Investment Rating for *Global X Southeast Asia ETF. The fund currently has a performance rating of D (Weak) based on an annualized return of -8.01% over the last three years and a total return of -19.65% year to date 2015. Factored into the performance evaluation is an expense ratio of 0.65% (very low).

The fund's risk rating is currently C+ (Fair). It carries a beta of 0.94, meaning that its performance tracks fairly well with that of the overall stock market. Volatility, as measured by both the semi-deviation and a drawdown factor, is considered low. As of December 31, 2015, *Global X Southeast Asia ETF traded at a discount of 1.30% below its net asset value, which is better than its one-year historical average discount of .37%.

Bruno Del Ama has been running the fund for 5 years and currently receives a manager quality ranking of 13 (0=worst, 99=best). This fund offers only a moderate level of risk but investors looking for strong performance are still waiting.

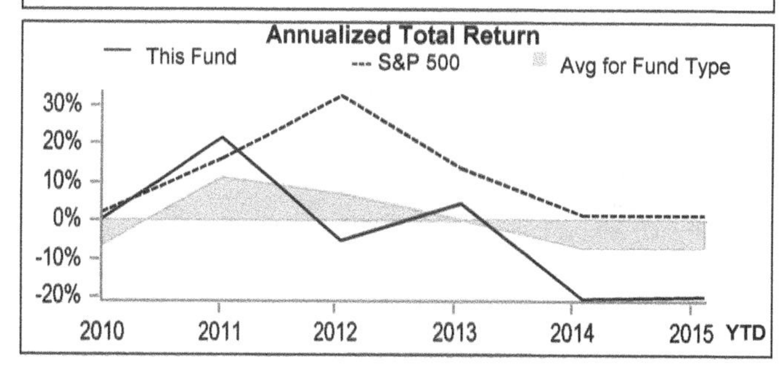

*Global X SuperDividend ETF (SDIV) C Fair

Fund Family: Global X Management Company LLC
Fund Type: Global
Inception Date: June 8, 2011

Data Date	Investment Rating	Net Assets ($Mil)	Price	Performance Rating/Pts	Total Return Y-T-D	Risk Rating/Pts
12-15	C	1,071.30	19.72	C / 4.4	-9.20%	B- / 7.3
2014	C+	1,071.30	23.07	C+ / 5.6	6.23%	B / 8.2
2013	B-	811.90	23.46	B- / 7.3	10.75%	B- / 7.7
2012	B	192.90	22.10	B / 8.2	17.79%	B- / 7.6

Major Rating Factors: Middle of the road best describes *Global X SuperDividend ETF whose TheStreet.com Investment Rating is currently a C (Fair). The fund currently has a performance rating of C (Fair) based on an annualized return of 2.27% over the last three years and a total return of -9.20% year to date 2015. Factored into the performance evaluation is an expense ratio of 0.58% (very low).

The fund's risk rating is currently B- (Good). It carries a beta of 1.34, meaning it is expected to move 13.4% for every 10% move in the market. Volatility, as measured by both the semi-deviation and a drawdown factor, is considered low. As of December 31, 2015, *Global X SuperDividend ETF traded at a discount of .60% below its net asset value, which is better than its one-year historical average discount of .02%.

Bruno Del Ama has been running the fund for 5 years and currently receives a manager quality ranking of 94 (0=worst, 99=best). If you desire an average level of risk, then this fund may be an option.

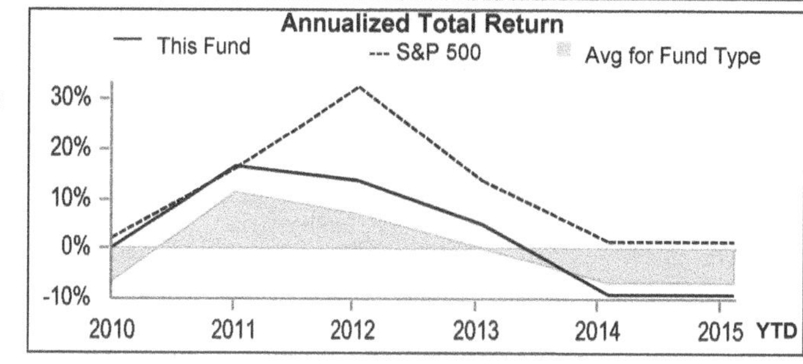

 * Denotes ETF Fund

*Global X SuperDividend US ETF (DIV) D+ Weak

Fund Family: Global X Management Company LLC
Fund Type: Income
Inception Date: March 11, 2013

Major Rating Factors:
Disappointing performance is the major factor driving the D+ (Weak) TheStreet.com Investment Rating for *Global X SuperDividend US ETF. The fund currently has a performance rating of D (Weak) based on an annualized return of 0.00% over the last three years and a total return of -11.84% year to date 2015. Factored into the performance evaluation is an expense ratio of 0.45% (very low).

The fund's risk rating is currently C+ (Fair). It carries a beta of 0.00, meaning the fund's expected move will be 0.0% for every 10% move in the market. Volatility, as measured by both the semi-deviation and a drawdown factor, is considered low. As of December 31, 2015, *Global X SuperDividend US ETF traded at a premium of .08% above its net asset value, which is worse than its one-year historical average premium of .01%.

Bruno Del Ama has been running the fund for 3 years and currently receives a manager quality ranking of 14 (0=worst, 99=best). This fund offers only a moderate level of risk but investors looking for strong performance are still waiting.

Data Date	Investment Rating	Net Assets ($Mil)	Price	Perfor-mance Rating/Pts	Total Return Y-T-D	Risk Rating/Pts
12-15	D+	210.60	23.94	D / 2.0	-11.84%	C+ / 6.3
2014	B	210.60	28.90	C+ / 6.9	18.63%	B / 8.5

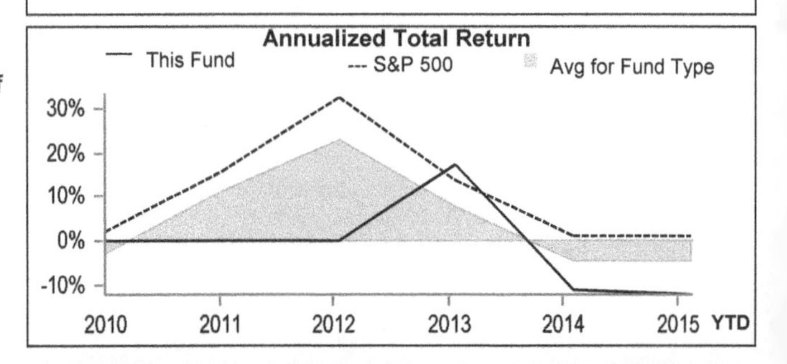

*Global X SuperIncome Preferred E (SPFF) C+ Fair

Fund Family: Global X Management Company LLC
Fund Type: Global
Inception Date: July 16, 2012

Major Rating Factors: Middle of the road best describes *Global X SuperIncome Preferred E whose TheStreet.com Investment Rating is currently a C+ (Fair). The fund currently has a performance rating of C (Fair) based on an annualized return of 2.32% over the last three years and a total return of -3.90% year to date 2015. Factored into the performance evaluation is an expense ratio of 0.58% (very low).

The fund's risk rating is currently B (Good). It carries a beta of 0.19, meaning the fund's expected move will be 1.9% for every 10% move in the market. Volatility, as measured by both the semi-deviation and a drawdown factor, is considered low. As of December 31, 2015, *Global X SuperIncome Preferred E traded at a discount of .30% below its net asset value, which is better than its one-year historical average premium of .03%.

Bruno Del Ama has been running the fund for 4 years and currently receives a manager quality ranking of 86 (0=worst, 99=best). If you desire an average level of risk, then this fund may be an option.

Data Date	Investment Rating	Net Assets ($Mil)	Price	Perfor-mance Rating/Pts	Total Return Y-T-D	Risk Rating/Pts
12-15	C+	144.50	13.15	C / 5.0	-3.90%	B / 8.8
2014	C+	144.50	14.54	C- / 3.9	5.72%	B+ / 9.3
2013	B-	67.60	14.59	C / 5.4	5.03%	B+ / 9.6

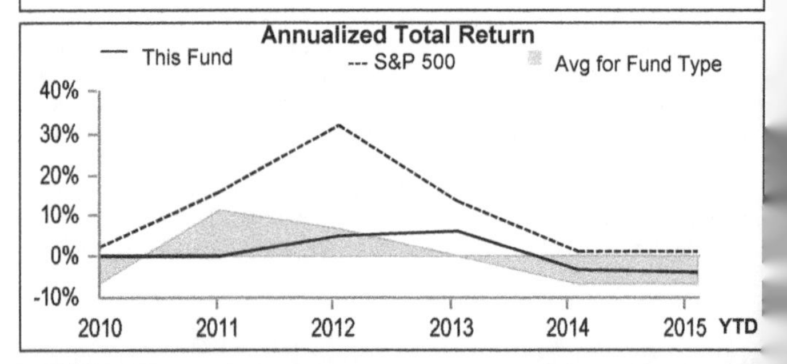

*Global X Uranium ETF (URA) E+ Very Weak

Fund Family: Global X Management Company LLC
Fund Type: Global
Inception Date: November 4, 2010

Major Rating Factors:
Very poor performance is the major factor driving the E+ (Very Weak) TheStreet.com Investment Rating for *Global X Uranium ETF. The fund currently has a performance rating of E (Very Weak) based on an annualized return of -28.02% over the last three years and a total return of -37.58% year to date 2015. Factored into the performance evaluation is an expense ratio of 0.69% (very low).

The fund's risk rating is currently C- (Fair). It carries a beta of 1.03, meaning its performance tracks fairly well with that of the overall stock market. Volatility, as measured by both the semi-deviation and a drawdown factor, is considered average. As of December 31, 2015, *Global X Uranium ETF traded at a discount of .71% below its net asset value, which is better than its one-year historical average discount of .19%.

Bruno Del Ama has been running the fund for 6 years and currently receives a manager quality ranking of 2 (0=worst, 99=best). This fund offers an average level of risk but investors looking for strong performance will be frustrated.

Data Date	Investment Rating	Net Assets ($Mil)	Price	Perfor-mance Rating/Pts	Total Return Y-T-D	Risk Rating/Pts
12-15	E+	238.50	13.99	E / 0.5	-37.58%	C- / 3.5
2014	E+	238.50	11.35	E+ / 0.6	-21.50%	C- / 4.0
2013	E-	135.00	15.27	E / 0.3	-24.44%	D+ / 2.5
2012	E-	133.00	6.51	E / 0.5	-22.62%	D+ / 2.6
2011	E-	164.00	8.15	E- / 0.1	-56.41%	D+ / 2.3

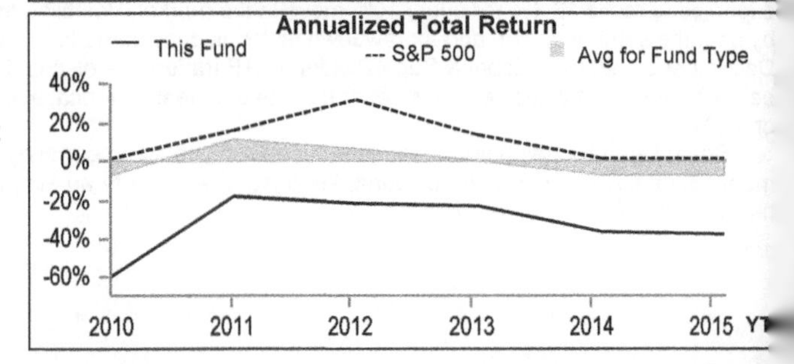

*GreenHaven Continuous Commodity (GCC) D Weak

Fund Family: Greenhaven Commodity Services LLC
Fund Type: Growth and Income
Inception Date: January 24, 2008

Major Rating Factors:
Disappointing performance is the major factor driving the D (Weak) TheStreet.com Investment Rating for *GreenHaven Continuous Commodity. The fund currently has a performance rating of D- (Weak) based on an annualized return of -13.59% over the last three years and a total return of -18.66% year to date 2015. Factored into the performance evaluation is an expense ratio of 1.05% (low).

The fund's risk rating is currently C+ (Fair). It carries a beta of 0.30, meaning the fund's expected move will be 3.0% for every 10% move in the market. Volatility, as measured by both the semi-deviation and a drawdown factor, is considered low. As of December 31, 2015, *GreenHaven Continuous Commodity traded at a discount of .22% below its net asset value, which is better than its one-year historical average discount of .02%.

Edgar Wachenheim, III currently receives a manager quality ranking of 9 (0=worst, 99=best). This fund offers only a moderate level of risk but investors looking for strong performance are still waiting.

Data Date	Investment Rating	Net Assets ($Mil)	Price	Performance Rating/Pts	Total Return Y-T-D	Risk Rating/Pts
12-15	D	321.00	18.52	D- / 1.3	-18.66%	C+ / 6.6
2014	D-	321.00	22.86	D- / 1.3	-11.15%	C / 5.3
2013	D	320.00	25.70	D- / 1.4	-10.16%	B- / 7.0
2012	D	474.60	28.83	D / 1.7	-4.65%	B- / 7.3
2011	C-	581.20	29.92	C- / 3.4	-6.48%	B / 8.1
2010	A	442.10	32.95	A / 9.5	25.19%	C+ / 5.7

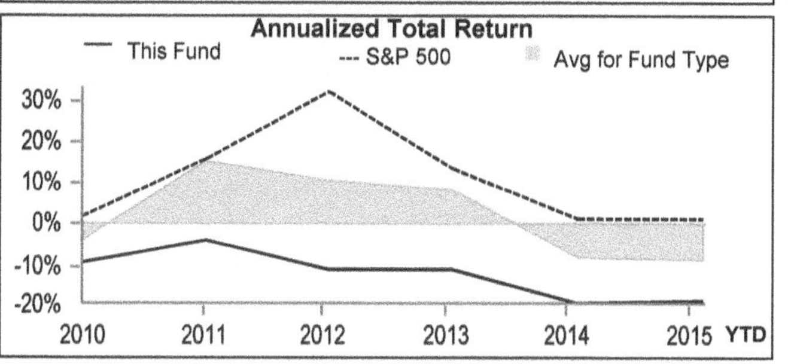

*GS Cnct S&P GSCI Enh Cmd TR Str (GSC) E+ Very Weak

Fund Family: Goldman Sachs & Co/GSAM
Fund Type: Growth
Inception Date: July 31, 2007

Major Rating Factors:
Very poor performance is the major factor driving the E+ (Very Weak) TheStreet.com Investment Rating for *GS Cnct S&P GSCI Enh Cmd TR Str. The fund currently has a performance rating of E (Very Weak) based on an annualized return of -25.19% over the last three years and a total return of -32.98% year to date 2015.

The fund's risk rating is currently C- (Fair). It carries a beta of 0.64, meaning the fund's expected move will be 6.4% for every 10% move in the market. Volatility, as measured by both the semi-deviation and a drawdown factor, is considered average. As of December 31, 2015, *GS Cnct S&P GSCI Enh Cmd TR Str traded at a price exactly equal to its net asset value, which is worse than its one-year historical average discount of .05%.

This fund has been team managed for 9 years and currently receives a manager quality ranking of 2 (0=worst, 99=best). This fund offers an average level of risk but investors looking for strong performance will be frustrated.

Data Date	Investment Rating	Net Assets ($Mil)	Price	Performance Rating/Pts	Total Return Y-T-D	Risk Rating/Pts
12-15	E+	0.00	20.08	E / 0.5	-32.98%	C- / 3.4
2014	E+	0.00	30.45	E+ / 0.6	-32.55%	C- / 3.5
2013	D	0.00	46.85	D / 2.1	-5.38%	B- / 7.2
2012	D	0.00	47.97	D / 1.9	-2.41%	B- / 7.1
2011	C-	0.00	48.88	C- / 4.2	4.26%	B- / 7.4
2010	D-	0.00	48.82	D- / 1.4	10.33%	C / 4.4

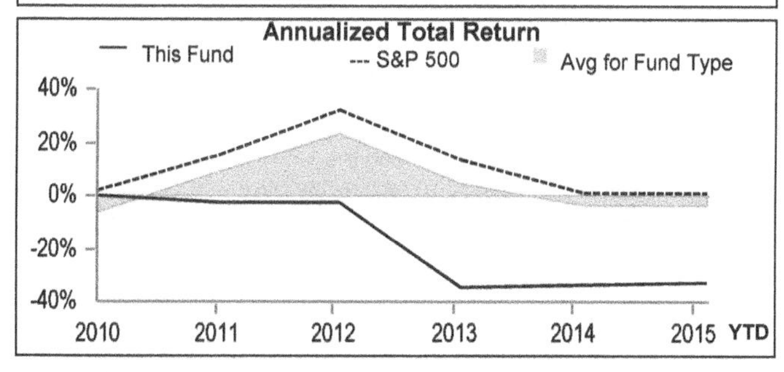

*Guggenheim Australian Dollar Tr (FXA) D Weak

Fund Family: Guggenheim Investments
Fund Type: Foreign
Inception Date: June 26, 2006

Major Rating Factors:
Disappointing performance is the major factor driving the D (Weak) TheStreet.com Investment Rating for *Guggenheim Australian Dollar Tr. The fund currently has a performance rating of D (Weak) based on an annualized return of -9.80% over the last three years and a total return of -8.61% year to date 2015. Factored into the performance evaluation is an expense ratio of 0.40% (very low).

The fund's risk rating is currently C (Fair). It carries a beta of 0.39, meaning the fund's expected move will be 3.9% for every 10% move in the market. Volatility, as measured by both the semi-deviation and a drawdown factor, is considered average. As of December 31, 2015, *Guggenheim Australian Dollar Tr traded at a premium of .18% above its net asset value, which is worse than its one-year historical average premium of .02%.

This fund has been team managed for 10 years and currently receives a manager quality ranking of 14 (0=worst, 99=best). This fund offers an average level of risk but investors looking for strong performance will be frustrated.

Data Date	Investment Rating	Net Assets ($Mil)	Price	Performance Rating/Pts	Total Return Y-T-D	Risk Rating/Pts
12-15	D	258.50	72.97	D / 2.1	-8.61%	C / 5.3
2014	D	258.50	81.73	D / 1.8	-6.87%	C+ / 5.7
2013	D+	353.90	89.43	D / 2.0	-13.12%	B / 8.0
2012	C-	582.50	104.15	C- / 3.2	5.21%	B / 8.5
2011	B-	784.40	102.62	C+ / 5.8	6.33%	B / 8.7
2010	B+	735.50	102.66	B / 7.7	18.23%	C+ / 6.4

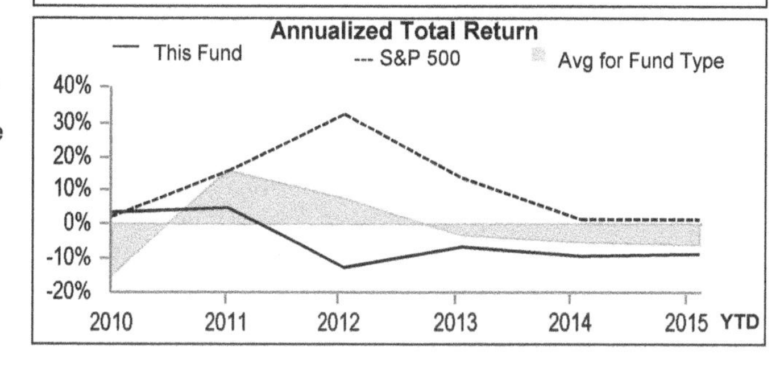

*Guggenheim BltShs 2016 Corp Bond (BSCG) B Good

Fund Family: Guggenheim Funds Investment Advisor
Fund Type: Corporate - Investment Grade
Inception Date: June 7, 2010

Major Rating Factors: *Guggenheim BltShs 2016 Corp Bond receives a TheStreet.com Investment Rating of B (Good). The fund currently has a performance rating of C (Fair) based on an annualized return of 1.20% over the last three years and a total return of 0.99% year to date 2015. Factored into the performance evaluation is an expense ratio of 0.24% (very low).

The fund's risk rating is currently B+ (Good). It carries a beta of 0.14, meaning the fund's expected move will be 1.4% for every 10% move in the market. Volatility, as measured by both the semi-deviation and a drawdown factor, is considered very low. As of December 31, 2015, *Guggenheim BltShs 2016 Corp Bond traded at a discount of .05% below its net asset value, which is better than its one-year historical average premium of .02%.

James R. King has been running the fund for 3 years and currently receives a manager quality ranking of 76 (0=worst, 99=best). If you desire an average level of risk, then this fund may be an option.

Data Date	Investment Rating	Net Assets ($Mil)	Price	Performance Rating/Pts	Total Return Y-T-D	Risk Rating/Pts
12-15	B	657.50	22.08	C / 4.9	0.99%	B+ / 9.9
2014	C+	657.50	22.10	C- / 3.5	0.56%	B+ / 9.8
2013	C+	486.40	22.29	C- / 4.2	2.18%	B+ / 9.8
2012	C	159.40	22.22	D+ / 2.7	7.03%	B+ / 9.7
2011	C	66.30	21.26	D+ / 2.9	4.99%	B+ / 9.8

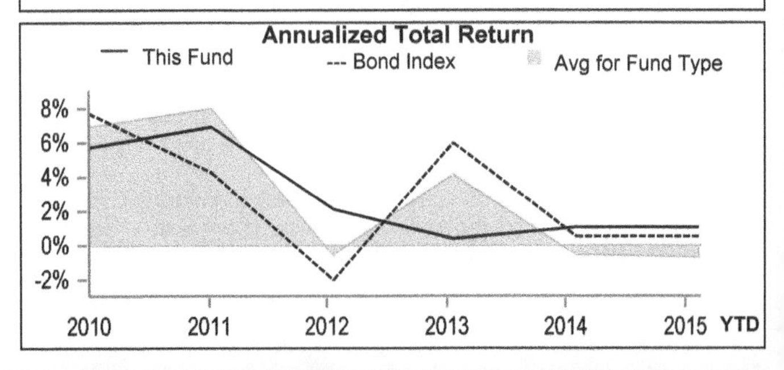

*Guggenheim BltShs 2016 Hi Yld Co (BSJG) B Good

Fund Family: Guggenheim Funds Investment Advisor
Fund Type: Corporate - High Yield
Inception Date: April 25, 2012

Major Rating Factors: *Guggenheim BltShs 2016 Hi Yld Co receives a TheStreet.com Investment Rating of B (Good). The fund currently has a performance rating of C+ (Fair) based on an annualized return of 3.15% over the last three years and a total return of 2.56% year to date 2015. Factored into the performance evaluation is an expense ratio of 0.43% (very low).

The fund's risk rating is currently B+ (Good). It carries a beta of 0.56, meaning the fund's expected move will be 5.6% for every 10% move in the market. Volatility, as measured by both the semi-deviation and a drawdown factor, is considered very low. As of December 31, 2015, *Guggenheim BltShs 2016 Hi Yld Co traded at a discount of .04% below its net asset value, which is in line with its one-year historical average discount of .04%.

James R. King has been running the fund for 3 years and currently receives a manager quality ranking of 82 (0=worst, 99=best). If you desire an average level of risk, then this fund may be an option.

Data Date	Investment Rating	Net Assets ($Mil)	Price	Performance Rating/Pts	Total Return Y-T-D	Risk Rating/Pts
12-15	B	617.10	25.87	C+ / 5.6	2.56%	B+ / 9.5
2014	C-	617.10	25.89	D+ / 2.3	-0.18%	B+ / 9.3
2013	B	374.20	27.02	C+ / 5.8	6.99%	B+ / 9.7

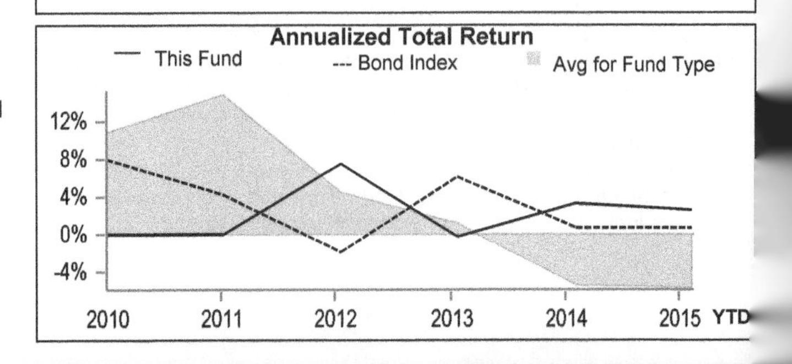

*Guggenheim BltShs 2017 Corp Bond (BSCH) B Good

Fund Family: Guggenheim Funds Investment Advisor
Fund Type: Corporate - Investment Grade
Inception Date: June 7, 2010

Major Rating Factors: *Guggenheim BltShs 2017 Corp Bond receives a TheStreet.com Investment Rating of B (Good). The fund currently has a performance rating of C (Fair) based on an annualized return of 1.26% over the last three years and a total return of 0.81% year to date 2015. Factored into the performance evaluation is an expense ratio of 0.24% (very low).

The fund's risk rating is currently B+ (Good). It carries a beta of 0.39, meaning the fund's expected move will be 3.9% for every 10% move in the market. Volatility, as measured by both the semi-deviation and a drawdown factor, is considered very low. As of December 31, 2015, *Guggenheim BltShs 2017 Corp Bond traded at a discount of .09% below its net asset value, which is better than its one-year historical average premium of .14%.

James R. King has been running the fund for 3 years and currently receives a manager quality ranking of 74 (0=worst, 99=best). If you desire an average level of risk, then this fund may be an option.

Data Date	Investment Rating	Net Assets ($Mil)	Price	Performance Rating/Pts	Total Return Y-T-D	Risk Rating/Pts
12-15	B	688.30	22.52	C / 4.9	0.81%	B+ / 9.8
2014	C-	688.30	22.71	C- / 3.8	1.66%	B- / 7.8
2013	C+	436.30	22.66	C / 4.5	1.20%	B+ / 9.7
2012	C	181.10	22.82	C- / 3.2	9.03%	B+ / 9.7
2011	C	53.90	21.32	C- / 3.0	4.99%	B+ / 9.8

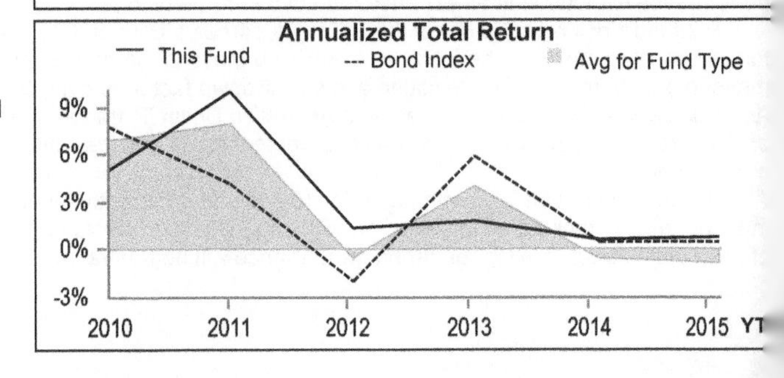

* Denotes ETF Fund

*Guggenheim BltShs 2017 Hi Yld Co (BSJH) B- Good

Fund Family: Guggenheim Funds Investment Advisor
Fund Type: Corporate - High Yield
Inception Date: April 25, 2012

Major Rating Factors: *Guggenheim BltShs 2017 Hi Yld Co receives a TheStreet.com Investment Rating of B- (Good). The fund currently has a performance rating of C (Fair) based on an annualized return of 2.13% over the last three years and a total return of -0.55% year to date 2015. Factored into the performance evaluation is an expense ratio of 0.43% (very low).

The fund's risk rating is currently B+ (Good). It carries a beta of 0.73, meaning the fund's expected move will be 7.3% for every 10% move in the market. Volatility, as measured by both the semi-deviation and a drawdown factor, is considered very low. As of December 31, 2015, *Guggenheim BltShs 2017 Hi Yld Co traded at a discount of .04% below its net asset value, which is better than its one-year historical average premium of .16%.

James R. King has been running the fund for 3 years and currently receives a manager quality ranking of 77 (0=worst, 99=best). If you desire an average level of risk, then this fund may be an option.

Data Date	Investment Rating	Net Assets ($Mil)	Price	Performance Rating/Pts	Total Return Y-T-D	Risk Rating/Pts
12-15	B-	362.50	24.96	C / 5.1	-0.55%	B+ / 9.2
2014	C-	362.50	25.95	D / 2.2	-0.48%	B+ / 9.3
2013	B	167.40	27.12	C+ / 5.9	7.29%	B+ / 9.7

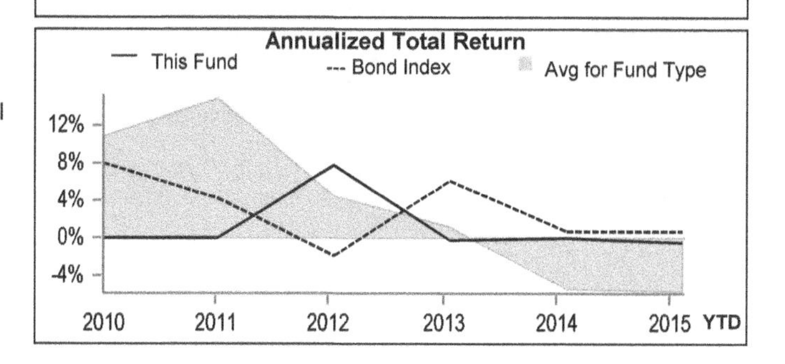

*Guggenheim BltShs 2018 Corp Bond (BSCI) C+ Fair

Fund Family: Guggenheim Funds Investment Advisor
Fund Type: Corporate - Investment Grade
Inception Date: March 28, 2012

Major Rating Factors: Middle of the road best describes *Guggenheim BltShs 2018 Corp Bond whose TheStreet.com Investment Rating is currently a C+ (Fair). The fund currently has a performance rating of C (Fair) based on an annualized return of 1.61% over the last three years and a total return of 1.40% year to date 2015. Factored into the performance evaluation is an expense ratio of 0.24% (very low).

The fund's risk rating is currently B- (Good). It carries a beta of 0.50, meaning the fund's expected move will be 5.0% for every 10% move in the market. Volatility, as measured by both the semi-deviation and a drawdown factor, is considered low. As of December 31, 2015, *Guggenheim BltShs 2018 Corp Bond traded at a premium of .29% above its net asset value, which is worse than its one-year historical average premium of .26%.

James R. King has been running the fund for 3 years and currently receives a manager quality ranking of 75 (0=worst, 99=best). If you desire an average level of risk, then this fund may be an option.

Data Date	Investment Rating	Net Assets ($Mil)	Price	Performance Rating/Pts	Total Return Y-T-D	Risk Rating/Pts
12-15	C+	410.60	21.02	C / 5.1	1.40%	B- / 7.9
2014	C-	410.60	21.12	C- / 3.3	2.37%	B- / 7.9
2013	C+	193.60	20.93	C- / 3.5	0.98%	B+ / 9.7

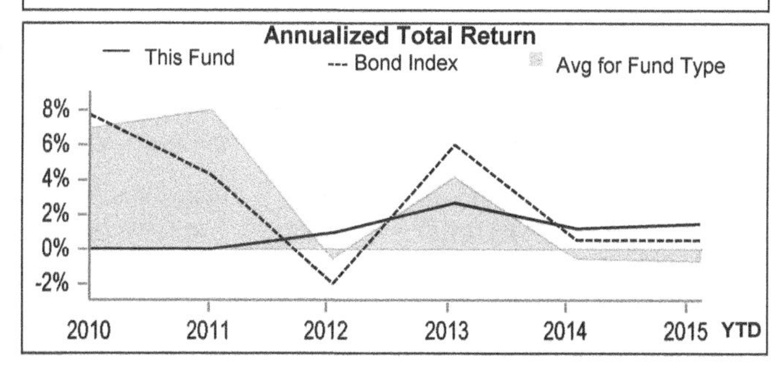

*Guggenheim BltShs 2018 Hi Yld Co (BSJI) C+ Fair

Fund Family: Guggenheim Funds Investment Advisor
Fund Type: Corporate - High Yield
Inception Date: April 25, 2012

Major Rating Factors: Middle of the road best describes *Guggenheim BltShs 2018 Hi Yld Co whose TheStreet.com Investment Rating is currently a C+ (Fair). The fund currently has a performance rating of C- (Fair) based on an annualized return of 1.19% over the last three years and a total return of -4.16% year to date 2015. Factored into the performance evaluation is an expense ratio of 0.43% (very low).

The fund's risk rating is currently B (Good). It carries a beta of 0.80, meaning the fund's expected move will be 8.0% for every 10% move in the market. Volatility, as measured by both the semi-deviation and a drawdown factor, is considered low. As of December 31, 2015, *Guggenheim BltShs 2018 Hi Yld Co traded at a discount of .38% below its net asset value, which is better than its one-year historical average premium of .18%.

Saroj Kanuri has been running the fund for 4 years and currently receives a manager quality ranking of 70 (0=worst, 99=best). If you desire an average level of risk, then this fund may be an option.

Data Date	Investment Rating	Net Assets ($Mil)	Price	Performance Rating/Pts	Total Return Y-T-D	Risk Rating/Pts
12-15	C+	271.50	23.66	C- / 4.1	-4.16%	B / 8.8
2013	B	150.30	26.96	C+ / 6.2	8.02%	B+ / 9.7

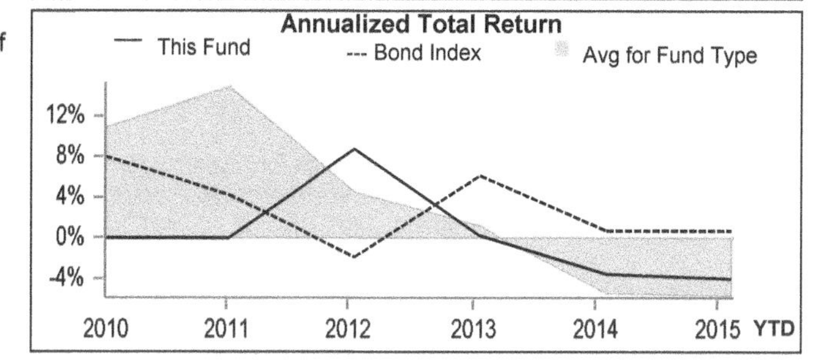

*Guggenheim BltShs 2019 Corp Bond (BSCJ) C+ Fair

Fund Family: Guggenheim Funds Investment Advisor
Fund Type: Corporate - Investment Grade
Inception Date: March 28, 2012

Major Rating Factors: Middle of the road best describes *Guggenheim BltShs 2019 Corp Bond whose TheStreet.com Investment Rating is currently a C+ (Fair). The fund currently has a performance rating of C (Fair) based on an annualized return of 1.77% over the last three years and a total return of 1.46% year to date 2015. Factored into the performance evaluation is an expense ratio of 0.24% (very low).

The fund's risk rating is currently B- (Good). It carries a beta of 0.67, meaning the fund's expected move will be 6.7% for every 10% move in the market. Volatility, as measured by both the semi-deviation and a drawdown factor, is considered low. As of December 31, 2015, *Guggenheim BltShs 2019 Corp Bond traded at a premium of .14% above its net asset value, which is better than its one-year historical average premium of .27%.

SAROJ KANURI has been running the fund for 4 years and currently receives a manager quality ranking of 75 (0=worst, 99=best). If you desire an average level of risk, then this fund may be an option.

Data Date	Investment Rating	Net Assets ($Mil)	Price	Perfor-mance Rating/Pts	Total Return Y-T-D	Risk Rating/Pts
12-15	C+	200.90	20.86	C / 5.2	1.46%	B- / 7.8
2014	C	200.90	20.91	C- / 3.4	3.46%	B+ / 9.6
2013	C	92.50	20.57	C- / 3.3	0.16%	B+ / 9.6

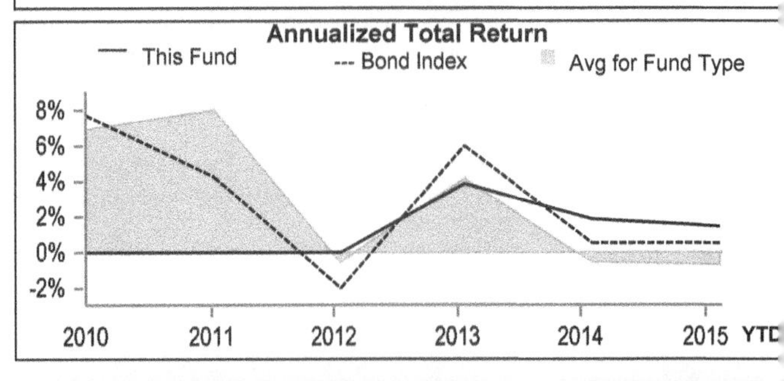

*Guggenheim BltShs 2019 Hi Yld Co (BSJJ) C- Fair

Fund Family: Guggenheim Funds Investment Advisor
Fund Type: Corporate - High Yield
Inception Date: September 24, 2013

Major Rating Factors:
Disappointing performance is the major factor driving the C- (Fair) TheStreet.com Investment Rating for *Guggenheim BltShs 2019 Hi Yld Co. The fund currently has a performance rating of D+ (Weak) based on an annualized return of 0.00% over the last three years and a total return of -4.80% year to date 2015. Factored into the performance evaluation is an expense ratio of 0.43% (very low).

The fund's risk rating is currently B (Good). It carries a beta of 0.00, meaning the fund's expected move will be 0.0% for every 10% move in the market. Volatility, as measured by both the semi-deviation and a drawdown factor, is considered low. As of December 31, 2015, *Guggenheim BltShs 2019 Hi Yld Co traded at a discount of .26% below its net asset value, which is better than its one-year historical average premium of .20%.

James R. King has been running the fund for 3 years and currently receives a manager quality ranking of 68 (0=worst, 99=best). This fund offers only a moderate level of risk but investors looking for strong performance are still waiting.

Data Date	Investment Rating	Net Assets ($Mil)	Price	Perfor-mance Rating/Pts	Total Return Y-T-D	Risk Rating/Pts
12-15	C-	71.80	22.73	D+ / 2.4	-4.80%	B / 8.6
2014	D+	71.80	24.90	D+ / 2.3	0.26%	B- / 7.8

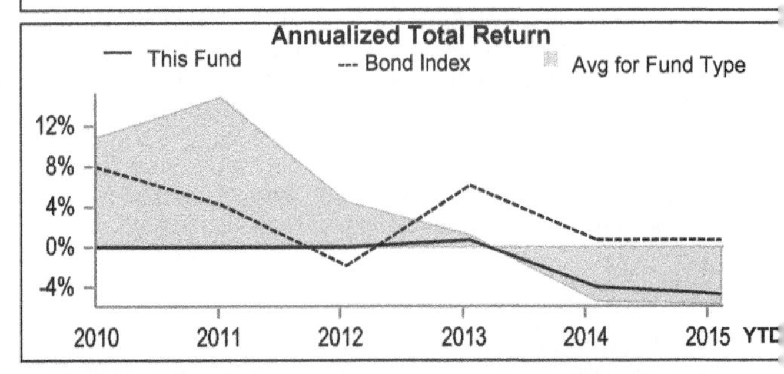

*Guggenheim BltShs 2020 Corp Bond (BSCK) C+ Fair

Fund Family: Guggenheim Funds Investment Advisor
Fund Type: Corporate - Investment Grade
Inception Date: March 28, 2012

Major Rating Factors: Middle of the road best describes *Guggenheim BltShs 2020 Corp Bond whose TheStreet.com Investment Rating is currently a C+ (Fair). The fund currently has a performance rating of C (Fair) based on an annualized return of 2.14% over the last three years and a total return of 1.39% year to date 2015. Factored into the performance evaluation is an expense ratio of 0.24% (very low).

The fund's risk rating is currently B- (Good). It carries a beta of 0.84, meaning the fund's expected move will be 8.4% for every 10% move in the market. Volatility, as measured by both the semi-deviation and a drawdown factor, is considered low. As of December 31, 2015, *Guggenheim BltShs 2020 Corp Bond traded at a premium of .24% above its net asset value, which is better than its one-year historical average premium of .29%.

James R. King has been running the fund for 3 years and currently receives a manager quality ranking of 74 (0=worst, 99=best). If you desire an average level of risk, then this fund may be an option.

Data Date	Investment Rating	Net Assets ($Mil)	Price	Perfor-mance Rating/Pts	Total Return Y-T-D	Risk Rating/Pts
12-15	C+	176.40	20.89	C / 5.2	1.39%	B- / 7.7
2014	C-	176.40	21.09	C- / 3.7	4.51%	B- / 7.6
2013	C	79.90	20.54	C- / 3.5	0.22%	B+ / 9.5

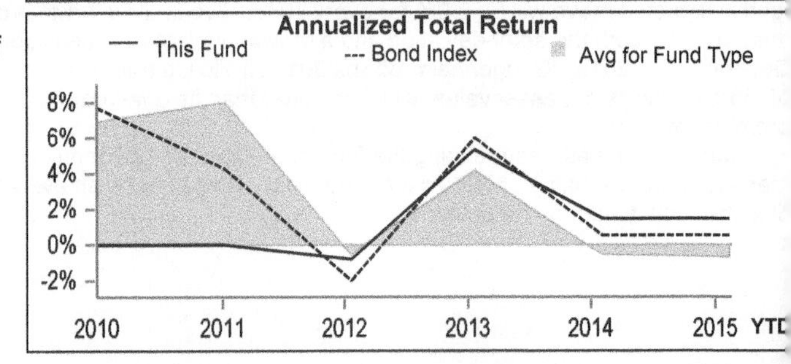

*Guggenheim BltShs 2020 Hi Yld Co (BSJK) C- Fair

Fund Family: Guggenheim Funds Investment Advisor
Fund Type: Corporate - High Yield
Inception Date: September 24, 2013

Data Date	Investment Rating	Net Assets ($Mil)	Price	Performance Rating/Pts	Total Return Y-T-D	Risk Rating/Pts
12-15	C-	33.50	22.52	D / 2.1	-6.03%	B / 8.5
2014	C-	33.50	25.00	D+ / 2.4	1.40%	B / 8.9

Major Rating Factors:
Disappointing performance is the major factor driving the C- (Fair) TheStreet.com Investment Rating for *Guggenheim BltShs 2020 Hi Yld Co. The fund currently has a performance rating of D (Weak) based on an annualized return of 0.00% over the last three years and a total return of -6.03% year to date 2015. Factored into the performance evaluation is an expense ratio of 0.43% (very low).

The fund's risk rating is currently B (Good). It carries a beta of 0.00, meaning the fund's expected move will be 0.0% for every 10% move in the market. Volatility, as measured by both the semi-deviation and a drawdown factor, is considered low. As of December 31, 2015, *Guggenheim BltShs 2020 Hi Yld Co traded at a discount of .27% below its net asset value, which is better than its one-year historical average premium of .25%.

James R. King has been running the fund for 3 years and currently receives a manager quality ranking of 67 (0=worst, 99=best). This fund offers only a moderate level of risk but investors looking for strong performance are still waiting.

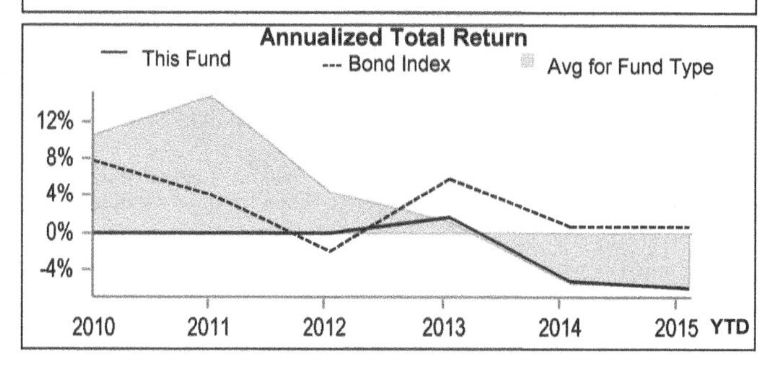

*Guggenheim BltShs 2021 Corp Bond (BSCL) C Fair

Fund Family: Guggenheim Funds Investment Advisor
Fund Type: Corporate - Investment Grade
Inception Date: July 17, 2013

Data Date	Investment Rating	Net Assets ($Mil)	Price	Performance Rating/Pts	Total Return Y-T-D	Risk Rating/Pts
12-15	C	68.40	20.52	C- / 4.2	0.47%	B- / 7.9
2014	C	68.40	20.86	C / 4.3	7.00%	B / 8.1

Major Rating Factors: Middle of the road best describes *Guggenheim BltShs 2021 Corp Bond whose TheStreet.com Investment Rating is currently a C (Fair). The fund currently has a performance rating of C- (Fair) based on an annualized return of 0.00% over the last three years and a total return of 0.47% year to date 2015. Factored into the performance evaluation is an expense ratio of 0.24% (very low).

The fund's risk rating is currently B- (Good). It carries a beta of 0.00, meaning the fund's expected move will be 0.0% for every 10% move in the market. Volatility, as measured by both the semi-deviation and a drawdown factor, is considered low. As of December 31, 2015, *Guggenheim BltShs 2021 Corp Bond traded at a premium of .39% above its net asset value, which is worse than its one-year historical average premium of .28%.

James R. King has been running the fund for 3 years and currently receives a manager quality ranking of 79 (0=worst, 99=best). If you desire an average level of risk, then this fund may be an option.

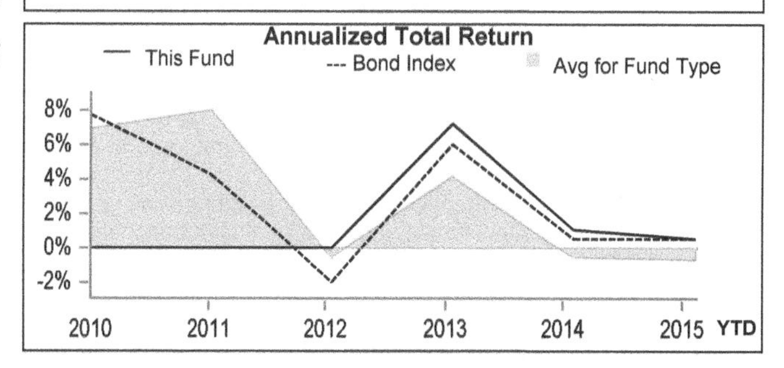

*Guggenheim BltShs 2021 Hi Yld Co (BSJL) C- Fair

Fund Family: Guggenheim Funds Investment Advisor
Fund Type: Corporate - High Yield
Inception Date: September 17, 2014

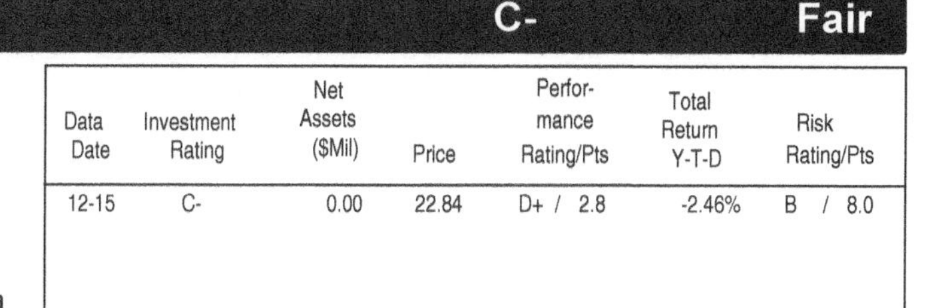

Data Date	Investment Rating	Net Assets ($Mil)	Price	Performance Rating/Pts	Total Return Y-T-D	Risk Rating/Pts
12-15	C-	0.00	22.84	D+ / 2.8	-2.46%	B / 8.0

Major Rating Factors:
Disappointing performance is the major factor driving the C- (Fair) TheStreet.com Investment Rating for *Guggenheim BltShs 2021 Hi Yld Co. The fund currently has a performance rating of D+ (Weak) based on an annualized return of 0.00% over the last three years and a total return of -2.46% year to date 2015. Factored into the performance evaluation is an expense ratio of 0.43% (very low).

The fund's risk rating is currently B (Good). It carries a beta of 0.00, meaning the fund's expected move will be 0.0% for every 10% move in the market. Volatility, as measured by both the semi-deviation and a drawdown factor, is considered low. As of December 31, 2015, *Guggenheim BltShs 2021 Hi Yld Co traded at a price exactly equal to its net asset value, which is better than its one-year historical average premium of .23%.

Michael P. Byrum currently receives a manager quality ranking of 84 (0=worst, 99=best). This fund offers only a moderate level of risk but investors looking for strong performance are still waiting.

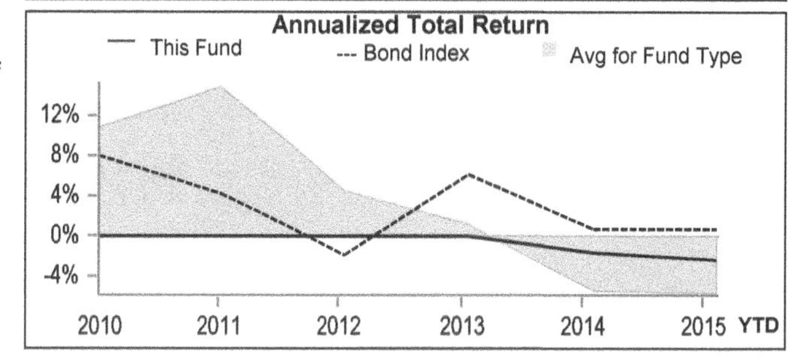

* Denotes ETF Fund

*Guggenheim BltShs 2022 Corp Bond (BSCM) C Fair

Fund Family: Guggenheim Funds Investment Advisor
Fund Type: Corporate - Investment Grade
Inception Date: July 17, 2013

Major Rating Factors: Middle of the road best describes *Guggenheim BltShs 2022 Corp Bond whose TheStreet.com Investment Rating is currently a C (Fair). The fund currently has a performance rating of C- (Fair) based on an annualized return of 0.00% over the last three years and a total return of 0.01% year to date 2015. Factored into the performance evaluation is an expense ratio of 0.24% (very low).

The fund's risk rating is currently B- (Good). It carries a beta of 0.00, meaning the fund's expected move will be 0.0% for every 10% move in the market. Volatility, as measured by both the semi-deviation and a drawdown factor, is considered low. As of December 31, 2015, *Guggenheim BltShs 2022 Corp Bond traded at a premium of .25% above its net asset value, which is worse than its one-year historical average premium of .18%.

James R. King has been running the fund for 3 years and currently receives a manager quality ranking of 76 (0=worst, 99=best). If you desire an average level of risk, then this fund may be an option.

Data Date	Investment Rating	Net Assets ($Mil)	Price	Performance Rating/Pts	Total Return Y-T-D	Risk Rating/Pts
12-15	C	55.60	20.29	C- / 4.0	0.01%	B- / 7.8
2014	C	55.60	20.79	C / 4.4	7.10%	B / 8.3

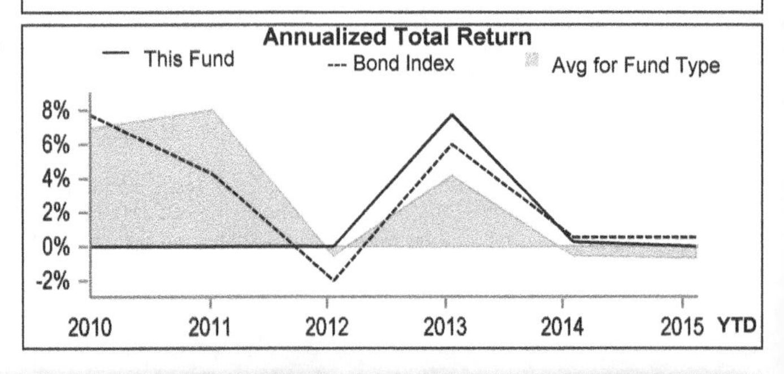

*Guggenheim BltShs 2022 Hi Yld Co (BSJM) C Fair

Fund Family: Guggenheim Funds Investment Advisor
Fund Type: Corporate - High Yield
Inception Date: September 17, 2014

Major Rating Factors:
Disappointing performance is the major factor driving the C (Fair) TheStreet.com Investment Rating for *Guggenheim BltShs 2022 Hi Yld Co. The fund currently has a performance rating of D+ (Weak) based on an annualized return of 0.00% over the last three years and a total return of -3.38% year to date 2015. Factored into the performance evaluation is an expense ratio of 0.43% (very low).

The fund's risk rating is currently B (Good). It carries a beta of 0.00, meaning the fund's expected move will be 0.0% for every 10% move in the market. Volatility, as measured by both the semi-deviation and a drawdown factor, is considered low. As of December 31, 2015, *Guggenheim BltShs 2022 Hi Yld Co traded at a discount of .44% below its net asset value, which is better than its one-year historical average premium of .22%.

Michael P. Byrum currently receives a manager quality ranking of 81 (0=worst, 99=best). This fund offers only a moderate level of risk but investors looking for strong performance are still waiting.

Data Date	Investment Rating	Net Assets ($Mil)	Price	Performance Rating/Pts	Total Return Y-T-D	Risk Rating/Pts
12-15	C	0.00	22.57	D+ / 2.6	-3.38%	B / 8.7

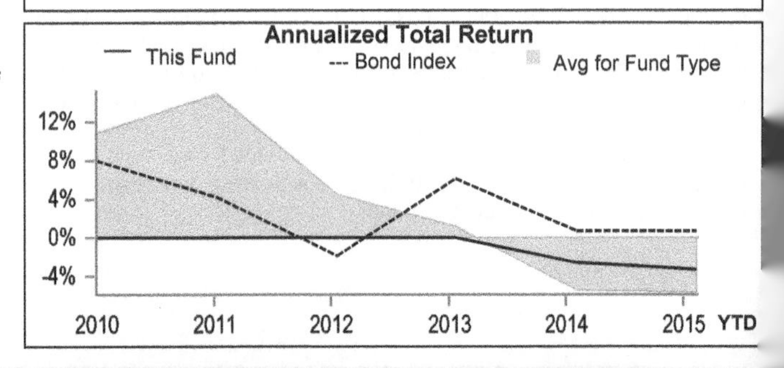

*Guggenheim BltShs 2023 Corp Bond (BSCN) C Fair

Fund Family: Guggenheim Funds Investment Advisor
Fund Type: Corporate - Investment Grade
Inception Date: September 17, 2014

Major Rating Factors: Middle of the road best describes *Guggenheim BltShs 2023 Corp Bond whose TheStreet.com Investment Rating is currently a C (Fair). The fund currently has a performance rating of C- (Fair) based on an annualized return of 0.00% over the last three years and a total return of -0.62% year to date 2015. Factored into the performance evaluation is an expense ratio of 0.24% (very low).

The fund's risk rating is currently B- (Good). It carries a beta of 0.00, meaning the fund's expected move will be 0.0% for every 10% move in the market. Volatility, as measured by both the semi-deviation and a drawdown factor, is considered low. As of December 31, 2015, *Guggenheim BltShs 2023 Corp Bond traded at a premium of .35% above its net asset value, which is better than its one-year historical average premium of .47%.

Jie Du has been running the fund for 2 years and currently receives a manager quality ranking of 79 (0=worst, 99=best). If you desire an average level of risk, then this fund may be an option.

Data Date	Investment Rating	Net Assets ($Mil)	Price	Performance Rating/Pts	Total Return Y-T-D	Risk Rating/Pts
12-15	C	0.00	19.93	C- / 3.9	-0.62%	B- / 7.8

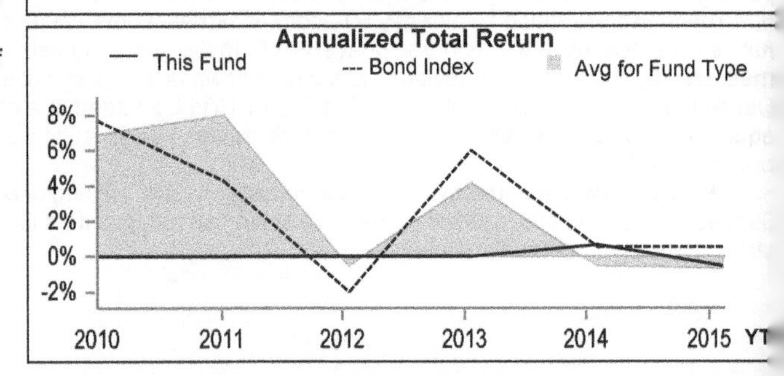

*Guggenheim BltShs 2024 Corp Bond (BSCO) C Fair

Fund Family: Guggenheim Funds Investment Advisor
Fund Type: Corporate - Investment Grade
Inception Date: September 17, 2014

Data Date	Investment Rating	Net Assets ($Mil)	Price	Performance Rating/Pts	Total Return Y-T-D	Risk Rating/Pts
12-15	C	0.00	19.77	C- / 3.8	-1.24%	B / 8.4

Major Rating Factors: Middle of the road best describes *Guggenheim BltShs 2024 Corp Bond whose TheStreet.com Investment Rating is currently a C (Fair). The fund currently has a performance rating of C- (Fair) based on an annualized return of 0.00% over the last three years and a total return of -1.24% year to date 2015. Factored into the performance evaluation is an expense ratio of 0.24% (very low).

The fund's risk rating is currently B (Good). It carries a beta of 0.00, meaning the fund's expected move will be 0.0% for every 10% move in the market. Volatility, as measured by both the semi-deviation and a drawdown factor, is considered low. As of December 31, 2015, *Guggenheim BltShs 2024 Corp Bond traded at a price exactly equal to its net asset value, which is better than its one-year historical average premium of .24%.

Jie Du has been running the fund for 2 years and currently receives a manager quality ranking of 75 (0=worst, 99=best). If you desire an average level of risk, then this fund may be an option.

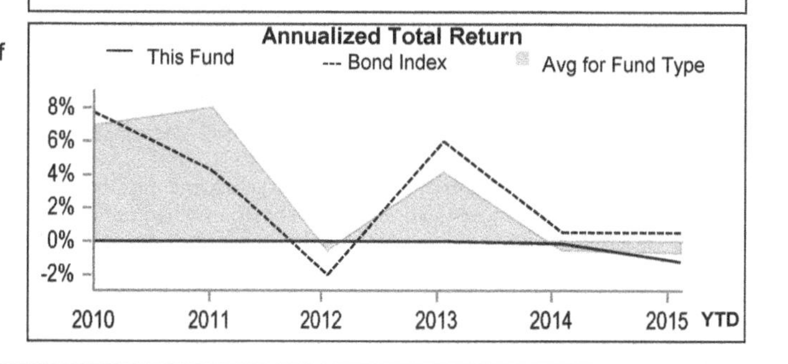

*Guggenheim BRIC ETF (EEB) D Weak

Fund Family: Guggenheim Funds Investment Advisor
Fund Type: Income
Inception Date: September 21, 2006

Data Date	Investment Rating	Net Assets ($Mil)	Price	Performance Rating/Pts	Total Return Y-T-D	Risk Rating/Pts
12-15	D	162.00	24.34	D / 1.8	-12.73%	C+ / 6.0
2014	D	162.00	28.57	D / 1.7	-10.69%	C+ / 6.0
2013	D	212.90	34.65	D / 1.6	-6.75%	C+ / 6.2
2012	D	320.50	36.02	D- / 1.4	1.18%	C+ / 6.5
2011	C-	418.90	35.03	C / 4.6	-17.98%	B- / 7.0
2010	D	1,054.70	46.14	C- / 3.5	10.49%	C- / 4.2

Major Rating Factors:
Disappointing performance is the major factor driving the D (Weak) TheStreet.com Investment Rating for *Guggenheim BRIC ETF. The fund currently has a performance rating of D (Weak) based on an annualized return of -10.58% over the last three years and a total return of -12.73% year to date 2015. Factored into the performance evaluation is an expense ratio of 0.64% (very low).

The fund's risk rating is currently C+ (Fair). It carries a beta of 1.23, meaning it is expected to move 12.3% for every 10% move in the market. Volatility, as measured by both the semi-deviation and a drawdown factor, is considered low. As of December 31, 2015, *Guggenheim BRIC ETF traded at a discount of .08% below its net asset value, which is worse than its one-year historical average discount of .23%.

James R. King has been running the fund for 3 years and currently receives a manager quality ranking of 5 (0=worst, 99=best). This fund offers only a moderate level of risk but investors looking for strong performance are still waiting.

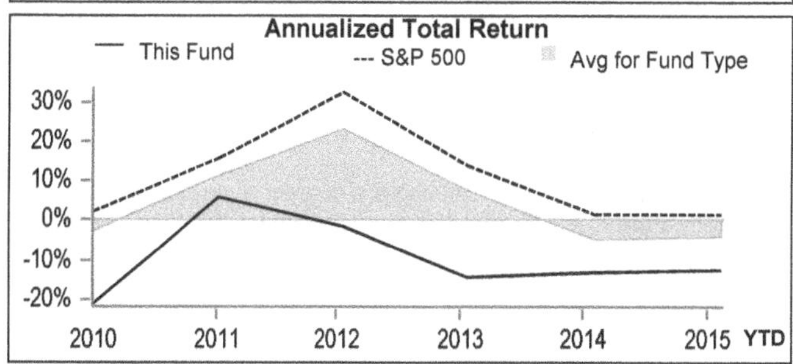

*Guggenheim British Pound Sterlin (FXB) C- Fair

Fund Family: Guggenheim Investments
Fund Type: Foreign
Inception Date: June 26, 2006

Data Date	Investment Rating	Net Assets ($Mil)	Price	Performance Rating/Pts	Total Return Y-T-D	Risk Rating/Pts
12-15	C-	87.70	144.32	C- / 3.1	-4.18%	B- / 7.7
2014	D+	87.70	153.06	D+ / 2.4	-5.34%	B- / 7.1
2013	C	57.10	163.30	C- / 3.4	1.70%	B+ / 9.0
2012	D+	64.30	160.71	D- / 1.4	4.88%	B / 8.9
2011	C-	92.50	154.10	D / 1.9	-1.00%	B / 8.8
2010	D+	124.50	155.77	D- / 1.0	-3.33%	B- / 7.1

Major Rating Factors: Middle of the road best describes *Guggenheim British Pound Sterlin whose TheStreet.com Investment Rating is currently a C- (Fair). The fund currently has a performance rating of C- (Fair) based on an annualized return of -3.18% over the last three years and a total return of -4.18% year to date 2015. Factored into the performance evaluation is an expense ratio of 0.40% (very low).

The fund's risk rating is currently B- (Good). It carries a beta of 0.29, meaning the fund's expected move will be 2.9% for every 10% move in the market. Volatility, as measured by both the semi-deviation and a drawdown factor, is considered low. As of December 31, 2015, *Guggenheim British Pound Sterlin traded at a premium of .01% above its net asset value, which is in line with its one-year historical average premium of .01%.

This fund has been team managed for 10 years and currently receives a manager quality ranking of 30 (0=worst, 99=best). If you desire an average level of risk, then this fund may be an option.

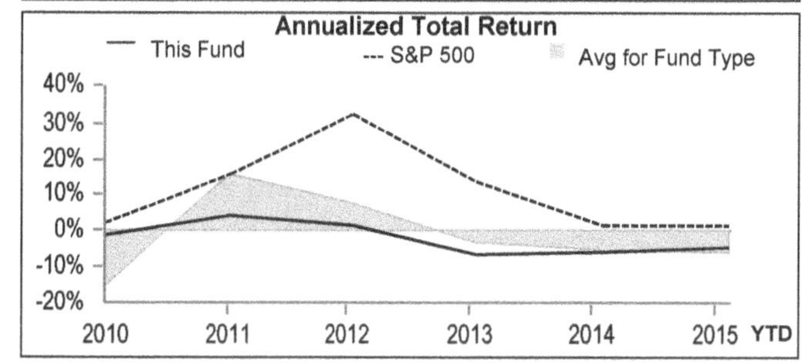

* Denotes ETF Fund

*Guggenheim Canadian Dollar Tr (FXC) D Weak

Fund Family: Guggenheim Investments
Fund Type: Foreign
Inception Date: June 26, 2006

Major Rating Factors:
Disappointing performance is the major factor driving the D (Weak) TheStreet.com Investment Rating for *Guggenheim Canadian Dollar Tr. The fund currently has a performance rating of D (Weak) based on an annualized return of -10.59% over the last three years and a total return of -15.21% year to date 2015. Factored into the performance evaluation is an expense ratio of 0.40% (very low).

The fund's risk rating is currently C+ (Fair). It carries a beta of 0.35, meaning the fund's expected move will be 3.5% for every 10% move in the market. Volatility, as measured by both the semi-deviation and a drawdown factor, is considered low. As of December 31, 2015, *Guggenheim Canadian Dollar Tr traded at a premium of .35% above its net asset value, which is worse than its one-year historical average discount of .01%.

This fund has been team managed for 10 years and currently receives a manager quality ranking of 13 (0=worst, 99=best). This fund offers only a moderate level of risk but investors looking for strong performance are still waiting.

Data Date	Investment Rating	Net Assets ($Mil)	Price	Performance Rating/Pts	Total Return Y-T-D	Risk Rating/Pts
12-15	D	258.10	71.67	D / 1.7	-15.21%	C+ / 5.7
2014	D	258.10	85.54	D / 2.0	-8.25%	C+ / 6.6
2013	C-	308.90	93.61	D / 2.0	-7.05%	B / 8.9
2012	C-	499.40	100.14	D / 1.8	4.00%	B+ / 9.0
2011	C-	576.20	97.62	D+ / 2.5	-3.32%	B+ / 9.0
2010	C	590.50	99.54	C- / 3.0	4.97%	B- / 7.4

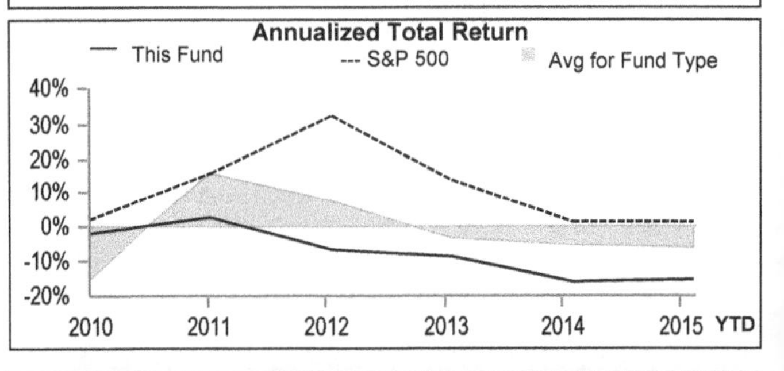

*Guggenheim Canadian Energy Inc E (ENY) E+ Very Weak

Fund Family: Guggenheim Funds Investment Advisor
Fund Type: Energy/Natural Resources
Inception Date: July 3, 2007

Major Rating Factors:
Very poor performance is the major factor driving the E+ (Very Weak) TheStreet.com Investment Rating for *Guggenheim Canadian Energy Inc E. The fund currently has a performance rating of E+ (Very Weak) based on an annualized return of -22.19% over the last three years and a total return of -40.25% year to date 2015. Factored into the performance evaluation is an expense ratio of 0.70% (very low).

The fund's risk rating is currently C- (Fair). It carries a beta of 1.23, meaning it is expected to move 12.3% for every 10% move in the market. Volatility, as measured by both the semi-deviation and a drawdown factor, is considered average. As of December 31, 2015, *Guggenheim Canadian Energy Inc E traded at a premium of .30% above its net asset value, which is worse than its one-year historical average discount of .08%.

Saroj Kanuri has been running the fund for 6 years and currently receives a manager quality ranking of 8 (0=worst, 99=best). This fund offers an average level of risk but investors looking for strong performance will be frustrated.

Data Date	Investment Rating	Net Assets ($Mil)	Price	Performance Rating/Pts	Total Return Y-T-D	Risk Rating/Pts
12-15	E+	40.80	6.77	E+ / 0.6	-40.25%	C- / 3.5
2014	D	40.80	11.75	D- / 1.0	-16.77%	C+ / 6.5
2013	D	46.10	14.71	D- / 1.5	-5.05%	C+ / 6.1
2012	D-	75.60	15.52	D- / 1.2	-3.91%	C+ / 6.3
2011	C-	114.70	16.85	C / 5.0	-12.19%	C+ / 6.4
2010	D	97.90	20.15	C- / 4.0	22.45%	C- / 3.6

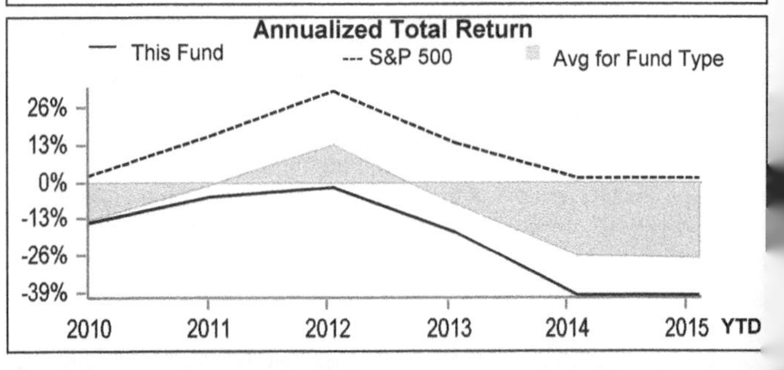

*Guggenheim China All-Cap ETF (YAO) C- Fair

Fund Family: Guggenheim Funds Investment Advisor
Fund Type: Foreign
Inception Date: October 19, 2009

Major Rating Factors: Middle of the road best describes *Guggenheim China All-Cap ETF whose TheStreet.com Investment Rating is currently a C- (Fair). The fund currently has a performance rating of C- (Fair) based on an annualized return of 0.66% over the last three years and a total return of -7.01% year to date 2015. Factored into the performance evaluation is an expense ratio of 0.70% (very low).

The fund's risk rating is currently C+ (Fair). It carries a beta of 1.00, meaning that its performance tracks fairly well with that of the overall stock market. Volatility, as measured by both the semi-deviation and a drawdown factor, is considered low. As of December 31, 2015, *Guggenheim China All-Cap ETF traded at a discount of .44% below its net asset value, which is better than its one-year historical average discount of .17%.

James R. King has been running the fund for 3 years and currently receives a manager quality ranking of 39 (0=worst, 99=best). If you desire an average level of risk, then this fund may be an option.

Data Date	Investment Rating	Net Assets ($Mil)	Price	Performance Rating/Pts	Total Return Y-T-D	Risk Rating/Pts
12-15	C-	51.10	24.95	C- / 3.8	-7.01%	C+ / 6.7
2014	C+	51.10	27.70	C+ / 5.8	6.42%	B- / 7.8
2013	D+	53.80	27.27	C- / 3.3	1.70%	C+ / 6.3
2012	D+	55.30	25.54	C- / 3.2	18.55%	C+ / 6.4
2011	D-	53.80	21.35	E+ / 0.8	-20.98%	C+ / 6.5
2010	A	84.10	27.16	B / 8.1	8.81%	B- / 7.9

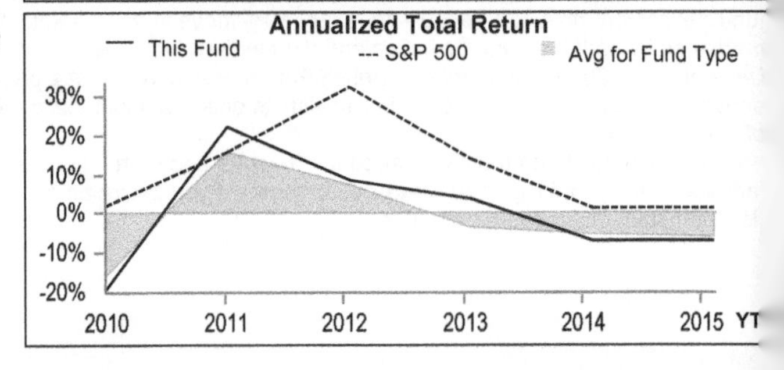

*Guggenheim China Real Estate ETF (TAO) C- Fair

Fund Family: Guggenheim Funds Investment Advisor
Fund Type: Growth and Income
Inception Date: December 18, 2007

Major Rating Factors: Middle of the road best describes *Guggenheim China Real Estate ETF whose TheStreet.com Investment Rating is currently a C- (Fair). The fund currently has a performance rating of C- (Fair) based on an annualized return of -2.23% over the last three years and a total return of -2.49% year to date 2015. Factored into the performance evaluation is an expense ratio of 0.70% (very low).

The fund's risk rating is currently B- (Good). It carries a beta of 0.68, meaning the fund's expected move will be 6.8% for every 10% move in the market. Volatility, as measured by both the semi-deviation and a drawdown factor, is considered low. As of December 31, 2015, *Guggenheim China Real Estate ETF traded at a discount of 1.49% below its net asset value, which is better than its one-year historical average discount of .38%.

Saroj Kanuri has been running the fund for 6 years and currently receives a manager quality ranking of 16 (0=worst, 99=best). If you desire an average level of risk, then this fund may be an option.

Data Date	Investment Rating	Net Assets ($Mil)	Price	Performance Rating/Pts	Total Return Y-T-D	Risk Rating/Pts
12-15	C-	38.10	19.80	C- / 3.4	-2.49%	B- / 7.1
2014	C+	38.10	20.87	B- / 7.0	8.96%	B- / 7.2
2013	D	32.20	20.06	D / 2.0	-14.35%	C+ / 5.9
2012	B	79.60	22.85	A / 9.3	57.22%	C+ / 6.0
2011	D	17.90	14.64	C- / 3.2	-29.69%	C+ / 6.1
2010	D-	65.40	19.94	D / 2.0	10.10%	C- / 4.0

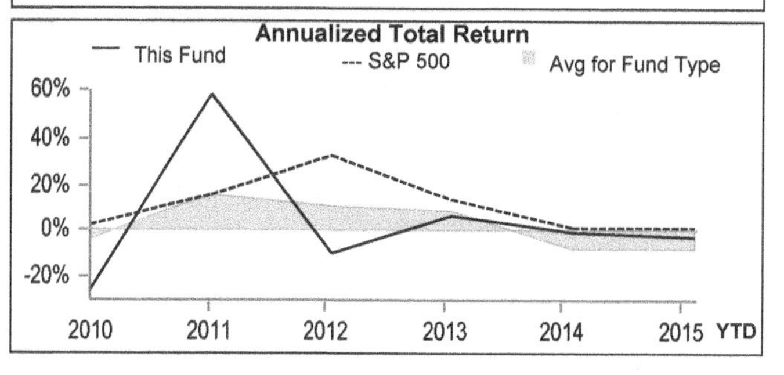

*Guggenheim China Small Cap ETF (HAO) C- Fair

Fund Family: Guggenheim Funds Investment Advisor
Fund Type: Foreign
Inception Date: January 30, 2008

Major Rating Factors: Middle of the road best describes *Guggenheim China Small Cap ETF whose TheStreet.com Investment Rating is currently a C- (Fair). The fund currently has a performance rating of C- (Fair) based on an annualized return of 1.43% over the last three years and a total return of -3.61% year to date 2015. Factored into the performance evaluation is an expense ratio of 0.75% (very low).

The fund's risk rating is currently C+ (Fair). It carries a beta of 0.92, meaning that its performance tracks fairly well with that of the overall stock market. Volatility, as measured by both the semi-deviation and a drawdown factor, is considered low. As of December 31, 2015, *Guggenheim China Small Cap ETF traded at a discount of .98% below its net asset value, which is better than its one-year historical average discount of .36%.

Saroj Kanuri has been running the fund for 6 years and currently receives a manager quality ranking of 52 (0=worst, 99=best). If you desire an average level of risk, then this fund may be an option.

Data Date	Investment Rating	Net Assets ($Mil)	Price	Performance Rating/Pts	Total Return Y-T-D	Risk Rating/Pts
12-15	C-	213.40	24.18	C- / 4.0	-3.61%	C+ / 6.3
2014	C+	213.40	25.99	C+ / 5.7	-1.53%	B- / 7.4
2013	D	265.10	26.60	D+ / 2.8	7.17%	C / 5.5
2012	D-	302.20	23.99	D+ / 2.8	28.51%	C / 4.3
2011	D-	142.00	19.30	C- / 3.2	-36.56%	C / 4.4
2010	B-	438.70	30.06	B+ / 8.9	15.32%	C- / 3.7

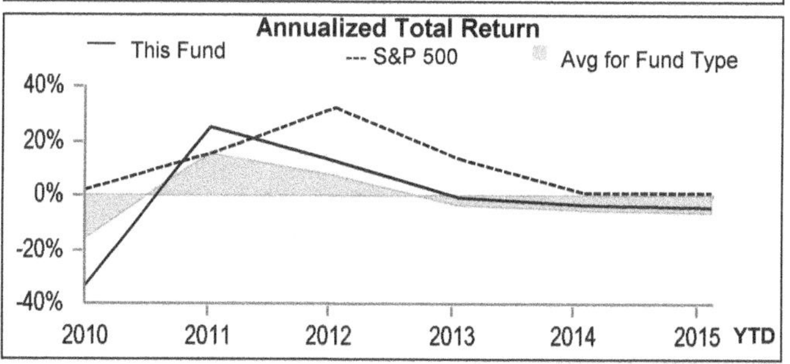

*Guggenheim China Technology ETF (CQQQ) B+ Good

Fund Family: Guggenheim Funds Investment Advisor
Fund Type: Foreign
Inception Date: December 8, 2009

Major Rating Factors:
Exceptional performance is the major factor driving the B+ (Good) TheStreet.com Investment Rating for *Guggenheim China Technology ETF. The fund currently has a performance rating of A (Excellent) based on an annualized return of 17.07% over the last three years and a total return of 6.28% year to date 2015. Factored into the performance evaluation is an expense ratio of 0.70% (very low).

The fund's risk rating is currently C+ (Fair). It carries a beta of 1.17, meaning it is expected to move 11.7% for every 10% move in the market. Volatility, as measured by both the semi-deviation and a drawdown factor, is considered low. As of December 31, 2015, *Guggenheim China Technology ETF traded at a discount of .55% below its net asset value, which is better than its one-year historical average discount of .33%.

James R. King has been running the fund for 3 years and currently receives a manager quality ranking of 96 (0=worst, 99=best). If you desire only a moderate level of risk and strong performance, then this fund is an excellent option.

Data Date	Investment Rating	Net Assets ($Mil)	Price	Performance Rating/Pts	Total Return Y-T-D	Risk Rating/Pts
12-15	B+	75.60	36.01	A / 9.3	6.28%	C+ / 6.3
2014	B-	75.60	34.67	B- / 7.4	-1.32%	B- / 7.4
2013	C+	67.80	35.07	B+ / 8.7	52.61%	C+ / 5.6
2012	D-	17.60	22.32	D / 1.8	12.58%	C+ / 5.6
2011	D-	21.60	20.43	E+ / 0.6	-27.17%	C+ / 5.8
2010	A	37.10	27.58	B / 8.0	7.08%	B- / 7.4

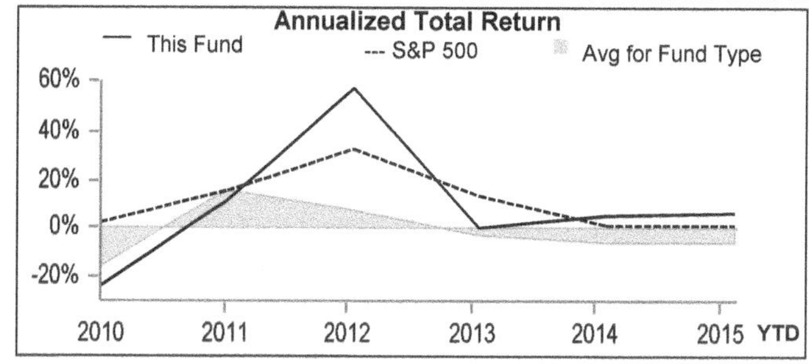

*Guggenheim Chinese Renminbi Tr (FXCH) C- Fair

Fund Family: Guggenheim Investments
Fund Type: Growth and Income
Inception Date: September 29, 2011

Major Rating Factors: Middle of the road best describes *Guggenheim Chinese Renminbi Tr whose TheStreet.com Investment Rating is currently a C- (Fair). The fund currently has a performance rating of C- (Fair) based on an annualized return of -1.50% over the last three years and a total return of -2.92% year to date 2015. Factored into the performance evaluation is an expense ratio of 0.40% (very low).

The fund's risk rating is currently B- (Good). It carries a beta of 0.06, meaning the fund's expected move will be 0.6% for every 10% move in the market. Volatility, as measured by both the semi-deviation and a drawdown factor, is considered low. As of December 31, 2015, *Guggenheim Chinese Renminbi Tr traded at a premium of 1.74% above its net asset value, which is worse than its one-year historical average premium of .07%.

Joseph Arruda has been running the fund for 5 years and currently receives a manager quality ranking of 48 (0=worst, 99=best). If you desire an average level of risk, then this fund may be an option.

Data Date	Investment Rating	Net Assets ($Mil)	Price	Performance Rating/Pts	Total Return Y-T-D	Risk Rating/Pts
12-15	C-	8.00	76.47	C- / 3.5	-2.92%	B- / 7.3
2014	C	8.00	78.77	D+ / 2.5	-2.98%	B+ / 9.4
2013	C	8.20	81.32	C- / 3.0	1.62%	B+ / 9.6
2012	C-	4.00	79.80	D / 1.7	0.14%	B+ / 9.8

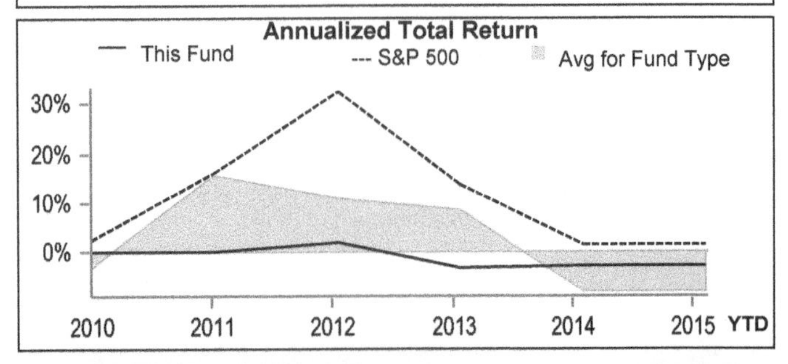

*Guggenheim Defensive Equity ETF (DEF) B Good

Fund Family: Guggenheim Funds Investment Advisor
Fund Type: Income
Inception Date: December 15, 2006

Major Rating Factors: *Guggenheim Defensive Equity ETF receives a TheStreet.com Investment Rating of B (Good). The fund currently has a performance rating of C+ (Fair) based on an annualized return of 8.74% over the last three years and a total return of -4.73% year to date 2015. Factored into the performance evaluation is an expense ratio of 0.65% (very low).

The fund's risk rating is currently B (Good). It carries a beta of 0.70, meaning the fund's expected move will be 7.0% for every 10% move in the market. Volatility, as measured by both the semi-deviation and a drawdown factor, is considered low. As of December 31, 2015, *Guggenheim Defensive Equity ETF traded at a price exactly equal to its net asset value, which is worse than its one-year historical average discount of .01%.

James R. King has been running the fund for 3 years and currently receives a manager quality ranking of 62 (0=worst, 99=best). If you desire an average level of risk, then this fund may be an option.

Data Date	Investment Rating	Net Assets ($Mil)	Price	Performance Rating/Pts	Total Return Y-T-D	Risk Rating/Pts
12-15	B	201.00	34.83	C+ / 6.8	-4.73%	B / 8.1
2014	A-	201.00	37.72	B- / 7.1	16.06%	B+ / 9.2
2013	B+	131.70	34.18	B- / 7.2	17.47%	B+ / 9.3
2012	B-	67.10	28.57	C / 5.4	11.55%	B+ / 9.2
2011	B-	47.60	27.34	C+ / 6.6	12.36%	B / 8.5
2010	C+	19.60	24.53	C / 5.4	18.77%	C+ / 6.0

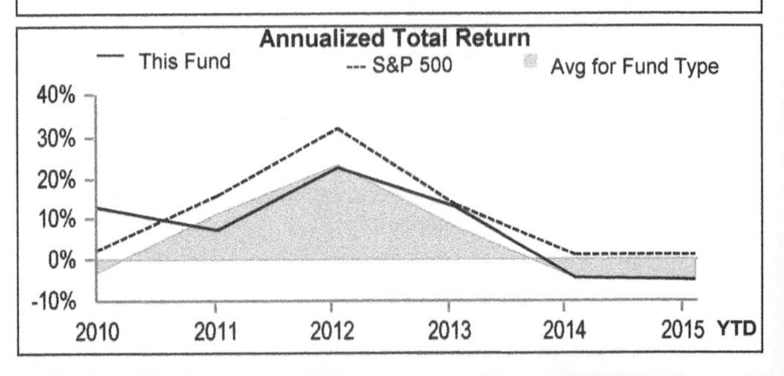

*Guggenheim Em Mkt RE ETF (EMRE) D+ Weak

Fund Family: Guggenheim Funds Investment Advisor
Fund Type: Growth and Income
Inception Date: September 29, 2014

Major Rating Factors:
Disappointing performance is the major factor driving the D+ (Weak) TheStreet.com Investment Rating for *Guggenheim Em Mkt RE ETF. The fund currently has a performance rating of D (Weak) based on an annualized return of 0.00% over the last three years and a total return of -10.42% year to date 2015. Factored into the performance evaluation is an expense ratio of 0.65% (very low).

The fund's risk rating is currently B- (Good). It carries a beta of 0.00, meaning the fund's expected move will be 0.0% for every 10% move in the market. Volatility, as measured by both the semi-deviation and a drawdown factor, is considered low. As of December 31, 2015, *Guggenheim Em Mkt RE ETF traded at a discount of .80% below its net asset value, which is better than its one-year historical average discount of .04%.

Michael P. Byrum currently receives a manager quality ranking of 14 (0=worst, 99=best). This fund offers only a moderate level of risk but investors looking for strong performance are still waiting.

Data Date	Investment Rating	Net Assets ($Mil)	Price	Performance Rating/Pts	Total Return Y-T-D	Risk Rating/Pts
12-15	D+	0.00	21.08	D / 1.7	-10.42%	B- / 7.0

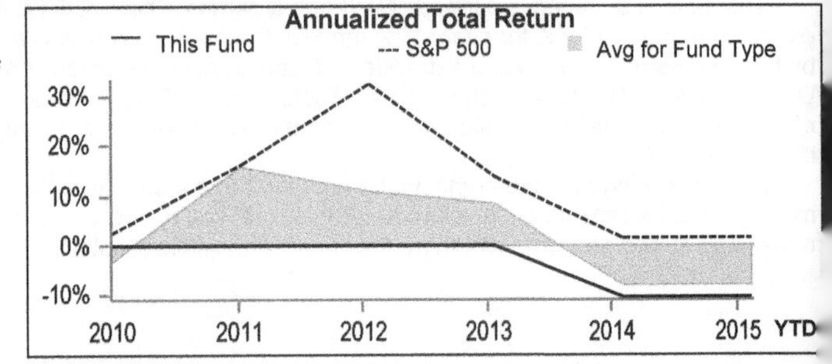

*Guggenheim Enhanced Short Dur (GSY) C+ Fair

und Family: Guggenheim Funds Investment Advisor
und Type: Growth
nception Date: February 12, 2008

ajor Rating Factors: Middle of the road best describes *Guggenheim Enhanced Short Dur whose TheStreet.com Investment Rating is currently a C+ (Fair). The fund currently has a performance rating of C (Fair) based on an annualized return of).98% over the last three years and a total return of 0.83% year to date 2015. actored into the performance evaluation is an expense ratio of 0.25% (very low).

The fund's risk rating is currently B (Good). It carries a beta of 0.01, meaning the und's expected move will be 0.1% for every 10% move in the market. Volatility, as neasured by both the semi-deviation and a drawdown factor, is considered low. As of December 31, 2015, *Guggenheim Enhanced Short Dur traded at a premium of .02% above its net asset value, which is worse than its one-year historical average discount of .01%.

Anne Walsh has been running the fund for 5 years and currently receives a nanager quality ranking of 75 (0=worst, 99=best). If you desire an average level of isk, then this fund may be an option.

Data Date	Investment Rating	Net Assets ($Mil)	Price	Perfor-mance Rating/Pts	Total Return Y-T-D	Risk Rating/Pts
12-15	C+	717.20	49.86	C / 4.8	0.83%	B / 8.4
2014	C	717.20	49.92	C- / 3.1	0.85%	B+ / 9.0
2013	C	466.60	50.17	D+ / 2.9	1.28%	B+ / 9.9
2012	C-	225.30	50.05	D- / 1.5	1.69%	B+ / 9.9
2011	C-	14.90	49.66	D / 2.0	0.05%	B+ / 9.9
2010	C	5.00	49.77	D / 2.2	-0.17%	B+ / 9.0

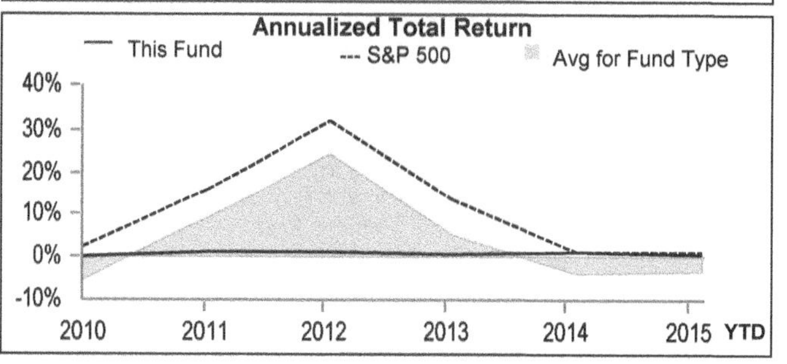

*Guggenheim Euro (FXE) D+ Weak

und Family: Guggenheim Investments
und Type: Foreign
nception Date: December 9, 2005

ajor Rating Factors:
Disappointing performance is the major factor driving the D+ (Weak) TheStreet.com nvestment Rating for *Guggenheim Euro. The fund currently has a performance ating of D+ (Weak) based on an annualized return of -6.41% over the last three ears and a total return of -9.98% year to date 2015. Factored into the performance valuation is an expense ratio of 0.40% (very low).

The fund's risk rating is currently C+ (Fair). It carries a beta of 0.23, meaning the und's expected move will be 2.3% for every 10% move in the market. Volatility, as neasured by both the semi-deviation and a drawdown factor, is considered low. As of December 31, 2015, *Guggenheim Euro traded at a premium of .06% above its net sset value, which is worse than its one-year historical average discount of .04%.

This fund has been team managed for 11 years and currently receives a nanager quality ranking of 20 (0=worst, 99=best). This fund offers only a moderate evel of risk but investors looking for strong performance are still waiting.

Data Date	Investment Rating	Net Assets ($Mil)	Price	Perfor-mance Rating/Pts	Total Return Y-T-D	Risk Rating/Pts
12-15	D+	217.90	106.40	D+ / 2.5	-9.98%	C+ / 6.2
2014	D	217.90	119.14	D / 2.1	-11.26%	C+ / 6.8
2013	C-	222.40	135.99	C- / 3.3	3.42%	B / 8.4
2012	D	222.40	130.96	D- / 1.3	4.77%	B / 8.2
2011	D+	278.00	128.92	D / 1.6	-1.25%	B / 8.2
2010	D+	354.10	133.09	D- / 1.5	-6.87%	B- / 7.2

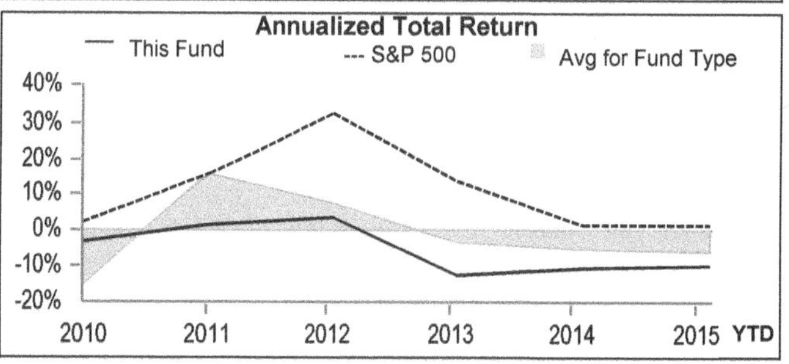

*Guggenheim Frontier Markets ETF (FRN) D Weak

und Family: Guggenheim Funds Investment Advisor
und Type: Global
nception Date: June 12, 2008

ajor Rating Factors:
Disappointing performance is the major factor driving the D (Weak) TheStreet.com nvestment Rating for *Guggenheim Frontier Markets ETF. The fund currently has a erformance rating of D- (Weak) based on an annualized return of -17.02% over the ast three years and a total return of -20.99% year to date 2015. Factored into the erformance evaluation is an expense ratio of 0.70% (very low).

The fund's risk rating is currently C (Fair). It carries a beta of 0.87, meaning the und's expected move will be 8.7% for every 10% move in the market. Volatility, as neasured by both the semi-deviation and a drawdown factor, is considered average. s of December 31, 2015, *Guggenheim Frontier Markets ETF traded at a discount f .74% below its net asset value, which is better than its one-year historical average iscount of .50%.

Saroj Kanuri has been running the fund for 6 years and currently receives a nanager quality ranking of 7 (0=worst, 99=best). This fund offers an average level of sk but investors looking for strong performance will be frustrated.

Data Date	Investment Rating	Net Assets ($Mil)	Price	Perfor-mance Rating/Pts	Total Return Y-T-D	Risk Rating/Pts
12-15	D	95.10	10.70	D- / 1.1	-20.99%	C / 5.5
2014	D-	95.10	13.88	D- / 1.5	-11.81%	C / 4.4
2013	D	85.10	16.23	D- / 1.1	-18.17%	C+ / 6.5
2012	D+	156.10	19.76	D+ / 2.9	11.24%	B- / 7.2
2011	C-	121.20	18.14	C / 4.4	-19.53%	B- / 7.3
2010	B+	242.00	24.44	A+ / 9.6	33.59%	C / 4.5

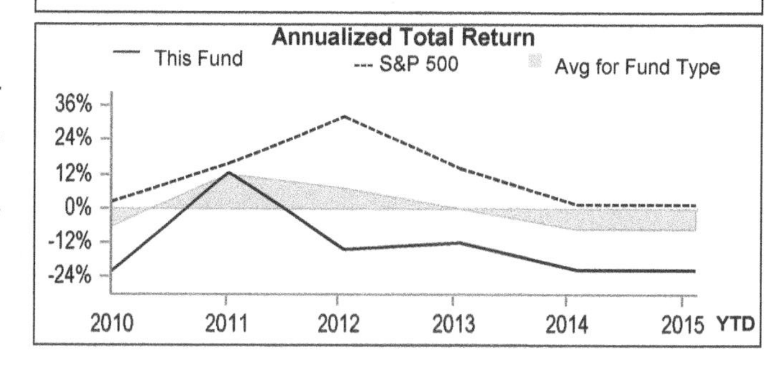

*Guggenheim Insider Sentiment ETF (NFO) B- Good

Fund Family: Guggenheim Funds Investment Advisor
Fund Type: Income
Inception Date: September 21, 2006

Major Rating Factors: Strong performance is the major factor driving the B- (Good) TheStreet.com Investment Rating for *Guggenheim Insider Sentiment ETF. The fund currently has a performance rating of B- (Good) based on an annualized return of 9.98% over the last three years and a total return of -3.59% year to date 2015. Factored into the performance evaluation is an expense ratio of 0.65% (very low).

The fund's risk rating is currently C+ (Fair). It carries a beta of 1.17, meaning it is expected to move 11.7% for every 10% move in the market. Volatility, as measured by both the semi-deviation and a drawdown factor, is considered low. As of December 31, 2015, *Guggenheim Insider Sentiment ETF traded at a premium of .19% above its net asset value, which is worse than its one-year historical average discount of .02%.

James R. King has been running the fund for 3 years and currently receives a manager quality ranking of 28 (0=worst, 99=best). If you desire only a moderate level of risk and strong performance, then this fund is an excellent option.

Data Date	Investment Rating	Net Assets ($Mil)	Price	Perfor-mance Rating/Pts	Total Return Y-T-D	Risk Rating/Pts
12-15	B-	166.10	46.54	B- / 7.3	-3.59%	C+ / 6.9
2014	B-	166.10	49.06	B- / 7.4	7.03%	C+ / 6.9
2013	B	203.70	46.87	B / 8.1	29.75%	B- / 7.5
2012	C+	96.00	34.75	C+ / 6.0	16.27%	B- / 7.6
2011	C+	97.00	30.79	C+ / 6.8	-2.20%	B- / 7.5
2010	B	127.00	32.65	B / 7.9	25.48%	C / 5.4

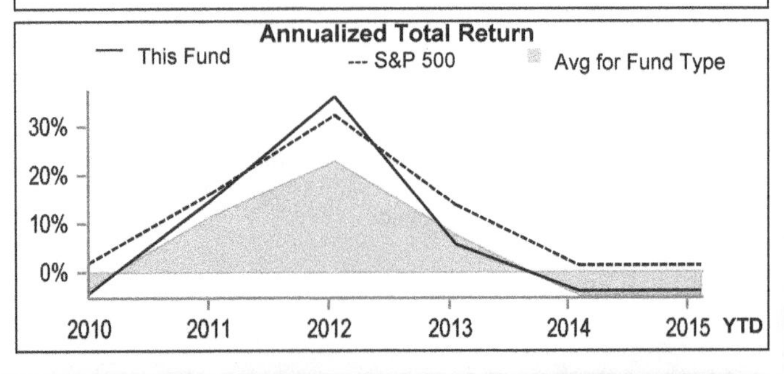

*Guggenheim Intl Multi-Asset Inc (HGI) C- Fair

Fund Family: Guggenheim Funds Investment Advisor
Fund Type: Foreign
Inception Date: July 11, 2007

Major Rating Factors:
Disappointing performance is the major factor driving the C- (Fair) TheStreet.com Investment Rating for *Guggenheim Intl Multi-Asset Inc. The fund currently has a performance rating of D+ (Weak) based on an annualized return of -2.20% over the last three years and a total return of -12.40% year to date 2015. Factored into the performance evaluation is an expense ratio of 0.70% (very low).

The fund's risk rating is currently B- (Good). It carries a beta of 0.96, meaning that its performance tracks fairly well with that of the overall stock market. Volatility, as measured by both the semi-deviation and a drawdown factor, is considered low. As of December 31, 2015, *Guggenheim Intl Multi-Asset Inc traded at a discount of .70% below its net asset value, which is better than its one-year historical average discount of .24%.

Saroj Kanuri has been running the fund for 6 years and currently receives a manager quality ranking of 24 (0=worst, 99=best). This fund offers only a moderate level of risk but investors looking for strong performance are still waiting.

Data Date	Investment Rating	Net Assets ($Mil)	Price	Perfor-mance Rating/Pts	Total Return Y-T-D	Risk Rating/Pts
12-15	C-	33.30	14.26	D+ / 2.9	-12.40%	B- / 7.6
2014	C-	33.30	16.89	C- / 3.4	-3.53%	B / 8.2
2013	C	114.80	18.48	C / 4.7	11.02%	B- / 7.6
2012	D+	118.90	16.84	D+ / 2.5	9.79%	B- / 7.6
2011	C-	85.70	16.22	C- / 4.2	-9.94%	B- / 7.3
2010	C-	80.30	19.24	C- / 3.8	12.13%	C / 5.4

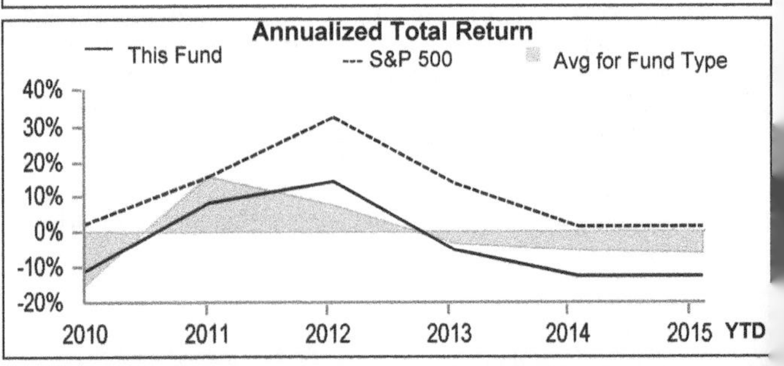

*Guggenheim Japanese Yen Trust (FXY) D Weak

Fund Family: Guggenheim Investments
Fund Type: Foreign
Inception Date: February 13, 2007

Major Rating Factors:
Disappointing performance is the major factor driving the D (Weak) TheStreet.com Investment Rating for *Guggenheim Japanese Yen Trust. The fund currently has a performance rating of D+ (Weak) based on an annualized return of -10.17% over the last three years and a total return of -0.11% year to date 2015. Factored into the performance evaluation is an expense ratio of 0.40% (very low).

The fund's risk rating is currently C+ (Fair). It carries a beta of -0.11, meaning the fund's expected move will be -1.1% for every 10% move in the market. Volatility, as measured by both the semi-deviation and a drawdown factor, is considered low. As of December 31, 2015, *Guggenheim Japanese Yen Trust traded at a premium of .10% above its net asset value, which is worse than its one-year historical average discount of .01%.

David C. Kwan has been running the fund for 8 years and currently receives a manager quality ranking of 16 (0=worst, 99=best). This fund offers only a moderate level of risk but investors looking for strong performance are still waiting.

Data Date	Investment Rating	Net Assets ($Mil)	Price	Perfor-mance Rating/Pts	Total Return Y-T-D	Risk Rating/Pts
12-15	D	66.60	80.63	D+ / 2.3	-0.11%	C+ / 5.8
2014	D-	66.60	81.21	D- / 1.0	-12.88%	C / 4.7
2013	D	176.60	92.76	D- / 1.2	-16.21%	B- / 7.6
2012	D+	124.80	113.03	D- / 1.0	-14.10%	B / 8.7
2011	C	729.50	127.93	C- / 3.1	7.44%	B+ / 9.0
2010	A	207.20	121.75	B- / 7.4	14.20%	B / 8.2

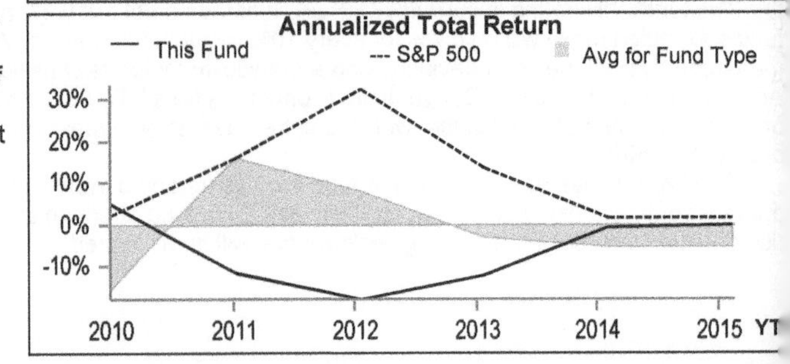

* Denotes ETF Fund

*Guggenheim Mid-Cap Core ETF (CZA) B+ Good

Fund Family: Guggenheim Funds Investment Advisor
Fund Type: Growth
Inception Date: April 2, 2007

Major Rating Factors: Strong performance is the major factor driving the B+ (Good) TheStreet.com Investment Rating for *Guggenheim Mid-Cap Core ETF. The fund currently has a performance rating of B (Good) based on an annualized return of 12.39% over the last three years and a total return of -1.73% year to date 2015. Factored into the performance evaluation is an expense ratio of 0.65% (very low).

The fund's risk rating is currently B- (Good). It carries a beta of 0.94, meaning that its performance tracks fairly well with that of the overall stock market. Volatility, as measured by both the semi-deviation and a drawdown factor, is considered low. As of December 31, 2015, *Guggenheim Mid-Cap Core ETF traded at a premium of .13% above its net asset value, which is worse than its one-year historical average premium of .10%.

James R. King has been running the fund for 3 years and currently receives a manager quality ranking of 64 (0=worst, 99=best). If you desire only a moderate level of risk and strong performance, then this fund is an excellent option.

Data Date	Investment Rating	Net Assets ($Mil)	Price	Performance Rating/Pts	Total Return Y-T-D	Risk Rating/Pts
12-15	B+	142.30	47.93	B / 8.0	-1.73%	B- / 7.3
2014	B+	142.30	49.52	B / 8.0	11.49%	B- / 7.6
2013	A-	113.60	45.54	B+ / 8.6	30.76%	B / 8.2
2012	B-	47.30	33.75	C+ / 6.8	16.92%	B / 8.1
2011	B-	26.70	29.75	B- / 7.1	4.16%	B / 8.0
2010	B+	11.50	28.75	B- / 7.1	22.60%	C+ / 6.4

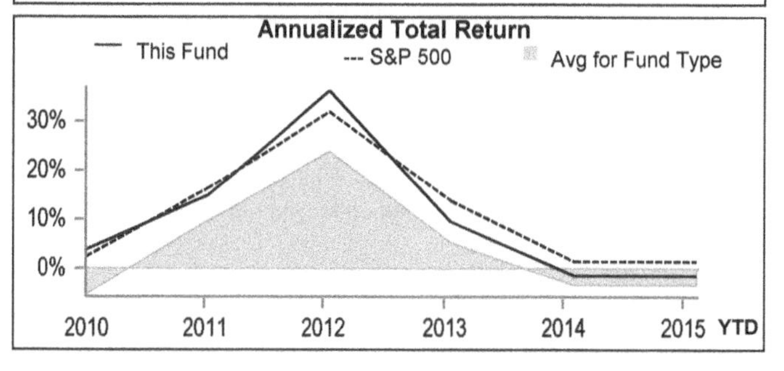

*Guggenheim MSCI EM Eq Cntry Weig (EWEM) D Weak

Fund Family: Guggenheim Investments
Fund Type: Emerging Market
Inception Date: December 3, 2010

Major Rating Factors:
Disappointing performance is the major factor driving the D (Weak) TheStreet.com Investment Rating for *Guggenheim MSCI EM Eq Cntry Weig. The fund currently has a performance rating of D (Weak) based on an annualized return of -8.99% over the last three years and a total return of -17.50% year to date 2015. Factored into the performance evaluation is an expense ratio of 0.60% (very low).

The fund's risk rating is currently C (Fair). It carries a beta of 0.98, meaning that its performance tracks fairly well with that of the overall stock market. Volatility, as measured by both the semi-deviation and a drawdown factor, is considered average. As of December 31, 2015, *Guggenheim MSCI EM Eq Cntry Weig traded at a premium of 1.57% above its net asset value, which is worse than its one-year historical average discount of .12%.

Michael P. Byrum has been running the fund for 6 years and currently receives a manager quality ranking of 47 (0=worst, 99=best). This fund offers an average level of risk but investors looking for strong performance will be frustrated.

Data Date	Investment Rating	Net Assets ($Mil)	Price	Performance Rating/Pts	Total Return Y-T-D	Risk Rating/Pts
12-15	D	13.60	25.89	D / 1.8	-17.50%	C / 5.1
2014	C-	13.60	32.36	C- / 3.1	0.03%	B- / 7.2
2013	D	9.90	33.61	D / 1.6	-8.27%	C+ / 6.1
2012	C+	14.20	35.73	B / 8.1	13.69%	C+ / 6.0
2011	D-	12.30	30.97	E+ / 0.7	-22.60%	C+ / 5.7

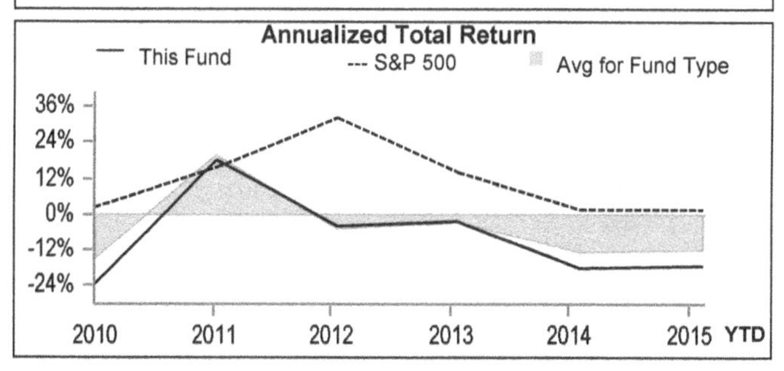

*Guggenheim Multi-Asset Income ET (CVY) C- Fair

Fund Family: Guggenheim Funds Investment Advisor
Fund Type: Income
Inception Date: September 21, 2006

Major Rating Factors: Middle of the road best describes *Guggenheim Multi-Asset Income ET whose TheStreet.com Investment Rating is currently a C- (Fair). The fund currently has a performance rating of C- (Fair) based on an annualized return of -1.71% over the last three years and a total return of -14.32% year to date 2015. Factored into the performance evaluation is an expense ratio of 0.65% (very low).

The fund's risk rating is currently B- (Good). It carries a beta of 0.95, meaning that its performance tracks fairly well with that of the overall stock market. Volatility, as measured by both the semi-deviation and a drawdown factor, is considered low. As of December 31, 2015, *Guggenheim Multi-Asset Income ET traded at a discount of .16% below its net asset value, which is better than its one-year historical average discount of .10%.

James R. King has been running the fund for 3 years and currently receives a manager quality ranking of 12 (0=worst, 99=best). If you desire an average level of risk, then this fund may be an option.

Data Date	Investment Rating	Net Assets ($Mil)	Price	Performance Rating/Pts	Total Return Y-T-D	Risk Rating/Pts
12-15	C-	1,299.80	18.18	C- / 3.0	-14.32%	B- / 7.4
2014	C	1,299.80	22.37	C / 4.3	-3.30%	B / 8.4
2013	B	1,165.20	24.77	B- / 7.2	15.08%	B / 8.5
2012	C+	794.00	21.92	C+ / 5.9	15.56%	B / 8.5
2011	B	474.80	20.45	B- / 7.5	9.03%	B / 8.0
2010	C	358.70	20.07	C+ / 5.7	16.98%	C / 4.9

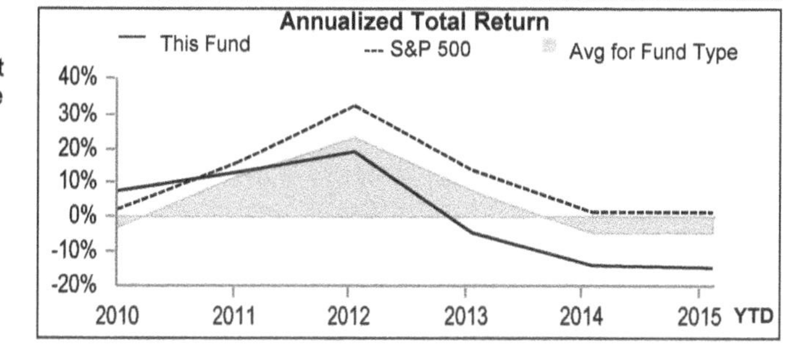

*Guggenheim Raymond James SB1 Eq (RYJ) C+ Fair

Fund Family: Guggenheim Funds Investment Advisor
Fund Type: Income
Inception Date: May 19, 2006

Major Rating Factors: Strong performance is the major factor driving the C+ (Fair) TheStreet.com Investment Rating for *Guggenheim Raymond James SB1 Eq. The fund currently has a performance rating of B- (Good) based on an annualized return of 10.74% over the last three years and a total return of -5.92% year to date 2015. Factored into the performance evaluation is an expense ratio of 0.75% (very low).

The fund's risk rating is currently C+ (Fair). It carries a beta of 1.03, meaning that its performance tracks fairly well with that of the overall stock market. Volatility, as measured by both the semi-deviation and a drawdown factor, is considered low. As of December 31, 2015, *Guggenheim Raymond James SB1 Eq traded at a premium of .03% above its net asset value, which is worse than its one-year historical average discount of .07%.

James R. King has been running the fund for 3 years and currently receives a manager quality ranking of 43 (0=worst, 99=best). If you desire only a moderate level of risk and strong performance, then this fund is an excellent option.

Data Date	Investment Rating	Net Assets ($Mil)	Price	Performance Rating/Pts	Total Return Y-T-D	Risk Rating/Pts
12-15	C+	255.30	32.57	B- / 7.2	-5.92%	C+ / 6.9
2014	A-	255.30	34.99	B / 7.6	5.97%	B / 8.7
2013	A-	237.30	33.53	B+ / 8.8	37.50%	B- / 7.7
2012	C+	101.50	23.47	C+ / 6.5	15.64%	B- / 7.6
2011	B-	82.50	20.53	B- / 7.3	-0.43%	B- / 7.6
2010	B-	63.40	21.03	B / 8.1	27.45%	C / 4.6

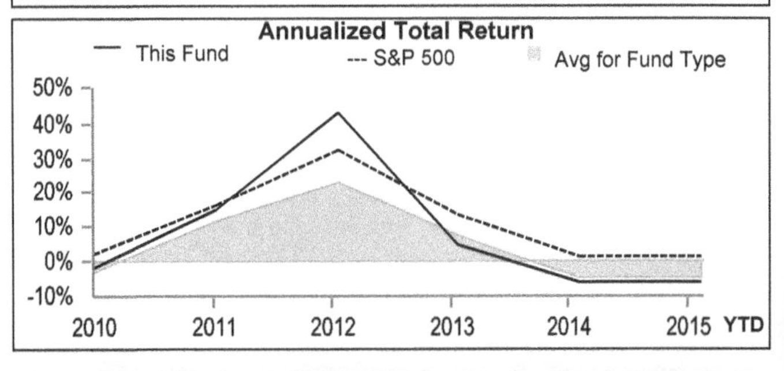

*Guggenheim Russ Top 50 Mega Cap (XLG) A+ Excellent

Fund Family: Guggenheim Investments
Fund Type: Income
Inception Date: May 4, 2005

Major Rating Factors:
Strong performance is the major factor driving the A+ (Excellent) TheStreet.com Investment Rating for *Guggenheim Russ Top 50 Mega Cap. The fund currently has a performance rating of B+ (Good) based on an annualized return of 13.38% over the last three years and a total return of 4.42% year to date 2015. Factored into the performance evaluation is an expense ratio of 0.20% (very low).

The fund's risk rating is currently B (Good). It carries a beta of 1.03, meaning that its performance tracks fairly well with that of the overall stock market. Volatility, as measured by both the semi-deviation and a drawdown factor, is considered low. As of December 31, 2015, *Guggenheim Russ Top 50 Mega Cap traded at a discount of .03% below its net asset value, which is better than its one-year historical average premium of .02%.

Michael P. Byrum has been running the fund for 11 years and currently receives a manager quality ranking of 59 (0=worst, 99=best). If you desire only a moderate level of risk and strong performance, then this fund is an excellent option.

Data Date	Investment Rating	Net Assets ($Mil)	Price	Performance Rating/Pts	Total Return Y-T-D	Risk Rating/Pts
12-15	A+	531.90	144.58	B+ / 8.9	4.42%	B / 8.5
2014	B	531.90	141.70	B / 7.8	13.56%	B- / 7.4
2013	B+	545.50	129.85	B / 8.0	24.53%	B / 8.3
2012	C	566.80	102.98	C / 4.4	17.01%	B / 8.0
2011	C	461.20	91.31	C / 4.8	4.54%	B- / 7.9
2010	D+	331.20	89.50	D+ / 2.4	9.32%	C+ / 6.2

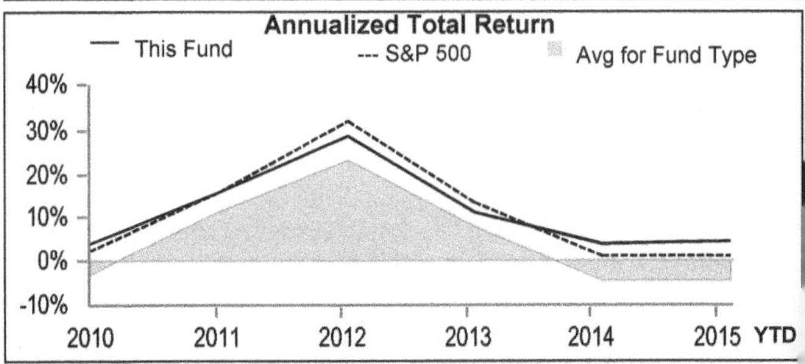

*Guggenheim Russell 1000 Eq Wght (EWRI) B Good

Fund Family: Guggenheim Investments
Fund Type: Growth
Inception Date: December 3, 2010

Major Rating Factors: Strong performance is the major factor driving the B (Good) TheStreet.com Investment Rating for *Guggenheim Russell 1000 Eq Wght. The fund currently has a performance rating of B (Good) based on an annualized return of 11.47% over the last three years and a total return of -3.95% year to date 2015. Factored into the performance evaluation is an expense ratio of 0.41% (very low).

The fund's risk rating is currently B- (Good). It carries a beta of 1.02, meaning that its performance tracks fairly well with that of the overall stock market. Volatility, as measured by both the semi-deviation and a drawdown factor, is considered low. As of December 31, 2015, *Guggenheim Russell 1000 Eq Wght traded at a premium of .31% above its net asset value, which is worse than its one-year historical average discount of .01%.

James R. King currently receives a manager quality ranking of 51 (0=worst, 99=best). If you desire only a moderate level of risk and strong performance, then this fund is an excellent option.

Data Date	Investment Rating	Net Assets ($Mil)	Price	Performance Rating/Pts	Total Return Y-T-D	Risk Rating/Pts
12-15	B	118.10	48.03	B / 7.7	-3.95%	B- / 7.0
2014	B	118.10	50.94	B / 8.1	12.49%	B- / 7.2
2013	B+	72.10	46.53	B+ / 8.3	29.19%	B- / 7.9
2012	B+	38.50	34.52	B+ / 8.3	16.66%	B- / 7.8
2011	D+	35.30	30.70	D+ / 2.3	1.59%	B- / 7.8

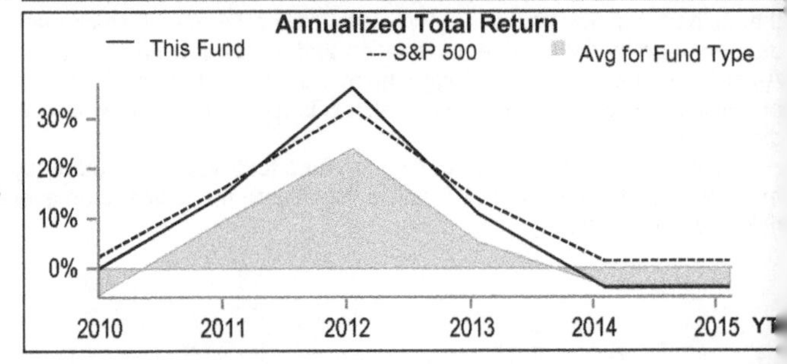

* Denotes ETF Fund

*Guggenheim Russell 2000 Eq Wght (EWRS) C+ Fair

Fund Family: Guggenheim Investments
Fund Type: Growth
Inception Date: December 3, 2010

Major Rating Factors: Middle of the road best describes *Guggenheim Russell 2000 Eq Wght whose TheStreet.com Investment Rating is currently a C+ (Fair). The fund currently has a performance rating of C+ (Fair) based on an annualized return of 6.98% over the last three years and a total return of -9.67% year to date 2015. Factored into the performance evaluation is an expense ratio of 0.42% (very low).

The fund's risk rating is currently B- (Good). It carries a beta of 1.12, meaning it is expected to move 11.2% for every 10% move in the market. Volatility, as measured by both the semi-deviation and a drawdown factor, is considered low. As of December 31, 2015, *Guggenheim Russell 2000 Eq Wght traded at a discount of .02% below its net asset value, which is worse than its one-year historical average discount of .03%.

James R. King currently receives a manager quality ranking of 23 (0=worst, 99=best). If you desire an average level of risk, then this fund may be an option.

Data Date	Investment Rating	Net Assets ($Mil)	Price	Performance Rating/Pts	Total Return Y-T-D	Risk Rating/Pts
12-15	C+	38.30	40.23	C+ / 5.9	-9.67%	B- / 7.6
2014	C+	38.30	45.59	B- / 7.1	1.68%	C+ / 6.6
2013	B	31.90	45.50	B+ / 8.4	35.01%	B- / 7.4
2012	C+	13.10	32.10	C+ / 6.8	13.77%	B- / 7.3
2011	D	17.60	29.36	D / 1.6	-4.82%	B- / 7.3

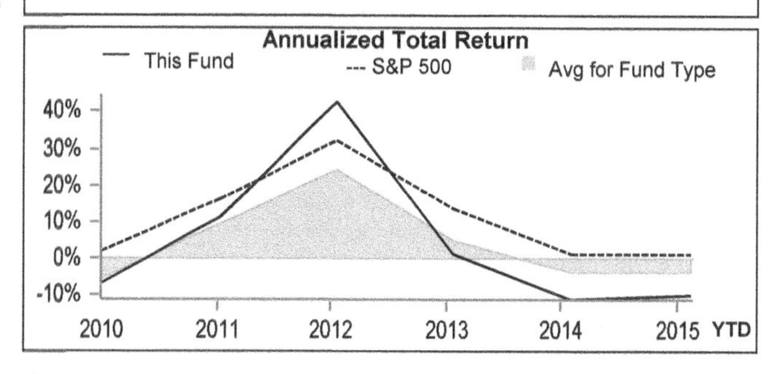

*Guggenheim Russell MC Eq Wght ET (EWRM) B+ Good

Fund Family: Guggenheim Investments
Fund Type: Growth
Inception Date: December 3, 2010

Major Rating Factors: Strong performance is the major factor driving the B+ (Good) TheStreet.com Investment Rating for *Guggenheim Russell MC Eq Wght ET. The fund currently has a performance rating of B- (Good) based on an annualized return of 10.85% over the last three years and a total return of -5.27% year to date 2015. Factored into the performance evaluation is an expense ratio of 0.41% (very low).

The fund's risk rating is currently B (Good). It carries a beta of 1.01, meaning that its performance tracks fairly well with that of the overall stock market. Volatility, as measured by both the semi-deviation and a drawdown factor, is considered low. As of December 31, 2015, *Guggenheim Russell MC Eq Wght ET traded at a discount of .02% below its net asset value, which is worse than its one-year historical average discount of .03%.

James R. King currently receives a manager quality ranking of 45 (0=worst, 99=best). If you desire only a moderate level of risk and strong performance, then this fund is an excellent option.

Data Date	Investment Rating	Net Assets ($Mil)	Price	Performance Rating/Pts	Total Return Y-T-D	Risk Rating/Pts
12-15	B+	142.80	47.39	B- / 7.4	-5.27%	B / 8.2
2014	B	142.80	50.69	B / 8.1	12.01%	B- / 7.4
2013	B+	91.00	46.60	B+ / 8.3	29.47%	B- / 7.9
2012	B+	52.80	35.19	B+ / 8.3	16.88%	B- / 7.8
2011	D+	49.20	30.78	D / 2.2	1.61%	B- / 7.7

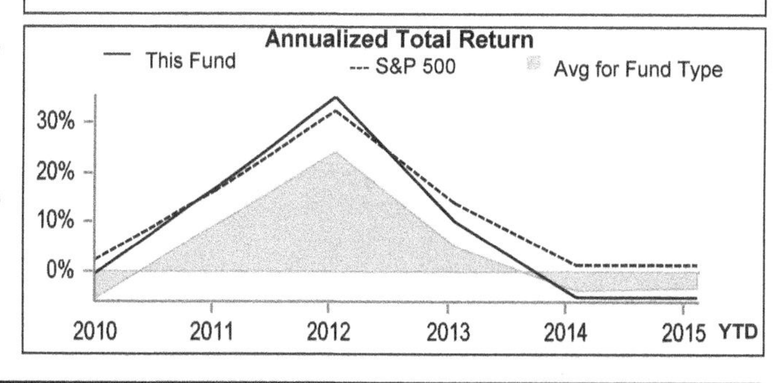

*Guggenheim S&P 500 Eq WgCon Dsc (RCD) A+ Excellent

Fund Family: Guggenheim Investments
Fund Type: Growth
Inception Date: November 1, 2006

Major Rating Factors:
Strong performance is the major factor driving the A+ (Excellent) TheStreet.com Investment Rating for *Guggenheim S&P 500 Eq WgCon Dsc. The fund currently has a performance rating of B+ (Good) based on an annualized return of 14.70% over the last three years and a total return of -2.36% year to date 2015. Factored into the performance evaluation is an expense ratio of 0.40% (very low).

The fund's risk rating is currently B (Good). It carries a beta of 1.15, meaning it is expected to move 11.5% for every 10% move in the market. Volatility, as measured by both the semi-deviation and a drawdown factor, is considered low. As of December 31, 2015, *Guggenheim S&P 500 Eq WgCon Dsc traded at a discount of .05% below its net asset value, which is better than its one-year historical average premium of .01%.

James R. King currently receives a manager quality ranking of 56 (0=worst, 99=best). If you desire only a moderate level of risk and strong performance, then this fund is an excellent option.

Data Date	Investment Rating	Net Assets ($Mil)	Price	Performance Rating/Pts	Total Return Y-T-D	Risk Rating/Pts
12-15	A+	108.40	84.69	B+ / 8.5	-2.36%	B / 8.7
2014	A-	108.40	88.60	A- / 9.2	12.37%	B- / 7.2
2013	A	156.50	80.09	A- / 9.2	38.90%	B / 8.0
2012	B	42.50	56.42	B / 7.8	20.84%	B- / 7.9
2011	B	26.00	47.32	B / 8.2	6.53%	B- / 7.7
2010	B+	27.50	45.86	B+ / 8.3	26.07%	C / 5.3

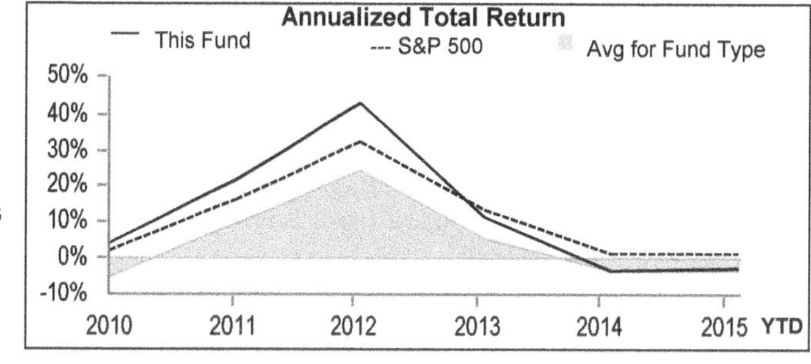

*Guggenheim S&P 500 Eq WgCon St E (RHS) A+ Excellent

Fund Family: Guggenheim Investments
Fund Type: Growth
Inception Date: November 1, 2006

Major Rating Factors:
Exceptional performance is the major factor driving the A+ (Excellent) TheStreet.com Investment Rating for *Guggenheim S&P 500 Eq WgCon St E. The fund currently has a performance rating of A+ (Excellent) based on an annualized return of 19.81% over the last three years and a total return of 13.70% year to date 2015. Factored into the performance evaluation is an expense ratio of 0.40% (very low).

The fund's risk rating is currently B- (Good). It carries a beta of 0.81, meaning the fund's expected move will be 8.1% for every 10% move in the market. Volatility, as measured by both the semi-deviation and a drawdown factor, is considered low. As of December 31, 2015, *Guggenheim S&P 500 Eq WgCon St E traded at a premium of .08% above its net asset value, which is worse than its one-year historical average premium of .04%.

James R. King currently receives a manager quality ranking of 93 (0=worst, 99=best). If you desire only a moderate level of risk and strong performance, then this fund is an excellent option.

Data Date	Investment Rating	Net Assets ($Mil)	Price	Performance Rating/Pts	Total Return Y-T-D	Risk Rating/Pts
12-15	A+	146.10	116.02	A+ / 9.6	13.70%	B- / 7.7
2014	A	146.10	104.48	A- / 9.1	20.96%	B- / 7.7
2013	A+	90.20	90.18	B+ / 8.7	27.62%	B+ / 9.1
2012	B-	41.50	69.18	C+ / 6.1	16.18%	B / 8.9
2011	B	28.40	63.25	C+ / 6.6	13.31%	B / 8.7
2010	A-	14.30	57.22	B- / 7.3	17.03%	B- / 7.1

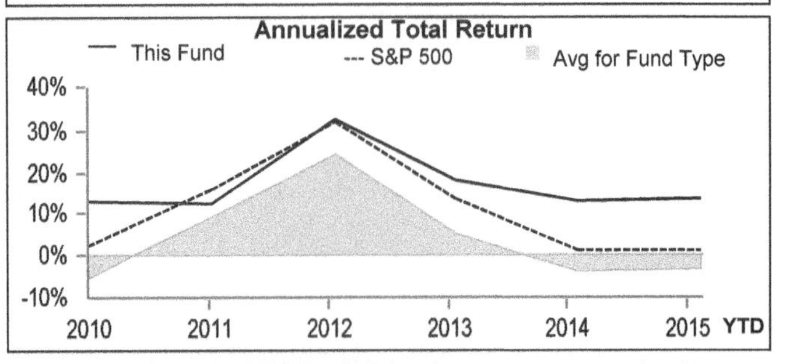

*Guggenheim S&P 500 Eq Wght Engy (RYE) D Weak

Fund Family: Guggenheim Investments
Fund Type: Energy/Natural Resources
Inception Date: November 1, 2006

Major Rating Factors:
Disappointing performance is the major factor driving the D (Weak) TheStreet.com Investment Rating for *Guggenheim S&P 500 Eq Wght Engy. The fund currently has a performance rating of D- (Weak) based on an annualized return of -9.51% over the last three years and a total return of -28.92% year to date 2015. Factored into the performance evaluation is an expense ratio of 0.40% (very low).

The fund's risk rating is currently C (Fair). It carries a beta of 1.14, meaning it is expected to move 11.4% for every 10% move in the market. Volatility, as measured by both the semi-deviation and a drawdown factor, is considered average. As of December 31, 2015, *Guggenheim S&P 500 Eq Wght Engy traded at a price exactly equal to its net asset value.

James R. King currently receives a manager quality ranking of 36 (0=worst, 99=best). This fund offers an average level of risk but investors looking for strong performance will be frustrated.

Data Date	Investment Rating	Net Assets ($Mil)	Price	Performance Rating/Pts	Total Return Y-T-D	Risk Rating/Pts
12-15	D	211.90	47.09	D- / 1.5	-28.92%	C / 5.2
2014	D+	211.90	67.63	D+ / 2.4	-12.80%	B- / 7.2
2013	C+	48.40	80.78	C+ / 6.7	20.07%	B- / 7.0
2012	D+	29.00	63.85	C- / 3.6	8.20%	C+ / 6.9
2011	C+	33.80	61.61	C+ / 6.6	1.15%	C+ / 6.9
2010	C	22.00	62.84	C+ / 6.0	26.08%	C / 4.9

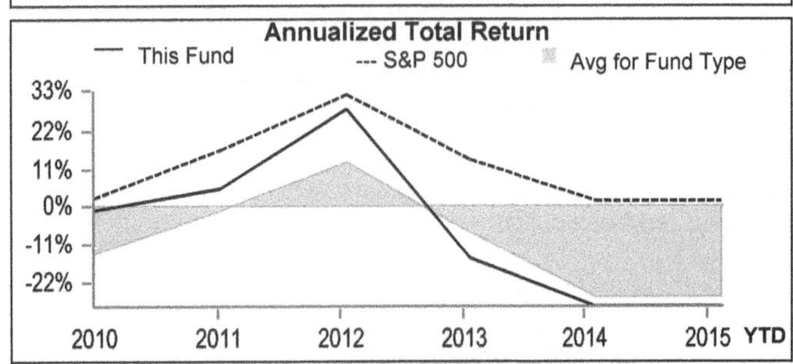

*Guggenheim S&P 500 Eq Wght Finl (RYF) A+ Excellent

Fund Family: Guggenheim Investments
Fund Type: Financial Services
Inception Date: November 1, 2006

Major Rating Factors:
Strong performance is the major factor driving the A+ (Excellent) TheStreet.com Investment Rating for *Guggenheim S&P 500 Eq Wght Finl. The fund currently has a performance rating of B+ (Good) based on an annualized return of 14.35% over the last three years and a total return of -1.46% year to date 2015. Factored into the performance evaluation is an expense ratio of 0.40% (very low).

The fund's risk rating is currently B (Good). It carries a beta of 1.02, meaning that its performance tracks fairly well with that of the overall stock market. Volatility, as measured by both the semi-deviation and a drawdown factor, is considered low. As of December 31, 2015, *Guggenheim S&P 500 Eq Wght Finl traded at a discount of .05% below its net asset value, which is better than its one-year historical average premium of .01%.

James R. King currently receives a manager quality ranking of 71 (0=worst, 99=best). If you desire only a moderate level of risk and strong performance, then this fund is an excellent option.

Data Date	Investment Rating	Net Assets ($Mil)	Price	Performance Rating/Pts	Total Return Y-T-D	Risk Rating/Pts
12-15	A+	133.00	43.20	B+ / 8.8	-1.46%	B / 8.9
2014	A+	133.00	44.77	A / 9.3	16.35%	B / 8.0
2013	B	69.40	39.66	B / 8.2	31.91%	B- / 7.7
2012	C+	13.20	29.16	C+ / 6.6	25.08%	B- / 7.5
2011	C-	15.60	23.99	C- / 4.1	-10.89%	C+ / 6.9
2010	D-	18.10	27.84	D / 1.8	22.41%	C / 4.3

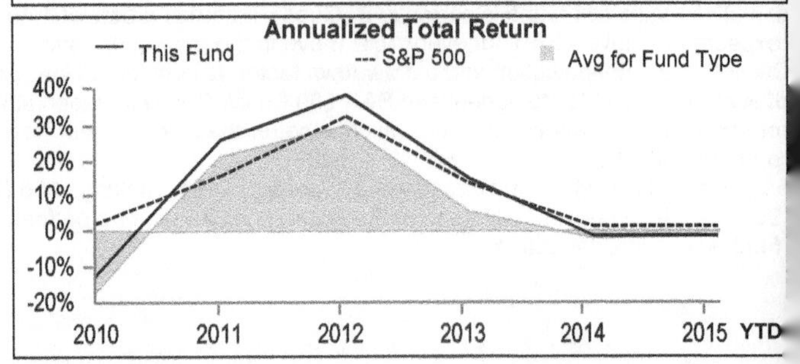

*Guggenheim S&P 500 Eq Wght HC ET (RYH) A+ Excellent

Fund Family: Guggenheim Investments
Fund Type: Growth
Inception Date: November 1, 2006

Major Rating Factors:
Exceptional performance is the major factor driving the A+ (Excellent) TheStreet.com Investment Rating for *Guggenheim S&P 500 Eq Wght HC ET. The fund currently has a performance rating of A+ (Excellent) based on an annualized return of 24.52% over the last three years and a total return of 7.93% year to date 2015. Factored into the performance evaluation is an expense ratio of 0.40% (very low).

The fund's risk rating is currently B- (Good). It carries a beta of 0.92, meaning that its performance tracks fairly well with that of the overall stock market. Volatility, as measured by both the semi-deviation and a drawdown factor, is considered low. As of December 31, 2015, *Guggenheim S&P 500 Eq Wght HC ET traded at a discount of .01% below its net asset value, which is better than its one-year historical average premium of .04%.

James R. King currently receives a manager quality ranking of 95 (0=worst, 99=best). If you desire only a moderate level of risk and strong performance, then this fund is an excellent option.

Data Date	Investment Rating	Net Assets ($Mil)	Price	Performance Rating/Pts	Total Return Y-T-D	Risk Rating/Pts
12-15	A+	335.10	153.49	A+ / 9.6	7.93%	B- / 7.5
2014	A+	335.10	142.57	A+ / 9.6	31.21%	B / 8.8
2013	A+	143.50	110.42	A- / 9.1	37.19%	B / 8.3
2012	B-	63.00	78.39	C+ / 6.6	22.02%	B / 8.2
2011	C+	46.60	66.44	C+ / 6.3	7.16%	B / 8.1
2010	C+	50.30	62.81	C+ / 6.1	10.67%	C+ / 6.7

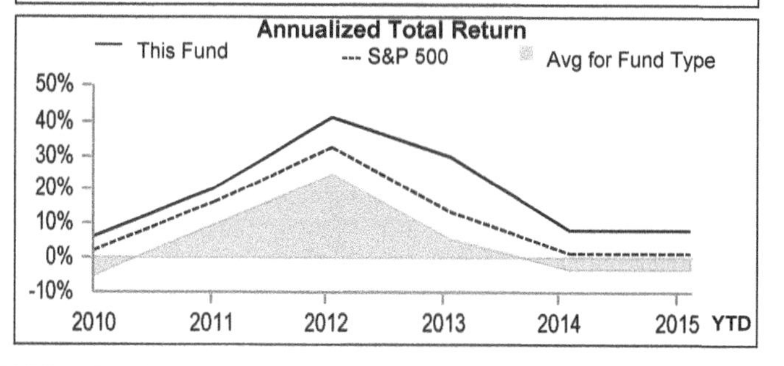

*Guggenheim S&P 500 Eq Wght Ind E (RGI) B Good

Fund Family: Guggenheim Investments
Fund Type: Growth
Inception Date: November 1, 2006

Major Rating Factors: Strong performance is the major factor driving the B (Good) TheStreet.com Investment Rating for *Guggenheim S&P 500 Eq Wght Ind E. The fund currently has a performance rating of B (Good) based on an annualized return of 12.09% over the last three years and a total return of -6.76% year to date 2015. Factored into the performance evaluation is an expense ratio of 0.40% (very low).

The fund's risk rating is currently B- (Good). It carries a beta of 1.09, meaning that its performance tracks fairly well with that of the overall stock market. Volatility, as measured by both the semi-deviation and a drawdown factor, is considered low. As of December 31, 2015, *Guggenheim S&P 500 Eq Wght Ind E traded at a premium of .25% above its net asset value, which is worse than its one-year historical average discount of .01%.

James R. King currently receives a manager quality ranking of 45 (0=worst, 99=best). If you desire only a moderate level of risk and strong performance, then this fund is an excellent option.

Data Date	Investment Rating	Net Assets ($Mil)	Price	Performance Rating/Pts	Total Return Y-T-D	Risk Rating/Pts
12-15	B	106.40	82.96	B / 7.8	-6.76%	B- / 7.1
2014	A-	106.40	90.45	B+ / 8.9	13.75%	B- / 7.4
2013	A-	77.80	81.85	B+ / 8.9	33.95%	B- / 7.9
2012	C+	17.80	59.03	C+ / 6.2	15.47%	B- / 7.7
2011	C+	13.00	52.03	C+ / 5.6	-0.99%	B- / 7.6
2010	C+	48.70	54.21	C+ / 6.5	26.13%	C / 5.5

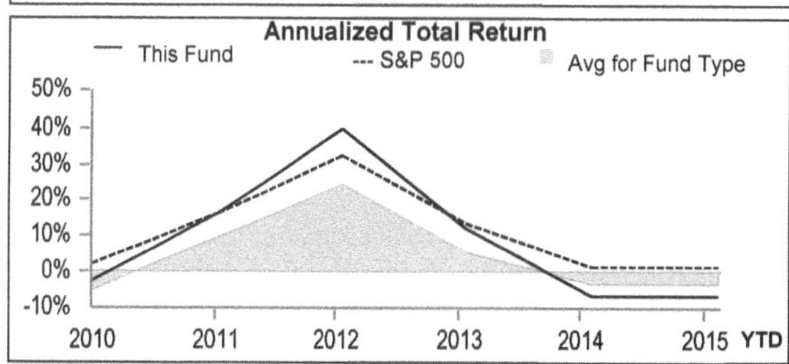

*Guggenheim S&P 500 Eq Wght Mat E (RTM) C Fair

Fund Family: Guggenheim Investments
Fund Type: Growth
Inception Date: November 1, 2006

Major Rating Factors: Middle of the road best describes *Guggenheim S&P 500 Eq Wght Mat E whose TheStreet.com Investment Rating is currently a C (Fair). The fund currently has a performance rating of C+ (Fair) based on an annualized return of 6.35% over the last three years and a total return of -7.48% year to date 2015. Factored into the performance evaluation is an expense ratio of 0.40% (very low).

The fund's risk rating is currently C+ (Fair). It carries a beta of 1.20, meaning it is expected to move 12.0% for every 10% move in the market. Volatility, as measured by both the semi-deviation and a drawdown factor, is considered low. As of December 31, 2015, *Guggenheim S&P 500 Eq Wght Mat E traded at a premium of .42% above its net asset value, which is worse than its one-year historical average premium of .04%.

James R. King currently receives a manager quality ranking of 17 (0=worst, 99=best). If you desire an average level of risk, then this fund may be an option.

Data Date	Investment Rating	Net Assets ($Mil)	Price	Performance Rating/Pts	Total Return Y-T-D	Risk Rating/Pts
12-15	C	79.30	76.43	C+ / 5.9	-7.48%	C+ / 6.6
2014	B-	79.30	84.25	B- / 7.0	9.01%	B- / 7.2
2013	C+	51.90	79.74	B- / 7.0	20.84%	B- / 7.4
2012	C	29.20	64.79	C / 4.8	14.12%	B- / 7.3
2011	C+	33.70	56.17	B- / 7.1	-6.27%	B- / 7.3
2010	B	40.90	63.00	B / 7.9	23.12%	C / 5.4

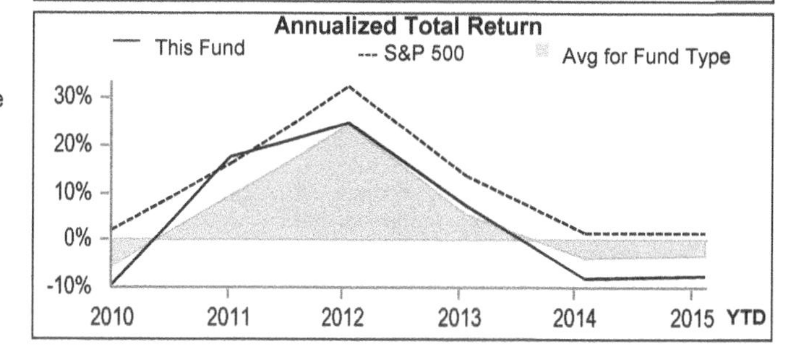

* Denotes ETF Fund

*Guggenheim S&P 500 Eq Wght Tech (RYT) A+ Excellent

Fund Family: Guggenheim Investments
Fund Type: Growth
Inception Date: November 1, 2006

Major Rating Factors:
Exceptional performance is the major factor driving the A+ (Excellent) TheStreet.com Investment Rating for *Guggenheim S&P 500 Eq Wght Tech. The fund currently has a performance rating of A (Excellent) based on an annualized return of 18.67% over the last three years and a total return of 2.90% year to date 2015. Factored into the performance evaluation is an expense ratio of 0.40% (very low).

The fund's risk rating is currently B (Good). It carries a beta of 1.12, meaning it is expected to move 11.2% for every 10% move in the market. Volatility, as measured by both the semi-deviation and a drawdown factor, is considered low. As of December 31, 2015, *Guggenheim S&P 500 Eq Wght Tech traded at a discount of .06% below its net asset value, which is better than its one-year historical average premium of .01%.

James R. King currently receives a manager quality ranking of 82 (0=worst, 99=best). If you desire only a moderate level of risk and strong performance, then this fund is an excellent option.

Data Date	Investment Rating	Net Assets ($Mil)	Price	Performance Rating/Pts	Total Return Y-T-D	Risk Rating/Pts
12-15	A+	620.30	92.27	A / 9.4	2.90%	B / 8.3
2014	B+	620.30	90.76	A- / 9.2	21.67%	C+ / 6.7
2013	B	342.90	77.07	B / 8.1	34.98%	B- / 7.6
2012	C-	91.50	55.27	C / 4.4	13.02%	B- / 7.2
2011	C+	102.40	49.99	C+ / 6.5	-7.30%	B- / 7.4
2010	B-	102.30	53.77	B- / 7.0	17.89%	C / 5.4

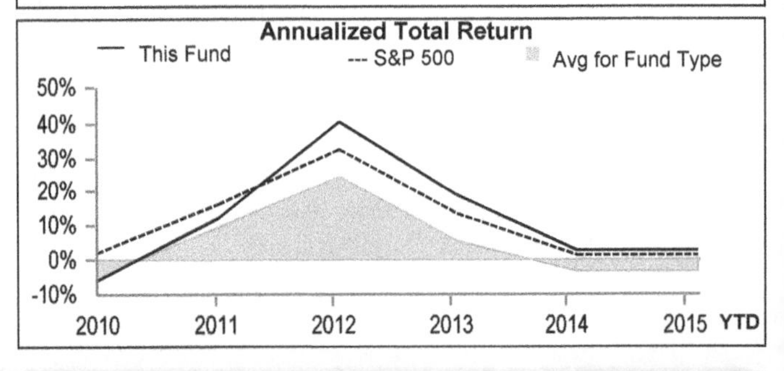

*Guggenheim S&P 500 Eq Wght Util (RYU) A- Excellent

Fund Family: Guggenheim Investments
Fund Type: Utilities
Inception Date: November 1, 2006

Major Rating Factors:
Strong performance is the major factor driving the A- (Excellent) TheStreet.com Investment Rating for *Guggenheim S&P 500 Eq Wght Util. The fund currently has a performance rating of B (Good) based on an annualized return of 10.72% over the last three years and a total return of -4.64% year to date 2015. Factored into the performance evaluation is an expense ratio of 0.40% (very low).

The fund's risk rating is currently B (Good). It carries a beta of 0.86, meaning the fund's expected move will be 8.6% for every 10% move in the market. Volatility, as measured by both the semi-deviation and a drawdown factor, is considered low. As of December 31, 2015, *Guggenheim S&P 500 Eq Wght Util traded at a discount of .03% below its net asset value, which is better than its one-year historical average discount of .01%.

Michael P. Byrum currently receives a manager quality ranking of 77 (0=worst, 99=best). If you desire only a moderate level of risk and strong performance, then this fund is an excellent option.

Data Date	Investment Rating	Net Assets ($Mil)	Price	Performance Rating/Pts	Total Return Y-T-D	Risk Rating/Pts
12-15	A-	82.40	72.35	B / 7.8	-4.64%	B / 8.4
2014	A+	82.40	78.57	A / 9.3	34.62%	B / 8.9
2013	B	50.70	63.26	C+ / 6.4	8.64%	B+ / 9.0
2012	C+	37.70	57.47	C / 4.7	14.01%	B+ / 9.2
2011	C+	33.30	55.53	C / 4.9	9.75%	B / 8.8
2010	C-	20.40	51.10	C- / 3.3	12.70%	C+ / 6.7

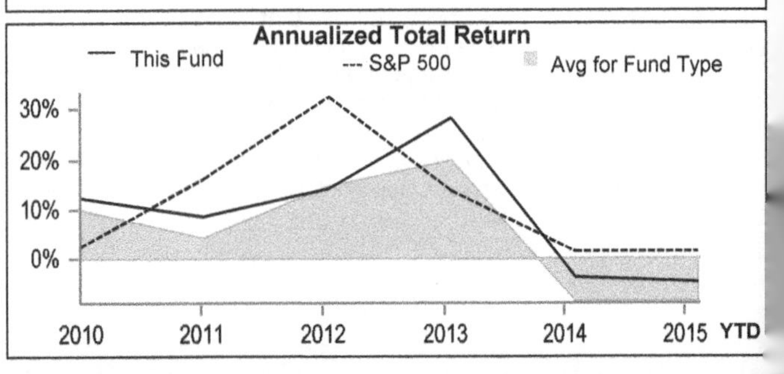

*Guggenheim S&P 500 Equal Wght (RSP) A+ Excellent

Fund Family: Guggenheim Investments
Fund Type: Income
Inception Date: April 24, 2003

Major Rating Factors:
Strong performance is the major factor driving the A+ (Excellent) TheStreet.com Investment Rating for *Guggenheim S&P 500 Equal Wght. The fund currently has a performance rating of B+ (Good) based on an annualized return of 13.42% over the last three years and a total return of -2.62% year to date 2015. Factored into the performance evaluation is an expense ratio of 0.40% (very low).

The fund's risk rating is currently B (Good). It carries a beta of 1.01, meaning that its performance tracks fairly well with that of the overall stock market. Volatility, as measured by both the semi-deviation and a drawdown factor, is considered low. As of December 31, 2015, *Guggenheim S&P 500 Equal Wght traded at a discount of .07% below its net asset value, which is better than its one-year historical average discount of .01%.

Michael P. Byrum currently receives a manager quality ranking of 62 (0=worst, 99=best). If you desire only a moderate level of risk and strong performance, then this fund is an excellent option.

Data Date	Investment Rating	Net Assets ($Mil)	Price	Performance Rating/Pts	Total Return Y-T-D	Risk Rating/Pts
12-15	A+	8,677.30	76.64	B+ / 8.4	-2.62%	B / 8.6
2014	A	8,677.30	80.05	B+ / 8.9	16.28%	B- / 7.6
2013	B+	6,556.30	71.25	B+ / 8.4	30.05%	B / 8.1
2012	C+	2,696.80	53.32	C+ / 6.3	17.68%	B- / 7.9
2011	C+	2,640.10	46.28	C+ / 6.5	0.24%	B- / 7.8
2010	C+	3,181.20	47.31	C+ / 6.6	21.39%	C+ / 5.7

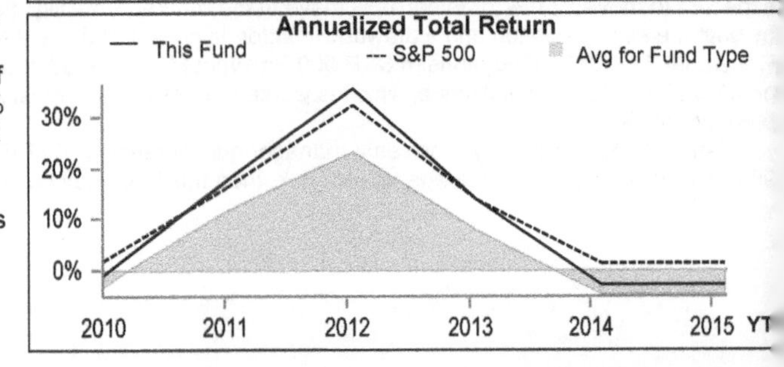

*Guggenheim S&P 500 Pure Growth (RPG) — A+ Excellent

Fund Family: Guggenheim Investments
Fund Type: Growth
Inception Date: March 1, 2006

Data Date	Investment Rating	Net Assets ($Mil)	Price	Performance Rating/Pts	Total Return Y-T-D	Risk Rating/Pts
12-15	A+	1,753.50	80.70	A- / 9.2	2.25%	B / 8.3
2014	A-	1,753.50	79.52	A- / 9.0	15.62%	B- / 7.4
2013	B+	934.60	70.30	A- / 9.0	38.21%	B- / 7.1
2012	C+	328.20	49.28	C+ / 6.5	15.59%	B- / 7.2
2011	C+	257.40	43.24	B- / 7.2	1.20%	B- / 7.0
2010	B	197.00	43.25	B / 7.8	26.91%	C / 5.3

Major Rating Factors:
Exceptional performance is the major factor driving the A+ (Excellent) TheStreet.com Investment Rating for *Guggenheim S&P 500 Pure Growth. The fund currently has a performance rating of A- (Excellent) based on an annualized return of 17.47% over the last three years and a total return of 2.25% year to date 2015. Factored into the performance evaluation is an expense ratio of 0.35% (very low).

The fund's risk rating is currently B (Good). It carries a beta of 1.01, meaning that its performance tracks fairly well with that of the overall stock market. Volatility, as measured by both the semi-deviation and a drawdown factor, is considered low. As of December 31, 2015, *Guggenheim S&P 500 Pure Growth traded at a discount of .06% below its net asset value, which is better than its one-year historical average premium of .02%.

Michael P. Byrum currently receives a manager quality ranking of 84 (0=worst, 99=best). If you desire only a moderate level of risk and strong performance, then this fund is an excellent option.

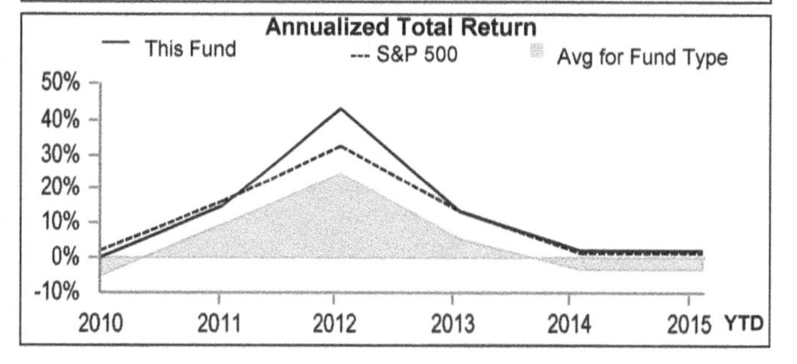

*Guggenheim S&P 500 Pure Value (RPV) — A Excellent

Fund Family: Guggenheim Investments
Fund Type: Income
Inception Date: March 1, 2006

Data Date	Investment Rating	Net Assets ($Mil)	Price	Performance Rating/Pts	Total Return Y-T-D	Risk Rating/Pts
12-15	A	1,326.30	49.20	B / 8.0	-8.26%	B / 8.6
2014	A	1,326.30	54.96	A / 9.4	14.84%	B- / 7.1
2013	A+	559.50	49.77	A- / 9.2	40.68%	B / 8.1
2012	B+	107.70	34.20	B / 8.0	23.82%	B / 8.0
2011	C+	77.80	27.81	C+ / 6.8	-1.15%	B- / 7.1
2010	C	62.90	28.59	C+ / 6.1	22.52%	C / 4.7

Major Rating Factors:
Strong performance is the major factor driving the A (Excellent) TheStreet.com Investment Rating for *Guggenheim S&P 500 Pure Value. The fund currently has a performance rating of B (Good) based on an annualized return of 13.58% over the last three years and a total return of -8.26% year to date 2015. Factored into the performance evaluation is an expense ratio of 0.35% (very low).

The fund's risk rating is currently B (Good). It carries a beta of 1.18, meaning it is expected to move 11.8% for every 10% move in the market. Volatility, as measured by both the semi-deviation and a drawdown factor, is considered low. As of December 31, 2015, *Guggenheim S&P 500 Pure Value traded at a discount of .08% below its net asset value, which is better than its one-year historical average discount of .01%.

James R. King currently receives a manager quality ranking of 45 (0=worst, 99=best). If you desire only a moderate level of risk and strong performance, then this fund is an excellent option.

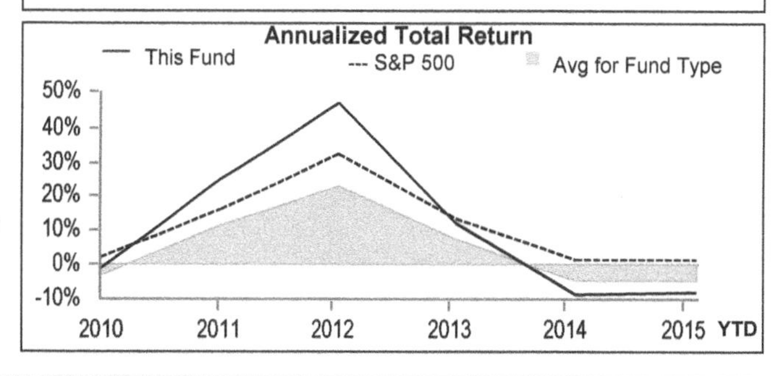

*Guggenheim S&P Gl Div Opps Idx E (LVL) — D+ Weak

Fund Family: Guggenheim Funds Investment Advisor
Fund Type: Income
Inception Date: June 25, 2007

Data Date	Investment Rating	Net Assets ($Mil)	Price	Performance Rating/Pts	Total Return Y-T-D	Risk Rating/Pts
12-15	D+	93.50	8.73	D / 1.9	-19.50%	C+ / 6.8
2014	C-	93.50	11.42	D+ / 2.5	-7.11%	B- / 7.8
2013	C-	88.20	13.24	C / 4.4	4.22%	B- / 7.6
2012	D+	50.70	13.14	D+ / 2.5	9.42%	B- / 7.1
2011	C	53.00	13.25	C / 5.1	-2.94%	B- / 7.5
2010	D	27.20	14.80	D+ / 2.4	6.00%	C- / 4.1

Major Rating Factors:
Disappointing performance is the major factor driving the D+ (Weak) TheStreet.com Investment Rating for *Guggenheim S&P Gl Div Opps Idx E. The fund currently has a performance rating of D (Weak) based on an annualized return of -8.17% over the last three years and a total return of -19.50% year to date 2015. Factored into the performance evaluation is an expense ratio of 0.65% (very low).

The fund's risk rating is currently C+ (Fair). It carries a beta of 1.06, meaning that its performance tracks fairly well with that of the overall stock market. Volatility, as measured by both the semi-deviation and a drawdown factor, is considered low. As of December 31, 2015, *Guggenheim S&P Gl Div Opps Idx E traded at a discount of .80% below its net asset value, which is better than its one-year historical average discount of .22%.

Saroj Kanuri has been running the fund for 6 years and currently receives a manager quality ranking of 7 (0=worst, 99=best). This fund offers only a moderate level of risk but investors looking for strong performance are still waiting.

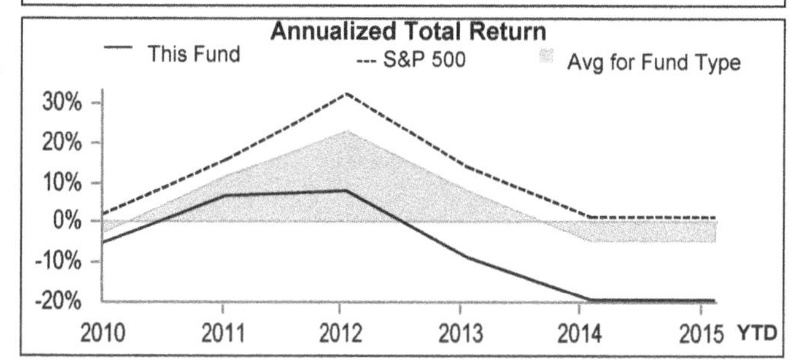

* Denotes ETF Fund

*Guggenheim S&P Global Water Idx (CGW) B Good

Fund Family: Guggenheim Funds Investment Advisor
Fund Type: Energy/Natural Resources
Inception Date: May 14, 2007

Major Rating Factors: *Guggenheim S&P Global Water Idx receives a TheStreet.com Investment Rating of B (Good). The fund currently has a performance rating of C+ (Fair) based on an annualized return of 8.07% over the last three years and a total return of -1.31% year to date 2015. Factored into the performance evaluation is an expense ratio of 0.64% (very low).

The fund's risk rating is currently B- (Good). It carries a beta of 0.48, meaning the fund's expected move will be 4.8% for every 10% move in the market. Volatility, as measured by both the semi-deviation and a drawdown factor, is considered low. As of December 31, 2015, *Guggenheim S&P Global Water Idx traded at a price exactly equal to its net asset value, which is better than its one-year historical average premium of .08%.

James R. King has been running the fund for 3 years and currently receives a manager quality ranking of 95 (0=worst, 99=best). If you desire an average level of risk, then this fund may be an option.

Data Date	Investment Rating	Net Assets ($Mil)	Price	Performance Rating/Pts	Total Return Y-T-D	Risk Rating/Pts
12-15	B	350.00	27.14	C+ / 6.8	-1.31%	B- / 7.8
2014	C+	350.00	28.06	B- / 7.1	5.55%	B- / 7.1
2013	B	311.60	27.65	B- / 7.5	22.38%	B / 8.2
2012	C	206.40	22.24	C / 5.2	21.16%	B / 8.0
2011	D+	179.80	18.74	C- / 3.8	-6.38%	C+ / 6.1
2010	D+	220.00	20.77	C- / 3.6	14.46%	C / 4.9

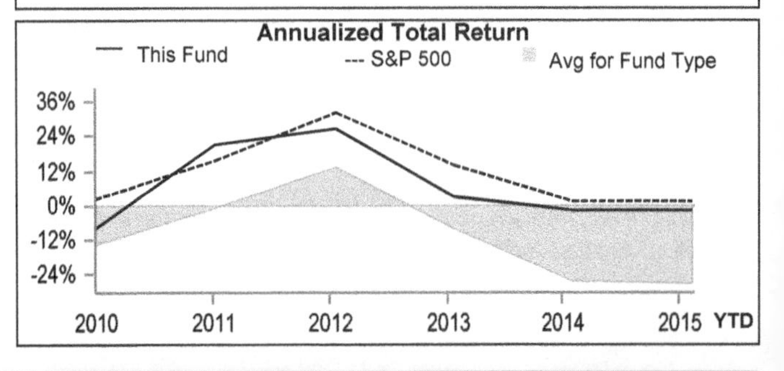

*Guggenheim S&P Mid Cap 400 Pure (RFV) C+ Fair

Fund Family: Guggenheim Investments
Fund Type: Growth
Inception Date: March 1, 2006

Major Rating Factors: Middle of the road best describes *Guggenheim S&P Mid Cap 400 Pure whose TheStreet.com Investment Rating is currently a C+ (Fair). The fund currently has a performance rating of C+ (Fair) based on an annualized return of 8.72% over the last three years and a total return of -10.58% year to date 2015. Factored into the performance evaluation is an expense ratio of 0.35% (very low).

The fund's risk rating is currently B- (Good). It carries a beta of 1.13, meaning it is expected to move 11.3% for every 10% move in the market. Volatility, as measured by both the semi-deviation and a drawdown factor, is considered low. As of December 31, 2015, *Guggenheim S&P Mid Cap 400 Pure traded at a premium of .02% above its net asset value, which is worse than its one-year historical average discount of .03%.

Michael P. Byrum currently receives a manager quality ranking of 26 (0=worst, 99=best). If you desire an average level of risk, then this fund may be an option.

Data Date	Investment Rating	Net Assets ($Mil)	Price	Performance Rating/Pts	Total Return Y-T-D	Risk Rating/Pts
12-15	C+	114.90	47.65	C+ / 6.2	-10.58%	B- / 7.2
2014	B+	114.90	54.36	B+ / 8.6	10.31%	B- / 7.1
2013	B+	88.80	50.75	B+ / 8.4	32.06%	B- / 7.9
2012	C+	37.00	36.93	C+ / 6.1	18.25%	B- / 7.7
2011	B-	39.60	31.66	C+ / 6.9	-4.40%	B- / 7.5
2010	B-	45.90	34.01	B- / 7.5	22.34%	C / 5.0

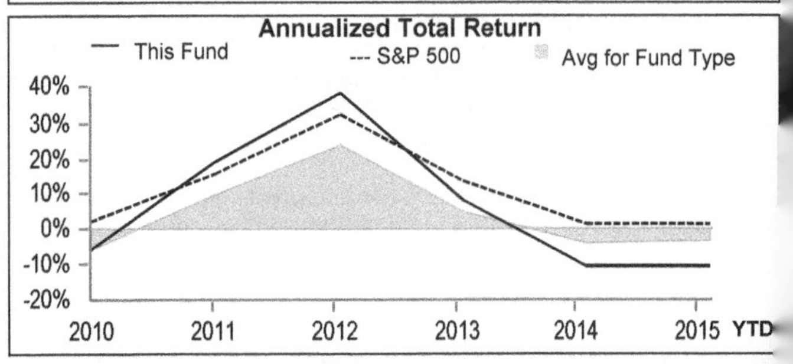

*Guggenheim S&P Mid Cap 400 Pure (RFG) B- Good

Fund Family: Guggenheim Investments
Fund Type: Growth
Inception Date: March 1, 2006

Major Rating Factors: Strong performance is the major factor driving the B- (Good) TheStreet.com Investment Rating for *Guggenheim S&P Mid Cap 400 Pure. The fund currently has a performance rating of B (Good) based on an annualized return of 10.50% over the last three years and a total return of 2.95% year to date 2015. Factored into the performance evaluation is an expense ratio of 0.35% (very low).

The fund's risk rating is currently C+ (Fair). It carries a beta of 1.05, meaning that its performance tracks fairly well with that of the overall stock market. Volatility, as measured by both the semi-deviation and a drawdown factor, is considered low. As of December 31, 2015, *Guggenheim S&P Mid Cap 400 Pure traded at a premium of .47% above its net asset value.

James R. King currently receives a manager quality ranking of 38 (0=worst, 99=best). If you desire only a moderate level of risk and strong performance, then this fund is an excellent option.

Data Date	Investment Rating	Net Assets ($Mil)	Price	Performance Rating/Pts	Total Return Y-T-D	Risk Rating/Pts
12-15	B-	776.80	124.69	B / 7.6	2.95%	C+ / 6.5
2014	B-	776.80	121.80	C+ / 6.9	1.34%	B- / 7.4
2013	B+	805.40	123.07	B+ / 8.6	30.52%	B- / 7.8
2012	B	534.00	91.26	B- / 7.5	15.86%	B- / 7.8
2011	B	514.80	78.48	B / 8.0	2.17%	B- / 7.6
2010	B+	477.40	78.35	B+ / 8.7	34.84%	C / 4.8

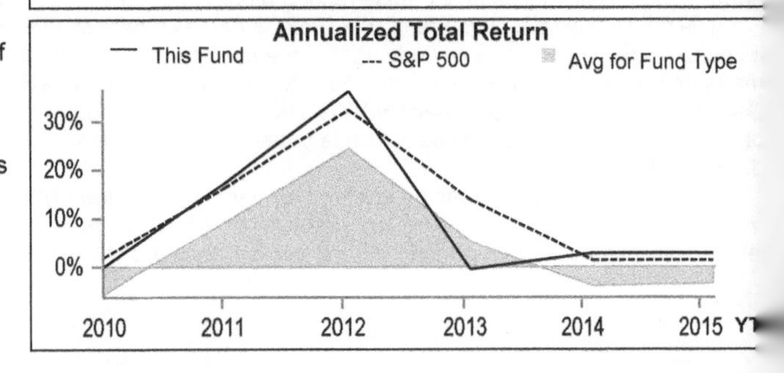

* Denotes ETF Fund

*Guggenheim S&P Sm Cap 600 Pure G (RZG) B- Good

Fund Family: Guggenheim Investments
Fund Type: Growth
Inception Date: March 1, 2006

Major Rating Factors: Strong performance is the major factor driving the B- (Good) TheStreet.com Investment Rating for *Guggenheim S&P Sm Cap 600 Pure G. The fund currently has a performance rating of B (Good) based on an annualized return of 12.39% over the last three years and a total return of 1.65% year to date 2015. Factored into the performance evaluation is an expense ratio of 0.35% (very low).

The fund's risk rating is currently C+ (Fair). It carries a beta of 1.05, meaning that its performance tracks fairly well with that of the overall stock market. Volatility, as measured by both the semi-deviation and a drawdown factor, is considered low. As of December 31, 2015, *Guggenheim S&P Sm Cap 600 Pure G traded at a premium of .05% above its net asset value, which is worse than its one-year historical average premium of .04%.

James R. King currently receives a manager quality ranking of 51 (0=worst, 99=best). If you desire only a moderate level of risk and strong performance, then this fund is an excellent option.

Data Date	Investment Rating	Net Assets ($Mil)	Price	Performance Rating/Pts	Total Return Y-T-D	Risk Rating/Pts
12-15	B-	98.30	80.86	B / 8.0	1.65%	C+ / 6.2
2014	C+	98.30	80.72	B- / 7.4	3.54%	C+ / 6.7
2013	B+	119.70	79.82	A- / 9.0	36.80%	B- / 7.2
2012	B-	72.60	55.82	B- / 7.0	16.06%	B- / 7.5
2011	C+	55.10	50.21	B- / 7.0	4.10%	C+ / 6.7
2010	B+	26.30	47.88	B / 8.0	28.38%	C / 5.3

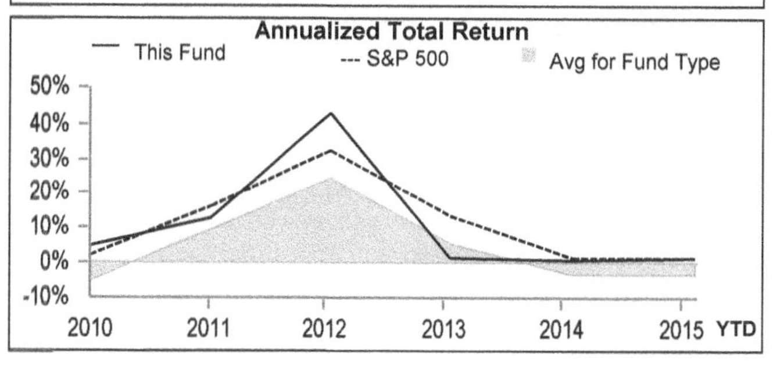

*Guggenheim S&P Sm Cap 600 Pure V (RZV) C+ Fair

Fund Family: Guggenheim Investments
Fund Type: Growth
Inception Date: March 1, 2006

Major Rating Factors: Middle of the road best describes *Guggenheim S&P Sm Cap 600 Pure V whose TheStreet.com Investment Rating is currently a C+ (Fair). The fund currently has a performance rating of C+ (Fair) based on an annualized return of 7.65% over the last three years and a total return of -12.11% year to date 2015. Factored into the performance evaluation is an expense ratio of 0.35% (very low).

The fund's risk rating is currently B (Good). It carries a beta of 1.25, meaning it is expected to move 12.5% for every 10% move in the market. Volatility, as measured by both the semi-deviation and a drawdown factor, is considered low. As of December 31, 2015, *Guggenheim S&P Sm Cap 600 Pure V traded at a discount of .24% below its net asset value, which is better than its one-year historical average discount of .03%.

Michael P. Byrum currently receives a manager quality ranking of 19 (0=worst, 99=best). If you desire an average level of risk, then this fund may be an option.

Data Date	Investment Rating	Net Assets ($Mil)	Price	Performance Rating/Pts	Total Return Y-T-D	Risk Rating/Pts
12-15	C+	169.80	54.82	C+ / 5.9	-12.11%	B / 8.0
2014	B	169.80	63.55	B+ / 8.3	3.65%	C+ / 6.9
2013	A-	155.60	62.30	A- / 9.0	38.18%	B- / 7.6
2012	C+	71.30	43.21	C+ / 6.9	20.39%	B- / 7.2
2011	C+	63.20	36.08	B- / 7.0	-6.64%	C+ / 6.3
2010	B	106.20	39.40	B+ / 8.4	28.57%	C / 4.4

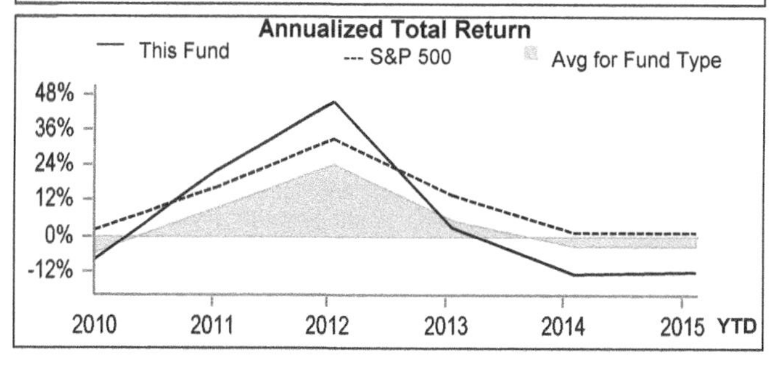

*Guggenheim Shipping ETF (SEA) D- Weak

Fund Family: Guggenheim Funds Investment Advisor
Fund Type: Global
Inception Date: June 11, 2010

Major Rating Factors:
Disappointing performance is the major factor driving the D- (Weak) TheStreet.com Investment Rating for *Guggenheim Shipping ETF. The fund currently has a performance rating of D (Weak) based on an annualized return of -4.61% over the last three years and a total return of -25.32% year to date 2015. Factored into the performance evaluation is an expense ratio of 0.65% (very low).

The fund's risk rating is currently C- (Fair). It carries a beta of 0.96, meaning that its performance tracks fairly well with that of the overall stock market. Volatility, as measured by both the semi-deviation and a drawdown factor, is considered average. As of December 31, 2015, *Guggenheim Shipping ETF traded at a premium of .16% above its net asset value, which is worse than its one-year historical average discount of .11%.

Saroj Kanuri has been running the fund for 8 years and currently receives a manager quality ranking of 20 (0=worst, 99=best). This fund offers an average level of risk but investors looking for strong performance will be frustrated.

Data Date	Investment Rating	Net Assets ($Mil)	Price	Performance Rating/Pts	Total Return Y-T-D	Risk Rating/Pts
12-15	D-	95.00	12.67	D / 2.0	-25.32%	C- / 3.9
2014	C-	95.00	18.44	C- / 4.2	-10.30%	B- / 7.5
2013	D	106.80	21.59	D+ / 2.7	29.02%	C / 5.2
2012	C+	27.20	16.10	B+ / 8.6	15.74%	C / 5.1
2011	E+	34.10	14.88	E- / 0.2	-45.68%	C / 5.1

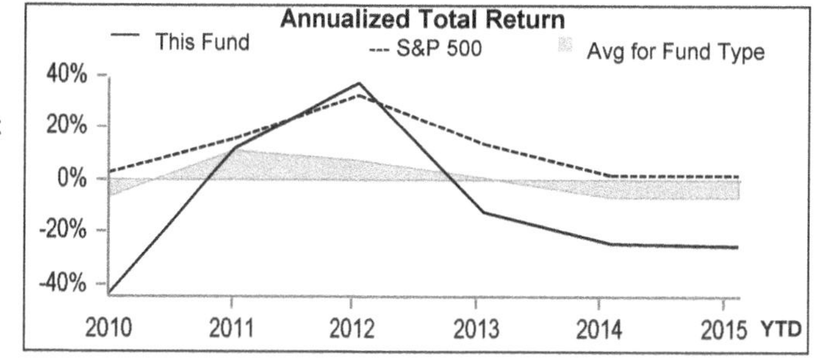

*Guggenheim Singapore Dollar Tr (FXSG) C- Fair

Fund Family: Guggenheim Investments
Fund Type: Global
Inception Date: February 12, 2013

Major Rating Factors:
Disappointing performance is the major factor driving the C- (Fair) TheStreet.com Investment Rating for *Guggenheim Singapore Dollar Tr. The fund currently has a performance rating of D (Weak) based on an annualized return of 0.00% over the last three years and a total return of -7.77% year to date 2015. Factored into the performance evaluation is an expense ratio of 0.40% (very low).

The fund's risk rating is currently B (Good). It carries a beta of 0.00, meaning the fund's expected move will be 0.0% for every 10% move in the market. Volatility, as measured by both the semi-deviation and a drawdown factor, is considered low. As of December 31, 2015, *Guggenheim Singapore Dollar Tr traded at a discount of .85% below its net asset value, which is better than its one-year historical average discount of .18%.

Michael P. Byrum currently receives a manager quality ranking of 29 (0=worst, 99=best). This fund offers only a moderate level of risk but investors looking for strong performance are still waiting.

Data Date	Investment Rating	Net Assets ($Mil)	Price	Performance Rating/Pts	Total Return Y-T-D	Risk Rating/Pts
12-15	C-	7.80	69.13	D / 2.2	-7.77%	B / 8.6
2014	D+	7.80	74.95	D / 1.7	-4.32%	B- / 7.3

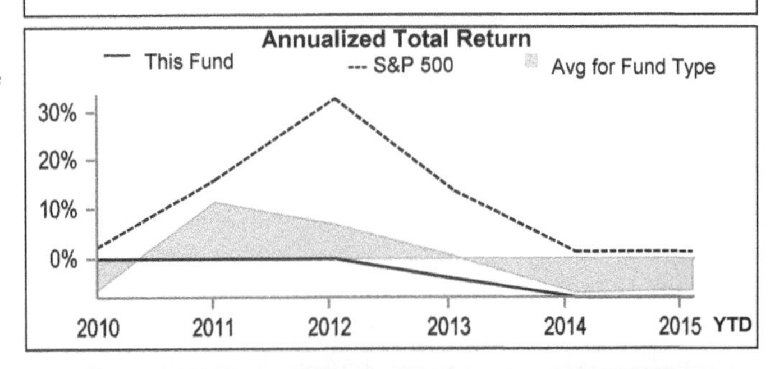

*Guggenheim Solar ETF (TAN) C Fair

Fund Family: Guggenheim Funds Investment Advisor
Fund Type: Energy/Natural Resources
Inception Date: April 15, 2008

Major Rating Factors:
Exceptional performance is the major factor driving the C (Fair) TheStreet.com Investment Rating for *Guggenheim Solar ETF. The fund currently has a performance rating of A (Excellent) based on an annualized return of 20.70% over the last three years and a total return of -8.39% year to date 2015. Factored into the performance evaluation is an expense ratio of 0.70% (very low).

The fund's risk rating is currently C- (Fair). It carries a beta of 0.92, meaning that its performance tracks fairly well with that of the overall stock market. Volatility, as measured by both the semi-deviation and a drawdown factor, is considered average. As of December 31, 2015, *Guggenheim Solar ETF traded at a premium of .10% above its net asset value, which is worse than its one-year historical average premium of .04%.

James R. King has been running the fund for 3 years and currently receives a manager quality ranking of 99 (0=worst, 99=best). If you desire an average level of risk and strong performance, then this fund is a good option.

Data Date	Investment Rating	Net Assets ($Mil)	Price	Performance Rating/Pts	Total Return Y-T-D	Risk Rating/Pts
12-15	C	395.20	30.64	A / 9.3	-8.39%	C- / 3.5
2014	D	395.20	34.10	C / 4.9	-10.34%	C- / 3.8
2013	D-	293.10	35.18	C / 5.0	111.99%	D / 2.2
2012	E	47.30	15.64	E / 0.3	-30.07%	C- / 3.6
2011	E	59.30	2.47	E / 0.4	-62.75%	C- / 3.7
2010	E	142.70	7.30	E / 0.5	-28.64%	D+ / 2.8

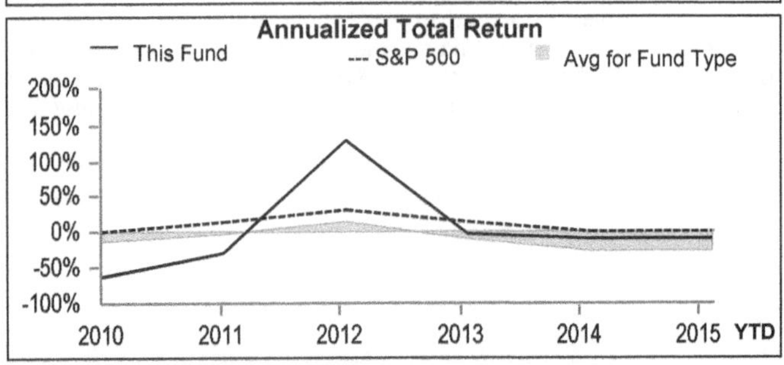

*Guggenheim Spin-Off ETF (CSD) C+ Fair

Fund Family: Guggenheim Funds Investment Advisor
Fund Type: Income
Inception Date: December 15, 2006

Major Rating Factors: Middle of the road best describes *Guggenheim Spin-Off ETF whose TheStreet.com Investment Rating is currently a C+ (Fair). The fund currently has a performance rating of C+ (Fair) based on an annualized return of 9.40% over the last three years and a total return of -12.00% year to date 2015. Factored into the performance evaluation is an expense ratio of 0.65% (very low).

The fund's risk rating is currently B- (Good). It carries a beta of 1.31, meaning it is expected to move 13.1% for every 10% move in the market. Volatility, as measured by both the semi-deviation and a drawdown factor, is considered low. As of December 31, 2015, *Guggenheim Spin-Off ETF traded at a discount of .05% below its net asset value, which is better than its one-year historical average discount of .02%.

James R. King has been running the fund for 3 years and currently receives a manager quality ranking of 20 (0=worst, 99=best). If you desire an average level of risk, then this fund may be an option.

Data Date	Investment Rating	Net Assets ($Mil)	Price	Performance Rating/Pts	Total Return Y-T-D	Risk Rating/Pts
12-15	C+	579.90	38.44	C+ / 6.4	-12.00%	B- / 7.5
2014	A+	579.90	44.79	B+ / 8.9	3.24%	B / 8.6
2013	A+	719.60	45.01	A / 9.4	45.65%	B / 8.4
2012	A-	65.30	29.64	B / 8.2	26.96%	B / 8.5
2011	B+	29.30	23.52	B / 8.0	6.00%	B / 8.4
2010	C-	15.90	22.78	C / 4.4	21.35%	C / 4.8

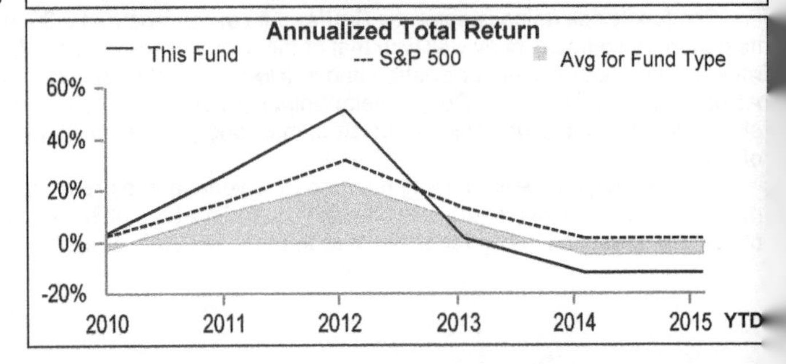

*Guggenheim Swedish Krona (FXS) C- Fair

Fund Family: Guggenheim Investments
Fund Type: Foreign
Inception Date: June 26, 2006

Major Rating Factors:
Disappointing performance is the major factor driving the C- (Fair) TheStreet.com Investment Rating for *Guggenheim Swedish Krona. The fund currently has a performance rating of D+ (Weak) based on an annualized return of -8.46% over the last three years and a total return of -7.38% year to date 2015. Factored into the performance evaluation is an expense ratio of 0.40% (very low).

The fund's risk rating is currently B- (Good). It carries a beta of 0.20, meaning the fund's expected move will be 2.0% for every 10% move in the market. Volatility, as measured by both the semi-deviation and a drawdown factor, is considered low. As of December 31, 2015, *Guggenheim Swedish Krona traded at a discount of .08% below its net asset value, which is better than its one-year historical average discount of .06%.

This fund has been team managed for 10 years and currently receives a manager quality ranking of 17 (0=worst, 99=best). This fund offers only a moderate level of risk but investors looking for strong performance are still waiting.

Data Date	Investment Rating	Net Assets ($Mil)	Price	Performance Rating/Pts	Total Return Y-T-D	Risk Rating/Pts
12-15	C-	34.50	116.47	D+ / 2.3	-7.38%	B- / 7.5
2014	D	34.50	126.83	D / 1.8	-16.67%	C+ / 6.2
2013	C-	54.20	154.56	C- / 3.5	0.26%	B / 8.2
2012	D+	68.90	153.14	D+ / 2.5	9.23%	B / 8.1
2011	C-	87.10	144.57	D+ / 2.6	0.80%	B / 8.5
2010	C-	51.80	148.96	D+ / 2.7	7.00%	C+ / 6.6

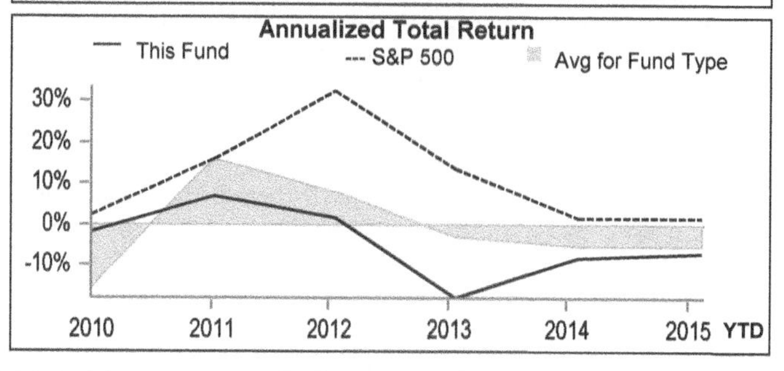

*Guggenheim Swiss Franc (FXF) C Fair

Fund Family: Guggenheim Investments
Fund Type: Foreign
Inception Date: June 26, 2006

Major Rating Factors: Middle of the road best describes *Guggenheim Swiss Franc whose TheStreet.com Investment Rating is currently a C (Fair). The fund currently has a performance rating of C- (Fair) based on an annualized return of -3.26% over the last three years and a total return of -1.07% year to date 2015. Factored into the performance evaluation is an expense ratio of 0.40% (very low).

The fund's risk rating is currently B (Good). It carries a beta of 0.22, meaning the fund's expected move will be 2.2% for every 10% move in the market. Volatility, as measured by both the semi-deviation and a drawdown factor, is considered low. As of December 31, 2015, *Guggenheim Swiss Franc traded at a discount of .10% below its net asset value, which is better than its one-year historical average discount of .05%.

This fund has been team managed for 10 years and currently receives a manager quality ranking of 32 (0=worst, 99=best). If you desire an average level of risk, then this fund may be an option.

Data Date	Investment Rating	Net Assets ($Mil)	Price	Performance Rating/Pts	Total Return Y-T-D	Risk Rating/Pts
12-15	C	204.50	96.37	C- / 3.1	-1.07%	B / 8.3
2014	D	204.50	98.16	D / 2.1	-9.25%	C+ / 6.7
2013	C-	269.90	109.82	C- / 3.3	1.62%	B / 8.0
2012	D+	338.50	107.46	D / 2.2	3.80%	B / 8.0
2011	C-	427.70	105.10	D+ / 2.4	0.83%	B / 8.4
2010	B-	393.60	106.25	C+ / 6.3	10.54%	B- / 7.7

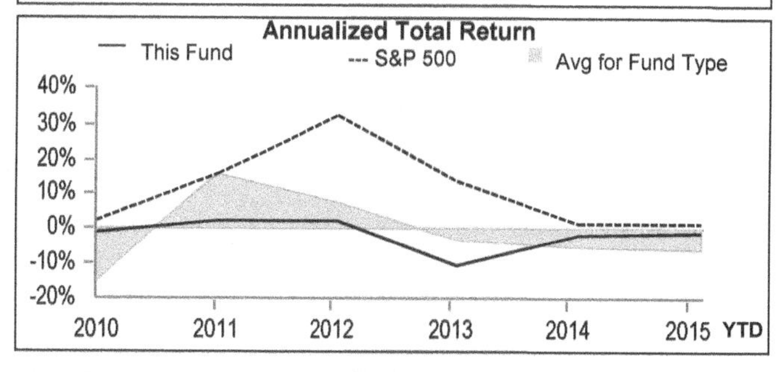

*Guggenheim Timber ETF (CUT) B- Good

Fund Family: Guggenheim Funds Investment Advisor
Fund Type: Global
Inception Date: November 9, 2007

Major Rating Factors: *Guggenheim Timber ETF receives a TheStreet.com Investment Rating of B- (Good). The fund currently has a performance rating of C+ (Fair) based on an annualized return of 5.83% over the last three years and a total return of -0.71% year to date 2015. Factored into the performance evaluation is an expense ratio of 0.70% (very low).

The fund's risk rating is currently B (Good). It carries a beta of 0.86, meaning the fund's expected move will be 8.6% for every 10% move in the market. Volatility, as measured by both the semi-deviation and a drawdown factor, is considered low. As of December 31, 2015, *Guggenheim Timber ETF traded at a discount of .51% below its net asset value, which is better than its one-year historical average discount of .10%.

Saroj Kanuri has been running the fund for 6 years and currently receives a manager quality ranking of 81 (0=worst, 99=best). If you desire an average level of risk, then this fund may be an option.

Data Date	Investment Rating	Net Assets ($Mil)	Price	Performance Rating/Pts	Total Return Y-T-D	Risk Rating/Pts
12-15	B-	224.00	23.57	C+ / 6.1	-0.71%	B / 8.4
2014	C+	224.00	24.24	C+ / 6.7	-1.69%	C+ / 6.6
2013	C+	279.20	25.90	B- / 7.1	22.74%	B- / 7.2
2012	C	195.70	20.44	C / 5.3	26.46%	B- / 7.0
2011	C-	103.60	16.54	C- / 3.8	-18.21%	B- / 7.1
2010	C-	142.80	20.63	C- / 3.8	17.21%	C / 5.2

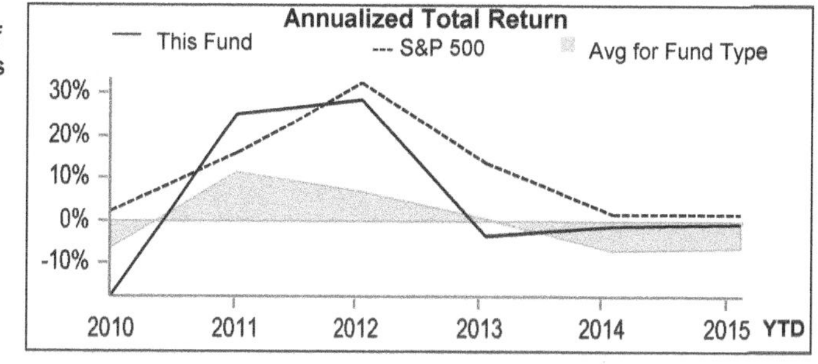

* Denotes ETF Fund

*Guggenheim Wilshire MicroCap ETF (WMCR) B Good

Fund Family: Guggenheim Funds Investment Advisor
Fund Type: Income
Inception Date: September 21, 2006

Major Rating Factors: Strong performance is the major factor driving the B (Good) TheStreet.com Investment Rating for *Guggenheim Wilshire MicroCap ETF. The fund currently has a performance rating of B (Good) based on an annualized return of 12.33% over the last three years and a total return of -3.53% year to date 2015. Factored into the performance evaluation is an expense ratio of 0.50% (very low).

The fund's risk rating is currently B- (Good). It carries a beta of 0.89, meaning the fund's expected move will be 8.9% for every 10% move in the market. Volatility, as measured by both the semi-deviation and a drawdown factor, is considered low. As of December 31, 2015, *Guggenheim Wilshire MicroCap ETF traded at a premium of .35% above its net asset value, which is worse than its one-year historical average premium of .01%.

James R. King has been running the fund for 3 years and currently receives a manager quality ranking of 71 (0=worst, 99=best). If you desire only a moderate level of risk and strong performance, then this fund is an excellent option.

Data Date	Investment Rating	Net Assets ($Mil)	Price	Performance Rating/Pts	Total Return Y-T-D	Risk Rating/Pts
12-15	B	15.60	25.51	B / 7.9	-3.53%	B- / 7.0
2014	B+	15.60	26.99	B+ / 8.6	3.68%	B- / 7.2
2013	B+	45.80	27.01	B+ / 8.7	42.20%	B- / 7.4
2012	C-	12.90	18.48	C / 4.8	20.97%	B- / 7.2
2011	D+	13.80	15.25	C- / 3.1	-15.76%	B- / 7.1
2010	C-	39.90	19.14	C / 5.0	24.27%	C / 5.2

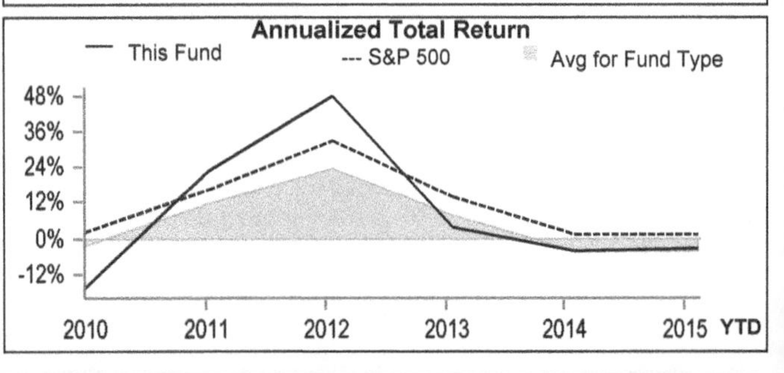

*Guggenheim Wilshire US REIT ETF (WREI) B Good

Fund Family: Guggenheim Funds Investment Advisor
Fund Type: Growth and Income
Inception Date: March 9, 2010

Major Rating Factors: Strong performance is the major factor driving the B (Good) TheStreet.com Investment Rating for *Guggenheim Wilshire US REIT ETF. The fund currently has a performance rating of B+ (Good) based on an annualized return of 11.16% over the last three years and a total return of 2.66% year to date 2015. Factored into the performance evaluation is an expense ratio of 0.32% (very low).

The fund's risk rating is currently C+ (Fair). It carries a beta of 0.42, meaning the fund's expected move will be 4.2% for every 10% move in the market. Volatility, as measured by both the semi-deviation and a drawdown factor, is considered low. As of December 31, 2015, *Guggenheim Wilshire US REIT ETF traded at a premium of .31% above its net asset value, which is worse than its one-year historical average discount of .04%.

James R. King has been running the fund for 3 years and currently receives a manager quality ranking of 90 (0=worst, 99=best). If you desire only a moderate level of risk and strong performance, then this fund is an excellent option.

Data Date	Investment Rating	Net Assets ($Mil)	Price	Performance Rating/Pts	Total Return Y-T-D	Risk Rating/Pts
12-15	B	17.90	45.82	B+ / 8.4	2.66%	C+ / 6.5
2014	B+	17.90	46.32	A- / 9.2	32.88%	C+ / 6.5
2013	C+	14.30	35.69	C+ / 5.6	1.16%	B- / 7.9
2012	B-	18.20	36.10	C+ / 6.6	19.83%	B / 8.0
2011	C	8.00	31.97	C- / 4.0	9.09%	B / 8.0

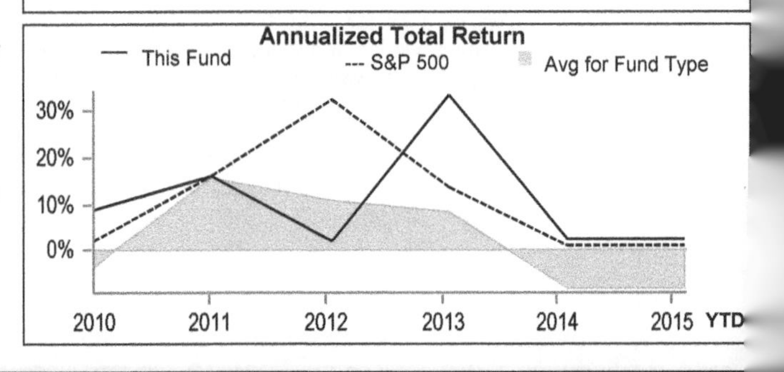

*Health Care Select Sector SPDR (XLV) A+ Excellent

Fund Family: SSgA Funds Management Inc
Fund Type: Health
Inception Date: December 16, 1998

Major Rating Factors:
Exceptional performance is the major factor driving the A+ (Excellent) TheStreet.com Investment Rating for *Health Care Select Sector SPDR. The fund currently has a performance rating of A+ (Excellent) based on an annualized return of 22.80% over the last three years and a total return of 6.93% year to date 2015. Factored into the performance evaluation is an expense ratio of 0.15% (very low).

The fund's risk rating is currently B (Good). It carries a beta of 0.96, meaning that its performance tracks fairly well with that of the overall stock market. Volatility, as measured by both the semi-deviation and a drawdown factor, is considered low. As of December 31, 2015, *Health Care Select Sector SPDR traded at a discount of .03% below its net asset value, which is better than its one-year historical average discount of .01%.

John A. Tucker has been running the fund for 18 years and currently receives a manager quality ranking of 93 (0=worst, 99=best). If you desire only a moderate level of risk and strong performance, then this fund is an excellent option.

Data Date	Investment Rating	Net Assets ($Mil)	Price	Performance Rating/Pts	Total Return Y-T-D	Risk Rating/Pts
12-15	A+	11,126.80	72.03	A+ / 9.6	6.93%	B / 8.1
2014	A+	11,126.80	68.38	A / 9.5	25.56%	B / 8.8
2013	A+	8,512.10	55.44	A- / 9.2	37.43%	B / 8.4
2012	C+	5,571.00	39.88	C+ / 5.6	20.36%	B / 8.4
2011	C	3,400.80	34.69	C / 4.9	11.77%	B / 8.2
2010	C-	2,705.80	31.50	D+ / 2.5	3.32%	C+ / 6.9

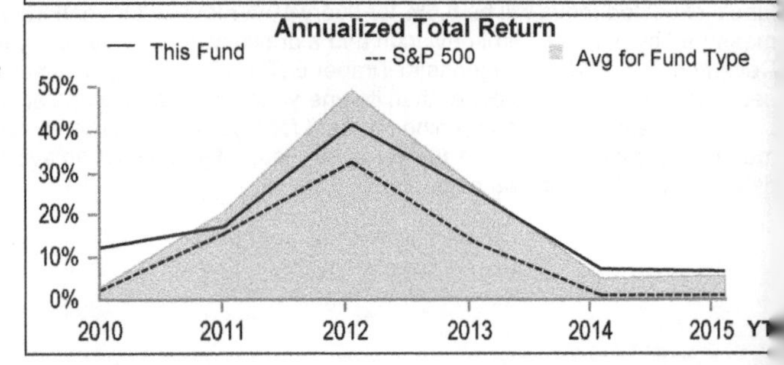

*Highland/iBoxx Senior Loan ETF (SNLN) C Fair

Fund Family: Highland Capital Mgmt Fund Advisors
Fund Type: Loan Participation
Inception Date: November 6, 2012

Data Date	Investment Rating	Net Assets ($Mil)	Price	Performance Rating/Pts	Total Return Y-T-D	Risk Rating/Pts
12-15	C	216.40	18.05	C / 4.3	-2.09%	B / 8.2
2014	C-	216.40	19.20	D+ / 2.5	0.29%	B+ / 9.3
2013	C+	127.80	19.93	C / 4.5	4.46%	B+ / 9.9

Major Rating Factors: Middle of the road best describes *Highland/iBoxx Senior Loan ETF whose TheStreet.com Investment Rating is currently a C (Fair). The fund currently has a performance rating of C (Fair) based on an annualized return of 0.88% over the last three years and a total return of -2.09% year to date 2015. Factored into the performance evaluation is an expense ratio of 0.55% (very low).

The fund's risk rating is currently B (Good). It carries a beta of 34.40, meaning it is expected to move 344.0% for every 10% move in the market. Volatility, as measured by both the semi-deviation and a drawdown factor, is considered low. As of December 31, 2015, *Highland/iBoxx Senior Loan ETF traded at a price exactly equal to its net asset value, which is worse than its one-year historical average discount of .15%.

Mark Okada currently receives a manager quality ranking of 79 (0=worst, 99=best). If you desire an average level of risk, then this fund may be an option.

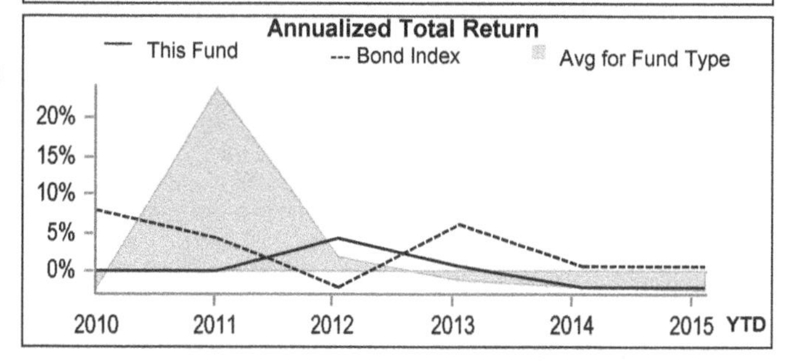

*Horizons Korea KOSPI 200 ETF (HKOR) C- Fair

Fund Family: Horizons ETFs Management (USA) LLC
Fund Type: Foreign
Inception Date: March 4, 2014

Data Date	Investment Rating	Net Assets ($Mil)	Price	Performance Rating/Pts	Total Return Y-T-D	Risk Rating/Pts
12-15	C-	5.40	28.17	D+ / 2.6	-5.25%	B- / 7.0

Major Rating Factors:
Disappointing performance is the major factor driving the C- (Fair) TheStreet.com Investment Rating for *Horizons Korea KOSPI 200 ETF. The fund currently has a performance rating of D+ (Weak) based on an annualized return of 0.00% over the last three years and a total return of -5.25% year to date 2015. Factored into the performance evaluation is an expense ratio of 0.38% (very low).

The fund's risk rating is currently B- (Good). It carries a beta of 0.00, meaning the fund's expected move will be 0.0% for every 10% move in the market. Volatility, as measured by both the semi-deviation and a drawdown factor, is considered low. As of December 31, 2015, *Horizons Korea KOSPI 200 ETF traded at a discount of 4.83% below its net asset value, which is better than its one-year historical average discount of .33%.

Laura Lui has been running the fund for 2 years and currently receives a manager quality ranking of 15 (0=worst, 99=best). This fund offers only a moderate level of risk but investors looking for strong performance are still waiting.

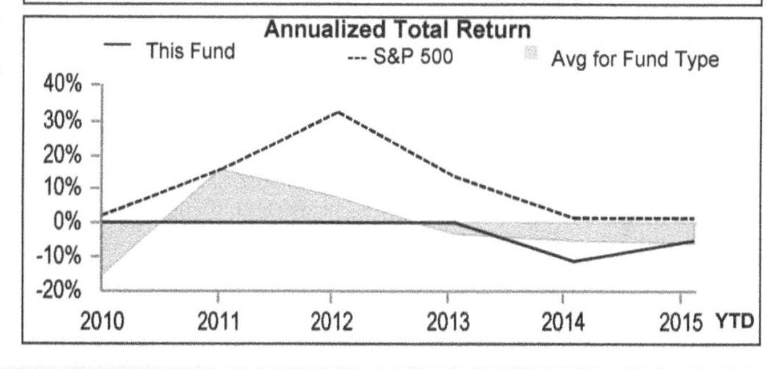

*Horizons S&P 500 Covered Call (HSPX) C Fair

Fund Family: Exchange Traded Concepts LLC
Fund Type: Growth
Inception Date: June 24, 2013

Data Date	Investment Rating	Net Assets ($Mil)	Price	Performance Rating/Pts	Total Return Y-T-D	Risk Rating/Pts
12-15	C	32.40	43.77	C+ / 5.8	1.29%	C+ / 6.9
2014	C+	32.40	45.60	C / 5.2	9.10%	B / 8.5

Major Rating Factors: Middle of the road best describes *Horizons S&P 500 Covered Call whose TheStreet.com Investment Rating is currently a C (Fair). The fund currently has a performance rating of C+ (Fair) based on an annualized return of 0.00% over the last three years and a total return of 1.29% year to date 2015. Factored into the performance evaluation is an expense ratio of 0.65% (very low).

The fund's risk rating is currently C+ (Fair). It carries a beta of 0.00, meaning the fund's expected move will be 0.0% for every 10% move in the market. Volatility, as measured by both the semi-deviation and a drawdown factor, is considered low. As of December 31, 2015, *Horizons S&P 500 Covered Call traded at a premium of .51% above its net asset value, which is worse than its one-year historical average discount of .06%.

Eden Rahim has been running the fund for 3 years and currently receives a manager quality ranking of 68 (0=worst, 99=best). If you desire an average level of risk, then this fund may be an option.

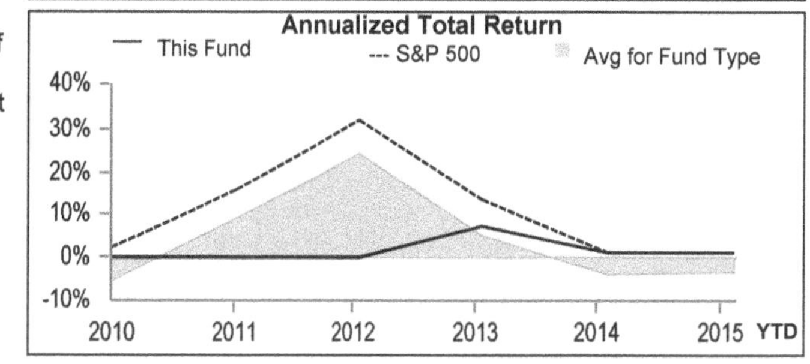

*Huntington EcoLogical Strategy E (HECO) B+ Good

Fund Family: Huntington Asset Advisors Inc
Fund Type: Global
Inception Date: June 18, 2012

Major Rating Factors: Strong performance is the major factor driving the B+ (Good) TheStreet.com Investment Rating for *Huntington EcoLogical Strategy E. The fund currently has a performance rating of B (Good) based on an annualized return of 11.47% over the last three years and a total return of 1.93% year to date 2015. Factored into the performance evaluation is an expense ratio of 0.95% (low).

The fund's risk rating is currently B- (Good). It carries a beta of 0.69, meaning the fund's expected move will be 6.9% for every 10% move in the market. Volatility, as measured by both the semi-deviation and a drawdown factor, is considered low. As of December 31, 2015, *Huntington EcoLogical Strategy E traded at a premium of .48% above its net asset value, which is worse than its one-year historical average discount of .02%.

Paul W. Attwood has been running the fund for 1 year and currently receives a manager quality ranking of 94 (0=worst, 99=best). If you desire only a moderate level of risk and strong performance, then this fund is an excellent option.

Data Date	Investment Rating	Net Assets ($Mil)	Price	Performance Rating/Pts	Total Return Y-T-D	Risk Rating/Pts
12-15	B+	10.90	35.65	B / 8.2	1.93%	B- / 7.0
2014	C+	10.90	37.08	C+ / 6.3	10.89%	B- / 7.7
2013	A+	16.40	34.36	A- / 9.1	24.61%	B+ / 9.6

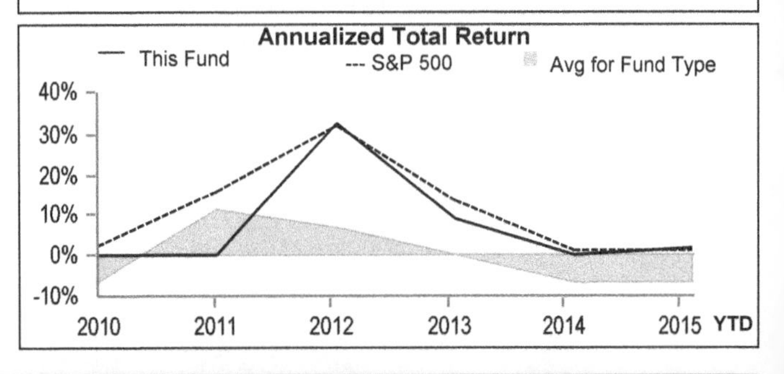

*Huntington US Eq Rotation Strat (HUSE) A- Excellent

Fund Family: Huntington Asset Advisors Inc
Fund Type: Income
Inception Date: July 23, 2012

Major Rating Factors:
Exceptional performance is the major factor driving the A- (Excellent) TheStreet.com Investment Rating for *Huntington US Eq Rotation Strat. The fund currently has a performance rating of A- (Excellent) based on an annualized return of 14.95% over the last three years and a total return of 4.40% year to date 2015. Factored into the performance evaluation is an expense ratio of 0.95% (low).

The fund's risk rating is currently B- (Good). It carries a beta of 0.98, meaning that its performance tracks fairly well with that of the overall stock market. Volatility, as measured by both the semi-deviation and a drawdown factor, is considered low. As of December 31, 2015, *Huntington US Eq Rotation Strat traded at a premium of 1.45% above its net asset value, which is worse than its one-year historical average discount of .10%.

Martina Cheung has been running the fund for 4 years and currently receives a manager quality ranking of 78 (0=worst, 99=best). If you desire only a moderate level of risk and strong performance, then this fund is an excellent option.

Data Date	Investment Rating	Net Assets ($Mil)	Price	Performance Rating/Pts	Total Return Y-T-D	Risk Rating/Pts
12-15	A-	11.20	37.89	A- / 9.0	4.40%	B- / 7.2
2014	B	11.20	37.99	B- / 7.4	14.49%	B- / 7.7
2013	A+	13.10	34.88	A / 9.4	28.76%	B+ / 9.7

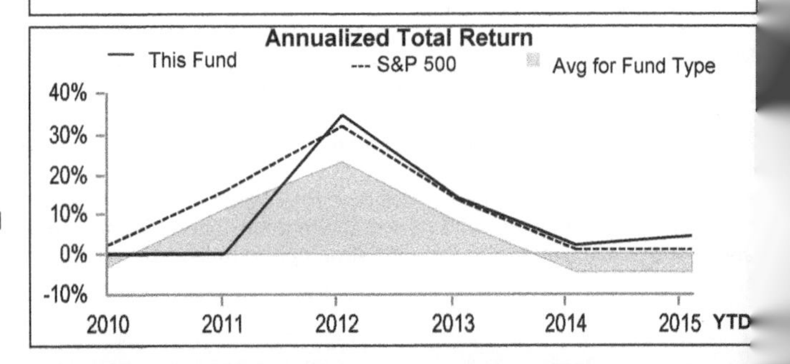

*Industrial Select Sector SPDR (XLI) A+ Excellent

Fund Family: SSgA Funds Management Inc
Fund Type: Growth
Inception Date: December 16, 1998

Major Rating Factors:
Strong performance is the major factor driving the A+ (Excellent) TheStreet.com Investment Rating for *Industrial Select Sector SPDR. The fund currently has a performance rating of B+ (Good) based on an annualized return of 13.10% over the last three years and a total return of -3.60% year to date 2015. Factored into the performance evaluation is an expense ratio of 0.15% (very low).

The fund's risk rating is currently B (Good). It carries a beta of 1.06, meaning that its performance tracks fairly well with that of the overall stock market. Volatility, as measured by both the semi-deviation and a drawdown factor, is considered low. As of December 31, 2015, *Industrial Select Sector SPDR traded at a discount of .04% below its net asset value, which is better than its one-year historical average discount of .01%.

John A. Tucker has been running the fund for 18 years and currently receives a manager quality ranking of 54 (0=worst, 99=best). If you desire only a moderate level of risk and strong performance, then this fund is an excellent option.

Data Date	Investment Rating	Net Assets ($Mil)	Price	Performance Rating/Pts	Total Return Y-T-D	Risk Rating/Pts
12-15	A+	8,692.50	53.01	B+ / 8.4	-3.60%	B / 8.7
2014	B+	8,692.50	56.58	B+ / 8.5	11.63%	B- / 7.5
2013	A-	9,866.00	52.26	B+ / 8.8	34.62%	B- / 7.9
2012	C	3,878.20	37.90	C+ / 5.6	12.73%	B- / 7.7
2011	C	2,711.00	33.75	C+ / 5.8	0.22%	B- / 7.3
2010	C	3,744.30	34.87	C+ / 5.8	27.85%	C / 5.4

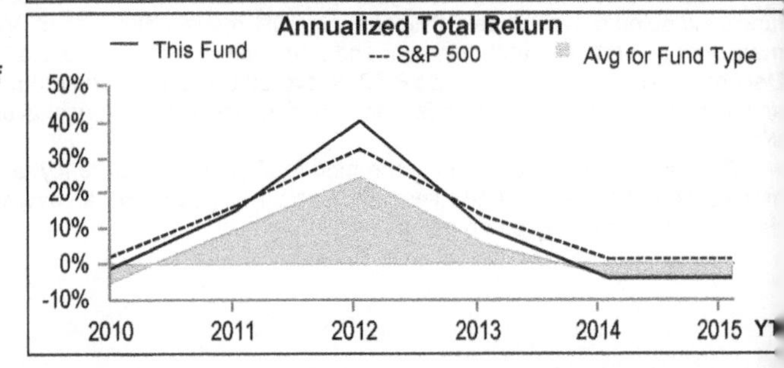

*iPath Bloomberg Agri SI TR A (JJA) E+ Very Weak

Fund Family: Barclays Bank PLC
Fund Type: Energy/Natural Resources
Inception Date: October 23, 2007

Major Rating Factors:
Disappointing performance is the major factor driving the E+ (Very Weak) TheStreet.com Investment Rating for *iPath Bloomberg Agri SI TR A. The fund currently has a performance rating of D- (Weak) based on an annualized return of -13.92% over the last three years and a total return of -16.26% year to date 2015. Factored into the performance evaluation is an expense ratio of 0.75% (very low).

The fund's risk rating is currently C- (Fair). It carries a beta of 0.26, meaning the fund's expected move will be 2.6% for every 10% move in the market. Volatility, as measured by both the semi-deviation and a drawdown factor, is considered average. As of December 31, 2015, *iPath Bloomberg Agri SI TR A traded at a discount of .29% below its net asset value, which is better than its one-year historical average premium of .01%.

This fund has been team managed for 9 years and currently receives a manager quality ranking of 12 (0=worst, 99=best). This fund offers an average level of risk but investors looking for strong performance will be frustrated.

Data Date	Investment Rating	Net Assets ($Mil)	Price	Performance Rating/Pts	Total Return Y-T-D	Risk Rating/Pts
12-15	E+	68.43	34.35	D- / 1.3	-16.26%	C- / 3.4
2014	D-	52.90	41.75	D / 1.7	-8.46%	C- / 4.1
2013	E+	68.43	46.53	D- / 1.1	-14.06%	C- / 4.1
2012	D-	68.43	55.14	D+ / 2.7	6.87%	C / 4.3
2011	D-	135.50	53.42	D+ / 2.8	-13.45%	C / 4.6
2010	C	142.20	63.07	B / 8.2	38.40%	D+ / 2.6

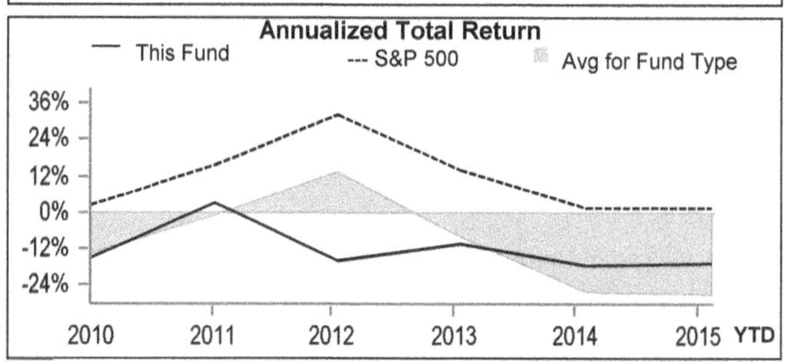

*iPath Bloomberg Almin SI TR A (JJU) E Very Weak

Fund Family: Barclays Bank PLC
Fund Type: Energy/Natural Resources
Inception Date: June 24, 2008

Major Rating Factors: *iPath Bloomberg Almin SI TR A has adopted a very risky asset allocation strategy and currently receives an overall TheStreet.com Investment Rating of E (Very Weak). The fund has a high level of volatility, as measured by both semi-deviation and drawdown factors. It carries a beta of 0.23, meaning the fund's expected move will be 2.3% for every 10% move in the market. As of December 31, 2015, *iPath Bloomberg Almin SI TR A traded at a premium of .89% above its net asset value, which is worse than its one-year historical average premium of .11%. Unfortunately, the high level of risk (D-, Weak) failed to pay off as investors endured poor performance.

The fund's performance rating is currently D- (Weak). It has registered an annualized return of -17.32% over the last three years and is down -25.88% year to date 2015. Factored into the performance evaluation is an expense ratio of 0.75% (very low).

This fund has been team managed for 8 years and currently receives a manager quality ranking of 9 (0=worst, 99=best). If you can tolerate very high levels of risk in the hope of improved future returns, holding this fund may be an option.

Data Date	Investment Rating	Net Assets ($Mil)	Price	Performance Rating/Pts	Total Return Y-T-D	Risk Rating/Pts
12-15	E	6.79	13.59	D- / 1.0	-25.88%	D- / 1.4
2014	E+	4.20	17.96	D- / 1.3	-3.06%	C- / 4.0
2013	E	6.79	18.64	E+ / 0.6	-22.40%	D+ / 2.9
2012	E	6.79	24.18	E+ / 0.8	-9.37%	C- / 3.5
2011	E+	4.50	25.30	D / 1.6	-22.88%	C- / 4.2
2010	C	11.60	33.10	B+ / 8.5	4.48%	D / 2.1

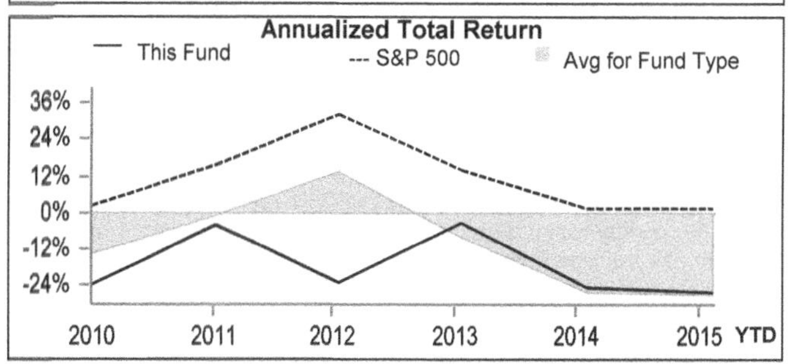

*iPath Bloomberg Cocoa SI TR A (NIB) C Fair

Fund Family: Barclays Bank PLC
Fund Type: Energy/Natural Resources
Inception Date: June 24, 2008

Major Rating Factors: Strong performance is the major factor driving the C (Fair) TheStreet.com Investment Rating for *iPath Bloomberg Cocoa SI TR A. The fund currently has a performance rating of B (Good) based on an annualized return of 11.05% over the last three years and a total return of 7.60% year to date 2015. Factored into the performance evaluation is an expense ratio of 0.75% (very low).

The fund's risk rating is currently C- (Fair). It carries a beta of 0.30, meaning the fund's expected move will be 3.0% for every 10% move in the market. Volatility, as measured by both the semi-deviation and a drawdown factor, is considered average. As of December 31, 2015, *iPath Bloomberg Cocoa SI TR A traded at a discount of .17% below its net asset value, which is better than its one-year historical average discount of .14%.

This fund has been team managed for 8 years and currently receives a manager quality ranking of 96 (0=worst, 99=best). If you desire an average level of risk and strong performance, then this fund is a good option.

Data Date	Investment Rating	Net Assets ($Mil)	Price	Performance Rating/Pts	Total Return Y-T-D	Risk Rating/Pts
12-15	C	27.73	41.32	B / 8.2	7.60%	C- / 4.2
2014	C+	23.50	37.98	C+ / 5.9	7.87%	B- / 7.3
2013	E+	27.73	35.80	D+ / 2.9	18.88%	C- / 3.0
2012	E	27.73	30.30	E+ / 0.6	-1.13%	D+ / 2.9
2011	E	17.60	28.75	E+ / 0.9	-31.94%	C- / 3.1
2010	E+	15.20	43.18	D- / 1.1	-11.66%	C- / 3.6

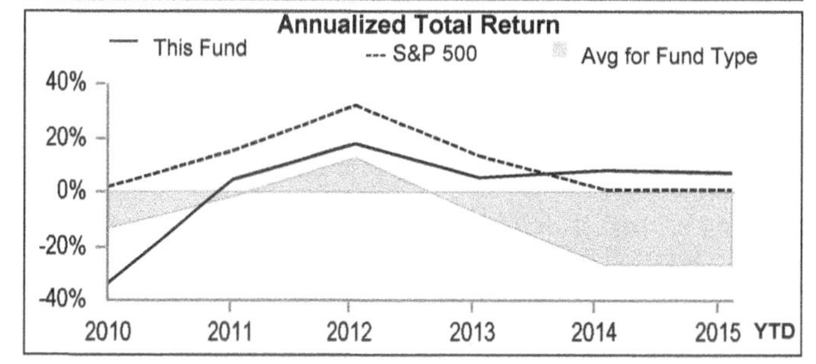

*iPath Bloomberg Coffee SI TR A (JO) E+ Very Weak

Fund Family: Barclays Bank PLC
Fund Type: Energy/Natural Resources
Inception Date: June 24, 2008

Major Rating Factors: *iPath Bloomberg Coffee SI TR A has adopted a risky asset allocation strategy and currently receives an overall TheStreet.com Investment Rating of E+ (Very Weak). The fund has an above average level of volatility, as measured by both semi-deviation and drawdown factors. It carries a beta of 0.13, meaning the fund's expected move will be 1.3% for every 10% move in the market. As of December 31, 2015, *iPath Bloomberg Coffee SI TR A traded at a discount of 1.05% below its net asset value, which is better than its one-year historical average premium of .23%. Unfortunately, the high level of risk (D+, Weak) failed to pay off as investors endured poor performance.

The fund's performance rating is currently D- (Weak). It has registered an annualized return of -15.92% over the last three years and is down -32.28% year to date 2015. Factored into the performance evaluation is an expense ratio of 0.75% (very low).

This fund has been team managed for 8 years and currently receives a manager quality ranking of 10 (0=worst, 99=best). If you can tolerate high levels of risk in the hope of improved future returns, holding this fund may be an option.

Data Date	Investment Rating	Net Assets ($Mil)	Price	Performance Rating/Pts	Total Return Y-T-D	Risk Rating/Pts
12-15	E+	7.89	19.70	D- / 1.1	-32.28%	D+ / 2.5
2014	E	89.60	30.48	D- / 1.0	29.23%	D / 2.0
2013	E-	7.89	21.70	E / 0.4	-30.41%	D / 1.9
2012	E-	7.89	32.37	E+ / 0.7	-38.91%	D / 2.1
2011	D	25.70	56.52	C- / 3.7	-12.01%	C- / 4.2
2010	B	34.50	64.03	A+ / 9.8	65.37%	C- / 3.5

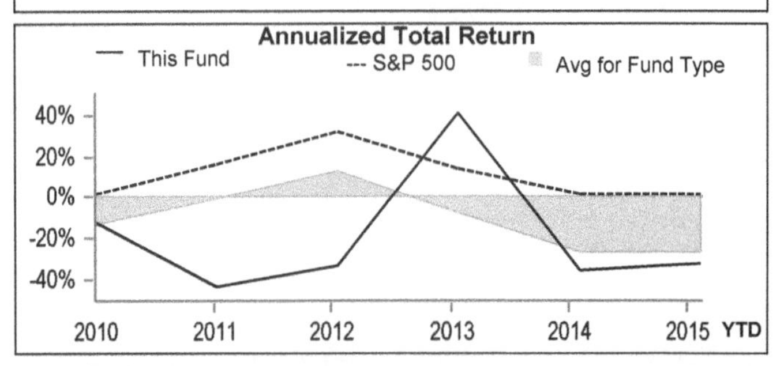

*iPath Bloomberg Commodity Index (DJP) D- Weak

Fund Family: Barclays Bank PLC
Fund Type: Growth
Inception Date: June 6, 2006

Major Rating Factors:
Very poor performance is the major factor driving the D- (Weak) TheStreet.com Investment Rating for *iPath Bloomberg Commodity Index. The fund currently has a performance rating of E+ (Very Weak) based on an annualized return of -19.36% over the last three years and a total return of -27.59% year to date 2015. Factored into the performance evaluation is an expense ratio of 0.75% (very low).

The fund's risk rating is currently C+ (Fair). It carries a beta of 0.34, meaning the fund's expected move will be 3.4% for every 10% move in the market. Volatility, as measured by both the semi-deviation and a drawdown factor, is considered low. As of December 31, 2015, *iPath Bloomberg Commodity Index traded at a discount of .05% below its net asset value, which is worse than its one-year historical average discount of 3.35%.

This fund has been team managed for 10 years and currently receives a manager quality ranking of 5 (0=worst, 99=best). This fund offers only a moderate level of risk but investors looking for strong performance are still waiting.

Data Date	Investment Rating	Net Assets ($Mil)	Price	Performance Rating/Pts	Total Return Y-T-D	Risk Rating/Pts
12-15	D-	1,897.33	21.47	E+ / 0.8	-27.59%	C+ / 5.7
2014	D-	1,453.10	29.91	D- / 1.0	-16.91%	C / 4.8
2013	D	1,897.33	36.75	D- / 1.2	-10.74%	C+ / 6.7
2012	D	1,897.33	41.35	D- / 1.2	-2.02%	B- / 7.0
2011	D+	2,581.80	42.24	D+ / 2.4	-10.98%	B- / 7.7
2010	D	2,854.70	49.12	C- / 3.0	16.23%	C / 4.9

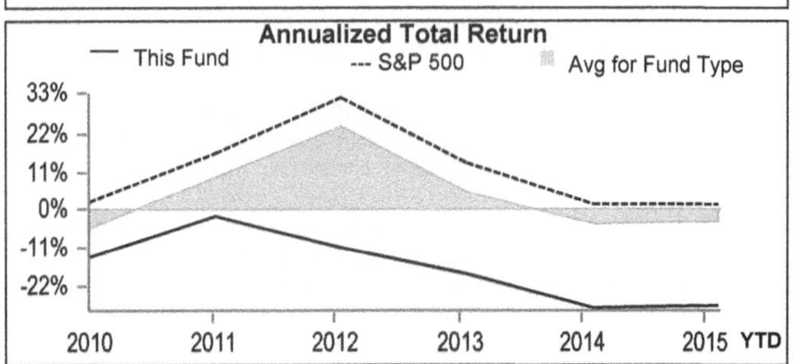

*iPath Bloomberg Copper SI TR A (JJC) E Very Weak

Fund Family: Barclays Bank PLC
Fund Type: Energy/Natural Resources
Inception Date: October 23, 2007

Major Rating Factors: *iPath Bloomberg Copper SI TR A has adopted a very risky asset allocation strategy and currently receives an overall TheStreet.com Investment Rating of E (Very Weak). The fund has a high level of volatility, as measured by both semi-deviation and drawdown factors. It carries a beta of 0.41, meaning the fund's expected move will be 4.1% for every 10% move in the market. As of December 31, 2015, *iPath Bloomberg Copper SI TR A traded at a premium of .12% above its net asset value, which is worse than its one-year historical average premium of .04%. Unfortunately, the high level of risk (D-, Weak) failed to pay off as investors endured very poor performance.

The fund's performance rating is currently E+ (Very Weak). It has registered an annualized return of -19.19% over the last three years and is down -27.21% year to date 2015. Factored into the performance evaluation is an expense ratio of 0.75% (very low).

This fund has been team managed for 9 years and currently receives a manager quality ranking of 8 (0=worst, 99=best). If you can tolerate very high levels of risk in the hope of improved future returns, holding this fund may be an option.

Data Date	Investment Rating	Net Assets ($Mil)	Price	Performance Rating/Pts	Total Return Y-T-D	Risk Rating/Pts
12-15	E	130.36	24.64	E+ / 0.8	-27.21%	D- / 1.4
2014	D-	63.30	33.96	D- / 1.3	-16.04%	C / 4.5
2013	E+	130.36	41.45	D- / 1.2	-12.38%	C- / 3.6
2012	E+	130.36	45.99	D- / 1.3	-1.87%	C- / 3.8
2011	D+	127.80	44.04	C+ / 6.4	-23.04%	C- / 4.0
2010	C	252.40	59.10	B+ / 8.6	29.04%	D / 1.8

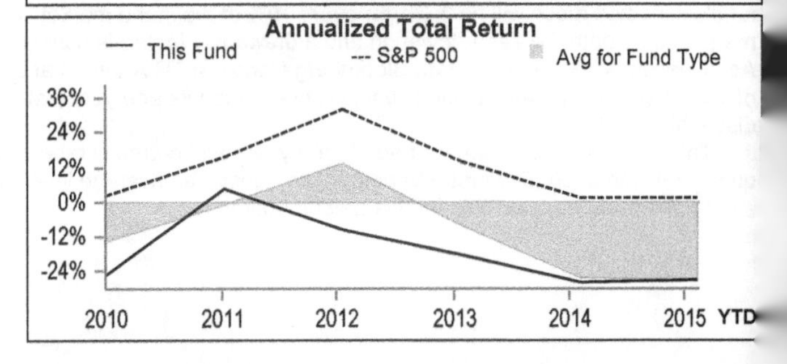

*iPath Bloomberg Cotton SI TR A (BAL) D- Weak

Fund Family: Barclays Bank PLC
Fund Type: Energy/Natural Resources
Inception Date: June 24, 2008

Major Rating Factors: *iPath Bloomberg Cotton SI TR A receives a TheStreet.com Investment Rating of D- (Weak). The fund currently has a performance rating of C- (Fair) based on an annualized return of -4.98% over the last three years and a total return of 3.65% year to date 2015. Factored into the performance evaluation is an expense ratio of 0.75% (very low).

The fund's risk rating is currently C- (Fair). It carries a beta of 0.43, meaning the fund's expected move will be 4.3% for every 10% move in the market. Volatility, as measured by both the semi-deviation and a drawdown factor, is considered average. As of December 31, 2015, *iPath Bloomberg Cotton SI TR A traded at a discount of .02% below its net asset value, which is better than its one-year historical average premium of .03%.

This fund has been team managed for 8 years and currently receives a manager quality ranking of 39 (0=worst, 99=best). If you desire an average level of risk, then this fund may be an option.

Data Date	Investment Rating	Net Assets ($Mil)	Price	Performance Rating/Pts	Total Return Y-T-D	Risk Rating/Pts
12-15	D-	22.72	42.04	C- / 3.1	3.65%	C- / 3.3
2014	E+	19.20	41.18	D- / 1.2	-19.06%	C- / 3.9
2013	E	22.72	53.18	D- / 1.3	6.83%	D+ / 2.3
2012	E+	22.72	49.14	C- / 3.4	-16.47%	D / 2.1
2011	D+	45.50	56.46	C+ / 6.6	-17.92%	C- / 3.1
2010	B-	56.40	73.05	A+ / 9.9	96.21%	D+ / 2.7

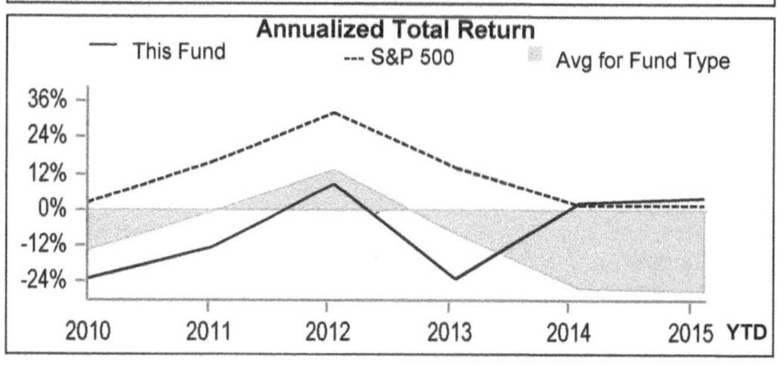

*iPath Bloomberg Energy SI TR A (JJE) E- Very Weak

Fund Family: Barclays Bank PLC
Fund Type: Energy/Natural Resources
Inception Date: October 23, 2007

Major Rating Factors: *iPath Bloomberg Energy SI TR A has adopted a very risky asset allocation strategy and currently receives an overall TheStreet.com Investment Rating of E- (Very Weak). The fund has a high level of volatility, as measured by both semi-deviation and drawdown factors. It carries a beta of 0.77, meaning the fund's expected move will be 7.7% for every 10% move in the market. As of December 31, 2015, *iPath Bloomberg Energy SI TR A traded at a premium of 1.07% above its net asset value, which is worse than its one-year historical average premium of .32%. Unfortunately, the high level of risk (E-, Very Weak) failed to pay off as investors endured very poor performance.

The fund's performance rating is currently E (Very Weak). It has registered an annualized return of -30.74% over the last three years and is down -44.34% year to date 2015. Factored into the performance evaluation is an expense ratio of 0.75% (very low).

This fund has been team managed for 9 years and currently receives a manager quality ranking of 3 (0=worst, 99=best). If you can tolerate very high levels of risk in the hope of improved future returns, holding this fund may be an option.

Data Date	Investment Rating	Net Assets ($Mil)	Price	Performance Rating/Pts	Total Return Y-T-D	Risk Rating/Pts
12-15	E-	10.54	5.66	E / 0.3	-44.34%	E- / 0.1
2014	E+	5.90	10.17	E / 0.5	-40.24%	C / 4.5
2013	E+	10.54	18.06	D- / 1.5	3.11%	C- / 3.5
2012	E	10.54	17.12	E+ / 0.7	-9.98%	C- / 3.4
2011	E+	19.00	19.15	D- / 1.2	-12.68%	C- / 4.0
2010	E-	15.60	23.21	E / 0.5	-11.92%	D- / 1.2

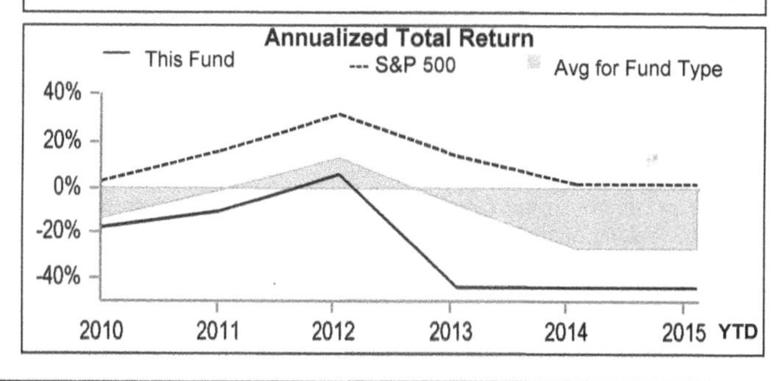

*iPath Bloomberg Grains SI TR A (JJG) E+ Very Weak

Fund Family: Barclays Bank PLC
Fund Type: Energy/Natural Resources
Inception Date: October 23, 2007

Major Rating Factors: *iPath Bloomberg Grains SI TR A has adopted a risky asset allocation strategy and currently receives an overall TheStreet.com Investment Rating of E+ (Very Weak). The fund has an above average level of volatility, as measured by both semi-deviation and drawdown factors. It carries a beta of 0.22, meaning the fund's expected move will be 2.2% for every 10% move in the market. As of December 31, 2015, *iPath Bloomberg Grains SI TR A traded at a discount of .10% below its net asset value, which is better than its one-year historical average discount of .03%. Unfortunately, the high level of risk (D+, Weak) failed to pay off as investors endured poor performance.

The fund's performance rating is currently D- (Weak). It has registered an annualized return of -16.13% over the last three years and is down -20.51% year to date 2015. Factored into the performance evaluation is an expense ratio of 0.75% (very low).

This fund has been team managed for 9 years and currently receives a manager quality ranking of 9 (0=worst, 99=best). If you can tolerate high levels of risk in the hope of improved future returns, holding this fund may be an option.

Data Date	Investment Rating	Net Assets ($Mil)	Price	Performance Rating/Pts	Total Return Y-T-D	Risk Rating/Pts
12-15	E+	57.16	30.35	D- / 1.1	-20.51%	D+ / 2.4
2014	E+	115.20	38.59	D / 2.2	-8.29%	C- / 3.1
2013	E+	57.16	43.13	D- / 1.3	-16.29%	C- / 4.0
2012	D	57.16	52.93	C- / 3.7	24.61%	C / 4.4
2011	D-	166.80	45.03	D / 1.8	-13.30%	C / 4.4
2010	D+	190.60	53.09	C+ / 5.9	29.87%	D+ / 2.4

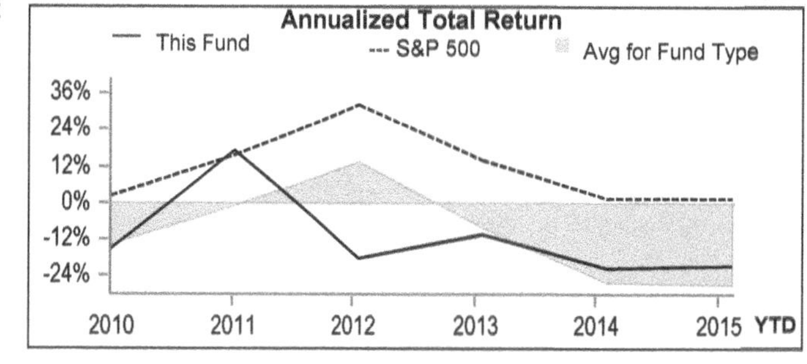

*iPath Bloomberg Ind Me SI TR A (JJM) E+ Very Weak

Fund Family: Barclays Bank PLC
Fund Type: Energy/Natural Resources
Inception Date: October 23, 2007

Major Rating Factors: *iPath Bloomberg Ind Me SI TR A has adopted a risky asset allocation strategy and currently receives an overall TheStreet.com Investment Rating of E+ (Very Weak). The fund has an above average level of volatility, as measured by both semi-deviation and drawdown factors. It carries a beta of 0.31, meaning the fund's expected move will be 3.1% for every 10% move in the market. As of December 31, 2015, *iPath Bloomberg Ind Me SI TR A traded at a discount of .26% below its net asset value, which is better than its one-year historical average discount of .13%. Unfortunately, the high level of risk (D+, Weak) failed to pay off as investors endured very poor performance.

The fund's performance rating is currently E+ (Very Weak). It has registered an annualized return of -18.32% over the last three years and is down -29.18% year to date 2015. Factored into the performance evaluation is an expense ratio of 0.75% (very low).

This fund has been team managed for 9 years and currently receives a manager quality ranking of 9 (0=worst, 99=best). If you can tolerate high levels of risk in the hope of improved future returns, holding this fund may be an option.

Data Date	Investment Rating	Net Assets ($Mil)	Price	Performance Rating/Pts	Total Return Y-T-D	Risk Rating/Pts
12-15	E+	49.69	19.10	E+ / 0.9	-29.18%	D+ / 2.8
2014	D-	13.00	27.03	D- / 1.5	-7.15%	C / 5.0
2013	E	49.69	29.66	E+ / 0.8	-16.72%	C- / 3.3
2012	E+	49.69	34.87	D- / 1.0	-4.88%	C- / 3.8
2011	D-	31.50	34.70	C- / 3.4	-23.79%	C- / 4.1
2010	D	71.70	46.87	C+ / 5.8	15.59%	D / 1.9

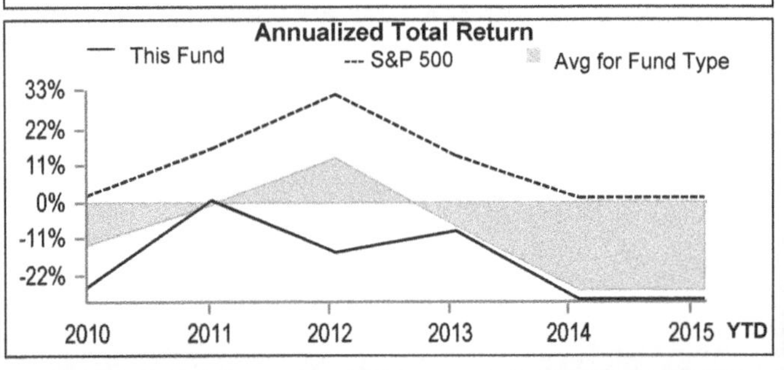

*iPath Bloomberg Lead SI TR A (LD) E+ Very Weak

Fund Family: Barclays Bank PLC
Fund Type: Energy/Natural Resources
Inception Date: June 24, 2008

Major Rating Factors:
Disappointing performance is the major factor driving the E+ (Very Weak) TheStreet.com Investment Rating for *iPath Bloomberg Lead SI TR A. The fund currently has a performance rating of D- (Weak) based on an annualized return of -14.38% over the last three years and a total return of -13.78% year to date 2015. Factored into the performance evaluation is an expense ratio of 0.75% (very low).

The fund's risk rating is currently C- (Fair). It carries a beta of 0.41, meaning the fund's expected move will be 4.1% for every 10% move in the market. Volatility, as measured by both the semi-deviation and a drawdown factor, is considered average. As of December 31, 2015, *iPath Bloomberg Lead SI TR A traded at a discount of 8.34% below its net asset value, which is better than its one-year historical average discount of .77%.

This fund has been team managed for 8 years and currently receives a manager quality ranking of 12 (0=worst, 99=best). This fund offers an average level of risk but investors looking for strong performance will be frustrated.

Data Date	Investment Rating	Net Assets ($Mil)	Price	Performance Rating/Pts	Total Return Y-T-D	Risk Rating/Pts
12-15	E+	13.63	35.59	D- / 1.4	-13.78%	C- / 3.3
2013	E+	13.63	49.45	D- / 1.3	-11.00%	C- / 3.9
2012	E+	13.63	56.32	D- / 1.4	11.16%	C- / 3.8
2011	D-	4.20	49.05	C- / 3.5	-25.01%	C- / 4.2
2010	C+	6.70	64.98	A / 9.3	3.22%	D / 2.2

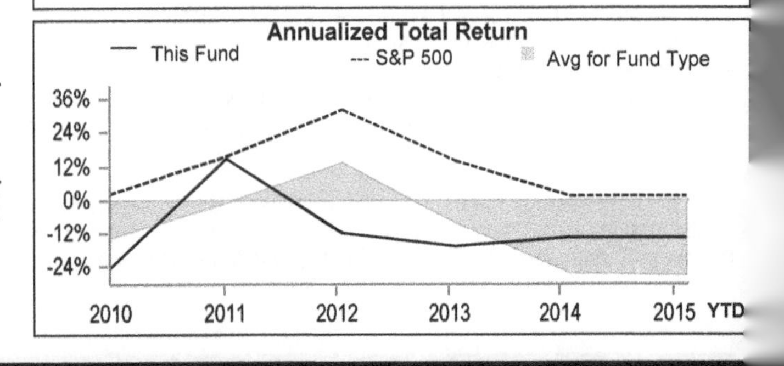

*iPath Bloomberg Live Stk SI TR A (COW) D- Weak

Fund Family: Barclays Bank PLC
Fund Type: Energy/Natural Resources
Inception Date: October 23, 2007

Major Rating Factors:
Disappointing performance is the major factor driving the D- (Weak) TheStreet.com Investment Rating for *iPath Bloomberg Live Stk SI TR A. The fund currently has a performance rating of D (Weak) based on an annualized return of -5.94% over the last three years and a total return of -21.64% year to date 2015. Factored into the performance evaluation is an expense ratio of 0.75% (very low).

The fund's risk rating is currently C- (Fair). It carries a beta of 0.06, meaning the fund's expected move will be 0.6% for every 10% move in the market. Volatility, as measured by both the semi-deviation and a drawdown factor, is considered average. As of December 31, 2015, *iPath Bloomberg Live Stk SI TR A traded at a discount of .25% below its net asset value.

This fund has been team managed for 9 years and currently receives a manager quality ranking of 28 (0=worst, 99=best). This fund offers an average level of risk but investors looking for strong performance will be frustrated.

Data Date	Investment Rating	Net Assets ($Mil)	Price	Performance Rating/Pts	Total Return Y-T-D	Risk Rating/Pts
12-15	D-	110.42	23.93	D / 2.2	-21.64%	C- / 3.6
2014	C-	43.00	30.40	D+ / 2.8	10.65%	B / 8.3
2013	D-	110.42	27.14	D / 1.9	-4.31%	C / 4.7
2012	D-	110.42	28.53	D- / 1.2	-5.81%	C / 4.9
2011	D-	99.20	29.76	D- / 1.5	-2.02%	C / 4.8
2010	E+	65.00	30.75	E+ / 0.8	9.20%	D+ / 2.9

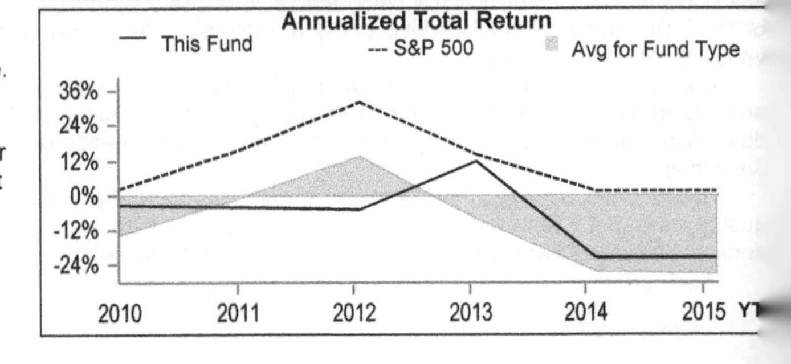

*iPath Bloomberg Nkl SI TR A (JJN) E- Very Weak

Fund Family: Barclays Bank PLC
Fund Type: Energy/Natural Resources
Inception Date: October 23, 2007

Major Rating Factors: *iPath Bloomberg Nkl SI TR A has adopted a very risky asset allocation strategy and currently receives an overall TheStreet.com Investment Rating of E- (Very Weak). The fund has a high level of volatility, as measured by both semi-deviation and drawdown factors. It carries a beta of 0.65, meaning the fund's expected move will be 6.5% for every 10% move in the market. As of December 31, 2015, *iPath Bloomberg Nkl SI TR A traded at a premium of 1.22% above its net asset value, which is worse than its one-year historical average premium of .50%. Unfortunately, the high level of risk (E+, Very Weak) failed to pay off as investors endured very poor performance.

The fund's performance rating is currently E (Very Weak). It has registered an annualized return of -23.93% over the last three years and is down -44.59% year to date 2015. Factored into the performance evaluation is an expense ratio of 0.75% (very low).

This fund has been team managed for 9 years and currently receives a manager quality ranking of 6 (0=worst, 99=best). If you can tolerate very high levels of risk in the hope of improved future returns, holding this fund may be an option.

Data Date	Investment Rating	Net Assets ($Mil)	Price	Performance Rating/Pts	Total Return Y-T-D	Risk Rating/Pts
12-15	E-	14.87	10.81	E / 0.5	-44.59%	E+ / 0.6
2014	E+	9.90	19.98	D- / 1.3	5.49%	D+ / 2.9
2013	E-	14.87	19.06	E+ / 0.6	-23.66%	D / 2.1
2012	E	14.87	24.10	D- / 1.0	-12.54%	D+ / 2.9
2011	D-	8.00	26.68	C- / 3.2	-25.20%	C- / 3.5
2010	E+	18.30	36.65	C- / 3.0	32.12%	D- / 1.5

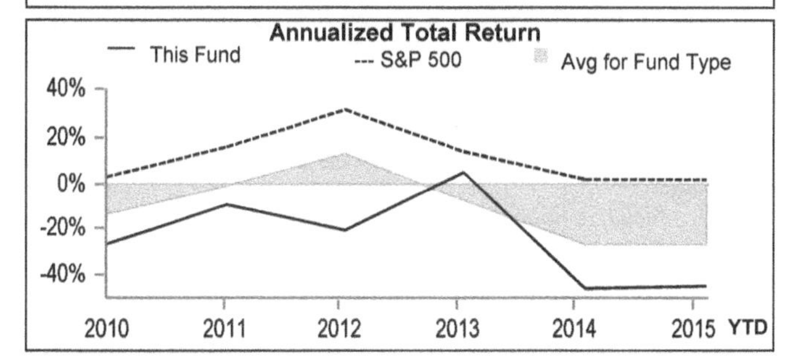

*iPath Bloomberg Ntrl Gas SI TR A (GAZ) E- Very Weak

Fund Family: Barclays Bank PLC
Fund Type: Energy/Natural Resources
Inception Date: October 23, 2007

Major Rating Factors: *iPath Bloomberg Ntrl Gas SI TR A has adopted a very risky asset allocation strategy and currently receives an overall TheStreet.com Investment Rating of E- (Very Weak). The fund has a high level of volatility, as measured by both semi-deviation and drawdown factors. It carries a beta of -0.23, meaning the fund's expected move will be -2.3% for every 10% move in the market. As of December 31, 2015, *iPath Bloomberg Ntrl Gas SI TR A traded at a premium of 33.33% above its net asset value, which is worse than its one-year historical average premium of 7.13%. Unfortunately, the high level of risk (E-, Very Weak) failed to pay off as investors endured very poor performance.

The fund's performance rating is currently E- (Very Weak). It has registered an annualized return of -35.40% over the last three years and is down -64.18% year to date 2015. Factored into the performance evaluation is an expense ratio of 0.75% (very low).

This fund has been team managed for 9 years and currently receives a manager quality ranking of 2 (0=worst, 99=best). If you can tolerate very high levels of risk in the hope of improved future returns, holding this fund may be an option.

Data Date	Investment Rating	Net Assets ($Mil)	Price	Performance Rating/Pts	Total Return Y-T-D	Risk Rating/Pts
12-15	E-	208.19	0.72	E- / 0.2	-64.18%	E- / 0.1
2014	E-	25.60	2.01	E+ / 0.7	-18.25%	D- / 1.0
2013	E-	208.19	2.52	E / 0.4	-1.50%	D / 1.9
2012	E-	208.19	2.69	E- / 0.1	-21.07%	D / 1.9
2011	E-	56.10	3.77	E- / 0.1	-53.56%	D / 1.9
2010	E-	119.30	8.05	E- / 0.2	-43.63%	D- / 1.0

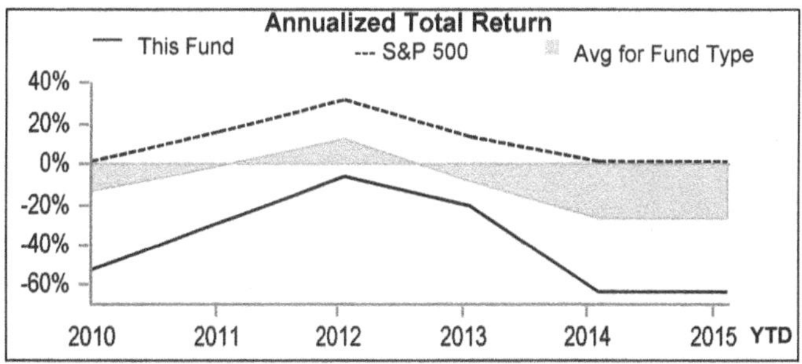

*iPath Bloomberg Platinum SI TR A (PGM) E Very Weak

Fund Family: Barclays Bank PLC
Fund Type: Energy/Natural Resources
Inception Date: June 24, 2008

Major Rating Factors: *iPath Bloomberg Platinum SI TR A has adopted a very risky asset allocation strategy and currently receives an overall TheStreet.com Investment Rating of E (Very Weak). The fund has a high level of volatility, as measured by both semi-deviation and drawdown factors. It carries a beta of 0.28, meaning the fund's expected move will be 2.8% for every 10% move in the market. As of December 31, 2015, *iPath Bloomberg Platinum SI TR A traded at a discount of .21% below its net asset value, which is worse than its one-year historical average discount of .89%. Unfortunately, the high level of risk (D, Weak) failed to pay off as investors endured very poor performance.

The fund's performance rating is currently E+ (Very Weak). It has registered an annualized return of -19.25% over the last three years and is down -28.29% year to date 2015. Factored into the performance evaluation is an expense ratio of 0.75% (very low).

This fund has been team managed for 8 years and currently receives a manager quality ranking of 8 (0=worst, 99=best). If you can tolerate very high levels of risk in the hope of improved future returns, holding this fund may be an option.

Data Date	Investment Rating	Net Assets ($Mil)	Price	Performance Rating/Pts	Total Return Y-T-D	Risk Rating/Pts
12-15	E	103.49	18.57	E+ / 0.9	-28.29%	D / 2.0
2014	D	14.70	25.90	D- / 1.5	-14.56%	C+ / 6.1
2013	E+	103.49	29.96	D- / 1.2	-12.53%	C- / 3.9
2012	E+	103.49	34.80	D- / 1.3	7.74%	C- / 4.2
2011	D-	30.80	32.03	D+ / 2.7	-20.15%	C / 4.3
2010	C-	78.00	41.85	B+ / 8.4	8.59%	D / 1.6

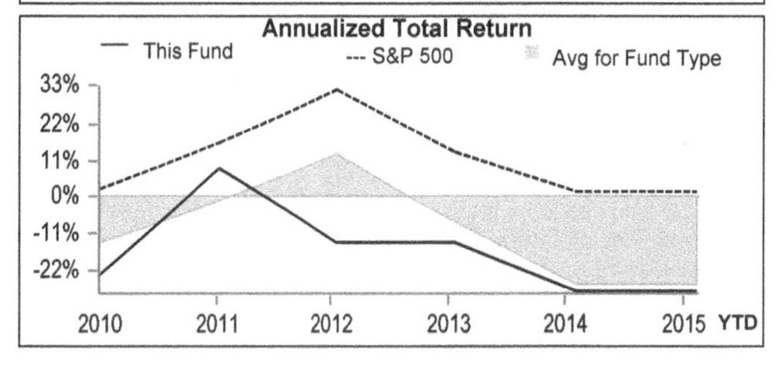

*iPath Bloomberg Prec Mtls SI TR (JJP) E+ Very Weak

Fund Family: Barclays Bank PLC
Fund Type: Energy/Natural Resources
Inception Date: June 24, 2008

Major Rating Factors: *iPath Bloomberg Prec Mtls SI TR has adopted a risky asset allocation strategy and currently receives an overall TheStreet.com Investment Rating of E+ (Very Weak). The fund has an above average level of volatility, as measured by both semi-deviation and drawdown factors. It carries a beta of 0.20, meaning the fund's expected move will be 2.0% for every 10% move in the market. As of December 31, 2015, *iPath Bloomberg Prec Mtls SI TR traded at a discount of .16% below its net asset value, which is better than its one-year historical average discount of .09%. Unfortunately, the high level of risk (D+, Weak) failed to pay off as investors endured poor performance.

The fund's performance rating is currently D- (Weak). It has registered an annualized return of -17.91% over the last three years and is down -13.87% year to date 2015. Factored into the performance evaluation is an expense ratio of 0.75% (very low).

This fund has been team managed for 8 years and currently receives a manager quality ranking of 8 (0=worst, 99=best). If you can tolerate high levels of risk in the hope of improved future returns, holding this fund may be an option.

Data Date	Investment Rating	Net Assets ($Mil)	Price	Performance Rating/Pts	Total Return Y-T-D	Risk Rating/Pts
12-15	E+	8.23	48.47	D- / 1.1	-13.87%	D+ / 2.8
2014	E+	10.30	56.05	D- / 1.1	-7.58%	C- / 3.5
2013	E+	8.23	60.61	D- / 1.1	-29.59%	C- / 3.3
2012	D	8.23	89.23	C / 4.4	0.10%	C / 4.7
2011	C	73.20	84.32	B / 7.8	13.19%	C / 4.8
2010	B+	28.40	81.64	A+ / 9.7	41.91%	C- / 3.7

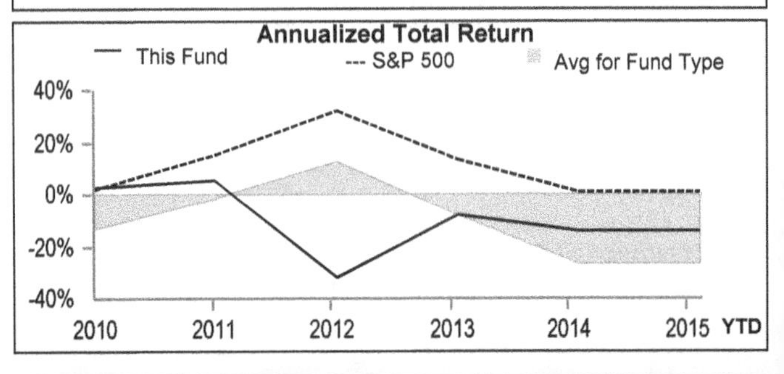

*iPath Bloomberg Softs SI TR A (JJS) E Very Weak

Fund Family: Barclays Bank PLC
Fund Type: Energy/Natural Resources
Inception Date: June 24, 2008

Major Rating Factors: *iPath Bloomberg Softs SI TR A has adopted a very risky asset allocation strategy and currently receives an overall TheStreet.com Investment Rating of E (Very Weak). The fund has a high level of volatility, as measured by both semi-deviation and drawdown factors. It carries a beta of 0.31, meaning the fund's expected move will be 3.1% for every 10% move in the market. As of December 31, 2015, *iPath Bloomberg Softs SI TR A traded at a premium of .35% above its net asset value, which is worse than its one-year historical average discount of .10%. Unfortunately, the high level of risk (D-, Weak) failed to pay off as investors endured poor performance.

The fund's performance rating is currently D (Weak). It has registered an annualized return of -13.48% over the last three years and is down -11.51% year to date 2015. Factored into the performance evaluation is an expense ratio of 0.75% (very low).

This fund has been team managed for 8 years and currently receives a manager quality ranking of 13 (0=worst, 99=best). If you can tolerate very high levels of risk in the hope of improved future returns, holding this fund may be an option.

Data Date	Investment Rating	Net Assets ($Mil)	Price	Performance Rating/Pts	Total Return Y-T-D	Risk Rating/Pts
12-15	E	4.67	34.15	D / 1.8	-11.51%	D- / 1.4
2014	E+	3.70	38.59	E+ / 0.8	-11.60%	C- / 3.6
2013	E-	4.67	43.41	E+ / 0.6	-17.92%	D+ / 2.6
2012	E	4.67	53.00	D- / 1.0	-24.35%	C- / 3.2
2011	C-	17.40	69.30	C+ / 6.0	-13.53%	C / 4.5
2010	B+	43.50	81.05	A+ / 9.9	58.86%	C- / 3.6

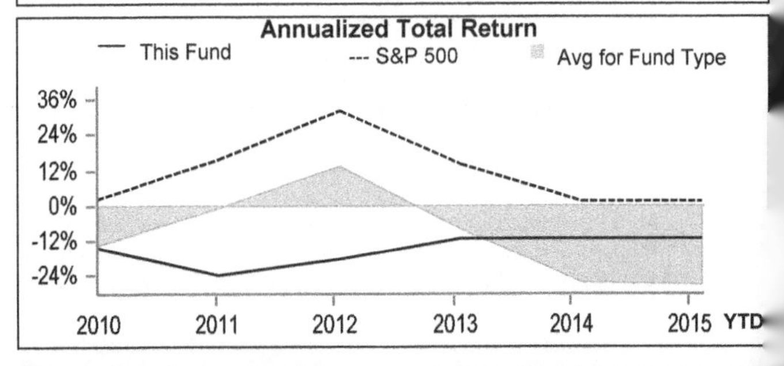

*iPath Bloomberg Sugar SI TR A (SGG) E Very Weak

Fund Family: Barclays Bank PLC
Fund Type: Energy/Natural Resources
Inception Date: June 24, 2008

Major Rating Factors: *iPath Bloomberg Sugar SI TR A has adopted a very risky asset allocation strategy and currently receives an overall TheStreet.com Investment Rating of E (Very Weak). The fund has a high level of volatility, as measured by both semi-deviation and drawdown factors. It carries a beta of 0.41, meaning the fund's expected move will be 4.1% for every 10% move in the market. As of December 31, 2015, *iPath Bloomberg Sugar SI TR A traded at a discount of .23% below its net asset value, which is better than its one-year historical average premium of .14%. Unfortunately, the high level of risk (D, Weak) failed to pay off as investors endured poor performance.

The fund's performance rating is currently D- (Weak). It has registered an annualized return of -20.07% over the last three years and is down -4.12% year to date 2015. Factored into the performance evaluation is an expense ratio of 0.75% (very low).

This fund has been team managed for 8 years and currently receives a manager quality ranking of 7 (0=worst, 99=best). If you can tolerate very high levels of risk in the hope of improved future returns, holding this fund may be an option.

Data Date	Investment Rating	Net Assets ($Mil)	Price	Performance Rating/Pts	Total Return Y-T-D	Risk Rating/Pts
12-15	E	26.55	34.69	D- / 1.3	-4.12%	D / 1.7
2014	E	38.60	37.03	E / 0.5	-31.39%	D / 2.2
2013	E	26.55	55.49	E+ / 0.6	-20.17%	C- / 3.1
2012	E	26.55	70.35	E+ / 0.8	-17.39%	D+ / 2.5
2011	D	32.90	81.80	C+ / 6.6	-11.44%	D+ / 2.7
2010	C+	81.10	93.55	A+ / 9.9	25.07%	D+ / 2.4

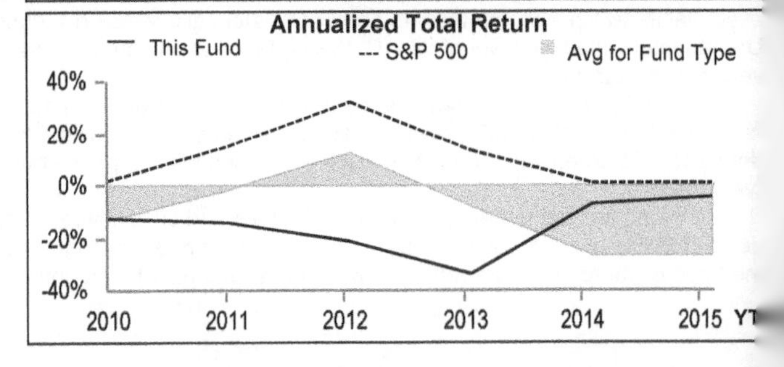

*iPath Bloomberg Tin SI TR A (JJT) E Very Weak

Fund Family: Barclays Bank PLC
Fund Type: Energy/Natural Resources
Inception Date: June 24, 2008

Major Rating Factors: *iPath Bloomberg Tin SI TR A has adopted a very risky asset allocation strategy and currently receives an overall TheStreet.com Investment Rating of E (Very Weak). The fund has a high level of volatility, as measured by both semi-deviation and drawdown factors. It carries a beta of 0.08, meaning the fund's expected move will be 0.8% for every 10% move in the market. As of December 31, 2015, *iPath Bloomberg Tin SI TR A traded at a premium of .16% above its net asset value, which is worse than its one-year historical average discount of .61%. Unfortunately, the high level of risk (D-, Weak) failed to pay off as investors endured poor performance.

The fund's performance rating is currently D- (Weak). It has registered an annualized return of -16.64% over the last three years and is down -24.76% year to date 2015. Factored into the performance evaluation is an expense ratio of 0.75% (very low).

This fund has been team managed for 8 years and currently receives a manager quality ranking of 10 (0=worst, 99=best). If you can tolerate very high levels of risk in the hope of improved future returns, holding this fund may be an option.

Data Date	Investment Rating	Net Assets ($Mil)	Price	Performance Rating/Pts	Total Return Y-T-D	Risk Rating/Pts
12-15	E	1.74	31.82	D- / 1.2	-24.76%	D- / 1.1
2014	D	4.90	42.49	D / 2.0	-10.96%	C+ / 6.5
2013	E	1.74	53.21	D- / 1.2	-12.58%	C- / 3.0
2012	D	1.74	53.86	C+ / 6.1	18.00%	D+ / 2.9
2011	D	7.50	43.71	C / 4.5	-27.52%	C- / 3.3
2010	C+	33.40	63.37	A+ / 9.8	58.74%	D+ / 2.4

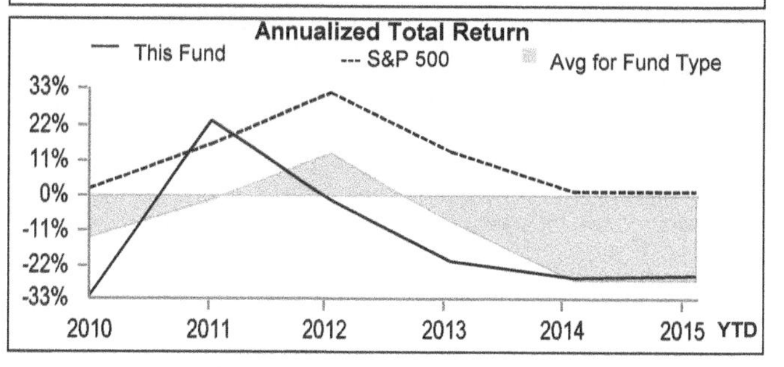

*iPath CBOE S&P 500 BuyWrite Idx (BWV) B Good

Fund Family: Barclays Bank PLC
Fund Type: Growth
Inception Date: May 22, 2007

Major Rating Factors: Strong performance is the major factor driving the B (Good) TheStreet.com Investment Rating for *iPath CBOE S&P 500 BuyWrite Idx. The fund currently has a performance rating of B- (Good) based on an annualized return of 7.24% over the last three years and a total return of 4.28% year to date 2015. Factored into the performance evaluation is an expense ratio of 0.75% (very low).

The fund's risk rating is currently B- (Good). It carries a beta of 0.52, meaning the fund's expected move will be 5.2% for every 10% move in the market. Volatility, as measured by both the semi-deviation and a drawdown factor, is considered low. As of December 31, 2015, *iPath CBOE S&P 500 BuyWrite Idx traded at a premium of .21% above its net asset value, which is worse than its one-year historical average discount of .11%.

This fund has been team managed for 9 years and currently receives a manager quality ranking of 72 (0=worst, 99=best). If you desire only a moderate level of risk and strong performance, then this fund is an excellent option.

Data Date	Investment Rating	Net Assets ($Mil)	Price	Performance Rating/Pts	Total Return Y-T-D	Risk Rating/Pts
12-15	B	10.45	65.38	B- / 7.0	4.28%	B- / 7.6
2014	C	10.90	62.70	C / 4.7	5.80%	B- / 7.6
2013	B-	10.45	58.67	C+ / 6.1	11.79%	B / 8.8
2012	C-	10.45	51.92	D+ / 2.4	4.84%	B / 8.6
2011	C+	18.80	50.40	C / 4.7	5.45%	B / 8.7
2010	C-	16.70	47.83	D+ / 2.8	4.80%	C+ / 6.4

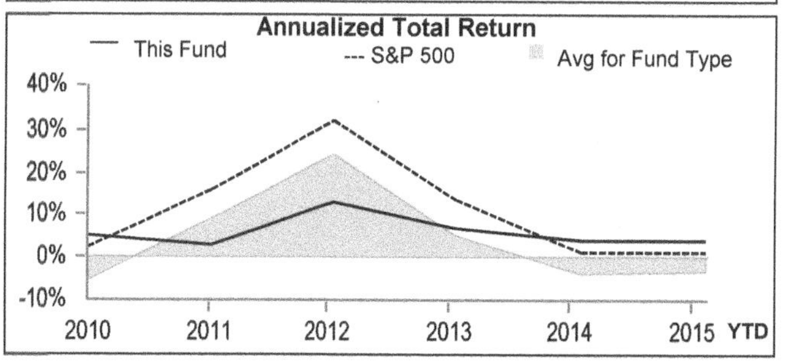

*iPath Cptl Glbl Carbon Tot Ret E (GRN) C- Fair

Fund Family: Barclays Bank PLC
Fund Type: Energy/Natural Resources
Inception Date: June 24, 2008

Major Rating Factors: *iPath Cptl Glbl Carbon Tot Ret E has adopted a very risky asset allocation strategy and currently receives an overall TheStreet.com Investment Rating of C- (Fair). The fund has shown a high level of volatility, as measured by both semi-deviation and drawdown factors. It carries a beta of -0.01, meaning the fund's expected move will be -0.1% for every 10% move in the market. As of December 31, 2015, *iPath Cptl Glbl Carbon Tot Ret E traded at a discount of .97% below its net asset value, which is better than its one-year historical average premium of .66%. The high level of risk (D, Weak) did however, reward investors with excellent performance.

The fund's performance rating is currently B (Good). It has registered an annualized return of 9.29% over the last three years and is up 8.38% year to date 2015. Factored into the performance evaluation is an expense ratio of 0.75% (very low).

This fund has been team managed for 8 years and currently receives a manager quality ranking of 94 (0=worst, 99=best). If you are comfortable owning a very high risk investment, this fund may be an option.

Data Date	Investment Rating	Net Assets ($Mil)	Price	Performance Rating/Pts	Total Return Y-T-D	Risk Rating/Pts
12-15	C-	4.10	10.21	B / 7.7	8.38%	D / 2.0
2014	E+	1.80	9.41	C / 5.1	56.17%	E- / 0
2013	E-	4.10	6.05	E- / 0.2	-23.27%	D / 1.9
2012	E-	4.10	7.82	E- / 0.2	-29.17%	D / 1.9
2011	E-	1.20	10.34	E / 0.4	-57.96%	D / 1.9
2010	E+	3.80	25.54	D+ / 2.4	11.67%	D- / 1.4

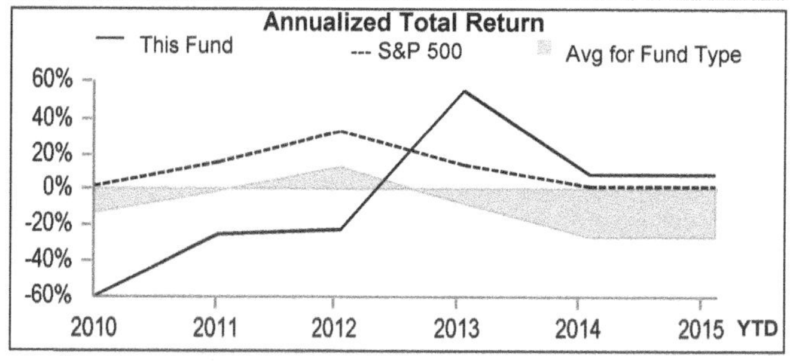

*iPath ETN US Treasury 5Yr Bear E (DFVS) D- Weak

Fund Family: Barclays Bank PLC
Fund Type: US Government/Agency
Inception Date: July 11, 2011

Data Date	Investment Rating	Net Assets ($Mil)	Price	Performance Rating/Pts	Total Return Y-T-D	Risk Rating/Pts
12-15	D-	5.90	31.91	D+ / 2.8	-8.96%	C- / 3.3
2014	D	5.90	35.63	D / 1.8	-14.08%	C+ / 5.6
2013	D+	5.90	42.24	C / 4.6	8.58%	C / 4.7
2012	E+	1.70	38.26	E+ / 0.9	-6.79%	C / 4.8

Major Rating Factors:
Disappointing performance is the major factor driving the D- (Weak) TheStreet.com Investment Rating for *iPath ETN US Treasury 5Yr Bear E. The fund currently has a performance rating of D+ (Weak) based on an annualized return of -6.30% over the last three years and a total return of -8.96% year to date 2015.

The fund's risk rating is currently C- (Fair). It carries a beta of -1.43, meaning the fund's expected move will be -14.3% for every 10% move in the market. Volatility, as measured by both the semi-deviation and a drawdown factor, is considered average. As of December 31, 2015, *iPath ETN US Treasury 5Yr Bear E traded at a discount of .44% below its net asset value, which is better than its one-year historical average premium of .04%.

This fund has been team managed for 5 years and currently receives a manager quality ranking of 47 (0=worst, 99=best). This fund offers an average level of risk but investors looking for strong performance will be frustrated.

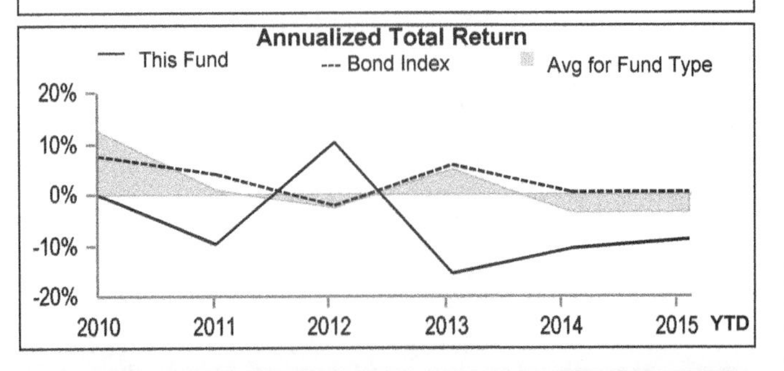

*iPath ETN US Treasury 5Yr Bull E (DFVL) D+ Weak

Fund Family: Barclays Bank PLC
Fund Type: US Government/Agency
Inception Date: July 11, 2011

Data Date	Investment Rating	Net Assets ($Mil)	Price	Performance Rating/Pts	Total Return Y-T-D	Risk Rating/Pts
12-15	D+	0.50	64.42	C / 5.3	6.44%	C- / 3.5
2013	D-	0.50	57.70	D / 1.9	-5.33%	C / 5.3

Major Rating Factors: *iPath ETN US Treasury 5Yr Bull E receives a TheStreet.com Investment Rating of D+ (Weak). The fund currently has a performance rating of C (Fair) based on an annualized return of 1.86% over the last three years and a total return of 6.44% year to date 2015.

The fund's risk rating is currently C- (Fair). It carries a beta of 0.53, meaning the fund's expected move will be 5.3% for every 10% move in the market. Volatility, as measured by both the semi-deviation and a drawdown factor, is considered average. As of December 31, 2015, *iPath ETN US Treasury 5Yr Bull E traded at a premium of .11% above its net asset value, which is worse than its one-year historical average discount of .07%.

This fund has been team managed for 5 years and currently receives a manager quality ranking of 73 (0=worst, 99=best). If you desire an average level of risk, then this fund may be an option.

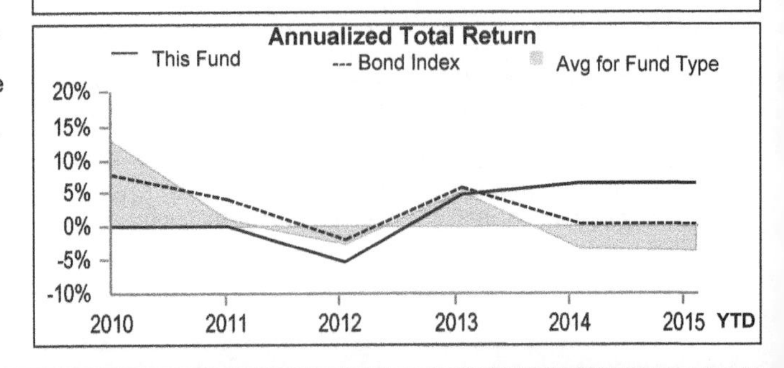

*iPath EUR/USD Exch Rate ETN (ERO) D+ Weak

Fund Family: Barclays Bank PLC
Fund Type: Foreign
Inception Date: May 8, 2007

Data Date	Investment Rating	Net Assets ($Mil)	Price	Performance Rating/Pts	Total Return Y-T-D	Risk Rating/Pts
12-15	D+	8.45	41.35	D+ / 2.4	-9.75%	C+ / 5.9
2014	C-	2.90	45.82	D / 2.1	-12.01%	B / 8.4
2013	C-	8.45	52.80	C- / 3.3	1.60%	B / 8.2
2012	D	8.45	51.97	D- / 1.2	3.00%	B / 8.1
2011	D+	4.80	50.34	D / 1.8	1.31%	B / 8.1
2010	D+	6.40	51.77	D- / 1.5	-7.50%	C+ / 6.8

Major Rating Factors:
Disappointing performance is the major factor driving the D+ (Weak) TheStreet.com Investment Rating for *iPath EUR/USD Exch Rate ETN. The fund currently has a performance rating of D+ (Weak) based on an annualized return of -7.34% over the last three years and a total return of -9.75% year to date 2015. Factored into the performance evaluation is an expense ratio of 0.40% (very low).

The fund's risk rating is currently C+ (Fair). It carries a beta of 0.19, meaning the fund's expected move will be 1.9% for every 10% move in the market. Volatility, as measured by both the semi-deviation and a drawdown factor, is considered low. As of December 31, 2015, *iPath EUR/USD Exch Rate ETN traded at a premium of .85% above its net asset value, which is worse than its one-year historical average discount of .21%.

This fund has been team managed for 9 years and currently receives a manager quality ranking of 19 (0=worst, 99=best). This fund offers only a moderate level of risk but investors looking for strong performance are still waiting.

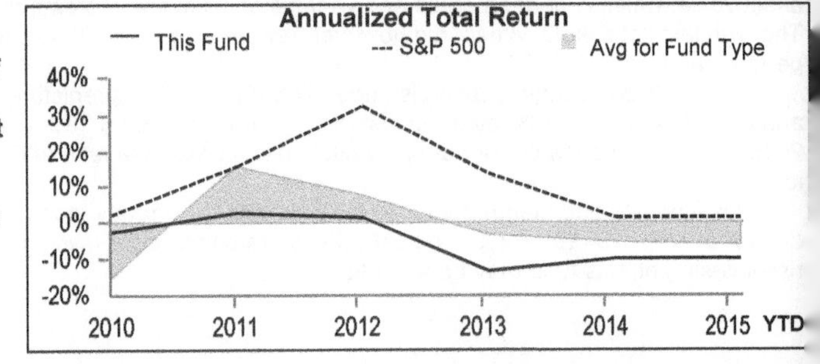

*iPath GBP/USD Exchange Rate ETN (GBB) C- Fair

Fund Family: Barclays Bank PLC
Fund Type: Growth
Inception Date: May 8, 2007

Major Rating Factors: Middle of the road best describes *iPath GBP/USD Exchange Rate ETN whose TheStreet.com Investment Rating is currently a C- (Fair). The fund currently has a performance rating of C- (Fair) based on an annualized return of -3.02% over the last three years and a total return of -3.50% year to date 2015. Factored into the performance evaluation is an expense ratio of 0.40% (very low).

The fund's risk rating is currently B (Good). It carries a beta of -0.11, meaning the fund's expected move will be -1.1% for every 10% move in the market. Volatility, as measured by both the semi-deviation and a drawdown factor, is considered low. As of December 31, 2015, *iPath GBP/USD Exchange Rate ETN traded at a discount of .87% below its net asset value, which is better than its one-year historical average discount of .32%.

This fund has been team managed for 9 years and currently receives a manager quality ranking of 51 (0=worst, 99=best). If you desire an average level of risk, then this fund may be an option.

Data Date	Investment Rating	Net Assets ($Mil)	Price	Performance Rating/Pts	Total Return Y-T-D	Risk Rating/Pts
12-15	C-	1.78	38.78	C- / 3.2	-3.50%	B / 8.0
2013	C	1.78	44.16	C- / 3.5	2.20%	B / 8.9
2012	D+	1.78	43.03	D- / 1.3	4.25%	B / 8.8
2011	C-	2.50	41.43	D+ / 2.3	2.04%	B / 8.7
2010	D	6.80	41.40	E+ / 0.9	-3.77%	C+ / 6.5

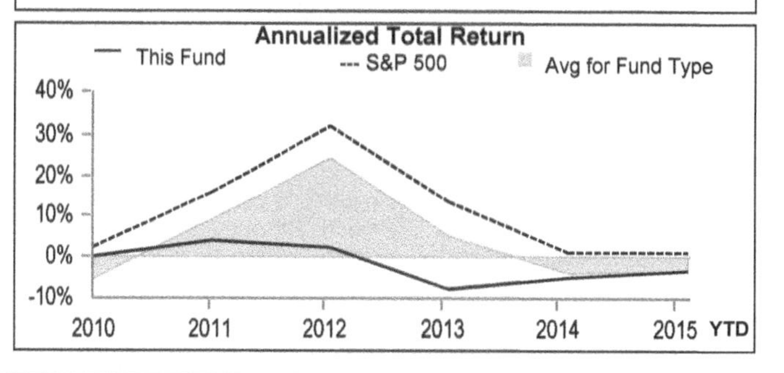

*iPath GEMS Asia 8 ETN (AYT) D Weak

Fund Family: Barclays Bank PLC
Fund Type: Foreign
Inception Date: April 2, 2008

Major Rating Factors: *iPath GEMS Asia 8 ETN receives a TheStreet.com Investment Rating of D (Weak). The fund currently has a performance rating of C- (Fair) based on an annualized return of -3.87% over the last three years and a total return of -4.64% year to date 2015.

The fund's risk rating is currently C (Fair). It carries a beta of 0.28, meaning the fund's expected move will be 2.8% for every 10% move in the market. Volatility, as measured by both the semi-deviation and a drawdown factor, is considered average. As of December 31, 2015, *iPath GEMS Asia 8 ETN traded at a discount of .57% below its net asset value, which is better than its one-year historical average discount of .36%.

This fund has been team managed for 8 years and currently receives a manager quality ranking of 28 (0=worst, 99=best). If you desire an average level of risk, then this fund may be an option.

Data Date	Investment Rating	Net Assets ($Mil)	Price	Performance Rating/Pts	Total Return Y-T-D	Risk Rating/Pts
12-15	D	3.50	40.24	C- / 3.0	-4.64%	C / 4.4
2014	C-	3.50	43.46	D+ / 2.4	-1.95%	B / 8.9
2013	D-	9.70	44.65	D / 2.2	-4.50%	C / 5.3
2012	D-	19.70	48.20	D / 1.8	3.54%	C / 5.5
2011	D-	18.40	47.01	D / 2.2	-2.40%	C+ / 5.6
2010	C+	10.00	48.99	C+ / 6.5	6.79%	C / 4.9

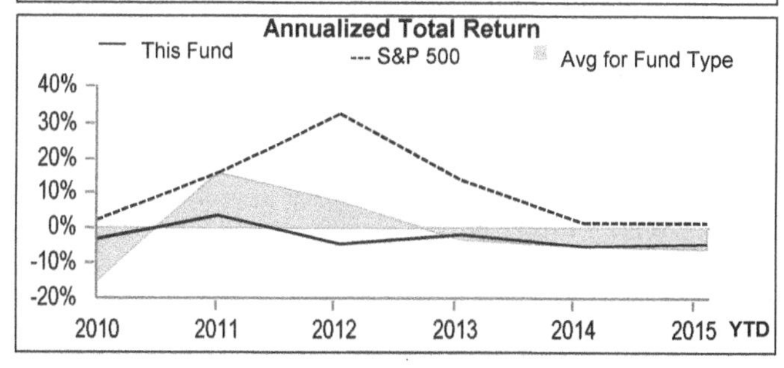

*iPath GEMS Index ETN (JEM) D- Weak

Fund Family: Barclays Bank PLC
Fund Type: Growth and Income
Inception Date: February 1, 2008

Major Rating Factors:
Disappointing performance is the major factor driving the D- (Weak) TheStreet.com Investment Rating for *iPath GEMS Index ETN. The fund currently has a performance rating of D+ (Weak) based on an annualized return of -6.52% over the last three years and a total return of -8.97% year to date 2015.

The fund's risk rating is currently C- (Fair). It carries a beta of 0.42, meaning the fund's expected move will be 4.2% for every 10% move in the market. Volatility, as measured by both the semi-deviation and a drawdown factor, is considered average. As of December 31, 2015, *iPath GEMS Index ETN traded at a discount of .10% below its net asset value, which is worse than its one-year historical average discount of .34%.

Barclays Capital has been running the fund for 8 years and currently receives a manager quality ranking of 14 (0=worst, 99=best). This fund offers an average level of risk but investors looking for strong performance will be frustrated.

Data Date	Investment Rating	Net Assets ($Mil)	Price	Performance Rating/Pts	Total Return Y-T-D	Risk Rating/Pts
12-15	D-	1.30	29.25	D+ / 2.5	-8.97%	C- / 3.1
2014	D	1.30	34.39	D / 2.2	-7.97%	C+ / 5.9
2013	D-	0.80	39.13	D+ / 2.4	-2.49%	C / 4.9
2012	D-	1.40	42.50	D / 1.7	6.17%	C / 5.1
2011	D-	1.40	42.00	D / 2.1	-7.28%	C / 5.3
2010	C	4.10	46.50	B- / 7.4	6.69%	C- / 3.7

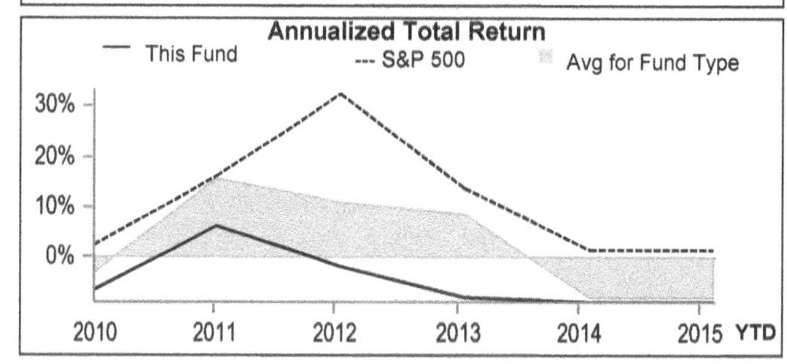

*iPath JPY/USD Exchange Rate ETN (JYN) D+ Weak

Fund Family: Barclays Bank PLC
Fund Type: Foreign
Inception Date: May 8, 2007

Major Rating Factors:
Disappointing performance is the major factor driving the D+ (Weak) TheStreet.com Investment Rating for *iPath JPY/USD Exchange Rate ETN. The fund currently has a performance rating of D (Weak) based on an annualized return of -13.19% over the last three years and a total return of -0.17% year to date 2015. Factored into the performance evaluation is an expense ratio of 0.40% (very low).

The fund's risk rating is currently C+ (Fair). It carries a beta of 0.10, meaning the fund's expected move will be 1.0% for every 10% move in the market. Volatility, as measured by both the semi-deviation and a drawdown factor, is considered low. As of December 31, 2015, *iPath JPY/USD Exchange Rate ETN traded at a discount of .21% below its net asset value, which is worse than its one-year historical average discount of .33%.

This fund has been team managed for 9 years and currently receives a manager quality ranking of 12 (0=worst, 99=best). This fund offers only a moderate level of risk but investors looking for strong performance are still waiting.

Data Date	Investment Rating	Net Assets ($Mil)	Price	Performance Rating/Pts	Total Return Y-T-D	Risk Rating/Pts
12-15	D+	11.27	47.06	D / 1.9	-0.17%	C+ / 6.8
2014	D-	1.60	47.14	E+ / 0.9	-12.44%	C+ / 6.2
2013	D	11.27	54.58	D- / 1.0	-24.13%	B- / 7.3
2012	D+	11.27	71.94	D- / 1.0	-15.52%	B+ / 9.1
2011	C	20.00	76.45	C- / 3.1	7.13%	B+ / 9.0
2010	B	8.90	72.80	B- / 7.3	14.09%	C+ / 5.9

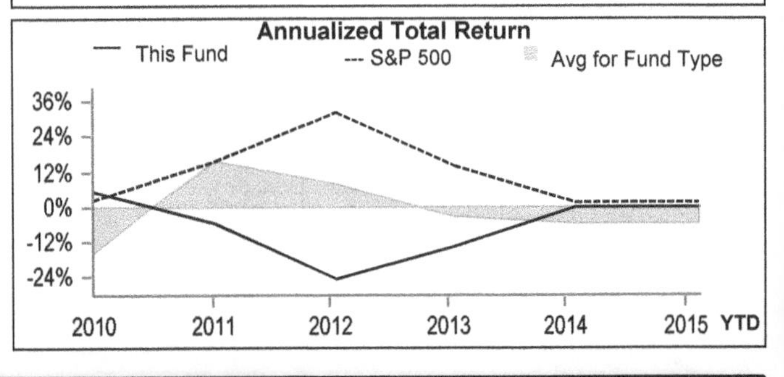

*iPath Long Ext S&P 500 TR Idx ET (SFLA) C+ Fair

Fund Family: Barclays Bank PLC
Fund Type: Income
Inception Date: November 29, 2010

Major Rating Factors:
Exceptional performance is the major factor driving the C+ (Fair) TheStreet.com Investment Rating for *iPath Long Ext S&P 500 TR Idx ET. The fund currently has a performance rating of A+ (Excellent) based on an annualized return of 25.80% over the last three years and a total return of 1.47% year to date 2015.

The fund's risk rating is currently C- (Fair). It carries a beta of 0.57, meaning the fund's expected move will be 5.7% for every 10% move in the market. Volatility, as measured by both the semi-deviation and a drawdown factor, is considered average. As of December 31, 2015, *iPath Long Ext S&P 500 TR Idx ET traded at a premium of .61% above its net asset value, which is worse than its one-year historical average discount of 4.87%.

This is team managed and currently receives a manager quality ranking of 98 (0=worst, 99=best). If you desire an average level of risk and strong performance, then this fund is a good option.

Data Date	Investment Rating	Net Assets ($Mil)	Price	Performance Rating/Pts	Total Return Y-T-D	Risk Rating/Pts
12-15	C+	6.70	181.63	A+ / 9.7	1.47%	C- / 4.0
2013	C	6.00	133.27	A+ / 9.7	57.83%	C- / 3.5
2012	C	3.60	85.71	A+ / 9.7	41.26%	C- / 3.4
2011	D	5.20	61.42	C / 5.0	5.71%	C- / 3.6

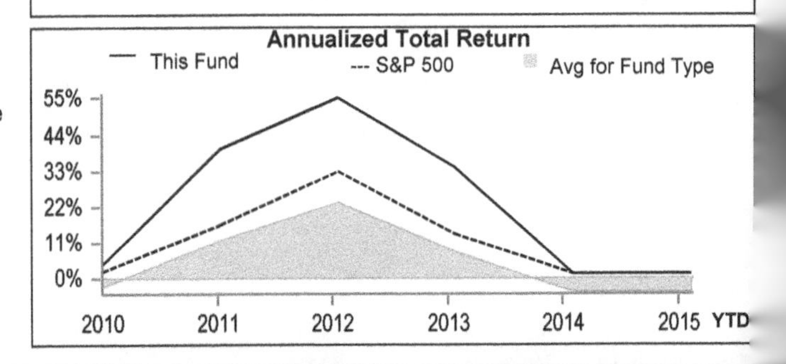

*iPath MSCI India Index ETN (INP) C- Fair

Fund Family: Barclays Bank PLC
Fund Type: Emerging Market
Inception Date: December 19, 2006

Major Rating Factors: Middle of the road best describes *iPath MSCI India Index ETN whose TheStreet.com Investment Rating is currently a C- (Fair). The fund currently has a performance rating of C- (Fair) based on an annualized return of 1.86% over the last three years and a total return of -9.40% year to date 2015. Factored into the performance evaluation is an expense ratio of 0.89% (low).

The fund's risk rating is currently C+ (Fair). It carries a beta of 0.69, meaning the fund's expected move will be 6.9% for every 10% move in the market. Volatility, as measured by both the semi-deviation and a drawdown factor, is considered low. As of December 31, 2015, *iPath MSCI India Index ETN traded at a discount of 1.04% below its net asset value, which is better than its one-year historical average premium of .20%.

This fund has been team managed for 10 years and currently receives a manager quality ranking of 93 (0=worst, 99=best). If you desire an average level of risk, then this fund may be an option.

Data Date	Investment Rating	Net Assets ($Mil)	Price	Performance Rating/Pts	Total Return Y-T-D	Risk Rating/Pts
12-15	C-	1,058.84	63.91	C- / 3.9	-9.40%	C+ / 6.9
2014	C+	384.60	69.65	C+ / 6.6	24.48%	C+ / 6.8
2013	D-	1,058.84	56.96	D- / 1.4	-7.94%	C+ / 5.8
2012	D-	1,058.84	59.33	D / 1.7	18.28%	C+ / 5.7
2011	D	454.00	46.62	C- / 3.4	-34.14%	C+ / 5.9
2010	D-	1,154.20	77.66	D / 2.1	21.23%	C- / 3.4

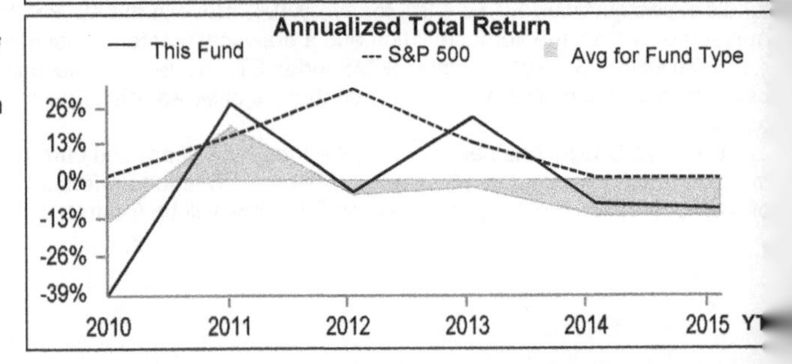

*iPath Pure Beta Agriculture ETN (DIRT) E+ Very Weak

Fund Family: Barclays Bank PLC
Fund Type: Income
Inception Date: April 20, 2011

Data Date	Investment Rating	Net Assets ($Mil)	Price	Performance Rating/Pts	Total Return Y-T-D	Risk Rating/Pts
12-15	E+	1.10	31.16	D- / 1.5	-16.62%	C- / 3.2
2014	D-	1.10	38.00	D / 1.9	-6.83%	C / 4.3
2013	E+	3.20	41.61	D- / 1.0	-10.52%	C / 4.5
2012	D-	3.20	47.35	D / 2.0	12.89%	C / 4.7

Major Rating Factors:
Disappointing performance is the major factor driving the E+ (Very Weak) TheStreet.com Investment Rating for *iPath Pure Beta Agriculture ETN. The fund currently has a performance rating of D- (Weak) based on an annualized return of -12.49% over the last three years and a total return of -16.62% year to date 2015.

The fund's risk rating is currently C- (Fair). It carries a beta of 0.30, meaning the fund's expected move will be 3.0% for every 10% move in the market. Volatility, as measured by both the semi-deviation and a drawdown factor, is considered average. As of December 31, 2015, *iPath Pure Beta Agriculture ETN traded at a discount of .06% below its net asset value, which is worse than its one-year historical average discount of .17%.

This fund has been team managed for 5 years and currently receives a manager quality ranking of 9 (0=worst, 99=best). This fund offers an average level of risk but investors looking for strong performance will be frustrated.

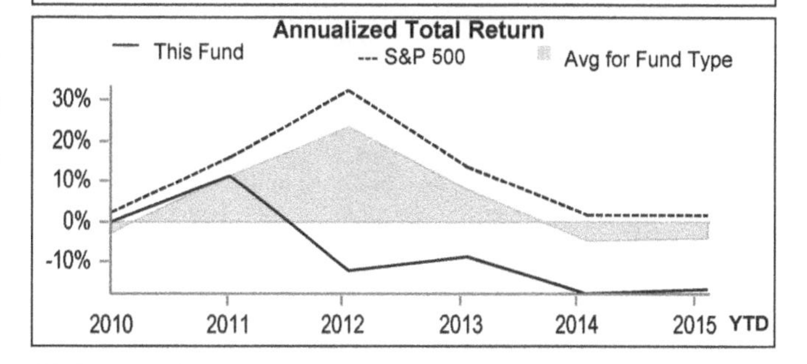

*iPath Pure Beta Aluminum ETN (FOIL) E Very Weak

Fund Family: Barclays Bank PLC
Fund Type: Income
Inception Date: April 20, 2011

Data Date	Investment Rating	Net Assets ($Mil)	Price	Performance Rating/Pts	Total Return Y-T-D	Risk Rating/Pts
12-15	E	3.20	21.69	D- / 1.2	-20.83%	D / 1.9
2014	D	3.20	27.40	D / 1.7	-3.50%	C+ / 6.5
2013	E	1.40	28.53	E+ / 0.8	-18.89%	C- / 3.3
2012	E+	1.40	34.53	E+ / 0.9	-9.98%	C- / 3.8

Major Rating Factors: *iPath Pure Beta Aluminum ETN has adopted a very risky asset allocation strategy and currently receives an overall TheStreet.com Investment Rating of E (Very Weak). The fund has a high level of volatility, as measured by both semi-deviation and drawdown factors. It carries a beta of 0.20, meaning the fund's expected move will be 2.0% for every 10% move in the market. As of December 31, 2015, *iPath Pure Beta Aluminum ETN traded at a premium of .70% above its net asset value, which is worse than its one-year historical average discount of .04%. Unfortunately, the high level of risk (D, Weak) failed to pay off as investors endured poor performance.

The fund's performance rating is currently D- (Weak). It has registered an annualized return of -14.87% over the last three years and is down -20.83% year to date 2015.

This fund has been team managed for 5 years and currently receives a manager quality ranking of 9 (0=worst, 99=best). If you can tolerate very high levels of risk in the hope of improved future returns, holding this fund may be an option.

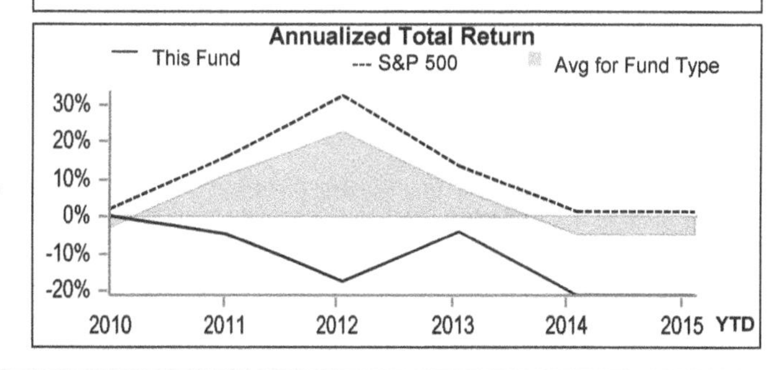

*iPath Pure Beta Broad Commodity (BCM) E Very Weak

Fund Family: Barclays Bank PLC
Fund Type: Income
Inception Date: April 20, 2011

Data Date	Investment Rating	Net Assets ($Mil)	Price	Performance Rating/Pts	Total Return Y-T-D	Risk Rating/Pts
12-15	E	17.50	23.69	E+ / 0.9	-25.92%	D- / 1.3
2014	D-	17.50	31.98	D- / 1.1	-17.46%	C / 4.9
2013	D-	21.50	39.51	D- / 1.3	-10.60%	C / 4.7
2012	D-	21.50	44.62	D- / 1.3	0.37%	C / 4.8

Major Rating Factors: *iPath Pure Beta Broad Commodity has adopted a very risky asset allocation strategy and currently receives an overall TheStreet.com Investment Rating of E (Very Weak). The fund has a high level of volatility, as measured by both semi-deviation and drawdown factors. It carries a beta of 0.39, meaning the fund's expected move will be 3.9% for every 10% move in the market. As of December 31, 2015, *iPath Pure Beta Broad Commodity traded at a premium of .17% above its net asset value, which is worse than its one-year historical average premium of .06%. Unfortunately, the high level of risk (D-, Weak) failed to pay off as investors endured very poor performance.

The fund's performance rating is currently E+ (Very Weak). It has registered an annualized return of -18.44% over the last three years and is down -25.92% year to date 2015.

This fund has been team managed for 5 years and currently receives a manager quality ranking of 5 (0=worst, 99=best). If you can tolerate very high levels of risk in the hope of improved future returns, holding this fund may be an option.

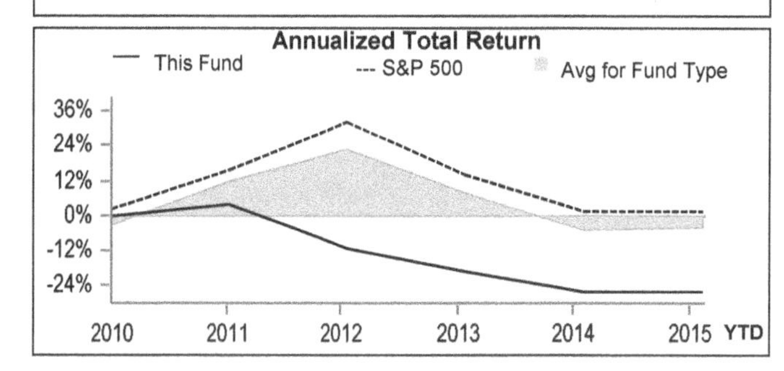

*iPath Pure Beta Cocoa ETN (CHOC) — C — Fair

Fund Family: Barclays Bank PLC
Fund Type: Income
Inception Date: April 20, 2011

Major Rating Factors: Strong performance is the major factor driving the C (Fair) TheStreet.com Investment Rating for *iPath Pure Beta Cocoa ETN. The fund currently has a performance rating of B+ (Good) based on an annualized return of 12.55% over the last three years and a total return of 12.58% year to date 2015.

The fund's risk rating is currently C- (Fair). It carries a beta of 0.37, meaning the fund's expected move will be 3.7% for every 10% move in the market. Volatility, as measured by both the semi-deviation and a drawdown factor, is considered average. As of December 31, 2015, *iPath Pure Beta Cocoa ETN traded at a premium of .36% above its net asset value, which is worse than its one-year historical average discount of .16%.

This fund has been team managed for 5 years and currently receives a manager quality ranking of 92 (0=worst, 99=best). If you desire an average level of risk and strong performance, then this fund is a good option.

Data Date	Investment Rating	Net Assets ($Mil)	Price	Performance Rating/Pts	Total Return Y-T-D	Risk Rating/Pts
12-15	C	10.00	47.69	B+ / 8.7	12.58%	C- / 3.3
2014	C-	10.00	42.36	C / 5.4	7.83%	C+ / 5.7
2013	C	6.10	39.88	A- / 9.1	19.13%	C- / 3.6
2012	E	3.00	33.58	E+ / 0.9	-4.83%	C- / 3.5

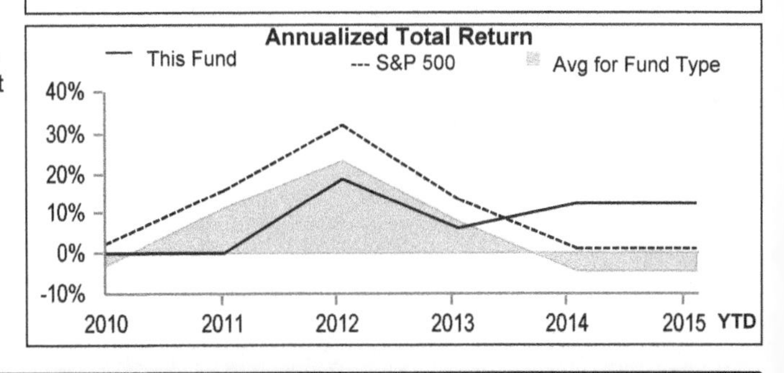

*iPath Pure Beta Coffee ETN (CAFE) — E+ — Very Weak

Fund Family: Barclays Bank PLC
Fund Type: Income
Inception Date: April 20, 2011

Major Rating Factors: *iPath Pure Beta Coffee ETN has adopted a risky asset allocation strategy and currently receives an overall TheStreet.com Investment Rating of E+ (Very Weak). The fund has an above average level of volatility, as measured by both semi-deviation and drawdown factors. It carries a beta of 0.05, meaning the fund's expected move will be 0.5% for every 10% move in the market. As of December 31, 2015, *iPath Pure Beta Coffee ETN traded at a discount of .72% below its net asset value, which is better than its one-year historical average premium of .08%. Unfortunately, the high level of risk (D+, Weak) failed to pay off as investors endured poor performance.

The fund's performance rating is currently D- (Weak). It has registered an annualized return of -14.31% over the last three years and is down -29.53% year to date 2015.

This fund has been team managed for 5 years and currently receives a manager quality ranking of 11 (0=worst, 99=best). If you can tolerate high levels of risk in the hope of improved future returns, holding this fund may be an option.

Data Date	Investment Rating	Net Assets ($Mil)	Price	Performance Rating/Pts	Total Return Y-T-D	Risk Rating/Pts
12-15	E+	7.50	13.71	D- / 1.2	-29.53%	D+ / 2.8
2014	E	7.50	20.47	D- / 1.1	29.62%	D / 2.2
2013	E-	8.80	14.69	E / 0.4	-29.12%	D / 1.9
2012	E-	2.00	21.23	E- / 0.2	-37.51%	D+ / 2.3

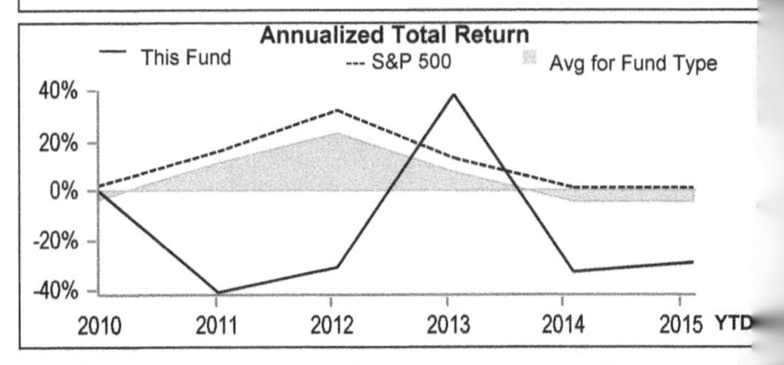

*iPath Pure Beta Crude Oil ETN (OLEM) — E- — Very Weak

Fund Family: Barclays Bank PLC
Fund Type: Income
Inception Date: April 20, 2011

Major Rating Factors: *iPath Pure Beta Crude Oil ETN has adopted a very risky asset allocation strategy and currently receives an overall TheStreet.com Investment Rating of E- (Very Weak). The fund has a high level of volatility, as measured by both semi-deviation and drawdown factors. It carries a beta of 0.59, meaning the fund's expected move will be 5.9% for every 10% move in the market. As of December 31, 2015, *iPath Pure Beta Crude Oil ETN traded at a discount of .13% below its net asset value, which is better than its one-year historical average premium of .02%. Unfortunately, the high level of risk (D-, Weak) failed to pay off as investors endured very poor performance.

The fund's performance rating is currently E (Very Weak). It has registered an annualized return of -27.39% over the last three years and is down -39.90% year to date 2015.

This fund has been team managed for 5 years and currently receives a manager quality ranking of 2 (0=worst, 99=best). If you can tolerate very high levels of risk in the hope of improved future returns, holding this fund may be an option.

Data Date	Investment Rating	Net Assets ($Mil)	Price	Performance Rating/Pts	Total Return Y-T-D	Risk Rating/Pts
12-15	E-	3.20	14.90	E / 0.4	-39.90%	D- / 1.1
2014	E	3.20	24.95	E / 0.5	-40.19%	D+ / 2.8
2013	D+	3.30	42.22	C / 5.3	8.47%	C / 4.6
2012	E+	2.10	38.48	E+ / 0.8	-12.49%	C / 4.6

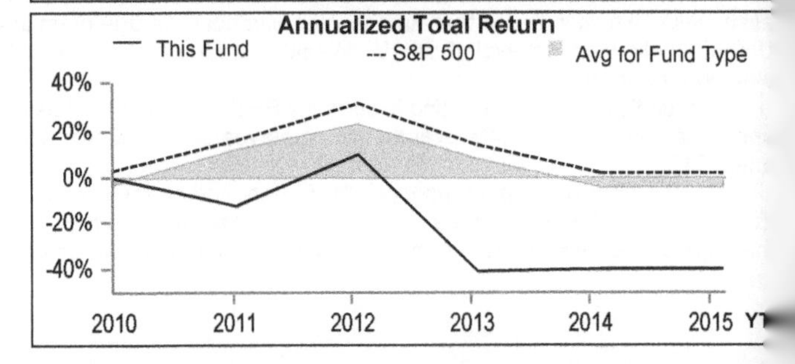

*iPath Pure Beta Energy ETN (ONG) E- Very Weak

Fund Family: Barclays Bank PLC
Fund Type: Energy/Natural Resources
Inception Date: April 20, 2011

Data Date	Investment Rating	Net Assets ($Mil)	Price	Perfor-mance Rating/Pts	Total Return Y-T-D	Risk Rating/Pts
12-15	E-	2.40	15.45	E / 0.4	-40.85%	E- / 0.2
2014	E	2.40	26.11	E- / 0	-37.60%	C- / 3.2

Major Rating Factors: *iPath Pure Beta Energy ETN has adopted a very risky asset allocation strategy and currently receives an overall TheStreet.com Investment Rating of E- (Very Weak). The fund has a high level of volatility, as measured by both semi-deviation and drawdown factors. It carries a beta of 0.97, meaning that its performance tracks fairly well with that of the overall stock market. As of December 31, 2015, *iPath Pure Beta Energy ETN traded at a premium of 1.38% above its net asset value, which is worse than its one-year historical average premium of .92%. Unfortunately, the high level of risk (E-, Very Weak) failed to pay off as investors endured very poor performance.

The fund's performance rating is currently E (Very Weak). It has registered an annualized return of -27.38% over the last three years and is down -40.85% year to date 2015.

This fund has been team managed for 5 years and currently receives a manager quality ranking of 4 (0=worst, 99=best). If you can tolerate very high levels of risk in the hope of improved future returns, holding this fund may be an option.

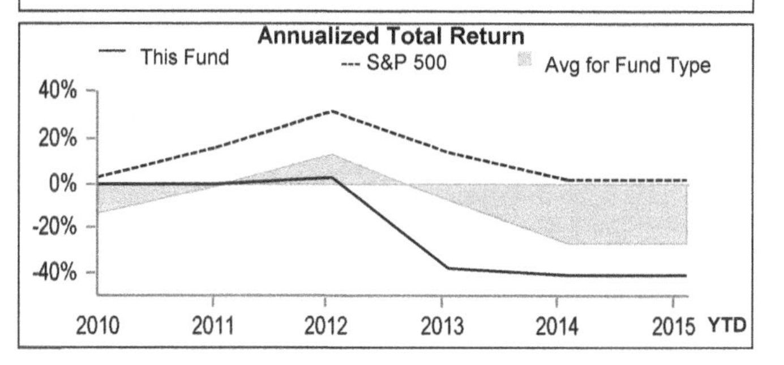

*iPath Pure Beta Grains ETN (WEET) E+ Very Weak

Fund Family: Barclays Bank PLC
Fund Type: Income
Inception Date: April 20, 2011

Data Date	Investment Rating	Net Assets ($Mil)	Price	Perfor-mance Rating/Pts	Total Return Y-T-D	Risk Rating/Pts
12-15	E+	0.80	32.91	D- / 1.4	-18.03%	D+ / 2.7
2014	D-	0.80	40.88	D+ / 2.7	-5.64%	C- / 4.1
2013	E+	2.90	44.06	D- / 1.0	-9.81%	C / 4.5
2012	D	2.80	50.44	C- / 4.0	19.74%	C / 4.5

Major Rating Factors: *iPath Pure Beta Grains ETN has adopted a risky asset allocation strategy and currently receives an overall TheStreet.com Investment Rating of E+ (Very Weak). The fund has an above average level of volatility, as measured by both semi-deviation and drawdown factors. It carries a beta of 0.29, meaning the fund's expected move will be 2.9% for every 10% move in the market. As of December 31, 2015, *iPath Pure Beta Grains ETN traded at a discount of .06% below its net asset value, which is better than its one-year historical average discount of .05%. Unfortunately, the high level of risk (D+, Weak) failed to pay off as investors endured poor performance.

The fund's performance rating is currently D- (Weak). It has registered an annualized return of -12.34% over the last three years and is down -18.03% year to date 2015.

This fund has been team managed for 5 years and currently receives a manager quality ranking of 9 (0=worst, 99=best). If you can tolerate high levels of risk in the hope of improved future returns, holding this fund may be an option.

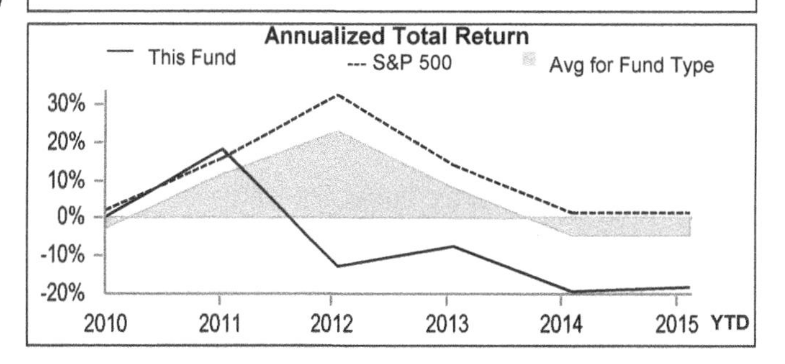

*iPath Pure Beta Lead ETN (LEDD) D- Weak

Fund Family: Barclays Bank PLC
Fund Type: Income
Inception Date: April 20, 2011

Data Date	Investment Rating	Net Assets ($Mil)	Price	Perfor-mance Rating/Pts	Total Return Y-T-D	Risk Rating/Pts
12-15	D-	1.90	29.22	D / 1.7	-8.89%	C- / 3.5
2014	D-	1.90	32.07	E / 0.5	-20.87%	C+ / 6.5
2013	E+	1.10	40.53	D / 1.9	-7.84%	C- / 3.7
2012	C-	0.70	43.98	B / 7.6	10.28%	C- / 3.6

Major Rating Factors:
Disappointing performance is the major factor driving the D- (Weak) TheStreet.com Investment Rating for *iPath Pure Beta Lead ETN. The fund currently has a performance rating of D (Weak) based on an annualized return of -12.74% over the last three years and a total return of -8.89% year to date 2015.

The fund's risk rating is currently C- (Fair). It carries a beta of 0.38, meaning the fund's expected move will be 3.8% for every 10% move in the market. Volatility, as measured by both the semi-deviation and a drawdown factor, is considered average. As of December 31, 2015, *iPath Pure Beta Lead ETN traded at a discount of 4.20% below its net asset value, which is better than its one-year historical average premium of .07%.

This fund has been team managed for 5 years and currently receives a manager quality ranking of 9 (0=worst, 99=best). This fund offers an average level of risk but investors looking for strong performance will be frustrated.

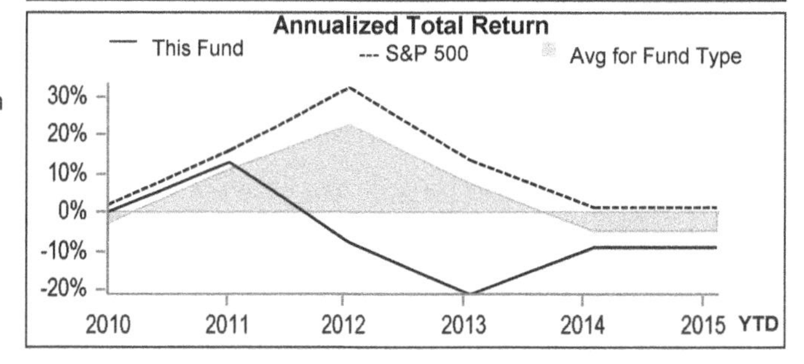

*iPath Pure Beta Livestock ETN (LSTK) D Weak

Fund Family: Barclays Bank PLC
Fund Type: Income
Inception Date: April 20, 2011

Major Rating Factors:
Disappointing performance is the major factor driving the D (Weak) TheStreet.com Investment Rating for *iPath Pure Beta Livestock ETN. The fund currently has a performance rating of D+ (Weak) based on an annualized return of -0.88% over the last three years and a total return of -21.23% year to date 2015.

The fund's risk rating is currently C- (Fair). It carries a beta of 0.18, meaning the fund's expected move will be 1.8% for every 10% move in the market. Volatility, as measured by both the semi-deviation and a drawdown factor, is considered average. As of December 31, 2015, *iPath Pure Beta Livestock ETN traded at a discount of 1.22% below its net asset value, which is better than its one-year historical average discount of .09%.

This fund has been team managed for 5 years and currently receives a manager quality ranking of 42 (0=worst, 99=best). This fund offers an average level of risk but investors looking for strong performance will be frustrated.

Data Date	Investment Rating	Net Assets ($Mil)	Price	Performance Rating/Pts	Total Return Y-T-D	Risk Rating/Pts
12-15	D	1.40	42.80	D+ / 2.9	-21.23%	C- / 4.0
2014	C	1.40	54.34	C- / 4.2	22.46%	B / 8.2
2013	D-	2.50	42.75	D / 2.1	-2.73%	C / 4.9

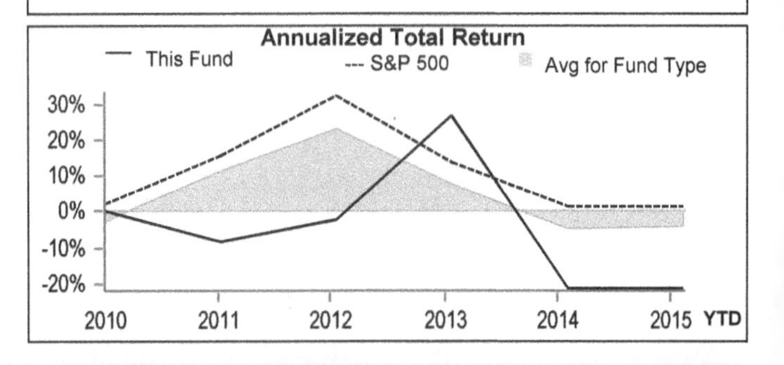

*iPath Pure Beta S&P GW ETN (SBV) E Very Weak

Fund Family: Barclays Bank PLC
Fund Type: Precious Metals
Inception Date: April 20, 2011

Major Rating Factors: *iPath Pure Beta S&P GW ETN has adopted a risky asset allocation strategy and currently receives an overall TheStreet.com Investment Rating of E (Very Weak). The fund has an above average level of volatility, as measured by both semi-deviation and drawdown factors. It carries a beta of 0.14, meaning the fund's expected move will be 1.4% for every 10% move in the market. As of December 31, 2015, *iPath Pure Beta S&P GW ETN traded at a discount of .62% below its net asset value, which is better than its one-year historical average discount of .09%. Unfortunately, the high level of risk (D+, Weak) failed to pay off as investors endured very poor performance.

The fund's performance rating is currently E+ (Very Weak). It has registered an annualized return of -22.55% over the last three years and is down -35.97% year to date 2015.

This fund has been team managed for 5 years and currently receives a manager quality ranking of 6 (0=worst, 99=best). If you can tolerate high levels of risk in the hope of improved future returns, holding this fund may be an option.

Data Date	Investment Rating	Net Assets ($Mil)	Price	Performance Rating/Pts	Total Return Y-T-D	Risk Rating/Pts
12-15	E	1.30	19.38	E+ / 0.6	-35.97%	D+ / 2.3
2014	E+	1.30	30.27	E- / 0.2	-25.66%	C / 4.5
2013	D-	1.30	41.85	D / 1.9	-2.40%	C / 5.4

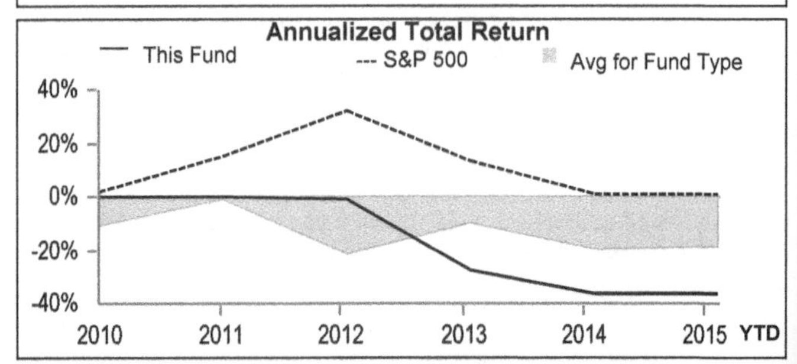

*iPath Pure Beta Softs ETN (GRWN) E+ Very Weak

Fund Family: Barclays Bank PLC
Fund Type: Income
Inception Date: April 20, 2011

Major Rating Factors: *iPath Pure Beta Softs ETN has adopted a risky asset allocation strategy and currently receives an overall TheStreet.com Investment Rating of E+ (Very Weak). The fund has an above average level of volatility, as measured by both semi-deviation and drawdown factors. It carries a beta of 0.70, meaning the fund's expected move will be 7.0% for every 10% move in the market. As of December 31, 2015, *iPath Pure Beta Softs ETN traded at a discount of 2.79% below its net asset value, which is better than its one-year historical average premium of .13%. Unfortunately, the high level of risk (D+, Weak) failed to pay off as investors endured poor performance.

The fund's performance rating is currently D (Weak). It has registered an annualized return of -13.63% over the last three years and is down -17.96% year to date 2015.

This fund has been team managed for 5 years and currently receives a manager quality ranking of 6 (0=worst, 99=best). If you can tolerate high levels of risk in the hope of improved future returns, holding this fund may be an option.

Data Date	Investment Rating	Net Assets ($Mil)	Price	Performance Rating/Pts	Total Return Y-T-D	Risk Rating/Pts
12-15	E+	0.90	21.24	D / 1.7	-17.96%	D+ / 2.3
2014	E+	0.90	25.89	E+ / 0.9	-3.86%	C- / 3.8
2013	E	0.70	26.93	E+ / 0.9	-18.32%	D+ / 2.8
2012	E	0.90	32.65	E / 0.4	-26.52%	C- / 3.4

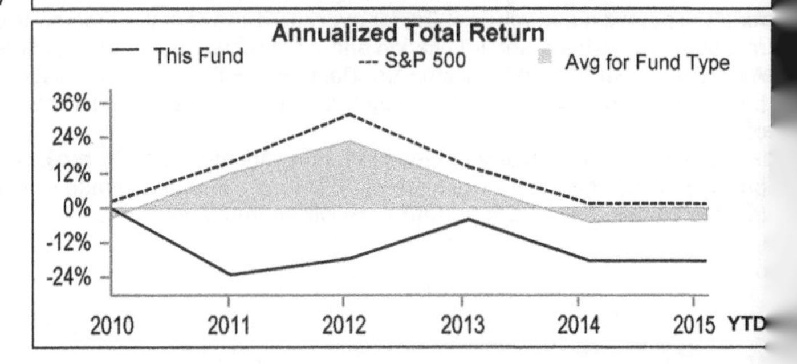

* Denotes ETF Fund

*iPath Pure Beta Sugar ETN (SGAR) E Very Weak

Fund Family: Barclays Bank PLC
Fund Type: Growth and Income
Inception Date: April 20, 2011

Major Rating Factors: *iPath Pure Beta Sugar ETN has adopted a very risky asset allocation strategy and currently receives an overall TheStreet.com Investment Rating of E (Very Weak). The fund has a high level of volatility, as measured by both semi-deviation and drawdown factors. It carries a beta of 0.45, meaning the fund's expected move will be 4.5% for every 10% move in the market. As of December 31, 2015, *iPath Pure Beta Sugar ETN traded at a discount of .34% below its net asset value, which is better than its one-year historical average discount of .05%. Unfortunately, the high level of risk (D, Weak) failed to pay off as investors endured poor performance.

The fund's performance rating is currently D- (Weak). It has registered an annualized return of -18.91% over the last three years and is down -11.58% year to date 2015.

This fund has been team managed for 5 years and currently receives a manager quality ranking of 5 (0=worst, 99=best). If you can tolerate very high levels of risk in the hope of improved future returns, holding this fund may be an option.

Data Date	Investment Rating	Net Assets ($Mil)	Price	Performance Rating/Pts	Total Return Y-T-D	Risk Rating/Pts
12-15	E	2.50	23.30	D- / 1.3	-11.58%	D / 1.7
2014	E	2.50	26.35	E+ / 0.6	-21.18%	D+ / 2.9
2013	E	2.40	34.38	E / 0.5	-21.31%	C- / 3.1
2012	E	2.70	43.69	E / 0.4	-18.07%	C- / 3.8

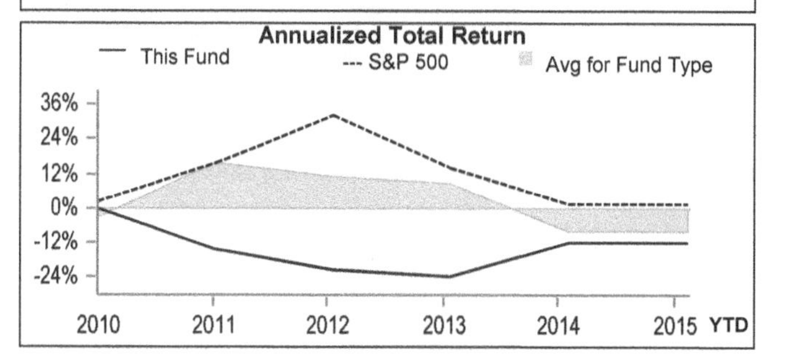

*IPath S&P 500 Dynamic VIX ETN (XVZ) E+ Very Weak

Fund Family: Barclays Bank PLC
Fund Type: Global
Inception Date: August 17, 2011

Major Rating Factors: *IPath S&P 500 Dynamic VIX ETN has adopted a risky asset allocation strategy and currently receives an overall TheStreet.com Investment Rating of E+ (Very Weak). The fund has an above average level of volatility, as measured by both semi-deviation and drawdown factors. It carries a beta of -0.76, meaning the fund's expected move will be -7.6% for every 10% move in the market. As of December 31, 2015, *IPath S&P 500 Dynamic VIX ETN traded at a discount of .04% below its net asset value, which is worse than its one-year historical average discount of .08%. Unfortunately, the high level of risk (D+, Weak) failed to pay off as investors endured poor performance.

The fund's performance rating is currently D- (Weak). It has registered an annualized return of -16.12% over the last three years and is down -9.83% year to date 2015.

This fund has been team managed for 5 years and currently receives a manager quality ranking of 11 (0=worst, 99=best). If you can tolerate high levels of risk in the hope of improved future returns, holding this fund may be an option.

Data Date	Investment Rating	Net Assets ($Mil)	Price	Performance Rating/Pts	Total Return Y-T-D	Risk Rating/Pts
12-15	E+	23.10	25.79	D- / 1.2	-9.83%	D+ / 2.4
2014	D-	23.10	28.48	E+ / 0.8	-16.23%	C / 5.2
2013	E	266.60	33.73	E / 0.3	-22.33%	C- / 3.3
2012	E+	266.60	46.04	E / 0.3	-22.83%	C / 4.6

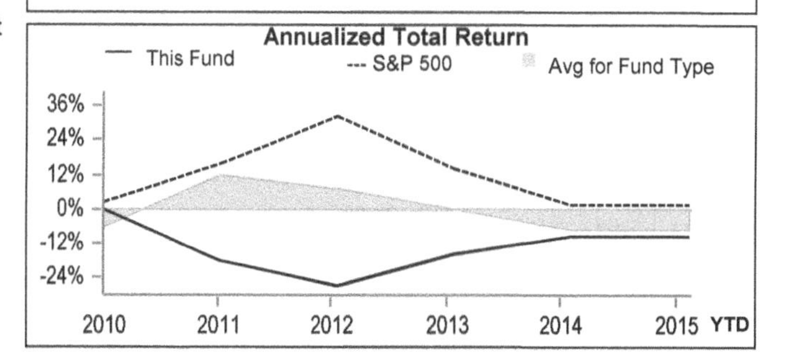

*IPath S&P 500 VIX Mid-Trm Futr E (VXZ) E- Very Weak

Fund Family: Barclays Bank PLC
Fund Type: Income
Inception Date: January 29, 2009

Major Rating Factors: *IPath S&P 500 VIX Mid-Trm Futr E has adopted a very risky asset allocation strategy and currently receives an overall TheStreet.com Investment Rating of E- (Very Weak). The fund has a high level of volatility, as measured by both semi-deviation and drawdown factors. It carries a beta of -2.21, meaning the fund's expected move will be -22.1% for every 10% move in the market. As of December 31, 2015, *IPath S&P 500 VIX Mid-Trm Futr E traded at a premium of .36% above its net asset value, which is worse than its one-year historical average premium of .03%. Unfortunately, the high level of risk (E+, Very Weak) failed to pay off as investors endured very poor performance.

The fund's performance rating is currently E+ (Very Weak). It has registered an annualized return of -24.46% over the last three years and is down -14.50% year to date 2015. Factored into the performance evaluation is an expense ratio of 0.89% (low).

This fund has been team managed for 7 years and currently receives a manager quality ranking of 72 (0=worst, 99=best). If you can tolerate very high levels of risk in the hope of improved future returns, holding this fund may be an option.

Data Date	Investment Rating	Net Assets ($Mil)	Price	Performance Rating/Pts	Total Return Y-T-D	Risk Rating/Pts
12-15	E-	28.95	11.14	E+ / 0.7	-14.50%	E+ / 0.8
2014	E	70.30	13.12	E- / 0.2	-20.80%	C- / 3.3
2013	E-	28.95	15.72	E- / 0.2	-38.43%	D / 1.9
2012	E-	28.95	27.95	E- / 0.2	-55.82%	D / 1.9
2011	E	186.50	60.66	D- / 1.5	-9.91%	D+ / 2.4
2010	E	702.60	65.76	E / 0.3	-14.43%	D+ / 2.9

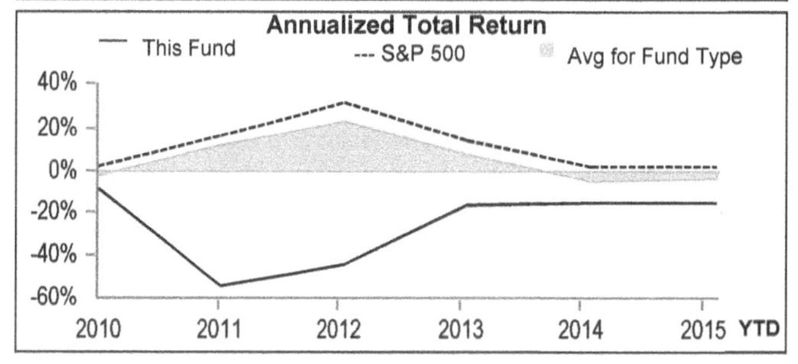

* Denotes ETF Fund

*IPath S&P 500 VIX Sm-Trm Futr ET (VXX) E- Very Weak

Fund Family: Barclays Bank PLC
Fund Type: Income
Inception Date: January 29, 2009

Major Rating Factors: *IPath S&P 500 VIX Sm-Trm Futr ET has adopted a very risky asset allocation strategy and currently receives an overall TheStreet.com Investment Rating of E- (Very Weak). The fund has a high level of volatility, as measured by both semi-deviation and drawdown factors. It carries a beta of -4.69, meaning the fund's expected move will be -46.9% for every 10% move in the market. As of December 31, 2015, *IPath S&P 500 VIX Sm-Trm Futr ET traded at a premium of .75% above its net asset value, which is worse than its one-year historical average premium of .22%. Unfortunately, the high level of risk (E+, Very Weak) failed to pay off as investors endured very poor performance.

The fund's performance rating is currently E- (Very Weak). It has registered an annualized return of -43.29% over the last three years and is down -35.14% year to date 2015. Factored into the performance evaluation is an expense ratio of 0.89% (low).

This fund has been team managed for 7 years and currently receives a manager quality ranking of 88 (0=worst, 99=best). If you can tolerate very high levels of risk in the hope of improved future returns, holding this fund may be an option.

Data Date	Investment Rating	Net Assets ($Mil)	Price	Performance Rating/Pts	Total Return Y-T-D	Risk Rating/Pts
12-15	E-	664.55	20.10	E- / 0.2	-35.14%	E+ / 0.6
2014	E-	1,362.60	31.51	E- / 0	-32.34%	E- / 0
2013	E-	664.55	42.55	E- / 0	-60.83%	D / 1.9
2012	E-	664.55	31.81	E- / 0	-78.99%	D / 1.9
2011	E+	791.90	35.53	C- / 3.2	-10.54%	D / 1.9
2010	E-	1,994.20	37.61	E- / 0	-72.40%	D- / 1.0

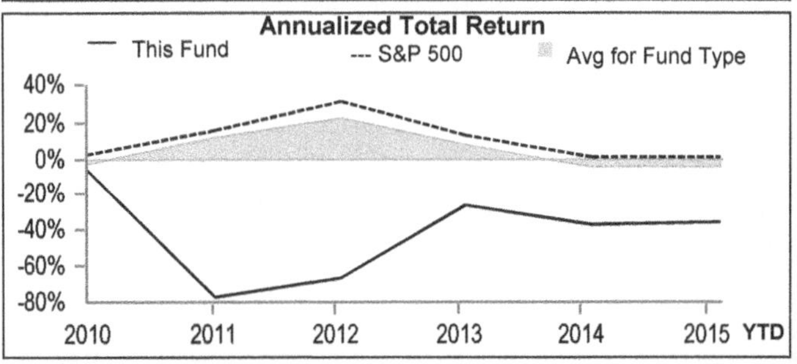

*iPath S&P GSCI Crude Oil TotRet (OIL) E- Very Weak

Fund Family: Barclays Bank PLC
Fund Type: Energy/Natural Resources
Inception Date: August 15, 2006

Major Rating Factors: *iPath S&P GSCI Crude Oil TotRet has adopted a very risky asset allocation strategy and currently receives an overall TheStreet.com Investment Rating of E- (Very Weak). The fund has a high level of volatility, as measured by both semi-deviation and drawdown factors. It carries a beta of 1.20, meaning it is expected to move 12.0% for every 10% move in the market. As of December 31, 2015, *iPath S&P GSCI Crude Oil TotRet traded at a premium of 8.73% above its net asset value, which is worse than its one-year historical average premium of 2.21%. Unfortunately, the high level of risk (D-, Weak) failed to pay off as investors endured very poor performance.

The fund's performance rating is currently E- (Very Weak). It has registered an annualized return of -34.48% over the last three years and is down -48.98% year to date 2015. Factored into the performance evaluation is an expense ratio of 0.75% (very low).

This fund has been team managed for 10 years and currently receives a manager quality ranking of 3 (0=worst, 99=best). If you can tolerate very high levels of risk in the hope of improved future returns, holding this fund may be an option.

Data Date	Investment Rating	Net Assets ($Mil)	Price	Performance Rating/Pts	Total Return Y-T-D	Risk Rating/Pts
12-15	E-	564.45	6.23	E- / 0.2	-48.98%	D- / 1.2
2014	E-	200.50	12.54	E / 0.4	-43.18%	D / 1.9
2013	D	564.45	23.12	D / 1.7	-0.68%	C+ / 6.1
2012	D-	564.45	21.79	E+ / 0.9	-11.55%	C+ / 5.9
2011	D+	436.60	25.12	C- / 3.6	4.56%	C+ / 6.4
2010	E	643.90	25.61	E+ / 0.6	-1.04%	D+ / 2.4

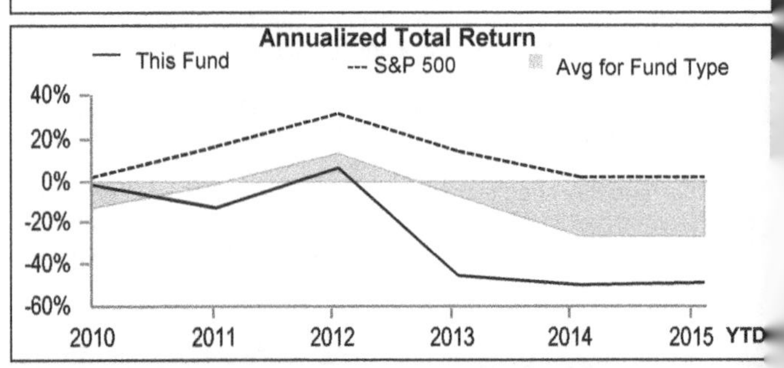

*iPath S&P GSCI Total Return ETN (GSP) E+ Very Weak

Fund Family: Barclays Bank PLC
Fund Type: Growth
Inception Date: June 6, 2006

Major Rating Factors:
Very poor performance is the major factor driving the E+ (Very Weak) TheStreet.com Investment Rating for *iPath S&P GSCI Total Return ETN. The fund currently has a performance rating of E (Very Weak) based on an annualized return of -26.89% over the last three years and a total return of -37.03% year to date 2015. Factored into the performance evaluation is an expense ratio of 0.75% (very low).

The fund's risk rating is currently C- (Fair). It carries a beta of 0.61, meaning the fund's expected move will be 6.1% for every 10% move in the market. Volatility, as measured by both the semi-deviation and a drawdown factor, is considered average. As of December 31, 2015, *iPath S&P GSCI Total Return ETN traded at a price exactly equal to its net asset value, which is worse than its one-year historical average discount of .04%.

This fund has been team managed for 10 years and currently receives a manager quality ranking of 2 (0=worst, 99=best). This fund offers an average level of risk but investors looking for strong performance will be frustrated.

Data Date	Investment Rating	Net Assets ($Mil)	Price	Performance Rating/Pts	Total Return Y-T-D	Risk Rating/Pts
12-15	E+	79.00	13.01	E / 0.4	-37.03%	C- / 3.1
2014	E+	89.70	21.10	E+ / 0.6	-33.15%	C- / 3.6
2013	D+	79.00	32.57	D / 2.0	-4.96%	B- / 7.2
2012	D	79.00	33.28	D / 1.8	-1.47%	B- / 7.1
2011	C-	97.60	33.75	C- / 3.6	3.48%	B- / 7.4
2010	E+	102.50	34.23	E+ / 0.9	8.36%	C- / 3.5

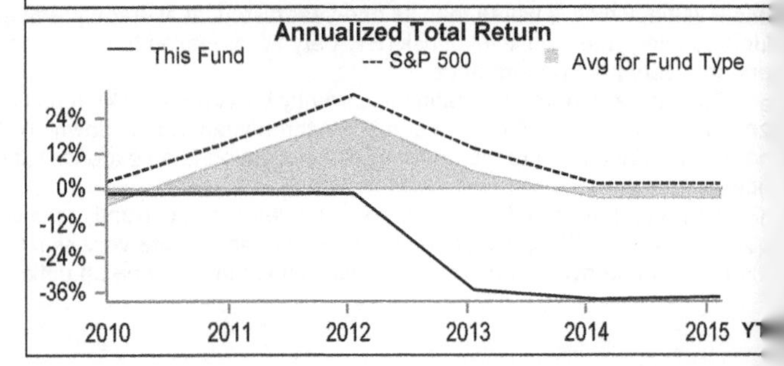

*iPath S&P MLP ETN (IMLP) E- Very Weak

Fund Family: Barclays Bank PLC
Fund Type: Energy/Natural Resources
Inception Date: January 3, 2013

Major Rating Factors: *iPath S&P MLP ETN has adopted a very risky asset allocation strategy and currently receives an overall TheStreet.com Investment Rating of E- (Very Weak). The fund has a high level of volatility, as measured by both semi-deviation and drawdown factors. It carries a beta of 0.00, meaning the fund's expected move will be 0.0% for every 10% move in the market. As of December 31, 2015, *iPath S&P MLP ETN traded at a premium of 2.23% above its net asset value, which is worse than its one-year historical average premium of .01%. Unfortunately, the high level of risk (D-, Weak) failed to pay off as investors endured very poor performance.

The fund's performance rating is currently E- (Very Weak). It has registered an annualized return of 0.00% over the last three years but is down -36.11% year to date 2015.

This fund has been team managed for 3 years and currently receives a manager quality ranking of 7 (0=worst, 99=best). If you can tolerate very high levels of risk in the hope of improved future returns, holding this fund may be an option.

Data Date	Investment Rating	Net Assets ($Mil)	Price	Perfor-mance Rating/Pts	Total Return Y-T-D	Risk Rating/Pts
12-15	E-	795.20	18.35	E- / 0.1	-36.11%	D- / 1.2
2014	C-	795.20	29.98	D / 2.2	7.75%	B / 8.1

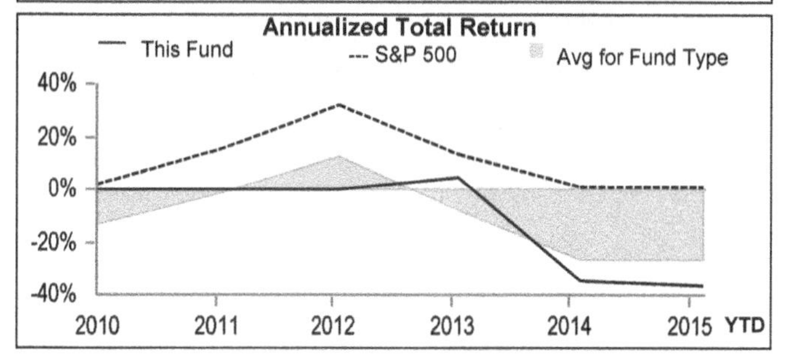

*iPath Seasonal Natural Gas ETN (DCNG) E- Very Weak

Fund Family: Barclays Bank PLC
Fund Type: Energy/Natural Resources
Inception Date: April 20, 2011

Major Rating Factors: *iPath Seasonal Natural Gas ETN has adopted a very risky asset allocation strategy and currently receives an overall TheStreet.com Investment Rating of E- (Very Weak). The fund has a high level of volatility, as measured by both semi-deviation and drawdown factors. It carries a beta of -0.03, meaning the fund's expected move will be -0.3% for every 10% move in the market. As of December 31, 2015, *iPath Seasonal Natural Gas ETN traded at a premium of .38% above its net asset value, which is better than its one-year historical average premium of .42%. Unfortunately, the high level of risk (D-, Weak) failed to pay off as investors endured very poor performance.

The fund's performance rating is currently E+ (Very Weak). It has registered an annualized return of -18.65% over the last three years and is down -28.57% year to date 2015.

This fund has been team managed for 5 years and currently receives a manager quality ranking of 8 (0=worst, 99=best). If you can tolerate very high levels of risk in the hope of improved future returns, holding this fund may be an option.

Data Date	Investment Rating	Net Assets ($Mil)	Price	Perfor-mance Rating/Pts	Total Return Y-T-D	Risk Rating/Pts
12-15	E-	1.40	15.90	E+ / 0.8	-28.57%	D- / 1.0
2014	E+	1.40	22.43	E / 0.3	-21.91%	C- / 4.0
2013	D	7.10	28.98	C / 5.1	1.62%	D+ / 2.8

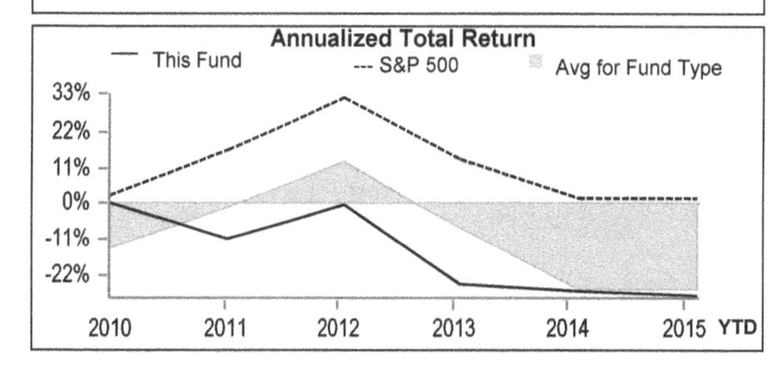

*iPath US Treas 10Yr Bear ETN (DTYS) D- Weak

Fund Family: Barclays Bank PLC
Fund Type: US Government/Agency
Inception Date: August 9, 2010

Major Rating Factors: *iPath US Treas 10Yr Bear ETN has adopted a risky asset allocation strategy and currently receives an overall TheStreet.com Investment Rating of D- (Weak). The fund has an above average level of volatility, as measured by both semi-deviation and drawdown factors. It carries a beta of -2.63, meaning the fund's expected move will be -26.3% for every 10% move in the market. As of December 31, 2015, *iPath US Treas 10Yr Bear ETN traded at a discount of .93% below its net asset value. Unfortunately, the high level of risk (D+, Weak) failed to pay off as investors endured poor performance.

The fund's performance rating is currently D+ (Weak). It has registered an annualized return of -9.98% over the last three years and is down -9.14% year to date 2015.

This fund has been team managed for 6 years and currently receives a manager quality ranking of 45 (0=worst, 99=best). If you can tolerate high levels of risk in the hope of improved future returns, holding this fund may be an option.

Data Date	Investment Rating	Net Assets ($Mil)	Price	Perfor-mance Rating/Pts	Total Return Y-T-D	Risk Rating/Pts
12-15	D-	100.60	20.27	D+ / 2.3	-9.14%	D+ / 2.9
2014	E+	100.60	22.88	D- / 1.0	-29.07%	C- / 4.0
2013	E	109.90	32.87	D- / 1.1	16.89%	D+ / 2.5
2012	E	106.20	26.75	E+ / 0.9	-13.91%	D+ / 2.5
2011	E	40.60	32.26	E / 0.3	-37.54%	C- / 3.5

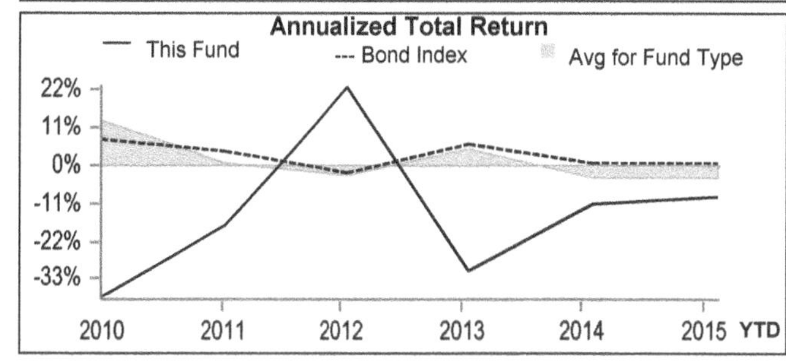

*iPath US Treas 10Yr Bull ETN (DTYL) C- Fair

Fund Family: Barclays Bank PLC
Fund Type: US Government/Agency
Inception Date: August 9, 2010

Major Rating Factors: Middle of the road best describes *iPath US Treas 10Yr Bull ETN whose TheStreet.com Investment Rating is currently a C- (Fair). The fund currently has a performance rating of C (Fair) based on an annualized return of 2.13% over the last three years and a total return of 1.64% year to date 2015.

The fund's risk rating is currently C (Fair). It carries a beta of 0.80, meaning the fund's expected move will be 8.0% for every 10% move in the market. Volatility, as measured by both the semi-deviation and a drawdown factor, is considered average. As of December 31, 2015, *iPath US Treas 10Yr Bull ETN traded at a discount of .53% below its net asset value, which is better than its one-year historical average premium of .06%.

This fund has been team managed for 6 years and currently receives a manager quality ranking of 62 (0=worst, 99=best). If you desire an average level of risk, then this fund may be an option.

Data Date	Investment Rating	Net Assets ($Mil)	Price	Performance Rating/Pts	Total Return Y-T-D	Risk Rating/Pts
12-15	C-	2.90	74.81	C / 5.2	1.64%	C / 5.1
2014	C	2.90	73.60	C / 4.3	12.76%	B / 8.6
2013	C-	2.50	64.68	C+ / 5.7	-7.90%	C / 5.2
2012	D-	5.70	71.70	D / 1.7	4.87%	C / 5.1
2011	B-	4.80	66.75	A+ / 9.8	40.23%	C / 5.2

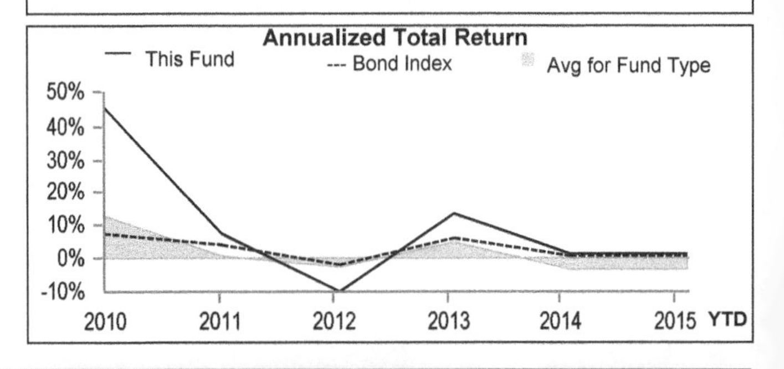

*iPath US Treas 2Yr Bear ETN (DTUS) D Weak

Fund Family: Barclays Bank PLC
Fund Type: US Government/Agency
Inception Date: August 9, 2010

Major Rating Factors:
Disappointing performance is the major factor driving the D (Weak) TheStreet.com Investment Rating for *iPath US Treas 2Yr Bear ETN. The fund currently has a performance rating of D+ (Weak) based on an annualized return of -6.48% over the last three years and a total return of -8.37% year to date 2015.

The fund's risk rating is currently C- (Fair). It carries a beta of -0.49, meaning the fund's expected move will be -4.9% for every 10% move in the market. Volatility, as measured by both the semi-deviation and a drawdown factor, is considered average. As of December 31, 2015, *iPath US Treas 2Yr Bear ETN traded at a discount of .24% below its net asset value, which is better than its one-year historical average premium of .19%.

This fund has been team managed for 6 years and currently receives a manager quality ranking of 29 (0=worst, 99=best). This fund offers an average level of risk but investors looking for strong performance will be frustrated.

Data Date	Investment Rating	Net Assets ($Mil)	Price	Performance Rating/Pts	Total Return Y-T-D	Risk Rating/Pts
12-15	D	20.50	33.17	D+ / 2.8	-8.37%	C- / 4.0
2014	D	20.50	36.11	D / 1.9	-8.52%	C+ / 6.5
2013	D-	15.70	39.42	D- / 1.5	-2.42%	C / 4.6
2012	E+	15.10	40.51	D- / 1.2	-1.39%	C / 4.7
2011	D-	13.00	41.51	D- / 1.1	-16.28%	C / 5.0

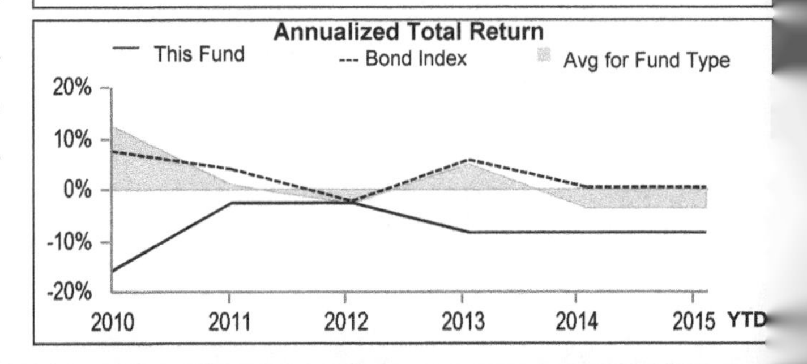

*iPath US Treas 2Yr Bull ETN (DTUL) D+ Weak

Fund Family: Barclays Bank PLC
Fund Type: US Government/Agency
Inception Date: August 9, 2010

Major Rating Factors: *iPath US Treas 2Yr Bull ETN receives a TheStreet.com Investment Rating of D+ (Weak). The fund currently has a performance rating of C (Fair) based on an annualized return of 2.90% over the last three years and a total return of 5.06% year to date 2015.

The fund's risk rating is currently C- (Fair). It carries a beta of 0.17, meaning the fund's expected move will be 1.7% for every 10% move in the market. Volatility, as measured by both the semi-deviation and a drawdown factor, is considered average. As of December 31, 2015, *iPath US Treas 2Yr Bull ETN traded at a premium of 1.51% above its net asset value, which is worse than its one-year historical average discount of .48%.

This fund has been team managed for 6 years and currently receives a manager quality ranking of 84 (0=worst, 99=best). If you desire an average level of risk, then this fund may be an option.

Data Date	Investment Rating	Net Assets ($Mil)	Price	Performance Rating/Pts	Total Return Y-T-D	Risk Rating/Pts
12-15	D+	1.90	63.37	C / 5.4	5.06%	C- / 4.0
2013	D+	4.10	58.63	C / 4.5	1.82%	C+ / 5.9
2011	C-	8.60	57.56	C / 4.8	14.12%	C+ / 5.8

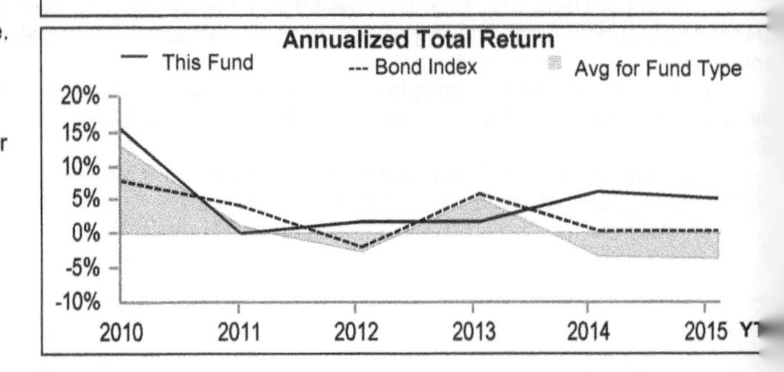

*iPath US Treas Flattener ETN (FLAT) D+ Weak

Fund Family: Barclays Bank PLC
Fund Type: US Government/Agency
Inception Date: August 9, 2010

Major Rating Factors: *iPath US Treas Flattener ETN receives a TheStreet.com Investment Rating of D+ (Weak). The fund currently has a performance rating of C- (Fair) based on an annualized return of -0.86% over the last three years and a total return of -2.70% year to date 2015.

The fund's risk rating is currently C (Fair). It carries a beta of 0.66, meaning the fund's expected move will be 6.6% for every 10% move in the market. Volatility, as measured by both the semi-deviation and a drawdown factor, is considered average. As of December 31, 2015, *iPath US Treas Flattener ETN traded at a discount of .43% below its net asset value, which is better than its one-year historical average discount of .07%.

This fund has been team managed for 6 years and currently receives a manager quality ranking of 43 (0=worst, 99=best). If you desire an average level of risk, then this fund may be an option.

Data Date	Investment Rating	Net Assets ($Mil)	Price	Perfor-mance Rating/Pts	Total Return Y-T-D	Risk Rating/Pts
12-15	D+	4.90	60.04	C- / 4.0	-2.70%	C / 5.0
2014	C	4.90	61.27	C- / 3.9	10.39%	B / 8.5
2013	D	4.60	55.43	C- / 3.7	-10.03%	C / 5.1
2012	D-	20.70	62.48	D- / 1.5	4.88%	C / 5.2
2011	C+	49.80	58.33	B+ / 8.4	24.07%	C / 5.3

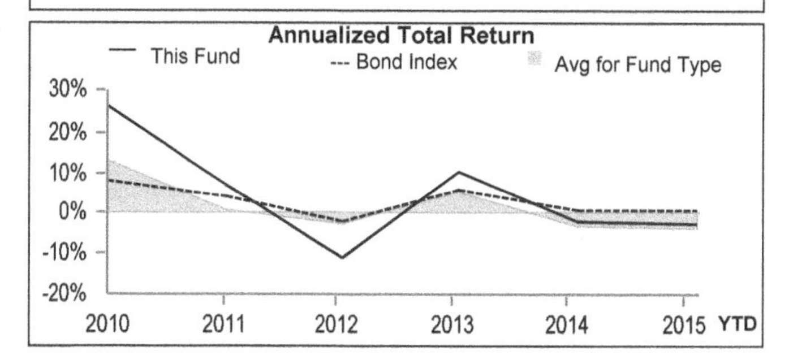

*iPath US Treas Lng Bd Bear ETN (DLBS) E Very Weak

Fund Family: Barclays Bank PLC
Fund Type: US Government/Agency
Inception Date: August 9, 2010

Major Rating Factors: *iPath US Treas Lng Bd Bear ETN has adopted a very risky asset allocation strategy and currently receives an overall TheStreet.com Investment Rating of E (Very Weak). The fund has a high level of volatility, as measured by both semi-deviation and drawdown factors. It carries a beta of -2.67, meaning the fund's expected move will be -26.7% for every 10% move in the market. As of December 31, 2015, *iPath US Treas Lng Bd Bear ETN traded at a premium of .46% above its net asset value, which is worse than its one-year historical average discount of .09%. Unfortunately, the high level of risk (E+, Very Weak) failed to pay off as investors endured poor performance.

The fund's performance rating is currently D (Weak). It has registered an annualized return of -10.28% over the last three years and is up 3.25% year to date 2015.

This fund has been team managed for 6 years and currently receives a manager quality ranking of 46 (0=worst, 99=best). If you can tolerate very high levels of risk in the hope of improved future returns, holding this fund may be an option.

Data Date	Investment Rating	Net Assets ($Mil)	Price	Perfor-mance Rating/Pts	Total Return Y-T-D	Risk Rating/Pts
12-15	E	44.00	21.62	D / 2.2	3.25%	E+ / 0.8
2014	E+	44.00	21.50	E+ / 0.7	-41.11%	C- / 3.4
2013	E	61.70	36.80	D- / 1.4	21.65%	D+ / 2.7
2012	E+	22.60	28.54	D / 1.9	-7.97%	D+ / 2.6
2011	E	18.80	31.97	E / 0.3	-37.49%	C- / 3.4

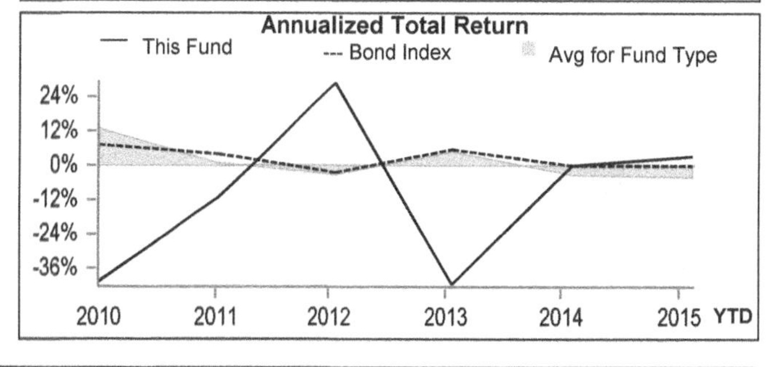

*iPath US Treas Lng Bd Bull ETN (DLBL) D+ Weak

Fund Family: Barclays Bank PLC
Fund Type: US Government/Agency
Inception Date: August 9, 2010

Major Rating Factors: *iPath US Treas Lng Bd Bull ETN receives a TheStreet.com Investment Rating of D+ (Weak). The fund currently has a performance rating of C (Fair) based on an annualized return of 2.99% over the last three years and a total return of 0.42% year to date 2015.

The fund's risk rating is currently C- (Fair). It carries a beta of 0.87, meaning the fund's expected move will be 8.7% for every 10% move in the market. Volatility, as measured by both the semi-deviation and a drawdown factor, is considered average. As of December 31, 2015, *iPath US Treas Lng Bd Bull ETN traded at a premium of 1.19% above its net asset value, which is worse than its one-year historical average premium of .07%.

This fund has been team managed for 6 years and currently receives a manager quality ranking of 67 (0=worst, 99=best). If you desire an average level of risk, then this fund may be an option.

Data Date	Investment Rating	Net Assets ($Mil)	Price	Perfor-mance Rating/Pts	Total Return Y-T-D	Risk Rating/Pts
12-15	D+	1.70	75.04	C / 5.5	0.42%	C- / 3.3
2014	C+	1.70	74.04	C / 5.4	22.16%	B / 8.3
2013	D+	1.50	60.61	C / 5.0	-10.96%	C / 5.0
2012	D-	3.00	70.33	D- / 1.2	2.89%	C / 5.0
2011	B-	10.70	66.82	A+ / 9.9	43.39%	C / 5.1

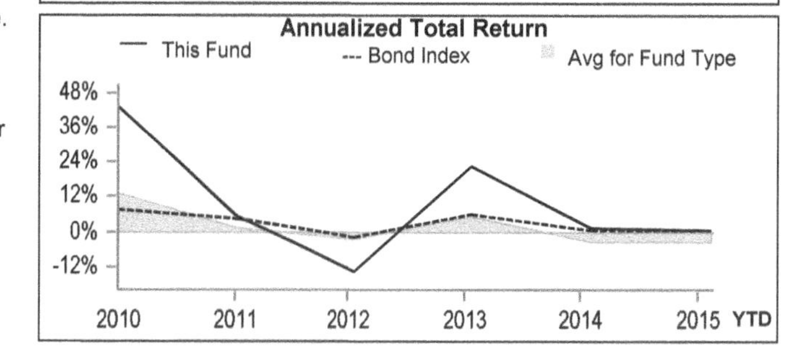

*iPath US Treas Steepen ETN (STPP) D- Weak

Fund Family: Barclays Bank PLC
Fund Type: US Government/Agency
Inception Date: August 9, 2010

Major Rating Factors: *iPath US Treas Steepen ETN has adopted a risky asset allocation strategy and currently receives an overall TheStreet.com Investment Rating of D- (Weak). The fund has an above average level of volatility, as measured by both semi-deviation and drawdown factors. It carries a beta of -1.17, meaning the fund's expected move will be -11.7% for every 10% move in the market. As of December 31, 2015, *iPath US Treas Steepen ETN traded at a premium of .55% above its net asset value, which is worse than its one-year historical average discount of .09%. Unfortunately, the high level of risk (D+, Weak) has only provided investors with average performance.

The fund's performance rating is currently C- (Fair). It has registered an annualized return of -1.21% over the last three years and is up 2.04% year to date 2015.

This fund has been team managed for 6 years and currently receives a manager quality ranking of 83 (0=worst, 99=best). If you are comfortable owning a high risk investment, then this fund may be an option.

Data Date	Investment Rating	Net Assets ($Mil)	Price	Performance Rating/Pts	Total Return Y-T-D	Risk Rating/Pts
12-15	D-	11.10	34.91	C- / 3.7	2.04%	D+ / 2.8
2014	D	11.10	34.59	D / 1.7	-16.23%	C+ / 5.9
2013	E+	16.80	42.05	D / 1.7	14.47%	C- / 3.5
2012	E+	7.80	35.12	E+ / 0.9	-11.46%	C- / 3.5
2011	E+	2.50	40.21	E+ / 0.7	-23.18%	C / 4.4

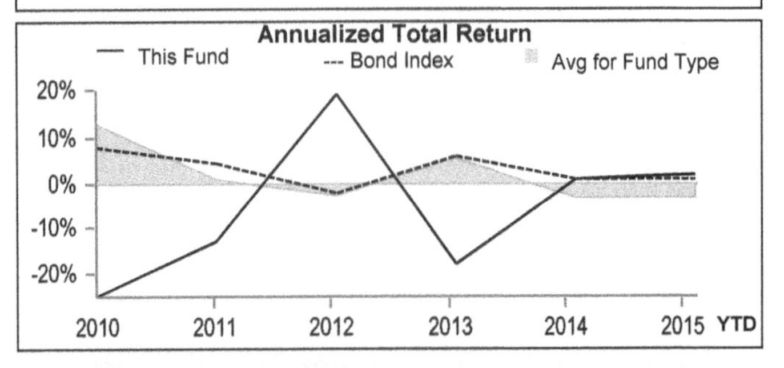

*IQ Australia Small Cap ETF (KROO) D Weak

Fund Family: New York Life Investment Management
Fund Type: Foreign
Inception Date: March 22, 2010

Major Rating Factors:
Disappointing performance is the major factor driving the D (Weak) TheStreet.com Investment Rating for *IQ Australia Small Cap ETF. The fund currently has a performance rating of D (Weak) based on an annualized return of -11.10% over the last three years and a total return of -9.52% year to date 2015. Factored into the performance evaluation is an expense ratio of 0.70% (very low).

The fund's risk rating is currently C (Fair). It carries a beta of 1.18, meaning it is expected to move 11.8% for every 10% move in the market. Volatility, as measured by both the semi-deviation and a drawdown factor, is considered average. As of December 31, 2015, *IQ Australia Small Cap ETF traded at a discount of 1.18% below its net asset value, which is better than its one-year historical average discount of .65%.

Greg Barrato has been running the fund for 5 years and currently receives a manager quality ranking of 10 (0=worst, 99=best). This fund offers an average level of risk but investors looking for strong performance will be frustrated.

Data Date	Investment Rating	Net Assets ($Mil)	Price	Performance Rating/Pts	Total Return Y-T-D	Risk Rating/Pts
12-15	D	7.10	13.39	D / 2.1	-9.52%	C / 5.4
2014	D-	7.10	15.55	D / 1.7	-10.01%	C+ / 5.6
2013	D-	9.10	18.12	D- / 1.2	-13.77%	C / 4.7
2012	C	13.80	21.57	C+ / 6.9	5.96%	C / 5.4
2011	D-	15.10	20.15	E+ / 0.8	-20.03%	C+ / 5.6

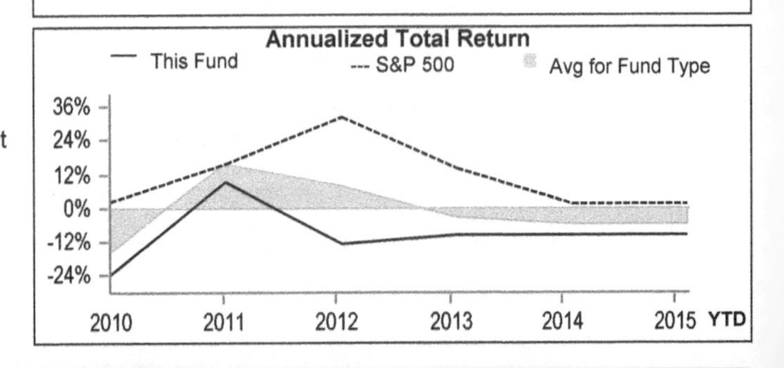

*IQ Canada Small Cap ETF (CNDA) E+ Very Weak

Fund Family: New York Life Investment Management
Fund Type: Foreign
Inception Date: March 22, 2010

Major Rating Factors:
Very poor performance is the major factor driving the E+ (Very Weak) TheStreet.com Investment Rating for *IQ Canada Small Cap ETF. The fund currently has a performance rating of E+ (Very Weak) based on an annualized return of -19.56% over the last three years and a total return of -35.83% year to date 2015. Factored into the performance evaluation is an expense ratio of 0.69% (very low).

The fund's risk rating is currently C- (Fair). It carries a beta of 1.04, meaning that its performance tracks fairly well with that of the overall stock market. Volatility, as measured by both the semi-deviation and a drawdown factor, is considered average. As of December 31, 2015, *IQ Canada Small Cap ETF traded at a price exactly equal to its net asset value, which is worse than its one-year historical average discount of .04%.

Greg Barrato has been running the fund for 5 years and currently receives a manager quality ranking of 6 (0=worst, 99=best). This fund offers an average level of risk but investors looking for strong performance will be frustrated.

Data Date	Investment Rating	Net Assets ($Mil)	Price	Performance Rating/Pts	Total Return Y-T-D	Risk Rating/Pts
12-15	E+	15.80	11.90	E+ / 0.7	-35.83%	C- / 3.8
2014	D-	15.80	18.75	D- / 1.2	-11.63%	C+ / 5.9
2013	D-	16.00	21.26	D- / 1.1	-8.50%	C / 5.2
2012	D-	19.80	23.15	D / 1.8	-5.59%	C+ / 5.7
2011	D-	31.80	25.33	E+ / 0.9	-19.98%	C+ / 6.2

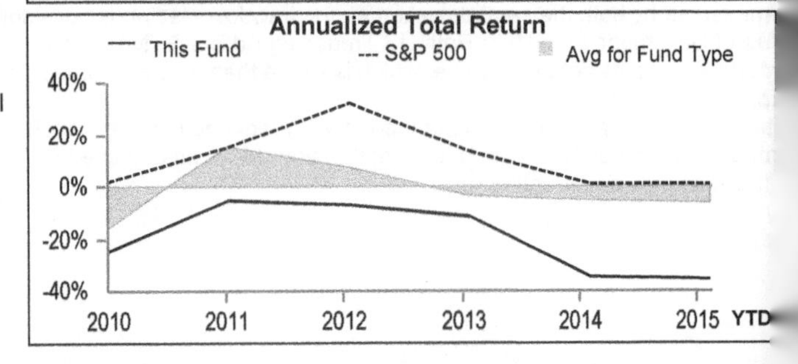

*IQ Global Agribusiness SmCp ETF (CROP) B+ Good

Fund Family: New York Life Investment Management
Fund Type: Global
Inception Date: March 21, 2011

Major Rating Factors: *IQ Global Agribusiness SmCp ETF receives a TheStreet.com Investment Rating of B+ (Good). The fund currently has a performance rating of C+ (Fair) based on an annualized return of 3.87% over the last three years and a total return of 13.66% year to date 2015. Factored into the performance evaluation is an expense ratio of 0.76% (very low).

The fund's risk rating is currently B (Good). It carries a beta of 0.61, meaning the fund's expected move will be 6.1% for every 10% move in the market. Volatility, as measured by both the semi-deviation and a drawdown factor, is considered low. As of December 31, 2015, *IQ Global Agribusiness SmCp ETF traded at a discount of 1.49% below its net asset value, which is better than its one-year historical average discount of .29%.

Greg Barrato has been running the fund for 5 years and currently receives a manager quality ranking of 77 (0=worst, 99=best). If you desire an average level of risk, then this fund may be an option.

Data Date	Investment Rating	Net Assets ($Mil)	Price	Performance Rating/Pts	Total Return Y-T-D	Risk Rating/Pts
12-15	B+	18.00	27.85	C+ / 6.9	13.66%	B / 8.6
2014	C	18.00	25.08	C- / 3.4	-6.16%	B / 8.6
2013	C+	37.10	27.50	C+ / 5.7	5.78%	B / 8.0
2012	B	36.90	25.58	B / 8.0	15.65%	B- / 7.8

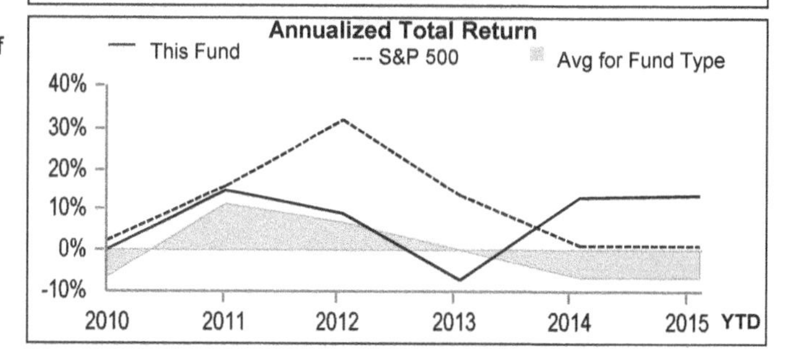

*IQ Global Oil Small Cap ETF (IOIL) D- Weak

Fund Family: New York Life Investment Management
Fund Type: Global
Inception Date: May 4, 2011

Major Rating Factors:
Disappointing performance is the major factor driving the D- (Weak) TheStreet.com Investment Rating for *IQ Global Oil Small Cap ETF. The fund currently has a performance rating of D- (Weak) based on an annualized return of -14.85% over the last three years and a total return of -33.29% year to date 2015. Factored into the performance evaluation is an expense ratio of 0.76% (very low).

The fund's risk rating is currently C- (Fair). It carries a beta of 1.45, meaning it is expected to move 14.5% for every 10% move in the market. Volatility, as measured by both the semi-deviation and a drawdown factor, is considered average. As of December 31, 2015, *IQ Global Oil Small Cap ETF traded at a discount of 1.09% below its net asset value, which is better than its one-year historical average discount of .02%.

Greg Barrato has been running the fund for 5 years and currently receives a manager quality ranking of 7 (0=worst, 99=best). This fund offers an average level of risk but investors looking for strong performance will be frustrated.

Data Date	Investment Rating	Net Assets ($Mil)	Price	Performance Rating/Pts	Total Return Y-T-D	Risk Rating/Pts
12-15	D-	2.10	9.96	D- / 1.0	-33.29%	C- / 4.1
2014	D	2.10	15.37	D / 1.8	-23.13%	C+ / 6.1
2013	C+	2.10	20.72	B / 7.8	19.68%	C+ / 6.3
2012	C+	2.60	16.75	B / 7.7	12.19%	C+ / 5.9

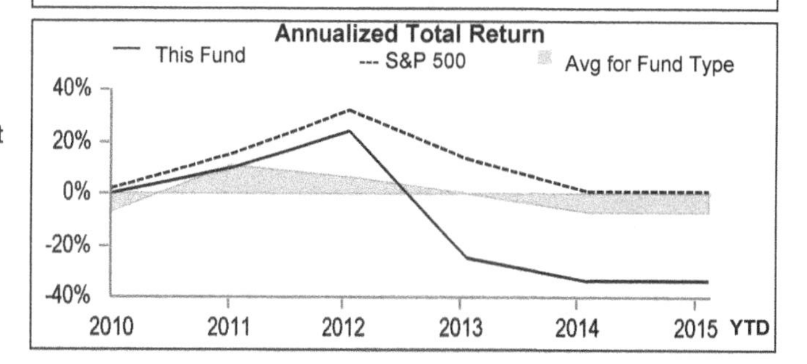

*IQ Global Resources ETF (GRES) D+ Weak

Fund Family: New York Life Investment Management
Fund Type: Energy/Natural Resources
Inception Date: October 26, 2009

Major Rating Factors:
Disappointing performance is the major factor driving the D+ (Weak) TheStreet.com Investment Rating for *IQ Global Resources ETF. The fund currently has a performance rating of D (Weak) based on an annualized return of -10.37% over the last three years and a total return of -19.66% year to date 2015. Factored into the performance evaluation is an expense ratio of 0.75% (very low).

The fund's risk rating is currently B- (Good). It carries a beta of 0.51, meaning the fund's expected move will be 5.1% for every 10% move in the market. Volatility, as measured by both the semi-deviation and a drawdown factor, is considered low. As of December 31, 2015, *IQ Global Resources ETF traded at a discount of .76% below its net asset value, which is better than its one-year historical average discount of .26%.

Greg Barrato has been running the fund for 5 years and currently receives a manager quality ranking of 19 (0=worst, 99=best). This fund offers only a moderate level of risk but investors looking for strong performance are still waiting.

Data Date	Investment Rating	Net Assets ($Mil)	Price	Performance Rating/Pts	Total Return Y-T-D	Risk Rating/Pts
12-15	D+	91.40	20.84	D / 1.6	-19.66%	B- / 7.2
2014	C-	91.40	26.64	D+ / 2.3	-5.61%	B / 8.4
2013	D+	81.40	28.42	D+ / 2.5	-5.03%	B- / 7.9
2012	C-	76.10	30.42	C- / 3.0	6.66%	B- / 7.8
2011	D	61.70	28.02	D- / 1.5	-5.74%	B- / 7.2
2010	A+	42.50	31.83	A / 9.3	23.38%	B / 8.3

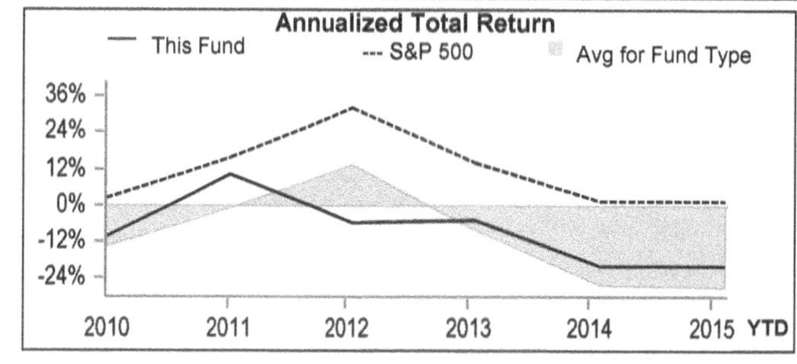

*IQ Hedge Macro Tracker ETF (MCRO) C- Fair

Fund Family: New York Life Investment Management
Fund Type: Global
Inception Date: June 8, 2009

Major Rating Factors: Middle of the road best describes *IQ Hedge Macro Tracker ETF whose TheStreet.com Investment Rating is currently a C- (Fair). The fund currently has a performance rating of C- (Fair) based on an annualized return of -3.24% over the last three years and a total return of -4.79% year to date 2015. Factored into the performance evaluation is an expense ratio of 0.75% (very low).

The fund's risk rating is currently B- (Good). It carries a beta of 0.23, meaning the fund's expected move will be 2.3% for every 10% move in the market. Volatility, as measured by both the semi-deviation and a drawdown factor, is considered low. As of December 31, 2015, *IQ Hedge Macro Tracker ETF traded at a premium of .25% above its net asset value, which is worse than its one-year historical average discount of .02%.

Denise Krisko has been running the fund for 7 years and currently receives a manager quality ranking of 35 (0=worst, 99=best). If you desire an average level of risk, then this fund may be an option.

Data Date	Investment Rating	Net Assets ($Mil)	Price	Perfor-mance Rating/Pts	Total Return Y-T-D	Risk Rating/Pts
12-15	C-	23.60	24.35	C- / 3.1	-4.79%	B- / 7.3
2014	D+	23.60	25.60	D+ / 2.6	-1.68%	B- / 7.2
2013	C-	34.20	26.24	D+ / 2.5	-3.11%	B+ / 9.1
2012	C-	38.30	27.40	D / 1.8	3.80%	B+ / 9.2
2011	C-	32.90	26.27	D / 1.6	-3.05%	B+ / 9.3
2010	B	24.70	27.54	C / 5.5	4.88%	B / 8.8

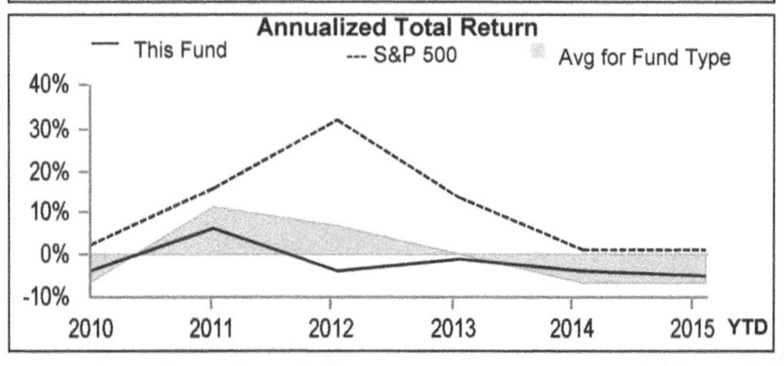

*IQ Hedge Market Neutral Tracker (QMN) C Fair

Fund Family: New York Life Investment Management
Fund Type: Precious Metals
Inception Date: October 4, 2012

Major Rating Factors: Middle of the road best describes *IQ Hedge Market Neutral Tracker whose TheStreet.com Investment Rating is currently a C (Fair). The fund currently has a performance rating of C- (Fair) based on an annualized return of 0.34% over the last three years and a total return of -1.46% year to date 2015. Factored into the performance evaluation is an expense ratio of 0.76% (very low).

The fund's risk rating is currently B- (Good). It carries a beta of 0.05, meaning the fund's expected move will be 0.5% for every 10% move in the market. Volatility, as measured by both the semi-deviation and a drawdown factor, is considered low. As of December 31, 2015, *IQ Hedge Market Neutral Tracker traded at a premium of .04% above its net asset value, which is worse than its one-year historical average discount of .04%.

Greg Barrato has been running the fund for 4 years and currently receives a manager quality ranking of 77 (0=worst, 99=best). If you desire an average level of risk, then this fund may be an option.

Data Date	Investment Rating	Net Assets ($Mil)	Price	Perfor-mance Rating/Pts	Total Return Y-T-D	Risk Rating/Pts
12-15	C	16.70	24.93	C- / 4.2	-1.46%	B- / 7.7
2014	C-	16.70	25.33	D+ / 2.8	0.90%	B- / 7.9
2013	C+	20.30	25.48	C- / 3.7	1.72%	B+ / 9.8

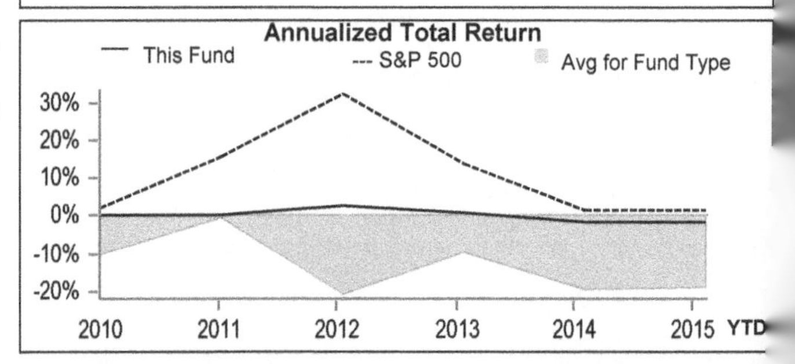

*IQ Hedge Multi-Strategy Tracker (QAI) C+ Fair

Fund Family: New York Life Investment Management
Fund Type: Global
Inception Date: March 24, 2009

Major Rating Factors: Middle of the road best describes *IQ Hedge Multi-Strategy Tracker whose TheStreet.com Investment Rating is currently a C+ (Fair). The fund currently has a performance rating of C (Fair) based on an annualized return of 1.66% over the last three years and a total return of -2.46% year to date 2015. Factored into the performance evaluation is an expense ratio of 0.76% (very low).

The fund's risk rating is currently B (Good). It carries a beta of 0.29, meaning the fund's expected move will be 2.9% for every 10% move in the market. Volatility, as measured by both the semi-deviation and a drawdown factor, is considered low. As of December 31, 2015, *IQ Hedge Multi-Strategy Tracker traded at a price exactly equal to its net asset value, which is better than its one-year historical average premium of .01%.

Donald J. Mulvihill has been running the fund for 8 years and currently receives a manager quality ranking of 70 (0=worst, 99=best). If you desire an average level of risk, then this fund may be an option.

Data Date	Investment Rating	Net Assets ($Mil)	Price	Perfor-mance Rating/Pts	Total Return Y-T-D	Risk Rating/Pts
12-15	C+	855.50	28.46	C / 4.7	-2.46%	B / 8.5
2014	C-	855.50	29.39	C- / 3.7	3.23%	B- / 7.8
2013	C+	629.30	28.97	C- / 3.9	4.57%	B+ / 9.7
2012	C-	314.80	27.81	D / 1.9	3.22%	B+ / 9.6
2011	C-	177.40	27.08	D / 2.0	0.51%	B+ / 9.6
2010	B	123.30	27.41	C- / 4.2	2.57%	B / 8.8

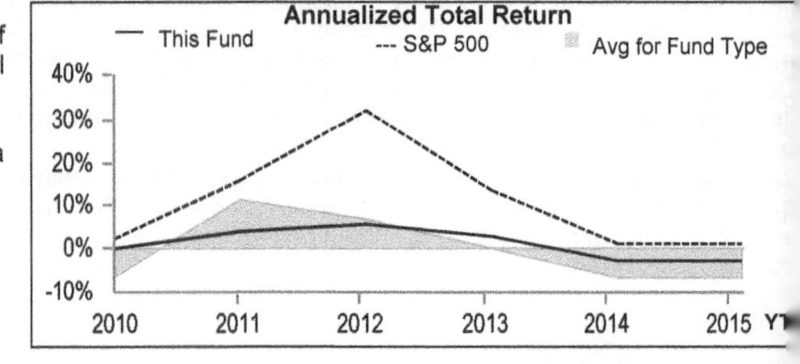

*IQ Merger Arbitrage ETF (MNA) — C+ — Fair

Fund Family: New York Life Investment Management
Fund Type: Global
Inception Date: November 16, 2009

Major Rating Factors: Middle of the road best describes *IQ Merger Arbitrage ETF whose TheStreet.com Investment Rating is currently a C+ (Fair). The fund currently has a performance rating of C+ (Fair) based on an annualized return of 4.20% over the last three years and a total return of 0.57% year to date 2015. Factored into the performance evaluation is an expense ratio of 0.76% (very low).

The fund's risk rating is currently B- (Good). It carries a beta of 0.08, meaning the fund's expected move will be 0.8% for every 10% move in the market. Volatility, as measured by both the semi-deviation and a drawdown factor, is considered low. As of December 31, 2015, *IQ Merger Arbitrage ETF traded at a premium of .21% above its net asset value, which is worse than its one-year historical average premium of .11%.

Greg Barrato has been running the fund for 5 years and currently receives a manager quality ranking of 87 (0=worst, 99=best). If you desire an average level of risk, then this fund may be an option.

Data Date	Investment Rating	Net Assets ($Mil)	Price	Performance Rating/Pts	Total Return Y-T-D	Risk Rating/Pts
12-15	C+	61.60	28.07	C+ / 5.7	0.57%	B- / 7.9
2014	C	61.60	27.91	C- / 3.9	5.16%	B+ / 9.1
2013	C	23.80	26.54	C- / 3.7	6.96%	B+ / 9.5
2012	D+	12.40	25.16	D- / 1.4	1.24%	B+ / 9.1
2011	C-	24.80	24.58	D / 2.0	-0.56%	B+ / 9.2
2010	C-	23.60	24.70	D- / 1.1	-3.05%	B / 8.6

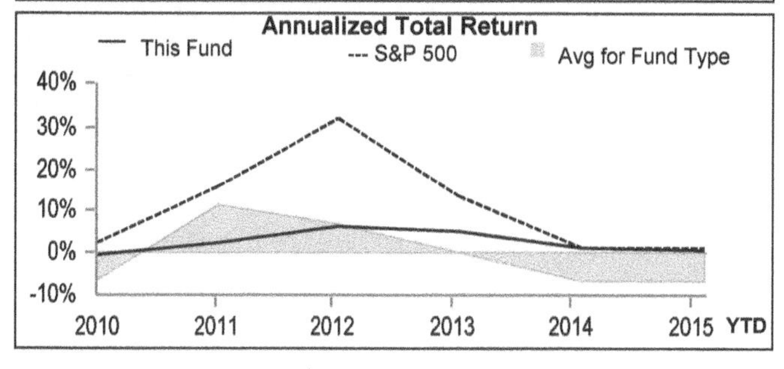

*IQ Real Return ETF (CPI) — C — Fair

Fund Family: New York Life Investment Management
Fund Type: Income
Inception Date: October 26, 2009

Major Rating Factors: Middle of the road best describes *IQ Real Return ETF whose TheStreet.com Investment Rating is currently a C (Fair). The fund currently has a performance rating of C (Fair) based on an annualized return of 0.38% over the last three years and a total return of 0.38% year to date 2015. Factored into the performance evaluation is an expense ratio of 0.48% (very low).

The fund's risk rating is currently B- (Good). It carries a beta of 0.17, meaning the fund's expected move will be 1.7% for every 10% move in the market. Volatility, as measured by both the semi-deviation and a drawdown factor, is considered low. As of December 31, 2015, *IQ Real Return ETF traded at a premium of .19% above its net asset value, which is worse than its one-year historical average discount of .01%.

Greg Barrato has been running the fund for 5 years and currently receives a manager quality ranking of 50 (0=worst, 99=best). If you desire an average level of risk, then this fund may be an option.

Data Date	Investment Rating	Net Assets ($Mil)	Price	Performance Rating/Pts	Total Return Y-T-D	Risk Rating/Pts
12-15	C	25.10	26.53	C / 4.5	0.38%	B- / 7.9
2014	C-	25.10	27.19	C- / 3.5	4.88%	B- / 7.9
2013	C	22.10	25.83	D+ / 2.8	-1.15%	B+ / 9.8
2012	C-	40.80	26.32	D / 1.7	1.25%	B+ / 9.9
2011	C	33.70	26.00	D+ / 2.6	2.69%	B+ / 9.9
2010	C+	12.70	25.48	C- / 3.2	1.57%	B / 8.3

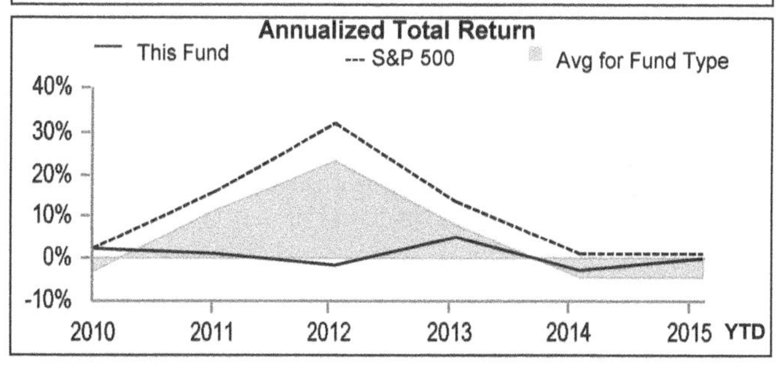

*IQ US Real Estate SmCp ETF (ROOF) — C+ — Fair

Fund Family: New York Life Investment Management
Fund Type: Growth and Income
Inception Date: June 13, 2011

Major Rating Factors: Middle of the road best describes *IQ US Real Estate SmCp ETF whose TheStreet.com Investment Rating is currently a C+ (Fair). The fund currently has a performance rating of C+ (Fair) based on an annualized return of 6.49% over the last three years and a total return of -11.21% year to date 2015. Factored into the performance evaluation is an expense ratio of 0.69% (very low).

The fund's risk rating is currently B (Good). It carries a beta of 0.82, meaning the fund's expected move will be 8.2% for every 10% move in the market. Volatility, as measured by both the semi-deviation and a drawdown factor, is considered low. As of December 31, 2015, *IQ US Real Estate SmCp ETF traded at a discount of .04% below its net asset value, which is better than its one-year historical average discount of .01%.

Greg Barrato has been running the fund for 5 years and currently receives a manager quality ranking of 40 (0=worst, 99=best). If you desire an average level of risk, then this fund may be an option.

Data Date	Investment Rating	Net Assets ($Mil)	Price	Performance Rating/Pts	Total Return Y-T-D	Risk Rating/Pts
12-15	C+	64.60	24.22	C+ / 5.9	-11.21%	B / 8.1
2014	A+	64.60	27.49	A- / 9.1	19.93%	B / 8.2
2013	B-	40.90	24.12	B- / 7.0	11.85%	B- / 7.6
2012	A	16.90	22.48	A+ / 9.7	36.39%	B- / 7.5

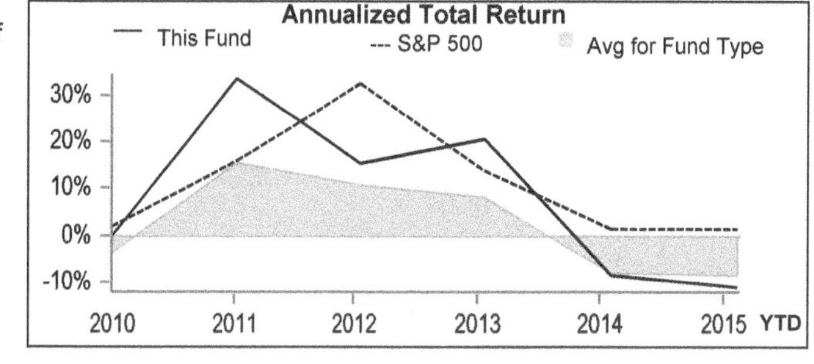

*iShares 0-5 Yr Hi Yld Corp Bd ET (SHYG) C- Fair

Fund Family: BlackRock Fund Advisors
Fund Type: Corporate - High Yield
Inception Date: October 15, 2013

Data Date	Investment Rating	Net Assets ($Mil)	Price	Perfor-mance Rating/Pts	Total Return Y-T-D	Risk Rating/Pts
12-15	C-	83.90	44.53	D+ / 2.9	-3.02%	B- / 7.1
2014	D-	83.90	48.57	D+ / 2.5	0.20%	C- / 4.2

Major Rating Factors:
Disappointing performance is the major factor driving the C- (Fair) TheStreet.com Investment Rating for *iShares 0-5 Yr Hi Yld Corp Bd ET. The fund currently has a performance rating of D+ (Weak) based on an annualized return of 0.00% over the last three years and a total return of -3.02% year to date 2015. Factored into the performance evaluation is an expense ratio of 0.38% (very low).

The fund's risk rating is currently B- (Good). It carries a beta of 0.00, meaning the fund's expected move will be 0.0% for every 10% move in the market. Volatility, as measured by both the semi-deviation and a drawdown factor, is considered low. As of December 31, 2015, *iShares 0-5 Yr Hi Yld Corp Bd ET traded at a premium of .45% above its net asset value, which is worse than its one-year historical average premium of .36%.

James J. Mauro has been running the fund for 3 years and currently receives a manager quality ranking of 65 (0=worst, 99=best). This fund offers only a moderate level of risk but investors looking for strong performance are still waiting.

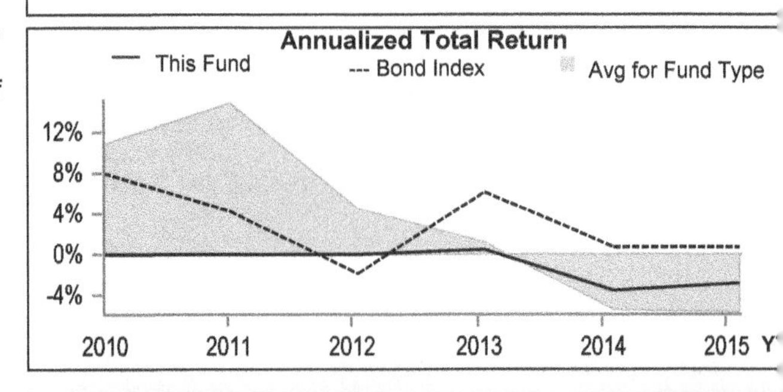

*iShares 0-5 Yr Invest Grde Corp (SLQD) C+ Fair

Fund Family: BlackRock Fund Advisors
Fund Type: Corporate - Investment Grade
Inception Date: October 15, 2013

Data Date	Investment Rating	Net Assets ($Mil)	Price	Perfor-mance Rating/Pts	Total Return Y-T-D	Risk Rating/Pts
12-15	C+	22.60	50.24	C / 5.1	1.25%	B / 8.1
2014	D	22.60	50.30	C- / 3.1	1.58%	C / 4.4

Major Rating Factors: Middle of the road best describes *iShares 0-5 Yr Invest Grde Corp whose TheStreet.com Investment Rating is currently a C+ (Fair). The fund currently has a performance rating of C (Fair) based on an annualized return of 0.00% over the last three years and a total return of 1.25% year to date 2015. Factored into the performance evaluation is an expense ratio of 0.15% (very low).

The fund's risk rating is currently B (Good). It carries a beta of 0.00, meaning the fund's expected move will be 0.0% for every 10% move in the market. Volatility, as measured by both the semi-deviation and a drawdown factor, is considered low. As of December 31, 2015, *iShares 0-5 Yr Invest Grde Corp traded at a premium of .58% above its net asset value, which is worse than its one-year historical average premium of .32%.

James J. Mauro has been running the fund for 3 years and currently receives a manager quality ranking of 79 (0=worst, 99=best). If you desire an average level of risk, then this fund may be an option.

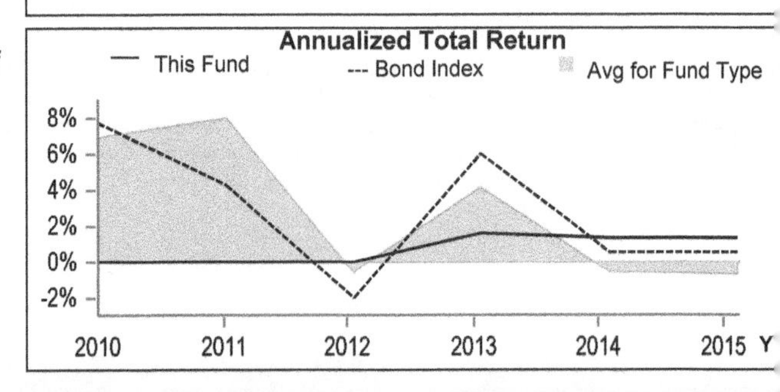

*iShares 0-5 Yr TIPS Bond ETF (STIP) C Fair

Fund Family: BlackRock Fund Advisors
Fund Type: US Government/Agency
Inception Date: December 1, 2010

Data Date	Investment Rating	Net Assets ($Mil)	Price	Perfor-mance Rating/Pts	Total Return Y-T-D	Risk Rating/Pts
12-15	C	517.50	98.92	C- / 3.9	-0.19%	B / 8.1
2014	C	517.50	99.06	D+ / 2.6	-1.17%	B+ / 9.7
2013	C	610.70	101.03	D+ / 2.8	-1.68%	B+ / 9.9
2012	C-	427.60	103.08	D / 1.7	1.79%	B+ / 9.9
2011	C	244.50	102.01	D+ / 2.6	4.28%	B+ / 9.9

Major Rating Factors: Middle of the road best describes *iShares 0-5 Yr TIPS Bond ETF whose TheStreet.com Investment Rating is currently a C (Fair). The fund currently has a performance rating of C- (Fair) based on an annualized return of -1.00% over the last three years and a total return of -0.19% year to date 2015. Factored into the performance evaluation is an expense ratio of 0.16% (very low).

The fund's risk rating is currently B (Good). It carries a beta of 0.04, meaning the fund's expected move will be 0.4% for every 10% move in the market. Volatility, as measured by both the semi-deviation and a drawdown factor, is considered low. As of December 31, 2015, *iShares 0-5 Yr TIPS Bond ETF traded at a premium of .09% above its net asset value, which is worse than its one-year historical average premium of .07%.

Scott F. Radell has been running the fund for 6 years and currently receives a manager quality ranking of 58 (0=worst, 99=best). If you desire an average level of risk, then this fund may be an option.

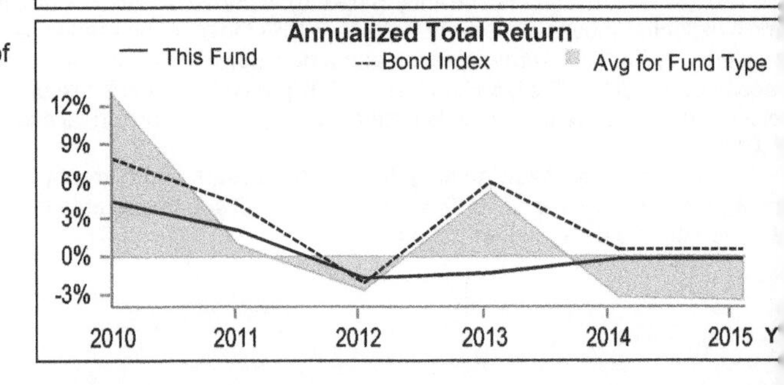

*iShares 1-3 Year Intl Treas Bd E (ISHG) D+ Weak

Fund Family: BlackRock Fund Advisors
Fund Type: Global
Inception Date: January 21, 2009

Major Rating Factors:
Disappointing performance is the major factor driving the D+ (Weak) TheStreet.com Investment Rating for *iShares 1-3 Year Intl Treas Bd E. The fund currently has a performance rating of D+ (Weak) based on an annualized return of -6.47% over the last three years and a total return of -6.94% year to date 2015. Factored into the performance evaluation is an expense ratio of 0.35% (very low).

The fund's risk rating is currently C+ (Fair). It carries a beta of 0.88, meaning the fund's expected move will be 8.8% for every 10% move in the market. Volatility, as measured by both the semi-deviation and a drawdown factor, is considered low. As of December 31, 2015, *iShares 1-3 Year Intl Treas Bd E traded at a premium of .08% above its net asset value, which is worse than its one-year historical average discount of .06%.

Scott F. Radell has been running the fund for 6 years and currently receives a manager quality ranking of 41 (0=worst, 99=best). This fund offers only a moderate level of risk but investors looking for strong performance are still waiting.

Data Date	Investment Rating	Net Assets ($Mil)	Price	Performance Rating/Pts	Total Return Y-T-D	Risk Rating/Pts
12-15	D+	178.60	77.92	D+ / 2.6	-6.94%	C+ / 6.4
2014	D	178.60	84.50	D / 1.9	-9.73%	C+ / 6.6
2013	C-	175.60	94.34	D+ / 2.4	-1.78%	B / 8.4
2012	D+	203.60	97.02	D- / 1.4	1.15%	B / 8.5
2011	D+	154.80	96.99	D- / 1.5	-0.99%	B / 8.7
2010	C+	114.70	104.21	C- / 4.1	0.99%	B / 8.1

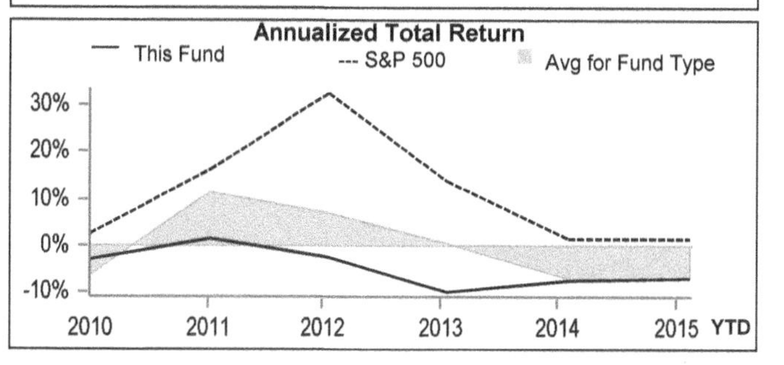

*iShares 1-3 Yr Credit Bd ETF (CSJ) C+ Fair

Fund Family: BlackRock Fund Advisors
Fund Type: Corporate - Investment Grade
Inception Date: January 5, 2007

Major Rating Factors: Middle of the road best describes *iShares 1-3 Yr Credit Bd ETF whose TheStreet.com Investment Rating is currently a C+ (Fair). The fund currently has a performance rating of C (Fair) based on an annualized return of 0.81% over the last three years and a total return of 0.68% year to date 2015. Factored into the performance evaluation is an expense ratio of 0.20% (very low).

The fund's risk rating is currently B (Good). It carries a beta of 0.09, meaning the fund's expected move will be 0.9% for every 10% move in the market. Volatility, as measured by both the semi-deviation and a drawdown factor, is considered low. As of December 31, 2015, *iShares 1-3 Yr Credit Bd ETF traded at a premium of .14% above its net asset value, which is worse than its one-year historical average premium of .08%.

Scott F. Radell has been running the fund for 6 years and currently receives a manager quality ranking of 74 (0=worst, 99=best). If you desire an average level of risk, then this fund may be an option.

Data Date	Investment Rating	Net Assets ($Mil)	Price	Performance Rating/Pts	Total Return Y-T-D	Risk Rating/Pts
12-15	C+	11,355.30	104.60	C / 4.7	0.68%	B / 8.1
2014	C-	11,355.30	105.18	C- / 3.1	0.78%	B / 8.0
2013	C	11,809.80	105.46	C- / 3.1	1.00%	B+ / 9.9
2012	C-	9,225.10	105.48	D / 1.9	2.94%	B+ / 9.8
2011	C	8,835.10	104.20	D+ / 2.5	1.67%	B+ / 9.9
2010	B	7,219.20	104.28	C / 4.3	2.88%	B / 8.8

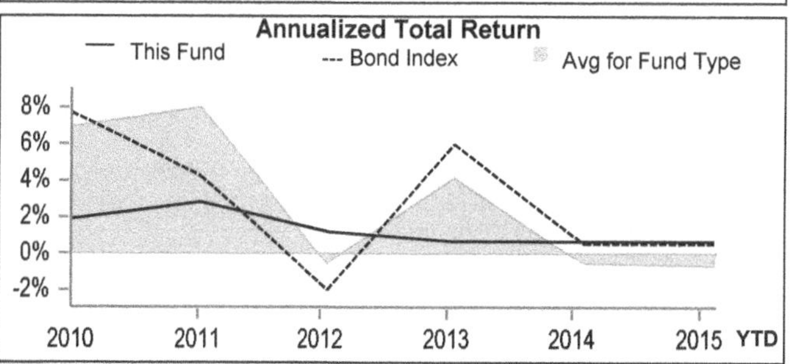

*iShares 1-3 Yr Treasury Bd ETF (SHY) B- Good

Fund Family: BlackRock Fund Advisors
Fund Type: US Government/Agency
Inception Date: July 22, 2002

Major Rating Factors: *iShares 1-3 Yr Treasury Bd ETF receives a TheStreet.com Investment Rating of B- (Good). The fund currently has a performance rating of C (Fair) based on an annualized return of 0.37% over the last three years and a total return of 0.33% year to date 2015. Factored into the performance evaluation is an expense ratio of 0.15% (very low).

The fund's risk rating is currently B+ (Good). It carries a beta of 0.04, meaning the fund's expected move will be 0.4% for every 10% move in the market. Volatility, as measured by both the semi-deviation and a drawdown factor, is considered very low. As of December 31, 2015, *iShares 1-3 Yr Treasury Bd ETF traded at a discount of .05% below its net asset value, which is better than its one-year historical average premium of .02%.

Scott F. Radell has been running the fund for 6 years and currently receives a manager quality ranking of 70 (0=worst, 99=best). If you desire an average level of risk, then this fund may be an option.

Data Date	Investment Rating	Net Assets ($Mil)	Price	Performance Rating/Pts	Total Return Y-T-D	Risk Rating/Pts
12-15	B-	8,221.00	84.36	C / 4.4	0.33%	B+ / 9.9
2014	C	8,221.00	84.45	D+ / 2.8	0.45%	B+ / 9.9
2013	C	8,211.20	84.38	D+ / 2.7	0.24%	B+ / 9.9
2012	C-	8,044.90	84.42	D / 1.6	0.25%	B+ / 9.9
2011	C	10,905.40	84.50	D / 2.2	1.37%	B+ / 9.9
2010	B-	8,102.10	83.98	C- / 3.6	2.28%	B+ / 9.1

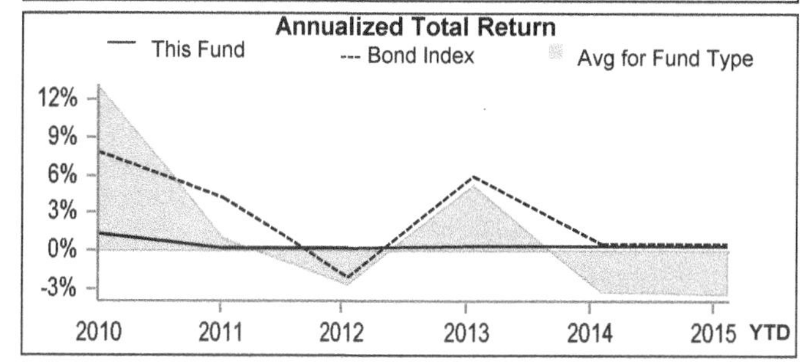

*iShares 10+ Year Credit Bond (CLY) C- Fair

Fund Family: BlackRock Fund Advisors
Fund Type: Global
Inception Date: December 8, 2009

Major Rating Factors: Middle of the road best describes *iShares 10+ Year Credit Bond whose TheStreet.com Investment Rating is currently a C- (Fair). The fund currently has a performance rating of C (Fair) based on an annualized return of 0.87% over the last three years and a total return of -6.07% year to date 2015. Factored into the performance evaluation is an expense ratio of 0.20% (very low).

The fund's risk rating is currently C+ (Fair). It carries a beta of 0.65, meaning the fund's expected move will be 6.5% for every 10% move in the market. Volatility, as measured by both the semi-deviation and a drawdown factor, is considered low. As of December 31, 2015, *iShares 10+ Year Credit Bond traded at a premium of .04% above its net asset value, which is better than its one-year historical average premium of .25%.

Scott F. Radell has been running the fund for 6 years and currently receives a manager quality ranking of 86 (0=worst, 99=best). If you desire an average level of risk, then this fund may be an option.

Data Date	Investment Rating	Net Assets ($Mil)	Price	Perfor-mance Rating/Pts	Total Return Y-T-D	Risk Rating/Pts
12-15	C-	547.80	55.68	C / 4.3	-6.07%	C+ / 6.6
2014	C	547.80	61.54	C / 5.3	15.88%	C+ / 6.7
2013	C+	259.10	55.08	C / 4.6	-6.33%	B / 8.7
2012	C+	448.30	62.67	C / 4.4	11.29%	B+ / 9.4
2011	B	340.40	59.02	C+ / 6.6	16.76%	B+ / 9.5
2010	B	15.80	52.98	C+ / 6.4	10.72%	B / 8.7

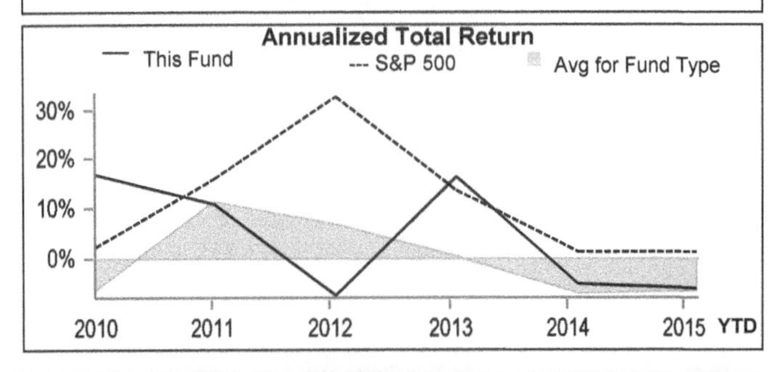

*iShares 10-20 Yr Treasury Bd ETF (TLH) B- Good

Fund Family: BlackRock Fund Advisors
Fund Type: US Government/Agency
Inception Date: January 5, 2007

Major Rating Factors: *iShares 10-20 Yr Treasury Bd ETF receives a TheStreet.com Investment Rating of B- (Good). The fund currently has a performance rating of C (Fair) based on an annualized return of 2.50% over the last three years and a total return of 0.60% year to date 2015. Factored into the performance evaluation is an expense ratio of 0.15% (very low).

The fund's risk rating is currently B (Good). It carries a beta of 0.64, meaning the fund's expected move will be 6.4% for every 10% move in the market. Volatility, as measured by both the semi-deviation and a drawdown factor, is considered low. As of December 31, 2015, *iShares 10-20 Yr Treasury Bd ETF traded at a discount of .12% below its net asset value, which is better than its one-year historical average premium of .05%.

Scott F. Radell has been running the fund for 6 years and currently receives a manager quality ranking of 72 (0=worst, 99=best). If you desire an average level of risk, then this fund may be an option.

Data Date	Investment Rating	Net Assets ($Mil)	Price	Perfor-mance Rating/Pts	Total Return Y-T-D	Risk Rating/Pts
12-15	B-	312.50	134.21	C / 5.4	0.60%	B / 8.9
2014	C+	312.50	135.17	C / 4.5	13.99%	B / 8.7
2013	C	217.90	120.92	C- / 3.8	-6.83%	B / 8.8
2012	C	609.00	134.86	C- / 3.4	2.83%	B+ / 9.1
2011	C+	505.20	132.93	C / 4.5	21.15%	B / 8.9
2010	B	248.10	112.70	C / 4.6	9.71%	B / 8.4

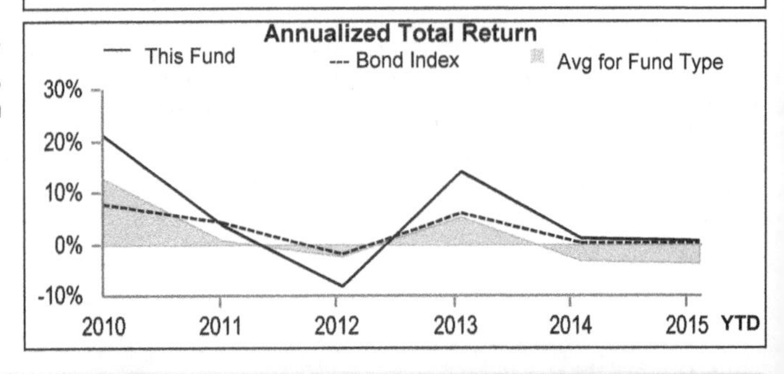

*iShares 20+ Yr Treasury Bd ETF (TLT) C+ Fair

Fund Family: BlackRock Fund Advisors
Fund Type: US Government/Agency
Inception Date: July 22, 2002

Major Rating Factors: Middle of the road best describes *iShares 20+ Yr Treasury Bd ETF whose TheStreet.com Investment Rating is currently a C+ (Fair). The fund currently has a performance rating of C+ (Fair) based on an annualized return of 3.51% over the last three years and a total return of -2.84% year to date 2015. Factored into the performance evaluation is an expense ratio of 0.15% (very low).

The fund's risk rating is currently B (Good). It carries a beta of 1.13, meaning it is expected to move 11.3% for every 10% move in the market. Volatility, as measured by both the semi-deviation and a drawdown factor, is considered low. As of December 31, 2015, *iShares 20+ Yr Treasury Bd ETF traded at a discount of .12% below its net asset value, which is better than its one-year historical average premium of .04%.

Scott F. Radell has been running the fund for 6 years and currently receives a manager quality ranking of 66 (0=worst, 99=best). If you desire an average level of risk, then this fund may be an option.

Data Date	Investment Rating	Net Assets ($Mil)	Price	Perfor-mance Rating/Pts	Total Return Y-T-D	Risk Rating/Pts
12-15	C+	4,010.30	120.58	C+ / 5.6	-2.84%	B / 8.2
2014	C+	4,010.30	125.92	C+ / 6.1	26.93%	B- / 7.8
2013	C-	2,178.50	101.86	C- / 4.1	-11.06%	B / 8.0
2012	C	3,193.10	121.18	C- / 4.2	1.84%	B / 8.4
2011	C+	3,382.10	121.25	C / 5.4	34.09%	B- / 7.9
2010	C+	2,726.90	94.12	C- / 3.4	9.06%	B / 8.0

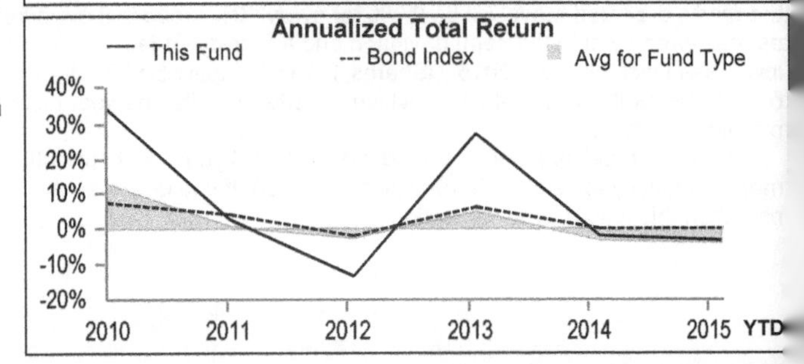

* Denotes ETF Fund

*iShares 3-7 Yr Treasury Bd ETF (IEI) C+ Fair

Fund Family: BlackRock Fund Advisors
Fund Type: US Government/Agency
Inception Date: January 5, 2007

Major Rating Factors: Middle of the road best describes *iShares 3-7 Yr Treasury Bd ETF whose TheStreet.com Investment Rating is currently a C+ (Fair). The fund currently has a performance rating of C (Fair) based on an annualized return of 1.07% over the last three years and a total return of 1.43% year to date 2015. Factored into the performance evaluation is an expense ratio of 0.15% (very low).

The fund's risk rating is currently B (Good). It carries a beta of 0.23, meaning the fund's expected move will be 2.3% for every 10% move in the market. Volatility, as measured by both the semi-deviation and a drawdown factor, is considered low. As of December 31, 2015, *iShares 3-7 Yr Treasury Bd ETF traded at a discount of .02% below its net asset value, which is better than its one-year historical average premium of .03%.

Scott F. Radell has been running the fund for 6 years and currently receives a manager quality ranking of 71 (0=worst, 99=best). If you desire an average level of risk, then this fund may be an option.

Data Date	Investment Rating	Net Assets ($Mil)	Price	Performance Rating/Pts	Total Return Y-T-D	Risk Rating/Pts
12-15	C+	3,407.20	122.61	C / 4.8	1.43%	B / 8.8
2014	C	3,407.20	122.31	C- / 3.2	3.15%	B+ / 9.6
2013	C	2,700.80	120.03	C- / 3.2	-1.53%	B+ / 9.8
2012	C	3,096.70	123.22	D+ / 2.3	1.58%	B+ / 9.7
2011	C	2,816.00	122.04	C- / 3.0	7.88%	B+ / 9.7
2010	B+	1,308.00	114.65	C / 4.6	6.32%	B+ / 9.0

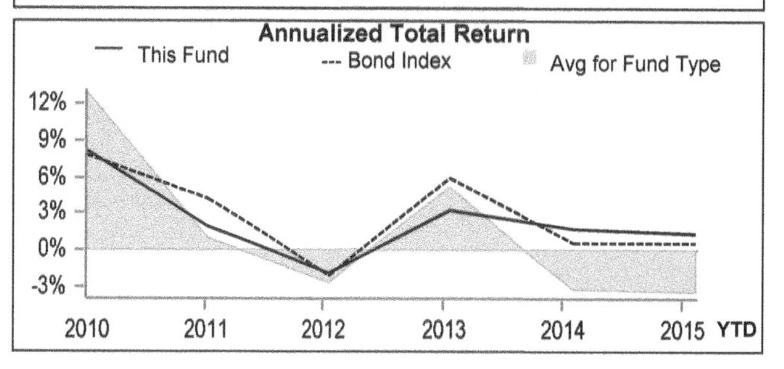

*iShares 7-10 Yr Treasury Bd ETF (IEF) B- Good

Fund Family: BlackRock Fund Advisors
Fund Type: US Government/Agency
Inception Date: July 22, 2002

Major Rating Factors: *iShares 7-10 Yr Treasury Bd ETF receives a TheStreet.com Investment Rating of B- (Good). The fund currently has a performance rating of C (Fair) based on an annualized return of 1.63% over the last three years and a total return of 1.01% year to date 2015. Factored into the performance evaluation is an expense ratio of 0.15% (very low).

The fund's risk rating is currently B+ (Good). It carries a beta of 0.49, meaning the fund's expected move will be 4.9% for every 10% move in the market. Volatility, as measured by both the semi-deviation and a drawdown factor, is considered very low. As of December 31, 2015, *iShares 7-10 Yr Treasury Bd ETF traded at a discount of .09% below its net asset value, which is better than its one-year historical average premium of .03%.

Scott F. Radell has been running the fund for 6 years and currently receives a manager quality ranking of 68 (0=worst, 99=best). If you desire an average level of risk, then this fund may be an option.

Data Date	Investment Rating	Net Assets ($Mil)	Price	Performance Rating/Pts	Total Return Y-T-D	Risk Rating/Pts
12-15	B-	4,897.50	105.59	C / 5.1	1.01%	B+ / 9.2
2014	C	4,897.50	105.99	C- / 3.9	8.72%	B+ / 9.1
2013	C	3,638.70	99.24	C- / 3.6	-4.89%	B+ / 9.2
2012	C	4,405.80	107.49	C- / 3.1	3.01%	B+ / 9.5
2011	C	4,795.30	105.57	C- / 3.8	15.00%	B+ / 9.2
2010	B+	3,039.30	93.82	C / 4.9	9.37%	B / 8.6

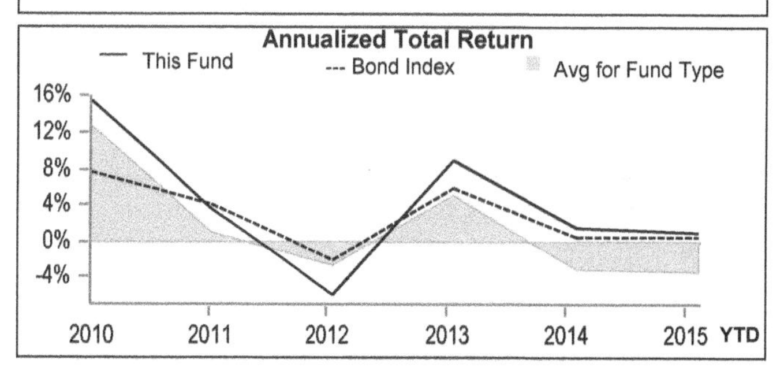

*iShares Aaa - A Rated Corporate (QLTA) B Good

Fund Family: BlackRock Fund Advisors
Fund Type: Corporate - Investment Grade
Inception Date: February 14, 2012

Major Rating Factors: *iShares Aaa - A Rated Corporate receives a TheStreet.com Investment Rating of B (Good). The fund currently has a performance rating of C (Fair) based on an annualized return of 1.55% over the last three years and a total return of 0.38% year to date 2015. Factored into the performance evaluation is an expense ratio of 0.15% (very low).

The fund's risk rating is currently B+ (Good). It carries a beta of 0.95, meaning that its performance tracks fairly well with that of the overall stock market. Volatility, as measured by both the semi-deviation and a drawdown factor, is considered very low. As of December 31, 2015, *iShares Aaa - A Rated Corporate traded at a discount of .12% below its net asset value, which is better than its one-year historical average discount of .09%.

James J. Mauro has been running the fund for 4 years and currently receives a manager quality ranking of 67 (0=worst, 99=best). If you desire an average level of risk, then this fund may be an option.

Data Date	Investment Rating	Net Assets ($Mil)	Price	Performance Rating/Pts	Total Return Y-T-D	Risk Rating/Pts
12-15	B	418.90	50.52	C / 5.2	0.38%	B+ / 9.4
2014	C+	418.90	51.78	C / 4.4	6.39%	B+ / 9.4
2013	C-	397.50	49.79	D+ / 2.5	-2.28%	B+ / 9.5

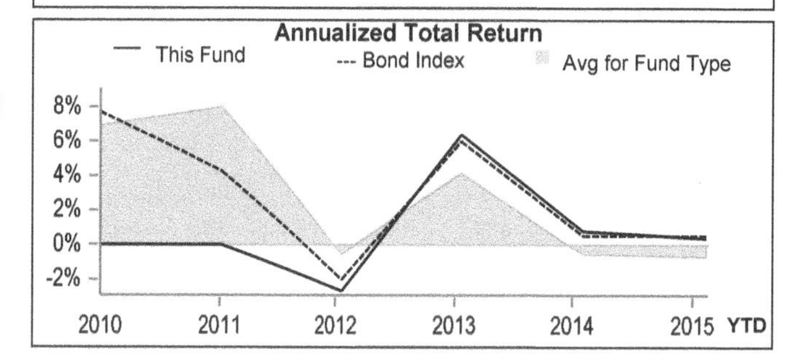

* Denotes ETF Fund

*iShares Agency Bond ETF (AGZ) C+ Fair

Fund Family: BlackRock Fund Advisors
Fund Type: US Government/Agency
Inception Date: November 5, 2008

Major Rating Factors: Middle of the road best describes *iShares Agency Bond ETF whose TheStreet.com Investment Rating is currently a C+ (Fair). The fund currently has a performance rating of C (Fair) based on an annualized return of 1.29% over the last three years and a total return of 1.09% year to date 2015. Factored into the performance evaluation is an expense ratio of 0.20% (very low).

The fund's risk rating is currently B (Good). It carries a beta of 0.16, meaning the fund's expected move will be 1.6% for every 10% move in the market. Volatility, as measured by both the semi-deviation and a drawdown factor, is considered low. As of December 31, 2015, *iShares Agency Bond ETF traded at a premium of .33% above its net asset value, which is worse than its one-year historical average premium of .11%.

Scott F. Radell has been running the fund for 6 years and currently receives a manager quality ranking of 75 (0=worst, 99=best). If you desire an average level of risk, then this fund may be an option.

Data Date	Investment Rating	Net Assets ($Mil)	Price	Performance Rating/Pts	Total Return Y-T-D	Risk Rating/Pts
12-15	C+	365.20	113.15	C / 5.0	1.09%	B / 8.0
2014	C+	365.20	113.10	C- / 3.3	3.67%	B+ / 9.8
2013	C	398.50	110.55	C- / 3.0	-1.11%	B+ / 9.9
2012	C-	425.60	113.30	D / 2.0	1.29%	B+ / 9.9
2011	C	360.50	112.95	D+ / 2.6	4.50%	B+ / 9.9
2010	B-	361.40	109.52	C- / 3.4	3.75%	B+ / 9.1

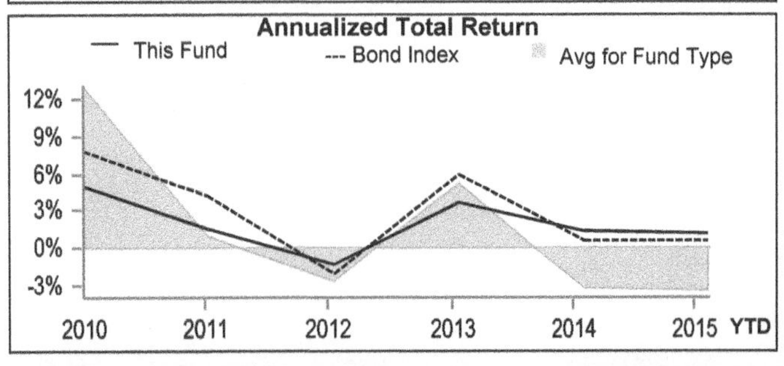

*iShares Asia 50 (AIA) C- Fair

Fund Family: BlackRock Fund Advisors
Fund Type: Foreign
Inception Date: November 13, 2007

Major Rating Factors: Middle of the road best describes *iShares Asia 50 whose TheStreet.com Investment Rating is currently a C- (Fair). The fund currently has a performance rating of C- (Fair) based on an annualized return of -1.54% over the last three years and a total return of -5.08% year to date 2015. Factored into the performance evaluation is an expense ratio of 0.50% (very low).

The fund's risk rating is currently B- (Good). It carries a beta of 0.84, meaning the fund's expected move will be 8.4% for every 10% move in the market. Volatility, as measured by both the semi-deviation and a drawdown factor, is considered low. As of December 31, 2015, *iShares Asia 50 traded at a discount of 1.05% below its net asset value, which is better than its one-year historical average discount of .05%.

Diane Hsiung has been running the fund for 8 years and currently receives a manager quality ranking of 27 (0=worst, 99=best). If you desire an average level of risk, then this fund may be an option.

Data Date	Investment Rating	Net Assets ($Mil)	Price	Performance Rating/Pts	Total Return Y-T-D	Risk Rating/Pts
12-15	C-	312.50	42.27	C- / 3.4	-5.08%	B- / 7.4
2014	C	312.50	47.05	C / 4.9	4.14%	B / 8.1
2013	D+	265.90	47.98	C- / 3.1	-2.88%	B- / 7.0
2012	C	227.10	48.15	C+ / 5.8	21.84%	B- / 7.1
2011	C	177.10	39.15	C / 5.2	-13.93%	B- / 7.3
2010	C	209.60	46.95	C+ / 6.3	19.62%	C / 4.9

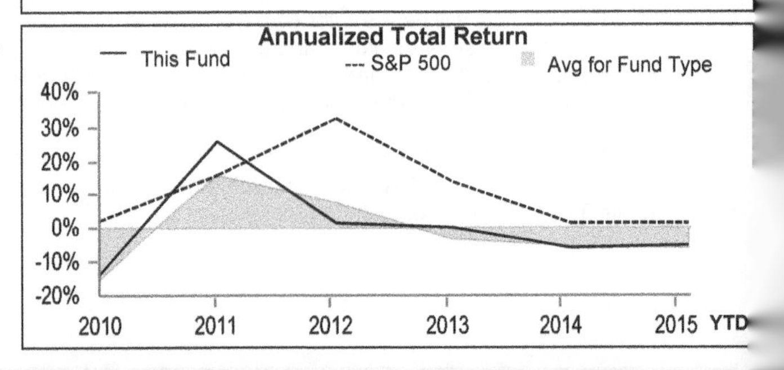

*iShares Asia/Pacific Dividend ET (DVYA) D+ Weak

Fund Family: BlackRock Fund Advisors
Fund Type: Foreign
Inception Date: February 23, 2012

Major Rating Factors:
Disappointing performance is the major factor driving the D+ (Weak) TheStreet.com Investment Rating for *iShares Asia/Pacific Dividend ET. The fund currently has a performance rating of D+ (Weak) based on an annualized return of -5.46% over the last three years and a total return of -16.49% year to date 2015. Factored into the performance evaluation is an expense ratio of 0.49% (very low).

The fund's risk rating is currently C+ (Fair). It carries a beta of 1.01, meaning that its performance tracks fairly well with that of the overall stock market. Volatility, as measured by both the semi-deviation and a drawdown factor, is considered low. As of December 31, 2015, *iShares Asia/Pacific Dividend ET traded at a discount of .61% below its net asset value, which is better than its one-year historical average discount of .28%.

Jennifer F.Y. Hsui has been running the fund for 4 years and currently receives a manager quality ranking of 16 (0=worst, 99=best). This fund offers only a moderate level of risk but investors looking for strong performance are still waiting.

Data Date	Investment Rating	Net Assets ($Mil)	Price	Performance Rating/Pts	Total Return Y-T-D	Risk Rating/Pts
12-15	D+	46.90	39.25	D+ / 2.5	-16.49%	C+ / 6.0
2014	D	46.90	49.80	D- / 1.4	-3.02%	C+ / 6.4
2013	C	43.20	54.20	C / 4.9	4.83%	B- / 7.9

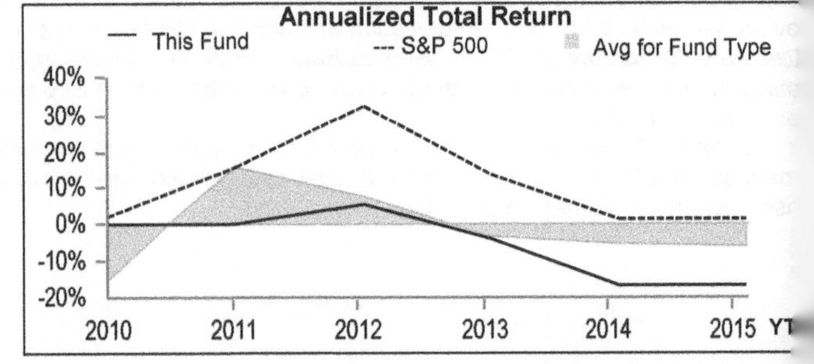

*iShares B - Ca Rated Corp Bond E (QLTC) C- Fair

Fund Family: BlackRock Fund Advisors
Fund Type: Corporate - Investment Grade
Inception Date: April 24, 2012

Major Rating Factors: Middle of the road best describes *iShares B - Ca Rated Corp Bond E whose TheStreet.com Investment Rating is currently a C- (Fair). The fund currently has a performance rating of C- (Fair) based on an annualized return of -1.29% over the last three years and a total return of -9.96% year to date 2015. Factored into the performance evaluation is an expense ratio of 0.55% (very low).

The fund's risk rating is currently B- (Good). It carries a beta of 0.48, meaning the fund's expected move will be 4.8% for every 10% move in the market. Volatility, as measured by both the semi-deviation and a drawdown factor, is considered low. As of December 31, 2015, *iShares B - Ca Rated Corp Bond E traded at a discount of 2.18% below its net asset value, which is better than its one-year historical average discount of .19%.

James J. Mauro has been running the fund for 4 years and currently receives a manager quality ranking of 54 (0=worst, 99=best). If you desire an average level of risk, then this fund may be an option.

Data Date	Investment Rating	Net Assets ($Mil)	Price	Perfor-mance Rating/Pts	Total Return Y-T-D	Risk Rating/Pts
12-15	C-	20.50	41.35	C- / 3.2	-9.96%	B- / 7.8
2014	D+	20.50	49.42	D / 2.1	-0.41%	B- / 7.3
2013	B+	10.40	52.31	C+ / 6.5	6.92%	B+ / 9.6

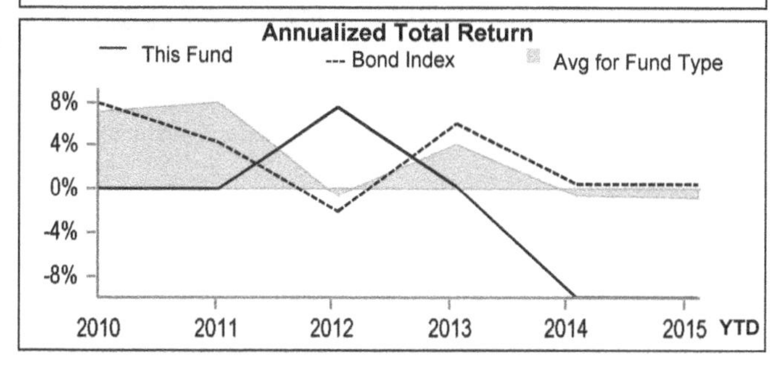

*iShares Baa - Ba Rated Corp Bd E (QLTB) C+ Fair

Fund Family: BlackRock Fund Advisors
Fund Type: Corporate - Investment Grade
Inception Date: April 24, 2012

Major Rating Factors: Middle of the road best describes *iShares Baa - Ba Rated Corp Bd E whose TheStreet.com Investment Rating is currently a C+ (Fair). The fund currently has a performance rating of C (Fair) based on an annualized return of 1.39% over the last three years and a total return of -4.22% year to date 2015. Factored into the performance evaluation is an expense ratio of 0.30% (very low).

The fund's risk rating is currently B (Good). It carries a beta of 1.11, meaning it is expected to move 11.1% for every 10% move in the market. Volatility, as measured by both the semi-deviation and a drawdown factor, is considered low. As of December 31, 2015, *iShares Baa - Ba Rated Corp Bd E traded at a discount of .45% below its net asset value, which is better than its one-year historical average premium of .22%.

James J. Mauro has been running the fund for 4 years and currently receives a manager quality ranking of 65 (0=worst, 99=best). If you desire an average level of risk, then this fund may be an option.

Data Date	Investment Rating	Net Assets ($Mil)	Price	Perfor-mance Rating/Pts	Total Return Y-T-D	Risk Rating/Pts
12-15	C+	26.10	48.63	C / 4.5	-4.22%	B / 8.9
2014	C	26.10	52.87	C / 5.0	9.81%	B- / 7.4
2013	C	20.30	49.82	C- / 3.1	-1.18%	B+ / 9.2

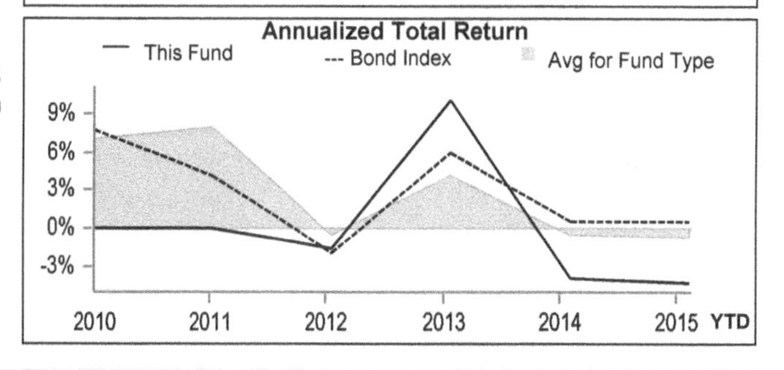

*iShares California AMT Free Muni (CMF) B- Good

Fund Family: BlackRock Fund Advisors
Fund Type: Municipal - Single State
Inception Date: October 4, 2007

Major Rating Factors: *iShares California AMT Free Muni receives a TheStreet.com Investment Rating of B- (Good). The fund currently has a performance rating of C+ (Fair) based on an annualized return of 3.78% over the last three years and a total return of 2.98% year to date 2015. Factored into the performance evaluation is an expense ratio of 0.25% (very low).

The fund's risk rating is currently B- (Good). It carries a beta of 1.32, meaning it is expected to move 13.2% for every 10% move in the market. Volatility, as measured by both the semi-deviation and a drawdown factor, is considered low. As of December 31, 2015, *iShares California AMT Free Muni traded at a premium of .23% above its net asset value, which is better than its one-year historical average premium of .24%.

Scott F. Radell has been running the fund for 6 years and currently receives a manager quality ranking of 64 (0=worst, 99=best). If you desire an average level of risk, then this fund may be an option.

Data Date	Investment Rating	Net Assets ($Mil)	Price	Perfor-mance Rating/Pts	Total Return Y-T-D	Risk Rating/Pts
12-15	B-	303.10	118.15	C+ / 6.6	2.98%	B- / 7.8
2014	C+	303.10	117.75	C+ / 5.6	10.83%	B- / 7.6
2013	B-	235.50	108.80	C+ / 5.8	-2.03%	B+ / 9.3
2012	C	282.10	115.30	C- / 3.9	5.23%	B+ / 9.1
2011	B-	193.00	110.79	C / 5.5	15.89%	B+ / 9.2
2010	C	225.30	98.85	D / 2.2	-2.64%	B / 8.5

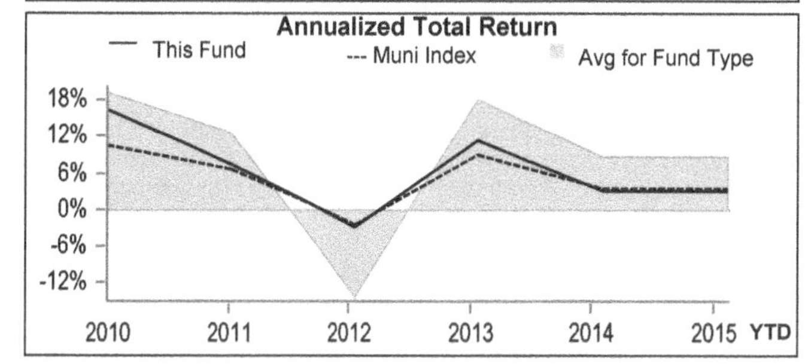

*iShares China Large-Cap ETF (FXI) D+ Weak

Fund Family: BlackRock Fund Advisors
Fund Type: Foreign
Inception Date: October 5, 2004

Data Date	Investment Rating	Net Assets ($Mil)	Price	Performance Rating/Pts	Total Return Y-T-D	Risk Rating/Pts
12-15	D+	5,505.00	35.29	D+ / 2.9	-11.20%	C+ / 6.4
2014	C+	5,505.00	41.62	C+ / 6.4	16.58%	B- / 7.1
2013	D	6,055.60	38.37	D / 2.0	-9.19%	C+ / 6.2
2012	D	8,478.30	40.45	D+ / 2.8	15.01%	C+ / 6.5
2011	D+	5,838.20	34.87	C- / 3.2	-17.93%	C+ / 6.8
2010	E	8,139.90	43.09	D- / 1.3	3.51%	D- / 1.5

Major Rating Factors:
Disappointing performance is the major factor driving the D+ (Weak) TheStreet.com Investment Rating for *iShares China Large-Cap ETF. The fund currently has a performance rating of D+ (Weak) based on an annualized return of -1.99% over the last three years and a total return of -11.20% year to date 2015. Factored into the performance evaluation is an expense ratio of 0.73% (very low).

The fund's risk rating is currently C+ (Fair). It carries a beta of 0.92, meaning that its performance tracks fairly well with that of the overall stock market. Volatility, as measured by both the semi-deviation and a drawdown factor, is considered low. As of December 31, 2015, *iShares China Large-Cap ETF traded at a discount of .65% below its net asset value, which is better than its one-year historical average discount of .10%.

Diane Hsiung has been running the fund for 8 years and currently receives a manager quality ranking of 26 (0=worst, 99=best). This fund offers only a moderate level of risk but investors looking for strong performance are still waiting.

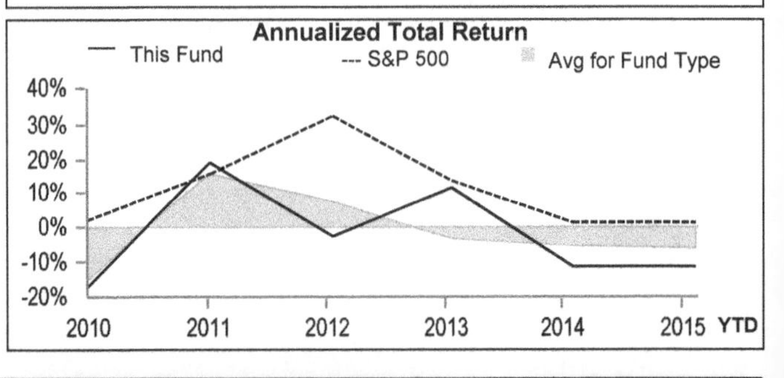

*iShares CMBS ETF (CMBS) C+ Fair

Fund Family: BlackRock Fund Advisors
Fund Type: Corporate - Investment Grade
Inception Date: February 14, 2012

Data Date	Investment Rating	Net Assets ($Mil)	Price	Performance Rating/Pts	Total Return Y-T-D	Risk Rating/Pts
12-15	C+	120.10	50.66	C / 5.0	0.68%	B- / 7.9
2014	C	120.10	51.19	C- / 3.3	2.31%	B+ / 9.7
2013	C	88.80	51.05	C- / 3.0	0.68%	B+ / 9.9

Major Rating Factors: Middle of the road best describes *iShares CMBS ETF whose TheStreet.com Investment Rating is currently a C+ (Fair). The fund currently has a performance rating of C (Fair) based on an annualized return of 1.40% over the last three years and a total return of 0.68% year to date 2015. Factored into the performance evaluation is an expense ratio of 0.25% (very low).

The fund's risk rating is currently B- (Good). It carries a beta of 0.47, meaning the fund's expected move will be 4.7% for every 10% move in the market. Volatility, as measured by both the semi-deviation and a drawdown factor, is considered low. As of December 31, 2015, *iShares CMBS ETF traded at a premium of .18% above its net asset value, which is better than its one-year historical average premium of .22%.

James J. Mauro has been running the fund for 4 years and currently receives a manager quality ranking of 74 (0=worst, 99=best). If you desire an average level of risk, then this fund may be an option.

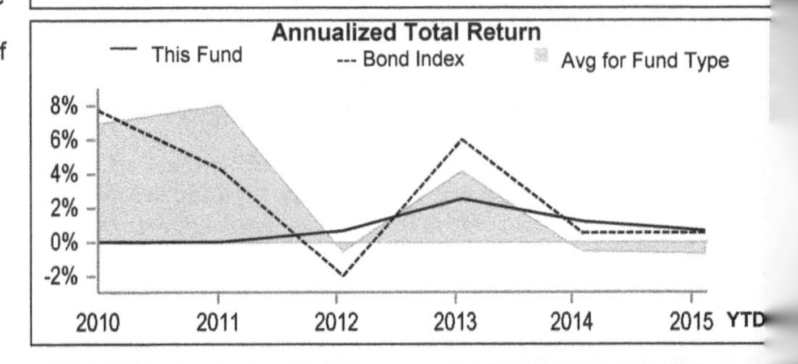

*iShares Cohen and Steers REIT ET (ICF) B Good

Fund Family: BlackRock Fund Advisors
Fund Type: Income
Inception Date: January 29, 2001

Data Date	Investment Rating	Net Assets ($Mil)	Price	Performance Rating/Pts	Total Return Y-T-D	Risk Rating/Pts
12-15	B	2,862.30	99.24	B+ / 8.7	5.50%	C+ / 6.4
2014	A	2,862.30	96.84	B+ / 8.9	33.24%	B- / 7.9
2013	C	2,340.50	74.72	C / 4.8	-2.66%	B- / 7.8
2012	B	2,705.30	78.54	B- / 7.5	16.69%	B- / 7.6
2011	C+	2,315.40	70.22	B / 7.8	10.06%	C+ / 6.1
2010	C	2,212.70	65.72	B- / 7.1	29.14%	C- / 3.9

Major Rating Factors: Strong performance is the major factor driving the B (Good) TheStreet.com Investment Rating for *iShares Cohen and Steers REIT ET. The fund currently has a performance rating of B+ (Good) based on an annualized return of 11.60% over the last three years and a total return of 5.50% year to date 2015. Factored into the performance evaluation is an expense ratio of 0.35% (very low).

The fund's risk rating is currently C+ (Fair). It carries a beta of 0.34, meaning the fund's expected move will be 3.4% for every 10% move in the market. Volatility, as measured by both the semi-deviation and a drawdown factor, is considered low. As of December 31, 2015, *iShares Cohen and Steers REIT ET traded at a premium of .03% above its net asset value.

Diane Hsiung has been running the fund for 8 years and currently receives a manager quality ranking of 92 (0=worst, 99=best). If you desire only a moderate level of risk and strong performance, then this fund is an excellent option.

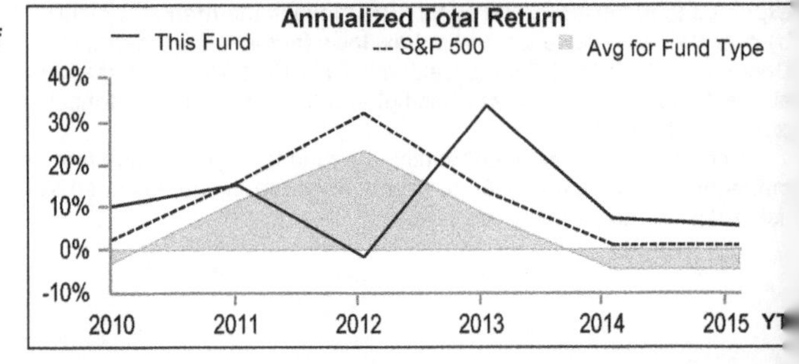

*iShares Commodities Select Strat (COMT) D- Weak

Fund Family: BlackRock Fund Advisors
Fund Type: Global
Inception Date: October 15, 2014

Data Date	Investment Rating	Net Assets ($Mil)	Price	Performance Rating/Pts	Total Return Y-T-D	Risk Rating/Pts
12-15	D-	0.00	28.44	E / 0.3	-30.13%	C / 4.8

Major Rating Factors:
Very poor performance is the major factor driving the D- (Weak) TheStreet.com Investment Rating for *iShares Commodities Select Strat. The fund currently has a performance rating of E (Very Weak) based on an annualized return of 0.00% over the last three years and a total return of -30.13% year to date 2015.

The fund's risk rating is currently C (Fair). It carries a beta of 0.00, meaning the fund's expected move will be 0.0% for every 10% move in the market. Volatility, as measured by both the semi-deviation and a drawdown factor, is considered average. As of December 31, 2015, *iShares Commodities Select Strat traded at a price exactly equal to its net asset value, which is worse than its one-year historical average discount of .09%.

Gregory R Savage has been running the fund for 2 years and currently receives a manager quality ranking of 3 (0=worst, 99=best). This fund offers an average level of risk but investors looking for strong performance will be frustrated.

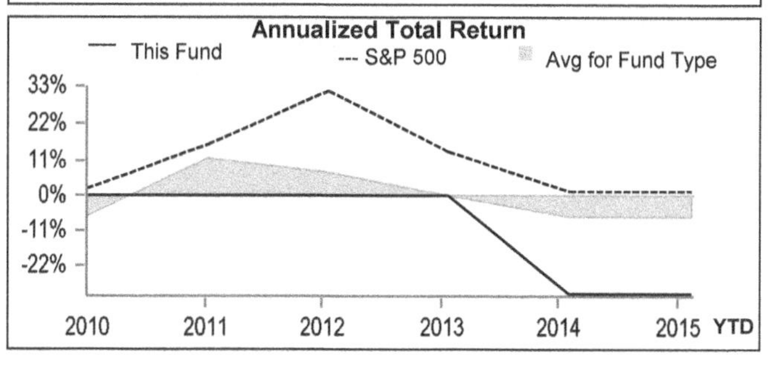

*iShares Commodity Optimized (CMDT) D Weak

Fund Family: BlackRock Fund Advisors
Fund Type: Global
Inception Date: August 8, 2013

Data Date	Investment Rating	Net Assets ($Mil)	Price	Performance Rating/Pts	Total Return Y-T-D	Risk Rating/Pts
12-15	D	0.00	32.03	E / 0.5	-24.33%	B- / 7.1
2014	D-	0.00	42.85	E+ / 0.6	-14.56%	C+ / 6.4

Major Rating Factors:
Very poor performance is the major factor driving the D (Weak) TheStreet.com Investment Rating for *iShares Commodity Optimized. The fund currently has a performance rating of E (Very Weak) based on an annualized return of 0.00% over the last three years and a total return of -24.33% year to date 2015. Factored into the performance evaluation is an expense ratio of 0.83% (very low).

The fund's risk rating is currently B- (Good). It carries a beta of 0.00, meaning the fund's expected move will be 0.0% for every 10% move in the market. Volatility, as measured by both the semi-deviation and a drawdown factor, is considered low. As of December 31, 2015, *iShares Commodity Optimized traded at a discount of .25% below its net asset value, which is better than its one-year historical average discount of .06%.

This fund offers only a moderate level of risk but investors looking for strong performance are still waiting.

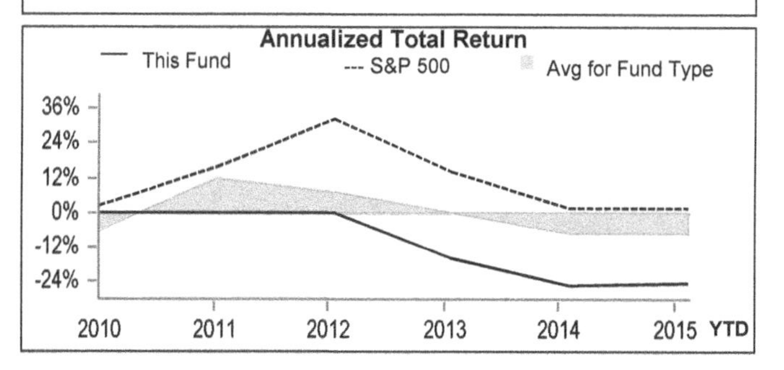

*iShares Core 1-5 Year USD Bond (ISTB) C+ Fair

Fund Family: BlackRock Fund Advisors
Fund Type: US Government/Agency
Inception Date: October 18, 2012

Data Date	Investment Rating	Net Assets ($Mil)	Price	Performance Rating/Pts	Total Return Y-T-D	Risk Rating/Pts
12-15	C+	189.70	99.27	C / 4.7	0.56%	B / 8.2
2014	C-	189.70	100.19	C- / 3.1	1.27%	B / 8.2
2013	C	94.70	100.11	D+ / 2.7	0.61%	B+ / 9.9

Major Rating Factors: Middle of the road best describes *iShares Core 1-5 Year USD Bond whose TheStreet.com Investment Rating is currently a C+ (Fair). The fund currently has a performance rating of C (Fair) based on an annualized return of 0.84% over the last three years and a total return of 0.56% year to date 2015. Factored into the performance evaluation is an expense ratio of 0.12% (very low).

The fund's risk rating is currently B (Good). It carries a beta of 0.07, meaning the fund's expected move will be 0.7% for every 10% move in the market. Volatility, as measured by both the semi-deviation and a drawdown factor, is considered low. As of December 31, 2015, *iShares Core 1-5 Year USD Bond traded at a premium of .31% above its net asset value, which is worse than its one-year historical average premium of .29%.

James J. Mauro has been running the fund for 4 years and currently receives a manager quality ranking of 73 (0=worst, 99=best). If you desire an average level of risk, then this fund may be an option.

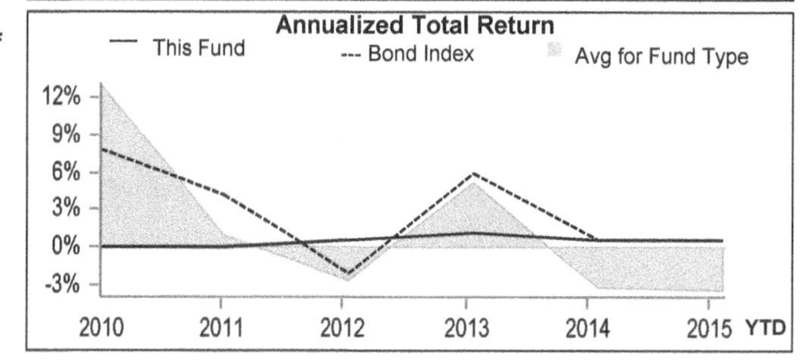

*iShares Core 10+ Year USD Bond (ILTB) C+ Fair

Fund Family: BlackRock Fund Advisors
Fund Type: Global
Inception Date: December 8, 2009

Major Rating Factors: Middle of the road best describes *iShares Core 10+ Year USD Bond whose TheStreet.com Investment Rating is currently a C+ (Fair). The fund currently has a performance rating of C (Fair) based on an annualized return of 2.03% over the last three years and a total return of -4.88% year to date 2015. Factored into the performance evaluation is an expense ratio of 0.12% (very low).

The fund's risk rating is currently B (Good). It carries a beta of 0.62, meaning the fund's expected move will be 6.2% for every 10% move in the market. Volatility, as measured by both the semi-deviation and a drawdown factor, is considered low. As of December 31, 2015, *iShares Core 10+ Year USD Bond traded at a discount of .07% below its net asset value, which is better than its one-year historical average premium of .33%.

Scott F. Radell has been running the fund for 6 years and currently receives a manager quality ranking of 87 (0=worst, 99=best). If you desire an average level of risk, then this fund may be an option.

Data Date	Investment Rating	Net Assets ($Mil)	Price	Performance Rating/Pts	Total Return Y-T-D	Risk Rating/Pts
12-15	C+	109.10	58.45	C / 5.0	-4.88%	B / 8.3
2014	C	109.10	63.52	C+ / 5.6	19.68%	C+ / 6.4
2013	C	27.70	54.84	C / 4.4	-7.39%	B / 8.4
2012	C+	206.30	63.78	C- / 4.2	6.72%	B+ / 9.2
2011	B+	24.30	60.74	B / 7.6	21.11%	B+ / 9.3
2010	B	15.60	52.27	C / 4.3	9.17%	B / 8.5

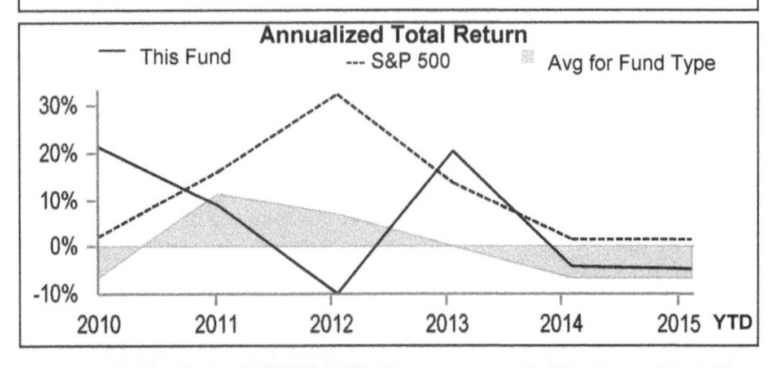

*iShares Core Aggressive Allocati (AOA) B+ Good

Fund Family: BlackRock Fund Advisors
Fund Type: Growth and Income
Inception Date: November 4, 2008

Major Rating Factors: *iShares Core Aggressive Allocati receives a TheStreet.com Investment Rating of B+ (Good). The fund currently has a performance rating of C+ (Fair) based on an annualized return of 7.96% over the last three years and a total return of -0.96% year to date 2015. Factored into the performance evaluation is an expense ratio of 0.11% (very low).

The fund's risk rating is currently B+ (Good). It carries a beta of 0.82, meaning the fund's expected move will be 8.2% for every 10% move in the market. Volatility, as measured by both the semi-deviation and a drawdown factor, is considered very low. As of December 31, 2015, *iShares Core Aggressive Allocati traded at a discount of .04% below its net asset value, which is better than its one-year historical average premium of .06%.

Diane Hsiung has been running the fund for 8 years and currently receives a manager quality ranking of 42 (0=worst, 99=best). If you desire an average level of risk, then this fund may be an option.

Data Date	Investment Rating	Net Assets ($Mil)	Price	Performance Rating/Pts	Total Return Y-T-D	Risk Rating/Pts
12-15	B+	273.30	44.84	C+ / 6.7	-0.96%	B+ / 9.0
2014	C+	273.30	46.28	C+ / 6.5	7.05%	B- / 7.2
2013	B	220.70	44.61	B- / 7.1	18.82%	B / 8.3
2012	C	105.90	37.17	C / 4.8	15.48%	B / 8.1
2011	C	82.50	33.05	C / 4.7	-0.71%	B / 8.1
2010	A+	56.70	34.37	A- / 9.2	16.77%	B- / 7.5

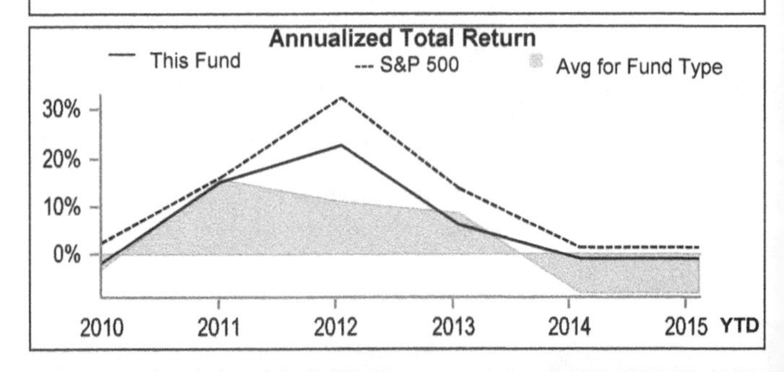

*iShares Core Conservative Alloc (AOK) C+ Fair

Fund Family: BlackRock Fund Advisors
Fund Type: Growth and Income
Inception Date: November 4, 2008

Major Rating Factors: Middle of the road best describes *iShares Core Conservative Alloc whose TheStreet.com Investment Rating is currently a C+ (Fair). The fund currently has a performance rating of C (Fair) based on an annualized return of 2.98% over the last three years and a total return of -1.07% year to date 2015. Factored into the performance evaluation is an expense ratio of 0.11% (very low).

The fund's risk rating is currently B- (Good). It carries a beta of 0.33, meaning the fund's expected move will be 3.3% for every 10% move in the market. Volatility, as measured by both the semi-deviation and a drawdown factor, is considered low. As of December 31, 2015, *iShares Core Conservative Alloc traded at a premium of .16% above its net asset value, which is worse than its one-year historical average premium of .01%.

Diane Hsiung has been running the fund for 8 years and currently receives a manager quality ranking of 54 (0=worst, 99=best). If you desire an average level of risk, then this fund may be an option.

Data Date	Investment Rating	Net Assets ($Mil)	Price	Performance Rating/Pts	Total Return Y-T-D	Risk Rating/Pts
12-15	C+	186.50	31.64	C / 5.4	-1.07%	B- / 7.6
2014	C	186.50	32.60	C- / 4.2	4.27%	B / 8.8
2013	B-	137.60	32.01	C / 5.0	5.79%	B+ / 9.8
2012	C	116.20	30.58	D+ / 2.7	6.57%	B+ / 9.8
2011	C	95.30	29.35	C- / 3.4	4.56%	B+ / 9.6
2010	B	44.60	28.79	C+ / 6.6	7.08%	B / 8.7

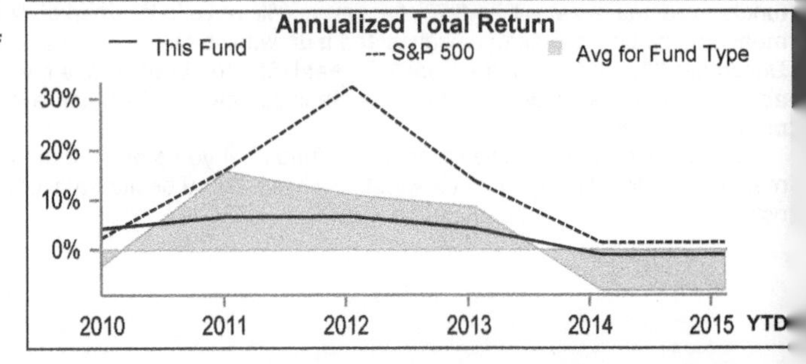

* Denotes ETF Fund

*iShares Core Dividend Growth ETF (DGRO) C Fair

Fund Family: BlackRock Fund Advisors
Fund Type: Income
Inception Date: June 12, 2014

Data Date	Investment Rating	Net Assets ($Mil)	Price	Performance Rating/Pts	Total Return Y-T-D	Risk Rating/Pts
12-15	C	71.20	25.69	C / 5.4	-0.08%	C+ / 6.9

Major Rating Factors: Middle of the road best describes *iShares Core Dividend Growth ETF whose TheStreet.com Investment Rating is currently a C (Fair). The fund currently has a performance rating of C (Fair) based on an annualized return of 0.00% over the last three years and a total return of -0.08% year to date 2015. Factored into the performance evaluation is an expense ratio of 0.05% (very low).

The fund's risk rating is currently C+ (Fair). It carries a beta of 0.00, meaning the fund's expected move will be 0.0% for every 10% move in the market. Volatility, as measured by both the semi-deviation and a drawdown factor, is considered low. As of December 31, 2015, *iShares Core Dividend Growth ETF traded at a premium of .08% above its net asset value, which is worse than its one-year historical average premium of .07%.

Diane Hsiung has been running the fund for 2 years and currently receives a manager quality ranking of 56 (0=worst, 99=best). If you desire an average level of risk, then this fund may be an option.

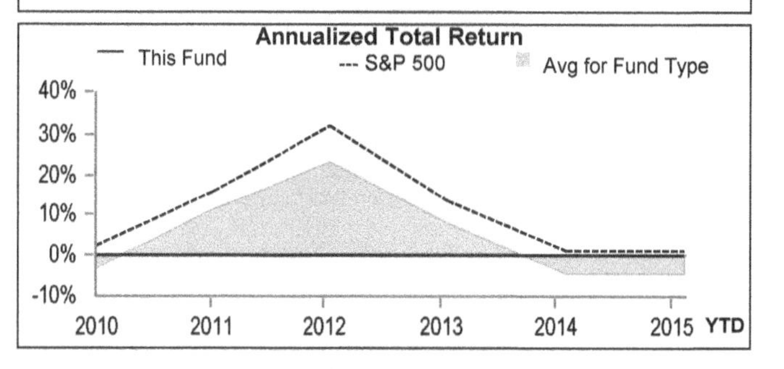

*iShares Core GNMA Bond ETF (GNMA) C Fair

Fund Family: BlackRock Fund Advisors
Fund Type: General - Investment Grade
Inception Date: February 14, 2012

Data Date	Investment Rating	Net Assets ($Mil)	Price	Performance Rating/Pts	Total Return Y-T-D	Risk Rating/Pts
12-15	C	39.90	50.11	C / 5.0	0.75%	B- / 7.8
2014	C	39.90	50.62	C / 4.6	6.53%	B- / 7.5
2013	C-	28.80	48.38	D / 2.1	-2.94%	B+ / 9.5

Major Rating Factors: Middle of the road best describes *iShares Core GNMA Bond ETF whose TheStreet.com Investment Rating is currently a C (Fair). The fund currently has a performance rating of C (Fair) based on an annualized return of 1.27% over the last three years and a total return of 0.75% year to date 2015. Factored into the performance evaluation is an expense ratio of 0.15% (very low).

The fund's risk rating is currently B- (Good). It carries a beta of 0.79, meaning the fund's expected move will be 7.9% for every 10% move in the market. Volatility, as measured by both the semi-deviation and a drawdown factor, is considered low. As of December 31, 2015, *iShares Core GNMA Bond ETF traded at a premium of .16% above its net asset value, which is worse than its one-year historical average premium of .12%.

James J. Mauro has been running the fund for 4 years and currently receives a manager quality ranking of 68 (0=worst, 99=best). If you desire an average level of risk, then this fund may be an option.

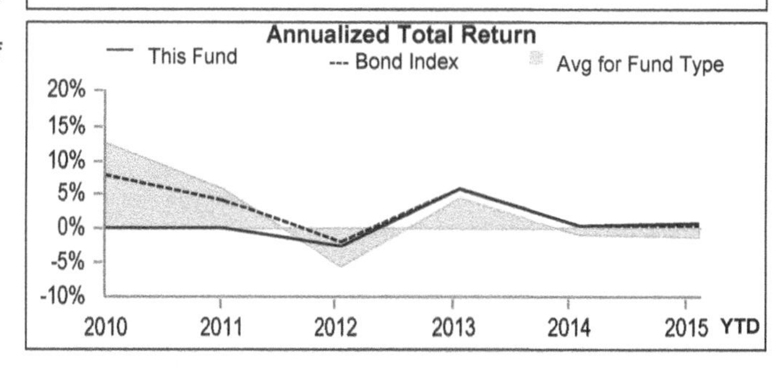

*iShares Core Growth Allocation (AOR) C+ Fair

Fund Family: BlackRock Fund Advisors
Fund Type: Growth and Income
Inception Date: November 4, 2008

Data Date	Investment Rating	Net Assets ($Mil)	Price	Performance Rating/Pts	Total Return Y-T-D	Risk Rating/Pts
12-15	C+	317.50	38.88	C+ / 6.2	-1.02%	B- / 7.5
2014	C+	317.50	40.12	C+ / 5.9	7.81%	B- / 7.7
2013	B	250.30	38.50	C+ / 6.4	13.37%	B / 8.9
2012	C	152.50	33.97	C- / 3.6	11.64%	B / 8.8
2011	C	118.20	31.14	C- / 4.0	1.90%	B / 8.8
2010	A+	81.90	31.54	B+ / 8.5	11.14%	B- / 7.8

Major Rating Factors: Middle of the road best describes *iShares Core Growth Allocation whose TheStreet.com Investment Rating is currently a C+ (Fair). The fund currently has a performance rating of C+ (Fair) based on an annualized return of 6.31% over the last three years and a total return of -1.02% year to date 2015. Factored into the performance evaluation is an expense ratio of 0.11% (very low).

The fund's risk rating is currently B- (Good). It carries a beta of 0.63, meaning the fund's expected move will be 6.3% for every 10% move in the market. Volatility, as measured by both the semi-deviation and a drawdown factor, is considered low. As of December 31, 2015, *iShares Core Growth Allocation traded at a premium of .18% above its net asset value, which is worse than its one-year historical average premium of .04%.

Diane Hsiung has been running the fund for 8 years and currently receives a manager quality ranking of 48 (0=worst, 99=best). If you desire an average level of risk, then this fund may be an option.

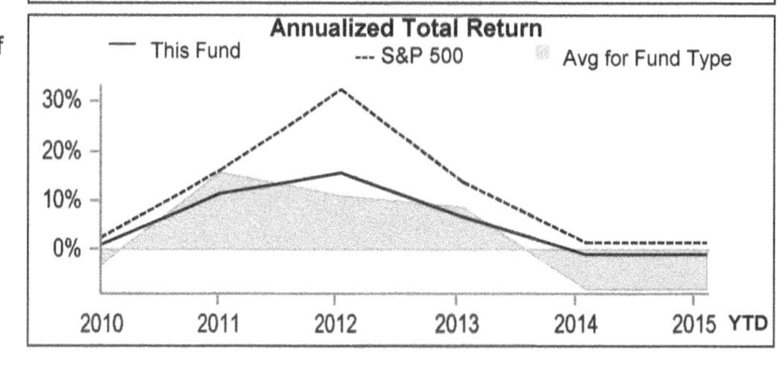

* Denotes ETF Fund

*iShares Core High Dividend (HDV) B+ Good

Fund Family: BlackRock Fund Advisors
Fund Type: Global
Inception Date: March 29, 2011

Major Rating Factors: Strong performance is the major factor driving the B+ (Good) TheStreet.com Investment Rating for *iShares Core High Dividend. The fund currently has a performance rating of B (Good) based on an annualized return of 10.93% over the last three years and a total return of 0.60% year to date 2015. Factored into the performance evaluation is an expense ratio of 0.14% (very low).

The fund's risk rating is currently B- (Good). It carries a beta of 0.52, meaning the fund's expected move will be 5.2% for every 10% move in the market. Volatility, as measured by both the semi-deviation and a drawdown factor, is considered low. As of December 31, 2015, *iShares Core High Dividend traded at a price exactly equal to its net asset value.

Diane Hsiung has been running the fund for 5 years and currently receives a manager quality ranking of 97 (0=worst, 99=best). If you desire only a moderate level of risk and strong performance, then this fund is an excellent option.

Data Date	Investment Rating	Net Assets ($Mil)	Price	Performance Rating/Pts	Total Return Y-T-D	Risk Rating/Pts
12-15	B+	4,432.90	73.41	B / 8.0	0.60%	B- / 7.9
2014	A	4,432.90	76.54	B- / 7.2	13.79%	B+ / 9.5
2013	A	3,253.20	70.25	B / 7.8	19.10%	B+ / 9.4
2012	C+	2,135.80	58.79	C / 4.5	14.15%	B+ / 9.4

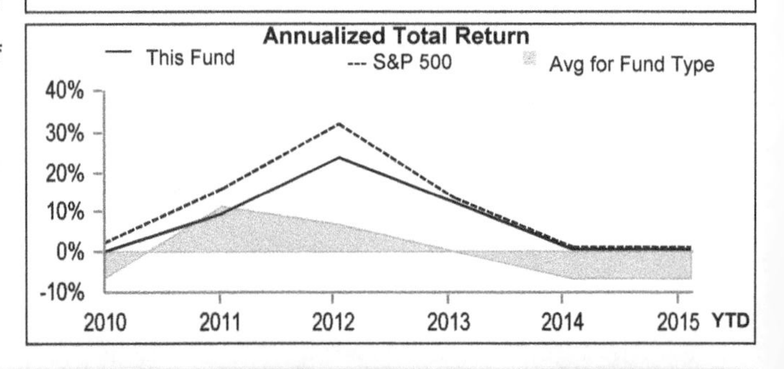

*iShares Core Moderate Allocation (AOM) C+ Fair

Fund Family: BlackRock Fund Advisors
Fund Type: Growth and Income
Inception Date: November 4, 2008

Major Rating Factors: Middle of the road best describes *iShares Core Moderate Allocation whose TheStreet.com Investment Rating is currently a C+ (Fair). The fund currently has a performance rating of C+ (Fair) based on an annualized return of 4.14% over the last three years and a total return of -1.18% year to date 2015. Factored into the performance evaluation is an expense ratio of 0.11% (very low).

The fund's risk rating is currently B- (Good). It carries a beta of 0.44, meaning the fund's expected move will be 4.4% for every 10% move in the market. Volatility, as measured by both the semi-deviation and a drawdown factor, is considered low. As of December 31, 2015, *iShares Core Moderate Allocation traded at a premium of .03% above its net asset value, which is better than its one-year historical average premium of .06%.

Diane Hsiung has been running the fund for 8 years and currently receives a manager quality ranking of 51 (0=worst, 99=best). If you desire an average level of risk, then this fund may be an option.

Data Date	Investment Rating	Net Assets ($Mil)	Price	Performance Rating/Pts	Total Return Y-T-D	Risk Rating/Pts
12-15	C+	254.70	34.05	C+ / 5.7	-1.18%	B- / 7.7
2014	C	254.70	35.17	C / 4.8	5.09%	B- / 7.7
2013	B-	214.50	34.31	C+ / 5.6	8.87%	B+ / 9.4
2012	C	145.80	31.73	C- / 3.0	8.65%	B+ / 9.3
2011	C	125.40	29.90	C- / 3.6	2.59%	B+ / 9.2
2010	A	74.80	29.92	B- / 7.5	7.90%	B / 8.4

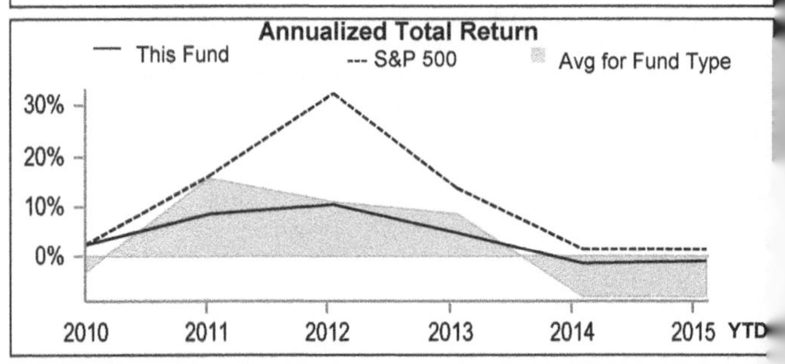

*iShares Core MSCI EAFE (IEFA) B- Good

Fund Family: BlackRock Fund Advisors
Fund Type: Emerging Market
Inception Date: October 18, 2012

Major Rating Factors: *iShares Core MSCI EAFE receives a TheStreet.com Investment Rating of B- (Good). The fund currently has a performance rating of C+ (Fair) based on an annualized return of 4.74% over the last three years and a total return of 1.75% year to date 2015. Factored into the performance evaluation is an expense ratio of 0.12% (very low).

The fund's risk rating is currently B (Good). It carries a beta of 0.64, meaning the fund's expected move will be 6.4% for every 10% move in the market. Volatility, as measured by both the semi-deviation and a drawdown factor, is considered low. As of December 31, 2015, *iShares Core MSCI EAFE traded at a discount of .53% below its net asset value, which is better than its one-year historical average premium of .18%.

Diane Hsiung has been running the fund for 4 years and currently receives a manager quality ranking of 95 (0=worst, 99=best). If you desire an average level of risk, then this fund may be an option.

Data Date	Investment Rating	Net Assets ($Mil)	Price	Performance Rating/Pts	Total Return Y-T-D	Risk Rating/Pts
12-15	B-	2,586.30	54.38	C+ / 5.9	1.75%	B / 8.2
2014	D+	2,586.30	55.32	D- / 1.4	-4.72%	B / 8.6
2013	A+	1,337.80	60.77	B+ / 8.8	18.77%	B+ / 9.2

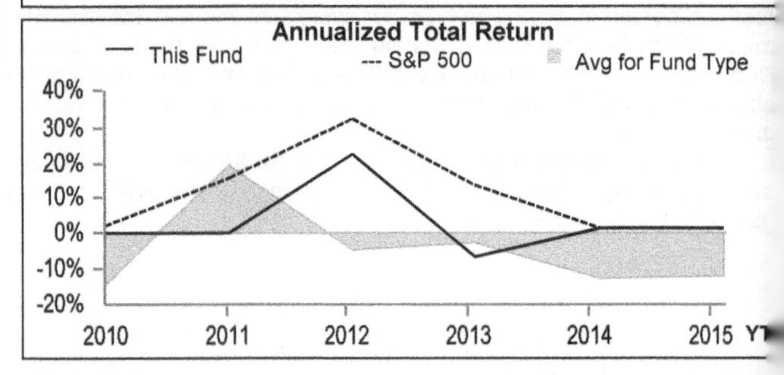

* Denotes ETF Fund

*iShares Core MSCI Emerging Marke (IEMG) D+ Weak

Fund Family: BlackRock Fund Advisors
Fund Type: Emerging Market
Inception Date: October 18, 2012

Data Date	Investment Rating	Net Assets ($Mil)	Price	Performance Rating/Pts	Total Return Y-T-D	Risk Rating/Pts
12-15	D+	5,706.10	39.39	D / 2.2	-12.33%	B- / 7.1
2014	D	5,706.10	47.03	D / 1.8	0.10%	C+ / 6.3
2013	D+	3,351.10	49.81	D / 2.1	-7.61%	B / 8.6

Major Rating Factors:
Disappointing performance is the major factor driving the D+ (Weak) TheStreet.com Investment Rating for *iShares Core MSCI Emerging Marke. The fund currently has a performance rating of D (Weak) based on an annualized return of -7.04% over the last three years and a total return of -12.33% year to date 2015. Factored into the performance evaluation is an expense ratio of 0.18% (very low).

The fund's risk rating is currently B- (Good). It carries a beta of 0.98, meaning that its performance tracks fairly well with that of the overall stock market. Volatility, as measured by both the semi-deviation and a drawdown factor, is considered low. As of December 31, 2015, *iShares Core MSCI Emerging Marke traded at a discount of .58% below its net asset value, which is better than its one-year historical average premium of .11%.

Diane Hsiung has been running the fund for 4 years and currently receives a manager quality ranking of 64 (0=worst, 99=best). This fund offers only a moderate level of risk but investors looking for strong performance are still waiting.

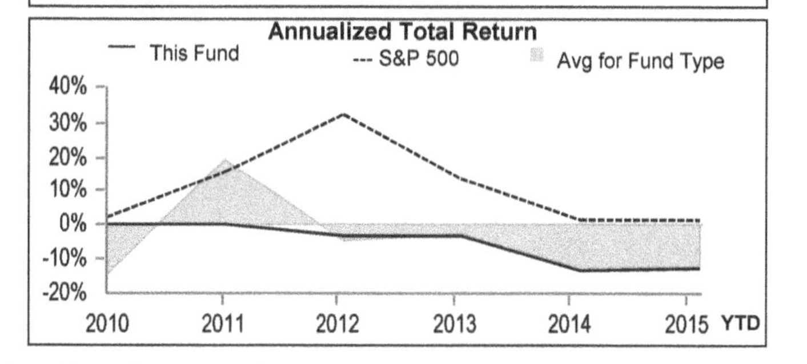

*iShares Core MSCI Europe ETF (IEUR) C Fair

Fund Family: BlackRock Fund Advisors
Fund Type: Foreign
Inception Date: June 12, 2014

Data Date	Investment Rating	Net Assets ($Mil)	Price	Performance Rating/Pts	Total Return Y-T-D	Risk Rating/Pts
12-15	C	165.50	42.24	C- / 3.4	0.32%	B / 8.0

Major Rating Factors: Middle of the road best describes *iShares Core MSCI Europe ETF whose TheStreet.com Investment Rating is currently a C (Fair). The fund currently has a performance rating of C- (Fair) based on an annualized return of 0.00% over the last three years and a total return of 0.32% year to date 2015. Factored into the performance evaluation is an expense ratio of 0.05% (very low).

The fund's risk rating is currently B (Good). It carries a beta of 0.00, meaning the fund's expected move will be 0.0% for every 10% move in the market. Volatility, as measured by both the semi-deviation and a drawdown factor, is considered low. As of December 31, 2015, *iShares Core MSCI Europe ETF traded at a discount of .07% below its net asset value, which is better than its one-year historical average premium of .31%.

Diane Hsiung has been running the fund for 2 years and currently receives a manager quality ranking of 68 (0=worst, 99=best). If you desire an average level of risk, then this fund may be an option.

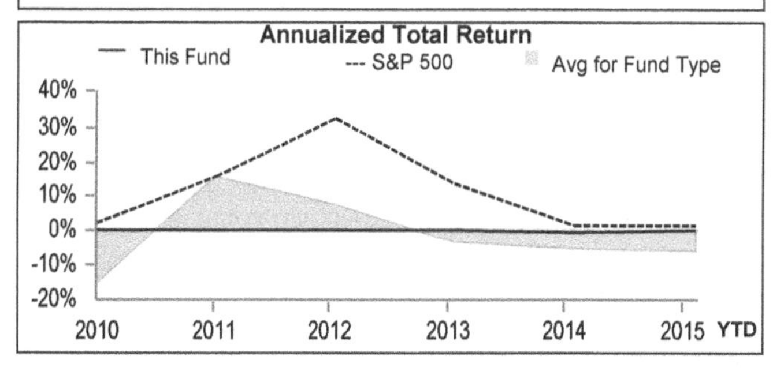

*iShares Core MSCI Pacific ETF (IPAC) C+ Fair

Fund Family: BlackRock Fund Advisors
Fund Type: Foreign
Inception Date: June 12, 2014

Data Date	Investment Rating	Net Assets ($Mil)	Price	Performance Rating/Pts	Total Return Y-T-D	Risk Rating/Pts
12-15	C+	187.10	47.72	C+ / 5.9	5.10%	B / 8.1

Major Rating Factors: Middle of the road best describes *iShares Core MSCI Pacific ETF whose TheStreet.com Investment Rating is currently a C+ (Fair). The fund currently has a performance rating of C+ (Fair) based on an annualized return of 0.00% over the last three years and a total return of 5.10% year to date 2015. Factored into the performance evaluation is an expense ratio of 0.05% (very low).

The fund's risk rating is currently B (Good). It carries a beta of 0.00, meaning the fund's expected move will be 0.0% for every 10% move in the market. Volatility, as measured by both the semi-deviation and a drawdown factor, is considered low. As of December 31, 2015, *iShares Core MSCI Pacific ETF traded at a discount of .81% below its net asset value, which is better than its one-year historical average premium of .04%.

Diane Hsiung has been running the fund for 2 years and currently receives a manager quality ranking of 90 (0=worst, 99=best). If you desire an average level of risk, then this fund may be an option.

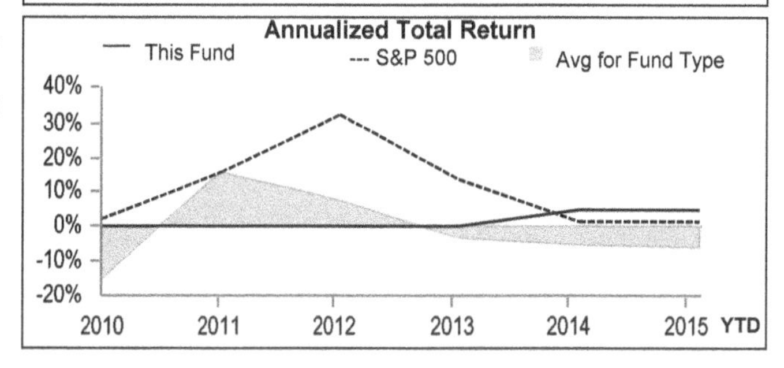

*iShares Core MSCI Total Intl Sto (IXUS) C Fair

Fund Family: BlackRock Fund Advisors
Fund Type: Emerging Market
Inception Date: October 18, 2012

Major Rating Factors: Middle of the road best describes *iShares Core MSCI Total Intl Sto whose TheStreet.com Investment Rating is currently a C (Fair). The fund currently has a performance rating of C (Fair) based on an annualized return of 1.16% over the last three years and a total return of -3.08% year to date 2015. Factored into the performance evaluation is an expense ratio of 0.14% (very low).

The fund's risk rating is currently B (Good). It carries a beta of 0.70, meaning the fund's expected move will be 7.0% for every 10% move in the market. Volatility, as measured by both the semi-deviation and a drawdown factor, is considered low. As of December 31, 2015, *iShares Core MSCI Total Intl Sto traded at a discount of .22% below its net asset value, which is better than its one-year historical average premium of .27%.

Diane Hsiung has been running the fund for 4 years and currently receives a manager quality ranking of 91 (0=worst, 99=best). If you desire an average level of risk, then this fund may be an option.

Data Date	Investment Rating	Net Assets ($Mil)	Price	Performance Rating/Pts	Total Return Y-T-D	Risk Rating/Pts
12-15	C	813.90	49.48	C / 4.3	-3.08%	B / 8.0
2014	D	813.90	53.27	D / 1.6	-3.22%	C+ / 6.8
2013	B+	428.50	57.65	B- / 7.2	10.93%	B+ / 9.1

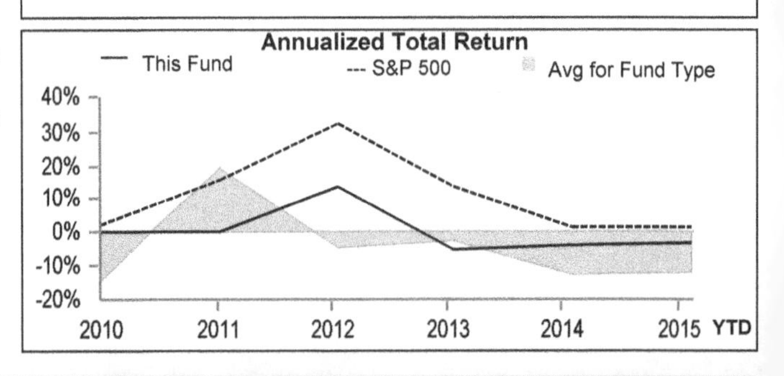

*iShares Core S&P 500 ETF (IVV) A+ Excellent

Fund Family: BlackRock Fund Advisors
Fund Type: Growth
Inception Date: May 15, 2000

Major Rating Factors:
Strong performance is the major factor driving the A+ (Excellent) TheStreet.com Investment Rating for *iShares Core S&P 500 ETF. The fund currently has a performance rating of B+ (Good) based on an annualized return of 14.20% over the last three years and a total return of 1.97% year to date 2015. Factored into the performance evaluation is an expense ratio of 0.07% (very low).

The fund's risk rating is currently B (Good). It carries a beta of 1.00, meaning that its performance tracks fairly well with that of the overall stock market. Volatility, as measured by both the semi-deviation and a drawdown factor, is considered low. As of December 31, 2015, *iShares Core S&P 500 ETF traded at a discount of .07% below its net asset value.

Diane Hsiung has been running the fund for 8 years and currently receives a manager quality ranking of 68 (0=worst, 99=best). If you desire only a moderate level of risk and strong performance, then this fund is an excellent option.

Data Date	Investment Rating	Net Assets ($Mil)	Price	Performance Rating/Pts	Total Return Y-T-D	Risk Rating/Pts
12-15	A+	61,119.00	204.87	B+ / 8.9	1.97%	B / 8.6
2014	A	61,119.00	206.87	B+ / 8.3	14.64%	B / 8.2
2013	B+	53,700.70	185.65	B / 8.2	27.49%	B / 8.2
2012	C	34,911.50	143.14	C / 5.2	16.64%	B / 8.0
2011	C+	26,208.70	125.96	C / 5.3	2.61%	B- / 7.9
2010	C-	25,763.50	126.25	C- / 3.9	15.11%	C+ / 6.0

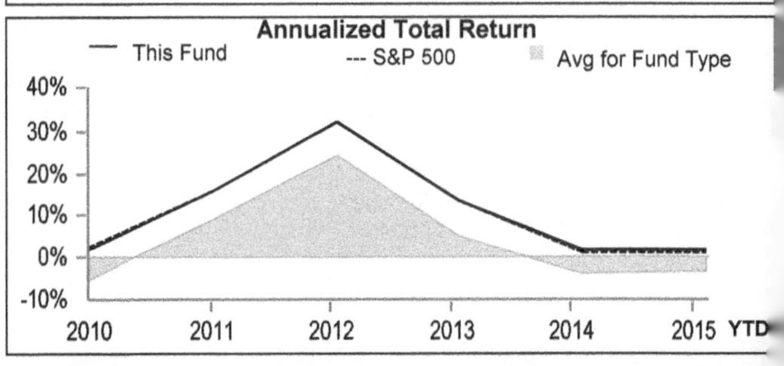

*iShares Core S&P Mid-Cap ETF (IJH) A- Excellent

Fund Family: BlackRock Fund Advisors
Fund Type: Growth
Inception Date: May 22, 2000

Major Rating Factors:
Strong performance is the major factor driving the A- (Excellent) TheStreet.com Investment Rating for *iShares Core S&P Mid-Cap ETF. The fund currently has a performance rating of B (Good) based on an annualized return of 11.52% over the last three years and a total return of -1.69% year to date 2015. Factored into the performance evaluation is an expense ratio of 0.13% (very low).

The fund's risk rating is currently B (Good). It carries a beta of 0.99, meaning that its performance tracks fairly well with that of the overall stock market. Volatility, as measured by both the semi-deviation and a drawdown factor, is considered low. As of December 31, 2015, *iShares Core S&P Mid-Cap ETF traded at a discount of .09% below its net asset value, which is better than its one-year historical average discount of .01%.

Diane Hsiung has been running the fund for 8 years and currently receives a manager quality ranking of 52 (0=worst, 99=best). If you desire only a moderate level of risk and strong performance, then this fund is an excellent option.

Data Date	Investment Rating	Net Assets ($Mil)	Price	Performance Rating/Pts	Total Return Y-T-D	Risk Rating/Pts
12-15	A-	23,367.60	139.32	B / 7.8	-1.69%	B / 8.5
2014	B	23,367.60	144.80	B / 7.9	10.38%	B- / 7.3
2013	B	22,730.70	133.81	B / 8.0	28.00%	B- / 7.8
2012	B-	13,558.40	101.70	C+ / 6.9	18.23%	B- / 7.7
2011	C+	9,297.30	87.61	C+ / 6.4	-0.90%	B- / 7.7
2010	B	9,360.60	90.69	B- / 7.4	26.73%	C+ / 5.7

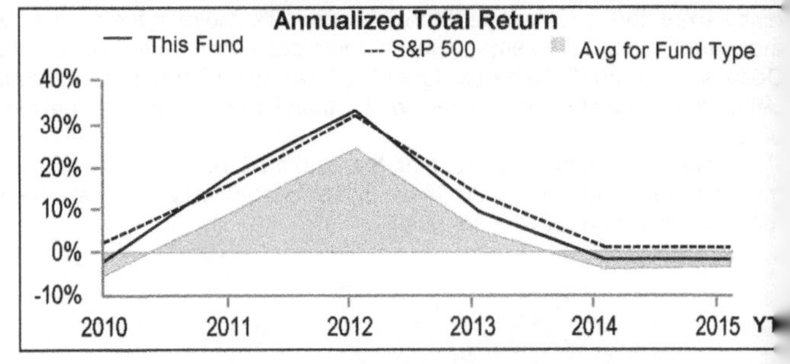

* Denotes ETF Fund

*iShares Core S&P Small-Cap ETF (IJR) A- Excellent

Fund Family: BlackRock Fund Advisors
Fund Type: Growth
Inception Date: May 22, 2000

Major Rating Factors:
Strong performance is the major factor driving the A- (Excellent) TheStreet.com Investment Rating for *iShares Core S&P Small-Cap ETF. The fund currently has a performance rating of B (Good) based on an annualized return of 12.47% over the last three years and a total return of -0.88% year to date 2015. Factored into the performance evaluation is an expense ratio of 0.13% (very low).

The fund's risk rating is currently B (Good). It carries a beta of 1.00, meaning that its performance tracks fairly well with that of the overall stock market. Volatility, as measured by both the semi-deviation and a drawdown factor, is considered low. As of December 31, 2015, *iShares Core S&P Small-Cap ETF traded at a discount of .03% below its net asset value.

Diane Hsiung has been running the fund for 8 years and currently receives a manager quality ranking of 58 (0=worst, 99=best). If you desire only a moderate level of risk and strong performance, then this fund is an excellent option.

Data Date	Investment Rating	Net Assets ($Mil)	Price	Performance Rating/Pts	Total Return Y-T-D	Risk Rating/Pts
12-15	A-	12,716.30	110.11	B / 8.2	-0.88%	B / 8.2
2014	B	12,716.30	114.06	B / 8.0	6.66%	B- / 7.0
2013	A-	14,258.80	109.13	B+ / 8.9	35.57%	B- / 7.6
2012	C+	8,090.60	78.10	C+ / 6.7	16.46%	B- / 7.5
2011	C+	6,915.20	68.30	C+ / 6.4	2.24%	B- / 7.5
2010	B	6,785.10	68.47	B- / 7.3	26.61%	C+ / 5.7

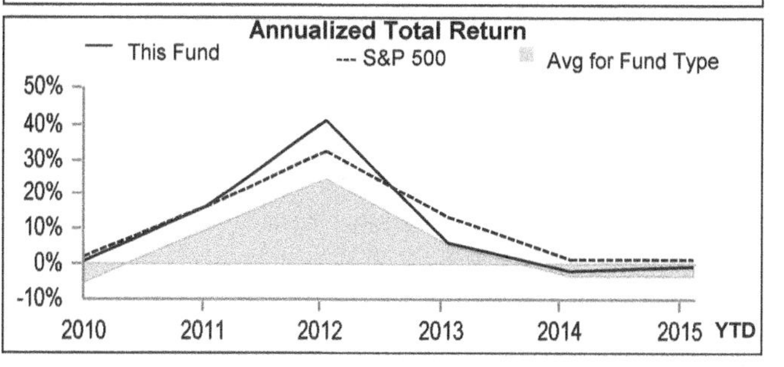

*iShares Core S&P Tot US Stk Mkt (ITOT) A- Excellent

Fund Family: BlackRock Fund Advisors
Fund Type: Income
Inception Date: January 20, 2004

Major Rating Factors:
Strong performance is the major factor driving the A- (Excellent) TheStreet.com Investment Rating for *iShares Core S&P Tot US Stk Mkt. The fund currently has a performance rating of B+ (Good) based on an annualized return of 13.93% over the last three years and a total return of 1.56% year to date 2015. Factored into the performance evaluation is an expense ratio of 0.07% (very low).

The fund's risk rating is currently B- (Good). It carries a beta of 1.00, meaning that its performance tracks fairly well with that of the overall stock market. Volatility, as measured by both the semi-deviation and a drawdown factor, is considered low. As of December 31, 2015, *iShares Core S&P Tot US Stk Mkt traded at a premium of .02% above its net asset value, which is better than its one-year historical average premium of .03%.

Diane Hsiung has been running the fund for 8 years and currently receives a manager quality ranking of 66 (0=worst, 99=best). If you desire only a moderate level of risk and strong performance, then this fund is an excellent option.

Data Date	Investment Rating	Net Assets ($Mil)	Price	Performance Rating/Pts	Total Return Y-T-D	Risk Rating/Pts
12-15	A-	1,380.30	92.86	B+ / 8.8	1.56%	B- / 7.5
2014	B+	1,380.30	93.89	B+ / 8.3	14.09%	B- / 7.3
2013	B+	1,035.30	84.60	B / 8.2	27.75%	B / 8.2
2012	C	434.80	64.94	C / 5.3	16.72%	B / 8.0
2011	C+	299.60	57.17	C / 5.3	2.26%	B- / 7.9
2010	D+	323.40	57.25	C- / 4.2	16.24%	C- / 3.7

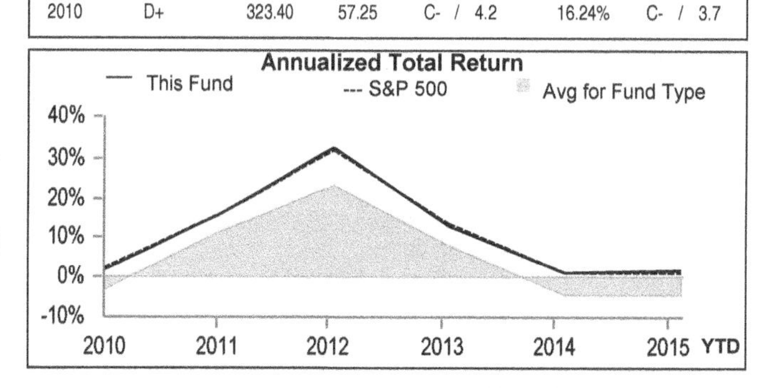

*iShares Core Total USD Bond Mark (IUSB) C Fair

Fund Family: BlackRock Fund Advisors
Fund Type: Global
Inception Date: June 12, 2014

Major Rating Factors: Middle of the road best describes *iShares Core Total USD Bond Mark whose TheStreet.com Investment Rating is currently a C (Fair). The fund currently has a performance rating of C- (Fair) based on an annualized return of 0.00% over the last three years and a total return of -0.03% year to date 2015.

The fund's risk rating is currently B (Good). It carries a beta of 0.00, meaning the fund's expected move will be 0.0% for every 10% move in the market. Volatility, as measured by both the semi-deviation and a drawdown factor, is considered low. As of December 31, 2015, *iShares Core Total USD Bond Mark traded at a premium of .10% above its net asset value, which is better than its one-year historical average premium of .38%.

James J. Mauro has been running the fund for 2 years and currently receives a manager quality ranking of 62 (0=worst, 99=best). If you desire an average level of risk, then this fund may be an option.

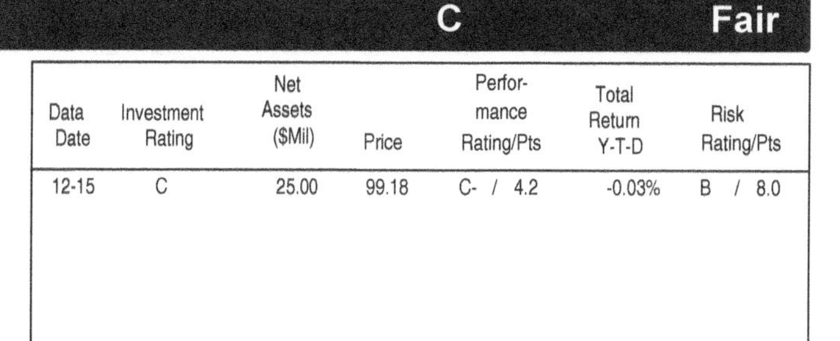

Data Date	Investment Rating	Net Assets ($Mil)	Price	Performance Rating/Pts	Total Return Y-T-D	Risk Rating/Pts
12-15	C	25.00	99.18	C- / 4.2	-0.03%	B / 8.0

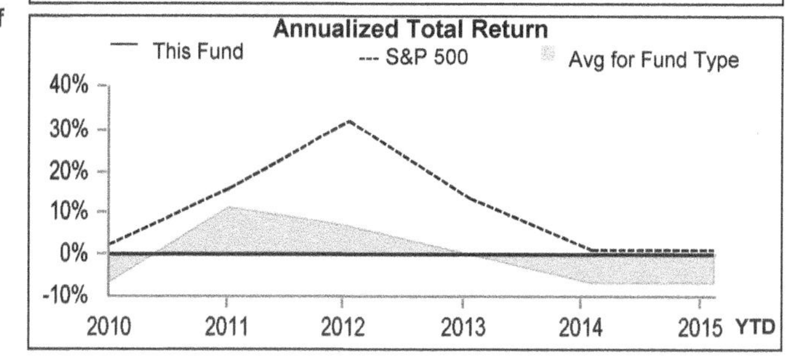

* Denotes ETF Fund

*iShares Core US Aggregate Bond E (AGG) C+ Fair

Fund Family: BlackRock Fund Advisors
Fund Type: General - Investment Grade
Inception Date: September 22, 2003

Major Rating Factors: Middle of the road best describes *iShares Core US Aggregate Bond E whose TheStreet.com Investment Rating is currently a C+ (Fair). The fund currently has a performance rating of C (Fair) based on an annualized return of 1.55% over the last three years and a total return of 0.21% year to date 2015. Factored into the performance evaluation is an expense ratio of 0.07% (very low).

The fund's risk rating is currently B- (Good). It carries a beta of 1.03, meaning that its performance tracks fairly well with that of the overall stock market. Volatility, as measured by both the semi-deviation and a drawdown factor, is considered low. As of December 31, 2015, *iShares Core US Aggregate Bond E traded at a premium of .18% above its net asset value, which is worse than its one-year historical average premium of .06%.

Scott F. Radell has been running the fund for 6 years and currently receives a manager quality ranking of 67 (0=worst, 99=best). If you desire an average level of risk, then this fund may be an option.

Data Date	Investment Rating	Net Assets ($Mil)	Price	Perfor-mance Rating/Pts	Total Return Y-T-D	Risk Rating/Pts
12-15	C+	18,853.10	108.01	C / 5.1	0.21%	B- / 7.8
2014	C+	18,853.10	110.12	C- / 3.7	5.90%	B+ / 9.5
2013	C	15,251.30	106.43	C- / 3.5	-1.61%	B+ / 9.7
2012	C	15,335.80	111.08	D+ / 2.4	3.26%	B+ / 9.8
2011	C+	14,146.60	110.25	C- / 3.4	7.81%	B+ / 9.8
2010	B+	11,219.50	105.75	C / 4.8	6.38%	B / 8.9

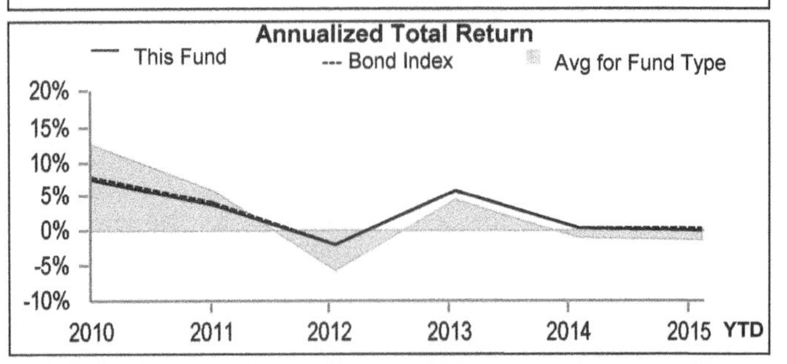

*iShares Core US Credit Bond (CRED) C Fair

Fund Family: BlackRock Fund Advisors
Fund Type: Corporate - Investment Grade
Inception Date: January 5, 2007

Major Rating Factors: Middle of the road best describes *iShares Core US Credit Bond whose TheStreet.com Investment Rating is currently a C (Fair). The fund currently has a performance rating of C (Fair) based on an annualized return of 1.43% over the last three years and a total return of -1.69% year to date 2015. Factored into the performance evaluation is an expense ratio of 0.16% (very low).

The fund's risk rating is currently B- (Good). It carries a beta of 1.04, meaning that its performance tracks fairly well with that of the overall stock market. Volatility, as measured by both the semi-deviation and a drawdown factor, is considered low. As of December 31, 2015, *iShares Core US Credit Bond traded at a premium of .18% above its net asset value, which is worse than its one-year historical average premium of .16%.

Scott F. Radell has been running the fund for 6 years and currently receives a manager quality ranking of 66 (0=worst, 99=best). If you desire an average level of risk, then this fund may be an option.

Data Date	Investment Rating	Net Assets ($Mil)	Price	Perfor-mance Rating/Pts	Total Return Y-T-D	Risk Rating/Pts
12-15	C	728.90	106.71	C / 4.9	-1.69%	B- / 7.5
2014	C-	728.90	111.81	C- / 4.2	7.94%	B- / 7.4
2013	C+	844.80	106.90	C- / 4.1	-1.92%	B+ / 9.5
2012	C	1,405.20	113.16	C- / 3.1	7.42%	B+ / 9.5
2011	C+	1,043.90	108.96	C- / 4.0	8.23%	B+ / 9.3
2010	B	727.30	104.13	C / 5.3	8.43%	B / 8.1

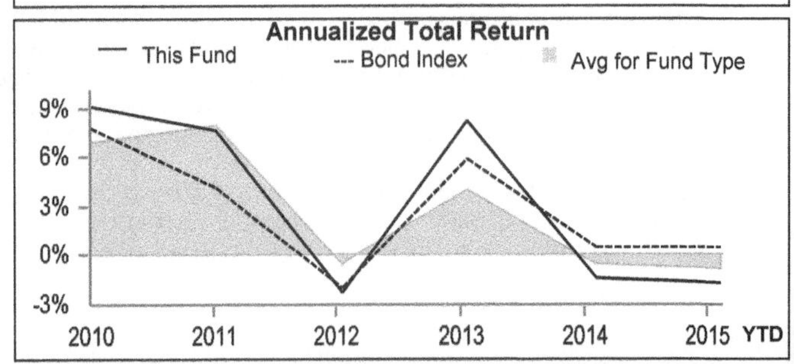

*iShares Core US Growth (IUSG) B+ Good

Fund Family: BlackRock Fund Advisors
Fund Type: Growth
Inception Date: July 24, 2000

Major Rating Factors:
Exceptional performance is the major factor driving the B+ (Good) TheStreet.com Investment Rating for *iShares Core US Growth. The fund currently has a performance rating of A- (Excellent) based on an annualized return of 15.60% over the last three years and a total return of 5.72% year to date 2015. Factored into the performance evaluation is an expense ratio of 0.12% (very low).

The fund's risk rating is currently C+ (Fair). It carries a beta of 1.02, meaning that its performance tracks fairly well with that of the overall stock market. Volatility, as measured by both the semi-deviation and a drawdown factor, is considered low. As of December 31, 2015, *iShares Core US Growth traded at a premium of .05% above its net asset value, which is worse than its one-year historical average premium of .01%.

Diane Hsiung has been running the fund for 8 years and currently receives a manager quality ranking of 76 (0=worst, 99=best). If you desire only a moderate level of risk and strong performance, then this fund is an excellent option.

Data Date	Investment Rating	Net Assets ($Mil)	Price	Perfor-mance Rating/Pts	Total Return Y-T-D	Risk Rating/Pts
12-15	B+	492.60	81.18	A- / 9.1	5.72%	C+ / 6.8
2014	B	492.60	78.34	B / 8.2	13.65%	B- / 7.1
2013	B+	486.90	70.58	B+ / 8.4	29.09%	B- / 7.9
2012	C	363.20	53.41	C / 5.2	15.74%	B- / 7.6
2011	C+	346.90	47.19	C+ / 6.2	2.55%	B- / 7.7
2010	C+	333.00	46.93	C / 5.5	17.42%	C+ / 5.9

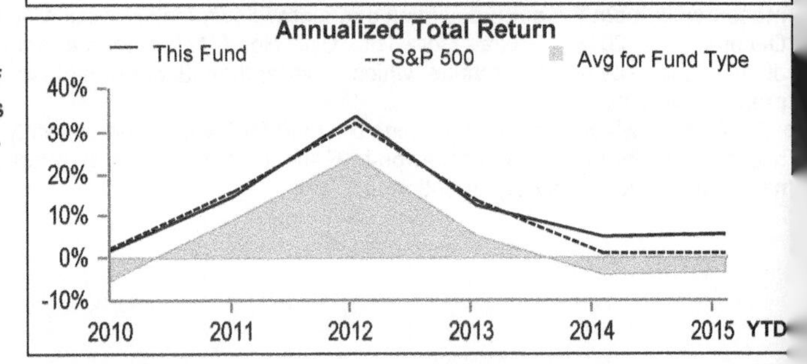

*iShares Core US Treasury Bond (GOVT) C Fair

Fund Family: BlackRock Fund Advisors
Fund Type: US Government/Agency
Inception Date: February 14, 2012

Data Date	Investment Rating	Net Assets ($Mil)	Price	Perfor-mance Rating/Pts	Total Return Y-T-D	Risk Rating/Pts
12-15	C	213.20	25.06	C / 4.8	0.22%	B- / 7.7
2014	C+	213.20	25.15	C- / 4.1	4.88%	B+ / 9.5
2013	C-	106.80	24.30	D / 2.2	-2.23%	B+ / 9.7

Major Rating Factors: Middle of the road best describes *iShares Core US Treasury Bond whose TheStreet.com Investment Rating is currently a C (Fair). The fund currently has a performance rating of C (Fair) based on an annualized return of 1.10% over the last three years and a total return of 0.22% year to date 2015. Factored into the performance evaluation is an expense ratio of 0.15% (very low).

The fund's risk rating is currently B- (Good). It carries a beta of 0.28, meaning the fund's expected move will be 2.8% for every 10% move in the market. Volatility, as measured by both the semi-deviation and a drawdown factor, is considered low. As of December 31, 2015, *iShares Core US Treasury Bond traded at a premium of .04% above its net asset value, which is better than its one-year historical average premium of .06%.

James J. Mauro has been running the fund for 4 years and currently receives a manager quality ranking of 70 (0=worst, 99=best). If you desire an average level of risk, then this fund may be an option.

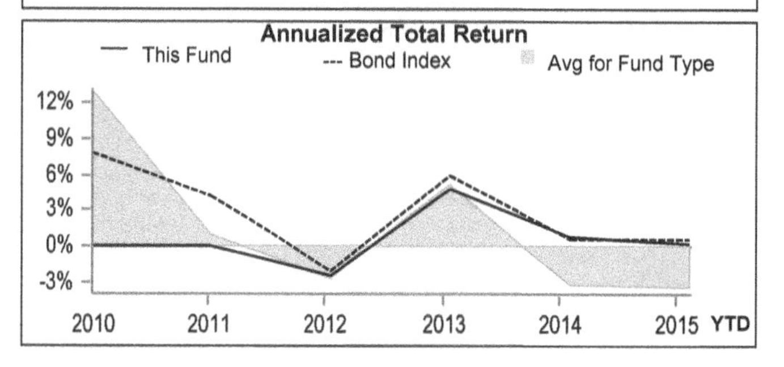

*iShares Core US Value (IUSV) A Excellent

Fund Family: BlackRock Fund Advisors
Fund Type: Income
Inception Date: July 24, 2000

Data Date	Investment Rating	Net Assets ($Mil)	Price	Perfor-mance Rating/Pts	Total Return Y-T-D	Risk Rating/Pts
12-15	A	715.60	127.39	B / 7.9	-3.34%	B / 8.7
2014	B+	715.60	136.49	B+ / 8.3	13.52%	B- / 7.5
2013	B+	574.10	123.40	B / 8.0	27.33%	B / 8.3
2012	C+	366.80	95.35	C / 5.5	17.89%	B / 8.1
2011	C	307.60	83.14	C / 4.6	0.22%	B- / 7.8
2010	C-	324.00	85.25	C- / 3.4	15.76%	C+ / 5.9

Major Rating Factors:
Strong performance is the major factor driving the A (Excellent) TheStreet.com Investment Rating for *iShares Core US Value. The fund currently has a performance rating of B (Good) based on an annualized return of 11.67% over the last three years and a total return of -3.34% year to date 2015. Factored into the performance evaluation is an expense ratio of 0.11% (very low).

The fund's risk rating is currently B (Good). It carries a beta of 1.00, meaning that its performance tracks fairly well with that of the overall stock market. Volatility, as measured by both the semi-deviation and a drawdown factor, is considered low. As of December 31, 2015, *iShares Core US Value traded at a discount of .03% below its net asset value, which is better than its one-year historical average premium of .01%.

Diane Hsiung has been running the fund for 8 years and currently receives a manager quality ranking of 51 (0=worst, 99=best). If you desire only a moderate level of risk and strong performance, then this fund is an excellent option.

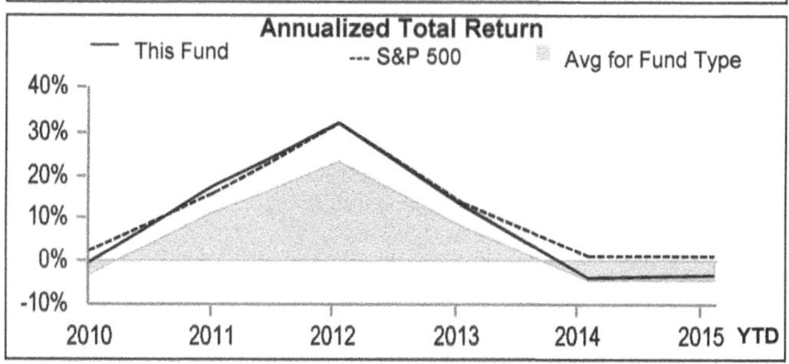

*iShares Curr Hedged MSCI EAFE ET (HEFA) C Fair

Fund Family: BlackRock Fund Advisors
Fund Type: Global
Inception Date: January 31, 2014

Data Date	Investment Rating	Net Assets ($Mil)	Price	Perfor-mance Rating/Pts	Total Return Y-T-D	Risk Rating/Pts
12-15	C	2.50	25.40	C+ / 5.7	4.96%	C+ / 6.4

Major Rating Factors: Middle of the road best describes *iShares Curr Hedged MSCI EAFE ET whose TheStreet.com Investment Rating is currently a C (Fair). The fund currently has a performance rating of C+ (Fair) based on an annualized return of 0.00% over the last three years and a total return of 4.96% year to date 2015. Factored into the performance evaluation is an expense ratio of 0.05% (very low).

The fund's risk rating is currently C+ (Fair). It carries a beta of 0.00, meaning the fund's expected move will be 0.0% for every 10% move in the market. Volatility, as measured by both the semi-deviation and a drawdown factor, is considered low. As of December 31, 2015, *iShares Curr Hedged MSCI EAFE ET traded at a premium of .20% above its net asset value, which is worse than its one-year historical average premium of .05%.

Greg Savage has been running the fund for 2 years and currently receives a manager quality ranking of 90 (0=worst, 99=best). If you desire an average level of risk, then this fund may be an option.

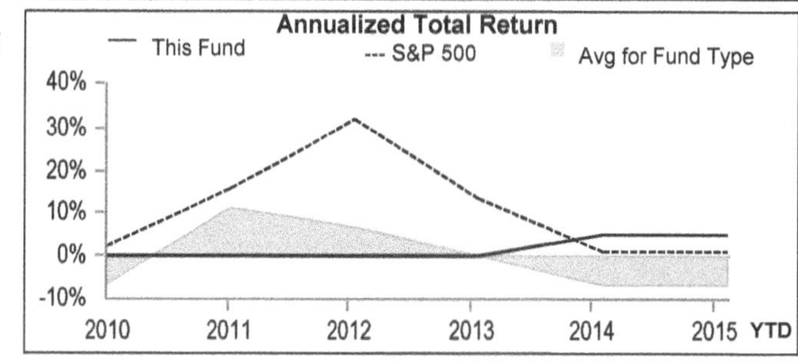

* Denotes ETF Fund

*iShares Curr Hedged MSCI Em Mkts (HEEM) D Weak

Fund Family: BlackRock Fund Advisors
Fund Type: Emerging Market
Inception Date: September 23, 2014

Data Date	Investment Rating	Net Assets ($Mil)	Price	Performance Rating/Pts	Total Return Y-T-D	Risk Rating/Pts
12-15	D	0.00	20.00	D+ / 2.4	-5.68%	C+ / 5.7

Major Rating Factors:
Disappointing performance is the major factor driving the D (Weak) TheStreet.com Investment Rating for *iShares Curr Hedged MSCI Em Mkts. The fund currently has a performance rating of D+ (Weak) based on an annualized return of 0.00% over the last three years and a total return of -5.68% year to date 2015. Factored into the performance evaluation is an expense ratio of 0.02% (very low).

The fund's risk rating is currently C+ (Fair). It carries a beta of 0.00, meaning the fund's expected move will be 0.0% for every 10% move in the market. Volatility, as measured by both the semi-deviation and a drawdown factor, is considered low. As of December 31, 2015, *iShares Curr Hedged MSCI Em Mkts traded at a premium of .25% above its net asset value, which is worse than its one-year historical average premium of .19%.

Jennifer F.Y. Hsui has been running the fund for 2 years and currently receives a manager quality ranking of 87 (0=worst, 99=best). This fund offers only a moderate level of risk but investors looking for strong performance are still waiting.

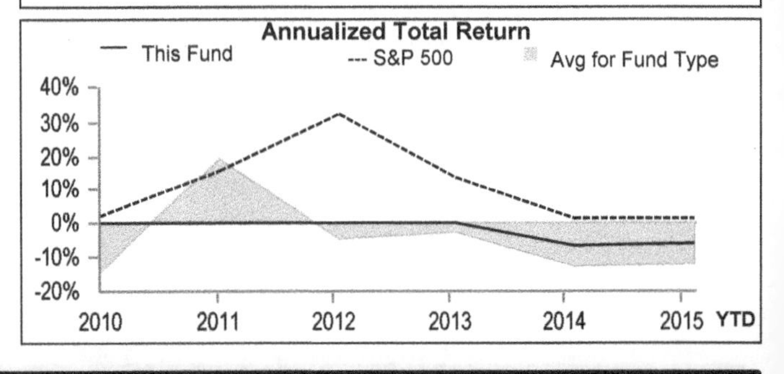

*iShares Curr Hedged MSCI Germany (HEWG) C+ Fair

Fund Family: BlackRock Fund Advisors
Fund Type: Foreign
Inception Date: January 31, 2014

Data Date	Investment Rating	Net Assets ($Mil)	Price	Performance Rating/Pts	Total Return Y-T-D	Risk Rating/Pts
12-15	C+	74.20	24.37	C+ / 6.8	6.93%	C+ / 6.6

Major Rating Factors: Middle of the road best describes *iShares Curr Hedged MSCI Germany whose TheStreet.com Investment Rating is currently a C+ (Fair). The fund currently has a performance rating of C+ (Fair) based on an annualized return of 0.00% over the last three years and a total return of 6.93% year to date 2015. Factored into the performance evaluation is an expense ratio of 0.05% (very low).

The fund's risk rating is currently C+ (Fair). It carries a beta of 0.00, meaning the fund's expected move will be 0.0% for every 10% move in the market. Volatility, as measured by both the semi-deviation and a drawdown factor, is considered low. As of December 31, 2015, *iShares Curr Hedged MSCI Germany traded at a price exactly equal to its net asset value, which is better than its one-year historical average premium of .03%.

Greg Savage has been running the fund for 2 years and currently receives a manager quality ranking of 93 (0=worst, 99=best). If you desire an average level of risk, then this fund may be an option.

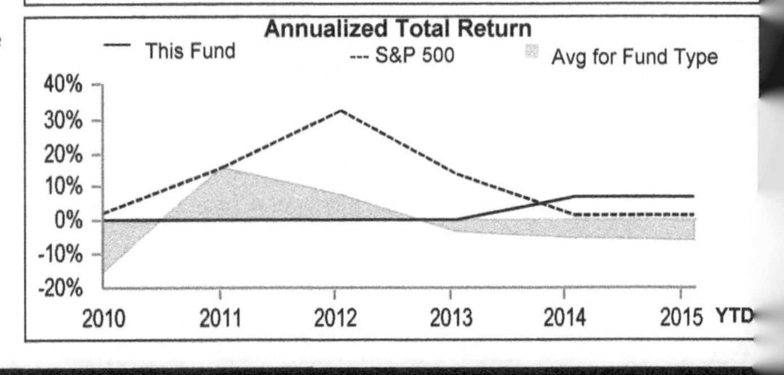

*iShares Curr Hedged MSCI Japan E (HEWJ) C Fair

Fund Family: BlackRock Fund Advisors
Fund Type: Foreign
Inception Date: January 31, 2014

Data Date	Investment Rating	Net Assets ($Mil)	Price	Performance Rating/Pts	Total Return Y-T-D	Risk Rating/Pts
12-15	C	43.30	28.67	C+ / 6.0	8.36%	C+ / 6.4

Major Rating Factors: Middle of the road best describes *iShares Curr Hedged MSCI Japan E whose TheStreet.com Investment Rating is currently a C (Fair). The fund currently has a performance rating of C+ (Fair) based on an annualized return of 0.00% over the last three years and a total return of 8.36% year to date 2015. Factored into the performance evaluation is an expense ratio of 0.01% (very low).

The fund's risk rating is currently C+ (Fair). It carries a beta of 0.00, meaning the fund's expected move will be 0.0% for every 10% move in the market. Volatility, as measured by both the semi-deviation and a drawdown factor, is considered low. As of December 31, 2015, *iShares Curr Hedged MSCI Japan E traded at a premium of .03% above its net asset value, which is worse than its one-year historical average premium of .02%.

Greg Savage has been running the fund for 2 years and currently receives a manager quality ranking of 94 (0=worst, 99=best). If you desire an average level of risk, then this fund may be an option.

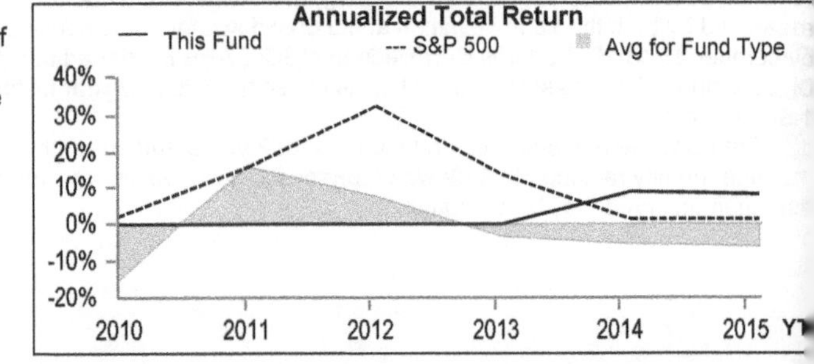

*iShares DJ US Index ETF (IYY) A- Excellent

Fund Family: BlackRock Fund Advisors
Fund Type: Income
Inception Date: June 12, 2000

Major Rating Factors:
Strong performance is the major factor driving the A- (Excellent) TheStreet.com Investment Rating for *iShares DJ US Index ETF. The fund currently has a performance rating of B+ (Good) based on an annualized return of 13.66% over the last three years and a total return of 1.13% year to date 2015. Factored into the performance evaluation is an expense ratio of 0.20% (very low).

The fund's risk rating is currently B- (Good). It carries a beta of 1.00, meaning that its performance tracks fairly well with that of the overall stock market. Volatility, as measured by both the semi-deviation and a drawdown factor, is considered low. As of December 31, 2015, *iShares DJ US Index ETF traded at a premium of .02% above its net asset value, which is worse than its one-year historical average discount of .01%.

Diane Hsiung has been running the fund for 8 years and currently receives a manager quality ranking of 64 (0=worst, 99=best). If you desire only a moderate level of risk and strong performance, then this fund is an excellent option.

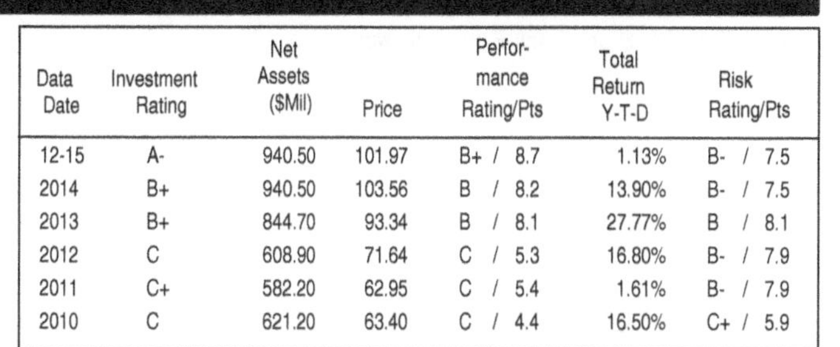

Data Date	Investment Rating	Net Assets ($Mil)	Price	Performance Rating/Pts	Total Return Y-T-D	Risk Rating/Pts
12-15	A-	940.50	101.97	B+ / 8.7	1.13%	B- / 7.5
2014	B+	940.50	103.56	B / 8.2	13.90%	B- / 7.5
2013	B+	844.70	93.34	B / 8.1	27.77%	B / 8.1
2012	C	608.90	71.64	C / 5.3	16.80%	B- / 7.9
2011	C+	582.20	62.95	C / 5.4	1.61%	B- / 7.9
2010	C	621.20	63.40	C / 4.4	16.50%	C+ / 5.9

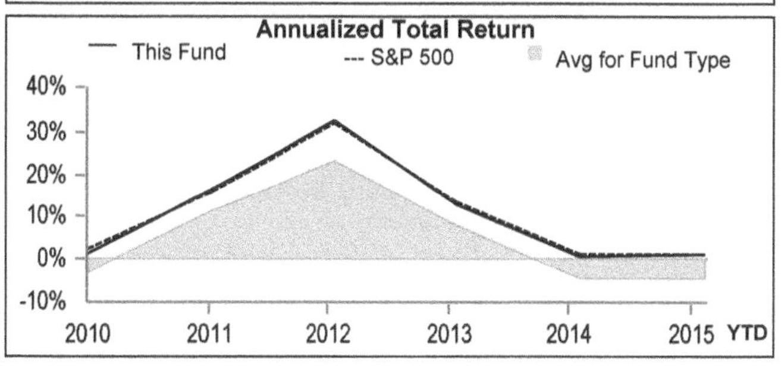

*iShares Emerging Markets Corp B (CEMB) C Fair

Fund Family: BlackRock Fund Advisors
Fund Type: Corporate - Investment Grade
Inception Date: April 17, 2012

Major Rating Factors: Middle of the road best describes *iShares Emerging Markets Corp B whose TheStreet.com Investment Rating is currently a C (Fair). The fund currently has a performance rating of C- (Fair) based on an annualized return of -0.96% over the last three years and a total return of -1.65% year to date 2015. Factored into the performance evaluation is an expense ratio of 0.60% (very low).

The fund's risk rating is currently B (Good). It carries a beta of 1.05, meaning that its performance tracks fairly well with that of the overall stock market. Volatility, as measured by both the semi-deviation and a drawdown factor, is considered low. As of December 31, 2015, *iShares Emerging Markets Corp B traded at a discount of .58% below its net asset value, which is better than its one-year historical average premium of .21%.

James J. Mauro has been running the fund for 4 years and currently receives a manager quality ranking of 47 (0=worst, 99=best). If you desire an average level of risk, then this fund may be an option.

Data Date	Investment Rating	Net Assets ($Mil)	Price	Performance Rating/Pts	Total Return Y-T-D	Risk Rating/Pts
12-15	C	25.40	46.06	C- / 3.7	-1.65%	B / 8.5
2014	D+	25.40	49.05	D+ / 2.9	5.03%	C+ / 6.8
2013	C-	29.70	49.09	D / 2.0	-5.91%	B / 8.8

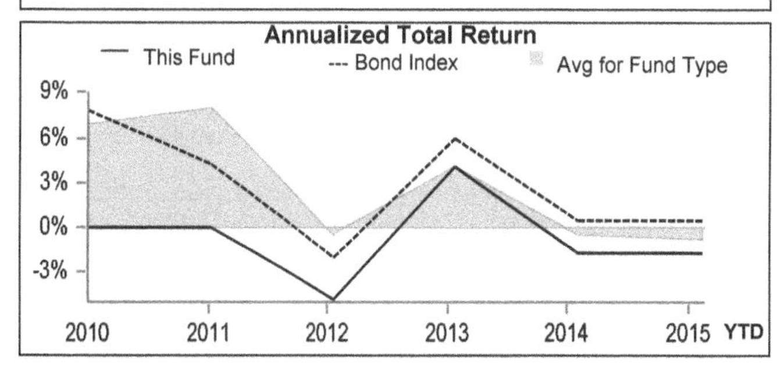

*iShares Emerging Markets Dividen (DVYE) D Weak

Fund Family: BlackRock Fund Advisors
Fund Type: Emerging Market
Inception Date: February 23, 2012

Major Rating Factors:
Disappointing performance is the major factor driving the D (Weak) TheStreet.com Investment Rating for *iShares Emerging Markets Dividen. The fund currently has a performance rating of D- (Weak) based on an annualized return of -15.23% over the last three years and a total return of -22.90% year to date 2015. Factored into the performance evaluation is an expense ratio of 0.49% (very low).

The fund's risk rating is currently C (Fair). It carries a beta of 1.14, meaning it is expected to move 11.4% for every 10% move in the market. Volatility, as measured by both the semi-deviation and a drawdown factor, is considered average. As of December 31, 2015, *iShares Emerging Markets Dividen traded at a discount of 1.05% below its net asset value, which is better than its one-year historical average discount of .09%.

Diane Hsiung has been running the fund for 4 years and currently receives a manager quality ranking of 19 (0=worst, 99=best). This fund offers an average level of risk but investors looking for strong performance will be frustrated.

Data Date	Investment Rating	Net Assets ($Mil)	Price	Performance Rating/Pts	Total Return Y-T-D	Risk Rating/Pts
12-15	D	281.90	30.11	D- / 1.1	-22.90%	C / 5.4
2014	D	281.90	41.82	D- / 1.0	-8.24%	C+ / 6.9
2013	D	173.90	48.78	D- / 1.1	-13.20%	B- / 7.9

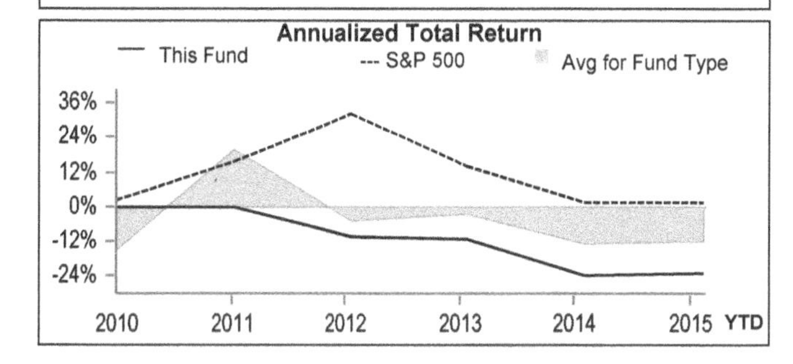

*iShares Emerging Markets HY Bd E (EMHY) C- Fair

Fund Family: BlackRock Fund Advisors
Fund Type: Emerging Market
Inception Date: April 3, 2012

Major Rating Factors: Middle of the road best describes *iShares Emerging Markets HY Bd E whose TheStreet.com Investment Rating is currently a C- (Fair). The fund currently has a performance rating of C- (Fair) based on an annualized return of -1.21% over the last three years and a total return of 1.93% year to date 2015. Factored into the performance evaluation is an expense ratio of 0.65% (very low).

The fund's risk rating is currently C+ (Fair). It carries a beta of 0.59, meaning the fund's expected move will be 5.9% for every 10% move in the market. Volatility, as measured by both the semi-deviation and a drawdown factor, is considered low. As of December 31, 2015, *iShares Emerging Markets HY Bd E traded at a premium of .16% above its net asset value, which is better than its one-year historical average premium of .21%.

James J. Mauro has been running the fund for 4 years and currently receives a manager quality ranking of 80 (0=worst, 99=best). If you desire an average level of risk, then this fund may be an option.

Data Date	Investment Rating	Net Assets ($Mil)	Price	Performance Rating/Pts	Total Return Y-T-D	Risk Rating/Pts
12-15	C-	202.20	45.05	C- / 3.9	1.93%	C+ / 6.3
2014	D+	202.20	47.21	D / 2.0	1.81%	B- / 7.9
2013	D+	191.70	49.29	D / 1.9	-7.37%	B / 8.6

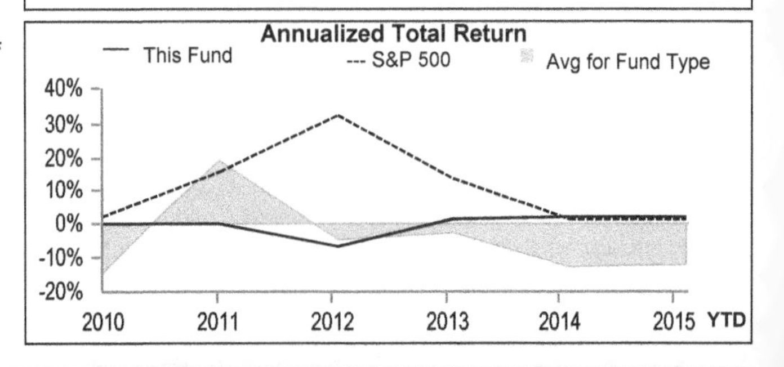

*iShares Emerging Markets Infr ET (EMIF) D+ Weak

Fund Family: BlackRock Fund Advisors
Fund Type: Global
Inception Date: June 16, 2009

Major Rating Factors:
Disappointing performance is the major factor driving the D+ (Weak) TheStreet.com Investment Rating for *iShares Emerging Markets Infr ET. The fund currently has a performance rating of D+ (Weak) based on an annualized return of -5.39% over the last three years and a total return of -12.81% year to date 2015. Factored into the performance evaluation is an expense ratio of 0.75% (very low).

The fund's risk rating is currently B- (Good). It carries a beta of 0.99, meaning that its performance tracks fairly well with that of the overall stock market. Volatility, as measured by both the semi-deviation and a drawdown factor, is considered low. As of December 31, 2015, *iShares Emerging Markets Infr ET traded at a discount of .69% below its net asset value, which is better than its one-year historical average discount of .34%.

Diane Hsiung has been running the fund for 7 years and currently receives a manager quality ranking of 17 (0=worst, 99=best). This fund offers only a moderate level of risk but investors looking for strong performance are still waiting.

Data Date	Investment Rating	Net Assets ($Mil)	Price	Performance Rating/Pts	Total Return Y-T-D	Risk Rating/Pts
12-15	D+	101.40	27.26	D+ / 2.4	-12.81%	B- / 7.0
2014	D+	101.40	32.41	C- / 4.0	0.57%	C+ / 6.2
2013	D+	134.60	34.13	C- / 3.2	-2.34%	C+ / 6.8
2012	C-	130.80	34.24	C / 4.3	20.15%	C+ / 6.9
2011	D	102.60	28.84	D- / 1.3	-12.27%	B- / 7.1
2010	A+	109.40	34.32	A- / 9.0	18.30%	B / 8.2

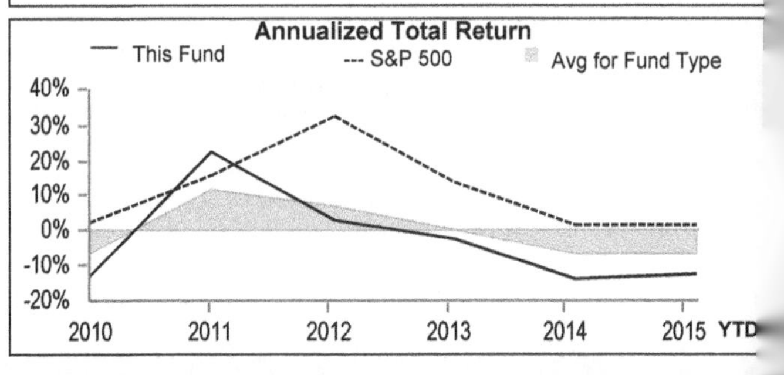

*iShares Emerging Mkts Loc Cur Bo (LEMB) D Weak

Fund Family: BlackRock Fund Advisors
Fund Type: Global
Inception Date: October 18, 2011

Major Rating Factors:
Disappointing performance is the major factor driving the D (Weak) TheStreet.com Investment Rating for *iShares Emerging Mkts Loc Cur Bo. The fund currently has a performance rating of D+ (Weak) based on an annualized return of -7.25% over the last three years and a total return of -11.30% year to date 2015. Factored into the performance evaluation is an expense ratio of 0.59% (very low).

The fund's risk rating is currently C+ (Fair). It carries a beta of 0.98, meaning that its performance tracks fairly well with that of the overall stock market. Volatility, as measured by both the semi-deviation and a drawdown factor, is considered low. As of December 31, 2015, *iShares Emerging Mkts Loc Cur Bo traded at a premium of .65% above its net asset value, which is worse than its one-year historical average discount of .03%.

James J. Mauro has been running the fund for 5 years and currently receives a manager quality ranking of 41 (0=worst, 99=best). This fund offers only a moderate level of risk but investors looking for strong performance are still waiting.

Data Date	Investment Rating	Net Assets ($Mil)	Price	Performance Rating/Pts	Total Return Y-T-D	Risk Rating/Pts
12-15	D	583.50	40.32	D+ / 2.3	-11.30%	C+ / 5.8
2014	D	583.50	46.14	D+ / 2.5	-2.29%	C+ / 6.4
2013	D+	606.10	48.82	D / 1.6	-7.06%	B / 8.6
2012	B-	381.00	53.86	C / 5.5	11.82%	B+ / 9.1

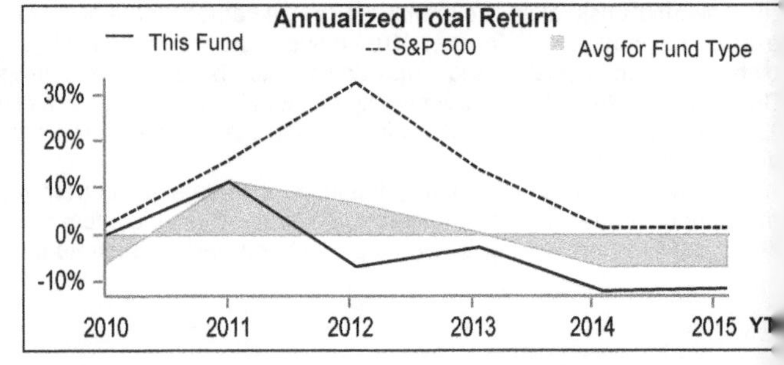

*iShares Enhanced Intl Large Cap (IEIL) C+ Fair

Fund Family: BlackRock Fund Advisors
Fund Type: Foreign
Inception Date: February 25, 2014

Data Date	Investment Rating	Net Assets ($Mil)	Price	Perfor-mance Rating/Pts	Total Return Y-T-D	Risk Rating/Pts
12-15	C+	63.10	22.90	C / 5.5	3.95%	B / 8.1

Major Rating Factors: Middle of the road best describes *iShares Enhanced Intl Large Cap whose TheStreet.com Investment Rating is currently a C+ (Fair). The fund currently has a performance rating of C (Fair) based on an annualized return of 0.00% over the last three years and a total return of 3.95% year to date 2015. Factored into the performance evaluation is an expense ratio of 0.35% (very low).

The fund's risk rating is currently B (Good). It carries a beta of 0.00, meaning the fund's expected move will be 0.0% for every 10% move in the market. Volatility, as measured by both the semi-deviation and a drawdown factor, is considered low. As of December 31, 2015, *iShares Enhanced Intl Large Cap traded at a discount of .35% below its net asset value, which is better than its one-year historical average premium of .26%.

Jennifer F.Y. Hsui currently receives a manager quality ranking of 88 (0=worst, 99=best). If you desire an average level of risk, then this fund may be an option.

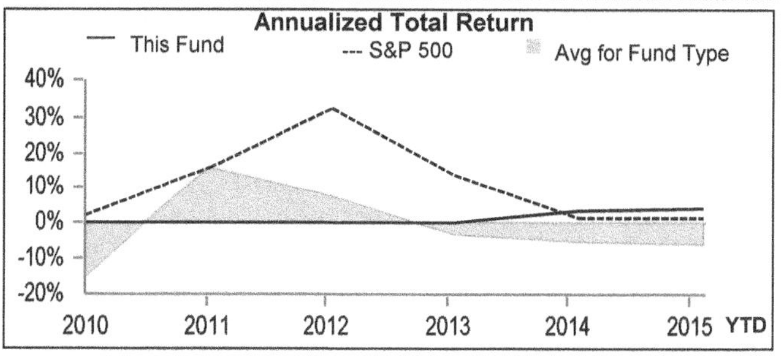

*iShares Enhanced Intl Small Cap (IEIS) C+ Fair

Fund Family: BlackRock Fund Advisors
Fund Type: Foreign
Inception Date: February 25, 2014

Data Date	Investment Rating	Net Assets ($Mil)	Price	Perfor-mance Rating/Pts	Total Return Y-T-D	Risk Rating/Pts
12-15	C+	9.20	22.77	C+ / 6.8	7.42%	C+ / 6.7

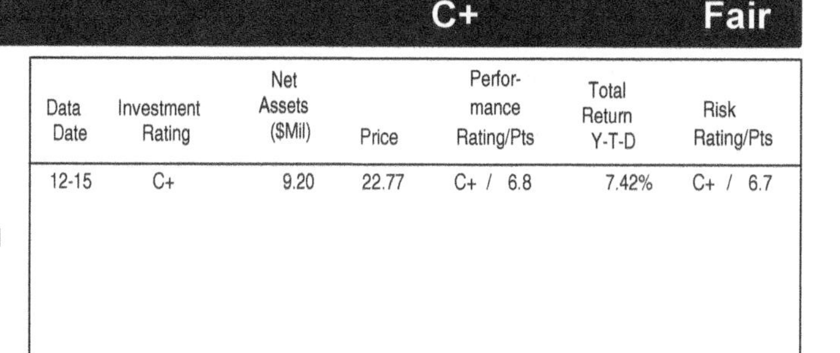

Major Rating Factors: Middle of the road best describes *iShares Enhanced Intl Small Cap whose TheStreet.com Investment Rating is currently a C+ (Fair). The fund currently has a performance rating of C+ (Fair) based on an annualized return of 0.00% over the last three years and a total return of 7.42% year to date 2015. Factored into the performance evaluation is an expense ratio of 0.49% (very low).

The fund's risk rating is currently C+ (Fair). It carries a beta of 0.00, meaning the fund's expected move will be 0.0% for every 10% move in the market. Volatility, as measured by both the semi-deviation and a drawdown factor, is considered low. As of December 31, 2015, *iShares Enhanced Intl Small Cap traded at a premium of .22% above its net asset value, which is better than its one-year historical average premium of .54%.

Jennifer F.Y. Hsui has been running the fund for 2 years and currently receives a manager quality ranking of 93 (0=worst, 99=best). If you desire an average level of risk, then this fund may be an option.

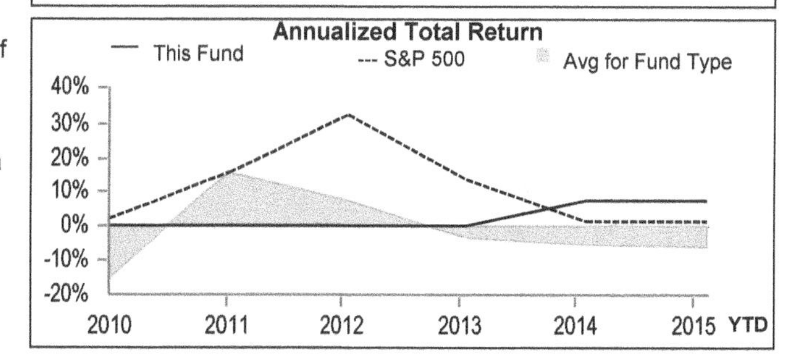

*iShares Enhanced US Large Cap ET (IELG) C Fair

Fund Family: BlackRock Fund Advisors
Fund Type: Growth
Inception Date: April 16, 2013

Data Date	Investment Rating	Net Assets ($Mil)	Price	Perfor-mance Rating/Pts	Total Return Y-T-D	Risk Rating/Pts
12-15	C	64.10	31.53	C / 5.1	1.09%	B- / 7.4
2014	B-	64.10	32.10	C+ / 6.9	13.06%	B- / 7.7

Major Rating Factors: Middle of the road best describes *iShares Enhanced US Large Cap ET whose TheStreet.com Investment Rating is currently a C (Fair). The fund currently has a performance rating of C (Fair) based on an annualized return of 0.00% over the last three years and a total return of 1.09% year to date 2015. Factored into the performance evaluation is an expense ratio of 0.18% (very low).

The fund's risk rating is currently B- (Good). It carries a beta of 0.00, meaning the fund's expected move will be 0.0% for every 10% move in the market. Volatility, as measured by both the semi-deviation and a drawdown factor, is considered low. As of December 31, 2015, *iShares Enhanced US Large Cap ET traded at a premium of .32% above its net asset value, which is worse than its one-year historical average premium of .04%.

Jennifer F.Y. Hsui has been running the fund for 3 years and currently receives a manager quality ranking of 65 (0=worst, 99=best). If you desire an average level of risk, then this fund may be an option.

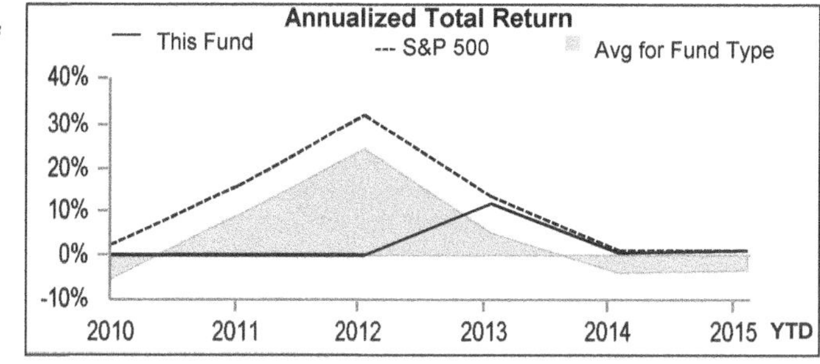

* Denotes ETF Fund

*iShares Enhanced US Small Cap ET (IESM) C- Fair

Fund Family: BlackRock Fund Advisors
Fund Type: Growth
Inception Date: April 16, 2013

Major Rating Factors:
Disappointing performance is the major factor driving the C- (Fair) TheStreet.com Investment Rating for *iShares Enhanced US Small Cap ET. The fund currently has a performance rating of D+ (Weak) based on an annualized return of 0.00% over the last three years and a total return of -3.52% year to date 2015. Factored into the performance evaluation is an expense ratio of 0.35% (very low).

The fund's risk rating is currently C+ (Fair). It carries a beta of 0.00, meaning the fund's expected move will be 0.0% for every 10% move in the market. Volatility, as measured by both the semi-deviation and a drawdown factor, is considered low. As of December 31, 2015, *iShares Enhanced US Small Cap ET traded at a premium of .44% above its net asset value, which is worse than its one-year historical average premium of .09%.

Jennifer F.Y. Hsui has been running the fund for 3 years and currently receives a manager quality ranking of 26 (0=worst, 99=best). This fund offers only a moderate level of risk but investors looking for strong performance are still waiting.

Data Date	Investment Rating	Net Assets ($Mil)	Price	Performance Rating/Pts	Total Return Y-T-D	Risk Rating/Pts
12-15	C-	16.10	29.62	D+ / 2.8	-3.52%	C+ / 6.9
2014	C+	16.10	31.93	C+ / 5.9	8.20%	B- / 7.5

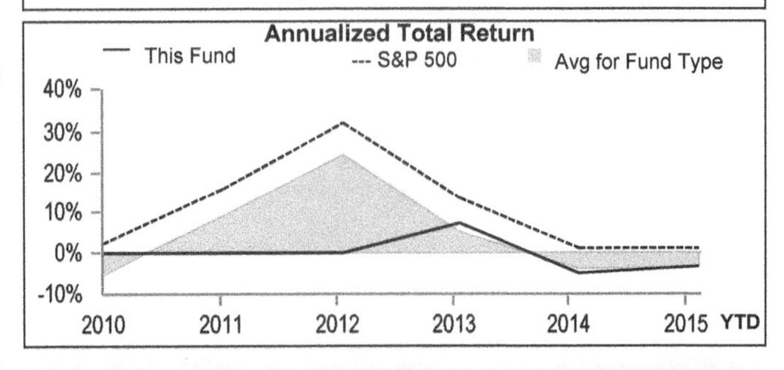

*iShares Europe (IEV) C+ Fair

Fund Family: BlackRock Fund Advisors
Fund Type: Foreign
Inception Date: July 25, 2000

Major Rating Factors: Middle of the road best describes *iShares Europe whose TheStreet.com Investment Rating is currently a C+ (Fair). The fund currently has a performance rating of C (Fair) based on an annualized return of 3.55% over the last three years and a total return of -2.19% year to date 2015. Factored into the performance evaluation is an expense ratio of 0.60% (very low).

The fund's risk rating is currently B- (Good). It carries a beta of 1.04, meaning that its performance tracks fairly well with that of the overall stock market. Volatility, as measured by both the semi-deviation and a drawdown factor, is considered low. As of December 31, 2015, *iShares Europe traded at a discount of .64% below its net asset value, which is better than its one-year historical average premium of .06%.

Diane Hsiung has been running the fund for 8 years and currently receives a manager quality ranking of 53 (0=worst, 99=best). If you desire an average level of risk, then this fund may be an option.

Data Date	Investment Rating	Net Assets ($Mil)	Price	Performance Rating/Pts	Total Return Y-T-D	Risk Rating/Pts
12-15	C+	3,123.50	40.11	C / 5.3	-2.19%	B- / 7.7
2014	C-	3,123.50	42.53	C / 5.2	-5.23%	C+ / 6.4
2013	C+	2,636.40	47.45	B- / 7.1	20.38%	B- / 7.0
2012	C-	1,200.90	39.30	C / 4.5	24.73%	C+ / 6.9
2011	D	915.60	33.74	D+ / 2.4	-10.74%	B- / 7.0
2010	E+	1,156.80	39.28	D- / 1.2	3.83%	C- / 3.0

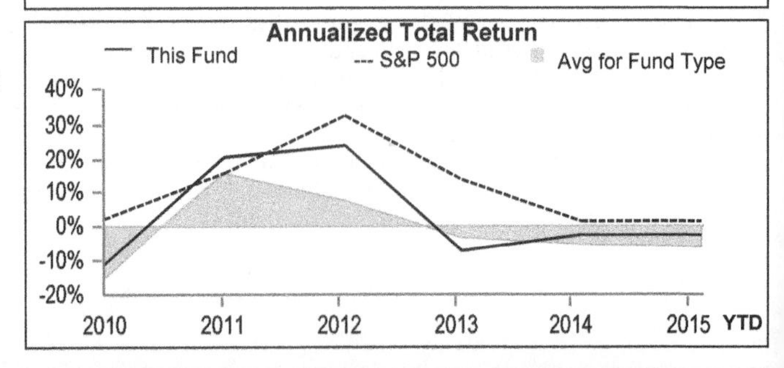

*iShares Europe Developed RE ETF (IFEU) B Good

Fund Family: BlackRock Fund Advisors
Fund Type: Growth and Income
Inception Date: November 12, 2007

Major Rating Factors: Strong performance is the major factor driving the B (Good) TheStreet.com Investment Rating for *iShares Europe Developed RE ETF. The fund currently has a performance rating of B (Good) based on an annualized return of 10.40% over the last three years and a total return of 8.46% year to date 2015. Factored into the performance evaluation is an expense ratio of 0.48% (very low).

The fund's risk rating is currently C+ (Fair). It carries a beta of 0.73, meaning the fund's expected move will be 7.3% for every 10% move in the market. Volatility, as measured by both the semi-deviation and a drawdown factor, is considered low. As of December 31, 2015, *iShares Europe Developed RE ETF traded at a premium of .70% above its net asset value, which is worse than its one-year historical average premium of .23%.

Diane Hsiung has been running the fund for 8 years and currently receives a manager quality ranking of 67 (0=worst, 99=best). If you desire only a moderate level of risk and strong performance, then this fund is an excellent option.

Data Date	Investment Rating	Net Assets ($Mil)	Price	Performance Rating/Pts	Total Return Y-T-D	Risk Rating/Pts
12-15	B	40.50	37.59	B / 8.1	8.46%	C+ / 6.8
2014	B-	40.50	36.50	B / 7.8	10.66%	C+ / 6.8
2013	C+	27.40	34.61	C+ / 6.7	12.69%	C+ / 6.8
2012	C	13.90	30.75	C+ / 6.0	34.75%	C+ / 6.6
2011	D	11.20	24.69	D / 1.8	-14.45%	C+ / 6.7
2010	E+	9.00	29.97	D- / 1.2	9.46%	C- / 3.6

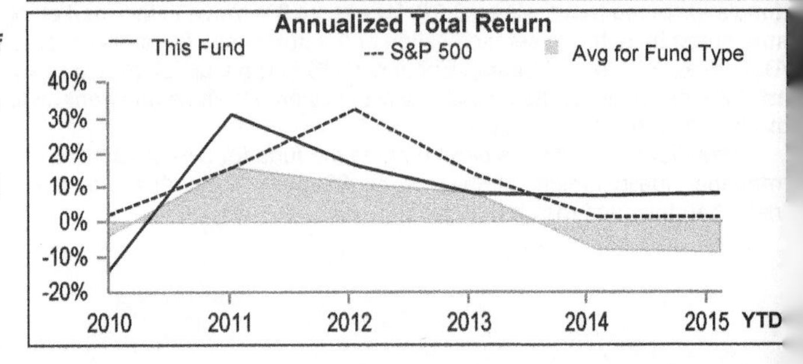

*iShares Floating Rate Bond ETF (FLOT) C Fair

Fund Family: BlackRock Fund Advisors
Fund Type: Corporate - Investment Grade
Inception Date: June 14, 2011

Data Date	Investment Rating	Net Assets ($Mil)	Price	Perfor-mance Rating/Pts	Total Return Y-T-D	Risk Rating/Pts
12-15	C	4,053.20	50.44	C / 4.5	0.44%	B / 8.0
2014	C	4,053.20	50.54	C- / 3.1	0.12%	B+ / 9.7
2013	C	3,616.90	50.72	D+ / 2.8	0.68%	B+ / 9.9
2012	C-	402.70	50.59	D / 2.2	4.00%	B+ / 9.9

Major Rating Factors: Middle of the road best describes *iShares Floating Rate Bond ETF whose TheStreet.com Investment Rating is currently a C (Fair). The fund currently has a performance rating of C (Fair) based on an annualized return of 0.38% over the last three years and a total return of 0.44% year to date 2015. Factored into the performance evaluation is an expense ratio of 0.20% (very low).

The fund's risk rating is currently B (Good). It carries a beta of -0.01, meaning the fund's expected move will be -0.1% for every 10% move in the market. Volatility, as measured by both the semi-deviation and a drawdown factor, is considered low. As of December 31, 2015, *iShares Floating Rate Bond ETF traded at a premium of .12% above its net asset value, which is worse than its one-year historical average premium of .01%.

James J. Mauro has been running the fund for 5 years and currently receives a manager quality ranking of 71 (0=worst, 99=best). If you desire an average level of risk, then this fund may be an option.

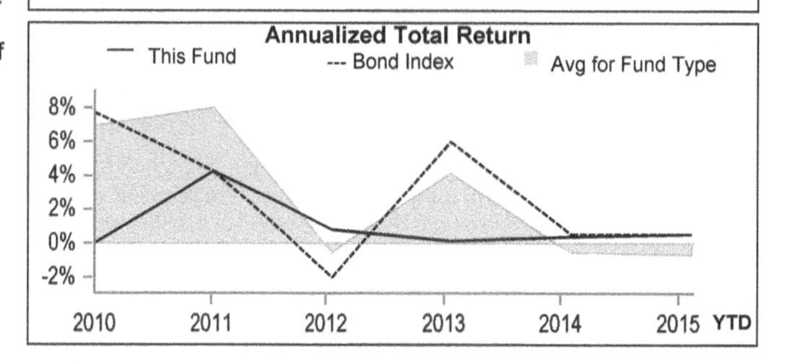

*iShares Glbl High Yield Corp Bd (GHYG) C Fair

Fund Family: BlackRock Fund Advisors
Fund Type: Global
Inception Date: April 3, 2012

Data Date	Investment Rating	Net Assets ($Mil)	Price	Perfor-mance Rating/Pts	Total Return Y-T-D	Risk Rating/Pts
12-15	C	98.20	44.62	C- / 3.6	-6.20%	B / 8.3
2014	C-	98.20	49.74	D / 1.8	-2.22%	B+ / 9.1
2013	B+	85.30	53.76	C+ / 6.2	6.96%	B+ / 9.6

Major Rating Factors: Middle of the road best describes *iShares Glbl High Yield Corp Bd whose TheStreet.com Investment Rating is currently a C (Fair). The fund currently has a performance rating of C- (Fair) based on an annualized return of -0.57% over the last three years and a total return of -6.20% year to date 2015. Factored into the performance evaluation is an expense ratio of 0.40% (very low).

The fund's risk rating is currently B (Good). It carries a beta of 0.44, meaning the fund's expected move will be 4.4% for every 10% move in the market. Volatility, as measured by both the semi-deviation and a drawdown factor, is considered low. As of December 31, 2015, *iShares Glbl High Yield Corp Bd traded at a discount of .76% below its net asset value, which is better than its one-year historical average premium of .49%.

James J. Mauro has been running the fund for 4 years and currently receives a manager quality ranking of 79 (0=worst, 99=best). If you desire an average level of risk, then this fund may be an option.

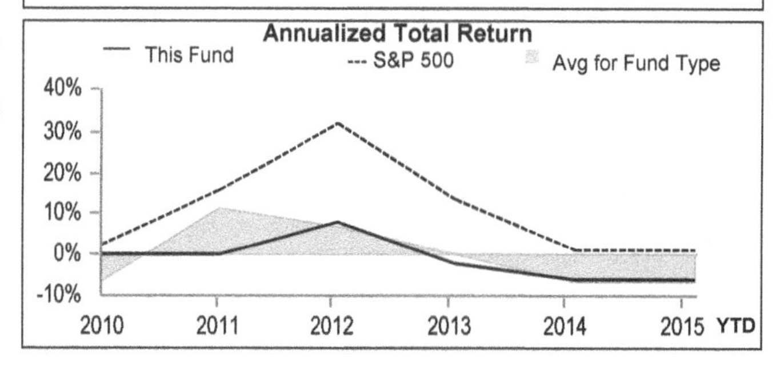

*iShares Global 100 (IOO) C+ Fair

Fund Family: BlackRock Fund Advisors
Fund Type: Growth
Inception Date: December 5, 2000

Data Date	Investment Rating	Net Assets ($Mil)	Price	Perfor-mance Rating/Pts	Total Return Y-T-D	Risk Rating/Pts
12-15	C+	1,745.60	72.83	C+ / 6.7	-0.46%	B- / 7.2
2014	C+	1,745.60	76.22	C+ / 6.0	3.46%	B- / 7.2
2013	B-	1,560.90	77.24	B- / 7.1	20.04%	B / 8.0
2012	C-	1,054.00	63.96	C- / 4.2	17.86%	B- / 7.9
2011	C-	975.50	57.94	C- / 3.5	-3.56%	B- / 7.8
2010	D+	953.10	62.27	D / 1.9	5.96%	C+ / 6.0

Major Rating Factors: Middle of the road best describes *iShares Global 100 whose TheStreet.com Investment Rating is currently a C+ (Fair). The fund currently has a performance rating of C+ (Fair) based on an annualized return of 7.25% over the last three years and a total return of -0.46% year to date 2015. Factored into the performance evaluation is an expense ratio of 0.40% (very low).

The fund's risk rating is currently B- (Good). It carries a beta of 1.05, meaning that its performance tracks fairly well with that of the overall stock market. Volatility, as measured by both the semi-deviation and a drawdown factor, is considered low. As of December 31, 2015, *iShares Global 100 traded at a premium of .03% above its net asset value, which is worse than its one-year historical average discount of .01%.

Diane Hsiung has been running the fund for 8 years and currently receives a manager quality ranking of 23 (0=worst, 99=best). If you desire an average level of risk, then this fund may be an option.

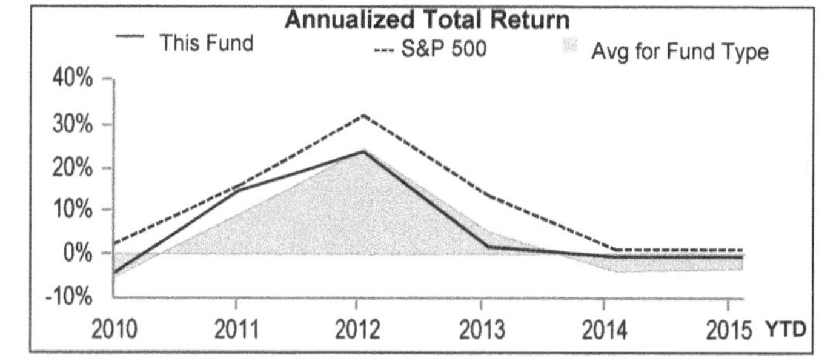

*iShares Global Clean Energy ETF (ICLN) B- Good

Fund Family: BlackRock Fund Advisors
Fund Type: Energy/Natural Resources
Inception Date: June 24, 2008

Data Date	Investment Rating	Net Assets ($Mil)	Price	Performance Rating/Pts	Total Return Y-T-D	Risk Rating/Pts
12-15	B-	66.00	9.84	B / 8.2	3.92%	C+ / 6.1
2014	D+	66.00	9.68	C- / 3.6	-6.83%	C+ / 6.6
2013	D-	46.70	10.44	D+ / 2.5	44.15%	C / 4.5
2012	E+	26.40	7.17	E / 0.4	-11.82%	C / 4.4
2011	E+	32.00	8.54	E+ / 0.6	-43.76%	C / 4.3
2010	E+	50.60	15.84	E / 0.5	-27.64%	C- / 3.5

Major Rating Factors: Strong performance is the major factor driving the B- (Good) TheStreet.com Investment Rating for *iShares Global Clean Energy ETF. The fund currently has a performance rating of B (Good) based on an annualized return of 12.02% over the last three years and a total return of 3.92% year to date 2015. Factored into the performance evaluation is an expense ratio of 0.47% (very low).

The fund's risk rating is currently C+ (Fair). It carries a beta of 0.57, meaning the fund's expected move will be 5.7% for every 10% move in the market. Volatility, as measured by both the semi-deviation and a drawdown factor, is considered low. As of December 31, 2015, *iShares Global Clean Energy ETF traded at a premium of .61% above its net asset value, which is worse than its one-year historical average premium of .28%.

Diane Hsiung has been running the fund for 8 years and currently receives a manager quality ranking of 98 (0=worst, 99=best). If you desire only a moderate level of risk and strong performance, then this fund is an excellent option.

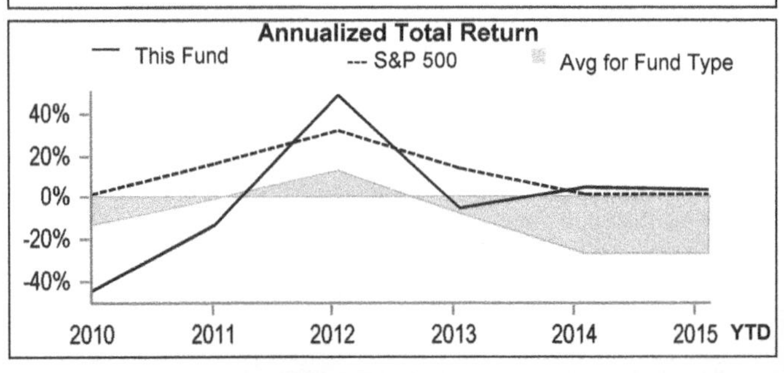

*iShares Global Consumer Discr (RXI) A Excellent

Fund Family: BlackRock Fund Advisors
Fund Type: Global
Inception Date: September 12, 2006

Data Date	Investment Rating	Net Assets ($Mil)	Price	Performance Rating/Pts	Total Return Y-T-D	Risk Rating/Pts
12-15	A	157.90	89.02	B+ / 8.9	6.74%	B- / 7.8
2014	B	157.90	85.14	B / 8.1	4.15%	C+ / 6.8
2013	B+	251.60	84.08	B+ / 8.8	33.65%	B- / 7.6
2012	B	162.80	61.71	B / 7.6	24.68%	B- / 7.8
2011	C	112.60	49.95	C / 5.3	-3.82%	B- / 7.8
2010	C+	130.60	53.41	C+ / 6.6	23.32%	C+ / 5.8

Major Rating Factors:
Strong performance is the major factor driving the A (Excellent) TheStreet.com Investment Rating for *iShares Global Consumer Discr. The fund currently has a performance rating of B+ (Good) based on an annualized return of 13.94% over the last three years and a total return of 6.74% year to date 2015. Factored into the performance evaluation is an expense ratio of 0.47% (very low).

The fund's risk rating is currently B- (Good). It carries a beta of 0.88, meaning the fund's expected move will be 8.8% for every 10% move in the market. Volatility, as measured by both the semi-deviation and a drawdown factor, is considered low. As of December 31, 2015, *iShares Global Consumer Discr traded at a discount of .34% below its net asset value, which is better than its one-year historical average premium of .02%.

Diane Hsiung has been running the fund for 8 years and currently receives a manager quality ranking of 94 (0=worst, 99=best). If you desire only a moderate level of risk and strong performance, then this fund is an excellent option.

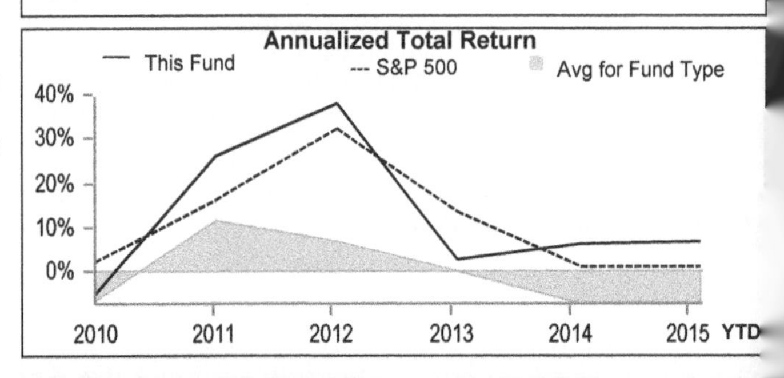

*iShares Global Consumer Staples (KXI) A+ Excellent

Fund Family: BlackRock Fund Advisors
Fund Type: Global
Inception Date: September 12, 2006

Data Date	Investment Rating	Net Assets ($Mil)	Price	Performance Rating/Pts	Total Return Y-T-D	Risk Rating/Pts
12-15	A+	600.90	93.03	B / 8.2	7.74%	B / 8.8
2014	C+	600.90	89.61	C+ / 6.5	7.94%	B- / 7.5
2013	B+	650.20	86.18	B- / 7.3	15.90%	B+ / 9.0
2012	C+	440.20	73.63	C+ / 5.6	19.05%	B / 8.9
2011	C+	465.70	66.56	C+ / 5.7	10.17%	B / 8.5
2010	C+	327.50	62.47	C / 5.4	13.19%	C+ / 6.9

Major Rating Factors:
Strong performance is the major factor driving the A+ (Excellent) TheStreet.com Investment Rating for *iShares Global Consumer Staples. The fund currently has a performance rating of B (Good) based on an annualized return of 10.26% over the last three years and a total return of 7.74% year to date 2015. Factored into the performance evaluation is an expense ratio of 0.47% (very low).

The fund's risk rating is currently B (Good). It carries a beta of 0.72, meaning the fund's expected move will be 7.2% for every 10% move in the market. Volatility, as measured by both the semi-deviation and a drawdown factor, is considered low. As of December 31, 2015, *iShares Global Consumer Staples traded at a discount of .20% below its net asset value, which is better than its one-year historical average premium of .01%.

Diane Hsiung has been running the fund for 8 years and currently receives a manager quality ranking of 92 (0=worst, 99=best). If you desire only a moderate level of risk and strong performance, then this fund is an excellent option.

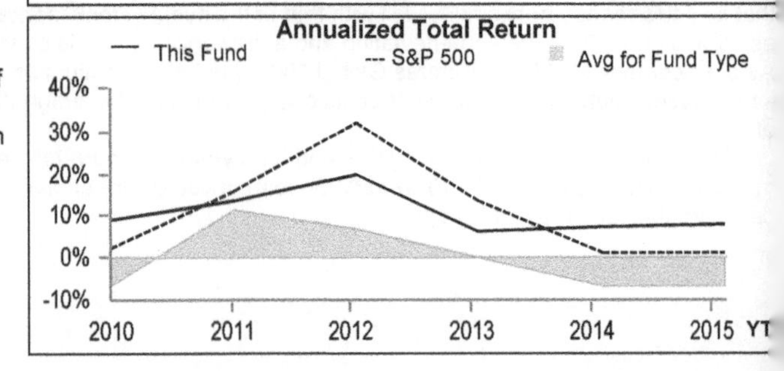

*iShares Global Energy (IXC) | D | Weak

Fund Family: BlackRock Fund Advisors
Fund Type: Energy/Natural Resources
Inception Date: November 12, 2001

Data Date	Investment Rating	Net Assets ($Mil)	Price	Performance Rating/Pts	Total Return Y-T-D	Risk Rating/Pts
12-15	D	1,001.00	28.03	D / 2.0	-20.67%	C / 5.0
2014	D+	1,001.00	37.19	D / 2.2	-10.44%	C+ / 6.9
2013	C	991.60	43.22	C / 5.4	11.27%	B- / 7.5
2012	D+	990.70	38.25	D+ / 2.5	5.33%	B- / 7.4
2011	C-	1,123.40	38.19	C / 4.3	1.57%	B- / 7.5
2010	D-	1,313.20	39.06	C- / 3.3	11.85%	D+ / 2.8

Major Rating Factors:
Disappointing performance is the major factor driving the D (Weak) TheStreet.com Investment Rating for *iShares Global Energy. The fund currently has a performance rating of D (Weak) based on an annualized return of -7.52% over the last three years and a total return of -20.67% year to date 2015. Factored into the performance evaluation is an expense ratio of 0.47% (very low).

The fund's risk rating is currently C (Fair). It carries a beta of 0.94, meaning that its performance tracks fairly well with that of the overall stock market. Volatility, as measured by both the semi-deviation and a drawdown factor, is considered average. As of December 31, 2015, *iShares Global Energy traded at a premium of .04% above its net asset value, which is better than its one-year historical average premium of .06%.

Diane Hsiung has been running the fund for 8 years and currently receives a manager quality ranking of 41 (0=worst, 99=best). This fund offers an average level of risk but investors looking for strong performance will be frustrated.

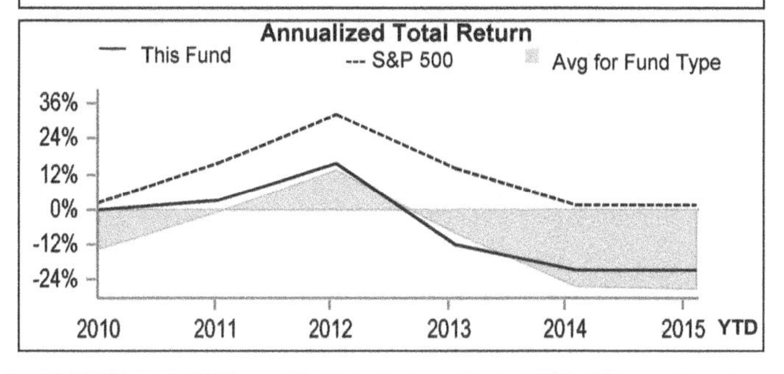

*iShares Global Financials (IXG) | C+ | Fair

Fund Family: BlackRock Fund Advisors
Fund Type: Financial Services
Inception Date: November 12, 2001

Data Date	Investment Rating	Net Assets ($Mil)	Price	Performance Rating/Pts	Total Return Y-T-D	Risk Rating/Pts
12-15	C+	312.60	52.99	C+ / 6.4	-2.34%	B- / 7.1
2014	B+	312.60	56.46	B- / 7.5	3.63%	B / 8.3
2013	C+	328.30	56.19	B- / 7.0	21.65%	B- / 7.2
2012	C	219.50	45.66	C / 5.4	32.05%	B- / 7.0
2011	D	147.40	35.78	D / 2.0	-19.50%	C+ / 6.8
2010	D-	287.80	46.13	E+ / 0.8	3.97%	C / 4.4

Major Rating Factors: Middle of the road best describes *iShares Global Financials whose TheStreet.com Investment Rating is currently a C+ (Fair). The fund currently has a performance rating of C+ (Fair) based on an annualized return of 7.15% over the last three years and a total return of -2.34% year to date 2015. Factored into the performance evaluation is an expense ratio of 0.47% (very low).

The fund's risk rating is currently B- (Good). It carries a beta of 0.93, meaning that its performance tracks fairly well with that of the overall stock market. Volatility, as measured by both the semi-deviation and a drawdown factor, is considered low. As of December 31, 2015, *iShares Global Financials traded at a premium of .34% above its net asset value, which is worse than its one-year historical average discount of .03%.

Diane Hsiung has been running the fund for 8 years and currently receives a manager quality ranking of 28 (0=worst, 99=best). If you desire an average level of risk, then this fund may be an option.

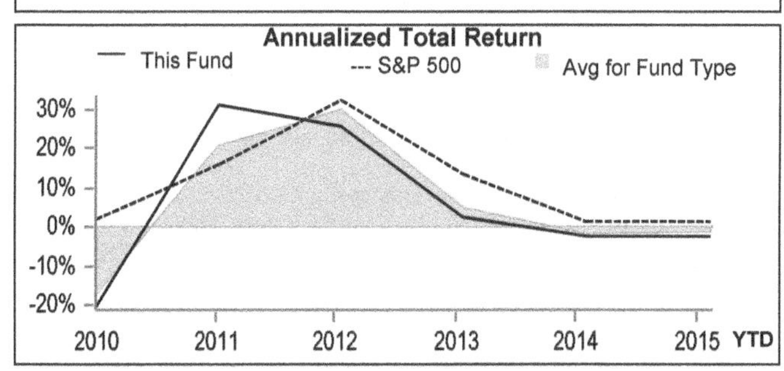

*iShares Global Healthcare (IXJ) | A+ | Excellent

Fund Family: BlackRock Fund Advisors
Fund Type: Health
Inception Date: November 13, 2001

Data Date	Investment Rating	Net Assets ($Mil)	Price	Performance Rating/Pts	Total Return Y-T-D	Risk Rating/Pts
12-15	A+	1,264.90	102.62	A / 9.4	7.57%	B / 8.2
2014	A+	1,264.90	99.56	A- / 9.0	17.62%	B / 8.6
2013	A	1,007.90	86.10	A- / 9.0	32.58%	B / 8.3
2012	C+	572.70	64.50	C+ / 5.7	21.92%	B / 8.3
2011	C	530.40	56.12	C / 4.4	10.62%	B- / 7.9
2010	C-	477.00	51.76	D+ / 2.4	1.91%	C+ / 6.8

Major Rating Factors:
Exceptional performance is the major factor driving the A+ (Excellent) TheStreet.com Investment Rating for *iShares Global Healthcare. The fund currently has a performance rating of A (Excellent) based on an annualized return of 18.92% over the last three years and a total return of 7.57% year to date 2015. Factored into the performance evaluation is an expense ratio of 0.47% (very low).

The fund's risk rating is currently B (Good). It carries a beta of 0.88, meaning the fund's expected move will be 8.8% for every 10% move in the market. Volatility, as measured by both the semi-deviation and a drawdown factor, is considered low. As of December 31, 2015, *iShares Global Healthcare traded at a discount of .30% below its net asset value, which is better than its one-year historical average premium of .04%.

Diane Hsiung has been running the fund for 8 years and currently receives a manager quality ranking of 90 (0=worst, 99=best). If you desire only a moderate level of risk and strong performance, then this fund is an excellent option.

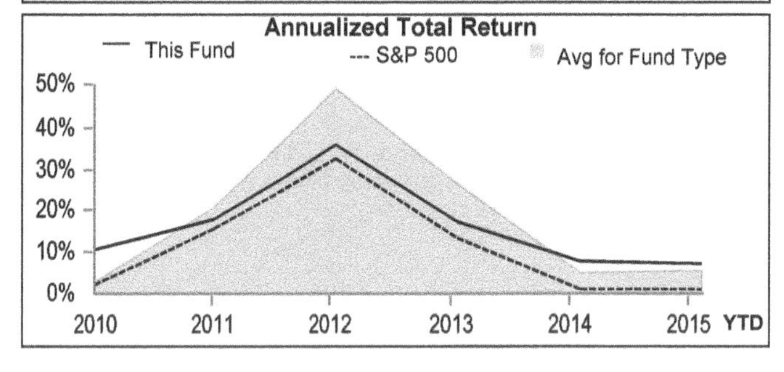

*iShares Global Industrials (EXI) B+ Good

Fund Family: BlackRock Fund Advisors
Fund Type: Global
Inception Date: September 12, 2006

Major Rating Factors: Strong performance is the major factor driving the B+ (Good) TheStreet.com Investment Rating for *iShares Global Industrials. The fund currently has a performance rating of B- (Good) based on an annualized return of 8.46% over the last three years and a total return of -1.44% year to date 2015. Factored into the performance evaluation is an expense ratio of 0.47% (very low).

The fund's risk rating is currently B (Good). It carries a beta of 0.84, meaning the fund's expected move will be 8.4% for every 10% move in the market. Volatility, as measured by both the semi-deviation and a drawdown factor, is considered low. As of December 31, 2015, *iShares Global Industrials traded at a discount of .53% below its net asset value, which is better than its one-year historical average discount of .12%.

Diane Hsiung has been running the fund for 8 years and currently receives a manager quality ranking of 89 (0=worst, 99=best). If you desire only a moderate level of risk and strong performance, then this fund is an excellent option.

Data Date	Investment Rating	Net Assets ($Mil)	Price	Performance Rating/Pts	Total Return Y-T-D	Risk Rating/Pts
12-15	B+	280.90	67.62	B- / 7.0	-1.44%	B / 8.5
2014	B	280.90	70.51	C+ / 6.6	1.99%	B / 8.8
2013	B	319.30	71.41	B / 7.7	26.97%	B- / 7.6
2012	C-	153.20	54.89	C / 4.5	16.08%	B- / 7.5
2011	C-	167.10	48.23	C- / 4.1	-7.32%	B- / 7.4
2010	C-	199.00	53.85	C / 4.6	23.33%	C / 5.3

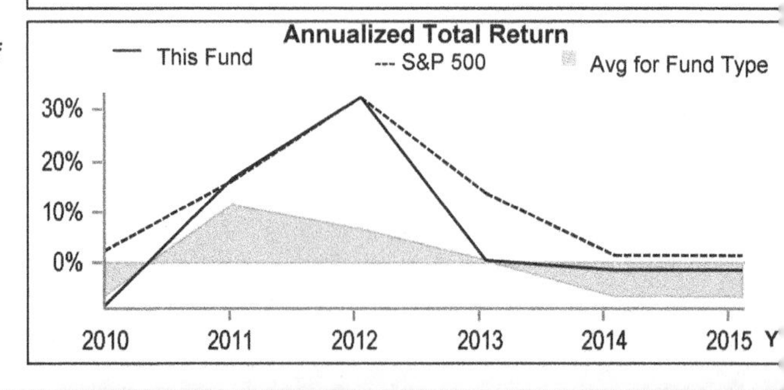

*iShares Global Inflation-Linked (GTIP) D+ Weak

Fund Family: BlackRock Fund Advisors
Fund Type: Global
Inception Date: May 18, 2011

Major Rating Factors:
Disappointing performance is the major factor driving the D+ (Weak) TheStreet.com Investment Rating for *iShares Global Inflation-Linked. The fund currently has a performance rating of D+ (Weak) based on an annualized return of -3.76% over the last three years and a total return of -7.15% year to date 2015. Factored into the performance evaluation is an expense ratio of 0.40% (very low).

The fund's risk rating is currently C+ (Fair). It carries a beta of 0.72, meaning the fund's expected move will be 7.2% for every 10% move in the market. Volatility, as measured by both the semi-deviation and a drawdown factor, is considered low. As of December 31, 2015, *iShares Global Inflation-Linked traded at a premium of .15% above its net asset value, which is worse than its one-year historical average premium of .03%.

James J. Mauro has been running the fund for 5 years and currently receives a manager quality ranking of 58 (0=worst, 99=best). This fund offers only a moderate level of risk but investors looking for strong performance are still waiting.

Data Date	Investment Rating	Net Assets ($Mil)	Price	Performance Rating/Pts	Total Return Y-T-D	Risk Rating/Pts
12-15	D+	25.20	46.02	D+ / 2.9	-7.15%	C+ / 6.6
2014	D+	25.20	49.79	C- / 3.1	3.09%	C+ / 6.7
2013	D+	24.90	49.69	D / 1.7	-6.72%	B / 8.7
2012	B	16.00	54.08	C+ / 6.0	11.11%	B+ / 9.2

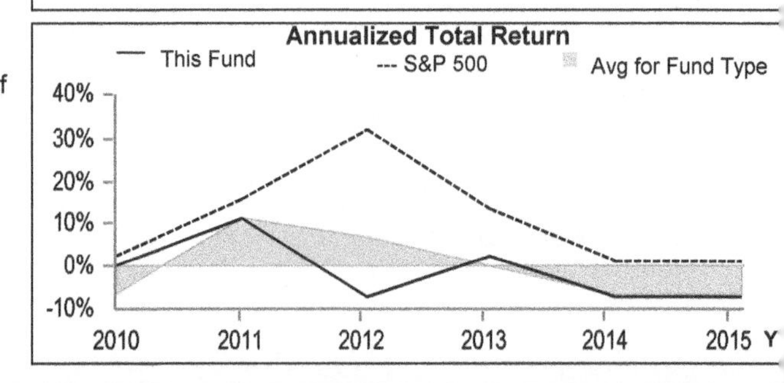

*iShares Global Infrastructure (IGF) C+ Fair

Fund Family: BlackRock Fund Advisors
Fund Type: Global
Inception Date: December 10, 2007

Major Rating Factors: Middle of the road best describes *iShares Global Infrastructure whose TheStreet.com Investment Rating is currently a C+ (Fair). The fund currently has a performance rating of C (Fair) based on an annualized return of 3.60% over the last three years and a total return of -10.73% year to date 2015. Factored into the performance evaluation is an expense ratio of 0.47% (very low).

The fund's risk rating is currently B (Good). It carries a beta of 0.71, meaning the fund's expected move will be 7.1% for every 10% move in the market. Volatility, as measured by both the semi-deviation and a drawdown factor, is considered low. As of December 31, 2015, *iShares Global Infrastructure traded at a discount of .44% below its net asset value, which is better than its one-year historical average premium of .05%.

Diane Hsiung has been running the fund for 8 years and currently receives a manager quality ranking of 69 (0=worst, 99=best). If you desire an average level of risk, then this fund may be an option.

Data Date	Investment Rating	Net Assets ($Mil)	Price	Performance Rating/Pts	Total Return Y-T-D	Risk Rating/Pts
12-15	C+	977.00	35.94	C / 4.7	-10.73%	B / 8.2
2014	B	977.00	42.15	C+ / 6.1	12.88%	B / 8.8
2013	C+	671.50	38.94	C+ / 5.9	10.16%	B / 8.4
2012	C-	357.10	35.71	C- / 3.1	13.81%	B / 8.2
2011	C-	415.10	33.20	C- / 3.3	-1.41%	B- / 7.8
2010	D	468.90	35.06	D- / 1.3	7.05%	C+ / 5.7

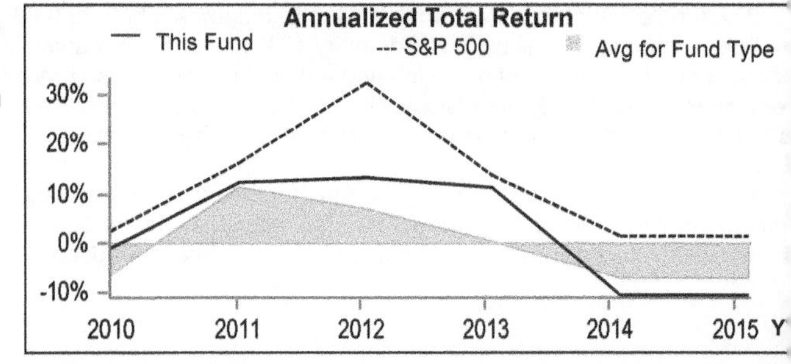

* Denotes ETF Fund

*iShares Global Materials (MXI) D+ Weak

Fund Family: BlackRock Fund Advisors
Fund Type: Global
Inception Date: September 12, 2006

Major Rating Factors:
Disappointing performance is the major factor driving the D+ (Weak) TheStreet.com Investment Rating for *iShares Global Materials. The fund currently has a performance rating of D (Weak) based on an annualized return of -8.10% over the last three years and a total return of -15.56% year to date 2015. Factored into the performance evaluation is an expense ratio of 0.47% (very low).

The fund's risk rating is currently B- (Good). It carries a beta of 1.03, meaning that its performance tracks fairly well with that of the overall stock market. Volatility, as measured by both the semi-deviation and a drawdown factor, is considered low. As of December 31, 2015, *iShares Global Materials traded at a discount of .60% below its net asset value, which is better than its one-year historical average discount of .09%.

Diane Hsiung has been running the fund for 8 years and currently receives a manager quality ranking of 13 (0=worst, 99=best). This fund offers only a moderate level of risk but investors looking for strong performance are still waiting.

Data Date	Investment Rating	Net Assets ($Mil)	Price	Perfor-mance Rating/Pts	Total Return Y-T-D	Risk Rating/Pts
12-15	D+	357.30	45.01	D / 2.1	-15.56%	B- / 7.1
2014	C-	357.30	55.91	D+ / 2.4	-7.06%	B- / 7.8
2013	D	401.30	62.33	D+ / 2.4	-0.86%	C+ / 6.8
2012	D	486.00	62.45	D+ / 2.3	7.07%	C+ / 6.6
2011	C-	476.20	57.20	C- / 4.2	-16.15%	C+ / 6.5
2010	C	777.40	73.25	C+ / 6.0	19.99%	C / 4.6

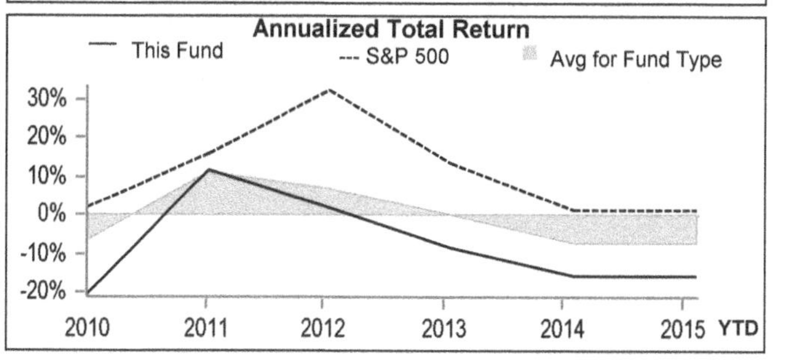

*iShares Global REIT ETF (REET) C+ Fair

Fund Family: BlackRock Fund Advisors
Fund Type: Growth and Income
Inception Date: July 8, 2014

Major Rating Factors: Middle of the road best describes *iShares Global REIT ETF whose TheStreet.com Investment Rating is currently a C+ (Fair). The fund currently has a performance rating of C+ (Fair) based on an annualized return of 0.00% over the last three years and a total return of 1.09% year to date 2015. Factored into the performance evaluation is an expense ratio of 0.14% (very low).

The fund's risk rating is currently C+ (Fair). It carries a beta of 0.00, meaning the fund's expected move will be 0.0% for every 10% move in the market. Volatility, as measured by both the semi-deviation and a drawdown factor, is considered low. As of December 31, 2015, *iShares Global REIT ETF traded at a premium of .96% above its net asset value, which is worse than its one-year historical average premium of .51%.

Jennifer F.Y. Hsui has been running the fund for 2 years and currently receives a manager quality ranking of 76 (0=worst, 99=best). If you desire an average level of risk, then this fund may be an option.

Data Date	Investment Rating	Net Assets ($Mil)	Price	Perfor-mance Rating/Pts	Total Return Y-T-D	Risk Rating/Pts
12-15	C+	0.00	25.25	C+ / 6.3	1.09%	C+ / 6.6

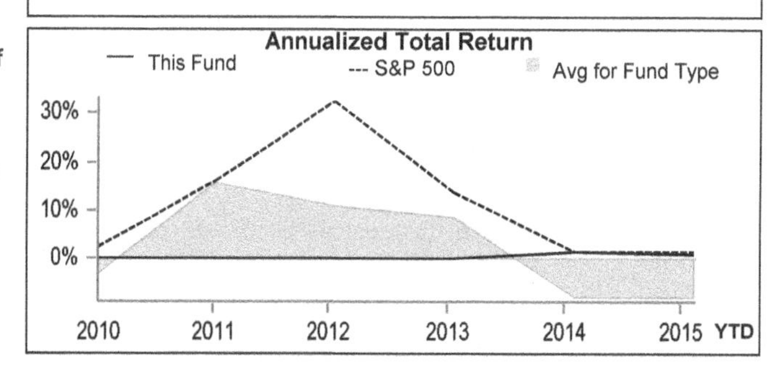

*iShares Global Tech (IXN) A+ Excellent

Fund Family: BlackRock Fund Advisors
Fund Type: Global
Inception Date: November 12, 2001

Major Rating Factors:
Strong performance is the major factor driving the A+ (Excellent) TheStreet.com Investment Rating for *iShares Global Tech. The fund currently has a performance rating of B+ (Good) based on an annualized return of 14.00% over the last three years and a total return of 4.87% year to date 2015. Factored into the performance evaluation is an expense ratio of 0.47% (very low).

The fund's risk rating is currently B (Good). It carries a beta of 0.73, meaning the fund's expected move will be 7.3% for every 10% move in the market. Volatility, as measured by both the semi-deviation and a drawdown factor, is considered low. As of December 31, 2015, *iShares Global Tech traded at a discount of .34% below its net asset value, which is better than its one-year historical average discount of .01%.

Diane Hsiung has been running the fund for 8 years and currently receives a manager quality ranking of 95 (0=worst, 99=best). If you desire only a moderate level of risk and strong performance, then this fund is an excellent option.

Data Date	Investment Rating	Net Assets ($Mil)	Price	Perfor-mance Rating/Pts	Total Return Y-T-D	Risk Rating/Pts
12-15	A+	749.70	97.52	B+ / 8.9	4.87%	B / 8.6
2014	B	749.70	94.88	B / 7.9	17.14%	B- / 7.0
2013	B-	702.20	83.29	B- / 7.3	21.00%	B- / 7.5
2012	D+	484.00	67.31	C- / 3.9	16.08%	C+ / 6.7
2011	C	475.80	58.71	C+ / 5.7	-3.22%	B- / 7.1
2010	C-	601.00	61.42	C / 4.7	10.48%	C / 5.4

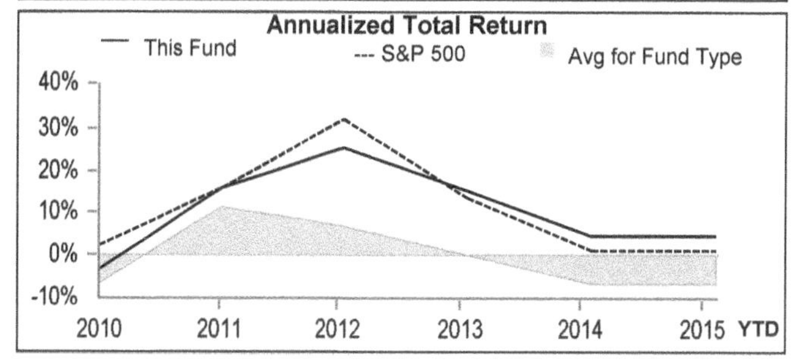

*iShares Global Telecom (IXP) B Good

Fund Family: BlackRock Fund Advisors
Fund Type: Global
Inception Date: November 12, 2001

Major Rating Factors: *iShares Global Telecom receives a TheStreet.com Investment Rating of B (Good). The fund currently has a performance rating of C+ (Fair) based on an annualized return of 6.81% over the last three years and a total return of 2.01% year to date 2015. Factored into the performance evaluation is an expense ratio of 0.47% (very low).

The fund's risk rating is currently B (Good). It carries a beta of 0.83, meaning the fund's expected move will be 8.3% for every 10% move in the market. Volatility, as measured by both the semi-deviation and a drawdown factor, is considered low. As of December 31, 2015, *iShares Global Telecom traded at a discount of .34% below its net asset value, which is better than its one-year historical average discount of .08%.

Diane Hsiung has been running the fund for 8 years and currently receives a manager quality ranking of 84 (0=worst, 99=best). If you desire an average level of risk, then this fund may be an option.

Data Date	Investment Rating	Net Assets ($Mil)	Price	Perfor-mance Rating/Pts	Total Return Y-T-D	Risk Rating/Pts
12-15	B	468.70	57.85	C+ / 6.6	2.01%	B / 8.0
2014	C+	468.70	60.09	C / 5.1	-0.12%	B / 8.3
2013	B	603.80	68.31	B- / 7.0	19.81%	B / 8.7
2012	C-	475.30	57.17	C- / 3.4	12.60%	B / 8.6
2011	C-	440.60	55.79	C- / 3.5	-0.66%	B / 8.5
2010	D+	409.50	58.27	D+ / 2.3	11.74%	C+ / 6.4

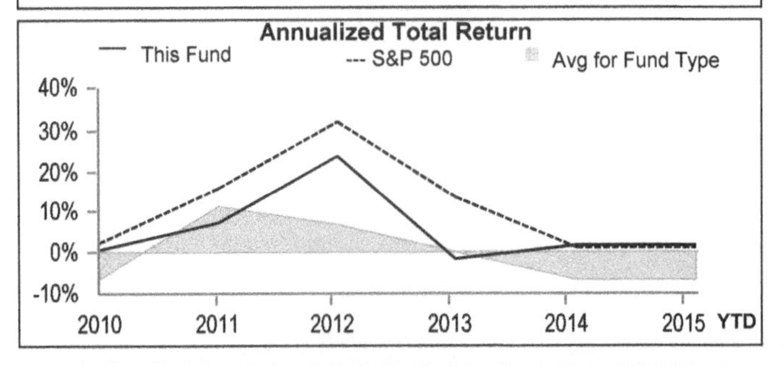

*iShares Global Timber&Forestry E (WOOD) C+ Fair

Fund Family: BlackRock Fund Advisors
Fund Type: Global
Inception Date: June 24, 2008

Major Rating Factors: Middle of the road best describes *iShares Global Timber&Forestry E whose TheStreet.com Investment Rating is currently a C+ (Fair). The fund currently has a performance rating of C (Fair) based on an annualized return of 3.08% over the last three years and a total return of -6.74% year to date 2015. Factored into the performance evaluation is an expense ratio of 0.47% (very low).

The fund's risk rating is currently B (Good). It carries a beta of 0.79, meaning the fund's expected move will be 7.9% for every 10% move in the market. Volatility, as measured by both the semi-deviation and a drawdown factor, is considered low. As of December 31, 2015, *iShares Global Timber&Forestry E traded at a discount of .41% below its net asset value, which is better than its one-year historical average discount of .14%.

Diane Hsiung has been running the fund for 8 years and currently receives a manager quality ranking of 67 (0=worst, 99=best). If you desire an average level of risk, then this fund may be an option.

Data Date	Investment Rating	Net Assets ($Mil)	Price	Perfor-mance Rating/Pts	Total Return Y-T-D	Risk Rating/Pts
12-15	C+	281.90	48.03	C / 5.2	-6.74%	B / 8.0
2014	B-	281.90	52.97	C+ / 6.5	3.22%	B / 8.2
2013	C	360.90	52.88	C+ / 5.7	13.77%	B- / 7.2
2012	C-	226.90	45.10	C / 4.5	22.86%	B- / 7.1
2011	C-	142.00	37.19	C- / 3.8	-16.43%	B- / 7.0
2010	B+	166.70	44.95	A- / 9.1	16.19%	C / 5.0

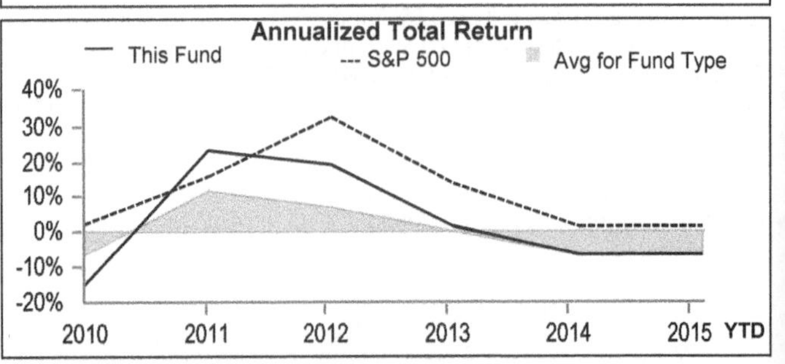

*iShares Global Utilities (JXI) B Good

Fund Family: BlackRock Fund Advisors
Fund Type: Utilities
Inception Date: September 12, 2006

Major Rating Factors: *iShares Global Utilities receives a TheStreet.com Investment Rating of B (Good). The fund currently has a performance rating of C+ (Fair) based on an annualized return of 6.33% over the last three years and a total return of -5.78% year to date 2015. Factored into the performance evaluation is an expense ratio of 0.47% (very low).

The fund's risk rating is currently B (Good). It carries a beta of 0.71, meaning the fund's expected move will be 7.1% for every 10% move in the market. Volatility, as measured by both the semi-deviation and a drawdown factor, is considered low. As of December 31, 2015, *iShares Global Utilities traded at a discount of .47% below its net asset value, which is better than its one-year historical average discount of .08%.

Diane Hsiung has been running the fund for 8 years and currently receives a manager quality ranking of 52 (0=worst, 99=best). If you desire an average level of risk, then this fund may be an option.

Data Date	Investment Rating	Net Assets ($Mil)	Price	Perfor-mance Rating/Pts	Total Return Y-T-D	Risk Rating/Pts
12-15	B	232.00	44.02	C+ / 6.2	-5.78%	B / 8.5
2014	C+	232.00	49.17	C+ / 6.1	17.30%	B- / 7.2
2013	C	213.70	44.18	C / 4.5	8.71%	B / 8.6
2012	D+	235.00	41.23	D- / 1.4	5.86%	B / 8.4
2011	D+	238.40	41.90	D / 1.9	-3.87%	B / 8.0
2010	D	252.70	45.08	E+ / 0.9	-1.70%	C+ / 6.3

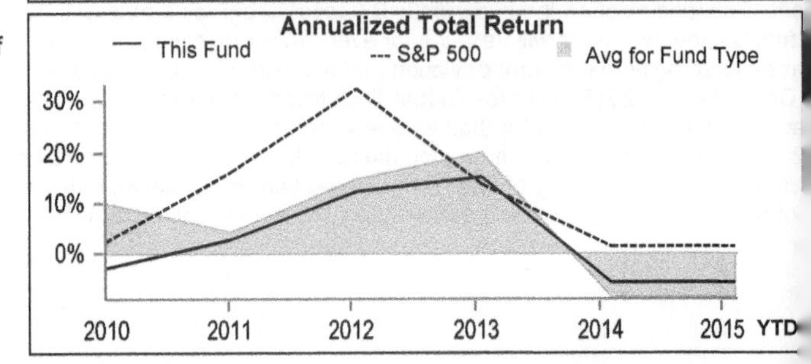

*iShares Gold Trust (IAU) D Weak

Fund Family: BlackRock Fund Advisors
Fund Type: Precious Metals
Inception Date: January 21, 2005

Major Rating Factors:
Disappointing performance is the major factor driving the D (Weak) TheStreet.com Investment Rating for *iShares Gold Trust. The fund currently has a performance rating of D- (Weak) based on an annualized return of -14.05% over the last three years and a total return of -11.04% year to date 2015. Factored into the performance evaluation is an expense ratio of 0.25% (very low).

The fund's risk rating is currently C+ (Fair). It carries a beta of 0.92, meaning that its performance tracks fairly well with that of the overall stock market. Volatility, as measured by both the semi-deviation and a drawdown factor, is considered low. As of December 31, 2015, *iShares Gold Trust traded at a discount of .20% below its net asset value, which is better than its one-year historical average premium of .11%.

Index Strategies Group has been running the fund for 11 years and currently receives a manager quality ranking of 53 (0=worst, 99=best). This fund offers only a moderate level of risk but investors looking for strong performance are still waiting.

Data Date	Investment Rating	Net Assets ($Mil)	Price	Performance Rating/Pts	Total Return Y-T-D	Risk Rating/Pts
12-15	D	6,351.50	10.23	D- / 1.4	-11.04%	C+ / 6.3
2014	D-	6,351.50	11.44	D- / 1.4	-4.75%	C / 4.5
2013	D	6,271.00	11.68	D- / 1.5	-25.46%	C+ / 6.4
2012	D-	11,645.30	16.28	C / 4.3	1.25%	D / 1.9
2011	D+	8,416.90	15.23	B / 7.6	17.74%	D / 1.9
2010	C-	5,316.70	13.90	B+ / 8.9	29.46%	D- / 1.0

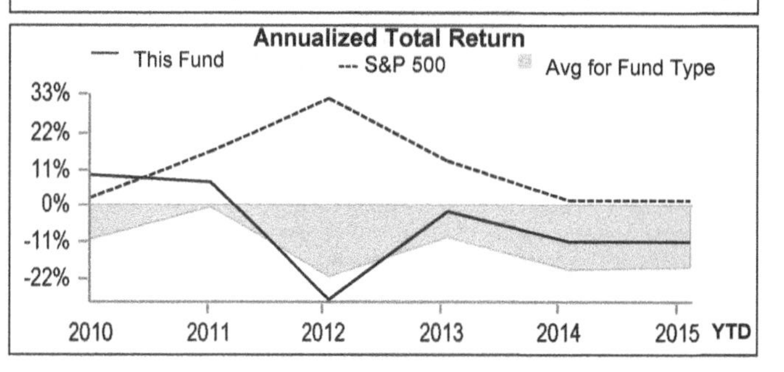

*iShares Govt/Credit Bond ETF (GBF) C Fair

Fund Family: BlackRock Fund Advisors
Fund Type: US Government/Agency
Inception Date: January 5, 2007

Major Rating Factors: Middle of the road best describes *iShares Govt/Credit Bond ETF whose TheStreet.com Investment Rating is currently a C (Fair). The fund currently has a performance rating of C (Fair) based on an annualized return of 1.25% over the last three years and a total return of -0.24% year to date 2015. Factored into the performance evaluation is an expense ratio of 0.20% (very low).

The fund's risk rating is currently B- (Good). It carries a beta of 0.29, meaning the fund's expected move will be 2.9% for every 10% move in the market. Volatility, as measured by both the semi-deviation and a drawdown factor, is considered low. As of December 31, 2015, *iShares Govt/Credit Bond ETF traded at a premium of .21% above its net asset value, which is worse than its one-year historical average premium of .19%.

Scott F. Radell has been running the fund for 6 years and currently receives a manager quality ranking of 72 (0=worst, 99=best). If you desire an average level of risk, then this fund may be an option.

Data Date	Investment Rating	Net Assets ($Mil)	Price	Performance Rating/Pts	Total Return Y-T-D	Risk Rating/Pts
12-15	C	123.70	111.70	C / 4.9	-0.24%	B- / 7.8
2014	C-	123.70	114.51	C- / 3.8	6.31%	B- / 7.6
2013	C	190.20	110.00	C- / 3.7	-1.94%	B+ / 9.6
2012	C	190.20	114.87	D+ / 2.5	3.29%	B+ / 9.7
2011	C+	113.10	113.83	C- / 3.5	9.33%	B+ / 9.7
2010	B	129.00	107.39	C / 4.5	5.72%	B / 8.8

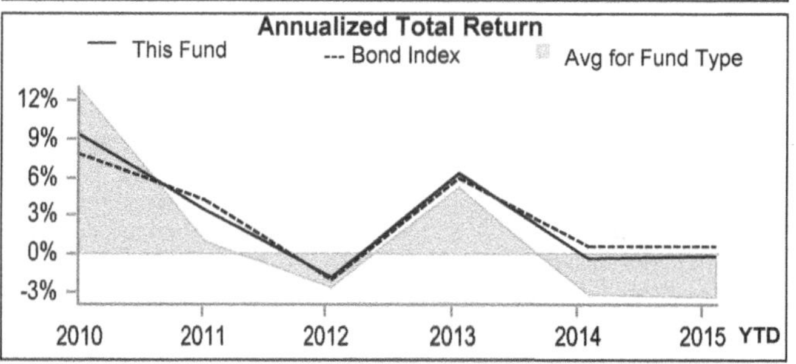

*iShares iBonds Dec 2016 Corporat (IBDF) D- Weak

Fund Family: BlackRock Fund Advisors
Fund Type: Corporate - Investment Grade
Inception Date: May 28, 2014

Major Rating Factors: *iShares iBonds Dec 2016 Corporat has adopted a very risky asset allocation strategy and currently receives an overall TheStreet.com Investment Rating of D- (Weak). The fund has a high level of volatility, as measured by both semi -deviation and drawdown factors. It carries a beta of 0.00, meaning the fund's expected move will be 0.0% for every 10% move in the market. As of December 31, 2015, *iShares iBonds Dec 2016 Corporat traded at a premium of .68% above its net asset value, which is worse than its one-year historical average premium of .53%. Unfortunately, the high level of risk (E-, Very Weak) has only provided investors with average performance.

The fund's performance rating is currently C (Fair). It has registered an annualized return of 0.00% over the last three years and is up 1.24% year to date 2015.

James J. Mauro currently receives a manager quality ranking of 79 (0=worst, 99=best). If you are comfortable owning a very high risk investment, then this fund may be an option.

Data Date	Investment Rating	Net Assets ($Mil)	Price	Performance Rating/Pts	Total Return Y-T-D	Risk Rating/Pts
12-15	D-	10.00	25.17	C / 5.0	1.24%	E- / 0.1

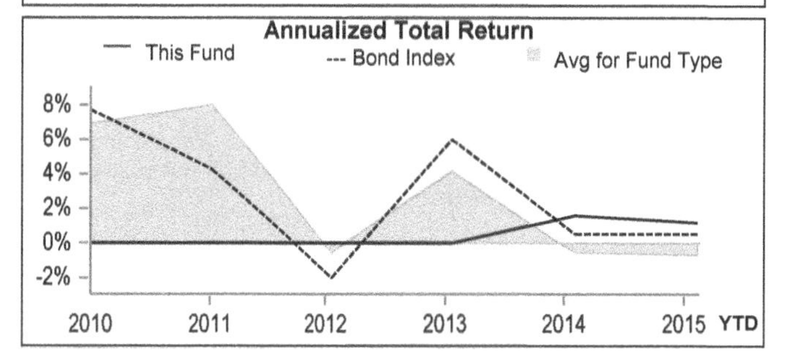

*iShares iBonds Dec 2018 Corporat (IBDH) D- Weak

Fund Family: BlackRock Fund Advisors
Fund Type: Corporate - Investment Grade
Inception Date: May 28, 2014

Data Date	Investment Rating	Net Assets ($Mil)	Price	Perfor-mance Rating/Pts	Total Return Y-T-D	Risk Rating/Pts
12-15	D-	9.90	24.98	C / 4.7	1.36%	E- / 0.1

Major Rating Factors: *iShares iBonds Dec 2018 Corporat has adopted a very risky asset allocation strategy and currently receives an overall TheStreet.com Investment Rating of D- (Weak). The fund has a high level of volatility, as measured by both semi -deviation and drawdown factors. It carries a beta of 0.00, meaning the fund's expected move will be 0.0% for every 10% move in the market. As of December 31, 2015, *iShares iBonds Dec 2018 Corporat traded at a premium of .52% above its net asset value, which is better than its one-year historical average premium of .64%. Unfortunately, the high level of risk (E-, Very Weak) has only provided investors with average performance.

The fund's performance rating is currently C (Fair). It has registered an annualized return of 0.00% over the last three years and is up 1.36% year to date 2015.

James J. Mauro has been running the fund for 2 years and currently receives a manager quality ranking of 80 (0=worst, 99=best). If you are comfortable owning a very high risk investment, then this fund may be an option.

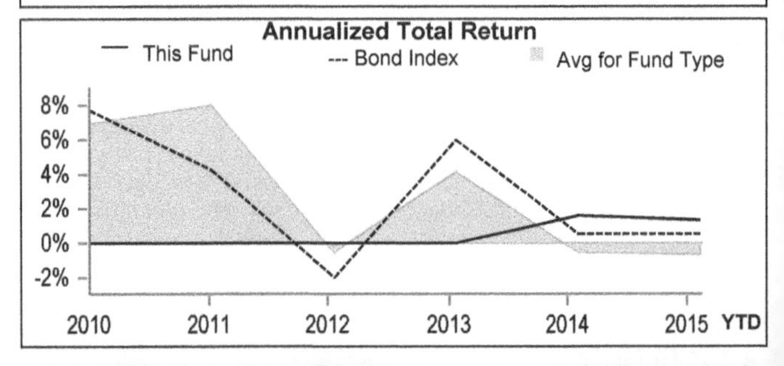

*iShares iBonds Dec 2020 Corporat (IBDL) D- Weak

Fund Family: BlackRock Fund Advisors
Fund Type: Corporate - Investment Grade
Inception Date: December 2, 2014

Data Date	Investment Rating	Net Assets ($Mil)	Price	Perfor-mance Rating/Pts	Total Return Y-T-D	Risk Rating/Pts
12-15	D-	0.00	24.95	C / 4.8	1.89%	E- / 0.2

Major Rating Factors: *iShares iBonds Dec 2020 Corporat has adopted a very risky asset allocation strategy and currently receives an overall TheStreet.com Investment Rating of D- (Weak). The fund has a high level of volatility, as measured by both semi -deviation and drawdown factors. It carries a beta of 0.00, meaning the fund's expected move will be 0.0% for every 10% move in the market. As of December 31, 2015, *iShares iBonds Dec 2020 Corporat traded at a premium of .56% above its net asset value, which is better than its one-year historical average premium of .69%. Unfortunately, the high level of risk (E-, Very Weak) has only provided investors with average performance.

The fund's performance rating is currently C (Fair). It has registered an annualized return of 0.00% over the last three years and is up 1.89% year to date 2015.

James J. Mauro has been running the fund for 2 years and currently receives a manager quality ranking of 83 (0=worst, 99=best). If you are comfortable owning a very high risk investment, then this fund may be an option.

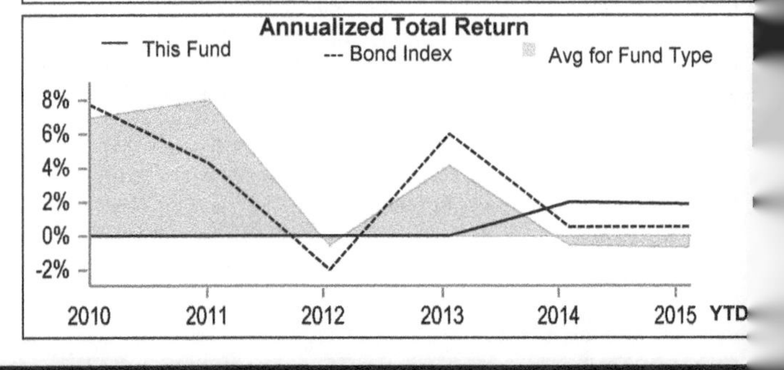

*iShares iBonds Mar 2016 Corp ex- (IBCB) B- Good

Fund Family: BlackRock Fund Advisors
Fund Type: Corporate - Investment Grade
Inception Date: April 17, 2013

Data Date	Investment Rating	Net Assets ($Mil)	Price	Perfor-mance Rating/Pts	Total Return Y-T-D	Risk Rating/Pts
12-15	B-	34.90	99.35	C / 4.4	0.04%	B+ / 9.9
2014	C-	34.90	99.61	D+ / 2.9	0.77%	B / 8.4

Major Rating Factors: *iShares iBonds Mar 2016 Corp ex- receives a TheStreet.com Investment Rating of B- (Good). The fund currently has a performance rating of C (Fair) based on an annualized return of 0.00% over the last three years and a total return of 0.04% year to date 2015. Factored into the performance evaluation is an expense ratio of 0.10% (very low).

The fund's risk rating is currently B+ (Good). It carries a beta of 0.00, meaning the fund's expected move will be 0.0% for every 10% move in the market. Volatility, as measured by both the semi-deviation and a drawdown factor, is considered very low. As of December 31, 2015, *iShares iBonds Mar 2016 Corp ex- traded at a discount of .12% below its net asset value.

James J. Mauro has been running the fund for 3 years and currently receives a manager quality ranking of 70 (0=worst, 99=best). If you desire an average level of risk, then this fund may be an option.

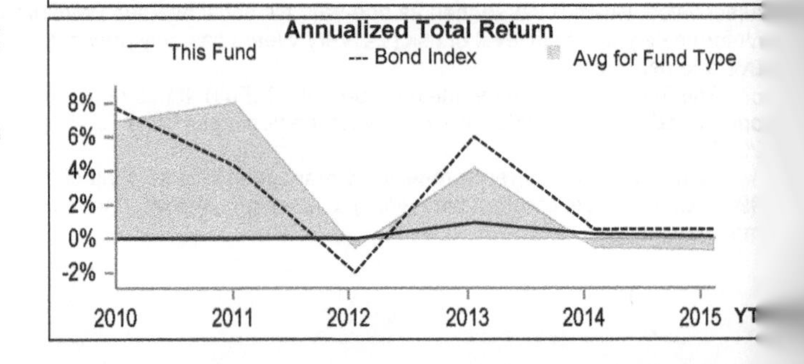

*iShares iBonds Mar 2016 Corporat (IBDA) C Fair

Fund Family: BlackRock Fund Advisors
Fund Type: Corporate - Investment Grade
Inception Date: July 9, 2013

Data Date	Investment Rating	Net Assets ($Mil)	Price	Perfor-mance Rating/Pts	Total Return Y-T-D	Risk Rating/Pts
12-15	C	40.40	100.90	C / 4.5	0.35%	B / 8.2
2014	C-	40.40	101.06	C- / 3.0	0.92%	B / 8.3

Major Rating Factors: Middle of the road best describes *iShares iBonds Mar 2016 Corporat whose TheStreet.com Investment Rating is currently a C (Fair). The fund currently has a performance rating of C (Fair) based on an annualized return of 0.00% over the last three years and a total return of 0.35% year to date 2015. Factored into the performance evaluation is an expense ratio of 0.07% (very low).

The fund's risk rating is currently B (Good). It carries a beta of 0.00, meaning the fund's expected move will be 0.0% for every 10% move in the market. Volatility, as measured by both the semi-deviation and a drawdown factor, is considered low. As of December 31, 2015, *iShares iBonds Mar 2016 Corporat traded at a premium of .13% above its net asset value, which is worse than its one-year historical average premium of .06%.

James J. Mauro has been running the fund for 3 years and currently receives a manager quality ranking of 71 (0=worst, 99=best). If you desire an average level of risk, then this fund may be an option.

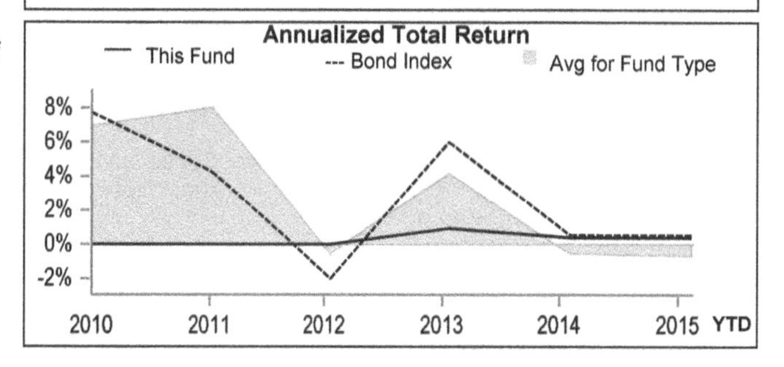

*iShares iBonds Mar 2018 Corp ex- (IBCC) C+ Fair

Fund Family: BlackRock Fund Advisors
Fund Type: Corporate - Investment Grade
Inception Date: April 17, 2013

Data Date	Investment Rating	Net Assets ($Mil)	Price	Perfor-mance Rating/Pts	Total Return Y-T-D	Risk Rating/Pts
12-15	C+	162.50	98.99	C / 4.8	1.11%	B / 8.0
2014	C-	162.50	98.87	C- / 3.3	2.28%	B / 8.2

Major Rating Factors: Middle of the road best describes *iShares iBonds Mar 2018 Corp ex- whose TheStreet.com Investment Rating is currently a C+ (Fair). The fund currently has a performance rating of C (Fair) based on an annualized return of 0.00% over the last three years and a total return of 1.11% year to date 2015. Factored into the performance evaluation is an expense ratio of 0.10% (very low).

The fund's risk rating is currently B (Good). It carries a beta of 0.00, meaning the fund's expected move will be 0.0% for every 10% move in the market. Volatility, as measured by both the semi-deviation and a drawdown factor, is considered low. As of December 31, 2015, *iShares iBonds Mar 2018 Corp ex- traded at a premium of .94% above its net asset value, which is worse than its one-year historical average premium of .66%.

James J. Mauro has been running the fund for 3 years and currently receives a manager quality ranking of 79 (0=worst, 99=best). If you desire an average level of risk, then this fund may be an option.

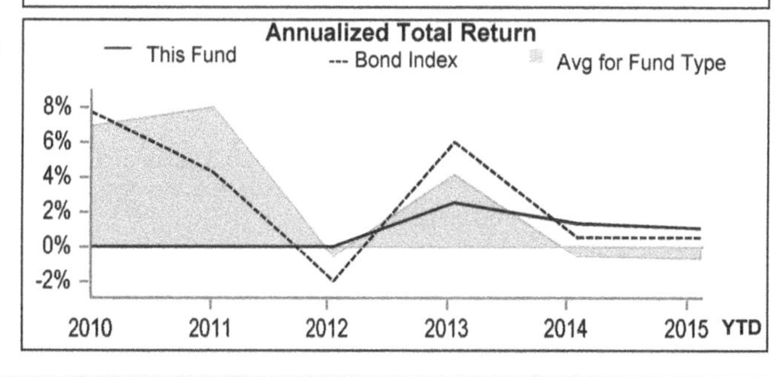

*iShares iBonds Mar 2018 Corporat (IBDB) C+ Fair

Fund Family: BlackRock Fund Advisors
Fund Type: Corporate - Investment Grade
Inception Date: July 9, 2013

Data Date	Investment Rating	Net Assets ($Mil)	Price	Perfor-mance Rating/Pts	Total Return Y-T-D	Risk Rating/Pts
12-15	C+	66.50	102.26	C / 5.0	1.38%	B / 8.1
2014	C-	66.50	102.73	C- / 3.2	2.19%	B / 8.4

Major Rating Factors: Middle of the road best describes *iShares iBonds Mar 2018 Corporat whose TheStreet.com Investment Rating is currently a C+ (Fair). The fund currently has a performance rating of C (Fair) based on an annualized return of 0.00% over the last three years and a total return of 1.38% year to date 2015. Factored into the performance evaluation is an expense ratio of 0.08% (very low).

The fund's risk rating is currently B (Good). It carries a beta of 0.00, meaning the fund's expected move will be 0.0% for every 10% move in the market. Volatility, as measured by both the semi-deviation and a drawdown factor, is considered low. As of December 31, 2015, *iShares iBonds Mar 2018 Corporat traded at a premium of .45% above its net asset value, which is worse than its one-year historical average premium of .35%.

James J. Mauro has been running the fund for 3 years and currently receives a manager quality ranking of 77 (0=worst, 99=best). If you desire an average level of risk, then this fund may be an option.

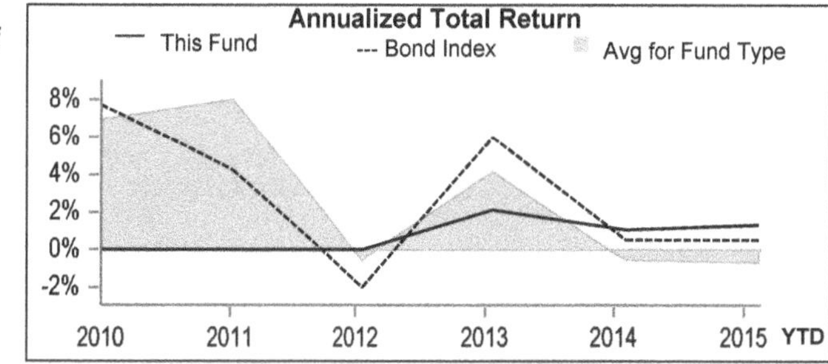

*iShares iBonds Mar 2020 Corp ex- (IBCD) C Fair

Fund Family: BlackRock Fund Advisors
Fund Type: Corporate - Investment Grade
Inception Date: April 17, 2013

Major Rating Factors: Middle of the road best describes *iShares iBonds Mar 2020 Corp ex- whose TheStreet.com Investment Rating is currently a C (Fair). The fund currently has a performance rating of C (Fair) based on an annualized return of 0.00% over the last three years and a total return of 0.88% year to date 2015. Factored into the performance evaluation is an expense ratio of 0.10% (very low).

The fund's risk rating is currently B- (Good). It carries a beta of 0.00, meaning the fund's expected move will be 0.0% for every 10% move in the market. Volatility, as measured by both the semi-deviation and a drawdown factor, is considered low. As of December 31, 2015, *iShares iBonds Mar 2020 Corp ex- traded at a premium of .44% above its net asset value, which is better than its one-year historical average premium of .49%.

James J. Mauro has been running the fund for 3 years and currently receives a manager quality ranking of 78 (0=worst, 99=best). If you desire an average level of risk, then this fund may be an option.

Data Date	Investment Rating	Net Assets ($Mil)	Price	Performance Rating/Pts	Total Return Y-T-D	Risk Rating/Pts
12-15	C	53.70	97.42	C / 4.6	0.88%	B- / 7.9
2014	C	53.70	98.40	C- / 3.9	4.57%	B / 8.1

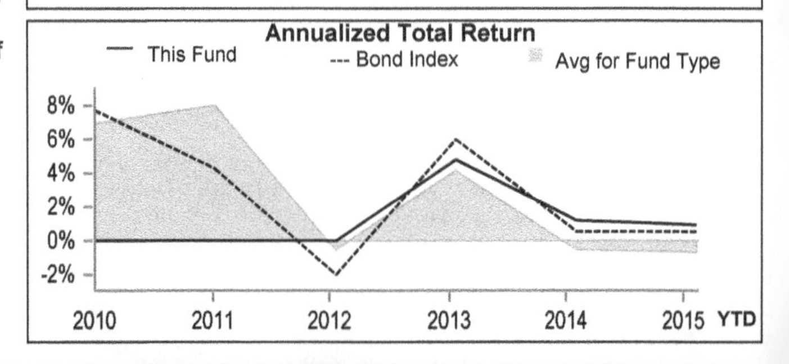

*iShares iBonds Mar 2020 Corporat (IBDC) C Fair

Fund Family: BlackRock Fund Advisors
Fund Type: Corporate - Investment Grade
Inception Date: July 9, 2013

Major Rating Factors: Middle of the road best describes *iShares iBonds Mar 2020 Corporat whose TheStreet.com Investment Rating is currently a C (Fair). The fund currently has a performance rating of C- (Fair) based on an annualized return of 0.00% over the last three years and a total return of 0.36% year to date 2015. Factored into the performance evaluation is an expense ratio of 0.08% (very low).

The fund's risk rating is currently B (Good). It carries a beta of 0.00, meaning the fund's expected move will be 0.0% for every 10% move in the market. Volatility, as measured by both the semi-deviation and a drawdown factor, is considered low. As of December 31, 2015, *iShares iBonds Mar 2020 Corporat traded at a premium of .52% above its net asset value, which is better than its one-year historical average premium of .59%.

James J. Mauro has been running the fund for 3 years and currently receives a manager quality ranking of 75 (0=worst, 99=best). If you desire an average level of risk, then this fund may be an option.

Data Date	Investment Rating	Net Assets ($Mil)	Price	Performance Rating/Pts	Total Return Y-T-D	Risk Rating/Pts
12-15	C	25.90	103.40	C- / 4.2	0.36%	B / 8.0
2014	C	25.90	105.16	C- / 4.2	5.66%	B / 8.3

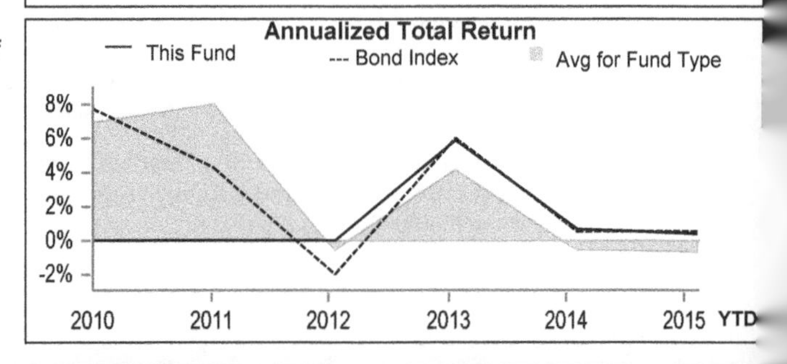

*iShares iBonds Mar 2023 Corp ex- (IBCE) C Fair

Fund Family: BlackRock Fund Advisors
Fund Type: Corporate - Investment Grade
Inception Date: April 17, 2013

Major Rating Factors: Middle of the road best describes *iShares iBonds Mar 2023 Corp ex- whose TheStreet.com Investment Rating is currently a C (Fair). The fund currently has a performance rating of C (Fair) based on an annualized return of 0.00% over the last three years and a total return of 1.28% year to date 2015. Factored into the performance evaluation is an expense ratio of 0.10% (very low).

The fund's risk rating is currently B- (Good). It carries a beta of 0.00, meaning the fund's expected move will be 0.0% for every 10% move in the market. Volatility, as measured by both the semi-deviation and a drawdown factor, is considered low. As of December 31, 2015, *iShares iBonds Mar 2023 Corp ex- traded at a premium of .26% above its net asset value, which is better than its one-year historical average premium of .57%.

James J. Mauro has been running the fund for 3 years and currently receives a manager quality ranking of 81 (0=worst, 99=best). If you desire an average level of risk, then this fund may be an option.

Data Date	Investment Rating	Net Assets ($Mil)	Price	Performance Rating/Pts	Total Return Y-T-D	Risk Rating/Pts
12-15	C	47.60	94.80	C / 4.8	1.28%	B- / 7.5
2014	C	47.60	96.43	C / 4.8	8.43%	B- / 7.6

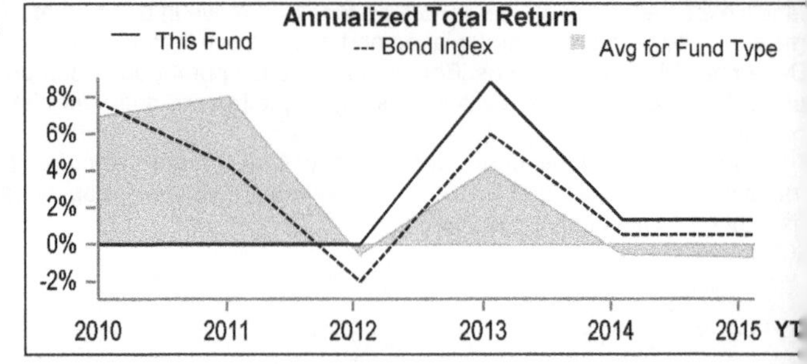

*iShares iBonds Mar 2023 Corporat (IBDD) C+ Fair

Fund Family: BlackRock Fund Advisors
Fund Type: Corporate - Investment Grade
Inception Date: July 9, 2013

Major Rating Factors: Middle of the road best describes *iShares iBonds Mar 2023 Corporat whose TheStreet.com Investment Rating is currently a C+ (Fair). The fund currently has a performance rating of C (Fair) based on an annualized return of 0.00% over the last three years and a total return of 0.48% year to date 2015. Factored into the performance evaluation is an expense ratio of 0.08% (very low).

The fund's risk rating is currently B- (Good). It carries a beta of 0.00, meaning the fund's expected move will be 0.0% for every 10% move in the market. Volatility, as measured by both the semi-deviation and a drawdown factor, is considered low. As of December 31, 2015, *iShares iBonds Mar 2023 Corporat traded at a premium of 1.94% above its net asset value, which is worse than its one-year historical average premium of .93%.

James J. Mauro has been running the fund for 3 years and currently receives a manager quality ranking of 81 (0=worst, 99=best). If you desire an average level of risk, then this fund may be an option.

Data Date	Investment Rating	Net Assets ($Mil)	Price	Performance Rating/Pts	Total Return Y-T-D	Risk Rating/Pts
12-15	C+	26.00	103.87	C / 5.1	0.48%	B- / 7.7
2014	C+	26.00	105.66	C / 5.4	9.94%	B / 8.2

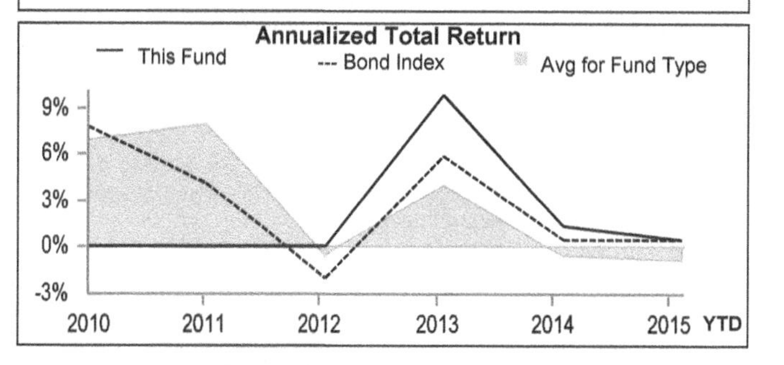

*iShares iBonds Sep 2016 AMT-Fr M (IBME) D+ Weak

Fund Family: BlackRock Fund Advisors
Fund Type: General - Investment Grade
Inception Date: January 7, 2010

Major Rating Factors: *iShares iBonds Sep 2016 AMT-Fr M receives a TheStreet.com Investment Rating of D+ (Weak). The fund currently has a performance rating of C (Fair) based on an annualized return of 0.63% over the last three years and a total return of 0.11% year to date 2015. Factored into the performance evaluation is an expense ratio of 0.20% (very low).

The fund's risk rating is currently C- (Fair). It carries a beta of -0.03, meaning the fund's expected move will be -0.3% for every 10% move in the market. Volatility, as measured by both the semi-deviation and a drawdown factor, is considered average. As of December 31, 2015, *iShares iBonds Sep 2016 AMT-Fr M traded at a discount of .04% below its net asset value, which is worse than its one-year historical average discount of .08%.

Scott F. Radell has been running the fund for 6 years and currently receives a manager quality ranking of 73 (0=worst, 99=best). If you desire an average level of risk, then this fund may be an option.

Data Date	Investment Rating	Net Assets ($Mil)	Price	Performance Rating/Pts	Total Return Y-T-D	Risk Rating/Pts
12-15	D+	128.30	26.52	C / 4.6	0.11%	C- / 3.9
2014	C	128.30	53.30	C- / 3.0	0.29%	B+ / 9.5
2013	C+	104.10	53.60	C- / 3.9	1.22%	B+ / 9.9
2012	C-	50.70	53.56	D / 1.6	1.43%	B+ / 9.7
2011	C+	26.50	53.26	C- / 3.9	8.75%	B+ / 9.8

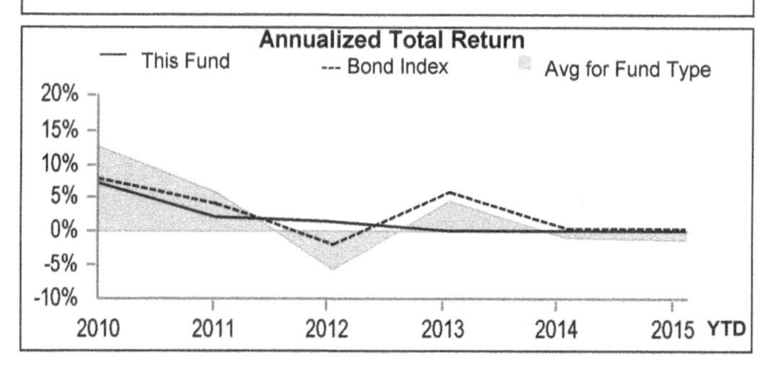

*iShares iBonds Sep 2017 AMT-Fr M (IBMF) D Weak

Fund Family: BlackRock Fund Advisors
Fund Type: General - Investment Grade
Inception Date: January 7, 2010

Major Rating Factors: *iShares iBonds Sep 2017 AMT-Fr M has adopted a very risky asset allocation strategy and currently receives an overall TheStreet.com Investment Rating of D (Weak). The fund has a high level of volatility, as measured by both semi-deviation and drawdown factors. It carries a beta of 0.39, meaning the fund's expected move will be 3.9% for every 10% move in the market. As of December 31, 2015, *iShares iBonds Sep 2017 AMT-Fr M traded at a premium of .07% above its net asset value, which is better than its one-year historical average premium of .09%. Unfortunately, the high level of risk (D, Weak) has only provided investors with average performance.

The fund's performance rating is currently C (Fair). It has registered an annualized return of 0.75% over the last three years and is up 0.56% year to date 2015. Factored into the performance evaluation is an expense ratio of 0.20% (very low).

Scott F. Radell has been running the fund for 6 years and currently receives a manager quality ranking of 69 (0=worst, 99=best). If you are comfortable owning a very high risk investment, then this fund may be an option.

Data Date	Investment Rating	Net Assets ($Mil)	Price	Performance Rating/Pts	Total Return Y-T-D	Risk Rating/Pts
12-15	D	146.20	27.35	C / 4.7	0.56%	D / 2.2
2014	C	146.20	54.92	C- / 3.1	0.82%	B+ / 9.4
2013	C+	112.60	54.96	C- / 4.1	0.88%	B+ / 9.7
2012	C-	66.10	55.29	D / 1.7	1.85%	B+ / 9.4
2011	C+	35.50	54.96	C / 4.4	10.54%	B+ / 9.5

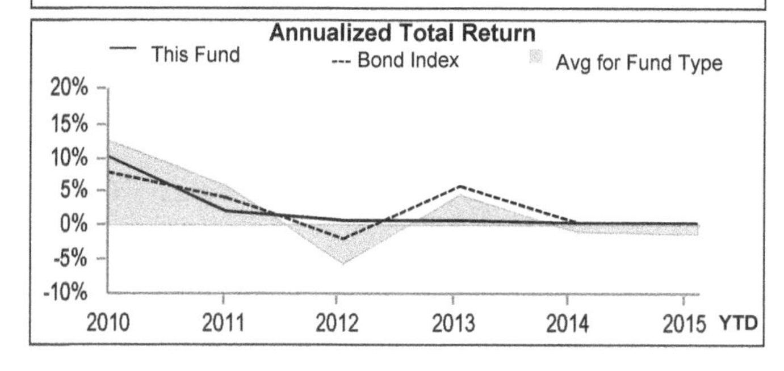

*iShares iBonds Sep 2018 AMT-Fr M (IBMG) C Fair

Fund Family: BlackRock Fund Advisors
Fund Type: Municipal - National
Inception Date: March 19, 2013

Major Rating Factors: Middle of the road best describes *iShares iBonds Sep 2018 AMT-Fr M whose TheStreet.com Investment Rating is currently a C (Fair). The fund currently has a performance rating of C (Fair) based on an annualized return of 0.00% over the last three years and a total return of 0.36% year to date 2015. Factored into the performance evaluation is an expense ratio of 0.19% (very low).

The fund's risk rating is currently B- (Good). It carries a beta of 0.00, meaning the fund's expected move will be 0.0% for every 10% move in the market. Volatility, as measured by both the semi-deviation and a drawdown factor, is considered low. As of December 31, 2015, *iShares iBonds Sep 2018 AMT-Fr M traded at a premium of .35% above its net asset value, which is worse than its one-year historical average premium of .23%.

James Mauro has been running the fund for 3 years and currently receives a manager quality ranking of 63 (0=worst, 99=best). If you desire an average level of risk, then this fund may be an option.

Data Date	Investment Rating	Net Assets ($Mil)	Price	Perfor-mance Rating/Pts	Total Return Y-T-D	Risk Rating/Pts
12-15	C	66.40	25.52	C / 4.6	0.36%	B- / 7.9
2014	C-	66.40	25.62	C- / 3.8	2.55%	B / 8.0

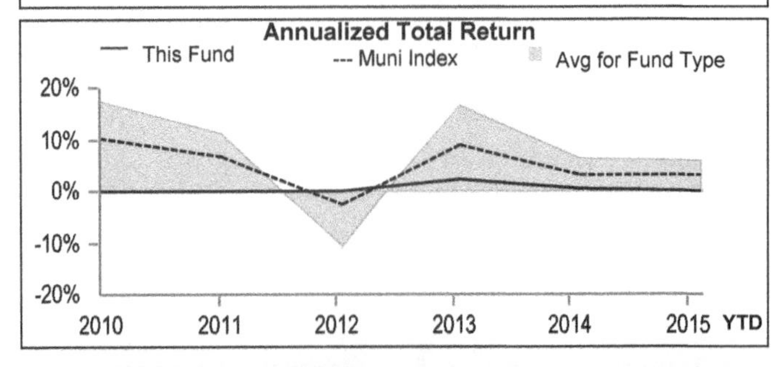

*iShares iBonds Sep 2019 AMT-Fr M (IBMH) C+ Fair

Fund Family: BlackRock Fund Advisors
Fund Type: Municipal - National
Inception Date: February 4, 2014

Major Rating Factors: Middle of the road best describes *iShares iBonds Sep 2019 AMT-Fr M whose TheStreet.com Investment Rating is currently a C+ (Fair). The fund currently has a performance rating of C+ (Fair) based on an annualized return of 0.00% over the last three years and a total return of 2.09% year to date 2015. Factored into the performance evaluation is an expense ratio of 0.19% (very low).

The fund's risk rating is currently B (Good). It carries a beta of 0.00, meaning the fund's expected move will be 0.0% for every 10% move in the market. Volatility, as measured by both the semi-deviation and a drawdown factor, is considered low. As of December 31, 2015, *iShares iBonds Sep 2019 AMT-Fr M traded at a premium of .71% above its net asset value, which is worse than its one-year historical average premium of .25%.

James J. Mauro has been running the fund for 2 years and currently receives a manager quality ranking of 59 (0=worst, 99=best). If you desire an average level of risk, then this fund may be an option.

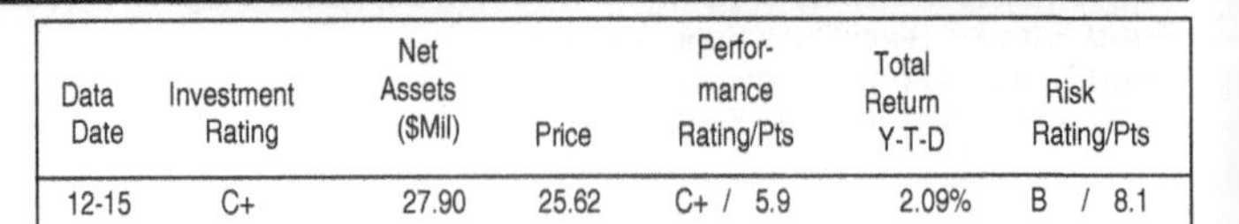

Data Date	Investment Rating	Net Assets ($Mil)	Price	Perfor-mance Rating/Pts	Total Return Y-T-D	Risk Rating/Pts
12-15	C+	27.90	25.62	C+ / 5.9	2.09%	B / 8.1

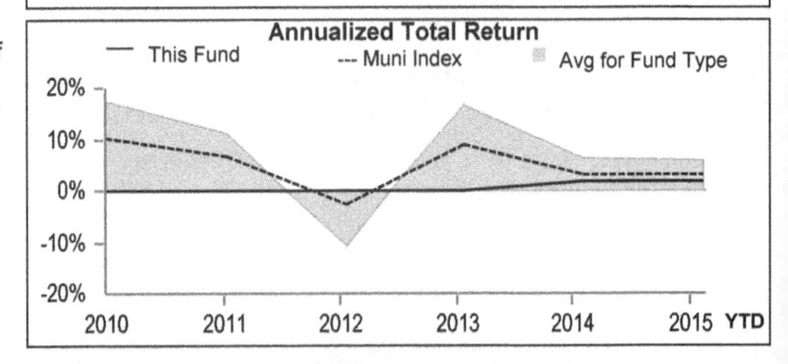

*iShares iBonds Sep 2020 AMT-Fr M (IBMI) C+ Fair

Fund Family: BlackRock Fund Advisors
Fund Type: Municipal - National
Inception Date: August 14, 2014

Major Rating Factors: Middle of the road best describes *iShares iBonds Sep 2020 AMT-Fr M whose TheStreet.com Investment Rating is currently a C+ (Fair). The fund currently has a performance rating of C+ (Fair) based on an annualized return of 0.00% over the last three years and a total return of 2.07% year to date 2015. Factored into the performance evaluation is an expense ratio of 0.18% (very low).

The fund's risk rating is currently B (Good). It carries a beta of 0.00, meaning the fund's expected move will be 0.0% for every 10% move in the market. Volatility, as measured by both the semi-deviation and a drawdown factor, is considered low. As of December 31, 2015, *iShares iBonds Sep 2020 AMT-Fr M traded at a premium of .20% above its net asset value, which is better than its one-year historical average premium of .23%.

James J. Mauro has been running the fund for 2 years and currently receives a manager quality ranking of 64 (0=worst, 99=best). If you desire an average level of risk, then this fund may be an option.

Data Date	Investment Rating	Net Assets ($Mil)	Price	Perfor-mance Rating/Pts	Total Return Y-T-D	Risk Rating/Pts
12-15	C+	0.00	25.53	C+ / 5.8	2.07%	B / 8.0

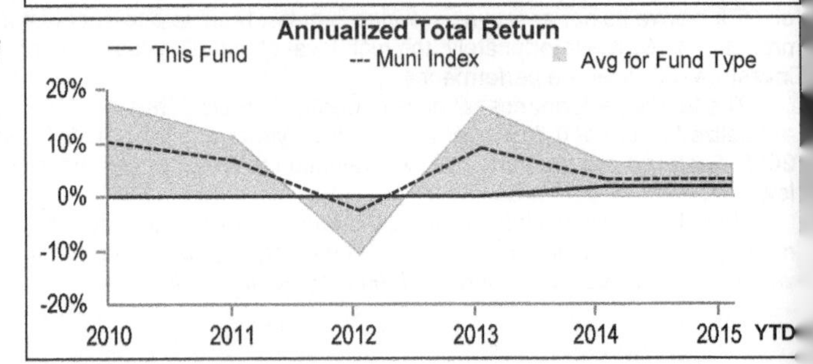

* Denotes ETF Fund

*iShares iBoxx $ Hi Yld Corp Bd E (HYG) C- Fair

Fund Family: BlackRock Fund Advisors
Fund Type: Corporate - High Yield
Inception Date: April 4, 2007

Major Rating Factors: Middle of the road best describes *iShares iBoxx $ Hi Yld Corp Bd E whose TheStreet.com Investment Rating is currently a C- (Fair). The fund currently has a performance rating of C- (Fair) based on an annualized return of 0.59% over the last three years and a total return of -4.93% year to date 2015. Factored into the performance evaluation is an expense ratio of 0.50% (very low).

The fund's risk rating is currently C+ (Fair). It carries a beta of 1.02, meaning that its performance tracks fairly well with that of the overall stock market. Volatility, as measured by both the semi-deviation and a drawdown factor, is considered low. As of December 31, 2015, *iShares iBoxx $ Hi Yld Corp Bd E traded at a premium of .76% above its net asset value, which is worse than its one-year historical average premium of .27%.

Scott F. Radell has been running the fund for 6 years and currently receives a manager quality ranking of 61 (0=worst, 99=best). If you desire an average level of risk, then this fund may be an option.

Data Date	Investment Rating	Net Assets ($Mil)	Price	Performance Rating/Pts	Total Return Y-T-D	Risk Rating/Pts
12-15	C-	12,411.50	80.58	C- / 4.0	-4.93%	C+ / 6.8
2014	C-	12,411.50	89.60	C- / 4.2	1.77%	B- / 7.4
2013	C+	15,087.50	92.88	C+ / 5.6	5.20%	B / 8.9
2012	C-	15,972.30	93.35	C / 4.4	13.60%	B- / 7.7
2011	C	10,636.60	89.43	C / 5.0	5.63%	B- / 7.0
2010	C+	7,273.10	90.29	C+ / 6.7	11.98%	C / 5.2

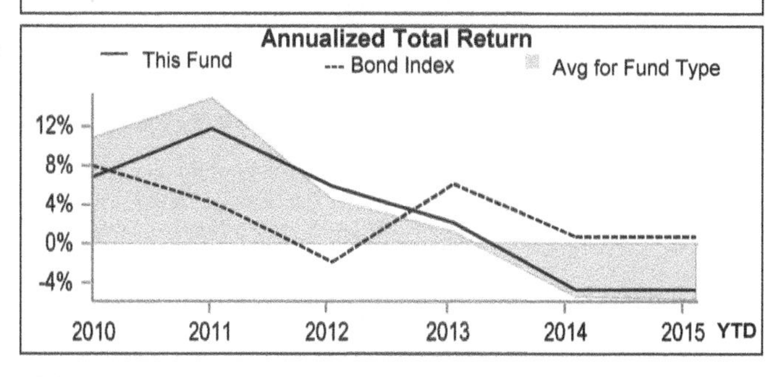

*iShares iBoxx $ Inv Grade Cor B (LQD) C+ Fair

Fund Family: BlackRock Fund Advisors
Fund Type: Corporate - Investment Grade
Inception Date: July 22, 2002

Major Rating Factors: Middle of the road best describes *iShares iBoxx $ Inv Grade Cor B whose TheStreet.com Investment Rating is currently a C+ (Fair). The fund currently has a performance rating of C (Fair) based on an annualized return of 1.69% over the last three years and a total return of -1.59% year to date 2015. Factored into the performance evaluation is an expense ratio of 0.15% (very low).

The fund's risk rating is currently B (Good). It carries a beta of 1.24, meaning it is expected to move 12.4% for every 10% move in the market. Volatility, as measured by both the semi-deviation and a drawdown factor, is considered low. As of December 31, 2015, *iShares iBoxx $ Inv Grade Cor B traded at a price exactly equal to its net asset value, which is better than its one-year historical average premium of .07%.

Scott F. Radell has been running the fund for 6 years and currently receives a manager quality ranking of 65 (0=worst, 99=best). If you desire an average level of risk, then this fund may be an option.

Data Date	Investment Rating	Net Assets ($Mil)	Price	Performance Rating/Pts	Total Return Y-T-D	Risk Rating/Pts
12-15	C+	17,377.20	114.01	C / 5.0	-1.59%	B / 8.3
2014	C+	17,377.20	119.41	C / 4.4	7.86%	B+ / 9.1
2013	C+	15,645.70	114.19	C / 4.6	-1.29%	B+ / 9.3
2012	C	25,350.40	120.99	C- / 3.5	9.98%	B+ / 9.4
2011	C+	16,990.80	113.76	C- / 4.0	9.22%	B+ / 9.2
2010	B	13,098.30	108.44	C / 5.5	9.35%	B / 8.5

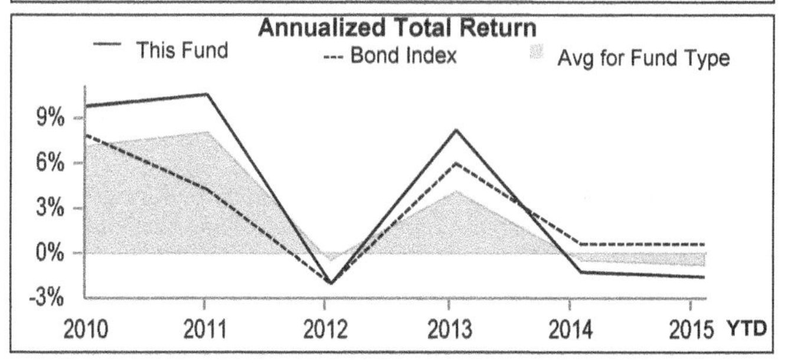

*iShares India 50 ETF (INDY) C- Fair

Fund Family: BlackRock Fund Advisors
Fund Type: Emerging Market
Inception Date: November 18, 2009

Major Rating Factors: Middle of the road best describes *iShares India 50 ETF whose TheStreet.com Investment Rating is currently a C- (Fair). The fund currently has a performance rating of C (Fair) based on an annualized return of 3.06% over the last three years and a total return of -9.85% year to date 2015. Factored into the performance evaluation is an expense ratio of 0.93% (low).

The fund's risk rating is currently C+ (Fair). It carries a beta of 0.76, meaning the fund's expected move will be 7.6% for every 10% move in the market. Volatility, as measured by both the semi-deviation and a drawdown factor, is considered low. As of December 31, 2015, *iShares India 50 ETF traded at a discount of .95% below its net asset value, which is better than its one-year historical average premium of .08%.

Diane Hsiung has been running the fund for 7 years and currently receives a manager quality ranking of 94 (0=worst, 99=best). If you desire an average level of risk, then this fund may be an option.

Data Date	Investment Rating	Net Assets ($Mil)	Price	Performance Rating/Pts	Total Return Y-T-D	Risk Rating/Pts
12-15	C-	672.00	27.20	C / 4.4	-9.85%	C+ / 6.8
2014	C+	672.00	29.90	B- / 7.3	31.78%	C+ / 6.7
2013	D-	449.80	23.47	D- / 1.4	-9.31%	C+ / 5.8
2012	D	358.40	24.97	D / 1.9	17.19%	C+ / 6.0
2011	D-	214.40	19.75	E / 0.4	-30.60%	C+ / 6.1
2010	A+	174.70	31.35	A- / 9.2	24.42%	B / 8.0

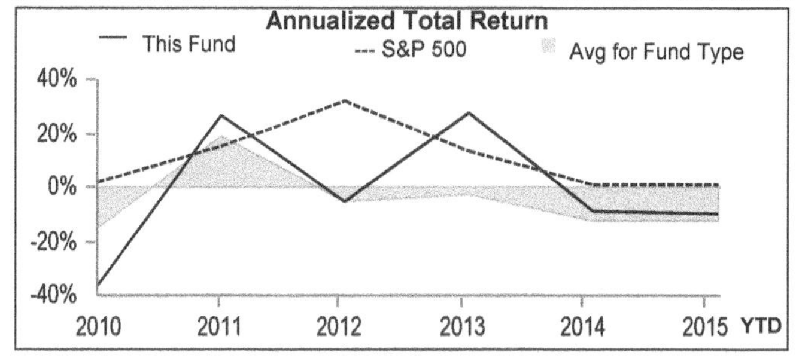

* Denotes ETF Fund

*iShares Interest Rate Hgd HY Bon (HYGH) C- Fair

Fund Family: BlackRock Fund Advisors
Fund Type: Corporate - High Yield
Inception Date: May 27, 2014

Data Date	Investment Rating	Net Assets ($Mil)	Price	Performance Rating/Pts	Total Return Y-T-D	Risk Rating/Pts
12-15	C-	43.70	83.05	D+ / 2.4	-6.62%	B / 8.3

Major Rating Factors:
Disappointing performance is the major factor driving the C- (Fair) TheStreet.com Investment Rating for *iShares Interest Rate Hgd HY Bon. The fund currently has a performance rating of D+ (Weak) based on an annualized return of 0.00% over the last three years and a total return of -6.62% year to date 2015.

The fund's risk rating is currently B (Good). It carries a beta of 0.00, meaning the fund's expected move will be 0.0% for every 10% move in the market. Volatility, as measured by both the semi-deviation and a drawdown factor, is considered low. As of December 31, 2015, *iShares Interest Rate Hgd HY Bon traded at a discount of .17% below its net asset value, which is better than its one-year historical average premium of .02%.

James J. Mauro has been running the fund for 2 years and currently receives a manager quality ranking of 55 (0=worst, 99=best). This fund offers only a moderate level of risk but investors looking for strong performance are still waiting.

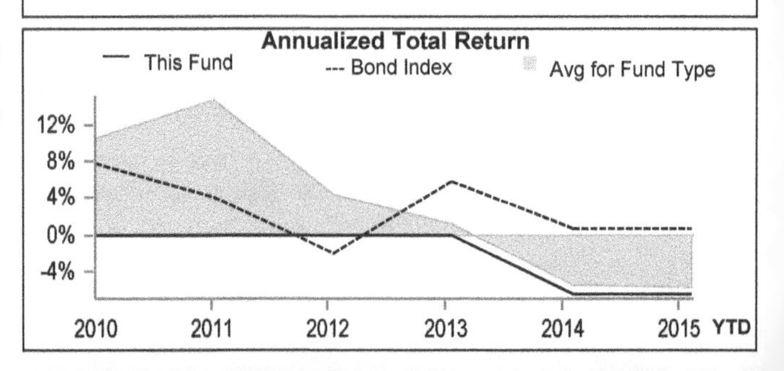

*iShares Internat Infl-Link Bd ET (ITIP) C- Fair

Fund Family: BlackRock Fund Advisors
Fund Type: Global
Inception Date: May 18, 2011

Data Date	Investment Rating	Net Assets ($Mil)	Price	Performance Rating/Pts	Total Return Y-T-D	Risk Rating/Pts
12-15	C-	124.50	39.01	D+ / 2.3	-11.50%	B- / 7.5
2014	D+	124.50	44.34	D+ / 2.7	-0.26%	C+ / 6.4
2013	D+	105.70	46.00	D- / 1.5	-8.85%	B / 8.4
2012	B	65.60	51.29	B- / 7.1	13.28%	B / 8.7

Major Rating Factors:
Disappointing performance is the major factor driving the C- (Fair) TheStreet.com Investment Rating for *iShares Internat Infl-Link Bd ET. The fund currently has a performance rating of D+ (Weak) based on an annualized return of -7.13% over the last three years and a total return of -11.50% year to date 2015. Factored into the performance evaluation is an expense ratio of 0.40% (very low).

The fund's risk rating is currently B- (Good). It carries a beta of 1.02, meaning that its performance tracks fairly well with that of the overall stock market. Volatility, as measured by both the semi-deviation and a drawdown factor, is considered low. As of December 31, 2015, *iShares Internat Infl-Link Bd ET traded at a discount of .03% below its net asset value, which is worse than its one-year historical average discount of .14%.

James J. Mauro has been running the fund for 5 years and currently receives a manager quality ranking of 42 (0=worst, 99=best). This fund offers only a moderate level of risk but investors looking for strong performance are still waiting.

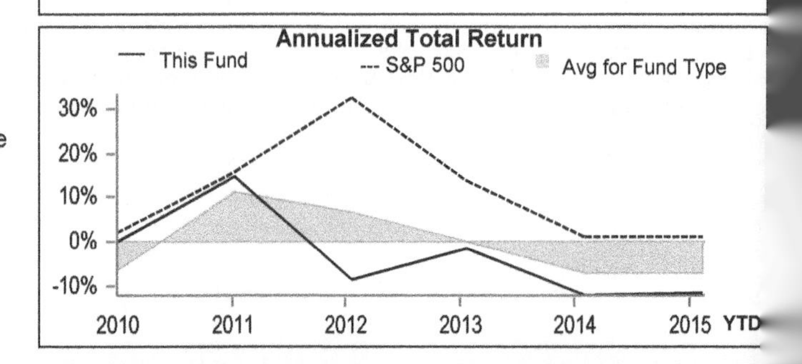

*iShares International High Yield (HYXU) C- Fair

Fund Family: BlackRock Fund Advisors
Fund Type: Global
Inception Date: April 3, 2012

Data Date	Investment Rating	Net Assets ($Mil)	Price	Performance Rating/Pts	Total Return Y-T-D	Risk Rating/Pts
12-15	C-	133.70	44.37	C- / 3.0	-9.60%	B- / 7.6
2014	D	133.70	50.74	D- / 1.2	-7.53%	C+ / 6.7
2013	A-	68.90	57.92	B- / 7.3	10.62%	B+ / 9.3

Major Rating Factors: Middle of the road best describes *iShares International High Yield whose TheStreet.com Investment Rating is currently a C- (Fair). The fund currently has a performance rating of C- (Fair) based on an annualized return of -2.75% over the last three years and a total return of -9.60% year to date 2015. Factored into the performance evaluation is an expense ratio of 0.40% (very low).

The fund's risk rating is currently B- (Good). It carries a beta of 1.05, meaning that its performance tracks fairly well with that of the overall stock market. Volatility, as measured by both the semi-deviation and a drawdown factor, is considered low. As of December 31, 2015, *iShares International High Yield traded at a discount of .49% below its net asset value, which is better than its one-year historical average premium of .27%.

James J. Mauro has been running the fund for 4 years and currently receives a manager quality ranking of 81 (0=worst, 99=best). If you desire an average level of risk, then this fund may be an option.

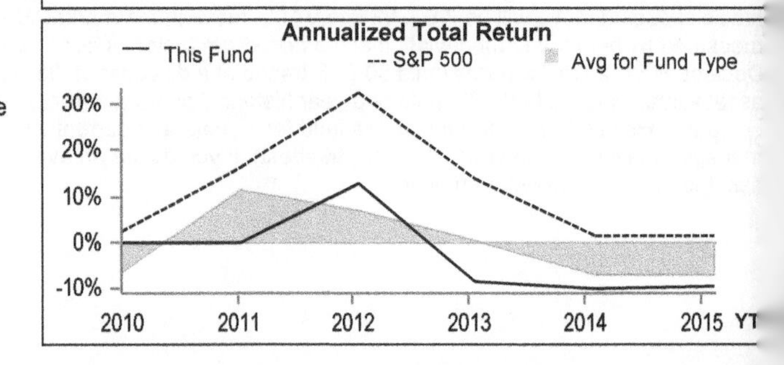

*iShares International Preferred (IPFF) D Weak

Fund Family: BlackRock Fund Advisors
Fund Type: Corporate - Investment Grade
Inception Date: November 15, 2011

Data Date	Investment Rating	Net Assets ($Mil)	Price	Performance Rating/Pts	Total Return Y-T-D	Risk Rating/Pts
12-15	D	38.80	16.08	D- / 1.5	-22.81%	C+ / 6.1
2014	D	38.80	22.51	D+ / 2.7	-2.12%	C+ / 6.2
2013	D+	32.50	23.97	D / 2.0	-6.47%	B / 8.6
2012	B	123.20	27.10	C+ / 6.1	12.72%	B+ / 9.1

Major Rating Factors:
Disappointing performance is the major factor driving the D (Weak) TheStreet.com Investment Rating for *iShares International Preferred. The fund currently has a performance rating of D- (Weak) based on an annualized return of -11.26% over the last three years and a total return of -22.81% year to date 2015. Factored into the performance evaluation is an expense ratio of 0.55% (very low).

The fund's risk rating is currently C+ (Fair). It carries a beta of 0.21, meaning the fund's expected move will be 2.1% for every 10% move in the market. Volatility, as measured by both the semi-deviation and a drawdown factor, is considered low. As of December 31, 2015, *iShares International Preferred traded at a discount of 1.11% below its net asset value, which is better than its one-year historical average discount of .56%.

Diane Hsiung has been running the fund for 5 years and currently receives a manager quality ranking of 14 (0=worst, 99=best). This fund offers only a moderate level of risk but investors looking for strong performance are still waiting.

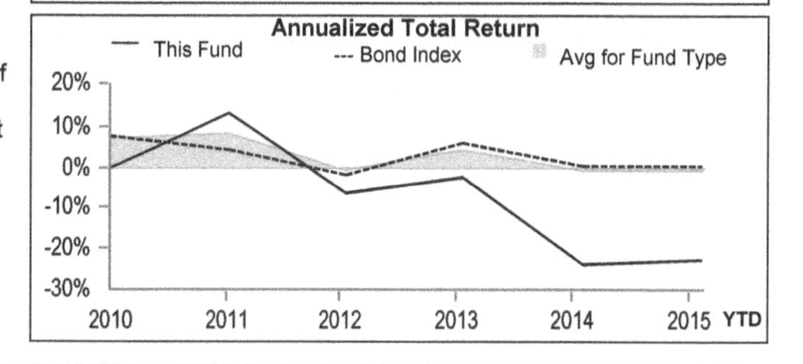

*iShares International Treas Bd E (IGOV) C- Fair

Fund Family: BlackRock Fund Advisors
Fund Type: Global
Inception Date: January 21, 2009

Data Date	Investment Rating	Net Assets ($Mil)	Price	Performance Rating/Pts	Total Return Y-T-D	Risk Rating/Pts
12-15	C-	541.20	89.67	C- / 3.1	-7.03%	C+ / 6.8
2014	D+	541.20	96.78	D+ / 2.8	-1.60%	B- / 7.2
2013	C	624.30	100.19	C- / 3.5	-0.69%	B / 8.8
2012	C-	365.00	102.93	D / 2.2	8.55%	B / 8.8
2011	C-	273.90	99.90	D / 1.8	2.71%	B / 8.8
2010	C+	163.30	102.27	C- / 3.3	1.40%	B / 8.1

Major Rating Factors: Middle of the road best describes *iShares International Treas Bd E whose TheStreet.com Investment Rating is currently a C- (Fair). The fund currently has a performance rating of C- (Fair) based on an annualized return of -3.22% over the last three years and a total return of -7.03% year to date 2015. Factored into the performance evaluation is an expense ratio of 0.35% (very low).

The fund's risk rating is currently C+ (Fair). It carries a beta of 0.98, meaning that its performance tracks fairly well with that of the overall stock market. Volatility, as measured by both the semi-deviation and a drawdown factor, is considered low. As of December 31, 2015, *iShares International Treas Bd E traded at a premium of .15% above its net asset value, which is worse than its one-year historical average discount of .01%.

Scott F. Radell has been running the fund for 6 years and currently receives a manager quality ranking of 73 (0=worst, 99=best). If you desire an average level of risk, then this fund may be an option.

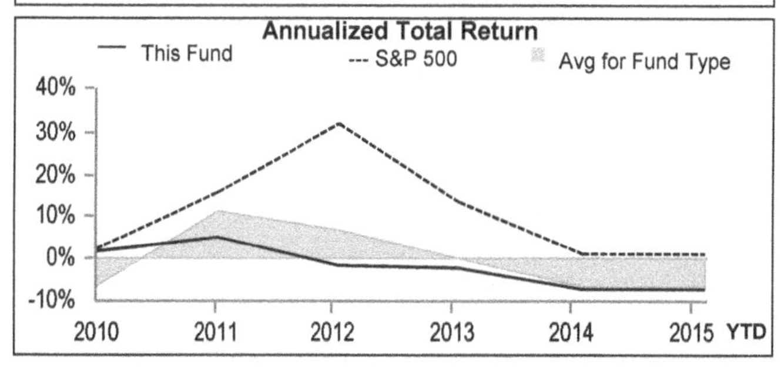

*iShares Interntl Developed RE ET (IFGL) C- Fair

Fund Family: BlackRock Fund Advisors
Fund Type: Growth and Income
Inception Date: November 12, 2007

Data Date	Investment Rating	Net Assets ($Mil)	Price	Performance Rating/Pts	Total Return Y-T-D	Risk Rating/Pts
12-15	C-	792.00	27.89	C- / 4.1	-3.51%	C+ / 6.2
2014	C-	792.00	30.04	C+ / 6.1	2.52%	C+ / 5.7
2013	D+	706.20	30.86	C / 4.8	2.29%	C / 5.5
2012	C	1,546.20	33.13	B- / 7.5	36.15%	C+ / 5.6
2011	D	336.00	25.25	C- / 3.1	-15.95%	C+ / 5.6
2010	E+	380.50	31.01	D / 1.6	14.55%	C- / 3.1

Major Rating Factors: Middle of the road best describes *iShares Interntl Developed RE ET whose TheStreet.com Investment Rating is currently a C- (Fair). The fund currently has a performance rating of C- (Fair) based on an annualized return of 0.47% over the last three years and a total return of -3.51% year to date 2015. Factored into the performance evaluation is an expense ratio of 0.48% (very low).

The fund's risk rating is currently C+ (Fair). It carries a beta of 0.65, meaning the fund's expected move will be 6.5% for every 10% move in the market. Volatility, as measured by both the semi-deviation and a drawdown factor, is considered low. As of December 31, 2015, *iShares Interntl Developed RE ET traded at a discount of .50% below its net asset value, which is better than its one-year historical average discount of .04%.

Diane Hsiung has been running the fund for 8 years and currently receives a manager quality ranking of 19 (0=worst, 99=best). If you desire an average level of risk, then this fund may be an option.

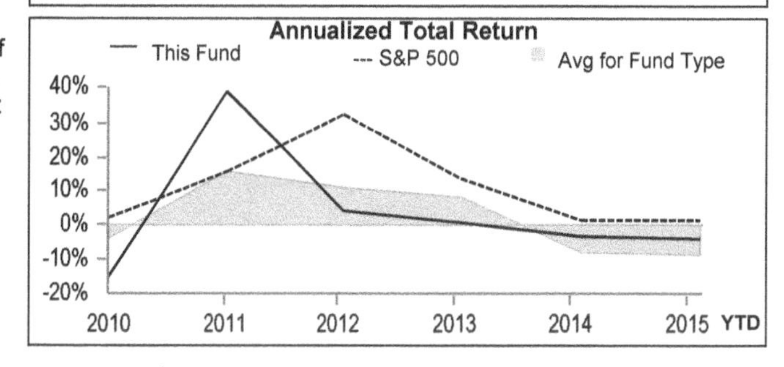

*iShares Intl Developed Property (WPS) C Fair

Fund Family: BlackRock Fund Advisors
Fund Type: Foreign
Inception Date: July 30, 2007

Data Date	Investment Rating	Net Assets ($Mil)	Price	Performance Rating/Pts	Total Return Y-T-D	Risk Rating/Pts
12-15	C	168.20	35.13	C / 5.4	0.66%	C+ / 6.8
2014	C	168.20	36.23	C+ / 6.3	2.29%	C+ / 6.0
2013	C-	181.30	37.38	C / 5.4	5.50%	C+ / 5.6
2012	C+	233.20	36.31	B / 7.8	38.20%	C+ / 5.6
2011	D	116.30	27.53	C- / 3.2	-15.78%	C / 5.5
2010	D-	143.30	34.25	D+ / 2.4	18.13%	C- / 3.1

Major Rating Factors: Middle of the road best describes *iShares Intl Developed Property whose TheStreet.com Investment Rating is currently a C (Fair). The fund currently has a performance rating of C (Fair) based on an annualized return of 2.91% over the last three years and a total return of 0.66% year to date 2015. Factored into the performance evaluation is an expense ratio of 0.48% (very low).

The fund's risk rating is currently C+ (Fair). It carries a beta of 0.79, meaning the fund's expected move will be 7.9% for every 10% move in the market. Volatility, as measured by both the semi-deviation and a drawdown factor, is considered low. As of December 31, 2015, *iShares Intl Developed Property traded at a discount of .54% below its net asset value, which is better than its one-year historical average discount of .22%.

Diane Hsiung has been running the fund for 8 years and currently receives a manager quality ranking of 57 (0=worst, 99=best). If you desire an average level of risk, then this fund may be an option.

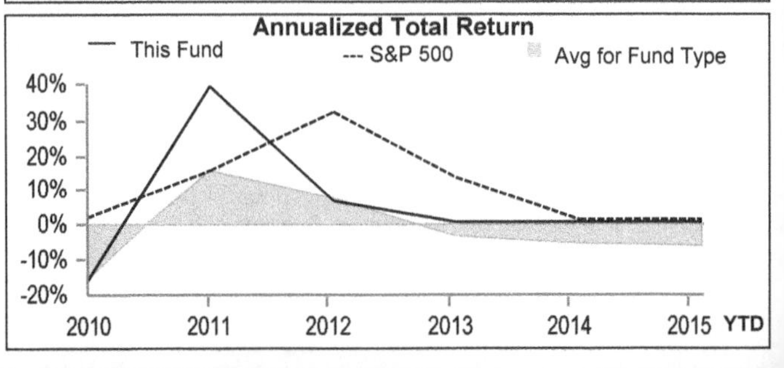

*iShares Intl Select Dividend ETF (IDV) C- Fair

Fund Family: BlackRock Fund Advisors
Fund Type: Foreign
Inception Date: June 11, 2007

Data Date	Investment Rating	Net Assets ($Mil)	Price	Performance Rating/Pts	Total Return Y-T-D	Risk Rating/Pts
12-15	C-	4,360.30	28.71	C- / 3.7	-9.19%	B- / 7.4
2014	C	4,360.30	33.69	C / 4.7	-4.51%	B / 8.2
2013	C+	3,191.50	37.94	C+ / 6.7	15.59%	B- / 7.7
2012	C	1,426.10	33.67	C / 5.1	22.58%	B- / 7.5
2011	C+	698.80	29.69	C+ / 5.6	-5.78%	B- / 7.7
2010	D	347.20	33.64	D+ / 2.6	11.82%	C / 4.9

Major Rating Factors: Middle of the road best describes *iShares Intl Select Dividend ETF whose TheStreet.com Investment Rating is currently a C- (Fair). The fund currently has a performance rating of C- (Fair) based on an annualized return of -0.10% over the last three years and a total return of -9.19% year to date 2015. Factored into the performance evaluation is an expense ratio of 0.50% (very low).

The fund's risk rating is currently B- (Good). It carries a beta of 1.06, meaning that its performance tracks fairly well with that of the overall stock market. Volatility, as measured by both the semi-deviation and a drawdown factor, is considered low. As of December 31, 2015, *iShares Intl Select Dividend ETF traded at a discount of .73% below its net asset value, which is better than its one-year historical average discount of .08%.

Diane Hsiung has been running the fund for 8 years and currently receives a manager quality ranking of 28 (0=worst, 99=best). If you desire an average level of risk, then this fund may be an option.

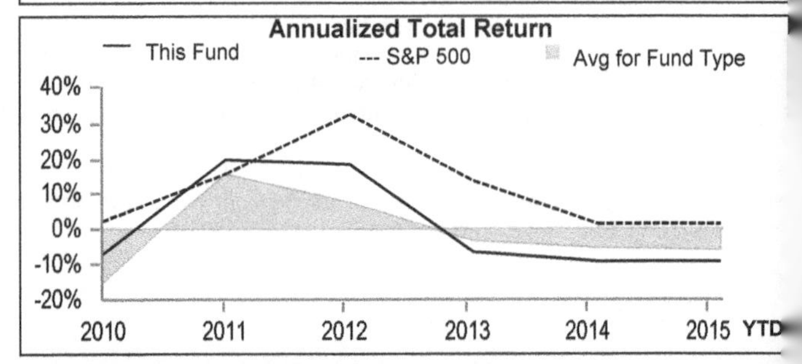

*iShares Intrm Credit Bond ETF (CIU) C+ Fair

Fund Family: BlackRock Fund Advisors
Fund Type: Corporate - Investment Grade
Inception Date: January 5, 2007

Data Date	Investment Rating	Net Assets ($Mil)	Price	Performance Rating/Pts	Total Return Y-T-D	Risk Rating/Pts
12-15	C+	6,213.00	107.28	C / 5.0	0.45%	B / 8.0
2014	C	6,213.00	109.33	C- / 3.7	3.74%	B / 8.7
2013	C+	5,371.60	107.88	C- / 3.9	0.09%	B+ / 9.7
2012	C	5,339.90	111.29	D+ / 2.7	7.00%	B+ / 9.7
2011	C	4,475.90	107.18	C- / 3.5	5.55%	B+ / 9.6
2010	B	2,950.70	105.18	C / 5.2	6.84%	B / 8.4

Major Rating Factors: Middle of the road best describes *iShares Intrm Credit Bond ETF whose TheStreet.com Investment Rating is currently a C+ (Fair). The fund currently has a performance rating of C (Fair) based on an annualized return of 1.47% over the last three years and a total return of 0.45% year to date 2015. Factored into the performance evaluation is an expense ratio of 0.20% (very low).

The fund's risk rating is currently B (Good). It carries a beta of 0.61, meaning the fund's expected move will be 6.1% for every 10% move in the market. Volatility, as measured by both the semi-deviation and a drawdown factor, is considered low. As of December 31, 2015, *iShares Intrm Credit Bond ETF traded at a premium of .09% above its net asset value, which is in line with its one-year historical average premium of .09%.

Scott F. Radell has been running the fund for 6 years and currently receives a manager quality ranking of 72 (0=worst, 99=best). If you desire an average level of risk, then this fund may be an option.

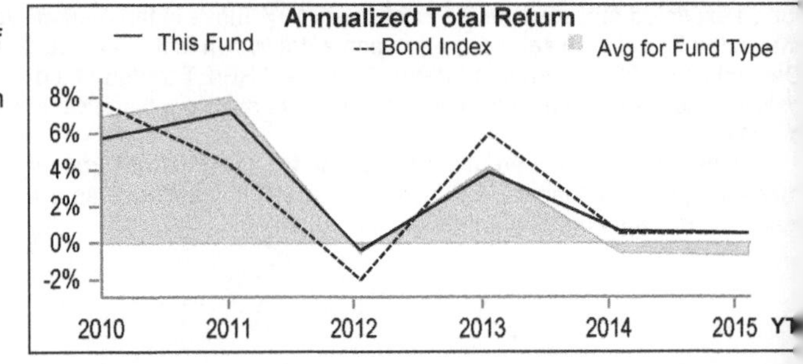

*iShares Intrm Govt/Crdt Bond ETF (GVI) C Fair

Fund Family: BlackRock Fund Advisors
Fund Type: General - Investment Grade
Inception Date: January 5, 2007

Major Rating Factors: Middle of the road best describes *iShares Intrm Govt/Crdt Bond ETF whose TheStreet.com Investment Rating is currently a C (Fair). The fund currently has a performance rating of C (Fair) based on an annualized return of 0.98% over the last three years and a total return of 0.53% year to date 2015. Factored into the performance evaluation is an expense ratio of 0.20% (very low).

The fund's risk rating is currently B- (Good). It carries a beta of 0.71, meaning the fund's expected move will be 7.1% for every 10% move in the market. Volatility, as measured by both the semi-deviation and a drawdown factor, is considered low. As of December 31, 2015, *iShares Intrm Govt/Crdt Bond ETF traded at a premium of .04% above its net asset value, which is better than its one-year historical average premium of .07%.

Scott F. Radell has been running the fund for 6 years and currently receives a manager quality ranking of 66 (0=worst, 99=best). If you desire an average level of risk, then this fund may be an option.

Data Date	Investment Rating	Net Assets ($Mil)	Price	Performance Rating/Pts	Total Return Y-T-D	Risk Rating/Pts
12-15	C	1,427.30	109.61	C / 4.8	0.53%	B- / 7.8
2014	C	1,427.30	110.65	C- / 3.3	2.90%	B+ / 9.4
2013	C	1,223.60	109.42	C- / 3.4	-0.73%	B+ / 9.8
2012	C	955.10	112.41	D / 2.2	3.15%	B+ / 9.8
2011	C	686.70	111.29	D+ / 2.9	5.79%	B+ / 9.8
2010	B+	538.40	107.88	C / 4.5	5.47%	B / 8.9

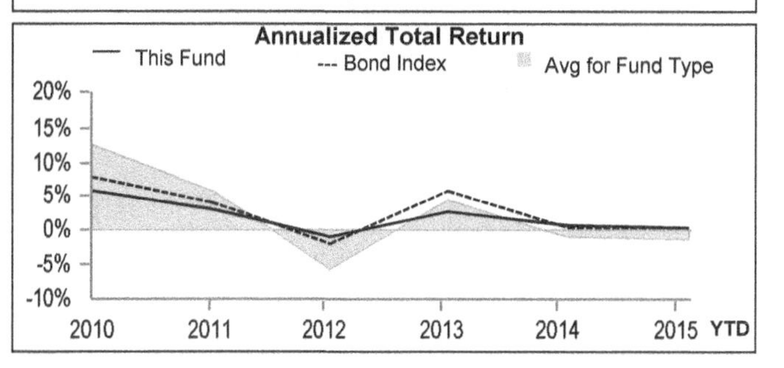

*iShares JPMorgan USD Emg Mkts B (EMB) C- Fair

Fund Family: BlackRock Fund Advisors
Fund Type: Emerging Market
Inception Date: December 17, 2007

Major Rating Factors: Middle of the road best describes *iShares JPMorgan USD Emg Mkts B whose TheStreet.com Investment Rating is currently a C- (Fair). The fund currently has a performance rating of C (Fair) based on an annualized return of -0.30% over the last three years and a total return of 1.54% year to date 2015. Factored into the performance evaluation is an expense ratio of 0.59% (very low).

The fund's risk rating is currently C+ (Fair). It carries a beta of 0.59, meaning the fund's expected move will be 5.9% for every 10% move in the market. Volatility, as measured by both the semi-deviation and a drawdown factor, is considered low. As of December 31, 2015, *iShares JPMorgan USD Emg Mkts B traded at a premium of .32% above its net asset value, which is better than its one-year historical average premium of .40%.

Scott F. Radell has been running the fund for 6 years and currently receives a manager quality ranking of 82 (0=worst, 99=best). If you desire an average level of risk, then this fund may be an option.

Data Date	Investment Rating	Net Assets ($Mil)	Price	Performance Rating/Pts	Total Return Y-T-D	Risk Rating/Pts
12-15	C-	4,422.20	105.78	C / 4.3	1.54%	C+ / 6.3
2014	C-	4,422.20	109.71	C- / 3.9	5.95%	B- / 7.6
2013	C-	3,461.60	108.16	C- / 4.0	-7.56%	B / 8.2
2012	C+	6,902.90	122.79	C / 4.6	17.25%	B / 8.9
2011	C+	3,554.20	109.75	C / 4.7	6.45%	B / 8.6
2010	C+	2,187.50	107.08	C+ / 6.4	10.89%	C+ / 6.8

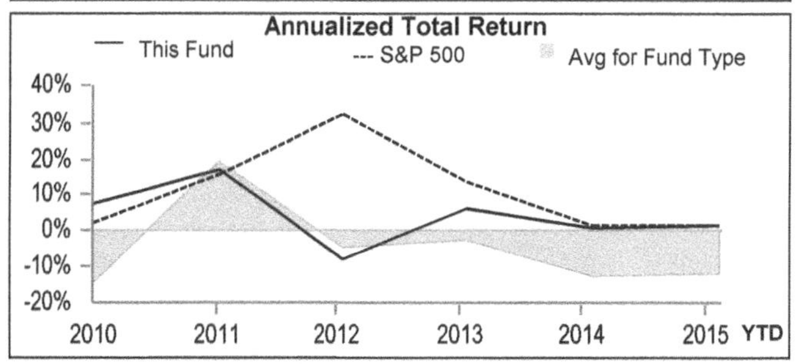

*iShares Latin America 40 (ILF) D- Weak

Fund Family: BlackRock Fund Advisors
Fund Type: Foreign
Inception Date: October 25, 2001

Major Rating Factors:
Very poor performance is the major factor driving the D- (Weak) TheStreet.com Investment Rating for *iShares Latin America 40. The fund currently has a performance rating of E+ (Very Weak) based on an annualized return of -19.92% over the last three years and a total return of -28.89% year to date 2015. Factored into the performance evaluation is an expense ratio of 0.49% (very low).

The fund's risk rating is currently C (Fair). It carries a beta of 1.16, meaning it is expected to move 11.6% for every 10% move in the market. Volatility, as measured by both the semi-deviation and a drawdown factor, is considered average. As of December 31, 2015, *iShares Latin America 40 traded at a discount of .66% below its net asset value, which is better than its one-year historical average discount of .13%.

Diane Hsiung has been running the fund for 8 years and currently receives a manager quality ranking of 5 (0=worst, 99=best). This fund offers an average level of risk but investors looking for strong performance will be frustrated.

Data Date	Investment Rating	Net Assets ($Mil)	Price	Performance Rating/Pts	Total Return Y-T-D	Risk Rating/Pts
12-15	D-	1,164.80	21.19	E+ / 0.7	-28.89%	C / 4.7
2014	D-	1,164.80	31.81	D- / 1.4	-9.31%	C / 4.7
2013	D-	958.90	37.04	D- / 1.0	-18.13%	C+ / 6.2
2012	D	1,603.20	43.84	D / 2.0	5.14%	C+ / 6.9
2011	C	1,733.60	42.57	C / 5.5	-16.22%	B- / 7.5
2010	C-	3,334.70	53.86	B- / 7.1	15.58%	D / 2.1

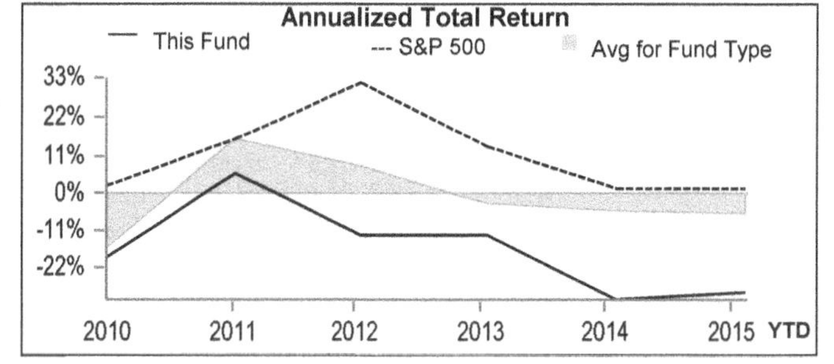

*iShares MBS ETF (MBB) B Good

Fund Family: BlackRock Fund Advisors
Fund Type: Mortgage
Inception Date: March 13, 2007

Major Rating Factors: *iShares MBS ETF receives a TheStreet.com Investment Rating of B (Good). The fund currently has a performance rating of C (Fair) based on an annualized return of 1.82% over the last three years and a total return of 1.33% year to date 2015. Factored into the performance evaluation is an expense ratio of 0.25% (very low).

The fund's risk rating is currently B+ (Good). It carries a beta of 1.08, meaning that its performance tracks fairly well with that of the overall stock market. Volatility, as measured by both the semi-deviation and a drawdown factor, is considered very low. As of December 31, 2015, *iShares MBS ETF traded at a discount of .06% below its net asset value, which is better than its one-year historical average premium of .03%.

Scott F. Radell has been running the fund for 6 years and currently receives a manager quality ranking of 65 (0=worst, 99=best). If you desire an average level of risk, then this fund may be an option.

Data Date	Investment Rating	Net Assets ($Mil)	Price	Performance Rating/Pts	Total Return Y-T-D	Risk Rating/Pts
12-15	B	6,288.40	107.70	C / 5.2	1.33%	B+ / 9.4
2014	C+	6,288.40	109.32	C- / 3.6	6.33%	B+ / 9.5
2013	C	5,183.40	104.57	C- / 3.0	-2.05%	B+ / 9.8
2012	C-	6,518.70	107.99	D / 2.2	1.71%	B+ / 9.7
2011	C	4,057.40	108.07	C- / 3.1	5.98%	B+ / 9.7
2010	B+	2,224.20	105.58	C / 5.1	5.58%	B / 8.9

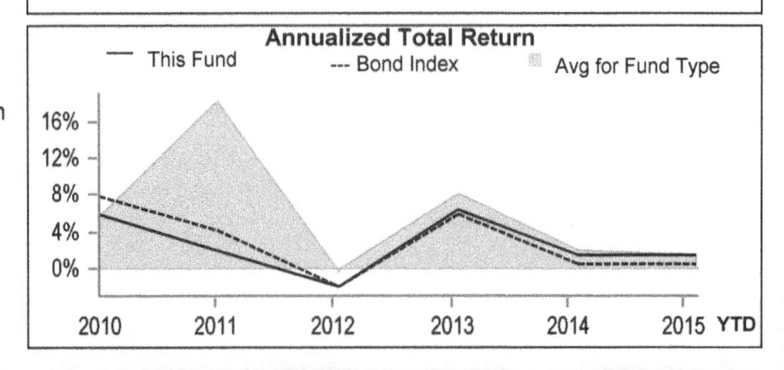

*iShares Micro Cap (IWC) B Good

Fund Family: BlackRock Fund Advisors
Fund Type: Growth
Inception Date: August 12, 2005

Major Rating Factors: Strong performance is the major factor driving the B (Good) TheStreet.com Investment Rating for *iShares Micro Cap. The fund currently has a performance rating of B (Good) based on an annualized return of 11.56% over the last three years and a total return of -4.23% year to date 2015. Factored into the performance evaluation is an expense ratio of 0.60% (very low).

The fund's risk rating is currently B- (Good). It carries a beta of 0.97, meaning that its performance tracks fairly well with that of the overall stock market. Volatility, as measured by both the semi-deviation and a drawdown factor, is considered low. As of December 31, 2015, *iShares Micro Cap traded at a price exactly equal to its net asset value, which is worse than its one-year historical average discount of .03%.

Diane Hsiung has been running the fund for 8 years and currently receives a manager quality ranking of 56 (0=worst, 99=best). If you desire only a moderate level of risk and strong performance, then this fund is an excellent option.

Data Date	Investment Rating	Net Assets ($Mil)	Price	Performance Rating/Pts	Total Return Y-T-D	Risk Rating/Pts
12-15	B	813.00	72.10	B / 7.6	-4.23%	B- / 7.5
2014	B	813.00	76.98	B+ / 8.3	3.66%	B- / 7.0
2013	B+	899.20	75.12	B+ / 8.9	40.21%	B- / 7.5
2012	C	460.60	52.32	C+ / 5.8	19.38%	B- / 7.3
2011	C-	388.90	44.65	C / 4.4	-9.31%	B- / 7.1
2010	C+	529.90	50.11	C+ / 6.6	29.55%	C / 5.5

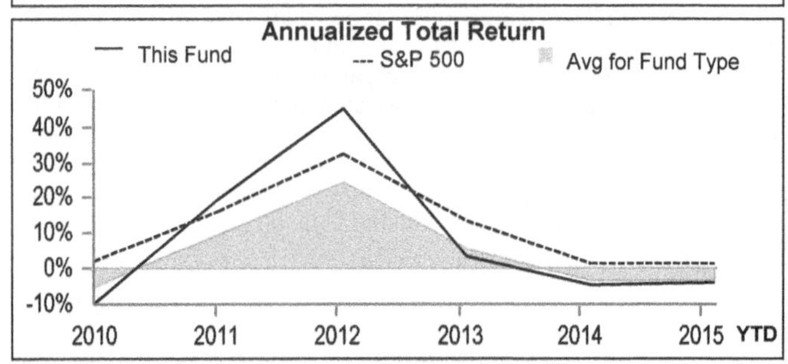

*iShares Morningstar Large-Cp ETF (JKD) A+ Excellent

Fund Family: BlackRock Fund Advisors
Fund Type: Growth
Inception Date: June 28, 2004

Major Rating Factors:
Strong performance is the major factor driving the A+ (Excellent) TheStreet.com Investment Rating for *iShares Morningstar Large-Cp ETF. The fund currently has a performance rating of B+ (Good) based on an annualized return of 14.86% over the last three years and a total return of -0.37% year to date 2015. Factored into the performance evaluation is an expense ratio of 0.20% (very low).

The fund's risk rating is currently B (Good). It carries a beta of 1.01, meaning that its performance tracks fairly well with that of the overall stock market. Volatility, as measured by both the semi-deviation and a drawdown factor, is considered low. As of December 31, 2015, *iShares Morningstar Large-Cp ETF traded at a discount of .07% below its net asset value.

Diane Hsiung has been running the fund for 8 years and currently receives a manager quality ranking of 73 (0=worst, 99=best). If you desire only a moderate level of risk and strong performance, then this fund is an excellent option.

Data Date	Investment Rating	Net Assets ($Mil)	Price	Performance Rating/Pts	Total Return Y-T-D	Risk Rating/Pts
12-15	A+	489.60	119.07	B+ / 8.9	-0.37%	B / 8.7
2014	A	489.60	123.53	A- / 9.0	17.65%	B- / 7.6
2013	A	441.80	107.84	B+ / 8.5	29.68%	B / 8.6
2012	C+	287.00	82.04	C / 5.5	18.05%	B / 8.4
2011	C	285.80	71.50	C / 4.9	4.32%	B / 8.0
2010	C-	275.90	70.70	C- / 3.8	12.68%	C+ / 6.2

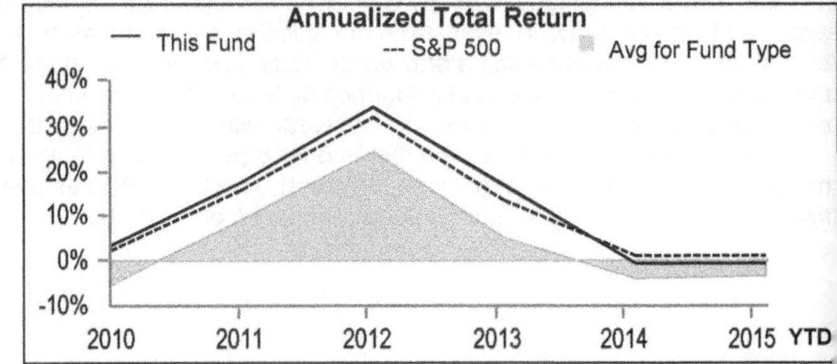

*iShares Morningstar Large-Cp Gr (JKE) B+ Good

Fund Family: BlackRock Fund Advisors
Fund Type: Growth
Inception Date: June 28, 2004

Data Date	Investment Rating	Net Assets ($Mil)	Price	Performance Rating/Pts	Total Return Y-T-D	Risk Rating/Pts
12-15	B+	570.80	120.29	A / 9.3	7.91%	C+ / 6.6
2014	B+	570.80	113.17	B+ / 8.6	15.74%	B- / 7.0
2013	B+	529.80	99.71	B+ / 8.4	27.34%	B- / 7.6
2012	C	447.50	76.50	C / 5.0	18.50%	B- / 7.1
2011	C+	355.30	65.95	C+ / 6.2	2.09%	B- / 7.4
2010	C-	370.40	65.53	C / 4.3	12.57%	C+ / 5.7

Major Rating Factors:
Exceptional performance is the major factor driving the B+ (Good) TheStreet.com Investment Rating for *iShares Morningstar Large-Cp Gr. The fund currently has a performance rating of A (Excellent) based on an annualized return of 16.64% over the last three years and a total return of 7.91% year to date 2015. Factored into the performance evaluation is an expense ratio of 0.25% (very low).

The fund's risk rating is currently C+ (Fair). It carries a beta of 1.02, meaning that its performance tracks fairly well with that of the overall stock market. Volatility, as measured by both the semi-deviation and a drawdown factor, is considered low. As of December 31, 2015, *iShares Morningstar Large-Cp Gr traded at a premium of .08% above its net asset value, which is worse than its one-year historical average premium of .04%.

Diane Hsiung has been running the fund for 8 years and currently receives a manager quality ranking of 80 (0=worst, 99=best). If you desire only a moderate level of risk and strong performance, then this fund is an excellent option.

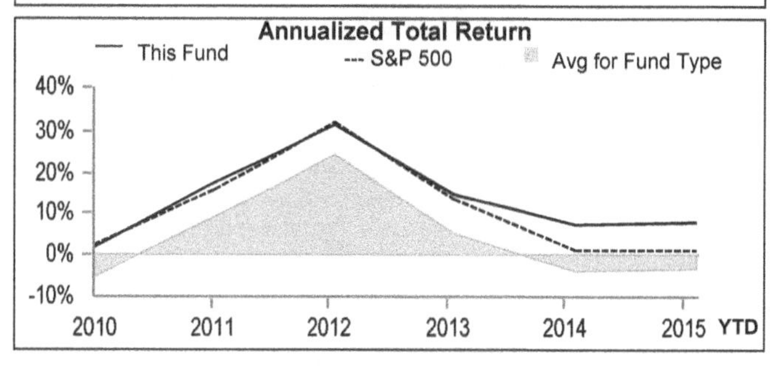

*iShares Morningstar Large-Cp V E (JKF) A Excellent

Fund Family: BlackRock Fund Advisors
Fund Type: Income
Inception Date: June 28, 2004

Data Date	Investment Rating	Net Assets ($Mil)	Price	Performance Rating/Pts	Total Return Y-T-D	Risk Rating/Pts
12-15	A	312.40	81.76	B / 7.8	-1.00%	B / 8.9
2014	B	312.40	86.20	B- / 7.2	10.32%	B- / 7.7
2013	B+	277.90	80.40	B / 7.6	23.84%	B / 8.4
2012	C	244.70	64.47	C / 4.4	14.06%	B / 8.2
2011	C	244.40	58.90	C- / 4.1	1.10%	B / 8.0
2010	D+	208.20	59.53	D / 2.1	14.57%	C+ / 6.1

Major Rating Factors:
Strong performance is the major factor driving the A (Excellent) TheStreet.com Investment Rating for *iShares Morningstar Large-Cp V E. The fund currently has a performance rating of B (Good) based on an annualized return of 10.42% over the last three years and a total return of -1.00% year to date 2015. Factored into the performance evaluation is an expense ratio of 0.25% (very low).

The fund's risk rating is currently B (Good). It carries a beta of 0.96, meaning that its performance tracks fairly well with that of the overall stock market. Volatility, as measured by both the semi-deviation and a drawdown factor, is considered low. As of December 31, 2015, *iShares Morningstar Large-Cp V E traded at a discount of .04% below its net asset value, which is better than its one-year historical average discount of .03%.

Diane Hsiung has been running the fund for 8 years and currently receives a manager quality ranking of 46 (0=worst, 99=best). If you desire only a moderate level of risk and strong performance, then this fund is an excellent option.

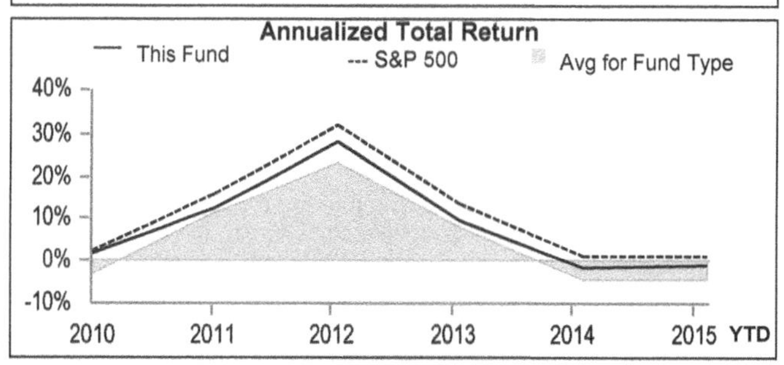

*iShares Morningstar Mid-Cp ETF (JKG) B+ Good

Fund Family: BlackRock Fund Advisors
Fund Type: Growth
Inception Date: June 28, 2004

Data Date	Investment Rating	Net Assets ($Mil)	Price	Performance Rating/Pts	Total Return Y-T-D	Risk Rating/Pts
12-15	B+	298.60	143.06	B+ / 8.5	-0.85%	B- / 7.3
2014	A+	298.60	147.42	B+ / 8.8	16.28%	B+ / 9.0
2013	A-	239.30	129.35	B+ / 8.4	27.89%	B / 8.0
2012	B	158.30	98.60	B- / 7.3	18.12%	B- / 7.8
2011	B-	140.60	85.15	B- / 7.0	3.18%	B- / 7.8
2010	B-	143.90	84.94	B- / 7.1	26.50%	C+ / 5.6

Major Rating Factors: Strong performance is the major factor driving the B+ (Good) TheStreet.com Investment Rating for *iShares Morningstar Mid-Cp ETF. The fund currently has a performance rating of B+ (Good) based on an annualized return of 13.75% over the last three years and a total return of -0.85% year to date 2015. Factored into the performance evaluation is an expense ratio of 0.25% (very low).

The fund's risk rating is currently B- (Good). It carries a beta of 1.01, meaning that its performance tracks fairly well with that of the overall stock market. Volatility, as measured by both the semi-deviation and a drawdown factor, is considered low. As of December 31, 2015, *iShares Morningstar Mid-Cp ETF traded at a premium of .03% above its net asset value, which is better than its one-year historical average premium of .04%.

Diane Hsiung has been running the fund for 8 years and currently receives a manager quality ranking of 66 (0=worst, 99=best). If you desire only a moderate level of risk and strong performance, then this fund is an excellent option.

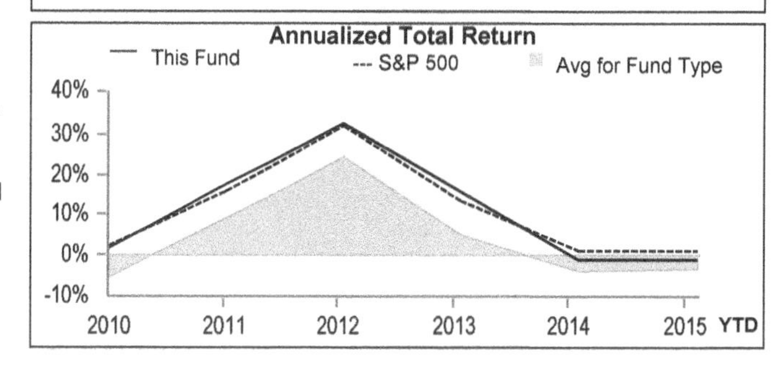

*iShares Morningstar Mid-Cp Gr ET (JKH) B Good

Fund Family: BlackRock Fund Advisors
Fund Type: Growth
Inception Date: June 28, 2004

Major Rating Factors: Strong performance is the major factor driving the B (Good) TheStreet.com Investment Rating for *iShares Morningstar Mid-Cp Gr ET. The fund currently has a performance rating of B (Good) based on an annualized return of 12.58% over the last three years and a total return of 0.49% year to date 2015. Factored into the performance evaluation is an expense ratio of 0.30% (very low).

The fund's risk rating is currently C+ (Fair). It carries a beta of 0.95, meaning that its performance tracks fairly well with that of the overall stock market. Volatility, as measured by both the semi-deviation and a drawdown factor, is considered low. As of December 31, 2015, *iShares Morningstar Mid-Cp Gr ET traded at a premium of .88% above its net asset value, which is worse than its one-year historical average discount of .02%.

Diane Hsiung has been running the fund for 8 years and currently receives a manager quality ranking of 63 (0=worst, 99=best). If you desire only a moderate level of risk and strong performance, then this fund is an excellent option.

Data Date	Investment Rating	Net Assets ($Mil)	Price	Performance Rating/Pts	Total Return Y-T-D	Risk Rating/Pts
12-15	B	199.40	154.55	B / 8.2	0.49%	C+ / 6.8
2014	B-	199.40	156.55	B / 7.9	11.35%	C+ / 6.8
2013	B	192.50	142.62	B / 7.8	29.08%	B- / 7.3
2012	C+	160.50	106.95	C+ / 6.2	15.47%	B- / 7.8
2011	C+	158.70	93.33	C+ / 6.5	-1.40%	B- / 7.5
2010	C	192.00	96.31	C+ / 6.1	27.84%	C / 4.9

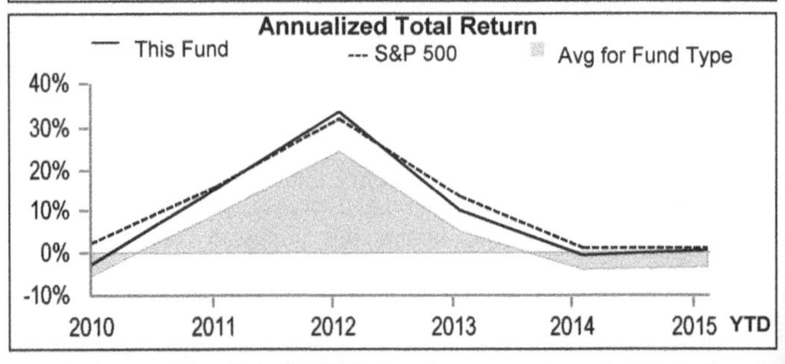

*iShares Morningstar Mid-Cp Val E (JKI) A- Excellent

Fund Family: BlackRock Fund Advisors
Fund Type: Growth
Inception Date: June 28, 2004

Major Rating Factors:
Strong performance is the major factor driving the A- (Excellent) TheStreet.com Investment Rating for *iShares Morningstar Mid-Cp Val E. The fund currently has a performance rating of B+ (Good) based on an annualized return of 14.33% over the last three years and a total return of -1.72% year to date 2015. Factored into the performance evaluation is an expense ratio of 0.30% (very low).

The fund's risk rating is currently B- (Good). It carries a beta of 0.99, meaning that its performance tracks fairly well with that of the overall stock market. Volatility, as measured by both the semi-deviation and a drawdown factor, is considered low. As of December 31, 2015, *iShares Morningstar Mid-Cp Val E traded at a premium of .36% above its net asset value, which is worse than its one-year historical average discount of .01%.

Diane Hsiung has been running the fund for 8 years and currently receives a manager quality ranking of 73 (0=worst, 99=best). If you desire only a moderate level of risk and strong performance, then this fund is an excellent option.

Data Date	Investment Rating	Net Assets ($Mil)	Price	Performance Rating/Pts	Total Return Y-T-D	Risk Rating/Pts
12-15	A-	215.50	118.84	B+ / 8.7	-1.72%	B- / 7.4
2014	A+	215.50	124.54	B+ / 8.8	12.17%	B / 8.7
2013	A-	165.80	114.33	B+ / 8.7	35.54%	B / 8.1
2012	C+	98.90	82.35	C+ / 6.1	18.04%	B- / 7.9
2011	C+	93.50	72.09	C+ / 5.7	-1.89%	B- / 7.7
2010	C+	109.70	75.75	C+ / 6.5	20.46%	C+ / 5.6

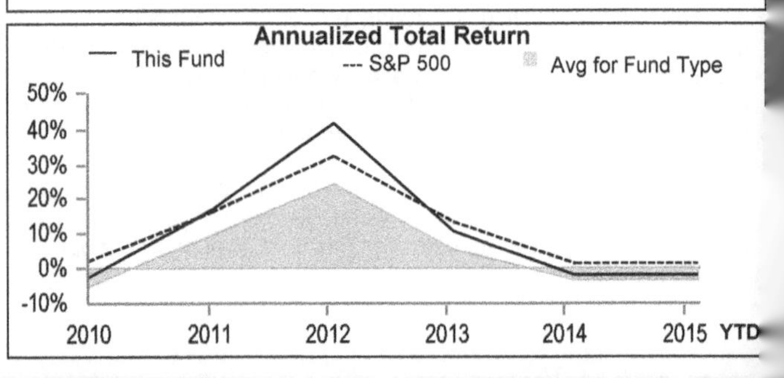

*iShares Morningstar MltAsst Inc (IYLD) C Fair

Fund Family: BlackRock Fund Advisors
Fund Type: Growth and Income
Inception Date: April 3, 2012

Major Rating Factors: Middle of the road best describes *iShares Morningstar MltAsst Inc whose TheStreet.com Investment Rating is currently a C (Fair). The fund currently has a performance rating of C (Fair) based on an annualized return of 1.63% over the last three years and a total return of -4.94% year to date 2015. Factored into the performance evaluation is an expense ratio of 0.24% (very low).

The fund's risk rating is currently C+ (Fair). It carries a beta of 0.39, meaning the fund's expected move will be 3.9% for every 10% move in the market. Volatility, as measured by both the semi-deviation and a drawdown factor, is considered low. As of December 31, 2015, *iShares Morningstar MltAsst Inc traded at a premium of .26% above its net asset value, which is worse than its one-year historical average premium of .03%.

James Mauro has been running the fund for 4 years and currently receives a manager quality ranking of 39 (0=worst, 99=best). If you desire an average level of risk, then this fund may be an option.

Data Date	Investment Rating	Net Assets ($Mil)	Price	Performance Rating/Pts	Total Return Y-T-D	Risk Rating/Pts
12-15	C	186.10	23.27	C / 4.6	-4.94%	C+ / 6.7
2014	C+	186.10	25.62	C / 4.9	10.02%	B / 8.7
2013	C	97.70	24.72	C- / 3.5	-0.24%	B / 8.9

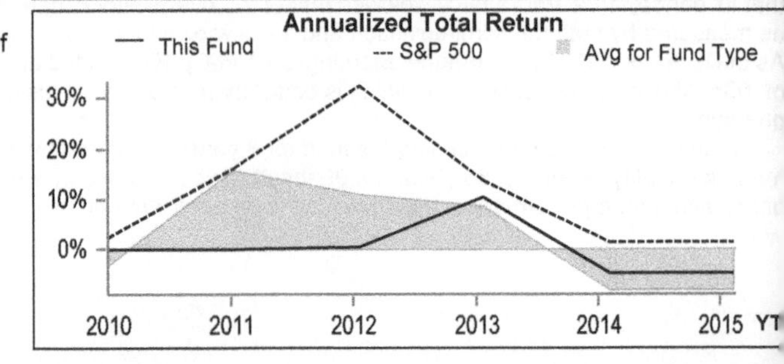

*iShares Morningstar Sm-Cp ETF (JKJ) B+ Good

Fund Family: BlackRock Fund Advisors
Fund Type: Growth
Inception Date: June 28, 2004

Data Date	Investment Rating	Net Assets ($Mil)	Price	Performance Rating/Pts	Total Return Y-T-D	Risk Rating/Pts
12-15	B+	206.40	128.49	B- / 7.2	-4.95%	B / 8.1
2014	B	206.40	138.64	B / 7.9	9.25%	B- / 7.2
2013	B	213.00	129.28	B / 8.1	31.14%	B- / 7.5
2012	C	134.10	95.27	C+ / 6.0	16.66%	B- / 7.2
2011	C+	138.30	83.78	C+ / 6.4	-3.41%	B- / 7.3
2010	B	173.60	89.11	B / 7.8	27.70%	C / 5.5

Major Rating Factors: Strong performance is the major factor driving the B+ (Good) TheStreet.com Investment Rating for *iShares Morningstar Sm-Cp ETF. The fund currently has a performance rating of B- (Good) based on an annualized return of 10.59% over the last three years and a total return of -4.95% year to date 2015. Factored into the performance evaluation is an expense ratio of 0.25% (very low).

The fund's risk rating is currently B (Good). It carries a beta of 1.06, meaning that its performance tracks fairly well with that of the overall stock market. Volatility, as measured by both the semi-deviation and a drawdown factor, is considered low. As of December 31, 2015, *iShares Morningstar Sm-Cp ETF traded at a discount of .18% below its net asset value, which is better than its one-year historical average discount of .02%.

Diane Hsiung has been running the fund for 8 years and currently receives a manager quality ranking of 39 (0=worst, 99=best). If you desire only a moderate level of risk and strong performance, then this fund is an excellent option.

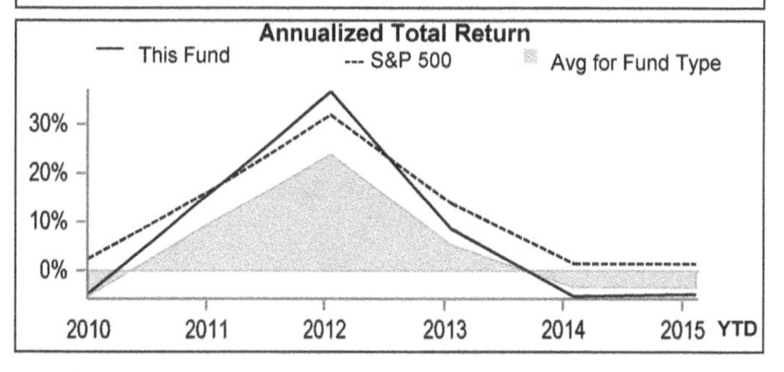

*iShares Morningstar Sm-Cp Gr ETF (JKK) B- Good

Fund Family: BlackRock Fund Advisors
Fund Type: Growth
Inception Date: June 28, 2004

Data Date	Investment Rating	Net Assets ($Mil)	Price	Performance Rating/Pts	Total Return Y-T-D	Risk Rating/Pts
12-15	B-	119.60	134.68	B / 8.2	1.21%	C+ / 6.3
2014	C+	119.60	135.12	B- / 7.5	3.39%	C+ / 5.9
2013	B-	139.10	132.48	B+ / 8.7	36.84%	C+ / 6.3
2012	C+	89.20	93.85	C+ / 6.6	15.44%	B- / 7.1
2011	C+	83.20	83.29	C+ / 6.4	-1.76%	C+ / 6.8
2010	B-	109.80	84.51	B- / 7.2	31.19%	C / 5.3

Major Rating Factors: Strong performance is the major factor driving the B- (Good) TheStreet.com Investment Rating for *iShares Morningstar Sm-Cp Gr ETF. The fund currently has a performance rating of B (Good) based on an annualized return of 12.44% over the last three years and a total return of 1.21% year to date 2015. Factored into the performance evaluation is an expense ratio of 0.30% (very low).

The fund's risk rating is currently C+ (Fair). It carries a beta of 1.01, meaning that its performance tracks fairly well with that of the overall stock market. Volatility, as measured by both the semi-deviation and a drawdown factor, is considered low. As of December 31, 2015, *iShares Morningstar Sm-Cp Gr ETF traded at a premium of .54% above its net asset value, which is worse than its one-year historical average discount of .07%.

Diane Hsiung has been running the fund for 8 years and currently receives a manager quality ranking of 55 (0=worst, 99=best). If you desire only a moderate level of risk and strong performance, then this fund is an excellent option.

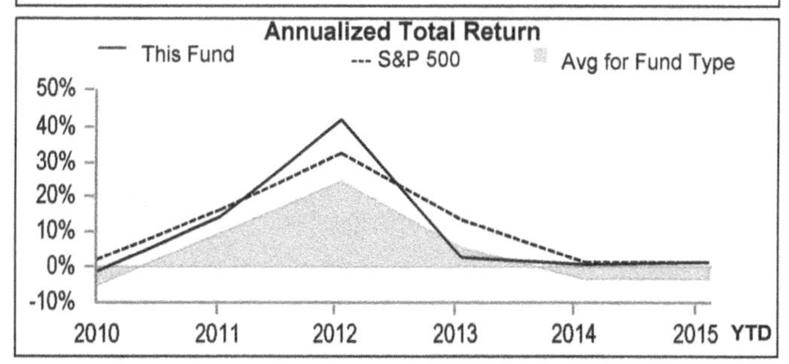

*iShares Morningstar Sm-Cp Val ET (JKL) B- Good

Fund Family: BlackRock Fund Advisors
Fund Type: Growth
Inception Date: June 28, 2004

Data Date	Investment Rating	Net Assets ($Mil)	Price	Performance Rating/Pts	Total Return Y-T-D	Risk Rating/Pts
12-15	B-	375.20	114.77	C+ / 6.9	-7.67%	B- / 7.1
2014	B+	375.20	128.97	B / 8.2	10.76%	B- / 7.4
2013	B+	348.80	120.26	B+ / 8.3	29.05%	B / 8.0
2012	C+	208.50	90.76	C+ / 6.7	18.71%	B- / 7.7
2011	C+	153.80	78.90	C+ / 6.7	-1.38%	B- / 7.5
2010	B+	185.90	82.67	B / 8.0	25.80%	C+ / 5.6

Major Rating Factors: *iShares Morningstar Sm-Cp Val ET receives a TheStreet.com Investment Rating of B- (Good). The fund currently has a performance rating of C+ (Fair) based on an annualized return of 9.52% over the last three years and a total return of -7.67% year to date 2015. Factored into the performance evaluation is an expense ratio of 0.30% (very low).

The fund's risk rating is currently B- (Good). It carries a beta of 1.08, meaning that its performance tracks fairly well with that of the overall stock market. Volatility, as measured by both the semi-deviation and a drawdown factor, is considered low. As of December 31, 2015, *iShares Morningstar Sm-Cp Val ET traded at a premium of .03% above its net asset value, which is worse than its one-year historical average discount of .02%.

Diane Hsiung has been running the fund for 8 years and currently receives a manager quality ranking of 32 (0=worst, 99=best). If you desire an average level of risk, then this fund may be an option.

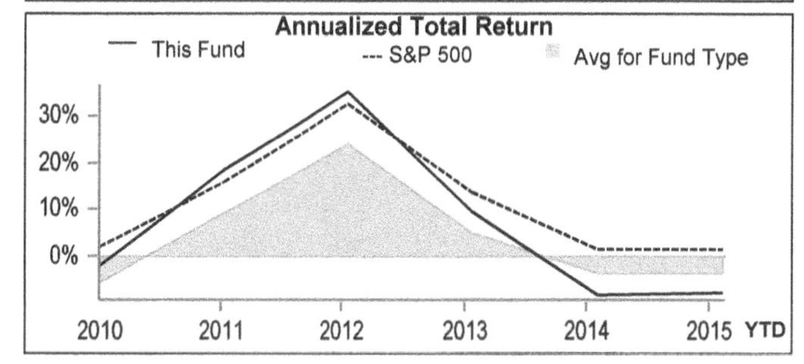

* Denotes ETF Fund

*iShares Mortgage Real Estate Cp (REM) C- Fair

Fund Family: BlackRock Fund Advisors
Fund Type: Income
Inception Date: May 1, 2007

Major Rating Factors: Middle of the road best describes *iShares Mortgage Real Estate Cp whose TheStreet.com Investment Rating is currently a C- (Fair). The fund currently has a performance rating of C- (Fair) based on an annualized return of 0.23% over the last three years and a total return of -8.15% year to date 2015. Factored into the performance evaluation is an expense ratio of 0.48% (very low).

The fund's risk rating is currently C+ (Fair). It carries a beta of 0.49, meaning the fund's expected move will be 4.9% for every 10% move in the market. Volatility, as measured by both the semi-deviation and a drawdown factor, is considered low. As of December 31, 2015, *iShares Mortgage Real Estate Cp traded at a price exactly equal to its net asset value, which is worse than its one-year historical average discount of .02%.

Diane Hsiung has been running the fund for 8 years and currently receives a manager quality ranking of 31 (0=worst, 99=best). If you desire an average level of risk, then this fund may be an option.

Data Date	Investment Rating	Net Assets ($Mil)	Price	Performance Rating/Pts	Total Return Y-T-D	Risk Rating/Pts
12-15	C-	1,215.10	9.56	C- / 3.9	-8.15%	C+ / 6.1
2014	C+	1,215.10	11.71	C+ / 6.1	15.27%	B- / 7.4
2013	C-	947.40	11.52	C- / 3.2	-6.58%	B- / 7.5
2012	C+	862.10	13.67	C+ / 5.8	26.26%	B / 8.1
2011	C-	215.00	12.66	D+ / 2.6	-8.62%	B / 8.0
2010	D-	102.10	15.59	D- / 1.5	16.49%	C- / 4.2

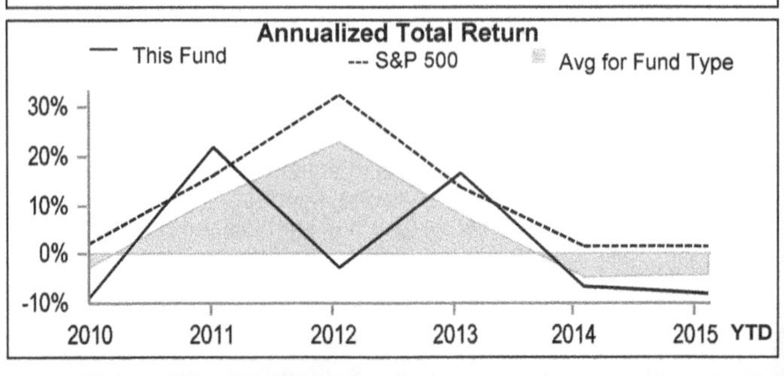

*iShares MSCI ACW Minimum Vol (ACWV) B+ Good

Fund Family: BlackRock Fund Advisors
Fund Type: Global
Inception Date: October 18, 2011

Major Rating Factors: Strong performance is the major factor driving the B+ (Good) TheStreet.com Investment Rating for *iShares MSCI ACW Minimum Vol. The fund currently has a performance rating of B (Good) based on an annualized return of 9.88% over the last three years and a total return of 4.44% year to date 2015. Factored into the performance evaluation is an expense ratio of 0.20% (very low).

The fund's risk rating is currently B (Good). It carries a beta of 0.59, meaning the fund's expected move will be 5.9% for every 10% move in the market. Volatility, as measured by both the semi-deviation and a drawdown factor, is considered low. As of December 31, 2015, *iShares MSCI ACW Minimum Vol traded at a discount of .01% below its net asset value, which is better than its one-year historical average premium of .12%.

Diane Hsiung has been running the fund for 5 years and currently receives a manager quality ranking of 92 (0=worst, 99=best). If you desire only a moderate level of risk and strong performance, then this fund is an excellent option.

Data Date	Investment Rating	Net Assets ($Mil)	Price	Performance Rating/Pts	Total Return Y-T-D	Risk Rating/Pts
12-15	B+	1,253.30	69.27	B / 7.8	4.44%	B / 8.1
2014	C+	1,253.30	68.84	C+ / 6.6	12.08%	B- / 7.2
2013	B+	1,120.60	63.67	B- / 7.0	13.63%	B+ / 9.3
2012	C+	648.00	55.63	C / 4.6	12.41%	B+ / 9.5

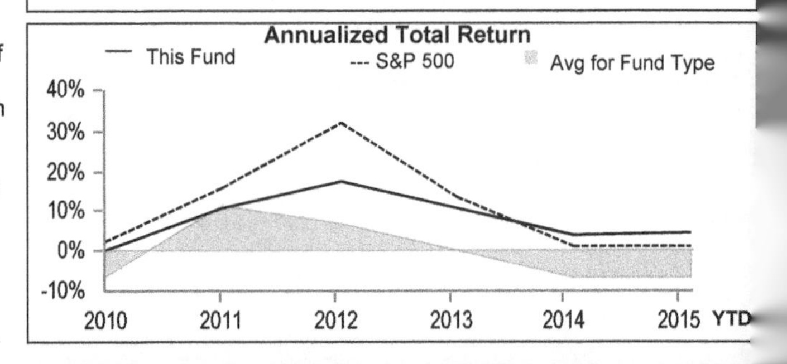

*iShares MSCI ACWI ETF (ACWI) B Good

Fund Family: BlackRock Fund Advisors
Fund Type: Global
Inception Date: March 26, 2008

Major Rating Factors: *iShares MSCI ACWI ETF receives a TheStreet.com Investment Rating of B (Good). The fund currently has a performance rating of C+ (Fair) based on an annualized return of 7.18% over the last three years and a total return of -0.82% year to date 2015. Factored into the performance evaluation is an expense ratio of 0.33% (very low).

The fund's risk rating is currently B (Good). It carries a beta of 0.82, meaning the fund's expected move will be 8.2% for every 10% move in the market. Volatility, as measured by both the semi-deviation and a drawdown factor, is considered low. As of December 31, 2015, *iShares MSCI ACWI ETF traded at a discount of .25% below its net asset value.

Diane Hsiung has been running the fund for 8 years and currently receives a manager quality ranking of 85 (0=worst, 99=best). If you desire an average level of risk, then this fund may be an option.

Data Date	Investment Rating	Net Assets ($Mil)	Price	Performance Rating/Pts	Total Return Y-T-D	Risk Rating/Pts
12-15	B	6,421.80	55.82	C+ / 6.5	-0.82%	B / 8.4
2014	B	6,421.80	58.50	C+ / 6.3	5.33%	B / 8.7
2013	B-	5,270.00	57.62	C+ / 6.9	18.16%	B- / 7.7
2012	C-	3,262.00	48.08	C- / 4.2	17.86%	B- / 7.5
2011	C-	2,189.90	42.17	C- / 4.0	-6.86%	B- / 7.6
2010	A-	1,501.30	46.81	A- / 9.0	12.82%	C+ / 5.6

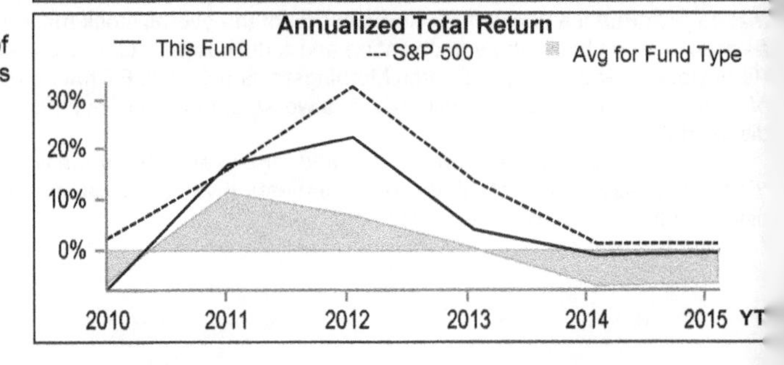

*iShares MSCI ACWI ex US ETF (ACWX) C Fair

Fund Family: BlackRock Fund Advisors
Fund Type: Foreign
Inception Date: March 26, 2008

Data Date	Investment Rating	Net Assets ($Mil)	Price	Performance Rating/Pts	Total Return Y-T-D	Risk Rating/Pts
12-15	C	1,701.60	39.61	C- / 4.0	-4.49%	B / 8.2
2014	C-	1,701.60	43.02	C / 4.3	-3.21%	C+ / 6.8
2013	C	1,696.50	46.67	C / 5.1	10.85%	B- / 7.6
2012	C-	1,276.00	41.88	C- / 3.7	18.92%	B- / 7.4
2011	D+	835.90	36.81	C- / 3.0	-13.57%	B- / 7.3
2010	B+	771.80	44.04	B+ / 8.9	10.44%	C / 5.0

Major Rating Factors: Middle of the road best describes *iShares MSCI ACWI ex US ETF whose TheStreet.com Investment Rating is currently a C (Fair). The fund currently has a performance rating of C- (Fair) based on an annualized return of 0.61% over the last three years and a total return of -4.49% year to date 2015. Factored into the performance evaluation is an expense ratio of 0.33% (very low).

The fund's risk rating is currently B (Good). It carries a beta of 0.95, meaning that its performance tracks fairly well with that of the overall stock market. Volatility, as measured by both the semi-deviation and a drawdown factor, is considered low. As of December 31, 2015, *iShares MSCI ACWI ex US ETF traded at a discount of .53% below its net asset value, which is better than its one-year historical average premium of .06%.

Diane Hsiung has been running the fund for 8 years and currently receives a manager quality ranking of 37 (0=worst, 99=best). If you desire an average level of risk, then this fund may be an option.

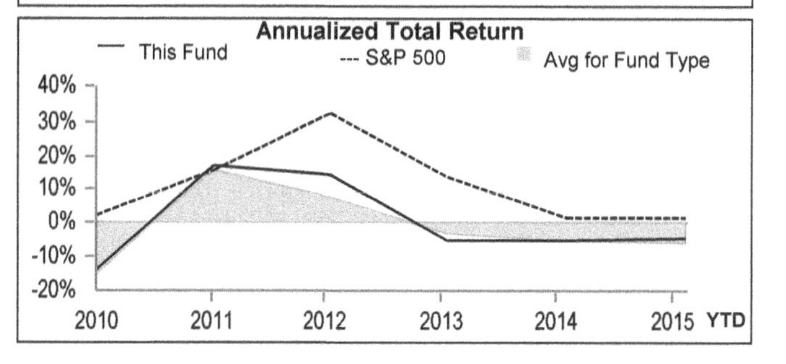

*iShares MSCI ACWI Low Carbon Tar (CRBN) D+ Weak

Fund Family: BlackRock Fund Advisors
Fund Type: Energy/Natural Resources
Inception Date: December 8, 2014

Data Date	Investment Rating	Net Assets ($Mil)	Price	Performance Rating/Pts	Total Return Y-T-D	Risk Rating/Pts
12-15	D+	0.00	93.03	C / 5.3	1.25%	C- / 3.4

Major Rating Factors: *iShares MSCI ACWI Low Carbon Tar receives a TheStreet.com Investment Rating of D+ (Weak). The fund currently has a performance rating of C (Fair) based on an annualized return of 0.00% over the last three years and a total return of 1.25% year to date 2015. Factored into the performance evaluation is an expense ratio of 0.20% (very low).

The fund's risk rating is currently C- (Fair). It carries a beta of 0.00, meaning the fund's expected move will be 0.0% for every 10% move in the market. Volatility, as measured by both the semi-deviation and a drawdown factor, is considered average. As of December 31, 2015, *iShares MSCI ACWI Low Carbon Tar traded at a premium of 1.19% above its net asset value, which is worse than its one-year historical average premium of .19%.

Gregory R Savage has been running the fund for 2 years and currently receives a manager quality ranking of 96 (0=worst, 99=best). If you desire an average level of risk, then this fund may be an option.

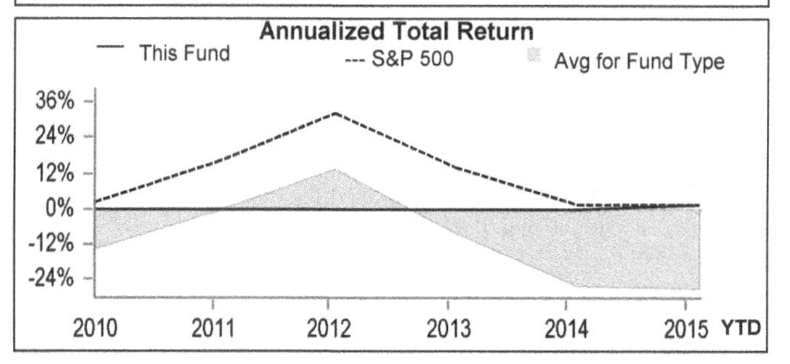

*iShares MSCI All Ctry Asia xJap (AAXJ) C- Fair

Fund Family: BlackRock Fund Advisors
Fund Type: Foreign
Inception Date: August 13, 2008

Data Date	Investment Rating	Net Assets ($Mil)	Price	Performance Rating/Pts	Total Return Y-T-D	Risk Rating/Pts
12-15	C-	2,731.10	53.41	C- / 3.1	-8.39%	B- / 7.4
2014	C+	2,731.10	60.93	C / 5.0	6.85%	B / 8.2
2013	D+	2,708.60	60.31	D+ / 2.3	-3.55%	C+ / 6.9
2012	C-	2,128.30	60.52	C- / 3.9	19.73%	C+ / 6.9
2011	C-	2,006.60	49.90	C / 4.5	-19.52%	B- / 7.1
2010	A-	2,657.90	63.70	A- / 9.0	16.22%	C+ / 6.0

Major Rating Factors: Middle of the road best describes *iShares MSCI All Ctry Asia xJap whose TheStreet.com Investment Rating is currently a C- (Fair). The fund currently has a performance rating of C- (Fair) based on an annualized return of -2.06% over the last three years and a total return of -8.39% year to date 2015. Factored into the performance evaluation is an expense ratio of 0.69% (very low).

The fund's risk rating is currently B- (Good). It carries a beta of 0.83, meaning the fund's expected move will be 8.3% for every 10% move in the market. Volatility, as measured by both the semi-deviation and a drawdown factor, is considered low. As of December 31, 2015, *iShares MSCI All Ctry Asia xJap traded at a discount of .67% below its net asset value, which is better than its one-year historical average discount of .10%.

Diane Hsiung has been running the fund for 8 years and currently receives a manager quality ranking of 26 (0=worst, 99=best). If you desire an average level of risk, then this fund may be an option.

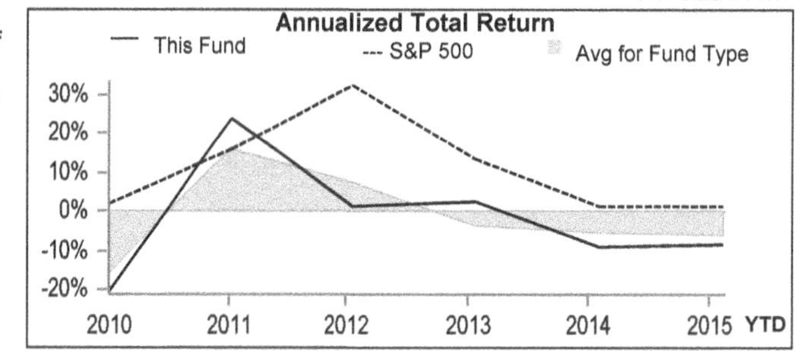

*iShares MSCI All Peru Capped ETF (EPU) D- Weak

Fund Family: BlackRock Fund Advisors
Fund Type: Foreign
Inception Date: June 19, 2009

Data Date	Investment Rating	Net Assets ($Mil)	Price	Performance Rating/Pts	Total Return Y-T-D	Risk Rating/Pts
12-15	D-	288.00	20.18	E+ / 0.6	-35.81%	C / 5.4
2014	D	288.00	31.96	D / 1.9	-3.33%	C+ / 6.7
2013	D-	313.50	33.66	D- / 1.0	-27.19%	C+ / 6.0
2012	C+	509.60	45.88	B / 7.7	21.53%	C+ / 6.7
2011	D	429.60	38.37	D- / 1.4	-16.95%	B- / 7.4
2010	A+	556.20	50.36	A+ / 9.8	57.46%	B / 8.3

Major Rating Factors:
Very poor performance is the major factor driving the D- (Weak) TheStreet.com Investment Rating for *iShares MSCI All Peru Capped ETF. The fund currently has a performance rating of E+ (Very Weak) based on an annualized return of -23.29% over the last three years and a total return of -35.81% year to date 2015. Factored into the performance evaluation is an expense ratio of 0.61% (very low).

The fund's risk rating is currently C (Fair). It carries a beta of 0.58, meaning the fund's expected move will be 5.8% for every 10% move in the market. Volatility, as measured by both the semi-deviation and a drawdown factor, is considered average. As of December 31, 2015, *iShares MSCI All Peru Capped ETF traded at a discount of .98% below its net asset value, which is better than its one-year historical average discount of .40%.

Diane Hsiung has been running the fund for 7 years and currently receives a manager quality ranking of 4 (0=worst, 99=best). This fund offers an average level of risk but investors looking for strong performance will be frustrated.

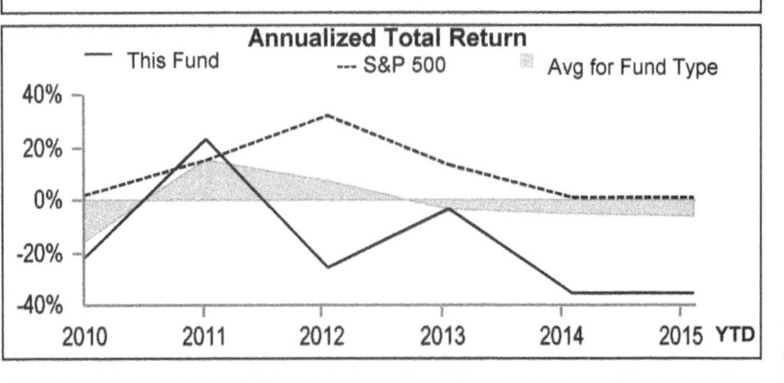

*iShares MSCI Asia ex-Japan Min V (AXJV) C- Fair

Fund Family: BlackRock Fund Advisors
Fund Type: Foreign
Inception Date: June 3, 2014

Data Date	Investment Rating	Net Assets ($Mil)	Price	Performance Rating/Pts	Total Return Y-T-D	Risk Rating/Pts
12-15	C-	5.20	45.91	D+ / 2.4	-4.12%	B- / 7.5

Major Rating Factors:
Disappointing performance is the major factor driving the C- (Fair) TheStreet.com Investment Rating for *iShares MSCI Asia ex-Japan Min V. The fund currently has a performance rating of D+ (Weak) based on an annualized return of 0.00% over the last three years and a total return of -4.12% year to date 2015. Factored into the performance evaluation is an expense ratio of 0.35% (very low).

The fund's risk rating is currently B- (Good). It carries a beta of 0.00, meaning the fund's expected move will be 0.0% for every 10% move in the market. Volatility, as measured by both the semi-deviation and a drawdown factor, is considered low. As of December 31, 2015, *iShares MSCI Asia ex-Japan Min V traded at a discount of 1.08% below its net asset value, which is better than its one-year historical average discount of .08%.

Jennifer F.Y. Hsui has been running the fund for 2 years and currently receives a manager quality ranking of 33 (0=worst, 99=best). This fund offers only a moderate level of risk but investors looking for strong performance are still waiting.

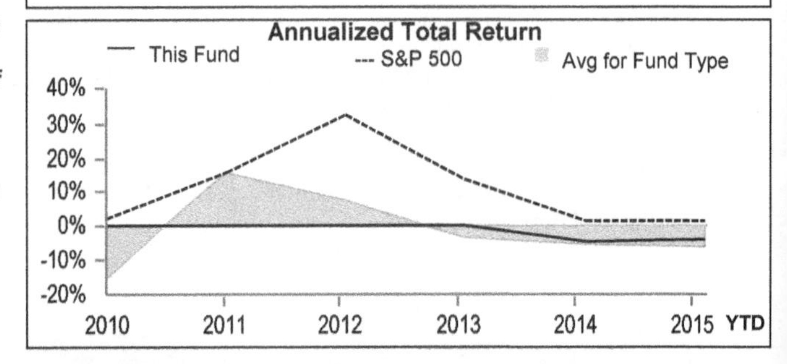

*iShares MSCI Australia (EWA) D+ Weak

Fund Family: BlackRock Fund Advisors
Fund Type: Foreign
Inception Date: March 12, 1996

Data Date	Investment Rating	Net Assets ($Mil)	Price	Performance Rating/Pts	Total Return Y-T-D	Risk Rating/Pts
12-15	D+	1,812.70	18.96	C- / 3.0	-7.28%	C+ / 6.1
2014	C-	1,812.70	22.17	C- / 3.5	-4.96%	B- / 7.0
2013	C-	1,924.10	24.37	C / 4.6	0.59%	C+ / 6.5
2012	C-	2,387.70	25.14	C / 4.3	20.88%	C+ / 6.6
2011	C+	2,637.80	21.44	C+ / 6.3	-6.55%	C+ / 6.9
2010	C-	2,958.40	25.44	C+ / 5.6	15.35%	C- / 4.1

Major Rating Factors: *iShares MSCI Australia receives a TheStreet.com Investment Rating of D+ (Weak). The fund currently has a performance rating of C- (Fair) based on an annualized return of -4.04% over the last three years and a total return of -7.28% year to date 2015. Factored into the performance evaluation is an expense ratio of 0.48% (very low).

The fund's risk rating is currently C+ (Fair). It carries a beta of 1.07, meaning that its performance tracks fairly well with that of the overall stock market. Volatility, as measured by both the semi-deviation and a drawdown factor, is considered low. As of December 31, 2015, *iShares MSCI Australia traded at a discount of .68% below its net asset value, which is better than its one-year historical average discount of .11%.

Diane Hsiung has been running the fund for 8 years and currently receives a manager quality ranking of 18 (0=worst, 99=best). If you desire an average level of risk, then this fund may be an option.

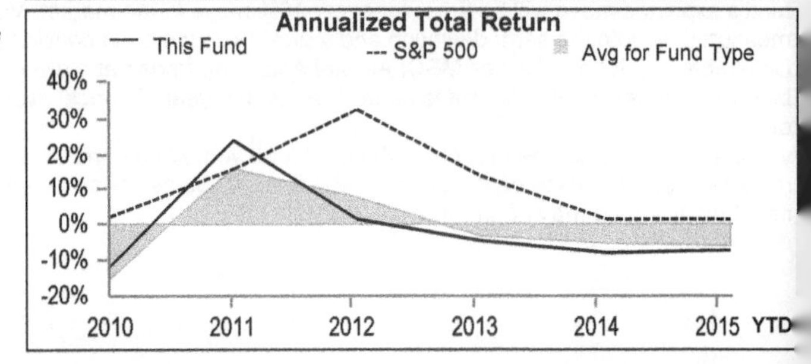

*iShares MSCI Austria Capped (EWO) C- Fair

Fund Family: BlackRock Fund Advisors
Fund Type: Foreign
Inception Date: March 12, 1996

Major Rating Factors: Middle of the road best describes *iShares MSCI Austria Capped whose TheStreet.com Investment Rating is currently a C- (Fair). The fund currently has a performance rating of C- (Fair) based on an annualized return of -2.76% over the last three years and a total return of 3.75% year to date 2015. Factored into the performance evaluation is an expense ratio of 0.48% (very low).

The fund's risk rating is currently C+ (Fair). It carries a beta of 1.10, meaning it is expected to move 11.0% for every 10% move in the market. Volatility, as measured by both the semi-deviation and a drawdown factor, is considered low. As of December 31, 2015, *iShares MSCI Austria Capped traded at a discount of .95% below its net asset value, which is better than its one-year historical average discount of .06%.

Diane Hsiung has been running the fund for 8 years and currently receives a manager quality ranking of 20 (0=worst, 99=best). If you desire an average level of risk, then this fund may be an option.

Data Date	Investment Rating	Net Assets ($Mil)	Price	Performance Rating/Pts	Total Return Y-T-D	Risk Rating/Pts
12-15	C-	58.30	15.65	C- / 3.7	3.75%	C+ / 6.9
2014	D+	58.30	15.18	D+ / 2.9	-19.83%	C+ / 6.9
2013	D	88.80	19.81	C- / 3.6	9.25%	C+ / 5.6
2012	D	121.30	18.19	D+ / 2.9	35.72%	C / 5.4
2011	D-	53.90	14.22	D / 1.6	-33.36%	C+ / 5.7
2010	E+	119.50	22.33	D- / 1.3	15.81%	D+ / 2.8

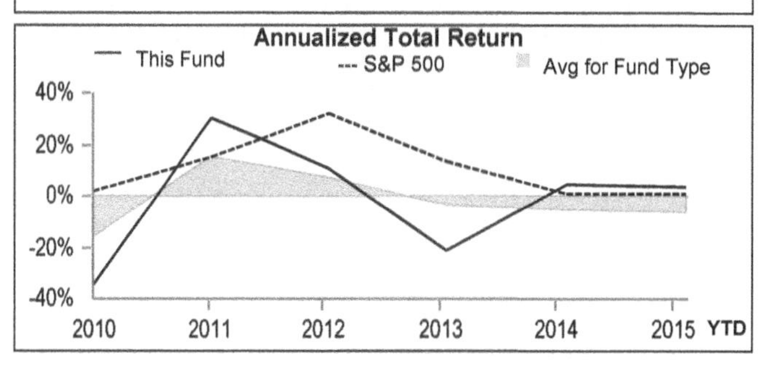

*iShares MSCI Belgium Capped (EWK) A+ Excellent

Fund Family: BlackRock Fund Advisors
Fund Type: Foreign
Inception Date: March 12, 1996

Major Rating Factors:
Exceptional performance is the major factor driving the A+ (Excellent) TheStreet.com Investment Rating for *iShares MSCI Belgium Capped. The fund currently has a performance rating of A- (Excellent) based on an annualized return of 12.85% over the last three years and a total return of 14.21% year to date 2015. Factored into the performance evaluation is an expense ratio of 0.48% (very low).

The fund's risk rating is currently B (Good). It carries a beta of 0.86, meaning the fund's expected move will be 8.6% for every 10% move in the market. Volatility, as measured by both the semi-deviation and a drawdown factor, is considered low. As of December 31, 2015, *iShares MSCI Belgium Capped traded at a discount of .39% below its net asset value, which is better than its one-year historical average premium of .05%.

Diane Hsiung has been running the fund for 8 years and currently receives a manager quality ranking of 93 (0=worst, 99=best). If you desire only a moderate level of risk and strong performance, then this fund is an excellent option.

Data Date	Investment Rating	Net Assets ($Mil)	Price	Performance Rating/Pts	Total Return Y-T-D	Risk Rating/Pts
12-15	A+	146.90	18.06	A- / 9.0	14.21%	B / 8.7
2014	B+	146.90	16.21	B- / 7.5	2.80%	B / 8.5
2013	C+	67.20	16.39	B / 7.7	22.31%	C+ / 6.8
2012	C	57.20	13.85	C+ / 6.4	38.55%	C+ / 6.6
2011	D+	23.40	10.59	D+ / 2.6	-14.35%	C+ / 6.8
2010	E+	50.40	13.13	E+ / 0.7	5.07%	C- / 3.3

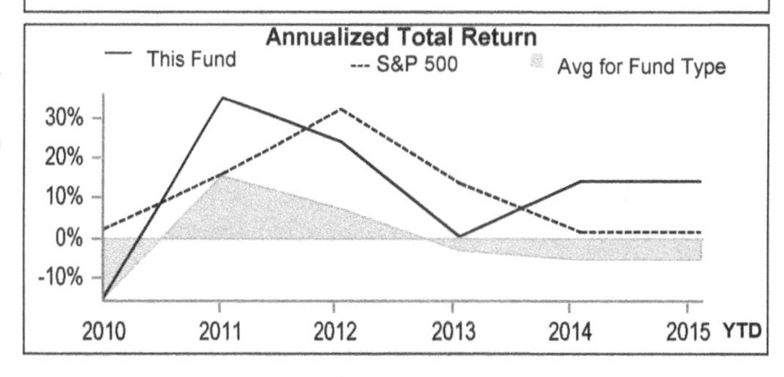

*iShares MSCI Brazil Capped (EWZ) E+ Very Weak

Fund Family: BlackRock Fund Advisors
Fund Type: Foreign
Inception Date: July 10, 2000

Major Rating Factors:
Very poor performance is the major factor driving the E+ (Very Weak) TheStreet.com Investment Rating for *iShares MSCI Brazil Capped. The fund currently has a performance rating of E (Very Weak) based on an annualized return of -26.23% over the last three years and a total return of -39.11% year to date 2015. Factored into the performance evaluation is an expense ratio of 0.62% (very low).

The fund's risk rating is currently C- (Fair). It carries a beta of 1.49, meaning it is expected to move 14.9% for every 10% move in the market. Volatility, as measured by both the semi-deviation and a drawdown factor, is considered average. As of December 31, 2015, *iShares MSCI Brazil Capped traded at a discount of 1.29% below its net asset value, which is better than its one-year historical average discount of .17%.

Diane Hsiung has been running the fund for 8 years and currently receives a manager quality ranking of 2 (0=worst, 99=best). This fund offers an average level of risk but investors looking for strong performance will be frustrated.

Data Date	Investment Rating	Net Assets ($Mil)	Price	Performance Rating/Pts	Total Return Y-T-D	Risk Rating/Pts
12-15	E+	5,099.40	20.68	E / 0.5	-39.11%	C- / 3.4
2014	E	5,099.40	36.57	D- / 1.0	-13.10%	D+ / 2.7
2013	E+	4,378.30	44.68	E+ / 0.7	-21.54%	C / 5.2
2012	D-	9,303.80	55.94	D- / 1.0	-5.20%	C+ / 6.2
2011	C-	9,346.00	57.39	C / 4.9	-21.34%	C+ / 6.5
2010	C-	11,699.30	77.40	C+ / 5.6	7.42%	C- / 3.6

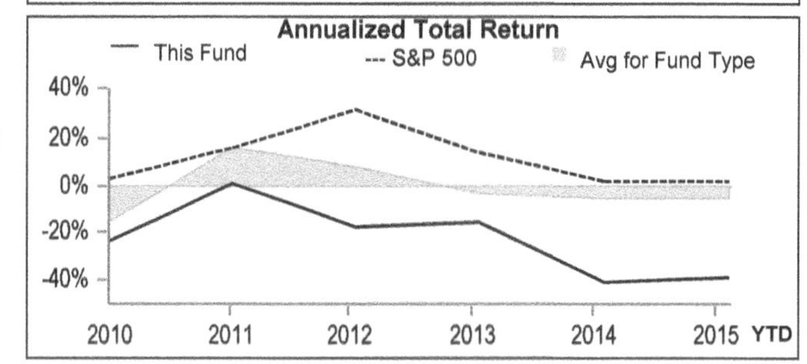

*iShares MSCI Brazil Small-Cap ET (EWZS) E+ Very Weak

Fund Family: BlackRock Fund Advisors
Fund Type: Foreign
Inception Date: September 28, 2010

Data Date	Investment Rating	Net Assets ($Mil)	Price	Performance Rating/Pts	Total Return Y-T-D	Risk Rating/Pts
12-15	E+	33.80	6.88	E- / 0.2	-48.26%	C- / 3.2
2014	E	33.80	14.28	E+ / 0.9	-24.82%	D+ / 2.5
2013	D-	34.70	19.82	E+ / 0.8	-28.62%	C+ / 5.6
2012	B	55.00	27.80	A / 9.5	21.15%	C+ / 6.1
2011	D-	45.30	22.41	E+ / 0.7	-22.60%	C+ / 6.1

Major Rating Factors:
Very poor performance is the major factor driving the E+ (Very Weak) TheStreet.com Investment Rating for *iShares MSCI Brazil Small-Cap ET. The fund currently has a performance rating of E- (Very Weak) based on an annualized return of -35.49% over the last three years and a total return of -48.26% year to date 2015. Factored into the performance evaluation is an expense ratio of 0.62% (very low).

The fund's risk rating is currently C- (Fair). It carries a beta of 1.44, meaning it is expected to move 14.4% for every 10% move in the market. Volatility, as measured by both the semi-deviation and a drawdown factor, is considered average. As of December 31, 2015, *iShares MSCI Brazil Small-Cap ET traded at a discount of 2.55% below its net asset value, which is better than its one-year historical average premium of .35%.

Diane Hsiung has been running the fund for 6 years and currently receives a manager quality ranking of 1 (0=worst, 99=best). This fund offers an average level of risk but investors looking for strong performance will be frustrated.

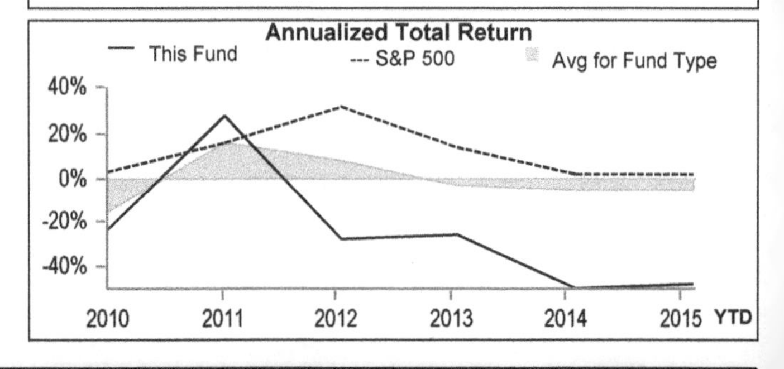

*iShares MSCI BRIC (BKF) D+ Weak

Fund Family: BlackRock Fund Advisors
Fund Type: Foreign
Inception Date: November 12, 2007

Data Date	Investment Rating	Net Assets ($Mil)	Price	Performance Rating/Pts	Total Return Y-T-D	Risk Rating/Pts
12-15	D+	364.10	29.27	D / 2.1	-12.23%	C+ / 6.6
2014	D+	364.10	35.03	D+ / 2.6	-1.13%	B- / 7.0
2013	D-	499.30	37.69	D- / 1.4	-10.91%	C+ / 6.2
2012	D	772.60	40.84	D / 1.8	10.32%	C+ / 6.4
2011	C-	683.90	36.27	C- / 4.0	-23.34%	C+ / 6.7
2010	D-	1,188.10	49.13	D / 2.2	9.13%	C- / 4.0

Major Rating Factors:
Disappointing performance is the major factor driving the D+ (Weak) TheStreet.com Investment Rating for *iShares MSCI BRIC. The fund currently has a performance rating of D (Weak) based on an annualized return of -8.31% over the last three years and a total return of -12.23% year to date 2015. Factored into the performance evaluation is an expense ratio of 0.69% (very low).

The fund's risk rating is currently C+ (Fair). It carries a beta of 1.03, meaning that its performance tracks fairly well with that of the overall stock market. Volatility, as measured by both the semi-deviation and a drawdown factor, is considered low. As of December 31, 2015, *iShares MSCI BRIC traded at a discount of .91% below its net asset value, which is better than its one-year historical average discount of .42%.

Diane Hsiung has been running the fund for 8 years and currently receives a manager quality ranking of 13 (0=worst, 99=best). This fund offers only a moderate level of risk but investors looking for strong performance are still waiting.

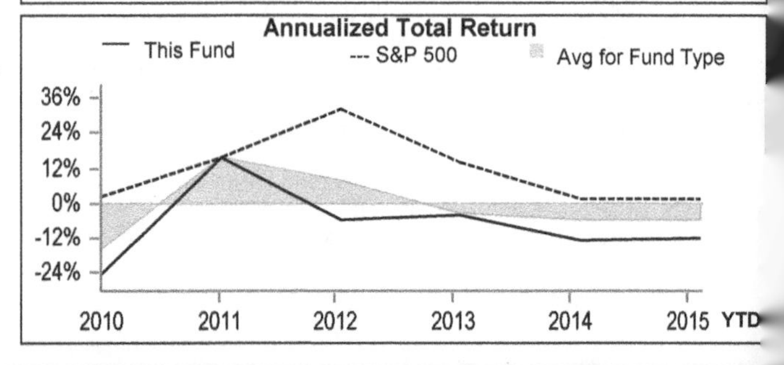

*iShares MSCI Canada (EWC) D Weak

Fund Family: BlackRock Fund Advisors
Fund Type: Foreign
Inception Date: March 12, 1996

Data Date	Investment Rating	Net Assets ($Mil)	Price	Performance Rating/Pts	Total Return Y-T-D	Risk Rating/Pts
12-15	D	3,500.90	21.50	D / 2.0	-22.44%	C+ / 5.8
2014	C-	3,500.90	28.86	C- / 3.5	1.79%	B- / 7.1
2013	C-	3,320.20	29.16	C- / 3.1	3.08%	B- / 7.7
2012	D+	4,733.20	28.40	D+ / 2.9	9.44%	B- / 7.5
2011	C	4,471.00	26.60	C / 4.6	-11.03%	B- / 7.4
2010	C	4,647.50	31.00	C+ / 5.6	19.80%	C / 5.0

Major Rating Factors:
Disappointing performance is the major factor driving the D (Weak) TheStreet.com Investment Rating for *iShares MSCI Canada. The fund currently has a performance rating of D (Weak) based on an annualized return of -6.82% over the last three years and a total return of -22.44% year to date 2015. Factored into the performance evaluation is an expense ratio of 0.48% (very low).

The fund's risk rating is currently C+ (Fair). It carries a beta of 0.77, meaning the fund's expected move will be 7.7% for every 10% move in the market. Volatility, as measured by both the semi-deviation and a drawdown factor, is considered low. As of December 31, 2015, *iShares MSCI Canada traded at a premium of .37% above its net asset value, which is worse than its one-year historical average discount of .03%.

Diane Hsiung has been running the fund for 8 years and currently receives a manager quality ranking of 16 (0=worst, 99=best). This fund offers only a moderate level of risk but investors looking for strong performance are still waiting.

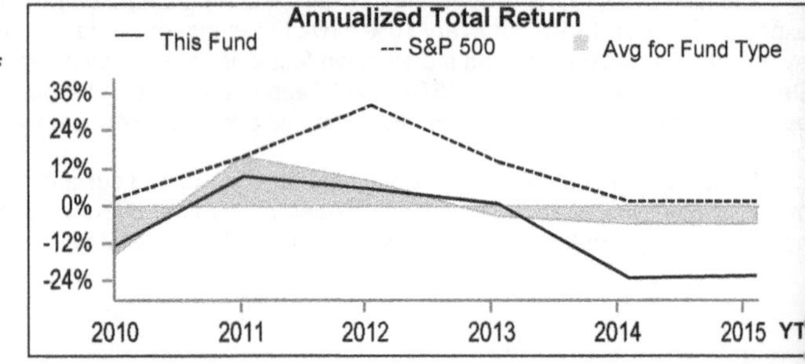

*iShares MSCI Chile Capped (ECH) D- Weak

Fund Family: BlackRock Fund Advisors
Fund Type: Foreign
Inception Date: November 12, 2007

Data Date	Investment Rating	Net Assets ($Mil)	Price	Performance Rating/Pts	Total Return Y-T-D	Risk Rating/Pts
12-15	D-	318.90	31.92	D- / 1.0	-17.20%	C / 5.1
2014	E+	318.90	39.89	D- / 1.2	-12.25%	C- / 3.7
2013	D-	365.30	47.51	E+ / 0.7	-27.75%	C+ / 5.7
2012	D	548.40	63.24	D+ / 2.7	10.29%	C+ / 6.4
2011	C+	505.80	57.71	C+ / 6.5	-18.08%	C+ / 6.7
2010	A-	1,006.80	79.60	A / 9.3	46.59%	C+ / 5.6

Major Rating Factors:
Disappointing performance is the major factor driving the D- (Weak) TheStreet.com Investment Rating for *iShares MSCI Chile Capped. The fund currently has a performance rating of D- (Weak) based on an annualized return of -19.66% over the last three years and a total return of -17.20% year to date 2015. Factored into the performance evaluation is an expense ratio of 0.62% (very low).

The fund's risk rating is currently C (Fair). It carries a beta of 0.81, meaning the fund's expected move will be 8.1% for every 10% move in the market. Volatility, as measured by both the semi-deviation and a drawdown factor, is considered average. As of December 31, 2015, *iShares MSCI Chile Capped traded at a discount of 1.48% below its net asset value, which is better than its one-year historical average discount of .14%.

Diane Hsiung has been running the fund for 8 years and currently receives a manager quality ranking of 6 (0=worst, 99=best). This fund offers an average level of risk but investors looking for strong performance will be frustrated.

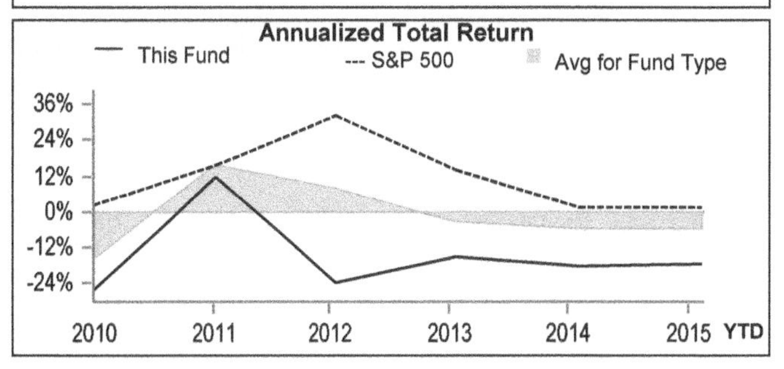

*iShares MSCI China ETF (MCHI) C- Fair

Fund Family: BlackRock Fund Advisors
Fund Type: Foreign
Inception Date: March 29, 2011

Data Date	Investment Rating	Net Assets ($Mil)	Price	Performance Rating/Pts	Total Return Y-T-D	Risk Rating/Pts
12-15	C-	1,163.50	44.62	C- / 3.3	-7.76%	C+ / 6.6
2014	C+	1,163.50	50.23	C+ / 6.1	11.06%	B- / 7.6
2013	D+	1,082.00	48.22	C- / 4.2	-4.28%	C+ / 6.4
2012	B	831.30	48.54	A+ / 9.6	20.53%	C+ / 6.3

Major Rating Factors: Middle of the road best describes *iShares MSCI China ETF whose TheStreet.com Investment Rating is currently a C- (Fair). The fund currently has a performance rating of C- (Fair) based on an annualized return of -0.63% over the last three years and a total return of -7.76% year to date 2015. Factored into the performance evaluation is an expense ratio of 0.62% (very low).

The fund's risk rating is currently C+ (Fair). It carries a beta of 0.90, meaning that its performance tracks fairly well with that of the overall stock market. Volatility, as measured by both the semi-deviation and a drawdown factor, is considered low. As of December 31, 2015, *iShares MSCI China ETF traded at a discount of .25% below its net asset value, which is better than its one-year historical average premium of .01%.

Diane Hsiung has been running the fund for 5 years and currently receives a manager quality ranking of 33 (0=worst, 99=best). If you desire an average level of risk, then this fund may be an option.

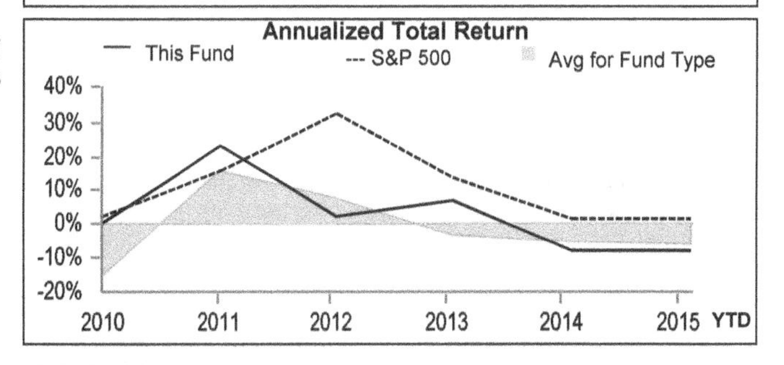

*iShares MSCI China Small-Cap ETF (ECNS) C Fair

Fund Family: BlackRock Fund Advisors
Fund Type: Foreign
Inception Date: September 28, 2010

Data Date	Investment Rating	Net Assets ($Mil)	Price	Performance Rating/Pts	Total Return Y-T-D	Risk Rating/Pts
12-15	C	33.20	44.55	C+ / 5.9	4.18%	C+ / 6.1
2014	C+	33.20	45.33	C+ / 6.2	0.35%	B- / 7.4
2013	D	32.30	46.44	D+ / 2.7	11.27%	C / 5.3
2012	B-	22.00	41.09	A+ / 9.8	31.87%	C / 5.2
2011	E+	15.10	33.19	E / 0.3	-40.13%	C / 5.2

Major Rating Factors: Middle of the road best describes *iShares MSCI China Small-Cap ETF whose TheStreet.com Investment Rating is currently a C (Fair). The fund currently has a performance rating of C+ (Fair) based on an annualized return of 4.83% over the last three years and a total return of 4.18% year to date 2015. Factored into the performance evaluation is an expense ratio of 0.62% (very low).

The fund's risk rating is currently C+ (Fair). It carries a beta of 0.95, meaning that its performance tracks fairly well with that of the overall stock market. Volatility, as measured by both the semi-deviation and a drawdown factor, is considered low. As of December 31, 2015, *iShares MSCI China Small-Cap ETF traded at a discount of 2.54% below its net asset value, which is better than its one-year historical average discount of .66%.

Diane Hsiung has been running the fund for 6 years and currently receives a manager quality ranking of 77 (0=worst, 99=best). If you desire an average level of risk, then this fund may be an option.

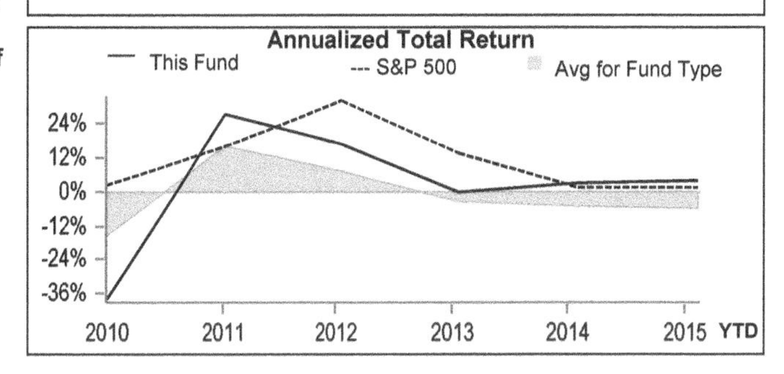

*iShares MSCI Colombia Capped (ICOL) E Very Weak

Fund Family: BlackRock Fund Advisors
Fund Type: General - Investment Grade
Inception Date: June 18, 2013

Major Rating Factors: *iShares MSCI Colombia Capped has adopted a very risky asset allocation strategy and currently receives an overall TheStreet.com Investment Rating of E (Very Weak). The fund has a high level of volatility, as measured by both semi-deviation and drawdown factors. It carries a beta of 0.00, meaning the fund's expected move will be 0.0% for every 10% move in the market. As of December 31, 2015, *iShares MSCI Colombia Capped traded at a premium of .28% above its net asset value, which is better than its one-year historical average premium of .94%. Unfortunately, the high level of risk (D, Weak) failed to pay off as investors endured very poor performance.

The fund's performance rating is currently E- (Very Weak). It has registered an annualized return of 0.00% over the last three years but is down -39.81% year to date 2015. Factored into the performance evaluation is an expense ratio of 0.61% (very low).

Thomas F. Cooper has been running the fund for 22 years and currently receives a manager quality ranking of 1 (0=worst, 99=best). If you can tolerate very high levels of risk in the hope of improved future returns, holding this fund may be an option.

Data Date	Investment Rating	Net Assets ($Mil)	Price	Performance Rating/Pts	Total Return Y-T-D	Risk Rating/Pts
12-15	E	22.50	10.57	E- / 0.1	-39.81%	D / 1.8
2014	E	22.50	18.14	E- / 0.1	-28.02%	C- / 3.5

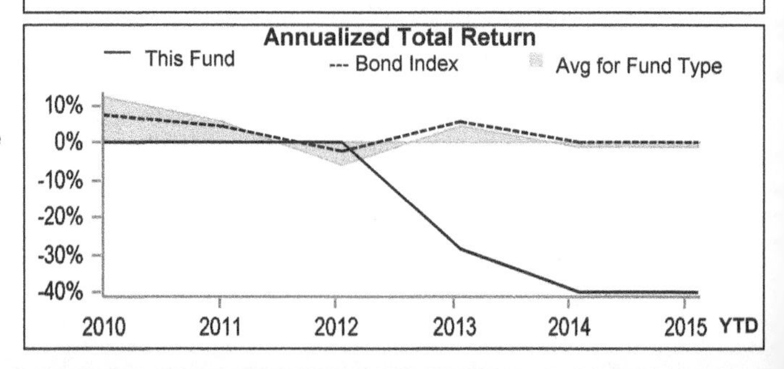

*iShares MSCI Denmark Capped ETF (EDEN) A+ Excellent

Fund Family: BlackRock Fund Advisors
Fund Type: Foreign
Inception Date: January 25, 2012

Major Rating Factors:
Exceptional performance is the major factor driving the A+ (Excellent) TheStreet.com Investment Rating for *iShares MSCI Denmark Capped ETF. The fund currently has a performance rating of A+ (Excellent) based on an annualized return of 21.52% over the last three years and a total return of 19.14% year to date 2015. Factored into the performance evaluation is an expense ratio of 0.53% (very low).

The fund's risk rating is currently B (Good). It carries a beta of 0.81, meaning the fund's expected move will be 8.1% for every 10% move in the market. Volatility, as measured by both the semi-deviation and a drawdown factor, is considered low. As of December 31, 2015, *iShares MSCI Denmark Capped ETF traded at a discount of .98% below its net asset value, which is better than its one-year historical average discount of .03%.

Jennifer F.Y. Hsui has been running the fund for 4 years and currently receives a manager quality ranking of 98 (0=worst, 99=best). If you desire only a moderate level of risk and strong performance, then this fund is an excellent option.

Data Date	Investment Rating	Net Assets ($Mil)	Price	Performance Rating/Pts	Total Return Y-T-D	Risk Rating/Pts
12-15	A+	56.70	55.85	A+ / 9.6	19.14%	B / 8.7
2014	C-	56.70	46.99	D / 2.2	5.41%	B / 8.1
2013	A+	17.90	45.00	A+ / 9.8	41.09%	B / 8.6

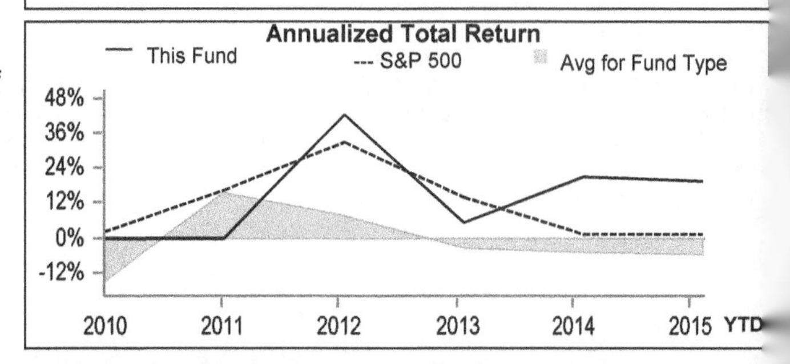

*iShares MSCI EAFE ETF (EFA) C+ Fair

Fund Family: BlackRock Fund Advisors
Fund Type: Foreign
Inception Date: August 14, 2001

Major Rating Factors: Middle of the road best describes *iShares MSCI EAFE ETF whose TheStreet.com Investment Rating is currently a C+ (Fair). The fund currently has a performance rating of C+ (Fair) based on an annualized return of 3.98% over the last three years and a total return of 0.31% year to date 2015. Factored into the performance evaluation is an expense ratio of 0.33% (very low).

The fund's risk rating is currently B- (Good). It carries a beta of 0.98, meaning that its performance tracks fairly well with that of the overall stock market. Volatility, as measured by both the semi-deviation and a drawdown factor, is considered low. As of December 31, 2015, *iShares MSCI EAFE ETF traded at a discount of .78% below its net asset value, which is better than its one-year historical average premium of .08%.

Diane Hsiung has been running the fund for 8 years and currently receives a manager quality ranking of 60 (0=worst, 99=best). If you desire an average level of risk, then this fund may be an option.

Data Date	Investment Rating	Net Assets ($Mil)	Price	Performance Rating/Pts	Total Return Y-T-D	Risk Rating/Pts
12-15	C+	53,613.30	58.72	C+ / 5.6	0.31%	B- / 7.9
2014	C	53,613.30	60.84	C / 4.9	-4.65%	B- / 7.4
2013	C+	52,823.40	67.10	C+ / 6.7	18.07%	B- / 7.4
2012	C-	38,814.70	56.86	C- / 4.1	21.12%	B- / 7.3
2011	D+	36,543.40	49.53	D+ / 2.6	-11.62%	B- / 7.4
2010	D	36,829.10	58.22	D / 1.7	8.25%	C / 5.2

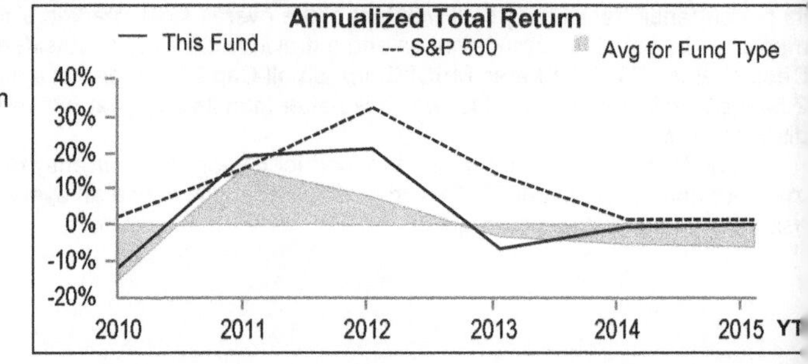

*iShares MSCI EAFE Growth ETF (EFG) B- Good

Fund Family: BlackRock Fund Advisors
Fund Type: Foreign
Inception Date: August 1, 2005

Major Rating Factors: *iShares MSCI EAFE Growth ETF receives a TheStreet.com Investment Rating of B- (Good). The fund currently has a performance rating of C+ (Fair) based on an annualized return of 5.67% over the last three years and a total return of 4.36% year to date 2015. Factored into the performance evaluation is an expense ratio of 0.40% (very low).

The fund's risk rating is currently B (Good). It carries a beta of 0.92, meaning that its performance tracks fairly well with that of the overall stock market. Volatility, as measured by both the semi-deviation and a drawdown factor, is considered low. As of December 31, 2015, *iShares MSCI EAFE Growth ETF traded at a discount of .59% below its net asset value, which is better than its one-year historical average premium of .09%.

Diane Hsiung has been running the fund for 8 years and currently receives a manager quality ranking of 76 (0=worst, 99=best). If you desire an average level of risk, then this fund may be an option.

Data Date	Investment Rating	Net Assets ($Mil)	Price	Performance Rating/Pts	Total Return Y-T-D	Risk Rating/Pts
12-15	B-	1,638.50	67.14	C+ / 6.3	4.36%	B / 8.1
2014	C-	1,638.50	65.81	C / 5.0	-4.37%	C+ / 6.7
2013	C+	1,731.30	71.48	C+ / 6.6	18.46%	B- / 7.4
2012	C-	1,375.90	60.04	C- / 3.9	19.10%	B- / 7.3
2011	D+	1,106.10	52.01	D+ / 2.8	-11.50%	B- / 7.4
2010	D	1,338.40	61.08	D+ / 2.3	13.12%	C / 5.3

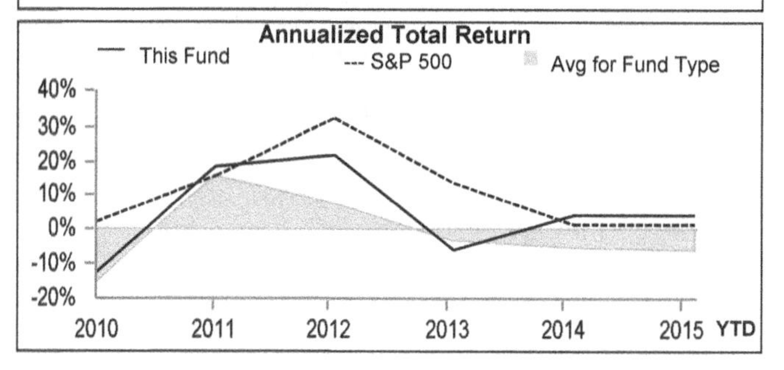

*iShares MSCI EAFE Minimum Vol ET (EFAV) A Excellent

Fund Family: BlackRock Fund Advisors
Fund Type: Foreign
Inception Date: October 18, 2011

Major Rating Factors:
Strong performance is the major factor driving the A (Excellent) TheStreet.com Investment Rating for *iShares MSCI EAFE Minimum Vol ET. The fund currently has a performance rating of B (Good) based on an annualized return of 9.10% over the last three years and a total return of 9.53% year to date 2015. Factored into the performance evaluation is an expense ratio of 0.20% (very low).

The fund's risk rating is currently B (Good). It carries a beta of 0.69, meaning the fund's expected move will be 6.9% for every 10% move in the market. Volatility, as measured by both the semi-deviation and a drawdown factor, is considered low. As of December 31, 2015, *iShares MSCI EAFE Minimum Vol ET traded at a discount of .45% below its net asset value, which is better than its one-year historical average premium of .17%.

Diane Hsiung has been running the fund for 5 years and currently receives a manager quality ranking of 90 (0=worst, 99=best). If you desire only a moderate level of risk and strong performance, then this fund is an excellent option.

Data Date	Investment Rating	Net Assets ($Mil)	Price	Performance Rating/Pts	Total Return Y-T-D	Risk Rating/Pts
12-15	A	1,135.40	64.87	B / 7.8	9.53%	B / 8.8
2014	C	1,135.40	61.70	C / 5.4	4.77%	B- / 7.0
2013	B+	937.40	61.60	B- / 7.1	13.87%	B+ / 9.0
2012	B-	210.60	54.68	C+ / 5.7	13.87%	B+ / 9.0

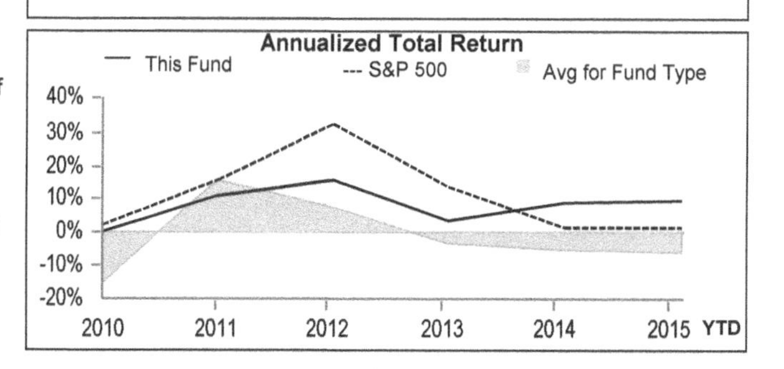

*iShares MSCI EAFE Small-Cap ETF (SCZ) A Excellent

Fund Family: BlackRock Fund Advisors
Fund Type: Foreign
Inception Date: December 10, 2007

Major Rating Factors:
Strong performance is the major factor driving the A (Excellent) TheStreet.com Investment Rating for *iShares MSCI EAFE Small-Cap ETF. The fund currently has a performance rating of B (Good) based on an annualized return of 9.55% over the last three years and a total return of 10.09% year to date 2015. Factored into the performance evaluation is an expense ratio of 0.40% (very low).

The fund's risk rating is currently B (Good). It carries a beta of 0.84, meaning the fund's expected move will be 8.4% for every 10% move in the market. Volatility, as measured by both the semi-deviation and a drawdown factor, is considered low. As of December 31, 2015, *iShares MSCI EAFE Small-Cap ETF traded at a discount of .52% below its net asset value, which is better than its one-year historical average premium of .25%.

Diane Hsiung has been running the fund for 8 years and currently receives a manager quality ranking of 89 (0=worst, 99=best). If you desire only a moderate level of risk and strong performance, then this fund is an excellent option.

Data Date	Investment Rating	Net Assets ($Mil)	Price	Performance Rating/Pts	Total Return Y-T-D	Risk Rating/Pts
12-15	A	3,672.40	49.95	B / 7.9	10.09%	B / 8.8
2014	C+	3,672.40	46.71	C+ / 5.6	-5.44%	B / 8.3
2013	B-	3,120.50	50.98	B- / 7.4	26.36%	B- / 7.4
2012	C	1,619.00	40.71	C / 5.5	22.33%	B- / 7.7
2011	C-	1,231.60	34.76	C- / 3.9	-14.12%	B- / 7.9
2010	C-	1,373.40	42.21	C / 4.4	21.51%	C / 5.3

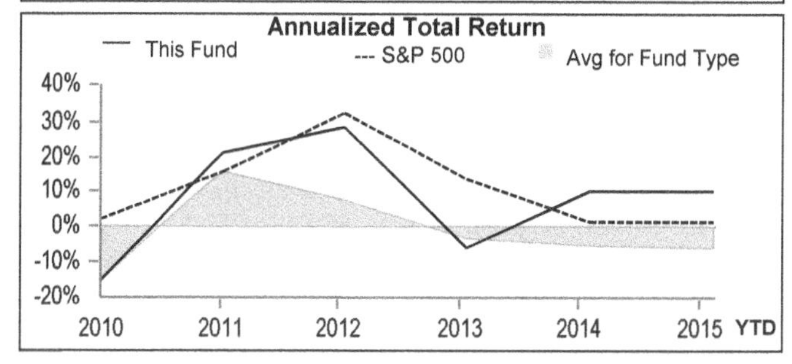

* Denotes ETF Fund

*iShares MSCI EAFE Value ETF (EFV) C Fair

Fund Family: BlackRock Fund Advisors
Fund Type: Foreign
Inception Date: August 1, 2005

Major Rating Factors: Middle of the road best describes *iShares MSCI EAFE Value ETF whose TheStreet.com Investment Rating is currently a C (Fair). The fund currently has a performance rating of C (Fair) based on an annualized return of 2.11% over the last three years and a total return of -4.57% year to date 2015. Factored into the performance evaluation is an expense ratio of 0.40% (very low).

The fund's risk rating is currently B- (Good). It carries a beta of 1.05, meaning that its performance tracks fairly well with that of the overall stock market. Volatility, as measured by both the semi-deviation and a drawdown factor, is considered low. As of December 31, 2015, *iShares MSCI EAFE Value ETF traded at a discount of .49% below its net asset value, which is better than its one-year historical average premium of .17%.

Diane Hsiung has been running the fund for 8 years and currently receives a manager quality ranking of 43 (0=worst, 99=best). If you desire an average level of risk, then this fund may be an option.

Data Date	Investment Rating	Net Assets ($Mil)	Price	Performance Rating/Pts	Total Return Y-T-D	Risk Rating/Pts
12-15	C	2,604.50	46.52	C / 4.5	-4.57%	B- / 7.6
2014	C-	2,604.50	51.03	C / 4.8	-5.08%	C+ / 6.2
2013	C+	2,431.70	57.20	C+ / 6.7	17.90%	B- / 7.1
2012	C-	1,613.90	48.64	C- / 4.2	23.23%	C+ / 6.9
2011	D+	1,210.30	42.70	D+ / 2.3	-12.50%	B- / 7.2
2010	D-	1,355.20	50.77	D- / 1.4	4.59%	C / 4.7

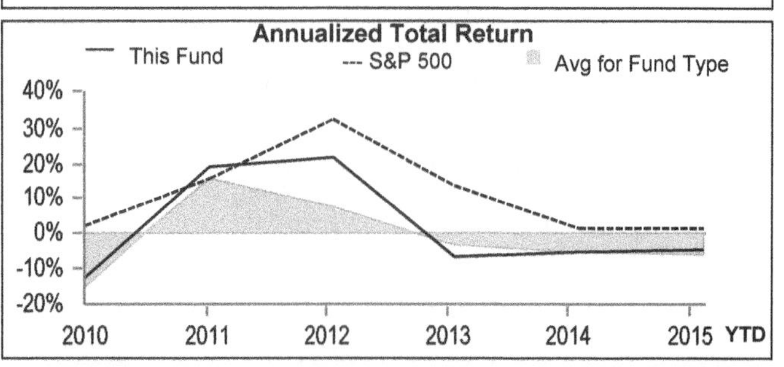

*iShares MSCI EM Asia ETF (EEMA) C- Fair

Fund Family: BlackRock Fund Advisors
Fund Type: Emerging Market
Inception Date: February 8, 2012

Major Rating Factors: Middle of the road best describes *iShares MSCI EM Asia ETF whose TheStreet.com Investment Rating is currently a C- (Fair). The fund currently has a performance rating of C- (Fair) based on an annualized return of -2.50% over the last three years and a total return of -9.05% year to date 2015. Factored into the performance evaluation is an expense ratio of 0.49% (very low).

The fund's risk rating is currently B- (Good). It carries a beta of 0.95, meaning that its performance tracks fairly well with that of the overall stock market. Volatility, as measured by both the semi-deviation and a drawdown factor, is considered low. As of December 31, 2015, *iShares MSCI EM Asia ETF traded at a discount of 1.08% below its net asset value, which is better than its one-year historical average premium of .05%.

Jennifer F.Y. Hsui has been running the fund for 4 years and currently receives a manager quality ranking of 88 (0=worst, 99=best). If you desire an average level of risk, then this fund may be an option.

Data Date	Investment Rating	Net Assets ($Mil)	Price	Performance Rating/Pts	Total Return Y-T-D	Risk Rating/Pts
12-15	C-	87.70	50.40	C- / 3.0	-9.05%	B- / 7.4
2014	C-	87.70	58.19	C- / 3.7	7.06%	C+ / 6.6
2013	C-	33.70	57.10	C- / 3.5	-3.85%	B / 8.5

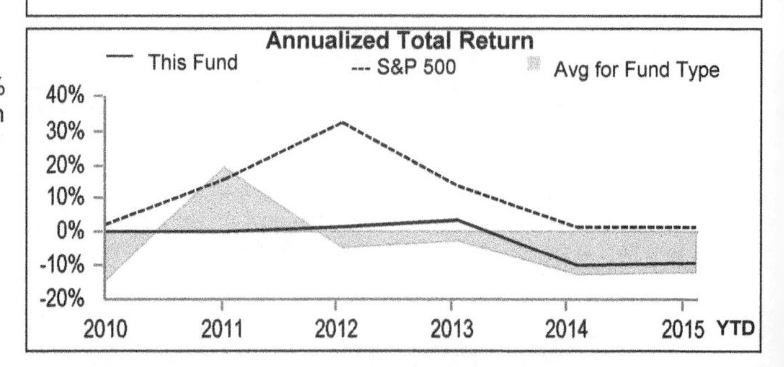

*iShares MSCI Em Mkts Lat Amer ET (EEML) D- Weak

Fund Family: BlackRock Fund Advisors
Fund Type: Foreign
Inception Date: January 18, 2012

Major Rating Factors:
Very poor performance is the major factor driving the D- (Weak) TheStreet.com Investment Rating for *iShares MSCI Em Mkts Lat Amer ET. The fund currently has a performance rating of E+ (Very Weak) based on an annualized return of -20.71% over the last three years and a total return of -27.86% year to date 2015. Factored into the performance evaluation is an expense ratio of 0.49% (very low).

The fund's risk rating is currently C (Fair). It carries a beta of 1.13, meaning it is expected to move 11.3% for every 10% move in the market. Volatility, as measured by both the semi-deviation and a drawdown factor, is considered average. As of December 31, 2015, *iShares MSCI Em Mkts Lat Amer ET traded at a discount of .08% below its net asset value, which is better than its one-year historical average discount of .06%.

Jennifer F.Y. Hsui has been running the fund for 4 years and currently receives a manager quality ranking of 4 (0=worst, 99=best). This fund offers an average level of risk but investors looking for strong performance will be frustrated.

Data Date	Investment Rating	Net Assets ($Mil)	Price	Performance Rating/Pts	Total Return Y-T-D	Risk Rating/Pts
12-15	D-	12.80	24.39	E+ / 0.7	-27.86%	C / 4.6
2014	E+	12.80	36.57	E+ / 0.7	-10.12%	C- / 3.9
2013	D-	12.80	42.74	E+ / 0.7	-19.97%	C+ / 6.7

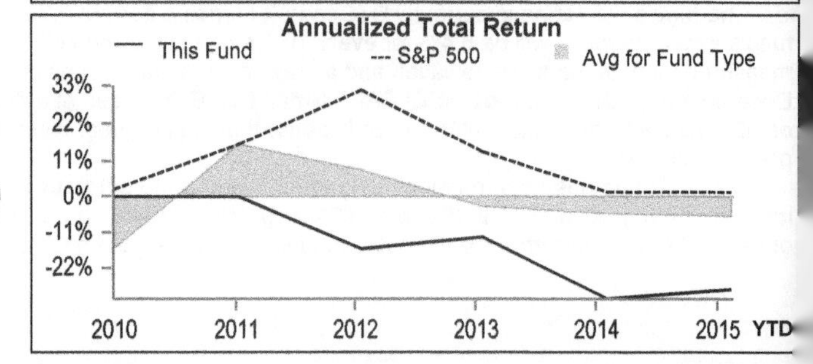

*iShares MSCI Emerging Markets (EEM) D+ Weak

Fund Family: BlackRock Fund Advisors
Fund Type: Emerging Market
Inception Date: April 7, 2003

Data Date	Investment Rating	Net Assets ($Mil)	Price	Performance Rating/Pts	Total Return Y-T-D	Risk Rating/Pts
12-15	D+	39,252.80	32.19	D / 2.1	-13.78%	B- / 7.3
2014	D+	39,252.80	39.29	C- / 3.2	0.05%	C+ / 6.3
2013	D	40,123.20	41.80	D / 1.9	-8.89%	C+ / 6.9
2012	D+	48,189.60	44.35	D+ / 2.9	15.33%	C+ / 6.8
2011	C-	32,493.30	37.94	C / 4.5	-17.54%	B- / 7.5
2010	D+	47,459.00	47.64	C / 5.3	16.47%	D+ / 2.7

Major Rating Factors:
Disappointing performance is the major factor driving the D+ (Weak) TheStreet.com Investment Rating for *iShares MSCI Emerging Markets. The fund currently has a performance rating of D (Weak) based on an annualized return of -8.12% over the last three years and a total return of -13.78% year to date 2015. Factored into the performance evaluation is an expense ratio of 0.69% (very low).

The fund's risk rating is currently B- (Good). It carries a beta of 0.99, meaning that its performance tracks fairly well with that of the overall stock market. Volatility, as measured by both the semi-deviation and a drawdown factor, is considered low. As of December 31, 2015, *iShares MSCI Emerging Markets traded at a discount of .83% below its net asset value, which is better than its one-year historical average discount of .14%.

Diane Hsiung has been running the fund for 8 years and currently receives a manager quality ranking of 56 (0=worst, 99=best). This fund offers only a moderate level of risk but investors looking for strong performance are still waiting.

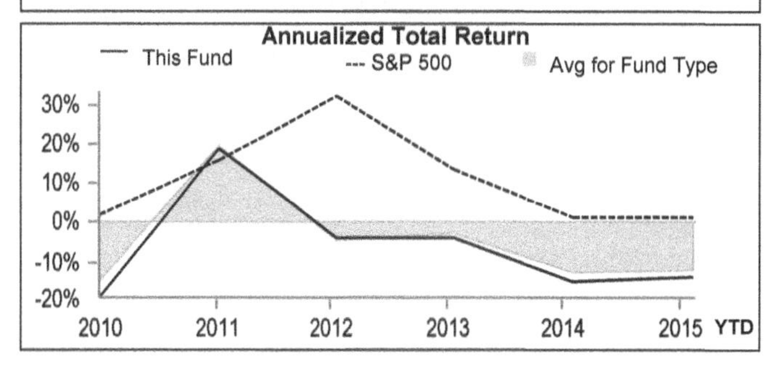

*iShares MSCI Emerging Mkts Min V (EEMV) C- Fair

Fund Family: BlackRock Fund Advisors
Fund Type: Emerging Market
Inception Date: October 18, 2011

Data Date	Investment Rating	Net Assets ($Mil)	Price	Performance Rating/Pts	Total Return Y-T-D	Risk Rating/Pts
12-15	C-	1,991.20	48.66	D+ / 2.6	-10.15%	B- / 7.5
2014	C	1,991.20	56.63	C- / 4.1	2.69%	B / 8.1
2013	D+	2,410.50	58.26	D / 1.8	-4.77%	B / 8.5
2012	A	846.60	60.56	B+ / 8.7	20.57%	B / 8.7

Major Rating Factors:
Disappointing performance is the major factor driving the C- (Fair) TheStreet.com Investment Rating for *iShares MSCI Emerging Mkts Min V. The fund currently has a performance rating of D+ (Weak) based on an annualized return of -4.49% over the last three years and a total return of -10.15% year to date 2015. Factored into the performance evaluation is an expense ratio of 0.25% (very low).

The fund's risk rating is currently B- (Good). It carries a beta of 0.81, meaning the fund's expected move will be 8.1% for every 10% move in the market. Volatility, as measured by both the semi-deviation and a drawdown factor, is considered low. As of December 31, 2015, *iShares MSCI Emerging Mkts Min V traded at a discount of .39% below its net asset value, which is better than its one-year historical average premium of .19%.

Diane Hsiung has been running the fund for 5 years and currently receives a manager quality ranking of 76 (0=worst, 99=best). This fund offers only a moderate level of risk but investors looking for strong performance are still waiting.

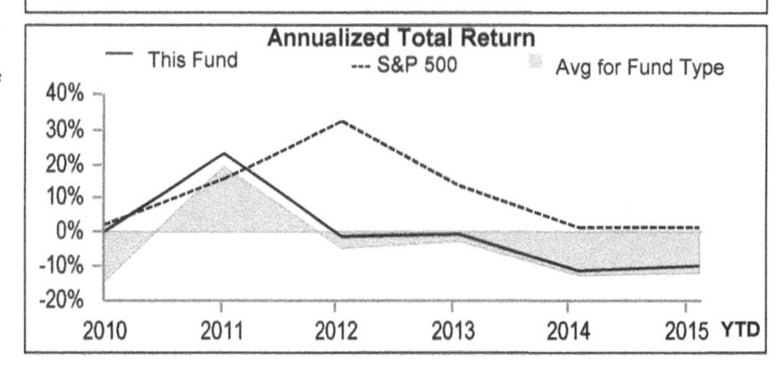

*iShares MSCI Emerging Mkts Sm-Ca (EEMS) D+ Weak

Fund Family: BlackRock Fund Advisors
Fund Type: Emerging Market
Inception Date: August 16, 2011

Data Date	Investment Rating	Net Assets ($Mil)	Price	Performance Rating/Pts	Total Return Y-T-D	Risk Rating/Pts
12-15	D+	41.70	40.95	C- / 3.1	-5.04%	C+ / 5.7
2014	C-	41.70	45.00	C- / 3.8	-0.84%	B- / 7.9
2013	C-	32.60	47.68	C- / 3.4	-1.73%	B- / 7.5
2012	B+	9.40	47.30	A / 9.3	20.19%	B- / 7.3

Major Rating Factors: *iShares MSCI Emerging Mkts Sm-Ca receives a TheStreet.com Investment Rating of D+ (Weak). The fund currently has a performance rating of C- (Fair) based on an annualized return of -2.76% over the last three years and a total return of -5.04% year to date 2015. Factored into the performance evaluation is an expense ratio of 0.69% (very low).

The fund's risk rating is currently C+ (Fair). It carries a beta of 0.96, meaning that its performance tracks fairly well with that of the overall stock market. Volatility, as measured by both the semi-deviation and a drawdown factor, is considered low. As of December 31, 2015, *iShares MSCI Emerging Mkts Sm-Ca traded at a premium of .29% above its net asset value, which is better than its one-year historical average premium of .34%.

Christopher R. Bliss has been running the fund for 5 years and currently receives a manager quality ranking of 88 (0=worst, 99=best). If you desire an average level of risk, then this fund may be an option.

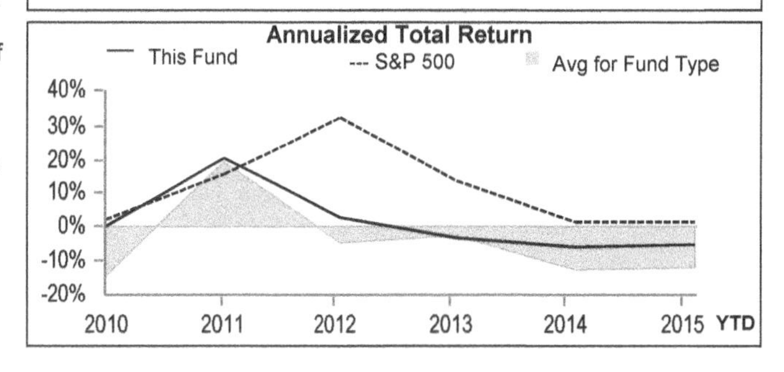

*iShares MSCI Emg Mkts Horizon ET (EMHZ) D Weak

Fund Family: BlackRock Fund Advisors
Fund Type: Emerging Market
Inception Date: October 14, 2014

Data Date	Investment Rating	Net Assets ($Mil)	Price	Performance Rating/Pts	Total Return Y-T-D	Risk Rating/Pts
12-15	D	0.00	17.47	E+ / 0.8	-21.22%	C+ / 6.9

Major Rating Factors:
Very poor performance is the major factor driving the D (Weak) TheStreet.com Investment Rating for *iShares MSCI Emg Mkts Horizon ET. The fund currently has a performance rating of E+ (Very Weak) based on an annualized return of 0.00% over the last three years and a total return of -21.22% year to date 2015. Factored into the performance evaluation is an expense ratio of 0.50% (very low).

The fund's risk rating is currently C+ (Fair). It carries a beta of 0.00, meaning the fund's expected move will be 0.0% for every 10% move in the market. Volatility, as measured by both the semi-deviation and a drawdown factor, is considered low. As of December 31, 2015, *iShares MSCI Emg Mkts Horizon ET traded at a discount of 1.69% below its net asset value, which is better than its one-year historical average discount of .62%.

Diane Hsiung has been running the fund for 2 years and currently receives a manager quality ranking of 13 (0=worst, 99=best). This fund offers only a moderate level of risk but investors looking for strong performance are still waiting.

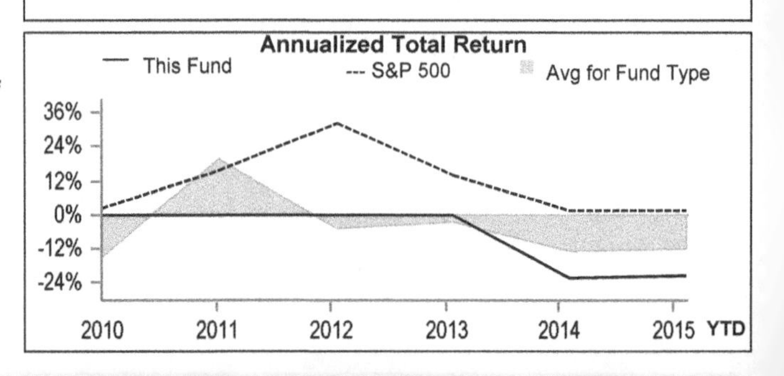

*iShares MSCI Europ Financials ET (EUFN) C Fair

Fund Family: BlackRock Fund Advisors
Fund Type: Financial Services
Inception Date: January 20, 2010

Data Date	Investment Rating	Net Assets ($Mil)	Price	Performance Rating/Pts	Total Return Y-T-D	Risk Rating/Pts
12-15	C	455.60	20.30	C / 5.0	-4.00%	B- / 7.5
2014	C+	455.60	21.98	C+ / 6.7	-7.26%	B- / 7.2
2013	C	362.90	25.12	B- / 7.1	23.70%	C / 5.4
2012	B-	33.00	19.80	A+ / 9.9	44.74%	C / 5.2
2011	E+	20.40	15.15	E / 0.4	-29.32%	C+ / 5.6

Major Rating Factors: Middle of the road best describes *iShares MSCI Europ Financials ET whose TheStreet.com Investment Rating is currently a C (Fair). The fund currently has a performance rating of C (Fair) based on an annualized return of 3.33% over the last three years and a total return of -4.00% year to date 2015. Factored into the performance evaluation is an expense ratio of 0.48% (very low).

The fund's risk rating is currently B- (Good). It carries a beta of 0.91, meaning that its performance tracks fairly well with that of the overall stock market. Volatility, as measured by both the semi-deviation and a drawdown factor, is considered low. As of December 31, 2015, *iShares MSCI Europ Financials ET traded at a discount of .68% below its net asset value, which is better than its one-year historical average premium of .03%.

Diane Hsiung has been running the fund for 6 years and currently receives a manager quality ranking of 18 (0=worst, 99=best). If you desire an average level of risk, then this fund may be an option.

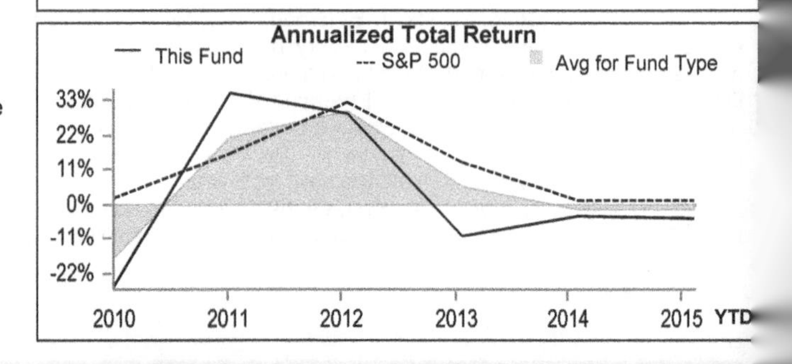

*iShares MSCI Europe Minimum Vol (EUMV) B Good

Fund Family: BlackRock Fund Advisors
Fund Type: Foreign
Inception Date: June 3, 2014

Data Date	Investment Rating	Net Assets ($Mil)	Price	Performance Rating/Pts	Total Return Y-T-D	Risk Rating/Pts
12-15	B	4.80	23.56	C+ / 6.1	5.30%	B / 8.6

Major Rating Factors: *iShares MSCI Europe Minimum Vol receives a TheStreet.com Investment Rating of B (Good). The fund currently has a performance rating of C+ (Fair) based on an annualized return of 0.00% over the last three years and a total return of 5.30% year to date 2015. Factored into the performance evaluation is an expense ratio of 0.25% (very low).

The fund's risk rating is currently B (Good). It carries a beta of 0.00, meaning the fund's expected move will be 0.0% for every 10% move in the market. Volatility, as measured by both the semi-deviation and a drawdown factor, is considered low. As of December 31, 2015, *iShares MSCI Europe Minimum Vol traded at a discount of .63% below its net asset value, which is better than its one-year historical average premium of .19%.

Jennifer F.Y. Hsui has been running the fund for 2 years and currently receives a manager quality ranking of 89 (0=worst, 99=best). If you desire an average level of risk, then this fund may be an option.

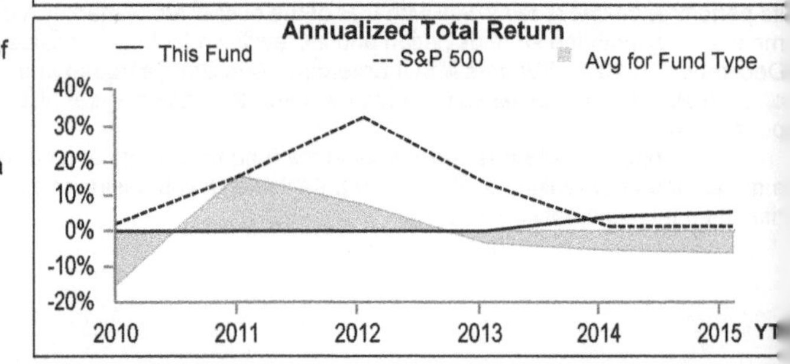

*iShares MSCI Europe Small-Cap (IEUS) A Excellent

Fund Family: BlackRock Fund Advisors
Fund Type: Foreign
Inception Date: November 12, 2007

Data Date	Investment Rating	Net Assets ($Mil)	Price	Perfor-mance Rating/Pts	Total Return Y-T-D	Risk Rating/Pts
12-15	A	36.50	45.28	B / 7.9	12.01%	B / 8.8
2014	C+	36.50	41.67	C+ / 5.8	-3.81%	B / 8.3
2013	C+	44.30	44.71	B- / 7.1	23.38%	B- / 7.2
2012	C	28.60	36.26	C / 5.1	22.98%	B- / 7.5
2011	C-	30.70	30.52	C- / 3.4	-17.16%	B- / 7.7
2010	C-	38.70	38.69	C- / 4.1	20.80%	C / 5.4

Major Rating Factors:
Strong performance is the major factor driving the A (Excellent) TheStreet.com Investment Rating for *iShares MSCI Europe Small-Cap. The fund currently has a performance rating of B (Good) based on an annualized return of 9.91% over the last three years and a total return of 12.01% year to date 2015. Factored into the performance evaluation is an expense ratio of 0.41% (very low).

The fund's risk rating is currently B (Good). It carries a beta of 0.89, meaning the fund's expected move will be 8.9% for every 10% move in the market. Volatility, as measured by both the semi-deviation and a drawdown factor, is considered low. As of December 31, 2015, *iShares MSCI Europe Small-Cap traded at a discount of .79% below its net asset value, which is better than its one-year historical average premium of .51%.

Diane Hsiung has been running the fund for 8 years and currently receives a manager quality ranking of 90 (0=worst, 99=best). If you desire only a moderate level of risk and strong performance, then this fund is an excellent option.

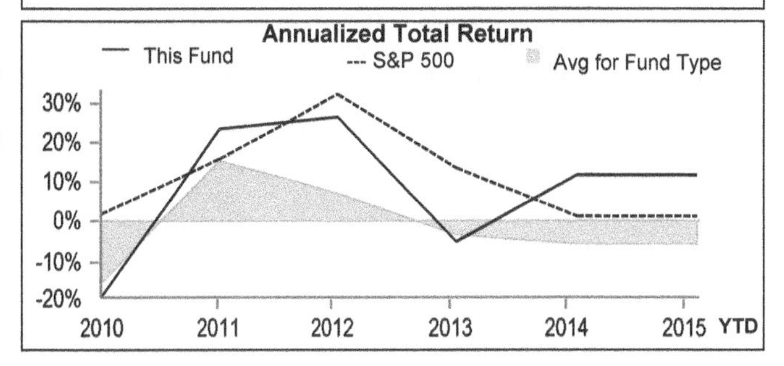

*iShares MSCI Eurozone (EZU) C+ Fair

Fund Family: BlackRock Fund Advisors
Fund Type: Foreign
Inception Date: July 25, 2000

Data Date	Investment Rating	Net Assets ($Mil)	Price	Perfor-mance Rating/Pts	Total Return Y-T-D	Risk Rating/Pts
12-15	C+	8,485.30	35.04	C / 5.5	-1.48%	B- / 7.6
2014	C	8,485.30	36.33	C / 5.3	-7.39%	B- / 7.6
2013	C+	8,312.70	41.38	B- / 7.0	23.28%	C+ / 6.4
2012	D	2,195.00	33.46	D+ / 2.9	27.79%	C+ / 6.1
2011	D	624.10	27.90	D- / 1.5	-17.17%	C+ / 6.4
2010	E	741.50	35.27	E+ / 0.8	-3.00%	D+ / 2.8

Major Rating Factors: Middle of the road best describes *iShares MSCI Eurozone whose TheStreet.com Investment Rating is currently a C+ (Fair). The fund currently has a performance rating of C (Fair) based on an annualized return of 4.04% over the last three years and a total return of -1.48% year to date 2015. Factored into the performance evaluation is an expense ratio of 0.48% (very low).

The fund's risk rating is currently B- (Good). It carries a beta of 1.10, meaning it is expected to move 11.0% for every 10% move in the market. Volatility, as measured by both the semi-deviation and a drawdown factor, is considered low. As of December 31, 2015, *iShares MSCI Eurozone traded at a discount of .88% below its net asset value, which is better than its one-year historical average premium of .11%.

Diane Hsiung has been running the fund for 8 years and currently receives a manager quality ranking of 53 (0=worst, 99=best). If you desire an average level of risk, then this fund may be an option.

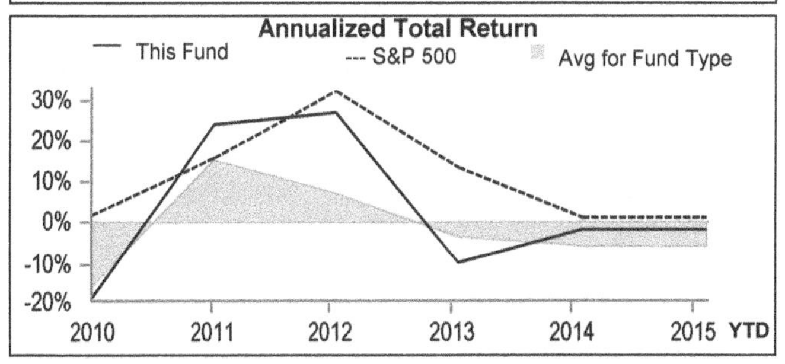

*iShares MSCI Finland Capped ETF (EFNL) B+ Good

Fund Family: BlackRock Fund Advisors
Fund Type: Foreign
Inception Date: January 25, 2012

Data Date	Investment Rating	Net Assets ($Mil)	Price	Perfor-mance Rating/Pts	Total Return Y-T-D	Risk Rating/Pts
12-15	B+	36.40	32.61	B / 7.6	2.45%	B / 8.0
2014	D	36.40	31.98	D / 1.6	-3.64%	B- / 7.3
2013	A	15.50	34.93	A+ / 9.7	30.79%	B- / 7.4

Major Rating Factors: Strong performance is the major factor driving the B+ (Good) TheStreet.com Investment Rating for *iShares MSCI Finland Capped ETF. The fund currently has a performance rating of B (Good) based on an annualized return of 9.29% over the last three years and a total return of 2.45% year to date 2015. Factored into the performance evaluation is an expense ratio of 0.53% (very low).

The fund's risk rating is currently B (Good). It carries a beta of 1.01, meaning that its performance tracks fairly well with that of the overall stock market. Volatility, as measured by both the semi-deviation and a drawdown factor, is considered low. As of December 31, 2015, *iShares MSCI Finland Capped ETF traded at a discount of 1.27% below its net asset value, which is better than its one-year historical average discount of .10%.

Jennifer F.Y. Hsui has been running the fund for 4 years and currently receives a manager quality ranking of 89 (0=worst, 99=best). If you desire only a moderate level of risk and strong performance, then this fund is an excellent option.

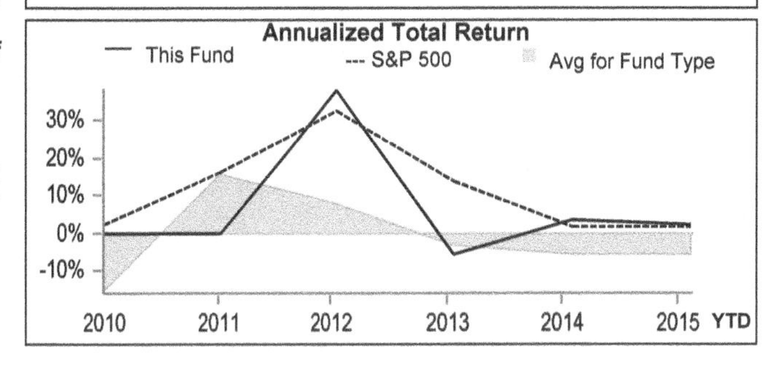

* Denotes ETF Fund

*iShares MSCI France (EWQ) C+ Fair

Fund Family: BlackRock Fund Advisors
Fund Type: Foreign
Inception Date: March 12, 1996

Major Rating Factors: Middle of the road best describes *iShares MSCI France whose TheStreet.com Investment Rating is currently a C+ (Fair). The fund currently has a performance rating of C+ (Fair) based on an annualized return of 3.77% over the last three years and a total return of 1.13% year to date 2015. Factored into the performance evaluation is an expense ratio of 0.48% (very low).

The fund's risk rating is currently B- (Good). It carries a beta of 1.10, meaning it is expected to move 11.0% for every 10% move in the market. Volatility, as measured by both the semi-deviation and a drawdown factor, is considered low. As of December 31, 2015, *iShares MSCI France traded at a discount of .25% below its net asset value, which is better than its one-year historical average premium of .13%.

Diane Hsiung has been running the fund for 8 years and currently receives a manager quality ranking of 49 (0=worst, 99=best). If you desire an average level of risk, then this fund may be an option.

Data Date	Investment Rating	Net Assets ($Mil)	Price	Performance Rating/Pts	Total Return Y-T-D	Risk Rating/Pts
12-15	C+	250.50	24.21	C+ / 5.6	1.13%	B- / 7.6
2014	C-	250.50	24.65	C / 5.1	-8.19%	C+ / 5.9
2013	C	425.50	28.45	C+ / 6.9	20.97%	C+ / 6.3
2012	D	448.20	23.59	D+ / 2.6	27.06%	C+ / 6.0
2011	D	251.40	19.58	D- / 1.5	-17.73%	C+ / 6.3
2010	D-	286.50	24.45	D- / 1.0	-2.38%	C / 4.3

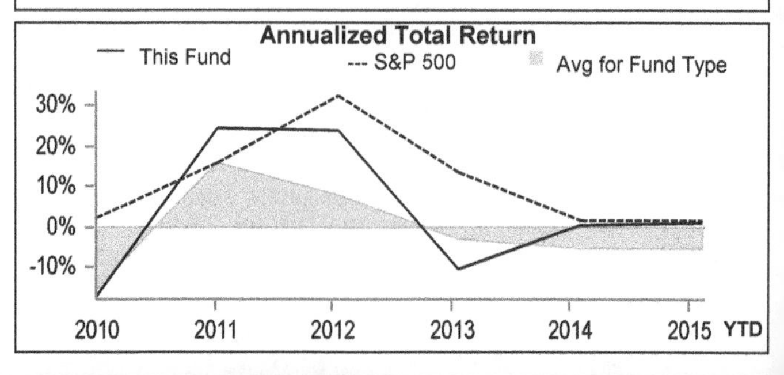

*iShares MSCI Frontier 100 ETF (FM) C- Fair

Fund Family: BlackRock Fund Advisors
Fund Type: Foreign
Inception Date: September 12, 2012

Major Rating Factors: Middle of the road best describes *iShares MSCI Frontier 100 ETF whose TheStreet.com Investment Rating is currently a C- (Fair). The fund currently has a performance rating of C- (Fair) based on an annualized return of 1.09% over the last three years and a total return of -16.01% year to date 2015. Factored into the performance evaluation is an expense ratio of 0.79% (very low).

The fund's risk rating is currently C+ (Fair). It carries a beta of 0.61, meaning the fund's expected move will be 6.1% for every 10% move in the market. Volatility, as measured by both the semi-deviation and a drawdown factor, is considered low. As of December 31, 2015, *iShares MSCI Frontier 100 ETF traded at a discount of 1.15% below its net asset value, which is better than its one-year historical average premium of .12%.

Jennifer Hsui has been running the fund for 4 years and currently receives a manager quality ranking of 55 (0=worst, 99=best). If you desire an average level of risk, then this fund may be an option.

Data Date	Investment Rating	Net Assets ($Mil)	Price	Performance Rating/Pts	Total Return Y-T-D	Risk Rating/Pts
12-15	C-	810.50	24.89	C- / 3.5	-16.01%	C+ / 6.5
2014	D	810.50	30.80	D / 1.6	2.30%	C+ / 5.7
2013	A+	430.60	33.74	A- / 9.0	21.57%	B / 8.9

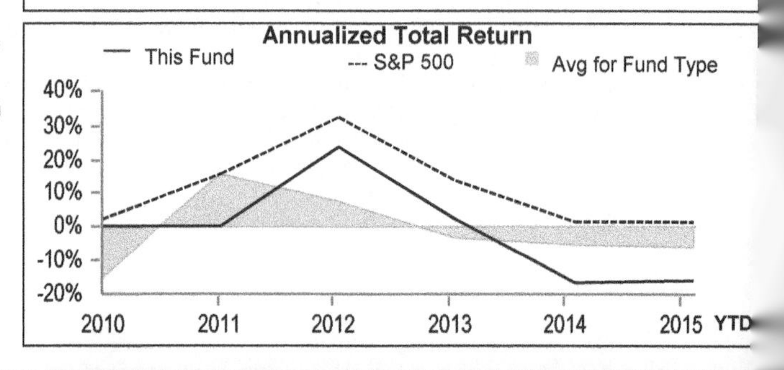

*iShares MSCI Germany (EWG) C+ Fair

Fund Family: BlackRock Fund Advisors
Fund Type: Foreign
Inception Date: March 12, 1996

Major Rating Factors: Middle of the road best describes *iShares MSCI Germany whose TheStreet.com Investment Rating is currently a C+ (Fair). The fund currently has a performance rating of C+ (Fair) based on an annualized return of 3.81% over the last three years and a total return of -2.27% year to date 2015. Factored into the performance evaluation is an expense ratio of 0.48% (very low).

The fund's risk rating is currently B- (Good). It carries a beta of 1.07, meaning that its performance tracks fairly well with that of the overall stock market. Volatility, as measured by both the semi-deviation and a drawdown factor, is considered low. As of December 31, 2015, *iShares MSCI Germany traded at a discount of 1.47% below its net asset value, which is better than its one-year historical average premium of .01%.

Diane Hsiung has been running the fund for 8 years and currently receives a manager quality ranking of 52 (0=worst, 99=best). If you desire an average level of risk, then this fund may be an option.

Data Date	Investment Rating	Net Assets ($Mil)	Price	Performance Rating/Pts	Total Return Y-T-D	Risk Rating/Pts
12-15	C+	4,819.20	26.19	C+ / 5.6	-2.27%	B- / 7.5
2014	C	4,819.20	27.41	C+ / 5.9	-8.77%	C+ / 6.3
2013	C+	6,249.90	31.76	B- / 7.5	26.06%	C+ / 6.3
2012	C	3,991.80	24.70	C+ / 6.4	31.89%	C+ / 6.2
2011	D	2,313.50	19.22	D / 2.0	-15.20%	C+ / 6.3
2010	D-	1,892.70	23.94	D- / 1.3	8.31%	C / 4.7

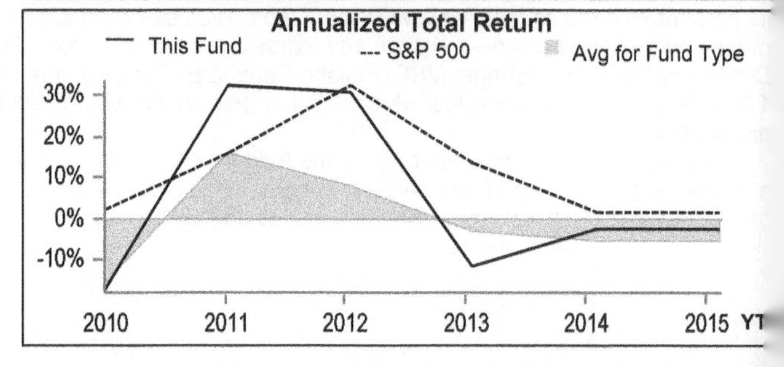

*iShares MSCI Germany Small-Cap (EWGS) A Excellent

Fund Family: BlackRock Fund Advisors
Fund Type: Foreign
Inception Date: January 25, 2012

Data Date	Investment Rating	Net Assets ($Mil)	Price	Performance Rating/Pts	Total Return Y-T-D	Risk Rating/Pts
12-15	A	35.10	41.35	B+ / 8.6	11.27%	B / 8.1
2014	D+	35.10	37.50	D / 1.6	-5.54%	B- / 7.8
2013	A+	30.30	40.77	A+ / 9.6	32.02%	B / 8.4

Major Rating Factors:
Strong performance is the major factor driving the A (Excellent) TheStreet.com Investment Rating for *iShares MSCI Germany Small-Cap. The fund currently has a performance rating of B+ (Good) based on an annualized return of 11.67% over the last three years and a total return of 11.27% year to date 2015. Factored into the performance evaluation is an expense ratio of 0.59% (very low).

The fund's risk rating is currently B (Good). It carries a beta of 0.74, meaning the fund's expected move will be 7.4% for every 10% move in the market. Volatility, as measured by both the semi-deviation and a drawdown factor, is considered low. As of December 31, 2015, *iShares MSCI Germany Small-Cap traded at a discount of .79% below its net asset value, which is better than its one-year historical average discount of .02%.

Jennifer F.Y. Hsui has been running the fund for 4 years and currently receives a manager quality ranking of 93 (0=worst, 99=best). If you desire only a moderate level of risk and strong performance, then this fund is an excellent option.

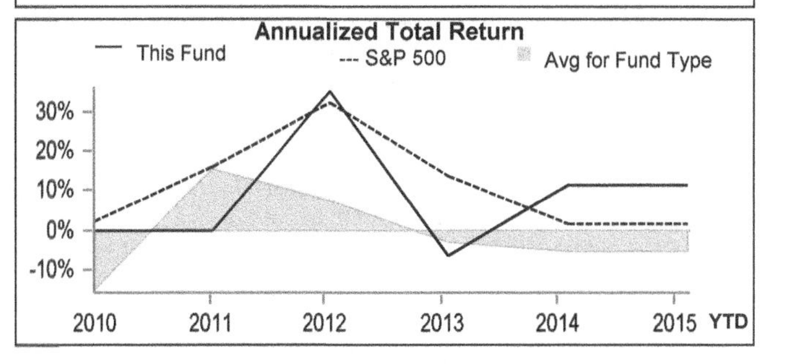

*iShares MSCI Gl Met&MP (PICK) E Very Weak

Fund Family: BlackRock Fund Advisors
Fund Type: Precious Metals
Inception Date: January 31, 2012

Data Date	Investment Rating	Net Assets ($Mil)	Price	Performance Rating/Pts	Total Return Y-T-D	Risk Rating/Pts
12-15	E	173.00	8.42	E+ / 0.6	-38.37%	D / 2.1
2014	E+	173.00	15.64	E / 0.4	-18.31%	C- / 4.1
2013	D+	139.70	20.00	C- / 3.8	-12.48%	C+ / 6.3

Major Rating Factors: *iShares MSCI Gl Met&MP has adopted a very risky asset allocation strategy and currently receives an overall TheStreet.com Investment Rating of E (Very Weak). The fund has a high level of volatility, as measured by both semi-deviation and drawdown factors. It carries a beta of 0.46, meaning the fund's expected move will be 4.6% for every 10% move in the market. As of December 31, 2015, *iShares MSCI Gl Met&MP traded at a premium of .48% above its net asset value, which is worse than its one-year historical average premium of .45%. Unfortunately, the high level of risk (D, Weak) failed to pay off as investors endured very poor performance.

The fund's performance rating is currently E+ (Very Weak). It has registered an annualized return of -24.11% over the last three years and is down -38.37% year to date 2015. Factored into the performance evaluation is an expense ratio of 0.39% (very low).

Jennifer F.Y. Hsui has been running the fund for 4 years and currently receives a manager quality ranking of 8 (0=worst, 99=best). If you can tolerate very high levels of risk in the hope of improved future returns, holding this fund may be an option.

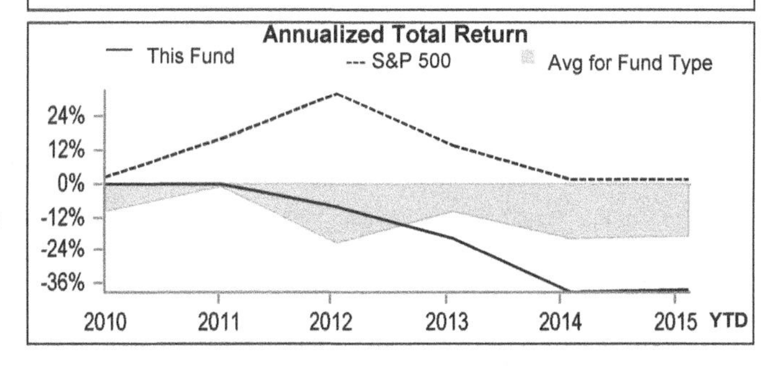

*iShares MSCI Glbl Agri Prod (VEGI) D+ Weak

Fund Family: BlackRock Fund Advisors
Fund Type: Global
Inception Date: January 31, 2012

Data Date	Investment Rating	Net Assets ($Mil)	Price	Performance Rating/Pts	Total Return Y-T-D	Risk Rating/Pts
12-15	D+	45.10	22.44	D+ / 2.7	-12.05%	C+ / 5.7
2014	D	45.10	26.55	D+ / 2.4	-0.72%	C+ / 6.5
2013	C	43.60	27.48	C / 4.6	0.89%	B / 8.5

Major Rating Factors:
Disappointing performance is the major factor driving the D+ (Weak) TheStreet.com Investment Rating for *iShares MSCI Glbl Agri Prod. The fund currently has a performance rating of D+ (Weak) based on an annualized return of -4.38% over the last three years and a total return of -12.05% year to date 2015. Factored into the performance evaluation is an expense ratio of 0.38% (very low).

The fund's risk rating is currently C+ (Fair). It carries a beta of 0.81, meaning the fund's expected move will be 8.1% for every 10% move in the market. Volatility, as measured by both the semi-deviation and a drawdown factor, is considered low. As of December 31, 2015, *iShares MSCI Glbl Agri Prod traded at a premium of .54% above its net asset value, which is worse than its one-year historical average discount of .22%.

Jennifer F.Y. Hsui has been running the fund for 4 years and currently receives a manager quality ranking of 20 (0=worst, 99=best). This fund offers only a moderate level of risk but investors looking for strong performance are still waiting.

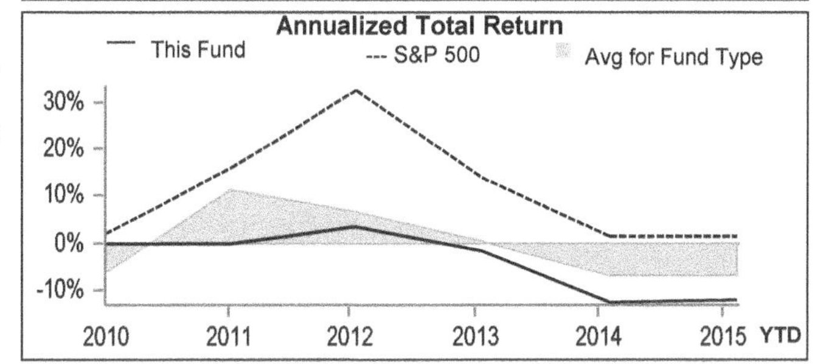

*iShares MSCI Global Engy Prod (FILL) D Weak

Fund Family: BlackRock Fund Advisors
Fund Type: Energy/Natural Resources
Inception Date: January 31, 2012

Major Rating Factors:
Disappointing performance is the major factor driving the D (Weak) TheStreet.com Investment Rating for *iShares MSCI Global Engy Prod. The fund currently has a performance rating of D (Weak) based on an annualized return of -9.21% over the last three years and a total return of -20.51% year to date 2015. Factored into the performance evaluation is an expense ratio of 0.39% (very low).

The fund's risk rating is currently C+ (Fair). It carries a beta of 0.98, meaning that its performance tracks fairly well with that of the overall stock market. Volatility, as measured by both the semi-deviation and a drawdown factor, is considered low. As of December 31, 2015, *iShares MSCI Global Engy Prod traded at a discount of .79% below its net asset value, which is better than its one-year historical average premium of .68%.

Jennifer F.Y. Hsui has been running the fund for 4 years and currently receives a manager quality ranking of 30 (0=worst, 99=best). This fund offers only a moderate level of risk but investors looking for strong performance are still waiting.

Data Date	Investment Rating	Net Assets ($Mil)	Price	Performance Rating/Pts	Total Return Y-T-D	Risk Rating/Pts
12-15	D	7.70	16.34	D / 1.7	-20.51%	C+ / 5.7
2014	D-	7.70	21.52	E / 0.5	-14.82%	C / 5.1
2013	B	5.20	26.12	B- / 7.2	10.45%	B / 8.1

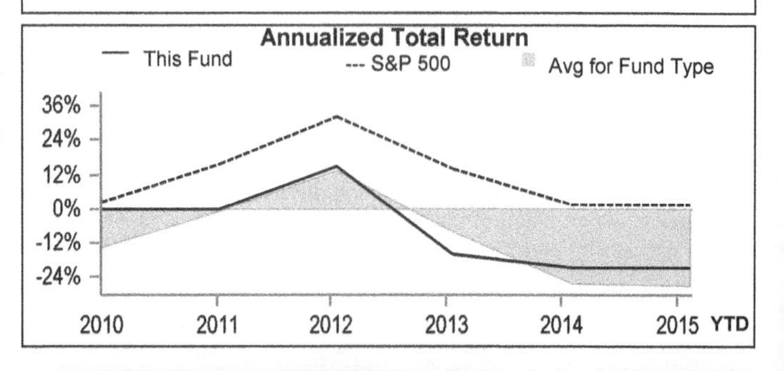

*iShares MSCI Global Gold Miners (RING) E- Very Weak

Fund Family: BlackRock Fund Advisors
Fund Type: Precious Metals
Inception Date: January 31, 2012

Major Rating Factors: *iShares MSCI Global Gold Miners has adopted a very risky asset allocation strategy and currently receives an overall TheStreet.com Investment Rating of E- (Very Weak). The fund has a high level of volatility, as measured by both semi-deviation and drawdown factors. It carries a beta of 1.85, meaning it is expected to move 18.5% for every 10% move in the market. As of December 31, 2015, *iShares MSCI Global Gold Miners traded at a premium of .92% above its net asset value, which is worse than its one-year historical average premium of .34%. Unfortunately, the high level of risk (E+, Very Weak) failed to pay off as investors endured very poor performance.

The fund's performance rating is currently E (Very Weak). It has registered an annualized return of -33.25% over the last three years and is down -27.29% year to date 2015. Factored into the performance evaluation is an expense ratio of 0.39% (very low).

Jennifer F.Y. Hsui has been running the fund for 4 years and currently receives a manager quality ranking of 13 (0=worst, 99=best). If you can tolerate very high levels of risk in the hope of improved future returns, holding this fund may be an option.

Data Date	Investment Rating	Net Assets ($Mil)	Price	Performance Rating/Pts	Total Return Y-T-D	Risk Rating/Pts
12-15	E-	55.50	5.48	E / 0.4	-27.29%	E+ / 0.9
2014	E	55.50	7.45	E / 0.3	-20.19%	D+ / 2.8
2013	E	41.10	9.11	E- / 0.2	-49.96%	C- / 3.3

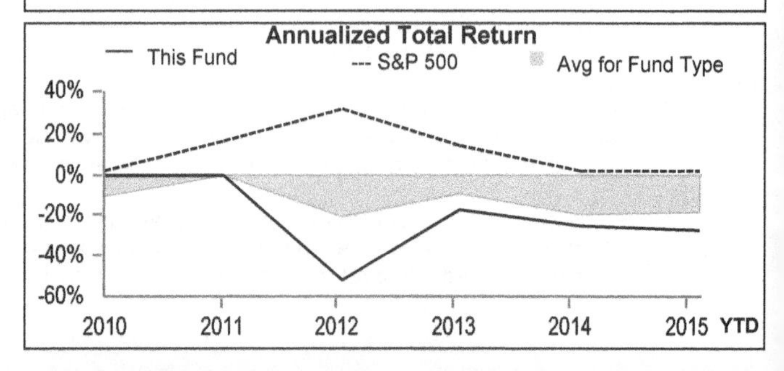

*iShares MSCI Global Silver Miner (SLVP) E Very Weak

Fund Family: BlackRock Fund Advisors
Fund Type: Precious Metals
Inception Date: January 31, 2012

Major Rating Factors: *iShares MSCI Global Silver Miner has adopted a very risky asset allocation strategy and currently receives an overall TheStreet.com Investment Rating of E (Very Weak). The fund has a high level of volatility, as measured by both semi-deviation and drawdown factors. It carries a beta of 1.86, meaning it is expected to move 18.6% for every 10% move in the market. As of December 31, 2015, *iShares MSCI Global Silver Miner traded at a price exactly equal to its net asset value, which is better than its one-year historical average premium of .50%. Unfortunately, the high level of risk (D, Weak) failed to pay off as investors endured very poor performance.

The fund's performance rating is currently E (Very Weak). It has registered an annualized return of -35.11% over the last three years and is down -36.28% year to date 2015. Factored into the performance evaluation is an expense ratio of 0.39% (very low).

Jennifer F.Y. Hsui has been running the fund for 4 years and currently receives a manager quality ranking of 11 (0=worst, 99=best). If you can tolerate very high levels of risk in the hope of improved future returns, holding this fund may be an option.

Data Date	Investment Rating	Net Assets ($Mil)	Price	Performance Rating/Pts	Total Return Y-T-D	Risk Rating/Pts
12-15	E	12.10	5.62	E / 0.3	-36.28%	D / 1.8
2014	E	12.10	8.76	E / 0.4	-18.98%	D+ / 2.7
2013	E	7.30	10.51	E- / 0.2	-47.74%	C- / 3.3

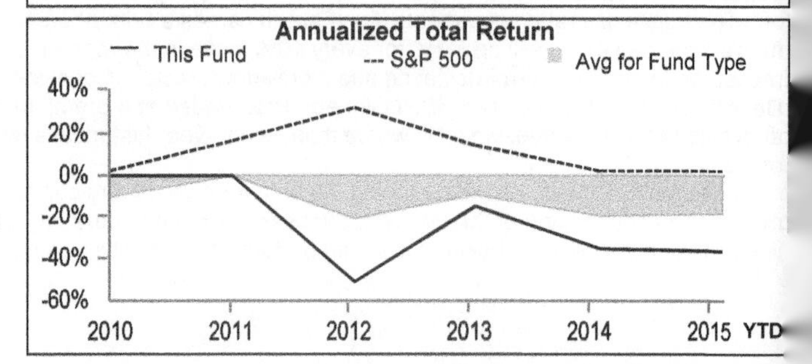

*iShares MSCI Hong Kong (EWH) C+ Fair

Fund Family: BlackRock Fund Advisors
Fund Type: Foreign
Inception Date: March 12, 1996

Major Rating Factors: Middle of the road best describes *iShares MSCI Hong Kong whose TheStreet.com Investment Rating is currently a C+ (Fair). The fund currently has a performance rating of C (Fair) based on an annualized return of 3.59% over the last three years and a total return of 0.01% year to date 2015. Factored into the performance evaluation is an expense ratio of 0.48% (very low).

The fund's risk rating is currently B- (Good). It carries a beta of 0.97, meaning that its performance tracks fairly well with that of the overall stock market. Volatility, as measured by both the semi-deviation and a drawdown factor, is considered low. As of December 31, 2015, *iShares MSCI Hong Kong traded at a discount of .40% below its net asset value, which is better than its one-year historical average discount of .03%.

Diane Hsiung has been running the fund for 8 years and currently receives a manager quality ranking of 58 (0=worst, 99=best). If you desire an average level of risk, then this fund may be an option.

Data Date	Investment Rating	Net Assets ($Mil)	Price	Performance Rating/Pts	Total Return Y-T-D	Risk Rating/Pts
12-15	C+	3,009.80	19.82	C / 5.4	0.01%	B- / 7.6
2014	B-	3,009.80	20.54	C+ / 6.2	5.72%	B / 8.1
2013	C-	2,270.90	20.60	C- / 4.2	5.25%	B- / 7.0
2012	B-	3,001.60	19.42	B- / 7.5	30.54%	B- / 7.1
2011	C-	1,814.00	15.47	C / 4.5	-19.53%	B- / 7.3
2010	C-	2,059.00	18.92	C / 4.7	24.16%	C / 5.0

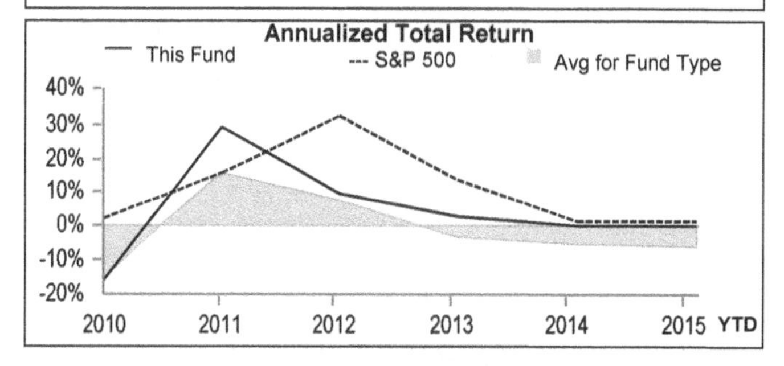

*iShares MSCI India ETF (INDA) C Fair

Fund Family: BlackRock Fund Advisors
Fund Type: Foreign
Inception Date: February 2, 2012

Major Rating Factors: Middle of the road best describes *iShares MSCI India ETF whose TheStreet.com Investment Rating is currently a C (Fair). The fund currently has a performance rating of C (Fair) based on an annualized return of 2.33% over the last three years and a total return of -7.80% year to date 2015. Factored into the performance evaluation is an expense ratio of 0.68% (very low).

The fund's risk rating is currently B- (Good). It carries a beta of 0.74, meaning the fund's expected move will be 7.4% for every 10% move in the market. Volatility, as measured by both the semi-deviation and a drawdown factor, is considered low. As of December 31, 2015, *iShares MSCI India ETF traded at a discount of .79% below its net asset value, which is better than its one-year historical average premium of .22%.

Jennifer F.Y. Hsui has been running the fund for 4 years and currently receives a manager quality ranking of 57 (0=worst, 99=best). If you desire an average level of risk, then this fund may be an option.

Data Date	Investment Rating	Net Assets ($Mil)	Price	Performance Rating/Pts	Total Return Y-T-D	Risk Rating/Pts
12-15	C	1,479.40	27.50	C / 4.3	-7.80%	B- / 7.0
2014	C+	1,479.40	29.95	B- / 7.4	25.07%	C+ / 6.8
2013	D	511.00	24.76	D / 2.2	-8.41%	C+ / 6.9

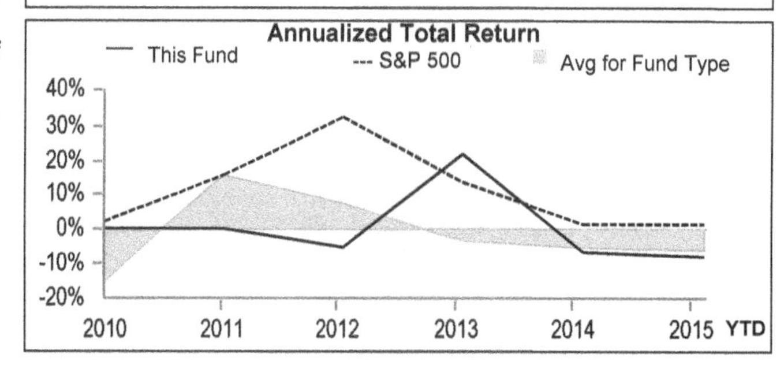

*iShares MSCI India Small-Cap (SMIN) C Fair

Fund Family: BlackRock Fund Advisors
Fund Type: Foreign
Inception Date: February 8, 2012

Major Rating Factors: Strong performance is the major factor driving the C (Fair) TheStreet.com Investment Rating for *iShares MSCI India Small-Cap. The fund currently has a performance rating of B- (Good) based on an annualized return of 9.08% over the last three years and a total return of -0.66% year to date 2015. Factored into the performance evaluation is an expense ratio of 0.74% (very low).

The fund's risk rating is currently C+ (Fair). It carries a beta of 0.87, meaning the fund's expected move will be 8.7% for every 10% move in the market. Volatility, as measured by both the semi-deviation and a drawdown factor, is considered low. As of December 31, 2015, *iShares MSCI India Small-Cap traded at a discount of 1.51% below its net asset value, which is better than its one-year historical average premium of .17%.

Jennifer F.Y. Hsui has been running the fund for 4 years and currently receives a manager quality ranking of 89 (0=worst, 99=best). If you desire only a moderate level of risk and strong performance, then this fund is an excellent option.

Data Date	Investment Rating	Net Assets ($Mil)	Price	Performance Rating/Pts	Total Return Y-T-D	Risk Rating/Pts
12-15	C	14.20	33.28	B- / 7.1	-0.66%	C+ / 5.6
2014	B-	14.20	33.64	A+ / 9.8	58.79%	C / 5.0
2013	D	5.40	22.16	D+ / 2.6	-18.83%	C / 5.3

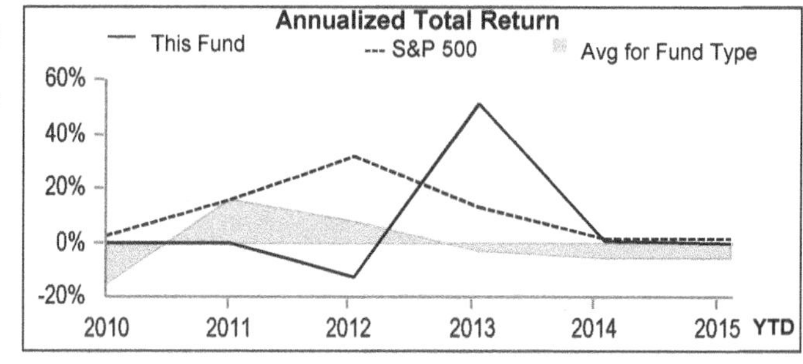

*iShares MSCI Indonesia ETF (EIDO) D Weak

Fund Family: BlackRock Fund Advisors
Fund Type: Foreign
Inception Date: May 5, 2010

Data Date	Investment Rating	Net Assets ($Mil)	Price	Performance Rating/Pts	Total Return Y-T-D	Risk Rating/Pts
12-15	D	540.30	20.87	D / 1.8	-20.74%	C / 4.7
2014	D	540.30	27.44	C- / 3.5	26.30%	C- / 3.9
2013	D-	328.00	22.84	E+ / 0.9	-27.32%	C+ / 5.6
2012	D	387.10	30.26	D- / 1.5	0.47%	C+ / 6.8
2011	D+	295.60	29.31	C- / 3.0	5.94%	C+ / 6.9

Major Rating Factors:
Disappointing performance is the major factor driving the D (Weak) TheStreet.com Investment Rating for *iShares MSCI Indonesia ETF. The fund currently has a performance rating of D (Weak) based on an annualized return of -10.79% over the last three years and a total return of -20.74% year to date 2015. Factored into the performance evaluation is an expense ratio of 0.62% (very low).

The fund's risk rating is currently C (Fair). It carries a beta of 0.82, meaning the fund's expected move will be 8.2% for every 10% move in the market. Volatility, as measured by both the semi-deviation and a drawdown factor, is considered average. As of December 31, 2015, *iShares MSCI Indonesia ETF traded at a discount of .81% below its net asset value, which is better than its one-year historical average discount of .27%.

Diane Hsiung has been running the fund for 6 years and currently receives a manager quality ranking of 11 (0=worst, 99=best). This fund offers an average level of risk but investors looking for strong performance will be frustrated.

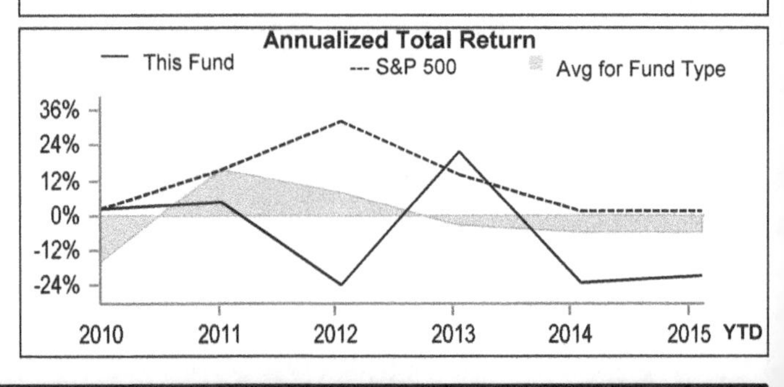

*iShares MSCI Ireland ETF (EIRL) A- Excellent

Fund Family: BlackRock Fund Advisors
Fund Type: Foreign
Inception Date: May 5, 2010

Data Date	Investment Rating	Net Assets ($Mil)	Price	Performance Rating/Pts	Total Return Y-T-D	Risk Rating/Pts
12-15	A-	118.80	41.56	A+ / 9.6	22.97%	C+ / 6.5
2014	A	118.80	34.43	B+ / 8.8	-1.02%	B- / 7.9
2013	A	123.20	35.85	A / 9.4	43.97%	B- / 7.6
2012	A	35.40	25.09	A+ / 9.8	37.24%	B- / 7.3
2011	D	7.60	18.99	D- / 1.3	-4.27%	B- / 7.3

Major Rating Factors:
Exceptional performance is the major factor driving the A- (Excellent) TheStreet.com Investment Rating for *iShares MSCI Ireland ETF. The fund currently has a performance rating of A+ (Excellent) based on an annualized return of 20.77% over the last three years and a total return of 22.97% year to date 2015. Factored into the performance evaluation is an expense ratio of 0.48% (very low).

The fund's risk rating is currently C+ (Fair). It carries a beta of 0.72, meaning the fund's expected move will be 7.2% for every 10% move in the market. Volatility, as measured by both the semi-deviation and a drawdown factor, is considered low. As of December 31, 2015, *iShares MSCI Ireland ETF traded at a premium of 1.27% above its net asset value, which is worse than its one-year historical average premium of .80%.

Diane Hsiung has been running the fund for 6 years and currently receives a manager quality ranking of 97 (0=worst, 99=best). If you desire only a moderate level of risk and strong performance, then this fund is an excellent option.

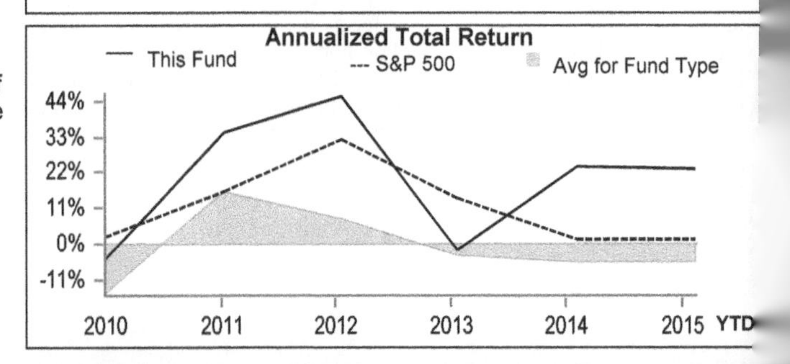

*iShares MSCI Israel Capped (EIS) B+ Good

Fund Family: BlackRock Fund Advisors
Fund Type: Foreign
Inception Date: March 26, 2008

Data Date	Investment Rating	Net Assets ($Mil)	Price	Performance Rating/Pts	Total Return Y-T-D	Risk Rating/Pts
12-15	B+	124.70	49.19	B- / 7.2	9.63%	B / 8.3
2014	D+	124.70	46.78	C- / 3.9	-0.27%	C+ / 6.1
2013	D	94.30	48.42	D+ / 2.3	15.08%	C+ / 6.1
2012	D-	79.50	41.90	D- / 1.1	6.01%	C+ / 5.9
2011	D+	75.20	39.56	D+ / 2.8	-30.74%	C+ / 6.6
2010	A-	141.30	60.52	A / 9.3	15.39%	C+ / 5.6

Major Rating Factors: Strong performance is the major factor driving the B+ (Good) TheStreet.com Investment Rating for *iShares MSCI Israel Capped. The fund currently has a performance rating of B- (Good) based on an annualized return of 7.80% over the last three years and a total return of 9.63% year to date 2015. Factored into the performance evaluation is an expense ratio of 0.62% (very low).

The fund's risk rating is currently B (Good). It carries a beta of 0.67, meaning the fund's expected move will be 6.7% for every 10% move in the market. Volatility, as measured by both the semi-deviation and a drawdown factor, is considered low. As of December 31, 2015, *iShares MSCI Israel Capped traded at a discount of .24% below its net asset value, which is better than its one-year historical average premium of .02%.

Diane Hsiung has been running the fund for 8 years and currently receives a manager quality ranking of 88 (0=worst, 99=best). If you desire only a moderate level of risk and strong performance, then this fund is an excellent option.

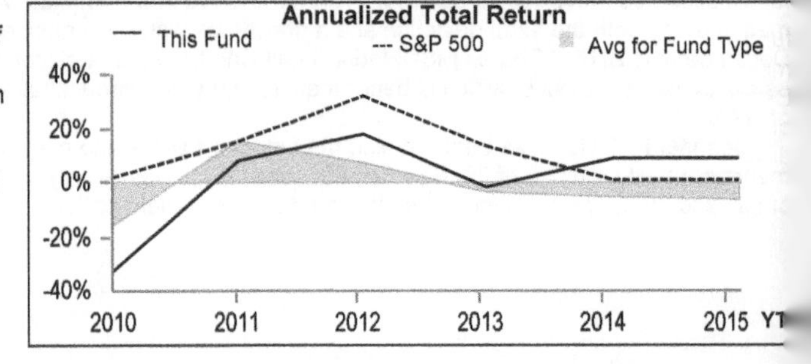

*iShares MSCI Italy Capped (EWI) C Fair

Fund Family: BlackRock Fund Advisors
Fund Type: Foreign
Inception Date: March 12, 1996

Major Rating Factors: Middle of the road best describes *iShares MSCI Italy Capped whose TheStreet.com Investment Rating is currently a C (Fair). The fund currently has a performance rating of C (Fair) based on an annualized return of 2.57% over the last three years and a total return of 3.26% year to date 2015. Factored into the performance evaluation is an expense ratio of 0.48% (very low).

The fund's risk rating is currently B- (Good). It carries a beta of 1.12, meaning it is expected to move 11.2% for every 10% move in the market. Volatility, as measured by both the semi-deviation and a drawdown factor, is considered low. As of December 31, 2015, *iShares MSCI Italy Capped traded at a discount of 1.29% below its net asset value, which is better than its one-year historical average premium of .06%.

Diane Hsiung has been running the fund for 8 years and currently receives a manager quality ranking of 44 (0=worst, 99=best). If you desire an average level of risk, then this fund may be an option.

Data Date	Investment Rating	Net Assets ($Mil)	Price	Performance Rating/Pts	Total Return Y-T-D	Risk Rating/Pts
12-15	C	1,388.80	13.74	C / 4.5	3.26%	B- / 7.0
2014	C-	1,388.80	13.60	C- / 3.7	-9.73%	C+ / 6.6
2013	D+	856.20	15.59	C / 4.8	15.52%	C / 4.8
2012	D-	384.40	13.45	D / 1.6	26.57%	C / 4.6
2011	D-	100.80	11.99	D- / 1.1	-26.93%	C / 5.5
2010	E+	95.80	16.38	E+ / 0.6	-14.12%	C- / 3.8

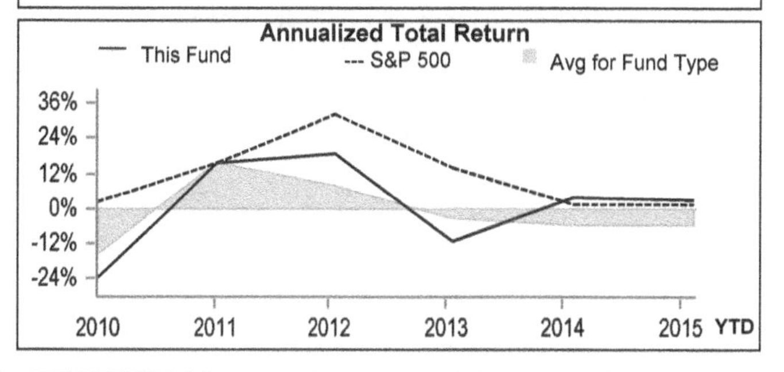

*iShares MSCI Japan (EWJ) B+ Good

Fund Family: BlackRock Fund Advisors
Fund Type: Foreign
Inception Date: March 12, 1996

Major Rating Factors: Strong performance is the major factor driving the B+ (Good) TheStreet.com Investment Rating for *iShares MSCI Japan. The fund currently has a performance rating of B- (Good) based on an annualized return of 8.68% over the last three years and a total return of 9.76% year to date 2015. Factored into the performance evaluation is an expense ratio of 0.48% (very low).

The fund's risk rating is currently B (Good). It carries a beta of 0.80, meaning the fund's expected move will be 8.0% for every 10% move in the market. Volatility, as measured by both the semi-deviation and a drawdown factor, is considered low. As of December 31, 2015, *iShares MSCI Japan traded at a discount of 1.30% below its net asset value, which is better than its one-year historical average discount of .01%.

Diane Hsiung has been running the fund for 8 years and currently receives a manager quality ranking of 88 (0=worst, 99=best). If you desire only a moderate level of risk and strong performance, then this fund is an excellent option.

Data Date	Investment Rating	Net Assets ($Mil)	Price	Performance Rating/Pts	Total Return Y-T-D	Risk Rating/Pts
12-15	B+	14,397.20	12.12	B- / 7.5	9.76%	B / 8.3
2014	C	14,397.20	11.24	C / 4.5	-5.23%	B / 8.2
2013	C	13,985.80	12.14	C+ / 5.7	23.21%	B- / 7.5
2012	D	5,156.00	9.75	D / 2.0	10.21%	B- / 7.5
2011	D+	5,345.00	9.11	D / 1.7	-15.76%	B- / 7.6
2010	D+	4,904.70	10.91	D+ / 2.4	13.61%	C+ / 5.6

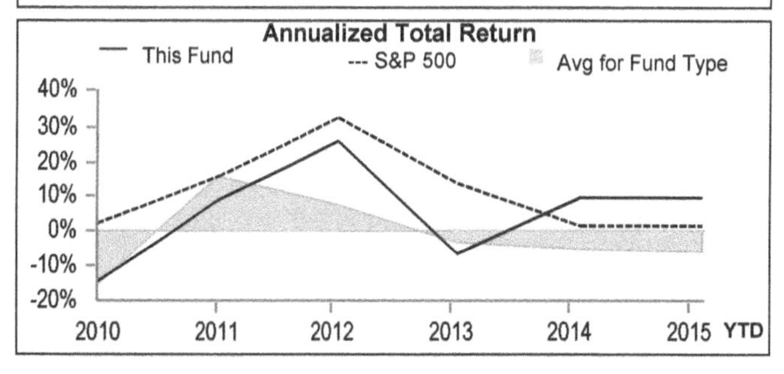

*iShares MSCI Japan Minimum Vol E (JPMV) A+ Excellent

Fund Family: BlackRock Fund Advisors
Fund Type: Foreign
Inception Date: June 3, 2014

Major Rating Factors:
Exceptional performance is the major factor driving the A+ (Excellent) TheStreet.com Investment Rating for *iShares MSCI Japan Minimum Vol E. The fund currently has a performance rating of A (Excellent) based on an annualized return of 0.00% over the last three years and a total return of 17.01% year to date 2015. Factored into the performance evaluation is an expense ratio of 0.30% (very low).

The fund's risk rating is currently B (Good). It carries a beta of 0.00, meaning the fund's expected move will be 0.0% for every 10% move in the market. Volatility, as measured by both the semi-deviation and a drawdown factor, is considered low. As of December 31, 2015, *iShares MSCI Japan Minimum Vol E traded at a discount of .89% below its net asset value, which is better than its one-year historical average discount of .03%.

Diane Hsiung has been running the fund for 2 years and currently receives a manager quality ranking of 98 (0=worst, 99=best). If you desire only a moderate level of risk and strong performance, then this fund is an excellent option.

Data Date	Investment Rating	Net Assets ($Mil)	Price	Performance Rating/Pts	Total Return Y-T-D	Risk Rating/Pts
12-15	A+	10.30	57.00	A / 9.3	17.01%	B / 8.8

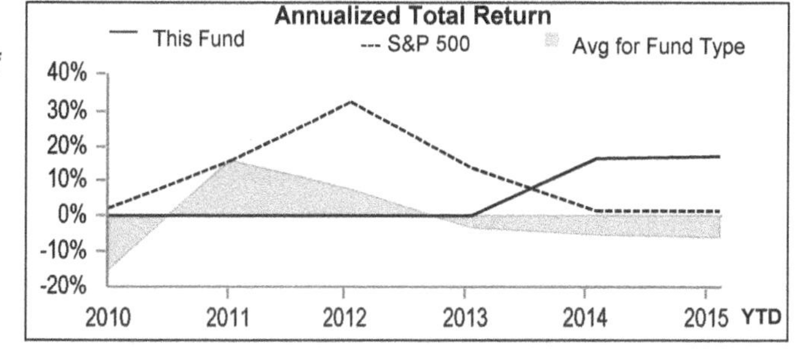

*iShares MSCI Japan Small Cap (SCJ) A+ Excellent

Fund Family: BlackRock Fund Advisors
Fund Type: Foreign
Inception Date: December 20, 2007

Data Date	Investment Rating	Net Assets ($Mil)	Price	Performance Rating/Pts	Total Return Y-T-D	Risk Rating/Pts
12-15	A+	158.60	58.45	B+ / 8.8	15.85%	B / 8.6
2014	C	158.60	51.66	C / 4.4	-1.46%	B / 8.4
2013	C+	140.30	54.28	C+ / 6.2	22.17%	B / 8.2
2012	C-	39.50	44.39	D+ / 2.6	6.72%	B / 8.3
2011	C-	52.20	43.33	C- / 3.0	-4.95%	B- / 7.8
2010	C	42.00	46.66	C / 4.3	19.07%	C+ / 6.1

Major Rating Factors:
Strong performance is the major factor driving the A+ (Excellent) TheStreet.com Investment Rating for *iShares MSCI Japan Small Cap. The fund currently has a performance rating of B+ (Good) based on an annualized return of 11.73% over the last three years and a total return of 15.85% year to date 2015. Factored into the performance evaluation is an expense ratio of 0.48% (very low).

The fund's risk rating is currently B (Good). It carries a beta of 0.58, meaning the fund's expected move will be 5.8% for every 10% move in the market. Volatility, as measured by both the semi-deviation and a drawdown factor, is considered low. As of December 31, 2015, *iShares MSCI Japan Small Cap traded at a discount of 1.07% below its net asset value, which is better than its one-year historical average premium of .09%.

Diane Hsiung has been running the fund for 8 years and currently receives a manager quality ranking of 94 (0=worst, 99=best). If you desire only a moderate level of risk and strong performance, then this fund is an excellent option.

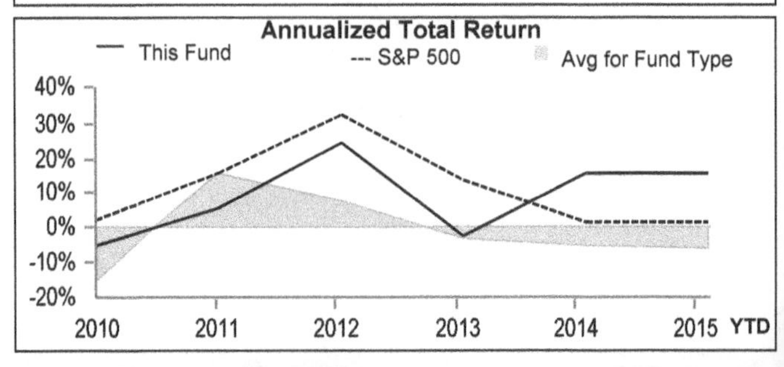

*iShares MSCI KLD 400 Social ETF (DSI) A Excellent

Fund Family: BlackRock Fund Advisors
Fund Type: Income
Inception Date: November 14, 2006

Data Date	Investment Rating	Net Assets ($Mil)	Price	Performance Rating/Pts	Total Return Y-T-D	Risk Rating/Pts
12-15	A	384.70	75.71	B+ / 8.8	0.83%	B- / 7.9
2014	B	384.70	76.59	B / 8.0	13.23%	B- / 7.3
2013	B+	304.00	69.10	B / 8.2	30.60%	B / 8.3
2012	C	165.50	51.74	C- / 4.2	13.81%	B / 8.2
2011	C	161.20	46.89	C / 5.1	1.78%	B / 8.0
2010	C-	140.70	46.91	C- / 4.0	11.42%	C+ / 6.0

Major Rating Factors:
Strong performance is the major factor driving the A (Excellent) TheStreet.com Investment Rating for *iShares MSCI KLD 400 Social ETF. The fund currently has a performance rating of B+ (Good) based on an annualized return of 14.22% over the last three years and a total return of 0.83% year to date 2015. Factored into the performance evaluation is an expense ratio of 0.50% (very low).

The fund's risk rating is currently B- (Good). It carries a beta of 1.01, meaning that its performance tracks fairly well with that of the overall stock market. Volatility, as measured by both the semi-deviation and a drawdown factor, is considered low. As of December 31, 2015, *iShares MSCI KLD 400 Social ETF traded at a discount of .01% below its net asset value, which is better than its one-year historical average premium of .05%.

Diane Hsiung has been running the fund for 8 years and currently receives a manager quality ranking of 68 (0=worst, 99=best). If you desire only a moderate level of risk and strong performance, then this fund is an excellent option.

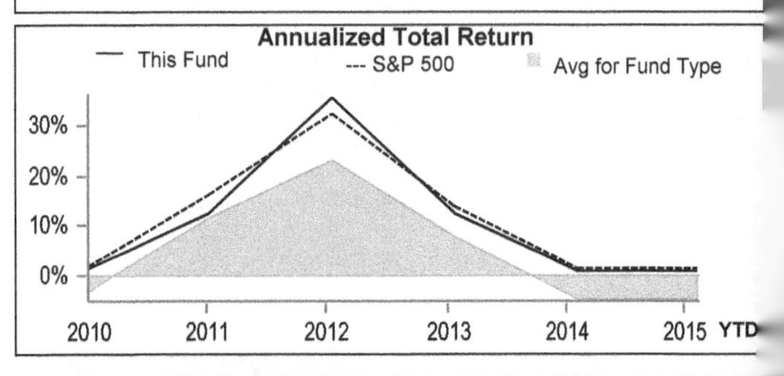

*iShares MSCI Kokusai ETF (TOK) B+ Good

Fund Family: BlackRock Fund Advisors
Fund Type: Global
Inception Date: December 10, 2007

Data Date	Investment Rating	Net Assets ($Mil)	Price	Performance Rating/Pts	Total Return Y-T-D	Risk Rating/Pts
12-15	B+	485.50	51.76	B- / 7.5	-0.02%	B- / 7.7
2014	C+	485.50	54.16	C+ / 6.9	6.87%	B- / 7.2
2013	B	471.80	52.68	B- / 7.5	23.95%	B- / 7.9
2012	C-	636.20	42.69	C- / 4.2	17.13%	B- / 7.7
2011	C	611.30	37.81	C / 4.3	-2.35%	B- / 7.7
2010	D+	287.30	40.24	D+ / 2.9	11.45%	C+ / 5.7

Major Rating Factors: Strong performance is the major factor driving the B+ (Good) TheStreet.com Investment Rating for *iShares MSCI Kokusai ETF. The fund currently has a performance rating of B- (Good) based on an annualized return of 9.73% over the last three years and a total return of -0.02% year to date 2015. Factored into the performance evaluation is an expense ratio of 0.25% (very low).

The fund's risk rating is currently B- (Good). It carries a beta of 0.81, meaning the fund's expected move will be 8.1% for every 10% move in the market. Volatility, as measured by both the semi-deviation and a drawdown factor, is considered low. As of December 31, 2015, *iShares MSCI Kokusai ETF traded at a price exactly equal to its net asset value, which is better than its one-year historical average premium of .12%.

Diane Hsiung has been running the fund for 8 years and currently receives a manager quality ranking of 90 (0=worst, 99=best). If you desire only a moderate level of risk and strong performance, then this fund is an excellent option.

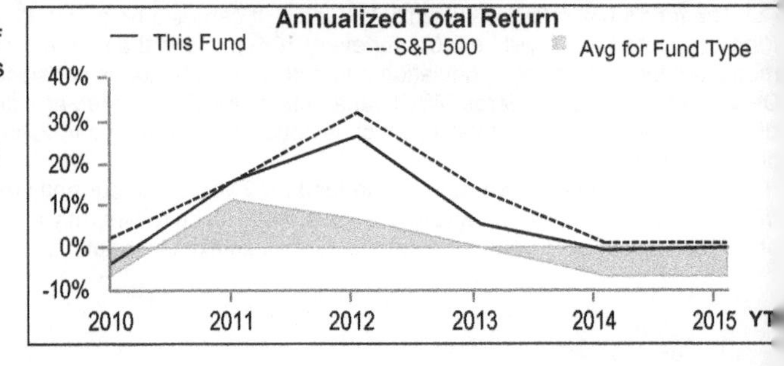

*iShares MSCI Malaysia (EWM) C- Fair

Fund Family: BlackRock Fund Advisors
Fund Type: Foreign
Inception Date: March 12, 1996

Data Date	Investment Rating	Net Assets ($Mil)	Price	Performance Rating/Pts	Total Return Y-T-D	Risk Rating/Pts
12-15	C-	741.90	7.74	C / 5.3	2.56%	C / 4.6
2014	D	741.90	13.48	D+ / 2.5	-8.76%	C+ / 6.2
2013	C-	835.40	15.82	C- / 4.1	3.65%	B- / 7.8
2012	C+	971.30	15.13	C+ / 5.9	13.75%	B- / 7.8
2011	B	855.70	13.40	B- / 7.4	-4.45%	B / 8.0
2010	B+	973.10	14.38	B+ / 8.4	38.97%	C+ / 5.7

Major Rating Factors: Middle of the road best describes *iShares MSCI Malaysia whose TheStreet.com Investment Rating is currently a C- (Fair). The fund currently has a performance rating of C (Fair) based on an annualized return of -1.78% over the last three years and a total return of 2.56% year to date 2015. Factored into the performance evaluation is an expense ratio of 0.48% (very low).

The fund's risk rating is currently C (Fair). It carries a beta of 0.72, meaning the fund's expected move will be 7.2% for every 10% move in the market. Volatility, as measured by both the semi-deviation and a drawdown factor, is considered average. As of December 31, 2015, *iShares MSCI Malaysia traded at a discount of .26% below its net asset value, which is better than its one-year historical average discount of .13%.

Diane Hsiung has been running the fund for 8 years and currently receives a manager quality ranking of 29 (0=worst, 99=best). If you desire an average level of risk, then this fund may be an option.

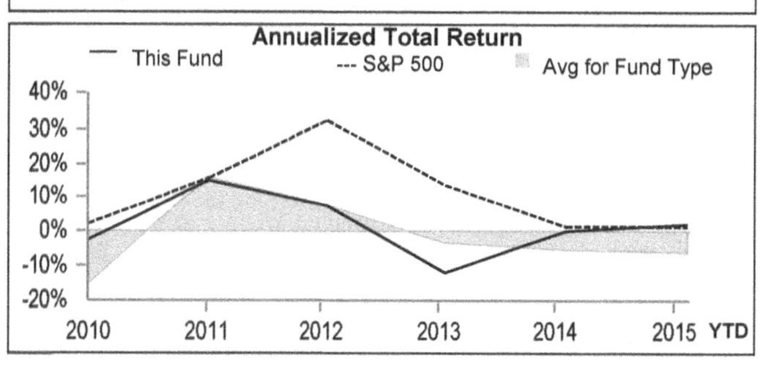

*iShares MSCI Mexico Capped (EWW) D+ Weak

Fund Family: BlackRock Fund Advisors
Fund Type: Foreign
Inception Date: March 12, 1996

Data Date	Investment Rating	Net Assets ($Mil)	Price	Performance Rating/Pts	Total Return Y-T-D	Risk Rating/Pts
12-15	D+	3,048.40	49.83	D / 1.9	-11.28%	C+ / 6.6
2014	D	3,048.40	59.39	D+ / 2.9	-9.07%	C / 5.5
2013	C-	2,642.10	68.00	C- / 3.5	-6.70%	B- / 7.2
2012	B	1,928.70	70.53	B+ / 8.4	36.35%	B- / 7.3
2011	C+	1,133.30	53.76	C+ / 6.1	-12.13%	B- / 7.3
2010	B-	1,720.10	61.92	B / 7.8	27.91%	C / 4.6

Major Rating Factors:
Disappointing performance is the major factor driving the D+ (Weak) TheStreet.com Investment Rating for *iShares MSCI Mexico Capped. The fund currently has a performance rating of D (Weak) based on an annualized return of -9.81% over the last three years and a total return of -11.28% year to date 2015. Factored into the performance evaluation is an expense ratio of 0.48% (very low).

The fund's risk rating is currently C+ (Fair). It carries a beta of 0.72, meaning the fund's expected move will be 7.2% for every 10% move in the market. Volatility, as measured by both the semi-deviation and a drawdown factor, is considered low. As of December 31, 2015, *iShares MSCI Mexico Capped traded at a discount of .44% below its net asset value, which is better than its one-year historical average discount of .12%.

Diane Hsiung has been running the fund for 8 years and currently receives a manager quality ranking of 13 (0=worst, 99=best). This fund offers only a moderate level of risk but investors looking for strong performance are still waiting.

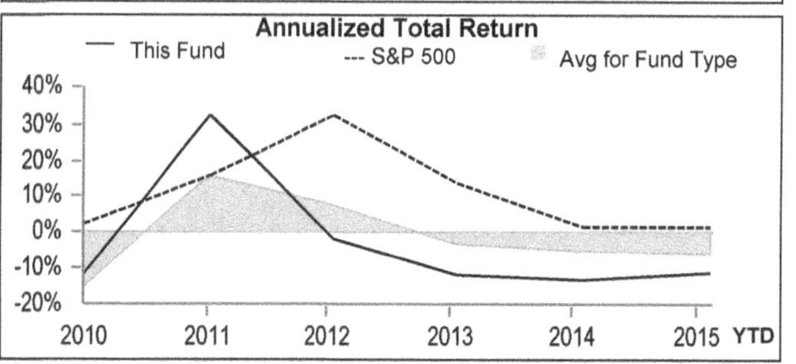

*iShares MSCI Netherlands (EWN) B Good

Fund Family: BlackRock Fund Advisors
Fund Type: Foreign
Inception Date: March 12, 1996

Data Date	Investment Rating	Net Assets ($Mil)	Price	Performance Rating/Pts	Total Return Y-T-D	Risk Rating/Pts
12-15	B	159.80	23.84	C+ / 6.6	2.59%	B / 8.2
2014	C	159.80	23.91	C+ / 6.2	-4.15%	C+ / 6.2
2013	C+	304.60	25.93	B- / 7.5	25.95%	C+ / 6.7
2012	C-	148.40	20.51	C / 4.7	29.11%	C+ / 6.5
2011	D	73.50	17.23	D / 2.2	-14.80%	C+ / 6.7
2010	D-	172.20	21.09	D- / 1.3	4.95%	C- / 4.1

Major Rating Factors: *iShares MSCI Netherlands receives a TheStreet.com Investment Rating of B (Good). The fund currently has a performance rating of C+ (Fair) based on an annualized return of 7.23% over the last three years and a total return of 2.59% year to date 2015. Factored into the performance evaluation is an expense ratio of 0.48% (very low).

The fund's risk rating is currently B (Good). It carries a beta of 1.01, meaning that its performance tracks fairly well with that of the overall stock market. Volatility, as measured by both the semi-deviation and a drawdown factor, is considered low. As of December 31, 2015, *iShares MSCI Netherlands traded at a discount of .46% below its net asset value, which is better than its one-year historical average premium of .02%.

Diane Hsiung has been running the fund for 8 years and currently receives a manager quality ranking of 80 (0=worst, 99=best). If you desire an average level of risk, then this fund may be an option.

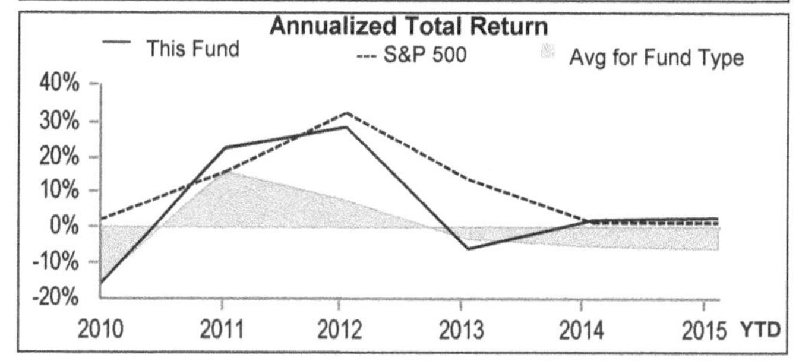

*iShares MSCI Norway Capped ETF (ENOR) D Weak

Fund Family: BlackRock Fund Advisors
Fund Type: Foreign
Inception Date: January 23, 2012

Data Date	Investment Rating	Net Assets ($Mil)	Price	Performance Rating/Pts	Total Return Y-T-D	Risk Rating/Pts
12-15	D	27.10	18.91	D / 1.6	-15.03%	C+ / 5.6
2014	D-	27.10	23.30	E / 0.3	-21.07%	C+ / 6.0
2013	C+	12.40	30.91	C+ / 6.6	5.62%	B- / 7.8

Major Rating Factors:
Disappointing performance is the major factor driving the D (Weak) TheStreet.com Investment Rating for *iShares MSCI Norway Capped ETF. The fund currently has a performance rating of D (Weak) based on an annualized return of -11.09% over the last three years and a total return of -15.03% year to date 2015. Factored into the performance evaluation is an expense ratio of 0.53% (very low).

The fund's risk rating is currently C+ (Fair). It carries a beta of 1.16, meaning it is expected to move 11.6% for every 10% move in the market. Volatility, as measured by both the semi-deviation and a drawdown factor, is considered low. As of December 31, 2015, *iShares MSCI Norway Capped ETF traded at a discount of 1.05% below its net asset value, which is better than its one-year historical average premium of .03%.

Jennifer F.Y. Hsui has been running the fund for 4 years and currently receives a manager quality ranking of 10 (0=worst, 99=best). This fund offers only a moderate level of risk but investors looking for strong performance are still waiting.

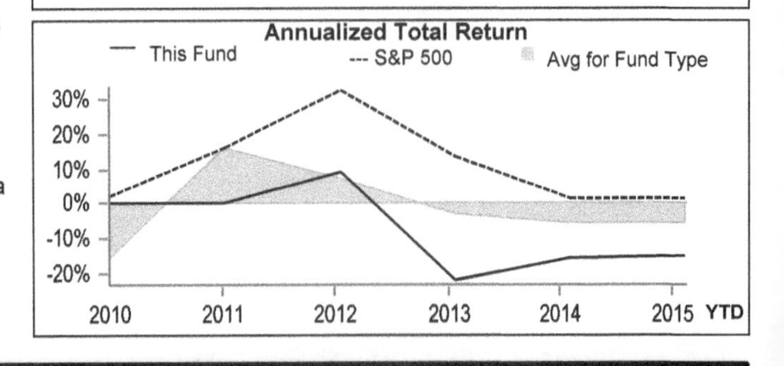

*iShares MSCI NZ Capped ETF (ENZL) B Good

Fund Family: BlackRock Fund Advisors
Fund Type: Foreign
Inception Date: September 1, 2010

Data Date	Investment Rating	Net Assets ($Mil)	Price	Performance Rating/Pts	Total Return Y-T-D	Risk Rating/Pts
12-15	B	138.60	37.48	B / 7.9	0.69%	B- / 7.1
2014	C+	138.60	39.98	B / 7.7	10.86%	C+ / 6.1
2013	B-	136.20	37.36	B- / 7.4	13.87%	B- / 7.7
2012	A+	157.20	34.58	A+ / 9.7	34.74%	B- / 7.8
2011	D	95.80	27.56	D- / 1.4	1.98%	B- / 7.9

Major Rating Factors: Strong performance is the major factor driving the B (Good) TheStreet.com Investment Rating for *iShares MSCI NZ Capped ETF. The fund currently has a performance rating of B (Good) based on an annualized return of 8.01% over the last three years and a total return of 0.69% year to date 2015. Factored into the performance evaluation is an expense ratio of 0.48% (very low).

The fund's risk rating is currently B- (Good). It carries a beta of 1.04, meaning that its performance tracks fairly well with that of the overall stock market. Volatility, as measured by both the semi-deviation and a drawdown factor, is considered low. As of December 31, 2015, *iShares MSCI NZ Capped ETF traded at a discount of 1.03% below its net asset value, which is better than its one-year historical average discount of .11%.

Diane Hsiung has been running the fund for 6 years and currently receives a manager quality ranking of 82 (0=worst, 99=best). If you desire only a moderate level of risk and strong performance, then this fund is an excellent option.

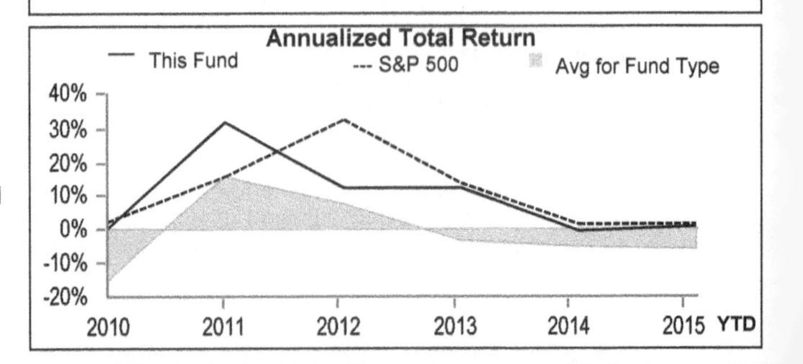

*iShares MSCI Pacific ex Japan (EPP) C- Fair

Fund Family: BlackRock Fund Advisors
Fund Type: Foreign
Inception Date: October 25, 2001

Data Date	Investment Rating	Net Assets ($Mil)	Price	Performance Rating/Pts	Total Return Y-T-D	Risk Rating/Pts
12-15	C-	3,141.20	38.39	C- / 3.4	-6.17%	C+ / 6.8
2014	C-	3,141.20	43.95	C / 4.3	-1.38%	B- / 7.5
2013	C-	3,249.10	46.73	C / 4.4	1.40%	C+ / 6.8
2012	C	3,798.50	47.14	C+ / 5.8	23.59%	C+ / 6.9
2011	C	3,099.70	38.93	C+ / 6.0	-10.68%	B- / 7.1
2010	D	4,319.90	46.98	C+ / 5.7	17.77%	D- / 1.4

Major Rating Factors: Middle of the road best describes *iShares MSCI Pacific ex Japan whose TheStreet.com Investment Rating is currently a C- (Fair). The fund currently has a performance rating of C- (Fair) based on an annualized return of -2.18% over the last three years and a total return of -6.17% year to date 2015. Factored into the performance evaluation is an expense ratio of 0.49% (very low).

The fund's risk rating is currently C+ (Fair). It carries a beta of 1.04, meaning that its performance tracks fairly well with that of the overall stock market. Volatility, as measured by both the semi-deviation and a drawdown factor, is considered low. As of December 31, 2015, *iShares MSCI Pacific ex Japan traded at a discount of .65% below its net asset value, which is better than its one-year historical average discount of .18%.

Diane Hsiung has been running the fund for 8 years and currently receives a manager quality ranking of 22 (0=worst, 99=best). If you desire an average level of risk, then this fund may be an option.

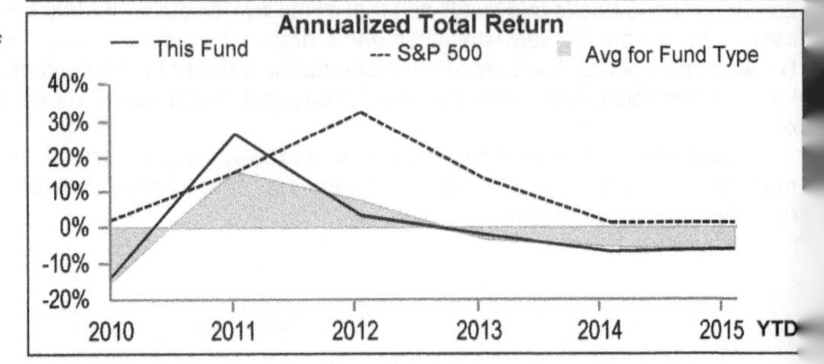

*iShares MSCI Philippines ETF (EPHE) C- Fair

Fund Family: BlackRock Fund Advisors
Fund Type: Foreign
Inception Date: September 28, 2010

Data Date	Investment Rating	Net Assets ($Mil)	Price	Performance Rating/Pts	Total Return Y-T-D	Risk Rating/Pts
12-15	C-	363.90	33.74	C- / 3.2	-10.32%	B- / 7.0
2014	B-	363.90	38.20	B / 7.8	24.25%	B- / 7.0
2013	C-	259.80	31.60	C- / 4.2	-11.92%	B- / 7.0
2012	A	218.40	34.55	A+ / 9.8	45.19%	B- / 7.5
2011	D+	69.80	23.57	D / 2.2	-1.29%	B- / 7.3

Major Rating Factors: Middle of the road best describes *iShares MSCI Philippines ETF whose TheStreet.com Investment Rating is currently a C- (Fair). The fund currently has a performance rating of C- (Fair) based on an annualized return of -0.70% over the last three years and a total return of -10.32% year to date 2015. Factored into the performance evaluation is an expense ratio of 0.62% (very low).

The fund's risk rating is currently B- (Good). It carries a beta of 0.82, meaning the fund's expected move will be 8.2% for every 10% move in the market. Volatility, as measured by both the semi-deviation and a drawdown factor, is considered low. As of December 31, 2015, *iShares MSCI Philippines ETF traded at a discount of 1.40% below its net asset value, which is better than its one-year historical average discount of .45%.

Diane Hsiung has been running the fund for 6 years and currently receives a manager quality ranking of 36 (0=worst, 99=best). If you desire an average level of risk, then this fund may be an option.

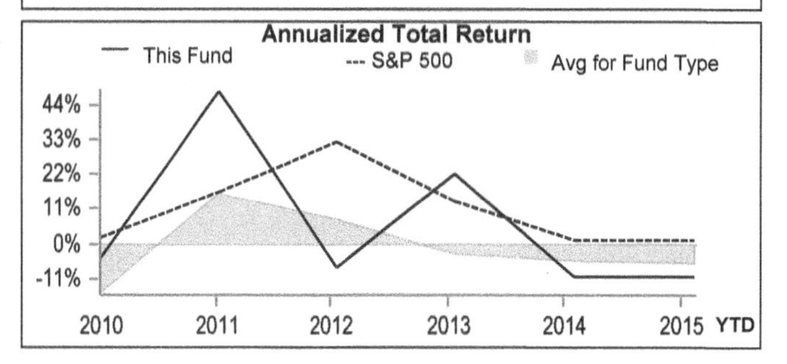

*iShares MSCI Poland Capped ETF (EPOL) D- Weak

Fund Family: BlackRock Fund Advisors
Fund Type: Foreign
Inception Date: May 25, 2010

Data Date	Investment Rating	Net Assets ($Mil)	Price	Performance Rating/Pts	Total Return Y-T-D	Risk Rating/Pts
12-15	D-	286.50	18.08	D- / 1.4	-20.87%	C / 4.3
2014	D	286.50	24.07	C- / 3.6	-14.13%	C / 4.9
2013	D	280.30	29.68	C- / 3.6	3.27%	C / 4.8
2012	B-	184.50	29.62	A+ / 9.8	39.88%	C / 4.8
2011	E+	109.80	21.64	E- / 0.2	-31.35%	C / 4.9

Major Rating Factors:
Disappointing performance is the major factor driving the D- (Weak) TheStreet.com Investment Rating for *iShares MSCI Poland Capped ETF. The fund currently has a performance rating of D- (Weak) based on an annualized return of -11.63% over the last three years and a total return of -20.87% year to date 2015. Factored into the performance evaluation is an expense ratio of 0.62% (very low).

The fund's risk rating is currently C (Fair). It carries a beta of 0.76, meaning the fund's expected move will be 7.6% for every 10% move in the market. Volatility, as measured by both the semi-deviation and a drawdown factor, is considered average. As of December 31, 2015, *iShares MSCI Poland Capped ETF traded at a premium of .06% above its net asset value.

Diane Hsiung has been running the fund for 6 years and currently receives a manager quality ranking of 10 (0=worst, 99=best). This fund offers an average level of risk but investors looking for strong performance will be frustrated.

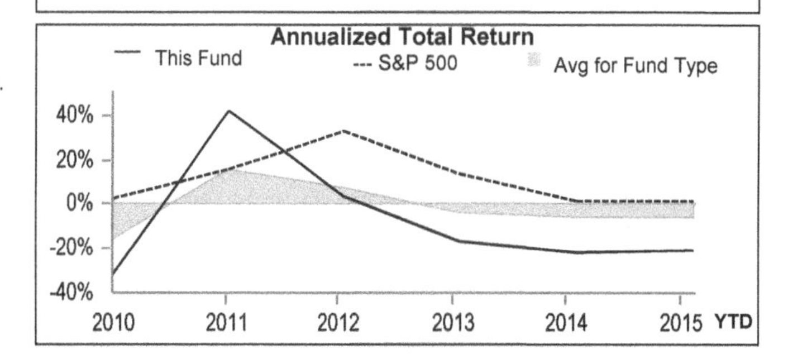

*iShares MSCI Qatar Capped ETF (QAT) D- Weak

Fund Family: BlackRock Fund Advisors
Fund Type: Emerging Market
Inception Date: April 29, 2014

Data Date	Investment Rating	Net Assets ($Mil)	Price	Performance Rating/Pts	Total Return Y-T-D	Risk Rating/Pts
12-15	D-	36.50	19.28	E+ / 0.8	-14.64%	C / 4.3

Major Rating Factors:
Very poor performance is the major factor driving the D- (Weak) TheStreet.com Investment Rating for *iShares MSCI Qatar Capped ETF. The fund currently has a performance rating of E+ (Very Weak) based on an annualized return of 0.00% over the last three years and a total return of -14.64% year to date 2015. Factored into the performance evaluation is an expense ratio of 0.62% (very low).

The fund's risk rating is currently C (Fair). It carries a beta of 0.00, meaning the fund's expected move will be 0.0% for every 10% move in the market. Volatility, as measured by both the semi-deviation and a drawdown factor, is considered average. As of December 31, 2015, *iShares MSCI Qatar Capped ETF traded at a premium of .16% above its net asset value, which is better than its one-year historical average premium of .46%.

Jennifer F.Y. Hsui has been running the fund for 2 years and currently receives a manager quality ranking of 17 (0=worst, 99=best). This fund offers an average level of risk but investors looking for strong performance will be frustrated.

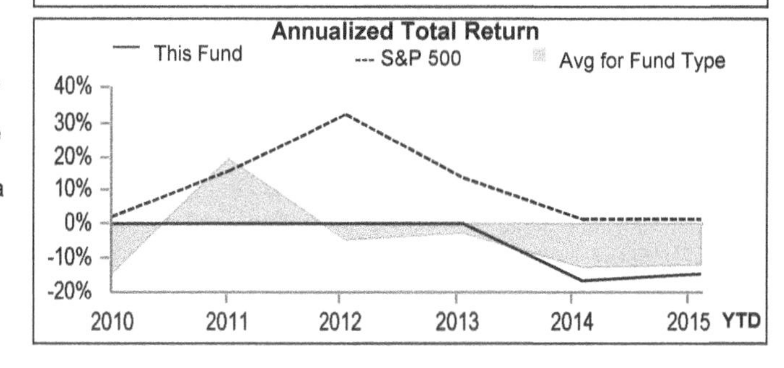

*iShares MSCI Russia Capped ETF (ERUS) D- Weak

Fund Family: BlackRock Fund Advisors
Fund Type: Foreign
Inception Date: November 9, 2010

Data Date	Investment Rating	Net Assets ($Mil)	Price	Performance Rating/Pts	Total Return Y-T-D	Risk Rating/Pts
12-15	D-	276.20	11.13	D- / 1.2	4.15%	C / 4.4
2014	E-	276.20	11.47	E / 0.5	-42.56%	D / 1.8
2013	D-	388.10	21.90	D / 1.6	-10.62%	C / 5.2
2012	C-	205.50	23.65	C+ / 6.8	10.94%	C / 5.1

Major Rating Factors:
Disappointing performance is the major factor driving the D- (Weak) TheStreet.com Investment Rating for *iShares MSCI Russia Capped ETF. The fund currently has a performance rating of D- (Weak) based on an annualized return of -18.86% over the last three years and a total return of 4.15% year to date 2015. Factored into the performance evaluation is an expense ratio of 0.62% (very low).

The fund's risk rating is currently C (Fair). It carries a beta of 1.18, meaning it is expected to move 11.8% for every 10% move in the market. Volatility, as measured by both the semi-deviation and a drawdown factor, is considered average. As of December 31, 2015, *iShares MSCI Russia Capped ETF traded at a discount of .09% below its net asset value, which is better than its one-year historical average discount of .04%.

Diane Hsiung has been running the fund for 6 years and currently receives a manager quality ranking of 6 (0=worst, 99=best). This fund offers an average level of risk but investors looking for strong performance will be frustrated.

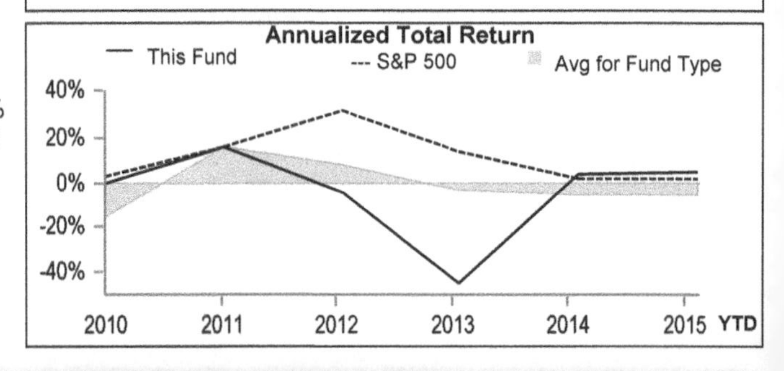

*iShares MSCI Singapore (EWS) D+ Weak

Fund Family: BlackRock Fund Advisors
Fund Type: Foreign
Inception Date: March 12, 1996

Data Date	Investment Rating	Net Assets ($Mil)	Price	Performance Rating/Pts	Total Return Y-T-D	Risk Rating/Pts
12-15	D+	936.20	10.28	D+ / 2.5	-15.70%	C+ / 6.8
2014	C-	936.20	13.08	C / 5.3	5.02%	C+ / 6.0
2013	D+	1,138.00	13.17	D+ / 2.9	-2.82%	B- / 7.0
2012	C	1,520.80	13.69	C / 5.5	24.38%	B- / 7.1
2011	C	1,282.60	10.83	C+ / 5.6	-17.03%	B- / 7.3
2010	C+	2,205.60	13.85	B / 7.7	24.51%	C / 4.5

Major Rating Factors:
Disappointing performance is the major factor driving the D+ (Weak) TheStreet.com Investment Rating for *iShares MSCI Singapore. The fund currently has a performance rating of D+ (Weak) based on an annualized return of -5.16% over the last three years and a total return of -15.70% year to date 2015. Factored into the performance evaluation is an expense ratio of 0.48% (very low).

The fund's risk rating is currently C+ (Fair). It carries a beta of 0.95, meaning that its performance tracks fairly well with that of the overall stock market. Volatility, as measured by both the semi-deviation and a drawdown factor, is considered low. As of December 31, 2015, *iShares MSCI Singapore traded at a discount of .48% below its net asset value, which is better than its one-year historical average discount of .07%.

Diane Hsiung has been running the fund for 8 years and currently receives a manager quality ranking of 17 (0=worst, 99=best). This fund offers only a moderate level of risk but investors looking for strong performance are still waiting.

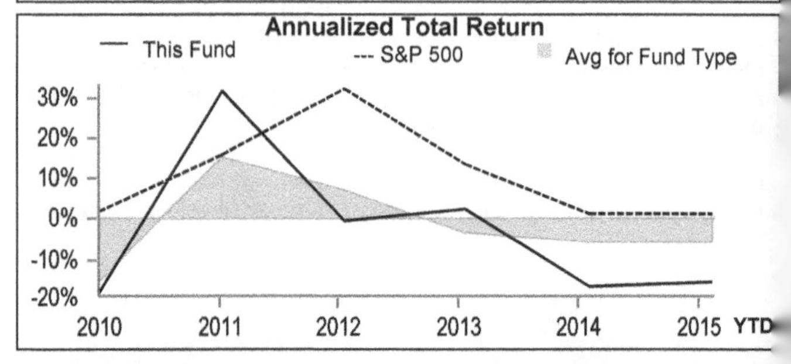

*iShares MSCI South Africa (EZA) D Weak

Fund Family: BlackRock Fund Advisors
Fund Type: Foreign
Inception Date: February 3, 2003

Data Date	Investment Rating	Net Assets ($Mil)	Price	Performance Rating/Pts	Total Return Y-T-D	Risk Rating/Pts
12-15	D	462.50	46.71	D- / 1.3	-23.24%	C+ / 6.2
2014	D+	462.50	64.82	C- / 3.9	7.08%	C+ / 5.6
2013	D	503.30	64.49	D / 2.1	-10.87%	B- / 7.0
2012	C-	533.50	71.58	C / 5.1	14.86%	C+ / 6.9
2011	C+	504.20	61.07	C+ / 6.2	-11.62%	B- / 7.1
2010	C	684.40	74.68	B+ / 8.5	36.91%	D+ / 2.3

Major Rating Factors:
Disappointing performance is the major factor driving the D (Weak) TheStreet.com Investment Rating for *iShares MSCI South Africa. The fund currently has a performance rating of D- (Weak) based on an annualized return of -10.46% over the last three years and a total return of -23.24% year to date 2015. Factored into the performance evaluation is an expense ratio of 0.62% (very low).

The fund's risk rating is currently C+ (Fair). It carries a beta of 0.87, meaning the fund's expected move will be 8.7% for every 10% move in the market. Volatility, as measured by both the semi-deviation and a drawdown factor, is considered low. As of December 31, 2015, *iShares MSCI South Africa traded at a discount of .66% below its net asset value, which is better than its one-year historical average premium of .01%.

Diane Hsiung has been running the fund for 8 years and currently receives a manager quality ranking of 11 (0=worst, 99=best). This fund offers only a moderate level of risk but investors looking for strong performance are still waiting.

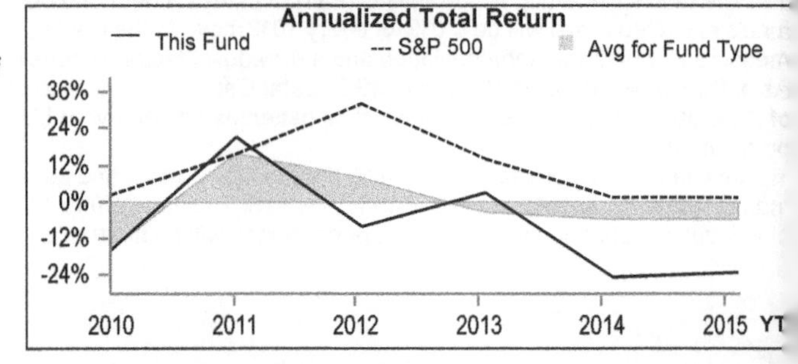

*iShares MSCI South Korea Capped (EWY) C- Fair

Fund Family: BlackRock Fund Advisors
Fund Type: Foreign
Inception Date: May 9, 2000

Major Rating Factors:
Disappointing performance is the major factor driving the C- (Fair) TheStreet.com Investment Rating for *iShares MSCI South Korea Capped. The fund currently has a performance rating of D+ (Weak) based on an annualized return of -5.66% over the last three years and a total return of -4.90% year to date 2015. Factored into the performance evaluation is an expense ratio of 0.62% (very low).

The fund's risk rating is currently B- (Good). It carries a beta of 0.76, meaning the fund's expected move will be 7.6% for every 10% move in the market. Volatility, as measured by both the semi-deviation and a drawdown factor, is considered low. As of December 31, 2015, *iShares MSCI South Korea Capped traded at a discount of 1.51% below its net asset value, which is better than its one-year historical average discount of .38%.

Diane Hsiung has been running the fund for 8 years and currently receives a manager quality ranking of 18 (0=worst, 99=best). This fund offers only a moderate level of risk but investors looking for strong performance are still waiting.

Data Date	Investment Rating	Net Assets ($Mil)	Price	Performance Rating/Pts	Total Return Y-T-D	Risk Rating/Pts
12-15	C-	4,724.80	49.67	D+ / 2.7	-4.90%	B- / 7.0
2014	D+	4,724.80	55.29	D+ / 2.7	-8.67%	C+ / 6.7
2013	D+	4,397.90	64.67	C- / 3.2	-2.32%	C+ / 6.3
2012	C-	3,344.80	63.35	C / 5.1	19.04%	C+ / 6.3
2011	C	3,038.60	52.26	C+ / 6.5	-14.56%	C+ / 6.3
2010	C	4,170.10	61.19	C+ / 6.7	29.58%	C- / 3.8

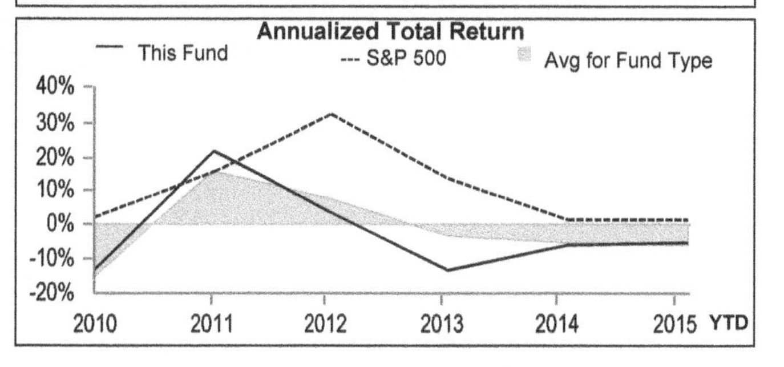

*iShares MSCI Spain Capped (EWP) C- Fair

Fund Family: BlackRock Fund Advisors
Fund Type: Foreign
Inception Date: March 12, 1996

Major Rating Factors: Middle of the road best describes *iShares MSCI Spain Capped whose TheStreet.com Investment Rating is currently a C- (Fair). The fund currently has a performance rating of C- (Fair) based on an annualized return of 1.65% over the last three years and a total return of -14.84% year to date 2015. Factored into the performance evaluation is an expense ratio of 0.48% (very low).

The fund's risk rating is currently C+ (Fair). It carries a beta of 1.31, meaning it is expected to move 13.1% for every 10% move in the market. Volatility, as measured by both the semi-deviation and a drawdown factor, is considered low. As of December 31, 2015, *iShares MSCI Spain Capped traded at a discount of .63% below its net asset value, which is better than its one-year historical average premium of .06%.

Diane Hsiung has been running the fund for 8 years and currently receives a manager quality ranking of 31 (0=worst, 99=best). If you desire an average level of risk, then this fund may be an option.

Data Date	Investment Rating	Net Assets ($Mil)	Price	Performance Rating/Pts	Total Return Y-T-D	Risk Rating/Pts
12-15	C-	2,349.70	28.27	C- / 3.6	-14.84%	C+ / 6.5
2014	C-	2,349.70	34.63	C / 4.8	-3.25%	C+ / 6.1
2013	C-	882.60	38.57	B- / 7.1	26.21%	C / 4.7
2012	E+	241.50	30.26	D / 1.7	16.00%	C / 4.4
2011	D-	99.70	30.27	D- / 1.5	-9.32%	C+ / 5.7
2010	E+	137.40	36.74	E+ / 0.7	-18.61%	C- / 4.2

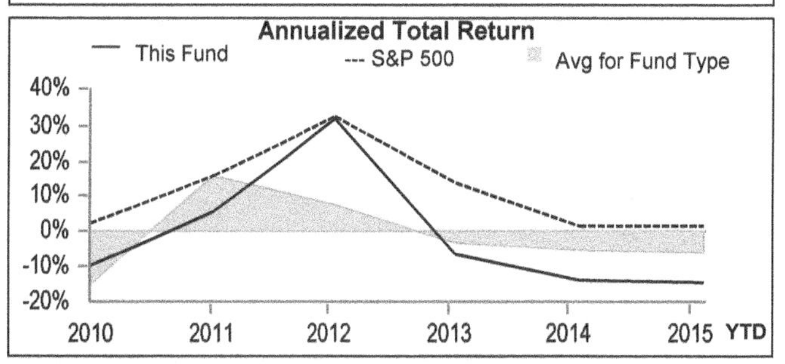

*iShares MSCI Sweden (EWD) C Fair

Fund Family: BlackRock Fund Advisors
Fund Type: Foreign
Inception Date: March 12, 1996

Major Rating Factors: Middle of the road best describes *iShares MSCI Sweden whose TheStreet.com Investment Rating is currently a C (Fair). The fund currently has a performance rating of C (Fair) based on an annualized return of 2.20% over the last three years and a total return of -3.72% year to date 2015. Factored into the performance evaluation is an expense ratio of 0.92% (low).

The fund's risk rating is currently B- (Good). It carries a beta of 0.94, meaning that its performance tracks fairly well with that of the overall stock market. Volatility, as measured by both the semi-deviation and a drawdown factor, is considered low. As of December 31, 2015, *iShares MSCI Sweden traded at a discount of 1.35% below its net asset value, which is better than its one-year historical average premium of .01%.

Diane Hsiung has been running the fund for 8 years and currently receives a manager quality ranking of 47 (0=worst, 99=best). If you desire an average level of risk, then this fund may be an option.

Data Date	Investment Rating	Net Assets ($Mil)	Price	Performance Rating/Pts	Total Return Y-T-D	Risk Rating/Pts
12-15	C	394.00	29.18	C / 4.7	-3.72%	B- / 7.6
2014	C-	394.00	31.67	C / 5.3	-5.92%	C+ / 5.8
2013	C	497.20	35.83	C+ / 6.9	18.64%	C+ / 6.2
2012	C	366.00	30.20	B- / 7.0	25.22%	C+ / 6.2
2011	C	267.20	25.14	C+ / 5.8	-13.65%	C+ / 6.5
2010	B-	421.90	31.23	B+ / 8.4	36.11%	C- / 4.1

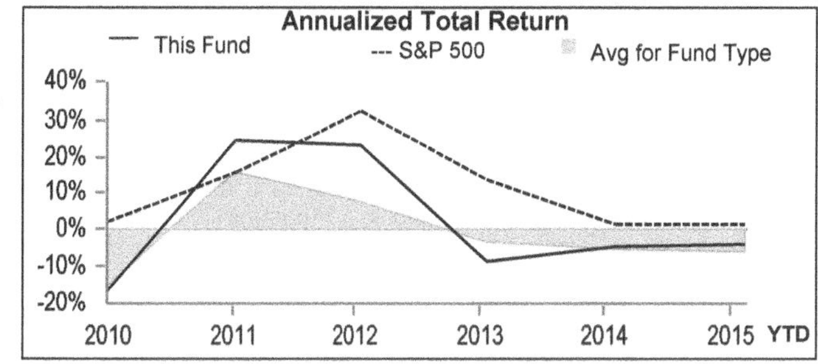

*iShares MSCI Switzerland Capped (EWL) B Good

Fund Family: BlackRock Fund Advisors
Fund Type: Foreign
Inception Date: March 12, 1996

Major Rating Factors: *iShares MSCI Switzerland Capped receives a TheStreet.com Investment Rating of B (Good). The fund currently has a performance rating of C+ (Fair) based on an annualized return of 6.85% over the last three years and a total return of 0.84% year to date 2015. Factored into the performance evaluation is an expense ratio of 0.48% (very low).

The fund's risk rating is currently B (Good). It carries a beta of 0.89, meaning the fund's expected move will be 8.9% for every 10% move in the market. Volatility, as measured by both the semi-deviation and a drawdown factor, is considered low. As of December 31, 2015, *iShares MSCI Switzerland Capped traded at a discount of .64% below its net asset value, which is better than its one-year historical average premium of .04%.

Diane Hsiung has been running the fund for 8 years and currently receives a manager quality ranking of 82 (0=worst, 99=best). If you desire an average level of risk, then this fund may be an option.

Data Date	Investment Rating	Net Assets ($Mil)	Price	Performance Rating/Pts	Total Return Y-T-D	Risk Rating/Pts
12-15	B	1,237.10	31.04	C+ / 6.4	0.84%	B / 8.3
2014	C	1,237.10	31.69	C+ / 6.2	-0.36%	C+ / 6.5
2013	B-	1,029.70	32.99	B- / 7.4	22.01%	B- / 7.5
2012	C+	698.90	26.80	C+ / 6.9	27.51%	B- / 7.4
2011	C-	475.80	22.62	C- / 3.4	-5.63%	B- / 7.5
2010	C	464.90	25.08	C / 5.2	14.48%	C / 5.5

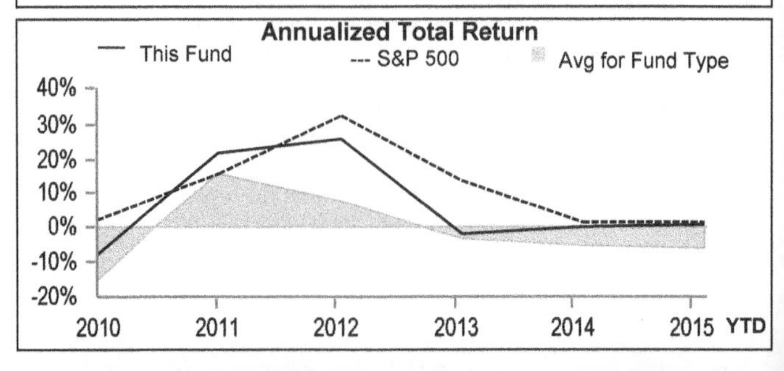

*iShares MSCI Taiwan (EWT) C- Fair

Fund Family: BlackRock Fund Advisors
Fund Type: Foreign
Inception Date: June 20, 2000

Major Rating Factors: Middle of the road best describes *iShares MSCI Taiwan whose TheStreet.com Investment Rating is currently a C- (Fair). The fund currently has a performance rating of C- (Fair) based on an annualized return of 1.07% over the last three years and a total return of -9.27% year to date 2015. Factored into the performance evaluation is an expense ratio of 0.62% (very low).

The fund's risk rating is currently B- (Good). It carries a beta of 0.75, meaning the fund's expected move will be 7.5% for every 10% move in the market. Volatility, as measured by both the semi-deviation and a drawdown factor, is considered low. As of December 31, 2015, *iShares MSCI Taiwan traded at a discount of 1.39% below its net asset value, which is better than its one-year historical average discount of .05%.

Diane Hsiung has been running the fund for 8 years and currently receives a manager quality ranking of 44 (0=worst, 99=best). If you desire an average level of risk, then this fund may be an option.

Data Date	Investment Rating	Net Assets ($Mil)	Price	Performance Rating/Pts	Total Return Y-T-D	Risk Rating/Pts
12-15	C-	3,069.50	12.77	C- / 3.7	-9.27%	B- / 7.5
2014	C+	3,069.50	15.11	C+ / 5.6	10.03%	B / 8.4
2013	D+	2,833.70	14.42	D+ / 2.9	4.60%	B- / 7.1
2012	D+	2,693.80	13.62	D+ / 2.9	14.96%	B- / 7.0
2011	C	2,193.10	11.71	C / 5.4	-18.43%	B- / 7.1
2010	B-	3,435.30	15.62	B / 8.0	22.70%	C / 4.5

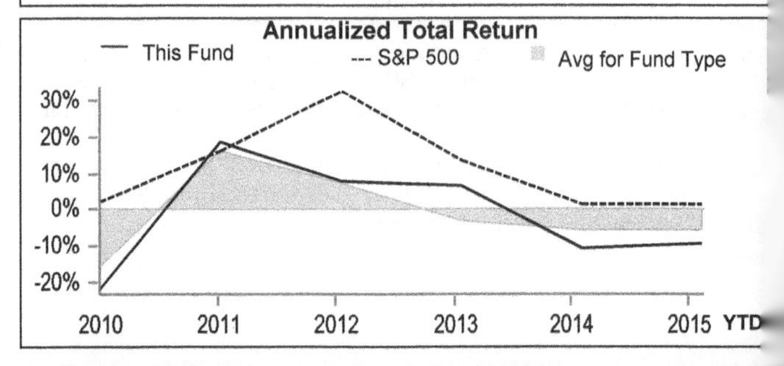

*iShares MSCI Thailand Capped (THD) D Weak

Fund Family: BlackRock Fund Advisors
Fund Type: Foreign
Inception Date: March 26, 2008

Major Rating Factors:
Disappointing performance is the major factor driving the D (Weak) TheStreet.com Investment Rating for *iShares MSCI Thailand Capped. The fund currently has a performance rating of D (Weak) based on an annualized return of -8.36% over the last three years and a total return of -20.37% year to date 2015. Factored into the performance evaluation is an expense ratio of 0.62% (very low).

The fund's risk rating is currently C+ (Fair). It carries a beta of 0.85, meaning the fund's expected move will be 8.5% for every 10% move in the market. Volatility, as measured by both the semi-deviation and a drawdown factor, is considered low. As of December 31, 2015, *iShares MSCI Thailand Capped traded at a discount of .85% below its net asset value, which is better than its one-year historical average discount of .03%.

Diane Hsiung has been running the fund for 8 years and currently receives a manager quality ranking of 13 (0=worst, 99=best). This fund offers only a moderate level of risk but investors looking for strong performance are still waiting.

Data Date	Investment Rating	Net Assets ($Mil)	Price	Performance Rating/Pts	Total Return Y-T-D	Risk Rating/Pts
12-15	D	565.40	58.64	D / 1.8	-20.37%	C+ / 6.0
2014	C-	565.40	77.46	C+ / 6.3	27.81%	C / 4.6
2013	D	506.00	68.65	D / 1.7	-23.50%	C+ / 6.3
2012	B+	788.90	82.49	A+ / 9.6	39.82%	C+ / 6.9
2011	B+	459.40	60.11	A / 9.3	-3.93%	B- / 7.2
2010	B+	694.00	64.61	A+ / 9.8	56.76%	C- / 4.2

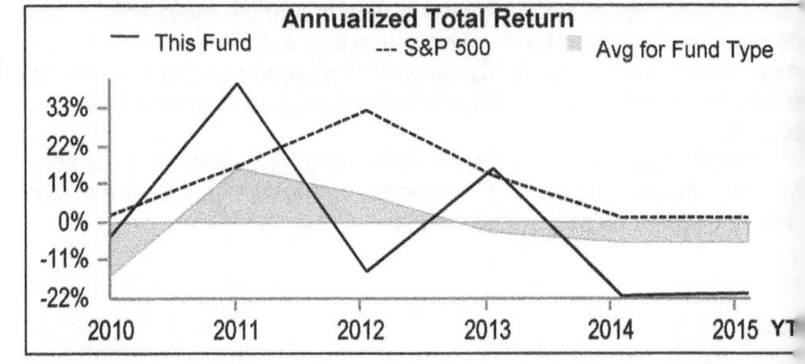

*iShares MSCI Turkey (TUR) D- Weak

Fund Family: BlackRock Fund Advisors
Fund Type: Foreign
Inception Date: March 26, 2008

Data Date	Investment Rating	Net Assets ($Mil)	Price	Performance Rating/Pts	Total Return Y-T-D	Risk Rating/Pts
12-15	D-	442.20	36.36	D- / 1.0	-30.75%	C / 4.5
2014	D+	442.20	54.31	B- / 7.1	21.04%	C- / 3.1
2013	D-	452.20	47.66	E+ / 0.7	-31.33%	C / 5.3
2012	B-	767.60	66.78	A- / 9.1	68.00%	C / 5.4
2011	D	352.10	41.14	C- / 3.3	-38.46%	C+ / 5.8
2010	B	787.90	66.21	A- / 9.1	25.64%	C- / 3.8

Major Rating Factors:
Disappointing performance is the major factor driving the D- (Weak) TheStreet.com Investment Rating for *iShares MSCI Turkey. The fund currently has a performance rating of D- (Weak) based on an annualized return of -17.07% over the last three years and a total return of -30.75% year to date 2015. Factored into the performance evaluation is an expense ratio of 0.62% (very low).

The fund's risk rating is currently C (Fair). It carries a beta of 1.08, meaning that its performance tracks fairly well with that of the overall stock market. Volatility, as measured by both the semi-deviation and a drawdown factor, is considered average. As of December 31, 2015, *iShares MSCI Turkey traded at a discount of .16% below its net asset value, which is better than its one-year historical average discount of .03%.

Diane Hsiung has been running the fund for 8 years and currently receives a manager quality ranking of 6 (0=worst, 99=best). This fund offers an average level of risk but investors looking for strong performance will be frustrated.

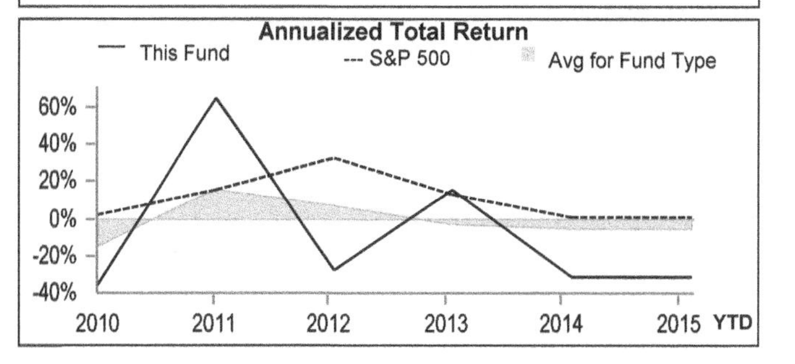

*iShares MSCI UAE Capped ETF (UAE) E+ Very Weak

Fund Family: BlackRock Fund Advisors
Fund Type: Emerging Market
Inception Date: April 29, 2014

Data Date	Investment Rating	Net Assets ($Mil)	Price	Performance Rating/Pts	Total Return Y-T-D	Risk Rating/Pts
12-15	E+	59.30	15.81	E+ / 0.7	-13.34%	C- / 3.7

Major Rating Factors:
Very poor performance is the major factor driving the E+ (Very Weak) TheStreet.com Investment Rating for *iShares MSCI UAE Capped ETF. The fund currently has a performance rating of E+ (Very Weak) based on an annualized return of 0.00% over the last three years and a total return of -13.34% year to date 2015. Factored into the performance evaluation is an expense ratio of 0.62% (very low).

The fund's risk rating is currently C- (Fair). It carries a beta of 0.00, meaning the fund's expected move will be 0.0% for every 10% move in the market. Volatility, as measured by both the semi-deviation and a drawdown factor, is considered average. As of December 31, 2015, *iShares MSCI UAE Capped ETF traded at a premium of .32% above its net asset value, which is worse than its one-year historical average discount of .15%.

Jennifer F.Y. Hsui has been running the fund for 2 years and currently receives a manager quality ranking of 40 (0=worst, 99=best). This fund offers an average level of risk but investors looking for strong performance will be frustrated.

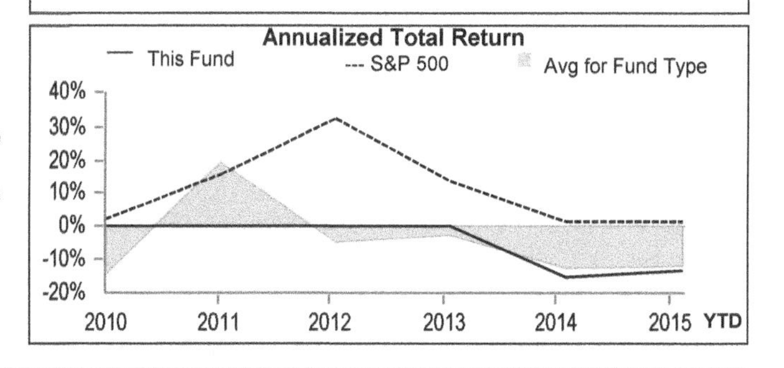

*iShares MSCI UK Small-Cap ETF (EWUS) A Excellent

Fund Family: BlackRock Fund Advisors
Fund Type: Foreign
Inception Date: January 25, 2012

Data Date	Investment Rating	Net Assets ($Mil)	Price	Performance Rating/Pts	Total Return Y-T-D	Risk Rating/Pts
12-15	A	28.80	39.54	B+ / 8.4	11.54%	B / 8.1
2014	D	28.80	37.49	D- / 1.5	-8.18%	C+ / 6.1
2013	A+	27.10	42.15	A+ / 9.8	37.69%	B / 8.5

Major Rating Factors:
Strong performance is the major factor driving the A (Excellent) TheStreet.com Investment Rating for *iShares MSCI UK Small-Cap ETF. The fund currently has a performance rating of B+ (Good) based on an annualized return of 11.63% over the last three years and a total return of 11.54% year to date 2015. Factored into the performance evaluation is an expense ratio of 0.59% (very low).

The fund's risk rating is currently B (Good). It carries a beta of 0.75, meaning the fund's expected move will be 7.5% for every 10% move in the market. Volatility, as measured by both the semi-deviation and a drawdown factor, is considered low. As of December 31, 2015, *iShares MSCI UK Small-Cap ETF traded at a discount of .38% below its net asset value, which is better than its one-year historical average discount of .03%.

Jennifer F.Y. Hsui has been running the fund for 4 years and currently receives a manager quality ranking of 93 (0=worst, 99=best). If you desire only a moderate level of risk and strong performance, then this fund is an excellent option.

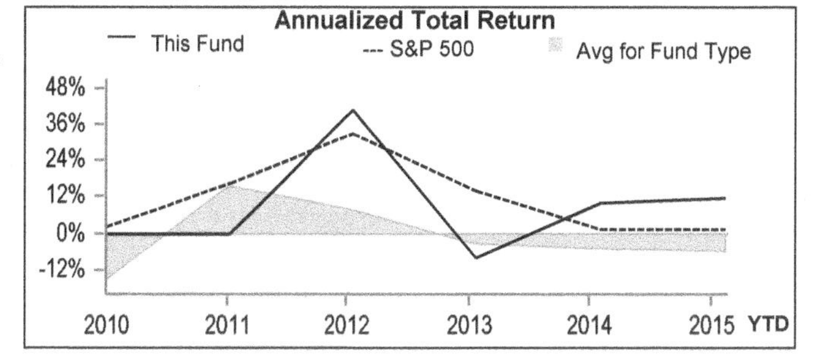

*iShares MSCI United Kingdom (EWU) C Fair

Fund Family: BlackRock Fund Advisors
Fund Type: Foreign
Inception Date: March 12, 1996

Data Date	Investment Rating	Net Assets ($Mil)	Price	Performance Rating/Pts	Total Return Y-T-D	Risk Rating/Pts
12-15	C	4,068.90	16.14	C- / 4.1	-4.35%	B- / 7.4
2014	D+	4,068.90	18.03	C- / 4.0	-6.62%	C+ / 5.9
2013	C+	3,621.70	20.88	C+ / 6.7	16.47%	B- / 7.6
2012	C-	1,423.50	17.94	C- / 4.1	17.92%	B- / 7.4
2011	C-	1,296.50	16.16	C- / 4.2	-2.62%	B- / 7.6
2010	D	1,143.80	17.37	D / 1.8	10.28%	C / 4.8

Major Rating Factors: Middle of the road best describes *iShares MSCI United Kingdom whose TheStreet.com Investment Rating is currently a C (Fair). The fund currently has a performance rating of C- (Fair) based on an annualized return of 1.00% over the last three years and a total return of -4.35% year to date 2015. Factored into the performance evaluation is an expense ratio of 0.48% (very low).

The fund's risk rating is currently B- (Good). It carries a beta of 1.01, meaning that its performance tracks fairly well with that of the overall stock market. Volatility, as measured by both the semi-deviation and a drawdown factor, is considered low. As of December 31, 2015, *iShares MSCI United Kingdom traded at a discount of .12% below its net asset value, which is better than its one-year historical average premium of .04%.

Diane Hsiung has been running the fund for 8 years and currently receives a manager quality ranking of 37 (0=worst, 99=best). If you desire an average level of risk, then this fund may be an option.

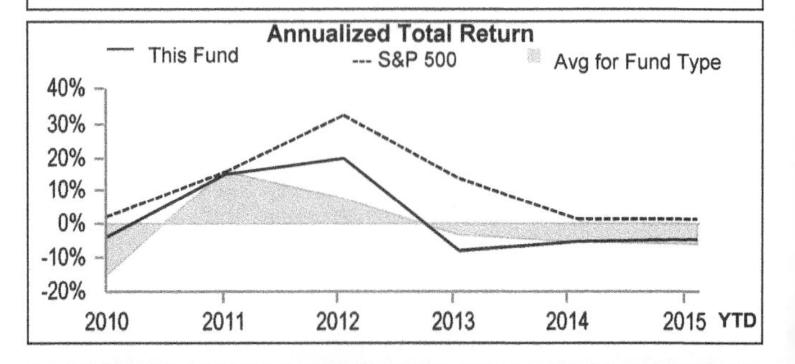

*iShares MSCI USA Equal Weighted (EUSA) B+ Good

Fund Family: BlackRock Fund Advisors
Fund Type: Income
Inception Date: May 5, 2010

Data Date	Investment Rating	Net Assets ($Mil)	Price	Performance Rating/Pts	Total Return Y-T-D	Risk Rating/Pts
12-15	B+	46.40	42.20	B+ / 8.3	-1.46%	B- / 7.4
2014	B+	46.40	44.34	B+ / 8.4	14.81%	B- / 7.5
2013	A-	140.90	39.64	B+ / 8.3	28.06%	B / 8.2
2012	B	150.10	30.68	B / 7.7	16.85%	B / 8.1
2011	C-	122.80	27.20	D+ / 2.9	2.51%	B / 8.1

Major Rating Factors: Strong performance is the major factor driving the B+ (Good) TheStreet.com Investment Rating for *iShares MSCI USA Equal Weighted. The fund currently has a performance rating of B+ (Good) based on an annualized return of 12.90% over the last three years and a total return of -1.46% year to date 2015. Factored into the performance evaluation is an expense ratio of 0.15% (very low).

The fund's risk rating is currently B- (Good). It carries a beta of 1.00, meaning that its performance tracks fairly well with that of the overall stock market. Volatility, as measured by both the semi-deviation and a drawdown factor, is considered low. As of December 31, 2015, *iShares MSCI USA Equal Weighted traded at a premium of .09% above its net asset value, which is worse than its one-year historical average premium of .06%.

Diane Hsiung has been running the fund for 6 years and currently receives a manager quality ranking of 59 (0=worst, 99=best). If you desire only a moderate level of risk and strong performance, then this fund is an excellent option.

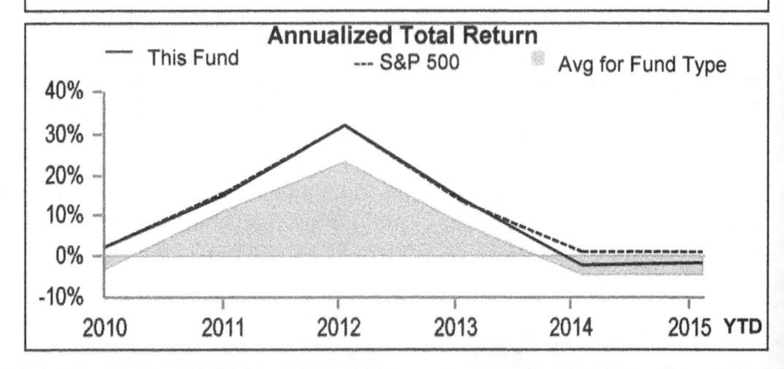

*iShares MSCI USA ESG Select ETF (KLD) B+ Good

Fund Family: BlackRock Fund Advisors
Fund Type: Growth
Inception Date: January 24, 2005

Data Date	Investment Rating	Net Assets ($Mil)	Price	Performance Rating/Pts	Total Return Y-T-D	Risk Rating/Pts
12-15	B+	275.10	83.38	B+ / 8.3	-1.32%	B- / 7.2
2014	B	275.10	86.11	B / 7.6	14.62%	B- / 7.3
2013	B+	245.70	76.73	B / 7.6	25.73%	B / 8.4
2012	C	172.60	59.33	C- / 4.1	11.30%	B / 8.1
2011	C+	164.80	55.03	C / 5.4	2.49%	B / 8.1
2010	C	145.50	54.91	C / 4.5	13.88%	C+ / 6.1

Major Rating Factors: Strong performance is the major factor driving the B+ (Good) TheStreet.com Investment Rating for *iShares MSCI USA ESG Select ETF. The fund currently has a performance rating of B+ (Good) based on an annualized return of 12.44% over the last three years and a total return of -1.32% year to date 2015. Factored into the performance evaluation is an expense ratio of 0.50% (very low).

The fund's risk rating is currently B- (Good). It carries a beta of 0.99, meaning that its performance tracks fairly well with that of the overall stock market. Volatility, as measured by both the semi-deviation and a drawdown factor, is considered low. As of December 31, 2015, *iShares MSCI USA ESG Select ETF traded at a premium of .16% above its net asset value, which is worse than its one-year historical average premium of .03%.

Diane Hsiung has been running the fund for 8 years and currently receives a manager quality ranking of 59 (0=worst, 99=best). If you desire only a moderate level of risk and strong performance, then this fund is an excellent option.

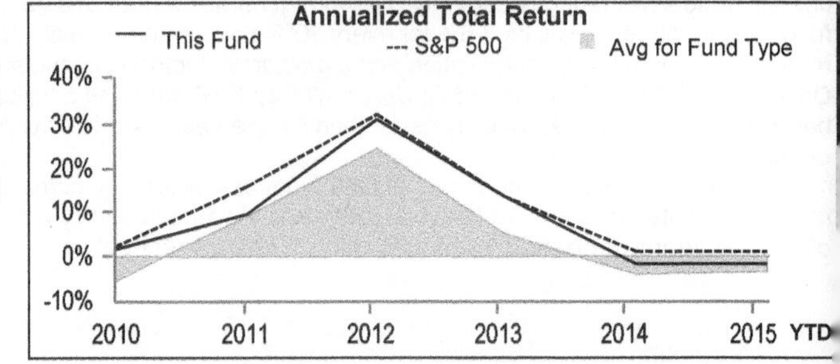

* Denotes ETF Fund

*iShares MSCI USA Minimum Vol ETF (USMV) A+ Excellent

Fund Family: BlackRock Fund Advisors
Fund Type: Income
Inception Date: October 18, 2011

Data Date	Investment Rating	Net Assets ($Mil)	Price	Performance Rating/Pts	Total Return Y-T-D	Risk Rating/Pts
12-15	A+	2,852.70	41.82	A- / 9.0	6.05%	B / 8.4
2014	A+	2,852.70	40.48	B / 8.0	17.52%	B+ / 9.4
2013	A+	2,416.20	35.50	B+ / 8.6	20.49%	B+ / 9.7
2012	B-	751.60	29.04	C / 4.8	14.08%	B+ / 9.8

Major Rating Factors:
Exceptional performance is the major factor driving the A+ (Excellent) TheStreet.com Investment Rating for *iShares MSCI USA Minimum Vol ETF. The fund currently has a performance rating of A- (Excellent) based on an annualized return of 14.54% over the last three years and a total return of 6.05% year to date 2015. Factored into the performance evaluation is an expense ratio of 0.15% (very low).

The fund's risk rating is currently B (Good). It carries a beta of 0.76, meaning the fund's expected move will be 7.6% for every 10% move in the market. Volatility, as measured by both the semi-deviation and a drawdown factor, is considered low. As of December 31, 2015, *iShares MSCI USA Minimum Vol ETF traded at a price exactly equal to its net asset value, which is better than its one-year historical average premium of .02%.

Diane Hsiung has been running the fund for 5 years and currently receives a manager quality ranking of 87 (0=worst, 99=best). If you desire only a moderate level of risk and strong performance, then this fund is an excellent option.

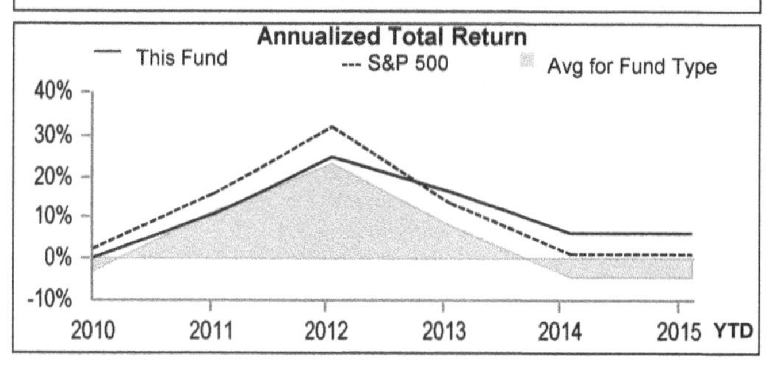

*iShares MSCI USA Momentum Factor (MTUM) B+ Good

Fund Family: BlackRock Fund Advisors
Fund Type: Growth
Inception Date: April 16, 2013

Data Date	Investment Rating	Net Assets ($Mil)	Price	Performance Rating/Pts	Total Return Y-T-D	Risk Rating/Pts
12-15	B+	363.40	73.29	B / 8.1	9.41%	B- / 7.4
2014	B	363.40	68.06	B- / 7.4	15.62%	B- / 7.7

Major Rating Factors: Strong performance is the major factor driving the B+ (Good) TheStreet.com Investment Rating for *iShares MSCI USA Momentum Factor. The fund currently has a performance rating of B (Good) based on an annualized return of 0.00% over the last three years and a total return of 9.41% year to date 2015. Factored into the performance evaluation is an expense ratio of 0.15% (very low).

The fund's risk rating is currently B- (Good). It carries a beta of 0.00, meaning the fund's expected move will be 0.0% for every 10% move in the market. Volatility, as measured by both the semi-deviation and a drawdown factor, is considered low. As of December 31, 2015, *iShares MSCI USA Momentum Factor traded at a premium of .03% above its net asset value, which is in line with its one-year historical average premium of .03%.

Matthew Goff has been running the fund for 3 years and currently receives a manager quality ranking of 93 (0=worst, 99=best). If you desire only a moderate level of risk and strong performance, then this fund is an excellent option.

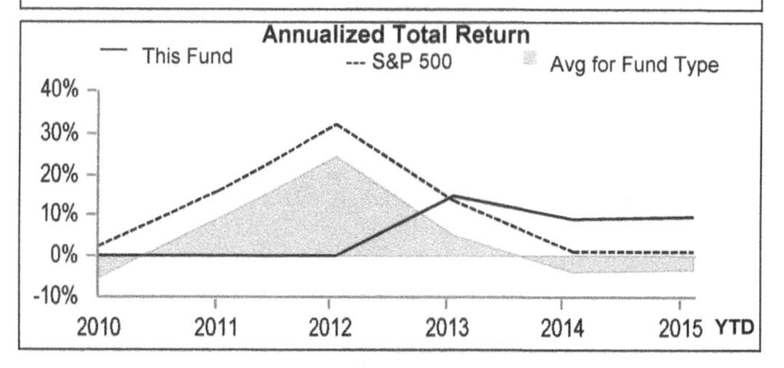

*iShares MSCI USA Quality Factor (QUAL) B+ Good

Fund Family: BlackRock Fund Advisors
Fund Type: Growth
Inception Date: July 16, 2013

Data Date	Investment Rating	Net Assets ($Mil)	Price	Performance Rating/Pts	Total Return Y-T-D	Risk Rating/Pts
12-15	B+	562.00	64.57	B- / 7.3	5.93%	B / 8.2
2014	B-	562.00	62.25	C+ / 6.8	12.77%	B- / 7.9

Major Rating Factors: Strong performance is the major factor driving the B+ (Good) TheStreet.com Investment Rating for *iShares MSCI USA Quality Factor. The fund currently has a performance rating of B- (Good) based on an annualized return of 0.00% over the last three years and a total return of 5.93% year to date 2015. Factored into the performance evaluation is an expense ratio of 0.15% (very low).

The fund's risk rating is currently B (Good). It carries a beta of 0.00, meaning the fund's expected move will be 0.0% for every 10% move in the market. Volatility, as measured by both the semi-deviation and a drawdown factor, is considered low. As of December 31, 2015, *iShares MSCI USA Quality Factor traded at a premium of .02% above its net asset value, which is better than its one-year historical average premium of .05%.

Matthew Goff has been running the fund for 3 years and currently receives a manager quality ranking of 88 (0=worst, 99=best). If you desire only a moderate level of risk and strong performance, then this fund is an excellent option.

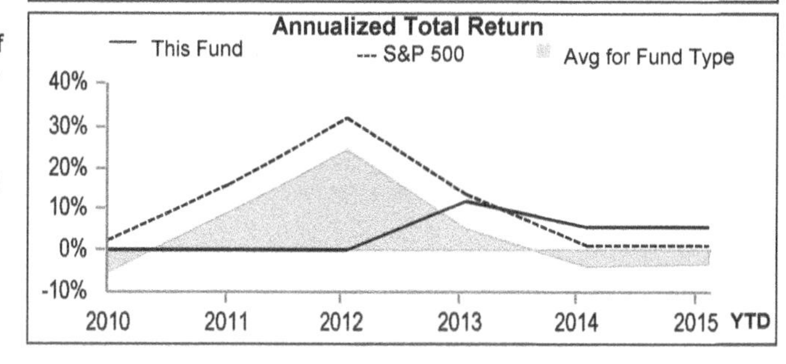

*iShares MSCI USA Size Factor ETF (SIZE) C+ Fair

Fund Family: BlackRock Fund Advisors
Fund Type: Growth
Inception Date: April 16, 2013

Data Date	Investment Rating	Net Assets ($Mil)	Price	Performance Rating/Pts	Total Return Y-T-D	Risk Rating/Pts
12-15	C+	162.50	65.29	C+ / 6.1	2.54%	B- / 7.3
2014	A-	162.50	65.53	B / 7.7	16.71%	B / 8.7

Major Rating Factors: Middle of the road best describes *iShares MSCI USA Size Factor ETF whose TheStreet.com Investment Rating is currently a C+ (Fair). The fund currently has a performance rating of C+ (Fair) based on an annualized return of 0.00% over the last three years and a total return of 2.54% year to date 2015. Factored into the performance evaluation is an expense ratio of 0.15% (very low).

The fund's risk rating is currently B- (Good). It carries a beta of 0.00, meaning the fund's expected move will be 0.0% for every 10% move in the market. Volatility, as measured by both the semi-deviation and a drawdown factor, is considered low. As of December 31, 2015, *iShares MSCI USA Size Factor ETF traded at a premium of 1.26% above its net asset value, which is worse than its one-year historical average premium of .06%.

Matthew Goff has been running the fund for 3 years and currently receives a manager quality ranking of 76 (0=worst, 99=best). If you desire an average level of risk, then this fund may be an option.

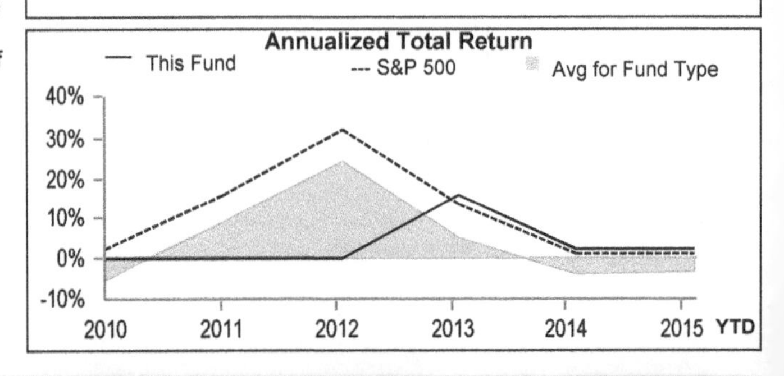

*iShares MSCI USA Value Factor ET (VLUE) C- Fair

Fund Family: BlackRock Fund Advisors
Fund Type: Growth
Inception Date: April 16, 2013

Data Date	Investment Rating	Net Assets ($Mil)	Price	Performance Rating/Pts	Total Return Y-T-D	Risk Rating/Pts
12-15	C-	332.50	62.24	C- / 3.8	-1.87%	B- / 7.0
2014	B-	332.50	66.01	C+ / 6.7	13.54%	B- / 7.7

Major Rating Factors: Middle of the road best describes *iShares MSCI USA Value Factor ET whose TheStreet.com Investment Rating is currently a C- (Fair). The fund currently has a performance rating of C- (Fair) based on an annualized return of 0.00% over the last three years and a total return of -1.87% year to date 2015. Factored into the performance evaluation is an expense ratio of 0.15% (very low).

The fund's risk rating is currently B- (Good). It carries a beta of 0.00, meaning the fund's expected move will be 0.0% for every 10% move in the market. Volatility, as measured by both the semi-deviation and a drawdown factor, is considered low. As of December 31, 2015, *iShares MSCI USA Value Factor ET traded at a premium of .34% above its net asset value, which is worse than its one-year historical average premium of .07%.

Matthew Goff has been running the fund for 3 years and currently receives a manager quality ranking of 36 (0=worst, 99=best). If you desire an average level of risk, then this fund may be an option.

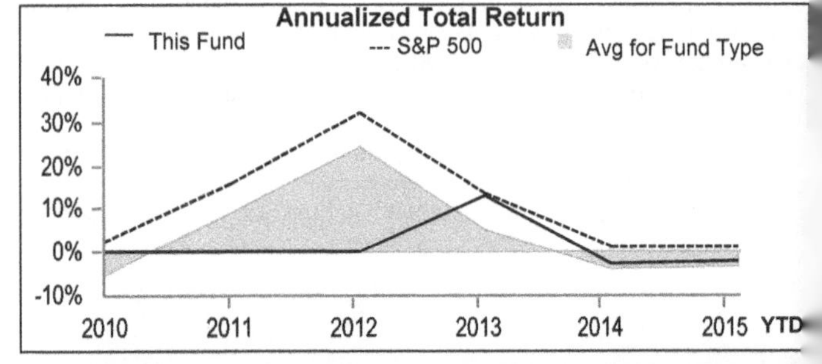

*iShares MSCI World (URTH) B- Good

Fund Family: BlackRock Fund Advisors
Fund Type: Global
Inception Date: January 10, 2012

Data Date	Investment Rating	Net Assets ($Mil)	Price	Performance Rating/Pts	Total Return Y-T-D	Risk Rating/Pts
12-15	B-	185.60	69.60	B- / 7.4	0.43%	C+ / 6.9
2014	C-	185.60	71.66	C- / 3.7	5.39%	B- / 7.0
2013	A+	125.30	70.27	A- / 9.1	23.77%	B / 8.9

Major Rating Factors: Strong performance is the major factor driving the B- (Good) TheStreet.com Investment Rating for *iShares MSCI World. The fund currently has a performance rating of B- (Good) based on an annualized return of 9.41% over the last three years and a total return of 0.43% year to date 2015. Factored into the performance evaluation is an expense ratio of 0.24% (very low).

The fund's risk rating is currently C+ (Fair). It carries a beta of 0.81, meaning the fund's expected move will be 8.1% for every 10% move in the market. Volatility, as measured by both the semi-deviation and a drawdown factor, is considered low. As of December 31, 2015, *iShares MSCI World traded at a premium of .37% above its net asset value, which is worse than its one-year historical average premium of .15%.

Jennifer F.Y. Hsui has been running the fund for 4 years and currently receives a manager quality ranking of 90 (0=worst, 99=best). If you desire only a moderate level of risk and strong performance, then this fund is an excellent option.

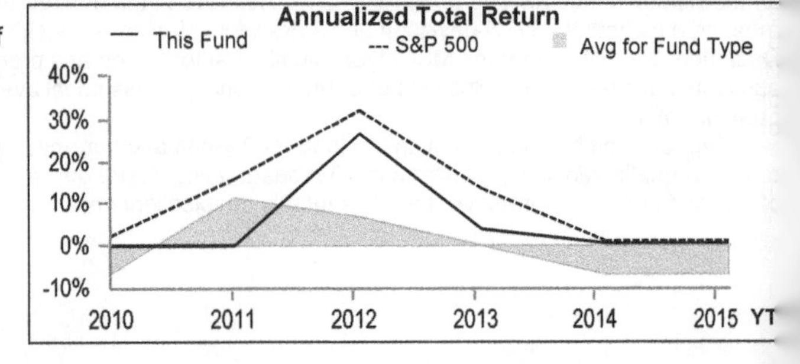

*iShares Nasdaq Biotechnology (IBB) B+ Good

Fund Family: BlackRock Fund Advisors
Fund Type: Health
Inception Date: February 5, 2001

Major Rating Factors:
Exceptional performance is the major factor driving the B+ (Good) TheStreet.com Investment Rating for *iShares Nasdaq Biotechnology. The fund currently has a performance rating of A+ (Excellent) based on an annualized return of 33.48% over the last three years and a total return of 10.48% year to date 2015. Factored into the performance evaluation is an expense ratio of 0.48% (very low).

The fund's risk rating is currently C+ (Fair). It carries a beta of 1.11, meaning it is expected to move 11.1% for every 10% move in the market. Volatility, as measured by both the semi-deviation and a drawdown factor, is considered low. As of December 31, 2015, *iShares Nasdaq Biotechnology traded at a discount of .03% below its net asset value, which is better than its one-year historical average premium of .02%.

Diane Hsiung has been running the fund for 8 years and currently receives a manager quality ranking of 97 (0=worst, 99=best). If you desire only a moderate level of risk and strong performance, then this fund is an excellent option.

Data Date	Investment Rating	Net Assets ($Mil)	Price	Performance Rating/Pts	Total Return Y-T-D	Risk Rating/Pts
12-15	B+	5,424.30	338.33	A+ / 9.8	10.48%	C+ / 5.6
2014	B+	5,424.30	303.35	A+ / 9.8	34.44%	C+ / 6.2
2013	B+	4,422.70	227.06	A+ / 9.7	58.55%	C+ / 6.4
2012	B-	2,145.90	137.22	B+ / 8.6	30.12%	C+ / 6.4
2011	C	1,393.90	104.35	C+ / 6.1	12.81%	C+ / 6.2
2010	C+	1,446.90	93.42	C+ / 6.8	14.84%	C+ / 5.9

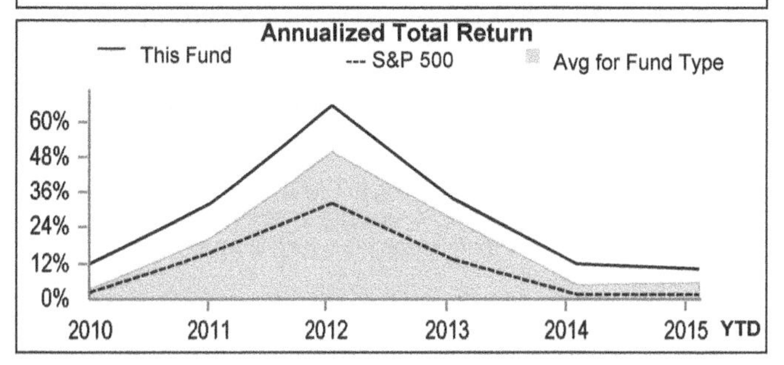

*iShares National AMT Free Muni B (MUB) C+ Fair

Fund Family: BlackRock Fund Advisors
Fund Type: Municipal - National
Inception Date: September 7, 2007

Major Rating Factors: Middle of the road best describes *iShares National AMT Free Muni B whose TheStreet.com Investment Rating is currently a C+ (Fair). The fund currently has a performance rating of C+ (Fair) based on an annualized return of 2.52% over the last three years and a total return of 3.16% year to date 2015. Factored into the performance evaluation is an expense ratio of 0.25% (very low).

The fund's risk rating is currently B- (Good). It carries a beta of 1.21, meaning it is expected to move 12.1% for every 10% move in the market. Volatility, as measured by both the semi-deviation and a drawdown factor, is considered low. As of December 31, 2015, *iShares National AMT Free Muni B traded at a premium of .34% above its net asset value, which is worse than its one-year historical average premium of .08%.

Scott F. Radell has been running the fund for 6 years and currently receives a manager quality ranking of 60 (0=worst, 99=best). If you desire an average level of risk, then this fund may be an option.

Data Date	Investment Rating	Net Assets ($Mil)	Price	Performance Rating/Pts	Total Return Y-T-D	Risk Rating/Pts
12-15	C+	3,659.40	110.71	C+ / 6.1	3.16%	B- / 7.8
2014	C	3,659.40	110.34	C / 4.6	9.01%	B- / 7.6
2013	C+	3,026.60	103.74	C / 4.8	-3.92%	B+ / 9.2
2012	C	3,476.20	110.64	C- / 3.6	4.56%	B+ / 9.4
2011	B	2,512.30	108.25	C+ / 5.8	15.36%	B+ / 9.5
2010	C+	1,975.60	99.18	C- / 3.2	-0.22%	B / 8.7

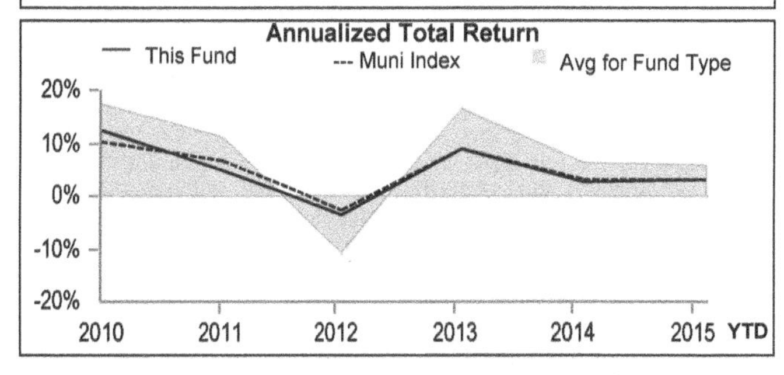

*iShares New York AMT Free Muni B (NYF) B- Good

Fund Family: BlackRock Fund Advisors
Fund Type: Municipal - Single State
Inception Date: October 4, 2007

Major Rating Factors: *iShares New York AMT Free Muni B receives a TheStreet.com Investment Rating of B- (Good). The fund currently has a performance rating of C+ (Fair) based on an annualized return of 2.91% over the last three years and a total return of 3.19% year to date 2015. Factored into the performance evaluation is an expense ratio of 0.25% (very low).

The fund's risk rating is currently B- (Good). It carries a beta of 1.32, meaning it is expected to move 13.2% for every 10% move in the market. Volatility, as measured by both the semi-deviation and a drawdown factor, is considered low. As of December 31, 2015, *iShares New York AMT Free Muni B traded at a premium of .21% above its net asset value, which is worse than its one-year historical average premium of .16%.

Scott F. Radell has been running the fund for 6 years and currently receives a manager quality ranking of 58 (0=worst, 99=best). If you desire an average level of risk, then this fund may be an option.

Data Date	Investment Rating	Net Assets ($Mil)	Price	Performance Rating/Pts	Total Return Y-T-D	Risk Rating/Pts
12-15	B-	155.10	111.93	C+ / 6.3	3.19%	B- / 7.8
2014	C	155.10	111.47	C / 5.2	9.75%	B- / 7.5
2013	C+	126.30	104.41	C / 4.8	-3.67%	B+ / 9.2
2012	C	128.00	111.52	C- / 3.6	5.65%	B+ / 9.4
2011	C+	97.10	108.23	C / 4.5	11.31%	B+ / 9.4
2010	C+	70.90	99.98	C- / 3.4	-0.26%	B / 8.6

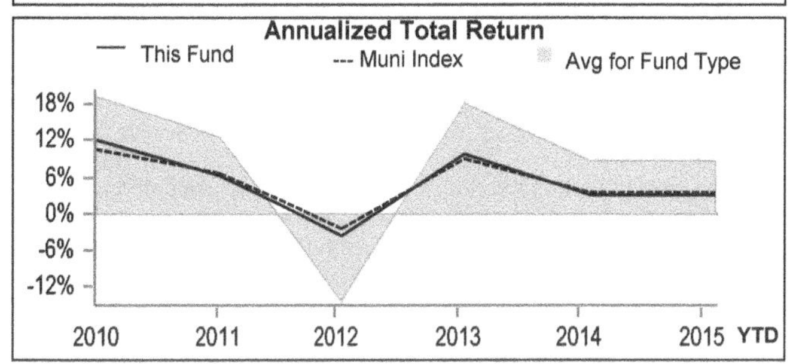

*iShares North Amer Tech Software (IGV) B+ Good

Fund Family: BlackRock Fund Advisors
Fund Type: Income
Inception Date: July 10, 2001

Major Rating Factors:
Exceptional performance is the major factor driving the B+ (Good) TheStreet.com Investment Rating for *iShares North Amer Tech Software. The fund currently has a performance rating of A (Excellent) based on an annualized return of 17.57% over the last three years and a total return of 12.78% year to date 2015. Factored into the performance evaluation is an expense ratio of 0.47% (very low).

The fund's risk rating is currently C+ (Fair). It carries a beta of 1.03, meaning that its performance tracks fairly well with that of the overall stock market. Volatility, as measured by both the semi-deviation and a drawdown factor, is considered low. As of December 31, 2015, *iShares North Amer Tech Software traded at a premium of .11% above its net asset value, which is worse than its one-year historical average premium of .01%.

Diane Hsiung has been running the fund for 8 years and currently receives a manager quality ranking of 82 (0=worst, 99=best). If you desire only a moderate level of risk and strong performance, then this fund is an excellent option.

Data Date	Investment Rating	Net Assets ($Mil)	Price	Performance Rating/Pts	Total Return Y-T-D	Risk Rating/Pts
12-15	B+	1,050.30	103.81	A / 9.4	12.78%	C+ / 6.2
2014	B-	1,050.30	92.80	B+ / 8.4	14.11%	C+ / 6.1
2013	C+	1,018.20	82.07	B- / 7.5	26.94%	B- / 7.0
2012	C-	640.60	63.03	C+ / 5.7	17.72%	C+ / 5.9
2011	C-	492.40	54.12	C+ / 5.6	-7.62%	C+ / 6.2
2010	C+	385.10	58.42	B- / 7.5	24.64%	C / 4.6

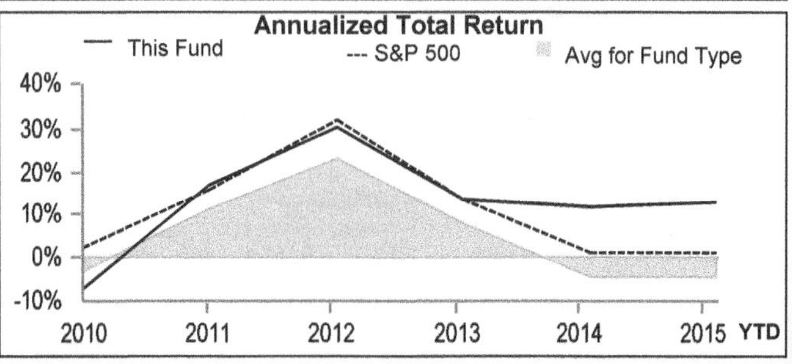

*iShares North Amer Tech-Mmedia N (IGN) B- Good

Fund Family: BlackRock Fund Advisors
Fund Type: Growth
Inception Date: July 10, 2001

Major Rating Factors: Strong performance is the major factor driving the B- (Good) TheStreet.com Investment Rating for *iShares North Amer Tech-Mmedia N. The fund currently has a performance rating of B- (Good) based on an annualized return of 9.20% over the last three years and a total return of 1.13% year to date 2015. Factored into the performance evaluation is an expense ratio of 0.47% (very low).

The fund's risk rating is currently B- (Good). It carries a beta of 0.94, meaning that its performance tracks fairly well with that of the overall stock market. Volatility, as measured by both the semi-deviation and a drawdown factor, is considered low. As of December 31, 2015, *iShares North Amer Tech-Mmedia N traded at a premium of .62% above its net asset value, which is worse than its one-year historical average discount of .01%.

Diane Hsiung has been running the fund for 8 years and currently receives a manager quality ranking of 40 (0=worst, 99=best). If you desire only a moderate level of risk and strong performance, then this fund is an excellent option.

Data Date	Investment Rating	Net Assets ($Mil)	Price	Performance Rating/Pts	Total Return Y-T-D	Risk Rating/Pts
12-15	B-	277.50	37.08	B- / 7.3	1.13%	B- / 7.2
2014	C	277.50	37.15	C+ / 6.7	16.34%	C+ / 6.1
2013	D+	227.80	32.29	D+ / 2.8	11.10%	C+ / 6.7
2012	D	253.60	28.14	D+ / 2.7	4.25%	C+ / 6.6
2011	C-	203.80	27.35	C / 4.3	-20.89%	C+ / 6.8
2010	C+	217.60	33.51	C+ / 6.8	24.30%	C / 5.2

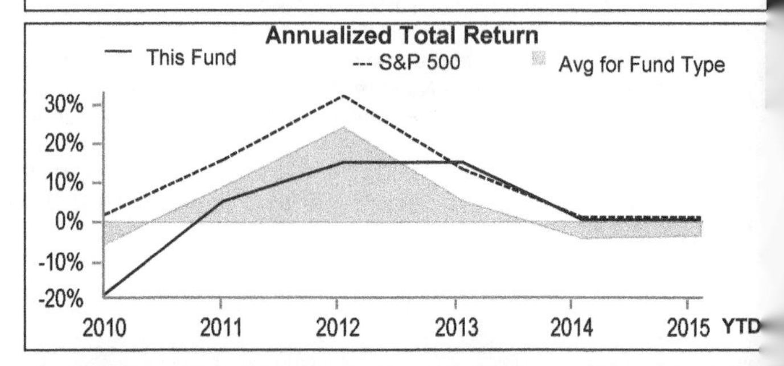

*iShares North American Natural R (IGE) D Weak

Fund Family: BlackRock Fund Advisors
Fund Type: Energy/Natural Resources
Inception Date: October 22, 2001

Major Rating Factors:
Disappointing performance is the major factor driving the D (Weak) TheStreet.com Investment Rating for *iShares North American Natural R. The fund currently has a performance rating of D (Weak) based on an annualized return of -8.31% over the last three years and a total return of -23.95% year to date 2015. Factored into the performance evaluation is an expense ratio of 0.47% (very low).

The fund's risk rating is currently C+ (Fair). It carries a beta of 0.99, meaning that its performance tracks fairly well with that of the overall stock market. Volatility, as measured by both the semi-deviation and a drawdown factor, is considered low. As of December 31, 2015, *iShares North American Natural R traded at a price exactly equal to its net asset value, which is worse than its one-year historical average discount of .01%.

Diane Hsiung has been running the fund for 8 years and currently receives a manager quality ranking of 36 (0=worst, 99=best). This fund offers only a moderate level of risk but investors looking for strong performance are still waiting.

Data Date	Investment Rating	Net Assets ($Mil)	Price	Performance Rating/Pts	Total Return Y-T-D	Risk Rating/Pts
12-15	D	2,213.70	28.14	D / 1.7	-23.95%	C+ / 5.7
2014	D+	2,213.70	38.32	D / 2.2	-8.84%	B- / 7.5
2013	C-	2,219.50	43.39	C / 4.8	10.71%	B- / 7.2
2012	D+	1,744.70	38.16	D+ / 2.5	2.92%	B- / 7.1
2011	C	1,816.50	38.00	C / 5.1	-4.25%	B- / 7.0
2010	D+	2,097.00	41.69	C+ / 5.8	23.35%	D+ / 2.6

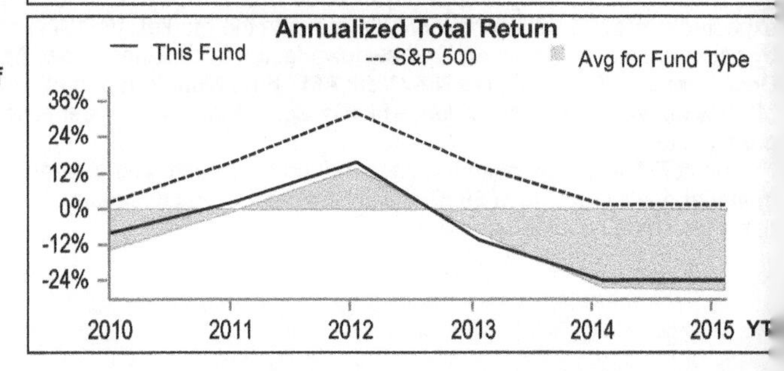

* Denotes ETF Fund

*iShares North American Tech (IGM) A- Excellent

Fund Family: BlackRock Fund Advisors
Fund Type: Growth
Inception Date: March 13, 2001

Major Rating Factors:
Exceptional performance is the major factor driving the A- (Excellent) TheStreet.com Investment Rating for *iShares North American Tech. The fund currently has a performance rating of A (Excellent) based on an annualized return of 18.09% over the last three years and a total return of 9.98% year to date 2015. Factored into the performance evaluation is an expense ratio of 0.47% (very low).

The fund's risk rating is currently C+ (Fair). It carries a beta of 1.06, meaning that its performance tracks fairly well with that of the overall stock market. Volatility, as measured by both the semi-deviation and a drawdown factor, is considered low. As of December 31, 2015, *iShares North American Tech traded at a premium of .11% above its net asset value, which is worse than its one-year historical average premium of .02%.

Diane Hsiung has been running the fund for 8 years and currently receives a manager quality ranking of 83 (0=worst, 99=best). If you desire only a moderate level of risk and strong performance, then this fund is an excellent option.

Data Date	Investment Rating	Net Assets ($Mil)	Price	Performance Rating/Pts	Total Return Y-T-D	Risk Rating/Pts
12-15	A-	742.80	110.69	A / 9.4	9.98%	C+ / 6.8
2014	B	742.80	101.92	B+ / 8.5	16.02%	C+ / 6.7
2013	B	690.00	89.58	B / 8.1	29.31%	B- / 7.4
2012	C-	493.80	67.46	C / 4.5	15.30%	B- / 7.3
2011	C+	365.20	59.41	C+ / 6.7	-1.45%	B- / 7.3
2010	C+	450.90	60.45	C+ / 6.0	11.98%	C / 5.5

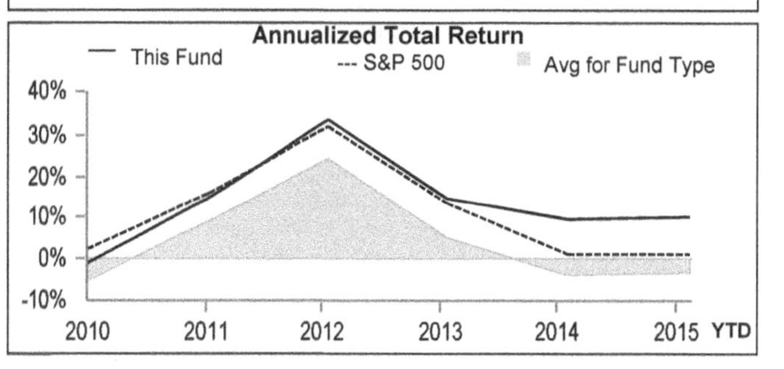

*iShares PHLX Semiconductor ETF (SOXX) B+ Good

Fund Family: BlackRock Fund Advisors
Fund Type: Income
Inception Date: July 10, 2001

Major Rating Factors:
Exceptional performance is the major factor driving the B+ (Good) TheStreet.com Investment Rating for *iShares PHLX Semiconductor ETF. The fund currently has a performance rating of A (Excellent) based on an annualized return of 20.34% over the last three years and a total return of -1.75% year to date 2015. Factored into the performance evaluation is an expense ratio of 0.47% (very low).

The fund's risk rating is currently C+ (Fair). It carries a beta of 1.19, meaning it is expected to move 11.9% for every 10% move in the market. Volatility, as measured by both the semi-deviation and a drawdown factor, is considered low. As of December 31, 2015, *iShares PHLX Semiconductor ETF traded at a premium of .03% above its net asset value, which is worse than its one-year historical average premium of .01%.

Diane Hsiung has been running the fund for 8 years and currently receives a manager quality ranking of 84 (0=worst, 99=best). If you desire only a moderate level of risk and strong performance, then this fund is an excellent option.

Data Date	Investment Rating	Net Assets ($Mil)	Price	Performance Rating/Pts	Total Return Y-T-D	Risk Rating/Pts
12-15	B+	542.60	89.79	A / 9.4	-1.75%	C+ / 6.6
2014	B+	542.60	92.90	A / 9.4	32.02%	C+ / 6.5
2013	B-	254.30	72.61	B- / 7.2	34.48%	B- / 7.5
2012	D+	216.30	52.04	C- / 3.2	6.31%	B- / 7.4
2011	C+	177.90	49.40	C+ / 6.3	-10.91%	B- / 7.4
2010	C	230.90	55.70	C+ / 6.0	14.35%	C / 5.2

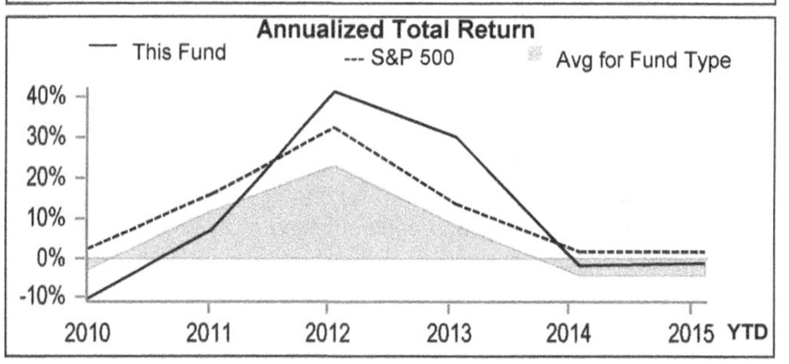

*iShares Real Estate 50 ETF (FTY) B- Good

Fund Family: BlackRock Fund Advisors
Fund Type: Income
Inception Date: May 1, 2007

Major Rating Factors: Strong performance is the major factor driving the B- (Good) TheStreet.com Investment Rating for *iShares Real Estate 50 ETF. The fund currently has a performance rating of B (Good) based on an annualized return of 9.60% over the last three years and a total return of 4.35% year to date 2015. Factored into the performance evaluation is an expense ratio of 0.48% (very low).

The fund's risk rating is currently C+ (Fair). It carries a beta of 0.46, meaning the fund's expected move will be 4.6% for every 10% move in the market. Volatility, as measured by both the semi-deviation and a drawdown factor, is considered low. As of December 31, 2015, *iShares Real Estate 50 ETF traded at a premium of .75% above its net asset value.

Diane Hsiung has been running the fund for 8 years and currently receives a manager quality ranking of 86 (0=worst, 99=best). If you desire only a moderate level of risk and strong performance, then this fund is an excellent option.

Data Date	Investment Rating	Net Assets ($Mil)	Price	Performance Rating/Pts	Total Return Y-T-D	Risk Rating/Pts
12-15	B-	76.10	47.33	B / 8.1	4.35%	C+ / 6.4
2014	A-	76.10	47.27	B+ / 8.3	28.10%	B / 8.0
2013	C	74.10	38.01	C / 5.1	-2.19%	B / 8.0
2012	B	69.80	39.82	B- / 7.5	19.33%	B- / 7.9
2011	C+	42.20	35.35	B- / 7.5	8.60%	C+ / 6.7
2010	C+	50.40	33.72	B- / 7.2	26.21%	C / 4.3

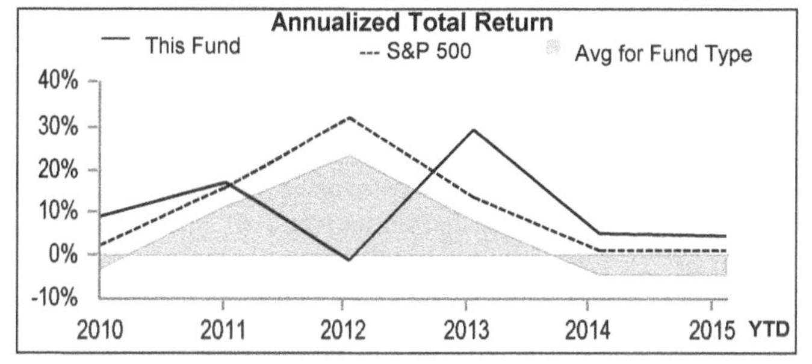

*iShares Residential Rl Est Cap E (REZ) B+ Good

Fund Family: BlackRock Fund Advisors
Fund Type: Income
Inception Date: May 1, 2007

Major Rating Factors:
Exceptional performance is the major factor driving the B+ (Good) TheStreet.com Investment Rating for *iShares Residential Rl Est Cap E. The fund currently has a performance rating of A- (Excellent) based on an annualized return of 12.97% over the last three years and a total return of 10.32% year to date 2015. Factored into the performance evaluation is an expense ratio of 0.48% (very low).

The fund's risk rating is currently C+ (Fair). It carries a beta of 0.16, meaning the fund's expected move will be 1.6% for every 10% move in the market. Volatility, as measured by both the semi-deviation and a drawdown factor, is considered low. As of December 31, 2015, *iShares Residential Rl Est Cap E traded at a premium of .09% above its net asset value.

Diane Hsiung has been running the fund for 8 years and currently receives a manager quality ranking of 95 (0=worst, 99=best). If you desire only a moderate level of risk and strong performance, then this fund is an excellent option.

Data Date	Investment Rating	Net Assets ($Mil)	Price	Performance Rating/Pts	Total Return Y-T-D	Risk Rating/Pts
12-15	B+	224.90	63.45	A- / 9.0	10.32%	C+ / 6.3
2014	A	224.90	58.91	B+ / 8.8	34.23%	B- / 7.7
2013	C	223.40	45.11	C / 4.8	-4.27%	B- / 7.8
2012	B+	257.20	48.47	B / 8.2	16.69%	B- / 7.9
2011	C+	143.50	44.22	B / 8.2	15.63%	C+ / 6.2
2010	B	70.90	39.39	B+ / 8.3	31.61%	C / 4.5

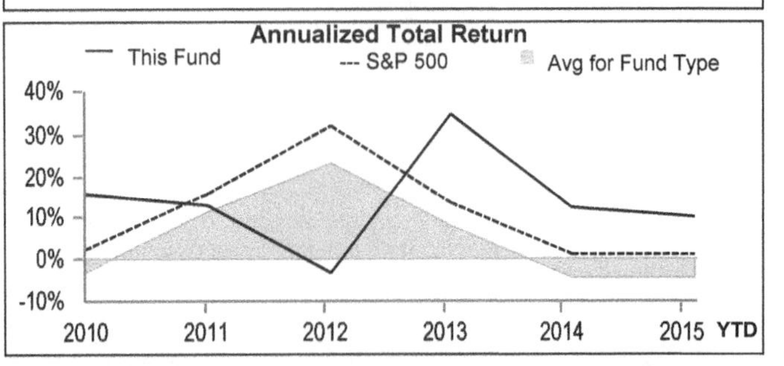

*iShares Russell 1000 ETF (IWB) A+ Excellent

Fund Family: BlackRock Fund Advisors
Fund Type: Growth
Inception Date: May 15, 2000

Major Rating Factors:
Strong performance is the major factor driving the A+ (Excellent) TheStreet.com Investment Rating for *iShares Russell 1000 ETF. The fund currently has a performance rating of B+ (Good) based on an annualized return of 13.94% over the last three years and a total return of 1.39% year to date 2015. Factored into the performance evaluation is an expense ratio of 0.15% (very low).

The fund's risk rating is currently B (Good). It carries a beta of 0.98, meaning that its performance tracks fairly well with that of the overall stock market. Volatility, as measured by both the semi-deviation and a drawdown factor, is considered low. As of December 31, 2015, *iShares Russell 1000 ETF traded at a discount of .04% below its net asset value.

Diane Hsiung has been running the fund for 8 years and currently receives a manager quality ranking of 69 (0=worst, 99=best). If you desire only a moderate level of risk and strong performance, then this fund is an excellent option.

Data Date	Investment Rating	Net Assets ($Mil)	Price	Performance Rating/Pts	Total Return Y-T-D	Risk Rating/Pts
12-15	A+	9,851.70	113.31	B+ / 8.8	1.39%	B / 8.8
2014	A	9,851.70	114.63	B+ / 8.3	14.09%	B / 8.2
2013	B+	8,712.40	103.17	B / 8.2	27.96%	B / 8.2
2012	C+	6,546.30	79.15	C / 5.4	16.95%	B / 8.0
2011	C+	6,300.80	69.37	C / 5.3	1.99%	B- / 7.9
2010	C-	6,452.00	69.86	C- / 4.2	16.02%	C+ / 5.9

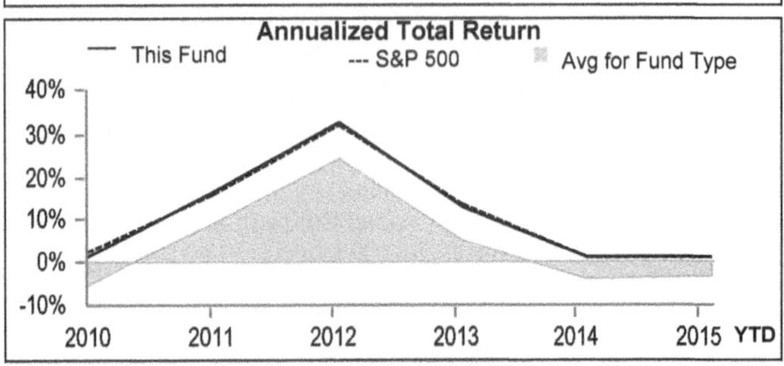

*iShares Russell 1000 Growth ETF (IWF) A Excellent

Fund Family: BlackRock Fund Advisors
Fund Type: Growth
Inception Date: May 22, 2000

Major Rating Factors:
Exceptional performance is the major factor driving the A (Excellent) TheStreet.com Investment Rating for *iShares Russell 1000 Growth ETF. The fund currently has a performance rating of A- (Excellent) based on an annualized return of 15.76% over the last three years and a total return of 6.01% year to date 2015. Factored into the performance evaluation is an expense ratio of 0.20% (very low).

The fund's risk rating is currently B- (Good). It carries a beta of 1.00, meaning that its performance tracks fairly well with that of the overall stock market. Volatility, as measured by both the semi-deviation and a drawdown factor, is considered low. As of December 31, 2015, *iShares Russell 1000 Growth ETF traded at a discount of .01% below its net asset value.

Diane Hsiung has been running the fund for 8 years and currently receives a manager quality ranking of 78 (0=worst, 99=best). If you desire only a moderate level of risk and strong performance, then this fund is an excellent option.

Data Date	Investment Rating	Net Assets ($Mil)	Price	Performance Rating/Pts	Total Return Y-T-D	Risk Rating/Pts
12-15	A	24,930.40	99.48	A- / 9.1	6.01%	B- / 7.7
2014	B	24,930.40	95.61	B / 8.1	13.93%	B- / 7.1
2013	B+	22,673.00	85.95	B+ / 8.3	28.56%	B- / 7.9
2012	C	16,907.00	65.49	C / 5.2	15.83%	B- / 7.6
2011	C+	14,210.50	57.79	C+ / 6.2	3.14%	B- / 7.7
2010	C	12,576.60	57.26	C / 5.3	16.48%	C+ / 5.9

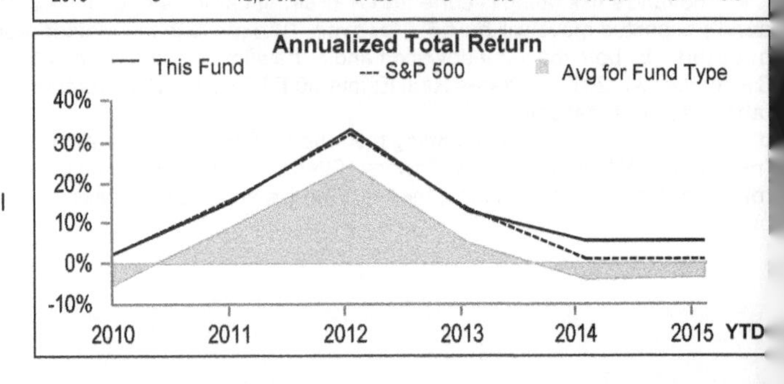

*iShares Russell 1000 Value ETF (IWD) B+ Good

und Family: BlackRock Fund Advisors
und Type: Income
nception Date: May 22, 2000

lajor Rating Factors: Strong performance is the major factor driving the B+ (Good) heStreet.com Investment Rating for *iShares Russell 1000 Value ETF. The fund urrently has a performance rating of B (Good) based on an annualized return of 1.93% over the last three years and a total return of -3.33% year to date 2015. actored into the performance evaluation is an expense ratio of 0.20% (very low).
The fund's risk rating is currently B (Good). It carries a beta of 1.00, meaning that s performance tracks fairly well with that of the overall stock market. Volatility, as neasured by both the semi-deviation and a drawdown factor, is considered low. As of)ecember 31, 2015, *iShares Russell 1000 Value ETF traded at a discount of .01% elow its net asset value, which is in line with its one-year historical average discount f .01%.
Diane Hsiung has been running the fund for 8 years and currently receives a nanager quality ranking of 54 (0=worst, 99=best). If you desire only a moderate level f risk and strong performance, then this fund is an excellent option.

Data Date	Investment Rating	Net Assets ($Mil)	Price	Perfor-mance Rating/Pts	Total Return Y-T-D	Risk Rating/Pts
12-15	B+	23,463.20	97.86	B / 8.0	-3.33%	B / 8.0
2014	A+	23,463.20	104.40	B+ / 8.4	14.02%	B+ / 9.2
2013	B+	20,723.70	94.17	B / 8.0	27.20%	B / 8.3
2012	C+	14,536.20	72.82	C / 5.5	17.84%	B / 8.2
2011	C	11,359.00	63.48	C / 4.6	0.79%	B- / 7.8
2010	C-	10,698.20	64.87	C- / 3.1	15.44%	C+ / 5.9

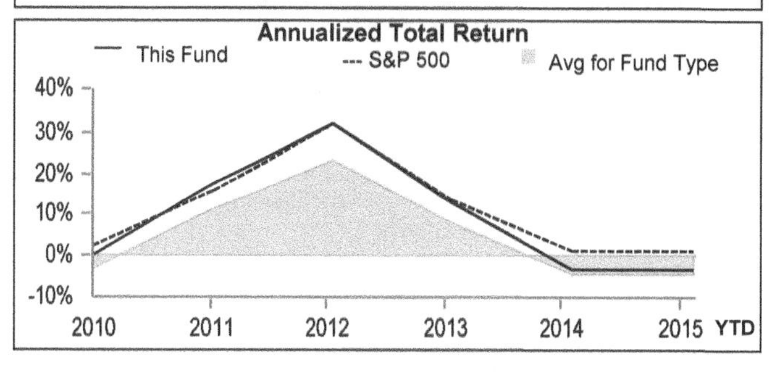

*iShares Russell 2000 ETF (IWM) B+ Good

und Family: BlackRock Fund Advisors
und Type: Growth
nception Date: May 22, 2000

lajor Rating Factors: Strong performance is the major factor driving the B+ (Good) heStreet.com Investment Rating for *iShares Russell 2000 ETF. The fund currently as a performance rating of B- (Good) based on an annualized return of 10.56% over ne last three years and a total return of -3.48% year to date 2015. Factored into the erformance evaluation is an expense ratio of 0.20% (very low).
The fund's risk rating is currently B (Good). It carries a beta of 1.06, meaning that s performance tracks fairly well with that of the overall stock market. Volatility, as neasured by both the semi-deviation and a drawdown factor, is considered low. As of)ecember 31, 2015, *iShares Russell 2000 ETF traded at a discount of .12% below s net asset value, which is better than its one-year historical average discount f .02%.
Diane Hsiung has been running the fund for 8 years and currently receives a nanager quality ranking of 38 (0=worst, 99=best). If you desire only a moderate level f risk and strong performance, then this fund is an excellent option.

Data Date	Investment Rating	Net Assets ($Mil)	Price	Perfor-mance Rating/Pts	Total Return Y-T-D	Risk Rating/Pts
12-15	B+	23,992.60	112.62	B- / 7.4	-3.48%	B / 8.2
2014	B-	23,992.60	119.62	B / 7.7	5.67%	B- / 7.0
2013	B+	27,514.30	115.36	B+ / 8.5	33.26%	B- / 7.5
2012	C+	15,997.10	84.32	C+ / 6.1	16.69%	B- / 7.3
2011	C	14,101.20	73.75	C+ / 5.6	-3.44%	B- / 7.2
2010	B	17,565.80	78.24	B- / 7.2	26.90%	C+ / 6.1

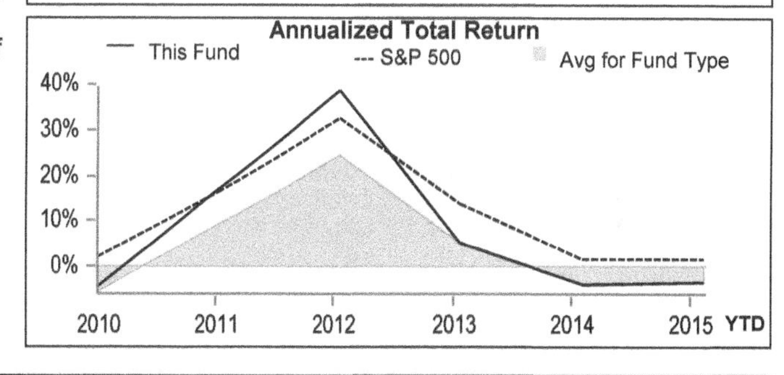

*iShares Russell 2000 Growth ETF (IWO) B+ Good

und Family: BlackRock Fund Advisors
und Type: Growth
nception Date: July 24, 2000

lajor Rating Factors: Strong performance is the major factor driving the B+ (Good) heStreet.com Investment Rating for *iShares Russell 2000 Growth ETF. The fund urrently has a performance rating of B+ (Good) based on an annualized return of 3.23% over the last three years and a total return of -0.35% year to date 2015. actored into the performance evaluation is an expense ratio of 0.25% (very low).
The fund's risk rating is currently B- (Good). It carries a beta of 1.10, meaning it is xpected to move 11.0% for every 10% move in the market. Volatility, as measured y both the semi-deviation and a drawdown factor, is considered low. As of)ecember 31, 2015, *iShares Russell 2000 Growth ETF traded at a discount of .16% elow its net asset value, which is better than its one-year historical average discount f .02%.
Diane Hsiung has been running the fund for 8 years and currently receives a nanager quality ranking of 51 (0=worst, 99=best). If you desire only a moderate level f risk and strong performance, then this fund is an excellent option.

Data Date	Investment Rating	Net Assets ($Mil)	Price	Perfor-mance Rating/Pts	Total Return Y-T-D	Risk Rating/Pts
12-15	B+	5,646.30	139.28	B+ / 8.3	-0.35%	B- / 7.5
2014	B-	5,646.30	142.38	B / 8.0	6.30%	C+ / 6.6
2013	B	6,316.90	135.51	B+ / 8.8	37.99%	B- / 7.1
2012	C	3,915.00	95.31	C+ / 6.2	15.53%	B- / 7.0
2011	C+	3,492.10	84.23	C+ / 6.3	-2.45%	C+ / 6.9
2010	B-	4,134.90	87.42	B- / 7.4	29.35%	C / 5.4

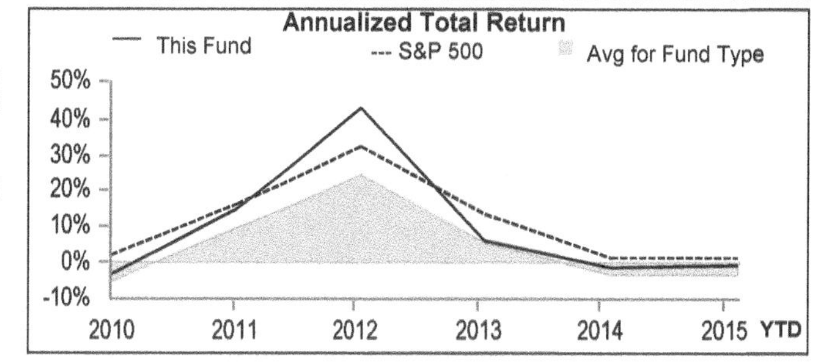

*iShares Russell 2000 Value ETF (IWN) B Good

Fund Family: BlackRock Fund Advisors
Fund Type: Growth
Inception Date: July 24, 2000

Major Rating Factors: *iShares Russell 2000 Value ETF receives a TheStreet.com Investment Rating of B (Good). The fund currently has a performance rating of C+ (Fair) based on an annualized return of 7.91% over the last three years and a total return of -6.59% year to date 2015. Factored into the performance evaluation is an expense ratio of 0.25% (very low).

The fund's risk rating is currently B (Good). It carries a beta of 1.02, meaning that its performance tracks fairly well with that of the overall stock market. Volatility, as measured by both the semi-deviation and a drawdown factor, is considered low. As of December 31, 2015, *iShares Russell 2000 Value ETF traded at a discount of .20% below its net asset value, which is better than its one-year historical average discount of .02%.

Diane Hsiung has been running the fund for 8 years and currently receives a manager quality ranking of 28 (0=worst, 99=best). If you desire an average level of risk, then this fund may be an option.

Data Date	Investment Rating	Net Assets ($Mil)	Price	Performance Rating/Pts	Total Return Y-T-D	Risk Rating/Pts
12-15	B	5,473.70	91.94	C+ / 6.4	-6.59%	B / 8.5
2014	B-	5,473.70	101.68	B- / 7.3	5.05%	B- / 7.1
2013	B	6,164.10	99.50	B / 7.9	28.69%	B- / 7.7
2012	C+	4,260.00	75.51	C+ / 5.9	17.97%	B- / 7.5
2011	C	3,887.90	65.64	C / 4.8	-4.48%	B- / 7.4
2010	B-	4,728.40	71.09	B- / 7.1	24.68%	C+ / 5.7

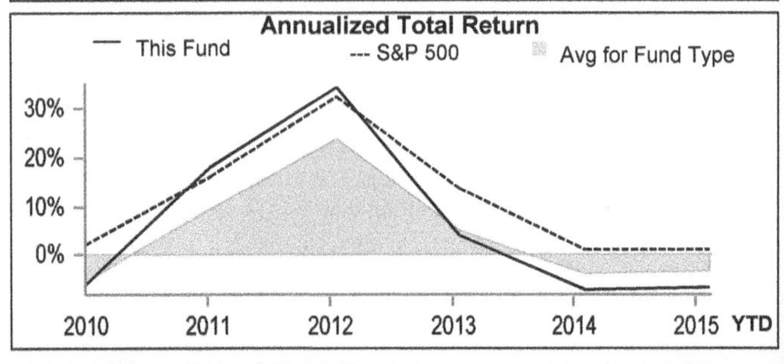

*iShares Russell 3000 (IWV) A Excellent

Fund Family: BlackRock Fund Advisors
Fund Type: Income
Inception Date: May 22, 2000

Major Rating Factors:
Strong performance is the major factor driving the A (Excellent) TheStreet.com Investment Rating for *iShares Russell 3000. The fund currently has a performance rating of B+ (Good) based on an annualized return of 13.63% over the last three years and a total return of 0.97% year to date 2015. Factored into the performance evaluation is an expense ratio of 0.20% (very low).

The fund's risk rating is currently B- (Good). It carries a beta of 1.00, meaning that its performance tracks fairly well with that of the overall stock market. Volatility, as measured by both the semi-deviation and a drawdown factor, is considered low. As of December 31, 2015, *iShares Russell 3000 traded at a discount of .01% below its net asset value.

Diane Hsiung has been running the fund for 8 years and currently receives a manager quality ranking of 65 (0=worst, 99=best). If you desire only a moderate level of risk and strong performance, then this fund is an excellent option.

Data Date	Investment Rating	Net Assets ($Mil)	Price	Performance Rating/Pts	Total Return Y-T-D	Risk Rating/Pts
12-15	A	5,658.70	120.31	B+ / 8.6	0.97%	B- / 7.9
2014	B+	5,658.70	122.29	B / 8.2	13.32%	B- / 7.4
2013	B+	5,412.10	110.65	B / 8.2	28.34%	B / 8.1
2012	C+	3,660.90	84.68	C / 5.4	16.89%	B- / 7.9
2011	C+	3,209.30	74.18	C / 5.3	1.44%	B- / 7.9
2010	C	3,250.80	74.95	C / 4.5	16.82%	C+ / 5.9

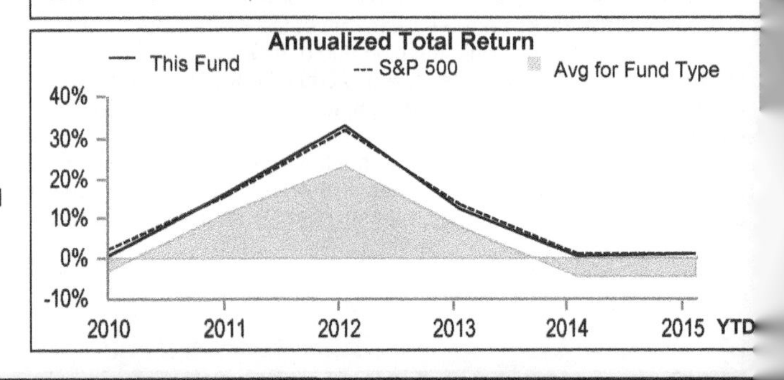

*iShares Russell Mid Cap (IWR) A Excellent

Fund Family: BlackRock Fund Advisors
Fund Type: Growth
Inception Date: July 17, 2001

Major Rating Factors:
Strong performance is the major factor driving the A (Excellent) TheStreet.com Investment Rating for *iShares Russell Mid Cap. The fund currently has a performance rating of B+ (Good) based on an annualized return of 13.00% over the last three years and a total return of -2.08% year to date 2015. Factored into the performance evaluation is an expense ratio of 0.20% (very low).

The fund's risk rating is currently B (Good). It carries a beta of 0.97, meaning that its performance tracks fairly well with that of the overall stock market. Volatility, as measured by both the semi-deviation and a drawdown factor, is considered low. As of December 31, 2015, *iShares Russell Mid Cap traded at a discount of .06% below its net asset value, which is better than its one-year historical average discount of .01%.

Diane Hsiung has been running the fund for 8 years and currently receives a manager quality ranking of 65 (0=worst, 99=best). If you desire only a moderate level of risk and strong performance, then this fund is an excellent option.

Data Date	Investment Rating	Net Assets ($Mil)	Price	Performance Rating/Pts	Total Return Y-T-D	Risk Rating/Pts
12-15	A	10,231.50	160.18	B+ / 8.3	-2.08%	B / 8.6
2014	A	10,231.50	167.04	B+ / 8.6	13.92%	B / 8.1
2013	B+	9,316.10	149.98	B / 8.1	29.33%	B / 8.0
2012	C+	6,523.60	113.10	C+ / 6.5	17.22%	B- / 7.9
2011	C+	6,009.40	98.42	C+ / 6.5	-0.83%	B- / 7.8
2010	C+	6,018.40	101.75	C+ / 6.6	25.31%	C / 5.5

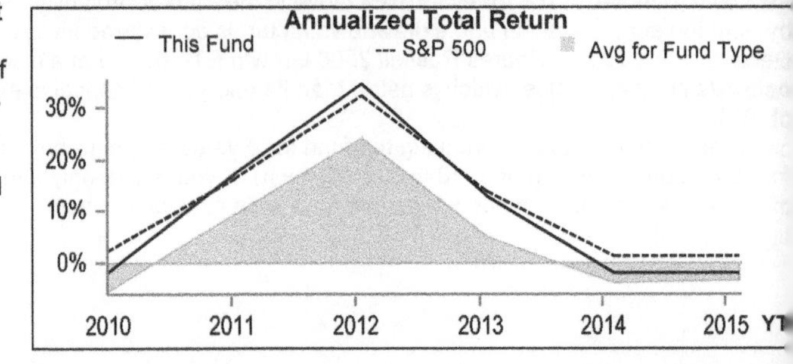

* Denotes ETF Fund

*iShares Russell Mid Cap Growth (IWP) A+ Excellent

Fund Family: BlackRock Fund Advisors
Fund Type: Growth
Inception Date: July 17, 2001

Major Rating Factors:
Strong performance is the major factor driving the A+ (Excellent) TheStreet.com Investment Rating for *iShares Russell Mid Cap Growth. The fund currently has a performance rating of B+ (Good) based on an annualized return of 13.60% over the last three years and a total return of 0.00% year to date 2015. Factored into the performance evaluation is an expense ratio of 0.25% (very low).

The fund's risk rating is currently B (Good). It carries a beta of 1.01, meaning that its performance tracks fairly well with that of the overall stock market. Volatility, as measured by both the semi-deviation and a drawdown factor, is considered low. As of December 31, 2015, *iShares Russell Mid Cap Growth traded at a discount of .04% below its net asset value.

Diane Hsiung has been running the fund for 8 years and currently receives a manager quality ranking of 64 (0=worst, 99=best). If you desire only a moderate level of risk and strong performance, then this fund is an excellent option.

Data Date	Investment Rating	Net Assets ($Mil)	Price	Performance Rating/Pts	Total Return Y-T-D	Risk Rating/Pts
12-15	A+	4,911.40	91.92	B+ / 8.5	0.00%	B / 8.6
2014	B	4,911.40	93.23	B / 8.2	12.59%	B- / 7.0
2013	B	4,766.00	84.36	B / 8.1	30.36%	B- / 7.7
2012	C+	3,289.00	62.80	C+ / 6.2	15.39%	B- / 7.7
2011	C+	2,896.90	55.05	C+ / 6.7	-0.85%	B- / 7.6
2010	C-	3,161.20	56.61	C+ / 6.7	26.03%	C- / 3.2

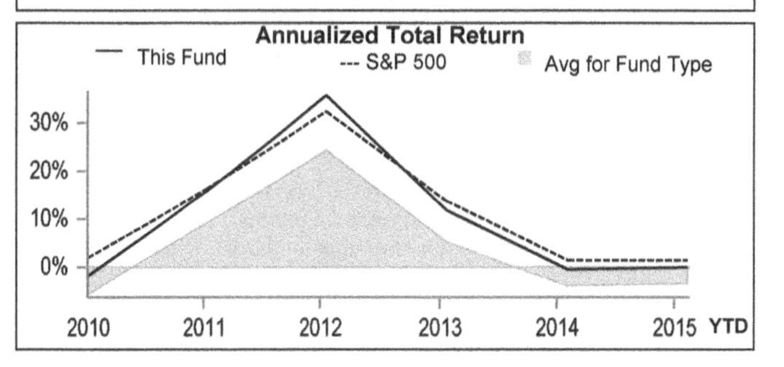

*iShares Russell Mid Cap Value (IWS) A Excellent

Fund Family: BlackRock Fund Advisors
Fund Type: Growth
Inception Date: July 17, 2001

Major Rating Factors:
Strong performance is the major factor driving the A (Excellent) TheStreet.com Investment Rating for *iShares Russell Mid Cap Value. The fund currently has a performance rating of B (Good) based on an annualized return of 12.20% over the last three years and a total return of -4.39% year to date 2015. Factored into the performance evaluation is an expense ratio of 0.25% (very low).

The fund's risk rating is currently B (Good). It carries a beta of 0.94, meaning that its performance tracks fairly well with that of the overall stock market. Volatility, as measured by both the semi-deviation and a drawdown factor, is considered low. As of December 31, 2015, *iShares Russell Mid Cap Value traded at a discount of .06% below its net asset value.

Diane Hsiung has been running the fund for 8 years and currently receives a manager quality ranking of 62 (0=worst, 99=best). If you desire only a moderate level of risk and strong performance, then this fund is an excellent option.

Data Date	Investment Rating	Net Assets ($Mil)	Price	Performance Rating/Pts	Total Return Y-T-D	Risk Rating/Pts
12-15	A	6,555.20	68.66	B / 7.9	-4.39%	B / 8.7
2014	A+	6,555.20	73.76	B+ / 8.8	15.49%	B+ / 9.1
2013	B+	5,506.00	65.71	B / 8.0	27.77%	B / 8.1
2012	B-	3,907.30	50.24	C+ / 6.6	18.68%	B- / 7.9
2011	C+	2,744.40	43.40	C+ / 6.1	-0.74%	B- / 7.9
2010	C-	3,100.30	45.01	C+ / 6.5	24.43%	D+ / 2.8

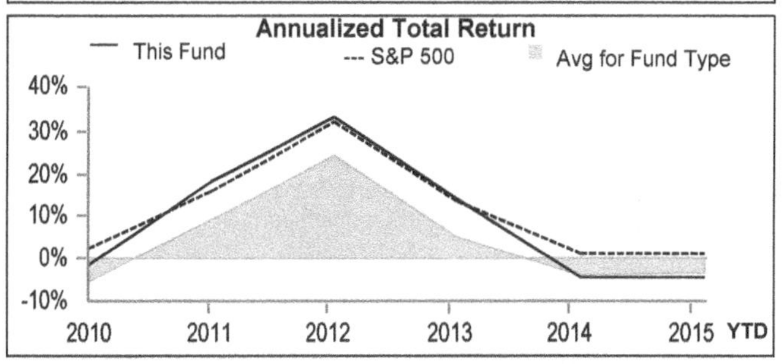

*iShares Russell Top 200 (IWL) A- Excellent

Fund Family: BlackRock Fund Advisors
Fund Type: Income
Inception Date: September 22, 2009

Major Rating Factors:
Exceptional performance is the major factor driving the A- (Excellent) TheStreet.com Investment Rating for *iShares Russell Top 200. The fund currently has a performance rating of A- (Excellent) based on an annualized return of 14.49% over the last three years and a total return of 3.34% year to date 2015. Factored into the performance evaluation is an expense ratio of 0.15% (very low).

The fund's risk rating is currently B- (Good). It carries a beta of 1.02, meaning that its performance tracks fairly well with that of the overall stock market. Volatility, as measured by both the semi-deviation and a drawdown factor, is considered low. As of December 31, 2015, *iShares Russell Top 200 traded at a premium of .51% above its net asset value, which is worse than its one-year historical average premium of .04%.

Diane Hsiung has been running the fund for 7 years and currently receives a manager quality ranking of 68 (0=worst, 99=best). If you desire only a moderate level of risk and strong performance, then this fund is an excellent option.

Data Date	Investment Rating	Net Assets ($Mil)	Price	Performance Rating/Pts	Total Return Y-T-D	Risk Rating/Pts
12-15	A-	89.90	46.99	A- / 9.0	3.34%	B- / 7.1
2014	B+	89.90	47.20	B+ / 8.4	14.91%	B- / 7.3
2013	A	73.70	42.00	B+ / 8.3	27.63%	B / 8.6
2012	C	52.00	32.50	C / 4.9	16.98%	B / 8.4
2011	C-	109.10	29.17	C- / 3.2	3.50%	B / 8.5
2010	A+	11.60	28.87	B+ / 8.9	11.26%	B- / 7.9

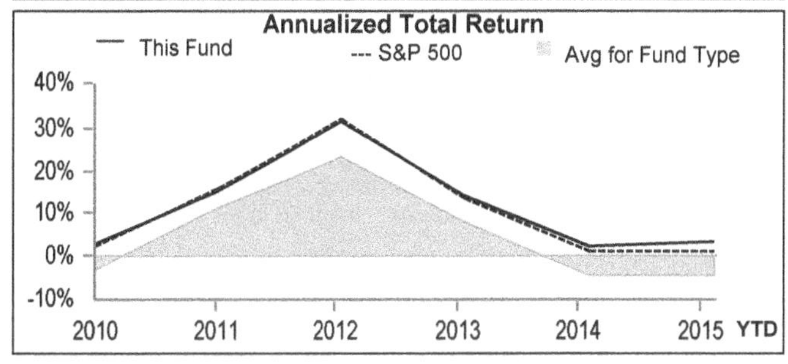

*iShares Russell Top 200 Growth (IWY) A+ Excellent

Fund Family: BlackRock Fund Advisors
Fund Type: Growth
Inception Date: September 22, 2009

Data Date	Investment Rating	Net Assets ($Mil)	Price	Performance Rating/Pts	Total Return Y-T-D	Risk Rating/Pts
12-15	A+	502.20	53.54	A / 9.3	8.51%	B- / 7.6
2014	B	502.20	50.43	B / 8.1	14.61%	B- / 7.3
2013	A	442.40	45.16	B+ / 8.5	27.79%	B / 8.7
2012	C+	352.30	34.71	C / 4.8	15.92%	B / 8.5
2011	C-	401.70	30.82	C- / 3.3	5.08%	B / 8.6
2010	A+	331.00	29.93	A- / 9.0	11.98%	B- / 7.8

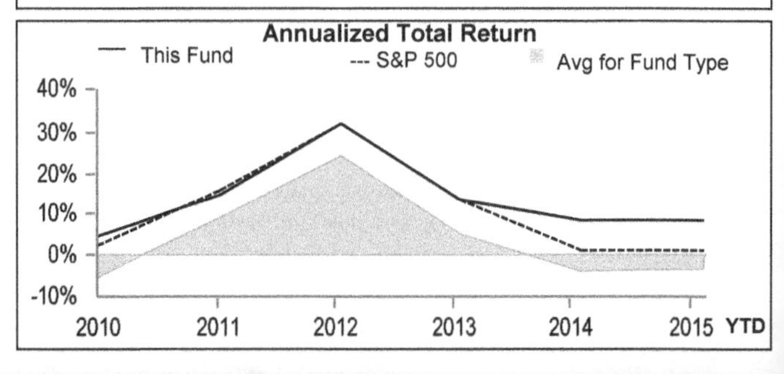

Major Rating Factors:
Exceptional performance is the major factor driving the A+ (Excellent) TheStreet.com Investment Rating for *iShares Russell Top 200 Growth. The fund currently has a performance rating of A (Excellent) based on an annualized return of 16.64% over the last three years and a total return of 8.51% year to date 2015. Factored into the performance evaluation is an expense ratio of 0.20% (very low).

The fund's risk rating is currently B- (Good). It carries a beta of 1.00, meaning that its performance tracks fairly well with that of the overall stock market. Volatility, as measured by both the semi-deviation and a drawdown factor, is considered low. As of December 31, 2015, *iShares Russell Top 200 Growth traded at a premium of .02% above its net asset value, which is better than its one-year historical average premium of .03%.

Diane Hsiung has been running the fund for 7 years and currently receives a manager quality ranking of 81 (0=worst, 99=best). If you desire only a moderate level of risk and strong performance, then this fund is an excellent option.

*iShares Russell Top 200 Value (IWX) B Good

Fund Family: BlackRock Fund Advisors
Fund Type: Income
Inception Date: September 22, 2009

Data Date	Investment Rating	Net Assets ($Mil)	Price	Performance Rating/Pts	Total Return Y-T-D	Risk Rating/Pts
12-15	B	151.40	41.72	B / 8.1	-2.72%	C+ / 6.9
2014	B+	151.40	44.52	B / 8.2	13.83%	B- / 7.3
2013	B+	128.80	40.24	B / 8.0	27.02%	B / 8.2
2012	C	79.50	31.17	C / 4.8	17.41%	B / 8.0
2011	C-	137.30	27.54	D+ / 2.9	1.09%	B / 8.1
2010	A+	212.20	27.94	B+ / 8.8	10.59%	B- / 7.8

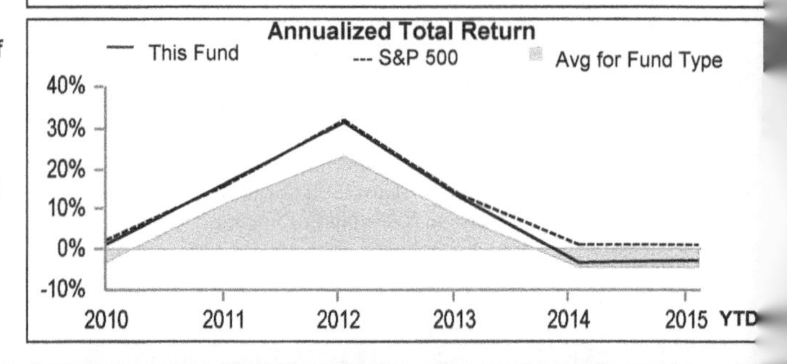

Major Rating Factors: Strong performance is the major factor driving the B (Good) TheStreet.com Investment Rating for *iShares Russell Top 200 Value. The fund currently has a performance rating of B (Good) based on an annualized return of 11.93% over the last three years and a total return of -2.72% year to date 2015. Factored into the performance evaluation is an expense ratio of 0.20% (very low).

The fund's risk rating is currently C+ (Fair). It carries a beta of 1.00, meaning that its performance tracks fairly well with that of the overall stock market. Volatility, as measured by both the semi-deviation and a drawdown factor, is considered low. As of December 31, 2015, *iShares Russell Top 200 Value traded at a premium of .34% above its net asset value, which is worse than its one-year historical average premium of .02%.

Diane Hsiung has been running the fund for 7 years and currently receives a manager quality ranking of 53 (0=worst, 99=best). If you desire only a moderate level of risk and strong performance, then this fund is an excellent option.

*iShares S&P 100 (OEF) A+ Excellent

Fund Family: BlackRock Fund Advisors
Fund Type: Growth
Inception Date: October 23, 2000

Data Date	Investment Rating	Net Assets ($Mil)	Price	Performance Rating/Pts	Total Return Y-T-D	Risk Rating/Pts
12-15	A+	4,493.00	91.17	B+ / 8.8	3.11%	B / 8.5
2014	B	4,493.00	90.94	B / 7.8	13.55%	B- / 7.5
2013	B+	3,940.10	82.35	B / 7.9	25.45%	B / 8.3
2012	C	3,940.10	64.69	C / 4.8	16.75%	B / 8.0
2011	C	2,878.00	57.03	C / 4.9	3.39%	B- / 7.9
2010	C-	2,415.40	56.67	C- / 3.2	12.48%	C+ / 6.1

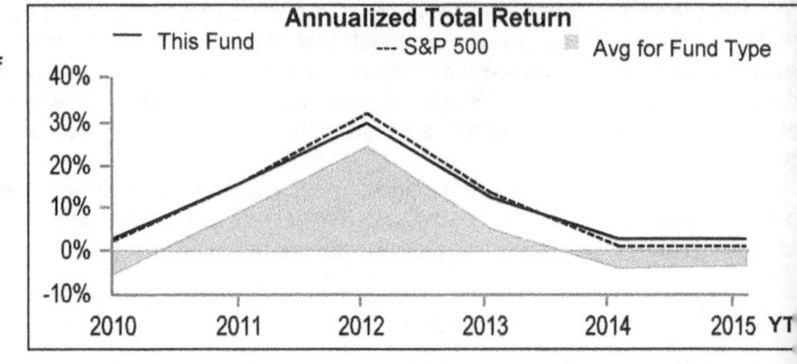

Major Rating Factors:
Strong performance is the major factor driving the A+ (Excellent) TheStreet.com Investment Rating for *iShares S&P 100. The fund currently has a performance rating of B+ (Good) based on an annualized return of 13.62% over the last three years and a total return of 3.11% year to date 2015. Factored into the performance evaluation is an expense ratio of 0.20% (very low).

The fund's risk rating is currently B (Good). It carries a beta of 1.02, meaning that its performance tracks fairly well with that of the overall stock market. Volatility, as measured by both the semi-deviation and a drawdown factor, is considered low. As of December 31, 2015, *iShares S&P 100 traded at a discount of .03% below its net asset value.

Diane Hsiung has been running the fund for 8 years and currently receives a manager quality ranking of 61 (0=worst, 99=best). If you desire only a moderate level of risk and strong performance, then this fund is an excellent option.

*iShares S&P 500 Growth (IVW) A+ Excellent

Fund Family: BlackRock Fund Advisors
Fund Type: Growth
Inception Date: May 22, 2000

Data Date	Investment Rating	Net Assets ($Mil)	Price	Performance Rating/Pts	Total Return Y-T-D	Risk Rating/Pts
12-15	A+	10,572.80	115.80	A- / 9.2	5.93%	B- / 7.8
2014	B+	10,572.80	111.60	B+ / 8.4	15.89%	B- / 7.5
2013	B+	9,189.90	98.75	B+ / 8.4	27.78%	B / 8.0
2012	C	6,644.40	75.74	C / 5.1	16.04%	B- / 7.8
2011	C+	6,403.90	67.43	C+ / 6.0	4.98%	B- / 7.8
2010	C	5,806.90	65.65	C / 5.0	14.91%	C+ / 6.1

Major Rating Factors:
Exceptional performance is the major factor driving the A+ (Excellent) TheStreet.com Investment Rating for *iShares S&P 500 Growth. The fund currently has a performance rating of A- (Excellent) based on an annualized return of 16.16% over the last three years and a total return of 5.93% year to date 2015. Factored into the performance evaluation is an expense ratio of 0.18% (very low).

The fund's risk rating is currently B- (Good). It carries a beta of 1.01, meaning that its performance tracks fairly well with that of the overall stock market. Volatility, as measured by both the semi-deviation and a drawdown factor, is considered low. As of December 31, 2015, *iShares S&P 500 Growth traded at a price exactly equal to its net asset value.

Diane Hsiung has been running the fund for 8 years and currently receives a manager quality ranking of 79 (0=worst, 99=best). If you desire only a moderate level of risk and strong performance, then this fund is an excellent option.

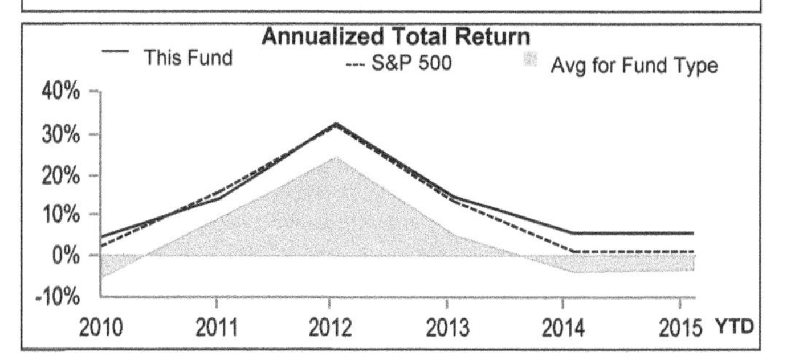

*iShares S&P 500 Value (IVE) A Excellent

Fund Family: BlackRock Fund Advisors
Fund Type: Income
Inception Date: May 22, 2000

Data Date	Investment Rating	Net Assets ($Mil)	Price	Performance Rating/Pts	Total Return Y-T-D	Risk Rating/Pts
12-15	A	8,086.00	88.53	B / 8.0	-2.59%	B / 8.7
2014	A-	8,086.00	93.77	B / 8.1	13.04%	B / 8.3
2013	B+	6,503.60	85.46	B / 7.9	26.79%	B / 8.3
2012	C+	4,830.60	66.39	C / 5.3	17.10%	B / 8.1
2011	C	3,901.70	57.83	C / 4.7	0.07%	B- / 7.8
2010	D+	4,115.90	59.59	D+ / 2.7	14.97%	C+ / 5.7

Major Rating Factors:
Strong performance is the major factor driving the A (Excellent) TheStreet.com Investment Rating for *iShares S&P 500 Value. The fund currently has a performance rating of B (Good) based on an annualized return of 11.75% over the last three years and a total return of -2.59% year to date 2015. Factored into the performance evaluation is an expense ratio of 0.18% (very low).

The fund's risk rating is currently B (Good). It carries a beta of 0.99, meaning that its performance tracks fairly well with that of the overall stock market. Volatility, as measured by both the semi-deviation and a drawdown factor, is considered low. As of December 31, 2015, *iShares S&P 500 Value traded at a discount of .03% below its net asset value, which is better than its one-year historical average discount of .01%.

Diane Hsiung has been running the fund for 8 years and currently receives a manager quality ranking of 52 (0=worst, 99=best). If you desire only a moderate level of risk and strong performance, then this fund is an excellent option.

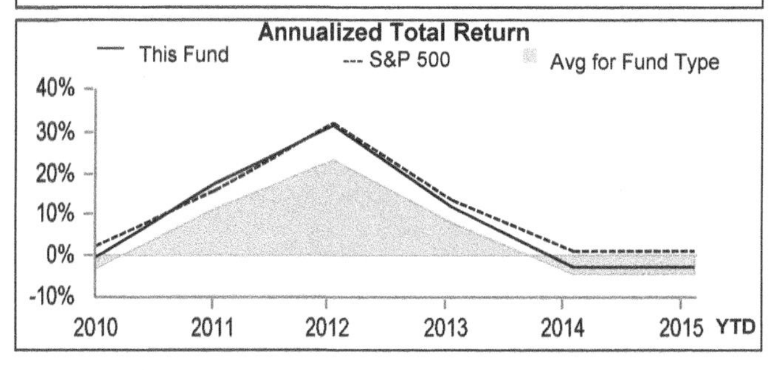

*iShares S&P GSCI Commodity-Index (GSG) E Very Weak

Fund Family: BlackRock Fund Advisors
Fund Type: Income
Inception Date: July 21, 2006

Data Date	Investment Rating	Net Assets ($Mil)	Price	Performance Rating/Pts	Total Return Y-T-D	Risk Rating/Pts
12-15	E	979.20	14.23	E+ / 0.6	-32.94%	D+ / 2.8
2014	E+	979.20	21.58	E+ / 0.7	-30.90%	C- / 3.9
2013	D+	1,171.10	32.19	D / 2.0	-4.38%	B- / 7.4
2012	D	1,167.60	32.79	D- / 1.5	-1.79%	B- / 7.3
2011	C-	1,313.30	32.98	C- / 3.2	1.80%	B- / 7.6
2010	E+	1,799.90	34.10	E+ / 0.8	7.17%	C- / 3.7

Major Rating Factors: *iShares S&P GSCI Commodity-Index has adopted a risky asset allocation strategy and currently receives an overall TheStreet.com Investment Rating of E (Very Weak). The fund has an above average level of volatility, as measured by both semi-deviation and drawdown factors. It carries a beta of 0.57, meaning the fund's expected move will be 5.7% for every 10% move in the market. As of December 31, 2015, *iShares S&P GSCI Commodity-Index traded at a premium of .14% above its net asset value, which is worse than its one-year historical average premium of .06%. Unfortunately, the high level of risk (D+, Weak) failed to pay off as investors endured very poor performance.

The fund's performance rating is currently E+ (Very Weak). It has registered an annualized return of -24.19% over the last three years and is down -32.94% year to date 2015. Factored into the performance evaluation is an expense ratio of 0.82% (very low).

Gregory R Savage currently receives a manager quality ranking of 3 (0=worst, 99=best). If you can tolerate high levels of risk in the hope of improved future returns, holding this fund may be an option.

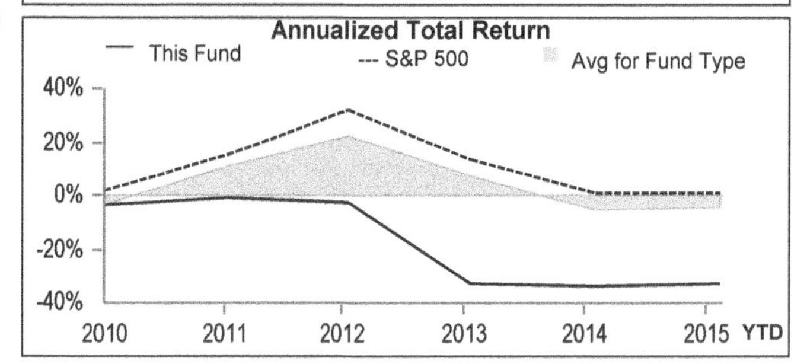

*iShares S&P Mid Cap 400 Grow (IJK) A- Excellent

Fund Family: BlackRock Fund Advisors
Fund Type: Growth
Inception Date: July 24, 2000

Major Rating Factors:
Strong performance is the major factor driving the A- (Excellent) TheStreet.com Investment Rating for *iShares S&P Mid Cap 400 Grow. The fund currently has a performance rating of B (Good) based on an annualized return of 12.03% over the last three years and a total return of 2.15% year to date 2015. Factored into the performance evaluation is an expense ratio of 0.25% (very low).

The fund's risk rating is currently B (Good). It carries a beta of 0.96, meaning that its performance tracks fairly well with that of the overall stock market. Volatility, as measured by both the semi-deviation and a drawdown factor, is considered low. As of December 31, 2015, *iShares S&P Mid Cap 400 Grow traded at a discount of .04% below its net asset value.

Diane Hsiung has been running the fund for 8 years and currently receives a manager quality ranking of 59 (0=worst, 99=best). If you desire only a moderate level of risk and strong performance, then this fund is an excellent option.

Data Date	Investment Rating	Net Assets ($Mil)	Price	Performance Rating/Pts	Total Return Y-T-D	Risk Rating/Pts
12-15	A-	4,487.80	160.96	B / 8.1	2.15%	B / 8.3
2014	B+	4,487.80	159.67	B- / 7.5	8.07%	B / 8.4
2013	B	4,538.60	150.19	B / 7.9	27.19%	B- / 7.8
2012	B-	3,117.10	114.41	B- / 7.3	17.85%	B- / 7.7
2011	B-	2,632.90	98.73	C+ / 6.9	-0.33%	B- / 7.7
2010	B	2,962.90	100.72	B / 7.7	30.44%	C / 5.5

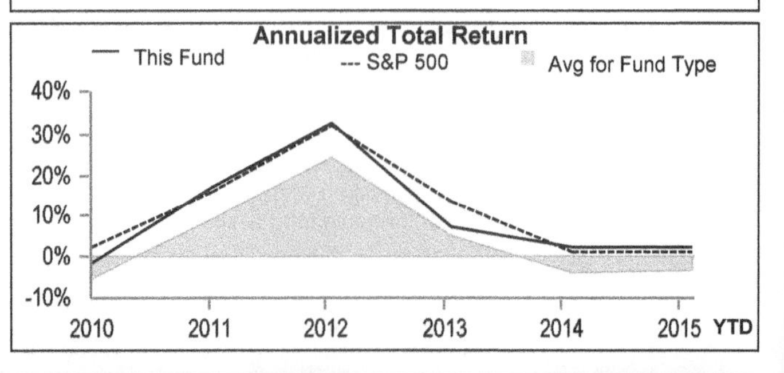

*iShares S&P Mid Cap 400 Value (IJJ) B- Good

Fund Family: BlackRock Fund Advisors
Fund Type: Growth
Inception Date: July 24, 2000

Major Rating Factors: Strong performance is the major factor driving the B- (Good) TheStreet.com Investment Rating for *iShares S&P Mid Cap 400 Value. The fund currently has a performance rating of B- (Good) based on an annualized return of 10.71% over the last three years and a total return of -6.00% year to date 2015. Factored into the performance evaluation is an expense ratio of 0.25% (very low).

The fund's risk rating is currently B- (Good). It carries a beta of 1.02, meaning that its performance tracks fairly well with that of the overall stock market. Volatility, as measured by both the semi-deviation and a drawdown factor, is considered low. As of December 31, 2015, *iShares S&P Mid Cap 400 Value traded at a premium of .04% above its net asset value.

Diane Hsiung has been running the fund for 8 years and currently receives a manager quality ranking of 44 (0=worst, 99=best). If you desire only a moderate level of risk and strong performance, then this fund is an excellent option.

Data Date	Investment Rating	Net Assets ($Mil)	Price	Performance Rating/Pts	Total Return Y-T-D	Risk Rating/Pts
12-15	B-	4,070.00	117.20	B- / 7.3	-6.00%	B- / 7.0
2014	B+	4,070.00	127.83	B+ / 8.4	12.49%	B- / 7.4
2013	B	3,563.50	116.23	B / 8.0	28.51%	B- / 7.8
2012	C+	2,253.60	88.14	C+ / 6.4	18.72%	B- / 7.6
2011	C+	1,988.30	75.98	C+ / 6.0	-1.40%	B- / 7.6
2010	C+	2,082.10	79.46	C+ / 6.8	22.58%	C+ / 5.8

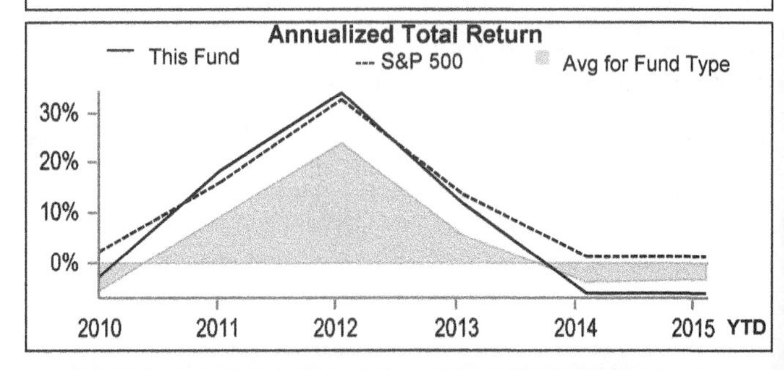

*iShares S&P Small Cap 600 Growth (IJT) B+ Good

Fund Family: BlackRock Fund Advisors
Fund Type: Growth
Inception Date: July 24, 2000

Major Rating Factors: Strong performance is the major factor driving the B+ (Good) TheStreet.com Investment Rating for *iShares S&P Small Cap 600 Growth. The fund currently has a performance rating of B+ (Good) based on an annualized return of 13.89% over the last three years and a total return of 3.77% year to date 2015. Factored into the performance evaluation is an expense ratio of 0.25% (very low).

The fund's risk rating is currently B- (Good). It carries a beta of 0.97, meaning that its performance tracks fairly well with that of the overall stock market. Volatility, as measured by both the semi-deviation and a drawdown factor, is considered low. As of December 31, 2015, *iShares S&P Small Cap 600 Growth traded at a premium of .01% above its net asset value.

Diane Hsiung has been running the fund for 8 years and currently receives a manager quality ranking of 71 (0=worst, 99=best). If you desire only a moderate level of risk and strong performance, then this fund is an excellent option.

Data Date	Investment Rating	Net Assets ($Mil)	Price	Performance Rating/Pts	Total Return Y-T-D	Risk Rating/Pts
12-15	B+	2,565.60	124.31	B+ / 8.7	3.77%	B- / 7.0
2014	B-	2,565.60	122.39	B / 7.6	4.68%	B- / 7.0
2013	B+	2,969.00	118.61	A- / 9.0	36.86%	B- / 7.1
2012	C+	1,606.40	84.04	B- / 7.0	16.37%	B- / 7.4
2011	C+	1,561.20	74.47	C+ / 6.8	3.60%	B- / 7.2
2010	C	1,885.30	72.59	B- / 7.4	28.24%	C- / 3.4

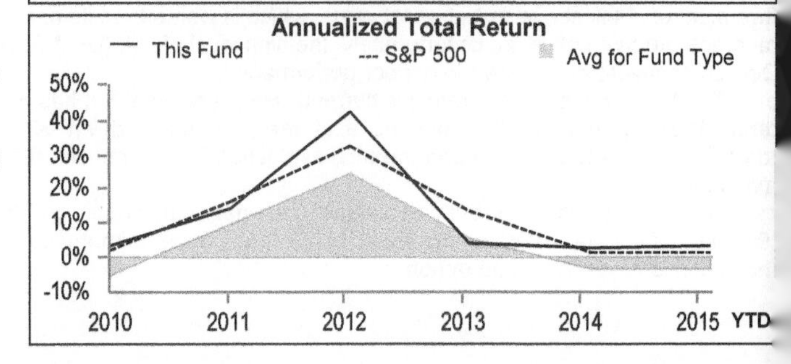

*iShares S&P Small Cap 600 Value (IJS) B Good

Fund Family: BlackRock Fund Advisors
Fund Type: Growth
Inception Date: July 24, 2000

Major Rating Factors: Strong performance is the major factor driving the B (Good) TheStreet.com Investment Rating for *iShares S&P Small Cap 600 Value. The fund currently has a performance rating of B- (Good) based on an annualized return of 10.66% over the last three years and a total return of -5.79% year to date 2015. Factored into the performance evaluation is an expense ratio of 0.25% (very low).

The fund's risk rating is currently B- (Good). It carries a beta of 1.04, meaning that its performance tracks fairly well with that of the overall stock market. Volatility, as measured by both the semi-deviation and a drawdown factor, is considered low. As of December 31, 2015, *iShares S&P Small Cap 600 Value traded at a price exactly equal to its net asset value.

Diane Hsiung has been running the fund for 8 years and currently receives a manager quality ranking of 40 (0=worst, 99=best). If you desire only a moderate level of risk and strong performance, then this fund is an excellent option.

Data Date	Investment Rating	Net Assets ($Mil)	Price	Performance Rating/Pts	Total Return Y-T-D	Risk Rating/Pts
12-15	B	2,863.80	108.16	B- / 7.3	-5.79%	B- / 7.8
2014	B	2,863.80	117.94	B / 8.2	8.10%	B- / 7.0
2013	A-	3,099.50	111.26	B+ / 8.8	34.06%	B- / 7.9
2012	C+	1,904.10	80.91	C+ / 6.4	16.69%	B- / 7.6
2011	C+	1,591.40	69.76	C+ / 6.1	0.69%	B- / 7.4
2010	B	1,792.50	71.89	B- / 7.2	24.70%	C+ / 5.7

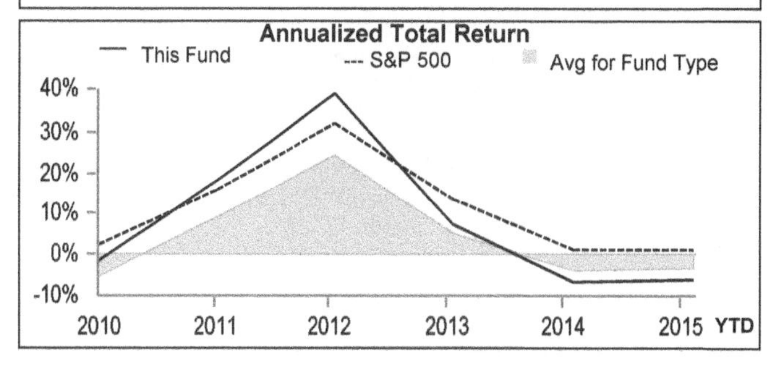

*iShares Select Dividend ETF (DVY) A Excellent

Fund Family: BlackRock Fund Advisors
Fund Type: Income
Inception Date: November 3, 2003

Major Rating Factors:
Strong performance is the major factor driving the A (Excellent) TheStreet.com Investment Rating for *iShares Select Dividend ETF. The fund currently has a performance rating of B+ (Good) based on an annualized return of 12.46% over the last three years and a total return of -1.20% year to date 2015. Factored into the performance evaluation is an expense ratio of 0.39% (very low).

The fund's risk rating is currently B (Good). It carries a beta of 0.77, meaning the fund's expected move will be 7.7% for every 10% move in the market. Volatility, as measured by both the semi-deviation and a drawdown factor, is considered low. As of December 31, 2015, *iShares Select Dividend ETF traded at a discount of .01% below its net asset value.

Diane Hsiung has been running the fund for 8 years and currently receives a manager quality ranking of 80 (0=worst, 99=best). If you desire only a moderate level of risk and strong performance, then this fund is an excellent option.

Data Date	Investment Rating	Net Assets ($Mil)	Price	Performance Rating/Pts	Total Return Y-T-D	Risk Rating/Pts
12-15	A	13,925.50	75.15	B+ / 8.3	-1.20%	B / 8.3
2014	A+	13,925.50	79.40	B / 7.9	16.46%	B+ / 9.0
2013	A	12,868.10	71.35	B / 8.0	23.56%	B+ / 9.0
2012	C+	10,371.70	57.24	C / 5.4	12.63%	B / 8.9
2011	C+	9,548.00	53.77	C+ / 5.8	11.92%	B- / 7.6
2010	C-	6,011.90	49.86	C- / 3.3	17.79%	C+ / 5.7

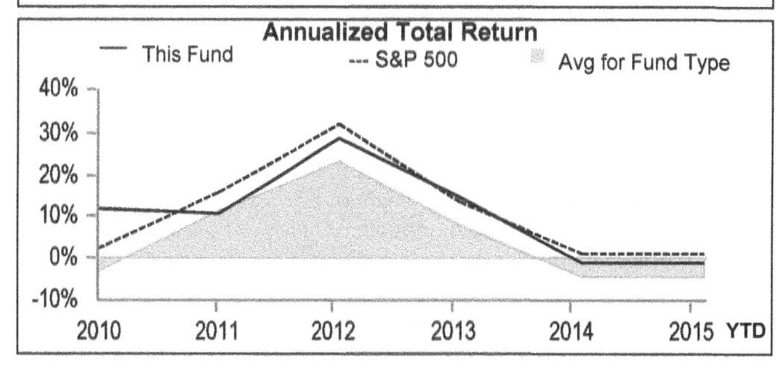

*iShares Sh-Term Natl AMT-Fr Muni (SUB) C+ Fair

Fund Family: BlackRock Fund Advisors
Fund Type: Municipal - National
Inception Date: November 5, 2008

Major Rating Factors: Middle of the road best describes *iShares Sh-Term Natl AMT-Fr Muni whose TheStreet.com Investment Rating is currently a C+ (Fair). The fund currently has a performance rating of C (Fair) based on an annualized return of 0.62% over the last three years and a total return of 0.65% year to date 2015. Factored into the performance evaluation is an expense ratio of 0.25% (very low).

The fund's risk rating is currently B (Good). It carries a beta of 0.14, meaning the fund's expected move will be 1.4% for every 10% move in the market. Volatility, as measured by both the semi-deviation and a drawdown factor, is considered low. As of December 31, 2015, *iShares Sh-Term Natl AMT-Fr Muni traded at a premium of .26% above its net asset value, which is worse than its one-year historical average discount of .01%.

Scott F. Radell has been running the fund for 6 years and currently receives a manager quality ranking of 69 (0=worst, 99=best). If you desire an average level of risk, then this fund may be an option.

Data Date	Investment Rating	Net Assets ($Mil)	Price	Performance Rating/Pts	Total Return Y-T-D	Risk Rating/Pts
12-15	C+	907.80	105.95	C / 4.9	0.65%	B / 8.1
2014	C-	907.80	105.92	C- / 3.0	0.41%	B / 8.1
2013	C+	800.30	106.22	C- / 3.6	0.71%	B+ / 9.9
2012	C-	621.00	106.23	D / 1.8	0.04%	B+ / 9.9
2011	C	472.60	106.73	D+ / 2.9	4.19%	B+ / 9.9
2010	C	449.90	104.10	D / 2.0	0.36%	B / 8.9

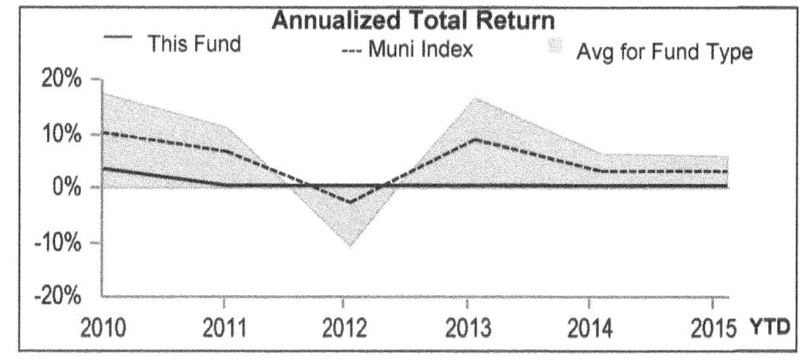

*iShares Short Maturity Bond (NEAR) C Fair

Fund Family: BlackRock Fund Advisors
Fund Type: General - Investment Grade
Inception Date: September 25, 2013

Major Rating Factors: Middle of the road best describes *iShares Short Maturity Bond whose TheStreet.com Investment Rating is currently a C (Fair). The fund currently has a performance rating of C (Fair) based on an annualized return of 0.00% over the last three years and a total return of 0.84% year to date 2015. Factored into the performance evaluation is an expense ratio of 0.25% (very low).

The fund's risk rating is currently B (Good). It carries a beta of 0.00, meaning the fund's expected move will be 0.0% for every 10% move in the market. Volatility, as measured by both the semi-deviation and a drawdown factor, is considered low. As of December 31, 2015, *iShares Short Maturity Bond traded at a premium of .12% above its net asset value, which is worse than its one-year historical average premium of .04%.

Scott F. Radell has been running the fund for 3 years and currently receives a manager quality ranking of 75 (0=worst, 99=best). If you desire an average level of risk, then this fund may be an option.

Data Date	Investment Rating	Net Assets ($Mil)	Price	Perfor-mance Rating/Pts	Total Return Y-T-D	Risk Rating/Pts
12-15	C	361.10	50.02	C / 4.8	0.84%	B / 8.0
2014	C	361.10	50.02	D+ / 2.9	0.61%	B+ / 9.4

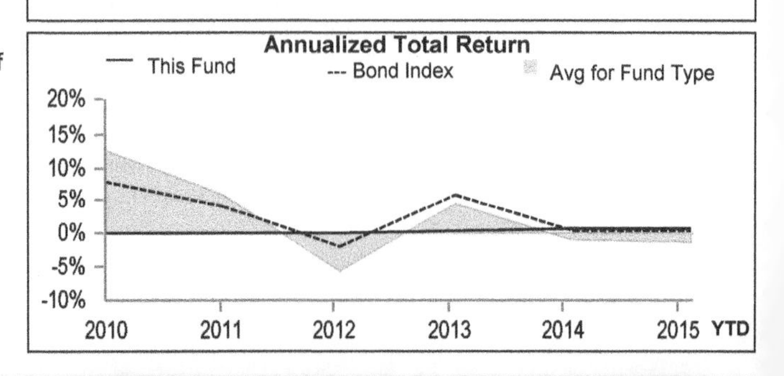

*iShares Short Treasury Bond ETF (SHV) C Fair

Fund Family: BlackRock Fund Advisors
Fund Type: US Government/Agency
Inception Date: January 5, 2007

Major Rating Factors: Middle of the road best describes *iShares Short Treasury Bond ETF whose TheStreet.com Investment Rating is currently a C (Fair). The fund currently has a performance rating of C (Fair) based on an annualized return of 0.01% over the last three years and a total return of 0.03% year to date 2015. Factored into the performance evaluation is an expense ratio of 0.08% (very low).

The fund's risk rating is currently B (Good). It carries a beta of 0.00, meaning the fund's expected move will be 0.0% for every 10% move in the market. Volatility, as measured by both the semi-deviation and a drawdown factor, is considered low. As of December 31, 2015, *iShares Short Treasury Bond ETF traded at a premium of .03% above its net asset value, which is worse than its one-year historical average premium of .02%.

Scott F. Radell has been running the fund for 6 years and currently receives a manager quality ranking of 67 (0=worst, 99=best). If you desire an average level of risk, then this fund may be an option.

Data Date	Investment Rating	Net Assets ($Mil)	Price	Perfor-mance Rating/Pts	Total Return Y-T-D	Risk Rating/Pts
12-15	C	2,348.60	110.22	C / 4.3	0.03%	B / 8.2
2014	C-	2,348.60	110.25	D+ / 2.8	0.00%	B+ / 9.0
2012	C-	2,579.10	110.26	D- / 1.3	0.02%	B+ / 9.9
2011	C-	2,589.70	110.23	D / 2.0	0.06%	B+ / 9.9
2010	C+	4,000.20	110.24	D+ / 2.5	0.12%	B+ / 9.1

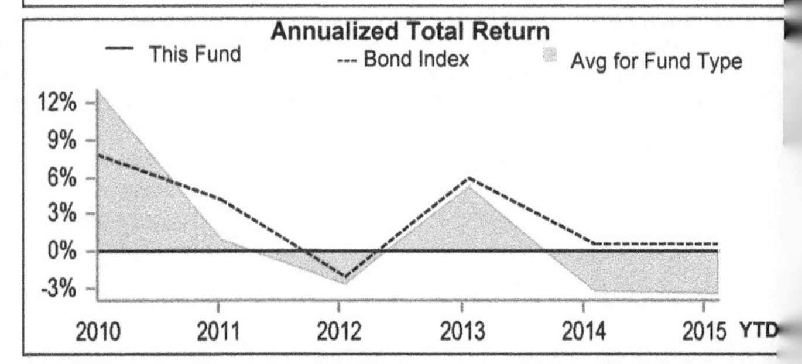

*iShares Silver Trust (SLV) E+ Very Weak

Fund Family: BlackRock Fund Advisors
Fund Type: Precious Metals
Inception Date: April 28, 2006

Major Rating Factors: *iShares Silver Trust has adopted a risky asset allocation strategy and currently receives an overall TheStreet.com Investment Rating of E+ (Very Weak). The fund has an above average level of volatility, as measured by both semi-deviation and drawdown factors. It carries a beta of 1.17, meaning it is expected to move 11.7% for every 10% move in the market. As of December 31, 2015, *iShares Silver Trust traded at a premium of .15% above its net asset value, which is better than its one-year historical average premium of .33%. Unfortunately, the high level of risk (D+, Weak) failed to pay off as investors endured very poor performance.

The fund's performance rating is currently E+ (Very Weak). It has registered an annualized return of -23.31% over the last three years and is down -12.71% year to date 2015. Factored into the performance evaluation is an expense ratio of 0.50% (very low).

This fund has been team managed for 10 years and currently receives a manager quality ranking of 18 (0=worst, 99=best). If you can tolerate high levels of risk in the hope of improved future returns, holding this fund may be an option.

Data Date	Investment Rating	Net Assets ($Mil)	Price	Perfor-mance Rating/Pts	Total Return Y-T-D	Risk Rating/Pts
12-15	E+	5,987.40	13.19	E+ / 0.8	-12.71%	D+ / 2.7
2014	E	5,987.40	15.06	E+ / 0.7	-22.45%	D / 2.0
2013	E	6,240.70	18.71	E+ / 0.8	-33.58%	C- / 3.2
2012	C-	9,706.70	29.37	C+ / 6.3	2.29%	C / 4.9
2011	C+	8,699.00	26.94	B+ / 8.5	-0.68%	C / 5.2
2010	C	10,750.90	30.18	A+ / 9.7	82.47%	D- / 1.0

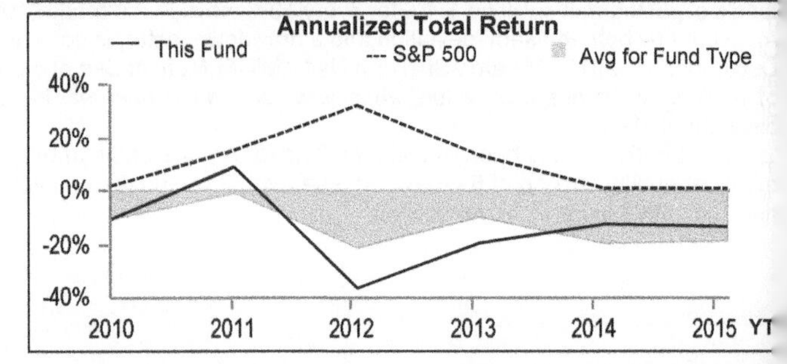

*iShares TIPS Bond ETF (TIP) — C — Fair

Fund Family: BlackRock Fund Advisors
Fund Type: US Government/Agency
Inception Date: December 4, 2003

Major Rating Factors: Middle of the road best describes *iShares TIPS Bond ETF whose TheStreet.com Investment Rating is currently a C (Fair). The fund currently has a performance rating of C- (Fair) based on an annualized return of -2.08% over the last three years and a total return of -2.38% year to date 2015. Factored into the performance evaluation is an expense ratio of 0.20% (very low).

The fund's risk rating is currently B+ (Good). It carries a beta of 0.37, meaning the fund's expected move will be 3.7% for every 10% move in the market. Volatility, as measured by both the semi-deviation and a drawdown factor, is considered very low. As of December 31, 2015, *iShares TIPS Bond ETF traded at a discount of .08% below its net asset value, which is better than its one-year historical average premium of .07%.

Scott F. Radell has been running the fund for 6 years and currently receives a manager quality ranking of 41 (0=worst, 99=best). If you desire an average level of risk, then this fund may be an option.

Data Date	Investment Rating	Net Assets ($Mil)	Price	Performance Rating/Pts	Total Return Y-T-D	Risk Rating/Pts
12-15	C	12,439.00	109.68	C- / 3.5	-2.38%	B+ / 9.0
2014	C-	12,439.00	112.01	D+ / 2.9	3.31%	B / 8.9
2013	C-	12,573.40	109.90	C- / 3.1	-7.50%	B+ / 9.1
2012	C	22,284.70	121.41	C- / 3.1	5.46%	B+ / 9.7
2011	C+	22,164.20	116.69	C / 4.4	13.87%	B+ / 9.7
2010	B-	19,351.30	107.52	C / 4.5	6.14%	B / 8.3

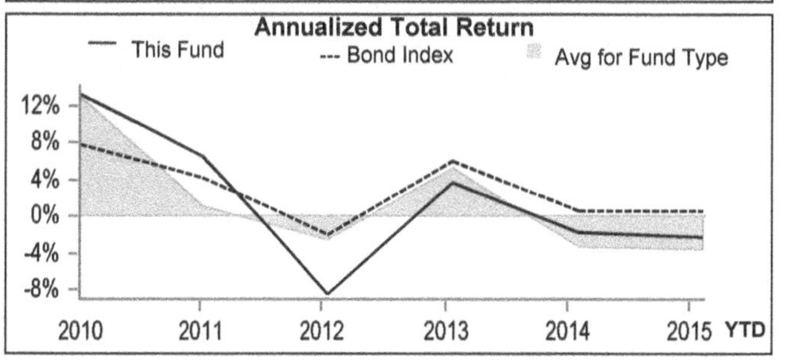

*iShares Transportation Average E (IYT) — B — Good

Fund Family: BlackRock Fund Advisors
Fund Type: Income
Inception Date: October 6, 2003

Major Rating Factors: Strong performance is the major factor driving the B (Good) TheStreet.com Investment Rating for *iShares Transportation Average E. The fund currently has a performance rating of B- (Good) based on an annualized return of 12.20% over the last three years and a total return of -16.24% year to date 2015. Factored into the performance evaluation is an expense ratio of 0.43% (very low).

The fund's risk rating is currently B- (Good). It carries a beta of 1.01, meaning that its performance tracks fairly well with that of the overall stock market. Volatility, as measured by both the semi-deviation and a drawdown factor, is considered low. As of December 31, 2015, *iShares Transportation Average E traded at a discount of .01% below its net asset value, which is in line with its one-year historical average discount of .01%.

Diane Hsiung has been running the fund for 8 years and currently receives a manager quality ranking of 57 (0=worst, 99=best). If you desire only a moderate level of risk and strong performance, then this fund is an excellent option.

Data Date	Investment Rating	Net Assets ($Mil)	Price	Performance Rating/Pts	Total Return Y-T-D	Risk Rating/Pts
12-15	B	1,471.20	134.73	B- / 7.1	-16.24%	B- / 7.5
2014	A	1,471.20	164.07	A / 9.3	26.30%	B- / 7.4
2013	B+	745.30	131.90	B+ / 8.3	34.13%	B- / 7.7
2012	C	594.40	94.35	C / 4.7	8.99%	B- / 7.6
2011	C	411.70	89.47	C / 5.0	-1.94%	B- / 7.2
2010	B+	673.20	92.32	B / 8.0	26.74%	C / 5.5

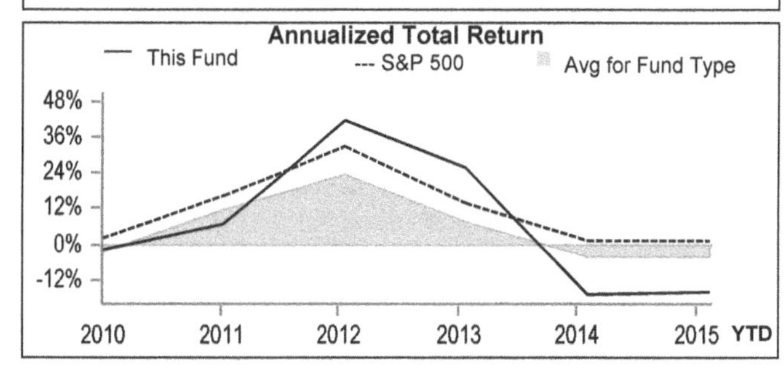

*iShares Treasury Floatg Rate Bd (TFLO) — C+ — Fair

Fund Family: BlackRock Fund Advisors
Fund Type: Loan Participation
Inception Date: February 3, 2014

Major Rating Factors: Middle of the road best describes *iShares Treasury Floatg Rate Bd whose TheStreet.com Investment Rating is currently a C+ (Fair). The fund currently has a performance rating of C (Fair) based on an annualized return of 0.00% over the last three years and a total return of 0.69% year to date 2015.

The fund's risk rating is currently B (Good). It carries a beta of 0.00, meaning the fund's expected move will be 0.0% for every 10% move in the market. Volatility, as measured by both the semi-deviation and a drawdown factor, is considered low. As of December 31, 2015, *iShares Treasury Floatg Rate Bd traded at a premium of .56% above its net asset value, which is worse than its one-year historical average premium of .05%.

James J. Mauro has been running the fund for 2 years and currently receives a manager quality ranking of 68 (0=worst, 99=best). If you desire an average level of risk, then this fund may be an option.

Data Date	Investment Rating	Net Assets ($Mil)	Price	Performance Rating/Pts	Total Return Y-T-D	Risk Rating/Pts
12-15	C+	10.00	50.34	C / 4.8	0.69%	B / 8.1

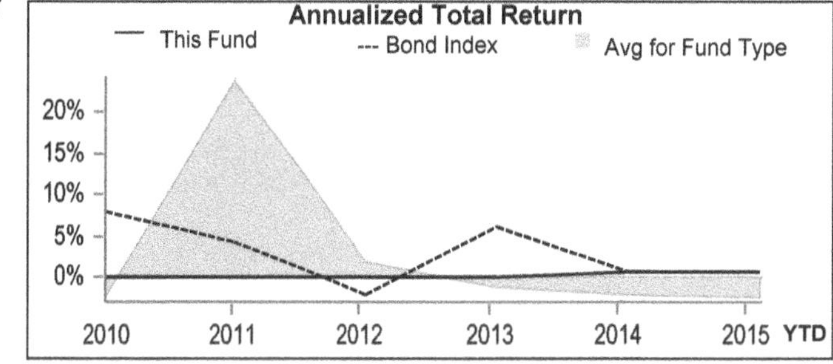

*iShares Ultra Short-Term Bond (ICSH) B- Good

Fund Family: BlackRock Fund Advisors
Fund Type: Corporate - Investment Grade
Inception Date: December 11, 2013

Data Date	Investment Rating	Net Assets ($Mil)	Price	Performance Rating/Pts	Total Return Y-T-D	Risk Rating/Pts
12-15	B-	20.00	49.73	C / 4.3	0.26%	B+ / 9.8
2014	D	20.00	49.89	D+ / 2.7	-0.04%	C / 5.4

Major Rating Factors: *iShares Ultra Short-Term Bond receives a TheStreet.com Investment Rating of B- (Good). The fund currently has a performance rating of C (Fair) based on an annualized return of 0.00% over the last three years and a total return of 0.26% year to date 2015. Factored into the performance evaluation is an expense ratio of 0.18% (very low).

The fund's risk rating is currently B+ (Good). It carries a beta of 0.00, meaning the fund's expected move will be 0.0% for every 10% move in the market. Volatility, as measured by both the semi-deviation and a drawdown factor, is considered very low. As of December 31, 2015, *iShares Ultra Short-Term Bond traded at a discount of .14% below its net asset value, which is better than its one-year historical average discount of .04%.

Richard Mejzak currently receives a manager quality ranking of 70 (0=worst, 99=best). If you desire an average level of risk, then this fund may be an option.

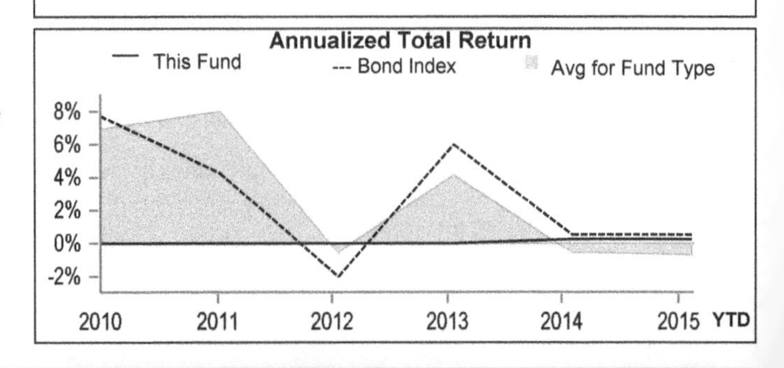

*iShares US Aerospace & Def ETF (ITA) A- Excellent

Fund Family: BlackRock Fund Advisors
Fund Type: Income
Inception Date: May 1, 2006

Data Date	Investment Rating	Net Assets ($Mil)	Price	Performance Rating/Pts	Total Return Y-T-D	Risk Rating/Pts
12-15	A-	338.60	118.22	A / 9.5	4.54%	B- / 7.0
2014	A-	338.60	114.69	A- / 9.2	10.63%	B- / 7.1
2013	A+	296.20	105.68	A / 9.4	50.80%	B / 8.1
2012	C	78.50	68.25	C / 5.1	12.55%	B- / 7.9
2011	C	106.90	61.19	C / 5.2	2.66%	B- / 7.5
2010	D+	147.10	58.85	C- / 3.4	16.60%	C / 5.5

Major Rating Factors:
Exceptional performance is the major factor driving the A- (Excellent) TheStreet.com Investment Rating for *iShares US Aerospace & Def ETF. The fund currently has a performance rating of A (Excellent) based on an annualized return of 20.29% over the last three years and a total return of 4.54% year to date 2015. Factored into the performance evaluation is an expense ratio of 0.43% (very low).

The fund's risk rating is currently B- (Good). It carries a beta of 0.92, meaning that its performance tracks fairly well with that of the overall stock market. Volatility, as measured by both the semi-deviation and a drawdown factor, is considered low. As of December 31, 2015, *iShares US Aerospace & Def ETF traded at a premium of .05% above its net asset value, which is worse than its one-year historical average premium of .01%.

Diane Hsiung has been running the fund for 8 years and currently receives a manager quality ranking of 92 (0=worst, 99=best). If you desire only a moderate level of risk and strong performance, then this fund is an excellent option.

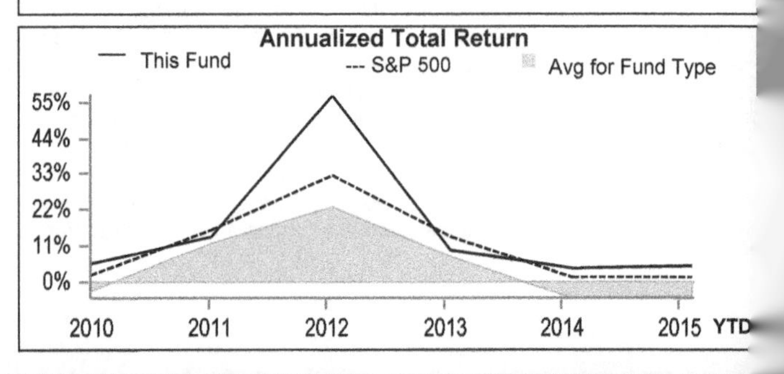

*iShares US Basic Material ETF (IYM) C- Fair

Fund Family: BlackRock Fund Advisors
Fund Type: Income
Inception Date: June 12, 2000

Data Date	Investment Rating	Net Assets ($Mil)	Price	Performance Rating/Pts	Total Return Y-T-D	Risk Rating/Pts
12-15	C-	920.60	70.53	C- / 4.1	-12.27%	C+ / 6.7
2014	C+	920.60	82.47	C / 5.1	3.86%	B / 8.3
2013	C-	830.90	81.43	C / 5.4	15.24%	C+ / 6.8
2012	D+	533.80	69.31	C- / 3.2	5.88%	C+ / 6.9
2011	C+	530.50	64.30	C+ / 6.4	-11.86%	C+ / 6.9
2010	C+	1,114.50	77.46	B- / 7.5	31.02%	C / 4.7

Major Rating Factors: Middle of the road best describes *iShares US Basic Material ETF whose TheStreet.com Investment Rating is currently a C- (Fair). The fund currently has a performance rating of C- (Fair) based on an annualized return of 1.67% over the last three years and a total return of -12.27% year to date 2015. Factored into the performance evaluation is an expense ratio of 0.43% (very low).

The fund's risk rating is currently C+ (Fair). It carries a beta of 1.23, meaning it is expected to move 12.3% for every 10% move in the market. Volatility, as measured by both the semi-deviation and a drawdown factor, is considered low. As of December 31, 2015, *iShares US Basic Material ETF traded at a price exactly equal to its net asset value, which is worse than its one-year historical average discount of .01%.

Diane Hsiung has been running the fund for 8 years and currently receives a manager quality ranking of 12 (0=worst, 99=best). If you desire an average level of risk, then this fund may be an option.

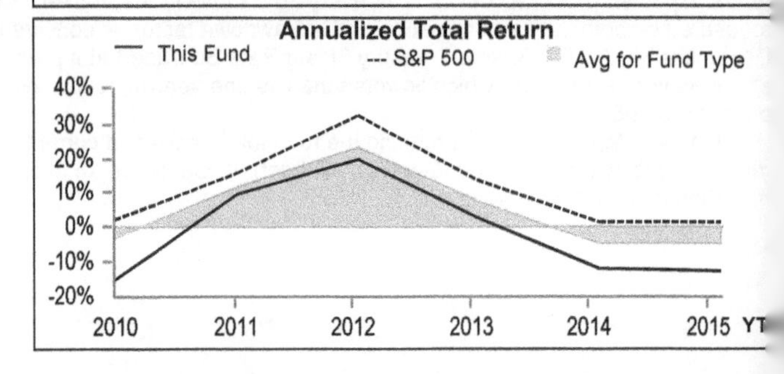

*iShares US Broker-Dealers ETF (IAI) A- Excellent

Fund Family: BlackRock Fund Advisors
Fund Type: Financial Services
Inception Date: May 1, 2006

Major Rating Factors:
Exceptional performance is the major factor driving the A- (Excellent) TheStreet.com Investment Rating for *iShares US Broker-Dealers ETF. The fund currently has a performance rating of A (Excellent) based on an annualized return of 20.43% over the last three years and a total return of -0.37% year to date 2015. Factored into the performance evaluation is an expense ratio of 0.43% (very low).

The fund's risk rating is currently B- (Good). It carries a beta of 1.23, meaning it is expected to move 12.3% for every 10% move in the market. Volatility, as measured by both the semi-deviation and a drawdown factor, is considered low. As of December 31, 2015, *iShares US Broker-Dealers ETF traded at a premium of .34% above its net asset value.

Diane Hsiung has been running the fund for 8 years and currently receives a manager quality ranking of 83 (0=worst, 99=best). If you desire only a moderate level of risk and strong performance, then this fund is an excellent option.

Data Date	Investment Rating	Net Assets ($Mil)	Price	Performance Rating/Pts	Total Return Y-T-D	Risk Rating/Pts
12-15	A-	239.40	41.52	A / 9.4	-0.37%	B- / 7.0
2014	A-	239.40	42.65	A / 9.5	11.46%	C+ / 6.6
2013	B+	224.00	38.64	A- / 9.1	57.95%	C+ / 6.8
2012	D	44.90	23.63	D / 2.0	17.23%	C+ / 6.7
2011	D	52.20	20.92	D / 1.9	-26.39%	C+ / 6.9
2010	D-	100.10	29.02	E+ / 0.8	4.89%	C / 4.7

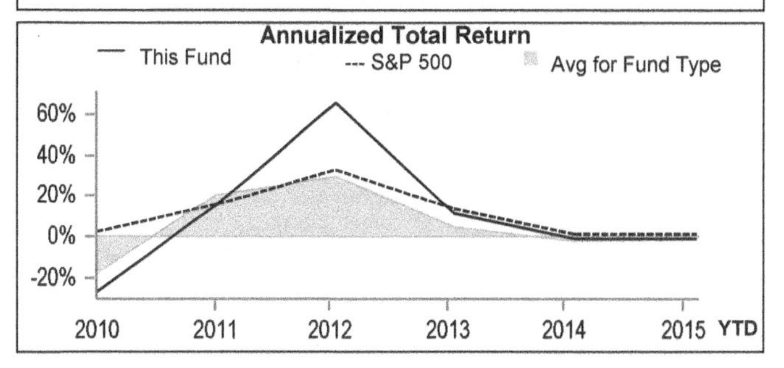

*iShares US Consumer Goods ETF (IYK) A Excellent

Fund Family: BlackRock Fund Advisors
Fund Type: Income
Inception Date: June 12, 2000

Major Rating Factors:
Exceptional performance is the major factor driving the A (Excellent) TheStreet.com Investment Rating for *iShares US Consumer Goods ETF. The fund currently has a performance rating of A- (Excellent) based on an annualized return of 14.50% over the last three years and a total return of 7.05% year to date 2015. Factored into the performance evaluation is an expense ratio of 0.43% (very low).

The fund's risk rating is currently B- (Good). It carries a beta of 0.92, meaning that its performance tracks fairly well with that of the overall stock market. Volatility, as measured by both the semi-deviation and a drawdown factor, is considered low. As of December 31, 2015, *iShares US Consumer Goods ETF traded at a premium of .12% above its net asset value.

Diane Hsiung has been running the fund for 8 years and currently receives a manager quality ranking of 79 (0=worst, 99=best). If you desire only a moderate level of risk and strong performance, then this fund is an excellent option.

Data Date	Investment Rating	Net Assets ($Mil)	Price	Performance Rating/Pts	Total Return Y-T-D	Risk Rating/Pts
12-15	A	473.70	108.43	A- / 9.0	7.05%	B- / 7.6
2014	B	473.70	104.76	B / 7.6	13.04%	B- / 7.6
2013	A	483.10	95.72	B / 7.9	24.77%	B+ / 9.0
2012	B-	394.30	74.99	C+ / 6.0	15.43%	B / 8.8
2011	B-	359.20	68.48	C+ / 6.1	8.96%	B / 8.5
2010	C+	306.70	64.55	C+ / 6.4	18.99%	C+ / 6.8

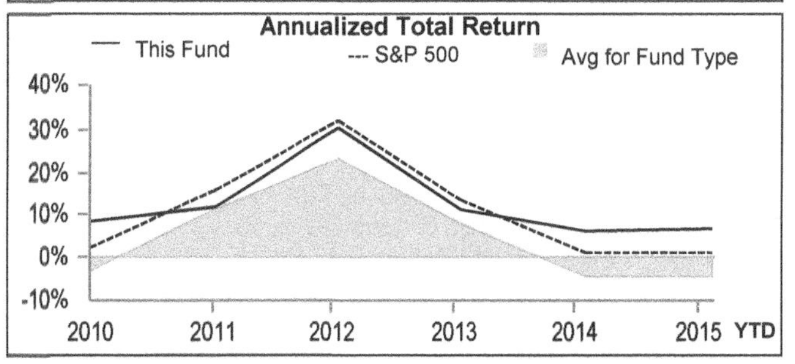

*iShares US Consumer Services ETF (IYC) A+ Excellent

Fund Family: BlackRock Fund Advisors
Fund Type: Income
Inception Date: June 12, 2000

Major Rating Factors:
Exceptional performance is the major factor driving the A+ (Excellent) TheStreet.com Investment Rating for *iShares US Consumer Services ETF. The fund currently has a performance rating of A (Excellent) based on an annualized return of 18.65% over the last three years and a total return of 7.18% year to date 2015. Factored into the performance evaluation is an expense ratio of 0.43% (very low).

The fund's risk rating is currently B- (Good). It carries a beta of 1.07, meaning that its performance tracks fairly well with that of the overall stock market. Volatility, as measured by both the semi-deviation and a drawdown factor, is considered low. As of December 31, 2015, *iShares US Consumer Services ETF traded at a discount of .02% below its net asset value, which is better than its one-year historical average premium of .01%.

Diane Hsiung has been running the fund for 8 years and currently receives a manager quality ranking of 85 (0=worst, 99=best). If you desire only a moderate level of risk and strong performance, then this fund is an excellent option.

Data Date	Investment Rating	Net Assets ($Mil)	Price	Performance Rating/Pts	Total Return Y-T-D	Risk Rating/Pts
12-15	A+	504.00	144.65	A / 9.4	7.18%	B- / 7.7
2014	A	504.00	137.76	A / 9.4	14.75%	B- / 7.1
2013	A+	523.60	121.39	A- / 9.2	36.84%	B / 8.1
2012	B+	334.30	86.80	B / 8.1	24.62%	B / 8.1
2011	B-	260.40	71.41	B- / 7.1	7.75%	B / 8.1
2010	B+	209.60	67.66	B- / 7.4	23.26%	C+ / 6.1

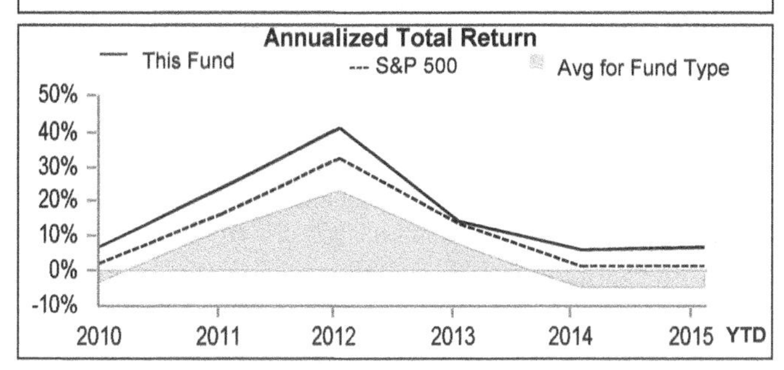

*iShares US Energy ETF (IYE) D Weak

Fund Family: BlackRock Fund Advisors
Fund Type: Energy/Natural Resources
Inception Date: June 12, 2000

Data Date	Investment Rating	Net Assets ($Mil)	Price	Performance Rating/Pts	Total Return Y-T-D	Risk Rating/Pts
12-15	D	1,190.70	33.86	D+ / 2.3	-21.92%	C / 5.3
2014	C-	1,190.70	44.81	C- / 3.0	-8.15%	B- / 7.8
2013	C+	1,653.90	50.49	C+ / 6.9	19.51%	B- / 7.6
2012	C-	817.00	40.84	C- / 3.6	7.75%	B- / 7.4
2011	C	945.90	39.83	C / 5.0	5.13%	B- / 7.2
2010	D	806.00	38.96	C / 4.3	19.00%	D+ / 2.8

Major Rating Factors:
Disappointing performance is the major factor driving the D (Weak) TheStreet.com Investment Rating for *iShares US Energy ETF. The fund currently has a performance rating of D+ (Weak) based on an annualized return of -4.86% over the last three years and a total return of -21.92% year to date 2015. Factored into the performance evaluation is an expense ratio of 0.43% (very low).

The fund's risk rating is currently C (Fair). It carries a beta of 0.99, meaning that its performance tracks fairly well with that of the overall stock market. Volatility, as measured by both the semi-deviation and a drawdown factor, is considered average. As of December 31, 2015, *iShares US Energy ETF traded at a premium of .03% above its net asset value, which is worse than its one-year historical average discount of .01%.

Diane Hsiung has been running the fund for 8 years and currently receives a manager quality ranking of 67 (0=worst, 99=best). This fund offers an average level of risk but investors looking for strong performance will be frustrated.

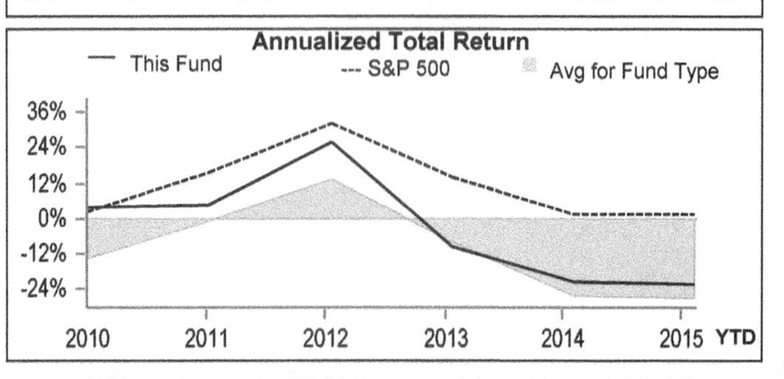

*iShares US Financial Services ET (IYG) A Excellent

Fund Family: BlackRock Fund Advisors
Fund Type: Financial Services
Inception Date: June 12, 2000

Data Date	Investment Rating	Net Assets ($Mil)	Price	Performance Rating/Pts	Total Return Y-T-D	Risk Rating/Pts
12-15	A	571.80	89.98	B+ / 8.8	-0.15%	B- / 7.9
2014	A-	571.80	91.83	A / 9.4	10.49%	C+ / 6.9
2013	B	603.00	83.74	B+ / 8.6	37.14%	B- / 7.2
2012	C	353.00	59.31	C / 5.1	29.73%	B- / 7.0
2011	D	172.10	45.27	D / 2.2	-19.00%	C+ / 6.8
2010	D-	221.50	57.57	E+ / 0.8	7.71%	C / 4.3

Major Rating Factors:
Strong performance is the major factor driving the A (Excellent) TheStreet.com Investment Rating for *iShares US Financial Services ET. The fund currently has a performance rating of B+ (Good) based on an annualized return of 14.75% over the last three years and a total return of -0.15% year to date 2015. Factored into the performance evaluation is an expense ratio of 0.43% (very low).

The fund's risk rating is currently B- (Good). It carries a beta of 1.19, meaning it is expected to move 11.9% for every 10% move in the market. Volatility, as measured by both the semi-deviation and a drawdown factor, is considered low. As of December 31, 2015, *iShares US Financial Services ET traded at a premium of .01% above its net asset value, which is better than its one-year historical average premium of .02%.

Diane Hsiung has been running the fund for 8 years and currently receives a manager quality ranking of 52 (0=worst, 99=best). If you desire only a moderate level of risk and strong performance, then this fund is an excellent option.

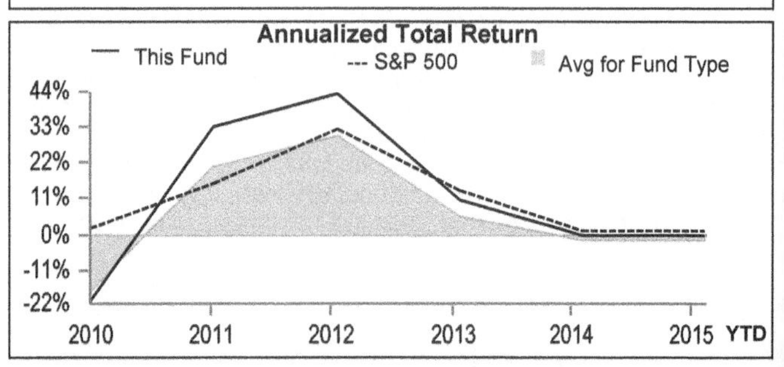

*iShares US Financials ETF (IYF) A+ Excellent

Fund Family: BlackRock Fund Advisors
Fund Type: Financial Services
Inception Date: May 22, 2000

Data Date	Investment Rating	Net Assets ($Mil)	Price	Performance Rating/Pts	Total Return Y-T-D	Risk Rating/Pts
12-15	A+	1,293.20	88.38	B+ / 8.6	0.05%	B / 8.7
2014	A+	1,293.20	90.20	A- / 9.1	14.20%	B / 8.7
2013	B	1,358.90	80.16	B / 7.7	28.39%	B- / 7.6
2012	C	614.90	60.70	C / 5.3	25.29%	B- / 7.4
2011	D+	380.20	49.05	C- / 3.1	-12.26%	C+ / 6.9
2010	D-	476.70	57.48	D- / 1.0	12.23%	C / 4.5

Major Rating Factors:
Strong performance is the major factor driving the A+ (Excellent) TheStreet.com Investment Rating for *iShares US Financials ETF. The fund currently has a performance rating of B+ (Good) based on an annualized return of 13.68% over the last three years and a total return of 0.05% year to date 2015. Factored into the performance evaluation is an expense ratio of 0.43% (very low).

The fund's risk rating is currently B (Good). It carries a beta of 1.01, meaning that its performance tracks fairly well with that of the overall stock market. Volatility, as measured by both the semi-deviation and a drawdown factor, is considered low. As of December 31, 2015, *iShares US Financials ETF traded at a discount of .03% below its net asset value.

Diane Hsiung has been running the fund for 8 years and currently receives a manager quality ranking of 65 (0=worst, 99=best). If you desire only a moderate level of risk and strong performance, then this fund is an excellent option.

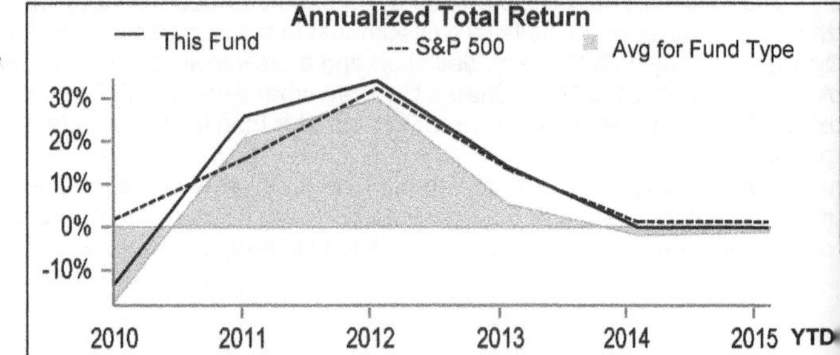

*iShares US Healthcare ETF (IYH) A+ Excellent

Fund Family: BlackRock Fund Advisors
Fund Type: Health
Inception Date: June 12, 2000

Data Date	Investment Rating	Net Assets ($Mil)	Price	Performance Rating/Pts	Total Return Y-T-D	Risk Rating/Pts
12-15	A+	2,658.20	150.01	A+ / 9.6	6.08%	B / 8.1
2014	A+	2,658.20	144.13	A / 9.5	25.54%	B / 8.6
2013	A+	1,928.70	116.49	A- / 9.1	37.31%	B / 8.2
2012	C+	705.70	83.51	C+ / 5.7	21.45%	B / 8.3
2011	C+	575.90	71.57	C / 5.0	10.67%	B / 8.2
2010	C-	552.10	65.37	D+ / 2.9	4.13%	B- / 7.0

Major Rating Factors:
Exceptional performance is the major factor driving the A+ (Excellent) TheStreet.com Investment Rating for *iShares US Healthcare ETF. The fund currently has a performance rating of A+ (Excellent) based on an annualized return of 22.48% over the last three years and a total return of 6.08% year to date 2015. Factored into the performance evaluation is an expense ratio of 0.43% (very low).

The fund's risk rating is currently B (Good). It carries a beta of 0.95, meaning that its performance tracks fairly well with that of the overall stock market. Volatility, as measured by both the semi-deviation and a drawdown factor, is considered low. As of December 31, 2015, *iShares US Healthcare ETF traded at a discount of .04% below its net asset value, which is better than its one-year historical average premium of .01%.

Diane Hsiung has been running the fund for 8 years and currently receives a manager quality ranking of 93 (0=worst, 99=best). If you desire only a moderate level of risk and strong performance, then this fund is an excellent option.

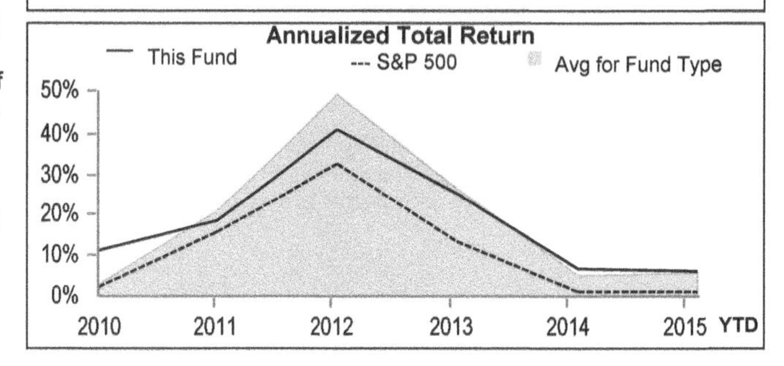

*iShares US Healthcare Providers (IHF) A+ Excellent

Fund Family: BlackRock Fund Advisors
Fund Type: Health
Inception Date: May 1, 2006

Data Date	Investment Rating	Net Assets ($Mil)	Price	Performance Rating/Pts	Total Return Y-T-D	Risk Rating/Pts
12-15	A+	614.20	124.35	A / 9.5	5.55%	B / 8.2
2014	A	614.20	118.37	A / 9.5	27.23%	B- / 7.2
2013	A	386.90	93.25	B+ / 8.8	36.02%	B / 8.0
2012	C	225.60	68.45	C / 4.8	15.86%	B- / 7.9
2011	B-	217.70	58.85	C+ / 6.9	9.57%	B- / 7.8
2010	D	110.40	53.87	D / 2.2	11.47%	C+ / 5.7

Major Rating Factors:
Exceptional performance is the major factor driving the A+ (Excellent) TheStreet.com Investment Rating for *iShares US Healthcare Providers. The fund currently has a performance rating of A (Excellent) based on an annualized return of 22.17% over the last three years and a total return of 5.55% year to date 2015. Factored into the performance evaluation is an expense ratio of 0.43% (very low).

The fund's risk rating is currently B (Good). It carries a beta of 0.64, meaning the fund's expected move will be 6.4% for every 10% move in the market. Volatility, as measured by both the semi-deviation and a drawdown factor, is considered low. As of December 31, 2015, *iShares US Healthcare Providers traded at a discount of .02% below its net asset value, which is better than its one-year historical average premium of .01%.

Diane Hsiung has been running the fund for 8 years and currently receives a manager quality ranking of 96 (0=worst, 99=best). If you desire only a moderate level of risk and strong performance, then this fund is an excellent option.

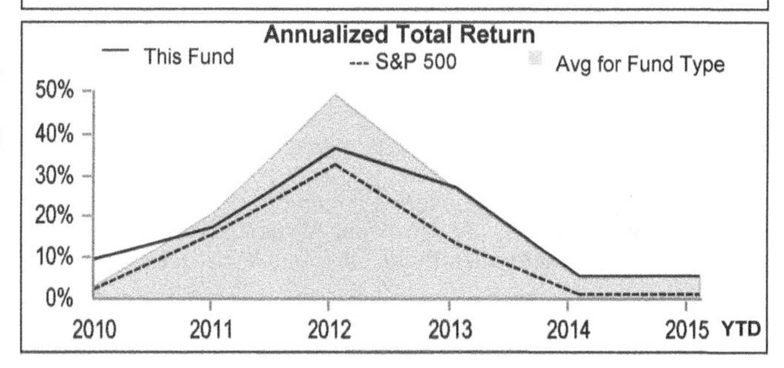

*iShares US Home Construction ETF (ITB) B Good

Fund Family: BlackRock Fund Advisors
Fund Type: Income
Inception Date: May 1, 2006

Data Date	Investment Rating	Net Assets ($Mil)	Price	Performance Rating/Pts	Total Return Y-T-D	Risk Rating/Pts
12-15	B	1,445.70	27.10	B- / 7.1	6.04%	B- / 7.9
2014	B+	1,445.70	25.88	A / 9.4	5.58%	C+ / 6.6
2013	B	1,723.20	24.82	B+ / 8.8	12.38%	B- / 7.1
2012	B+	1,627.60	21.16	A+ / 9.7	69.50%	C+ / 6.4
2011	D+	374.60	11.88	C- / 3.6	-8.89%	C+ / 6.4
2010	D	505.20	13.18	D+ / 2.4	10.43%	C / 4.5

Major Rating Factors: Strong performance is the major factor driving the B (Good) TheStreet.com Investment Rating for *iShares US Home Construction ETF. The fund currently has a performance rating of B- (Good) based on an annualized return of 7.66% over the last three years and a total return of 6.04% year to date 2015. Factored into the performance evaluation is an expense ratio of 0.43% (very low).

The fund's risk rating is currently B- (Good). It carries a beta of 1.15, meaning it is expected to move 11.5% for every 10% move in the market. Volatility, as measured by both the semi-deviation and a drawdown factor, is considered low. As of December 31, 2015, *iShares US Home Construction ETF traded at a discount of .07% below its net asset value, which is better than its one-year historical average discount of .01%.

Diane Hsiung has been running the fund for 8 years and currently receives a manager quality ranking of 21 (0=worst, 99=best). If you desire only a moderate level of risk and strong performance, then this fund is an excellent option.

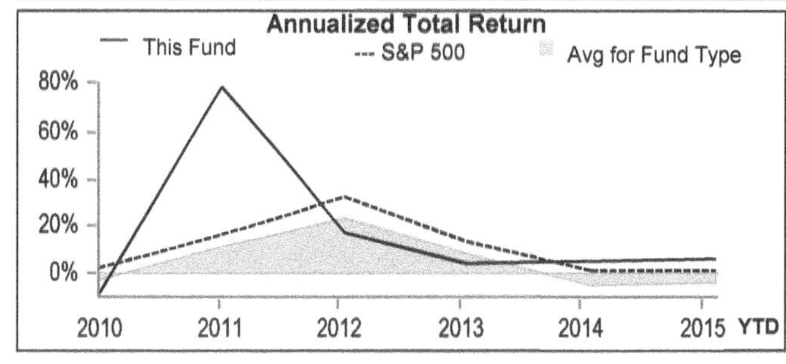

* Denotes ETF Fund

*iShares US Industrials ETF (IYJ) B+ Good

Fund Family: BlackRock Fund Advisors
Fund Type: Income
Inception Date: June 12, 2000

Data Date	Investment Rating	Net Assets ($Mil)	Price	Performance Rating/Pts	Total Return Y-T-D	Risk Rating/Pts
12-15	B+	1,748.70	102.92	B+ / 8.3	-1.38%	B- / 7.3
2014	B	1,748.70	106.59	B / 8.0	8.11%	B- / 7.5
2013	A-	1,640.70	101.38	B+ / 8.8	34.00%	B- / 7.8
2012	C+	689.30	73.33	C+ / 6.4	15.34%	B- / 7.6
2011	C	343.20	63.62	C+ / 5.6	-0.19%	B- / 7.5
2010	C	369.30	65.40	C+ / 5.7	25.49%	C / 5.4

Major Rating Factors: Strong performance is the major factor driving the B+ (Good) TheStreet.com Investment Rating for *iShares US Industrials ETF. The fund currently has a performance rating of B+ (Good) based on an annualized return of 12.56% over the last three years and a total return of -1.38% year to date 2015. Factored into the performance evaluation is an expense ratio of 0.43% (very low).

The fund's risk rating is currently B- (Good). It carries a beta of 1.10, meaning it is expected to move 11.0% for every 10% move in the market. Volatility, as measured by both the semi-deviation and a drawdown factor, is considered low. As of December 31, 2015, *iShares US Industrials ETF traded at a premium of .10% above its net asset value.

Diane Hsiung has been running the fund for 8 years and currently receives a manager quality ranking of 46 (0=worst, 99=best). If you desire only a moderate level of risk and strong performance, then this fund is an excellent option.

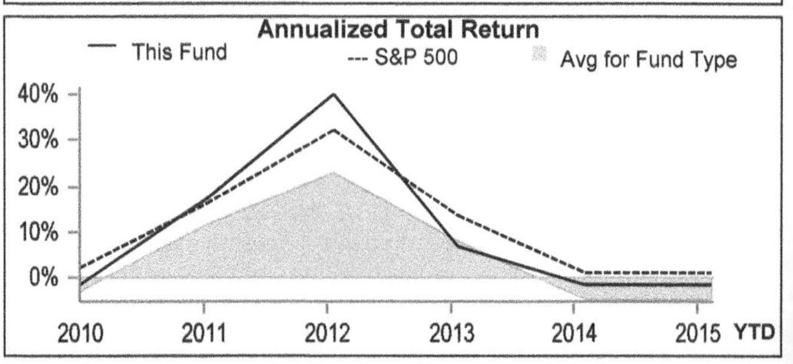

*iShares US Insurance ETF (IAK) A Excellent

Fund Family: BlackRock Fund Advisors
Fund Type: Income
Inception Date: May 1, 2006

Data Date	Investment Rating	Net Assets ($Mil)	Price	Performance Rating/Pts	Total Return Y-T-D	Risk Rating/Pts
12-15	A	122.50	51.15	A- / 9.1	4.82%	B- / 7.4
2014	A-	122.50	50.01	B+ / 8.7	8.82%	B- / 7.4
2013	A-	165.70	47.37	B+ / 8.6	37.55%	B / 8.0
2012	C	79.20	32.99	C / 5.4	19.08%	B- / 7.8
2011	C-	59.80	28.57	C- / 3.7	-6.96%	B- / 7.0
2010	D-	81.50	31.34	D- / 1.1	20.03%	C / 4.5

Major Rating Factors:
Exceptional performance is the major factor driving the A (Excellent) TheStreet.com Investment Rating for *iShares US Insurance ETF. The fund currently has a performance rating of A- (Excellent) based on an annualized return of 16.08% over the last three years and a total return of 4.82% year to date 2015. Factored into the performance evaluation is an expense ratio of 0.43% (very low).

The fund's risk rating is currently B- (Good). It carries a beta of 1.18, meaning it is expected to move 11.8% for every 10% move in the market. Volatility, as measured by both the semi-deviation and a drawdown factor, is considered low. As of December 31, 2015, *iShares US Insurance ETF traded at a premium of .10% above its net asset value, which is worse than its one-year historical average discount of .02%.

Diane Hsiung has been running the fund for 8 years and currently receives a manager quality ranking of 65 (0=worst, 99=best). If you desire only a moderate level of risk and strong performance, then this fund is an excellent option.

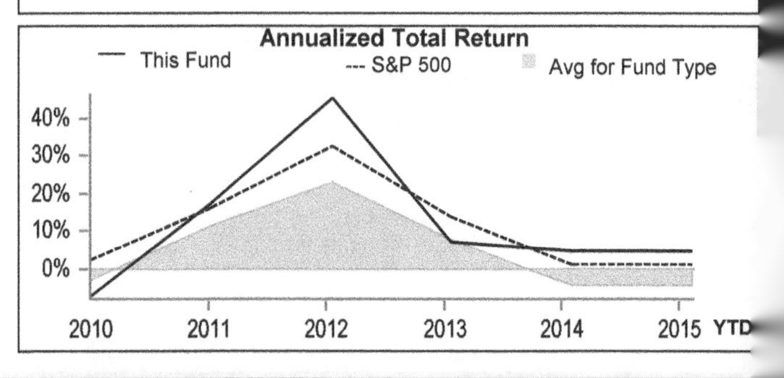

*iShares US Medical Devices ETF (IHI) A+ Excellent

Fund Family: BlackRock Fund Advisors
Fund Type: Health
Inception Date: May 1, 2006

Data Date	Investment Rating	Net Assets ($Mil)	Price	Performance Rating/Pts	Total Return Y-T-D	Risk Rating/Pts
12-15	A+	735.60	122.48	A+ / 9.6	10.75%	B- / 7.5
2014	A	735.60	113.11	A / 9.4	23.22%	B- / 7.2
2013	B+	459.70	92.81	B+ / 8.7	34.20%	B- / 7.6
2012	C-	274.00	67.60	C / 4.9	18.76%	B- / 7.0
2011	C	331.90	58.76	C / 5.3	1.63%	C+ / 6.9
2010	C-	338.80	58.91	C- / 3.7	11.35%	C+ / 5.6

Major Rating Factors:
Exceptional performance is the major factor driving the A+ (Excellent) TheStreet.com Investment Rating for *iShares US Medical Devices ETF. The fund currently has a performance rating of A+ (Excellent) based on an annualized return of 22.31% over the last three years and a total return of 10.75% year to date 2015. Factored into the performance evaluation is an expense ratio of 0.43% (very low).

The fund's risk rating is currently B- (Good). It carries a beta of 0.92, meaning that its performance tracks fairly well with that of the overall stock market. Volatility, as measured by both the semi-deviation and a drawdown factor, is considered low. As of December 31, 2015, *iShares US Medical Devices ETF traded at a premium of .01% above its net asset value, which is in line with its one-year historical average premium of .01%.

Diane Hsiung has been running the fund for 8 years and currently receives a manager quality ranking of 93 (0=worst, 99=best). If you desire only a moderate level of risk and strong performance, then this fund is an excellent option.

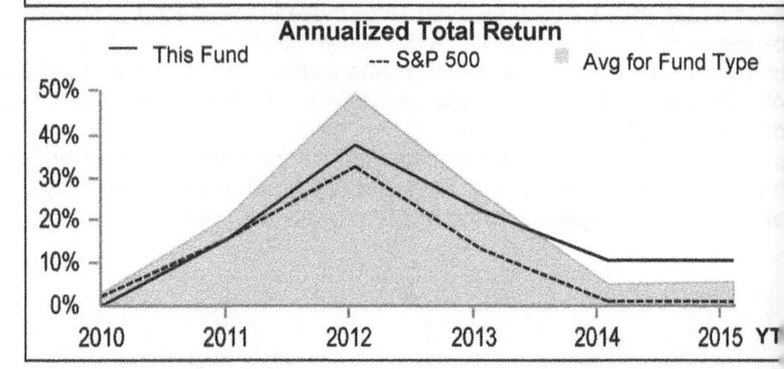

*iShares US Oil & Gas Exp & Pro E (IEO) D Weak

Fund Family: BlackRock Fund Advisors
Fund Type: Energy/Natural Resources
Inception Date: May 1, 2006

Data Date	Investment Rating	Net Assets ($Mil)	Price	Performance Rating/Pts	Total Return Y-T-D	Risk Rating/Pts
12-15	D	534.50	52.95	D / 2.0	-24.70%	C / 4.7
2014	D+	534.50	71.43	D+ / 2.7	-10.18%	B- / 7.2
2013	C+	431.90	82.32	C+ / 6.7	23.41%	C+ / 6.9
2012	D+	314.70	63.54	C- / 3.0	6.29%	C+ / 6.8
2011	C	343.80	61.42	C+ / 6.0	0.08%	C+ / 6.9
2010	C	427.70	63.85	C / 5.5	18.64%	C / 4.9

Major Rating Factors:
Disappointing performance is the major factor driving the D (Weak) TheStreet.com Investment Rating for *iShares US Oil & Gas Exp & Pro E. The fund currently has a performance rating of D (Weak) based on an annualized return of -5.65% over the last three years and a total return of -24.70% year to date 2015. Factored into the performance evaluation is an expense ratio of 0.43% (very low).

The fund's risk rating is currently C (Fair). It carries a beta of 1.17, meaning it is expected to move 11.7% for every 10% move in the market. Volatility, as measured by both the semi-deviation and a drawdown factor, is considered average. As of December 31, 2015, *iShares US Oil & Gas Exp & Pro E traded at a premium of .08% above its net asset value, which is worse than its one-year historical average premium of .01%.

Diane Hsiung has been running the fund for 8 years and currently receives a manager quality ranking of 65 (0=worst, 99=best). This fund offers an average level of risk but investors looking for strong performance will be frustrated.

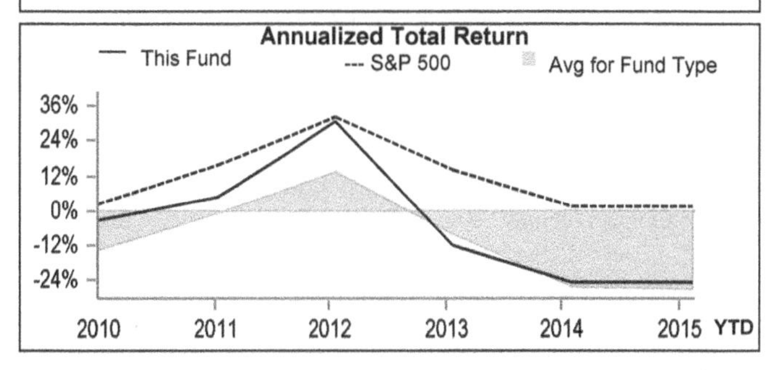

*iShares US Oil Equip & Svcs ETF (IEZ) D- Weak

Fund Family: BlackRock Fund Advisors
Fund Type: Energy/Natural Resources
Inception Date: May 1, 2006

Data Date	Investment Rating	Net Assets ($Mil)	Price	Performance Rating/Pts	Total Return Y-T-D	Risk Rating/Pts
12-15	D-	530.50	35.78	D- / 1.3	-26.87%	C / 4.7
2014	D	530.50	49.96	D / 1.6	-20.71%	C+ / 6.5
2013	C-	525.60	64.81	C+ / 5.8	19.64%	C+ / 6.4
2012	D	324.10	51.01	D+ / 2.8	3.36%	C+ / 6.2
2011	C+	417.80	51.92	B- / 7.1	-2.95%	C+ / 6.3
2010	C-	495.60	56.35	C+ / 5.9	31.77%	C- / 4.2

Major Rating Factors:
Disappointing performance is the major factor driving the D- (Weak) TheStreet.com Investment Rating for *iShares US Oil Equip & Svcs ETF. The fund currently has a performance rating of D- (Weak) based on an annualized return of -11.34% over the last three years and a total return of -26.87% year to date 2015. Factored into the performance evaluation is an expense ratio of 0.43% (very low).

The fund's risk rating is currently C (Fair). It carries a beta of 1.32, meaning it is expected to move 13.2% for every 10% move in the market. Volatility, as measured by both the semi-deviation and a drawdown factor, is considered average. As of December 31, 2015, *iShares US Oil Equip & Svcs ETF traded at a price exactly equal to its net asset value.

Diane Hsiung has been running the fund for 8 years and currently receives a manager quality ranking of 30 (0=worst, 99=best). This fund offers an average level of risk but investors looking for strong performance will be frustrated.

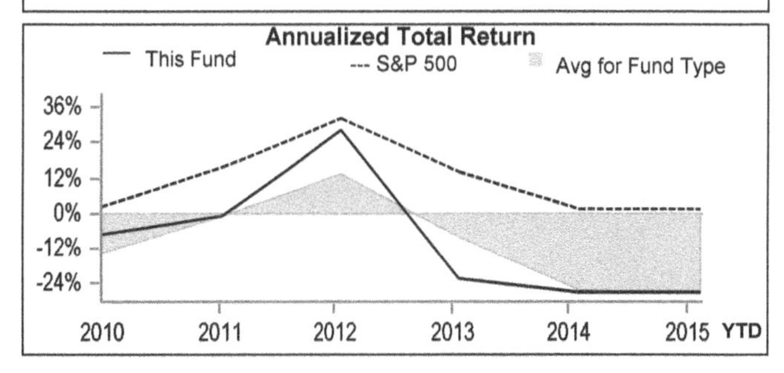

*iShares US Pharmaceuticals ETF (IHE) B- Good

Fund Family: BlackRock Fund Advisors
Fund Type: Health
Inception Date: May 1, 2006

Data Date	Investment Rating	Net Assets ($Mil)	Price	Performance Rating/Pts	Total Return Y-T-D	Risk Rating/Pts
12-15	B-	737.50	161.69	A+ / 9.6	8.46%	C / 4.7
2014	A+	737.50	151.40	A / 9.5	30.28%	B- / 7.4
2013	A	572.80	118.10	A / 9.3	35.31%	B / 8.0
2012	B-	348.70	85.02	C+ / 6.7	18.29%	B / 8.0
2011	B-	344.10	76.45	B / 7.6	19.16%	B- / 7.3
2010	B+	159.80	64.04	B- / 7.1	12.72%	C+ / 6.7

Major Rating Factors:
Exceptional performance is the major factor driving the B- (Good) TheStreet.com Investment Rating for *iShares US Pharmaceuticals ETF. The fund currently has a performance rating of A+ (Excellent) based on an annualized return of 24.27% over the last three years and a total return of 8.46% year to date 2015. Factored into the performance evaluation is an expense ratio of 0.43% (very low).

The fund's risk rating is currently C (Fair). It carries a beta of 1.02, meaning that its performance tracks fairly well with that of the overall stock market. Volatility, as measured by both the semi-deviation and a drawdown factor, is considered average. As of December 31, 2015, *iShares US Pharmaceuticals ETF traded at a premium of .13% above its net asset value, which is worse than its one-year historical average premium of .01%.

Diane Hsiung has been running the fund for 8 years and currently receives a manager quality ranking of 94 (0=worst, 99=best). If you desire an average level of risk and strong performance, then this fund is a good option.

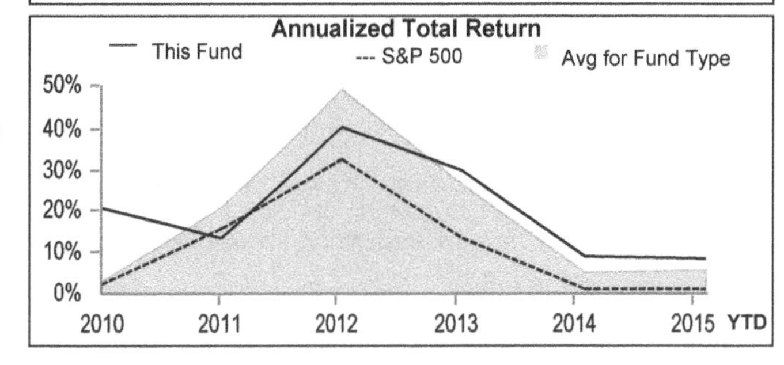

* Denotes ETF Fund

*iShares US Preferred Stock (PFF) B+ Good

Fund Family: BlackRock Fund Advisors
Fund Type: Income
Inception Date: March 26, 2007

Major Rating Factors: *iShares US Preferred Stock receives a TheStreet.com Investment Rating of B+ (Good). The fund currently has a performance rating of C+ (Fair) based on an annualized return of 5.54% over the last three years and a total return of 4.67% year to date 2015. Factored into the performance evaluation is an expense ratio of 0.47% (very low).

The fund's risk rating is currently B+ (Good). It carries a beta of 0.16, meaning the fund's expected move will be 1.6% for every 10% move in the market. Volatility, as measured by both the semi-deviation and a drawdown factor, is considered very low. As of December 31, 2015, *iShares US Preferred Stock traded at a discount of .08% below its net asset value, which is better than its one-year historical average premium of .04%.

Diane Hsiung has been running the fund for 8 years and currently receives a manager quality ranking of 86 (0=worst, 99=best). If you desire an average level of risk, then this fund may be an option.

Data Date	Investment Rating	Net Assets ($Mil)	Price	Performance Rating/Pts	Total Return Y-T-D	Risk Rating/Pts
12-15	B+	10,397.80	38.85	C+ / 6.5	4.67%	B+ / 9.1
2014	B-	10,397.80	39.44	C+ / 5.6	12.75%	B+ / 9.0
2013	C	8,338.90	36.83	C / 4.3	-0.81%	B / 8.9
2012	C	10,747.30	39.62	C- / 4.0	15.27%	B / 8.9
2011	C-	6,979.90	35.62	C / 4.7	0.55%	C+ / 6.6
2010	C	6,127.40	38.80	C+ / 6.2	13.87%	C / 4.4

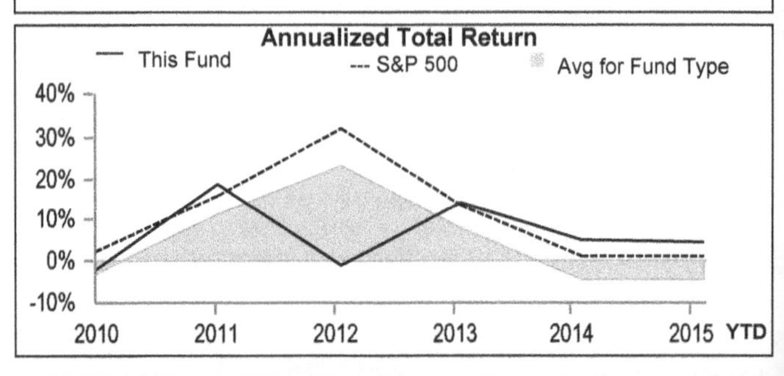

*iShares US Real Estate ETF (IYR) B- Good

Fund Family: BlackRock Fund Advisors
Fund Type: Income
Inception Date: June 12, 2000

Major Rating Factors: Strong performance is the major factor driving the B- (Good) TheStreet.com Investment Rating for *iShares US Real Estate ETF. The fund currently has a performance rating of B (Good) based on an annualized return of 8.85% over the last three years and a total return of 1.67% year to date 2015. Factored into the performance evaluation is an expense ratio of 0.43% (very low).

The fund's risk rating is currently C+ (Fair). It carries a beta of 0.50, meaning the fund's expected move will be 5.0% for every 10% move in the market. Volatility, as measured by both the semi-deviation and a drawdown factor, is considered low. As of December 31, 2015, *iShares US Real Estate ETF traded at a premium of .05% above its net asset value, which is worse than its one-year historical average discount of .01%.

Diane Hsiung has been running the fund for 8 years and currently receives a manager quality ranking of 81 (0=worst, 99=best). If you desire only a moderate level of risk and strong performance, then this fund is an excellent option.

Data Date	Investment Rating	Net Assets ($Mil)	Price	Performance Rating/Pts	Total Return Y-T-D	Risk Rating/Pts
12-15	B-	4,679.00	75.08	B / 7.7	1.67%	C+ / 6.7
2014	A-	4,679.00	76.84	B / 8.1	26.15%	B / 8.0
2013	C	3,665.30	63.08	C / 5.2	-0.66%	B- / 7.8
2012	B-	4,590.90	64.67	B- / 7.4	19.70%	B- / 7.7
2011	C+	3,294.80	56.81	B- / 7.4	5.93%	C+ / 6.6
2010	C+	3,080.10	55.96	B- / 7.1	26.59%	C / 4.3

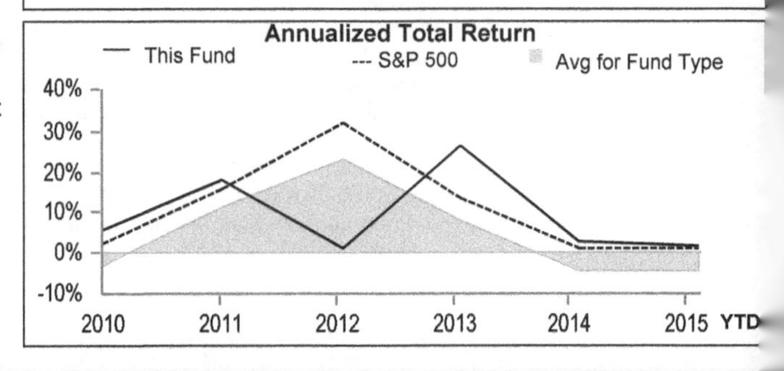

*iShares US Regional Banks ETF (IAT) A Excellent

Fund Family: BlackRock Fund Advisors
Fund Type: Financial Services
Inception Date: May 1, 2006

Major Rating Factors:
Strong performance is the major factor driving the A (Excellent) TheStreet.com Investment Rating for *iShares US Regional Banks ETF. The fund currently has a performance rating of B+ (Good) based on an annualized return of 13.09% over the last three years and a total return of 2.98% year to date 2015. Factored into the performance evaluation is an expense ratio of 0.43% (very low).

The fund's risk rating is currently B (Good). It carries a beta of 1.03, meaning that its performance tracks fairly well with that of the overall stock market. Volatility, as measured by both the semi-deviation and a drawdown factor, is considered low. As of December 31, 2015, *iShares US Regional Banks ETF traded at a price exactly equal to its net asset value, which is better than its one-year historical average premium of .01%.

Diane Hsiung has been running the fund for 8 years and currently receives a manager quality ranking of 60 (0=worst, 99=best). If you desire only a moderate level of risk and strong performance, then this fund is an excellent option.

Data Date	Investment Rating	Net Assets ($Mil)	Price	Performance Rating/Pts	Total Return Y-T-D	Risk Rating/Pts
12-15	A	471.90	34.96	B+ / 8.5	2.98%	B / 8.1
2014	B	471.90	34.95	B / 7.7	8.52%	B- / 7.7
2013	B	494.30	33.06	B / 7.6	30.21%	B- / 7.7
2012	D+	173.60	24.43	C- / 3.0	12.77%	B- / 7.3
2011	D+	95.10	21.16	D+ / 2.4	-8.36%	C+ / 6.9
2010	D	135.90	24.74	D / 1.6	20.25%	C / 4.7

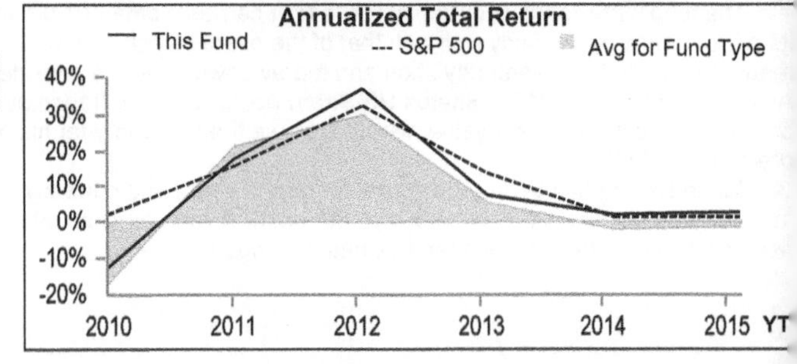

*iShares US Technology ETF (IYW) A+ Excellent

Fund Family: BlackRock Fund Advisors
Fund Type: Growth
Inception Date: May 15, 2000

Major Rating Factors:
Exceptional performance is the major factor driving the A+ (Excellent) TheStreet.com Investment Rating for *iShares US Technology ETF. The fund currently has a performance rating of A- (Excellent) based on an annualized return of 15.66% over the last three years and a total return of 4.38% year to date 2015. Factored into the performance evaluation is an expense ratio of 0.43% (very low).

The fund's risk rating is currently B- (Good). It carries a beta of 1.03, meaning that its performance tracks fairly well with that of the overall stock market. Volatility, as measured by both the semi-deviation and a drawdown factor, is considered low. As of December 31, 2015, *iShares US Technology ETF traded at a premium of .01% above its net asset value.

Diane Hsiung has been running the fund for 8 years and currently receives a manager quality ranking of 73 (0=worst, 99=best). If you desire only a moderate level of risk and strong performance, then this fund is an excellent option.

Data Date	Investment Rating	Net Assets ($Mil)	Price	Performance Rating/Pts	Total Return Y-T-D	Risk Rating/Pts
12-15	A+	4,115.10	107.03	A- / 9.1	4.38%	B- / 7.8
2014	B	4,115.10	104.40	B / 8.1	21.25%	C+ / 6.8
2013	B-	3,081.70	88.44	B- / 7.4	22.65%	B- / 7.5
2012	D+	1,514.40	70.72	C- / 3.4	10.94%	C+ / 6.9
2011	C+	1,300.00	63.90	B- / 7.1	0.03%	B- / 7.3
2010	C+	1,451.40	64.38	C+ / 6.3	12.42%	C+ / 5.6

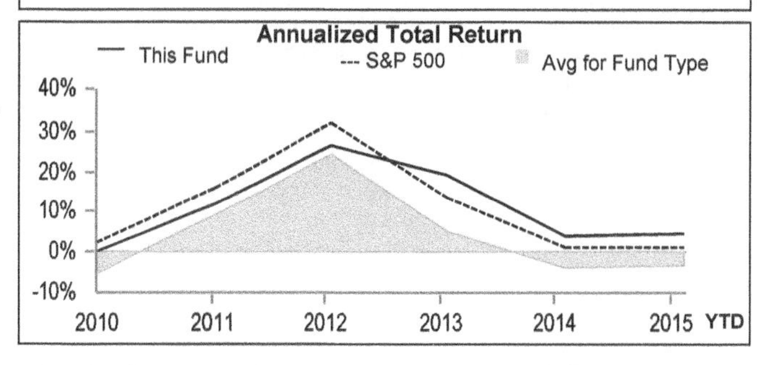

*iShares US Telecommunications ET (IYZ) B+ Good

Fund Family: BlackRock Fund Advisors
Fund Type: Income
Inception Date: May 22, 2000

Major Rating Factors: *iShares US Telecommunications ET receives a TheStreet.com Investment Rating of B+ (Good). The fund currently has a performance rating of C+ (Fair) based on an annualized return of 7.48% over the last three years and a total return of 0.18% year to date 2015. Factored into the performance evaluation is an expense ratio of 0.43% (very low).

The fund's risk rating is currently B (Good). It carries a beta of 0.89, meaning the fund's expected move will be 8.9% for every 10% move in the market. Volatility, as measured by both the semi-deviation and a drawdown factor, is considered low. As of December 31, 2015, *iShares US Telecommunications ET traded at a discount of .17% below its net asset value, which is better than its one-year historical average discount of .02%.

Diane Hsiung has been running the fund for 8 years and currently receives a manager quality ranking of 34 (0=worst, 99=best). If you desire an average level of risk, then this fund may be an option.

Data Date	Investment Rating	Net Assets ($Mil)	Price	Performance Rating/Pts	Total Return Y-T-D	Risk Rating/Pts
12-15	B+	574.70	28.79	C+ / 6.9	0.18%	B / 8.6
2014	B+	574.70	29.28	C+ / 6.4	2.05%	B+ / 9.1
2013	B	440.40	29.73	B- / 7.2	21.17%	B / 8.2
2012	C+	479.30	24.26	C / 5.2	19.22%	B / 8.2
2011	C-	512.30	21.00	C- / 3.5	-8.08%	B / 8.1
2010	C-	761.10	23.37	C- / 3.8	20.72%	C+ / 6.1

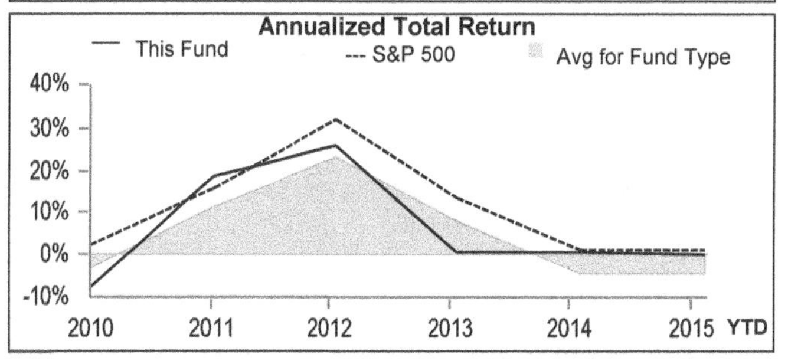

*iShares US Utilities ETF (IDU) B Good

Fund Family: BlackRock Fund Advisors
Fund Type: Utilities
Inception Date: June 12, 2000

Major Rating Factors: Strong performance is the major factor driving the B (Good) TheStreet.com Investment Rating for *iShares US Utilities ETF. The fund currently has a performance rating of B (Good) based on an annualized return of 11.28% over the last three years and a total return of -3.99% year to date 2015. Factored into the performance evaluation is an expense ratio of 0.43% (very low).

The fund's risk rating is currently C+ (Fair). It carries a beta of 0.97, meaning that its performance tracks fairly well with that of the overall stock market. Volatility, as measured by both the semi-deviation and a drawdown factor, is considered low. As of December 31, 2015, *iShares US Utilities ETF traded at a premium of .05% above its net asset value.

Diane Hsiung has been running the fund for 8 years and currently receives a manager quality ranking of 67 (0=worst, 99=best). If you desire only a moderate level of risk and strong performance, then this fund is an excellent option.

Data Date	Investment Rating	Net Assets ($Mil)	Price	Performance Rating/Pts	Total Return Y-T-D	Risk Rating/Pts
12-15	B	652.50	107.92	B / 8.0	-3.99%	C+ / 6.8
2014	A+	652.50	118.27	B+ / 8.6	29.63%	B / 8.7
2013	B	618.10	95.82	C+ / 6.3	9.95%	B+ / 9.0
2012	C	838.40	86.36	C- / 3.2	5.85%	B+ / 9.2
2011	C+	772.40	88.32	C / 4.9	14.44%	B / 8.6
2010	D+	497.30	77.10	D / 1.6	7.21%	C+ / 6.6

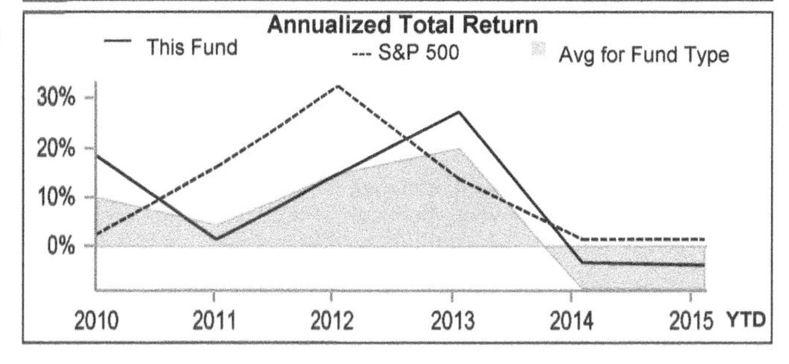

*iShares Yield Optimized Bond ETF (BYLD) C+ Fair

Fund Family: BlackRock Fund Advisors
Fund Type: General Bond
Inception Date: April 24, 2014

Major Rating Factors: Middle of the road best describes *iShares Yield Optimized Bond ETF whose TheStreet.com Investment Rating is currently a C+ (Fair). The fund currently has a performance rating of C- (Fair) based on an annualized return of 0.00% over the last three years and a total return of -1.37% year to date 2015. Factored into the performance evaluation is an expense ratio of 0.01% (very low).

The fund's risk rating is currently B+ (Good). It carries a beta of 0.00, meaning the fund's expected move will be 0.0% for every 10% move in the market. Volatility, as measured by both the semi-deviation and a drawdown factor, is considered very low. As of December 31, 2015, *iShares Yield Optimized Bond ETF traded at a discount of .37% below its net asset value, which is better than its one-year historical average premium of .04%.

James J. Mauro has been running the fund for 2 years and currently receives a manager quality ranking of 54 (0=worst, 99=best). If you desire an average level of risk, then this fund may be an option.

Data Date	Investment Rating	Net Assets ($Mil)	Price	Performance Rating/Pts	Total Return Y-T-D	Risk Rating/Pts
12-15	C+	8.80	24.01	C- / 3.5	-1.37%	B+ / 9.4

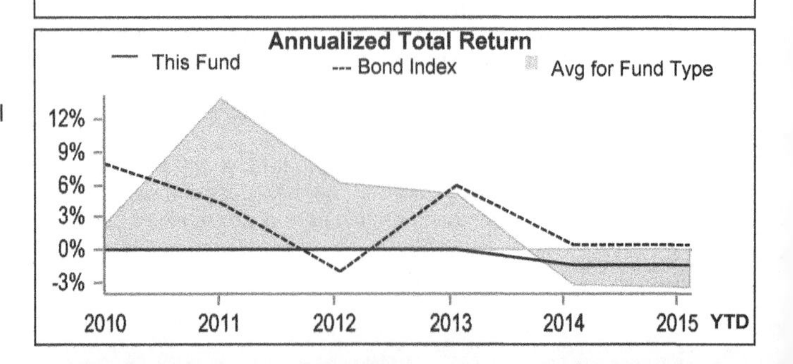

*Janus Eq Risk Weighted LC (ERW) C Fair

Fund Family: Exchange Traded Concepts LLC
Fund Type: Growth
Inception Date: July 29, 2013

Major Rating Factors: Middle of the road best describes *Janus Eq Risk Weighted LC whose TheStreet.com Investment Rating is currently a C (Fair). The fund currently has a performance rating of C- (Fair) based on an annualized return of 0.00% over the last three years and a total return of -1.59% year to date 2015. Factored into the performance evaluation is an expense ratio of 0.65% (very low).

The fund's risk rating is currently B (Good). It carries a beta of 0.00, meaning the fund's expected move will be 0.0% for every 10% move in the market. Volatility, as measured by both the semi-deviation and a drawdown factor, is considered low. As of December 31, 2015, *Janus Eq Risk Weighted LC traded at a discount of .14% below its net asset value, which is better than its one-year historical average premium of .45%.

Denise M. Krisko has been running the fund for 1 year and currently receives a manager quality ranking of 53 (0=worst, 99=best). If you desire an average level of risk, then this fund may be an option.

Data Date	Investment Rating	Net Assets ($Mil)	Price	Performance Rating/Pts	Total Return Y-T-D	Risk Rating/Pts
12-15	C	8.40	50.04	C- / 3.1	-1.59%	B / 8.5
2014	B-	8.40	51.55	C+ / 6.2	11.50%	B / 8.2

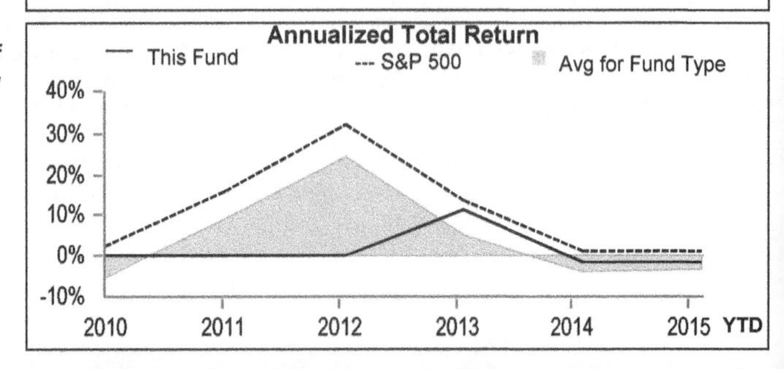

*JPMorgan Alerian MLP Idx ETN (AMJ) E+ Very Weak

Fund Family: JP Morgan Investment Management Inc
Fund Type: Energy/Natural Resources
Inception Date: April 2, 2009

Major Rating Factors: *JPMorgan Alerian MLP Idx ETN has adopted a very risky asset allocation strategy and currently receives an overall TheStreet.com Investment Rating of E+ (Very Weak). The fund has a high level of volatility, as measured by both semi-deviation and drawdown factors. It carries a beta of 0.70, meaning the fund's expected move will be 7.0% for every 10% move in the market. As of December 31, 2015, *JPMorgan Alerian MLP Idx ETN traded at a premium of .03% above its net asset value, which is worse than its one-year historical average discount of .04%. Unfortunately, the high level of risk (D, Weak) failed to pay off as investors endured poor performance.

The fund's performance rating is currently D (Weak). It has registered an annualized return of -5.57% over the last three years and is down -34.10% year to date 2015.

This fund has been team managed for 7 years and currently receives a manager quality ranking of 57 (0=worst, 99=best). If you can tolerate very high levels of risk in the hope of improved future returns, holding this fund may be an option.

Data Date	Investment Rating	Net Assets ($Mil)	Price	Performance Rating/Pts	Total Return Y-T-D	Risk Rating/Pts
12-15	E+	6,715.90	28.97	D / 1.8	-34.10%	D / 1.9
2014	C+	6,715.90	45.95	C / 5.0	5.44%	B / 8.2
2013	C	5,863.30	46.35	B- / 7.0	18.69%	C / 5.2
2012	C	4,869.00	38.46	B- / 7.0	10.78%	C / 5.1
2011	C	3,639.00	38.97	B- / 7.2	13.98%	C / 5.2
2010	A-	2,271.30	36.35	A / 9.5	34.55%	C / 4.7

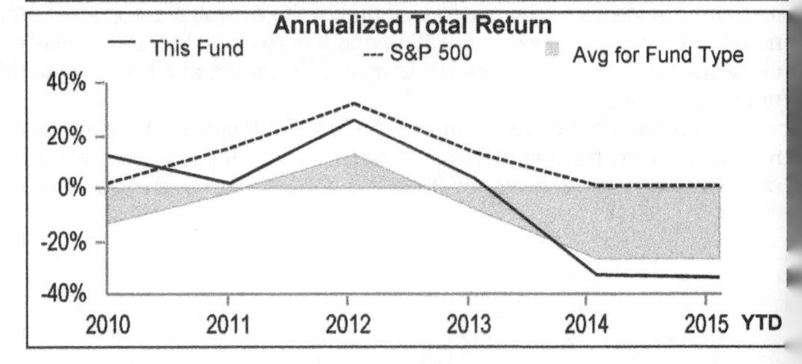

* Denotes ETF Fund

*JPMorgan Diversified Ret Glbl Eq (JPGE) C+ Fair

Fund Family: JP Morgan Investment Management Inc
Fund Type: Global
Inception Date: June 17, 2014

Major Rating Factors: Middle of the road best describes *JPMorgan Diversified Ret Glbl Eq whose TheStreet.com Investment Rating is currently a C+ (Fair). The fund currently has a performance rating of C+ (Fair) based on an annualized return of 0.00% over the last three years and a total return of 4.03% year to date 2015. Factored into the performance evaluation is an expense ratio of 0.38% (very low).

The fund's risk rating is currently B- (Good). It carries a beta of 0.00, meaning the fund's expected move will be 0.0% for every 10% move in the market. Volatility, as measured by both the semi-deviation and a drawdown factor, is considered low. As of December 31, 2015, *JPMorgan Diversified Ret Glbl Eq traded at a premium of .57% above its net asset value, which is worse than its one-year historical average premium of .22%.

Ido Eisenberg has been running the fund for 2 years and currently receives a manager quality ranking of 86 (0=worst, 99=best). If you desire an average level of risk, then this fund may be an option.

Data Date	Investment Rating	Net Assets ($Mil)	Price	Perfor-mance Rating/Pts	Total Return Y-T-D	Risk Rating/Pts
12-15	C+	0.00	49.31	C+ / 6.0	4.03%	B- / 7.1

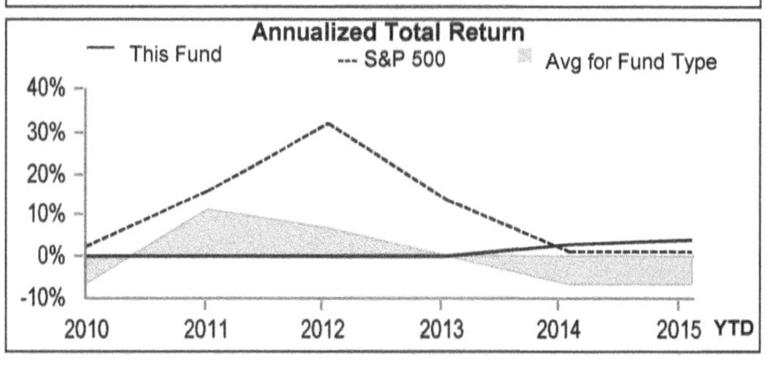

*JPMorgan Diversified Ret Intl Eq (JPIN) D+ Weak

Fund Family: JP Morgan Investment Management Inc
Fund Type: Global
Inception Date: November 5, 2014

Major Rating Factors: *JPMorgan Diversified Ret Intl Eq receives a TheStreet.com Investment Rating of D+ (Weak). The fund currently has a performance rating of C (Fair) based on an annualized return of 0.00% over the last three years and a total return of 2.60% year to date 2015.

The fund's risk rating is currently C- (Fair). It carries a beta of 0.00, meaning the fund's expected move will be 0.0% for every 10% move in the market. Volatility, as measured by both the semi-deviation and a drawdown factor, is considered average. As of December 31, 2015, *JPMorgan Diversified Ret Intl Eq traded at a premium of .26% above its net asset value, which is better than its one-year historical average premium of .35%.

Christopher T. Blum currently receives a manager quality ranking of 84 (0=worst, 99=best). If you desire an average level of risk, then this fund may be an option.

Data Date	Investment Rating	Net Assets ($Mil)	Price	Perfor-mance Rating/Pts	Total Return Y-T-D	Risk Rating/Pts
12-15	D+	0.00	49.30	C / 4.9	2.60%	C- / 3.6

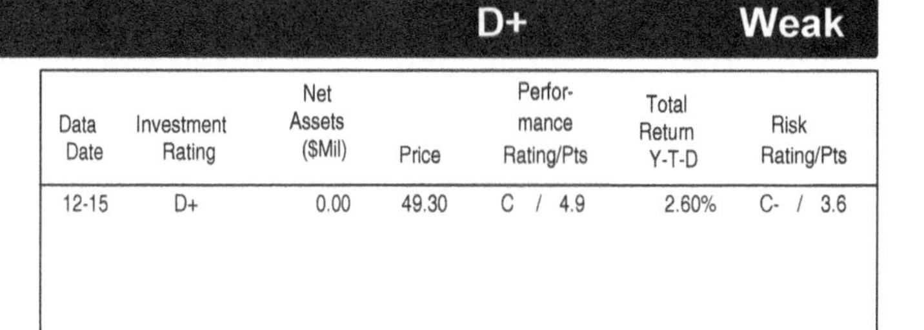

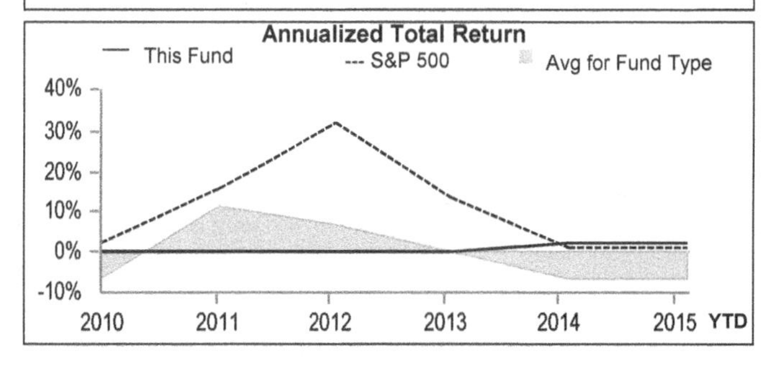

*KraneShares Bosera MSCI China A (KBA) D Weak

Fund Family: Krane Funds Advisors LLC
Fund Type: Foreign
Inception Date: March 4, 2014

Major Rating Factors:
Disappointing performance is the major factor driving the D (Weak) TheStreet.com Investment Rating for *KraneShares Bosera MSCI China A. The fund currently has a performance rating of D+ (Weak) based on an annualized return of 0.00% over the last three years and a total return of -4.85% year to date 2015. Factored into the performance evaluation is an expense ratio of 1.31% (average).

The fund's risk rating is currently C (Fair). It carries a beta of 0.00, meaning the fund's expected move will be 0.0% for every 10% move in the market. Volatility, as measured by both the semi-deviation and a drawdown factor, is considered average. As of December 31, 2015, *KraneShares Bosera MSCI China A traded at a discount of 1.30% below its net asset value, which is better than its one-year historical average discount of .92%.

Jean Kong has been running the fund for 2 years and currently receives a manager quality ranking of 38 (0=worst, 99=best). This fund offers an average level of risk but investors looking for strong performance will be frustrated.

Data Date	Investment Rating	Net Assets ($Mil)	Price	Perfor-mance Rating/Pts	Total Return Y-T-D	Risk Rating/Pts
12-15	D	3.50	34.85	D+ / 2.3	-4.85%	C / 4.5

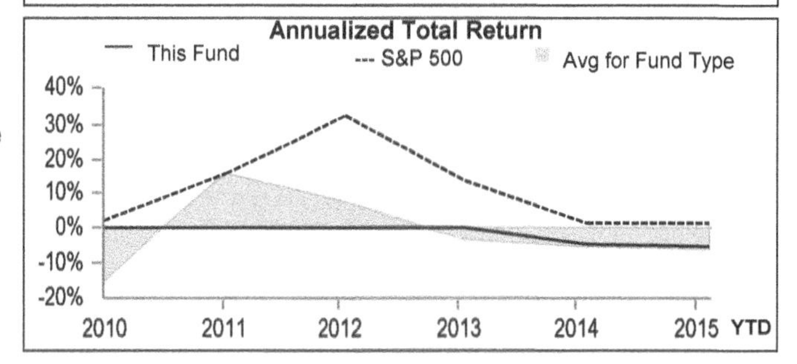

* Denotes ETF Fund

*KraneShares E Fd China Comm Pape (KCNY) D Weak

Fund Family: Krane Funds Advisors LLC
Fund Type: Foreign
Inception Date: December 2, 2014

Data Date	Investment Rating	Net Assets ($Mil)	Price	Performance Rating/Pts	Total Return Y-T-D	Risk Rating/Pts
12-15	D	0.00	33.96	C- / 3.4	-1.12%	C- / 3.9

Major Rating Factors: *KraneShares E Fd China Comm Pape receives a TheStreet.com Investment Rating of D (Weak). The fund currently has a performance rating of C- (Fair) based on an annualized return of 0.00% over the last three years and a total return of -1.12% year to date 2015.

The fund's risk rating is currently C- (Fair). It carries a beta of 0.00, meaning the fund's expected move will be 0.0% for every 10% move in the market. Volatility, as measured by both the semi-deviation and a drawdown factor, is considered average. As of December 31, 2015, *KraneShares E Fd China Comm Pape traded at a premium of .27% above its net asset value, which is worse than its one-year historical average discount of .19%.

Xiaochen Wang has been running the fund for 2 years and currently receives a manager quality ranking of 58 (0=worst, 99=best). If you desire an average level of risk, then this fund may be an option.

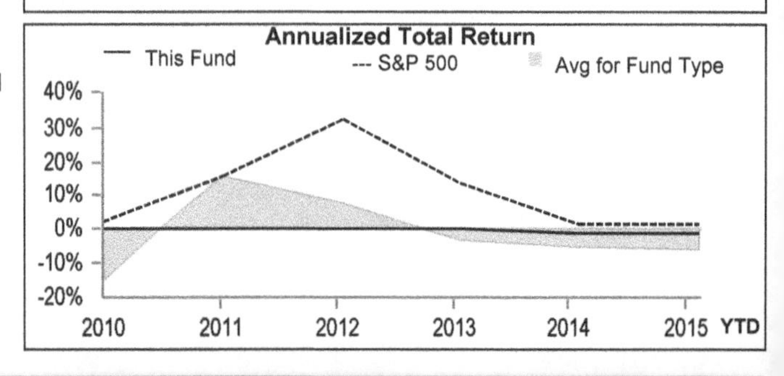

*KraneShares New China (KFYP) B- Good

Fund Family: Krane Funds Advisors LLC
Fund Type: Foreign
Inception Date: July 22, 2013

Data Date	Investment Rating	Net Assets ($Mil)	Price	Performance Rating/Pts	Total Return Y-T-D	Risk Rating/Pts
12-15	B-	3.30	63.40	A / 9.5	6.65%	C / 4.9
2014	D+	3.30	65.50	C- / 3.1	2.34%	B- / 7.0

Major Rating Factors:
Exceptional performance is the major factor driving the B- (Good) TheStreet.com Investment Rating for *KraneShares New China. The fund currently has a performance rating of A (Excellent) based on an annualized return of 0.00% over the last three years and a total return of 6.65% year to date 2015. Factored into the performance evaluation is an expense ratio of 0.71% (very low).

The fund's risk rating is currently C (Fair). It carries a beta of 0.00, meaning the fund's expected move will be 0.0% for every 10% move in the market. Volatility, as measured by both the semi-deviation and a drawdown factor, is considered average. As of December 31, 2015, *KraneShares New China traded at a premium of 8.75% above its net asset value, which is worse than its one-year historical average discount of 1.33%.

Mark R. Schlarbaum has been running the fund for 1 year and currently receives a manager quality ranking of 92 (0=worst, 99=best). If you desire an average level of risk and strong performance, then this fund is a good option.

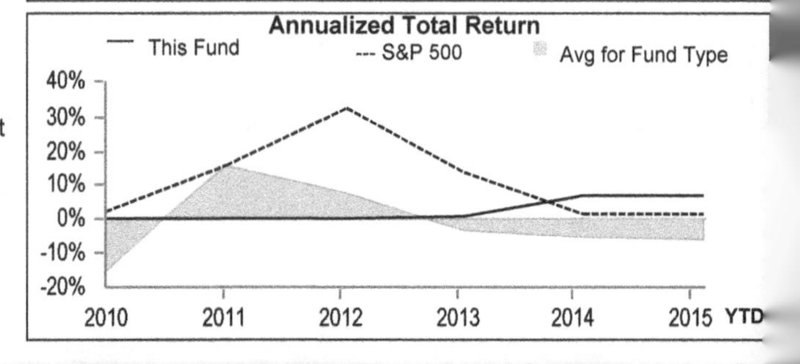

*Madrona Domestic ETF (FWDD) B Good

Fund Family: AdvisorShares Investments LLC
Fund Type: Growth
Inception Date: June 20, 2011

Data Date	Investment Rating	Net Assets ($Mil)	Price	Performance Rating/Pts	Total Return Y-T-D	Risk Rating/Pts
12-15	B	28.70	41.28	B / 8.2	-4.22%	C+ / 6.9
2014	B+	28.70	43.10	B+ / 8.8	12.54%	B- / 7.1
2013	A+	22.00	38.42	A+ / 9.6	34.34%	B / 8.2
2012	B+	15.20	27.80	B+ / 8.5	17.09%	B- / 7.9

Major Rating Factors: Strong performance is the major factor driving the B (Good) TheStreet.com Investment Rating for *Madrona Domestic ETF. The fund currently has a performance rating of B (Good) based on an annualized return of 13.13% over the last three years and a total return of -4.22% year to date 2015. Factored into the performance evaluation is an expense ratio of 1.25% (average).

The fund's risk rating is currently C+ (Fair). It carries a beta of 1.15, meaning it is expected to move 11.5% for every 10% move in the market. Volatility, as measured by both the semi-deviation and a drawdown factor, is considered low. As of December 31, 2015, *Madrona Domestic ETF traded at a premium of .68% above its net asset value, which is worse than its one-year historical average discount of .01%.

Brian K. Evans has been running the fund for 5 years and currently receives a manager quality ranking of 46 (0=worst, 99=best). If you desire only a moderate level of risk and strong performance, then this fund is an excellent option.

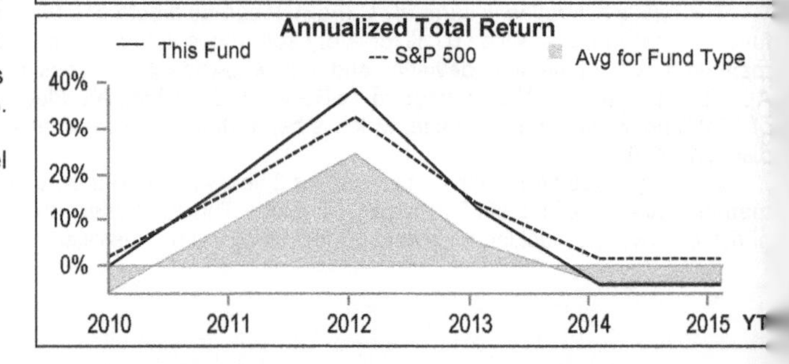

* Denotes ETF Fund

*Madrona Global Bond ETF (FWDB) C Fair

Fund Family: AdvisorShares Investments LLC
Fund Type: Global
Inception Date: June 21, 2011

Major Rating Factors: Middle of the road best describes *Madrona Global Bond ETF whose TheStreet.com Investment Rating is currently a C (Fair). The fund currently has a performance rating of C- (Fair) based on an annualized return of 0.17% over the last three years and a total return of -2.34% year to date 2015. Factored into the performance evaluation is an expense ratio of 0.95% (low).

The fund's risk rating is currently B- (Good). It carries a beta of 0.43, meaning the fund's expected move will be 4.3% for every 10% move in the market. Volatility, as measured by both the semi-deviation and a drawdown factor, is considered low. As of December 31, 2015, *Madrona Global Bond ETF traded at a premium of .29% above its net asset value, which is worse than its one-year historical average discount of .10%.

Brian K. Evans currently receives a manager quality ranking of 81 (0=worst, 99=best). If you desire an average level of risk, then this fund may be an option.

Data Date	Investment Rating	Net Assets ($Mil)	Price	Performance Rating/Pts	Total Return Y-T-D	Risk Rating/Pts
12-15	C	25.80	24.47	C- / 4.1	-2.34%	B- / 7.5
2014	C-	25.80	25.60	C- / 3.6	4.91%	B- / 7.3
2013	C-	22.00	25.13	D+ / 2.7	-1.92%	B+ / 9.4
2012	C	23.20	26.55	C- / 3.1	7.64%	B+ / 9.8

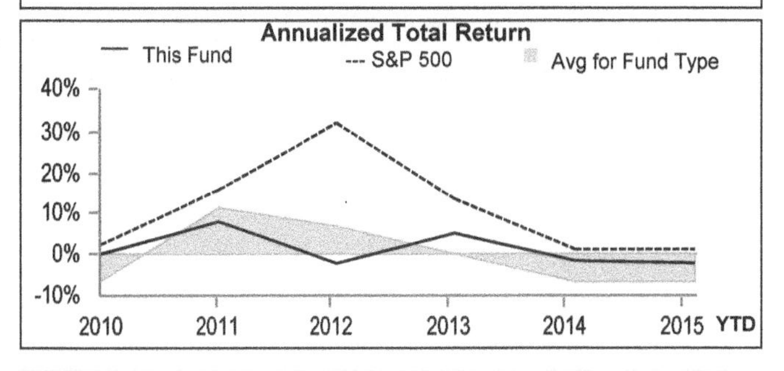

*Madrona International ETF (FWDI) C- Fair

Fund Family: AdvisorShares Investments LLC
Fund Type: Foreign
Inception Date: June 21, 2011

Major Rating Factors: Middle of the road best describes *Madrona International ETF whose TheStreet.com Investment Rating is currently a C- (Fair). The fund currently has a performance rating of C- (Fair) based on an annualized return of 0.65% over the last three years and a total return of -7.75% year to date 2015. Factored into the performance evaluation is an expense ratio of 1.25% (average).

The fund's risk rating is currently C+ (Fair). It carries a beta of 1.08, meaning that its performance tracks fairly well with that of the overall stock market. Volatility, as measured by both the semi-deviation and a drawdown factor, is considered low. As of December 31, 2015, *Madrona International ETF traded at a premium of 1.18% above its net asset value, which is worse than its one-year historical average premium of .21%.

Brian K. Evans has been running the fund for 5 years and currently receives a manager quality ranking of 35 (0=worst, 99=best). If you desire an average level of risk, then this fund may be an option.

Data Date	Investment Rating	Net Assets ($Mil)	Price	Performance Rating/Pts	Total Return Y-T-D	Risk Rating/Pts
12-15	C-	18.20	23.93	C- / 3.8	-7.75%	C+ / 5.9
2014	C-	18.20	25.97	C / 4.4	-6.46%	C+ / 6.1
2013	B+	18.50	28.50	A- / 9.0	18.29%	B- / 7.0
2012	B+	15.00	24.03	A / 9.5	19.96%	C+ / 6.7

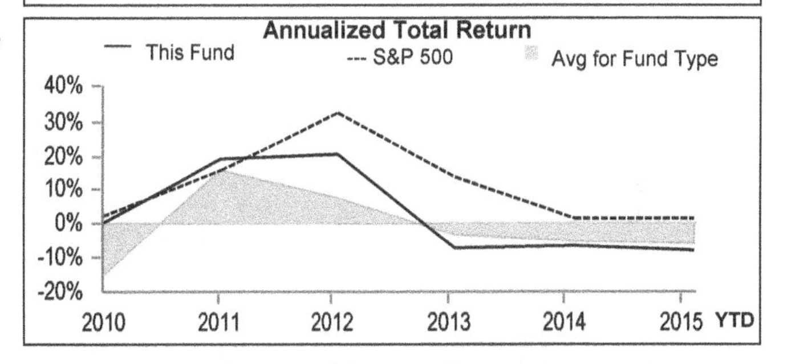

*Market Vectors Africa Index ETF (AFK) D Weak

Fund Family: Van Eck Associates Corporation
Fund Type: Foreign
Inception Date: July 10, 2008

Major Rating Factors:
Disappointing performance is the major factor driving the D (Weak) TheStreet.com Investment Rating for *Market Vectors Africa Index ETF. The fund currently has a performance rating of D- (Weak) based on an annualized return of -15.35% over the last three years and a total return of -30.25% year to date 2015. Factored into the performance evaluation is an expense ratio of 0.78% (very low).

The fund's risk rating is currently C+ (Fair). It carries a beta of 0.87, meaning the fund's expected move will be 8.7% for every 10% move in the market. Volatility, as measured by both the semi-deviation and a drawdown factor, is considered low. As of December 31, 2015, *Market Vectors Africa Index ETF traded at a discount of 1.77% below its net asset value, which is better than its one-year historical average discount of .14%.

George Chao has been running the fund for 8 years and currently receives a manager quality ranking of 8 (0=worst, 99=best). This fund offers only a moderate level of risk but investors looking for strong performance are still waiting.

Data Date	Investment Rating	Net Assets ($Mil)	Price	Performance Rating/Pts	Total Return Y-T-D	Risk Rating/Pts
12-15	D	120.20	17.79	D- / 1.0	-30.25%	C+ / 6.3
2014	D+	120.20	25.94	D+ / 2.5	-10.51%	B- / 7.7
2013	D+	108.20	30.92	D+ / 2.4	-2.11%	B- / 7.7
2012	C-	84.60	31.35	C- / 3.8	22.68%	B- / 7.6
2011	C-	63.80	25.75	D+ / 2.9	-23.32%	B- / 7.7
2010	B	107.50	35.18	A / 9.4	25.26%	C- / 3.4

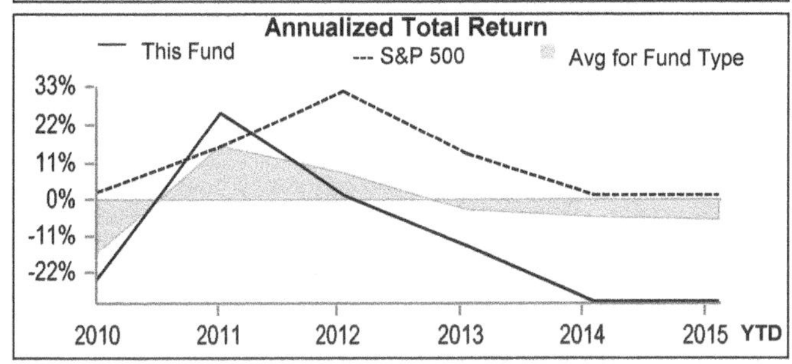

*Market Vectors Agribusiness ETF (MOO) C- Fair

Fund Family: Van Eck Associates Corporation
Fund Type: Global
Inception Date: August 31, 2007

Major Rating Factors: Middle of the road best describes *Market Vectors Agribusiness ETF whose TheStreet.com Investment Rating is currently a C- (Fair). The fund currently has a performance rating of C- (Fair) based on an annualized return of -2.51% over the last three years and a total return of -8.88% year to date 2015. Factored into the performance evaluation is an expense ratio of 0.56% (very low).

The fund's risk rating is currently B- (Good). It carries a beta of 0.76, meaning the fund's expected move will be 7.6% for every 10% move in the market. Volatility, as measured by both the semi-deviation and a drawdown factor, is considered low. As of December 31, 2015, *Market Vectors Agribusiness ETF traded at a discount of .13% below its net asset value, which is better than its one-year historical average discount of .11%.

Hao-Hung Liao has been running the fund for 9 years and currently receives a manager quality ranking of 28 (0=worst, 99=best). If you desire an average level of risk, then this fund may be an option.

Data Date	Investment Rating	Net Assets ($Mil)	Price	Performance Rating/Pts	Total Return Y-T-D	Risk Rating/Pts
12-15	C-	1,576.10	46.49	C- / 3.0	-8.88%	B- / 7.8
2014	C	1,576.10	52.53	C- / 4.0	1.43%	B / 8.2
2013	C-	4,635.30	54.49	C- / 3.2	1.08%	B- / 7.4
2012	C-	5,667.20	52.76	C- / 3.6	11.78%	B- / 7.2
2011	C	5,530.60	47.15	C+ / 5.6	-9.74%	B- / 7.3
2010	C	2,624.20	53.54	C+ / 5.8	23.02%	C / 4.7

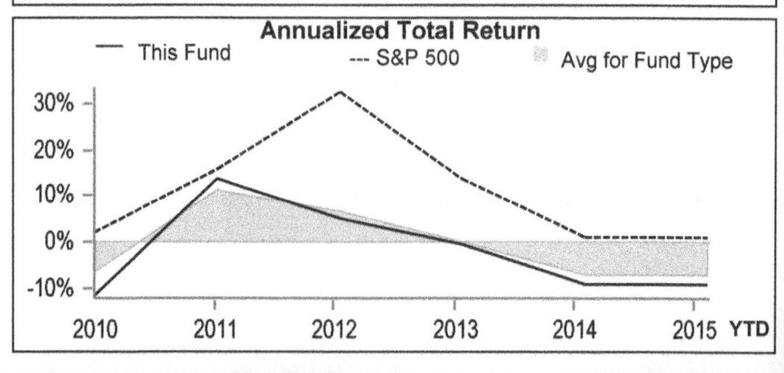

*Market Vectors BDC Income ETF (BIZD) D+ Weak

Fund Family: Van Eck Associates Corporation
Fund Type: Growth
Inception Date: February 11, 2013

Major Rating Factors:
Disappointing performance is the major factor driving the D+ (Weak) TheStreet.com Investment Rating for *Market Vectors BDC Income ETF. The fund currently has a performance rating of D+ (Weak) based on an annualized return of 0.00% over the last three years and a total return of -5.33% year to date 2015. Factored into the performance evaluation is an expense ratio of 0.40% (very low).

The fund's risk rating is currently C (Fair). It carries a beta of 0.00, meaning the fund's expected move will be 0.0% for every 10% move in the market. Volatility, as measured by both the semi-deviation and a drawdown factor, is considered average. As of December 31, 2015, *Market Vectors BDC Income ETF traded at a premium of .25% above its net asset value, which is worse than its one-year historical average premium of .06%.

George Cao has been running the fund for 3 years and currently receives a manager quality ranking of 30 (0=worst, 99=best). This fund offers an average level of risk but investors looking for strong performance will be frustrated.

Data Date	Investment Rating	Net Assets ($Mil)	Price	Performance Rating/Pts	Total Return Y-T-D	Risk Rating/Pts
12-15	D+	45.90	15.77	D+ / 2.8	-5.33%	C / 5.5
2014	D	45.90	17.93	D- / 1.2	-7.30%	B- / 7.7

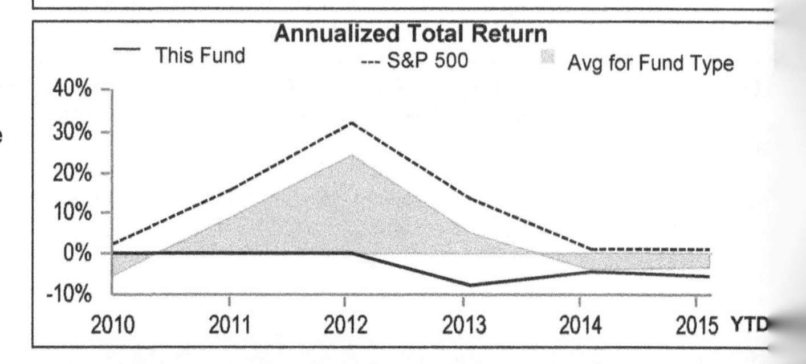

*Market Vectors Biotech ETF (BBH) B+ Good

Fund Family: Van Eck Associates Corporation
Fund Type: Income
Inception Date: December 20, 2011

Major Rating Factors:
Exceptional performance is the major factor driving the B+ (Good) TheStreet.com Investment Rating for *Market Vectors Biotech ETF. The fund currently has a performance rating of A+ (Excellent) based on an annualized return of 31.90% over the last three years and a total return of 9.32% year to date 2015. Factored into the performance evaluation is an expense ratio of 0.35% (very low).

The fund's risk rating is currently C+ (Fair). It carries a beta of 1.06, meaning that its performance tracks fairly well with that of the overall stock market. Volatility, as measured by both the semi-deviation and a drawdown factor, is considered low. As of December 31, 2015, *Market Vectors Biotech ETF traded at a premium of .10% above its net asset value, which is worse than its one-year historical average premium of .01%.

George Chao has been running the fund for 5 years and currently receives a manager quality ranking of 97 (0=worst, 99=best). If you desire only a moderate level of risk and strong performance, then this fund is an excellent option.

Data Date	Investment Rating	Net Assets ($Mil)	Price	Performance Rating/Pts	Total Return Y-T-D	Risk Rating/Pts
12-15	B+	539.40	126.95	A+ / 9.8	9.32%	C+ / 6.1
2014	A+	539.40	115.38	A+ / 9.8	31.68%	B / 8.2
2013	B	473.30	88.52	A+ / 9.8	58.79%	C+ / 5.8
2012	B	146.90	53.50	A+ / 9.8	42.75%	C+ / 6.1

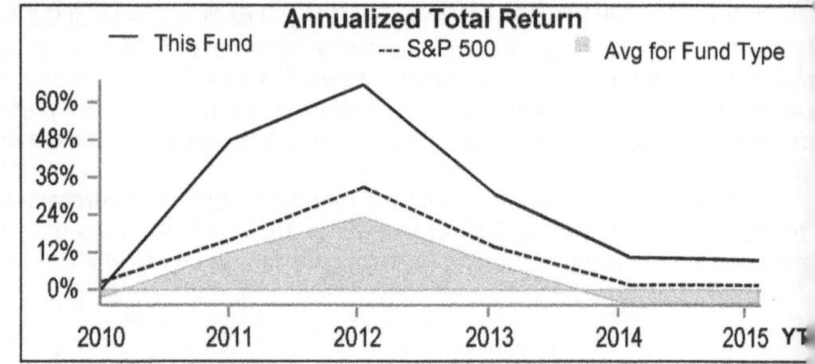

*Market Vectors Brazil Small-Cap (BRF) E Very Weak

Fund Family: Van Eck Associates Corporation
Fund Type: Foreign
Inception Date: May 12, 2009

Data Date	Investment Rating	Net Assets ($Mil)	Price	Performance Rating/Pts	Total Return Y-T-D	Risk Rating/Pts
12-15	E	130.10	10.38	E- / 0.2	-47.30%	C- / 3.2
2014	E	130.10	21.07	E+ / 0.8	-24.08%	D / 2.1
2013	E+	196.90	29.62	E+ / 0.6	-30.84%	C / 4.6
2012	D	552.80	42.62	D+ / 2.5	10.45%	C / 5.4
2011	D-	512.60	36.44	E+ / 0.6	-26.12%	C+ / 5.7
2010	A+	1,078.10	57.68	A / 9.5	24.05%	C+ / 6.6

Major Rating Factors: Very poor performance is the major factor driving the E (Very Weak) TheStreet.com Investment Rating for *Market Vectors Brazil Small-Cap. The fund currently has a performance rating of E- (Very Weak) based on an annualized return of -35.60% over the last three years and a total return of -47.30% year to date 2015. Factored into the performance evaluation is an expense ratio of 0.59% (very low).

The fund's risk rating is currently C- (Fair). It carries a beta of 1.49, meaning it is expected to move 14.9% for every 10% move in the market. Volatility, as measured by both the semi-deviation and a drawdown factor, is considered average. As of December 31, 2015, *Market Vectors Brazil Small-Cap traded at a discount of .57% below its net asset value, which is better than its one-year historical average premium of .37%.

George Chao has been running the fund for 7 years and currently receives a manager quality ranking of 1 (0=worst, 99=best). This fund offers an average level of risk but investors looking for strong performance will be frustrated.

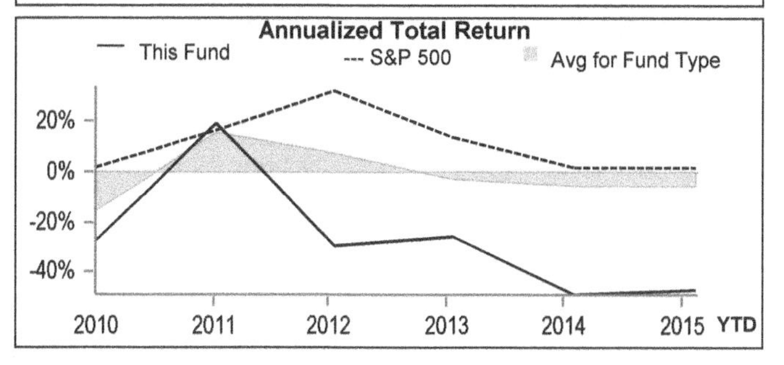

*Market Vectors CEF Muni Inc ETF (XMPT) C+ Fair

Fund Family: Van Eck Associates Corporation
Fund Type: Municipal - National
Inception Date: July 12, 2011

Data Date	Investment Rating	Net Assets ($Mil)	Price	Performance Rating/Pts	Total Return Y-T-D	Risk Rating/Pts
12-15	C+	34.60	26.86	C+ / 6.9	7.32%	C+ / 6.2
2014	C+	34.60	26.13	C+ / 6.5	17.96%	B- / 7.6
2013	D	22.20	23.40	D- / 1.0	-15.27%	B- / 7.8
2012	A+	15.60	28.30	B+ / 8.6	15.31%	B+ / 9.2

Major Rating Factors: Middle of the road best describes *Market Vectors CEF Muni Inc ETF whose TheStreet.com Investment Rating is currently a C+ (Fair). The fund currently has a performance rating of C+ (Fair) based on an annualized return of 2.53% over the last three years and a total return of 7.32% year to date 2015. Factored into the performance evaluation is an expense ratio of 0.40% (very low).

The fund's risk rating is currently C+ (Fair). It carries a beta of 2.22, meaning it is expected to move 22.2% for every 10% move in the market. Volatility, as measured by both the semi-deviation and a drawdown factor, is considered low. As of December 31, 2015, *Market Vectors CEF Muni Inc ETF traded at a premium of .49% above its net asset value, which is worse than its one-year historical average premium of .09%.

Hao-Hung Liao has been running the fund for 5 years and currently receives a manager quality ranking of 44 (0=worst, 99=best). If you desire an average level of risk, then this fund may be an option.

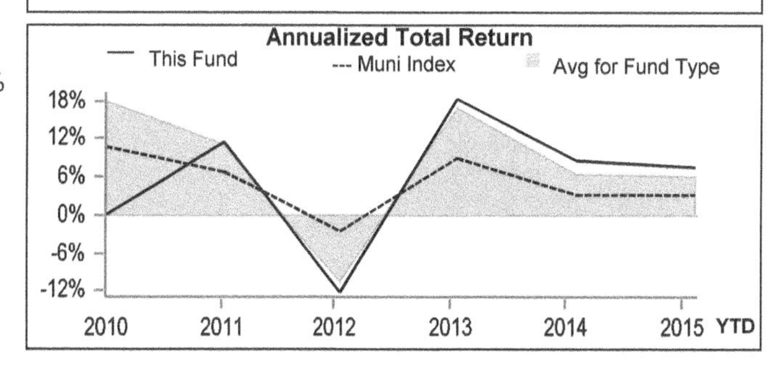

*Market Vectors ChinaAMC A-Share (PEK) C Fair

Fund Family: Van Eck Associates Corporation
Fund Type: Foreign
Inception Date: October 13, 2010

Data Date	Investment Rating	Net Assets ($Mil)	Price	Performance Rating/Pts	Total Return Y-T-D	Risk Rating/Pts
12-15	C	29.30	44.08	C+ / 6.6	-1.41%	C+ / 5.9
2014	B+	29.30	46.02	A / 9.3	44.07%	C+ / 6.7
2013	D-	29.30	31.82	D- / 1.0	-14.03%	C+ / 6.1
2012	C	33.20	36.50	C+ / 6.8	9.00%	C+ / 6.2
2011	D-	15.10	31.64	E / 0.4	-31.54%	C+ / 6.4

Major Rating Factors: Middle of the road best describes *Market Vectors ChinaAMC A-Share whose TheStreet.com Investment Rating is currently a C (Fair). The fund currently has a performance rating of C+ (Fair) based on an annualized return of 8.02% over the last three years and a total return of -1.41% year to date 2015. Factored into the performance evaluation is an expense ratio of 0.72% (very low).

The fund's risk rating is currently C+ (Fair). It carries a beta of 0.57, meaning the fund's expected move will be 5.7% for every 10% move in the market. Volatility, as measured by both the semi-deviation and a drawdown factor, is considered low. As of December 31, 2015, *Market Vectors ChinaAMC A-Share traded at a discount of 1.52% below its net asset value, which is better than its one-year historical average discount of .54%.

George Chao has been running the fund for 6 years and currently receives a manager quality ranking of 89 (0=worst, 99=best). If you desire an average level of risk, then this fund may be an option.

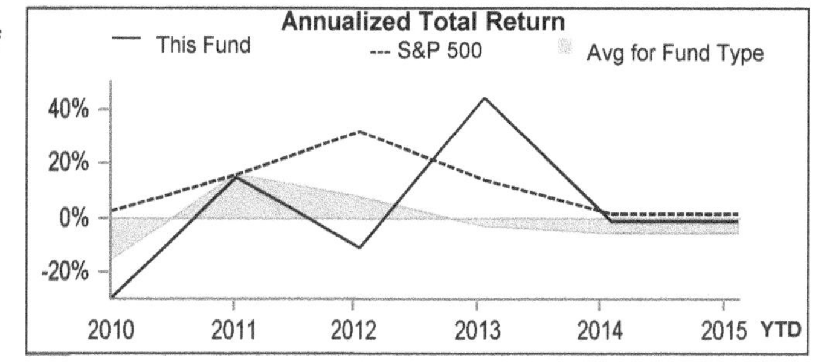

*Market Vectors ChinaAMC China Bo (CBON) D+ Weak

Fund Family: Van Eck Associates Corporation
Fund Type: Foreign
Inception Date: November 10, 2014

Major Rating Factors: *Market Vectors ChinaAMC China Bo receives a TheStreet.com Investment Rating of D+ (Weak). The fund currently has a performance rating of C- (Fair) based on an annualized return of 0.00% over the last three years and a total return of 0.60% year to date 2015.

The fund's risk rating is currently C+ (Fair). It carries a beta of 0.00, meaning the fund's expected move will be 0.0% for every 10% move in the market. Volatility, as measured by both the semi-deviation and a drawdown factor, is considered low. As of December 31, 2015, *Market Vectors ChinaAMC China Bo traded at a discount of 1.19% below its net asset value, which is better than its one-year historical average discount of .76%.

David Lai has been running the fund for 2 years and currently receives a manager quality ranking of 74 (0=worst, 99=best). If you desire an average level of risk, then this fund may be an option.

Data Date	Investment Rating	Net Assets ($Mil)	Price	Performance Rating/Pts	Total Return Y-T-D	Risk Rating/Pts
12-15	D+	0.00	24.18	C- / 3.9	0.60%	C+ / 5.6

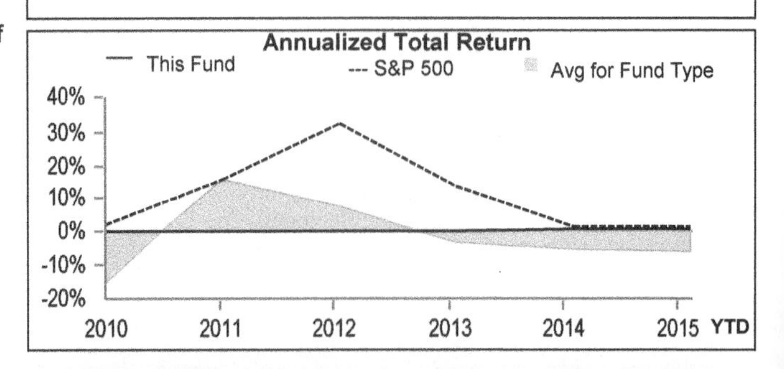

*Market Vectors ChinaAMC SME-ChiN (CNXT) B- Good

Fund Family: Van Eck Associates Corporation
Fund Type: Foreign
Inception Date: July 23, 2014

Major Rating Factors:
Exceptional performance is the major factor driving the B- (Good) TheStreet.com Investment Rating for *Market Vectors ChinaAMC SME-ChiN. The fund currently has a performance rating of A+ (Excellent) based on an annualized return of 0.00% over the last three years and a total return of 42.39% year to date 2015.

The fund's risk rating is currently C (Fair). It carries a beta of 0.00, meaning the fund's expected move will be 0.0% for every 10% move in the market. Volatility, as measured by both the semi-deviation and a drawdown factor, is considered average. As of December 31, 2015, *Market Vectors ChinaAMC SME-ChiN traded at a discount of 1.08% below its net asset value, which is better than its one-year historical average discount of .45%.

George Chao has been running the fund for 2 years and currently receives a manager quality ranking of 99 (0=worst, 99=best). If you desire an average level of risk and strong performance, then this fund is a good option.

Data Date	Investment Rating	Net Assets ($Mil)	Price	Performance Rating/Pts	Total Return Y-T-D	Risk Rating/Pts
12-15	B-	0.00	41.29	A+ / 9.8	42.39%	C / 4.6

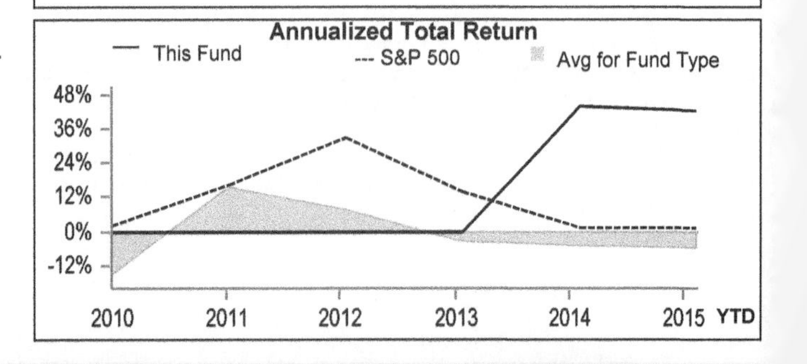

*Market Vectors Chinese RMB USD E (CNY) C+ Fair

Fund Family: Morgan Stanley Investment Managemen
Fund Type: Foreign
Inception Date: March 14, 2008

Major Rating Factors: Middle of the road best describes *Market Vectors Chinese RMB USD E whose TheStreet.com Investment Rating is currently a C+ (Fair). The fund currently has a performance rating of C- (Fair) based on an annualized return of -0.27% over the last three years and a total return of -2.32% year to date 2015. Factored into the performance evaluation is an expense ratio of 0.55% (very low).

The fund's risk rating is currently B+ (Good). It carries a beta of 0.07, meaning the fund's expected move will be 0.7% for every 10% move in the market. Volatility, as measured by both the semi-deviation and a drawdown factor, is considered very low. As of December 31, 2015, *Market Vectors Chinese RMB USD E traded at a discount of 1.06% below its net asset value, which is better than its one-year historical average discount of .77%.

This fund has been team managed for 8 years and currently receives a manager quality ranking of 61 (0=worst, 99=best). If you desire an average level of risk, then this fund may be an option.

Data Date	Investment Rating	Net Assets ($Mil)	Price	Performance Rating/Pts	Total Return Y-T-D	Risk Rating/Pts
12-15	C+	27.05	41.22	C- / 3.9	-2.32%	B+ / 9.4
2014	C	31.80	42.02	D+ / 2.8	-2.28%	B+ / 9.6
2013	C+	27.05	43.05	C- / 3.5	3.47%	B+ / 9.9
2012	C-	27.05	41.62	D / 1.7	1.84%	B+ / 9.9
2011	C	27.05	40.95	D / 2.2	1.61%	B+ / 9.8
2010	C+	27.05	40.57	D+ / 2.9	0.87%	B / 8.8

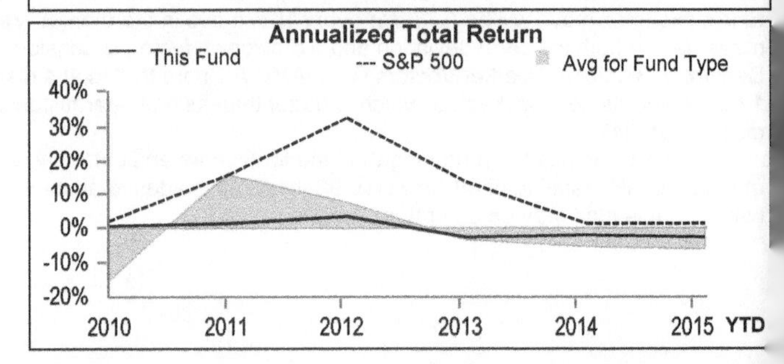

*Market Vectors Coal ETF (KOL) E+ Very Weak

Fund Family: Van Eck Associates Corporation
Fund Type: Energy/Natural Resources
Inception Date: January 10, 2008

Major Rating Factors:
Very poor performance is the major factor driving the E+ (Very Weak) TheStreet.com Investment Rating for *Market Vectors Coal ETF. The fund currently has a performance rating of E- (Very Weak) based on an annualized return of -36.11% over the last three years and a total return of -55.17% year to date 2015. Factored into the performance evaluation is an expense ratio of 0.59% (very low).

The fund's risk rating is currently C (Fair). It carries a beta of 0.87, meaning the fund's expected move will be 8.7% for every 10% move in the market. Volatility, as measured by both the semi-deviation and a drawdown factor, is considered average. As of December 31, 2015, *Market Vectors Coal ETF traded at a discount of .48% below its net asset value, which is better than its one-year historical average discount of .35%.

George Chao has been running the fund for 8 years and currently receives a manager quality ranking of 2 (0=worst, 99=best). This fund offers an average level of risk but investors looking for strong performance will be frustrated.

Data Date	Investment Rating	Net Assets ($Mil)	Price	Perfor-mance Rating/Pts	Total Return Y-T-D	Risk Rating/Pts
12-15	E+	157.60	6.25	E- / 0.2	-55.17%	C / 4.5
2014	D-	157.60	14.67	E+ / 0.6	-20.69%	C / 4.9
2013	E+	155.00	19.44	E / 0.4	-26.46%	C / 4.4
2012	E+	235.40	25.14	E+ / 0.7	-22.64%	C / 4.9
2011	C	314.40	32.25	B- / 7.1	-30.06%	C+ / 5.9
2010	B	529.60	47.24	A+ / 9.8	31.33%	C- / 3.1

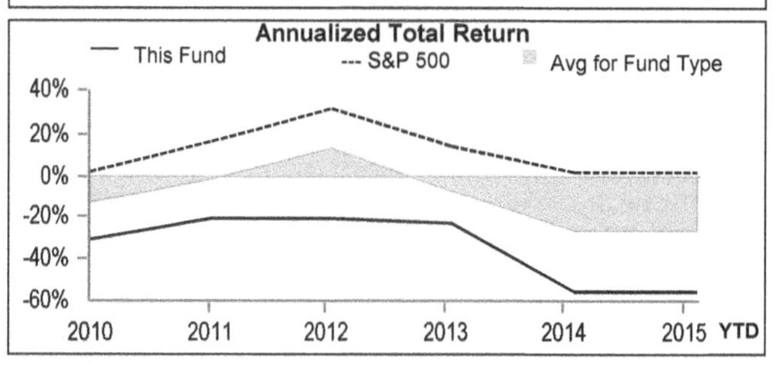

*Market Vectors Double Long Euro (URR) D Weak

Fund Family: Morgan Stanley Investment Managemen
Fund Type: Foreign
Inception Date: May 7, 2008

Major Rating Factors:
Disappointing performance is the major factor driving the D (Weak) TheStreet.com Investment Rating for *Market Vectors Double Long Euro. The fund currently has a performance rating of D- (Weak) based on an annualized return of -12.85% over the last three years and a total return of -22.52% year to date 2015. Factored into the performance evaluation is an expense ratio of 0.65% (very low).

The fund's risk rating is currently C+ (Fair). It carries a beta of 0.33, meaning the fund's expected move will be 3.3% for every 10% move in the market. Volatility, as measured by both the semi-deviation and a drawdown factor, is considered low. As of December 31, 2015, *Market Vectors Double Long Euro traded at a discount of .35% below its net asset value, which is better than its one-year historical average discount of .24%.

This fund has been team managed for 8 years and currently receives a manager quality ranking of 10 (0=worst, 99=best). This fund offers only a moderate level of risk but investors looking for strong performance are still waiting.

Data Date	Investment Rating	Net Assets ($Mil)	Price	Perfor-mance Rating/Pts	Total Return Y-T-D	Risk Rating/Pts
12-15	D	4.84	17.00	D- / 1.4	-22.52%	C+ / 5.6
2014	D-	0.90	22.28	D- / 1.5	-23.93%	C / 5.3
2013	C-	4.84	29.29	C / 4.6	14.06%	C+ / 6.6
2012	D-	4.84	27.00	E+ / 0.8	1.32%	C+ / 6.4
2011	D-	4.84	26.24	D- / 1.3	-4.98%	C+ / 6.4
2010	D	4.84	29.10	D- / 1.1	-14.24%	C / 5.3

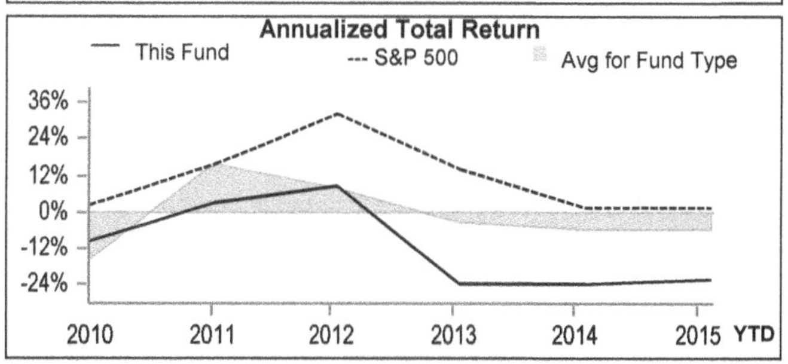

*Market Vectors Double Shrt Euro (DRR) A Excellent

Fund Family: Morgan Stanley Investment Managemen
Fund Type: Foreign
Inception Date: May 7, 2008

Major Rating Factors:
Strong performance is the major factor driving the A (Excellent) TheStreet.com Investment Rating for *Market Vectors Double Shrt Euro. The fund currently has a performance rating of B+ (Good) based on an annualized return of 10.83% over the last three years and a total return of 17.82% year to date 2015. Factored into the performance evaluation is an expense ratio of 0.65% (very low).

The fund's risk rating is currently B (Good). It carries a beta of -0.50, meaning the fund's expected move will be -5.0% for every 10% move in the market. Volatility, as measured by both the semi-deviation and a drawdown factor, is considered low. As of December 31, 2015, *Market Vectors Double Shrt Euro traded at a discount of .38% below its net asset value, which is better than its one-year historical average discount of .08%.

This fund has been team managed for 8 years and currently receives a manager quality ranking of 97 (0=worst, 99=best). If you desire only a moderate level of risk and strong performance, then this fund is an excellent option.

Data Date	Investment Rating	Net Assets ($Mil)	Price	Perfor-mance Rating/Pts	Total Return Y-T-D	Risk Rating/Pts
12-15	A	28.43	59.70	B+ / 8.8	17.82%	B / 8.0
2014	C	38.40	49.76	C / 4.9	25.53%	B- / 7.4
2013	D	28.43	38.45	D- / 1.3	-9.60%	B- / 7.5
2012	D-	28.43	43.15	D- / 1.1	-11.69%	C+ / 6.3
2011	D	28.43	45.66	D / 2.0	-2.93%	C+ / 6.4
2010	C-	28.43	45.64	C- / 3.2	9.24%	C+ / 5.9

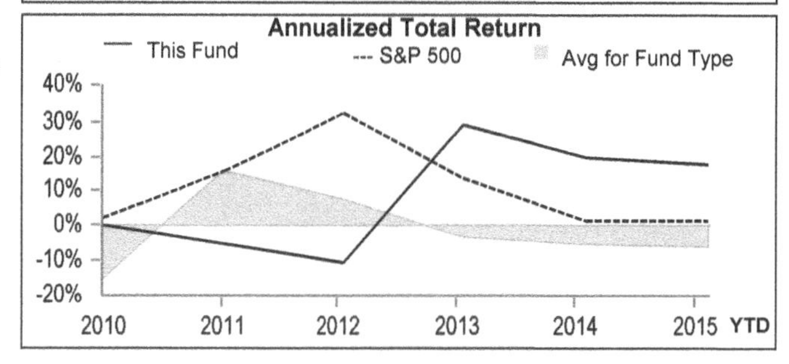

*Market Vectors Egypt Index ETF (EGPT) D- Weak

Fund Family: Van Eck Associates Corporation
Fund Type: Emerging Market
Inception Date: February 16, 2010

Data Date	Investment Rating	Net Assets ($Mil)	Price	Performance Rating/Pts	Total Return Y-T-D	Risk Rating/Pts
12-15	D-	97.70	38.21	D / 1.6	-33.79%	C / 4.8
2014	C+	97.70	58.30	B / 7.9	14.87%	C+ / 6.1
2013	D-	48.60	53.63	D / 1.8	3.71%	C / 4.9
2012	C+	36.30	13.08	A+ / 9.6	39.59%	C- / 4.2
2011	E+	36.20	9.46	E- / 0	-52.05%	C / 4.4

Major Rating Factors:
Disappointing performance is the major factor driving the D- (Weak) TheStreet.com Investment Rating for *Market Vectors Egypt Index ETF. The fund currently has a performance rating of D (Weak) based on an annualized return of -8.02% over the last three years and a total return of -33.79% year to date 2015. Factored into the performance evaluation is an expense ratio of 0.92% (low).

The fund's risk rating is currently C (Fair). It carries a beta of 0.66, meaning the fund's expected move will be 6.6% for every 10% move in the market. Volatility, as measured by both the semi-deviation and a drawdown factor, is considered average. As of December 31, 2015, *Market Vectors Egypt Index ETF traded at a discount of 2.05% below its net asset value, which is better than its one-year historical average discount of .31%.

George Chao has been running the fund for 6 years and currently receives a manager quality ranking of 40 (0=worst, 99=best). This fund offers an average level of risk but investors looking for strong performance will be frustrated.

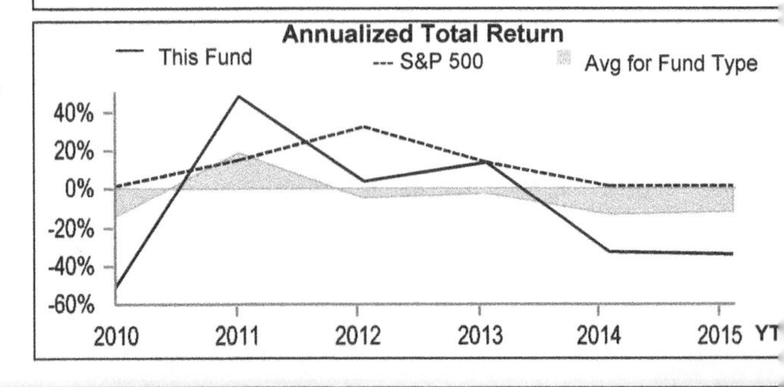

*Market Vectors EM Aggregate Bd E (EMAG) C- Fair

Fund Family: Van Eck Associates Corporation
Fund Type: General - Investment Grade
Inception Date: May 11, 2011

Data Date	Investment Rating	Net Assets ($Mil)	Price	Performance Rating/Pts	Total Return Y-T-D	Risk Rating/Pts
12-15	C-	17.60	19.81	D+ / 2.7	-7.79%	B- / 7.7
2014	D+	17.60	22.23	C- / 3.2	1.15%	C+ / 6.6
2013	C-	16.50	23.57	D / 2.1	-6.35%	B / 8.5
2012	B	7.50	26.15	C+ / 6.5	15.41%	B / 8.9

Major Rating Factors:
Disappointing performance is the major factor driving the C- (Fair) TheStreet.com Investment Rating for *Market Vectors EM Aggregate Bd E. The fund currently has a performance rating of D+ (Weak) based on an annualized return of -4.96% over the last three years and a total return of -7.79% year to date 2015. Factored into the performance evaluation is an expense ratio of 0.49% (very low).

The fund's risk rating is currently B- (Good). It carries a beta of 1.53, meaning it is expected to move 15.3% for every 10% move in the market. Volatility, as measured by both the semi-deviation and a drawdown factor, is considered low. As of December 31, 2015, *Market Vectors EM Aggregate Bd E traded at a discount of 2.08% below its net asset value, which is better than its one-year historical average discount of .57%.

Francis G. Rodilosso has been running the fund for 4 years and currently receives a manager quality ranking of 23 (0=worst, 99=best). This fund offers only a moderate level of risk but investors looking for strong performance are still waiting.

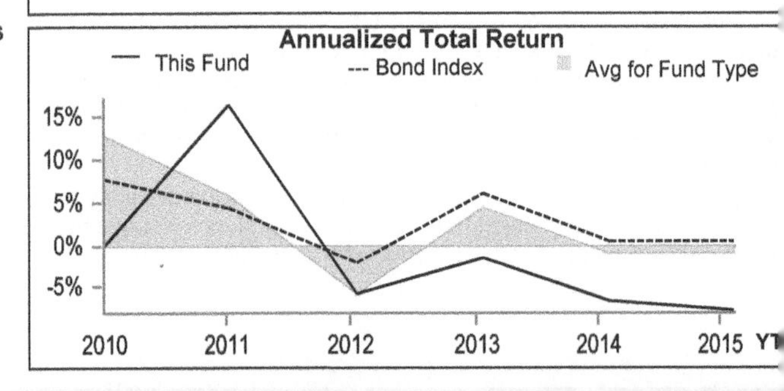

*Market Vectors Emg Mkts Hi Yld B (HYEM) C Fair

Fund Family: Van Eck Associates Corporation
Fund Type: Emerging Market
Inception Date: May 8, 2012

Data Date	Investment Rating	Net Assets ($Mil)	Price	Performance Rating/Pts	Total Return Y-T-D	Risk Rating/Pts
12-15	C	432.60	22.12	C- / 4.0	2.84%	B / 8.1
2014	D+	432.60	22.97	D- / 1.5	-2.19%	B / 8.3
2013	C	222.50	25.03	C- / 3.0	-2.08%	B+ / 9.2

Major Rating Factors: Middle of the road best describes *Market Vectors Emg Mkts Hi Yld B whose TheStreet.com Investment Rating is currently a C (Fair). The fund currently has a performance rating of C- (Fair) based on an annualized return of -0.70% over the last three years and a total return of 2.84% year to date 2015. Factored into the performance evaluation is an expense ratio of 0.40% (very low).

The fund's risk rating is currently B (Good). It carries a beta of 0.26, meaning the fund's expected move will be 2.6% for every 10% move in the market. Volatility, as measured by both the semi-deviation and a drawdown factor, is considered low. As of December 31, 2015, *Market Vectors Emg Mkts Hi Yld B traded at a discount of .67% below its net asset value, which is better than its one-year historical average discount of .57%.

Francis G. Rodilosso has been running the fund for 4 years and currently receives a manager quality ranking of 76 (0=worst, 99=best). If you desire an average level of risk, then this fund may be an option.

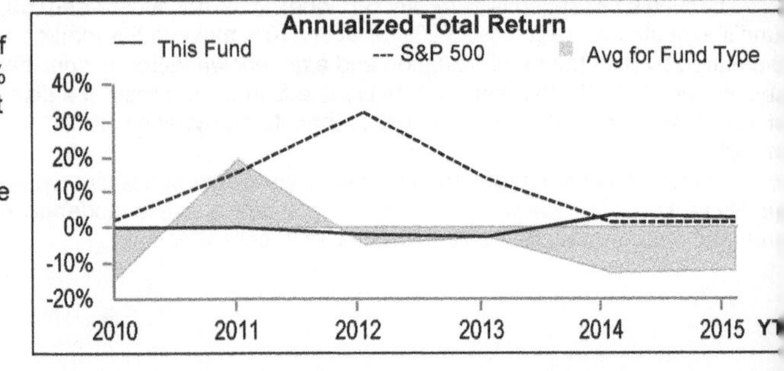

* Denotes ETF Fund

*Market Vectors Environment Svc E (EVX) C Fair

Fund Family: Van Eck Associates Corporation
Fund Type: Income
Inception Date: October 10, 2006

Major Rating Factors: Middle of the road best describes *Market Vectors Environment Svc E whose TheStreet.com Investment Rating is currently a C (Fair). The fund currently has a performance rating of C+ (Fair) based on an annualized return of 5.24% over the last three years and a total return of -9.50% year to date 2015. Factored into the performance evaluation is an expense ratio of 0.55% (very low).

The fund's risk rating is currently C+ (Fair). It carries a beta of 0.88, meaning the fund's expected move will be 8.8% for every 10% move in the market. Volatility, as measured by both the semi-deviation and a drawdown factor, is considered low. As of December 31, 2015, *Market Vectors Environment Svc E traded at a premium of .43% above its net asset value, which is worse than its one-year historical average discount of .02%.

Hao-Hung Liao has been running the fund for 10 years and currently receives a manager quality ranking of 25 (0=worst, 99=best). If you desire an average level of risk, then this fund may be an option.

Data Date	Investment Rating	Net Assets ($Mil)	Price	Performance Rating/Pts	Total Return Y-T-D	Risk Rating/Pts
12-15	C	16.10	58.67	C+ / 5.6	-9.50%	C+ / 6.9
2014	C+	16.10	66.72	C+ / 6.5	4.69%	C+ / 6.9
2013	B	19.60	65.43	B- / 7.2	24.57%	B / 8.1
2012	C-	20.50	50.97	C- / 3.6	11.69%	B- / 7.8
2011	C-	23.30	46.59	C- / 3.4	-5.73%	B- / 7.1
2010	C+	30.90	51.60	C+ / 6.2	22.10%	C / 5.3

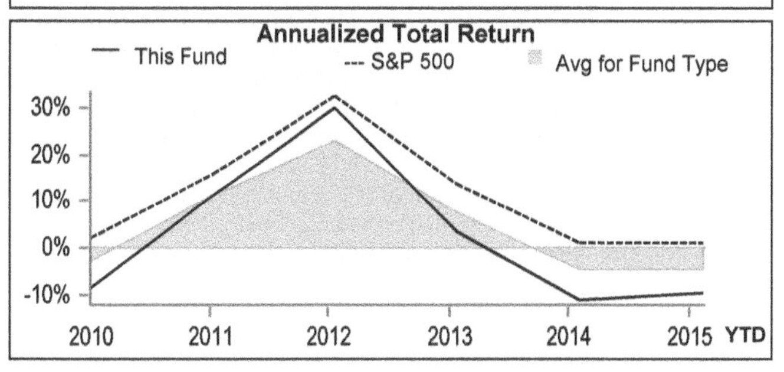

*Market Vectors FA Hi Yld Bd ETF (ANGL) C+ Fair

Fund Family: Van Eck Associates Corporation
Fund Type: General - Investment Grade
Inception Date: April 10, 2012

Major Rating Factors: Middle of the road best describes *Market Vectors FA Hi Yld Bd ETF whose TheStreet.com Investment Rating is currently a C+ (Fair). The fund currently has a performance rating of C (Fair) based on an annualized return of 2.54% over the last three years and a total return of -1.16% year to date 2015. Factored into the performance evaluation is an expense ratio of 0.40% (very low).

The fund's risk rating is currently B (Good). It carries a beta of 0.88, meaning the fund's expected move will be 8.8% for every 10% move in the market. Volatility, as measured by both the semi-deviation and a drawdown factor, is considered low. As of December 31, 2015, *Market Vectors FA Hi Yld Bd ETF traded at a discount of .12% below its net asset value, which is better than its one-year historical average discount of .05%.

Francis G. Rodilosso has been running the fund for 4 years and currently receives a manager quality ranking of 79 (0=worst, 99=best). If you desire an average level of risk, then this fund may be an option.

Data Date	Investment Rating	Net Assets ($Mil)	Price	Performance Rating/Pts	Total Return Y-T-D	Risk Rating/Pts
12-15	C+	16.50	24.33	C / 4.9	-1.16%	B / 8.6
2014	C-	16.50	26.04	D+ / 2.5	3.55%	B+ / 9.0
2013	B	16.10	27.04	C+ / 5.9	6.22%	B+ / 9.5

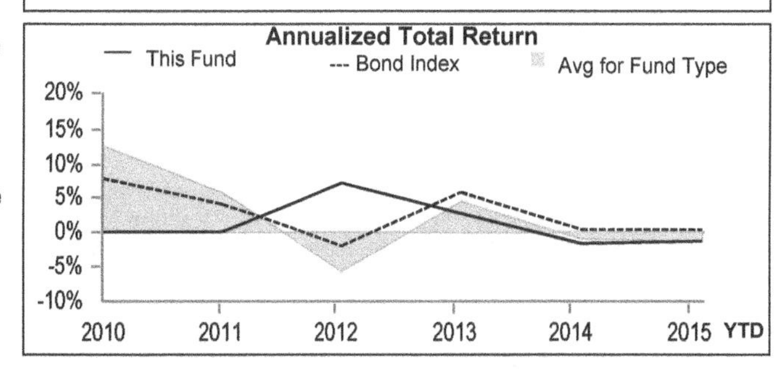

*Market Vectors Gaming ETF (BJK) D Weak

Fund Family: Van Eck Associates Corporation
Fund Type: Global
Inception Date: January 22, 2008

Major Rating Factors: *Market Vectors Gaming ETF receives a TheStreet.com Investment Rating of D (Weak). The fund currently has a performance rating of C- (Fair) based on an annualized return of -2.15% over the last three years and a total return of -12.46% year to date 2015. Factored into the performance evaluation is an expense ratio of 0.65% (very low).

The fund's risk rating is currently C (Fair). It carries a beta of 1.37, meaning it is expected to move 13.7% for every 10% move in the market. Volatility, as measured by both the semi-deviation and a drawdown factor, is considered average. As of December 31, 2015, *Market Vectors Gaming ETF traded at a premium of .44% above its net asset value, which is worse than its one-year historical average discount of .08%.

George Chao has been running the fund for 8 years and currently receives a manager quality ranking of 21 (0=worst, 99=best). If you desire an average level of risk, then this fund may be an option.

Data Date	Investment Rating	Net Assets ($Mil)	Price	Performance Rating/Pts	Total Return Y-T-D	Risk Rating/Pts
12-15	D	43.40	31.73	C- / 3.1	-12.46%	C / 4.6
2014	D+	43.40	38.47	C- / 4.1	-24.31%	C / 5.3
2013	A-	82.40	53.40	A / 9.3	43.65%	B- / 7.3
2012	B	60.80	35.45	B+ / 8.5	26.54%	B- / 7.2
2011	C-	96.70	30.07	C+ / 6.1	-5.67%	C / 5.5
2010	B+	129.10	31.49	A+ / 9.7	37.89%	C / 4.4

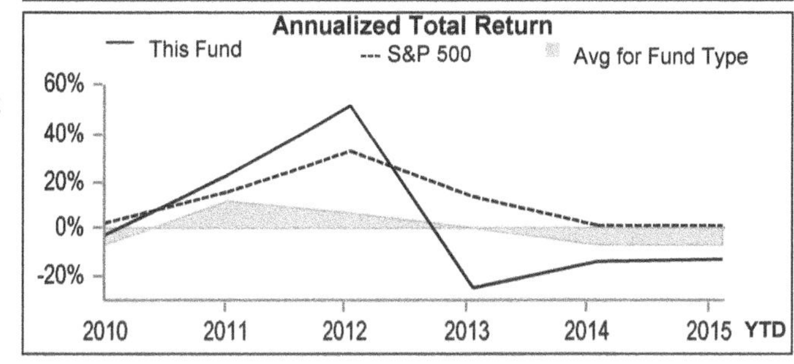

*Market Vectors Global Alt Enrgy (GEX) B Good

Fund Family: Van Eck Associates Corporation
Fund Type: Energy/Natural Resources
Inception Date: May 3, 2007

Major Rating Factors:
Exceptional performance is the major factor driving the B (Good) TheStreet.com Investment Rating for *Market Vectors Global Alt Enrgy. The fund currently has a performance rating of A- (Excellent) based on an annualized return of 17.30% over the last three years and a total return of 1.42% year to date 2015. Factored into the performance evaluation is an expense ratio of 0.62% (very low).

The fund's risk rating is currently C+ (Fair). It carries a beta of 0.65, meaning the fund's expected move will be 6.5% for every 10% move in the market. Volatility, as measured by both the semi-deviation and a drawdown factor, is considered low. As of December 31, 2015, *Market Vectors Global Alt Enrgy traded at a premium of .44% above its net asset value, which is worse than its one-year historical average premium of .06%.

Hao-Hung Liao has been running the fund for 9 years and currently receives a manager quality ranking of 98 (0=worst, 99=best). If you desire only a moderate level of risk and strong performance, then this fund is an excellent option.

Data Date	Investment Rating	Net Assets ($Mil)	Price	Performance Rating/Pts	Total Return Y-T-D	Risk Rating/Pts
12-15	B	100.20	54.81	A- / 9.1	1.42%	C+ / 6.0
2014	C+	100.20	53.98	C+ / 6.8	-4.34%	B- / 7.4
2013	C-	91.30	55.96	B- / 7.2	65.33%	C / 4.9
2012	E+	46.00	11.04	E+ / 0.6	3.66%	C / 4.7
2011	E+	58.60	10.91	E+ / 0.6	-43.40%	C / 4.8
2010	E+	134.50	20.01	E / 0.4	-19.20%	C- / 3.5

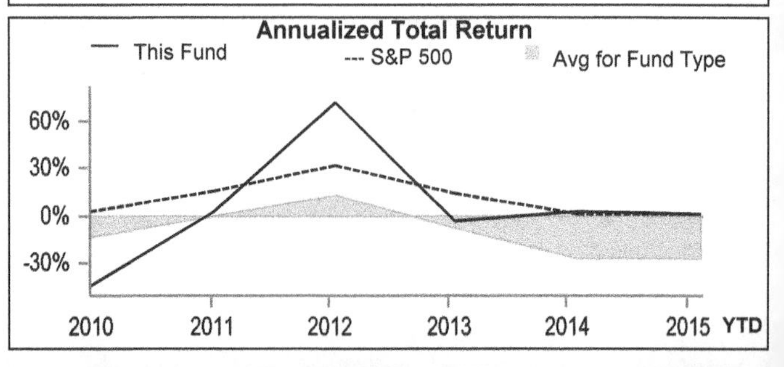

*Market Vectors Gold Miners ETF (GDX) E+ Very Weak

Fund Family: Van Eck Associates Corporation
Fund Type: Precious Metals
Inception Date: May 16, 2006

Major Rating Factors:
Very poor performance is the major factor driving the E+ (Very Weak) TheStreet.com Investment Rating for *Market Vectors Gold Miners ETF. The fund currently has a performance rating of E (Very Weak) based on an annualized return of -32.31% over the last three years and a total return of -26.95% year to date 2015. Factored into the performance evaluation is an expense ratio of 0.53% (very low).

The fund's risk rating is currently C- (Fair). It carries a beta of 1.84, meaning it is expected to move 18.4% for every 10% move in the market. Volatility, as measured by both the semi-deviation and a drawdown factor, is considered average. As of December 31, 2015, *Market Vectors Gold Miners ETF traded at a price exactly equal to its net asset value, which is worse than its one-year historical average discount of .01%.

Hao-Hung Liao has been running the fund for 10 years and currently receives a manager quality ranking of 14 (0=worst, 99=best). This fund offers an average level of risk but investors looking for strong performance will be frustrated.

Data Date	Investment Rating	Net Assets ($Mil)	Price	Performance Rating/Pts	Total Return Y-T-D	Risk Rating/Pts
12-15	E+	6,704.20	13.72	E / 0.4	-26.95%	C- / 3.1
2014	E+	6,704.20	18.38	E / 0.4	-14.91%	C- / 3.9
2013	E+	6,652.60	21.13	E / 0.3	-51.40%	C- / 4.1
2012	D-	9,406.10	46.39	D- / 1.1	-15.17%	C / 5.1
2011	C	8,772.70	51.43	C+ / 6.0	-5.70%	B- / 7.1
2010	C+	7,677.40	61.47	B+ / 8.4	33.90%	C- / 3.3

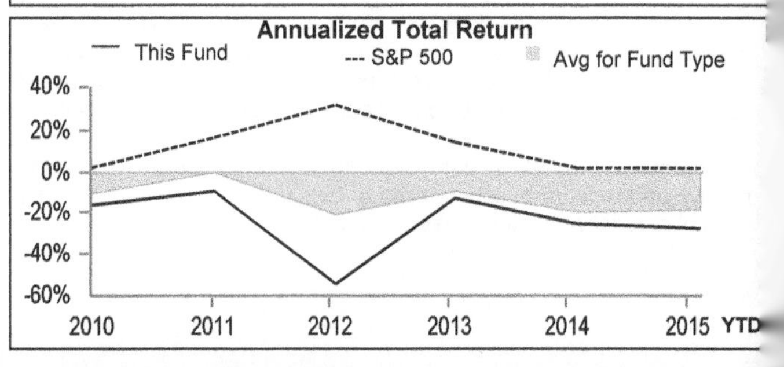

*Market Vectors Gulf States Idx E (MES) C Fair

Fund Family: Van Eck Associates Corporation
Fund Type: Foreign
Inception Date: July 22, 2008

Major Rating Factors: Middle of the road best describes *Market Vectors Gulf States Idx E whose TheStreet.com Investment Rating is currently a C (Fair). The fund currently has a performance rating of C (Fair) based on an annualized return of 5.91% over the last three years and a total return of -11.92% year to date 2015. Factored into the performance evaluation is an expense ratio of 0.98% (low).

The fund's risk rating is currently C+ (Fair). It carries a beta of 0.55, meaning the fund's expected move will be 5.5% for every 10% move in the market. Volatility, as measured by both the semi-deviation and a drawdown factor, is considered low. As of December 31, 2015, *Market Vectors Gulf States Idx E traded at a discount of .41% below its net asset value, which is worse than its one-year historical average discount of 1.25%.

George Chao has been running the fund for 8 years and currently receives a manager quality ranking of 86 (0=worst, 99=best). If you desire an average level of risk, then this fund may be an option.

Data Date	Investment Rating	Net Assets ($Mil)	Price	Performance Rating/Pts	Total Return Y-T-D	Risk Rating/Pts
12-15	C	27.20	22.10	C / 5.2	-11.92%	C+ / 6.1
2014	C	27.20	26.37	C+ / 5.6	1.05%	C+ / 6.9
2013	B	16.30	26.96	B- / 7.4	36.21%	B / 8.1
2012	C-	10.30	20.25	C- / 3.6	14.48%	B- / 7.9
2011	D+	14.10	19.56	D+ / 2.4	-15.84%	B- / 7.3
2010	B	22.10	23.81	A / 9.4	23.81%	C- / 3.8

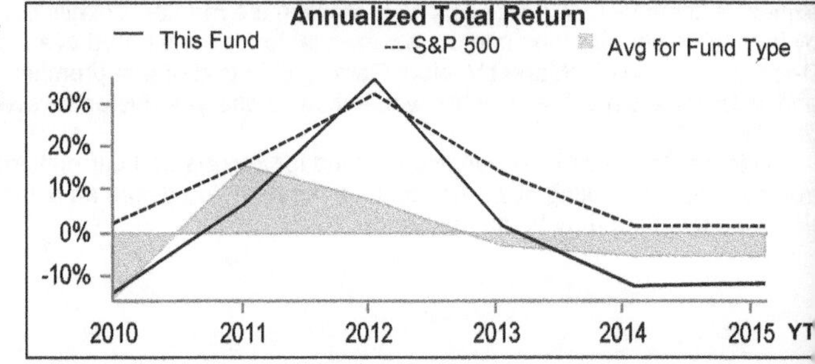

*Market Vectors Hi-Yld Mun Idx ET (HYD) C+ Fair

Fund Family: Van Eck Associates Corporation
Fund Type: Municipal - High Yield
Inception Date: February 4, 2009

Major Rating Factors: Middle of the road best describes *Market Vectors Hi-Yld Mun Idx ET whose TheStreet.com Investment Rating is currently a C+ (Fair). The fund currently has a performance rating of C+ (Fair) based on an annualized return of 3.15% over the last three years and a total return of 4.48% year to date 2015. Factored into the performance evaluation is an expense ratio of 0.35% (very low).

The fund's risk rating is currently C+ (Fair). It carries a beta of 1.89, meaning it is expected to move 18.9% for every 10% move in the market. Volatility, as measured by both the semi-deviation and a drawdown factor, is considered low. As of December 31, 2015, *Market Vectors Hi-Yld Mun Idx ET traded at a premium of .32% above its net asset value, which is worse than its one-year historical average discount of .17%.

Jeffrey A. Herrmann has been running the fund for 8 years and currently receives a manager quality ranking of 46 (0=worst, 99=best). If you desire an average level of risk, then this fund may be an option.

Data Date	Investment Rating	Net Assets ($Mil)	Price	Performance Rating/Pts	Total Return Y-T-D	Risk Rating/Pts
12-15	C+	1,231.20	30.88	C+ / 6.5	4.48%	C+ / 6.8
2014	B-	1,231.20	30.85	C+ / 6.9	14.52%	B- / 7.4
2013	C+	794.90	28.26	C / 4.9	-8.21%	B / 8.6
2012	B	1,044.10	32.84	C+ / 6.1	14.47%	B+ / 9.1
2011	B	340.80	29.80	C+ / 6.8	11.68%	B+ / 9.1
2010	C-	175.50	28.51	D- / 1.0	-0.40%	B / 8.4

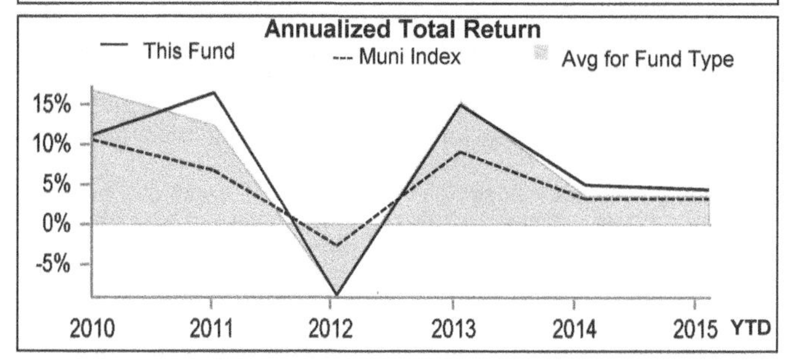

*Market Vectors India Small-Cap E (SCIF) C- Fair

Fund Family: Van Eck Associates Corporation
Fund Type: Foreign
Inception Date: August 24, 2010

Major Rating Factors: Middle of the road best describes *Market Vectors India Small-Cap E whose TheStreet.com Investment Rating is currently a C- (Fair). The fund currently has a performance rating of C- (Fair) based on an annualized return of -0.88% over the last three years and a total return of -2.60% year to date 2015. Factored into the performance evaluation is an expense ratio of 0.85% (very low).

The fund's risk rating is currently C+ (Fair). It carries a beta of 1.17, meaning it is expected to move 11.7% for every 10% move in the market. Volatility, as measured by both the semi-deviation and a drawdown factor, is considered low. As of December 31, 2015, *Market Vectors India Small-Cap E traded at a discount of .89% below its net asset value, which is better than its one-year historical average discount of .21%.

George Chao has been running the fund for 6 years and currently receives a manager quality ranking of 28 (0=worst, 99=best). If you desire an average level of risk, then this fund may be an option.

Data Date	Investment Rating	Net Assets ($Mil)	Price	Performance Rating/Pts	Total Return Y-T-D	Risk Rating/Pts
12-15	C-	294.80	43.27	C- / 4.0	-2.60%	C+ / 6.3
2014	C-	294.80	44.69	C+ / 5.9	43.40%	C / 5.4
2013	E+	110.40	31.70	E / 0.5	-32.40%	C- / 3.8
2012	D	81.10	11.12	C / 4.9	9.08%	C- / 3.3
2011	E	30.90	8.73	E- / 0	-50.66%	C- / 3.3

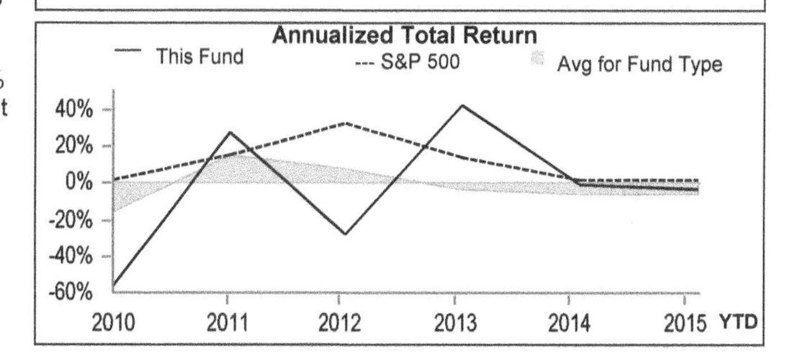

*Market Vectors Indian Rupee USD (INR) C+ Fair

Fund Family: Morgan Stanley Investment Managemen
Fund Type: Foreign
Inception Date: March 14, 2008

Major Rating Factors: Middle of the road best describes *Market Vectors Indian Rupee USD whose TheStreet.com Investment Rating is currently a C+ (Fair). The fund currently has a performance rating of C (Fair) based on an annualized return of 0.11% over the last three years and a total return of 4.74% year to date 2015. Factored into the performance evaluation is an expense ratio of 0.55% (very low).

The fund's risk rating is currently B (Good). It carries a beta of 0.05, meaning the fund's expected move will be 0.5% for every 10% move in the market. Volatility, as measured by both the semi-deviation and a drawdown factor, is considered low. As of December 31, 2015, *Market Vectors Indian Rupee USD traded at a discount of .78% below its net asset value, which is worse than its one-year historical average discount of .86%.

This fund has been team managed for 8 years and currently receives a manager quality ranking of 66 (0=worst, 99=best). If you desire an average level of risk, then this fund may be an option.

Data Date	Investment Rating	Net Assets ($Mil)	Price	Performance Rating/Pts	Total Return Y-T-D	Risk Rating/Pts
12-15	C+	6.60	36.87	C / 4.8	4.74%	B / 8.1
2014	C-	1.70	35.73	C- / 3.3	13.07%	B- / 7.7
2013	D	6.60	31.60	D- / 1.1	-14.01%	B- / 7.5
2012	D	6.60	36.75	D- / 1.2	1.72%	B / 8.2
2011	D+	6.60	35.70	D / 1.6	-11.95%	B / 8.5
2010	A-	6.60	40.85	B- / 7.0	7.78%	B- / 7.8

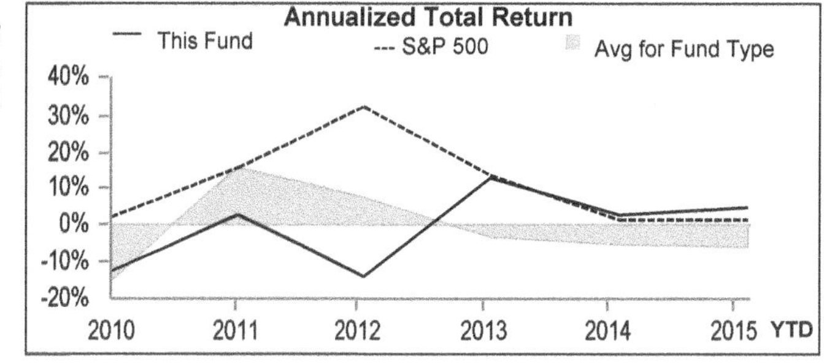

*Market Vectors Indonesia Idx ETF (IDX) D- Weak

Fund Family: Van Eck Associates Corporation
Fund Type: Foreign
Inception Date: January 15, 2009

Major Rating Factors:
Disappointing performance is the major factor driving the D- (Weak) TheStreet.com Investment Rating for *Market Vectors Indonesia Idx ETF. The fund currently has a performance rating of D (Weak) based on an annualized return of -11.80% over the last three years and a total return of -21.01% year to date 2015. Factored into the performance evaluation is an expense ratio of 0.57% (very low).

The fund's risk rating is currently C- (Fair). It carries a beta of 0.89, meaning the fund's expected move will be 8.9% for every 10% move in the market. Volatility, as measured by both the semi-deviation and a drawdown factor, is considered average. As of December 31, 2015, *Market Vectors Indonesia Idx ETF traded at a premium of .27% above its net asset value, which is worse than its one-year historical average discount of .26%.

George Chao has been running the fund for 7 years and currently receives a manager quality ranking of 10 (0=worst, 99=best). This fund offers an average level of risk but investors looking for strong performance will be frustrated.

Data Date	Investment Rating	Net Assets ($Mil)	Price	Performance Rating/Pts	Total Return Y-T-D	Risk Rating/Pts
12-15	D-	214.30	18.41	D / 1.7	-21.01%	C- / 3.2
2014	D-	214.30	24.29	D+ / 2.7	21.57%	C- / 3.9
2013	E+	183.60	21.26	E+ / 0.9	-27.36%	C- / 3.6
2012	D-	405.10	28.64	C- / 3.1	-1.76%	C / 4.5
2011	D-	471.30	28.47	D+ / 2.5	3.98%	C / 4.9
2010	A+	623.50	87.31	A / 9.5	41.77%	B- / 7.9

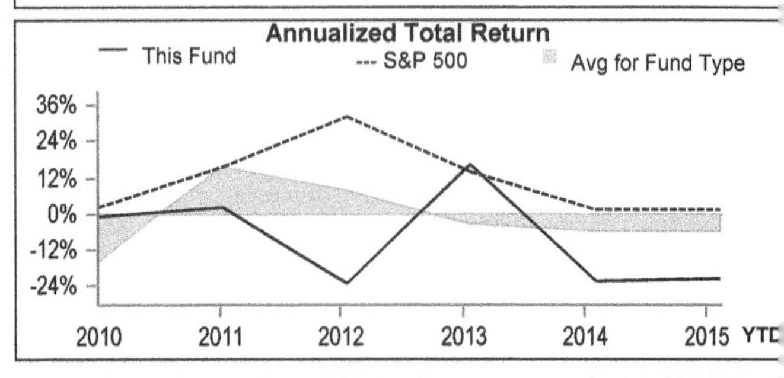

*Market Vectors Indonesia SC ETF (IDXJ) E+ Very Weak

Fund Family: Van Eck Associates Corporation
Fund Type: Foreign
Inception Date: March 20, 2012

Major Rating Factors:
Very poor performance is the major factor driving the E+ (Very Weak) TheStreet.com Investment Rating for *Market Vectors Indonesia SC ETF. The fund currently has a performance rating of E+ (Very Weak) based on an annualized return of -18.14% over the last three years and a total return of -42.19% year to date 2015. Factored into the performance evaluation is an expense ratio of 0.61% (very low).

The fund's risk rating is currently C- (Fair). It carries a beta of 1.24, meaning it is expected to move 12.4% for every 10% move in the market. Volatility, as measured by both the semi-deviation and a drawdown factor, is considered average. As of December 31, 2015, *Market Vectors Indonesia SC ETF traded at a discount of .38% below its net asset value, which is better than its one-year historical average premium of 1.31%.

George Cao has been running the fund for 4 years and currently receives a manager quality ranking of 6 (0=worst, 99=best). This fund offers an average level of risk but investors looking for strong performance will be frustrated.

Data Date	Investment Rating	Net Assets ($Mil)	Price	Performance Rating/Pts	Total Return Y-T-D	Risk Rating/Pts
12-15	E+	7.80	7.90	E+ / 0.8	-42.19%	C- / 3.4
2014	C+	7.80	13.68	A / 9.5	27.36%	C / 4.3
2013	E+	5.30	11.90	E- / 0.2	-24.37%	C / 4.4

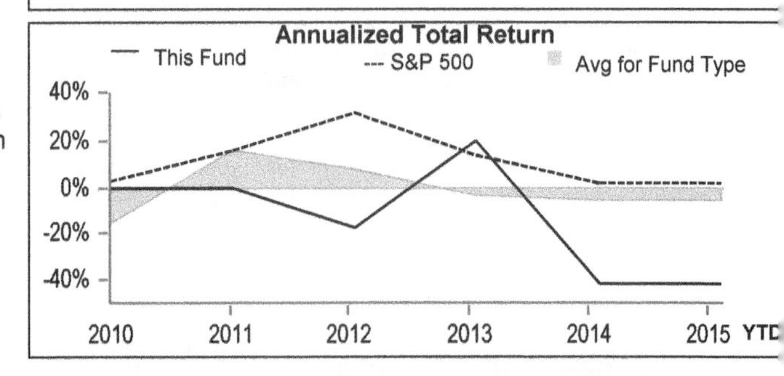

*Market Vectors Interm Muni Idx E (ITM) B- Good

Fund Family: Van Eck Associates Corporation
Fund Type: Municipal - National
Inception Date: December 4, 2007

Major Rating Factors: *Market Vectors Interm Muni Idx E receives a TheStreet.com Investment Rating of B- (Good). The fund currently has a performance rating of C+ (Fair) based on an annualized return of 2.99% over the last three years and a total return of 3.45% year to date 2015. Factored into the performance evaluation is an expense ratio of 0.24% (very low).

The fund's risk rating is currently B- (Good). It carries a beta of 1.42, meaning it is expected to move 14.2% for every 10% move in the market. Volatility, as measured by both the semi-deviation and a drawdown factor, is considered low. As of December 31, 2015, *Market Vectors Interm Muni Idx E traded at a premium of .38% above its net asset value, which is worse than its one-year historical average premium of .11%.

James T. Colby, III has been running the fund for 9 years and currently receives a manager quality ranking of 56 (0=worst, 99=best). If you desire an average level of risk, then this fund may be an option.

Data Date	Investment Rating	Net Assets ($Mil)	Price	Performance Rating/Pts	Total Return Y-T-D	Risk Rating/Pts
12-15	B-	736.00	23.97	C+ / 6.3	3.45%	B- / 7.8
2014	C	736.00	23.67	C / 5.0	9.45%	B- / 7.6
2013	C+	561.20	22.00	C / 4.8	-3.64%	B+ / 9.2
2012	C+	690.00	23.64	C- / 4.0	5.23%	B+ / 9.4
2011	B-	351.40	22.86	C+ / 5.8	13.47%	B+ / 9.4
2010	D	209.70	20.89	C- / 4.1	1.47%	D+ / 2.7

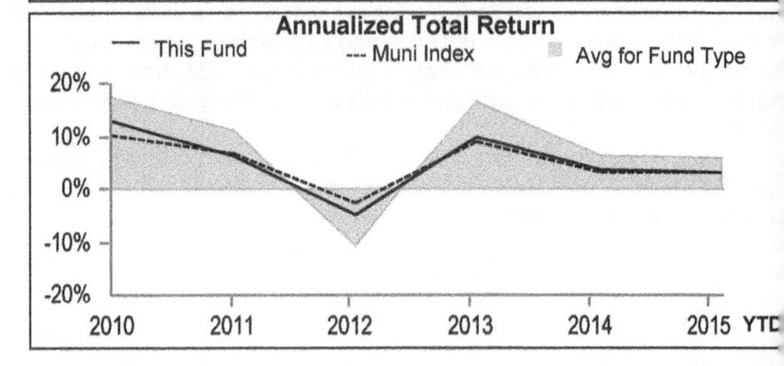

*Market Vectors Intl Hi Yld Bond (IHY) C Fair

Fund Family: Van Eck Associates Corporation
Fund Type: Global
Inception Date: April 2, 2012

Major Rating Factors: Middle of the road best describes *Market Vectors Intl Hi Yld Bond whose TheStreet.com Investment Rating is currently a C (Fair). The fund currently has a performance rating of C- (Fair) based on an annualized return of -0.93% over the last three years and a total return of -4.93% year to date 2015. Factored into the performance evaluation is an expense ratio of 0.40% (very low).

The fund's risk rating is currently B (Good). It carries a beta of 0.61, meaning the fund's expected move will be 6.1% for every 10% move in the market. Volatility, as measured by both the semi-deviation and a drawdown factor, is considered low. As of December 31, 2015, *Market Vectors Intl Hi Yld Bond traded at a discount of 1.01% below its net asset value, which is better than its one-year historical average discount of .16%.

Francis G. Rodilosso has been running the fund for 4 years and currently receives a manager quality ranking of 81 (0=worst, 99=best). If you desire an average level of risk, then this fund may be an option.

Data Date	Investment Rating	Net Assets ($Mil)	Price	Performance Rating/Pts	Total Return Y-T-D	Risk Rating/Pts
12-15	C	206.00	22.50	C- / 3.5	-4.93%	B / 8.1
2014	D+	206.00	24.53	D / 1.6	-3.63%	B / 8.6
2013	B	135.60	27.25	C+ / 6.4	5.82%	B+ / 9.2

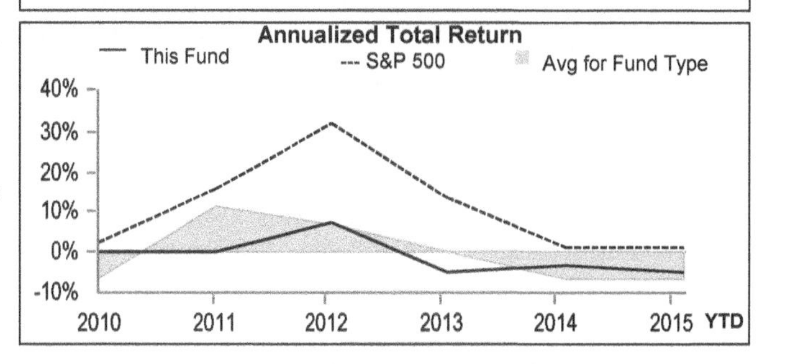

*Market Vectors Invest Grade FR E (FLTR) B- Good

Fund Family: Van Eck Associates Corporation
Fund Type: Corporate - Investment Grade
Inception Date: April 25, 2011

Major Rating Factors: *Market Vectors Invest Grade FR E receives a TheStreet.com Investment Rating of B- (Good). The fund currently has a performance rating of C (Fair) based on an annualized return of 0.57% over the last three years and a total return of -0.45% year to date 2015. Factored into the performance evaluation is an expense ratio of 0.17% (very low).

The fund's risk rating is currently B+ (Good). It carries a beta of 0.02, meaning the fund's expected move will be 0.2% for every 10% move in the market. Volatility, as measured by both the semi-deviation and a drawdown factor, is considered very low. As of December 31, 2015, *Market Vectors Invest Grade FR E traded at a discount of .24% below its net asset value, which is better than its one-year historical average discount of .10%.

Francis G. Rodilosso has been running the fund for 4 years and currently receives a manager quality ranking of 73 (0=worst, 99=best). If you desire an average level of risk, then this fund may be an option.

Data Date	Investment Rating	Net Assets ($Mil)	Price	Performance Rating/Pts	Total Return Y-T-D	Risk Rating/Pts
12-15	B-	90.30	24.67	C / 4.5	-0.45%	B+ / 9.7
2014	C-	90.30	24.93	C- / 3.4	-0.03%	B / 8.0
2013	C	97.30	24.97	C- / 3.0	1.70%	B+ / 9.5
2012	C	7.30	24.72	C- / 3.1	8.14%	B+ / 9.4

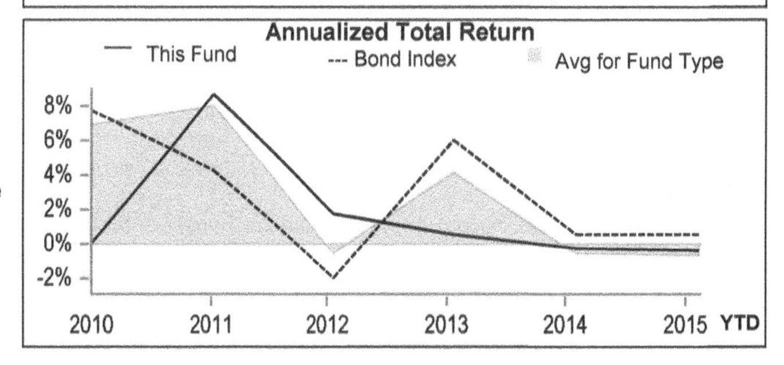

*Market Vectors Israel ETF (ISRA) C- Fair

Fund Family: Van Eck Associates Corporation
Fund Type: Foreign
Inception Date: June 25, 2013

Major Rating Factors:
Disappointing performance is the major factor driving the C- (Fair) TheStreet.com Investment Rating for *Market Vectors Israel ETF. The fund currently has a performance rating of D+ (Weak) based on an annualized return of 0.00% over the last three years and a total return of -0.45% year to date 2015. Factored into the performance evaluation is an expense ratio of 0.59% (very low).

The fund's risk rating is currently B (Good). It carries a beta of 0.00, meaning the fund's expected move will be 0.0% for every 10% move in the market. Volatility, as measured by both the semi-deviation and a drawdown factor, is considered low. As of December 31, 2015, *Market Vectors Israel ETF traded at a discount of .17% below its net asset value, which is better than its one-year historical average premium of .02%.

George Chao has been running the fund for 3 years and currently receives a manager quality ranking of 58 (0=worst, 99=best). This fund offers only a moderate level of risk but investors looking for strong performance are still waiting.

Data Date	Investment Rating	Net Assets ($Mil)	Price	Performance Rating/Pts	Total Return Y-T-D	Risk Rating/Pts
12-15	C-	51.10	28.76	D+ / 2.6	-0.45%	B / 8.2
2014	D+	51.10	29.57	D / 2.0	-0.12%	B- / 7.4

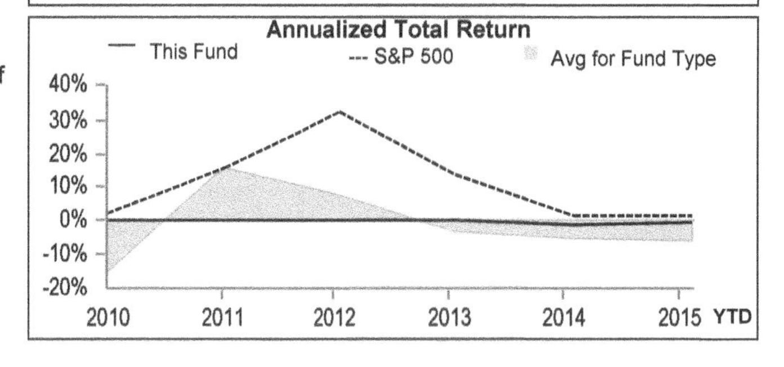

*Market Vectors JP Morgan EM LC B (EMLC) D Weak

Fund Family: Van Eck Associates Corporation
Fund Type: Global
Inception Date: July 22, 2010

Major Rating Factors:
Disappointing performance is the major factor driving the D (Weak) TheStreet.com Investment Rating for *Market Vectors JP Morgan EM LC B. The fund currently has a performance rating of D (Weak) based on an annualized return of -10.13% over the last three years and a total return of -14.85% year to date 2015. Factored into the performance evaluation is an expense ratio of 0.47% (very low).

The fund's risk rating is currently C+ (Fair). It carries a beta of 0.87, meaning the fund's expected move will be 8.7% for every 10% move in the market. Volatility, as measured by both the semi-deviation and a drawdown factor, is considered low. As of December 31, 2015, *Market Vectors JP Morgan EM LC B traded at a price exactly equal to its net asset value, which is worse than its one-year historical average discount of .06%.

Francis G. Rodilosso has been running the fund for 4 years and currently receives a manager quality ranking of 24 (0=worst, 99=best). This fund offers only a moderate level of risk but investors looking for strong performance are still waiting.

Data Date	Investment Rating	Net Assets ($Mil)	Price	Perfor-mance Rating/Pts	Total Return Y-T-D	Risk Rating/Pts
12-15	D	890.80	17.00	D / 1.8	-14.85%	C+ / 5.7
2014	D	890.80	21.17	D+ / 2.4	-4.11%	C+ / 5.6
2013	D+	919.20	23.55	D+ / 2.4	-10.05%	B / 8.0
2012	B	927.00	27.45	B- / 7.1	16.43%	B / 8.4
2011	D+	491.80	24.51	D- / 1.3	-4.26%	B / 8.5

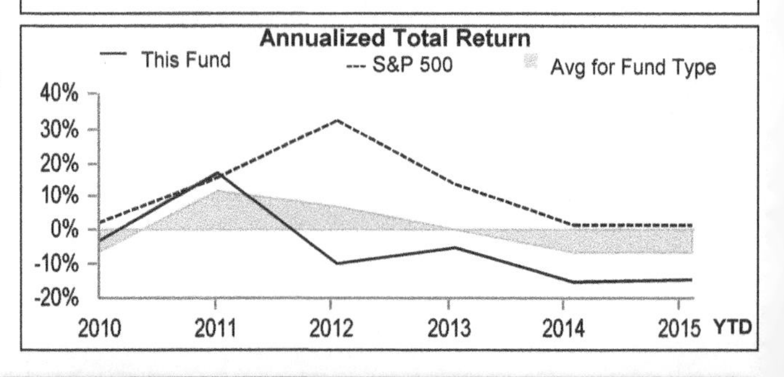

*Market Vectors Junior Gold Mnrs (GDXJ) E Very Weak

Fund Family: Van Eck Associates Corporation
Fund Type: Precious Metals
Inception Date: November 10, 2009

Major Rating Factors: *Market Vectors Junior Gold Mnrs has adopted a very risky asset allocation strategy and currently receives an overall TheStreet.com Investment Rating of E (Very Weak). The fund has a high level of volatility, as measured by both semi-deviation and drawdown factors. It carries a beta of 2.31, meaning it is expected to move 23.1% for every 10% move in the market. As of December 31, 2015, *Market Vectors Junior Gold Mnrs traded at a discount of .05% below its net asset value, which is better than its one-year historical average premium of .05%. Unfortunately, the high level of risk (D, Weak) failed to pay off as investors endured very poor performance.

The fund's performance rating is currently E (Very Weak). It has registered an annualized return of -37.65% over the last three years and is down -22.49% year to date 2015. Factored into the performance evaluation is an expense ratio of 0.54% (very low).

George Chao has been running the fund for 7 years and currently receives a manager quality ranking of 14 (0=worst, 99=best). If you can tolerate very high levels of risk in the hope of improved future returns, holding this fund may be an option.

Data Date	Investment Rating	Net Assets ($Mil)	Price	Perfor-mance Rating/Pts	Total Return Y-T-D	Risk Rating/Pts
12-15	E	2,330.80	19.21	E / 0.3	-22.49%	D / 2.1
2014	E-	2,330.80	23.93	E- / 0.2	-25.55%	D / 2.2
2013	E-	1,136.80	31.05	E- / 0.1	-59.41%	D+ / 2.4
2012	E+	2,537.20	19.80	E+ / 0.9	-20.49%	C- / 4.1
2011	E+	1,922.70	24.70	E+ / 0.6	-24.60%	C / 5.2
2010	A+	2,123.90	39.89	A+ / 9.9	66.53%	B- / 7.6

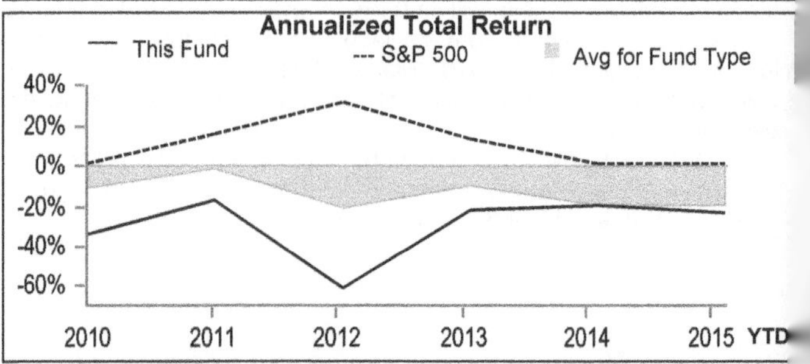

*Market Vectors Long Muni Index E (MLN) C+ Fair

Fund Family: Van Eck Associates Corporation
Fund Type: Municipal - National
Inception Date: January 2, 2008

Major Rating Factors: Middle of the road best describes *Market Vectors Long Muni Index E whose TheStreet.com Investment Rating is currently a C+ (Fair). The fund currently has a performance rating of C+ (Fair) based on an annualized return of 3.47% over the last three years and a total return of 3.58% year to date 2015. Factored into the performance evaluation is an expense ratio of 0.24% (very low).

The fund's risk rating is currently C+ (Fair). It carries a beta of 2.26, meaning it is expected to move 22.6% for every 10% move in the market. Volatility, as measured by both the semi-deviation and a drawdown factor, is considered low. As of December 31, 2015, *Market Vectors Long Muni Index E traded at a premium of .10% above its net asset value, which is worse than its one-year historical average discount of .11%.

James T. Colby, III has been running the fund for 8 years and currently receives a manager quality ranking of 40 (0=worst, 99=best). If you desire an average level of risk, then this fund may be an option.

Data Date	Investment Rating	Net Assets ($Mil)	Price	Perfor-mance Rating/Pts	Total Return Y-T-D	Risk Rating/Pts
12-15	C+	86.90	19.92	C+ / 6.6	3.58%	C+ / 6.8
2014	C+	86.90	19.85	C+ / 6.4	17.13%	B- / 7.0
2013	C	72.00	17.54	C / 4.6	-8.94%	B / 8.6
2012	C+	119.60	20.12	C / 4.9	8.34%	B+ / 9.0
2011	B	67.30	19.03	C+ / 6.9	17.62%	B+ / 9.1
2010	E	56.00	17.17	E+ / 0.9	-1.26%	D+ / 2.7

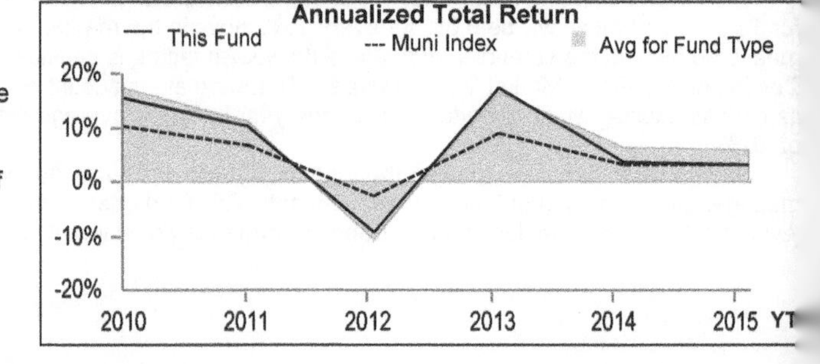

*Market Vectors MS Wide Moat ETF (MOAT) B+ Good

Fund Family: Van Eck Associates Corporation
Fund Type: Income
Inception Date: April 24, 2012

Major Rating Factors: Strong performance is the major factor driving the B+ (Good) TheStreet.com Investment Rating for *Market Vectors MS Wide Moat ETF. The fund currently has a performance rating of B- (Good) based on an annualized return of 9.35% over the last three years and a total return of -4.97% year to date 2015. Factored into the performance evaluation is an expense ratio of 0.49% (very low).

The fund's risk rating is currently B (Good). It carries a beta of 1.06, meaning that its performance tracks fairly well with that of the overall stock market. Volatility, as measured by both the semi-deviation and a drawdown factor, is considered low. As of December 31, 2015, *Market Vectors MS Wide Moat ETF traded at a discount of .03% below its net asset value, which is in line with its one-year historical average discount of .03%.

George Chao has been running the fund for 4 years and currently receives a manager quality ranking of 33 (0=worst, 99=best). If you desire only a moderate level of risk and strong performance, then this fund is an excellent option.

Data Date	Investment Rating	Net Assets ($Mil)	Price	Performance Rating/Pts	Total Return Y-T-D	Risk Rating/Pts
12-15	B+	853.60	28.91	B- / 7.1	-4.97%	B / 8.3
2014	B	853.60	31.08	C+ / 5.7	11.57%	B+ / 9.5
2013	A+	541.70	28.84	A- / 9.2	24.44%	B+ / 9.3

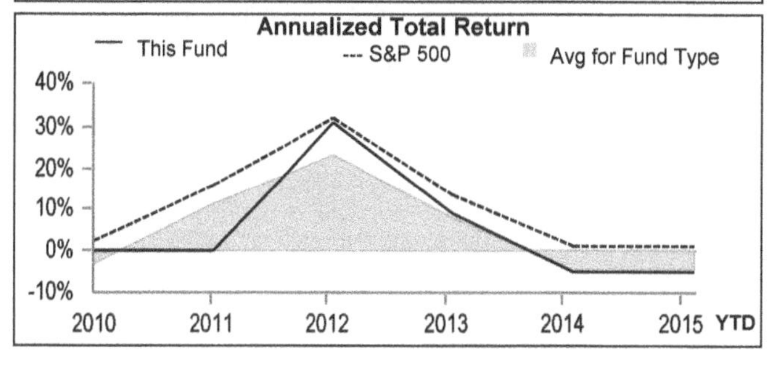

*Market Vectors Mtge REIT Income (MORT) D+ Weak

Fund Family: Van Eck Associates Corporation
Fund Type: Mortgage
Inception Date: August 16, 2011

Major Rating Factors: *Market Vectors Mtge REIT Income receives a TheStreet.com Investment Rating of D+ (Weak). The fund currently has a performance rating of C- (Fair) based on an annualized return of -0.22% over the last three years and a total return of -13.29% year to date 2015. Factored into the performance evaluation is an expense ratio of 0.40% (very low).

The fund's risk rating is currently C (Fair). It carries a beta of 3.69, meaning it is expected to move 36.9% for every 10% move in the market. Volatility, as measured by both the semi-deviation and a drawdown factor, is considered average. As of December 31, 2015, *Market Vectors Mtge REIT Income traded at a premium of .46% above its net asset value.

George Chao has been running the fund for 5 years and currently receives a manager quality ranking of 32 (0=worst, 99=best). If you desire an average level of risk, then this fund may be an option.

Data Date	Investment Rating	Net Assets ($Mil)	Price	Performance Rating/Pts	Total Return Y-T-D	Risk Rating/Pts
12-15	D+	118.00	19.53	C- / 3.3	-13.29%	C / 4.9
2014	C+	118.00	23.70	C+ / 6.9	17.63%	B- / 7.1
2013	D+	90.70	22.17	C- / 3.3	-2.82%	B- / 7.3
2012	A+	79.30	25.18	A- / 9.1	26.96%	B / 8.8

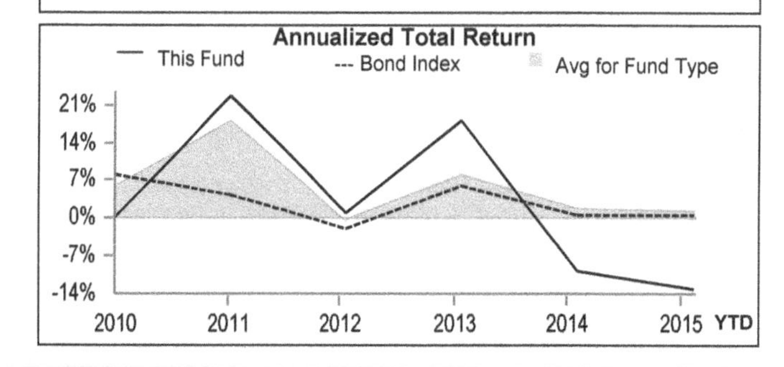

*Market Vectors Natural Resources (HAP) D+ Weak

Fund Family: Van Eck Associates Corporation
Fund Type: Global
Inception Date: August 29, 2008

Major Rating Factors:
Disappointing performance is the major factor driving the D+ (Weak) TheStreet.com Investment Rating for *Market Vectors Natural Resources. The fund currently has a performance rating of D (Weak) based on an annualized return of -8.13% over the last three years and a total return of -19.93% year to date 2015. Factored into the performance evaluation is an expense ratio of 0.49% (very low).

The fund's risk rating is currently B- (Good). It carries a beta of 0.96, meaning that its performance tracks fairly well with that of the overall stock market. Volatility, as measured by both the semi-deviation and a drawdown factor, is considered low. As of December 31, 2015, *Market Vectors Natural Resources traded at a discount of .15% below its net asset value, which is better than its one-year historical average premium of .05%.

George Chao has been running the fund for 8 years and currently receives a manager quality ranking of 13 (0=worst, 99=best). This fund offers only a moderate level of risk but investors looking for strong performance are still waiting.

Data Date	Investment Rating	Net Assets ($Mil)	Price	Performance Rating/Pts	Total Return Y-T-D	Risk Rating/Pts
12-15	D+	96.80	26.34	D / 1.9	-19.93%	B- / 7.0
2014	D+	96.80	33.88	D+ / 2.5	-6.24%	C+ / 6.5
2013	D+	101.10	37.44	C- / 3.3	3.43%	B- / 7.2
2012	D+	122.20	35.85	D+ / 2.5	7.09%	B- / 7.0
2011	C-	158.70	33.73	C- / 4.2	-9.56%	B- / 7.1
2010	A+	209.70	38.95	A / 9.5	16.52%	C+ / 6.9

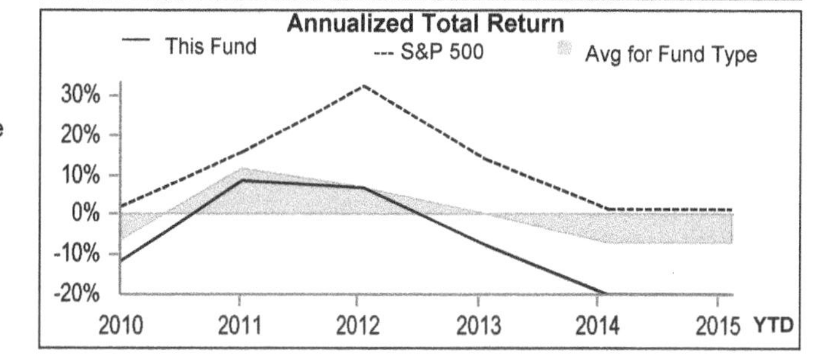

*Market Vectors Oil Services ETF (OIH) D- Weak

Fund Family: Van Eck Associates Corporation
Fund Type: Income
Inception Date: December 20, 2011

Major Rating Factors:
Disappointing performance is the major factor driving the D- (Weak) TheStreet.com Investment Rating for *Market Vectors Oil Services ETF. The fund currently has a performance rating of D- (Weak) based on an annualized return of -11.65% over the last three years and a total return of -24.70% year to date 2015. Factored into the performance evaluation is an expense ratio of 0.35% (very low).

The fund's risk rating is currently C- (Fair). It carries a beta of 1.19, meaning it is expected to move 11.9% for every 10% move in the market. Volatility, as measured by both the semi-deviation and a drawdown factor, is considered average. As of December 31, 2015, *Market Vectors Oil Services ETF traded at a price exactly equal to its net asset value, which is worse than its one-year historical average discount of .02%.

George Chao has been running the fund for 5 years and currently receives a manager quality ranking of 5 (0=worst, 99=best). This fund offers an average level of risk but investors looking for strong performance will be frustrated.

Data Date	Investment Rating	Net Assets ($Mil)	Price	Performance Rating/Pts	Total Return Y-T-D	Risk Rating/Pts
12-15	D-	1,170.80	26.45	D- / 1.4	-24.70%	C- / 3.7
2014	E	1,170.80	35.92	D / 1.6	-21.57%	D / 1.9
2013	D+	1,482.10	48.07	B- / 7.4	17.61%	D / 1.9
2012	D-	1,283.30	38.63	C / 4.5	5.73%	D / 1.9

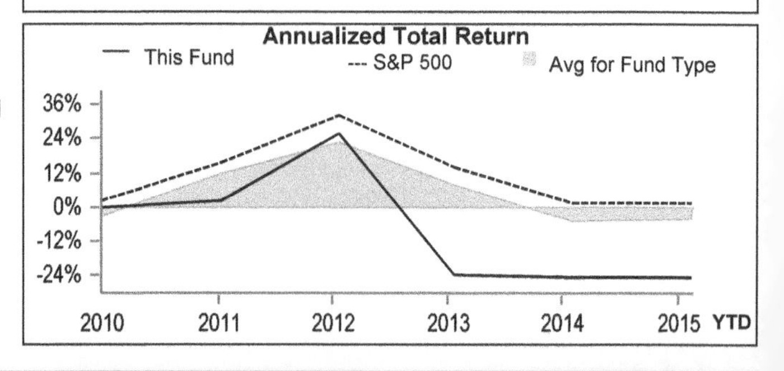

*Market Vectors Pharmaceutical ET (PPH) B+ Good

Fund Family: Van Eck Associates Corporation
Fund Type: Income
Inception Date: December 20, 2011

Major Rating Factors:
Exceptional performance is the major factor driving the B+ (Good) TheStreet.com Investment Rating for *Market Vectors Pharmaceutical ET. The fund currently has a performance rating of A (Excellent) based on an annualized return of 19.13% over the last three years and a total return of 3.20% year to date 2015. Factored into the performance evaluation is an expense ratio of 0.35% (very low).

The fund's risk rating is currently C+ (Fair). It carries a beta of 0.91, meaning that its performance tracks fairly well with that of the overall stock market. Volatility, as measured by both the semi-deviation and a drawdown factor, is considered low. As of December 31, 2015, *Market Vectors Pharmaceutical ET traded at a premium of .11% above its net asset value, which is worse than its one-year historical average premium of .01%.

George Chao has been running the fund for 5 years and currently receives a manager quality ranking of 90 (0=worst, 99=best). If you desire only a moderate level of risk and strong performance, then this fund is an excellent option.

Data Date	Investment Rating	Net Assets ($Mil)	Price	Performance Rating/Pts	Total Return Y-T-D	Risk Rating/Pts
12-15	B+	405.90	65.31	A / 9.3	3.20%	C+ / 6.6
2014	A+	405.90	64.27	A- / 9.2	24.49%	B / 8.3
2013	B+	262.50	53.11	A / 9.5	32.37%	C+ / 6.9
2012	B-	164.40	39.73	B / 7.9	18.04%	B- / 7.1

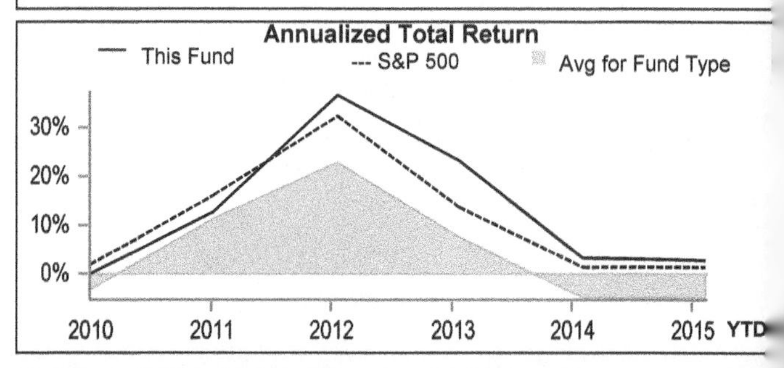

*Market Vectors Poland ETF (PLND) D- Weak

Fund Family: Van Eck Associates Corporation
Fund Type: Emerging Market
Inception Date: November 24, 2009

Major Rating Factors:
Disappointing performance is the major factor driving the D- (Weak) TheStreet.com Investment Rating for *Market Vectors Poland ETF. The fund currently has a performance rating of D- (Weak) based on an annualized return of -12.71% over the last three years and a total return of -23.48% year to date 2015. Factored into the performance evaluation is an expense ratio of 0.60% (very low).

The fund's risk rating is currently C- (Fair). It carries a beta of 0.76, meaning the fund's expected move will be 7.6% for every 10% move in the market. Volatility, as measured by both the semi-deviation and a drawdown factor, is considered average. As of December 31, 2015, *Market Vectors Poland ETF traded at a premium of .15% above its net asset value, which is worse than its one-year historical average premium of .01%.

George Chao has been running the fund for 7 years and currently receives a manager quality ranking of 19 (0=worst, 99=best). This fund offers an average level of risk but investors looking for strong performance will be frustrated.

Data Date	Investment Rating	Net Assets ($Mil)	Price	Performance Rating/Pts	Total Return Y-T-D	Risk Rating/Pts
12-15	D-	26.10	13.30	D- / 1.2	-23.48%	C- / 3.8
2014	D	26.10	18.07	C- / 3.3	-14.81%	C / 4.7
2013	D-	30.50	22.86	D+ / 2.8	3.62%	C / 4.8
2012	D-	32.30	22.47	D+ / 2.9	35.16%	C / 4.8
2011	E+	31.00	17.18	E- / 0.2	-33.68%	C / 5.1
2010	A	52.80	27.02	A- / 9.1	12.50%	C+ / 6.5

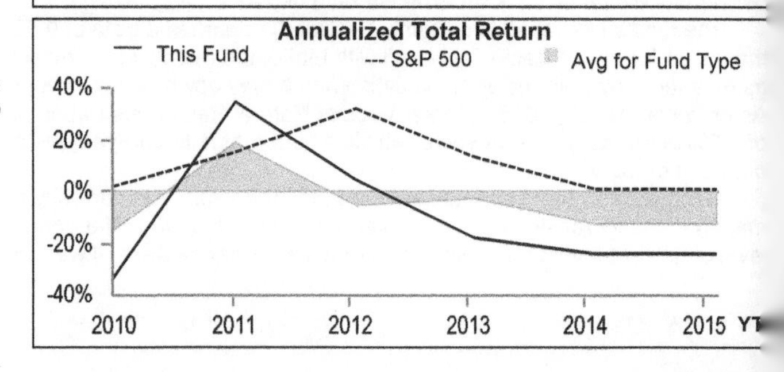

* Denotes ETF Fund

*Market Vectors Pre-Refnded Muni (PRB) C+ Fair

Fund Family: Van Eck Associates Corporation
Fund Type: Municipal - National
Inception Date: February 2, 2009

Major Rating Factors: Middle of the road best describes *Market Vectors Pre-Refnded Muni whose TheStreet.com Investment Rating is currently a C+ (Fair). The fund currently has a performance rating of C (Fair) based on an annualized return of -0.07% over the last three years and a total return of 1.52% year to date 2015. Factored into the performance evaluation is an expense ratio of 0.24% (very low).

The fund's risk rating is currently B+ (Good). It carries a beta of 0.48, meaning the fund's expected move will be 4.8% for every 10% move in the market. Volatility, as measured by both the semi-deviation and a drawdown factor, is considered very low. As of December 31, 2015, *Market Vectors Pre-Refnded Muni traded at a discount of .20% below its net asset value, which is worse than its one-year historical average discount of .69%.

Christian Andreach has been running the fund for 8 years and currently receives a manager quality ranking of 55 (0=worst, 99=best). If you desire an average level of risk, then this fund may be an option.

Data Date	Investment Rating	Net Assets ($Mil)	Price	Performance Rating/Pts	Total Return Y-T-D	Risk Rating/Pts
12-15	C+	29.60	24.55	C / 4.5	1.52%	B+ / 9.4
2014	C	29.60	24.24	D+ / 2.7	-0.02%	B+ / 9.4
2013	C	34.50	24.49	D+ / 2.8	-2.01%	B+ / 9.6
2012	C-	36.00	25.36	D / 1.9	1.58%	B+ / 9.7
2011	C	35.40	25.20	C- / 3.1	3.35%	B+ / 9.8
2010	D	37.20	24.76	D / 2.0	0.49%	C / 4.9

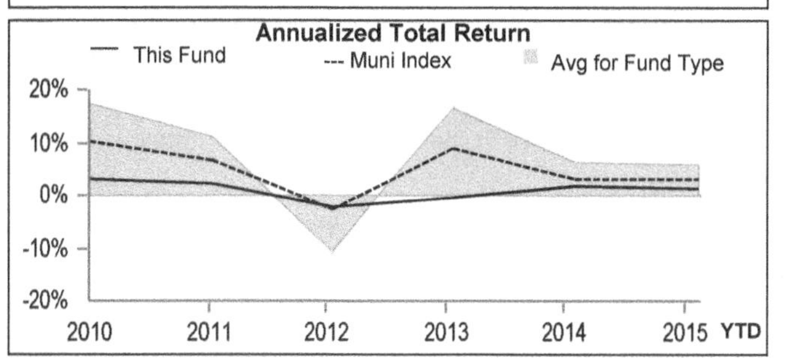

*Market Vectors Prfrd Secs ex Fin (PFXF) B- Good

Fund Family: Van Eck Associates Corporation
Fund Type: Corporate - Investment Grade
Inception Date: July 16, 2012

Major Rating Factors: *Market Vectors Prfrd Secs ex Fin receives a TheStreet.com Investment Rating of B- (Good). The fund currently has a performance rating of C (Fair) based on an annualized return of 3.20% over the last three years and a total return of -2.86% year to date 2015. Factored into the performance evaluation is an expense ratio of 0.40% (very low).

The fund's risk rating is currently B+ (Good). It carries a beta of 0.94, meaning that its performance tracks fairly well with that of the overall stock market. Volatility, as measured by both the semi-deviation and a drawdown factor, is considered very low. As of December 31, 2015, *Market Vectors Prfrd Secs ex Fin traded at a discount of .62% below its net asset value, which is better than its one-year historical average discount of .02%.

George Chao has been running the fund for 4 years and currently receives a manager quality ranking of 82 (0=worst, 99=best). If you desire an average level of risk, then this fund may be an option.

Data Date	Investment Rating	Net Assets ($Mil)	Price	Performance Rating/Pts	Total Return Y-T-D	Risk Rating/Pts
12-15	B-	175.50	19.15	C / 5.3	-2.86%	B+ / 9.0
2014	B+	175.50	20.59	B- / 7.0	15.93%	B / 8.9
2013	C-	123.90	18.85	D+ / 2.4	-2.16%	B+ / 9.1

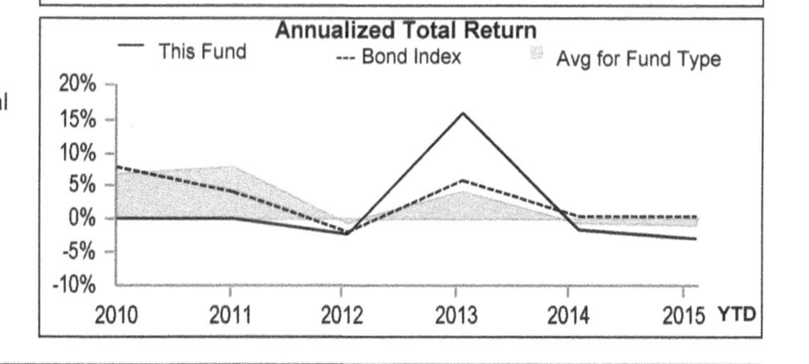

*Market Vectors Retail ETF (RTH) A+ Excellent

Fund Family: Van Eck Associates Corporation
Fund Type: Income
Inception Date: December 20, 2011

Major Rating Factors:
Exceptional performance is the major factor driving the A+ (Excellent) TheStreet.com Investment Rating for *Market Vectors Retail ETF. The fund currently has a performance rating of A+ (Excellent) based on an annualized return of 21.88% over the last three years and a total return of 11.37% year to date 2015. Factored into the performance evaluation is an expense ratio of 0.35% (very low).

The fund's risk rating is currently B (Good). It carries a beta of 0.94, meaning that its performance tracks fairly well with that of the overall stock market. Volatility, as measured by both the semi-deviation and a drawdown factor, is considered low. As of December 31, 2015, *Market Vectors Retail ETF traded at a premium of .01% above its net asset value, which is better than its one-year historical average premium of .02%.

George Chao has been running the fund for 5 years and currently receives a manager quality ranking of 92 (0=worst, 99=best). If you desire only a moderate level of risk and strong performance, then this fund is an excellent option.

Data Date	Investment Rating	Net Assets ($Mil)	Price	Performance Rating/Pts	Total Return Y-T-D	Risk Rating/Pts
12-15	A+	66.70	77.72	A+ / 9.6	11.37%	B / 8.1
2014	A	66.70	71.65	A / 9.5	19.23%	B- / 7.2
2013	B	40.90	60.85	A+ / 9.6	37.49%	C+ / 5.9
2012	C+	33.80	43.83	B- / 7.4	20.32%	C+ / 6.3

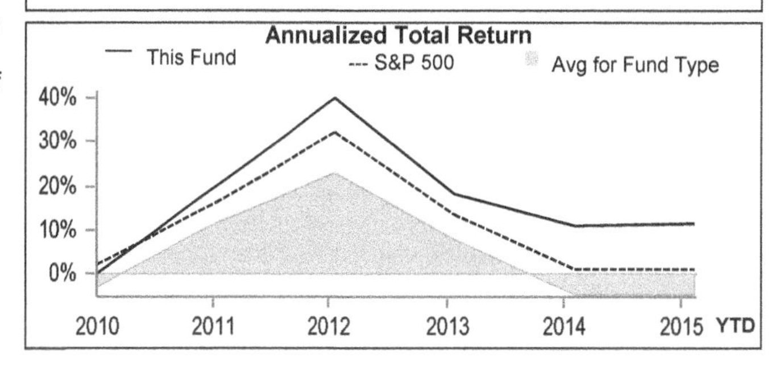

*Market Vectors Russia ETF (RSX) D- Weak

Fund Family: Van Eck Associates Corporation
Fund Type: Foreign
Inception Date: April 24, 2007

Data Date	Investment Rating	Net Assets ($Mil)	Price	Perfor-mance Rating/Pts	Total Return Y-T-D	Risk Rating/Pts
12-15	D-	1,906.50	14.65	D- / 1.2	2.60%	C / 4.3
2014	E+	1,906.50	14.63	E+ / 0.6	-41.48%	C- / 3.6
2013	D-	1,187.90	28.87	D- / 1.5	-6.82%	C / 5.0
2012	D-	1,634.20	29.90	D / 1.6	9.61%	C / 5.0
2011	C-	1,557.00	26.65	C+ / 6.2	-27.27%	C+ / 5.8
2010	E+	2,609.60	37.91	D / 2.0	22.14%	D+ / 2.3

Major Rating Factors:
Disappointing performance is the major factor driving the D- (Weak) TheStreet.com Investment Rating for *Market Vectors Russia ETF. The fund currently has a performance rating of D- (Weak) based on an annualized return of -18.95% over the last three years and a total return of 2.60% year to date 2015. Factored into the performance evaluation is an expense ratio of 0.61% (very low).

The fund's risk rating is currently C (Fair). It carries a beta of 1.27, meaning it is expected to move 12.7% for every 10% move in the market. Volatility, as measured by both the semi-deviation and a drawdown factor, is considered average. As of December 31, 2015, *Market Vectors Russia ETF traded at a discount of .27% below its net asset value, which is better than its one-year historical average discount of .02%.

Hao-Hung Liao has been running the fund for 9 years and currently receives a manager quality ranking of 5 (0=worst, 99=best). This fund offers an average level of risk but investors looking for strong performance will be frustrated.

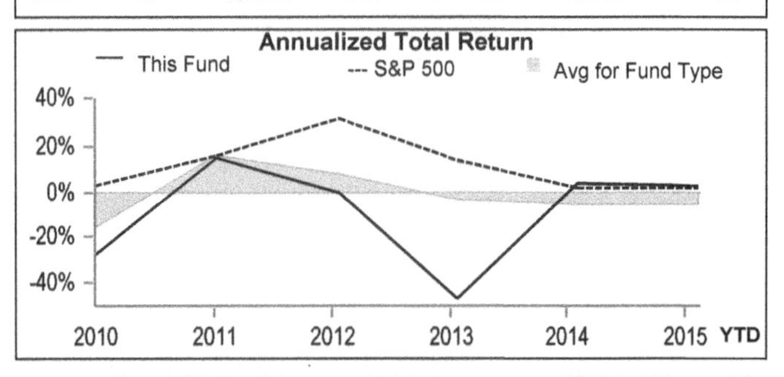

*Market Vectors Russia SmallCap E (RSXJ) D- Weak

Fund Family: Van Eck Associates Corporation
Fund Type: Foreign
Inception Date: April 13, 2011

Data Date	Investment Rating	Net Assets ($Mil)	Price	Perfor-mance Rating/Pts	Total Return Y-T-D	Risk Rating/Pts
12-15	D-	74.10	19.10	E+ / 0.9	-3.02%	C- / 4.0
2014	E-	74.10	19.85	E / 0.4	-50.07%	D / 1.8
2013	D-	16.20	42.58	D / 2.1	-7.35%	C / 5.1
2012	E+	8.30	15.24	D- / 1.3	-6.32%	C / 4.8

Major Rating Factors:
Very poor performance is the major factor driving the D- (Weak) TheStreet.com Investment Rating for *Market Vectors Russia SmallCap E. The fund currently has a performance rating of E+ (Very Weak) based on an annualized return of -23.69% over the last three years and a total return of -3.02% year to date 2015. Factored into the performance evaluation is an expense ratio of 0.67% (very low).

The fund's risk rating is currently C- (Fair). It carries a beta of 1.53, meaning it is expected to move 15.3% for every 10% move in the market. Volatility, as measured by both the semi-deviation and a drawdown factor, is considered average. As of December 31, 2015, *Market Vectors Russia SmallCap E traded at a discount of 1.09% below its net asset value, which is better than its one-year historical average discount of .24%.

George Chao has been running the fund for 5 years and currently receives a manager quality ranking of 3 (0=worst, 99=best). This fund offers an average level of risk but investors looking for strong performance will be frustrated.

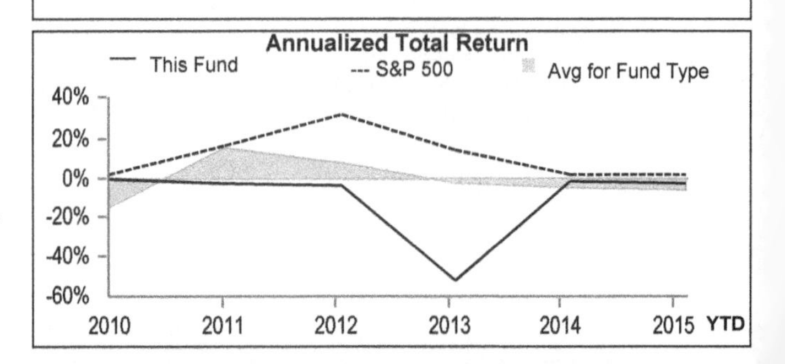

*Market Vectors Semiconductor ETF (SMH) A+ Excellent

Fund Family: Van Eck Associates Corporation
Fund Type: Income
Inception Date: December 20, 2011

Data Date	Investment Rating	Net Assets ($Mil)	Price	Perfor-mance Rating/Pts	Total Return Y-T-D	Risk Rating/Pts
12-15	A+	415.00	53.28	A / 9.4	-0.16%	B / 8.1
2014	A-	415.00	54.62	A+ / 9.6	32.51%	C+ / 6.5
2013	A+	304.40	42.43	A- / 9.2	27.90%	B / 8.3

Major Rating Factors:
Exceptional performance is the major factor driving the A+ (Excellent) TheStreet.com Investment Rating for *Market Vectors Semiconductor ETF. The fund currently has a performance rating of A (Excellent) based on an annualized return of 18.91% over the last three years and a total return of -0.16% year to date 2015. Factored into the performance evaluation is an expense ratio of 0.35% (very low).

The fund's risk rating is currently B (Good). It carries a beta of 1.08, meaning that its performance tracks fairly well with that of the overall stock market. Volatility, as measured by both the semi-deviation and a drawdown factor, is considered low. As of December 31, 2015, *Market Vectors Semiconductor ETF traded at a discount of .15% below its net asset value, which is better than its one-year historical average premium of .01%.

George Chao has been running the fund for 5 years and currently receives a manager quality ranking of 85 (0=worst, 99=best). If you desire only a moderate level of risk and strong performance, then this fund is an excellent option.

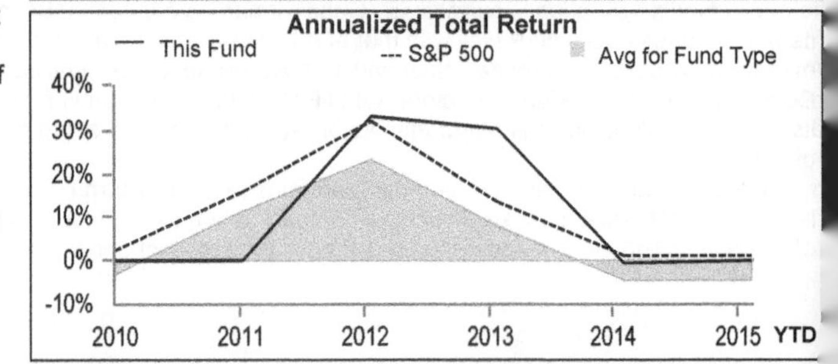

*Market Vectors Short HY Muni Ind (SHYD) — C+ Fair

Fund Family: Van Eck Associates Corporation
Fund Type: Municipal - High Yield
Inception Date: January 13, 2014

Data Date	Investment Rating	Net Assets ($Mil)	Price	Performance Rating/Pts	Total Return Y-T-D	Risk Rating/Pts
12-15	C+	71.00	24.53	C- / 3.9	-0.57%	B+ / 9.5

Major Rating Factors: Middle of the road best describes *Market Vectors Short HY Muni Ind whose TheStreet.com Investment Rating is currently a C+ (Fair). The fund currently has a performance rating of C- (Fair) based on an annualized return of 0.00% over the last three years and a total return of -0.57% year to date 2015. Factored into the performance evaluation is an expense ratio of 0.35% (very low).

The fund's risk rating is currently B+ (Good). It carries a beta of 0.00, meaning the fund's expected move will be 0.0% for every 10% move in the market. Volatility, as measured by both the semi-deviation and a drawdown factor, is considered very low. As of December 31, 2015, *Market Vectors Short HY Muni Ind traded at a discount of 1.72% below its net asset value, which is better than its one-year historical average discount of .30%.

James T. Colby III has been running the fund for 2 years and currently receives a manager quality ranking of 49 (0=worst, 99=best). If you desire an average level of risk, then this fund may be an option.

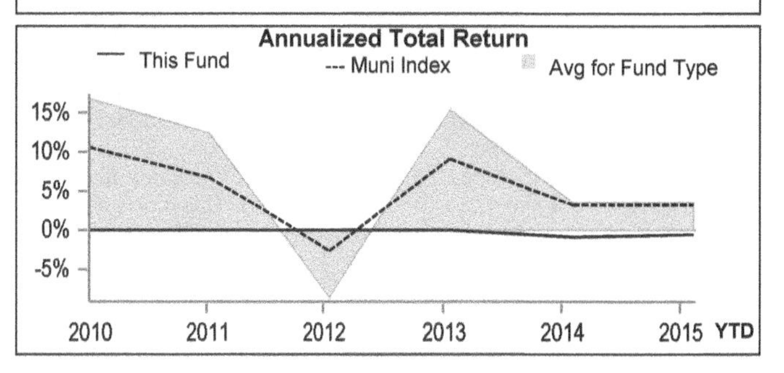

*Market Vectors Short Muni Index (SMB) — B Good

Fund Family: Van Eck Associates Corporation
Fund Type: Municipal - National
Inception Date: February 22, 2008

Data Date	Investment Rating	Net Assets ($Mil)	Price	Performance Rating/Pts	Total Return Y-T-D	Risk Rating/Pts
12-15	B	258.40	17.53	C / 5.1	1.10%	B+ / 9.6
2014	C	258.40	17.54	C- / 3.1	0.93%	B+ / 9.7
2013	C+	221.60	17.58	C- / 3.9	0.30%	B+ / 9.8
2012	C-	177.40	17.68	D / 2.2	1.85%	B+ / 9.7
2011	C+	113.80	17.71	C- / 3.6	5.61%	B+ / 9.7
2010	D-	102.40	17.12	D / 2.0	0.86%	C- / 3.8

Major Rating Factors: *Market Vectors Short Muni Index receives a TheStreet.com Investment Rating of B (Good). The fund currently has a performance rating of C (Fair) based on an annualized return of 0.81% over the last three years and a total return of 1.10% year to date 2015. Factored into the performance evaluation is an expense ratio of 0.20% (very low).

The fund's risk rating is currently B+ (Good). It carries a beta of 0.37, meaning the fund's expected move will be 3.7% for every 10% move in the market. Volatility, as measured by both the semi-deviation and a drawdown factor, is considered very low. As of December 31, 2015, *Market Vectors Short Muni Index traded at a discount of .06% below its net asset value, which is worse than its one-year historical average discount of .26%.

James T. Colby, III has been running the fund for 8 years and currently receives a manager quality ranking of 65 (0=worst, 99=best). If you desire an average level of risk, then this fund may be an option.

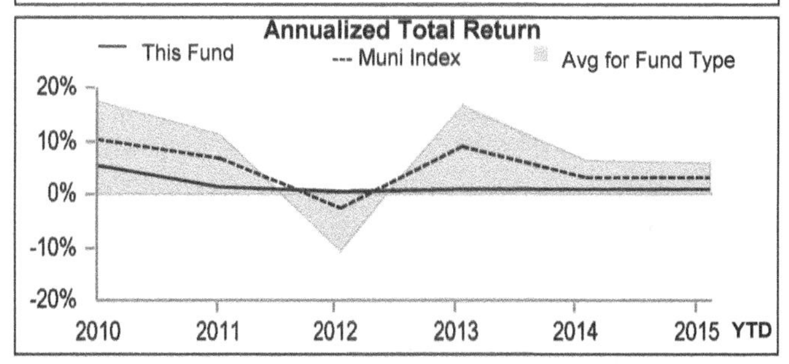

*Market Vectors Solar Energy ETF (KWT) — C+ Fair

Fund Family: Van Eck Associates Corporation
Fund Type: Energy/Natural Resources
Inception Date: April 21, 2008

Data Date	Investment Rating	Net Assets ($Mil)	Price	Performance Rating/Pts	Total Return Y-T-D	Risk Rating/Pts
12-15	C+	23.30	61.38	B+ / 8.3	-7.78%	C / 5.2
2014	D-	23.30	67.14	C- / 3.1	-13.30%	C- / 4.1
2013	E+	21.80	72.80	D+ / 2.4	84.16%	D / 2.2
2012	E	10.90	35.83	E / 0.3	-29.44%	C- / 3.6
2011	E	9.90	3.69	E / 0.3	-63.93%	C- / 3.8
2010	E	24.90	10.99	E / 0.5	-28.71%	C- / 3.0

Major Rating Factors: Strong performance is the major factor driving the C+ (Fair) TheStreet.com Investment Rating for *Market Vectors Solar Energy ETF. The fund currently has a performance rating of B+ (Good) based on an annualized return of 14.20% over the last three years and a total return of -7.78% year to date 2015. Factored into the performance evaluation is an expense ratio of 0.65% (very low).

The fund's risk rating is currently C (Fair). It carries a beta of 1.02, meaning that its performance tracks fairly well with that of the overall stock market. Volatility, as measured by both the semi-deviation and a drawdown factor, is considered average. As of December 31, 2015, *Market Vectors Solar Energy ETF traded at a discount of .42% below its net asset value, which is worse than its one-year historical average discount of .50%.

George Chao has been running the fund for 8 years and currently receives a manager quality ranking of 99 (0=worst, 99=best). If you desire an average level of risk and strong performance, then this fund is a good option.

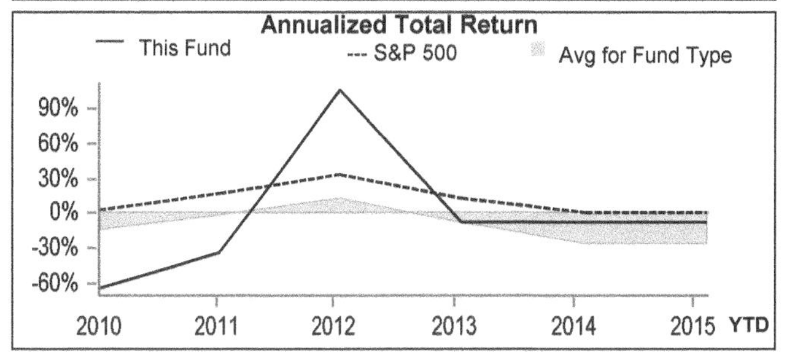

* Denotes ETF Fund

*Market Vectors Steel Index ETF (SLX) D- Weak

Fund Family: Van Eck Associates Corporation
Fund Type: Income
Inception Date: October 10, 2006

Major Rating Factors:
Very poor performance is the major factor driving the D- (Weak) TheStreet.com Investment Rating for *Market Vectors Steel Index ETF. The fund currently has a performance rating of E (Very Weak) based on an annualized return of -24.49% over the last three years and a total return of -41.43% year to date 2015. Factored into the performance evaluation is an expense ratio of 0.55% (very low).

The fund's risk rating is currently C (Fair). It carries a beta of 1.35, meaning it is expected to move 13.5% for every 10% move in the market. Volatility, as measured by both the semi-deviation and a drawdown factor, is considered average. As of December 31, 2015, *Market Vectors Steel Index ETF traded at a discount of .10% below its net asset value.

Hao-Hung Liao has been running the fund for 10 years and currently receives a manager quality ranking of 1 (0=worst, 99=best). This fund offers an average level of risk but investors looking for strong performance will be frustrated.

Data Date	Investment Rating	Net Assets ($Mil)	Price	Performance Rating/Pts	Total Return Y-T-D	Risk Rating/Pts
12-15	D-	102.70	19.50	E / 0.5	-41.43%	C / 4.9
2014	D-	102.70	35.47	D- / 1.1	-24.12%	C / 4.9
2013	D-	144.30	49.72	D / 1.6	-1.30%	C+ / 5.6
2012	D-	153.90	48.69	D- / 1.0	-2.75%	C+ / 5.9
2011	C-	181.00	47.55	C- / 4.2	-29.78%	C+ / 6.3
2010	C-	279.10	72.58	C / 5.4	19.65%	C- / 3.7

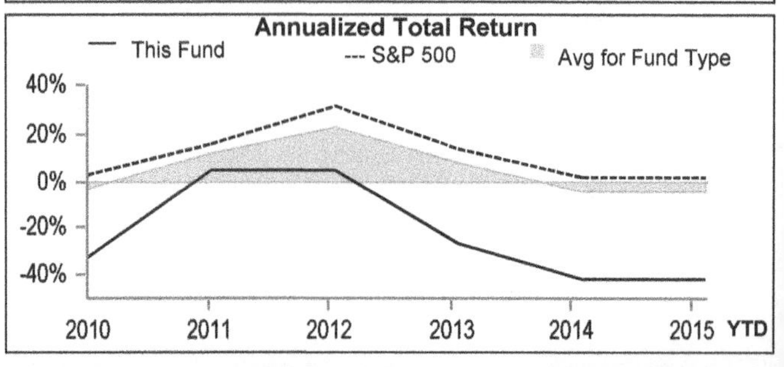

*Market Vectors Trs Hdg Hi Yld Bd (THHY) C- Fair

Fund Family: Van Eck Associates Corporation
Fund Type: Corporate - High Yield
Inception Date: March 21, 2013

Major Rating Factors:
Disappointing performance is the major factor driving the C- (Fair) TheStreet.com Investment Rating for *Market Vectors Trs Hdg Hi Yld Bd. The fund currently has a performance rating of D+ (Weak) based on an annualized return of 0.00% over the last three years and a total return of -7.74% year to date 2015. Factored into the performance evaluation is an expense ratio of 0.50% (very low).

The fund's risk rating is currently B (Good). It carries a beta of 0.00, meaning the fund's expected move will be 0.0% for every 10% move in the market. Volatility, as measured by both the semi-deviation and a drawdown factor, is considered low. As of December 31, 2015, *Market Vectors Trs Hdg Hi Yld Bd traded at a discount of .64% below its net asset value, which is better than its one-year historical average premium of .14%.

Francis G. Rodilosso has been running the fund for 3 years and currently receives a manager quality ranking of 39 (0=worst, 99=best). This fund offers only a moderate level of risk but investors looking for strong performance are still waiting.

Data Date	Investment Rating	Net Assets ($Mil)	Price	Performance Rating/Pts	Total Return Y-T-D	Risk Rating/Pts
12-15	C-	10.00	21.85	D+ / 2.4	-7.74%	B / 8.2
2014	C-	10.00	24.75	C- / 3.2	1.98%	B- / 7.2

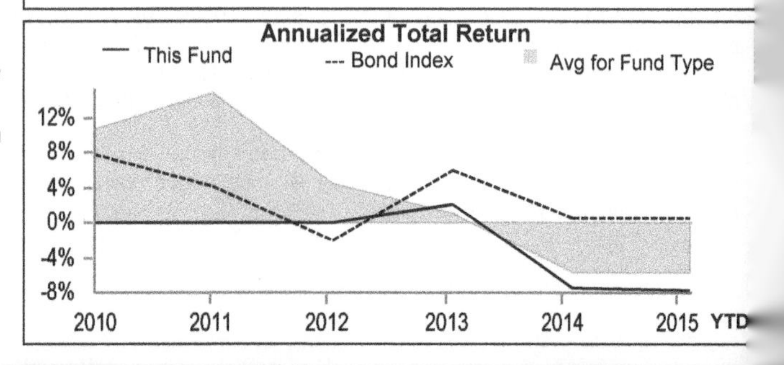

*Market Vectors Uranium+Nuc Engy (NLR) C+ Fair

Fund Family: Van Eck Associates Corporation
Fund Type: Global
Inception Date: August 13, 2007

Major Rating Factors: Middle of the road best describes *Market Vectors Uranium+Nuc Engy whose TheStreet.com Investment Rating is currently a C+ (Fair). The fund currently has a performance rating of C (Fair) based on an annualized return of 4.40% over the last three years and a total return of -9.10% year to date 2015. Factored into the performance evaluation is an expense ratio of 0.60% (very low).

The fund's risk rating is currently B (Good). It carries a beta of 0.54, meaning the fund's expected move will be 5.4% for every 10% move in the market. Volatility, as measured by both the semi-deviation and a drawdown factor, is considered low. As of December 31, 2015, *Market Vectors Uranium+Nuc Engy traded at a discount of .40% below its net asset value, which is better than its one-year historical average discount of .29%.

Hao-Hung Liao has been running the fund for 9 years and currently receives a manager quality ranking of 81 (0=worst, 99=best). If you desire an average level of risk, then this fund may be an option.

Data Date	Investment Rating	Net Assets ($Mil)	Price	Performance Rating/Pts	Total Return Y-T-D	Risk Rating/Pts
12-15	C+	69.40	45.07	C / 5.4	-9.10%	B / 8.5
2014	C+	69.40	51.43	C+ / 5.6	12.86%	B- / 7.9
2013	D-	77.80	48.09	D / 1.8	13.18%	C+ / 5.7
2012	D-	78.60	13.76	E+ / 0.8	-4.67%	C+ / 5.7
2011	D-	86.70	14.84	D- / 1.3	-32.61%	C+ / 5.8
2010	D	260.40	25.35	D+ / 2.3	16.59%	C / 5.1

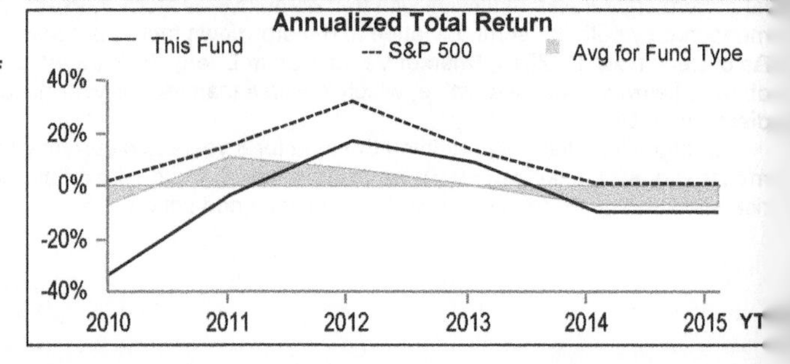

*Market Vectors Vietnam ETF (VNM) D Weak

Fund Family: Van Eck Associates Corporation
Fund Type: Foreign
Inception Date: August 11, 2009

Major Rating Factors:
Disappointing performance is the major factor driving the D (Weak) TheStreet.com Investment Rating for *Market Vectors Vietnam ETF. The fund currently has a performance rating of D (Weak) based on an annualized return of -5.38% over the last three years and a total return of -19.46% year to date 2015. Factored into the performance evaluation is an expense ratio of 0.65% (very low).

The fund's risk rating is currently C (Fair). It carries a beta of 0.92, meaning that its performance tracks fairly well with that of the overall stock market. Volatility, as measured by both the semi-deviation and a drawdown factor, is considered average. As of December 31, 2015, *Market Vectors Vietnam ETF traded at a price exactly equal to its net asset value, which is better than its one-year historical average premium of .18%.

George Chao has been running the fund for 7 years and currently receives a manager quality ranking of 20 (0=worst, 99=best). This fund offers an average level of risk but investors looking for strong performance will be frustrated.

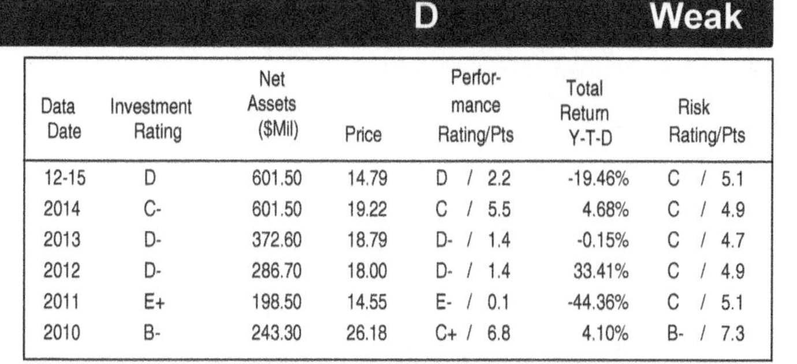

Data Date	Investment Rating	Net Assets ($Mil)	Price	Performance Rating/Pts	Total Return Y-T-D	Risk Rating/Pts
12-15	D	601.50	14.79	D / 2.2	-19.46%	C / 5.1
2014	C-	601.50	19.22	C / 5.5	4.68%	C / 4.9
2013	D-	372.60	18.79	D- / 1.4	-0.15%	C / 4.7
2012	D-	286.70	18.00	D- / 1.4	33.41%	C / 4.9
2011	E+	198.50	14.55	E- / 0.1	-44.36%	C / 5.1
2010	B-	243.30	26.18	C+ / 6.8	4.10%	B- / 7.3

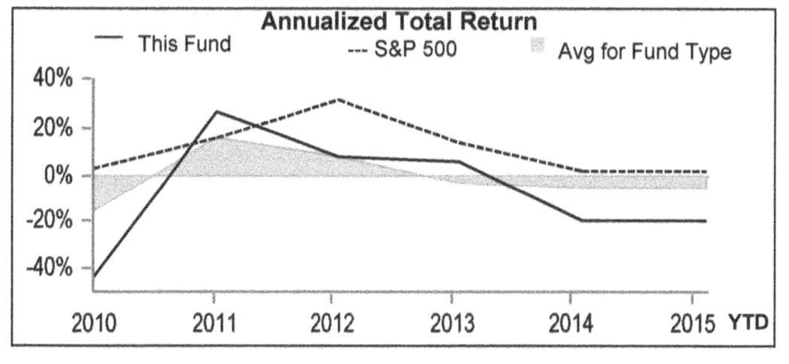

*Materials Select Sector SPDR (XLB) C+ Fair

Fund Family: SSgA Funds Management Inc
Fund Type: Growth
Inception Date: December 16, 1998

Major Rating Factors: Middle of the road best describes *Materials Select Sector SPDR whose TheStreet.com Investment Rating is currently a C+ (Fair). The fund currently has a performance rating of C+ (Fair) based on an annualized return of 6.45% over the last three years and a total return of -8.12% year to date 2015. Factored into the performance evaluation is an expense ratio of 0.15% (very low).

The fund's risk rating is currently B- (Good). It carries a beta of 1.19, meaning it is expected to move 11.9% for every 10% move in the market. Volatility, as measured by both the semi-deviation and a drawdown factor, is considered low. As of December 31, 2015, *Materials Select Sector SPDR traded at a discount of .09% below its net asset value, which is better than its one-year historical average discount of .01%.

John A. Tucker has been running the fund for 18 years and currently receives a manager quality ranking of 18 (0=worst, 99=best). If you desire an average level of risk, then this fund may be an option.

Data Date	Investment Rating	Net Assets ($Mil)	Price	Performance Rating/Pts	Total Return Y-T-D	Risk Rating/Pts
12-15	C+	5,107.90	43.42	C+ / 6.0	-8.12%	B- / 7.7
2014	B	5,107.90	48.58	C+ / 6.6	8.30%	B / 8.7
2013	C+	4,264.90	46.22	B- / 7.1	21.04%	B- / 7.3
2012	C-	2,445.50	37.54	C- / 3.6	10.61%	B- / 7.1
2011	C	1,635.40	33.50	C / 5.3	-7.30%	B- / 7.1
2010	C+	2,594.70	38.41	C+ / 6.4	20.56%	C / 5.3

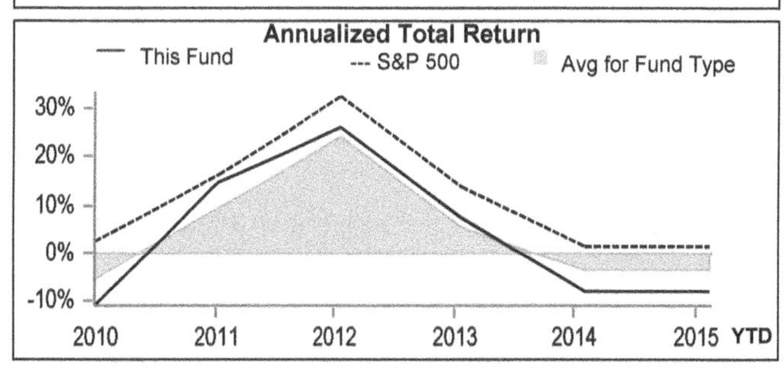

*Meidell Tactical Advantage ETF (MATH) C Fair

Fund Family: AdvisorShares Investments LLC
Fund Type: Growth and Income
Inception Date: June 23, 2011

Major Rating Factors: Middle of the road best describes *Meidell Tactical Advantage ETF whose TheStreet.com Investment Rating is currently a C (Fair). The fund currently has a performance rating of C (Fair) based on an annualized return of 2.28% over the last three years and a total return of -6.52% year to date 2015. Factored into the performance evaluation is an expense ratio of 1.35% (average).

The fund's risk rating is currently B- (Good). It carries a beta of 0.52, meaning the fund's expected move will be 5.2% for every 10% move in the market. Volatility, as measured by both the semi-deviation and a drawdown factor, is considered low. As of December 31, 2015, *Meidell Tactical Advantage ETF traded at a premium of 1.01% above its net asset value, which is worse than its one-year historical average premium of .27%.

Laif Meidell has been running the fund for 5 years and currently receives a manager quality ranking of 34 (0=worst, 99=best). If you desire an average level of risk, then this fund may be an option.

Data Date	Investment Rating	Net Assets ($Mil)	Price	Performance Rating/Pts	Total Return Y-T-D	Risk Rating/Pts
12-15	C	15.40	28.07	C / 4.4	-6.52%	B- / 7.2
2014	C	15.40	30.45	C / 4.8	2.71%	B- / 7.4
2013	B+	15.70	30.04	C+ / 6.8	12.57%	B+ / 9.3
2012	C+	7.10	25.93	C- / 4.0	7.08%	B+ / 9.3

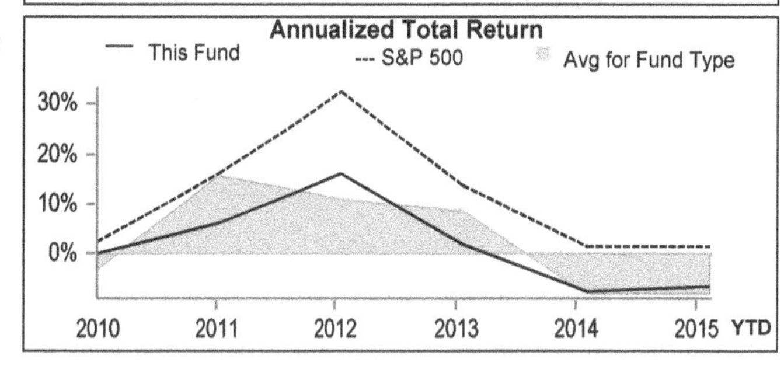

*Merk Gold (OUNZ) D+ Weak

Fund Family: Merk Investments LLC
Fund Type: Global
Inception Date: May 16, 2014

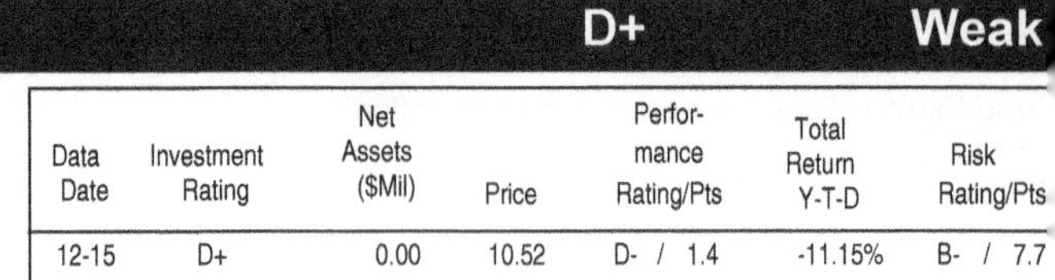

Data Date	Investment Rating	Net Assets ($Mil)	Price	Perfor-mance Rating/Pts	Total Return Y-T-D	Risk Rating/Pts
12-15	D+	0.00	10.52	D- / 1.4	-11.15%	B- / 7.7

Major Rating Factors:
Disappointing performance is the major factor driving the D+ (Weak) TheStreet.com Investment Rating for *Merk Gold. The fund currently has a performance rating of D- (Weak) based on an annualized return of 0.00% over the last three years and a total return of -11.15% year to date 2015. Factored into the performance evaluation is an expense ratio of 0.40% (very low).

The fund's risk rating is currently B- (Good). It carries a beta of 0.00, meaning the fund's expected move will be 0.0% for every 10% move in the market. Volatility, as measured by both the semi-deviation and a drawdown factor, is considered low. As of December 31, 2015, *Merk Gold traded at a discount of .28% below its net asset value, which is better than its one-year historical average premium of .14%.

Alexander G. Merk currently receives a manager quality ranking of 15 (0=worst, 99=best). This fund offers only a moderate level of risk but investors looking for strong performance are still waiting.

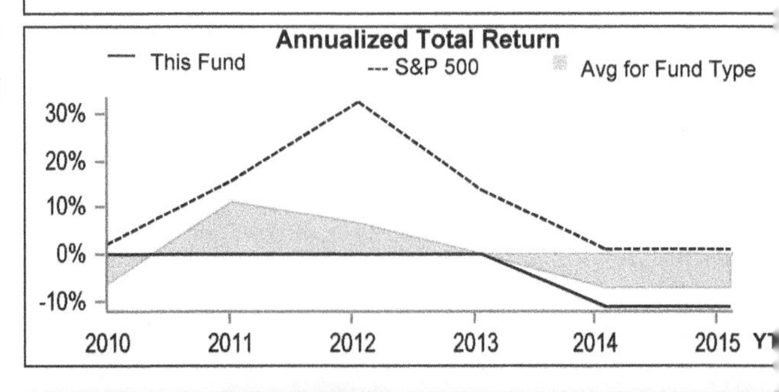

*Mk Vectors Unconv O&G ETF (FRAK) E Very Weak

Fund Family: Van Eck Associates Corporation
Fund Type: Energy/Natural Resources
Inception Date: February 14, 2012

Data Date	Investment Rating	Net Assets ($Mil)	Price	Perfor-mance Rating/Pts	Total Return Y-T-D	Risk Rating/Pts
12-15	E	89.70	13.28	E+ / 0.8	-38.69%	D / 2.1
2014	D-	89.70	22.05	E- / 0.2	-19.50%	C+ / 5.8
2013	B	46.90	28.42	B / 7.6	19.92%	B- / 7.9

Major Rating Factors: *Mk Vectors Unconv O&G ETF has adopted a very risky asset allocation strategy and currently receives an overall TheStreet.com Investment Rating of E (Very Weak). The fund has a high level of volatility, as measured by both semi-deviation and drawdown factors. It carries a beta of 1.40, meaning it is expected to move 14.0% for every 10% move in the market. As of December 31, 2015, *Mk Vectors Unconv O&G ETF traded at a premium of .30% above its net asset value, which is worse than its one-year historical average discount of .01%. Unfortunately, the high level of risk (D, Weak) failed to pay off as investors endured very poor performance.

The fund's performance rating is currently E+ (Very Weak). It has registered an annualized return of -15.93% over the last three years and is down -38.69% year to date 2015. Factored into the performance evaluation is an expense ratio of 0.54% (very low).

George Chao has been running the fund for 4 years and currently receives a manager quality ranking of 16 (0=worst, 99=best). If you can tolerate very high levels of risk in the hope of improved future returns, holding this fund may be an option.

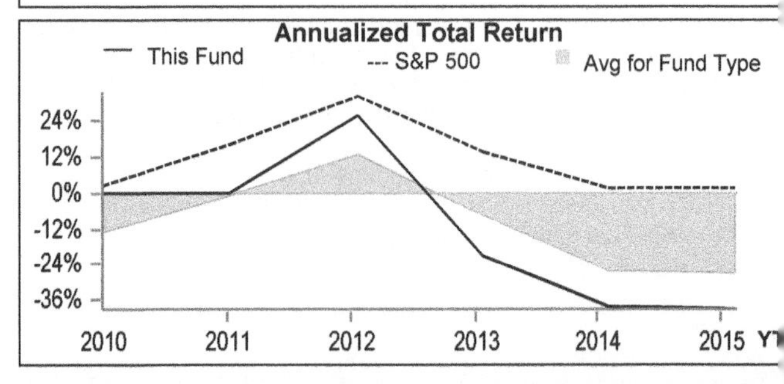

*Morgan Creek Global Tact ETF Fun (GTAA) C- Fair

Fund Family: AdvisorShares Investments LLC
Fund Type: Growth and Income
Inception Date: October 26, 2010

Data Date	Investment Rating	Net Assets ($Mil)	Price	Perfor-mance Rating/Pts	Total Return Y-T-D	Risk Rating/Pts
12-15	C-	20.20	22.49	C- / 3.3	-9.00%	C+ / 6.9
2014	C	20.20	24.94	C- / 3.7	3.73%	B+ / 9.0
2013	C-	44.80	24.75	D+ / 2.6	-0.12%	B / 8.7
2012	C	63.60	24.31	C- / 4.0	8.40%	B / 8.7
2011	D+	140.70	23.49	D- / 1.2	-7.19%	B / 8.8

Major Rating Factors: Middle of the road best describes *Morgan Creek Global Tact ETF Fun whose TheStreet.com Investment Rating is currently a C- (Fair). The fund currently has a performance rating of C- (Fair) based on an annualized return of -1.75% over the last three years and a total return of -9.00% year to date 2015. Factored into the performance evaluation is an expense ratio of 1.25% (average).

The fund's risk rating is currently C+ (Fair). It carries a beta of 0.54, meaning the fund's expected move will be 5.4% for every 10% move in the market. Volatility, as measured by both the semi-deviation and a drawdown factor, is considered low. As of December 31, 2015, *Morgan Creek Global Tact ETF Fun traded at a premium of .13% above its net asset value, which is worse than its one-year historical average discount of .09%.

Eric W. Richardson currently receives a manager quality ranking of 19 (0=worst, 99=best). If you desire an average level of risk, then this fund may be an option.

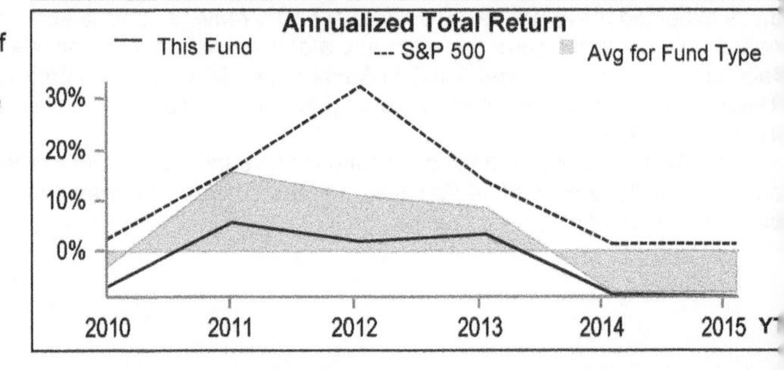

*Morgan Stanley Technology ETF (MTK) C Fair

Fund Family: SSgA Funds Management Inc
Fund Type: Growth
Inception Date: September 25, 2000

Major Rating Factors: *Morgan Stanley Technology ETF has adopted a very risky asset allocation strategy and currently receives an overall TheStreet.com Investment Rating of C (Fair). The fund has shown a high level of volatility, as measured by both semi-deviation and drawdown factors. It carries a beta of 1.06, meaning that its performance tracks fairly well with that of the overall stock market. As of December 31, 2015, *Morgan Stanley Technology ETF traded at a premium of .37% above its net asset value, which is worse than its one-year historical average premium of .06%. The high level of risk (D, Weak) did however, reward investors with excellent performance.

The fund's performance rating is currently A (Excellent). It has registered an annualized return of 16.83% over the last three years and is up 8.76% year to date 2015. Factored into the performance evaluation is an expense ratio of 0.42% (very low).

John A. Tucker has been running the fund for 16 years and currently receives a manager quality ranking of 78 (0=worst, 99=best). If you are comfortable owning a very high risk investment, this fund may be an option.

Data Date	Investment Rating	Net Assets ($Mil)	Price	Perfor-mance Rating/Pts	Total Return Y-T-D	Risk Rating/Pts
12-15	C	227.60	54.08	A / 9.4	8.76%	D / 2.2
2014	B	227.60	101.80	B+ / 8.7	15.96%	C+ / 6.1
2013	B-	215.70	89.59	B- / 7.5	27.85%	B- / 7.4
2012	C-	163.80	68.37	C / 5.0	18.18%	C+ / 6.5
2011	C	155.30	58.66	C+ / 5.7	-10.97%	B- / 7.0
2010	C+	218.00	66.08	C+ / 6.9	15.31%	C / 4.7

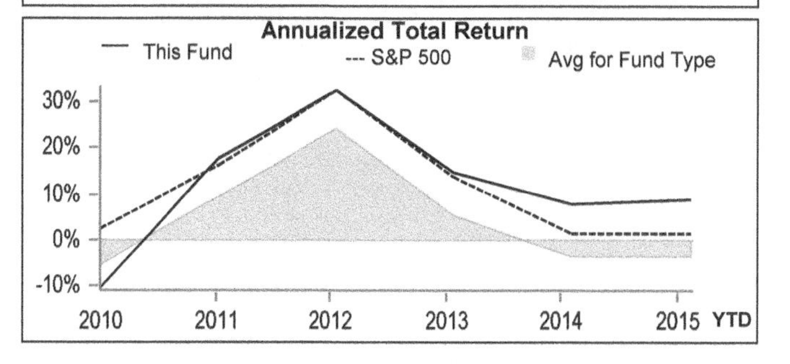

*Mrkt Vectors Rare Earth/Str Met (REMX) E+ Very Weak

Fund Family: Van Eck Associates Corporation
Fund Type: Growth
Inception Date: October 27, 2010

Major Rating Factors:
Very poor performance is the major factor driving the E+ (Very Weak) TheStreet.com Investment Rating for *Mrkt Vectors Rare Earth/Str Met. The fund currently has a performance rating of E- (Very Weak) based on an annualized return of -35.94% over the last three years and a total return of -44.57% year to date 2015. Factored into the performance evaluation is an expense ratio of 0.57% (very low).

The fund's risk rating is currently C- (Fair). It carries a beta of 1.13, meaning it is expected to move 11.3% for every 10% move in the market. Volatility, as measured by both the semi-deviation and a drawdown factor, is considered average. As of December 31, 2015, *Mrkt Vectors Rare Earth/Str Met traded at a discount of 1.97% below its net asset value, which is better than its one-year historical average discount of .50%.

George Chao has been running the fund for 6 years and currently receives a manager quality ranking of 0 (0=worst, 99=best). This fund offers an average level of risk but investors looking for strong performance will be frustrated.

Data Date	Investment Rating	Net Assets ($Mil)	Price	Perfor-mance Rating/Pts	Total Return Y-T-D	Risk Rating/Pts
12-15	E+	75.30	13.41	E- / 0.2	-44.57%	C- / 3.4
2014	D-	75.30	25.19	E / 0.4	-29.37%	C / 5.2
2013	E	96.20	35.77	E / 0.4	-33.65%	C- / 3.4
2012	E+	174.60	13.16	E+ / 0.9	-15.70%	C- / 3.8
2011	E+	198.50	14.92	E / 0.5	-29.00%	C / 4.3

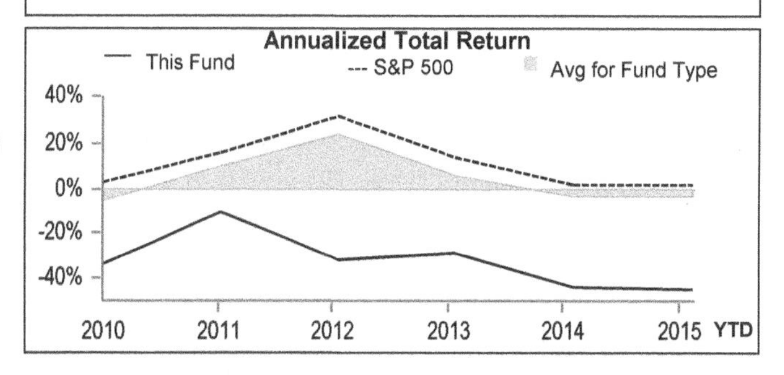

*Nashville Area ETF (NASH) D Weak

Fund Family: LocalShares Inc
Fund Type: Growth
Inception Date: July 31, 2013

Major Rating Factors:
Disappointing performance is the major factor driving the D (Weak) TheStreet.com Investment Rating for *Nashville Area ETF. The fund currently has a performance rating of D- (Weak) based on an annualized return of 0.00% over the last three years and a total return of -13.08% year to date 2015. Factored into the performance evaluation is an expense ratio of 0.49% (very low).

The fund's risk rating is currently C+ (Fair). It carries a beta of 0.00, meaning the fund's expected move will be 0.0% for every 10% move in the market. Volatility, as measured by both the semi-deviation and a drawdown factor, is considered low. As of December 31, 2015, *Nashville Area ETF traded at a premium of .50% above its net asset value, which is worse than its one-year historical average premium of .30%.

William S. Decker has been running the fund for 3 years and currently receives a manager quality ranking of 11 (0=worst, 99=best). This fund offers only a moderate level of risk but investors looking for strong performance are still waiting.

Data Date	Investment Rating	Net Assets ($Mil)	Price	Perfor-mance Rating/Pts	Total Return Y-T-D	Risk Rating/Pts
12-15	D	8.60	25.94	D- / 1.1	-13.08%	C+ / 6.0
2014	A+	8.60	31.51	A- / 9.1	16.75%	B- / 7.8

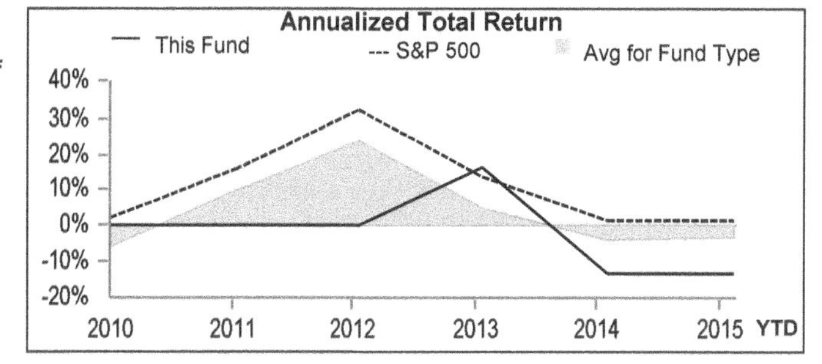

*Newfleet Multi-Sector Income ETF (MINC) C Fair

Fund Family: AdvisorShares Investments LLC
Fund Type: General Bond
Inception Date: March 19, 2013

Major Rating Factors: Middle of the road best describes *Newfleet Multi-Sector Income ETF whose TheStreet.com Investment Rating is currently a C (Fair). The fund currently has a performance rating of C (Fair) based on an annualized return of 0.00% over the last three years and a total return of 0.96% year to date 2015. Factored into the performance evaluation is an expense ratio of 0.75% (very low).

The fund's risk rating is currently B- (Good). It carries a beta of 0.00, meaning the fund's expected move will be 0.0% for every 10% move in the market. Volatility, as measured by both the semi-deviation and a drawdown factor, is considered low. As of December 31, 2015, *Newfleet Multi-Sector Income ETF traded at a premium of .04% above its net asset value, which is worse than its one-year historical average premium of .03%.

David L. Albrycht currently receives a manager quality ranking of 74 (0=worst, 99=best). If you desire an average level of risk, then this fund may be an option.

Data Date	Investment Rating	Net Assets ($Mil)	Price	Performance Rating/Pts	Total Return Y-T-D	Risk Rating/Pts
12-15	C	173.00	48.37	C / 4.5	0.96%	B- / 7.8
2014	C-	173.00	49.16	C- / 3.2	2.26%	B / 8.1

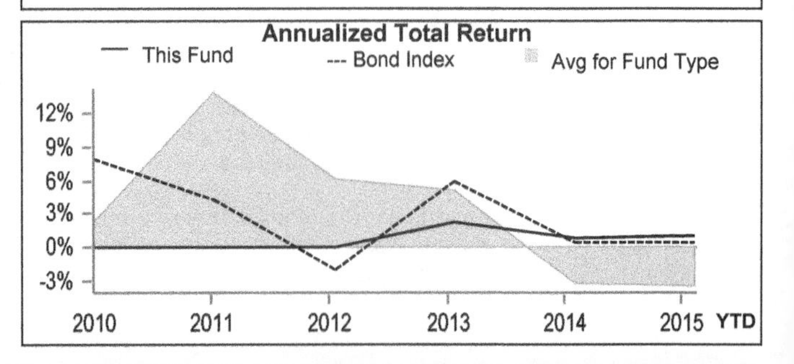

*Nuveen Diversified Commodity (CFD) D- Weak

Fund Family: Nuveen Commodities Asset Management
Fund Type: Growth
Inception Date: September 28, 2010

Major Rating Factors:
Disappointing performance is the major factor driving the D- (Weak) TheStreet.com Investment Rating for *Nuveen Diversified Commodity. The fund currently has a performance rating of D- (Weak) based on an annualized return of -15.71% over the last three years and a total return of -21.90% year to date 2015. Factored into the performance evaluation is an expense ratio of 1.81% (above average).

The fund's risk rating is currently C- (Fair). It carries a beta of 0.35, meaning the fund's expected move will be 3.5% for every 10% move in the market. Volatility, as measured by both the semi-deviation and a drawdown factor, is considered average. As of December 31, 2015, *Nuveen Diversified Commodity traded at a discount of 4.75% below its net asset value, which is worse than its one-year historical average discount of 4.93%.

Douglas M. Baker currently receives a manager quality ranking of 7 (0=worst, 99=best). This fund offers an average level of risk but investors looking for strong performance will be frustrated.

Data Date	Investment Rating	Net Assets ($Mil)	Price	Performance Rating/Pts	Total Return Y-T-D	Risk Rating/Pts
12-15	D-	147.90	9.02	D- / 1.1	-21.90%	C- / 3.9
2014	D-	147.90	12.83	D / 1.6	-6.44%	C / 5.3
2013	D-	167.20	15.17	D- / 1.1	-17.21%	C / 5.1
2012	D	197.10	19.97	D / 1.7	2.93%	C+ / 6.3
2011	D-	214.30	20.30	D- / 1.0	-13.03%	C+ / 6.6

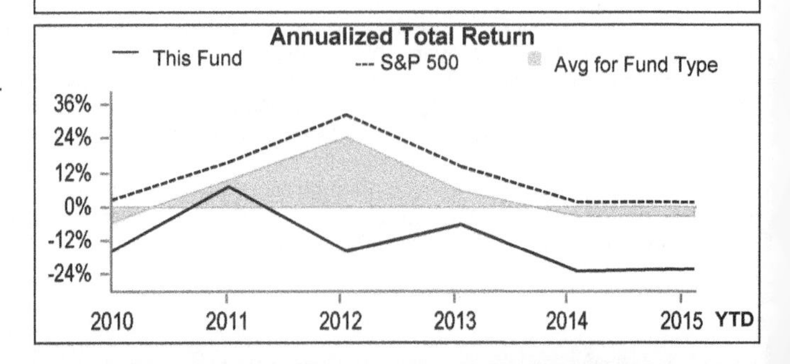

*Nuveen Long/Short Commodity Tot (CTF) C- Fair

Fund Family: Nuveen Commodities Asset Management
Fund Type: Global
Inception Date: October 26, 2012

Major Rating Factors: Middle of the road best describes *Nuveen Long/Short Commodity Tot whose TheStreet.com Investment Rating is currently a C- (Fair). The fund currently has a performance rating of C- (Fair) based on an annualized return of -4.18% over the last three years and a total return of 0.90% year to date 2015. Factored into the performance evaluation is an expense ratio of 1.73% (above average).

The fund's risk rating is currently C+ (Fair). It carries a beta of -0.19, meaning the fund's expected move will be -1.9% for every 10% move in the market. Volatility, as measured by both the semi-deviation and a drawdown factor, is considered low. As of December 31, 2015, *Nuveen Long/Short Commodity Tot traded at a discount of 5.53% below its net asset value, which is better than its one-year historical average discount of 5.02%.

Douglas M. Baker currently receives a manager quality ranking of 57 (0=worst, 99=best). If you desire an average level of risk, then this fund may be an option.

Data Date	Investment Rating	Net Assets ($Mil)	Price	Performance Rating/Pts	Total Return Y-T-D	Risk Rating/Pts
12-15	C-	320.50	15.54	C- / 3.2	0.90%	C+ / 6.7
2014	B	320.50	16.60	B- / 7.5	9.30%	B- / 7.5
2013	D	364.60	17.22	E+ / 0.7	-20.71%	B- / 7.4

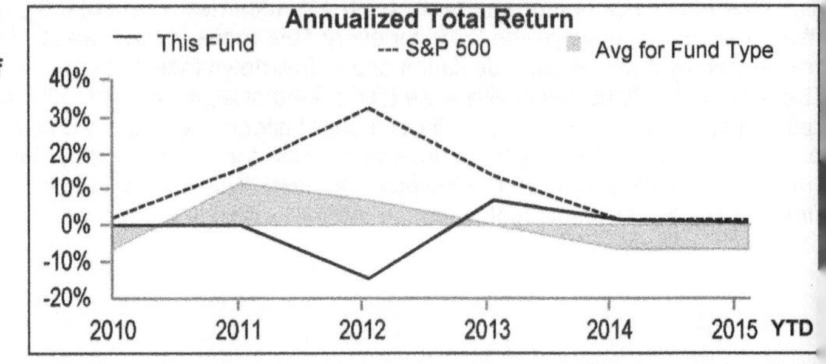

*Oppenheimer ADR Revenue ETF (RTR) D+ Weak

Fund Family: VTL Associates LLC
Fund Type: Income
Inception Date: November 18, 2008

Major Rating Factors:
Disappointing performance is the major factor driving the D+ (Weak) TheStreet.com Investment Rating for *Oppenheimer ADR Revenue ETF. The fund currently has a performance rating of D+ (Weak) based on an annualized return of -3.72% over the last three years and a total return of -15.55% year to date 2015. Factored into the performance evaluation is an expense ratio of 0.49% (very low).

The fund's risk rating is currently B- (Good). It carries a beta of 1.17, meaning it is expected to move 11.7% for every 10% move in the market. Volatility, as measured by both the semi-deviation and a drawdown factor, is considered low. As of December 31, 2015, *Oppenheimer ADR Revenue ETF traded at a discount of .34% below its net asset value, which is better than its one-year historical average premium of .01%.

Vincent T. Lowry currently receives a manager quality ranking of 8 (0=worst, 99=best). This fund offers only a moderate level of risk but investors looking for strong performance are still waiting.

Data Date	Investment Rating	Net Assets ($Mil)	Price	Performance Rating/Pts	Total Return Y-T-D	Risk Rating/Pts
12-15	D+	21.70	29.48	D+ / 2.5	-15.55%	B- / 7.0
2014	D+	21.70	35.91	C- / 3.7	-2.93%	C+ / 6.0
2013	C-	23.50	39.09	C / 4.7	9.76%	B- / 7.1
2012	D+	26.50	35.29	D+ / 2.7	14.74%	C+ / 6.9
2011	C-	38.10	31.71	C- / 3.2	-10.85%	B- / 7.4
2010	A	59.10	38.13	B+ / 8.6	6.85%	B- / 7.1

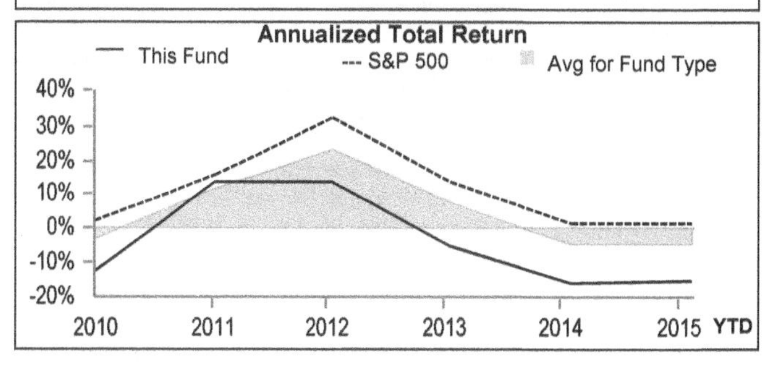

*Oppenheimer Financials Sector Re (RWW) B+ Good

Fund Family: VTL Associates LLC
Fund Type: Financial Services
Inception Date: November 10, 2008

Major Rating Factors: Strong performance is the major factor driving the B+ (Good) TheStreet.com Investment Rating for *Oppenheimer Financials Sector Re. The fund currently has a performance rating of B+ (Good) based on an annualized return of 13.83% over the last three years and a total return of -3.31% year to date 2015. Factored into the performance evaluation is an expense ratio of 0.49% (very low).

The fund's risk rating is currently C+ (Fair). It carries a beta of 1.17, meaning it is expected to move 11.7% for every 10% move in the market. Volatility, as measured by both the semi-deviation and a drawdown factor, is considered low. As of December 31, 2015, *Oppenheimer Financials Sector Re traded at a premium of .46% above its net asset value, which is worse than its one-year historical average premium of .02%.

Justin V. Lowry has been running the fund for 2 years and currently receives a manager quality ranking of 50 (0=worst, 99=best). If you desire only a moderate level of risk and strong performance, then this fund is an excellent option.

Data Date	Investment Rating	Net Assets ($Mil)	Price	Performance Rating/Pts	Total Return Y-T-D	Risk Rating/Pts
12-15	B+	33.40	48.09	B+ / 8.5	-3.31%	C+ / 6.8
2014	B+	33.40	50.68	A / 9.5	13.51%	C+ / 6.4
2013	B-	29.40	45.13	B / 8.0	35.67%	C+ / 6.8
2012	C	9.60	32.04	C+ / 5.9	31.49%	C+ / 6.6
2011	D	7.20	23.91	D / 2.1	-23.94%	C+ / 6.1
2010	A-	20.70	31.84	A- / 9.0	15.52%	C / 5.3

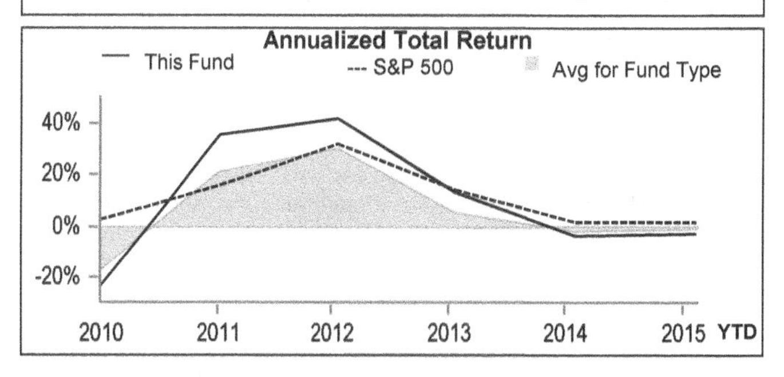

*Oppenheimer Large Cap Revenue (RWL) A+ Excellent

Fund Family: VTL Associates LLC
Fund Type: Growth
Inception Date: February 22, 2008

Major Rating Factors:
Strong performance is the major factor driving the A+ (Excellent) TheStreet.com Investment Rating for *Oppenheimer Large Cap Revenue. The fund currently has a performance rating of B+ (Good) based on an annualized return of 14.15% over the last three years and a total return of -1.93% year to date 2015. Factored into the performance evaluation is an expense ratio of 0.49% (very low).

The fund's risk rating is currently B (Good). It carries a beta of 1.01, meaning that its performance tracks fairly well with that of the overall stock market. Volatility, as measured by both the semi-deviation and a drawdown factor, is considered low. As of December 31, 2015, *Oppenheimer Large Cap Revenue traded at a discount of .03% below its net asset value, which is better than its one-year historical average premium of .01%.

Justin V. Lowry has been running the fund for 2 years and currently receives a manager quality ranking of 70 (0=worst, 99=best). If you desire only a moderate level of risk and strong performance, then this fund is an excellent option.

Data Date	Investment Rating	Net Assets ($Mil)	Price	Performance Rating/Pts	Total Return Y-T-D	Risk Rating/Pts
12-15	A+	258.90	39.44	B+ / 8.6	-1.93%	B / 8.7
2014	A-	258.90	40.77	B+ / 8.9	14.35%	B- / 7.4
2013	A	207.80	36.48	B+ / 8.7	32.74%	B / 8.3
2012	C+	151.00	26.92	C+ / 5.7	18.30%	B / 8.1
2011	C	162.90	23.27	C / 5.1	0.60%	B / 8.0
2010	B-	188.90	23.64	A- / 9.2	16.38%	C- / 3.6

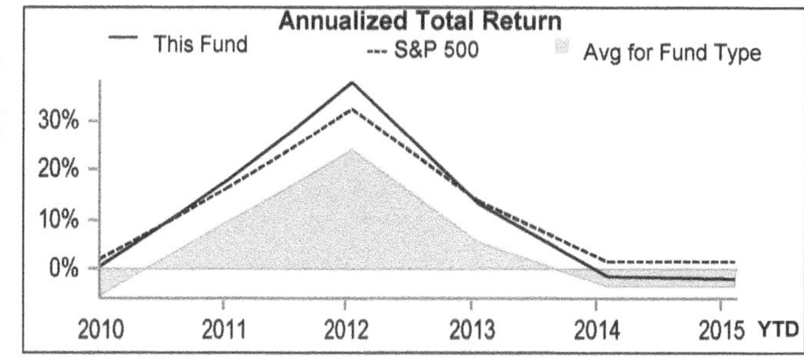

*Oppenheimer Mid Cap Revenue (RWK) B Good

Fund Family: VTL Associates LLC
Fund Type: Growth
Inception Date: February 22, 2008

Major Rating Factors: Strong performance is the major factor driving the B (Good) TheStreet.com Investment Rating for *Oppenheimer Mid Cap Revenue. The fund currently has a performance rating of B (Good) based on an annualized return of 11.74% over the last three years and a total return of -5.44% year to date 2015. Factored into the performance evaluation is an expense ratio of 0.54% (very low).

The fund's risk rating is currently B- (Good). It carries a beta of 1.12, meaning it is expected to move 11.2% for every 10% move in the market. Volatility, as measured by both the semi-deviation and a drawdown factor, is considered low. As of December 31, 2015, *Oppenheimer Mid Cap Revenue traded at a premium of .35% above its net asset value, which is worse than its one-year historical average premium of .04%.

Justin V. Lowry has been running the fund for 2 years and currently receives a manager quality ranking of 42 (0=worst, 99=best). If you desire only a moderate level of risk and strong performance, then this fund is an excellent option.

Data Date	Investment Rating	Net Assets ($Mil)	Price	Perfor-mance Rating/Pts	Total Return Y-T-D	Risk Rating/Pts
12-15	B	209.10	45.29	B / 7.6	-5.44%	B- / 7.2
2014	B+	209.10	48.42	B+ / 8.4	10.31%	B- / 7.1
2013	B+	167.30	44.65	B+ / 8.7	34.32%	B- / 7.7
2012	C+	104.60	32.08	C+ / 6.9	17.09%	B- / 7.6
2011	B-	126.70	28.16	C+ / 6.9	-0.21%	B- / 7.6
2010	B-	138.60	29.51	A / 9.4	23.00%	C- / 3.3

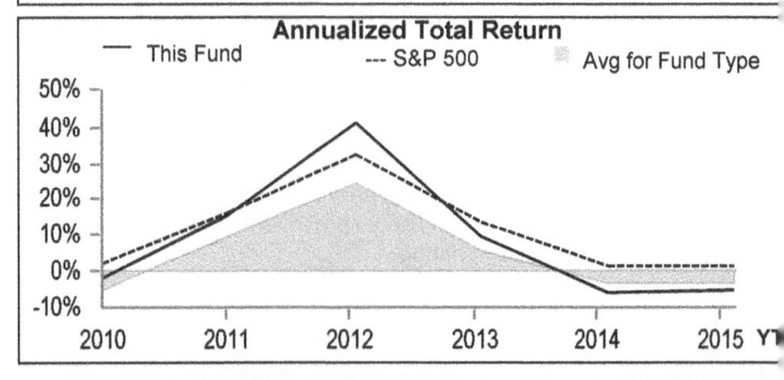

*Oppenheimer Navellier Overall A1 (RWV) C+ Fair

Fund Family: VTL Associates LLC
Fund Type: Income
Inception Date: January 21, 2009

Major Rating Factors: Strong performance is the major factor driving the C+ (Fair) TheStreet.com Investment Rating for *Oppenheimer Navellier Overall A1. The fund currently has a performance rating of B (Good) based on an annualized return of 12.58% over the last three years and a total return of -2.08% year to date 2015. Factored into the performance evaluation is an expense ratio of 0.60% (very low).

The fund's risk rating is currently C+ (Fair). It carries a beta of 0.98, meaning that its performance tracks fairly well with that of the overall stock market. Volatility, as measured by both the semi-deviation and a drawdown factor, is considered low. As of December 31, 2015, *Oppenheimer Navellier Overall A1 traded at a premium of .09% above its net asset value, which is better than its one-year historical average premium of .21%.

Vincent T. Lowry currently receives a manager quality ranking of 67 (0=worst, 99=best). If you desire only a moderate level of risk and strong performance, then this fund is an excellent option.

Data Date	Investment Rating	Net Assets ($Mil)	Price	Perfor-mance Rating/Pts	Total Return Y-T-D	Risk Rating/Pts
12-15	C+	8.20	46.77	B / 7.9	-2.08%	C+ / 5.9
2014	C+	8.20	48.64	B / 7.6	12.62%	C+ / 6.1
2013	B	7.70	51.44	B / 7.6	27.99%	B- / 7.8
2012	C	8.00	39.66	C / 4.4	14.00%	B- / 7.8
2011	D	9.00	35.93	D- / 1.4	-4.24%	B- / 7.9
2010	A+	9.60	38.66	A / 9.5	21.99%	B- / 7.8

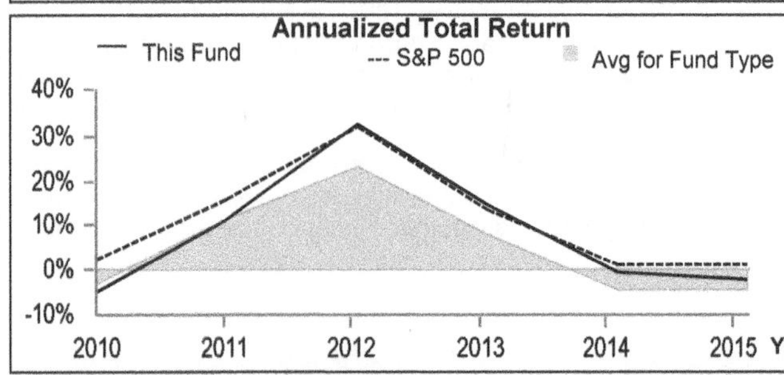

*Oppenheimer Small Cap Revenue (RWJ) B+ Good

Fund Family: VTL Associates LLC
Fund Type: Growth
Inception Date: February 22, 2008

Major Rating Factors: Strong performance is the major factor driving the B+ (Good) TheStreet.com Investment Rating for *Oppenheimer Small Cap Revenue. The fund currently has a performance rating of B- (Good) based on an annualized return of 10.90% over the last three years and a total return of -8.12% year to date 2015. Factored into the performance evaluation is an expense ratio of 0.54% (very low).

The fund's risk rating is currently B (Good). It carries a beta of 1.21, meaning it is expected to move 12.1% for every 10% move in the market. Volatility, as measured by both the semi-deviation and a drawdown factor, is considered low. As of December 31, 2015, *Oppenheimer Small Cap Revenue traded at a discount of .19% below its net asset value, which is better than its one-year historical average premium of .02%.

Justin V. Lowry has been running the fund for 2 years and currently receives a manager quality ranking of 29 (0=worst, 99=best). If you desire only a moderate level of risk and strong performance, then this fund is an excellent option.

Data Date	Investment Rating	Net Assets ($Mil)	Price	Perfor-mance Rating/Pts	Total Return Y-T-D	Risk Rating/Pts
12-15	B+	275.00	51.70	B- / 7.1	-8.12%	B / 8.3
2014	B+	275.00	57.06	B+ / 8.7	7.41%	B- / 7.0
2013	A	253.20	53.89	A- / 9.1	39.41%	B- / 7.8
2012	C+	122.00	37.44	B- / 7.0	16.99%	B- / 7.5
2011	B-	104.30	32.07	B- / 7.3	0.68%	B- / 7.4
2010	B	128.20	32.49	A / 9.5	25.66%	C- / 3.3

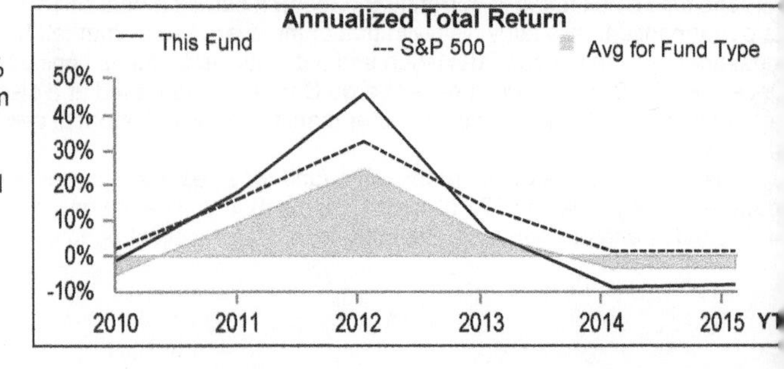

*Oppenheimer Ultra Dividend Reven (RDIV) C- Fair

Fund Family: VTL Associates LLC
Fund Type: Income
Inception Date: September 30, 2013

Data Date	Investment Rating	Net Assets ($Mil)	Price	Performance Rating/Pts	Total Return Y-T-D	Risk Rating/Pts
12-15	C-	26.80	27.63	D+ / 2.9	-5.51%	B- / 7.1
2014	B-	26.80	30.33	A / 9.4	23.11%	C / 5.3

Major Rating Factors:
Disappointing performance is the major factor driving the C- (Fair) TheStreet.com Investment Rating for *Oppenheimer Ultra Dividend Reven. The fund currently has a performance rating of D+ (Weak) based on an annualized return of 0.00% over the last three years and a total return of -5.51% year to date 2015. Factored into the performance evaluation is an expense ratio of 0.49% (very low).

The fund's risk rating is currently B- (Good). It carries a beta of 0.00, meaning the fund's expected move will be 0.0% for every 10% move in the market. Volatility, as measured by both the semi-deviation and a drawdown factor, is considered low. As of December 31, 2015, *Oppenheimer Ultra Dividend Reven traded at a premium of .29% above its net asset value, which is worse than its one-year historical average premium of .02%.

Justin V. Lowry has been running the fund for 2 years and currently receives a manager quality ranking of 27 (0=worst, 99=best). This fund offers only a moderate level of risk but investors looking for strong performance are still waiting.

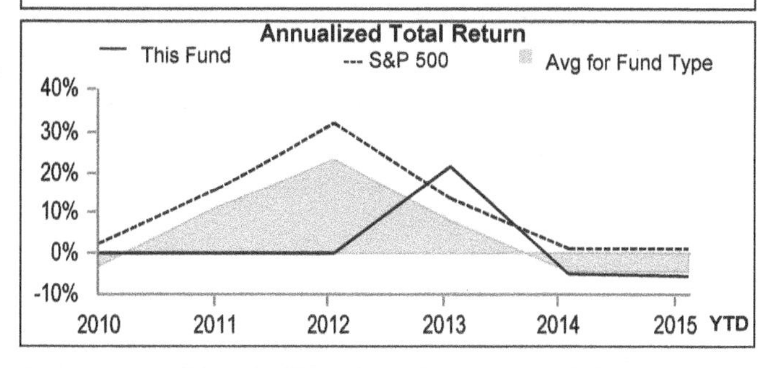

*Peritus High Yield ETF (HYLD) D+ Weak

Fund Family: AdvisorShares Investments LLC
Fund Type: Corporate - High Yield
Inception Date: December 1, 2010

Data Date	Investment Rating	Net Assets ($Mil)	Price	Performance Rating/Pts	Total Return Y-T-D	Risk Rating/Pts
12-15	D+	748.80	32.64	D / 2.2	-14.14%	C+ / 6.5
2014	D+	748.80	41.15	D+ / 2.4	-13.67%	B- / 7.7
2013	B-	459.90	51.72	C+ / 6.1	10.55%	B+ / 9.1
2012	B	177.20	50.07	C+ / 6.3	15.04%	B+ / 9.0
2011	C-	61.40	47.52	D / 1.9	-0.21%	B+ / 9.0

Major Rating Factors:
Disappointing performance is the major factor driving the D+ (Weak) TheStreet.com Investment Rating for *Peritus High Yield ETF. The fund currently has a performance rating of D (Weak) based on an annualized return of -6.28% over the last three years and a total return of -14.14% year to date 2015. Factored into the performance evaluation is an expense ratio of 1.23% (average).

The fund's risk rating is currently C+ (Fair). It carries a beta of 1.36, meaning it is expected to move 13.6% for every 10% move in the market. Volatility, as measured by both the semi-deviation and a drawdown factor, is considered low. As of December 31, 2015, *Peritus High Yield ETF traded at a discount of 1.33% below its net asset value, which is better than its one-year historical average discount of .63%.

Dave Flaherty currently receives a manager quality ranking of 20 (0=worst, 99=best). This fund offers only a moderate level of risk but investors looking for strong performance are still waiting.

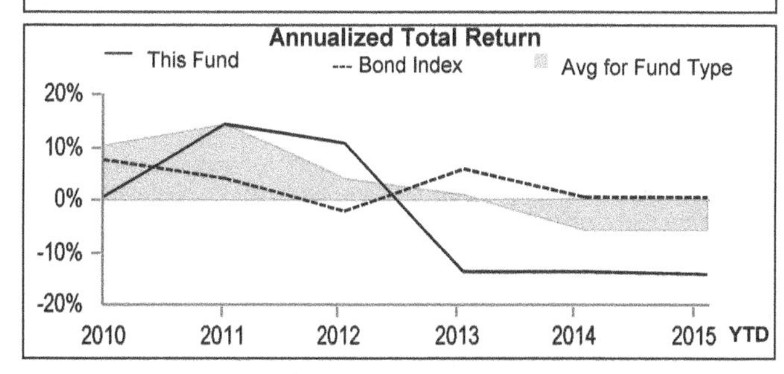

*PIMCO 0-5 Year Hi Yield Corp Bd (HYS) C Fair

Fund Family: PIMCO
Fund Type: Corporate - Investment Grade
Inception Date: June 16, 2011

Data Date	Investment Rating	Net Assets ($Mil)	Price	Performance Rating/Pts	Total Return Y-T-D	Risk Rating/Pts
12-15	C	3,867.60	91.62	C- / 4.0	-5.22%	B / 8.7
2014	C+	3,867.60	100.83	C- / 4.1	-0.09%	B+ / 9.4
2013	B	3,618.20	106.36	C+ / 5.9	7.61%	B+ / 9.6
2012	B-	791.70	103.43	C / 5.0	11.95%	B+ / 9.6

Major Rating Factors: Middle of the road best describes *PIMCO 0-5 Year Hi Yield Corp Bd whose TheStreet.com Investment Rating is currently a C (Fair). The fund currently has a performance rating of C- (Fair) based on an annualized return of 0.70% over the last three years and a total return of -5.22% year to date 2015. Factored into the performance evaluation is an expense ratio of 0.55% (very low).

The fund's risk rating is currently B (Good). It carries a beta of 0.45, meaning the fund's expected move will be 4.5% for every 10% move in the market. Volatility, as measured by both the semi-deviation and a drawdown factor, is considered low. As of December 31, 2015, *PIMCO 0-5 Year Hi Yield Corp Bd traded at a discount of .43% below its net asset value, which is better than its one-year historical average discount of .21%.

Andrew R. Jessop has been running the fund for 1 year and currently receives a manager quality ranking of 69 (0=worst, 99=best). If you desire an average level of risk, then this fund may be an option.

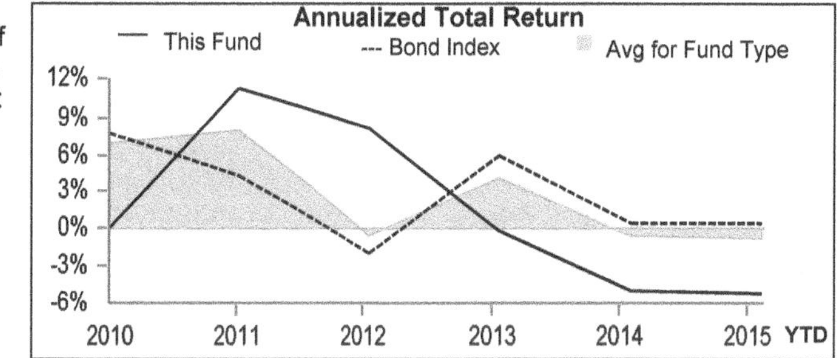

*PIMCO 1-3 Year US Treasury Idx E (TUZ) B- Good

Fund Family: PIMCO
Fund Type: US Government/Agency
Inception Date: June 1, 2009

Major Rating Factors: *PIMCO 1-3 Year US Treasury Idx E receives a TheStreet.com Investment Rating of B- (Good). The fund currently has a performance rating of C (Fair) based on an annualized return of 0.33% over the last three years and a total return of 0.18% year to date 2015. Factored into the performance evaluation is an expense ratio of 0.14% (very low).

The fund's risk rating is currently B+ (Good). It carries a beta of 0.03, meaning the fund's expected move will be 0.3% for every 10% move in the market. Volatility, as measured by both the semi-deviation and a drawdown factor, is considered very low. As of December 31, 2015, *PIMCO 1-3 Year US Treasury Idx E traded at a discount of .16% below its net asset value, which is better than its one-year historical average discount of .01%.

Chris Caltagirone has been running the fund for 1 year and currently receives a manager quality ranking of 70 (0=worst, 99=best). If you desire an average level of risk, then this fund may be an option.

Data Date	Investment Rating	Net Assets ($Mil)	Price	Performance Rating/Pts	Total Return Y-T-D	Risk Rating/Pts
12-15	B-	127.30	50.66	C / 4.4	0.18%	B+ / 9.9
2014	C-	127.30	50.98	C- / 3.0	0.93%	B / 8.1
2013	C	122.10	50.87	D+ / 2.7	0.25%	B+ / 9.9
2012	C-	122.20	50.85	D / 1.6	0.28%	B+ / 9.9
2011	C	143.10	51.12	D / 2.2	1.52%	B+ / 9.9
2010	C+	106.80	50.92	C- / 3.1	2.37%	B+ / 9.0

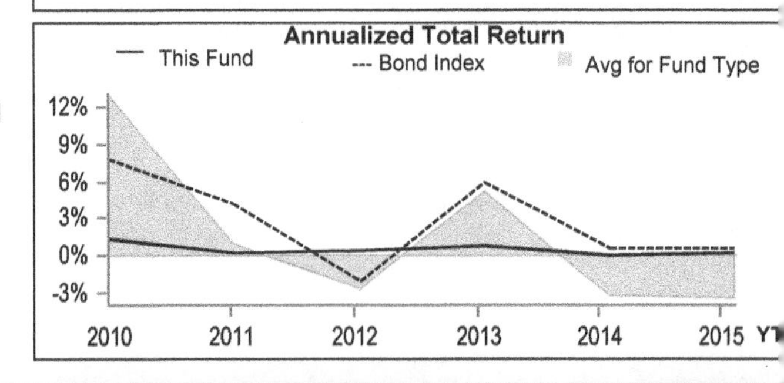

*PIMCO 1-5 Year US TIPS Index ETF (STPZ) C Fair

Fund Family: PIMCO
Fund Type: US Government/Agency
Inception Date: August 20, 2009

Major Rating Factors: Middle of the road best describes *PIMCO 1-5 Year US TIPS Index ETF whose TheStreet.com Investment Rating is currently a C (Fair). The fund currently has a performance rating of C- (Fair) based on an annualized return of -1.22% over the last three years and a total return of -0.45% year to date 2015. Factored into the performance evaluation is an expense ratio of 0.20% (very low).

The fund's risk rating is currently B- (Good). It carries a beta of 0.07, meaning the fund's expected move will be 0.7% for every 10% move in the market. Volatility, as measured by both the semi-deviation and a drawdown factor, is considered low. As of December 31, 2015, *PIMCO 1-5 Year US TIPS Index ETF traded at a premium of .20% above its net asset value, which is worse than its one-year historical average premium of .01%.

Jeremie Banet has been running the fund for 1 year and currently receives a manager quality ranking of 56 (0=worst, 99=best). If you desire an average level of risk, then this fund may be an option.

Data Date	Investment Rating	Net Assets ($Mil)	Price	Performance Rating/Pts	Total Return Y-T-D	Risk Rating/Pts
12-15	C	1,407.00	51.33	C- / 3.8	-0.45%	B- / 7.8
2014	C	1,407.00	51.73	D+ / 2.5	-1.43%	B+ / 9.7
2013	C	1,298.30	52.82	D+ / 2.9	-1.93%	B+ / 9.9
2012	C-	992.70	54.06	D / 2.1	2.01%	B+ / 9.9
2011	C	933.90	53.34	D+ / 2.8	4.95%	B+ / 9.9
2010	B	672.80	52.58	C- / 4.0	3.40%	B+ / 9.0

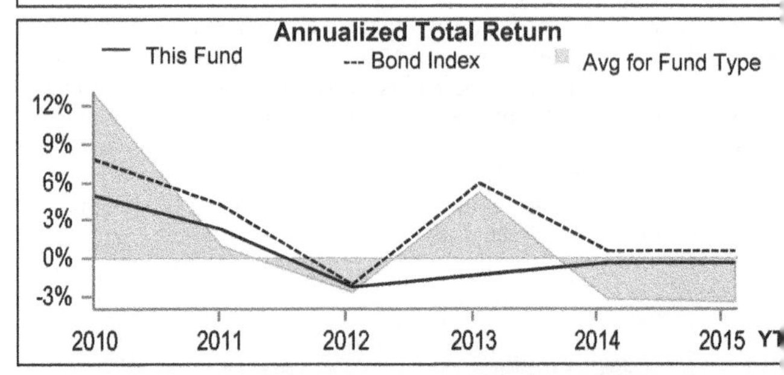

*PIMCO 15 Plus Year US TIPS Idx E (LTPZ) D+ Weak

Fund Family: PIMCO
Fund Type: US Government/Agency
Inception Date: September 3, 2009

Major Rating Factors:
Disappointing performance is the major factor driving the D+ (Weak) TheStreet.com Investment Rating for *PIMCO 15 Plus Year US TIPS Idx E. The fund currently has a performance rating of D+ (Weak) based on an annualized return of -3.52% over the last three years and a total return of -10.16% year to date 2015. Factored into the performance evaluation is an expense ratio of 0.21% (very low).

The fund's risk rating is currently C+ (Fair). It carries a beta of 0.99, meaning that its performance tracks fairly well with that of the overall stock market. Volatility, as measured by both the semi-deviation and a drawdown factor, is considered low. As of December 31, 2015, *PIMCO 15 Plus Year US TIPS Idx E traded at a premium of .35% above its net asset value.

Jeremie Banet has been running the fund for 1 year and currently receives a manager quality ranking of 24 (0=worst, 99=best). This fund offers only a moderate level of risk but investors looking for strong performance are still waiting.

Data Date	Investment Rating	Net Assets ($Mil)	Price	Performance Rating/Pts	Total Return Y-T-D	Risk Rating/Pts
12-15	D+	77.40	60.86	D+ / 2.9	-10.16%	C+ / 6.1
2014	C	77.40	67.21	C / 4.6	18.49%	B- / 7.7
2013	C-	72.50	57.19	C- / 3.0	-16.86%	B / 8.0
2012	C+	155.90	71.65	C / 5.3	9.54%	B+ / 9.1
2011	A	360.50	65.25	B+ / 8.7	27.59%	B+ / 9.1
2010	B	250.80	54.35	C / 5.2	8.49%	B / 8.4

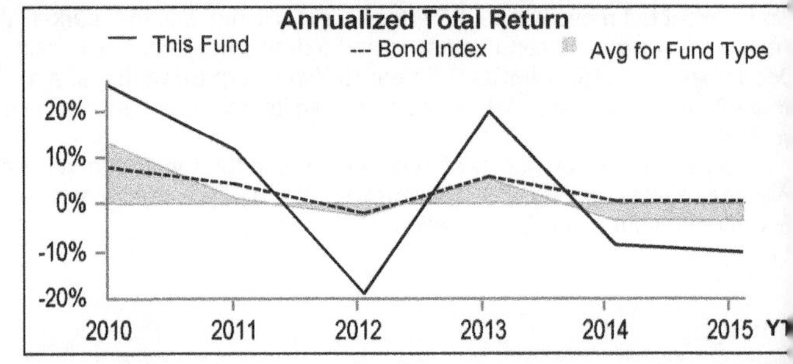

*PIMCO 25+ Year Zero Coupon US Tr (ZROZ) C Fair

Fund Family: PIMCO
Fund Type: US Government/Agency
Inception Date: October 30, 2009

Major Rating Factors: Middle of the road best describes *PIMCO 25+ Year Zero Coupon US Tr whose TheStreet.com Investment Rating is currently a C (Fair). The fund currently has a performance rating of C+ (Fair) based on an annualized return of 4.48% over the last three years and a total return of -8.14% year to date 2015. Factored into the performance evaluation is an expense ratio of 0.16% (very low).

The fund's risk rating is currently B- (Good). It carries a beta of 1.81, meaning it is expected to move 18.1% for every 10% move in the market. Volatility, as measured by both the semi-deviation and a drawdown factor, is considered low. As of December 31, 2015, *PIMCO 25+ Year Zero Coupon US Tr traded at a discount of .84% below its net asset value, which is better than its one-year historical average premium of .03%.

Chris Caltagirone has been running the fund for 1 year and currently receives a manager quality ranking of 56 (0=worst, 99=best). If you desire an average level of risk, then this fund may be an option.

Data Date	Investment Rating	Net Assets ($Mil)	Price	Performance Rating/Pts	Total Return Y-T-D	Risk Rating/Pts
12-15	C	64.80	109.31	C+ / 5.6	-8.14%	B- / 7.2
2014	B	64.80	119.90	B+ / 8.4	48.47%	C+ / 6.6
2013	C-	55.20	83.00	C / 5.0	-17.46%	C+ / 6.8
2012	C+	100.90	109.12	C+ / 6.5	0.81%	B- / 7.1
2011	B+	64.50	111.50	A+ / 9.9	63.48%	B- / 7.2
2010	D	53.50	72.30	D- / 1.0	8.61%	C+ / 6.8

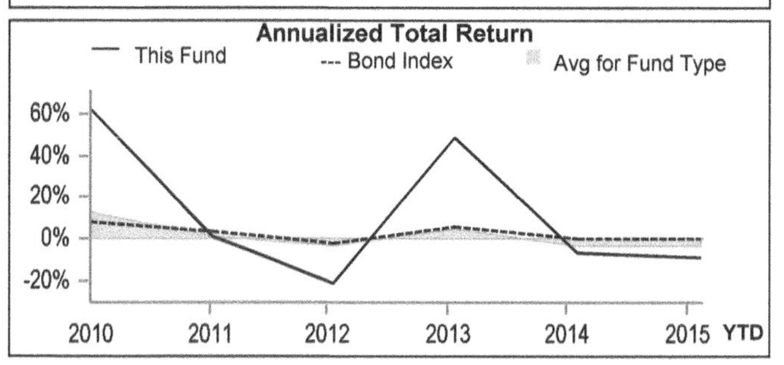

*PIMCO Broad US TIPS Index ETF (TIPZ) C Fair

Fund Family: PIMCO
Fund Type: US Government/Agency
Inception Date: September 3, 2009

Major Rating Factors: Middle of the road best describes *PIMCO Broad US TIPS Index ETF whose TheStreet.com Investment Rating is currently a C (Fair). The fund currently has a performance rating of C- (Fair) based on an annualized return of -2.27% over the last three years and a total return of -3.22% year to date 2015. Factored into the performance evaluation is an expense ratio of 0.21% (very low).

The fund's risk rating is currently B (Good). It carries a beta of 0.40, meaning the fund's expected move will be 4.0% for every 10% move in the market. Volatility, as measured by both the semi-deviation and a drawdown factor, is considered low. As of December 31, 2015, *PIMCO Broad US TIPS Index ETF traded at a discount of .20% below its net asset value, which is better than its one-year historical average discount of .01%.

Jeremie Banet has been running the fund for 1 year and currently receives a manager quality ranking of 38 (0=worst, 99=best). If you desire an average level of risk, then this fund may be an option.

Data Date	Investment Rating	Net Assets ($Mil)	Price	Performance Rating/Pts	Total Return Y-T-D	Risk Rating/Pts
12-15	C	123.70	55.25	C- / 3.4	-3.22%	B / 8.8
2014	C-	123.70	56.97	C- / 3.0	4.14%	B / 8.9
2013	C-	51.20	55.23	C- / 3.1	-8.08%	B+ / 9.1
2012	C	136.50	61.20	C- / 3.1	5.62%	B+ / 9.7
2011	B	95.00	58.29	C+ / 5.7	14.80%	B+ / 9.7
2010	B	38.80	53.13	C / 4.5	5.94%	B / 8.8

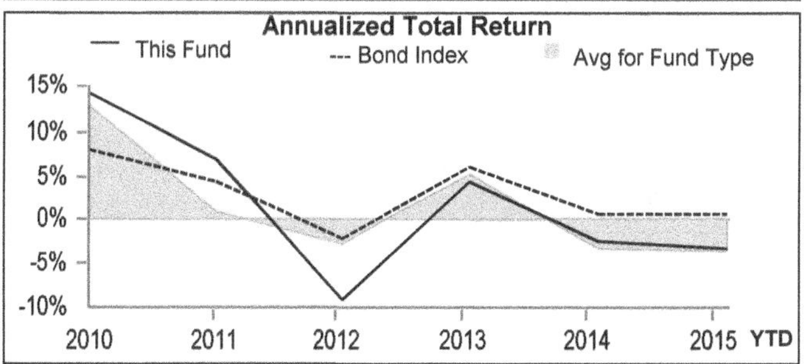

*PIMCO Dvsfd Inc Active Exch Trad (DI) C Fair

Fund Family: PIMCO
Fund Type: General Bond
Inception Date: January 22, 2014

Major Rating Factors: Middle of the road best describes *PIMCO Dvsfd Inc Active Exch Trad whose TheStreet.com Investment Rating is currently a C (Fair). The fund currently has a performance rating of C- (Fair) based on an annualized return of 0.00% over the last three years and a total return of -0.97% year to date 2015. Factored into the performance evaluation is an expense ratio of 0.85% (very low).

The fund's risk rating is currently B (Good). It carries a beta of 0.00, meaning the fund's expected move will be 0.0% for every 10% move in the market. Volatility, as measured by both the semi-deviation and a drawdown factor, is considered low. As of December 31, 2015, *PIMCO Dvsfd Inc Active Exch Trad traded at a discount of .43% below its net asset value, which is better than its one-year historical average premium of .75%.

Curtis A. Mewbourne, II has been running the fund for 2 years and currently receives a manager quality ranking of 51 (0=worst, 99=best). If you desire an average level of risk, then this fund may be an option.

Data Date	Investment Rating	Net Assets ($Mil)	Price	Performance Rating/Pts	Total Return Y-T-D	Risk Rating/Pts
12-15	C	43.30	45.83	C- / 3.6	-0.97%	B / 8.7

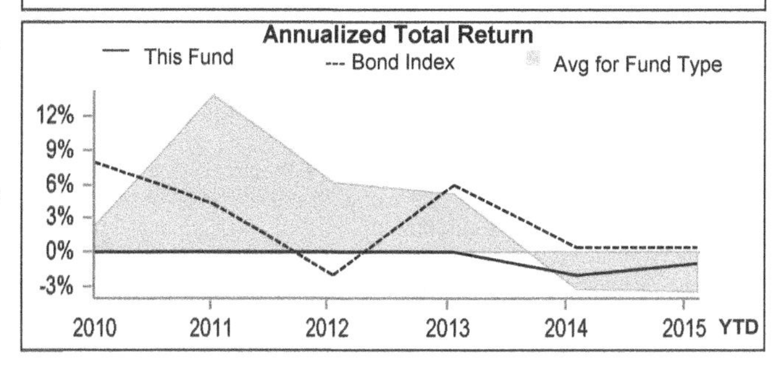

*PIMCO Enhanced Sht Maturity Act (MINT) B- Good

Fund Family: PIMCO
Fund Type: Corporate - Investment Grade
Inception Date: November 16, 2009

Major Rating Factors: *PIMCO Enhanced Sht Maturity Act receives a TheStreet.com Investment Rating of B- (Good). The fund currently has a performance rating of C (Fair) based on an annualized return of 0.58% over the last three years and a total return of 0.35% year to date 2015. Factored into the performance evaluation is an expense ratio of 0.35% (very low).

The fund's risk rating is currently B+ (Good). It carries a beta of 0.04, meaning the fund's expected move will be 0.4% for every 10% move in the market. Volatility, as measured by both the semi-deviation and a drawdown factor, is considered very low. As of December 31, 2015, *PIMCO Enhanced Sht Maturity Act traded at a discount of .06% below its net asset value, which is better than its one-year historical average discount of .03%.

Jerome M. Schneider has been running the fund for 7 years and currently receives a manager quality ranking of 72 (0=worst, 99=best). If you desire an average level of risk, then this fund may be an option.

Data Date	Investment Rating	Net Assets ($Mil)	Price	Performance Rating/Pts	Total Return Y-T-D	Risk Rating/Pts
12-15	B-	3,722.80	100.61	C / 4.6	0.35%	B+ / 9.7
2014	C	3,722.80	101.06	C- / 3.1	0.66%	B+ / 9.0
2013	C	3,874.90	101.30	D+ / 2.9	0.72%	B+ / 9.9
2012	C-	2,169.30	101.48	D / 1.7	2.31%	B+ / 9.9
2011	C-	1,803.30	100.16	D / 2.0	0.45%	B+ / 9.9
2010	C+	785.20	100.71	C- / 3.0	1.61%	B+ / 9.0

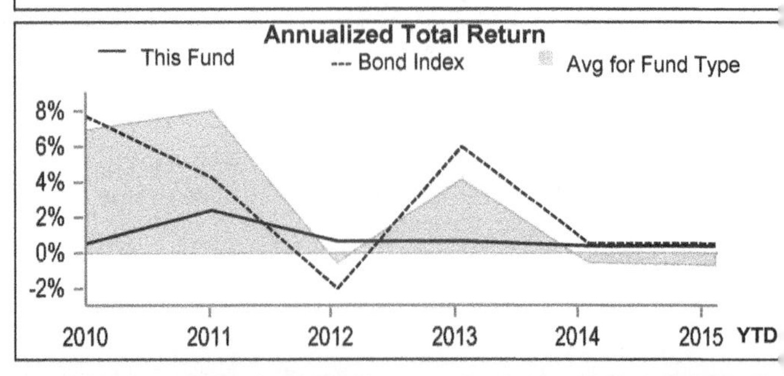

*PIMCO Global Adv Infl-Link Bond (ILB) C- Fair

Fund Family: PIMCO
Fund Type: Global
Inception Date: April 30, 2012

Major Rating Factors:
Disappointing performance is the major factor driving the C- (Fair) TheStreet.com Investment Rating for *PIMCO Global Adv Infl-Link Bond. The fund currently has a performance rating of D+ (Weak) based on an annualized return of -7.70% over the last three years and a total return of -10.01% year to date 2015. Factored into the performance evaluation is an expense ratio of 0.61% (very low).

The fund's risk rating is currently B- (Good). It carries a beta of 0.99, meaning that its performance tracks fairly well with that of the overall stock market. Volatility, as measured by both the semi-deviation and a drawdown factor, is considered low. As of December 31, 2015, *PIMCO Global Adv Infl-Link Bond traded at a discount of .47% below its net asset value, which is worse than its one-year historical average discount of .74%.

Mihir Worah has been running the fund for 4 years and currently receives a manager quality ranking of 36 (0=worst, 99=best). This fund offers only a moderate level of risk but investors looking for strong performance are still waiting.

Data Date	Investment Rating	Net Assets ($Mil)	Price	Performance Rating/Pts	Total Return Y-T-D	Risk Rating/Pts
12-15	C-	123.40	40.05	D+ / 2.3	-10.01%	B- / 7.4
2014	D	123.40	45.81	D / 1.9	-0.39%	C+ / 6.3
2013	D+	98.70	47.65	D- / 1.3	-11.00%	B / 8.5

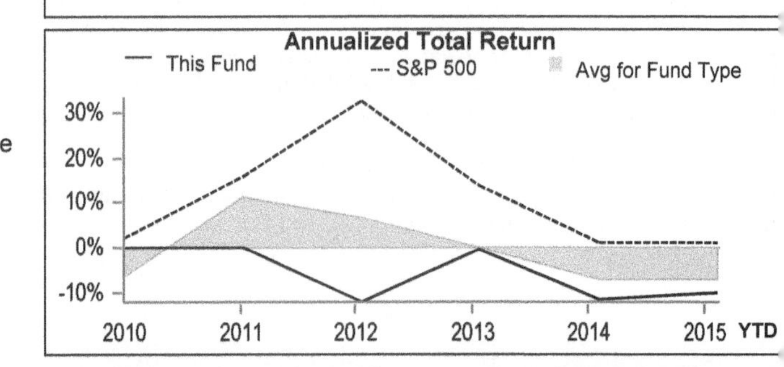

*PIMCO Intermediate Muni Bd Act E (MUNI) C+ Fair

Fund Family: PIMCO
Fund Type: Municipal - National
Inception Date: November 30, 2009

Major Rating Factors: Middle of the road best describes *PIMCO Intermediate Muni Bd Act E whose TheStreet.com Investment Rating is currently a C+ (Fair). The fund currently has a performance rating of C+ (Fair) based on an annualized return of 1.89% over the last three years and a total return of 2.48% year to date 2015. Factored into the performance evaluation is an expense ratio of 0.35% (very low).

The fund's risk rating is currently B- (Good). It carries a beta of 0.95, meaning that its performance tracks fairly well with that of the overall stock market. Volatility, as measured by both the semi-deviation and a drawdown factor, is considered low. As of December 31, 2015, *PIMCO Intermediate Muni Bd Act E traded at a premium of .37% above its net asset value, which is worse than its one-year historical average discount of .03%.

Joseph P. Deane has been running the fund for 5 years and currently receives a manager quality ranking of 59 (0=worst, 99=best). If you desire an average level of risk, then this fund may be an option.

Data Date	Investment Rating	Net Assets ($Mil)	Price	Performance Rating/Pts	Total Return Y-T-D	Risk Rating/Pts
12-15	C+	217.00	53.97	C+ / 5.8	2.48%	B- / 7.7
2014	C	217.00	53.68	C- / 4.1	5.42%	B / 8.4
2013	C+	195.00	51.77	C- / 4.2	-2.23%	B+ / 9.5
2012	C	204.20	54.37	C- / 3.3	4.22%	B+ / 9.7
2011	B	98.60	53.12	C+ / 5.6	8.67%	B+ / 9.8
2010	C+	63.40	50.37	C- / 3.4	3.50%	B / 8.9

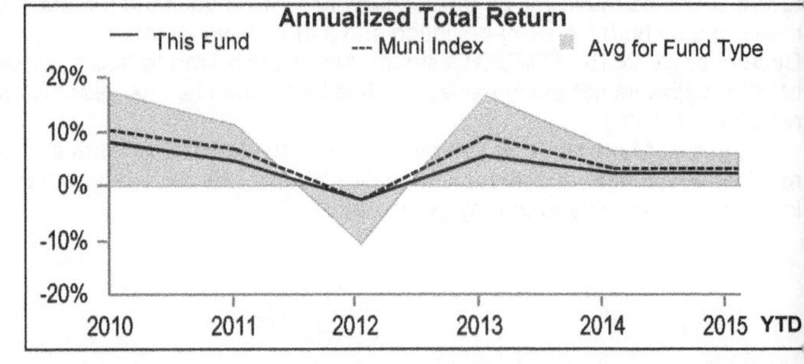

* Denotes ETF Fund

*PIMCO Investment Grade Crp Bond (CORP) C+ Fair

Fund Family: PIMCO
Fund Type: Corporate - Investment Grade
Inception Date: September 20, 2010

Data Date	Investment Rating	Net Assets ($Mil)	Price	Performance Rating/Pts	Total Return Y-T-D	Risk Rating/Pts
12-15	C+	238.30	98.98	C / 4.8	-1.62%	B / 8.9
2014	C+	238.30	102.95	C / 4.4	7.59%	B / 8.7
2013	C+	176.30	99.00	C / 4.3	-2.32%	B+ / 9.2
2011	C+	186.40	100.71	C- / 3.4	6.76%	B+ / 9.8

Major Rating Factors: Middle of the road best describes *PIMCO Investment Grade Crp Bond whose TheStreet.com Investment Rating is currently a C+ (Fair). The fund currently has a performance rating of C (Fair) based on an annualized return of 1.29% over the last three years and a total return of -1.62% year to date 2015. Factored into the performance evaluation is an expense ratio of 0.20% (very low).

The fund's risk rating is currently B (Good). It carries a beta of 1.04, meaning that its performance tracks fairly well with that of the overall stock market. Volatility, as measured by both the semi-deviation and a drawdown factor, is considered low. As of December 31, 2015, *PIMCO Investment Grade Crp Bond traded at a discount of .13% below its net asset value, which is better than its one-year historical average discount of .02%.

Chris Caltagirone has been running the fund for 1 year and currently receives a manager quality ranking of 65 (0=worst, 99=best). If you desire an average level of risk, then this fund may be an option.

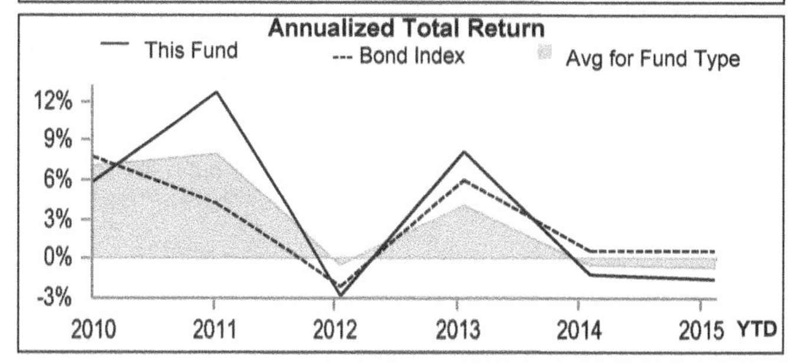

*PIMCO Low Duration Active Exch T (LDUR) C+ Fair

Fund Family: PIMCO
Fund Type: Corporate - Investment Grade
Inception Date: January 22, 2014

Data Date	Investment Rating	Net Assets ($Mil)	Price	Performance Rating/Pts	Total Return Y-T-D	Risk Rating/Pts
12-15	C+	144.90	99.67	C / 5.3	2.16%	B / 8.0

Major Rating Factors: Middle of the road best describes *PIMCO Low Duration Active Exch T whose TheStreet.com Investment Rating is currently a C+ (Fair). The fund currently has a performance rating of C (Fair) based on an annualized return of 0.00% over the last three years and a total return of 2.16% year to date 2015. Factored into the performance evaluation is an expense ratio of 0.50% (very low).

The fund's risk rating is currently B (Good). It carries a beta of 0.00, meaning the fund's expected move will be 0.0% for every 10% move in the market. Volatility, as measured by both the semi-deviation and a drawdown factor, is considered low. As of December 31, 2015, *PIMCO Low Duration Active Exch T traded at a premium of .34% above its net asset value, which is worse than its one-year historical average premium of .04%.

Jerome M. Schneider has been running the fund for 2 years and currently receives a manager quality ranking of 82 (0=worst, 99=best). If you desire an average level of risk, then this fund may be an option.

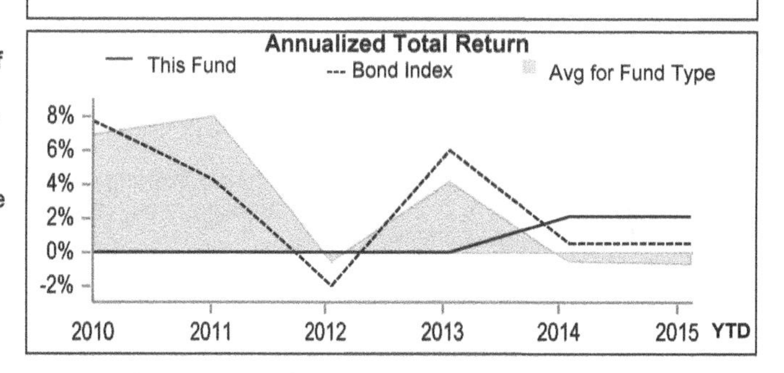

*PIMCO Short Term Muni Bd Act ETF (SMMU) B Good

Fund Family: PIMCO
Fund Type: Municipal - National
Inception Date: February 1, 2010

Data Date	Investment Rating	Net Assets ($Mil)	Price	Performance Rating/Pts	Total Return Y-T-D	Risk Rating/Pts
12-15	B	76.20	50.27	C / 4.9	0.89%	B+ / 9.9
2014	C	76.20	50.17	C- / 3.0	0.46%	B+ / 9.9
2013	C	78.40	50.22	C- / 3.1	0.39%	B+ / 9.9
2012	C-	58.40	50.42	D- / 1.5	0.68%	B+ / 9.9
2011	C	38.30	50.44	D+ / 2.4	1.99%	B+ / 9.9

Major Rating Factors: *PIMCO Short Term Muni Bd Act ETF receives a TheStreet.com Investment Rating of B (Good). The fund currently has a performance rating of C (Fair) based on an annualized return of 0.62% over the last three years and a total return of 0.89% year to date 2015. Factored into the performance evaluation is an expense ratio of 0.35% (very low).

The fund's risk rating is currently B+ (Good). It carries a beta of 0.13, meaning the fund's expected move will be 1.3% for every 10% move in the market. Volatility, as measured by both the semi-deviation and a drawdown factor, is considered very low. As of December 31, 2015, *PIMCO Short Term Muni Bd Act ETF traded at a discount of .12% below its net asset value, which is better than its one-year historical average discount of .09%.

Julie P. Callahan has been running the fund for 2 years and currently receives a manager quality ranking of 69 (0=worst, 99=best). If you desire an average level of risk, then this fund may be an option.

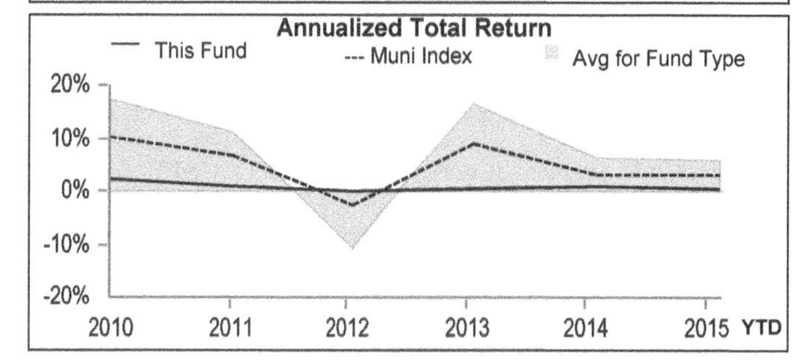

*PIMCO Total Return Active Exch T (BOND) C+ Fair

Fund Family: PIMCO
Fund Type: Corporate - Investment Grade
Inception Date: February 29, 2012

Major Rating Factors: Middle of the road best describes *PIMCO Total Return Active Exch T whose TheStreet.com Investment Rating is currently a C+ (Fair). The fund currently has a performance rating of C (Fair) based on an annualized return of 2.21% over the last three years and a total return of 0.36% year to date 2015. Factored into the performance evaluation is an expense ratio of 0.55% (very low).

The fund's risk rating is currently B- (Good). It carries a beta of 0.82, meaning the fund's expected move will be 8.2% for every 10% move in the market. Volatility, as measured by both the semi-deviation and a drawdown factor, is considered low. As of December 31, 2015, *PIMCO Total Return Active Exch T traded at a premium of .26% above its net asset value, which is worse than its one-year historical average discount of .03%.

Scott A. Mather currently receives a manager quality ranking of 75 (0=worst, 99=best). If you desire an average level of risk, then this fund may be an option.

Data Date	Investment Rating	Net Assets ($Mil)	Price	Performance Rating/Pts	Total Return Y-T-D	Risk Rating/Pts
12-15	C+	3,010.20	104.22	C / 5.3	0.36%	B- / 7.7
2014	C+	3,010.20	107.21	C / 4.5	6.52%	B+ / 9.4
2013	C-	3,511.30	104.74	D+ / 2.7	-0.67%	B+ / 9.5

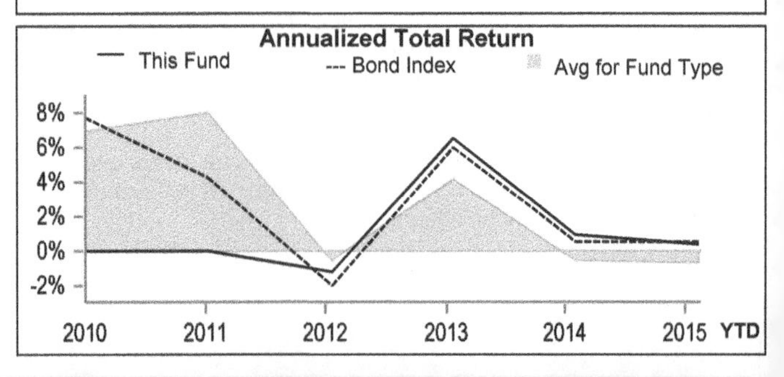

*PowerShares 1-30 Laddered Treasu (PLW) C Fair

Fund Family: Invesco Powershares Capital Mgmt LL
Fund Type: US Government/Agency
Inception Date: October 11, 2007

Major Rating Factors: Middle of the road best describes *PowerShares 1-30 Laddered Treasu whose TheStreet.com Investment Rating is currently a C (Fair). The fund currently has a performance rating of C (Fair) based on an annualized return of 2.37% over the last three years and a total return of -0.75% year to date 2015. Factored into the performance evaluation is an expense ratio of 0.25% (very low).

The fund's risk rating is currently B- (Good). It carries a beta of 0.67, meaning the fund's expected move will be 6.7% for every 10% move in the market. Volatility, as measured by both the semi-deviation and a drawdown factor, is considered low. As of December 31, 2015, *PowerShares 1-30 Laddered Treasu traded at a premium of .09% above its net asset value, which is worse than its one-year historical average premium of .02%.

Peter Hubbard has been running the fund for 9 years and currently receives a manager quality ranking of 70 (0=worst, 99=best). If you desire an average level of risk, then this fund may be an option.

Data Date	Investment Rating	Net Assets ($Mil)	Price	Performance Rating/Pts	Total Return Y-T-D	Risk Rating/Pts
12-15	C	268.60	32.28	C / 5.3	-0.75%	B- / 7.3
2014	C+	268.60	32.92	C / 4.7	14.56%	B / 8.7
2013	C	144.00	29.33	C- / 3.7	-6.49%	B / 8.9
2012	C	167.00	32.60	C- / 3.2	2.02%	B+ / 9.2
2011	C	0.00	32.47	C- / 4.2	20.23%	B / 8.8
2010	B-	280.30	27.95	C / 4.4	9.11%	B / 8.3

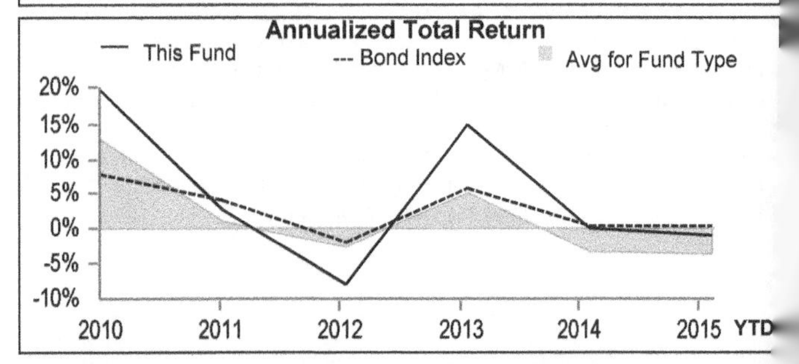

*PowerShares Act US Real Estate (PSR) B- Good

Fund Family: Invesco Powershares Capital Mgmt LL
Fund Type: Growth and Income
Inception Date: November 19, 2008

Major Rating Factors: Strong performance is the major factor driving the B- (Good) TheStreet.com Investment Rating for *PowerShares Act US Real Estate. The fund currently has a performance rating of B (Good) based on an annualized return of 10.19% over the last three years and a total return of 1.26% year to date 2015. Factored into the performance evaluation is an expense ratio of 0.80% (very low).

The fund's risk rating is currently C+ (Fair). It carries a beta of 0.49, meaning the fund's expected move will be 4.9% for every 10% move in the market. Volatility, as measured by both the semi-deviation and a drawdown factor, is considered low. As of December 31, 2015, *PowerShares Act US Real Estate traded at a premium of .44% above its net asset value, which is worse than its one-year historical average premium of .03%.

Joseph V. Rodriguez, Jr. has been running the fund for 8 years and currently receives a manager quality ranking of 86 (0=worst, 99=best). If you desire only a moderate level of risk and strong performance, then this fund is an excellent option.

Data Date	Investment Rating	Net Assets ($Mil)	Price	Performance Rating/Pts	Total Return Y-T-D	Risk Rating/Pts
12-15	B-	38.60	72.75	B / 8.0	1.26%	C+ / 6.5
2014	B+	38.60	74.43	A- / 9.0	32.11%	C+ / 6.6
2013	C+	31.30	56.81	C / 5.5	0.32%	B / 8.1
2012	B	17.20	56.83	B / 7.7	17.47%	B- / 7.8
2011	C+	20.10	50.42	B / 7.6	11.41%	C+ / 6.8
2010	A	16.00	45.81	A / 9.4	26.87%	C+ / 6.6

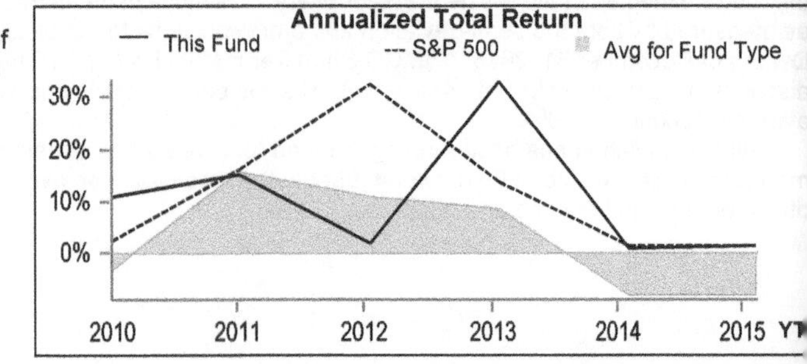

*PowerShares Aerospace & Defense (PPA) A+ Excellent

Fund Family: Invesco Powershares Capital Mgmt LL
Fund Type: Income
Inception Date: October 26, 2005

Major Rating Factors:
Exceptional performance is the major factor driving the A+ (Excellent) TheStreet.com Investment Rating for *PowerShares Aerospace & Defense. The fund currently has a performance rating of A (Excellent) based on an annualized return of 19.67% over the last three years and a total return of 4.24% year to date 2015. Factored into the performance evaluation is an expense ratio of 0.66% (very low).

The fund's risk rating is currently B (Good). It carries a beta of 0.93, meaning that its performance tracks fairly well with that of the overall stock market. Volatility, as measured by both the semi-deviation and a drawdown factor, is considered low. As of December 31, 2015, *PowerShares Aerospace & Defense traded at a discount of .06% below its net asset value, which is better than its one-year historical average discount of .02%.

Peter Hubbard has been running the fund for 9 years and currently receives a manager quality ranking of 91 (0=worst, 99=best). If you desire only a moderate level of risk and strong performance, then this fund is an excellent option.

Data Date	Investment Rating	Net Assets ($Mil)	Price	Performance Rating/Pts	Total Return Y-T-D	Risk Rating/Pts
12-15	A+	151.80	35.64	A / 9.5	4.24%	B / 8.7
2014	A	151.80	34.75	A / 9.3	13.57%	B- / 7.4
2013	A+	92.90	31.03	A- / 9.2	45.05%	B / 8.1
2012	C	46.20	20.94	C / 5.0	16.71%	B- / 7.9
2011	C-	53.70	18.20	C- / 3.7	-3.51%	B- / 7.7
2010	D+	110.40	18.71	D+ / 2.3	10.93%	C+ / 5.8

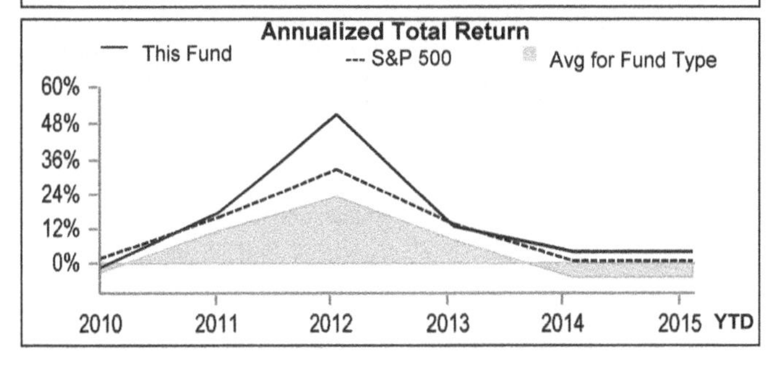

*PowerShares Build America Bond (BAB) B- Good

Fund Family: Invesco Powershares Capital Mgmt LL
Fund Type: US Government/Agency
Inception Date: November 17, 2009

Major Rating Factors: *PowerShares Build America Bond receives a TheStreet.com Investment Rating of B- (Good). The fund currently has a performance rating of C+ (Fair) based on an annualized return of 3.74% over the last three years and a total return of -0.62% year to date 2015. Factored into the performance evaluation is an expense ratio of 0.27% (very low).

The fund's risk rating is currently B (Good). It carries a beta of 0.54, meaning the fund's expected move will be 5.4% for every 10% move in the market. Volatility, as measured by both the semi-deviation and a drawdown factor, is considered low. As of December 31, 2015, *PowerShares Build America Bond traded at a discount of .48% below its net asset value, which is better than its one-year historical average discount of .33%.

Peter Hubbard has been running the fund for 7 years and currently receives a manager quality ranking of 80 (0=worst, 99=best). If you desire an average level of risk, then this fund may be an option.

Data Date	Investment Rating	Net Assets ($Mil)	Price	Performance Rating/Pts	Total Return Y-T-D	Risk Rating/Pts
12-15	B-	682.70	28.99	C+ / 5.7	-0.62%	B / 8.7
2014	C	682.70	30.44	C+ / 5.6	16.56%	C+ / 6.9
2013	C+	599.00	27.29	C / 5.2	-3.96%	B / 8.9
2012	C+	1,124.00	30.24	C / 4.6	9.09%	B+ / 9.3
2011	B+	777.10	28.70	B- / 7.2	21.19%	B+ / 9.4
2010	B-	606.70	25.08	C- / 4.0	8.81%	B / 8.6

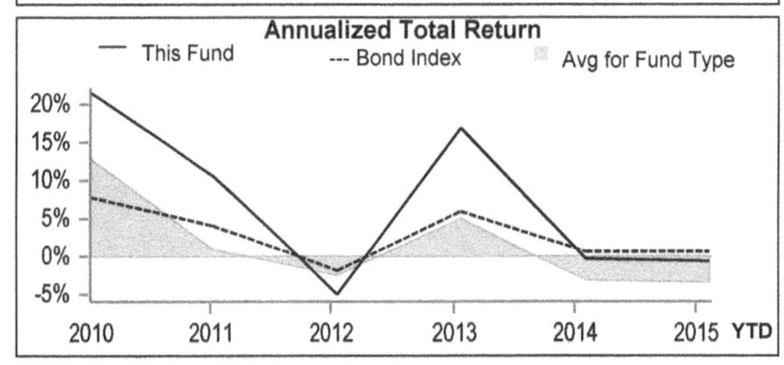

*PowerShares Buyback Achievers (PKW) B+ Good

Fund Family: Invesco Powershares Capital Mgmt LL
Fund Type: Income
Inception Date: December 20, 2006

Major Rating Factors: Strong performance is the major factor driving the B+ (Good) TheStreet.com Investment Rating for *PowerShares Buyback Achievers. The fund currently has a performance rating of B+ (Good) based on an annualized return of 15.23% over the last three years and a total return of -4.07% year to date 2015. Factored into the performance evaluation is an expense ratio of 0.63% (very low).

The fund's risk rating is currently B- (Good). It carries a beta of 1.11, meaning it is expected to move 11.1% for every 10% move in the market. Volatility, as measured by both the semi-deviation and a drawdown factor, is considered low. As of December 31, 2015, *PowerShares Buyback Achievers traded at a premium of .04% above its net asset value, which is worse than its one-year historical average discount of .03%.

Peter Hubbard has been running the fund for 9 years and currently receives a manager quality ranking of 63 (0=worst, 99=best). If you desire only a moderate level of risk and strong performance, then this fund is an excellent option.

Data Date	Investment Rating	Net Assets ($Mil)	Price	Performance Rating/Pts	Total Return Y-T-D	Risk Rating/Pts
12-15	B+	2,739.40	45.46	B+ / 8.7	-4.07%	B- / 7.0
2014	A	2,739.40	48.05	A- / 9.0	13.88%	B- / 7.5
2013	A+	2,502.50	43.08	A- / 9.2	40.42%	B / 8.7
2012	B-	214.30	29.80	C+ / 6.3	15.47%	B / 8.5
2011	B-	74.20	26.53	C+ / 6.9	11.02%	B / 8.1
2010	C+	35.20	24.32	C+ / 6.1	18.11%	C / 5.2

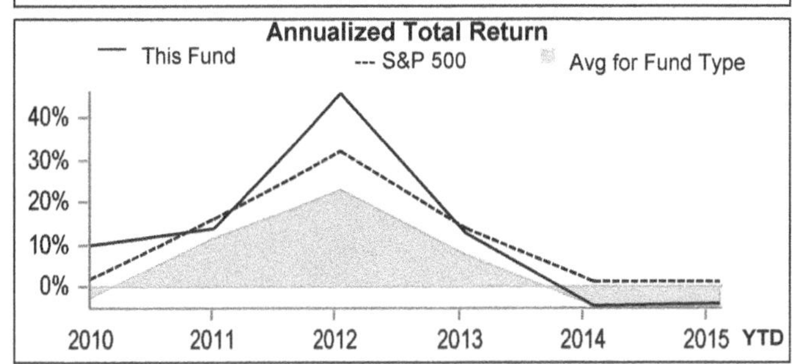

*PowerShares CA AMT-Free Muni Bon (PWZ) B Good

Fund Family: Invesco Powershares Capital Mgmt LL
Fund Type: Municipal - National
Inception Date: October 11, 2007

Major Rating Factors: Strong performance is the major factor driving the B (Good) TheStreet.com Investment Rating for *PowerShares CA AMT-Free Muni Bon. The fund currently has a performance rating of B- (Good) based on an annualized return of 4.59% over the last three years and a total return of 3.23% year to date 2015. Factored into the performance evaluation is an expense ratio of 0.26% (very low).

The fund's risk rating is currently B- (Good). It carries a beta of 1.31, meaning it is expected to move 13.1% for every 10% move in the market. Volatility, as measured by both the semi-deviation and a drawdown factor, is considered low. As of December 31, 2015, *PowerShares CA AMT-Free Muni Bon traded at a premium of .31% above its net asset value, which is worse than its one-year historical average premium of .24%.

Peter Hubbard has been running the fund for 9 years and currently receives a manager quality ranking of 72 (0=worst, 99=best). If you desire only a moderate level of risk and strong performance, then this fund is an excellent option.

Data Date	Investment Rating	Net Assets ($Mil)	Price	Performance Rating/Pts	Total Return Y-T-D	Risk Rating/Pts
12-15	B	59.70	25.88	B- / 7.1	3.23%	B- / 7.8
2014	C+	59.70	25.77	C+ / 6.3	15.17%	B- / 7.6
2013	C+	47.80	23.18	C / 5.2	-4.22%	B+ / 9.2
2012	C+	72.10	25.26	C- / 4.2	7.22%	B+ / 9.3
2011	B-	39.90	24.21	C+ / 5.9	13.94%	B+ / 9.3
2010	C	38.30	22.57	D+ / 2.4	1.06%	B / 8.1

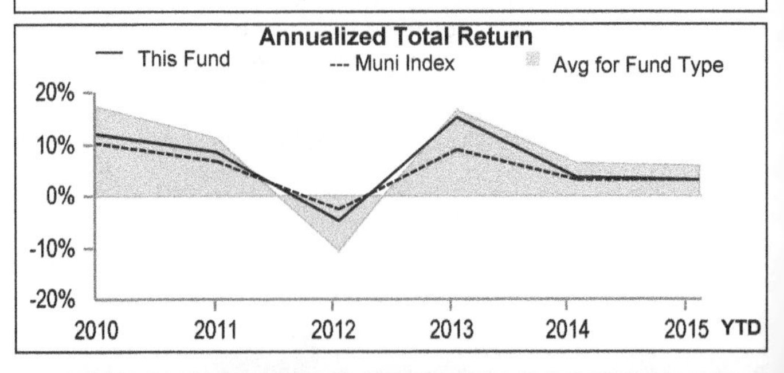

*PowerShares CEF Inc Composite Po (PCEF) C Fair

Fund Family: Invesco Powershares Capital Mgmt LL
Fund Type: Income
Inception Date: February 18, 2010

Major Rating Factors: Middle of the road best describes *PowerShares CEF Inc Composite Po whose TheStreet.com Investment Rating is currently a C (Fair). The fund currently has a performance rating of C (Fair) based on an annualized return of 1.88% over the last three years and a total return of -1.68% year to date 2015. Factored into the performance evaluation is an expense ratio of 0.50% (very low).

The fund's risk rating is currently C+ (Fair). It carries a beta of 0.52, meaning the fund's expected move will be 5.2% for every 10% move in the market. Volatility, as measured by both the semi-deviation and a drawdown factor, is considered low. As of December 31, 2015, *PowerShares CEF Inc Composite Po traded at a premium of .14% above its net asset value, which is worse than its one-year historical average premium of .01%.

This fund has been team managed for 6 years and currently receives a manager quality ranking of 32 (0=worst, 99=best). If you desire an average level of risk, then this fund may be an option.

Data Date	Investment Rating	Net Assets ($Mil)	Price	Performance Rating/Pts	Total Return Y-T-D	Risk Rating/Pts
12-15	C	618.80	21.34	C / 5.1	-1.68%	C+ / 6.4
2014	C+	618.80	23.61	C / 4.6	5.06%	B / 8.8
2013	C+	488.60	24.34	C / 5.1	2.15%	B / 8.7
2012	B	394.30	25.14	C+ / 6.7	16.55%	B / 8.6
2011	C-	233.40	23.51	D+ / 2.6	2.81%	B / 8.6

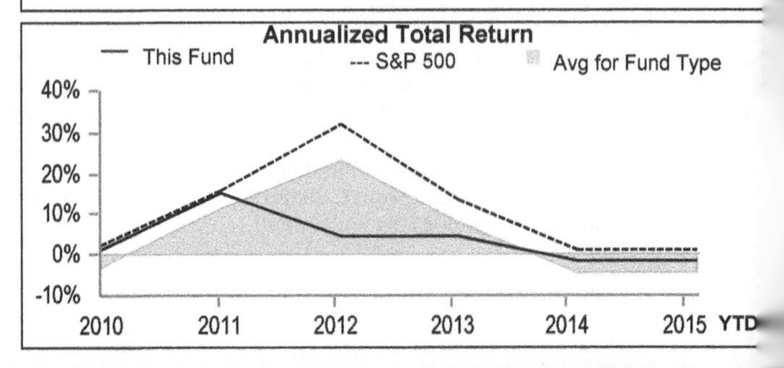

*PowerShares China A Shares Port (CHNA) C- Fair

Fund Family: Invesco Powershares Capital Mgmt LL
Fund Type: Foreign
Inception Date: October 8, 2013

Major Rating Factors: Middle of the road best describes *PowerShares China A Shares Port whose TheStreet.com Investment Rating is currently a C- (Fair). The fund currently has a performance rating of C+ (Fair) based on an annualized return of 0.00% over the last three years and a total return of 0.50% year to date 2015. Factored into the performance evaluation is an expense ratio of 0.43% (very low).

The fund's risk rating is currently C- (Fair). It carries a beta of 0.00, meaning the fund's expected move will be 0.0% for every 10% move in the market. Volatility, as measured by both the semi-deviation and a drawdown factor, is considered average. As of December 31, 2015, *PowerShares China A Shares Port traded at a premium of .57% above its net asset value, which is worse than its one-year historical average premium of .09%.

Richard Ose has been running the fund for 3 years and currently receives a manager quality ranking of 77 (0=worst, 99=best). If you desire an average level of risk, then this fund may be an option.

Data Date	Investment Rating	Net Assets ($Mil)	Price	Performance Rating/Pts	Total Return Y-T-D	Risk Rating/Pts
12-15	C-	2.40	28.03	C+ / 6.2	0.50%	C- / 3.5
2014	B-	2.40	38.80	A+ / 9.9	60.55%	C / 4.3

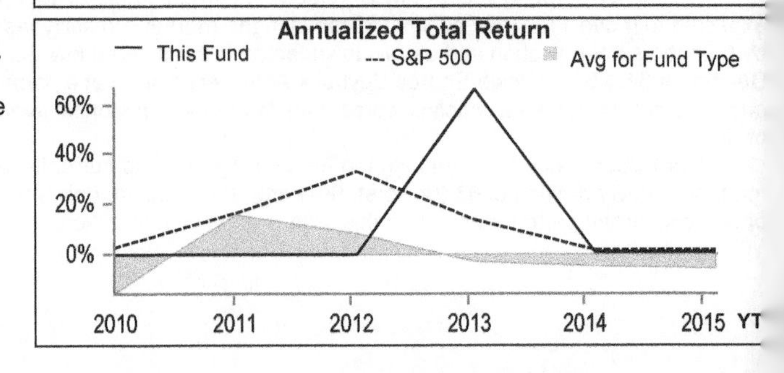

*PowerShares Chinese YDS Bd (DSUM) C Fair

Fund Family: Invesco Powershares Capital Mgmt LL
Fund Type: Global
Inception Date: September 23, 2011

Data Date	Investment Rating	Net Assets ($Mil)	Price	Performance Rating/Pts	Total Return Y-T-D	Risk Rating/Pts
12-15	C	186.10	22.71	C- / 3.8	-3.91%	B / 8.8
2014	C+	186.10	24.31	C- / 3.6	-1.76%	B+ / 9.5
2013	B	153.40	25.52	C+ / 5.6	6.12%	B+ / 9.7
2012	C+	35.70	24.79	C- / 3.8	8.09%	B+ / 9.8

Major Rating Factors: Middle of the road best describes *PowerShares Chinese YDS Bd whose TheStreet.com Investment Rating is currently a C (Fair). The fund currently has a performance rating of C- (Fair) based on an annualized return of 0.17% over the last three years and a total return of -3.91% year to date 2015. Factored into the performance evaluation is an expense ratio of 0.45% (very low).

The fund's risk rating is currently B (Good). It carries a beta of -0.10, meaning the fund's expected move will be -1.0% for every 10% move in the market. Volatility, as measured by both the semi-deviation and a drawdown factor, is considered low. As of December 31, 2015, *PowerShares Chinese YDS Bd traded at a discount of 1.17% below its net asset value, which is better than its one-year historical average discount of .45%.

Peter Hubbard has been running the fund for 5 years and currently receives a manager quality ranking of 66 (0=worst, 99=best). If you desire an average level of risk, then this fund may be an option.

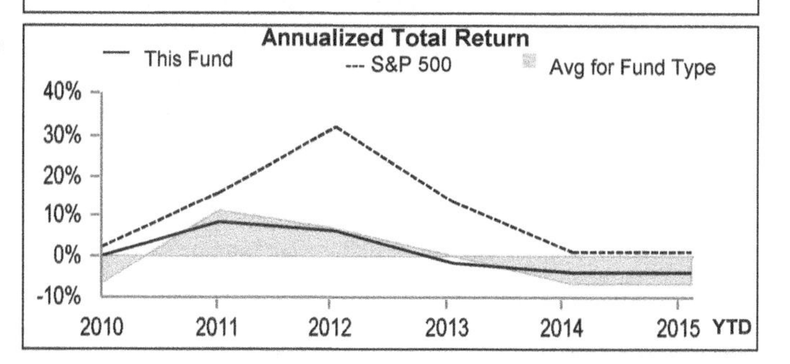

*PowerShares Cleantech Portfolio (PZD) C+ Fair

Fund Family: Invesco Powershares Capital Mgmt LL
Fund Type: Income
Inception Date: October 24, 2006

Data Date	Investment Rating	Net Assets ($Mil)	Price	Performance Rating/Pts	Total Return Y-T-D	Risk Rating/Pts
12-15	C+	74.80	29.40	B- / 7.3	2.71%	C+ / 6.6
2014	C-	74.80	28.95	C / 5.0	-7.52%	C+ / 6.6
2013	C+	83.80	31.77	B- / 7.4	34.58%	B- / 7.0
2012	D	66.10	23.12	D / 2.1	8.58%	C+ / 6.8
2011	D	97.30	21.51	D / 2.2	-17.03%	C+ / 6.5
2010	D-	147.10	26.40	D- / 1.5	7.61%	C / 4.4

Major Rating Factors: Strong performance is the major factor driving the C+ (Fair) TheStreet.com Investment Rating for *PowerShares Cleantech Portfolio. The fund currently has a performance rating of B- (Good) based on an annualized return of 8.41% over the last three years and a total return of 2.71% year to date 2015. Factored into the performance evaluation is an expense ratio of 0.67% (very low).

The fund's risk rating is currently C+ (Fair). It carries a beta of 1.28, meaning it is expected to move 12.8% for every 10% move in the market. Volatility, as measured by both the semi-deviation and a drawdown factor, is considered low. As of December 31, 2015, *PowerShares Cleantech Portfolio traded at a premium of .10% above its net asset value, which is worse than its one-year historical average discount of .16%.

Peter Hubbard has been running the fund for 9 years and currently receives a manager quality ranking of 19 (0=worst, 99=best). If you desire only a moderate level of risk and strong performance, then this fund is an excellent option.

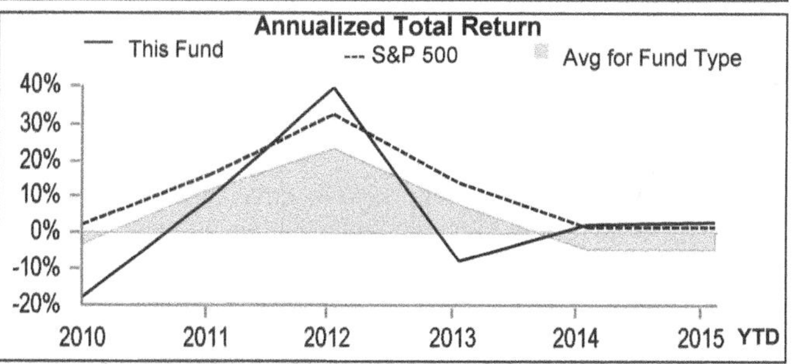

*PowerShares Contrarian Opptys (CNTR) D+ Weak

Fund Family: Invesco Powershares Capital Mgmt LL
Fund Type: Global
Inception Date: January 13, 2014

Data Date	Investment Rating	Net Assets ($Mil)	Price	Performance Rating/Pts	Total Return Y-T-D	Risk Rating/Pts
12-15	D+	3.80	24.44	D / 2.2	-9.32%	C+ / 6.6

Major Rating Factors:
Disappointing performance is the major factor driving the D+ (Weak) TheStreet.com Investment Rating for *PowerShares Contrarian Opptys. The fund currently has a performance rating of D (Weak) based on an annualized return of 0.00% over the last three years and a total return of -9.32% year to date 2015. Factored into the performance evaluation is an expense ratio of 0.50% (very low).

The fund's risk rating is currently C+ (Fair). It carries a beta of 0.00, meaning the fund's expected move will be 0.0% for every 10% move in the market. Volatility, as measured by both the semi-deviation and a drawdown factor, is considered low. As of December 31, 2015, *PowerShares Contrarian Opptys traded at a premium of 2.00% above its net asset value, which is worse than its one-year historical average discount of .16%.

Michael C. Jeanette has been running the fund for 2 years and currently receives a manager quality ranking of 18 (0=worst, 99=best). This fund offers only a moderate level of risk but investors looking for strong performance are still waiting.

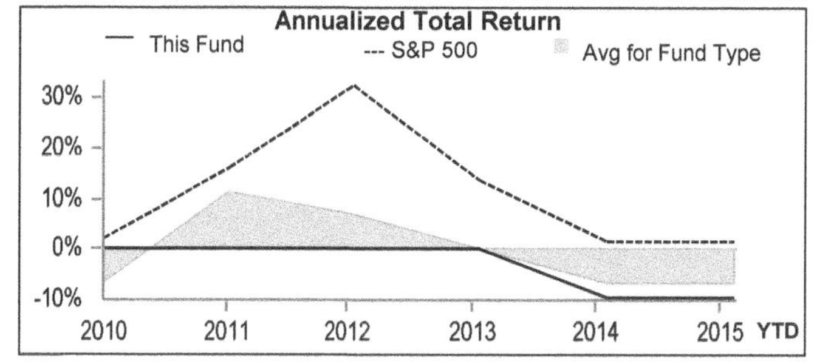

*PowerShares DB Agriculture Fund (DBA) D+ Weak

Fund Family: Invesco Powershares Capital Mgmt LL
Fund Type: Income
Inception Date: January 3, 2007

Data Date	Investment Rating	Net Assets ($Mil)	Price	Performance Rating/Pts	Total Return Y-T-D	Risk Rating/Pts
12-15	D+	1,164.60	20.61	D / 1.9	-16.36%	B- / 7.1
2014	D	1,164.60	24.89	D / 2.1	1.84%	C+ / 6.0
2013	D	1,219.00	24.25	D- / 1.2	-11.58%	B- / 7.1
2012	D	1,661.30	27.95	D- / 1.5	-2.97%	B- / 7.5
2011	D+	2,034.30	28.88	D / 1.8	-10.37%	B / 8.1
2010	C	2,712.70	32.35	C / 5.3	22.35%	C+ / 5.6

Major Rating Factors:
Disappointing performance is the major factor driving the D+ (Weak) TheStreet.com Investment Rating for *PowerShares DB Agriculture Fund. The fund currently has a performance rating of D (Weak) based on an annualized return of -9.32% over the last three years and a total return of -16.36% year to date 2015. Factored into the performance evaluation is an expense ratio of 0.93% (low).

The fund's risk rating is currently B- (Good). It carries a beta of 0.18, meaning the fund's expected move will be 1.8% for every 10% move in the market. Volatility, as measured by both the semi-deviation and a drawdown factor, is considered low. As of December 31, 2015, *PowerShares DB Agriculture Fund traded at a discount of .29% below its net asset value, which is better than its one-year historical average discount of .05%.

Peter Hubbard has been running the fund for 9 years and currently receives a manager quality ranking of 14 (0=worst, 99=best). This fund offers only a moderate level of risk but investors looking for strong performance are still waiting.

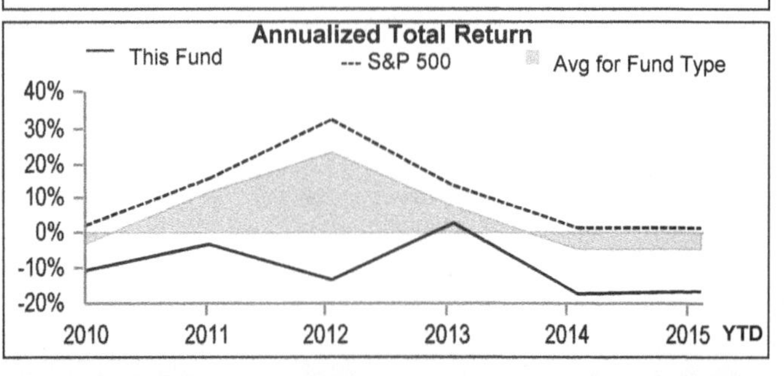

*PowerShares DB Base Metals Fund (DBB) D- Weak

Fund Family: Invesco Powershares Capital Mgmt LL
Fund Type: Income
Inception Date: January 3, 2007

Data Date	Investment Rating	Net Assets ($Mil)	Price	Performance Rating/Pts	Total Return Y-T-D	Risk Rating/Pts
12-15	D-	329.40	11.88	D- / 1.1	-25.38%	C / 4.5
2014	D	329.40	15.90	D / 1.8	-4.22%	B- / 7.1
2013	D-	234.90	16.86	E+ / 0.9	-13.18%	C+ / 6.0
2012	D-	310.00	19.28	D- / 1.0	-3.84%	C+ / 6.5
2011	C-	366.90	18.65	C- / 3.4	-22.17%	B- / 7.0
2010	C	511.70	24.43	C+ / 6.1	8.58%	C / 4.4

Major Rating Factors:
Disappointing performance is the major factor driving the D- (Weak) TheStreet.com Investment Rating for *PowerShares DB Base Metals Fund. The fund currently has a performance rating of D- (Weak) based on an annualized return of -14.67% over the last three years and a total return of -25.38% year to date 2015. Factored into the performance evaluation is an expense ratio of 0.78% (very low).

The fund's risk rating is currently C (Fair). It carries a beta of 0.28, meaning the fund's expected move will be 2.8% for every 10% move in the market. Volatility, as measured by both the semi-deviation and a drawdown factor, is considered average. As of December 31, 2015, *PowerShares DB Base Metals Fund traded at a premium of .08% above its net asset value, which is worse than its one-year historical average premium of .01%.

James T. Anderson currently receives a manager quality ranking of 8 (0=worst, 99=best). This fund offers an average level of risk but investors looking for strong performance will be frustrated.

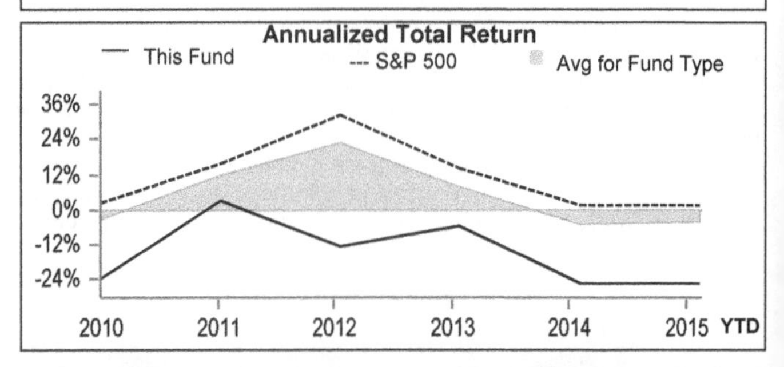

*PowerShares DB Commodity Idx Tra (DBC) E+ Very Weak

Fund Family: Invesco Powershares Capital Mgmt LL
Fund Type: Growth
Inception Date: February 3, 2006

Data Date	Investment Rating	Net Assets ($Mil)	Price	Performance Rating/Pts	Total Return Y-T-D	Risk Rating/Pts
12-15	E+	4,997.10	13.36	E+ / 0.7	-26.71%	C- / 3.5
2014	E+	4,997.10	18.45	E+ / 0.9	-26.58%	C / 4.3
2013	D+	5,697.20	25.66	D / 1.9	-8.72%	B- / 7.5
2012	D+	6,607.50	27.78	D / 2.2	1.10%	B- / 7.5
2011	C-	5,456.80	26.84	C- / 3.6	1.73%	B- / 7.8
2010	D	5,106.80	27.55	D+ / 2.7	11.90%	C / 4.7

Major Rating Factors:
Very poor performance is the major factor driving the E+ (Very Weak) TheStreet.com Investment Rating for *PowerShares DB Commodity Idx Tra. The fund currently has a performance rating of E+ (Very Weak) based on an annualized return of -21.42% over the last three years and a total return of -26.71% year to date 2015. Factored into the performance evaluation is an expense ratio of 0.88% (low).

The fund's risk rating is currently C- (Fair). It carries a beta of 0.44, meaning the fund's expected move will be 4.4% for every 10% move in the market. Volatility, as measured by both the semi-deviation and a drawdown factor, is considered average. As of December 31, 2015, *PowerShares DB Commodity Idx Tra traded at a premium of .07% above its net asset value, which is worse than its one-year historical average discount of .08%.

James T. Anderson currently receives a manager quality ranking of 4 (0=worst, 99=best). This fund offers an average level of risk but investors looking for strong performance will be frustrated.

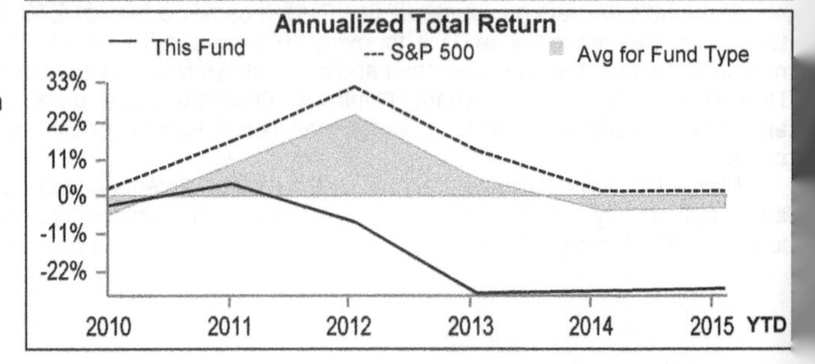

* Denotes ETF Fund

*PowerShares DB Energy Fund (DBE) E Very Weak

Fund Family: Invesco Powershares Capital Mgmt LL
Fund Type: Energy/Natural Resources
Inception Date: January 3, 2007

Major Rating Factors: *PowerShares DB Energy Fund has adopted a very risky asset allocation strategy and currently receives an overall TheStreet.com Investment Rating of E (Very Weak). The fund has a high level of volatility, as measured by both semi-deviation and drawdown factors. It carries a beta of 0.91, meaning that its performance tracks fairly well with that of the overall stock market. As of December 31, 2015, *PowerShares DB Energy Fund traded at a premium of .45% above its net asset value, which is worse than its one-year historical average discount of .09%. Unfortunately, the high level of risk (D, Weak) failed to pay off as investors endured very poor performance.

The fund's performance rating is currently E (Very Weak). It has registered an annualized return of -26.29% over the last three years and is down -33.86% year to date 2015. Factored into the performance evaluation is an expense ratio of 0.78% (very low).

James T. Anderson currently receives a manager quality ranking of 5 (0=worst, 99=best). If you can tolerate very high levels of risk in the hope of improved future returns, holding this fund may be an option.

Data Date	Investment Rating	Net Assets ($Mil)	Price	Performance Rating/Pts	Total Return Y-T-D	Risk Rating/Pts
12-15	E	279.40	11.20	E / 0.5	-33.86%	D / 2.1
2014	E	279.40	17.47	E / 0.5	-38.18%	C- / 3.3
2013	D+	268.30	29.15	C- / 3.1	1.07%	B- / 7.2
2012	D	139.90	27.94	D / 2.0	-0.99%	B- / 7.1
2011	C	149.10	27.62	C / 4.6	9.52%	B- / 7.5
2010	E+	161.40	26.88	D- / 1.2	2.63%	C- / 3.8

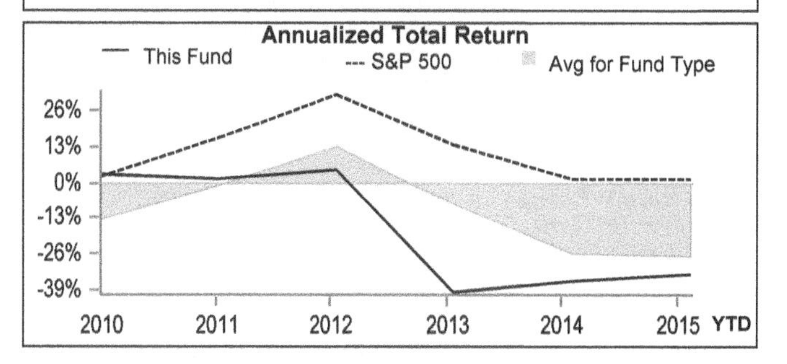

*PowerShares DB G10 Currency Harv (DBV) C- Fair

Fund Family: Invesco Powershares Capital Mgmt LL
Fund Type: Income
Inception Date: September 18, 2006

Major Rating Factors: Middle of the road best describes *PowerShares DB G10 Currency Harv whose TheStreet.com Investment Rating is currently a C- (Fair). The fund currently has a performance rating of C- (Fair) based on an annualized return of -4.08% over the last three years and a total return of -7.71% year to date 2015. Factored into the performance evaluation is an expense ratio of 0.81% (very low).

The fund's risk rating is currently C+ (Fair). It carries a beta of 0.55, meaning the fund's expected move will be 5.5% for every 10% move in the market. Volatility, as measured by both the semi-deviation and a drawdown factor, is considered low. As of December 31, 2015, *PowerShares DB G10 Currency Harv traded at a premium of .21% above its net asset value, which is worse than its one-year historical average discount of .05%.

James T. Anderson currently receives a manager quality ranking of 15 (0=worst, 99=best). If you desire an average level of risk, then this fund may be an option.

Data Date	Investment Rating	Net Assets ($Mil)	Price	Performance Rating/Pts	Total Return Y-T-D	Risk Rating/Pts
12-15	C-	97.80	23.34	C- / 3.0	-7.71%	C+ / 6.5
2014	D+	97.80	25.54	C- / 3.2	0.35%	B- / 7.0
2013	C-	193.20	25.42	C- / 3.0	-3.78%	B+ / 9.0
2012	C-	345.10	26.15	D+ / 2.8	10.43%	B / 8.9
2011	C	286.00	23.76	C- / 3.2	1.44%	B+ / 9.0
2010	D+	356.10	23.74	D / 1.6	0.85%	C+ / 6.7

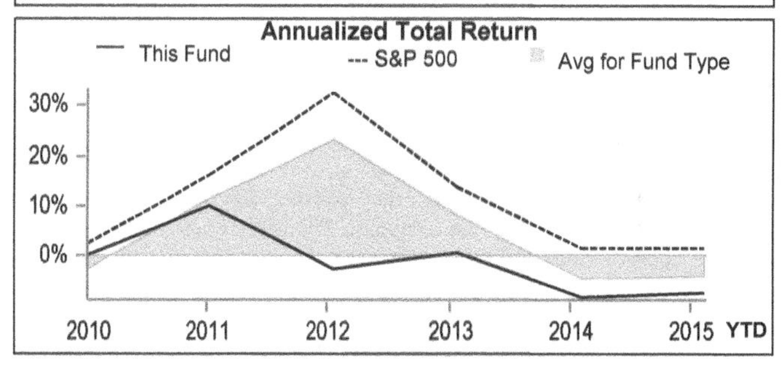

*PowerShares DB Gold Fund (DGL) D Weak

Fund Family: Invesco Powershares Capital Mgmt LL
Fund Type: Precious Metals
Inception Date: January 3, 2007

Major Rating Factors:
Disappointing performance is the major factor driving the D (Weak) TheStreet.com Investment Rating for *PowerShares DB Gold Fund. The fund currently has a performance rating of D- (Weak) based on an annualized return of -15.15% over the last three years and a total return of -11.60% year to date 2015. Factored into the performance evaluation is an expense ratio of 0.80% (very low).

The fund's risk rating is currently C+ (Fair). It carries a beta of 0.95, meaning that its performance tracks fairly well with that of the overall stock market. Volatility, as measured by both the semi-deviation and a drawdown factor, is considered low. As of December 31, 2015, *PowerShares DB Gold Fund traded at a discount of .09% below its net asset value, which is better than its one-year historical average premium of .04%.

James T. Anderson currently receives a manager quality ranking of 45 (0=worst, 99=best). This fund offers only a moderate level of risk but investors looking for strong performance are still waiting.

Data Date	Investment Rating	Net Assets ($Mil)	Price	Performance Rating/Pts	Total Return Y-T-D	Risk Rating/Pts
12-15	D	144.80	34.66	D- / 1.3	-11.60%	C+ / 6.2
2014	D-	144.80	39.14	D- / 1.2	-5.69%	C+ / 6.0
2013	D-	145.20	40.36	D- / 1.3	-26.86%	C+ / 6.3
2012	C-	516.90	57.35	C- / 3.8	-0.02%	B / 8.1
2011	B	458.10	54.45	B- / 7.3	16.47%	B / 8.2
2010	A	331.30	50.16	B+ / 8.7	27.89%	C+ / 6.9

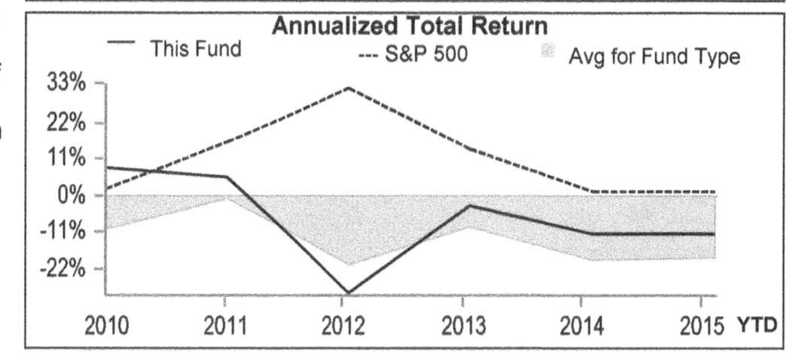

*PowerShares DB Oil Fund (DBO) E+ Very Weak

Fund Family: Invesco Powershares Capital Mgmt LL
Fund Type: Energy/Natural Resources
Inception Date: January 3, 2007

Data Date	Investment Rating	Net Assets ($Mil)	Price	Perfor-mance Rating/Pts	Total Return Y-T-D	Risk Rating/Pts
12-15	E+	243.30	9.05	E / 0.3	-40.77%	C- / 3.3
2014	E	243.30	15.70	E / 0.4	-41.04%	D+ / 2.4
2013	D	310.20	27.70	D+ / 2.3	1.76%	C+ / 6.3
2012	D-	774.50	25.94	D- / 1.2	-8.57%	C+ / 6.2
2011	C	508.40	28.57	C / 5.4	6.68%	C+ / 6.7
2010	D-	597.80	28.22	D- / 1.4	2.36%	C- / 3.7

Major Rating Factors:
Very poor performance is the major factor driving the E+ (Very Weak) TheStreet.com Investment Rating for *PowerShares DB Oil Fund. The fund currently has a performance rating of E (Very Weak) based on an annualized return of -29.81% over the last three years and a total return of -40.77% year to date 2015. Factored into the performance evaluation is an expense ratio of 0.78% (very low).

The fund's risk rating is currently C- (Fair). It carries a beta of 1.04, meaning that its performance tracks fairly well with that of the overall stock market. Volatility, as measured by both the semi-deviation and a drawdown factor, is considered average. As of December 31, 2015, *PowerShares DB Oil Fund traded at a discount of .22% below its net asset value, which is better than its one-year historical average discount of .14%.

James T. Anderson currently receives a manager quality ranking of 4 (0=worst, 99=best). This fund offers an average level of risk but investors looking for strong performance will be frustrated.

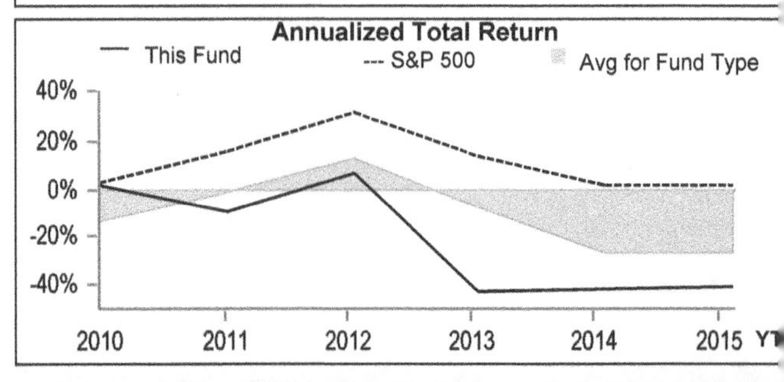

*PowerShares DB Opt Yld Dvsd Comd (PDBC) E Very Weak

Fund Family: Invesco Powershares Capital Mgmt LL
Fund Type: Global
Inception Date: November 6, 2014

Data Date	Investment Rating	Net Assets ($Mil)	Price	Perfor-mance Rating/Pts	Total Return Y-T-D	Risk Rating/Pts
12-15	E	0.00	15.61	E / 0.4	-26.23%	D+ / 2.9

Major Rating Factors: *PowerShares DB Opt Yld Dvsd Comd has adopted a risky asset allocation strategy and currently receives an overall TheStreet.com Investment Rating of E (Very Weak). The fund has an above average level of volatility, as measured by both semi-deviation and drawdown factors. It carries a beta of 0.00, meaning the fund's expected move will be 0.0% for every 10% move in the market. As of December 31, 2015, *PowerShares DB Opt Yld Dvsd Comd traded at a premium of .71% above its net asset value, which is worse than its one-year historical average premium of .05%. Unfortunately, the high level of risk (D+, Weak) failed to pay off as investors endured very poor performance.

The fund's performance rating is currently E (Very Weak). It has registered an annualized return of 0.00% over the last three years but is down -26.23% year to date 2015.

Peter Hubbard has been running the fund for 2 years and currently receives a manager quality ranking of 4 (0=worst, 99=best). If you can tolerate high levels of risk in the hope of improved future returns, holding this fund may be an option.

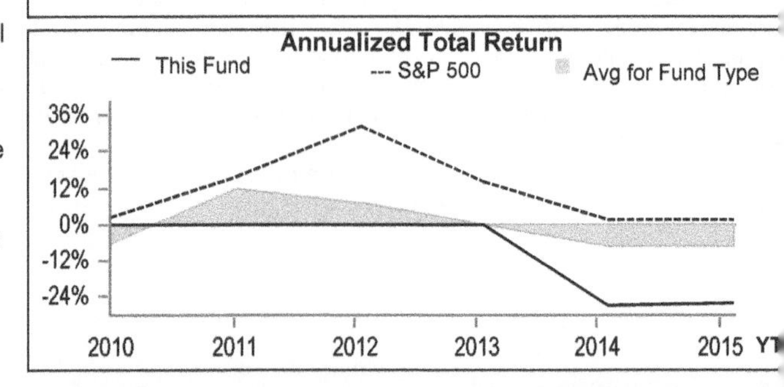

*PowerShares DB Precious Metals F (DBP) D Weak

Fund Family: Invesco Powershares Capital Mgmt LL
Fund Type: Precious Metals
Inception Date: January 3, 2007

Data Date	Investment Rating	Net Assets ($Mil)	Price	Perfor-mance Rating/Pts	Total Return Y-T-D	Risk Rating/Pts
12-15	D	167.50	32.22	D- / 1.1	-12.35%	C+ / 5.7
2014	D-	167.50	36.65	D- / 1.1	-9.25%	C / 5.5
2013	D-	180.20	39.19	D- / 1.2	-28.60%	C+ / 5.7
2012	C-	354.00	57.09	C- / 4.2	0.21%	B- / 7.5
2011	B-	454.10	53.88	B- / 7.5	12.39%	B- / 7.7
2010	A	404.20	51.82	A- / 9.1	37.56%	C+ / 6.5

Major Rating Factors:
Disappointing performance is the major factor driving the D (Weak) TheStreet.com Investment Rating for *PowerShares DB Precious Metals F. The fund currently has a performance rating of D- (Weak) based on an annualized return of -17.11% over the last three years and a total return of -12.35% year to date 2015. Factored into the performance evaluation is an expense ratio of 0.79% (very low).

The fund's risk rating is currently C+ (Fair). It carries a beta of 1.00, meaning that its performance tracks fairly well with that of the overall stock market. Volatility, as measured by both the semi-deviation and a drawdown factor, is considered low. As of December 31, 2015, *PowerShares DB Precious Metals F traded at a discount of .19% below its net asset value, which is better than its one-year historical average discount of .01%.

James T. Anderson currently receives a manager quality ranking of 36 (0=worst, 99=best). This fund offers only a moderate level of risk but investors looking for strong performance are still waiting.

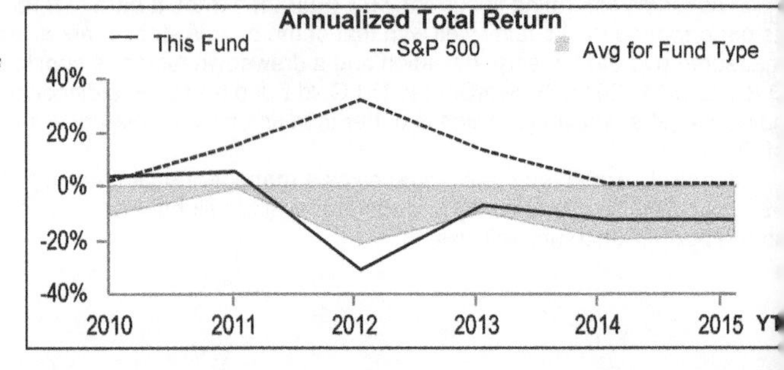

*PowerShares DB Silver Fund (DBS) E+ Very Weak

Fund Family: Invesco Powershares Capital Mgmt LL
Fund Type: Precious Metals
Inception Date: January 3, 2007

Major Rating Factors:
Very poor performance is the major factor driving the E+ (Very Weak) TheStreet.com Investment Rating for *PowerShares DB Silver Fund. The fund currently has a performance rating of E+ (Very Weak) based on an annualized return of -25.09% over the last three years and a total return of -13.93% year to date 2015. Factored into the performance evaluation is an expense ratio of 0.76% (very low).

The fund's risk rating is currently C- (Fair). It carries a beta of 1.25, meaning it is expected to move 12.5% for every 10% move in the market. Volatility, as measured by both the semi-deviation and a drawdown factor, is considered average. As of December 31, 2015, *PowerShares DB Silver Fund traded at a discount of .14% below its net asset value, which is better than its one-year historical average discount of .04%.

James T. Anderson currently receives a manager quality ranking of 17 (0=worst, 99=best). This fund offers an average level of risk but investors looking for strong performance will be frustrated.

Data Date	Investment Rating	Net Assets ($Mil)	Price	Performance Rating/Pts	Total Return Y-T-D	Risk Rating/Pts
12-15	E+	22.20	21.87	E+ / 0.7	-13.93%	C- / 4.1
2014	E+	22.20	25.27	E+ / 0.6	-24.59%	C- / 3.6
2013	E	32.20	32.29	E+ / 0.7	-34.89%	C- / 3.0
2012	D+	62.30	52.35	C+ / 5.8	1.53%	C / 4.8
2011	C+	77.70	47.99	B+ / 8.4	-1.77%	C / 5.1
2010	A-	207.60	54.51	A+ / 9.7	81.16%	C / 4.8

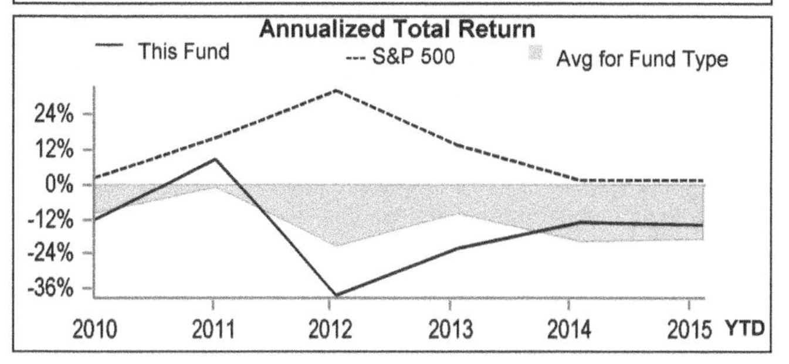

*PowerShares DB US Dollar Bearish (UDN) D+ Weak

Fund Family: Invesco Powershares Capital Mgmt LL
Fund Type: Growth
Inception Date: February 15, 2007

Major Rating Factors:
Disappointing performance is the major factor driving the D+ (Weak) TheStreet.com Investment Rating for *PowerShares DB US Dollar Bearish. The fund currently has a performance rating of D+ (Weak) based on an annualized return of -7.23% over the last three years and a total return of -8.62% year to date 2015. Factored into the performance evaluation is an expense ratio of 0.81% (very low).

The fund's risk rating is currently B- (Good). It carries a beta of 0.14, meaning the fund's expected move will be 1.4% for every 10% move in the market. Volatility, as measured by both the semi-deviation and a drawdown factor, is considered low. As of December 31, 2015, *PowerShares DB US Dollar Bearish traded at a price exactly equal to its net asset value, which is worse than its one-year historical average discount of .02%.

James T. Anderson currently receives a manager quality ranking of 17 (0=worst, 99=best). This fund offers only a moderate level of risk but investors looking for strong performance are still waiting.

Data Date	Investment Rating	Net Assets ($Mil)	Price	Performance Rating/Pts	Total Return Y-T-D	Risk Rating/Pts
12-15	D+	45.20	21.42	D+ / 2.4	-8.62%	B- / 7.1
2014	D	45.20	23.76	D / 1.9	-11.28%	C+ / 6.7
2013	C-	65.00	27.06	D+ / 2.8	-0.63%	B / 8.9
2012	D+	92.50	27.21	D- / 1.4	2.94%	B / 8.8
2011	C-	102.20	26.85	D / 2.0	0.65%	B / 8.7
2010	C-	151.50	27.10	D / 2.1	-1.60%	B- / 7.8

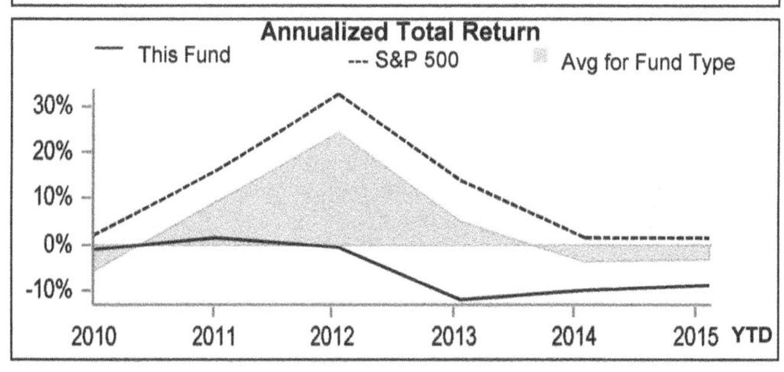

*PowerShares DB US Dollar Bullish (UUP) B Good

Fund Family: Invesco Powershares Capital Mgmt LL
Fund Type: Growth
Inception Date: February 15, 2007

Major Rating Factors: *PowerShares DB US Dollar Bullish receives a TheStreet.com Investment Rating of B (Good). The fund currently has a performance rating of C+ (Fair) based on an annualized return of 5.09% over the last three years and a total return of 5.45% year to date 2015. Factored into the performance evaluation is an expense ratio of 0.81% (very low).

The fund's risk rating is currently B (Good). It carries a beta of -0.13, meaning the fund's expected move will be -1.3% for every 10% move in the market. Volatility, as measured by both the semi-deviation and a drawdown factor, is considered low. As of December 31, 2015, *PowerShares DB US Dollar Bullish traded at a price exactly equal to its net asset value, which is better than its one-year historical average premium of .02%.

James T. Anderson currently receives a manager quality ranking of 93 (0=worst, 99=best). If you desire an average level of risk, then this fund may be an option.

Data Date	Investment Rating	Net Assets ($Mil)	Price	Performance Rating/Pts	Total Return Y-T-D	Risk Rating/Pts
12-15	B	713.30	25.65	C+ / 6.3	5.45%	B / 8.4
2014	C+	713.30	23.97	C- / 3.9	10.26%	B+ / 9.2
2013	C-	689.10	21.52	D / 2.1	-1.14%	B+ / 9.3
2012	D+	689.10	21.81	D- / 1.1	-4.44%	B / 8.4
2011	D+	0.00	22.47	D / 1.7	-2.75%	B / 8.2
2010	C-	997.50	22.71	D / 1.8	-1.60%	B- / 7.8

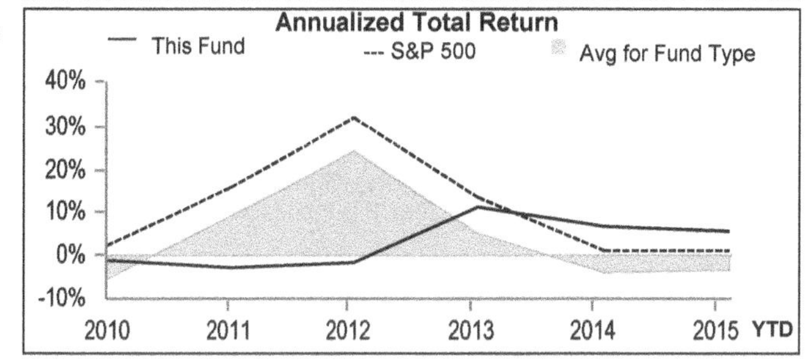

*PowerShares Div Achievers (PFM) B Good

Fund Family: Invesco Powershares Capital Mgmt LL
Fund Type: Income
Inception Date: September 15, 2005

Major Rating Factors: Strong performance is the major factor driving the B (Good) TheStreet.com Investment Rating for *PowerShares Div Achievers. The fund currently has a performance rating of B (Good) based on an annualized return of 10.11% over the last three years and a total return of -3.12% year to date 2015. Factored into the performance evaluation is an expense ratio of 0.55% (very low).

The fund's risk rating is currently B- (Good). It carries a beta of 0.93, meaning that its performance tracks fairly well with that of the overall stock market. Volatility, as measured by both the semi-deviation and a drawdown factor, is considered low. As of December 31, 2015, *PowerShares Div Achievers traded at a premium of .15% above its net asset value, which is worse than its one-year historical average discount of .06%.

Peter Hubbard has been running the fund for 9 years and currently receives a manager quality ranking of 47 (0=worst, 99=best). If you desire only a moderate level of risk and strong performance, then this fund is an excellent option.

Data Date	Investment Rating	Net Assets ($Mil)	Price	Perfor-mance Rating/Pts	Total Return Y-T-D	Risk Rating/Pts
12-15	B	354.20	20.55	B / 7.6	-3.12%	B- / 7.3
2014	B	354.20	21.70	B- / 7.2	12.14%	B- / 7.8
2013	A-	343.50	19.91	B / 7.7	22.01%	B / 8.9
2012	C+	254.70	16.16	C / 5.1	13.95%	B / 8.8
2011	C	256.30	14.96	C / 5.0	9.43%	B / 8.0
2010	C-	193.50	14.02	C- / 3.5	15.87%	C+ / 6.1

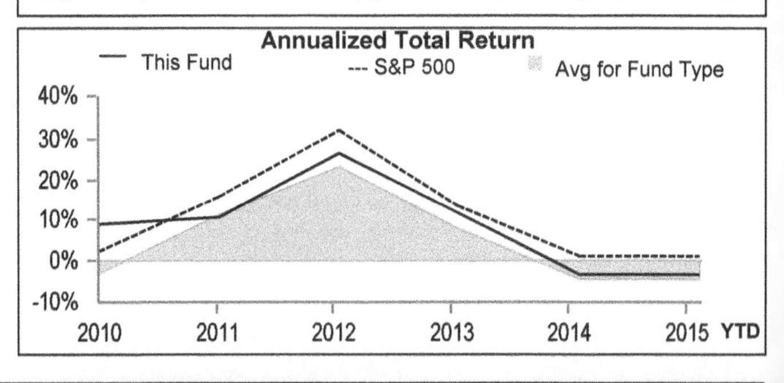

*PowerShares DWA Basic Materials (PYZ) C Fair

Fund Family: Invesco Powershares Capital Mgmt LL
Fund Type: Income
Inception Date: October 12, 2006

Major Rating Factors: Middle of the road best describes *PowerShares DWA Basic Materials whose TheStreet.com Investment Rating is currently a C (Fair). The fund currently has a performance rating of C+ (Fair) based on an annualized return of 6.34% over the last three years and a total return of -5.83% year to date 2015. Factored into the performance evaluation is an expense ratio of 0.60% (very low).

The fund's risk rating is currently C+ (Fair). It carries a beta of 1.19, meaning it is expected to move 11.9% for every 10% move in the market. Volatility, as measured by both the semi-deviation and a drawdown factor, is considered low. As of December 31, 2015, *PowerShares DWA Basic Materials traded at a premium of .39% above its net asset value, which is worse than its one-year historical average discount of .08%.

Peter Hubbard has been running the fund for 9 years and currently receives a manager quality ranking of 18 (0=worst, 99=best). If you desire an average level of risk, then this fund may be an option.

Data Date	Investment Rating	Net Assets ($Mil)	Price	Perfor-mance Rating/Pts	Total Return Y-T-D	Risk Rating/Pts
12-15	C	118.50	48.83	C+ / 6.1	-5.83%	C+ / 6.4
2014	B-	118.50	52.50	B- / 7.1	4.81%	B- / 7.3
2013	B-	84.10	50.98	B / 7.8	21.81%	C+ / 6.9
2012	B	70.60	40.45	B+ / 8.5	24.47%	C+ / 6.8
2011	C+	54.40	32.03	C+ / 6.7	-5.25%	B- / 7.0
2010	B-	76.20	35.44	B / 7.7	30.88%	C / 4.9

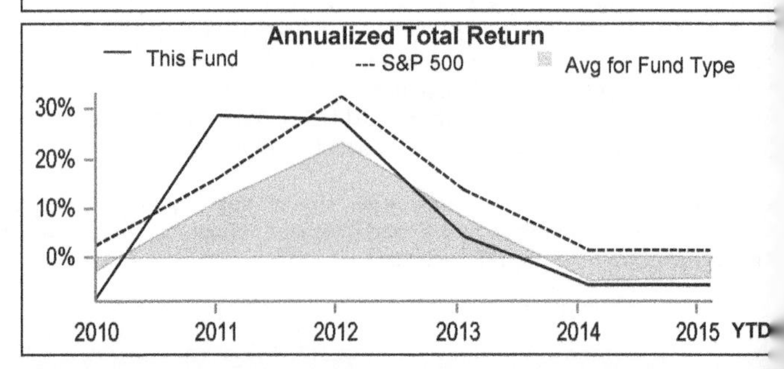

*PowerShares DWA Con Cyc Mom (PEZ) B+ Good

Fund Family: Invesco Powershares Capital Mgmt LL
Fund Type: Income
Inception Date: October 12, 2006

Major Rating Factors: Strong performance is the major factor driving the B+ (Good) TheStreet.com Investment Rating for *PowerShares DWA Con Cyc Mom. The fund currently has a performance rating of B+ (Good) based on an annualized return of 13.65% over the last three years and a total return of -0.05% year to date 2015. Factored into the performance evaluation is an expense ratio of 0.60% (very low).

The fund's risk rating is currently B- (Good). It carries a beta of 0.93, meaning that its performance tracks fairly well with that of the overall stock market. Volatility, as measured by both the semi-deviation and a drawdown factor, is considered low. As of December 31, 2015, *PowerShares DWA Con Cyc Mom traded at a premium of .05% above its net asset value, which is in line with its one-year historical average premium of .05%.

Peter Hubbard has been running the fund for 9 years and currently receives a manager quality ranking of 72 (0=worst, 99=best). If you desire only a moderate level of risk and strong performance, then this fund is an excellent option.

Data Date	Investment Rating	Net Assets ($Mil)	Price	Perfor-mance Rating/Pts	Total Return Y-T-D	Risk Rating/Pts
12-15	B+	48.80	44.04	B+ / 8.3	-0.05%	B- / 7.0
2014	B	48.80	44.66	B+ / 8.5	8.85%	C+ / 6.3
2013	A	24.80	41.19	B+ / 8.7	35.93%	B / 8.4
2012	C+	31.20	29.74	C+ / 6.4	17.08%	B- / 7.9
2011	C+	17.70	25.52	C+ / 6.2	2.30%	B- / 7.8
2010	B+	22.80	25.42	B / 7.6	29.87%	C+ / 6.2

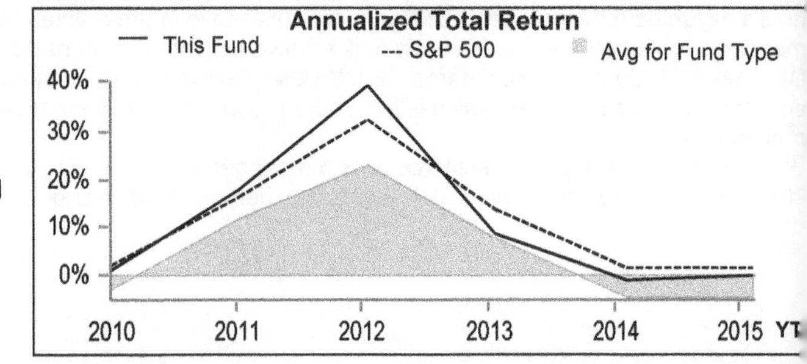

* Denotes ETF Fund

*PowerShares DWA Cons Staples Mom (PSL) A- Excellent

Fund Family: Invesco Powershares Capital Mgmt LL
Fund Type: Income
Inception Date: October 12, 2006

Major Rating Factors:
Exceptional performance is the major factor driving the A- (Excellent) TheStreet.com Investment Rating for *PowerShares DWA Cons Staples Mom. The fund currently has a performance rating of A+ (Excellent) based on an annualized return of 20.12% over the last three years and a total return of 14.58% year to date 2015. Factored into the performance evaluation is an expense ratio of 0.60% (very low).

The fund's risk rating is currently C+ (Fair). It carries a beta of 0.90, meaning that its performance tracks fairly well with that of the overall stock market. Volatility, as measured by both the semi-deviation and a drawdown factor, is considered low. As of December 31, 2015, *PowerShares DWA Cons Staples Mom traded at a premium of .04% above its net asset value, which is worse than its one-year historical average premium of .02%.

Peter Hubbard has been running the fund for 9 years and currently receives a manager quality ranking of 92 (0=worst, 99=best). If you desire only a moderate level of risk and strong performance, then this fund is an excellent option.

Data Date	Investment Rating	Net Assets ($Mil)	Price	Perfor-mance Rating/Pts	Total Return Y-T-D	Risk Rating/Pts
12-15	A-	40.10	56.79	A+ / 9.6	14.58%	C+ / 6.9
2014	B+	40.10	50.94	B+ / 8.8	17.72%	B- / 7.2
2013	A+	39.80	44.11	B+ / 8.5	30.46%	B / 8.8
2012	C+	33.30	33.22	C / 5.4	13.52%	B / 8.7
2011	B-	38.80	31.12	C+ / 6.0	9.95%	B / 8.4
2010	C+	40.40	28.98	C+ / 6.8	20.56%	C+ / 6.9

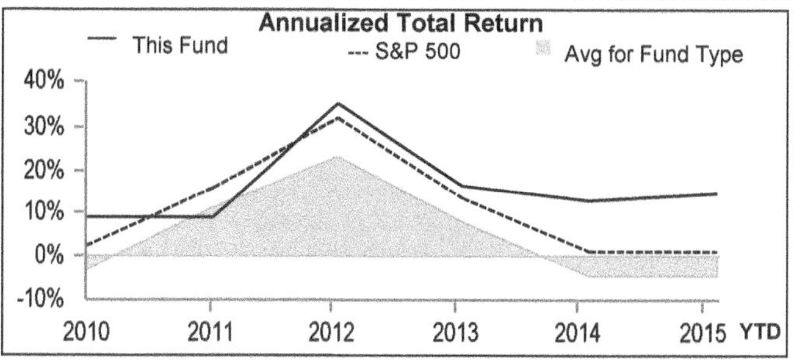

*PowerShares DWA Dev Mkt Momentum (PIZ) B Good

Fund Family: Invesco Powershares Capital Mgmt LL
Fund Type: Foreign
Inception Date: December 27, 2007

Major Rating Factors: *PowerShares DWA Dev Mkt Momentum receives a TheStreet.com Investment Rating of B (Good). The fund currently has a performance rating of C+ (Fair) based on an annualized return of 7.48% over the last three years and a total return of -0.10% year to date 2015. Factored into the performance evaluation is an expense ratio of 0.80% (very low).

The fund's risk rating is currently B (Good). It carries a beta of 0.93, meaning that its performance tracks fairly well with that of the overall stock market. Volatility, as measured by both the semi-deviation and a drawdown factor, is considered low. As of December 31, 2015, *PowerShares DWA Dev Mkt Momentum traded at a discount of .71% below its net asset value, which is better than its one-year historical average discount of .13%.

Peter Hubbard has been running the fund for 9 years and currently receives a manager quality ranking of 82 (0=worst, 99=best). If you desire an average level of risk, then this fund may be an option.

Data Date	Investment Rating	Net Assets ($Mil)	Price	Perfor-mance Rating/Pts	Total Return Y-T-D	Risk Rating/Pts
12-15	B	500.70	23.70	C+ / 6.8	-0.10%	B / 8.0
2014	C+	500.70	24.03	C+ / 5.7	-7.02%	B- / 7.9
2013	C	596.30	26.50	B / 7.7	33.95%	C / 5.1
2012	D+	101.40	20.14	C- / 3.9	19.18%	C+ / 6.8
2011	D+	54.30	17.47	C- / 3.3	-17.64%	C+ / 6.9
2010	C-	120.70	22.15	C / 4.4	21.32%	C / 5.3

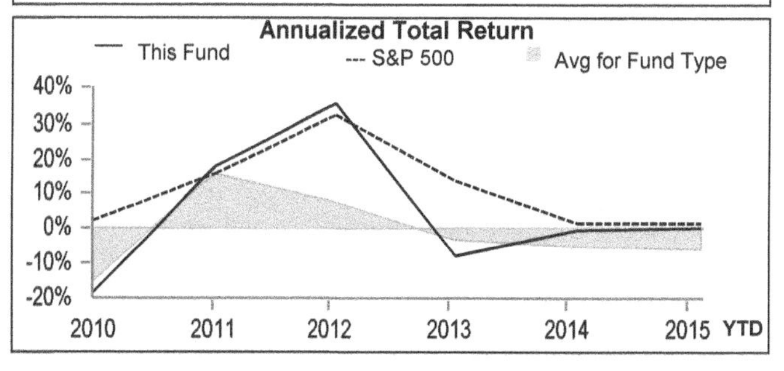

*PowerShares DWA Emg Mkts Momentu (PIE) D+ Weak

Fund Family: Invesco Powershares Capital Mgmt LL
Fund Type: Emerging Market
Inception Date: December 27, 2007

Major Rating Factors:
Disappointing performance is the major factor driving the D+ (Weak) TheStreet.com Investment Rating for *PowerShares DWA Emg Mkts Momentu. The fund currently has a performance rating of D (Weak) based on an annualized return of -6.43% over the last three years and a total return of -13.21% year to date 2015. Factored into the performance evaluation is an expense ratio of 0.90% (low).

The fund's risk rating is currently C+ (Fair). It carries a beta of 0.92, meaning that its performance tracks fairly well with that of the overall stock market. Volatility, as measured by both the semi-deviation and a drawdown factor, is considered low. As of December 31, 2015, *PowerShares DWA Emg Mkts Momentu traded at a discount of 1.19% below its net asset value, which is better than its one-year historical average discount of .31%.

Peter Hubbard has been running the fund for 9 years and currently receives a manager quality ranking of 65 (0=worst, 99=best). This fund offers only a moderate level of risk but investors looking for strong performance are still waiting.

Data Date	Investment Rating	Net Assets ($Mil)	Price	Perfor-mance Rating/Pts	Total Return Y-T-D	Risk Rating/Pts
12-15	D+	407.00	14.95	D / 2.2	-13.21%	C+ / 6.8
2014	D+	407.00	17.56	C- / 3.4	-1.11%	C+ / 6.4
2013	D	348.20	18.17	D+ / 2.4	-3.44%	C+ / 6.7
2012	C-	239.40	18.59	C / 4.6	16.22%	C+ / 6.9
2011	C	147.90	15.94	C+ / 6.0	-11.95%	B- / 7.0
2010	D-	392.00	18.37	D / 1.7	25.56%	C- / 3.8

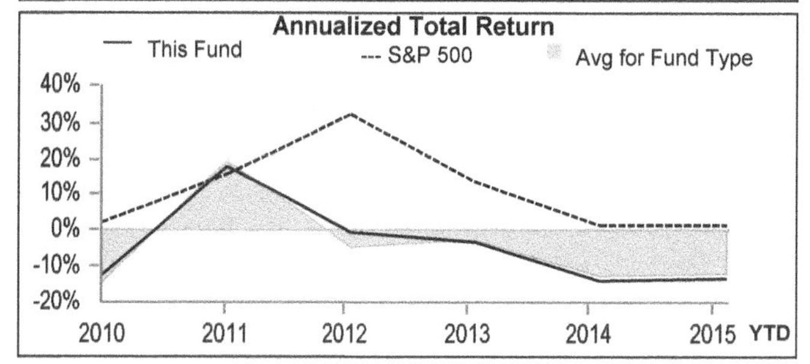

*PowerShares DWA Energy Momentum (PXI) D- Weak

Fund Family: Invesco Powershares Capital Mgmt LL
Fund Type: Energy/Natural Resources
Inception Date: October 12, 2006

Major Rating Factors:
Disappointing performance is the major factor driving the D- (Weak) TheStreet.com Investment Rating for *PowerShares DWA Energy Momentum. The fund currently has a performance rating of D (Weak) based on an annualized return of -7.75% over the last three years and a total return of -24.29% year to date 2015. Factored into the performance evaluation is an expense ratio of 0.60% (very low).

The fund's risk rating is currently C (Fair). It carries a beta of 1.23, meaning it is expected to move 12.3% for every 10% move in the market. Volatility, as measured by both the semi-deviation and a drawdown factor, is considered average. As of December 31, 2015, *PowerShares DWA Energy Momentum traded at a premium of .12% above its net asset value, which is worse than its one-year historical average discount of .04%.

Peter Hubbard has been running the fund for 9 years and currently receives a manager quality ranking of 50 (0=worst, 99=best). This fund offers an average level of risk but investors looking for strong performance will be frustrated.

Data Date	Investment Rating	Net Assets ($Mil)	Price	Performance Rating/Pts	Total Return Y-T-D	Risk Rating/Pts
12-15	D-	246.00	33.57	D / 1.7	-24.29%	C / 4.4
2014	D+	246.00	44.81	D+ / 2.4	-17.15%	C+ / 6.9
2013	B-	172.30	55.49	B / 7.8	24.35%	B- / 7.1
2012	B-	113.70	42.89	B / 7.8	16.26%	B- / 7.1
2011	B-	135.50	38.15	B / 7.9	6.26%	B- / 7.1
2010	B-	106.50	37.41	B / 7.6	40.04%	C / 4.9

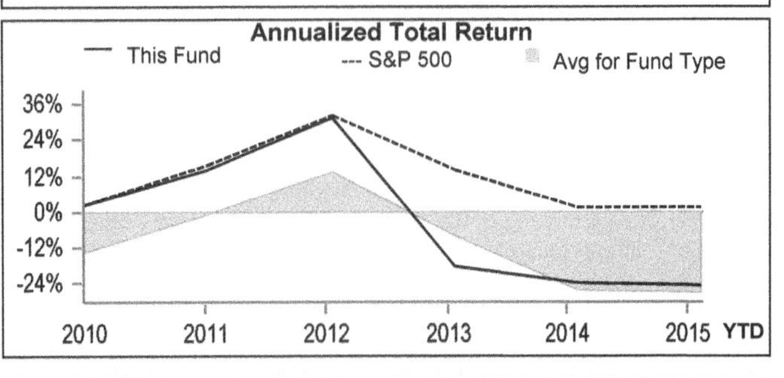

*PowerShares DWA Financial Moment (PFI) B+ Good

Fund Family: Invesco Powershares Capital Mgmt LL
Fund Type: Financial Services
Inception Date: October 12, 2006

Major Rating Factors: Strong performance is the major factor driving the B+ (Good) TheStreet.com Investment Rating for *PowerShares DWA Financial Moment. The fund currently has a performance rating of B+ (Good) based on an annualized return of 13.51% over the last three years and a total return of 1.37% year to date 2015. Factored into the performance evaluation is an expense ratio of 0.60% (very low).

The fund's risk rating is currently B- (Good). It carries a beta of 0.96, meaning that its performance tracks fairly well with that of the overall stock market. Volatility, as measured by both the semi-deviation and a drawdown factor, is considered low. As of December 31, 2015, *PowerShares DWA Financial Moment traded at a premium of .26% above its net asset value, which is worse than its one-year historical average discount of .10%.

Peter Hubbard has been running the fund for 9 years and currently receives a manager quality ranking of 69 (0=worst, 99=best). If you desire only a moderate level of risk and strong performance, then this fund is an excellent option.

Data Date	Investment Rating	Net Assets ($Mil)	Price	Performance Rating/Pts	Total Return Y-T-D	Risk Rating/Pts
12-15	B+	32.70	30.69	B+ / 8.7	1.37%	B- / 7.2
2014	A+	32.70	30.75	B+ / 8.5	7.48%	B / 8.9
2013	A	27.80	29.26	B+ / 8.8	34.35%	B / 8.0
2012	C+	19.10	21.15	C+ / 5.8	20.09%	B- / 7.9
2011	D+	17.00	17.93	D+ / 2.7	-3.01%	B- / 7.5
2010	D+	19.00	19.01	D / 2.2	15.84%	C+ / 6.0

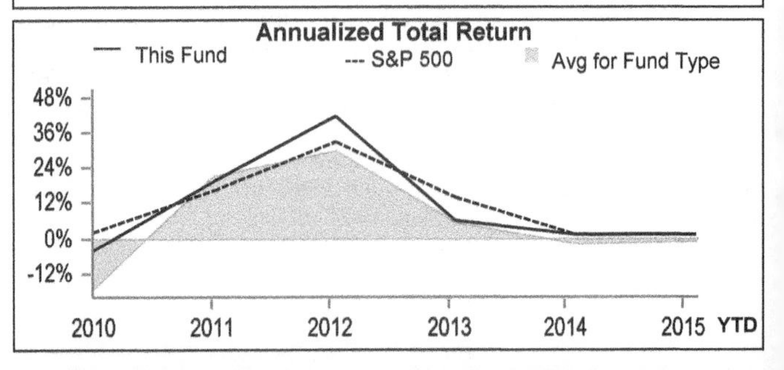

*PowerShares DWA Healthcare Momen (PTH) A+ Excellent

Fund Family: Invesco Powershares Capital Mgmt LL
Fund Type: Health
Inception Date: October 12, 2006

Major Rating Factors:
Exceptional performance is the major factor driving the A+ (Excellent) TheStreet.com Investment Rating for *PowerShares DWA Healthcare Momen. The fund currently has a performance rating of A- (Excellent) based on an annualized return of 17.83% over the last three years and a total return of 2.06% year to date 2015. Factored into the performance evaluation is an expense ratio of 0.60% (very low).

The fund's risk rating is currently B- (Good). It carries a beta of 0.95, meaning that its performance tracks fairly well with that of the overall stock market. Volatility, as measured by both the semi-deviation and a drawdown factor, is considered low. As of December 31, 2015, *PowerShares DWA Healthcare Momen traded at a discount of .07% below its net asset value, which is better than its one-year historical average premium of .03%.

Peter Hubbard has been running the fund for 9 years and currently receives a manager quality ranking of 87 (0=worst, 99=best). If you desire only a moderate level of risk and strong performance, then this fund is an excellent option.

Data Date	Investment Rating	Net Assets ($Mil)	Price	Performance Rating/Pts	Total Return Y-T-D	Risk Rating/Pts
12-15	A+	79.10	55.11	A- / 9.1	2.06%	B- / 7.9
2014	B+	79.10	54.29	A- / 9.2	14.74%	C+ / 6.4
2013	B+	90.10	47.31	A- / 9.2	40.47%	B- / 7.2
2012	C	49.50	32.82	C / 5.5	18.86%	B- / 7.1
2011	C+	45.90	28.69	C+ / 5.6	8.32%	B- / 7.8
2010	D+	49.70	26.85	D+ / 2.7	13.58%	C+ / 5.9

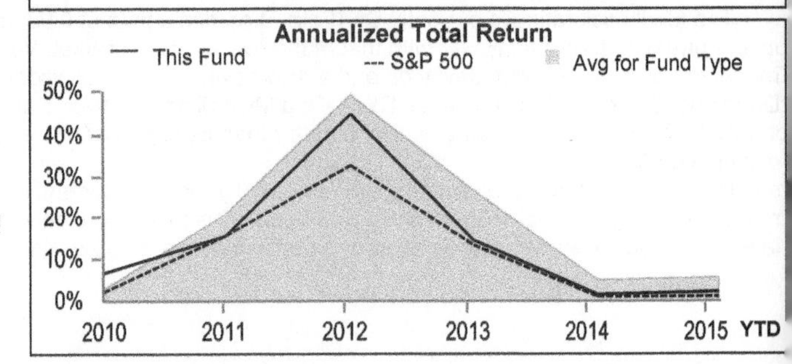

*PowerShares DWA Industrials Mome (PRN) B- Good

Fund Family: Invesco Powershares Capital Mgmt LL
Fund Type: Income
Inception Date: October 12, 2006

Major Rating Factors: Strong performance is the major factor driving the B- (Good) TheStreet.com Investment Rating for *PowerShares DWA Industrials Mome. The fund currently has a performance rating of B (Good) based on an annualized return of 10.74% over the last three years and a total return of -5.09% year to date 2015. Factored into the performance evaluation is an expense ratio of 0.60% (very low).

The fund's risk rating is currently C+ (Fair). It carries a beta of 1.26, meaning it is expected to move 12.6% for every 10% move in the market. Volatility, as measured by both the semi-deviation and a drawdown factor, is considered low. As of December 31, 2015, *PowerShares DWA Industrials Mome traded at a premium of .27% above its net asset value, which is worse than its one-year historical average premium of .01%.

Peter Hubbard has been running the fund for 9 years and currently receives a manager quality ranking of 26 (0=worst, 99=best). If you desire only a moderate level of risk and strong performance, then this fund is an excellent option.

Data Date	Investment Rating	Net Assets ($Mil)	Price	Performance Rating/Pts	Total Return Y-T-D	Risk Rating/Pts
12-15	B-	130.50	44.58	B / 7.6	-5.09%	C+ / 6.7
2014	B	130.50	47.41	B / 7.8	0.37%	B- / 7.3
2013	A-	128.80	47.71	A- / 9.1	43.27%	B- / 7.5
2012	B	29.00	31.82	B / 7.8	18.81%	B- / 7.4
2011	C-	46.30	27.31	C / 4.4	-4.87%	B- / 7.2
2010	B-	55.60	29.35	B- / 7.0	33.38%	C / 5.5

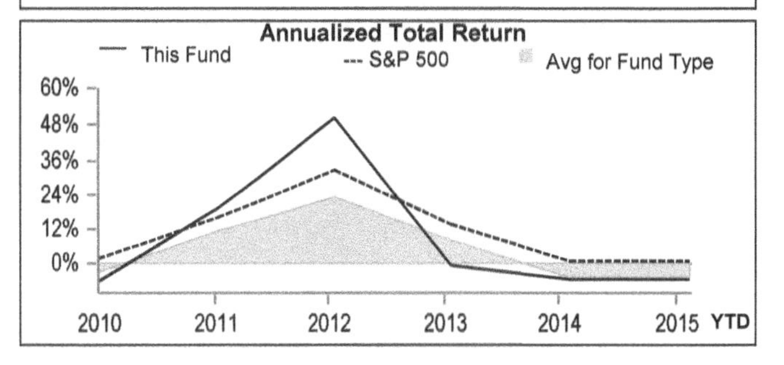

*PowerShares DWA Momentum (PDP) A Excellent

Fund Family: Invesco Powershares Capital Mgmt LL
Fund Type: Income
Inception Date: March 1, 2007

Major Rating Factors:
Strong performance is the major factor driving the A (Excellent) TheStreet.com Investment Rating for *PowerShares DWA Momentum. The fund currently has a performance rating of B+ (Good) based on an annualized return of 13.39% over the last three years and a total return of 1.56% year to date 2015. Factored into the performance evaluation is an expense ratio of 0.63% (very low).

The fund's risk rating is currently B (Good). It carries a beta of 0.92, meaning that its performance tracks fairly well with that of the overall stock market. Volatility, as measured by both the semi-deviation and a drawdown factor, is considered low. As of December 31, 2015, *PowerShares DWA Momentum traded at a discount of .07% below its net asset value.

Peter Hubbard has been running the fund for 9 years and currently receives a manager quality ranking of 72 (0=worst, 99=best). If you desire only a moderate level of risk and strong performance, then this fund is an excellent option.

Data Date	Investment Rating	Net Assets ($Mil)	Price	Performance Rating/Pts	Total Return Y-T-D	Risk Rating/Pts
12-15	A	1,313.40	41.37	B+ / 8.5	1.56%	B / 8.2
2014	B	1,313.40	41.06	B+ / 8.4	13.57%	B- / 7.1
2013	B	1,190.90	36.65	B / 8.1	26.93%	B- / 7.5
2012	B-	721.00	27.92	C+ / 6.9	18.12%	B- / 7.8
2011	C+	441.40	23.83	C+ / 6.2	1.64%	B- / 7.3
2010	D+	323.90	23.51	C- / 4.2	26.79%	C / 4.6

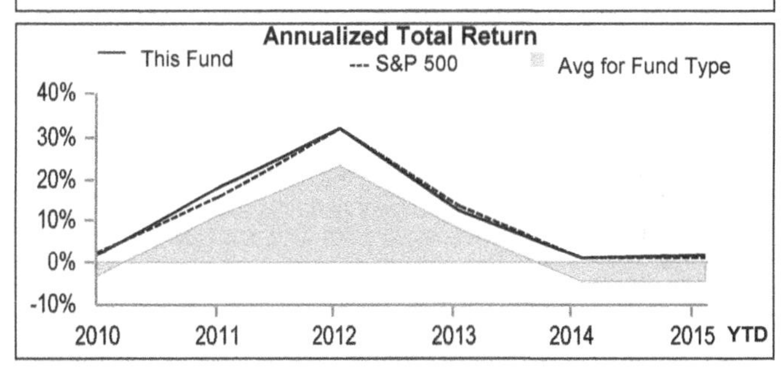

*PowerShares DWA NASDAQ Momentum (DWAQ) B Good

Fund Family: Invesco Powershares Capital Mgmt LL
Fund Type: Growth
Inception Date: May 1, 2003

Major Rating Factors: Strong performance is the major factor driving the B (Good) TheStreet.com Investment Rating for *PowerShares DWA NASDAQ Momentum. The fund currently has a performance rating of B+ (Good) based on an annualized return of 14.69% over the last three years and a total return of 6.02% year to date 2015. Factored into the performance evaluation is an expense ratio of 0.60% (very low).

The fund's risk rating is currently C+ (Fair). It carries a beta of 1.10, meaning it is expected to move 11.0% for every 10% move in the market. Volatility, as measured by both the semi-deviation and a drawdown factor, is considered low. As of December 31, 2015, *PowerShares DWA NASDAQ Momentum traded at a premium of .63% above its net asset value, which is worse than its one-year historical average premium of .06%.

Peter Hubbard has been running the fund for 9 years and currently receives a manager quality ranking of 62 (0=worst, 99=best). If you desire only a moderate level of risk and strong performance, then this fund is an excellent option.

Data Date	Investment Rating	Net Assets ($Mil)	Price	Performance Rating/Pts	Total Return Y-T-D	Risk Rating/Pts
12-15	B	26.70	74.53	B+ / 8.9	6.02%	C+ / 6.2
2014	C	26.70	71.46	B- / 7.2	3.93%	C+ / 5.6
2013	B+	24.30	69.30	B+ / 8.3	39.10%	B- / 7.6
2012	D+	21.80	48.10	C- / 3.3	8.38%	B- / 7.1
2011	C-	27.20	45.44	C- / 3.9	-6.58%	B- / 7.4
2010	C+	37.20	49.80	C / 5.5	23.64%	C+ / 6.0

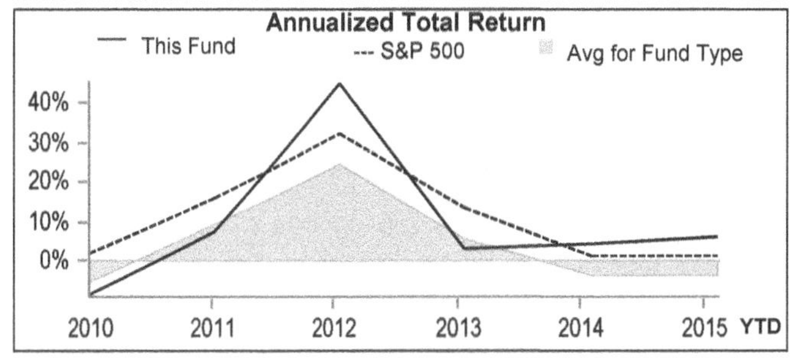

*PowerShares DWA SmallCap Momentu (DWAS) B+ Good

Fund Family: Invesco Powershares Capital Mgmt LL
Fund Type: Income
Inception Date: July 19, 2012

Major Rating Factors: Strong performance is the major factor driving the B+ (Good) TheStreet.com Investment Rating for *PowerShares DWA SmallCap Momentu. The fund currently has a performance rating of B- (Good) based on an annualized return of 11.04% over the last three years and a total return of -2.33% year to date 2015. Factored into the performance evaluation is an expense ratio of 0.60% (very low).

The fund's risk rating is currently B (Good). It carries a beta of 1.12, meaning it is expected to move 11.2% for every 10% move in the market. Volatility, as measured by both the semi-deviation and a drawdown factor, is considered low. As of December 31, 2015, *PowerShares DWA SmallCap Momentu traded at a discount of .16% below its net asset value, which is better than its one-year historical average premium of .01%.

Joshua Betts has been running the fund for 9 years and currently receives a manager quality ranking of 37 (0=worst, 99=best). If you desire only a moderate level of risk and strong performance, then this fund is an excellent option.

Data Date	Investment Rating	Net Assets ($Mil)	Price	Performance Rating/Pts	Total Return Y-T-D	Risk Rating/Pts
12-15	B+	359.10	37.60	B- / 7.5	-2.33%	B / 8.2
2014	C-	359.10	39.04	C- / 3.8	0.48%	C+ / 6.6
2013	A+	637.10	39.69	A+ / 9.7	42.48%	B+ / 9.7

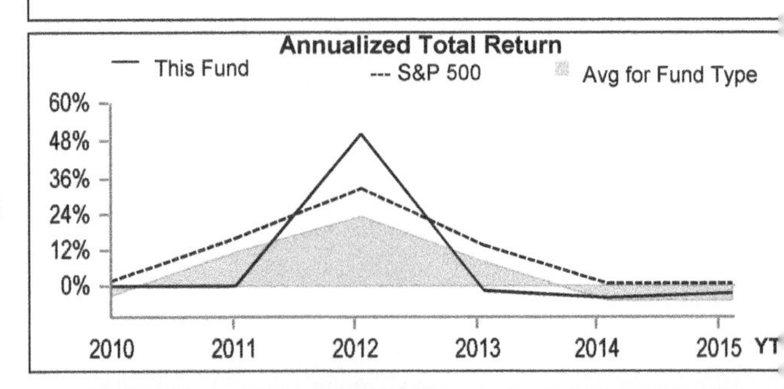

*PowerShares DWA Technology Momen (PTF) B- Good

Fund Family: Invesco Powershares Capital Mgmt LL
Fund Type: Growth
Inception Date: October 12, 2006

Major Rating Factors: Strong performance is the major factor driving the B- (Good) TheStreet.com Investment Rating for *PowerShares DWA Technology Momen. The fund currently has a performance rating of B+ (Good) based on an annualized return of 13.66% over the last three years and a total return of 5.08% year to date 2015. Factored into the performance evaluation is an expense ratio of 0.60% (very low).

The fund's risk rating is currently C+ (Fair). It carries a beta of 1.15, meaning it is expected to move 11.5% for every 10% move in the market. Volatility, as measured by both the semi-deviation and a drawdown factor, is considered low. As of December 31, 2015, *PowerShares DWA Technology Momen traded at a price exactly equal to its net asset value, which is worse than its one-year historical average discount of .04%.

Peter Hubbard has been running the fund for 9 years and currently receives a manager quality ranking of 51 (0=worst, 99=best). If you desire only a moderate level of risk and strong performance, then this fund is an excellent option.

Data Date	Investment Rating	Net Assets ($Mil)	Price	Performance Rating/Pts	Total Return Y-T-D	Risk Rating/Pts
12-15	B-	58.80	39.69	B+ / 8.6	5.08%	C+ / 5.6
2014	B-	58.80	38.37	B / 7.9	9.43%	C+ / 6.4
2013	B-	39.00	35.49	B- / 7.5	29.73%	B- / 7.5
2012	D+	29.00	26.17	C- / 3.9	15.18%	C+ / 6.8
2011	C-	27.70	23.28	C- / 4.0	-9.93%	B- / 7.1
2010	C	42.30	25.63	C / 4.9	11.21%	C+ / 5.7

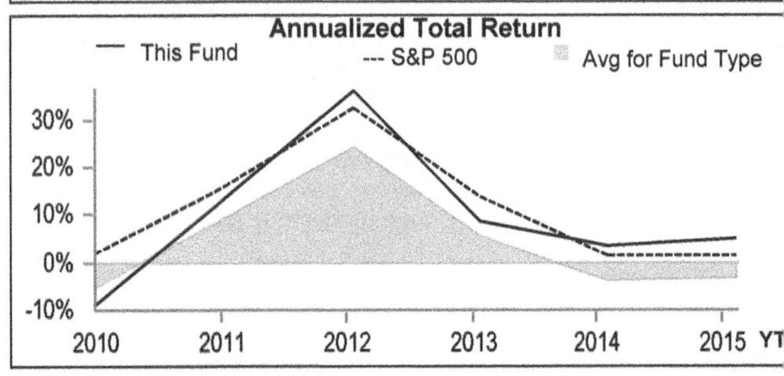

*PowerShares DWA Utilities Moment (PUI) B Good

Fund Family: Invesco Powershares Capital Mgmt LL
Fund Type: Utilities
Inception Date: October 26, 2005

Major Rating Factors: Strong performance is the major factor driving the B (Good) TheStreet.com Investment Rating for *PowerShares DWA Utilities Moment. The fund currently has a performance rating of B (Good) based on an annualized return of 11.05% over the last three years and a total return of -2.76% year to date 2015. Factored into the performance evaluation is an expense ratio of 0.60% (very low).

The fund's risk rating is currently B- (Good). It carries a beta of 0.80, meaning the fund's expected move will be 8.0% for every 10% move in the market. Volatility, as measured by both the semi-deviation and a drawdown factor, is considered low. As of December 31, 2015, *PowerShares DWA Utilities Moment traded at a premium of .72% above its net asset value, which is worse than its one-year historical average discount of .07%.

Peter Hubbard has been running the fund for 9 years and currently receives a manager quality ranking of 80 (0=worst, 99=best). If you desire only a moderate level of risk and strong performance, then this fund is an excellent option.

Data Date	Investment Rating	Net Assets ($Mil)	Price	Performance Rating/Pts	Total Return Y-T-D	Risk Rating/Pts
12-15	B	39.50	22.41	B / 8.1	-2.76%	B- / 7.1
2014	A	39.50	23.71	B / 7.9	19.28%	B / 8.8
2013	B+	38.20	20.64	B- / 7.1	18.03%	B / 8.9
2012	C	38.20	17.31	C- / 3.7	12.42%	B / 8.8
2011	C-	47.10	16.25	C- / 3.2	4.71%	B / 8.3
2010	C-	41.30	15.59	D+ / 2.3	8.56%	C+ / 6.8

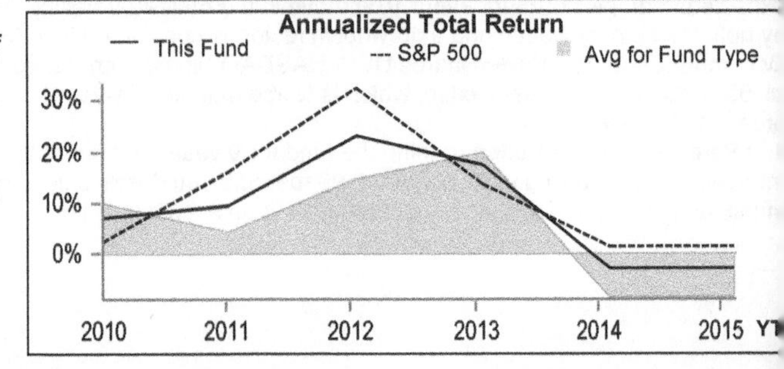

* Denotes ETF Fund

*PowerShares Dynamic Biotech&Geno (PBE) B+ Good

Fund Family: Invesco Powershares Capital Mgmt LL
Fund Type: Health
Inception Date: June 23, 2005

Major Rating Factors:
Exceptional performance is the major factor driving the B+ (Good) TheStreet.com Investment Rating for *PowerShares Dynamic Biotech&Geno. The fund currently has a performance rating of A+ (Excellent) based on an annualized return of 29.56% over the last three years and a total return of 1.40% year to date 2015. Factored into the performance evaluation is an expense ratio of 0.57% (very low).

The fund's risk rating is currently C (Fair). It carries a beta of 1.10, meaning it is expected to move 11.0% for every 10% move in the market. Volatility, as measured by both the semi-deviation and a drawdown factor, is considered average. As of December 31, 2015, *PowerShares Dynamic Biotech&Geno traded at a discount of .08% below its net asset value, which is better than its one-year historical average discount of .02%.

Peter Hubbard has been running the fund for 9 years and currently receives a manager quality ranking of 96 (0=worst, 99=best). If you desire an average level of risk and strong performance, then this fund is a good option.

Data Date	Investment Rating	Net Assets ($Mil)	Price	Performance Rating/Pts	Total Return Y-T-D	Risk Rating/Pts
12-15	B+	395.00	50.52	A+ / 9.7	1.40%	C / 5.5
2014	B+	395.00	50.20	A+ / 9.7	37.64%	C+ / 6.3
2013	B-	288.30	37.05	A- / 9.2	55.25%	C+ / 5.9
2012	D+	126.90	22.84	C / 4.7	14.24%	C+ / 5.8
2011	C-	135.40	20.06	C / 4.8	-4.41%	C+ / 5.8
2010	B	205.30	21.89	B+ / 8.4	31.47%	C / 4.5

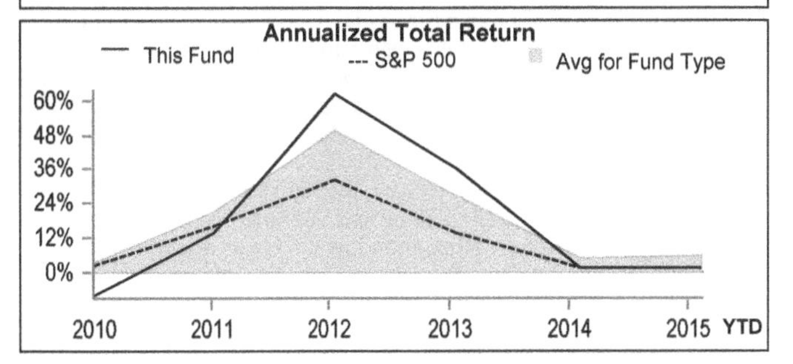

*PowerShares Dynamic Bldg & Cons (PKB) B Good

Fund Family: Invesco Powershares Capital Mgmt LL
Fund Type: Income
Inception Date: October 26, 2005

Major Rating Factors: Strong performance is the major factor driving the B (Good) TheStreet.com Investment Rating for *PowerShares Dynamic Bldg & Cons. The fund currently has a performance rating of B (Good) based on an annualized return of 10.12% over the last three years and a total return of 11.08% year to date 2015. Factored into the performance evaluation is an expense ratio of 0.63% (very low).

The fund's risk rating is currently B- (Good). It carries a beta of 1.15, meaning it is expected to move 11.5% for every 10% move in the market. Volatility, as measured by both the semi-deviation and a drawdown factor, is considered low. As of December 31, 2015, *PowerShares Dynamic Bldg & Cons traded at a premium of .13% above its net asset value, which is worse than its one-year historical average discount of .02%.

Peter Hubbard has been running the fund for 9 years and currently receives a manager quality ranking of 27 (0=worst, 99=best). If you desire only a moderate level of risk and strong performance, then this fund is an excellent option.

Data Date	Investment Rating	Net Assets ($Mil)	Price	Performance Rating/Pts	Total Return Y-T-D	Risk Rating/Pts
12-15	B	108.90	23.80	B / 8.1	11.08%	B- / 7.0
2014	B-	108.90	21.60	B / 7.7	-2.47%	C+ / 6.9
2013	B+	100.70	22.41	B+ / 8.8	24.13%	B- / 7.2
2012	B+	65.90	17.41	A / 9.4	41.98%	B- / 7.1
2011	D+	25.80	11.98	D+ / 2.9	-6.79%	C+ / 6.9
2010	D+	42.50	13.00	C- / 3.5	22.05%	C / 5.1

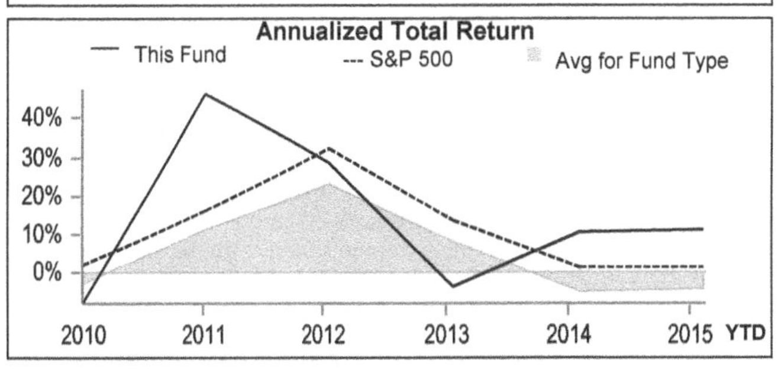

*PowerShares Dynamic Enrg Exp & P (PXE) D Weak

Fund Family: Invesco Powershares Capital Mgmt LL
Fund Type: Energy/Natural Resources
Inception Date: October 26, 2005

Major Rating Factors:
Disappointing performance is the major factor driving the D (Weak) TheStreet.com Investment Rating for *PowerShares Dynamic Enrg Exp & P. The fund currently has a performance rating of D (Weak) based on an annualized return of -5.71% over the last three years and a total return of -19.91% year to date 2015. Factored into the performance evaluation is an expense ratio of 0.64% (very low).

The fund's risk rating is currently C (Fair). It carries a beta of 1.26, meaning it is expected to move 12.6% for every 10% move in the market. Volatility, as measured by both the semi-deviation and a drawdown factor, is considered average. As of December 31, 2015, *PowerShares Dynamic Enrg Exp & P traded at a premium of .05% above its net asset value, which is worse than its one-year historical average discount of .06%.

Peter Hubbard has been running the fund for 9 years and currently receives a manager quality ranking of 96 (0=worst, 99=best). This fund offers an average level of risk but investors looking for strong performance will be frustrated.

Data Date	Investment Rating	Net Assets ($Mil)	Price	Performance Rating/Pts	Total Return Y-T-D	Risk Rating/Pts
12-15	D	128.40	21.91	D / 2.1	-19.91%	C / 4.6
2014	C-	128.40	27.74	C- / 3.2	-16.79%	B- / 7.2
2013	B	115.80	34.45	B+ / 8.3	24.68%	B- / 7.0
2012	B	65.10	26.97	B+ / 8.7	24.36%	B- / 7.1
2011	C+	67.30	22.43	C+ / 6.2	2.05%	B- / 7.0
2010	C+	76.10	23.07	C+ / 6.8	40.36%	C / 4.9

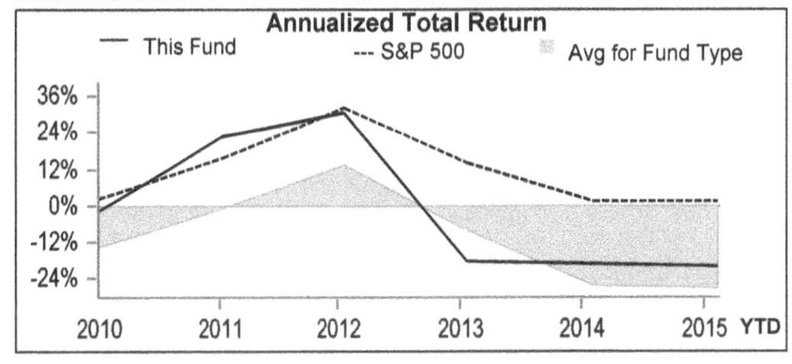

*PowerShares Dynamic Food & Bever (PBJ) A+ Excellent

Fund Family: Invesco Powershares Capital Mgmt LL
Fund Type: Income
Inception Date: June 23, 2005

Data Date	Investment Rating	Net Assets ($Mil)	Price	Performance Rating/Pts	Total Return Y-T-D	Risk Rating/Pts
12-15	A+	245.70	32.20	A / 9.3	7.18%	B- / 7.7
2014	A-	245.70	30.49	B+ / 8.4	18.65%	B- / 7.7
2013	B+	230.70	26.34	B / 7.6	28.68%	B / 8.9
2012	C+	102.70	19.91	C+ / 5.6	9.53%	B / 8.8
2011	C+	190.90	19.17	C / 5.5	6.23%	B / 8.5
2010	A	126.70	18.23	B / 8.2	30.78%	B- / 7.0

Major Rating Factors:
Exceptional performance is the major factor driving the A+ (Excellent) TheStreet.com Investment Rating for *PowerShares Dynamic Food & Bever. The fund currently has a performance rating of A (Excellent) based on an annualized return of 17.75% over the last three years and a total return of 7.18% year to date 2015. Factored into the performance evaluation is an expense ratio of 0.58% (very low).

The fund's risk rating is currently B- (Good). It carries a beta of 0.93, meaning that its performance tracks fairly well with that of the overall stock market. Volatility, as measured by both the semi-deviation and a drawdown factor, is considered low. As of December 31, 2015, *PowerShares Dynamic Food & Bever traded at a premium of .03% above its net asset value, which is worse than its one-year historical average discount of .01%.

Peter Hubbard has been running the fund for 9 years and currently receives a manager quality ranking of 88 (0=worst, 99=best). If you desire only a moderate level of risk and strong performance, then this fund is an excellent option.

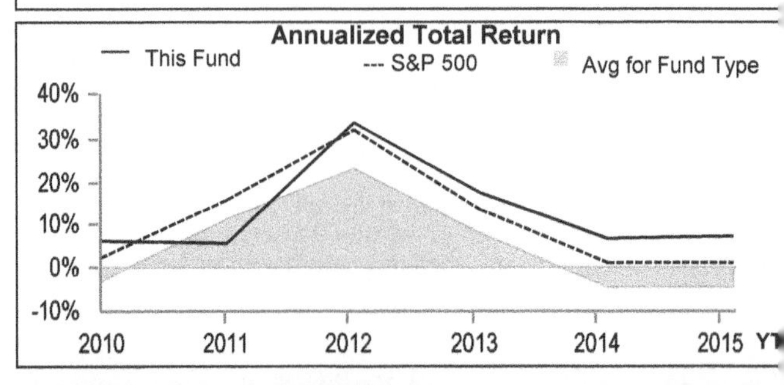

*PowerShares Dynamic Large Cap Gr (PWB) A+ Excellent

Fund Family: Invesco Powershares Capital Mgmt LL
Fund Type: Growth
Inception Date: March 3, 2005

Data Date	Investment Rating	Net Assets ($Mil)	Price	Performance Rating/Pts	Total Return Y-T-D	Risk Rating/Pts
12-15	A+	275.00	31.29	A / 9.4	7.97%	B- / 7.5
2014	A-	275.00	29.26	A- / 9.0	14.19%	B- / 7.2
2013	A-	266.30	25.88	B+ / 8.8	33.19%	B- / 7.8
2012	C+	188.20	18.93	C+ / 5.7	21.29%	B- / 7.6
2011	C	163.70	16.12	C / 5.1	0.46%	B- / 7.5
2010	C-	215.50	16.25	C- / 3.6	14.11%	C+ / 5.9

Major Rating Factors:
Exceptional performance is the major factor driving the A+ (Excellent) TheStreet.com Investment Rating for *PowerShares Dynamic Large Cap Gr. The fund currently has a performance rating of A (Excellent) based on an annualized return of 17.87% over the last three years and a total return of 7.97% year to date 2015. Factored into the performance evaluation is an expense ratio of 0.58% (very low).

The fund's risk rating is currently B- (Good). It carries a beta of 0.89, meaning the fund's expected move will be 8.9% for every 10% move in the market. Volatility, as measured by both the semi-deviation and a drawdown factor, is considered low. As of December 31, 2015, *PowerShares Dynamic Large Cap Gr traded at a premium of .03% above its net asset value, which is worse than its one-year historical average premium of .01%.

Peter Hubbard has been running the fund for 9 years and currently receives a manager quality ranking of 89 (0=worst, 99=best). If you desire only a moderate level of risk and strong performance, then this fund is an excellent option.

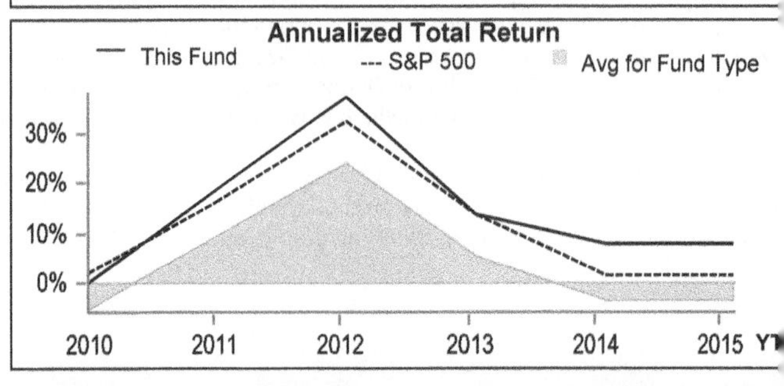

*PowerShares Dynamic Large Cap Va (PWV) B+ Good

Fund Family: Invesco Powershares Capital Mgmt LL
Fund Type: Income
Inception Date: March 3, 2005

Data Date	Investment Rating	Net Assets ($Mil)	Price	Performance Rating/Pts	Total Return Y-T-D	Risk Rating/Pts
12-15	B+	907.90	29.09	B / 7.7	-4.82%	B / 8.0
2014	A+	907.90	31.27	B / 8.2	13.15%	B+ / 9.3
2013	A	759.50	28.41	B+ / 8.6	28.96%	B / 8.7
2012	C+	459.60	21.85	C+ / 6.0	17.96%	B / 8.5
2011	C+	393.90	19.28	C / 5.1	6.12%	B / 8.1
2010	C	374.50	18.53	C / 4.6	14.34%	C+ / 6.6

Major Rating Factors: Strong performance is the major factor driving the B+ (Good) TheStreet.com Investment Rating for *PowerShares Dynamic Large Cap Va. The fund currently has a performance rating of B (Good) based on an annualized return of 11.60% over the last three years and a total return of -4.82% year to date 2015. Factored into the performance evaluation is an expense ratio of 0.57% (very low).

The fund's risk rating is currently B (Good). It carries a beta of 0.98, meaning that its performance tracks fairly well with that of the overall stock market. Volatility, as measured by both the semi-deviation and a drawdown factor, is considered low. As of December 31, 2015, *PowerShares Dynamic Large Cap Va traded at a price exactly equal to its net asset value, which is worse than its one-year historical average discount of .02%.

Peter Hubbard has been running the fund for 9 years and currently receives a manager quality ranking of 51 (0=worst, 99=best). If you desire only a moderate level of risk and strong performance, then this fund is an excellent option.

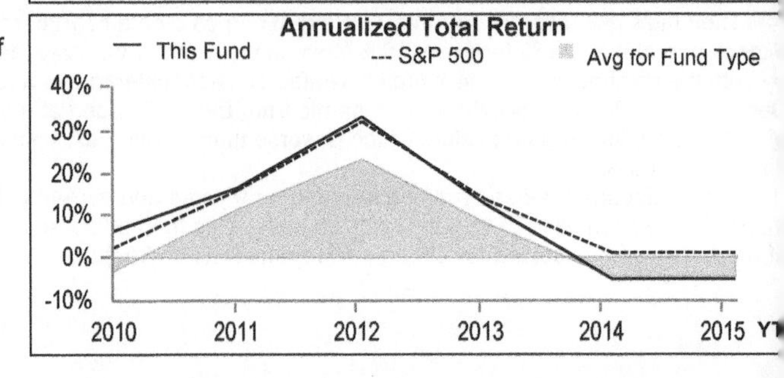

*PowerShares Dynamic Leisure&Ente (PEJ) A+ Excellent

Fund Family: Invesco Powershares Capital Mgmt LL
Fund Type: Income
Inception Date: June 23, 2005

Major Rating Factors:
Exceptional performance is the major factor driving the A+ (Excellent) TheStreet.com Investment Rating for *PowerShares Dynamic Leisure&Ente. The fund currently has a performance rating of A- (Excellent) based on an annualized return of 15.86% over the last three years and a total return of 4.11% year to date 2015. Factored into the performance evaluation is an expense ratio of 0.63% (very low).

The fund's risk rating is currently B (Good). It carries a beta of 1.00, meaning that its performance tracks fairly well with that of the overall stock market. Volatility, as measured by both the semi-deviation and a drawdown factor, is considered low. As of December 31, 2015, *PowerShares Dynamic Leisure&Ente traded at a discount of .03% below its net asset value, which is better than its one-year historical average premium of .05%.

Peter Hubbard has been running the fund for 9 years and currently receives a manager quality ranking of 81 (0=worst, 99=best). If you desire only a moderate level of risk and strong performance, then this fund is an excellent option.

Data Date	Investment Rating	Net Assets ($Mil)	Price	Performance Rating/Pts	Total Return Y-T-D	Risk Rating/Pts
12-15	A+	148.20	36.76	A- / 9.1	4.11%	B / 8.5
2014	A	148.20	35.73	A- / 9.1	6.36%	B- / 7.4
2013	A	197.60	34.11	A- / 9.2	41.40%	B / 8.0
2012	A-	58.50	22.95	B+ / 8.8	25.82%	B / 8.0
2011	B	35.50	18.69	B / 7.7	0.84%	B- / 7.6
2010	A-	66.30	18.47	B+ / 8.8	39.93%	C+ / 5.6

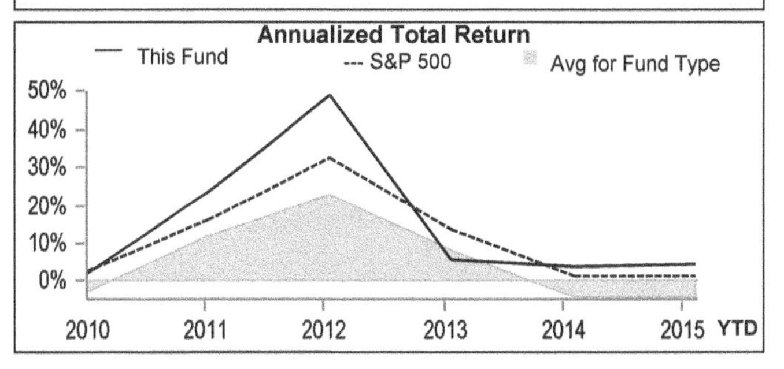

*PowerShares Dynamic Market (PWC) A- Excellent

Fund Family: Invesco Powershares Capital Mgmt LL
Fund Type: Growth
Inception Date: May 1, 2003

Major Rating Factors:
Strong performance is the major factor driving the A- (Excellent) TheStreet.com Investment Rating for *PowerShares Dynamic Market. The fund currently has a performance rating of B+ (Good) based on an annualized return of 14.50% over the last three years and a total return of 0.77% year to date 2015. Factored into the performance evaluation is an expense ratio of 0.59% (very low).

The fund's risk rating is currently B- (Good). It carries a beta of 1.06, meaning that its performance tracks fairly well with that of the overall stock market. Volatility, as measured by both the semi-deviation and a drawdown factor, is considered low. As of December 31, 2015, *PowerShares Dynamic Market traded at a premium of .78% above its net asset value, which is worse than its one-year historical average discount of .04%.

Peter Hubbard has been running the fund for 9 years and currently receives a manager quality ranking of 64 (0=worst, 99=best). If you desire only a moderate level of risk and strong performance, then this fund is an excellent option.

Data Date	Investment Rating	Net Assets ($Mil)	Price	Performance Rating/Pts	Total Return Y-T-D	Risk Rating/Pts
12-15	A-	186.60	73.22	B+ / 8.8	0.77%	B- / 7.4
2014	B+	186.60	73.86	B+ / 8.8	10.31%	B- / 7.1
2013	A-	170.70	68.26	B+ / 8.9	35.88%	B- / 7.6
2012	C+	132.10	48.78	C+ / 6.0	22.57%	B- / 7.6
2011	C-	131.10	41.02	C- / 3.7	-5.02%	B- / 7.7
2010	C-	195.80	44.01	C- / 3.8	18.15%	C+ / 6.3

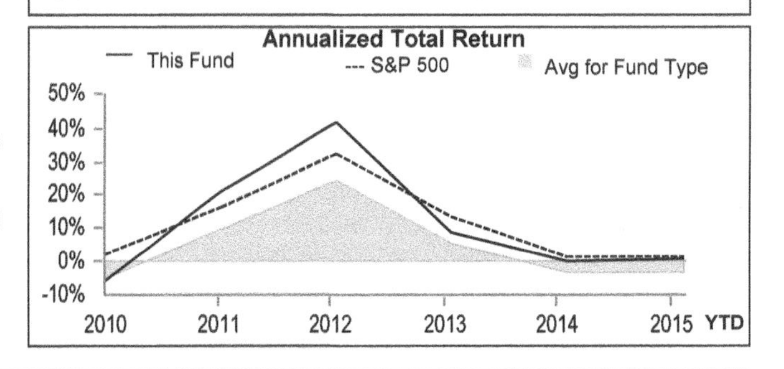

*PowerShares Dynamic Media (PBS) B+ Good

Fund Family: Invesco Powershares Capital Mgmt LL
Fund Type: Income
Inception Date: June 23, 2005

Major Rating Factors: Strong performance is the major factor driving the B+ (Good) TheStreet.com Investment Rating for *PowerShares Dynamic Media. The fund currently has a performance rating of B+ (Good) based on an annualized return of 14.52% over the last three years and a total return of 0.53% year to date 2015. Factored into the performance evaluation is an expense ratio of 0.59% (very low).

The fund's risk rating is currently C+ (Fair). It carries a beta of 1.27, meaning it is expected to move 12.7% for every 10% move in the market. Volatility, as measured by both the semi-deviation and a drawdown factor, is considered low. As of December 31, 2015, *PowerShares Dynamic Media traded at a premium of .44% above its net asset value, which is worse than its one-year historical average discount of .01%.

Peter Hubbard has been running the fund for 9 years and currently receives a manager quality ranking of 39 (0=worst, 99=best). If you desire only a moderate level of risk and strong performance, then this fund is an excellent option.

Data Date	Investment Rating	Net Assets ($Mil)	Price	Performance Rating/Pts	Total Return Y-T-D	Risk Rating/Pts
12-15	B+	150.60	25.14	B+ / 8.7	0.53%	C+ / 6.9
2014	C+	150.60	25.58	B+ / 8.8	-2.72%	C / 5.0
2013	B	326.20	26.63	A / 9.5	55.41%	C+ / 6.2
2012	B-	84.50	16.69	B- / 7.5	26.49%	B- / 7.4
2011	B-	124.00	13.25	B- / 7.0	-4.00%	B- / 7.5
2010	C+	84.10	13.92	C+ / 6.1	20.54%	C / 5.4

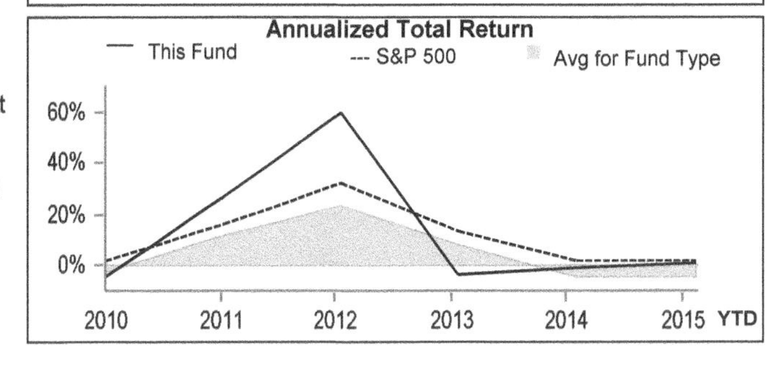

*PowerShares Dynamic Networking (PXQ) B Good

Fund Family: Invesco Powershares Capital Mgmt LL
Fund Type: Growth
Inception Date: June 23, 2005

Major Rating Factors: Strong performance is the major factor driving the B (Good) TheStreet.com Investment Rating for *PowerShares Dynamic Networking. The fund currently has a performance rating of B (Good) based on an annualized return of 10.53% over the last three years and a total return of 0.56% year to date 2015. Factored into the performance evaluation is an expense ratio of 0.63% (very low).

The fund's risk rating is currently B- (Good). It carries a beta of 1.09, meaning that its performance tracks fairly well with that of the overall stock market. Volatility, as measured by both the semi-deviation and a drawdown factor, is considered low. As of December 31, 2015, *PowerShares Dynamic Networking traded at a premium of .46% above its net asset value, which is worse than its one-year historical average discount of .04%.

Peter Hubbard has been running the fund for 9 years and currently receives a manager quality ranking of 33 (0=worst, 99=best). If you desire only a moderate level of risk and strong performance, then this fund is an excellent option.

Data Date	Investment Rating	Net Assets ($Mil)	Price	Performance Rating/Pts	Total Return Y-T-D	Risk Rating/Pts
12-15	B	27.60	34.62	B / 7.7	0.56%	B- / 7.0
2014	C	27.60	34.94	C+ / 6.8	12.71%	C+ / 6.1
2013	C	31.60	31.59	C+ / 6.1	20.90%	B- / 7.0
2012	C-	39.40	25.33	C / 5.0	2.93%	C+ / 6.9
2011	B-	81.40	24.29	B / 7.6	-9.79%	B- / 7.0
2010	A	116.10	26.46	A- / 9.2	47.05%	C+ / 5.8

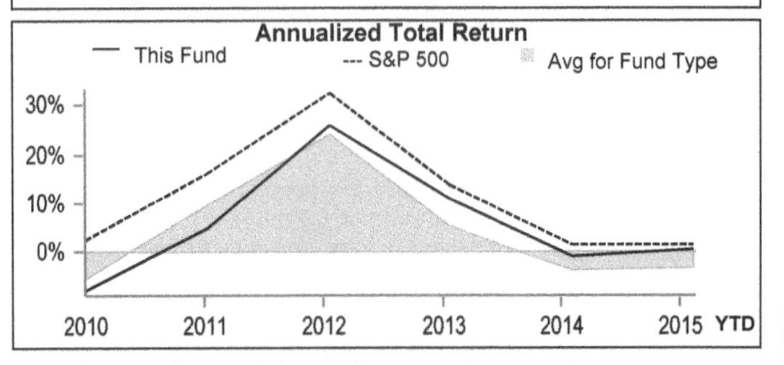

*PowerShares Dynamic Oil & Gas Sv (PXJ) E+ Very Weak

Fund Family: Invesco Powershares Capital Mgmt LL
Fund Type: Energy/Natural Resources
Inception Date: October 26, 2005

Major Rating Factors:
Very poor performance is the major factor driving the E+ (Very Weak) TheStreet.com Investment Rating for *PowerShares Dynamic Oil & Gas Sv. The fund currently has a performance rating of E+ (Very Weak) based on an annualized return of -17.09% over the last three years and a total return of -31.06% year to date 2015. Factored into the performance evaluation is an expense ratio of 0.63% (very low).

The fund's risk rating is currently C- (Fair). It carries a beta of 1.42, meaning it is expected to move 14.2% for every 10% move in the market. Volatility, as measured by both the semi-deviation and a drawdown factor, is considered average. As of December 31, 2015, *PowerShares Dynamic Oil & Gas Sv traded at a premium of .08% above its net asset value, which is worse than its one-year historical average discount of .10%.

Peter Hubbard has been running the fund for 9 years and currently receives a manager quality ranking of 15 (0=worst, 99=best). This fund offers an average level of risk but investors looking for strong performance will be frustrated.

Data Date	Investment Rating	Net Assets ($Mil)	Price	Performance Rating/Pts	Total Return Y-T-D	Risk Rating/Pts
12-15	E+	102.30	11.83	E+ / 0.9	-31.06%	C- / 3.4
2014	D-	102.30	17.52	D- / 1.1	-30.70%	C+ / 6.0
2013	C-	126.70	25.84	C+ / 6.1	19.42%	C+ / 6.1
2012	D	113.00	20.34	C- / 3.3	6.34%	C+ / 6.0
2011	C	169.50	20.16	C+ / 6.6	-1.74%	C+ / 6.0
2010	D+	199.50	21.83	C- / 4.0	29.63%	C- / 4.1

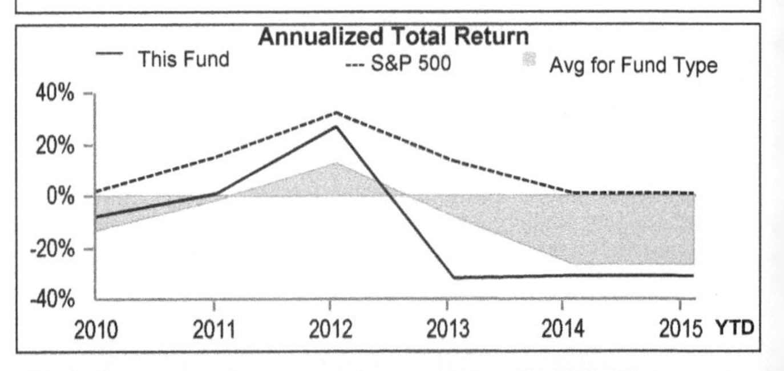

*PowerShares Dynamic Pharmaceutic (PJP) B Good

Fund Family: Invesco Powershares Capital Mgmt LL
Fund Type: Health
Inception Date: June 23, 2005

Major Rating Factors:
Exceptional performance is the major factor driving the B (Good) TheStreet.com Investment Rating for *PowerShares Dynamic Pharmaceutic. The fund currently has a performance rating of A+ (Excellent) based on an annualized return of 30.56% over the last three years and a total return of 14.64% year to date 2015. Factored into the performance evaluation is an expense ratio of 0.56% (very low).

The fund's risk rating is currently C (Fair). It carries a beta of 1.08, meaning that its performance tracks fairly well with that of the overall stock market. Volatility, as measured by both the semi-deviation and a drawdown factor, is considered average. As of December 31, 2015, *PowerShares Dynamic Pharmaceutic traded at a discount of .01% below its net asset value.

Peter Hubbard has been running the fund for 9 years and currently receives a manager quality ranking of 96 (0=worst, 99=best). If you desire an average level of risk and strong performance, then this fund is a good option.

Data Date	Investment Rating	Net Assets ($Mil)	Price	Performance Rating/Pts	Total Return Y-T-D	Risk Rating/Pts
12-15	B	1,262.90	69.97	A+ / 9.8	14.64%	C / 5.2
2014	A	1,262.90	66.53	A+ / 9.6	28.30%	C+ / 6.9
2013	A-	943.40	53.48	A+ / 9.7	51.10%	C+ / 6.9
2012	B+	316.00	34.53	A / 9.3	28.77%	B- / 7.1
2011	B	182.80	28.18	B / 7.9	21.18%	B- / 7.5
2010	A-	94.60	23.64	B+ / 8.3	27.81%	C+ / 5.9

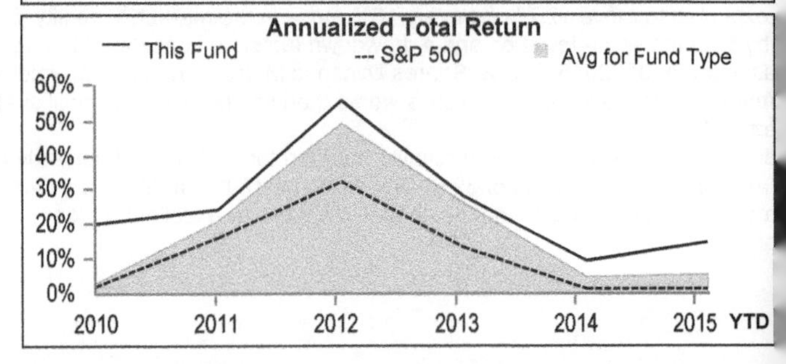

*PowerShares Dynamic Retail (PMR) B+ Good

Fund Family: Invesco Powershares Capital Mgmt LL
Fund Type: Income
Inception Date: October 26, 2005

Major Rating Factors: Strong performance is the major factor driving the B+ (Good) TheStreet.com Investment Rating for *PowerShares Dynamic Retail. The fund currently has a performance rating of B+ (Good) based on an annualized return of 14.68% over the last three years and a total return of -2.77% year to date 2015. Factored into the performance evaluation is an expense ratio of 0.63% (very low).

The fund's risk rating is currently C+ (Fair). It carries a beta of 1.04, meaning that its performance tracks fairly well with that of the overall stock market. Volatility, as measured by both the semi-deviation and a drawdown factor, is considered low. As of December 31, 2015, *PowerShares Dynamic Retail traded at a premium of .68% above its net asset value, which is worse than its one-year historical average discount of .04%.

Peter Hubbard has been running the fund for 9 years and currently receives a manager quality ranking of 61 (0=worst, 99=best). If you desire only a moderate level of risk and strong performance, then this fund is an excellent option.

Data Date	Investment Rating	Net Assets ($Mil)	Price	Performance Rating/Pts	Total Return Y-T-D	Risk Rating/Pts
12-15	B+	21.40	37.21	B+ / 8.6	-2.77%	C+ / 6.9
2014	A-	21.40	39.03	A- / 9.2	12.98%	B- / 7.0
2013	A+	41.90	34.89	A- / 9.2	38.93%	B / 8.7
2012	B	53.00	25.22	B- / 7.2	14.43%	B / 8.2
2011	B	29.70	21.96	B / 8.0	19.06%	B / 8.0
2010	A-	13.60	19.45	B+ / 8.3	24.90%	C+ / 6.7

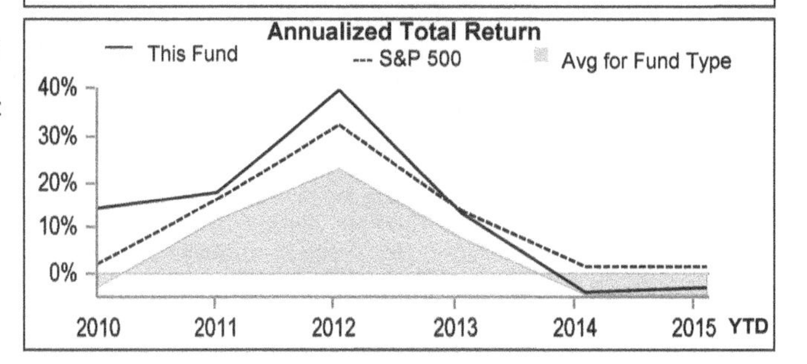

*PowerShares Dynamic Semiconducto (PSI) B+ Good

Fund Family: Invesco Powershares Capital Mgmt LL
Fund Type: Income
Inception Date: June 23, 2005

Major Rating Factors:
Exceptional performance is the major factor driving the B+ (Good) TheStreet.com Investment Rating for *PowerShares Dynamic Semiconducto. The fund currently has a performance rating of A (Excellent) based on an annualized return of 20.48% over the last three years and a total return of -0.43% year to date 2015. Factored into the performance evaluation is an expense ratio of 0.63% (very low).

The fund's risk rating is currently C+ (Fair). It carries a beta of 1.16, meaning it is expected to move 11.6% for every 10% move in the market. Volatility, as measured by both the semi-deviation and a drawdown factor, is considered low. As of December 31, 2015, *PowerShares Dynamic Semiconducto traded at a premium of .20% above its net asset value, which is worse than its one-year historical average premium of .01%.

Peter Hubbard has been running the fund for 9 years and currently receives a manager quality ranking of 86 (0=worst, 99=best). If you desire only a moderate level of risk and strong performance, then this fund is an excellent option.

Data Date	Investment Rating	Net Assets ($Mil)	Price	Performance Rating/Pts	Total Return Y-T-D	Risk Rating/Pts
12-15	B+	28.70	25.23	A / 9.4	-0.43%	C+ / 6.4
2014	B+	28.70	25.46	A / 9.5	39.32%	C+ / 6.5
2013	C+	16.10	18.88	C+ / 6.5	26.47%	C+ / 6.9
2012	D	15.90	14.40	D+ / 2.7	3.68%	C+ / 6.7
2011	C-	22.30	13.89	C / 4.4	-15.24%	C+ / 6.7
2010	C+	37.40	16.28	C+ / 6.6	20.74%	C / 5.3

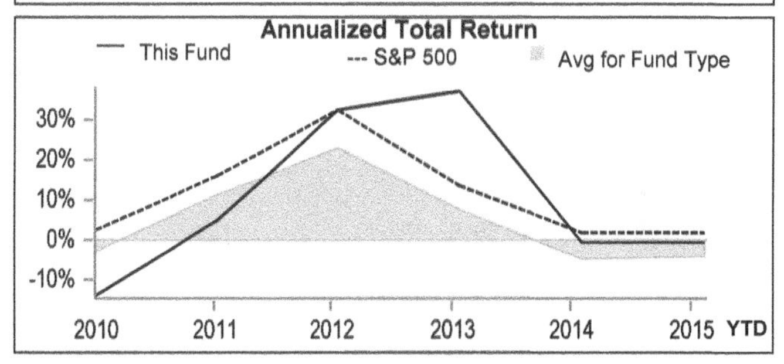

*PowerShares Dynamic Software (PSJ) A Excellent

Fund Family: Invesco Powershares Capital Mgmt LL
Fund Type: Growth
Inception Date: June 23, 2005

Major Rating Factors:
Exceptional performance is the major factor driving the A (Excellent) TheStreet.com Investment Rating for *PowerShares Dynamic Software. The fund currently has a performance rating of A- (Excellent) based on an annualized return of 15.14% over the last three years and a total return of 7.85% year to date 2015. Factored into the performance evaluation is an expense ratio of 0.63% (very low).

The fund's risk rating is currently B- (Good). It carries a beta of 1.02, meaning that its performance tracks fairly well with that of the overall stock market. Volatility, as measured by both the semi-deviation and a drawdown factor, is considered low. As of December 31, 2015, *PowerShares Dynamic Software traded at a price exactly equal to its net asset value, which is worse than its one-year historical average discount of .03%.

Peter Hubbard has been running the fund for 9 years and currently receives a manager quality ranking of 72 (0=worst, 99=best). If you desire only a moderate level of risk and strong performance, then this fund is an excellent option.

Data Date	Investment Rating	Net Assets ($Mil)	Price	Performance Rating/Pts	Total Return Y-T-D	Risk Rating/Pts
12-15	A	47.70	42.27	A- / 9.0	7.85%	B- / 7.6
2014	B	47.70	39.95	B+ / 8.5	10.84%	C+ / 6.7
2013	B-	57.80	36.12	B / 7.9	29.96%	B- / 7.2
2012	C-	44.80	27.14	C / 4.9	21.13%	C+ / 6.8
2011	C+	50.20	23.45	C+ / 5.9	-7.60%	B- / 7.4
2010	A-	66.00	24.96	B / 7.9	20.06%	C+ / 6.4

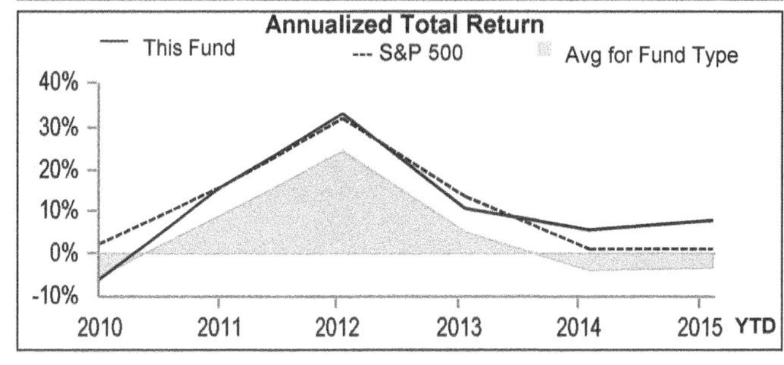

* Denotes ETF Fund

*PowerShares Emg Mkts Infrastruct (PXR) D Weak

Fund Family: Invesco Powershares Capital Mgmt LL
Fund Type: Emerging Market
Inception Date: October 15, 2008

Major Rating Factors:
Disappointing performance is the major factor driving the D (Weak) TheStreet.com Investment Rating for *PowerShares Emg Mkts Infrastruct. The fund currently has a performance rating of D- (Weak) based on an annualized return of -13.39% over the last three years and a total return of -22.40% year to date 2015. Factored into the performance evaluation is an expense ratio of 0.76% (very low).

The fund's risk rating is currently C+ (Fair). It carries a beta of 0.94, meaning that its performance tracks fairly well with that of the overall stock market. Volatility, as measured by both the semi-deviation and a drawdown factor, is considered low. As of December 31, 2015, *PowerShares Emg Mkts Infrastruct traded at a discount of .73% below its net asset value, which is better than its one-year historical average discount of .45%.

Peter Hubbard has been running the fund for 8 years and currently receives a manager quality ranking of 22 (0=worst, 99=best). This fund offers only a moderate level of risk but investors looking for strong performance are still waiting.

Data Date	Investment Rating	Net Assets ($Mil)	Price	Performance Rating/Pts	Total Return Y-T-D	Risk Rating/Pts
12-15	D	38.20	27.35	D- / 1.2	-22.40%	C+ / 6.8
2014	C-	38.20	35.96	D+ / 2.7	-1.41%	B- / 7.5
2013	D-	59.10	38.14	D- / 1.1	-14.76%	C+ / 6.2
2012	D	101.10	43.21	D+ / 2.5	15.10%	C+ / 6.2
2011	C-	112.20	37.13	C- / 4.1	-29.12%	C+ / 6.4
2010	A+	192.00	53.62	A+ / 9.6	27.00%	B- / 7.6

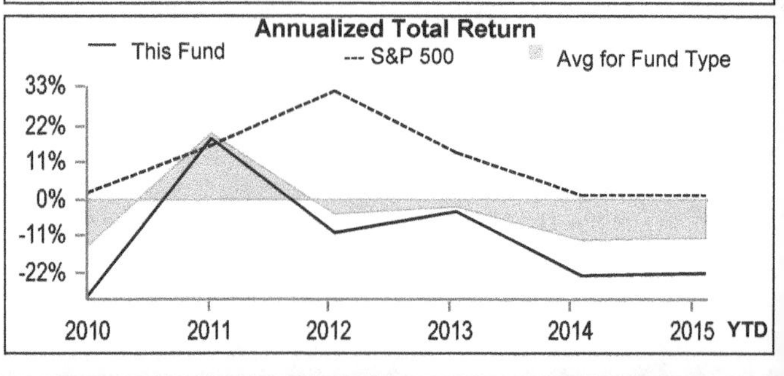

*PowerShares Emrg Mkt Sovereign D (PCY) C- Fair

Fund Family: Invesco Powershares Capital Mgmt LL
Fund Type: Emerging Market
Inception Date: October 11, 2007

Major Rating Factors: Middle of the road best describes *PowerShares Emrg Mkt Sovereign D whose TheStreet.com Investment Rating is currently a C- (Fair). The fund currently has a performance rating of C (Fair) based on an annualized return of -0.02% over the last three years and a total return of 2.67% year to date 2015. Factored into the performance evaluation is an expense ratio of 0.50% (very low).

The fund's risk rating is currently C+ (Fair). It carries a beta of 0.80, meaning the fund's expected move will be 8.0% for every 10% move in the market. Volatility, as measured by both the semi-deviation and a drawdown factor, is considered low. As of December 31, 2015, *PowerShares Emrg Mkt Sovereign D traded at a price exactly equal to its net asset value, which is worse than its one-year historical average discount of .09%.

Peter Hubbard has been running the fund for 9 years and currently receives a manager quality ranking of 86 (0=worst, 99=best). If you desire an average level of risk, then this fund may be an option.

Data Date	Investment Rating	Net Assets ($Mil)	Price	Performance Rating/Pts	Total Return Y-T-D	Risk Rating/Pts
12-15	C-	2,328.80	27.31	C / 4.5	2.67%	C+ / 6.7
2014	C-	2,328.80	28.16	C / 4.4	9.12%	B- / 7.1
2013	C-	1,851.70	27.00	C- / 3.8	-10.43%	B- / 7.9
2012	B-	3,032.70	31.45	C+ / 5.8	21.90%	B / 8.9
2011	C+	1,405.50	27.36	C / 5.2	7.33%	B / 8.8
2010	C+	893.80	26.67	C+ / 6.4	11.40%	C+ / 6.2

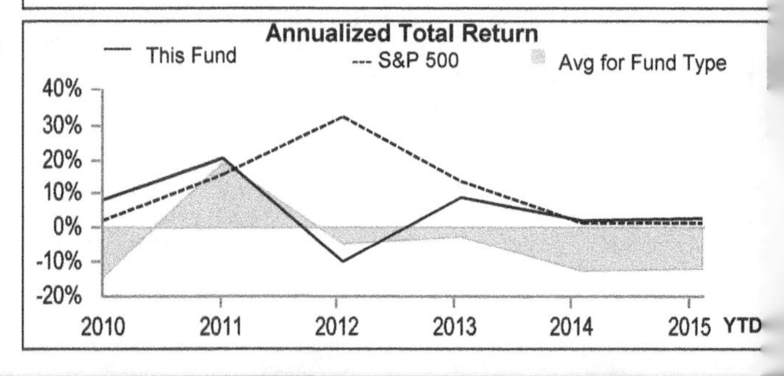

*PowerShares Financial Preferred (PGF) B Good

Fund Family: Invesco Powershares Capital Mgmt LL
Fund Type: Financial Services
Inception Date: December 1, 2006

Major Rating Factors: Strong performance is the major factor driving the B (Good) TheStreet.com Investment Rating for *PowerShares Financial Preferred. The fund currently has a performance rating of B- (Good) based on an annualized return of 6.85% over the last three years and a total return of 8.51% year to date 2015. Factored into the performance evaluation is an expense ratio of 0.63% (very low).

The fund's risk rating is currently B- (Good). It carries a beta of 0.05, meaning the fund's expected move will be 0.5% for every 10% move in the market. Volatility, as measured by both the semi-deviation and a drawdown factor, is considered low. As of December 31, 2015, *PowerShares Financial Preferred traded at a premium of .05% above its net asset value.

Jeffrey W. Kernagis has been running the fund for 9 years and currently receives a manager quality ranking of 91 (0=worst, 99=best). If you desire only a moderate level of risk and strong performance, then this fund is an excellent option.

Data Date	Investment Rating	Net Assets ($Mil)	Price	Performance Rating/Pts	Total Return Y-T-D	Risk Rating/Pts
12-15	B	1,395.30	18.83	B- / 7.5	8.51%	B- / 7.7
2014	B	1,395.30	18.26	C+ / 5.8	13.18%	B+ / 9.2
2013	C	1,411.50	16.94	C / 4.4	-1.27%	B / 8.8
2012	C	1,720.40	18.28	C / 4.4	16.96%	B / 8.8
2011	D+	1,423.20	16.12	C / 4.6	1.94%	C+ / 5.6
2010	C-	1,735.70	17.61	C+ / 5.6	16.71%	C- / 3.4

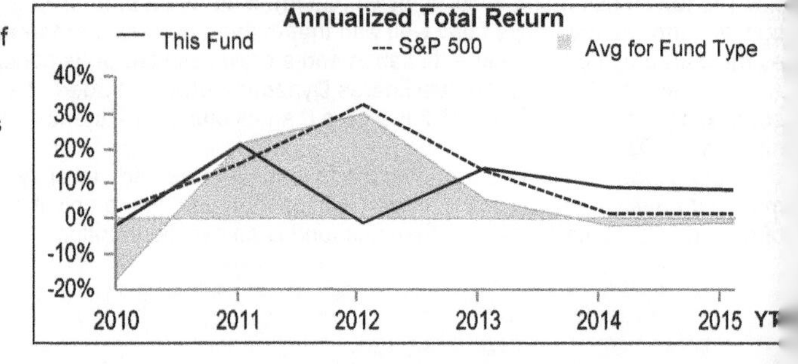

*PowerShares FTSE RAFI Asia Pac E (PAF) D+ Weak

Fund Family: Invesco Powershares Capital Mgmt LL
Fund Type: Foreign
Inception Date: June 25, 2007

Major Rating Factors:
Disappointing performance is the major factor driving the D+ (Weak) TheStreet.com Investment Rating for *PowerShares FTSE RAFI Asia Pac E. The fund currently has a performance rating of D+ (Weak) based on an annualized return of -5.86% over the last three years and a total return of -11.08% year to date 2015. Factored into the performance evaluation is an expense ratio of 0.49% (very low).

The fund's risk rating is currently C+ (Fair). It carries a beta of 1.03, meaning that its performance tracks fairly well with that of the overall stock market. Volatility, as measured by both the semi-deviation and a drawdown factor, is considered low. As of December 31, 2015, *PowerShares FTSE RAFI Asia Pac E traded at a discount of .46% below its net asset value, which is better than its one-year historical average discount of .25%.

Peter Hubbard currently receives a manager quality ranking of 16 (0=worst, 99=best). This fund offers only a moderate level of risk but investors looking for strong performance are still waiting.

Data Date	Investment Rating	Net Assets ($Mil)	Price	Performance Rating/Pts	Total Return Y-T-D	Risk Rating/Pts
12-15	D+	43.60	43.07	D+ / 2.5	-11.08%	C+ / 6.6
2014	C-	43.60	50.38	C- / 3.6	-4.44%	B- / 7.5
2013	D+	50.60	56.17	C- / 3.8	-1.20%	C+ / 6.7
2012	C+	65.10	57.17	C+ / 6.7	24.02%	C+ / 6.7
2011	C+	53.70	46.53	C+ / 6.2	-12.26%	B- / 7.0
2010	C+	49.50	55.67	B- / 7.2	23.18%	C / 4.6

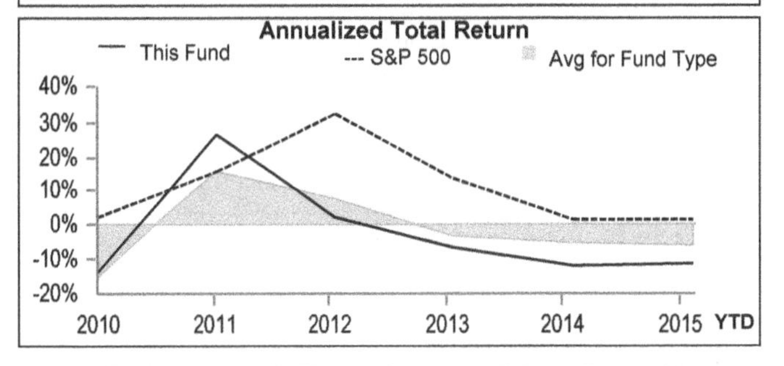

*PowerShares FTSE RAFI DM exUS Sm (PDN) C+ Fair

Fund Family: Invesco Powershares Capital Mgmt LL
Fund Type: Foreign
Inception Date: September 27, 2007

Major Rating Factors: Middle of the road best describes *PowerShares FTSE RAFI DM exUS Sm whose TheStreet.com Investment Rating is currently a C+ (Fair). The fund currently has a performance rating of C+ (Fair) based on an annualized return of 4.89% over the last three years and a total return of 2.02% year to date 2015. Factored into the performance evaluation is an expense ratio of 0.49% (very low).

The fund's risk rating is currently B (Good). It carries a beta of 0.81, meaning the fund's expected move will be 8.1% for every 10% move in the market. Volatility, as measured by both the semi-deviation and a drawdown factor, is considered low. As of December 31, 2015, *PowerShares FTSE RAFI DM exUS Sm traded at a discount of .73% below its net asset value, which is better than its one-year historical average premium of .53%.

Peter Hubbard has been running the fund for 9 years and currently receives a manager quality ranking of 77 (0=worst, 99=best). If you desire an average level of risk, then this fund may be an option.

Data Date	Investment Rating	Net Assets ($Mil)	Price	Performance Rating/Pts	Total Return Y-T-D	Risk Rating/Pts
12-15	C+	108.70	25.92	C+ / 5.9	2.02%	B / 8.1
2014	C-	108.70	26.00	C / 4.9	-3.84%	C+ / 6.5
2013	C+	104.30	27.91	C+ / 6.4	17.99%	B- / 7.6
2012	D+	62.70	23.50	C- / 3.8	19.68%	C+ / 6.6
2011	C-	60.30	20.56	C / 4.6	-13.69%	C+ / 6.6
2010	C+	70.20	24.49	C+ / 6.9	20.35%	C / 5.3

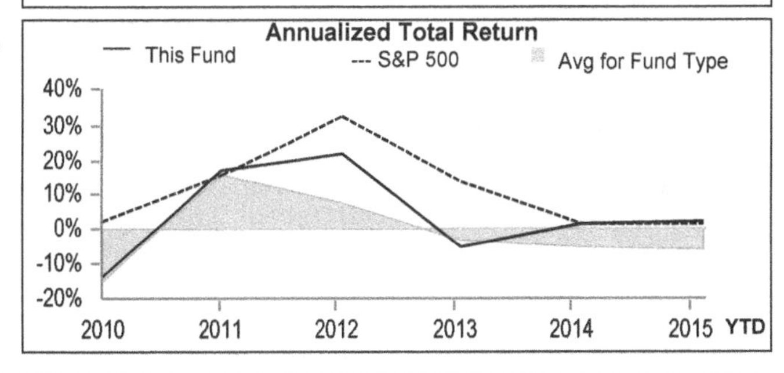

*PowerShares FTSE RAFI Dvlp Mkt e (PXF) C Fair

Fund Family: Invesco Powershares Capital Mgmt LL
Fund Type: Foreign
Inception Date: June 25, 2007

Major Rating Factors: Middle of the road best describes *PowerShares FTSE RAFI Dvlp Mkt e whose TheStreet.com Investment Rating is currently a C (Fair). The fund currently has a performance rating of C (Fair) based on an annualized return of 2.64% over the last three years and a total return of -5.36% year to date 2015. Factored into the performance evaluation is an expense ratio of 0.45% (very low).

The fund's risk rating is currently B (Good). It carries a beta of 1.04, meaning that its performance tracks fairly well with that of the overall stock market. Volatility, as measured by both the semi-deviation and a drawdown factor, is considered low. As of December 31, 2015, *PowerShares FTSE RAFI Dvlp Mkt e traded at a discount of .82% below its net asset value, which is better than its one-year historical average premium of .04%.

Peter Hubbard has been running the fund for 9 years and currently receives a manager quality ranking of 48 (0=worst, 99=best). If you desire an average level of risk, then this fund may be an option.

Data Date	Investment Rating	Net Assets ($Mil)	Price	Performance Rating/Pts	Total Return Y-T-D	Risk Rating/Pts
12-15	C	831.30	36.20	C / 4.7	-5.36%	B / 8.0
2014	C-	831.30	39.50	C / 4.8	-5.35%	C+ / 6.8
2013	C+	711.10	43.97	C+ / 6.7	21.12%	B- / 7.3
2012	D+	301.20	36.45	D+ / 2.8	20.24%	B- / 7.0
2011	D+	229.70	32.15	D+ / 2.5	-16.32%	B- / 7.2
2010	D	214.60	39.41	D+ / 2.5	8.95%	C / 5.4

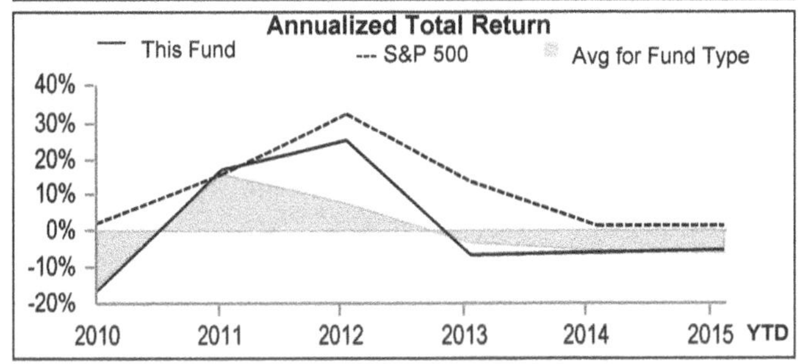

*PowerShares FTSE RAFI Emg Mkts (PXH) D Weak

Fund Family: Invesco Powershares Capital Mgmt LL
Fund Type: Emerging Market
Inception Date: September 27, 2007

Major Rating Factors:
Disappointing performance is the major factor driving the D (Weak) TheStreet.com Investment Rating for *PowerShares FTSE RAFI Emg Mkts. The fund currently has a performance rating of D- (Weak) based on an annualized return of -12.80% over the last three years and a total return of -21.85% year to date 2015. Factored into the performance evaluation is an expense ratio of 0.49% (very low).

The fund's risk rating is currently C+ (Fair). It carries a beta of 1.25, meaning it is expected to move 12.5% for every 10% move in the market. Volatility, as measured by both the semi-deviation and a drawdown factor, is considered low. As of December 31, 2015, *PowerShares FTSE RAFI Emg Mkts traded at a discount of .85% below its net asset value, which is better than its one-year historical average discount of .14%.

Peter Hubbard has been running the fund for 9 years and currently receives a manager quality ranking of 31 (0=worst, 99=best). This fund offers only a moderate level of risk but investors looking for strong performance are still waiting.

Data Date	Investment Rating	Net Assets ($Mil)	Price	Performance Rating/Pts	Total Return Y-T-D	Risk Rating/Pts
12-15	D	382.10	13.94	D- / 1.3	-21.85%	C+ / 5.9
2014	D	382.10	18.63	D+ / 2.3	-2.96%	C / 5.3
2013	D	362.20	20.49	D- / 1.5	-11.51%	C+ / 6.6
2012	D	384.30	22.82	D+ / 2.3	10.98%	C+ / 6.7
2011	C-	327.50	20.23	C / 4.4	-18.35%	B- / 7.0
2010	C	533.90	25.78	C+ / 5.9	14.23%	C / 4.6

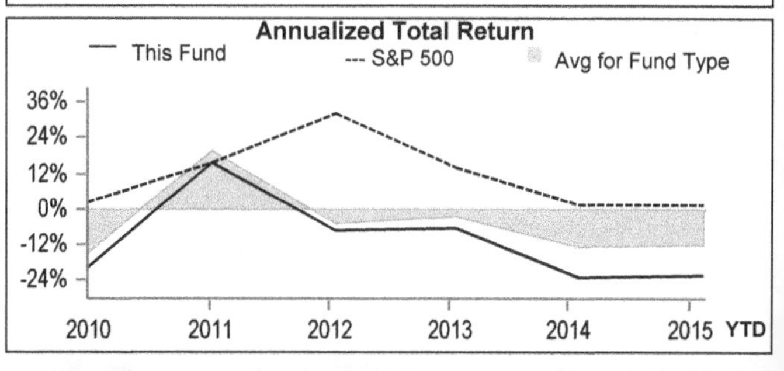

*PowerShares FTSE RAFI US 1000 (PRF) A- Excellent

Fund Family: Invesco Powershares Capital Mgmt LL
Fund Type: Income
Inception Date: December 19, 2005

Major Rating Factors:
Strong performance is the major factor driving the A- (Excellent) TheStreet.com Investment Rating for *PowerShares FTSE RAFI US 1000. The fund currently has a performance rating of B (Good) based on an annualized return of 12.77% over the last three years and a total return of -2.81% year to date 2015. Factored into the performance evaluation is an expense ratio of 0.39% (very low).

The fund's risk rating is currently B (Good). It carries a beta of 1.01, meaning that its performance tracks fairly well with that of the overall stock market. Volatility, as measured by both the semi-deviation and a drawdown factor, is considered low. As of December 31, 2015, *PowerShares FTSE RAFI US 1000 traded at a discount of .01% below its net asset value, which is worse than its one-year historical average discount of .03%.

Peter Hubbard has been running the fund for 9 years and currently receives a manager quality ranking of 58 (0=worst, 99=best). If you desire only a moderate level of risk and strong performance, then this fund is an excellent option.

Data Date	Investment Rating	Net Assets ($Mil)	Price	Performance Rating/Pts	Total Return Y-T-D	Risk Rating/Pts
12-15	A-	3,816.70	86.83	B / 8.2	-2.81%	B / 8.0
2014	B+	3,816.70	91.43	B+ / 8.5	13.15%	B- / 7.4
2013	A-	2,810.20	82.94	B+ / 8.4	30.51%	B / 8.3
2012	C+	1,479.00	62.43	C+ / 5.8	17.73%	B / 8.1
2011	B-	1,164.80	54.58	C+ / 6.5	-0.17%	B- / 7.9
2010	C+	927.40	55.95	C+ / 6.1	20.41%	C+ / 5.8

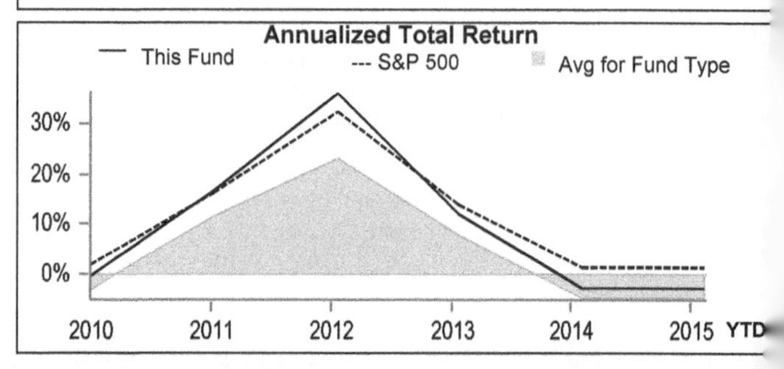

*PowerShares FTSE RAFI US 1500 Sm (PRFZ) B- Good

Fund Family: Invesco Powershares Capital Mgmt LL
Fund Type: Income
Inception Date: September 20, 2006

Major Rating Factors: Strong performance is the major factor driving the B- (Good) TheStreet.com Investment Rating for *PowerShares FTSE RAFI US 1500 Sm. The fund currently has a performance rating of B- (Good) based on an annualized return of 10.50% over the last three years and a total return of -5.02% year to date 2015. Factored into the performance evaluation is an expense ratio of 0.39% (very low).

The fund's risk rating is currently B- (Good). It carries a beta of 1.05, meaning that its performance tracks fairly well with that of the overall stock market. Volatility, as measured by both the semi-deviation and a drawdown factor, is considered low. As of December 31, 2015, *PowerShares FTSE RAFI US 1500 Sm traded at a premium of .05% above its net asset value, which is worse than its one-year historical average discount of .02%.

Peter Hubbard has been running the fund for 9 years and currently receives a manager quality ranking of 38 (0=worst, 99=best). If you desire only a moderate level of risk and strong performance, then this fund is an excellent option.

Data Date	Investment Rating	Net Assets ($Mil)	Price	Performance Rating/Pts	Total Return Y-T-D	Risk Rating/Pts
12-15	B-	958.90	93.89	B- / 7.2	-5.02%	B- / 7.1
2014	B	958.90	100.74	B / 7.8	5.13%	B- / 7.0
2013	B+	893.60	97.73	B+ / 8.7	35.85%	B- / 7.6
2012	C+	487.20	69.54	C+ / 6.5	18.31%	B- / 7.3
2011	B-	344.40	60.00	B- / 7.4	-5.32%	B- / 7.2
2010	B+	389.60	64.47	B+ / 8.3	28.81%	C / 5.4

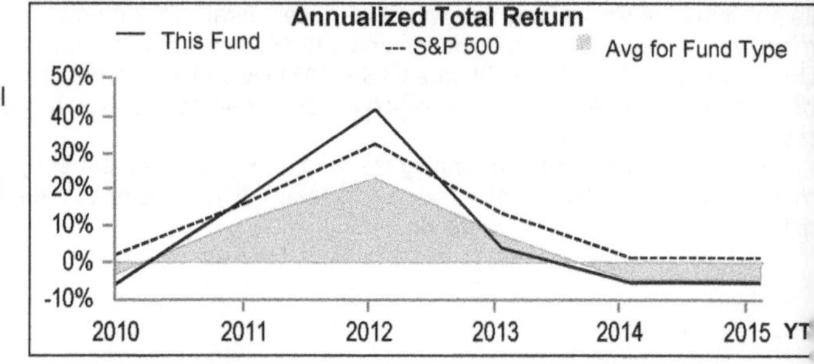

* Denotes ETF Fund

*PowerShares Fundamental High Yie (PHB) C+ Fair

Fund Family: Invesco Powershares Capital Mgmt LL
Fund Type: Corporate - High Yield
Inception Date: November 13, 2007

Major Rating Factors: Middle of the road best describes *PowerShares Fundamental High Yie whose TheStreet.com Investment Rating is currently a C+ (Fair). The fund currently has a performance rating of C- (Fair) based on an annualized return of 0.82% over the last three years and a total return of -2.99% year to date 2015. Factored into the performance evaluation is an expense ratio of 0.50% (very low).

The fund's risk rating is currently B (Good). It carries a beta of 0.90, meaning that its performance tracks fairly well with that of the overall stock market. Volatility, as measured by both the semi-deviation and a drawdown factor, is considered low. As of December 31, 2015, *PowerShares Fundamental High Yie traded at a discount of .11% below its net asset value, which is better than its one-year historical average discount of .04%.

Peter Hubbard has been running the fund for 9 years and currently receives a manager quality ranking of 65 (0=worst, 99=best). If you desire an average level of risk, then this fund may be an option.

Data Date	Investment Rating	Net Assets ($Mil)	Price	Performance Rating/Pts	Total Return Y-T-D	Risk Rating/Pts
12-15	C+	610.30	17.44	C- / 4.2	-2.99%	B / 8.9
2014	C-	610.30	18.80	C- / 4.1	2.07%	B- / 7.5
2013	B-	643.70	19.19	C / 5.3	3.56%	B+ / 9.4
2012	C-	845.30	19.25	C- / 3.7	11.36%	B / 8.1
2011	C	637.10	18.47	C / 4.7	5.75%	B- / 7.7
2010	D	407.30	18.19	D+ / 2.5	9.83%	C / 5.2

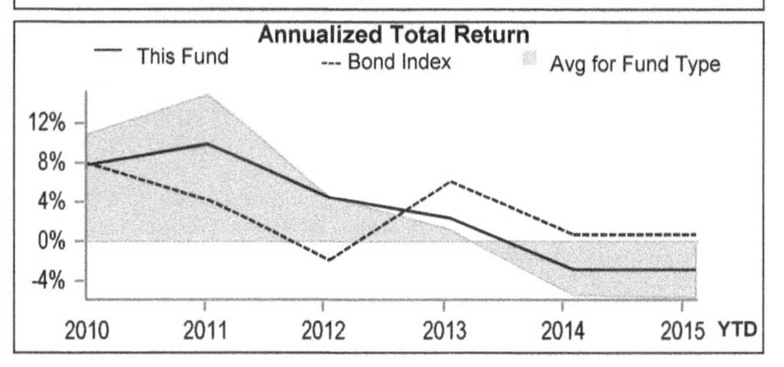

*PowerShares Fundmntl Em Loc Dbt (PFEM) D Weak

Fund Family: Invesco Powershares Capital Mgmt LL
Fund Type: Emerging Market
Inception Date: May 9, 2013

Major Rating Factors:
Disappointing performance is the major factor driving the D (Weak) TheStreet.com Investment Rating for *PowerShares Fundmntl Em Loc Dbt. The fund currently has a performance rating of D (Weak) based on an annualized return of 0.00% over the last three years and a total return of -13.66% year to date 2015. Factored into the performance evaluation is an expense ratio of 0.50% (very low).

The fund's risk rating is currently C+ (Fair). It carries a beta of 0.00, meaning the fund's expected move will be 0.0% for every 10% move in the market. Volatility, as measured by both the semi-deviation and a drawdown factor, is considered low. As of December 31, 2015, *PowerShares Fundmntl Em Loc Dbt traded at a premium of 1.10% above its net asset value, which is worse than its one-year historical average discount of .12%.

Philip P. Fang has been running the fund for 3 years and currently receives a manager quality ranking of 14 (0=worst, 99=best). This fund offers only a moderate level of risk but investors looking for strong performance are still waiting.

Data Date	Investment Rating	Net Assets ($Mil)	Price	Performance Rating/Pts	Total Return Y-T-D	Risk Rating/Pts
12-15	D	5.20	16.54	D / 1.6	-13.66%	C+ / 5.6
2014	D	5.20	20.19	D / 1.9	-1.80%	C+ / 6.9

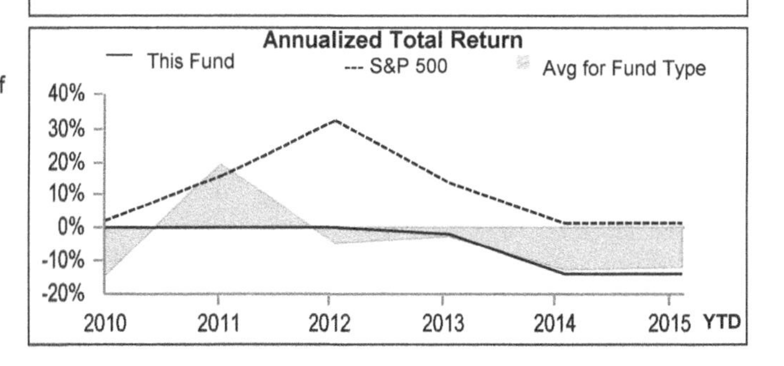

*PowerShares Fundmntl Inv Gr Corp (PFIG) C+ Fair

Fund Family: Invesco Powershares Capital Mgmt LL
Fund Type: Corporate - Investment Grade
Inception Date: September 15, 2011

Major Rating Factors: Middle of the road best describes *PowerShares Fundmntl Inv Gr Corp whose TheStreet.com Investment Rating is currently a C+ (Fair). The fund currently has a performance rating of C (Fair) based on an annualized return of 1.53% over the last three years and a total return of 0.91% year to date 2015. Factored into the performance evaluation is an expense ratio of 0.22% (very low).

The fund's risk rating is currently B- (Good). It carries a beta of 0.76, meaning the fund's expected move will be 7.6% for every 10% move in the market. Volatility, as measured by both the semi-deviation and a drawdown factor, is considered low. As of December 31, 2015, *PowerShares Fundmntl Inv Gr Corp traded at a premium of .32% above its net asset value, which is worse than its one-year historical average premium of .11%.

Peter Hubbard has been running the fund for 5 years and currently receives a manager quality ranking of 71 (0=worst, 99=best). If you desire an average level of risk, then this fund may be an option.

Data Date	Investment Rating	Net Assets ($Mil)	Price	Performance Rating/Pts	Total Return Y-T-D	Risk Rating/Pts
12-15	C+	27.90	25.02	C / 5.1	0.91%	B- / 7.8
2014	C	27.90	25.37	C- / 3.5	4.39%	B+ / 9.5
2013	C	34.80	24.84	D+ / 2.7	-0.88%	B+ / 9.6
2012	C	33.40	25.69	D / 2.2	5.04%	B+ / 9.9

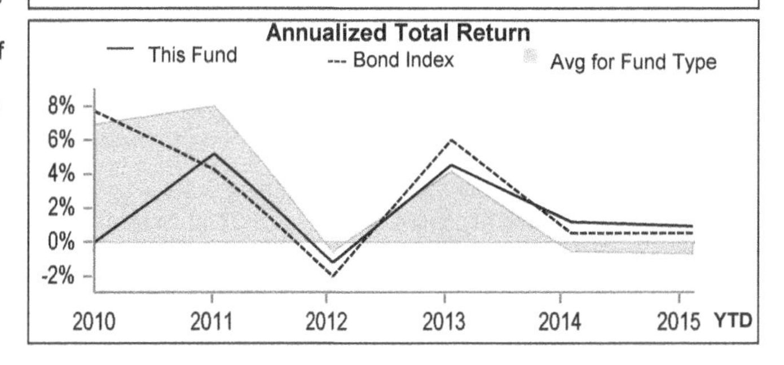

*PowerShares Glb Gold & Precious (PSAU) E+ Very Weak

Fund Family: Invesco Powershares Capital Mgmt LL
Fund Type: Precious Metals
Inception Date: September 16, 2008

Data Date	Investment Rating	Net Assets ($Mil)	Price	Performance Rating/Pts	Total Return Y-T-D	Risk Rating/Pts
12-15	E+	21.90	11.75	E / 0.4	-27.45%	C- / 4.0
2014	E+	21.90	16.00	E / 0.5	-15.73%	C- / 4.0
2013	E+	21.10	18.50	E / 0.4	-47.39%	C- / 4.1
2012	E+	36.70	37.08	D- / 1.1	-12.62%	C / 4.7
2011	C-	47.80	39.81	C+ / 5.7	-10.86%	C / 5.4
2010	A-	67.50	50.01	A+ / 9.6	37.48%	C / 5.3

Major Rating Factors:
Very poor performance is the major factor driving the E+ (Very Weak) TheStreet.com Investment Rating for *PowerShares Glb Gold & Precious. The fund currently has a performance rating of E (Very Weak) based on an annualized return of -31.07% over the last three years and a total return of -27.45% year to date 2015. Factored into the performance evaluation is an expense ratio of 0.75% (very low).

The fund's risk rating is currently C- (Fair). It carries a beta of 1.74, meaning it is expected to move 17.4% for every 10% move in the market. Volatility, as measured by both the semi-deviation and a drawdown factor, is considered average. As of December 31, 2015, *PowerShares Glb Gold & Precious traded at a discount of .84% below its net asset value, which is better than its one-year historical average discount of .12%.

Peter Hubbard has been running the fund for 8 years and currently receives a manager quality ranking of 15 (0=worst, 99=best). This fund offers an average level of risk but investors looking for strong performance will be frustrated.

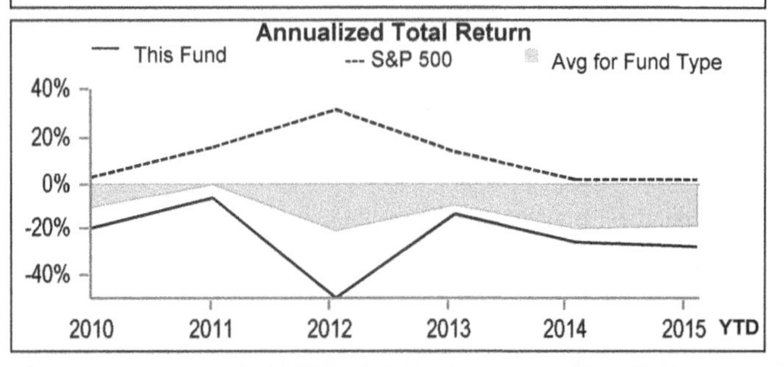

*PowerShares Glbl Sh Tm Hi Yld (PGHY) C+ Fair

Fund Family: Invesco Powershares Capital Mgmt LL
Fund Type: Global
Inception Date: June 20, 2013

Data Date	Investment Rating	Net Assets ($Mil)	Price	Performance Rating/Pts	Total Return Y-T-D	Risk Rating/Pts
12-15	C+	37.40	22.92	C / 5.5	3.41%	B- / 7.5
2014	C-	37.40	23.30	D / 2.0	-2.63%	B / 8.9

Major Rating Factors: Middle of the road best describes *PowerShares Glbl Sh Tm Hi Yld whose TheStreet.com Investment Rating is currently a C+ (Fair). The fund currently has a performance rating of C (Fair) based on an annualized return of 0.00% over the last three years and a total return of 3.41% year to date 2015. Factored into the performance evaluation is an expense ratio of 0.35% (very low).

The fund's risk rating is currently B- (Good). It carries a beta of 0.00, meaning the fund's expected move will be 0.0% for every 10% move in the market. Volatility, as measured by both the semi-deviation and a drawdown factor, is considered low. As of December 31, 2015, *PowerShares Glbl Sh Tm Hi Yld traded at a premium of .22% above its net asset value, which is worse than its one-year historical average discount of .22%.

Philip P. Fang has been running the fund for 3 years and currently receives a manager quality ranking of 86 (0=worst, 99=best). If you desire an average level of risk, then this fund may be an option.

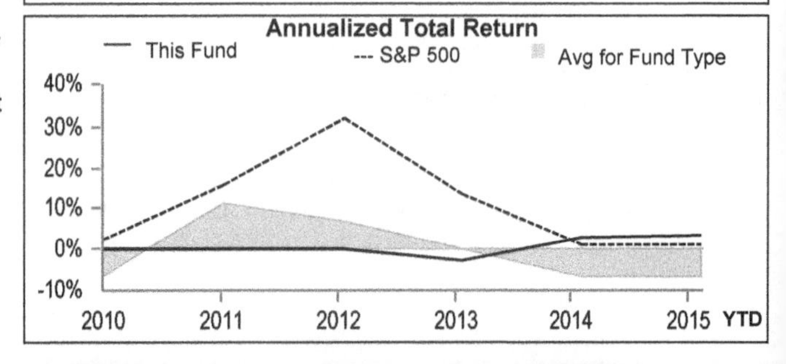

*PowerShares Global Agriculture P (PAGG) D Weak

Fund Family: Invesco Powershares Capital Mgmt LL
Fund Type: Global
Inception Date: September 16, 2008

Data Date	Investment Rating	Net Assets ($Mil)	Price	Performance Rating/Pts	Total Return Y-T-D	Risk Rating/Pts
12-15	D	59.90	23.18	D / 2.0	-17.95%	C+ / 5.9
2014	C-	59.90	29.24	C- / 3.5	0.96%	B / 8.0
2013	D+	88.70	29.91	D / 2.2	-4.03%	B- / 7.2
2012	D+	109.40	30.73	C- / 3.5	13.55%	B- / 7.0
2011	C-	106.40	26.88	C / 4.4	-14.73%	C+ / 6.9
2010	A	68.50	32.03	A+ / 9.7	21.91%	C+ / 6.2

Major Rating Factors:
Disappointing performance is the major factor driving the D (Weak) TheStreet.com Investment Rating for *PowerShares Global Agriculture P. The fund currently has a performance rating of D (Weak) based on an annualized return of -7.51% over the last three years and a total return of -17.95% year to date 2015. Factored into the performance evaluation is an expense ratio of 0.75% (very low).

The fund's risk rating is currently C+ (Fair). It carries a beta of 0.80, meaning the fund's expected move will be 8.0% for every 10% move in the market. Volatility, as measured by both the semi-deviation and a drawdown factor, is considered low. As of December 31, 2015, *PowerShares Global Agriculture P traded at a premium of .35% above its net asset value, which is worse than its one-year historical average discount of .16%.

Peter Hubbard has been running the fund for 8 years and currently receives a manager quality ranking of 15 (0=worst, 99=best). This fund offers only a moderate level of risk but investors looking for strong performance are still waiting.

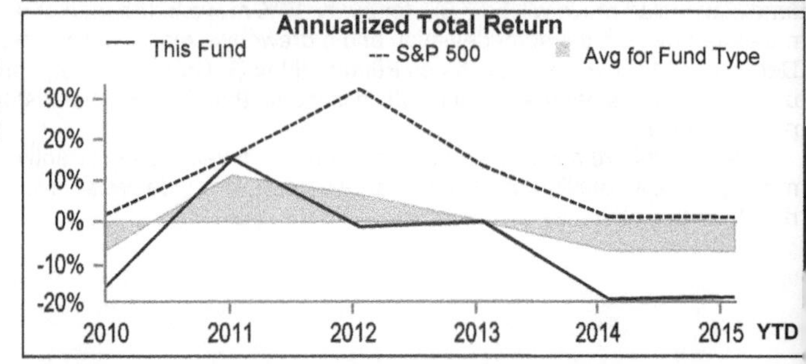

*PowerShares Global Clean Energy (PBD) B+ Good

Fund Family: Invesco Powershares Capital Mgmt LL
Fund Type: Energy/Natural Resources
Inception Date: June 13, 2007

Major Rating Factors: Strong performance is the major factor driving the B+ (Good) TheStreet.com Investment Rating for *PowerShares Global Clean Energy. The fund currently has a performance rating of B (Good) based on an annualized return of 12.59% over the last three years and a total return of -0.09% year to date 2015. Factored into the performance evaluation is an expense ratio of 0.76% (very low).

The fund's risk rating is currently B- (Good). It carries a beta of 0.64, meaning the fund's expected move will be 6.4% for every 10% move in the market. Volatility, as measured by both the semi-deviation and a drawdown factor, is considered low. As of December 31, 2015, *PowerShares Global Clean Energy traded at a discount of .35% below its net asset value.

Peter Hubbard has been running the fund for 9 years and currently receives a manager quality ranking of 98 (0=worst, 99=best). If you desire only a moderate level of risk and strong performance, then this fund is an excellent option.

Data Date	Investment Rating	Net Assets ($Mil)	Price	Performance Rating/Pts	Total Return Y-T-D	Risk Rating/Pts
12-15	B+	81.80	11.42	B / 8.2	-0.09%	B- / 7.1
2014	C	81.80	11.52	C / 5.2	-5.79%	B- / 7.1
2013	D+	86.80	12.07	C / 5.2	51.00%	C / 5.1
2012	E+	57.30	7.89	E+ / 0.6	-0.36%	C / 4.9
2011	D-	97.00	8.23	E+ / 0.9	-40.09%	C / 5.4
2010	E+	147.40	13.96	E / 0.5	-15.98%	C- / 4.0

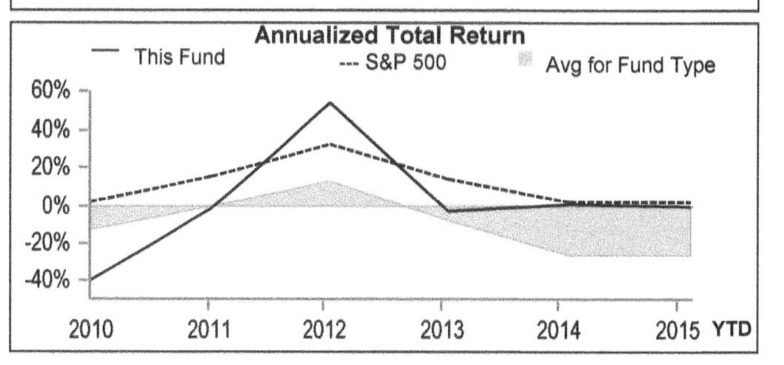

*PowerShares Global Listed Priv E (PSP) B+ Good

Fund Family: Invesco Powershares Capital Mgmt LL
Fund Type: Income
Inception Date: October 24, 2006

Major Rating Factors: Strong performance is the major factor driving the B+ (Good) TheStreet.com Investment Rating for *PowerShares Global Listed Priv E. The fund currently has a performance rating of B- (Good) based on an annualized return of 10.12% over the last three years and a total return of 1.67% year to date 2015. Factored into the performance evaluation is an expense ratio of 0.64% (very low).

The fund's risk rating is currently B (Good). It carries a beta of 1.03, meaning that its performance tracks fairly well with that of the overall stock market. Volatility, as measured by both the semi-deviation and a drawdown factor, is considered low. As of December 31, 2015, *PowerShares Global Listed Priv E traded at a discount of .09% below its net asset value, which is better than its one-year historical average discount of .06%.

Peter Hubbard has been running the fund for 9 years and currently receives a manager quality ranking of 36 (0=worst, 99=best). If you desire only a moderate level of risk and strong performance, then this fund is an excellent option.

Data Date	Investment Rating	Net Assets ($Mil)	Price	Performance Rating/Pts	Total Return Y-T-D	Risk Rating/Pts
12-15	B+	551.60	10.52	B- / 7.3	1.67%	B / 8.2
2014	B+	551.60	10.98	B- / 7.3	-3.89%	B / 8.4
2013	B-	494.50	12.10	B+ / 8.4	37.02%	C+ / 6.7
2012	C+	300.60	10.12	B- / 7.5	31.96%	C+ / 6.0
2011	D	240.60	7.99	D / 2.0	-20.54%	C+ / 6.4
2010	E+	309.90	10.75	D- / 1.3	30.23%	C- / 3.5

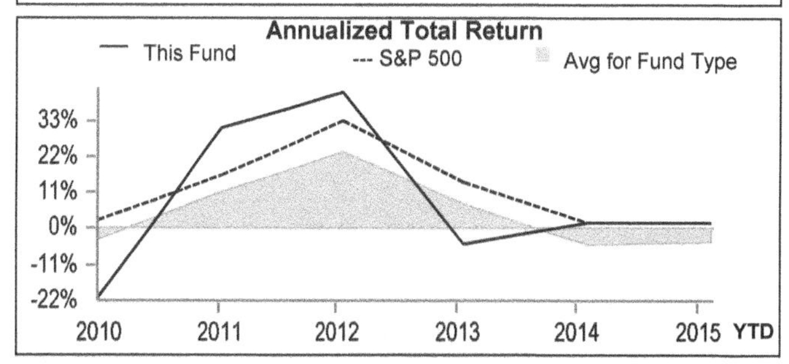

*PowerShares Global Water Portfol (PIO) C+ Fair

Fund Family: Invesco Powershares Capital Mgmt LL
Fund Type: Energy/Natural Resources
Inception Date: June 13, 2007

Major Rating Factors: Middle of the road best describes *PowerShares Global Water Portfol whose TheStreet.com Investment Rating is currently a C+ (Fair). The fund currently has a performance rating of C+ (Fair) based on an annualized return of 6.38% over the last three years and a total return of -7.15% year to date 2015. Factored into the performance evaluation is an expense ratio of 0.76% (very low).

The fund's risk rating is currently B- (Good). It carries a beta of 0.55, meaning the fund's expected move will be 5.5% for every 10% move in the market. Volatility, as measured by both the semi-deviation and a drawdown factor, is considered low. As of December 31, 2015, *PowerShares Global Water Portfol traded at a discount of .29% below its net asset value, which is better than its one-year historical average discount of .21%.

Peter Hubbard has been running the fund for 9 years and currently receives a manager quality ranking of 94 (0=worst, 99=best). If you desire an average level of risk, then this fund may be an option.

Data Date	Investment Rating	Net Assets ($Mil)	Price	Performance Rating/Pts	Total Return Y-T-D	Risk Rating/Pts
12-15	C+	280.90	20.93	C+ / 5.8	-7.15%	B- / 7.7
2014	B-	280.90	22.96	C+ / 6.6	1.50%	B / 8.1
2013	C+	246.70	23.10	B- / 7.2	28.14%	B- / 7.2
2012	D	196.90	18.01	D+ / 2.9	16.46%	C+ / 6.6
2011	D	234.10	15.59	D+ / 2.4	-19.45%	C / 5.5
2010	D	352.70	20.01	D+ / 2.5	11.80%	C / 4.3

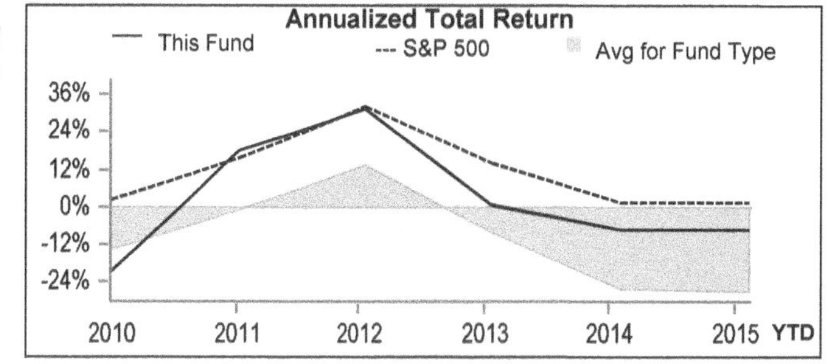

*PowerShares Golden Dragon China (PGJ) B+ Good

Fund Family: Invesco Powershares Capital Mgmt LL
Fund Type: Global
Inception Date: December 9, 2004

Data Date	Investment Rating	Net Assets ($Mil)	Price	Performance Rating/Pts	Total Return Y-T-D	Risk Rating/Pts
12-15	B+	290.10	32.90	A+ / 9.6	17.00%	C+ / 5.8
2014	C	290.10	27.85	C / 5.4	-6.76%	B- / 7.2
2013	C+	323.10	30.32	B / 8.2	54.57%	C+ / 5.9
2012	D-	196.90	19.16	D- / 1.1	-1.34%	C+ / 5.9
2011	D+	228.90	19.61	C- / 3.1	-25.46%	C+ / 6.3
2010	D-	450.30	26.64	D / 1.7	11.77%	C / 4.4

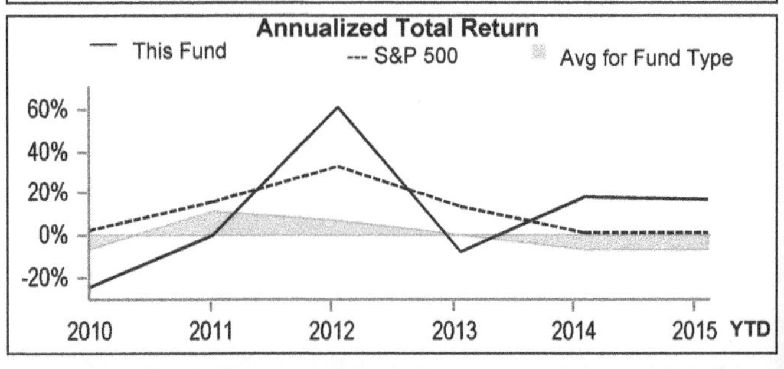

Major Rating Factors:
Exceptional performance is the major factor driving the B+ (Good) TheStreet.com Investment Rating for *PowerShares Golden Dragon China. The fund currently has a performance rating of A+ (Excellent) based on an annualized return of 19.56% over the last three years and a total return of 17.00% year to date 2015. Factored into the performance evaluation is an expense ratio of 0.70% (very low).

The fund's risk rating is currently C+ (Fair). It carries a beta of 1.19, meaning it is expected to move 11.9% for every 10% move in the market. Volatility, as measured by both the semi-deviation and a drawdown factor, is considered low. As of December 31, 2015, *PowerShares Golden Dragon China traded at a premium of .15% above its net asset value, which is worse than its one-year historical average discount of .14%.

Peter Hubbard has been running the fund for 9 years and currently receives a manager quality ranking of 97 (0=worst, 99=best). If you desire only a moderate level of risk and strong performance, then this fund is an excellent option.

*PowerShares High Yld Eq Div Ach (PEY) A Excellent

Fund Family: Invesco Powershares Capital Mgmt LL
Fund Type: Income
Inception Date: December 9, 2004

Data Date	Investment Rating	Net Assets ($Mil)	Price	Performance Rating/Pts	Total Return Y-T-D	Risk Rating/Pts
12-15	A	432.20	13.35	A- / 9.0	3.12%	B- / 7.8
2014	B+	432.20	13.50	B+ / 8.3	19.27%	B- / 7.7
2013	A	364.40	11.85	B / 7.7	24.44%	B+ / 9.2
2012	C+	276.40	9.41	C / 4.6	9.52%	B+ / 9.1
2011	C	357.50	9.25	C / 5.3	8.67%	C+ / 6.9
2010	D	182.60	8.86	D / 1.9	21.32%	C / 4.7

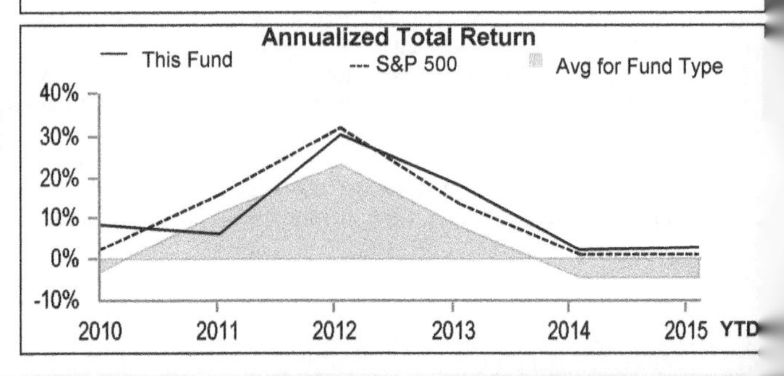

Major Rating Factors:
Exceptional performance is the major factor driving the A (Excellent) TheStreet.com Investment Rating for *PowerShares High Yld Eq Div Ach. The fund currently has a performance rating of A- (Excellent) based on an annualized return of 14.96% over the last three years and a total return of 3.12% year to date 2015. Factored into the performance evaluation is an expense ratio of 0.54% (very low).

The fund's risk rating is currently B- (Good). It carries a beta of 0.84, meaning the fund's expected move will be 8.4% for every 10% move in the market. Volatility, as measured by both the semi-deviation and a drawdown factor, is considered low. As of December 31, 2015, *PowerShares High Yld Eq Div Ach traded at a premium of .07% above its net asset value, which is worse than its one-year historical average discount of .01%.

Peter Hubbard has been running the fund for 9 years and currently receives a manager quality ranking of 85 (0=worst, 99=best). If you desire only a moderate level of risk and strong performance, then this fund is an excellent option.

*PowerShares India Portfolio (PIN) C- Fair

Fund Family: Invesco Powershares Capital Mgmt LL
Fund Type: Foreign
Inception Date: March 4, 2008

Data Date	Investment Rating	Net Assets ($Mil)	Price	Performance Rating/Pts	Total Return Y-T-D	Risk Rating/Pts
12-15	C-	547.20	19.52	C- / 4.2	-8.18%	B- / 7.0
2014	C	547.20	20.99	C / 5.4	23.56%	C+ / 6.7
2013	D-	364.40	17.62	D- / 1.2	-7.08%	C+ / 5.8
2012	D-	406.80	18.36	D- / 1.1	7.30%	C+ / 6.0
2011	D	286.00	16.30	D+ / 2.9	-30.14%	C+ / 6.4
2010	B-	566.00	25.42	B+ / 8.5	16.25%	C- / 4.2

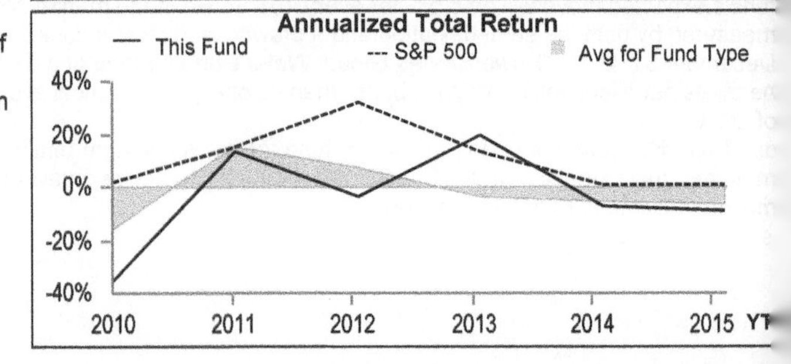

Major Rating Factors: Middle of the road best describes *PowerShares India Portfolio whose TheStreet.com Investment Rating is currently a C- (Fair). The fund currently has a performance rating of C- (Fair) based on an annualized return of 2.40% over the last three years and a total return of -8.18% year to date 2015. Factored into the performance evaluation is an expense ratio of 0.85% (very low).

The fund's risk rating is currently B- (Good). It carries a beta of 0.79, meaning the fund's expected move will be 7.9% for every 10% move in the market. Volatility, as measured by both the semi-deviation and a drawdown factor, is considered low. As of December 31, 2015, *PowerShares India Portfolio traded at a discount of 1.06% below its net asset value, which is better than its one-year historical average premium of .04%.

Peter Hubbard has been running the fund for 8 years and currently receives a manager quality ranking of 57 (0=worst, 99=best). If you desire an average level of risk, then this fund may be an option.

*PowerShares International Corp B (PICB) C- Fair

Fund Family: Invesco Powershares Capital Mgmt LL
Fund Type: Global
Inception Date: June 2, 2010

Major Rating Factors: Middle of the road best describes *PowerShares International Corp B whose TheStreet.com Investment Rating is currently a C- (Fair). The fund currently has a performance rating of C- (Fair) based on an annualized return of -2.40% over the last three years and a total return of -8.37% year to date 2015. Factored into the performance evaluation is an expense ratio of 0.50% (very low).

The fund's risk rating is currently C+ (Fair). It carries a beta of 0.93, meaning that its performance tracks fairly well with that of the overall stock market. Volatility, as measured by both the semi-deviation and a drawdown factor, is considered low. As of December 31, 2015, *PowerShares International Corp B traded at a premium of .24% above its net asset value, which is worse than its one-year historical average discount of .04%.

Peter Hubbard has been running the fund for 6 years and currently receives a manager quality ranking of 77 (0=worst, 99=best). If you desire an average level of risk, then this fund may be an option.

Data Date	Investment Rating	Net Assets ($Mil)	Price	Performance Rating/Pts	Total Return Y-T-D	Risk Rating/Pts
12-15	C-	244.90	25.23	C- / 3.2	-8.37%	C+ / 6.7
2014	C-	244.90	28.44	C- / 4.0	-0.20%	B- / 7.2
2013	C+	167.70	29.51	C / 5.3	2.62%	B / 8.8
2012	B+	133.10	29.61	B / 7.8	17.65%	B / 8.7
2011	C-	77.50	26.46	D / 1.9	3.18%	B / 8.7

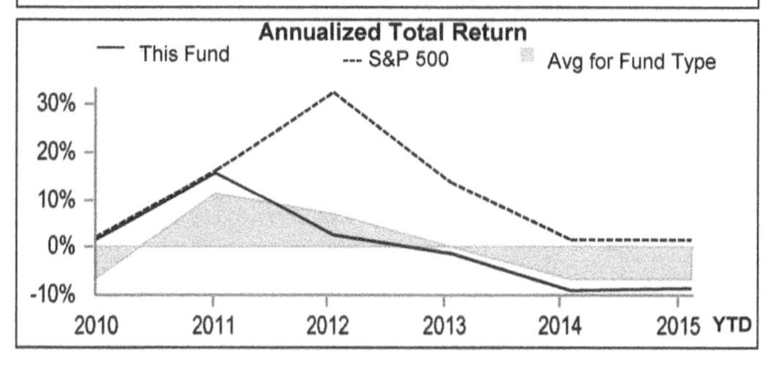

*PowerShares Intl BuyBack Achieve (IPKW) B- Good

Fund Family: Invesco Powershares Capital Mgmt LL
Fund Type: Foreign
Inception Date: February 27, 2014

Major Rating Factors: *PowerShares Intl BuyBack Achieve receives a TheStreet.com Investment Rating of B- (Good). The fund currently has a performance rating of C+ (Fair) based on an annualized return of 0.00% over the last three years and a total return of 7.30% year to date 2015. Factored into the performance evaluation is an expense ratio of 0.55% (very low).

The fund's risk rating is currently B (Good). It carries a beta of 0.00, meaning the fund's expected move will be 0.0% for every 10% move in the market. Volatility, as measured by both the semi-deviation and a drawdown factor, is considered low. As of December 31, 2015, *PowerShares Intl BuyBack Achieve traded at a discount of .46% below its net asset value, which is better than its one-year historical average premium of .24%.

Jonathan Nixon has been running the fund for 2 years and currently receives a manager quality ranking of 92 (0=worst, 99=best). If you desire an average level of risk, then this fund may be an option.

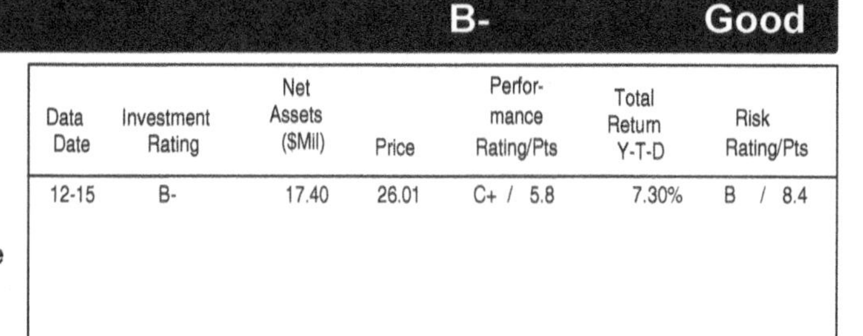

Data Date	Investment Rating	Net Assets ($Mil)	Price	Performance Rating/Pts	Total Return Y-T-D	Risk Rating/Pts
12-15	B-	17.40	26.01	C+ / 5.8	7.30%	B / 8.4

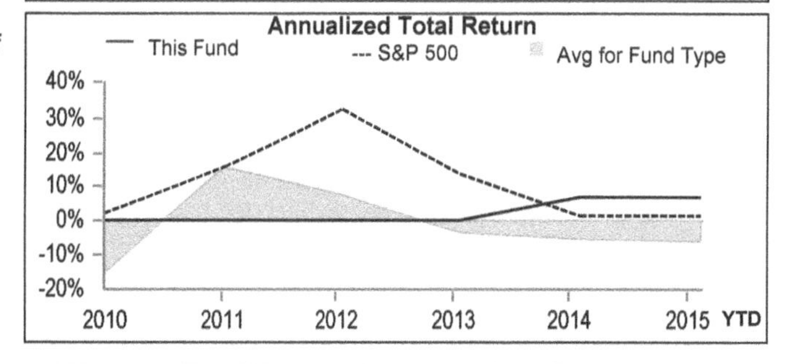

*PowerShares Intl Dividend Ach (PID) C- Fair

Fund Family: Invesco Powershares Capital Mgmt LL
Fund Type: Foreign
Inception Date: September 15, 2005

Major Rating Factors:
Disappointing performance is the major factor driving the C- (Fair) TheStreet.com Investment Rating for *PowerShares Intl Dividend Ach. The fund currently has a performance rating of D+ (Weak) based on an annualized return of -2.09% over the last three years and a total return of -18.95% year to date 2015. Factored into the performance evaluation is an expense ratio of 0.55% (very low).

The fund's risk rating is currently B- (Good). It carries a beta of 0.92, meaning that its performance tracks fairly well with that of the overall stock market. Volatility, as measured by both the semi-deviation and a drawdown factor, is considered low. As of December 31, 2015, *PowerShares Intl Dividend Ach traded at a discount of .29% below its net asset value, which is better than its one-year historical average discount of .09%.

Peter Hubbard has been running the fund for 9 years and currently receives a manager quality ranking of 25 (0=worst, 99=best). This fund offers only a moderate level of risk but investors looking for strong performance are still waiting.

Data Date	Investment Rating	Net Assets ($Mil)	Price	Performance Rating/Pts	Total Return Y-T-D	Risk Rating/Pts
12-15	C-	1,348.30	13.58	D+ / 2.6	-18.95%	B- / 7.3
2014	C-	1,348.30	17.51	C / 4.8	0.25%	B- / 7.0
2013	B-	1,086.90	18.42	C+ / 6.7	16.08%	B / 8.2
2012	C	738.10	15.83	C / 4.3	14.78%	B / 8.0
2011	C	585.20	14.57	C / 4.8	-1.36%	B / 8.0
2010	D	468.80	15.40	D+ / 2.4	15.04%	C / 5.1

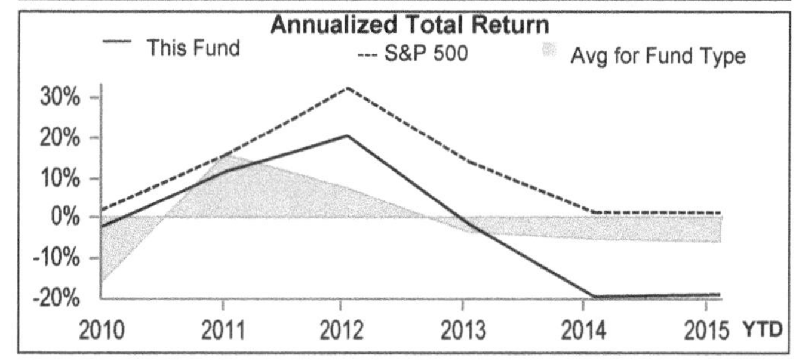

*PowerShares KBW Bank (KBWB) B Good

Fund Family: Invesco Powershares Capital Mgmt LL
Fund Type: Income
Inception Date: November 1, 2011

Data Date	Investment Rating	Net Assets ($Mil)	Price	Performance Rating/Pts	Total Return Y-T-D	Risk Rating/Pts
12-15	B	233.60	37.59	B+ / 8.4	0.34%	C+ / 6.8
2014	B+	233.60	38.21	A- / 9.1	9.86%	C+ / 6.8
2013	A+	156.30	35.52	A / 9.4	32.15%	B / 8.7
2012	A+	38.70	26.27	A / 9.4	24.09%	B / 8.6

Major Rating Factors: Strong performance is the major factor driving the B (Good) TheStreet.com Investment Rating for *PowerShares KBW Bank. The fund currently has a performance rating of B+ (Good) based on an annualized return of 12.86% over the last three years and a total return of 0.34% year to date 2015. Factored into the performance evaluation is an expense ratio of 0.35% (very low).

The fund's risk rating is currently C+ (Fair). It carries a beta of 0.99, meaning that its performance tracks fairly well with that of the overall stock market. Volatility, as measured by both the semi-deviation and a drawdown factor, is considered low. As of December 31, 2015, *PowerShares KBW Bank traded at a premium of .03% above its net asset value, which is worse than its one-year historical average discount of .01%.

Michael C. Jeanette has been running the fund for 5 years and currently receives a manager quality ranking of 65 (0=worst, 99=best). If you desire only a moderate level of risk and strong performance, then this fund is an excellent option.

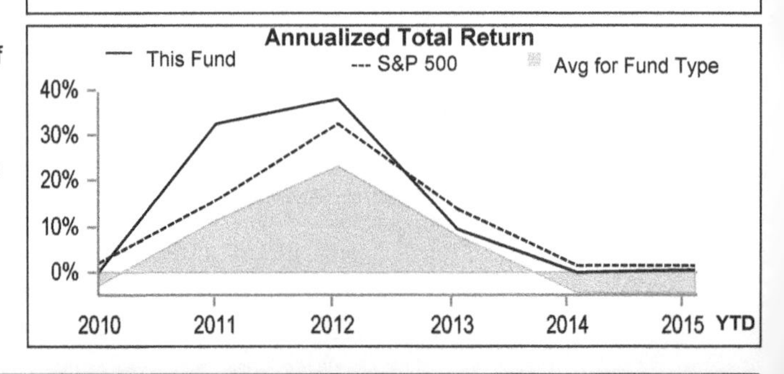

*PowerShares KBW Capital Markets (KBWC) B+ Good

Fund Family: Invesco Powershares Capital Mgmt LL
Fund Type: Income
Inception Date: November 1, 2011

Data Date	Investment Rating	Net Assets ($Mil)	Price	Performance Rating/Pts	Total Return Y-T-D	Risk Rating/Pts
12-15	B+	5.10	52.75	A / 9.3	-2.39%	C+ / 6.6
2014	B	5.10	55.27	B+ / 8.9	14.43%	C+ / 6.0
2013	A+	12.50	50.06	A+ / 9.9	54.81%	B / 8.0
2012	A	1.70	32.72	A / 9.3	22.28%	B- / 7.8

Major Rating Factors:
Exceptional performance is the major factor driving the B+ (Good) TheStreet.com Investment Rating for *PowerShares KBW Capital Markets. The fund currently has a performance rating of A (Excellent) based on an annualized return of 19.31% over the last three years and a total return of -2.39% year to date 2015. Factored into the performance evaluation is an expense ratio of 0.35% (very low).

The fund's risk rating is currently C+ (Fair). It carries a beta of 1.23, meaning it is expected to move 12.3% for every 10% move in the market. Volatility, as measured by both the semi-deviation and a drawdown factor, is considered low. As of December 31, 2015, *PowerShares KBW Capital Markets traded at a premium of .32% above its net asset value, which is worse than its one-year historical average discount of .03%.

Michael C. Jeanette has been running the fund for 5 years and currently receives a manager quality ranking of 71 (0=worst, 99=best). If you desire only a moderate level of risk and strong performance, then this fund is an excellent option.

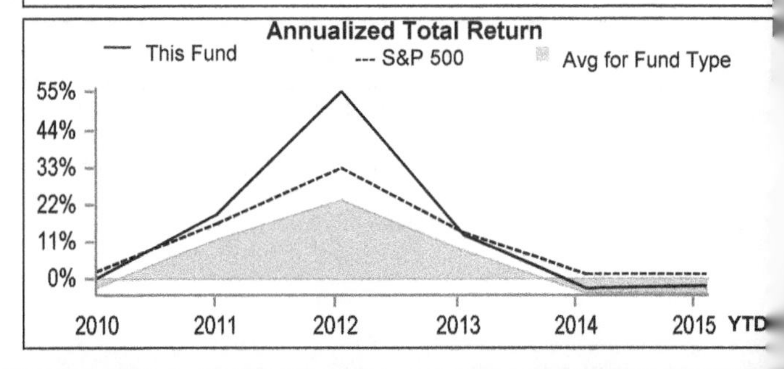

*PowerShares KBW High Div Yield F (KBWD) C Fair

Fund Family: Invesco Powershares Capital Mgmt LL
Fund Type: Growth and Income
Inception Date: December 1, 2010

Data Date	Investment Rating	Net Assets ($Mil)	Price	Performance Rating/Pts	Total Return Y-T-D	Risk Rating/Pts
12-15	C	260.20	20.99	C / 4.4	-10.89%	B- / 7.0
2014	B	260.20	25.29	C+ / 6.5	8.26%	B / 8.8
2013	B-	229.40	25.37	C+ / 6.8	12.85%	B / 8.4
2012	C+	169.10	23.15	C+ / 5.6	15.91%	B / 8.4
2011	C-	33.60	21.76	C- / 3.1	2.58%	B / 8.3

Major Rating Factors: Middle of the road best describes *PowerShares KBW High Div Yield F whose TheStreet.com Investment Rating is currently a C (Fair). The fund currently has a performance rating of C (Fair) based on an annualized return of 3.12% over the last three years and a total return of -10.89% year to date 2015. Factored into the performance evaluation is an expense ratio of 0.35% (very low).

The fund's risk rating is currently B- (Good). It carries a beta of 0.77, meaning the fund's expected move will be 7.7% for every 10% move in the market. Volatility, as measured by both the semi-deviation and a drawdown factor, is considered low. As of December 31, 2015, *PowerShares KBW High Div Yield F traded at a price exactly equal to its net asset value, which is worse than its one-year historical average discount of .01%.

Michael C. Jeanette has been running the fund for 6 years and currently receives a manager quality ranking of 26 (0=worst, 99=best). If you desire an average level of risk, then this fund may be an option.

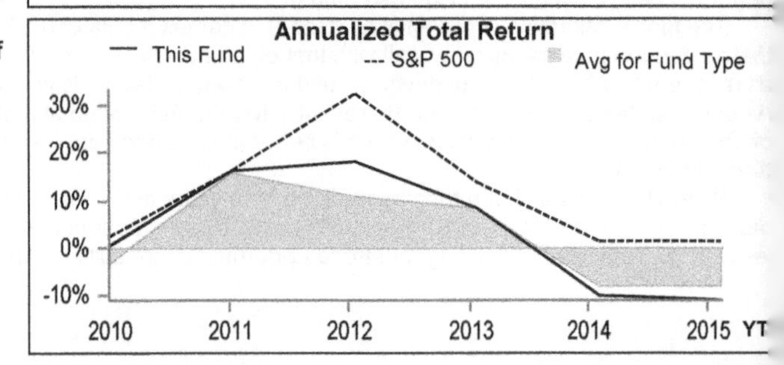

*PowerShares KBW Insurance (KBWI) A- Excellent

Fund Family: Invesco Powershares Capital Mgmt LL
Fund Type: Income
Inception Date: November 1, 2011

Major Rating Factors:
Exceptional performance is the major factor driving the A- (Excellent) TheStreet.com Investment Rating for *PowerShares KBW Insurance. The fund currently has a performance rating of A (Excellent) based on an annualized return of 18.04% over the last three years and a total return of 0.77% year to date 2015. Factored into the performance evaluation is an expense ratio of 0.35% (very low).

The fund's risk rating is currently B- (Good). It carries a beta of 1.20, meaning it is expected to move 12.0% for every 10% move in the market. Volatility, as measured by both the semi-deviation and a drawdown factor, is considered low. As of December 31, 2015, *PowerShares KBW Insurance traded at a premium of .20% above its net asset value, which is worse than its one-year historical average discount of .05%.

Michael C. Jeanette has been running the fund for 5 years and currently receives a manager quality ranking of 76 (0=worst, 99=best). If you desire only a moderate level of risk and strong performance, then this fund is an excellent option.

Data Date	Investment Rating	Net Assets ($Mil)	Price	Performance Rating/Pts	Total Return Y-T-D	Risk Rating/Pts
12-15	A-	6.50	69.14	A / 9.3	0.77%	B- / 7.0
2014	B+	6.50	69.86	A / 9.3	10.65%	C+ / 6.7
2013	A+	13.20	66.18	A+ / 9.8	49.57%	B / 8.7

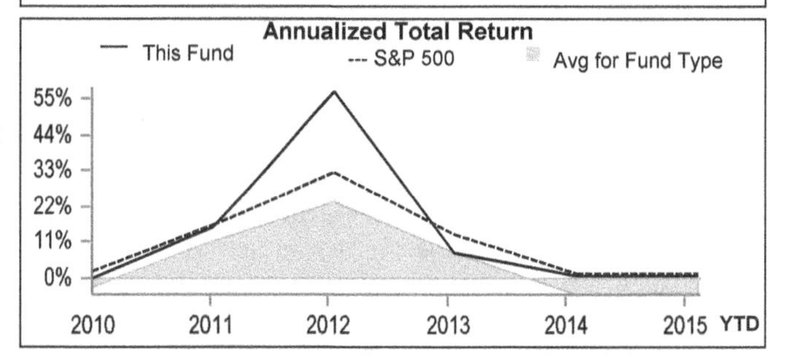

*PowerShares KBW Premium Yld Eq R (KBWY) C Fair

Fund Family: Invesco Powershares Capital Mgmt LL
Fund Type: Income
Inception Date: December 1, 2010

Major Rating Factors: Middle of the road best describes *PowerShares KBW Premium Yld Eq R whose TheStreet.com Investment Rating is currently a C (Fair). The fund currently has a performance rating of C+ (Fair) based on an annualized return of 6.85% over the last three years and a total return of -9.36% year to date 2015. Factored into the performance evaluation is an expense ratio of 0.35% (very low).

The fund's risk rating is currently C+ (Fair). It carries a beta of 0.70, meaning the fund's expected move will be 7.0% for every 10% move in the market. Volatility, as measured by both the semi-deviation and a drawdown factor, is considered low. As of December 31, 2015, *PowerShares KBW Premium Yld Eq R traded at a premium of .13% above its net asset value, which is worse than its one-year historical average discount of .03%.

Michael C. Jeanette has been running the fund for 6 years and currently receives a manager quality ranking of 49 (0=worst, 99=best). If you desire an average level of risk, then this fund may be an option.

Data Date	Investment Rating	Net Assets ($Mil)	Price	Performance Rating/Pts	Total Return Y-T-D	Risk Rating/Pts
12-15	C	89.50	30.45	C+ / 6.2	-9.36%	C+ / 6.0
2014	A+	89.50	34.98	A- / 9.1	23.61%	B / 8.2
2013	C+	63.80	29.71	C+ / 6.2	7.45%	B- / 7.6
2012	A	29.60	28.10	A / 9.4	27.82%	B- / 7.7
2011	D+	6.90	23.04	D / 2.1	-1.53%	B- / 7.6

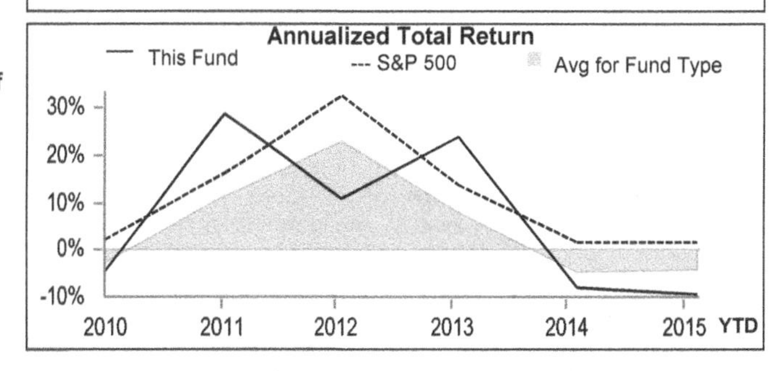

*PowerShares KBW Prop & Casualty (KBWP) A Excellent

Fund Family: Invesco Powershares Capital Mgmt LL
Fund Type: Growth
Inception Date: December 1, 2010

Major Rating Factors:
Exceptional performance is the major factor driving the A (Excellent) TheStreet.com Investment Rating for *PowerShares KBW Prop & Casualty. The fund currently has a performance rating of A (Excellent) based on an annualized return of 19.06% over the last three years and a total return of 16.26% year to date 2015. Factored into the performance evaluation is an expense ratio of 0.35% (very low).

The fund's risk rating is currently B- (Good). It carries a beta of 0.83, meaning the fund's expected move will be 8.3% for every 10% move in the market. Volatility, as measured by both the semi-deviation and a drawdown factor, is considered low. As of December 31, 2015, *PowerShares KBW Prop & Casualty traded at a premium of .63% above its net asset value, which is worse than its one-year historical average premium of .04%.

Michael C. Jeanette has been running the fund for 6 years and currently receives a manager quality ranking of 92 (0=worst, 99=best). If you desire only a moderate level of risk and strong performance, then this fund is an excellent option.

Data Date	Investment Rating	Net Assets ($Mil)	Price	Performance Rating/Pts	Total Return Y-T-D	Risk Rating/Pts
12-15	A	9.80	48.06	A / 9.5	16.26%	B- / 7.2
2014	B+	9.80	42.52	A- / 9.0	14.71%	B- / 7.1
2013	B+	21.60	39.17	B+ / 8.3	26.88%	B / 8.2

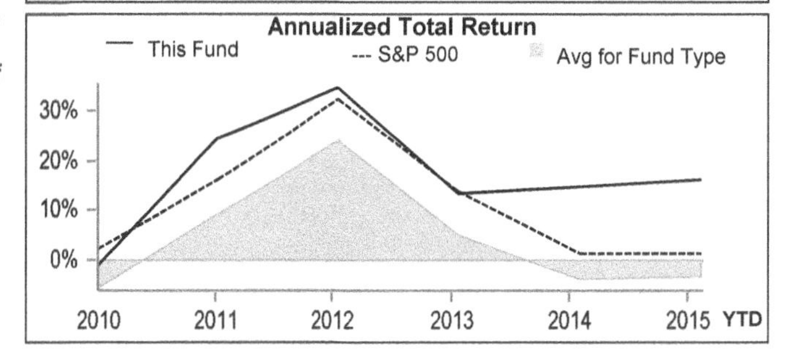

*PowerShares KBW Regional Banking (KBWR) A- Excellent

Fund Family: Invesco Powershares Capital Mgmt LL
Fund Type: Income
Inception Date: November 1, 2011

Data Date	Investment Rating	Net Assets ($Mil)	Price	Performance Rating/Pts	Total Return Y-T-D	Risk Rating/Pts
12-15	A-	32.90	41.11	B+ / 8.9	6.66%	B- / 7.4
2014	B-	32.90	39.99	B- / 7.5	4.58%	C+ / 6.8
2013	A+	45.60	39.65	A+ / 9.6	37.52%	B+ / 9.2
2012	C	20.70	27.35	C- / 3.4	9.33%	B+ / 9.2

Major Rating Factors:
Strong performance is the major factor driving the A- (Excellent) TheStreet.com Investment Rating for *PowerShares KBW Regional Banking. The fund currently has a performance rating of B+ (Good) based on an annualized return of 14.44% over the last three years and a total return of 6.66% year to date 2015. Factored into the performance evaluation is an expense ratio of 0.35% (very low).

The fund's risk rating is currently B- (Good). It carries a beta of 1.02, meaning that its performance tracks fairly well with that of the overall stock market. Volatility, as measured by both the semi-deviation and a drawdown factor, is considered low. As of December 31, 2015, *PowerShares KBW Regional Banking traded at a price exactly equal to its net asset value, which is worse than its one-year historical average discount of .03%.

Michael C. Jeanette has been running the fund for 5 years and currently receives a manager quality ranking of 77 (0=worst, 99=best). If you desire only a moderate level of risk and strong performance, then this fund is an excellent option.

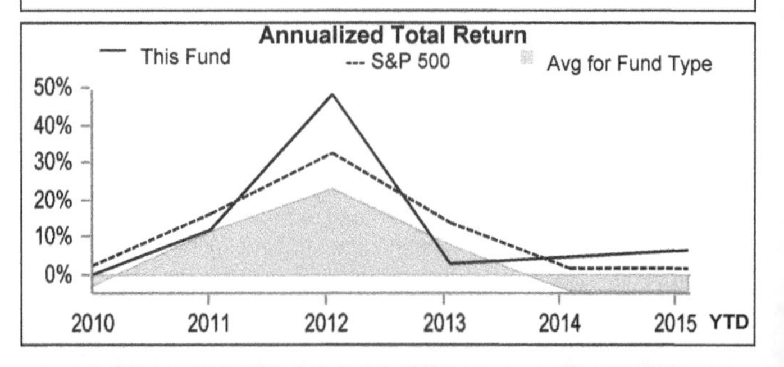

*PowerShares Multi-Strategy Alt (LALT) C- Fair

Fund Family: Invesco Powershares Capital Mgmt LL
Fund Type: Growth and Income
Inception Date: May 28, 2014

Data Date	Investment Rating	Net Assets ($Mil)	Price	Performance Rating/Pts	Total Return Y-T-D	Risk Rating/Pts
12-15	C-	22.00	22.24	D+ / 2.3	-8.10%	B / 8.9

Major Rating Factors:
Disappointing performance is the major factor driving the C- (Fair) TheStreet.com Investment Rating for *PowerShares Multi-Strategy Alt. The fund currently has a performance rating of D+ (Weak) based on an annualized return of 0.00% over the last three years and a total return of -8.10% year to date 2015.

The fund's risk rating is currently B (Good). It carries a beta of 0.00, meaning the fund's expected move will be 0.0% for every 10% move in the market. Volatility, as measured by both the semi-deviation and a drawdown factor, is considered low. As of December 31, 2015, *PowerShares Multi-Strategy Alt traded at a discount of .45% below its net asset value, which is better than its one-year historical average discount of .06%.

Duy Nguyen has been running the fund for 2 years and currently receives a manager quality ranking of 20 (0=worst, 99=best). This fund offers only a moderate level of risk but investors looking for strong performance are still waiting.

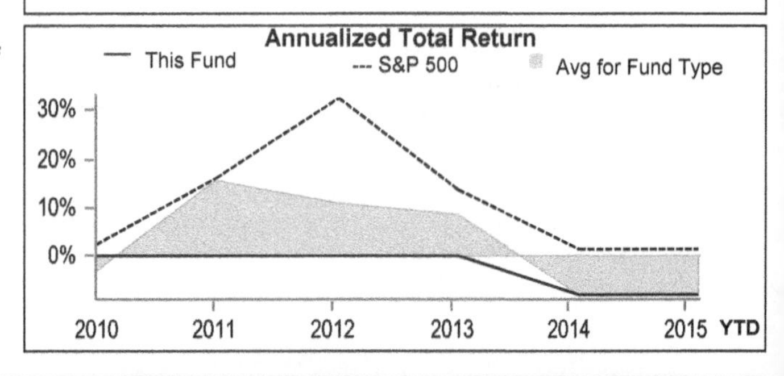

*PowerShares NASDAQ Internet Port (PNQI) B- Good

Fund Family: Invesco Powershares Capital Mgmt LL
Fund Type: Income
Inception Date: June 10, 2008

Data Date	Investment Rating	Net Assets ($Mil)	Price	Performance Rating/Pts	Total Return Y-T-D	Risk Rating/Pts
12-15	B-	314.20	80.23	A+ / 9.7	19.71%	C / 4.8
2014	C+	314.20	67.09	B+ / 8.6	-0.43%	C / 4.8
2013	B	286.50	68.47	A / 9.5	57.14%	C+ / 5.7
2012	B-	48.20	41.46	B+ / 8.4	22.28%	C+ / 6.3
2011	B	53.50	34.54	B+ / 8.8	-1.71%	C+ / 6.5
2010	B+	31.10	34.69	A+ / 9.6	34.20%	C- / 3.9

Major Rating Factors:
Exceptional performance is the major factor driving the B- (Good) TheStreet.com Investment Rating for *PowerShares NASDAQ Internet Port. The fund currently has a performance rating of A+ (Excellent) based on an annualized return of 23.22% over the last three years and a total return of 19.71% year to date 2015. Factored into the performance evaluation is an expense ratio of 0.60% (very low).

The fund's risk rating is currently C (Fair). It carries a beta of 1.15, meaning it is expected to move 11.5% for every 10% move in the market. Volatility, as measured by both the semi-deviation and a drawdown factor, is considered average. As of December 31, 2015, *PowerShares NASDAQ Internet Port traded at a premium of .14% above its net asset value, which is worse than its one-year historical average discount of .01%.

Peter Hubbard has been running the fund for 8 years and currently receives a manager quality ranking of 91 (0=worst, 99=best). If you desire an average level of risk and strong performance, then this fund is a good option.

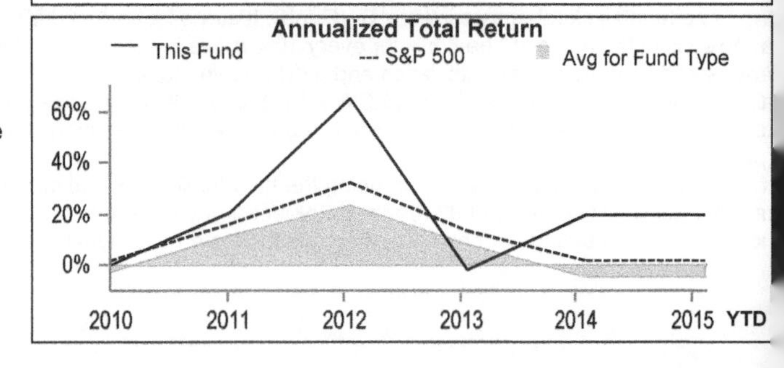

* Denotes ETF Fund

*PowerShares Natl AMT-Free Muni B (PZA) B- Good

Fund Family: Invesco Powershares Capital Mgmt LL
Fund Type: Municipal - National
Inception Date: October 11, 2007

Major Rating Factors: *PowerShares Natl AMT-Free Muni B receives a TheStreet.com Investment Rating of B- (Good). The fund currently has a performance rating of C+ (Fair) based on an annualized return of 3.70% over the last three years and a total return of 3.65% year to date 2015. Factored into the performance evaluation is an expense ratio of 0.28% (very low).

The fund's risk rating is currently B- (Good). It carries a beta of 1.51, meaning it is expected to move 15.1% for every 10% move in the market. Volatility, as measured by both the semi-deviation and a drawdown factor, is considered low. As of December 31, 2015, *PowerShares Natl AMT-Free Muni B traded at a premium of .28% above its net asset value, which is worse than its one-year historical average premium of .14%.

Peter Hubbard has been running the fund for 9 years and currently receives a manager quality ranking of 59 (0=worst, 99=best). If you desire an average level of risk, then this fund may be an option.

Data Date	Investment Rating	Net Assets ($Mil)	Price	Perfor-mance Rating/Pts	Total Return Y-T-D	Risk Rating/Pts
12-15	B-	706.20	25.47	C+ / 6.7	3.65%	B- / 7.6
2014	C+	706.20	25.41	C+ / 6.1	15.05%	B- / 7.4
2013	C+	534.00	22.96	C / 4.8	-6.75%	B+ / 9.0
2012	C+	982.20	25.75	C / 4.6	7.77%	B+ / 9.3
2011	B	588.30	24.45	C+ / 6.4	14.87%	B+ / 9.3
2010	C	507.10	22.54	D / 2.2	-0.09%	B / 8.2

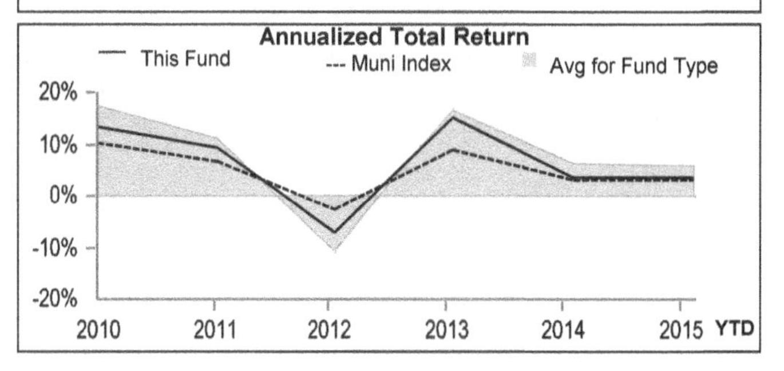

*PowerShares NY AMT-Free Muni Bon (PZT) B+ Good

Fund Family: Invesco Powershares Capital Mgmt LL
Fund Type: Municipal - National
Inception Date: October 11, 2007

Major Rating Factors: *PowerShares NY AMT-Free Muni Bon receives a TheStreet.com Investment Rating of B+ (Good). The fund currently has a performance rating of C+ (Fair) based on an annualized return of 3.48% over the last three years and a total return of 2.74% year to date 2015. Factored into the performance evaluation is an expense ratio of 0.26% (very low).

The fund's risk rating is currently B (Good). It carries a beta of 1.41, meaning it is expected to move 14.1% for every 10% move in the market. Volatility, as measured by both the semi-deviation and a drawdown factor, is considered low. As of December 31, 2015, *PowerShares NY AMT-Free Muni Bon traded at a discount of .61% below its net asset value, which is better than its one-year historical average premium of .03%.

Peter Hubbard has been running the fund for 9 years and currently receives a manager quality ranking of 60 (0=worst, 99=best). If you desire an average level of risk, then this fund may be an option.

Data Date	Investment Rating	Net Assets ($Mil)	Price	Perfor-mance Rating/Pts	Total Return Y-T-D	Risk Rating/Pts
12-15	B+	47.30	24.31	C+ / 6.5	2.74%	B / 8.9
2014	C+	47.30	24.45	C+ / 5.9	15.10%	B- / 7.4
2013	C	43.20	21.98	C- / 4.2	-6.43%	B+ / 9.0
2012	C	68.80	24.57	C- / 3.8	5.66%	B+ / 9.3
2011	B	40.60	23.90	C+ / 6.1	13.66%	B+ / 9.4
2010	C-	37.80	22.15	D / 2.1	0.22%	B / 8.1

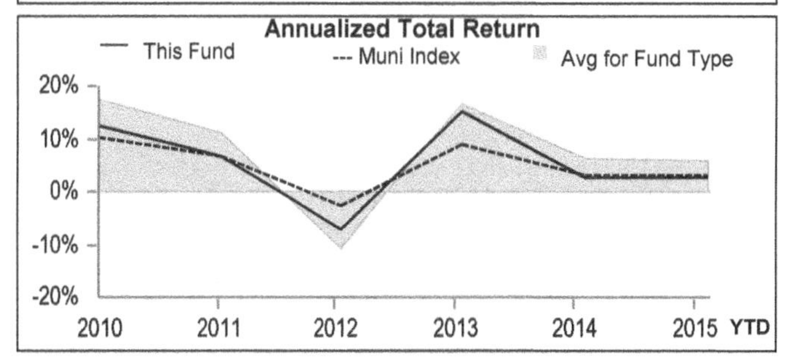

*PowerShares Preferred Port (PGX) B- Good

Fund Family: Invesco Powershares Capital Mgmt LL
Fund Type: General - Investment Grade
Inception Date: January 28, 2008

Major Rating Factors: Strong performance is the major factor driving the B- (Good) TheStreet.com Investment Rating for *PowerShares Preferred Port. The fund currently has a performance rating of B- (Good) based on an annualized return of 6.65% over the last three years and a total return of 7.53% year to date 2015. Factored into the performance evaluation is an expense ratio of 0.50% (very low).

The fund's risk rating is currently B- (Good). It carries a beta of 1.08, meaning that its performance tracks fairly well with that of the overall stock market. Volatility, as measured by both the semi-deviation and a drawdown factor, is considered low. As of December 31, 2015, *PowerShares Preferred Port traded at a premium of .27% above its net asset value, which is worse than its one-year historical average premium of .10%.

Peter Hubbard has been running the fund for 8 years and currently receives a manager quality ranking of 90 (0=worst, 99=best). If you desire only a moderate level of risk and strong performance, then this fund is an excellent option.

Data Date	Investment Rating	Net Assets ($Mil)	Price	Perfor-mance Rating/Pts	Total Return Y-T-D	Risk Rating/Pts
12-15	B-	2,257.80	14.95	B- / 7.3	7.53%	B- / 7.3
2014	B-	2,257.80	14.70	C+ / 5.6	14.52%	B+ / 9.1
2013	C+	1,971.10	13.44	C / 4.3	-1.82%	B+ / 9.1
2012	C+	2,149.00	14.68	C- / 4.0	13.12%	B+ / 9.4
2011	C-	1,359.70	13.69	C- / 3.8	5.97%	C+ / 6.8
2010	C+	1,353.90	14.12	B- / 7.3	12.18%	C / 4.4

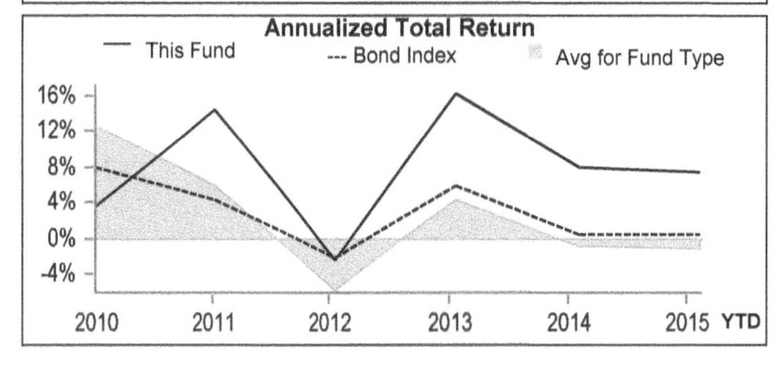

*PowerShares QQQ (QQQ) A Excellent

Fund Family: Bank of New York Mellon
Fund Type: Growth
Inception Date: March 10, 1999

Major Rating Factors:
Exceptional performance is the major factor driving the A (Excellent) TheStreet.com Investment Rating for *PowerShares QQQ. The fund currently has a performance rating of A (Excellent) based on an annualized return of 20.21% over the last three years and a total return of 9.50% year to date 2015. Factored into the performance evaluation is an expense ratio of 0.20% (very low).

The fund's risk rating is currently B- (Good). It carries a beta of 1.08, meaning that its performance tracks fairly well with that of the overall stock market. Volatility, as measured by both the semi-deviation and a drawdown factor, is considered low. As of December 31, 2015, *PowerShares QQQ traded at a discount of .01% below its net asset value, which is in line with its one-year historical average discount of .01%.

Steven M. Hill currently receives a manager quality ranking of 87 (0=worst, 99=best). If you desire only a moderate level of risk and strong performance, then this fund is an excellent option.

Data Date	Investment Rating	Net Assets ($Mil)	Price	Performance Rating/Pts	Total Return Y-T-D	Risk Rating/Pts
12-15	A	42,596.10	111.86	A / 9.5	9.50%	B- / 7.3
2014	B+	42,596.10	103.25	A- / 9.2	22.26%	C+ / 6.7
2013	B+	45,337.80	87.96	B+ / 8.8	31.49%	B- / 7.4
2012	C	30,416.90	65.13	C+ / 6.0	17.07%	B- / 7.1
2011	B	25,574.40	55.83	B- / 7.5	3.82%	B / 8.6
2010	C+	22,061.00	54.46	C+ / 6.9	20.16%	C+ / 5.6

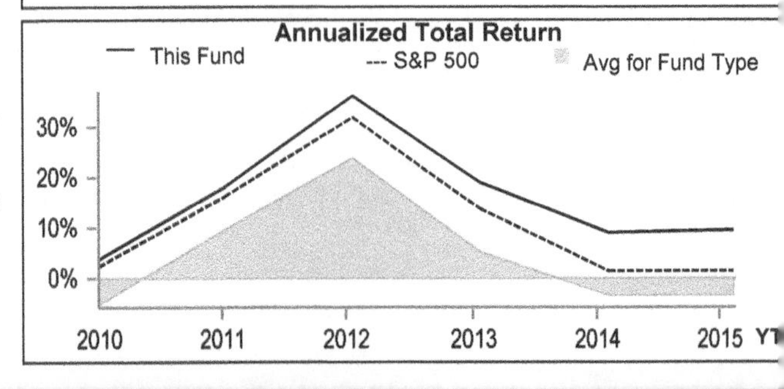

*PowerShares Rus 1000 Equal Weigh (EQAL) D- Weak

Fund Family: Invesco Powershares Capital Mgmt LL
Fund Type: Growth
Inception Date: December 23, 2014

Major Rating Factors:
Disappointing performance is the major factor driving the D- (Weak) TheStreet.com Investment Rating for *PowerShares Rus 1000 Equal Weigh. The fund currently has a performance rating of D+ (Weak) based on an annualized return of 0.00% over the last three years and a total return of -3.66% year to date 2015.

The fund's risk rating is currently C- (Fair). It carries a beta of 0.00, meaning the fund's expected move will be 0.0% for every 10% move in the market. Volatility, as measured by both the semi-deviation and a drawdown factor, is considered average. As of December 31, 2015, *PowerShares Rus 1000 Equal Weigh traded at a premium of .51% above its net asset value, which is worse than its one-year historical average discount of .05%.

Brian Picken has been running the fund for 2 years and currently receives a manager quality ranking of 25 (0=worst, 99=best). This fund offers an average level of risk but investors looking for strong performance will be frustrated.

Data Date	Investment Rating	Net Assets ($Mil)	Price	Performance Rating/Pts	Total Return Y-T-D	Risk Rating/Pts
12-15	D-	0.00	23.66	D+ / 2.9	-3.66%	C- / 3.5

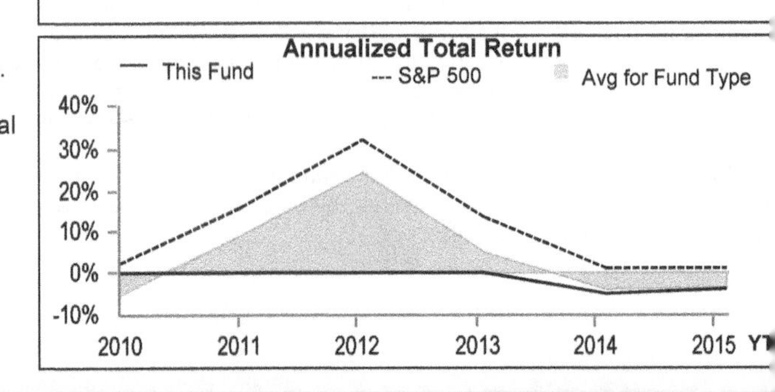

*PowerShares Russell 2000 Equal W (EQWS) C+ Fair

Fund Family: Invesco Powershares Capital Mgmt LL
Fund Type: Growth
Inception Date: December 1, 2006

Major Rating Factors: Middle of the road best describes *PowerShares Russell 2000 Equal W whose TheStreet.com Investment Rating is currently a C+ (Fair). The fund currently has a performance rating of C+ (Fair) based on an annualized return of 9.43% over the last three years and a total return of -7.60% year to date 2015. Factored into the performance evaluation is an expense ratio of 0.39% (very low).

The fund's risk rating is currently B- (Good). It carries a beta of 1.06, meaning that its performance tracks fairly well with that of the overall stock market. Volatility, as measured by both the semi-deviation and a drawdown factor, is considered low. As of December 31, 2015, *PowerShares Russell 2000 Equal W traded at a premium of .06% above its net asset value, which is better than its one-year historical average premium of .07%.

Peter Hubbard has been running the fund for 9 years and currently receives a manager quality ranking of 34 (0=worst, 99=best). If you desire an average level of risk, then this fund may be an option.

Data Date	Investment Rating	Net Assets ($Mil)	Price	Performance Rating/Pts	Total Return Y-T-D	Risk Rating/Pts
12-15	C+	14.60	31.89	C+ / 6.7	-7.60%	B- / 7.0
2014	B	14.60	35.75	B / 8.0	10.21%	C+ / 6.9
2013	B+	16.40	32.88	B / 8.2	31.03%	B- / 7.8
2012	C	13.40	24.26	C+ / 5.8	15.82%	B- / 7.5
2011	C-	14.20	21.98	C / 4.5	-0.54%	B- / 7.4
2010	C	17.80	22.45	C+ / 5.6	23.30%	C+ / 5.6

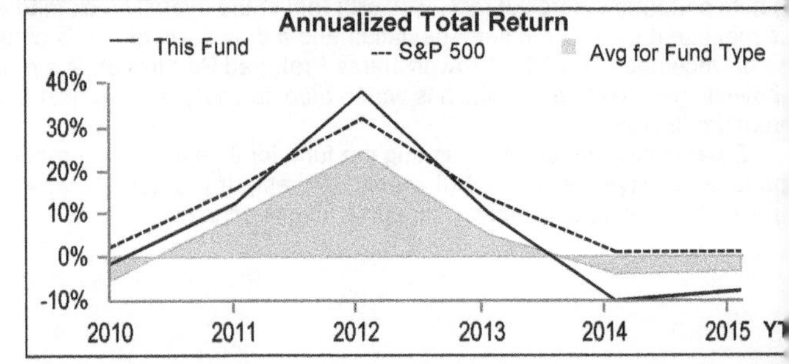

*PowerShares Russell 2000 Pure Gr (PXSG) C+ Fair

Fund Family: Invesco Powershares Capital Mgmt LL
Fund Type: Growth
Inception Date: March 3, 2005

Major Rating Factors: Strong performance is the major factor driving the C+ (Fair) TheStreet.com Investment Rating for *PowerShares Russell 2000 Pure Gr. The fund currently has a performance rating of B (Good) based on an annualized return of 10.77% over the last three years and a total return of 1.03% year to date 2015. Factored into the performance evaluation is an expense ratio of 0.39% (very low).

The fund's risk rating is currently C+ (Fair). It carries a beta of 0.92, meaning that its performance tracks fairly well with that of the overall stock market. Volatility, as measured by both the semi-deviation and a drawdown factor, is considered low. As of December 31, 2015, *PowerShares Russell 2000 Pure Gr traded at a premium of .57% above its net asset value, which is worse than its one-year historical average discount of .03%.

Peter Hubbard has been running the fund for 9 years and currently receives a manager quality ranking of 55 (0=worst, 99=best). If you desire only a moderate level of risk and strong performance, then this fund is an excellent option.

Data Date	Investment Rating	Net Assets ($Mil)	Price	Performance Rating/Pts	Total Return Y-T-D	Risk Rating/Pts
12-15	C+	29.40	24.51	B / 7.8	1.03%	C+ / 6.2
2014	C+	29.40	24.70	B- / 7.2	6.68%	C+ / 6.5
2013	B-	29.50	23.66	B / 7.7	27.98%	C+ / 6.9
2012	C	27.20	17.93	C+ / 6.1	14.63%	C+ / 6.9
2011	C-	33.30	15.91	C / 5.0	-1.47%	C+ / 6.8
2010	C+	38.70	16.13	C+ / 5.7	27.31%	C+ / 5.8

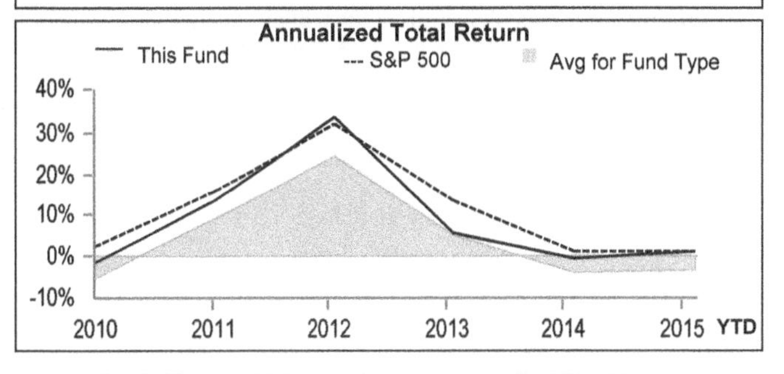

*PowerShares Russell 2000 Pure Va (PXSV) B Good

Fund Family: Invesco Powershares Capital Mgmt LL
Fund Type: Growth
Inception Date: March 3, 2005

Major Rating Factors: *PowerShares Russell 2000 Pure Va receives a TheStreet.com Investment Rating of B (Good). The fund currently has a performance rating of C+ (Fair) based on an annualized return of 10.19% over the last three years and a total return of -8.33% year to date 2015. Factored into the performance evaluation is an expense ratio of 0.39% (very low).

The fund's risk rating is currently B- (Good). It carries a beta of 1.09, meaning that its performance tracks fairly well with that of the overall stock market. Volatility, as measured by both the semi-deviation and a drawdown factor, is considered low. As of December 31, 2015, *PowerShares Russell 2000 Pure Va traded at a price exactly equal to its net asset value, which is worse than its one-year historical average discount of .02%.

Peter Hubbard has been running the fund for 9 years and currently receives a manager quality ranking of 35 (0=worst, 99=best). If you desire an average level of risk, then this fund may be an option.

Data Date	Investment Rating	Net Assets ($Mil)	Price	Performance Rating/Pts	Total Return Y-T-D	Risk Rating/Pts
12-15	B	62.80	22.93	C+ / 6.9	-8.33%	B- / 7.7
2014	B+	62.80	25.84	B+ / 8.7	6.20%	B- / 7.2
2013	A-	60.90	24.85	A- / 9.1	38.37%	B- / 7.7
2012	C+	44.80	17.47	B- / 7.0	20.93%	B- / 7.5
2011	C	52.30	14.74	C / 4.6	-0.48%	B- / 7.4
2010	C+	65.60	15.08	C+ / 5.8	19.92%	C+ / 5.7

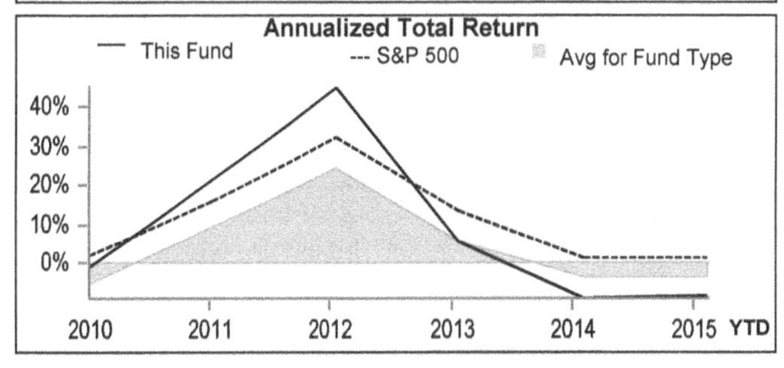

*PowerShares Russell Midcap Equal (EQWM) B- Good

Fund Family: Invesco Powershares Capital Mgmt LL
Fund Type: Growth
Inception Date: December 1, 2006

Major Rating Factors: Strong performance is the major factor driving the B- (Good) TheStreet.com Investment Rating for *PowerShares Russell Midcap Equal. The fund currently has a performance rating of B- (Good) based on an annualized return of 11.10% over the last three years and a total return of -6.51% year to date 2015. Factored into the performance evaluation is an expense ratio of 0.39% (very low).

The fund's risk rating is currently B- (Good). It carries a beta of 1.02, meaning that its performance tracks fairly well with that of the overall stock market. Volatility, as measured by both the semi-deviation and a drawdown factor, is considered low. As of December 31, 2015, *PowerShares Russell Midcap Equal traded at a premium of .38% above its net asset value, which is worse than its one-year historical average premium of .01%.

Peter Hubbard has been running the fund for 9 years and currently receives a manager quality ranking of 45 (0=worst, 99=best). If you desire only a moderate level of risk and strong performance, then this fund is an excellent option.

Data Date	Investment Rating	Net Assets ($Mil)	Price	Performance Rating/Pts	Total Return Y-T-D	Risk Rating/Pts
12-15	B-	31.60	36.55	B- / 7.4	-6.51%	B- / 7.0
2014	B	31.60	39.61	B / 8.1	14.09%	B- / 7.2
2013	B+	30.20	35.49	B / 7.9	28.53%	B / 8.2
2012	C+	17.30	26.92	C / 5.5	14.68%	B / 8.0
2011	C+	20.50	24.16	C / 5.5	0.29%	B- / 7.8
2010	C	22.20	24.76	C / 4.7	21.78%	C+ / 5.8

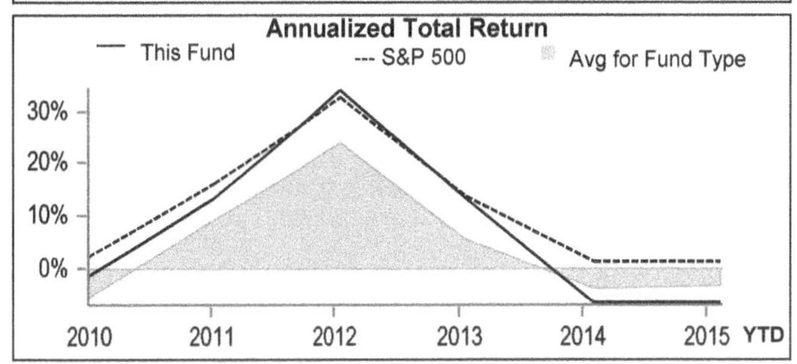

* Denotes ETF Fund

*PowerShares Russell Midcap Pure (PXMG) C Fair

Fund Family: Invesco Powershares Capital Mgmt LL
Fund Type: Growth
Inception Date: March 3, 2005

Data Date	Investment Rating	Net Assets ($Mil)	Price	Perfor-mance Rating/Pts	Total Return Y-T-D	Risk Rating/Pts
12-15	C	89.30	30.08	B- / 7.0	-3.74%	C / 5.5
2014	B-	89.30	31.71	B- / 7.4	11.46%	B- / 7.2
2013	B-	90.00	29.03	B- / 7.2	23.08%	B- / 7.6
2012	C+	75.40	23.09	C+ / 6.2	14.82%	B- / 7.4
2011	C	86.40	20.35	C / 4.9	-3.58%	B- / 7.5
2010	C-	131.10	21.66	C / 5.1	29.95%	C / 4.6

Major Rating Factors: Strong performance is the major factor driving the C (Fair) TheStreet.com Investment Rating for *PowerShares Russell Midcap Pure. The fund currently has a performance rating of B- (Good) based on an annualized return of 9.40% over the last three years and a total return of -3.74% year to date 2015. Factored into the performance evaluation is an expense ratio of 0.39% (very low).

The fund's risk rating is currently C (Fair). It carries a beta of 0.97, meaning that its performance tracks fairly well with that of the overall stock market. Volatility, as measured by both the semi-deviation and a drawdown factor, is considered average. As of December 31, 2015, *PowerShares Russell Midcap Pure traded at a premium of .77% above its net asset value, which is worse than its one-year historical average discount of .02%.

Peter Hubbard has been running the fund for 9 years and currently receives a manager quality ranking of 39 (0=worst, 99=best). If you desire an average level of risk and strong performance, then this fund is a good option.

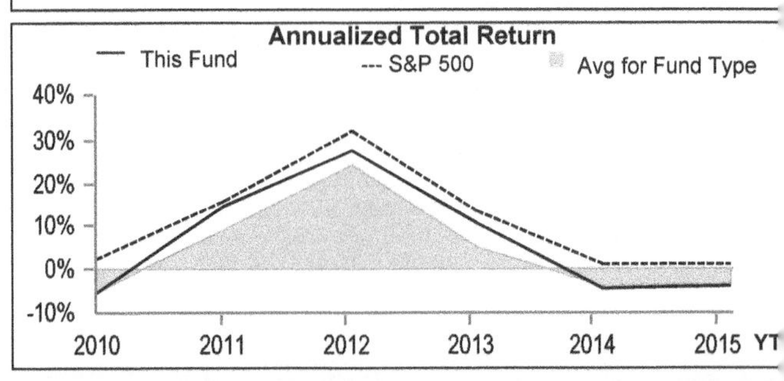

*PowerShares Russell Midcap Pure (PXMV) A Excellent

Fund Family: Invesco Powershares Capital Mgmt LL
Fund Type: Growth
Inception Date: March 3, 2005

Data Date	Investment Rating	Net Assets ($Mil)	Price	Perfor-mance Rating/Pts	Total Return Y-T-D	Risk Rating/Pts
12-15	A	48.20	24.78	B / 7.7	-7.21%	B / 8.8
2014	A	48.20	27.62	A- / 9.1	13.77%	B- / 7.4
2013	A	39.70	24.86	B+ / 8.9	35.45%	B / 8.1
2012	C+	27.40	17.82	C+ / 6.2	19.97%	B / 8.0
2011	C	32.30	15.42	C / 4.7	-0.49%	B- / 7.8
2010	C-	39.40	15.79	C- / 3.6	15.31%	C+ / 5.7

Major Rating Factors:
Strong performance is the major factor driving the A (Excellent) TheStreet.com Investment Rating for *PowerShares Russell Midcap Pure. The fund currently has a performance rating of B (Good) based on an annualized return of 12.35% over the last three years and a total return of -7.21% year to date 2015. Factored into the performance evaluation is an expense ratio of 0.39% (very low).

The fund's risk rating is currently B (Good). It carries a beta of 1.08, meaning that its performance tracks fairly well with that of the overall stock market. Volatility, as measured by both the semi-deviation and a drawdown factor, is considered low. As of December 31, 2015, *PowerShares Russell Midcap Pure traded at a discount of .04% below its net asset value, which is better than its one-year historical average discount of .02%.

Peter Hubbard has been running the fund for 9 years and currently receives a manager quality ranking of 49 (0=worst, 99=best). If you desire only a moderate level of risk and strong performance, then this fund is an excellent option.

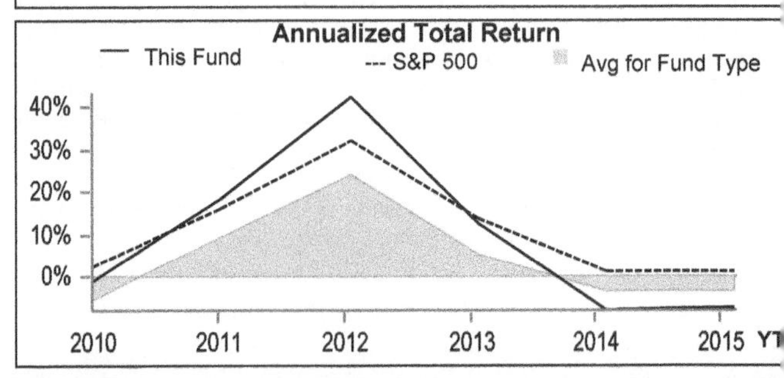

*PowerShares Russell Top 200 Eq W (EQWL) B+ Good

Fund Family: Invesco Powershares Capital Mgmt LL
Fund Type: Growth
Inception Date: December 1, 2006

Data Date	Investment Rating	Net Assets ($Mil)	Price	Perfor-mance Rating/Pts	Total Return Y-T-D	Risk Rating/Pts
12-15	B+	42.40	38.91	B+ / 8.7	-1.54%	B- / 7.1
2014	A	42.40	40.63	B+ / 8.7	15.71%	B- / 7.8
2013	A	37.80	35.94	B+ / 8.5	31.51%	B / 8.7
2012	C+	25.40	26.64	C / 5.0	14.44%	B / 8.5
2011	C+	23.20	24.44	C / 4.8	3.30%	B / 8.3
2010	C-	32.80	24.27	C- / 3.8	14.84%	C+ / 6.3

Major Rating Factors: Strong performance is the major factor driving the B+ (Good) TheStreet.com Investment Rating for *PowerShares Russell Top 200 Eq W. The fund currently has a performance rating of B+ (Good) based on an annualized return of 14.14% over the last three years and a total return of -1.54% year to date 2015. Factored into the performance evaluation is an expense ratio of 0.39% (very low).

The fund's risk rating is currently B- (Good). It carries a beta of 1.06, meaning that its performance tracks fairly well with that of the overall stock market. Volatility, as measured by both the semi-deviation and a drawdown factor, is considered low. As of December 31, 2015, *PowerShares Russell Top 200 Eq W traded at a premium of .26% above its net asset value, which is worse than its one-year historical average discount of .05%.

Peter Hubbard has been running the fund for 9 years and currently receives a manager quality ranking of 65 (0=worst, 99=best). If you desire only a moderate level of risk and strong performance, then this fund is an excellent option.

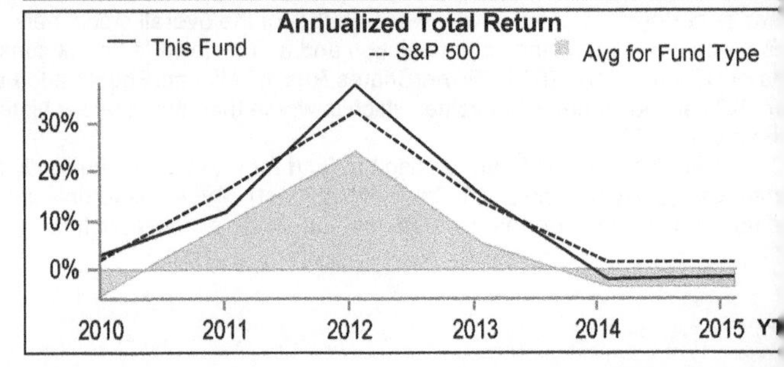

*PowerShares Russell Top 200 Pure (PXLG) A- Excellent

Fund Family: Invesco Powershares Capital Mgmt LL
Fund Type: Growth
Inception Date: June 16, 2011

Major Rating Factors:
Exceptional performance is the major factor driving the A- (Excellent) TheStreet.com Investment Rating for *PowerShares Russell Top 200 Pure. The fund currently has a performance rating of A- (Excellent) based on an annualized return of 15.76% over the last three years and a total return of 6.63% year to date 2015. Factored into the performance evaluation is an expense ratio of 0.39% (very low).

The fund's risk rating is currently B- (Good). It carries a beta of 0.95, meaning that its performance tracks fairly well with that of the overall stock market. Volatility, as measured by both the semi-deviation and a drawdown factor, is considered low. As of December 31, 2015, *PowerShares Russell Top 200 Pure traded at a premium of .56% above its net asset value, which is worse than its one-year historical average discount of .04%.

Michael C. Jeanette has been running the fund for 5 years and currently receives a manager quality ranking of 82 (0=worst, 99=best). If you desire only a moderate level of risk and strong performance, then this fund is an excellent option.

Data Date	Investment Rating	Net Assets ($Mil)	Price	Performance Rating/Pts	Total Return Y-T-D	Risk Rating/Pts
12-15	A-	123.80	34.30	A- / 9.1	6.63%	B- / 7.2
2014	B+	123.80	32.63	B+ / 8.6	18.73%	B- / 7.4
2013	A+	99.60	28.52	A / 9.3	25.22%	B / 8.7
2012	B	5.60	22.47	C+ / 6.6	17.52%	B / 8.5

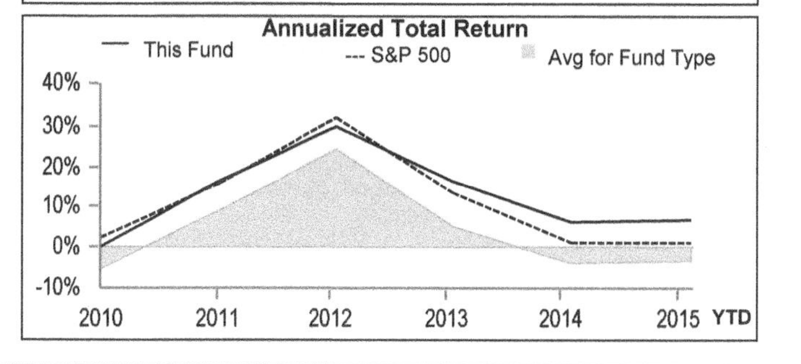

*PowerShares Russell Top200 Pure (PXLV) B- Good

Fund Family: Invesco Powershares Capital Mgmt LL
Fund Type: Growth
Inception Date: June 16, 2011

Major Rating Factors: Strong performance is the major factor driving the B- (Good) TheStreet.com Investment Rating for *PowerShares Russell Top200 Pure. The fund currently has a performance rating of B- (Good) based on an annualized return of 10.69% over the last three years and a total return of -4.76% year to date 2015. Factored into the performance evaluation is an expense ratio of 0.39% (very low).

The fund's risk rating is currently C+ (Fair). It carries a beta of 1.00, meaning that its performance tracks fairly well with that of the overall stock market. Volatility, as measured by both the semi-deviation and a drawdown factor, is considered low. As of December 31, 2015, *PowerShares Russell Top200 Pure traded at a premium of .28% above its net asset value, which is worse than its one-year historical average premium of .01%.

Michael C. Jeanette has been running the fund for 5 years and currently receives a manager quality ranking of 44 (0=worst, 99=best). If you desire only a moderate level of risk and strong performance, then this fund is an excellent option.

Data Date	Investment Rating	Net Assets ($Mil)	Price	Performance Rating/Pts	Total Return Y-T-D	Risk Rating/Pts
12-15	B-	34.50	28.66	B- / 7.5	-4.76%	C+ / 6.9
2014	B	34.50	31.11	B+ / 8.5	11.87%	C+ / 6.9
2013	A+	14.30	28.65	A / 9.4	29.19%	B / 8.3
2012	A	5.50	21.86	B+ / 8.9	19.60%	B / 8.1

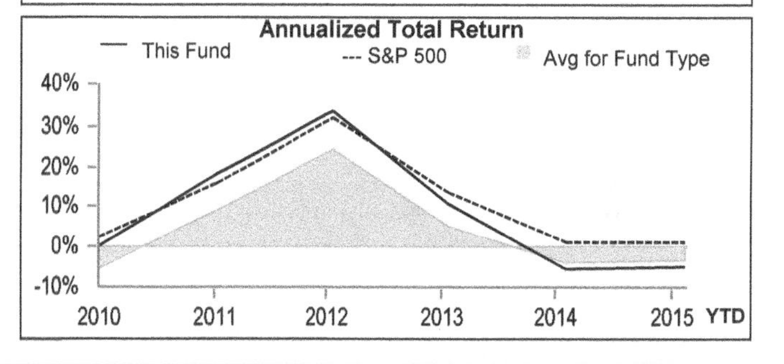

*PowerShares S&P 500 BuyWrite Por (PBP) C+ Fair

Fund Family: Invesco Powershares Capital Mgmt LL
Fund Type: Income
Inception Date: December 20, 2007

Major Rating Factors: Middle of the road best describes *PowerShares S&P 500 BuyWrite Por whose TheStreet.com Investment Rating is currently a C+ (Fair). The fund currently has a performance rating of C+ (Fair) based on an annualized return of 6.74% over the last three years and a total return of 4.53% year to date 2015. Factored into the performance evaluation is an expense ratio of 0.75% (very low).

The fund's risk rating is currently B- (Good). It carries a beta of 0.55, meaning the fund's expected move will be 5.5% for every 10% move in the market. Volatility, as measured by both the semi-deviation and a drawdown factor, is considered low. As of December 31, 2015, *PowerShares S&P 500 BuyWrite Por traded at a premium of .05% above its net asset value, which is worse than its one-year historical average premium of .04%.

Peter Hubbard has been running the fund for 9 years and currently receives a manager quality ranking of 61 (0=worst, 99=best). If you desire an average level of risk, then this fund may be an option.

Data Date	Investment Rating	Net Assets ($Mil)	Price	Performance Rating/Pts	Total Return Y-T-D	Risk Rating/Pts
12-15	C+	378.30	20.51	C+ / 6.8	4.53%	B- / 7.2
2014	C	378.30	20.73	C / 4.5	5.16%	B- / 7.5
2013	B-	199.60	20.75	C+ / 6.5	12.63%	B / 8.4
2012	C-	274.90	19.65	D+ / 2.9	5.20%	B / 8.2
2011	C+	89.50	19.62	C+ / 5.8	10.77%	B / 8.2
2010	C-	140.70	20.89	D+ / 2.8	5.51%	C+ / 6.4

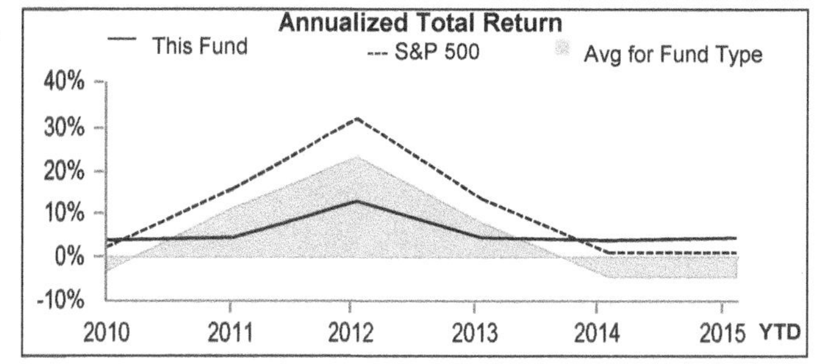

*PowerShares S&P 500 Downside Hed (PHDG) C Fair

Fund Family: Invesco Powershares Capital Mgmt LL
Fund Type: Growth and Income
Inception Date: December 6, 2012

Major Rating Factors: Middle of the road best describes *PowerShares S&P 500 Downside Hed whose TheStreet.com Investment Rating is currently a C (Fair). The fund currently has a performance rating of C (Fair) based on an annualized return of 2.05% over the last three years and a total return of -9.87% year to date 2015. Factored into the performance evaluation is an expense ratio of 0.36% (very low).

The fund's risk rating is currently B (Good). It carries a beta of 0.57, meaning the fund's expected move will be 5.7% for every 10% move in the market. Volatility, as measured by both the semi-deviation and a drawdown factor, is considered low. As of December 31, 2015, *PowerShares S&P 500 Downside Hed traded at a discount of .08% below its net asset value, which is better than its one-year historical average premium of .01%.

Peter Hubbard has been running the fund for 4 years and currently receives a manager quality ranking of 28 (0=worst, 99=best). If you desire an average level of risk, then this fund may be an option.

Data Date	Investment Rating	Net Assets ($Mil)	Price	Performance Rating/Pts	Total Return Y-T-D	Risk Rating/Pts
12-15	C	421.70	24.68	C / 4.5	-9.87%	B / 8.1
2014	C-	421.70	27.83	C / 4.4	5.97%	B- / 7.2
2013	B+	112.80	27.89	C+ / 6.4	11.09%	B+ / 9.7

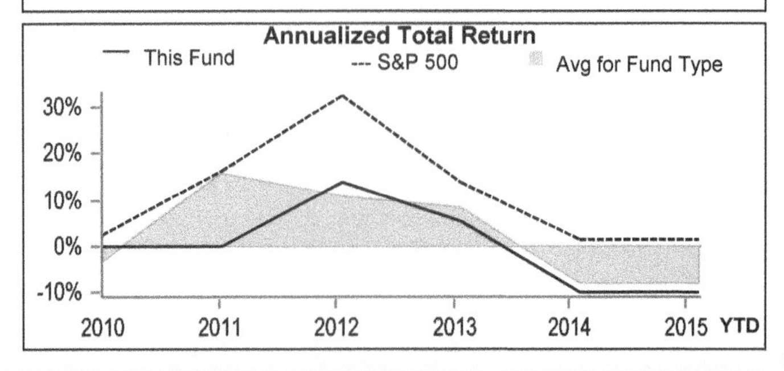

*PowerShares S&P 500 Hi Div Low V (SPHD) A Excellent

Fund Family: Invesco Powershares Capital Mgmt LL
Fund Type: Corporate - High Yield
Inception Date: October 18, 2012

Major Rating Factors:
Exceptional performance is the major factor driving the A (Excellent) TheStreet.com Investment Rating for *PowerShares S&P 500 Hi Div Low V. The fund currently has a performance rating of A- (Excellent) based on an annualized return of 13.96% over the last three years and a total return of 4.86% year to date 2015. Factored into the performance evaluation is an expense ratio of 0.30% (very low).

The fund's risk rating is currently B- (Good). It carries a beta of 1.10, meaning it is expected to move 11.0% for every 10% move in the market. Volatility, as measured by both the semi-deviation and a drawdown factor, is considered low. As of December 31, 2015, *PowerShares S&P 500 Hi Div Low V traded at a premium of .06% above its net asset value, which is worse than its one-year historical average discount of .01%.

Brian Picken has been running the fund for 4 years and currently receives a manager quality ranking of 97 (0=worst, 99=best). If you desire only a moderate level of risk and strong performance, then this fund is an excellent option.

Data Date	Investment Rating	Net Assets ($Mil)	Price	Performance Rating/Pts	Total Return Y-T-D	Risk Rating/Pts
12-15	A	177.00	33.34	A- / 9.0	4.86%	B- / 7.7
2014	A+	177.00	32.85	A- / 9.2	22.70%	B / 8.9
2013	A-	141.80	28.36	B- / 7.3	16.00%	B+ / 9.3

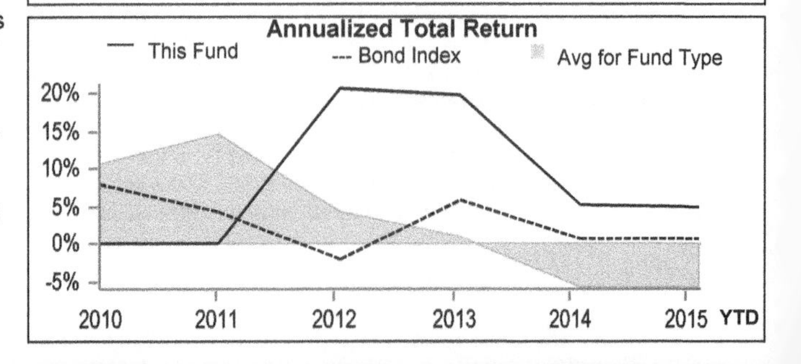

*Powershares S&P 500 High Beta Po (SPHB) B- Good

Fund Family: Invesco Powershares Capital Mgmt LL
Fund Type: Income
Inception Date: May 5, 2011

Major Rating Factors: *Powershares S&P 500 High Beta Po receives a TheStreet.com Investment Rating of B- (Good). The fund currently has a performance rating of C+ (Fair) based on an annualized return of 9.86% over the last three years and a total return of -12.66% year to date 2015. Factored into the performance evaluation is an expense ratio of 0.25% (very low).

The fund's risk rating is currently B- (Good). It carries a beta of 1.27, meaning it is expected to move 12.7% for every 10% move in the market. Volatility, as measured by both the semi-deviation and a drawdown factor, is considered low. As of December 31, 2015, *Powershares S&P 500 High Beta Po traded at a discount of .03% below its net asset value, which is worse than its one-year historical average discount of .05%.

Michael C. Jeanette has been running the fund for 5 years and currently receives a manager quality ranking of 23 (0=worst, 99=best). If you desire an average level of risk, then this fund may be an option.

Data Date	Investment Rating	Net Assets ($Mil)	Price	Performance Rating/Pts	Total Return Y-T-D	Risk Rating/Pts
12-15	B-	289.90	29.28	C+ / 6.5	-12.66%	B- / 7.8
2014	B	289.90	34.13	B+ / 8.7	13.91%	C+ / 6.2
2013	A	519.90	30.60	A+ / 9.6	33.50%	B- / 7.5
2012	B+	119.30	21.92	A- / 9.1	14.61%	B- / 7.2

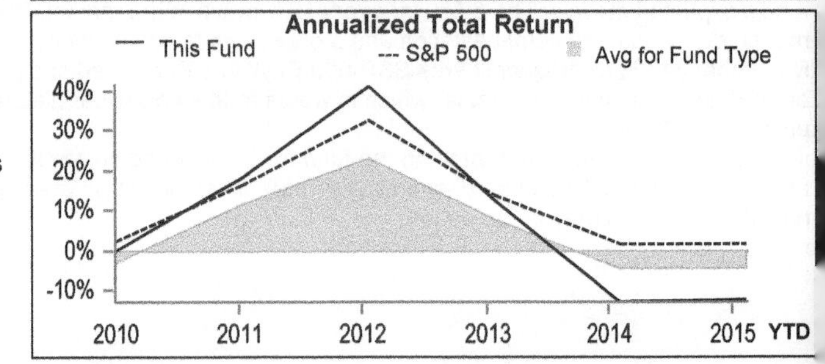

*PowerShares S&P 500 High Quality (SPHQ) A- Excellent

Fund Family: Invesco Powershares Capital Mgmt LL
Fund Type: Income
Inception Date: December 6, 2005

Major Rating Factors:
Exceptional performance is the major factor driving the A- (Excellent) TheStreet.com Investment Rating for *PowerShares S&P 500 High Quality. The fund currently has a performance rating of A- (Excellent) based on an annualized return of 15.06% over the last three years and a total return of 1.80% year to date 2015. Factored into the performance evaluation is an expense ratio of 0.29% (very low).

The fund's risk rating is currently B- (Good). It carries a beta of 0.92, meaning that its performance tracks fairly well with that of the overall stock market. Volatility, as measured by both the semi-deviation and a drawdown factor, is considered low. As of December 31, 2015, *PowerShares S&P 500 High Quality traded at a premium of .04% above its net asset value.

Peter Hubbard has been running the fund for 9 years and currently receives a manager quality ranking of 81 (0=worst, 99=best). If you desire only a moderate level of risk and strong performance, then this fund is an excellent option.

Data Date	Investment Rating	Net Assets ($Mil)	Price	Performance Rating/Pts	Total Return Y-T-D	Risk Rating/Pts
12-15	A-	398.80	23.13	A- / 9.0	1.80%	B- / 7.4
2014	A	398.80	23.28	B+ / 8.8	17.12%	B- / 7.6
2013	A	323.40	20.41	B+ / 8.5	27.94%	B / 8.7
2012	B-	175.70	15.72	C+ / 6.5	15.42%	B / 8.6
2011	C+	134.50	14.03	C / 5.1	7.33%	B / 8.4
2010	D	108.80	13.44	D / 1.7	21.20%	C+ / 6.0

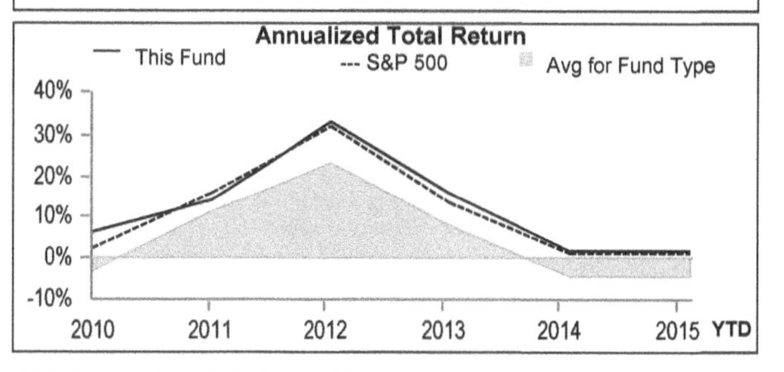

*Powershares S&P 500 Low Vol Port (SPLV) A- Excellent

Fund Family: Invesco Powershares Capital Mgmt LL
Fund Type: Growth
Inception Date: May 5, 2011

Major Rating Factors:
Strong performance is the major factor driving the A- (Excellent) TheStreet.com Investment Rating for *Powershares S&P 500 Low Vol Port. The fund currently has a performance rating of B+ (Good) based on an annualized return of 13.50% over the last three years and a total return of 3.90% year to date 2015. Factored into the performance evaluation is an expense ratio of 0.25% (very low).

The fund's risk rating is currently B- (Good). It carries a beta of 0.77, meaning the fund's expected move will be 7.7% for every 10% move in the market. Volatility, as measured by both the semi-deviation and a drawdown factor, is considered low. As of December 31, 2015, *Powershares S&P 500 Low Vol Port traded at a premium of .03% above its net asset value, which is worse than its one-year historical average discount of .04%.

Michael C. Jeanette has been running the fund for 5 years and currently receives a manager quality ranking of 83 (0=worst, 99=best). If you desire only a moderate level of risk and strong performance, then this fund is an excellent option.

Data Date	Investment Rating	Net Assets ($Mil)	Price	Performance Rating/Pts	Total Return Y-T-D	Risk Rating/Pts
12-15	A-	4,547.40	38.57	B+ / 8.9	3.90%	B- / 7.5
2014	A+	4,547.40	37.96	B / 8.0	18.69%	B+ / 9.3
2013	A	3,916.60	33.16	B / 7.9	18.45%	B+ / 9.4
2012	C+	3,092.20	27.68	C / 4.5	13.46%	B+ / 9.7

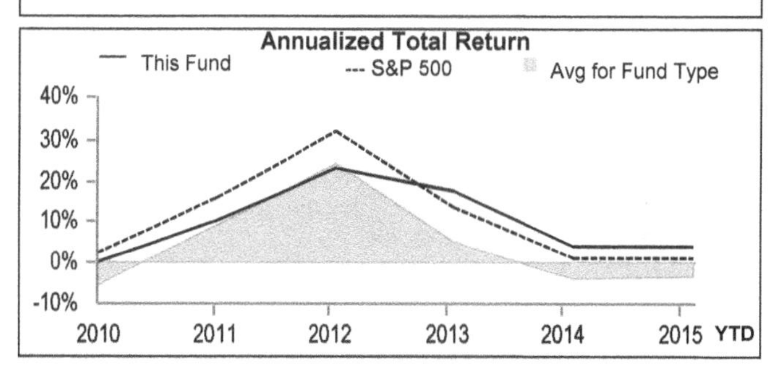

*PowerShares S&P EM High Beta (EEHB) D Weak

Fund Family: Invesco Powershares Capital Mgmt LL
Fund Type: Emerging Market
Inception Date: February 24, 2012

Major Rating Factors:
Disappointing performance is the major factor driving the D (Weak) TheStreet.com Investment Rating for *PowerShares S&P EM High Beta. The fund currently has a performance rating of D- (Weak) based on an annualized return of -15.05% over the last three years and a total return of -28.89% year to date 2015. Factored into the performance evaluation is an expense ratio of 0.29% (very low).

The fund's risk rating is currently C (Fair). It carries a beta of 1.19, meaning it is expected to move 11.9% for every 10% move in the market. Volatility, as measured by both the semi-deviation and a drawdown factor, is considered average. As of December 31, 2015, *PowerShares S&P EM High Beta traded at a discount of .42% below its net asset value, which is worse than its one-year historical average discount of .47%.

Joshua Betts has been running the fund for 4 years and currently receives a manager quality ranking of 24 (0=worst, 99=best). This fund offers an average level of risk but investors looking for strong performance will be frustrated.

Data Date	Investment Rating	Net Assets ($Mil)	Price	Performance Rating/Pts	Total Return Y-T-D	Risk Rating/Pts
12-15	D	6.30	14.21	D- / 1.1	-28.89%	C / 5.5
2014	D+	6.30	21.04	C- / 3.9	8.08%	C / 5.1
2013	D	4.10	20.44	D- / 1.1	-19.03%	B- / 7.2

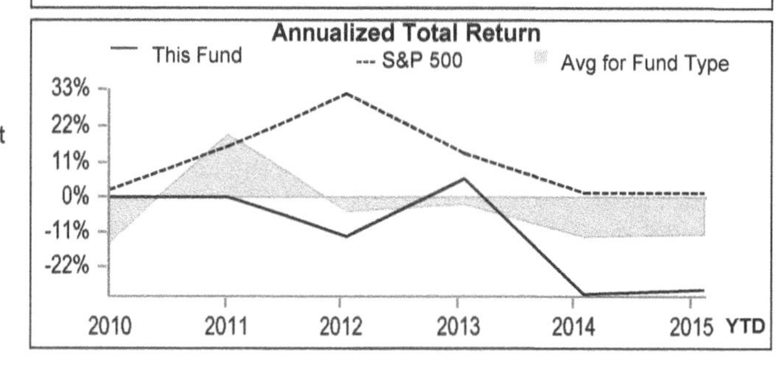

*PowerShares S&P EM Low Vol (EELV) D+ Weak

Fund Family: Invesco Powershares Capital Mgmt LL
Fund Type: Emerging Market
Inception Date: January 13, 2012

Data Date	Investment Rating	Net Assets ($Mil)	Price	Performance Rating/Pts	Total Return Y-T-D	Risk Rating/Pts
12-15	D+	233.30	20.29	D / 1.8	-17.65%	C+ / 6.8
2014	D	233.30	25.57	D- / 1.5	-3.14%	C+ / 6.2
2013	D+	226.00	27.74	D / 1.9	-4.64%	B / 8.7

Major Rating Factors:
Disappointing performance is the major factor driving the D+ (Weak) TheStreet.com Investment Rating for *PowerShares S&P EM Low Vol. The fund currently has a performance rating of D (Weak) based on an annualized return of -8.81% over the last three years and a total return of -17.65% year to date 2015. Factored into the performance evaluation is an expense ratio of 0.29% (very low).

The fund's risk rating is currently C+ (Fair). It carries a beta of 0.84, meaning the fund's expected move will be 8.4% for every 10% move in the market. Volatility, as measured by both the semi-deviation and a drawdown factor, is considered low. As of December 31, 2015, *PowerShares S&P EM Low Vol traded at a discount of 1.31% below its net asset value, which is better than its one-year historical average discount of .17%.

Joshua Betts has been running the fund for 4 years and currently receives a manager quality ranking of 41 (0=worst, 99=best). This fund offers only a moderate level of risk but investors looking for strong performance are still waiting.

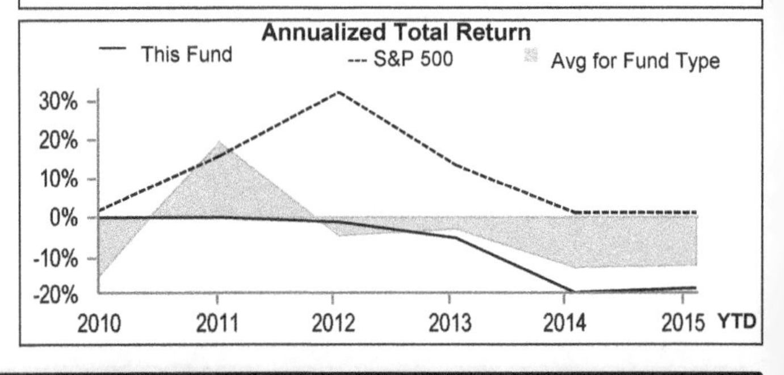

*PowerShares S&P Intl Dev Hi Beta (IDHB) D+ Weak

Fund Family: Invesco Powershares Capital Mgmt LL
Fund Type: Foreign
Inception Date: February 24, 2012

Data Date	Investment Rating	Net Assets ($Mil)	Price	Performance Rating/Pts	Total Return Y-T-D	Risk Rating/Pts
12-15	D+	4.30	23.37	C- / 3.1	-11.57%	C / 5.2
2014	D	4.30	27.06	D- / 1.2	-4.83%	B- / 7.2
2013	B+	5.90	29.74	A- / 9.1	16.72%	B- / 7.3

Major Rating Factors: *PowerShares S&P Intl Dev Hi Beta receives a TheStreet.com Investment Rating of D+ (Weak). The fund currently has a performance rating of C- (Fair) based on an annualized return of -0.76% over the last three years and a total return of -11.57% year to date 2015. Factored into the performance evaluation is an expense ratio of 0.26% (very low).

The fund's risk rating is currently C (Fair). It carries a beta of 1.36, meaning it is expected to move 13.6% for every 10% move in the market. Volatility, as measured by both the semi-deviation and a drawdown factor, is considered average. As of December 31, 2015, *PowerShares S&P Intl Dev Hi Beta traded at a premium of .30% above its net asset value, which is better than its one-year historical average premium of .96%.

Joshua Betts has been running the fund for 4 years and currently receives a manager quality ranking of 22 (0=worst, 99=best). If you desire an average level of risk, then this fund may be an option.

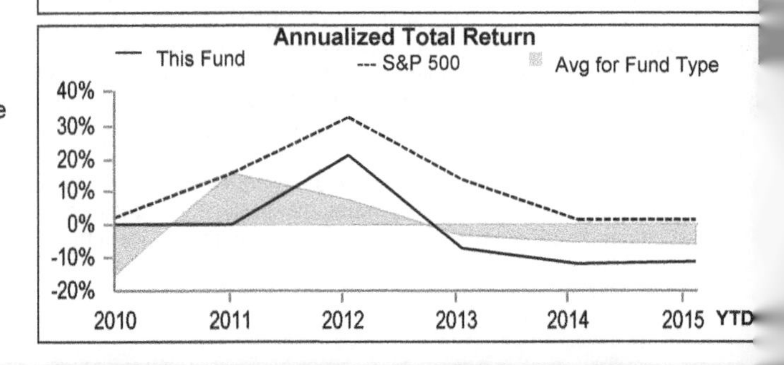

*PowerShares S&P Intl Dev High Qu (IDHQ) B Good

Fund Family: Invesco Powershares Capital Mgmt LL
Fund Type: Foreign
Inception Date: June 13, 2007

Data Date	Investment Rating	Net Assets ($Mil)	Price	Performance Rating/Pts	Total Return Y-T-D	Risk Rating/Pts
12-15	B	16.50	20.15	B- / 7.0	8.51%	B- / 7.6
2014	C	16.50	19.06	C / 5.5	-1.17%	C+ / 6.9
2013	C+	21.70	19.85	C+ / 6.0	15.65%	B- / 7.7
2012	C-	18.90	17.33	C / 4.3	23.03%	B- / 7.5
2011	C-	17.70	14.57	C- / 3.3	-16.27%	B- / 7.5
2010	D	31.70	17.48	D+ / 2.5	16.28%	C / 4.7

Major Rating Factors: Strong performance is the major factor driving the B (Good) TheStreet.com Investment Rating for *PowerShares S&P Intl Dev High Qu. The fund currently has a performance rating of B- (Good) based on an annualized return of 7.12% over the last three years and a total return of 8.51% year to date 2015. Factored into the performance evaluation is an expense ratio of 0.47% (very low).

The fund's risk rating is currently B- (Good). It carries a beta of 0.68, meaning the fund's expected move will be 6.8% for every 10% move in the market. Volatility, as measured by both the semi-deviation and a drawdown factor, is considered low. As of December 31, 2015, *PowerShares S&P Intl Dev High Qu traded at a premium of .15% above its net asset value, which is better than its one-year historical average premium of .45%.

Peter Hubbard has been running the fund for 9 years and currently receives a manager quality ranking of 86 (0=worst, 99=best). If you desire only a moderate level of risk and strong performance, then this fund is an excellent option.

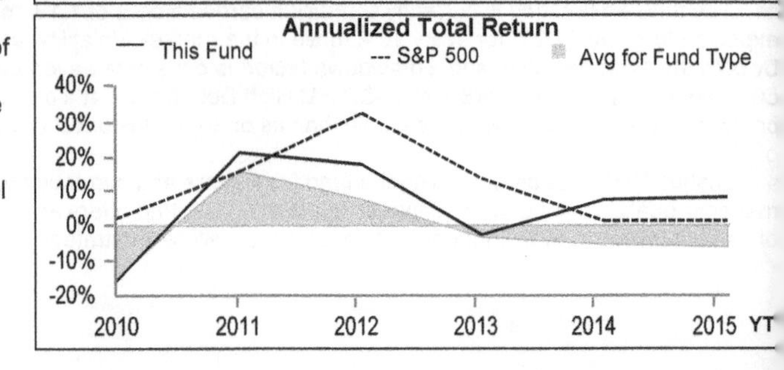

*PowerShares S&P Intl Dev Low Vol (IDLV) C+ Fair

Fund Family: Invesco Powershares Capital Mgmt LL
Fund Type: Foreign
Inception Date: January 13, 2012

Major Rating Factors: Middle of the road best describes *PowerShares S&P Intl Dev Low Vol whose TheStreet.com Investment Rating is currently a C+ (Fair). The fund currently has a performance rating of C (Fair) based on an annualized return of 3.99% over the last three years and a total return of -3.48% year to date 2015. Factored into the performance evaluation is an expense ratio of 0.25% (very low).

The fund's risk rating is currently B (Good). It carries a beta of 0.78, meaning the fund's expected move will be 7.8% for every 10% move in the market. Volatility, as measured by both the semi-deviation and a drawdown factor, is considered low. As of December 31, 2015, *PowerShares S&P Intl Dev Low Vol traded at a discount of .24% below its net asset value, which is better than its one-year historical average premium of .06%.

Joshua Betts has been running the fund for 4 years and currently receives a manager quality ranking of 66 (0=worst, 99=best). If you desire an average level of risk, then this fund may be an option.

Data Date	Investment Rating	Net Assets ($Mil)	Price	Performance Rating/Pts	Total Return Y-T-D	Risk Rating/Pts
12-15	C+	254.30	28.60	C / 5.5	-3.48%	B / 8.1
2014	D+	254.30	30.94	D+ / 2.5	2.90%	C+ / 6.7
2013	B+	151.10	31.52	B- / 7.5	14.48%	B / 8.7

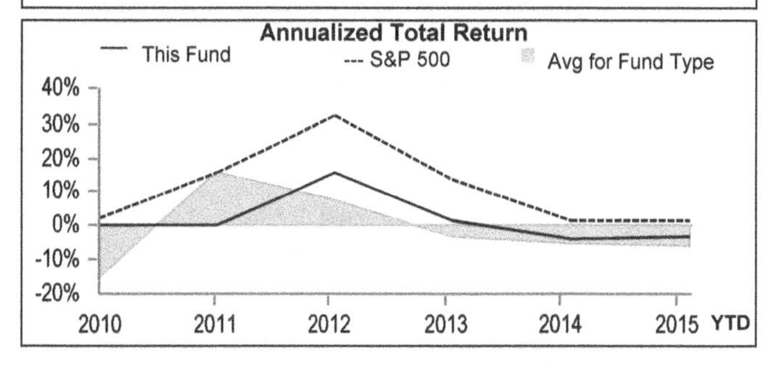

*PowerShares S&P MidCap Low Vol (XMLV) B- Good

Fund Family: Invesco Powershares Capital Mgmt LL
Fund Type: Growth
Inception Date: February 15, 2013

Major Rating Factors: *PowerShares S&P MidCap Low Vol receives a TheStreet.com Investment Rating of B- (Good). The fund currently has a performance rating of C+ (Fair) based on an annualized return of 0.00% over the last three years and a total return of 5.17% year to date 2015. Factored into the performance evaluation is an expense ratio of 0.25% (very low).

The fund's risk rating is currently B- (Good). It carries a beta of 0.00, meaning the fund's expected move will be 0.0% for every 10% move in the market. Volatility, as measured by both the semi-deviation and a drawdown factor, is considered low. As of December 31, 2015, *PowerShares S&P MidCap Low Vol traded at a premium of .06% above its net asset value, which is worse than its one-year historical average premium of .01%.

Michael C. Jeanette has been running the fund for 3 years and currently receives a manager quality ranking of 88 (0=worst, 99=best). If you desire an average level of risk, then this fund may be an option.

Data Date	Investment Rating	Net Assets ($Mil)	Price	Performance Rating/Pts	Total Return Y-T-D	Risk Rating/Pts
12-15	B-	38.60	34.01	C+ / 6.9	5.17%	B- / 7.4
2014	A+	38.60	32.88	A- / 9.2	20.74%	B / 8.7

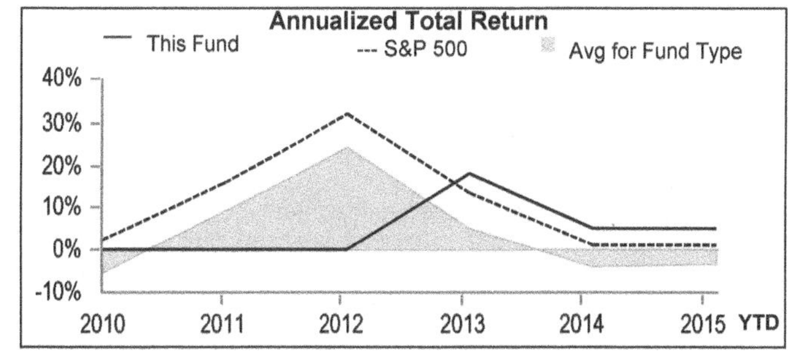

*PowerShares S&P SC Cnsmr Discr (PSCD) C+ Fair

Fund Family: Invesco Powershares Capital Mgmt LL
Fund Type: Growth
Inception Date: April 6, 2010

Major Rating Factors: Middle of the road best describes *PowerShares S&P SC Cnsmr Discr whose TheStreet.com Investment Rating is currently a C+ (Fair). The fund currently has a performance rating of C+ (Fair) based on an annualized return of 10.98% over the last three years and a total return of -7.96% year to date 2015. Factored into the performance evaluation is an expense ratio of 0.29% (very low).

The fund's risk rating is currently C+ (Fair). It carries a beta of 1.09, meaning that its performance tracks fairly well with that of the overall stock market. Volatility, as measured by both the semi-deviation and a drawdown factor, is considered low. As of December 31, 2015, *PowerShares S&P SC Cnsmr Discr traded at a premium of .26% above its net asset value, which is worse than its one-year historical average premium of .03%.

Michael C. Jeanette has been running the fund for 6 years and currently receives a manager quality ranking of 39 (0=worst, 99=best). If you desire an average level of risk, then this fund may be an option.

Data Date	Investment Rating	Net Assets ($Mil)	Price	Performance Rating/Pts	Total Return Y-T-D	Risk Rating/Pts
12-15	C+	103.80	45.92	C+ / 6.8	-7.96%	C+ / 6.3
2014	B+	103.80	50.71	A- / 9.1	4.61%	C+ / 6.7
2013	A	119.80	49.09	A / 9.3	42.85%	B- / 7.9
2012	B+	63.00	32.98	A- / 9.1	23.09%	B- / 7.4
2011	D	43.30	27.10	D / 1.8	-1.00%	B- / 7.3

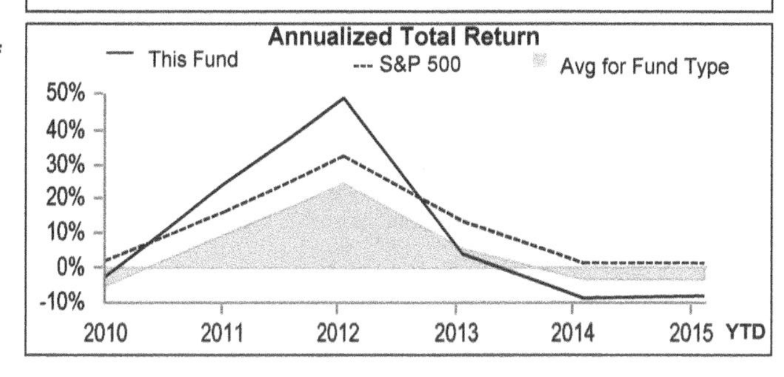

*PowerShares S&P SC Cnsmr Staples (PSCC) A- Excellent

Fund Family: Invesco Powershares Capital Mgmt LL
Fund Type: Growth
Inception Date: April 6, 2010

Major Rating Factors:
Exceptional performance is the major factor driving the A- (Excellent) TheStreet.com Investment Rating for *PowerShares S&P SC Cnsmr Staples. The fund currently has a performance rating of A- (Excellent) based on an annualized return of 16.75% over the last three years and a total return of 3.33% year to date 2015. Factored into the performance evaluation is an expense ratio of 0.29% (very low).

The fund's risk rating is currently B- (Good). It carries a beta of 0.87, meaning the fund's expected move will be 8.7% for every 10% move in the market. Volatility, as measured by both the semi-deviation and a drawdown factor, is considered low. As of December 31, 2015, *PowerShares S&P SC Cnsmr Staples traded at a premium of .62% above its net asset value, which is worse than its one-year historical average discount of .03%.

Michael C. Jeanette has been running the fund for 6 years and currently receives a manager quality ranking of 89 (0=worst, 99=best). If you desire only a moderate level of risk and strong performance, then this fund is an excellent option.

Data Date	Investment Rating	Net Assets ($Mil)	Price	Performance Rating/Pts	Total Return Y-T-D	Risk Rating/Pts
12-15	A-	17.80	54.90	A- / 9.1	3.33%	B- / 7.2
2014	A-	17.80	54.47	A- / 9.0	13.28%	B- / 7.2
2013	A+	59.70	49.83	A- / 9.1	37.52%	B / 8.8
2012	C+	27.70	34.44	C / 4.9	14.97%	B / 8.7
2011	C	20.30	31.45	C- / 3.3	8.98%	B / 8.7

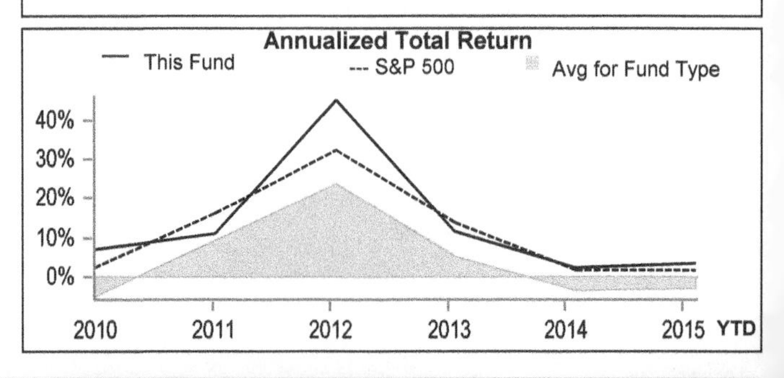

*PowerShares S&P SC Energy (PSCE) E Very Weak

Fund Family: Invesco Powershares Capital Mgmt LL
Fund Type: Growth
Inception Date: April 6, 2010

Major Rating Factors: *PowerShares S&P SC Energy has adopted a risky asset allocation strategy and currently receives an overall TheStreet.com Investment Rating of E (Very Weak). The fund has an above average level of volatility, as measured by both semi-deviation and drawdown factors. It carries a beta of 1.55, meaning it is expected to move 15.5% for every 10% move in the market. As of December 31, 2015, *PowerShares S&P SC Energy traded at a discount of .07% below its net asset value, which is better than its one-year historical average discount of .03%. Unfortunately, the high level of risk (D+, Weak) failed to pay off as investors endured very poor performance.

The fund's performance rating is currently E (Very Weak). It has registered an annualized return of -23.73% over the last three years and is down -48.26% year to date 2015. Factored into the performance evaluation is an expense ratio of 0.29% (very low).

Michael C. Jeanette has been running the fund for 6 years and currently receives a manager quality ranking of 1 (0=worst, 99=best). If you can tolerate high levels of risk in the hope of improved future returns, holding this fund may be an option.

Data Date	Investment Rating	Net Assets ($Mil)	Price	Performance Rating/Pts	Total Return Y-T-D	Risk Rating/Pts
12-15	E	34.50	15.37	E / 0.5	-48.26%	D+ / 2.9
2014	D-	34.50	29.68	D- / 1.0	-34.31%	C / 4.7
2013	C	48.60	46.34	B- / 7.2	29.53%	C+ / 5.9
2012	D	30.30	33.64	C- / 3.1	2.20%	C+ / 5.7
2011	D+	54.80	34.30	C- / 4.0	7.21%	C+ / 5.8

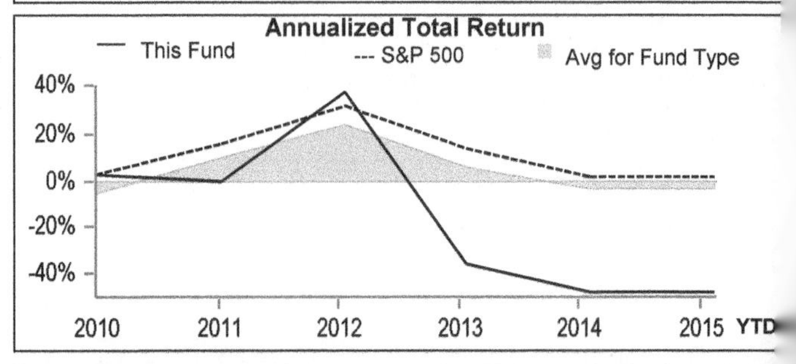

*PowerShares S&P SC Financials (PSCF) B Good

Fund Family: Invesco Powershares Capital Mgmt LL
Fund Type: Growth
Inception Date: April 6, 2010

Major Rating Factors: Strong performance is the major factor driving the B (Good) TheStreet.com Investment Rating for *PowerShares S&P SC Financials. The fund currently has a performance rating of B (Good) based on an annualized return of 11.28% over the last three years and a total return of 0.46% year to date 2015. Factored into the performance evaluation is an expense ratio of 0.29% (very low).

The fund's risk rating is currently B- (Good). It carries a beta of 0.87, meaning the fund's expected move will be 8.7% for every 10% move in the market. Volatility, as measured by both the semi-deviation and a drawdown factor, is considered low. As of December 31, 2015, *PowerShares S&P SC Financials traded at a premium of .10% above its net asset value, which is worse than its one-year historical average discount of .08%.

Michael C. Jeanette has been running the fund for 6 years and currently receives a manager quality ranking of 63 (0=worst, 99=best). If you desire only a moderate level of risk and strong performance, then this fund is an excellent option.

Data Date	Investment Rating	Net Assets ($Mil)	Price	Performance Rating/Pts	Total Return Y-T-D	Risk Rating/Pts
12-15	B	104.40	40.78	B / 7.9	0.46%	B- / 7.2
2014	B	104.40	41.70	B / 7.7	8.54%	B- / 7.2
2013	B+	106.90	39.71	B / 8.2	26.56%	B / 8.1
2012	B-	74.10	30.89	B- / 7.1	17.63%	B- / 7.8
2011	C	62.00	27.04	C / 4.3	4.16%	B- / 7.8

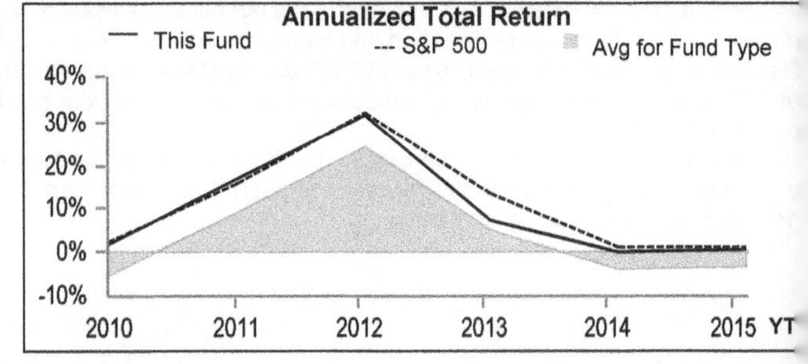

*PowerShares S&P SC Health Care (PSCH) A Excellent

Fund Family: Invesco Powershares Capital Mgmt LL
Fund Type: Growth
Inception Date: April 6, 2010

Major Rating Factors:
Exceptional performance is the major factor driving the A (Excellent) TheStreet.com Investment Rating for *PowerShares S&P SC Health Care. The fund currently has a performance rating of A+ (Excellent) based on an annualized return of 26.28% over the last three years and a total return of 21.58% year to date 2015. Factored into the performance evaluation is an expense ratio of 0.29% (very low).

The fund's risk rating is currently C+ (Fair). It carries a beta of 0.78, meaning the fund's expected move will be 7.8% for every 10% move in the market. Volatility, as measured by both the semi-deviation and a drawdown factor, is considered low. As of December 31, 2015, *PowerShares S&P SC Health Care traded at a premium of .11% above its net asset value, which is worse than its one-year historical average premium of .05%.

Michael C. Jeanette has been running the fund for 6 years and currently receives a manager quality ranking of 97 (0=worst, 99=best). If you desire only a moderate level of risk and strong performance, then this fund is an excellent option.

Data Date	Investment Rating	Net Assets ($Mil)	Price	Performance Rating/Pts	Total Return Y-T-D	Risk Rating/Pts
12-15	A	150.90	71.87	A+ / 9.7	21.58%	C+ / 6.9
2014	A-	150.90	59.76	A / 9.3	12.48%	B- / 7.1
2013	A+	201.10	55.12	A / 9.5	50.00%	B / 8.0
2012	C+	109.80	35.35	C+ / 6.2	17.04%	B- / 7.9
2011	C	103.80	31.53	C- / 4.1	12.05%	B / 8.0

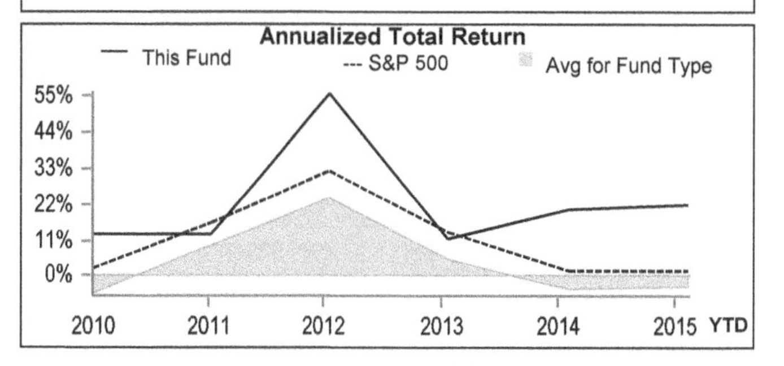

*PowerShares S&P SC Industrials (PSCI) C+ Fair

Fund Family: Invesco Powershares Capital Mgmt LL
Fund Type: Growth
Inception Date: April 6, 2010

Major Rating Factors: Strong performance is the major factor driving the C+ (Fair) TheStreet.com Investment Rating for *PowerShares S&P SC Industrials. The fund currently has a performance rating of B- (Good) based on an annualized return of 9.70% over the last three years and a total return of -3.36% year to date 2015. Factored into the performance evaluation is an expense ratio of 0.29% (very low).

The fund's risk rating is currently C+ (Fair). It carries a beta of 1.28, meaning it is expected to move 12.8% for every 10% move in the market. Volatility, as measured by both the semi-deviation and a drawdown factor, is considered low. As of December 31, 2015, *PowerShares S&P SC Industrials traded at a premium of .07% above its net asset value, which is worse than its one-year historical average discount of .09%.

Michael C. Jeanette has been running the fund for 6 years and currently receives a manager quality ranking of 23 (0=worst, 99=best). If you desire only a moderate level of risk and strong performance, then this fund is an excellent option.

Data Date	Investment Rating	Net Assets ($Mil)	Price	Performance Rating/Pts	Total Return Y-T-D	Risk Rating/Pts
12-15	C+	103.90	43.23	B- / 7.1	-3.36%	C+ / 6.6
2014	B-	103.90	46.69	B / 8.1	4.21%	C+ / 6.7
2013	B+	93.30	45.72	A- / 9.0	35.48%	B- / 7.5
2012	B+	24.30	32.03	A / 9.5	20.37%	B- / 7.2
2011	D	25.90	27.38	D / 1.9	-3.50%	B- / 7.2

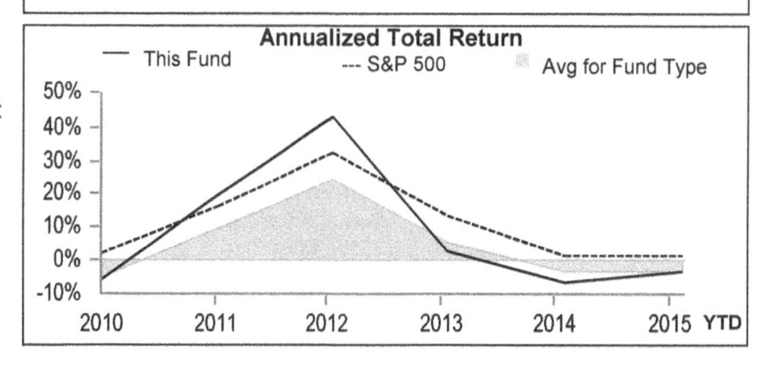

*PowerShares S&P SC Information T (PSCT) A Excellent

Fund Family: Invesco Powershares Capital Mgmt LL
Fund Type: Growth
Inception Date: April 6, 2010

Major Rating Factors:
Exceptional performance is the major factor driving the A (Excellent) TheStreet.com Investment Rating for *PowerShares S&P SC Information T. The fund currently has a performance rating of A (Excellent) based on an annualized return of 18.25% over the last three years and a total return of 5.74% year to date 2015. Factored into the performance evaluation is an expense ratio of 0.29% (very low).

The fund's risk rating is currently B- (Good). It carries a beta of 0.99, meaning that its performance tracks fairly well with that of the overall stock market. Volatility, as measured by both the semi-deviation and a drawdown factor, is considered low. As of December 31, 2015, *PowerShares S&P SC Information T traded at a premium of .10% above its net asset value, which is worse than its one-year historical average premium of .02%.

Michael C. Jeanette has been running the fund for 6 years and currently receives a manager quality ranking of 87 (0=worst, 99=best). If you desire only a moderate level of risk and strong performance, then this fund is an excellent option.

Data Date	Investment Rating	Net Assets ($Mil)	Price	Performance Rating/Pts	Total Return Y-T-D	Risk Rating/Pts
12-15	A	214.60	52.32	A / 9.4	5.74%	B- / 7.2
2014	B+	214.60	50.22	A- / 9.0	13.91%	C+ / 6.7
2013	B+	231.30	44.53	B+ / 8.7	39.12%	B- / 7.2
2012	B	84.90	30.69	B / 8.2	12.31%	B- / 7.0
2011	D	78.10	28.03	D / 1.7	-4.76%	B- / 7.0

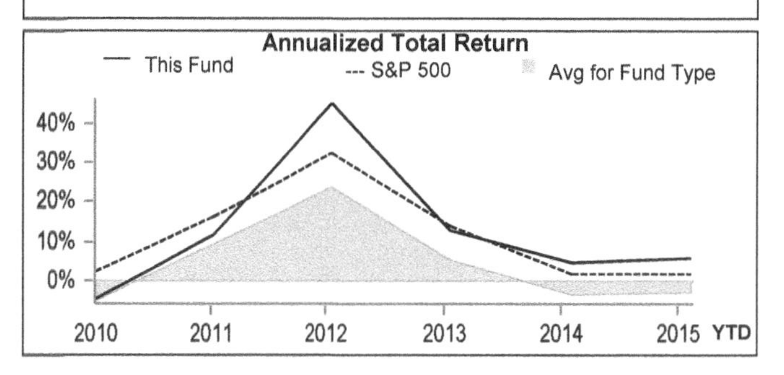

*PowerShares S&P SC Materials (PSCM) D Weak

Fund Family: Invesco Powershares Capital Mgmt LL
Fund Type: Growth
Inception Date: April 6, 2010

Major Rating Factors:
Disappointing performance is the major factor driving the D (Weak) TheStreet.com Investment Rating for *PowerShares S&P SC Materials. The fund currently has a performance rating of D+ (Weak) based on an annualized return of -1.47% over the last three years and a total return of -25.54% year to date 2015. Factored into the performance evaluation is an expense ratio of 0.29% (very low).

The fund's risk rating is currently C (Fair). It carries a beta of 1.46, meaning it is expected to move 14.6% for every 10% move in the market. Volatility, as measured by both the semi-deviation and a drawdown factor, is considered average. As of December 31, 2015, *PowerShares S&P SC Materials traded at a premium of .16% above its net asset value, which is worse than its one-year historical average discount of .15%.

Michael C. Jeanette has been running the fund for 6 years and currently receives a manager quality ranking of 8 (0=worst, 99=best). This fund offers an average level of risk but investors looking for strong performance will be frustrated.

Data Date	Investment Rating	Net Assets ($Mil)	Price	Performance Rating/Pts	Total Return Y-T-D	Risk Rating/Pts
12-15	D	58.40	31.32	D+ / 2.6	-25.54%	C / 4.7
2014	C+	58.40	42.72	B- / 7.2	0.67%	C+ / 6.4
2013	B+	21.50	43.15	B+ / 8.6	28.02%	B- / 7.5
2012	B+	6.40	31.49	B+ / 8.8	25.18%	B- / 7.2
2011	D	3.90	25.84	D- / 1.4	-6.25%	B- / 7.2

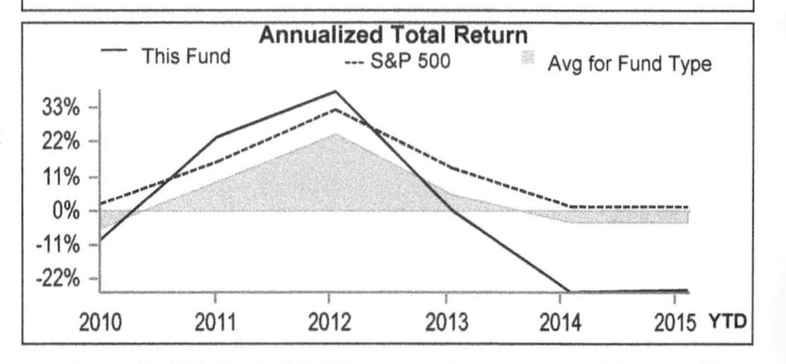

*PowerShares S&P SC Utilities (PSCU) A- Excellent

Fund Family: Invesco Powershares Capital Mgmt LL
Fund Type: Growth
Inception Date: April 6, 2010

Major Rating Factors:
Exceptional performance is the major factor driving the A- (Excellent) TheStreet.com Investment Rating for *PowerShares S&P SC Utilities. The fund currently has a performance rating of A- (Excellent) based on an annualized return of 13.70% over the last three years and a total return of 8.09% year to date 2015. Factored into the performance evaluation is an expense ratio of 0.29% (very low).

The fund's risk rating is currently B- (Good). It carries a beta of 0.85, meaning the fund's expected move will be 8.5% for every 10% move in the market. Volatility, as measured by both the semi-deviation and a drawdown factor, is considered low. As of December 31, 2015, *PowerShares S&P SC Utilities traded at a premium of .07% above its net asset value, which is worse than its one-year historical average discount of .08%.

Michael C. Jeanette has been running the fund for 6 years and currently receives a manager quality ranking of 81 (0=worst, 99=best). If you desire only a moderate level of risk and strong performance, then this fund is an excellent option.

Data Date	Investment Rating	Net Assets ($Mil)	Price	Performance Rating/Pts	Total Return Y-T-D	Risk Rating/Pts
12-15	A-	35.40	41.17	A- / 9.1	8.09%	B- / 7.1
2014	B-	35.40	40.15	B / 7.9	19.65%	C+ / 6.9
2013	B	34.90	35.02	C+ / 6.9	16.12%	B / 8.9
2012	D+	28.40	29.56	D- / 1.5	3.67%	B / 8.9
2011	C+	46.10	30.75	C / 4.8	11.07%	B+ / 9.0

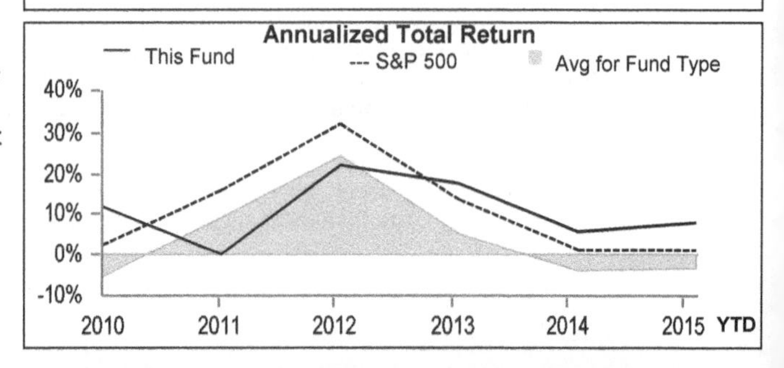

*PowerShares S&P SmallCap Low Vol (XSLV) C+ Fair

Fund Family: Invesco Powershares Capital Mgmt LL
Fund Type: Growth
Inception Date: February 15, 2013

Major Rating Factors: Middle of the road best describes *PowerShares S&P SmallCap Low Vol whose TheStreet.com Investment Rating is currently a C+ (Fair). The fund currently has a performance rating of C+ (Fair) based on an annualized return of 0.00% over the last three years and a total return of 3.05% year to date 2015. Factored into the performance evaluation is an expense ratio of 0.25% (very low).

The fund's risk rating is currently B- (Good). It carries a beta of 0.00, meaning the fund's expected move will be 0.0% for every 10% move in the market. Volatility, as measured by both the semi-deviation and a drawdown factor, is considered low. As of December 31, 2015, *PowerShares S&P SmallCap Low Vol traded at a premium of .09% above its net asset value, which is worse than its one-year historical average premium of .05%.

Michael C. Jeanette has been running the fund for 3 years and currently receives a manager quality ranking of 80 (0=worst, 99=best). If you desire an average level of risk, then this fund may be an option.

Data Date	Investment Rating	Net Assets ($Mil)	Price	Performance Rating/Pts	Total Return Y-T-D	Risk Rating/Pts
12-15	C+	55.40	33.75	C+ / 6.4	3.05%	B- / 7.1
2014	B	55.40	33.60	B / 7.7	12.74%	B- / 7.3

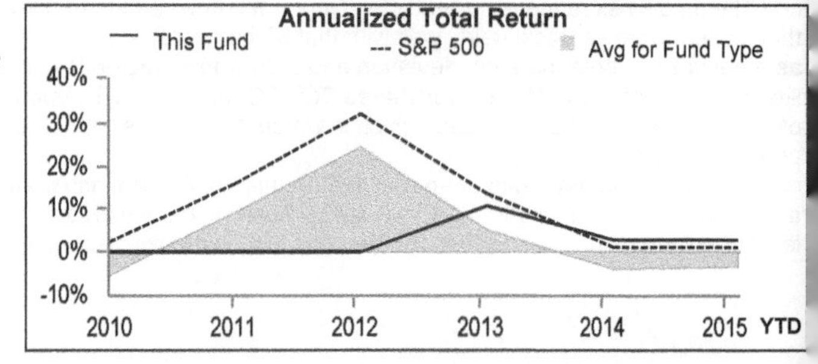

*PowerShares Senior Loan (BKLN) C+ Fair

Fund Family: Invesco Powershares Capital Mgmt LL
Fund Type: Loan Participation
Inception Date: March 1, 2011

Major Rating Factors: Middle of the road best describes *PowerShares Senior Loan whose TheStreet.com Investment Rating is currently a C+ (Fair). The fund currently has a performance rating of C- (Fair) based on an annualized return of 0.37% over the last three years and a total return of -2.89% year to date 2015. Factored into the performance evaluation is an expense ratio of 0.64% (very low).

The fund's risk rating is currently B+ (Good). It carries a beta of 1.95, meaning it is expected to move 19.5% for every 10% move in the market. Volatility, as measured by both the semi-deviation and a drawdown factor, is considered very low. As of December 31, 2015, *PowerShares Senior Loan traded at a discount of .13% below its net asset value, which is in line with its one-year historical average discount of .13%.

Peter Hubbard has been running the fund for 5 years and currently receives a manager quality ranking of 72 (0=worst, 99=best). If you desire an average level of risk, then this fund may be an option.

Data Date	Investment Rating	Net Assets ($Mil)	Price	Performance Rating/Pts	Total Return Y-T-D	Risk Rating/Pts
12-15	C+	6,475.00	22.40	C- / 4.0	-2.89%	B+ / 9.0
2014	C	6,475.00	24.03	C- / 3.7	0.46%	B / 8.7
2013	C+	6,439.70	24.88	C / 4.4	3.82%	B+ / 9.6
2012	C	1,499.40	24.98	C- / 3.7	9.36%	B+ / 9.6

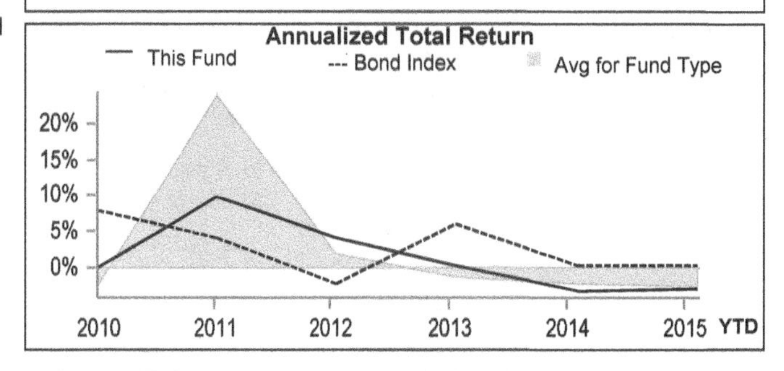

*PowerShares Variable Rate Prefer (VRP) C+ Fair

Fund Family: Invesco Powershares Capital Mgmt LL
Fund Type: Global
Inception Date: May 1, 2014

Major Rating Factors: Middle of the road best describes *PowerShares Variable Rate Prefer whose TheStreet.com Investment Rating is currently a C+ (Fair). The fund currently has a performance rating of C (Fair) based on an annualized return of 0.00% over the last three years and a total return of 2.65% year to date 2015. Factored into the performance evaluation is an expense ratio of 0.50% (very low).

The fund's risk rating is currently B- (Good). It carries a beta of 0.00, meaning the fund's expected move will be 0.0% for every 10% move in the market. Volatility, as measured by both the semi-deviation and a drawdown factor, is considered low. As of December 31, 2015, *PowerShares Variable Rate Prefer traded at a premium of .41% above its net asset value, which is worse than its one-year historical average premium of .27%.

Peter Hubbard has been running the fund for 2 years and currently receives a manager quality ranking of 86 (0=worst, 99=best). If you desire an average level of risk, then this fund may be an option.

Data Date	Investment Rating	Net Assets ($Mil)	Price	Performance Rating/Pts	Total Return Y-T-D	Risk Rating/Pts
12-15	C+	79.50	24.26	C / 5.5	2.65%	B- / 7.8

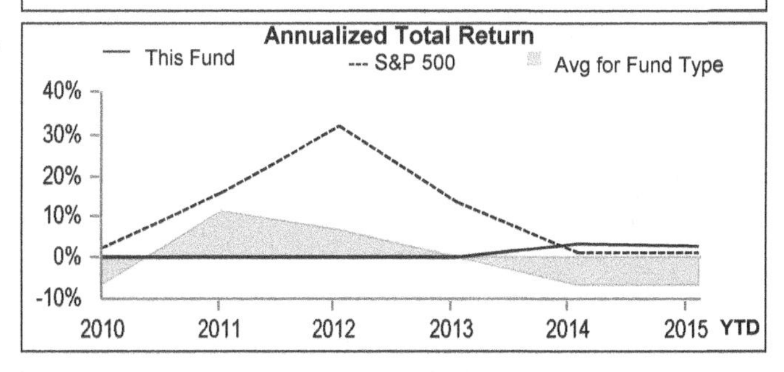

*PowerShares VRDO Tax-Free Weekly (PVI) B- Good

Fund Family: Invesco Powershares Capital Mgmt LL
Fund Type: Municipal - High Yield
Inception Date: November 14, 2007

Major Rating Factors: *PowerShares VRDO Tax-Free Weekly receives a TheStreet.com Investment Rating of B- (Good). The fund currently has a performance rating of C- (Fair) based on an annualized return of -0.08% over the last three years and a total return of -0.18% year to date 2015. Factored into the performance evaluation is an expense ratio of 0.25% (very low).

The fund's risk rating is currently B+ (Good). It carries a beta of -0.02, meaning the fund's expected move will be -0.2% for every 10% move in the market. Volatility, as measured by both the semi-deviation and a drawdown factor, is considered very low. As of December 31, 2015, *PowerShares VRDO Tax-Free Weekly traded at a discount of .04% below its net asset value, which is better than its one-year historical average discount of .02%.

Peter Hubbard has been running the fund for 9 years and currently receives a manager quality ranking of 67 (0=worst, 99=best). If you desire an average level of risk, then this fund may be an option.

Data Date	Investment Rating	Net Assets ($Mil)	Price	Performance Rating/Pts	Total Return Y-T-D	Risk Rating/Pts
12-15	B-	123.60	24.91	C- / 4.2	-0.18%	B+ / 9.9
2014	C	123.60	24.96	D+ / 2.8	-0.08%	B+ / 9.1
2013	C	176.20	24.98	D+ / 2.6	0.03%	B+ / 9.9
2012	C-	274.90	24.99	D- / 1.4	0.13%	B+ / 9.9
2011	C	436.20	25.02	D / 2.1	0.47%	B+ / 9.9
2010	B-	566.30	24.99	C- / 3.3	0.32%	B+ / 9.1

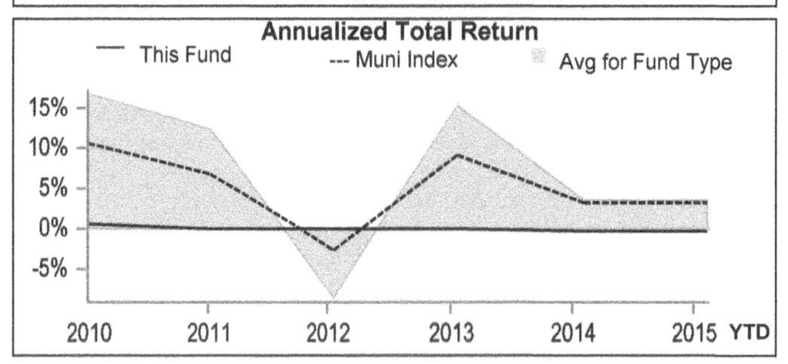

*PowerShares Water Resources (PHO) C- Fair

Fund Family: Invesco Powershares Capital Mgmt LL
Fund Type: Income
Inception Date: December 6, 2005

Major Rating Factors: Middle of the road best describes *PowerShares Water Resources whose TheStreet.com Investment Rating is currently a C- (Fair). The fund currently has a performance rating of C- (Fair) based on an annualized return of 1.45% over the last three years and a total return of -15.21% year to date 2015. Factored into the performance evaluation is an expense ratio of 0.61% (very low).

The fund's risk rating is currently B- (Good). It carries a beta of 1.27, meaning it is expected to move 12.7% for every 10% move in the market. Volatility, as measured by both the semi-deviation and a drawdown factor, is considered low. As of December 31, 2015, *PowerShares Water Resources traded at a discount of .09% below its net asset value, which is better than its one-year historical average discount of .08%.

Peter Hubbard has been running the fund for 9 years and currently receives a manager quality ranking of 11 (0=worst, 99=best). If you desire an average level of risk, then this fund may be an option.

Data Date	Investment Rating	Net Assets ($Mil)	Price	Performance Rating/Pts	Total Return Y-T-D	Risk Rating/Pts
12-15	C-	918.50	21.67	C- / 3.7	-15.21%	B- / 7.3
2014	C+	918.50	25.75	C+ / 6.6	0.17%	B- / 7.6
2013	B-	1,004.90	26.22	B / 7.6	23.00%	B- / 7.3
2012	C	823.70	20.75	C+ / 5.9	23.06%	C+ / 6.8
2011	D+	808.80	16.85	C- / 3.1	-7.86%	C+ / 6.4
2010	D+	1,162.50	18.99	C- / 3.9	13.73%	C / 5.0

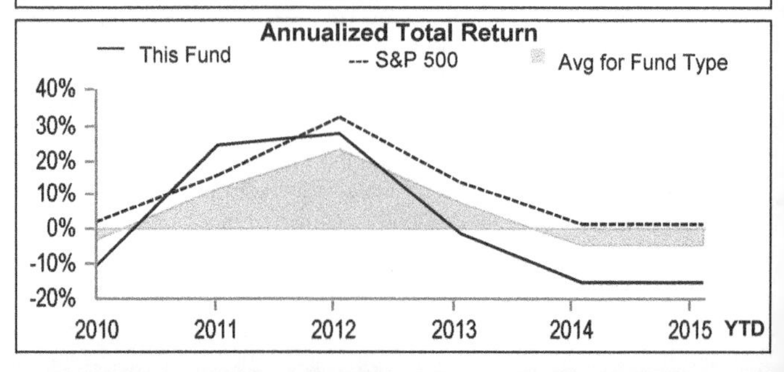

*PowerShares Wilder Clean Energy (PBW) C Fair

Fund Family: Invesco Powershares Capital Mgmt LL
Fund Type: Energy/Natural Resources
Inception Date: March 3, 2005

Major Rating Factors: Middle of the road best describes *PowerShares Wilder Clean Energy whose TheStreet.com Investment Rating is currently a C (Fair). The fund currently has a performance rating of C+ (Fair) based on an annualized return of 5.00% over the last three years and a total return of -8.54% year to date 2015. Factored into the performance evaluation is an expense ratio of 0.70% (very low).

The fund's risk rating is currently C+ (Fair). It carries a beta of 0.74, meaning the fund's expected move will be 7.4% for every 10% move in the market. Volatility, as measured by both the semi-deviation and a drawdown factor, is considered low. As of December 31, 2015, *PowerShares Wilder Clean Energy traded at a discount of .21% below its net asset value, which is better than its one-year historical average discount of .10%.

Peter Hubbard has been running the fund for 9 years and currently receives a manager quality ranking of 95 (0=worst, 99=best). If you desire an average level of risk, then this fund may be an option.

Data Date	Investment Rating	Net Assets ($Mil)	Price	Performance Rating/Pts	Total Return Y-T-D	Risk Rating/Pts
12-15	C	174.40	4.74	C+ / 5.7	-8.54%	C+ / 6.0
2014	D	174.40	5.27	D+ / 2.3	-18.33%	C+ / 5.6
2013	D-	208.40	6.39	D+ / 2.3	55.27%	C / 4.4
2012	E+	123.10	4.08	E / 0.4	-20.14%	C / 4.5
2011	E+	194.50	5.07	E+ / 0.8	-49.81%	C / 4.8
2010	E+	547.20	10.39	E / 0.5	-5.55%	C- / 3.7

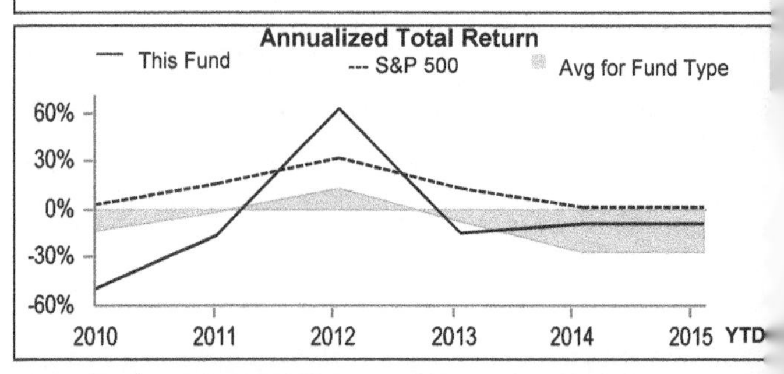

*PowerShares WilderHill Progr Ene (PUW) D Weak

Fund Family: Invesco Powershares Capital Mgmt LL
Fund Type: Energy/Natural Resources
Inception Date: October 24, 2006

Major Rating Factors:
Disappointing performance is the major factor driving the D (Weak) TheStreet.com Investment Rating for *PowerShares WilderHill Progr Ene. The fund currently has a performance rating of D (Weak) based on an annualized return of -8.27% over the last three years and a total return of -25.08% year to date 2015. Factored into the performance evaluation is an expense ratio of 0.70% (very low).

The fund's risk rating is currently C+ (Fair). It carries a beta of 0.96, meaning that its performance tracks fairly well with that of the overall stock market. Volatility, as measured by both the semi-deviation and a drawdown factor, is considered low. As of December 31, 2015, *PowerShares WilderHill Progr Ene traded at a discount of .10% below its net asset value, which is better than its one-year historical average discount of .06%.

Peter Hubbard has been running the fund for 9 years and currently receives a manager quality ranking of 37 (0=worst, 99=best). This fund offers only a moderate level of risk but investors looking for strong performance are still waiting.

Data Date	Investment Rating	Net Assets ($Mil)	Price	Performance Rating/Pts	Total Return Y-T-D	Risk Rating/Pts
12-15	D	37.30	19.46	D / 1.6	-25.08%	C+ / 6.1
2014	D+	37.30	26.44	D+ / 2.9	-15.63%	C+ / 6.1
2013	C+	41.70	32.11	C+ / 6.6	22.60%	C+ / 6.7
2012	D	37.20	25.58	D+ / 2.6	12.24%	C+ / 6.7
2011	C-	43.90	22.53	C / 4.3	-16.09%	C+ / 6.8
2010	C	61.70	28.13	C+ / 5.8	20.44%	C / 5.1

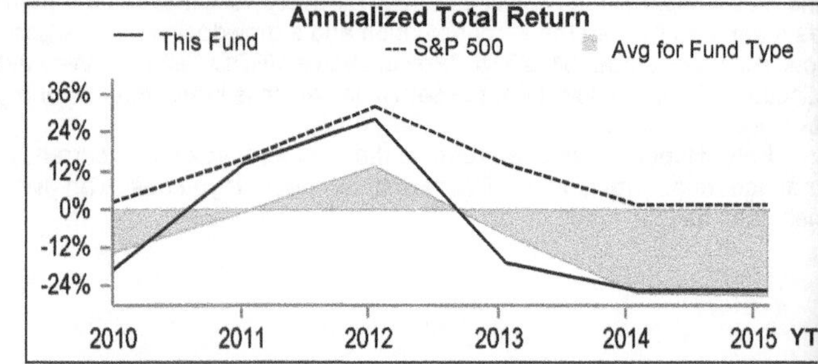

*PowerShares Zacks Micro Cap (PZI) B- Good

Fund Family: Invesco Powershares Capital Mgmt LL
Fund Type: Growth
Inception Date: August 18, 2005

Major Rating Factors: Strong performance is the major factor driving the B- (Good) TheStreet.com Investment Rating for *PowerShares Zacks Micro Cap. The fund currently has a performance rating of B- (Good) based on an annualized return of 9.36% over the last three years and a total return of -2.80% year to date 2015. Factored into the performance evaluation is an expense ratio of 0.70% (very low).

The fund's risk rating is currently C+ (Fair). It carries a beta of 1.05, meaning that its performance tracks fairly well with that of the overall stock market. Volatility, as measured by both the semi-deviation and a drawdown factor, is considered low. As of December 31, 2015, *PowerShares Zacks Micro Cap traded at a premium of .32% above its net asset value, which is worse than its one-year historical average discount of .18%.

Peter Hubbard has been running the fund for 9 years and currently receives a manager quality ranking of 35 (0=worst, 99=best). If you desire only a moderate level of risk and strong performance, then this fund is an excellent option.

Data Date	Investment Rating	Net Assets ($Mil)	Price	Performance Rating/Pts	Total Return Y-T-D	Risk Rating/Pts
12-15	B-	33.20	15.48	B- / 7.2	-2.80%	C+ / 6.9
2014	B-	33.20	16.20	B- / 7.2	-1.40%	B- / 7.1
2013	B	57.60	16.94	B+ / 8.3	37.48%	B- / 7.3
2012	C	29.20	11.83	C / 5.0	19.79%	B- / 7.1
2011	D+	31.60	10.19	D+ / 2.9	-13.44%	C+ / 6.8
2010	C-	110.70	12.01	C- / 4.0	23.70%	C / 5.3

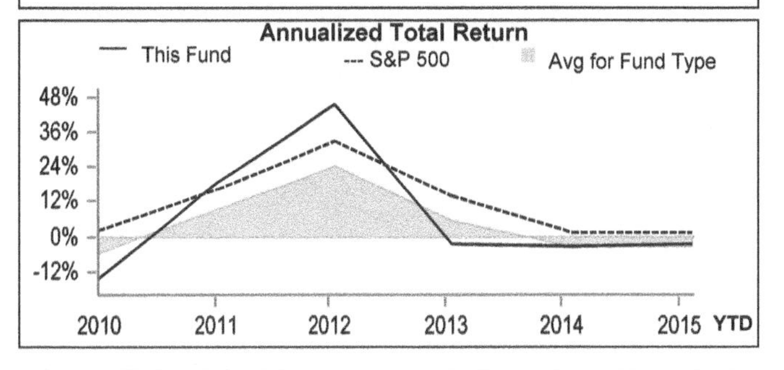

*Precidian Maxis Nikkei 225 Index (NKY) B+ Good

Fund Family: Precidian Funds LLC
Fund Type: Global
Inception Date: July 8, 2011

Major Rating Factors: Strong performance is the major factor driving the B+ (Good) TheStreet.com Investment Rating for *Precidian Maxis Nikkei 225 Index. The fund currently has a performance rating of B (Good) based on an annualized return of 9.42% over the last three years and a total return of 8.42% year to date 2015. Factored into the performance evaluation is an expense ratio of 0.50% (very low).

The fund's risk rating is currently B (Good). It carries a beta of 0.10, meaning the fund's expected move will be 1.0% for every 10% move in the market. Volatility, as measured by both the semi-deviation and a drawdown factor, is considered low. As of December 31, 2015, *Precidian Maxis Nikkei 225 Index traded at a discount of 1.65% below its net asset value, which is better than its one-year historical average discount of .10%.

Jordan Dekhayser has been running the fund for 5 years and currently receives a manager quality ranking of 95 (0=worst, 99=best). If you desire only a moderate level of risk and strong performance, then this fund is an excellent option.

Data Date	Investment Rating	Net Assets ($Mil)	Price	Performance Rating/Pts	Total Return Y-T-D	Risk Rating/Pts
12-15	B+	120.20	18.48	B / 7.7	8.42%	B / 8.4
2014	C+	190.40	17.07	C / 5.3	-4.64%	B / 8.3
2013	A+	192.90	18.53	A- / 9.1	26.99%	B / 8.4
2012	B+	192.90	14.45	B / 7.9	13.48%	B / 8.3

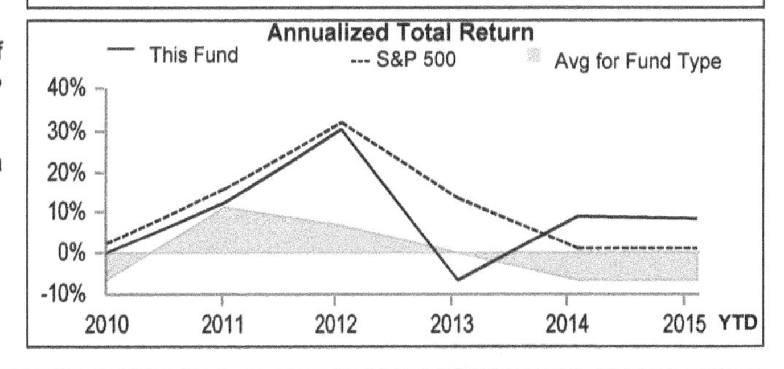

*ProShares 30 Year TIPS TSY Sprea (RINF) D+ Weak

Fund Family: ProShare Advisors LLC
Fund Type: General - Investment Grade
Inception Date: January 10, 2012

Major Rating Factors:
Disappointing performance is the major factor driving the D+ (Weak) TheStreet.com Investment Rating for *ProShares 30 Year TIPS TSY Sprea. The fund currently has a performance rating of D (Weak) based on an annualized return of -10.23% over the last three years and a total return of -8.77% year to date 2015. Factored into the performance evaluation is an expense ratio of 0.75% (very low).

The fund's risk rating is currently B- (Good). It carries a beta of -0.71, meaning the fund's expected move will be -7.1% for every 10% move in the market. Volatility, as measured by both the semi-deviation and a drawdown factor, is considered low. As of December 31, 2015, *ProShares 30 Year TIPS TSY Sprea traded at a discount of .18% below its net asset value, which is better than its one-year historical average premium of .14%.

Michelle Liu has been running the fund for 4 years and currently receives a manager quality ranking of 17 (0=worst, 99=best). This fund offers only a moderate level of risk but investors looking for strong performance are still waiting.

Data Date	Investment Rating	Net Assets ($Mil)	Price	Performance Rating/Pts	Total Return Y-T-D	Risk Rating/Pts
12-15	D+	5.00	28.24	D / 2.0	-8.77%	B- / 7.1
2014	D-	5.00	31.53	E+ / 0.9	-11.90%	C+ / 5.9
2013	D+	3.70	36.25	D- / 1.3	-10.00%	B / 8.7

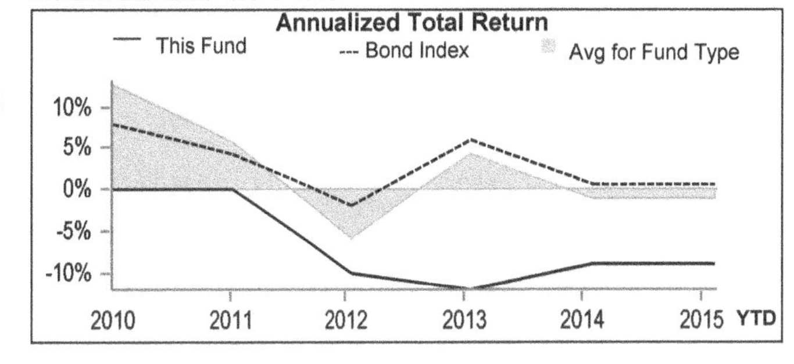

*ProShares CDS N Amer HY Credit (TYTE) C Fair

Fund Family: ProShare Advisors LLC
Fund Type: Corporate - High Yield
Inception Date: August 5, 2014

Major Rating Factors: Middle of the road best describes *ProShares CDS N Amer HY Credit whose TheStreet.com Investment Rating is currently a C (Fair). The fund currently has a performance rating of C- (Fair) based on an annualized return of 0.00% over the last three years and a total return of -2.15% year to date 2015. Factored into the performance evaluation is an expense ratio of 0.50% (very low).

The fund's risk rating is currently B- (Good). It carries a beta of 0.00, meaning the fund's expected move will be 0.0% for every 10% move in the market. Volatility, as measured by both the semi-deviation and a drawdown factor, is considered low. As of December 31, 2015, *ProShares CDS N Amer HY Credit traded at a premium of 1.30% above its net asset value, which is worse than its one-year historical average premium of .19%.

Jeff Ploshnick has been running the fund for 2 years and currently receives a manager quality ranking of 77 (0=worst, 99=best). If you desire an average level of risk, then this fund may be an option.

Data Date	Investment Rating	Net Assets ($Mil)	Price	Performance Rating/Pts	Total Return Y-T-D	Risk Rating/Pts
12-15	C	0.00	39.05	C- / 3.8	-2.15%	B- / 7.6

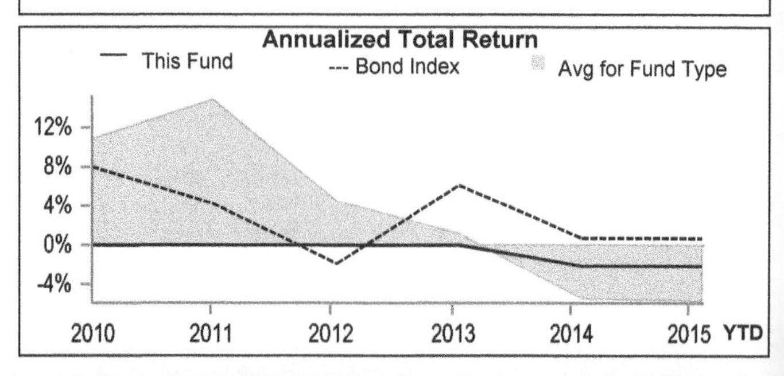

*ProShares CDS Short NA HY Credit (WYDE) C Fair

Fund Family: ProShare Advisors LLC
Fund Type: Global
Inception Date: August 5, 2014

Major Rating Factors: Middle of the road best describes *ProShares CDS Short NA HY Credit whose TheStreet.com Investment Rating is currently a C (Fair). The fund currently has a performance rating of C- (Fair) based on an annualized return of 0.00% over the last three years and a total return of -2.81% year to date 2015. Factored into the performance evaluation is an expense ratio of 0.50% (very low).

The fund's risk rating is currently B+ (Good). It carries a beta of 0.00, meaning the fund's expected move will be 0.0% for every 10% move in the market. Volatility, as measured by both the semi-deviation and a drawdown factor, is considered very low. As of December 31, 2015, *ProShares CDS Short NA HY Credit traded at a discount of .47% below its net asset value, which is better than its one-year historical average discount of .08%.

Jeff Ploshnick has been running the fund for 2 years and currently receives a manager quality ranking of 40 (0=worst, 99=best). If you desire an average level of risk, then this fund may be an option.

Data Date	Investment Rating	Net Assets ($Mil)	Price	Performance Rating/Pts	Total Return Y-T-D	Risk Rating/Pts
12-15	C	0.00	38.09	C- / 3.1	-2.81%	B+ / 9.4

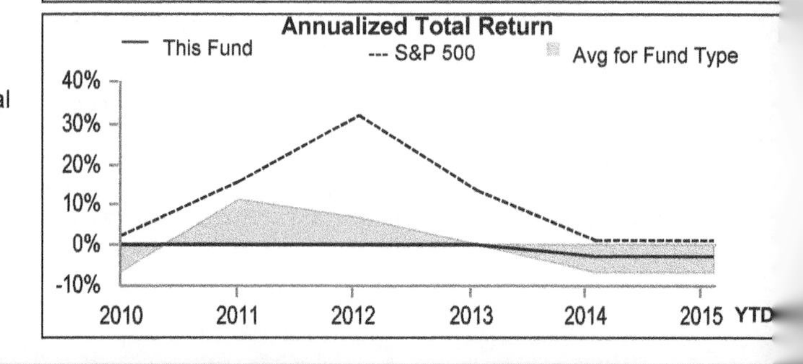

*ProShares DJ Brookfield Global I (TOLZ) D+ Weak

Fund Family: ProShare Advisors LLC
Fund Type: Global
Inception Date: March 25, 2014

Major Rating Factors:
Disappointing performance is the major factor driving the D+ (Weak) TheStreet.com Investment Rating for *ProShares DJ Brookfield Global I. The fund currently has a performance rating of D- (Weak) based on an annualized return of 0.00% over the last three years and a total return of -14.12% year to date 2015. Factored into the performance evaluation is an expense ratio of 0.45% (very low).

The fund's risk rating is currently B- (Good). It carries a beta of 0.00, meaning the fund's expected move will be 0.0% for every 10% move in the market. Volatility, as measured by both the semi-deviation and a drawdown factor, is considered low. As of December 31, 2015, *ProShares DJ Brookfield Global I traded at a discount of .31% below its net asset value, which is better than its one-year historical average premium of .05%.

Alexander Ilyasov has been running the fund for 2 years and currently receives a manager quality ranking of 11 (0=worst, 99=best). This fund offers only a moderate level of risk but investors looking for strong performance are still waiting.

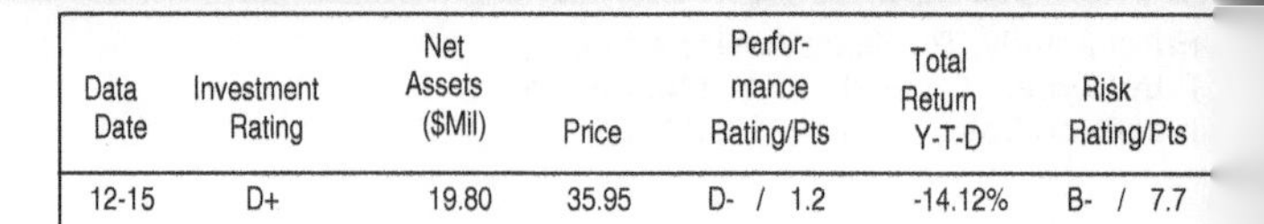

Data Date	Investment Rating	Net Assets ($Mil)	Price	Performance Rating/Pts	Total Return Y-T-D	Risk Rating/Pts
12-15	D+	19.80	35.95	D- / 1.2	-14.12%	B- / 7.7

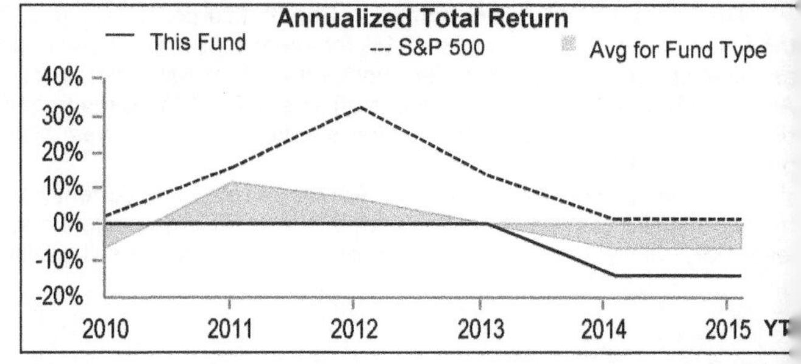

*ProShares German Sovereign Sub S (GGOV) D+ Weak

Fund Family: ProShare Advisors LLC
Fund Type: Global
Inception Date: January 24, 2012

Data Date	Investment Rating	Net Assets ($Mil)	Price	Performance Rating/Pts	Total Return Y-T-D	Risk Rating/Pts
12-15	D+	6.10	35.51	D+ / 2.8	-8.65%	C+ / 6.4
2014	D+	6.10	40.00	D / 1.7	-4.80%	B- / 7.3
2013	C+	4.30	42.66	C / 4.3	2.94%	B+ / 9.3

Major Rating Factors:
Disappointing performance is the major factor driving the D+ (Weak) TheStreet.com Investment Rating for *ProShares German Sovereign Sub S. The fund currently has a performance rating of D+ (Weak) based on an annualized return of -4.22% over the last three years and a total return of -8.65% year to date 2015. Factored into the performance evaluation is an expense ratio of 0.45% (very low).

The fund's risk rating is currently C+ (Fair). It carries a beta of 0.68, meaning the fund's expected move will be 6.8% for every 10% move in the market. Volatility, as measured by both the semi-deviation and a drawdown factor, is considered low. As of December 31, 2015, *ProShares German Sovereign Sub S traded at a premium of .34% above its net asset value, which is better than its one-year historical average premium of .80%.

Alexander V. Ilyasov has been running the fund for 4 years and currently receives a manager quality ranking of 57 (0=worst, 99=best). This fund offers only a moderate level of risk but investors looking for strong performance are still waiting.

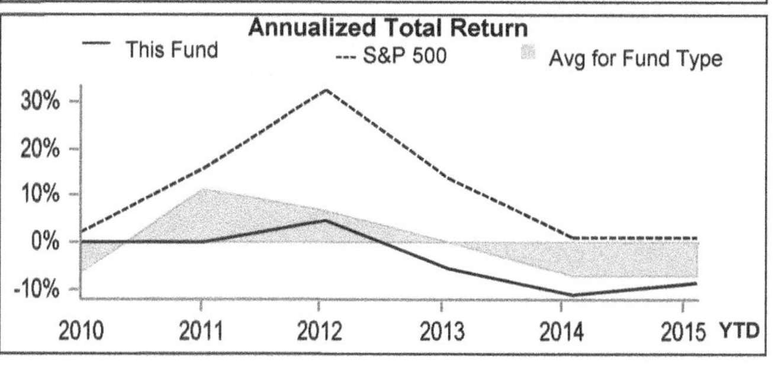

*ProShares Glb Lstd Priv Eqty (PEX) C Fair

Fund Family: ProShare Advisors LLC
Fund Type: Global
Inception Date: February 26, 2013

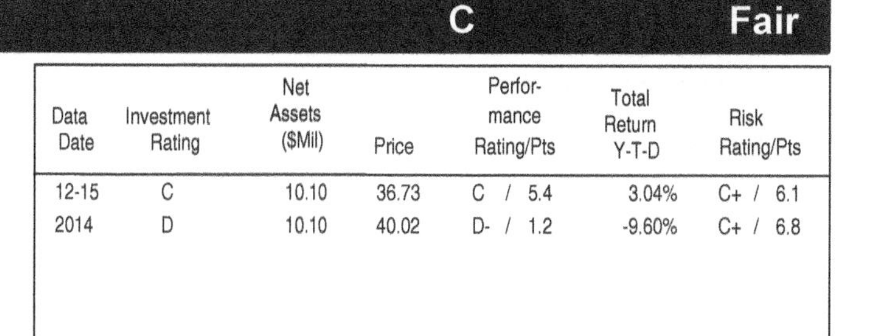

Data Date	Investment Rating	Net Assets ($Mil)	Price	Performance Rating/Pts	Total Return Y-T-D	Risk Rating/Pts
12-15	C	10.10	36.73	C / 5.4	3.04%	C+ / 6.1
2014	D	10.10	40.02	D- / 1.2	-9.60%	C+ / 6.8

Major Rating Factors: Middle of the road best describes *ProShares Glb Lstd Priv Eqty whose TheStreet.com Investment Rating is currently a C (Fair). The fund currently has a performance rating of C (Fair) based on an annualized return of 0.00% over the last three years and a total return of 3.04% year to date 2015. Factored into the performance evaluation is an expense ratio of 0.60% (very low).

The fund's risk rating is currently C+ (Fair). It carries a beta of 0.00, meaning the fund's expected move will be 0.0% for every 10% move in the market. Volatility, as measured by both the semi-deviation and a drawdown factor, is considered low. As of December 31, 2015, *ProShares Glb Lstd Priv Eqty traded at a premium of .38% above its net asset value, which is worse than its one-year historical average premium of .12%.

Alexander Ilyasov has been running the fund for 3 years and currently receives a manager quality ranking of 80 (0=worst, 99=best). If you desire an average level of risk, then this fund may be an option.

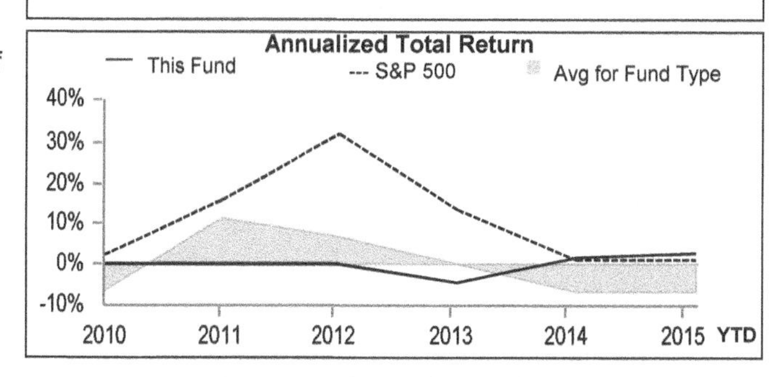

*ProShares Hedge Replication ETF (HDG) C+ Fair

Fund Family: ProShare Advisors LLC
Fund Type: Global
Inception Date: July 12, 2011

Data Date	Investment Rating	Net Assets ($Mil)	Price	Performance Rating/Pts	Total Return Y-T-D	Risk Rating/Pts
12-15	C+	33.50	42.09	C / 5.0	-0.05%	B- / 7.9
2014	C-	33.50	42.29	C- / 3.4	1.90%	B- / 7.6
2013	C+	35.50	41.72	C- / 4.1	3.03%	B+ / 9.5
2012	C-	22.00	39.89	D+ / 2.5	3.63%	B+ / 9.4

Major Rating Factors: Middle of the road best describes *ProShares Hedge Replication ETF whose TheStreet.com Investment Rating is currently a C+ (Fair). The fund currently has a performance rating of C (Fair) based on an annualized return of 1.47% over the last three years and a total return of -0.05% year to date 2015. Factored into the performance evaluation is an expense ratio of 0.95% (low).

The fund's risk rating is currently B- (Good). It carries a beta of 0.28, meaning the fund's expected move will be 2.8% for every 10% move in the market. Volatility, as measured by both the semi-deviation and a drawdown factor, is considered low. As of December 31, 2015, *ProShares Hedge Replication ETF traded at a premium of .17% above its net asset value, which is worse than its one-year historical average premium of .01%.

Charles Lowery has been running the fund for 3 years and currently receives a manager quality ranking of 70 (0=worst, 99=best). If you desire an average level of risk, then this fund may be an option.

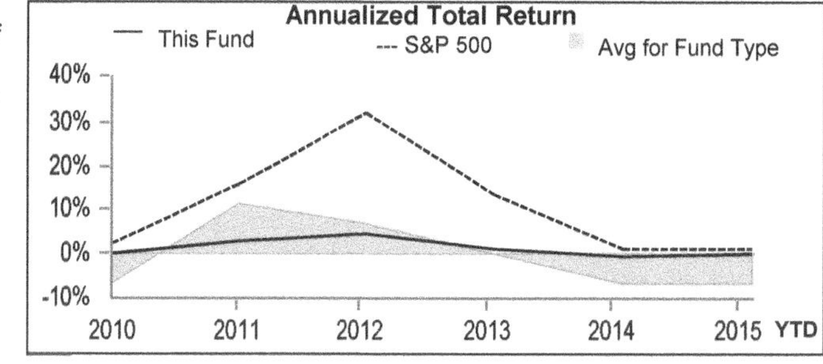

*ProShares Hi Yld-Int Rte Hdgd (HYHG) C- Fair

Fund Family: ProShare Advisors LLC
Fund Type: Corporate - High Yield
Inception Date: May 21, 2013

Major Rating Factors:
Disappointing performance is the major factor driving the C- (Fair) TheStreet.com Investment Rating for *ProShares Hi Yld-Int Rte Hdgd. The fund currently has a performance rating of D (Weak) based on an annualized return of 0.00% over the last three years and a total return of -9.65% year to date 2015. Factored into the performance evaluation is an expense ratio of 0.50% (very low).

The fund's risk rating is currently B- (Good). It carries a beta of 0.00, meaning the fund's expected move will be 0.0% for every 10% move in the market. Volatility, as measured by both the semi-deviation and a drawdown factor, is considered low. As of December 31, 2015, *ProShares Hi Yld-Int Rte Hdgd traded at a discount of .68% below its net asset value, which is better than its one-year historical average premium of .06%.

Jeff Ploshnick has been running the fund for 3 years and currently receives a manager quality ranking of 38 (0=worst, 99=best). This fund offers only a moderate level of risk but investors looking for strong performance are still waiting.

Data Date	Investment Rating	Net Assets ($Mil)	Price	Performance Rating/Pts	Total Return Y-T-D	Risk Rating/Pts
12-15	C-	173.00	62.57	D / 1.7	-9.65%	B- / 7.9
2014	C-	173.00	73.25	D / 1.7	-4.02%	B / 8.7

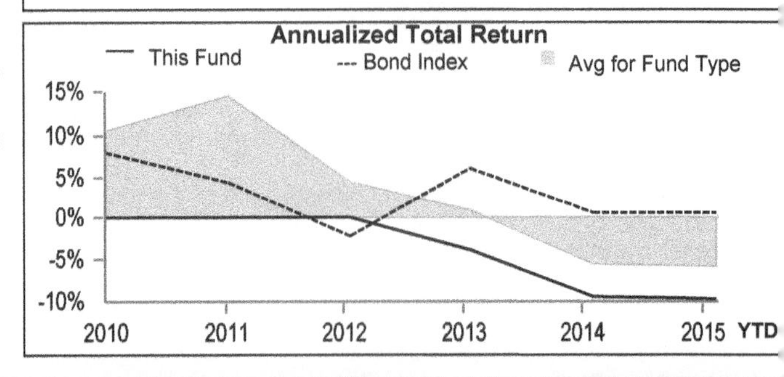

*ProShares Investment Grd-Int Rte (IGHG) C- Fair

Fund Family: ProShare Advisors LLC
Fund Type: General - Investment Grade
Inception Date: November 5, 2013

Major Rating Factors: Middle of the road best describes *ProShares Investment Grd-Int Rte whose TheStreet.com Investment Rating is currently a C- (Fair). The fund currently has a performance rating of C- (Fair) based on an annualized return of 0.00% over the last three years and a total return of -1.45% year to date 2015. Factored into the performance evaluation is an expense ratio of 0.30% (very low).

The fund's risk rating is currently B- (Good). It carries a beta of 0.00, meaning the fund's expected move will be 0.0% for every 10% move in the market. Volatility, as measured by both the semi-deviation and a drawdown factor, is considered low. As of December 31, 2015, *ProShares Investment Grd-Int Rte traded at a premium of .30% above its net asset value, which is worse than its one-year historical average premium of .16%.

Jeff Ploshnick has been running the fund for 3 years and currently receives a manager quality ranking of 54 (0=worst, 99=best). If you desire an average level of risk, then this fund may be an option.

Data Date	Investment Rating	Net Assets ($Mil)	Price	Performance Rating/Pts	Total Return Y-T-D	Risk Rating/Pts
12-15	C-	123.60	73.21	C- / 3.7	-1.45%	B- / 7.3
2014	D-	123.60	77.36	D / 1.9	-3.45%	C- / 4.2

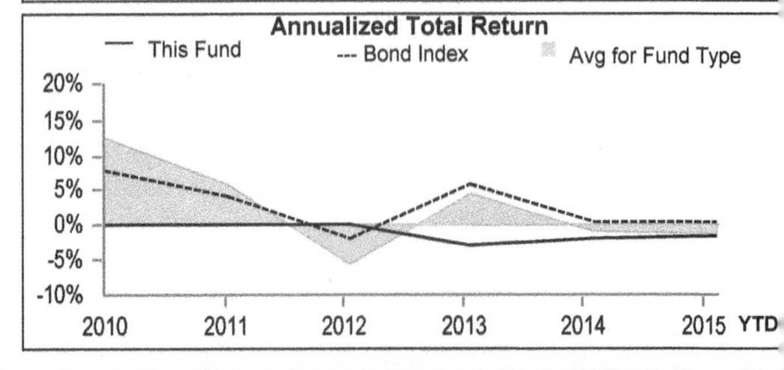

*ProShares Large Cap Core Plus (CSM) C- Fair

Fund Family: ProShare Advisors LLC
Fund Type: Income
Inception Date: July 13, 2009

Major Rating Factors: *ProShares Large Cap Core Plus has adopted a very risky asset allocation strategy and currently receives an overall TheStreet.com Investment Rating of C- (Fair). The fund has shown a high level of volatility, as measured by both semi-deviation and drawdown factors. It carries a beta of 1.04, meaning that its performance tracks fairly well with that of the overall stock market. As of December 31, 2015, *ProShares Large Cap Core Plus traded at a premium of .10% above its net asset value, which is worse than its one-year historical average discount of .01%. The high level of risk (D, Weak) did however, reward investors with excellent performance.

The fund's performance rating is currently B+ (Good). It has registered an annualized return of 14.92% over the last three years but is down -1.03% year to date 2015. Factored into the performance evaluation is an expense ratio of 0.45% (very low).

Charles Lowery has been running the fund for 3 years and currently receives a manager quality ranking of 69 (0=worst, 99=best). If you are comfortable owning a very high risk investment, this fund may be an option.

Data Date	Investment Rating	Net Assets ($Mil)	Price	Performance Rating/Pts	Total Return Y-T-D	Risk Rating/Pts
12-15	C-	379.10	49.36	B+ / 8.9	-1.03%	D / 1.9
2014	A-	379.10	100.91	A- / 9.0	17.03%	B- / 7.3
2013	A	228.90	87.91	B+ / 8.5	31.08%	B / 8.3
2012	C	75.60	65.83	C / 5.1	18.27%	B / 8.1
2011	D+	91.00	56.77	D / 2.1	0.30%	B / 8.2
2010	A+	62.70	57.03	A- / 9.0	14.17%	B- / 7.9

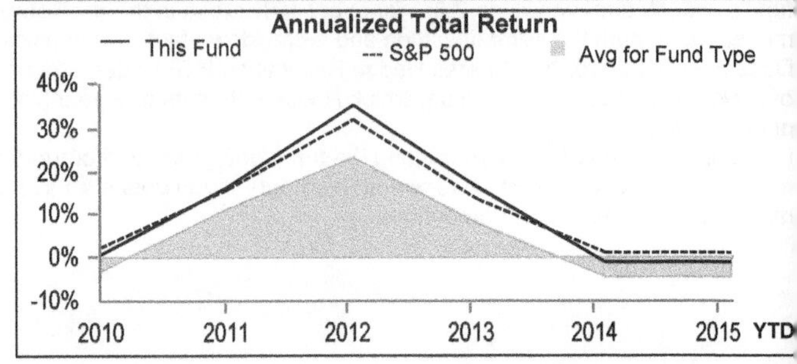

*ProShares Managed Futures Strate (FUTS) D Weak

Fund Family: ProShare Advisors LLC
Fund Type: Income
Inception Date: October 1, 2014

Major Rating Factors: *ProShares Managed Futures Strate receives a TheStreet.com Investment Rating of D (Weak). The fund currently has a performance rating of C- (Fair) based on an annualized return of 0.00% over the last three years and a total return of -2.63% year to date 2015.

The fund's risk rating is currently C (Fair). It carries a beta of 0.00, meaning the fund's expected move will be 0.0% for every 10% move in the market. Volatility, as measured by both the semi-deviation and a drawdown factor, is considered average. As of December 31, 2015, *ProShares Managed Futures Strate traded at a premium of 1.12% above its net asset value, which is worse than its one-year historical average premium of .85%.

Hratch Najarian has been running the fund for 2 years and currently receives a manager quality ranking of 51 (0=worst, 99=best). If you desire an average level of risk, then this fund may be an option.

Data Date	Investment Rating	Net Assets ($Mil)	Price	Performance Rating/Pts	Total Return Y-T-D	Risk Rating/Pts
12-15	D	0.00	20.76	C- / 3.4	-2.63%	C / 4.3

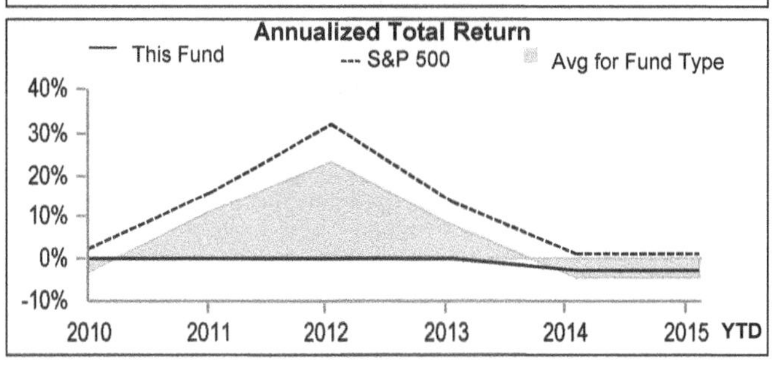

*ProShares Merger ETF (MRGR) C- Fair

Fund Family: ProShare Advisors LLC
Fund Type: Global
Inception Date: December 11, 2012

Major Rating Factors: Middle of the road best describes *ProShares Merger ETF whose TheStreet.com Investment Rating is currently a C- (Fair). The fund currently has a performance rating of C- (Fair) based on an annualized return of -2.28% over the last three years and a total return of -0.69% year to date 2015. Factored into the performance evaluation is an expense ratio of 0.75% (very low).

The fund's risk rating is currently B- (Good). It carries a beta of -0.06, meaning the fund's expected move will be -0.6% for every 10% move in the market. Volatility, as measured by both the semi-deviation and a drawdown factor, is considered low. As of December 31, 2015, *ProShares Merger ETF traded at a premium of .39% above its net asset value, which is better than its one-year historical average premium of .47%.

Alexander V. Ilyasov has been running the fund for 3 years and currently receives a manager quality ranking of 50 (0=worst, 99=best). If you desire an average level of risk, then this fund may be an option.

Data Date	Investment Rating	Net Assets ($Mil)	Price	Performance Rating/Pts	Total Return Y-T-D	Risk Rating/Pts
12-15	C-	1.80	36.40	C- / 3.6	-0.69%	B- / 7.5
2014	C-	1.80	36.31	D+ / 2.4	-1.12%	B+ / 9.2
2013	C-	3.80	37.65	D / 1.8	-5.68%	B+ / 9.4

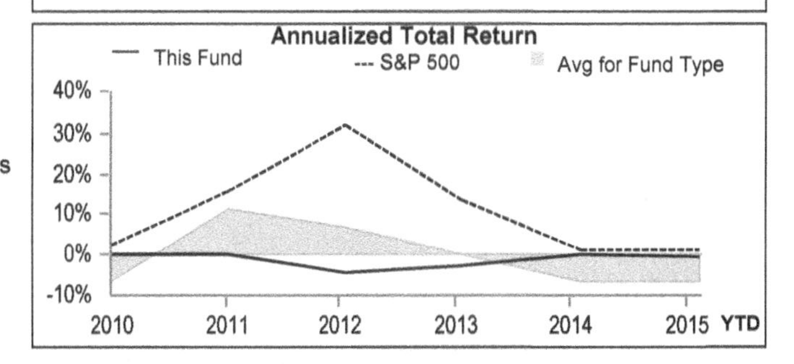

*ProShares Mornstr Alt Solutiion (ALTS) C- Fair

Fund Family: ProShare Advisors LLC
Fund Type: Global
Inception Date: October 8, 2014

Major Rating Factors:
Disappointing performance is the major factor driving the C- (Fair) TheStreet.com Investment Rating for *ProShares Mornstr Alt Solutiion. The fund currently has a performance rating of D+ (Weak) based on an annualized return of 0.00% over the last three years and a total return of -5.73% year to date 2015. Factored into the performance evaluation is an expense ratio of 0.16% (very low).

The fund's risk rating is currently B- (Good). It carries a beta of 0.00, meaning the fund's expected move will be 0.0% for every 10% move in the market. Volatility, as measured by both the semi-deviation and a drawdown factor, is considered low. As of December 31, 2015, *ProShares Mornstr Alt Solutiion traded at a premium of .81% above its net asset value, which is worse than its one-year historical average premium of .31%.

Todd B. Johnson currently receives a manager quality ranking of 27 (0=worst, 99=best). This fund offers only a moderate level of risk but investors looking for strong performance are still waiting.

Data Date	Investment Rating	Net Assets ($Mil)	Price	Performance Rating/Pts	Total Return Y-T-D	Risk Rating/Pts
12-15	C-	0.00	38.47	D+ / 2.7	-5.73%	B- / 7.6

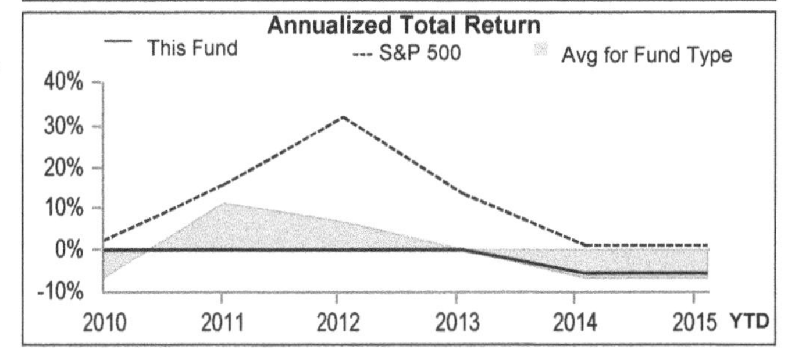

*ProShares MSCI EAFE Div Grower (EFAD) C- Fair

Fund Family: ProShare Advisors LLC
Fund Type: Foreign
Inception Date: August 19, 2014

Major Rating Factors: Middle of the road best describes *ProShares MSCI EAFE Div Grower whose TheStreet.com Investment Rating is currently a C- (Fair). The fund currently has a performance rating of C- (Fair) based on an annualized return of 0.00% over the last three years and a total return of 1.08% year to date 2015. Factored into the performance evaluation is an expense ratio of 0.50% (very low).

The fund's risk rating is currently C+ (Fair). It carries a beta of 0.00, meaning the fund's expected move will be 0.0% for every 10% move in the market. Volatility, as measured by both the semi-deviation and a drawdown factor, is considered low. As of December 31, 2015, *ProShares MSCI EAFE Div Grower traded at a premium of .55% above its net asset value, which is worse than its one-year historical average premium of .50%.

Alexander V. Ilyasov has been running the fund for 2 years and currently receives a manager quality ranking of 75 (0=worst, 99=best). If you desire an average level of risk, then this fund may be an option.

Data Date	Investment Rating	Net Assets ($Mil)	Price	Performance Rating/Pts	Total Return Y-T-D	Risk Rating/Pts
12-15	C-	0.00	36.24	C- / 4.0	1.08%	C+ / 6.6

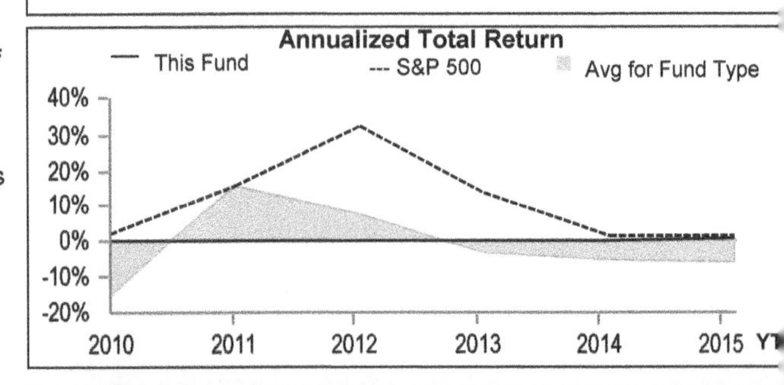

*ProShares RAFI Long/Short (RALS) C Fair

Fund Family: ProShare Advisors LLC
Fund Type: Income
Inception Date: December 2, 2010

Major Rating Factors: Middle of the road best describes *ProShares RAFI Long/Short whose TheStreet.com Investment Rating is currently a C (Fair). The fund currently has a performance rating of C (Fair) based on an annualized return of 1.75% over the last three years and a total return of -6.40% year to date 2015. Factored into the performance evaluation is an expense ratio of 0.95% (low).

The fund's risk rating is currently B- (Good). It carries a beta of 0.08, meaning the fund's expected move will be 0.8% for every 10% move in the market. Volatility, as measured by both the semi-deviation and a drawdown factor, is considered low. As of December 31, 2015, *ProShares RAFI Long/Short traded at a premium of .34% above its net asset value, which is worse than its one-year historical average premium of .01%.

Charles Lowery has been running the fund for 3 years and currently receives a manager quality ranking of 71 (0=worst, 99=best). If you desire an average level of risk, then this fund may be an option.

Data Date	Investment Rating	Net Assets ($Mil)	Price	Performance Rating/Pts	Total Return Y-T-D	Risk Rating/Pts
12-15	C	63.10	38.91	C / 4.5	-6.40%	B- / 7.3
2014	C-	63.10	42.15	C- / 3.8	-0.10%	B- / 7.4
2013	C	11.70	42.57	C- / 4.1	12.44%	B / 8.8
2012	C-	11.70	38.82	D+ / 2.4	0.83%	B / 8.7
2011	C-	15.40	38.37	D- / 1.4	-8.00%	B+ / 9.1

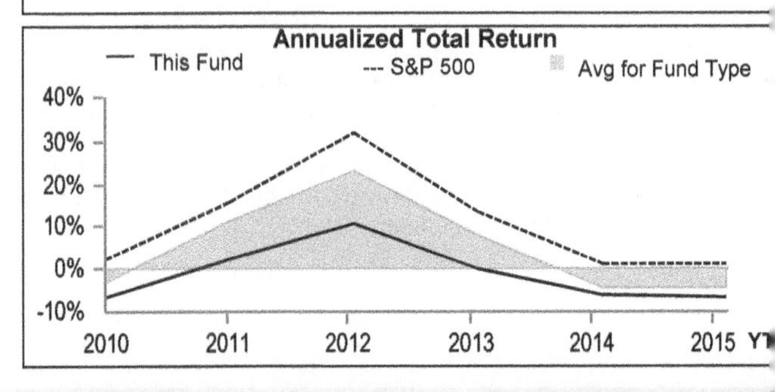

*ProShares S&P 500 Div Aristocrat (NOBL) C Fair

Fund Family: ProShare Advisors LLC
Fund Type: Growth
Inception Date: October 8, 2013

Major Rating Factors: Middle of the road best describes *ProShares S&P 500 Div Aristocrat whose TheStreet.com Investment Rating is currently a C (Fair). The fund currently has a performance rating of C (Fair) based on an annualized return of 0.00% over the last three years and a total return of 0.51% year to date 2015. Factored into the performance evaluation is an expense ratio of 0.35% (very low).

The fund's risk rating is currently B- (Good). It carries a beta of 0.00, meaning the fund's expected move will be 0.0% for every 10% move in the market. Volatility, as measured by both the semi-deviation and a drawdown factor, is considered low. As of December 31, 2015, *ProShares S&P 500 Div Aristocrat traded at a premium of .10% above its net asset value, which is worse than its one-year historical average premium of .02%.

Michael Neches has been running the fund for 3 years and currently receives a manager quality ranking of 61 (0=worst, 99=best). If you desire an average level of risk, then this fund may be an option.

Data Date	Investment Rating	Net Assets ($Mil)	Price	Performance Rating/Pts	Total Return Y-T-D	Risk Rating/Pts
12-15	C	259.30	49.33	C / 5.5	0.51%	B- / 7.3
2014	C	259.30	50.12	B / 8.2	16.42%	C / 4.3

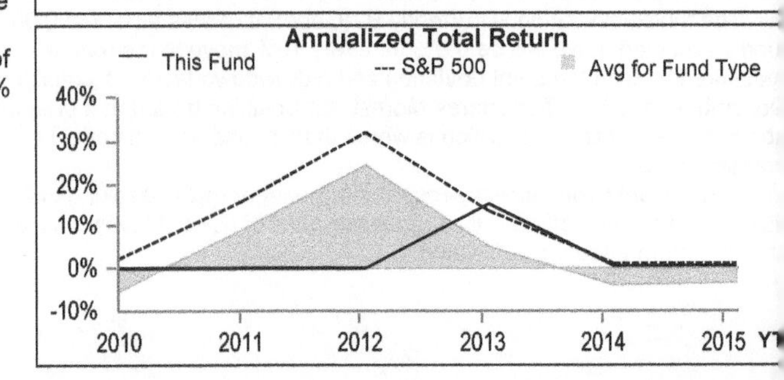

*ProShares Sh Trm USD Em Mkts Bd (EMSH) A Excellent

Fund Family: ProShare Advisors LLC
Fund Type: Emerging Market
Inception Date: November 19, 2013

Data Date	Investment Rating	Net Assets ($Mil)	Price	Performance Rating/Pts	Total Return Y-T-D	Risk Rating/Pts
12-15	A	8.00	75.60	B- / 7.5	10.19%	B+ / 9.1
2014	D-	8.00	75.39	D / 1.8	-3.03%	C- / 4.1

Major Rating Factors:
Strong performance is the major factor driving the A (Excellent) TheStreet.com Investment Rating for *ProShares Sh Trm USD Em Mkts Bd. The fund currently has a performance rating of B- (Good) based on an annualized return of 0.00% over the last three years and a total return of 10.19% year to date 2015. Factored into the performance evaluation is an expense ratio of 0.50% (very low).

The fund's risk rating is currently B+ (Good). It carries a beta of 0.00, meaning the fund's expected move will be 0.0% for every 10% move in the market. Volatility, as measured by both the semi-deviation and a drawdown factor, is considered very low. As of December 31, 2015, *ProShares Sh Trm USD Em Mkts Bd traded at a discount of .15% below its net asset value, which is worse than its one-year historical average discount of .46%.

Alexander V. Ilyasov currently receives a manager quality ranking of 92 (0=worst, 99=best). If you desire only a moderate level of risk and strong performance, then this fund is an excellent option.

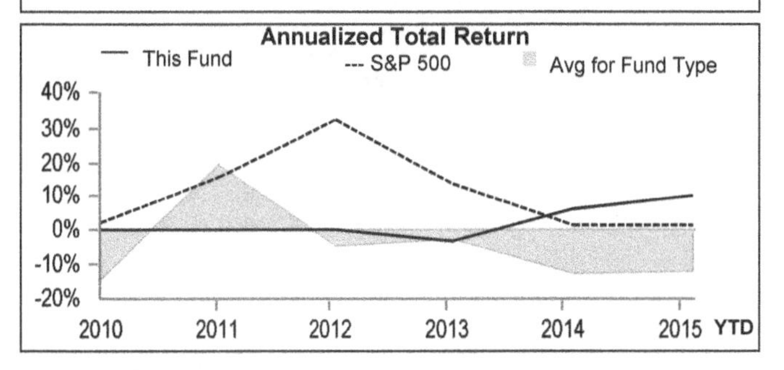

*ProShares Short 20+ Year Treas (TBF) D Weak

Fund Family: ProShare Advisors LLC
Fund Type: US Government/Agency
Inception Date: August 18, 2009

Data Date	Investment Rating	Net Assets ($Mil)	Price	Performance Rating/Pts	Total Return Y-T-D	Risk Rating/Pts
12-15	D	1,513.50	24.73	D+ / 2.7	-0.72%	C / 5.3
2014	D-	1,513.50	25.15	D- / 1.2	-23.35%	C+ / 5.6
2013	D	1,714.80	32.89	D- / 1.4	9.18%	C+ / 6.4
2012	D-	780.60	29.38	E+ / 0.6	-5.00%	C+ / 5.9
2011	D-	712.30	31.17	E / 0.5	-29.04%	C+ / 6.5
2010	D+	812.00	44.25	D- / 1.4	-12.39%	B- / 7.3

Major Rating Factors:
Disappointing performance is the major factor driving the D (Weak) TheStreet.com Investment Rating for *ProShares Short 20+ Year Treas. The fund currently has a performance rating of D+ (Weak) based on an annualized return of -6.29% over the last three years and a total return of -0.72% year to date 2015. Factored into the performance evaluation is an expense ratio of 0.95% (low).

The fund's risk rating is currently C (Fair). It carries a beta of -1.13, meaning the fund's expected move will be -11.3% for every 10% move in the market. Volatility, as measured by both the semi-deviation and a drawdown factor, is considered average. As of December 31, 2015, *ProShares Short 20+ Year Treas traded at a premium of .04% above its net asset value, which is worse than its one-year historical average discount of .03%.

Michelle Liu has been running the fund for 7 years and currently receives a manager quality ranking of 44 (0=worst, 99=best). This fund offers an average level of risk but investors looking for strong performance will be frustrated.

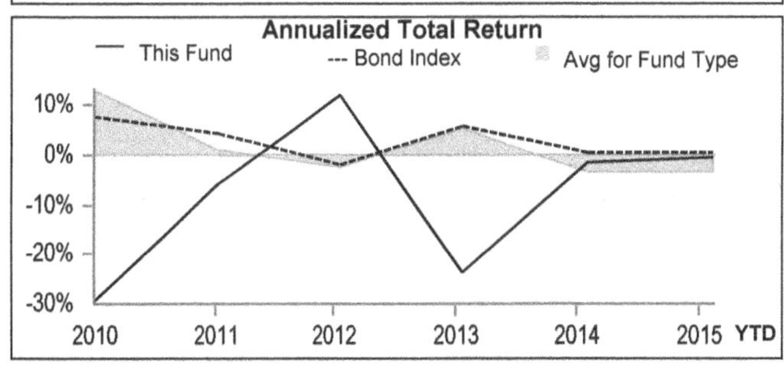

*ProShares Short 7-10 Year Treasu (TBX) C- Fair

Fund Family: ProShare Advisors LLC
Fund Type: General - Investment Grade
Inception Date: April 4, 2011

Data Date	Investment Rating	Net Assets ($Mil)	Price	Performance Rating/Pts	Total Return Y-T-D	Risk Rating/Pts
12-15	C-	71.00	29.52	C- / 3.2	-2.91%	B- / 7.8
2014	D+	71.00	30.50	D / 2.0	-9.50%	B- / 7.1
2013	C-	81.00	33.92	C- / 3.3	3.15%	B / 8.4
2012	D	15.30	32.42	D- / 1.1	-4.37%	B / 8.4

Major Rating Factors: Middle of the road best describes *ProShares Short 7-10 Year Treasu whose TheStreet.com Investment Rating is currently a C- (Fair). The fund currently has a performance rating of C- (Fair) based on an annualized return of -3.33% over the last three years and a total return of -2.91% year to date 2015. Factored into the performance evaluation is an expense ratio of 0.95% (low).

The fund's risk rating is currently B- (Good). It carries a beta of -1.86, meaning the fund's expected move will be -18.6% for every 10% move in the market. Volatility, as measured by both the semi-deviation and a drawdown factor, is considered low. As of December 31, 2015, *ProShares Short 7-10 Year Treasu traded at a price exactly equal to its net asset value, which is worse than its one-year historical average discount of .06%.

Michelle Liu has been running the fund for 5 years and currently receives a manager quality ranking of 63 (0=worst, 99=best). If you desire an average level of risk, then this fund may be an option.

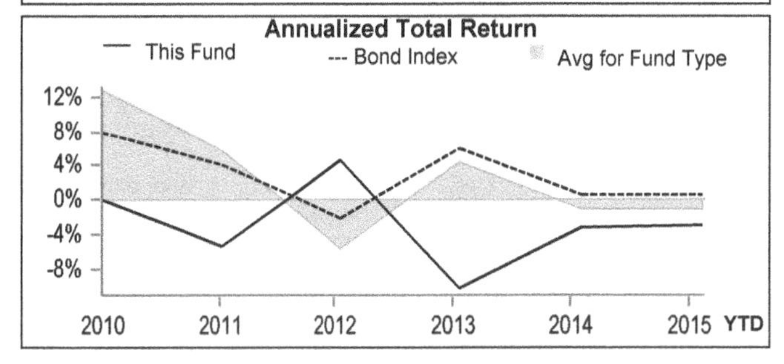

*ProShares Short Dow30 (DOG) D Weak

Fund Family: ProShare Advisors LLC
Fund Type: Growth
Inception Date: June 19, 2006

Major Rating Factors:
Disappointing performance is the major factor driving the D (Weak) TheStreet.com Investment Rating for *ProShares Short Dow30. The fund currently has a performance rating of D (Weak) based on an annualized return of -12.36% over the last three years and a total return of -2.92% year to date 2015. Factored into the performance evaluation is an expense ratio of 0.95% (low).

The fund's risk rating is currently C (Fair). It carries a beta of -0.99, meaning the fund's expected move will be -9.9% for every 10% move in the market. Volatility, as measured by both the semi-deviation and a drawdown factor, is considered average. As of December 31, 2015, *ProShares Short Dow30 traded at a premium of .04% above its net asset value.

Michael Neches has been running the fund for 3 years and currently receives a manager quality ranking of 67 (0=worst, 99=best). This fund offers an average level of risk but investors looking for strong performance will be frustrated.

Data Date	Investment Rating	Net Assets ($Mil)	Price	Performance Rating/Pts	Total Return Y-T-D	Risk Rating/Pts
12-15	D	284.90	22.60	D / 1.8	-2.92%	C / 5.0
2014	D-	284.90	23.28	D- / 1.0	-11.35%	C+ / 5.6
2013	D-	262.30	26.11	E+ / 0.6	-21.78%	C+ / 6.5
2012	D-	260.80	34.40	E+ / 0.6	-12.31%	C+ / 6.6
2011	D-	293.90	38.80	D- / 1.0	-12.94%	C / 5.5
2010	D	246.20	44.33	E+ / 0.8	-15.29%	C+ / 5.7

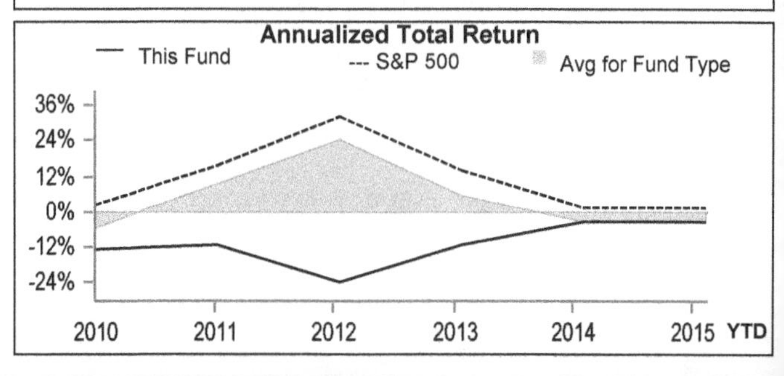

*ProShares Short Euro (EUFX) B+ Good

Fund Family: ProShare Advisors LLC
Fund Type: Growth and Income
Inception Date: June 26, 2012

Major Rating Factors: *ProShares Short Euro receives a TheStreet.com Investment Rating of B+ (Good). The fund currently has a performance rating of C+ (Fair) based on an annualized return of 4.76% over the last three years and a total return of 8.45% year to date 2015. Factored into the performance evaluation is an expense ratio of 0.96% (low).

The fund's risk rating is currently B (Good). It carries a beta of -0.15, meaning the fund's expected move will be -1.5% for every 10% move in the market. Volatility, as measured by both the semi-deviation and a drawdown factor, is considered low. As of December 31, 2015, *ProShares Short Euro traded at a discount of .09% below its net asset value.

Jeff Ploshnick has been running the fund for 4 years and currently receives a manager quality ranking of 93 (0=worst, 99=best). If you desire an average level of risk, then this fund may be an option.

Data Date	Investment Rating	Net Assets ($Mil)	Price	Performance Rating/Pts	Total Return Y-T-D	Risk Rating/Pts
12-15	B+	17.30	43.74	C+ / 6.4	8.45%	B / 8.8
2014	B+	17.30	40.03	B- / 7.1	12.25%	B / 8.6
2013	D+	8.90	35.66	D- / 1.3	-6.26%	B / 8.9

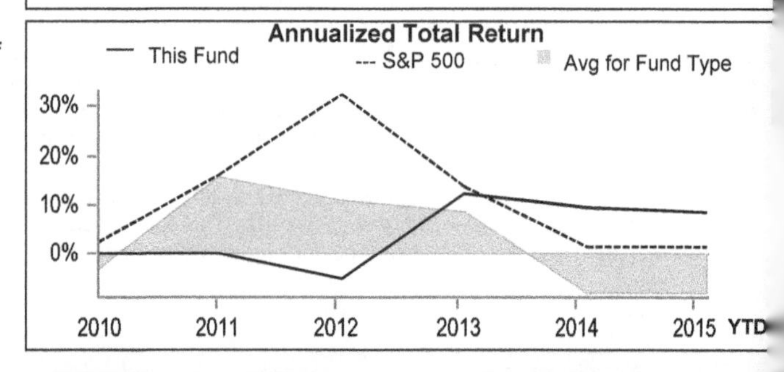

*ProShares Short Financials (SEF) D Weak

Fund Family: ProShare Advisors LLC
Fund Type: Financial Services
Inception Date: June 10, 2008

Major Rating Factors:
Disappointing performance is the major factor driving the D (Weak) TheStreet.com Investment Rating for *ProShares Short Financials. The fund currently has a performance rating of D- (Weak) based on an annualized return of -14.84% over the last three years and a total return of -3.65% year to date 2015. Factored into the performance evaluation is an expense ratio of 0.95% (low).

The fund's risk rating is currently C+ (Fair). It carries a beta of -0.98, meaning the fund's expected move will be -9.8% for every 10% move in the market. Volatility, as measured by both the semi-deviation and a drawdown factor, is considered low. As of December 31, 2015, *ProShares Short Financials traded at a discount of .41% below its net asset value, which is better than its one-year historical average discount of .01%.

Charles Lowery has been running the fund for 3 years and currently receives a manager quality ranking of 41 (0=worst, 99=best). This fund offers only a moderate level of risk but investors looking for strong performance are still waiting.

Data Date	Investment Rating	Net Assets ($Mil)	Price	Performance Rating/Pts	Total Return Y-T-D	Risk Rating/Pts
12-15	D	20.10	16.87	D- / 1.5	-3.65%	C+ / 6.4
2014	E+	20.10	17.54	E+ / 0.7	-14.73%	C / 4.5
2013	E+	29.40	20.61	E+ / 0.6	-24.69%	C / 5.3
2012	D-	70.40	28.39	E / 0.5	-23.32%	C+ / 6.3
2011	E+	131.90	37.38	E+ / 0.8	0.89%	C- / 3.9
2010	E+	96.30	36.66	E / 0.4	-17.43%	C- / 3.7

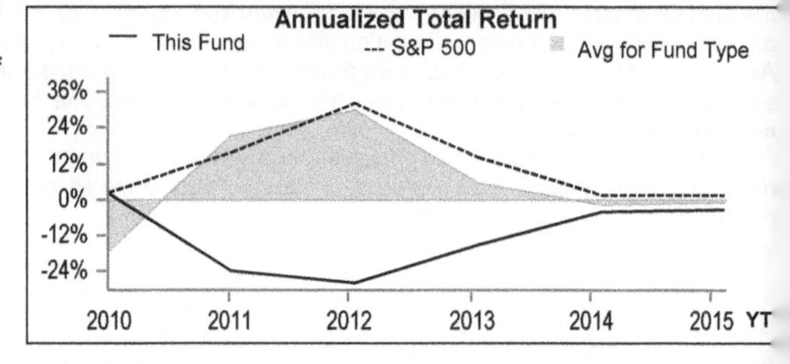

*ProShares Short FTSE China 50 (YXI) D+ Weak

Fund Family: ProShare Advisors LLC
Fund Type: Foreign
Inception Date: March 16, 2010

Major Rating Factors: *ProShares Short FTSE China 50 receives a TheStreet.com Investment Rating of D+ (Weak). The fund currently has a performance rating of C- (Fair) based on an annualized return of -5.36% over the last three years and a total return of 3.96% year to date 2015. Factored into the performance evaluation is an expense ratio of 0.95% (low).

The fund's risk rating is currently C+ (Fair). It carries a beta of -0.91, meaning the fund's expected move will be -9.1% for every 10% move in the market. Volatility, as measured by both the semi-deviation and a drawdown factor, is considered low. As of December 31, 2015, *ProShares Short FTSE China 50 traded at a discount of .17% below its net asset value, which is better than its one-year historical average premium of .19%.

Alexander V. Ilyasov has been running the fund for 6 years and currently receives a manager quality ranking of 53 (0=worst, 99=best). If you desire an average level of risk, then this fund may be an option.

Data Date	Investment Rating	Net Assets ($Mil)	Price	Performance Rating/Pts	Total Return Y-T-D	Risk Rating/Pts
12-15	D+	4.80	29.13	C- / 3.4	3.96%	C+ / 5.6
2014	D-	4.80	28.04	E+ / 0.9	-20.26%	C+ / 6.0
2013	D-	3.40	33.56	D- / 1.5	2.33%	C+ / 5.9
2012	D-	8.80	35.50	E / 0.3	-19.26%	C+ / 6.3
2011	D+	11.30	45.31	D / 2.1	5.05%	B- / 7.4

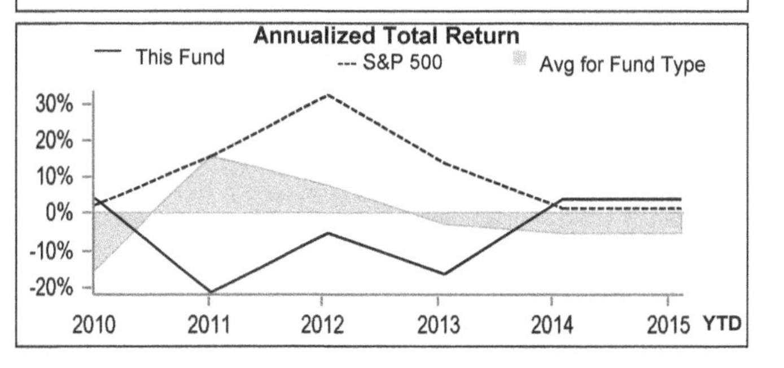

*ProShares Short High Yield (SJB) C- Fair

Fund Family: ProShare Advisors LLC
Fund Type: General - Investment Grade
Inception Date: March 21, 2011

Major Rating Factors: Middle of the road best describes *ProShares Short High Yield whose TheStreet.com Investment Rating is currently a C- (Fair). The fund currently has a performance rating of C- (Fair) based on an annualized return of -3.55% over the last three years and a total return of 2.36% year to date 2015. Factored into the performance evaluation is an expense ratio of 0.95% (low).

The fund's risk rating is currently B- (Good). It carries a beta of -0.81, meaning the fund's expected move will be -8.1% for every 10% move in the market. Volatility, as measured by both the semi-deviation and a drawdown factor, is considered low. As of December 31, 2015, *ProShares Short High Yield traded at a price exactly equal to its net asset value, which is worse than its one-year historical average discount of .01%.

Jeff Ploshnick has been running the fund for 5 years and currently receives a manager quality ranking of 45 (0=worst, 99=best). If you desire an average level of risk, then this fund may be an option.

Data Date	Investment Rating	Net Assets ($Mil)	Price	Performance Rating/Pts	Total Return Y-T-D	Risk Rating/Pts
12-15	C-	79.90	28.65	C- / 3.5	2.36%	B- / 7.7
2014	D+	79.90	27.99	D / 1.6	-4.52%	B- / 7.8
2013	D	51.50	29.40	D- / 1.0	-8.19%	B- / 7.5
2012	D	40.20	32.15	E / 0.5	-14.63%	B- / 7.8

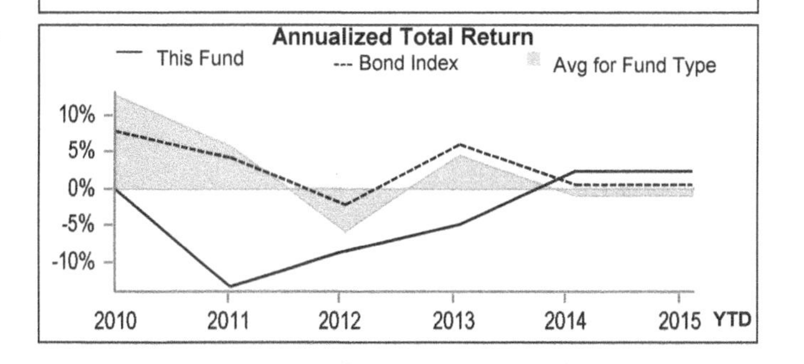

*ProShares Short Inv Grade Corp (IGS) C Fair

Fund Family: ProShare Advisors LLC
Fund Type: Corporate - Investment Grade
Inception Date: March 28, 2011

Major Rating Factors: Middle of the road best describes *ProShares Short Inv Grade Corp whose TheStreet.com Investment Rating is currently a C (Fair). The fund currently has a performance rating of C- (Fair) based on an annualized return of -4.20% over the last three years and a total return of -0.45% year to date 2015. Factored into the performance evaluation is an expense ratio of 0.95% (low).

The fund's risk rating is currently B (Good). It carries a beta of -1.15, meaning the fund's expected move will be -11.5% for every 10% move in the market. Volatility, as measured by both the semi-deviation and a drawdown factor, is considered low. As of December 31, 2015, *ProShares Short Inv Grade Corp traded at a discount of .14% below its net asset value, which is better than its one-year historical average premium of .21%.

Jeff Ploshnick has been running the fund for 5 years and currently receives a manager quality ranking of 48 (0=worst, 99=best). If you desire an average level of risk, then this fund may be an option.

Data Date	Investment Rating	Net Assets ($Mil)	Price	Performance Rating/Pts	Total Return Y-T-D	Risk Rating/Pts
12-15	C	2.90	28.34	C- / 3.1	-0.45%	B / 8.5
2014	D	2.90	28.62	D / 1.6	-9.53%	C+ / 6.3
2013	D+	3.20	32.03	D / 1.6	-1.69%	B / 8.3
2012	D	4.80	31.90	E+ / 0.7	-10.86%	B / 8.3

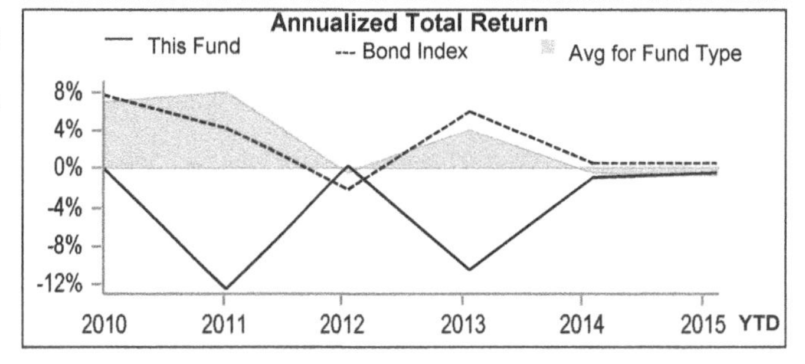

*ProShares Short Midcap 400 (MYY) D Weak

Fund Family: ProShare Advisors LLC
Fund Type: Growth
Inception Date: June 19, 2006

Major Rating Factors:
Disappointing performance is the major factor driving the D (Weak) TheStreet.com Investment Rating for *ProShares Short Midcap 400. The fund currently has a performance rating of D (Weak) based on an annualized return of -12.69% over the last three years and a total return of -0.85% year to date 2015. Factored into the performance evaluation is an expense ratio of 0.95% (low).

The fund's risk rating is currently C+ (Fair). It carries a beta of -0.99, meaning the fund's expected move will be -9.9% for every 10% move in the market. Volatility, as measured by both the semi-deviation and a drawdown factor, is considered low. As of December 31, 2015, *ProShares Short Midcap 400 traded at a price exactly equal to its net asset value.

Michael Neches has been running the fund for 3 years and currently receives a manager quality ranking of 60 (0=worst, 99=best). This fund offers only a moderate level of risk but investors looking for strong performance are still waiting.

Data Date	Investment Rating	Net Assets ($Mil)	Price	Performance Rating/Pts	Total Return Y-T-D	Risk Rating/Pts
12-15	D	133.80	16.26	D / 1.9	-0.85%	C+ / 5.7
2014	D-	133.80	16.39	E+ / 0.9	-11.88%	C+ / 5.9
2013	D-	23.60	18.48	E / 0.5	-23.86%	C+ / 5.7
2012	D-	19.00	25.35	E / 0.5	-18.29%	C+ / 5.8
2011	E+	32.40	30.85	E+ / 0.8	-8.07%	C / 4.5
2010	D-	32.40	33.15	E / 0.5	-25.40%	C / 4.5

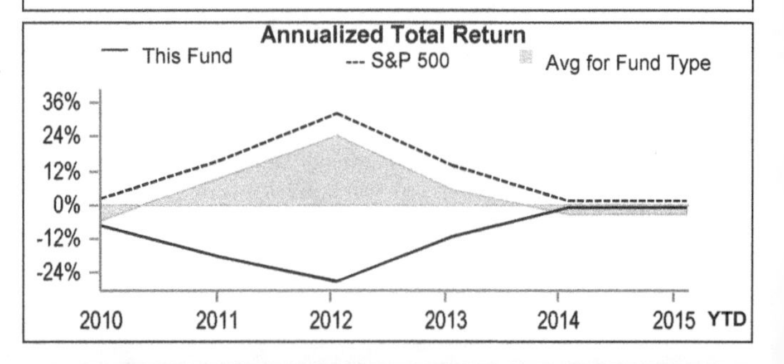

*ProShares Short MSCI EAFE (EFZ) C- Fair

Fund Family: ProShare Advisors LLC
Fund Type: Foreign
Inception Date: October 23, 2007

Major Rating Factors:
Disappointing performance is the major factor driving the C- (Fair) TheStreet.com Investment Rating for *ProShares Short MSCI EAFE. The fund currently has a performance rating of D+ (Weak) based on an annualized return of -6.64% over the last three years and a total return of -3.43% year to date 2015. Factored into the performance evaluation is an expense ratio of 0.95% (low).

The fund's risk rating is currently B- (Good). It carries a beta of -0.98, meaning the fund's expected move will be -9.8% for every 10% move in the market. Volatility, as measured by both the semi-deviation and a drawdown factor, is considered low. As of December 31, 2015, *ProShares Short MSCI EAFE traded at a discount of .24% below its net asset value, which is better than its one-year historical average discount of .02%.

Alexander V. Ilyasov has been running the fund for 7 years and currently receives a manager quality ranking of 50 (0=worst, 99=best). This fund offers only a moderate level of risk but investors looking for strong performance are still waiting.

Data Date	Investment Rating	Net Assets ($Mil)	Price	Performance Rating/Pts	Total Return Y-T-D	Risk Rating/Pts
12-15	C-	227.60	33.47	D+ / 2.7	-3.43%	B- / 7.4
2014	D	227.60	34.51	D- / 1.4	2.25%	C+ / 6.1
2013	D-	42.40	33.20	E+ / 0.8	-17.94%	C+ / 6.3
2012	D-	134.20	41.51	E+ / 0.6	-20.76%	C+ / 6.4
2011	D-	251.10	51.50	D- / 1.2	1.98%	C / 4.9
2010	D-	105.20	50.06	E+ / 0.8	-14.24%	C / 4.6

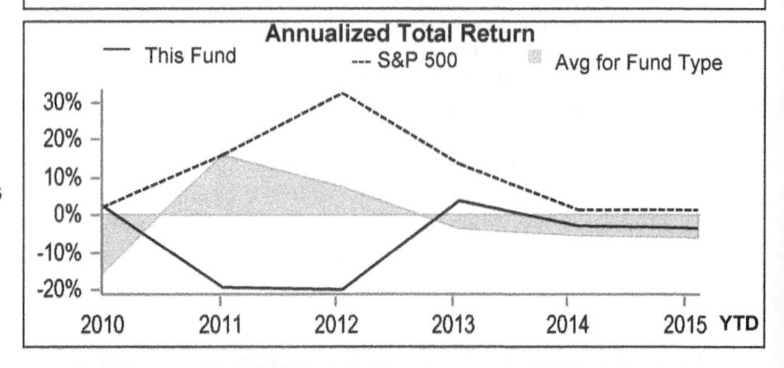

*ProShares Short MSCI Emg Mkts (EUM) C+ Fair

Fund Family: ProShare Advisors LLC
Fund Type: Emerging Market
Inception Date: October 30, 2007

Major Rating Factors: Middle of the road best describes *ProShares Short MSCI Emg Mkts whose TheStreet.com Investment Rating is currently a C+ (Fair). The fund currently has a performance rating of C+ (Fair) based on an annualized return of 3.87% over the last three years and a total return of 10.67% year to date 2015. Factored into the performance evaluation is an expense ratio of 0.95% (low).

The fund's risk rating is currently C+ (Fair). It carries a beta of -0.98, meaning the fund's expected move will be -9.8% for every 10% move in the market. Volatility, as measured by both the semi-deviation and a drawdown factor, is considered low. As of December 31, 2015, *ProShares Short MSCI Emg Mkts traded at a price exactly equal to its net asset value, which is worse than its one-year historical average discount of .03%.

Alexander V. Ilyasov has been running the fund for 7 years and currently receives a manager quality ranking of 41 (0=worst, 99=best). If you desire an average level of risk, then this fund may be an option.

Data Date	Investment Rating	Net Assets ($Mil)	Price	Performance Rating/Pts	Total Return Y-T-D	Risk Rating/Pts
12-15	C+	233.50	29.46	C+ / 6.6	10.67%	C+ / 6.9
2014	D+	233.50	26.33	D / 1.9	-3.80%	B- / 7.1
2013	D	187.70	26.30	D / 1.9	4.11%	C+ / 6.7
2012	D-	214.10	26.68	E+ / 0.6	-17.45%	C+ / 6.1
2011	E+	280.80	33.39	E+ / 0.9	6.99%	C- / 4.0
2010	E+	200.20	30.66	E / 0.4	-20.92%	C- / 3.7

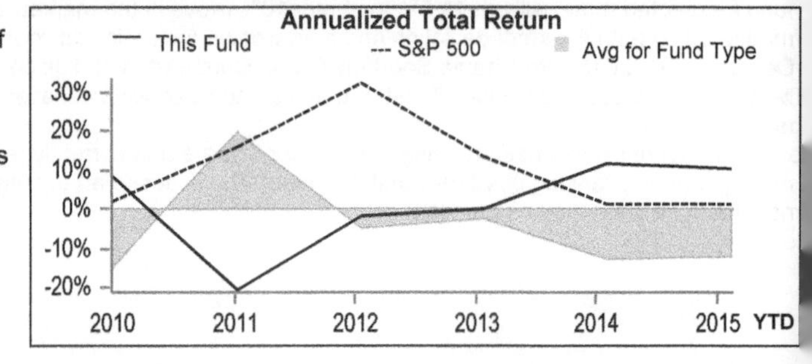

*ProShares Short Oil and Gas (DDG) C+ Fair

Fund Family: ProShare Advisors LLC
Fund Type: Income
Inception Date: June 10, 2008

Major Rating Factors: Middle of the road best describes *ProShares Short Oil and Gas whose TheStreet.com Investment Rating is currently a C+ (Fair). The fund currently has a performance rating of C+ (Fair) based on an annualized return of 0.14% over the last three years and a total return of 19.35% year to date 2015. Factored into the performance evaluation is an expense ratio of 0.95% (low).

The fund's risk rating is currently C+ (Fair). It carries a beta of -1.18, meaning the fund's expected move will be -11.8% for every 10% move in the market. Volatility, as measured by both the semi-deviation and a drawdown factor, is considered low. As of December 31, 2015, *ProShares Short Oil and Gas traded at a discount of .10% below its net asset value, which is better than its one-year historical average premium of .01%.

Charles Lowery has been running the fund for 3 years and currently receives a manager quality ranking of 98 (0=worst, 99=best). If you desire an average level of risk, then this fund may be an option.

Data Date	Investment Rating	Net Assets ($Mil)	Price	Performance Rating/Pts	Total Return Y-T-D	Risk Rating/Pts
12-15	C+	1.70	31.03	C+ / 6.6	19.35%	C+ / 6.5
2014	D-	1.70	26.15	D / 2.1	8.55%	C- / 4.1
2013	D-	1.90	24.09	E+ / 0.6	-22.04%	C+ / 5.9
2012	D-	4.80	32.08	E+ / 0.6	-11.48%	C+ / 5.7
2011	D-	7.90	34.85	E+ / 0.9	-15.38%	C / 5.2
2010	E+	12.10	40.38	E / 0.3	-21.02%	C / 4.5

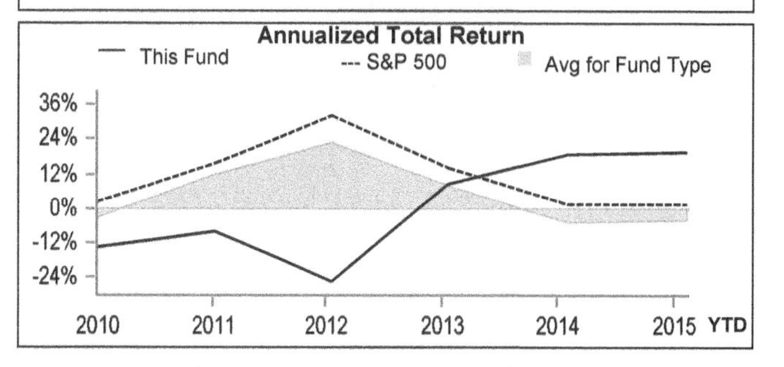

*ProShares Short QQQ (PSQ) D Weak

Fund Family: ProShare Advisors LLC
Fund Type: Growth
Inception Date: June 19, 2006

Major Rating Factors:
Disappointing performance is the major factor driving the D (Weak) TheStreet.com Investment Rating for *ProShares Short QQQ. The fund currently has a performance rating of D- (Weak) based on an annualized return of -19.43% over the last three years and a total return of -12.46% year to date 2015. Factored into the performance evaluation is an expense ratio of 0.95% (low).

The fund's risk rating is currently C+ (Fair). It carries a beta of -1.05, meaning the fund's expected move will be -10.5% for every 10% move in the market. Volatility, as measured by both the semi-deviation and a drawdown factor, is considered low. As of December 31, 2015, *ProShares Short QQQ traded at a discount of .04% below its net asset value.

Michael Neches has been running the fund for 3 years and currently receives a manager quality ranking of 21 (0=worst, 99=best). This fund offers only a moderate level of risk but investors looking for strong performance are still waiting.

Data Date	Investment Rating	Net Assets ($Mil)	Price	Performance Rating/Pts	Total Return Y-T-D	Risk Rating/Pts
12-15	D	257.40	52.20	D- / 1.0	-12.46%	C+ / 6.4
2014	D-	257.40	59.48	E+ / 0.7	-19.64%	C+ / 5.6
2013	D-	139.50	18.25	E / 0.5	-25.83%	C+ / 5.9
2012	D-	184.10	25.57	E / 0.5	-17.51%	C+ / 5.6
2011	E+	293.30	31.29	E+ / 0.8	-10.56%	C / 4.8
2010	D-	200.30	34.67	E+ / 0.6	-20.61%	C / 4.9

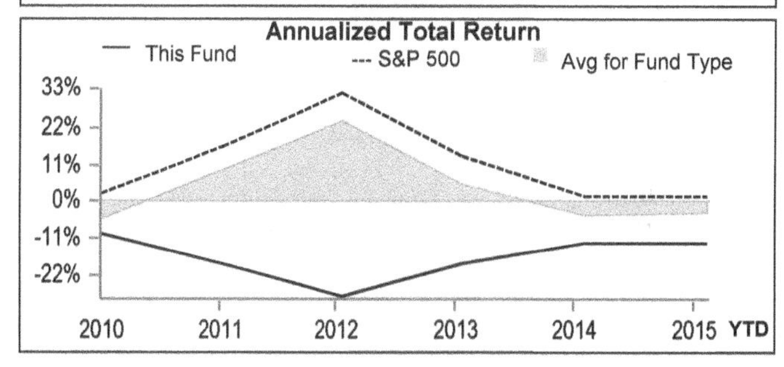

*ProShares Short Real Estate (REK) D+ Weak

Fund Family: ProShare Advisors LLC
Fund Type: Growth and Income
Inception Date: March 16, 2010

Major Rating Factors:
Disappointing performance is the major factor driving the D+ (Weak) TheStreet.com Investment Rating for *ProShares Short Real Estate. The fund currently has a performance rating of D (Weak) based on an annualized return of -11.00% over the last three years and a total return of -4.73% year to date 2015. Factored into the performance evaluation is an expense ratio of 0.95% (low).

The fund's risk rating is currently C+ (Fair). It carries a beta of -0.45, meaning the fund's expected move will be -4.5% for every 10% move in the market. Volatility, as measured by both the semi-deviation and a drawdown factor, is considered low. As of December 31, 2015, *ProShares Short Real Estate traded at a discount of .46% below its net asset value, which is better than its one-year historical average discount of .03%.

Charles Lowery has been running the fund for 3 years and currently receives a manager quality ranking of 26 (0=worst, 99=best). This fund offers only a moderate level of risk but investors looking for strong performance are still waiting.

Data Date	Investment Rating	Net Assets ($Mil)	Price	Performance Rating/Pts	Total Return Y-T-D	Risk Rating/Pts
12-15	D+	39.30	19.28	D / 1.9	-4.73%	C+ / 6.9
2014	D-	39.30	20.16	E+ / 0.8	-23.46%	C+ / 6.5
2013	D-	34.50	26.55	E+ / 0.9	-3.69%	C+ / 6.3
2012	D-	28.00	28.00	E / 0.5	-19.29%	C+ / 5.9
2011	D-	42.90	34.29	D- / 1.0	-14.56%	C+ / 6.8

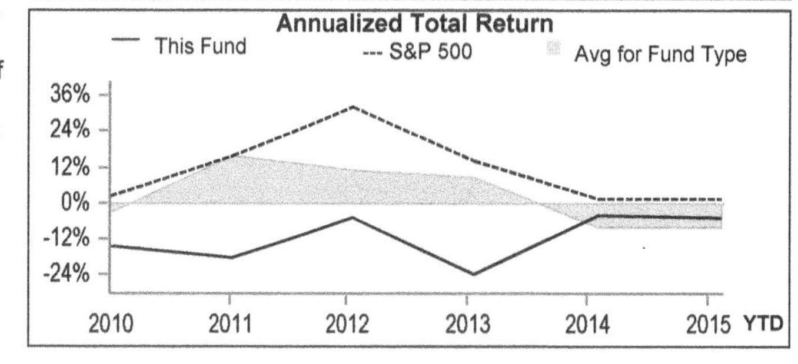

*ProShares Short Russell 2000 (RWM) D Weak

Fund Family: ProShare Advisors LLC
Fund Type: Growth
Inception Date: January 23, 2007

Major Rating Factors:
Disappointing performance is the major factor driving the D (Weak) TheStreet.com Investment Rating for *ProShares Short Russell 2000. The fund currently has a performance rating of D (Weak) based on an annualized return of -12.90% over the last three years and a total return of 0.05% year to date 2015. Factored into the performance evaluation is an expense ratio of 0.95% (low).

The fund's risk rating is currently C (Fair). It carries a beta of -1.06, meaning the fund's expected move will be -10.6% for every 10% move in the market. Volatility, as measured by both the semi-deviation and a drawdown factor, is considered average. As of December 31, 2015, *ProShares Short Russell 2000 traded at a premium of .10% above its net asset value, which is worse than its one-year historical average premium of .02%.

Michael Neches has been running the fund for 3 years and currently receives a manager quality ranking of 66 (0=worst, 99=best). This fund offers an average level of risk but investors looking for strong performance will be frustrated.

Data Date	Investment Rating	Net Assets ($Mil)	Price	Performance Rating/Pts	Total Return Y-T-D	Risk Rating/Pts
12-15	D	946.20	62.11	D / 1.9	0.05%	C / 4.8
2014	D-	946.20	15.45	E+ / 0.8	-8.96%	C+ / 5.7
2013	E+	478.20	16.88	E / 0.5	-27.79%	C / 5.2
2012	E+	437.30	24.32	E / 0.5	-18.17%	C / 5.5
2011	E+	475.30	29.68	E+ / 0.8	-8.71%	C / 4.3
2010	E+	224.60	32.18	E / 0.5	-27.39%	C- / 3.7

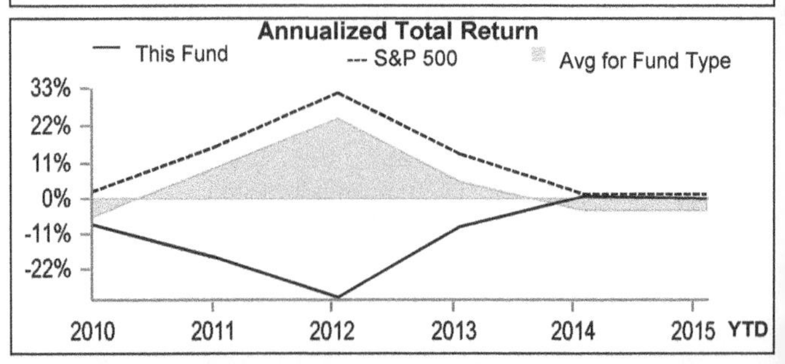

*ProShares Short S&P500 (SH) D+ Weak

Fund Family: ProShare Advisors LLC
Fund Type: Growth
Inception Date: June 19, 2006

Major Rating Factors:
Disappointing performance is the major factor driving the D+ (Weak) TheStreet.com Investment Rating for *ProShares Short S&P500. The fund currently has a performance rating of D (Weak) based on an annualized return of -14.21% over the last three years and a total return of -4.31% year to date 2015. Factored into the performance evaluation is an expense ratio of 0.90% (low).

The fund's risk rating is currently C+ (Fair). It carries a beta of -0.99, meaning the fund's expected move will be -9.9% for every 10% move in the market. Volatility, as measured by both the semi-deviation and a drawdown factor, is considered low. As of December 31, 2015, *ProShares Short S&P500 traded at a discount of .05% below its net asset value, which is better than its one-year historical average discount of .01%.

Michael Neches has been running the fund for 3 years and currently receives a manager quality ranking of 48 (0=worst, 99=best). This fund offers only a moderate level of risk but investors looking for strong performance are still waiting.

Data Date	Investment Rating	Net Assets ($Mil)	Price	Performance Rating/Pts	Total Return Y-T-D	Risk Rating/Pts
12-15	D+	1,641.80	20.87	D / 1.6	-4.31%	C+ / 6.7
2014	D-	1,641.80	21.78	E+ / 0.8	-14.52%	C+ / 5.9
2013	D-	1,402.80	25.23	E+ / 0.6	-22.90%	C+ / 6.1
2012	D-	1,849.60	34.03	E+ / 0.6	-16.33%	C+ / 6.4
2011	D-	2,366.70	40.41	D- / 1.0	-8.46%	C / 5.4
2010	D-	1,553.90	43.84	E+ / 0.7	-16.59%	C / 5.4

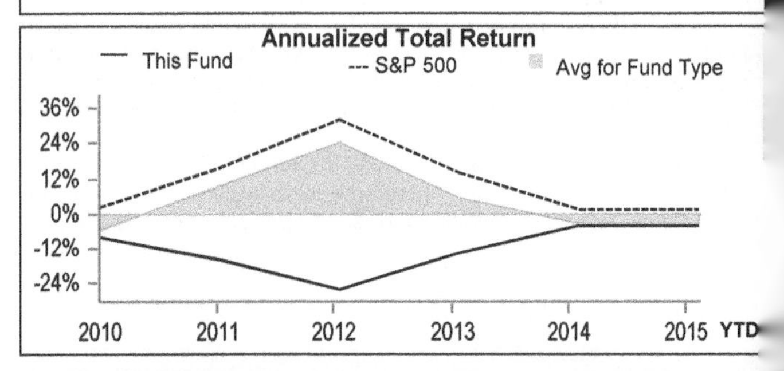

*ProShares Short Small Cap 600 (SBB) D Weak

Fund Family: ProShare Advisors LLC
Fund Type: Growth
Inception Date: January 23, 2007

Major Rating Factors:
Disappointing performance is the major factor driving the D (Weak) TheStreet.com Investment Rating for *ProShares Short Small Cap 600. The fund currently has a performance rating of D (Weak) based on an annualized return of -13.92% over the last three years and a total return of -2.41% year to date 2015. Factored into the performance evaluation is an expense ratio of 0.95% (low).

The fund's risk rating is currently C (Fair). It carries a beta of -1.02, meaning the fund's expected move will be -10.2% for every 10% move in the market. Volatility, as measured by both the semi-deviation and a drawdown factor, is considered average. As of December 31, 2015, *ProShares Short Small Cap 600 traded at a premium of .06% above its net asset value, which is worse than its one-year historical average discount of .24%.

Michael Neches has been running the fund for 3 years and currently receives a manager quality ranking of 52 (0=worst, 99=best). This fund offers an average level of risk but investors looking for strong performance will be frustrated.

Data Date	Investment Rating	Net Assets ($Mil)	Price	Performance Rating/Pts	Total Return Y-T-D	Risk Rating/Pts
12-15	D	9.90	51.77	D / 1.7	-2.41%	C / 5.3
2014	E+	9.90	53.02	E+ / 0.8	-9.15%	C- / 4.2
2013	E+	10.80	14.40	E / 0.5	-28.10%	C / 5.3
2012	E+	15.80	20.97	E / 0.4	-17.81%	C / 5.4
2011	E+	28.60	25.37	E+ / 0.7	-12.77%	C / 4.3
2010	E+	23.80	28.76	E / 0.5	-26.33%	C- / 3.3

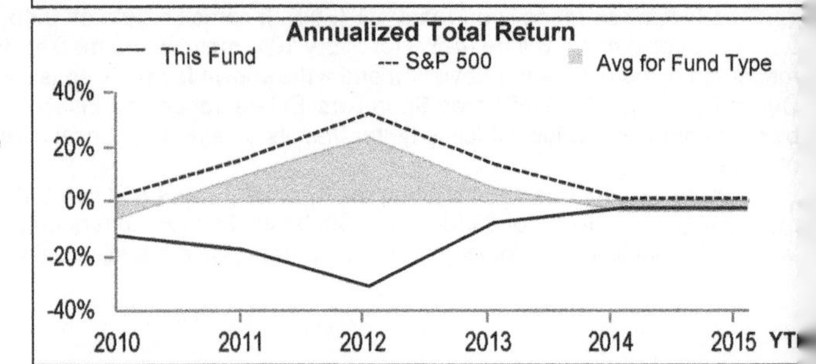

*ProShares Short VIX Sh-Tm Fut ET (SVXY) D Weak

Fund Family: ProShare Advisors LLC
Fund Type: Growth and Income
Inception Date: October 3, 2011

Data Date	Investment Rating	Net Assets ($Mil)	Price	Performance Rating/Pts	Total Return Y-T-D	Risk Rating/Pts
12-15	D	276.90	50.45	C+ / 5.8	-18.98%	D / 1.8
2014	C-	276.90	61.16	A+ / 9.8	-8.05%	D / 1.9
2013	C	141.70	134.94	A+ / 9.9	78.97%	D+ / 2.6
2012	C	79.40	65.45	A+ / 9.9	164.27%	D+ / 2.5

Major Rating Factors: *ProShares Short VIX Sh-Tm Fut ET has adopted a very risky asset allocation strategy and currently receives an overall TheStreet.com Investment Rating of D (Weak). The fund has a high level of volatility, as measured by both semi-deviation and drawdown factors. It carries a beta of 5.02, meaning it is expected to move 50.2% for every 10% move in the market. As of December 31, 2015, *ProShares Short VIX Sh-Tm Fut ET traded at a discount of .73% below its net asset value, which is better than its one-year historical average discount of .20%. Unfortunately, the high level of risk (D, Weak) has only provided investors with average performance.

The fund's performance rating is currently C+ (Fair). It has registered an annualized return of 10.72% over the last three years but is down -18.98% year to date 2015. Factored into the performance evaluation is an expense ratio of 1.49% (average).

Todd B. Johnson currently receives a manager quality ranking of 1 (0=worst, 99=best). If you are comfortable owning a very high risk investment, then this fund may be an option.

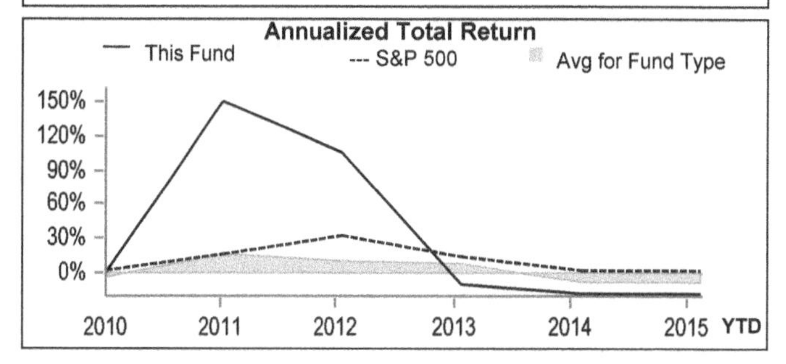

*ProShares Ult Telecommunications (LTL) B Good

Fund Family: ProShare Advisors LLC
Fund Type: Income
Inception Date: March 25, 2008

Data Date	Investment Rating	Net Assets ($Mil)	Price	Performance Rating/Pts	Total Return Y-T-D	Risk Rating/Pts
12-15	B	6.90	83.01	B / 7.9	-5.87%	C+ / 6.9
2014	B	6.90	89.72	A- / 9.2	-0.91%	C+ / 6.2
2013	B+	6.80	91.21	A / 9.4	49.29%	C+ / 6.8
2012	B	4.50	58.58	B+ / 8.8	37.61%	C+ / 6.9
2011	C-	3.30	43.59	C- / 3.7	-20.15%	C+ / 6.7
2010	B+	8.20	54.58	A+ / 9.8	40.39%	C- / 3.6

Major Rating Factors: Strong performance is the major factor driving the B (Good) TheStreet.com Investment Rating for *ProShares Ult Telecommunications. The fund currently has a performance rating of B (Good) based on an annualized return of 11.58% over the last three years and a total return of -5.87% year to date 2015. Factored into the performance evaluation is an expense ratio of 0.95% (low).

The fund's risk rating is currently C+ (Fair). It carries a beta of 1.46, meaning it is expected to move 14.6% for every 10% move in the market. Volatility, as measured by both the semi-deviation and a drawdown factor, is considered low. As of December 31, 2015, *ProShares Ult Telecommunications traded at a discount of 1.59% below its net asset value, which is better than its one-year historical average discount of .73%.

Charles Lowery has been running the fund for 3 years and currently receives a manager quality ranking of 21 (0=worst, 99=best). If you desire only a moderate level of risk and strong performance, then this fund is an excellent option.

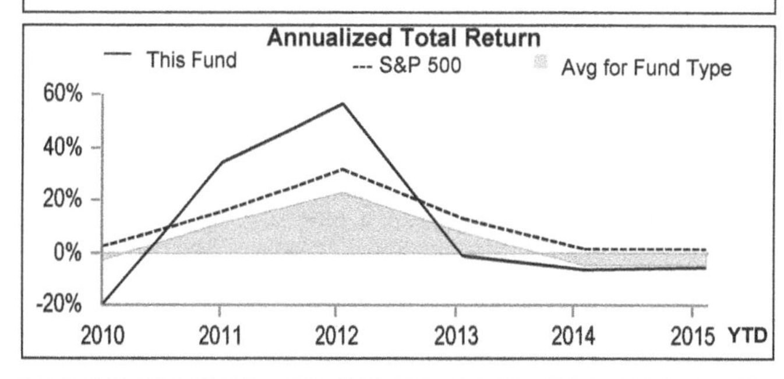

*ProShares Ultra 20+ Year Treasur (UBT) C Fair

Fund Family: ProShare Advisors LLC
Fund Type: US Government/Agency
Inception Date: January 19, 2010

Data Date	Investment Rating	Net Assets ($Mil)	Price	Performance Rating/Pts	Total Return Y-T-D	Risk Rating/Pts
12-15	C	33.90	73.26	C / 5.5	-9.46%	C+ / 6.6
2014	C	33.90	80.79	A- / 9.2	59.03%	C- / 3.0
2013	D	17.80	50.83	C / 4.7	-22.23%	C- / 3.2
2012	E+	14.10	69.53	E+ / 0.8	0.39%	C / 4.4
2011	B+	33.90	135.46	A+ / 9.9	71.45%	B- / 7.2

Major Rating Factors: Middle of the road best describes *ProShares Ultra 20+ Year Treasur whose TheStreet.com Investment Rating is currently a C (Fair). The fund currently has a performance rating of C (Fair) based on an annualized return of 4.43% over the last three years and a total return of -9.46% year to date 2015. Factored into the performance evaluation is an expense ratio of 0.95% (low).

The fund's risk rating is currently C+ (Fair). It carries a beta of 2.29, meaning it is expected to move 22.9% for every 10% move in the market. Volatility, as measured by both the semi-deviation and a drawdown factor, is considered low. As of December 31, 2015, *ProShares Ultra 20+ Year Treasur traded at a discount of 1.11% below its net asset value, which is better than its one-year historical average discount of .02%.

Michelle Liu has been running the fund for 6 years and currently receives a manager quality ranking of 44 (0=worst, 99=best). If you desire an average level of risk, then this fund may be an option.

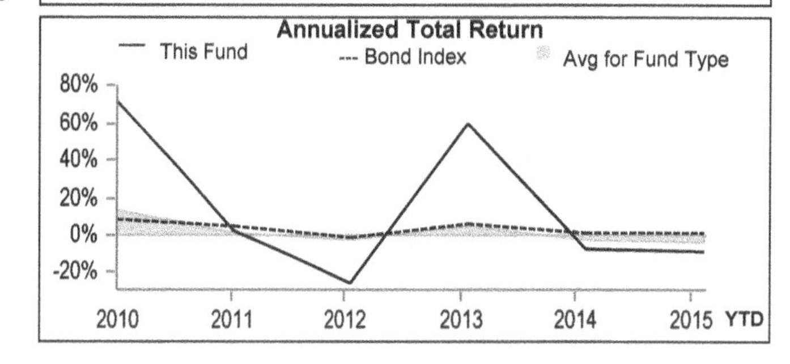

*ProShares Ultra 7-10 Year Treasu (UST) C+ Fair

Fund Family: ProShare Advisors LLC
Fund Type: US Government/Agency
Inception Date: January 19, 2010

Major Rating Factors: Middle of the road best describes *ProShares Ultra 7-10 Year Treasu whose TheStreet.com Investment Rating is currently a C+ (Fair). The fund currently has a performance rating of C (Fair) based on an annualized return of 2.22% over the last three years and a total return of 0.96% year to date 2015. Factored into the performance evaluation is an expense ratio of 0.95% (low).

The fund's risk rating is currently B (Good). It carries a beta of 0.98, meaning that its performance tracks fairly well with that of the overall stock market. Volatility, as measured by both the semi-deviation and a drawdown factor, is considered low. As of December 31, 2015, *ProShares Ultra 7-10 Year Treasu traded at a discount of .12% below its net asset value, which is better than its one-year historical average premium of .01%.

Michelle Liu has been running the fund for 6 years and currently receives a manager quality ranking of 60 (0=worst, 99=best). If you desire an average level of risk, then this fund may be an option.

Data Date	Investment Rating	Net Assets ($Mil)	Price	Performance Rating/Pts	Total Return Y-T-D	Risk Rating/Pts
12-15	C+	21.20	56.13	C / 5.3	0.96%	B / 8.4
2014	D	21.20	55.49	C / 4.9	16.97%	C- / 3.2
2013	D	14.90	49.63	C / 4.3	-10.41%	C- / 3.7
2012	E+	741.30	56.75	D / 1.6	4.73%	C / 4.3
2011	A+	181.10	106.40	A- / 9.1	30.60%	B+ / 9.1

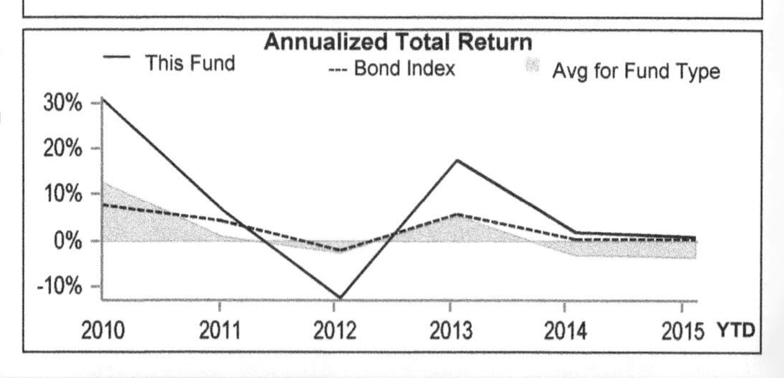

*ProShares Ultra Basic Materials (UYM) D Weak

Fund Family: ProShare Advisors LLC
Fund Type: Income
Inception Date: January 30, 2007

Major Rating Factors:
Disappointing performance is the major factor driving the D (Weak) TheStreet.com Investment Rating for *ProShares Ultra Basic Materials. The fund currently has a performance rating of D+ (Weak) based on an annualized return of -0.84% over the last three years and a total return of -27.32% year to date 2015. Factored into the performance evaluation is an expense ratio of 0.95% (low).

The fund's risk rating is currently C (Fair). It carries a beta of 2.49, meaning it is expected to move 24.9% for every 10% move in the market. Volatility, as measured by both the semi-deviation and a drawdown factor, is considered average. As of December 31, 2015, *ProShares Ultra Basic Materials traded at a premium of .39% above its net asset value, which is worse than its one-year historical average discount of .03%.

Charles Lowery has been running the fund for 3 years and currently receives a manager quality ranking of 3 (0=worst, 99=best). This fund offers an average level of risk but investors looking for strong performance will be frustrated.

Data Date	Investment Rating	Net Assets ($Mil)	Price	Performance Rating/Pts	Total Return Y-T-D	Risk Rating/Pts
12-15	D	101.90	36.18	D+ / 2.8	-27.32%	C / 4.3
2014	C+	101.90	49.82	C+ / 6.3	4.71%	B- / 7.0
2013	C+	120.40	48.59	A+ / 9.8	27.73%	C / 4.4
2012	D-	157.40	36.68	C- / 3.2	7.04%	C / 4.4
2011	C	224.00	32.12	B / 7.6	-31.61%	C / 4.5
2010	D+	368.30	50.65	C+ / 5.8	57.39%	D+ / 2.3

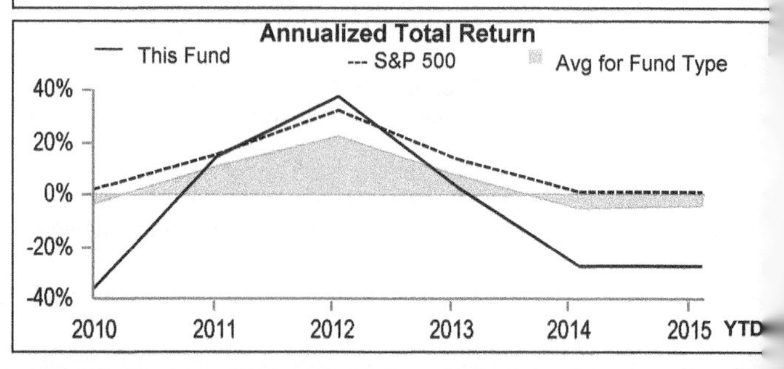

*ProShares Ultra Bloomberg Commod (UCD) E+ Very Weak

Fund Family: ProShare Advisors LLC
Fund Type: Income
Inception Date: November 25, 2008

Major Rating Factors:
Very poor performance is the major factor driving the E+ (Very Weak) TheStreet.com Investment Rating for *ProShares Ultra Bloomberg Commod. The fund currently has a performance rating of E (Very Weak) based on an annualized return of -33.10% over the last three years and a total return of -45.56% year to date 2015. Factored into the performance evaluation is an expense ratio of 0.95% (low).

The fund's risk rating is currently C- (Fair). It carries a beta of 0.89, meaning the fund's expected move will be 8.9% for every 10% move in the market. Volatility, as measured by both the semi-deviation and a drawdown factor, is considered average. As of December 31, 2015, *ProShares Ultra Bloomberg Commod traded at a discount of 1.27% below its net asset value, which is better than its one-year historical average premium of .28%.

Michael Neches currently receives a manager quality ranking of 1 (0=worst, 99=best). This fund offers an average level of risk but investors looking for strong performance will be frustrated.

Data Date	Investment Rating	Net Assets ($Mil)	Price	Performance Rating/Pts	Total Return Y-T-D	Risk Rating/Pts
12-15	E+	3.40	28.07	E / 0.3	-45.56%	C- / 4.0
2014	E+	3.40	12.86	E / 0.5	-32.78%	C- / 3.8
2013	E+	2.90	19.13	E+ / 0.6	-18.35%	C- / 3.9
2012	E+	6.10	23.93	E+ / 0.8	-7.97%	C / 4.5
2011	D-	9.10	25.64	D / 2.0	-22.79%	C+ / 5.6
2010	A+	18.20	36.27	A+ / 9.8	27.58%	C+ / 6.6

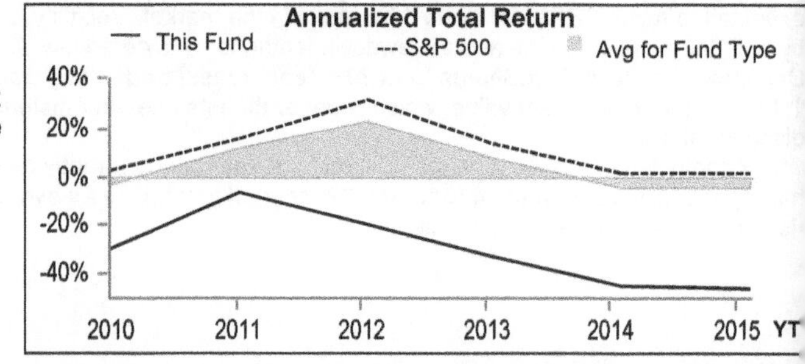

*ProShares Ultra Bloomberg Crude (UCO) E- Very Weak

Fund Family: ProShare Advisors LLC
Fund Type: Energy/Natural Resources
Inception Date: November 25, 2008

Major Rating Factors: *ProShares Ultra Bloomberg Crude has adopted a very risky asset allocation strategy and currently receives an overall TheStreet.com Investment Rating of E- (Very Weak). The fund has a high level of volatility, as measured by both semi-deviation and drawdown factors. It carries a beta of 2.20, meaning it is expected to move 22.0% for every 10% move in the market. As of December 31, 2015, *ProShares Ultra Bloomberg Crude traded at a discount of .32% below its net asset value, which is better than its one-year historical average discount of .17%. Unfortunately, the high level of risk (D, Weak) failed to pay off as investors endured very poor performance.

The fund's performance rating is currently E- (Very Weak). It has registered an annualized return of -56.35% over the last three years and is down -74.69% year to date 2015. Factored into the performance evaluation is an expense ratio of 0.99% (low).

Michael Neches currently receives a manager quality ranking of 0 (0=worst, 99=best). If you can tolerate very high levels of risk in the hope of improved future returns, holding this fund may be an option.

Data Date	Investment Rating	Net Assets ($Mil)	Price	Performance Rating/Pts	Total Return Y-T-D	Risk Rating/Pts
12-15	E-	183.70	12.54	E- / 0	-74.69%	D / 1.8
2014	E-	183.70	10.37	E- / 0.1	-64.75%	E- / 0.1
2013	E	142.80	32.22	E+ / 0.7	-2.42%	D+ / 2.8
2012	E	495.20	29.32	E+ / 0.6	-25.69%	D+ / 2.8
2011	E+	251.40	40.94	D / 1.7	-8.11%	C- / 3.4
2010	B-	228.10	12.50	A- / 9.2	-1.42%	C- / 3.2

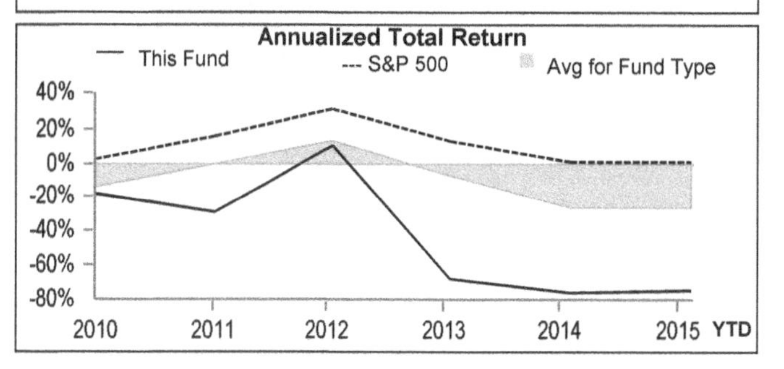

*ProShares Ultra Bloomberg Nat Ga (BOIL) E- Very Weak

Fund Family: ProShare Advisors LLC
Fund Type: Energy/Natural Resources
Inception Date: October 6, 2011

Major Rating Factors: *ProShares Ultra Bloomberg Nat Ga has adopted a very risky asset allocation strategy and currently receives an overall TheStreet.com Investment Rating of E- (Very Weak). The fund has a high level of volatility, as measured by both semi-deviation and drawdown factors. It carries a beta of -0.07, meaning the fund's expected move will be -0.7% for every 10% move in the market. As of December 31, 2015, *ProShares Ultra Bloomberg Nat Ga traded at a discount of .48% below its net asset value, which is better than its one-year historical average discount of .05%. Unfortunately, the high level of risk (D, Weak) failed to pay off as investors endured very poor performance.

The fund's performance rating is currently E- (Very Weak). It has registered an annualized return of -50.14% over the last three years and is down -71.16% year to date 2015. Factored into the performance evaluation is an expense ratio of 1.13% (low).

Michael Neches currently receives a manager quality ranking of 0 (0=worst, 99=best). If you can tolerate very high levels of risk in the hope of improved future returns, holding this fund may be an option.

Data Date	Investment Rating	Net Assets ($Mil)	Price	Performance Rating/Pts	Total Return Y-T-D	Risk Rating/Pts
12-15	E-	71.30	18.48	E- / 0	-71.16%	D / 1.8
2014	E-	71.30	15.78	E- / 0	-61.34%	D / 1.9
2013	C-	62.90	39.28	B+ / 8.9	9.52%	D / 1.9
2012	E-	73.00	39.24	E- / 0	-51.80%	D / 1.9

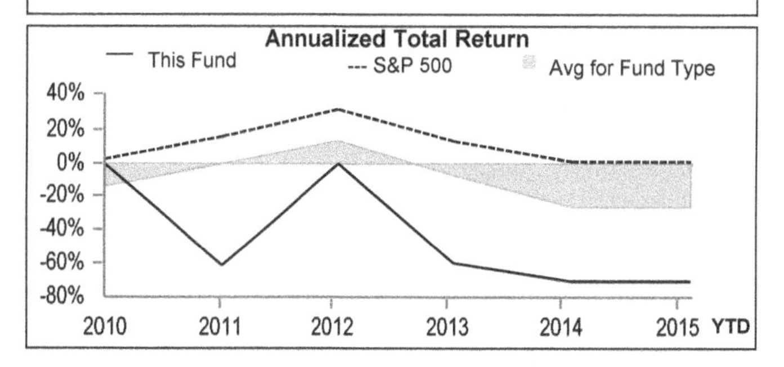

*ProShares Ultra Consumer Goods (UGE) C+ Fair

Fund Family: ProShare Advisors LLC
Fund Type: Income
Inception Date: January 30, 2007

Major Rating Factors:
Exceptional performance is the major factor driving the C+ (Fair) TheStreet.com Investment Rating for *ProShares Ultra Consumer Goods. The fund currently has a performance rating of A+ (Excellent) based on an annualized return of 28.20% over the last three years and a total return of 11.83% year to date 2015. Factored into the performance evaluation is an expense ratio of 0.95% (low).

The fund's risk rating is currently C- (Fair). It carries a beta of 1.98, meaning it is expected to move 19.8% for every 10% move in the market. Volatility, as measured by both the semi-deviation and a drawdown factor, is considered average. As of December 31, 2015, *ProShares Ultra Consumer Goods traded at a premium of 1.12% above its net asset value, which is worse than its one-year historical average discount of .07%.

Charles Lowery has been running the fund for 3 years and currently receives a manager quality ranking of 65 (0=worst, 99=best). If you desire an average level of risk and strong performance, then this fund is a good option.

Data Date	Investment Rating	Net Assets ($Mil)	Price	Performance Rating/Pts	Total Return Y-T-D	Risk Rating/Pts
12-15	C+	25.70	105.50	A+ / 9.8	11.83%	C- / 3.1
2014	C	25.70	98.81	A+ / 9.7	26.67%	D+ / 2.7
2013	C+	11.90	79.35	A+ / 9.7	54.81%	C / 4.6
2012	A	14.50	94.10	A / 9.4	29.99%	B- / 7.9
2011	B+	11.80	78.34	B+ / 8.9	14.43%	B- / 7.4
2010	C+	20.80	69.61	B- / 7.4	36.67%	C / 4.8

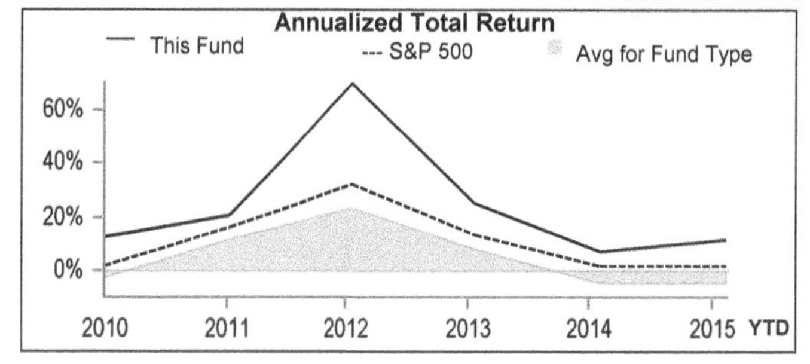

*ProShares Ultra Consumer Service (UCC) C Fair

Fund Family: ProShare Advisors LLC
Fund Type: Income
Inception Date: January 30, 2007

Major Rating Factors: *ProShares Ultra Consumer Service has adopted a risky asset allocation strategy and currently receives an overall TheStreet.com Investment Rating of C (Fair). The fund has shown an above average level of volatility, as measured by both semi-deviation and drawdown factors. It carries a beta of 2.19, meaning it is expected to move 21.9% for every 10% move in the market. As of December 31, 2015, *ProShares Ultra Consumer Service traded at a premium of .04% above its net asset value, which is worse than its one-year historical average discount of .04%. The high level of risk (D+, Weak) did however, reward investors with excellent performance.

The fund's performance rating is currently A+ (Excellent). It has registered an annualized return of 37.33% over the last three years and is up 9.62% year to date 2015. Factored into the performance evaluation is an expense ratio of 0.95% (low).

Charles Lowery has been running the fund for 3 years and currently receives a manager quality ranking of 83 (0=worst, 99=best). If you are comfortable owning a high risk investment, this fund may be an option.

Data Date	Investment Rating	Net Assets ($Mil)	Price	Performance Rating/Pts	Total Return Y-T-D	Risk Rating/Pts
12-15	C	24.10	106.68	A+ / 9.8	9.62%	D+ / 2.9
2014	C	24.10	98.44	A+ / 9.8	29.02%	D+ / 2.7
2013	C+	28.90	77.34	A+ / 9.9	84.97%	C / 4.6
2012	A-	11.80	78.44	A+ / 9.8	52.14%	B- / 7.1
2011	B+	7.90	52.93	A / 9.5	9.61%	B- / 7.1
2010	C+	11.00	49.20	B / 8.1	46.07%	C- / 3.8

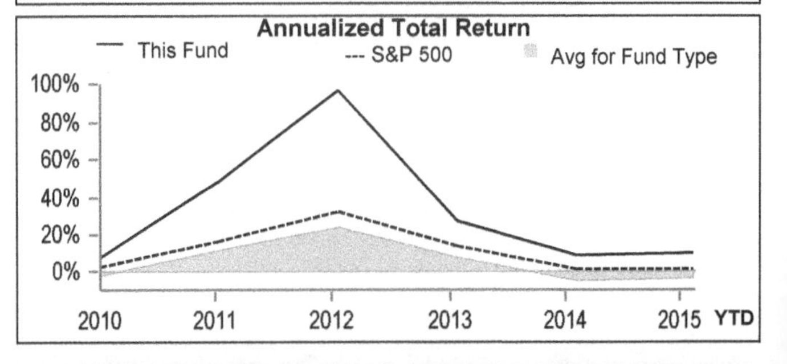

*ProShares Ultra Dow30 (DDM) C Fair

Fund Family: ProShare Advisors LLC
Fund Type: Growth
Inception Date: June 19, 2006

Major Rating Factors: *ProShares Ultra Dow30 has adopted a risky asset allocation strategy and currently receives an overall TheStreet.com Investment Rating of C (Fair). The fund has shown an above average level of volatility, as measured by both semi-deviation and drawdown factors. It carries a beta of 2.06, meaning it is expected to move 20.6% for every 10% move in the market. As of December 31, 2015, *ProShares Ultra Dow30 traded at a discount of .03% below its net asset value. The high level of risk (D+, Weak) did however, reward investors with excellent performance.

The fund's performance rating is currently A (Excellent). It has registered an annualized return of 21.17% over the last three years but is down -3.48% year to date 2015. Factored into the performance evaluation is an expense ratio of 0.95% (low).

Howard Rubin has been running the fund for 9 years and currently receives a manager quality ranking of 21 (0=worst, 99=best). If you are comfortable owning a high risk investment, this fund may be an option.

Data Date	Investment Rating	Net Assets ($Mil)	Price	Performance Rating/Pts	Total Return Y-T-D	Risk Rating/Pts
12-15	C	285.90	64.30	A / 9.5	-3.48%	D+ / 2.9
2014	A+	285.90	134.63	A+ / 9.6	19.50%	B / 8.0
2013	A-	302.30	115.11	A+ / 9.6	53.90%	B- / 7.0
2012	B-	217.10	70.23	B / 8.1	21.02%	C+ / 6.8
2011	B-	269.80	59.89	B / 8.2	11.60%	C+ / 6.2
2010	E+	314.20	54.52	D / 1.9	25.37%	C- / 3.0

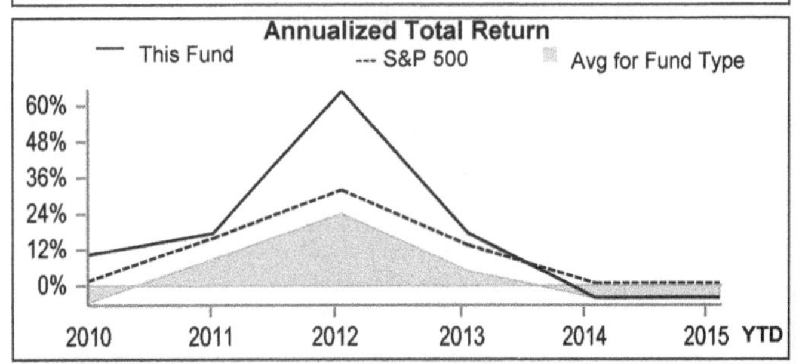

*ProShares Ultra Euro (ULE) D- Weak

Fund Family: ProShare Advisors LLC
Fund Type: Foreign
Inception Date: November 25, 2008

Major Rating Factors:
Disappointing performance is the major factor driving the D- (Weak) TheStreet.com Investment Rating for *ProShares Ultra Euro. The fund currently has a performance rating of D- (Weak) based on an annualized return of -13.69% over the last three years and a total return of -20.91% year to date 2015. Factored into the performance evaluation is an expense ratio of 0.95% (low).

The fund's risk rating is currently C (Fair). It carries a beta of 0.48, meaning the fund's expected move will be 4.8% for every 10% move in the market. Volatility, as measured by both the semi-deviation and a drawdown factor, is considered average. As of December 31, 2015, *ProShares Ultra Euro traded at a price exactly equal to its net asset value, which is better than its one-year historical average premium of .03%.

Michael Neches currently receives a manager quality ranking of 10 (0=worst, 99=best). This fund offers an average level of risk but investors looking for strong performance will be frustrated.

Data Date	Investment Rating	Net Assets ($Mil)	Price	Performance Rating/Pts	Total Return Y-T-D	Risk Rating/Pts
12-15	D-	2.20	15.51	D- / 1.3	-20.91%	C / 4.9
2014	D-	2.20	19.80	D- / 1.5	-21.83%	C / 5.1
2013	D+	2.60	25.98	C- / 3.7	5.02%	C+ / 6.6
2012	D-	4.90	24.32	D- / 1.1	7.81%	C+ / 6.3
2011	D-	9.60	23.87	D- / 1.3	-3.95%	C+ / 6.5
2010	D	7.70	25.86	D- / 1.0	-14.29%	C+ / 5.9

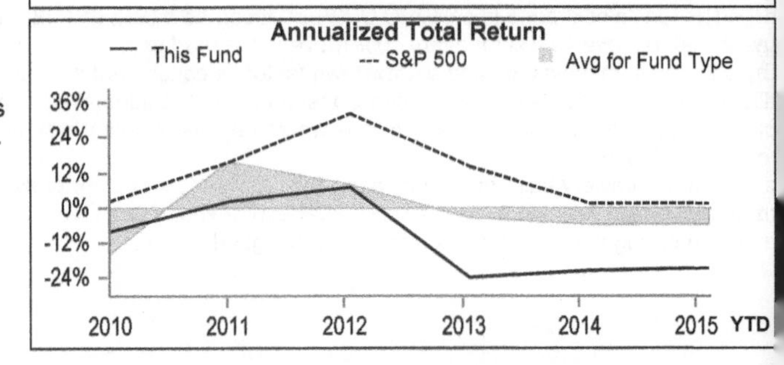

*ProShares Ultra Financials (UYG) C+ Fair

Fund Family: ProShare Advisors LLC
Fund Type: Financial Services
Inception Date: January 30, 2007

Major Rating Factors:
Exceptional performance is the major factor driving the C+ (Fair) TheStreet.com Investment Rating for *ProShares Ultra Financials. The fund currently has a performance rating of A+ (Excellent) based on an annualized return of 25.43% over the last three years and a total return of -4.45% year to date 2015. Factored into the performance evaluation is an expense ratio of 0.95% (low).

The fund's risk rating is currently C- (Fair). It carries a beta of 2.03, meaning it is expected to move 20.3% for every 10% move in the market. Volatility, as measured by both the semi-deviation and a drawdown factor, is considered average. As of December 31, 2015, *ProShares Ultra Financials traded at a discount of .01% below its net asset value, which is worse than its one-year historical average discount of .02%.

Charles Lowery has been running the fund for 3 years and currently receives a manager quality ranking of 37 (0=worst, 99=best). If you desire an average level of risk and strong performance, then this fund is a good option.

Data Date	Investment Rating	Net Assets ($Mil)	Price	Performance Rating/Pts	Total Return Y-T-D	Risk Rating/Pts
12-15	C+	786.60	71.00	A+ / 9.6	-4.45%	C- / 3.5
2014	A+	786.60	149.11	A+ / 9.8	27.61%	B- / 7.8
2013	B-	861.00	117.76	A / 9.4	61.19%	C / 5.4
2012	C+	754.80	67.81	B+ / 8.4	51.91%	C / 5.1
2011	E+	770.40	44.37	D- / 1.4	-31.54%	C- / 4.2
2010	E	1,372.70	66.38	E / 0.3	18.04%	D+ / 2.4

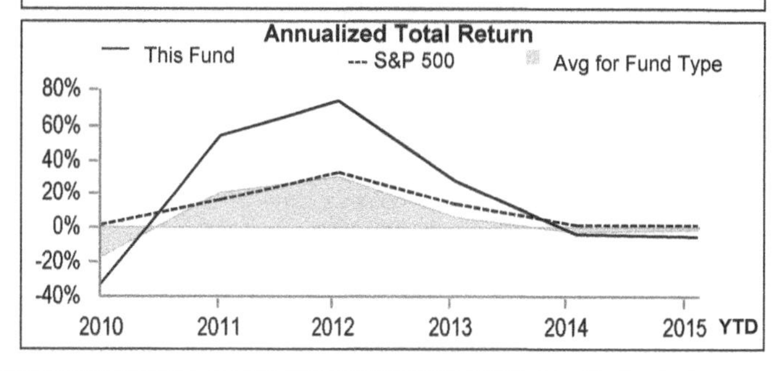

*ProShares Ultra FTSE China 50 (XPP) E Very Weak

Fund Family: ProShare Advisors LLC
Fund Type: Foreign
Inception Date: June 2, 2009

Major Rating Factors: *ProShares Ultra FTSE China 50 has adopted a very risky asset allocation strategy and currently receives an overall TheStreet.com Investment Rating of E (Very Weak). The fund has a high level of volatility, as measured by both semi-deviation and drawdown factors. It carries a beta of 1.89, meaning it is expected to move 18.9% for every 10% move in the market. As of December 31, 2015, *ProShares Ultra FTSE China 50 traded at a premium of .04% above its net asset value, which is in line with its one-year historical average premium of .04%. Unfortunately, the high level of risk (D, Weak) failed to pay off as investors endured poor performance.

The fund's performance rating is currently D- (Weak). It has registered an annualized return of -9.84% over the last three years and is down -30.36% year to date 2015. Factored into the performance evaluation is an expense ratio of 0.95% (low).

Alexander V. Ilyasov has been running the fund for 7 years and currently receives a manager quality ranking of 9 (0=worst, 99=best). If you can tolerate very high levels of risk in the hope of improved future returns, holding this fund may be an option.

Data Date	Investment Rating	Net Assets ($Mil)	Price	Performance Rating/Pts	Total Return Y-T-D	Risk Rating/Pts
12-15	E	49.10	48.35	D- / 1.3	-30.36%	D / 1.7
2014	C+	49.10	69.24	A- / 9.1	31.19%	C / 4.7
2013	E+	40.50	57.88	D- / 1.1	-19.99%	C- / 3.2
2012	D-	43.70	62.37	C- / 3.3	27.68%	C- / 3.6
2011	E+	24.90	45.40	E / 0.5	-38.74%	C- / 4.0
2010	B+	47.50	73.12	B- / 7.5	2.74%	C+ / 6.3

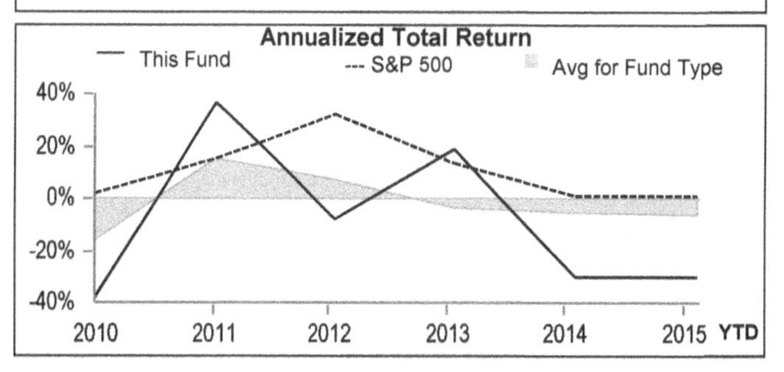

*ProShares Ultra FTSR Europe (UPV) C- Fair

Fund Family: ProShare Advisors LLC
Fund Type: Foreign
Inception Date: April 27, 2010

Major Rating Factors: Middle of the road best describes *ProShares Ultra FTSR Europe whose TheStreet.com Investment Rating is currently a C- (Fair). The fund currently has a performance rating of C (Fair) based on an annualized return of 5.16% over the last three years and a total return of -5.87% year to date 2015. Factored into the performance evaluation is an expense ratio of 0.95% (low).

The fund's risk rating is currently C (Fair). It carries a beta of 2.11, meaning it is expected to move 21.1% for every 10% move in the market. Volatility, as measured by both the semi-deviation and a drawdown factor, is considered average. As of December 31, 2015, *ProShares Ultra FTSR Europe traded at a premium of .43% above its net asset value, which is worse than its one-year historical average premium of .02%.

Alexander V. Ilyasov has been running the fund for 7 years and currently receives a manager quality ranking of 30 (0=worst, 99=best). If you desire an average level of risk, then this fund may be an option.

Data Date	Investment Rating	Net Assets ($Mil)	Price	Performance Rating/Pts	Total Return Y-T-D	Risk Rating/Pts
12-15	C-	21.40	39.96	C / 5.4	-5.87%	C / 4.6
2014	C-	21.40	43.05	B- / 7.1	-12.06%	C / 4.3
2013	C	25.60	51.09	B+ / 8.6	42.46%	C- / 4.1
2012	C+	8.40	33.44	A+ / 9.9	50.40%	C- / 3.7
2011	E	2.40	23.87	E / 0.4	-29.69%	C- / 3.8

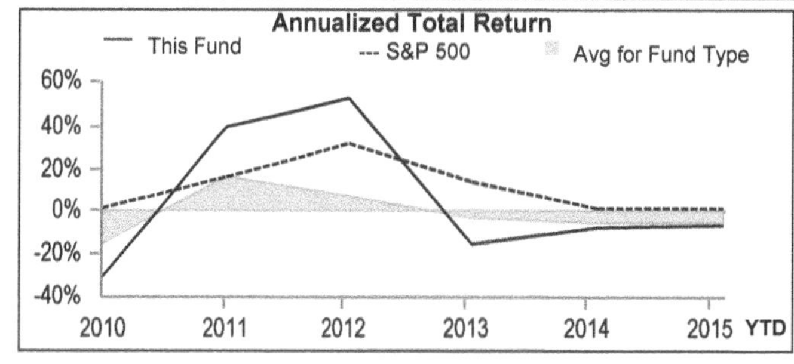

*ProShares Ultra Gold (UGL) E Very Weak

Fund Family: ProShare Advisors LLC
Fund Type: Precious Metals
Inception Date: December 2, 2008

Major Rating Factors: *ProShares Ultra Gold has adopted a risky asset allocation strategy and currently receives an overall TheStreet.com Investment Rating of E (Very Weak). The fund has an above average level of volatility, as measured by both semi-deviation and drawdown factors. It carries a beta of 1.85, meaning it is expected to move 18.5% for every 10% move in the market. As of December 31, 2015, *ProShares Ultra Gold traded at a price exactly equal to its net asset value, which is better than its one-year historical average premium of .20%. Unfortunately, the high level of risk (D+, Weak) failed to pay off as investors endured very poor performance.

The fund's performance rating is currently E (Very Weak). It has registered an annualized return of -29.12% over the last three years and is down -23.18% year to date 2015. Factored into the performance evaluation is an expense ratio of 0.95% (low).

Michael Neches currently receives a manager quality ranking of 22 (0=worst, 99=best). If you can tolerate high levels of risk in the hope of improved future returns, holding this fund may be an option.

Data Date	Investment Rating	Net Assets ($Mil)	Price	Performance Rating/Pts	Total Return Y-T-D	Risk Rating/Pts
12-15	E	113.00	29.73	E / 0.5	-23.18%	D+ / 2.3
2014	E-	113.00	38.41	E+ / 0.6	-11.74%	D- / 1.4
2013	E	364.40	41.26	E+ / 0.6	-47.87%	C- / 3.1
2012	C	364.40	85.26	B- / 7.0	-2.60%	C+ / 5.9
2011	B	322.60	79.01	A+ / 9.8	28.65%	C+ / 6.3
2010	A+	252.80	70.72	A+ / 9.8	58.28%	B- / 7.1

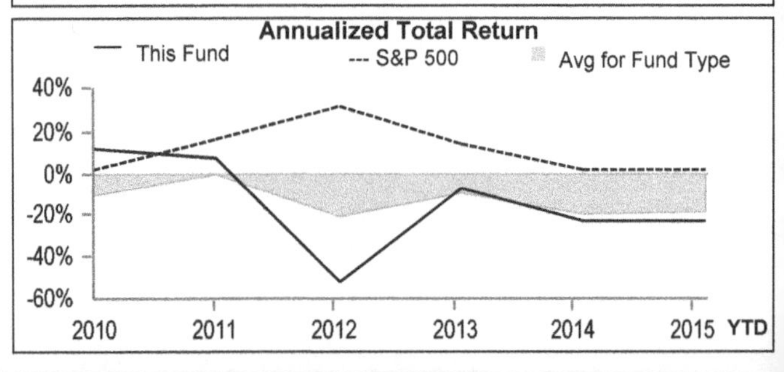

*ProShares Ultra Health Care (RXL) C Fair

Fund Family: ProShare Advisors LLC
Fund Type: Health
Inception Date: January 30, 2007

Major Rating Factors: *ProShares Ultra Health Care has adopted a very risky asset allocation strategy and currently receives an overall TheStreet.com Investment Rating of C (Fair). The fund has shown a high level of volatility, as measured by both semi-deviation and drawdown factors. It carries a beta of 1.97, meaning it is expected to move 19.7% for every 10% move in the market. As of December 31, 2015, *ProShares Ultra Health Care traded at a discount of .02% below its net asset value, which is better than its one-year historical average discount of .01%. The high level of risk (D, Weak) did however, reward investors with excellent performance.

The fund's performance rating is currently A+ (Excellent). It has registered an annualized return of 44.94% over the last three years and is up 7.32% year to date 2015. Factored into the performance evaluation is an expense ratio of 0.95% (low).

Charles Lowery has been running the fund for 3 years and currently receives a manager quality ranking of 96 (0=worst, 99=best). If you are comfortable owning a very high risk investment, this fund may be an option.

Data Date	Investment Rating	Net Assets ($Mil)	Price	Performance Rating/Pts	Total Return Y-T-D	Risk Rating/Pts
12-15	C	121.00	65.98	A+ / 9.9	7.32%	D / 2.1
2014	C+	121.00	123.89	A+ / 9.9	53.68%	C- / 3.7
2013	C+	97.60	81.10	A+ / 9.9	84.31%	C- / 4.1
2012	B+	44.00	83.83	A / 9.3	44.11%	B- / 7.2
2011	B-	36.60	60.90	B- / 7.5	17.11%	B- / 7.1
2010	D	46.80	52.02	D- / 1.5	5.01%	C / 4.9

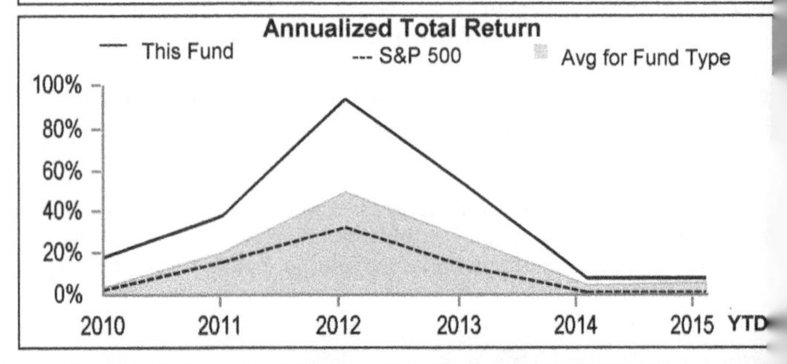

*ProShares Ultra High Yield (UJB) C- Fair

Fund Family: ProShare Advisors LLC
Fund Type: Corporate - High Yield
Inception Date: April 13, 2011

Major Rating Factors: Middle of the road best describes *ProShares Ultra High Yield whose TheStreet.com Investment Rating is currently a C- (Fair). The fund currently has a performance rating of C- (Fair) based on an annualized return of -1.20% over the last three years and a total return of -13.40% year to date 2015. Factored into the performance evaluation is an expense ratio of 0.95% (low).

The fund's risk rating is currently B- (Good). It carries a beta of 2.23, meaning it is expected to move 22.3% for every 10% move in the market. Volatility, as measured by both the semi-deviation and a drawdown factor, is considered low. As of December 31, 2015, *ProShares Ultra High Yield traded at a discount of 2.53% below its net asset value, which is better than its one-year historical average discount of .35%.

Jeff Ploshnick has been running the fund for 5 years and currently receives a manager quality ranking of 36 (0=worst, 99=best). If you desire an average level of risk, then this fund may be an option.

Data Date	Investment Rating	Net Assets ($Mil)	Price	Performance Rating/Pts	Total Return Y-T-D	Risk Rating/Pts
12-15	C-	2.90	47.78	C- / 3.0	-13.40%	B- / 7.5
2014	C	2.90	57.02	C+ / 5.7	3.93%	B- / 7.0
2013	B-	2.80	55.29	C+ / 6.7	7.67%	B / 8.3
2012	A+	5.10	50.37	A / 9.3	25.48%	B / 8.2

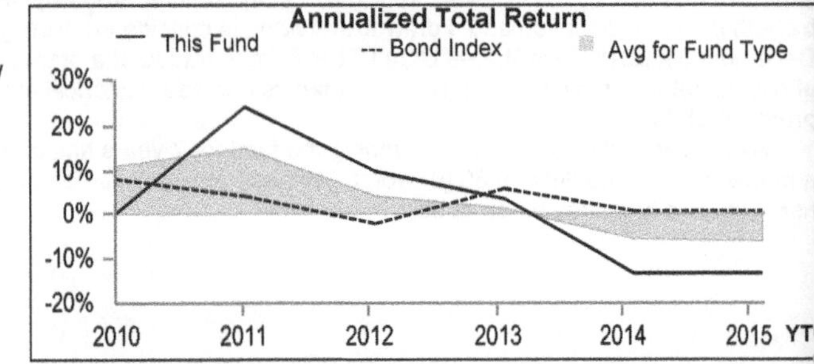

* Denotes ETF Fund

*ProShares Ultra Industrials (UXI) B+ Good

Fund Family: ProShare Advisors LLC
Fund Type: Income
Inception Date: January 30, 2007

Major Rating Factors:
Exceptional performance is the major factor driving the B+ (Good) TheStreet.com Investment Rating for *ProShares Ultra Industrials. The fund currently has a performance rating of A (Excellent) based on an annualized return of 22.78% over the last three years and a total return of -6.70% year to date 2015. Factored into the performance evaluation is an expense ratio of 0.95% (low).

The fund's risk rating is currently C+ (Fair). It carries a beta of 2.30, meaning it is expected to move 23.0% for every 10% move in the market. Volatility, as measured by both the semi-deviation and a drawdown factor, is considered low. As of December 31, 2015, *ProShares Ultra Industrials traded at a premium of .10% above its net asset value, which is worse than its one-year historical average premium of .03%.

Charles Lowery has been running the fund for 3 years and currently receives a manager quality ranking of 18 (0=worst, 99=best). If you desire only a moderate level of risk and strong performance, then this fund is an excellent option.

Data Date	Investment Rating	Net Assets ($Mil)	Price	Performance Rating/Pts	Total Return Y-T-D	Risk Rating/Pts
12-15	B+	31.20	106.85	A / 9.5	-6.70%	C+ / 5.9
2014	A-	31.20	117.79	A+ / 9.7	15.03%	C+ / 6.5
2013	B	31.40	104.50	A+ / 9.8	76.68%	C+ / 5.9
2012	C+	20.60	54.60	A- / 9.0	28.53%	C / 5.5
2011	C	24.80	41.42	B- / 7.3	-8.30%	C / 5.4
2010	D	34.70	46.31	C- / 3.9	49.21%	D+ / 2.9

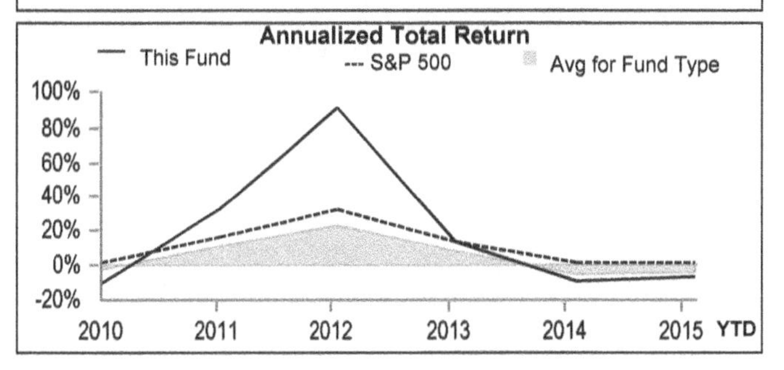

*ProShares Ultra Invest Grade Cor (IGU) C Fair

Fund Family: ProShare Advisors LLC
Fund Type: Corporate - Investment Grade
Inception Date: April 13, 2011

Major Rating Factors: Middle of the road best describes *ProShares Ultra Invest Grade Cor whose TheStreet.com Investment Rating is currently a C (Fair). The fund currently has a performance rating of C (Fair) based on an annualized return of 1.86% over the last three years and a total return of -2.07% year to date 2015. Factored into the performance evaluation is an expense ratio of 0.95% (low).

The fund's risk rating is currently C+ (Fair). It carries a beta of 2.39, meaning it is expected to move 23.9% for every 10% move in the market. Volatility, as measured by both the semi-deviation and a drawdown factor, is considered low. As of December 31, 2015, *ProShares Ultra Invest Grade Cor traded at a premium of .54% above its net asset value, which is worse than its one-year historical average discount of .37%.

Jeff Ploshnick has been running the fund for 5 years and currently receives a manager quality ranking of 52 (0=worst, 99=best). If you desire an average level of risk, then this fund may be an option.

Data Date	Investment Rating	Net Assets ($Mil)	Price	Performance Rating/Pts	Total Return Y-T-D	Risk Rating/Pts
12-15	C	2.90	57.38	C / 5.1	-2.07%	C+ / 6.8
2014	C+	2.90	59.56	C+ / 5.6	13.55%	B / 8.4
2013	C-	2.60	52.36	D+ / 2.9	-4.96%	B / 8.5
2012	B	5.60	55.58	C+ / 6.0	19.16%	B+ / 9.2

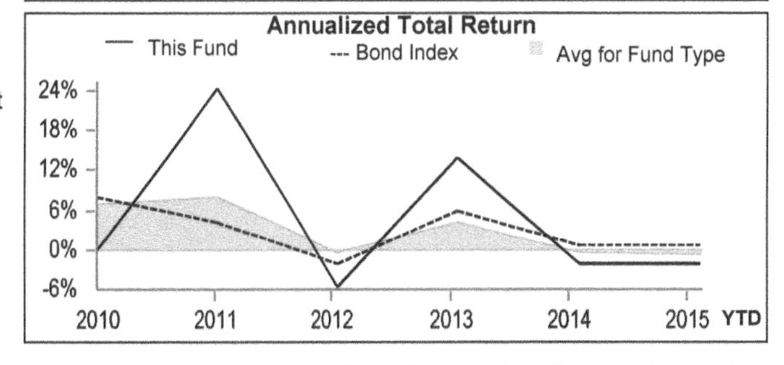

*ProShares Ultra MidCap 400 (MVV) C Fair

Fund Family: ProShare Advisors LLC
Fund Type: Growth
Inception Date: June 19, 2006

Major Rating Factors: *ProShares Ultra MidCap 400 has adopted a risky asset allocation strategy and currently receives an overall TheStreet.com Investment Rating of C (Fair). The fund has shown an above average level of volatility, as measured by both semi-deviation and drawdown factors. It carries a beta of 1.99, meaning it is expected to move 19.9% for every 10% move in the market. As of December 31, 2015, *ProShares Ultra MidCap 400 traded at a premium of .21% above its net asset value, which is worse than its one-year historical average discount of .02%. The high level of risk (D+, Weak) did however, reward investors with excellent performance.

The fund's performance rating is currently A- (Excellent). It has registered an annualized return of 19.69% over the last three years but is down -7.38% year to date 2015. Factored into the performance evaluation is an expense ratio of 0.95% (low).

Michael Neches has been running the fund for 3 years and currently receives a manager quality ranking of 21 (0=worst, 99=best). If you are comfortable owning a high risk investment, this fund may be an option.

Data Date	Investment Rating	Net Assets ($Mil)	Price	Performance Rating/Pts	Total Return Y-T-D	Risk Rating/Pts
12-15	C	773.50	67.86	A- / 9.1	-7.38%	D+ / 2.6
2014	C-	773.50	73.60	A+ / 9.7	17.37%	D / 2.1
2013	B	1,799.50	126.90	A / 9.5	58.17%	C+ / 5.9
2012	B	644.40	74.05	A / 9.5	34.56%	C+ / 5.7
2011	C+	91.50	55.36	B / 8.2	-10.60%	C+ / 5.9
2010	C	137.90	63.68	B- / 7.4	52.88%	C- / 3.1

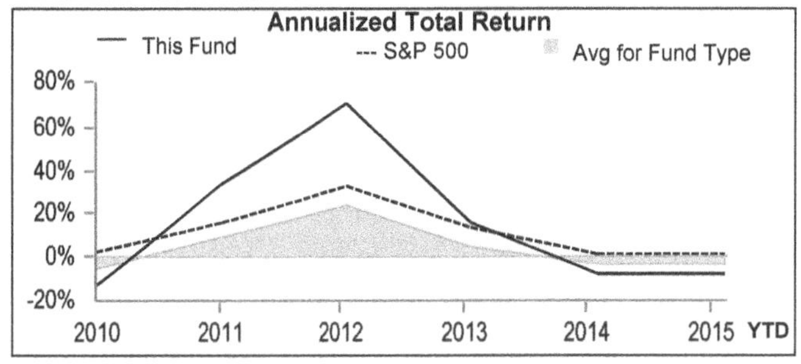

*ProShares Ultra MSCI Brazil Capp (UBR) E- Very Weak

Fund Family: ProShare Advisors LLC
Fund Type: Foreign
Inception Date: April 27, 2010

Major Rating Factors: *ProShares Ultra MSCI Brazil Capp has adopted a very risky asset allocation strategy and currently receives an overall TheStreet.com Investment Rating of E- (Very Weak). The fund has a high level of volatility, as measured by both semi-deviation and drawdown factors. It carries a beta of 2.98, meaning it is expected to move 29.8% for every 10% move in the market. As of December 31, 2015, *ProShares Ultra MSCI Brazil Capp traded at a discount of 2.75% below its net asset value, which is better than its one-year historical average premium of .07%. Unfortunately, the high level of risk (D, Weak) failed to pay off as investors endured very poor performance.

The fund's performance rating is currently E- (Very Weak). It has registered an annualized return of -51.29% over the last three years and is down -68.36% year to date 2015. Factored into the performance evaluation is an expense ratio of 0.95% (low).

Alexander V. Ilyasov has been running the fund for 6 years and currently receives a manager quality ranking of 0 (0=worst, 99=best). If you can tolerate very high levels of risk in the hope of improved future returns, holding this fund may be an option.

Data Date	Investment Rating	Net Assets ($Mil)	Price	Perfor-mance Rating/Pts	Total Return Y-T-D	Risk Rating/Pts
12-15	E-	12.60	25.45	E- / 0	-68.36%	D / 1.8
2014	E-	12.60	28.81	E / 0.3	-32.21%	E- / 0
2013	E-	6.80	44.77	E / 0.3	-42.11%	D+ / 2.5
2012	E+	14.10	70.24	D / 1.8	-16.02%	D+ / 2.6
2011	E	10.30	18.66	E- / 0.2	-45.39%	C- / 3.0

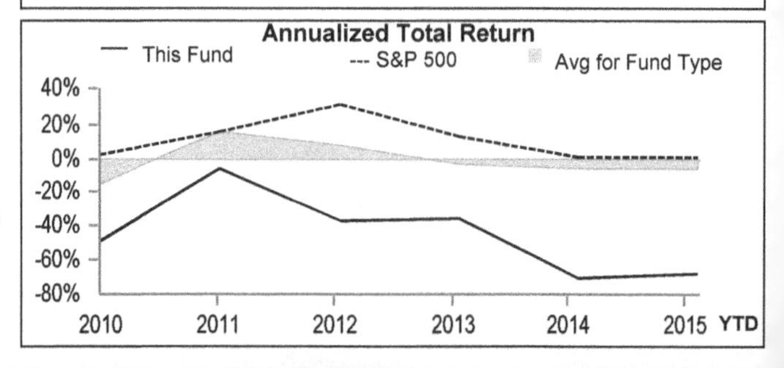

*ProShares Ultra MSCI EAFE (EFO) C- Fair

Fund Family: ProShare Advisors LLC
Fund Type: Income
Inception Date: June 2, 2009

Major Rating Factors: Middle of the road best describes *ProShares Ultra MSCI EAFE whose TheStreet.com Investment Rating is currently a C- (Fair). The fund currently has a performance rating of C (Fair) based on an annualized return of 3.70% over the last three years and a total return of -6.37% year to date 2015. Factored into the performance evaluation is an expense ratio of 0.95% (low).

The fund's risk rating is currently C (Fair). It carries a beta of 2.21, meaning it is expected to move 22.1% for every 10% move in the market. Volatility, as measured by both the semi-deviation and a drawdown factor, is considered average. As of December 31, 2015, *ProShares Ultra MSCI EAFE traded at a premium of .40% above its net asset value, which is better than its one-year historical average premium of .78%.

Alexander V. Ilyasov has been running the fund for 7 years and currently receives a manager quality ranking of 5 (0=worst, 99=best). If you desire an average level of risk, then this fund may be an option.

Data Date	Investment Rating	Net Assets ($Mil)	Price	Perfor-mance Rating/Pts	Total Return Y-T-D	Risk Rating/Pts
12-15	C-	47.40	90.02	C / 5.1	-6.37%	C / 4.6
2014	C-	47.40	96.14	C+ / 6.2	-12.21%	C / 4.6
2013	C	16.90	112.49	B / 8.0	35.65%	C / 4.6
2012	C+	11.90	78.88	A+ / 9.9	40.38%	C / 4.4
2011	E+	5.90	58.18	E / 0.4	-30.21%	C / 5.0
2010	A	8.50	85.89	A / 9.5	9.53%	C+ / 5.9

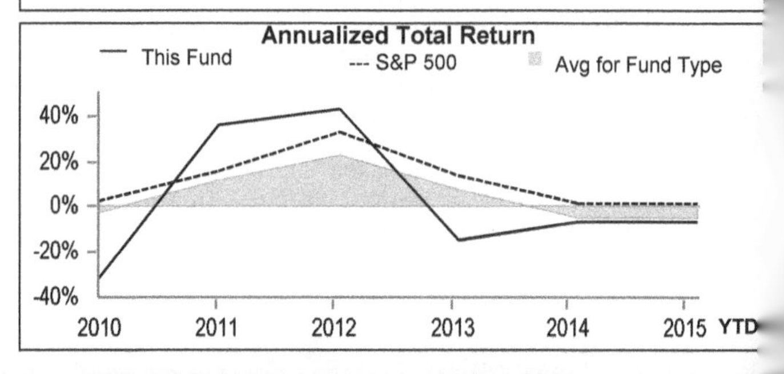

*ProShares Ultra MSCI Emerging Mk (EET) E+ Very Weak

Fund Family: ProShare Advisors LLC
Fund Type: Emerging Market
Inception Date: June 2, 2009

Major Rating Factors: *ProShares Ultra MSCI Emerging Mk has adopted a risky asset allocation strategy and currently receives an overall TheStreet.com Investment Rating of E+ (Very Weak). The fund has an above average level of volatility, as measured by both semi-deviation and drawdown factors. It carries a beta of 2.06, meaning it is expected to move 20.6% for every 10% move in the market. As of December 31, 2015, *ProShares Ultra MSCI Emerging Mk traded at a premium of .22% above its net asset value, which is worse than its one-year historical average premium of .05%. Unfortunately, the high level of risk (D+, Weak) failed to pay off as investors endured very poor performance.

The fund's performance rating is currently E+ (Very Weak). It has registered an annualized return of -20.07% over the last three years and is down -31.27% year to date 2015. Factored into the performance evaluation is an expense ratio of 0.95% (low).

Alexander V. Ilyasov has been running the fund for 7 years and currently receives a manager quality ranking of 21 (0=worst, 99=best). If you can tolerate high levels of risk in the hope of improved future returns, holding this fund may be an option.

Data Date	Investment Rating	Net Assets ($Mil)	Price	Perfor-mance Rating/Pts	Total Return Y-T-D	Risk Rating/Pts
12-15	E+	44.60	44.98	E+ / 0.7	-31.27%	D+ / 2.8
2014	D-	44.60	67.56	D+ / 2.4	-3.55%	C- / 4.0
2013	E+	45.60	75.89	E+ / 0.8	-20.47%	C- / 3.8
2012	D-	42.80	85.62	D+ / 2.7	26.98%	C- / 3.8
2011	E	22.20	63.92	E- / 0.2	-40.18%	C- / 4.1
2010	A	43.80	109.55	A+ / 9.6	25.18%	C+ / 6.3

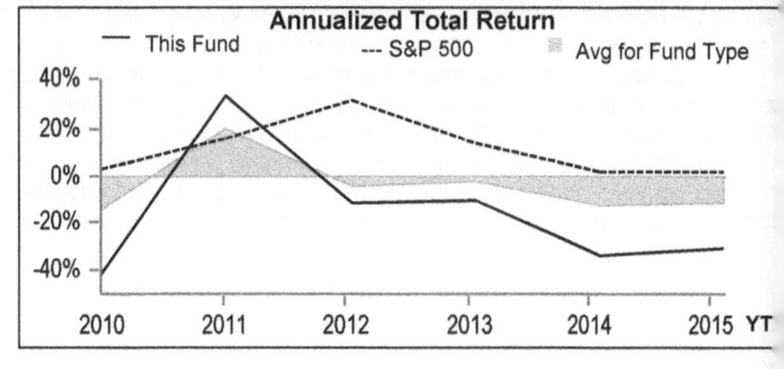

*ProShares Ultra MSCI Japan (EZJ) C+ Fair

Fund Family: ProShare Advisors LLC
Fund Type: Foreign
Inception Date: June 2, 2009

Major Rating Factors: Strong performance is the major factor driving the C+ (Fair) TheStreet.com Investment Rating for *ProShares Ultra MSCI Japan. The fund currently has a performance rating of B+ (Good) based on an annualized return of 12.54% over the last three years and a total return of 13.77% year to date 2015. Factored into the performance evaluation is an expense ratio of 0.95% (low).

The fund's risk rating is currently C (Fair). It carries a beta of 1.61, meaning it is expected to move 16.1% for every 10% move in the market. Volatility, as measured by both the semi-deviation and a drawdown factor, is considered average. As of December 31, 2015, *ProShares Ultra MSCI Japan traded at a premium of .70% above its net asset value, which is worse than its one-year historical average discount of .01%.

Alexander V. Ilyasov has been running the fund for 7 years and currently receives a manager quality ranking of 87 (0=worst, 99=best). If you desire an average level of risk and strong performance, then this fund is a good option.

Data Date	Investment Rating	Net Assets ($Mil)	Price	Performance Rating/Pts	Total Return Y-T-D	Risk Rating/Pts
12-15	C+	25.40	88.18	B+ / 8.5	13.77%	C / 5.0
2014	C-	25.40	77.04	C / 5.3	-13.22%	C+ / 6.4
2013	C-	31.80	90.99	C+ / 6.6	43.52%	C / 5.0
2012	D-	18.10	60.62	D / 1.7	17.55%	C / 5.1
2011	D-	23.60	52.38	E / 0.4	-34.56%	C+ / 5.7
2010	A+	11.70	78.49	A+ / 9.6	24.81%	C+ / 6.8

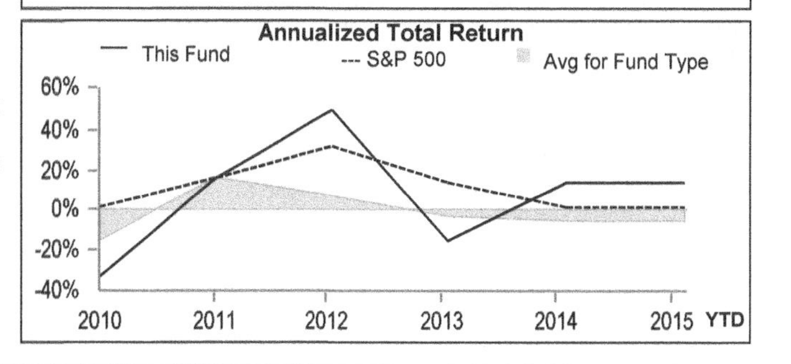

*ProShares Ultra MSCI Mex Cap IMI (UMX) E Very Weak

Fund Family: ProShare Advisors LLC
Fund Type: Foreign
Inception Date: April 27, 2010

Major Rating Factors: *ProShares Ultra MSCI Mex Cap IMI has adopted a very risky asset allocation strategy and currently receives an overall TheStreet.com Investment Rating of E (Very Weak). The fund has a high level of volatility, as measured by both semi-deviation and drawdown factors. It carries a beta of 1.61, meaning it is expected to move 16.1% for every 10% move in the market. As of December 31, 2015, *ProShares Ultra MSCI Mex Cap IMI traded at a premium of 1.09% above its net asset value, which is worse than its one-year historical average discount of .12%. Unfortunately, the high level of risk (D, Weak) failed to pay off as investors endured very poor performance.

The fund's performance rating is currently E+ (Very Weak). It has registered an annualized return of -22.43% over the last three years and is down -27.79% year to date 2015. Factored into the performance evaluation is an expense ratio of 0.95% (low).

Alexander V. Ilyasov has been running the fund for 6 years and currently receives a manager quality ranking of 3 (0=worst, 99=best). If you can tolerate very high levels of risk in the hope of improved future returns, holding this fund may be an option.

Data Date	Investment Rating	Net Assets ($Mil)	Price	Performance Rating/Pts	Total Return Y-T-D	Risk Rating/Pts
12-15	E	6.80	24.12	E+ / 0.7	-27.79%	D / 2.2
2014	D-	6.80	34.17	D+ / 2.3	-19.73%	C- / 3.2
2013	D-	4.50	44.38	D+ / 2.3	-17.61%	C / 4.5
2012	C+	2.50	49.02	A+ / 9.9	74.42%	C / 4.6
2011	E+	1.50	29.11	E+ / 0.6	-30.29%	C / 4.5

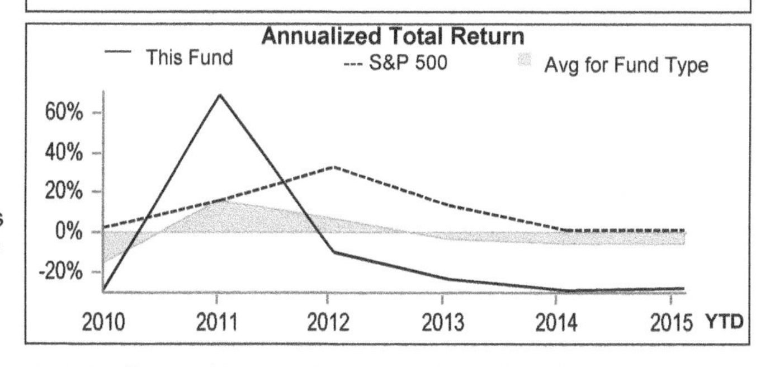

*ProShares Ultra MSCI Pacific ex- (UXJ) D- Weak

Fund Family: ProShare Advisors LLC
Fund Type: Foreign
Inception Date: April 27, 2010

Major Rating Factors:
Disappointing performance is the major factor driving the D- (Weak) TheStreet.com Investment Rating for *ProShares Ultra MSCI Pacific ex-. The fund currently has a performance rating of D (Weak) based on an annualized return of -9.21% over the last three years and a total return of -20.32% year to date 2015. Factored into the performance evaluation is an expense ratio of 0.95% (low).

The fund's risk rating is currently C (Fair). It carries a beta of 1.97, meaning it is expected to move 19.7% for every 10% move in the market. Volatility, as measured by both the semi-deviation and a drawdown factor, is considered average. As of December 31, 2015, *ProShares Ultra MSCI Pacific ex- traded at a discount of 3.99% below its net asset value, which is better than its one-year historical average premium of .61%.

Alexander V. Ilyasov has been running the fund for 6 years and currently receives a manager quality ranking of 7 (0=worst, 99=best). This fund offers an average level of risk but investors looking for strong performance will be frustrated.

Data Date	Investment Rating	Net Assets ($Mil)	Price	Performance Rating/Pts	Total Return Y-T-D	Risk Rating/Pts
12-15	D-	1.90	27.43	D / 1.8	-20.32%	C / 4.3
2014	D	1.90	36.57	C / 5.1	-5.74%	C- / 3.7
2013	D	2.00	38.54	C- / 3.9	-0.36%	C- / 4.0
2012	C+	3.80	37.92	A+ / 9.9	44.88%	C- / 4.0
2011	E+	2.50	24.98	E / 0.5	-28.99%	C- / 4.0

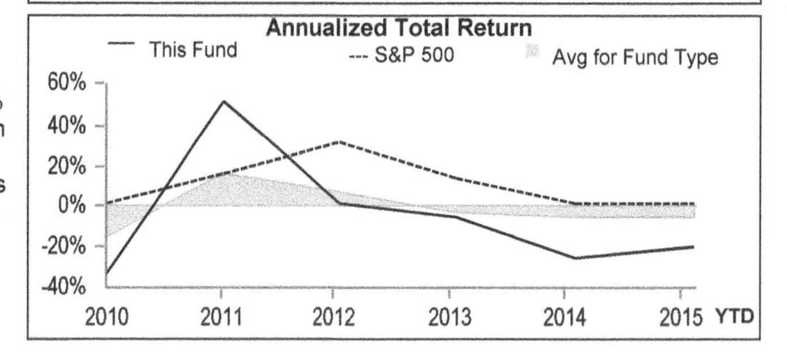

*ProShares Ultra Nasdaq Biotech (BIB) C- Fair

Fund Family: ProShare Advisors LLC
Fund Type: Health
Inception Date: April 7, 2010

Major Rating Factors: *ProShares Ultra Nasdaq Biotech has adopted a very risky asset allocation strategy and currently receives an overall TheStreet.com Investment Rating of C- (Fair). The fund has shown a high level of volatility, as measured by both semi-deviation and drawdown factors. It carries a beta of 2.31, meaning it is expected to move 23.1% for every 10% move in the market. As of December 31, 2015, *ProShares Ultra Nasdaq Biotech traded at a premium of .08% above its net asset value, which is worse than its one-year historical average premium of .02%. The high level of risk (E-, Very Weak) did however, reward investors with excellent performance.

The fund's performance rating is currently A+ (Excellent). It has registered an annualized return of 65.97% over the last three years and is up 11.86% year to date 2015. Factored into the performance evaluation is an expense ratio of 0.95% (low).

Charles Lowery has been running the fund for 3 years and currently receives a manager quality ranking of 98 (0=worst, 99=best). If you are comfortable owning a very high risk investment, this fund may be an option.

Data Date	Investment Rating	Net Assets ($Mil)	Price	Performance Rating/Pts	Total Return Y-T-D	Risk Rating/Pts
12-15	C-	327.00	71.49	A+ / 9.9	11.86%	E- / 0.2
2014	C	327.00	125.50	A+ / 9.9	68.26%	D / 2.0
2013	C	225.90	150.49	A+ / 9.9	138.48%	D+ / 2.7
2012	C	37.60	57.97	A+ / 9.9	62.43%	D+ / 2.6
2011	C+	13.90	69.52	B- / 7.1	18.85%	C+ / 6.2

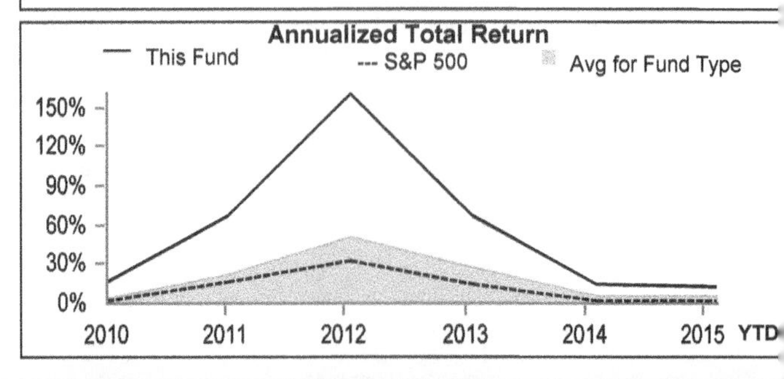

*ProShares Ultra Oil and Gas (DIG) D- Weak

Fund Family: ProShare Advisors LLC
Fund Type: Energy/Natural Resources
Inception Date: January 30, 2007

Major Rating Factors:
Very poor performance is the major factor driving the D- (Weak) TheStreet.com Investment Rating for *ProShares Ultra Oil and Gas. The fund currently has a performance rating of E+ (Very Weak) based on an annualized return of -14.45% over the last three years and a total return of -44.45% year to date 2015. Factored into the performance evaluation is an expense ratio of 0.95% (low).

The fund's risk rating is currently C- (Fair). It carries a beta of 2.04, meaning it is expected to move 20.4% for every 10% move in the market. Volatility, as measured by both the semi-deviation and a drawdown factor, is considered average. As of December 31, 2015, *ProShares Ultra Oil and Gas traded at a discount of .03% below its net asset value, which is better than its one-year historical average discount of .01%.

Charles Lowery has been running the fund for 3 years and currently receives a manager quality ranking of 28 (0=worst, 99=best). This fund offers an average level of risk but investors looking for strong performance will be frustrated.

Data Date	Investment Rating	Net Assets ($Mil)	Price	Performance Rating/Pts	Total Return Y-T-D	Risk Rating/Pts
12-15	D-	136.50	29.93	E+ / 0.9	-44.45%	C- / 4.1
2014	D	136.50	54.01	D+ / 2.4	-19.24%	C+ / 5.8
2013	C+	146.20	69.67	B+ / 8.6	38.38%	C / 5.3
2012	D	192.00	45.73	C / 4.6	10.97%	C- / 4.2
2011	D+	254.00	43.91	C / 5.5	-1.11%	C / 4.5
2010	E	366.70	45.81	D- / 1.1	33.69%	D / 1.7

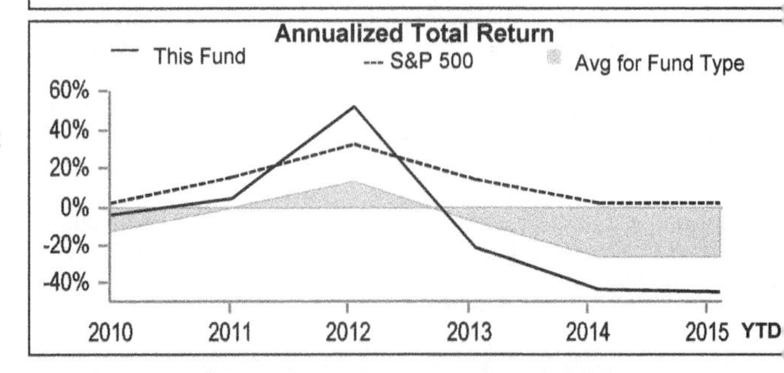

*ProShares Ultra QQQ (QLD) C Fair

Fund Family: ProShare Advisors LLC
Fund Type: Growth
Inception Date: June 19, 2006

Major Rating Factors: *ProShares Ultra QQQ has adopted a very risky asset allocation strategy and currently receives an overall TheStreet.com Investment Rating of C (Fair). The fund has shown a high level of volatility, as measured by both semi-deviation and drawdown factors. It carries a beta of 2.19, meaning it is expected to move 21.9% for every 10% move in the market. As of December 31, 2015, *ProShares Ultra QQQ traded at a premium of .04% above its net asset value, which is worse than its one-year historical average premium of .01%. The high level of risk (D, Weak) did however, reward investors with excellent performance.

The fund's performance rating is currently A+ (Excellent). It has registered an annualized return of 40.03% over the last three years and is up 15.22% year to date 2015. Factored into the performance evaluation is an expense ratio of 0.95% (low).

Michael Neches has been running the fund for 3 years and currently receives a manager quality ranking of 88 (0=worst, 99=best). If you are comfortable owning a very high risk investment, this fund may be an option.

Data Date	Investment Rating	Net Assets ($Mil)	Price	Performance Rating/Pts	Total Return Y-T-D	Risk Rating/Pts
12-15	C	904.30	78.36	A+ / 9.9	15.22%	D / 2.1
2014	C-	904.30	136.74	A+ / 9.8	41.74%	D- / 1.5
2013	C	784.40	99.60	A+ / 9.8	68.82%	D+ / 2.8
2012	C-	671.10	54.81	A / 9.3	32.54%	D+ / 2.8
2011	B+	678.20	81.46	A+ / 9.8	1.76%	C+ / 6.8
2010	C-	842.00	81.43	C+ / 6.8	36.90%	C- / 3.1

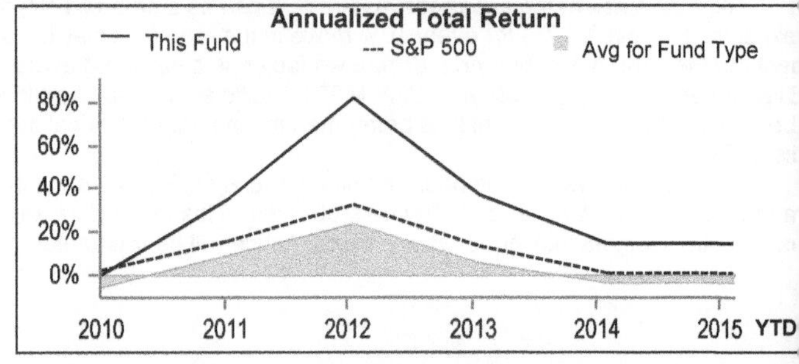

*ProShares Ultra Real Estate (URE) C+ Fair

Fund Family: ProShare Advisors LLC
Fund Type: Income
Inception Date: January 30, 2007

Major Rating Factors:
Exceptional performance is the major factor driving the C+ (Fair) TheStreet.com Investment Rating for *ProShares Ultra Real Estate. The fund currently has a performance rating of A- (Excellent) based on an annualized return of 14.50% over the last three years and a total return of -2.74% year to date 2015. Factored into the performance evaluation is an expense ratio of 0.95% (low).

The fund's risk rating is currently C (Fair). It carries a beta of 1.03, meaning that its performance tracks fairly well with that of the overall stock market. Volatility, as measured by both the semi-deviation and a drawdown factor, is considered average. As of December 31, 2015, *ProShares Ultra Real Estate traded at a premium of .09% above its net asset value, which is worse than its one-year historical average discount of .01%.

Charles Lowery has been running the fund for 3 years and currently receives a manager quality ranking of 72 (0=worst, 99=best). If you desire an average level of risk and strong performance, then this fund is a good option.

Data Date	Investment Rating	Net Assets ($Mil)	Price	Performance Rating/Pts	Total Return Y-T-D	Risk Rating/Pts
12-15	C+	257.00	104.54	A- / 9.0	-2.74%	C / 5.0
2014	A-	257.00	105.65	A+ / 9.7	56.41%	C+ / 6.7
2013	C-	322.90	67.87	C+ / 6.1	-3.82%	C+ / 6.0
2012	B	349.60	69.09	A+ / 9.6	40.33%	C+ / 6.0
2011	C	353.40	51.00	B / 7.9	3.00%	C- / 4.2
2010	E	535.30	50.62	E+ / 0.7	48.36%	D / 2.1

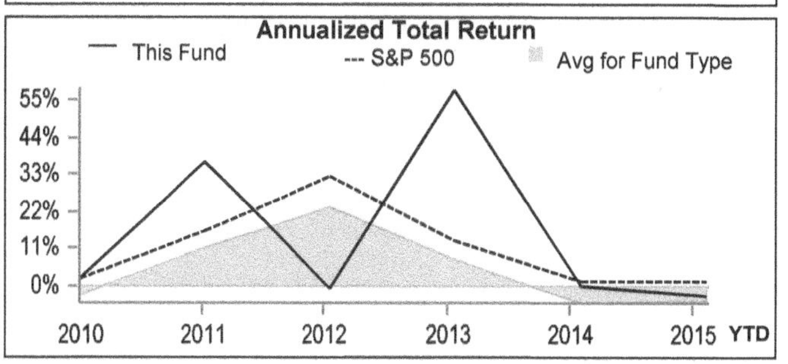

*ProShares Ultra Russell2000 (UWM) B+ Good

Fund Family: ProShare Advisors LLC
Fund Type: Growth
Inception Date: January 23, 2007

Major Rating Factors: Strong performance is the major factor driving the B+ (Good) TheStreet.com Investment Rating for *ProShares Ultra Russell2000. The fund currently has a performance rating of B+ (Good) based on an annualized return of 17.65% over the last three years and a total return of -11.30% year to date 2015. Factored into the performance evaluation is an expense ratio of 0.95% (low).

The fund's risk rating is currently C+ (Fair). It carries a beta of 2.15, meaning it is expected to move 21.5% for every 10% move in the market. Volatility, as measured by both the semi-deviation and a drawdown factor, is considered low. As of December 31, 2015, *ProShares Ultra Russell2000 traded at a discount of .25% below its net asset value, which is better than its one-year historical average discount of .04%.

Michael Neches has been running the fund for 3 years and currently receives a manager quality ranking of 15 (0=worst, 99=best). If you desire only a moderate level of risk and strong performance, then this fund is an excellent option.

Data Date	Investment Rating	Net Assets ($Mil)	Price	Performance Rating/Pts	Total Return Y-T-D	Risk Rating/Pts
12-15	B+	524.00	79.14	B+ / 8.8	-11.30%	C+ / 6.9
2014	B+	524.00	90.43	A+ / 9.6	7.63%	C+ / 5.9
2013	B-	1,807.40	85.10	A+ / 9.7	72.50%	C / 5.3
2012	C+	126.60	45.52	A- / 9.0	31.48%	C / 5.1
2011	C-	204.40	34.86	C+ / 6.6	-16.85%	C / 5.2
2010	C-	275.70	42.69	C+ / 6.5	50.63%	C- / 3.0

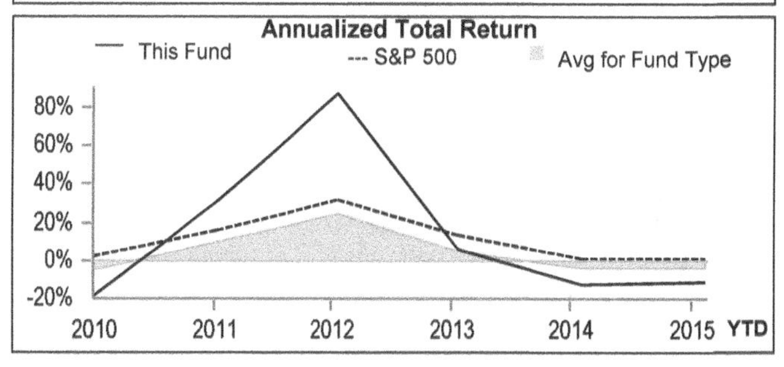

*ProShares Ultra S&P Regional Ban (KRU) B Good

Fund Family: ProShare Advisors LLC
Fund Type: Financial Services
Inception Date: April 20, 2010

Major Rating Factors:
Exceptional performance is the major factor driving the B (Good) TheStreet.com Investment Rating for *ProShares Ultra S&P Regional Ban. The fund currently has a performance rating of A+ (Excellent) based on an annualized return of 26.05% over the last three years and a total return of 13.18% year to date 2015. Factored into the performance evaluation is an expense ratio of 0.95% (low).

The fund's risk rating is currently C (Fair). It carries a beta of 2.35, meaning it is expected to move 23.5% for every 10% move in the market. Volatility, as measured by both the semi-deviation and a drawdown factor, is considered average. As of December 31, 2015, *ProShares Ultra S&P Regional Ban traded at a premium of 2.45% above its net asset value, which is worse than its one-year historical average discount of .13%.

Charles Lowery has been running the fund for 3 years and currently receives a manager quality ranking of 23 (0=worst, 99=best). If you desire an average level of risk and strong performance, then this fund is a good option.

Data Date	Investment Rating	Net Assets ($Mil)	Price	Performance Rating/Pts	Total Return Y-T-D	Risk Rating/Pts
12-15	B	7.80	98.88	A+ / 9.7	13.18%	C / 5.0
2014	B	7.80	93.35	A+ / 9.6	4.59%	C / 5.3
2013	C+	27.80	92.98	A+ / 9.7	79.26%	C / 4.4
2012	D	2.30	45.21	C / 4.9	13.34%	C- / 3.8
2011	D-	3.80	38.20	C- / 3.9	-12.95%	D+ / 2.8

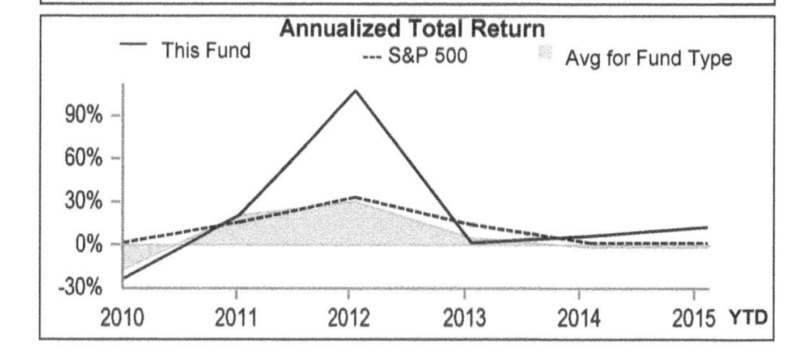

*ProShares Ultra S&P500 (SSO) C+ Fair

Fund Family: ProShare Advisors LLC
Fund Type: Growth
Inception Date: June 19, 2006

Data Date	Investment Rating	Net Assets ($Mil)	Price	Performance Rating/Pts	Total Return Y-T-D	Risk Rating/Pts
12-15	C+	2,127.40	63.00	A+ / 9.7	-1.06%	C- / 3.3
2014	A-	2,127.40	128.31	A+ / 9.7	28.16%	C+ / 6.4
2013	B+	1,542.10	102.56	A+ / 9.6	58.61%	C+ / 6.8
2012	B-	1,279.30	60.35	B+ / 8.7	32.03%	C+ / 6.4
2011	C+	1,654.20	46.39	B- / 7.4	-1.51%	C+ / 6.5
2010	D-	1,589.60	48.05	D / 1.6	26.86%	C- / 3.5

Major Rating Factors:
Exceptional performance is the major factor driving the C+ (Fair) TheStreet.com Investment Rating for *ProShares Ultra S&P500. The fund currently has a performance rating of A+ (Excellent) based on an annualized return of 26.17% over the last three years and a total return of -1.06% year to date 2015. Factored into the performance evaluation is an expense ratio of 0.89% (low).

The fund's risk rating is currently C- (Fair). It carries a beta of 2.03, meaning it is expected to move 20.3% for every 10% move in the market. Volatility, as measured by both the semi-deviation and a drawdown factor, is considered average. As of December 31, 2015, *ProShares Ultra S&P500 traded at a discount of .05% below its net asset value, which is better than its one-year historical average discount of .02%.

Michael Neches has been running the fund for 3 years and currently receives a manager quality ranking of 38 (0=worst, 99=best). If you desire an average level of risk and strong performance, then this fund is a good option.

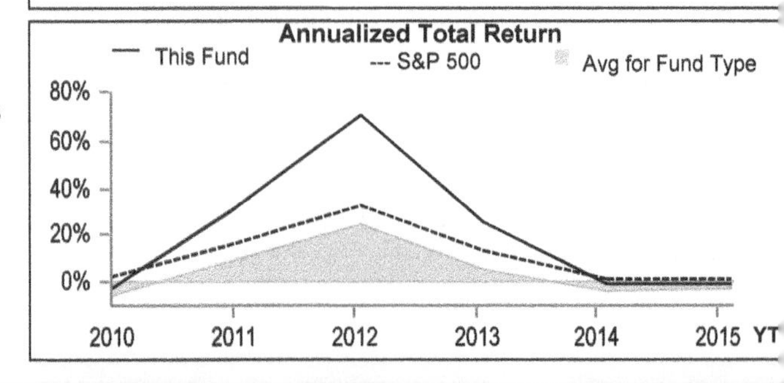

*ProShares Ultra Semiconductors (USD) B- Good

Fund Family: ProShare Advisors LLC
Fund Type: Income
Inception Date: January 30, 2007

Data Date	Investment Rating	Net Assets ($Mil)	Price	Performance Rating/Pts	Total Return Y-T-D	Risk Rating/Pts
12-15	B-	43.60	86.62	A+ / 9.8	-7.94%	C / 4.5
2014	B	43.60	94.02	A+ / 9.8	81.41%	C+ / 5.6
2013	C+	32.10	53.34	B+ / 8.9	63.75%	C / 5.3
2012	D-	38.70	30.25	D / 1.9	-8.80%	C / 4.9
2011	C+	43.30	33.90	B+ / 8.8	-12.50%	C / 5.3
2010	E+	74.60	39.82	D+ / 2.6	19.43%	D / 1.6

Major Rating Factors:
Exceptional performance is the major factor driving the B- (Good) TheStreet.com Investment Rating for *ProShares Ultra Semiconductors. The fund currently has a performance rating of A+ (Excellent) based on an annualized return of 40.06% over the last three years and a total return of -7.94% year to date 2015. Factored into the performance evaluation is an expense ratio of 0.95% (low).

The fund's risk rating is currently C (Fair). It carries a beta of 2.13, meaning it is expected to move 21.3% for every 10% move in the market. Volatility, as measured by both the semi-deviation and a drawdown factor, is considered average. As of December 31, 2015, *ProShares Ultra Semiconductors traded at a premium of .52% above its net asset value, which is worse than its one-year historical average discount of .09%.

Charles Lowery has been running the fund for 3 years and currently receives a manager quality ranking of 91 (0=worst, 99=best). If you desire an average level of risk and strong performance, then this fund is a good option.

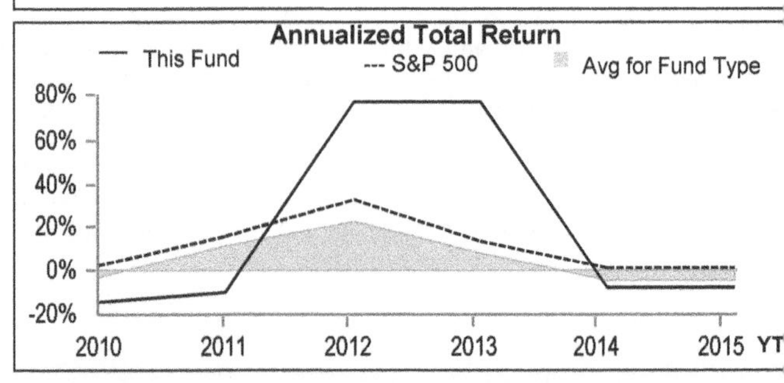

*ProShares Ultra Silver (AGQ) E- Very Weak

Fund Family: ProShare Advisors LLC
Fund Type: Energy/Natural Resources
Inception Date: December 2, 2008

Data Date	Investment Rating	Net Assets ($Mil)	Price	Performance Rating/Pts	Total Return Y-T-D	Risk Rating/Pts
12-15	E-	357.20	27.08	E- / 0.1	-29.52%	E / 0.3
2014	E-	357.20	38.05	E- / 0.1	-43.81%	D / 1.9
2013	E-	465.50	15.76	E- / 0.2	-61.07%	D / 1.9
2012	E+	745.50	44.10	C- / 3.0	-6.80%	D / 1.9
2011	D+	600.40	41.65	B / 8.2	-34.79%	D / 1.9
2010	A	546.70	158.59	A+ / 9.9	182.44%	C+ / 5.8

Major Rating Factors: *ProShares Ultra Silver has adopted a very risky asset allocation strategy and currently receives an overall TheStreet.com Investment Rating of E- (Very Weak). The fund has a high level of volatility, as measured by both semi-deviation and drawdown factors. It carries a beta of 0.62, meaning the fund's expected move will be 6.2% for every 10% move in the market. As of December 31, 2015, *ProShares Ultra Silver traded at a premium of .07% above its net asset value, which is better than its one-year historical average premium of .60%. Unfortunately, the high level of risk (E, Very Weak) failed to pay off as investors endured very poor performance.

The fund's performance rating is currently E- (Very Weak). It has registered an annualized return of -46.21% over the last three years and is down -29.52% year to date 2015. Factored into the performance evaluation is an expense ratio of 0.95% (low).

Michael Neches currently receives a manager quality ranking of 0 (0=worst, 99=best). If you can tolerate very high levels of risk in the hope of improved future returns, holding this fund may be an option.

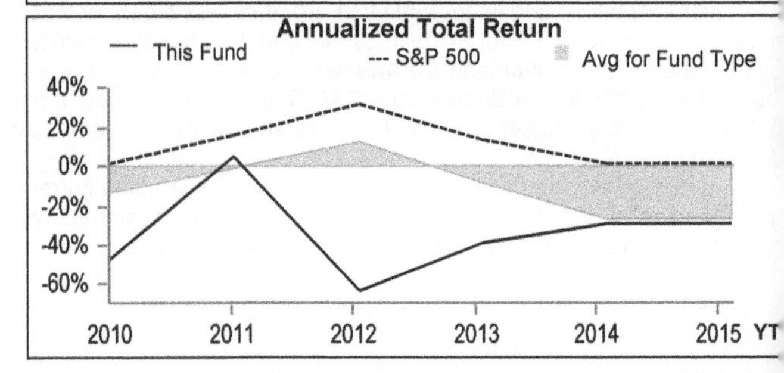

*ProShares Ultra SmallCap 600 (SAA) C Fair

Fund Family: ProShare Advisors LLC
Fund Type: Growth
Inception Date: January 23, 2007

Data Date	Investment Rating	Net Assets ($Mil)	Price	Performance Rating/Pts	Total Return Y-T-D	Risk Rating/Pts
12-15	C	21.60	53.85	A / 9.5	-3.21%	D / 2.2
2014	B+	21.60	114.11	A+ / 9.7	9.63%	C+ / 6.1
2013	B	31.80	105.96	A+ / 9.8	77.93%	C+ / 5.7
2012	B-	20.60	54.60	A / 9.3	31.00%	C / 5.5
2011	C+	37.90	41.99	B / 7.8	-6.86%	C+ / 5.6
2010	C-	48.50	46.37	B- / 7.1	49.95%	C- / 3.0

Major Rating Factors: *ProShares Ultra SmallCap 600 has adopted a very risky asset allocation strategy and currently receives an overall TheStreet.com Investment Rating of C (Fair). The fund has shown a high level of volatility, as measured by both semi-deviation and drawdown factors. It carries a beta of 2.10, meaning it is expected to move 21.0% for every 10% move in the market. As of December 31, 2015, *ProShares Ultra SmallCap 600 traded at a premium of 1.68% above its net asset value, which is worse than its one-year historical average discount of .08%. The high level of risk (D, Weak) did however, reward investors with excellent performance.

The fund's performance rating is currently A (Excellent). It has registered an annualized return of 22.56% over the last three years but is down -3.21% year to date 2015. Factored into the performance evaluation is an expense ratio of 0.95% (low).

Michael Neches has been running the fund for 3 years and currently receives a manager quality ranking of 24 (0=worst, 99=best). If you are comfortable owning a very high risk investment, this fund may be an option.

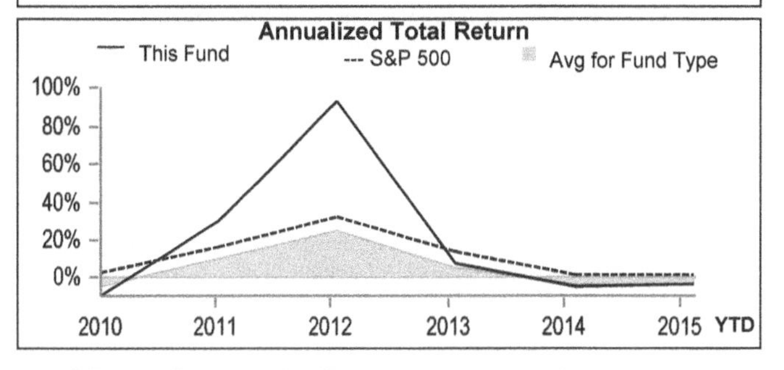

*ProShares Ultra Technology (ROM) C Fair

Fund Family: ProShare Advisors LLC
Fund Type: Growth
Inception Date: January 30, 2007

Data Date	Investment Rating	Net Assets ($Mil)	Price	Performance Rating/Pts	Total Return Y-T-D	Risk Rating/Pts
12-15	C	170.80	78.74	A+ / 9.8	4.04%	D+ / 2.5
2014	B+	170.80	152.22	A+ / 9.7	41.82%	C+ / 5.8
2013	B	140.20	109.84	A / 9.4	47.74%	C+ / 6.2
2012	D+	74.10	70.01	C / 4.8	17.88%	C / 5.4
2011	B	88.10	58.71	A / 9.4	-6.99%	C+ / 6.5
2010	D+	151.80	63.37	C / 5.4	19.91%	C- / 3.2

Major Rating Factors: *ProShares Ultra Technology has adopted a risky asset allocation strategy and currently receives an overall TheStreet.com Investment Rating of C (Fair). The fund has shown an above average level of volatility, as measured by both semi-deviation and drawdown factors. It carries a beta of 2.09, meaning it is expected to move 20.9% for every 10% move in the market. As of December 31, 2015, *ProShares Ultra Technology traded at a premium of .61% above its net asset value, which is worse than its one-year historical average discount of .06%. The high level of risk (D+, Weak) did however, reward investors with excellent performance.

The fund's performance rating is currently A+ (Excellent). It has registered an annualized return of 29.47% over the last three years and is up 4.04% year to date 2015. Factored into the performance evaluation is an expense ratio of 0.95% (low).

Charles Lowery has been running the fund for 3 years and currently receives a manager quality ranking of 48 (0=worst, 99=best). If you are comfortable owning a high risk investment, this fund may be an option.

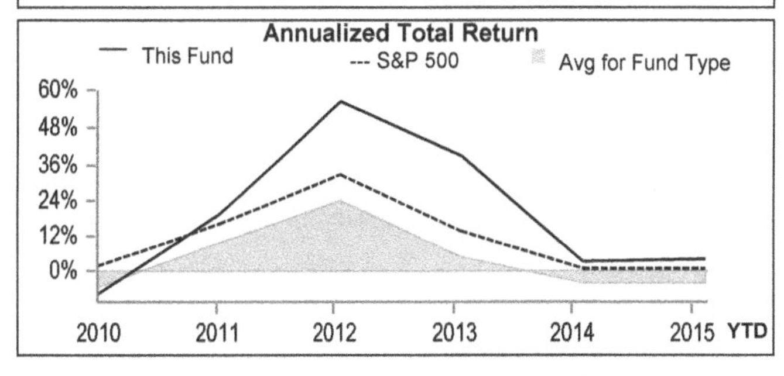

*ProShares Ultra Utilities (UPW) B Good

Fund Family: ProShare Advisors LLC
Fund Type: Utilities
Inception Date: January 30, 2007

Data Date	Investment Rating	Net Assets ($Mil)	Price	Performance Rating/Pts	Total Return Y-T-D	Risk Rating/Pts
12-15	B	25.30	92.00	A / 9.3	-13.27%	C / 5.5
2014	A+	25.30	107.56	A+ / 9.8	65.38%	B- / 7.6
2013	B	10.30	68.60	B / 7.7	18.44%	B- / 7.9
2012	C+	16.40	54.01	C / 5.3	8.98%	B / 8.3
2011	B-	20.80	55.62	B- / 7.5	25.92%	B- / 7.3
2010	D-	22.10	42.00	E+ / 0.7	11.49%	C / 4.4

Major Rating Factors:
Exceptional performance is the major factor driving the B (Good) TheStreet.com Investment Rating for *ProShares Ultra Utilities. The fund currently has a performance rating of A (Excellent) based on an annualized return of 19.65% over the last three years and a total return of -13.27% year to date 2015. Factored into the performance evaluation is an expense ratio of 0.95% (low).

The fund's risk rating is currently C (Fair). It carries a beta of 1.96, meaning it is expected to move 19.6% for every 10% move in the market. Volatility, as measured by both the semi-deviation and a drawdown factor, is considered average. As of December 31, 2015, *ProShares Ultra Utilities traded at a premium of 1.10% above its net asset value, which is worse than its one-year historical average discount of .04%.

Charles Lowery has been running the fund for 3 years and currently receives a manager quality ranking of 42 (0=worst, 99=best). If you desire an average level of risk and strong performance, then this fund is a good option.

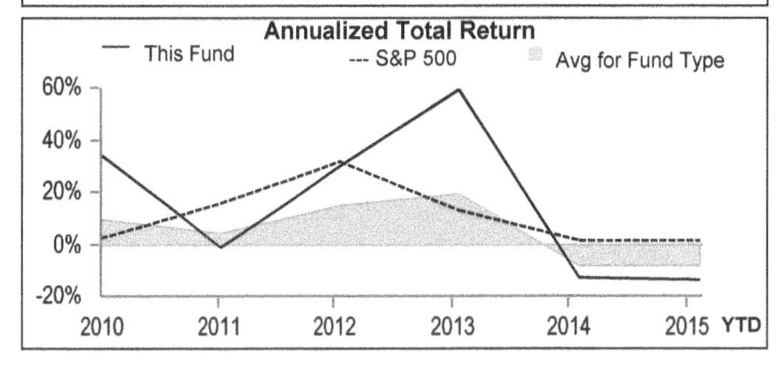

*ProShares Ultra VIX Sh-Tm Fut ET (UVXY) E- Very Weak

Fund Family: ProShare Advisors LLC
Fund Type: Growth and Income
Inception Date: October 3, 2011

Major Rating Factors: *ProShares Ultra VIX Sh-Tm Fut ET has adopted a very risky asset allocation strategy and currently receives an overall TheStreet.com Investment Rating of E- (Very Weak). The fund has a high level of volatility, as measured by both semi-deviation and drawdown factors. It carries a beta of -9.17, meaning the fund's expected move will be -91.7% for every 10% move in the market. As of December 31, 2015, *ProShares Ultra VIX Sh-Tm Fut ET traded at a premium of .93% above its net asset value, which is worse than its one-year historical average premium of .36%. Unfortunately, the high level of risk (E-, Very Weak) failed to pay off as investors endured very poor performance.

The fund's performance rating is currently E- (Very Weak). It has registered an annualized return of -79.00% over the last three years and is down -76.70% year to date 2015. Factored into the performance evaluation is an expense ratio of 1.80% (above average).

Todd B. Johnson currently receives a manager quality ranking of 2 (0=worst, 99=best). If you can tolerate very high levels of risk in the hope of improved future returns, holding this fund may be an option.

Data Date	Investment Rating	Net Assets ($Mil)	Price	Performance Rating/Pts	Total Return Y-T-D	Risk Rating/Pts
12-15	E-	283.50	28.35	E- / 0	-76.70%	E- / 0.1
2014	E-	283.50	25.15	E- / 0	-63.59%	E- / 0.1
2013	E-	215.30	16.78	E- / 0	-88.73%	D / 1.9
2012	E-	72.60	20.90	E- / 0	-97.51%	D / 1.9

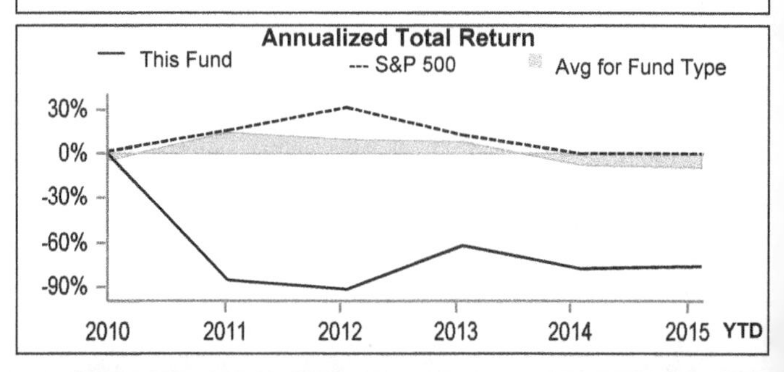

*ProShares Ultra Yen (YCL) D- Weak

Fund Family: ProShare Advisors LLC
Fund Type: Foreign
Inception Date: November 25, 2008

Major Rating Factors:
Disappointing performance is the major factor driving the D- (Weak) TheStreet.com Investment Rating for *ProShares Ultra Yen. The fund currently has a performance rating of D- (Weak) based on an annualized return of -20.53% over the last three years and a total return of -2.39% year to date 2015. Factored into the performance evaluation is an expense ratio of 0.95% (low).

The fund's risk rating is currently C (Fair). It carries a beta of -0.25, meaning the fund's expected move will be -2.5% for every 10% move in the market. Volatility, as measured by both the semi-deviation and a drawdown factor, is considered average. As of December 31, 2015, *ProShares Ultra Yen traded at a discount of .09% below its net asset value, which is better than its one-year historical average discount of .03%.

Michael Neches currently receives a manager quality ranking of 7 (0=worst, 99=best). This fund offers an average level of risk but investors looking for strong performance will be frustrated.

Data Date	Investment Rating	Net Assets ($Mil)	Price	Performance Rating/Pts	Total Return Y-T-D	Risk Rating/Pts
12-15	D-	1.70	54.70	D- / 1.2	-2.39%	C / 5.3
2014	E-	1.70	14.12	E / 0.4	-25.17%	D+ / 2.3
2013	E+	2.80	18.61	E+ / 0.6	-30.75%	C / 5.4
2012	D	4.20	28.28	E+ / 0.8	-27.05%	B- / 7.3
2011	C-	5.50	36.50	C- / 4.0	13.90%	B- / 7.8
2010	A+	5.00	33.29	A- / 9.1	25.24%	B- / 7.0

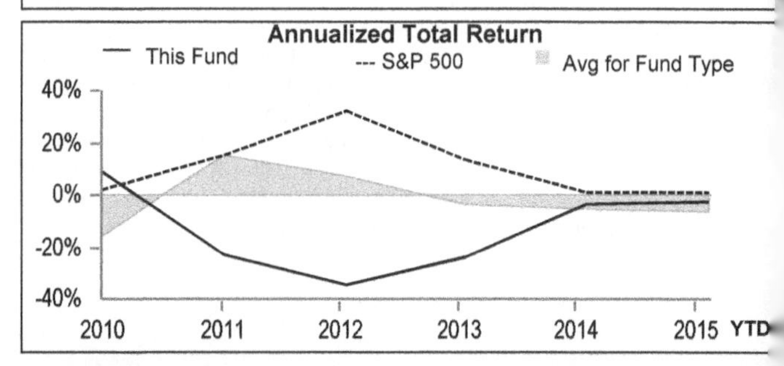

*ProShares UltraPro Dow30 (UDOW) C+ Fair

Fund Family: ProShare Advisors LLC
Fund Type: Growth
Inception Date: February 9, 2010

Major Rating Factors:
Exceptional performance is the major factor driving the C+ (Fair) TheStreet.com Investment Rating for *ProShares UltraPro Dow30. The fund currently has a performance rating of A+ (Excellent) based on an annualized return of 30.37% over the last three years and a total return of -8.48% year to date 2015. Factored into the performance evaluation is an expense ratio of 0.95% (low).

The fund's risk rating is currently C- (Fair). It carries a beta of 3.09, meaning it is expected to move 30.9% for every 10% move in the market. Volatility, as measured by both the semi-deviation and a drawdown factor, is considered average. As of December 31, 2015, *ProShares UltraPro Dow30 traded at a discount of .03% below its net asset value.

Michael Neches has been running the fund for 3 years and currently receives a manager quality ranking of 12 (0=worst, 99=best). If you desire an average level of risk and strong performance, then this fund is a good option.

Data Date	Investment Rating	Net Assets ($Mil)	Price	Performance Rating/Pts	Total Return Y-T-D	Risk Rating/Pts
12-15	C+	111.50	64.54	A+ / 9.7	-8.48%	C- / 3.5
2014	C	111.50	141.46	A+ / 9.8	28.36%	D+ / 2.3
2013	C	118.50	112.86	A+ / 9.9	88.78%	C- / 3.1
2012	C	46.60	54.82	A+ / 9.6	30.56%	C- / 3.1
2011	C-	58.80	130.31	C+ / 5.7	10.33%	C+ / 5.7

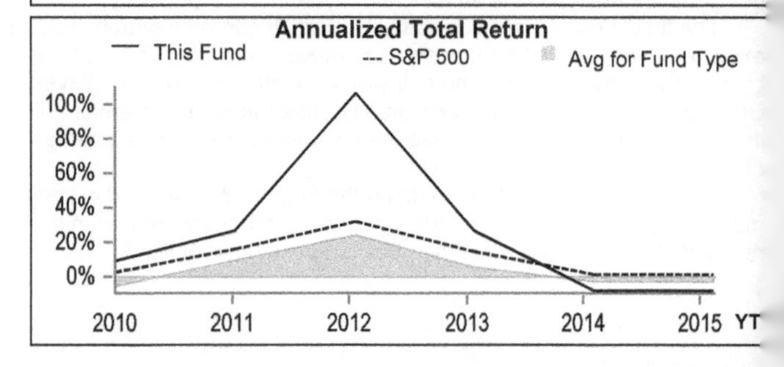

*ProShares UltraPro Finl Sel Sect (FINU) C- Fair

Fund Family: ProShare Advisors LLC
Fund Type: Growth and Income
Inception Date: July 10, 2012

Major Rating Factors: *ProShares UltraPro Finl Sel Sect has adopted a very risky asset allocation strategy and currently receives an overall TheStreet.com Investment Rating of C- (Fair). The fund has shown a high level of volatility, as measured by both semi-deviation and drawdown factors. It carries a beta of 3.04, meaning it is expected to move 30.4% for every 10% move in the market. As of December 31, 2015, *ProShares UltraPro Finl Sel Sect traded at a premium of 2.52% above its net asset value, which is worse than its one-year historical average premium of .12%. The high level of risk (D-, Weak) did however, reward investors with excellent performance.

The fund's performance rating is currently A+ (Excellent). It has registered an annualized return of 37.28% over the last three years but is down -8.19% year to date 2015. Factored into the performance evaluation is an expense ratio of 0.95% (low).

Charles Lowery has been running the fund for 3 years and currently receives a manager quality ranking of 24 (0=worst, 99=best). If you are comfortable owning a very high risk investment, this fund may be an option.

Data Date	Investment Rating	Net Assets ($Mil)	Price	Performance Rating/Pts	Total Return Y-T-D	Risk Rating/Pts
12-15	C-	10.60	80.27	A+ / 9.8	-8.19%	D- / 1.0
2014	C-	10.60	88.16	A+ / 9.8	41.10%	E / 0.5
2013	A+	25.00	124.12	A+ / 9.9	100.64%	B- / 7.9

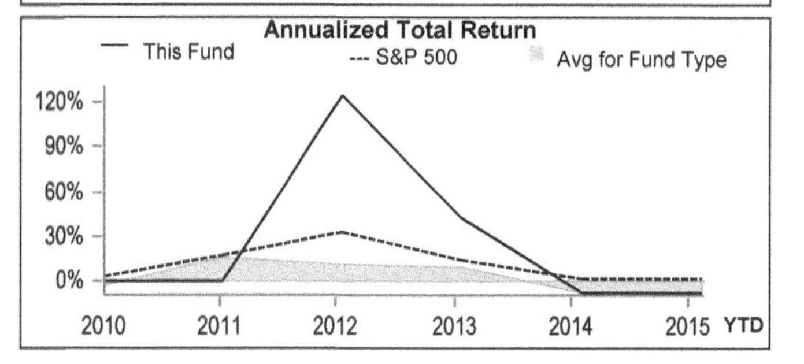

*ProShares UltraPro MidCap400 (UMDD) C- Fair

Fund Family: ProShare Advisors LLC
Fund Type: Growth
Inception Date: February 9, 2010

Major Rating Factors: *ProShares UltraPro MidCap400 has adopted a very risky asset allocation strategy and currently receives an overall TheStreet.com Investment Rating of C- (Fair). The fund has shown a high level of volatility, as measured by both semi-deviation and drawdown factors. It carries a beta of 3.00, meaning it is expected to move 30.0% for every 10% move in the market. As of December 31, 2015, *ProShares UltraPro MidCap400 traded at a premium of 1.56% above its net asset value, which is worse than its one-year historical average premium of .01%. The high level of risk (E-, Very Weak) did however, reward investors with excellent performance.

The fund's performance rating is currently A+ (Excellent). It has registered an annualized return of 28.74% over the last three years but is down -12.65% year to date 2015. Factored into the performance evaluation is an expense ratio of 0.95% (low).

Hratch Najarian has been running the fund for 6 years and currently receives a manager quality ranking of 13 (0=worst, 99=best). If you are comfortable owning a very high risk investment, this fund may be an option.

Data Date	Investment Rating	Net Assets ($Mil)	Price	Performance Rating/Pts	Total Return Y-T-D	Risk Rating/Pts
12-15	C-	44.00	50.01	A+ / 9.6	-12.65%	E- / 0.1
2014	C-	44.00	115.10	A+ / 9.9	25.55%	E+ / 0.6
2013	C-	37.40	93.48	A+ / 9.8	95.48%	D / 1.9
2012	C-	25.50	84.85	A+ / 9.9	51.19%	D / 2.1
2011	E-	34.00	56.60	E+ / 0.7	-25.05%	D / 1.9

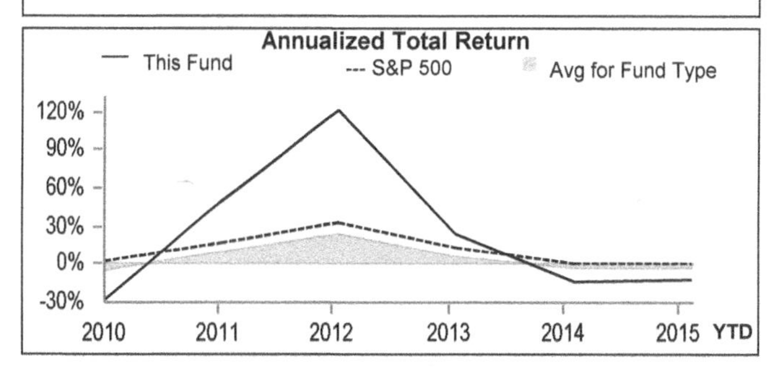

*ProShares UltraPro QQQ (TQQQ) C Fair

Fund Family: ProShare Advisors LLC
Fund Type: Growth
Inception Date: February 9, 2010

Major Rating Factors: *ProShares UltraPro QQQ has adopted a risky asset allocation strategy and currently receives an overall TheStreet.com Investment Rating of C (Fair). The fund has shown an above average level of volatility, as measured by both semi-deviation and drawdown factors. It carries a beta of 3.31, meaning it is expected to move 33.1% for every 10% move in the market. As of December 31, 2015, *ProShares UltraPro QQQ traded at a discount of .03% below its net asset value, which is better than its one-year historical average premium of .01%. The high level of risk (D+, Weak) did however, reward investors with excellent performance.

The fund's performance rating is currently A+ (Excellent). It has registered an annualized return of 60.47% over the last three years and is up 17.94% year to date 2015. Factored into the performance evaluation is an expense ratio of 0.95% (low).

Michael Neches has been running the fund for 3 years and currently receives a manager quality ranking of 85 (0=worst, 99=best). If you are comfortable owning a high risk investment, this fund may be an option.

Data Date	Investment Rating	Net Assets ($Mil)	Price	Performance Rating/Pts	Total Return Y-T-D	Risk Rating/Pts
12-15	C	834.30	114.14	A+ / 9.9	17.94%	D+ / 2.9
2014	D+	834.30	97.36	A+ / 9.9	64.17%	E- / 0
2013	C-	558.30	124.10	A+ / 9.9	114.72%	D / 1.9
2012	C-	317.90	51.69	A+ / 9.8	47.95%	D / 1.9
2011	E	183.70	67.97	D- / 1.5	-5.52%	D / 2.1

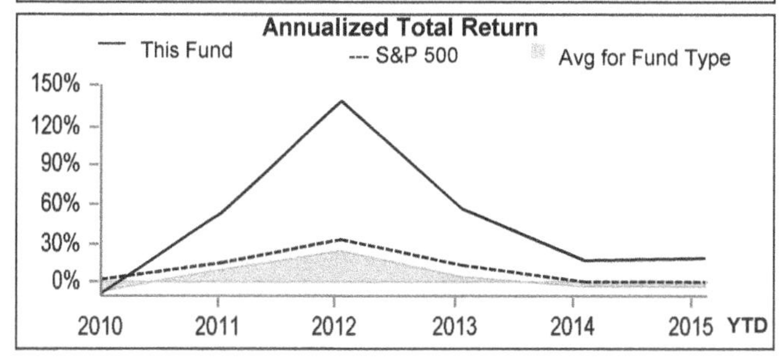

*ProShares UltraPro Russell2000 (URTY) C Fair

Fund Family: ProShare Advisors LLC
Fund Type: Growth
Inception Date: February 9, 2010

Major Rating Factors: *ProShares UltraPro Russell2000 has adopted a risky asset allocation strategy and currently receives an overall TheStreet.com Investment Rating of C (Fair). The fund has shown an above average level of volatility, as measured by both semi-deviation and drawdown factors. It carries a beta of 3.25, meaning it is expected to move 32.5% for every 10% move in the market. As of December 31, 2015, *ProShares UltraPro Russell2000 traded at a discount of .36% below its net asset value, which is better than its one-year historical average discount of .05%. The high level of risk (D+, Weak) did however, reward investors with excellent performance.

The fund's performance rating is currently A- (Excellent). It has registered an annualized return of 23.43% over the last three years but is down -19.62% year to date 2015. Factored into the performance evaluation is an expense ratio of 0.95% (low).

Michael Neches has been running the fund for 3 years and currently receives a manager quality ranking of 7 (0=worst, 99=best). If you are comfortable owning a high risk investment, this fund may be an option.

Data Date	Investment Rating	Net Assets ($Mil)	Price	Performance Rating/Pts	Total Return Y-T-D	Risk Rating/Pts
12-15	C	174.90	74.12	A- / 9.2	-19.62%	D+ / 2.6
2014	C-	174.90	93.78	A+ / 9.8	7.83%	E / 0.5
2013	C-	208.50	88.55	A+ / 9.8	120.65%	D / 1.9
2012	C-	67.90	71.13	A+ / 9.9	45.22%	D / 1.9
2011	E-	99.40	49.48	E+ / 0.6	-35.74%	D / 1.9

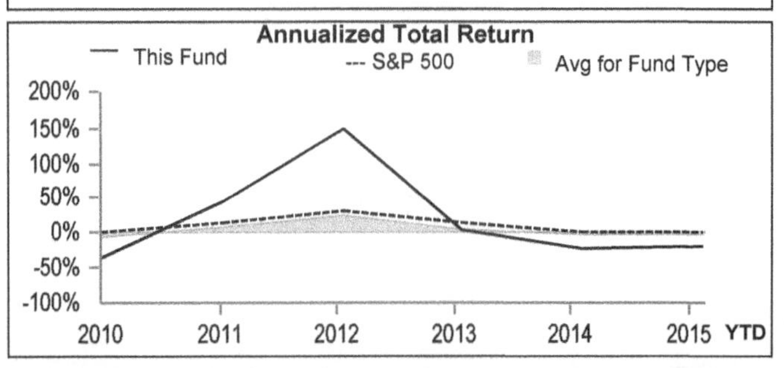

*ProShares UltraPro S&P500 (UPRO) C Fair

Fund Family: ProShare Advisors LLC
Fund Type: Income
Inception Date: June 23, 2009

Major Rating Factors: *ProShares UltraPro S&P500 has adopted a very risky asset allocation strategy and currently receives an overall TheStreet.com Investment Rating of C (Fair). The fund has shown a high level of volatility, as measured by both semi-deviation and drawdown factors. It carries a beta of 3.09, meaning it is expected to move 30.9% for every 10% move in the market. As of December 31, 2015, *ProShares UltraPro S&P500 traded at a discount of .22% below its net asset value, which is better than its one-year historical average discount of .03%. The high level of risk (D, Weak) did however, reward investors with excellent performance.

The fund's performance rating is currently A+ (Excellent). It has registered an annualized return of 38.19% over the last three years but is down -5.08% year to date 2015. Factored into the performance evaluation is an expense ratio of 0.95% (low).

Michael Neches has been running the fund for 3 years and currently receives a manager quality ranking of 20 (0=worst, 99=best). If you are comfortable owning a very high risk investment, this fund may be an option.

Data Date	Investment Rating	Net Assets ($Mil)	Price	Performance Rating/Pts	Total Return Y-T-D	Risk Rating/Pts
12-15	C	768.20	62.56	A+ / 9.8	-5.08%	D / 1.9
2014	C-	768.20	132.61	A+ / 9.9	42.31%	D- / 1.0
2013	C-	683.20	96.33	A+ / 9.9	95.91%	D / 1.9
2012	C-	365.80	87.86	A+ / 9.6	48.56%	D / 1.9
2011	E	343.60	60.15	D- / 1.4	-10.05%	D / 1.9
2010	A-	204.50	204.91	A+ / 9.9	36.37%	C / 5.1

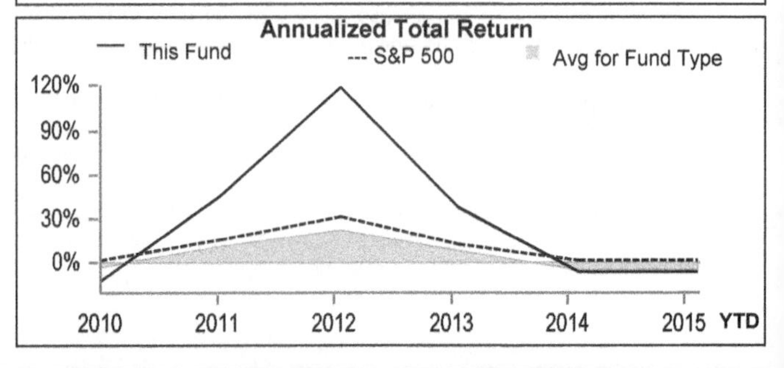

*ProShares UltraPro Short Dow30 (SDOW) E+ Very Weak

Fund Family: ProShare Advisors LLC
Fund Type: Growth
Inception Date: February 9, 2010

Major Rating Factors:
Very poor performance is the major factor driving the E+ (Very Weak) TheStreet.com Investment Rating for *ProShares UltraPro Short Dow30. The fund currently has a performance rating of E (Very Weak) based on an annualized return of -34.65% over the last three years and a total return of -13.85% year to date 2015. Factored into the performance evaluation is an expense ratio of 0.95% (low).

The fund's risk rating is currently C- (Fair). It carries a beta of -2.92, meaning the fund's expected move will be -29.2% for every 10% move in the market. Volatility, as measured by both the semi-deviation and a drawdown factor, is considered average. As of December 31, 2015, *ProShares UltraPro Short Dow30 traded at a discount of .06% below its net asset value, which is better than its one-year historical average discount of .03%.

Michael Neches has been running the fund for 3 years and currently receives a manager quality ranking of 36 (0=worst, 99=best). This fund offers an average level of risk but investors looking for strong performance will be frustrated.

Data Date	Investment Rating	Net Assets ($Mil)	Price	Performance Rating/Pts	Total Return Y-T-D	Risk Rating/Pts
12-15	E+	133.20	17.72	E / 0.4	-13.85%	C- / 3.1
2014	E-	133.20	20.56	E- / 0.2	-31.42%	D- / 1.3
2013	E	101.60	29.49	E- / 0.1	-52.77%	C- / 3.3
2012	E	82.10	68.47	E- / 0.2	-34.23%	C- / 3.1
2011	E	68.00	25.21	E- / 0.1	-41.15%	D+ / 2.9

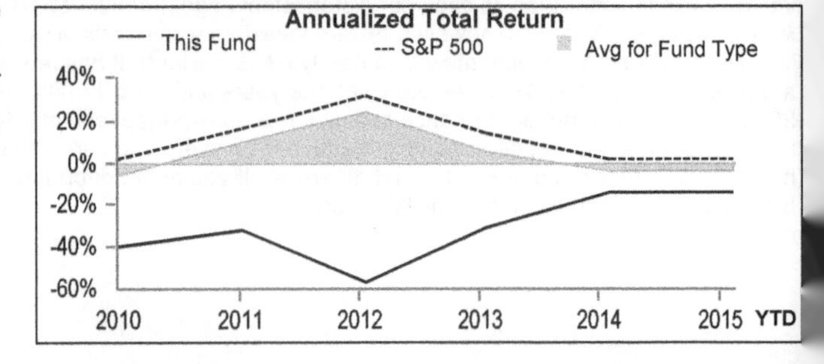

*ProShares UltraPro Short MidCap4 (SMDD) E+ Very Weak

Fund Family: ProShare Advisors LLC
Fund Type: Growth
Inception Date: February 9, 2010

Major Rating Factors:
Very poor performance is the major factor driving the E+ (Very Weak) TheStreet.com Investment Rating for *ProShares UltraPro Short MidCap4. The fund currently has a performance rating of E (Very Weak) based on an annualized return of -36.22% over the last three years and a total return of -7.80% year to date 2015. Factored into the performance evaluation is an expense ratio of 0.95% (low).

The fund's risk rating is currently C- (Fair). It carries a beta of -2.91, meaning the fund's expected move will be -29.1% for every 10% move in the market. Volatility, as measured by both the semi-deviation and a drawdown factor, is considered average. As of December 31, 2015, *ProShares UltraPro Short MidCap4 traded at a discount of .17% below its net asset value, which is better than its one-year historical average premium of .04%.

Michael Neches has been running the fund for 3 years and currently receives a manager quality ranking of 21 (0=worst, 99=best). This fund offers an average level of risk but investors looking for strong performance will be frustrated.

Data Date	Investment Rating	Net Assets ($Mil)	Price	Performance Rating/Pts	Total Return Y-T-D	Risk Rating/Pts
12-15	E+	7.80	34.28	E / 0.5	-7.80%	C- / 3.0
2014	E	7.80	37.08	E- / 0.1	-33.83%	D+ / 2.6
2013	E-	5.20	13.75	E- / 0	-57.58%	D / 2.2
2012	E-	6.40	36.87	E- / 0	-48.24%	D / 2.2
2011	E-	11.40	17.57	E- / 0.2	-38.19%	D / 1.9

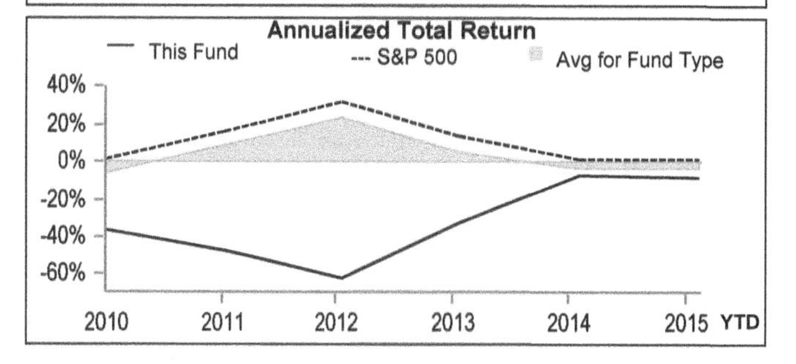

*ProShares UltraPro Short QQQ (SQQQ) E- Very Weak

Fund Family: ProShare Advisors LLC
Fund Type: Growth
Inception Date: February 9, 2010

Major Rating Factors: *ProShares UltraPro Short QQQ has adopted a very risky asset allocation strategy and currently receives an overall TheStreet.com Investment Rating of E- (Very Weak). The fund has a high level of volatility, as measured by both semi-deviation and drawdown factors. It carries a beta of -3.07, meaning the fund's expected move will be -30.7% for every 10% move in the market. As of December 31, 2015, *ProShares UltraPro Short QQQ traded at a premium of .11% above its net asset value, which is worse than its one-year historical average discount of .01%. Unfortunately, the high level of risk (E+, Very Weak) failed to pay off as investors endured very poor performance.

The fund's performance rating is currently E- (Very Weak). It has registered an annualized return of -50.09% over the last three years and is down -37.77% year to date 2015. Factored into the performance evaluation is an expense ratio of 0.95% (low).

Hratch Najarian has been running the fund for 7 years and currently receives a manager quality ranking of 4 (0=worst, 99=best). If you can tolerate very high levels of risk in the hope of improved future returns, holding this fund may be an option.

Data Date	Investment Rating	Net Assets ($Mil)	Price	Performance Rating/Pts	Total Return Y-T-D	Risk Rating/Pts
12-15	E-	328.90	18.72	E- / 0.1	-37.77%	E+ / 0.6
2014	E-	328.90	29.87	E- / 0.1	-50.22%	D / 2.2
2013	E-	181.50	14.35	E- / 0	-60.15%	D+ / 2.4
2012	E-	134.00	40.55	E- / 0.1	-47.23%	D / 2.2
2011	E-	94.50	19.69	E- / 0.1	-38.46%	D+ / 2.3

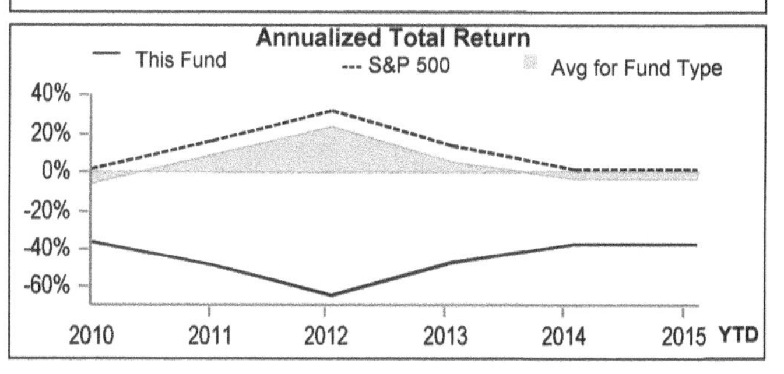

*ProShares UltraPro Short S&P500 (SPXU) E- Very Weak

Fund Family: ProShare Advisors LLC
Fund Type: Growth
Inception Date: June 23, 2009

Major Rating Factors: *ProShares UltraPro Short S&P500 has adopted a very risky asset allocation strategy and currently receives an overall TheStreet.com Investment Rating of E- (Very Weak). The fund has a high level of volatility, as measured by both semi-deviation and drawdown factors. It carries a beta of -2.92, meaning the fund's expected move will be -29.2% for every 10% move in the market. As of December 31, 2015, *ProShares UltraPro Short S&P500 traded at a premium of .16% above its net asset value, which is worse than its one-year historical average premium of .01%. Unfortunately, the high level of risk (D, Weak) failed to pay off as investors endured very poor performance.

The fund's performance rating is currently E (Very Weak). It has registered an annualized return of -38.84% over the last three years and is down -16.75% year to date 2015. Factored into the performance evaluation is an expense ratio of 0.93% (low).

Michael Neches has been running the fund for 3 years and currently receives a manager quality ranking of 16 (0=worst, 99=best). If you can tolerate very high levels of risk in the hope of improved future returns, holding this fund may be an option.

Data Date	Investment Rating	Net Assets ($Mil)	Price	Performance Rating/Pts	Total Return Y-T-D	Risk Rating/Pts
12-15	E-	515.20	31.71	E / 0.3	-16.75%	D / 1.6
2014	E	515.20	38.01	E- / 0.1	-38.85%	C- / 3.0
2013	E-	413.30	15.07	E- / 0.1	-55.16%	D+ / 2.8
2012	E-	462.00	37.86	E- / 0.1	-43.52%	D+ / 2.8
2011	E-	596.80	13.13	E- / 0.2	-33.78%	D+ / 2.6
2010	E-	290.10	19.41	E- / 0	-46.51%	D+ / 2.3

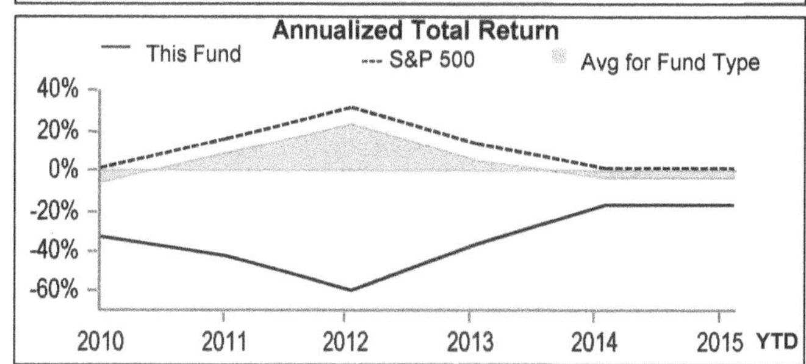

*ProShares UltraPro Shrt Russell2 (SRTY) E- Very Weak

Fund Family: ProShare Advisors LLC
Fund Type: Growth
Inception Date: February 9, 2010

Major Rating Factors: *ProShares UltraPro Shrt Russell2 has adopted a very risky asset allocation strategy and currently receives an overall TheStreet.com Investment Rating of E- (Very Weak). The fund has a high level of volatility, as measured by both semi-deviation and drawdown factors. It carries a beta of -3.09, meaning the fund's expected move will be -30.9% for every 10% move in the market. As of December 31, 2015, *ProShares UltraPro Shrt Russell2 traded at a premium of .38% above its net asset value, which is worse than its one-year historical average premium of .08%. Unfortunately, the high level of risk (E+, Very Weak) failed to pay off as investors endured very poor performance.

The fund's performance rating is currently E (Very Weak). It has registered an annualized return of -37.67% over the last three years and is down -6.42% year to date 2015. Factored into the performance evaluation is an expense ratio of 0.95% (low).

Michael Neches has been running the fund for 3 years and currently receives a manager quality ranking of 22 (0=worst, 99=best). If you can tolerate very high levels of risk in the hope of improved future returns, holding this fund may be an option.

Data Date	Investment Rating	Net Assets ($Mil)	Price	Performance Rating/Pts	Total Return Y-T-D	Risk Rating/Pts
12-15	E-	123.50	29.32	E / 0.4	-6.42%	E+ / 0.8
2014	E-	123.50	30.90	E- / 0.1	-29.32%	D / 2.1
2013	E-	53.30	10.75	E- / 0	-63.89%	D / 1.9
2012	E-	61.40	33.74	E- / 0	-49.17%	D / 1.9
2011	E-	66.90	13.12	E- / 0	-44.09%	D / 1.9

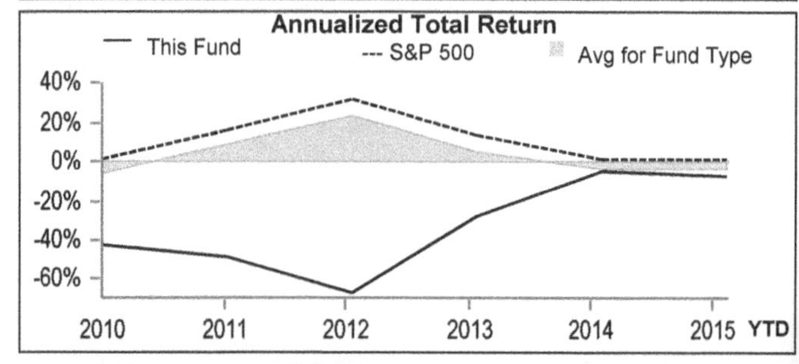

*ProShares UltraPro Sht 20+ Yr Tr (TTT) E Very Weak

Fund Family: ProShare Advisors LLC
Fund Type: US Government/Agency
Inception Date: March 27, 2012

Major Rating Factors: *ProShares UltraPro Sht 20+ Yr Tr has adopted a very risky asset allocation strategy and currently receives an overall TheStreet.com Investment Rating of E (Very Weak). The fund has a high level of volatility, as measured by both semi-deviation and drawdown factors. It carries a beta of -3.36, meaning the fund's expected move will be -33.6% for every 10% move in the market. As of December 31, 2015, *ProShares UltraPro Sht 20+ Yr Tr traded at a premium of .40% above its net asset value, which is worse than its one-year historical average discount of .08%. Unfortunately, the high level of risk (D-, Weak) failed to pay off as investors endured poor performance.

The fund's performance rating is currently D- (Weak). It has registered an annualized return of -20.22% over the last three years and is down -7.63% year to date 2015. Factored into the performance evaluation is an expense ratio of 0.95% (low).

Michelle Liu has been running the fund for 4 years and currently receives a manager quality ranking of 15 (0=worst, 99=best). If you can tolerate very high levels of risk in the hope of improved future returns, holding this fund may be an option.

Data Date	Investment Rating	Net Assets ($Mil)	Price	Performance Rating/Pts	Total Return Y-T-D	Risk Rating/Pts
12-15	E	119.90	37.65	D- / 1.0	-7.63%	D- / 1.5
2014	E-	119.90	42.06	E- / 0	-55.21%	D / 1.6
2013	C+	121.00	94.82	B+ / 8.6	26.67%	C+ / 5.8

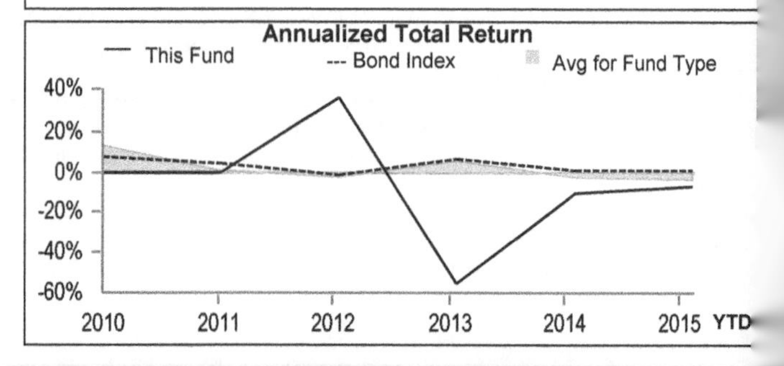

*ProShares UltraPro Sht Finl Sel (FINZ) E- Very Weak

Fund Family: ProShare Advisors LLC
Fund Type: Growth and Income
Inception Date: July 10, 2012

Major Rating Factors: *ProShares UltraPro Sht Finl Sel has adopted a very risky asset allocation strategy and currently receives an overall TheStreet.com Investment Rating of E- (Very Weak). The fund has a high level of volatility, as measured by both semi-deviation and drawdown factors. It carries a beta of -2.64, meaning the fund's expected move will be -26.4% for every 10% move in the market. As of December 31, 2015, *ProShares UltraPro Sht Finl Sel traded at a premium of 7.04% above its net asset value, which is worse than its one-year historical average premium of .26%. Unfortunately, the high level of risk (D-, Weak) failed to pay off as investors endured very poor performance.

The fund's performance rating is currently E- (Very Weak). It has registered an annualized return of -41.46% over the last three years and is down -16.02% year to date 2015. Factored into the performance evaluation is an expense ratio of 0.95% (low).

Charles Lowery has been running the fund for 3 years and currently receives a manager quality ranking of 9 (0=worst, 99=best). If you can tolerate very high levels of risk in the hope of improved future returns, holding this fund may be an option.

Data Date	Investment Rating	Net Assets ($Mil)	Price	Performance Rating/Pts	Total Return Y-T-D	Risk Rating/Pts
12-15	E-	4.10	20.08	E- / 0.2	-16.02%	D- / 1.5
2014	E-	4.10	22.35	E- / 0.1	-40.95%	D+ / 2.5
2013	E-	3.30	42.50	E- / 0	-59.56%	D+ / 2.6

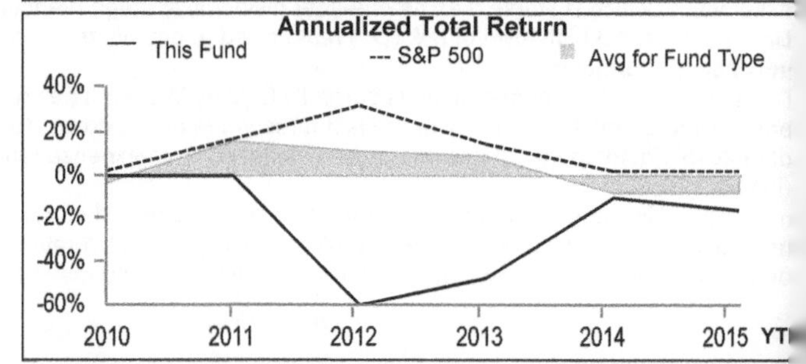

*ProShares UltraShort 20+ Year Tr (TBT) D- Weak

Fund Family: ProShare Advisors LLC
Fund Type: Income
Inception Date: April 29, 2008

Data Date	Investment Rating	Net Assets ($Mil)	Price	Perfor-mance Rating/Pts	Total Return Y-T-D	Risk Rating/Pts
12-15	D-	4,256.60	44.07	D / 1.7	-3.08%	C- / 3.2
2014	E	4,256.60	46.39	E+ / 0.7	-41.12%	C- / 3.4
2013	E+	4,594.60	79.20	E+ / 0.8	18.78%	C- / 3.6
2012	E	2,902.10	63.45	E / 0.4	-10.91%	C- / 3.6
2011	E+	3,106.50	18.07	E+ / 0.6	-50.91%	C- / 3.9
2010	E+	5,392.20	37.04	E+ / 0.8	-25.74%	C- / 4.2

Major Rating Factors:
Disappointing performance is the major factor driving the D- (Weak) TheStreet.com Investment Rating for *ProShares UltraShort 20+ Year Tr. The fund currently has a performance rating of D (Weak) based on an annualized return of -12.74% over the last three years and a total return of -3.08% year to date 2015. Factored into the performance evaluation is an expense ratio of 0.93% (low).

The fund's risk rating is currently C- (Fair). It carries a beta of 0.50, meaning the fund's expected move will be 5.0% for every 10% move in the market. Volatility, as measured by both the semi-deviation and a drawdown factor, is considered average. As of December 31, 2015, *ProShares UltraShort 20+ Year Tr traded at a premium of .25% above its net asset value, which is worse than its one-year historical average discount of .06%.

Michelle Liu has been running the fund for 8 years and currently receives a manager quality ranking of 8 (0=worst, 99=best). This fund offers an average level of risk but investors looking for strong performance will be frustrated.

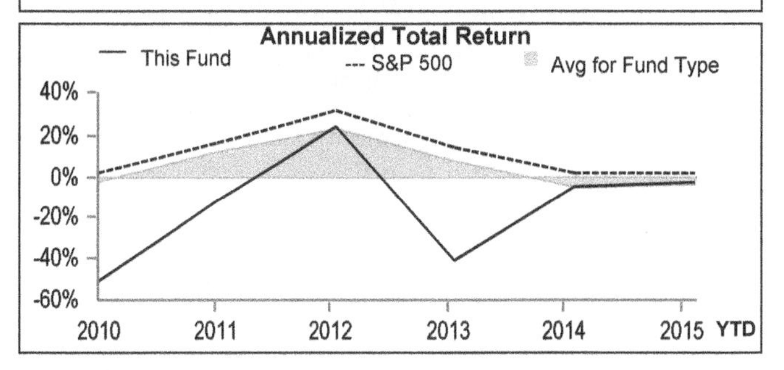

*ProShares UltraShort 3-7 Yr Trea (TBZ) C- Fair

Fund Family: ProShare Advisors LLC
Fund Type: General - Investment Grade
Inception Date: April 4, 2011

Data Date	Investment Rating	Net Assets ($Mil)	Price	Perfor-mance Rating/Pts	Total Return Y-T-D	Risk Rating/Pts
12-15	C-	3.90	28.54	C- / 3.1	-4.89%	C+ / 6.9
2014	D+	3.90	30.01	D / 2.0	-7.66%	B- / 7.1
2013	C-	4.10	32.45	D+ / 2.6	1.43%	B / 8.6
2012	D	4.80	31.94	D- / 1.0	-4.91%	B / 8.5

Major Rating Factors: Middle of the road best describes *ProShares UltraShort 3-7 Yr Trea whose TheStreet.com Investment Rating is currently a C- (Fair). The fund currently has a performance rating of C- (Fair) based on an annualized return of -3.78% over the last three years and a total return of -4.89% year to date 2015. Factored into the performance evaluation is an expense ratio of 0.95% (low).

The fund's risk rating is currently C+ (Fair). It carries a beta of -1.56, meaning the fund's expected move will be -15.6% for every 10% move in the market. Volatility, as measured by both the semi-deviation and a drawdown factor, is considered low. As of December 31, 2015, *ProShares UltraShort 3-7 Yr Trea traded at a premium of .74% above its net asset value, which is worse than its one-year historical average premium of .14%.

Michelle Liu has been running the fund for 5 years and currently receives a manager quality ranking of 55 (0=worst, 99=best). If you desire an average level of risk, then this fund may be an option.

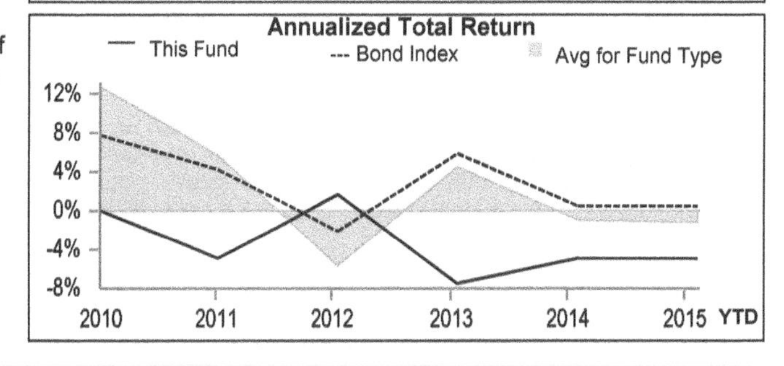

*ProShares UltraShort 7-10 Year T (PST) C- Fair

Fund Family: ProShare Advisors LLC
Fund Type: Income
Inception Date: April 29, 2008

Data Date	Investment Rating	Net Assets ($Mil)	Price	Perfor-mance Rating/Pts	Total Return Y-T-D	Risk Rating/Pts
12-15	C-	298.80	23.24	D+ / 2.6	-5.33%	B- / 7.6
2014	D-	298.80	24.77	D- / 1.4	-17.76%	C+ / 5.9
2013	D	310.50	30.30	D- / 1.3	7.23%	C+ / 6.7
2012	D-	292.50	27.60	E / 0.5	-8.39%	C+ / 5.9
2011	D-	380.80	30.51	E+ / 0.9	-27.05%	C+ / 6.2
2010	D	451.30	42.34	E+ / 0.6	-21.51%	C+ / 5.8

Major Rating Factors:
Disappointing performance is the major factor driving the C- (Fair) TheStreet.com Investment Rating for *ProShares UltraShort 7-10 Year T. The fund currently has a performance rating of D+ (Weak) based on an annualized return of -6.12% over the last three years and a total return of -5.33% year to date 2015. Factored into the performance evaluation is an expense ratio of 0.95% (low).

The fund's risk rating is currently B- (Good). It carries a beta of 0.17, meaning the fund's expected move will be 1.7% for every 10% move in the market. Volatility, as measured by both the semi-deviation and a drawdown factor, is considered low. As of December 31, 2015, *ProShares UltraShort 7-10 Year T traded at a discount of .30% below its net asset value, which is better than its one-year historical average discount of .08%.

Michelle Liu has been running the fund for 8 years and currently receives a manager quality ranking of 20 (0=worst, 99=best). This fund offers only a moderate level of risk but investors looking for strong performance are still waiting.

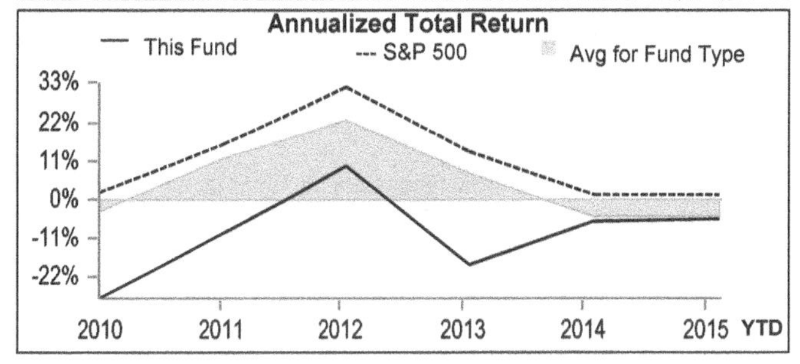

*ProShares UltraShort Basic Mater (SMN) D Weak

Fund Family: ProShare Advisors LLC
Fund Type: Income
Inception Date: January 30, 2007

Data Date	Investment Rating	Net Assets ($Mil)	Price	Performance Rating/Pts	Total Return Y-T-D	Risk Rating/Pts
12-15	D	14.10	34.32	D+ / 2.4	16.14%	C / 4.5
2014	E	14.10	29.63	E+ / 0.6	-14.86%	D+ / 2.4
2013	E+	19.40	34.23	E / 0.4	-30.79%	C- / 4.0
2012	E-	30.40	53.77	E / 0.3	-21.94%	D+ / 2.7
2011	E-	64.50	18.63	E- / 0.1	-10.74%	D / 1.9
2010	E-	73.90	19.24	E- / 0.1	-54.68%	D- / 1.0

Major Rating Factors:
Disappointing performance is the major factor driving the D (Weak) TheStreet.com Investment Rating for *ProShares UltraShort Basic Mater. The fund currently has a performance rating of D+ (Weak) based on an annualized return of -11.95% over the last three years and a total return of 16.14% year to date 2015. Factored into the performance evaluation is an expense ratio of 0.95% (low).

The fund's risk rating is currently C (Fair). It carries a beta of -2.45, meaning the fund's expected move will be -24.5% for every 10% move in the market. Volatility, as measured by both the semi-deviation and a drawdown factor, is considered average. As of December 31, 2015, *ProShares UltraShort Basic Mater traded at a discount of .15% below its net asset value, which is better than its one-year historical average discount of .02%.

Charles Lowery has been running the fund for 3 years and currently receives a manager quality ranking of 98 (0=worst, 99=best). This fund offers an average level of risk but investors looking for strong performance will be frustrated.

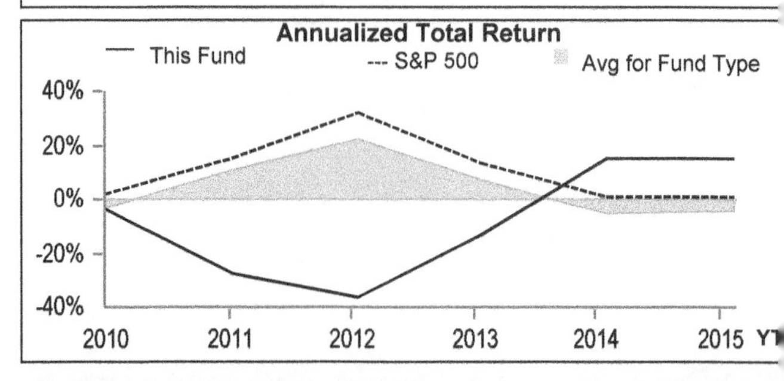

*ProShares UltraShort Blmbrg Nat (KOLD) C- Fair

Fund Family: ProShare Advisors LLC
Fund Type: Income
Inception Date: October 6, 2011

Data Date	Investment Rating	Net Assets ($Mil)	Price	Performance Rating/Pts	Total Return Y-T-D	Risk Rating/Pts
12-15	C-	19.70	139.66	A+ / 9.8	75.01%	E / 0.5
2014	D-	19.70	82.03	C+ / 6.9	23.67%	E- / 0
2013	E-	22.70	69.36	E- / 0.1	-37.40%	D / 1.9
2012	E-	12.80	25.41	D- / 1.1	-14.01%	D / 1.9

Major Rating Factors: *ProShares UltraShort Blmbrg Nat has adopted a very risky asset allocation strategy and currently receives an overall TheStreet.com Investment Rating of C- (Fair). The fund has shown a high level of volatility, as measured by both semi-deviation and drawdown factors. It carries a beta of 0.06, meaning the fund's expected move will be 0.6% for every 10% move in the market. As of December 31, 2015, *ProShares UltraShort Blmbrg Nat traded at a premium of .04% above its net asset value, which is better than its one-year historical average premium of .05%. The high level of risk (E, Very Weak) did however, reward investors with excellent performance.

The fund's performance rating is currently A+ (Excellent). It has registered an annualized return of 9.64% over the last three years and is up 75.01% year to date 2015. Factored into the performance evaluation is an expense ratio of 1.18% (low).

Michael Neches currently receives a manager quality ranking of 95 (0=worst, 99=best). If you are comfortable owning a very high risk investment, this fund may be an option.

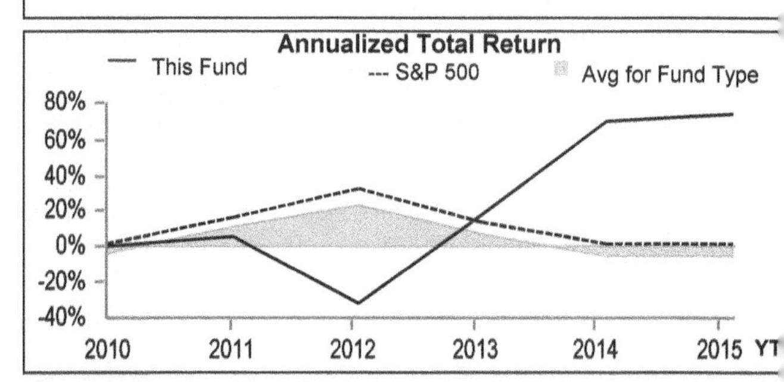

*ProShares UltraShort Bloomberg C (CMD) A+ Excellent

Fund Family: ProShare Advisors LLC
Fund Type: Income
Inception Date: November 25, 2008

Data Date	Investment Rating	Net Assets ($Mil)	Price	Performance Rating/Pts	Total Return Y-T-D	Risk Rating/Pts
12-15	A+	4.10	140.41	A+ / 9.9	59.72%	B- / 7.3
2014	B+	4.10	87.44	A / 9.4	39.90%	C+ / 6.5
2013	C	3.80	58.41	C+ / 5.9	18.89%	C+ / 6.6
2012	E+	3.20	51.64	E+ / 0.8	-4.22%	C / 5.0
2011	E+	9.10	56.19	E+ / 0.9	8.13%	C- / 3.8
2010	E	1.40	9.66	E- / 0.1	-34.06%	C- / 3.5

Major Rating Factors:
Exceptional performance is the major factor driving the A+ (Excellent) TheStreet.com Investment Rating for *ProShares UltraShort Bloomberg C. The fund currently has a performance rating of A+ (Excellent) based on an annualized return of 38.75% over the last three years and a total return of 59.72% year to date 2015. Factored into the performance evaluation is an expense ratio of 0.95% (low).

The fund's risk rating is currently B- (Good). It carries a beta of -0.77, meaning the fund's expected move will be -7.7% for every 10% move in the market. Volatility, as measured by both the semi-deviation and a drawdown factor, is considered low. As of December 31, 2015, *ProShares UltraShort Bloomberg C traded at a discount of 1.05% below its net asset value, which is better than its one-year historical average discount of .42%.

Michael Neches currently receives a manager quality ranking of 99 (0=worst, 99=best). If you desire only a moderate level of risk and strong performance, then this fund is an excellent option.

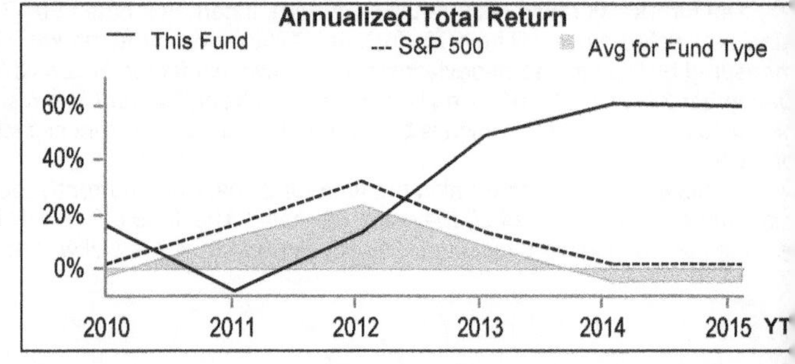

*ProShares UltraShort Bloomberg C (SCO) C Fair

Fund Family: ProShare Advisors LLC
Fund Type: Energy/Natural Resources
Inception Date: November 25, 2008

Major Rating Factors: *ProShares UltraShort Bloomberg C has adopted a risky asset allocation strategy and currently receives an overall TheStreet.com Investment Rating of C (Fair). The fund has shown an above average level of volatility, as measured by both semi-deviation and drawdown factors. It carries a beta of -2.03, meaning the fund's expected move will be -20.3% for every 10% move in the market. As of December 31, 2015, *ProShares UltraShort Bloomberg C traded at a premium of .32% above its net asset value, which is worse than its one-year historical average premium of .18%. The high level of risk (D+, Weak) did however, reward investors with excellent performance.

The fund's performance rating is currently A+ (Excellent). It has registered an annualized return of 50.45% over the last three years and is up 67.26% year to date 2015. Factored into the performance evaluation is an expense ratio of 0.98% (low).

Michael Neches currently receives a manager quality ranking of 99 (0=worst, 99=best). If you are comfortable owning a high risk investment, this fund may be an option.

Data Date	Investment Rating	Net Assets ($Mil)	Price	Performance Rating/Pts	Total Return Y-T-D	Risk Rating/Pts
12-15	C	196.10	133.64	A+ / 9.9	67.26%	D+ / 2.8
2014	C+	196.10	76.52	A+ / 9.9	122.31%	C- / 3.9
2013	E	256.00	31.58	D- / 1.0	-12.28%	C- / 3.1
2012	E	85.40	40.44	E / 0.5	1.26%	C- / 3.7
2011	E-	144.40	38.69	E / 0.3	-32.33%	D+ / 2.4
2010	E-	132.20	10.17	E- / 0.2	-25.49%	D / 1.9

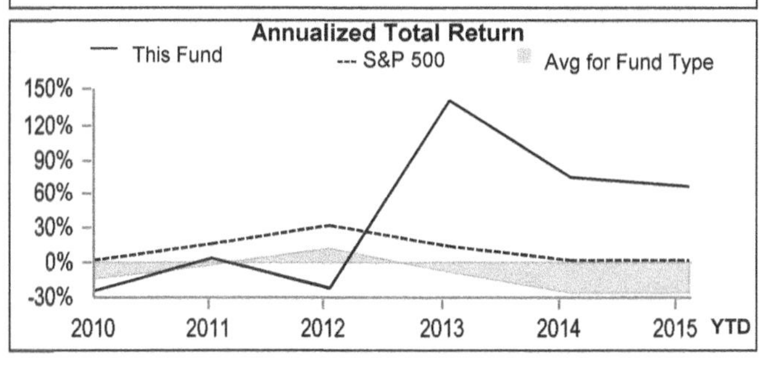

*ProShares UltraShort Consumer Go (SZK) E+ Very Weak

Fund Family: ProShare Advisors LLC
Fund Type: Income
Inception Date: January 30, 2007

Major Rating Factors:
Very poor performance is the major factor driving the E+ (Very Weak) TheStreet.com Investment Rating for *ProShares UltraShort Consumer Go. The fund currently has a performance rating of E (Very Weak) based on an annualized return of -28.75% over the last three years and a total return of -22.68% year to date 2015. Factored into the performance evaluation is an expense ratio of 0.95% (low).

The fund's risk rating is currently C- (Fair). It carries a beta of -1.60, meaning the fund's expected move will be -16.0% for every 10% move in the market. Volatility, as measured by both the semi-deviation and a drawdown factor, is considered average. As of December 31, 2015, *ProShares UltraShort Consumer Go traded at a discount of 2.23% below its net asset value, which is better than its one-year historical average premium of .43%.

Charles Lowery has been running the fund for 3 years and currently receives a manager quality ranking of 13 (0=worst, 99=best). This fund offers an average level of risk but investors looking for strong performance will be frustrated.

Data Date	Investment Rating	Net Assets ($Mil)	Price	Performance Rating/Pts	Total Return Y-T-D	Risk Rating/Pts
12-15	E+	3.50	21.51	E / 0.5	-22.68%	C- / 4.0
2014	E-	3.50	27.82	E / 0.4	-20.24%	D / 2.1
2013	E+	3.90	34.88	E- / 0.2	-41.34%	C / 5.1
2012	E+	2.40	62.39	E / 0.3	-27.84%	C- / 4.2
2011	E	4.70	20.84	E / 0.5	-25.60%	C- / 3.8
2010	E+	8.30	27.52	E / 0.4	-34.86%	C- / 3.3

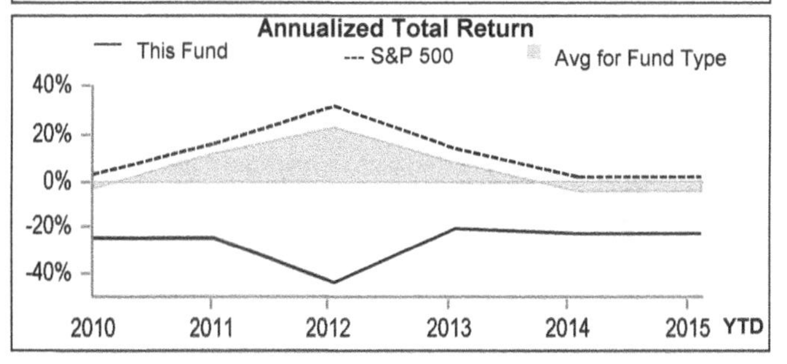

*ProShares UltraShort Consumer Se (SCC) E Very Weak

Fund Family: ProShare Advisors LLC
Fund Type: Income
Inception Date: January 30, 2007

Major Rating Factors: *ProShares UltraShort Consumer Se has adopted a very risky asset allocation strategy and currently receives an overall TheStreet.com Investment Rating of E (Very Weak). The fund has a high level of volatility, as measured by both semi-deviation and drawdown factors. It carries a beta of -2.07, meaning the fund's expected move will be -20.7% for every 10% move in the market. As of December 31, 2015, *ProShares UltraShort Consumer Se traded at a premium of .99% above its net asset value, which is worse than its one-year historical average premium of .26%. Unfortunately, the high level of risk (D, Weak) failed to pay off as investors endured very poor performance.

The fund's performance rating is currently E (Very Weak). It has registered an annualized return of -33.78% over the last three years and is down -20.40% year to date 2015. Factored into the performance evaluation is an expense ratio of 0.95% (low).

Charles Lowery has been running the fund for 3 years and currently receives a manager quality ranking of 12 (0=worst, 99=best). If you can tolerate very high levels of risk in the hope of improved future returns, holding this fund may be an option.

Data Date	Investment Rating	Net Assets ($Mil)	Price	Performance Rating/Pts	Total Return Y-T-D	Risk Rating/Pts
12-15	E	7.40	42.66	E / 0.4	-20.40%	D / 1.9
2014	E	7.40	12.75	E- / 0.2	-30.37%	C- / 3.6
2013	E	4.10	18.24	E- / 0.1	-50.13%	C- / 3.6
2012	E	5.80	39.00	E- / 0.2	-40.22%	C- / 3.6
2011	E	12.00	15.94	E / 0.3	-28.53%	C- / 3.2
2010	E-	22.90	21.81	E / 0.3	-42.09%	D / 2.0

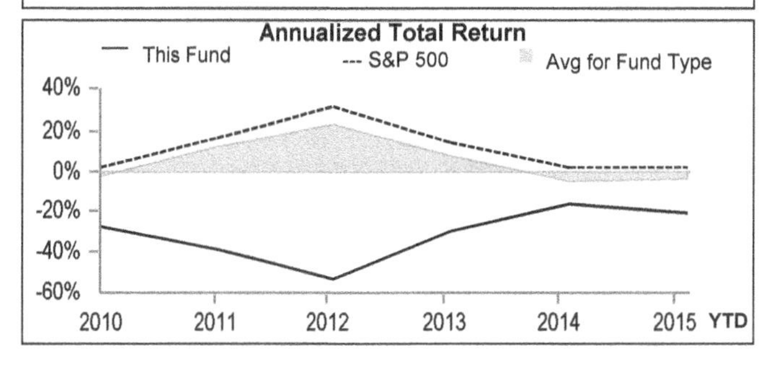

*ProShares UltraShort Dow30 (DXD) D- Weak

Fund Family: ProShare Advisors LLC
Fund Type: Growth
Inception Date: July 11, 2006

Major Rating Factors:
Very poor performance is the major factor driving the D- (Weak) TheStreet.com Investment Rating for *ProShares UltraShort Dow30. The fund currently has a performance rating of E+ (Very Weak) based on an annualized return of -23.74% over the last three years and a total return of -7.27% year to date 2015. Factored into the performance evaluation is an expense ratio of 0.95% (low).

The fund's risk rating is currently C (Fair). It carries a beta of -1.96, meaning the fund's expected move will be -19.6% for every 10% move in the market. Volatility, as measured by both the semi-deviation and a drawdown factor, is considered average. As of December 31, 2015, *ProShares UltraShort Dow30 traded at a discount of .05% below its net asset value, which is better than its one-year historical average discount of .01%.

Michael Neches has been running the fund for 3 years and currently receives a manager quality ranking of 58 (0=worst, 99=best). This fund offers an average level of risk but investors looking for strong performance will be frustrated.

Data Date	Investment Rating	Net Assets ($Mil)	Price	Performance Rating/Pts	Total Return Y-T-D	Risk Rating/Pts
12-15	D-	218.40	20.16	E+ / 0.8	-7.27%	C / 4.6
2014	E	218.40	21.76	E / 0.4	-21.67%	D+ / 2.5
2013	E+	272.40	27.42	E / 0.3	-38.88%	C / 4.7
2012	E+	272.40	47.78	E / 0.4	-23.78%	C- / 4.1
2011	E	288.20	15.31	E / 0.5	-26.78%	C- / 3.6
2010	E	379.70	20.70	E / 0.4	-29.76%	C- / 3.1

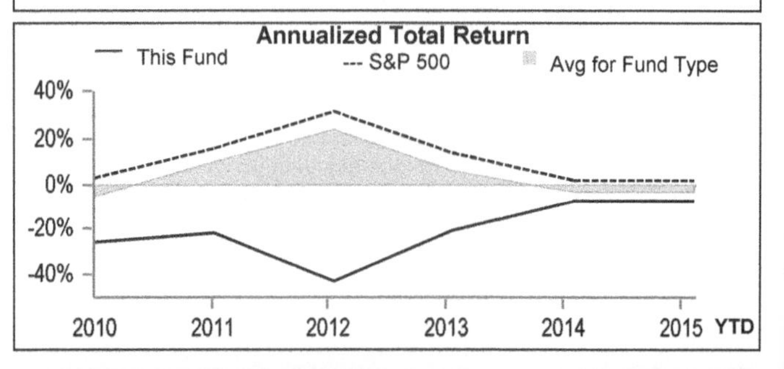

*ProShares UltraShort Euro (EUO) A Excellent

Fund Family: ProShare Advisors LLC
Fund Type: Foreign
Inception Date: November 25, 2008

Major Rating Factors:
Strong performance is the major factor driving the A (Excellent) TheStreet.com Investment Rating for *ProShares UltraShort Euro. The fund currently has a performance rating of B+ (Good) based on an annualized return of 9.72% over the last three years and a total return of 16.31% year to date 2015. Factored into the performance evaluation is an expense ratio of 0.95% (low).

The fund's risk rating is currently B (Good). It carries a beta of -0.46, meaning the fund's expected move will be -4.6% for every 10% move in the market. Volatility, as measured by both the semi-deviation and a drawdown factor, is considered low. As of December 31, 2015, *ProShares UltraShort Euro traded at a discount of .04% below its net asset value.

Michael Neches currently receives a manager quality ranking of 97 (0=worst, 99=best). If you desire only a moderate level of risk and strong performance, then this fund is an excellent option.

Data Date	Investment Rating	Net Assets ($Mil)	Price	Performance Rating/Pts	Total Return Y-T-D	Risk Rating/Pts
12-15	A	478.40	25.53	B+ / 8.4	16.31%	B / 8.2
2014	C	478.40	21.61	C / 4.5	23.56%	B- / 7.4
2013	D	423.90	17.06	D- / 1.3	-9.52%	B- / 7.6
2012	D-	530.60	19.01	D- / 1.1	-12.02%	C+ / 6.5
2011	D	1,095.10	20.35	D / 2.0	-3.31%	C+ / 6.6
2010	D+	444.40	20.31	D+ / 2.8	8.61%	C+ / 5.9

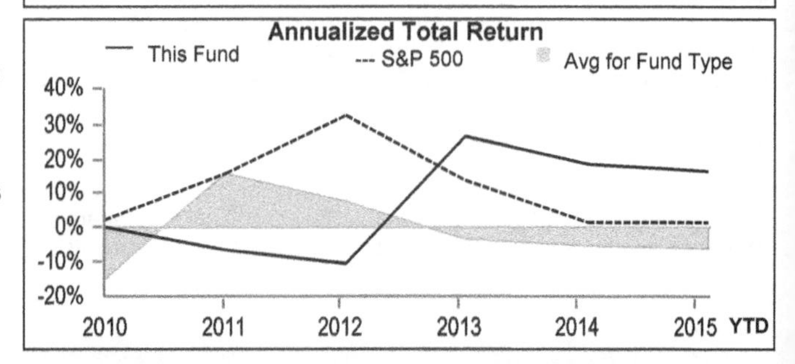

*ProShares UltraShort Financials (SKF) D- Weak

Fund Family: ProShare Advisors LLC
Fund Type: Financial Services
Inception Date: January 30, 2007

Major Rating Factors:
Very poor performance is the major factor driving the D- (Weak) TheStreet.com Investment Rating for *ProShares UltraShort Financials. The fund currently has a performance rating of E+ (Very Weak) based on an annualized return of -28.12% over the last three years and a total return of -8.42% year to date 2015. Factored into the performance evaluation is an expense ratio of 0.95% (low).

The fund's risk rating is currently C (Fair). It carries a beta of -1.96, meaning the fund's expected move will be -19.6% for every 10% move in the market. Volatility, as measured by both the semi-deviation and a drawdown factor, is considered average. As of December 31, 2015, *ProShares UltraShort Financials traded at a discount of .20% below its net asset value.

Charles Lowery has been running the fund for 3 years and currently receives a manager quality ranking of 21 (0=worst, 99=best). This fund offers an average level of risk but investors looking for strong performance will be frustrated.

Data Date	Investment Rating	Net Assets ($Mil)	Price	Performance Rating/Pts	Total Return Y-T-D	Risk Rating/Pts
12-15	D-	71.70	45.87	E+ / 0.6	-8.42%	C / 4.4
2014	E-	71.70	50.19	E- / 0.2	-28.05%	D / 2.0
2013	E	92.40	17.42	E- / 0.2	-43.52%	C- / 3.3
2012	E	168.90	33.54	E- / 0.2	-42.43%	C- / 3.3
2011	E-	350.30	59.32	E- / 0.2	-7.58%	D / 1.9
2010	E-	389.10	15.67	E- / 0.2	-35.33%	D- / 1.0

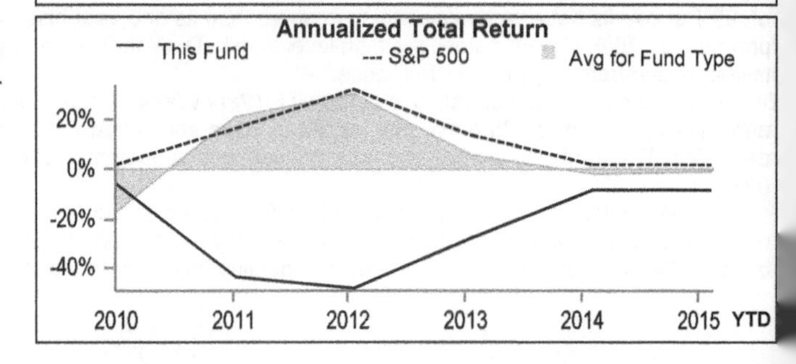

*ProShares UltraShort FTSE China (FXP) D- Weak

Fund Family: ProShare Advisors LLC
Fund Type: Foreign
Inception Date: November 6, 2007

Major Rating Factors: *ProShares UltraShort FTSE China has adopted a risky asset allocation strategy and currently receives an overall TheStreet.com Investment Rating of D- (Weak). The fund has an above average level of volatility, as measured by both semi-deviation and drawdown factors. It carries a beta of -1.79, meaning the fund's expected move will be -17.9% for every 10% move in the market. As of December 31, 2015, *ProShares UltraShort FTSE China traded at a discount of .17% below its net asset value, which is better than its one-year historical average discount of .01%. Unfortunately, the high level of risk (D+, Weak) failed to pay off as investors endured poor performance.

The fund's performance rating is currently D (Weak). It has registered an annualized return of -14.10% over the last three years and is down -0.52% year to date 2015. Factored into the performance evaluation is an expense ratio of 0.95% (low).

Alexander V. Ilyasov has been running the fund for 7 years and currently receives a manager quality ranking of 21 (0=worst, 99=best). If you can tolerate high levels of risk in the hope of improved future returns, holding this fund may be an option.

Data Date	Investment Rating	Net Assets ($Mil)	Price	Performance Rating/Pts	Total Return Y-T-D	Risk Rating/Pts
12-15	D-	81.60	41.94	D / 2.2	-0.52%	D+ / 2.9
2014	E-	81.60	42.27	E / 0.3	-36.61%	D / 1.8
2013	E	92.60	15.28	E+ / 0.7	0.79%	D+ / 2.8
2012	E	111.50	17.58	E / 0.3	-37.35%	C- / 3.0
2011	E-	192.70	30.37	E / 0.4	1.85%	D / 2.2
2010	E-	211.10	30.08	E- / 0.1	-28.29%	D- / 1.0

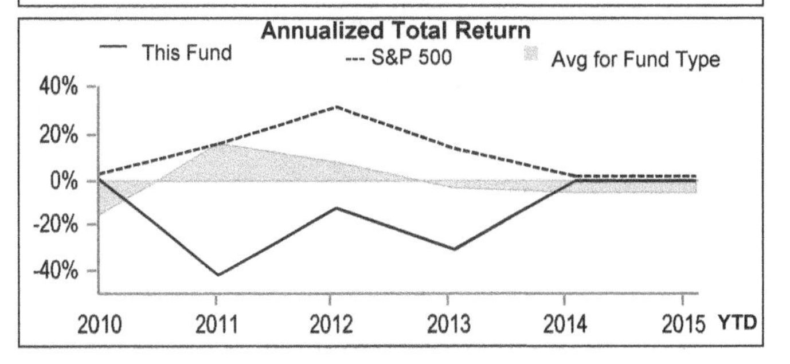

*ProShares UltraShort FTSE Europe (EPV) D Weak

Fund Family: ProShare Advisors LLC
Fund Type: Foreign
Inception Date: June 16, 2009

Major Rating Factors:
Disappointing performance is the major factor driving the D (Weak) TheStreet.com Investment Rating for *ProShares UltraShort FTSE Europe. The fund currently has a performance rating of D- (Weak) based on an annualized return of -17.07% over the last three years and a total return of -8.57% year to date 2015. Factored into the performance evaluation is an expense ratio of 0.95% (low).

The fund's risk rating is currently C (Fair). It carries a beta of -2.02, meaning the fund's expected move will be -20.2% for every 10% move in the market. Volatility, as measured by both the semi-deviation and a drawdown factor, is considered average. As of December 31, 2015, *ProShares UltraShort FTSE Europe traded at a discount of .09% below its net asset value, which is better than its one-year historical average discount of .03%.

Alexander V. Ilyasov has been running the fund for 7 years and currently receives a manager quality ranking of 19 (0=worst, 99=best). This fund offers an average level of risk but investors looking for strong performance will be frustrated.

Data Date	Investment Rating	Net Assets ($Mil)	Price	Performance Rating/Pts	Total Return Y-T-D	Risk Rating/Pts
12-15	D	39.60	58.54	D- / 1.4	-8.57%	C / 5.4
2014	E	39.60	63.46	E+ / 0.6	1.05%	C- / 3.4
2013	E	34.00	15.08	E- / 0.2	-38.82%	C- / 3.1
2012	E	84.80	26.10	E- / 0.2	-46.89%	C- / 3.1
2011	E	149.20	46.60	D- / 1.0	-20.82%	C- / 3.3
2010	E	51.40	14.29	E- / 0.1	-34.66%	C- / 3.2

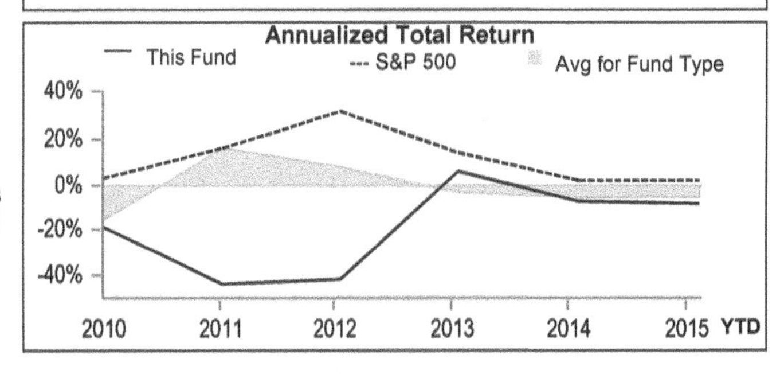

*ProShares UltraShort Gold (GLL) A- Excellent

Fund Family: ProShare Advisors LLC
Fund Type: Energy/Natural Resources
Inception Date: December 2, 2008

Major Rating Factors:
Exceptional performance is the major factor driving the A- (Excellent) TheStreet.com Investment Rating for *ProShares UltraShort Gold. The fund currently has a performance rating of A+ (Excellent) based on an annualized return of 22.06% over the last three years and a total return of 16.22% year to date 2015. Factored into the performance evaluation is an expense ratio of 0.95% (low).

The fund's risk rating is currently C+ (Fair). It carries a beta of -0.28, meaning the fund's expected move will be -2.8% for every 10% move in the market. Volatility, as measured by both the semi-deviation and a drawdown factor, is considered low. As of December 31, 2015, *ProShares UltraShort Gold traded at a discount of .04% below its net asset value, which is worse than its one-year historical average discount of .21%.

Michael Neches currently receives a manager quality ranking of 98 (0=worst, 99=best). If you desire only a moderate level of risk and strong performance, then this fund is an excellent option.

Data Date	Investment Rating	Net Assets ($Mil)	Price	Performance Rating/Pts	Total Return Y-T-D	Risk Rating/Pts
12-15	A-	82.10	115.83	A+ / 9.7	16.22%	C+ / 6.7
2014	C	82.10	100.22	C+ / 6.0	2.29%	C+ / 6.4
2013	D-	94.40	103.53	D+ / 2.9	53.84%	C- / 3.6
2012	E	94.40	62.60	E / 0.4	-11.64%	C- / 3.4
2011	E	194.20	19.81	E / 0.3	-38.52%	C- / 3.4
2010	E+	81.10	27.80	E- / 0.1	-46.28%	C / 4.5

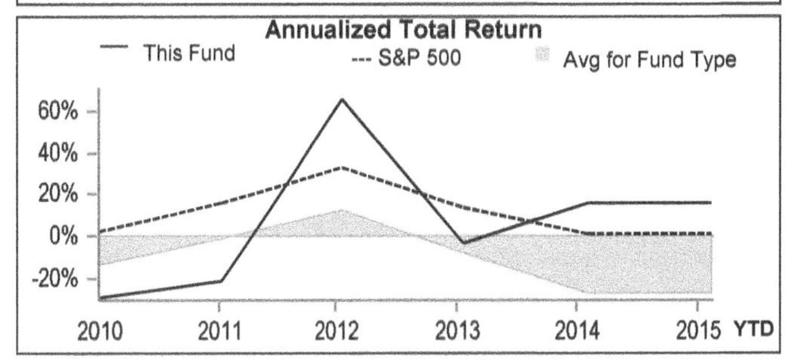

*ProShares UltraShort Health Care (RXD) E+ Very Weak

Fund Family: ProShare Advisors LLC
Fund Type: Health
Inception Date: January 30, 2007

Major Rating Factors:
Very poor performance is the major factor driving the E+ (Very Weak) TheStreet.com Investment Rating for *ProShares UltraShort Health Care. The fund currently has a performance rating of E (Very Weak) based on an annualized return of -39.10% over the last three years and a total return of -21.23% year to date 2015. Factored into the performance evaluation is an expense ratio of 0.95% (low).

The fund's risk rating is currently C- (Fair). It carries a beta of -1.76, meaning the fund's expected move will be -17.6% for every 10% move in the market. Volatility, as measured by both the semi-deviation and a drawdown factor, is considered average. As of December 31, 2015, *ProShares UltraShort Health Care traded at a discount of .84% below its net asset value, which is better than its one-year historical average premium of .05%.

Charles Lowery has been running the fund for 3 years and currently receives a manager quality ranking of 5 (0=worst, 99=best). This fund offers an average level of risk but investors looking for strong performance will be frustrated.

Data Date	Investment Rating	Net Assets ($Mil)	Price	Performance Rating/Pts	Total Return Y-T-D	Risk Rating/Pts
12-15	E+	1.70	47.39	E / 0.3	-21.23%	C- / 3.6
2014	E-	1.70	15.14	E- / 0.2	-41.79%	D / 1.6
2013	E+	2.40	25.99	E- / 0.1	-50.41%	C- / 4.2
2012	E+	5.20	56.06	E / 0.3	-36.15%	C- / 4.2
2011	E+	3.10	20.55	E / 0.5	-29.20%	C- / 4.0
2010	E	4.40	29.22	E+ / 0.6	-15.62%	D+ / 2.8

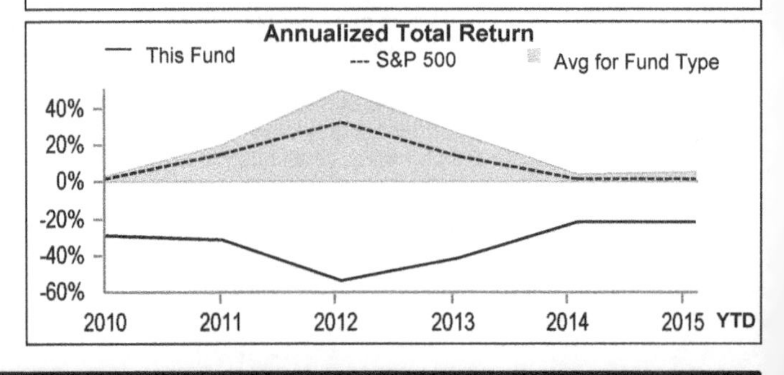

*ProShares UltraShort Industrials (SIJ) D- Weak

Fund Family: ProShare Advisors LLC
Fund Type: Income
Inception Date: January 30, 2007

Major Rating Factors:
Very poor performance is the major factor driving the D- (Weak) TheStreet.com Investment Rating for *ProShares UltraShort Industrials. The fund currently has a performance rating of E+ (Very Weak) based on an annualized return of -26.95% over the last three years and a total return of -4.71% year to date 2015. Factored into the performance evaluation is an expense ratio of 0.95% (low).

The fund's risk rating is currently C (Fair). It carries a beta of -2.11, meaning the fund's expected move will be -21.1% for every 10% move in the market. Volatility, as measured by both the semi-deviation and a drawdown factor, is considered average. As of December 31, 2015, *ProShares UltraShort Industrials traded at a discount of .37% below its net asset value, which is better than its one-year historical average premium of .26%.

Charles Lowery has been running the fund for 3 years and currently receives a manager quality ranking of 36 (0=worst, 99=best). This fund offers an average level of risk but investors looking for strong performance will be frustrated.

Data Date	Investment Rating	Net Assets ($Mil)	Price	Performance Rating/Pts	Total Return Y-T-D	Risk Rating/Pts
12-15	D-	3.00	40.27	E+ / 0.7	-4.71%	C / 4.5
2014	E	3.00	42.37	E / 0.3	-19.44%	C- / 3.7
2013	E	3.20	13.15	E- / 0.1	-49.07%	C- / 3.4
2012	E	6.70	27.63	E- / 0.2	-31.41%	C- / 3.6
2011	E-	7.00	41.56	E / 0.3	-22.46%	D+ / 2.6
2010	E-	8.90	13.07	E / 0.3	-46.26%	D- / 1.3

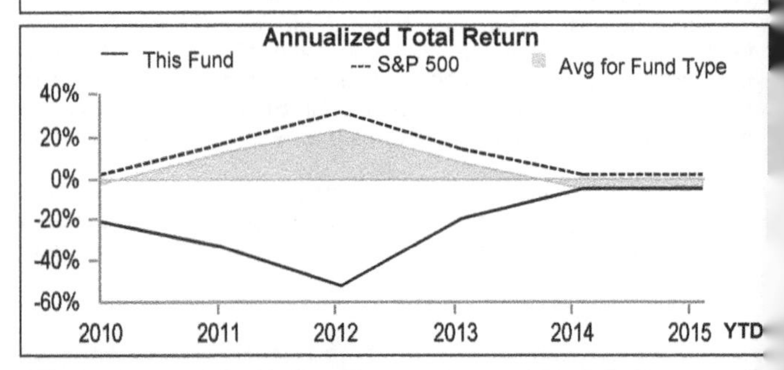

*ProShares UltraShort MidCap 400 (MZZ) D- Weak

Fund Family: ProShare Advisors LLC
Fund Type: Growth
Inception Date: July 11, 2006

Major Rating Factors:
Very poor performance is the major factor driving the D- (Weak) TheStreet.com Investment Rating for *ProShares UltraShort MidCap 400. The fund currently has a performance rating of E+ (Very Weak) based on an annualized return of -24.56% over the last three years and a total return of -3.34% year to date 2015. Factored into the performance evaluation is an expense ratio of 0.95% (low).

The fund's risk rating is currently C (Fair). It carries a beta of -1.93, meaning the fund's expected move will be -19.3% for every 10% move in the market. Volatility, as measured by both the semi-deviation and a drawdown factor, is considered average. As of December 31, 2015, *ProShares UltraShort MidCap 400 traded at a discount of .05% below its net asset value, which is better than its one-year historical average premium of .04%.

Howard Rubin has been running the fund for 9 years and currently receives a manager quality ranking of 39 (0=worst, 99=best). This fund offers an average level of risk but investors looking for strong performance will be frustrated.

Data Date	Investment Rating	Net Assets ($Mil)	Price	Performance Rating/Pts	Total Return Y-T-D	Risk Rating/Pts
12-15	D-	14.70	40.53	E+ / 0.9	-3.34%	C / 5.2
2014	E	14.70	41.77	E / 0.3	-22.82%	C- / 3.7
2013	E	12.30	13.36	E- / 0.2	-42.67%	C- / 3.5
2012	E	25.20	25.31	E- / 0.2	-34.17%	C- / 4.0
2011	E	40.80	38.03	E / 0.3	-21.38%	D+ / 2.9
2010	E-	19.60	11.89	E- / 0.2	-46.22%	D / 1.8

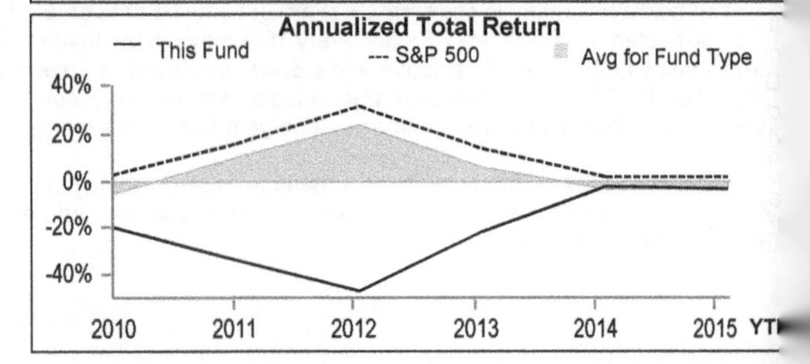

*ProShares UltraShort MSCI Br Cap (BZQ) C Fair

Fund Family: ProShare Advisors LLC
Fund Type: Foreign
Inception Date: June 16, 2009

Major Rating Factors: *ProShares UltraShort MSCI Br Cap has adopted a risky asset allocation strategy and currently receives an overall TheStreet.com Investment Rating of C (Fair). The fund has shown an above average level of volatility, as measured by both semi-deviation and drawdown factors. It carries a beta of -2.84, meaning the fund's expected move will be -28.4% for every 10% move in the market. As of December 31, 2015, *ProShares UltraShort MSCI Br Cap traded at a discount of .37% below its net asset value, which is better than its one-year historical average discount of .02%. The high level of risk (D+, Weak) did however, reward investors with excellent performance.

The fund's performance rating is currently A+ (Excellent). It has registered an annualized return of 38.82% over the last three years and is up 85.40% year to date 2015. Factored into the performance evaluation is an expense ratio of 0.95% (low).

Alexander V. Ilyasov has been running the fund for 7 years and currently receives a manager quality ranking of 99 (0=worst, 99=best). If you are comfortable owning a high risk investment, this fund may be an option.

Data Date	Investment Rating	Net Assets ($Mil)	Price	Performance Rating/Pts	Total Return Y-T-D	Risk Rating/Pts
12-15	C	19.20	81.13	A+ / 9.9	85.40%	D+ / 2.3
2014	D	19.20	82.01	C / 5.0	-2.94%	C- / 3.3
2013	C-	14.00	80.07	B- / 7.3	39.28%	C- / 3.4
2012	E	14.20	63.59	E+ / 0.6	-5.17%	D+ / 2.8
2011	D-	17.00	18.95	C- / 3.9	16.43%	D+ / 2.4
2010	E-	18.80	15.06	E- / 0.2	-34.97%	D / 1.9

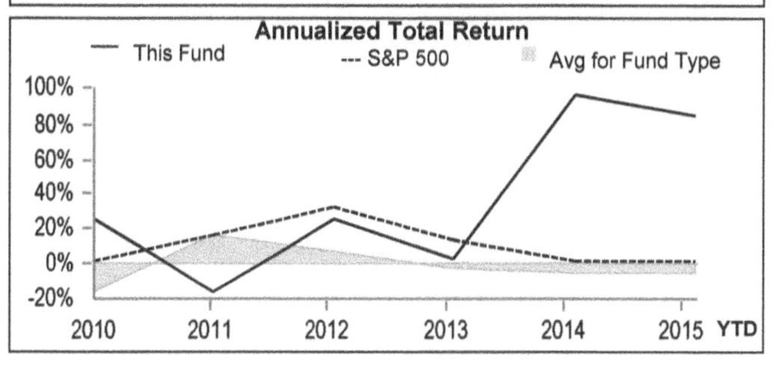

*ProShares UltraShort MSCI EAFE (EFU) D Weak

Fund Family: ProShare Advisors LLC
Fund Type: Foreign
Inception Date: October 23, 2007

Major Rating Factors:
Disappointing performance is the major factor driving the D (Weak) TheStreet.com Investment Rating for *ProShares UltraShort MSCI EAFE. The fund currently has a performance rating of D (Weak) based on an annualized return of -13.95% over the last three years and a total return of -8.40% year to date 2015. Factored into the performance evaluation is an expense ratio of 0.95% (low).

The fund's risk rating is currently C+ (Fair). It carries a beta of -1.92, meaning the fund's expected move will be -19.2% for every 10% move in the market. Volatility, as measured by both the semi-deviation and a drawdown factor, is considered low. As of December 31, 2015, *ProShares UltraShort MSCI EAFE traded at a discount of .05% below its net asset value, which is better than its one-year historical average premium of .05%.

Alexander V. Ilyasov has been running the fund for 7 years and currently receives a manager quality ranking of 28 (0=worst, 99=best). This fund offers only a moderate level of risk but investors looking for strong performance are still waiting.

Data Date	Investment Rating	Net Assets ($Mil)	Price	Performance Rating/Pts	Total Return Y-T-D	Risk Rating/Pts
12-15	D	7.80	41.11	D / 1.7	-8.40%	C+ / 5.7
2014	E+	7.80	44.60	E+ / 0.8	3.17%	C / 4.5
2013	E+	4.70	41.74	E / 0.3	-33.00%	C- / 4.0
2012	E	11.20	16.47	E / 0.4	-38.66%	C- / 3.4
2011	E	27.20	25.94	E+ / 0.6	-4.58%	D+ / 2.9
2010	E-	18.00	26.70	E / 0.3	-30.72%	D / 1.9

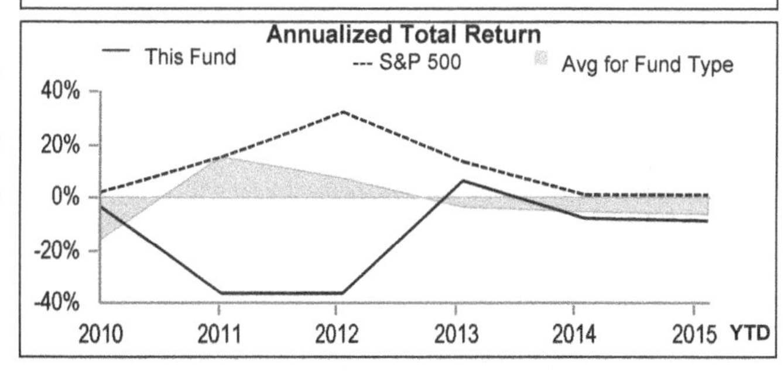

*ProShares UltraShort MSCI Emg Mk (EEV) C+ Fair

Fund Family: ProShare Advisors LLC
Fund Type: Emerging Market
Inception Date: October 30, 2007

Major Rating Factors: Strong performance is the major factor driving the C+ (Fair) TheStreet.com Investment Rating for *ProShares UltraShort MSCI Emg Mk. The fund currently has a performance rating of B (Good) based on an annualized return of 5.08% over the last three years and a total return of 17.85% year to date 2015. Factored into the performance evaluation is an expense ratio of 0.95% (low).

The fund's risk rating is currently C+ (Fair). It carries a beta of -1.95, meaning the fund's expected move will be -19.5% for every 10% move in the market. Volatility, as measured by both the semi-deviation and a drawdown factor, is considered low. As of December 31, 2015, *ProShares UltraShort MSCI Emg Mk traded at a discount of .13% below its net asset value, which is better than its one-year historical average discount of .04%.

Alexander V. Ilyasov has been running the fund for 7 years and currently receives a manager quality ranking of 19 (0=worst, 99=best). If you desire only a moderate level of risk and strong performance, then this fund is an excellent option.

Data Date	Investment Rating	Net Assets ($Mil)	Price	Performance Rating/Pts	Total Return Y-T-D	Risk Rating/Pts
12-15	C+	41.50	23.85	B / 7.8	17.85%	C+ / 5.8
2014	D-	41.50	19.78	D- / 1.1	-8.97%	C / 4.4
2013	E+	47.80	20.13	D- / 1.0	5.69%	C- / 3.6
2012	E	48.60	21.18	E / 0.3	-33.78%	D+ / 3.0
2011	E-	91.60	34.32	E / 0.3	4.32%	D / 2.0
2010	E-	103.80	31.71	E- / 0.1	-41.82%	D- / 1.2

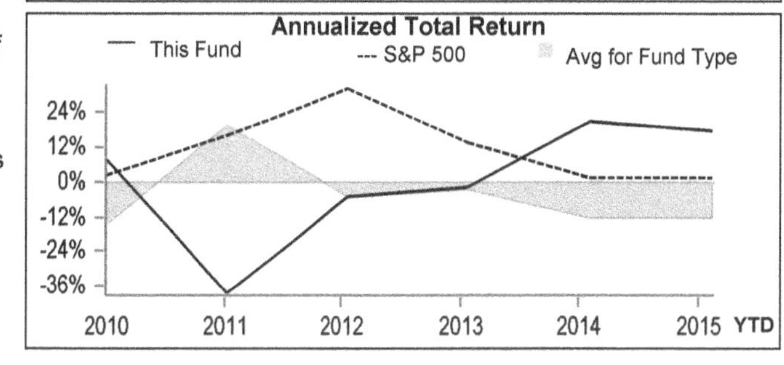

*ProShares UltraShort MSCI Japan (EWV) D- Weak

Fund Family: ProShare Advisors LLC
Fund Type: Foreign
Inception Date: November 6, 2007

Data Date	Investment Rating	Net Assets ($Mil)	Price	Performance Rating/Pts	Total Return Y-T-D	Risk Rating/Pts
12-15	D-	9.40	48.79	E+ / 0.7	-24.88%	C / 4.7
2014	E-	9.40	65.32	E+ / 0.8	1.30%	D / 1.8
2013	E	9.50	15.79	E / 0.4	-43.06%	C- / 3.9
2012	E+	10.90	29.01	E / 0.5	-25.20%	C / 5.3
2011	E+	17.10	37.92	D- / 1.1	13.33%	C- / 3.9
2010	E	12.80	34.00	E / 0.4	-30.85%	C- / 3.2

Major Rating Factors:
Very poor performance is the major factor driving the D- (Weak) TheStreet.com Investment Rating for *ProShares UltraShort MSCI Japan. The fund currently has a performance rating of E+ (Very Weak) based on an annualized return of -24.47% over the last three years and a total return of -24.88% year to date 2015. Factored into the performance evaluation is an expense ratio of 0.95% (low).

The fund's risk rating is currently C (Fair). It carries a beta of -1.54, meaning the fund's expected move will be -15.4% for every 10% move in the market. Volatility, as measured by both the semi-deviation and a drawdown factor, is considered average. As of December 31, 2015, *ProShares UltraShort MSCI Japan traded at a discount of .14% below its net asset value, which is better than its one-year historical average premium of .09%.

Alexander V. Ilyasov has been running the fund for 7 years and currently receives a manager quality ranking of 8 (0=worst, 99=best). This fund offers an average level of risk but investors looking for strong performance will be frustrated.

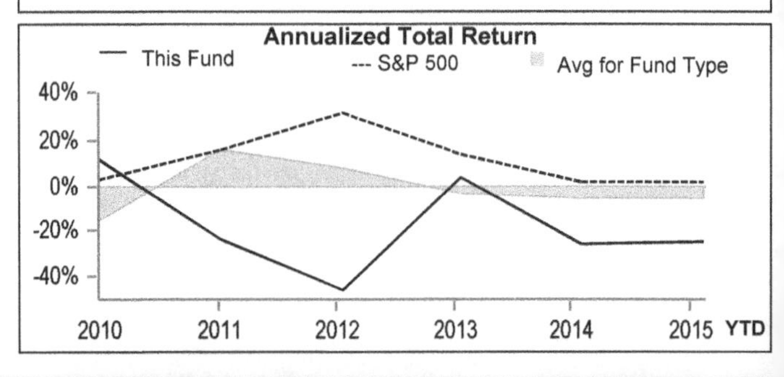

*ProShares UltraShort MSCI PXJ (JPX) D Weak

Fund Family: ProShare Advisors LLC
Fund Type: Foreign
Inception Date: June 16, 2009

Data Date	Investment Rating	Net Assets ($Mil)	Price	Performance Rating/Pts	Total Return Y-T-D	Risk Rating/Pts
12-15	D	2.40	26.11	D+ / 2.7	1.04%	C- / 3.8
2014	E+	2.40	23.70	E+ / 0.8	-6.95%	C- / 3.6
2013	E	1.20	25.37	E / 0.5	-11.96%	C- / 3.1
2012	E	1.50	30.19	E- / 0.2	-40.10%	C- / 3.4
2011	E	2.60	52.11	D- / 1.1	-10.02%	D+ / 2.7
2010	E	2.70	10.88	E- / 0.1	-43.22%	D+ / 2.4

Major Rating Factors:
Disappointing performance is the major factor driving the D (Weak) TheStreet.com Investment Rating for *ProShares UltraShort MSCI PXJ. The fund currently has a performance rating of D+ (Weak) based on an annualized return of -5.54% over the last three years and a total return of 1.04% year to date 2015. Factored into the performance evaluation is an expense ratio of 0.95% (low).

The fund's risk rating is currently C- (Fair). It carries a beta of -1.92, meaning the fund's expected move will be -19.2% for every 10% move in the market. Volatility, as measured by both the semi-deviation and a drawdown factor, is considered average. As of December 31, 2015, *ProShares UltraShort MSCI PXJ traded at a premium of 4.31% above its net asset value, which is worse than its one-year historical average discount of .48%.

Alexander V. Ilyasov has been running the fund for 7 years and currently receives a manager quality ranking of 90 (0=worst, 99=best). This fund offers an average level of risk but investors looking for strong performance will be frustrated.

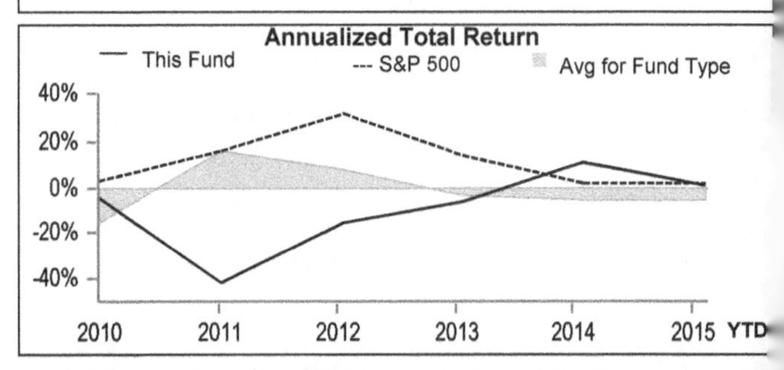

*ProShares UltraShort Nasdaq Biot (BIS) E Very Weak

Fund Family: ProShare Advisors LLC
Fund Type: Health
Inception Date: April 7, 2010

Data Date	Investment Rating	Net Assets ($Mil)	Price	Performance Rating/Pts	Total Return Y-T-D	Risk Rating/Pts
12-15	E	74.50	28.71	E- / 0.1	-36.47%	D / 2.0
2014	E-	74.50	46.00	E- / 0	-55.68%	E- / 0.3
2013	E-	7.80	20.64	E- / 0	-66.02%	D+ / 2.6
2012	E	5.00	66.33	E- / 0.1	-47.85%	C- / 3.4
2011	E	1.60	32.60	E / 0.3	-36.62%	C- / 4.0

Major Rating Factors: *ProShares UltraShort Nasdaq Biot has adopted a very risky asset allocation strategy and currently receives an overall TheStreet.com Investment Rating of E (Very Weak). The fund has a high level of volatility, as measured by both semi-deviation and drawdown factors. It carries a beta of -2.15, meaning the fund's expected move will be -21.5% for every 10% move in the market. As of December 31, 2015, *ProShares UltraShort Nasdaq Biot traded at a discount of .14% below its net asset value. Unfortunately, the high level of risk (D, Weak) failed to pay off as investors endured very poor performance.

The fund's performance rating is currently E- (Very Weak). It has registered an annualized return of -54.53% over the last three years and is down -36.47% year to date 2015. Factored into the performance evaluation is an expense ratio of 0.95% (low).

Charles Lowery has been running the fund for 3 years and currently receives a manager quality ranking of 1 (0=worst, 99=best). If you can tolerate very high levels of risk in the hope of improved future returns, holding this fund may be an option.

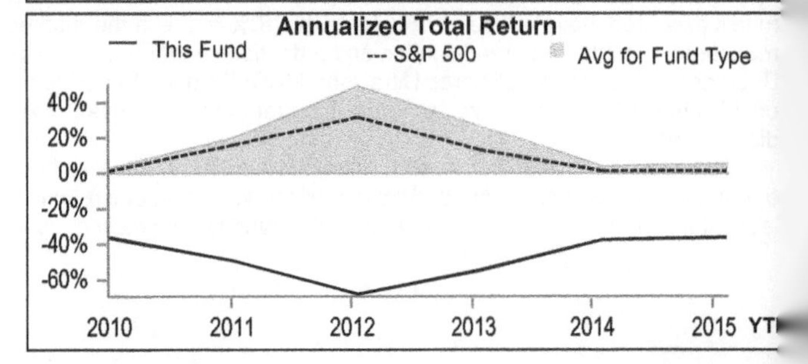

*ProShares UltraShort Oil & Gas (DUG) D+ Weak

Fund Family: ProShare Advisors LLC
Fund Type: Energy/Natural Resources
Inception Date: January 30, 2007

Major Rating Factors: *ProShares UltraShort Oil & Gas receives a TheStreet.com Investment Rating of D+ (Weak). The fund currently has a performance rating of C+ (Fair) based on an annualized return of -2.86% over the last three years and a total return of 35.94% year to date 2015. Factored into the performance evaluation is an expense ratio of 0.95% (low).

The fund's risk rating is currently C- (Fair). It carries a beta of -1.94, meaning the fund's expected move will be -19.4% for every 10% move in the market. Volatility, as measured by both the semi-deviation and a drawdown factor, is considered average. As of December 31, 2015, *ProShares UltraShort Oil & Gas traded at a premium of .03% above its net asset value.

Charles Lowery has been running the fund for 3 years and currently receives a manager quality ranking of 14 (0=worst, 99=best). If you desire an average level of risk, then this fund may be an option.

Data Date	Investment Rating	Net Assets ($Mil)	Price	Performance Rating/Pts	Total Return Y-T-D	Risk Rating/Pts
12-15	D+	48.80	71.87	C+ / 6.2	35.94%	C- / 3.4
2014	E+	48.80	53.34	D- / 1.4	4.98%	D+ / 2.8
2013	E	51.30	49.21	E / 0.3	-35.19%	C- / 3.4
2012	E	57.70	21.04	E / 0.3	-22.81%	C- / 3.1
2011	E	89.50	25.63	E / 0.3	-33.65%	C- / 3.0
2010	E	86.20	37.42	E- / 0.2	-41.26%	D+ / 2.6

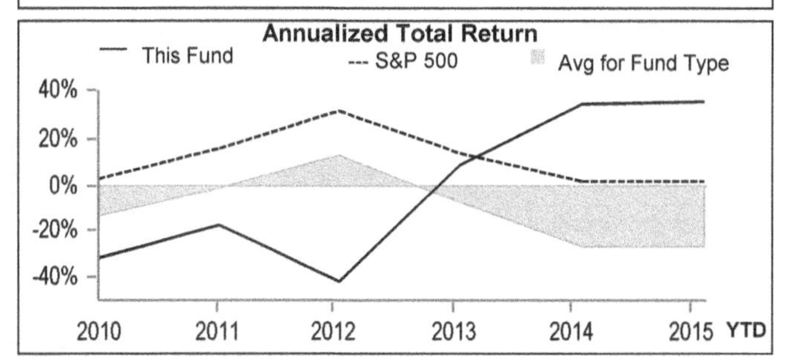

*ProShares UltraShort QQQ (QID) E+ Very Weak

Fund Family: ProShare Advisors LLC
Fund Type: Growth
Inception Date: July 11, 2006

Major Rating Factors:
Very poor performance is the major factor driving the E+ (Very Weak) TheStreet.com Investment Rating for *ProShares UltraShort QQQ. The fund currently has a performance rating of E (Very Weak) based on an annualized return of -35.91% over the last three years and a total return of -25.09% year to date 2015. Factored into the performance evaluation is an expense ratio of 0.95% (low).

The fund's risk rating is currently C- (Fair). It carries a beta of -2.07, meaning the fund's expected move will be -20.7% for every 10% move in the market. Volatility, as measured by both the semi-deviation and a drawdown factor, is considered average. As of December 31, 2015, *ProShares UltraShort QQQ traded at a discount of .07% below its net asset value, which is better than its one-year historical average discount of .01%.

Howard Rubin has been running the fund for 9 years and currently receives a manager quality ranking of 10 (0=worst, 99=best). This fund offers an average level of risk but investors looking for strong performance will be frustrated.

Data Date	Investment Rating	Net Assets ($Mil)	Price	Performance Rating/Pts	Total Return Y-T-D	Risk Rating/Pts
12-15	E+	383.40	29.71	E / 0.3	-25.09%	C- / 4.1
2014	E	383.40	39.48	E- / 0.2	-36.12%	C- / 3.6
2013	E	358.50	14.99	E- / 0.2	-45.23%	C- / 3.6
2012	E	377.30	29.65	E / 0.3	-33.29%	C- / 4.2
2011	E	601.70	45.13	E- / 0.2	-23.75%	C- / 3.1
2010	E	629.70	11.63	E / 0.3	-38.92%	D / 2.2

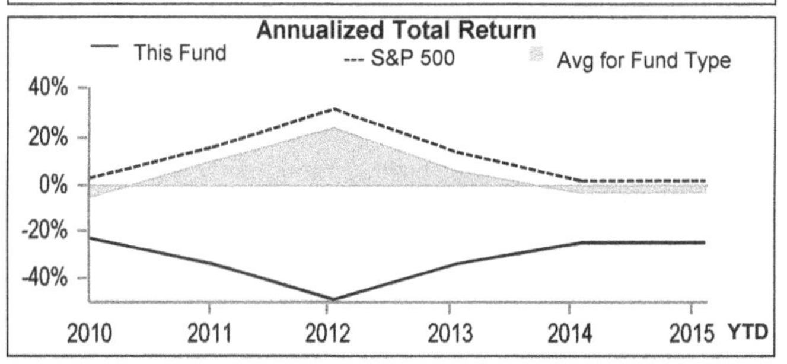

*ProShares UltraShort Real Estate (SRS) D- Weak

Fund Family: ProShare Advisors LLC
Fund Type: Income
Inception Date: January 30, 2007

Major Rating Factors:
Very poor performance is the major factor driving the D- (Weak) TheStreet.com Investment Rating for *ProShares UltraShort Real Estate. The fund currently has a performance rating of E+ (Very Weak) based on an annualized return of -21.62% over the last three years and a total return of -9.59% year to date 2015. Factored into the performance evaluation is an expense ratio of 0.95% (low).

The fund's risk rating is currently C (Fair). It carries a beta of -0.98, meaning the fund's expected move will be -9.8% for every 10% move in the market. Volatility, as measured by both the semi-deviation and a drawdown factor, is considered average. As of December 31, 2015, *ProShares UltraShort Real Estate traded at a discount of .11% below its net asset value, which is better than its one-year historical average premium of .01%.

Charles Lowery has been running the fund for 3 years and currently receives a manager quality ranking of 15 (0=worst, 99=best). This fund offers an average level of risk but investors looking for strong performance will be frustrated.

Data Date	Investment Rating	Net Assets ($Mil)	Price	Performance Rating/Pts	Total Return Y-T-D	Risk Rating/Pts
12-15	D-	48.70	44.81	E+ / 0.8	-9.59%	C / 4.5
2014	E-	48.70	12.73	E / 0.3	-40.40%	D / 2.0
2013	E+	54.80	21.59	E / 0.4	-8.17%	C / 4.6
2012	E	108.90	24.26	E- / 0.1	-35.57%	C- / 4.2
2011	E-	134.80	36.76	E- / 0	-32.93%	D / 1.9
2010	E-	242.40	18.14	E- / 0	-51.63%	D- / 1.0

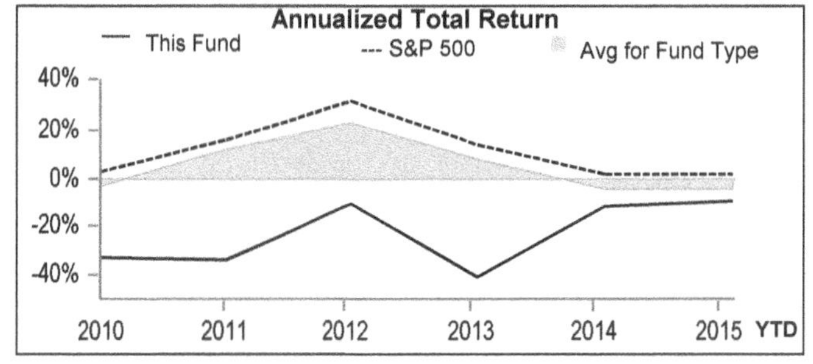

* Denotes ETF Fund

*ProShares UltraShort Russell2000 (TWM) E+ Very Weak

Fund Family: ProShare Advisors LLC
Fund Type: Growth
Inception Date: January 23, 2007

Major Rating Factors: *ProShares UltraShort Russell2000 has adopted a risky asset allocation strategy and currently receives an overall TheStreet.com Investment Rating of E+ (Very Weak). The fund has an above average level of volatility, as measured by both semi-deviation and drawdown factors. It carries a beta of -2.09, meaning the fund's expected move will be -20.9% for every 10% move in the market. As of December 31, 2015, *ProShares UltraShort Russell2000 traded at a premium of .18% above its net asset value, which is worse than its one-year historical average premium of .03%. Unfortunately, the high level of risk (D+, Weak) failed to pay off as investors endured very poor performance.

The fund's performance rating is currently E+ (Very Weak). It has registered an annualized return of -25.32% over the last three years and is down -1.85% year to date 2015. Factored into the performance evaluation is an expense ratio of 0.95% (low).

Michael Neches has been running the fund for 3 years and currently receives a manager quality ranking of 49 (0=worst, 99=best). If you can tolerate high levels of risk in the hope of improved future returns, holding this fund may be an option.

Data Date	Investment Rating	Net Assets ($Mil)	Price	Performance Rating/Pts	Total Return Y-T-D	Risk Rating/Pts
12-15	E+	342.40	39.29	E+ / 0.9	-1.85%	D+ / 2.7
2014	E	342.40	39.59	E / 0.3	-18.61%	C- / 3.5
2013	E	250.70	12.03	E- / 0.1	-48.43%	C- / 3.2
2012	E	264.30	25.35	E- / 0.2	-34.57%	C- / 3.4
2011	E-	297.60	38.61	E- / 0.2	-24.64%	D+ / 2.6
2010	E-	299.00	12.56	E- / 0.2	-50.14%	D / 1.6

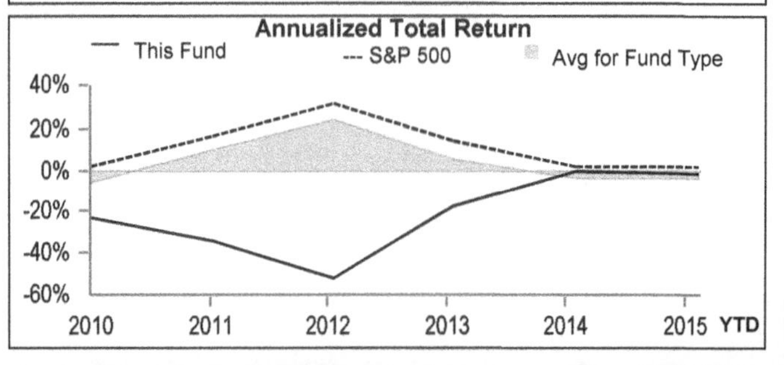

*ProShares UltraShort S&P500 (SDS) E+ Very Weak

Fund Family: ProShare Advisors LLC
Fund Type: Growth
Inception Date: July 11, 2006

Major Rating Factors:
Very poor performance is the major factor driving the E+ (Very Weak) TheStreet.com Investment Rating for *ProShares UltraShort S&P500. The fund currently has a performance rating of E+ (Very Weak) based on an annualized return of -26.97% over the last three years and a total return of -9.61% year to date 2015. Factored into the performance evaluation is an expense ratio of 0.91% (low).

The fund's risk rating is currently C- (Fair). It carries a beta of -1.96, meaning the fund's expected move will be -19.6% for every 10% move in the market. Volatility, as measured by both the semi-deviation and a drawdown factor, is considered average. As of December 31, 2015, *ProShares UltraShort S&P500 traded at a price exactly equal to its net asset value.

Michael Neches has been running the fund for 3 years and currently receives a manager quality ranking of 27 (0=worst, 99=best). This fund offers an average level of risk but investors looking for strong performance will be frustrated.

Data Date	Investment Rating	Net Assets ($Mil)	Price	Performance Rating/Pts	Total Return Y-T-D	Risk Rating/Pts
12-15	E+	1,548.20	19.93	E+ / 0.6	-9.61%	C- / 3.2
2014	E+	1,548.20	22.05	E / 0.3	-27.16%	C- / 3.9
2013	E+	1,368.10	29.66	E / 0.3	-40.84%	C / 4.9
2012	E	1,561.00	54.11	E / 0.3	-30.65%	C- / 3.8
2011	E	2,013.10	19.29	E / 0.5	-20.03%	C- / 3.4
2010	E	2,052.80	23.76	E / 0.4	-32.21%	D+ / 2.9

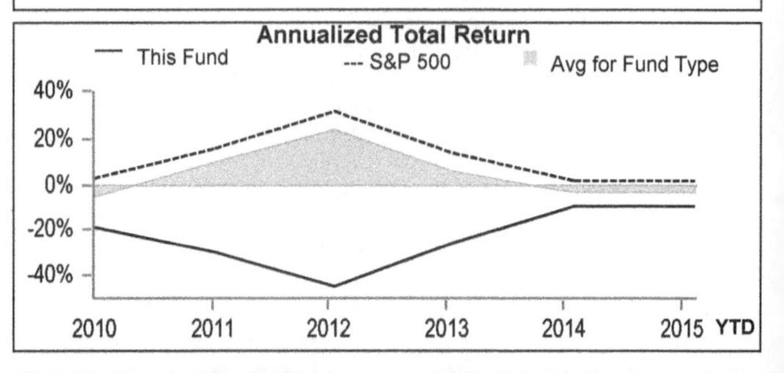

*ProShares UltraShort Semiconduct (SSG) E Very Weak

Fund Family: ProShare Advisors LLC
Fund Type: Income
Inception Date: January 30, 2007

Major Rating Factors: Very poor performance is the major factor driving the E (Very Weak) TheStreet.com Investment Rating for *ProShares UltraShort Semiconduct. The fund currently has a performance rating of E- (Very Weak) based on an annualized return of -41.22% over the last three years and a total return of -19.03% year to date 2015. Factored into the performance evaluation is an expense ratio of 0.95% (low).

The fund's risk rating is currently C- (Fair). It carries a beta of -2.01, meaning the fund's expected move will be -20.1% for every 10% move in the market. Volatility, as measured by both the semi-deviation and a drawdown factor, is considered average. As of December 31, 2015, *ProShares UltraShort Semiconduct traded at a discount of 4.96% below its net asset value, which is better than its one-year historical average premium of .03%.

Charles Lowery has been running the fund for 3 years and currently receives a manager quality ranking of 5 (0=worst, 99=best). This fund offers an average level of risk but investors looking for strong performance will be frustrated.

Data Date	Investment Rating	Net Assets ($Mil)	Price	Performance Rating/Pts	Total Return Y-T-D	Risk Rating/Pts
12-15	E	3.90	39.50	E- / 0.2	-19.03%	C- / 3.1
2014	E	3.90	47.82	E- / 0.2	-53.82%	C- / 3.5
2013	E	5.20	20.25	E / 0.3	-46.75%	C- / 3.3
2012	E	10.60	41.56	E / 0.4	-10.12%	C- / 3.5
2011	E-	15.00	45.59	E- / 0.1	-20.50%	D+ / 2.3
2010	E-	20.10	11.17	E- / 0.2	-38.59%	D- / 1.1

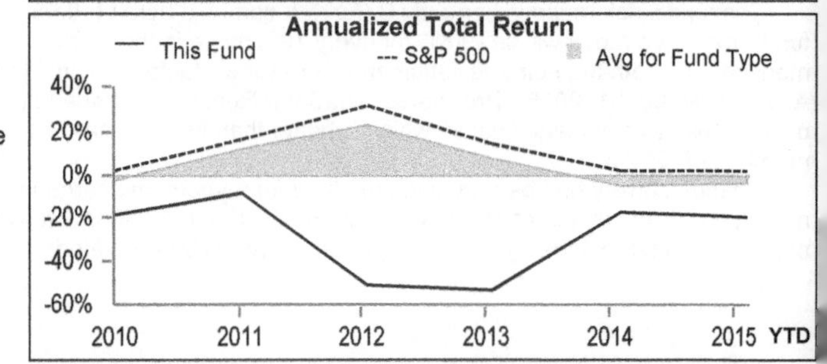

*ProShares UltraShort Silver (ZSL) C+ Fair

Fund Family: ProShare Advisors LLC
Fund Type: Energy/Natural Resources
Inception Date: December 2, 2008

Data Date	Investment Rating	Net Assets ($Mil)	Price	Performance Rating/Pts	Total Return Y-T-D	Risk Rating/Pts
12-15	C+	59.80	64.55	A+ / 9.9	9.61%	C- / 3.2
2014	C	59.80	119.39	A / 9.4	42.95%	D+ / 2.8
2013	E-	113.00	90.19	E+ / 0.7	67.78%	D / 1.9
2012	E-	105.80	50.07	E- / 0	-28.31%	D / 1.9
2011	E-	245.30	15.87	E- / 0	-67.29%	D / 1.9
2010	E-	99.10	9.82	E- / 0	-79.50%	D- / 1.4

Major Rating Factors:
Exceptional performance is the major factor driving the C+ (Fair) TheStreet.com Investment Rating for *ProShares UltraShort Silver. The fund currently has a performance rating of A+ (Excellent) based on an annualized return of 37.39% over the last three years and a total return of 9.61% year to date 2015. Factored into the performance evaluation is an expense ratio of 0.95% (low).

The fund's risk rating is currently C- (Fair). It carries a beta of -0.63, meaning the fund's expected move will be -6.3% for every 10% move in the market. Volatility, as measured by both the semi-deviation and a drawdown factor, is considered average. As of December 31, 2015, *ProShares UltraShort Silver traded at a discount of .05% below its net asset value, which is worse than its one-year historical average discount of .62%.

Michael Neches currently receives a manager quality ranking of 99 (0=worst, 99=best). If you desire an average level of risk and strong performance, then this fund is a good option.

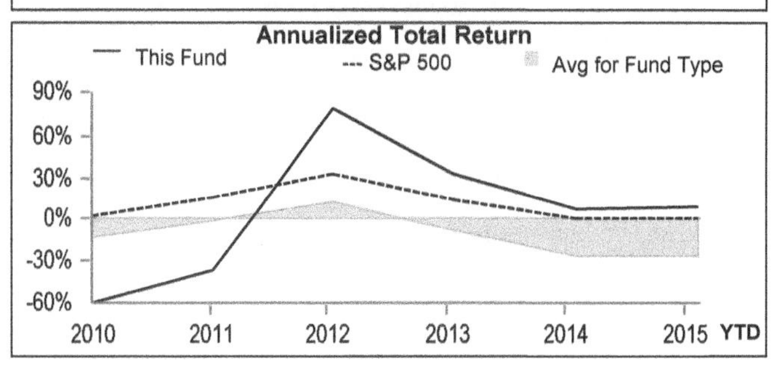

*ProShares UltraShort SmallCap 60 (SDD) D- Weak

Fund Family: ProShare Advisors LLC
Fund Type: Growth
Inception Date: January 23, 2007

Data Date	Investment Rating	Net Assets ($Mil)	Price	Performance Rating/Pts	Total Return Y-T-D	Risk Rating/Pts
12-15	D-	8.40	37.17	E+ / 0.7	-7.54%	C / 4.3
2014	E	8.40	38.81	E- / 0.2	-20.80%	C- / 3.6
2013	E	4.70	11.94	E- / 0.1	-49.38%	C- / 3.3
2012	E	8.30	25.80	E- / 0.2	-33.79%	C- / 3.4
2011	E-	18.10	38.51	E- / 0.1	-30.59%	D+ / 2.6
2010	E-	15.30	13.59	E- / 0.2	-48.39%	D- / 1.5

Major Rating Factors:
Very poor performance is the major factor driving the D- (Weak) TheStreet.com Investment Rating for *ProShares UltraShort SmallCap 60. The fund currently has a performance rating of E+ (Very Weak) based on an annualized return of -27.32% over the last three years and a total return of -7.54% year to date 2015. Factored into the performance evaluation is an expense ratio of 0.95% (low).

The fund's risk rating is currently C (Fair). It carries a beta of -1.95, meaning the fund's expected move will be -19.5% for every 10% move in the market. Volatility, as measured by both the semi-deviation and a drawdown factor, is considered average. As of December 31, 2015, *ProShares UltraShort SmallCap 60 traded at a discount of .35% below its net asset value, which is better than its one-year historical average premium of .11%.

Michael Neches has been running the fund for 3 years and currently receives a manager quality ranking of 24 (0=worst, 99=best). This fund offers an average level of risk but investors looking for strong performance will be frustrated.

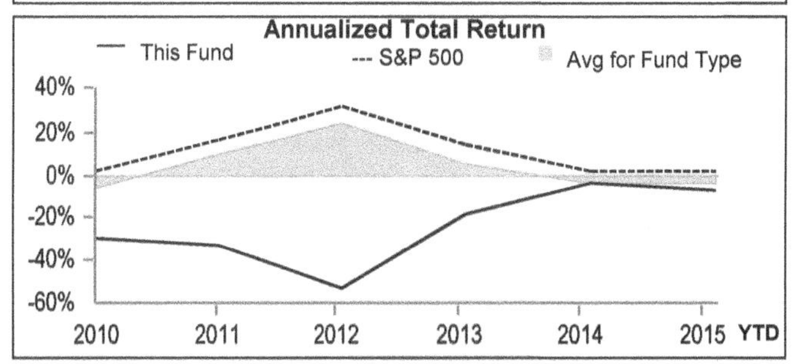

*ProShares UltraShort Technology (REW) E+ Very Weak

Fund Family: ProShare Advisors LLC
Fund Type: Growth
Inception Date: January 30, 2007

Data Date	Investment Rating	Net Assets ($Mil)	Price	Performance Rating/Pts	Total Return Y-T-D	Risk Rating/Pts
12-15	E+	4.10	45.91	E / 0.5	-18.25%	C- / 3.7
2014	E	4.10	54.76	E- / 0.2	-38.11%	C- / 3.8
2013	E	5.60	21.64	E / 0.3	-37.76%	C- / 3.6
2012	E+	12.50	37.00	E / 0.4	-26.81%	C- / 4.2
2011	E	13.40	51.06	E / 0.3	-17.88%	C- / 3.0
2010	E-	18.60	15.51	E / 0.3	-30.82%	D / 2.0

Major Rating Factors:
Very poor performance is the major factor driving the E+ (Very Weak) TheStreet.com Investment Rating for *ProShares UltraShort Technology. The fund currently has a performance rating of E (Very Weak) based on an annualized return of -31.39% over the last three years and a total return of -18.25% year to date 2015. Factored into the performance evaluation is an expense ratio of 0.95% (low).

The fund's risk rating is currently C- (Fair). It carries a beta of -2.01, meaning the fund's expected move will be -20.1% for every 10% move in the market. Volatility, as measured by both the semi-deviation and a drawdown factor, is considered average. As of December 31, 2015, *ProShares UltraShort Technology traded at a discount of .02% below its net asset value, which is better than its one-year historical average premium of .02%.

Charles Lowery has been running the fund for 3 years and currently receives a manager quality ranking of 16 (0=worst, 99=best). This fund offers an average level of risk but investors looking for strong performance will be frustrated.

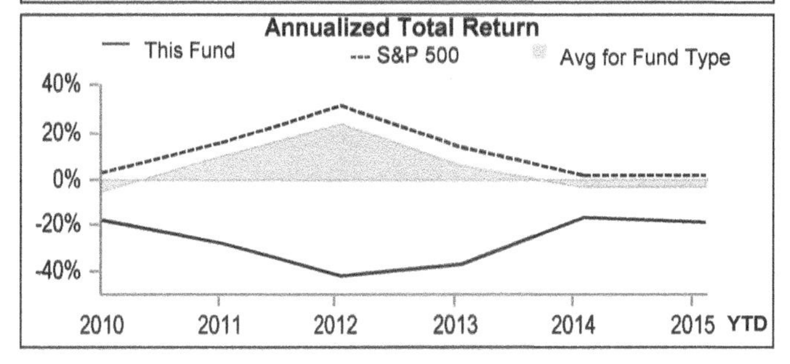

*ProShares UltraShort TIPS (TPS) C Fair

Fund Family: ProShare Advisors LLC
Fund Type: Growth
Inception Date: February 9, 2011

Major Rating Factors: Middle of the road best describes *ProShares UltraShort TIPS whose TheStreet.com Investment Rating is currently a C (Fair). The fund currently has a performance rating of C+ (Fair) based on an annualized return of 2.47% over the last three years and a total return of 2.10% year to date 2015. Factored into the performance evaluation is an expense ratio of 0.95% (low).

The fund's risk rating is currently B- (Good). It carries a beta of -0.09, meaning the fund's expected move will be -0.9% for every 10% move in the market. Volatility, as measured by both the semi-deviation and a drawdown factor, is considered low. As of December 31, 2015, *ProShares UltraShort TIPS traded at a premium of .57% above its net asset value, which is worse than its one-year historical average discount of .12%.

Michelle Liu has been running the fund for 5 years and currently receives a manager quality ranking of 88 (0=worst, 99=best). If you desire an average level of risk, then this fund may be an option.

Data Date	Investment Rating	Net Assets ($Mil)	Price	Performance Rating/Pts	Total Return Y-T-D	Risk Rating/Pts
12-15	C	12.50	28.18	C+ / 5.6	2.10%	B- / 7.0
2014	D+	12.50	27.65	D+ / 2.3	-7.51%	C+ / 6.7
2013	C+	13.60	30.16	C+ / 6.4	14.17%	B- / 7.5
2012	D	3.80	25.57	E+ / 0.7	-11.71%	B- / 7.4

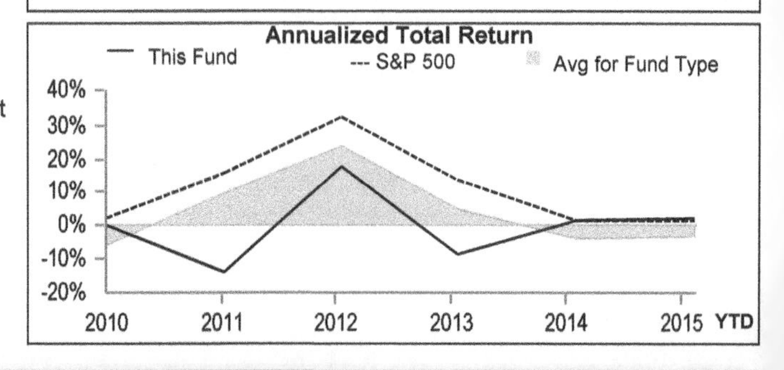

*ProShares UltraShort Utilities (SDP) D- Weak

Fund Family: ProShare Advisors LLC
Fund Type: Utilities
Inception Date: January 30, 2007

Major Rating Factors:
Very poor performance is the major factor driving the D- (Weak) TheStreet.com Investment Rating for *ProShares UltraShort Utilities. The fund currently has a performance rating of E+ (Very Weak) based on an annualized return of -24.56% over the last three years and a total return of 0.90% year to date 2015. Factored into the performance evaluation is an expense ratio of 0.95% (low).

The fund's risk rating is currently C (Fair). It carries a beta of -1.91, meaning the fund's expected move will be -19.1% for every 10% move in the market. Volatility, as measured by both the semi-deviation and a drawdown factor, is considered average. As of December 31, 2015, *ProShares UltraShort Utilities traded at a discount of .23% below its net asset value, which is better than its one-year historical average premium of .02%.

Charles Lowery has been running the fund for 3 years and currently receives a manager quality ranking of 21 (0=worst, 99=best). This fund offers an average level of risk but investors looking for strong performance will be frustrated.

Data Date	Investment Rating	Net Assets ($Mil)	Price	Performance Rating/Pts	Total Return Y-T-D	Risk Rating/Pts
12-15	D-	6.30	47.72	E+ / 0.8	0.90%	C / 4.4
2014	E-	6.30	47.50	E / 0.3	-44.69%	D / 1.8
2013	D-	2.90	20.95	E / 0.4	-22.74%	C+ / 5.6
2012	D-	2.90	29.74	E / 0.4	-15.41%	C+ / 5.8
2011	E+	3.10	31.14	E+ / 0.6	-31.70%	C- / 3.8
2010	E	6.20	16.44	E+ / 0.7	-19.80%	D+ / 2.4

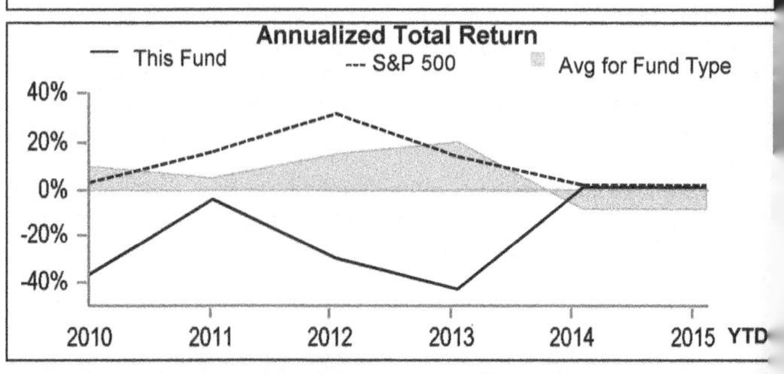

*ProShares UltraShort Yen (YCS) A+ Excellent

Fund Family: ProShare Advisors LLC
Fund Type: Foreign
Inception Date: November 25, 2008

Major Rating Factors:
Exceptional performance is the major factor driving the A+ (Excellent) TheStreet.com Investment Rating for *ProShares UltraShort Yen. The fund currently has a performance rating of A- (Excellent) based on an annualized return of 18.84% over the last three years and a total return of -2.78% year to date 2015. Factored into the performance evaluation is an expense ratio of 0.95% (low).

The fund's risk rating is currently B (Good). It carries a beta of 0.24, meaning the fund's expected move will be 2.4% for every 10% move in the market. Volatility, as measured by both the semi-deviation and a drawdown factor, is considered low. As of December 31, 2015, *ProShares UltraShort Yen traded at a discount of .07% below its net asset value, which is better than its one-year historical average discount of .01%.

Michael Neches currently receives a manager quality ranking of 98 (0=worst, 99=best). If you desire only a moderate level of risk and strong performance, then this fund is an excellent option.

Data Date	Investment Rating	Net Assets ($Mil)	Price	Performance Rating/Pts	Total Return Y-T-D	Risk Rating/Pts
12-15	A+	424.10	87.89	A- / 9.2	-2.78%	B / 8.7
2014	A+	424.10	89.30	A+ / 9.6	27.26%	B / 8.5
2013	B+	588.10	70.91	B / 7.8	33.99%	B / 8.2
2012	D	400.90	50.77	D+ / 2.4	31.05%	C+ / 6.5
2011	D-	221.20	40.95	D- / 1.1	-16.65%	C+ / 6.0
2010	D	207.70	15.67	E / 0.3	-26.43%	C+ / 6.0

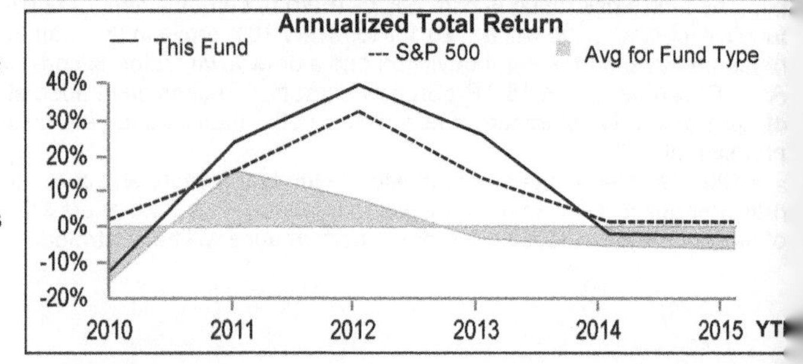

*ProShares UltraSht Australian DI (CROC) A+ Excellent

Fund Family: ProShare Advisors LLC
Fund Type: Growth and Income
Inception Date: July 17, 2012

Major Rating Factors:
Exceptional performance is the major factor driving the A+ (Excellent) TheStreet.com Investment Rating for *ProShares UltraSht Australian DI. The fund currently has a performance rating of A- (Excellent) based on an annualized return of 16.14% over the last three years and a total return of 11.33% year to date 2015. Factored into the performance evaluation is an expense ratio of 1.01% (low).

The fund's risk rating is currently B- (Good). It carries a beta of -0.63, meaning the fund's expected move will be -6.3% for every 10% move in the market. Volatility, as measured by both the semi-deviation and a drawdown factor, is considered low. As of December 31, 2015, *ProShares UltraSht Australian DI traded at a discount of .67% below its net asset value, which is better than its one-year historical average discount of .01%.

Todd B. Johnson currently receives a manager quality ranking of 99 (0=worst, 99=best). If you desire only a moderate level of risk and strong performance, then this fund is an excellent option.

Data Date	Investment Rating	Net Assets ($Mil)	Price	Performance Rating/Pts	Total Return Y-T-D	Risk Rating/Pts
12-15	A+	20.60	58.15	A- / 9.1	11.33%	B- / 7.9
2014	A+	20.60	51.37	A / 9.3	11.50%	B- / 7.7
2013	B+	28.00	46.66	B / 8.0	24.11%	B / 8.3

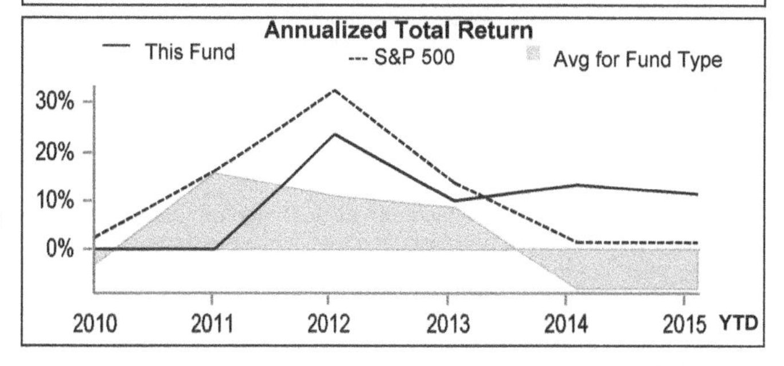

*ProShares UltraSht MSCI Mex Cap (SMK) C Fair

Fund Family: ProShare Advisors LLC
Fund Type: Foreign
Inception Date: June 16, 2009

Major Rating Factors: Middle of the road best describes *ProShares UltraSht MSCI Mex Cap whose TheStreet.com Investment Rating is currently a C (Fair). The fund currently has a performance rating of C+ (Fair) based on an annualized return of 4.58% over the last three years and a total return of 10.36% year to date 2015. Factored into the performance evaluation is an expense ratio of 0.95% (low).

The fund's risk rating is currently C+ (Fair). It carries a beta of -1.20, meaning the fund's expected move will be -12.0% for every 10% move in the market. Volatility, as measured by both the semi-deviation and a drawdown factor, is considered low. As of December 31, 2015, *ProShares UltraSht MSCI Mex Cap traded at a discount of 6.40% below its net asset value, which is better than its one-year historical average discount of .03%.

Alexander V. Ilyasov has been running the fund for 7 years and currently receives a manager quality ranking of 94 (0=worst, 99=best). If you desire an average level of risk, then this fund may be an option.

Data Date	Investment Rating	Net Assets ($Mil)	Price	Performance Rating/Pts	Total Return Y-T-D	Risk Rating/Pts
12-15	C	1.00	26.90	C+ / 6.5	10.36%	C+ / 5.8
2014	E+	1.00	24.38	D- / 1.2	11.50%	C- / 3.4
2013	E	1.10	21.76	E / 0.4	-7.04%	C- / 3.2
2012	E-	1.20	24.81	E- / 0.1	-53.40%	C- / 3.0
2011	E	2.50	49.44	D- / 1.2	-5.56%	C- / 3.1
2010	E	2.60	13.26	E- / 0.1	-49.66%	D+ / 2.5

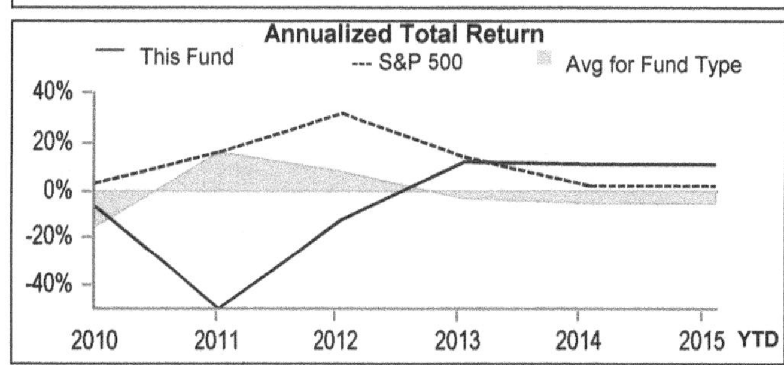

*ProShares USD Covered Bond (COBO) C+ Fair

Fund Family: ProShare Advisors LLC
Fund Type: Global
Inception Date: May 21, 2012

Major Rating Factors: Middle of the road best describes *ProShares USD Covered Bond whose TheStreet.com Investment Rating is currently a C+ (Fair). The fund currently has a performance rating of C (Fair) based on an annualized return of -0.01% over the last three years and a total return of -0.40% year to date 2015. Factored into the performance evaluation is an expense ratio of 0.35% (very low).

The fund's risk rating is currently B+ (Good). It carries a beta of 0.16, meaning the fund's expected move will be 1.6% for every 10% move in the market. Volatility, as measured by both the semi-deviation and a drawdown factor, is considered very low. As of December 31, 2015, *ProShares USD Covered Bond traded at a discount of 1.76% below its net asset value, which is better than its one-year historical average discount of 1.68%.

Alexander V. Ilyasov has been running the fund for 3 years and currently receives a manager quality ranking of 73 (0=worst, 99=best). If you desire an average level of risk, then this fund may be an option.

Data Date	Investment Rating	Net Assets ($Mil)	Price	Performance Rating/Pts	Total Return Y-T-D	Risk Rating/Pts
12-15	C+	6.60	98.52	C / 4.3	-0.40%	B+ / 9.3
2014	C	6.60	100.18	C- / 3.0	1.42%	B+ / 9.7
2013	C-	6.60	99.69	D+ / 2.3	-1.02%	B+ / 9.9

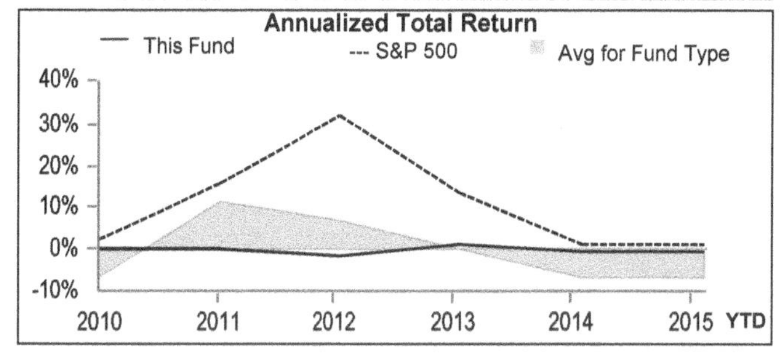

*ProShares VIX Mid-Term Futures E (VIXM) E+ Very Weak

Fund Family: ProShare Advisors LLC
Fund Type: General - Investment Grade
Inception Date: January 3, 2011

Major Rating Factors: *ProShares VIX Mid-Term Futures E has adopted a risky asset allocation strategy and currently receives an overall TheStreet.com Investment Rating of E+ (Very Weak). The fund has an above average level of volatility, as measured by both semi-deviation and drawdown factors. It carries a beta of -0.44, meaning the fund's expected move will be -4.4% for every 10% move in the market. As of December 31, 2015, *ProShares VIX Mid-Term Futures E traded at a premium of .15% above its net asset value, which is worse than its one-year historical average discount of .10%. Unfortunately, the high level of risk (D+, Weak) failed to pay off as investors endured very poor performance.

The fund's performance rating is currently E+ (Very Weak). It has registered an annualized return of -24.76% over the last three years and is down -14.72% year to date 2015. Factored into the performance evaluation is an expense ratio of 0.87% (low).

Todd B. Johnson currently receives a manager quality ranking of 4 (0=worst, 99=best). If you can tolerate high levels of risk in the hope of improved future returns, holding this fund may be an option.

Data Date	Investment Rating	Net Assets ($Mil)	Price	Performance Rating/Pts	Total Return Y-T-D	Risk Rating/Pts
12-15	E+	45.60	54.04	E+ / 0.7	-14.72%	D+ / 2.7
2014	E	45.60	63.89	E / 0.3	-18.05%	C- / 3.2
2013	E	55.00	19.29	E- / 0.1	-38.56%	C- / 3.2
2012	E	37.30	34.22	E- / 0	-55.69%	C- / 3.6

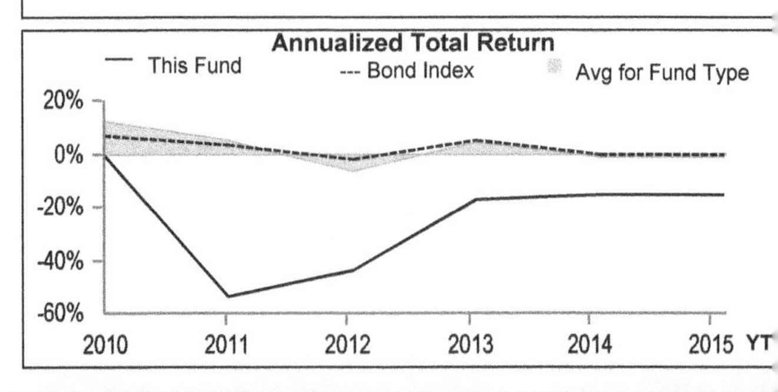

*ProShares VIX Short-Term Futures (VIXY) E- Very Weak

Fund Family: ProShare Advisors LLC
Fund Type: General - Investment Grade
Inception Date: January 3, 2011

Major Rating Factors: *ProShares VIX Short-Term Futures has adopted a very risky asset allocation strategy and currently receives an overall TheStreet.com Investment Rating of E- (Very Weak). The fund has a high level of volatility, as measured by both semi-deviation and drawdown factors. It carries a beta of -0.80, meaning the fund's expected move will be -8.0% for every 10% move in the market. As of December 31, 2015, *ProShares VIX Short-Term Futures traded at a premium of .68% above its net asset value, which is worse than its one-year historical average premium of .21%. Unfortunately, the high level of risk (E-, Very Weak) failed to pay off as investors endured very poor performance.

The fund's performance rating is currently E- (Very Weak). It has registered an annualized return of -43.47% over the last three years and is down -35.32% year to date 2015. Factored into the performance evaluation is an expense ratio of 0.92% (low).

Todd B. Johnson currently receives a manager quality ranking of 0 (0=worst, 99=best). If you can tolerate very high levels of risk in the hope of improved future returns, holding this fund may be an option.

Data Date	Investment Rating	Net Assets ($Mil)	Price	Performance Rating/Pts	Total Return Y-T-D	Risk Rating/Pts
12-15	E-	137.90	13.33	E- / 0.2	-35.32%	E- / 0.1
2014	E-	137.90	20.99	E- / 0.1	-27.42%	E- / 0
2013	E-	279.00	28.53	E- / 0	-60.81%	D / 1.9
2012	E-	147.70	17.01	E- / 0	-78.89%	D / 1.9

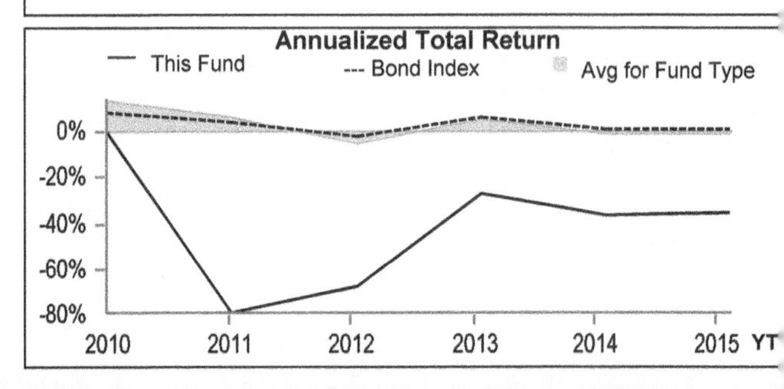

*PureFunds ISE Cyber Security ETF (HACK) D Weak

Fund Family: Factor Advisors LLC
Fund Type: Growth
Inception Date: November 11, 2014

Major Rating Factors:
Disappointing performance is the major factor driving the D (Weak) TheStreet.com Investment Rating for *PureFunds ISE Cyber Security ETF. The fund currently has a performance rating of D (Weak) based on an annualized return of 0.00% over the last three years and a total return of -1.07% year to date 2015. Factored into the performance evaluation is an expense ratio of 0.75% (very low).

The fund's risk rating is currently C (Fair). It carries a beta of 0.00, meaning the fund's expected move will be 0.0% for every 10% move in the market. Volatility, as measured by both the semi-deviation and a drawdown factor, is considered average. As of December 31, 2015, *PureFunds ISE Cyber Security ETF traded at a discount of .31% below its net asset value, which is better than its one-year historical average premium of .03%.

Dustin Lewellyn, CFA has been running the fund for 2 years and currently receives a manager quality ranking of 35 (0=worst, 99=best). This fund offers an average level of risk but investors looking for strong performance will be frustrated.

Data Date	Investment Rating	Net Assets ($Mil)	Price	Performance Rating/Pts	Total Return Y-T-D	Risk Rating/Pts
12-15	D	0.00	25.90	D / 2.2	-1.07%	C / 5.1

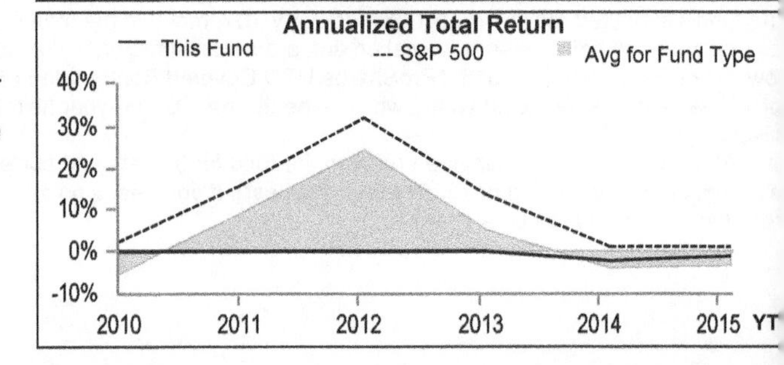

*PureFunds ISE Jr Silver SCM/E ET (SILJ) E- Very Weak

Fund Family: Factor Advisors LLC
Fund Type: Global
Inception Date: November 28, 2012

Data Date	Investment Rating	Net Assets ($Mil)	Price	Performance Rating/Pts	Total Return Y-T-D	Risk Rating/Pts
12-15	E-	7.00	5.07	E- / 0.2	-38.70%	E+ / 0.6
2014	E-	7.00	8.22	E / 0.3	-17.22%	D / 1.7
2013	E-	1.40	9.33	E- / 0.2	-52.14%	D+ / 2.8

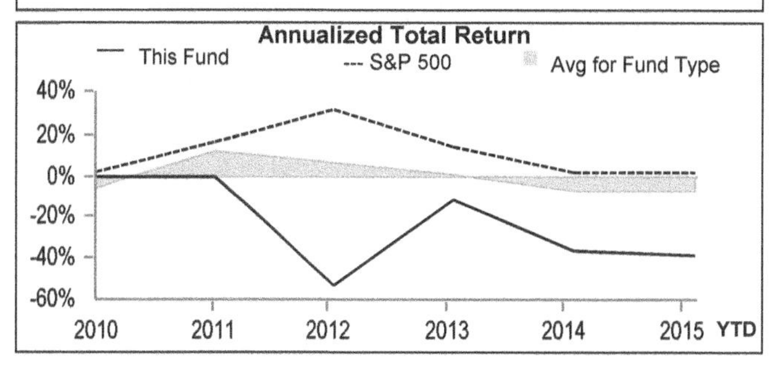

Major Rating Factors: *PureFunds ISE Jr Silver SCM/E ET has adopted a very risky asset allocation strategy and currently receives an overall TheStreet.com Investment Rating of E- (Very Weak). The fund has a high level of volatility, as measured by both semi-deviation and drawdown factors. It carries a beta of 0.68, meaning the fund's expected move will be 6.8% for every 10% move in the market. As of December 31, 2015, *PureFunds ISE Jr Silver SCM/E ET traded at a premium of .40% above its net asset value, which is better than its one-year historical average premium of .71%. Unfortunately, the high level of risk (E+, Very Weak) failed to pay off as investors endured very poor performance.

The fund's performance rating is currently E- (Very Weak). It has registered an annualized return of -36.99% over the last three years and is down -38.70% year to date 2015. Factored into the performance evaluation is an expense ratio of 0.69% (very low).

William D. Martin has been running the fund for 4 years and currently receives a manager quality ranking of 1 (0=worst, 99=best). If you can tolerate very high levels of risk in the hope of improved future returns, holding this fund may be an option.

*QAM Equity Hedge ETF (QEH) C Fair

Fund Family: AdvisorShares Investments LLC
Fund Type: Global
Inception Date: August 7, 2012

Data Date	Investment Rating	Net Assets ($Mil)	Price	Performance Rating/Pts	Total Return Y-T-D	Risk Rating/Pts
12-15	C	7.00	27.32	C / 5.2	-2.57%	B- / 7.3
2014	C-	7.00	28.34	C- / 3.4	2.47%	B- / 7.8
2013	B+	7.00	28.01	C+ / 6.5	9.12%	B+ / 9.6

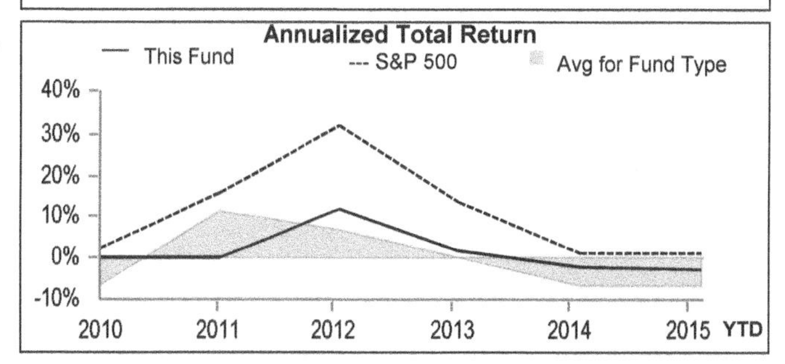

Major Rating Factors: Middle of the road best describes *QAM Equity Hedge ETF whose TheStreet.com Investment Rating is currently a C (Fair). The fund currently has a performance rating of C (Fair) based on an annualized return of 2.54% over the last three years and a total return of -2.57% year to date 2015. Factored into the performance evaluation is an expense ratio of 1.50% (average).

The fund's risk rating is currently B- (Good). It carries a beta of 0.44, meaning the fund's expected move will be 4.4% for every 10% move in the market. Volatility, as measured by both the semi-deviation and a drawdown factor, is considered low. As of December 31, 2015, *QAM Equity Hedge ETF traded at a premium of 2.05% above its net asset value, which is worse than its one-year historical average discount of .27%.

Akos Belezany currently receives a manager quality ranking of 77 (0=worst, 99=best). If you desire an average level of risk, then this fund may be an option.

*QuantShares US Market Neutral Si (SIZ) C- Fair

Fund Family: FFCM LLC
Fund Type: Growth
Inception Date: September 6, 2011

Data Date	Investment Rating	Net Assets ($Mil)	Price	Performance Rating/Pts	Total Return Y-T-D	Risk Rating/Pts
12-15	C-	1.20	21.35	D+ / 2.5	-11.12%	B / 8.3
2014	C-	1.20	24.21	D+ / 2.3	-4.91%	B / 8.9
2013	C	1.30	25.46	D+ / 2.7	1.03%	B+ / 9.5
2012	C-	5.00	25.12	D / 1.6	-0.30%	B+ / 9.5

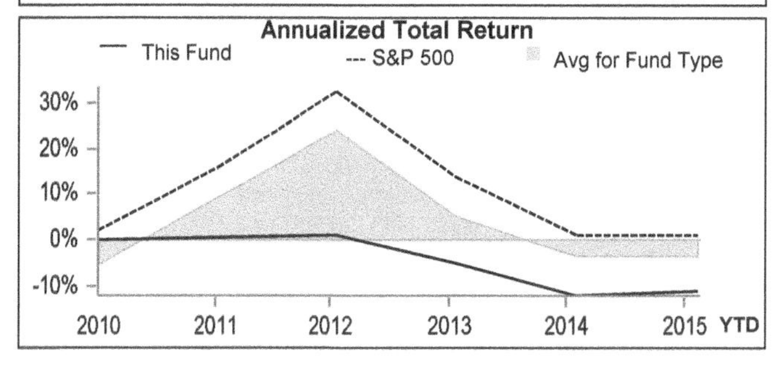

Major Rating Factors:
Disappointing performance is the major factor driving the C- (Fair) TheStreet.com Investment Rating for *QuantShares US Market Neutral Si. The fund currently has a performance rating of D+ (Weak) based on an annualized return of -5.38% over the last three years and a total return of -11.12% year to date 2015. Factored into the performance evaluation is an expense ratio of 1.49% (average).

The fund's risk rating is currently B (Good). It carries a beta of -0.02, meaning the fund's expected move will be -0.2% for every 10% move in the market. Volatility, as measured by both the semi-deviation and a drawdown factor, is considered low. As of December 31, 2015, *QuantShares US Market Neutral Si traded at a discount of .28% below its net asset value, which is better than its one-year historical average discount of .05%.

Charles Martin has been running the fund for 5 years and currently receives a manager quality ranking of 30 (0=worst, 99=best). This fund offers only a moderate level of risk but investors looking for strong performance are still waiting.

*QuantShares US Market Neutral Va (CHEP) C Fair

Fund Family: FFCM LLC
Fund Type: Income
Inception Date: September 12, 2011

Data Date	Investment Rating	Net Assets ($Mil)	Price	Perfor-mance Rating/Pts	Total Return Y-T-D	Risk Rating/Pts
12-15	C	2.80	24.18	C- / 3.3	-10.44%	B / 8.4
2014	C-	2.80	27.12	C- / 3.2	-2.00%	B- / 7.3
2013	B+	1.40	27.53	C+ / 6.7	11.05%	B+ / 9.2
2012	D+	3.70	24.57	D- / 1.5	-4.30%	B+ / 9.1

Major Rating Factors: Middle of the road best describes *QuantShares US Market Neutral Va whose TheStreet.com Investment Rating is currently a C (Fair). The fund currently has a performance rating of C- (Fair) based on an annualized return of -1.00% over the last three years and a total return of -10.44% year to date 2015. Factored into the performance evaluation is an expense ratio of 1.49% (average).

The fund's risk rating is currently B (Good). It carries a beta of 0.31, meaning the fund's expected move will be 3.1% for every 10% move in the market. Volatility, as measured by both the semi-deviation and a drawdown factor, is considered low. As of December 31, 2015, *QuantShares US Market Neutral Va traded at a discount of .21% below its net asset value, which is better than its one-year historical average discount of .08%.

Charles Martin has been running the fund for 5 years and currently receives a manager quality ranking of 31 (0=worst, 99=best). If you desire an average level of risk, then this fund may be an option.

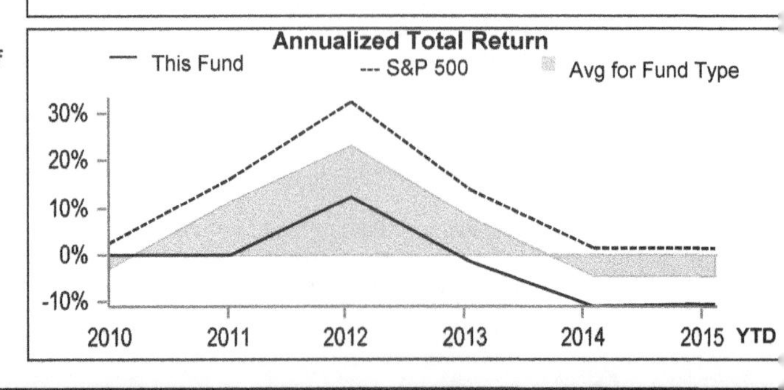

*QuantShares US Mkt Neut Anti-Bet (BTAL) C Fair

Fund Family: FFCM LLC
Fund Type: Growth
Inception Date: September 12, 2011

Data Date	Investment Rating	Net Assets ($Mil)	Price	Perfor-mance Rating/Pts	Total Return Y-T-D	Risk Rating/Pts
12-15	C	2.90	20.68	C / 4.3	4.33%	B / 8.3
2014	D	2.90	20.65	D+ / 2.6	7.78%	C+ / 6.1
2013	D	2.90	19.00	E+ / 0.9	-10.68%	B- / 7.6
2012	D	17.40	22.04	E+ / 0.7	-5.78%	B / 8.1

Major Rating Factors: Middle of the road best describes *QuantShares US Mkt Neut Anti-Bet whose TheStreet.com Investment Rating is currently a C (Fair). The fund currently has a performance rating of C (Fair) based on an annualized return of -1.21% over the last three years and a total return of 4.33% year to date 2015. Factored into the performance evaluation is an expense ratio of 0.99% (low).

The fund's risk rating is currently B (Good). It carries a beta of -0.50, meaning the fund's expected move will be -5.0% for every 10% move in the market. Volatility, as measured by both the semi-deviation and a drawdown factor, is considered low. As of December 31, 2015, *QuantShares US Mkt Neut Anti-Bet traded at a discount of .14% below its net asset value, which is better than its one-year historical average premium of .07%.

Charles Martin has been running the fund for 5 years and currently receives a manager quality ranking of 89 (0=worst, 99=best). If you desire an average level of risk, then this fund may be an option.

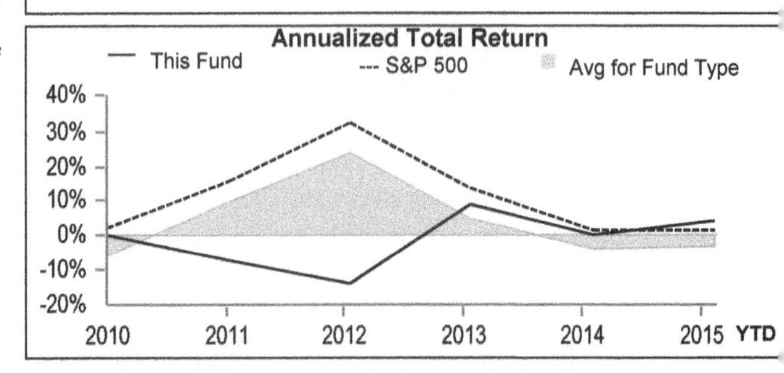

*QuantShares US Mkt Neutral Momen (MOM) B+ Good

Fund Family: FFCM LLC
Fund Type: Growth
Inception Date: September 6, 2011

Data Date	Investment Rating	Net Assets ($Mil)	Price	Perfor-mance Rating/Pts	Total Return Y-T-D	Risk Rating/Pts
12-15	B+	1.20	27.62	B- / 7.0	15.07%	B / 8.7
2014	C-	1.20	23.52	D / 1.9	-7.83%	B / 8.7
2013	B-	1.30	25.69	C+ / 5.9	4.50%	B / 8.7
2012	D	1.20	24.42	E+ / 0.7	-7.01%	B / 8.6

Major Rating Factors: Strong performance is the major factor driving the B+ (Good) TheStreet.com Investment Rating for *QuantShares US Mkt Neutral Momen. The fund currently has a performance rating of B- (Good) based on an annualized return of 4.19% over the last three years and a total return of 15.07% year to date 2015. Factored into the performance evaluation is an expense ratio of 1.49% (average).

The fund's risk rating is currently B (Good). It carries a beta of -0.26, meaning the fund's expected move will be -2.6% for every 10% move in the market. Volatility, as measured by both the semi-deviation and a drawdown factor, is considered low. As of December 31, 2015, *QuantShares US Mkt Neutral Momen traded at a discount of .47% below its net asset value, which is better than its one-year historical average premium of .64%.

Charles Martin has been running the fund for 5 years and currently receives a manager quality ranking of 93 (0=worst, 99=best). If you desire only a moderate level of risk and strong performance, then this fund is an excellent option.

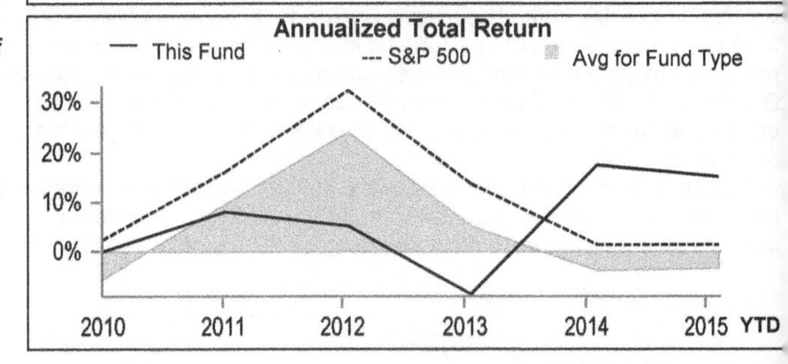

* Denotes ETF Fund

*Ranger Equity Bear ETF (HDGE) D- Weak

Fund Family: AdvisorShares Investments LLC
Fund Type: Growth
Inception Date: January 27, 2011

Major Rating Factors:
Disappointing performance is the major factor driving the D- (Weak) TheStreet.com Investment Rating for *Ranger Equity Bear ETF. The fund currently has a performance rating of D- (Weak) based on an annualized return of -15.40% over the last three years and a total return of -6.27% year to date 2015. Factored into the performance evaluation is an expense ratio of 1.65% (above average).

The fund's risk rating is currently C (Fair). It carries a beta of -1.03, meaning the fund's expected move will be -10.3% for every 10% move in the market. Volatility, as measured by both the semi-deviation and a drawdown factor, is considered average. As of December 31, 2015, *Ranger Equity Bear ETF traded at a premium of .09% above its net asset value.

Brad H. Lamensdorf currently receives a manager quality ranking of 42 (0=worst, 99=best). This fund offers an average level of risk but investors looking for strong performance will be frustrated.

Data Date	Investment Rating	Net Assets ($Mil)	Price	Performance Rating/Pts	Total Return Y-T-D	Risk Rating/Pts
12-15	D-	181.50	10.76	D- / 1.5	-6.27%	C / 4.6
2014	D-	181.50	11.43	E+ / 0.7	-10.84%	C / 4.9
2013	E+	130.90	12.76	E / 0.3	-27.86%	C / 4.9
2012	D-	218.90	18.28	E- / 0.2	-24.95%	C+ / 6.2

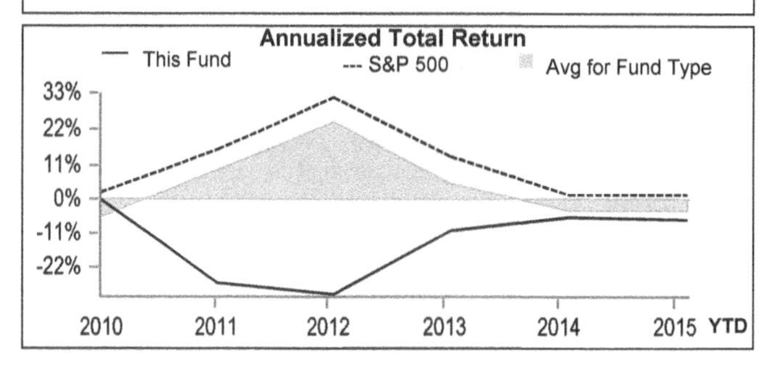

*Reality Shares DIVS ETF (DIVY) C- Fair

Fund Family: Reality Shares Advisors LLC
Fund Type: Global
Inception Date: December 18, 2014

Major Rating Factors: Middle of the road best describes *Reality Shares DIVS ETF whose TheStreet.com Investment Rating is currently a C- (Fair). The fund currently has a performance rating of C (Fair) based on an annualized return of 0.00% over the last three years and a total return of 0.14% year to date 2015.

The fund's risk rating is currently C+ (Fair). It carries a beta of 0.00, meaning the fund's expected move will be 0.0% for every 10% move in the market. Volatility, as measured by both the semi-deviation and a drawdown factor, is considered low. As of December 31, 2015, *Reality Shares DIVS ETF traded at a discount of .13% below its net asset value, which is better than its one-year historical average premium of .42%.

Eric R. Ervin has been running the fund for 2 years and currently receives a manager quality ranking of 71 (0=worst, 99=best). If you desire an average level of risk, then this fund may be an option.

Data Date	Investment Rating	Net Assets ($Mil)	Price	Performance Rating/Pts	Total Return Y-T-D	Risk Rating/Pts
12-15	C-	0.00	23.32	C / 4.7	0.14%	C+ / 5.7

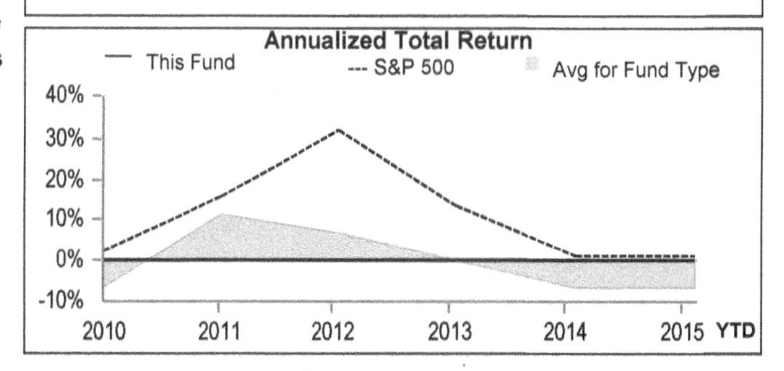

*Recon Cap NASDAQ 100 Cov Call (QYLD) C- Fair

Fund Family: Recon Capital Advisors LLC
Fund Type: Growth
Inception Date: December 12, 2013

Major Rating Factors: Middle of the road best describes *Recon Cap NASDAQ 100 Cov Call whose TheStreet.com Investment Rating is currently a C- (Fair). The fund currently has a performance rating of C (Fair) based on an annualized return of 0.00% over the last three years and a total return of -1.69% year to date 2015. Factored into the performance evaluation is an expense ratio of 0.60% (very low).

The fund's risk rating is currently C+ (Fair). It carries a beta of 0.00, meaning the fund's expected move will be 0.0% for every 10% move in the market. Volatility, as measured by both the semi-deviation and a drawdown factor, is considered low. As of December 31, 2015, *Recon Cap NASDAQ 100 Cov Call traded at a premium of .77% above its net asset value, which is worse than its one-year historical average premium of .17%.

Garrett Paolella has been running the fund for 3 years and currently receives a manager quality ranking of 39 (0=worst, 99=best). If you desire an average level of risk, then this fund may be an option.

Data Date	Investment Rating	Net Assets ($Mil)	Price	Performance Rating/Pts	Total Return Y-T-D	Risk Rating/Pts
12-15	C-	12.40	23.41	C / 4.4	-1.69%	C+ / 6.8
2014	D-	12.40	24.01	D / 1.6	-5.55%	C / 4.3

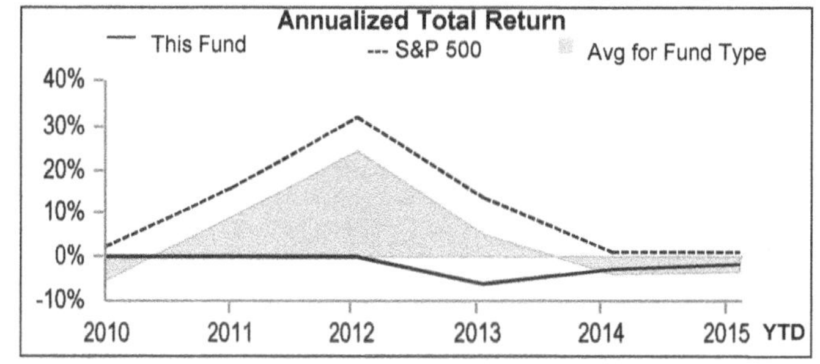

*Recon Capital DAX Germany (DAX) C- Fair

Fund Family: Recon Capital Advisors LLC
Fund Type: Foreign
Inception Date: October 22, 2014

Major Rating Factors: Middle of the road best describes *Recon Capital DAX Germany whose TheStreet.com Investment Rating is currently a C- (Fair). The fund currently has a performance rating of C- (Fair) based on an annualized return of 0.00% over the last three years and a total return of -4.87% year to date 2015.

The fund's risk rating is currently B- (Good). It carries a beta of 0.00, meaning the fund's expected move will be 0.0% for every 10% move in the market. Volatility, as measured by both the semi-deviation and a drawdown factor, is considered low. As of December 31, 2015, *Recon Capital DAX Germany traded at a discount of .72% below its net asset value, which is better than its one-year historical average premium of .01%.

Garrett Paolella currently receives a manager quality ranking of 33 (0=worst, 99=best). If you desire an average level of risk, then this fund may be an option.

Data Date	Investment Rating	Net Assets ($Mil)	Price	Performance Rating/Pts	Total Return Y-T-D	Risk Rating/Pts
12-15	C-	0.00	24.89	C- / 3.1	-4.87%	B- / 7.8

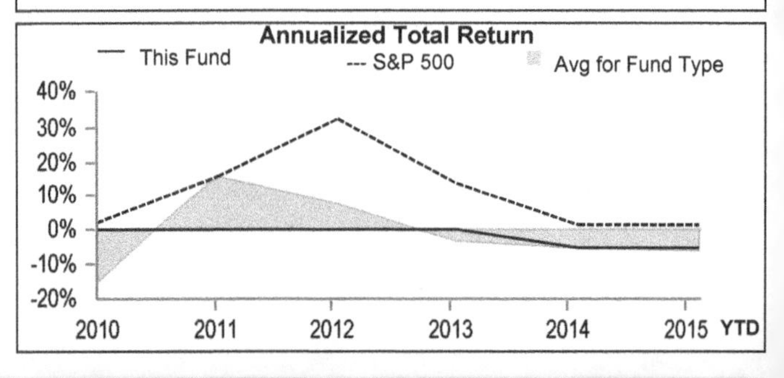

*Renaissance International IPO ET (IPOS) C- Fair

Fund Family: Renaissance Capital LLC
Fund Type: Foreign
Inception Date: October 1, 2014

Major Rating Factors:
Disappointing performance is the major factor driving the C- (Fair) TheStreet.com Investment Rating for *Renaissance International IPO ET. The fund currently has a performance rating of D+ (Weak) based on an annualized return of 0.00% over the last three years and a total return of -2.82% year to date 2015. Factored into the performance evaluation is an expense ratio of 0.80% (very low).

The fund's risk rating is currently B- (Good). It carries a beta of 0.00, meaning the fund's expected move will be 0.0% for every 10% move in the market. Volatility, as measured by both the semi-deviation and a drawdown factor, is considered low. As of December 31, 2015, *Renaissance International IPO ET traded at a discount of .92% below its net asset value, which is better than its one-year historical average premium of .67%.

Linda R. Killian currently receives a manager quality ranking of 52 (0=worst, 99=best). This fund offers only a moderate level of risk but investors looking for strong performance are still waiting.

Data Date	Investment Rating	Net Assets ($Mil)	Price	Performance Rating/Pts	Total Return Y-T-D	Risk Rating/Pts
12-15	C-	0.00	19.48	D+ / 2.6	-2.82%	B- / 7.9

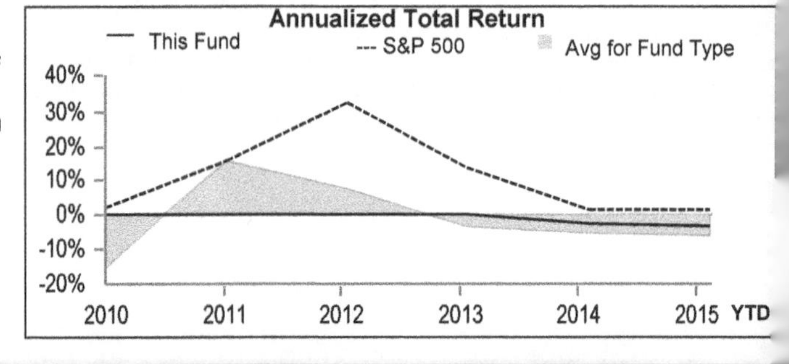

*Renaissance IPO ETF (IPO) D Weak

Fund Family: Renaissance Capital LLC
Fund Type: Growth
Inception Date: October 14, 2013

Major Rating Factors:
Disappointing performance is the major factor driving the D (Weak) TheStreet.com Investment Rating for *Renaissance IPO ETF. The fund currently has a performance rating of D (Weak) based on an annualized return of 0.00% over the last three years and a total return of -7.90% year to date 2015. Factored into the performance evaluation is an expense ratio of 0.60% (very low).

The fund's risk rating is currently C+ (Fair). It carries a beta of 0.00, meaning the fund's expected move will be 0.0% for every 10% move in the market. Volatility, as measured by both the semi-deviation and a drawdown factor, is considered low. As of December 31, 2015, *Renaissance IPO ETF traded at a premium of .24% above its net asset value, which is worse than its one-year historical average discount of .09%.

Linda R. Killian has been running the fund for 3 years and currently receives a manager quality ranking of 17 (0=worst, 99=best). This fund offers only a moderate level of risk but investors looking for strong performance are still waiting.

Data Date	Investment Rating	Net Assets ($Mil)	Price	Performance Rating/Pts	Total Return Y-T-D	Risk Rating/Pts
12-15	D	33.30	20.89	D / 1.9	-7.90%	C+ / 6.0
2014	D+	33.30	22.82	C / 4.4	6.94%	C / 4.9

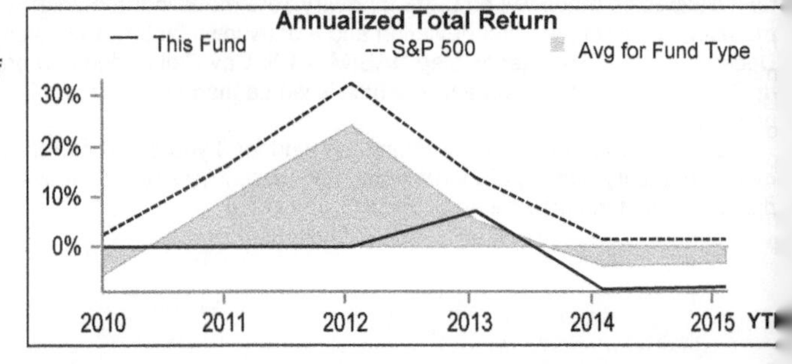

*ROBO Glbl Robots and Auto Index (ROBO) C- Fair

Fund Family: Exchange Traded Concepts LLC
Fund Type: Growth
Inception Date: October 21, 2013

Major Rating Factors: Middle of the road best describes *ROBO Glbl Robots and Auto Index whose TheStreet.com Investment Rating is currently a C- (Fair). The fund currently has a performance rating of C- (Fair) based on an annualized return of 0.00% over the last three years and a total return of -5.24% year to date 2015. Factored into the performance evaluation is an expense ratio of 0.95% (low).

The fund's risk rating is currently B- (Good). It carries a beta of 0.00, meaning the fund's expected move will be 0.0% for every 10% move in the market. Volatility, as measured by both the semi-deviation and a drawdown factor, is considered low. As of December 31, 2015, *ROBO Glbl Robots and Auto Index traded at a discount of .62% below its net asset value, which is better than its one-year historical average discount of .06%.

Denise M. Krisko has been running the fund for 1 year and currently receives a manager quality ranking of 23 (0=worst, 99=best). If you desire an average level of risk, then this fund may be an option.

Data Date	Investment Rating	Net Assets ($Mil)	Price	Perfor-mance Rating/Pts	Total Return Y-T-D	Risk Rating/Pts
12-15	C-	102.30	24.20	C- / 3.0	-5.24%	B- / 7.8
2014	D-	102.30	25.70	D / 1.7	-4.60%	C- / 3.9

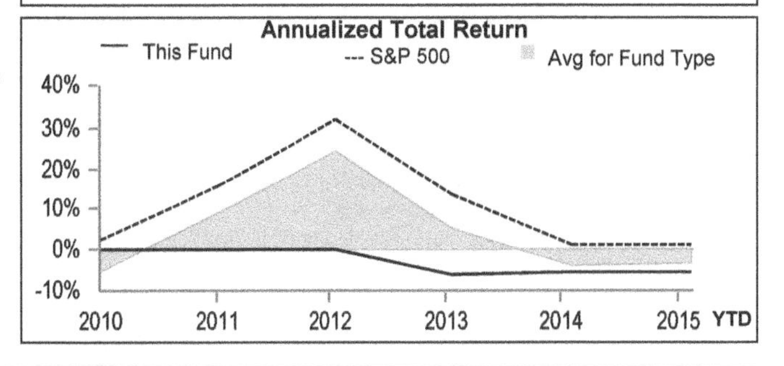

*Schwab Emerging Markets Equity E (SCHE) D+ Weak

Fund Family: Charles Schwab Investment Managemen
Fund Type: Foreign
Inception Date: January 13, 2010

Major Rating Factors:
Disappointing performance is the major factor driving the D+ (Weak) TheStreet.com Investment Rating for *Schwab Emerging Markets Equity E. The fund currently has a performance rating of D (Weak) based on an annualized return of -7.62% over the last three years and a total return of -15.72% year to date 2015. Factored into the performance evaluation is an expense ratio of 0.14% (very low).

The fund's risk rating is currently C+ (Fair). It carries a beta of 0.92, meaning that its performance tracks fairly well with that of the overall stock market. Volatility, as measured by both the semi-deviation and a drawdown factor, is considered low. As of December 31, 2015, *Schwab Emerging Markets Equity E traded at a discount of .41% below its net asset value, which is better than its one-year historical average premium of .34%.

Agnes Hong has been running the fund for 6 years and currently receives a manager quality ranking of 14 (0=worst, 99=best). This fund offers only a moderate level of risk but investors looking for strong performance are still waiting.

Data Date	Investment Rating	Net Assets ($Mil)	Price	Perfor-mance Rating/Pts	Total Return Y-T-D	Risk Rating/Pts
12-15	D+	1,211.60	19.51	D / 2.0	-15.72%	C+ / 6.9
2014	D+	1,211.60	23.90	C- / 3.6	3.39%	C+ / 5.9
2013	D	895.60	24.60	D / 1.9	-8.83%	C+ / 6.9
2012	B+	694.10	26.39	A- / 9.0	16.40%	C+ / 6.9
2011	D	0.00	22.87	D- / 1.0	-17.07%	B- / 7.0

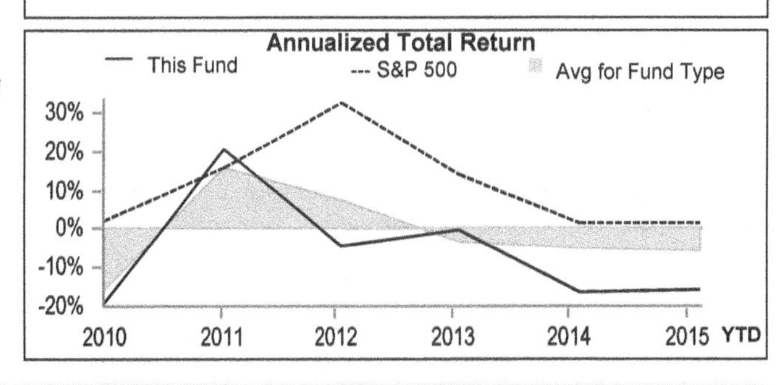

*Schwab Fndmtl EM Lrg Compny Idx (FNDE) D Weak

Fund Family: Charles Schwab Investment Managemen
Fund Type: Emerging Market
Inception Date: August 14, 2013

Major Rating Factors:
Very poor performance is the major factor driving the D (Weak) TheStreet.com Investment Rating for *Schwab Fndmtl EM Lrg Compny Idx. The fund currently has a performance rating of E+ (Very Weak) based on an annualized return of 0.00% over the last three years and a total return of -19.32% year to date 2015. Factored into the performance evaluation is an expense ratio of 0.46% (very low).

The fund's risk rating is currently C+ (Fair). It carries a beta of 0.00, meaning the fund's expected move will be 0.0% for every 10% move in the market. Volatility, as measured by both the semi-deviation and a drawdown factor, is considered low. As of December 31, 2015, *Schwab Fndmtl EM Lrg Compny Idx traded at a discount of .43% below its net asset value, which is better than its one-year historical average premium of .28%.

Agnes Hong has been running the fund for 3 years and currently receives a manager quality ranking of 36 (0=worst, 99=best). This fund offers only a moderate level of risk but investors looking for strong performance are still waiting.

Data Date	Investment Rating	Net Assets ($Mil)	Price	Perfor-mance Rating/Pts	Total Return Y-T-D	Risk Rating/Pts
12-15	D	41.60	18.33	E+ / 0.6	-19.32%	C+ / 6.2
2014	D-	41.60	23.42	E+ / 0.9	-8.49%	C+ / 5.8

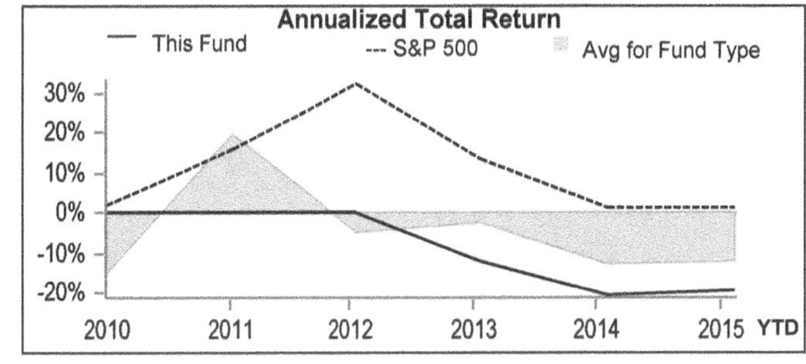

*Schwab Fndmtl Intl Lrg Co Idx ET (FNDF) C- Fair

Fund Family: Charles Schwab Investment Managemen
Fund Type: Foreign
Inception Date: August 14, 2013

Data Date	Investment Rating	Net Assets ($Mil)	Price	Performance Rating/Pts	Total Return Y-T-D	Risk Rating/Pts
12-15	C-	137.70	23.82	D+ / 2.3	-5.14%	B- / 7.8
2014	D	137.70	25.67	D- / 1.3	-4.78%	C+ / 6.8

Major Rating Factors:
Disappointing performance is the major factor driving the C- (Fair) TheStreet.com Investment Rating for *Schwab Fndmtl Intl Lrg Co Idx ET. The fund currently has a performance rating of D+ (Weak) based on an annualized return of 0.00% over the last three years and a total return of -5.14% year to date 2015. Factored into the performance evaluation is an expense ratio of 0.32% (very low).

The fund's risk rating is currently B- (Good). It carries a beta of 0.00, meaning the fund's expected move will be 0.0% for every 10% move in the market. Volatility, as measured by both the semi-deviation and a drawdown factor, is considered low. As of December 31, 2015, *Schwab Fndmtl Intl Lrg Co Idx ET traded at a discount of .33% below its net asset value, which is better than its one-year historical average premium of .39%.

Agnes Hong has been running the fund for 3 years and currently receives a manager quality ranking of 30 (0=worst, 99=best). This fund offers only a moderate level of risk but investors looking for strong performance are still waiting.

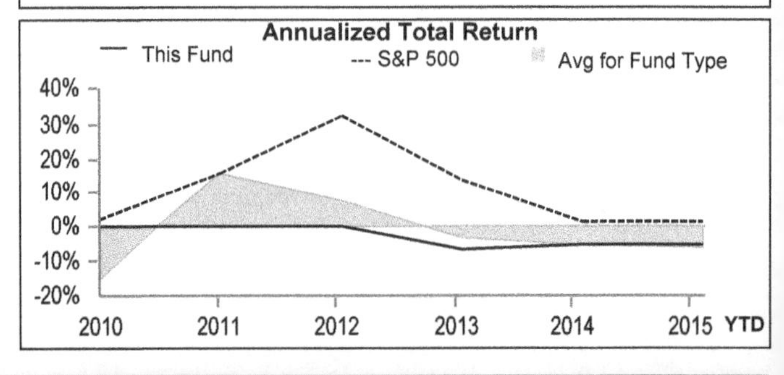

*Schwab Fndmtl Intl Sm Co Idx ETF (FNDC) C Fair

Fund Family: Charles Schwab Investment Managemen
Fund Type: Foreign
Inception Date: August 14, 2013

Data Date	Investment Rating	Net Assets ($Mil)	Price	Performance Rating/Pts	Total Return Y-T-D	Risk Rating/Pts
12-15	C	37.50	26.61	C+ / 5.7	5.24%	C+ / 6.8
2014	D	37.50	25.70	D- / 1.5	-4.17%	B- / 7.1

Major Rating Factors: Middle of the road best describes *Schwab Fndmtl Intl Sm Co Idx ETF whose TheStreet.com Investment Rating is currently a C (Fair). The fund currently has a performance rating of C+ (Fair) based on an annualized return of 0.00% over the last three years and a total return of 5.24% year to date 2015. Factored into the performance evaluation is an expense ratio of 0.46% (very low).

The fund's risk rating is currently C+ (Fair). It carries a beta of 0.00, meaning the fund's expected move will be 0.0% for every 10% move in the market. Volatility, as measured by both the semi-deviation and a drawdown factor, is considered low. As of December 31, 2015, *Schwab Fndmtl Intl Sm Co Idx ETF traded at a premium of .04% above its net asset value, which is better than its one-year historical average premium of .53%.

Agnes Hong has been running the fund for 3 years and currently receives a manager quality ranking of 90 (0=worst, 99=best). If you desire an average level of risk, then this fund may be an option.

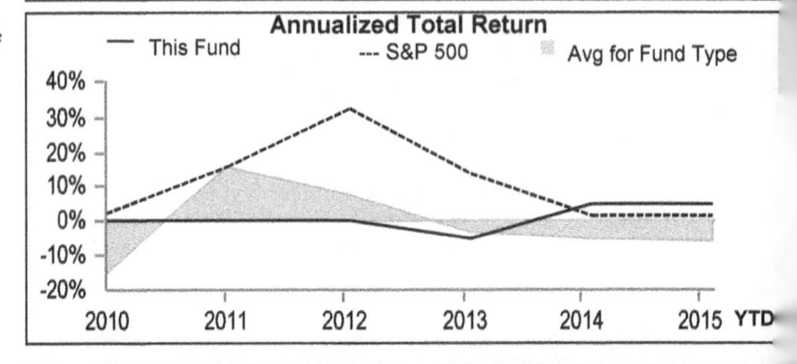

*Schwab Fndmtl US Broad Mkt Idx E (FNDB) C- Fair

Fund Family: Charles Schwab Investment Managemen
Fund Type: Growth and Income
Inception Date: August 14, 2013

Data Date	Investment Rating	Net Assets ($Mil)	Price	Performance Rating/Pts	Total Return Y-T-D	Risk Rating/Pts
12-15	C-	139.60	28.54	C- / 3.6	-2.95%	B- / 7.0
2014	B-	139.60	30.10	C+ / 6.5	12.92%	B- / 7.8

Major Rating Factors: Middle of the road best describes *Schwab Fndmtl US Broad Mkt Idx E whose TheStreet.com Investment Rating is currently a C- (Fair). The fund currently has a performance rating of C- (Fair) based on an annualized return of 0.00% over the last three years and a total return of -2.95% year to date 2015. Factored into the performance evaluation is an expense ratio of 0.32% (very low).

The fund's risk rating is currently B- (Good). It carries a beta of 0.00, meaning the fund's expected move will be 0.0% for every 10% move in the market. Volatility, as measured by both the semi-deviation and a drawdown factor, is considered low. As of December 31, 2015, *Schwab Fndmtl US Broad Mkt Idx E traded at a premium of .28% above its net asset value, which is worse than its one-year historical average premium of .03%.

Agnes Hong has been running the fund for 3 years and currently receives a manager quality ranking of 34 (0=worst, 99=best). If you desire an average level of risk, then this fund may be an option.

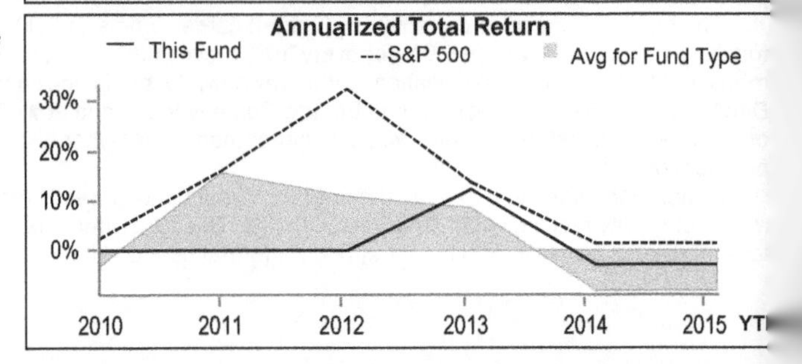

*Schwab Fndmtl US Lrg Compny Idx (FNDX) C- Fair

Fund Family: Charles Schwab Investment Managemen
Fund Type: Growth and Income
Inception Date: August 14, 2013

Major Rating Factors: Middle of the road best describes *Schwab Fndmtl US Lrg Compny Idx whose TheStreet.com Investment Rating is currently a C- (Fair). The fund currently has a performance rating of C- (Fair) based on an annualized return of 0.00% over the last three years and a total return of -2.99% year to date 2015. Factored into the performance evaluation is an expense ratio of 0.32% (very low).

The fund's risk rating is currently B- (Good). It carries a beta of 0.00, meaning the fund's expected move will be 0.0% for every 10% move in the market. Volatility, as measured by both the semi-deviation and a drawdown factor, is considered low. As of December 31, 2015, *Schwab Fndmtl US Lrg Compny Idx traded at a premium of .07% above its net asset value, which is worse than its one-year historical average premium of .03%.

Agnes Hong has been running the fund for 3 years and currently receives a manager quality ranking of 35 (0=worst, 99=best). If you desire an average level of risk, then this fund may be an option.

Data Date	Investment Rating	Net Assets ($Mil)	Price	Performance Rating/Pts	Total Return Y-T-D	Risk Rating/Pts
12-15	C-	176.40	28.64	C- / 3.6	-2.99%	B- / 7.1
2014	B-	176.40	30.12	C+ / 6.6	13.47%	B- / 7.9

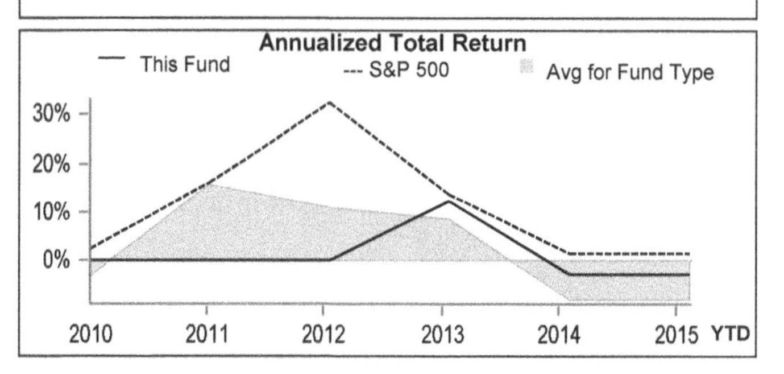

*Schwab Fndmtl US Sm Compny Idx E (FNDA) D+ Weak

Fund Family: Charles Schwab Investment Managemen
Fund Type: Growth and Income
Inception Date: August 14, 2013

Major Rating Factors:
Disappointing performance is the major factor driving the D+ (Weak) TheStreet.com Investment Rating for *Schwab Fndmtl US Sm Compny Idx E. The fund currently has a performance rating of D+ (Weak) based on an annualized return of 0.00% over the last three years and a total return of -4.70% year to date 2015. Factored into the performance evaluation is an expense ratio of 0.32% (very low).

The fund's risk rating is currently C+ (Fair). It carries a beta of 0.00, meaning the fund's expected move will be 0.0% for every 10% move in the market. Volatility, as measured by both the semi-deviation and a drawdown factor, is considered low. As of December 31, 2015, *Schwab Fndmtl US Sm Compny Idx E traded at a premium of .11% above its net asset value, which is worse than its one-year historical average premium of .03%.

Agnes Hong has been running the fund for 3 years and currently receives a manager quality ranking of 25 (0=worst, 99=best). This fund offers only a moderate level of risk but investors looking for strong performance are still waiting.

Data Date	Investment Rating	Net Assets ($Mil)	Price	Performance Rating/Pts	Total Return Y-T-D	Risk Rating/Pts
12-15	D+	93.90	27.97	D+ / 2.7	-4.70%	C+ / 6.7
2014	C	93.90	29.85	C / 5.5	8.38%	B- / 7.3

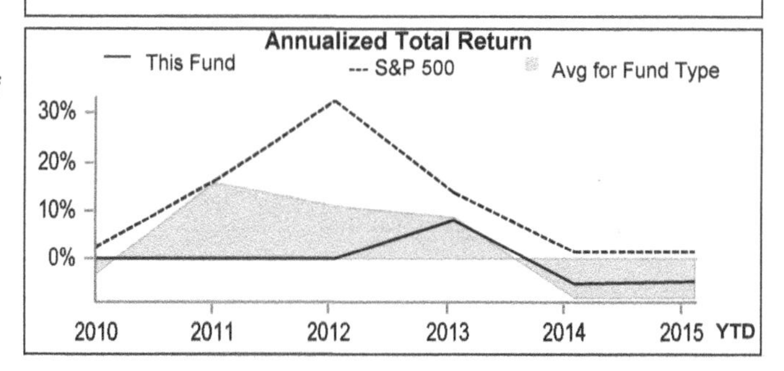

*Schwab International Equity ETF (SCHF) C+ Fair

Fund Family: Charles Schwab Investment Managemen
Fund Type: Foreign
Inception Date: October 30, 2009

Major Rating Factors: Middle of the road best describes *Schwab International Equity ETF whose TheStreet.com Investment Rating is currently a C+ (Fair). The fund currently has a performance rating of C (Fair) based on an annualized return of 2.70% over the last three years and a total return of -2.12% year to date 2015. Factored into the performance evaluation is an expense ratio of 0.08% (very low).

The fund's risk rating is currently B (Good). It carries a beta of 0.93, meaning that its performance tracks fairly well with that of the overall stock market. Volatility, as measured by both the semi-deviation and a drawdown factor, is considered low. As of December 31, 2015, *Schwab International Equity ETF traded at a discount of .36% below its net asset value, which is better than its one-year historical average premium of .25%.

Agnes Hong has been running the fund for 7 years and currently receives a manager quality ranking of 51 (0=worst, 99=best). If you desire an average level of risk, then this fund may be an option.

Data Date	Investment Rating	Net Assets ($Mil)	Price	Performance Rating/Pts	Total Return Y-T-D	Risk Rating/Pts
12-15	C+	2,660.40	27.57	C / 5.1	-2.12%	B / 8.3
2014	C	2,660.40	28.91	C / 5.0	-3.98%	B- / 7.0
2013	C+	1,895.70	31.53	C+ / 6.6	15.68%	B- / 7.7
2012	C	979.30	27.10	C / 5.0	23.10%	B- / 7.5
2011	D	632.50	23.43	D- / 1.1	-10.90%	B- / 7.4
2010	A+	359.70	27.69	B+ / 8.7	9.26%	B- / 7.7

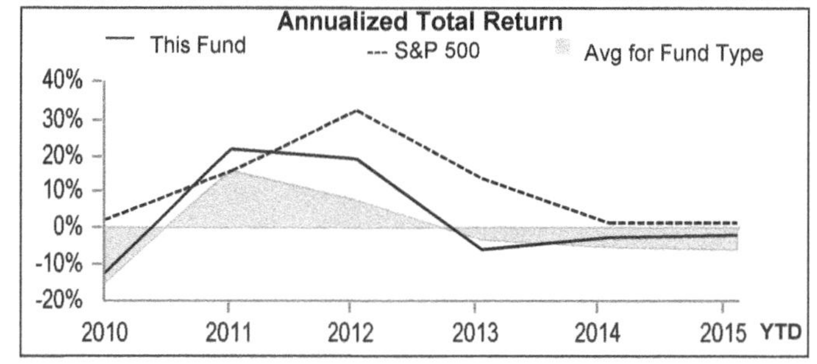

*Schwab Intl Small-Cap Equity ETF (SCHC) C Fair

Fund Family: Charles Schwab Investment Managemen
Fund Type: Foreign
Inception Date: January 13, 2010

Major Rating Factors: Middle of the road best describes *Schwab Intl Small-Cap Equity ETF whose TheStreet.com Investment Rating is currently a C (Fair). The fund currently has a performance rating of C+ (Fair) based on an annualized return of 4.28% over the last three years and a total return of 2.17% year to date 2015. Factored into the performance evaluation is an expense ratio of 0.18% (very low).

The fund's risk rating is currently C+ (Fair). It carries a beta of 0.84, meaning the fund's expected move will be 8.4% for every 10% move in the market. Volatility, as measured by both the semi-deviation and a drawdown factor, is considered low. As of December 31, 2015, *Schwab Intl Small-Cap Equity ETF traded at a premium of .21% above its net asset value, which is better than its one-year historical average premium of .49%.

Agnes Hong has been running the fund for 6 years and currently receives a manager quality ranking of 70 (0=worst, 99=best). If you desire an average level of risk, then this fund may be an option.

Data Date	Investment Rating	Net Assets ($Mil)	Price	Performance Rating/Pts	Total Return Y-T-D	Risk Rating/Pts
12-15	C	383.50	28.87	C+ / 5.8	2.17%	C+ / 6.8
2014	C	383.50	28.85	C / 4.8	-6.09%	B- / 7.7
2013	C+	343.90	31.92	C+ / 6.3	17.91%	B- / 7.1
2012	B	205.00	27.05	A+ / 9.7	24.30%	C+ / 6.0
2011	D-	137.80	23.38	E+ / 0.9	-15.30%	C+ / 6.1

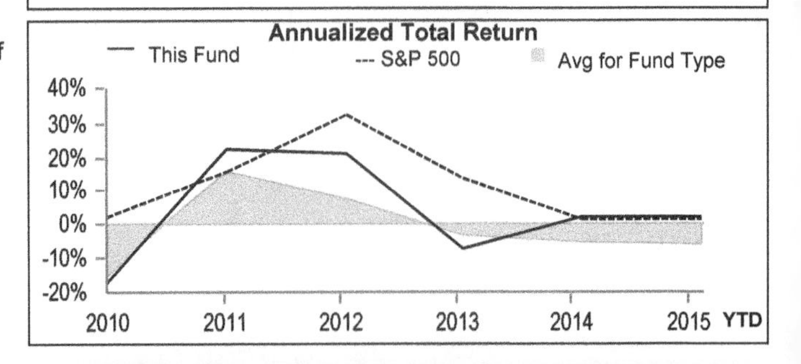

*Schwab Intmdt-Term US Treasury E (SCHR) C+ Fair

Fund Family: Charles Schwab Investment Managemen
Fund Type: US Government/Agency
Inception Date: August 4, 2010

Major Rating Factors: Middle of the road best describes *Schwab Intmdt-Term US Treasury E whose TheStreet.com Investment Rating is currently a C+ (Fair). The fund currently has a performance rating of C (Fair) based on an annualized return of 1.17% over the last three years and a total return of 1.28% year to date 2015. Factored into the performance evaluation is an expense ratio of 0.10% (very low).

The fund's risk rating is currently B (Good). It carries a beta of 0.27, meaning the fund's expected move will be 2.7% for every 10% move in the market. Volatility, as measured by both the semi-deviation and a drawdown factor, is considered low. As of December 31, 2015, *Schwab Intmdt-Term US Treasury E traded at a premium of .09% above its net asset value, which is worse than its one-year historical average premium of .02%.

Matthew Hastings has been running the fund for 6 years and currently receives a manager quality ranking of 71 (0=worst, 99=best). If you desire an average level of risk, then this fund may be an option.

Data Date	Investment Rating	Net Assets ($Mil)	Price	Performance Rating/Pts	Total Return Y-T-D	Risk Rating/Pts
12-15	C+	230.10	53.60	C / 4.8	1.28%	B / 8.0
2014	C	230.10	53.60	C- / 3.3	4.36%	B+ / 9.6
2013	C	242.20	52.07	C- / 3.3	-2.19%	B+ / 9.7
2012	C-	216.70	54.08	D / 1.6	1.96%	B+ / 9.7
2011	C+	117.50	53.52	C- / 4.1	9.68%	B+ / 9.7

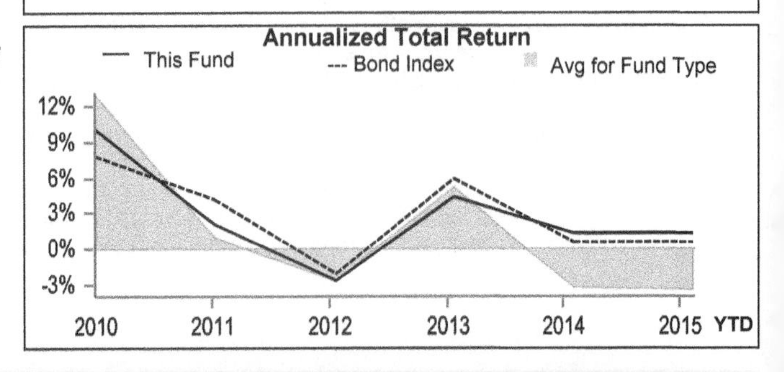

*Schwab Short-Term US Treas ETF (SCHO) C+ Fair

Fund Family: Charles Schwab Investment Managemen
Fund Type: US Government/Agency
Inception Date: August 4, 2010

Major Rating Factors: Middle of the road best describes *Schwab Short-Term US Treas ETF whose TheStreet.com Investment Rating is currently a C+ (Fair). The fund currently has a performance rating of C (Fair) based on an annualized return of 0.42% over the last three years and a total return of 0.38% year to date 2015. Factored into the performance evaluation is an expense ratio of 0.08% (very low).

The fund's risk rating is currently B (Good). It carries a beta of 0.03, meaning the fund's expected move will be 0.3% for every 10% move in the market. Volatility, as measured by both the semi-deviation and a drawdown factor, is considered low. As of December 31, 2015, *Schwab Short-Term US Treas ETF traded at a premium of .02% above its net asset value, which is worse than its one-year historical average premium of .01%.

Matthew Hastings has been running the fund for 6 years and currently receives a manager quality ranking of 71 (0=worst, 99=best). If you desire an average level of risk, then this fund may be an option.

Data Date	Investment Rating	Net Assets ($Mil)	Price	Performance Rating/Pts	Total Return Y-T-D	Risk Rating/Pts
12-15	C+	616.80	50.44	C / 4.5	0.38%	B / 8.4
2014	C-	616.80	50.58	D+ / 2.9	0.61%	B / 8.3
2013	C	431.90	50.55	D+ / 2.7	0.29%	B+ / 9.9
2012	C-	250.10	50.49	D- / 1.4	0.25%	B+ / 9.9
2011	C	197.00	50.54	D / 2.2	1.29%	B+ / 9.9

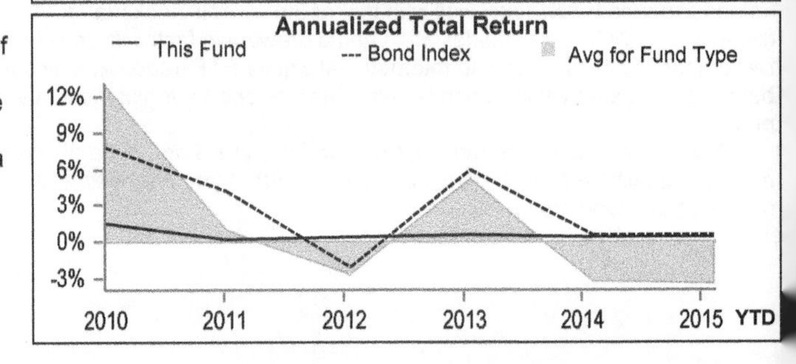

*Schwab US Aggregate Bond ETF (SCHZ) C Fair

Fund Family: Charles Schwab Investment Managemen
Fund Type: General Bond
Inception Date: July 13, 2011

Major Rating Factors: Middle of the road best describes *Schwab US Aggregate Bond ETF whose TheStreet.com Investment Rating is currently a C (Fair). The fund currently has a performance rating of C (Fair) based on an annualized return of 1.54% over the last three years and a total return of 0.08% year to date 2015. Factored into the performance evaluation is an expense ratio of 0.05% (very low).

The fund's risk rating is currently B- (Good). It carries a beta of 1.00, meaning that its performance tracks fairly well with that of the overall stock market. Volatility, as measured by both the semi-deviation and a drawdown factor, is considered low. As of December 31, 2015, *Schwab US Aggregate Bond ETF traded at a premium of .16% above its net asset value, which is worse than its one-year historical average premium of .09%.

Matthew Hastings has been running the fund for 5 years and currently receives a manager quality ranking of 67 (0=worst, 99=best). If you desire an average level of risk, then this fund may be an option.

Data Date	Investment Rating	Net Assets ($Mil)	Price	Performance Rating/Pts	Total Return Y-T-D	Risk Rating/Pts
12-15	C	898.80	51.49	C / 5.1	0.08%	B- / 7.7
2014	C-	898.80	52.36	C- / 3.7	6.05%	B- / 7.7
2013	C-	497.80	50.29	D+ / 2.5	-1.52%	B+ / 9.7
2012	C-	388.00	52.34	D / 1.8	2.77%	B+ / 9.9

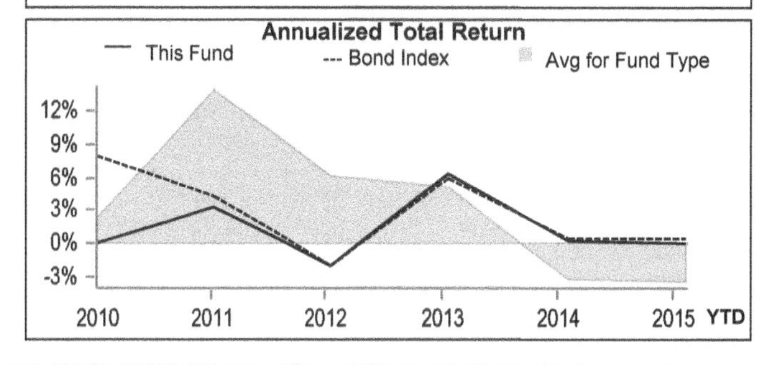

*Schwab US Broad Market ETF (SCHB) A+ Excellent

Fund Family: Charles Schwab Investment Managemen
Fund Type: Income
Inception Date: October 30, 2009

Major Rating Factors:
Strong performance is the major factor driving the A+ (Excellent) TheStreet.com Investment Rating for *Schwab US Broad Market ETF. The fund currently has a performance rating of B+ (Good) based on an annualized return of 13.57% over the last three years and a total return of 0.51% year to date 2015. Factored into the performance evaluation is an expense ratio of 0.04% (very low).

The fund's risk rating is currently B (Good). It carries a beta of 1.00, meaning that its performance tracks fairly well with that of the overall stock market. Volatility, as measured by both the semi-deviation and a drawdown factor, is considered low. As of December 31, 2015, *Schwab US Broad Market ETF traded at a discount of .02% below its net asset value, which is better than its one-year historical average premium of .01%.

Agnes Hong has been running the fund for 7 years and currently receives a manager quality ranking of 64 (0=worst, 99=best). If you desire only a moderate level of risk and strong performance, then this fund is an excellent option.

Data Date	Investment Rating	Net Assets ($Mil)	Price	Performance Rating/Pts	Total Return Y-T-D	Risk Rating/Pts
12-15	A+	3,614.80	49.04	B+ / 8.6	0.51%	B / 8.5
2014	B+	3,614.80	49.82	B+ / 8.4	13.72%	B- / 7.4
2013	A-	2,908.70	45.01	B+ / 8.4	28.28%	B / 8.2
2012	C+	1,334.50	34.41	C+ / 5.8	17.97%	B / 8.1
2011	C-	815.30	30.22	D+ / 2.8	2.61%	B / 8.1
2010	A+	405.40	30.38	A- / 9.2	17.11%	B- / 7.8

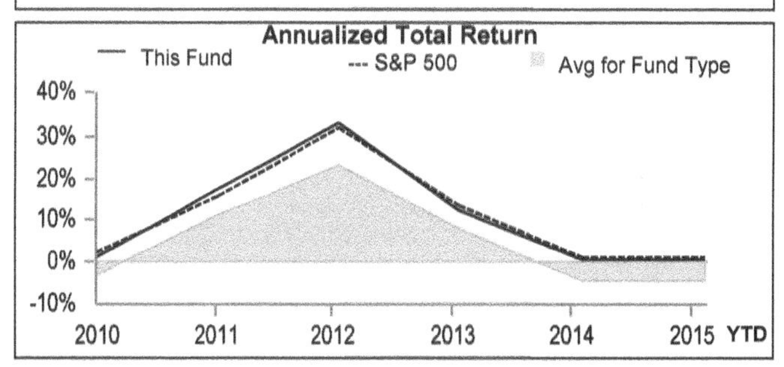

*Schwab US Dividend Equity ETF (SCHD) A+ Excellent

Fund Family: Charles Schwab Investment Managemen
Fund Type: Growth and Income
Inception Date: October 19, 2011

Major Rating Factors:
Strong performance is the major factor driving the A+ (Excellent) TheStreet.com Investment Rating for *Schwab US Dividend Equity ETF. The fund currently has a performance rating of B+ (Good) based on an annualized return of 12.98% over the last three years and a total return of -0.19% year to date 2015. Factored into the performance evaluation is an expense ratio of 0.07% (very low).

The fund's risk rating is currently B (Good). It carries a beta of 0.97, meaning that its performance tracks fairly well with that of the overall stock market. Volatility, as measured by both the semi-deviation and a drawdown factor, is considered low. As of December 31, 2015, *Schwab US Dividend Equity ETF traded at a discount of .05% below its net asset value, which is better than its one-year historical average premium of .02%.

Agnes Hong has been running the fund for 5 years and currently receives a manager quality ranking of 62 (0=worst, 99=best). If you desire only a moderate level of risk and strong performance, then this fund is an excellent option.

Data Date	Investment Rating	Net Assets ($Mil)	Price	Performance Rating/Pts	Total Return Y-T-D	Risk Rating/Pts
12-15	A+	2,135.00	38.56	B+ / 8.5	-0.19%	B / 8.8
2014	B	2,135.00	39.85	B / 7.8	12.64%	B- / 7.4
2013	A+	1,506.10	36.66	A / 9.3	28.40%	B+ / 9.6
2012	B+	575.00	28.34	C+ / 6.4	15.37%	B+ / 9.6

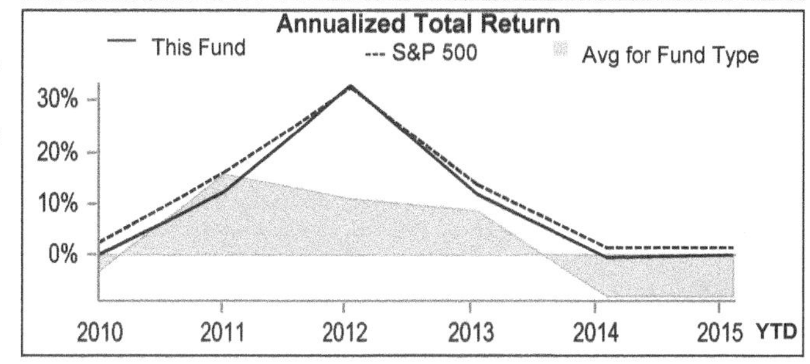

*Schwab US Large-Cap ETF (SCHX) A Excellent

Fund Family: Charles Schwab Investment Managemen
Fund Type: Income
Inception Date: October 30, 2009

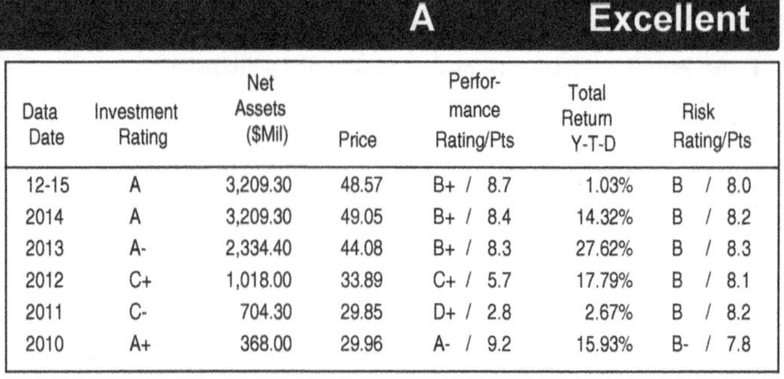

Data Date	Investment Rating	Net Assets ($Mil)	Price	Performance Rating/Pts	Total Return Y-T-D	Risk Rating/Pts
12-15	A	3,209.30	48.57	B+ / 8.7	1.03%	B / 8.0
2014	A	3,209.30	49.05	B+ / 8.4	14.32%	B / 8.2
2013	A-	2,334.40	44.08	B+ / 8.3	27.62%	B / 8.3
2012	C+	1,018.00	33.89	C+ / 5.7	17.79%	B / 8.1
2011	C-	704.30	29.85	D+ / 2.8	2.67%	B / 8.2
2010	A+	368.00	29.96	A- / 9.2	15.93%	B- / 7.8

Major Rating Factors:
Strong performance is the major factor driving the A (Excellent) TheStreet.com Investment Rating for *Schwab US Large-Cap ETF. The fund currently has a performance rating of B+ (Good) based on an annualized return of 13.81% over the last three years and a total return of 1.03% year to date 2015. Factored into the performance evaluation is an expense ratio of 0.04% (very low).

The fund's risk rating is currently B (Good). It carries a beta of 0.99, meaning that its performance tracks fairly well with that of the overall stock market. Volatility, as measured by both the semi-deviation and a drawdown factor, is considered low. As of December 31, 2015, *Schwab US Large-Cap ETF traded at a price exactly equal to its net asset value, which is better than its one-year historical average premium of .02%.

Agnes Hong has been running the fund for 7 years and currently receives a manager quality ranking of 66 (0=worst, 99=best). If you desire only a moderate level of risk and strong performance, then this fund is an excellent option.

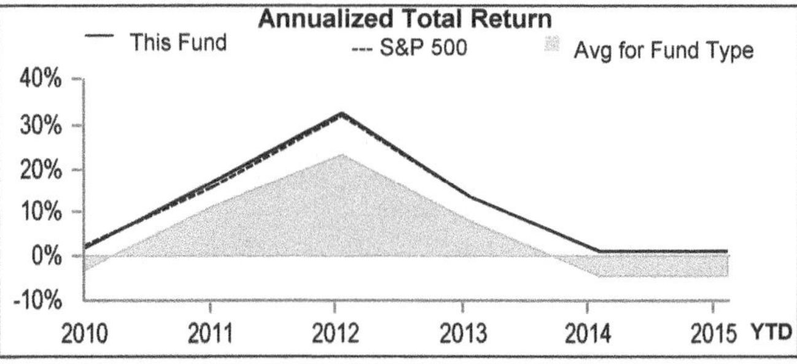

*Schwab US Large-Cap Growth ETF (SCHG) A Excellent

Fund Family: Charles Schwab Investment Managemen
Fund Type: Growth
Inception Date: December 9, 2009

Data Date	Investment Rating	Net Assets ($Mil)	Price	Performance Rating/Pts	Total Return Y-T-D	Risk Rating/Pts
12-15	A	1,496.10	52.83	A- / 9.0	3.41%	B- / 7.5
2014	A-	1,496.10	51.79	B+ / 8.9	16.92%	B- / 7.3
2013	A-	1,108.50	45.23	B+ / 8.4	29.10%	B / 8.2
2012	C+	528.30	34.15	C / 5.5	17.77%	B / 8.0
2011	D+	324.40	29.63	D+ / 2.3	0.84%	B / 8.0
2010	A+	162.30	30.16	A- / 9.2	16.85%	B- / 7.6

Major Rating Factors:
Exceptional performance is the major factor driving the A (Excellent) TheStreet.com Investment Rating for *Schwab US Large-Cap Growth ETF. The fund currently has a performance rating of A- (Excellent) based on an annualized return of 15.94% over the last three years and a total return of 3.41% year to date 2015. Factored into the performance evaluation is an expense ratio of 0.07% (very low).

The fund's risk rating is currently B- (Good). It carries a beta of 1.00, meaning that its performance tracks fairly well with that of the overall stock market. Volatility, as measured by both the semi-deviation and a drawdown factor, is considered low. As of December 31, 2015, *Schwab US Large-Cap Growth ETF traded at a premium of .02% above its net asset value, which is in line with its one-year historical average premium of .02%.

Agnes Hong has been running the fund for 7 years and currently receives a manager quality ranking of 79 (0=worst, 99=best). If you desire only a moderate level of risk and strong performance, then this fund is an excellent option.

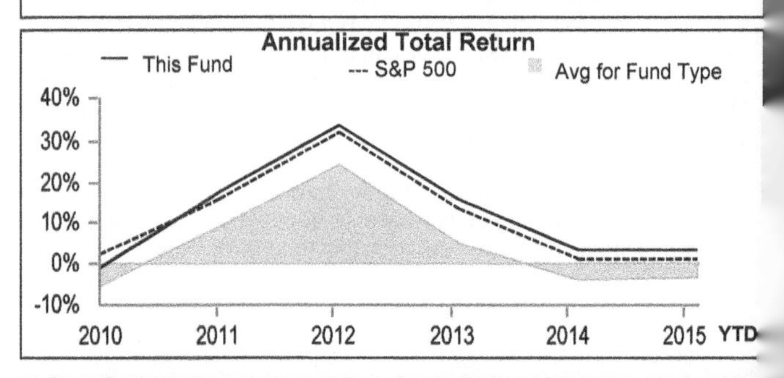

*Schwab US Large-Cap Value ETF (SCHV) B+ Good

Fund Family: Charles Schwab Investment Managemen
Fund Type: Income
Inception Date: December 9, 2009

Data Date	Investment Rating	Net Assets ($Mil)	Price	Performance Rating/Pts	Total Return Y-T-D	Risk Rating/Pts
12-15	B+	1,155.70	42.44	B / 8.1	-1.23%	B- / 7.9
2014	A+	1,155.70	44.09	B / 7.8	11.89%	B+ / 9.2
2013	B+	820.00	40.69	B / 8.1	25.97%	B / 8.4
2012	C+	420.00	31.83	C+ / 5.7	17.53%	B / 8.2
2011	C-	256.50	28.49	C- / 3.4	4.13%	B / 8.3
2010	A+	114.10	28.25	A- / 9.0	14.86%	B- / 7.8

Major Rating Factors: Strong performance is the major factor driving the B+ (Good) TheStreet.com Investment Rating for *Schwab US Large-Cap Value ETF. The fund currently has a performance rating of B (Good) based on an annualized return of 11.70% over the last three years and a total return of -1.23% year to date 2015. Factored into the performance evaluation is an expense ratio of 0.07% (very low).

The fund's risk rating is currently B- (Good). It carries a beta of 1.01, meaning that its performance tracks fairly well with that of the overall stock market. Volatility, as measured by both the semi-deviation and a drawdown factor, is considered low. As of December 31, 2015, *Schwab US Large-Cap Value ETF traded at a price exactly equal to its net asset value, which is better than its one-year historical average premium of .03%.

Agnes Hong has been running the fund for 7 years and currently receives a manager quality ranking of 50 (0=worst, 99=best). If you desire only a moderate level of risk and strong performance, then this fund is an excellent option.

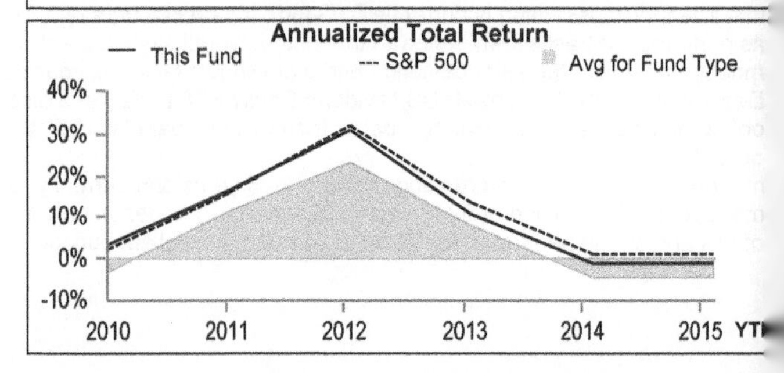

*Schwab US Mid-Cap ETF (SCHM) B+ Good

Fund Family: Charles Schwab Investment Managemen
Fund Type: Growth
Inception Date: January 12, 2011

Major Rating Factors: Strong performance is the major factor driving the B+ (Good) TheStreet.com Investment Rating for *Schwab US Mid-Cap ETF. The fund currently has a performance rating of B+ (Good) based on an annualized return of 13.28% over the last three years and a total return of 0.02% year to date 2015. Factored into the performance evaluation is an expense ratio of 0.07% (very low).

The fund's risk rating is currently B- (Good). It carries a beta of 1.00, meaning that its performance tracks fairly well with that of the overall stock market. Volatility, as measured by both the semi-deviation and a drawdown factor, is considered low. As of December 31, 2015, *Schwab US Mid-Cap ETF traded at a premium of .02% above its net asset value, which is better than its one-year historical average premium of .03%.

Agnes Hong has been running the fund for 5 years and currently receives a manager quality ranking of 63 (0=worst, 99=best). If you desire only a moderate level of risk and strong performance, then this fund is an excellent option.

Data Date	Investment Rating	Net Assets ($Mil)	Price	Perfor-mance Rating/Pts	Total Return Y-T-D	Risk Rating/Pts
12-15	B+	1,169.70	40.07	B+ / 8.4	0.02%	B- / 7.4
2014	B+	1,169.70	40.68	B+ / 8.3	11.03%	B- / 7.2
2013	A	866.90	37.44	A / 9.4	30.96%	B- / 7.7
2012	B+	292.60	27.87	B+ / 8.8	18.38%	B- / 7.5

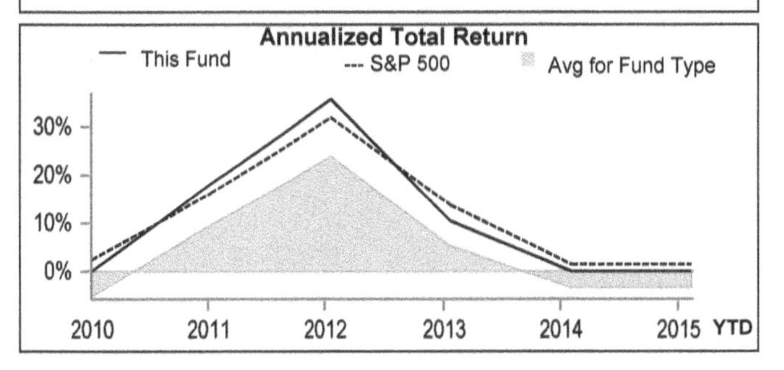

*Schwab US REIT ETF (SCHH) B Good

Fund Family: Charles Schwab Investment Managemen
Fund Type: Growth and Income
Inception Date: January 12, 2011

Major Rating Factors: Strong performance is the major factor driving the B (Good) TheStreet.com Investment Rating for *Schwab US REIT ETF. The fund currently has a performance rating of B+ (Good) based on an annualized return of 11.10% over the last three years and a total return of 1.90% year to date 2015. Factored into the performance evaluation is an expense ratio of 0.07% (very low).

The fund's risk rating is currently C+ (Fair). It carries a beta of 0.45, meaning the fund's expected move will be 4.5% for every 10% move in the market. Volatility, as measured by both the semi-deviation and a drawdown factor, is considered low. As of December 31, 2015, *Schwab US REIT ETF traded at a premium of .05% above its net asset value, which is worse than its one-year historical average premium of .03%.

Agnes Hong has been running the fund for 5 years and currently receives a manager quality ranking of 89 (0=worst, 99=best). If you desire only a moderate level of risk and strong performance, then this fund is an excellent option.

Data Date	Investment Rating	Net Assets ($Mil)	Price	Perfor-mance Rating/Pts	Total Return Y-T-D	Risk Rating/Pts
12-15	B	967.80	39.64	B+ / 8.3	1.90%	C+ / 6.3
2014	A+	967.80	38.95	A- / 9.0	31.04%	B / 8.2
2013	D+	560.80	30.25	D / 2.2	0.25%	B- / 7.8
2012	B-	372.50	30.64	B- / 7.0	19.50%	B- / 7.9

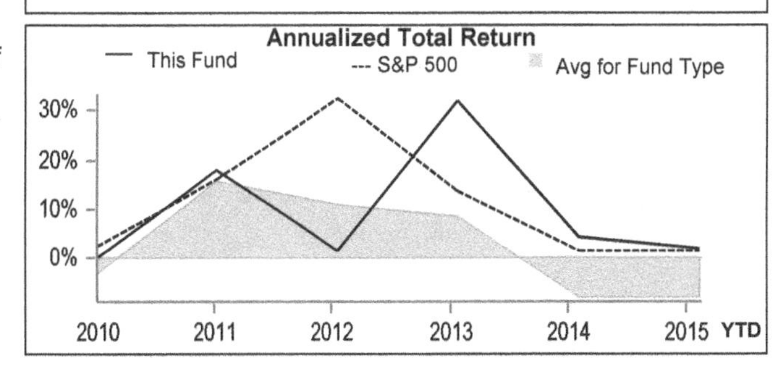

*Schwab US Small-Cap ETF (SCHA) B Good

Fund Family: Charles Schwab Investment Managemen
Fund Type: Growth
Inception Date: October 30, 2009

Major Rating Factors: Strong performance is the major factor driving the B (Good) TheStreet.com Investment Rating for *Schwab US Small-Cap ETF. The fund currently has a performance rating of B- (Good) based on an annualized return of 11.22% over the last three years and a total return of -3.91% year to date 2015. Factored into the performance evaluation is an expense ratio of 0.08% (very low).

The fund's risk rating is currently B- (Good). It carries a beta of 1.05, meaning that its performance tracks fairly well with that of the overall stock market. Volatility, as measured by both the semi-deviation and a drawdown factor, is considered low. As of December 31, 2015, *Schwab US Small-Cap ETF traded at a premium of .02% above its net asset value, which is in line with its one-year historical average premium of .02%.

Agnes Hong has been running the fund for 7 years and currently receives a manager quality ranking of 43 (0=worst, 99=best). If you desire only a moderate level of risk and strong performance, then this fund is an excellent option.

Data Date	Investment Rating	Net Assets ($Mil)	Price	Perfor-mance Rating/Pts	Total Return Y-T-D	Risk Rating/Pts
12-15	B	1,996.40	52.08	B- / 7.5	-3.91%	B- / 7.1
2014	B	1,996.40	55.12	B / 8.1	7.11%	C+ / 6.9
2013	B+	1,883.10	52.50	B+ / 8.7	34.05%	B- / 7.6
2012	B-	707.10	38.12	B- / 7.2	19.62%	B- / 7.4
2011	D	506.10	32.84	D / 1.9	-1.60%	B- / 7.4
2010	A+	277.00	34.30	A+ / 9.6	28.64%	B- / 7.5

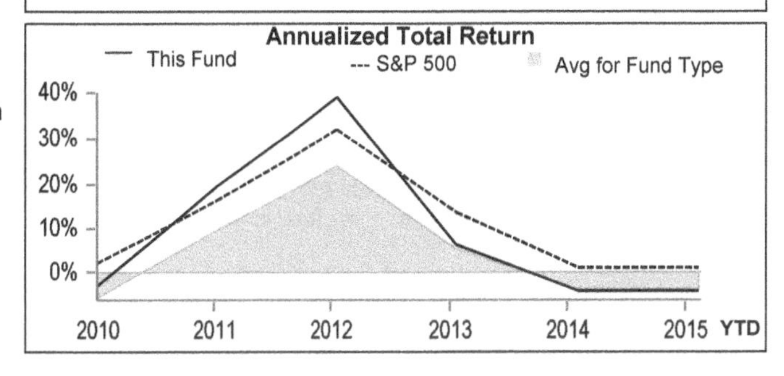

*Schwab US TIPS ETF (SCHP) C Fair

Fund Family: Charles Schwab Investment Managemen
Fund Type: General - Investment Grade
Inception Date: August 4, 2010

Major Rating Factors: Middle of the road best describes *Schwab US TIPS ETF whose TheStreet.com Investment Rating is currently a C (Fair). The fund currently has a performance rating of C- (Fair) based on an annualized return of -2.08% over the last three years and a total return of -2.26% year to date 2015. Factored into the performance evaluation is an expense ratio of 0.07% (very low).

The fund's risk rating is currently B+ (Good). It carries a beta of 1.61, meaning it is expected to move 16.1% for every 10% move in the market. Volatility, as measured by both the semi-deviation and a drawdown factor, is considered very low. As of December 31, 2015, *Schwab US TIPS ETF traded at a discount of .04% below its net asset value, which is better than its one-year historical average premium of .05%.

Matthew Hastings has been running the fund for 6 years and currently receives a manager quality ranking of 33 (0=worst, 99=best). If you desire an average level of risk, then this fund may be an option.

Data Date	Investment Rating	Net Assets ($Mil)	Price	Performance Rating/Pts	Total Return Y-T-D	Risk Rating/Pts
12-15	C	490.40	53.13	C- / 3.5	-2.26%	B+ / 9.1
2014	C-	490.40	54.24	D+ / 2.9	3.58%	B / 8.9
2013	C-	399.60	52.77	C- / 3.1	-7.71%	B+ / 9.1
2012	C-	571.40	58.30	D / 2.2	5.44%	B+ / 9.7
2011	B-	288.40	55.62	C / 4.9	12.69%	B+ / 9.8

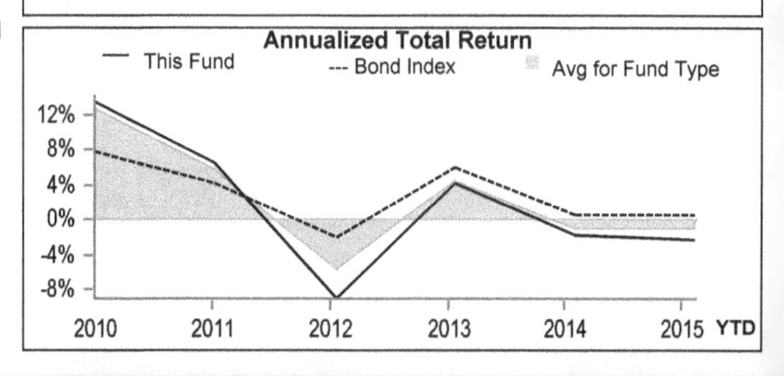

*Shares JPX-Nikkei 400 (JPXN) B+ Good

Fund Family: BlackRock Fund Advisors
Fund Type: Foreign
Inception Date: October 23, 2001

Major Rating Factors: Strong performance is the major factor driving the B+ (Good) TheStreet.com Investment Rating for *Shares JPX-Nikkei 400. The fund currently has a performance rating of B- (Good) based on an annualized return of 8.26% over the last three years and a total return of 11.25% year to date 2015. Factored into the performance evaluation is an expense ratio of 0.50% (very low).

The fund's risk rating is currently B (Good). It carries a beta of 0.77, meaning the fund's expected move will be 7.7% for every 10% move in the market. Volatility, as measured by both the semi-deviation and a drawdown factor, is considered low. As of December 31, 2015, *Shares JPX-Nikkei 400 traded at a discount of 1.17% below its net asset value, which is better than its one-year historical average premium of .34%.

Diane Hsiung has been running the fund for 8 years and currently receives a manager quality ranking of 88 (0=worst, 99=best). If you desire only a moderate level of risk and strong performance, then this fund is an excellent option.

Data Date	Investment Rating	Net Assets ($Mil)	Price	Performance Rating/Pts	Total Return Y-T-D	Risk Rating/Pts
12-15	B+	75.70	52.54	B- / 7.5	11.25%	B / 8.3
2014	C	75.70	48.48	C / 4.6	-5.18%	B / 8.3
2013	C	93.80	52.67	C+ / 5.7	20.98%	B- / 7.4
2012	D+	72.10	42.45	D / 2.2	12.71%	B- / 7.4
2011	D	70.50	38.68	D / 1.7	-16.76%	B- / 7.6
2010	D-	100.20	47.53	D+ / 2.4	14.07%	D+ / 2.7

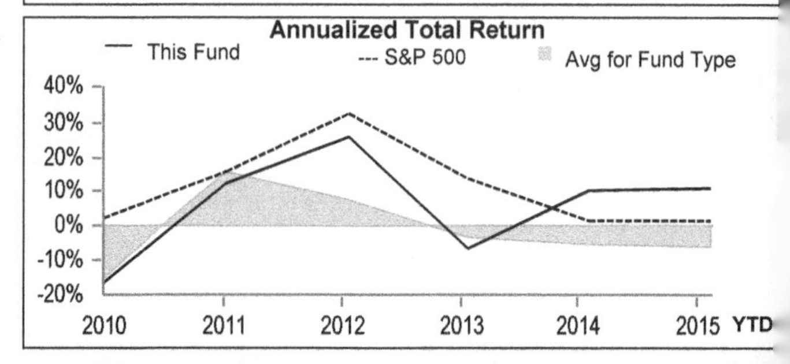

*SP Bank ETF (KBE) A+ Excellent

Fund Family: SSgA Funds Management Inc
Fund Type: Financial Services
Inception Date: November 8, 2005

Major Rating Factors:
Strong performance is the major factor driving the A+ (Excellent) TheStreet.com Investment Rating for *SP Bank ETF. The fund currently has a performance rating of B+ (Good) based on an annualized return of 12.53% over the last three years and a total return of 3.82% year to date 2015. Factored into the performance evaluation is an expense ratio of 0.35% (very low).

The fund's risk rating is currently B (Good). It carries a beta of 1.14, meaning it is expected to move 11.4% for every 10% move in the market. Volatility, as measured by both the semi-deviation and a drawdown factor, is considered low. As of December 31, 2015, *SP Bank ETF traded at a discount of .09% below its net asset value.

John A. Tucker has been running the fund for 11 years and currently receives a manager quality ranking of 44 (0=worst, 99=best). If you desire only a moderate level of risk and strong performance, then this fund is an excellent option.

Data Date	Investment Rating	Net Assets ($Mil)	Price	Performance Rating/Pts	Total Return Y-T-D	Risk Rating/Pts
12-15	A+	2,569.90	33.82	B+ / 8.4	3.82%	B / 8.7
2014	B	2,569.90	33.55	B / 7.6	3.77%	B- / 7.4
2013	B-	2,520.40	33.17	B- / 7.4	33.27%	B- / 7.2
2012	D+	1,678.90	23.83	C- / 3.3	17.30%	C+ / 6.9
2011	D	1,140.60	19.83	D / 2.1	-19.29%	C+ / 6.4
2010	D-	1,988.30	25.91	D- / 1.0	23.06%	C- / 4.0

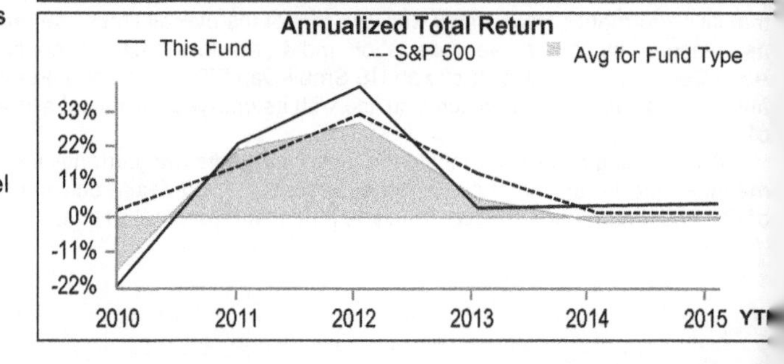

*SP Capital Markets ETF (KCE) C+ Fair

Fund Family: SSgA Funds Management Inc
Fund Type: Financial Services
Inception Date: November 8, 2005

Major Rating Factors: Middle of the road best describes *SP Capital Markets ETF whose TheStreet.com Investment Rating is currently a C+ (Fair). The fund currently has a performance rating of C+ (Fair) based on an annualized return of 9.24% over the last three years and a total return of -11.01% year to date 2015. Factored into the performance evaluation is an expense ratio of 0.35% (very low).

The fund's risk rating is currently C+ (Fair). It carries a beta of 1.44, meaning it is expected to move 14.4% for every 10% move in the market. Volatility, as measured by both the semi-deviation and a drawdown factor, is considered low. As of December 31, 2015, *SP Capital Markets ETF traded at a premium of .65% above its net asset value, which is worse than its one-year historical average discount of .05%.

John A. Tucker has been running the fund for 11 years and currently receives a manager quality ranking of 17 (0=worst, 99=best). If you desire an average level of risk, then this fund may be an option.

Data Date	Investment Rating	Net Assets ($Mil)	Price	Performance Rating/Pts	Total Return Y-T-D	Risk Rating/Pts
12-15	C+	186.90	43.60	C+ / 6.5	-11.01%	C+ / 6.5
2014	B+	186.90	50.86	B+ / 8.9	3.36%	C+ / 6.9
2013	B	122.80	50.10	B+ / 8.8	42.85%	C+ / 6.9
2012	C-	20.40	34.11	C / 4.3	26.88%	C+ / 6.7
2011	D	22.40	27.95	D / 2.2	-23.00%	C+ / 6.9
2010	D-	76.80	38.39	E+ / 0.9	6.23%	C / 4.8

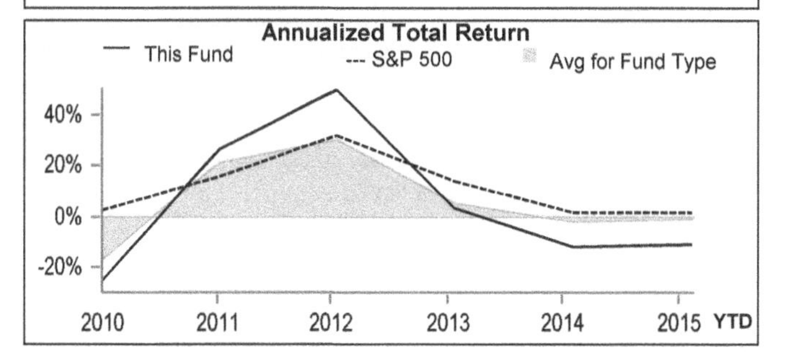

*SP Insurance ETF (KIE) A+ Excellent

Fund Family: SSgA Funds Management Inc
Fund Type: Income
Inception Date: November 8, 2005

Major Rating Factors:
Exceptional performance is the major factor driving the A+ (Excellent) TheStreet.com Investment Rating for *SP Insurance ETF. The fund currently has a performance rating of A (Excellent) based on an annualized return of 17.07% over the last three years and a total return of 7.22% year to date 2015. Factored into the performance evaluation is an expense ratio of 0.35% (very low).

The fund's risk rating is currently B (Good). It carries a beta of 1.05, meaning that its performance tracks fairly well with that of the overall stock market. Volatility, as measured by both the semi-deviation and a drawdown factor, is considered low. As of December 31, 2015, *SP Insurance ETF traded at a price exactly equal to its net asset value.

John A. Tucker has been running the fund for 11 years and currently receives a manager quality ranking of 82 (0=worst, 99=best). If you desire only a moderate level of risk and strong performance, then this fund is an excellent option.

Data Date	Investment Rating	Net Assets ($Mil)	Price	Performance Rating/Pts	Total Return Y-T-D	Risk Rating/Pts
12-15	A+	299.20	69.50	A / 9.3	7.22%	B / 8.1
2014	A-	299.20	66.69	A- / 9.0	9.90%	B- / 7.4
2013	B	476.50	63.09	B+ / 8.4	36.99%	B- / 7.5
2012	C	143.10	44.00	C+ / 5.9	22.93%	B- / 7.3
2011	C-	120.90	37.21	C / 4.3	-12.73%	C+ / 6.7
2010	D+	236.80	43.03	C- / 3.7	26.06%	C / 4.5

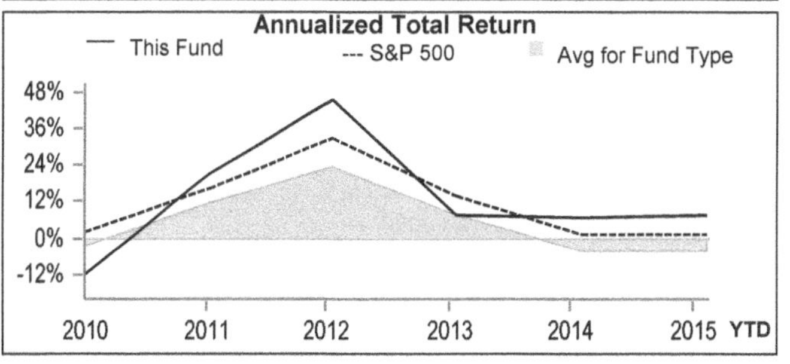

*SP Regional Banking ETF (KRE) A+ Excellent

Fund Family: SSgA Funds Management Inc
Fund Type: Financial Services
Inception Date: June 19, 2006

Major Rating Factors:
Strong performance is the major factor driving the A+ (Excellent) TheStreet.com Investment Rating for *SP Regional Banking ETF. The fund currently has a performance rating of B+ (Good) based on an annualized return of 14.50% over the last three years and a total return of 6.67% year to date 2015. Factored into the performance evaluation is an expense ratio of 0.35% (very low).

The fund's risk rating is currently B (Good). It carries a beta of 1.18, meaning it is expected to move 11.8% for every 10% move in the market. Volatility, as measured by both the semi-deviation and a drawdown factor, is considered low. As of December 31, 2015, *SP Regional Banking ETF traded at a discount of .05% below its net asset value, which is better than its one-year historical average discount of .01%.

John A. Tucker has been running the fund for 10 years and currently receives a manager quality ranking of 55 (0=worst, 99=best). If you desire only a moderate level of risk and strong performance, then this fund is an excellent option.

Data Date	Investment Rating	Net Assets ($Mil)	Price	Performance Rating/Pts	Total Return Y-T-D	Risk Rating/Pts
12-15	A+	2,197.20	41.92	B+ / 8.9	6.67%	B / 8.6
2014	B	2,197.20	40.70	B / 7.6	3.33%	B- / 7.3
2013	A-	2,901.00	40.61	B+ / 8.9	37.82%	B- / 7.7
2012	C-	1,147.00	27.97	C- / 3.8	12.58%	B- / 7.3
2011	D+	721.40	24.41	D+ / 2.9	0.95%	C+ / 6.8
2010	D	793.50	26.45	D+ / 2.3	20.66%	C / 5.3

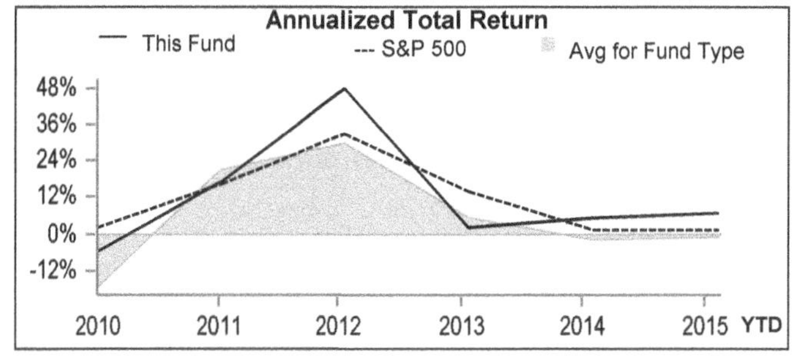

*SPDR Barclays 0-5 Year TIPS ETF (SIPE) C Fair

Fund Family: SSgA Funds Management Inc
Fund Type: General - Investment Grade
Inception Date: February 26, 2014

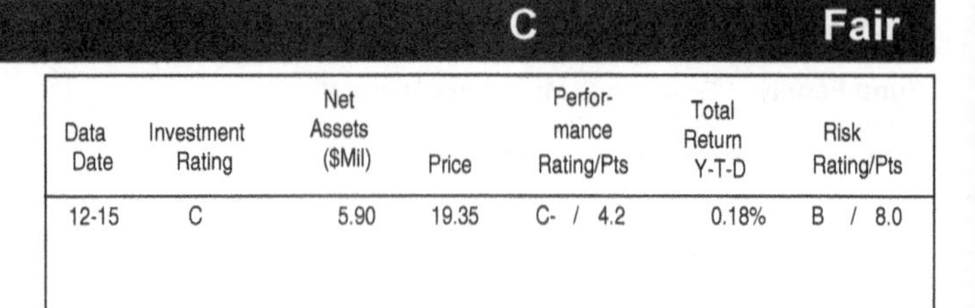

Data Date	Investment Rating	Net Assets ($Mil)	Price	Performance Rating/Pts	Total Return Y-T-D	Risk Rating/Pts
12-15	C	5.90	19.35	C- / 4.2	0.18%	B / 8.0

Major Rating Factors: Middle of the road best describes *SPDR Barclays 0-5 Year TIPS ETF whose TheStreet.com Investment Rating is currently a C (Fair). The fund currently has a performance rating of C- (Fair) based on an annualized return of 0.00% over the last three years and a total return of 0.18% year to date 2015. Factored into the performance evaluation is an expense ratio of 0.15% (very low).

The fund's risk rating is currently B (Good). It carries a beta of 0.00, meaning the fund's expected move will be 0.0% for every 10% move in the market. Volatility, as measured by both the semi-deviation and a drawdown factor, is considered low. As of December 31, 2015, *SPDR Barclays 0-5 Year TIPS ETF traded at a premium of .21% above its net asset value.

Mahesh Jayakumar has been running the fund for 2 years and currently receives a manager quality ranking of 67 (0=worst, 99=best). If you desire an average level of risk, then this fund may be an option.

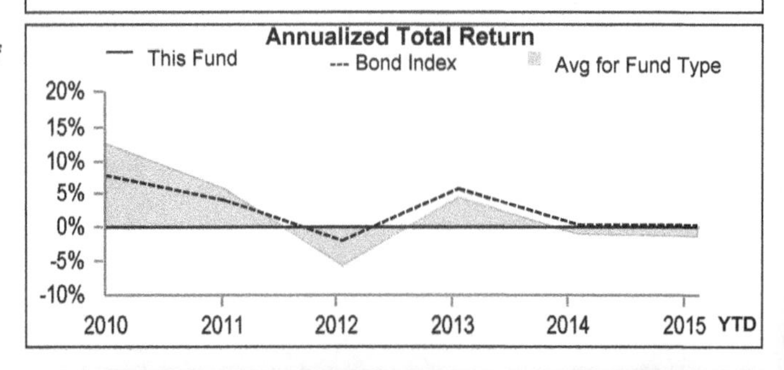

*SPDR Barclays 1-10 Year TIPS ETF (TIPX) C Fair

Fund Family: SSgA Funds Management Inc
Fund Type: General - Investment Grade
Inception Date: May 29, 2013

Data Date	Investment Rating	Net Assets ($Mil)	Price	Performance Rating/Pts	Total Return Y-T-D	Risk Rating/Pts
12-15	C	9.70	19.18	C- / 4.1	-0.07%	B- / 7.7
2014	C-	9.70	19.06	D+ / 2.4	0.44%	B+ / 9.2

Major Rating Factors: Middle of the road best describes *SPDR Barclays 1-10 Year TIPS ETF whose TheStreet.com Investment Rating is currently a C (Fair). The fund currently has a performance rating of C- (Fair) based on an annualized return of 0.00% over the last three years and a total return of -0.07% year to date 2015. Factored into the performance evaluation is an expense ratio of 0.15% (very low).

The fund's risk rating is currently B- (Good). It carries a beta of 0.00, meaning the fund's expected move will be 0.0% for every 10% move in the market. Volatility, as measured by both the semi-deviation and a drawdown factor, is considered low. As of December 31, 2015, *SPDR Barclays 1-10 Year TIPS ETF traded at a premium of 1.11% above its net asset value, which is worse than its one-year historical average premium of .09%.

Mahesh Jayakumar has been running the fund for 3 years and currently receives a manager quality ranking of 70 (0=worst, 99=best). If you desire an average level of risk, then this fund may be an option.

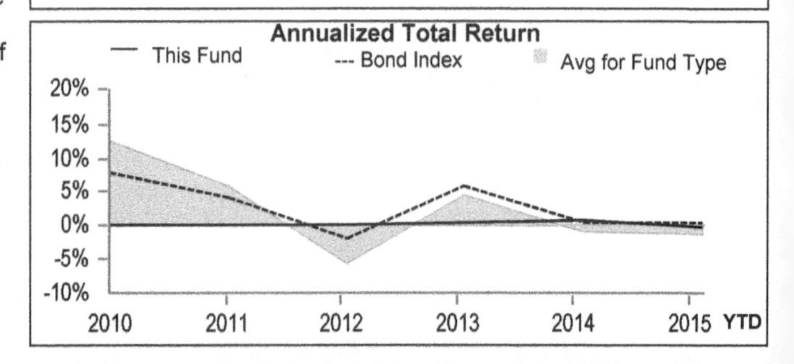

*SPDR Barclays 1-3 Month T-Bill E (BIL) C+ Fair

Fund Family: SSgA Funds Management Inc
Fund Type: US Government/Agency
Inception Date: May 25, 2007

Data Date	Investment Rating	Net Assets ($Mil)	Price	Performance Rating/Pts	Total Return Y-T-D	Risk Rating/Pts
12-15	C+	947.00	45.68	C- / 4.2	-0.11%	B / 8.9
2014	C-	947.00	45.74	D+ / 2.7	-0.09%	B+ / 9.0
2013	C	1,071.30	45.77	D+ / 2.5	-0.09%	B+ / 9.9
2012	C-	1,296.50	45.81	D- / 1.3	-0.04%	B+ / 9.9
2011	C-	1,654.50	45.83	D / 1.9	-0.06%	B+ / 9.9
2010	C	1,013.40	45.85	D+ / 2.3	-0.04%	B+ / 9.0

Major Rating Factors: Middle of the road best describes *SPDR Barclays 1-3 Month T-Bill E whose TheStreet.com Investment Rating is currently a C+ (Fair). The fund currently has a performance rating of C- (Fair) based on an annualized return of -0.10% over the last three years and a total return of -0.11% year to date 2015. Factored into the performance evaluation is an expense ratio of 0.14% (very low).

The fund's risk rating is currently B (Good). It carries a beta of 0.00, meaning the fund's expected move will be 0.0% for every 10% move in the market. Volatility, as measured by both the semi-deviation and a drawdown factor, is considered low. As of December 31, 2015, *SPDR Barclays 1-3 Month T-Bill E traded at a price exactly equal to its net asset value.

Jeffrey A. St. Peters currently receives a manager quality ranking of 66 (0=worst, 99=best). If you desire an average level of risk, then this fund may be an option.

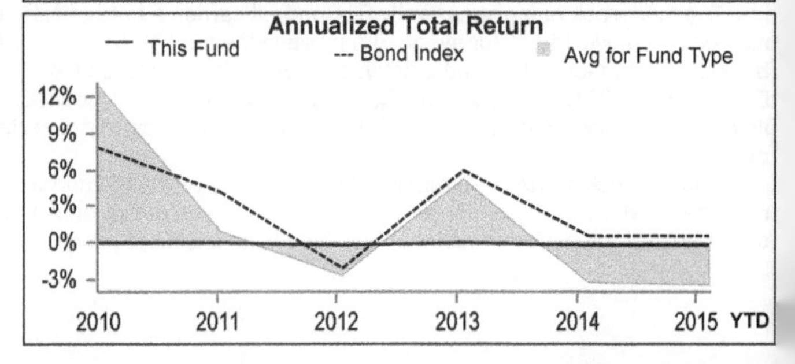

*SPDR Barclays Conv Sec ETF (CWB) C+ Fair

Fund Family: SSgA Funds Management Inc
Fund Type: Growth and Income
Inception Date: April 14, 2009

Major Rating Factors: Middle of the road best describes *SPDR Barclays Conv Sec ETF whose TheStreet.com Investment Rating is currently a C+ (Fair). The fund currently has a performance rating of C+ (Fair) based on an annualized return of 8.31% over the last three years and a total return of -0.86% year to date 2015. Factored into the performance evaluation is an expense ratio of 0.40% (very low).

The fund's risk rating is currently C+ (Fair). It carries a beta of 0.61, meaning the fund's expected move will be 6.1% for every 10% move in the market. Volatility, as measured by both the semi-deviation and a drawdown factor, is considered low. As of December 31, 2015, *SPDR Barclays Conv Sec ETF traded at a premium of .28% above its net asset value, which is worse than its one-year historical average premium of .07%.

Mahesh Jayakumar currently receives a manager quality ranking of 66 (0=worst, 99=best). If you desire an average level of risk, then this fund may be an option.

Data Date	Investment Rating	Net Assets ($Mil)	Price	Perfor-mance Rating/Pts	Total Return Y-T-D	Risk Rating/Pts
12-15	C+	2,940.10	43.28	C+ / 6.9	-0.86%	C+ / 6.7
2014	C+	2,940.10	46.89	C+ / 6.4	8.28%	B- / 7.1
2013	B-	2,018.10	46.73	C+ / 6.6	18.22%	B / 8.4
2012	C	918.40	40.30	C- / 3.9	14.25%	B / 8.3
2011	D+	680.90	36.17	D- / 1.5	-5.95%	B / 8.5
2010	A+	532.30	41.05	B+ / 8.6	13.01%	B / 8.4

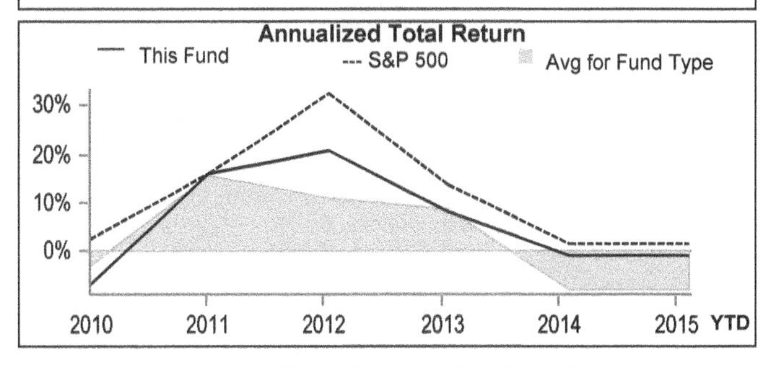

*SPDR Barclays Em Mkt Local Bond (EBND) C- Fair

Fund Family: SSgA Funds Management Inc
Fund Type: Growth and Income
Inception Date: February 23, 2011

Major Rating Factors:
Disappointing performance is the major factor driving the C- (Fair) TheStreet.com Investment Rating for *SPDR Barclays Em Mkt Local Bond. The fund currently has a performance rating of D (Weak) based on an annualized return of -7.56% over the last three years and a total return of -12.32% year to date 2015. Factored into the performance evaluation is an expense ratio of 0.50% (very low).

The fund's risk rating is currently B- (Good). It carries a beta of 0.50, meaning the fund's expected move will be 5.0% for every 10% move in the market. Volatility, as measured by both the semi-deviation and a drawdown factor, is considered low. As of December 31, 2015, *SPDR Barclays Em Mkt Local Bond traded at a discount of .28% below its net asset value, which is worse than its one-year historical average discount of .37%.

Abhishek Kumar has been running the fund for 5 years and currently receives a manager quality ranking of 11 (0=worst, 99=best). This fund offers only a moderate level of risk but investors looking for strong performance are still waiting.

Data Date	Investment Rating	Net Assets ($Mil)	Price	Perfor-mance Rating/Pts	Total Return Y-T-D	Risk Rating/Pts
12-15	C-	112.90	24.76	D / 2.2	-12.32%	B- / 7.5
2014	D+	112.90	28.43	D+ / 2.6	-2.81%	C+ / 6.4
2013	D+	176.70	29.75	D / 1.7	-6.69%	B / 8.4
2012	C+	150.50	32.29	C+ / 5.8	13.19%	B / 8.7

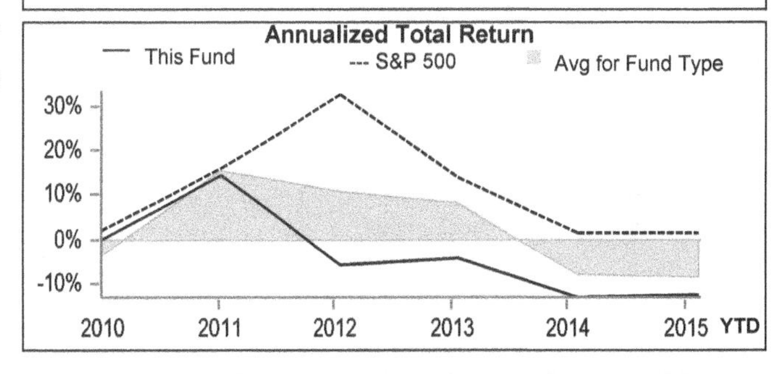

*SPDR Barclays High Yield Bond ET (JNK) C- Fair

Fund Family: SSgA Funds Management Inc
Fund Type: Corporate - High Yield
Inception Date: November 28, 2007

Major Rating Factors: Middle of the road best describes *SPDR Barclays High Yield Bond ET whose TheStreet.com Investment Rating is currently a C- (Fair). The fund currently has a performance rating of C- (Fair) based on an annualized return of -0.23% over the last three years and a total return of -6.91% year to date 2015. Factored into the performance evaluation is an expense ratio of 0.40% (very low).

The fund's risk rating is currently C+ (Fair). It carries a beta of 1.14, meaning it is expected to move 11.4% for every 10% move in the market. Volatility, as measured by both the semi-deviation and a drawdown factor, is considered low. As of December 31, 2015, *SPDR Barclays High Yield Bond ET traded at a premium of .47% above its net asset value, which is worse than its one-year historical average premium of .25%.

Michael J. Brunell currently receives a manager quality ranking of 52 (0=worst, 99=best). If you desire an average level of risk, then this fund may be an option.

Data Date	Investment Rating	Net Assets ($Mil)	Price	Perfor-mance Rating/Pts	Total Return Y-T-D	Risk Rating/Pts
12-15	C-	8,896.70	33.91	C- / 3.6	-6.91%	C+ / 6.6
2014	C+	8,896.70	38.61	C- / 4.2	1.28%	B / 8.9
2013	C	9,965.10	40.56	C+ / 5.7	5.14%	B- / 7.5
2012	C-	12,502.30	40.71	C / 4.5	14.40%	B- / 7.3
2011	B-	8,852.60	38.45	C+ / 6.1	5.78%	B / 8.6
2010	C+	6,315.30	39.71	C+ / 6.1	11.68%	C+ / 6.0

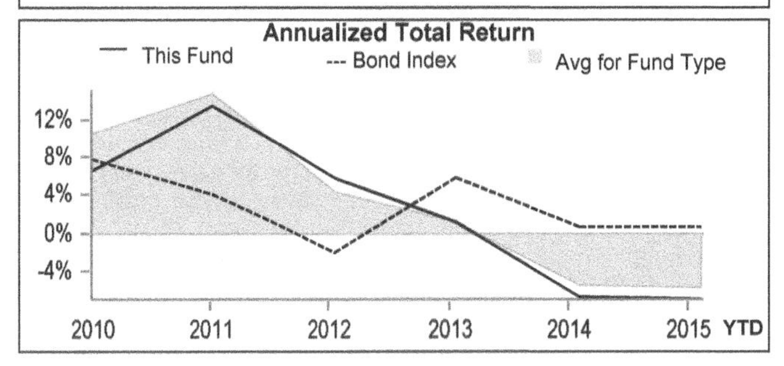

*SPDR Barclays Int Term Crp Bond (ITR) C+ Fair

Fund Family: SSgA Funds Management Inc
Fund Type: General - Investment Grade
Inception Date: February 10, 2009

Major Rating Factors: Middle of the road best describes *SPDR Barclays Int Term Crp Bond whose TheStreet.com Investment Rating is currently a C+ (Fair). The fund currently has a performance rating of C (Fair) based on an annualized return of 1.58% over the last three years and a total return of 0.17% year to date 2015. Factored into the performance evaluation is an expense ratio of 0.14% (very low).

The fund's risk rating is currently B (Good). It carries a beta of 0.94, meaning that its performance tracks fairly well with that of the overall stock market. Volatility, as measured by both the semi-deviation and a drawdown factor, is considered low. As of December 31, 2015, *SPDR Barclays Int Term Crp Bond traded at a price exactly equal to its net asset value, which is better than its one-year historical average premium of .21%.

Kyle Kelly has been running the fund for 4 years and currently receives a manager quality ranking of 69 (0=worst, 99=best). If you desire an average level of risk, then this fund may be an option.

Data Date	Investment Rating	Net Assets ($Mil)	Price	Performance Rating/Pts	Total Return Y-T-D	Risk Rating/Pts
12-15	C+	466.40	33.43	C / 5.0	0.17%	B / 8.7
2014	C-	466.40	34.18	C- / 3.9	4.38%	B- / 7.8
2013	C+	432.70	33.60	C- / 4.1	-0.04%	B+ / 9.7
2012	C	349.80	34.82	D+ / 2.8	7.25%	B+ / 9.7
2011	C	217.60	33.21	C- / 3.1	5.67%	B+ / 9.8
2010	B	143.10	32.56	C- / 4.2	6.35%	B / 8.9

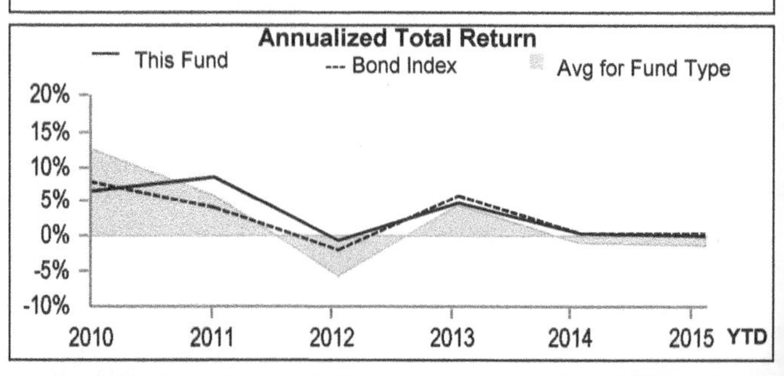

*SPDR Barclays Int Tr Treas ETF (ITE) C+ Fair

Fund Family: SSgA Funds Management Inc
Fund Type: US Government/Agency
Inception Date: May 23, 2007

Major Rating Factors: Middle of the road best describes *SPDR Barclays Int Tr Treas ETF whose TheStreet.com Investment Rating is currently a C+ (Fair). The fund currently has a performance rating of C (Fair) based on an annualized return of 1.03% over the last three years and a total return of 1.54% year to date 2015. Factored into the performance evaluation is an expense ratio of 0.12% (very low).

The fund's risk rating is currently B (Good). It carries a beta of 0.17, meaning the fund's expected move will be 1.7% for every 10% move in the market. Volatility, as measured by both the semi-deviation and a drawdown factor, is considered low. As of December 31, 2015, *SPDR Barclays Int Tr Treas ETF traded at a premium of .60% above its net asset value, which is worse than its one-year historical average premium of .03%.

Joanna Mauro has been running the fund for 2 years and currently receives a manager quality ranking of 73 (0=worst, 99=best). If you desire an average level of risk, then this fund may be an option.

Data Date	Investment Rating	Net Assets ($Mil)	Price	Performance Rating/Pts	Total Return Y-T-D	Risk Rating/Pts
12-15	C+	172.70	60.19	C / 4.9	1.54%	B / 8.0
2014	C	172.70	59.95	C- / 3.2	2.62%	B+ / 9.2
2013	C	165.40	59.12	C- / 3.1	-1.10%	B+ / 9.8
2012	C-	170.30	60.72	D / 2.1	1.31%	B+ / 9.8
2011	C	226.10	61.05	D+ / 2.8	6.45%	B+ / 9.8
2010	B	205.30	58.57	C- / 3.9	4.53%	B+ / 9.1

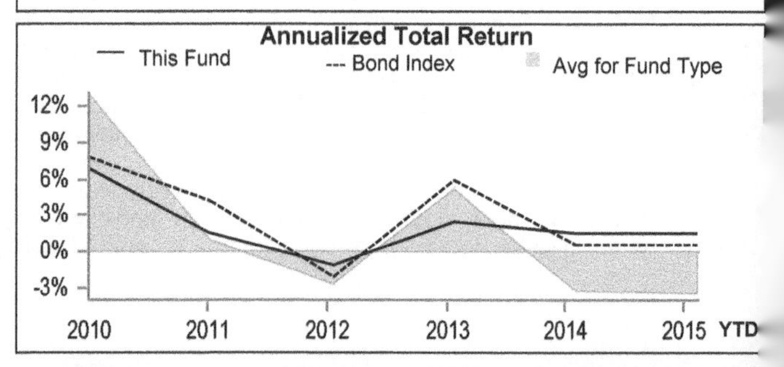

*SPDR Barclays Intl Corporate Bd (IBND) C- Fair

Fund Family: SSgA Funds Management Inc
Fund Type: Corporate - Investment Grade
Inception Date: May 19, 2010

Major Rating Factors: Middle of the road best describes *SPDR Barclays Intl Corporate Bd whose TheStreet.com Investment Rating is currently a C- (Fair). The fund currently has a performance rating of C- (Fair) based on an annualized return of -3.13% over the last three years and a total return of -9.99% year to date 2015. Factored into the performance evaluation is an expense ratio of 0.54% (very low).

The fund's risk rating is currently C+ (Fair). It carries a beta of 0.18, meaning the fund's expected move will be 1.8% for every 10% move in the market. Volatility, as measured by both the semi-deviation and a drawdown factor, is considered low. As of December 31, 2015, *SPDR Barclays Intl Corporate Bd traded at a premium of .06% above its net asset value, which is worse than its one-year historical average discount of .05%.

Stephen Yeats has been running the fund for 4 years and currently receives a manager quality ranking of 37 (0=worst, 99=best). If you desire an average level of risk, then this fund may be an option.

Data Date	Investment Rating	Net Assets ($Mil)	Price	Performance Rating/Pts	Total Return Y-T-D	Risk Rating/Pts
12-15	C-	311.70	30.80	C- / 3.0	-9.99%	C+ / 6.7
2014	C-	311.70	34.37	C- / 3.5	-3.69%	B- / 7.1
2013	C+	229.90	36.70	C / 4.9	5.29%	B / 8.7
2012	B+	116.10	35.40	B- / 7.3	15.22%	B / 8.7
2011	D+	53.60	31.52	D- / 1.4	-1.99%	B / 8.7

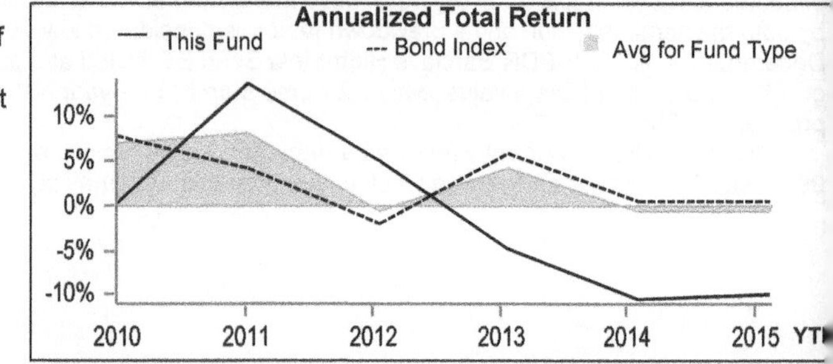

*SPDR Barclays Intl High Yld Bd E (IJNK) C- Fair

Fund Family: SSgA Funds Management Inc
Fund Type: Global
Inception Date: March 12, 2014

Major Rating Factors: Middle of the road best describes *SPDR Barclays Intl High Yld Bd E whose TheStreet.com Investment Rating is currently a C- (Fair). The fund currently has a performance rating of C- (Fair) based on an annualized return of 0.00% over the last three years and a total return of -4.47% year to date 2015. Factored into the performance evaluation is an expense ratio of 0.40% (very low).

The fund's risk rating is currently C+ (Fair). It carries a beta of 0.00, meaning the fund's expected move will be 0.0% for every 10% move in the market. Volatility, as measured by both the semi-deviation and a drawdown factor, is considered low. As of December 31, 2015, *SPDR Barclays Intl High Yld Bd E traded at a premium of 1.84% above its net asset value, which is worse than its one-year historical average discount of .55%.

Kyle Kelly has been running the fund for 2 years and currently receives a manager quality ranking of 45 (0=worst, 99=best). If you desire an average level of risk, then this fund may be an option.

Data Date	Investment Rating	Net Assets ($Mil)	Price	Performance Rating/Pts	Total Return Y-T-D	Risk Rating/Pts
12-15	C-	33.70	21.63	C- / 3.1	-4.47%	C+ / 6.8

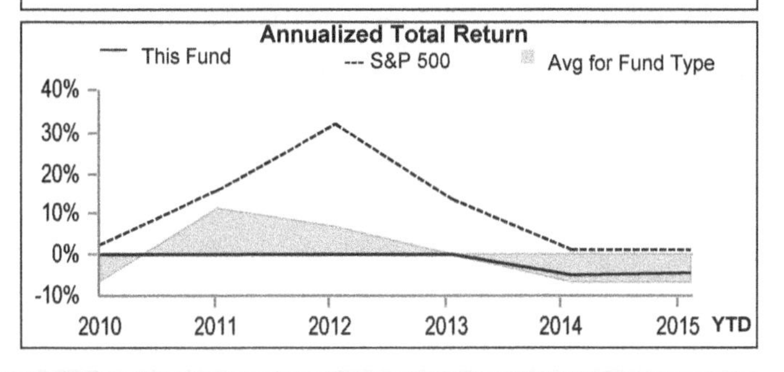

*SPDR Barclays Intl Treasury Bd E (BWX) C- Fair

Fund Family: SSgA Funds Management Inc
Fund Type: Global
Inception Date: October 2, 2007

Major Rating Factors: Middle of the road best describes *SPDR Barclays Intl Treasury Bd E whose TheStreet.com Investment Rating is currently a C- (Fair). The fund currently has a performance rating of C- (Fair) based on an annualized return of -3.74% over the last three years and a total return of -6.28% year to date 2015. Factored into the performance evaluation is an expense ratio of 0.50% (very low).

The fund's risk rating is currently B- (Good). It carries a beta of 1.00, meaning that its performance tracks fairly well with that of the overall stock market. Volatility, as measured by both the semi-deviation and a drawdown factor, is considered low. As of December 31, 2015, *SPDR Barclays Intl Treasury Bd E traded at a premium of .47% above its net asset value, which is worse than its one-year historical average discount of .03%.

Mahesh Jayakumar has been running the fund for 4 years and currently receives a manager quality ranking of 67 (0=worst, 99=best). If you desire an average level of risk, then this fund may be an option.

Data Date	Investment Rating	Net Assets ($Mil)	Price	Performance Rating/Pts	Total Return Y-T-D	Risk Rating/Pts
12-15	C-	2,221.70	51.63	C- / 3.0	-6.28%	B- / 7.3
2014	D+	2,221.70	55.33	D+ / 2.6	-1.53%	B- / 7.5
2013	C	2,040.60	57.74	C- / 3.3	-2.93%	B+ / 9.1
2012	C-	1,975.10	61.01	D / 2.2	6.27%	B+ / 9.3
2011	C-	1,616.60	58.83	D+ / 2.6	5.66%	B / 8.8
2010	C+	1,342.40	58.46	C- / 4.1	3.17%	B- / 7.8

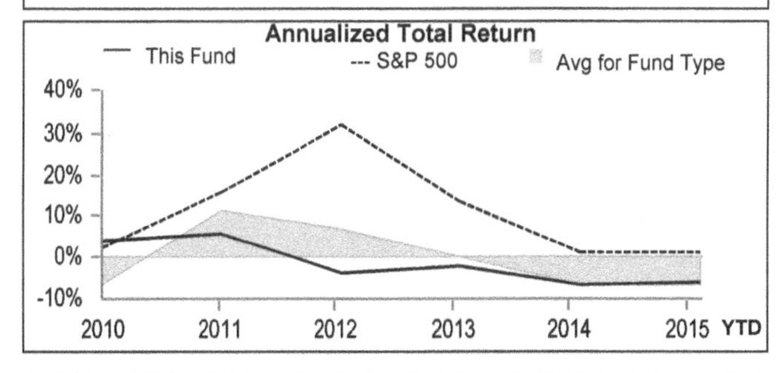

*SPDR Barclays Invest Grade FlRt (FLRN) C Fair

Fund Family: SSgA Funds Management Inc
Fund Type: Corporate - Investment Grade
Inception Date: December 1, 2011

Major Rating Factors: Middle of the road best describes *SPDR Barclays Invest Grade FlRt whose TheStreet.com Investment Rating is currently a C (Fair). The fund currently has a performance rating of C (Fair) based on an annualized return of 0.34% over the last three years and a total return of 0.47% year to date 2015. Factored into the performance evaluation is an expense ratio of 0.15% (very low).

The fund's risk rating is currently B (Good). It carries a beta of 0.00, meaning the fund's expected move will be 0.0% for every 10% move in the market. Volatility, as measured by both the semi-deviation and a drawdown factor, is considered low. As of December 31, 2015, *SPDR Barclays Invest Grade FlRt traded at a premium of .07% above its net asset value, which is worse than its one-year historical average premium of .03%.

Thomas Connelley has been running the fund for 5 years and currently receives a manager quality ranking of 71 (0=worst, 99=best). If you desire an average level of risk, then this fund may be an option.

Data Date	Investment Rating	Net Assets ($Mil)	Price	Performance Rating/Pts	Total Return Y-T-D	Risk Rating/Pts
12-15	C	395.30	30.42	C / 4.4	0.47%	B / 8.2
2014	C	395.30	30.48	C- / 3.1	-0.05%	B+ / 9.5
2013	C	354.60	30.67	D+ / 2.7	0.63%	B+ / 9.7
2012	C-	15.20	30.66	D / 2.1	3.04%	B+ / 9.6

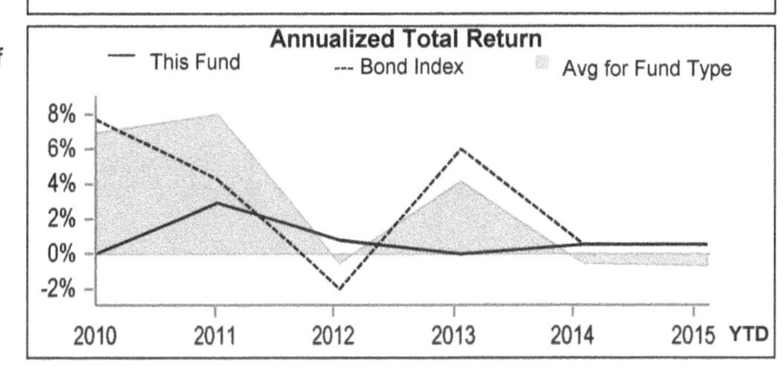

*SPDR Barclays Iss Sco Corp Bond (CBND) C Fair

Fund Family: SSgA Funds Management Inc
Fund Type: Corporate - Investment Grade
Inception Date: April 6, 2011

Major Rating Factors: Middle of the road best describes *SPDR Barclays Iss Sco Corp Bond whose TheStreet.com Investment Rating is currently a C (Fair). The fund currently has a performance rating of C (Fair) based on an annualized return of 1.59% over the last three years and a total return of -1.58% year to date 2015. Factored into the performance evaluation is an expense ratio of 0.16% (very low).

The fund's risk rating is currently B- (Good). It carries a beta of 1.00, meaning that its performance tracks fairly well with that of the overall stock market. Volatility, as measured by both the semi-deviation and a drawdown factor, is considered low. As of December 31, 2015, *SPDR Barclays Iss Sco Corp Bond traded at a premium of .42% above its net asset value, which is worse than its one-year historical average premium of .39%.

Patrick Bresnehan has been running the fund for 5 years and currently receives a manager quality ranking of 70 (0=worst, 99=best). If you desire an average level of risk, then this fund may be an option.

Data Date	Investment Rating	Net Assets ($Mil)	Price	Performance Rating/Pts	Total Return Y-T-D	Risk Rating/Pts
12-15	C	12.80	30.99	C / 4.9	-1.58%	B- / 7.6
2014	C-	12.80	32.42	C / 4.3	8.00%	B- / 7.4
2013	C	27.90	30.94	D+ / 2.9	-1.44%	B+ / 9.4
2012	C	29.30	32.58	D+ / 2.8	7.08%	B+ / 9.9

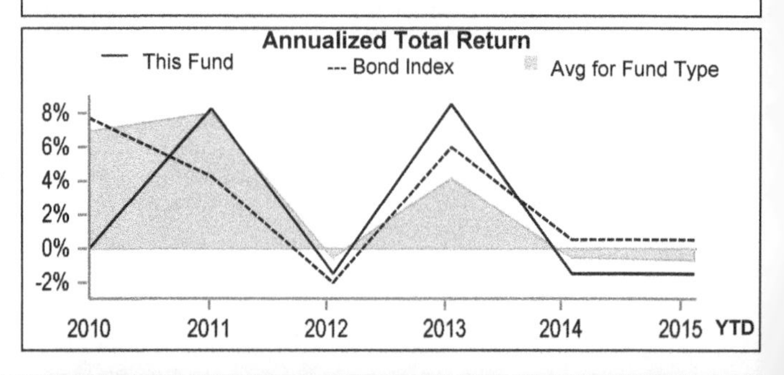

*SPDR Barclays LongTerm Treasury (TLO) C+ Fair

Fund Family: SSgA Funds Management Inc
Fund Type: US Government/Agency
Inception Date: May 23, 2007

Major Rating Factors: Middle of the road best describes *SPDR Barclays LongTerm Treasury whose TheStreet.com Investment Rating is currently a C+ (Fair). The fund currently has a performance rating of C+ (Fair) based on an annualized return of 3.43% over the last three years and a total return of -2.24% year to date 2015. Factored into the performance evaluation is an expense ratio of 0.11% (very low).

The fund's risk rating is currently B (Good). It carries a beta of 1.04, meaning that its performance tracks fairly well with that of the overall stock market. Volatility, as measured by both the semi-deviation and a drawdown factor, is considered low. As of December 31, 2015, *SPDR Barclays LongTerm Treasury traded at a discount of .09% below its net asset value, which is better than its one-year historical average discount of .01%.

Karen Tsang has been running the fund for 6 years and currently receives a manager quality ranking of 68 (0=worst, 99=best). If you desire an average level of risk, then this fund may be an option.

Data Date	Investment Rating	Net Assets ($Mil)	Price	Performance Rating/Pts	Total Return Y-T-D	Risk Rating/Pts
12-15	C+	108.10	69.88	C+ / 5.6	-2.24%	B / 8.4
2014	C+	108.10	72.87	C+ / 6.0	25.13%	B / 8.0
2013	C-	35.90	59.84	C- / 3.9	-10.11%	B / 8.2
2012	C	42.40	70.11	C- / 3.9	1.83%	B / 8.7
2011	C+	56.00	69.93	C / 5.5	30.10%	B / 8.5
2010	C+	27.90	55.55	C- / 3.6	8.41%	B / 8.1

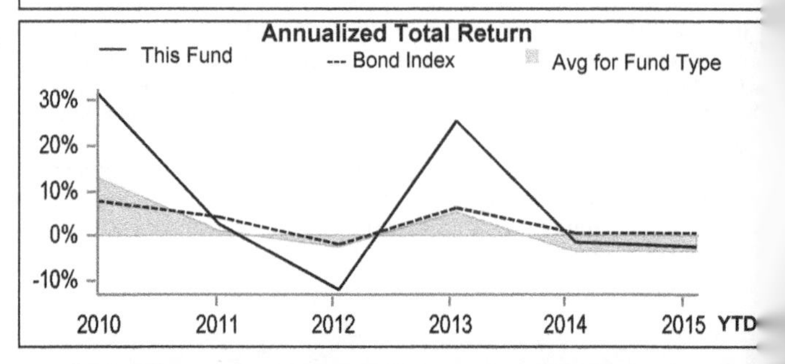

*SPDR Barclays LongTrm Corp Bond (LWC) C Fair

Fund Family: SSgA Funds Management Inc
Fund Type: General - Investment Grade
Inception Date: March 10, 2009

Major Rating Factors: Middle of the road best describes *SPDR Barclays LongTrm Corp Bond whose TheStreet.com Investment Rating is currently a C (Fair). The fund currently has a performance rating of C (Fair) based on an annualized return of 1.86% over the last three years and a total return of -5.87% year to date 2015. Factored into the performance evaluation is an expense ratio of 0.14% (very low).

The fund's risk rating is currently C+ (Fair). It carries a beta of 2.67, meaning it is expected to move 26.7% for every 10% move in the market. Volatility, as measured by both the semi-deviation and a drawdown factor, is considered low. As of December 31, 2015, *SPDR Barclays LongTrm Corp Bond traded at a premium of .37% above its net asset value, which is worse than its one-year historical average premium of .25%.

John P. Kirby currently receives a manager quality ranking of 50 (0=worst, 99=best). If you desire an average level of risk, then this fund may be an option.

Data Date	Investment Rating	Net Assets ($Mil)	Price	Performance Rating/Pts	Total Return Y-T-D	Risk Rating/Pts
12-15	C	212.00	37.58	C / 4.8	-5.87%	C+ / 6.8
2014	C	212.00	41.36	C / 5.4	16.15%	C+ / 6.9
2013	C+	81.50	37.12	C / 5.0	-4.29%	B / 8.7
2012	C	128.00	41.14	C- / 3.8	9.21%	B+ / 9.0
2011	B	65.90	39.49	C+ / 6.8	17.49%	B+ / 9.1
2010	C+	28.40	35.65	D+ / 2.9	6.18%	B / 8.5

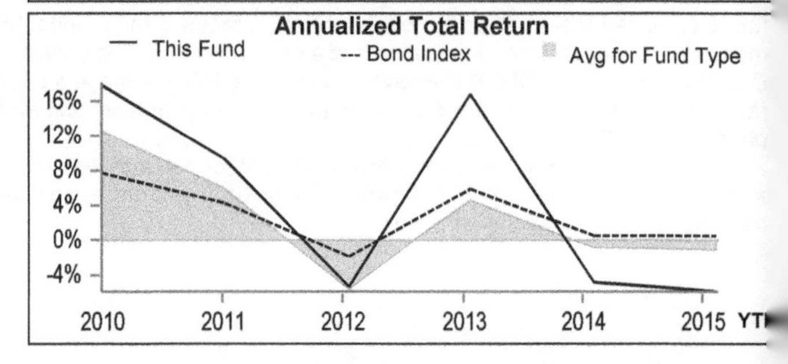

*SPDR Barclays Mortg Backed Bond (MBG) C+ Fair

Fund Family: SSgA Funds Management Inc
Fund Type: Mortgage
Inception Date: January 15, 2009

Major Rating Factors: Middle of the road best describes *SPDR Barclays Mortg Backed Bond whose TheStreet.com Investment Rating is currently a C+ (Fair). The fund currently has a performance rating of C (Fair) based on an annualized return of 2.01% over the last three years and a total return of 2.05% year to date 2015. Factored into the performance evaluation is an expense ratio of 0.20% (very low).

The fund's risk rating is currently B- (Good). It carries a beta of 1.07, meaning that its performance tracks fairly well with that of the overall stock market. Volatility, as measured by both the semi-deviation and a drawdown factor, is considered low. As of December 31, 2015, *SPDR Barclays Mortg Backed Bond traded at a premium of .34% above its net asset value, which is worse than its one-year historical average premium of .18%.

Karen Tsang currently receives a manager quality ranking of 66 (0=worst, 99=best). If you desire an average level of risk, then this fund may be an option.

Data Date	Investment Rating	Net Assets ($Mil)	Price	Performance Rating/Pts	Total Return Y-T-D	Risk Rating/Pts
12-15	C+	122.70	26.82	C / 5.3	2.05%	B- / 7.9
2014	C+	122.70	27.17	C- / 3.5	5.93%	B+ / 9.6
2013	C	111.80	26.56	C- / 3.2	-1.51%	B+ / 9.7
2012	C-	35.50	27.31	D / 2.1	1.76%	B+ / 9.6
2011	C	41.10	27.38	C- / 3.5	7.10%	B+ / 9.6
2010	C	32.20	26.44	D / 1.9	2.55%	B / 8.8

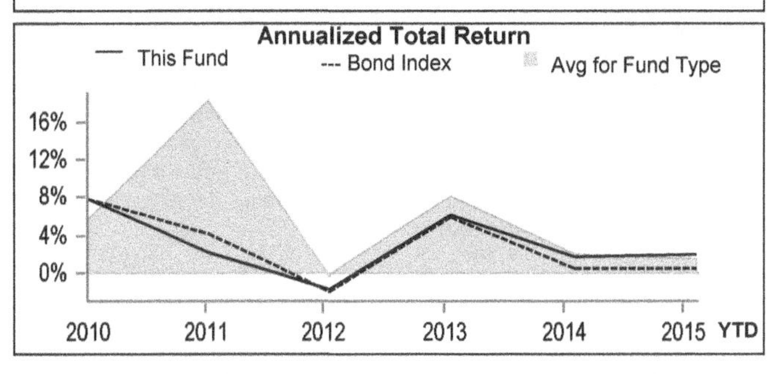

*SPDR Barclays Short Term HiYld B (SJNK) C- Fair

Fund Family: SSgA Funds Management Inc
Fund Type: Corporate - High Yield
Inception Date: March 14, 2012

Major Rating Factors: Middle of the road best describes *SPDR Barclays Short Term HiYld B whose TheStreet.com Investment Rating is currently a C- (Fair). The fund currently has a performance rating of C- (Fair) based on an annualized return of -0.42% over the last three years and a total return of -6.61% year to date 2015. Factored into the performance evaluation is an expense ratio of 0.40% (very low).

The fund's risk rating is currently C+ (Fair). It carries a beta of 0.78, meaning the fund's expected move will be 7.8% for every 10% move in the market. Volatility, as measured by both the semi-deviation and a drawdown factor, is considered low. As of December 31, 2015, *SPDR Barclays Short Term HiYld B traded at a premium of .27% above its net asset value, which is worse than its one-year historical average premium of .21%.

Michael J. Brunell currently receives a manager quality ranking of 55 (0=worst, 99=best). If you desire an average level of risk, then this fund may be an option.

Data Date	Investment Rating	Net Assets ($Mil)	Price	Performance Rating/Pts	Total Return Y-T-D	Risk Rating/Pts
12-15	C-	3,936.40	25.69	C- / 3.5	-6.61%	C+ / 6.8
2014	C-	3,936.40	28.91	D / 2.2	-0.91%	B+ / 9.2
2013	B	3,045.50	30.85	C+ / 5.7	6.31%	B+ / 9.8

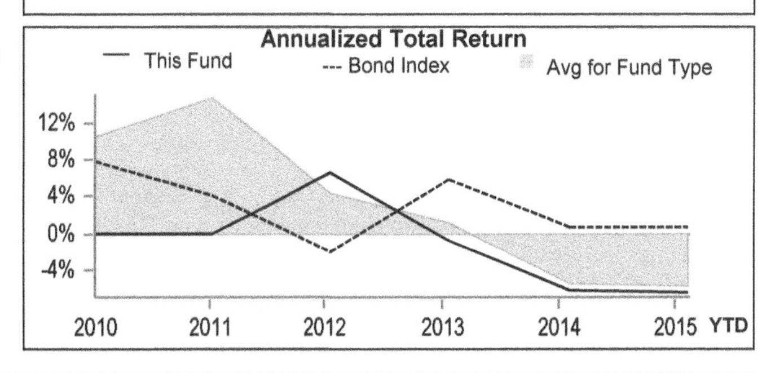

*SPDR Barclays Sht Trm Corp Bond (SCPB) C+ Fair

Fund Family: SSgA Funds Management Inc
Fund Type: Corporate - Investment Grade
Inception Date: December 16, 2009

Major Rating Factors: Middle of the road best describes *SPDR Barclays Sht Trm Corp Bond whose TheStreet.com Investment Rating is currently a C+ (Fair). The fund currently has a performance rating of C (Fair) based on an annualized return of 1.05% over the last three years and a total return of 0.87% year to date 2015. Factored into the performance evaluation is an expense ratio of 0.12% (very low).

The fund's risk rating is currently B (Good). It carries a beta of 0.15, meaning the fund's expected move will be 1.5% for every 10% move in the market. Volatility, as measured by both the semi-deviation and a drawdown factor, is considered low. As of December 31, 2015, *SPDR Barclays Sht Trm Corp Bond traded at a premium of .20% above its net asset value, which is worse than its one-year historical average premium of .08%.

Patrick Bresnehan has been running the fund for 6 years and currently receives a manager quality ranking of 75 (0=worst, 99=best). If you desire an average level of risk, then this fund may be an option.

Data Date	Investment Rating	Net Assets ($Mil)	Price	Performance Rating/Pts	Total Return Y-T-D	Risk Rating/Pts
12-15	C+	3,685.50	30.40	C / 4.9	0.87%	B / 8.0
2014	C-	3,685.50	30.59	C- / 3.2	1.08%	B- / 7.9
2013	C	2,926.80	30.69	C- / 3.2	1.25%	B+ / 9.9
2012	C-	1,723.10	30.72	D / 2.0	2.97%	B+ / 9.9
2011	C	390.60	30.11	D+ / 2.3	2.08%	B+ / 9.9
2010	B-	196.40	30.25	C- / 3.4	2.52%	B+ / 9.0

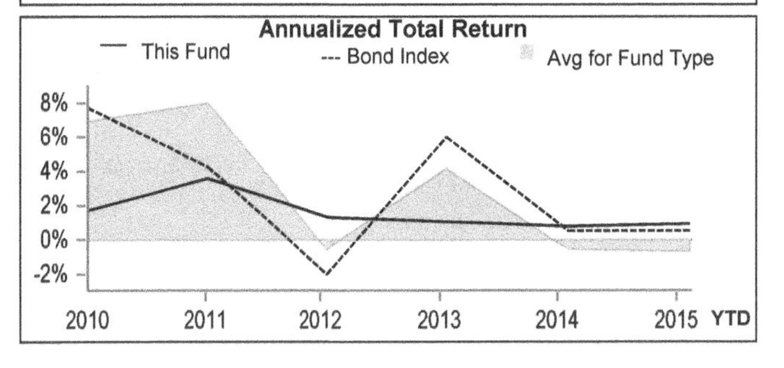

*SPDR Barclays Sht Trm Treasury E (SST) C Fair

Fund Family: SSgA Funds Management Inc
Fund Type: US Government/Agency
Inception Date: December 1, 2011

Major Rating Factors: Middle of the road best describes *SPDR Barclays Sht Trm Treasury E whose TheStreet.com Investment Rating is currently a C (Fair). The fund currently has a performance rating of C (Fair) based on an annualized return of 0.62% over the last three years and a total return of 0.83% year to date 2015. Factored into the performance evaluation is an expense ratio of 0.11% (very low).

The fund's risk rating is currently B- (Good). It carries a beta of 0.18, meaning the fund's expected move will be 1.8% for every 10% move in the market. Volatility, as measured by both the semi-deviation and a drawdown factor, is considered low. As of December 31, 2015, *SPDR Barclays Sht Trm Treasury E traded at a premium of .10% above its net asset value, which is worse than its one-year historical average premium of .02%.

Karen Tsang has been running the fund for 5 years and currently receives a manager quality ranking of 68 (0=worst, 99=best). If you desire an average level of risk, then this fund may be an option.

Data Date	Investment Rating	Net Assets ($Mil)	Price	Performance Rating/Pts	Total Return Y-T-D	Risk Rating/Pts
12-15	C	12.00	30.10	C / 4.6	0.83%	B- / 7.8
2014	C	12.00	30.08	C- / 3.0	0.90%	B / 8.9
2013	C	21.00	29.93	D+ / 2.7	0.06%	B+ / 9.9
2012	C-	3.00	30.17	D- / 1.5	0.77%	B+ / 9.9

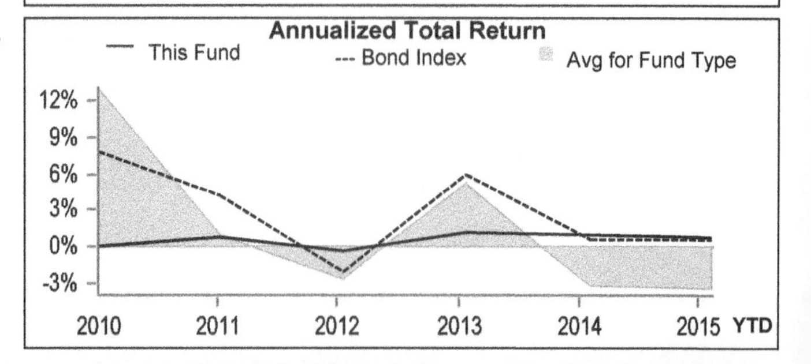

*SPDR Barclays ST Intl Treas Bd E (BWZ) C- Fair

Fund Family: SSgA Funds Management Inc
Fund Type: Global
Inception Date: January 15, 2009

Major Rating Factors:
Disappointing performance is the major factor driving the C- (Fair) TheStreet.com Investment Rating for *SPDR Barclays ST Intl Treas Bd E. The fund currently has a performance rating of D+ (Weak) based on an annualized return of -6.43% over the last three years and a total return of -6.54% year to date 2015. Factored into the performance evaluation is an expense ratio of 0.35% (very low).

The fund's risk rating is currently B (Good). It carries a beta of 0.83, meaning the fund's expected move will be 8.3% for every 10% move in the market. Volatility, as measured by both the semi-deviation and a drawdown factor, is considered low. As of December 31, 2015, *SPDR Barclays ST Intl Treas Bd E traded at a discount of .03% below its net asset value, which is worse than its one-year historical average discount of .12%.

Mahesh Jayakumar has been running the fund for 6 years and currently receives a manager quality ranking of 42 (0=worst, 99=best). This fund offers only a moderate level of risk but investors looking for strong performance are still waiting.

Data Date	Investment Rating	Net Assets ($Mil)	Price	Performance Rating/Pts	Total Return Y-T-D	Risk Rating/Pts
12-15	C-	265.80	29.75	D+ / 2.6	-6.54%	B / 8.2
2014	D	265.80	32.26	D / 2.0	-8.98%	C+ / 6.9
2013	C-	239.50	35.82	D+ / 2.6	-2.46%	B / 8.7
2012	D+	256.50	36.65	D / 1.7	2.84%	B / 8.7
2011	C-	218.90	35.59	D / 1.6	1.02%	B / 8.9
2010	B	166.60	37.00	C / 4.7	1.59%	B / 8.2

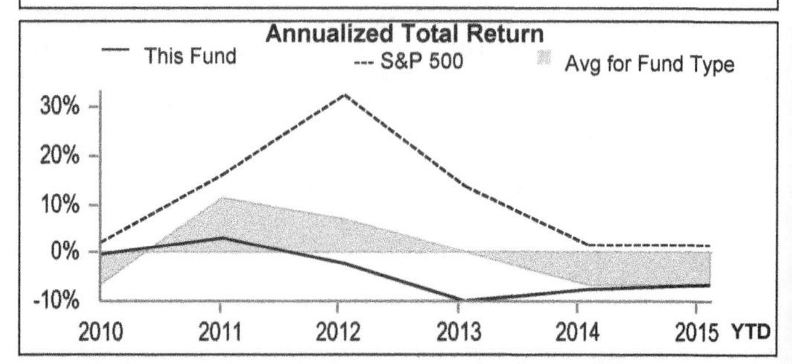

*SPDR Barclays TIPS ETF (IPE) C Fair

Fund Family: SSgA Funds Management Inc
Fund Type: US Government/Agency
Inception Date: May 25, 2007

Major Rating Factors: Middle of the road best describes *SPDR Barclays TIPS ETF whose TheStreet.com Investment Rating is currently a C (Fair). The fund currently has a performance rating of C- (Fair) based on an annualized return of -2.22% over the last three years and a total return of -3.18% year to date 2015. Factored into the performance evaluation is an expense ratio of 0.17% (very low).

The fund's risk rating is currently B (Good). It carries a beta of 0.41, meaning the fund's expected move will be 4.1% for every 10% move in the market. Volatility, as measured by both the semi-deviation and a drawdown factor, is considered low. As of December 31, 2015, *SPDR Barclays TIPS ETF traded at a discount of .18% below its net asset value, which is better than its one-year historical average discount of .01%.

Mahesh Jayakumar has been running the fund for 8 years and currently receives a manager quality ranking of 39 (0=worst, 99=best). If you desire an average level of risk, then this fund may be an option.

Data Date	Investment Rating	Net Assets ($Mil)	Price	Performance Rating/Pts	Total Return Y-T-D	Risk Rating/Pts
12-15	C	596.30	54.63	C- / 3.4	-3.18%	B / 8.8
2014	C-	596.30	55.98	C- / 3.0	4.18%	B / 8.8
2013	C	577.20	54.41	C- / 3.2	-8.18%	B+ / 9.0
2012	C	771.60	60.72	C- / 3.3	6.31%	B+ / 9.7
2011	B-	613.60	58.02	C / 4.7	15.28%	B+ / 9.7
2010	B-	360.60	53.12	C / 4.3	6.03%	B / 8.3

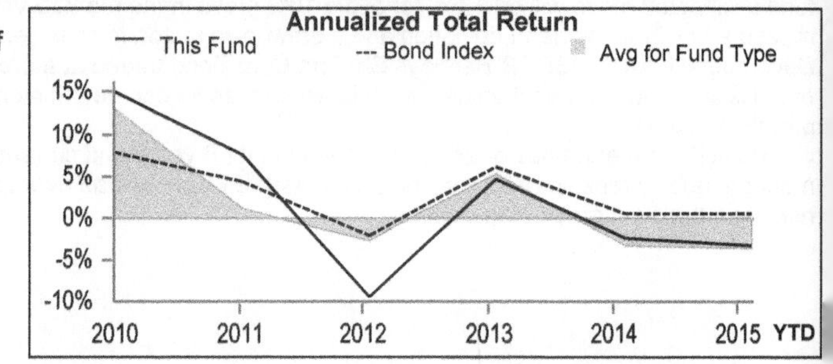

*SPDR Blackstone/GSO Senior Loan (SRLN) C Fair

Fund Family: SSgA Funds Management Inc
Fund Type: Loan Participation
Inception Date: April 3, 2013

Major Rating Factors: Middle of the road best describes *SPDR Blackstone/GSO Senior Loan whose TheStreet.com Investment Rating is currently a C (Fair). The fund currently has a performance rating of C- (Fair) based on an annualized return of 0.00% over the last three years and a total return of -1.15% year to date 2015. Factored into the performance evaluation is an expense ratio of 0.71% (very low).

The fund's risk rating is currently B+ (Good). It carries a beta of 0.00, meaning the fund's expected move will be 0.0% for every 10% move in the market. Volatility, as measured by both the semi-deviation and a drawdown factor, is considered very low. As of December 31, 2015, *SPDR Blackstone/GSO Senior Loan traded at a discount of .15% below its net asset value, which is better than its one-year historical average discount of .02%.

Lee Shaiman has been running the fund for 3 years and currently receives a manager quality ranking of 67 (0=worst, 99=best). If you desire an average level of risk, then this fund may be an option.

Data Date	Investment Rating	Net Assets ($Mil)	Price	Performance Rating/Pts	Total Return Y-T-D	Risk Rating/Pts
12-15	C	0.00	46.13	C- / 3.2	-1.15%	B+ / 9.4
2014	D	0.00	48.75	C- / 3.0	1.19%	C / 4.7

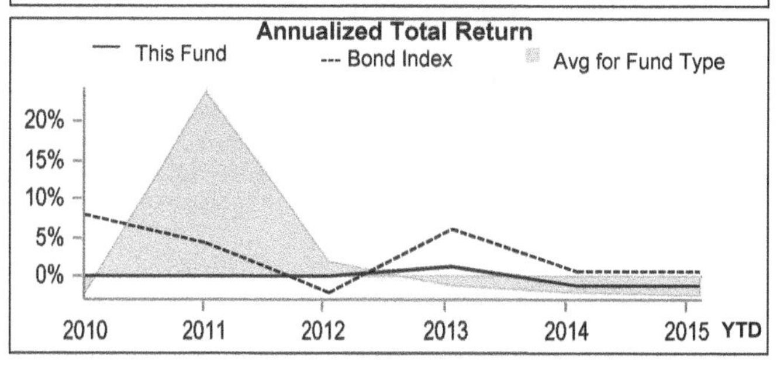

*SPDR BofA Merrill Lynch Em Mkt C (EMCD) C- Fair

Fund Family: SSgA Funds Management Inc
Fund Type: Emerging Market
Inception Date: June 19, 2012

Major Rating Factors: Middle of the road best describes *SPDR BofA Merrill Lynch Em Mkt C whose TheStreet.com Investment Rating is currently a C- (Fair). The fund currently has a performance rating of C- (Fair) based on an annualized return of -0.58% over the last three years and a total return of -0.45% year to date 2015. Factored into the performance evaluation is an expense ratio of 0.50% (very low).

The fund's risk rating is currently C+ (Fair). It carries a beta of 0.43, meaning the fund's expected move will be 4.3% for every 10% move in the market. Volatility, as measured by both the semi-deviation and a drawdown factor, is considered low. As of December 31, 2015, *SPDR BofA Merrill Lynch Em Mkt C traded at a premium of .30% above its net asset value, which is worse than its one-year historical average discount of .48%.

Michael J. Brunell currently receives a manager quality ranking of 78 (0=worst, 99=best). If you desire an average level of risk, then this fund may be an option.

Data Date	Investment Rating	Net Assets ($Mil)	Price	Performance Rating/Pts	Total Return Y-T-D	Risk Rating/Pts
12-15	C-	24.00	26.99	C- / 3.9	-0.45%	C+ / 6.7
2014	C-	24.00	28.55	D+ / 2.3	2.26%	B / 8.6
2013	C-	14.60	29.16	D+ / 2.5	-3.00%	B+ / 9.0

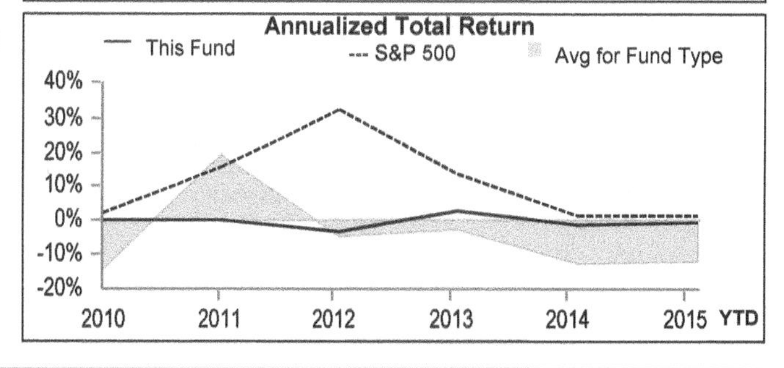

*SPDR DB Intl Gvt Inflation Pt Bo (WIP) C- Fair

Fund Family: SSgA Funds Management Inc
Fund Type: Global
Inception Date: March 13, 2008

Major Rating Factors:
Disappointing performance is the major factor driving the C- (Fair) TheStreet.com Investment Rating for *SPDR DB Intl Gvt Inflation Pt Bo. The fund currently has a performance rating of D+ (Weak) based on an annualized return of -5.15% over the last three years and a total return of -9.68% year to date 2015. Factored into the performance evaluation is an expense ratio of 0.50% (very low).

The fund's risk rating is currently B (Good). It carries a beta of 1.02, meaning that its performance tracks fairly well with that of the overall stock market. Volatility, as measured by both the semi-deviation and a drawdown factor, is considered low. As of December 31, 2015, *SPDR DB Intl Gvt Inflation Pt Bo traded at a discount of .55% below its net asset value, which is better than its one-year historical average discount of .16%.

Peter R. Breault has been running the fund for 4 years and currently receives a manager quality ranking of 57 (0=worst, 99=best). This fund offers only a moderate level of risk but investors looking for strong performance are still waiting.

Data Date	Investment Rating	Net Assets ($Mil)	Price	Performance Rating/Pts	Total Return Y-T-D	Risk Rating/Pts
12-15	C-	892.10	50.36	D+ / 2.6	-9.68%	B / 8.3
2014	C-	892.10	56.95	C- / 3.2	0.71%	B- / 7.4
2013	C	952.50	58.45	C- / 3.6	-5.26%	B / 8.8
2012	C	1,426.90	63.54	C- / 3.6	14.58%	B / 8.8
2011	C	1,171.50	56.75	C- / 3.4	4.79%	B / 8.8
2010	C+	893.40	58.11	C+ / 6.2	4.78%	C+ / 6.8

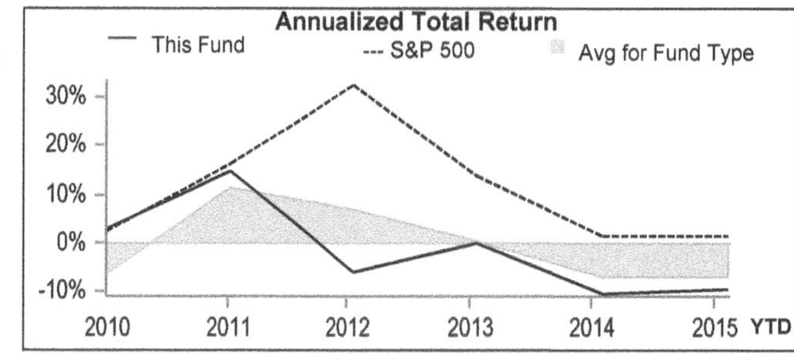

*SPDR DJ REIT ETF (RWR) B Good

Fund Family: SSgA Funds Management Inc
Fund Type: Income
Inception Date: April 23, 2001

Major Rating Factors: Strong performance is the major factor driving the B (Good) TheStreet.com Investment Rating for *SPDR DJ REIT ETF. The fund currently has a performance rating of B+ (Good) based on an annualized return of 11.24% over the last three years and a total return of 3.72% year to date 2015. Factored into the performance evaluation is an expense ratio of 0.25% (very low).

The fund's risk rating is currently C+ (Fair). It carries a beta of 0.42, meaning the fund's expected move will be 4.2% for every 10% move in the market. Volatility, as measured by both the semi-deviation and a drawdown factor, is considered low. As of December 31, 2015, *SPDR DJ REIT ETF traded at a premium of .04% above its net asset value.

Karl A. Schneider has been running the fund for 2 years and currently receives a manager quality ranking of 90 (0=worst, 99=best). If you desire only a moderate level of risk and strong performance, then this fund is an excellent option.

Data Date	Investment Rating	Net Assets ($Mil)	Price	Performance Rating/Pts	Total Return Y-T-D	Risk Rating/Pts
12-15	B	2,620.10	91.63	B+ / 8.5	3.72%	C+ / 6.4
2014	A+	2,620.10	90.90	B+ / 8.9	30.95%	B / 8.0
2013	C	2,091.00	71.27	C / 5.4	-0.10%	B- / 7.8
2012	B	1,892.20	72.97	B / 7.6	18.20%	B- / 7.6
2011	C+	1,513.00	64.40	B / 7.9	9.54%	C+ / 6.3
2010	C+	1,367.30	61.02	B- / 7.4	28.03%	C- / 4.1

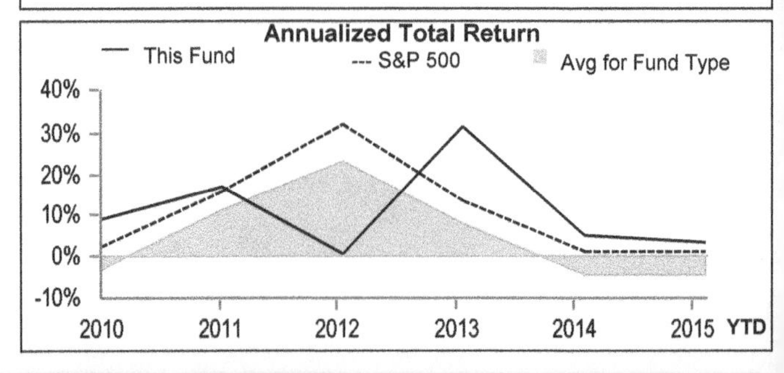

*SPDR DJ Wilshire Glb Real Est ET (RWO) C+ Fair

Fund Family: SSgA Funds Management Inc
Fund Type: Growth and Income
Inception Date: May 7, 2008

Major Rating Factors: Middle of the road best describes *SPDR DJ Wilshire Glb Real Est ET whose TheStreet.com Investment Rating is currently a C+ (Fair). The fund currently has a performance rating of C+ (Fair) based on an annualized return of 7.03% over the last three years and a total return of 1.32% year to date 2015. Factored into the performance evaluation is an expense ratio of 0.50% (very low).

The fund's risk rating is currently C+ (Fair). It carries a beta of 0.55, meaning the fund's expected move will be 5.5% for every 10% move in the market. Volatility, as measured by both the semi-deviation and a drawdown factor, is considered low. As of December 31, 2015, *SPDR DJ Wilshire Glb Real Est ET traded at a premium of .02% above its net asset value, which is better than its one-year historical average premium of .09%.

Amos J. Rogers III has been running the fund for 8 years and currently receives a manager quality ranking of 62 (0=worst, 99=best). If you desire an average level of risk, then this fund may be an option.

Data Date	Investment Rating	Net Assets ($Mil)	Price	Performance Rating/Pts	Total Return Y-T-D	Risk Rating/Pts
12-15	C+	1,464.30	46.80	C+ / 6.9	1.32%	C+ / 6.8
2014	B+	1,464.30	47.73	B- / 7.5	19.10%	B / 8.1
2013	C	984.80	41.53	C / 5.2	0.97%	B- / 7.7
2012	B	685.10	42.12	B- / 7.4	25.71%	B- / 7.8
2011	C	323.70	34.89	C+ / 5.9	-1.97%	B- / 7.0
2010	B	162.20	37.07	A / 9.3	24.01%	C- / 4.0

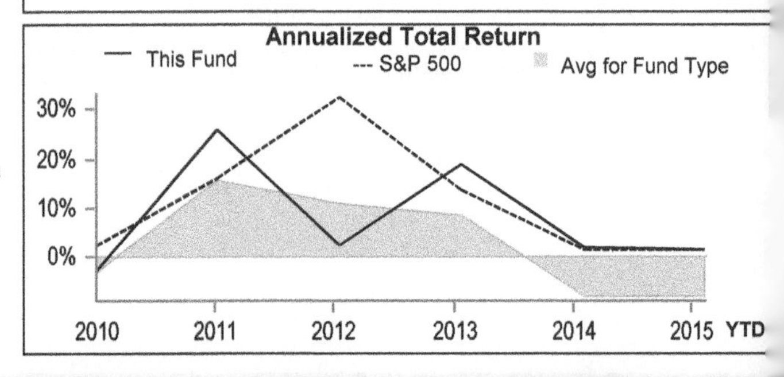

*SPDR DJ Wilshire Intl Real Estat (RWX) C+ Fair

Fund Family: SSgA Funds Management Inc
Fund Type: Foreign
Inception Date: December 15, 2006

Major Rating Factors: Middle of the road best describes *SPDR DJ Wilshire Intl Real Estat whose TheStreet.com Investment Rating is currently a C+ (Fair). The fund currently has a performance rating of C (Fair) based on an annualized return of 2.08% over the last three years and a total return of -2.44% year to date 2015. Factored into the performance evaluation is an expense ratio of 0.60% (very low).

The fund's risk rating is currently B (Good). It carries a beta of 0.82, meaning the fund's expected move will be 8.2% for every 10% move in the market. Volatility, as measured by both the semi-deviation and a drawdown factor, is considered low. As of December 31, 2015, *SPDR DJ Wilshire Intl Real Estat traded at a discount of .56% below its net asset value, which is better than its one-year historical average premium of .04%.

John A. Tucker currently receives a manager quality ranking of 47 (0=worst, 99=best). If you desire an average level of risk, then this fund may be an option.

Data Date	Investment Rating	Net Assets ($Mil)	Price	Performance Rating/Pts	Total Return Y-T-D	Risk Rating/Pts
12-15	C+	4,902.20	39.12	C / 4.9	-2.44%	B / 8.0
2014	C+	4,902.20	41.57	C+ / 6.6	5.78%	B- / 7.4
2013	C-	4,145.70	41.20	C / 5.2	3.28%	C+ / 6.7
2012	C	3,452.60	41.35	B / 7.7	35.27%	C+ / 5.6
2011	D	2,007.70	31.83	C- / 3.4	-13.23%	C+ / 5.6
2010	D	1,430.50	38.93	D+ / 2.8	21.77%	C- / 3.9

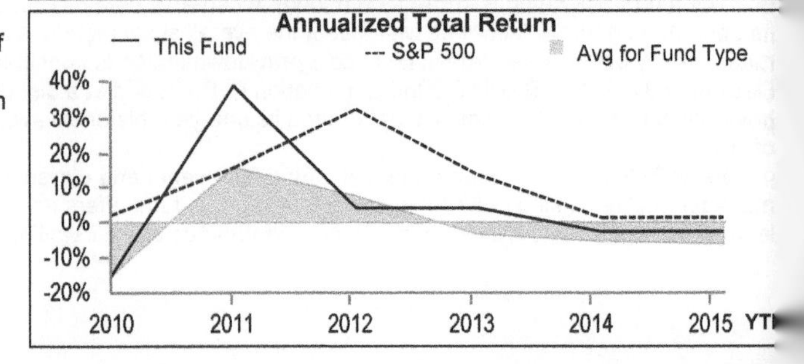

* Denotes ETF Fund

*SPDR Dow Jones Industrial Averag (DIA) A- Excellent

Fund Family: State Street Bank and Trust Company
Fund Type: Growth
Inception Date: January 14, 1998

Data Date	Investment Rating	Net Assets ($Mil)	Price	Performance Rating/Pts	Total Return Y-T-D	Risk Rating/Pts
12-15	A-	11,861.10	173.99	B / 8.2	0.40%	B / 8.1
2014	A-	11,861.10	177.88	B- / 7.2	10.55%	B+ / 9.1
2013	A-	12,593.90	165.47	B / 7.9	25.58%	B / 8.6
2012	C	10,923.40	130.58	C / 4.4	11.31%	B / 8.5
2011	C+	10,842.40	121.85	C+ / 6.0	8.64%	B / 8.1
2010	C	8,721.10	115.63	C- / 4.1	14.26%	C+ / 6.3

Major Rating Factors:
Strong performance is the major factor driving the A- (Excellent) TheStreet.com Investment Rating for *SPDR Dow Jones Industrial Averag. The fund currently has a performance rating of B (Good) based on an annualized return of 11.72% over the last three years and a total return of 0.40% year to date 2015. Factored into the performance evaluation is an expense ratio of 0.17% (very low).

The fund's risk rating is currently B (Good). It carries a beta of 1.01, meaning that its performance tracks fairly well with that of the overall stock market. Volatility, as measured by both the semi-deviation and a drawdown factor, is considered low. As of December 31, 2015, *SPDR Dow Jones Industrial Averag traded at a discount of .01% below its net asset value.

David K. Chin currently receives a manager quality ranking of 49 (0=worst, 99=best). If you desire only a moderate level of risk and strong performance, then this fund is an excellent option.

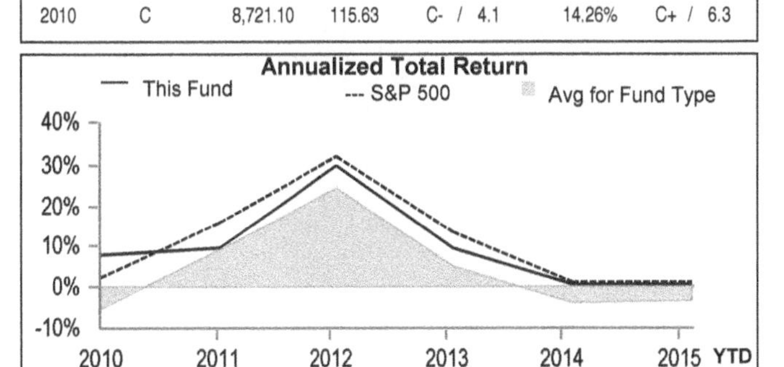

*SPDR Euro STOXX 50 ETF (FEZ) C Fair

Fund Family: SSgA Funds Management Inc
Fund Type: Foreign
Inception Date: October 15, 2002

Data Date	Investment Rating	Net Assets ($Mil)	Price	Performance Rating/Pts	Total Return Y-T-D	Risk Rating/Pts
12-15	C	4,977.40	34.43	C / 5.2	-3.44%	B- / 7.3
2014	C-	4,977.40	36.86	C / 5.2	-6.70%	C+ / 5.7
2013	C	4,918.70	42.20	C+ / 6.8	21.32%	C+ / 5.9
2012	D	1,304.60	34.66	D+ / 2.7	27.78%	C+ / 5.7
2011	D-	138.40	29.51	D- / 1.5	-16.12%	C+ / 6.2
2010	E+	163.70	36.84	E+ / 0.8	-7.75%	C- / 4.2

Major Rating Factors: Middle of the road best describes *SPDR Euro STOXX 50 ETF whose TheStreet.com Investment Rating is currently a C (Fair). The fund currently has a performance rating of C (Fair) based on an annualized return of 2.98% over the last three years and a total return of -3.44% year to date 2015. Factored into the performance evaluation is an expense ratio of 0.29% (very low).

The fund's risk rating is currently B- (Good). It carries a beta of 1.16, meaning it is expected to move 11.6% for every 10% move in the market. Volatility, as measured by both the semi-deviation and a drawdown factor, is considered low. As of December 31, 2015, *SPDR Euro STOXX 50 ETF traded at a discount of .43% below its net asset value, which is better than its one-year historical average premium of .05%.

John A. Tucker has been running the fund for 14 years and currently receives a manager quality ranking of 43 (0=worst, 99=best). If you desire an average level of risk, then this fund may be an option.

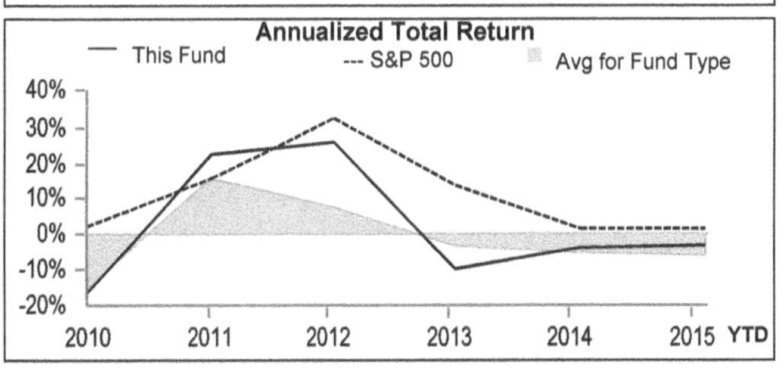

*SPDR EURO STOXX Small Cap ETF (SMEZ) C Fair

Fund Family: SSgA Funds Management Inc
Fund Type: Foreign
Inception Date: June 5, 2014

Data Date	Investment Rating	Net Assets ($Mil)	Price	Performance Rating/Pts	Total Return Y-T-D	Risk Rating/Pts
12-15	C	7.60	48.38	C- / 3.9	1.58%	B / 8.0

Major Rating Factors: Middle of the road best describes *SPDR EURO STOXX Small Cap ETF whose TheStreet.com Investment Rating is currently a C (Fair). The fund currently has a performance rating of C- (Fair) based on an annualized return of 0.00% over the last three years and a total return of 1.58% year to date 2015. Factored into the performance evaluation is an expense ratio of 0.46% (very low).

The fund's risk rating is currently B (Good). It carries a beta of 0.00, meaning the fund's expected move will be 0.0% for every 10% move in the market. Volatility, as measured by both the semi-deviation and a drawdown factor, is considered low. As of December 31, 2015, *SPDR EURO STOXX Small Cap ETF traded at a discount of .58% below its net asset value, which is better than its one-year historical average premium of .18%.

John A. Tucker currently receives a manager quality ranking of 82 (0=worst, 99=best). If you desire an average level of risk, then this fund may be an option.

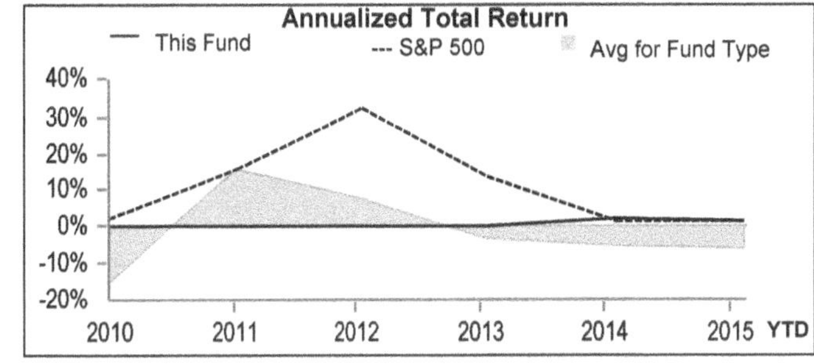

* Denotes ETF Fund

*SPDR Global Dow ETF (DGT) B- Good

Fund Family: SSgA Funds Management Inc
Fund Type: Global
Inception Date: September 25, 2000

Data Date	Investment Rating	Net Assets ($Mil)	Price	Performance Rating/Pts	Total Return Y-T-D	Risk Rating/Pts
12-15	B-	112.40	64.67	C+ / 6.3	-3.31%	B / 8.3
2014	C+	112.40	69.06	C+ / 6.2	4.08%	C+ / 6.9
2013	C+	103.70	69.19	C+ / 6.8	21.56%	B- / 7.6
2012	D+	89.30	56.18	D+ / 2.7	16.63%	B- / 7.5
2011	D+	98.20	50.18	D+ / 2.3	-11.90%	B- / 7.6
2010	D	122.50	58.46	D / 1.6	4.99%	C+ / 5.9

Major Rating Factors: *SPDR Global Dow ETF receives a TheStreet.com Investment Rating of B- (Good). The fund currently has a performance rating of C+ (Fair) based on an annualized return of 6.81% over the last three years and a total return of -3.31% year to date 2015. Factored into the performance evaluation is an expense ratio of 0.50% (very low).

The fund's risk rating is currently B (Good). It carries a beta of 0.90, meaning that its performance tracks fairly well with that of the overall stock market. Volatility, as measured by both the semi-deviation and a drawdown factor, is considered low. As of December 31, 2015, *SPDR Global Dow ETF traded at a discount of .03% below its net asset value, which is worse than its one-year historical average discount of .05%.

John A. Tucker has been running the fund for 16 years and currently receives a manager quality ranking of 83 (0=worst, 99=best). If you desire an average level of risk, then this fund may be an option.

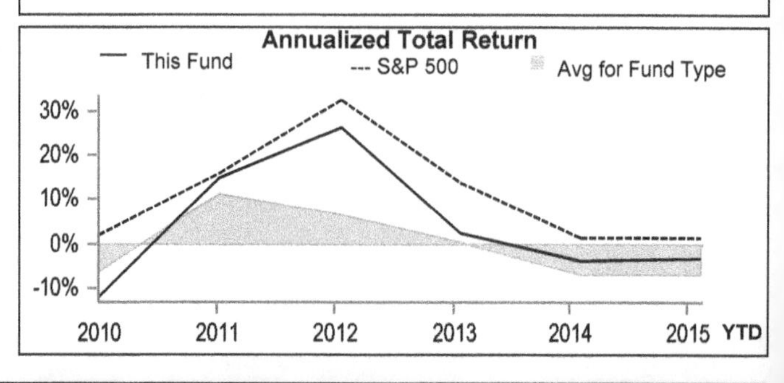

*SPDR Gold Shares (GLD) D Weak

Fund Family: SSgA Funds Management Inc
Fund Type: Precious Metals
Inception Date: November 18, 2004

Data Date	Investment Rating	Net Assets ($Mil)	Price	Performance Rating/Pts	Total Return Y-T-D	Risk Rating/Pts
12-15	D	30,096.90	101.46	D- / 1.4	-11.06%	C+ / 6.2
2014	D-	30,096.90	113.58	D- / 1.3	-4.79%	C / 4.5
2013	D	30,822.00	116.12	D- / 1.5	-25.65%	C+ / 6.4
2012	C	72,239.30	162.02	C / 4.3	1.13%	B / 8.1
2011	B	63,484.30	151.99	B- / 7.5	17.68%	B / 8.3
2010	A	57,210.20	138.72	B+ / 8.8	29.27%	C+ / 6.9

Major Rating Factors:
Disappointing performance is the major factor driving the D (Weak) TheStreet.com Investment Rating for *SPDR Gold Shares. The fund currently has a performance rating of D- (Weak) based on an annualized return of -14.17% over the last three years and a total return of -11.06% year to date 2015. Factored into the performance evaluation is an expense ratio of 0.40% (very low).

The fund's risk rating is currently C+ (Fair). It carries a beta of 0.93, meaning that its performance tracks fairly well with that of the overall stock market. Volatility, as measured by both the semi-deviation and a drawdown factor, is considered low. As of December 31, 2015, *SPDR Gold Shares traded at a discount of .17% below its net asset value, which is better than its one-year historical average premium of .10%.

Kent A. Finkle currently receives a manager quality ranking of 53 (0=worst, 99=best). This fund offers only a moderate level of risk but investors looking for strong performance are still waiting.

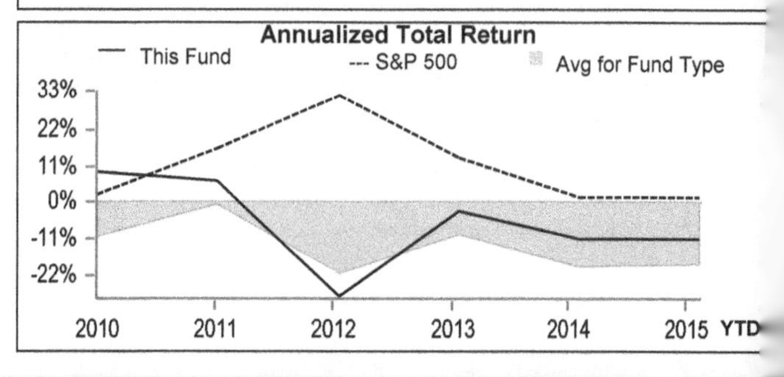

*SPDR MFS Systematic Core Equity (SYE) B Good

Fund Family: SSgA Funds Management Inc
Fund Type: Growth
Inception Date: January 8, 2014

Data Date	Investment Rating	Net Assets ($Mil)	Price	Performance Rating/Pts	Total Return Y-T-D	Risk Rating/Pts
12-15	B	2.70	58.95	B / 7.8	7.68%	B- / 7.2

Major Rating Factors: Strong performance is the major factor driving the B (Good) TheStreet.com Investment Rating for *SPDR MFS Systematic Core Equity. The fund currently has a performance rating of B (Good) based on an annualized return of 0.00% over the last three years and a total return of 7.68% year to date 2015. Factored into the performance evaluation is an expense ratio of 0.60% (very low).

The fund's risk rating is currently B- (Good). It carries a beta of 0.00, meaning the fund's expected move will be 0.0% for every 10% move in the market. Volatility, as measured by both the semi-deviation and a drawdown factor, is considered low. As of December 31, 2015, *SPDR MFS Systematic Core Equity traded at a premium of 1.69% above its net asset value.

Matthew Krummell has been running the fund for 2 years and currently receives a manager quality ranking of 91 (0=worst, 99=best). If you desire only a moderate level of risk and strong performance, then this fund is an excellent option.

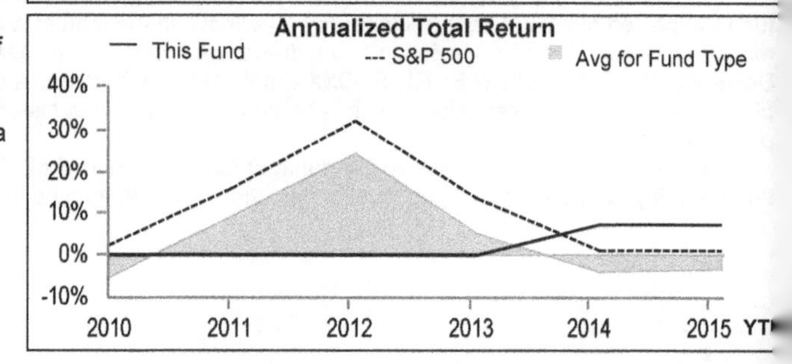

*SPDR MFS Systematic Gro Equity E (SYG) B Good

Fund Family: SSgA Funds Management Inc
Fund Type: Growth
Inception Date: January 8, 2014

Data Date	Investment Rating	Net Assets ($Mil)	Price	Performance Rating/Pts	Total Return Y-T-D	Risk Rating/Pts
12-15	B	2.80	60.34	B / 7.8	8.54%	B- / 7.2

Major Rating Factors: Strong performance is the major factor driving the B (Good) TheStreet.com Investment Rating for *SPDR MFS Systematic Gro Equity E. The fund currently has a performance rating of B (Good) based on an annualized return of 0.00% over the last three years and a total return of 8.54% year to date 2015. Factored into the performance evaluation is an expense ratio of 0.60% (very low).

The fund's risk rating is currently B- (Good). It carries a beta of 0.00, meaning the fund's expected move will be 0.0% for every 10% move in the market. Volatility, as measured by both the semi-deviation and a drawdown factor, is considered low. As of December 31, 2015, *SPDR MFS Systematic Gro Equity E traded at a premium of .35% above its net asset value, which is worse than its one-year historical average premium of .11%.

Matthew Krummell has been running the fund for 2 years and currently receives a manager quality ranking of 91 (0=worst, 99=best). If you desire only a moderate level of risk and strong performance, then this fund is an excellent option.

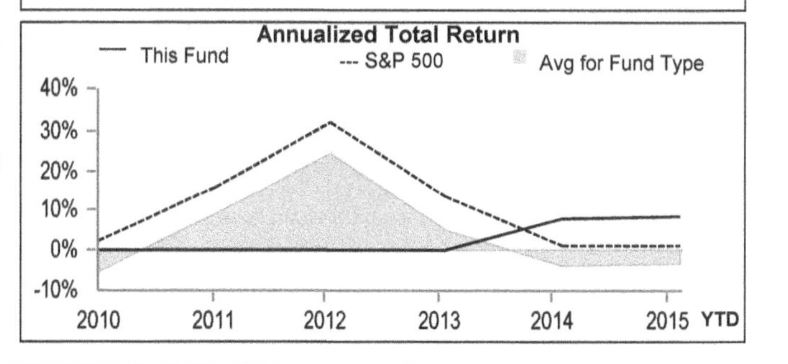

*SPDR MFS Systematic Value Eqty E (SYV) C- Fair

Fund Family: SSgA Funds Management Inc
Fund Type: Growth
Inception Date: January 8, 2014

Data Date	Investment Rating	Net Assets ($Mil)	Price	Performance Rating/Pts	Total Return Y-T-D	Risk Rating/Pts
12-15	C-	2.70	52.64	C- / 4.1	-1.37%	C+ / 6.7

Major Rating Factors: Middle of the road best describes *SPDR MFS Systematic Value Eqty E whose TheStreet.com Investment Rating is currently a C- (Fair). The fund currently has a performance rating of C- (Fair) based on an annualized return of 0.00% over the last three years and a total return of -1.37% year to date 2015. Factored into the performance evaluation is an expense ratio of 0.60% (very low).

The fund's risk rating is currently C+ (Fair). It carries a beta of 0.00, meaning the fund's expected move will be 0.0% for every 10% move in the market. Volatility, as measured by both the semi-deviation and a drawdown factor, is considered low. As of December 31, 2015, *SPDR MFS Systematic Value Eqty E traded at a premium of .15% above its net asset value, which is worse than its one-year historical average premium of .12%.

Jonathan W. Sage has been running the fund for 2 years and currently receives a manager quality ranking of 45 (0=worst, 99=best). If you desire an average level of risk, then this fund may be an option.

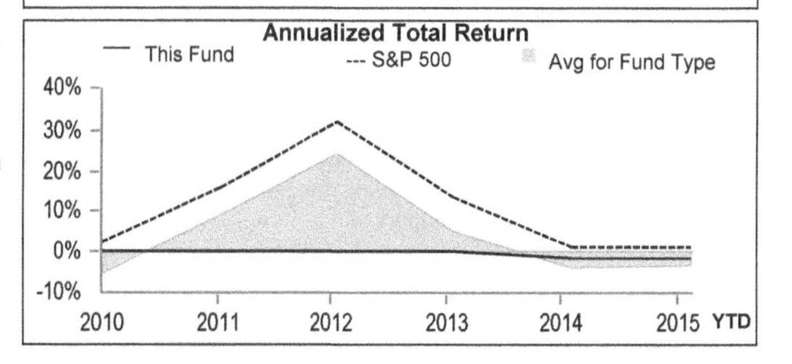

*SPDR MSCI ACWI ex-US ETF (CWI) C Fair

Fund Family: SSgA Funds Management Inc
Fund Type: Global
Inception Date: January 10, 2007

Data Date	Investment Rating	Net Assets ($Mil)	Price	Performance Rating/Pts	Total Return Y-T-D	Risk Rating/Pts
12-15	C	575.50	30.80	C / 4.3	-3.72%	B / 8.2
2014	C-	575.50	33.46	C / 4.6	-1.12%	C+ / 6.9
2013	C	495.90	35.63	C / 4.9	9.98%	B- / 7.6
2012	C-	368.30	32.19	C- / 3.7	18.18%	B- / 7.3
2011	C-	527.50	28.46	C- / 3.3	-13.27%	B- / 7.5
2010	D+	410.90	33.91	C- / 3.0	11.59%	C / 5.5

Major Rating Factors: Middle of the road best describes *SPDR MSCI ACWI ex-US ETF whose TheStreet.com Investment Rating is currently a C (Fair). The fund currently has a performance rating of C (Fair) based on an annualized return of 1.30% over the last three years and a total return of -3.72% year to date 2015. Factored into the performance evaluation is an expense ratio of 0.32% (very low).

The fund's risk rating is currently B (Good). It carries a beta of 0.94, meaning that its performance tracks fairly well with that of the overall stock market. Volatility, as measured by both the semi-deviation and a drawdown factor, is considered low. As of December 31, 2015, *SPDR MSCI ACWI ex-US ETF traded at a discount of .39% below its net asset value, which is better than its one-year historical average premium of .07%.

John A. Tucker currently receives a manager quality ranking of 41 (0=worst, 99=best). If you desire an average level of risk, then this fund may be an option.

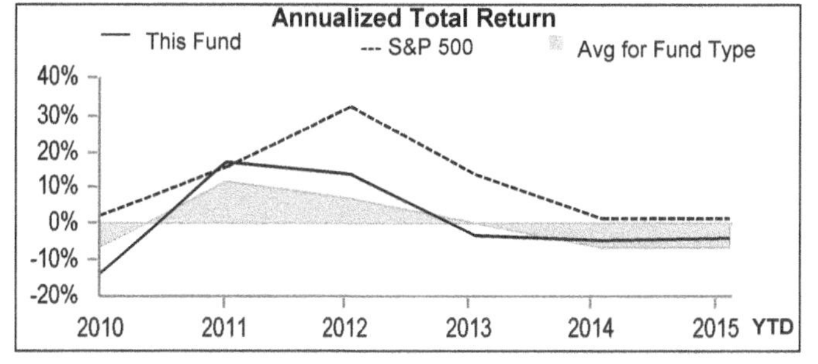

*SPDR MSCI ACWI IMI ETF (ACIM) B- Good

Fund Family: SSgA Funds Management Inc
Fund Type: Global
Inception Date: February 27, 2012

Major Rating Factors: Strong performance is the major factor driving the B- (Good) TheStreet.com Investment Rating for *SPDR MSCI ACWI IMI ETF. The fund currently has a performance rating of B- (Good) based on an annualized return of 9.44% over the last three years and a total return of -0.23% year to date 2015. Factored into the performance evaluation is an expense ratio of 0.25% (very low).

The fund's risk rating is currently B- (Good). It carries a beta of 0.65, meaning the fund's expected move will be 6.5% for every 10% move in the market. Volatility, as measured by both the semi-deviation and a drawdown factor, is considered low. As of December 31, 2015, *SPDR MSCI ACWI IMI ETF traded at a premium of 1.15% above its net asset value, which is worse than its one-year historical average premium of 1.14%.

John A. Tucker has been running the fund for 4 years and currently receives a manager quality ranking of 92 (0=worst, 99=best). If you desire only a moderate level of risk and strong performance, then this fund is an excellent option.

Data Date	Investment Rating	Net Assets ($Mil)	Price	Performance Rating/Pts	Total Return Y-T-D	Risk Rating/Pts
12-15	B-	57.40	61.50	B- / 7.4	-0.23%	B- / 7.1
2014	C-	57.40	64.97	C / 4.7	7.95%	B- / 7.1
2013	A+	12.40	61.22	A- / 9.1	21.73%	B+ / 9.0

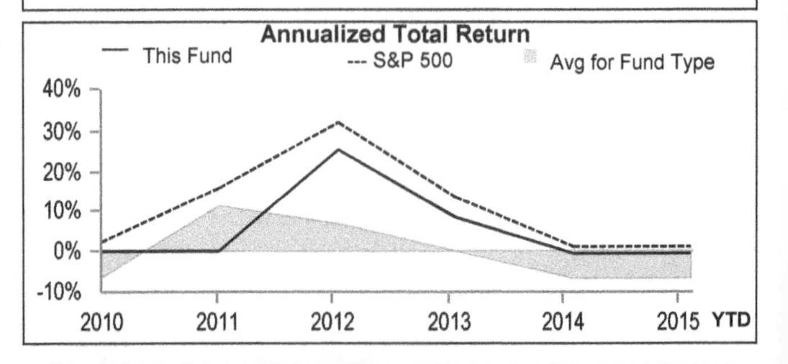

*SPDR MSCI ACWI Low Carbon Target (LOWC) D+ Weak

Fund Family: SSgA Funds Management Inc
Fund Type: Energy/Natural Resources
Inception Date: November 26, 2014

Major Rating Factors: *SPDR MSCI ACWI Low Carbon Target receives a TheStreet.com Investment Rating of D+ (Weak). The fund currently has a performance rating of C- (Fair) based on an annualized return of 0.00% over the last three years and a total return of -1.04% year to date 2015. Factored into the performance evaluation is an expense ratio of 0.20% (very low).

The fund's risk rating is currently C (Fair). It carries a beta of 0.00, meaning the fund's expected move will be 0.0% for every 10% move in the market. Volatility, as measured by both the semi-deviation and a drawdown factor, is considered average. As of December 31, 2015, *SPDR MSCI ACWI Low Carbon Target traded at a discount of .28% below its net asset value, which is better than its one-year historical average premium of .22%.

John A. Tucker has been running the fund for 2 years and currently receives a manager quality ranking of 96 (0=worst, 99=best). If you desire an average level of risk, then this fund may be an option.

Data Date	Investment Rating	Net Assets ($Mil)	Price	Performance Rating/Pts	Total Return Y-T-D	Risk Rating/Pts
12-15	D+	0.00	70.36	C- / 4.1	-1.04%	C / 5.0

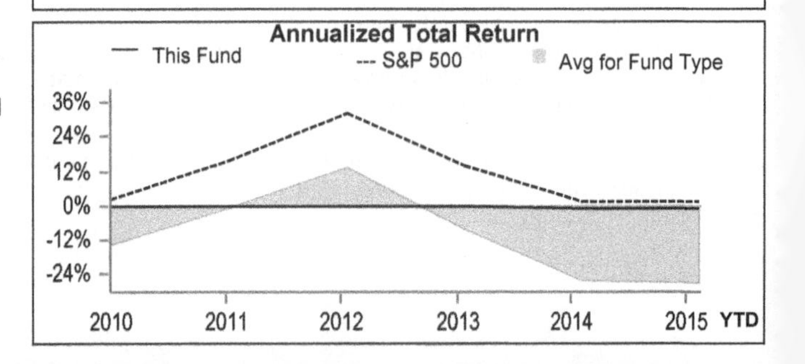

*SPDR MSCI Australia Quality Mix (QAUS) D Weak

Fund Family: SSgA Funds Management Inc
Fund Type: Foreign
Inception Date: June 12, 2014

Major Rating Factors: *SPDR MSCI Australia Quality Mix receives a TheStreet.com Investment Rating of D (Weak). The fund currently has a performance rating of C- (Fair) based on an annualized return of 0.00% over the last three years and a total return of -6.93% year to date 2015. Factored into the performance evaluation is an expense ratio of 0.30% (very low).

The fund's risk rating is currently C (Fair). It carries a beta of 0.00, meaning the fund's expected move will be 0.0% for every 10% move in the market. Volatility, as measured by both the semi-deviation and a drawdown factor, is considered average. As of December 31, 2015, *SPDR MSCI Australia Quality Mix traded at a premium of .27% above its net asset value, which is worse than its one-year historical average discount of .07%.

John A. Tucker currently receives a manager quality ranking of 24 (0=worst, 99=best). If you desire an average level of risk, then this fund may be an option.

Data Date	Investment Rating	Net Assets ($Mil)	Price	Performance Rating/Pts	Total Return Y-T-D	Risk Rating/Pts
12-15	D	5.60	45.04	C- / 3.5	-6.93%	C / 4.7

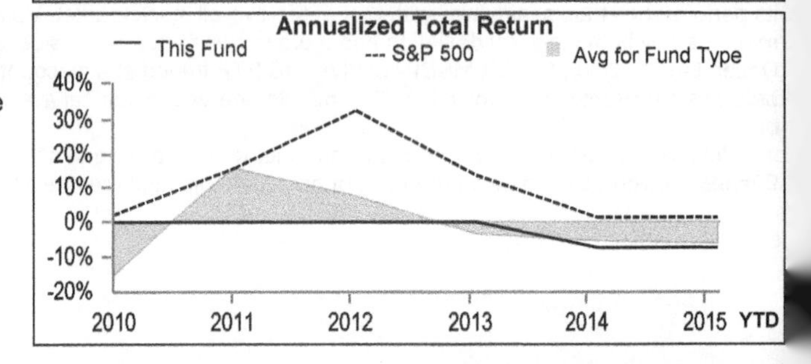

* Denotes ETF Fund

*SPDR MSCI Canada Quality Mix ETF (QCAN) D- Weak

Fund Family: SSgA Funds Management Inc
Fund Type: Foreign
Inception Date: June 12, 2014

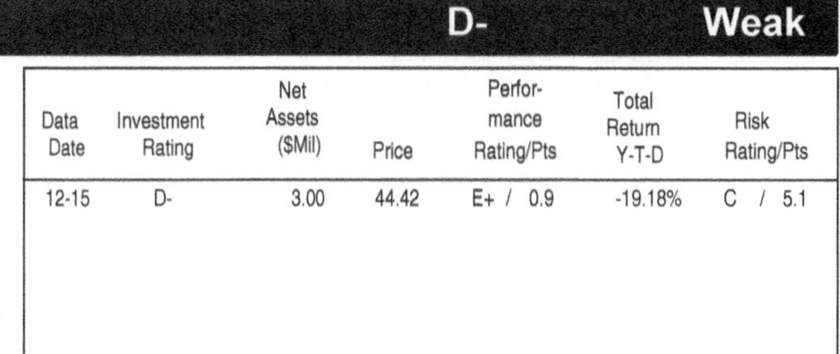

Data Date	Investment Rating	Net Assets ($Mil)	Price	Perfor-mance Rating/Pts	Total Return Y-T-D	Risk Rating/Pts
12-15	D-	3.00	44.42	E+ / 0.9	-19.18%	C / 5.1

Major Rating Factors:
Very poor performance is the major factor driving the D- (Weak) TheStreet.com Investment Rating for *SPDR MSCI Canada Quality Mix ETF. The fund currently has a performance rating of E+ (Very Weak) based on an annualized return of 0.00% over the last three years and a total return of -19.18% year to date 2015. Factored into the performance evaluation is an expense ratio of 0.30% (very low).

The fund's risk rating is currently C (Fair). It carries a beta of 0.00, meaning the fund's expected move will be 0.0% for every 10% move in the market. Volatility, as measured by both the semi-deviation and a drawdown factor, is considered average. As of December 31, 2015, *SPDR MSCI Canada Quality Mix ETF traded at a premium of .43% above its net asset value, which is worse than its one-year historical average premium of .18%.

John A. Tucker currently receives a manager quality ranking of 7 (0=worst, 99=best). This fund offers an average level of risk but investors looking for strong performance will be frustrated.

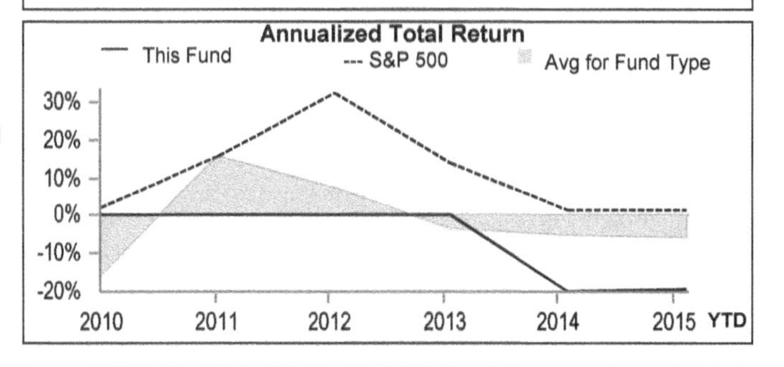

*SPDR MSCI EAFE Quality Mix ETF (QEFA) C Fair

Fund Family: SSgA Funds Management Inc
Fund Type: Foreign
Inception Date: June 5, 2014

Data Date	Investment Rating	Net Assets ($Mil)	Price	Perfor-mance Rating/Pts	Total Return Y-T-D	Risk Rating/Pts
12-15	C	5.70	54.96	C+ / 5.8	4.30%	C+ / 6.7

Major Rating Factors: Middle of the road best describes *SPDR MSCI EAFE Quality Mix ETF whose TheStreet.com Investment Rating is currently a C (Fair). The fund currently has a performance rating of C+ (Fair) based on an annualized return of 0.00% over the last three years and a total return of 4.30% year to date 2015. Factored into the performance evaluation is an expense ratio of 0.30% (very low).

The fund's risk rating is currently C+ (Fair). It carries a beta of 0.00, meaning the fund's expected move will be 0.0% for every 10% move in the market. Volatility, as measured by both the semi-deviation and a drawdown factor, is considered low. As of December 31, 2015, *SPDR MSCI EAFE Quality Mix ETF traded at a premium of .66% above its net asset value, which is worse than its one-year historical average premium of .37%.

John A. Tucker currently receives a manager quality ranking of 85 (0=worst, 99=best). If you desire an average level of risk, then this fund may be an option.

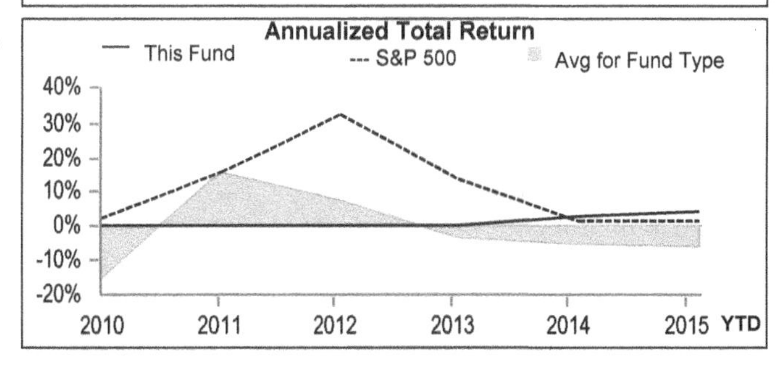

*SPDR MSCI EM 50 ETF (EMFT) D+ Weak

Fund Family: SSgA Funds Management Inc
Fund Type: Emerging Market
Inception Date: February 27, 2012

Data Date	Investment Rating	Net Assets ($Mil)	Price	Perfor-mance Rating/Pts	Total Return Y-T-D	Risk Rating/Pts
12-15	D+	2.40	37.25	D / 2.2	-15.28%	C+ / 6.5
2014	D	2.40	45.93	D / 2.2	0.95%	C+ / 6.0
2013	D+	2.40	48.63	D / 1.7	-5.23%	B / 8.2

Major Rating Factors:
Disappointing performance is the major factor driving the D+ (Weak) TheStreet.com Investment Rating for *SPDR MSCI EM 50 ETF. The fund currently has a performance rating of D (Weak) based on an annualized return of -6.77% over the last three years and a total return of -15.28% year to date 2015. Factored into the performance evaluation is an expense ratio of 0.50% (very low).

The fund's risk rating is currently C+ (Fair). It carries a beta of 1.17, meaning it is expected to move 11.7% for every 10% move in the market. Volatility, as measured by both the semi-deviation and a drawdown factor, is considered low. As of December 31, 2015, *SPDR MSCI EM 50 ETF traded at a discount of 1.87% below its net asset value, which is better than its one-year historical average premium of .68%.

John A. Tucker has been running the fund for 4 years and currently receives a manager quality ranking of 74 (0=worst, 99=best). This fund offers only a moderate level of risk but investors looking for strong performance are still waiting.

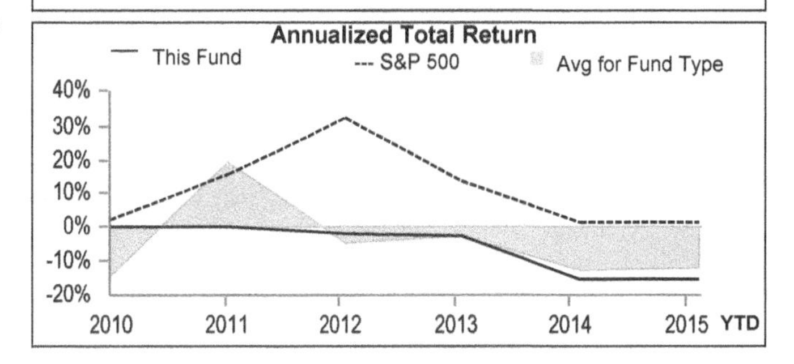

*SPDR MSCI EM Beyond BRIC ETF (EMBB) D Weak

Fund Family: SSgA Funds Management Inc
Fund Type: Emerging Market
Inception Date: December 4, 2013

Data Date	Investment Rating	Net Assets ($Mil)	Price	Performance Rating/Pts	Total Return Y-T-D	Risk Rating/Pts
12-15	D	3.10	46.20	D- / 1.0	-16.47%	C+ / 6.7
2014	D-	3.10	57.38	D / 1.8	-0.60%	C / 4.6

Major Rating Factors:
Disappointing performance is the major factor driving the D (Weak) TheStreet.com Investment Rating for *SPDR MSCI EM Beyond BRIC ETF. The fund currently has a performance rating of D- (Weak) based on an annualized return of 0.00% over the last three years and a total return of -16.47% year to date 2015. Factored into the performance evaluation is an expense ratio of 0.52% (very low).

The fund's risk rating is currently C+ (Fair). It carries a beta of 0.00, meaning the fund's expected move will be 0.0% for every 10% move in the market. Volatility, as measured by both the semi-deviation and a drawdown factor, is considered low. As of December 31, 2015, *SPDR MSCI EM Beyond BRIC ETF traded at a discount of .79% below its net asset value, which is better than its one-year historical average discount of .25%.

John A. Tucker has been running the fund for 3 years and currently receives a manager quality ranking of 37 (0=worst, 99=best). This fund offers only a moderate level of risk but investors looking for strong performance are still waiting.

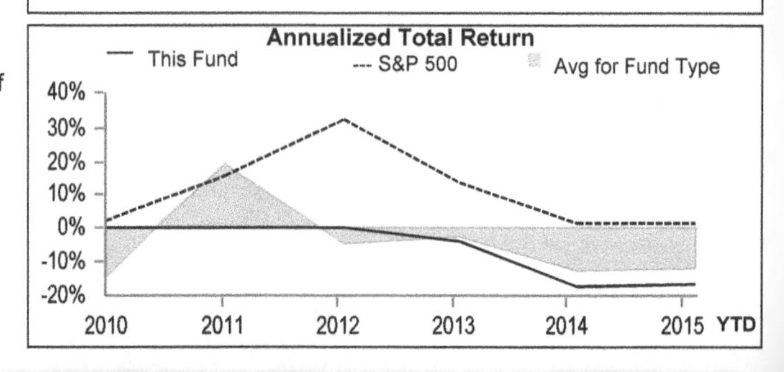

*SPDR MSCI Emerg Markets QI Mix E (QEMM) D Weak

Fund Family: SSgA Funds Management Inc
Fund Type: Emerging Market
Inception Date: June 5, 2014

Data Date	Investment Rating	Net Assets ($Mil)	Price	Performance Rating/Pts	Total Return Y-T-D	Risk Rating/Pts
12-15	D	6.00	47.43	D- / 1.3	-12.05%	C / 5.4

Major Rating Factors:
Disappointing performance is the major factor driving the D (Weak) TheStreet.com Investment Rating for *SPDR MSCI Emerg Markets QI Mix E. The fund currently has a performance rating of D- (Weak) based on an annualized return of 0.00% over the last three years and a total return of -12.05% year to date 2015. Factored into the performance evaluation is an expense ratio of 0.30% (very low).

The fund's risk rating is currently C (Fair). It carries a beta of 0.00, meaning the fund's expected move will be 0.0% for every 10% move in the market. Volatility, as measured by both the semi-deviation and a drawdown factor, is considered average. As of December 31, 2015, *SPDR MSCI Emerg Markets QI Mix E traded at a premium of 1.00% above its net asset value, which is worse than its one-year historical average premium of .66%.

John A. Tucker currently receives a manager quality ranking of 68 (0=worst, 99=best). This fund offers an average level of risk but investors looking for strong performance will be frustrated.

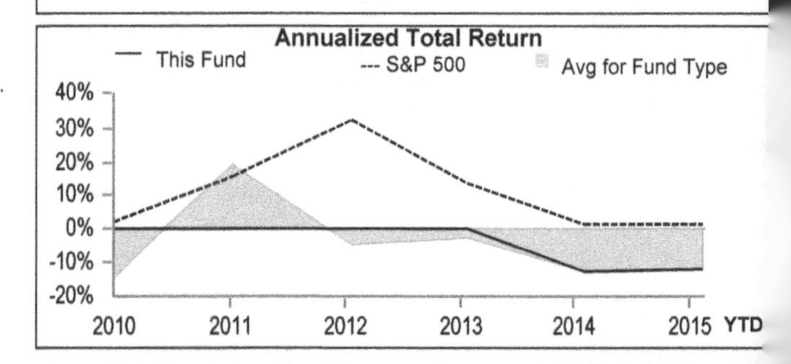

*SPDR MSCI Germany Quality Mix ET (QDEU) C Fair

Fund Family: SSgA Funds Management Inc
Fund Type: Foreign
Inception Date: June 12, 2014

Data Date	Investment Rating	Net Assets ($Mil)	Price	Performance Rating/Pts	Total Return Y-T-D	Risk Rating/Pts
12-15	C	5.40	51.62	C / 4.4	-0.42%	B / 8.0

Major Rating Factors: Middle of the road best describes *SPDR MSCI Germany Quality Mix ET whose TheStreet.com Investment Rating is currently a C (Fair). The fund currently has a performance rating of C (Fair) based on an annualized return of 0.00% over the last three years and a total return of -0.42% year to date 2015. Factored into the performance evaluation is an expense ratio of 0.30% (very low).

The fund's risk rating is currently B (Good). It carries a beta of 0.00, meaning the fund's expected move will be 0.0% for every 10% move in the market. Volatility, as measured by both the semi-deviation and a drawdown factor, is considered low. As of December 31, 2015, *SPDR MSCI Germany Quality Mix ET traded at a discount of .88% below its net asset value, which is better than its one-year historical average premium of .05%.

John A. Tucker currently receives a manager quality ranking of 49 (0=worst, 99=best). If you desire an average level of risk, then this fund may be an option.

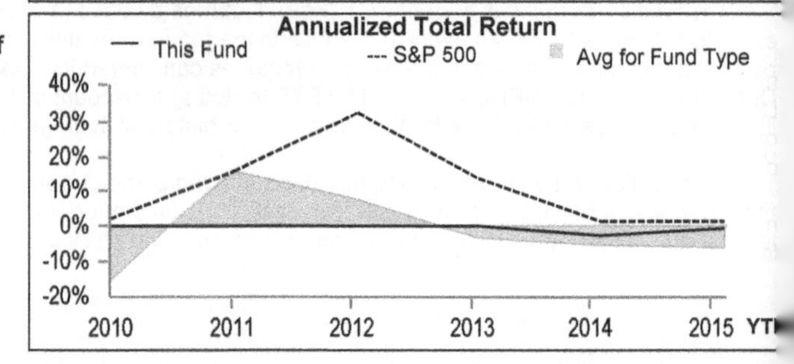

*SPDR MSCI Japan Quality Mix ETF (QJPN) A Excellent

Fund Family: SSgA Funds Management Inc
Fund Type: Foreign
Inception Date: June 12, 2014

Data Date	Investment Rating	Net Assets ($Mil)	Price	Performance Rating/Pts	Total Return Y-T-D	Risk Rating/Pts
12-15	A	6.00	64.48	B+ / 8.4	11.23%	B / 8.5

Major Rating Factors:
Strong performance is the major factor driving the A (Excellent) TheStreet.com Investment Rating for *SPDR MSCI Japan Quality Mix ETF. The fund currently has a performance rating of B+ (Good) based on an annualized return of 0.00% over the last three years and a total return of 11.23% year to date 2015. Factored into the performance evaluation is an expense ratio of 0.30% (very low).

The fund's risk rating is currently B (Good). It carries a beta of 0.00, meaning the fund's expected move will be 0.0% for every 10% move in the market. Volatility, as measured by both the semi-deviation and a drawdown factor, is considered low. As of December 31, 2015, *SPDR MSCI Japan Quality Mix ETF traded at a discount of 1.23% below its net asset value, which is better than its one-year historical average discount of .23%.

John A. Tucker currently receives a manager quality ranking of 96 (0=worst, 99=best). If you desire only a moderate level of risk and strong performance, then this fund is an excellent option.

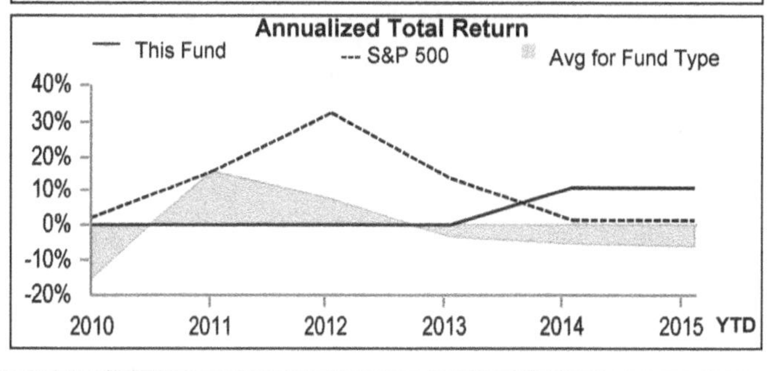

*SPDR MSCI Mexico Quality Mix ETF (QMEX) D Weak

Fund Family: SSgA Funds Management Inc
Fund Type: Foreign
Inception Date: September 18, 2014

Data Date	Investment Rating	Net Assets ($Mil)	Price	Performance Rating/Pts	Total Return Y-T-D	Risk Rating/Pts
12-15	D	0.00	22.15	D / 1.9	-9.62%	C+ / 6.2

Major Rating Factors:
Disappointing performance is the major factor driving the D (Weak) TheStreet.com Investment Rating for *SPDR MSCI Mexico Quality Mix ETF. The fund currently has a performance rating of D (Weak) based on an annualized return of 0.00% over the last three years and a total return of -9.62% year to date 2015. Factored into the performance evaluation is an expense ratio of 0.40% (very low).

The fund's risk rating is currently C+ (Fair). It carries a beta of 0.00, meaning the fund's expected move will be 0.0% for every 10% move in the market. Volatility, as measured by both the semi-deviation and a drawdown factor, is considered low. As of December 31, 2015, *SPDR MSCI Mexico Quality Mix ETF traded at a premium of .45% above its net asset value, which is worse than its one-year historical average premium of .41%.

John A. Tucker has been running the fund for 2 years and currently receives a manager quality ranking of 17 (0=worst, 99=best). This fund offers only a moderate level of risk but investors looking for strong performance are still waiting.

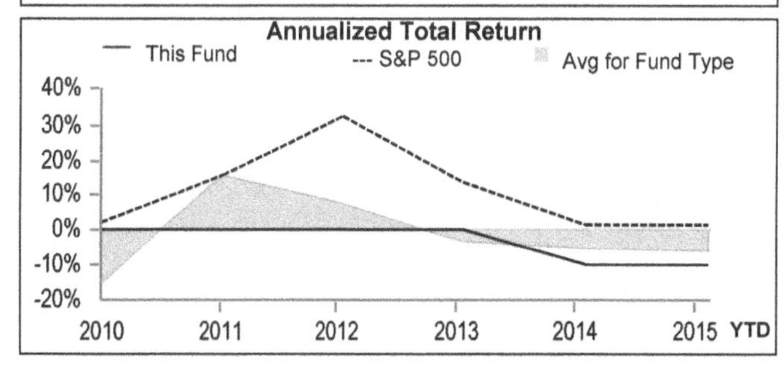

*SPDR MSCI South Korea Quality Mi (QKOR) D+ Weak

Fund Family: SSgA Funds Management Inc
Fund Type: Foreign
Inception Date: September 18, 2014

Data Date	Investment Rating	Net Assets ($Mil)	Price	Performance Rating/Pts	Total Return Y-T-D	Risk Rating/Pts
12-15	D+	0.00	25.01	D+ / 2.8	-7.47%	C+ / 5.7

Major Rating Factors:
Disappointing performance is the major factor driving the D+ (Weak) TheStreet.com Investment Rating for *SPDR MSCI South Korea Quality Mi. The fund currently has a performance rating of D+ (Weak) based on an annualized return of 0.00% over the last three years and a total return of -7.47% year to date 2015. Factored into the performance evaluation is an expense ratio of 0.40% (very low).

The fund's risk rating is currently C+ (Fair). It carries a beta of 0.00, meaning the fund's expected move will be 0.0% for every 10% move in the market. Volatility, as measured by both the semi-deviation and a drawdown factor, is considered low. As of December 31, 2015, *SPDR MSCI South Korea Quality Mi traded at a premium of .97% above its net asset value, which is worse than its one-year historical average premium of .47%.

John A. Tucker has been running the fund for 2 years and currently receives a manager quality ranking of 22 (0=worst, 99=best). This fund offers only a moderate level of risk but investors looking for strong performance are still waiting.

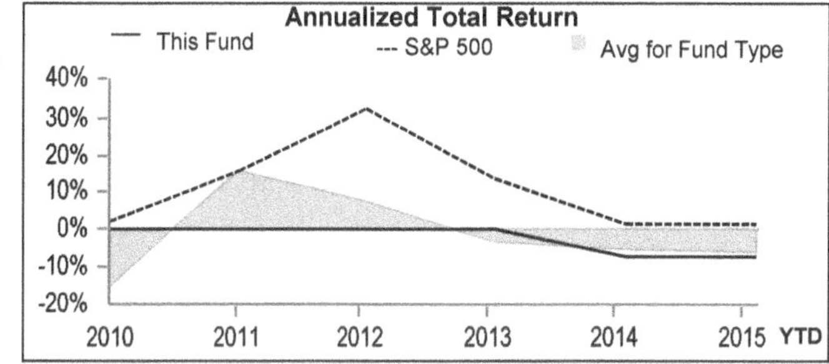

*SPDR MSCI Spain Quality Mix ETF (QESP) D Weak

Fund Family: SSgA Funds Management Inc
Fund Type: Foreign
Inception Date: June 12, 2014

Data Date	Investment Rating	Net Assets ($Mil)	Price	Performance Rating/Pts	Total Return Y-T-D	Risk Rating/Pts
12-15	D	8.30	42.98	D / 2.0	-9.06%	C / 5.4

Major Rating Factors:
Disappointing performance is the major factor driving the D (Weak) TheStreet.com Investment Rating for *SPDR MSCI Spain Quality Mix ETF. The fund currently has a performance rating of D (Weak) based on an annualized return of 0.00% over the last three years and a total return of -9.06% year to date 2015. Factored into the performance evaluation is an expense ratio of 0.30% (very low).

The fund's risk rating is currently C (Fair). It carries a beta of 0.00, meaning the fund's expected move will be 0.0% for every 10% move in the market. Volatility, as measured by both the semi-deviation and a drawdown factor, is considered average. As of December 31, 2015, *SPDR MSCI Spain Quality Mix ETF traded at a premium of .28% above its net asset value.

John A. Tucker currently receives a manager quality ranking of 19 (0=worst, 99=best). This fund offers an average level of risk but investors looking for strong performance will be frustrated.

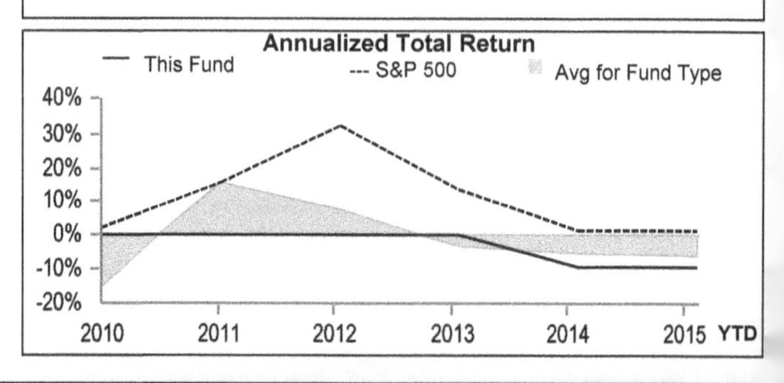

*SPDR MSCI United Kingdom Qual Mi (QGBR) C- Fair

Fund Family: SSgA Funds Management Inc
Fund Type: Foreign
Inception Date: June 12, 2014

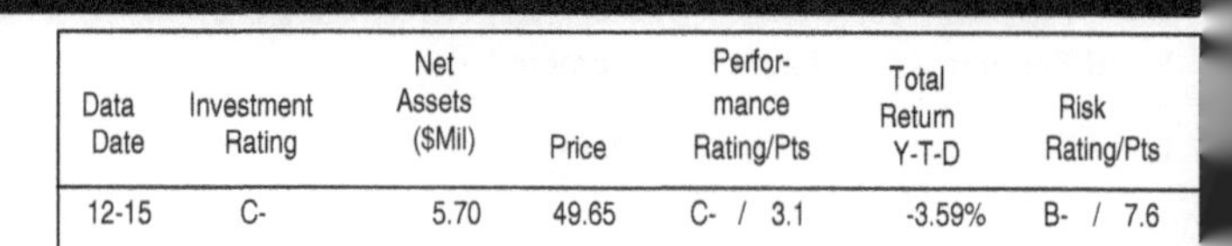

Data Date	Investment Rating	Net Assets ($Mil)	Price	Performance Rating/Pts	Total Return Y-T-D	Risk Rating/Pts
12-15	C-	5.70	49.65	C- / 3.1	-3.59%	B- / 7.6

Major Rating Factors: Middle of the road best describes *SPDR MSCI United Kingdom Qual Mi whose TheStreet.com Investment Rating is currently a C- (Fair). The fund currently has a performance rating of C- (Fair) based on an annualized return of 0.00% over the last three years and a total return of -3.59% year to date 2015. Factored into the performance evaluation is an expense ratio of 0.30% (very low).

The fund's risk rating is currently B- (Good). It carries a beta of 0.00, meaning the fund's expected move will be 0.0% for every 10% move in the market. Volatility, as measured by both the semi-deviation and a drawdown factor, is considered low. As of December 31, 2015, *SPDR MSCI United Kingdom Qual Mi traded at a discount of .18% below its net asset value, which is better than its one-year historical average premium of .43%.

John A. Tucker currently receives a manager quality ranking of 41 (0=worst, 99=best). If you desire an average level of risk, then this fund may be an option.

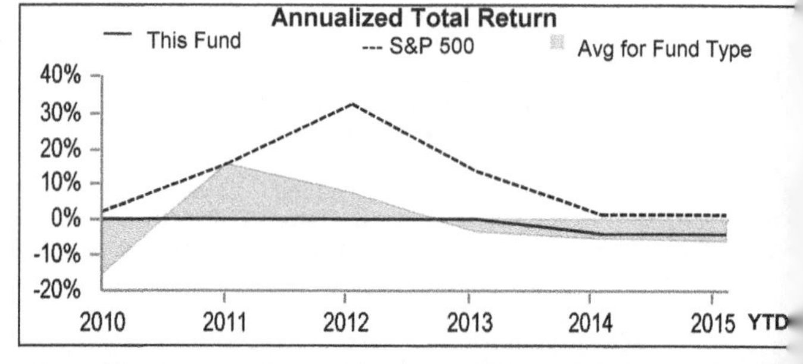

*SPDR MSCI World Quality Mix ETF (QWLD) B+ Good

Fund Family: SSgA Funds Management Inc
Fund Type: Global
Inception Date: June 5, 2014

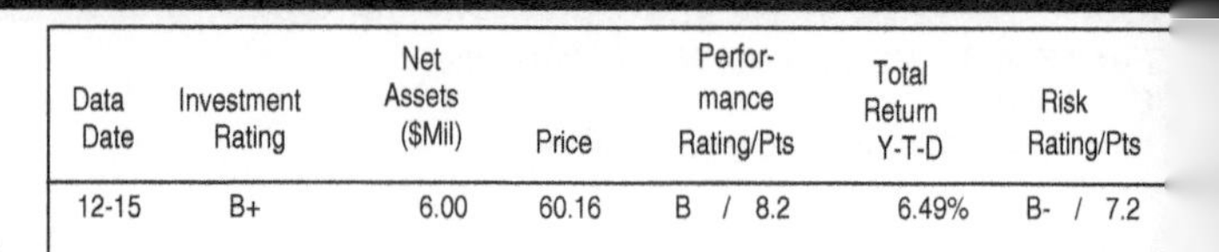

Data Date	Investment Rating	Net Assets ($Mil)	Price	Performance Rating/Pts	Total Return Y-T-D	Risk Rating/Pts
12-15	B+	6.00	60.16	B / 8.2	6.49%	B- / 7.2

Major Rating Factors: Strong performance is the major factor driving the B+ (Good) TheStreet.com Investment Rating for *SPDR MSCI World Quality Mix ETF. The fund currently has a performance rating of B (Good) based on an annualized return of 0.00% over the last three years and a total return of 6.49% year to date 2015. Factored into the performance evaluation is an expense ratio of 0.30% (very low).

The fund's risk rating is currently B- (Good). It carries a beta of 0.00, meaning the fund's expected move will be 0.0% for every 10% move in the market. Volatility, as measured by both the semi-deviation and a drawdown factor, is considered low. As of December 31, 2015, *SPDR MSCI World Quality Mix ETF traded at a premium of .32% above its net asset value, which is worse than its one-year historical average discount of .22%.

John A. Tucker currently receives a manager quality ranking of 92 (0=worst, 99=best). If you desire only a moderate level of risk and strong performance, then this fund is an excellent option.

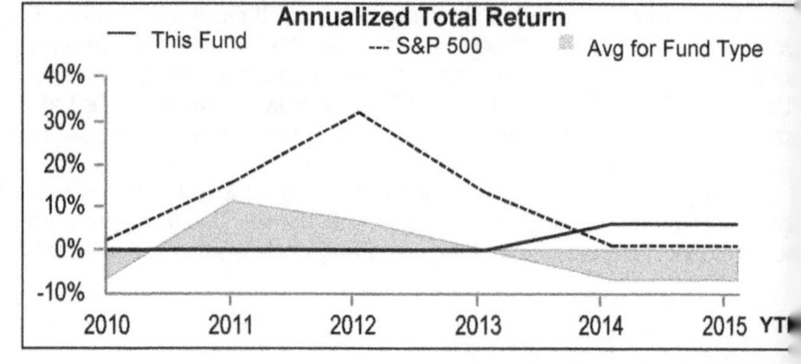

* Denotes ETF Fund

*SPDR Nuveen Barclays Bld Amr Bd (BABS) B Good

Fund Family: SSgA Funds Management Inc
Fund Type: Municipal - National
Inception Date: May 12, 2010

Major Rating Factors: *SPDR Nuveen Barclays Bld Amr Bd receives a TheStreet.com Investment Rating of B (Good). The fund currently has a performance rating of C+ (Fair) based on an annualized return of 3.84% over the last three years and a total return of -2.30% year to date 2015. Factored into the performance evaluation is an expense ratio of 0.35% (very low).

The fund's risk rating is currently B (Good). It carries a beta of 2.34, meaning it is expected to move 23.4% for every 10% move in the market. Volatility, as measured by both the semi-deviation and a drawdown factor, is considered low. As of December 31, 2015, *SPDR Nuveen Barclays Bld Amr Bd traded at a discount of 1.18% below its net asset value, which is better than its one-year historical average discount of 1.15%.

Daniel J. Close currently receives a manager quality ranking of 37 (0=worst, 99=best). If you desire an average level of risk, then this fund may be an option.

Data Date	Investment Rating	Net Assets ($Mil)	Price	Performance Rating/Pts	Total Return Y-T-D	Risk Rating/Pts
12-15	B	73.00	59.62	C+ / 6.3	-2.30%	B / 8.3
2014	A	73.00	63.13	B / 8.2	22.08%	B / 8.3
2013	B-	43.60	53.83	C+ / 6.6	-6.66%	B / 8.4
2012	B-	104.90	61.55	C+ / 5.6	10.82%	B+ / 9.0
2011	A	39.90	56.90	A- / 9.1	23.04%	B+ / 9.0

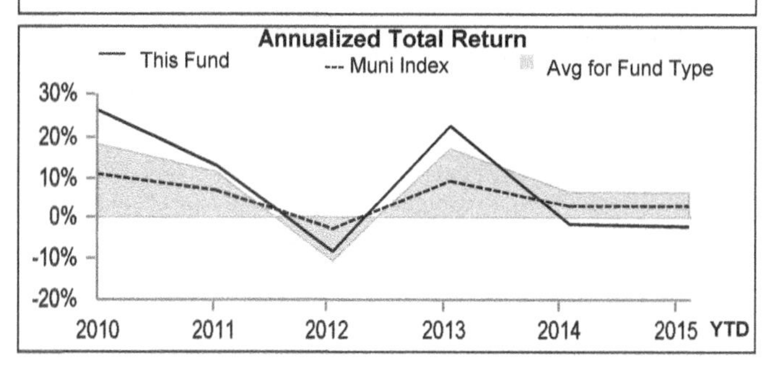

*SPDR Nuveen Barclays CA Muni Bd (CXA) B- Good

Fund Family: SSgA Funds Management Inc
Fund Type: Municipal - National
Inception Date: October 10, 2007

Major Rating Factors: *SPDR Nuveen Barclays CA Muni Bd receives a TheStreet.com Investment Rating of B- (Good). The fund currently has a performance rating of C+ (Fair) based on an annualized return of 3.71% over the last three years and a total return of 4.12% year to date 2015. Factored into the performance evaluation is an expense ratio of 0.20% (very low).

The fund's risk rating is currently B- (Good). It carries a beta of 1.72, meaning it is expected to move 17.2% for every 10% move in the market. Volatility, as measured by both the semi-deviation and a drawdown factor, is considered low. As of December 31, 2015, *SPDR Nuveen Barclays CA Muni Bd traded at a premium of .08% above its net asset value.

Steven M. Hlavin currently receives a manager quality ranking of 54 (0=worst, 99=best). If you desire an average level of risk, then this fund may be an option.

Data Date	Investment Rating	Net Assets ($Mil)	Price	Performance Rating/Pts	Total Return Y-T-D	Risk Rating/Pts
12-15	B-	78.50	24.26	C+ / 6.7	4.12%	B- / 7.6
2014	B-	78.50	23.84	C / 5.5	11.36%	B / 8.8
2013	B-	77.70	21.93	C+ / 5.9	-4.02%	B / 8.9
2012	C+	99.60	24.18	C / 4.7	7.23%	B+ / 9.0
2011	B	75.10	23.44	C+ / 6.4	19.12%	B+ / 9.0
2010	C	65.60	20.76	D / 2.0	-2.80%	B / 8.5

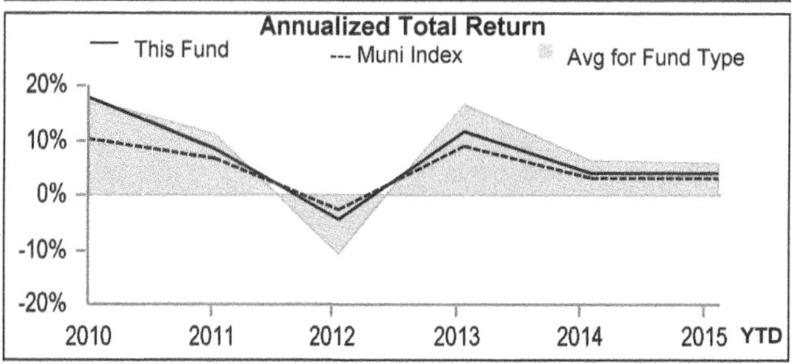

*SPDR Nuveen Barclays Muni Bond E (TFI) B- Good

Fund Family: SSgA Funds Management Inc
Fund Type: Municipal - National
Inception Date: September 11, 2007

Major Rating Factors: *SPDR Nuveen Barclays Muni Bond E receives a TheStreet.com Investment Rating of B- (Good). The fund currently has a performance rating of C+ (Fair) based on an annualized return of 3.03% over the last three years and a total return of 3.31% year to date 2015. Factored into the performance evaluation is an expense ratio of 0.23% (very low).

The fund's risk rating is currently B- (Good). It carries a beta of 1.22, meaning it is expected to move 12.2% for every 10% move in the market. Volatility, as measured by both the semi-deviation and a drawdown factor, is considered low. As of December 31, 2015, *SPDR Nuveen Barclays Muni Bond E traded at a premium of .21% above its net asset value, which is worse than its one-year historical average discount of .07%.

Steven M. Hlavin currently receives a manager quality ranking of 61 (0=worst, 99=best). If you desire an average level of risk, then this fund may be an option.

Data Date	Investment Rating	Net Assets ($Mil)	Price	Performance Rating/Pts	Total Return Y-T-D	Risk Rating/Pts
12-15	B-	1,079.30	24.38	C+ / 6.3	3.31%	B- / 7.9
2014	B-	1,079.30	24.16	C / 5.2	9.70%	B+ / 9.2
2013	C+	907.10	22.55	C / 5.1	-3.59%	B+ / 9.3
2012	C	1,216.70	24.24	C- / 3.7	5.24%	B+ / 9.3
2011	B-	982.20	23.74	C / 5.2	13.96%	B+ / 9.4
2010	C+	862.00	21.63	D+ / 2.8	-1.42%	B / 8.6

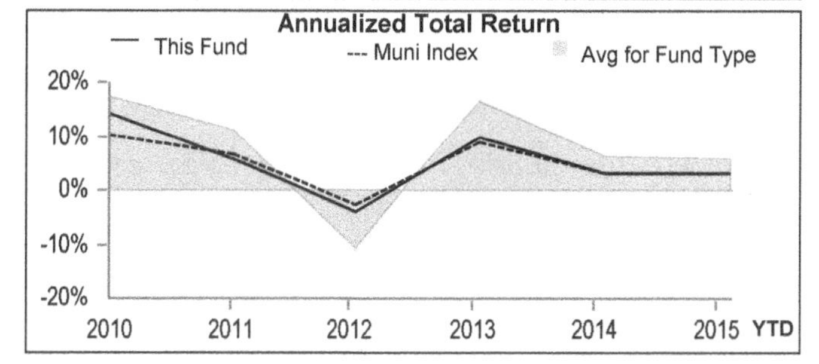

*SPDR Nuveen Barclays NY Muni Bd (INY) B- Good

Fund Family: SSgA Funds Management Inc
Fund Type: Municipal - National
Inception Date: October 11, 2007

Major Rating Factors: *SPDR Nuveen Barclays NY Muni Bd receives a TheStreet.com Investment Rating of B- (Good). The fund currently has a performance rating of C+ (Fair) based on an annualized return of 3.55% over the last three years and a total return of 2.97% year to date 2015. Factored into the performance evaluation is an expense ratio of 0.20% (very low).

The fund's risk rating is currently B- (Good). It carries a beta of 1.33, meaning it is expected to move 13.3% for every 10% move in the market. Volatility, as measured by both the semi-deviation and a drawdown factor, is considered low. As of December 31, 2015, *SPDR Nuveen Barclays NY Muni Bd traded at a premium of 1.02% above its net asset value, which is worse than its one-year historical average discount of .28%.

Steven M. Hlavin currently receives a manager quality ranking of 63 (0=worst, 99=best). If you desire an average level of risk, then this fund may be an option.

Data Date	Investment Rating	Net Assets ($Mil)	Price	Performance Rating/Pts	Total Return Y-T-D	Risk Rating/Pts
12-15	B-	25.60	23.77	C+ / 6.7	2.97%	B- / 7.7
2014	C+	25.60	23.68	C+ / 5.7	11.73%	B- / 7.3
2013	C+	24.10	21.65	C / 5.1	-3.94%	B+ / 9.0
2012	C	31.20	23.95	C- / 3.9	6.68%	B+ / 9.2
2011	B-	25.70	23.34	C+ / 5.8	14.61%	B+ / 9.3
2010	C	26.00	21.42	D+ / 2.8	-0.91%	B / 8.3

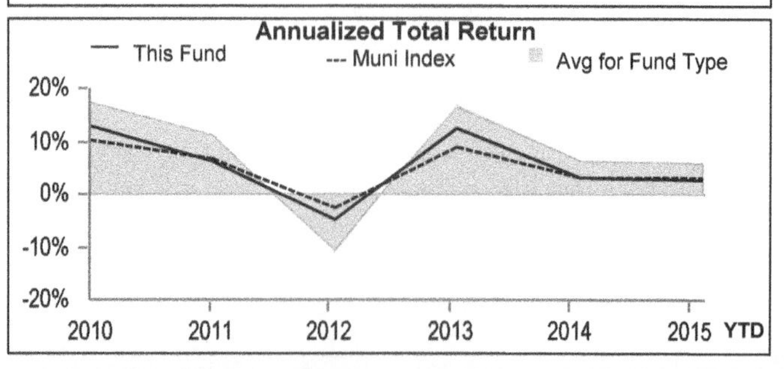

*SPDR Nuveen Barclays ST Muni Bd (SHM) C+ Fair

Fund Family: SSgA Funds Management Inc
Fund Type: Municipal - National
Inception Date: October 10, 2007

Major Rating Factors: Middle of the road best describes *SPDR Nuveen Barclays ST Muni Bd whose TheStreet.com Investment Rating is currently a C+ (Fair). The fund currently has a performance rating of C (Fair) based on an annualized return of 1.16% over the last three years and a total return of 1.13% year to date 2015. Factored into the performance evaluation is an expense ratio of 0.20% (very low).

The fund's risk rating is currently B (Good). It carries a beta of 0.32, meaning the fund's expected move will be 3.2% for every 10% move in the market. Volatility, as measured by both the semi-deviation and a drawdown factor, is considered low. As of December 31, 2015, *SPDR Nuveen Barclays ST Muni Bd traded at a premium of .29% above its net asset value, which is worse than its one-year historical average discount of .02%.

Steven M. Hlavin currently receives a manager quality ranking of 67 (0=worst, 99=best). If you desire an average level of risk, then this fund may be an option.

Data Date	Investment Rating	Net Assets ($Mil)	Price	Performance Rating/Pts	Total Return Y-T-D	Risk Rating/Pts
12-15	C+	2,351.10	24.36	C / 5.3	1.13%	B / 8.4
2014	C-	2,351.10	24.29	C- / 3.2	1.11%	B / 8.5
2013	C+	2,097.60	24.29	C- / 3.8	1.15%	B+ / 9.9
2012	C-	1,614.10	24.31	D / 1.9	1.07%	B+ / 9.8
2011	C	1,455.50	24.34	C- / 3.0	4.48%	B+ / 9.9
2010	B+	1,300.60	23.81	C / 4.3	0.59%	B+ / 9.1

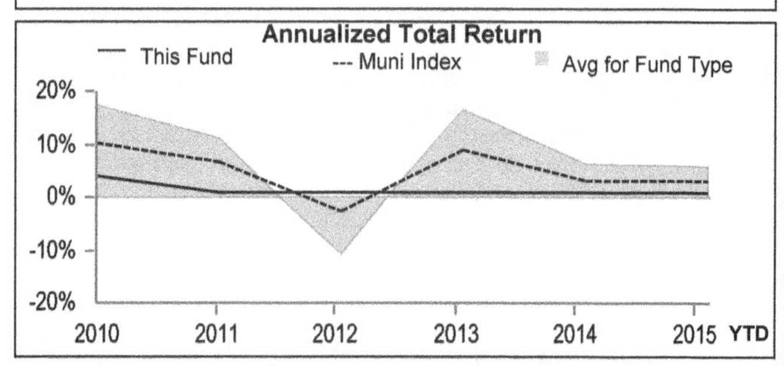

*SPDR Nuveen S&P Hi Yld Muni Bd E (HYMB) C Fair

Fund Family: SSgA Funds Management Inc
Fund Type: Corporate - High Yield
Inception Date: April 13, 2011

Major Rating Factors: Middle of the road best describes *SPDR Nuveen S&P Hi Yld Muni Bd E whose TheStreet.com Investment Rating is currently a C (Fair). The fund currently has a performance rating of C+ (Fair) based on an annualized return of 4.14% over the last three years and a total return of 3.74% year to date 2015. Factored into the performance evaluation is an expense ratio of 0.45% (very low).

The fund's risk rating is currently C+ (Fair). It carries a beta of 0.37, meaning the fund's expected move will be 3.7% for every 10% move in the market. Volatility, as measured by both the semi-deviation and a drawdown factor, is considered low. As of December 31, 2015, *SPDR Nuveen S&P Hi Yld Muni Bd E traded at a premium of .16% above its net asset value, which is worse than its one-year historical average discount of .33%.

Steven M. Hlavin currently receives a manager quality ranking of 87 (0=worst, 99=best). If you desire an average level of risk, then this fund may be an option.

Data Date	Investment Rating	Net Assets ($Mil)	Price	Performance Rating/Pts	Total Return Y-T-D	Risk Rating/Pts
12-15	C	295.70	57.05	C+ / 6.1	3.74%	C+ / 6.7
2014	C	295.70	57.67	C+ / 5.9	18.64%	C+ / 6.7
2013	D+	175.80	51.05	D / 1.6	-8.06%	B / 8.5
2012	B+	192.50	58.00	C+ / 6.5	16.79%	B+ / 9.8

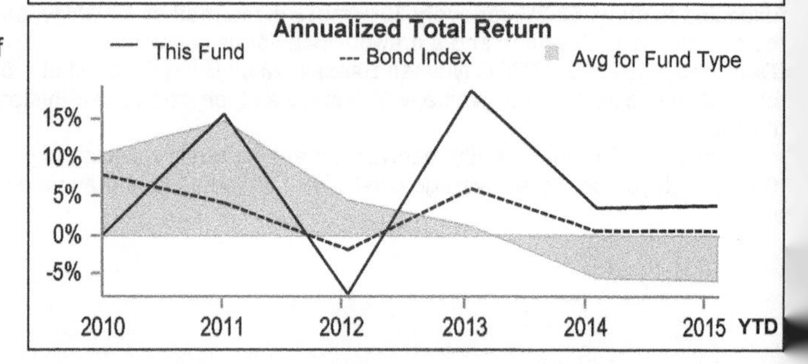

*SPDR Russell 1000 ETF (ONEK) A- Excellent

Fund Family: SSgA Funds Management Inc
Fund Type: Growth
Inception Date: November 8, 2005

Major Rating Factors:
Strong performance is the major factor driving the A- (Excellent) TheStreet.com Investment Rating for *SPDR Russell 1000 ETF. The fund currently has a performance rating of B+ (Good) based on an annualized return of 14.27% over the last three years and a total return of 1.98% year to date 2015. Factored into the performance evaluation is an expense ratio of 0.11% (very low).

The fund's risk rating is currently B- (Good). It carries a beta of 1.01, meaning that its performance tracks fairly well with that of the overall stock market. Volatility, as measured by both the semi-deviation and a drawdown factor, is considered low. As of December 31, 2015, *SPDR Russell 1000 ETF traded at a premium of .52% above its net asset value, which is worse than its one-year historical average premium of .07%.

John A. Tucker has been running the fund for 11 years and currently receives a manager quality ranking of 70 (0=worst, 99=best). If you desire only a moderate level of risk and strong performance, then this fund is an excellent option.

Data Date	Investment Rating	Net Assets ($Mil)	Price	Performance Rating/Pts	Total Return Y-T-D	Risk Rating/Pts
12-15	A-	51.00	96.05	B+ / 8.9	1.98%	B- / 7.2
2014	B+	51.00	96.84	B+ / 8.3	14.26%	B- / 7.5
2013	A-	43.50	86.78	B / 8.2	28.31%	B / 8.4
2012	C+	43.40	66.40	C / 5.2	17.04%	B / 8.2
2011	C+	35.30	58.88	C / 5.2	2.06%	B / 8.0
2010	C-	41.30	59.00	C- / 4.0	15.91%	C+ / 6.0

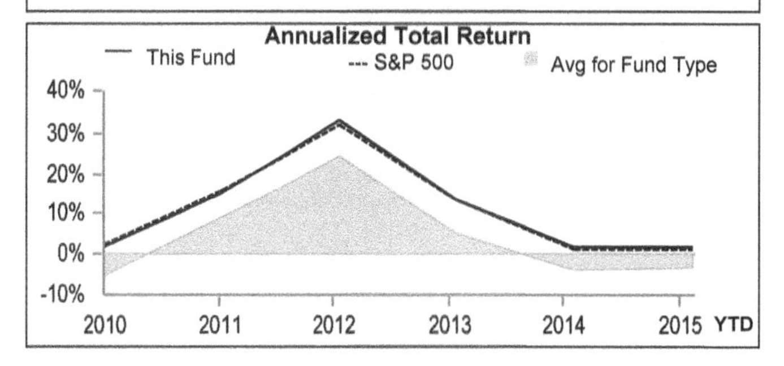

*SPDR Russell 1000 Low Volatility (LGLV) B+ Good

Fund Family: SSgA Funds Management Inc
Fund Type: Growth
Inception Date: February 20, 2013

Major Rating Factors: Strong performance is the major factor driving the B+ (Good) TheStreet.com Investment Rating for *SPDR Russell 1000 Low Volatility. The fund currently has a performance rating of B (Good) based on an annualized return of 0.00% over the last three years and a total return of 5.30% year to date 2015. Factored into the performance evaluation is an expense ratio of 0.15% (very low).

The fund's risk rating is currently B- (Good). It carries a beta of 0.00, meaning the fund's expected move will be 0.0% for every 10% move in the market. Volatility, as measured by both the semi-deviation and a drawdown factor, is considered low. As of December 31, 2015, *SPDR Russell 1000 Low Volatility traded at a premium of .20% above its net asset value, which is worse than its one-year historical average premium of .04%.

Michael J. Feehily has been running the fund for 3 years and currently receives a manager quality ranking of 86 (0=worst, 99=best). If you desire only a moderate level of risk and strong performance, then this fund is an excellent option.

Data Date	Investment Rating	Net Assets ($Mil)	Price	Performance Rating/Pts	Total Return Y-T-D	Risk Rating/Pts
12-15	B+	10.90	73.99	B / 8.2	5.30%	B- / 7.1
2014	A-	10.90	74.59	B+ / 8.6	18.21%	B- / 7.7

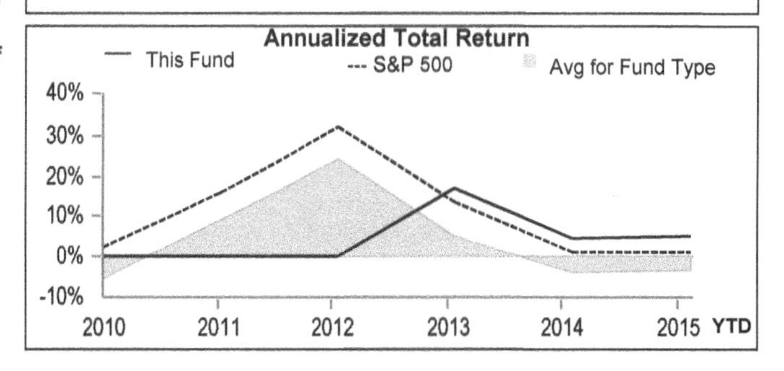

*SPDR Russell 2000 ETF (TWOK) C- Fair

Fund Family: SSgA Funds Management Inc
Fund Type: Growth
Inception Date: July 8, 2013

Major Rating Factors: Middle of the road best describes *SPDR Russell 2000 ETF whose TheStreet.com Investment Rating is currently a C- (Fair). The fund currently has a performance rating of C- (Fair) based on an annualized return of 0.00% over the last three years and a total return of -0.57% year to date 2015. Factored into the performance evaluation is an expense ratio of 0.12% (very low).

The fund's risk rating is currently C+ (Fair). It carries a beta of 0.00, meaning the fund's expected move will be 0.0% for every 10% move in the market. Volatility, as measured by both the semi-deviation and a drawdown factor, is considered low. As of December 31, 2015, *SPDR Russell 2000 ETF traded at a premium of 1.17% above its net asset value, which is worse than its one-year historical average premium of .05%.

John A. Tucker has been running the fund for 3 years and currently receives a manager quality ranking of 47 (0=worst, 99=best). If you desire an average level of risk, then this fund may be an option.

Data Date	Investment Rating	Net Assets ($Mil)	Price	Performance Rating/Pts	Total Return Y-T-D	Risk Rating/Pts
12-15	C-	59.00	67.42	C- / 4.1	-0.57%	C+ / 6.6
2014	C	59.00	71.35	C / 5.1	5.57%	B- / 7.1

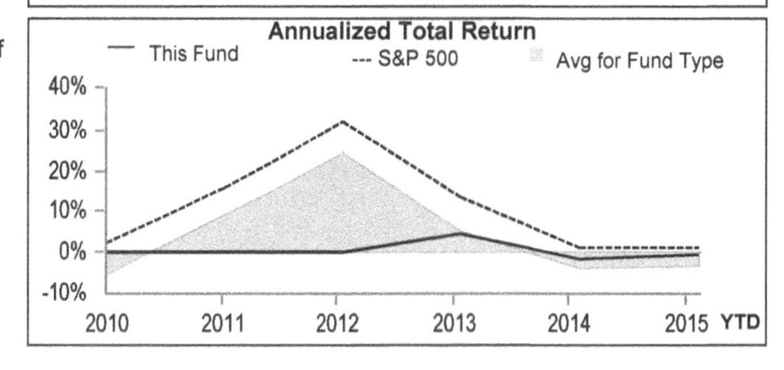

*SPDR Russell 2000 Low Volatility (SMLV) C Fair

Fund Family: SSgA Funds Management Inc
Fund Type: Growth
Inception Date: February 20, 2013

Major Rating Factors: Middle of the road best describes *SPDR Russell 2000 Low Volatility whose TheStreet.com Investment Rating is currently a C (Fair). The fund currently has a performance rating of C+ (Fair) based on an annualized return of 0.00% over the last three years and a total return of 0.19% year to date 2015. Factored into the performance evaluation is an expense ratio of 0.18% (very low).

The fund's risk rating is currently B- (Good). It carries a beta of 0.00, meaning the fund's expected move will be 0.0% for every 10% move in the market. Volatility, as measured by both the semi-deviation and a drawdown factor, is considered low. As of December 31, 2015, *SPDR Russell 2000 Low Volatility traded at a premium of .92% above its net asset value, which is worse than its one-year historical average premium of .06%.

Michael J. Feehily has been running the fund for 3 years and currently receives a manager quality ranking of 55 (0=worst, 99=best). If you desire an average level of risk, then this fund may be an option.

Data Date	Investment Rating	Net Assets ($Mil)	Price	Performance Rating/Pts	Total Return Y-T-D	Risk Rating/Pts
12-15	C	13.90	74.67	C+ / 5.6	0.19%	B- / 7.0
2014	B+	13.90	77.97	B / 8.1	15.14%	B- / 7.4

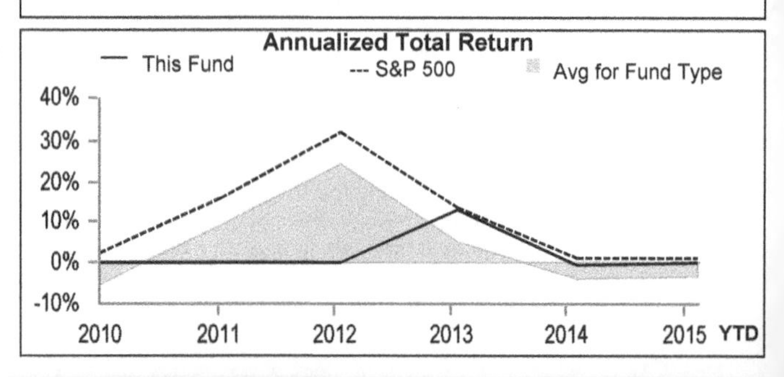

*SPDR Russell 3000 ETF (THRK) B+ Good

Fund Family: SSgA Funds Management Inc
Fund Type: Growth
Inception Date: October 4, 2000

Major Rating Factors: Strong performance is the major factor driving the B+ (Good) TheStreet.com Investment Rating for *SPDR Russell 3000 ETF. The fund currently has a performance rating of B+ (Good) based on an annualized return of 14.00% over the last three years and a total return of 1.57% year to date 2015. Factored into the performance evaluation is an expense ratio of 0.11% (very low).

The fund's risk rating is currently B- (Good). It carries a beta of 1.00, meaning that its performance tracks fairly well with that of the overall stock market. Volatility, as measured by both the semi-deviation and a drawdown factor, is considered low. As of December 31, 2015, *SPDR Russell 3000 ETF traded at a premium of .64% above its net asset value, which is worse than its one-year historical average premium of .08%.

John A. Tucker has been running the fund for 16 years and currently receives a manager quality ranking of 68 (0=worst, 99=best). If you desire only a moderate level of risk and strong performance, then this fund is an excellent option.

Data Date	Investment Rating	Net Assets ($Mil)	Price	Performance Rating/Pts	Total Return Y-T-D	Risk Rating/Pts
12-15	B+	198.60	152.18	B+ / 8.8	1.57%	B- / 7.2
2014	B+	198.60	154.72	B+ / 8.4	14.13%	B- / 7.4
2013	B+	564.40	139.37	B+ / 8.3	28.82%	B / 8.2
2012	C+	431.10	106.26	C / 5.4	16.66%	B / 8.0
2011	C+	163.90	93.54	C / 5.4	1.66%	B- / 7.9
2010	C	202.90	94.54	C / 4.7	17.34%	C+ / 5.9

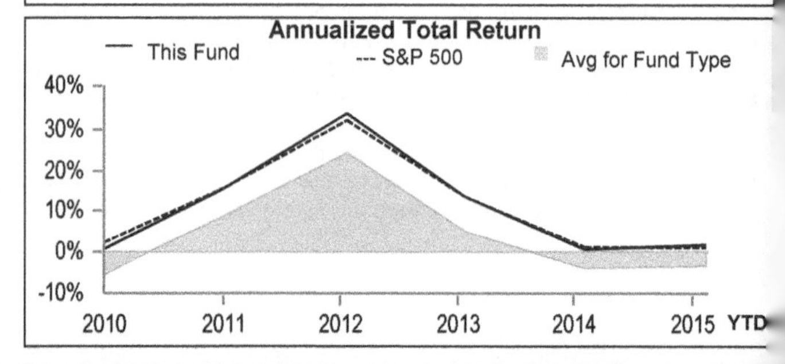

*SPDR Russell Small Cap Completen (RSCO) B Good

Fund Family: SSgA Funds Management Inc
Fund Type: Growth
Inception Date: November 8, 2005

Major Rating Factors: Strong performance is the major factor driving the B (Good) TheStreet.com Investment Rating for *SPDR Russell Small Cap Completen. The fund currently has a performance rating of B+ (Good) based on an annualized return of 13.00% over the last three years and a total return of 1.11% year to date 2015. Factored into the performance evaluation is an expense ratio of 0.10% (very low).

The fund's risk rating is currently C+ (Fair). It carries a beta of 1.02, meaning that its performance tracks fairly well with that of the overall stock market. Volatility, as measured by both the semi-deviation and a drawdown factor, is considered low. As of December 31, 2015, *SPDR Russell Small Cap Completen traded at a premium of .14% above its net asset value, which is worse than its one-year historical average discount of .14%.

John A. Tucker has been running the fund for 11 years and currently receives a manager quality ranking of 59 (0=worst, 99=best). If you desire only a moderate level of risk and strong performance, then this fund is an excellent option.

Data Date	Investment Rating	Net Assets ($Mil)	Price	Performance Rating/Pts	Total Return Y-T-D	Risk Rating/Pts
12-15	B	74.10	76.78	B+ / 8.5	1.11%	C+ / 6.7
2014	B	74.10	84.38	B / 8.0	8.82%	B- / 7.0
2013	B+	82.40	82.55	B+ / 8.7	33.11%	B- / 7.6
2012	C+	76.10	66.09	C+ / 6.7	17.25%	B- / 7.6
2011	B-	66.60	57.95	C+ / 6.8	0.52%	B- / 7.6
2010	B	59.10	59.43	B- / 7.3	24.63%	C+ / 5.8

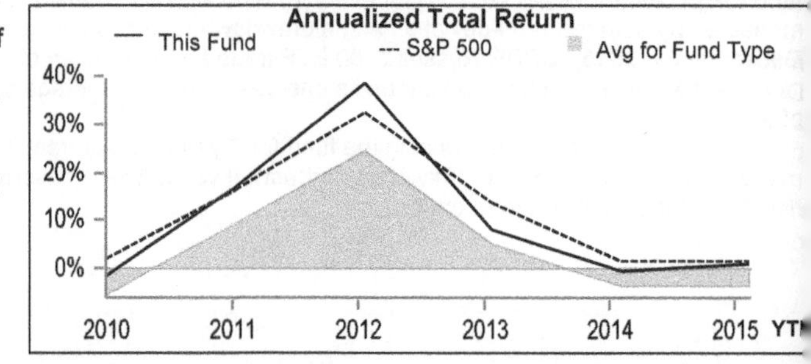

*SPDR Russell/Nomura PRIME Japan (JPP) A- Excellent

Fund Family: SSgA Funds Management Inc
Fund Type: Foreign
Inception Date: November 9, 2006

Data Date	Investment Rating	Net Assets ($Mil)	Price	Performance Rating/Pts	Total Return Y-T-D	Risk Rating/Pts
12-15	A-	27.10	46.16	B / 7.8	11.24%	B / 8.3
2014	C	27.10	42.35	C / 4.4	-4.42%	B / 8.0
2013	C	137.80	46.46	C+ / 5.8	21.54%	B- / 7.4
2012	D+	14.70	37.10	D / 2.2	9.02%	B- / 7.5
2011	D+	14.10	35.45	D / 1.9	-12.57%	B- / 7.6
2010	D+	8.30	41.07	D+ / 2.5	12.14%	C+ / 5.7

Major Rating Factors:
Strong performance is the major factor driving the A- (Excellent) TheStreet.com Investment Rating for *SPDR Russell/Nomura PRIME Japan. The fund currently has a performance rating of B (Good) based on an annualized return of 8.97% over the last three years and a total return of 11.24% year to date 2015. Factored into the performance evaluation is an expense ratio of 0.37% (very low).

The fund's risk rating is currently B (Good). It carries a beta of 0.75, meaning the fund's expected move will be 7.5% for every 10% move in the market. Volatility, as measured by both the semi-deviation and a drawdown factor, is considered low. As of December 31, 2015, *SPDR Russell/Nomura PRIME Japan traded at a discount of 1.22% below its net asset value, which is better than its one-year historical average premium of .12%.

John A. Tucker currently receives a manager quality ranking of 90 (0=worst, 99=best). If you desire only a moderate level of risk and strong performance, then this fund is an excellent option.

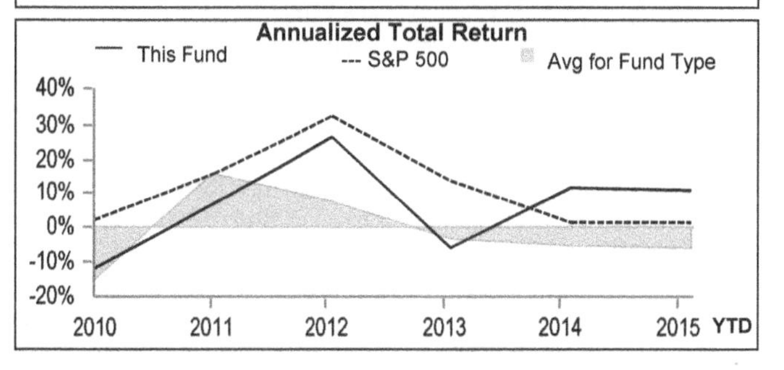

*SPDR Russell/Nomura Small Cap Ja (JSC) A+ Excellent

Fund Family: SSgA Funds Management Inc
Fund Type: Foreign
Inception Date: November 9, 2006

Data Date	Investment Rating	Net Assets ($Mil)	Price	Performance Rating/Pts	Total Return Y-T-D	Risk Rating/Pts
12-15	A+	72.80	54.28	B+ / 8.5	16.01%	B / 8.5
2014	C	72.80	47.94	C- / 4.0	-2.77%	B / 8.3
2013	C+	87.50	50.20	C+ / 5.9	19.39%	B / 8.3
2012	C-	60.70	42.35	D+ / 2.6	6.26%	B / 8.4
2011	C-	88.90	41.09	C- / 3.2	-3.53%	B- / 7.6
2010	C+	69.30	43.12	C+ / 6.4	17.94%	C+ / 6.1

Major Rating Factors:
Strong performance is the major factor driving the A+ (Excellent) TheStreet.com Investment Rating for *SPDR Russell/Nomura Small Cap Ja. The fund currently has a performance rating of B+ (Good) based on an annualized return of 10.32% over the last three years and a total return of 16.01% year to date 2015. Factored into the performance evaluation is an expense ratio of 0.45% (very low).

The fund's risk rating is currently B (Good). It carries a beta of 0.59, meaning the fund's expected move will be 5.9% for every 10% move in the market. Volatility, as measured by both the semi-deviation and a drawdown factor, is considered low. As of December 31, 2015, *SPDR Russell/Nomura Small Cap Ja traded at a discount of .80% below its net asset value, which is better than its one-year historical average discount of .30%.

John A. Tucker currently receives a manager quality ranking of 92 (0=worst, 99=best). If you desire only a moderate level of risk and strong performance, then this fund is an excellent option.

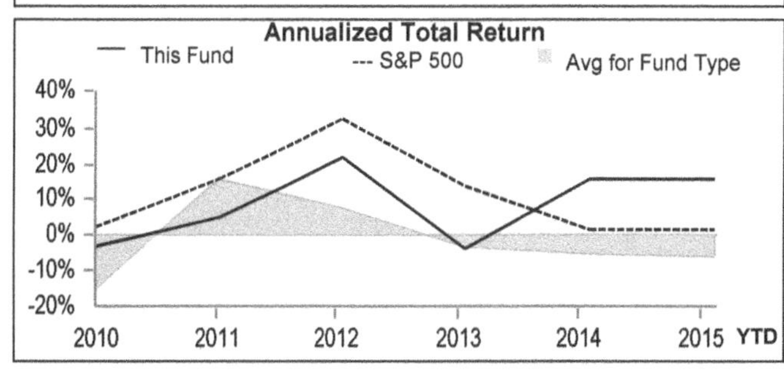

*SPDR S&P 1500 Momentum TILT ETF (MMTM) A- Excellent

Fund Family: SSgA Funds Management Inc
Fund Type: Income
Inception Date: October 24, 2012

Data Date	Investment Rating	Net Assets ($Mil)	Price	Performance Rating/Pts	Total Return Y-T-D	Risk Rating/Pts
12-15	A-	16.70	90.07	A- / 9.2	6.02%	B- / 7.3
2014	B	16.70	88.30	B- / 7.2	14.57%	B- / 7.9
2013	A+	11.80	78.60	A- / 9.0	28.68%	B+ / 9.7

Major Rating Factors:
Exceptional performance is the major factor driving the A- (Excellent) TheStreet.com Investment Rating for *SPDR S&P 1500 Momentum TILT ETF. The fund currently has a performance rating of A- (Excellent) based on an annualized return of 15.42% over the last three years and a total return of 6.02% year to date 2015. Factored into the performance evaluation is an expense ratio of 0.25% (very low).

The fund's risk rating is currently B- (Good). It carries a beta of 0.88, meaning the fund's expected move will be 8.8% for every 10% move in the market. Volatility, as measured by both the semi-deviation and a drawdown factor, is considered low. As of December 31, 2015, *SPDR S&P 1500 Momentum TILT ETF traded at a premium of 2.15% above its net asset value, which is worse than its one-year historical average premium of .22%.

Michael J. Feehily has been running the fund for 4 years and currently receives a manager quality ranking of 84 (0=worst, 99=best). If you desire only a moderate level of risk and strong performance, then this fund is an excellent option.

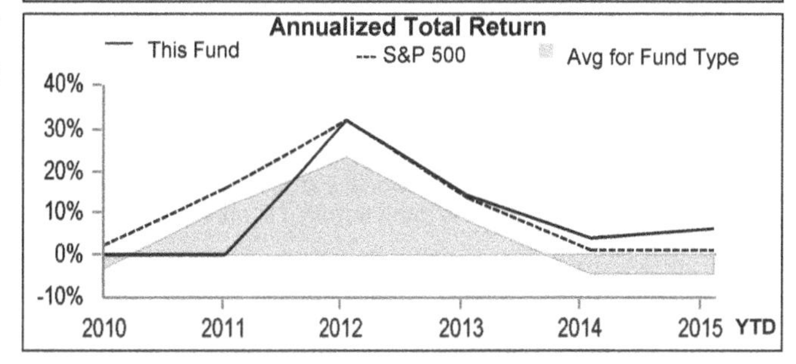

*SPDR S&P 1500 Value TILT ETF (VLU) B+ Good

Fund Family: SSgA Funds Management Inc
Fund Type: Income
Inception Date: October 24, 2012

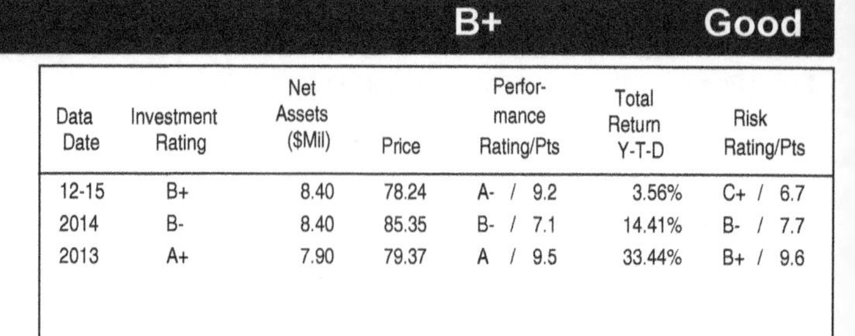

Data Date	Investment Rating	Net Assets ($Mil)	Price	Performance Rating/Pts	Total Return Y-T-D	Risk Rating/Pts
12-15	B+	8.40	78.24	A- / 9.2	3.56%	C+ / 6.7
2014	B-	8.40	85.35	B- / 7.1	14.41%	B- / 7.7
2013	A+	7.90	79.37	A / 9.5	33.44%	B+ / 9.6

Major Rating Factors:
Exceptional performance is the major factor driving the B+ (Good) TheStreet.com Investment Rating for *SPDR S&P 1500 Value TILT ETF. The fund currently has a performance rating of A- (Excellent) based on an annualized return of 15.86% over the last three years and a total return of 3.56% year to date 2015. Factored into the performance evaluation is an expense ratio of 0.24% (very low).

The fund's risk rating is currently C+ (Fair). It carries a beta of 0.93, meaning that its performance tracks fairly well with that of the overall stock market. Volatility, as measured by both the semi-deviation and a drawdown factor, is considered low. As of December 31, 2015, *SPDR S&P 1500 Value TILT ETF traded at a premium of 1.91% above its net asset value, which is worse than its one-year historical average discount of .52%.

Michael J. Feehily has been running the fund for 4 years and currently receives a manager quality ranking of 79 (0=worst, 99=best). If you desire only a moderate level of risk and strong performance, then this fund is an excellent option.

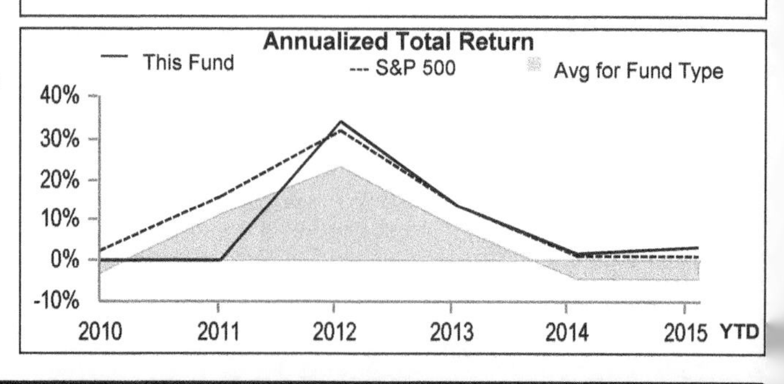

*SPDR S&P 400 Mid Cap Growth ETF (MDYG) A- Excellent

Fund Family: SSgA Funds Management Inc
Fund Type: Growth
Inception Date: November 8, 2005

Data Date	Investment Rating	Net Assets ($Mil)	Price	Performance Rating/Pts	Total Return Y-T-D	Risk Rating/Pts
12-15	A-	174.70	117.45	B+ / 8.8	5.79%	B- / 7.4
2014	B	174.70	118.14	B- / 7.5	8.22%	B- / 7.7
2013	B	145.20	111.91	B / 7.9	27.20%	B- / 7.8
2012	B-	68.10	85.22	B- / 7.0	17.83%	B- / 7.7
2011	B-	58.80	73.69	B- / 7.2	-0.13%	B- / 7.7
2010	B+	71.00	75.32	B / 7.9	27.62%	C / 5.5

Major Rating Factors:
Strong performance is the major factor driving the A- (Excellent) TheStreet.com Investment Rating for *SPDR S&P 400 Mid Cap Growth ETF. The fund currently has a performance rating of B+ (Good) based on an annualized return of 13.40% over the last three years and a total return of 5.79% year to date 2015. Factored into the performance evaluation is an expense ratio of 0.21% (very low).

The fund's risk rating is currently B- (Good). It carries a beta of 0.91, meaning that its performance tracks fairly well with that of the overall stock market. Volatility, as measured by both the semi-deviation and a drawdown factor, is considered low. As of December 31, 2015, *SPDR S&P 400 Mid Cap Growth ETF traded at a premium of .02% above its net asset value, which is better than its one-year historical average premium of .07%.

John A. Tucker has been running the fund for 11 years and currently receives a manager quality ranking of 75 (0=worst, 99=best). If you desire only a moderate level of risk and strong performance, then this fund is an excellent option.

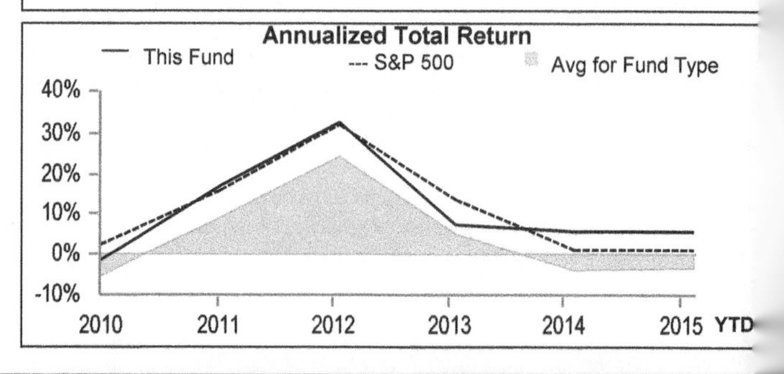

*SPDR S&P 400 Mid Cap Value ETF (MDYV) B Good

Fund Family: SSgA Funds Management Inc
Fund Type: Growth
Inception Date: November 8, 2005

Data Date	Investment Rating	Net Assets ($Mil)	Price	Performance Rating/Pts	Total Return Y-T-D	Risk Rating/Pts
12-15	B	106.40	76.12	B / 7.8	-3.89%	B- / 7.0
2014	B+	106.40	85.29	B+ / 8.5	12.96%	B- / 7.3
2013	B	75.10	79.06	B / 8.0	28.49%	B- / 7.9
2012	C+	24.00	59.85	C+ / 6.3	18.88%	B- / 7.7
2011	C+	25.90	51.91	C+ / 5.7	-1.08%	B- / 7.7
2010	C+	27.10	54.48	C+ / 6.2	21.37%	C+ / 5.7

Major Rating Factors: Strong performance is the major factor driving the B (Good) TheStreet.com Investment Rating for *SPDR S&P 400 Mid Cap Value ETF. The fund currently has a performance rating of B (Good) based on an annualized return of 11.54% over the last three years and a total return of -3.89% year to date 2015. Factored into the performance evaluation is an expense ratio of 0.21% (very low).

The fund's risk rating is currently B- (Good). It carries a beta of 1.00, meaning that its performance tracks fairly well with that of the overall stock market. Volatility, as measured by both the semi-deviation and a drawdown factor, is considered low. As of December 31, 2015, *SPDR S&P 400 Mid Cap Value ETF traded at a premium of .22% above its net asset value, which is worse than its one-year historical average premium of .08%.

John A. Tucker has been running the fund for 11 years and currently receives a manager quality ranking of 51 (0=worst, 99=best). If you desire only a moderate level of risk and strong performance, then this fund is an excellent option.

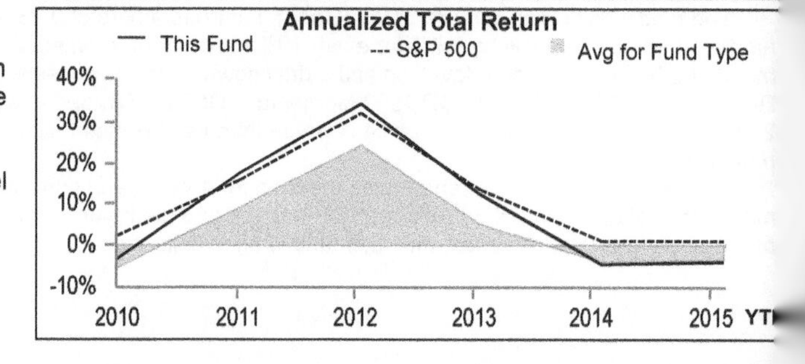

* Denotes ETF Fund

*SPDR S&P 500 ETF (SPY) A+ Excellent

Fund Family: State Street Bank and Trust Company
Fund Type: Growth
Inception Date: January 22, 1993

Data Date	Investment Rating	Net Assets ($Mil)	Price	Performance Rating/Pts	Total Return Y-T-D	Risk Rating/Pts
12-15	A+	180,378.10	203.87	B+ / 8.9	1.89%	B / 8.6
2014	B+	180,378.10	205.54	B+ / 8.3	14.58%	B- / 7.7
2013	B+	174,850.00	184.69	B / 8.1	27.47%	B / 8.2
2012	C	123,000.90	142.41	C / 5.2	16.70%	B / 8.0
2011	C	95,397.40	125.50	C / 5.2	2.54%	B- / 7.9
2010	C-	89,875.00	125.75	C- / 3.8	15.08%	C+ / 6.0

Major Rating Factors:
Strong performance is the major factor driving the A+ (Excellent) TheStreet.com Investment Rating for *SPDR S&P 500 ETF. The fund currently has a performance rating of B+ (Good) based on an annualized return of 14.16% over the last three years and a total return of 1.89% year to date 2015. Factored into the performance evaluation is an expense ratio of 0.09% (very low).

The fund's risk rating is currently B (Good). It carries a beta of 1.00, meaning that its performance tracks fairly well with that of the overall stock market. Volatility, as measured by both the semi-deviation and a drawdown factor, is considered low. As of December 31, 2015, *SPDR S&P 500 ETF traded at a discount of .07% below its net asset value, which is better than its one-year historical average premium of .01%.

David K. Chin currently receives a manager quality ranking of 68 (0=worst, 99=best). If you desire only a moderate level of risk and strong performance, then this fund is an excellent option.

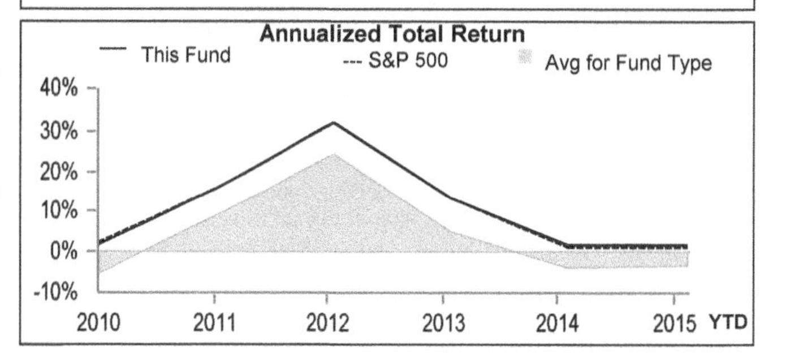

*SPDR S&P 500 Growth ETF (SPYG) A+ Excellent

Fund Family: SSgA Funds Management Inc
Fund Type: Growth
Inception Date: September 25, 2000

Data Date	Investment Rating	Net Assets ($Mil)	Price	Performance Rating/Pts	Total Return Y-T-D	Risk Rating/Pts
12-15	A+	424.70	100.09	A- / 9.2	5.79%	B / 8.4
2014	B+	424.70	96.64	B+ / 8.4	15.88%	B- / 7.2
2013	A-	324.70	85.59	B+ / 8.4	27.88%	B / 8.1
2012	C	216.40	65.56	C / 5.2	15.99%	B- / 7.8
2011	C+	207.30	58.47	C+ / 6.3	5.11%	B- / 7.8
2010	C+	190.40	56.94	C / 5.5	16.50%	C+ / 5.8

Major Rating Factors:
Exceptional performance is the major factor driving the A+ (Excellent) TheStreet.com Investment Rating for *SPDR S&P 500 Growth ETF. The fund currently has a performance rating of A- (Excellent) based on an annualized return of 16.15% over the last three years and a total return of 5.79% year to date 2015. Factored into the performance evaluation is an expense ratio of 0.18% (very low).

The fund's risk rating is currently B (Good). It carries a beta of 1.02, meaning that its performance tracks fairly well with that of the overall stock market. Volatility, as measured by both the semi-deviation and a drawdown factor, is considered low. As of December 31, 2015, *SPDR S&P 500 Growth ETF traded at a discount of .06% below its net asset value, which is better than its one-year historical average premium of .04%.

John A. Tucker has been running the fund for 16 years and currently receives a manager quality ranking of 78 (0=worst, 99=best). If you desire only a moderate level of risk and strong performance, then this fund is an excellent option.

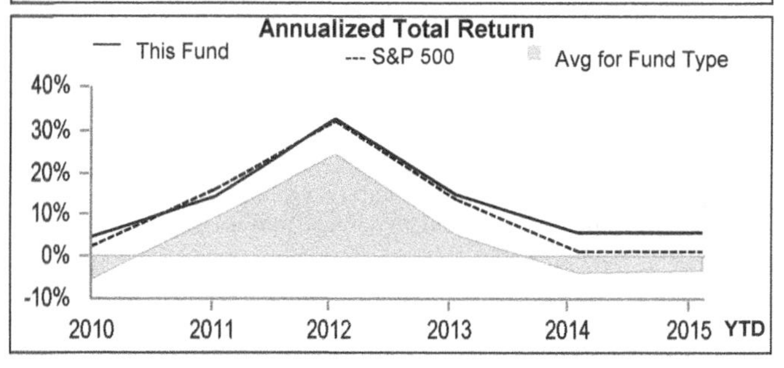

*SPDR S&P 500 Value ETF (SPYV) B Good

Fund Family: SSgA Funds Management Inc
Fund Type: Income
Inception Date: September 25, 2000

Data Date	Investment Rating	Net Assets ($Mil)	Price	Performance Rating/Pts	Total Return Y-T-D	Risk Rating/Pts
12-15	B	219.70	95.94	B / 8.0	-2.30%	B- / 7.2
2014	A+	219.70	101.55	B / 8.0	12.71%	B+ / 9.1
2013	B+	176.20	92.60	B / 7.9	27.12%	B / 8.3
2012	C+	115.10	71.79	C / 5.4	17.94%	B / 8.1
2011	C	160.30	62.80	C / 4.4	0.40%	B / 8.0
2010	D+	168.20	64.69	D+ / 2.8	15.51%	C+ / 6.0

Major Rating Factors: Strong performance is the major factor driving the B (Good) TheStreet.com Investment Rating for *SPDR S&P 500 Value ETF. The fund currently has a performance rating of B (Good) based on an annualized return of 11.81% over the last three years and a total return of -2.30% year to date 2015. Factored into the performance evaluation is an expense ratio of 0.18% (very low).

The fund's risk rating is currently B- (Good). It carries a beta of 1.03, meaning that its performance tracks fairly well with that of the overall stock market. Volatility, as measured by both the semi-deviation and a drawdown factor, is considered low. As of December 31, 2015, *SPDR S&P 500 Value ETF traded at a premium of .04% above its net asset value.

John A. Tucker has been running the fund for 16 years and currently receives a manager quality ranking of 49 (0=worst, 99=best). If you desire only a moderate level of risk and strong performance, then this fund is an excellent option.

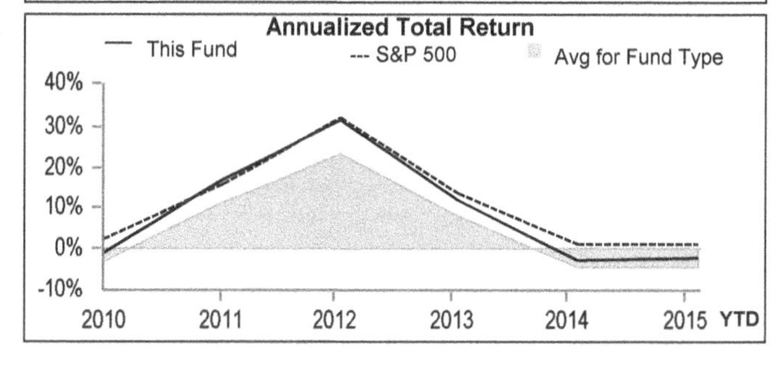

*SPDR S&P 600 Small Cap ETF (SLY) B+ Good

Fund Family: SSgA Funds Management Inc
Fund Type: Growth
Inception Date: November 8, 2005

Major Rating Factors: Strong performance is the major factor driving the B+ (Good) TheStreet.com Investment Rating for *SPDR S&P 600 Small Cap ETF. The fund currently has a performance rating of B (Good) based on an annualized return of 12.04% over the last three years and a total return of -1.42% year to date 2015. Factored into the performance evaluation is an expense ratio of 0.18% (very low).

The fund's risk rating is currently B (Good). It carries a beta of 1.03, meaning that its performance tracks fairly well with that of the overall stock market. Volatility, as measured by both the semi-deviation and a drawdown factor, is considered low. As of December 31, 2015, *SPDR S&P 600 Small Cap ETF traded at a discount of .03% below its net asset value, which is better than its one-year historical average premium of .08%.

John A. Tucker has been running the fund for 11 years and currently receives a manager quality ranking of 51 (0=worst, 99=best). If you desire only a moderate level of risk and strong performance, then this fund is an excellent option.

Data Date	Investment Rating	Net Assets ($Mil)	Price	Performance Rating/Pts	Total Return Y-T-D	Risk Rating/Pts
12-15	B+	313.60	98.88	B / 7.9	-1.42%	B / 8.1
2014	B-	313.60	104.73	B / 7.8	6.58%	B- / 7.0
2013	B+	421.20	102.69	B+ / 8.9	34.92%	B- / 7.6
2012	C+	229.20	75.11	C+ / 6.7	16.46%	B- / 7.5
2011	B-	72.40	66.07	B- / 7.3	2.74%	B- / 7.5
2010	B	62.60	66.87	B / 7.8	28.92%	C / 5.4

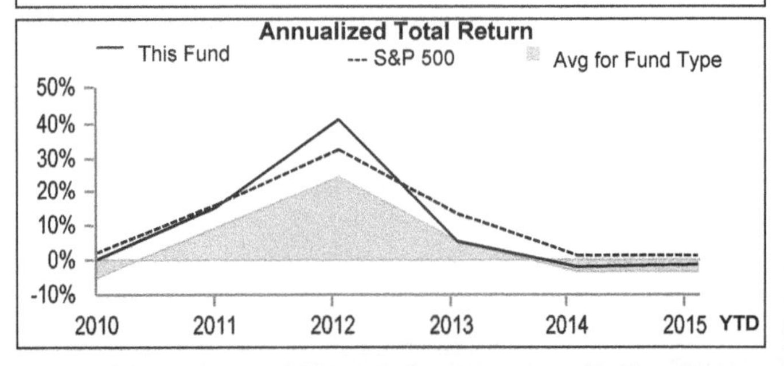

*SPDR S&P 600 Small Cap Growth ET (SLYG) B Good

Fund Family: SSgA Funds Management Inc
Fund Type: Growth
Inception Date: September 25, 2000

Major Rating Factors: Strong performance is the major factor driving the B (Good) TheStreet.com Investment Rating for *SPDR S&P 600 Small Cap Growth ET. The fund currently has a performance rating of B+ (Good) based on an annualized return of 13.65% over the last three years and a total return of 3.66% year to date 2015. Factored into the performance evaluation is an expense ratio of 0.20% (very low).

The fund's risk rating is currently C+ (Fair). It carries a beta of 0.97, meaning that its performance tracks fairly well with that of the overall stock market. Volatility, as measured by both the semi-deviation and a drawdown factor, is considered low. As of December 31, 2015, *SPDR S&P 600 Small Cap Growth ET traded at a premium of .13% above its net asset value, which is worse than its one-year historical average premium of .07%.

John A. Tucker has been running the fund for 16 years and currently receives a manager quality ranking of 70 (0=worst, 99=best). If you desire only a moderate level of risk and strong performance, then this fund is an excellent option.

Data Date	Investment Rating	Net Assets ($Mil)	Price	Performance Rating/Pts	Total Return Y-T-D	Risk Rating/Pts
12-15	B	372.20	172.78	B+ / 8.6	3.66%	C+ / 6.3
2014	B-	372.20	177.74	B / 7.6	4.52%	B- / 7.0
2013	B+	348.80	179.12	A- / 9.0	36.79%	B- / 7.1
2012	B-	164.40	126.35	B- / 7.1	16.70%	B- / 7.4
2011	B-	145.80	112.28	B / 7.7	4.08%	B- / 7.2
2010	B	174.60	110.57	B / 8.0	32.09%	C / 5.2

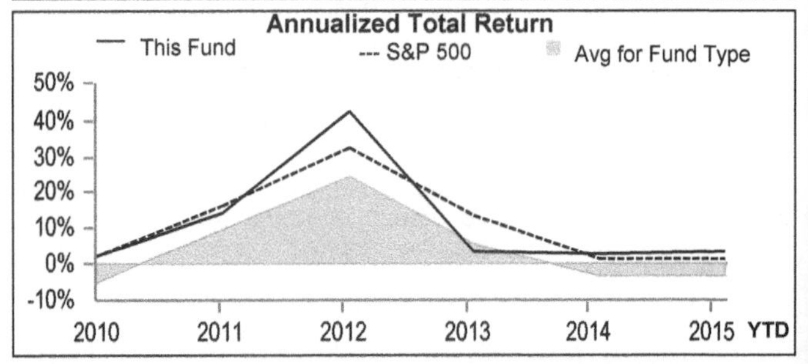

*SPDR S&P 600 Small Cap Value ETF (SLYV) B Good

Fund Family: SSgA Funds Management Inc
Fund Type: Growth
Inception Date: September 25, 2000

Major Rating Factors: Strong performance is the major factor driving the B (Good) TheStreet.com Investment Rating for *SPDR S&P 600 Small Cap Value ETF. The fund currently has a performance rating of B+ (Good) based on an annualized return of 12.28% over the last three years and a total return of -1.56% year to date 2015. Factored into the performance evaluation is an expense ratio of 0.21% (very low).

The fund's risk rating is currently C+ (Fair). It carries a beta of 1.03, meaning that its performance tracks fairly well with that of the overall stock market. Volatility, as measured by both the semi-deviation and a drawdown factor, is considered low. As of December 31, 2015, *SPDR S&P 600 Small Cap Value ETF traded at a premium of .06% above its net asset value, which is in line with its one-year historical average premium of .06%.

John A. Tucker has been running the fund for 16 years and currently receives a manager quality ranking of 55 (0=worst, 99=best). If you desire only a moderate level of risk and strong performance, then this fund is an excellent option.

Data Date	Investment Rating	Net Assets ($Mil)	Price	Performance Rating/Pts	Total Return Y-T-D	Risk Rating/Pts
12-15	B	286.70	92.97	B+ / 8.3	-1.56%	C+ / 6.9
2014	B	286.70	105.74	B / 8.0	7.47%	C+ / 6.9
2013	A-	250.10	106.46	B+ / 8.8	34.22%	B- / 7.8
2012	C+	131.80	77.01	C+ / 6.3	16.90%	B- / 7.6
2011	B-	114.00	66.98	C+ / 6.9	1.33%	B- / 7.5
2010	B	134.50	69.75	B / 7.6	25.97%	C+ / 5.6

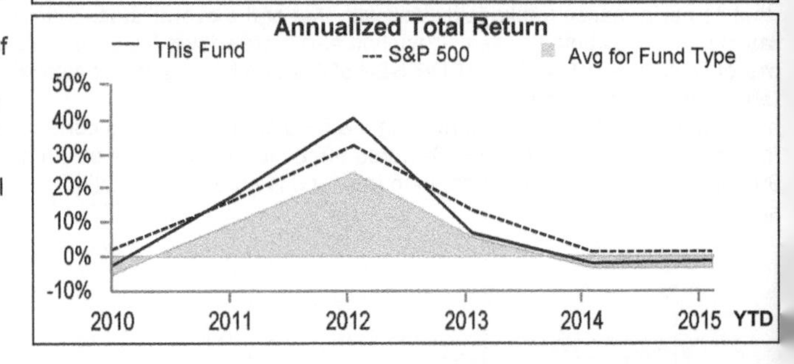

*SPDR S&P Aerospace & Defense ETF (XAR) C- Fair

Fund Family: SSgA Funds Management Inc
Fund Type: Income
Inception Date: September 29, 2011

Major Rating Factors: *SPDR S&P Aerospace & Defense ETF has adopted a very risky asset allocation strategy and currently receives an overall TheStreet.com Investment Rating of C- (Fair). The fund has shown a high level of volatility, as measured by both semi-deviation and drawdown factors. It carries a beta of 1.00, meaning that its performance tracks fairly well with that of the overall stock market. As of December 31, 2015, *SPDR S&P Aerospace & Defense ETF traded at a premium of .08% above its net asset value, which is worse than its one-year historical average premium of .04%. The high level of risk (D-, Weak) did however, reward investors with excellent performance.

The fund's performance rating is currently A (Excellent). It has registered an annualized return of 20.75% over the last three years and is up 4.14% year to date 2015. Factored into the performance evaluation is an expense ratio of 0.35% (very low).

John A. Tucker has been running the fund for 5 years and currently receives a manager quality ranking of 92 (0=worst, 99=best). If you are comfortable owning a very high risk investment, this fund may be an option.

Data Date	Investment Rating	Net Assets ($Mil)	Price	Performance Rating/Pts	Total Return Y-T-D	Risk Rating/Pts
12-15	C-	60.00	52.88	A / 9.5	4.14%	D- / 1.4
2014	A	60.00	109.25	A / 9.5	12.72%	B- / 7.2
2013	A+	34.70	99.02	A+ / 9.9	51.49%	B+ / 9.3
2012	A+	12.80	62.80	B+ / 8.7	17.14%	B+ / 9.1

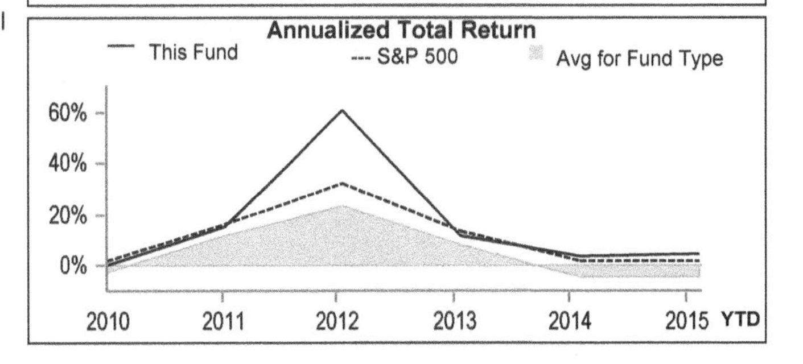

*SPDR S&P Biotech ETF (XBI) C- Fair

Fund Family: SSgA Funds Management Inc
Fund Type: Health
Inception Date: January 31, 2006

Major Rating Factors: *SPDR S&P Biotech ETF has adopted a very risky asset allocation strategy and currently receives an overall TheStreet.com Investment Rating of C- (Fair). The fund has shown a high level of volatility, as measured by both semi-deviation and drawdown factors. It carries a beta of 1.20, meaning it is expected to move 12.0% for every 10% move in the market. As of December 31, 2015, *SPDR S&P Biotech ETF traded at a price exactly equal to its net asset value, which is worse than its one-year historical average discount of .06%. The high level of risk (E+, Very Weak) did however, reward investors with excellent performance.

The fund's performance rating is currently A+ (Excellent). It has registered an annualized return of 32.53% over the last three years and is up 12.66% year to date 2015. Factored into the performance evaluation is an expense ratio of 0.35% (very low).

John A. Tucker has been running the fund for 10 years and currently receives a manager quality ranking of 97 (0=worst, 99=best). If you are comfortable owning a very high risk investment, this fund may be an option.

Data Date	Investment Rating	Net Assets ($Mil)	Price	Performance Rating/Pts	Total Return Y-T-D	Risk Rating/Pts
12-15	C-	1,191.70	70.20	A+ / 9.8	12.66%	E+ / 0.9
2014	B	1,191.70	186.46	A+ / 9.8	44.77%	C / 5.4
2013	B-	997.90	130.20	A / 9.3	41.25%	C+ / 5.8
2012	B-	629.20	87.91	B+ / 8.4	29.71%	C+ / 6.5
2011	D+	418.20	66.40	C- / 4.1	9.18%	C+ / 6.0
2010	C+	491.90	63.08	C+ / 5.9	17.60%	C+ / 6.0

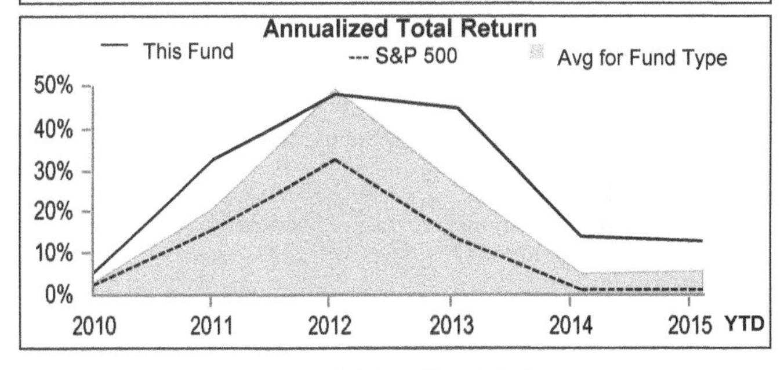

*SPDR S&P BRIC 40 ETF (BIK) D+ Weak

Fund Family: SSgA Funds Management Inc
Fund Type: Foreign
Inception Date: June 19, 2007

Major Rating Factors:
Disappointing performance is the major factor driving the D+ (Weak) TheStreet.com Investment Rating for *SPDR S&P BRIC 40 ETF. The fund currently has a performance rating of D+ (Weak) based on an annualized return of -6.09% over the last three years and a total return of -10.29% year to date 2015. Factored into the performance evaluation is an expense ratio of 0.50% (very low).

The fund's risk rating is currently C+ (Fair). It carries a beta of 1.08, meaning that its performance tracks fairly well with that of the overall stock market. Volatility, as measured by both the semi-deviation and a drawdown factor, is considered low. As of December 31, 2015, *SPDR S&P BRIC 40 ETF traded at a discount of .75% below its net asset value, which is better than its one-year historical average discount of .25%.

John A. Tucker currently receives a manager quality ranking of 16 (0=worst, 99=best). This fund offers only a moderate level of risk but investors looking for strong performance are still waiting.

Data Date	Investment Rating	Net Assets ($Mil)	Price	Performance Rating/Pts	Total Return Y-T-D	Risk Rating/Pts
12-15	D+	155.70	18.61	D+ / 2.4	-10.29%	C+ / 6.8
2014	D+	155.70	21.83	D+ / 2.9	-1.32%	B- / 7.1
2013	D	236.40	23.72	D / 2.0	-6.23%	C+ / 6.5
2012	D	320.30	24.40	D+ / 2.5	9.81%	C+ / 6.6
2011	C-	342.00	21.92	C / 4.9	-16.09%	C+ / 6.9
2010	D	503.00	27.43	C- / 3.1	11.36%	C- / 4.2

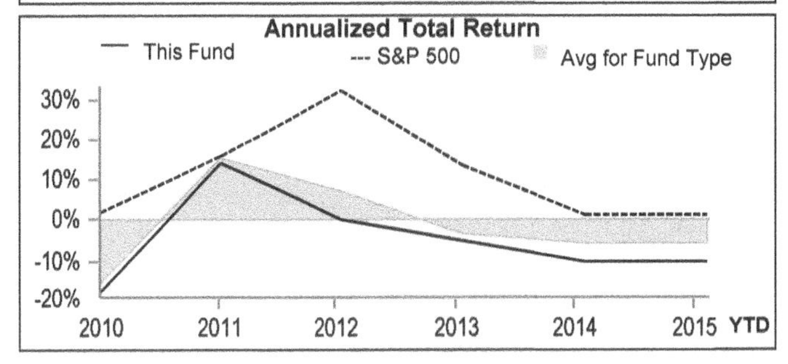

* Denotes ETF Fund

*SPDR S&P China ETF (GXC) C Fair

Fund Family: SSgA Funds Management Inc
Fund Type: Foreign
Inception Date: March 20, 2007

Major Rating Factors: Middle of the road best describes *SPDR S&P China ETF whose TheStreet.com Investment Rating is currently a C (Fair). The fund currently has a performance rating of C (Fair) based on an annualized return of 1.99% over the last three years and a total return of -3.37% year to date 2015. Factored into the performance evaluation is an expense ratio of 0.59% (very low).

The fund's risk rating is currently B- (Good). It carries a beta of 0.97, meaning that its performance tracks fairly well with that of the overall stock market. Volatility, as measured by both the semi-deviation and a drawdown factor, is considered low. As of December 31, 2015, *SPDR S&P China ETF traded at a discount of .41% below its net asset value, which is better than its one-year historical average discount of .14%.

John A. Tucker currently receives a manager quality ranking of 49 (0=worst, 99=best). If you desire an average level of risk, then this fund may be an option.

Data Date	Investment Rating	Net Assets ($Mil)	Price	Performance Rating/Pts	Total Return Y-T-D	Risk Rating/Pts
12-15	C	947.60	73.49	C / 4.6	-3.37%	B- / 7.0
2014	C+	947.60	79.64	C+ / 5.9	8.05%	B- / 7.9
2013	D+	888.80	77.93	C- / 3.5	1.57%	C+ / 6.3
2012	D+	1,067.30	74.09	C- / 3.2	18.11%	C+ / 6.4
2011	D+	584.70	62.30	C- / 4.0	-18.20%	C+ / 6.1
2010	D	703.70	76.24	D / 2.1	7.57%	C / 4.6

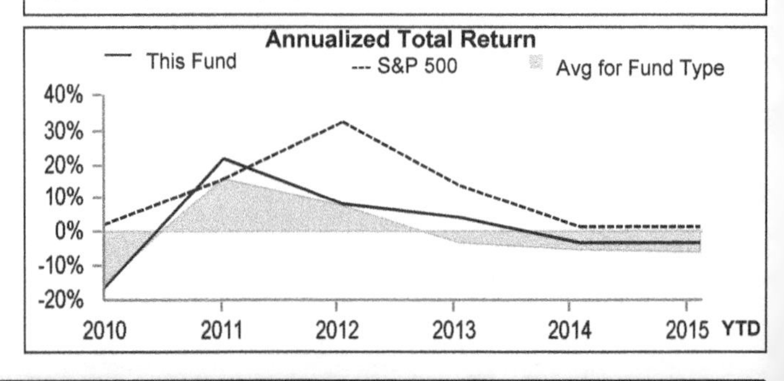

*SPDR S&P Dividend ETF (SDY) A- Excellent

Fund Family: SSgA Funds Management Inc
Fund Type: Income
Inception Date: November 8, 2005

Major Rating Factors:
Exceptional performance is the major factor driving the A- (Excellent) TheStreet.com Investment Rating for *SPDR S&P Dividend ETF. The fund currently has a performance rating of A- (Excellent) based on an annualized return of 14.00% over the last three years and a total return of 3.22% year to date 2015. Factored into the performance evaluation is an expense ratio of 0.35% (very low).

The fund's risk rating is currently B- (Good). It carries a beta of 0.91, meaning that its performance tracks fairly well with that of the overall stock market. Volatility, as measured by both the semi-deviation and a drawdown factor, is considered low. As of December 31, 2015, *SPDR S&P Dividend ETF traded at a premium of .03% above its net asset value, which is worse than its one-year historical average discount of .01%.

John A. Tucker has been running the fund for 11 years and currently receives a manager quality ranking of 77 (0=worst, 99=best). If you desire only a moderate level of risk and strong performance, then this fund is an excellent option.

Data Date	Investment Rating	Net Assets ($Mil)	Price	Performance Rating/Pts	Total Return Y-T-D	Risk Rating/Pts
12-15	A-	12,668.40	73.57	A- / 9.0	3.22%	B- / 7.4
2014	B+	12,668.40	78.80	B / 8.0	14.83%	B- / 7.8
2013	A-	12,553.60	72.62	B / 7.9	25.03%	B / 8.9
2012	C+	9,399.00	58.16	C / 5.5	14.33%	B / 8.7
2011	C+	8,252.90	53.87	C / 5.5	7.76%	B- / 7.8
2010	C+	5,031.90	51.98	C+ / 6.0	16.43%	C+ / 6.1

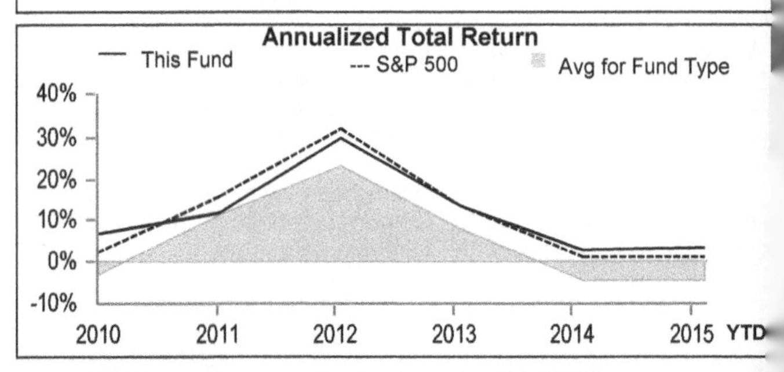

*SPDR S&P Emerg Middle East&Afric (GAF) D Weak

Fund Family: SSgA Funds Management Inc
Fund Type: Emerging Market
Inception Date: March 20, 2007

Major Rating Factors:
Disappointing performance is the major factor driving the D (Weak) TheStreet.com Investment Rating for *SPDR S&P Emerg Middle East&Afric. The fund currently has a performance rating of D (Weak) based on an annualized return of -9.19% over the last three years and a total return of -20.76% year to date 2015. Factored into the performance evaluation is an expense ratio of 0.53% (very low).

The fund's risk rating is currently C+ (Fair). It carries a beta of 0.99, meaning that its performance tracks fairly well with that of the overall stock market. Volatility, as measured by both the semi-deviation and a drawdown factor, is considered low. As of December 31, 2015, *SPDR S&P Emerg Middle East&Afric traded at a discount of .70% below its net asset value, which is worse than its one-year historical average discount of .85%.

John A. Tucker currently receives a manager quality ranking of 44 (0=worst, 99=best). This fund offers only a moderate level of risk but investors looking for strong performance are still waiting.

Data Date	Investment Rating	Net Assets ($Mil)	Price	Performance Rating/Pts	Total Return Y-T-D	Risk Rating/Pts
12-15	D	63.10	49.79	D / 1.6	-20.76%	C+ / 6.4
2014	C-	63.10	67.00	C- / 3.8	4.14%	B- / 7.6
2013	D+	67.80	68.55	D / 2.2	-8.48%	B- / 7.3
2012	C-	94.90	73.91	C / 4.3	16.43%	B- / 7.2
2011	C	94.70	62.75	C / 5.0	-14.64%	B- / 7.4
2010	B+	181.70	79.59	B / 8.1	30.45%	C+ / 5.8

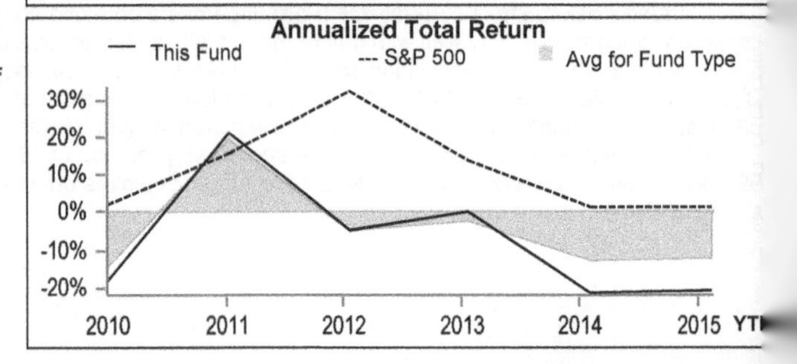

*SPDR S&P Emerging Asia Pacific E (GMF) — C — Fair

Fund Family: SSgA Funds Management Inc
Fund Type: Emerging Market
Inception Date: March 20, 2007

Major Rating Factors: Middle of the road best describes *SPDR S&P Emerging Asia Pacific E whose TheStreet.com Investment Rating is currently a C (Fair). The fund currently has a performance rating of C- (Fair) based on an annualized return of 1.25% over the last three years and a total return of -5.63% year to date 2015. Factored into the performance evaluation is an expense ratio of 0.53% (very low).

The fund's risk rating is currently B- (Good). It carries a beta of 0.92, meaning that its performance tracks fairly well with that of the overall stock market. Volatility, as measured by both the semi-deviation and a drawdown factor, is considered low. As of December 31, 2015, *SPDR S&P Emerging Asia Pacific E traded at a discount of .93% below its net asset value, which is better than its one-year historical average discount of .18%.

John A. Tucker currently receives a manager quality ranking of 94 (0=worst, 99=best). If you desire an average level of risk, then this fund may be an option.

Data Date	Investment Rating	Net Assets ($Mil)	Price	Performance Rating/Pts	Total Return Y-T-D	Risk Rating/Pts
12-15	C	687.50	73.60	C- / 4.2	-5.63%	B- / 7.6
2014	C+	687.50	83.41	C / 5.5	12.77%	B / 8.2
2013	D+	391.60	77.15	D+ / 2.4	-2.52%	C+ / 6.9
2012	D+	481.60	77.49	C- / 3.2	15.56%	B- / 7.0
2011	C-	450.30	65.99	C / 5.2	-17.24%	C+ / 6.5
2010	C	770.30	84.75	C+ / 5.9	19.44%	C / 4.8

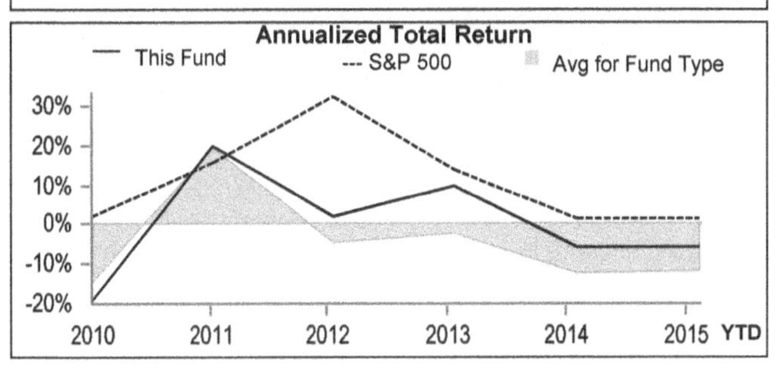

*SPDR S&P Emerging Europe ETF (GUR) — D — Weak

Fund Family: SSgA Funds Management Inc
Fund Type: Emerging Market
Inception Date: March 20, 2007

Major Rating Factors:
Disappointing performance is the major factor driving the D (Weak) TheStreet.com Investment Rating for *SPDR S&P Emerging Europe ETF. The fund currently has a performance rating of D- (Weak) based on an annualized return of -16.86% over the last three years and a total return of -13.60% year to date 2015. Factored into the performance evaluation is an expense ratio of 0.53% (very low).

The fund's risk rating is currently C+ (Fair). It carries a beta of 1.09, meaning that its performance tracks fairly well with that of the overall stock market. Volatility, as measured by both the semi-deviation and a drawdown factor, is considered low. As of December 31, 2015, *SPDR S&P Emerging Europe ETF traded at a discount of .66% below its net asset value, which is better than its one-year historical average discount of .13%.

John A. Tucker currently receives a manager quality ranking of 16 (0=worst, 99=best). This fund offers only a moderate level of risk but investors looking for strong performance are still waiting.

Data Date	Investment Rating	Net Assets ($Mil)	Price	Performance Rating/Pts	Total Return Y-T-D	Risk Rating/Pts
12-15	D	66.90	22.48	D- / 1.1	-13.60%	C+ / 5.9
2014	D	66.90	27.31	D- / 1.2	-27.01%	C+ / 6.2
2013	D-	83.90	40.25	D / 1.6	-9.55%	C / 5.4
2012	D	94.90	43.95	C- / 3.4	21.40%	C / 5.4
2011	D+	86.00	35.99	C- / 3.6	-24.61%	C+ / 6.1
2010	E+	217.30	49.55	D- / 1.4	15.70%	C- / 3.2

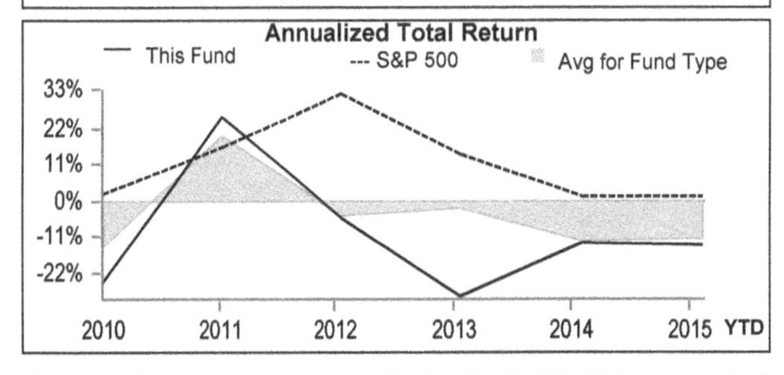

*SPDR S&P Emerging Latin America (GML) — D- — Weak

Fund Family: SSgA Funds Management Inc
Fund Type: Emerging Market
Inception Date: March 20, 2007

Major Rating Factors:
Very poor performance is the major factor driving the D- (Weak) TheStreet.com Investment Rating for *SPDR S&P Emerging Latin America. The fund currently has a performance rating of E+ (Very Weak) based on an annualized return of -20.33% over the last three years and a total return of -28.72% year to date 2015. Factored into the performance evaluation is an expense ratio of 0.53% (very low).

The fund's risk rating is currently C- (Fair). It carries a beta of 1.32, meaning it is expected to move 13.2% for every 10% move in the market. Volatility, as measured by both the semi-deviation and a drawdown factor, is considered average. As of December 31, 2015, *SPDR S&P Emerging Latin America traded at a premium of .03% above its net asset value, which is worse than its one-year historical average discount of .11%.

John A. Tucker currently receives a manager quality ranking of 13 (0=worst, 99=best). This fund offers an average level of risk but investors looking for strong performance will be frustrated.

Data Date	Investment Rating	Net Assets ($Mil)	Price	Performance Rating/Pts	Total Return Y-T-D	Risk Rating/Pts
12-15	D-	49.20	35.16	E+ / 0.7	-28.72%	C- / 4.1
2014	D-	49.20	52.41	D- / 1.4	-11.37%	C / 4.7
2013	D-	56.10	62.24	D- / 1.0	-18.17%	C+ / 6.5
2012	D	110.80	74.30	D / 2.0	6.48%	C+ / 6.7
2011	C	117.20	68.99	C+ / 5.7	-18.29%	C+ / 6.9
2010	C+	276.80	89.74	B- / 7.2	15.38%	C / 4.5

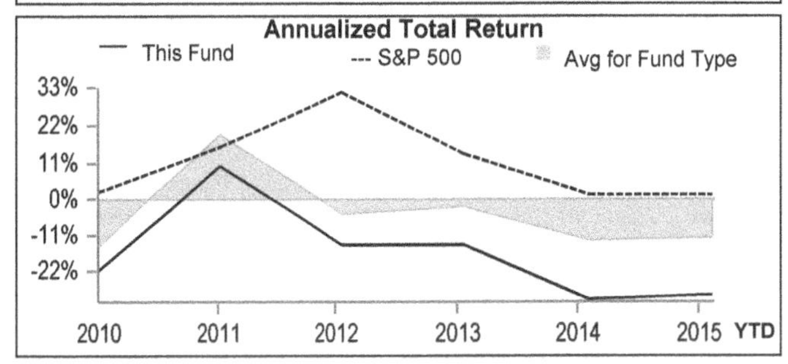

* Denotes ETF Fund

*SPDR S&P Emerging Markets ETF (GMM) C- Fair

Fund Family: SSgA Funds Management Inc
Fund Type: Emerging Market
Inception Date: March 20, 2007

Major Rating Factors:
Disappointing performance is the major factor driving the C- (Fair) TheStreet.com Investment Rating for *SPDR S&P Emerging Markets ETF. The fund currently has a performance rating of D+ (Weak) based on an annualized return of -6.22% over the last three years and a total return of -13.40% year to date 2015. Factored into the performance evaluation is an expense ratio of 0.59% (very low).

The fund's risk rating is currently B- (Good). It carries a beta of 1.01, meaning that its performance tracks fairly well with that of the overall stock market. Volatility, as measured by both the semi-deviation and a drawdown factor, is considered low. As of December 31, 2015, *SPDR S&P Emerging Markets ETF traded at a discount of .71% below its net asset value, which is better than its one-year historical average discount of .10%.

John A. Tucker currently receives a manager quality ranking of 75 (0=worst, 99=best). This fund offers only a moderate level of risk but investors looking for strong performance are still waiting.

Data Date	Investment Rating	Net Assets ($Mil)	Price	Performance Rating/Pts	Total Return Y-T-D	Risk Rating/Pts
12-15	C-	285.30	52.08	D+ / 2.3	-13.40%	B- / 7.4
2014	C-	285.30	62.84	C- / 3.5	2.80%	B- / 7.8
2013	D	236.30	64.66	D / 2.0	-6.71%	B- / 7.1
2012	D+	159.10	67.22	C- / 3.0	14.50%	B- / 7.0
2011	C	139.10	58.21	C / 5.1	-17.11%	B- / 7.1
2010	C	237.10	74.37	C+ / 5.9	18.75%	C / 5.0

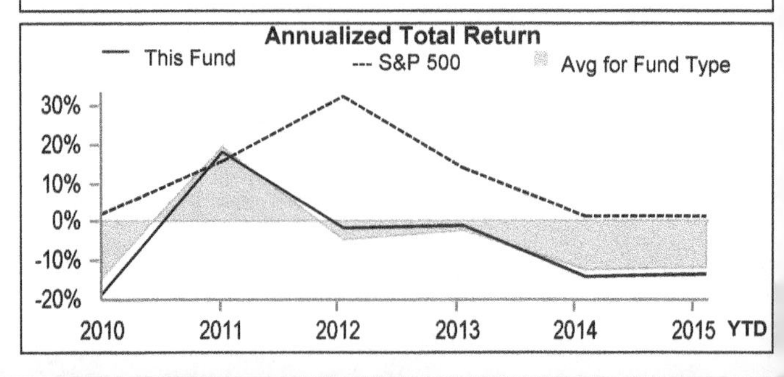

*SPDR S&P Emg Markets Dividend ET (EDIV) D- Weak

Fund Family: SSgA Funds Management Inc
Fund Type: Growth and Income
Inception Date: February 23, 2011

Major Rating Factors:
Disappointing performance is the major factor driving the D- (Weak) TheStreet.com Investment Rating for *SPDR S&P Emg Markets Dividend ET. The fund currently has a performance rating of D- (Weak) based on an annualized return of -16.85% over the last three years and a total return of -26.50% year to date 2015. Factored into the performance evaluation is an expense ratio of 0.53% (very low).

The fund's risk rating is currently C (Fair). It carries a beta of 0.97, meaning that its performance tracks fairly well with that of the overall stock market. Volatility, as measured by both the semi-deviation and a drawdown factor, is considered average. As of December 31, 2015, *SPDR S&P Emg Markets Dividend ET traded at a discount of 1.08% below its net asset value, which is better than its one-year historical average discount of .14%.

John A. Tucker currently receives a manager quality ranking of 3 (0=worst, 99=best). This fund offers an average level of risk but investors looking for strong performance will be frustrated.

Data Date	Investment Rating	Net Assets ($Mil)	Price	Performance Rating/Pts	Total Return Y-T-D	Risk Rating/Pts
12-15	D-	491.20	23.72	D- / 1.0	-26.50%	C / 5.2
2014	D	491.20	34.11	D / 1.7	-6.59%	C+ / 6.0
2013	D-	508.80	39.06	E+ / 0.9	-15.81%	C+ / 6.5
2012	C-	358.30	47.18	C / 4.8	4.30%	B- / 7.1

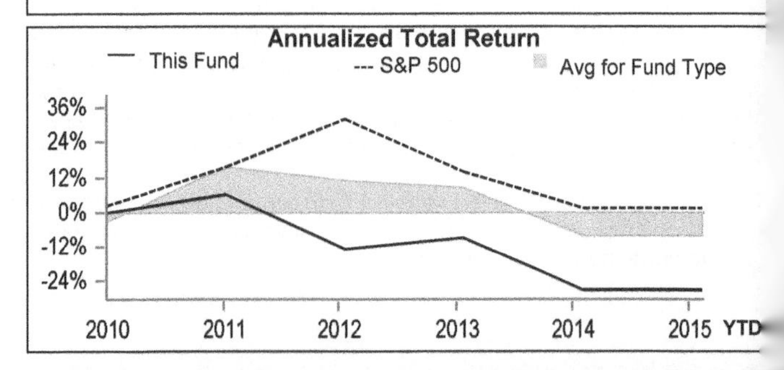

*SPDR S&P Emg Markets Sm Cap ETF (EWX) C- Fair

Fund Family: SSgA Funds Management Inc
Fund Type: Global
Inception Date: May 12, 2008

Major Rating Factors:
Disappointing performance is the major factor driving the C- (Fair) TheStreet.com Investment Rating for *SPDR S&P Emg Markets Sm Cap ETF. The fund currently has a performance rating of D+ (Weak) based on an annualized return of -4.33% over the last three years and a total return of -9.75% year to date 2015. Factored into the performance evaluation is an expense ratio of 0.65% (very low).

The fund's risk rating is currently B- (Good). It carries a beta of 0.90, meaning that its performance tracks fairly well with that of the overall stock market. Volatility, as measured by both the semi-deviation and a drawdown factor, is considered low. As of December 31, 2015, *SPDR S&P Emg Markets Sm Cap ETF traded at a discount of .50% below its net asset value, which is better than its one-year historical average discount of .26%.

John A. Tucker currently receives a manager quality ranking of 20 (0=worst, 99=best). This fund offers only a moderate level of risk but investors looking for strong performance are still waiting.

Data Date	Investment Rating	Net Assets ($Mil)	Price	Performance Rating/Pts	Total Return Y-T-D	Risk Rating/Pts
12-15	C-	608.60	37.71	D+ / 2.7	-9.75%	B- / 7.5
2014	C	608.60	44.34	C- / 4.1	-0.11%	B / 8.4
2013	D	718.50	46.41	D / 1.9	-2.12%	C+ / 6.1
2012	D+	875.30	46.64	C- / 3.9	25.12%	C+ / 5.9
2011	D+	736.60	37.73	C / 4.7	-28.69%	C / 5.0
2010	B+	1,245.10	57.01	A / 9.3	23.48%	C / 4.8

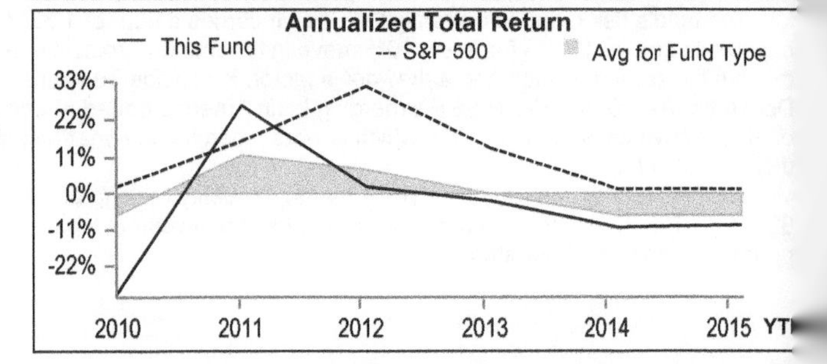

*SPDR S&P Glbl Natural Resources (GNR) D- Weak

Fund Family: SSgA Funds Management Inc
Fund Type: Energy/Natural Resources
Inception Date: September 13, 2010

Major Rating Factors:
Disappointing performance is the major factor driving the D- (Weak) TheStreet.com Investment Rating for *SPDR S&P Glbl Natural Resources. The fund currently has a performance rating of D- (Weak) based on an annualized return of -12.09% over the last three years and a total return of -22.50% year to date 2015. Factored into the performance evaluation is an expense ratio of 0.40% (very low).

The fund's risk rating is currently C (Fair). It carries a beta of 0.73, meaning the fund's expected move will be 7.3% for every 10% move in the market. Volatility, as measured by both the semi-deviation and a drawdown factor, is considered average. As of December 31, 2015, *SPDR S&P Glbl Natural Resources traded at a premium of .06% above its net asset value, which is better than its one-year historical average premium of .09%.

John A. Tucker currently receives a manager quality ranking of 18 (0=worst, 99=best). This fund offers an average level of risk but investors looking for strong performance will be frustrated.

Data Date	Investment Rating	Net Assets ($Mil)	Price	Performance Rating/Pts	Total Return Y-T-D	Risk Rating/Pts
12-15	D-	573.70	32.10	D- / 1.4	-22.50%	C / 4.6
2014	D	573.70	44.00	D / 2.0	-9.27%	C+ / 5.8
2013	D	497.10	50.24	D / 2.1	-3.18%	C+ / 6.7
2012	C-	490.30	51.56	C / 4.7	5.16%	C+ / 6.7
2011	D	171.40	49.02	D- / 1.1	-12.99%	C+ / 6.8

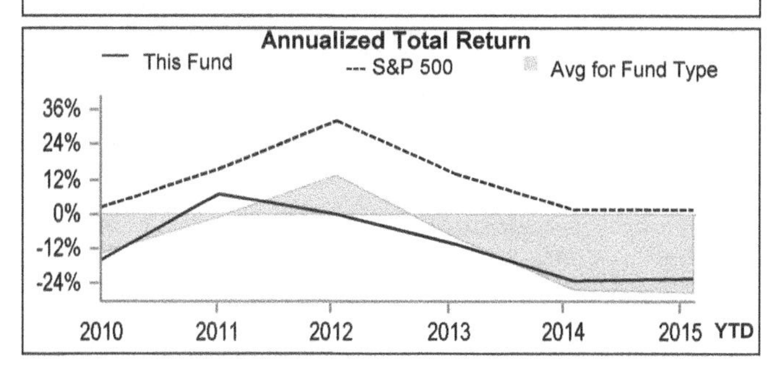

*SPDR S&P Global Dividend ETF (WDIV) D+ Weak

Fund Family: SSgA Funds Management Inc
Fund Type: Global
Inception Date: May 29, 2013

Major Rating Factors:
Disappointing performance is the major factor driving the D+ (Weak) TheStreet.com Investment Rating for *SPDR S&P Global Dividend ETF. The fund currently has a performance rating of D+ (Weak) based on an annualized return of 0.00% over the last three years and a total return of -4.94% year to date 2015. Factored into the performance evaluation is an expense ratio of 0.40% (very low).

The fund's risk rating is currently C+ (Fair). It carries a beta of 0.00, meaning the fund's expected move will be 0.0% for every 10% move in the market. Volatility, as measured by both the semi-deviation and a drawdown factor, is considered low. As of December 31, 2015, *SPDR S&P Global Dividend ETF traded at a premium of .04% above its net asset value, which is better than its one-year historical average premium of .24%.

John A. Tucker currently receives a manager quality ranking of 28 (0=worst, 99=best). This fund offers only a moderate level of risk but investors looking for strong performance are still waiting.

Data Date	Investment Rating	Net Assets ($Mil)	Price	Performance Rating/Pts	Total Return Y-T-D	Risk Rating/Pts
12-15	D+	29.20	56.96	D+ / 2.5	-4.94%	C+ / 6.1
2014	C-	29.20	64.74	C- / 3.6	6.40%	B- / 7.2

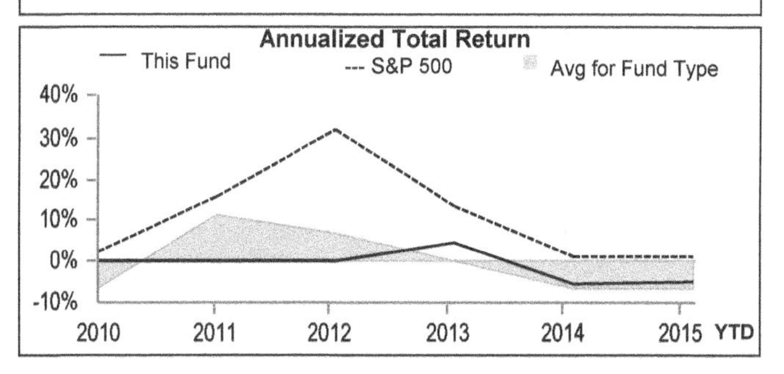

*SPDR S&P Global Infrastructure (GII) C Fair

Fund Family: SSgA Funds Management Inc
Fund Type: Global
Inception Date: January 25, 2007

Major Rating Factors: Middle of the road best describes *SPDR S&P Global Infrastructure whose TheStreet.com Investment Rating is currently a C (Fair). The fund currently has a performance rating of C (Fair) based on an annualized return of 4.92% over the last three years and a total return of -9.65% year to date 2015. Factored into the performance evaluation is an expense ratio of 0.40% (very low).

The fund's risk rating is currently C+ (Fair). It carries a beta of 0.73, meaning the fund's expected move will be 7.3% for every 10% move in the market. Volatility, as measured by both the semi-deviation and a drawdown factor, is considered low. As of December 31, 2015, *SPDR S&P Global Infrastructure traded at a premium of .19% above its net asset value, which is worse than its one-year historical average discount of .05%.

John A. Tucker currently receives a manager quality ranking of 78 (0=worst, 99=best). If you desire an average level of risk, then this fund may be an option.

Data Date	Investment Rating	Net Assets ($Mil)	Price	Performance Rating/Pts	Total Return Y-T-D	Risk Rating/Pts
12-15	C	112.30	41.54	C / 5.4	-9.65%	C+ / 6.8
2014	B-	112.30	48.48	C+ / 5.8	13.49%	B / 8.9
2013	B-	75.90	44.67	C+ / 6.0	12.70%	B / 8.7
2012	C-	59.60	40.26	D / 2.2	8.22%	B / 8.6
2011	C-	35.70	39.51	D+ / 2.6	0.80%	B / 8.1
2010	D	49.70	41.32	D- / 1.0	1.22%	C+ / 6.3

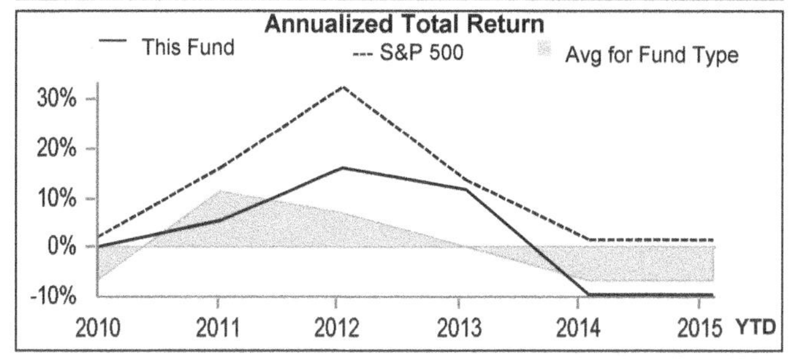

*SPDR S&P Health Care Equipment E (XHE) C- Fair

Fund Family: SSgA Funds Management Inc
Fund Type: Health
Inception Date: January 26, 2011

Major Rating Factors: *SPDR S&P Health Care Equipment E has adopted a very risky asset allocation strategy and currently receives an overall TheStreet.com Investment Rating of C- (Fair). The fund has shown a high level of volatility, as measured by both semi-deviation and drawdown factors. It carries a beta of 0.67, meaning the fund's expected move will be 6.7% for every 10% move in the market. As of December 31, 2015, *SPDR S&P Health Care Equipment E traded at a premium of .65% above its net asset value, which is worse than its one-year historical average premium of .10%. The high level of risk (D-, Weak) did however, reward investors with excellent performance.

The fund's performance rating is currently A+ (Excellent). It has registered an annualized return of 21.90% over the last three years and is up 17.93% year to date 2015. Factored into the performance evaluation is an expense ratio of 0.35% (very low).

John A. Tucker has been running the fund for 5 years and currently receives a manager quality ranking of 96 (0=worst, 99=best). If you are comfortable owning a very high risk investment, this fund may be an option.

Data Date	Investment Rating	Net Assets ($Mil)	Price	Performance Rating/Pts	Total Return Y-T-D	Risk Rating/Pts
12-15	C-	33.70	44.57	A+ / 9.7	17.93%	D- / 1.4
2014	B+	33.70	86.99	A- / 9.2	16.69%	C+ / 6.8
2013	A+	26.70	76.40	A+ / 9.6	32.72%	B / 8.2
2012	B-	19.70	54.90	B- / 7.1	19.17%	B / 8.1

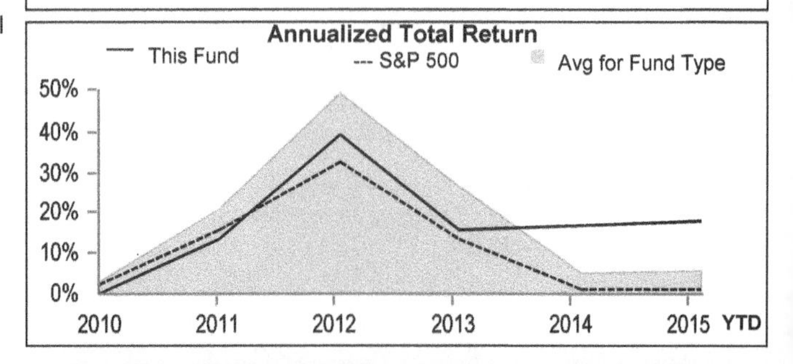

*SPDR S&P Health Care Services ET (XHS) C- Fair

Fund Family: SSgA Funds Management Inc
Fund Type: Health
Inception Date: September 29, 2011

Major Rating Factors: *SPDR S&P Health Care Services ET has adopted a very risky asset allocation strategy and currently receives an overall TheStreet.com Investment Rating of C- (Fair). The fund has shown a high level of volatility, as measured by both semi-deviation and drawdown factors. It carries a beta of 0.69, meaning the fund's expected move will be 6.9% for every 10% move in the market. As of December 31, 2015, *SPDR S&P Health Care Services ET traded at a premium of .07% above its net asset value, which is worse than its one-year historical average premium of .03%. The high level of risk (D-, Weak) did however, reward investors with excellent performance.

The fund's performance rating is currently A (Excellent). It has registered an annualized return of 21.19% over the last three years and is up 6.19% year to date 2015. Factored into the performance evaluation is an expense ratio of 0.35% (very low).

John A. Tucker has been running the fund for 5 years and currently receives a manager quality ranking of 95 (0=worst, 99=best). If you are comfortable owning a very high risk investment, this fund may be an option.

Data Date	Investment Rating	Net Assets ($Mil)	Price	Performance Rating/Pts	Total Return Y-T-D	Risk Rating/Pts
12-15	C-	117.60	57.38	A / 9.5	6.19%	D- / 1.5
2014	A-	117.60	112.13	A / 9.4	24.69%	C+ / 6.9
2013	A+	63.40	90.64	A / 9.5	34.99%	B+ / 9.0
2012	A+	13.30	66.30	A- / 9.2	24.71%	B / 8.9

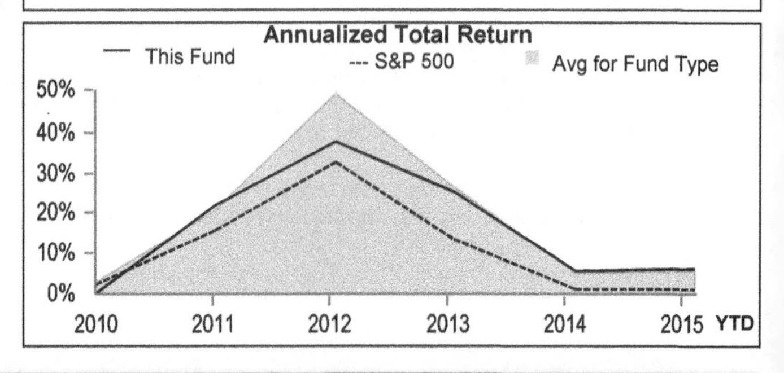

*SPDR S&P Homebuilders ETF (XHB) C+ Fair

Fund Family: SSgA Funds Management Inc
Fund Type: Income
Inception Date: January 31, 2006

Major Rating Factors: Middle of the road best describes *SPDR S&P Homebuilders ETF whose TheStreet.com Investment Rating is currently a C+ (Fair). The fund currently has a performance rating of C+ (Fair) based on an annualized return of 7.93% over the last three years and a total return of 1.75% year to date 2015. Factored into the performance evaluation is an expense ratio of 0.35% (very low).

The fund's risk rating is currently C+ (Fair). It carries a beta of 1.12, meaning it is expected to move 11.2% for every 10% move in the market. Volatility, as measured by both the semi-deviation and a drawdown factor, is considered low. As of December 31, 2015, *SPDR S&P Homebuilders ETF traded at a premium of .03% above its net asset value, which is worse than its one-year historical average discount of .01%.

John A. Tucker has been running the fund for 10 years and currently receives a manager quality ranking of 23 (0=worst, 99=best). If you desire an average level of risk, then this fund may be an option.

Data Date	Investment Rating	Net Assets ($Mil)	Price	Performance Rating/Pts	Total Return Y-T-D	Risk Rating/Pts
12-15	C+	1,452.90	34.18	C+ / 6.7	1.75%	C+ / 6.9
2014	B+	1,452.90	34.12	A- / 9.1	3.52%	C+ / 6.8
2013	A-	2,014.80	33.30	A- / 9.1	20.45%	B- / 7.4
2012	A-	2,206.30	26.60	A+ / 9.6	52.39%	B- / 7.1
2011	C	876.90	17.10	C+ / 5.8	1.86%	B- / 7.0
2010	C	874.70	17.39	C+ / 6.1	17.40%	C / 4.9

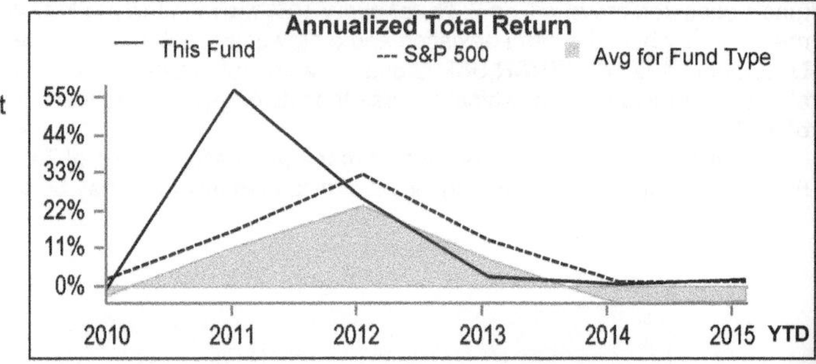

*SPDR S&P International Div ETF (DWX) D+ Weak

Fund Family: SSgA Funds Management Inc
Fund Type: Emerging Market
Inception Date: February 12, 2008

Data Date	Investment Rating	Net Assets ($Mil)	Price	Performance Rating/Pts	Total Return Y-T-D	Risk Rating/Pts
12-15	D+	1,450.20	33.36	D+ / 2.3	-14.92%	B- / 7.0
2014	C-	1,450.20	42.02	D+ / 2.8	-5.46%	B- / 7.7
2013	D+	1,324.50	47.45	C- / 3.6	2.92%	B- / 7.0
2012	D	1,146.80	48.11	D+ / 2.4	13.40%	C+ / 6.4
2011	C-	603.60	46.49	C- / 4.2	-9.24%	B- / 7.1
2010	B	351.30	56.00	B+ / 8.6	7.87%	C / 4.7

Major Rating Factors:
Disappointing performance is the major factor driving the D+ (Weak) TheStreet.com Investment Rating for *SPDR S&P International Div ETF. The fund currently has a performance rating of D+ (Weak) based on an annualized return of -6.16% over the last three years and a total return of -14.92% year to date 2015. Factored into the performance evaluation is an expense ratio of 0.46% (very low).

The fund's risk rating is currently B- (Good). It carries a beta of 0.95, meaning that its performance tracks fairly well with that of the overall stock market. Volatility, as measured by both the semi-deviation and a drawdown factor, is considered low. As of December 31, 2015, *SPDR S&P International Div ETF traded at a discount of .77% below its net asset value, which is better than its one-year historical average discount of .10%.

John A. Tucker currently receives a manager quality ranking of 73 (0=worst, 99=best). This fund offers only a moderate level of risk but investors looking for strong performance are still waiting.

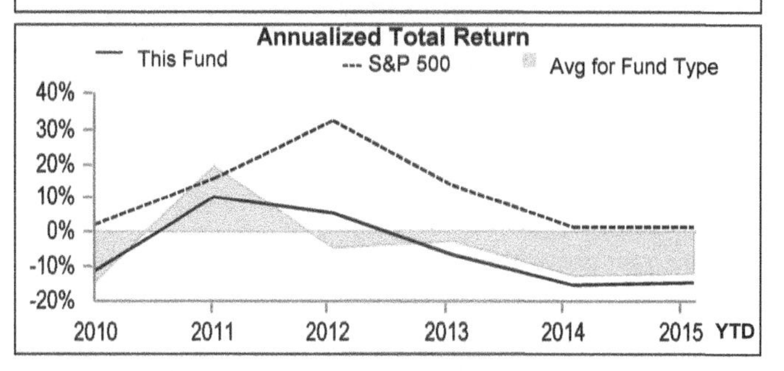

*SPDR S&P International Mid Cap E (MDD) C+ Fair

Fund Family: SSgA Funds Management Inc
Fund Type: Global
Inception Date: May 7, 2008

Data Date	Investment Rating	Net Assets ($Mil)	Price	Performance Rating/Pts	Total Return Y-T-D	Risk Rating/Pts
12-15	C+	70.40	29.79	B- / 7.2	8.62%	C+ / 6.6
2014	C	70.40	28.30	C / 5.0	-4.98%	B- / 7.7
2013	C+	51.50	32.65	C+ / 6.7	20.49%	B- / 7.1
2012	C-	34.30	28.69	C / 4.9	19.82%	B- / 7.1
2011	C-	35.10	24.88	C- / 3.5	-13.56%	B- / 7.4
2010	B+	40.10	31.00	A / 9.4	23.05%	C / 4.3

Major Rating Factors: Strong performance is the major factor driving the C+ (Fair) TheStreet.com Investment Rating for *SPDR S&P International Mid Cap E. The fund currently has a performance rating of B- (Good) based on an annualized return of 7.46% over the last three years and a total return of 8.62% year to date 2015. Factored into the performance evaluation is an expense ratio of 0.45% (very low).

The fund's risk rating is currently C+ (Fair). It carries a beta of 0.89, meaning the fund's expected move will be 8.9% for every 10% move in the market. Volatility, as measured by both the semi-deviation and a drawdown factor, is considered low. As of December 31, 2015, *SPDR S&P International Mid Cap E traded at a premium of 1.50% above its net asset value, which is worse than its one-year historical average premium of .42%.

John A. Tucker currently receives a manager quality ranking of 85 (0=worst, 99=best). If you desire only a moderate level of risk and strong performance, then this fund is an excellent option.

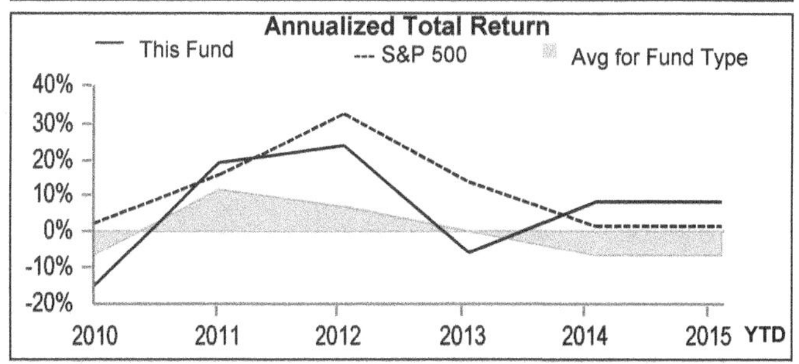

*SPDR S&P International Small Cap (GWX) B- Good

Fund Family: SSgA Funds Management Inc
Fund Type: Foreign
Inception Date: April 20, 2007

Data Date	Investment Rating	Net Assets ($Mil)	Price	Performance Rating/Pts	Total Return Y-T-D	Risk Rating/Pts
12-15	B-	792.80	28.23	C+ / 6.3	6.36%	B- / 7.8
2014	C-	792.80	27.31	C- / 4.2	-6.87%	B- / 7.6
2013	C+	832.10	33.57	C+ / 6.4	19.02%	B- / 7.6
2012	C	694.20	28.45	C / 4.6	18.55%	B- / 7.6
2011	C-	656.90	25.17	C- / 3.9	-14.79%	B- / 7.7
2010	C	806.70	30.84	C / 5.4	24.94%	C / 5.4

Major Rating Factors: *SPDR S&P International Small Cap receives a TheStreet.com Investment Rating of B- (Good). The fund currently has a performance rating of C+ (Fair) based on an annualized return of 5.73% over the last three years and a total return of 6.36% year to date 2015. Factored into the performance evaluation is an expense ratio of 0.47% (very low).

The fund's risk rating is currently B- (Good). It carries a beta of 0.81, meaning the fund's expected move will be 8.1% for every 10% move in the market. Volatility, as measured by both the semi-deviation and a drawdown factor, is considered low. As of December 31, 2015, *SPDR S&P International Small Cap traded at a discount of .46% below its net asset value, which is better than its one-year historical average premium of .03%.

John A. Tucker currently receives a manager quality ranking of 79 (0=worst, 99=best). If you desire an average level of risk, then this fund may be an option.

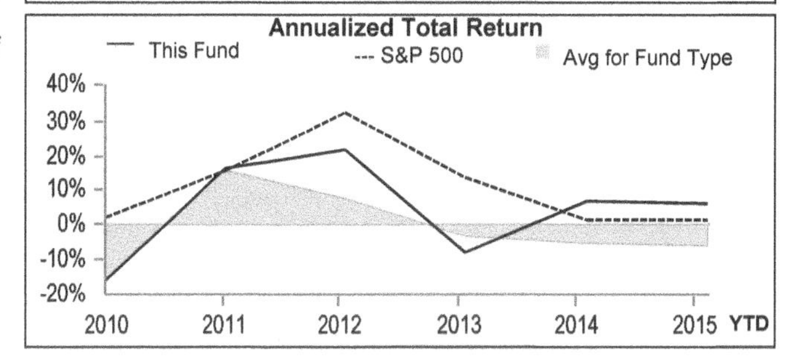

*SPDR S&P Metals & Mining ETF (XME) E+ Very Weak

Fund Family: SSgA Funds Management Inc
Fund Type: Income
Inception Date: June 19, 2006

Data Date	Investment Rating	Net Assets ($Mil)	Price	Performance Rating/Pts	Total Return Y-T-D	Risk Rating/Pts
12-15	E+	500.10	14.95	E / 0.3	-50.06%	C- / 3.8
2014	D-	500.10	30.86	E+ / 0.8	-25.55%	C / 5.4
2013	D-	1,004.30	42.08	D- / 1.2	-7.98%	C / 5.1
2012	D-	1,004.30	45.13	E+ / 0.9	-11.36%	C+ / 5.6
2011	C-	707.50	48.99	C / 5.1	-24.85%	C+ / 6.2
2010	C+	1,220.90	68.78	B / 7.8	34.14%	C- / 3.7

Major Rating Factors:
Very poor performance is the major factor driving the E+ (Very Weak) TheStreet.com Investment Rating for *SPDR S&P Metals & Mining ETF. The fund currently has a performance rating of E (Very Weak) based on an annualized return of -30.05% over the last three years and a total return of -50.06% year to date 2015. Factored into the performance evaluation is an expense ratio of 0.35% (very low).

The fund's risk rating is currently C- (Fair). It carries a beta of 1.25, meaning it is expected to move 12.5% for every 10% move in the market. Volatility, as measured by both the semi-deviation and a drawdown factor, is considered average. As of December 31, 2015, *SPDR S&P Metals & Mining ETF traded at a price exactly equal to its net asset value, which is worse than its one-year historical average discount of .02%.

John A. Tucker has been running the fund for 10 years and currently receives a manager quality ranking of 1 (0=worst, 99=best). This fund offers an average level of risk but investors looking for strong performance will be frustrated.

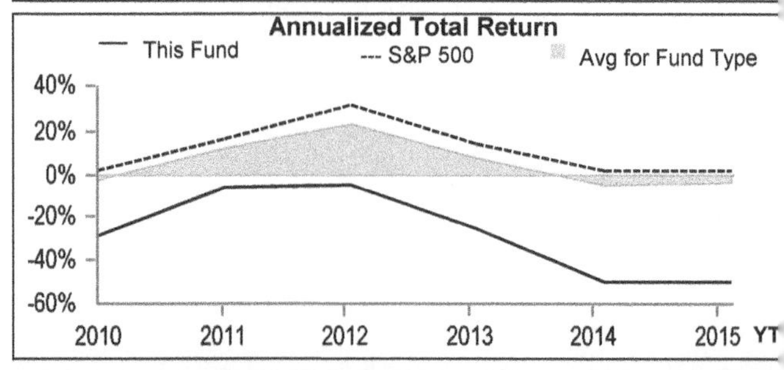

*SPDR S&P MidCap 400 ETF (MDY) B+ Good

Fund Family: Bank of New York Mellon
Fund Type: Growth
Inception Date: April 28, 1995

Data Date	Investment Rating	Net Assets ($Mil)	Price	Performance Rating/Pts	Total Return Y-T-D	Risk Rating/Pts
12-15	B+	14,017.10	254.04	B / 7.7	-1.95%	B / 8.2
2014	B	14,017.10	263.97	B / 7.9	10.19%	B- / 7.3
2013	B	15,305.80	244.20	B / 7.9	27.70%	B- / 7.8
2012	C+	10,616.80	185.71	C+ / 6.8	17.70%	B- / 7.7
2011	C+	0.00	159.49	C+ / 6.4	-1.00%	B- / 7.7
2010	B-	10,875.80	164.68	B- / 7.2	25.93%	C / 5.5

Major Rating Factors: Strong performance is the major factor driving the B+ (Good) TheStreet.com Investment Rating for *SPDR S&P MidCap 400 ETF. The fund currently has a performance rating of B (Good) based on an annualized return of 11.26% over the last three years and a total return of -1.95% year to date 2015. Factored into the performance evaluation is an expense ratio of 0.25% (very low).

The fund's risk rating is currently B (Good). It carries a beta of 0.99, meaning that its performance tracks fairly well with that of the overall stock market. Volatility, as measured by both the semi-deviation and a drawdown factor, is considered low. As of December 31, 2015, *SPDR S&P MidCap 400 ETF traded at a discount of .09% below its net asset value, which is better than its one-year historical average discount of .02%.

Lynn S. Blake currently receives a manager quality ranking of 49 (0=worst, 99=best). If you desire only a moderate level of risk and strong performance, then this fund is an excellent option.

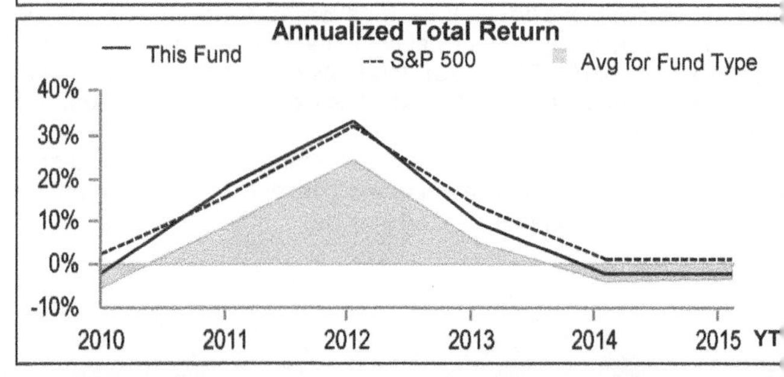

*SPDR S&P Oil & Gas Equip & Serv (XES) D- Weak

Fund Family: SSgA Funds Management Inc
Fund Type: Energy/Natural Resources
Inception Date: June 19, 2006

Data Date	Investment Rating	Net Assets ($Mil)	Price	Performance Rating/Pts	Total Return Y-T-D	Risk Rating/Pts
12-15	D-	250.90	17.54	E+ / 0.7	-36.75%	C / 4.3
2014	D-	250.90	28.21	D- / 1.0	-33.76%	C+ / 5.8
2013	C	310.20	43.72	C+ / 6.0	18.94%	C+ / 6.4
2012	D+	277.10	34.62	C- / 3.3	5.58%	C+ / 6.3
2011	C+	341.50	34.66	B- / 7.5	-0.87%	C+ / 6.3
2010	C-	451.20	36.71	C+ / 6.0	30.10%	C- / 4.2

Major Rating Factors:
Very poor performance is the major factor driving the D- (Weak) TheStreet.com Investment Rating for *SPDR S&P Oil & Gas Equip & Serv. The fund currently has a performance rating of E+ (Very Weak) based on an annualized return of -20.51% over the last three years and a total return of -36.75% year to date 2015. Factored into the performance evaluation is an expense ratio of 0.35% (very low).

The fund's risk rating is currently C (Fair). It carries a beta of 1.55, meaning it is expected to move 15.5% for every 10% move in the market. Volatility, as measured by both the semi-deviation and a drawdown factor, is considered average. As of December 31, 2015, *SPDR S&P Oil & Gas Equip & Serv traded at a discount of .06% below its net asset value.

John A. Tucker has been running the fund for 10 years and currently receives a manager quality ranking of 11 (0=worst, 99=best). This fund offers an average level of risk but investors looking for strong performance will be frustrated.

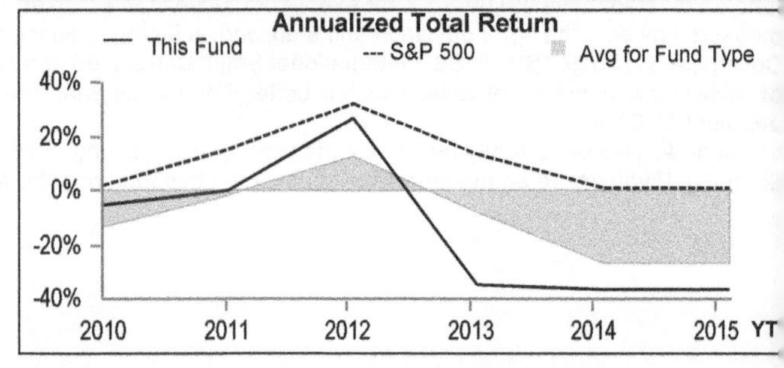

*SPDR S&P Oil & Gas Expl & Prod (XOP) — D- Weak

Fund Family: SSgA Funds Management Inc
Fund Type: Income
Inception Date: June 19, 2006

Major Rating Factors:
Very poor performance is the major factor driving the D- (Weak) TheStreet.com Investment Rating for *SPDR S&P Oil & Gas Expl & Prod. The fund currently has a performance rating of E+ (Very Weak) based on an annualized return of -17.44% over the last three years and a total return of -36.09% year to date 2015. Factored into the performance evaluation is an expense ratio of 0.35% (very low).

The fund's risk rating is currently C (Fair). It carries a beta of 1.32, meaning it is expected to move 13.2% for every 10% move in the market. Volatility, as measured by both the semi-deviation and a drawdown factor, is considered average. As of December 31, 2015, *SPDR S&P Oil & Gas Expl & Prod traded at a discount of .03% below its net asset value, which is better than its one-year historical average discount of .02%.

John A. Tucker has been running the fund for 10 years and currently receives a manager quality ranking of 3 (0=worst, 99=best). This fund offers an average level of risk but investors looking for strong performance will be frustrated.

Data Date	Investment Rating	Net Assets ($Mil)	Price	Performance Rating/Pts	Total Return Y-T-D	Risk Rating/Pts
12-15	D-	1,383.70	30.22	E+ / 0.8	-36.09%	C / 4.5
2014	D-	1,383.70	47.86	D- / 1.2	-27.27%	C+ / 5.9
2013	C	894.40	68.53	C+ / 6.5	19.83%	C+ / 6.7
2012	C-	721.90	54.08	C- / 4.2	7.85%	C+ / 6.7
2011	C+	776.50	52.69	B- / 7.1	4.18%	C+ / 6.7
2010	C+	722.10	52.75	B- / 7.0	28.57%	C / 4.8

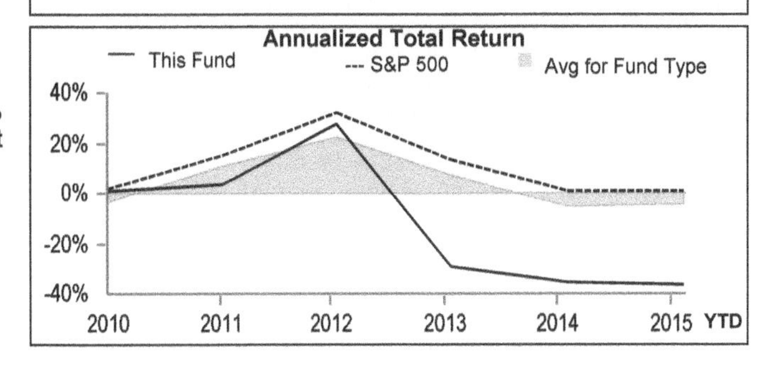

*SPDR S&P Pharmaceuticals ETF (XPH) — C- Fair

Fund Family: SSgA Funds Management Inc
Fund Type: Health
Inception Date: June 19, 2006

Major Rating Factors: *SPDR S&P Pharmaceuticals ETF has adopted a very risky asset allocation strategy and currently receives an overall TheStreet.com Investment Rating of C- (Fair). The fund has shown a high level of volatility, as measured by both semi-deviation and drawdown factors. It carries a beta of 1.19, meaning it is expected to move 11.9% for every 10% move in the market. As of December 31, 2015, *SPDR S&P Pharmaceuticals ETF traded at a discount of .02% below its net asset value, which is better than its one-year historical average premium of .01%. The high level of risk (D-, Weak) did however, reward investors with excellent performance.

The fund's performance rating is currently A+ (Excellent). It has registered an annualized return of 29.49% over the last three years and is up 7.81% year to date 2015. Factored into the performance evaluation is an expense ratio of 0.35% (very low).

John A. Tucker has been running the fund for 10 years and currently receives a manager quality ranking of 95 (0=worst, 99=best). If you are comfortable owning a very high risk investment, this fund may be an option.

Data Date	Investment Rating	Net Assets ($Mil)	Price	Performance Rating/Pts	Total Return Y-T-D	Risk Rating/Pts
12-15	C-	974.90	51.20	A+ / 9.8	7.81%	D- / 1.5
2014	A-	974.90	107.96	A+ / 9.6	29.65%	C+ / 6.5
2013	B+	708.10	87.97	A / 9.5	55.45%	C+ / 6.6
2012	C+	307.70	55.91	C+ / 6.3	14.43%	B- / 7.3
2011	C+	289.90	51.33	B- / 7.3	11.86%	C+ / 6.3
2010	B+	209.50	46.09	B+ / 8.5	22.48%	C / 5.4

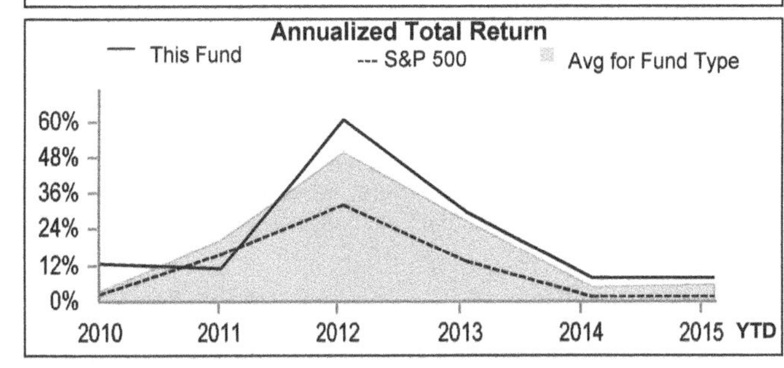

*SPDR S&P Retail ETF (XRT) — C- Fair

Fund Family: SSgA Funds Management Inc
Fund Type: Income
Inception Date: June 19, 2006

Major Rating Factors: Strong performance is the major factor driving the C- (Fair) TheStreet.com Investment Rating for *SPDR S&P Retail ETF. The fund currently has a performance rating of B- (Good) based on an annualized return of 11.71% over the last three years and a total return of -7.90% year to date 2015. Factored into the performance evaluation is an expense ratio of 0.35% (very low).

The fund's risk rating is currently C- (Fair). It carries a beta of 1.11, meaning it is expected to move 11.1% for every 10% move in the market. Volatility, as measured by both the semi-deviation and a drawdown factor, is considered average. As of December 31, 2015, *SPDR S&P Retail ETF traded at a discount of .09% below its net asset value.

John A. Tucker has been running the fund for 10 years and currently receives a manager quality ranking of 38 (0=worst, 99=best). If you desire an average level of risk and strong performance, then this fund is a good option.

Data Date	Investment Rating	Net Assets ($Mil)	Price	Performance Rating/Pts	Total Return Y-T-D	Risk Rating/Pts
12-15	C-	646.20	43.24	B- / 7.2	-7.90%	C- / 3.8
2014	A-	646.20	96.01	A- / 9.2	10.48%	C+ / 6.9
2013	A+	1,224.20	88.10	A- / 9.2	37.96%	B / 8.1
2012	B+	536.40	62.38	B+ / 8.6	21.55%	B / 8.0
2011	A-	614.50	52.55	A / 9.3	12.03%	B / 8.1
2010	A-	976.70	48.36	A- / 9.2	37.38%	C / 5.3

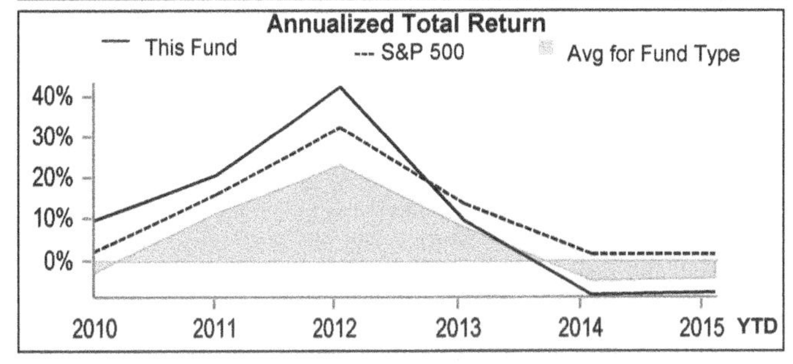

* Denotes ETF Fund

*SPDR S&P Russia (RBL) D- Weak

Fund Family: SSgA Funds Management Inc
Fund Type: Emerging Market
Inception Date: March 10, 2010

Data Date	Investment Rating	Net Assets ($Mil)	Price	Performance Rating/Pts	Total Return Y-T-D	Risk Rating/Pts
12-15	D-	23.10	13.85	D- / 1.3	5.37%	C- / 4.1
2014	E	23.10	14.36	E / 0.5	-44.04%	C- / 3.6
2013	D-	33.40	28.02	D / 1.6	-6.20%	C / 5.3
2012	C-	37.20	29.11	C+ / 6.1	9.23%	C / 5.3
2011	D-	35.20	26.32	E+ / 0.7	-24.16%	C+ / 5.6

Major Rating Factors:
Disappointing performance is the major factor driving the D- (Weak) TheStreet.com Investment Rating for *SPDR S&P Russia. The fund currently has a performance rating of D- (Weak) based on an annualized return of -17.84% over the last three years and a total return of 5.37% year to date 2015. Factored into the performance evaluation is an expense ratio of 0.59% (very low).

The fund's risk rating is currently C- (Fair). It carries a beta of 1.18, meaning it is expected to move 11.8% for every 10% move in the market. Volatility, as measured by both the semi-deviation and a drawdown factor, is considered average. As of December 31, 2015, *SPDR S&P Russia traded at a discount of .07% below its net asset value, which is better than its one-year historical average premium of .03%.

John A. Tucker currently receives a manager quality ranking of 16 (0=worst, 99=best). This fund offers an average level of risk but investors looking for strong performance will be frustrated.

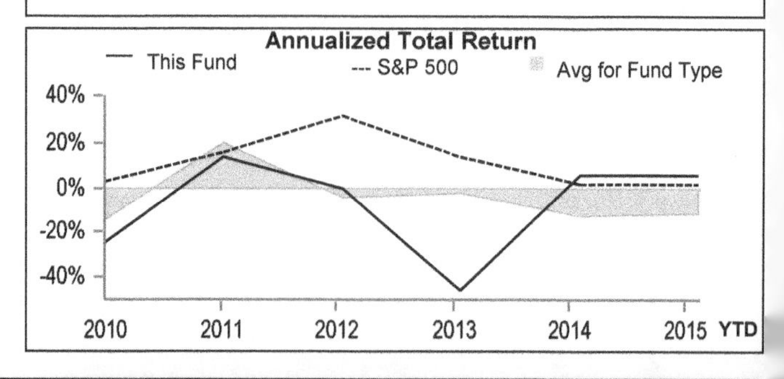

*SPDR S&P Semiconductor ETF (XSD) C+ Fair

Fund Family: SSgA Funds Management Inc
Fund Type: Income
Inception Date: January 31, 2006

Data Date	Investment Rating	Net Assets ($Mil)	Price	Performance Rating/Pts	Total Return Y-T-D	Risk Rating/Pts
12-15	C+	176.20	43.68	A+ / 9.7	10.31%	C- / 3.8
2014	A+	176.20	79.73	A- / 9.2	32.44%	B- / 7.6
2013	C	97.90	61.11	C+ / 5.8	29.96%	C+ / 6.9
2012	D	33.90	45.07	D+ / 2.3	1.95%	C+ / 6.8
2011	C	33.20	44.32	C+ / 6.2	-20.86%	C+ / 6.7
2010	B	109.20	54.60	B / 8.1	15.71%	C / 5.0

Major Rating Factors:
Exceptional performance is the major factor driving the C+ (Fair) TheStreet.com Investment Rating for *SPDR S&P Semiconductor ETF. The fund currently has a performance rating of A+ (Excellent) based on an annualized return of 23.86% over the last three years and a total return of 10.31% year to date 2015. Factored into the performance evaluation is an expense ratio of 0.35% (very low).

The fund's risk rating is currently C- (Fair). It carries a beta of 1.21, meaning it is expected to move 12.1% for every 10% move in the market. Volatility, as measured by both the semi-deviation and a drawdown factor, is considered average. As of December 31, 2015, *SPDR S&P Semiconductor ETF traded at a discount of .07% below its net asset value.

John A. Tucker has been running the fund for 10 years and currently receives a manager quality ranking of 90 (0=worst, 99=best). If you desire an average level of risk and strong performance, then this fund is a good option.

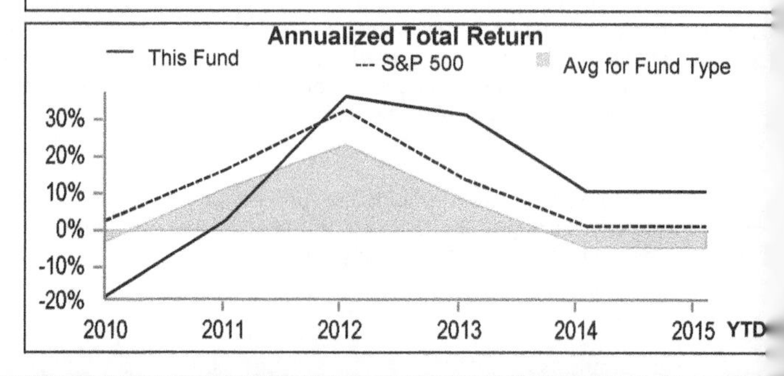

*SPDR S&P Software & Services ETF (XSW) C- Fair

Fund Family: SSgA Funds Management Inc
Fund Type: Growth
Inception Date: September 28, 2011

Data Date	Investment Rating	Net Assets ($Mil)	Price	Performance Rating/Pts	Total Return Y-T-D	Risk Rating/Pts
12-15	C-	25.80	50.72	A / 9.4	10.39%	D / 1.7
2014	B	25.80	95.21	B+ / 8.7	6.66%	C+ / 6.5
2013	A+	31.70	90.50	A+ / 9.7	42.47%	B+ / 9.1
2012	A	12.50	62.39	B+ / 8.3	18.88%	B / 8.9

Major Rating Factors: *SPDR S&P Software & Services ETF has adopted a very risky asset allocation strategy and currently receives an overall TheStreet.com Investment Rating of C- (Fair). The fund has shown a high level of volatility, as measured by both semi-deviation and drawdown factors. It carries a beta of 1.05, meaning that its performance tracks fairly well with that of the overall stock market. As of December 31, 2015, *SPDR S&P Software & Services ETF traded at a premium of .92% above its net asset value, which is worse than its one-year historical average discount of .05%. The high level of risk (D, Weak) did however, reward investors with excellent performance.

The fund's performance rating is currently A (Excellent). It has registered an annualized return of 17.77% over the last three years and is up 10.39% year to date 2015. Factored into the performance evaluation is an expense ratio of 0.35% (very low).

John A. Tucker has been running the fund for 5 years and currently receives a manager quality ranking of 83 (0=worst, 99=best). If you are comfortable owning a very high risk investment, this fund may be an option.

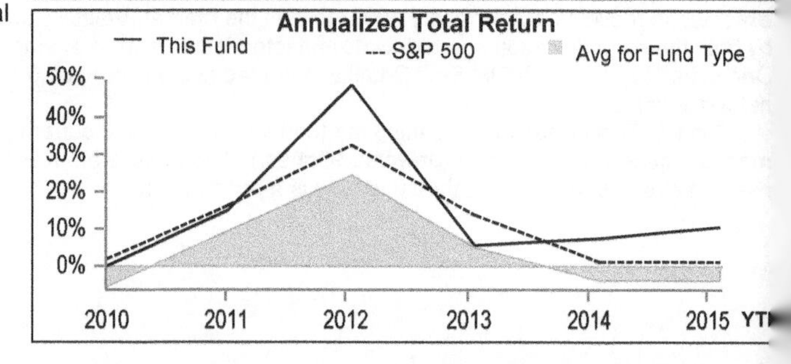

*SPDR S&P Telecom ETF (XTL) C+ Fair

Fund Family: SSgA Funds Management Inc
Fund Type: Growth
Inception Date: January 26, 2011

Major Rating Factors: Middle of the road best describes *SPDR S&P Telecom ETF whose TheStreet.com Investment Rating is currently a C+ (Fair). The fund currently has a performance rating of C+ (Fair) based on an annualized return of 7.32% over the last three years and a total return of -1.02% year to date 2015. Factored into the performance evaluation is an expense ratio of 0.35% (very low).

The fund's risk rating is currently C+ (Fair). It carries a beta of 0.89, meaning the fund's expected move will be 8.9% for every 10% move in the market. Volatility, as measured by both the semi-deviation and a drawdown factor, is considered low. As of December 31, 2015, *SPDR S&P Telecom ETF traded at a premium of .48% above its net asset value, which is worse than its one-year historical average premium of .07%.

John A. Tucker has been running the fund for 5 years and currently receives a manager quality ranking of 35 (0=worst, 99=best). If you desire an average level of risk, then this fund may be an option.

Data Date	Investment Rating	Net Assets ($Mil)	Price	Performance Rating/Pts	Total Return Y-T-D	Risk Rating/Pts
12-15	C+	24.80	56.22	C+ / 6.8	-1.02%	C+ / 6.9
2014	C	24.80	57.74	C+ / 6.4	5.52%	C+ / 6.1
2013	B	13.90	55.33	B+ / 8.4	18.18%	B- / 7.0
2012	B-	4.50	45.20	B / 7.9	10.03%	C+ / 6.8

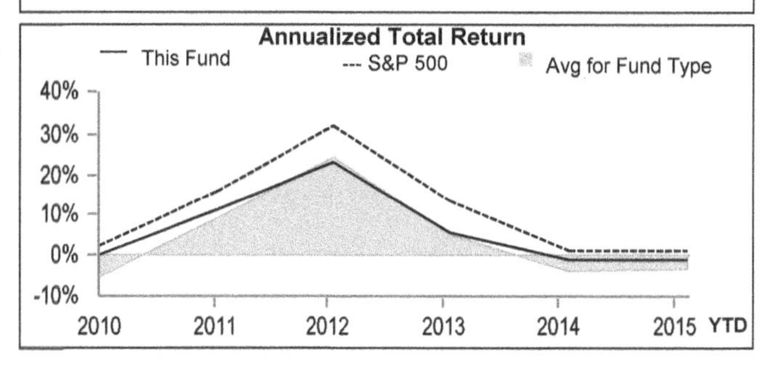

*SPDR S&P Transportation ETF (XTN) C- Fair

Fund Family: SSgA Funds Management Inc
Fund Type: Utilities
Inception Date: January 26, 2011

Major Rating Factors: *SPDR S&P Transportation ETF has adopted a very risky asset allocation strategy and currently receives an overall TheStreet.com Investment Rating of C- (Fair). The fund has shown a high level of volatility, as measured by both semi-deviation and drawdown factors. It carries a beta of 0.19, meaning the fund's expected move will be 1.9% for every 10% move in the market. As of December 31, 2015, *SPDR S&P Transportation ETF traded at a premium of .02% above its net asset value, which is worse than its one-year historical average discount of .03%. The high level of risk (D-, Weak) did however, reward investors with excellent performance.

The fund's performance rating is currently B+ (Good). It has registered an annualized return of 16.25% over the last three years but is down -18.64% year to date 2015. Factored into the performance evaluation is an expense ratio of 0.35% (very low).

John A. Tucker has been running the fund for 5 years and currently receives a manager quality ranking of 97 (0=worst, 99=best). If you are comfortable owning a very high risk investment, this fund may be an option.

Data Date	Investment Rating	Net Assets ($Mil)	Price	Performance Rating/Pts	Total Return Y-T-D	Risk Rating/Pts
12-15	C-	274.20	42.85	B+ / 8.3	-18.64%	D- / 1.5
2014	A+	274.20	108.50	A+ / 9.7	33.34%	B- / 7.4
2013	A	73.30	81.37	A+ / 9.8	45.49%	B- / 7.2
2012	B+	13.50	53.78	A / 9.4	21.40%	B- / 7.1

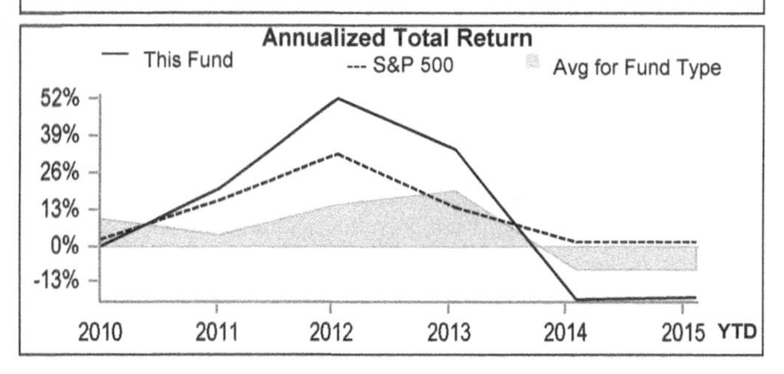

*SPDR S&P WORLD EX-US ETF (GWL) C+ Fair

Fund Family: SSgA Funds Management Inc
Fund Type: Global
Inception Date: April 20, 2007

Major Rating Factors: Middle of the road best describes *SPDR S&P WORLD EX-US ETF whose TheStreet.com Investment Rating is currently a C+ (Fair). The fund currently has a performance rating of C+ (Fair) based on an annualized return of 3.60% over the last three years and a total return of 0.37% year to date 2015. Factored into the performance evaluation is an expense ratio of 0.34% (very low).

The fund's risk rating is currently B (Good). It carries a beta of 0.93, meaning that its performance tracks fairly well with that of the overall stock market. Volatility, as measured by both the semi-deviation and a drawdown factor, is considered low. As of December 31, 2015, *SPDR S&P WORLD EX-US ETF traded at a discount of .43% below its net asset value, which is better than its one-year historical average premium of .15%.

John A. Tucker currently receives a manager quality ranking of 59 (0=worst, 99=best). If you desire an average level of risk, then this fund may be an option.

Data Date	Investment Rating	Net Assets ($Mil)	Price	Performance Rating/Pts	Total Return Y-T-D	Risk Rating/Pts
12-15	C+	825.40	25.75	C+ / 5.6	0.37%	B / 8.3
2014	C-	825.40	26.90	C / 4.8	-3.70%	B- / 7.0
2013	C+	826.50	29.34	C+ / 6.3	15.63%	B- / 7.6
2012	C-	460.00	25.33	C- / 4.2	21.29%	B- / 7.3
2011	D+	140.20	21.79	D+ / 2.7	-12.67%	B- / 7.2
2010	D	118.30	25.95	D+ / 2.3	11.26%	C / 5.4

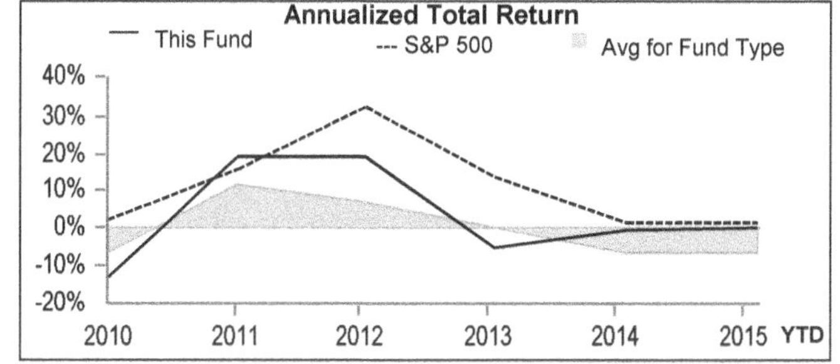

*SPDR SP Intl Con Disc Sect ETF (IPD) B+ Good

Fund Family: SSgA Funds Management Inc
Fund Type: Global
Inception Date: July 16, 2008

Data Date	Investment Rating	Net Assets ($Mil)	Price	Performance Rating/Pts	Total Return Y-T-D	Risk Rating/Pts
12-15	B+	18.40	36.80	B- / 7.0	2.27%	B / 8.6
2014	C+	18.40	37.12	C+ / 6.7	-5.35%	C+ / 6.7
2013	B	21.80	40.60	B / 8.1	32.29%	B- / 7.5
2012	C+	6.00	30.32	C+ / 6.7	25.38%	B- / 7.5
2011	C	4.90	24.37	C / 5.0	-13.57%	B- / 7.9
2010	A	22.00	29.34	A / 9.3	19.59%	C+ / 6.2

Major Rating Factors: Strong performance is the major factor driving the B+ (Good) TheStreet.com Investment Rating for *SPDR SP Intl Con Disc Sect ETF. The fund currently has a performance rating of B- (Good) based on an annualized return of 8.37% over the last three years and a total return of 2.27% year to date 2015. Factored into the performance evaluation is an expense ratio of 0.44% (very low).

The fund's risk rating is currently B (Good). It carries a beta of 0.88, meaning the fund's expected move will be 8.8% for every 10% move in the market. Volatility, as measured by both the semi-deviation and a drawdown factor, is considered low. As of December 31, 2015, *SPDR SP Intl Con Disc Sect ETF traded at a discount of .92% below its net asset value, which is better than its one-year historical average discount of .07%.

John A. Tucker currently receives a manager quality ranking of 87 (0=worst, 99=best). If you desire only a moderate level of risk and strong performance, then this fund is an excellent option.

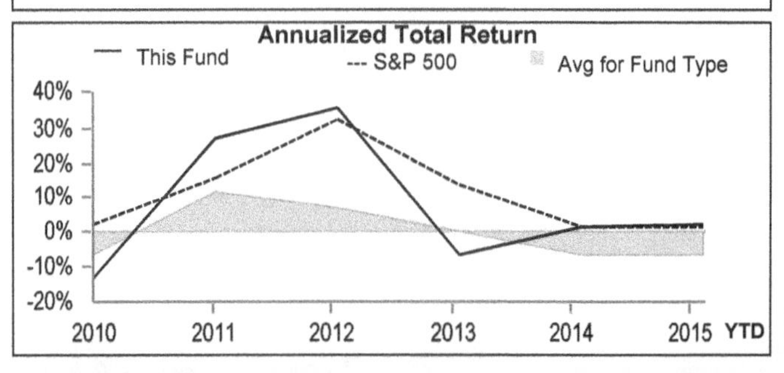

*SPDR SP Intl Con Stap Sect ETF (IPS) B Good

Fund Family: SSgA Funds Management Inc
Fund Type: Global
Inception Date: July 16, 2008

Data Date	Investment Rating	Net Assets ($Mil)	Price	Performance Rating/Pts	Total Return Y-T-D	Risk Rating/Pts
12-15	B	42.90	41.47	B / 7.7	12.75%	B- / 7.4
2014	C	42.90	38.12	C / 4.9	-1.31%	B- / 7.2
2013	B	37.90	40.06	B- / 7.0	12.79%	B / 8.7
2012	C+	19.40	35.67	C+ / 5.6	22.46%	B / 8.6
2011	C+	17.20	31.31	C / 4.9	5.68%	B / 8.3
2010	A	12.40	30.95	B+ / 8.6	11.72%	C+ / 6.8

Major Rating Factors: Strong performance is the major factor driving the B (Good) TheStreet.com Investment Rating for *SPDR SP Intl Con Stap Sect ETF. The fund currently has a performance rating of B (Good) based on an annualized return of 7.38% over the last three years and a total return of 12.75% year to date 2015. Factored into the performance evaluation is an expense ratio of 0.43% (very low).

The fund's risk rating is currently B- (Good). It carries a beta of 0.82, meaning the fund's expected move will be 8.2% for every 10% move in the market. Volatility, as measured by both the semi-deviation and a drawdown factor, is considered low. As of December 31, 2015, *SPDR SP Intl Con Stap Sect ETF traded at a premium of .22% above its net asset value, which is worse than its one-year historical average premium of .01%.

John A. Tucker has been running the fund for 8 years and currently receives a manager quality ranking of 84 (0=worst, 99=best). If you desire only a moderate level of risk and strong performance, then this fund is an excellent option.

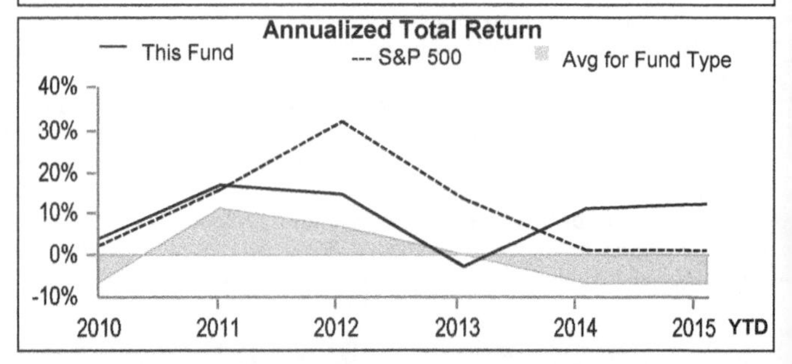

*SPDR SP Intl Energy Sector ETF (IPW) D- Weak

Fund Family: SSgA Funds Management Inc
Fund Type: Energy/Natural Resources
Inception Date: July 16, 2008

Data Date	Investment Rating	Net Assets ($Mil)	Price	Performance Rating/Pts	Total Return Y-T-D	Risk Rating/Pts
12-15	D-	19.30	15.32	D- / 1.4	-21.17%	C / 4.7
2014	D-	19.30	20.62	D- / 1.5	-16.76%	C+ / 5.6
2013	C-	13.00	26.07	C- / 3.6	4.35%	B- / 7.4
2012	D	11.10	24.96	D / 2.0	6.14%	B- / 7.3
2011	C-	10.20	25.25	C- / 3.7	-2.52%	B- / 7.4
2010	A-	15.00	27.44	B+ / 8.9	4.68%	C+ / 6.1

Major Rating Factors:
Disappointing performance is the major factor driving the D- (Weak) TheStreet.com Investment Rating for *SPDR SP Intl Energy Sector ETF. The fund currently has a performance rating of D- (Weak) based on an annualized return of -11.96% over the last three years and a total return of -21.17% year to date 2015. Factored into the performance evaluation is an expense ratio of 0.43% (very low).

The fund's risk rating is currently C (Fair). It carries a beta of 0.92, meaning that its performance tracks fairly well with that of the overall stock market. Volatility, as measured by both the semi-deviation and a drawdown factor, is considered average. As of December 31, 2015, *SPDR SP Intl Energy Sector ETF traded at a premium of .99% above its net asset value, which is worse than its one-year historical average premium of .31%.

John A. Tucker currently receives a manager quality ranking of 19 (0=worst, 99=best). This fund offers an average level of risk but investors looking for strong performance will be frustrated.

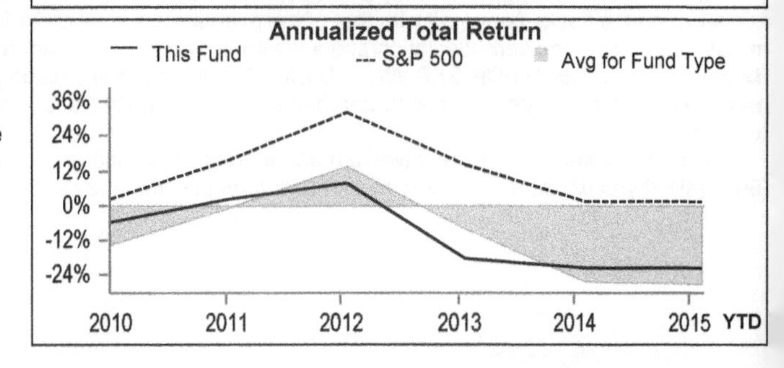

*SPDR SP Intl Finl Sector ETF (IPF) C+ Fair

Fund Family: SSgA Funds Management Inc
Fund Type: Financial Services
Inception Date: July 16, 2008

Major Rating Factors: Middle of the road best describes *SPDR SP Intl Finl Sector ETF whose TheStreet.com Investment Rating is currently a C+ (Fair). The fund currently has a performance rating of C+ (Fair) based on an annualized return of 4.51% over the last three years and a total return of 0.87% year to date 2015. Factored into the performance evaluation is an expense ratio of 0.44% (very low).

The fund's risk rating is currently C+ (Fair). It carries a beta of 0.71, meaning the fund's expected move will be 7.1% for every 10% move in the market. Volatility, as measured by both the semi-deviation and a drawdown factor, is considered low. As of December 31, 2015, *SPDR SP Intl Finl Sector ETF traded at a premium of 2.53% above its net asset value, which is worse than its one-year historical average premium of .25%.

John A. Tucker currently receives a manager quality ranking of 29 (0=worst, 99=best). If you desire an average level of risk, then this fund may be an option.

Data Date	Investment Rating	Net Assets ($Mil)	Price	Performance Rating/Pts	Total Return Y-T-D	Risk Rating/Pts
12-15	C+	10.90	19.82	C+ / 6.0	0.87%	C+ / 6.9
2014	C+	10.90	20.73	C+ / 6.1	-6.67%	B / 8.0
2013	C+	7.90	23.35	C+ / 6.9	21.18%	B- / 7.2
2012	D+	5.70	19.33	C- / 3.1	35.80%	B- / 7.0
2011	D	4.60	15.05	D / 1.7	-21.27%	B- / 7.1
2010	C+	6.00	19.81	B- / 7.0	0.56%	C / 5.1

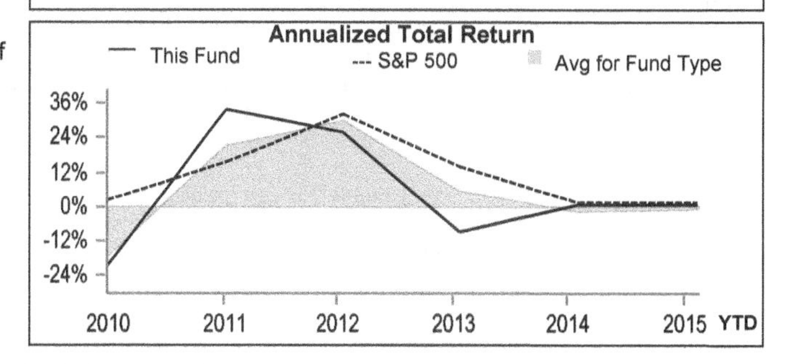

*SPDR SP Intl Health Care ETF (IRY) A Excellent

Fund Family: SSgA Funds Management Inc
Fund Type: Health
Inception Date: July 16, 2008

Major Rating Factors:
Strong performance is the major factor driving the A (Excellent) TheStreet.com Investment Rating for *SPDR SP Intl Health Care ETF. The fund currently has a performance rating of B+ (Good) based on an annualized return of 13.76% over the last three years and a total return of 10.22% year to date 2015. Factored into the performance evaluation is an expense ratio of 0.44% (very low).

The fund's risk rating is currently B- (Good). It carries a beta of 0.69, meaning the fund's expected move will be 6.9% for every 10% move in the market. Volatility, as measured by both the semi-deviation and a drawdown factor, is considered low. As of December 31, 2015, *SPDR SP Intl Health Care ETF traded at a discount of .40% below its net asset value, which is better than its one-year historical average premium of .01%.

John A. Tucker currently receives a manager quality ranking of 87 (0=worst, 99=best). If you desire only a moderate level of risk and strong performance, then this fund is an excellent option.

Data Date	Investment Rating	Net Assets ($Mil)	Price	Performance Rating/Pts	Total Return Y-T-D	Risk Rating/Pts
12-15	A	66.10	50.37	B+ / 8.9	10.22%	B- / 7.9
2014	B	66.10	46.76	B- / 7.1	7.31%	B / 8.3
2013	A-	60.30	44.77	B / 8.2	24.88%	B / 8.4
2012	C+	30.20	35.81	C+ / 5.7	22.07%	B / 8.2
2011	C-	15.50	31.00	C- / 3.7	5.53%	B / 8.1
2010	C+	12.10	30.12	C+ / 6.9	3.51%	C+ / 6.5

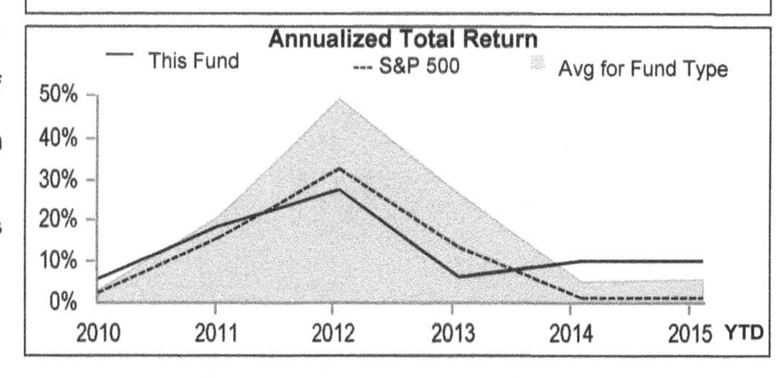

*SPDR SP Intl Industrial ETF (IPN) C+ Fair

Fund Family: SSgA Funds Management Inc
Fund Type: Global
Inception Date: July 16, 2008

Major Rating Factors: Middle of the road best describes *SPDR SP Intl Industrial ETF whose TheStreet.com Investment Rating is currently a C+ (Fair). The fund currently has a performance rating of C (Fair) based on an annualized return of 3.45% over the last three years and a total return of -0.85% year to date 2015. Factored into the performance evaluation is an expense ratio of 0.45% (very low).

The fund's risk rating is currently B (Good). It carries a beta of 0.90, meaning that its performance tracks fairly well with that of the overall stock market. Volatility, as measured by both the semi-deviation and a drawdown factor, is considered low. As of December 31, 2015, *SPDR SP Intl Industrial ETF traded at a discount of .86% below its net asset value, which is better than its one-year historical average discount of .08%.

John A. Tucker currently receives a manager quality ranking of 60 (0=worst, 99=best). If you desire an average level of risk, then this fund may be an option.

Data Date	Investment Rating	Net Assets ($Mil)	Price	Performance Rating/Pts	Total Return Y-T-D	Risk Rating/Pts
12-15	C+	24.30	27.75	C / 5.5	-0.85%	B / 8.3
2014	C	24.30	28.74	C / 4.6	-7.30%	B / 8.4
2013	C+	25.40	32.00	C+ / 6.6	20.45%	B- / 7.6
2012	C-	6.50	26.35	C- / 3.6	19.30%	B- / 7.4
2011	C-	12.80	23.02	C- / 3.0	-16.18%	B- / 7.6
2010	A-	28.30	28.28	A / 9.3	20.35%	C+ / 5.7

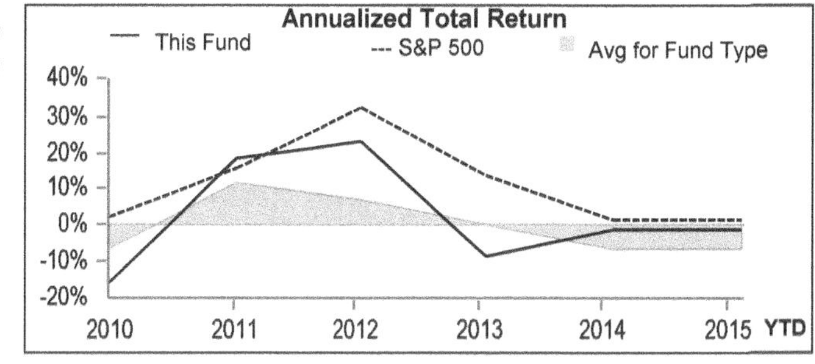

*SPDR SP Intl Materials Sec ETF (IRV) D Weak

Fund Family: SSgA Funds Management Inc
Fund Type: Global
Inception Date: July 16, 2008

Major Rating Factors:
Disappointing performance is the major factor driving the D (Weak) TheStreet.com Investment Rating for *SPDR SP Intl Materials Sec ETF. The fund currently has a performance rating of D (Weak) based on an annualized return of -10.51% over the last three years and a total return of -12.82% year to date 2015. Factored into the performance evaluation is an expense ratio of 0.45% (very low).

The fund's risk rating is currently C+ (Fair). It carries a beta of 1.01, meaning that its performance tracks fairly well with that of the overall stock market. Volatility, as measured by both the semi-deviation and a drawdown factor, is considered low. As of December 31, 2015, *SPDR SP Intl Materials Sec ETF traded at a premium of .83% above its net asset value, which is worse than its one-year historical average discount of .02%.

John A. Tucker currently receives a manager quality ranking of 11 (0=worst, 99=best). This fund offers only a moderate level of risk but investors looking for strong performance are still waiting.

Data Date	Investment Rating	Net Assets ($Mil)	Price	Performance Rating/Pts	Total Return Y-T-D	Risk Rating/Pts
12-15	D	7.60	16.93	D / 1.7	-12.82%	C+ / 5.6
2014	D+	7.60	20.20	D / 1.9	-10.63%	B- / 7.4
2013	D	9.40	23.40	D / 1.7	-7.53%	C+ / 6.4
2012	D	9.90	24.87	D / 2.0	6.21%	C+ / 5.9
2011	D	12.80	23.06	C- / 3.5	-19.62%	C+ / 5.8
2010	B	35.40	30.94	A+ / 9.6	21.94%	C- / 3.6

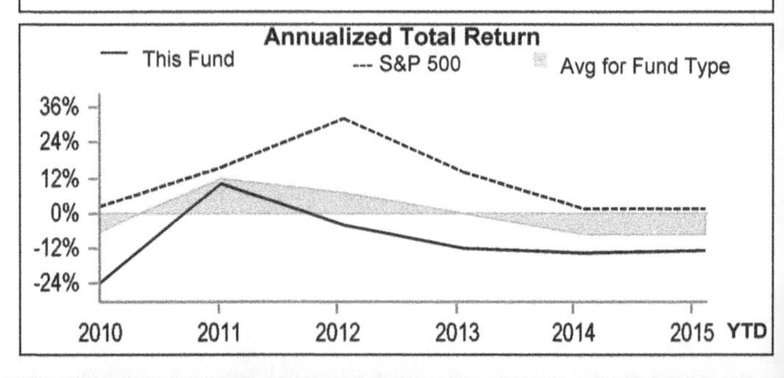

*SPDR SP Intl Tech Sector ETF (IPK) B- Good

Fund Family: SSgA Funds Management Inc
Fund Type: Global
Inception Date: July 16, 2008

Major Rating Factors: *SPDR SP Intl Tech Sector ETF receives a TheStreet.com Investment Rating of B- (Good). The fund currently has a performance rating of C+ (Fair) based on an annualized return of 6.25% over the last three years and a total return of 1.43% year to date 2015. Factored into the performance evaluation is an expense ratio of 0.45% (very low).

The fund's risk rating is currently B- (Good). It carries a beta of 0.83, meaning the fund's expected move will be 8.3% for every 10% move in the market. Volatility, as measured by both the semi-deviation and a drawdown factor, is considered low. As of December 31, 2015, *SPDR SP Intl Tech Sector ETF traded at a discount of .89% below its net asset value, which is better than its one-year historical average discount of .06%.

John A. Tucker currently receives a manager quality ranking of 80 (0=worst, 99=best). If you desire an average level of risk, then this fund may be an option.

Data Date	Investment Rating	Net Assets ($Mil)	Price	Performance Rating/Pts	Total Return Y-T-D	Risk Rating/Pts
12-15	B-	12.60	31.20	C+ / 6.6	1.43%	B- / 7.9
2014	C+	12.60	31.40	C+ / 6.0	1.50%	B / 8.0
2013	C	14.30	32.00	C+ / 6.0	16.69%	C+ / 6.4
2012	D+	11.90	27.11	C- / 3.7	23.98%	C+ / 6.7
2011	D+	12.50	22.55	C- / 3.1	-16.41%	C+ / 6.6
2010	A-	26.40	27.79	A- / 9.1	15.11%	C / 5.3

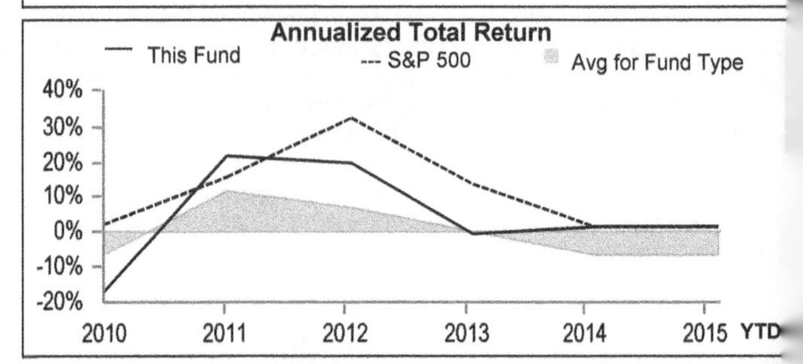

*SPDR SP Intl Telecom Sect ETF (IST) B+ Good

Fund Family: SSgA Funds Management Inc
Fund Type: Global
Inception Date: July 16, 2008

Major Rating Factors: Strong performance is the major factor driving the B+ (Good) TheStreet.com Investment Rating for *SPDR SP Intl Telecom Sect ETF. The fund currently has a performance rating of B (Good) based on an annualized return of 11.45% over the last three years and a total return of 4.66% year to date 2015. Factored into the performance evaluation is an expense ratio of 0.44% (very low).

The fund's risk rating is currently B- (Good). It carries a beta of 1.02, meaning that its performance tracks fairly well with that of the overall stock market. Volatility, as measured by both the semi-deviation and a drawdown factor, is considered low. As of December 31, 2015, *SPDR SP Intl Telecom Sect ETF traded at a price exactly equal to its net asset value, which is worse than its one-year historical average discount of .11%.

John A. Tucker currently receives a manager quality ranking of 91 (0=worst, 99=best). If you desire only a moderate level of risk and strong performance, then this fund is an excellent option.

Data Date	Investment Rating	Net Assets ($Mil)	Price	Performance Rating/Pts	Total Return Y-T-D	Risk Rating/Pts
12-15	B+	43.60	25.08	B / 8.2	4.66%	B- / 7.4
2014	C	43.60	25.07	C / 5.4	-2.95%	B- / 7.0
2013	B+	39.80	29.67	B+ / 8.4	36.37%	B- / 7.9
2012	D+	25.10	22.00	D+ / 2.6	9.23%	B- / 7.6
2011	C-	14.80	22.59	D+ / 2.9	-2.35%	B- / 7.9
2010	B	15.90	24.45	B+ / 8.3	9.02%	C / 4.7

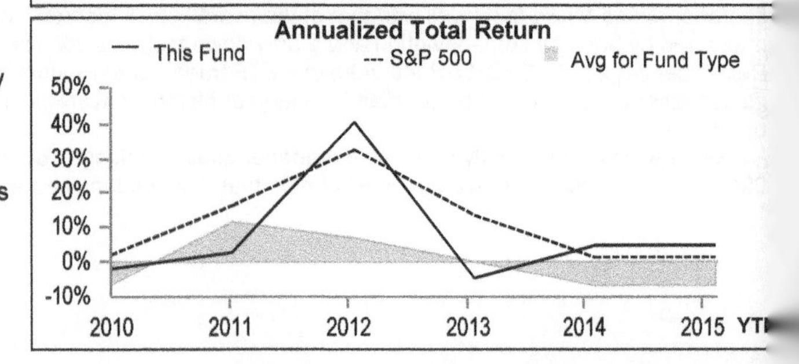

*SPDR SP Intl Utils Sector ETF (IPU) C+ Fair

Fund Family: SSgA Funds Management Inc
Fund Type: Utilities
Inception Date: July 16, 2008

Major Rating Factors: Middle of the road best describes *SPDR SP Intl Utils Sector ETF whose TheStreet.com Investment Rating is currently a C+ (Fair). The fund currently has a performance rating of C (Fair) based on an annualized return of 2.27% over the last three years and a total return of -5.05% year to date 2015. Factored into the performance evaluation is an expense ratio of 0.45% (very low).

The fund's risk rating is currently B (Good). It carries a beta of 0.42, meaning the fund's expected move will be 4.2% for every 10% move in the market. Volatility, as measured by both the semi-deviation and a drawdown factor, is considered low. As of December 31, 2015, *SPDR SP Intl Utils Sector ETF traded at a discount of .86% below its net asset value, which is better than its one-year historical average discount of .20%.

John A. Tucker currently receives a manager quality ranking of 48 (0=worst, 99=best). If you desire an average level of risk, then this fund may be an option.

Data Date	Investment Rating	Net Assets ($Mil)	Price	Performance Rating/Pts	Total Return Y-T-D	Risk Rating/Pts
12-15	C+	69.60	16.08	C / 4.9	-5.05%	B / 8.0
2014	C-	69.60	17.70	C- / 4.1	3.78%	C+ / 7.0
2013	D+	52.90	18.14	C- / 3.0	8.97%	B- / 7.4
2012	D	27.20	16.73	D- / 1.1	8.09%	B- / 7.2
2011	D	11.60	16.50	D- / 1.3	-15.71%	B- / 7.4
2010	C-	8.40	20.86	C- / 3.8	-5.61%	C+ / 6.2

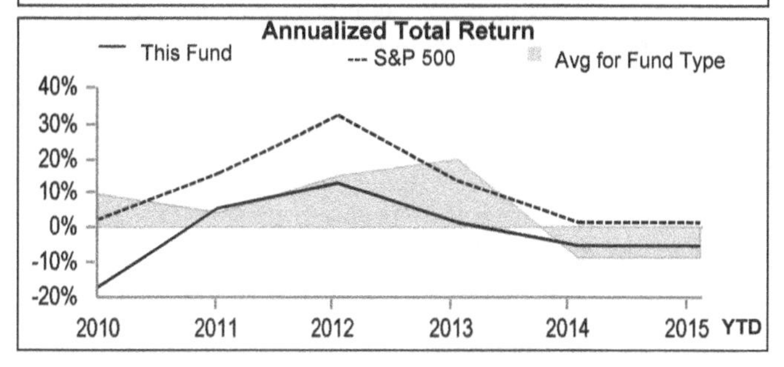

*SPDR SSgA Global Allocation ETF (GAL) C+ Fair

Fund Family: SSgA Funds Management Inc
Fund Type: Growth and Income
Inception Date: April 25, 2012

Major Rating Factors: Middle of the road best describes *SPDR SSgA Global Allocation ETF whose TheStreet.com Investment Rating is currently a C+ (Fair). The fund currently has a performance rating of C+ (Fair) based on an annualized return of 4.37% over the last three years and a total return of -3.22% year to date 2015. Factored into the performance evaluation is an expense ratio of 0.05% (very low).

The fund's risk rating is currently B- (Good). It carries a beta of 0.67, meaning the fund's expected move will be 6.7% for every 10% move in the market. Volatility, as measured by both the semi-deviation and a drawdown factor, is considered low. As of December 31, 2015, *SPDR SSgA Global Allocation ETF traded at a premium of .21% above its net asset value, which is worse than its one-year historical average premium of .04%.

Christopher J. Goolgasian currently receives a manager quality ranking of 32 (0=worst, 99=best). If you desire an average level of risk, then this fund may be an option.

Data Date	Investment Rating	Net Assets ($Mil)	Price	Performance Rating/Pts	Total Return Y-T-D	Risk Rating/Pts
12-15	C+	112.00	32.87	C+ / 5.7	-3.22%	B- / 7.2
2014	C-	112.00	34.70	C- / 4.2	6.62%	B- / 7.5
2013	B+	64.70	34.04	C+ / 6.8	10.10%	B+ / 9.3

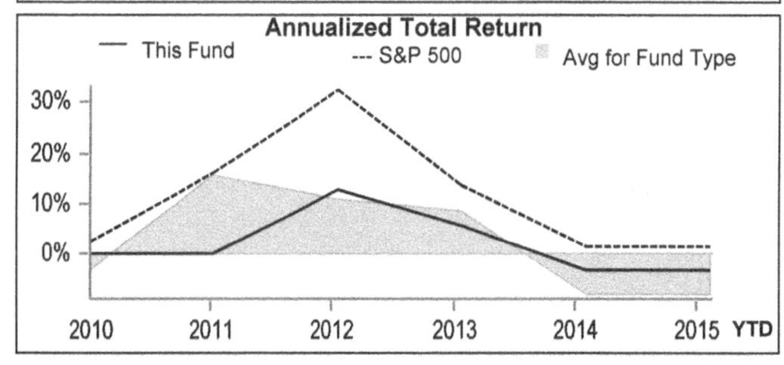

*SPDR SSgA Income Allocation ETF (INKM) C Fair

Fund Family: SSgA Funds Management Inc
Fund Type: Growth and Income
Inception Date: April 25, 2012

Major Rating Factors: Middle of the road best describes *SPDR SSgA Income Allocation ETF whose TheStreet.com Investment Rating is currently a C (Fair). The fund currently has a performance rating of C (Fair) based on an annualized return of 1.55% over the last three years and a total return of -5.74% year to date 2015. Factored into the performance evaluation is an expense ratio of 0.35% (very low).

The fund's risk rating is currently B- (Good). It carries a beta of 0.52, meaning the fund's expected move will be 5.2% for every 10% move in the market. Volatility, as measured by both the semi-deviation and a drawdown factor, is considered low. As of December 31, 2015, *SPDR SSgA Income Allocation ETF traded at a price exactly equal to its net asset value.

Jeremiah K. Holly currently receives a manager quality ranking of 28 (0=worst, 99=best). If you desire an average level of risk, then this fund may be an option.

Data Date	Investment Rating	Net Assets ($Mil)	Price	Performance Rating/Pts	Total Return Y-T-D	Risk Rating/Pts
12-15	C	105.90	29.58	C / 4.5	-5.74%	B- / 7.9
2014	C+	105.90	32.12	C / 5.0	9.13%	B / 8.7
2013	C	99.60	30.56	C- / 4.2	1.70%	B+ / 9.0

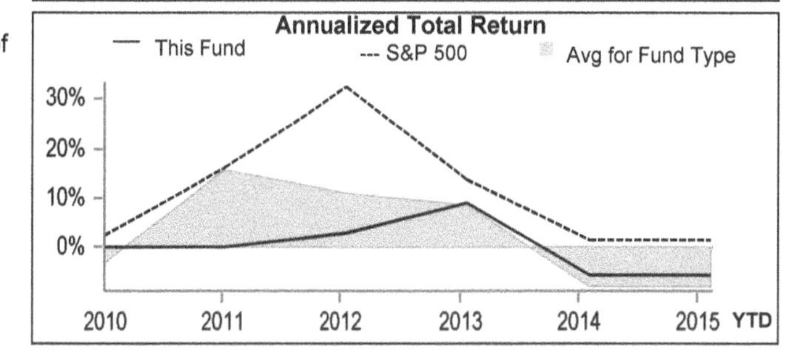

*SPDR SSgA Multi Asset Real Retur (RLY) D Weak

Fund Family: SSgA Funds Management Inc
Fund Type: Growth and Income
Inception Date: April 25, 2012

Major Rating Factors:
Disappointing performance is the major factor driving the D (Weak) TheStreet.com Investment Rating for *SPDR SSgA Multi Asset Real Retur. The fund currently has a performance rating of D (Weak) based on an annualized return of -8.89% over the last three years and a total return of -15.75% year to date 2015. Factored into the performance evaluation is an expense ratio of 0.23% (very low).

The fund's risk rating is currently C (Fair). It carries a beta of 0.65, meaning the fund's expected move will be 6.5% for every 10% move in the market. Volatility, as measured by both the semi-deviation and a drawdown factor, is considered average. As of December 31, 2015, *SPDR SSgA Multi Asset Real Retur traded at a premium of .09% above its net asset value, which is worse than its one-year historical average discount of .02%.

Christopher J. Goolgasian currently receives a manager quality ranking of 9 (0=worst, 99=best). This fund offers an average level of risk but investors looking for strong performance will be frustrated.

Data Date	Investment Rating	Net Assets ($Mil)	Price	Performance Rating/Pts	Total Return Y-T-D	Risk Rating/Pts
12-15	D	167.80	22.25	D / 1.9	-15.75%	C / 5.5
2014	D+	167.80	26.63	D- / 1.2	-5.81%	B / 8.2
2013	C-	55.10	29.06	D+ / 2.4	-4.74%	B / 8.7

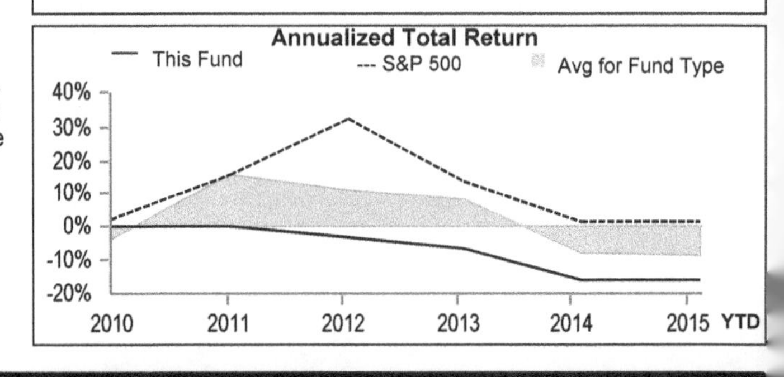

*SPDR SSgA Ultra Short Term Bond (ULST) B- Good

Fund Family: SSgA Funds Management Inc
Fund Type: General - Investment Grade
Inception Date: October 10, 2013

Major Rating Factors: *SPDR SSgA Ultra Short Term Bond receives a TheStreet.com Investment Rating of B- (Good). The fund currently has a performance rating of C- (Fair) based on an annualized return of 0.00% over the last three years and a total return of 0.14% year to date 2015. Factored into the performance evaluation is an expense ratio of 0.20% (very low).

The fund's risk rating is currently B+ (Good). It carries a beta of 0.00, meaning the fund's expected move will be 0.0% for every 10% move in the market. Volatility, as measured by both the semi-deviation and a drawdown factor, is considered very low. As of December 31, 2015, *SPDR SSgA Ultra Short Term Bond traded at a discount of .05% below its net asset value, which is better than its one-year historical average premium of .01%.

Lee Shaiman currently receives a manager quality ranking of 68 (0=worst, 99=best). If you desire an average level of risk, then this fund may be an option.

Data Date	Investment Rating	Net Assets ($Mil)	Price	Performance Rating/Pts	Total Return Y-T-D	Risk Rating/Pts
12-15	B-	18.00	39.90	C- / 4.2	0.14%	B+ / 9.9
2014	D	18.00	39.98	D+ / 2.7	0.15%	C / 5.4

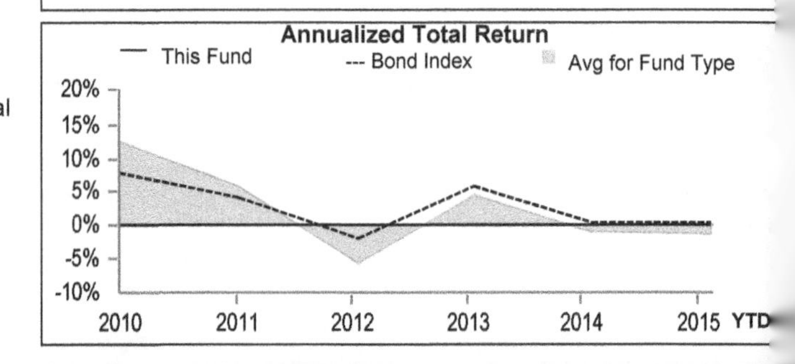

*SPDR STOXX Europe 50 ETF (FEU) C Fair

Fund Family: SSgA Funds Management Inc
Fund Type: Foreign
Inception Date: October 15, 2002

Major Rating Factors: Middle of the road best describes *SPDR STOXX Europe 50 ETF whose TheStreet.com Investment Rating is currently a C (Fair). The fund currently has a performance rating of C (Fair) based on an annualized return of 2.03% over the last three years and a total return of -3.03% year to date 2015. Factored into the performance evaluation is an expense ratio of 0.29% (very low).

The fund's risk rating is currently B- (Good). It carries a beta of 1.02, meaning that its performance tracks fairly well with that of the overall stock market. Volatility, as measured by both the semi-deviation and a drawdown factor, is considered low. As of December 31, 2015, *SPDR STOXX Europe 50 ETF traded at a discount of .34% below its net asset value, which is better than its one-year historical average premium of .11%.

John A. Tucker has been running the fund for 14 years and currently receives a manager quality ranking of 43 (0=worst, 99=best). If you desire an average level of risk, then this fund may be an option.

Data Date	Investment Rating	Net Assets ($Mil)	Price	Performance Rating/Pts	Total Return Y-T-D	Risk Rating/Pts
12-15	C	261.70	31.82	C / 4.7	-3.03%	B- / 7.6
2014	C-	261.70	34.22	C / 4.3	-6.21%	C+ / 6.2
2013	C+	183.30	39.33	C+ / 6.6	17.18%	B- / 7.1
2012	D+	44.60	33.62	C- / 3.5	21.10%	C+ / 6.9
2011	D+	28.40	29.79	D+ / 2.3	-7.73%	B- / 7.0
2010	D-	39.00	33.80	E+ / 0.9	-3.15%	C / 4.7

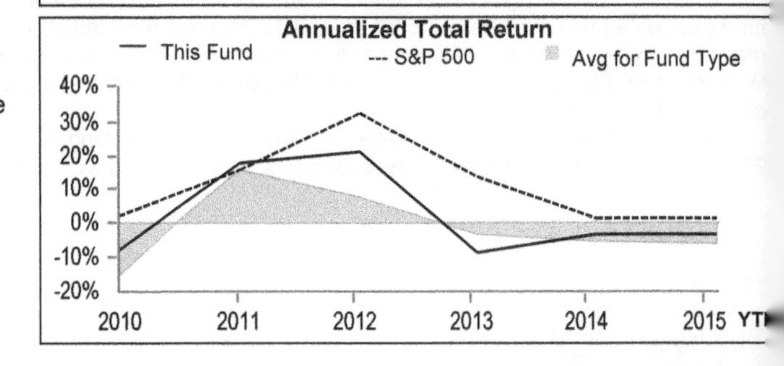

*SPDR Wells Fargo Preferred Stk E (PSK) B- Good

Fund Family: SSgA Funds Management Inc
Fund Type: Income
Inception Date: September 16, 2009

Major Rating Factors: Strong performance is the major factor driving the B- (Good) TheStreet.com Investment Rating for *SPDR Wells Fargo Preferred Stk E. The fund currently has a performance rating of B (Good) based on an annualized return of 6.48% over the last three years and a total return of 9.28% year to date 2015. Factored into the performance evaluation is an expense ratio of 0.45% (very low).

The fund's risk rating is currently C+ (Fair). It carries a beta of 0.06, meaning the fund's expected move will be 0.6% for every 10% move in the market. Volatility, as measured by both the semi-deviation and a drawdown factor, is considered low. As of December 31, 2015, *SPDR Wells Fargo Preferred Stk E traded at a premium of .18% above its net asset value, which is worse than its one-year historical average premium of .04%.

John A. Tucker has been running the fund for 7 years and currently receives a manager quality ranking of 90 (0=worst, 99=best). If you desire only a moderate level of risk and strong performance, then this fund is an excellent option.

Data Date	Investment Rating	Net Assets ($Mil)	Price	Performance Rating/Pts	Total Return Y-T-D	Risk Rating/Pts
12-15	B-	252.20	44.69	B / 7.6	9.28%	C+ / 6.9
2014	C+	252.20	43.78	C / 5.4	15.81%	B / 8.6
2013	C-	219.60	39.42	C- / 3.1	-4.94%	B / 8.6
2012	C	321.40	44.98	C- / 3.5	11.16%	B+ / 9.1
2011	C-	126.40	42.17	D+ / 2.6	3.56%	B+ / 9.2
2010	A+	102.80	44.59	B / 7.9	13.95%	B / 8.9

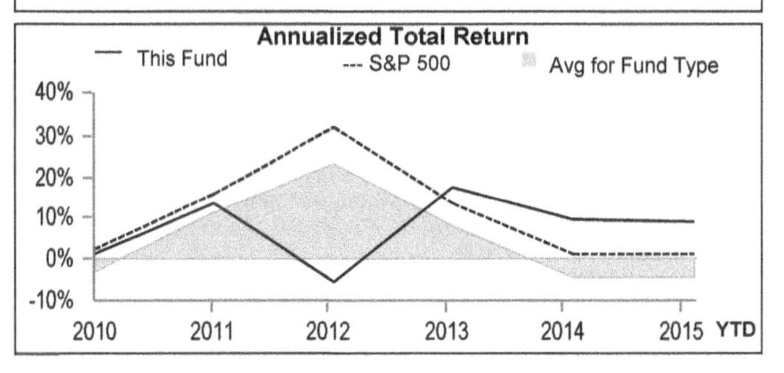

*Star Global Buy Write ETF (VEGA) C+ Fair

Fund Family: AdvisorShares Investments LLC
Fund Type: Growth and Income
Inception Date: September 17, 2012

Major Rating Factors: Middle of the road best describes *Star Global Buy Write ETF whose TheStreet.com Investment Rating is currently a C+ (Fair). The fund currently has a performance rating of C (Fair) based on an annualized return of 1.44% over the last three years and a total return of -1.86% year to date 2015. Factored into the performance evaluation is an expense ratio of 1.85% (above average).

The fund's risk rating is currently B+ (Good). It carries a beta of 0.57, meaning the fund's expected move will be 5.7% for every 10% move in the market. Volatility, as measured by both the semi-deviation and a drawdown factor, is considered very low. As of December 31, 2015, *Star Global Buy Write ETF traded at a discount of .27% below its net asset value, which is better than its one-year historical average discount of .10%.

Kenneth R. Hyman has been running the fund for 4 years and currently receives a manager quality ranking of 25 (0=worst, 99=best). If you desire an average level of risk, then this fund may be an option.

Data Date	Investment Rating	Net Assets ($Mil)	Price	Performance Rating/Pts	Total Return Y-T-D	Risk Rating/Pts
12-15	C+	26.10	25.88	C / 4.8	-1.86%	B+ / 9.1
2014	C	26.10	26.51	C- / 4.2	6.34%	B- / 7.7
2013	C+	25.00	25.00	C- / 4.2	0.56%	B+ / 9.6

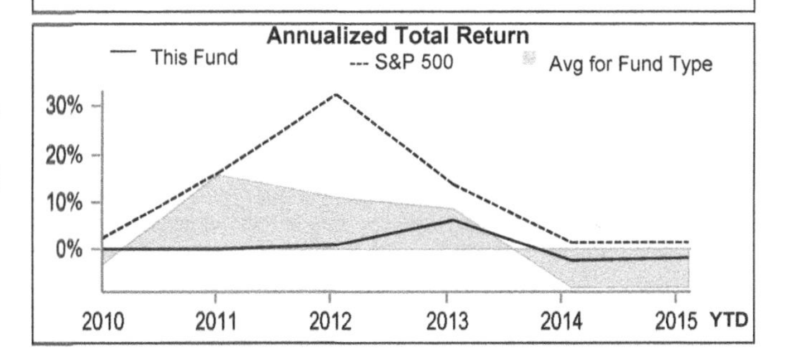

*Stock Split Index (TOFR) C- Fair

Fund Family: USCF Advisers LLC
Fund Type: Financial Services
Inception Date: September 15, 2014

Major Rating Factors: Middle of the road best describes *Stock Split Index whose TheStreet.com Investment Rating is currently a C- (Fair). The fund currently has a performance rating of C- (Fair) based on an annualized return of 0.00% over the last three years and a total return of 1.13% year to date 2015. Factored into the performance evaluation is an expense ratio of 0.55% (very low).

The fund's risk rating is currently C+ (Fair). It carries a beta of 0.00, meaning the fund's expected move will be 0.0% for every 10% move in the market. Volatility, as measured by both the semi-deviation and a drawdown factor, is considered low. As of December 31, 2015, *Stock Split Index traded at a premium of .67% above its net asset value, which is worse than its one-year historical average premium of .14%.

Andrew F. Ngim has been running the fund for 2 years and currently receives a manager quality ranking of 71 (0=worst, 99=best). If you desire an average level of risk, then this fund may be an option.

Data Date	Investment Rating	Net Assets ($Mil)	Price	Performance Rating/Pts	Total Return Y-T-D	Risk Rating/Pts
12-15	C-	0.00	15.01	C- / 4.1	1.13%	C+ / 6.9

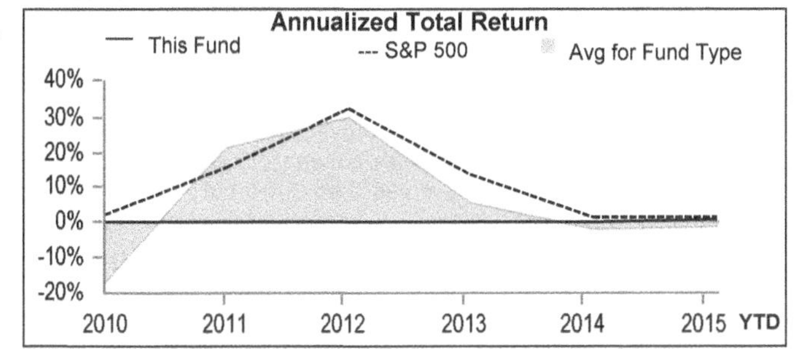

*Technology Select Sector SPDR (XLK) A+ Excellent

Fund Family: SSgA Funds Management Inc
Fund Type: Growth
Inception Date: December 16, 1998

Major Rating Factors:
Exceptional performance is the major factor driving the A+ (Excellent) TheStreet.com Investment Rating for *Technology Select Sector SPDR. The fund currently has a performance rating of A- (Excellent) based on an annualized return of 15.54% over the last three years and a total return of 6.23% year to date 2015. Factored into the performance evaluation is an expense ratio of 0.15% (very low).

The fund's risk rating is currently B (Good). It carries a beta of 0.99, meaning that its performance tracks fairly well with that of the overall stock market. Volatility, as measured by both the semi-deviation and a drawdown factor, is considered low. As of December 31, 2015, *Technology Select Sector SPDR traded at a discount of .07% below its net asset value.

John A. Tucker has been running the fund for 18 years and currently receives a manager quality ranking of 78 (0=worst, 99=best). If you desire only a moderate level of risk and strong performance, then this fund is an excellent option.

Data Date	Investment Rating	Net Assets ($Mil)	Price	Performance Rating/Pts	Total Return Y-T-D	Risk Rating/Pts
12-15	A+	13,858.40	42.83	A- / 9.2	6.23%	B / 8.6
2014	B+	13,858.40	41.35	B+ / 8.4	19.59%	B- / 7.3
2013	B	13,141.60	35.74	B / 7.6	21.66%	B- / 7.9
2012	C-	8,283.80	28.85	C / 4.4	15.41%	B- / 7.2
2011	C+	8,195.60	25.45	C+ / 6.6	2.41%	B- / 7.5
2010	C	5,849.30	25.19	C / 5.1	11.41%	C+ / 5.7

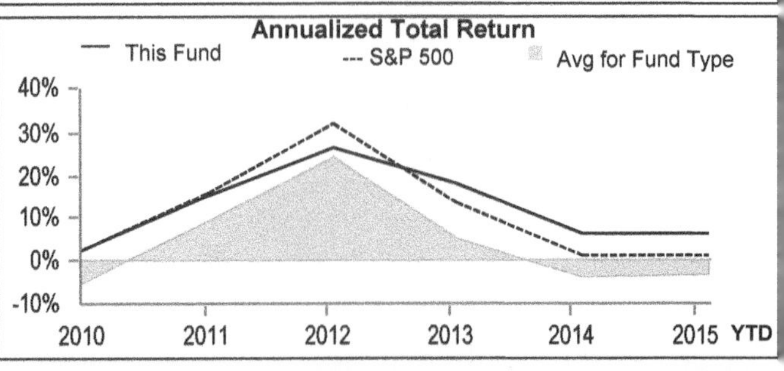

*Teucrium Agricultural Fund (TAGS) D- Weak

Fund Family: Teucrium Trading LLC
Fund Type: Global
Inception Date: March 28, 2012

Major Rating Factors:
Disappointing performance is the major factor driving the D- (Weak) TheStreet.com Investment Rating for *Teucrium Agricultural Fund. The fund currently has a performance rating of D- (Weak) based on an annualized return of -18.25% over the last three years and a total return of -19.91% year to date 2015. Factored into the performance evaluation is an expense ratio of 0.50% (very low).

The fund's risk rating is currently C (Fair). It carries a beta of 0.20, meaning the fund's expected move will be 2.0% for every 10% move in the market. Volatility, as measured by both the semi-deviation and a drawdown factor, is considered average. As of December 31, 2015, *Teucrium Agricultural Fund traded at a discount of .45% below its net asset value, which is worse than its one-year historical average discount of 1.87%.

Sal A. Gilbertie currently receives a manager quality ranking of 7 (0=worst, 99=best). This fund offers an average level of risk but investors looking for strong performance will be frustrated.

Data Date	Investment Rating	Net Assets ($Mil)	Price	Performance Rating/Pts	Total Return Y-T-D	Risk Rating/Pts
12-15	D-	1.50	26.47	D- / 1.0	-19.91%	C / 5.3
2014	D-	1.50	33.05	D+ / 2.4	-4.20%	C / 4.4
2013	D-	1.90	34.00	E / 0.3	-28.78%	C+ / 6.1

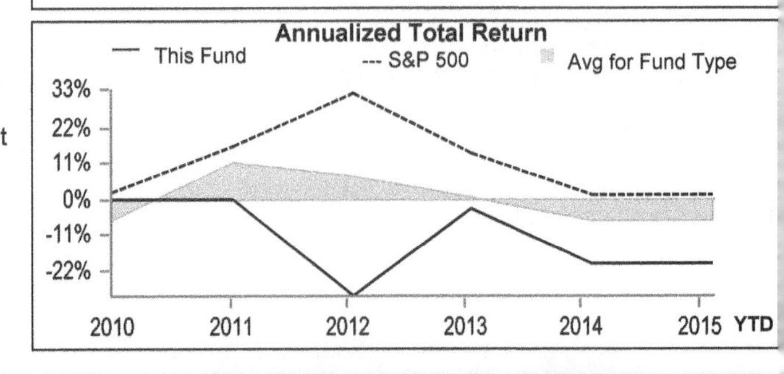

*Teucrium Corn (CORN) D- Weak

Fund Family: Teucrium Trading LLC
Fund Type: Growth
Inception Date: June 9, 2010

Major Rating Factors:
Very poor performance is the major factor driving the D- (Weak) TheStreet.com Investment Rating for *Teucrium Corn. The fund currently has a performance rating of E+ (Very Weak) based on an annualized return of -20.83% over the last three years and a total return of -19.86% year to date 2015. Factored into the performance evaluation is an expense ratio of 3.57% (high).

The fund's risk rating is currently C (Fair). It carries a beta of 0.09, meaning the fund's expected move will be 0.9% for every 10% move in the market. Volatility, as measured by both the semi-deviation and a drawdown factor, is considered average. As of December 31, 2015, *Teucrium Corn traded at a discount of .09% below its net asset value, which is better than its one-year historical average discount of .04%.

Sal A. Gilbertie currently receives a manager quality ranking of 6 (0=worst, 99=best). This fund offers an average level of risk but investors looking for strong performance will be frustrated.

Data Date	Investment Rating	Net Assets ($Mil)	Price	Performance Rating/Pts	Total Return Y-T-D	Risk Rating/Pts
12-15	D-	104.30	21.22	E+ / 0.8	-19.86%	C / 4.6
2014	E	104.30	26.64	D- / 1.2	-13.39%	D+ / 2.5
2013	D-	47.50	30.58	D- / 1.0	-28.08%	C+ / 5.6
2012	D	37.70	44.32	D / 1.6	12.25%	C+ / 6.6
2011	D+	71.30	41.98	C- / 3.2	10.47%	B- / 7.0

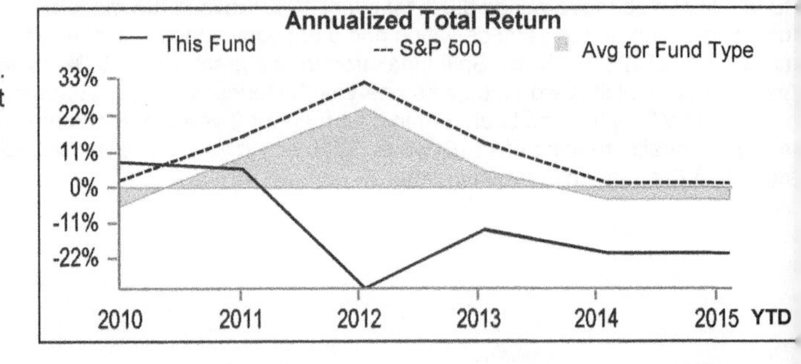

*Teucrium Soybean (SOYB) D+ Weak

Fund Family: Teucrium Trading LLC
Fund Type: Global
Inception Date: September 19, 2011

Major Rating Factors:
Disappointing performance is the major factor driving the D+ (Weak) TheStreet.com Investment Rating for *Teucrium Soybean. The fund currently has a performance rating of D (Weak) based on an annualized return of -9.59% over the last three years and a total return of -15.26% year to date 2015. Factored into the performance evaluation is an expense ratio of 3.87% (high).

The fund's risk rating is currently C+ (Fair). It carries a beta of 0.14, meaning the fund's expected move will be 1.4% for every 10% move in the market. Volatility, as measured by both the semi-deviation and a drawdown factor, is considered low. As of December 31, 2015, *Teucrium Soybean traded at a discount of .06% below its net asset value, which is in line with its one-year historical average discount of .06%.

Sal A. Gilbertie currently receives a manager quality ranking of 15 (0=worst, 99=best). This fund offers only a moderate level of risk but investors looking for strong performance are still waiting.

Data Date	Investment Rating	Net Assets ($Mil)	Price	Performance Rating/Pts	Total Return Y-T-D	Risk Rating/Pts
12-15	D+	4.30	17.33	D / 1.8	-15.26%	C+ / 6.4
2014	D-	4.30	20.76	D+ / 2.3	-8.47%	C / 4.6
2013	D+	4.00	22.81	D / 1.7	-3.28%	B- / 7.7
2012	D	6.60	24.07	D- / 1.2	10.95%	B / 8.0

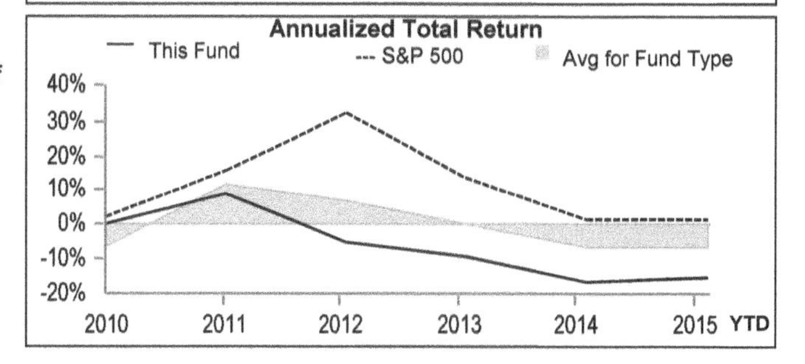

*Teucrium Sugar (CANE) D- Weak

Fund Family: Teucrium Trading LLC
Fund Type: Global
Inception Date: September 19, 2011

Major Rating Factors:
Disappointing performance is the major factor driving the D- (Weak) TheStreet.com Investment Rating for *Teucrium Sugar. The fund currently has a performance rating of D- (Weak) based on an annualized return of -16.63% over the last three years and a total return of -13.20% year to date 2015. Factored into the performance evaluation is an expense ratio of 1.88% (above average).

The fund's risk rating is currently C- (Fair). It carries a beta of 0.50, meaning the fund's expected move will be 5.0% for every 10% move in the market. Volatility, as measured by both the semi-deviation and a drawdown factor, is considered average. As of December 31, 2015, *Teucrium Sugar traded at a premium of .40% above its net asset value, which is worse than its one-year historical average premium of .16%.

Sal A. Gilbertie currently receives a manager quality ranking of 7 (0=worst, 99=best). This fund offers an average level of risk but investors looking for strong performance will be frustrated.

Data Date	Investment Rating	Net Assets ($Mil)	Price	Performance Rating/Pts	Total Return Y-T-D	Risk Rating/Pts
12-15	D-	2.60	10.06	D- / 1.5	-13.20%	C- / 3.3
2014	E	2.60	11.88	E+ / 0.7	-14.53%	C- / 3.3
2013	D-	2.50	14.05	E / 0.5	-19.93%	C+ / 5.8
2012	D-	2.20	17.84	E / 0.4	-23.01%	C+ / 6.6

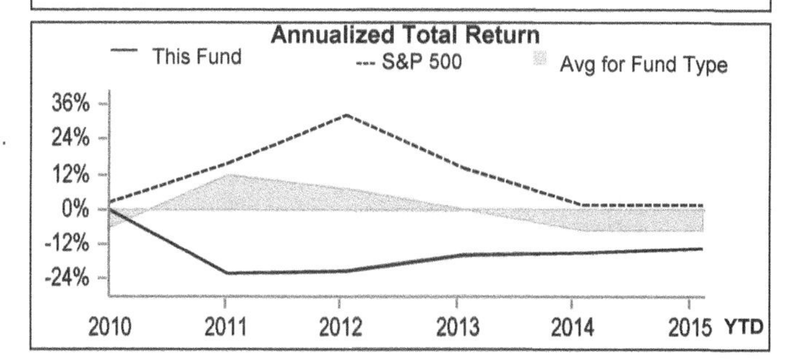

*Teucrium Wheat (WEAT) E+ Very Weak

Fund Family: Teucrium Trading LLC
Fund Type: Global
Inception Date: September 19, 2011

Major Rating Factors:
Very poor performance is the major factor driving the E+ (Very Weak) TheStreet.com Investment Rating for *Teucrium Wheat. The fund currently has a performance rating of E+ (Very Weak) based on an annualized return of -23.51% over the last three years and a total return of -27.11% year to date 2015. Factored into the performance evaluation is an expense ratio of 3.74% (high).

The fund's risk rating is currently C- (Fair). It carries a beta of 0.23, meaning the fund's expected move will be 2.3% for every 10% move in the market. Volatility, as measured by both the semi-deviation and a drawdown factor, is considered average. As of December 31, 2015, *Teucrium Wheat traded at a discount of .11% below its net asset value, which is better than its one-year historical average discount of .02%.

Sal A. Gilbertie currently receives a manager quality ranking of 4 (0=worst, 99=best). This fund offers an average level of risk but investors looking for strong performance will be frustrated.

Data Date	Investment Rating	Net Assets ($Mil)	Price	Performance Rating/Pts	Total Return Y-T-D	Risk Rating/Pts
12-15	E+	27.00	9.14	E+ / 0.6	-27.11%	C- / 4.0
2014	E	27.00	12.74	D- / 1.0	-13.65%	D+ / 2.3
2013	D-	7.00	14.75	E / 0.3	-27.77%	C+ / 6.1
2012	D	3.70	21.32	E+ / 0.6	-1.64%	B / 8.1

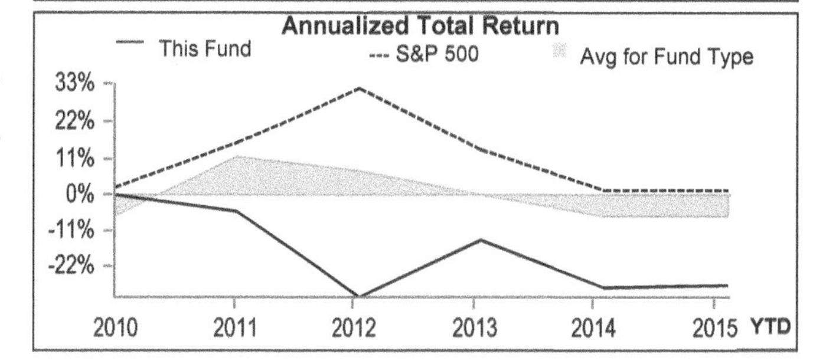

*TrimTabs Float Shrink ETF (TTFS) A+ Excellent

Fund Family: AdvisorShares Investments LLC
Fund Type: Income
Inception Date: October 5, 2011

Data Date	Investment Rating	Net Assets ($Mil)	Price	Performance Rating/Pts	Total Return Y-T-D	Risk Rating/Pts
12-15	A+	147.40	54.09	B+ / 8.9	-1.31%	B / 8.0
2014	A-	147.40	55.37	A- / 9.1	16.00%	B- / 7.2
2013	A+	98.10	48.49	A+ / 9.6	36.63%	B+ / 9.0
2012	B	11.10	33.89	C+ / 6.5	15.40%	B / 8.8

Major Rating Factors:
Strong performance is the major factor driving the A+ (Excellent) TheStreet.com Investment Rating for *TrimTabs Float Shrink ETF. The fund currently has a performance rating of B+ (Good) based on an annualized return of 15.98% over the last three years and a total return of -1.31% year to date 2015. Factored into the performance evaluation is an expense ratio of 0.99% (low).

The fund's risk rating is currently B (Good). It carries a beta of 1.04, meaning that its performance tracks fairly well with that of the overall stock market. Volatility, as measured by both the semi-deviation and a drawdown factor, is considered low. As of December 31, 2015, *TrimTabs Float Shrink ETF traded at a price exactly equal to its net asset value, which is better than its one-year historical average premium of .03%.

Theodore M. Theodore has been running the fund for 1 year and currently receives a manager quality ranking of 79 (0=worst, 99=best). If you desire only a moderate level of risk and strong performance, then this fund is an excellent option.

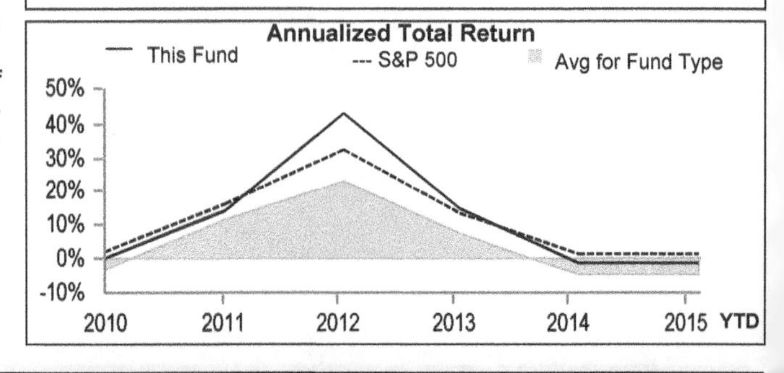

*UBS AG FI Enhanced BC Growth ETN (FBG) C+ Fair

Fund Family: UBS AG
Fund Type: Income
Inception Date: June 11, 2012

Data Date	Investment Rating	Net Assets ($Mil)	Price	Performance Rating/Pts	Total Return Y-T-D	Risk Rating/Pts
12-15	C+	129.80	59.39	A+ / 9.7	8.10%	C- / 3.7
2014	A-	129.80	55.16	A- / 9.1	22.17%	B- / 7.3
2013	B	1,063.80	45.73	A+ / 9.9	52.79%	C+ / 5.7

Major Rating Factors:
Exceptional performance is the major factor driving the C+ (Fair) TheStreet.com Investment Rating for *UBS AG FI Enhanced BC Growth ETN. The fund currently has a performance rating of A+ (Excellent) based on an annualized return of 26.20% over the last three years and a total return of 8.10% year to date 2015.

The fund's risk rating is currently C- (Fair). It carries a beta of 1.53, meaning it is expected to move 15.3% for every 10% move in the market. Volatility, as measured by both the semi-deviation and a drawdown factor, is considered average. As of December 31, 2015, *UBS AG FI Enhanced BC Growth ETN traded at a premium of .25% above its net asset value, which is worse than its one-year historical average discount of .03%.

This fund has been team managed for 4 years and currently receives a manager quality ranking of 86 (0=worst, 99=best). If you desire an average level of risk and strong performance, then this fund is a good option.

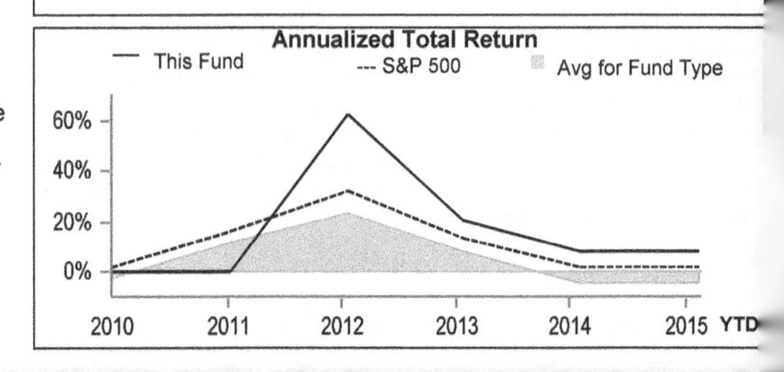

*UBS AG FI Enhanced Large Cap Gro (FBGX) C Fair

Fund Family: UBS Asset Mgmt (Americas) Inc
Fund Type: Growth
Inception Date: June 10, 2014

Data Date	Investment Rating	Net Assets ($Mil)	Price	Performance Rating/Pts	Total Return Y-T-D	Risk Rating/Pts
12-15	C	571.10	124.19	B+ / 8.6	9.83%	C- / 3.2

Major Rating Factors: Strong performance is the major factor driving the C (Fair) TheStreet.com Investment Rating for *UBS AG FI Enhanced Large Cap Gro. The fund currently has a performance rating of B+ (Good) based on an annualized return of 0.00% over the last three years and a total return of 9.83% year to date 2015.

The fund's risk rating is currently C- (Fair). It carries a beta of 0.00, meaning the fund's expected move will be 0.0% for every 10% move in the market. Volatility, as measured by both the semi-deviation and a drawdown factor, is considered average. As of December 31, 2015, *UBS AG FI Enhanced Large Cap Gro traded at a premium of .61% above its net asset value, which is worse than its one-year historical average discount of .01%.

If you desire an average level of risk and strong performance, then this fund is a good option.

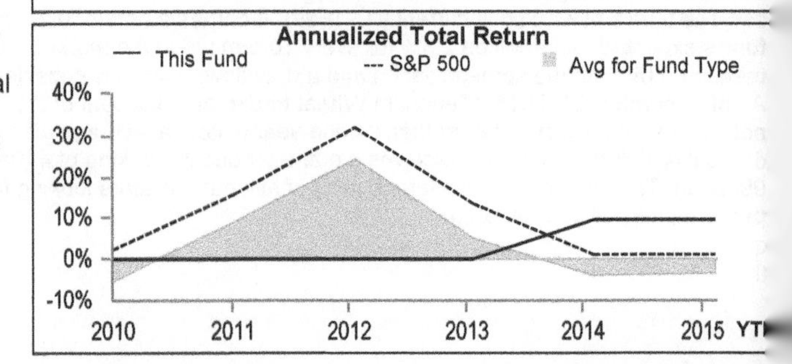

*UBS E Tracs Alerian MLP Infrast (MLPI) — E+ Very Weak

Fund Family: UBS Asset Mgmt (Americas) Inc
Fund Type: Income
Inception Date: April 1, 2010

Major Rating Factors: *UBS E Tracs Alerian MLP Infrast has adopted a very risky asset allocation strategy and currently receives an overall TheStreet.com Investment Rating of E+ (Very Weak). The fund has a high level of volatility, as measured by both semi-deviation and drawdown factors. It carries a beta of 1.08, meaning that its performance tracks fairly well with that of the overall stock market. As of December 31, 2015, *UBS E Tracs Alerian MLP Infrast traded at a premium of .23% above its net asset value, which is worse than its one-year historical average premium of .03%. Unfortunately, the high level of risk (D-, Weak) failed to pay off as investors endured poor performance.

The fund's performance rating is currently D (Weak). It has registered an annualized return of -4.28% over the last three years and is down -33.00% year to date 2015.

This fund has been team managed for 6 years and currently receives a manager quality ranking of 9 (0=worst, 99=best). If you can tolerate very high levels of risk in the hope of improved future returns, holding this fund may be an option.

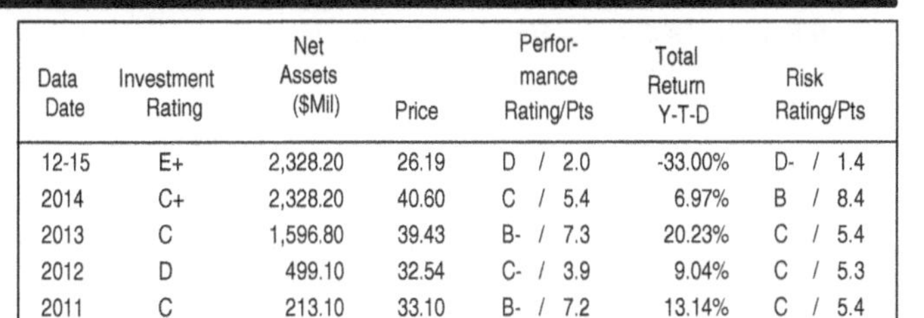

Data Date	Investment Rating	Net Assets ($Mil)	Price	Performance Rating/Pts	Total Return Y-T-D	Risk Rating/Pts
12-15	E+	2,328.20	26.19	D / 2.0	-33.00%	D- / 1.4
2014	C+	2,328.20	40.60	C / 5.4	6.97%	B / 8.4
2013	C	1,596.80	39.43	B- / 7.3	20.23%	C / 5.4
2012	D	499.10	32.54	C- / 3.9	9.04%	C / 5.3
2011	C	213.10	33.10	B- / 7.2	13.14%	C / 5.4

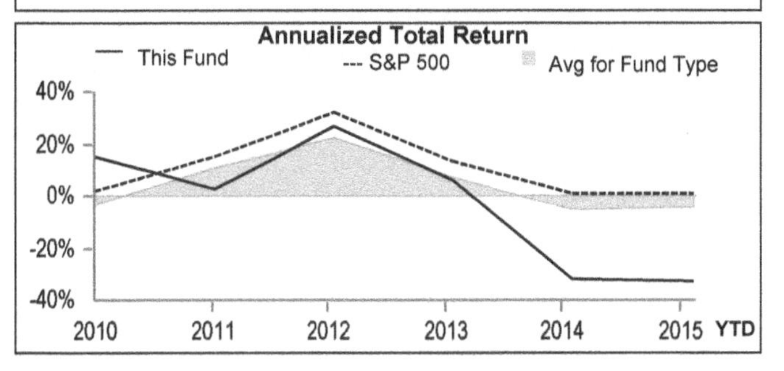

*UBS E Tracs CMCI Agriculture TR (UAG) — D- Weak

Fund Family: UBS Asset Mgmt (Americas) Inc
Fund Type: Growth
Inception Date: April 1, 2008

Major Rating Factors:
Disappointing performance is the major factor driving the D- (Weak) TheStreet.com Investment Rating for *UBS E Tracs CMCI Agriculture TR. The fund currently has a performance rating of D- (Weak) based on an annualized return of -13.53% over the last three years and a total return of -15.52% year to date 2015. Factored into the performance evaluation is an expense ratio of 0.65% (very low).

The fund's risk rating is currently C- (Fair). It carries a beta of 0.42, meaning the fund's expected move will be 4.2% for every 10% move in the market. Volatility, as measured by both the semi-deviation and a drawdown factor, is considered average. As of December 31, 2015, *UBS E Tracs CMCI Agriculture TR traded at a discount of 1.63% below its net asset value, which is better than its one-year historical average premium of .17%.

This fund has been team managed for 8 years and currently receives a manager quality ranking of 7 (0=worst, 99=best). This fund offers an average level of risk but investors looking for strong performance will be frustrated.

Data Date	Investment Rating	Net Assets ($Mil)	Price	Performance Rating/Pts	Total Return Y-T-D	Risk Rating/Pts
12-15	D-	3.43	18.08	D- / 1.4	-15.52%	C- / 3.3
2014	D-	15.30	21.98	D / 1.6	-10.65%	C / 4.4
2013	E+	3.43	24.60	D- / 1.4	-12.52%	C / 4.3
2012	D	3.43	28.82	C- / 3.2	5.69%	C / 4.5
2011	D	13.50	27.67	C- / 3.7	-8.44%	C / 4.7
2010	B	3.43	30.40	A+ / 9.8	35.17%	C- / 3.4

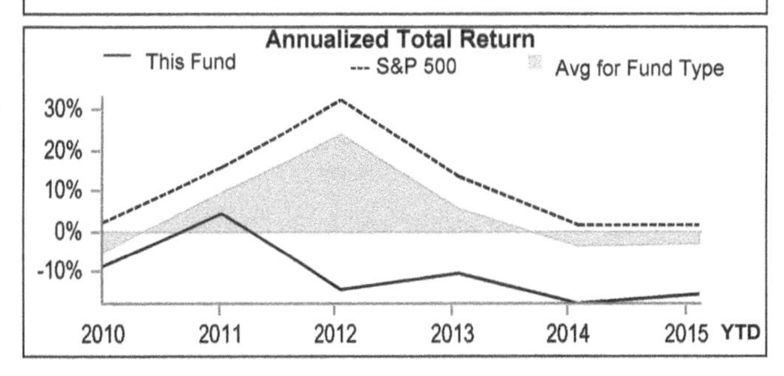

*UBS E Tracs CMCI Energy TR (UBN) — E Very Weak

Fund Family: UBS Asset Mgmt (Americas) Inc
Fund Type: Growth
Inception Date: April 1, 2008

Major Rating Factors: *UBS E Tracs CMCI Energy TR has adopted a very risky asset allocation strategy and currently receives an overall TheStreet.com Investment Rating of E (Very Weak). The fund has a high level of volatility, as measured by both semi-deviation and drawdown factors. It carries a beta of 0.43, meaning the fund's expected move will be 4.3% for every 10% move in the market. As of December 31, 2015, *UBS E Tracs CMCI Energy TR traded at a discount of 2.28% below its net asset value, which is better than its one-year historical average discount of .25%. Unfortunately, the high level of risk (D, Weak) failed to pay off as investors endured very poor performance.

The fund's performance rating is currently E (Very Weak). It has registered an annualized return of -26.68% over the last three years and is down -41.63% year to date 2015. Factored into the performance evaluation is an expense ratio of 0.65% (very low).

This fund has been team managed for 8 years and currently receives a manager quality ranking of 3 (0=worst, 99=best). If you can tolerate very high levels of risk in the hope of improved future returns, holding this fund may be an option.

Data Date	Investment Rating	Net Assets ($Mil)	Price	Performance Rating/Pts	Total Return Y-T-D	Risk Rating/Pts
12-15	E	4.37	6.00	E / 0.4	-41.63%	D / 1.8
2014	E+	6.80	10.28	E+ / 0.7	-35.14%	C- / 3.7
2013	D-	4.37	15.85	C- / 3.1	4.11%	C / 4.3
2011	D	3.10	15.45	C- / 3.2	4.70%	C / 4.6
2010	D+	4.37	15.21	C+ / 6.2	-0.59%	D / 1.9

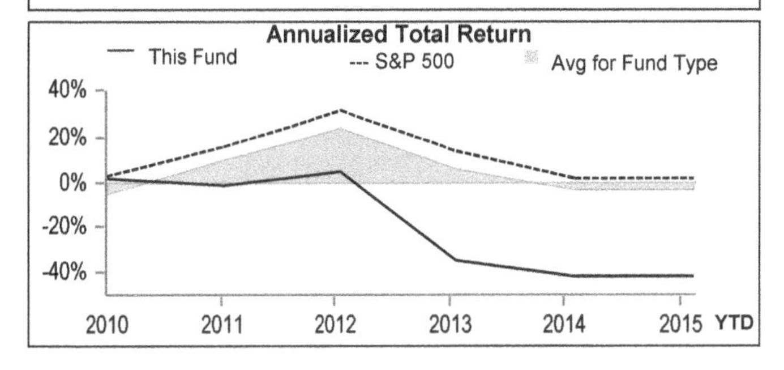

* Denotes ETF Fund

*UBS E Tracs CMCI Food Tr (FUD) D- Weak

Fund Family: UBS Asset Mgmt (Americas) Inc
Fund Type: Growth
Inception Date: April 1, 2008

Major Rating Factors:
Disappointing performance is the major factor driving the D- (Weak) TheStreet.com Investment Rating for *UBS E Tracs CMCI Food Tr. The fund currently has a performance rating of D- (Weak) based on an annualized return of -12.49% over the last three years and a total return of -16.82% year to date 2015. Factored into the performance evaluation is an expense ratio of 0.65% (very low).

The fund's risk rating is currently C- (Fair). It carries a beta of 0.29, meaning the fund's expected move will be 2.9% for every 10% move in the market. Volatility, as measured by both the semi-deviation and a drawdown factor, is considered average. As of December 31, 2015, *UBS E Tracs CMCI Food Tr traded at a discount of .32% below its net asset value, which is better than its one-year historical average premium of .07%.

This fund has been team managed for 8 years and currently receives a manager quality ranking of 9 (0=worst, 99=best). This fund offers an average level of risk but investors looking for strong performance will be frustrated.

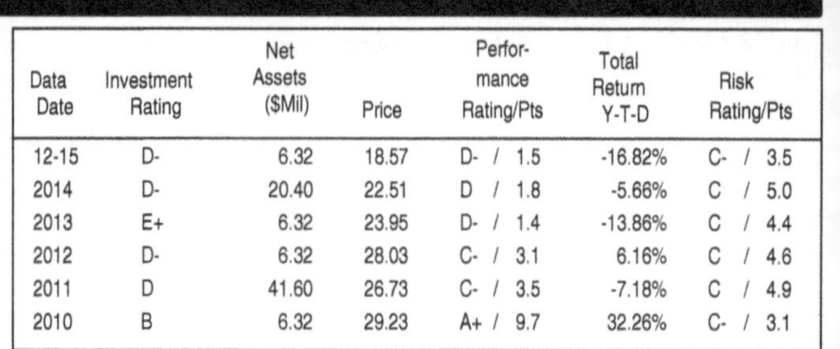

Data Date	Investment Rating	Net Assets ($Mil)	Price	Performance Rating/Pts	Total Return Y-T-D	Risk Rating/Pts
12-15	D-	6.32	18.57	D- / 1.5	-16.82%	C- / 3.5
2014	D-	20.40	22.51	D / 1.8	-5.66%	C / 5.0
2013	E+	6.32	23.95	D- / 1.4	-13.86%	C / 4.4
2012	D-	6.32	28.03	C- / 3.1	6.16%	C / 4.6
2011	D	41.60	26.73	C- / 3.5	-7.18%	C / 4.9
2010	B	6.32	29.23	A+ / 9.7	32.26%	C- / 3.1

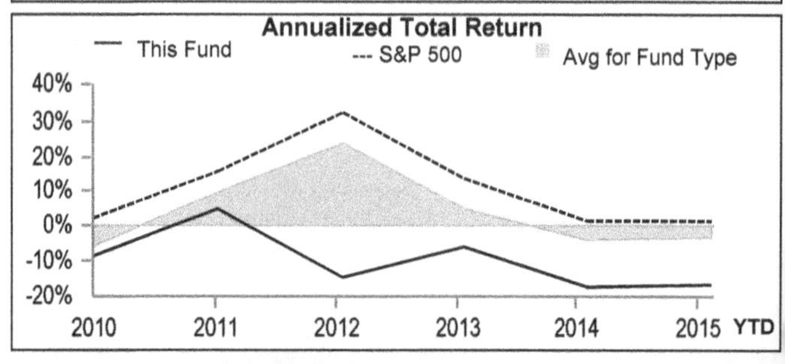

*UBS E Tracs CMCI Gold TR (UBG) E+ Very Weak

Fund Family: UBS Asset Mgmt (Americas) Inc
Fund Type: Growth
Inception Date: April 1, 2008

Major Rating Factors: *UBS E Tracs CMCI Gold TR has adopted a risky asset allocation strategy and currently receives an overall TheStreet.com Investment Rating of E+ (Very Weak). The fund has an above average level of volatility, as measured by both semi-deviation and drawdown factors. It carries a beta of 0.02, meaning the fund's expected move will be 0.2% for every 10% move in the market. As of December 31, 2015, *UBS E Tracs CMCI Gold TR traded at a discount of .22% below its net asset value, which is better than its one-year historical average discount of .04%. Unfortunately, the high level of risk (D+, Weak) failed to pay off as investors endured poor performance.

The fund's performance rating is currently D- (Weak). It has registered an annualized return of -14.77% over the last three years and is down -12.18% year to date 2015. Factored into the performance evaluation is an expense ratio of 0.30% (very low).

This fund has been team managed for 8 years and currently receives a manager quality ranking of 10 (0=worst, 99=best). If you can tolerate high levels of risk in the hope of improved future returns, holding this fund may be an option.

Data Date	Investment Rating	Net Assets ($Mil)	Price	Performance Rating/Pts	Total Return Y-T-D	Risk Rating/Pts
12-15	E+	4.56	27.15	D- / 1.3	-12.18%	D+ / 2.9
2014	D	12.30	30.67	D- / 1.3	-5.08%	C+ / 6.2
2013	E+	4.56	31.44	D- / 1.4	-26.32%	C- / 3.7
2012	D	4.56	44.34	C- / 3.7	0.11%	C / 5.0
2011	C	8.00	41.78	B- / 7.5	17.50%	C / 5.1
2010	B	4.56	38.25	A / 9.3	28.05%	C- / 3.9

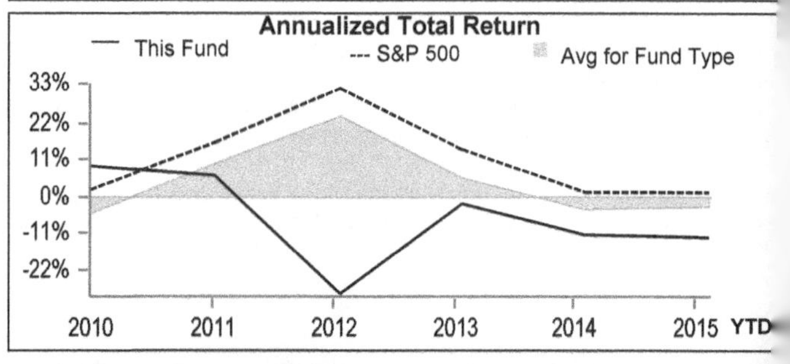

*UBS E Tracs CMCI Industrial Meta (UBM) E Very Weak

Fund Family: UBS Asset Mgmt (Americas) Inc
Fund Type: Growth
Inception Date: April 1, 2008

Major Rating Factors: *UBS E Tracs CMCI Industrial Meta has adopted a very risky asset allocation strategy and currently receives an overall TheStreet.com Investment Rating of E (Very Weak). The fund has a high level of volatility, as measured by both semi-deviation and drawdown factors. It carries a beta of 0.43, meaning the fund's expected move will be 4.3% for every 10% move in the market. As of December 31, 2015, *UBS E Tracs CMCI Industrial Meta traded at a premium of .52% above its net asset value, which is worse than its one-year historical average discount of .15%. Unfortunately, the high level of risk (D, Weak) failed to pay off as investors endured poor performance.

The fund's performance rating is currently D- (Weak). It has registered an annualized return of -16.09% over the last three years and is down -25.94% year to date 2015. Factored into the performance evaluation is an expense ratio of 0.65% (very low).

This fund has been team managed for 8 years and currently receives a manager quality ranking of 7 (0=worst, 99=best). If you can tolerate very high levels of risk in the hope of improved future returns, holding this fund may be an option.

Data Date	Investment Rating	Net Assets ($Mil)	Price	Performance Rating/Pts	Total Return Y-T-D	Risk Rating/Pts
12-15	E	3.90	11.68	D- / 1.1	-25.94%	D / 1.6
2014	D	4.50	15.77	D / 1.6	-8.79%	C+ / 6.8
2013	E+	3.90	17.46	D- / 1.1	-12.54%	C- / 3.7
2012	E+	3.90	19.77	D- / 1.2	-2.55%	C- / 4.1
2011	D	5.20	19.47	C- / 3.7	-20.04%	C / 4.5
2010	C+	3.90	25.16	A+ / 9.6	18.46%	D+ / 2.4

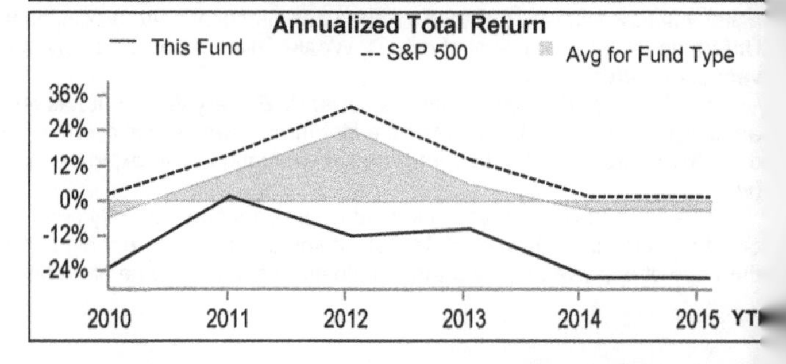

* Denotes ETF Fund

*UBS E Tracs CMCI Livestock Tr (UBC) D Weak

Fund Family: UBS Asset Mgmt (Americas) Inc
Fund Type: Growth
Inception Date: April 1, 2008

Data Date	Investment Rating	Net Assets ($Mil)	Price	Perfor-mance Rating/Pts	Total Return Y-T-D	Risk Rating/Pts
12-15	D	7.84	18.73	D+ / 2.7	-21.40%	C- / 4.0
2014	C	5.80	23.64	C- / 4.0	21.04%	B / 8.3
2013	D-	7.84	19.53	D / 2.2	-1.81%	C / 4.7
2012	D-	7.84	19.68	D- / 1.2	-8.20%	C / 4.8
2011	D-	5.00	21.09	D / 1.8	-0.62%	C / 4.6
2010	C+	7.84	21.14	B+ / 8.6	16.60%	C- / 3.1

Major Rating Factors:
Disappointing performance is the major factor driving the D (Weak) TheStreet.com Investment Rating for *UBS E Tracs CMCI Livestock Tr. The fund currently has a performance rating of D+ (Weak) based on an annualized return of -1.98% over the last three years and a total return of -21.40% year to date 2015. Factored into the performance evaluation is an expense ratio of 0.65% (very low).

The fund's risk rating is currently C- (Fair). It carries a beta of 0.23, meaning the fund's expected move will be 2.3% for every 10% move in the market. Volatility, as measured by both the semi-deviation and a drawdown factor, is considered average. As of December 31, 2015, *UBS E Tracs CMCI Livestock Tr traded at a discount of .64% below its net asset value, which is better than its one-year historical average premium of .09%.

This fund has been team managed for 8 years and currently receives a manager quality ranking of 31 (0=worst, 99=best). This fund offers an average level of risk but investors looking for strong performance will be frustrated.

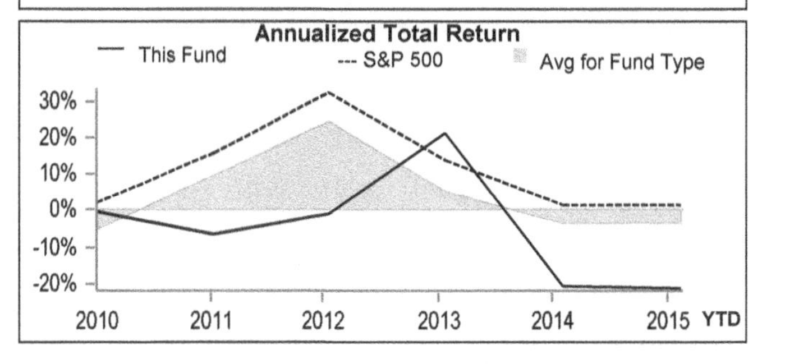

*UBS E Tracs CMCI Silver TR (USV) E- Very Weak

Fund Family: UBS Asset Mgmt (Americas) Inc
Fund Type: Growth
Inception Date: April 1, 2008

Data Date	Investment Rating	Net Assets ($Mil)	Price	Perfor-mance Rating/Pts	Total Return Y-T-D	Risk Rating/Pts
12-15	E-	3.74	18.71	E+ / 0.8	-11.62%	E / 0.5
2014	E+	9.30	21.05	E+ / 0.6	-24.06%	C- / 3.8
2013	E-	3.74	26.77	E+ / 0.8	-34.41%	D / 2.1
2012	D	3.74	41.96	C / 5.5	0.86%	C- / 3.0
2011	C	6.10	39.02	B+ / 8.7	1.03%	C- / 3.3
2010	B-	3.74	44.05	A+ / 9.9	80.74%	D+ / 2.7

Major Rating Factors: *UBS E Tracs CMCI Silver TR has adopted a very risky asset allocation strategy and currently receives an overall TheStreet.com Investment Rating of E- (Very Weak). The fund has a high level of volatility, as measured by both semi-deviation and drawdown factors. It carries a beta of 0.03, meaning the fund's expected move will be 0.3% for every 10% move in the market. As of December 31, 2015, *UBS E Tracs CMCI Silver TR traded at a premium of 3.48% above its net asset value, which is worse than its one-year historical average premium of .10%. Unfortunately, the high level of risk (E, Very Weak) failed to pay off as investors endured very poor performance.

The fund's performance rating is currently E+ (Very Weak). It has registered an annualized return of -23.78% over the last three years and is down -11.62% year to date 2015. Factored into the performance evaluation is an expense ratio of 0.40% (very low).

This fund has been team managed for 8 years and currently receives a manager quality ranking of 5 (0=worst, 99=best). If you can tolerate very high levels of risk in the hope of improved future returns, holding this fund may be an option.

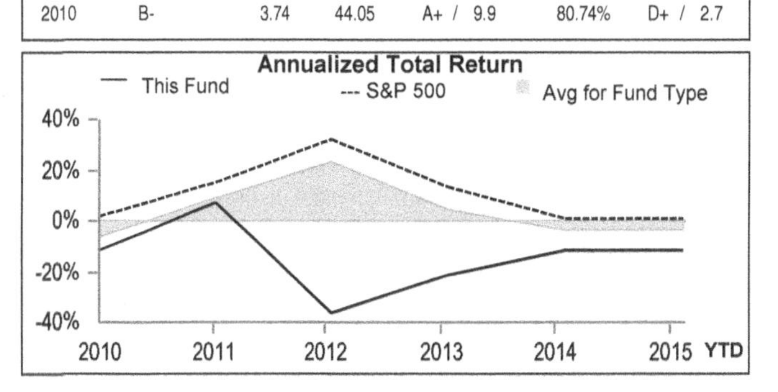

*UBS E Tracs CMCI Total Return (UCI) E+ Very Weak

Fund Family: UBS Asset Mgmt (Americas) Inc
Fund Type: Growth
Inception Date: April 1, 2008

Data Date	Investment Rating	Net Assets ($Mil)	Price	Perfor-mance Rating/Pts	Total Return Y-T-D	Risk Rating/Pts
12-15	E+	11.63	12.07	E+ / 0.9	-25.67%	D+ / 2.9
2014	D-	152.20	16.36	D- / 1.1	-18.65%	C / 5.0
2013	D-	11.63	20.46	D / 1.7	-8.34%	C / 4.6
2012	D-	11.63	22.06	D / 2.0	0.92%	C / 4.6
2011	D	137.50	21.56	C- / 3.9	-5.06%	C / 4.9
2010	C+	11.63	23.61	A / 9.4	18.61%	D+ / 2.5

Major Rating Factors: *UBS E Tracs CMCI Total Return has adopted a risky asset allocation strategy and currently receives an overall TheStreet.com Investment Rating of E+ (Very Weak). The fund has an above average level of volatility, as measured by both semi-deviation and drawdown factors. It carries a beta of 0.46, meaning the fund's expected move will be 4.6% for every 10% move in the market. As of December 31, 2015, *UBS E Tracs CMCI Total Return traded at a discount of .25% below its net asset value. Unfortunately, the high level of risk (D+, Weak) failed to pay off as investors endured very poor performance.

The fund's performance rating is currently E+ (Very Weak). It has registered an annualized return of -18.06% over the last three years and is down -25.67% year to date 2015. Factored into the performance evaluation is an expense ratio of 0.65% (very low).

This fund has been team managed for 8 years and currently receives a manager quality ranking of 5 (0=worst, 99=best). If you can tolerate high levels of risk in the hope of improved future returns, holding this fund may be an option.

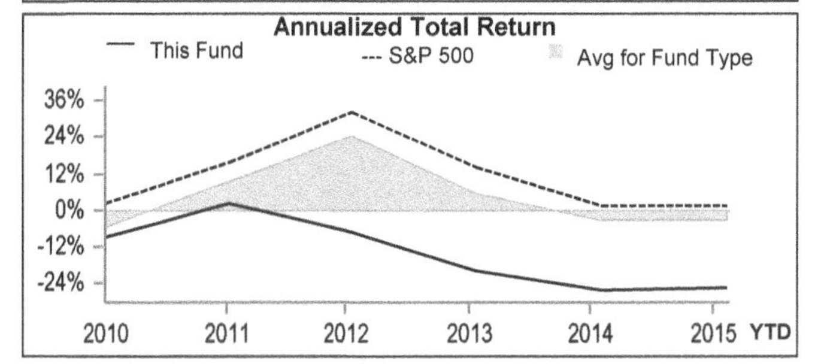

*UBS E Tracs DJ-UBS Comm Idx Tot (DJCI) E Very Weak

Fund Family: UBS Asset Mgmt (Americas) Inc
Fund Type: Income
Inception Date: October 29, 2009

Data Date	Investment Rating	Net Assets ($Mil)	Price	Performance Rating/Pts	Total Return Y-T-D	Risk Rating/Pts
12-15	E	118.60	14.22	E+ / 0.9	-25.59%	D / 1.7
2014	D-	118.60	19.25	D- / 1.0	-17.17%	C / 4.9
2013	E+	63.10	23.31	D- / 1.3	-9.84%	C- / 4.1
2012	E+	70.30	26.03	D- / 1.2	-2.48%	C- / 4.2
2011	E+	22.00	26.45	D- / 1.2	-10.40%	C / 4.7
2010	B+	13.80	30.60	A / 9.3	14.86%	C / 4.7

Major Rating Factors: *UBS E Tracs DJ-UBS Comm Idx Tot has adopted a very risky asset allocation strategy and currently receives an overall TheStreet.com Investment Rating of E (Very Weak). The fund has a high level of volatility, as measured by both semi-deviation and drawdown factors. It carries a beta of 0.33, meaning the fund's expected move will be 3.3% for every 10% move in the market. As of December 31, 2015, *UBS E Tracs DJ-UBS Comm Idx Tot traded at a premium of .07% above its net asset value, which is worse than its one-year historical average premium of .01%. Unfortunately, the high level of risk (D, Weak) failed to pay off as investors endured very poor performance.

The fund's performance rating is currently E+ (Very Weak). It has registered an annualized return of -17.98% over the last three years and is down -25.59% year to date 2015.

This fund has been team managed for 7 years and currently receives a manager quality ranking of 6 (0=worst, 99=best). If you can tolerate very high levels of risk in the hope of improved future returns, holding this fund may be an option.

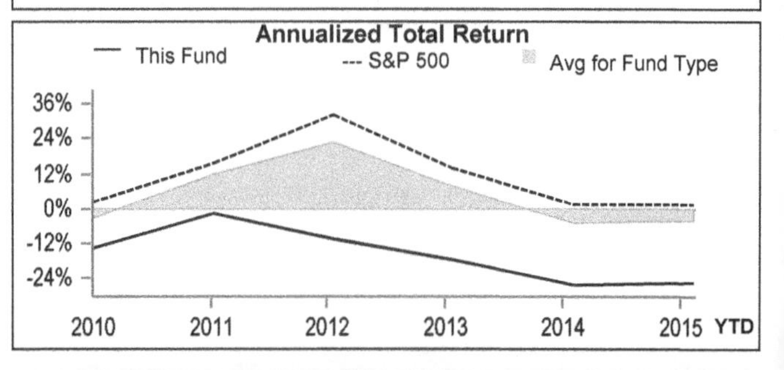

*UBS E Tracs Long Platinum ETN (PTM) E Very Weak

Fund Family: UBS Asset Mgmt (Americas) Inc
Fund Type: Growth
Inception Date: May 8, 2008

Data Date	Investment Rating	Net Assets ($Mil)	Price	Performance Rating/Pts	Total Return Y-T-D	Risk Rating/Pts
12-15	E	66.49	9.44	E+ / 0.9	-27.60%	D+ / 2.5
2014	E+	28.70	13.27	D- / 1.4	-15.91%	C- / 3.9
2013	E+	66.49	15.28	D- / 1.3	-11.55%	C- / 3.8
2012	E+	66.49	17.59	D- / 1.3	-0.64%	C- / 4.0
2011	D-	32.20	16.12	D+ / 2.5	-19.61%	C- / 4.1
2010	C	66.49	20.92	B+ / 8.7	13.70%	D+ / 2.5

Major Rating Factors: *UBS E Tracs Long Platinum ETN has adopted a risky asset allocation strategy and currently receives an overall TheStreet.com Investment Rating of E (Very Weak). The fund has an above average level of volatility, as measured by both semi-deviation and drawdown factors. It carries a beta of 0.40, meaning the fund's expected move will be 4.0% for every 10% move in the market. As of December 31, 2015, *UBS E Tracs Long Platinum ETN traded at a discount of .53% below its net asset value, which is better than its one-year historical average premium of .07%. Unfortunately, the high level of risk (D+, Weak) failed to pay off as investors endured very poor performance.

The fund's performance rating is currently E+ (Very Weak). It has registered an annualized return of -19.11% over the last three years and is down -27.60% year to date 2015. Factored into the performance evaluation is an expense ratio of 0.65% (very low).

This fund has been team managed for 8 years and currently receives a manager quality ranking of 5 (0=worst, 99=best). If you can tolerate high levels of risk in the hope of improved future returns, holding this fund may be an option.

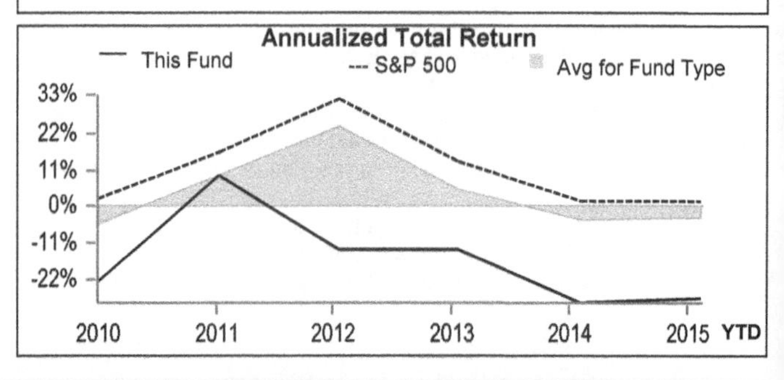

*UBS E-TRACS 1xMo Sht Alerian MLP (MLPS) C- Fair

Fund Family: UBS Asset Mgmt (Americas) Inc
Fund Type: Growth
Inception Date: September 28, 2010

Data Date	Investment Rating	Net Assets ($Mil)	Price	Performance Rating/Pts	Total Return Y-T-D	Risk Rating/Pts
12-15	C-	4.00	15.30	B- / 7.0	42.19%	C- / 3.6
2014	D	4.00	10.90	D / 2.2	-13.08%	C+ / 6.2

Major Rating Factors: Strong performance is the major factor driving the C- (Fair) TheStreet.com Investment Rating for *UBS E-TRACS 1xMo Sht Alerian MLP. The fund currently has a performance rating of B- (Good) based on an annualized return of -1.44% over the last three years and a total return of 42.19% year to date 2015.

The fund's risk rating is currently C- (Fair). It carries a beta of -1.21, meaning the fund's expected move will be -12.1% for every 10% move in the market. Volatility, as measured by both the semi-deviation and a drawdown factor, is considered average. As of December 31, 2015, *UBS E-TRACS 1xMo Sht Alerian MLP traded at a premium of 4.08% above its net asset value, which is worse than its one-year historical average premium of .41%.

If you desire an average level of risk and strong performance, then this fund is a good option.

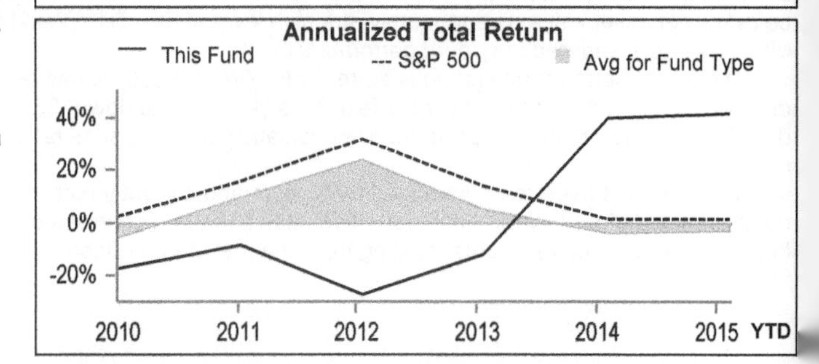

*UBS E-TRACS 2x Levd Lng Alerian (MLPL) E Very Weak

Fund Family: UBS Asset Mgmt (Americas) Inc
Fund Type: Energy/Natural Resources
Inception Date: July 7, 2010

Major Rating Factors: *UBS E-TRACS 2x Levd Lng Alerian has adopted a very risky asset allocation strategy and currently receives an overall TheStreet.com Investment Rating of E (Very Weak). The fund has a high level of volatility, as measured by both semi-deviation and drawdown factors. It carries a beta of 1.33, meaning it is expected to move 13.3% for every 10% move in the market. As of December 31, 2015, *UBS E -TRACS 2x Levd Lng Alerian traded at a price exactly equal to its net asset value, which is better than its one-year historical average premium of .42%. Unfortunately, the high level of risk (D-, Weak) failed to pay off as investors endured very poor performance.

The fund's performance rating is currently E+ (Very Weak). It has registered an annualized return of -10.22% over the last three years and is down -57.47% year to date 2015.

This fund has been team managed for 6 years and currently receives a manager quality ranking of 47 (0=worst, 99=best). If you can tolerate very high levels of risk in the hope of improved future returns, holding this fund may be an option.

Data Date	Investment Rating	Net Assets ($Mil)	Price	Performance Rating/Pts	Total Return Y-T-D	Risk Rating/Pts
12-15	E	312.00	22.16	E+ / 0.9	-57.47%	D- / 1.1
2014	B	312.00	57.50	B / 8.2	14.94%	C+ / 6.8
2013	C+	225.00	56.35	A / 9.4	42.26%	C / 4.7
2012	C+	127.50	38.55	B+ / 8.8	19.74%	C / 4.6
2011	B-	93.90	40.70	A+ / 9.8	23.74%	C / 4.8

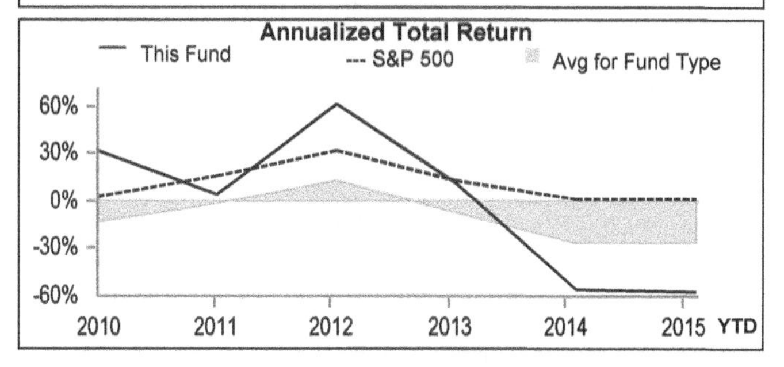

*UBS E-TRACS 2x Levd Long WF BDC (BDCL) E+ Very Weak

Fund Family: UBS Asset Mgmt (Americas) Inc
Fund Type: Growth
Inception Date: May 25, 2011

Major Rating Factors: *UBS E-TRACS 2x Levd Long WF BDC has adopted a very risky asset allocation strategy and currently receives an overall TheStreet.com Investment Rating of E+ (Very Weak). The fund has a high level of volatility, as measured by both semi-deviation and drawdown factors. It carries a beta of 1.38, meaning it is expected to move 13.8% for every 10% move in the market. As of December 31, 2015, *UBS E-TRACS 2x Levd Long WF BDC traded at a premium of .88% above its net asset value, which is worse than its one-year historical average discount of .01%. Unfortunately, the high level of risk (D-, Weak) failed to pay off as investors endured poor performance.

The fund's performance rating is currently D+ (Weak). It has registered an annualized return of -3.57% over the last three years and is down -11.76% year to date 2015.

This fund has been team managed for 5 years and currently receives a manager quality ranking of 8 (0=worst, 99=best). If you can tolerate very high levels of risk in the hope of improved future returns, holding this fund may be an option.

Data Date	Investment Rating	Net Assets ($Mil)	Price	Performance Rating/Pts	Total Return Y-T-D	Risk Rating/Pts
12-15	E+	221.50	15.98	D+ / 2.8	-11.76%	D- / 1.1
2014	C	221.50	21.43	C+ / 6.5	-18.96%	C+ / 6.3
2013	C+	151.90	29.80	A / 9.4	24.25%	C / 4.3
2012	C+	73.60	26.06	A+ / 9.9	60.83%	C- / 4.2

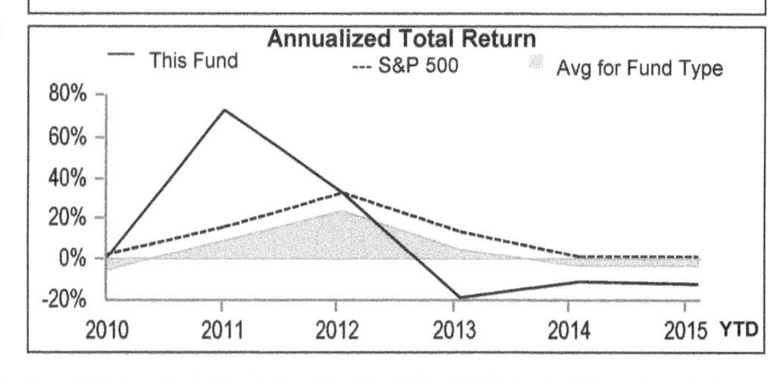

*UBS E-TRACS Alerian MLP Index ET (AMU) E+ Very Weak

Fund Family: UBS Asset Mgmt (Americas) Inc
Fund Type: Energy/Natural Resources
Inception Date: July 17, 2012

Major Rating Factors: *UBS E-TRACS Alerian MLP Index ET has adopted a risky asset allocation strategy and currently receives an overall TheStreet.com Investment Rating of E+ (Very Weak). The fund has an above average level of volatility, as measured by both semi-deviation and drawdown factors. It carries a beta of 0.70, meaning the fund's expected move will be 7.0% for every 10% move in the market. As of December 31, 2015, *UBS E-TRACS Alerian MLP Index ET traded at a discount of .11% below its net asset value. Unfortunately, the high level of risk (D+, Weak) failed to pay off as investors endured poor performance.

The fund's performance rating is currently D (Weak). It has registered an annualized return of -5.59% over the last three years and is down -34.27% year to date 2015.

This fund has been team managed for 4 years and currently receives a manager quality ranking of 56 (0=worst, 99=best). If you can tolerate high levels of risk in the hope of improved future returns, holding this fund may be an option.

Data Date	Investment Rating	Net Assets ($Mil)	Price	Performance Rating/Pts	Total Return Y-T-D	Risk Rating/Pts
12-15	E+	354.20	18.22	D / 1.7	-34.27%	D+ / 2.8
2014	D+	354.20	29.00	D / 1.9	5.56%	B / 8.2
2013	C+	214.40	29.11	B- / 7.5	18.81%	C+ / 5.7

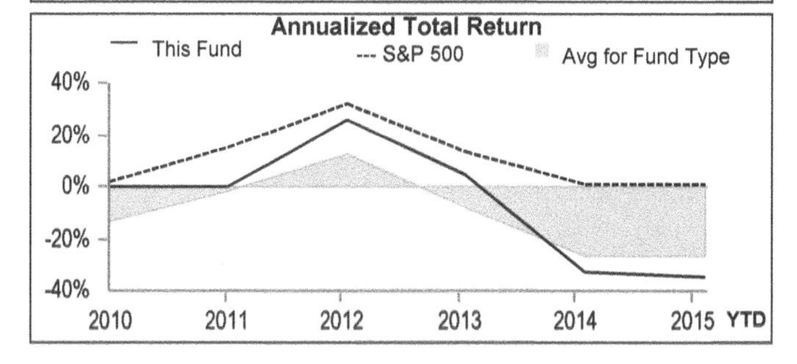

*UBS E-TRACS Alerian Nat Gas MLP (MLPG) E+ Very Weak

Fund Family: UBS Asset Mgmt (Americas) Inc
Fund Type: Energy/Natural Resources
Inception Date: July 14, 2010

Major Rating Factors: *UBS E-TRACS Alerian Nat Gas MLP has adopted a very risky asset allocation strategy and currently receives an overall TheStreet.com Investment Rating of E+ (Very Weak). The fund has a high level of volatility, as measured by both semi-deviation and drawdown factors. It carries a beta of 0.71, meaning the fund's expected move will be 7.1% for every 10% move in the market. As of December 31, 2015, *UBS E-TRACS Alerian Nat Gas MLP traded at a premium of .48% above its net asset value, which is worse than its one-year historical average discount of .05%. Unfortunately, the high level of risk (D-, Weak) failed to pay off as investors endured poor performance.

The fund's performance rating is currently D (Weak). It has registered an annualized return of -4.06% over the last three years and is down -32.59% year to date 2015.

This fund has been team managed for 6 years and currently receives a manager quality ranking of 71 (0=worst, 99=best). If you can tolerate very high levels of risk in the hope of improved future returns, holding this fund may be an option.

Data Date	Investment Rating	Net Assets ($Mil)	Price	Performance Rating/Pts	Total Return Y-T-D	Risk Rating/Pts
12-15	E+	37.80	22.96	D / 2.1	-32.59%	D- / 1.3
2014	C	37.80	35.69	C / 4.7	0.79%	B / 8.0
2013	C	33.30	37.06	B- / 7.5	28.17%	C / 5.1
2012	D-	25.70	28.56	D+ / 2.6	5.17%	C / 5.1
2011	D+	14.90	29.71	C / 5.1	8.04%	C / 5.2

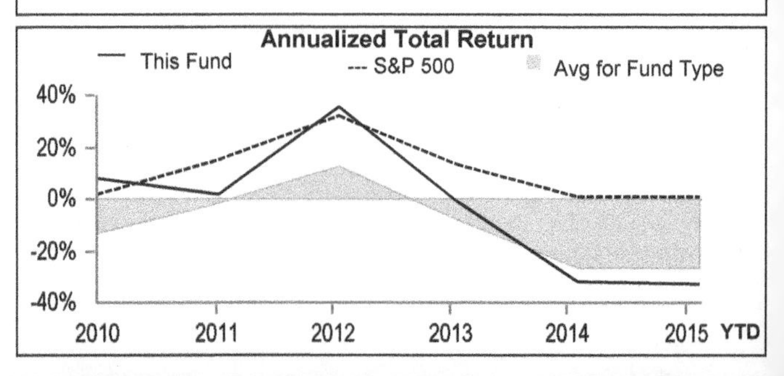

*UBS E-TRACS Daily Long-Sht VIX E (XVIX) D- Weak

Fund Family: UBS Asset Mgmt (Americas) Inc
Fund Type: Growth
Inception Date: November 30, 2010

Major Rating Factors:
Disappointing performance is the major factor driving the D- (Weak) TheStreet.com Investment Rating for *UBS E-TRACS Daily Long-Sht VIX E. The fund currently has a performance rating of D+ (Weak) based on an annualized return of -6.03% over the last three years and a total return of -0.83% year to date 2015.

The fund's risk rating is currently C- (Fair). It carries a beta of 0.20, meaning the fund's expected move will be 2.0% for every 10% move in the market. Volatility, as measured by both the semi-deviation and a drawdown factor, is considered average. As of December 31, 2015, *UBS E-TRACS Daily Long-Sht VIX E traded at a premium of 1.72% above its net asset value, which is worse than its one-year historical average discount of .20%.

This fund offers an average level of risk but investors looking for strong performance will be frustrated.

Data Date	Investment Rating	Net Assets ($Mil)	Price	Performance Rating/Pts	Total Return Y-T-D	Risk Rating/Pts
12-15	D-	0.00	15.95	D+ / 2.7	-0.83%	C- / 3.7

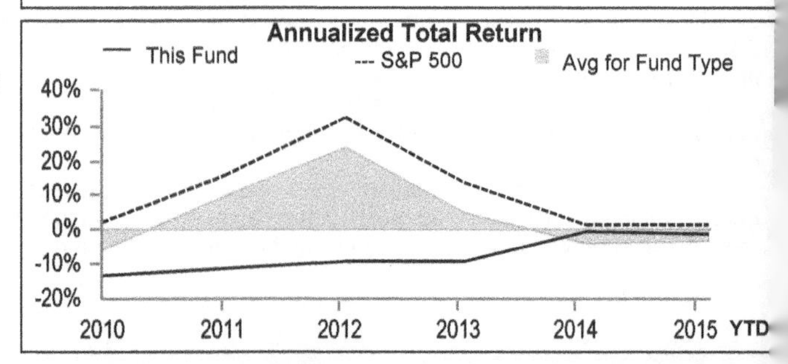

*UBS E-TRACS Diversified Hi Inc E (DVHI) D- Weak

Fund Family: UBS Asset Mgmt (Americas) Inc
Fund Type: Income
Inception Date: September 19, 2013

Major Rating Factors:
Disappointing performance is the major factor driving the D- (Weak) TheStreet.com Investment Rating for *UBS E-TRACS Diversified Hi Inc E. The fund currently has a performance rating of D- (Weak) based on an annualized return of 0.00% over the last three years and a total return of -15.08% year to date 2015.

The fund's risk rating is currently C (Fair). It carries a beta of 0.00, meaning the fund's expected move will be 0.0% for every 10% move in the market. Volatility, as measured by both the semi-deviation and a drawdown factor, is considered average. As of December 31, 2015, *UBS E-TRACS Diversified Hi Inc E traded at a discount of .62% below its net asset value, which is better than its one-year historical average premium of .05%.

This fund offers an average level of risk but investors looking for strong performance will be frustrated.

Data Date	Investment Rating	Net Assets ($Mil)	Price	Performance Rating/Pts	Total Return Y-T-D	Risk Rating/Pts
12-15	D-	25.90	20.73	D- / 1.5	-15.08%	C / 4.5
2014	D-	25.90	24.36	D / 2.2	2.27%	C / 4.7

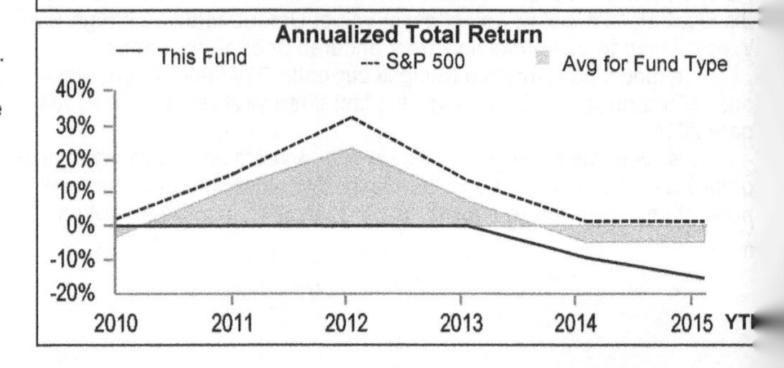

*UBS E-TRACS Mnth Pay 2xL DJ SDI (DVYL) C Fair

Fund Family: UBS Asset Mgmt (Americas) Inc
Fund Type: Income
Inception Date: May 22, 2012

Major Rating Factors:
Exceptional performance is the major factor driving the C (Fair) TheStreet.com Investment Rating for *UBS E-TRACS Mnth Pay 2xL DJ SDI. The fund currently has a performance rating of A+ (Excellent) based on an annualized return of 24.00% over the last three years and a total return of -3.65% year to date 2015.

The fund's risk rating is currently C- (Fair). It carries a beta of 1.58, meaning it is expected to move 15.8% for every 10% move in the market. Volatility, as measured by both the semi-deviation and a drawdown factor, is considered average. As of December 31, 2015, *UBS E-TRACS Mnth Pay 2xL DJ SDI traded at a premium of .27% above its net asset value, which is worse than its one-year historical average discount of .09%.

This fund has been team managed for 4 years and currently receives a manager quality ranking of 77 (0=worst, 99=best). If you desire an average level of risk and strong performance, then this fund is a good option.

Data Date	Investment Rating	Net Assets ($Mil)	Price	Performance Rating/Pts	Total Return Y-T-D	Risk Rating/Pts
12-15	C	17.60	44.78	A+ / 9.6	-3.65%	C- / 3.1
2014	A+	17.60	50.55	A+ / 9.6	32.20%	B / 8.4
2013	B	16.70	41.72	A+ / 9.8	51.31%	C / 5.4

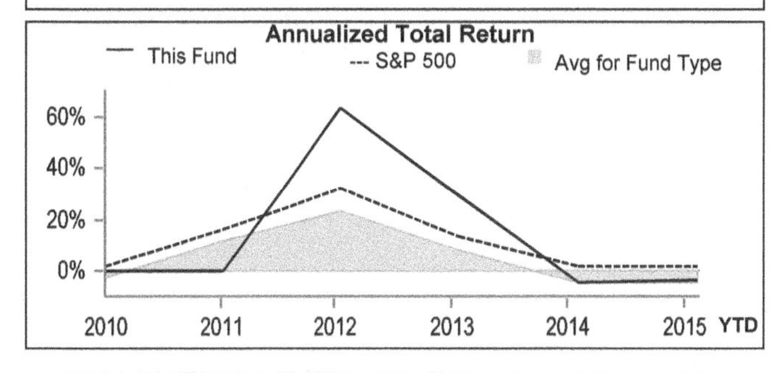

*UBS E-TRACS Mnth Pay 2xLev CE (CEFL) E+ Very Weak

Fund Family: UBS Asset Mgmt (Americas) Inc
Fund Type: Growth
Inception Date: December 10, 2013

Major Rating Factors: *UBS E-TRACS Mnth Pay 2xLev CE has adopted a risky asset allocation strategy and currently receives an overall TheStreet.com Investment Rating of E+ (Very Weak). The fund has an above average level of volatility, as measured by both semi-deviation and drawdown factors. It carries a beta of 0.00, meaning the fund's expected move will be 0.0% for every 10% move in the market. As of December 31, 2015, *UBS E-TRACS Mnth Pay 2xLev CE traded at a discount of 1.35% below its net asset value, which is better than its one-year historical average premium of .05%. Unfortunately, the high level of risk (D+, Weak) failed to pay off as investors endured poor performance.

The fund's performance rating is currently D- (Weak). It has registered an annualized return of 0.00% over the last three years but is down -16.24% year to date 2015.

If you can tolerate high levels of risk in the hope of improved future returns, holding this fund may be an option.

Data Date	Investment Rating	Net Assets ($Mil)	Price	Performance Rating/Pts	Total Return Y-T-D	Risk Rating/Pts
12-15	E+	183.90	15.35	D- / 1.2	-16.24%	D+ / 2.9
2014	E+	183.90	23.34	D / 1.6	2.85%	C- / 3.3

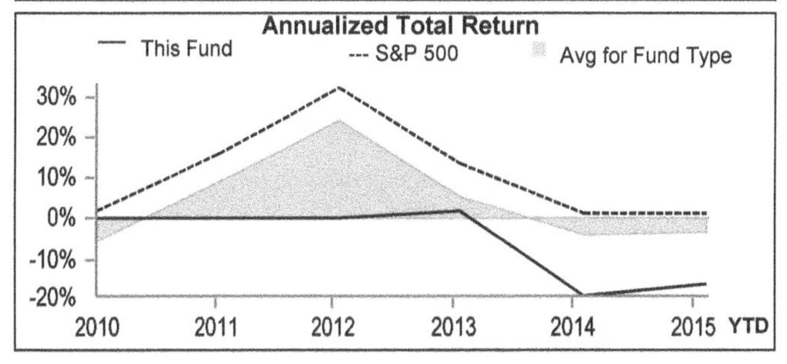

*UBS E-TRACS Mnth Pay 2xLev Dvs H (DVHL) E Very Weak

Fund Family: UBS Asset Mgmt (Americas) Inc
Fund Type: Global
Inception Date: November 13, 2013

Major Rating Factors: *UBS E-TRACS Mnth Pay 2xLev Dvs H has adopted a very risky asset allocation strategy and currently receives an overall TheStreet.com Investment Rating of E (Very Weak). The fund has a high level of volatility, as measured by both semi-deviation and drawdown factors. It carries a beta of 0.00, meaning the fund's expected move will be 0.0% for every 10% move in the market. As of December 31, 2015, *UBS E-TRACS Mnth Pay 2xLev Dvs H traded at a premium of .30% above its net asset value, which is worse than its one-year historical average premium of .06%. Unfortunately, the high level of risk (D, Weak) failed to pay off as investors endured poor performance.

The fund's performance rating is currently D- (Weak). It has registered an annualized return of 0.00% over the last three years but is down -16.87% year to date 2015.

This is team managed and currently receives a manager quality ranking of 8 (0=worst, 99=best). If you can tolerate very high levels of risk in the hope of improved future returns, holding this fund may be an option.

Data Date	Investment Rating	Net Assets ($Mil)	Price	Performance Rating/Pts	Total Return Y-T-D	Risk Rating/Pts
12-15	E	0.00	16.91	D- / 1.0	-16.87%	D / 2.2

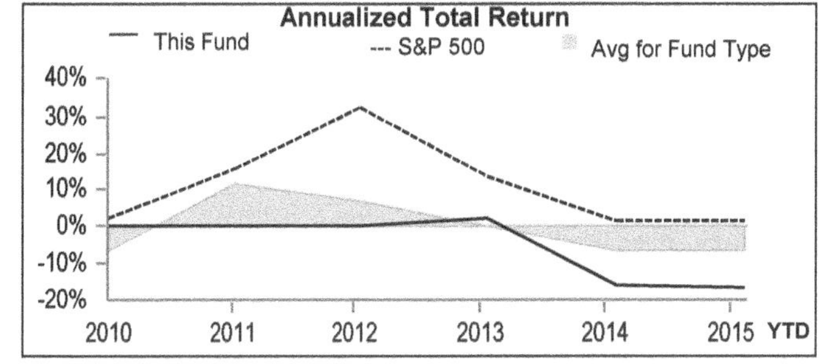

*UBS E-TRACS MnthPay 2xL S&P Div (SDYL) C Fair

Fund Family: UBS Asset Mgmt (Americas) Inc
Fund Type: Income
Inception Date: May 22, 2012

Major Rating Factors:
Exceptional performance is the major factor driving the C (Fair) TheStreet.com Investment Rating for *UBS E-TRACS MnthPay 2xL S&P Div. The fund currently has a performance rating of A+ (Excellent) based on an annualized return of 26.09% over the last three years and a total return of 0.04% year to date 2015.

The fund's risk rating is currently C- (Fair). It carries a beta of 1.84, meaning it is expected to move 18.4% for every 10% move in the market. Volatility, as measured by both the semi-deviation and a drawdown factor, is considered average. As of December 31, 2015, *UBS E-TRACS MnthPay 2xL S&P Div traded at a premium of 3.25% above its net asset value, which is worse than its one-year historical average discount of .01%.

This fund has been team managed for 4 years and currently receives a manager quality ranking of 61 (0=worst, 99=best). If you desire an average level of risk and strong performance, then this fund is a good option.

Data Date	Investment Rating	Net Assets ($Mil)	Price	Performance Rating/Pts	Total Return Y-T-D	Risk Rating/Pts
12-15	C	19.20	52.45	A+ / 9.7	0.04%	C- / 3.0
2014	A-	19.20	56.45	A+ / 9.7	32.45%	C+ / 6.6
2013	B	18.20	45.70	A+ / 9.8	53.85%	C / 5.4

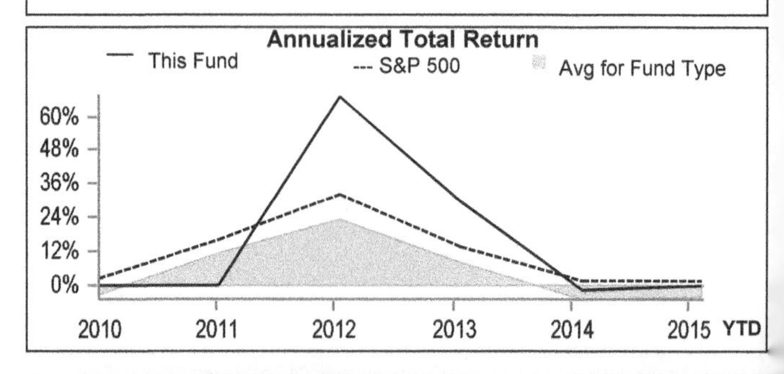

*UBS E-TRACS Mo Pay 2xLevd WF MLP (LMLP) E Very Weak

Fund Family: UBS Asset Mgmt (Americas) Inc
Fund Type: Growth
Inception Date: June 24, 2014

Major Rating Factors: *UBS E-TRACS Mo Pay 2xLevd WF MLP has adopted a risky asset allocation strategy and currently receives an overall TheStreet.com Investment Rating of E (Very Weak). The fund has an above average level of volatility, as measured by both semi-deviation and drawdown factors. It carries a beta of 0.00, meaning the fund's expected move will be 0.0% for every 10% move in the market. As of December 31, 2015, *UBS E-TRACS Mo Pay 2xLevd WF MLP traded at a discount of .16% below its net asset value, which is better than its one-year historical average premium of .01%. Unfortunately, the high level of risk (D+, Weak) failed to pay off as investors endured very poor performance.

The fund's performance rating is currently E- (Very Weak). It has registered an annualized return of 0.00% over the last three years but is down -33.93% year to date 2015.

If you can tolerate high levels of risk in the hope of improved future returns, holding this fund may be an option.

Data Date	Investment Rating	Net Assets ($Mil)	Price	Performance Rating/Pts	Total Return Y-T-D	Risk Rating/Pts
12-15	E	22.50	12.67	E- / 0.1	-33.93%	D+ / 2.7

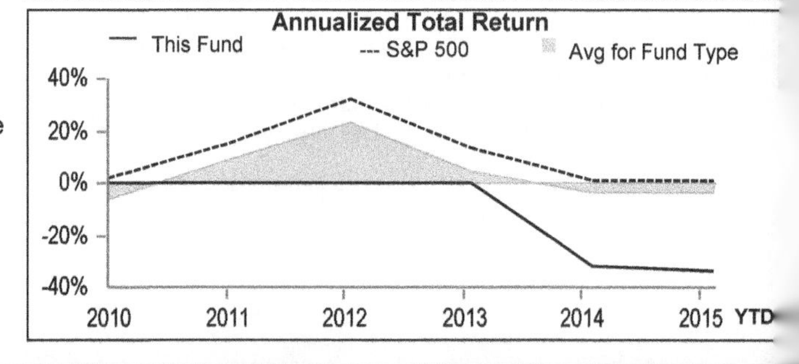

*UBS E-TRACS Mo Py 2x Levd DJ Int (RWXL) D Weak

Fund Family: UBS Asset Mgmt (Americas) Inc
Fund Type: Foreign
Inception Date: March 21, 2012

Major Rating Factors: *UBS E-TRACS Mo Py 2x Levd DJ Int has adopted a risky asset allocation strategy and currently receives an overall TheStreet.com Investment Rating of D (Weak). The fund has an above average level of volatility, as measured by both semi-deviation and drawdown factors. It carries a beta of 1.73, meaning it is expected to move 17.3% for every 10% move in the market. As of December 31, 2015, *UBS E-TRACS Mo Py 2x Levd DJ Int traded at a premium of .34% above its net asset value, which is worse than its one-year historical average premium of .23%. Unfortunately, the high level of risk (D+, Weak) has only provided investors with average performance.

The fund's performance rating is currently C (Fair). It has registered an annualized return of 1.81% over the last three years but is down -7.68% year to date 2015.

This fund has been team managed for 4 years and currently receives a manager quality ranking of 23 (0=worst, 99=best). If you are comfortable owning a high risk investment, then this fund may be an option.

Data Date	Investment Rating	Net Assets ($Mil)	Price	Performance Rating/Pts	Total Return Y-T-D	Risk Rating/Pts
12-15	D	13.30	29.52	C / 4.5	-7.68%	D+ / 2.9
2014	D+	13.30	33.65	C / 4.3	11.38%	C+ / 5.7
2013	D	13.00	32.03	C- / 3.6	2.36%	C- / 4.2

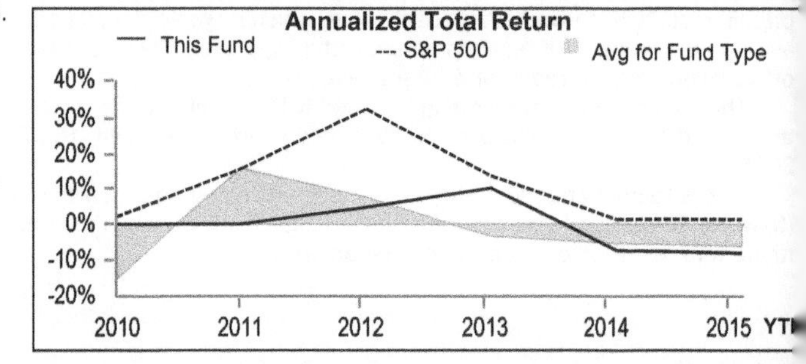

*UBS E-TRACS Mo Py 2x Levd Mort R (MORL) E Very Weak

Fund Family: UBS Asset Mgmt (Americas) Inc
Fund Type: Global
Inception Date: October 16, 2012

Data Date	Investment Rating	Net Assets ($Mil)	Price	Performance Rating/Pts	Total Return Y-T-D	Risk Rating/Pts
12-15	E	266.10	13.28	D+ / 2.5	-22.81%	E / 0.5
2014	C+	266.10	21.04	A- / 9.2	26.77%	C- / 4.2
2013	D-	112.60	19.00	D+ / 2.8	-9.10%	C- / 3.2

Major Rating Factors: *UBS E-TRACS Mo Py 2x Levd Mort R has adopted a very risky asset allocation strategy and currently receives an overall TheStreet.com Investment Rating of E (Very Weak). The fund has a high level of volatility, as measured by both semi-deviation and drawdown factors. It carries a beta of 1.13, meaning it is expected to move 11.3% for every 10% move in the market. As of December 31, 2015, *UBS E-TRACS Mo Py 2x Levd Mort R traded at a premium of .23% above its net asset value, which is worse than its one-year historical average premium of .12%. Unfortunately, the high level of risk (E, Very Weak) failed to pay off as investors endured poor performance.

The fund's performance rating is currently D+ (Weak). It has registered an annualized return of -3.01% over the last three years and is down -22.81% year to date 2015.

This fund has been team managed for 4 years and currently receives a manager quality ranking of 27 (0=worst, 99=best). If you can tolerate very high levels of risk in the hope of improved future returns, holding this fund may be an option.

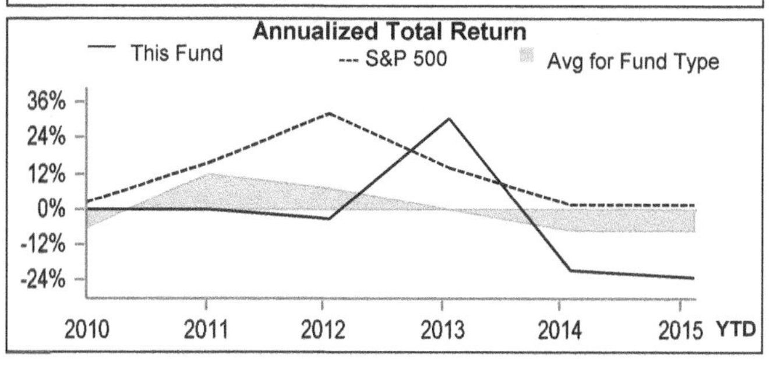

*UBS E-TRACS Mo Rst 2xLevd SP500 (SPLX) C- Fair

Fund Family: UBS Asset Mgmt (Americas) Inc
Fund Type: Growth
Inception Date: March 25, 2014

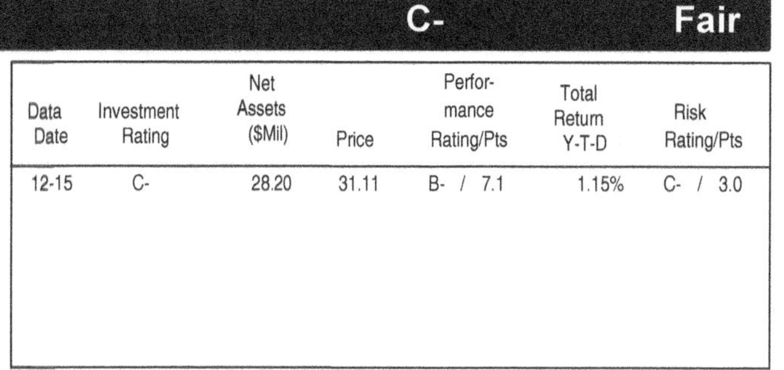

Data Date	Investment Rating	Net Assets ($Mil)	Price	Performance Rating/Pts	Total Return Y-T-D	Risk Rating/Pts
12-15	C-	28.20	31.11	B- / 7.1	1.15%	C- / 3.0

Major Rating Factors: Strong performance is the major factor driving the C- (Fair) TheStreet.com Investment Rating for *UBS E-TRACS Mo Rst 2xLevd SP500. The fund currently has a performance rating of B- (Good) based on an annualized return of 0.00% over the last three years and a total return of 1.15% year to date 2015.

The fund's risk rating is currently C- (Fair). It carries a beta of 0.00, meaning the fund's expected move will be 0.0% for every 10% move in the market. Volatility, as measured by both the semi-deviation and a drawdown factor, is considered average. As of December 31, 2015, *UBS E-TRACS Mo Rst 2xLevd SP500 traded at a premium of 1.01% above its net asset value, which is worse than its one-year historical average discount of .15%.

If you desire an average level of risk and strong performance, then this fund is a good option.

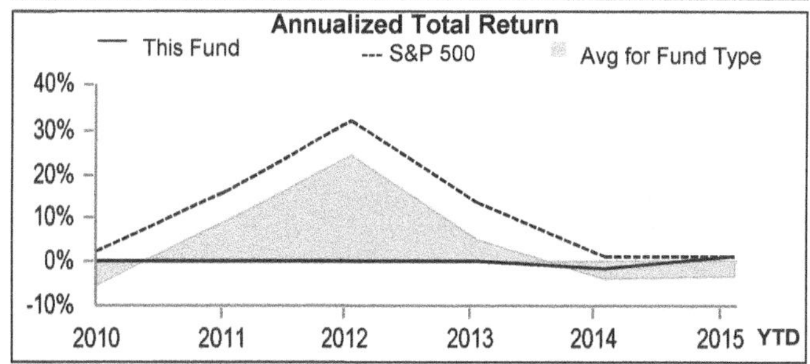

*UBS E-TRACS S&P 500 Gold Hedged (SPGH) D- Weak

Fund Family: UBS Asset Mgmt (Americas) Inc
Fund Type: Precious Metals
Inception Date: January 28, 2010

Data Date	Investment Rating	Net Assets ($Mil)	Price	Performance Rating/Pts	Total Return Y-T-D	Risk Rating/Pts
12-15	D-	19.30	48.74	C- / 3.1	-9.95%	D+ / 2.7
2014	D+	19.30	54.13	C / 4.7	10.94%	C / 4.5
2013	D+	17.80	48.45	C+ / 5.8	-6.55%	C- / 4.2
2012	C	18.90	50.99	B / 7.9	17.25%	C / 4.8
2011	C-	15.80	42.60	C+ / 6.4	19.41%	C / 4.9

Major Rating Factors: *UBS E-TRACS S&P 500 Gold Hedged has adopted a risky asset allocation strategy and currently receives an overall TheStreet.com Investment Rating of D- (Weak). The fund has an above average level of volatility, as measured by both semi-deviation and drawdown factors. It carries a beta of 1.13, meaning it is expected to move 11.3% for every 10% move in the market. As of December 31, 2015, *UBS E-TRACS S&P 500 Gold Hedged traded at a premium of 1.33% above its net asset value, which is worse than its one-year historical average premium of .36%. Unfortunately, the high level of risk (D+, Weak) has only provided investors with average performance.

The fund's performance rating is currently C- (Fair). It has registered an annualized return of -2.26% over the last three years and is down -9.95% year to date 2015.

This fund has been team managed for 6 years and currently receives a manager quality ranking of 98 (0=worst, 99=best). If you are comfortable owning a high risk investment, then this fund may be an option.

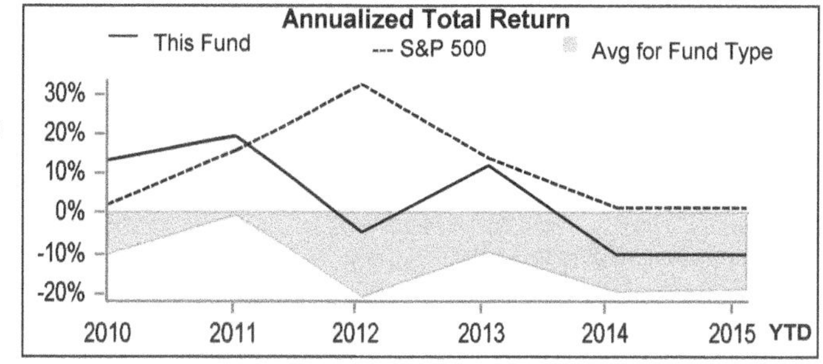

*UBS E-TRACS Wells Fargo BDC Inde (BDCS) D- Weak

Fund Family: UBS Asset Mgmt (Americas) Inc
Fund Type: Growth
Inception Date: April 27, 2011

Data Date	Investment Rating	Net Assets ($Mil)	Price	Perfor-mance Rating/Pts	Total Return Y-T-D	Risk Rating/Pts
12-15	D-	67.70	20.19	C- / 3.6	-5.01%	D+ / 2.5
2014	C	67.70	22.87	C / 4.4	-9.69%	B / 8.3
2013	C-	54.80	26.98	B- / 7.0	11.25%	C / 4.8
2012	C+	21.10	25.12	A / 9.4	27.58%	C / 4.7

Major Rating Factors: *UBS E-TRACS Wells Fargo BDC Inde has adopted a risky asset allocation strategy and currently receives an overall TheStreet.com Investment Rating of D- (Weak). The fund has an above average level of volatility, as measured by both semi-deviation and drawdown factors. It carries a beta of 0.68, meaning the fund's expected move will be 6.8% for every 10% move in the market. As of December 31, 2015, *UBS E-TRACS Wells Fargo BDC Inde traded at a premium of .45% above its net asset value, which is worse than its one-year historical average premium of .01%. Unfortunately, the high level of risk (D+, Weak) has only provided investors with average performance.

The fund's performance rating is currently C- (Fair). It has registered an annualized return of -1.24% over the last three years and is down -5.01% year to date 2015.

This fund has been team managed for 5 years and currently receives a manager quality ranking of 17 (0=worst, 99=best). If you are comfortable owning a high risk investment, then this fund may be an option.

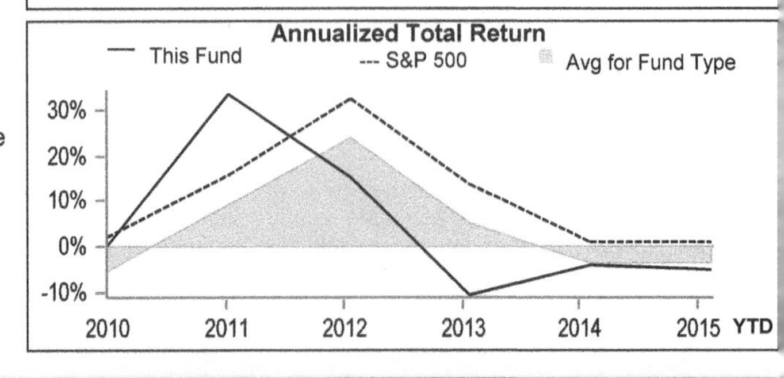

*UBS E-TRACS Wells Fargo MLP ex-E (FMLP) E Very Weak

Fund Family: UBS Asset Mgmt (Americas) Inc
Fund Type: Global
Inception Date: June 10, 2014

Data Date	Investment Rating	Net Assets ($Mil)	Price	Perfor-mance Rating/Pts	Total Return Y-T-D	Risk Rating/Pts
12-15	E	0.00	18.25	E+ / 0.6	-17.57%	D+ / 2.4

Major Rating Factors: *UBS E-TRACS Wells Fargo MLP ex-E has adopted a risky asset allocation strategy and currently receives an overall TheStreet.com Investment Rating of E (Very Weak). The fund has an above average level of volatility, as measured by both semi-deviation and drawdown factors. It carries a beta of 0.00, meaning the fund's expected move will be 0.0% for every 10% move in the market. As of December 31, 2015, *UBS E-TRACS Wells Fargo MLP ex-E traded at a premium of .22% above its net asset value, which is better than its one-year historical average premium of .48%. Unfortunately, the high level of risk (D+, Weak) failed to pay off as investors endured very poor performance.

The fund's performance rating is currently E+ (Very Weak). It has registered an annualized return of 0.00% over the last three years but is down -17.57% year to date 2015.

If you can tolerate high levels of risk in the hope of improved future returns, holding this fund may be an option.

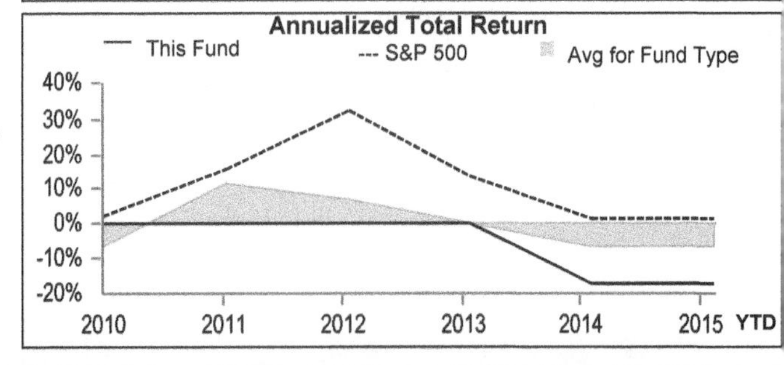

*UBS E-TRACS Wells Fargo MLP Inde (MLPW) E+ Very Weak

Fund Family: UBS Asset Mgmt (Americas) Inc
Fund Type: Energy/Natural Resources
Inception Date: November 1, 2010

Data Date	Investment Rating	Net Assets ($Mil)	Price	Perfor-mance Rating/Pts	Total Return Y-T-D	Risk Rating/Pts
12-15	E+	15.80	21.56	D / 1.7	-35.69%	D+ / 2.5
2014	C+	15.80	34.69	C+ / 5.6	7.07%	B / 8.4
2013	C	13.50	33.86	B- / 7.4	20.58%	C / 5.3
2012	D+	10.90	28.71	C / 4.6	10.98%	C / 5.2
2011	C-	19.00	27.21	C+ / 5.9	9.95%	C / 5.3

Major Rating Factors: *UBS E-TRACS Wells Fargo MLP Inde has adopted a risky asset allocation strategy and currently receives an overall TheStreet.com Investment Rating of E+ (Very Weak). The fund has an above average level of volatility, as measured by both semi-deviation and drawdown factors. It carries a beta of 0.74, meaning the fund's expected move will be 7.4% for every 10% move in the market. As of December 31, 2015, *UBS E-TRACS Wells Fargo MLP Inde traded at a discount of .09% below its net asset value, which is worse than its one-year historical average discount of .13%. Unfortunately, the high level of risk (D+, Weak) failed to pay off as investors endured poor performance.

The fund's performance rating is currently D (Weak). It has registered an annualized return of -5.30% over the last three years and is down -35.69% year to date 2015.

This is team managed and currently receives a manager quality ranking of 49 (0=worst, 99=best). If you can tolerate high levels of risk in the hope of improved future returns, holding this fund may be an option.

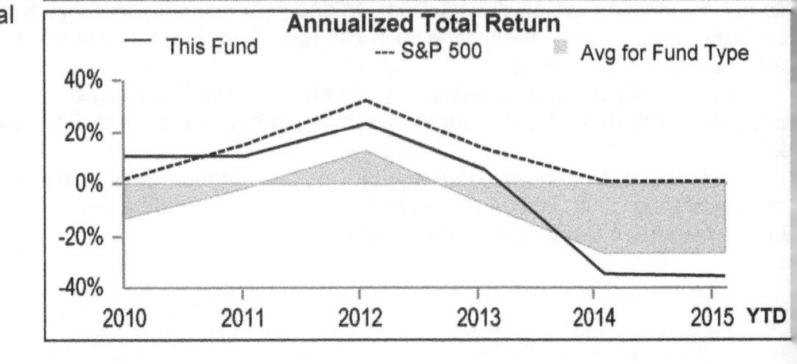

* Denotes ETF Fund

*United States 12 Month Oil Fund (USL) E Very Weak

Fund Family: United States Commodity Funds LLC
Fund Type: Energy/Natural Resources
Inception Date: December 6, 2007

Major Rating Factors: *United States 12 Month Oil Fund has adopted a very risky asset allocation strategy and currently receives an overall TheStreet.com Investment Rating of E (Very Weak). The fund has a high level of volatility, as measured by both semi-deviation and drawdown factors. It carries a beta of 0.98, meaning that its performance tracks fairly well with that of the overall stock market. As of December 31, 2015, *United States 12 Month Oil Fund traded at a premium of .12% above its net asset value, which is worse than its one-year historical average discount of .14%. Unfortunately, the high level of risk (D, Weak) failed to pay off as investors endured very poor performance.

The fund's performance rating is currently E (Very Weak). It has registered an annualized return of -24.84% over the last three years and is down -35.41% year to date 2015. Factored into the performance evaluation is an expense ratio of 0.93% (low).

John T. Hyland currently receives a manager quality ranking of 6 (0=worst, 99=best). If you can tolerate very high levels of risk in the hope of improved future returns, holding this fund may be an option.

Data Date	Investment Rating	Net Assets ($Mil)	Price	Performance Rating/Pts	Total Return Y-T-D	Risk Rating/Pts
12-15	E	48.10	17.02	E / 0.5	-35.41%	D / 1.9
2014	E	48.10	26.82	E+ / 0.6	-35.03%	C- / 3.2
2013	D	64.20	42.88	D+ / 2.4	2.99%	C+ / 6.5
2012	D-	99.50	39.67	D- / 1.3	-8.27%	C+ / 6.4
2011	C	169.50	43.48	C / 5.5	6.88%	C+ / 6.8
2010	D-	180.20	43.10	D- / 1.4	6.52%	C- / 3.6

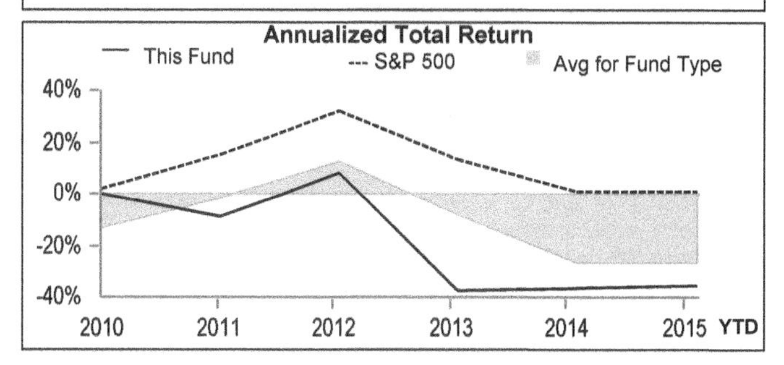

*United States Agriculture Index (USAG) D+ Weak

Fund Family: United States Commodity Funds LLC
Fund Type: Global
Inception Date: April 12, 2012

Major Rating Factors:
Disappointing performance is the major factor driving the D+ (Weak) TheStreet.com Investment Rating for *United States Agriculture Index. The fund currently has a performance rating of D (Weak) based on an annualized return of -8.84% over the last three years and a total return of -14.09% year to date 2015. Factored into the performance evaluation is an expense ratio of 0.88% (low).

The fund's risk rating is currently C+ (Fair). It carries a beta of 0.50, meaning the fund's expected move will be 5.0% for every 10% move in the market. Volatility, as measured by both the semi-deviation and a drawdown factor, is considered low. As of December 31, 2015, *United States Agriculture Index traded at a discount of 2.02% below its net asset value, which is worse than its one-year historical average discount of 2.76%.

John T. Hyland currently receives a manager quality ranking of 15 (0=worst, 99=best). This fund offers only a moderate level of risk but investors looking for strong performance are still waiting.

Data Date	Investment Rating	Net Assets ($Mil)	Price	Performance Rating/Pts	Total Return Y-T-D	Risk Rating/Pts
12-15	D+	2.30	19.39	D / 2.1	-14.09%	C+ / 6.5
2014	D	2.30	22.57	D / 2.2	1.44%	C+ / 5.9
2013	D-	2.30	22.35	E+ / 0.9	-13.06%	C+ / 6.1

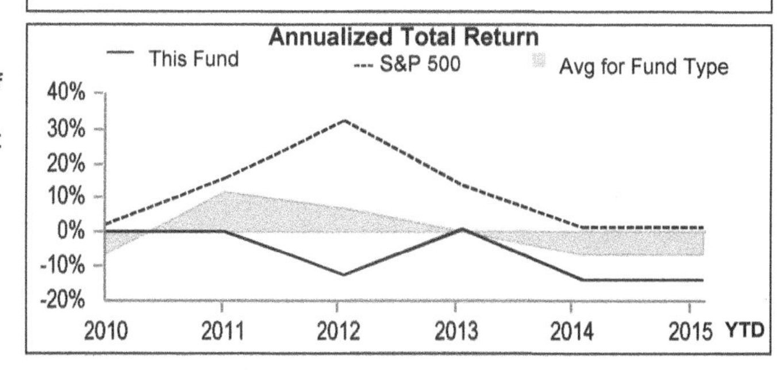

*United States Brent Oil Fund (BNO) E- Very Weak

Fund Family: United States Commodity Funds LLC
Fund Type: Energy/Natural Resources
Inception Date: June 1, 2010

Major Rating Factors: *United States Brent Oil Fund has adopted a very risky asset allocation strategy and currently receives an overall TheStreet.com Investment Rating of E- (Very Weak). The fund has a high level of volatility, as measured by both semi-deviation and drawdown factors. It carries a beta of 1.21, meaning it is expected to move 12.1% for every 10% move in the market. As of December 31, 2015, *United States Brent Oil Fund traded at a premium of .16% above its net asset value, which is worse than its one-year historical average discount of .12%. Unfortunately, the high level of risk (E, Very Weak) failed to pay off as investors endured very poor performance.

The fund's performance rating is currently E- (Very Weak). It has registered an annualized return of -33.19% over the last three years and is down -44.41% year to date 2015. Factored into the performance evaluation is an expense ratio of 0.92% (low).

John T. Hyland currently receives a manager quality ranking of 3 (0=worst, 99=best). If you can tolerate very high levels of risk in the hope of improved future returns, holding this fund may be an option.

Data Date	Investment Rating	Net Assets ($Mil)	Price	Performance Rating/Pts	Total Return Y-T-D	Risk Rating/Pts
12-15	E-	39.60	12.24	E- / 0.2	-44.41%	E / 0.3
2014	E-	39.60	22.70	E / 0.5	-46.30%	E / 0.4
2013	D+	28.50	44.54	C+ / 6.1	2.98%	C- / 3.7
2012	C-	45.10	82.07	C- / 3.7	5.90%	B- / 7.6
2011	B	37.30	74.64	B / 7.7	26.63%	B- / 7.9

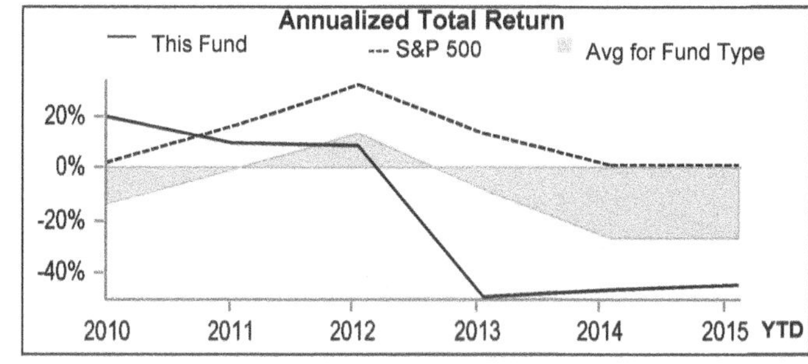

*United States Commodity Index (USCI) D+ Weak

Fund Family: United States Commodity Funds LLC
Fund Type: Income
Inception Date: August 9, 2010

Data Date	Investment Rating	Net Assets ($Mil)	Price	Performance Rating/Pts	Total Return Y-T-D	Risk Rating/Pts
12-15	D+	835.00	40.47	D / 1.6	-15.90%	B- / 7.0
2014	D-	835.00	48.29	D- / 1.4	-12.77%	C+ / 5.6
2013	D	513.00	56.08	D / 1.8	-4.60%	B- / 7.4
2012	D	485.20	58.63	D- / 1.0	-2.73%	B- / 7.7
2011	D	350.80	58.37	D- / 1.4	-5.07%	B- / 7.9

Major Rating Factors:
Disappointing performance is the major factor driving the D+ (Weak) TheStreet.com Investment Rating for *United States Commodity Index. The fund currently has a performance rating of D (Weak) based on an annualized return of -11.32% over the last three years and a total return of -15.90% year to date 2015. Factored into the performance evaluation is an expense ratio of 1.04% (low).

The fund's risk rating is currently B- (Good). It carries a beta of 0.29, meaning the fund's expected move will be 2.9% for every 10% move in the market. Volatility, as measured by both the semi-deviation and a drawdown factor, is considered low. As of December 31, 2015, *United States Commodity Index traded at a discount of .12% below its net asset value, which is better than its one-year historical average premium of .01%.

John T. Hyland currently receives a manager quality ranking of 10 (0=worst, 99=best). This fund offers only a moderate level of risk but investors looking for strong performance are still waiting.

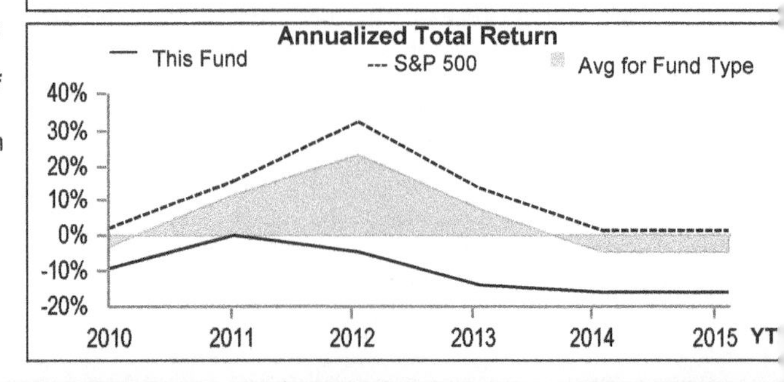

*United States Copper Index (CPER) D- Weak

Fund Family: United States Commodity Funds LLC
Fund Type: Income
Inception Date: November 14, 2011

Data Date	Investment Rating	Net Assets ($Mil)	Price	Performance Rating/Pts	Total Return Y-T-D	Risk Rating/Pts
12-15	D-	3.00	14.27	D- / 1.0	-24.97%	C- / 3.8
2014	D	3.00	19.02	D- / 1.3	-16.10%	C+ / 6.5
2013	D	2.30	22.90	D / 1.6	-12.00%	B- / 7.4
2012	D+	2.50	25.01	D / 1.7	-0.11%	B / 8.1

Major Rating Factors:
Disappointing performance is the major factor driving the D- (Weak) TheStreet.com Investment Rating for *United States Copper Index. The fund currently has a performance rating of D- (Weak) based on an annualized return of -17.87% over the last three years and a total return of -24.97% year to date 2015. Factored into the performance evaluation is an expense ratio of 0.82% (very low).

The fund's risk rating is currently C- (Fair). It carries a beta of 0.45, meaning the fund's expected move will be 4.5% for every 10% move in the market. Volatility, as measured by both the semi-deviation and a drawdown factor, is considered average. As of December 31, 2015, *United States Copper Index traded at a premium of .21% above its net asset value, which is worse than its one-year historical average premium of .03%.

John T. Hyland currently receives a manager quality ranking of 6 (0=worst, 99=best). This fund offers an average level of risk but investors looking for strong performance will be frustrated.

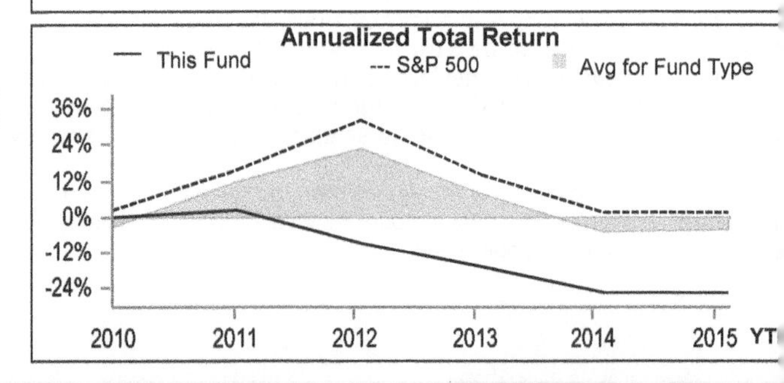

*United States Diesel-Heating Oil (UHN) E+ Very Weak

Fund Family: United States Commodity Funds LLC
Fund Type: Energy/Natural Resources
Inception Date: April 9, 2008

Data Date	Investment Rating	Net Assets ($Mil)	Price	Performance Rating/Pts	Total Return Y-T-D	Risk Rating/Pts
12-15	E+	3.00	12.45	E / 0.3	-41.36%	C- / 3.4
2014	E+	3.00	21.58	E+ / 0.7	-32.33%	C- / 3.7
2013	D+	5.00	33.03	C- / 3.0	-4.98%	B- / 7.5
2012	D+	6.80	33.73	D+ / 2.8	-2.32%	B- / 7.4
2011	C+	9.80	32.87	C+ / 5.7	17.61%	B- / 7.8
2010	C+	11.90	29.86	B+ / 8.8	8.15%	C- / 3.3

Major Rating Factors:
Very poor performance is the major factor driving the E+ (Very Weak) TheStreet.com Investment Rating for *United States Diesel-Heating Oil. The fund currently has a performance rating of E (Very Weak) based on an annualized return of -28.15% over the last three years and a total return of -41.36% year to date 2015. Factored into the performance evaluation is an expense ratio of 0.85% (very low).

The fund's risk rating is currently C- (Fair). It carries a beta of 0.92, meaning that its performance tracks fairly well with that of the overall stock market. Volatility, as measured by both the semi-deviation and a drawdown factor, is considered average. As of December 31, 2015, *United States Diesel-Heating Oil traded at a discount of .24% below its net asset value, which is better than its one-year historical average premium of .09%.

John T. Hyland currently receives a manager quality ranking of 4 (0=worst, 99=best). This fund offers an average level of risk but investors looking for strong performance will be frustrated.

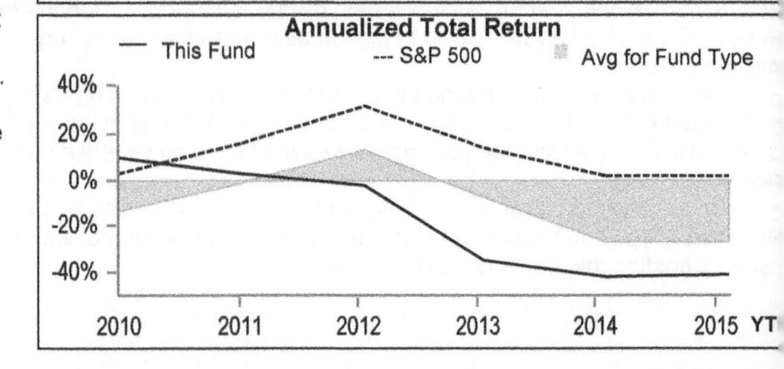

*United States Gasoline Fund LP (UGA) D- Weak

Fund Family: United States Commodity Funds LLC
Fund Type: Energy/Natural Resources
Inception Date: February 26, 2008

Data Date	Investment Rating	Net Assets ($Mil)	Price	Performance Rating/Pts	Total Return Y-T-D	Risk Rating/Pts
12-15	D-	51.70	29.26	E+ / 0.9	-11.92%	C / 4.3
2014	E	51.70	34.15	E+ / 0.6	-40.22%	D+ / 2.8
2013	C+	56.90	59.93	C+ / 5.8	-2.17%	B- / 7.5
2012	C+	64.20	58.44	C+ / 6.8	15.34%	B- / 7.3
2011	B+	77.40	48.32	A- / 9.0	19.61%	B- / 7.6
2010	C+	67.30	42.11	A / 9.3	15.12%	C- / 3.0

Major Rating Factors:
Very poor performance is the major factor driving the D- (Weak) TheStreet.com Investment Rating for *United States Gasoline Fund LP. The fund currently has a performance rating of E+ (Very Weak) based on an annualized return of -20.58% over the last three years and a total return of -11.92% year to date 2015. Factored into the performance evaluation is an expense ratio of 0.82% (very low).

The fund's risk rating is currently C (Fair). It carries a beta of 0.88, meaning the fund's expected move will be 8.8% for every 10% move in the market. Volatility, as measured by both the semi-deviation and a drawdown factor, is considered average. As of December 31, 2015, *United States Gasoline Fund LP traded at a discount of .14% below its net asset value, which is better than its one-year historical average discount of .03%.

John T. Hyland currently receives a manager quality ranking of 8 (0=worst, 99=best). This fund offers an average level of risk but investors looking for strong performance will be frustrated.

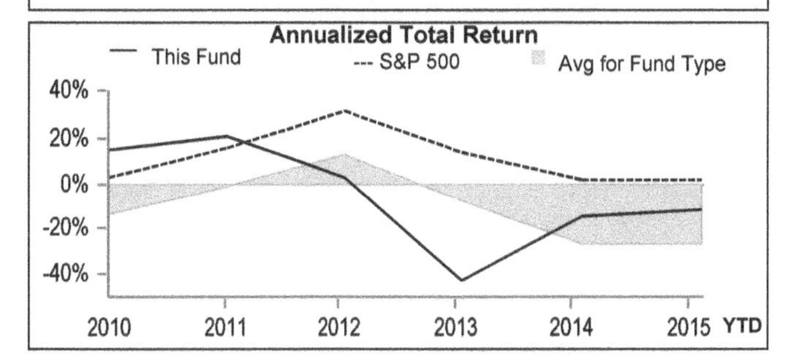

*United States Natural Gas Fund (UNG) E+ Very Weak

Fund Family: United States Commodity Funds LLC
Fund Type: Energy/Natural Resources
Inception Date: April 18, 2007

Data Date	Investment Rating	Net Assets ($Mil)	Price	Performance Rating/Pts	Total Return Y-T-D	Risk Rating/Pts
12-15	E+	721.90	8.67	E+ / 0.6	-42.04%	C- / 3.2
2014	E+	721.90	14.77	E / 0.5	-29.87%	C- / 3.9
2013	E+	843.70	20.69	E+ / 0.7	14.33%	C- / 3.6
2012	E	1,175.00	18.90	E- / 0.2	-17.46%	C- / 3.4
2011	E	1,072.10	6.46	E- / 0.1	-44.94%	C- / 3.4
2010	E-	2,724.40	5.99	E- / 0.2	-40.58%	D / 2.1

Major Rating Factors:
Very poor performance is the major factor driving the E+ (Very Weak) TheStreet.com Investment Rating for *United States Natural Gas Fund. The fund currently has a performance rating of E+ (Very Weak) based on an annualized return of -22.21% over the last three years and a total return of -42.04% year to date 2015. Factored into the performance evaluation is an expense ratio of 1.14% (low).

The fund's risk rating is currently C- (Fair). It carries a beta of -0.03, meaning the fund's expected move will be -0.3% for every 10% move in the market. Volatility, as measured by both the semi-deviation and a drawdown factor, is considered average. As of December 31, 2015, *United States Natural Gas Fund traded at a discount of .23% below its net asset value, which is better than its one-year historical average discount of .01%.

John T. Hyland currently receives a manager quality ranking of 6 (0=worst, 99=best). This fund offers an average level of risk but investors looking for strong performance will be frustrated.

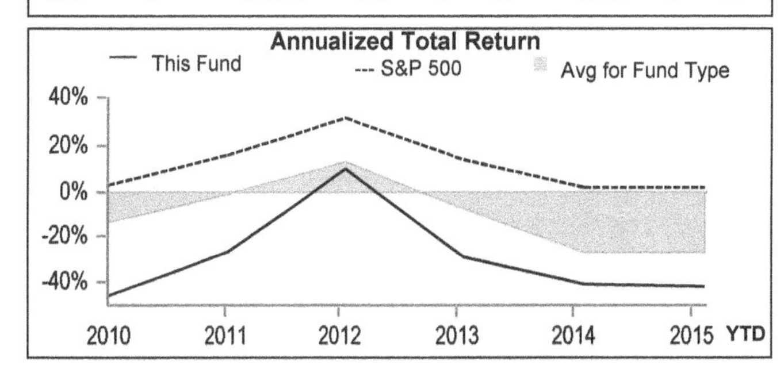

*United States Oil Fund (USO) E Very Weak

Fund Family: United States Commodity Funds LLC
Fund Type: Energy/Natural Resources
Inception Date: April 10, 2006

Data Date	Investment Rating	Net Assets ($Mil)	Price	Performance Rating/Pts	Total Return Y-T-D	Risk Rating/Pts
12-15	E	651.90	11.00	E / 0.3	-44.70%	C- / 3.1
2014	E	651.90	20.36	E / 0.4	-39.67%	D+ / 2.4
2013	D	528.50	35.32	D / 1.7	-0.38%	C+ / 6.3
2012	D-	1,199.80	33.37	D- / 1.0	-10.74%	C+ / 6.1
2011	D+	1,134.60	38.11	C- / 3.7	4.11%	C+ / 6.6
2010	E	1,819.80	39.00	E+ / 0.6	-0.71%	D+ / 2.7

Major Rating Factors: Very poor performance is the major factor driving the E (Very Weak) TheStreet.com Investment Rating for *United States Oil Fund. The fund currently has a performance rating of E (Very Weak) based on an annualized return of -31.27% over the last three years and a total return of -44.70% year to date 2015. Factored into the performance evaluation is an expense ratio of 0.72% (very low).

The fund's risk rating is currently C- (Fair). It carries a beta of 1.06, meaning that its performance tracks fairly well with that of the overall stock market. Volatility, as measured by both the semi-deviation and a drawdown factor, is considered average. As of December 31, 2015, *United States Oil Fund traded at a discount of .18% below its net asset value, which is better than its one-year historical average discount of .09%.

John T. Hyland currently receives a manager quality ranking of 3 (0=worst, 99=best). This fund offers an average level of risk but investors looking for strong performance will be frustrated.

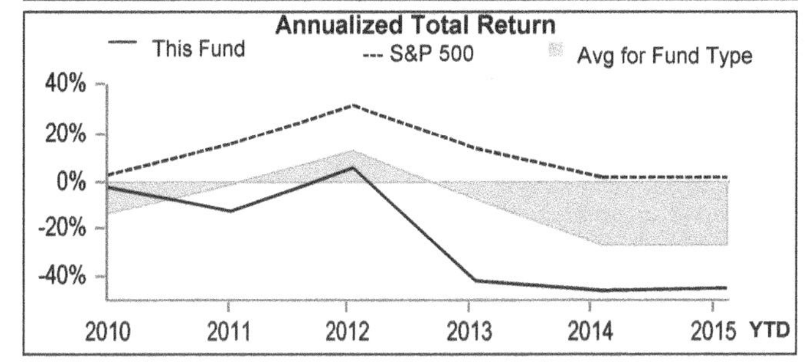

*United States Short Oil Fund (DNO) B+ Good

Fund Family: United States Commodity Funds LLC
Fund Type: Energy/Natural Resources
Inception Date: September 23, 2009

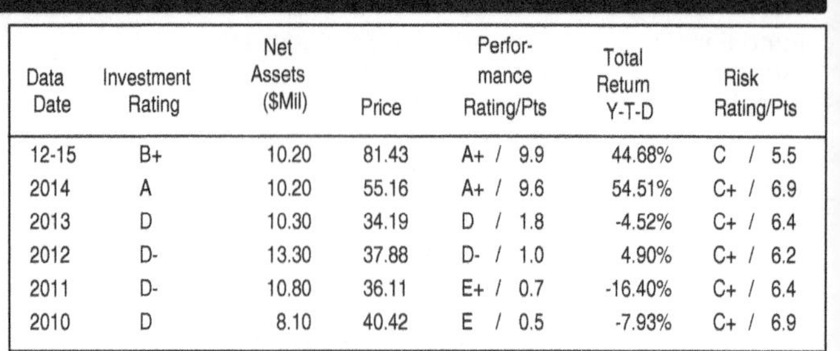

Data Date	Investment Rating	Net Assets ($Mil)	Price	Performance Rating/Pts	Total Return Y-T-D	Risk Rating/Pts
12-15	B+	10.20	81.43	A+ / 9.9	44.68%	C / 5.5
2014	A	10.20	55.16	A+ / 9.6	54.51%	C+ / 6.9
2013	D	10.30	34.19	D / 1.8	-4.52%	C+ / 6.4
2012	D-	13.30	37.88	D- / 1.0	4.90%	C+ / 6.2
2011	D-	10.80	36.11	E+ / 0.7	-16.40%	C+ / 6.4
2010	D	8.10	40.42	E / 0.5	-7.93%	C+ / 6.9

Major Rating Factors:
Exceptional performance is the major factor driving the B+ (Good) TheStreet.com Investment Rating for *United States Short Oil Fund. The fund currently has a performance rating of A+ (Excellent) based on an annualized return of 29.62% over the last three years and a total return of 44.68% year to date 2015. Factored into the performance evaluation is an expense ratio of 0.80% (very low).

The fund's risk rating is currently C (Fair). It carries a beta of -1.01, meaning the fund's expected move will be -10.1% for every 10% move in the market. Volatility, as measured by both the semi-deviation and a drawdown factor, is considered average. As of December 31, 2015, *United States Short Oil Fund traded at a premium of .23% above its net asset value, which is worse than its one-year historical average premium of .12%.

John T. Hyland currently receives a manager quality ranking of 98 (0=worst, 99=best). If you desire an average level of risk and strong performance, then this fund is a good option.

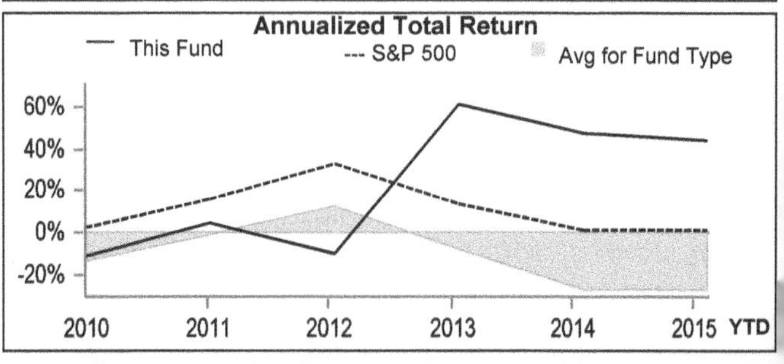

*US 12 Month Natural Gas Fund (UNL) D- Weak

Fund Family: United States Commodity Funds LLC
Fund Type: Energy/Natural Resources
Inception Date: November 19, 2009

Data Date	Investment Rating	Net Assets ($Mil)	Price	Performance Rating/Pts	Total Return Y-T-D	Risk Rating/Pts
12-15	D-	16.20	9.70	E+ / 0.9	-29.99%	C / 4.7
2014	D-	16.20	13.81	E+ / 0.8	-25.75%	C+ / 5.6
2013	E+	27.50	18.35	E+ / 0.8	9.54%	C / 4.7
2012	E	43.10	17.24	E / 0.3	-11.66%	C- / 4.1
2011	E+	21.20	21.12	E- / 0.1	-38.03%	C / 4.7
2010	D-	35.00	34.97	E / 0.3	-35.48%	C+ / 6.0

Major Rating Factors:
Very poor performance is the major factor driving the D- (Weak) TheStreet.com Investment Rating for *US 12 Month Natural Gas Fund. The fund currently has a performance rating of E+ (Very Weak) based on an annualized return of -17.03% over the last three years and a total return of -29.99% year to date 2015. Factored into the performance evaluation is an expense ratio of 0.93% (low).

The fund's risk rating is currently C (Fair). It carries a beta of 0.07, meaning the fund's expected move will be 0.7% for every 10% move in the market. Volatility, as measured by both the semi-deviation and a drawdown factor, is considered average. As of December 31, 2015, *US 12 Month Natural Gas Fund traded at a discount of .21% below its net asset value, which is better than its one-year historical average discount of .10%.

John T. Hyland currently receives a manager quality ranking of 9 (0=worst, 99=best). This fund offers an average level of risk but investors looking for strong performance will be frustrated.

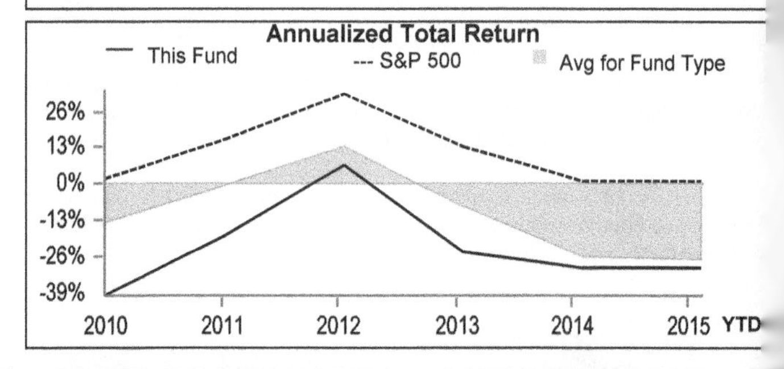

*Utilities Select Sector SPDR (XLU) B+ Good

Fund Family: SSgA Funds Management Inc
Fund Type: Utilities
Inception Date: December 16, 1998

Data Date	Investment Rating	Net Assets ($Mil)	Price	Performance Rating/Pts	Total Return Y-T-D	Risk Rating/Pts
12-15	B+	5,487.20	43.28	B / 7.8	-4.40%	B / 8.1
2014	A+	5,487.20	47.22	B+ / 8.6	31.10%	B / 8.6
2013	B-	4,501.40	37.97	C+ / 6.1	8.39%	B / 8.9
2012	C	5,457.90	34.92	C- / 3.1	5.64%	B+ / 9.1
2011	C+	7,662.30	35.98	C / 5.0	15.44%	B / 8.6
2010	D+	3,756.60	31.34	D- / 1.5	5.35%	C+ / 6.7

Major Rating Factors: Strong performance is the major factor driving the B+ (Good) TheStreet.com Investment Rating for *Utilities Select Sector SPDR. The fund currently has a performance rating of B (Good) based on an annualized return of 10.92% over the last three years and a total return of -4.40% year to date 2015. Factored into the performance evaluation is an expense ratio of 0.15% (very low).

The fund's risk rating is currently B (Good). It carries a beta of 0.98, meaning that its performance tracks fairly well with that of the overall stock market. Volatility, as measured by both the semi-deviation and a drawdown factor, is considered low. As of December 31, 2015, *Utilities Select Sector SPDR traded at a discount of .02% below its net asset value, which is better than its one-year historical average discount of .01%.

John A. Tucker has been running the fund for 18 years and currently receives a manager quality ranking of 63 (0=worst, 99=best). If you desire only a moderate level of risk and strong performance, then this fund is an excellent option.

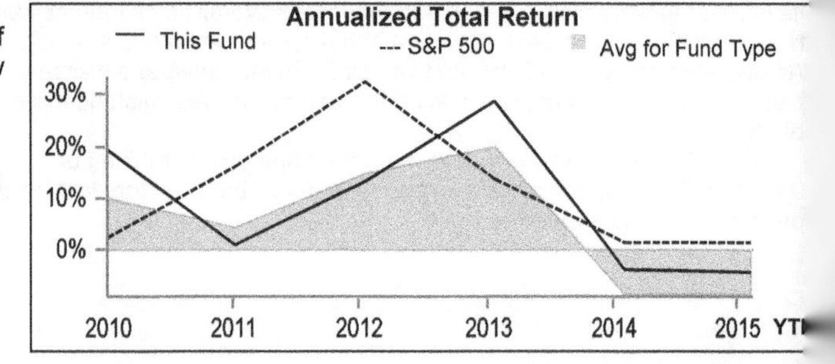

* Denotes ETF Fund

*Validea Market Legends (VALX) D- Weak

Fund Family: Validea Capital Management LLC
Fund Type: Growth
Inception Date: December 9, 2014

Data Date	Investment Rating	Net Assets ($Mil)	Price	Performance Rating/Pts	Total Return Y-T-D	Risk Rating/Pts
12-15	D-	0.00	23.06	D / 1.8	-7.97%	C- / 3.6

Major Rating Factors:
Disappointing performance is the major factor driving the D- (Weak) TheStreet.com Investment Rating for *Validea Market Legends. The fund currently has a performance rating of D (Weak) based on an annualized return of 0.00% over the last three years and a total return of -7.97% year to date 2015.

The fund's risk rating is currently C- (Fair). It carries a beta of 0.00, meaning the fund's expected move will be 0.0% for every 10% move in the market. Volatility, as measured by both the semi-deviation and a drawdown factor, is considered average. As of December 31, 2015, *Validea Market Legends traded at a premium of .09% above its net asset value, which is in line with its one-year historical average premium of .09%.

Jack M. Forehand currently receives a manager quality ranking of 17 (0=worst, 99=best). This fund offers an average level of risk but investors looking for strong performance will be frustrated.

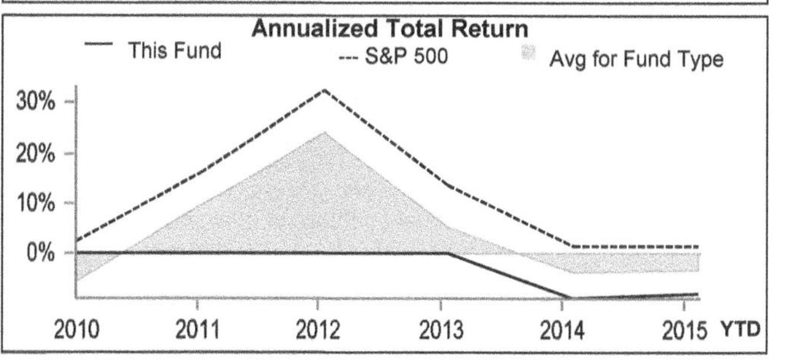

*ValueShares Intl Quantitative Va (IVAL) D Weak

Fund Family: Empowered Funds LLC
Fund Type: Foreign
Inception Date: December 17, 2014

Data Date	Investment Rating	Net Assets ($Mil)	Price	Performance Rating/Pts	Total Return Y-T-D	Risk Rating/Pts
12-15	D	0.00	23.95	D+ / 2.9	-2.94%	C / 4.8

Major Rating Factors:
Disappointing performance is the major factor driving the D (Weak) TheStreet.com Investment Rating for *ValueShares Intl Quantitative Va. The fund currently has a performance rating of D+ (Weak) based on an annualized return of 0.00% over the last three years and a total return of -2.94% year to date 2015.

The fund's risk rating is currently C (Fair). It carries a beta of 0.00, meaning the fund's expected move will be 0.0% for every 10% move in the market. Volatility, as measured by both the semi-deviation and a drawdown factor, is considered average. As of December 31, 2015, *ValueShares Intl Quantitative Va traded at a discount of .66% below its net asset value.

Wesley R. Gray currently receives a manager quality ranking of 43 (0=worst, 99=best). This fund offers an average level of risk but investors looking for strong performance will be frustrated.

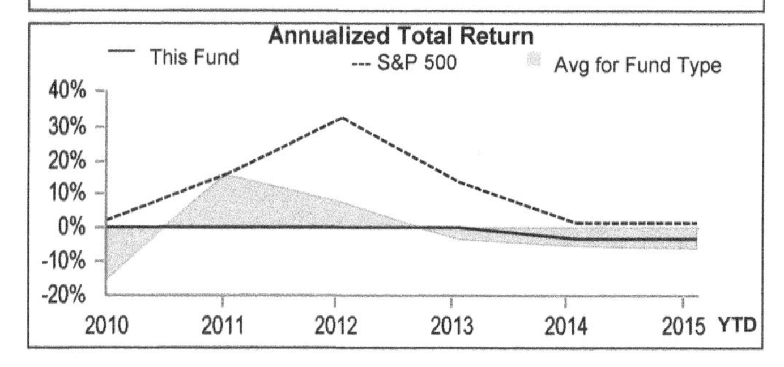

*ValueShares US Quantitative Valu (QVAL) D Weak

Fund Family: Empowered Funds LLC
Fund Type: Growth
Inception Date: October 22, 2014

Data Date	Investment Rating	Net Assets ($Mil)	Price	Performance Rating/Pts	Total Return Y-T-D	Risk Rating/Pts
12-15	D	0.00	22.20	D- / 1.1	-12.67%	C+ / 6.1

Major Rating Factors:
Disappointing performance is the major factor driving the D (Weak) TheStreet.com Investment Rating for *ValueShares US Quantitative Valu. The fund currently has a performance rating of D- (Weak) based on an annualized return of 0.00% over the last three years and a total return of -12.67% year to date 2015.

The fund's risk rating is currently C+ (Fair). It carries a beta of 0.00, meaning the fund's expected move will be 0.0% for every 10% move in the market. Volatility, as measured by both the semi-deviation and a drawdown factor, is considered low. As of December 31, 2015, *ValueShares US Quantitative Valu traded at a premium of .18% above its net asset value, which is worse than its one-year historical average premium of .04%.

Tao Wang has been running the fund for 2 years and currently receives a manager quality ranking of 11 (0=worst, 99=best). This fund offers only a moderate level of risk but investors looking for strong performance are still waiting.

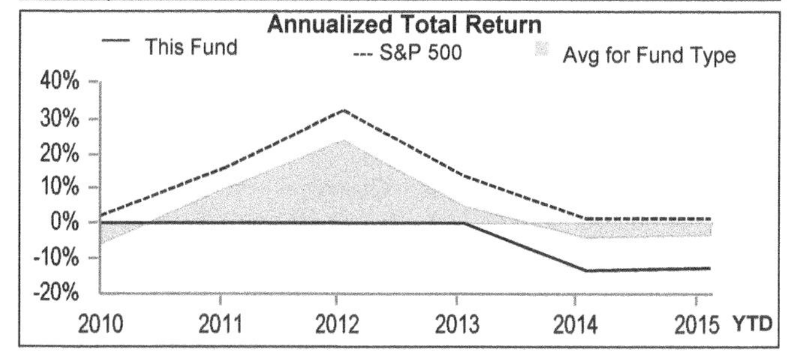

* Denotes ETF Fund

*Vanguard 500 Index ETF (VOO) A+ Excellent

Fund Family: Vanguard Group Inc
Fund Type: Income
Inception Date: September 7, 2010

Major Rating Factors:
Strong performance is the major factor driving the A+ (Excellent) TheStreet.com Investment Rating for *Vanguard 500 Index ETF. The fund currently has a performance rating of B+ (Good) based on an annualized return of 14.22% over the last three years and a total return of 1.92% year to date 2015. Factored into the performance evaluation is an expense ratio of 0.05% (very low).

The fund's risk rating is currently B (Good). It carries a beta of 0.98, meaning that its performance tracks fairly well with that of the overall stock market. Volatility, as measured by both the semi-deviation and a drawdown factor, is considered low. As of December 31, 2015, *Vanguard 500 Index ETF traded at a discount of .06% below its net asset value, which is better than its one-year historical average discount of .01%.

Michael H. Buek has been running the fund for 25 years and currently receives a manager quality ranking of 71 (0=worst, 99=best). If you desire only a moderate level of risk and strong performance, then this fund is an excellent option.

Data Date	Investment Rating	Net Assets ($Mil)	Price	Performance Rating/Pts	Total Return Y-T-D	Risk Rating/Pts
12-15	A+	21,814.20	186.93	B+ / 8.9	1.92%	B / 8.6
2014	A	21,814.20	188.45	B+ / 8.3	14.71%	B / 8.2
2013	A	15,036.50	169.15	B / 8.1	27.51%	B+ / 9.0
2011	C	2,365.60	57.45	C- / 3.0	2.85%	B+ / 9.4

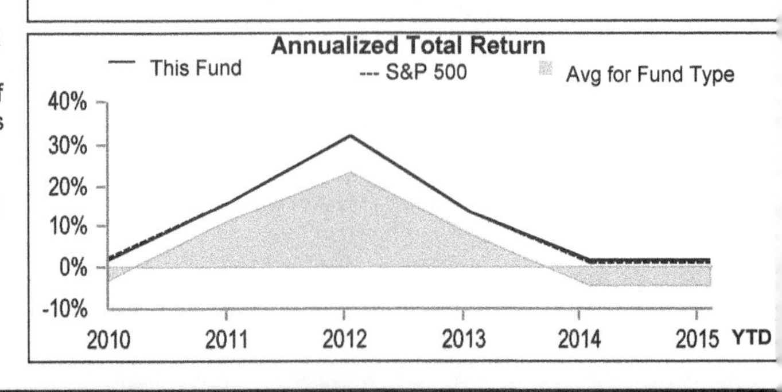

*Vanguard Consumer Discret ETF (VCR) A- Excellent

Fund Family: Vanguard Group Inc
Fund Type: Income
Inception Date: January 26, 2004

Major Rating Factors:
Exceptional performance is the major factor driving the A- (Excellent) TheStreet.com Investment Rating for *Vanguard Consumer Discret ETF. The fund currently has a performance rating of A (Excellent) based on an annualized return of 17.54% over the last three years and a total return of 7.19% year to date 2015. Factored into the performance evaluation is an expense ratio of 0.10% (very low).

The fund's risk rating is currently B- (Good). It carries a beta of 1.11, meaning it is expected to move 11.1% for every 10% move in the market. Volatility, as measured by both the semi-deviation and a drawdown factor, is considered low. As of December 31, 2015, *Vanguard Consumer Discret ETF traded at a premium of .01% above its net asset value, which is better than its one-year historical average premium of .02%.

Michael A. Johnson has been running the fund for 6 years and currently receives a manager quality ranking of 79 (0=worst, 99=best). If you desire only a moderate level of risk and strong performance, then this fund is an excellent option.

Data Date	Investment Rating	Net Assets ($Mil)	Price	Performance Rating/Pts	Total Return Y-T-D	Risk Rating/Pts
12-15	A-	1,259.50	122.55	A / 9.3	7.19%	B- / 7.2
2014	A-	1,259.50	116.88	A- / 9.1	10.19%	B- / 7.0
2013	A	1,373.50	108.06	A- / 9.2	38.63%	B- / 7.9
2012	B+	572.80	75.87	B+ / 8.5	23.94%	B- / 7.9
2011	B	346.20	61.81	B / 7.9	5.59%	B- / 7.9
2010	B+	362.70	60.47	B / 8.2	30.57%	C+ / 5.6

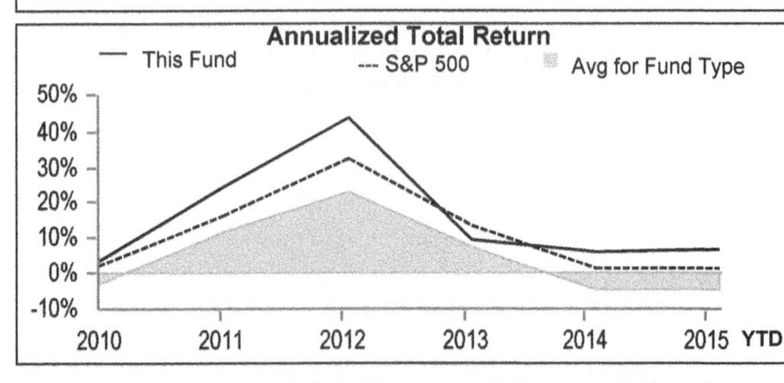

*Vanguard Consumer Staples ETF (VDC) A+ Excellent

Fund Family: Vanguard Group Inc
Fund Type: Income
Inception Date: January 26, 2004

Major Rating Factors:
Exceptional performance is the major factor driving the A+ (Excellent) TheStreet.com Investment Rating for *Vanguard Consumer Staples ETF. The fund currently has a performance rating of A- (Excellent) based on an annualized return of 15.19% over the last three years and a total return of 6.49% year to date 2015. Factored into the performance evaluation is an expense ratio of 0.10% (very low).

The fund's risk rating is currently B (Good). It carries a beta of 0.88, meaning the fund's expected move will be 8.8% for every 10% move in the market. Volatility, as measured by both the semi-deviation and a drawdown factor, is considered low. As of December 31, 2015, *Vanguard Consumer Staples ETF traded at a premium of .02% above its net asset value, which is worse than its one-year historical average premium of .01%.

Michael A. Johnson has been running the fund for 6 years and currently receives a manager quality ranking of 83 (0=worst, 99=best). If you desire only a moderate level of risk and strong performance, then this fund is an excellent option.

Data Date	Investment Rating	Net Assets ($Mil)	Price	Performance Rating/Pts	Total Return Y-T-D	Risk Rating/Pts
12-15	A+	1,976.40	129.07	A- / 9.1	6.49%	B / 8.2
2014	B+	1,976.40	125.24	B+ / 8.3	17.35%	B- / 7.5
2013	A	1,675.20	110.08	B / 8.1	23.04%	B+ / 9.2
2012	C+	1,202.60	87.91	C / 5.4	15.59%	B+ / 9.0
2011	B-	879.50	81.47	C+ / 6.0	13.52%	B / 8.6
2010	B-	608.70	73.39	C+ / 6.2	14.62%	B- / 7.3

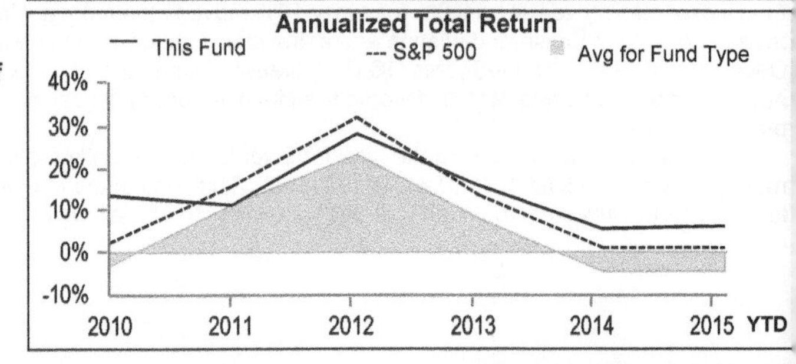

*Vanguard Div Appreciation ETF (VIG) A- Excellent

Fund Family: Vanguard Group Inc
Fund Type: Growth
Inception Date: April 21, 2006

Major Rating Factors:
Strong performance is the major factor driving the A- (Excellent) TheStreet.com Investment Rating for *Vanguard Div Appreciation ETF. The fund currently has a performance rating of B (Good) based on an annualized return of 10.63% over the last three years and a total return of -1.75% year to date 2015. Factored into the performance evaluation is an expense ratio of 0.10% (very low).

The fund's risk rating is currently B (Good). It carries a beta of 1.01, meaning that its performance tracks fairly well with that of the overall stock market. Volatility, as measured by both the semi-deviation and a drawdown factor, is considered low. As of December 31, 2015, *Vanguard Div Appreciation ETF traded at a discount of .03% below its net asset value.

Ryan E. Ludt has been running the fund for 10 years and currently receives a manager quality ranking of 42 (0=worst, 99=best). If you desire only a moderate level of risk and strong performance, then this fund is an excellent option.

Data Date	Investment Rating	Net Assets ($Mil)	Price	Performance Rating/Pts	Total Return Y-T-D	Risk Rating/Pts
12-15	A-	19,920.90	77.76	B / 7.7	-1.75%	B / 8.6
2014	B	19,920.90	81.16	B- / 7.3	10.98%	B- / 7.7
2013	A-	19,473.60	75.24	B / 7.8	24.39%	B / 8.7
2012	C+	12,040.10	59.57	C / 5.1	14.16%	B / 8.4
2011	C+	8,964.40	54.65	C / 5.3	7.26%	B / 8.2
2010	C+	4,606.30	52.63	C / 5.0	14.76%	C+ / 6.6

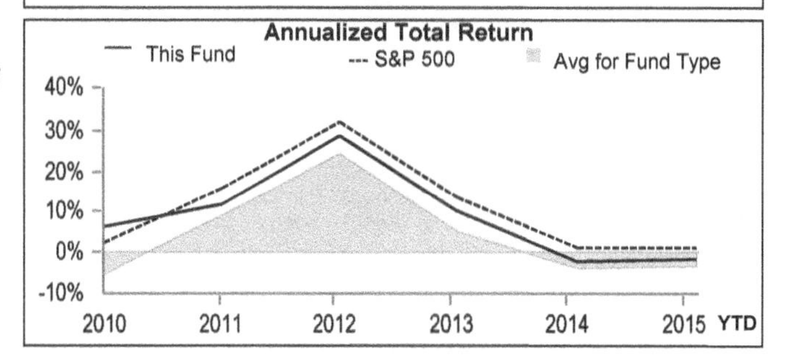

*Vanguard Em Mkt Govt Bd Idx ETF (VWOB) C Fair

Fund Family: Vanguard Group Inc
Fund Type: Emerging Market
Inception Date: May 31, 2013

Major Rating Factors: Middle of the road best describes *Vanguard Em Mkt Govt Bd Idx ETF whose TheStreet.com Investment Rating is currently a C (Fair). The fund currently has a performance rating of C (Fair) based on an annualized return of 0.00% over the last three years and a total return of 1.61% year to date 2015. Factored into the performance evaluation is an expense ratio of 0.34% (very low).

The fund's risk rating is currently B- (Good). It carries a beta of 0.00, meaning the fund's expected move will be 0.0% for every 10% move in the market. Volatility, as measured by both the semi-deviation and a drawdown factor, is considered low. As of December 31, 2015, *Vanguard Em Mkt Govt Bd Idx ETF traded at a premium of .37% above its net asset value, which is better than its one-year historical average premium of .46%.

Joshua C. Barrickman has been running the fund for 3 years and currently receives a manager quality ranking of 76 (0=worst, 99=best). If you desire an average level of risk, then this fund may be an option.

Data Date	Investment Rating	Net Assets ($Mil)	Price	Performance Rating/Pts	Total Return Y-T-D	Risk Rating/Pts
12-15	C	235.80	73.96	C / 4.6	1.61%	B- / 7.4
2014	C-	235.80	76.36	C- / 3.0	4.31%	B- / 7.8

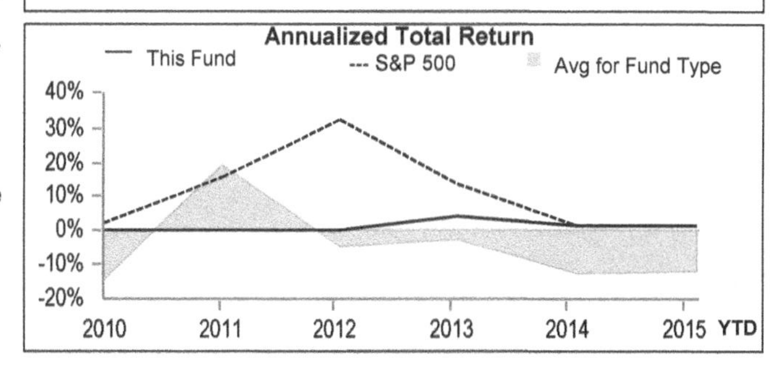

*Vanguard Energy ETF (VDE) D+ Weak

Fund Family: Vanguard Group Inc
Fund Type: Energy/Natural Resources
Inception Date: September 23, 2004

Major Rating Factors:
Disappointing performance is the major factor driving the D+ (Weak) TheStreet.com Investment Rating for *Vanguard Energy ETF. The fund currently has a performance rating of D (Weak) based on an annualized return of -5.61% over the last three years and a total return of -23.55% year to date 2015. Factored into the performance evaluation is an expense ratio of 0.10% (very low).

The fund's risk rating is currently C+ (Fair). It carries a beta of 1.02, meaning that its performance tracks fairly well with that of the overall stock market. Volatility, as measured by both the semi-deviation and a drawdown factor, is considered low. As of December 31, 2015, *Vanguard Energy ETF traded at a discount of .05% below its net asset value, which is better than its one-year historical average premium of .01%.

Jeffrey D. Miller has been running the fund for 6 years and currently receives a manager quality ranking of 61 (0=worst, 99=best). This fund offers only a moderate level of risk but investors looking for strong performance are still waiting.

Data Date	Investment Rating	Net Assets ($Mil)	Price	Performance Rating/Pts	Total Return Y-T-D	Risk Rating/Pts
12-15	D+	3,180.90	83.12	D / 2.1	-23.55%	C+ / 6.6
2014	C-	3,180.90	111.62	D+ / 2.8	-8.46%	B- / 7.7
2013	C+	2,574.60	126.43	C+ / 6.8	19.56%	B- / 7.5
2012	C-	1,880.60	102.26	C- / 3.5	6.58%	B- / 7.3
2011	C	1,728.20	100.81	C+ / 5.6	4.45%	B- / 7.1
2010	C-	1,548.60	99.67	C / 5.0	21.05%	C / 4.8

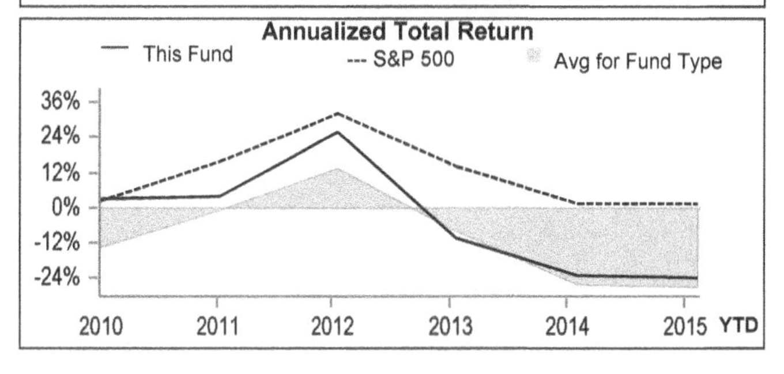

*Vanguard Extended Market Index E (VXF) B+ Good

Fund Family: Vanguard Group Inc
Fund Type: Growth
Inception Date: December 27, 2001

Major Rating Factors: Strong performance is the major factor driving the B+ (Good) TheStreet.com Investment Rating for *Vanguard Extended Market Index E. The fund currently has a performance rating of B (Good) based on an annualized return of 11.62% over the last three years and a total return of -3.03% year to date 2015. Factored into the performance evaluation is an expense ratio of 0.10% (very low).

The fund's risk rating is currently B- (Good). It carries a beta of 1.03, meaning that its performance tracks fairly well with that of the overall stock market. Volatility, as measured by both the semi-deviation and a drawdown factor, is considered low. As of December 31, 2015, *Vanguard Extended Market Index E traded at a price exactly equal to its net asset value, which is better than its one-year historical average premium of .01%.

Donald M. Butler has been running the fund for 19 years and currently receives a manager quality ranking of 48 (0=worst, 99=best). If you desire only a moderate level of risk and strong performance, then this fund is an excellent option.

Data Date	Investment Rating	Net Assets ($Mil)	Price	Perfor-mance Rating/Pts	Total Return Y-T-D	Risk Rating/Pts
12-15	B+	3,412.30	83.80	B / 7.7	-3.03%	B- / 7.6
2014	B	3,412.30	87.79	B / 8.1	8.19%	B- / 7.1
2013	B+	3,104.60	82.70	B+ / 8.6	32.81%	B- / 7.6
2012	C+	1,400.70	60.50	C+ / 6.9	18.78%	B- / 7.5
2011	C+	1,148.20	51.84	C+ / 6.1	-3.98%	B- / 7.4
2010	C	1,112.90	54.41	B- / 7.3	27.62%	C- / 3.2

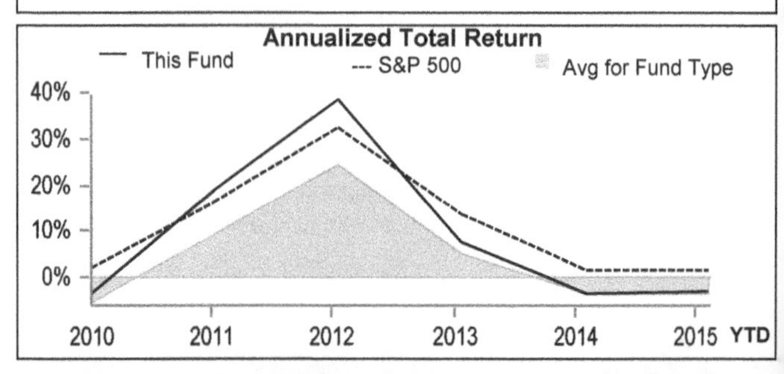

*Vanguard Extnd Durtn Trea Idx ET (EDV) C Fair

Fund Family: Vanguard Group Inc
Fund Type: US Government/Agency
Inception Date: December 6, 2007

Major Rating Factors: Middle of the road best describes *Vanguard Extnd Durtn Trea Idx ET whose TheStreet.com Investment Rating is currently a C (Fair). The fund currently has a performance rating of C+ (Fair) based on an annualized return of 4.71% over the last three years and a total return of -6.52% year to date 2015. Factored into the performance evaluation is an expense ratio of 0.10% (very low).

The fund's risk rating is currently C+ (Fair). It carries a beta of 1.68, meaning it is expected to move 16.8% for every 10% move in the market. Volatility, as measured by both the semi-deviation and a drawdown factor, is considered low. As of December 31, 2015, *Vanguard Extnd Durtn Trea Idx ET traded at a premium of .14% above its net asset value, which is better than its one-year historical average premium of .45%.

Joshua C. Barrickman has been running the fund for 3 years and currently receives a manager quality ranking of 60 (0=worst, 99=best). If you desire an average level of risk, then this fund may be an option.

Data Date	Investment Rating	Net Assets ($Mil)	Price	Perfor-mance Rating/Pts	Total Return Y-T-D	Risk Rating/Pts
12-15	C	256.20	113.20	C+ / 5.8	-6.52%	C+ / 5.6
2014	B-	256.20	123.94	B / 7.9	44.11%	C+ / 6.5
2013	C-	127.20	88.77	C / 4.9	-16.33%	B- / 7.2
2012	C+	176.60	116.00	C+ / 6.4	1.38%	B- / 7.7
2011	C+	187.90	121.94	B- / 7.2	58.00%	C+ / 6.3
2010	D+	132.00	82.80	D / 2.0	9.79%	C+ / 5.9

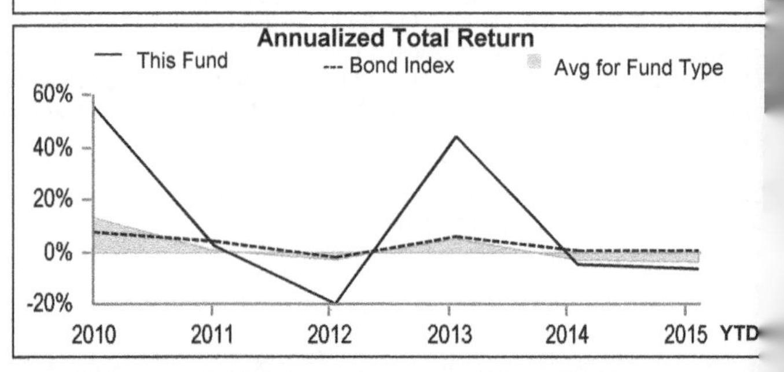

*Vanguard Financials ETF (VFH) A+ Excellent

Fund Family: Vanguard Group Inc
Fund Type: Financial Services
Inception Date: January 26, 2004

Major Rating Factors:
Strong performance is the major factor driving the A+ (Excellent) TheStreet.com Investment Rating for *Vanguard Financials ETF. The fund currently has a performance rating of B+ (Good) based on an annualized return of 13.20% over the last three years and a total return of -0.59% year to date 2015. Factored into the performance evaluation is an expense ratio of 0.10% (very low).

The fund's risk rating is currently B (Good). It carries a beta of 0.99, meaning that its performance tracks fairly well with that of the overall stock market. Volatility, as measured by both the semi-deviation and a drawdown factor, is considered low. As of December 31, 2015, *Vanguard Financials ETF traded at a discount of .02% below its net asset value, which is better than its one-year historical average premium of .02%.

Jeffrey D. Miller has been running the fund for 6 years and currently receives a manager quality ranking of 63 (0=worst, 99=best). If you desire only a moderate level of risk and strong performance, then this fund is an excellent option.

Data Date	Investment Rating	Net Assets ($Mil)	Price	Perfor-mance Rating/Pts	Total Return Y-T-D	Risk Rating/Pts
12-15	A+	2,227.30	48.45	B+ / 8.5	-0.59%	B / 8.5
2014	A+	2,227.30	49.71	A- / 9.1	14.01%	B / 8.6
2013	B	1,724.00	44.42	B / 7.6	27.96%	B- / 7.5
2012	C	850.50	34.10	C / 5.5	25.33%	B- / 7.4
2011	D+	534.20	27.62	C- / 3.0	-13.22%	C+ / 6.8
2010	D-	576.20	32.88	D- / 1.1	14.83%	C / 4.5

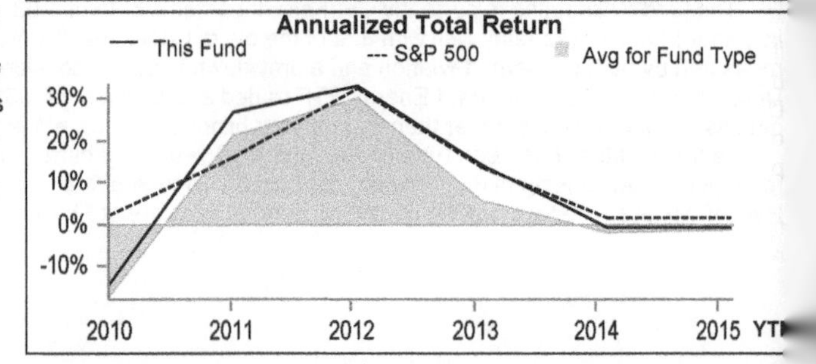

*Vanguard FTSE All-Wld ex-US S/C (VSS) C Fair

Fund Family: Vanguard Group Inc
Fund Type: Foreign
Inception Date: April 2, 2009

Major Rating Factors: Middle of the road best describes *Vanguard FTSE All-Wld ex-US S/C whose TheStreet.com Investment Rating is currently a C (Fair). The fund currently has a performance rating of C (Fair) based on an annualized return of 3.37% over the last three years and a total return of 1.28% year to date 2015. Factored into the performance evaluation is an expense ratio of 0.19% (very low).

The fund's risk rating is currently C+ (Fair). It carries a beta of 0.83, meaning the fund's expected move will be 8.3% for every 10% move in the market. Volatility, as measured by both the semi-deviation and a drawdown factor, is considered low. As of December 31, 2015, *Vanguard FTSE All-Wld ex-US S/C traded at a premium of .13% above its net asset value, which is better than its one-year historical average premium of .20%.

Jeffrey D. Miller has been running the fund for 1 year and currently receives a manager quality ranking of 62 (0=worst, 99=best). If you desire an average level of risk, then this fund may be an option.

Data Date	Investment Rating	Net Assets ($Mil)	Price	Performance Rating/Pts	Total Return Y-T-D	Risk Rating/Pts
12-15	C	2,015.30	92.87	C / 5.5	1.28%	C+ / 6.7
2014	C-	2,015.30	95.31	C / 4.6	-4.20%	B- / 7.0
2013	C	1,709.10	102.94	C / 5.3	13.96%	C+ / 6.9
2012	C-	1,067.20	90.89	C / 4.9	21.70%	C+ / 6.1
2011	D-	814.40	77.57	E+ / 0.8	-17.12%	C+ / 6.3
2010	A+	673.30	99.62	A / 9.5	25.62%	B- / 7.8

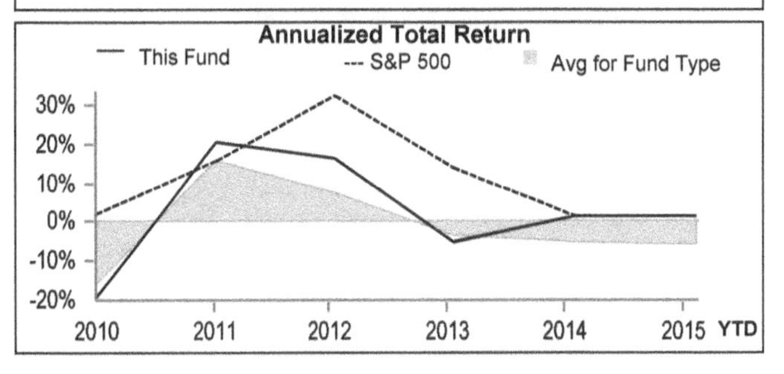

*Vanguard FTSE All-World ex-US ET (VEU) C Fair

Fund Family: Vanguard Group Inc
Fund Type: Foreign
Inception Date: March 2, 2007

Major Rating Factors: Middle of the road best describes *Vanguard FTSE All-World ex-US ET whose TheStreet.com Investment Rating is currently a C (Fair). The fund currently has a performance rating of C- (Fair) based on an annualized return of 1.10% over the last three years and a total return of -3.67% year to date 2015. Factored into the performance evaluation is an expense ratio of 0.14% (very low).

The fund's risk rating is currently B- (Good). It carries a beta of 0.96, meaning that its performance tracks fairly well with that of the overall stock market. Volatility, as measured by both the semi-deviation and a drawdown factor, is considered low. As of December 31, 2015, *Vanguard FTSE All-World ex-US ET traded at a discount of .09% below its net asset value, which is better than its one-year historical average premium of .08%.

Ryan E. Ludt has been running the fund for 8 years and currently receives a manager quality ranking of 39 (0=worst, 99=best). If you desire an average level of risk, then this fund may be an option.

Data Date	Investment Rating	Net Assets ($Mil)	Price	Performance Rating/Pts	Total Return Y-T-D	Risk Rating/Pts
12-15	C	12,524.20	43.41	C- / 4.2	-3.67%	B- / 7.7
2014	C-	12,524.20	46.86	C / 4.5	-2.59%	C+ / 6.8
2013	C	11,522.30	50.73	C / 5.2	10.57%	B- / 7.6
2012	C-	7,829.50	45.75	C- / 4.1	19.73%	B- / 7.3
2011	C-	5,864.70	39.65	C- / 3.3	-12.99%	B- / 7.3
2010	D+	6,174.60	47.73	D+ / 2.7	11.80%	C / 5.3

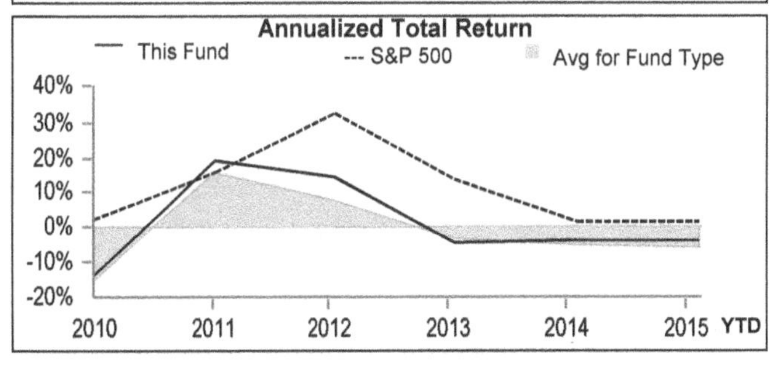

*Vanguard FTSE Developed Markets (VEA) C+ Fair

Fund Family: Vanguard Group Inc
Fund Type: Foreign
Inception Date: July 20, 2007

Major Rating Factors: Middle of the road best describes *Vanguard FTSE Developed Markets whose TheStreet.com Investment Rating is currently a C+ (Fair). The fund currently has a performance rating of C+ (Fair) based on an annualized return of 4.29% over the last three years and a total return of 0.75% year to date 2015. Factored into the performance evaluation is an expense ratio of 0.09% (very low).

The fund's risk rating is currently B (Good). It carries a beta of 0.97, meaning that its performance tracks fairly well with that of the overall stock market. Volatility, as measured by both the semi-deviation and a drawdown factor, is considered low. As of December 31, 2015, *Vanguard FTSE Developed Markets traded at a discount of .08% below its net asset value, which is better than its one-year historical average premium of .12%.

Christine Franquin has been running the fund for 3 years and currently receives a manager quality ranking of 63 (0=worst, 99=best). If you desire an average level of risk, then this fund may be an option.

Data Date	Investment Rating	Net Assets ($Mil)	Price	Performance Rating/Pts	Total Return Y-T-D	Risk Rating/Pts
12-15	C+	23,071.60	36.72	C+ / 5.7	0.75%	B / 8.1
2014	C-	23,071.60	37.88	C / 5.0	-4.40%	C+ / 6.7
2013	C+	19,020.60	41.68	C+ / 6.7	18.35%	B- / 7.4
2012	D	10,212.70	35.23	C- / 4.1	20.86%	C / 5.4
2011	D+	6,435.30	30.63	D+ / 2.6	-11.64%	B- / 7.4
2010	D-	4,829.40	36.15	D / 1.8	8.33%	C- / 3.6

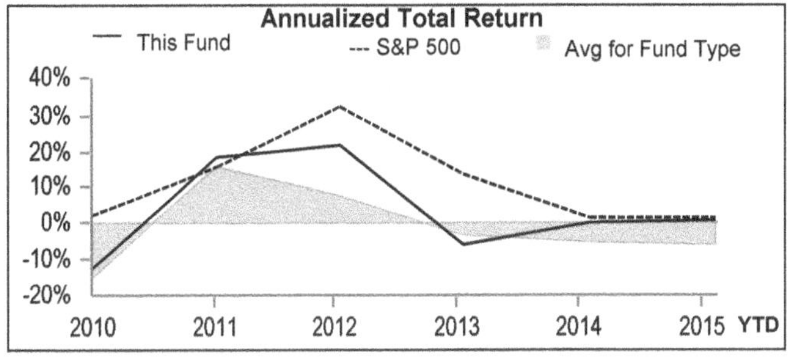

*Vanguard FTSE Emerging Markets E (VWO) D+ Weak

Fund Family: Vanguard Group Inc
Fund Type: Emerging Market
Inception Date: March 4, 2005

Major Rating Factors:
Disappointing performance is the major factor driving the D+ (Weak) TheStreet.com Investment Rating for *Vanguard FTSE Emerging Markets E. The fund currently has a performance rating of D (Weak) based on an annualized return of -7.56% over the last three years and a total return of -14.45% year to date 2015. Factored into the performance evaluation is an expense ratio of 0.15% (very low).

The fund's risk rating is currently B- (Good). It carries a beta of 1.02, meaning that its performance tracks fairly well with that of the overall stock market. Volatility, as measured by both the semi-deviation and a drawdown factor, is considered low. As of December 31, 2015, *Vanguard FTSE Emerging Markets E traded at a discount of .46% below its net asset value, which is better than its one-year historical average discount of .09%.

Michael Perre has been running the fund for 8 years and currently receives a manager quality ranking of 63 (0=worst, 99=best). This fund offers only a moderate level of risk but investors looking for strong performance are still waiting.

Data Date	Investment Rating	Net Assets ($Mil)	Price	Performance Rating/Pts	Total Return Y-T-D	Risk Rating/Pts
12-15	D+	46,906.60	32.71	D / 2.1	-14.45%	B- / 7.1
2014	D+	46,906.60	40.02	C- / 3.5	3.72%	C+ / 6.0
2013	D	46,553.60	41.14	D / 1.8	-9.94%	C+ / 6.7
2012	D+	56,968.50	44.53	C- / 3.1	15.78%	C+ / 6.8
2011	C	42,454.50	38.21	C / 5.2	-17.29%	B- / 7.0
2010	D+	44,730.40	48.15	C / 5.3	19.46%	C- / 3.0

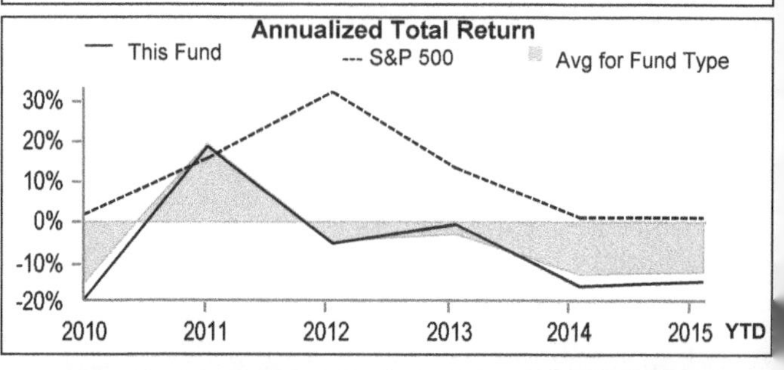

*Vanguard FTSE Europe ETF (VGK) C+ Fair

Fund Family: Vanguard Group Inc
Fund Type: Foreign
Inception Date: March 4, 2005

Major Rating Factors: Middle of the road best describes *Vanguard FTSE Europe ETF whose TheStreet.com Investment Rating is currently a C+ (Fair). The fund currently has a performance rating of C+ (Fair) based on an annualized return of 4.10% over the last three years and a total return of -0.98% year to date 2015. Factored into the performance evaluation is an expense ratio of 0.12% (very low).

The fund's risk rating is currently B- (Good). It carries a beta of 1.03, meaning that its performance tracks fairly well with that of the overall stock market. Volatility, as measured by both the semi-deviation and a drawdown factor, is considered low. As of December 31, 2015, *Vanguard FTSE Europe ETF traded at a discount of .20% below its net asset value, which is better than its one-year historical average premium of .10%.

Gerard C. O'Reilly has been running the fund for 8 years and currently receives a manager quality ranking of 58 (0=worst, 99=best). If you desire an average level of risk, then this fund may be an option.

Data Date	Investment Rating	Net Assets ($Mil)	Price	Performance Rating/Pts	Total Return Y-T-D	Risk Rating/Pts
12-15	C+	14,084.20	49.88	C+ / 5.6	-0.98%	B- / 7.7
2014	C-	14,084.20	52.41	C / 5.3	-5.10%	C+ / 6.5
2013	C+	13,653.70	58.80	B- / 7.3	20.67%	B- / 7.0
2012	D+	4,379.10	48.84	C / 4.9	25.59%	C / 5.1
2011	D+	2,220.40	41.43	D+ / 2.7	-10.46%	B- / 7.1
2010	E+	2,784.40	49.09	D- / 1.4	6.05%	C- / 3.4

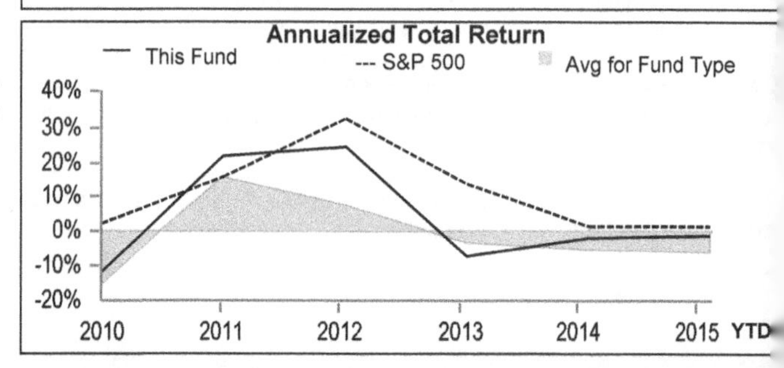

*Vanguard FTSE Pacific Fund ETF (VPL) C+ Fair

Fund Family: Vanguard Group Inc
Fund Type: Foreign
Inception Date: March 4, 2005

Major Rating Factors: Middle of the road best describes *Vanguard FTSE Pacific Fund ETF whose TheStreet.com Investment Rating is currently a C+ (Fair). The fund currently has a performance rating of C+ (Fair) based on an annualized return of 4.50% over the last three years and a total return of 3.40% year to date 2015. Factored into the performance evaluation is an expense ratio of 0.12% (very low).

The fund's risk rating is currently B- (Good). It carries a beta of 0.87, meaning the fund's expected move will be 8.7% for every 10% move in the market. Volatility, as measured by both the semi-deviation and a drawdown factor, is considered low. As of December 31, 2015, *Vanguard FTSE Pacific Fund ETF traded at a discount of .02% below its net asset value, which is better than its one-year historical average premium of .04%.

Michael H. Buek has been running the fund for 19 years and currently receives a manager quality ranking of 69 (0=worst, 99=best). If you desire an average level of risk, then this fund may be an option.

Data Date	Investment Rating	Net Assets ($Mil)	Price	Performance Rating/Pts	Total Return Y-T-D	Risk Rating/Pts
12-15	C+	2,703.90	56.67	C+ / 6.0	3.40%	B- / 7.8
2014	C-	2,703.90	56.87	C / 4.5	-3.45%	C+ / 6.5
2013	C	2,641.80	61.30	C / 5.5	14.60%	B- / 7.7
2012	C-	1,599.30	53.39	C- / 3.4	15.88%	B- / 7.7
2011	C-	1,415.50	47.59	D+ / 2.7	-13.38%	B- / 7.8
2010	C-	1,548.70	57.04	C- / 3.7	15.50%	C / 5.3

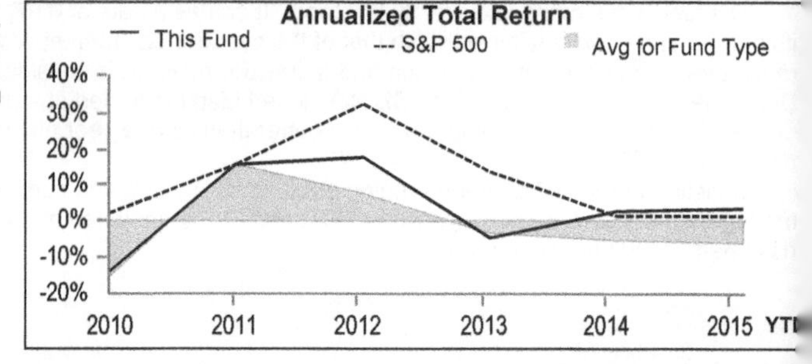

* Denotes ETF Fund

*Vanguard Global ex-US RE ETF (VNQI) C Fair

Fund Family: Vanguard Group Inc
Fund Type: Global
Inception Date: November 1, 2010

Major Rating Factors: Middle of the road best describes *Vanguard Global ex-US RE ETF whose TheStreet.com Investment Rating is currently a C (Fair). The fund currently has a performance rating of C- (Fair) based on an annualized return of 0.69% over the last three years and a total return of -2.31% year to date 2015. Factored into the performance evaluation is an expense ratio of 0.24% (very low).

The fund's risk rating is currently B (Good). It carries a beta of 0.82, meaning the fund's expected move will be 8.2% for every 10% move in the market. Volatility, as measured by both the semi-deviation and a drawdown factor, is considered low. As of December 31, 2015, *Vanguard Global ex-US RE ETF traded at a discount of .58% below its net asset value, which is better than its one-year historical average premium of .19%.

Justin E Hales has been running the fund for 1 year and currently receives a manager quality ranking of 39 (0=worst, 99=best). If you desire an average level of risk, then this fund may be an option.

Data Date	Investment Rating	Net Assets ($Mil)	Price	Performance Rating/Pts	Total Return Y-T-D	Risk Rating/Pts
12-15	C	2,099.10	51.11	C- / 4.2	-2.31%	B / 8.0
2014	B	2,099.10	53.51	C+ / 6.4	4.30%	B / 8.4
2013	C-	1,263.00	54.48	C / 4.6	0.34%	B- / 7.3
2012	A	423.30	55.03	A+ / 9.8	40.47%	B- / 7.3
2011	D	166.70	40.70	D- / 1.0	-15.59%	B- / 7.2

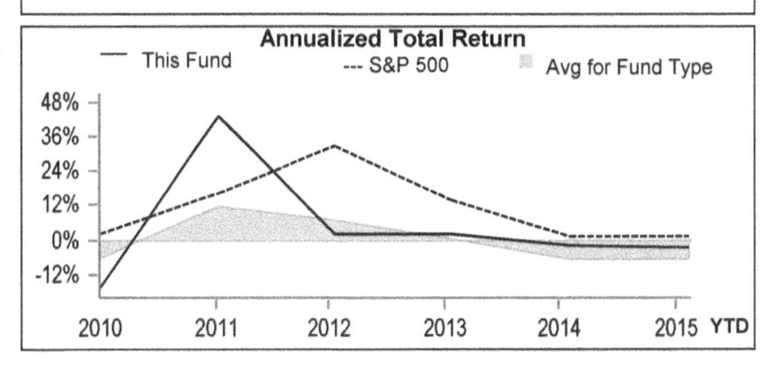

*Vanguard Growth ETF (VUG) A- Excellent

Fund Family: Vanguard Group Inc
Fund Type: Growth
Inception Date: January 26, 2004

Major Rating Factors:
Exceptional performance is the major factor driving the A- (Excellent) TheStreet.com Investment Rating for *Vanguard Growth ETF. The fund currently has a performance rating of A- (Excellent) based on an annualized return of 14.82% over the last three years and a total return of 3.40% year to date 2015. Factored into the performance evaluation is an expense ratio of 0.09% (very low).

The fund's risk rating is currently B- (Good). It carries a beta of 1.06, meaning that its performance tracks fairly well with that of the overall stock market. Volatility, as measured by both the semi-deviation and a drawdown factor, is considered low. As of December 31, 2015, *Vanguard Growth ETF traded at a discount of .01% below its net asset value, which is better than its one-year historical average premium of .01%.

Gerard C. O'Reilly has been running the fund for 22 years and currently receives a manager quality ranking of 65 (0=worst, 99=best). If you desire only a moderate level of risk and strong performance, then this fund is an excellent option.

Data Date	Investment Rating	Net Assets ($Mil)	Price	Performance Rating/Pts	Total Return Y-T-D	Risk Rating/Pts
12-15	A-	15,547.30	106.39	A- / 9.0	3.40%	B- / 7.5
2014	B	15,547.30	104.39	B+ / 8.5	14.94%	B- / 7.0
2013	B+	13,264.90	93.05	B+ / 8.3	27.54%	B- / 7.7
2012	C	8,446.50	71.18	C+ / 5.7	17.58%	B- / 7.6
2011	C+	6,045.60	61.76	C+ / 6.2	2.83%	B- / 7.7
2010	C+	5,099.50	61.42	C / 5.5	17.23%	C+ / 5.9

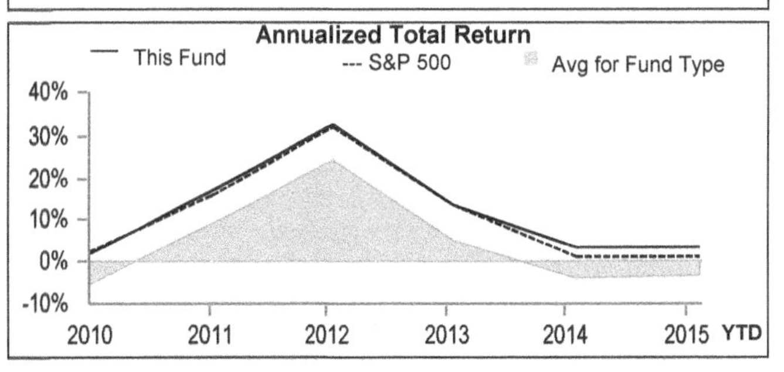

*Vanguard HealthCare Index ETF (VHT) A+ Excellent

Fund Family: Vanguard Group Inc
Fund Type: Health
Inception Date: January 26, 2004

Major Rating Factors:
Exceptional performance is the major factor driving the A+ (Excellent) TheStreet.com Investment Rating for *Vanguard HealthCare Index ETF. The fund currently has a performance rating of A+ (Excellent) based on an annualized return of 23.17% over the last three years and a total return of 6.95% year to date 2015. Factored into the performance evaluation is an expense ratio of 0.09% (very low).

The fund's risk rating is currently B- (Good). It carries a beta of 0.95, meaning that its performance tracks fairly well with that of the overall stock market. Volatility, as measured by both the semi-deviation and a drawdown factor, is considered low. As of December 31, 2015, *Vanguard HealthCare Index ETF traded at a discount of .02% below its net asset value, which is better than its one-year historical average premium of .02%.

Ryan E. Ludt has been running the fund for 12 years and currently receives a manager quality ranking of 94 (0=worst, 99=best). If you desire only a moderate level of risk and strong performance, then this fund is an excellent option.

Data Date	Investment Rating	Net Assets ($Mil)	Price	Performance Rating/Pts	Total Return Y-T-D	Risk Rating/Pts
12-15	A+	3,453.10	132.88	A+ / 9.6	6.95%	B- / 7.7
2014	A+	3,453.10	125.59	A / 9.5	25.85%	B / 8.7
2013	A+	2,398.40	101.10	A- / 9.2	38.51%	B / 8.3
2012	C+	1,014.30	71.67	C+ / 5.9	21.78%	B / 8.4
2011	C+	728.90	61.21	C / 5.2	10.15%	B / 8.2
2010	C	614.30	56.25	C- / 3.4	5.60%	C+ / 6.9

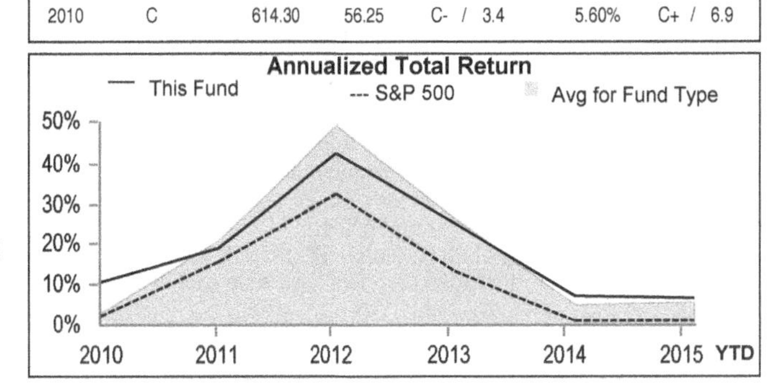

*Vanguard High Dividend Yield ETF (VYM) A+ Excellent

Fund Family: Vanguard Group Inc
Fund Type: Income
Inception Date: November 10, 2006

Major Rating Factors:
Strong performance is the major factor driving the A+ (Excellent) TheStreet.com Investment Rating for *Vanguard High Dividend Yield ETF. The fund currently has a performance rating of B+ (Good) based on an annualized return of 13.34% over the last three years and a total return of 1.21% year to date 2015. Factored into the performance evaluation is an expense ratio of 0.10% (very low).

The fund's risk rating is currently B (Good). It carries a beta of 0.95, meaning that its performance tracks fairly well with that of the overall stock market. Volatility, as measured by both the semi-deviation and a drawdown factor, is considered low. As of December 31, 2015, *Vanguard High Dividend Yield ETF traded at a discount of .03% below its net asset value, which is better than its one-year historical average premium of .01%.

Michael Perre has been running the fund for 10 years and currently receives a manager quality ranking of 68 (0=worst, 99=best). If you desire only a moderate level of risk and strong performance, then this fund is an excellent option.

Data Date	Investment Rating	Net Assets ($Mil)	Price	Performance Rating/Pts	Total Return Y-T-D	Risk Rating/Pts
12-15	A+	9,132.30	66.75	B+ / 8.7	1.21%	B / 8.7
2014	B+	9,132.30	68.75	B / 7.8	14.60%	B- / 7.7
2013	A	7,275.90	62.32	B / 8.2	25.57%	B / 8.9
2012	C+	4,230.70	49.38	C / 5.3	14.52%	B / 8.7
2011	C+	2,407.50	45.26	C+ / 5.9	10.69%	B- / 7.8
2010	C-	931.40	42.22	C- / 3.5	14.25%	C+ / 6.0

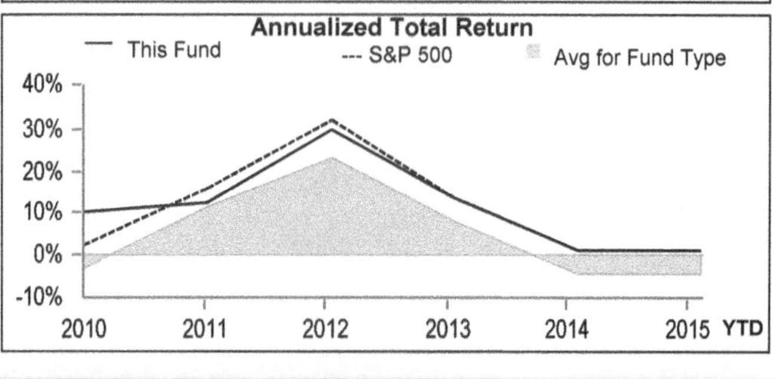

*Vanguard Industrials Index ETF (VIS) B+ Good

Fund Family: Vanguard Group Inc
Fund Type: Income
Inception Date: September 23, 2004

Major Rating Factors: Strong performance is the major factor driving the B+ (Good) TheStreet.com Investment Rating for *Vanguard Industrials Index ETF. The fund currently has a performance rating of B+ (Good) based on an annualized return of 12.88% over the last three years and a total return of -3.30% year to date 2015. Factored into the performance evaluation is an expense ratio of 0.10% (very low).

The fund's risk rating is currently B- (Good). It carries a beta of 1.10, meaning it is expected to move 11.0% for every 10% move in the market. Volatility, as measured by both the semi-deviation and a drawdown factor, is considered low. As of December 31, 2015, *Vanguard Industrials Index ETF traded at a premium of .09% above its net asset value, which is worse than its one-year historical average premium of .01%.

Jeffrey D. Miller has been running the fund for 6 years and currently receives a manager quality ranking of 48 (0=worst, 99=best). If you desire only a moderate level of risk and strong performance, then this fund is an excellent option.

Data Date	Investment Rating	Net Assets ($Mil)	Price	Performance Rating/Pts	Total Return Y-T-D	Risk Rating/Pts
12-15	B+	1,856.70	101.03	B+ / 8.3	-3.30%	B- / 7.1
2014	B+	1,856.70	106.82	B+ / 8.5	9.44%	B- / 7.5
2013	A-	1,551.20	100.03	A- / 9.0	36.16%	B- / 7.8
2012	C+	515.50	71.25	C+ / 6.4	15.01%	B- / 7.6
2011	C	435.10	62.09	C / 5.3	-1.03%	B- / 7.3
2010	C	440.40	64.82	C / 5.5	27.32%	C / 5.3

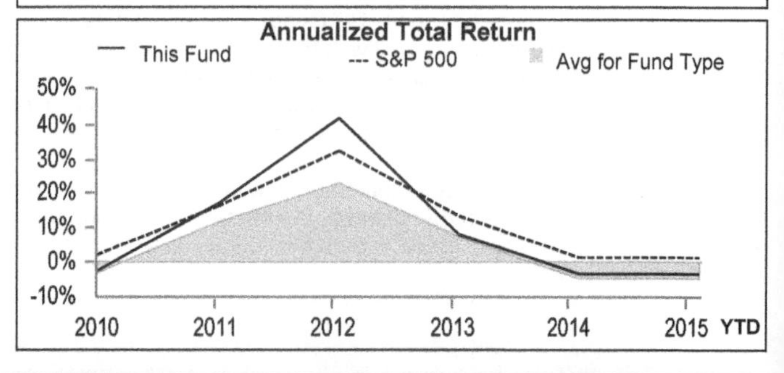

*Vanguard Info Tech Ind ETF (VGT) A Excellent

Fund Family: Vanguard Group Inc
Fund Type: Growth
Inception Date: January 26, 2004

Major Rating Factors:
Exceptional performance is the major factor driving the A (Excellent) TheStreet.com Investment Rating for *Vanguard Info Tech Ind ETF. The fund currently has a performance rating of A (Excellent) based on an annualized return of 16.74% over the last three years and a total return of 5.32% year to date 2015. Factored into the performance evaluation is an expense ratio of 0.10% (very low).

The fund's risk rating is currently B- (Good). It carries a beta of 1.04, meaning that its performance tracks fairly well with that of the overall stock market. Volatility, as measured by both the semi-deviation and a drawdown factor, is considered low. As of December 31, 2015, *Vanguard Info Tech Ind ETF traded at a premium of .02% above its net asset value, which is worse than its one-year historical average premium of .01%.

Jeffrey D. Miller has been running the fund for 6 years and currently receives a manager quality ranking of 78 (0=worst, 99=best). If you desire only a moderate level of risk and strong performance, then this fund is an excellent option.

Data Date	Investment Rating	Net Assets ($Mil)	Price	Performance Rating/Pts	Total Return Y-T-D	Risk Rating/Pts
12-15	A	5,947.60	108.29	A / 9.3	5.32%	B- / 7.5
2014	B+	5,947.60	104.48	B+ / 8.7	19.60%	B- / 7.0
2013	B	4,497.60	89.54	B / 7.8	26.59%	B- / 7.6
2012	C-	2,484.10	69.11	C- / 4.2	13.91%	B- / 7.0
2011	C+	1,891.00	61.37	B- / 7.0	0.26%	B- / 7.3
2010	C+	1,501.60	61.52	C+ / 6.3	12.78%	C+ / 5.6

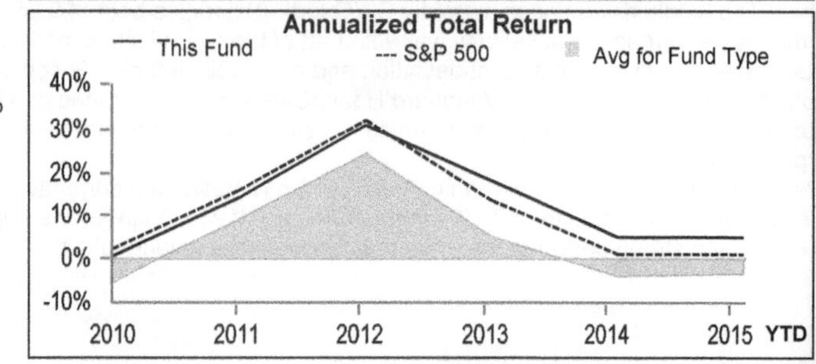

*Vanguard Intermediate Term Bond (BIV) C Fair

Fund Family: Vanguard Group Inc
Fund Type: General - Investment Grade
Inception Date: April 3, 2007

Major Rating Factors: Middle of the road best describes *Vanguard Intermediate Term Bond whose TheStreet.com Investment Rating is currently a C (Fair). The fund currently has a performance rating of C (Fair) based on an annualized return of 1.66% over the last three years and a total return of 0.83% year to date 2015. Factored into the performance evaluation is an expense ratio of 0.10% (very low).

The fund's risk rating is currently B- (Good). It carries a beta of 1.49, meaning it is expected to move 14.9% for every 10% move in the market. Volatility, as measured by both the semi-deviation and a drawdown factor, is considered low. As of December 31, 2015, *Vanguard Intermediate Term Bond traded at a premium of .13% above its net asset value, which is better than its one-year historical average premium of .15%.

Joshua C. Barrickman has been running the fund for 8 years and currently receives a manager quality ranking of 62 (0=worst, 99=best). If you desire an average level of risk, then this fund may be an option.

Data Date	Investment Rating	Net Assets ($Mil)	Price	Performance Rating/Pts	Total Return Y-T-D	Risk Rating/Pts
12-15	C	4,183.20	83.06	C / 5.1	0.83%	B- / 7.6
2014	C	4,183.20	84.68	C- / 4.0	6.92%	B / 8.1
2013	C	3,695.20	81.70	C- / 3.9	-2.77%	B+ / 9.3
2012	C	4,368.20	88.25	C- / 3.1	6.13%	B+ / 9.5
2011	C+	2,780.90	86.97	C- / 3.9	9.82%	B+ / 9.6
2010	B	1,931.90	82.49	C / 5.4	9.13%	B / 8.6

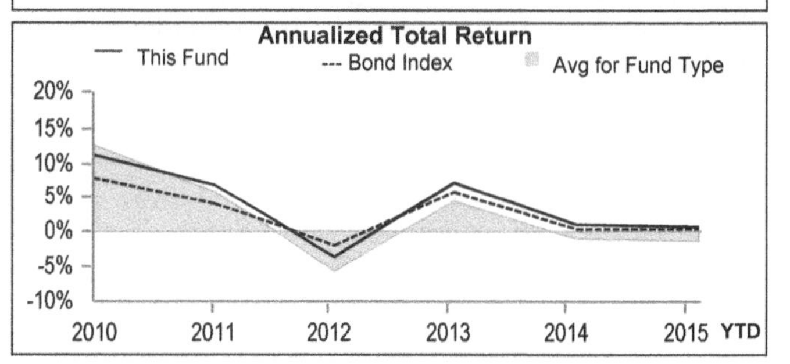

*Vanguard Intm-Term Corp Bd Idx E (VCIT) C+ Fair

Fund Family: Vanguard Group Inc
Fund Type: Corporate - Investment Grade
Inception Date: November 19, 2009

Major Rating Factors: Middle of the road best describes *Vanguard Intm-Term Corp Bd Idx E whose TheStreet.com Investment Rating is currently a C+ (Fair). The fund currently has a performance rating of C (Fair) based on an annualized return of 2.09% over the last three years and a total return of 0.62% year to date 2015. Factored into the performance evaluation is an expense ratio of 0.10% (very low).

The fund's risk rating is currently B- (Good). It carries a beta of 1.07, meaning that its performance tracks fairly well with that of the overall stock market. Volatility, as measured by both the semi-deviation and a drawdown factor, is considered low. As of December 31, 2015, *Vanguard Intm-Term Corp Bd Idx E traded at a premium of .43% above its net asset value, which is worse than its one-year historical average premium of .19%.

Joshua C. Barrickman has been running the fund for 7 years and currently receives a manager quality ranking of 73 (0=worst, 99=best). If you desire an average level of risk, then this fund may be an option.

Data Date	Investment Rating	Net Assets ($Mil)	Price	Performance Rating/Pts	Total Return Y-T-D	Risk Rating/Pts
12-15	C+	4,032.10	84.10	C / 5.3	0.62%	B- / 7.6
2014	C-	4,032.10	86.13	C / 4.3	7.42%	B- / 7.4
2013	C+	3,169.80	82.66	C / 4.5	-1.85%	B+ / 9.4
2012	C	3,222.70	87.66	C- / 3.5	10.02%	B+ / 9.7
2011	C+	953.70	82.37	C- / 4.0	8.69%	B+ / 9.7
2010	B	386.10	78.68	C+ / 6.2	9.96%	B / 8.9

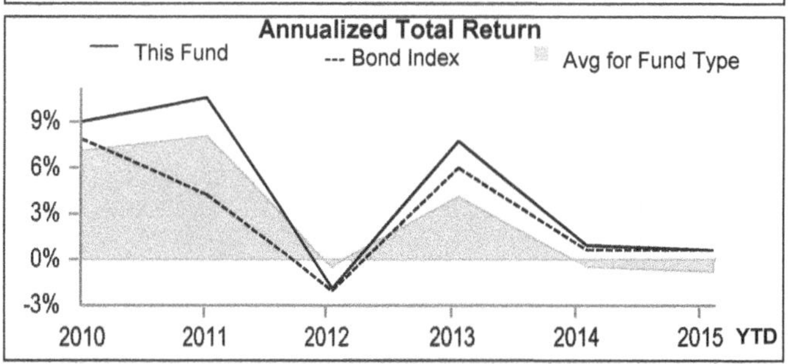

*Vanguard Intm-Term Govt Bd Idx E (VGIT) C Fair

Fund Family: Vanguard Group Inc
Fund Type: US Government/Agency
Inception Date: November 19, 2009

Major Rating Factors: Middle of the road best describes *Vanguard Intm-Term Govt Bd Idx E whose TheStreet.com Investment Rating is currently a C (Fair). The fund currently has a performance rating of C (Fair) based on an annualized return of 1.27% over the last three years and a total return of 1.34% year to date 2015. Factored into the performance evaluation is an expense ratio of 0.10% (very low).

The fund's risk rating is currently B- (Good). It carries a beta of 0.28, meaning the fund's expected move will be 2.8% for every 10% move in the market. Volatility, as measured by both the semi-deviation and a drawdown factor, is considered low. As of December 31, 2015, *Vanguard Intm-Term Govt Bd Idx E traded at a premium of .23% above its net asset value, which is worse than its one-year historical average premium of .07%.

Joshua C. Barrickman has been running the fund for 3 years and currently receives a manager quality ranking of 72 (0=worst, 99=best). If you desire an average level of risk, then this fund may be an option.

Data Date	Investment Rating	Net Assets ($Mil)	Price	Performance Rating/Pts	Total Return Y-T-D	Risk Rating/Pts
12-15	C	172.00	64.44	C / 4.9	1.34%	B- / 7.8
2014	C	172.00	64.49	C- / 3.4	4.31%	B / 8.5
2013	C	119.10	62.64	C- / 3.4	-2.02%	B+ / 9.6
2012	C-	126.30	65.41	D+ / 2.4	1.96%	B+ / 9.6
2011	C+	81.80	65.66	C- / 4.0	9.39%	B+ / 9.6
2010	B	34.70	61.23	C / 4.5	7.51%	B / 8.8

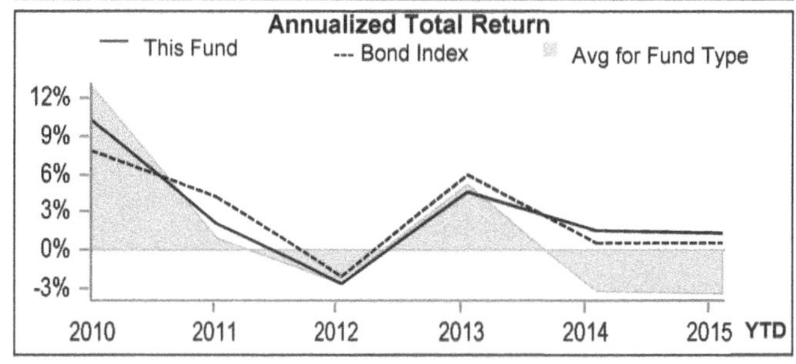

*Vanguard Large Cap ETF (VV) A+ Excellent

Fund Family: Vanguard Group Inc
Fund Type: Growth
Inception Date: January 27, 2004

Major Rating Factors:
Strong performance is the major factor driving the A+ (Excellent) TheStreet.com Investment Rating for *Vanguard Large Cap ETF. The fund currently has a performance rating of B+ (Good) based on an annualized return of 13.87% over the last three years and a total return of 1.10% year to date 2015. Factored into the performance evaluation is an expense ratio of 0.09% (very low).

The fund's risk rating is currently B (Good). It carries a beta of 1.00, meaning that its performance tracks fairly well with that of the overall stock market. Volatility, as measured by both the semi-deviation and a drawdown factor, is considered low. As of December 31, 2015, *Vanguard Large Cap ETF traded at a discount of .02% below its net asset value.

Ryan E. Ludt has been running the fund for 12 years and currently receives a manager quality ranking of 66 (0=worst, 99=best). If you desire only a moderate level of risk and strong performance, then this fund is an excellent option.

Data Date	Investment Rating	Net Assets ($Mil)	Price	Performance Rating/Pts	Total Return Y-T-D	Risk Rating/Pts
12-15	A+	5,194.80	93.50	B+ / 8.7	1.10%	B / 8.4
2014	B+	5,194.80	94.39	B+ / 8.3	14.47%	B- / 7.7
2013	B+	4,706.80	84.80	B / 8.2	27.70%	B / 8.2
2012	C	3,559.80	65.16	C / 5.3	16.77%	B / 8.0
2011	C+	3,020.90	57.30	C / 5.3	2.12%	B- / 7.9
2010	C-	2,857.80	57.61	C- / 4.2	15.93%	C+ / 6.0

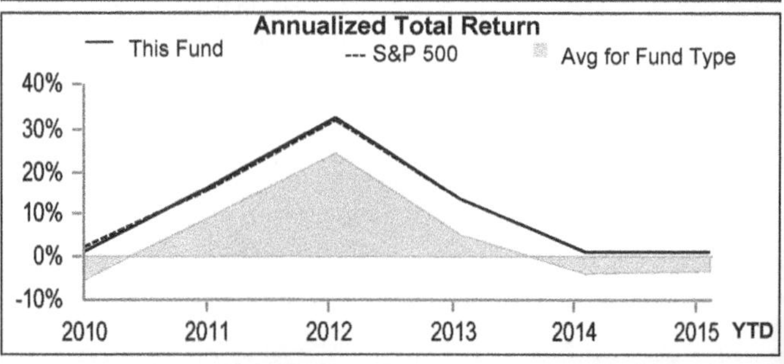

*Vanguard Long Term Bd Idx ETF (BLV) C Fair

Fund Family: Vanguard Group Inc
Fund Type: General - Investment Grade
Inception Date: April 3, 2007

Major Rating Factors: Middle of the road best describes *Vanguard Long Term Bd Idx ETF whose TheStreet.com Investment Rating is currently a C (Fair). The fund currently has a performance rating of C (Fair) based on an annualized return of 2.22% over the last three years and a total return of -4.67% year to date 2015. Factored into the performance evaluation is an expense ratio of 0.10% (very low).

The fund's risk rating is currently B- (Good). It carries a beta of 3.01, meaning it is expected to move 30.1% for every 10% move in the market. Volatility, as measured by both the semi-deviation and a drawdown factor, is considered low. As of December 31, 2015, *Vanguard Long Term Bd Idx ETF traded at a premium of .01% above its net asset value, which is better than its one-year historical average premium of .19%.

Joshua C. Barrickman has been running the fund for 3 years and currently receives a manager quality ranking of 46 (0=worst, 99=best). If you desire an average level of risk, then this fund may be an option.

Data Date	Investment Rating	Net Assets ($Mil)	Price	Performance Rating/Pts	Total Return Y-T-D	Risk Rating/Pts
12-15	C	872.70	86.81	C / 5.0	-4.67%	B- / 7.6
2014	C+	872.70	94.27	C+ / 5.6	19.66%	B / 8.2
2013	C	488.70	81.65	C / 4.5	-7.05%	B / 8.6
2012	C+	832.40	93.87	C / 4.4	7.10%	B+ / 9.1
2011	B-	511.80	92.01	C / 5.5	21.52%	B+ / 9.1
2010	B	324.20	79.09	C / 5.1	10.01%	B / 8.2

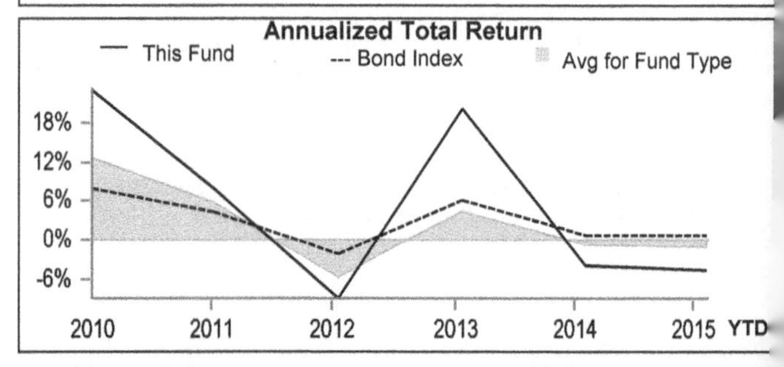

*Vanguard Long-Term Corp Bd Idx E (VCLT) C Fair

Fund Family: Vanguard Group Inc
Fund Type: Corporate - Investment Grade
Inception Date: November 19, 2009

Major Rating Factors: Middle of the road best describes *Vanguard Long-Term Corp Bd Idx E whose TheStreet.com Investment Rating is currently a C (Fair). The fund currently has a performance rating of C (Fair) based on an annualized return of 2.09% over the last three years and a total return of -5.23% year to date 2015. Factored into the performance evaluation is an expense ratio of 0.10% (very low).

The fund's risk rating is currently C+ (Fair). It carries a beta of 2.04, meaning it is expected to move 20.4% for every 10% move in the market. Volatility, as measured by both the semi-deviation and a drawdown factor, is considered low. As of December 31, 2015, *Vanguard Long-Term Corp Bd Idx E traded at a premium of .65% above its net asset value, which is worse than its one-year historical average premium of .20%.

Joshua C. Barrickman has been running the fund for 7 years and currently receives a manager quality ranking of 57 (0=worst, 99=best). If you desire an average level of risk, then this fund may be an option.

Data Date	Investment Rating	Net Assets ($Mil)	Price	Performance Rating/Pts	Total Return Y-T-D	Risk Rating/Pts
12-15	C	895.50	84.19	C / 4.9	-5.23%	C+ / 6.8
2014	C+	895.50	92.37	C / 5.5	15.60%	B / 8.5
2013	C+	574.90	82.99	C / 5.2	-3.46%	B / 8.7
2012	C+	1,164.00	91.70	C / 4.5	10.39%	B+ / 9.2
2011	B+	401.30	86.70	B- / 7.0	17.78%	B+ / 9.3
2010	B	54.90	77.52	C+ / 6.2	10.62%	B / 8.6

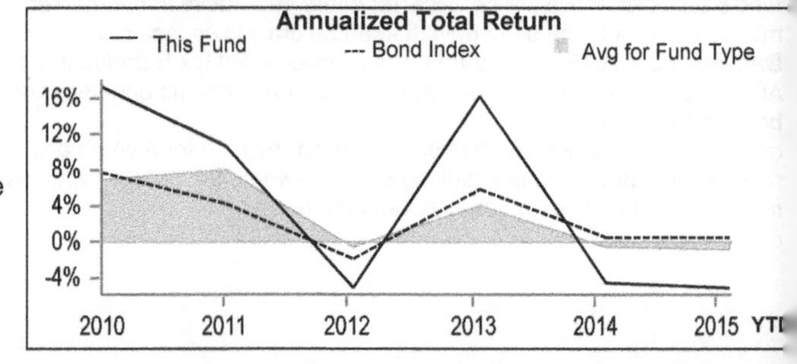

*Vanguard Long-Term Govt Bd Idx E (VGLT) C Fair

Fund Family: Vanguard Group Inc
Fund Type: US Government/Agency
Inception Date: November 19, 2009

Major Rating Factors: Middle of the road best describes *Vanguard Long-Term Govt Bd Idx E whose TheStreet.com Investment Rating is currently a C (Fair). The fund currently has a performance rating of C (Fair) based on an annualized return of 3.33% over the last three years and a total return of -2.17% year to date 2015. Factored into the performance evaluation is an expense ratio of 0.10% (very low).

The fund's risk rating is currently C+ (Fair). It carries a beta of 1.03, meaning that its performance tracks fairly well with that of the overall stock market. Volatility, as measured by both the semi-deviation and a drawdown factor, is considered low. As of December 31, 2015, *Vanguard Long-Term Govt Bd Idx E traded at a premium of .13% above its net asset value, which is worse than its one-year historical average premium of .10%.

Joshua C. Barrickman has been running the fund for 3 years and currently receives a manager quality ranking of 67 (0=worst, 99=best). If you desire an average level of risk, then this fund may be an option.

Data Date	Investment Rating	Net Assets ($Mil)	Price	Performance Rating/Pts	Total Return Y-T-D	Risk Rating/Pts
12-15	C	126.60	74.62	C / 5.5	-2.17%	C+ / 6.7
2014	C+	126.60	77.77	C+ / 5.9	24.42%	B / 8.0
2013	C-	70.40	64.01	C- / 3.8	-10.08%	B / 8.2
2012	C	81.20	75.30	C- / 3.8	2.03%	B / 8.7
2011	A	63.90	75.11	A- / 9.0	29.23%	B / 8.8
2010	C	72.30	60.27	D+ / 2.9	8.98%	B / 8.1

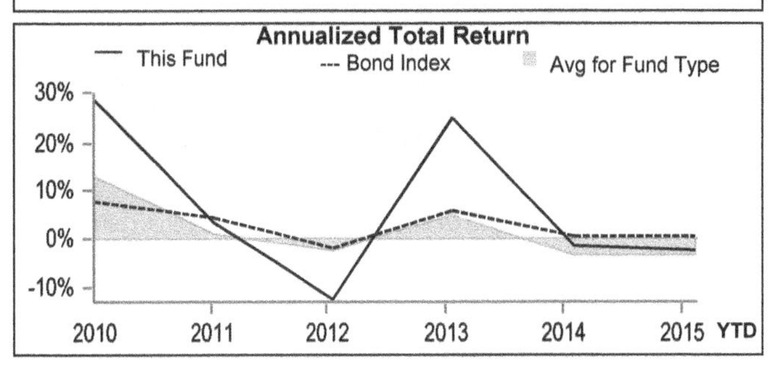

*Vanguard Materials ETF (VAW) C+ Fair

Fund Family: Vanguard Group Inc
Fund Type: Income
Inception Date: January 26, 2004

Major Rating Factors: Middle of the road best describes *Vanguard Materials ETF whose TheStreet.com Investment Rating is currently a C+ (Fair). The fund currently has a performance rating of C (Fair) based on an annualized return of 4.79% over the last three years and a total return of -10.42% year to date 2015. Factored into the performance evaluation is an expense ratio of 0.10% (very low).

The fund's risk rating is currently B- (Good). It carries a beta of 1.21, meaning it is expected to move 12.1% for every 10% move in the market. Volatility, as measured by both the semi-deviation and a drawdown factor, is considered low. As of December 31, 2015, *Vanguard Materials ETF traded at a discount of .04% below its net asset value.

William Coleman has been running the fund for 1 year and currently receives a manager quality ranking of 15 (0=worst, 99=best). If you desire an average level of risk, then this fund may be an option.

Data Date	Investment Rating	Net Assets ($Mil)	Price	Performance Rating/Pts	Total Return Y-T-D	Risk Rating/Pts
12-15	C+	1,371.10	94.19	C / 5.4	-10.42%	B- / 7.9
2014	B	1,371.10	107.39	C+ / 6.5	6.77%	B / 8.4
2013	C+	954.60	103.25	B- / 7.2	19.90%	B- / 7.2
2012	C-	700.40	84.21	C / 4.8	13.21%	B- / 7.1
2011	C+	530.10	73.13	C+ / 6.2	-5.84%	B- / 7.0
2010	C+	614.30	82.60	C+ / 6.7	24.46%	C / 5.0

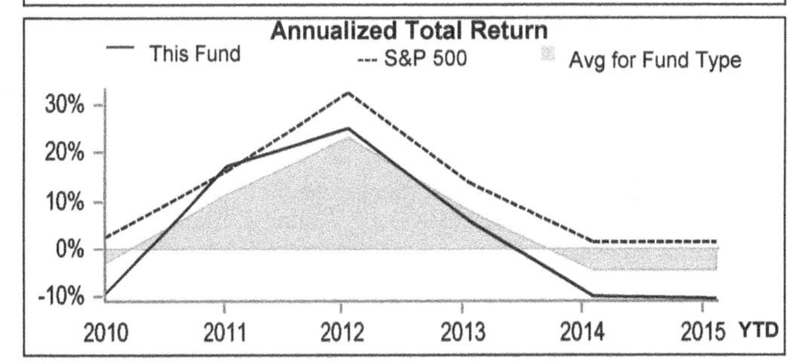

*Vanguard Mega Cap ETF (MGC) A Excellent

Fund Family: Vanguard Group Inc
Fund Type: Income
Inception Date: December 17, 2007

Major Rating Factors:
Strong performance is the major factor driving the A (Excellent) TheStreet.com Investment Rating for *Vanguard Mega Cap ETF. The fund currently has a performance rating of B+ (Good) based on an annualized return of 13.89% over the last three years and a total return of 1.57% year to date 2015. Factored into the performance evaluation is an expense ratio of 0.09% (very low).

The fund's risk rating is currently B- (Good). It carries a beta of 1.02, meaning that its performance tracks fairly well with that of the overall stock market. Volatility, as measured by both the semi-deviation and a drawdown factor, is considered low. As of December 31, 2015, *Vanguard Mega Cap ETF traded at a discount of .01% below its net asset value, which is better than its one-year historical average premium of .02%.

Ryan E. Ludt has been running the fund for 9 years and currently receives a manager quality ranking of 63 (0=worst, 99=best). If you desire only a moderate level of risk and strong performance, then this fund is an excellent option.

Data Date	Investment Rating	Net Assets ($Mil)	Price	Performance Rating/Pts	Total Return Y-T-D	Risk Rating/Pts
12-15	A	823.60	69.76	B+ / 8.8	1.57%	B- / 7.9
2014	B+	823.60	70.25	B / 8.2	14.41%	B- / 7.3
2013	B+	669.20	63.16	B / 8.2	27.31%	B / 8.3
2012	C	454.00	48.83	C / 5.1	16.81%	B / 8.0
2011	C	331.00	43.01	C / 5.1	2.79%	B- / 7.9
2010	C-	246.60	42.92	C- / 3.7	13.77%	C+ / 6.1

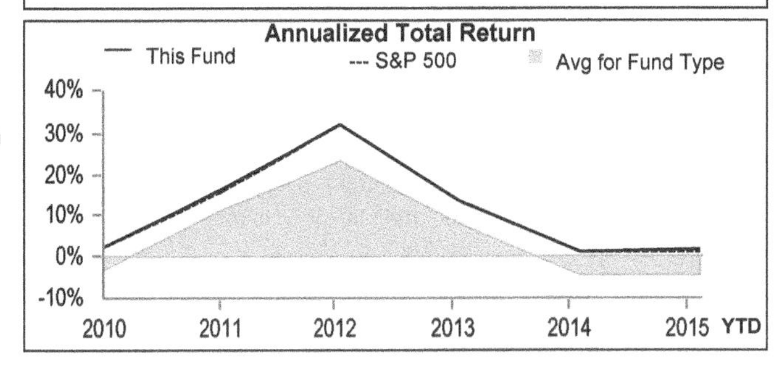

*Vanguard Mega Cap Growth ETF (MGK) A+ Excellent

Fund Family: Vanguard Group Inc
Fund Type: Growth
Inception Date: December 17, 2007

Major Rating Factors:
Exceptional performance is the major factor driving the A+ (Excellent) TheStreet.com Investment Rating for *Vanguard Mega Cap Growth ETF. The fund currently has a performance rating of A- (Excellent) based on an annualized return of 15.03% over the last three years and a total return of 3.91% year to date 2015. Factored into the performance evaluation is an expense ratio of 0.09% (very low).

The fund's risk rating is currently B (Good). It carries a beta of 1.05, meaning that its performance tracks fairly well with that of the overall stock market. Volatility, as measured by both the semi-deviation and a drawdown factor, is considered low. As of December 31, 2015, *Vanguard Mega Cap Growth ETF traded at a discount of .04% below its net asset value, which is better than its one-year historical average premium of .02%.

Gerard C. O'Reilly has been running the fund for 1 year and currently receives a manager quality ranking of 81 (0=worst, 99=best). If you desire only a moderate level of risk and strong performance, then this fund is an excellent option.

Data Date	Investment Rating	Net Assets ($Mil)	Price	Performance Rating/Pts	Total Return Y-T-D	Risk Rating/Pts
12-15	A+	1,515.90	83.04	A- / 9.0	3.91%	B / 8.3
2014	B+	1,515.90	81.27	B+ / 8.5	15.02%	B- / 7.1
2013	A	1,231.10	72.48	B+ / 8.5	27.68%	B / 8.6
2012	C	779.70	55.46	C / 5.4	18.08%	B- / 7.6
2011	C+	533.90	48.10	C+ / 6.1	3.75%	B- / 7.7
2010	C	346.90	47.31	C / 5.1	14.53%	C+ / 6.1

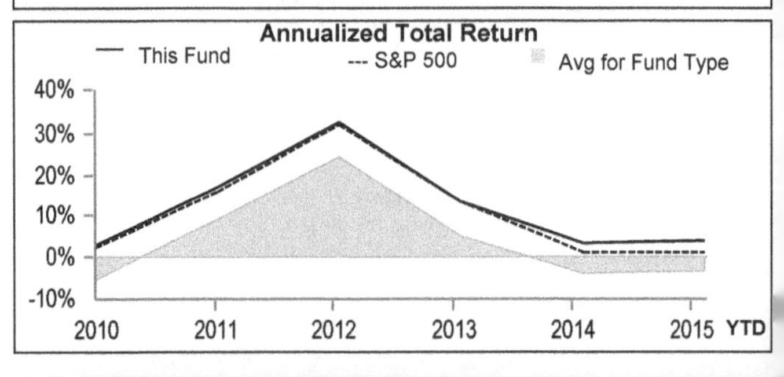

*Vanguard Mega Cap Value ETF (MGV) A Excellent

Fund Family: Vanguard Group Inc
Fund Type: Income
Inception Date: December 17, 2007

Major Rating Factors:
Strong performance is the major factor driving the A (Excellent) TheStreet.com Investment Rating for *Vanguard Mega Cap Value ETF. The fund currently has a performance rating of B+ (Good) based on an annualized return of 13.05% over the last three years and a total return of -0.15% year to date 2015. Factored into the performance evaluation is an expense ratio of 0.09% (very low).

The fund's risk rating is currently B (Good). It carries a beta of 0.97, meaning that its performance tracks fairly well with that of the overall stock market. Volatility, as measured by both the semi-deviation and a drawdown factor, is considered low. As of December 31, 2015, *Vanguard Mega Cap Value ETF traded at a premium of .02% above its net asset value, which is better than its one-year historical average premium of .03%.

Gerard C. O'Reilly has been running the fund for 1 year and currently receives a manager quality ranking of 64 (0=worst, 99=best). If you desire only a moderate level of risk and strong performance, then this fund is an excellent option.

Data Date	Investment Rating	Net Assets ($Mil)	Price	Performance Rating/Pts	Total Return Y-T-D	Risk Rating/Pts
12-15	A	867.80	59.03	B+ / 8.5	-0.15%	B / 8.1
2014	A+	867.80	60.69	B / 8.0	13.75%	B+ / 9.1
2013	B+	670.70	55.01	B / 7.9	27.23%	B / 8.4
2012	C	430.70	42.67	C / 4.8	15.83%	B / 8.2
2011	C	347.40	38.17	C / 4.3	1.43%	B- / 7.8
2010	D+	259.50	38.72	D+ / 2.4	13.16%	C+ / 6.0

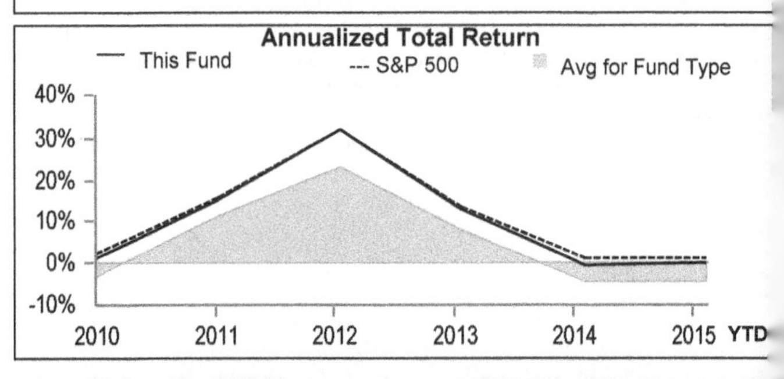

*Vanguard Mid Cap ETF (VO) B+ Good

Fund Family: Vanguard Group Inc
Fund Type: Growth
Inception Date: January 26, 2004

Major Rating Factors: Strong performance is the major factor driving the B+ (Good) TheStreet.com Investment Rating for *Vanguard Mid Cap ETF. The fund currently has a performance rating of B+ (Good) based on an annualized return of 13.75% over the last three years and a total return of -1.33% year to date 2015. Factored into the performance evaluation is an expense ratio of 0.09% (very low).

The fund's risk rating is currently B- (Good). It carries a beta of 0.95, meaning that its performance tracks fairly well with that of the overall stock market. Volatility, as measured by both the semi-deviation and a drawdown factor, is considered low. As of December 31, 2015, *Vanguard Mid Cap ETF traded at a premium of .03% above its net asset value, which is worse than its one-year historical average premium of .02%.

Donald M. Butler has been running the fund for 18 years and currently receives a manager quality ranking of 73 (0=worst, 99=best). If you desire only a moderate level of risk and strong performance, then this fund is an excellent option.

Data Date	Investment Rating	Net Assets ($Mil)	Price	Performance Rating/Pts	Total Return Y-T-D	Risk Rating/Pts
12-15	B+	8,568.60	120.11	B+ / 8.4	-1.33%	B- / 7.3
2014	A	8,568.60	123.56	B+ / 8.7	14.85%	B / 8.1
2013	B+	6,727.60	110.02	B / 8.1	29.86%	B- / 7.9
2012	C+	3,828.60	82.44	C+ / 6.3	16.17%	B- / 7.8
2011	C+	3,241.00	71.94	C+ / 6.5	-0.69%	B- / 7.7
2010	C+	3,356.30	74.46	C+ / 6.7	25.68%	C / 5.4

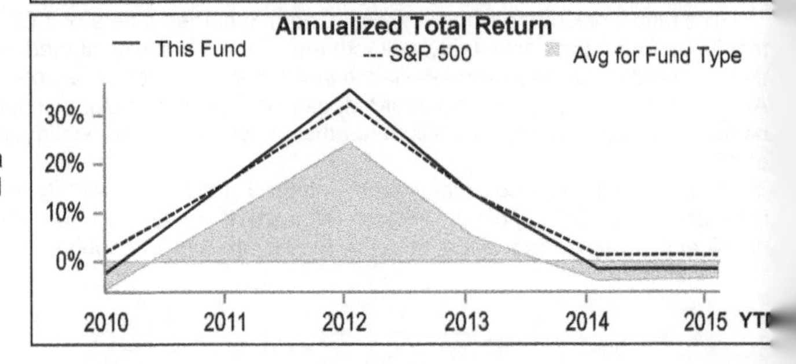

*Vanguard Mid Cap Growth ETF (VOT) A Excellent

Fund Family: Vanguard Group Inc
Fund Type: Growth
Inception Date: August 17, 2006

Major Rating Factors:
Strong performance is the major factor driving the A (Excellent) TheStreet.com Investment Rating for *Vanguard Mid Cap Growth ETF. The fund currently has a performance rating of B (Good) based on an annualized return of 12.90% over the last three years and a total return of -1.03% year to date 2015. Factored into the performance evaluation is an expense ratio of 0.09% (very low).

The fund's risk rating is currently B (Good). It carries a beta of 0.97, meaning that its performance tracks fairly well with that of the overall stock market. Volatility, as measured by both the semi-deviation and a drawdown factor, is considered low. As of December 31, 2015, *Vanguard Mid Cap Growth ETF traded at a discount of .04% below its net asset value, which is better than its one-year historical average premium of .01%.

Donald M. Butler has been running the fund for 3 years and currently receives a manager quality ranking of 64 (0=worst, 99=best). If you desire only a moderate level of risk and strong performance, then this fund is an excellent option.

Data Date	Investment Rating	Net Assets ($Mil)	Price	Performance Rating/Pts	Total Return Y-T-D	Risk Rating/Pts
12-15	A	2,276.00	99.71	B / 8.2	-1.03%	B / 8.6
2014	A	2,276.00	101.61	B+ / 8.3	14.55%	B / 8.5
2013	B	1,895.80	90.25	B / 7.6	26.96%	B- / 7.8
2012	C+	1,165.30	68.58	C+ / 6.4	15.64%	B- / 7.7
2011	C+	1,095.50	59.54	C+ / 6.6	-2.13%	B- / 7.5
2010	C+	913.50	62.30	C+ / 6.5	29.14%	C / 5.1

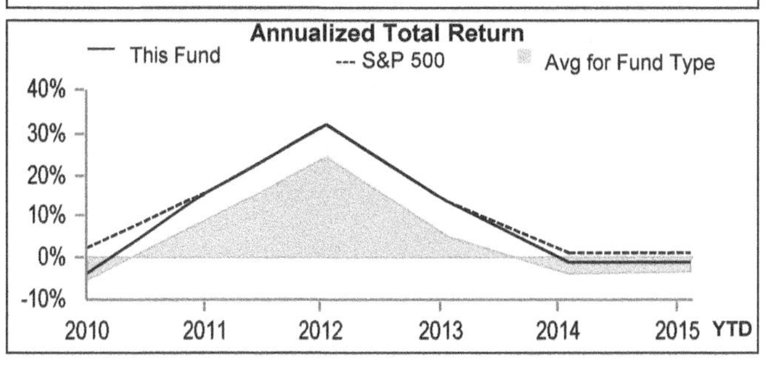

*Vanguard Mid Cap Value Index ETF (VOE) A+ Excellent

Fund Family: Vanguard Group Inc
Fund Type: Growth
Inception Date: August 17, 2006

Major Rating Factors:
Strong performance is the major factor driving the A+ (Excellent) TheStreet.com Investment Rating for *Vanguard Mid Cap Value Index ETF. The fund currently has a performance rating of B+ (Good) based on an annualized return of 14.30% over the last three years and a total return of -1.85% year to date 2015. Factored into the performance evaluation is an expense ratio of 0.09% (very low).

The fund's risk rating is currently B+ (Good). It carries a beta of 0.98, meaning that its performance tracks fairly well with that of the overall stock market. Volatility, as measured by both the semi-deviation and a drawdown factor, is considered very low. As of December 31, 2015, *Vanguard Mid Cap Value Index ETF traded at a discount of .05% below its net asset value, which is better than its one-year historical average premium of .01%.

Donald M. Butler has been running the fund for 10 years and currently receives a manager quality ranking of 74 (0=worst, 99=best). If you desire only a moderate level of risk and strong performance, then this fund is an excellent option.

Data Date	Investment Rating	Net Assets ($Mil)	Price	Performance Rating/Pts	Total Return Y-T-D	Risk Rating/Pts
12-15	A+	3,033.00	85.95	B+ / 8.6	-1.85%	B+ / 9.0
2014	A+	3,033.00	89.43	B+ / 8.9	15.06%	B / 8.3
2013	A-	2,256.30	79.78	B+ / 8.6	32.22%	B / 8.2
2012	C+	1,123.40	58.81	C+ / 6.0	16.69%	B / 8.0
2011	C+	784.60	51.67	C+ / 6.3	0.44%	B- / 7.9
2010	C+	688.10	53.01	C+ / 6.7	21.76%	C+ / 5.7

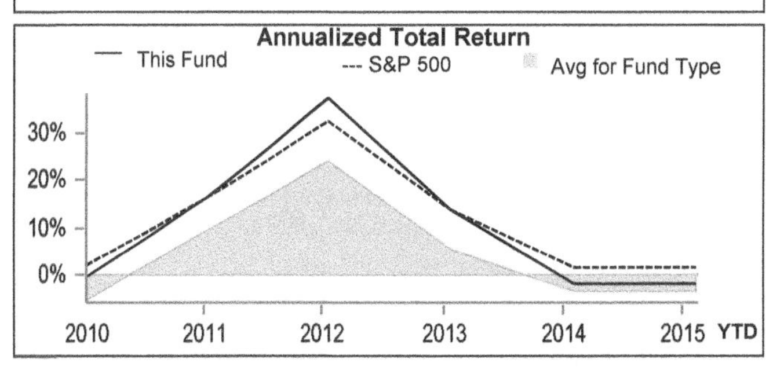

*Vanguard Mort-Backed Secs Idx ET (VMBS) C+ Fair

Fund Family: Vanguard Group Inc
Fund Type: Mortgage
Inception Date: November 19, 2009

Major Rating Factors: Middle of the road best describes *Vanguard Mort-Backed Secs Idx ET whose TheStreet.com Investment Rating is currently a C+ (Fair). The fund currently has a performance rating of C (Fair) based on an annualized return of 1.93% over the last three years and a total return of 1.30% year to date 2015. Factored into the performance evaluation is an expense ratio of 0.10% (very low).

The fund's risk rating is currently B (Good). It carries a beta of 0.95, meaning that its performance tracks fairly well with that of the overall stock market. Volatility, as measured by both the semi-deviation and a drawdown factor, is considered low. As of December 31, 2015, *Vanguard Mort-Backed Secs Idx ET traded at a premium of .08% above its net asset value, which is worse than its one-year historical average premium of .07%.

William D. Baird has been running the fund for 7 years and currently receives a manager quality ranking of 68 (0=worst, 99=best). If you desire an average level of risk, then this fund may be an option.

Data Date	Investment Rating	Net Assets ($Mil)	Price	Performance Rating/Pts	Total Return Y-T-D	Risk Rating/Pts
12-15	C+	542.40	52.72	C / 5.3	1.30%	B / 8.0
2014	C+	542.40	53.01	C- / 3.6	5.87%	B+ / 9.5
2013	C	377.70	51.03	C- / 3.1	-1.39%	B+ / 9.8
2012	C-	288.60	52.20	D / 2.1	1.73%	B+ / 9.8
2011	C+	129.50	51.88	C- / 3.3	5.97%	B+ / 9.9
2010	B	36.00	50.28	C / 4.4	5.44%	B / 8.9

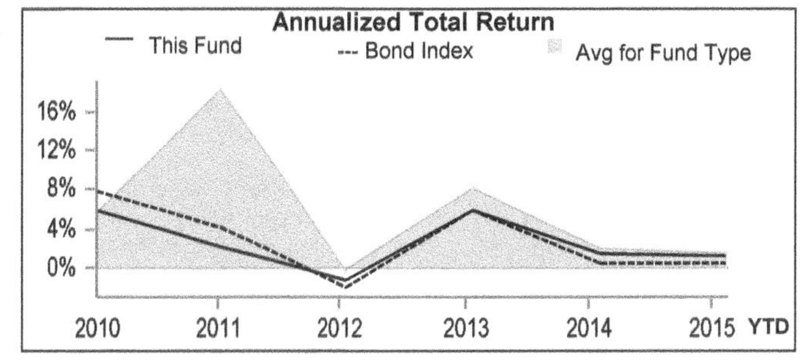

*Vanguard REIT ETF (VNQ) B Good

Fund Family: Vanguard Group Inc
Fund Type: Income
Inception Date: September 23, 2004

Major Rating Factors: Strong performance is the major factor driving the B (Good) TheStreet.com Investment Rating for *Vanguard REIT ETF. The fund currently has a performance rating of B (Good) based on an annualized return of 10.32% over the last three years and a total return of 0.91% year to date 2015. Factored into the performance evaluation is an expense ratio of 0.12% (very low).

The fund's risk rating is currently B- (Good). It carries a beta of 0.46, meaning the fund's expected move will be 4.6% for every 10% move in the market. Volatility, as measured by both the semi-deviation and a drawdown factor, is considered low. As of December 31, 2015, *Vanguard REIT ETF traded at a premium of .01% above its net asset value.

Gerard C. O'Reilly has been running the fund for 20 years and currently receives a manager quality ranking of 87 (0=worst, 99=best). If you desire only a moderate level of risk and strong performance, then this fund is an excellent option.

Data Date	Investment Rating	Net Assets ($Mil)	Price	Performance Rating/Pts	Total Return Y-T-D	Risk Rating/Pts
12-15	B	22,958.30	79.73	B / 8.0	0.91%	B- / 7.2
2014	A+	22,958.30	81.00	B+ / 8.8	29.61%	B / 8.0
2013	C+	17,392.40	64.56	C+ / 5.6	1.13%	B- / 7.8
2012	B	14,609.30	65.80	B / 7.6	19.22%	B- / 7.6
2011	C+	9,307.90	58.00	B / 7.8	7.88%	C+ / 6.4
2010	C+	7,532.70	55.37	B / 7.7	28.43%	C- / 4.2

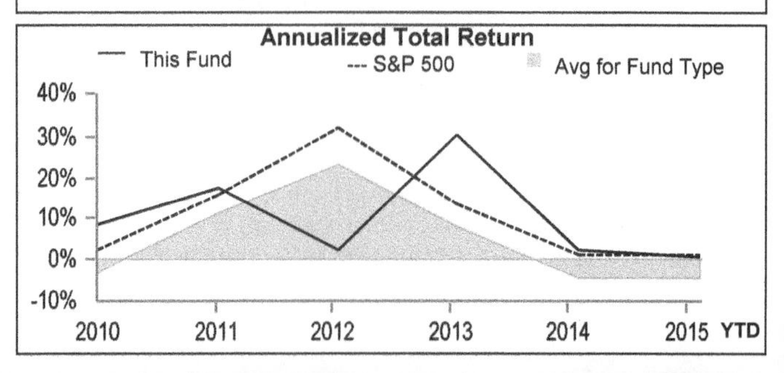

*Vanguard Russell 1000 Gro Idx ET (VONG) A- Excellent

Fund Family: Vanguard Group Inc
Fund Type: Growth
Inception Date: September 20, 2010

Major Rating Factors:
Exceptional performance is the major factor driving the A- (Excellent) TheStreet.com Investment Rating for *Vanguard Russell 1000 Gro Idx ET. The fund currently has a performance rating of A- (Excellent) based on an annualized return of 15.67% over the last three years and a total return of 5.58% year to date 2015. Factored into the performance evaluation is an expense ratio of 0.12% (very low).

The fund's risk rating is currently B- (Good). It carries a beta of 1.00, meaning that its performance tracks fairly well with that of the overall stock market. Volatility, as measured by both the semi-deviation and a drawdown factor, is considered low. As of December 31, 2015, *Vanguard Russell 1000 Gro Idx ET traded at a premium of .03% above its net asset value.

Michael A. Johnson has been running the fund for 6 years and currently receives a manager quality ranking of 78 (0=worst, 99=best). If you desire only a moderate level of risk and strong performance, then this fund is an excellent option.

Data Date	Investment Rating	Net Assets ($Mil)	Price	Performance Rating/Pts	Total Return Y-T-D	Risk Rating/Pts
12-15	A-	298.70	102.00	A- / 9.1	5.58%	B- / 7.3
2014	B+	298.70	98.06	B+ / 8.5	15.29%	B- / 7.4
2013	A-	231.50	88.15	B+ / 8.3	28.38%	B / 8.5
2012	B	82.90	67.12	C+ / 6.8	16.06%	B / 8.4
2011	C-	53.40	59.26	D+ / 2.7	2.76%	B / 8.5

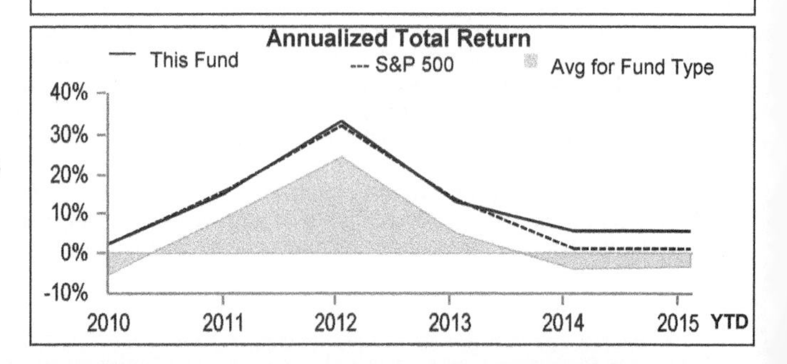

*Vanguard Russell 1000 Index ETF (VONE) A Excellent

Fund Family: Vanguard Group Inc
Fund Type: Growth
Inception Date: September 20, 2010

Major Rating Factors:
Strong performance is the major factor driving the A (Excellent) TheStreet.com Investment Rating for *Vanguard Russell 1000 Index ETF. The fund currently has a performance rating of B+ (Good) based on an annualized return of 13.75% over the last three years and a total return of 0.75% year to date 2015. Factored into the performance evaluation is an expense ratio of 0.12% (very low).

The fund's risk rating is currently B (Good). It carries a beta of 1.04, meaning that its performance tracks fairly well with that of the overall stock market. Volatility, as measured by both the semi-deviation and a drawdown factor, is considered low. As of December 31, 2015, *Vanguard Russell 1000 Index ETF traded at a premium of .01% above its net asset value, which is worse than its one-year historical average discount of .01%.

Jeffrey D. Miller has been running the fund for 6 years and currently receives a manager quality ranking of 61 (0=worst, 99=best). If you desire only a moderate level of risk and strong performance, then this fund is an excellent option.

Data Date	Investment Rating	Net Assets ($Mil)	Price	Performance Rating/Pts	Total Return Y-T-D	Risk Rating/Pts
12-15	A	385.50	93.63	B+ / 8.6	0.75%	B / 8.0
2014	B+	385.50	94.77	B+ / 8.6	15.05%	B- / 7.3
2013	A-	246.80	85.17	B+ / 8.3	28.18%	B / 8.3
2012	B	175.60	65.21	B / 7.6	17.38%	B / 8.2
2011	C-	34.40	57.25	D+ / 2.8	1.93%	B / 8.3

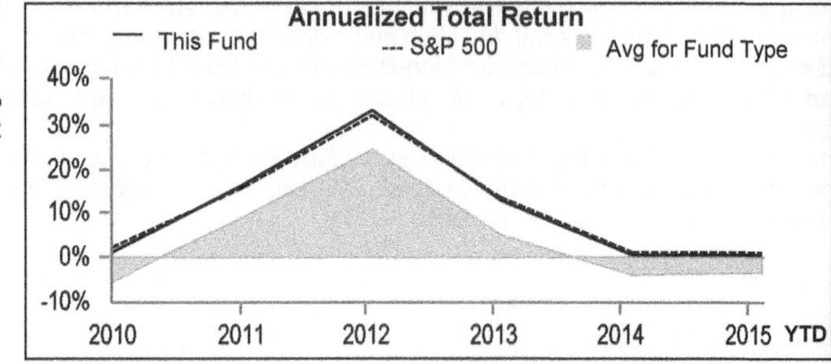

* Denotes ETF Fund

*Vanguard Russell 1000 Val Index (VONV) B Good

Fund Family: Vanguard Group Inc
Fund Type: Growth
Inception Date: September 20, 2010

Major Rating Factors: Strong performance is the major factor driving the B (Good) TheStreet.com Investment Rating for *Vanguard Russell 1000 Val Index. The fund currently has a performance rating of B (Good) based on an annualized return of 11.77% over the last three years and a total return of -4.04% year to date 2015. Factored into the performance evaluation is an expense ratio of 0.12% (very low).

The fund's risk rating is currently B- (Good). It carries a beta of 1.02, meaning that its performance tracks fairly well with that of the overall stock market. Volatility, as measured by both the semi-deviation and a drawdown factor, is considered low. As of December 31, 2015, *Vanguard Russell 1000 Val Index traded at a premium of .02% above its net asset value, which is in line with its one-year historical average premium of .02%.

Michael A. Johnson has been running the fund for 6 years and currently receives a manager quality ranking of 50 (0=worst, 99=best). If you desire only a moderate level of risk and strong performance, then this fund is an excellent option.

Data Date	Investment Rating	Net Assets ($Mil)	Price	Performance Rating/Pts	Total Return Y-T-D	Risk Rating/Pts
12-15	B	297.50	85.66	B / 7.9	-4.04%	B- / 7.3
2014	A+	297.50	91.17	B+ / 8.7	15.43%	B+ / 9.2
2013	B+	181.00	82.32	B / 8.0	27.27%	B / 8.1
2012	B+	47.00	63.35	B / 8.2	18.23%	B / 8.1
2011	C-	36.00	55.54	D+ / 2.8	1.08%	B / 8.1

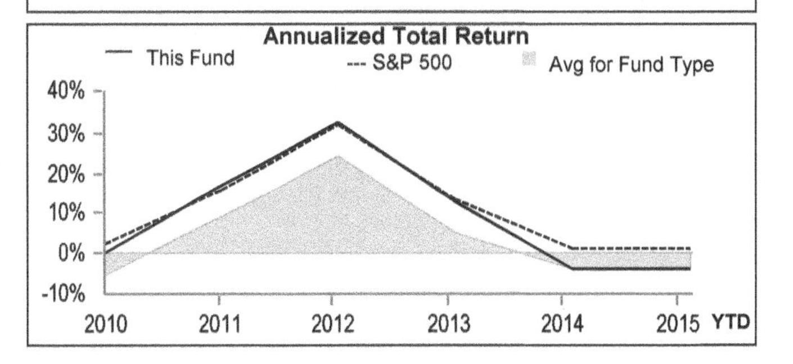

*Vanguard Russell 2000 Gro Idx ET (VTWG) B Good

Fund Family: Vanguard Group Inc
Fund Type: Growth
Inception Date: September 20, 2010

Major Rating Factors: Strong performance is the major factor driving the B (Good) TheStreet.com Investment Rating for *Vanguard Russell 2000 Gro Idx ET. The fund currently has a performance rating of B+ (Good) based on an annualized return of 13.34% over the last three years and a total return of 0.19% year to date 2015. Factored into the performance evaluation is an expense ratio of 0.20% (very low).

The fund's risk rating is currently C+ (Fair). It carries a beta of 1.11, meaning it is expected to move 11.1% for every 10% move in the market. Volatility, as measured by both the semi-deviation and a drawdown factor, is considered low. As of December 31, 2015, *Vanguard Russell 2000 Gro Idx ET traded at a premium of .79% above its net asset value, which is worse than its one-year historical average premium of .05%.

Walter Nejman has been running the fund for 1 year and currently receives a manager quality ranking of 51 (0=worst, 99=best). If you desire only a moderate level of risk and strong performance, then this fund is an excellent option.

Data Date	Investment Rating	Net Assets ($Mil)	Price	Performance Rating/Pts	Total Return Y-T-D	Risk Rating/Pts
12-15	B	94.50	102.06	B+ / 8.4	0.19%	C+ / 6.6
2014	B	94.50	103.98	B / 8.2	6.70%	C+ / 6.8
2013	B+	108.30	98.53	B+ / 8.8	37.97%	B- / 7.5
2012	B	47.40	69.11	B / 7.8	16.25%	B- / 7.4
2011	D	12.20	60.93	D / 1.8	-2.33%	B- / 7.4

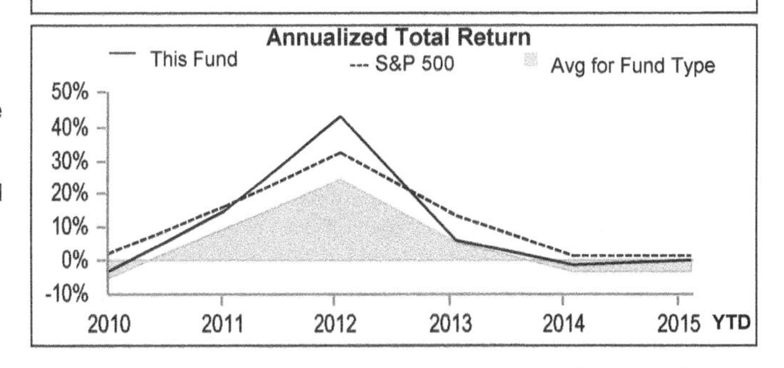

*Vanguard Russell 2000 Idx ETF (VTWO) B+ Good

Fund Family: Vanguard Group Inc
Fund Type: Growth
Inception Date: September 20, 2010

Major Rating Factors: Strong performance is the major factor driving the B+ (Good) TheStreet.com Investment Rating for *Vanguard Russell 2000 Idx ETF. The fund currently has a performance rating of B- (Good) based on an annualized return of 10.34% over the last three years and a total return of -4.00% year to date 2015. Factored into the performance evaluation is an expense ratio of 0.15% (very low).

The fund's risk rating is currently B (Good). It carries a beta of 1.06, meaning that its performance tracks fairly well with that of the overall stock market. Volatility, as measured by both the semi-deviation and a drawdown factor, is considered low. As of December 31, 2015, *Vanguard Russell 2000 Idx ETF traded at a discount of .10% below its net asset value.

Walter Nejman has been running the fund for 1 year and currently receives a manager quality ranking of 37 (0=worst, 99=best). If you desire only a moderate level of risk and strong performance, then this fund is an excellent option.

Data Date	Investment Rating	Net Assets ($Mil)	Price	Performance Rating/Pts	Total Return Y-T-D	Risk Rating/Pts
12-15	B+	352.30	90.14	B- / 7.2	-4.00%	B / 8.2
2014	B-	352.30	95.55	B / 7.7	6.25%	C+ / 6.9
2013	B+	350.00	92.01	B+ / 8.5	33.23%	B- / 7.6
2012	B	164.40	67.00	B / 8.0	16.75%	B- / 7.5
2011	D	52.70	58.53	D / 1.7	-3.28%	B- / 7.5

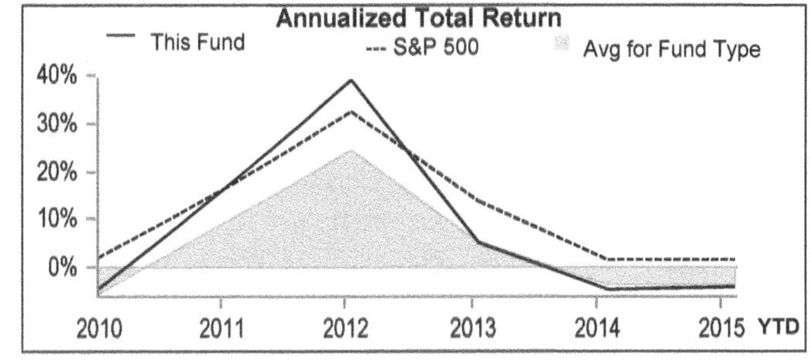

* Denotes ETF Fund

*Vanguard Russell 2000 Val Index (VTWV) C+ Fair

Fund Family: Vanguard Group Inc
Fund Type: Growth
Inception Date: September 20, 2010

Major Rating Factors: Middle of the road best describes *Vanguard Russell 2000 Val Index whose TheStreet.com Investment Rating is currently a C+ (Fair). The fund currently has a performance rating of C+ (Fair) based on an annualized return of 7.60% over the last three years and a total return of -7.09% year to date 2015. Factored into the performance evaluation is an expense ratio of 0.20% (very low).

The fund's risk rating is currently C+ (Fair). It carries a beta of 1.04, meaning that its performance tracks fairly well with that of the overall stock market. Volatility, as measured by both the semi-deviation and a drawdown factor, is considered low. As of December 31, 2015, *Vanguard Russell 2000 Val Index traded at a premium of .11% above its net asset value, which is worse than its one-year historical average discount of .01%.

Walter Nejman has been running the fund for 1 year and currently receives a manager quality ranking of 27 (0=worst, 99=best). If you desire an average level of risk, then this fund may be an option.

Data Date	Investment Rating	Net Assets ($Mil)	Price	Performance Rating/Pts	Total Return Y-T-D	Risk Rating/Pts
12-15	C+	65.50	79.76	C+ / 6.2	-7.09%	C+ / 6.6
2014	B-	65.50	88.03	B- / 7.4	5.95%	C+ / 6.9
2013	B	60.20	85.95	B / 7.9	28.23%	B- / 7.5
2012	B	19.10	64.62	B+ / 8.3	18.18%	B- / 7.5
2011	D+	11.20	56.67	D / 1.9	-4.01%	B- / 7.5

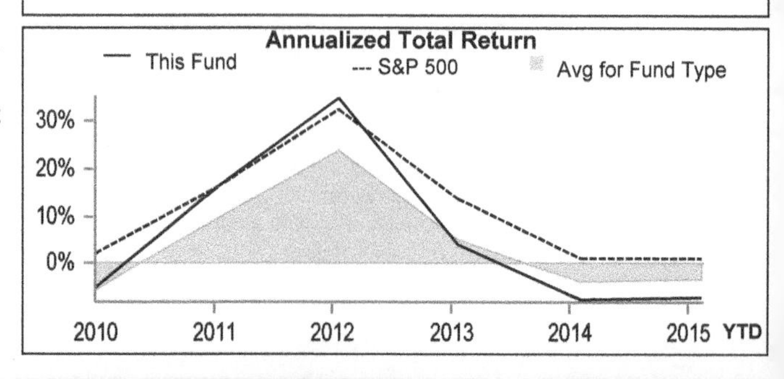

*Vanguard Russell 3000 Index ETF (VTHR) B- Good

Fund Family: Vanguard Group Inc
Fund Type: Growth
Inception Date: September 20, 2010

Major Rating Factors: Strong performance is the major factor driving the B- (Good) TheStreet.com Investment Rating for *Vanguard Russell 3000 Index ETF. The fund currently has a performance rating of B+ (Good) based on an annualized return of 13.61% over the last three years and a total return of -0.48% year to date 2015. Factored into the performance evaluation is an expense ratio of 0.15% (very low).

The fund's risk rating is currently C+ (Fair). It carries a beta of 0.97, meaning that its performance tracks fairly well with that of the overall stock market. Volatility, as measured by both the semi-deviation and a drawdown factor, is considered low. As of December 31, 2015, *Vanguard Russell 3000 Index ETF traded at a premium of .28% above its net asset value, which is worse than its one-year historical average premium of .06%.

Jeffrey D. Miller has been running the fund for 6 years and currently receives a manager quality ranking of 69 (0=worst, 99=best). If you desire only a moderate level of risk and strong performance, then this fund is an excellent option.

Data Date	Investment Rating	Net Assets ($Mil)	Price	Performance Rating/Pts	Total Return Y-T-D	Risk Rating/Pts
12-15	B-	108.60	93.59	B+ / 8.6	-0.48%	C+ / 5.7
2014	B-	108.60	95.77	B+ / 8.6	14.48%	C+ / 5.8
2013	B+	85.70	85.42	B+ / 8.3	28.70%	B / 8.2
2012	B	39.00	65.22	B / 7.7	16.91%	B / 8.2
2011	C-	22.90	57.42	D+ / 2.5	1.70%	B / 8.2

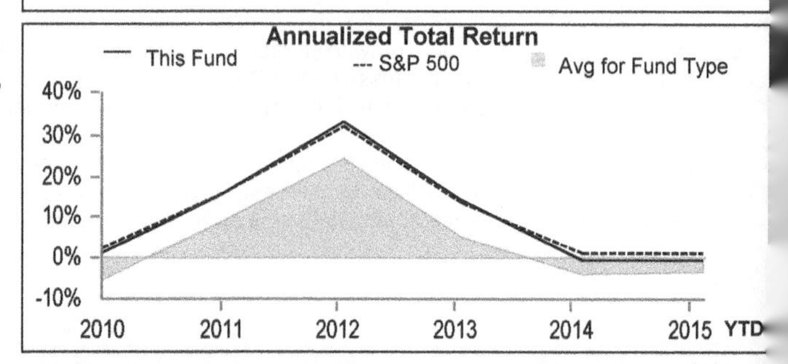

*Vanguard S&P 500 G Indx ETF (VOOG) A Excellent

Fund Family: Vanguard Group Inc
Fund Type: Growth
Inception Date: September 7, 2010

Major Rating Factors:
Exceptional performance is the major factor driving the A (Excellent) TheStreet.com Investment Rating for *Vanguard S&P 500 G Indx ETF. The fund currently has a performance rating of A- (Excellent) based on an annualized return of 16.06% over the last three years and a total return of 5.39% year to date 2015. Factored into the performance evaluation is an expense ratio of 0.15% (very low).

The fund's risk rating is currently B- (Good). It carries a beta of 1.00, meaning that its performance tracks fairly well with that of the overall stock market. Volatility, as measured by both the semi-deviation and a drawdown factor, is considered low. As of December 31, 2015, *Vanguard S&P 500 G Indx ETF traded at a premium of .02% above its net asset value, which is better than its one-year historical average premium of .07%.

Michael A. Johnson has been running the fund for 3 years and currently receives a manager quality ranking of 79 (0=worst, 99=best). If you desire only a moderate level of risk and strong performance, then this fund is an excellent option.

Data Date	Investment Rating	Net Assets ($Mil)	Price	Performance Rating/Pts	Total Return Y-T-D	Risk Rating/Pts
12-15	A	334.60	103.80	A- / 9.2	5.39%	B- / 7.6
2014	A-	334.60	100.17	B+ / 8.7	17.15%	B- / 7.3
2013	A	198.80	88.37	B+ / 8.5	27.91%	B / 8.7
2011	C-	51.20	60.37	C- / 3.2	5.15%	B / 8.8

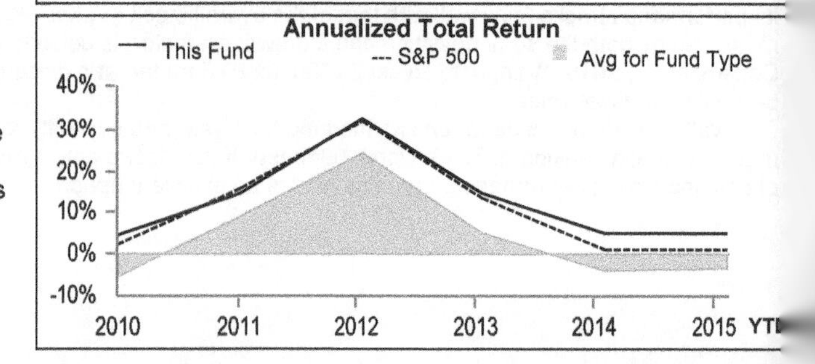

*Vanguard S&P 500 Val Indx ETF (VOOV) B+ Good

Fund Family: Vanguard Group Inc
Fund Type: Growth
Inception Date: September 7, 2010

Major Rating Factors: Strong performance is the major factor driving the B+ (Good) TheStreet.com Investment Rating for *Vanguard S&P 500 Val Indx ETF. The fund currently has a performance rating of B (Good) based on an annualized return of 11.52% over the last three years and a total return of -3.27% year to date 2015. Factored into the performance evaluation is an expense ratio of 0.15% (very low).

The fund's risk rating is currently B- (Good). It carries a beta of 1.00, meaning that its performance tracks fairly well with that of the overall stock market. Volatility, as measured by both the semi-deviation and a drawdown factor, is considered low. As of December 31, 2015, *Vanguard S&P 500 Val Indx ETF traded at a premium of .01% above its net asset value, which is better than its one-year historical average premium of .05%.

Michael A. Johnson has been running the fund for 3 years and currently receives a manager quality ranking of 50 (0=worst, 99=best). If you desire only a moderate level of risk and strong performance, then this fund is an excellent option.

Data Date	Investment Rating	Net Assets ($Mil)	Price	Perfor-mance Rating/Pts	Total Return Y-T-D	Risk Rating/Pts
12-15	B+	207.70	85.25	B / 7.8	-3.27%	B- / 7.8
2014	B+	207.70	90.23	B+ / 8.4	14.24%	B- / 7.1
2013	B+	139.40	82.03	B / 7.9	26.79%	B / 8.1
2012	B+	62.60	63.61	B / 8.2	17.89%	B / 8.0
2011	C-	33.20	55.53	D+ / 2.7	0.20%	B / 8.0

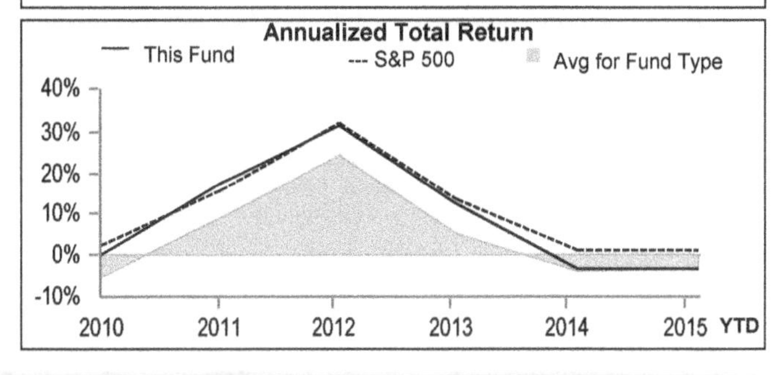

*Vanguard S&P Mid-Cap 400 Gro ETF (IVOG) B Good

Fund Family: Vanguard Group Inc
Fund Type: Growth
Inception Date: September 7, 2010

Major Rating Factors: Strong performance is the major factor driving the B (Good) TheStreet.com Investment Rating for *Vanguard S&P Mid-Cap 400 Gro ETF. The fund currently has a performance rating of B (Good) based on an annualized return of 11.90% over the last three years and a total return of 1.83% year to date 2015. Factored into the performance evaluation is an expense ratio of 0.20% (very low).

The fund's risk rating is currently C+ (Fair). It carries a beta of 0.98, meaning that its performance tracks fairly well with that of the overall stock market. Volatility, as measured by both the semi-deviation and a drawdown factor, is considered low. As of December 31, 2015, *Vanguard S&P Mid-Cap 400 Gro ETF traded at a premium of .05% above its net asset value, which is worse than its one-year historical average premium of .04%.

Christine Franquin has been running the fund for 3 years and currently receives a manager quality ranking of 56 (0=worst, 99=best). If you desire only a moderate level of risk and strong performance, then this fund is an excellent option.

Data Date	Investment Rating	Net Assets ($Mil)	Price	Perfor-mance Rating/Pts	Total Return Y-T-D	Risk Rating/Pts
12-15	B	280.60	98.97	B / 8.0	1.83%	C+ / 6.9
2014	B+	280.60	98.19	B / 7.8	9.25%	B / 8.1
2013	B+	234.90	92.15	B / 8.0	27.24%	B- / 7.9
2012	A-	97.40	69.97	B+ / 8.8	18.78%	B- / 7.9
2011	D+	30.10	60.35	D / 1.7	-0.31%	B- / 7.9

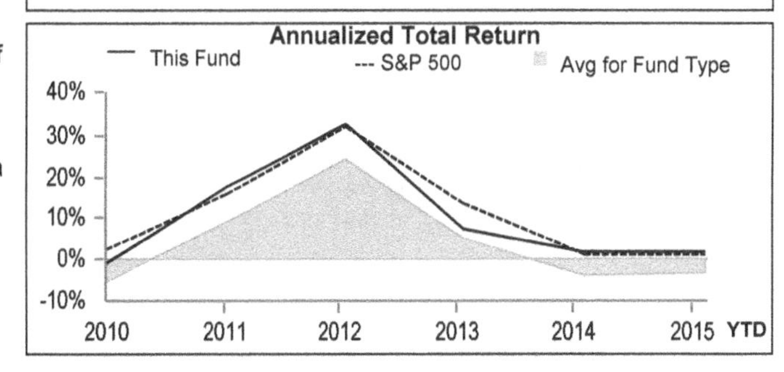

*Vanguard S&P Mid-Cap 400 Index E (IVOO) B Good

Fund Family: Vanguard Group Inc
Fund Type: Growth
Inception Date: September 7, 2010

Major Rating Factors: Strong performance is the major factor driving the B (Good) TheStreet.com Investment Rating for *Vanguard S&P Mid-Cap 400 Index E. The fund currently has a performance rating of B (Good) based on an annualized return of 11.30% over the last three years and a total return of -2.11% year to date 2015. Factored into the performance evaluation is an expense ratio of 0.15% (very low).

The fund's risk rating is currently B- (Good). It carries a beta of 1.00, meaning that its performance tracks fairly well with that of the overall stock market. Volatility, as measured by both the semi-deviation and a drawdown factor, is considered low. As of December 31, 2015, *Vanguard S&P Mid-Cap 400 Index E traded at a premium of .02% above its net asset value.

Christine Franquin has been running the fund for 3 years and currently receives a manager quality ranking of 49 (0=worst, 99=best). If you desire only a moderate level of risk and strong performance, then this fund is an excellent option.

Data Date	Investment Rating	Net Assets ($Mil)	Price	Perfor-mance Rating/Pts	Total Return Y-T-D	Risk Rating/Pts
12-15	B	329.40	93.84	B / 7.7	-2.11%	B- / 7.3
2014	B	329.40	97.40	B / 8.1	11.49%	B- / 7.1
2013	B+	260.90	90.09	B / 8.0	27.88%	B- / 7.9
2012	B+	101.10	68.07	B+ / 8.6	18.42%	B- / 7.8
2011	D+	26.30	58.66	D / 1.8	-0.69%	B- / 7.8

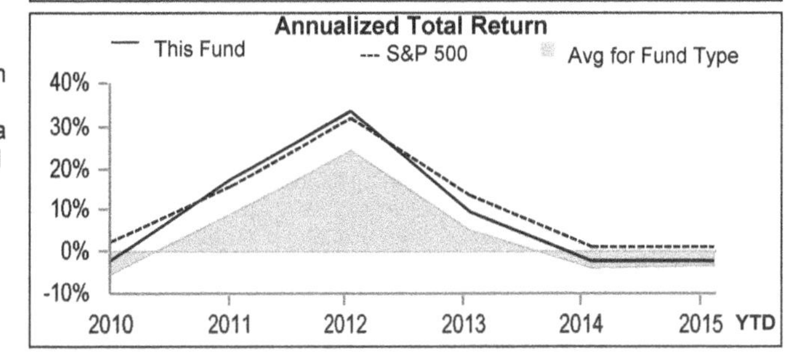

* Denotes ETF Fund

*Vanguard S&P Mid-Cap 400 Value E (IVOV) B Good

Fund Family: Vanguard Group Inc
Fund Type: Growth
Inception Date: September 7, 2010

Major Rating Factors: Strong performance is the major factor driving the B (Good) TheStreet.com Investment Rating for *Vanguard S&P Mid-Cap 400 Value E. The fund currently has a performance rating of B- (Good) based on an annualized return of 10.43% over the last three years and a total return of -6.63% year to date 2015. Factored into the performance evaluation is an expense ratio of 0.20% (very low).

The fund's risk rating is currently B- (Good). It carries a beta of 1.01, meaning that its performance tracks fairly well with that of the overall stock market. Volatility, as measured by both the semi-deviation and a drawdown factor, is considered low. As of December 31, 2015, *Vanguard S&P Mid-Cap 400 Value E traded at a premium of .01% above its net asset value, which is better than its one-year historical average premium of .04%.

Christine Franquin has been running the fund for 3 years and currently receives a manager quality ranking of 43 (0=worst, 99=best). If you desire only a moderate level of risk and strong performance, then this fund is an excellent option.

Data Date	Investment Rating	Net Assets ($Mil)	Price	Performance Rating/Pts	Total Return Y-T-D	Risk Rating/Pts
12-15	B	87.00	88.41	B- / 7.1	-6.63%	B- / 7.7
2014	B+	87.00	96.48	B+ / 8.8	13.79%	B- / 7.2
2013	B	9.70	87.44	B / 8.1	28.64%	B- / 7.6
2012	B+	9.70	65.63	B+ / 8.8	18.81%	B- / 7.6
2011	D	11.30	56.91	D / 1.7	-3.41%	B- / 7.6

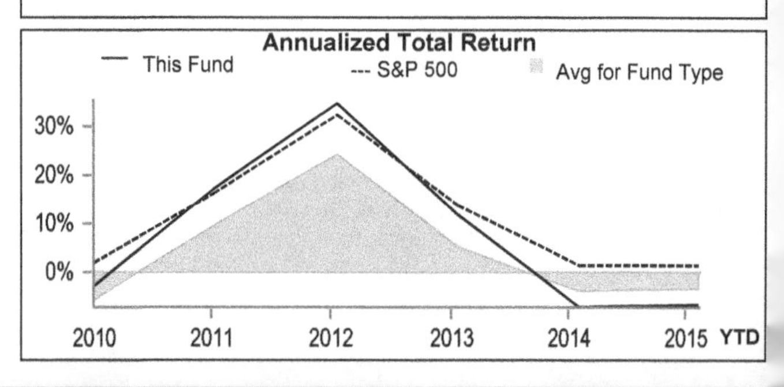

*Vanguard S&P SC 600 G Indx ETF (VIOG) B+ Good

Fund Family: Vanguard Group Inc
Fund Type: Growth
Inception Date: September 7, 2010

Major Rating Factors: Strong performance is the major factor driving the B+ (Good) TheStreet.com Investment Rating for *Vanguard S&P SC 600 G Indx ETF. The fund currently has a performance rating of B+ (Good) based on an annualized return of 13.83% over the last three years and a total return of 3.81% year to date 2015. Factored into the performance evaluation is an expense ratio of 0.20% (very low).

The fund's risk rating is currently C+ (Fair). It carries a beta of 0.97, meaning that its performance tracks fairly well with that of the overall stock market. Volatility, as measured by both the semi-deviation and a drawdown factor, is considered low. As of December 31, 2015, *Vanguard S&P SC 600 G Indx ETF traded at a premium of .52% above its net asset value, which is worse than its one-year historical average premium of .01%.

William Coleman has been running the fund for 3 years and currently receives a manager quality ranking of 72 (0=worst, 99=best). If you desire only a moderate level of risk and strong performance, then this fund is an excellent option.

Data Date	Investment Rating	Net Assets ($Mil)	Price	Performance Rating/Pts	Total Return Y-T-D	Risk Rating/Pts
12-15	B+	58.00	106.86	B+ / 8.7	3.81%	C+ / 6.9
2014	B	58.00	104.86	B / 7.7	5.39%	B- / 7.1
2013	A	40.70	101.80	A- / 9.0	36.74%	B / 8.0
2012	B	14.10	71.64	B / 7.7	16.50%	B- / 7.9
2011	C-	19.10	63.82	D+ / 2.7	3.79%	B- / 7.9

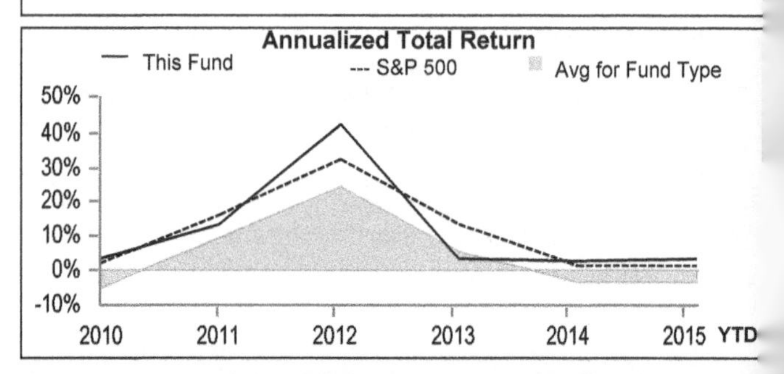

*Vanguard S&P SC 600 Indx ETF (VIOO) A- Excellent

Fund Family: Vanguard Group Inc
Fund Type: Growth
Inception Date: September 7, 2010

Major Rating Factors:
Strong performance is the major factor driving the A- (Excellent) TheStreet.com Investment Rating for *Vanguard S&P SC 600 Indx ETF. The fund currently has a performance rating of B (Good) based on an annualized return of 12.12% over the last three years and a total return of -1.47% year to date 2015. Factored into the performance evaluation is an expense ratio of 0.15% (very low).

The fund's risk rating is currently B (Good). It carries a beta of 1.03, meaning that its performance tracks fairly well with that of the overall stock market. Volatility, as measured by both the semi-deviation and a drawdown factor, is considered low. As of December 31, 2015, *Vanguard S&P SC 600 Indx ETF traded at a discount of .10% below its net asset value, which is better than its one-year historical average premium of .03%.

William Coleman has been running the fund for 3 years and currently receives a manager quality ranking of 52 (0=worst, 99=best). If you desire only a moderate level of risk and strong performance, then this fund is an excellent option.

Data Date	Investment Rating	Net Assets ($Mil)	Price	Performance Rating/Pts	Total Return Y-T-D	Risk Rating/Pts
12-15	A-	151.10	99.15	B / 8.0	-1.47%	B / 8.5
2014	B	151.10	102.63	B / 8.0	7.14%	B- / 7.0
2013	A-	127.70	98.39	B+ / 8.9	35.37%	B- / 7.9
2012	B	48.30	70.25	B / 8.1	16.69%	B- / 7.8
2011	D+	12.30	61.80	D+ / 2.5	1.25%	B- / 7.8

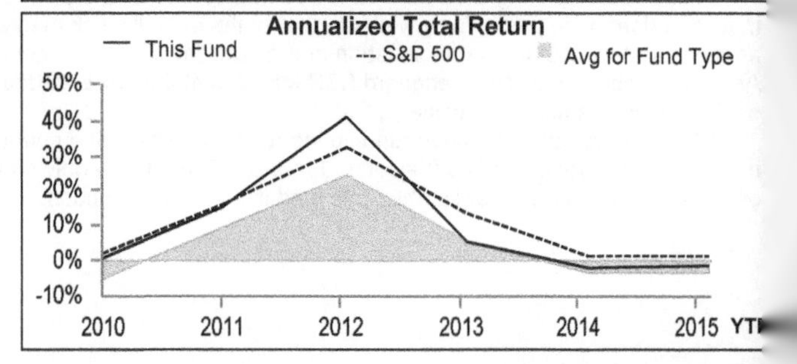

*Vanguard S&P SC 600 Val Indx ETF (VIOV) B+ Good

Fund Family: Vanguard Group Inc
Fund Type: Growth
Inception Date: September 7, 2010

Major Rating Factors: Strong performance is the major factor driving the B+ (Good) TheStreet.com Investment Rating for *Vanguard S&P SC 600 Val Indx ETF. The fund currently has a performance rating of B- (Good) based on an annualized return of 10.45% over the last three years and a total return of -6.04% year to date 2015. Factored into the performance evaluation is an expense ratio of 0.20% (very low).

The fund's risk rating is currently B (Good). It carries a beta of 1.03, meaning that its performance tracks fairly well with that of the overall stock market. Volatility, as measured by both the semi-deviation and a drawdown factor, is considered low. As of December 31, 2015, *Vanguard S&P SC 600 Val Indx ETF traded at a discount of .02% below its net asset value, which is better than its one-year historical average premium of .01%.

William Coleman has been running the fund for 3 years and currently receives a manager quality ranking of 40 (0=worst, 99=best). If you desire only a moderate level of risk and strong performance, then this fund is an excellent option.

Data Date	Investment Rating	Net Assets ($Mil)	Price	Performance Rating/Pts	Total Return Y-T-D	Risk Rating/Pts
12-15	B+	83.60	93.09	B- / 7.3	-6.04%	B / 8.1
2014	B	83.60	101.31	B+ / 8.5	8.61%	C+ / 6.8
2013	A-	47.80	95.61	B+ / 8.8	34.15%	B- / 7.8
2012	B+	16.90	69.17	B+ / 8.3	17.30%	B- / 7.7
2011	D+	14.80	59.59	D+ / 2.5	-0.43%	B- / 7.7

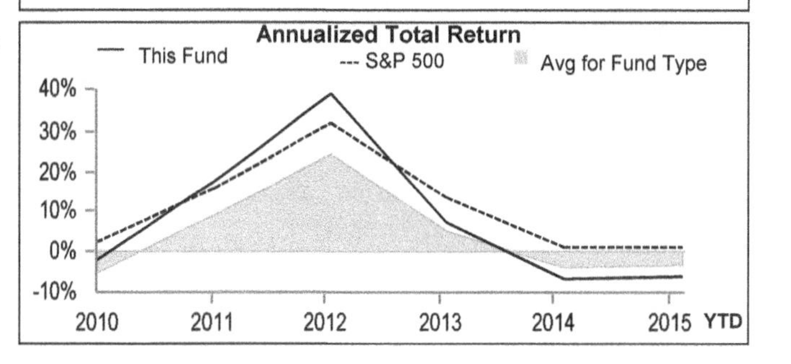

*Vanguard Short-Term Bd Idx ETF (BSV) C+ Fair

Fund Family: Vanguard Group Inc
Fund Type: General - Investment Grade
Inception Date: April 3, 2007

Major Rating Factors: Middle of the road best describes *Vanguard Short-Term Bd Idx ETF whose TheStreet.com Investment Rating is currently a C+ (Fair). The fund currently has a performance rating of C (Fair) based on an annualized return of 0.83% over the last three years and a total return of 0.92% year to date 2015. Factored into the performance evaluation is an expense ratio of 0.10% (very low).

The fund's risk rating is currently B (Good). It carries a beta of 0.36, meaning the fund's expected move will be 3.6% for every 10% move in the market. Volatility, as measured by both the semi-deviation and a drawdown factor, is considered low. As of December 31, 2015, *Vanguard Short-Term Bd Idx ETF traded at a premium of .10% above its net asset value, which is worse than its one-year historical average premium of .06%.

Joshua C. Barrickman has been running the fund for 3 years and currently receives a manager quality ranking of 70 (0=worst, 99=best). If you desire an average level of risk, then this fund may be an option.

Data Date	Investment Rating	Net Assets ($Mil)	Price	Performance Rating/Pts	Total Return Y-T-D	Risk Rating/Pts
12-15	C+	14,944.10	79.57	C / 4.6	0.92%	B / 8.2
2014	C-	14,944.10	79.95	C- / 3.1	1.40%	B / 8.3
2013	C	13,925.60	79.93	C- / 3.0	0.17%	B+ / 9.8
2012	C-	9,274.40	80.99	D / 1.9	1.94%	B+ / 9.8
2011	C	7,481.70	80.84	D+ / 2.5	2.49%	B+ / 9.8
2010	B	5,640.40	80.46	C / 4.3	3.89%	B / 8.9

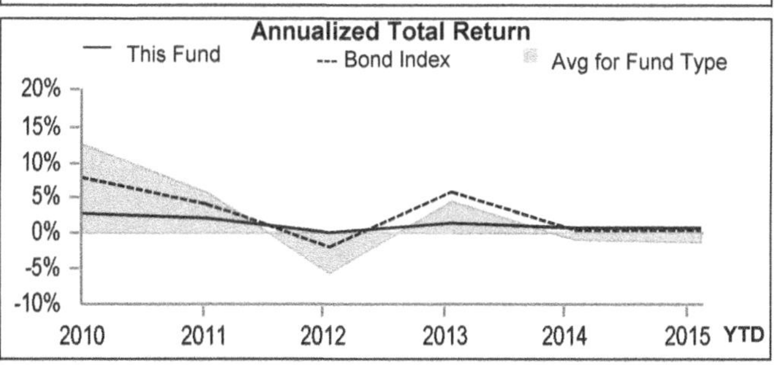

*Vanguard Short-Term Crp Bd Idx E (VCSH) C+ Fair

Fund Family: Vanguard Group Inc
Fund Type: Corporate - Investment Grade
Inception Date: November 19, 2009

Major Rating Factors: Middle of the road best describes *Vanguard Short-Term Crp Bd Idx E whose TheStreet.com Investment Rating is currently a C+ (Fair). The fund currently has a performance rating of C (Fair) based on an annualized return of 1.59% over the last three years and a total return of 1.36% year to date 2015. Factored into the performance evaluation is an expense ratio of 0.10% (very low).

The fund's risk rating is currently B (Good). It carries a beta of 0.31, meaning the fund's expected move will be 3.1% for every 10% move in the market. Volatility, as measured by both the semi-deviation and a drawdown factor, is considered low. As of December 31, 2015, *Vanguard Short-Term Crp Bd Idx E traded at a premium of .28% above its net asset value, which is worse than its one-year historical average premium of .12%.

Joshua C. Barrickman has been running the fund for 7 years and currently receives a manager quality ranking of 76 (0=worst, 99=best). If you desire an average level of risk, then this fund may be an option.

Data Date	Investment Rating	Net Assets ($Mil)	Price	Performance Rating/Pts	Total Return Y-T-D	Risk Rating/Pts
12-15	C+	8,660.00	78.98	C / 5.1	1.36%	B / 8.1
2014	C-	8,660.00	79.63	C- / 3.5	1.89%	B / 8.0
2013	C+	7,397.80	79.76	C- / 3.7	1.63%	B+ / 9.9
2012	C	4,648.50	80.33	D+ / 2.3	5.34%	B+ / 9.9
2011	C	2,230.20	77.83	D+ / 2.4	3.00%	B+ / 9.9
2010	B+	940.80	77.41	C / 4.5	5.27%	B+ / 9.0

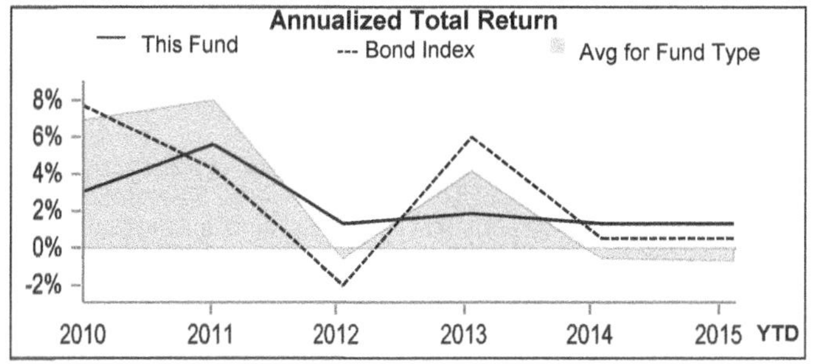

*Vanguard Short-Term Gvt Bd Idx E (VGSH) C Fair

Fund Family: Vanguard Group Inc
Fund Type: US Government/Agency
Inception Date: November 19, 2009

Major Rating Factors: Middle of the road best describes *Vanguard Short-Term Gvt Bd Idx E whose TheStreet.com Investment Rating is currently a C (Fair). The fund currently has a performance rating of C (Fair) based on an annualized return of 0.46% over the last three years and a total return of 0.46% year to date 2015. Factored into the performance evaluation is an expense ratio of 0.10% (very low).

The fund's risk rating is currently B- (Good). It carries a beta of 0.03, meaning the fund's expected move will be 0.3% for every 10% move in the market. Volatility, as measured by both the semi-deviation and a drawdown factor, is considered low. As of December 31, 2015, *Vanguard Short-Term Gvt Bd Idx E traded at a premium of .05% above its net asset value, which is worse than its one-year historical average premium of .03%.

Joshua C. Barrickman has been running the fund for 3 years and currently receives a manager quality ranking of 71 (0=worst, 99=best). If you desire an average level of risk, then this fund may be an option.

Data Date	Investment Rating	Net Assets ($Mil)	Price	Perfor-mance Rating/Pts	Total Return Y-T-D	Risk Rating/Pts
12-15	C	511.50	60.76	C / 4.5	0.46%	B- / 7.9
2014	C-	511.50	60.88	D+ / 2.9	0.54%	B / 8.5
2013	C	377.00	60.88	D+ / 2.7	0.32%	B+ / 9.9
2012	C-	225.50	60.89	D / 1.6	0.46%	B+ / 9.9
2011	C	170.60	60.98	D / 2.2	1.28%	B+ / 9.9
2010	C+	82.00	60.56	C- / 3.1	2.29%	B+ / 9.0

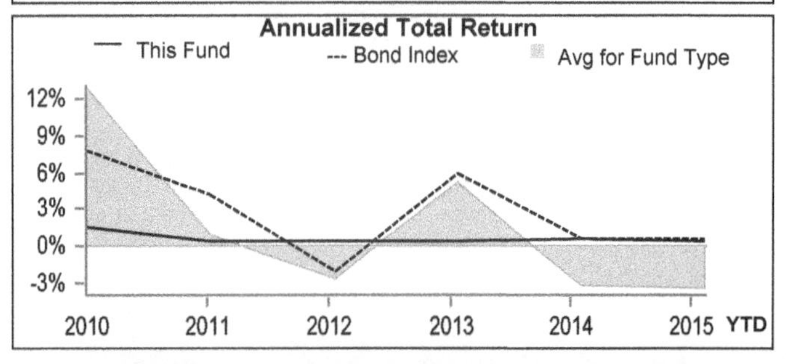

*Vanguard Small Cap ETF (VB) B+ Good

Fund Family: Vanguard Group Inc
Fund Type: Growth
Inception Date: January 26, 2004

Major Rating Factors: Strong performance is the major factor driving the B+ (Good) TheStreet.com Investment Rating for *Vanguard Small Cap ETF. The fund currently has a performance rating of B (Good) based on an annualized return of 11.26% over the last three years and a total return of -3.43% year to date 2015. Factored into the performance evaluation is an expense ratio of 0.09% (very low).

The fund's risk rating is currently B (Good). It carries a beta of 1.03, meaning that its performance tracks fairly well with that of the overall stock market. Volatility, as measured by both the semi-deviation and a drawdown factor, is considered low. As of December 31, 2015, *Vanguard Small Cap ETF traded at a discount of .06% below its net asset value.

Michael H. Buek has been running the fund for 25 years and currently receives a manager quality ranking of 46 (0=worst, 99=best). If you desire only a moderate level of risk and strong performance, then this fund is an excellent option.

Data Date	Investment Rating	Net Assets ($Mil)	Price	Perfor-mance Rating/Pts	Total Return Y-T-D	Risk Rating/Pts
12-15	B+	8,744.80	110.64	B / 7.6	-3.43%	B / 8.3
2014	B	8,744.80	116.66	B / 8.0	8.16%	B- / 7.1
2013	B+	8,217.50	109.95	B+ / 8.6	32.30%	B- / 7.6
2012	C+	4,491.00	80.90	C+ / 6.9	18.62%	B- / 7.4
2011	C+	3,683.00	69.67	C+ / 6.5	-1.97%	B- / 7.3
2010	B	4,843.10	72.63	B- / 7.5	28.12%	C / 5.5

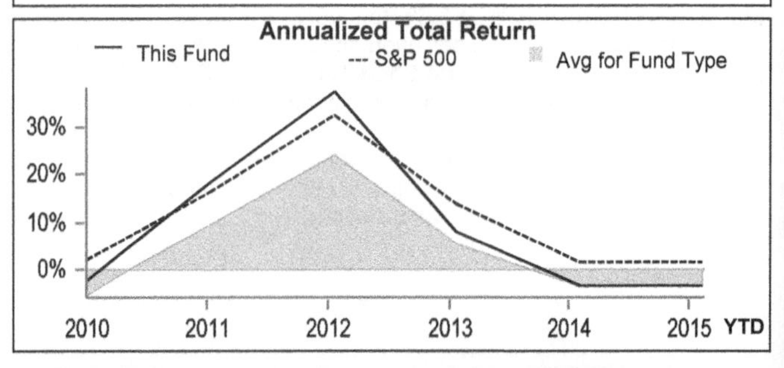

*Vanguard Small Cap Growth ETF (VBK) B Good

Fund Family: Vanguard Group Inc
Fund Type: Growth
Inception Date: January 26, 2004

Major Rating Factors: Strong performance is the major factor driving the B (Good) TheStreet.com Investment Rating for *Vanguard Small Cap Growth ETF. The fund currently has a performance rating of B- (Good) based on an annualized return of 10.69% over the last three years and a total return of -2.38% year to date 2015. Factored into the performance evaluation is an expense ratio of 0.09% (very low).

The fund's risk rating is currently B- (Good). It carries a beta of 1.00, meaning that its performance tracks fairly well with that of the overall stock market. Volatility, as measured by both the semi-deviation and a drawdown factor, is considered low. As of December 31, 2015, *Vanguard Small Cap Growth ETF traded at a discount of .07% below its net asset value, which is better than its one-year historical average premium of .01%.

Gerard C. O'Reilly has been running the fund for 12 years and currently receives a manager quality ranking of 44 (0=worst, 99=best). If you desire only a moderate level of risk and strong performance, then this fund is an excellent option.

Data Date	Investment Rating	Net Assets ($Mil)	Price	Perfor-mance Rating/Pts	Total Return Y-T-D	Risk Rating/Pts
12-15	B	3,642.00	121.44	B- / 7.4	-2.38%	B- / 7.4
2014	C+	3,642.00	125.94	B- / 7.5	4.48%	C+ / 6.6
2013	B	3,637.30	122.30	B+ / 8.6	33.29%	B- / 7.1
2012	C+	2,101.10	89.03	B- / 7.2	18.40%	B- / 7.0
2011	C+	1,857.30	76.36	B- / 7.0	-1.51%	C+ / 6.9
2010	B	1,841.90	78.04	B / 7.8	30.95%	C / 5.3

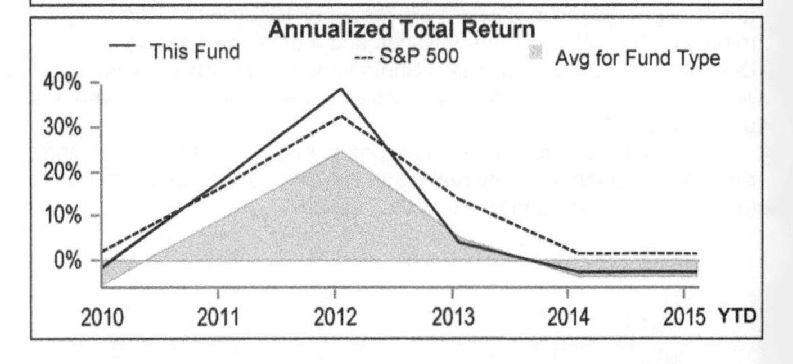

*Vanguard Small Cap Value ETF (VBR) A- Excellent

Fund Family: Vanguard Group Inc
Fund Type: Growth
Inception Date: January 26, 2004

Major Rating Factors:
Strong performance is the major factor driving the A- (Excellent) TheStreet.com Investment Rating for *Vanguard Small Cap Value ETF. The fund currently has a performance rating of B (Good) based on an annualized return of 11.48% over the last three years and a total return of -4.42% year to date 2015. Factored into the performance evaluation is an expense ratio of 0.09% (very low).

The fund's risk rating is currently B (Good). It carries a beta of 1.07, meaning that its performance tracks fairly well with that of the overall stock market. Volatility, as measured by both the semi-deviation and a drawdown factor, is considered low. As of December 31, 2015, *Vanguard Small Cap Value ETF traded at a discount of .04% below its net asset value, which is better than its one-year historical average premium of .01%.

Michael H. Buek has been running the fund for 18 years and currently receives a manager quality ranking of 44 (0=worst, 99=best). If you desire only a moderate level of risk and strong performance, then this fund is an excellent option.

Data Date	Investment Rating	Net Assets ($Mil)	Price	Performance Rating/Pts	Total Return Y-T-D	Risk Rating/Pts
12-15	A-	4,256.50	98.77	B / 7.6	-4.42%	B / 8.7
2014	B+	4,256.50	105.77	B+ / 8.5	11.36%	B- / 7.4
2013	B+	3,908.20	97.37	B+ / 8.4	30.60%	B- / 7.9
2012	C+	2,169.90	72.65	C+ / 6.4	18.68%	B- / 7.6
2011	C	1,755.20	62.67	C / 5.4	-4.50%	B- / 7.5
2010	B	1,851.20	66.86	B- / 7.4	25.12%	C / 5.5

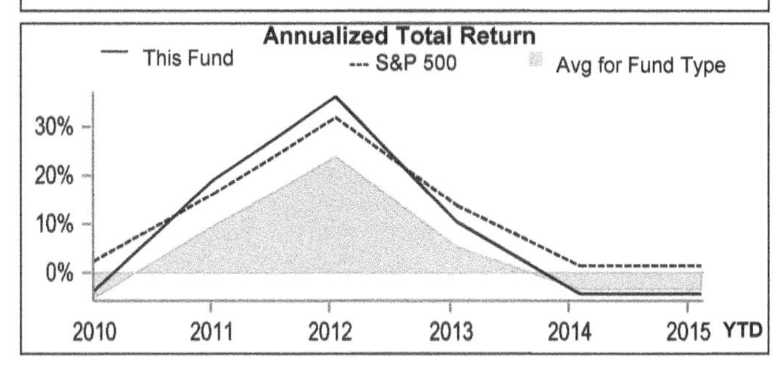

*Vanguard ST Inf Prot Sec Idx ETF (VTIP) C Fair

Fund Family: Vanguard Group Inc
Fund Type: General - Investment Grade
Inception Date: October 12, 2012

Major Rating Factors: Middle of the road best describes *Vanguard ST Inf Prot Sec Idx ETF whose TheStreet.com Investment Rating is currently a C (Fair). The fund currently has a performance rating of C- (Fair) based on an annualized return of -0.84% over the last three years and a total return of 0.04% year to date 2015. Factored into the performance evaluation is an expense ratio of 0.08% (very low).

The fund's risk rating is currently B- (Good). It carries a beta of 0.34, meaning the fund's expected move will be 3.4% for every 10% move in the market. Volatility, as measured by both the semi-deviation and a drawdown factor, is considered low. As of December 31, 2015, *Vanguard ST Inf Prot Sec Idx ETF traded at a premium of .35% above its net asset value, which is worse than its one-year historical average premium of .10%.

Gemma Wright-Casparius has been running the fund for 4 years and currently receives a manager quality ranking of 56 (0=worst, 99=best). If you desire an average level of risk, then this fund may be an option.

Data Date	Investment Rating	Net Assets ($Mil)	Price	Performance Rating/Pts	Total Return Y-T-D	Risk Rating/Pts
12-15	C	1,336.00	48.35	C- / 4.0	0.04%	B- / 7.9
2014	C-	1,336.00	48.24	D / 2.2	-1.53%	B+ / 9.4
2013	C	1,085.00	49.33	D+ / 2.3	-1.42%	B+ / 9.9

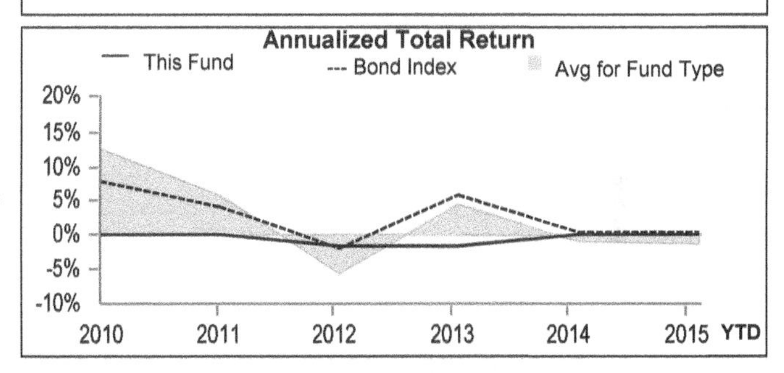

*Vanguard Telecom Serv ETF (VOX) A- Excellent

Fund Family: Vanguard Group Inc
Fund Type: Income
Inception Date: September 23, 2004

Major Rating Factors:
Strong performance is the major factor driving the A- (Excellent) TheStreet.com Investment Rating for *Vanguard Telecom Serv ETF. The fund currently has a performance rating of B (Good) based on an annualized return of 8.92% over the last three years and a total return of 2.62% year to date 2015. Factored into the performance evaluation is an expense ratio of 0.10% (very low).

The fund's risk rating is currently B (Good). It carries a beta of 0.75, meaning the fund's expected move will be 7.5% for every 10% move in the market. Volatility, as measured by both the semi-deviation and a drawdown factor, is considered low. As of December 31, 2015, *Vanguard Telecom Serv ETF traded at a discount of .04% below its net asset value, which is better than its one-year historical average premium of .01%.

Ryan E. Ludt has been running the fund for 12 years and currently receives a manager quality ranking of 58 (0=worst, 99=best). If you desire only a moderate level of risk and strong performance, then this fund is an excellent option.

Data Date	Investment Rating	Net Assets ($Mil)	Price	Performance Rating/Pts	Total Return Y-T-D	Risk Rating/Pts
12-15	A-	749.10	83.91	B / 7.6	2.62%	B / 8.8
2014	B+	749.10	84.72	C+ / 6.7	5.14%	B+ / 9.1
2013	B	569.20	83.66	B- / 7.1	19.57%	B / 8.6
2012	C+	484.90	70.01	C / 5.3	18.47%	B / 8.6
2011	C	373.10	62.17	C / 4.3	-4.14%	B / 8.4
2010	C	315.30	65.63	C / 4.7	19.52%	C+ / 6.4

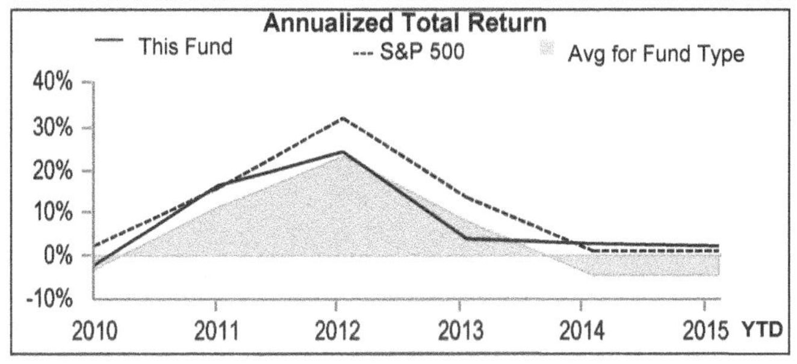

 * Denotes ETF Fund

*Vanguard Tot Stk Mkt Idx ETF (VTI) A+ Excellent

Fund Family: Vanguard Group Inc
Fund Type: Growth and Income
Inception Date: May 24, 2001

Major Rating Factors:
Strong performance is the major factor driving the A+ (Excellent) TheStreet.com Investment Rating for *Vanguard Tot Stk Mkt Idx ETF. The fund currently has a performance rating of B+ (Good) based on an annualized return of 13.76% over the last three years and a total return of 0.99% year to date 2015. Factored into the performance evaluation is an expense ratio of 0.05% (very low).

The fund's risk rating is currently B (Good). It carries a beta of 1.01, meaning that its performance tracks fairly well with that of the overall stock market. Volatility, as measured by both the semi-deviation and a drawdown factor, is considered low. As of December 31, 2015, *Vanguard Tot Stk Mkt Idx ETF traded at a discount of .04% below its net asset value.

Gerard C. O'Reilly has been running the fund for 22 years and currently receives a manager quality ranking of 64 (0=worst, 99=best). If you desire only a moderate level of risk and strong performance, then this fund is an excellent option.

Data Date	Investment Rating	Net Assets ($Mil)	Price	Performance Rating/Pts	Total Return Y-T-D	Risk Rating/Pts
12-15	A+	45,764.00	104.30	B+ / 8.7	0.99%	B / 8.7
2014	B+	45,764.00	106.00	B+ / 8.3	13.56%	B- / 7.4
2013	B+	39,164.90	95.92	B+ / 8.3	28.46%	B / 8.1
2012	C+	23,383.20	73.28	C / 5.5	17.04%	B- / 7.9
2011	C+	19,521.40	64.30	C / 5.5	1.69%	B- / 7.9
2010	D+	17,930.40	64.93	C / 4.8	17.45%	C- / 3.5

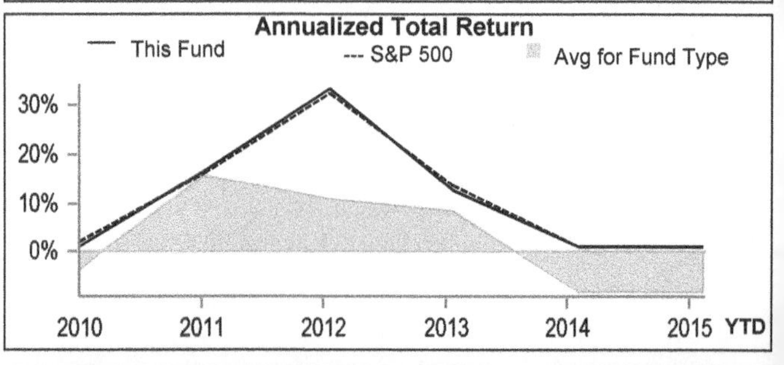

*Vanguard Total Bond Market ETF (BND) C Fair

Fund Family: Vanguard Group Inc
Fund Type: General - Investment Grade
Inception Date: April 3, 2007

Major Rating Factors: Middle of the road best describes *Vanguard Total Bond Market ETF whose TheStreet.com Investment Rating is currently a C (Fair). The fund currently has a performance rating of C (Fair) based on an annualized return of 1.48% over the last three years and a total return of 0.23% year to date 2015. Factored into the performance evaluation is an expense ratio of 0.07% (very low).

The fund's risk rating is currently B- (Good). It carries a beta of 1.08, meaning that its performance tracks fairly well with that of the overall stock market. Volatility, as measured by both the semi-deviation and a drawdown factor, is considered low. As of December 31, 2015, *Vanguard Total Bond Market ETF traded at a premium of .22% above its net asset value, which is worse than its one-year historical average premium of .07%.

Kenneth E. Volpert has been running the fund for 24 years and currently receives a manager quality ranking of 66 (0=worst, 99=best). If you desire an average level of risk, then this fund may be an option.

Data Date	Investment Rating	Net Assets ($Mil)	Price	Performance Rating/Pts	Total Return Y-T-D	Risk Rating/Pts
12-15	C	22,814.40	80.76	C / 5.0	0.23%	B- / 7.8
2014	C	22,814.40	82.37	C- / 3.6	5.72%	B+ / 9.4
2013	C	17,637.50	80.05	C- / 3.5	-1.71%	B+ / 9.6
2012	C	17,720.50	84.03	D+ / 2.4	3.45%	B+ / 9.8
2011	C	14,595.70	83.54	C- / 3.3	6.94%	B+ / 9.7
2010	B+	9,047.80	80.27	C / 4.8	6.20%	B / 8.9

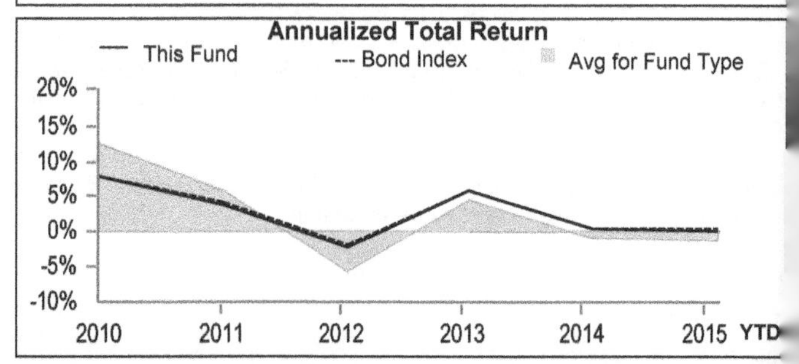

*Vanguard Total Internatl Bd Idx (BNDX) C+ Fair

Fund Family: Vanguard Group Inc
Fund Type: Global
Inception Date: May 31, 2013

Major Rating Factors: Middle of the road best describes *Vanguard Total Internatl Bd Idx whose TheStreet.com Investment Rating is currently a C+ (Fair). The fund currently has a performance rating of C (Fair) based on an annualized return of 0.00% over the last three years and a total return of 0.74% year to date 2015. Factored into the performance evaluation is an expense ratio of 0.19% (very low).

The fund's risk rating is currently B (Good). It carries a beta of 0.00, meaning the fund's expected move will be 0.0% for every 10% move in the market. Volatility, as measured by both the semi-deviation and a drawdown factor, is considered low. As of December 31, 2015, *Vanguard Total Internatl Bd Idx traded at a premium of .36% above its net asset value, which is worse than its one-year historical average premium of .20%.

Joshua C. Barrickman has been running the fund for 3 years and currently receives a manager quality ranking of 73 (0=worst, 99=best). If you desire an average level of risk, then this fund may be an option.

Data Date	Investment Rating	Net Assets ($Mil)	Price	Performance Rating/Pts	Total Return Y-T-D	Risk Rating/Pts
12-15	C+	2,022.10	52.88	C / 5.2	0.74%	B / 8.0
2014	B-	2,022.10	53.11	C / 5.5	8.85%	B+ / 9.0

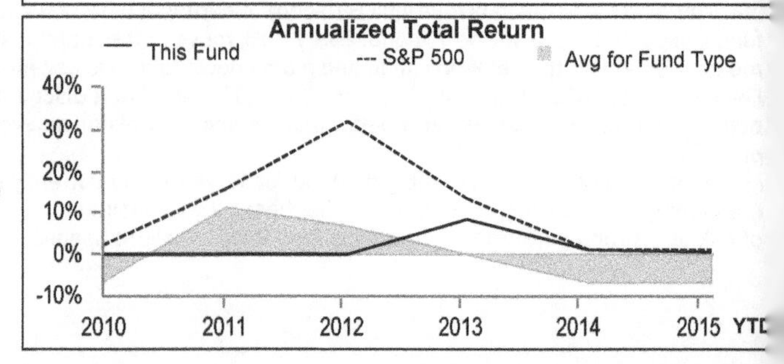

*Vanguard Total Intl Stock Index (VXUS) C- Fair

Fund Family: Vanguard Group Inc
Fund Type: Global
Inception Date: January 26, 2011

Major Rating Factors: Middle of the road best describes *Vanguard Total Intl Stock Index whose TheStreet.com Investment Rating is currently a C- (Fair). The fund currently has a performance rating of C- (Fair) based on an annualized return of 1.16% over the last three years and a total return of -3.89% year to date 2015. Factored into the performance evaluation is an expense ratio of 0.14% (very low).

The fund's risk rating is currently C+ (Fair). It carries a beta of 0.93, meaning that its performance tracks fairly well with that of the overall stock market. Volatility, as measured by both the semi-deviation and a drawdown factor, is considered low. As of December 31, 2015, *Vanguard Total Intl Stock Index traded at a premium of .09% above its net asset value, which is better than its one-year historical average premium of .23%.

Michael Perre has been running the fund for 8 years and currently receives a manager quality ranking of 40 (0=worst, 99=best). If you desire an average level of risk, then this fund may be an option.

Data Date	Investment Rating	Net Assets ($Mil)	Price	Performance Rating/Pts	Total Return Y-T-D	Risk Rating/Pts
12-15	C-	3,160.10	45.12	C- / 4.1	-3.89%	C+ / 6.7
2014	C-	3,160.10	48.32	C / 4.5	-2.53%	C+ / 6.8
2013	B-	2,331.00	52.43	B- / 7.3	11.22%	B- / 7.6
2012	B+	1,065.70	46.96	A- / 9.2	19.12%	B- / 7.2

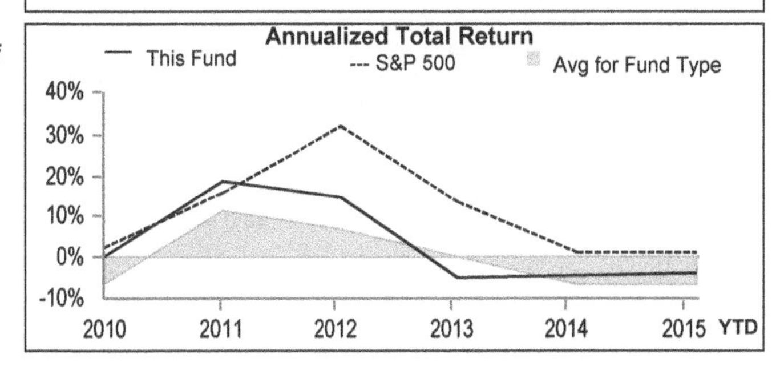

*Vanguard Total World Stock ETF (VT) C+ Fair

Fund Family: Vanguard Group Inc
Fund Type: Emerging Market
Inception Date: June 24, 2008

Major Rating Factors: Middle of the road best describes *Vanguard Total World Stock ETF whose TheStreet.com Investment Rating is currently a C+ (Fair). The fund currently has a performance rating of C+ (Fair) based on an annualized return of 7.22% over the last three years and a total return of -0.97% year to date 2015. Factored into the performance evaluation is an expense ratio of 0.17% (very low).

The fund's risk rating is currently B- (Good). It carries a beta of 0.60, meaning the fund's expected move will be 6.0% for every 10% move in the market. Volatility, as measured by both the semi-deviation and a drawdown factor, is considered low. As of December 31, 2015, *Vanguard Total World Stock ETF traded at a premium of .14% above its net asset value, which is worse than its one-year historical average premium of .13%.

Christine Franquin has been running the fund for 3 years and currently receives a manager quality ranking of 96 (0=worst, 99=best). If you desire an average level of risk, then this fund may be an option.

Data Date	Investment Rating	Net Assets ($Mil)	Price	Performance Rating/Pts	Total Return Y-T-D	Risk Rating/Pts
12-15	C+	3,603.90	57.62	C+ / 6.5	-0.97%	B- / 7.0
2014	C+	3,603.90	60.12	C+ / 6.3	5.12%	B- / 7.0
2013	B-	3,103.60	59.40	B- / 7.0	18.71%	B- / 7.7
2012	C-	1,559.60	49.42	C / 4.4	18.18%	B- / 7.4
2011	C-	1,050.20	43.18	C- / 4.1	-6.01%	B- / 7.7
2010	A-	742.10	47.80	A- / 9.0	13.09%	C+ / 5.9

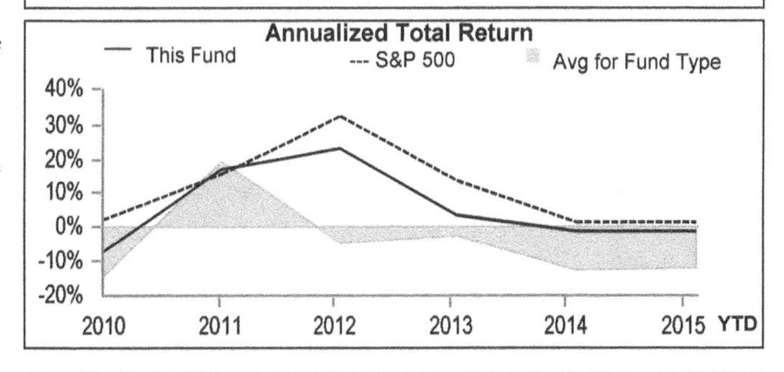

*Vanguard Utilities Index ETF (VPU) B+ Good

Fund Family: Vanguard Group Inc
Fund Type: Utilities
Inception Date: January 26, 2004

Major Rating Factors: Strong performance is the major factor driving the B+ (Good) TheStreet.com Investment Rating for *Vanguard Utilities Index ETF. The fund currently has a performance rating of B (Good) based on an annualized return of 10.64% over the last three years and a total return of -5.35% year to date 2015. Factored into the performance evaluation is an expense ratio of 0.10% (very low).

The fund's risk rating is currently B- (Good). It carries a beta of 0.97, meaning that its performance tracks fairly well with that of the overall stock market. Volatility, as measured by both the semi-deviation and a drawdown factor, is considered low. As of December 31, 2015, *Vanguard Utilities Index ETF traded at a price exactly equal to its net asset value.

Michael A. Johnson has been running the fund for 1 year and currently receives a manager quality ranking of 63 (0=worst, 99=best). If you desire only a moderate level of risk and strong performance, then this fund is an excellent option.

Data Date	Investment Rating	Net Assets ($Mil)	Price	Performance Rating/Pts	Total Return Y-T-D	Risk Rating/Pts
12-15	B+	1,604.50	93.93	B / 7.7	-5.35%	B- / 7.7
2014	A+	1,604.50	102.35	B+ / 8.6	29.19%	B / 8.7
2013	B	1,323.20	83.28	C+ / 6.4	10.16%	B+ / 9.0
2012	C	1,129.80	75.30	C- / 3.4	6.67%	B+ / 9.2
2011	C+	1,048.80	76.89	C / 4.9	14.47%	B / 8.5
2010	D+	647.00	67.08	D / 1.7	7.05%	C+ / 6.7

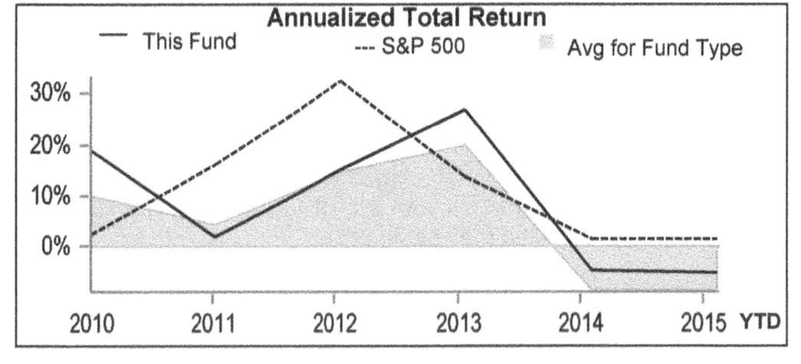

*Vanguard Value ETF (VTV) A+ Excellent

Fund Family: Vanguard Group Inc
Fund Type: Income
Inception Date: January 26, 2004

Data Date	Investment Rating	Net Assets ($Mil)	Price	Performance Rating/Pts	Total Return Y-T-D	Risk Rating/Pts
12-15	A+	15,471.20	81.52	B+ / 8.6	-0.30%	B+ / 9.0
2014	A	15,471.20	84.49	B / 8.2	14.11%	B / 8.4
2013	B+	12,460.90	76.39	B / 8.0	28.06%	B / 8.4
2012	C	6,758.20	58.80	C / 5.0	15.96%	B / 8.2
2011	C	5,049.00	52.49	C / 4.6	1.38%	B- / 7.9
2010	C-	4,330.00	53.33	C- / 3.1	14.57%	C+ / 6.0

Major Rating Factors:
Strong performance is the major factor driving the A+ (Excellent) TheStreet.com Investment Rating for *Vanguard Value ETF. The fund currently has a performance rating of B+ (Good) based on an annualized return of 13.37% over the last three years and a total return of -0.30% year to date 2015. Factored into the performance evaluation is an expense ratio of 0.09% (very low).

The fund's risk rating is currently B+ (Good). It carries a beta of 0.98, meaning that its performance tracks fairly well with that of the overall stock market. Volatility, as measured by both the semi-deviation and a drawdown factor, is considered very low. As of December 31, 2015, *Vanguard Value ETF traded at a discount of .05% below its net asset value.

Gerard C. O'Reilly has been running the fund for 22 years and currently receives a manager quality ranking of 65 (0=worst, 99=best). If you desire only a moderate level of risk and strong performance, then this fund is an excellent option.

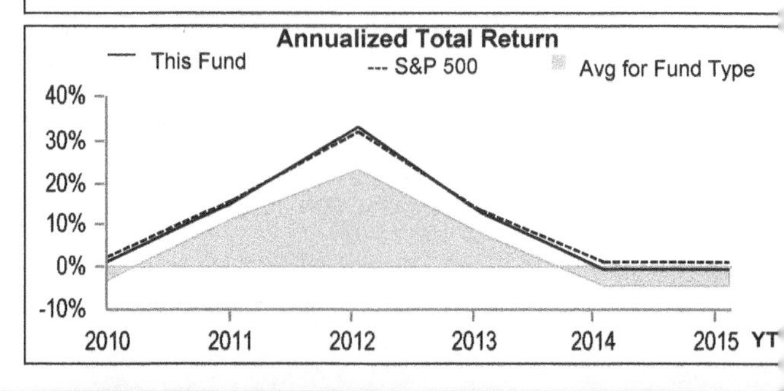

*VelocityShares 3x Inv Nat Gas ET (DGAZ) D Weak

Fund Family: Credit Suisse AG
Fund Type: Global
Inception Date: February 7, 2012

Data Date	Investment Rating	Net Assets ($Mil)	Price	Performance Rating/Pts	Total Return Y-T-D	Risk Rating/Pts
12-15	D	228.30	12.52	B- / 7.0	62.60%	E- / 0.1
2014	D+	228.30	8.04	A+ / 9.9	-3.83%	E- / 0.1
2013	E-	94.40	8.84	E- / 0	-61.95%	D / 1.9

Major Rating Factors: *VelocityShares 3x Inv Nat Gas ET has adopted a very risky asset allocation strategy and currently receives an overall TheStreet.com Investment Rating of D (Weak). The fund has shown a high level of volatility, as measured by both semi-deviation and drawdown factors. It carries a beta of -0.80, meaning the fund's expected move will be -8.0% for every 10% move in the market. As of December 31, 2015, *VelocityShares 3x Inv Nat Gas ET traded at a premium of .97% above its net asset value. The high level of risk (E-, Very Weak) did however, reward investors with excellent performance.

The fund's performance rating is currently B- (Good). It has registered an annualized return of -17.09% over the last three years and is up 62.60% year to date 2015.

This fund has been team managed for 4 years and currently receives a manager quality ranking of 14 (0=worst, 99=best). If you are comfortable owning a very high risk investment, this fund may be an option.

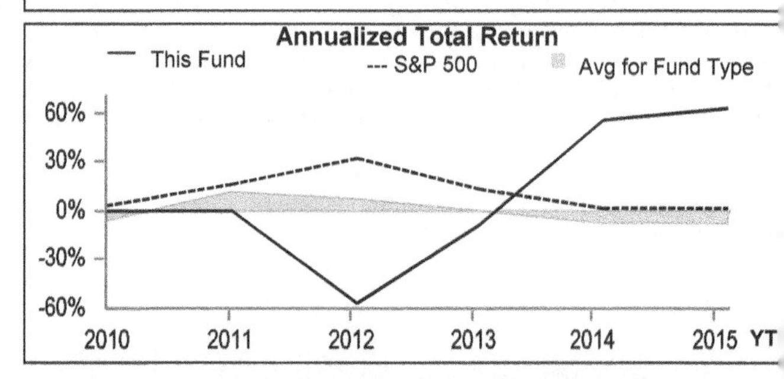

*VelocityShares 3x Inverse Crude (DWTI) C- Fair

Fund Family: Credit Suisse AG
Fund Type: Global
Inception Date: February 7, 2012

Data Date	Investment Rating	Net Assets ($Mil)	Price	Performance Rating/Pts	Total Return Y-T-D	Risk Rating/Pts
12-15	C-	3.40	199.79	A+ / 9.9	59.26%	E+ / 0.9
2014	C	3.40	117.19	A+ / 9.9	219.49%	D+ / 2.3
2013	E+	5.50	32.47	C- / 3.9	-20.61%	D / 2.0

Major Rating Factors: *VelocityShares 3x Inverse Crude has adopted a very risky asset allocation strategy and currently receives an overall TheStreet.com Investment Rating of C- (Fair). The fund has shown a high level of volatility, as measured by both semi-deviation and drawdown factors. It carries a beta of -1.78, meaning the fund's expected move will be -17.8% for every 10% move in the market. As of December 31, 2015, *VelocityShares 3x Inverse Crude traded at a premium of .51% above its net asset value, which is worse than its one-year historical average premium of .28%. The high level of risk (E+, Very Weak) did however, reward investors with excellent performance.

The fund's performance rating is currently A+ (Excellent). It has registered an annualized return of 62.92% over the last three years and is up 59.26% year to date 2015.

This fund has been team managed for 4 years and currently receives a manager quality ranking of 99 (0=worst, 99=best). If you are comfortable owning a very high risk investment, this fund may be an option.

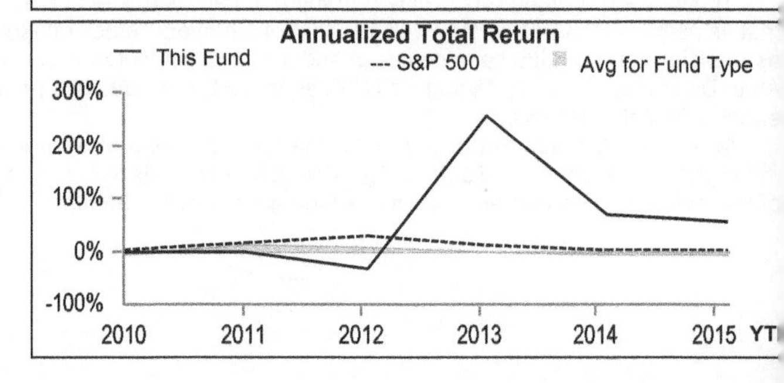

* Denotes ETF Fund

*VelocityShares 3x Inverse Gold E (DGLD) C Fair

Fund Family: Credit Suisse AG
Fund Type: Global
Inception Date: October 14, 2011

Major Rating Factors: *VelocityShares 3x Inverse Gold E has adopted a risky asset allocation strategy and currently receives an overall TheStreet.com Investment Rating of C (Fair). The fund has shown an above average level of volatility, as measured by both semi-deviation and drawdown factors. It carries a beta of -0.41, meaning the fund's expected move will be -4.1% for every 10% move in the market. As of December 31, 2015, *VelocityShares 3x Inverse Gold E traded at a premium of .14% above its net asset value, which is worse than its one-year historical average discount of .21%. The high level of risk (D+, Weak) did however, reward investors with excellent performance.

The fund's performance rating is currently A+ (Excellent). It has registered an annualized return of 30.74% over the last three years and is up 23.84% year to date 2015.

This fund has been team managed for 5 years and currently receives a manager quality ranking of 99 (0=worst, 99=best). If you are comfortable owning a high risk investment, this fund may be an option.

Data Date	Investment Rating	Net Assets ($Mil)	Price	Performance Rating/Pts	Total Return Y-T-D	Risk Rating/Pts
12-15	C	10.30	94.84	A+ / 9.8	23.84%	D+ / 2.9
2014	D+	10.30	77.17	C+ / 6.9	0.82%	C- / 3.2
2013	C+	46.90	76.09	A+ / 9.8	79.29%	C- / 3.6
2012	E	5.60	41.24	E+ / 0.6	-17.35%	C- / 3.5

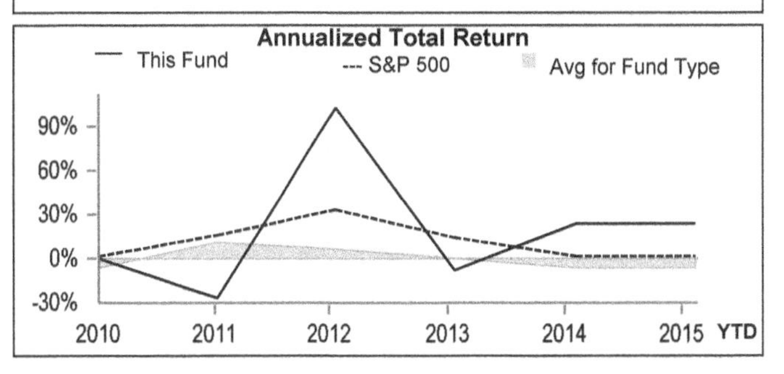

*VelocityShares 3x Inverse Silver (DSLV) C Fair

Fund Family: Credit Suisse AG
Fund Type: Global
Inception Date: October 14, 2011

Major Rating Factors: *VelocityShares 3x Inverse Silver has adopted a very risky asset allocation strategy and currently receives an overall TheStreet.com Investment Rating of C (Fair). The fund has shown a high level of volatility, as measured by both semi-deviation and drawdown factors. It carries a beta of -1.09, meaning the fund's expected move will be -10.9% for every 10% move in the market. As of December 31, 2015, *VelocityShares 3x Inverse Silver traded at a discount of .31% below its net asset value, which is better than its one-year historical average discount of .12%. The high level of risk (D, Weak) did however, reward investors with excellent performance.

The fund's performance rating is currently A+ (Excellent). It has registered an annualized return of 38.29% over the last three years but is down -0.26% year to date 2015.

This fund has been team managed for 5 years and currently receives a manager quality ranking of 99 (0=worst, 99=best). If you are comfortable owning a very high risk investment, this fund may be an option.

Data Date	Investment Rating	Net Assets ($Mil)	Price	Performance Rating/Pts	Total Return Y-T-D	Risk Rating/Pts
12-15	C	16.20	71.69	A+ / 9.9	-0.26%	D / 1.9
2014	D+	16.20	72.98	A / 9.3	52.93%	E- / 0.2
2013	C-	23.90	52.58	A+ / 9.9	93.95%	D / 1.9
2012	E-	16.90	26.91	E- / 0.1	-44.91%	D / 1.9

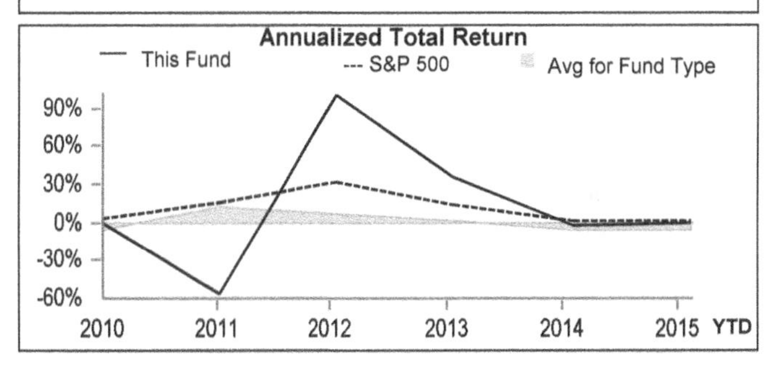

*VelocityShares 3x Long Crude ETN (UWTI) E- Very Weak

Fund Family: Credit Suisse AG
Fund Type: Global
Inception Date: February 7, 2012

Major Rating Factors: *VelocityShares 3x Long Crude ETN has adopted a very risky asset allocation strategy and currently receives an overall TheStreet.com Investment Rating of E- (Very Weak). The fund has a high level of volatility, as measured by both semi-deviation and drawdown factors. It carries a beta of 2.23, meaning it is expected to move 22.3% for every 10% move in the market. As of December 31, 2015, *VelocityShares 3x Long Crude ETN traded at a discount of 1.00% below its net asset value, which is better than its one-year historical average discount of .36%. Unfortunately, the high level of risk (D, Weak) failed to pay off as investors endured very poor performance.

The fund's performance rating is currently E- (Very Weak). It has registered an annualized return of -76.34% over the last three years and is down -91.38% year to date 2015.

This fund has been team managed for 4 years and currently receives a manager quality ranking of 0 (0=worst, 99=best). If you can tolerate very high levels of risk in the hope of improved future returns, holding this fund may be an option.

Data Date	Investment Rating	Net Assets ($Mil)	Price	Performance Rating/Pts	Total Return Y-T-D	Risk Rating/Pts
12-15	E-	6.70	3.95	E- / 0	-91.38%	D / 1.7
2014	E-	6.70	4.89	E- / 0	-81.76%	E- / 0.1
2013	E-	3.20	30.88	E / 0.3	-10.09%	D+ / 2.5

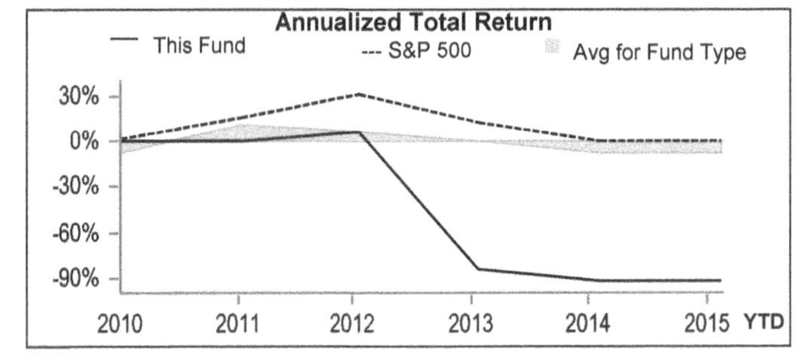

*VelocityShares 3x Long Gold ETN (UGLD) E- Very Weak

Fund Family: Credit Suisse AG
Fund Type: Global
Inception Date: October 14, 2011

Data Date	Investment Rating	Net Assets ($Mil)	Price	Performance Rating/Pts	Total Return Y-T-D	Risk Rating/Pts
12-15	E-	45.60	7.37	E- / 0.1	-35.12%	E+ / 0.9
2014	E-	45.60	11.22	E- / 0.2	-19.45%	D / 2.0
2013	E-	24.50	14.63	E- / 0.1	-63.92%	D / 1.9
2012	E+	42.40	41.86	E+ / 0.8	-7.11%	C- / 3.7

Major Rating Factors: *VelocityShares 3x Long Gold ETN has adopted a very risky asset allocation strategy and currently receives an overall TheStreet.com Investment Rating of E- (Very Weak). The fund has a high level of volatility, as measured by both semi-deviation and drawdown factors. It carries a beta of 0.25, meaning the fund's expected move will be 2.5% for every 10% move in the market. As of December 31, 2015, *VelocityShares 3x Long Gold ETN traded at a price exactly equal to its net asset value, which is better than its one-year historical average premium of .21%. Unfortunately, the high level of risk (E+, Very Weak) failed to pay off as investors endured very poor performance.

The fund's performance rating is currently E- (Very Weak). It has registered an annualized return of -43.36% over the last three years and is down -35.12% year to date 2015.

This fund has been team managed for 5 years and currently receives a manager quality ranking of 0 (0=worst, 99=best). If you can tolerate very high levels of risk in the hope of improved future returns, holding this fund may be an option.

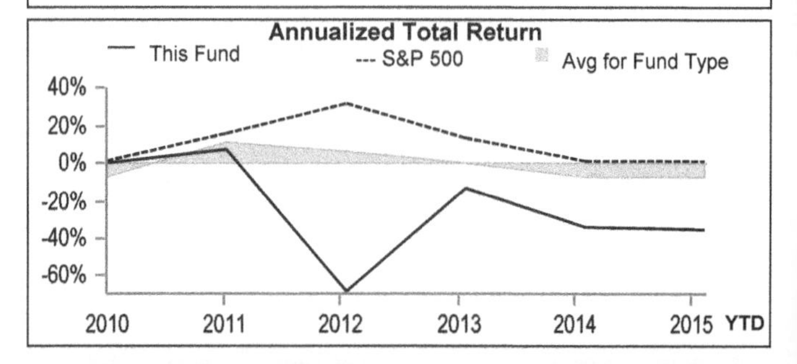

*VelocityShares 3x Long Nat Gas E (UGAZ) E- Very Weak

Fund Family: Credit Suisse AG
Fund Type: Global
Inception Date: February 7, 2012

Data Date	Investment Rating	Net Assets ($Mil)	Price	Performance Rating/Pts	Total Return Y-T-D	Risk Rating/Pts
12-15	E-	233.80	2.44	E- / 0	-88.07%	D / 1.8
2014	E-	233.80	3.98	E- / 0	-82.27%	D / 1.8
2013	C-	88.80	21.38	A+ / 9.6	11.58%	D / 1.9

Major Rating Factors: *VelocityShares 3x Long Nat Gas E has adopted a very risky asset allocation strategy and currently receives an overall TheStreet.com Investment Rating of E- (Very Weak). The fund has a high level of volatility, as measured by both semi-deviation and drawdown factors. It carries a beta of 1.15, meaning it is expected to move 11.5% for every 10% move in the market. As of December 31, 2015, *VelocityShares 3x Long Nat Gas E traded at a discount of 1.21% below its net asset value, which is better than its one-year historical average discount of .02%. Unfortunately, the high level of risk (D, Weak) failed to pay off as investors endured very poor performance.

The fund's performance rating is currently E- (Very Weak). It has registered an annualized return of -71.05% over the last three years and is down -88.07% year to date 2015.

This fund has been team managed for 4 years and currently receives a manager quality ranking of 0 (0=worst, 99=best). If you can tolerate very high levels of risk in the hope of improved future returns, holding this fund may be an option.

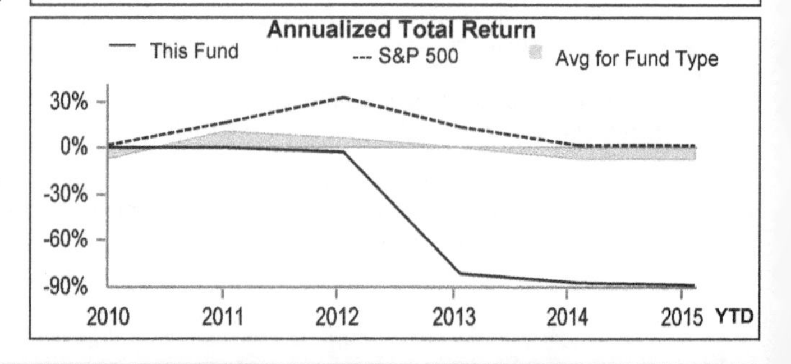

*VelocityShares 3x Long Silver ET (USLV) E- Very Weak

Fund Family: Credit Suisse AG
Fund Type: Global
Inception Date: October 14, 2011

Data Date	Investment Rating	Net Assets ($Mil)	Price	Performance Rating/Pts	Total Return Y-T-D	Risk Rating/Pts
12-15	E-	134.10	9.81	E- / 0	-49.12%	E+ / 0.8
2014	E-	134.10	18.99	E- / 0	-62.39%	D / 1.9
2013	E-	118.30	51.22	E- / 0	-79.98%	D / 1.9
2012	E-	121.20	26.11	E / 0.5	-21.10%	D / 2.2

Major Rating Factors: *VelocityShares 3x Long Silver ET has adopted a very risky asset allocation strategy and currently receives an overall TheStreet.com Investment Rating of E- (Very Weak). The fund has a high level of volatility, as measured by both semi-deviation and drawdown factors. It carries a beta of 0.77, meaning the fund's expected move will be 7.7% for every 10% move in the market. As of December 31, 2015, *VelocityShares 3x Long Silver ET traded at a premium of .41% above its net asset value, which is worse than its one-year historical average premium of .09%. Unfortunately, the high level of risk (E+, Very Weak) failed to pay off as investors endured very poor performance.

The fund's performance rating is currently E- (Very Weak). It has registered an annualized return of -66.28% over the last three years and is down -49.12% year to date 2015.

This fund has been team managed for 5 years and currently receives a manager quality ranking of 0 (0=worst, 99=best). If you can tolerate very high levels of risk in the hope of improved future returns, holding this fund may be an option.

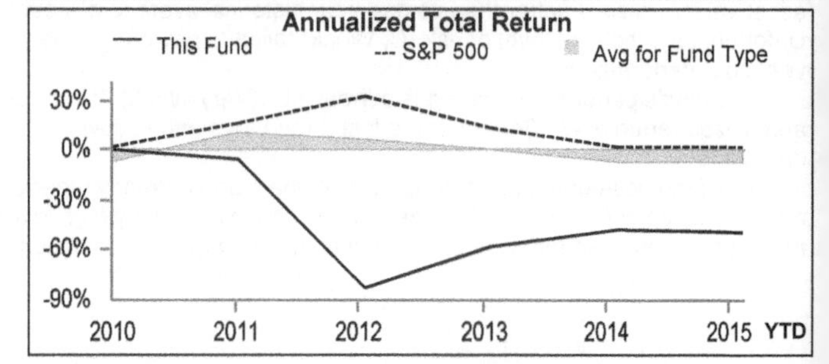

*VelocityShares Daily 2x VIX S-T (TVIX) E- Very Weak

Fund Family: Credit Suisse AG
Fund Type: Income
Inception Date: November 29, 2010

Major Rating Factors: *VelocityShares Daily 2x VIX S-T has adopted a very risky asset allocation strategy and currently receives an overall TheStreet.com Investment Rating of E- (Very Weak). The fund has a high level of volatility, as measured by both semi-deviation and drawdown factors. It carries a beta of -8.71, meaning the fund's expected move will be -87.1% for every 10% move in the market. As of December 31, 2015, *VelocityShares Daily 2x VIX S-T traded at a premium of 1.79% above its net asset value, which is better than its one-year historical average premium of 1.80%. Unfortunately, the high level of risk (E+, Very Weak) failed to pay off as investors endured very poor performance.

The fund's performance rating is currently E- (Very Weak). It has registered an annualized return of -79.26% over the last three years and is down -76.44% year to date 2015.

This fund has been team managed for 6 years and currently receives a manager quality ranking of 2 (0=worst, 99=best). If you can tolerate very high levels of risk in the hope of improved future returns, holding this fund may be an option.

Data Date	Investment Rating	Net Assets ($Mil)	Price	Performance Rating/Pts	Total Return Y-T-D	Risk Rating/Pts
12-15	E-	263.90	6.27	E- / 0	-76.44%	E+ / 0.6
2014	E-	263.90	2.77	E- / 0	-63.56%	E- / 0
2013	E-	98.00	7.50	E- / 0	-89.21%	D / 1.9
2012	E-	117.80	9.34	E- / 0	-97.36%	D / 1.9

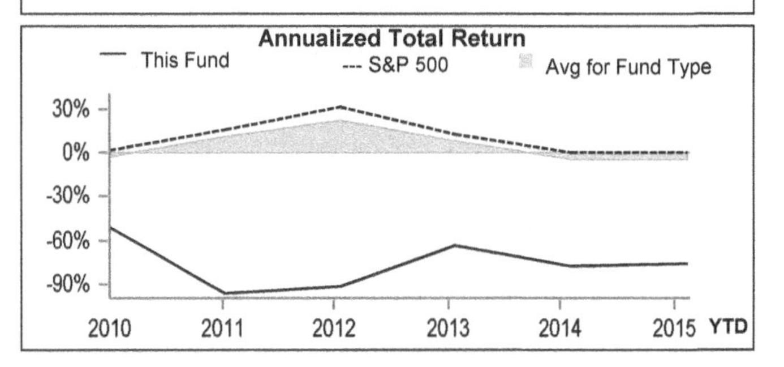

*VelocityShares Dly 2x VIX Med-T (TVIZ) E- Very Weak

Fund Family: Credit Suisse AG
Fund Type: Income
Inception Date: November 29, 2010

Major Rating Factors: *VelocityShares Dly 2x VIX Med-T has adopted a very risky asset allocation strategy and currently receives an overall TheStreet.com Investment Rating of E- (Very Weak). The fund has a high level of volatility, as measured by both semi-deviation and drawdown factors. It carries a beta of -4.45, meaning the fund's expected move will be -44.5% for every 10% move in the market. As of December 31, 2015, *VelocityShares Dly 2x VIX Med-T traded at a discount of 2.06% below its net asset value, which is better than its one-year historical average discount of .32%. Unfortunately, the high level of risk (D, Weak) failed to pay off as investors endured very poor performance.

The fund's performance rating is currently E- (Very Weak). It has registered an annualized return of -48.83% over the last three years and is down -38.59% year to date 2015.

This fund has been team managed for 6 years and currently receives a manager quality ranking of 18 (0=worst, 99=best). If you can tolerate very high levels of risk in the hope of improved future returns, holding this fund may be an option.

Data Date	Investment Rating	Net Assets ($Mil)	Price	Performance Rating/Pts	Total Return Y-T-D	Risk Rating/Pts
12-15	E-	1.00	13.32	E- / 0.1	-38.59%	D / 1.7
2014	E-	1.00	22.00	E- / 0	-37.47%	D / 1.9
2013	E-	1.80	34.45	E- / 0	-64.61%	D / 1.9
2012	E-	2.10	11.48	E- / 0	-82.86%	D / 1.9

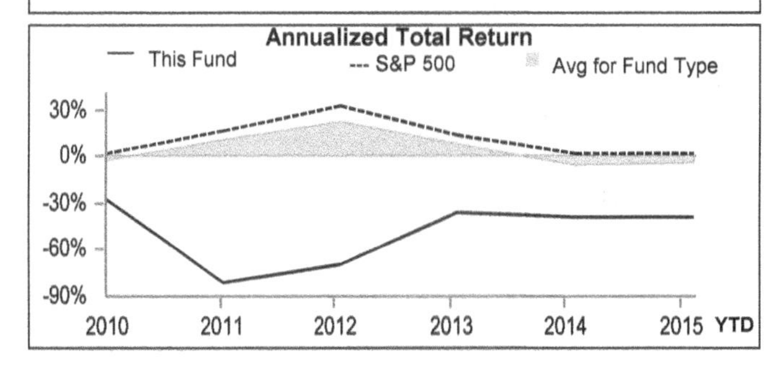

*VelocityShares Dly Invs VIX M-T (ZIV) C Fair

Fund Family: Credit Suisse AG
Fund Type: General - Investment Grade
Inception Date: November 29, 2010

Major Rating Factors:
Exceptional performance is the major factor driving the C (Fair) TheStreet.com Investment Rating for *VelocityShares Dly Invs VIX M-T. The fund currently has a performance rating of A- (Excellent) based on an annualized return of 17.62% over the last three years and a total return of -1.03% year to date 2015.

The fund's risk rating is currently C- (Fair). It carries a beta of 0.17, meaning the fund's expected move will be 1.7% for every 10% move in the market. Volatility, as measured by both the semi-deviation and a drawdown factor, is considered average. As of December 31, 2015, *VelocityShares Dly Invs VIX M-T traded at a discount of .22% below its net asset value, which is better than its one-year historical average premium of .04%.

This fund has been team managed for 6 years and currently receives a manager quality ranking of 98 (0=worst, 99=best). If you desire an average level of risk and strong performance, then this fund is a good option.

Data Date	Investment Rating	Net Assets ($Mil)	Price	Performance Rating/Pts	Total Return Y-T-D	Risk Rating/Pts
12-15	C	139.30	41.49	A- / 9.1	-1.03%	C- / 3.7
2014	B+	139.30	41.78	A+ / 9.7	9.06%	C+ / 6.0
2013	B-	74.10	38.70	A+ / 9.8	50.24%	C / 5.1
2012	B	15.70	23.77	A+ / 9.9	99.69%	C / 5.3
2011	D-	7.10	12.46	D- / 1.3	-5.51%	C / 5.4

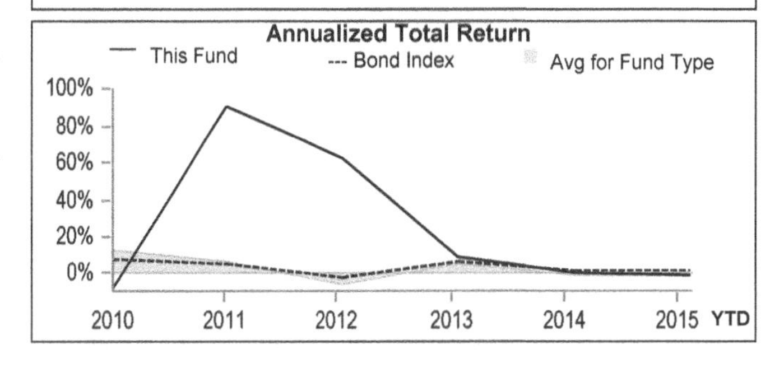

*VelocityShares Dly Invs VIX ST E (XIV) D+ Weak

Fund Family: Credit Suisse AG
Fund Type: Growth and Income
Inception Date: November 29, 2010

Data Date	Investment Rating	Net Assets ($Mil)	Price	Performance Rating/Pts	Total Return Y-T-D	Risk Rating/Pts
12-15	D+	590.50	25.78	C+ / 5.9	-18.73%	D+ / 2.4
2014	B-	590.50	31.14	A+ / 9.8	-8.22%	C / 5.0
2013	C-	407.40	34.42	A+ / 9.9	80.19%	D / 1.9
2012	C-	346.60	16.57	A+ / 9.9	168.59%	D / 1.9
2011	E-	387.60	6.51	E- / 0.2	-42.04%	D / 1.9

Major Rating Factors: *VelocityShares Dly Invs VIX ST E has adopted a risky asset allocation strategy and currently receives an overall TheStreet.com Investment Rating of D+ (Weak). The fund has an above average level of volatility, as measured by both semi-deviation and drawdown factors. It carries a beta of 5.01, meaning it is expected to move 50.1% for every 10% move in the market. As of December 31, 2015, *VelocityShares Dly Invs VIX ST E traded at a discount of .81% below its net asset value, which is better than its one-year historical average discount of .20%. Unfortunately, the high level of risk (D+, Weak) has only provided investors with average performance.

The fund's performance rating is currently C+ (Fair). It has registered an annualized return of 11.04% over the last three years but is down -18.73% year to date 2015.

This fund has been team managed for 6 years and currently receives a manager quality ranking of 1 (0=worst, 99=best). If you are comfortable owning a high risk investment, then this fund may be an option.

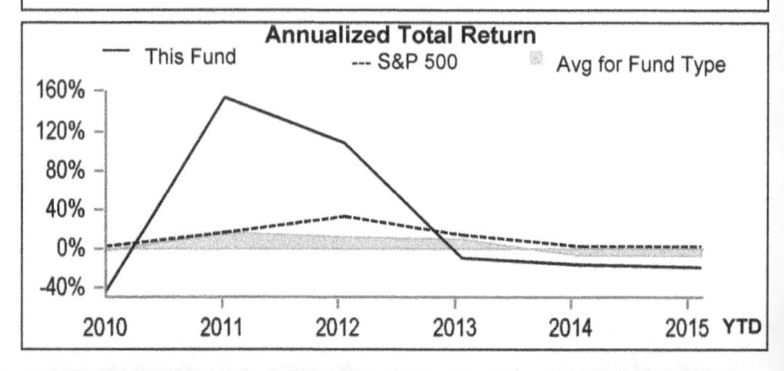

*VelocityShares VIX Medium-Term E (VIIZ) E- Very Weak

Fund Family: Credit Suisse AG
Fund Type: Growth and Income
Inception Date: November 29, 2010

Data Date	Investment Rating	Net Assets ($Mil)	Price	Performance Rating/Pts	Total Return Y-T-D	Risk Rating/Pts
12-15	E-	1.60	15.44	E+ / 0.7	-14.55%	E+ / 0.7
2014	E	1.60	17.83	E / 0.3	-18.77%	C- / 3.3
2013	E-	2.00	21.85	E- / 0.2	-38.84%	D / 1.9
2012	E-	4.90	38.65	E- / 0	-54.85%	D / 1.9
2011	D-	8.30	83.32	D- / 1.3	-11.04%	C / 4.7

Major Rating Factors: *VelocityShares VIX Medium-Term E has adopted a very risky asset allocation strategy and currently receives an overall TheStreet.com Investment Rating of E- (Very Weak). The fund has a high level of volatility, as measured by both semi-deviation and drawdown factors. It carries a beta of -2.26, meaning the fund's expected move will be -22.6% for every 10% move in the market. As of December 31, 2015, *VelocityShares VIX Medium-Term E traded at a premium of .32% above its net asset value, which is worse than its one-year historical average discount of .11%. Unfortunately, the high level of risk (E+, Very Weak) failed to pay off as investors endured very poor performance.

The fund's performance rating is currently E+ (Very Weak). It has registered an annualized return of -24.51% over the last three years and is down -14.55% year to date 2015.

This fund has been team managed for 6 years and currently receives a manager quality ranking of 77 (0=worst, 99=best). If you can tolerate very high levels of risk in the hope of improved future returns, holding this fund may be an option.

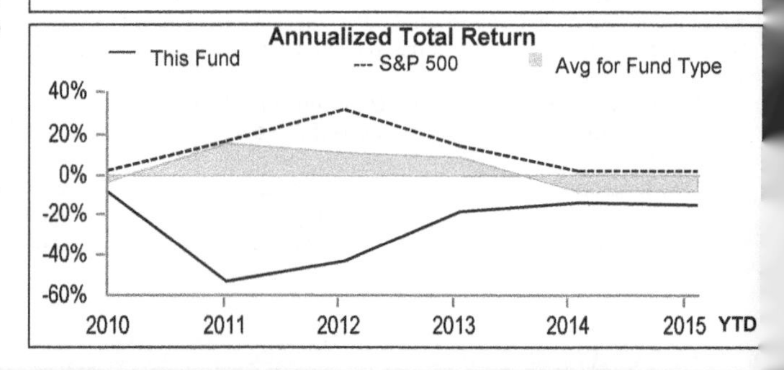

*VelocityShares VIX Short-Term ET (VIIX) E- Very Weak

Fund Family: Credit Suisse AG
Fund Type: Growth and Income
Inception Date: November 29, 2010

Data Date	Investment Rating	Net Assets ($Mil)	Price	Performance Rating/Pts	Total Return Y-T-D	Risk Rating/Pts
12-15	E-	8.20	27.12	E- / 0.2	-35.14%	E+ / 0.6
2014	E-	8.20	42.70	E- / 0.1	-26.83%	E- / 0
2013	E-	9.70	57.65	E- / 0	-60.75%	D / 1.9
2012	E-	13.60	17.19	E- / 0	-79.00%	D / 1.9
2011	D-	32.20	76.68	D+ / 2.5	-11.84%	C- / 3.9

Major Rating Factors: *VelocityShares VIX Short-Term ET has adopted a very risky asset allocation strategy and currently receives an overall TheStreet.com Investment Rating of E- (Very Weak). The fund has a high level of volatility, as measured by both semi-deviation and drawdown factors. It carries a beta of -4.68, meaning the fund's expected move will be -46.8% for every 10% move in the market. As of December 31, 2015, *VelocityShares VIX Short-Term ET traded at a premium of .59% above its net asset value, which is worse than its one-year historical average premium of .18%. Unfortunately, the high level of risk (E+, Very Weak) failed to pay off as investors endured very poor performance.

The fund's performance rating is currently E- (Very Weak). It has registered an annualized return of -43.29% over the last three years and is down -35.14% year to date 2015.

This fund has been team managed for 6 years and currently receives a manager quality ranking of 88 (0=worst, 99=best). If you can tolerate very high levels of risk in the hope of improved future returns, holding this fund may be an option.

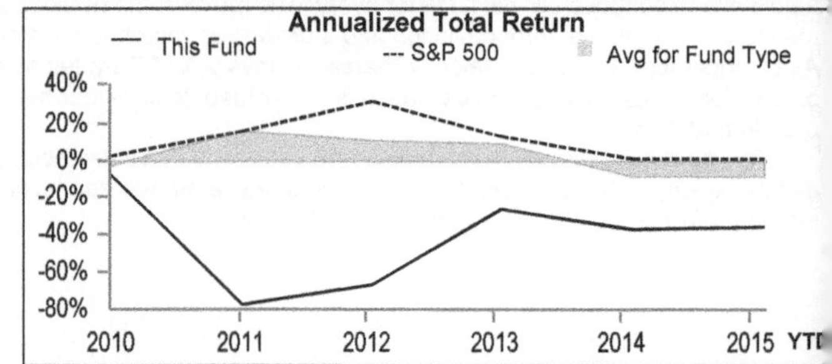

*Victory CEMP Develop Enh Vol Wtd (CIZ) C- Fair

Fund Family: Victory Capital Management Inc
Fund Type: Foreign
Inception Date: October 1, 2014

Data Date	Investment Rating	Net Assets ($Mil)	Price	Performance Rating/Pts	Total Return Y-T-D	Risk Rating/Pts
12-15	C-	0.00	31.35	D / 1.8	-7.91%	B / 8.1

Major Rating Factors:
Disappointing performance is the major factor driving the C- (Fair) TheStreet.com Investment Rating for *Victory CEMP Develop Enh Vol Wtd. The fund currently has a performance rating of D (Weak) based on an annualized return of 0.00% over the last three years and a total return of -7.91% year to date 2015. Factored into the performance evaluation is an expense ratio of 0.63% (very low).

The fund's risk rating is currently B (Good). It carries a beta of 0.00, meaning the fund's expected move will be 0.0% for every 10% move in the market. Volatility, as measured by both the semi-deviation and a drawdown factor, is considered low. As of December 31, 2015, *Victory CEMP Develop Enh Vol Wtd traded at a discount of .22% below its net asset value, which is better than its one-year historical average premium of .61%.

Stephen M. Hammers currently receives a manager quality ranking of 24 (0=worst, 99=best). This fund offers only a moderate level of risk but investors looking for strong performance are still waiting.

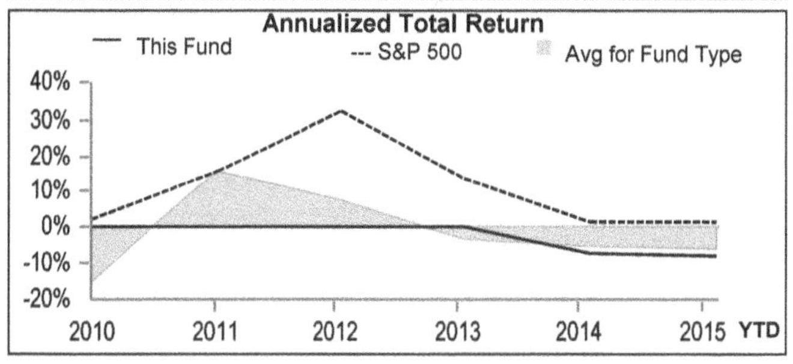

*Victory CEMP US 500 Enh Vol Wtd (CFO) C- Fair

Fund Family: Victory Capital Management Inc
Fund Type: Growth
Inception Date: July 1, 2014

Data Date	Investment Rating	Net Assets ($Mil)	Price	Performance Rating/Pts	Total Return Y-T-D	Risk Rating/Pts
12-15	C-	0.00	35.76	C- / 4.1	-0.69%	B- / 7.2

Major Rating Factors: Middle of the road best describes *Victory CEMP US 500 Enh Vol Wtd whose TheStreet.com Investment Rating is currently a C- (Fair). The fund currently has a performance rating of C- (Fair) based on an annualized return of 0.00% over the last three years and a total return of -0.69% year to date 2015. Factored into the performance evaluation is an expense ratio of 0.59% (very low).

The fund's risk rating is currently B- (Good). It carries a beta of 0.00, meaning the fund's expected move will be 0.0% for every 10% move in the market. Volatility, as measured by both the semi-deviation and a drawdown factor, is considered low. As of December 31, 2015, *Victory CEMP US 500 Enh Vol Wtd traded at a premium of .03% above its net asset value, which is better than its one-year historical average premium of .04%.

Stephen M. Hammers currently receives a manager quality ranking of 47 (0=worst, 99=best). If you desire an average level of risk, then this fund may be an option.

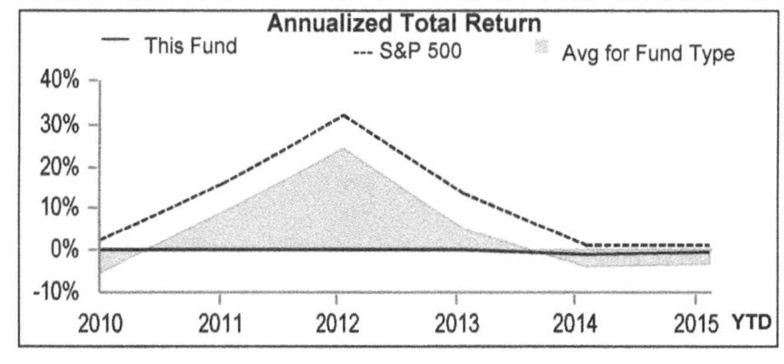

*Victory CEMP US 500 Volatility W (CFA) C Fair

Fund Family: Victory Capital Management Inc
Fund Type: Growth
Inception Date: July 1, 2014

Data Date	Investment Rating	Net Assets ($Mil)	Price	Performance Rating/Pts	Total Return Y-T-D	Risk Rating/Pts
12-15	C	0.00	35.80	C / 4.4	0.12%	B- / 7.3

Major Rating Factors: Middle of the road best describes *Victory CEMP US 500 Volatility W whose TheStreet.com Investment Rating is currently a C (Fair). The fund currently has a performance rating of C (Fair) based on an annualized return of 0.00% over the last three years and a total return of 0.12% year to date 2015. Factored into the performance evaluation is an expense ratio of 0.54% (very low).

The fund's risk rating is currently B- (Good). It carries a beta of 0.00, meaning the fund's expected move will be 0.0% for every 10% move in the market. Volatility, as measured by both the semi-deviation and a drawdown factor, is considered low. As of December 31, 2015, *Victory CEMP US 500 Volatility W traded at a premium of .06% above its net asset value, which is better than its one-year historical average premium of .07%.

Robert J. Bateman currently receives a manager quality ranking of 55 (0=worst, 99=best). If you desire an average level of risk, then this fund may be an option.

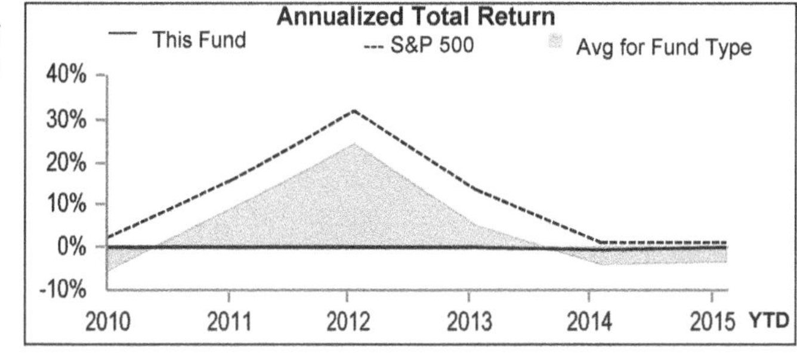

 * Denotes ETF Fund

*Victory CEMP US Discovery Enh Vo (CSF) D+ Weak

Fund Family: Victory Capital Management Inc
Fund Type: General - Investment Grade
Inception Date: August 1, 2014

Data Date	Investment Rating	Net Assets ($Mil)	Price	Perfor-mance Rating/Pts	Total Return Y-T-D	Risk Rating/Pts
12-15	D+	0.00	34.55	D / 1.8	-7.42%	C+ / 6.7

Major Rating Factors:
Disappointing performance is the major factor driving the D+ (Weak) TheStreet.com Investment Rating for *Victory CEMP US Discovery Enh Vo. The fund currently has a performance rating of D (Weak) based on an annualized return of 0.00% over the last three years and a total return of -7.42% year to date 2015. Factored into the performance evaluation is an expense ratio of 0.59% (very low).

The fund's risk rating is currently C+ (Fair). It carries a beta of 0.00, meaning the fund's expected move will be 0.0% for every 10% move in the market. Volatility, as measured by both the semi-deviation and a drawdown factor, is considered low. As of December 31, 2015, *Victory CEMP US Discovery Enh Vo traded at a premium of .17% above its net asset value, which is worse than its one-year historical average premium of .06%.

Stephen M. Hammers currently receives a manager quality ranking of 20 (0=worst, 99=best). This fund offers only a moderate level of risk but investors looking for strong performance are still waiting.

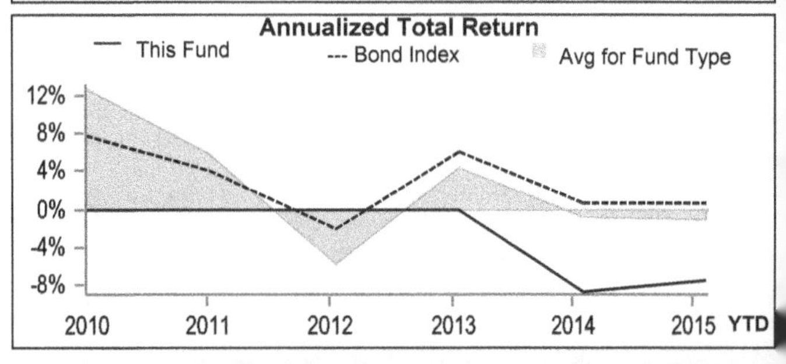

*Victory CEMP US EQ Inc Enh Vol W (CDC) C Fair

Fund Family: Victory Capital Management Inc
Fund Type: Growth
Inception Date: July 1, 2014

Data Date	Investment Rating	Net Assets ($Mil)	Price	Perfor-mance Rating/Pts	Total Return Y-T-D	Risk Rating/Pts
12-15	C	24.20	35.51	C / 5.2	-0.32%	B- / 7.3

Major Rating Factors: Middle of the road best describes *Victory CEMP US EQ Inc Enh Vol W whose TheStreet.com Investment Rating is currently a C (Fair). The fund currently has a performance rating of C (Fair) based on an annualized return of 0.00% over the last three years and a total return of -0.32% year to date 2015. Factored into the performance evaluation is an expense ratio of 0.59% (very low).

The fund's risk rating is currently B- (Good). It carries a beta of 0.00, meaning the fund's expected move will be 0.0% for every 10% move in the market. Volatility, as measured by both the semi-deviation and a drawdown factor, is considered low. As of December 31, 2015, *Victory CEMP US EQ Inc Enh Vol W traded at a premium of .40% above its net asset value, which is worse than its one-year historical average premium of .05%.

Stephen M. Hammers currently receives a manager quality ranking of 55 (0=worst, 99=best). If you desire an average level of risk, then this fund may be an option.

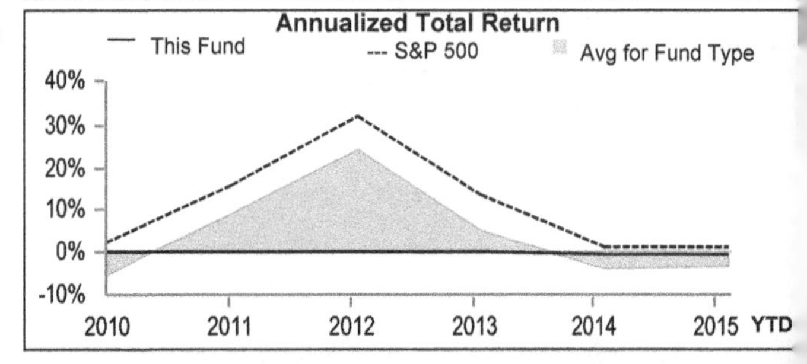

*Vident Core US Bond Strategy (VBND) C+ Fair

Fund Family: Exchange Traded Concepts LLC
Fund Type: Corporate - Investment Grade
Inception Date: October 15, 2014

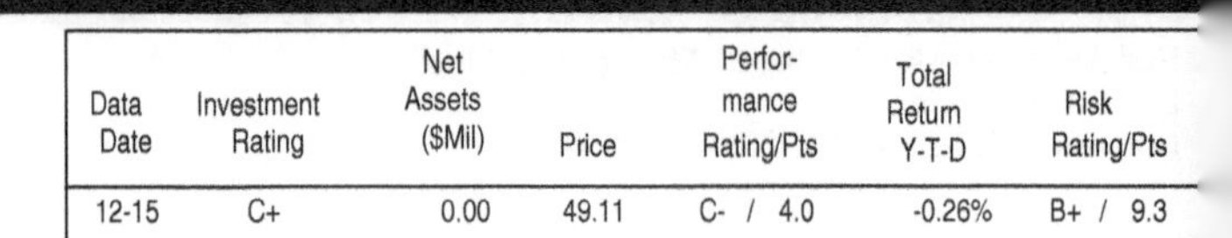

Data Date	Investment Rating	Net Assets ($Mil)	Price	Perfor-mance Rating/Pts	Total Return Y-T-D	Risk Rating/Pts
12-15	C+	0.00	49.11	C- / 4.0	-0.26%	B+ / 9.3

Major Rating Factors: Middle of the road best describes *Vident Core US Bond Strategy whose TheStreet.com Investment Rating is currently a C+ (Fair). The fund currently has a performance rating of C- (Fair) based on an annualized return of 0.00% over the last three years and a total return of -0.26% year to date 2015. Factored into the performance evaluation is an expense ratio of 0.45% (very low).

The fund's risk rating is currently B+ (Good). It carries a beta of 0.00, meaning the fund's expected move will be 0.0% for every 10% move in the market. Volatility, as measured by both the semi-deviation and a drawdown factor, is considered very low. As of December 31, 2015, *Vident Core US Bond Strategy traded at a discount of .02% below its net asset value.

Denise M. Krisko has been running the fund for 2 years and currently receives a manager quality ranking of 73 (0=worst, 99=best). If you desire an average level of risk, then this fund may be an option.

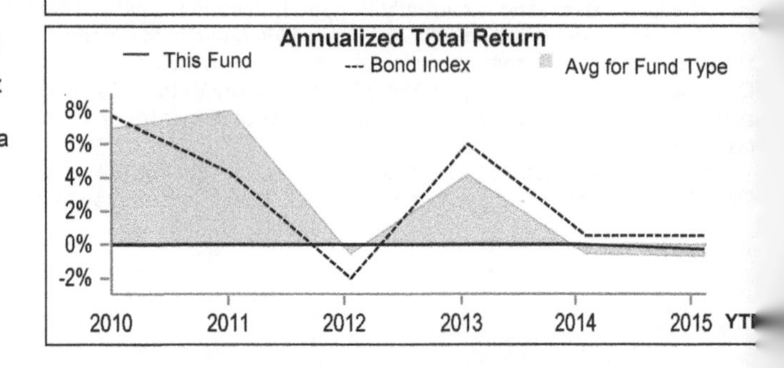

* Denotes ETF Fund

*Vident Core US Equity (VUSE) D+ Weak

Fund Family: Exchange Traded Concepts LLC
Fund Type: Growth
Inception Date: January 21, 2014

Data Date	Investment Rating	Net Assets ($Mil)	Price	Performance Rating/Pts	Total Return Y-T-D	Risk Rating/Pts
12-15	D+	175.10	24.81	D+ / 2.6	-5.69%	C+ / 6.7

Major Rating Factors:
Disappointing performance is the major factor driving the D+ (Weak) TheStreet.com Investment Rating for *Vident Core US Equity. The fund currently has a performance rating of D+ (Weak) based on an annualized return of 0.00% over the last three years and a total return of -5.69% year to date 2015. Factored into the performance evaluation is an expense ratio of 0.55% (very low).

The fund's risk rating is currently C+ (Fair). It carries a beta of 0.00, meaning the fund's expected move will be 0.0% for every 10% move in the market. Volatility, as measured by both the semi-deviation and a drawdown factor, is considered low. As of December 31, 2015, *Vident Core US Equity traded at a premium of .12% above its net asset value, which is worse than its one-year historical average premium of .03%.

Denise M. Krisko has been running the fund for 2 years and currently receives a manager quality ranking of 22 (0=worst, 99=best). This fund offers only a moderate level of risk but investors looking for strong performance are still waiting.

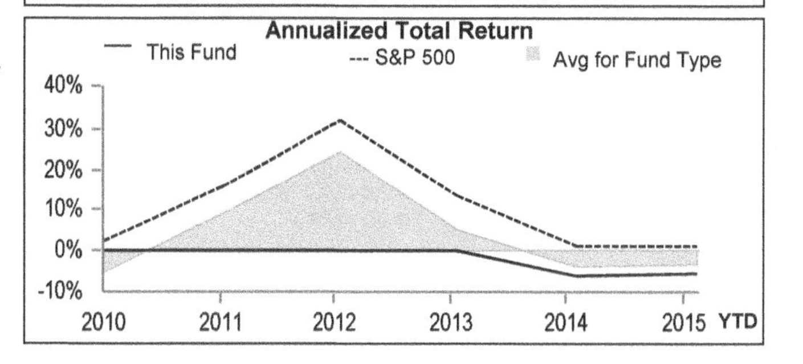

*Vident International Equity (VIDI) D+ Weak

Fund Family: Exchange Traded Concepts LLC
Fund Type: Foreign
Inception Date: October 29, 2013

Data Date	Investment Rating	Net Assets ($Mil)	Price	Performance Rating/Pts	Total Return Y-T-D	Risk Rating/Pts
12-15	D+	716.90	20.08	D- / 1.5	-10.91%	B- / 7.5
2014	E+	716.90	23.15	D / 1.7	-1.56%	C- / 3.7

Major Rating Factors:
Disappointing performance is the major factor driving the D+ (Weak) TheStreet.com Investment Rating for *Vident International Equity. The fund currently has a performance rating of D- (Weak) based on an annualized return of 0.00% over the last three years and a total return of -10.91% year to date 2015. Factored into the performance evaluation is an expense ratio of 0.71% (very low).

The fund's risk rating is currently B- (Good). It carries a beta of 0.00, meaning the fund's expected move will be 0.0% for every 10% move in the market. Volatility, as measured by both the semi-deviation and a drawdown factor, is considered low. As of December 31, 2015, *Vident International Equity traded at a discount of 1.38% below its net asset value, which is better than its one-year historical average discount of .16%.

Denise M. Krisko has been running the fund for 1 year and currently receives a manager quality ranking of 15 (0=worst, 99=best). This fund offers only a moderate level of risk but investors looking for strong performance are still waiting.

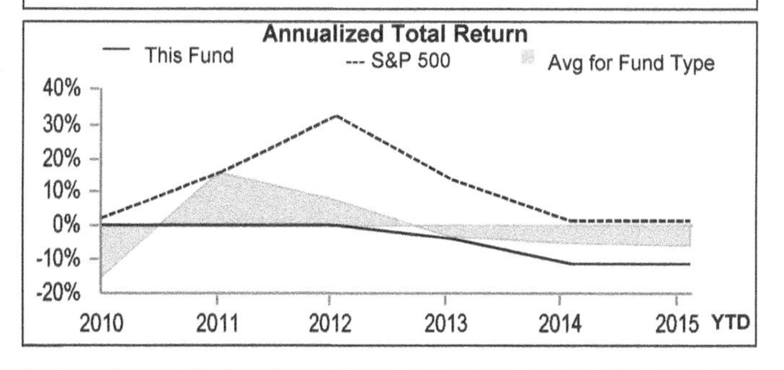

*WBI Tactical High Income (WBIH) C- Fair

Fund Family: Millington Securities Inc
Fund Type: Growth and Income
Inception Date: August 25, 2014

Data Date	Investment Rating	Net Assets ($Mil)	Price	Performance Rating/Pts	Total Return Y-T-D	Risk Rating/Pts
12-15	C-	0.00	23.32	D+ / 2.8	-4.17%	B- / 7.5

Major Rating Factors:
Disappointing performance is the major factor driving the C- (Fair) TheStreet.com Investment Rating for *WBI Tactical High Income. The fund currently has a performance rating of D+ (Weak) based on an annualized return of 0.00% over the last three years and a total return of -4.17% year to date 2015. Factored into the performance evaluation is an expense ratio of 0.98% (low).

The fund's risk rating is currently B- (Good). It carries a beta of 0.00, meaning the fund's expected move will be 0.0% for every 10% move in the market. Volatility, as measured by both the semi-deviation and a drawdown factor, is considered low. As of December 31, 2015, *WBI Tactical High Income traded at a premium of .13% above its net asset value, which is worse than its one-year historical average premium of .08%.

Donald R. Schreiber, Jr. has been running the fund for 2 years and currently receives a manager quality ranking of 33 (0=worst, 99=best). This fund offers only a moderate level of risk but investors looking for strong performance are still waiting.

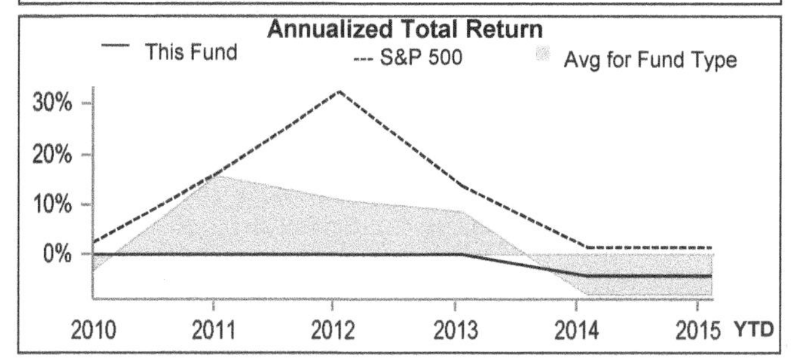

* Denotes ETF Fund

*WBI Tactical Income (WBII) C+ Fair

Fund Family: Millington Securities Inc
Fund Type: Growth and Income
Inception Date: August 25, 2014

Major Rating Factors: Middle of the road best describes *WBI Tactical Income whose TheStreet.com Investment Rating is currently a C+ (Fair). The fund currently has a performance rating of C- (Fair) based on an annualized return of 0.00% over the last three years and a total return of -0.78% year to date 2015. Factored into the performance evaluation is an expense ratio of 0.99% (low).

The fund's risk rating is currently B+ (Good). It carries a beta of 0.00, meaning the fund's expected move will be 0.0% for every 10% move in the market. Volatility, as measured by both the semi-deviation and a drawdown factor, is considered very low. As of December 31, 2015, *WBI Tactical Income traded at a discount of .08% below its net asset value, which is better than its one-year historical average premium of .06%.

Donald R. Schreiber, Jr. has been running the fund for 2 years and currently receives a manager quality ranking of 59 (0=worst, 99=best). If you desire an average level of risk, then this fund may be an option.

Data Date	Investment Rating	Net Assets ($Mil)	Price	Performance Rating/Pts	Total Return Y-T-D	Risk Rating/Pts
12-15	C+	0.00	24.51	C- / 3.4	-0.78%	B+ / 9.5

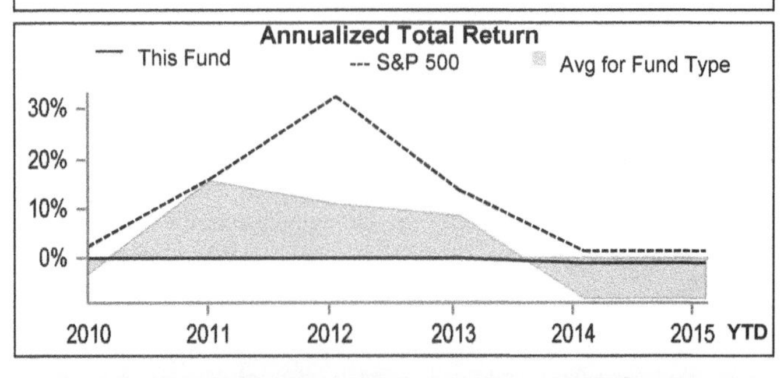

*WBI Tactical LCG (WBIE) D+ Weak

Fund Family: Millington Securities Inc
Fund Type: Global
Inception Date: August 25, 2014

Major Rating Factors:
Disappointing performance is the major factor driving the D+ (Weak) TheStreet.com Investment Rating for *WBI Tactical LCG. The fund currently has a performance rating of D+ (Weak) based on an annualized return of 0.00% over the last three years and a total return of -7.00% year to date 2015. Factored into the performance evaluation is an expense ratio of 1.02% (low).

The fund's risk rating is currently C+ (Fair). It carries a beta of 0.00, meaning the fund's expected move will be 0.0% for every 10% move in the market. Volatility, as measured by both the semi-deviation and a drawdown factor, is considered low. As of December 31, 2015, *WBI Tactical LCG traded at a premium of .30% above its net asset value, which is worse than its one-year historical average premium of .05%.

Donald R. Schreiber, Jr. has been running the fund for 2 years and currently receives a manager quality ranking of 22 (0=worst, 99=best). This fund offers only a moderate level of risk but investors looking for strong performance are still waiting.

Data Date	Investment Rating	Net Assets ($Mil)	Price	Performance Rating/Pts	Total Return Y-T-D	Risk Rating/Pts
12-15	D+	0.00	23.11	D+ / 2.5	-7.00%	C+ / 6.7

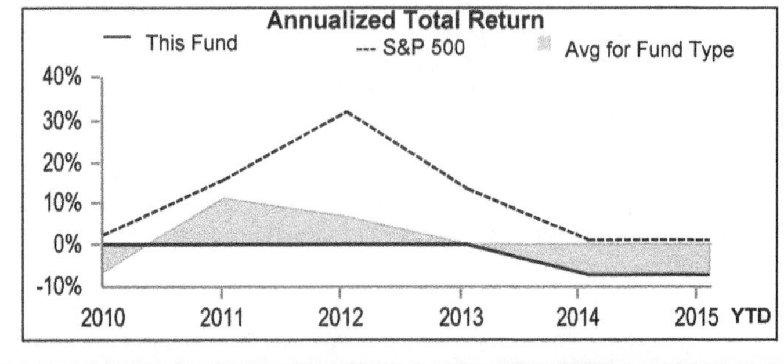

*WBI Tactical LCS (WBIL) D+ Weak

Fund Family: Millington Securities Inc
Fund Type: Global
Inception Date: August 25, 2014

Major Rating Factors:
Disappointing performance is the major factor driving the D+ (Weak) TheStreet.com Investment Rating for *WBI Tactical LCS. The fund currently has a performance rating of D+ (Weak) based on an annualized return of 0.00% over the last three years and a total return of -6.91% year to date 2015. Factored into the performance evaluation is an expense ratio of 1.02% (low).

The fund's risk rating is currently B- (Good). It carries a beta of 0.00, meaning the fund's expected move will be 0.0% for every 10% move in the market. Volatility, as measured by both the semi-deviation and a drawdown factor, is considered low. As of December 31, 2015, *WBI Tactical LCS traded at a premium of .27% above its net asset value, which is worse than its one-year historical average premium of .08%.

Donald R. Schreiber, Jr. has been running the fund for 2 years and currently receives a manager quality ranking of 22 (0=worst, 99=best). This fund offers only a moderate level of risk but investors looking for strong performance are still waiting.

Data Date	Investment Rating	Net Assets ($Mil)	Price	Performance Rating/Pts	Total Return Y-T-D	Risk Rating/Pts
12-15	D+	0.00	22.48	D+ / 2.4	-6.91%	B- / 7.1

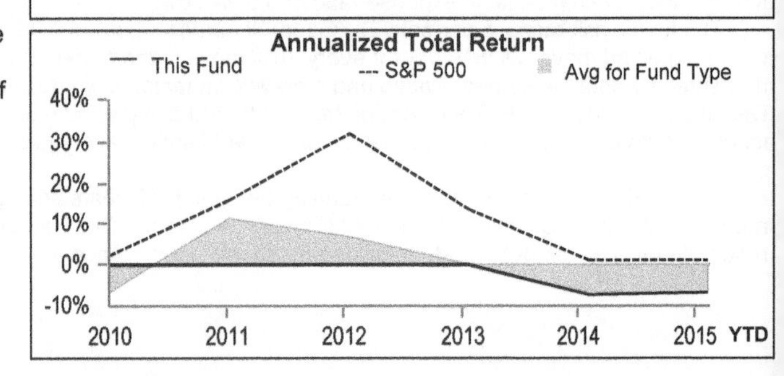

*WBI Tactical LCV (WBIF) C- Fair

Fund Family: Millington Securities Inc
Fund Type: Global
Inception Date: August 25, 2014

Data Date	Investment Rating	Net Assets ($Mil)	Price	Performance Rating/Pts	Total Return Y-T-D	Risk Rating/Pts
12-15	C-	0.00	22.84	D+ / 2.8	-4.12%	C+ / 6.9

Major Rating Factors:
Disappointing performance is the major factor driving the C- (Fair) TheStreet.com Investment Rating for *WBI Tactical LCV. The fund currently has a performance rating of D+ (Weak) based on an annualized return of 0.00% over the last three years and a total return of -4.12% year to date 2015. Factored into the performance evaluation is an expense ratio of 1.04% (low).

The fund's risk rating is currently C+ (Fair). It carries a beta of 0.00, meaning the fund's expected move will be 0.0% for every 10% move in the market. Volatility, as measured by both the semi-deviation and a drawdown factor, is considered low. As of December 31, 2015, *WBI Tactical LCV traded at a premium of .26% above its net asset value, which is worse than its one-year historical average premium of .10%.

Donald R. Schreiber, Jr. has been running the fund for 2 years and currently receives a manager quality ranking of 32 (0=worst, 99=best). This fund offers only a moderate level of risk but investors looking for strong performance are still waiting.

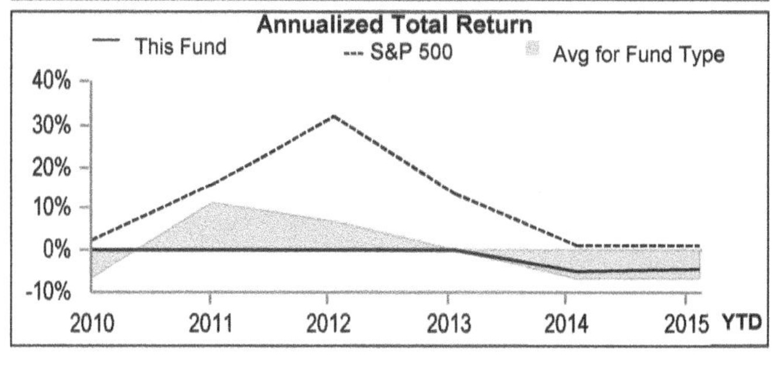

*WBI Tactical LCY (WBIG) D+ Weak

Fund Family: Millington Securities Inc
Fund Type: Global
Inception Date: August 25, 2014

Data Date	Investment Rating	Net Assets ($Mil)	Price	Performance Rating/Pts	Total Return Y-T-D	Risk Rating/Pts
12-15	D+	0.00	21.67	D / 1.8	-10.25%	C+ / 6.7

Major Rating Factors:
Disappointing performance is the major factor driving the D+ (Weak) TheStreet.com Investment Rating for *WBI Tactical LCY. The fund currently has a performance rating of D (Weak) based on an annualized return of 0.00% over the last three years and a total return of -10.25% year to date 2015. Factored into the performance evaluation is an expense ratio of 1.02% (low).

The fund's risk rating is currently C+ (Fair). It carries a beta of 0.00, meaning the fund's expected move will be 0.0% for every 10% move in the market. Volatility, as measured by both the semi-deviation and a drawdown factor, is considered low. As of December 31, 2015, *WBI Tactical LCY traded at a premium of .28% above its net asset value, which is worse than its one-year historical average premium of .09%.

Donald R. Schreiber, Jr. has been running the fund for 2 years and currently receives a manager quality ranking of 16 (0=worst, 99=best). This fund offers only a moderate level of risk but investors looking for strong performance are still waiting.

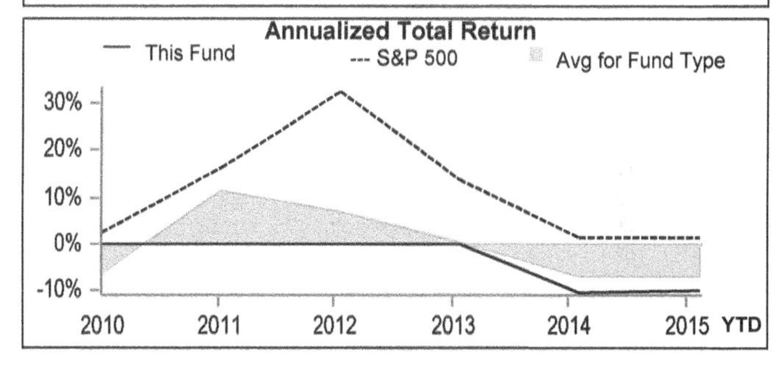

*WBI Tactical SMG (WBIA) C- Fair

Fund Family: Millington Securities Inc
Fund Type: Global
Inception Date: August 25, 2014

Data Date	Investment Rating	Net Assets ($Mil)	Price	Performance Rating/Pts	Total Return Y-T-D	Risk Rating/Pts
12-15	C-	0.00	22.60	D / 2.2	-8.93%	B / 8.0

Major Rating Factors:
Disappointing performance is the major factor driving the C- (Fair) TheStreet.com Investment Rating for *WBI Tactical SMG. The fund currently has a performance rating of D (Weak) based on an annualized return of 0.00% over the last three years and a total return of -8.93% year to date 2015. Factored into the performance evaluation is an expense ratio of 1.03% (low).

The fund's risk rating is currently B (Good). It carries a beta of 0.00, meaning the fund's expected move will be 0.0% for every 10% move in the market. Volatility, as measured by both the semi-deviation and a drawdown factor, is considered low. As of December 31, 2015, *WBI Tactical SMG traded at a discount of .04% below its net asset value, which is better than its one-year historical average premium of .03%.

Donald R. Schreiber, Jr. has been running the fund for 2 years and currently receives a manager quality ranking of 17 (0=worst, 99=best). This fund offers only a moderate level of risk but investors looking for strong performance are still waiting.

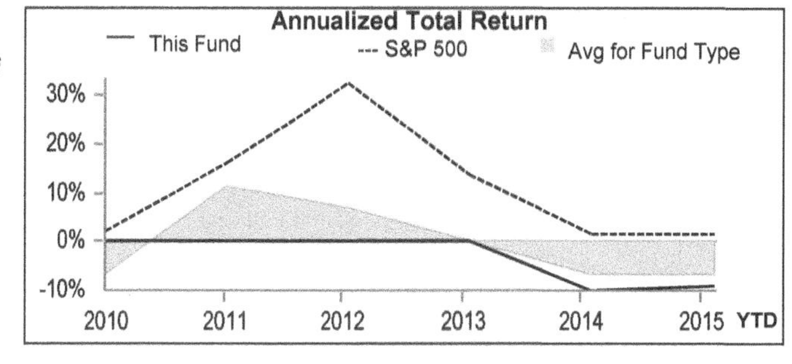

*WBI Tactical SMS (WBID) D+ Weak

Fund Family: Millington Securities Inc
Fund Type: Global
Inception Date: August 25, 2014

Data Date	Investment Rating	Net Assets ($Mil)	Price	Performance Rating/Pts	Total Return Y-T-D	Risk Rating/Pts
12-15	D+	0.00	21.30	D / 1.7	-10.68%	C+ / 6.6

Major Rating Factors:
Disappointing performance is the major factor driving the D+ (Weak) TheStreet.com Investment Rating for *WBI Tactical SMS. The fund currently has a performance rating of D (Weak) based on an annualized return of 0.00% over the last three years and a total return of -10.68% year to date 2015. Factored into the performance evaluation is an expense ratio of 1.06% (low).

The fund's risk rating is currently C+ (Fair). It carries a beta of 0.00, meaning the fund's expected move will be 0.0% for every 10% move in the market. Volatility, as measured by both the semi-deviation and a drawdown factor, is considered low. As of December 31, 2015, *WBI Tactical SMS traded at a premium of .33% above its net asset value, which is worse than its one-year historical average premium of .06%.

Donald R. Schreiber, Jr. has been running the fund for 2 years and currently receives a manager quality ranking of 15 (0=worst, 99=best). This fund offers only a moderate level of risk but investors looking for strong performance are still waiting.

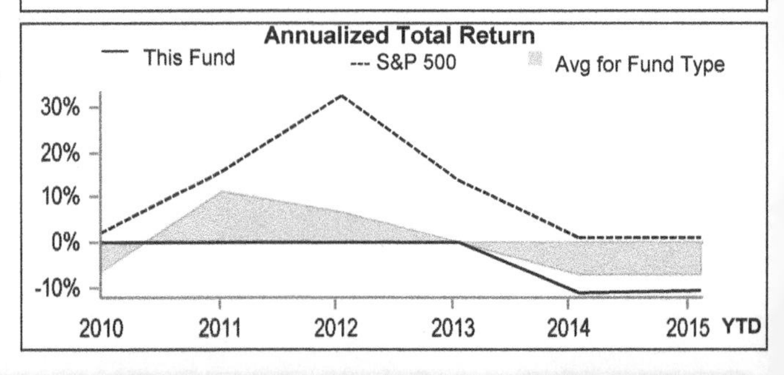

*WBI Tactical SMV (WBIB) D+ Weak

Fund Family: Millington Securities Inc
Fund Type: Global
Inception Date: August 25, 2014

Data Date	Investment Rating	Net Assets ($Mil)	Price	Performance Rating/Pts	Total Return Y-T-D	Risk Rating/Pts
12-15	D+	0.00	22.89	D+ / 2.5	-4.28%	B- / 7.0

Major Rating Factors:
Disappointing performance is the major factor driving the D+ (Weak) TheStreet.com Investment Rating for *WBI Tactical SMV. The fund currently has a performance rating of D+ (Weak) based on an annualized return of 0.00% over the last three years and a total return of -4.28% year to date 2015. Factored into the performance evaluation is an expense ratio of 1.07% (low).

The fund's risk rating is currently B- (Good). It carries a beta of 0.00, meaning the fund's expected move will be 0.0% for every 10% move in the market. Volatility, as measured by both the semi-deviation and a drawdown factor, is considered low. As of December 31, 2015, *WBI Tactical SMV traded at a premium of .39% above its net asset value, which is worse than its one-year historical average premium of .07%.

Donald R. Schreiber, Jr. has been running the fund for 2 years and currently receives a manager quality ranking of 29 (0=worst, 99=best). This fund offers only a moderate level of risk but investors looking for strong performance are still waiting.

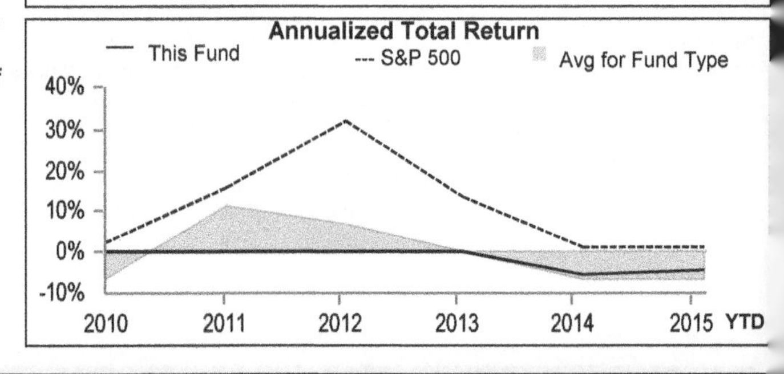

*WBI Tactical SMY (WBIC) D+ Weak

Fund Family: Millington Securities Inc
Fund Type: Global
Inception Date: August 25, 2014

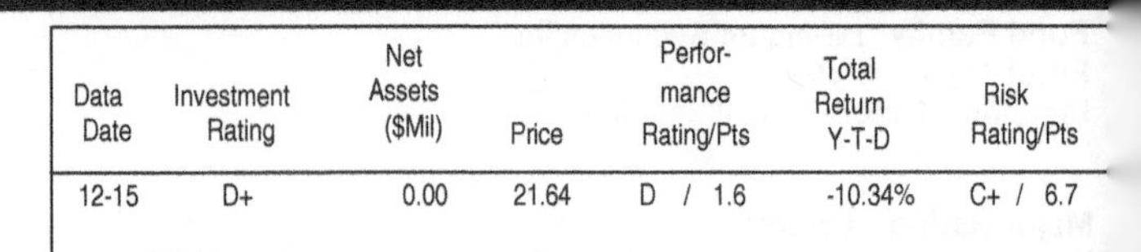

Data Date	Investment Rating	Net Assets ($Mil)	Price	Performance Rating/Pts	Total Return Y-T-D	Risk Rating/Pts
12-15	D+	0.00	21.64	D / 1.6	-10.34%	C+ / 6.7

Major Rating Factors:
Disappointing performance is the major factor driving the D+ (Weak) TheStreet.com Investment Rating for *WBI Tactical SMY. The fund currently has a performance rating of D (Weak) based on an annualized return of 0.00% over the last three years and a total return of -10.34% year to date 2015. Factored into the performance evaluation is an expense ratio of 1.03% (low).

The fund's risk rating is currently C+ (Fair). It carries a beta of 0.00, meaning the fund's expected move will be 0.0% for every 10% move in the market. Volatility, as measured by both the semi-deviation and a drawdown factor, is considered low. As of December 31, 2015, *WBI Tactical SMY traded at a premium of .37% above its net asset value, which is worse than its one-year historical average premium of .07%.

Donald R. Schreiber, Jr. has been running the fund for 2 years and currently receives a manager quality ranking of 15 (0=worst, 99=best). This fund offers only a moderate level of risk but investors looking for strong performance are still waiting.

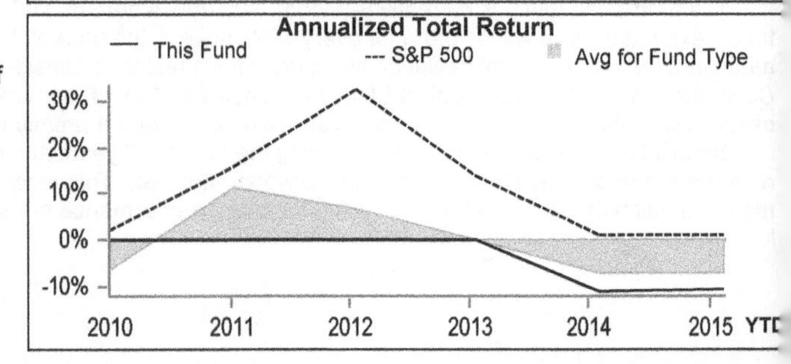

*WCM/BNY Mellon Focused Gro ADR E (AADR) C+ Fair

Fund Family: AdvisorShares Investments LLC
Fund Type: Global
Inception Date: July 21, 2010

Major Rating Factors: Strong performance is the major factor driving the C+ (Fair) TheStreet.com Investment Rating for *WCM/BNY Mellon Focused Gro ADR E. The fund currently has a performance rating of B- (Good) based on an annualized return of 7.39% over the last three years and a total return of 5.72% year to date 2015. Factored into the performance evaluation is an expense ratio of 1.25% (average).

The fund's risk rating is currently C+ (Fair). It carries a beta of 0.97, meaning that its performance tracks fairly well with that of the overall stock market. Volatility, as measured by both the semi-deviation and a drawdown factor, is considered low. As of December 31, 2015, *WCM/BNY Mellon Focused Gro ADR E traded at a premium of .31% above its net asset value, which is worse than its one-year historical average premium of .11%.

Kurt R. Winrich currently receives a manager quality ranking of 84 (0=worst, 99=best). If you desire only a moderate level of risk and strong performance, then this fund is an excellent option.

Data Date	Investment Rating	Net Assets ($Mil)	Price	Performance Rating/Pts	Total Return Y-T-D	Risk Rating/Pts
12-15	C+	13.90	38.53	B- / 7.1	5.72%	C+ / 6.9
2014	C	13.90	37.45	C / 5.3	0.72%	B- / 7.0
2013	B-	10.30	37.47	C+ / 6.8	18.87%	B- / 7.8
2012	B+	7.00	30.74	B+ / 8.5	15.42%	B- / 7.8
2011	D	6.30	28.11	D- / 1.4	-5.13%	B- / 7.8

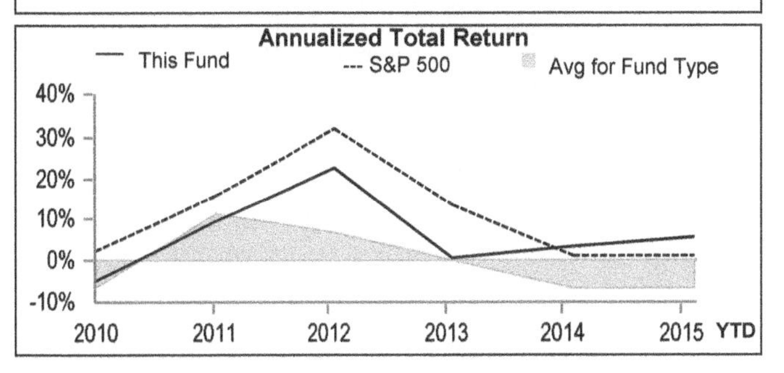

*WisdomTree Asia Local Debt (ALD) C- Fair

Fund Family: WisdomTree Asset Management Inc
Fund Type: Global
Inception Date: March 17, 2011

Major Rating Factors:
Disappointing performance is the major factor driving the C- (Fair) TheStreet.com Investment Rating for *WisdomTree Asia Local Debt. The fund currently has a performance rating of D+ (Weak) based on an annualized return of -4.56% over the last three years and a total return of -5.84% year to date 2015. Factored into the performance evaluation is an expense ratio of 0.55% (very low).

The fund's risk rating is currently B (Good). It carries a beta of 0.59, meaning the fund's expected move will be 5.9% for every 10% move in the market. Volatility, as measured by both the semi-deviation and a drawdown factor, is considered low. As of December 31, 2015, *WisdomTree Asia Local Debt traded at a discount of .51% below its net asset value, which is better than its one-year historical average discount of .44%.

Stephanie Shu has been running the fund for 5 years and currently receives a manager quality ranking of 50 (0=worst, 99=best). This fund offers only a moderate level of risk but investors looking for strong performance are still waiting.

Data Date	Investment Rating	Net Assets ($Mil)	Price	Performance Rating/Pts	Total Return Y-T-D	Risk Rating/Pts
12-15	C-	318.50	42.98	D+ / 2.9	-5.84%	B / 8.2
2014	C-	318.50	46.93	D+ / 2.6	-0.37%	B / 8.7
2013	D+	515.00	47.81	D / 1.6	-7.01%	B / 8.7
2012	C	456.60	52.55	C- / 3.1	6.66%	B+ / 9.1

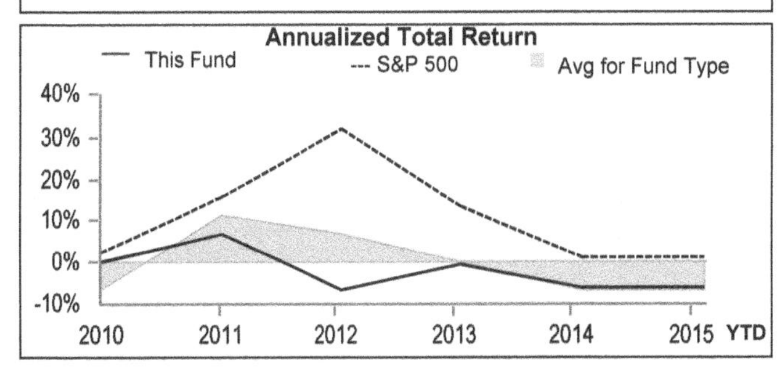

*WisdomTree Asia Pacific ex-Japan (AXJL) C- Fair

Fund Family: WisdomTree Asset Management Inc
Fund Type: Foreign
Inception Date: June 16, 2006

Major Rating Factors:
Disappointing performance is the major factor driving the C- (Fair) TheStreet.com Investment Rating for *WisdomTree Asia Pacific ex-Japan. The fund currently has a performance rating of D+ (Weak) based on an annualized return of -4.47% over the last three years and a total return of -12.83% year to date 2015. Factored into the performance evaluation is an expense ratio of 0.49% (very low).

The fund's risk rating is currently B- (Good). It carries a beta of 0.91, meaning that its performance tracks fairly well with that of the overall stock market. Volatility, as measured by both the semi-deviation and a drawdown factor, is considered low. As of December 31, 2015, *WisdomTree Asia Pacific ex-Japan traded at a discount of 1.11% below its net asset value, which is better than its one-year historical average discount of .20%.

Karen Q. Wong has been running the fund for 8 years and currently receives a manager quality ranking of 18 (0=worst, 99=best). This fund offers only a moderate level of risk but investors looking for strong performance are still waiting.

Data Date	Investment Rating	Net Assets ($Mil)	Price	Performance Rating/Pts	Total Return Y-T-D	Risk Rating/Pts
12-15	C-	46.80	54.59	D+ / 2.5	-12.83%	B- / 7.2
2014	C	46.80	65.24	C / 4.5	4.39%	B / 8.0
2013	C-	66.30	66.86	C- / 3.6	-3.67%	B- / 7.3
2012	C	91.80	69.06	C / 5.2	20.13%	B- / 7.2
2011	C+	72.50	58.05	C+ / 5.7	-6.17%	B- / 7.5
2010	C-	89.80	66.42	C / 4.6	15.09%	C / 4.5

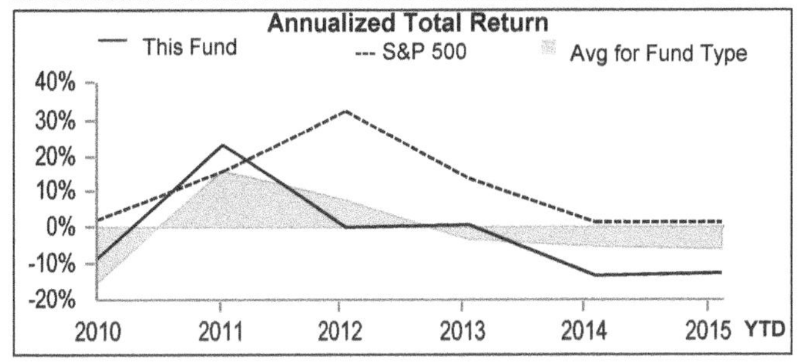

*WisdomTree Australia and NZ Debt (AUNZ) C- Fair

Fund Family: WisdomTree Asset Management Inc
Fund Type: Foreign
Inception Date: June 25, 2008

Major Rating Factors:
Disappointing performance is the major factor driving the C- (Fair) TheStreet.com Investment Rating for *WisdomTree Australia and NZ Debt. The fund currently has a performance rating of D+ (Weak) based on an annualized return of -7.22% over the last three years and a total return of -7.13% year to date 2015. Factored into the performance evaluation is an expense ratio of 0.45% (very low).

The fund's risk rating is currently B- (Good). It carries a beta of 0.46, meaning the fund's expected move will be 4.6% for every 10% move in the market. Volatility, as measured by both the semi-deviation and a drawdown factor, is considered low. As of December 31, 2015, *WisdomTree Australia and NZ Debt traded at a discount of .70% below its net asset value, which is worse than its one-year historical average discount of .89%.

Paul Benson has been running the fund for 1 year and currently receives a manager quality ranking of 17 (0=worst, 99=best). This fund offers only a moderate level of risk but investors looking for strong performance are still waiting.

Data Date	Investment Rating	Net Assets ($Mil)	Price	Perfor-mance Rating/Pts	Total Return Y-T-D	Risk Rating/Pts
12-15	C-	31.60	16.94	D+ / 2.5	-7.13%	B- / 7.2
2014	D+	31.60	18.96	D+ / 2.3	-0.99%	B- / 7.8
2013	D	37.20	19.43	D / 1.7	-11.99%	B- / 7.2
2012	D+	63.40	22.74	D+ / 2.4	8.73%	B- / 7.8
2011	C-	25.90	21.50	D+ / 2.9	-4.91%	B / 8.0
2010	A-	28.40	23.66	B+ / 8.3	9.97%	C+ / 6.5

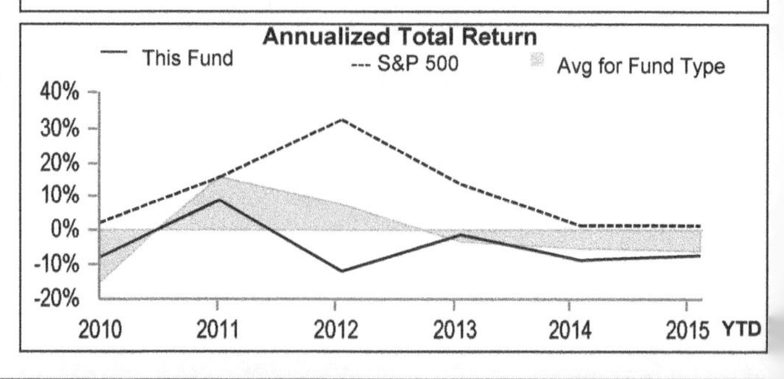

*WisdomTree Australia Divide (AUSE) D+ Weak

Fund Family: WisdomTree Asset Management Inc
Fund Type: Foreign
Inception Date: June 16, 2006

Major Rating Factors:
Disappointing performance is the major factor driving the D+ (Weak) TheStreet.com Investment Rating for *WisdomTree Australia Divide. The fund currently has a performance rating of D+ (Weak) based on an annualized return of -5.12% over the last three years and a total return of -10.82% year to date 2015. Factored into the performance evaluation is an expense ratio of 0.59% (very low).

The fund's risk rating is currently C+ (Fair). It carries a beta of 1.17, meaning it is expected to move 11.7% for every 10% move in the market. Volatility, as measured by both the semi-deviation and a drawdown factor, is considered low. As of December 31, 2015, *WisdomTree Australia Divide traded at a discount of 1.35% below its net asset value, which is better than its one-year historical average discount of .25%.

Karen Q. Wong has been running the fund for 8 years and currently receives a manager quality ranking of 16 (0=worst, 99=best). This fund offers only a moderate level of risk but investors looking for strong performance are still waiting.

Data Date	Investment Rating	Net Assets ($Mil)	Price	Perfor-mance Rating/Pts	Total Return Y-T-D	Risk Rating/Pts
12-15	D+	47.60	44.61	D+ / 2.6	-10.82%	C+ / 6.1
2014	C-	47.60	52.00	C- / 3.3	-7.33%	B- / 7.0
2013	C-	55.60	58.57	C / 4.8	3.21%	C+ / 6.6
2012	C-	69.00	58.17	C / 4.5	22.23%	C+ / 6.7
2011	C+	50.70	50.74	C+ / 6.6	-6.45%	B- / 7.0
2010	C-	78.50	60.41	C+ / 6.2	12.82%	C- / 4.0

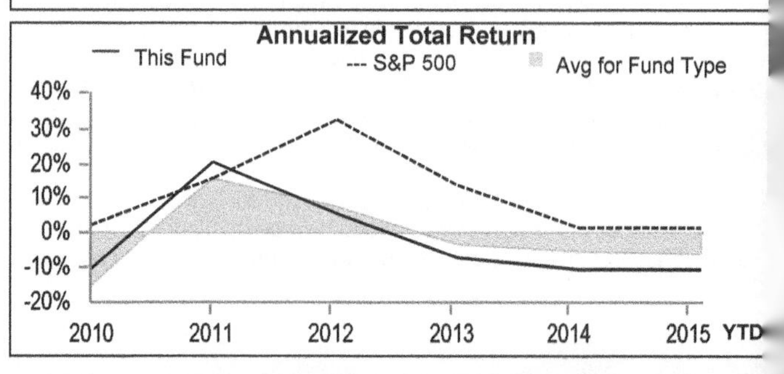

*WisdomTree Barclays US AB Neg Du (AGND) C Fair

Fund Family: WisdomTree Asset Management Inc
Fund Type: Corporate - Investment Grade
Inception Date: December 18, 2013

Major Rating Factors: Middle of the road best describes *WisdomTree Barclays US AB Neg Du whose TheStreet.com Investment Rating is currently a C (Fair). The fund currently has a performance rating of C- (Fair) based on an annualized return of 0.00% over the last three years and a total return of -0.31% year to date 2015. Factored into the performance evaluation is an expense ratio of 0.28% (very low).

The fund's risk rating is currently B+ (Good). It carries a beta of 0.00, meaning the fund's expected move will be 0.0% for every 10% move in the market. Volatility, as measured by both the semi-deviation and a drawdown factor, is considered very low. As of December 31, 2015, *WisdomTree Barclays US AB Neg Du traded at a discount of .23% below its net asset value, which is better than its one-year historical average discount of .10%.

David C. Kwan has been running the fund for 3 years and currently receives a manager quality ranking of 59 (0=worst, 99=best). If you desire an average level of risk, then this fund may be an option.

Data Date	Investment Rating	Net Assets ($Mil)	Price	Perfor-mance Rating/Pts	Total Return Y-T-D	Risk Rating/Pts
12-15	C	23.50	44.17	C- / 3.7	-0.31%	B+ / 9.0
2014	D-	23.50	45.04	D- / 1.4	-8.69%	C / 5.0

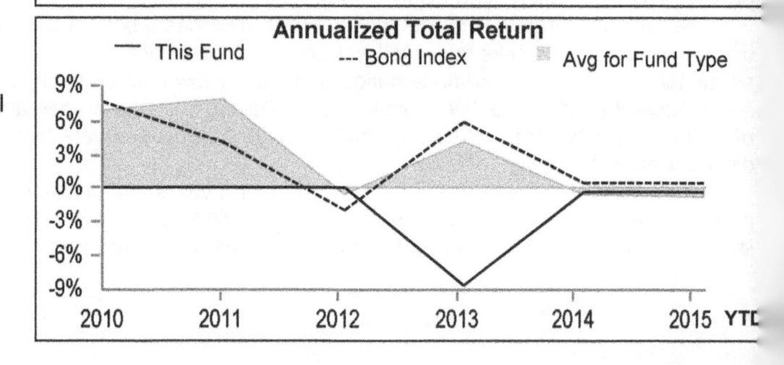

* Denotes ETF Fund

*WisdomTree Barclays US AB Zero D (AGZD) C Fair

Fund Family: WisdomTree Asset Management Inc
Fund Type: Corporate - Investment Grade
Inception Date: December 18, 2013

Major Rating Factors: Middle of the road best describes *WisdomTree Barclays US AB Zero D whose TheStreet.com Investment Rating is currently a C (Fair). The fund currently has a performance rating of C- (Fair) based on an annualized return of 0.00% over the last three years and a total return of -0.79% year to date 2015. Factored into the performance evaluation is an expense ratio of 0.23% (very low).

The fund's risk rating is currently B (Good). It carries a beta of 0.00, meaning the fund's expected move will be 0.0% for every 10% move in the market. Volatility, as measured by both the semi-deviation and a drawdown factor, is considered low. As of December 31, 2015, *WisdomTree Barclays US AB Zero D traded at a premium of .21% above its net asset value, which is worse than its one-year historical average discount of .16%.

David C. Kwan has been running the fund for 3 years and currently receives a manager quality ranking of 59 (0=worst, 99=best). If you desire an average level of risk, then this fund may be an option.

Data Date	Investment Rating	Net Assets ($Mil)	Price	Performance Rating/Pts	Total Return Y-T-D	Risk Rating/Pts
12-15	C	59.70	48.10	C- / 4.1	-0.79%	B / 8.0
2014	D	59.70	49.34	D+ / 2.7	0.49%	C / 5.3

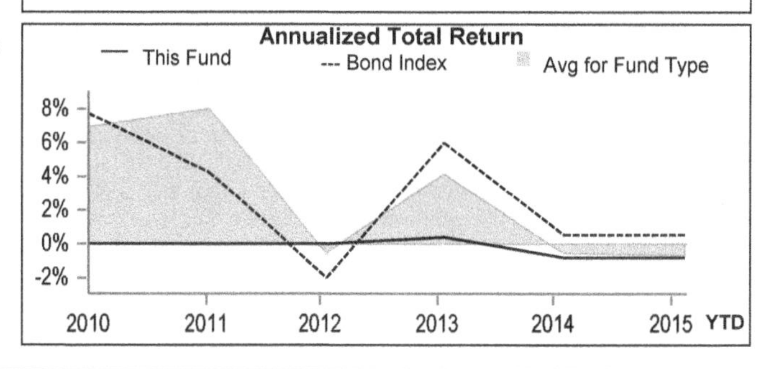

*WisdomTree Bloomberg Float Rt Tr (USFR) C+ Fair

Fund Family: WisdomTree Asset Management Inc
Fund Type: Loan Participation
Inception Date: February 4, 2014

Major Rating Factors: Middle of the road best describes *WisdomTree Bloomberg Float Rt Tr whose TheStreet.com Investment Rating is currently a C+ (Fair). The fund currently has a performance rating of C- (Fair) based on an annualized return of 0.00% over the last three years and a total return of -0.12% year to date 2015. Factored into the performance evaluation is an expense ratio of 0.15% (very low).

The fund's risk rating is currently B+ (Good). It carries a beta of 0.00, meaning the fund's expected move will be 0.0% for every 10% move in the market. Volatility, as measured by both the semi-deviation and a drawdown factor, is considered very low. As of December 31, 2015, *WisdomTree Bloomberg Float Rt Tr traded at a discount of .44% below its net asset value, which is better than its one-year historical average discount of .20%.

Paul Benson has been running the fund for 1 year and currently receives a manager quality ranking of 68 (0=worst, 99=best). If you desire an average level of risk, then this fund may be an option.

Data Date	Investment Rating	Net Assets ($Mil)	Price	Performance Rating/Pts	Total Return Y-T-D	Risk Rating/Pts
12-15	C+	2.50	24.85	C- / 4.1	-0.12%	B+ / 9.8

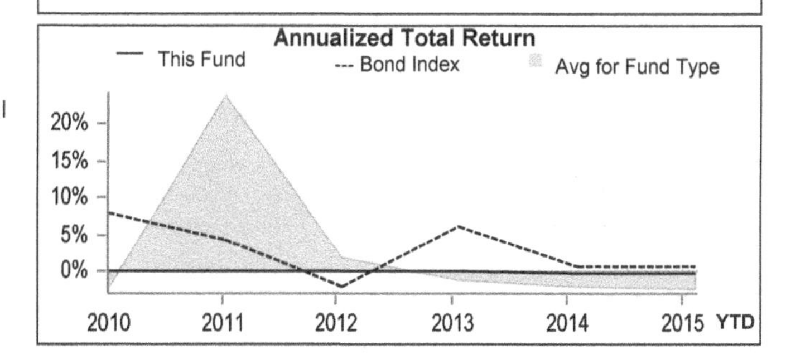

*WisdomTree Bloomberg US Dollar B (USDU) A+ Excellent

Fund Family: WisdomTree Asset Management Inc
Fund Type: General - Investment Grade
Inception Date: December 18, 2013

Major Rating Factors:
Exceptional performance is the major factor driving the A+ (Excellent) TheStreet.com Investment Rating for *WisdomTree Bloomberg US Dollar B. The fund currently has a performance rating of A+ (Excellent) based on an annualized return of 0.00% over the last three years and a total return of 19.69% year to date 2015. Factored into the performance evaluation is an expense ratio of 0.50% (very low).

The fund's risk rating is currently B+ (Good). It carries a beta of 0.00, meaning the fund's expected move will be 0.0% for every 10% move in the market. Volatility, as measured by both the semi-deviation and a drawdown factor, is considered very low. As of December 31, 2015, *WisdomTree Bloomberg US Dollar B traded at a discount of .11% below its net asset value, which is better than its one-year historical average premium of .04%.

Paul Benson has been running the fund for 1 year and currently receives a manager quality ranking of 98 (0=worst, 99=best). If you desire only a moderate level of risk and strong performance, then this fund is an excellent option.

Data Date	Investment Rating	Net Assets ($Mil)	Price	Performance Rating/Pts	Total Return Y-T-D	Risk Rating/Pts
12-15	A+	57.30	27.36	A+ / 9.8	19.69%	B+ / 9.0
2014	C	57.30	27.07	B- / 7.4	10.69%	C / 5.4

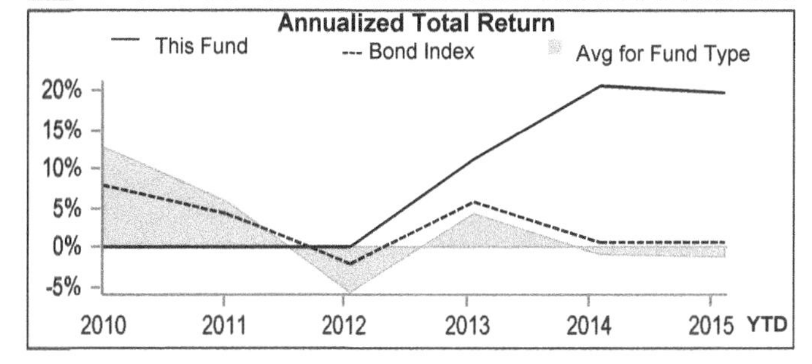

* Denotes ETF Fund

*WisdomTree BofA ML HY Bd Neg Dur (HYND) C- Fair

Fund Family: WisdomTree Asset Management Inc
Fund Type: Corporate - High Yield
Inception Date: December 18, 2013

Major Rating Factors:
Disappointing performance is the major factor driving the C- (Fair) TheStreet.com Investment Rating for *WisdomTree BofA ML HY Bd Neg Dur. The fund currently has a performance rating of D (Weak) based on an annualized return of 0.00% over the last three years and a total return of -5.42% year to date 2015. Factored into the performance evaluation is an expense ratio of 0.48% (very low).

The fund's risk rating is currently B (Good). It carries a beta of 0.00, meaning the fund's expected move will be 0.0% for every 10% move in the market. Volatility, as measured by both the semi-deviation and a drawdown factor, is considered low. As of December 31, 2015, *WisdomTree BofA ML HY Bd Neg Dur traded at a discount of 1.67% below its net asset value, which is better than its one-year historical average premium of .41%.

Paul Benson has been running the fund for 1 year and currently receives a manager quality ranking of 60 (0=worst, 99=best). This fund offers only a moderate level of risk but investors looking for strong performance are still waiting.

Data Date	Investment Rating	Net Assets ($Mil)	Price	Performance Rating/Pts	Total Return Y-T-D	Risk Rating/Pts
12-15	C-	11.40	19.39	D / 2.1	-5.42%	B / 8.0
2014	D-	11.40	21.38	D- / 1.0	-11.80%	C / 4.7

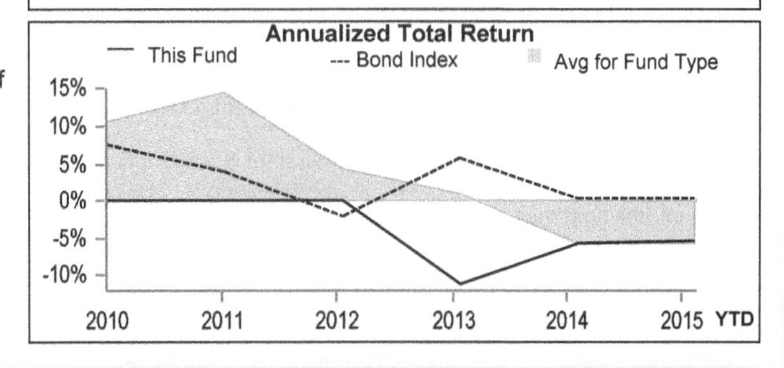

*WisdomTree BofA ML HY Bd Zero Du (HYZD) C- Fair

Fund Family: WisdomTree Asset Management Inc
Fund Type: Corporate - High Yield
Inception Date: December 18, 2013

Major Rating Factors: Middle of the road best describes *WisdomTree BofA ML HY Bd Zero Du whose TheStreet.com Investment Rating is currently a C- (Fair). The fund currently has a performance rating of C- (Fair) based on an annualized return of 0.00% over the last three years and a total return of -1.05% year to date 2015. Factored into the performance evaluation is an expense ratio of 0.43% (very low).

The fund's risk rating is currently C+ (Fair). It carries a beta of 0.00, meaning the fund's expected move will be 0.0% for every 10% move in the market. Volatility, as measured by both the semi-deviation and a drawdown factor, is considered low. As of December 31, 2015, *WisdomTree BofA ML HY Bd Zero Du traded at a premium of .05% above its net asset value, which is worse than its one-year historical average discount of .35%.

Paul Benson has been running the fund for 1 year and currently receives a manager quality ranking of 84 (0=worst, 99=best). If you desire an average level of risk, then this fund may be an option.

Data Date	Investment Rating	Net Assets ($Mil)	Price	Performance Rating/Pts	Total Return Y-T-D	Risk Rating/Pts
12-15	C-	22.10	21.92	C- / 3.0	-1.05%	C+ / 6.8
2014	D-	22.10	23.08	D- / 1.5	-4.71%	C / 4.9

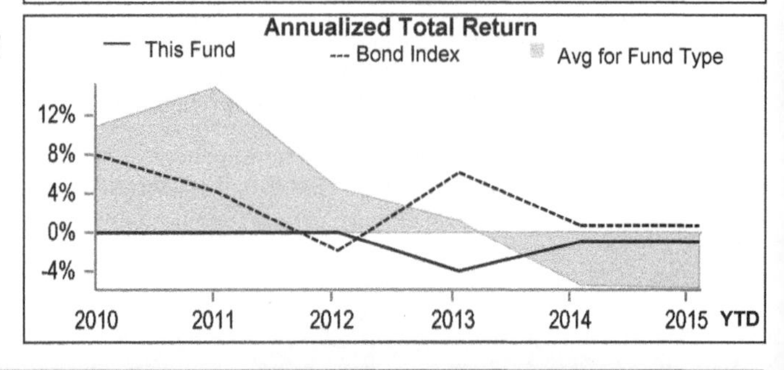

*WisdomTree Brazilian Real Strate (BZF) D Weak

Fund Family: WisdomTree Asset Management Inc
Fund Type: Foreign
Inception Date: May 14, 2008

Major Rating Factors:
Disappointing performance is the major factor driving the D (Weak) TheStreet.com Investment Rating for *WisdomTree Brazilian Real Strate. The fund currently has a performance rating of D- (Weak) based on an annualized return of -12.80% over the last three years and a total return of -24.53% year to date 2015. Factored into the performance evaluation is an expense ratio of 0.45% (very low).

The fund's risk rating is currently C+ (Fair). It carries a beta of 0.60, meaning the fund's expected move will be 6.0% for every 10% move in the market. Volatility, as measured by both the semi-deviation and a drawdown factor, is considered low. As of December 31, 2015, *WisdomTree Brazilian Real Strate traded at a discount of 1.33% below its net asset value, which is better than its one-year historical average discount of .22%.

Christopher N. Orndorff has been running the fund for 2 years and currently receives a manager quality ranking of 10 (0=worst, 99=best). This fund offers only a moderate level of risk but investors looking for strong performance are still waiting.

Data Date	Investment Rating	Net Assets ($Mil)	Price	Performance Rating/Pts	Total Return Y-T-D	Risk Rating/Pts
12-15	D	28.70	12.60	D- / 1.3	-24.53%	C+ / 6.3
2014	D	28.70	16.93	D / 1.9	-1.40%	C+ / 5.8
2013	D-	518.50	17.30	D- / 1.5	-9.63%	C / 5.4
2012	D	60.60	18.91	D / 2.2	-6.51%	C+ / 5.8
2011	C-	81.90	19.47	C / 5.4	-3.12%	C+ / 6.4
2010	A	132.80	26.55	A / 9.4	24.53%	C+ / 6.4

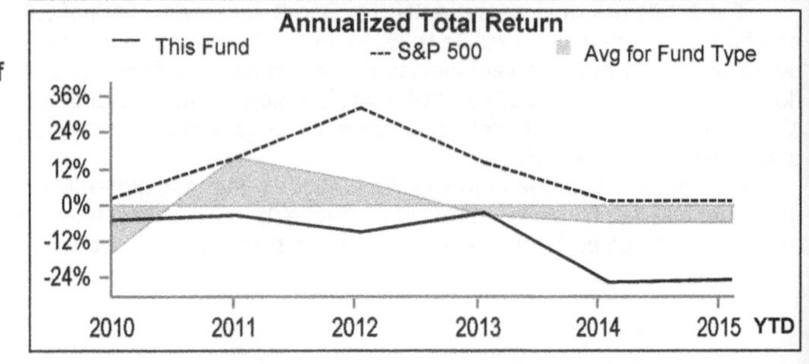

*WisdomTree China ex-State-Owned (CXSE) C- Fair

Fund Family: WisdomTree Asset Management Inc
Fund Type: Foreign
Inception Date: September 19, 2012

Major Rating Factors: Middle of the road best describes *WisdomTree China ex-State-Owned whose TheStreet.com Investment Rating is currently a C- (Fair). The fund currently has a performance rating of C- (Fair) based on an annualized return of -2.40% over the last three years and a total return of -3.26% year to date 2015. Factored into the performance evaluation is an expense ratio of 0.64% (very low).

The fund's risk rating is currently C+ (Fair). It carries a beta of 0.95, meaning that its performance tracks fairly well with that of the overall stock market. Volatility, as measured by both the semi-deviation and a drawdown factor, is considered low. As of December 31, 2015, *WisdomTree China ex-State-Owned traded at a discount of 2.08% below its net asset value, which is better than its one-year historical average discount of .82%.

Richard A. Brown has been running the fund for 2 years and currently receives a manager quality ranking of 24 (0=worst, 99=best). If you desire an average level of risk, then this fund may be an option.

Data Date	Investment Rating	Net Assets ($Mil)	Price	Performance Rating/Pts	Total Return Y-T-D	Risk Rating/Pts
12-15	C-	18.30	49.04	C- / 3.5	-3.26%	C+ / 6.4
2014	C-	18.30	52.00	C- / 3.4	3.70%	B- / 7.5
2013	C-	21.00	52.45	C- / 3.8	-7.24%	B / 8.0

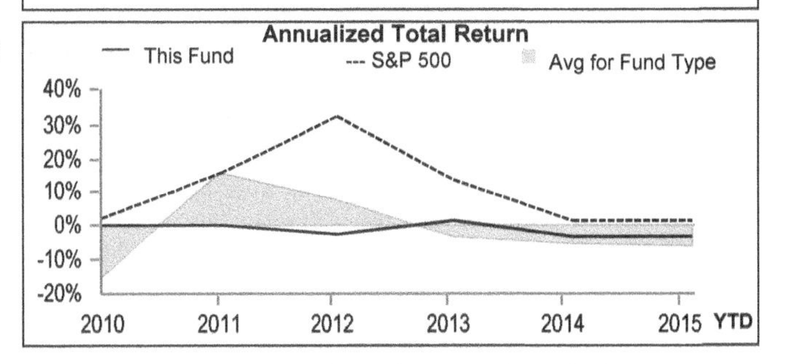

*WisdomTree Chinese Yuan Strategy (CYB) C+ Fair

Fund Family: WisdomTree Asset Management Inc
Fund Type: Foreign
Inception Date: May 14, 2008

Major Rating Factors: Middle of the road best describes *WisdomTree Chinese Yuan Strategy whose TheStreet.com Investment Rating is currently a C+ (Fair). The fund currently has a performance rating of C (Fair) based on an annualized return of 1.35% over the last three years and a total return of -3.34% year to date 2015. Factored into the performance evaluation is an expense ratio of 0.45% (very low).

The fund's risk rating is currently B+ (Good). It carries a beta of 0.12, meaning the fund's expected move will be 1.2% for every 10% move in the market. Volatility, as measured by both the semi-deviation and a drawdown factor, is considered very low. As of December 31, 2015, *WisdomTree Chinese Yuan Strategy traded at a discount of .16% below its net asset value, which is better than its one-year historical average discount of .15%.

Paul Benson has been running the fund for 1 year and currently receives a manager quality ranking of 75 (0=worst, 99=best). If you desire an average level of risk, then this fund may be an option.

Data Date	Investment Rating	Net Assets ($Mil)	Price	Performance Rating/Pts	Total Return Y-T-D	Risk Rating/Pts
12-15	C+	152.00	24.31	C / 4.3	-3.34%	B+ / 9.1
2014	C	152.00	25.13	C- / 3.4	-0.65%	B+ / 9.5
2013	B-	214.30	25.48	C / 5.2	8.30%	B+ / 9.7
2012	C-	240.30	25.53	D / 2.0	2.33%	B+ / 9.8
2011	C	448.50	25.19	C- / 3.0	6.67%	B+ / 9.8
2010	B-	639.60	25.37	C- / 3.6	1.79%	B / 8.9

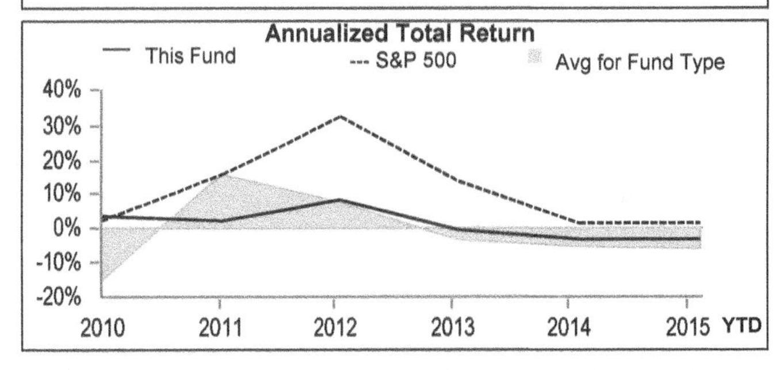

*WisdomTree Commodity Country Equ (CCXE) D Weak

Fund Family: WisdomTree Asset Management Inc
Fund Type: Foreign
Inception Date: October 13, 2006

Major Rating Factors:
Disappointing performance is the major factor driving the D (Weak) TheStreet.com Investment Rating for *WisdomTree Commodity Country Equ. The fund currently has a performance rating of D- (Weak) based on an annualized return of -11.60% over the last three years and a total return of -18.53% year to date 2015. Factored into the performance evaluation is an expense ratio of 0.59% (very low).

The fund's risk rating is currently C+ (Fair). It carries a beta of 1.13, meaning it is expected to move 11.3% for every 10% move in the market. Volatility, as measured by both the semi-deviation and a drawdown factor, is considered low. As of December 31, 2015, *WisdomTree Commodity Country Equ traded at a discount of 1.21% below its net asset value, which is better than its one-year historical average discount of .79%.

Karen Q. Wong has been running the fund for 8 years and currently receives a manager quality ranking of 9 (0=worst, 99=best). This fund offers only a moderate level of risk but investors looking for strong performance are still waiting.

Data Date	Investment Rating	Net Assets ($Mil)	Price	Performance Rating/Pts	Total Return Y-T-D	Risk Rating/Pts
12-15	D	16.10	19.62	D- / 1.5	-18.53%	C+ / 6.6
2014	D	16.10	25.55	D+ / 2.3	-11.07%	C+ / 6.0
2013	C-	21.30	30.35	C- / 3.7	-3.10%	B- / 7.3
2012	C-	26.90	31.83	C / 4.6	18.54%	B- / 7.2
2011	C	30.80	28.00	C / 5.2	-5.58%	B- / 7.3
2010	C-	41.90	32.15	C / 5.1	16.76%	C- / 3.9

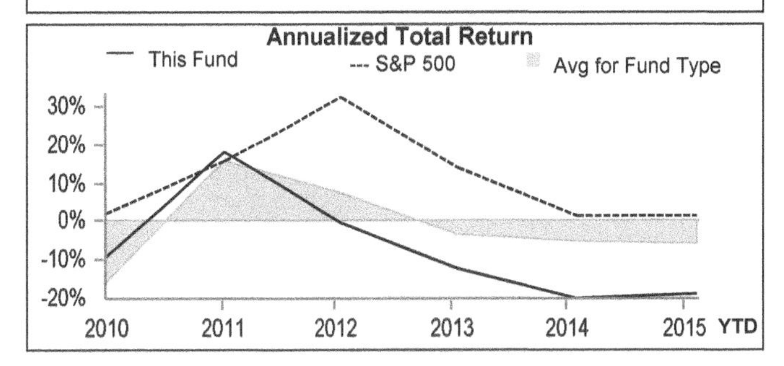

* Denotes ETF Fund

*WisdomTree Commodity Curr Str (CCX) D Weak

Fund Family: WisdomTree Asset Management Inc
Fund Type: Global
Inception Date: September 24, 2010

Data Date	Investment Rating	Net Assets ($Mil)	Price	Performance Rating/Pts	Total Return Y-T-D	Risk Rating/Pts
12-15	D	11.50	15.26	D / 1.8	-12.15%	C+ / 5.6
2014	D	11.50	17.56	D / 1.7	-11.71%	C+ / 6.0
2013	D	16.00	19.94	D / 2.2	-6.84%	C+ / 6.6
2012	D	23.60	21.48	D+ / 2.9	5.43%	C+ / 6.6
2011	D-	38.60	20.31	D- / 1.0	-10.03%	C+ / 6.5

Major Rating Factors:
Disappointing performance is the major factor driving the D (Weak) TheStreet.com Investment Rating for *WisdomTree Commodity Curr Str. The fund currently has a performance rating of D (Weak) based on an annualized return of -10.59% over the last three years and a total return of -12.15% year to date 2015. Factored into the performance evaluation is an expense ratio of 0.55% (very low).

The fund's risk rating is currently C+ (Fair). It carries a beta of 0.48, meaning the fund's expected move will be 4.8% for every 10% move in the market. Volatility, as measured by both the semi-deviation and a drawdown factor, is considered low. As of December 31, 2015, *WisdomTree Commodity Curr Str traded at a premium of 1.13% above its net asset value, which is worse than its one-year historical average discount of .20%.

Paul Benson has been running the fund for 1 year and currently receives a manager quality ranking of 12 (0=worst, 99=best). This fund offers only a moderate level of risk but investors looking for strong performance are still waiting.

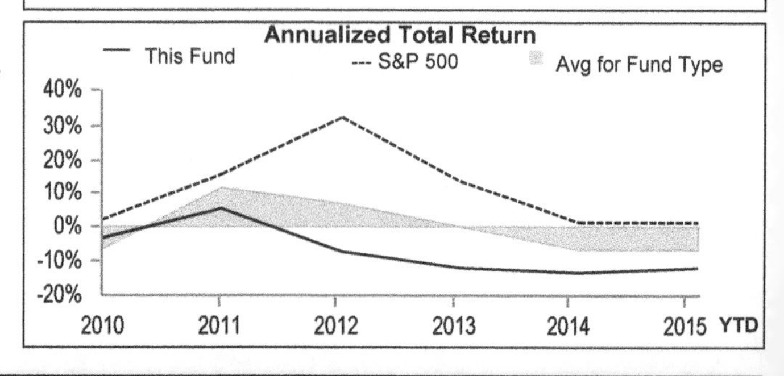

*WisdomTree Dividend Ex-Financial (DTN) B Good

Fund Family: WisdomTree Asset Management Inc
Fund Type: Income
Inception Date: June 16, 2006

Data Date	Investment Rating	Net Assets ($Mil)	Price	Performance Rating/Pts	Total Return Y-T-D	Risk Rating/Pts
12-15	B	1,187.40	70.29	B / 7.6	-5.35%	B- / 7.2
2014	A	1,187.40	76.70	B / 8.0	16.46%	B / 8.5
2013	A	1,148.50	68.77	B / 8.2	23.70%	B+ / 9.0
2012	B	1,080.80	55.58	C+ / 6.6	13.44%	B / 8.9
2011	B-	1,010.40	52.00	B- / 7.2	12.90%	B- / 7.7
2010	C	343.00	48.02	C / 5.4	21.44%	C+ / 5.6

Major Rating Factors: Strong performance is the major factor driving the B (Good) TheStreet.com Investment Rating for *WisdomTree Dividend Ex-Financial. The fund currently has a performance rating of B (Good) based on an annualized return of 10.91% over the last three years and a total return of -5.35% year to date 2015. Factored into the performance evaluation is an expense ratio of 0.39% (very low).

The fund's risk rating is currently B- (Good). It carries a beta of 0.93, meaning that its performance tracks fairly well with that of the overall stock market. Volatility, as measured by both the semi-deviation and a drawdown factor, is considered low. As of December 31, 2015, *WisdomTree Dividend Ex-Financial traded at a premium of .04% above its net asset value, which is worse than its one-year historical average discount of .01%.

Karen Q. Wong has been running the fund for 8 years and currently receives a manager quality ranking of 52 (0=worst, 99=best). If you desire only a moderate level of risk and strong performance, then this fund is an excellent option.

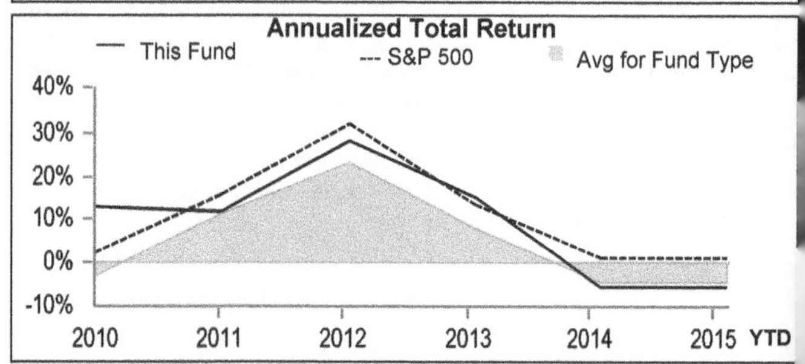

*WisdomTree Earnings 500 Fund (EPS) B+ Good

Fund Family: WisdomTree Asset Management Inc
Fund Type: Income
Inception Date: February 23, 2007

Data Date	Investment Rating	Net Assets ($Mil)	Price	Performance Rating/Pts	Total Return Y-T-D	Risk Rating/Pts
12-15	B+	113.50	69.36	B+ / 8.4	-1.35%	B- / 7.3
2014	B+	113.50	71.98	B / 8.2	14.13%	B- / 7.5
2013	A	90.20	64.47	B+ / 8.5	28.73%	B / 8.4
2012	C+	56.90	49.36	C / 5.2	15.60%	B / 8.2
2011	C+	61.50	44.03	C / 5.5	5.02%	B / 8.1
2010	C-	69.30	43.34	C- / 3.5	13.28%	C+ / 6.1

Major Rating Factors: Strong performance is the major factor driving the B+ (Good) TheStreet.com Investment Rating for *WisdomTree Earnings 500 Fund. The fund currently has a performance rating of B+ (Good) based on an annualized return of 13.09% over the last three years and a total return of -1.35% year to date 2015. Factored into the performance evaluation is an expense ratio of 0.29% (very low).

The fund's risk rating is currently B- (Good). It carries a beta of 1.04, meaning that its performance tracks fairly well with that of the overall stock market. Volatility, as measured by both the semi-deviation and a drawdown factor, is considered low. As of December 31, 2015, *WisdomTree Earnings 500 Fund traded at a premium of .19% above its net asset value.

Karen Q. Wong has been running the fund for 8 years and currently receives a manager quality ranking of 58 (0=worst, 99=best). If you desire only a moderate level of risk and strong performance, then this fund is an excellent option.

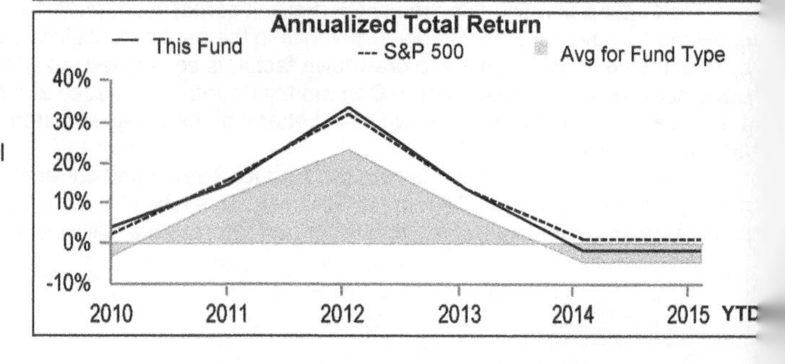

*WisdomTree EM Corporate Bond (EMCB) C Fair

Fund Family: WisdomTree Asset Management Inc
Fund Type: Emerging Market
Inception Date: March 8, 2012

Data Date	Investment Rating	Net Assets ($Mil)	Price	Performance Rating/Pts	Total Return Y-T-D	Risk Rating/Pts
12-15	C	113.80	65.58	C- / 3.3	-3.66%	B / 8.1
2014	D+	113.80	72.12	D / 2.2	1.76%	C+ / 6.8
2013	C-	111.60	74.41	D+ / 2.6	-3.64%	B+ / 9.0

Major Rating Factors: Middle of the road best describes *WisdomTree EM Corporate Bond whose TheStreet.com Investment Rating is currently a C (Fair). The fund currently has a performance rating of C- (Fair) based on an annualized return of -2.10% over the last three years and a total return of -3.66% year to date 2015. Factored into the performance evaluation is an expense ratio of 0.60% (very low).

The fund's risk rating is currently B (Good). It carries a beta of 0.48, meaning the fund's expected move will be 4.8% for every 10% move in the market. Volatility, as measured by both the semi-deviation and a drawdown factor, is considered low. As of December 31, 2015, *WisdomTree EM Corporate Bond traded at a discount of .56% below its net asset value, which is worse than its one-year historical average discount of .70%.

Keith J. Gardner has been running the fund for 4 years and currently receives a manager quality ranking of 69 (0=worst, 99=best). If you desire an average level of risk, then this fund may be an option.

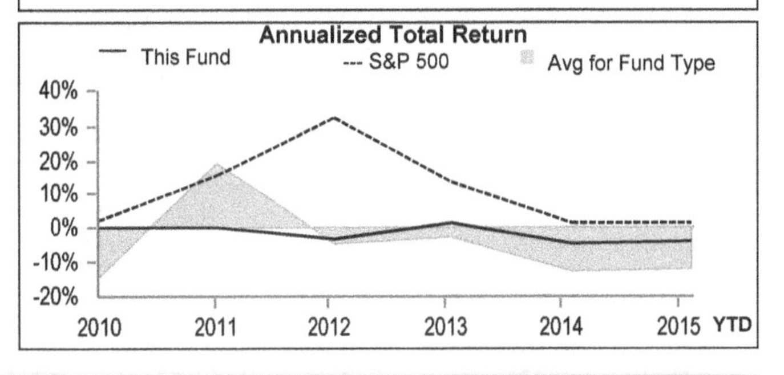

*WisdomTree EM ex-State-Owned Ent (XSOE) D- Weak

Fund Family: WisdomTree Asset Management Inc
Fund Type: Emerging Market
Inception Date: December 10, 2014

Data Date	Investment Rating	Net Assets ($Mil)	Price	Performance Rating/Pts	Total Return Y-T-D	Risk Rating/Pts
12-15	D-	0.00	20.43	D / 1.6	-11.81%	C- / 4.1

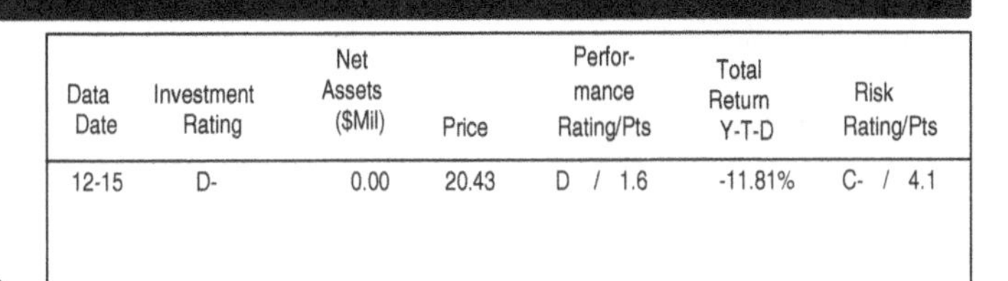

Major Rating Factors:
Disappointing performance is the major factor driving the D- (Weak) TheStreet.com Investment Rating for *WisdomTree EM ex-State-Owned Ent. The fund currently has a performance rating of D (Weak) based on an annualized return of 0.00% over the last three years and a total return of -11.81% year to date 2015.

The fund's risk rating is currently C- (Fair). It carries a beta of 0.00, meaning the fund's expected move will be 0.0% for every 10% move in the market. Volatility, as measured by both the semi-deviation and a drawdown factor, is considered average. As of December 31, 2015, *WisdomTree EM ex-State-Owned Ent traded at a discount of 1.16% below its net asset value, which is better than its one-year historical average discount of .11%.

Karen Q. Wong has been running the fund for 2 years and currently receives a manager quality ranking of 82 (0=worst, 99=best). This fund offers an average level of risk but investors looking for strong performance will be frustrated.

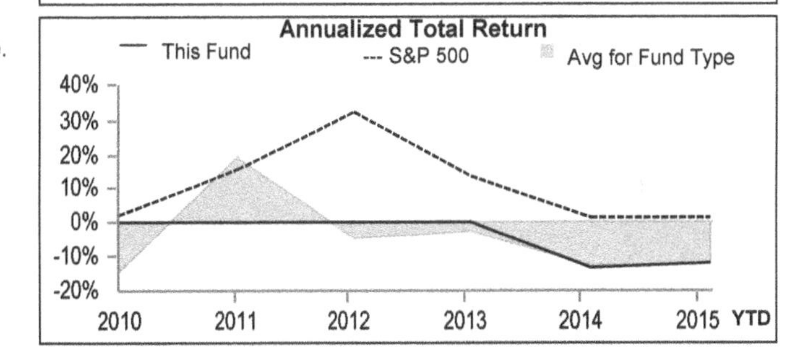

*WisdomTree Em Mkts Cons Gro (EMCG) D Weak

Fund Family: WisdomTree Asset Management Inc
Fund Type: Emerging Market
Inception Date: September 26, 2013

Data Date	Investment Rating	Net Assets ($Mil)	Price	Performance Rating/Pts	Total Return Y-T-D	Risk Rating/Pts
12-15	D	20.10	19.33	E+ / 0.7	-19.63%	C+ / 6.9
2014	D+	20.10	24.93	C- / 3.6	5.21%	C+ / 6.4

Major Rating Factors:
Very poor performance is the major factor driving the D (Weak) TheStreet.com Investment Rating for *WisdomTree Em Mkts Cons Gro. The fund currently has a performance rating of E+ (Very Weak) based on an annualized return of 0.00% over the last three years and a total return of -19.63% year to date 2015. Factored into the performance evaluation is an expense ratio of 0.64% (very low).

The fund's risk rating is currently C+ (Fair). It carries a beta of 0.00, meaning the fund's expected move will be 0.0% for every 10% move in the market. Volatility, as measured by both the semi-deviation and a drawdown factor, is considered low. As of December 31, 2015, *WisdomTree Em Mkts Cons Gro traded at a discount of .15% below its net asset value, which is worse than its one-year historical average discount of .26%.

Richard A. Brown has been running the fund for 3 years and currently receives a manager quality ranking of 22 (0=worst, 99=best). This fund offers only a moderate level of risk but investors looking for strong performance are still waiting.

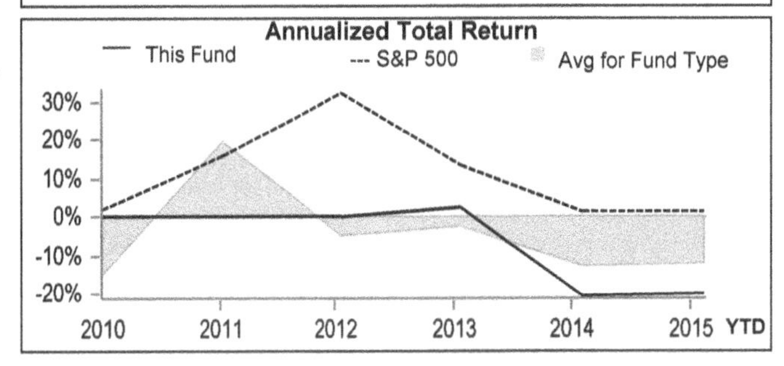

* Denotes ETF Fund

*WisdomTree Em Mkts Qual Div Gro (DGRE) D Weak

Fund Family: WisdomTree Asset Management Inc
Fund Type: Emerging Market
Inception Date: August 1, 2013

Data Date	Investment Rating	Net Assets ($Mil)	Price	Performance Rating/Pts	Total Return Y-T-D	Risk Rating/Pts
12-15	D	30.70	19.36	E+ / 0.9	-16.47%	C+ / 6.8
2014	D	30.70	24.43	D+ / 2.3	3.80%	C+ / 6.4

Major Rating Factors:
Very poor performance is the major factor driving the D (Weak) TheStreet.com Investment Rating for *WisdomTree Em Mkts Qual Div Gro. The fund currently has a performance rating of E+ (Very Weak) based on an annualized return of 0.00% over the last three years and a total return of -16.47% year to date 2015. Factored into the performance evaluation is an expense ratio of 0.64% (very low).

The fund's risk rating is currently C+ (Fair). It carries a beta of 0.00, meaning the fund's expected move will be 0.0% for every 10% move in the market. Volatility, as measured by both the semi-deviation and a drawdown factor, is considered low. As of December 31, 2015, *WisdomTree Em Mkts Qual Div Gro traded at a discount of 1.53% below its net asset value, which is better than its one-year historical average premium of .23%.

Karen Q. Wong has been running the fund for 3 years and currently receives a manager quality ranking of 22 (0=worst, 99=best). This fund offers only a moderate level of risk but investors looking for strong performance are still waiting.

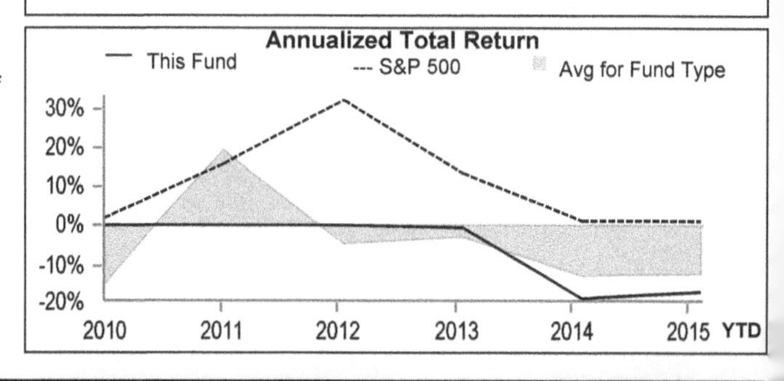

*WisdomTree Emerging Currency Str (CEW) D+ Weak

Fund Family: WisdomTree Asset Management Inc
Fund Type: Foreign
Inception Date: May 6, 2009

Data Date	Investment Rating	Net Assets ($Mil)	Price	Performance Rating/Pts	Total Return Y-T-D	Risk Rating/Pts
12-15	D+	86.80	16.80	D+ / 2.3	-9.43%	C+ / 6.5
2014	D	86.80	18.59	D / 2.1	-6.30%	C+ / 6.6
2013	D+	168.00	20.06	D+ / 2.3	-6.15%	B / 8.2
2012	D+	271.60	21.09	D+ / 2.3	5.84%	B / 8.2
2011	D+	344.00	19.70	D / 1.8	-1.30%	B / 8.4
2010	B	296.90	22.56	C+ / 6.9	6.40%	B / 8.8

Major Rating Factors:
Disappointing performance is the major factor driving the D+ (Weak) TheStreet.com Investment Rating for *WisdomTree Emerging Currency Str. The fund currently has a performance rating of D+ (Weak) based on an annualized return of -7.37% over the last three years and a total return of -9.43% year to date 2015. Factored into the performance evaluation is an expense ratio of 0.55% (very low).

The fund's risk rating is currently C+ (Fair). It carries a beta of 0.38, meaning the fund's expected move will be 3.8% for every 10% move in the market. Volatility, as measured by both the semi-deviation and a drawdown factor, is considered low. As of December 31, 2015, *WisdomTree Emerging Currency Str traded at a premium of .24% above its net asset value, which is worse than its one-year historical average discount of .19%.

Paul Benson has been running the fund for 1 year and currently receives a manager quality ranking of 18 (0=worst, 99=best). This fund offers only a moderate level of risk but investors looking for strong performance are still waiting.

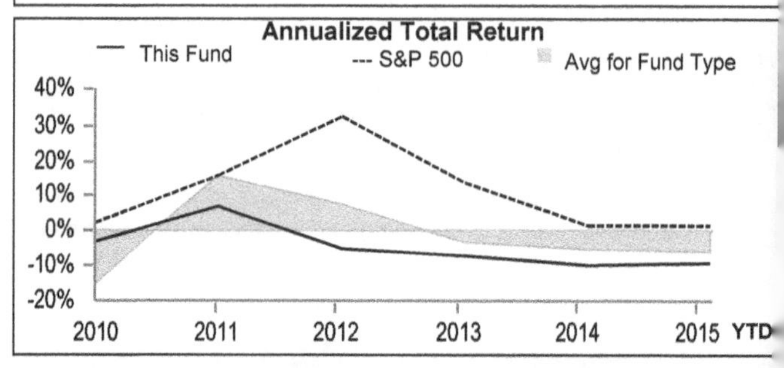

*WisdomTree Emg Mkts High Dividen (DEM) D Weak

Fund Family: WisdomTree Asset Management Inc
Fund Type: Emerging Market
Inception Date: July 13, 2007

Data Date	Investment Rating	Net Assets ($Mil)	Price	Performance Rating/Pts	Total Return Y-T-D	Risk Rating/Pts
12-15	D	3,437.10	31.64	D- / 1.2	-20.81%	C+ / 5.6
2014	D	3,437.10	42.16	D / 1.9	-9.96%	C+ / 6.8
2013	D	4,603.10	51.03	D / 2.1	-9.25%	B- / 7.0
2012	C-	4,866.00	57.19	C- / 3.8	12.48%	B- / 7.1
2011	C+	2,144.70	51.27	C+ / 6.4	-8.68%	B- / 7.3
2010	B+	1,166.90	59.69	B+ / 8.3	25.43%	C / 5.2

Major Rating Factors:
Disappointing performance is the major factor driving the D (Weak) TheStreet.com Investment Rating for *WisdomTree Emg Mkts High Dividen. The fund currently has a performance rating of D- (Weak) based on an annualized return of -14.39% over the last three years and a total return of -20.81% year to date 2015. Factored into the performance evaluation is an expense ratio of 0.64% (very low).

The fund's risk rating is currently C+ (Fair). It carries a beta of 1.12, meaning it is expected to move 11.2% for every 10% move in the market. Volatility, as measured by both the semi-deviation and a drawdown factor, is considered low. As of December 31, 2015, *WisdomTree Emg Mkts High Dividen traded at a discount of .82% below its net asset value, which is better than its one-year historical average discount of .26%.

Karen Q. Wong has been running the fund for 8 years and currently receives a manager quality ranking of 21 (0=worst, 99=best). This fund offers only a moderate level of risk but investors looking for strong performance are still waiting.

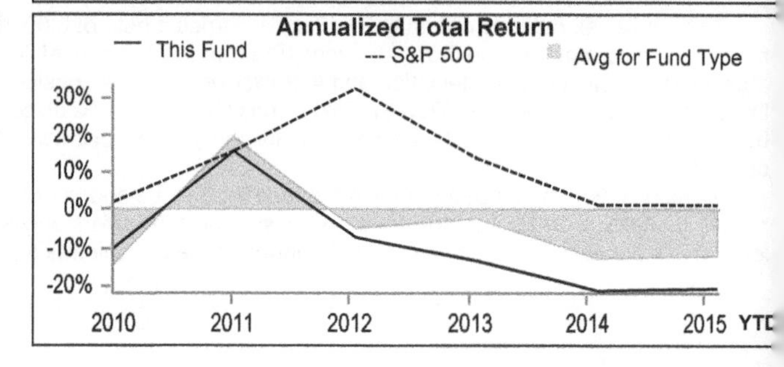

* Denotes ETF Fund

*WisdomTree Emg Mkts Local Debt F (ELD) D Weak

Fund Family: WisdomTree Asset Management Inc
Fund Type: Emerging Market
Inception Date: August 9, 2010

Major Rating Factors:
Disappointing performance is the major factor driving the D (Weak) TheStreet.com Investment Rating for *WisdomTree Emg Mkts Local Debt F. The fund currently has a performance rating of D (Weak) based on an annualized return of -9.81% over the last three years and a total return of -12.80% year to date 2015. Factored into the performance evaluation is an expense ratio of 0.55% (very low).

The fund's risk rating is currently C+ (Fair). It carries a beta of 0.85, meaning the fund's expected move will be 8.5% for every 10% move in the market. Volatility, as measured by both the semi-deviation and a drawdown factor, is considered low. As of December 31, 2015, *WisdomTree Emg Mkts Local Debt F traded at a price exactly equal to its net asset value, which is worse than its one-year historical average discount of .20%.

Stephanie Shu has been running the fund for 6 years and currently receives a manager quality ranking of 24 (0=worst, 99=best). This fund offers only a moderate level of risk but investors looking for strong performance are still waiting.

Data Date	Investment Rating	Net Assets ($Mil)	Price	Performance Rating/Pts	Total Return Y-T-D	Risk Rating/Pts
12-15	D	778.80	34.28	D / 1.9	-12.80%	C+ / 5.9
2014	D	778.80	41.60	D / 2.2	-5.11%	C+ / 5.8
2013	D+	1,184.60	46.02	D / 2.2	-10.77%	B / 8.2
2012	C+	1,497.50	53.46	C+ / 5.6	12.93%	B / 8.6
2011	D+	1,078.10	48.64	D- / 1.5	-1.63%	B / 8.6

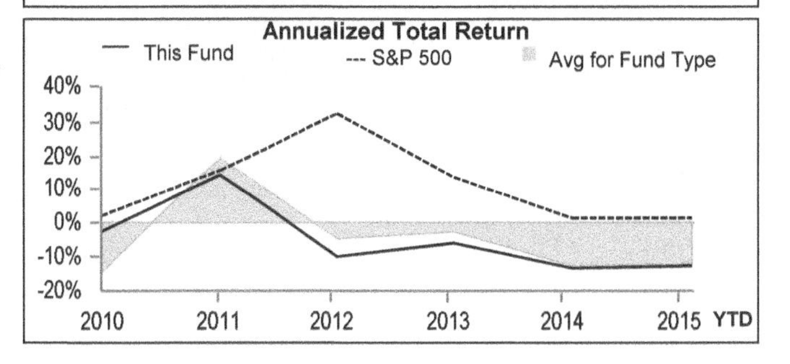

*WisdomTree Emg Mkts SmCap Div Fd (DGS) D+ Weak

Fund Family: WisdomTree Asset Management Inc
Fund Type: Emerging Market
Inception Date: October 30, 2007

Major Rating Factors:
Disappointing performance is the major factor driving the D+ (Weak) TheStreet.com Investment Rating for *WisdomTree Emg Mkts SmCap Div Fd. The fund currently has a performance rating of D (Weak) based on an annualized return of -8.16% over the last three years and a total return of -15.55% year to date 2015. Factored into the performance evaluation is an expense ratio of 0.64% (very low).

The fund's risk rating is currently C+ (Fair). It carries a beta of 0.90, meaning that its performance tracks fairly well with that of the overall stock market. Volatility, as measured by both the semi-deviation and a drawdown factor, is considered low. As of December 31, 2015, *WisdomTree Emg Mkts SmCap Div Fd traded at a discount of 1.41% below its net asset value, which is better than its one-year historical average discount of .50%.

Karen Q. Wong has been running the fund for 8 years and currently receives a manager quality ranking of 49 (0=worst, 99=best). This fund offers only a moderate level of risk but investors looking for strong performance are still waiting.

Data Date	Investment Rating	Net Assets ($Mil)	Price	Performance Rating/Pts	Total Return Y-T-D	Risk Rating/Pts
12-15	D+	1,939.40	35.06	D / 1.9	-15.55%	C+ / 6.6
2014	C-	1,939.40	43.16	C- / 3.4	-1.71%	B- / 7.6
2013	D	1,743.90	46.09	D / 2.0	-5.87%	C+ / 6.5
2012	C	1,191.60	49.44	C / 5.5	21.30%	C+ / 6.6
2011	C+	739.40	41.34	C+ / 6.5	-19.79%	C+ / 6.9
2010	B	929.70	54.50	B+ / 8.4	30.88%	C / 4.9

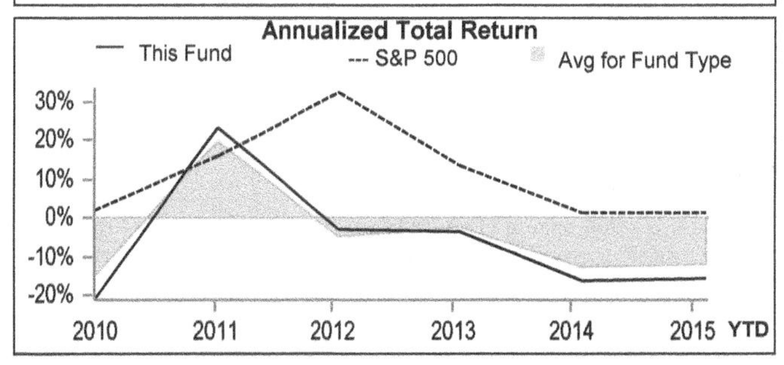

*WisdomTree Europe Hedged Equity (HEDJ) B Good

Fund Family: WisdomTree Asset Management Inc
Fund Type: Foreign
Inception Date: December 31, 2009

Major Rating Factors: Strong performance is the major factor driving the B (Good) TheStreet.com Investment Rating for *WisdomTree Europe Hedged Equity. The fund currently has a performance rating of B- (Good) based on an annualized return of 9.47% over the last three years and a total return of 5.05% year to date 2015. Factored into the performance evaluation is an expense ratio of 0.59% (very low).

The fund's risk rating is currently B- (Good). It carries a beta of 0.90, meaning that its performance tracks fairly well with that of the overall stock market. Volatility, as measured by both the semi-deviation and a drawdown factor, is considered low. As of December 31, 2015, *WisdomTree Europe Hedged Equity traded at a discount of .81% below its net asset value, which is better than its one-year historical average premium of .13%.

Karen Q. Wong has been running the fund for 7 years and currently receives a manager quality ranking of 89 (0=worst, 99=best). If you desire only a moderate level of risk and strong performance, then this fund is an excellent option.

Data Date	Investment Rating	Net Assets ($Mil)	Price	Performance Rating/Pts	Total Return Y-T-D	Risk Rating/Pts
12-15	B	2,932.60	53.81	B- / 7.5	5.05%	B- / 7.5
2014	B	2,932.60	55.62	C+ / 6.5	6.53%	B / 8.5
2013	B-	659.30	56.11	C+ / 6.6	16.57%	B / 8.2
2012	C	35.10	47.67	C- / 4.0	20.60%	B / 8.2
2011	D+	18.40	41.20	D- / 1.3	-8.83%	B / 8.2
2010	A-	21.00	46.85	B- / 7.1	3.53%	B- / 7.8

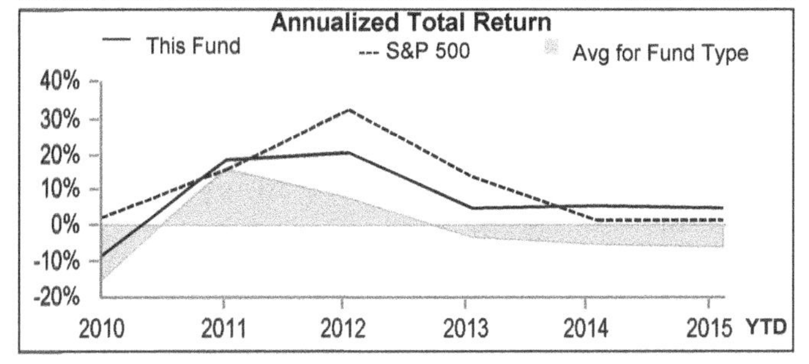

*WisdomTree Europe Quality Div Gr (EUDG) C+ Fair

Fund Family: WisdomTree Asset Management Inc
Fund Type: Foreign
Inception Date: May 7, 2014

Major Rating Factors: Middle of the road best describes *WisdomTree Europe Quality Div Gr whose TheStreet.com Investment Rating is currently a C+ (Fair). The fund currently has a performance rating of C+ (Fair) based on an annualized return of 0.00% over the last three years and a total return of 4.19% year to date 2015. Factored into the performance evaluation is an expense ratio of 0.58% (very low).

The fund's risk rating is currently B (Good). It carries a beta of 0.00, meaning the fund's expected move will be 0.0% for every 10% move in the market. Volatility, as measured by both the semi-deviation and a drawdown factor, is considered low. As of December 31, 2015, *WisdomTree Europe Quality Div Gr traded at a discount of .13% below its net asset value, which is better than its one-year historical average premium of .35%.

Karen Q. Wong has been running the fund for 2 years and currently receives a manager quality ranking of 86 (0=worst, 99=best). If you desire an average level of risk, then this fund may be an option.

Data Date	Investment Rating	Net Assets ($Mil)	Price	Performance Rating/Pts	Total Return Y-T-D	Risk Rating/Pts
12-15	C+	14.00	22.50	C+ / 5.8	4.19%	B / 8.1

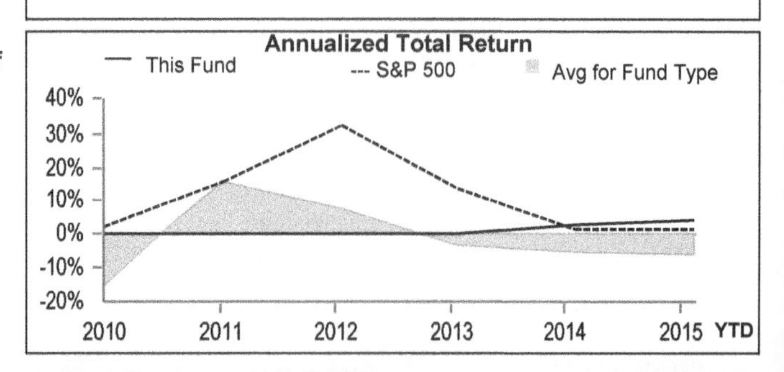

*WisdomTree Europe Small Cap Div (DFE) A+ Excellent

Fund Family: WisdomTree Asset Management Inc
Fund Type: Foreign
Inception Date: June 16, 2006

Major Rating Factors:
Strong performance is the major factor driving the A+ (Excellent) TheStreet.com Investment Rating for *WisdomTree Europe Small Cap Div. The fund currently has a performance rating of B+ (Good) based on an annualized return of 13.77% over the last three years and a total return of 11.27% year to date 2015. Factored into the performance evaluation is an expense ratio of 0.59% (very low).

The fund's risk rating is currently B (Good). It carries a beta of 0.92, meaning that its performance tracks fairly well with that of the overall stock market. Volatility, as measured by both the semi-deviation and a drawdown factor, is considered low. As of December 31, 2015, *WisdomTree Europe Small Cap Div traded at a discount of .52% below its net asset value, which is better than its one-year historical average premium of .12%.

Karen Q. Wong has been running the fund for 8 years and currently receives a manager quality ranking of 94 (0=worst, 99=best). If you desire only a moderate level of risk and strong performance, then this fund is an excellent option.

Data Date	Investment Rating	Net Assets ($Mil)	Price	Performance Rating/Pts	Total Return Y-T-D	Risk Rating/Pts
12-15	A+	1,009.10	56.00	B+ / 8.9	11.27%	B / 8.1
2014	B	1,009.10	51.47	B- / 7.2	-7.70%	B- / 7.8
2013	B	642.40	57.86	A- / 9.2	42.74%	C+ / 6.7
2012	C+	34.10	41.08	B / 7.7	34.63%	C+ / 6.5
2011	D+	21.20	32.65	C- / 3.4	-17.42%	C+ / 6.8
2010	D	29.80	42.55	C- / 3.4	19.92%	C- / 4.1

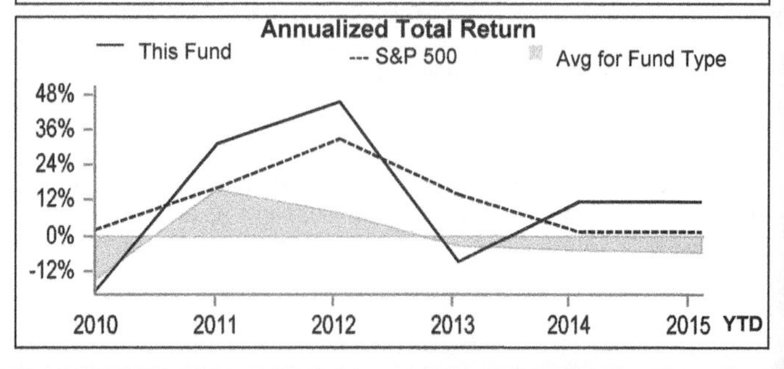

*WisdomTree Germany Hedged Equity (DXGE) B- Good

Fund Family: WisdomTree Asset Management Inc
Fund Type: Foreign
Inception Date: October 17, 2013

Major Rating Factors: *WisdomTree Germany Hedged Equity receives a TheStreet.com Investment Rating of B- (Good). The fund currently has a performance rating of C+ (Fair) based on an annualized return of 0.00% over the last three years and a total return of 6.87% year to date 2015. Factored into the performance evaluation is an expense ratio of 0.49% (very low).

The fund's risk rating is currently B- (Good). It carries a beta of 0.00, meaning the fund's expected move will be 0.0% for every 10% move in the market. Volatility, as measured by both the semi-deviation and a drawdown factor, is considered low. As of December 31, 2015, *WisdomTree Germany Hedged Equity traded at a discount of 1.52% below its net asset value, which is better than its one-year historical average premium of .09%.

Karen Q. Wong has been running the fund for 3 years and currently receives a manager quality ranking of 93 (0=worst, 99=best). If you desire an average level of risk, then this fund may be an option.

Data Date	Investment Rating	Net Assets ($Mil)	Price	Performance Rating/Pts	Total Return Y-T-D	Risk Rating/Pts
12-15	B-	14.50	26.62	C+ / 6.6	6.87%	B- / 7.5
2014	D	14.50	26.12	C- / 4.0	5.03%	C- / 4.1

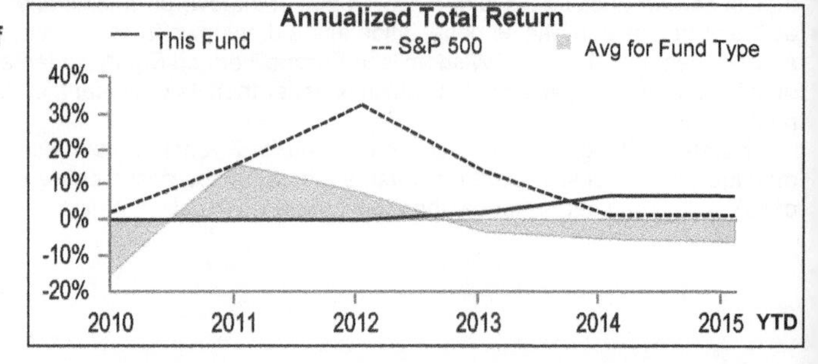

*WisdomTree Global ex-US Qual Div (DNL) C- Fair

Fund Family: WisdomTree Asset Management Inc
Fund Type: Global
Inception Date: June 16, 2006

Major Rating Factors: Middle of the road best describes *WisdomTree Global ex-US Qual Div whose TheStreet.com Investment Rating is currently a C- (Fair). The fund currently has a performance rating of C- (Fair) based on an annualized return of -3.19% over the last three years and a total return of -5.70% year to date 2015. Factored into the performance evaluation is an expense ratio of 0.59% (very low).

The fund's risk rating is currently B (Good). It carries a beta of 0.85, meaning the fund's expected move will be 8.5% for every 10% move in the market. Volatility, as measured by both the semi-deviation and a drawdown factor, is considered low. As of December 31, 2015, *WisdomTree Global ex-US Qual Div traded at a discount of .07% below its net asset value, which is better than its one-year historical average discount of .03%.

Karen Q. Wong has been running the fund for 8 years and currently receives a manager quality ranking of 22 (0=worst, 99=best). If you desire an average level of risk, then this fund may be an option.

Data Date	Investment Rating	Net Assets ($Mil)	Price	Performance Rating/Pts	Total Return Y-T-D	Risk Rating/Pts
12-15	C-	65.80	45.27	C- / 3.0	-5.70%	B / 8.0
2014	C-	65.80	49.62	C- / 3.7	1.81%	C+ / 6.7
2013	D+	61.00	50.81	D+ / 2.7	-4.13%	B- / 7.3
2012	D+	67.60	52.94	C- / 3.3	15.71%	C+ / 6.7
2011	D+	55.50	46.37	D+ / 2.8	-9.50%	B- / 7.4
2010	C+	37.80	54.19	C+ / 6.5	14.05%	C+ / 6.6

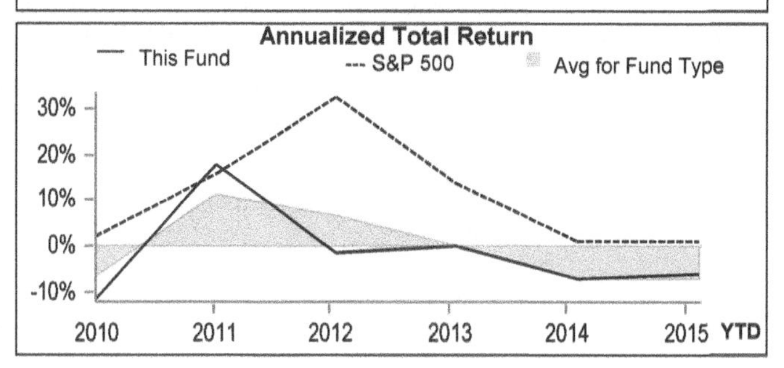

*WisdomTree Global ex-US Real Est (DRW) C- Fair

Fund Family: WisdomTree Asset Management Inc
Fund Type: Foreign
Inception Date: June 5, 2007

Major Rating Factors: Middle of the road best describes *WisdomTree Global ex-US Real Est whose TheStreet.com Investment Rating is currently a C- (Fair). The fund currently has a performance rating of C- (Fair) based on an annualized return of -0.14% over the last three years and a total return of -2.80% year to date 2015. Factored into the performance evaluation is an expense ratio of 0.59% (very low).

The fund's risk rating is currently B- (Good). It carries a beta of 0.88, meaning the fund's expected move will be 8.8% for every 10% move in the market. Volatility, as measured by both the semi-deviation and a drawdown factor, is considered low. As of December 31, 2015, *WisdomTree Global ex-US Real Est traded at a discount of .87% below its net asset value, which is better than its one-year historical average discount of .21%.

Karen Q. Wong has been running the fund for 8 years and currently receives a manager quality ranking of 34 (0=worst, 99=best). If you desire an average level of risk, then this fund may be an option.

Data Date	Investment Rating	Net Assets ($Mil)	Price	Performance Rating/Pts	Total Return Y-T-D	Risk Rating/Pts
12-15	C-	118.10	26.12	C- / 3.9	-2.80%	B- / 7.1
2014	C	118.10	28.15	C+ / 6.2	9.48%	C+ / 6.6
2013	D+	130.20	27.52	C- / 3.5	-6.22%	C+ / 6.0
2012	C+	108.00	29.97	B+ / 8.4	36.67%	C / 5.3
2011	D	102.80	23.21	C- / 3.9	-13.51%	C / 5.3
2010	D	118.60	28.63	D+ / 2.8	24.49%	C- / 3.9

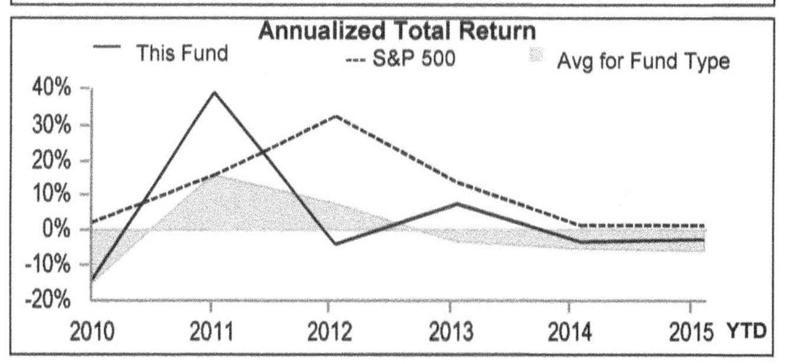

*WisdomTree Global ex-US Utilitie (DBU) C- Fair

Fund Family: WisdomTree Asset Management Inc
Fund Type: Utilities
Inception Date: October 13, 2006

Major Rating Factors:
Disappointing performance is the major factor driving the C- (Fair) TheStreet.com Investment Rating for *WisdomTree Global ex-US Utilitie. The fund currently has a performance rating of D+ (Weak) based on an annualized return of -2.28% over the last three years and a total return of -12.32% year to date 2015. Factored into the performance evaluation is an expense ratio of 0.59% (very low).

The fund's risk rating is currently B- (Good). It carries a beta of 0.40, meaning the fund's expected move will be 4.0% for every 10% move in the market. Volatility, as measured by both the semi-deviation and a drawdown factor, is considered low. As of December 31, 2015, *WisdomTree Global ex-US Utilitie traded at a discount of 1.10% below its net asset value, which is better than its one-year historical average discount of .20%.

Karen Q. Wong has been running the fund for 8 years and currently receives a manager quality ranking of 24 (0=worst, 99=best). This fund offers only a moderate level of risk but investors looking for strong performance are still waiting.

Data Date	Investment Rating	Net Assets ($Mil)	Price	Performance Rating/Pts	Total Return Y-T-D	Risk Rating/Pts
12-15	C-	24.00	15.25	D+ / 2.9	-12.32%	B- / 7.8
2014	C-	24.00	18.11	C- / 3.9	4.89%	B- / 7.0
2013	C-	29.30	18.30	C- / 3.5	2.31%	B- / 7.8
2012	D	37.10	18.40	D- / 1.5	8.64%	B- / 7.5
2011	D	30.30	17.78	D / 1.7	-5.09%	B- / 7.4
2010	D-	36.30	20.14	E+ / 0.8	-4.91%	C / 5.1

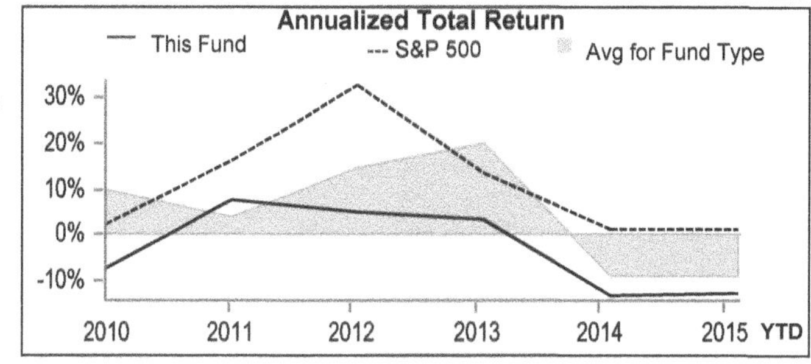

*WisdomTree Global High Dividend (DEW) C Fair

Fund Family: WisdomTree Asset Management Inc
Fund Type: Global
Inception Date: June 16, 2006

Major Rating Factors: Middle of the road best describes *WisdomTree Global High Dividend whose TheStreet.com Investment Rating is currently a C (Fair). The fund currently has a performance rating of C- (Fair) based on an annualized return of 0.63% over the last three years and a total return of -6.28% year to date 2015. Factored into the performance evaluation is an expense ratio of 0.59% (very low).

The fund's risk rating is currently B- (Good). It carries a beta of 0.96, meaning that its performance tracks fairly well with that of the overall stock market. Volatility, as measured by both the semi-deviation and a drawdown factor, is considered low. As of December 31, 2015, *WisdomTree Global High Dividend traded at a discount of .10% below its net asset value, which is better than its one-year historical average discount of .06%.

Karen Q. Wong has been running the fund for 8 years and currently receives a manager quality ranking of 38 (0=worst, 99=best). If you desire an average level of risk, then this fund may be an option.

Data Date	Investment Rating	Net Assets ($Mil)	Price	Performance Rating/Pts	Total Return Y-T-D	Risk Rating/Pts
12-15	C	116.10	39.37	C- / 4.0	-6.28%	B- / 7.8
2014	C	116.10	43.94	C / 4.5	-1.56%	B- / 7.8
2013	C+	120.60	47.85	C+ / 6.2	10.94%	B / 8.0
2012	C-	98.60	43.27	C- / 4.1	18.19%	B- / 7.8
2011	C-	70.20	39.31	C- / 3.9	-1.57%	B- / 7.7
2010	D	69.30	42.15	D- / 1.3	5.82%	C / 5.3

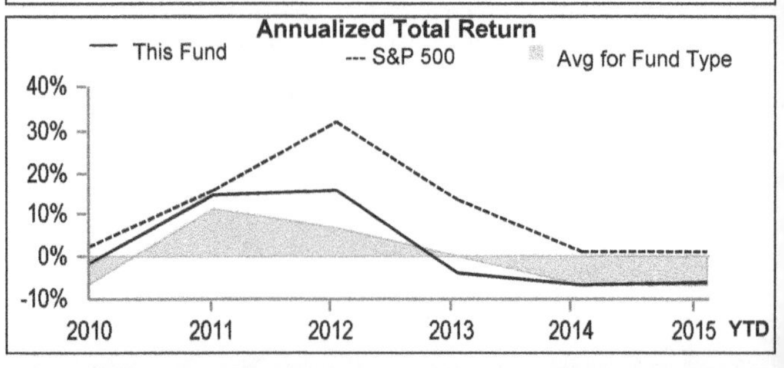

*WisdomTree Global Natural Resour (GNAT) D- Weak

Fund Family: WisdomTree Asset Management Inc
Fund Type: Energy/Natural Resources
Inception Date: October 13, 2006

Major Rating Factors:
Very poor performance is the major factor driving the D- (Weak) TheStreet.com Investment Rating for *WisdomTree Global Natural Resour. The fund currently has a performance rating of E+ (Very Weak) based on an annualized return of -20.69% over the last three years and a total return of -30.01% year to date 2015. Factored into the performance evaluation is an expense ratio of 0.59% (very low).

The fund's risk rating is currently C (Fair). It carries a beta of 0.90, meaning that its performance tracks fairly well with that of the overall stock market. Volatility, as measured by both the semi-deviation and a drawdown factor, is considered average. As of December 31, 2015, *WisdomTree Global Natural Resour traded at a discount of .27% below its net asset value, which is better than its one-year historical average premium of .10%.

Karen Q. Wong has been running the fund for 8 years and currently receives a manager quality ranking of 8 (0=worst, 99=best). This fund offers an average level of risk but investors looking for strong performance will be frustrated.

Data Date	Investment Rating	Net Assets ($Mil)	Price	Performance Rating/Pts	Total Return Y-T-D	Risk Rating/Pts
12-15	D-	21.30	11.01	E+ / 0.7	-30.01%	C / 5.4
2014	D	21.30	16.46	D- / 1.1	-18.88%	C+ / 6.4
2013	D	23.70	21.51	D / 1.8	-11.91%	C+ / 6.5
2012	D	27.90	24.54	D / 2.1	5.89%	C+ / 6.8
2011	C-	30.60	23.50	C- / 3.6	-5.88%	C+ / 6.9
2010	D	52.20	26.65	C- / 3.0	7.25%	C / 4.7

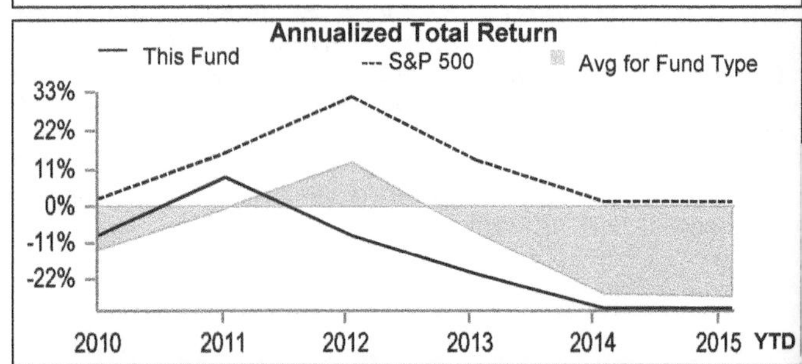

*WisdomTree Global Real Return Fu (RRF) C- Fair

Fund Family: WisdomTree Asset Management Inc
Fund Type: Growth and Income
Inception Date: July 14, 2011

Major Rating Factors: Middle of the road best describes *WisdomTree Global Real Return Fu whose TheStreet.com Investment Rating is currently a C- (Fair). The fund currently has a performance rating of C- (Fair) based on an annualized return of -3.41% over the last three years and a total return of -3.07% year to date 2015. Factored into the performance evaluation is an expense ratio of 0.60% (very low).

The fund's risk rating is currently C+ (Fair). It carries a beta of 0.33, meaning the fund's expected move will be 3.3% for every 10% move in the market. Volatility, as measured by both the semi-deviation and a drawdown factor, is considered low. As of December 31, 2015, *WisdomTree Global Real Return Fu traded at a premium of .76% above its net asset value, which is worse than its one-year historical average discount of .90%.

Christopher N. Orndorff has been running the fund for 3 years and currently receives a manager quality ranking of 19 (0=worst, 99=best). If you desire an average level of risk, then this fund may be an option.

Data Date	Investment Rating	Net Assets ($Mil)	Price	Performance Rating/Pts	Total Return Y-T-D	Risk Rating/Pts
12-15	C-	4.50	38.48	C- / 3.2	-3.07%	C+ / 6.4
2014	C-	4.50	41.03	D / 2.2	-4.44%	B / 8.3
2013	C-	4.60	44.63	C- / 3.0	-2.34%	B / 8.4
2012	D+	4.90	47.79	D / 1.8	1.78%	B / 8.8

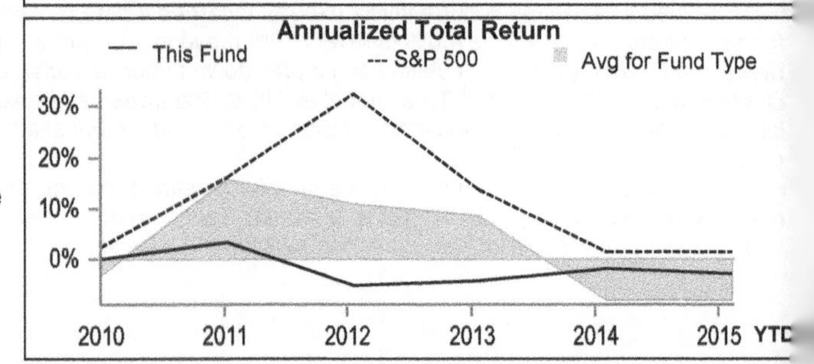

*WisdomTree High Dividend (DHS) B+ Good

Fund Family: WisdomTree Asset Management Inc
Fund Type: Growth and Income
Inception Date: June 16, 2006

Major Rating Factors: Strong performance is the major factor driving the B+ (Good) TheStreet.com Investment Rating for *WisdomTree High Dividend. The fund currently has a performance rating of B (Good) based on an annualized return of 11.73% over the last three years and a total return of -0.84% year to date 2015. Factored into the performance evaluation is an expense ratio of 0.39% (very low).

The fund's risk rating is currently B- (Good). It carries a beta of 0.83, meaning the fund's expected move will be 8.3% for every 10% move in the market. Volatility, as measured by both the semi-deviation and a drawdown factor, is considered low. As of December 31, 2015, *WisdomTree High Dividend traded at a premium of .07% above its net asset value, which is worse than its one-year historical average premium of .01%.

Karen Q. Wong has been running the fund for 8 years and currently receives a manager quality ranking of 71 (0=worst, 99=best). If you desire only a moderate level of risk and strong performance, then this fund is an excellent option.

Data Date	Investment Rating	Net Assets ($Mil)	Price	Performance Rating/Pts	Total Return Y-T-D	Risk Rating/Pts
12-15	B+	911.80	59.09	B / 8.2	-0.84%	B- / 7.6
2014	A+	911.80	61.58	B / 7.6	16.19%	B+ / 9.4
2013	A	760.40	55.12	B / 7.8	20.83%	B+ / 9.2
2012	B	535.90	45.80	C+ / 6.2	14.10%	B+ / 9.0
2011	C+	366.20	42.92	C+ / 6.8	14.49%	B- / 7.4
2010	D	169.40	38.91	D+ / 2.6	17.63%	C / 5.1

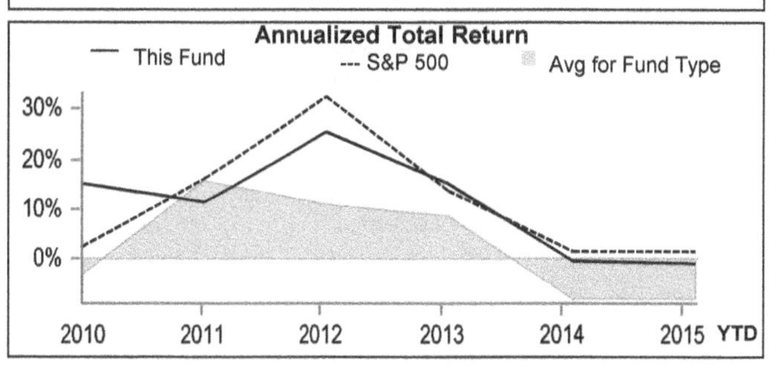

*WisdomTree India Earnings Fund (EPI) C- Fair

Fund Family: WisdomTree Asset Management Inc
Fund Type: Foreign
Inception Date: February 22, 2008

Major Rating Factors: Middle of the road best describes *WisdomTree India Earnings Fund whose TheStreet.com Investment Rating is currently a C- (Fair). The fund currently has a performance rating of C- (Fair) based on an annualized return of 1.11% over the last three years and a total return of -10.02% year to date 2015. Factored into the performance evaluation is an expense ratio of 0.84% (very low).

The fund's risk rating is currently C+ (Fair). It carries a beta of 0.88, meaning the fund's expected move will be 8.8% for every 10% move in the market. Volatility, as measured by both the semi-deviation and a drawdown factor, is considered low. As of December 31, 2015, *WisdomTree India Earnings Fund traded at a discount of 1.05% below its net asset value, which is better than its one-year historical average premium of .06%.

Karen Q. Wong has been running the fund for 8 years and currently receives a manager quality ranking of 44 (0=worst, 99=best). If you desire an average level of risk, then this fund may be an option.

Data Date	Investment Rating	Net Assets ($Mil)	Price	Performance Rating/Pts	Total Return Y-T-D	Risk Rating/Pts
12-15	C-	1,992.20	19.86	C- / 3.8	-10.02%	C+ / 6.5
2014	C	1,992.20	22.05	C+ / 6.8	32.07%	C+ / 6.2
2013	D-	1,022.00	17.44	D- / 1.0	-14.11%	C / 5.2
2012	D-	1,232.30	19.37	D- / 1.3	15.27%	C / 5.5
2011	D	714.70	15.60	C- / 3.0	-34.62%	C+ / 5.8
2010	B-	1,662.90	26.39	B+ / 8.7	20.34%	C- / 3.9

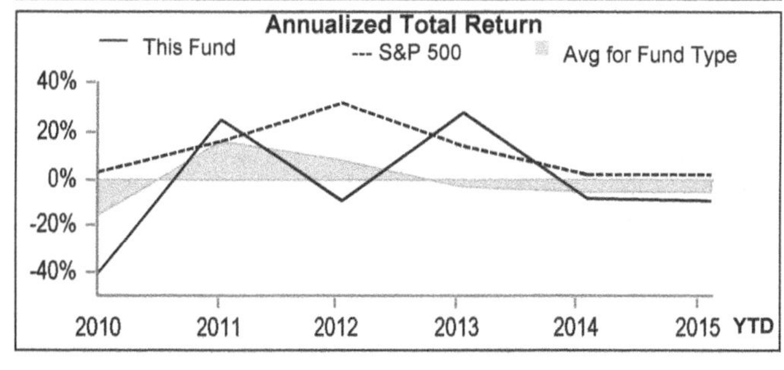

*WisdomTree Indian Rupee Strategy (ICN) C Fair

Fund Family: WisdomTree Asset Management Inc
Fund Type: Foreign
Inception Date: May 14, 2008

Major Rating Factors: Middle of the road best describes *WisdomTree Indian Rupee Strategy whose TheStreet.com Investment Rating is currently a C (Fair). The fund currently has a performance rating of C (Fair) based on an annualized return of 0.48% over the last three years and a total return of 1.28% year to date 2015. Factored into the performance evaluation is an expense ratio of 0.45% (very low).

The fund's risk rating is currently B (Good). It carries a beta of 0.31, meaning the fund's expected move will be 3.1% for every 10% move in the market. Volatility, as measured by both the semi-deviation and a drawdown factor, is considered low. As of December 31, 2015, *WisdomTree Indian Rupee Strategy traded at a discount of .33% below its net asset value, which is better than its one-year historical average discount of .32%.

Paul Benson has been running the fund for 1 year and currently receives a manager quality ranking of 52 (0=worst, 99=best). If you desire an average level of risk, then this fund may be an option.

Data Date	Investment Rating	Net Assets ($Mil)	Price	Performance Rating/Pts	Total Return Y-T-D	Risk Rating/Pts
12-15	C	25.30	20.97	C / 4.4	1.28%	B / 8.3
2014	C-	25.30	20.74	D+ / 2.9	4.67%	B / 8.0
2013	D	30.00	19.94	D / 1.8	-4.16%	C+ / 6.5
2012	D	14.70	21.09	D- / 1.3	1.30%	B- / 7.0
2011	D	16.10	20.12	D / 1.8	-9.72%	B- / 7.4
2010	A-	21.20	26.58	B- / 7.0	7.89%	B / 8.0

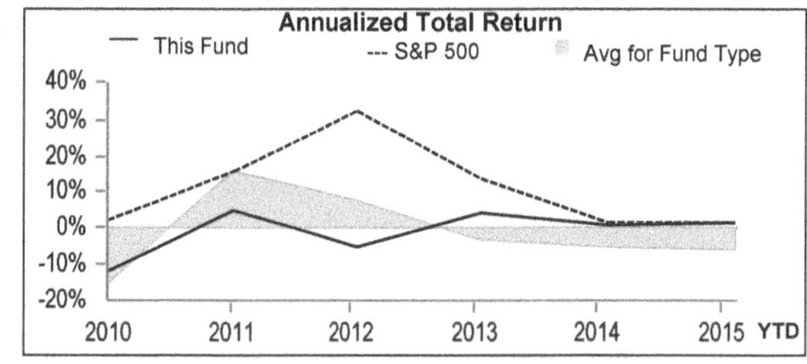

*WisdomTree International Equity (DWM) C+ Fair

Fund Family: WisdomTree Asset Management Inc
Fund Type: Foreign
Inception Date: June 16, 2006

Major Rating Factors: Middle of the road best describes *WisdomTree International Equity whose TheStreet.com Investment Rating is currently a C+ (Fair). The fund currently has a performance rating of C (Fair) based on an annualized return of 3.68% over the last three years and a total return of -2.73% year to date 2015. Factored into the performance evaluation is an expense ratio of 0.49% (very low).

The fund's risk rating is currently B- (Good). It carries a beta of 1.02, meaning that its performance tracks fairly well with that of the overall stock market. Volatility, as measured by both the semi-deviation and a drawdown factor, is considered low. As of December 31, 2015, *WisdomTree International Equity traded at a discount of .77% below its net asset value, which is better than its one-year historical average premium of .20%.

Richard A. Brown has been running the fund for 8 years and currently receives a manager quality ranking of 57 (0=worst, 99=best). If you desire an average level of risk, then this fund may be an option.

Data Date	Investment Rating	Net Assets ($Mil)	Price	Performance Rating/Pts	Total Return Y-T-D	Risk Rating/Pts
12-15	C+	578.80	46.59	C / 5.3	-2.73%	B- / 7.8
2014	C-	578.80	49.59	C / 5.2	-3.35%	C+ / 6.4
2013	C+	557.90	54.46	B- / 7.0	18.76%	B- / 7.3
2012	C-	418.20	46.47	C- / 4.0	21.28%	B- / 7.1
2011	D+	326.30	40.92	D+ / 2.7	-8.34%	B- / 7.4
2010	D-	426.80	47.37	D- / 1.4	5.19%	C / 4.8

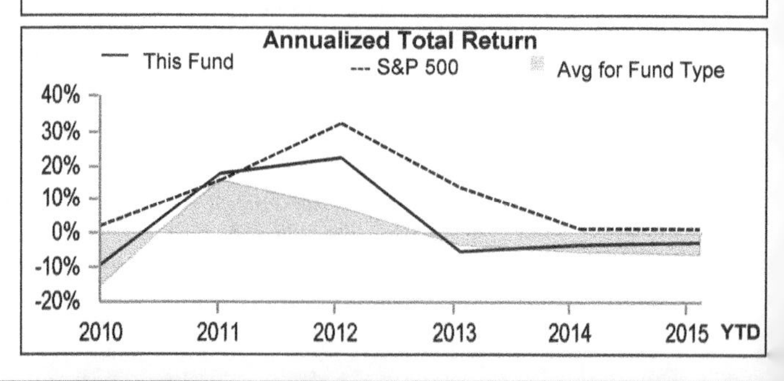

*WisdomTree International Hi Div (DTH) C Fair

Fund Family: WisdomTree Asset Management Inc
Fund Type: Foreign
Inception Date: June 16, 2006

Major Rating Factors: Middle of the road best describes *WisdomTree International Hi Div whose TheStreet.com Investment Rating is currently a C (Fair). The fund currently has a performance rating of C (Fair) based on an annualized return of 2.04% over the last three years and a total return of -6.78% year to date 2015. Factored into the performance evaluation is an expense ratio of 0.59% (very low).

The fund's risk rating is currently B- (Good). It carries a beta of 1.06, meaning that its performance tracks fairly well with that of the overall stock market. Volatility, as measured by both the semi-deviation and a drawdown factor, is considered low. As of December 31, 2015, *WisdomTree International Hi Div traded at a discount of .87% below its net asset value, which is better than its one-year historical average premium of .10%.

Karen Q. Wong has been running the fund for 8 years and currently receives a manager quality ranking of 42 (0=worst, 99=best). If you desire an average level of risk, then this fund may be an option.

Data Date	Investment Rating	Net Assets ($Mil)	Price	Performance Rating/Pts	Total Return Y-T-D	Risk Rating/Pts
12-15	C	326.70	37.74	C / 4.3	-6.78%	B- / 7.4
2014	C-	326.70	42.31	C / 4.8	-3.96%	C+ / 6.4
2013	C+	284.40	47.43	B- / 7.1	19.17%	B- / 7.1
2012	D+	183.50	40.43	C- / 3.8	20.80%	C+ / 6.9
2011	D+	145.60	36.56	D+ / 2.8	-4.91%	B- / 7.3
2010	D-	120.50	41.10	D- / 1.0	-0.99%	C / 4.5

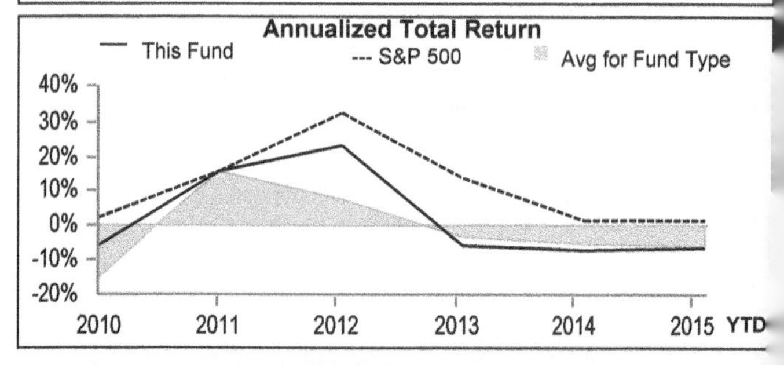

*WisdomTree Intl Div Ex-Financial (DOO) C- Fair

Fund Family: WisdomTree Asset Management Inc
Fund Type: Foreign
Inception Date: June 16, 2006

Major Rating Factors: Middle of the road best describes *WisdomTree Intl Div Ex-Financial whose TheStreet.com Investment Rating is currently a C- (Fair). The fund currently has a performance rating of C- (Fair) based on an annualized return of 0.85% over the last three years and a total return of -7.71% year to date 2015. Factored into the performance evaluation is an expense ratio of 0.59% (very low).

The fund's risk rating is currently B- (Good). It carries a beta of 1.02, meaning that its performance tracks fairly well with that of the overall stock market. Volatility, as measured by both the semi-deviation and a drawdown factor, is considered low. As of December 31, 2015, *WisdomTree Intl Div Ex-Financial traded at a discount of .89% below its net asset value, which is better than its one-year historical average discount of .03%.

Karen Q. Wong has been running the fund for 8 years and currently receives a manager quality ranking of 35 (0=worst, 99=best). If you desire an average level of risk, then this fund may be an option.

Data Date	Investment Rating	Net Assets ($Mil)	Price	Performance Rating/Pts	Total Return Y-T-D	Risk Rating/Pts
12-15	C-	393.40	38.04	C- / 3.8	-7.71%	B- / 7.4
2014	C	393.40	43.01	C- / 4.1	-3.45%	B- / 7.9
2013	C+	348.60	47.62	C+ / 6.4	15.59%	B- / 7.3
2012	D+	347.00	41.90	D+ / 2.9	14.99%	B- / 7.1
2011	C-	264.50	39.58	C- / 3.5	-4.36%	B- / 7.5
2010	D-	171.80	44.16	D- / 1.3	5.70%	C- / 4.2

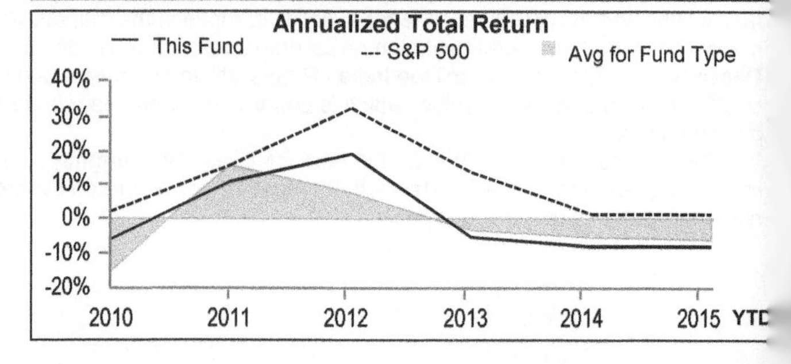

* Denotes ETF Fund

*WisdomTree Intl Hdgd Qual Div Gr (IHDG) A Excellent

Fund Family: WisdomTree Asset Management Inc
Fund Type: Foreign
Inception Date: May 7, 2014

Data Date	Investment Rating	Net Assets ($Mil)	Price	Performance Rating/Pts	Total Return Y-T-D	Risk Rating/Pts
12-15	A	7.50	26.43	B+ / 8.4	11.70%	B / 8.4

Major Rating Factors:
Strong performance is the major factor driving the A (Excellent) TheStreet.com Investment Rating for *WisdomTree Intl Hdgd Qual Div Gr. The fund currently has a performance rating of B+ (Good) based on an annualized return of 0.00% over the last three years and a total return of 11.70% year to date 2015. Factored into the performance evaluation is an expense ratio of 0.58% (very low).

The fund's risk rating is currently B (Good). It carries a beta of 0.00, meaning the fund's expected move will be 0.0% for every 10% move in the market. Volatility, as measured by both the semi-deviation and a drawdown factor, is considered low. As of December 31, 2015, *WisdomTree Intl Hdgd Qual Div Gr traded at a discount of .30% below its net asset value, which is better than its one-year historical average premium of .36%.

Luciano Siracusano, III currently receives a manager quality ranking of 96 (0=worst, 99=best). If you desire only a moderate level of risk and strong performance, then this fund is an excellent option.

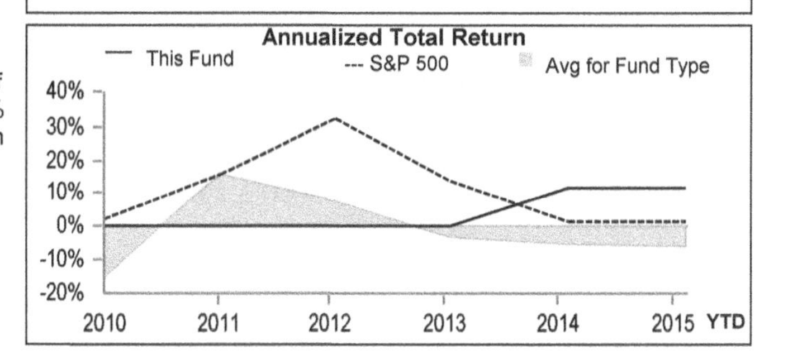

*WisdomTree Intl LargeCap Dividen (DOL) C Fair

Fund Family: WisdomTree Asset Management Inc
Fund Type: Foreign
Inception Date: June 16, 2006

Data Date	Investment Rating	Net Assets ($Mil)	Price	Performance Rating/Pts	Total Return Y-T-D	Risk Rating/Pts
12-15	C	339.40	43.16	C / 4.7	-4.14%	B- / 7.7
2014	C	339.40	46.73	C / 4.6	-4.13%	B / 8.1
2013	C+	294.00	51.97	C+ / 6.6	17.11%	B- / 7.3
2012	C-	199.20	44.93	C- / 3.6	19.66%	B- / 7.1
2011	D+	127.70	40.00	D+ / 2.6	-6.31%	B- / 7.3
2010	D-	149.30	45.49	D- / 1.2	1.87%	C / 4.8

Major Rating Factors: Middle of the road best describes *WisdomTree Intl LargeCap Dividen whose TheStreet.com Investment Rating is currently a C (Fair). The fund currently has a performance rating of C (Fair) based on an annualized return of 2.35% over the last three years and a total return of -4.14% year to date 2015. Factored into the performance evaluation is an expense ratio of 0.49% (very low).

The fund's risk rating is currently B- (Good). It carries a beta of 1.03, meaning that its performance tracks fairly well with that of the overall stock market. Volatility, as measured by both the semi-deviation and a drawdown factor, is considered low. As of December 31, 2015, *WisdomTree Intl LargeCap Dividen traded at a discount of .64% below its net asset value, which is better than its one-year historical average premium of .23%.

Karen Q. Wong has been running the fund for 8 years and currently receives a manager quality ranking of 45 (0=worst, 99=best). If you desire an average level of risk, then this fund may be an option.

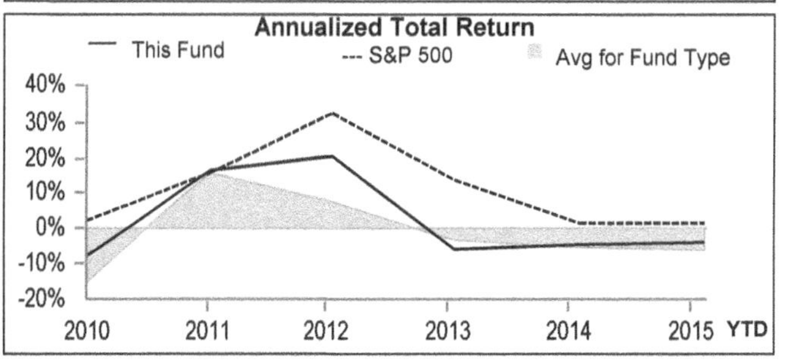

*WisdomTree Intl MidCap Dividend (DIM) B Good

Fund Family: WisdomTree Asset Management Inc
Fund Type: Foreign
Inception Date: June 16, 2006

Data Date	Investment Rating	Net Assets ($Mil)	Price	Performance Rating/Pts	Total Return Y-T-D	Risk Rating/Pts
12-15	B	144.80	55.50	C+ / 6.3	2.73%	B / 8.3
2014	C+	144.80	55.61	C+ / 5.6	-1.33%	B / 8.2
2013	C+	137.70	59.13	C+ / 6.8	18.28%	B- / 7.3
2012	C	104.60	50.29	C / 5.0	23.49%	B- / 7.1
2011	C-	112.60	43.05	C- / 3.0	-12.10%	B- / 7.4
2010	D	153.40	51.85	D+ / 2.7	11.31%	C / 4.7

Major Rating Factors: *WisdomTree Intl MidCap Dividend receives a TheStreet.com Investment Rating of B (Good). The fund currently has a performance rating of C+ (Fair) based on an annualized return of 6.16% over the last three years and a total return of 2.73% year to date 2015. Factored into the performance evaluation is an expense ratio of 0.59% (very low).

The fund's risk rating is currently B (Good). It carries a beta of 0.94, meaning that its performance tracks fairly well with that of the overall stock market. Volatility, as measured by both the semi-deviation and a drawdown factor, is considered low. As of December 31, 2015, *WisdomTree Intl MidCap Dividend traded at a discount of .63% below its net asset value, which is better than its one-year historical average premium of .23%.

Karen Q. Wong has been running the fund for 8 years and currently receives a manager quality ranking of 79 (0=worst, 99=best). If you desire an average level of risk, then this fund may be an option.

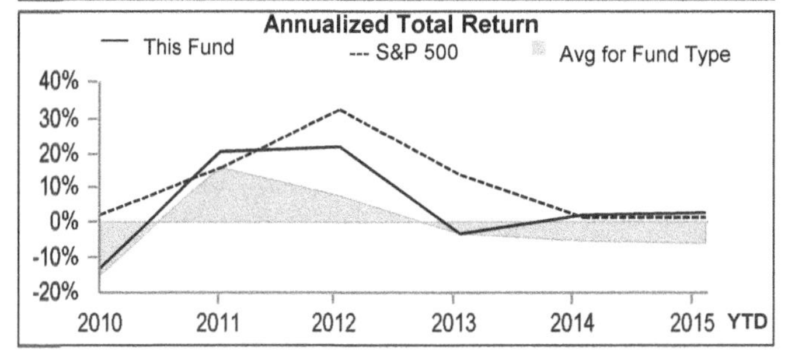

*WisdomTree Intl Small Cap Divide (DLS) B Good

Fund Family: WisdomTree Asset Management Inc
Fund Type: Foreign
Inception Date: June 16, 2006

Major Rating Factors: *WisdomTree Intl Small Cap Divide receives a TheStreet.com Investment Rating of B (Good). The fund currently has a performance rating of C+ (Fair) based on an annualized return of 7.22% over the last three years and a total return of 7.26% year to date 2015. Factored into the performance evaluation is an expense ratio of 0.59% (very low).

The fund's risk rating is currently B (Good). It carries a beta of 0.87, meaning the fund's expected move will be 8.7% for every 10% move in the market. Volatility, as measured by both the semi-deviation and a drawdown factor, is considered low. As of December 31, 2015, *WisdomTree Intl Small Cap Divide traded at a discount of .50% below its net asset value, which is better than its one-year historical average premium of .14%.

Karen Q. Wong has been running the fund for 8 years and currently receives a manager quality ranking of 83 (0=worst, 99=best). If you desire an average level of risk, then this fund may be an option.

Data Date	Investment Rating	Net Assets ($Mil)	Price	Performance Rating/Pts	Total Return Y-T-D	Risk Rating/Pts
12-15	B	930.80	58.10	C+ / 6.9	7.26%	B / 8.2
2014	C+	930.80	55.52	C / 5.2	-8.13%	B / 8.1
2013	B	807.50	63.01	B / 7.6	24.83%	B- / 7.7
2012	C+	483.50	52.13	C+ / 6.8	26.39%	B- / 7.5
2011	C-	363.80	43.73	C- / 3.9	-10.03%	B- / 7.7
2010	D+	471.20	51.77	C- / 3.9	19.41%	C / 4.6

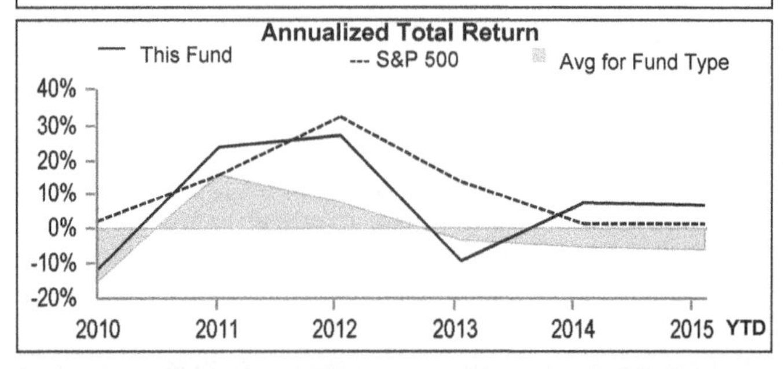

*WisdomTree Japan Hedged Cap Good (DXJC) C- Fair

Fund Family: WisdomTree Asset Management Inc
Fund Type: Foreign
Inception Date: April 8, 2014

Major Rating Factors: Middle of the road best describes *WisdomTree Japan Hedged Cap Good whose TheStreet.com Investment Rating is currently a C- (Fair). The fund currently has a performance rating of C- (Fair) based on an annualized return of 0.00% over the last three years and a total return of 0.34% year to date 2015. Factored into the performance evaluation is an expense ratio of 0.43% (very low).

The fund's risk rating is currently C+ (Fair). It carries a beta of 0.00, meaning the fund's expected move will be 0.0% for every 10% move in the market. Volatility, as measured by both the semi-deviation and a drawdown factor, is considered low. As of December 31, 2015, *WisdomTree Japan Hedged Cap Good traded at a discount of .76% below its net asset value, which is better than its one-year historical average premium of .01%.

Karen Q. Wong has been running the fund for 2 years and currently receives a manager quality ranking of 75 (0=worst, 99=best). If you desire an average level of risk, then this fund may be an option.

Data Date	Investment Rating	Net Assets ($Mil)	Price	Performance Rating/Pts	Total Return Y-T-D	Risk Rating/Pts
12-15	C-	2.80	24.70	C- / 4.2	0.34%	C+ / 6.8

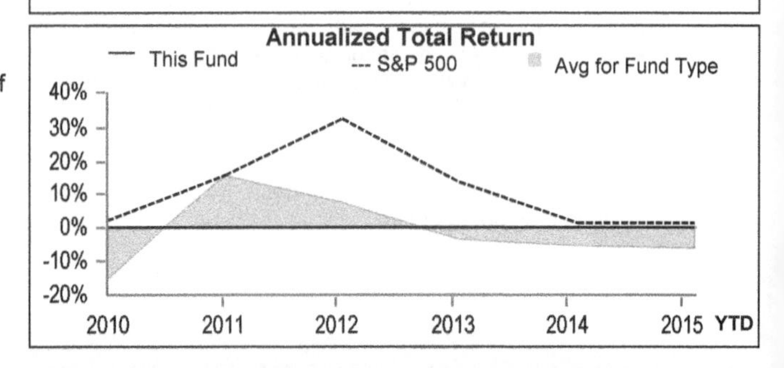

*WisdomTree Japan Hedged Equity (DXJ) A Excellent

Fund Family: WisdomTree Asset Management Inc
Fund Type: Foreign
Inception Date: June 16, 2006

Major Rating Factors:
Exceptional performance is the major factor driving the A (Excellent) TheStreet.com Investment Rating for *WisdomTree Japan Hedged Equity. The fund currently has a performance rating of A- (Excellent) based on an annualized return of 17.61% over the last three years and a total return of 6.83% year to date 2015. Factored into the performance evaluation is an expense ratio of 0.49% (very low).

The fund's risk rating is currently B- (Good). It carries a beta of 0.96, meaning that its performance tracks fairly well with that of the overall stock market. Volatility, as measured by both the semi-deviation and a drawdown factor, is considered low. As of December 31, 2015, *WisdomTree Japan Hedged Equity traded at a discount of 1.42% below its net asset value.

Karen Q. Wong has been running the fund for 8 years and currently receives a manager quality ranking of 96 (0=worst, 99=best). If you desire only a moderate level of risk and strong performance, then this fund is an excellent option.

Data Date	Investment Rating	Net Assets ($Mil)	Price	Performance Rating/Pts	Total Return Y-T-D	Risk Rating/Pts
12-15	A	10,863.40	50.08	A- / 9.2	6.83%	B- / 7.6
2014	A	10,863.40	49.23	B+ / 8.9	9.90%	B- / 7.7
2013	B	12,610.50	50.84	B / 7.8	37.46%	B- / 7.6
2012	D+	1,222.70	36.88	D+ / 2.6	23.92%	B- / 7.2
2011	D	399.20	31.34	D- / 1.4	-16.88%	B- / 7.4
2010	D	121.80	38.17	D- / 1.2	-1.78%	C+ / 5.8

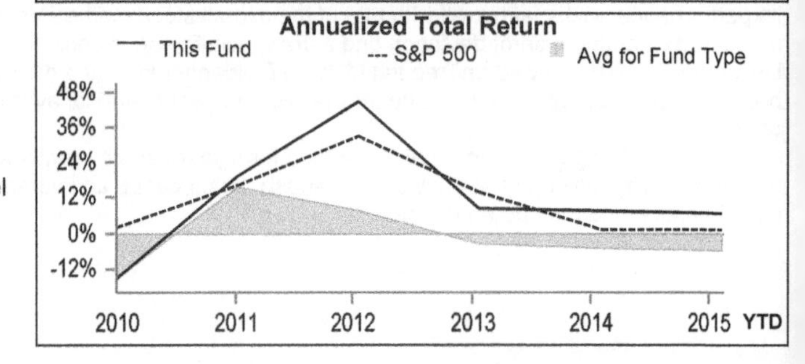

*WisdomTree Japan Hedged Financia (DXJF) C Fair

Fund Family: WisdomTree Asset Management Inc
Fund Type: Foreign
Inception Date: April 8, 2014

Major Rating Factors: Middle of the road best describes *WisdomTree Japan Hedged Financia whose TheStreet.com Investment Rating is currently a C (Fair). The fund currently has a performance rating of C (Fair) based on an annualized return of 0.00% over the last three years and a total return of 8.96% year to date 2015. Factored into the performance evaluation is an expense ratio of 0.43% (very low).

The fund's risk rating is currently B- (Good). It carries a beta of 0.00, meaning the fund's expected move will be 0.0% for every 10% move in the market. Volatility, as measured by both the semi-deviation and a drawdown factor, is considered low. As of December 31, 2015, *WisdomTree Japan Hedged Financia traded at a discount of 1.48% below its net asset value, which is better than its one-year historical average premium of .10%.

Karen Q. Wong has been running the fund for 2 years and currently receives a manager quality ranking of 95 (0=worst, 99=best). If you desire an average level of risk, then this fund may be an option.

Data Date	Investment Rating	Net Assets ($Mil)	Price	Performance Rating/Pts	Total Return Y-T-D	Risk Rating/Pts
12-15	C	7.90	26.01	C / 4.3	8.96%	B- / 7.3

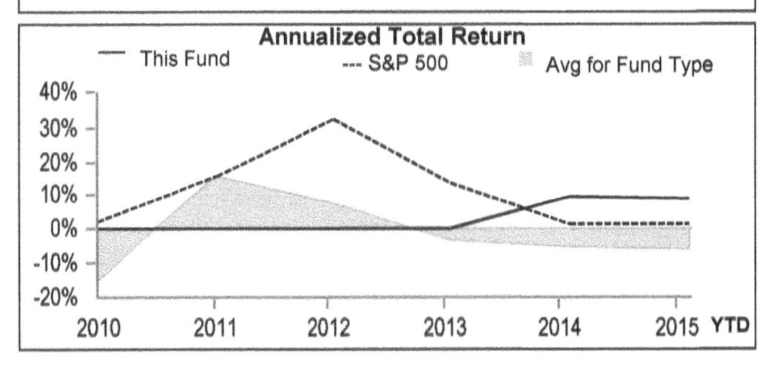

*WisdomTree Japan Hedged Health C (DXJH) A+ Excellent

Fund Family: WisdomTree Asset Management Inc
Fund Type: Foreign
Inception Date: April 8, 2014

Major Rating Factors:
Exceptional performance is the major factor driving the A+ (Excellent) TheStreet.com Investment Rating for *WisdomTree Japan Hedged Health C. The fund currently has a performance rating of A+ (Excellent) based on an annualized return of 0.00% over the last three years and a total return of 35.61% year to date 2015. Factored into the performance evaluation is an expense ratio of 0.43% (very low).

The fund's risk rating is currently B- (Good). It carries a beta of 0.00, meaning the fund's expected move will be 0.0% for every 10% move in the market. Volatility, as measured by both the semi-deviation and a drawdown factor, is considered low. As of December 31, 2015, *WisdomTree Japan Hedged Health C traded at a discount of 1.00% below its net asset value.

Luciano Siracusano, III currently receives a manager quality ranking of 99 (0=worst, 99=best). If you desire only a moderate level of risk and strong performance, then this fund is an excellent option.

Data Date	Investment Rating	Net Assets ($Mil)	Price	Performance Rating/Pts	Total Return Y-T-D	Risk Rating/Pts
12-15	A+	1.40	34.70	A+ / 9.9	35.61%	B- / 7.9

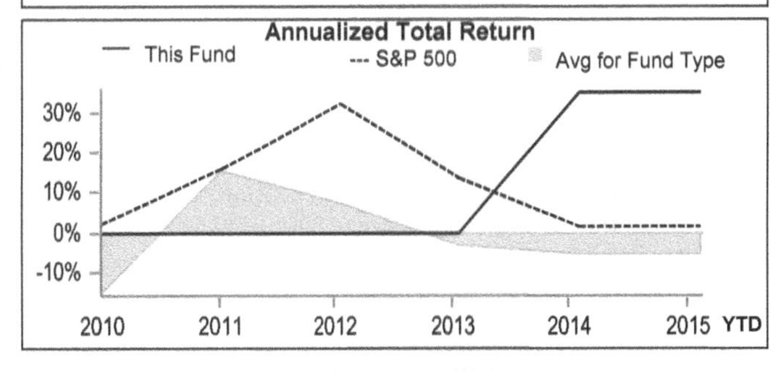

*WisdomTree Japan Hedged Real Est (DXJR) C+ Fair

Fund Family: WisdomTree Asset Management Inc
Fund Type: Foreign
Inception Date: April 8, 2014

Major Rating Factors: Middle of the road best describes *WisdomTree Japan Hedged Real Est whose TheStreet.com Investment Rating is currently a C+ (Fair). The fund currently has a performance rating of C (Fair) based on an annualized return of 0.00% over the last three years and a total return of 2.88% year to date 2015. Factored into the performance evaluation is an expense ratio of 0.43% (very low).

The fund's risk rating is currently B (Good). It carries a beta of 0.00, meaning the fund's expected move will be 0.0% for every 10% move in the market. Volatility, as measured by both the semi-deviation and a drawdown factor, is considered low. As of December 31, 2015, *WisdomTree Japan Hedged Real Est traded at a discount of 1.43% below its net asset value, which is better than its one-year historical average discount of .01%.

Karen Q. Wong has been running the fund for 2 years and currently receives a manager quality ranking of 86 (0=worst, 99=best). If you desire an average level of risk, then this fund may be an option.

Data Date	Investment Rating	Net Assets ($Mil)	Price	Performance Rating/Pts	Total Return Y-T-D	Risk Rating/Pts
12-15	C+	20.20	26.13	C / 4.8	2.88%	B / 8.1

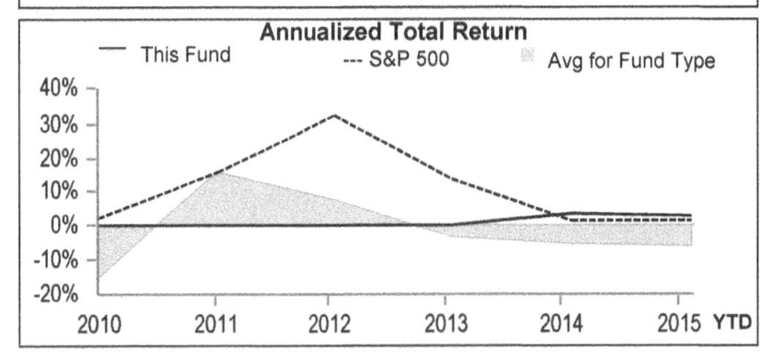

* Denotes ETF Fund

*WisdomTree Japan Hedged SmallCap (DXJS) A+ Excellent

Fund Family: WisdomTree Asset Management Inc
Fund Type: Foreign
Inception Date: June 28, 2013

Data Date	Investment Rating	Net Assets ($Mil)	Price	Performance Rating/Pts	Total Return Y-T-D	Risk Rating/Pts
12-15	A+	88.20	34.02	B+ / 8.5	15.70%	B / 8.6
2014	C-	88.20	30.44	C+ / 6.5	10.68%	C / 5.0

Major Rating Factors:
Strong performance is the major factor driving the A+ (Excellent) TheStreet.com Investment Rating for *WisdomTree Japan Hedged SmallCap. The fund currently has a performance rating of B+ (Good) based on an annualized return of 0.00% over the last three years and a total return of 15.70% year to date 2015. Factored into the performance evaluation is an expense ratio of 0.59% (very low).

The fund's risk rating is currently B (Good). It carries a beta of 0.00, meaning the fund's expected move will be 0.0% for every 10% move in the market. Volatility, as measured by both the semi-deviation and a drawdown factor, is considered low. As of December 31, 2015, *WisdomTree Japan Hedged SmallCap traded at a discount of 1.68% below its net asset value, which is better than its one-year historical average premium of .07%.

Richard A. Brown has been running the fund for 3 years and currently receives a manager quality ranking of 97 (0=worst, 99=best). If you desire only a moderate level of risk and strong performance, then this fund is an excellent option.

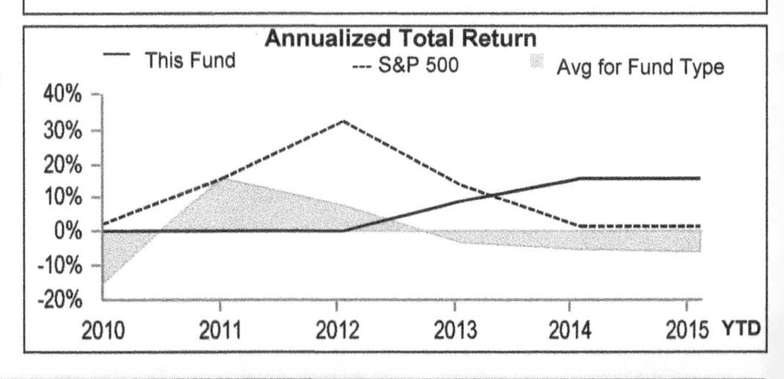

*WisdomTree Japan Hedged TM & Tel (DXJT) C Fair

Fund Family: WisdomTree Asset Management Inc
Fund Type: Foreign
Inception Date: April 8, 2014

Data Date	Investment Rating	Net Assets ($Mil)	Price	Performance Rating/Pts	Total Return Y-T-D	Risk Rating/Pts
12-15	C	2.70	26.40	C+ / 6.7	7.88%	C / 5.5

Major Rating Factors: Middle of the road best describes *WisdomTree Japan Hedged TM & Tel whose TheStreet.com Investment Rating is currently a C (Fair). The fund currently has a performance rating of C+ (Fair) based on an annualized return of 0.00% over the last three years and a total return of 7.88% year to date 2015. Factored into the performance evaluation is an expense ratio of 0.43% (very low).

The fund's risk rating is currently C (Fair). It carries a beta of 0.00, meaning the fund's expected move will be 0.0% for every 10% move in the market. Volatility, as measured by both the semi-deviation and a drawdown factor, is considered average. As of December 31, 2015, *WisdomTree Japan Hedged TM & Tel traded at a premium of .04% above its net asset value, which is better than its one-year historical average premium of .14%.

Karen Q. Wong has been running the fund for 2 years and currently receives a manager quality ranking of 94 (0=worst, 99=best). If you desire an average level of risk, then this fund may be an option.

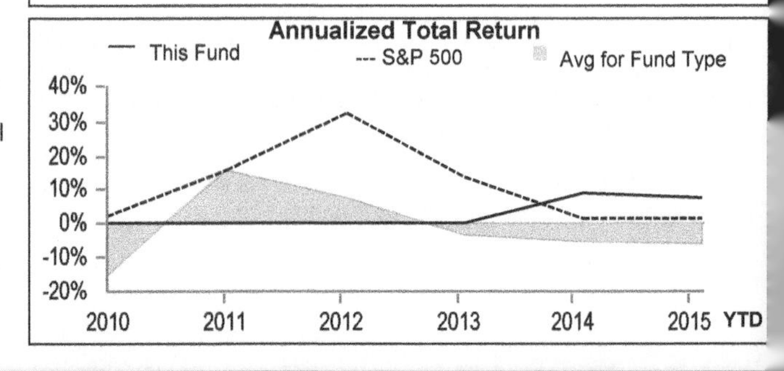

*WisdomTree Japan Interest Rate S (JGBB) C+ Fair

Fund Family: WisdomTree Asset Management Inc
Fund Type: Global
Inception Date: December 18, 2013

Data Date	Investment Rating	Net Assets ($Mil)	Price	Performance Rating/Pts	Total Return Y-T-D	Risk Rating/Pts
12-15	C+	5.00	48.53	C+ / 5.6	2.03%	B- / 7.6
2014	D	5.00	48.53	D+ / 2.5	-1.93%	C / 5.2

Major Rating Factors: Middle of the road best describes *WisdomTree Japan Interest Rate S whose TheStreet.com Investment Rating is currently a C+ (Fair). The fund currently has a performance rating of C+ (Fair) based on an annualized return of 0.00% over the last three years and a total return of 2.03% year to date 2015. Factored into the performance evaluation is an expense ratio of 0.50% (very low).

The fund's risk rating is currently B- (Good). It carries a beta of 0.00, meaning the fund's expected move will be 0.0% for every 10% move in the market. Volatility, as measured by both the semi-deviation and a drawdown factor, is considered low. As of December 31, 2015, *WisdomTree Japan Interest Rate S traded at a premium of 2.21% above its net asset value, which is worse than its one-year historical average discount of .33%.

Kazuto Doi has been running the fund for 3 years and currently receives a manager quality ranking of 65 (0=worst, 99=best). If you desire an average level of risk, then this fund may be an option.

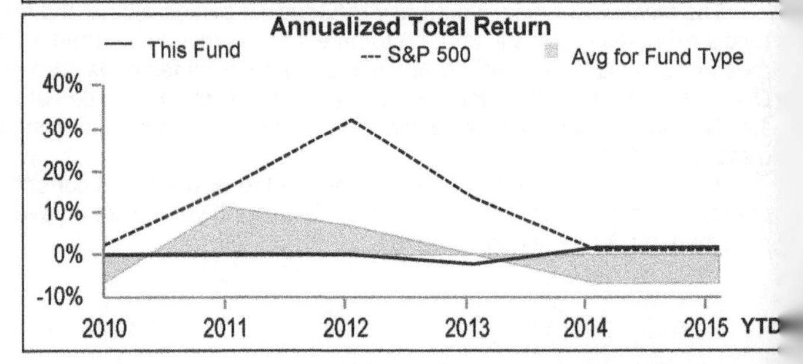

*WisdomTree Japan SmallCap Div Fd (DFJ) A+ Excellent

Fund Family: WisdomTree Asset Management Inc
Fund Type: Foreign
Inception Date: June 16, 2006

Major Rating Factors:
Strong performance is the major factor driving the A+ (Excellent) TheStreet.com Investment Rating for *WisdomTree Japan SmallCap Div Fd. The fund currently has a performance rating of B+ (Good) based on an annualized return of 11.06% over the last three years and a total return of 18.01% year to date 2015. Factored into the performance evaluation is an expense ratio of 0.59% (very low).

The fund's risk rating is currently B (Good). It carries a beta of 0.53, meaning the fund's expected move will be 5.3% for every 10% move in the market. Volatility, as measured by both the semi-deviation and a drawdown factor, is considered low. As of December 31, 2015, *WisdomTree Japan SmallCap Div Fd traded at a discount of .75% below its net asset value, which is better than its one-year historical average premium of .09%.

Karen Q. Wong has been running the fund for 8 years and currently receives a manager quality ranking of 93 (0=worst, 99=best). If you desire only a moderate level of risk and strong performance, then this fund is an excellent option.

Data Date	Investment Rating	Net Assets ($Mil)	Price	Performance Rating/Pts	Total Return Y-T-D	Risk Rating/Pts
12-15	A+	300.70	56.56	B+ / 8.8	18.01%	B / 8.5
2014	C	300.70	48.52	C- / 4.2	-2.21%	B / 8.4
2013	B-	283.20	51.01	C+ / 6.1	18.71%	B / 8.5
2012	C-	176.80	43.70	C- / 3.0	7.40%	B / 8.6
2011	C-	184.10	41.65	C- / 3.1	-3.18%	B- / 7.8
2010	C+	121.60	44.20	C+ / 6.3	17.37%	C+ / 6.3

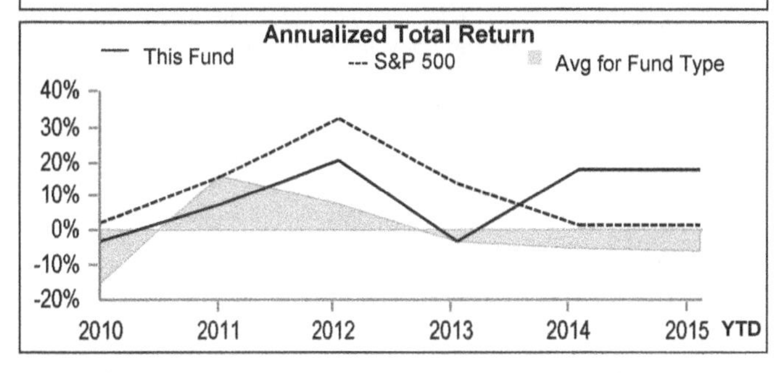

*WisdomTree Korea Hedged Equity (DXKW) C- Fair

Fund Family: WisdomTree Asset Management Inc
Fund Type: Foreign
Inception Date: November 7, 2013

Major Rating Factors: Middle of the road best describes *WisdomTree Korea Hedged Equity whose TheStreet.com Investment Rating is currently a C- (Fair). The fund currently has a performance rating of C- (Fair) based on an annualized return of 0.00% over the last three years and a total return of -2.55% year to date 2015. Factored into the performance evaluation is an expense ratio of 0.59% (very low).

The fund's risk rating is currently B- (Good). It carries a beta of 0.00, meaning the fund's expected move will be 0.0% for every 10% move in the market. Volatility, as measured by both the semi-deviation and a drawdown factor, is considered low. As of December 31, 2015, *WisdomTree Korea Hedged Equity traded at a discount of 1.34% below its net asset value, which is better than its one-year historical average discount of .23%.

Karen Q. Wong has been running the fund for 3 years and currently receives a manager quality ranking of 48 (0=worst, 99=best). If you desire an average level of risk, then this fund may be an option.

Data Date	Investment Rating	Net Assets ($Mil)	Price	Performance Rating/Pts	Total Return Y-T-D	Risk Rating/Pts
12-15	C-	8.80	19.94	C- / 3.3	-2.55%	B- / 7.7
2014	E+	8.80	20.50	D- / 1.0	-11.66%	C- / 3.6

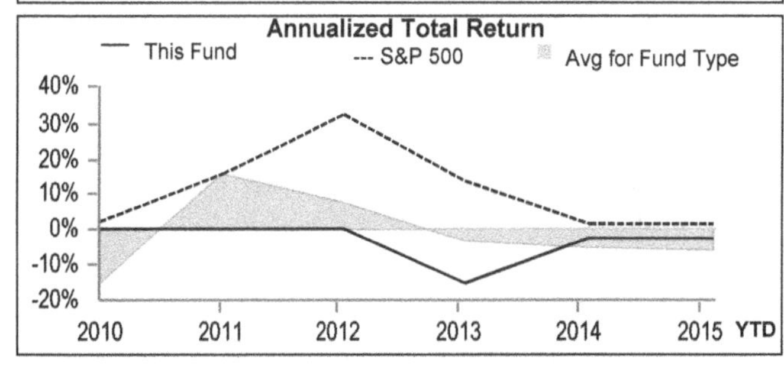

*WisdomTree LargeCap Dividend Fun (DLN) A Excellent

Fund Family: WisdomTree Asset Management Inc
Fund Type: Growth and Income
Inception Date: June 16, 2006

Major Rating Factors:
Strong performance is the major factor driving the A (Excellent) TheStreet.com Investment Rating for *WisdomTree LargeCap Dividend Fun. The fund currently has a performance rating of B (Good) based on an annualized return of 11.94% over the last three years and a total return of -1.36% year to date 2015. Factored into the performance evaluation is an expense ratio of 0.29% (very low).

The fund's risk rating is currently B (Good). It carries a beta of 0.95, meaning that its performance tracks fairly well with that of the overall stock market. Volatility, as measured by both the semi-deviation and a drawdown factor, is considered low. As of December 31, 2015, *WisdomTree LargeCap Dividend Fun traded at a discount of .03% below its net asset value, which is better than its one-year historical average discount of .01%.

Karen Q. Wong has been running the fund for 8 years and currently receives a manager quality ranking of 58 (0=worst, 99=best). If you desire only a moderate level of risk and strong performance, then this fund is an excellent option.

Data Date	Investment Rating	Net Assets ($Mil)	Price	Performance Rating/Pts	Total Return Y-T-D	Risk Rating/Pts
12-15	A	1,836.10	71.14	B / 8.1	-1.36%	B / 8.7
2014	B	1,836.10	74.16	B / 7.8	15.27%	B- / 7.6
2013	A	1,777.50	66.54	B / 8.0	23.41%	B / 8.8
2012	C+	1,239.60	53.64	C / 5.5	14.25%	B / 8.7
2011	C+	930.90	49.03	C+ / 6.1	10.90%	B- / 7.9
2010	C-	554.90	46.10	C- / 3.0	14.98%	C+ / 5.9

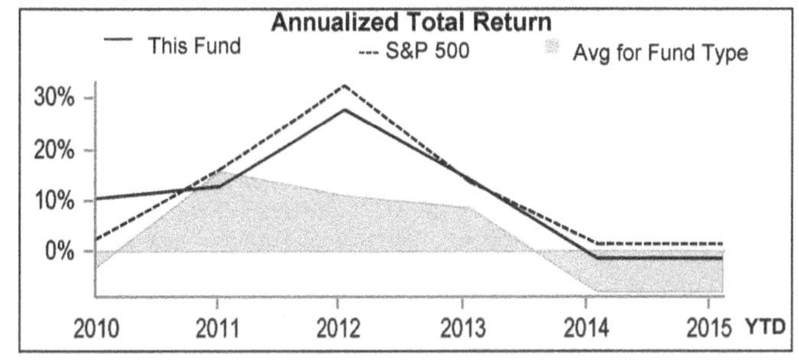

*WisdomTree LargeCap Value Fund (EZY) B+ Good

Fund Family: WisdomTree Asset Management Inc
Fund Type: Income
Inception Date: February 23, 2007

Major Rating Factors: Strong performance is the major factor driving the B+ (Good) TheStreet.com Investment Rating for *WisdomTree LargeCap Value Fund. The fund currently has a performance rating of B+ (Good) based on an annualized return of 13.25% over the last three years and a total return of -0.28% year to date 2015. Factored into the performance evaluation is an expense ratio of 0.39% (very low).

The fund's risk rating is currently B- (Good). It carries a beta of 1.05, meaning that its performance tracks fairly well with that of the overall stock market. Volatility, as measured by both the semi-deviation and a drawdown factor, is considered low. As of December 31, 2015, *WisdomTree LargeCap Value Fund traded at a premium of .55% above its net asset value, which is worse than its one-year historical average premium of .06%.

Karen Q. Wong has been running the fund for 8 years and currently receives a manager quality ranking of 56 (0=worst, 99=best). If you desire only a moderate level of risk and strong performance, then this fund is an excellent option.

Data Date	Investment Rating	Net Assets ($Mil)	Price	Performance Rating/Pts	Total Return Y-T-D	Risk Rating/Pts
12-15	B+	27.50	63.70	B+ / 8.4	-0.28%	B- / 7.3
2014	B	27.50	65.12	B / 7.9	14.49%	B- / 7.5
2013	A-	28.90	57.61	B+ / 8.4	27.70%	B / 8.4
2012	C-	29.10	44.65	C- / 4.1	11.55%	B- / 7.8
2011	C+	30.70	41.06	C+ / 5.7	6.11%	B- / 7.9
2010	C-	23.80	39.68	C- / 3.4	14.24%	C+ / 5.7

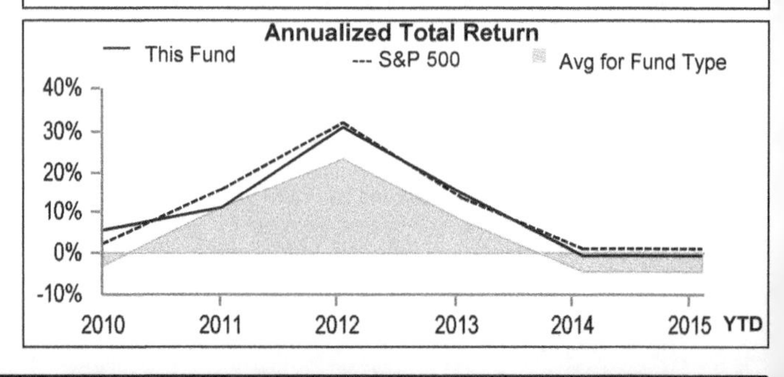

*WisdomTree Mgd Futures Strategy (WDTI) C Fair

Fund Family: WisdomTree Asset Management Inc
Fund Type: Growth
Inception Date: January 5, 2011

Major Rating Factors: Middle of the road best describes *WisdomTree Mgd Futures Strategy whose TheStreet.com Investment Rating is currently a C (Fair). The fund currently has a performance rating of C (Fair) based on an annualized return of 1.17% over the last three years and a total return of -3.51% year to date 2015. Factored into the performance evaluation is an expense ratio of 0.95% (low).

The fund's risk rating is currently B- (Good). It carries a beta of -0.05, meaning the fund's expected move will be -0.5% for every 10% move in the market. Volatility, as measured by both the semi-deviation and a drawdown factor, is considered low. As of December 31, 2015, *WisdomTree Mgd Futures Strategy traded at a premium of .65% above its net asset value, which is worse than its one-year historical average premium of .02%.

Vassilis Dagioglu has been running the fund for 5 years and currently receives a manager quality ranking of 81 (0=worst, 99=best). If you desire an average level of risk, then this fund may be an option.

Data Date	Investment Rating	Net Assets ($Mil)	Price	Performance Rating/Pts	Total Return Y-T-D	Risk Rating/Pts
12-15	C	178.30	42.07	C / 4.6	-3.51%	B- / 7.6
2014	C-	178.30	43.57	D+ / 2.7	6.19%	B+ / 9.0
2013	D+	153.40	41.54	D / 2.2	0.98%	B- / 7.9
2012	D	117.00	40.30	E+ / 0.8	-10.74%	B- / 7.8

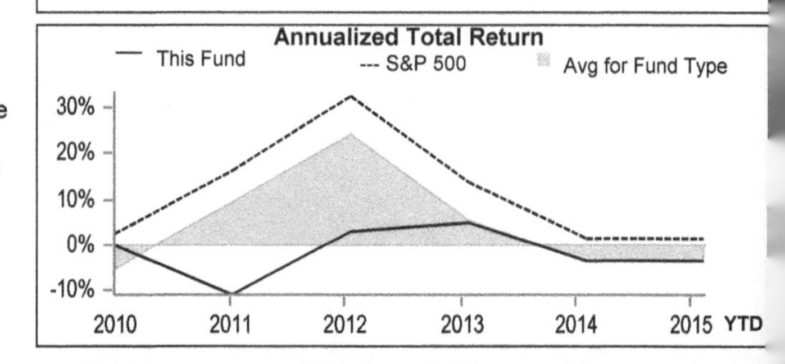

*WisdomTree MidCap Dividend Fund (DON) A Excellent

Fund Family: WisdomTree Asset Management Inc
Fund Type: Growth
Inception Date: June 16, 2006

Major Rating Factors:
Strong performance is the major factor driving the A (Excellent) TheStreet.com Investment Rating for *WisdomTree MidCap Dividend Fund. The fund currently has a performance rating of B+ (Good) based on an annualized return of 13.77% over the last three years and a total return of -1.15% year to date 2015. Factored into the performance evaluation is an expense ratio of 0.39% (very low).

The fund's risk rating is currently B (Good). It carries a beta of 0.93, meaning that its performance tracks fairly well with that of the overall stock market. Volatility, as measured by both the semi-deviation and a drawdown factor, is considered low. As of December 31, 2015, *WisdomTree MidCap Dividend Fund traded at a discount of .01% below its net asset value, which is better than its one-year historical average premium of .03%.

Karen Q. Wong has been running the fund for 8 years and currently receives a manager quality ranking of 76 (0=worst, 99=best). If you desire only a moderate level of risk and strong performance, then this fund is an excellent option.

Data Date	Investment Rating	Net Assets ($Mil)	Price	Performance Rating/Pts	Total Return Y-T-D	Risk Rating/Pts
12-15	A	1,126.40	80.51	B+ / 8.5	-1.15%	B / 8.1
2014	A+	1,126.40	83.74	B+ / 8.7	16.16%	B / 8.3
2013	A	913.30	74.61	B+ / 8.5	28.19%	B / 8.4
2012	B-	390.90	57.41	C+ / 6.6	16.25%	B / 8.2
2011	B-	288.30	52.07	C+ / 6.9	5.99%	B- / 7.6
2010	C+	233.00	50.70	C+ / 6.8	21.65%	C+ / 5.6

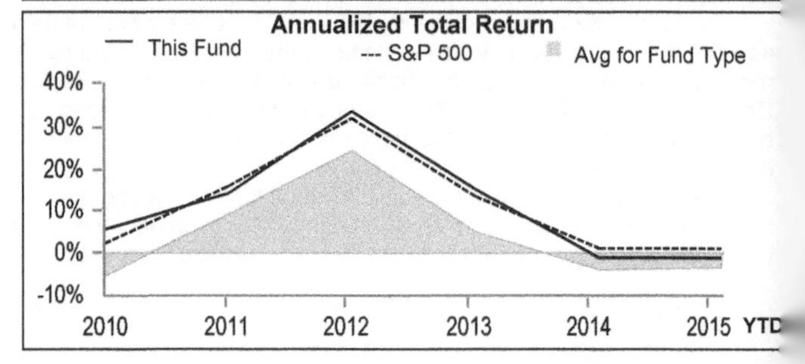

*WisdomTree MidCap Earnings Fund (EZM) A- Excellent

Fund Family: WisdomTree Asset Management Inc
Fund Type: Growth
Inception Date: February 23, 2007

Major Rating Factors:
Strong performance is the major factor driving the A- (Excellent) TheStreet.com Investment Rating for *WisdomTree MidCap Earnings Fund. The fund currently has a performance rating of B (Good) based on an annualized return of 11.91% over the last three years and a total return of -4.54% year to date 2015. Factored into the performance evaluation is an expense ratio of 0.39% (very low).

The fund's risk rating is currently B (Good). It carries a beta of 1.10, meaning it is expected to move 11.0% for every 10% move in the market. Volatility, as measured by both the semi-deviation and a drawdown factor, is considered low. As of December 31, 2015, *WisdomTree MidCap Earnings Fund traded at a discount of .07% below its net asset value, which is better than its one-year historical average premium of .03%.

Karen Q. Wong has been running the fund for 8 years and currently receives a manager quality ranking of 43 (0=worst, 99=best). If you desire only a moderate level of risk and strong performance, then this fund is an excellent option.

Data Date	Investment Rating	Net Assets ($Mil)	Price	Performance Rating/Pts	Total Return Y-T-D	Risk Rating/Pts
12-15	A-	590.80	87.14	B / 7.7	-4.54%	B / 8.4
2014	B	590.80	92.65	B+ / 8.3	9.20%	B- / 7.1
2013	A-	444.90	86.50	B+ / 8.9	34.78%	B- / 7.8
2012	B	165.10	62.38	B- / 7.5	17.84%	B- / 7.7
2011	B-	121.20	53.95	B- / 7.4	3.04%	B- / 7.5
2010	B+	93.90	53.99	B / 8.0	25.60%	C+ / 5.8

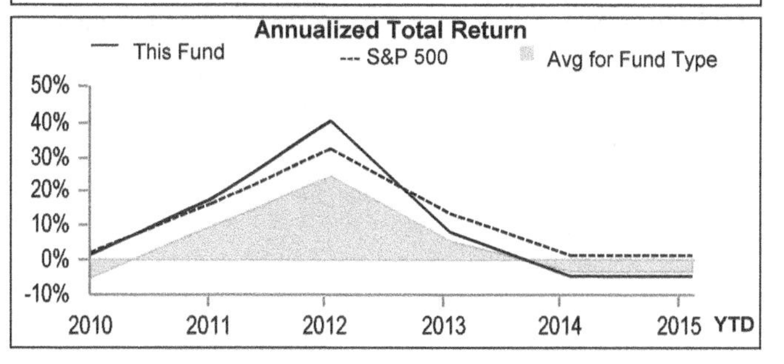

*WisdomTree Middle East Dividend (GULF) C Fair

Fund Family: WisdomTree Asset Management Inc
Fund Type: Foreign
Inception Date: July 16, 2008

Major Rating Factors: Middle of the road best describes *WisdomTree Middle East Dividend whose TheStreet.com Investment Rating is currently a C (Fair). The fund currently has a performance rating of C (Fair) based on an annualized return of 7.52% over the last three years and a total return of -14.54% year to date 2015. Factored into the performance evaluation is an expense ratio of 0.89% (low).

The fund's risk rating is currently C+ (Fair). It carries a beta of 0.47, meaning the fund's expected move will be 4.7% for every 10% move in the market. Volatility, as measured by both the semi-deviation and a drawdown factor, is considered low. As of December 31, 2015, *WisdomTree Middle East Dividend traded at a discount of 1.71% below its net asset value, which is better than its one-year historical average discount of 1.13%.

Jeffrey Zhang currently receives a manager quality ranking of 89 (0=worst, 99=best). If you desire an average level of risk, then this fund may be an option.

Data Date	Investment Rating	Net Assets ($Mil)	Price	Performance Rating/Pts	Total Return Y-T-D	Risk Rating/Pts
12-15	C	57.70	16.65	C / 5.5	-14.54%	C+ / 6.8
2014	B-	57.70	20.42	C+ / 6.6	5.74%	B- / 7.9
2013	B+	25.70	20.00	B / 7.8	38.63%	B / 8.1
2012	C-	11.90	14.99	C- / 4.1	13.59%	B / 8.0
2011	C-	14.70	14.63	D+ / 2.8	-11.53%	B / 8.0
2010	A-	20.30	17.04	A- / 9.2	22.43%	C / 5.0

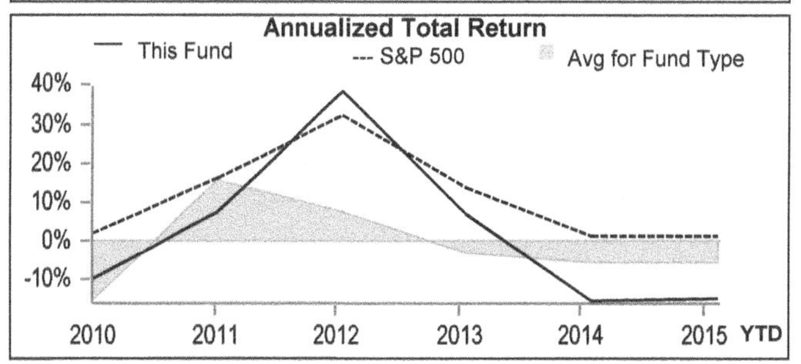

*WisdomTree SmallCap Dividend Fd (DES) B+ Good

Fund Family: WisdomTree Asset Management Inc
Fund Type: Growth
Inception Date: June 16, 2006

Major Rating Factors: Strong performance is the major factor driving the B+ (Good) TheStreet.com Investment Rating for *WisdomTree SmallCap Dividend Fd. The fund currently has a performance rating of B- (Good) based on an annualized return of 10.57% over the last three years and a total return of -5.30% year to date 2015. Factored into the performance evaluation is an expense ratio of 0.39% (very low).

The fund's risk rating is currently B (Good). It carries a beta of 1.03, meaning that its performance tracks fairly well with that of the overall stock market. Volatility, as measured by both the semi-deviation and a drawdown factor, is considered low. As of December 31, 2015, *WisdomTree SmallCap Dividend Fd traded at a discount of .12% below its net asset value, which is better than its one-year historical average premium of .04%.

Karen Q. Wong has been running the fund for 8 years and currently receives a manager quality ranking of 40 (0=worst, 99=best). If you desire only a moderate level of risk and strong performance, then this fund is an excellent option.

Data Date	Investment Rating	Net Assets ($Mil)	Price	Performance Rating/Pts	Total Return Y-T-D	Risk Rating/Pts
12-15	B+	981.10	64.93	B- / 7.3	-5.30%	B / 8.6
2014	B+	981.10	70.92	B / 8.1	8.45%	B- / 7.4
2013	A	1,043.60	67.79	B+ / 8.7	32.22%	B / 8.2
2012	B-	402.10	50.95	C+ / 6.6	18.12%	B / 8.0
2011	C	242.00	44.89	C / 5.2	0.87%	B- / 7.1
2010	B+	224.20	47.41	B / 8.2	27.05%	C / 5.4

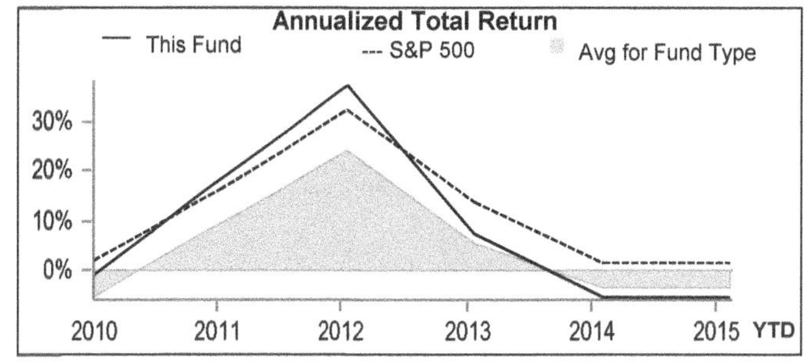

* Denotes ETF Fund

*WisdomTree SmallCap Earnings Fun (EES) C+ Fair

Fund Family: WisdomTree Asset Management Inc
Fund Type: Growth
Inception Date: February 23, 2007

Major Rating Factors: Strong performance is the major factor driving the C+ (Fair) TheStreet.com Investment Rating for *WisdomTree SmallCap Earnings Fun. The fund currently has a performance rating of B- (Good) based on an annualized return of 10.01% over the last three years and a total return of -6.18% year to date 2015. Factored into the performance evaluation is an expense ratio of 0.39% (very low).

The fund's risk rating is currently C+ (Fair). It carries a beta of 1.09, meaning that its performance tracks fairly well with that of the overall stock market. Volatility, as measured by both the semi-deviation and a drawdown factor, is considered low. As of December 31, 2015, *WisdomTree SmallCap Earnings Fun traded at a premium of .07% above its net asset value, which is worse than its one-year historical average discount of .02%.

Karen Q. Wong has been running the fund for 8 years and currently receives a manager quality ranking of 33 (0=worst, 99=best). If you desire only a moderate level of risk and strong performance, then this fund is an excellent option.

Data Date	Investment Rating	Net Assets ($Mil)	Price	Performance Rating/Pts	Total Return Y-T-D	Risk Rating/Pts
12-15	C+	395.80	75.80	B- / 7.0	-6.18%	C+ / 6.9
2014	B-	395.80	82.73	B / 7.6	3.34%	B- / 7.1
2013	A	404.20	81.63	A- / 9.0	38.77%	B- / 7.9
2012	C+	155.80	56.71	C+ / 5.9	14.06%	B- / 7.6
2011	B-	120.30	50.31	B- / 7.2	0.00%	B- / 7.4
2010	B+	116.40	51.95	B+ / 8.4	26.97%	C+ / 5.7

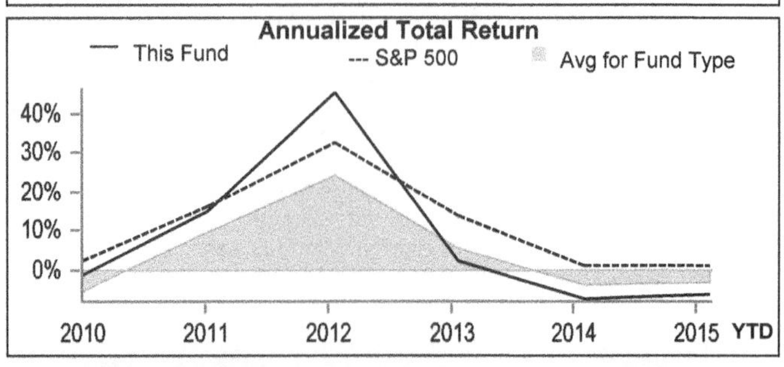

*WisdomTree Strategic Corporate B (CRDT) C+ Fair

Fund Family: WisdomTree Asset Management Inc
Fund Type: Global
Inception Date: January 31, 2013

Major Rating Factors: Middle of the road best describes *WisdomTree Strategic Corporate B whose TheStreet.com Investment Rating is currently a C+ (Fair). The fund currently has a performance rating of C- (Fair) based on an annualized return of 0.00% over the last three years and a total return of -0.31% year to date 2015. Factored into the performance evaluation is an expense ratio of 0.45% (very low).

The fund's risk rating is currently B+ (Good). It carries a beta of 0.00, meaning the fund's expected move will be 0.0% for every 10% move in the market. Volatility, as measured by both the semi-deviation and a drawdown factor, is considered very low. As of December 31, 2015, *WisdomTree Strategic Corporate B traded at a discount of .51% below its net asset value, which is better than its one-year historical average discount of .40%.

Paul Shuttleworth has been running the fund for 3 years and currently receives a manager quality ranking of 60 (0=worst, 99=best). If you desire an average level of risk, then this fund may be an option.

Data Date	Investment Rating	Net Assets ($Mil)	Price	Performance Rating/Pts	Total Return Y-T-D	Risk Rating/Pts
12-15	C+	7.50	71.54	C- / 4.0	-0.31%	B+ / 9.3
2014	C	7.50	74.95	C- / 4.0	5.09%	B+ / 9.0

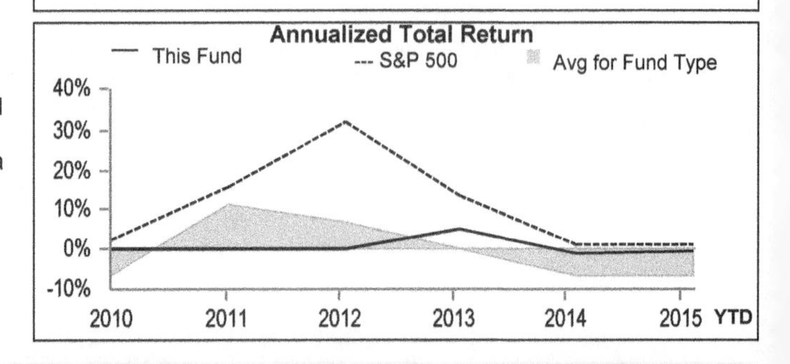

*WisdomTree Total Dividend (DTD) B+ Good

Fund Family: WisdomTree Asset Management Inc
Fund Type: Income
Inception Date: June 16, 2006

Major Rating Factors: Strong performance is the major factor driving the B+ (Good) TheStreet.com Investment Rating for *WisdomTree Total Dividend. The fund currently has a performance rating of B (Good) based on an annualized return of 12.08% over the last three years and a total return of -1.39% year to date 2015. Factored into the performance evaluation is an expense ratio of 0.29% (very low).

The fund's risk rating is currently B- (Good). It carries a beta of 0.95, meaning that its performance tracks fairly well with that of the overall stock market. Volatility, as measured by both the semi-deviation and a drawdown factor, is considered low. As of December 31, 2015, *WisdomTree Total Dividend traded at a premium of .04% above its net asset value.

Karen Q. Wong has been running the fund for 8 years and currently receives a manager quality ranking of 59 (0=worst, 99=best). If you desire only a moderate level of risk and strong performance, then this fund is an excellent option.

Data Date	Investment Rating	Net Assets ($Mil)	Price	Performance Rating/Pts	Total Return Y-T-D	Risk Rating/Pts
12-15	B+	516.20	71.66	B / 8.2	-1.39%	B- / 7.3
2014	B+	516.20	74.76	B / 7.9	15.02%	B- / 7.6
2013	A	392.60	67.12	B / 8.1	24.23%	B / 8.7
2012	C+	266.30	53.79	C+ / 5.6	14.48%	B / 8.6
2011	C+	206.00	49.05	C+ / 6.1	9.77%	B- / 7.9
2010	C-	155.80	46.59	C- / 3.7	16.32%	C+ / 5.9

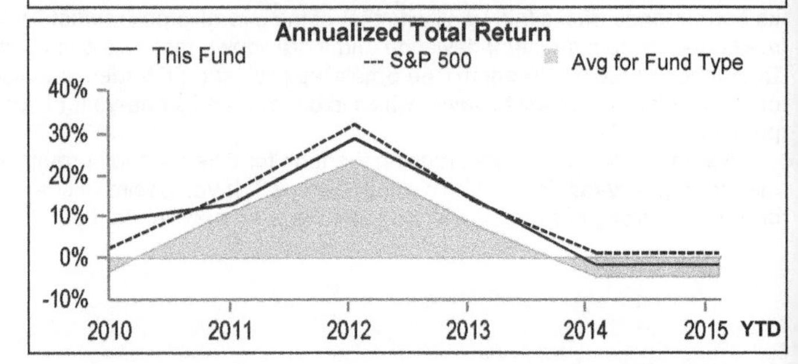

*WisdomTree Total Earnings Fund (EXT) B+ Good

Fund Family: WisdomTree Asset Management Inc
Fund Type: Income
Inception Date: February 23, 2007

Major Rating Factors: Strong performance is the major factor driving the B+ (Good) TheStreet.com Investment Rating for *WisdomTree Total Earnings Fund. The fund currently has a performance rating of B+ (Good) based on an annualized return of 13.21% over the last three years and a total return of -1.40% year to date 2015. Factored into the performance evaluation is an expense ratio of 0.29% (very low).

The fund's risk rating is currently B- (Good). It carries a beta of 1.04, meaning that its performance tracks fairly well with that of the overall stock market. Volatility, as measured by both the semi-deviation and a drawdown factor, is considered low. As of December 31, 2015, *WisdomTree Total Earnings Fund traded at a premium of .25% above its net asset value, which is worse than its one-year historical average discount of .02%.

Karen Q. Wong has been running the fund for 8 years and currently receives a manager quality ranking of 58 (0=worst, 99=best). If you desire only a moderate level of risk and strong performance, then this fund is an excellent option.

Data Date	Investment Rating	Net Assets ($Mil)	Price	Performance Rating/Pts	Total Return Y-T-D	Risk Rating/Pts
12-15	B+	95.40	71.09	B+ / 8.5	-1.40%	B- / 7.3
2014	B+	95.40	74.35	B+ / 8.4	14.01%	B- / 7.5
2013	A	63.50	66.82	B+ / 8.6	30.23%	B / 8.3
2012	C+	48.30	50.39	C / 5.4	15.90%	B / 8.1
2011	C+	33.70	45.01	C+ / 6.0	5.13%	B / 8.0
2010	C-	51.20	44.62	C- / 4.1	13.78%	C+ / 5.9

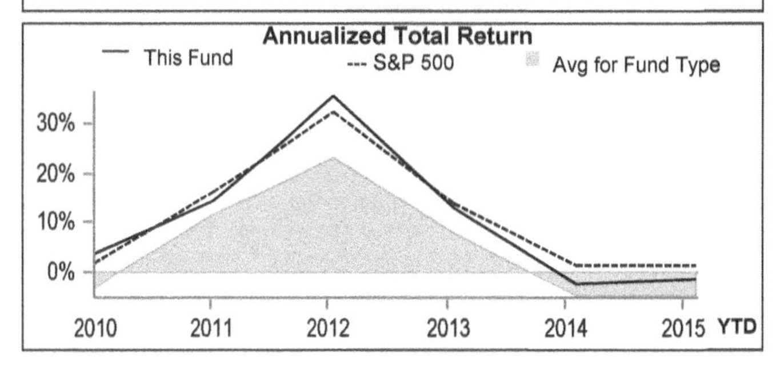

*WisdomTree United Kingdom Hedged (DXPS) C- Fair

Fund Family: WisdomTree Asset Management Inc
Fund Type: Foreign
Inception Date: June 28, 2013

Major Rating Factors:
Disappointing performance is the major factor driving the C- (Fair) TheStreet.com Investment Rating for *WisdomTree United Kingdom Hedged. The fund currently has a performance rating of D+ (Weak) based on an annualized return of 0.00% over the last three years and a total return of -3.97% year to date 2015. Factored into the performance evaluation is an expense ratio of 0.49% (very low).

The fund's risk rating is currently B- (Good). It carries a beta of 0.00, meaning the fund's expected move will be 0.0% for every 10% move in the market. Volatility, as measured by both the semi-deviation and a drawdown factor, is considered low. As of December 31, 2015, *WisdomTree United Kingdom Hedged traded at a discount of .65% below its net asset value, which is better than its one-year historical average premium of .47%.

Richard A. Brown has been running the fund for 3 years and currently receives a manager quality ranking of 39 (0=worst, 99=best). This fund offers only a moderate level of risk but investors looking for strong performance are still waiting.

Data Date	Investment Rating	Net Assets ($Mil)	Price	Performance Rating/Pts	Total Return Y-T-D	Risk Rating/Pts
12-15	C-	21.50	23.06	D+ / 2.6	-3.97%	B- / 7.9
2014	D+	21.50	25.05	D+ / 2.6	1.10%	B- / 7.1

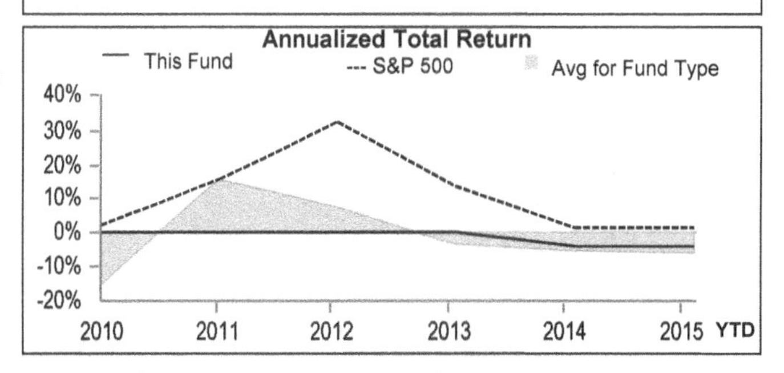

*WisdomTree US Dividend Growth (DGRW) C Fair

Fund Family: WisdomTree Asset Management Inc
Fund Type: Income
Inception Date: May 22, 2013

Major Rating Factors: Middle of the road best describes *WisdomTree US Dividend Growth whose TheStreet.com Investment Rating is currently a C (Fair). The fund currently has a performance rating of C (Fair) based on an annualized return of 0.00% over the last three years and a total return of 0.16% year to date 2015. Factored into the performance evaluation is an expense ratio of 0.29% (very low).

The fund's risk rating is currently B- (Good). It carries a beta of 0.00, meaning the fund's expected move will be 0.0% for every 10% move in the market. Volatility, as measured by both the semi-deviation and a drawdown factor, is considered low. As of December 31, 2015, *WisdomTree US Dividend Growth traded at a premium of .03% above its net asset value, which is better than its one-year historical average premium of .05%.

Richard A. Brown has been running the fund for 3 years and currently receives a manager quality ranking of 54 (0=worst, 99=best). If you desire an average level of risk, then this fund may be an option.

Data Date	Investment Rating	Net Assets ($Mil)	Price	Performance Rating/Pts	Total Return Y-T-D	Risk Rating/Pts
12-15	C	133.00	30.35	C / 5.0	0.16%	B- / 7.1
2014	B	133.00	31.09	B- / 7.4	14.90%	B- / 7.8

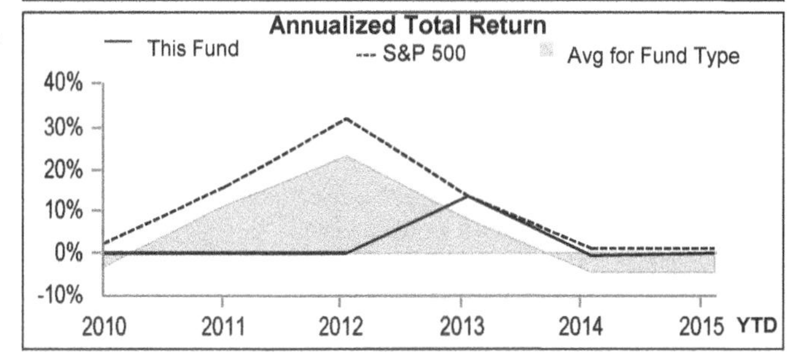

* Denotes ETF Fund

*WisdomTree US SmCp Qual Dividend (DGRS) C- Fair

Fund Family: WisdomTree Asset Management Inc
Fund Type: Income
Inception Date: July 25, 2013

Data Date	Investment Rating	Net Assets ($Mil)	Price	Perfor-mance Rating/Pts	Total Return Y-T-D	Risk Rating/Pts
12-15	C-	24.10	26.53	D+ / 2.4	-6.31%	B- / 7.4
2014	D+	24.10	29.26	C / 5.4	5.79%	C- / 4.2

Major Rating Factors:
Disappointing performance is the major factor driving the C- (Fair) TheStreet.com Investment Rating for *WisdomTree US SmCp Qual Dividend. The fund currently has a performance rating of D+ (Weak) based on an annualized return of 0.00% over the last three years and a total return of -6.31% year to date 2015. Factored into the performance evaluation is an expense ratio of 0.39% (very low).

The fund's risk rating is currently B- (Good). It carries a beta of 0.00, meaning the fund's expected move will be 0.0% for every 10% move in the market. Volatility, as measured by both the semi-deviation and a drawdown factor, is considered low. As of December 31, 2015, *WisdomTree US SmCp Qual Dividend traded at a price exactly equal to its net asset value, which is better than its one-year historical average premium of .01%.

Richard A. Brown has been running the fund for 3 years and currently receives a manager quality ranking of 20 (0=worst, 99=best). This fund offers only a moderate level of risk but investors looking for strong performance are still waiting.

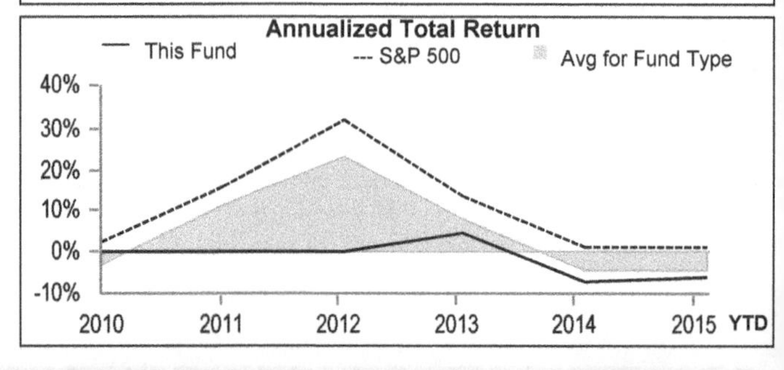

*YieldShares High Income ETF (YYY) C Fair

Fund Family: Exchange Traded Concepts LLC
Fund Type: Global
Inception Date: June 12, 2012

Data Date	Investment Rating	Net Assets ($Mil)	Price	Perfor-mance Rating/Pts	Total Return Y-T-D	Risk Rating/Pts
12-15	C	72.40	17.82	C- / 4.0	-7.93%	B- / 7.3
2014	D	72.40	21.60	D / 2.1	1.87%	C+ / 6.6
2013	B	20.80	23.25	C+ / 6.8	10.84%	B / 8.9

Major Rating Factors: Middle of the road best describes *YieldShares High Income ETF whose TheStreet.com Investment Rating is currently a C (Fair). The fund currently has a performance rating of C- (Fair) based on an annualized return of 0.88% over the last three years and a total return of -7.93% year to date 2015. Factored into the performance evaluation is an expense ratio of 0.50% (very low).

The fund's risk rating is currently B- (Good). It carries a beta of 0.65, meaning the fund's expected move will be 6.5% for every 10% move in the market. Volatility, as measured by both the semi-deviation and a drawdown factor, is considered low. As of December 31, 2015, *YieldShares High Income ETF traded at a discount of .11% below its net asset value, which is better than its one-year historical average discount of .01%.

Denise M. Krisko has been running the fund for 4 years and currently receives a manager quality ranking of 46 (0=worst, 99=best). If you desire an average level of risk, then this fund may be an option.

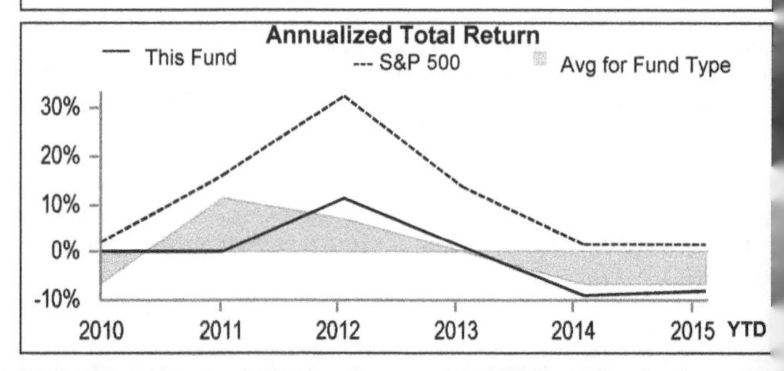

*Yorkville High Income Infras MLP (YMLI) E+ Very Weak

Fund Family: Exchange Traded Concepts LLC
Fund Type: Energy/Natural Resources
Inception Date: February 11, 2013

Data Date	Investment Rating	Net Assets ($Mil)	Price	Perfor-mance Rating/Pts	Total Return Y-T-D	Risk Rating/Pts
12-15	E+	45.80	12.62	E- / 0.1	-36.61%	C- / 3.8
2014	C-	45.80	21.04	D+ / 2.8	6.82%	B / 8.7

Major Rating Factors:
Very poor performance is the major factor driving the E+ (Very Weak) TheStreet.com Investment Rating for *Yorkville High Income Infras MLP. The fund currently has a performance rating of E- (Very Weak) based on an annualized return of 0.00% over the last three years and a total return of -36.61% year to date 2015. Factored into the performance evaluation is an expense ratio of 0.84% (very low).

The fund's risk rating is currently C- (Fair). It carries a beta of 0.00, meaning the fund's expected move will be 0.0% for every 10% move in the market. Volatility, as measured by both the semi-deviation and a drawdown factor, is considered average. As of December 31, 2015, *Yorkville High Income Infras MLP traded at a premium of .16% above its net asset value, which is worse than its one-year historical average discount of .04%.

Dustin Lewellyn has been running the fund for 1 year and currently receives a manager quality ranking of 5 (0=worst, 99=best). This fund offers an average level of risk but investors looking for strong performance will be frustrated.

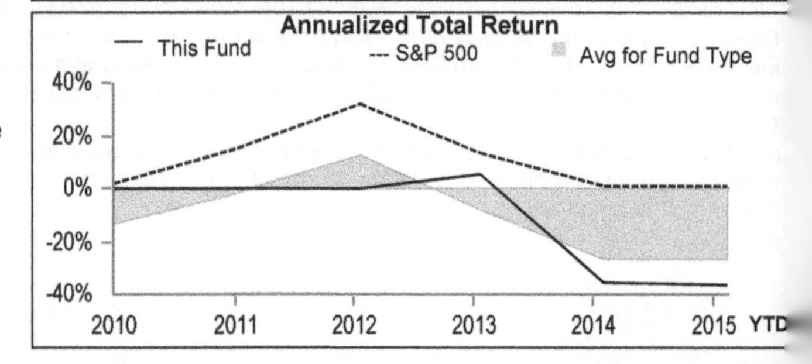

*Yorkville High Income MLP ETF (YMLP) E Very Weak

Fund Family: Exchange Traded Concepts LLC
Fund Type: Global
Inception Date: March 12, 2012

Major Rating Factors: Very poor performance is the major factor driving the E (Very Weak) TheStreet.com Investment Rating for *Yorkville High Income MLP ETF. The fund currently has a performance rating of E- (Very Weak) based on an annualized return of -29.51% over the last three years and a total return of -58.52% year to date 2015. Factored into the performance evaluation is an expense ratio of 0.83% (very low).

The fund's risk rating is currently C- (Fair). It carries a beta of 1.24, meaning it is expected to move 12.4% for every 10% move in the market. Volatility, as measured by both the semi-deviation and a drawdown factor, is considered average. As of December 31, 2015, *Yorkville High Income MLP ETF traded at a discount of .43% below its net asset value, which is better than its one-year historical average discount of .01%.

Dustin Lewellyn has been running the fund for 1 year and currently receives a manager quality ranking of 2 (0=worst, 99=best). This fund offers an average level of risk but investors looking for strong performance will be frustrated.

Data Date	Investment Rating	Net Assets ($Mil)	Price	Performance Rating/Pts	Total Return Y-T-D	Risk Rating/Pts
12-15	E	330.90	4.68	E- / 0.2	-58.52%	C- / 3.0
2014	D-	330.90	12.50	E- / 0.2	-25.70%	C+ / 5.7
2013	C+	257.60	18.44	C+ / 6.3	9.51%	B / 8.1

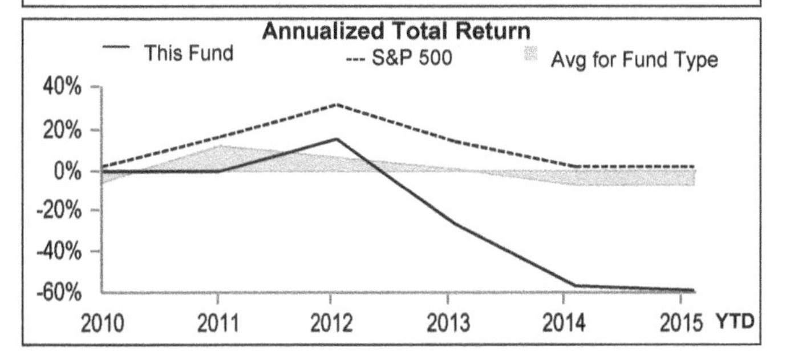

Aberdeen Asia-Pacific Income Fund (FAX) D+ Weak

Fund Family: Aberdeen Asset Management Asia Ltd
Fund Type: Global
Inception Date: April 17, 1986

Major Rating Factors:
Disappointing performance is the major factor driving the D+ (Weak) TheStreet.com Investment Rating for Aberdeen Asia-Pacific Income Fund. The fund currently has a performance rating of D (Weak) based on an annualized return of -10.34% over the last three years and a total return of -10.73% year to date 2015. Factored into the performance evaluation is an expense ratio of 1.97% (above average).

The fund's risk rating is currently C+ (Fair). It carries a beta of 1.32, meaning it is expected to move 13.2% for every 10% move in the market. Volatility, as measured by both the semi-deviation and a drawdown factor, is considered low. As of December 31, 2015, Aberdeen Asia-Pacific Income Fund traded at a discount of 16.76% below its net asset value, which is better than its one-year historical average discount of 14.10%.

Anthony Michael currently receives a manager quality ranking of 34 (0=worst, 99=best). This fund offers only a moderate level of risk but investors looking for strong performance are still waiting.

Data Date	Investment Rating	Net Assets ($Mil)	Price	Performance Rating/Pts	Total Return Y-T-D	Risk Rating/Pts
12-15	D+	1,718.94	4.57	D / 2.1	-10.73%	C+ / 6.2
2014	D+	1,709.10	5.55	D / 2.1	2.07%	B- / 7.2
2013	D+	2,072.10	5.76	D+ / 2.3	-20.88%	B- / 7.5
2012	C+	1,951.74	7.74	C / 5.3	12.62%	B / 8.6
2011	B+	1,917.40	7.33	B / 8.0	19.28%	B / 8.6
2010	B+	1,777.77	6.75	B / 8.1	15.66%	C+ / 6.0

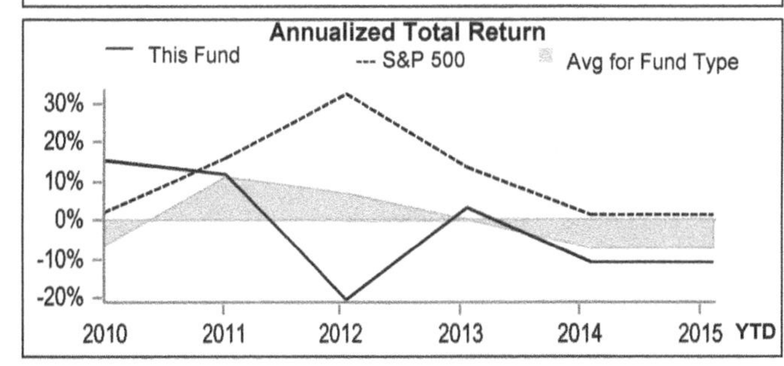

Aberdeen Australia Equity Fund (IAF) D Weak

Fund Family: Aberdeen Asset Management Asia Ltd
Fund Type: Foreign
Inception Date: December 12, 1985

Major Rating Factors:
Disappointing performance is the major factor driving the D (Weak) TheStreet.com Investment Rating for Aberdeen Australia Equity Fund. The fund currently has a performance rating of D (Weak) based on an annualized return of -10.22% over the last three years and a total return of -9.28% year to date 2015. Factored into the performance evaluation is an expense ratio of 1.48% (average).

The fund's risk rating is currently C (Fair). It carries a beta of 0.63, meaning the fund's expected move will be 6.3% for every 10% move in the market. Volatility, as measured by both the semi-deviation and a drawdown factor, is considered average. As of December 31, 2015, Aberdeen Australia Equity Fund traded at a discount of 11.53% below its net asset value, which is better than its one-year historical average discount of 9.15%.

Mark Daniels currently receives a manager quality ranking of 12 (0=worst, 99=best). This fund offers an average level of risk but investors looking for strong performance will be frustrated.

Data Date	Investment Rating	Net Assets ($Mil)	Price	Performance Rating/Pts	Total Return Y-T-D	Risk Rating/Pts
12-15	D	189.78	5.45	D / 2.0	-9.28%	C / 4.9
2014	D	183.70	6.86	D / 2.1	-10.81%	C / 5.5
2013	D	238.02	8.44	D / 2.2	-10.02%	C+ / 6.2
2012	D+	229.62	10.44	C- / 3.9	21.74%	C+ / 6.6
2011	C-	207.70	9.05	C / 5.0	-7.40%	C+ / 6.6
2010	C-	219.93	11.98	C / 4.8	8.15%	C / 4.4

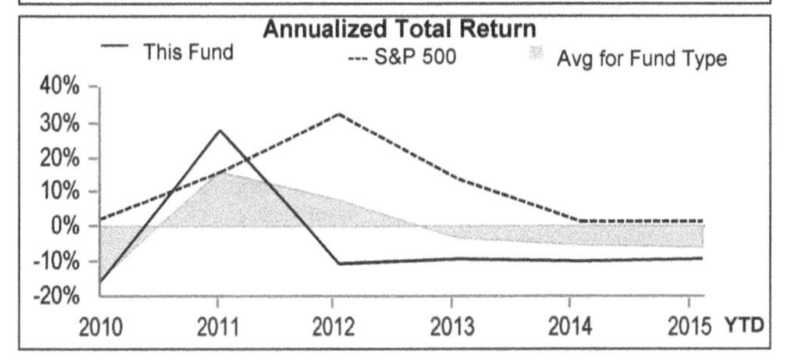

* Denotes ETF Fund

Aberdeen Chile Fund (CH) E+ Very Weak

Fund Family: Aberdeen Asset Managers Ltd
Fund Type: Foreign
Inception Date: September 27, 1989

Major Rating Factors:
Very poor performance is the major factor driving the E+ (Very Weak) TheStreet.com Investment Rating for Aberdeen Chile Fund. The fund currently has a performance rating of E+ (Very Weak) based on an annualized return of -20.34% over the last three years and a total return of -16.07% year to date 2015. Factored into the performance evaluation is an expense ratio of 2.58% (high).

The fund's risk rating is currently C- (Fair). It carries a beta of 0.19, meaning the fund's expected move will be 1.9% for every 10% move in the market. Volatility, as measured by both the semi-deviation and a drawdown factor, is considered average. As of December 31, 2015, Aberdeen Chile Fund traded at a discount of 13.49% below its net asset value, which is better than its one-year historical average discount of 10.36%.

Fiona Manning has been running the fund for 7 years and currently receives a manager quality ranking of 7 (0=worst, 99=best). This fund offers an average level of risk but investors looking for strong performance will be frustrated.

Data Date	Investment Rating	Net Assets ($Mil)	Price	Performance Rating/Pts	Total Return Y-T-D	Risk Rating/Pts
12-15	E+	77.47	5.58	E+ / 0.9	-16.07%	C- / 3.7
2014	E+	83.60	7.44	E+ / 0.9	-21.48%	C- / 3.8
2013	E+	119.81	10.55	E+ / 0.9	-22.52%	C- / 4.1
2012	D	142.16	15.09	C- / 3.7	5.23%	C / 5.4
2011	C+	134.50	15.04	B / 8.2	-10.43%	C+ / 5.9
2010	B+	190.85	22.67	A- / 9.1	48.63%	C / 4.7

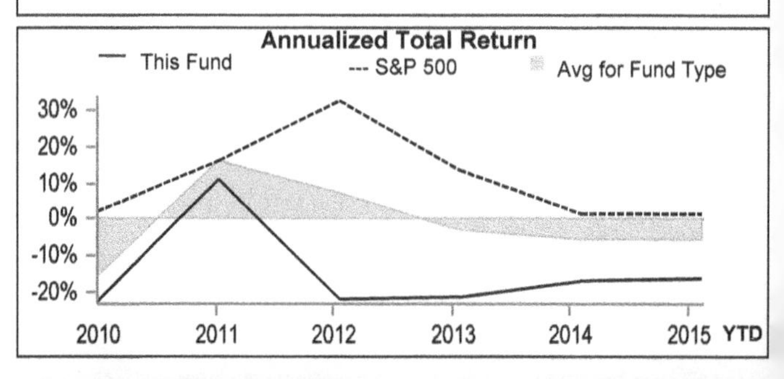

Aberdeen Emerging Mkt Sm Co Opptys (ETF) D- Weak

Fund Family: Aberdeen Asset Managers Ltd
Fund Type: Emerging Market
Inception Date: June 17, 1992

Major Rating Factors:
Disappointing performance is the major factor driving the D- (Weak) TheStreet.com Investment Rating for Aberdeen Emerging Mkt Sm Co Opptys. The fund currently has a performance rating of D (Weak) based on an annualized return of -8.37% over the last three years and a total return of -16.76% year to date 2015. Factored into the performance evaluation is an expense ratio of 1.61% (above average).

The fund's risk rating is currently C- (Fair). It carries a beta of 1.01, meaning that its performance tracks fairly well with that of the overall stock market. Volatility, as measured by both the semi-deviation and a drawdown factor, is considered average. As of December 31, 2015, Aberdeen Emerging Mkt Sm Co Opptys traded at a discount of 14.22% below its net asset value, which is better than its one-year historical average discount of 12.37%.

Devan Kaloo currently receives a manager quality ranking of 53 (0=worst, 99=best). This fund offers an average level of risk but investors looking for strong performance will be frustrated.

Data Date	Investment Rating	Net Assets ($Mil)	Price	Performance Rating/Pts	Total Return Y-T-D	Risk Rating/Pts
12-15	D-	153.22	10.86	D / 2.0	-16.76%	C- / 4.0
2014	D	153.20	13.08	C- / 3.4	-3.38%	C / 4.7
2013	D	198.37	13.80	C- / 3.1	-7.75%	C+ / 5.7
2012	B-	165.08	21.50	C+ / 6.7	24.99%	B / 8.3
2011	C	161.40	17.53	C- / 4.2	-4.92%	B / 8.0
2010	D-	157.63	19.36	D / 2.2	20.26%	C- / 3.3

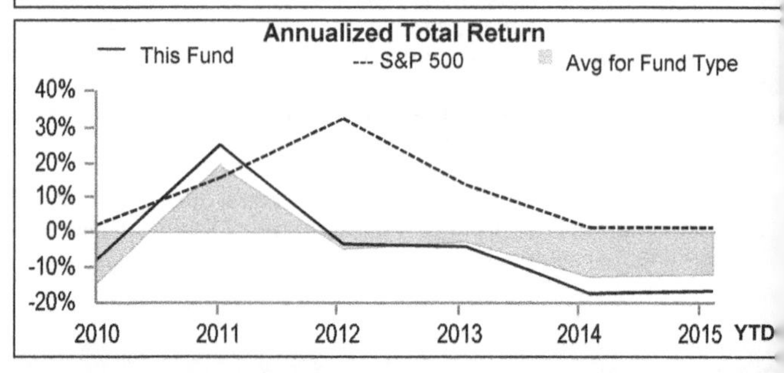

Aberdeen Global Income Fund (FCO) D Weak

Fund Family: Aberdeen Asset Management Asia Ltd
Fund Type: Global
Inception Date: February 20, 1992

Major Rating Factors:
Disappointing performance is the major factor driving the D (Weak) TheStreet.com Investment Rating for Aberdeen Global Income Fund. The fund currently has a performance rating of D (Weak) based on an annualized return of -11.23% over the last three years and a total return of -11.87% year to date 2015. Factored into the performance evaluation is an expense ratio of 2.18% (high).

The fund's risk rating is currently C+ (Fair). It carries a beta of 1.63, meaning it is expected to move 16.3% for every 10% move in the market. Volatility, as measured by both the semi-deviation and a drawdown factor, is considered low. As of December 31, 2015, Aberdeen Global Income Fund traded at a discount of 14.37% below its net asset value, which is better than its one-year historical average discount of 13.63%.

Anthony Michael currently receives a manager quality ranking of 32 (0=worst, 99=best). This fund offers only a moderate level of risk but investors looking for strong performance are still waiting.

Data Date	Investment Rating	Net Assets ($Mil)	Price	Performance Rating/Pts	Total Return Y-T-D	Risk Rating/Pts
12-15	D	105.65	7.69	D / 1.9	-11.87%	C+ / 5.9
2014	D	105.50	9.61	D / 1.8	-0.21%	B- / 7.0
2013	D+	130.70	10.40	D+ / 2.5	-20.59%	B- / 7.4
2012	C+	121.65	14.22	C / 5.2	8.45%	B / 8.5
2011	B+	119.80	13.90	B+ / 8.6	25.62%	B / 8.3
2010	B	108.85	12.31	B- / 7.5	5.93%	C+ / 5.6

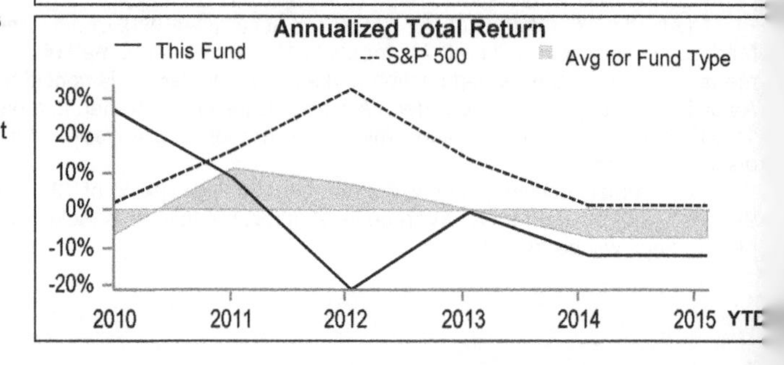

Aberdeen Greater China (GCH) D+ Weak

Fund Family: Aberdeen Asset Management Asia Ltd
Fund Type: Foreign
Inception Date: July 15, 1992

Major Rating Factors:
Disappointing performance is the major factor driving the D+ (Weak) TheStreet.com Investment Rating for Aberdeen Greater China. The fund currently has a performance rating of D+ (Weak) based on an annualized return of -7.01% over the last three years and a total return of -9.36% year to date 2015. Factored into the performance evaluation is an expense ratio of 1.99% (high).

The fund's risk rating is currently C+ (Fair). It carries a beta of 0.93, meaning that its performance tracks fairly well with that of the overall stock market. Volatility, as measured by both the semi-deviation and a drawdown factor, is considered low. As of December 31, 2015, Aberdeen Greater China traded at a discount of 15.00% below its net asset value, which is better than its one-year historical average discount of 13.88%.

Hugh Young currently receives a manager quality ranking of 15 (0=worst, 99=best). This fund offers only a moderate level of risk but investors looking for strong performance are still waiting.

Data Date	Investment Rating	Net Assets ($Mil)	Price	Performance Rating/Pts	Total Return Y-T-D	Risk Rating/Pts
12-15	D+	103.67	8.56	D+ / 2.4	-9.36%	C+ / 6.3
2014	C-	106.50	9.93	C- / 3.6	1.75%	B- / 7.0
2013	D	105.96	10.19	D- / 1.5	-14.32%	C+ / 6.8
2012	D+	282.12	12.88	D+ / 2.6	25.37%	B- / 7.1
2011	D	273.60	10.07	D+ / 2.5	-23.75%	C+ / 6.4
2010	E+	368.48	13.15	D- / 1.4	-5.41%	C- / 3.1

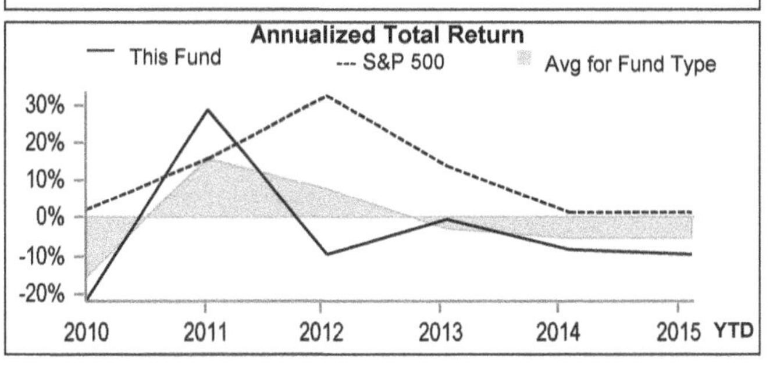

Aberdeen Indonesia Fund (IF) D- Weak

Fund Family: Aberdeen Asset Management Asia Ltd
Fund Type: Emerging Market
Inception Date: March 9, 1990

Major Rating Factors:
Disappointing performance is the major factor driving the D- (Weak) TheStreet.com Investment Rating for Aberdeen Indonesia Fund. The fund currently has a performance rating of D- (Weak) based on an annualized return of -16.33% over the last three years and a total return of -32.92% year to date 2015. Factored into the performance evaluation is an expense ratio of 1.53% (average).

The fund's risk rating is currently C- (Fair). It carries a beta of 0.87, meaning the fund's expected move will be 8.7% for every 10% move in the market. Volatility, as measured by both the semi-deviation and a drawdown factor, is considered average. As of December 31, 2015, Aberdeen Indonesia Fund traded at a discount of 15.08% below its net asset value, which is better than its one-year historical average discount of 12.13%.

Hugh Young has been running the fund for 7 years and currently receives a manager quality ranking of 16 (0=worst, 99=best). This fund offers an average level of risk but investors looking for strong performance will be frustrated.

Data Date	Investment Rating	Net Assets ($Mil)	Price	Performance Rating/Pts	Total Return Y-T-D	Risk Rating/Pts
12-15	D-	88.21	5.52	D- / 1.1	-32.92%	C- / 3.8
2014	D	100.90	8.41	C- / 3.2	9.86%	C / 5.2
2013	D-	126.47	8.26	D / 1.6	-21.96%	C / 5.5
2012	B	116.42	11.67	B / 8.0	18.78%	B- / 7.3
2011	B+	106.50	11.78	A+ / 9.7	-0.11%	B- / 7.5
2010	C+	84.14	13.31	B+ / 8.8	51.47%	D+ / 2.6

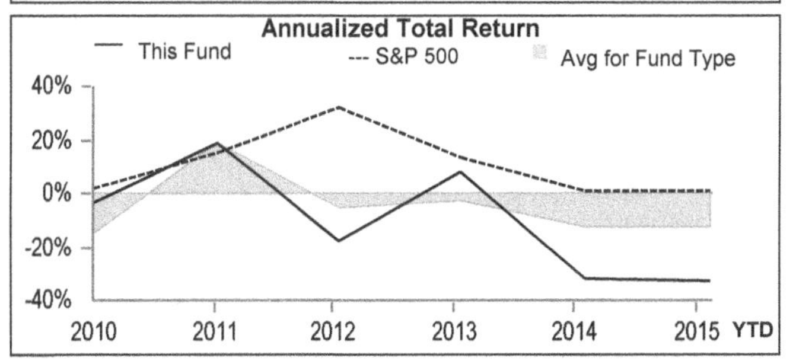

Aberdeen Israel Fund (ISL) B+ Good

Fund Family: Aberdeen Asset Managers Ltd
Fund Type: Foreign
Inception Date: October 22, 1992

Major Rating Factors: Strong performance is the major factor driving the B+ (Good) TheStreet.com Investment Rating for Aberdeen Israel Fund. The fund currently has a performance rating of B (Good) based on an annualized return of 10.54% over the last three years and a total return of 5.24% year to date 2015. Factored into the performance evaluation is an expense ratio of 1.55% (average).

The fund's risk rating is currently B (Good). It carries a beta of 0.43, meaning the fund's expected move will be 4.3% for every 10% move in the market. Volatility, as measured by both the semi-deviation and a drawdown factor, is considered low. As of December 31, 2015, Aberdeen Israel Fund traded at a discount of 16.38% below its net asset value, which is better than its one-year historical average discount of 14.31%.

Devan Kaloo has been running the fund for 7 years and currently receives a manager quality ranking of 94 (0=worst, 99=best). If you desire only a moderate level of risk and strong performance, then this fund is an excellent option.

Data Date	Investment Rating	Net Assets ($Mil)	Price	Performance Rating/Pts	Total Return Y-T-D	Risk Rating/Pts
12-15	B+	78.63	17.26	B / 7.7	5.24%	B / 8.1
2014	C+	80.90	16.60	C+ / 5.8	3.95%	B / 8.2
2013	C	70.76	16.86	C+ / 6.1	25.05%	C+ / 6.9
2012	D	60.30	13.10	D / 2.0	8.85%	C+ / 6.7
2011	C-	62.40	12.75	C / 4.7	-21.56%	B- / 7.1
2010	C-	70.25	17.40	C- / 4.2	16.96%	C / 5.4

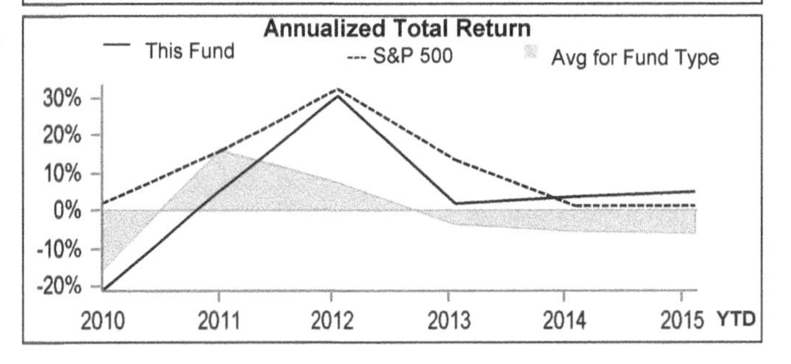

Aberdeen Japan Equity (JEQ) A- Excellent

Fund Family: Aberdeen Asset Management Asia Ltd
Fund Type: Foreign
Inception Date: July 24, 1992

Major Rating Factors:
Exceptional performance is the major factor driving the A- (Excellent) TheStreet.com Investment Rating for Aberdeen Japan Equity. The fund currently has a performance rating of A- (Excellent) based on an annualized return of 12.60% over the last three years and a total return of 17.25% year to date 2015. Factored into the performance evaluation is an expense ratio of 1.04% (low).

The fund's risk rating is currently B- (Good). It carries a beta of 0.75, meaning the fund's expected move will be 7.5% for every 10% move in the market. Volatility, as measured by both the semi-deviation and a drawdown factor, is considered low. As of December 31, 2015, Aberdeen Japan Equity traded at a discount of 9.20% below its net asset value, which is worse than its one-year historical average discount of 11.47%.

Chern-Yeh Kwok currently receives a manager quality ranking of 95 (0=worst, 99=best). If you desire only a moderate level of risk and strong performance, then this fund is an excellent option.

Data Date	Investment Rating	Net Assets ($Mil)	Price	Performance Rating/Pts	Total Return Y-T-D	Risk Rating/Pts
12-15	A-	113.70	7.70	A- / 9.1	17.25%	B- / 7.4
2014	C+	111.90	6.77	C / 5.4	0.23%	B / 8.4
2013	C	105.30	6.99	C / 5.5	20.31%	B- / 7.6
2012	D+	86.90	5.57	D+ / 2.9	15.58%	B- / 7.4
2011	D	82.40	5.00	D / 1.7	-15.71%	B- / 7.4
2010	D+	94.00	6.12	D+ / 2.6	17.85%	C+ / 6.3

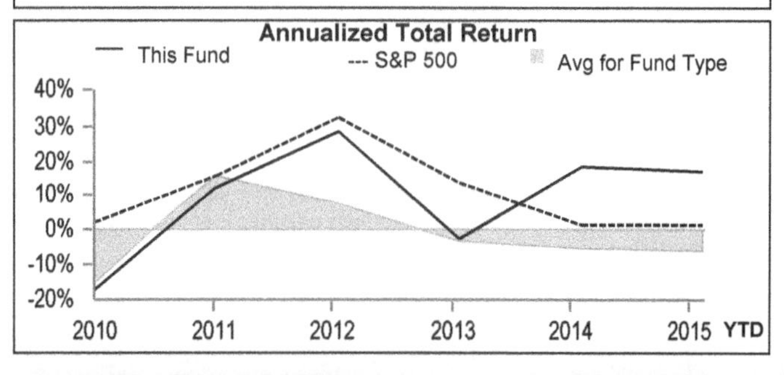

Aberdeen Latin America Equity Fund (LAQ) E+ Very Weak

Fund Family: Aberdeen Asset Managers Ltd
Fund Type: Foreign
Inception Date: October 30, 1991

Major Rating Factors:
Very poor performance is the major factor driving the E+ (Very Weak) TheStreet.com Investment Rating for Aberdeen Latin America Equity Fund. The fund currently has a performance rating of E+ (Very Weak) based on an annualized return of -21.34% over the last three years and a total return of -29.29% year to date 2015. Factored into the performance evaluation is an expense ratio of 1.26% (average).

The fund's risk rating is currently C- (Fair). It carries a beta of 1.20, meaning it is expected to move 12.0% for every 10% move in the market. Volatility, as measured by both the semi-deviation and a drawdown factor, is considered average. As of December 31, 2015, Aberdeen Latin America Equity Fund traded at a discount of 11.65% below its net asset value, which is better than its one-year historical average discount of 10.42%.

Devan Kaloo has been running the fund for 7 years and currently receives a manager quality ranking of 4 (0=worst, 99=best). This fund offers an average level of risk but investors looking for strong performance will be frustrated.

Data Date	Investment Rating	Net Assets ($Mil)	Price	Performance Rating/Pts	Total Return Y-T-D	Risk Rating/Pts
12-15	E+	228.97	15.25	E+ / 0.7	-29.29%	C- / 3.7
2014	D-	224.70	22.58	D / 1.7	-14.25%	C / 5.3
2013	D	257.40	28.05	D- / 1.5	-17.96%	C+ / 6.5
2012	C	264.11	36.24	C+ / 6.0	22.29%	C+ / 6.6
2011	B-	247.50	30.10	B / 7.6	-15.09%	C+ / 6.8
2010	C	265.10	38.72	B / 8.1	26.93%	D+ / 2.7

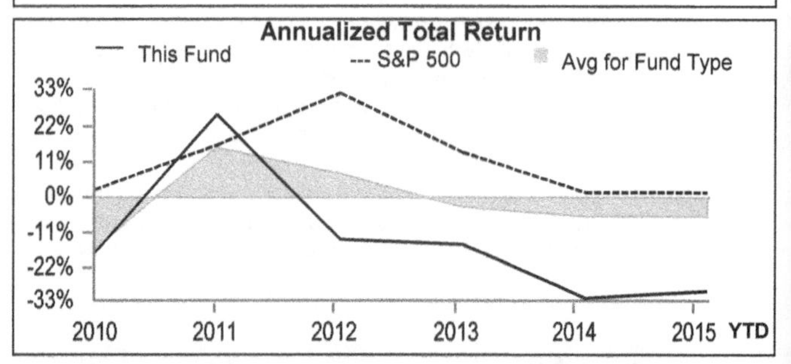

Aberdeen Singapore (SGF) D Weak

Fund Family: Aberdeen Asset Management Asia Ltd
Fund Type: Foreign
Inception Date: July 31, 1990

Major Rating Factors:
Disappointing performance is the major factor driving the D (Weak) TheStreet.com Investment Rating for Aberdeen Singapore. The fund currently has a performance rating of D+ (Weak) based on an annualized return of -6.38% over the last three years and a total return of -17.48% year to date 2015. Factored into the performance evaluation is an expense ratio of 1.47% (average).

The fund's risk rating is currently C+ (Fair). It carries a beta of 0.87, meaning the fund's expected move will be 8.7% for every 10% move in the market. Volatility, as measured by both the semi-deviation and a drawdown factor, is considered low. As of December 31, 2015, Aberdeen Singapore traded at a discount of 14.49% below its net asset value, which is better than its one-year historical average discount of 13.05%.

Hugh Young has been running the fund for 5 years and currently receives a manager quality ranking of 16 (0=worst, 99=best). This fund offers only a moderate level of risk but investors looking for strong performance are still waiting.

Data Date	Investment Rating	Net Assets ($Mil)	Price	Performance Rating/Pts	Total Return Y-T-D	Risk Rating/Pts
12-15	D	106.60	8.56	D+ / 2.3	-17.48%	C+ / 5.6
2014	C	107.60	11.92	C / 5.1	2.31%	B- / 7.8
2013	D	123.50	12.77	D+ / 2.3	-2.81%	C+ / 6.8
2012	C	137.50	13.98	C+ / 6.0	29.60%	C+ / 6.5
2011	C-	119.40	10.91	C / 5.0	-24.72%	C+ / 6.6
2010	C	146.90	15.19	B- / 7.3	28.33%	C- / 3.5

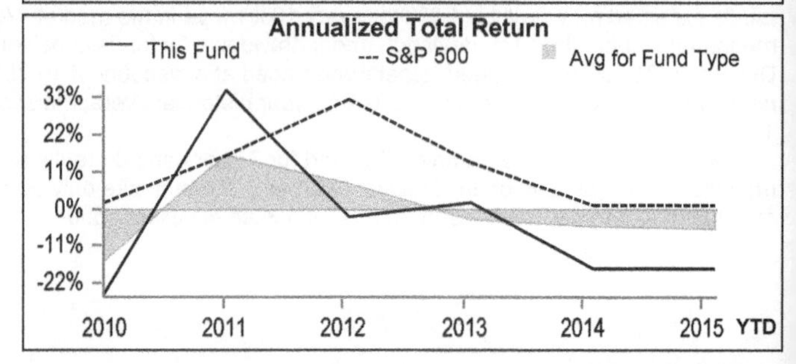

Adams Diversified Equity (ADX) A- Excellent

Fund Family: Adams Express Company
Fund Type: Income
Inception Date: N/A

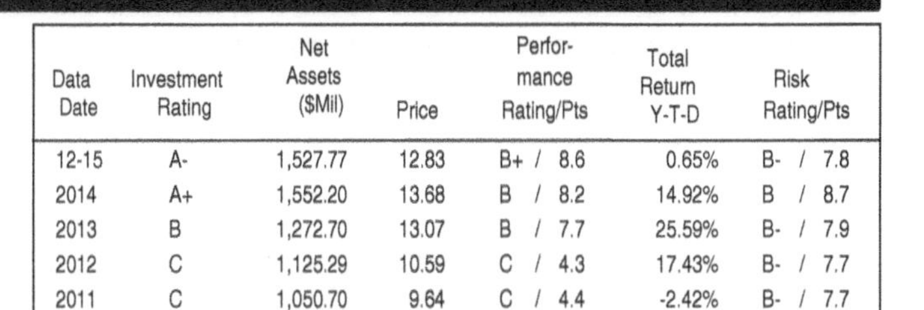

Data Date	Investment Rating	Net Assets ($Mil)	Price	Performance Rating/Pts	Total Return Y-T-D	Risk Rating/Pts
12-15	A-	1,527.77	12.83	B+ / 8.6	0.65%	B- / 7.8
2014	A+	1,552.20	13.68	B / 8.2	14.92%	B / 8.7
2013	B	1,272.70	13.07	B / 7.7	25.59%	B- / 7.9
2012	C	1,125.29	10.59	C / 4.3	17.43%	B- / 7.7
2011	C	1,050.70	9.64	C / 4.4	-2.42%	B- / 7.7
2010	C	939.67	10.74	C- / 3.9	11.85%	C+ / 6.7

Major Rating Factors:
Strong performance is the major factor driving the A- (Excellent) TheStreet.com Investment Rating for Adams Diversified Equity. The fund currently has a performance rating of B+ (Good) based on an annualized return of 13.38% over the last three years and a total return of 0.65% year to date 2015. Factored into the performance evaluation is an expense ratio of 0.58% (very low).

The fund's risk rating is currently B- (Good). It carries a beta of 1.06, meaning that its performance tracks fairly well with that of the overall stock market. Volatility, as measured by both the semi-deviation and a drawdown factor, is considered low. As of December 31, 2015, Adams Diversified Equity traded at a discount of 14.69% below its net asset value, which is better than its one-year historical average discount of 14.43%.

Nancy J.F. Prue has been running the fund for 6 years and currently receives a manager quality ranking of 57 (0=worst, 99=best). If you desire only a moderate level of risk and strong performance, then this fund is an excellent option.

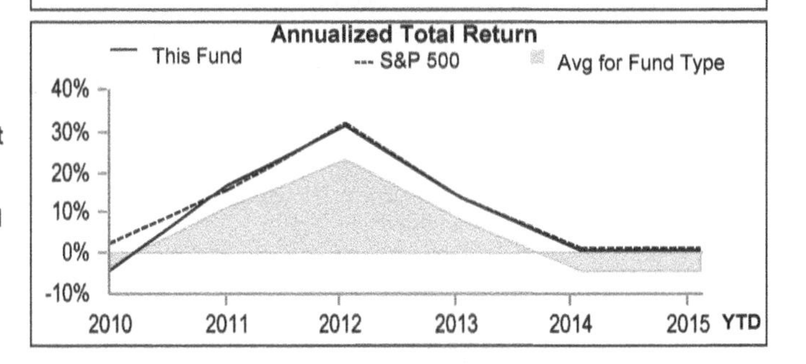

Adams Natural Resources (PEO) D+ Weak

Fund Family: Petroleum & Resources Corporation
Fund Type: Energy/Natural Resources
Inception Date: N/A

Data Date	Investment Rating	Net Assets ($Mil)	Price	Performance Rating/Pts	Total Return Y-T-D	Risk Rating/Pts
12-15	D+	754.51	17.74	D+ / 2.5	-19.75%	C+ / 5.9
2014	C-	970.10	23.84	C- / 3.2	-5.07%	B- / 7.5
2013	C+	776.23	27.38	C+ / 6.2	15.86%	B- / 7.4
2012	D+	710.41	23.92	C- / 3.3	7.74%	B- / 7.3
2011	C	732.80	24.48	C / 4.7	-1.36%	B- / 7.4
2010	C	650.72	27.02	C / 4.6	19.58%	C+ / 5.8

Major Rating Factors:
Disappointing performance is the major factor driving the D+ (Weak) TheStreet.com Investment Rating for Adams Natural Resources. The fund currently has a performance rating of D+ (Weak) based on an annualized return of -4.06% over the last three years and a total return of -19.75% year to date 2015. Factored into the performance evaluation is an expense ratio of 0.63% (very low).

The fund's risk rating is currently C+ (Fair). It carries a beta of 0.92, meaning that its performance tracks fairly well with that of the overall stock market. Volatility, as measured by both the semi-deviation and a drawdown factor, is considered low. As of December 31, 2015, Adams Natural Resources traded at a discount of 14.46% below its net asset value, which is better than its one-year historical average discount of 13.88%.

Mark E. Stoeckle has been running the fund for 3 years and currently receives a manager quality ranking of 74 (0=worst, 99=best). This fund offers only a moderate level of risk but investors looking for strong performance are still waiting.

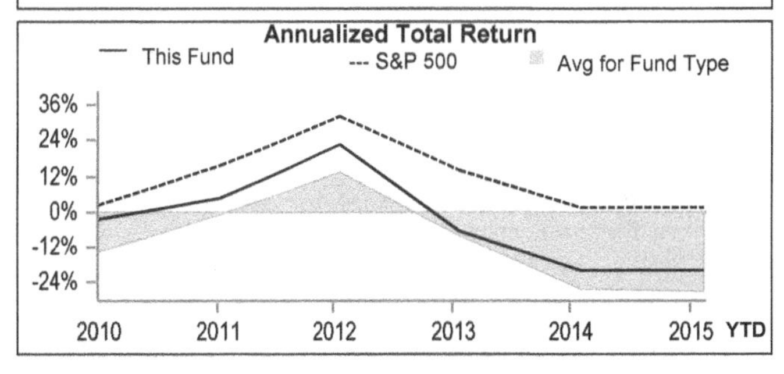

Advent Claymore Cnv Sec & Inc (AVK) C- Fair

Fund Family: Advent Capital Management LLC
Fund Type: Growth and Income
Inception Date: April 30, 2003

Data Date	Investment Rating	Net Assets ($Mil)	Price	Performance Rating/Pts	Total Return Y-T-D	Risk Rating/Pts
12-15	C-	448.03	13.52	C- / 3.4	-10.94%	C+ / 6.7
2014	C	447.20	16.35	C- / 4.1	-5.71%	B / 8.2
2013	C+	444.81	18.53	C+ / 6.6	17.58%	C+ / 6.8
2012	C-	413.04	16.12	C / 4.3	13.66%	C+ / 6.7
2011	C	390.20	14.73	C+ / 6.2	-6.03%	C+ / 6.6
2010	C	456.14	18.09	C+ / 6.9	27.15%	C- / 3.6

Major Rating Factors: Middle of the road best describes Advent Claymore Cnv Sec & Inc whose TheStreet.com Investment Rating is currently a C- (Fair). The fund currently has a performance rating of C- (Fair) based on an annualized return of -0.46% over the last three years and a total return of -10.94% year to date 2015. Factored into the performance evaluation is an expense ratio of 2.32% (high).

The fund's risk rating is currently C+ (Fair). It carries a beta of 1.02, meaning that its performance tracks fairly well with that of the overall stock market. Volatility, as measured by both the semi-deviation and a drawdown factor, is considered low. As of December 31, 2015, Advent Claymore Cnv Sec & Inc traded at a discount of 16.80% below its net asset value, which is better than its one-year historical average discount of 12.95%.

Paul L. Latronica currently receives a manager quality ranking of 12 (0=worst, 99=best). If you desire an average level of risk, then this fund may be an option.

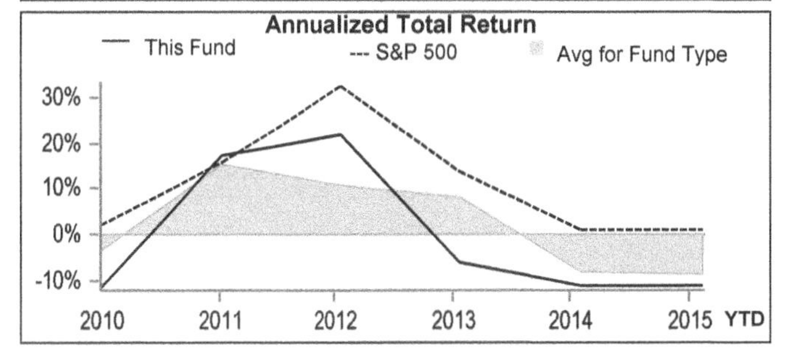

* Denotes ETF Fund

Advent Claymore Enhanced Gr & Inc (LCM) C Fair

Fund Family: Guggenheim Funds Investment Advisor
Fund Type: Global
Inception Date: January 26, 2005

Major Rating Factors: Middle of the road best describes Advent Claymore Enhanced Gr & Inc whose TheStreet.com Investment Rating is currently a C (Fair). The fund currently has a performance rating of C+ (Fair) based on an annualized return of 3.61% over the last three years and a total return of 1.77% year to date 2015. Factored into the performance evaluation is an expense ratio of 2.10% (high).

The fund's risk rating is currently C+ (Fair). It carries a beta of 0.73, meaning the fund's expected move will be 7.3% for every 10% move in the market. Volatility, as measured by both the semi-deviation and a drawdown factor, is considered low. As of December 31, 2015, Advent Claymore Enhanced Gr & Inc traded at a discount of 13.67% below its net asset value, which is better than its one-year historical average discount of 13.47%.

Paul L. Latronica has been running the fund for 9 years and currently receives a manager quality ranking of 75 (0=worst, 99=best). If you desire an average level of risk, then this fund may be an option.

Data Date	Investment Rating	Net Assets ($Mil)	Price	Performance Rating/Pts	Total Return Y-T-D	Risk Rating/Pts
12-15	C	147.82	8.27	C+ / 5.7	1.77%	C+ / 6.8
2014	C-	148.10	8.90	C- / 3.9	-4.23%	B- / 7.5
2013	C-	152.56	10.13	C / 4.8	13.86%	C+ / 6.7
2012	D+	144.53	9.10	D+ / 2.9	13.30%	C+ / 6.7
2011	C-	138.80	8.98	C- / 3.8	-14.53%	B- / 7.3
2010	C-	171.50	11.80	C / 5.0	15.91%	C / 4.3

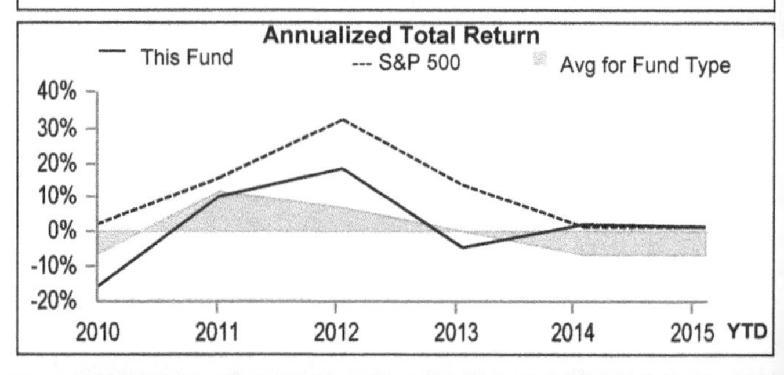

Advent/Claymore Con Sec & Inc (AGC) C- Fair

Fund Family: Guggenheim Funds Investment Advisor
Fund Type: Growth and Income
Inception Date: May 25, 2007

Major Rating Factors: Middle of the road best describes Advent/Claymore Con Sec & Inc whose TheStreet.com Investment Rating is currently a C- (Fair). The fund currently has a performance rating of C (Fair) based on an annualized return of 1.73% over the last three years and a total return of -3.30% year to date 2015. Factored into the performance evaluation is an expense ratio of 3.06% (high).

The fund's risk rating is currently C+ (Fair). It carries a beta of 1.02, meaning that its performance tracks fairly well with that of the overall stock market. Volatility, as measured by both the semi-deviation and a drawdown factor, is considered low. As of December 31, 2015, Advent/Claymore Con Sec & Inc traded at a discount of 17.29% below its net asset value, which is better than its one-year historical average discount of 15.34%.

Paul L. Latronica has been running the fund for 9 years and currently receives a manager quality ranking of 15 (0=worst, 99=best). If you desire an average level of risk, then this fund may be an option.

Data Date	Investment Rating	Net Assets ($Mil)	Price	Performance Rating/Pts	Total Return Y-T-D	Risk Rating/Pts
12-15	C-	246.13	5.55	C / 4.7	-3.30%	C+ / 6.3
2014	C-	247.60	6.30	C- / 3.8	-6.51%	B- / 7.8
2013	D+	253.36	7.28	C / 4.5	16.64%	C+ / 6.0
2012	D	238.69	6.48	D+ / 2.4	12.71%	C+ / 6.0
2011	D+	224.90	6.30	C- / 3.6	-24.11%	C+ / 6.1
2010	E+	300.46	9.17	D / 1.9	22.95%	C- / 3.0

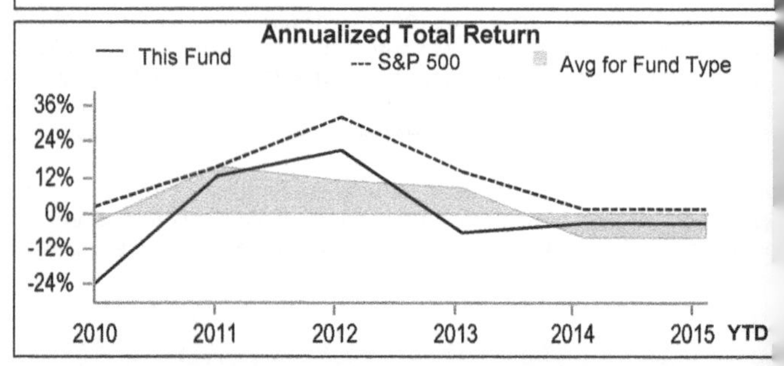

Alliance CA Municipal Income Fund (AKP) B+ Good

Fund Family: AllianceBernstein LP
Fund Type: Municipal - Single State
Inception Date: January 28, 2002

Major Rating Factors: Strong performance is the major factor driving the B+ (Good) TheStreet.com Investment Rating for Alliance CA Municipal Income Fund. The fund currently has a performance rating of B (Good) based on an annualized return of 3.51% over the last three years and a total return of 9.55% year to date 2015. Factored into the performance evaluation is an expense ratio of 1.44% (average).

The fund's risk rating is currently B- (Good). It carries a beta of 2.02, meaning it is expected to move 20.2% for every 10% move in the market. Volatility, as measured by both the semi-deviation and a drawdown factor, is considered low. As of December 31, 2015, Alliance CA Municipal Income Fund traded at a discount of 8.68% below its net asset value, which is better than its one-year historical average discount of 8.16%.

Michael G. Brooks currently receives a manager quality ranking of 52 (0=worst, 99=best). If you desire only a moderate level of risk and strong performance, then this fund is an excellent option.

Data Date	Investment Rating	Net Assets ($Mil)	Price	Performance Rating/Pts	Total Return Y-T-D	Risk Rating/Pts
12-15	B+	128.34	14.09	B / 7.7	9.55%	B- / 7.6
2014	C+	127.50	13.56	C+ / 5.9	17.42%	B- / 7.6
2013	C-	128.71	12.13	C- / 3.9	-13.89%	B- / 7.9
2012	B+	119.97	14.65	B- / 7.1	8.84%	B / 8.8
2011	A	115.27	14.51	B+ / 8.9	20.16%	B+ / 9.0
2010	C+	121.80	13.18	C / 4.8	10.12%	C+ / 6.5

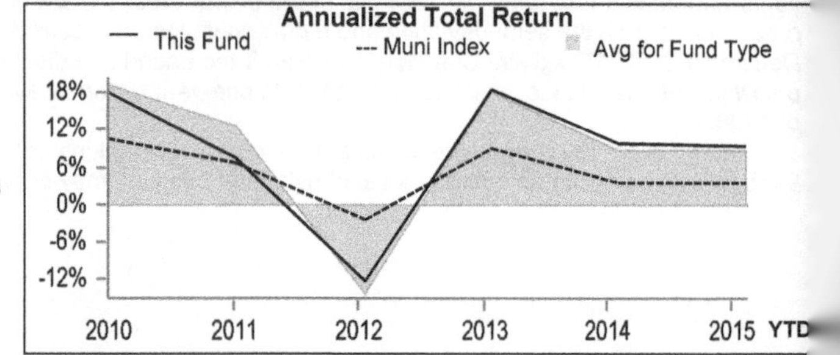

AllianceBernstein Global High Inc (AWF) C- Fair

Fund Family: AllianceBernstein LP
Fund Type: Global
Inception Date: July 23, 1993

Major Rating Factors: Middle of the road best describes AllianceBernstein Global High Inc whose TheStreet.com Investment Rating is currently a C- (Fair). The fund currently has a performance rating of C- (Fair) based on an annualized return of -2.70% over the last three years and a total return of -4.80% year to date 2015. Factored into the performance evaluation is an expense ratio of 1.01% (low).

The fund's risk rating is currently C+ (Fair). It carries a beta of 0.53, meaning the fund's expected move will be 5.3% for every 10% move in the market. Volatility, as measured by both the semi-deviation and a drawdown factor, is considered low. As of December 31, 2015, AllianceBernstein Global High Inc traded at a discount of 12.36% below its net asset value, which is better than its one-year historical average discount of 12.32%.

Paul J. DeNoon has been running the fund for 24 years and currently receives a manager quality ranking of 69 (0=worst, 99=best). If you desire an average level of risk, then this fund may be an option.

Data Date	Investment Rating	Net Assets ($Mil)	Price	Performance Rating/Pts	Total Return Y-T-D	Risk Rating/Pts
12-15	C-	1,207.98	10.78	C- / 3.3	-4.80%	C+ / 6.4
2014	C-	1,284.50	12.43	C- / 3.7	-3.92%	B- / 7.4
2013	C+	1,352.23	14.28	C+ / 6.3	-0.08%	B / 8.3
2012	B	1,267.20	15.65	B / 7.9	24.71%	B- / 7.7
2011	B+	1,186.30	14.17	B+ / 8.9	13.15%	B / 8.1
2010	B	1,232.80	14.30	B+ / 8.3	16.34%	C / 5.0

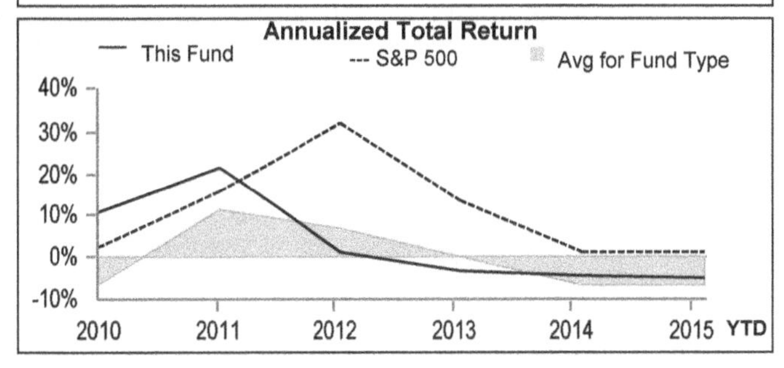

AllianceBernstein Income Fund (ACG) C+ Fair

Fund Family: AllianceBernstein LP
Fund Type: Global
Inception Date: August 21, 1987

Major Rating Factors: Middle of the road best describes AllianceBernstein Income Fund whose TheStreet.com Investment Rating is currently a C+ (Fair). The fund currently has a performance rating of C+ (Fair) based on an annualized return of 4.35% over the last three years and a total return of 9.42% year to date 2015. Factored into the performance evaluation is an expense ratio of 0.67% (very low).

The fund's risk rating is currently B- (Good). It carries a beta of 0.44, meaning the fund's expected move will be 4.4% for every 10% move in the market. Volatility, as measured by both the semi-deviation and a drawdown factor, is considered low. As of December 31, 2015, AllianceBernstein Income Fund traded at a discount of 2.42% below its net asset value, which is worse than its one-year historical average discount of 7.03%.

Douglas J. Peebles has been running the fund for 29 years and currently receives a manager quality ranking of 91 (0=worst, 99=best). If you desire an average level of risk, then this fund may be an option.

Data Date	Investment Rating	Net Assets ($Mil)	Price	Performance Rating/Pts	Total Return Y-T-D	Risk Rating/Pts
12-15	C+	1.90	7.67	C+ / 6.5	9.42%	B- / 7.3
2014	C	1,979.60	7.47	C / 4.6	11.47%	B / 8.0
2013	C	2,034.00	7.13	C- / 4.1	-7.06%	B / 8.2
2012	C	2.24	8.10	C- / 4.1	13.28%	B+ / 9.1
2011	C+	2,168.20	8.07	C / 4.5	11.75%	B+ / 9.2
2010	B	2,099.85	7.93	C / 4.7	2.11%	B / 8.3

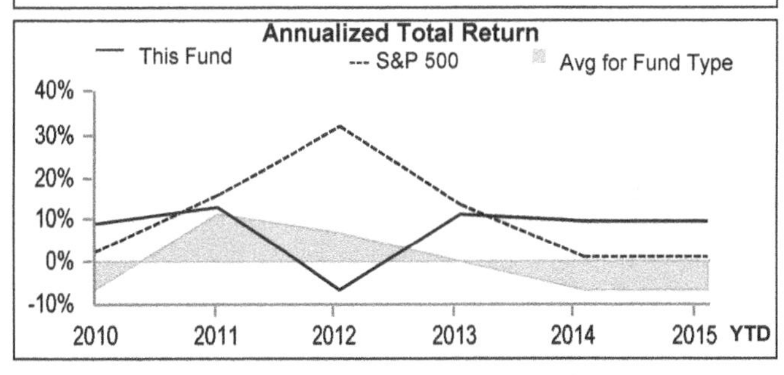

AllianceBernstein Nat Muni Inc Fun (AFB) C+ Fair

Fund Family: AllianceBernstein LP
Fund Type: Municipal - National
Inception Date: January 28, 2002

Major Rating Factors: Middle of the road best describes AllianceBernstein Nat Muni Inc Fun whose TheStreet.com Investment Rating is currently a C+ (Fair). The fund currently has a performance rating of C+ (Fair) based on an annualized return of 0.84% over the last three years and a total return of 6.57% year to date 2015. Factored into the performance evaluation is an expense ratio of 1.17% (low).

The fund's risk rating is currently B- (Good). It carries a beta of 2.65, meaning it is expected to move 26.5% for every 10% move in the market. Volatility, as measured by both the semi-deviation and a drawdown factor, is considered low. As of December 31, 2015, AllianceBernstein Nat Muni Inc Fun traded at a discount of 8.84% below its net asset value, which is better than its one-year historical average discount of 8.23%.

Michael G. Brooks currently receives a manager quality ranking of 27 (0=worst, 99=best). If you desire an average level of risk, then this fund may be an option.

Data Date	Investment Rating	Net Assets ($Mil)	Price	Performance Rating/Pts	Total Return Y-T-D	Risk Rating/Pts
12-15	C+	425.08	13.81	C+ / 5.9	6.57%	B- / 7.6
2014	C+	422.30	13.77	C+ / 5.8	16.60%	B- / 7.7
2013	C	434.21	12.53	C / 4.7	-17.37%	B / 8.0
2012	A+	409.20	15.55	A- / 9.1	19.71%	B / 8.8
2011	A+	386.44	14.78	A / 9.5	26.13%	B / 8.9
2010	C	403.45	12.94	C / 4.5	3.32%	C+ / 6.1

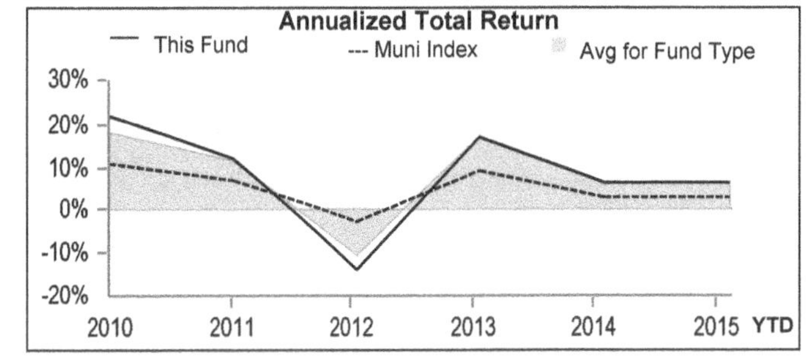

AllianzGI Convertible & Income II (NCZ) D- Weak

Fund Family: Allianz Global Investors Fund Mgmt
Fund Type: Growth and Income
Inception Date: July 28, 2003

Data Date	Investment Rating	Net Assets ($Mil)	Price	Performance Rating/Pts	Total Return Y-T-D	Risk Rating/Pts
12-15	D-	559.34	5.05	D / 1.6	-37.87%	C / 4.8
2014	C+	588.40	8.91	C+ / 6.9	9.40%	C+ / 6.5
2013	B-	569.13	8.98	B- / 7.3	23.68%	B- / 7.5
2012	C-	472.61	7.93	C- / 4.2	13.72%	B- / 7.4
2011	B	449.50	7.87	A- / 9.0	-3.45%	B- / 7.0
2010	C-	487.13	9.37	B- / 7.2	24.41%	D / 1.8

Major Rating Factors:
Disappointing performance is the major factor driving the D- (Weak) TheStreet.com Investment Rating for AllianzGI Convertible & Income II. The fund currently has a performance rating of D (Weak) based on an annualized return of -6.10% over the last three years and a total return of -37.87% year to date 2015. Factored into the performance evaluation is an expense ratio of 1.19% (average).

The fund's risk rating is currently C (Fair). It carries a beta of 0.92, meaning that its performance tracks fairly well with that of the overall stock market. Volatility, as measured by both the semi-deviation and a drawdown factor, is considered average. As of December 31, 2015, AllianzGI Convertible & Income II traded at a discount of 9.01% below its net asset value, which is better than its one-year historical average premium of 2.03%.

Douglas G. Forsyth has been running the fund for 13 years and currently receives a manager quality ranking of 10 (0=worst, 99=best). This fund offers an average level of risk but investors looking for strong performance will be frustrated.

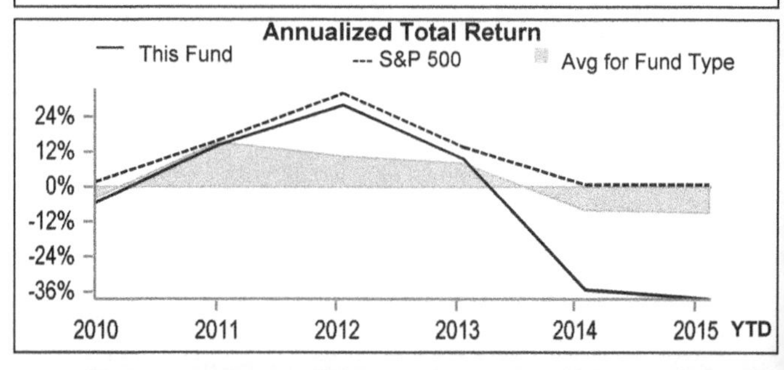

AllianzGI Convertible and Income (NCV) D Weak

Fund Family: Allianz Global Investors Fund Mgmt
Fund Type: Growth and Income
Inception Date: March 26, 2003

Data Date	Investment Rating	Net Assets ($Mil)	Price	Performance Rating/Pts	Total Return Y-T-D	Risk Rating/Pts
12-15	D	739.98	5.54	D / 2.1	-32.44%	C / 5.2
2014	C+	775.90	9.42	C+ / 6.6	7.79%	C+ / 6.7
2013	B-	728.37	9.71	B- / 7.1	21.31%	B- / 7.5
2012	C-	627.09	8.69	C / 4.5	13.04%	B- / 7.2
2011	B	595.10	8.45	B+ / 8.8	-4.14%	C+ / 6.5
2010	C-	644.41	10.24	B / 7.9	24.09%	D / 1.7

Major Rating Factors:
Disappointing performance is the major factor driving the D (Weak) TheStreet.com Investment Rating for AllianzGI Convertible and Income. The fund currently has a performance rating of D (Weak) based on an annualized return of -4.30% over the last three years and a total return of -32.44% year to date 2015. Factored into the performance evaluation is an expense ratio of 1.23% (average).

The fund's risk rating is currently C (Fair). It carries a beta of 1.05, meaning that its performance tracks fairly well with that of the overall stock market. Volatility, as measured by both the semi-deviation and a drawdown factor, is considered average. As of December 31, 2015, AllianzGI Convertible and Income traded at a discount of 11.22% below its net asset value, which is better than its one-year historical average premium of .08%.

Douglas G. Forsyth has been running the fund for 13 years and currently receives a manager quality ranking of 9 (0=worst, 99=best). This fund offers an average level of risk but investors looking for strong performance will be frustrated.

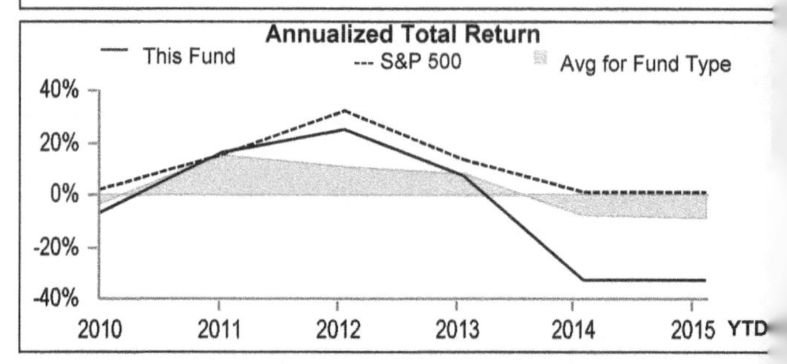

AllianzGI Equity and Conv Inc (NIE) B- Good

Fund Family: Allianz Global Investors Fund Mgmt
Fund Type: Income
Inception Date: February 27, 2007

Data Date	Investment Rating	Net Assets ($Mil)	Price	Performance Rating/Pts	Total Return Y-T-D	Risk Rating/Pts
12-15	B-	613.13	17.96	B- / 7.0	-5.40%	B- / 7.5
2014	B+	624.60	20.68	B- / 7.4	13.45%	B / 8.5
2013	B-	448.38	19.52	C+ / 6.9	21.16%	B- / 7.7
2012	C-	416.87	16.64	C- / 3.4	12.13%	B- / 7.5
2011	C-	403.70	15.60	C- / 4.1	-6.88%	B- / 7.4
2010	C	392.09	18.21	C+ / 5.6	15.68%	C / 5.1

Major Rating Factors: Strong performance is the major factor driving the B- (Good) TheStreet.com Investment Rating for AllianzGI Equity and Conv Inc. The fund currently has a performance rating of B- (Good) based on an annualized return of 8.98% over the last three years and a total return of -5.40% year to date 2015. Factored into the performance evaluation is an expense ratio of 1.13% (low).

The fund's risk rating is currently B- (Good). It carries a beta of 1.00, meaning that its performance tracks fairly well with that of the overall stock market. Volatility, as measured by both the semi-deviation and a drawdown factor, is considered low. As of December 31, 2015, AllianzGI Equity and Conv Inc traded at a discount of 14.07% below its net asset value, which is better than its one-year historical average discount of 12.83%.

Douglas G. Forsyth currently receives a manager quality ranking of 35 (0=worst, 99=best). If you desire only a moderate level of risk and strong performance, then this fund is an excellent option.

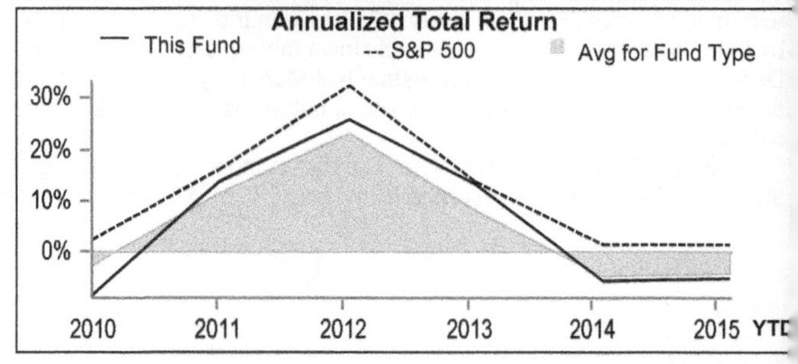

AllianzGI NFJ Div Int and Prem Str (NFJ) C- Fair

Fund Family: Allianz Global Investors Fund Mgmt
Fund Type: Growth and Income
Inception Date: February 23, 2005

Major Rating Factors: Middle of the road best describes AllianzGI NFJ Div Int and Prem Str whose TheStreet.com Investment Rating is currently a C- (Fair). The fund currently has a performance rating of C- (Fair) based on an annualized return of 1.72% over the last three years and a total return of -14.31% year to date 2015. Factored into the performance evaluation is an expense ratio of 0.96% (low).

The fund's risk rating is currently C+ (Fair). It carries a beta of 0.61, meaning the fund's expected move will be 6.1% for every 10% move in the market. Volatility, as measured by both the semi-deviation and a drawdown factor, is considered low. As of December 31, 2015, AllianzGI NFJ Div Int and Prem Str traded at a discount of 13.30% below its net asset value, which is better than its one-year historical average discount of 9.81%.

Benno J. Fischer currently receives a manager quality ranking of 27 (0=worst, 99=best). If you desire an average level of risk, then this fund may be an option.

Data Date	Investment Rating	Net Assets ($Mil)	Price	Performance Rating/Pts	Total Return Y-T-D	Risk Rating/Pts
12-15	C-	1,606.72	12.39	C- / 3.7	-14.31%	C+ / 6.8
2014	C	1,703.70	16.00	C / 4.5	-0.31%	B / 8.1
2013	B-	1,692.66	17.71	B- / 7.2	21.91%	B- / 7.7
2012	C-	1,644.18	15.60	C- / 3.8	6.22%	B- / 7.7
2011	C-	1,661.60	16.02	C / 4.4	4.29%	B- / 7.5
2010	C-	1,635.73	17.51	C- / 4.2	22.29%	C+ / 5.8

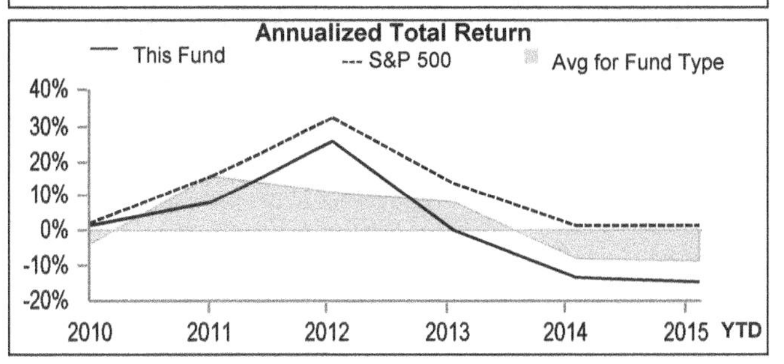

Alpine Global Dynamic Div Fd (AGD) C Fair

Fund Family: Alpine Woods Capital Investors LLC
Fund Type: Global
Inception Date: July 26, 2006

Major Rating Factors: Middle of the road best describes Alpine Global Dynamic Div Fd whose TheStreet.com Investment Rating is currently a C (Fair). The fund currently has a performance rating of C (Fair) based on an annualized return of 0.98% over the last three years and a total return of -2.50% year to date 2015. Factored into the performance evaluation is an expense ratio of 1.42% (average).

The fund's risk rating is currently B- (Good). It carries a beta of 0.73, meaning the fund's expected move will be 7.3% for every 10% move in the market. Volatility, as measured by both the semi-deviation and a drawdown factor, is considered low. As of December 31, 2015, Alpine Global Dynamic Div Fd traded at a discount of 15.07% below its net asset value, which is better than its one-year historical average discount of 13.64%.

Samuel A. Lieber currently receives a manager quality ranking of 55 (0=worst, 99=best). If you desire an average level of risk, then this fund may be an option.

Data Date	Investment Rating	Net Assets ($Mil)	Price	Performance Rating/Pts	Total Return Y-T-D	Risk Rating/Pts
12-15	C	140.71	8.85	C / 4.4	-2.50%	B- / 7.8
2014	C	140.60	9.84	C / 4.7	5.35%	B- / 7.4
2013	D	135.31	5.10	D+ / 2.3	0.25%	C+ / 6.1
2012	E+	142.83	5.23	E+ / 0.9	13.20%	C / 4.6
2011	D-	192.55	5.17	D / 1.6	-23.82%	C / 4.8
2010	D-	177.05	7.29	E+ / 0.6	-17.71%	C / 4.6

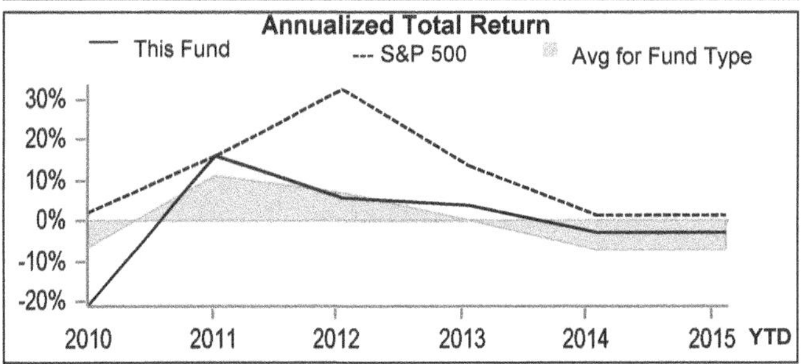

Alpine Global Premier Properties F (AWP) C- Fair

Fund Family: Alpine Woods Capital Investors LLC
Fund Type: Growth and Income
Inception Date: April 25, 2007

Major Rating Factors: Middle of the road best describes Alpine Global Premier Properties F whose TheStreet.com Investment Rating is currently a C- (Fair). The fund currently has a performance rating of C- (Fair) based on an annualized return of -0.05% over the last three years and a total return of -11.03% year to date 2015. Factored into the performance evaluation is an expense ratio of 1.29% (average).

The fund's risk rating is currently C+ (Fair). It carries a beta of 1.14, meaning it is expected to move 11.4% for every 10% move in the market. Volatility, as measured by both the semi-deviation and a drawdown factor, is considered low. As of December 31, 2015, Alpine Global Premier Properties F traded at a discount of 17.45% below its net asset value, which is better than its one-year historical average discount of 14.78%.

Samuel A. Lieber has been running the fund for 9 years and currently receives a manager quality ranking of 11 (0=worst, 99=best). If you desire an average level of risk, then this fund may be an option.

Data Date	Investment Rating	Net Assets ($Mil)	Price	Performance Rating/Pts	Total Return Y-T-D	Risk Rating/Pts
12-15	C-	672.13	5.77	C- / 3.7	-11.03%	C+ / 6.3
2014	B+	666.40	7.21	B / 8.0	9.67%	B- / 7.6
2013	C	764.99	7.19	C+ / 5.7	3.46%	B- / 7.0
2012	B	758.72	7.28	B+ / 8.8	51.27%	C+ / 6.8
2011	C	956.40	5.30	C / 5.5	-15.95%	C+ / 6.7
2010	D-	794.94	7.09	D / 1.9	21.04%	C / 4.3

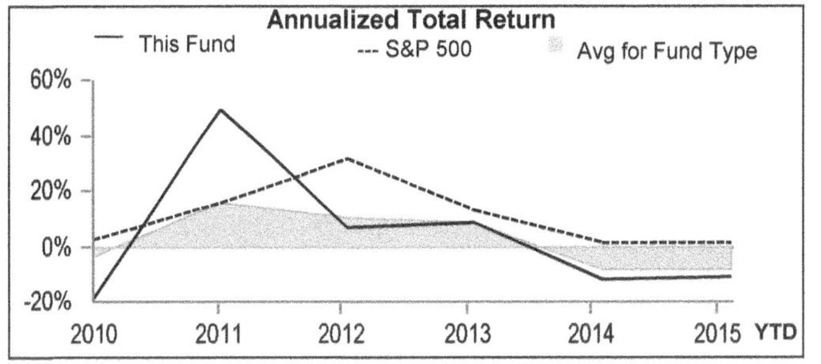

Alpine Total Dynamic Dividend Fund (AOD) C+ Fair

Fund Family: Alpine Woods Capital Investors LLC
Fund Type: Global
Inception Date: January 26, 2007

Major Rating Factors: Middle of the road best describes Alpine Total Dynamic Dividend Fund whose TheStreet.com Investment Rating is currently a C+ (Fair). The fund currently has a performance rating of C+ (Fair) based on an annualized return of 5.64% over the last three years and a total return of -3.30% year to date 2015. Factored into the performance evaluation is an expense ratio of 1.14% (low).

The fund's risk rating is currently B- (Good). It carries a beta of 0.77, meaning the fund's expected move will be 7.7% for every 10% move in the market. Volatility, as measured by both the semi-deviation and a drawdown factor, is considered low. As of December 31, 2015, Alpine Total Dynamic Dividend Fund traded at a discount of 16.61% below its net asset value, which is better than its one-year historical average discount of 14.86%.

Samuel A. Lieber currently receives a manager quality ranking of 83 (0=worst, 99=best). If you desire an average level of risk, then this fund may be an option.

Data Date	Investment Rating	Net Assets ($Mil)	Price	Performance Rating/Pts	Total Return Y-T-D	Risk Rating/Pts
12-15	C+	1,077.05	7.68	C+ / 5.9	-3.30%	B- / 7.8
2014	C+	1,071.90	8.49	C / 5.4	9.08%	B / 8.0
2013	D+	1,052.90	4.19	C- / 3.5	10.08%	C+ / 6.5
2012	E+	1,134.04	4.03	E+ / 0.8	7.99%	C / 4.7
2011	D-	1,504.33	4.38	D / 1.6	-16.45%	C / 5.0
2010	D-	1,424.57	5.92	E+ / 0.7	-22.17%	C / 4.6

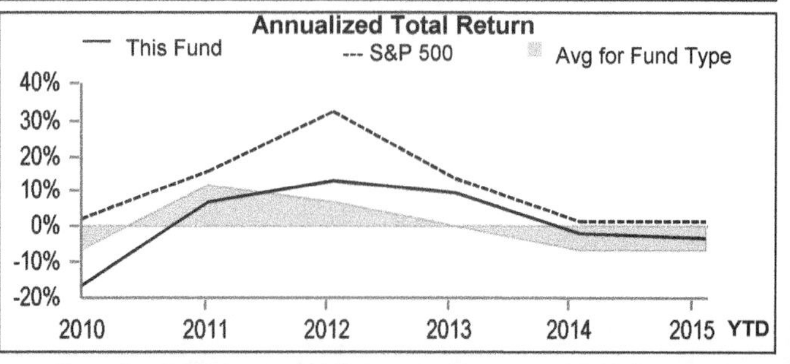

Apollo Senior Floating Rate Fd Inc (AFT) C- Fair

Fund Family: Apollo Credit Management LLC
Fund Type: Loan Participation
Inception Date: February 24, 2011

Major Rating Factors: Middle of the road best describes Apollo Senior Floating Rate Fd Inc whose TheStreet.com Investment Rating is currently a C- (Fair). The fund currently has a performance rating of C- (Fair) based on an annualized return of -0.48% over the last three years and a total return of -2.63% year to date 2015. Factored into the performance evaluation is an expense ratio of 3.07% (high).

The fund's risk rating is currently B- (Good). It carries a beta of -126.88, meaning the fund's expected move will be -1268.8% for every 10% move in the market. Volatility, as measured by both the semi-deviation and a drawdown factor, is considered low. As of December 31, 2015, Apollo Senior Floating Rate Fd Inc traded at a discount of 10.51% below its net asset value, which is better than its one-year historical average discount of 7.15%.

Joseph A. Moroney currently receives a manager quality ranking of 43 (0=worst, 99=best). If you desire an average level of risk, then this fund may be an option.

Data Date	Investment Rating	Net Assets ($Mil)	Price	Performance Rating/Pts	Total Return Y-T-D	Risk Rating/Pts
12-15	C-	284.99	15.15	C- / 3.6	-2.63%	B- / 7.2
2014	C	293.60	16.63	C / 4.3	-1.47%	B / 8.2
2013	C-	290.82	18.10	C- / 3.6	2.43%	B- / 7.9
2012	B+	283.96	18.77	B / 8.2	23.59%	B- / 7.8

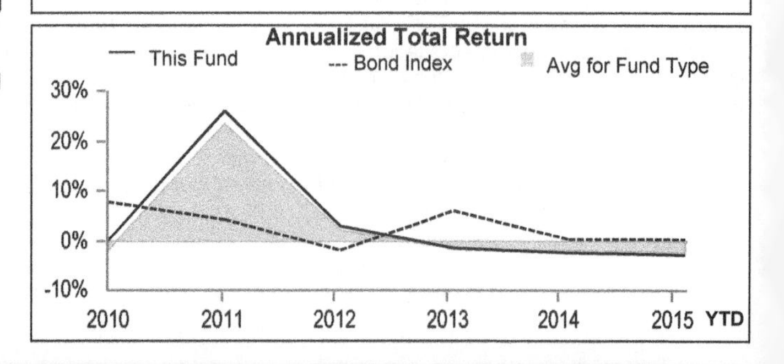

Apollo Tactical Income Fund Inc (AIF) C- Fair

Fund Family: Apollo Credit Management LLC
Fund Type: General - Investment Grade
Inception Date: February 26, 2013

Major Rating Factors:
Disappointing performance is the major factor driving the C- (Fair) TheStreet.com Investment Rating for Apollo Tactical Income Fund Inc. The fund currently has a performance rating of D+ (Weak) based on an annualized return of 0.00% over the last three years and a total return of -4.55% year to date 2015. Factored into the performance evaluation is an expense ratio of 2.90% (high).

The fund's risk rating is currently B- (Good). It carries a beta of 0.00, meaning the fund's expected move will be 0.0% for every 10% move in the market. Volatility, as measured by both the semi-deviation and a drawdown factor, is considered low. As of December 31, 2015, Apollo Tactical Income Fund Inc traded at a discount of 13.73% below its net asset value, which is better than its one-year historical average discount of 13.26%.

Bret Leas currently receives a manager quality ranking of 37 (0=worst, 99=best). This fund offers only a moderate level of risk but investors looking for strong performance are still waiting.

Data Date	Investment Rating	Net Assets ($Mil)	Price	Performance Rating/Pts	Total Return Y-T-D	Risk Rating/Pts
12-15	C-	263.43	13.89	D+ / 2.5	-4.55%	B- / 7.2
2014	D+	281.00	15.96	D / 1.7	-2.59%	B- / 7.5

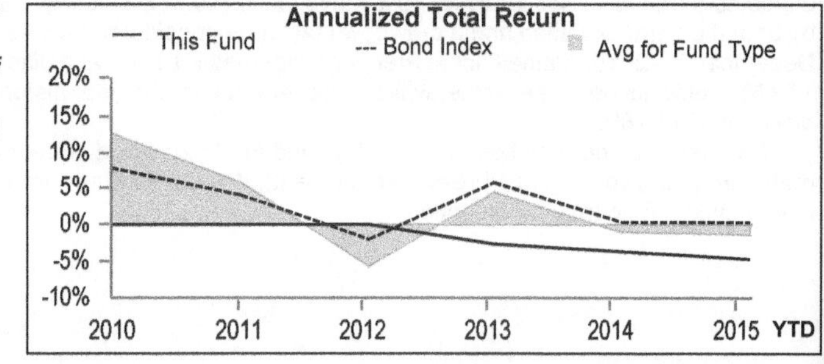

Ares Dynamic Credit Allocation Fun (ARDC) D+ Weak

Fund Family: Ares Capital Management II LLC
Fund Type: Corporate - High Yield
Inception Date: November 27, 2012

Data Date	Investment Rating	Net Assets ($Mil)	Price	Performance Rating/Pts	Total Return Y-T-D	Risk Rating/Pts
12-15	D+	321.37	13.36	D+ / 2.5	-8.63%	B- / 7.0
2014	D+	325.90	15.82	D- / 1.4	-5.03%	B- / 7.9
2013	C-	335.20	17.98	D / 2.0	-3.99%	B+ / 9.0

Major Rating Factors:
Disappointing performance is the major factor driving the D+ (Weak) TheStreet.com Investment Rating for Ares Dynamic Credit Allocation Fun. The fund currently has a performance rating of D+ (Weak) based on an annualized return of -5.73% over the last three years and a total return of -8.63% year to date 2015. Factored into the performance evaluation is an expense ratio of 2.58% (high).

The fund's risk rating is currently B- (Good). It carries a beta of 1.11, meaning it is expected to move 11.1% for every 10% move in the market. Volatility, as measured by both the semi-deviation and a drawdown factor, is considered low. As of December 31, 2015, Ares Dynamic Credit Allocation Fun traded at a discount of 14.74% below its net asset value, which is better than its one-year historical average discount of 13.78%.

John Leupp has been running the fund for 1 year and currently receives a manager quality ranking of 22 (0=worst, 99=best). This fund offers only a moderate level of risk but investors looking for strong performance are still waiting.

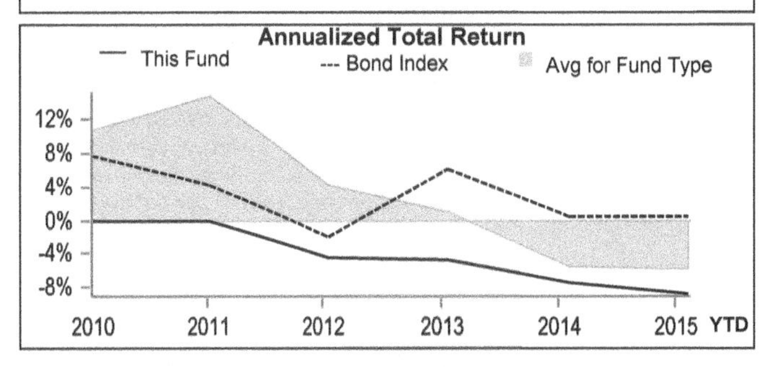

ASA Gold & Precious Metals Ltd (ASA) E+ Very Weak

Fund Family: ASA Limited
Fund Type: Precious Metals
Inception Date: N/A

Data Date	Investment Rating	Net Assets ($Mil)	Price	Performance Rating/Pts	Total Return Y-T-D	Risk Rating/Pts
12-15	E+	221.80	7.17	E / 0.4	-30.86%	C- / 3.7
2014	E+	253.10	10.11	E / 0.4	-18.33%	C / 4.3
2013	E+	302.36	12.26	E / 0.4	-41.92%	C / 4.7
2012	E	455.24	21.53	E+ / 0.9	-17.80%	D+ / 2.8
2011	D	549.40	26.19	C+ / 6.3	-10.24%	D+ / 2.5
2010	C	580.36	34.71	B+ / 8.9	35.98%	D / 1.6

Major Rating Factors:
Very poor performance is the major factor driving the E+ (Very Weak) TheStreet.com Investment Rating for ASA Gold & Precious Metals Ltd. The fund currently has a performance rating of E (Very Weak) based on an annualized return of -30.34% over the last three years and a total return of -30.86% year to date 2015. Factored into the performance evaluation is an expense ratio of 1.37% (average).

The fund's risk rating is currently C- (Fair). It carries a beta of 1.48, meaning it is expected to move 14.8% for every 10% move in the market. Volatility, as measured by both the semi-deviation and a drawdown factor, is considered average. As of December 31, 2015, ASA Gold & Precious Metals Ltd traded at a discount of 13.93% below its net asset value, which is better than its one-year historical average discount of 10.75%.

David J. Christensen currently receives a manager quality ranking of 12 (0=worst, 99=best). This fund offers an average level of risk but investors looking for strong performance will be frustrated.

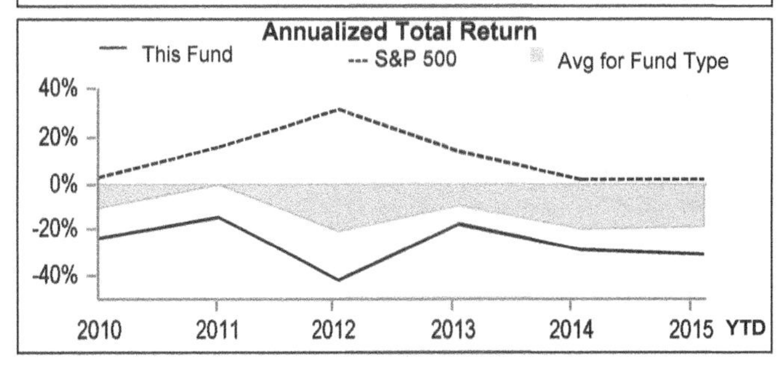

Asia Pacific Fund (APB) C- Fair

Fund Family: Value Partners Hong Kong Limited
Fund Type: Foreign
Inception Date: April 24, 1987

Data Date	Investment Rating	Net Assets ($Mil)	Price	Performance Rating/Pts	Total Return Y-T-D	Risk Rating/Pts
12-15	C-	135.24	10.07	C- / 3.2	-5.00%	C+ / 6.8
2014	C	135.40	11.28	C / 4.6	10.05%	B / 8.0
2013	D	123.27	10.51	D / 1.6	-7.91%	B- / 7.1
2012	D+	120.72	10.82	D+ / 2.5	13.03%	B- / 7.1
2011	C-	107.30	9.40	C- / 3.6	-21.08%	B- / 7.2
2010	D	113.44	11.95	C / 4.6	14.90%	C- / 3.3

Major Rating Factors: Middle of the road best describes Asia Pacific Fund whose TheStreet.com Investment Rating is currently a C- (Fair). The fund currently has a performance rating of C- (Fair) based on an annualized return of -1.64% over the last three years and a total return of -5.00% year to date 2015. Factored into the performance evaluation is an expense ratio of 2.05% (high).

The fund's risk rating is currently C+ (Fair). It carries a beta of 0.80, meaning the fund's expected move will be 8.0% for every 10% move in the market. Volatility, as measured by both the semi-deviation and a drawdown factor, is considered low. As of December 31, 2015, Asia Pacific Fund traded at a discount of 14.44% below its net asset value, which is better than its one-year historical average discount of 12.61%.

Norman M. K. Ho has been running the fund for 2 years and currently receives a manager quality ranking of 31 (0=worst, 99=best). If you desire an average level of risk, then this fund may be an option.

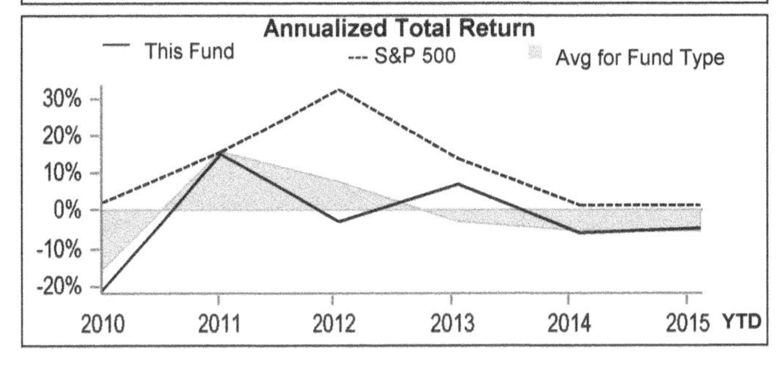

Asia Tigers Fund (GRR) D+ Weak

Fund Family: Aberdeen Asset Management Asia Ltd
Fund Type: Foreign
Inception Date: November 29, 1993

Major Rating Factors:
Disappointing performance is the major factor driving the D+ (Weak) TheStreet.com Investment Rating for Asia Tigers Fund. The fund currently has a performance rating of D (Weak) based on an annualized return of -7.90% over the last three years and a total return of -17.10% year to date 2015. Factored into the performance evaluation is an expense ratio of 2.33% (high).

The fund's risk rating is currently B- (Good). It carries a beta of 0.83, meaning the fund's expected move will be 8.3% for every 10% move in the market. Volatility, as measured by both the semi-deviation and a drawdown factor, is considered low. As of December 31, 2015, Asia Tigers Fund traded at a discount of 14.69% below its net asset value, which is better than its one-year historical average discount of 12.77%.

Gregory S. Geiling currently receives a manager quality ranking of 14 (0=worst, 99=best). This fund offers only a moderate level of risk but investors looking for strong performance are still waiting.

Data Date	Investment Rating	Net Assets ($Mil)	Price	Perfor-mance Rating/Pts	Total Return Y-T-D	Risk Rating/Pts
12-15	D+	47.64	9.06	D / 2.0	-17.10%	B- / 7.0
2014	C-	47.30	11.21	C- / 4.1	4.82%	B- / 7.2
2013	D-	54.78	11.29	D / 1.6	-9.68%	C / 5.1
2012	D-	57.14	12.59	D / 2.2	22.72%	C / 5.2
2011	D	79.92	12.01	C- / 3.3	-22.84%	C / 5.5
2010	D-	77.15	19.68	D- / 1.3	2.50%	C- / 3.7

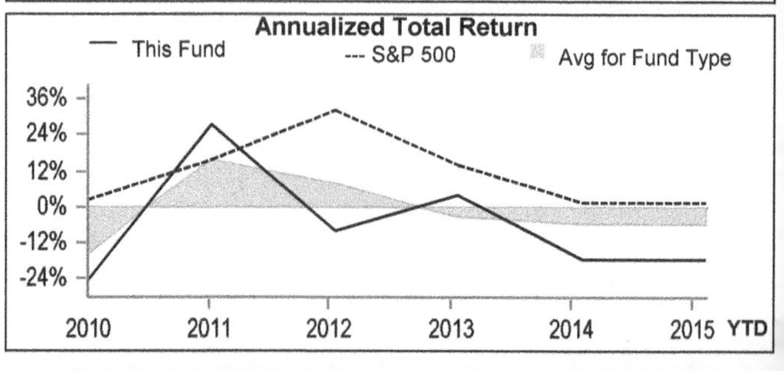

Avenue Income Credit Strategies (ACP) D Weak

Fund Family: Avenue Capital Management II LP
Fund Type: Loan Participation
Inception Date: January 27, 2011

Major Rating Factors:
Disappointing performance is the major factor driving the D (Weak) TheStreet.com Investment Rating for Avenue Income Credit Strategies. The fund currently has a performance rating of D (Weak) based on an annualized return of -6.04% over the last three years and a total return of -16.71% year to date 2015. Factored into the performance evaluation is an expense ratio of 2.89% (high).

The fund's risk rating is currently C+ (Fair). Volatility, as measured by both the semi-deviation and a drawdown factor, is considered low. As of December 31, 2015, Avenue Income Credit Strategies traded at a discount of 11.33% below its net asset value, which is better than its one-year historical average discount of 10.75%.

Robert T. Symington currently receives a manager quality ranking of 39 (0=worst, 99=best). This fund offers only a moderate level of risk but investors looking for strong performance are still waiting.

Data Date	Investment Rating	Net Assets ($Mil)	Price	Perfor-mance Rating/Pts	Total Return Y-T-D	Risk Rating/Pts
12-15	D	235.81	11.35	D / 2.1	-16.71%	C+ / 5.8
2014	C-	240.50	15.11	C- / 4.0	-4.84%	B- / 7.6
2013	C+	193.27	17.58	C+ / 6.3	2.30%	B- / 7.4
2012	A-	126.59	18.17	A+ / 9.6	25.54%	B- / 7.3

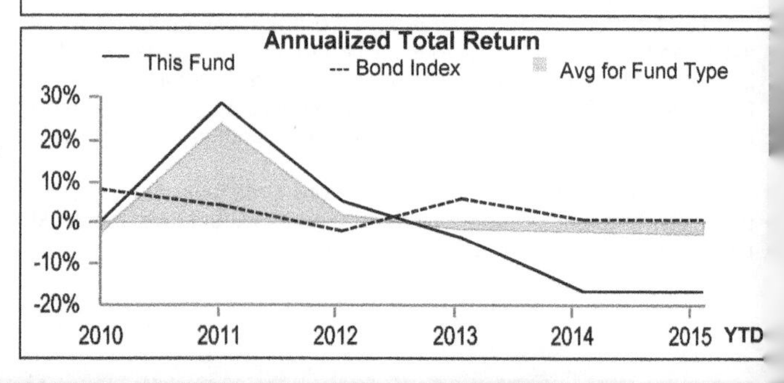

Babson Capital Corporate Investors (MCI) A+ Excellent

Fund Family: Babson Capital Management LLC
Fund Type: General - Investment Grade
Inception Date: August 25, 1971

Major Rating Factors:
Exceptional performance is the major factor driving the A+ (Excellent) TheStreet.com Investment Rating for Babson Capital Corporate Investors. The fund currently has a performance rating of A+ (Excellent) based on an annualized return of 0.00% over the last three years and a total return of 17.03% year to date 2015. Factored into the performance evaluation is an expense ratio of 2.22% (high).

The fund's risk rating is currently B- (Good). It carries a beta of 0.00, meaning the fund's expected move will be 0.0% for every 10% move in the market. Volatility, as measured by both the semi-deviation and a drawdown factor, is considered low. As of December 31, 2015, Babson Capital Corporate Investors traded at a premium of 17.35% above its net asset value, which is worse than its one-year historical average premium of 9.68%.

Michael L. Klofas currently receives a manager quality ranking of 98 (0=worst, 99=best). If you desire only a moderate level of risk and strong performance, then this fund is an excellent option.

Data Date	Investment Rating	Net Assets ($Mil)	Price	Perfor-mance Rating/Pts	Total Return Y-T-D	Risk Rating/Pts
12-15	A+	280.13	17.25	A+ / 9.6	17.03%	B- / 7.3
2014	C-	287.55	15.89	B- / 7.1	13.00%	C- / 4.1

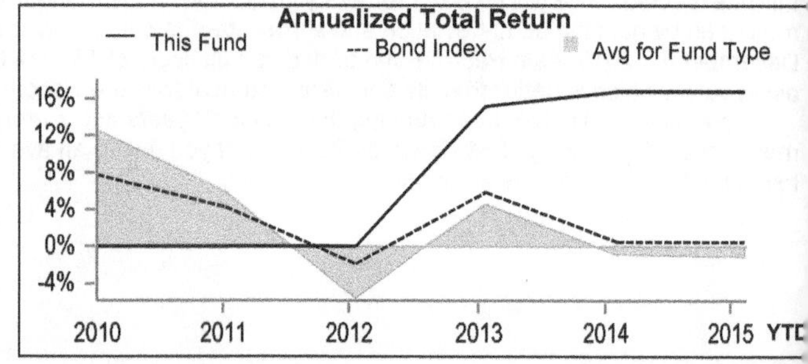

Babson Capital Glb Sht Dur Hi Yiel (BGH) C- Fair

Fund Family: Babson Capital Management LLC
Fund Type: Global
Inception Date: October 26, 2012

Major Rating Factors: Middle of the road best describes Babson Capital Glb Sht Dur Hi Yiel whose TheStreet.com Investment Rating is currently a C- (Fair). The fund currently has a performance rating of C- (Fair) based on an annualized return of -1.94% over the last three years and a total return of -9.82% year to date 2015. Factored into the performance evaluation is an expense ratio of 2.20% (high).

The fund's risk rating is currently C+ (Fair). It carries a beta of 0.45, meaning the fund's expected move will be 4.5% for every 10% move in the market. Volatility, as measured by both the semi-deviation and a drawdown factor, is considered low. As of December 31, 2015, Babson Capital Glb Sht Dur Hi Yiel traded at a discount of 10.67% below its net asset value, which is better than its one-year historical average discount of 9.51%.

Gideon Z. Summerscale has been running the fund for 4 years and currently receives a manager quality ranking of 74 (0=worst, 99=best). If you desire an average level of risk, then this fund may be an option.

Data Date	Investment Rating	Net Assets ($Mil)	Price	Performance Rating/Pts	Total Return Y-T-D	Risk Rating/Pts
12-15	C-	441.23	16.49	C- / 3.0	-9.82%	C+ / 6.5
2014	D+	493.20	20.19	D- / 1.4	-3.71%	B- / 7.5
2013	B	487.56	23.12	C+ / 6.7	7.68%	B / 8.6

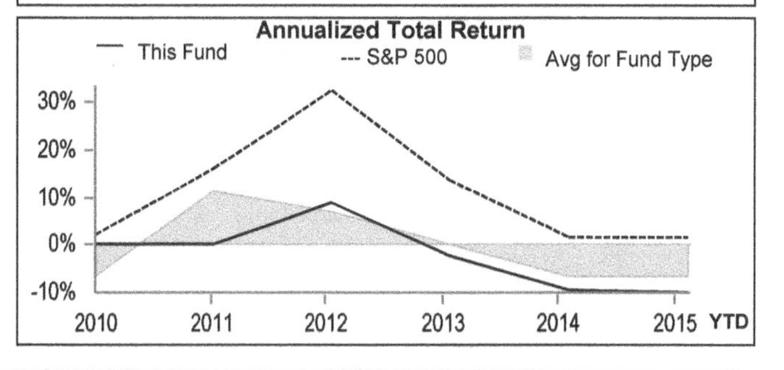

Babson Capital Participation Inv (MPV) A- Excellent

Fund Family: Babson Capital Management LLC
Fund Type: General - Investment Grade
Inception Date: October 21, 1988

Major Rating Factors:
Exceptional performance is the major factor driving the A- (Excellent) TheStreet.com Investment Rating for Babson Capital Participation Inv. The fund currently has a performance rating of A+ (Excellent) based on an annualized return of 0.00% over the last three years and a total return of 12.54% year to date 2015. Factored into the performance evaluation is an expense ratio of 1.94% (above average).

The fund's risk rating is currently C+ (Fair). It carries a beta of 0.00, meaning the fund's expected move will be 0.0% for every 10% move in the market. Volatility, as measured by both the semi-deviation and a drawdown factor, is considered low. As of December 31, 2015, Babson Capital Participation Inv traded at a premium of .81% above its net asset value, which is worse than its one-year historical average discount of 5.61%.

Michael L. Klofas currently receives a manager quality ranking of 96 (0=worst, 99=best). If you desire only a moderate level of risk and strong performance, then this fund is an excellent option.

Data Date	Investment Rating	Net Assets ($Mil)	Price	Performance Rating/Pts	Total Return Y-T-D	Risk Rating/Pts
12-15	A-	137.57	13.75	A+ / 9.6	12.54%	C+ / 6.8
2014	D+	139.69	13.23	C / 4.5	9.09%	C / 5.0

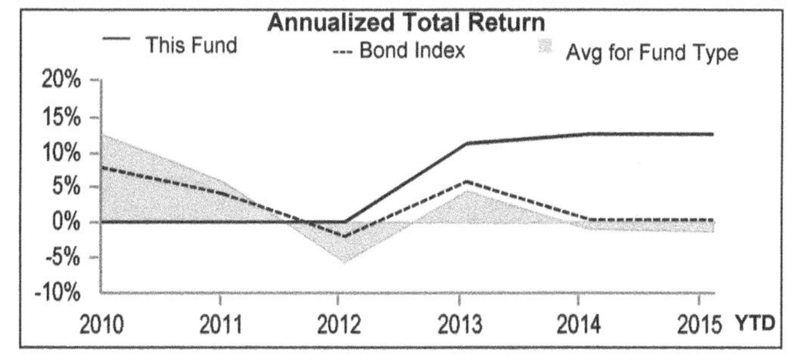

Bancroft Fund Ltd. (BCV) B- Good

Fund Family: Dinsmore Capital Management Co
Fund Type: Growth and Income
Inception Date: April 20, 1971

Major Rating Factors: Bancroft Fund Ltd. receives a TheStreet.com Investment Rating of B- (Good). The fund currently has a performance rating of C+ (Fair) based on an annualized return of 7.90% over the last three years and a total return of -0.21% year to date 2015. Factored into the performance evaluation is an expense ratio of 1.10% (low).

The fund's risk rating is currently B- (Good). It carries a beta of 0.66, meaning the fund's expected move will be 6.6% for every 10% move in the market. Volatility, as measured by both the semi-deviation and a drawdown factor, is considered low. As of December 31, 2015, Bancroft Fund Ltd. traded at a discount of 16.17% below its net asset value, which is better than its one-year historical average discount of 15.18%.

Thomas H. Dinsmore has been running the fund for 20 years and currently receives a manager quality ranking of 60 (0=worst, 99=best). If you desire an average level of risk, then this fund may be an option.

Data Date	Investment Rating	Net Assets ($Mil)	Price	Performance Rating/Pts	Total Return Y-T-D	Risk Rating/Pts
12-15	B-	123.67	18.20	C+ / 6.6	-0.21%	B- / 7.7
2014	B+	121.60	20.06	C+ / 6.3	11.01%	B+ / 9.3
2013	C+	110.69	18.60	C+ / 5.9	13.80%	B / 8.3
2012	C-	98.21	16.40	C- / 3.5	11.58%	B / 8.2
2011	C	95.00	15.12	C- / 4.2	-6.23%	B / 8.3
2010	C	97.60	16.92	C / 4.9	17.38%	C+ / 5.7

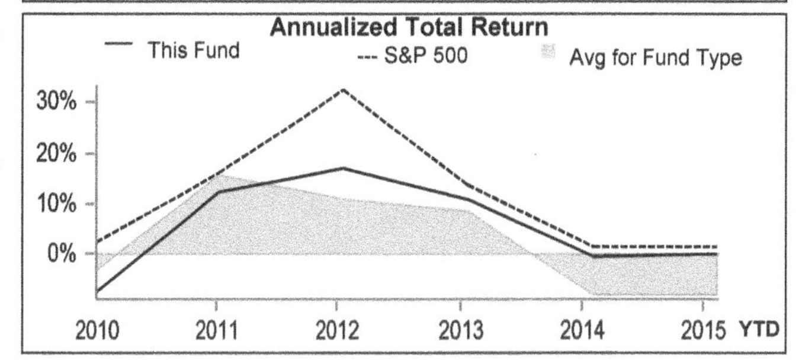

BlackRock CA Muni 2018 Income Trus (BJZ) C+ Fair

Fund Family: BlackRock Inc
Fund Type: Municipal - Single State
Inception Date: October 25, 2001

Major Rating Factors: Middle of the road best describes BlackRock CA Muni 2018 Income Trus whose TheStreet.com Investment Rating is currently a C+ (Fair). The fund currently has a performance rating of C (Fair) based on an annualized return of 0.89% over the last three years and a total return of 0.43% year to date 2015. Factored into the performance evaluation is an expense ratio of 0.57% (very low).

The fund's risk rating is currently B (Good). It carries a beta of 0.27, meaning the fund's expected move will be 2.7% for every 10% move in the market. Volatility, as measured by both the semi-deviation and a drawdown factor, is considered low. As of December 31, 2015, BlackRock CA Muni 2018 Income Trus traded at a discount of .73% below its net asset value, which is worse than its one-year historical average discount of 1.22%.

Theodore R. Jaeckel, Jr. has been running the fund for 10 years and currently receives a manager quality ranking of 66 (0=worst, 99=best). If you desire an average level of risk, then this fund may be an option.

Data Date	Investment Rating	Net Assets ($Mil)	Price	Performance Rating/Pts	Total Return Y-T-D	Risk Rating/Pts
12-15	C+	98.44	15.04	C / 5.2	0.43%	B / 8.6
2014	C	99.20	15.24	C- / 3.4	0.20%	B+ / 9.1
2013	B	101.73	15.77	C+ / 6.1	1.26%	B+ / 9.3
2012	C+	100.60	16.21	C / 4.7	3.00%	B+ / 9.4
2011	B	100.30	16.34	C+ / 6.7	14.84%	B+ / 9.4
2010	C+	94.69	15.38	C+ / 6.9	8.02%	C+ / 6.8

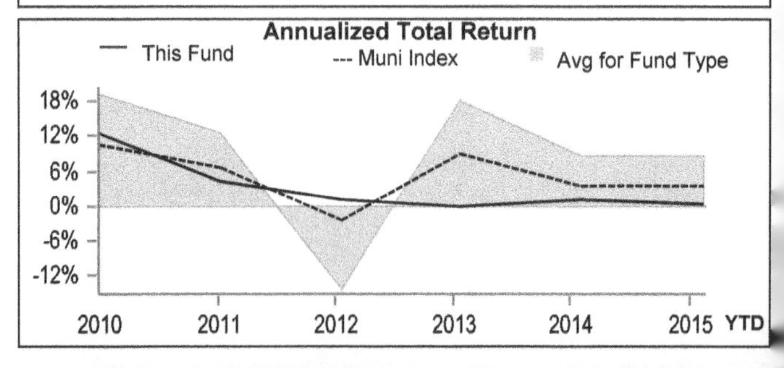

BlackRock CA Municipal Income Trus (BFZ) B+ Good

Fund Family: BlackRock Inc
Fund Type: Municipal - Single State
Inception Date: July 26, 2001

Major Rating Factors: Strong performance is the major factor driving the B+ (Good) TheStreet.com Investment Rating for BlackRock CA Municipal Income Trus. The fund currently has a performance rating of B+ (Good) based on an annualized return of 3.78% over the last three years and a total return of 12.49% year to date 2015. Factored into the performance evaluation is an expense ratio of 1.53% (average).

The fund's risk rating is currently C+ (Fair). It carries a beta of 2.31, meaning it is expected to move 23.1% for every 10% move in the market. Volatility, as measured by both the semi-deviation and a drawdown factor, is considered low. As of December 31, 2015, BlackRock CA Municipal Income Trus traded at a discount of .25% below its net asset value, which is worse than its one-year historical average discount of 4.39%.

Theodore R. Jaeckel, Jr. has been running the fund for 10 years and currently receives a manager quality ranking of 50 (0=worst, 99=best). If you desire only a moderate level of risk and strong performance, then this fund is an excellent option.

Data Date	Investment Rating	Net Assets ($Mil)	Price	Performance Rating/Pts	Total Return Y-T-D	Risk Rating/Pts
12-15	B+	504.97	15.95	B+ / 8.6	12.49%	C+ / 6.7
2014	C+	513.10	14.98	C+ / 6.8	16.22%	B- / 7.4
2013	C+	462.27	13.68	C+ / 6.1	-14.61%	B- / 7.7
2012	A+	519.58	16.34	A / 9.5	22.89%	B / 8.4
2011	A	472.90	14.71	A / 9.3	27.68%	B / 8.4
2010	D+	454.30	12.80	D / 1.7	3.76%	C+ / 6.7

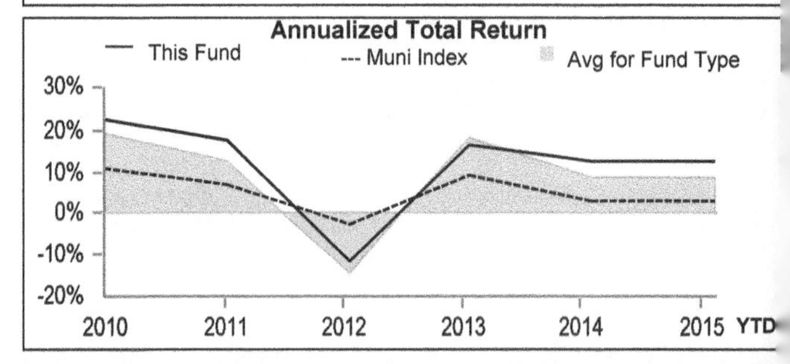

BlackRock Core Bond Trust (BHK) C Fair

Fund Family: BlackRock Inc
Fund Type: General - Investment Grade
Inception Date: November 27, 2001

Major Rating Factors: Middle of the road best describes BlackRock Core Bond Trust whose TheStreet.com Investment Rating is currently a C (Fair). The fund currently has a performance rating of C (Fair) based on an annualized return of 0.58% over the last three years and a total return of 2.01% year to date 2015. Factored into the performance evaluation is an expense ratio of 0.95% (low).

The fund's risk rating is currently B- (Good). It carries a beta of 2.28, meaning it is expected to move 22.8% for every 10% move in the market. Volatility, as measured by both the semi-deviation and a drawdown factor, is considered low. As of December 31, 2015, BlackRock Core Bond Trust traded at a discount of 8.93% below its net asset value, which is worse than its one-year historical average discount of 9.98%.

James E. Keenan has been running the fund for 9 years and currently receives a manager quality ranking of 55 (0=worst, 99=best). If you desire an average level of risk, then this fund may be an option.

Data Date	Investment Rating	Net Assets ($Mil)	Price	Performance Rating/Pts	Total Return Y-T-D	Risk Rating/Pts
12-15	C	770.82	12.64	C / 4.8	2.01%	B- / 7.4
2014	C	401.80	13.20	C / 4.8	10.21%	B- / 7.9
2013	C	379.91	12.88	C / 5.1	-9.89%	B / 8.1
2012	B-	411.14	14.90	C+ / 6.1	17.36%	B / 8.8
2011	B-	382.30	13.52	C+ / 6.3	16.31%	B / 8.8
2010	C+	383.54	12.52	C+ / 6.1	12.69%	C+ / 6.6

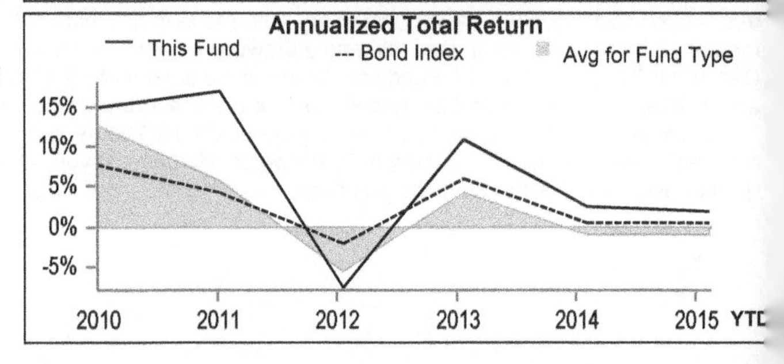

BlackRock Corporate High Yield (HYT) C- Fair

Fund Family: BlackRock Inc
Fund Type: Corporate - High Yield
Inception Date: May 28, 2003

Major Rating Factors: Middle of the road best describes BlackRock Corporate High Yield whose TheStreet.com Investment Rating is currently a C- (Fair). The fund currently has a performance rating of C- (Fair) based on an annualized return of 0.25% over the last three years and a total return of -4.99% year to date 2015. Factored into the performance evaluation is an expense ratio of 1.37% (average).

The fund's risk rating is currently B- (Good). It carries a beta of 1.29, meaning it is expected to move 12.9% for every 10% move in the market. Volatility, as measured by both the semi-deviation and a drawdown factor, is considered low. As of December 31, 2015, BlackRock Corporate High Yield traded at a discount of 9.78% below its net asset value, which is worse than its one-year historical average discount of 12.43%.

James E. Keenan has been running the fund for 10 years and currently receives a manager quality ranking of 59 (0=worst, 99=best). If you desire an average level of risk, then this fund may be an option.

Data Date	Investment Rating	Net Assets ($Mil)	Price	Performance Rating/Pts	Total Return Y-T-D	Risk Rating/Pts
12-15	C-	1,527.31	9.78	C- / 4.1	-4.99%	B- / 7.1
2014	C+	1,659.30	11.40	C / 4.7	1.16%	B / 8.5
2013	C+	446.85	12.17	C+ / 6.6	4.64%	B- / 7.3
2012	C+	435.96	12.39	C+ / 6.8	21.72%	B- / 7.2
2011	B	399.40	11.38	B+ / 8.7	9.06%	B- / 7.1
2010	C+	401.76	11.63	B+ / 8.3	19.98%	C- / 3.7

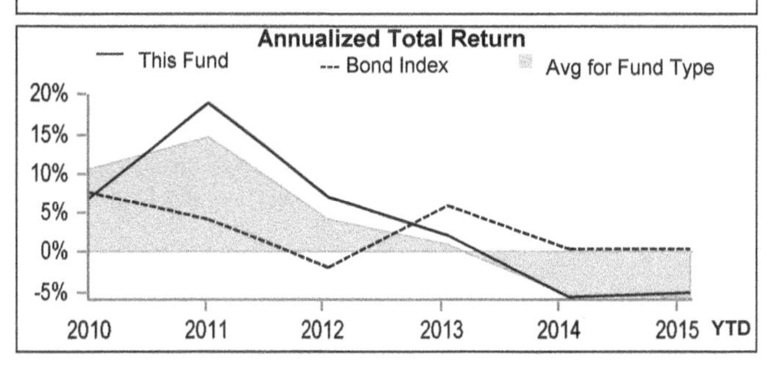

BlackRock Credit Alloc Inc Tr (BTZ) C+ Fair

Fund Family: BlackRock Inc
Fund Type: Income
Inception Date: December 27, 2006

Major Rating Factors: Middle of the road best describes BlackRock Credit Alloc Inc Tr whose TheStreet.com Investment Rating is currently a C+ (Fair). The fund currently has a performance rating of C+ (Fair) based on an annualized return of 3.34% over the last three years and a total return of 2.10% year to date 2015. Factored into the performance evaluation is an expense ratio of 1.16% (low).

The fund's risk rating is currently B- (Good). It carries a beta of 0.29, meaning the fund's expected move will be 2.9% for every 10% move in the market. Volatility, as measured by both the semi-deviation and a drawdown factor, is considered low. As of December 31, 2015, BlackRock Credit Alloc Inc Tr traded at a discount of 10.25% below its net asset value, which is worse than its one-year historical average discount of 12.94%.

Mitchell S. Garfin has been running the fund for 5 years and currently receives a manager quality ranking of 64 (0=worst, 99=best). If you desire an average level of risk, then this fund may be an option.

Data Date	Investment Rating	Net Assets ($Mil)	Price	Performance Rating/Pts	Total Return Y-T-D	Risk Rating/Pts
12-15	C+	1,549.12	12.34	C+ / 5.8	2.10%	B- / 7.7
2014	C+	1,649.50	12.92	C / 5.3	6.08%	B / 8.5
2013	B-	1,696.77	13.06	C+ / 6.2	0.96%	B / 8.7
2012	B	722.34	13.73	C+ / 6.6	22.18%	B / 8.8
2011	C+	708.60	12.15	B- / 7.5	9.66%	C+ / 6.8
2010	D	723.87	12.10	D+ / 2.8	14.66%	C / 4.4

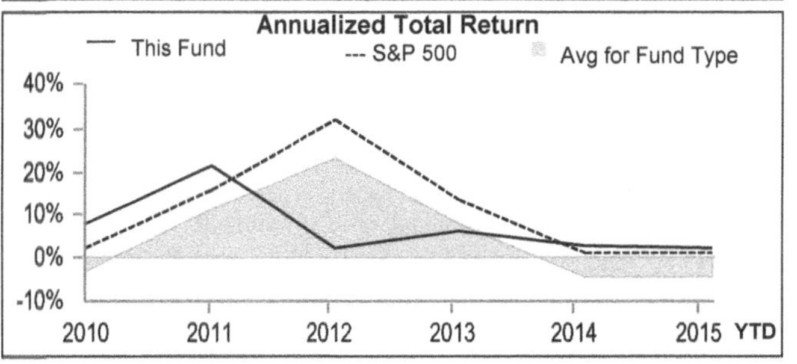

BlackRock Debt Strategies Fund Inc (DSU) C- Fair

Fund Family: BlackRock Inc
Fund Type: Corporate - High Yield
Inception Date: March 24, 1998

Major Rating Factors: Middle of the road best describes BlackRock Debt Strategies Fund Inc whose TheStreet.com Investment Rating is currently a C- (Fair). The fund currently has a performance rating of C- (Fair) based on an annualized return of -0.61% over the last three years and a total return of -1.16% year to date 2015. Factored into the performance evaluation is an expense ratio of 1.24% (average).

The fund's risk rating is currently B- (Good). It carries a beta of 1.10, meaning it is expected to move 11.0% for every 10% move in the market. Volatility, as measured by both the semi-deviation and a drawdown factor, is considered low. As of December 31, 2015, BlackRock Debt Strategies Fund Inc traded at a discount of 12.47% below its net asset value, which is worse than its one-year historical average discount of 13.59%.

Leland T. Hart has been running the fund for 7 years and currently receives a manager quality ranking of 50 (0=worst, 99=best). If you desire an average level of risk, then this fund may be an option.

Data Date	Investment Rating	Net Assets ($Mil)	Price	Performance Rating/Pts	Total Return Y-T-D	Risk Rating/Pts
12-15	C-	801.89	3.37	C- / 4.0	-1.16%	B- / 7.0
2014	C	806.50	3.72	C- / 4.0	-0.01%	B / 8.0
2013	C+	467.95	3.99	C+ / 6.0	0.43%	B / 8.5
2012	B+	453.44	4.30	B- / 7.4	22.22%	B / 8.6
2011	C	428.20	3.88	B- / 7.2	12.67%	C / 5.0
2010	D	431.56	3.81	D+ / 2.6	14.79%	C- / 3.7

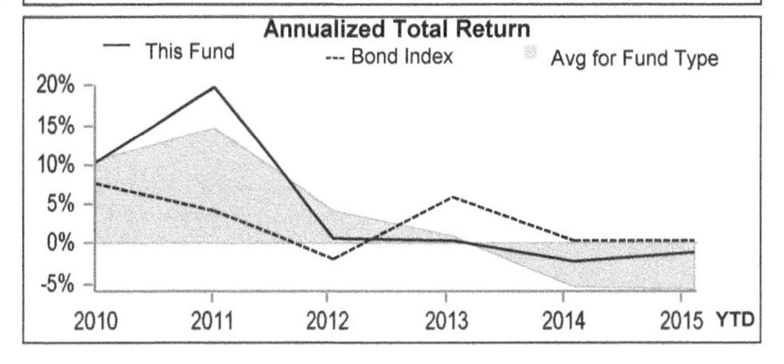

BlackRock Defined Opp Credit Trust (BHL) C+ Fair

Fund Family: BlackRock Inc
Fund Type: Loan Participation
Inception Date: January 31, 2008

Major Rating Factors: Middle of the road best describes BlackRock Defined Opp Credit Trust whose TheStreet.com Investment Rating is currently a C+ (Fair). The fund currently has a performance rating of C+ (Fair) based on an annualized return of 3.47% over the last three years and a total return of 6.03% year to date 2015. Factored into the performance evaluation is an expense ratio of 2.01% (high).

The fund's risk rating is currently B- (Good). It carries a beta of -2.52, meaning the fund's expected move will be -25.2% for every 10% move in the market. Volatility, as measured by both the semi-deviation and a drawdown factor, is considered low. As of December 31, 2015, BlackRock Defined Opp Credit Trust traded at a discount of 1.51% below its net asset value, which is worse than its one-year historical average discount of 4.73%.

James E. Keenan currently receives a manager quality ranking of 85 (0=worst, 99=best). If you desire an average level of risk, then this fund may be an option.

Data Date	Investment Rating	Net Assets ($Mil)	Price	Perfor-mance Rating/Pts	Total Return Y-T-D	Risk Rating/Pts
12-15	C+	125.18	13.02	C+ / 6.0	6.03%	B- / 7.5
2014	C	128.50	12.78	C- / 3.9	-0.60%	B / 8.3
2013	C	130.60	13.61	C / 4.6	2.23%	B / 8.2
2012	C+	127.46	14.18	C / 5.3	18.06%	B / 8.2
2011	C	121.10	12.45	C / 4.8	-1.86%	B / 8.2
2010	A	122.06	13.51	B+ / 8.7	19.14%	C+ / 6.8

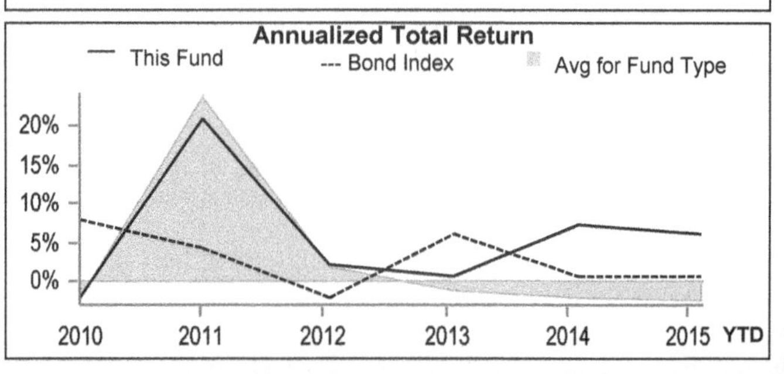

BlackRock Energy & Resources (BGR) D- Weak

Fund Family: BlackRock Inc
Fund Type: Energy/Natural Resources
Inception Date: December 23, 2004

Major Rating Factors:
Disappointing performance is the major factor driving the D- (Weak) TheStreet.com Investment Rating for BlackRock Energy & Resources. The fund currently has a performance rating of D- (Weak) based on an annualized return of -9.61% over the last three years and a total return of -32.98% year to date 2015. Factored into the performance evaluation is an expense ratio of 1.26% (average).

The fund's risk rating is currently C (Fair). It carries a beta of 1.01, meaning that its performance tracks fairly well with that of the overall stock market. Volatility, as measured by both the semi-deviation and a drawdown factor, is considered average. As of December 31, 2015, BlackRock Energy & Resources traded at a discount of 10.82% below its net asset value, which is better than its one-year historical average discount of 3.29%.

Christopher M. Accettella has been running the fund for 4 years and currently receives a manager quality ranking of 31 (0=worst, 99=best). This fund offers an average level of risk but investors looking for strong performance will be frustrated.

Data Date	Investment Rating	Net Assets ($Mil)	Price	Perfor-mance Rating/Pts	Total Return Y-T-D	Risk Rating/Pts
12-15	D-	741.11	12.53	D- / 1.3	-32.98%	C / 5.1
2014	D+	797.70	19.95	D+ / 2.7	-7.28%	B- / 7.2
2013	C	834.29	24.30	C / 5.5	16.21%	B- / 7.1
2012	D+	843.33	23.55	D+ / 2.5	2.75%	B- / 7.1
2011	C+	794.70	24.45	B- / 7.0	-5.45%	B- / 7.1
2010	C	795.72	28.74	B- / 7.2	19.58%	C- / 3.9

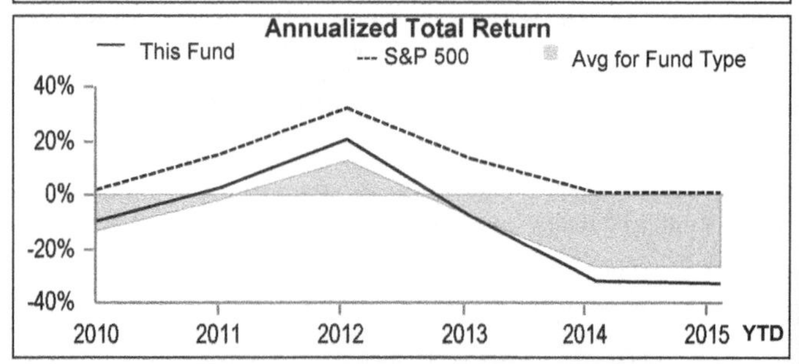

BlackRock Enhanced Capital and Inc (CII) A Excellent

Fund Family: BlackRock Inc
Fund Type: Growth and Income
Inception Date: April 30, 2004

Major Rating Factors:
Strong performance is the major factor driving the A (Excellent) TheStreet.com Investment Rating for BlackRock Enhanced Capital and Inc. The fund currently has a performance rating of B+ (Good) based on an annualized return of 12.57% over the last three years and a total return of 8.19% year to date 2015. Factored into the performance evaluation is an expense ratio of 0.93% (low).

The fund's risk rating is currently B- (Good). It carries a beta of 1.03, meaning that its performance tracks fairly well with that of the overall stock market. Volatility, as measured by both the semi-deviation and a drawdown factor, is considered low. As of December 31, 2015, BlackRock Enhanced Capital and Inc traded at a discount of 6.42% below its net asset value, which is worse than its one-year historical average discount of 6.46%.

Christopher M. Accettella has been running the fund for 4 years and currently receives a manager quality ranking of 54 (0=worst, 99=best). If you desire only a moderate level of risk and strong performance, then this fund is an excellent option.

Data Date	Investment Rating	Net Assets ($Mil)	Price	Perfor-mance Rating/Pts	Total Return Y-T-D	Risk Rating/Pts
12-15	A	682.49	14.14	B+ / 8.8	8.19%	B- / 7.8
2014	B	680.40	13.97	C+ / 6.3	11.56%	B / 8.6
2013	C+	639.91	13.67	C+ / 6.4	16.37%	B- / 7.5
2012	D+	612.15	12.42	D+ / 2.9	11.02%	B- / 7.8
2011	C	614.10	12.30	C / 5.1	-4.69%	B- / 7.6
2010	C	659.60	14.85	C+ / 5.7	8.97%	C / 4.9

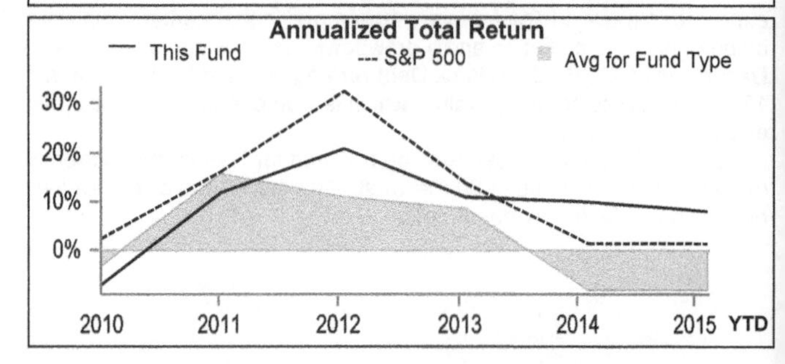

BlackRock Enhanced Equity Div (BDJ) B+ Good

Fund Family: BlackRock Inc
Fund Type: Income
Inception Date: August 31, 2005

Major Rating Factors: Strong performance is the major factor driving the B+ (Good) TheStreet.com Investment Rating for BlackRock Enhanced Equity Div. The fund currently has a performance rating of B- (Good) based on an annualized return of 8.71% over the last three years and a total return of 1.29% year to date 2015. Factored into the performance evaluation is an expense ratio of 0.86% (very low).

The fund's risk rating is currently B (Good). It carries a beta of 0.86, meaning the fund's expected move will be 8.6% for every 10% move in the market. Volatility, as measured by both the semi-deviation and a drawdown factor, is considered low. As of December 31, 2015, BlackRock Enhanced Equity Div traded at a discount of 12.53% below its net asset value, which is better than its one-year historical average discount of 11.41%.

Kathleen M. Anderson has been running the fund for 6 years and currently receives a manager quality ranking of 43 (0=worst, 99=best). If you desire only a moderate level of risk and strong performance, then this fund is an excellent option.

Data Date	Investment Rating	Net Assets ($Mil)	Price	Perfor-mance Rating/Pts	Total Return Y-T-D	Risk Rating/Pts
12-15	B+	1,648.68	7.61	B- / 7.4	1.29%	B / 8.1
2014	B	1,649.80	8.12	C+ / 6.2	9.56%	B+ / 9.1
2013	C+	1,560.14	7.94	C+ / 5.8	15.78%	B / 8.1
2012	D+	575.71	7.18	D+ / 2.6	12.61%	B- / 7.9
2011	D+	578.80	7.07	D+ / 2.7	-9.39%	B- / 7.2
2010	C	603.70	8.70	C+ / 5.8	11.31%	C / 4.9

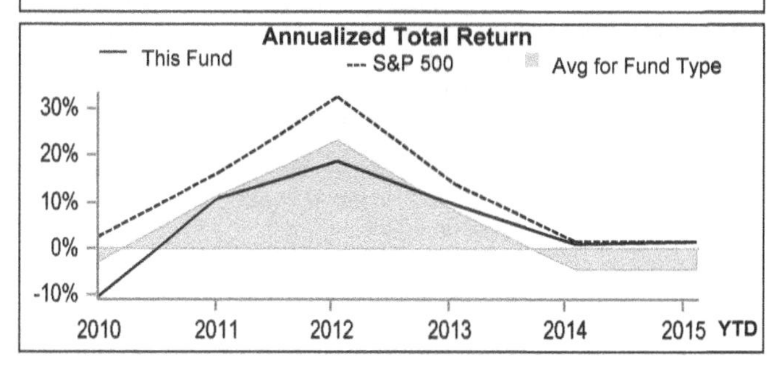

BlackRock Enhanced Government (EGF) C Fair

Fund Family: BlackRock Inc
Fund Type: US Government/Agency
Inception Date: October 27, 2005

Major Rating Factors: Middle of the road best describes BlackRock Enhanced Government whose TheStreet.com Investment Rating is currently a C (Fair). The fund currently has a performance rating of C (Fair) based on an annualized return of 0.11% over the last three years and a total return of 0.13% year to date 2015. Factored into the performance evaluation is an expense ratio of 1.20% (average).

The fund's risk rating is currently B- (Good). It carries a beta of 0.23, meaning the fund's expected move will be 2.3% for every 10% move in the market. Volatility, as measured by both the semi-deviation and a drawdown factor, is considered low. As of December 31, 2015, BlackRock Enhanced Government traded at a discount of 4.48% below its net asset value, which is worse than its one-year historical average discount of 5.93%.

Stuart Spodek currently receives a manager quality ranking of 64 (0=worst, 99=best). If you desire an average level of risk, then this fund may be an option.

Data Date	Investment Rating	Net Assets ($Mil)	Price	Perfor-mance Rating/Pts	Total Return Y-T-D	Risk Rating/Pts
12-15	C	120.05	13.65	C / 4.5	0.13%	B- / 7.9
2014	C	133.90	14.26	C- / 3.8	6.67%	B / 8.9
2013	C-	159.47	13.95	D+ / 2.9	-6.05%	B+ / 9.0
2012	C-	177.92	15.63	D+ / 2.3	7.24%	B+ / 9.1
2011	C-	187.90	15.25	D+ / 2.9	4.40%	B / 8.8
2010	C+	196.51	15.51	C- / 3.8	-4.02%	B / 8.2

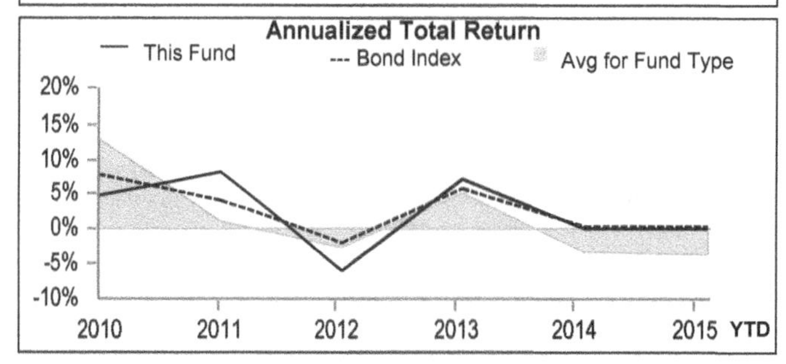

BlackRock FL Muni 2020 Term Tr (BFO) B- Good

Fund Family: BlackRock Inc
Fund Type: Municipal - Single State
Inception Date: September 26, 2003

Major Rating Factors: BlackRock FL Muni 2020 Term Tr receives a TheStreet.com Investment Rating of B- (Good). The fund currently has a performance rating of C (Fair) based on an annualized return of 1.29% over the last three years and a total return of 1.97% year to date 2015. Factored into the performance evaluation is an expense ratio of 0.68% (very low).

The fund's risk rating is currently B (Good). It carries a beta of 0.23, meaning the fund's expected move will be 2.3% for every 10% move in the market. Volatility, as measured by both the semi-deviation and a drawdown factor, is considered low. As of December 31, 2015, BlackRock FL Muni 2020 Term Tr traded at a discount of 2.23% below its net asset value, which is worse than its one-year historical average discount of 2.68%.

Theodore R. Jaeckel, Jr. has been running the fund for 10 years and currently receives a manager quality ranking of 78 (0=worst, 99=best). If you desire an average level of risk, then this fund may be an option.

Data Date	Investment Rating	Net Assets ($Mil)	Price	Perfor-mance Rating/Pts	Total Return Y-T-D	Risk Rating/Pts
12-15	B-	85.51	14.94	C / 5.5	1.97%	B / 8.9
2014	C+	86.00	15.02	C / 4.4	2.90%	B+ / 9.3
2013	B	85.14	15.11	C+ / 6.3	-1.30%	B+ / 9.4
2012	B+	89.25	15.64	B- / 7.1	9.70%	B+ / 9.3
2011	B+	86.30	15.20	B / 7.9	15.55%	B+ / 9.4
2010	C+	82.93	13.62	C+ / 6.0	7.01%	C+ / 6.6

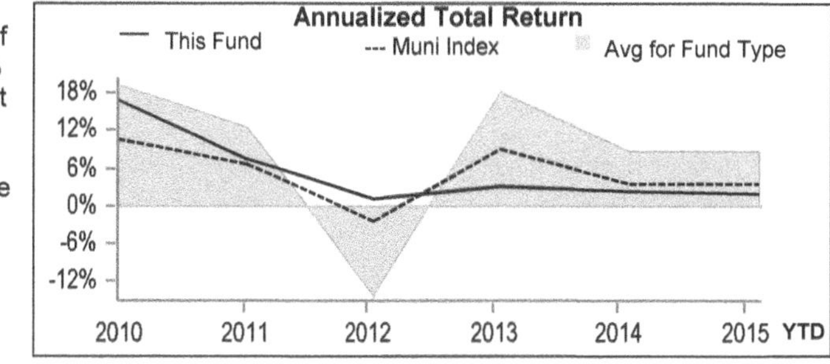

BlackRock Floating Rate Inc Strat (FRA) C Fair

Fund Family: BlackRock Inc
Fund Type: Loan Participation
Inception Date: October 28, 2003

Major Rating Factors: Middle of the road best describes BlackRock Floating Rate Inc Strat whose TheStreet.com Investment Rating is currently a C (Fair). The fund currently has a performance rating of C (Fair) based on an annualized return of 0.13% over the last three years and a total return of 2.34% year to date 2015. Factored into the performance evaluation is an expense ratio of 1.56% (average).

The fund's risk rating is currently B- (Good). It carries a beta of -59.03, meaning the fund's expected move will be -590.3% for every 10% move in the market. Volatility, as measured by both the semi-deviation and a drawdown factor, is considered low. As of December 31, 2015, BlackRock Floating Rate Inc Strat traded at a discount of 9.54% below its net asset value, which is worse than its one-year historical average discount of 10.55%.

C. Adrian Marshall has been running the fund for 7 years and currently receives a manager quality ranking of 62 (0=worst, 99=best). If you desire an average level of risk, then this fund may be an option.

Data Date	Investment Rating	Net Assets ($Mil)	Price	Performance Rating/Pts	Total Return Y-T-D	Risk Rating/Pts
12-15	C	555.10	12.90	C / 4.6	2.34%	B- / 7.6
2014	C	564.20	13.39	C- / 3.8	-2.25%	B / 8.3
2013	C	571.80	14.61	C / 4.6	0.43%	B- / 7.9
2012	C	276.99	15.15	C / 5.1	22.18%	B- / 7.5
2011	C+	263.10	13.36	C+ / 6.7	-0.80%	B- / 7.6
2010	C-	264.38	14.88	C+ / 5.9	10.94%	C- / 4.2

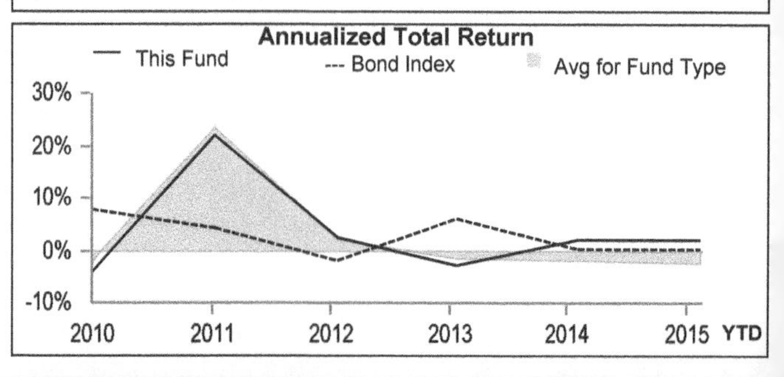

BlackRock Floating Rt Income (BGT) C Fair

Fund Family: BlackRock Inc
Fund Type: Loan Participation
Inception Date: August 30, 2004

Major Rating Factors: Middle of the road best describes BlackRock Floating Rt Income whose TheStreet.com Investment Rating is currently a C (Fair). The fund currently has a performance rating of C (Fair) based on an annualized return of -0.56% over the last three years and a total return of 2.39% year to date 2015. Factored into the performance evaluation is an expense ratio of 1.55% (average).

The fund's risk rating is currently B- (Good). It carries a beta of -23.07, meaning the fund's expected move will be -230.7% for every 10% move in the market. Volatility, as measured by both the semi-deviation and a drawdown factor, is considered low. As of December 31, 2015, BlackRock Floating Rt Income traded at a discount of 9.22% below its net asset value, which is worse than its one-year historical average discount of 9.40%.

C. Adrian Marshall has been running the fund for 7 years and currently receives a manager quality ranking of 62 (0=worst, 99=best). If you desire an average level of risk, then this fund may be an option.

Data Date	Investment Rating	Net Assets ($Mil)	Price	Performance Rating/Pts	Total Return Y-T-D	Risk Rating/Pts
12-15	C	335.44	12.50	C / 4.3	2.39%	B- / 7.5
2014	C-	344.40	12.85	C- / 3.5	-2.71%	B / 8.2
2013	C-	351.50	13.96	C- / 3.4	-2.21%	B / 8.0
2012	C	329.83	15.05	C+ / 5.6	22.71%	B- / 7.6
2011	B-	320.00	13.47	B- / 7.1	-7.82%	B- / 7.7
2010	B	337.34	16.55	B+ / 8.6	27.16%	C- / 4.2

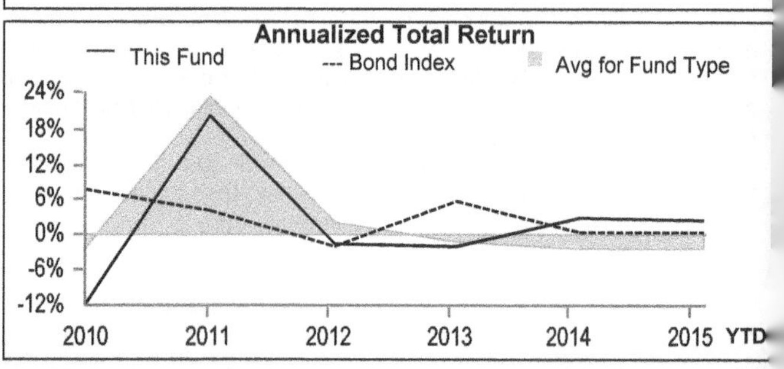

BlackRock Global Opportunities Eq (BOE) C+ Fair

Fund Family: BlackRock Inc
Fund Type: Global
Inception Date: May 26, 2005

Major Rating Factors: Middle of the road best describes BlackRock Global Opportunities Eq whose TheStreet.com Investment Rating is currently a C+ (Fair). The fund currently has a performance rating of C+ (Fair) based on an annualized return of 5.88% over the last three years and a total return of 5.71% year to date 2015. Factored into the performance evaluation is an expense ratio of 1.08% (low).

The fund's risk rating is currently B- (Good). It carries a beta of 0.89, meaning the fund's expected move will be 8.9% for every 10% move in the market. Volatility, as measured by both the semi-deviation and a drawdown factor, is considered low. As of December 31, 2015, BlackRock Global Opportunities Eq traded at a discount of 10.46% below its net asset value, which is worse than its one-year historical average discount of 11.57%.

Kyle G. McClements has been running the fund for 7 years and currently receives a manager quality ranking of 81 (0=worst, 99=best). If you desire an average level of risk, then this fund may be an option.

Data Date	Investment Rating	Net Assets ($Mil)	Price	Performance Rating/Pts	Total Return Y-T-D	Risk Rating/Pts
12-15	C+	1,079.86	12.76	C+ / 6.5	5.71%	B- / 7.3
2014	C-	1,088.80	13.13	C- / 4.2	-3.06%	B- / 7.7
2013	C-	1,101.89	14.96	C / 5.5	15.48%	C+ / 6.4
2012	D	1,113.92	13.20	D+ / 2.6	13.65%	C+ / 6.2
2011	D+	1,056.00	13.21	D+ / 2.8	-13.63%	C+ / 6.7
2010	D+	1,316.01	18.35	C- / 3.5	10.46%	C / 5.1

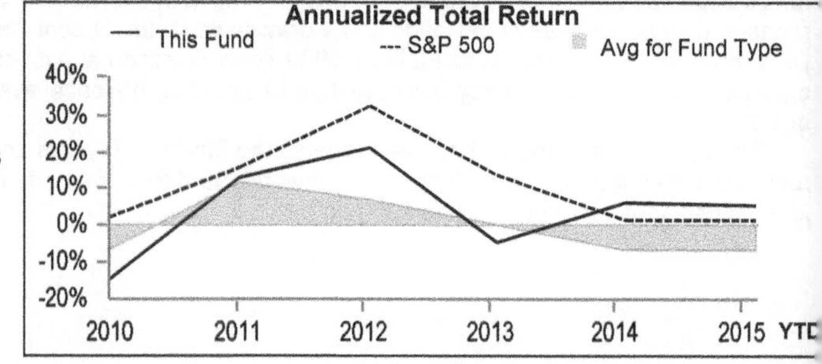

BlackRock Health Sciences Trust (BME) B+ Good

Fund Family: BlackRock Inc
Fund Type: Health
Inception Date: March 31, 2005

Major Rating Factors:
Exceptional performance is the major factor driving the B+ (Good) TheStreet.com Investment Rating for BlackRock Health Sciences Trust. The fund currently has a performance rating of A+ (Excellent) based on an annualized return of 25.19% over the last three years and a total return of 10.11% year to date 2015. Factored into the performance evaluation is an expense ratio of 1.11% (low).

The fund's risk rating is currently C+ (Fair). It carries a beta of 0.97, meaning that its performance tracks fairly well with that of the overall stock market. Volatility, as measured by both the semi-deviation and a drawdown factor, is considered low. As of December 31, 2015, BlackRock Health Sciences Trust traded at a premium of 8.79% above its net asset value, which is worse than its one-year historical average premium of 3.01%.

Kyle G. McClements has been running the fund for 11 years and currently receives a manager quality ranking of 95 (0=worst, 99=best). If you desire only a moderate level of risk and strong performance, then this fund is an excellent option.

Data Date	Investment Rating	Net Assets ($Mil)	Price	Performance Rating/Pts	Total Return Y-T-D	Risk Rating/Pts
12-15	B+	313.93	39.35	A+ / 9.7	10.11%	C+ / 6.2
2014	A-	301.60	42.70	A+ / 9.7	35.98%	C+ / 6.5
2013	A-	247.41	35.44	A- / 9.0	32.50%	B- / 7.7
2012	C+	202.68	28.02	B- / 7.4	22.56%	B- / 7.1
2011	C+	196.00	25.13	C+ / 5.9	4.03%	B- / 7.6
2010	C+	213.38	26.22	C+ / 6.6	8.94%	C+ / 5.7

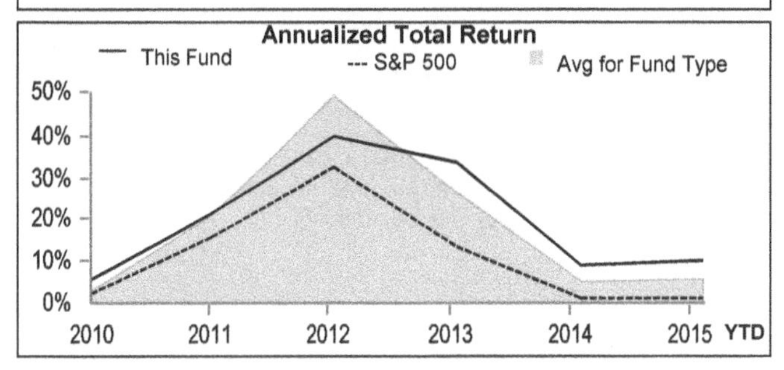

BlackRock Income Trust (BKT) C+ Fair

Fund Family: BlackRock Inc
Fund Type: Mortgage
Inception Date: July 22, 1988

Major Rating Factors: Middle of the road best describes BlackRock Income Trust whose TheStreet.com Investment Rating is currently a C+ (Fair). The fund currently has a performance rating of C+ (Fair) based on an annualized return of 1.55% over the last three years and a total return of 5.23% year to date 2015. Factored into the performance evaluation is an expense ratio of 0.99% (low).

The fund's risk rating is currently B- (Good). It carries a beta of 1.79, meaning it is expected to move 17.9% for every 10% move in the market. Volatility, as measured by both the semi-deviation and a drawdown factor, is considered low. As of December 31, 2015, BlackRock Income Trust traded at a discount of 8.07% below its net asset value, which is worse than its one-year historical average discount of 9.86%.

Robert S. Kapito has been running the fund for 28 years and currently receives a manager quality ranking of 52 (0=worst, 99=best). If you desire an average level of risk, then this fund may be an option.

Data Date	Investment Rating	Net Assets ($Mil)	Price	Performance Rating/Pts	Total Return Y-T-D	Risk Rating/Pts
12-15	C+	452.62	6.38	C+ / 5.6	5.23%	B- / 7.6
2014	C-	461.40	6.40	C- / 3.5	4.75%	B / 8.1
2013	C	467.95	6.48	C- / 3.9	-5.44%	B / 8.4
2012	C	507.85	7.35	C- / 3.5	5.06%	B+ / 9.6
2011	C+	509.30	7.33	C / 4.8	14.08%	B+ / 9.6
2010	A	496.26	6.84	B- / 7.2	11.86%	B / 8.1

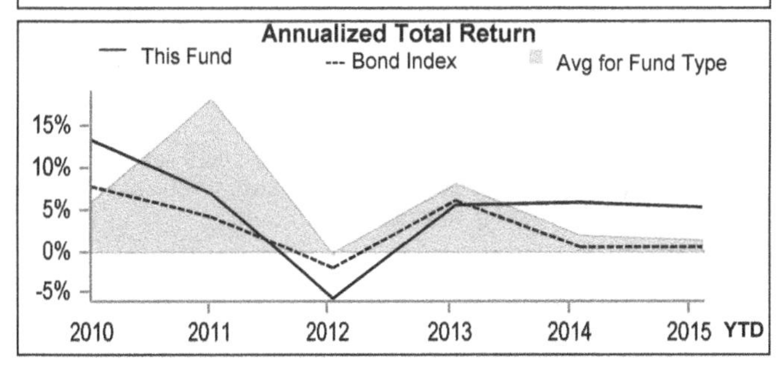

BlackRock Intl Grth and Inc Tr (BGY) C Fair

Fund Family: BlackRock Inc
Fund Type: Foreign
Inception Date: May 30, 2007

Major Rating Factors: Middle of the road best describes BlackRock Intl Grth and Inc Tr whose TheStreet.com Investment Rating is currently a C (Fair). The fund currently has a performance rating of C (Fair) based on an annualized return of 2.24% over the last three years and a total return of 1.23% year to date 2015. Factored into the performance evaluation is an expense ratio of 1.05% (low).

The fund's risk rating is currently B- (Good). It carries a beta of 1.03, meaning that its performance tracks fairly well with that of the overall stock market. Volatility, as measured by both the semi-deviation and a drawdown factor, is considered low. As of December 31, 2015, BlackRock Intl Grth and Inc Tr traded at a discount of 10.09% below its net asset value, which is better than its one-year historical average discount of 8.67%.

Ian Jamieson has been running the fund for 9 years and currently receives a manager quality ranking of 48 (0=worst, 99=best). If you desire an average level of risk, then this fund may be an option.

Data Date	Investment Rating	Net Assets ($Mil)	Price	Performance Rating/Pts	Total Return Y-T-D	Risk Rating/Pts
12-15	C	867.99	6.24	C / 5.2	1.23%	B- / 7.0
2014	C-	897.50	6.74	C- / 3.6	-7.97%	B- / 7.7
2013	C-	954.86	8.13	C / 5.2	15.07%	C+ / 6.6
2012	D-	959.15	7.35	D / 2.1	16.50%	C / 4.6
2011	D	890.80	7.16	D+ / 2.5	-19.20%	C+ / 6.5
2010	D	1,158.58	10.17	D+ / 2.4	1.66%	C / 4.6

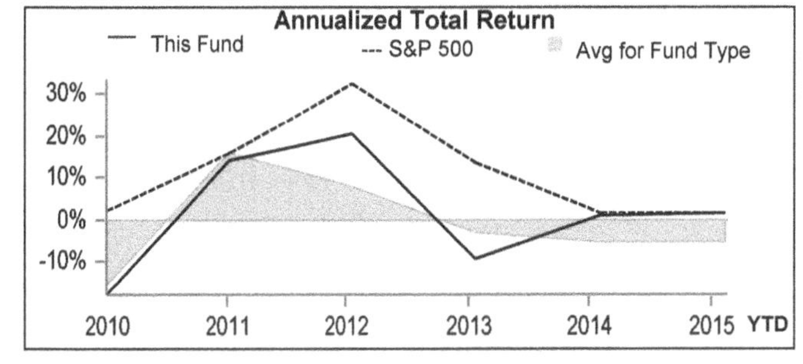

BlackRock Investment Qual Muni Tr (BKN) C+ Fair

Fund Family: BlackRock Inc
Fund Type: Municipal - National
Inception Date: February 19, 1993

Major Rating Factors: Middle of the road best describes BlackRock Investment Qual Muni Tr whose TheStreet.com Investment Rating is currently a C+ (Fair). The fund currently has a performance rating of C+ (Fair) based on an annualized return of 2.73% over the last three years and a total return of -0.50% year to date 2015. Factored into the performance evaluation is an expense ratio of 1.45% (average).

The fund's risk rating is currently B- (Good). It carries a beta of 2.03, meaning it is expected to move 20.3% for every 10% move in the market. Volatility, as measured by both the semi-deviation and a drawdown factor, is considered low. As of December 31, 2015, BlackRock Investment Qual Muni Tr traded at a discount of 5.76% below its net asset value, which is better than its one-year historical average discount of 4.84%.

Theodore R. Jaeckel, Jr. has been running the fund for 10 years and currently receives a manager quality ranking of 50 (0=worst, 99=best). If you desire an average level of risk, then this fund may be an option.

Data Date	Investment Rating	Net Assets ($Mil)	Price	Performance Rating/Pts	Total Return Y-T-D	Risk Rating/Pts
12-15	C+	276.31	15.39	C+ / 6.2	-0.50%	B- / 7.2
2014	C+	274.70	16.43	B+ / 8.7	20.96%	C / 5.5
2013	C+	280.51	14.24	C+ / 6.9	-9.86%	B- / 7.6
2012	A	263.38	16.34	B+ / 8.7	14.87%	B / 8.4
2011	A+	247.10	15.02	A+ / 9.8	28.20%	B / 8.6
2010	C-	232.47	13.14	D+ / 2.5	5.52%	C+ / 6.9

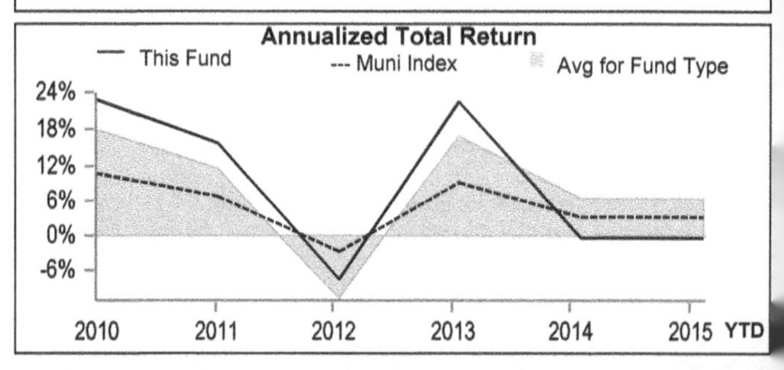

BlackRock Limited Duration Income (BLW) C Fair

Fund Family: BlackRock Inc
Fund Type: General Bond
Inception Date: July 30, 2003

Major Rating Factors: Middle of the road best describes BlackRock Limited Duration Income whose TheStreet.com Investment Rating is currently a C (Fair). The fund currently has a performance rating of C (Fair) based on an annualized return of 0.04% over the last three years and a total return of 0.62% year to date 2015. Factored into the performance evaluation is an expense ratio of 1.15% (low).

The fund's risk rating is currently B- (Good). It carries a beta of 0.59, meaning the fund's expected move will be 5.9% for every 10% move in the market. Volatility, as measured by both the semi-deviation and a drawdown factor, is considered low. As of December 31, 2015, BlackRock Limited Duration Income traded at a discount of 9.78% below its net asset value, which is worse than its one-year historical average discount of 11.24%.

James E. Keenan has been running the fund for 9 years and currently receives a manager quality ranking of 63 (0=worst, 99=best). If you desire an average level of risk, then this fund may be an option.

Data Date	Investment Rating	Net Assets ($Mil)	Price	Performance Rating/Pts	Total Return Y-T-D	Risk Rating/Pts
12-15	C	630.39	14.58	C / 4.6	0.62%	B- / 7.4
2014	C	656.50	15.72	C- / 4.0	-1.50%	B / 8.3
2013	B-	649.12	17.12	C+ / 6.1	0.61%	B / 8.7
2012	B-	642.39	18.17	B- / 7.2	21.54%	B- / 7.4
2011	B	603.70	15.97	B- / 7.1	9.27%	B / 8.7
2010	C+	619.38	16.30	C+ / 6.7	17.46%	C+ / 5.8

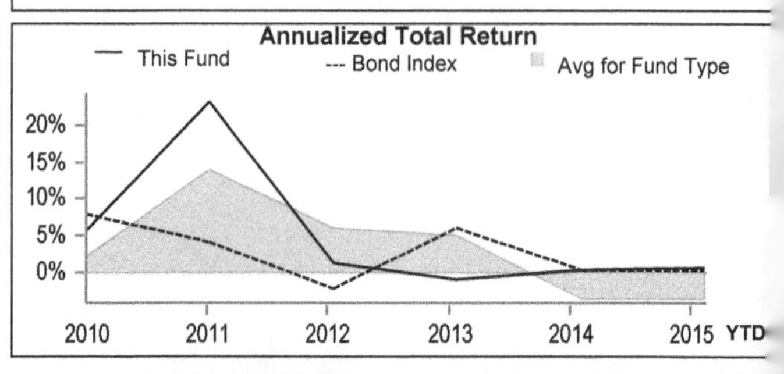

BlackRock Long Term Muni Adv (BTA) C+ Fair

Fund Family: BlackRock Inc
Fund Type: Municipal - National
Inception Date: February 27, 2006

Major Rating Factors: Middle of the road best describes BlackRock Long Term Muni Adv whose TheStreet.com Investment Rating is currently a C+ (Fair). The fund currently has a performance rating of C+ (Fair) based on an annualized return of 2.15% over the last three years and a total return of 8.26% year to date 2015. Factored into the performance evaluation is an expense ratio of 1.47% (average).

The fund's risk rating is currently B- (Good). It carries a beta of 2.35, meaning it is expected to move 23.5% for every 10% move in the market. Volatility, as measured by both the semi-deviation and a drawdown factor, is considered low. As of December 31, 2015, BlackRock Long Term Muni Adv traded at a discount of 8.59% below its net asset value, which is worse than its one-year historical average discount of 10.32%.

Theodore R. Jaeckel, Jr. has been running the fund for 10 years and currently receives a manager quality ranking of 37 (0=worst, 99=best). If you desire an average level of risk, then this fund may be an option.

Data Date	Investment Rating	Net Assets ($Mil)	Price	Performance Rating/Pts	Total Return Y-T-D	Risk Rating/Pts
12-15	C+	167.93	11.50	C+ / 6.8	8.26%	B- / 7.1
2014	C+	167.50	11.30	C+ / 6.3	17.15%	B- / 7.4
2013	C	172.43	10.20	C / 5.4	-15.96%	B- / 7.7
2012	A	163.22	12.59	A- / 9.0	18.14%	B / 8.3
2011	A+	154.80	11.67	A+ / 9.7	28.27%	B / 8.4
2010	D	150.36	10.08	D / 1.8	5.39%	C+ / 5.9

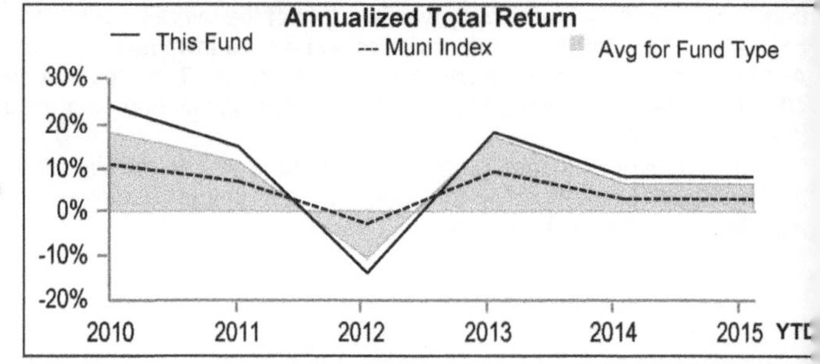

BlackRock Massachusetts Tax-Exempt (MHE) C Fair

Fund Family: BlackRock Inc
Fund Type: Municipal - Single State
Inception Date: July 23, 1993

Major Rating Factors: Middle of the road best describes BlackRock Massachusetts Tax-Exempt whose TheStreet.com Investment Rating is currently a C (Fair). The fund currently has a performance rating of C (Fair) based on an annualized return of 0.60% over the last three years and a total return of -1.56% year to date 2015. Factored into the performance evaluation is an expense ratio of 1.71% (above average).

The fund's risk rating is currently B- (Good). It carries a beta of 2.21, meaning it is expected to move 22.1% for every 10% move in the market. Volatility, as measured by both the semi-deviation and a drawdown factor, is considered low. As of December 31, 2015, BlackRock Massachusetts Tax-Exempt traded at a discount of 5.44% below its net asset value, which is better than its one-year historical average discount of 1.91%.

Robert D. Sneeden has been running the fund for 11 years and currently receives a manager quality ranking of 31 (0=worst, 99=best). If you desire an average level of risk, then this fund may be an option.

Data Date	Investment Rating	Net Assets ($Mil)	Price	Performance Rating/Pts	Total Return Y-T-D	Risk Rating/Pts
12-15	C	32.86	13.38	C / 5.0	-1.56%	B- / 7.6
2014	C+	33.10	14.35	B- / 7.0	28.32%	C+ / 6.0
2013	D+	29.16	11.80	D+ / 2.5	-19.15%	B- / 7.8
2012	A-	33.85	14.85	B / 8.0	7.83%	B / 8.8
2011	A+	32.00	14.60	A+ / 9.7	22.90%	B+ / 9.0
2010	A-	31.74	13.29	B+ / 8.5	18.59%	C+ / 6.3

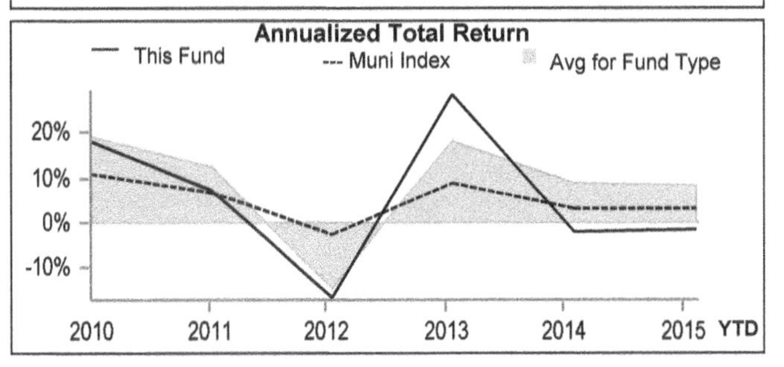

BlackRock MD Muni Bond Trust (BZM) C Fair

Fund Family: BlackRock Inc
Fund Type: Municipal - Single State
Inception Date: April 26, 2002

Major Rating Factors: Middle of the road best describes BlackRock MD Muni Bond Trust whose TheStreet.com Investment Rating is currently a C (Fair). The fund currently has a performance rating of C+ (Fair) based on an annualized return of 0.84% over the last three years and a total return of 7.42% year to date 2015. Factored into the performance evaluation is an expense ratio of 1.88% (above average).

The fund's risk rating is currently C+ (Fair). It carries a beta of 2.86, meaning it is expected to move 28.6% for every 10% move in the market. Volatility, as measured by both the semi-deviation and a drawdown factor, is considered low. As of December 31, 2015, BlackRock MD Muni Bond Trust traded at a discount of 2.03% below its net asset value, which is better than its one-year historical average discount of 2.00%.

Theodore R. Jaeckel, Jr. has been running the fund for 10 years and currently receives a manager quality ranking of 24 (0=worst, 99=best). If you desire an average level of risk, then this fund may be an option.

Data Date	Investment Rating	Net Assets ($Mil)	Price	Performance Rating/Pts	Total Return Y-T-D	Risk Rating/Pts
12-15	C	31.07	14.95	C+ / 6.2	7.42%	C+ / 5.8
2014	C-	31.50	14.55	C / 5.0	21.27%	C+ / 5.8
2013	D	27.64	12.63	D / 1.9	-21.28%	C+ / 6.1
2012	C+	32.32	16.17	C+ / 6.4	5.59%	B- / 7.9
2011	B+	30.80	16.61	B+ / 8.4	19.54%	B / 8.5
2010	C	31.35	14.67	C- / 3.0	8.04%	B- / 7.7

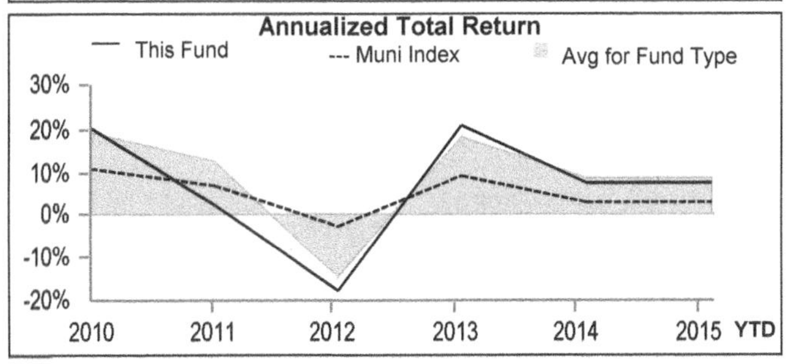

BlackRock Multi-Sector Income Trus (BIT) C+ Fair

Fund Family: BlackRock Fund Advisors
Fund Type: General - Investment Grade
Inception Date: February 26, 2013

Major Rating Factors: Middle of the road best describes BlackRock Multi-Sector Income Trus whose TheStreet.com Investment Rating is currently a C+ (Fair). The fund currently has a performance rating of C+ (Fair) based on an annualized return of 0.00% over the last three years and a total return of 2.87% year to date 2015. Factored into the performance evaluation is an expense ratio of 2.09% (high).

The fund's risk rating is currently B- (Good). It carries a beta of 0.00, meaning the fund's expected move will be 0.0% for every 10% move in the market. Volatility, as measured by both the semi-deviation and a drawdown factor, is considered low. As of December 31, 2015, BlackRock Multi-Sector Income Trus traded at a discount of 13.27% below its net asset value, which is better than its one-year historical average discount of 13.24%.

Akiva J. Dickstein currently receives a manager quality ranking of 83 (0=worst, 99=best). If you desire an average level of risk, then this fund may be an option.

Data Date	Investment Rating	Net Assets ($Mil)	Price	Performance Rating/Pts	Total Return Y-T-D	Risk Rating/Pts
12-15	C+	726.43	15.81	C+ / 6.0	2.87%	B- / 7.7
2014	D+	0.10	16.77	D+ / 2.8	5.37%	B- / 7.3

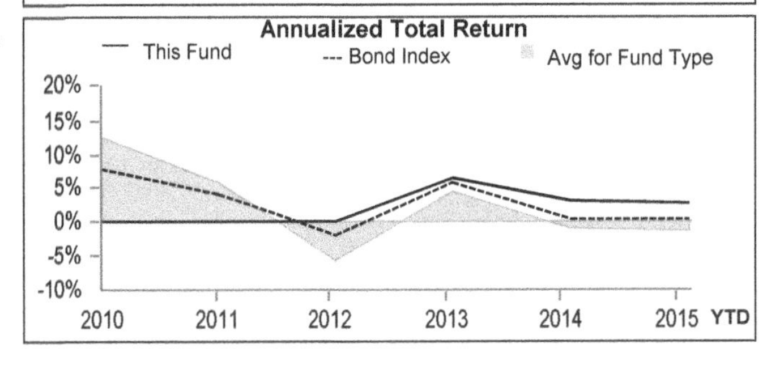

BlackRock Muni 2020 Term Trust (BKK) B- Good

Fund Family: BlackRock Inc
Fund Type: Municipal - National
Inception Date: September 26, 2003

Major Rating Factors: BlackRock Muni 2020 Term Trust receives a TheStreet.com Investment Rating of B- (Good). The fund currently has a performance rating of C+ (Fair) based on an annualized return of 2.05% over the last three years and a total return of 0.62% year to date 2015. Factored into the performance evaluation is an expense ratio of 0.72% (very low).

The fund's risk rating is currently B (Good). It carries a beta of 0.75, meaning the fund's expected move will be 7.5% for every 10% move in the market. Volatility, as measured by both the semi-deviation and a drawdown factor, is considered low. As of December 31, 2015, BlackRock Muni 2020 Term Trust traded at a discount of 1.86% below its net asset value, which is better than its one-year historical average discount of 1.76%.

Theodore R. Jaeckel, Jr. has been running the fund for 10 years and currently receives a manager quality ranking of 73 (0=worst, 99=best). If you desire an average level of risk, then this fund may be an option.

Data Date	Investment Rating	Net Assets ($Mil)	Price	Performance Rating/Pts	Total Return Y-T-D	Risk Rating/Pts
12-15	B-	329.81	15.86	C+ / 5.8	0.62%	B / 8.7
2014	B	331.10	16.38	C+ / 6.0	9.02%	B+ / 9.1
2013	B-	340.99	15.75	C+ / 5.9	-3.01%	B+ / 9.2
2012	B+	331.06	16.70	B- / 7.1	13.78%	B+ / 9.4
2011	B+	320.80	15.77	B / 8.0	13.26%	B+ / 9.3
2010	B-	293.55	14.67	C+ / 6.6	5.70%	B- / 7.1

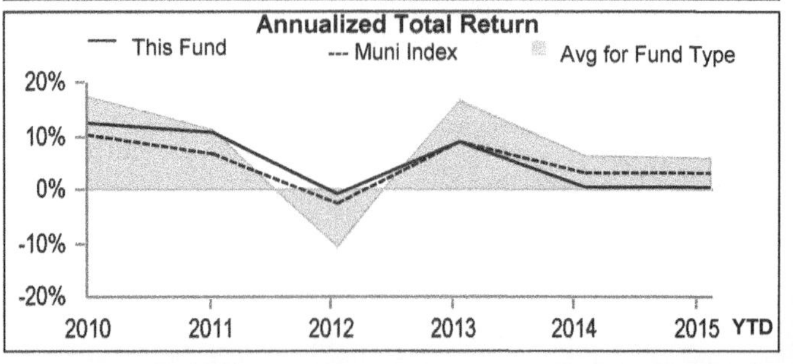

BlackRock Muni Bond Invt Trust (BIE) C+ Fair

Fund Family: BlackRock Inc
Fund Type: Municipal - Single State
Inception Date: April 26, 2002

Major Rating Factors: Middle of the road best describes BlackRock Muni Bond Invt Trust whose TheStreet.com Investment Rating is currently a C+ (Fair). The fund currently has a performance rating of C+ (Fair) based on an annualized return of 0.34% over the last three years and a total return of 7.65% year to date 2015. Factored into the performance evaluation is an expense ratio of 1.84% (above average).

The fund's risk rating is currently B- (Good). It carries a beta of 2.19, meaning it is expected to move 21.9% for every 10% move in the market. Volatility, as measured by both the semi-deviation and a drawdown factor, is considered low. As of December 31, 2015, BlackRock Muni Bond Invt Trust traded at a discount of 7.31% below its net asset value, which is worse than its one-year historical average discount of 9.61%.

Robert S. Kapito currently receives a manager quality ranking of 29 (0=worst, 99=best). If you desire an average level of risk, then this fund may be an option.

Data Date	Investment Rating	Net Assets ($Mil)	Price	Performance Rating/Pts	Total Return Y-T-D	Risk Rating/Pts
12-15	C+	53.25	14.97	C+ / 5.9	7.65%	B- / 7.4
2014	C+	54.40	14.83	C+ / 6.4	17.14%	B- / 7.7
2013	C	47.65	13.38	C / 4.3	-19.72%	B- / 7.9
2012	A+	56.33	17.18	A- / 9.0	17.68%	B / 8.6
2011	A	51.10	15.17	A- / 9.1	23.61%	B / 8.6
2010	C-	51.71	13.28	D / 2.0	6.26%	B- / 7.2

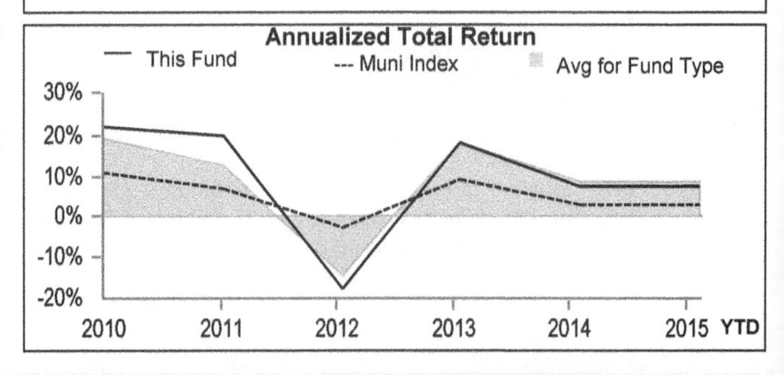

BlackRock Muni Interm Duration (MUI) C Fair

Fund Family: BlackRock Inc
Fund Type: Municipal - National
Inception Date: August 1, 2003

Major Rating Factors: Middle of the road best describes BlackRock Muni Interm Duration whose TheStreet.com Investment Rating is currently a C (Fair). The fund currently has a performance rating of C (Fair) based on an annualized return of -0.74% over the last three years and a total return of 4.96% year to date 2015. Factored into the performance evaluation is an expense ratio of 1.52% (average).

The fund's risk rating is currently B- (Good). It carries a beta of 1.77, meaning it is expected to move 17.7% for every 10% move in the market. Volatility, as measured by both the semi-deviation and a drawdown factor, is considered low. As of December 31, 2015, BlackRock Muni Interm Duration traded at a discount of 10.49% below its net asset value, which is worse than its one-year historical average discount of 10.82%.

Theodore R. Jaeckel, Jr. has been running the fund for 10 years and currently receives a manager quality ranking of 33 (0=worst, 99=best). If you desire an average level of risk, then this fund may be an option.

Data Date	Investment Rating	Net Assets ($Mil)	Price	Performance Rating/Pts	Total Return Y-T-D	Risk Rating/Pts
12-15	C	607.44	14.17	C / 5.2	4.96%	B- / 7.3
2014	C	613.40	14.40	C / 4.7	8.32%	B- / 7.4
2013	C	635.65	13.90	C / 5.4	-14.34%	B- / 7.7
2012	A+	617.44	16.63	A- / 9.1	15.74%	B / 8.8
2011	A	596.00	15.32	A- / 9.1	22.29%	B+ / 9.0
2010	C+	561.14	13.79	C+ / 5.7	10.91%	C+ / 6.4

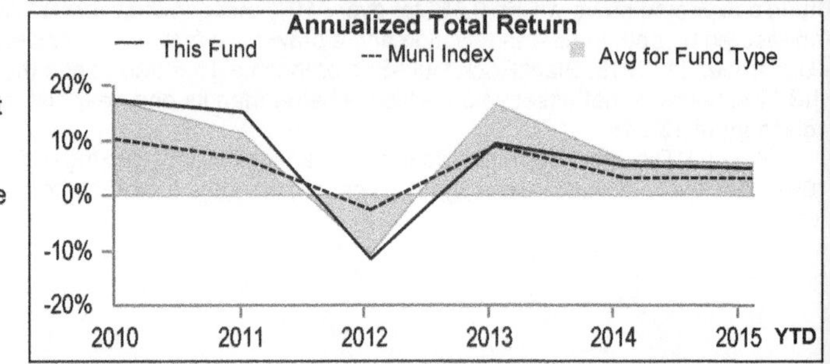

BlackRock Muni NY Interm Duration (MNE) A- Excellent

Fund Family: BlackRock Inc
Fund Type: Municipal - Single State
Inception Date: August 1, 2003

Major Rating Factors:
Strong performance is the major factor driving the A- (Excellent) TheStreet.com Investment Rating for BlackRock Muni NY Interm Duration. The fund currently has a performance rating of B+ (Good) based on an annualized return of 3.37% over the last three years and a total return of 13.89% year to date 2015. Factored into the performance evaluation is an expense ratio of 1.74% (above average).

The fund's risk rating is currently B- (Good). It carries a beta of 1.86, meaning it is expected to move 18.6% for every 10% move in the market. Volatility, as measured by both the semi-deviation and a drawdown factor, is considered low. As of December 31, 2015, BlackRock Muni NY Interm Duration traded at a discount of 3.74% below its net asset value, which is worse than its one-year historical average discount of 8.82%.

Timothy T. Browse has been running the fund for 12 years and currently receives a manager quality ranking of 57 (0=worst, 99=best). If you desire only a moderate level of risk and strong performance, then this fund is an excellent option.

Data Date	Investment Rating	Net Assets ($Mil)	Price	Performance Rating/Pts	Total Return Y-T-D	Risk Rating/Pts
12-15	A-	64.72	15.18	B+ / 8.6	13.89%	B- / 7.5
2014	C+	65.50	14.03	C / 5.5	13.37%	B / 8.0
2013	C	61.21	13.14	C- / 4.1	-14.22%	B / 8.2
2012	A+	67.16	15.44	B+ / 8.8	15.95%	B+ / 9.1
2011	A+	63.40	14.38	A / 9.3	20.03%	B+ / 9.1
2010	C+	61.01	12.85	C+ / 5.8	11.07%	C+ / 6.1

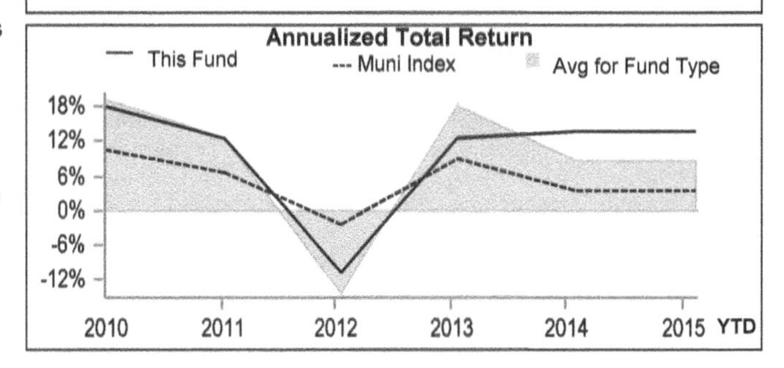

BlackRock MuniAssets Fund (MUA) B+ Good

Fund Family: BlackRock Inc
Fund Type: Municipal - National
Inception Date: June 18, 1993

Major Rating Factors: Strong performance is the major factor driving the B+ (Good) TheStreet.com Investment Rating for BlackRock MuniAssets Fund. The fund currently has a performance rating of B+ (Good) based on an annualized return of 5.27% over the last three years and a total return of 9.14% year to date 2015. Factored into the performance evaluation is an expense ratio of 0.82% (very low).

The fund's risk rating is currently B- (Good). It carries a beta of 2.30, meaning it is expected to move 23.0% for every 10% move in the market. Volatility, as measured by both the semi-deviation and a drawdown factor, is considered low. As of December 31, 2015, BlackRock MuniAssets Fund traded at a premium of .56% above its net asset value, which is worse than its one-year historical average discount of 2.12%.

Theodore R. Jaeckel, Jr. has been running the fund for 10 years and currently receives a manager quality ranking of 61 (0=worst, 99=best). If you desire only a moderate level of risk and strong performance, then this fund is an excellent option.

Data Date	Investment Rating	Net Assets ($Mil)	Price	Performance Rating/Pts	Total Return Y-T-D	Risk Rating/Pts
12-15	B+	505.34	14.27	B+ / 8.7	9.14%	B- / 7.1
2014	A	499.80	13.79	B+ / 8.8	26.05%	B- / 7.9
2013	C	513.92	11.55	C- / 4.2	-15.31%	B / 8.1
2012	A-	481.60	13.92	B / 8.1	17.37%	B / 8.6
2011	B+	456.80	12.53	B+ / 8.3	16.39%	B / 8.5
2010	C-	266.83	11.64	D+ / 2.9	1.63%	B- / 7.3

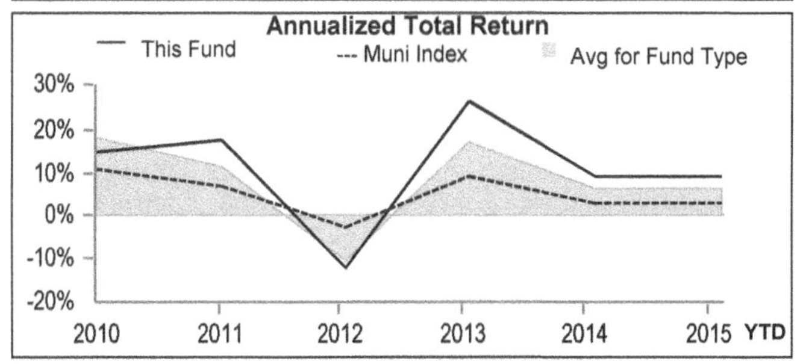

BlackRock Municipal 2018 Income Tr (BPK) C+ Fair

Fund Family: BlackRock Inc
Fund Type: Municipal - National
Inception Date: October 25, 2001

Major Rating Factors: Middle of the road best describes BlackRock Municipal 2018 Income Tr whose TheStreet.com Investment Rating is currently a C+ (Fair). The fund currently has a performance rating of C (Fair) based on an annualized return of 1.18% over the last three years and a total return of 0.10% year to date 2015. Factored into the performance evaluation is an expense ratio of 0.64% (very low).

The fund's risk rating is currently B (Good). It carries a beta of 0.49, meaning the fund's expected move will be 4.9% for every 10% move in the market. Volatility, as measured by both the semi-deviation and a drawdown factor, is considered low. As of December 31, 2015, BlackRock Municipal 2018 Income Tr traded at a premium of 1.04% above its net asset value, which is worse than its one-year historical average premium of .40%.

Theodore R. Jaeckel, Jr. has been running the fund for 10 years and currently receives a manager quality ranking of 72 (0=worst, 99=best). If you desire an average level of risk, then this fund may be an option.

Data Date	Investment Rating	Net Assets ($Mil)	Price	Performance Rating/Pts	Total Return Y-T-D	Risk Rating/Pts
12-15	C+	250.75	15.50	C / 5.3	0.10%	B / 8.0
2014	C	252.20	16.13	C / 4.8	4.65%	B- / 7.1
2013	B-	255.71	15.94	C+ / 5.7	-0.92%	B+ / 9.1
2012	B-	254.59	16.56	C+ / 5.6	7.94%	B+ / 9.3
2011	B	249.10	16.59	C+ / 6.7	12.14%	B+ / 9.4
2010	A-	235.85	15.72	B- / 7.1	10.28%	B- / 7.4

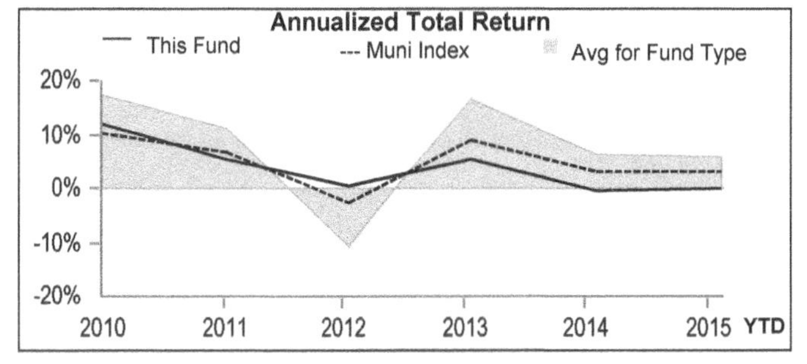

BlackRock Municipal Bond Trust (BBK) B- Good

Fund Family: BlackRock Inc
Fund Type: Municipal - National
Inception Date: April 26, 2002

Major Rating Factors: Strong performance is the major factor driving the B- (Good) TheStreet.com Investment Rating for BlackRock Municipal Bond Trust. The fund currently has a performance rating of B- (Good) based on an annualized return of 3.28% over the last three years and a total return of 7.76% year to date 2015. Factored into the performance evaluation is an expense ratio of 1.73% (above average).

The fund's risk rating is currently C+ (Fair). It carries a beta of 2.56, meaning it is expected to move 25.6% for every 10% move in the market. Volatility, as measured by both the semi-deviation and a drawdown factor, is considered low. As of December 31, 2015, BlackRock Municipal Bond Trust traded at a discount of 4.44% below its net asset value, which is worse than its one-year historical average discount of 4.93%.

Theodore R. Jaeckel, Jr. has been running the fund for 10 years and currently receives a manager quality ranking of 40 (0=worst, 99=best). If you desire only a moderate level of risk and strong performance, then this fund is an excellent option.

Data Date	Investment Rating	Net Assets ($Mil)	Price	Perfor-mance Rating/Pts	Total Return Y-T-D	Risk Rating/Pts
12-15	B-	173.36	16.14	B- / 7.2	7.76%	C+ / 6.9
2014	B-	174.30	15.90	B- / 7.3	23.14%	B- / 7.0
2013	C	149.00	13.71	C / 5.1	-17.00%	B- / 7.3
2012	A+	176.22	17.00	A- / 9.1	18.70%	B / 8.4
2011	A+	159.40	15.72	A / 9.5	26.50%	B / 8.6
2010	C-	159.22	13.73	D+ / 2.9	6.18%	B- / 7.1

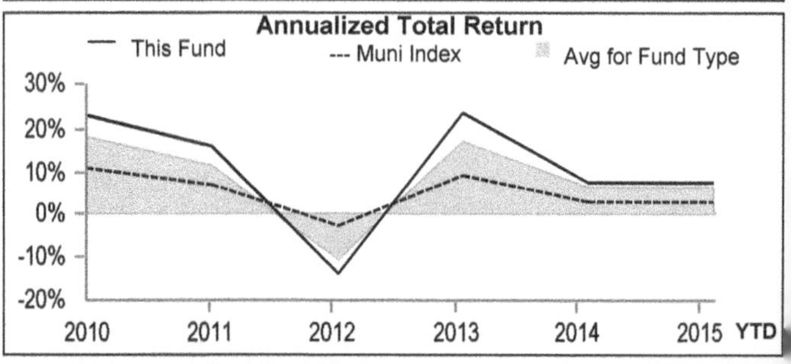

BlackRock Municipal Income Inv Qly (BAF) C+ Fair

Fund Family: BlackRock Inc
Fund Type: Municipal - Single State
Inception Date: October 28, 2002

Major Rating Factors: Middle of the road best describes BlackRock Municipal Income Inv Qly whose TheStreet.com Investment Rating is currently a C+ (Fair). The fund currently has a performance rating of C+ (Fair) based on an annualized return of 0.95% over the last three years and a total return of 8.33% year to date 2015. Factored into the performance evaluation is an expense ratio of 1.50% (average).

The fund's risk rating is currently C+ (Fair). It carries a beta of 2.24, meaning it is expected to move 22.4% for every 10% move in the market. Volatility, as measured by both the semi-deviation and a drawdown factor, is considered low. As of December 31, 2015, BlackRock Municipal Income Inv Qly traded at a discount of 8.37% below its net asset value, which is worse than its one-year historical average discount of 9.95%.

Robert D. Sneeden has been running the fund for 10 years and currently receives a manager quality ranking of 32 (0=worst, 99=best). If you desire an average level of risk, then this fund may be an option.

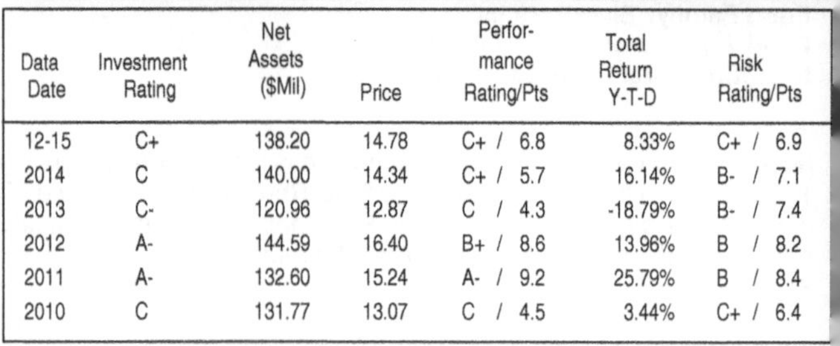

Data Date	Investment Rating	Net Assets ($Mil)	Price	Perfor-mance Rating/Pts	Total Return Y-T-D	Risk Rating/Pts
12-15	C+	138.20	14.78	C+ / 6.8	8.33%	C+ / 6.9
2014	C	140.00	14.34	C+ / 5.7	16.14%	B- / 7.1
2013	C-	120.96	12.87	C / 4.3	-18.79%	B- / 7.4
2012	A-	144.59	16.40	B+ / 8.6	13.96%	B / 8.2
2011	A-	132.60	15.24	A- / 9.2	25.79%	B / 8.4
2010	C	131.77	13.07	C / 4.5	3.44%	C+ / 6.4

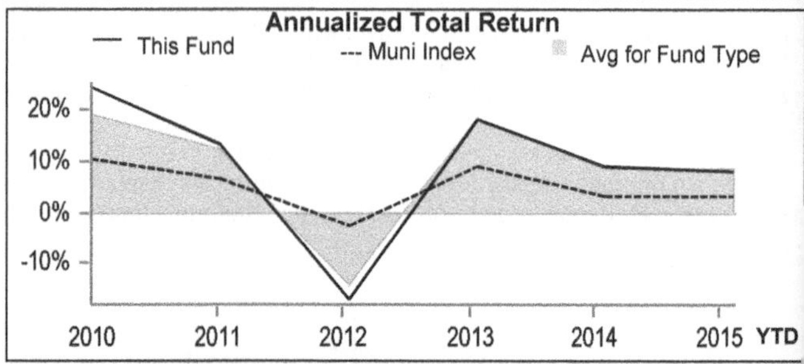

BlackRock Municipal Income Invt Tr (BBF) B- Good

Fund Family: BlackRock Inc
Fund Type: Municipal - Single State
Inception Date: July 26, 2001

Major Rating Factors: Strong performance is the major factor driving the B- (Good) TheStreet.com Investment Rating for BlackRock Municipal Income Invt Tr. The fund currently has a performance rating of B- (Good) based on an annualized return of 2.54% over the last three years and a total return of 10.98% year to date 2015. Factored into the performance evaluation is an expense ratio of 1.76% (above average).

The fund's risk rating is currently C+ (Fair). It carries a beta of 2.42, meaning it is expected to move 24.2% for every 10% move in the market. Volatility, as measured by both the semi-deviation and a drawdown factor, is considered low. As of December 31, 2015, BlackRock Municipal Income Invt Tr traded at a discount of 4.33% below its net asset value, which is worse than its one-year historical average discount of 9.16%.

Robert D. Sneeden has been running the fund for 10 years and currently receives a manager quality ranking of 36 (0=worst, 99=best). If you desire only a moderate level of risk and strong performance, then this fund is an excellent option.

Data Date	Investment Rating	Net Assets ($Mil)	Price	Perfor-mance Rating/Pts	Total Return Y-T-D	Risk Rating/Pts
12-15	B-	101.51	14.60	B- / 7.4	10.98%	C+ / 6.7
2014	C+	103.30	13.97	C+ / 6.6	18.62%	B- / 7.3
2013	C	93.15	12.48	C / 4.7	-18.29%	B- / 7.5
2012	A	106.63	15.87	A- / 9.1	20.61%	B / 8.2
2011	B+	96.10	14.30	B+ / 8.6	25.13%	B / 8.2
2010	C-	93.07	12.34	D / 1.8	3.01%	B- / 7.5

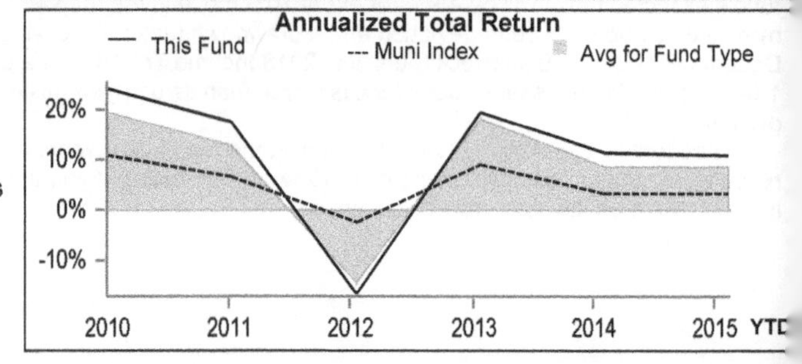

BlackRock Municipal Income Quality (BYM) C+ Fair

Fund Family: BlackRock Inc
Fund Type: Municipal - National
Inception Date: October 28, 2002

Major Rating Factors: Middle of the road best describes BlackRock Municipal Income Quality whose TheStreet.com Investment Rating is currently a C+ (Fair). The fund currently has a performance rating of C+ (Fair) based on an annualized return of 1.55% over the last three years and a total return of 10.15% year to date 2015. Factored into the performance evaluation is an expense ratio of 1.47% (average).

The fund's risk rating is currently C+ (Fair). It carries a beta of 2.69, meaning it is expected to move 26.9% for every 10% move in the market. Volatility, as measured by both the semi-deviation and a drawdown factor, is considered low. As of December 31, 2015, BlackRock Municipal Income Quality traded at a discount of 4.62% below its net asset value, which is worse than its one-year historical average discount of 8.93%.

Michael A. Kalinoski has been running the fund for 10 years and currently receives a manager quality ranking of 31 (0=worst, 99=best). If you desire an average level of risk, then this fund may be an option.

Data Date	Investment Rating	Net Assets ($Mil)	Price	Perfor-mance Rating/Pts	Total Return Y-T-D	Risk Rating/Pts
12-15	C+	401.54	14.88	C+ / 6.9	10.15%	C+ / 6.8
2014	C+	410.70	14.38	B- / 7.0	19.11%	B- / 7.2
2013	C-	355.37	12.68	C- / 4.1	-20.02%	B- / 7.4
2012	A+	424.79	16.20	A / 9.4	22.96%	B / 8.2
2011	B+	388.20	14.84	B+ / 8.5	22.46%	B / 8.5
2010	D+	384.56	12.95	D / 1.6	1.32%	C+ / 6.9

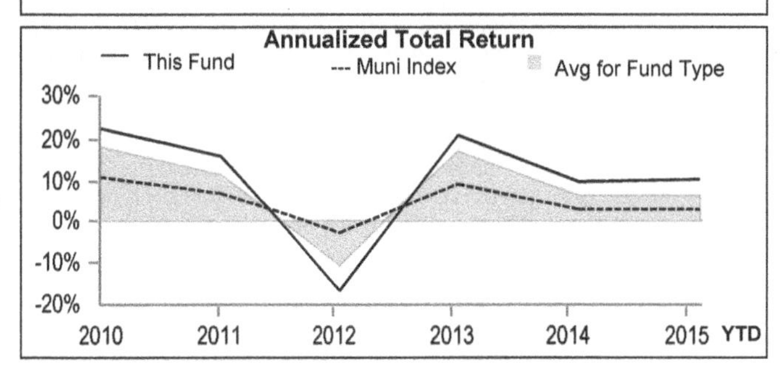

BlackRock Municipal Income Trust (BFK) B- Good

Fund Family: BlackRock Inc
Fund Type: Municipal - National
Inception Date: July 27, 2001

Major Rating Factors: Strong performance is the major factor driving the B- (Good) TheStreet.com Investment Rating for BlackRock Municipal Income Trust. The fund currently has a performance rating of B (Good) based on an annualized return of 3.31% over the last three years and a total return of 10.49% year to date 2015. Factored into the performance evaluation is an expense ratio of 1.60% (above average).

The fund's risk rating is currently C+ (Fair). It carries a beta of 2.57, meaning it is expected to move 25.7% for every 10% move in the market. Volatility, as measured by both the semi-deviation and a drawdown factor, is considered low. As of December 31, 2015, BlackRock Municipal Income Trust traded at a discount of 1.21% below its net asset value, which is worse than its one-year historical average discount of 4.65%.

Theodore R. Jaeckel, Jr. has been running the fund for 10 years and currently receives a manager quality ranking of 41 (0=worst, 99=best). If you desire only a moderate level of risk and strong performance, then this fund is an excellent option.

Data Date	Investment Rating	Net Assets ($Mil)	Price	Perfor-mance Rating/Pts	Total Return Y-T-D	Risk Rating/Pts
12-15	B-	667.06	14.75	B / 7.6	10.49%	C+ / 6.6
2014	C+	664.70	14.18	B- / 7.0	17.39%	B- / 7.1
2013	C+	688.71	12.70	C+ / 5.9	-15.27%	B- / 7.4
2012	A	648.50	15.52	B+ / 8.6	17.48%	B / 8.4
2011	A+	609.10	13.95	A+ / 9.7	28.32%	B / 8.5
2010	C	587.25	12.69	C- / 3.5	6.50%	C+ / 6.8

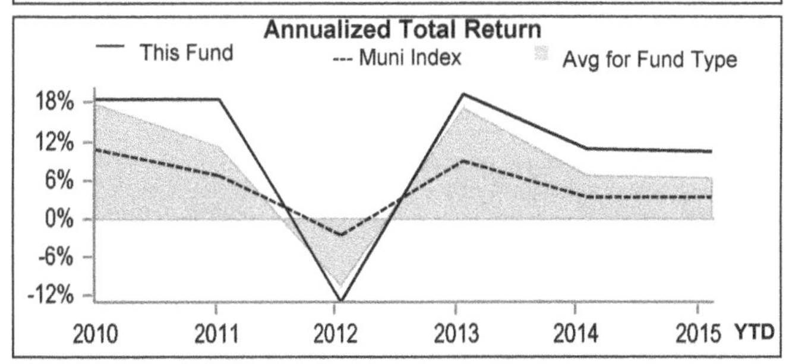

BlackRock Municipal Income Trust I (BLE) C+ Fair

Fund Family: BlackRock Inc
Fund Type: Municipal - National
Inception Date: July 25, 2002

Major Rating Factors: Middle of the road best describes BlackRock Municipal Income Trust I whose TheStreet.com Investment Rating is currently a C+ (Fair). The fund currently has a performance rating of C+ (Fair) based on an annualized return of 2.76% over the last three years and a total return of 2.16% year to date 2015. Factored into the performance evaluation is an expense ratio of 1.55% (average).

The fund's risk rating is currently C+ (Fair). It carries a beta of 3.17, meaning it is expected to move 31.7% for every 10% move in the market. Volatility, as measured by both the semi-deviation and a drawdown factor, is considered low. As of December 31, 2015, BlackRock Municipal Income Trust I traded at a discount of 1.67% below its net asset value, which is worse than its one-year historical average discount of 3.85%.

Theodore R. Jaeckel, Jr. has been running the fund for 10 years and currently receives a manager quality ranking of 30 (0=worst, 99=best). If you desire an average level of risk, then this fund may be an option.

Data Date	Investment Rating	Net Assets ($Mil)	Price	Perfor-mance Rating/Pts	Total Return Y-T-D	Risk Rating/Pts
12-15	C+	357.87	15.31	C+ / 6.7	2.16%	C+ / 6.7
2014	B-	363.40	15.88	A- / 9.1	27.80%	C / 5.4
2013	C	312.33	13.22	C / 5.2	-17.37%	B- / 7.5
2012	A+	376.77	16.21	A- / 9.0	18.50%	B / 8.4
2011	A+	340.50	15.21	A+ / 9.8	29.15%	B / 8.7
2010	C	340.27	13.10	C- / 3.2	2.63%	B- / 7.1

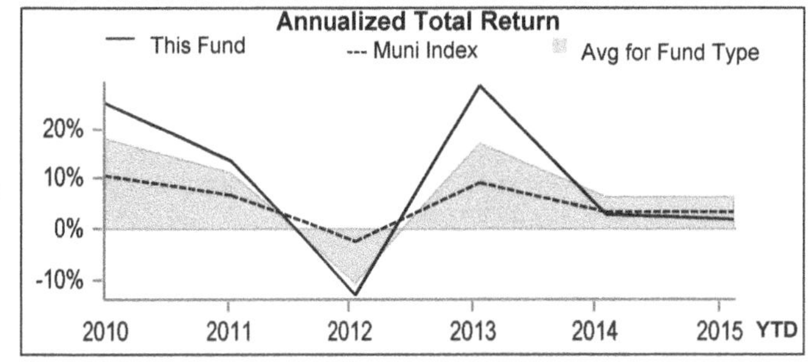

BlackRock Municipal Target Term (BTT) C+ Fair

Fund Family: BlackRock Fund Advisors
Fund Type: Municipal - National
Inception Date: August 30, 2012

Major Rating Factors: Strong performance is the major factor driving the C+ (Fair) TheStreet.com Investment Rating for BlackRock Municipal Target Term. The fund currently has a performance rating of B- (Good) based on an annualized return of 0.99% over the last three years and a total return of 11.81% year to date 2015. Factored into the performance evaluation is an expense ratio of 1.06% (low).

The fund's risk rating is currently C+ (Fair). It carries a beta of 3.32, meaning it is expected to move 33.2% for every 10% move in the market. Volatility, as measured by both the semi-deviation and a drawdown factor, is considered low. As of December 31, 2015, BlackRock Municipal Target Term traded at a discount of 9.26% below its net asset value, which is worse than its one-year historical average discount of 10.02%.

This fund has been team managed for 4 years and currently receives a manager quality ranking of 21 (0=worst, 99=best). If you desire only a moderate level of risk and strong performance, then this fund is an excellent option.

Data Date	Investment Rating	Net Assets ($Mil)	Price	Performance Rating/Pts	Total Return Y-T-D	Risk Rating/Pts
12-15	C+	1,602.41	21.57	B- / 7.2	11.81%	C+ / 6.5
2014	A-	1,600.50	20.09	A / 9.5	20.45%	C+ / 6.6
2013	D-	1,321.84	17.12	E / 0.5	-23.93%	C+ / 6.7

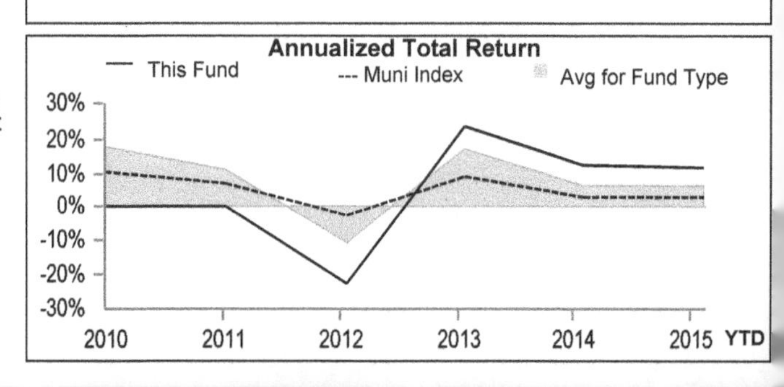

BlackRock MuniEnhanced Fund (MEN) B+ Good

Fund Family: BlackRock Inc
Fund Type: Municipal - National
Inception Date: February 23, 1989

Major Rating Factors: Strong performance is the major factor driving the B+ (Good) TheStreet.com Investment Rating for BlackRock MuniEnhanced Fund. The fund currently has a performance rating of B (Good) based on an annualized return of 4.15% over the last three years and a total return of 10.38% year to date 2015. Factored into the performance evaluation is an expense ratio of 1.43% (average).

The fund's risk rating is currently B- (Good). It carries a beta of 2.13, meaning it is expected to move 21.3% for every 10% move in the market. Volatility, as measured by both the semi-deviation and a drawdown factor, is considered low. As of December 31, 2015, BlackRock MuniEnhanced Fund traded at a discount of 3.81% below its net asset value, which is worse than its one-year historical average discount of 6.15%.

Michael A. Kalinoski has been running the fund for 27 years and currently receives a manager quality ranking of 54 (0=worst, 99=best). If you desire only a moderate level of risk and strong performance, then this fund is an excellent option.

Data Date	Investment Rating	Net Assets ($Mil)	Price	Performance Rating/Pts	Total Return Y-T-D	Risk Rating/Pts
12-15	B+	362.70	11.85	B / 7.8	10.38%	B- / 7.6
2014	B-	363.70	11.40	C+ / 6.8	16.75%	B / 8.0
2013	C	373.26	10.40	C / 5.0	-12.55%	B / 8.2
2012	A-	357.02	12.29	B+ / 8.4	15.42%	B / 8.6
2011	A	339.70	11.64	A- / 9.1	19.40%	B / 8.8
2010	C+	320.08	10.45	C / 5.4	7.20%	C+ / 6.3

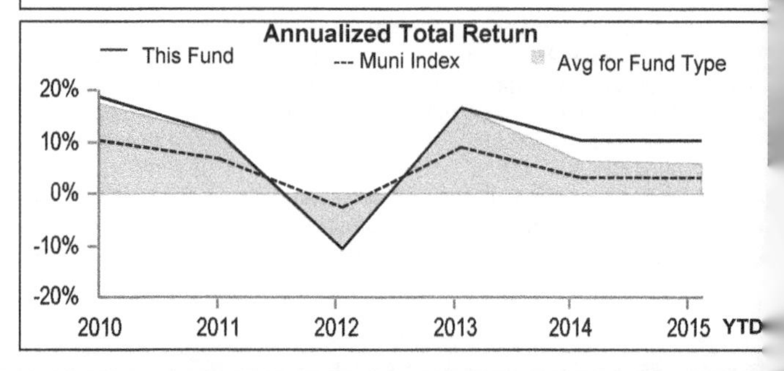

BlackRock MuniHoldings CA Qly (MUC) C+ Fair

Fund Family: BlackRock Inc
Fund Type: Municipal - Single State
Inception Date: February 27, 1998

Major Rating Factors: Middle of the road best describes BlackRock MuniHoldings CA Qly whose TheStreet.com Investment Rating is currently a C+ (Fair). The fund currently has a performance rating of C+ (Fair) based on an annualized return of 1.43% over the last three years and a total return of 8.33% year to date 2015. Factored into the performance evaluation is an expense ratio of 1.45% (average).

The fund's risk rating is currently B- (Good). It carries a beta of 2.19, meaning it is expected to move 21.9% for every 10% move in the market. Volatility, as measured by both the semi-deviation and a drawdown factor, is considered low. As of December 31, 2015, BlackRock MuniHoldings CA Qly traded at a discount of 7.36% below its net asset value, which is worse than its one-year historical average discount of 8.57%.

Walter O'Connor has been running the fund for 18 years and currently receives a manager quality ranking of 35 (0=worst, 99=best). If you desire an average level of risk, then this fund may be an option.

Data Date	Investment Rating	Net Assets ($Mil)	Price	Performance Rating/Pts	Total Return Y-T-D	Risk Rating/Pts
12-15	C+	646.90	14.85	C+ / 6.3	8.33%	B- / 7.0
2014	C+	656.50	14.47	C+ / 6.0	15.20%	B- / 7.3
2013	C	595.27	13.22	C / 5.0	-16.51%	B- / 7.5
2012	A+	671.08	16.34	A / 9.5	18.55%	B / 8.6
2011	A	618.00	14.88	A / 9.3	24.33%	B / 8.7
2010	C+	254.00	13.05	C+ / 5.7	10.47%	C+ / 6.4

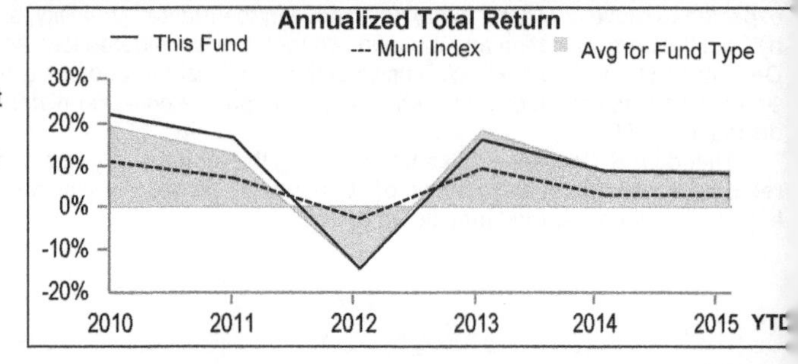

* Denotes ETF Fund

BlackRock MuniHoldings Fund (MHD) C+ Fair

Fund Family: BlackRock Inc
Fund Type: Municipal - National
Inception Date: April 29, 1997

Major Rating Factors: Middle of the road best describes BlackRock MuniHoldings Fund whose TheStreet.com Investment Rating is currently a C+ (Fair). The fund currently has a performance rating of C+ (Fair) based on an annualized return of 2.99% over the last three years and a total return of 5.96% year to date 2015. Factored into the performance evaluation is an expense ratio of 1.50% (average).

The fund's risk rating is currently B- (Good). It carries a beta of 2.33, meaning it is expected to move 23.3% for every 10% move in the market. Volatility, as measured by both the semi-deviation and a drawdown factor, is considered low. As of December 31, 2015, BlackRock MuniHoldings Fund traded at a discount of 3.11% below its net asset value, which is worse than its one-year historical average discount of 3.94%.

Theodore R. Jaeckel, Jr. has been running the fund for 10 years and currently receives a manager quality ranking of 42 (0=worst, 99=best). If you desire an average level of risk, then this fund may be an option.

Data Date	Investment Rating	Net Assets ($Mil)	Price	Performance Rating/Pts	Total Return Y-T-D	Risk Rating/Pts
12-15	C+	248.65	17.11	C+ / 6.8	5.96%	B- / 7.1
2014	B+	247.90	17.12	B+ / 8.6	24.54%	B- / 7.5
2013	C-	255.91	14.50	C / 4.3	-17.61%	B- / 7.7
2012	A+	243.99	18.36	A+ / 9.6	23.49%	B / 8.7
2011	A+	229.90	16.58	A / 9.5	21.38%	B / 8.9
2010	C+	219.13	15.03	C+ / 6.7	11.71%	C+ / 5.9

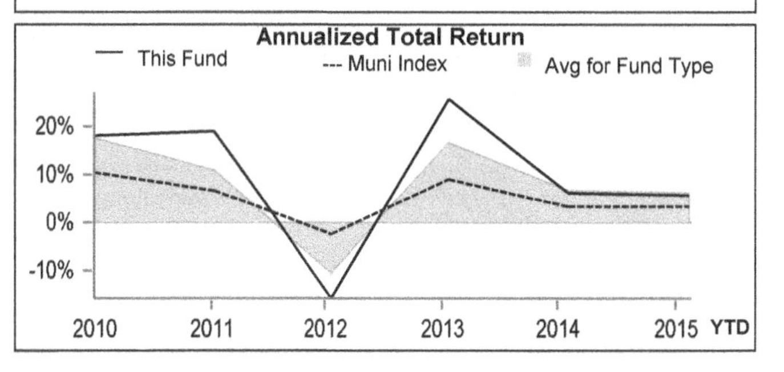

BlackRock MuniHoldings Fund II (MUH) C+ Fair

Fund Family: BlackRock Inc
Fund Type: Municipal - National
Inception Date: February 24, 1998

Major Rating Factors: Middle of the road best describes BlackRock MuniHoldings Fund II whose TheStreet.com Investment Rating is currently a C+ (Fair). The fund currently has a performance rating of C+ (Fair) based on an annualized return of 2.39% over the last three years and a total return of 4.21% year to date 2015. Factored into the performance evaluation is an expense ratio of 1.48% (average).

The fund's risk rating is currently B- (Good). It carries a beta of 2.75, meaning it is expected to move 27.5% for every 10% move in the market. Volatility, as measured by both the semi-deviation and a drawdown factor, is considered low. As of December 31, 2015, BlackRock MuniHoldings Fund II traded at a discount of 5.71% below its net asset value, which is worse than its one-year historical average discount of 6.84%.

Theodore R. Jaeckel, Jr. has been running the fund for 10 years and currently receives a manager quality ranking of 33 (0=worst, 99=best). If you desire an average level of risk, then this fund may be an option.

Data Date	Investment Rating	Net Assets ($Mil)	Price	Performance Rating/Pts	Total Return Y-T-D	Risk Rating/Pts
12-15	C+	183.21	15.35	C+ / 6.5	4.21%	B- / 7.3
2014	B	182.90	15.67	B / 7.8	23.85%	B- / 7.5
2013	C	191.37	13.35	C / 4.8	-16.82%	B- / 7.7
2012	A+	182.62	16.64	A- / 9.2	18.29%	B / 8.5
2011	A+	172.60	15.49	A+ / 9.6	24.54%	B / 8.7
2010	C+	163.72	13.66	C+ / 5.6	8.03%	C+ / 6.0

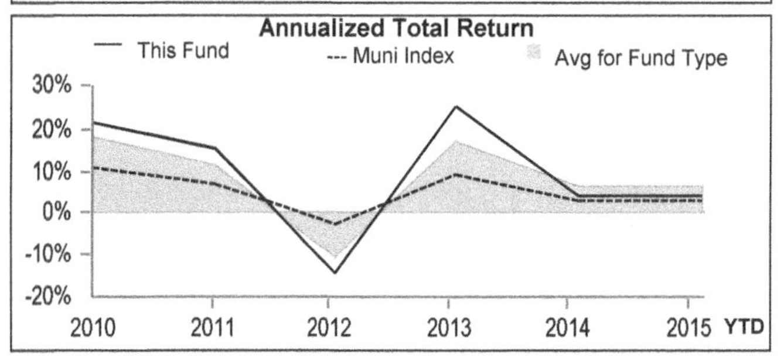

BlackRock MuniHoldings Inv Quality (MFL) C+ Fair

Fund Family: BlackRock Inc
Fund Type: Municipal - Single State
Inception Date: September 23, 1997

Major Rating Factors: Middle of the road best describes BlackRock MuniHoldings Inv Quality whose TheStreet.com Investment Rating is currently a C+ (Fair). The fund currently has a performance rating of C+ (Fair) based on an annualized return of 1.81% over the last three years and a total return of 7.20% year to date 2015. Factored into the performance evaluation is an expense ratio of 1.49% (average).

The fund's risk rating is currently C+ (Fair). It carries a beta of 2.27, meaning it is expected to move 22.7% for every 10% move in the market. Volatility, as measured by both the semi-deviation and a drawdown factor, is considered low. As of December 31, 2015, BlackRock MuniHoldings Inv Quality traded at a discount of 6.20% below its net asset value, which is worse than its one-year historical average discount of 7.60%.

Timothy T. Browse currently receives a manager quality ranking of 34 (0=worst, 99=best). If you desire an average level of risk, then this fund may be an option.

Data Date	Investment Rating	Net Assets ($Mil)	Price	Performance Rating/Pts	Total Return Y-T-D	Risk Rating/Pts
12-15	C+	573.89	14.53	C+ / 6.3	7.20%	C+ / 6.6
2014	C+	585.90	14.28	B- / 7.0	19.74%	B- / 7.0
2013	C-	501.81	12.52	C / 4.4	-18.41%	B- / 7.3
2012	A+	602.78	16.10	A- / 9.2	20.17%	B / 8.5
2011	A	550.70	14.61	A- / 9.2	24.85%	B / 8.7
2010	C+	553.37	12.78	C+ / 5.8	4.98%	C+ / 6.3

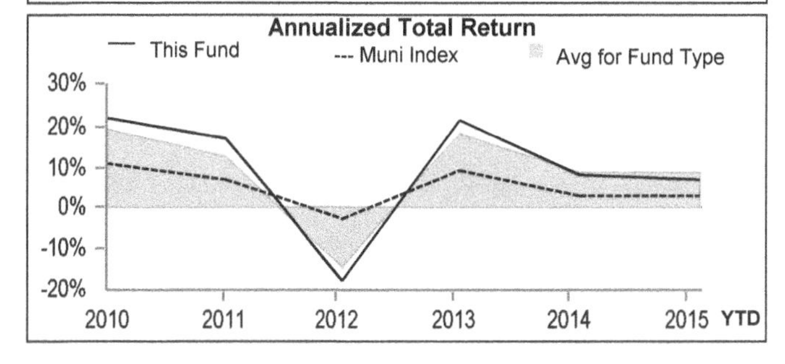

BlackRock MuniHoldings New York QI (MHN) B- Good

Fund Family: BlackRock Inc
Fund Type: Municipal - Single State
Inception Date: September 16, 1997

Major Rating Factors: Strong performance is the major factor driving the B- (Good) TheStreet.com Investment Rating for BlackRock MuniHoldings New York QI. The fund currently has a performance rating of B- (Good) based on an annualized return of 1.82% over the last three years and a total return of 9.35% year to date 2015. Factored into the performance evaluation is an expense ratio of 1.52% (average).

The fund's risk rating is currently B- (Good). It carries a beta of 1.87, meaning it is expected to move 18.7% for every 10% move in the market. Volatility, as measured by both the semi-deviation and a drawdown factor, is considered low. As of December 31, 2015, BlackRock MuniHoldings New York QI traded at a discount of 3.83% below its net asset value, which is worse than its one-year historical average discount of 6.21%.

Robert M. Shearer currently receives a manager quality ranking of 41 (0=worst, 99=best). If you desire only a moderate level of risk and strong performance, then this fund is an excellent option.

Data Date	Investment Rating	Net Assets ($Mil)	Price	Performance Rating/Pts	Total Return Y-T-D	Risk Rating/Pts
12-15	B-	461.16	14.56	B- / 7.5	9.35%	B- / 7.0
2014	C+	465.60	13.99	C+ / 6.1	17.55%	B- / 7.3
2013	C-	408.94	12.49	C- / 3.1	-18.56%	B- / 7.6
2012	A	485.45	16.15	B+ / 8.7	14.81%	B / 8.4
2011	A+	459.90	15.16	A / 9.5	20.74%	B / 8.7
2010	C+	464.85	13.46	C+ / 5.7	8.10%	C+ / 6.1

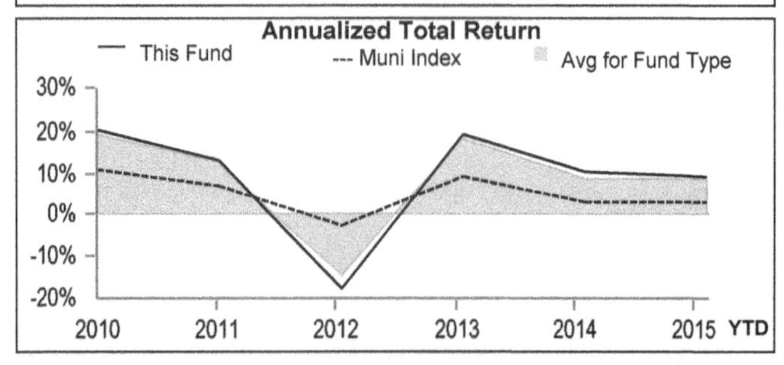

BlackRock MuniHoldings NJ Qly (MUJ) C+ Fair

Fund Family: BlackRock Inc
Fund Type: Municipal - Single State
Inception Date: March 6, 1998

Major Rating Factors: Middle of the road best describes BlackRock MuniHoldings NJ Qly whose TheStreet.com Investment Rating is currently a C+ (Fair). The fund currently has a performance rating of C+ (Fair) based on an annualized return of 0.76% over the last three years and a total return of 5.66% year to date 2015. Factored into the performance evaluation is an expense ratio of 1.57% (above average).

The fund's risk rating is currently B- (Good). It carries a beta of 1.91, meaning it is expected to move 19.1% for every 10% move in the market. Volatility, as measured by both the semi-deviation and a drawdown factor, is considered low. As of December 31, 2015, BlackRock MuniHoldings NJ Qly traded at a discount of 9.36% below its net asset value, which is worse than its one-year historical average discount of 11.01%.

Theodore R. Jaeckel, Jr. has been running the fund for 10 years and currently receives a manager quality ranking of 33 (0=worst, 99=best). If you desire an average level of risk, then this fund may be an option.

Data Date	Investment Rating	Net Assets ($Mil)	Price	Performance Rating/Pts	Total Return Y-T-D	Risk Rating/Pts
12-15	C+	470.95	14.43	C+ / 6.1	5.66%	B- / 7.5
2014	C+	341.90	14.47	C+ / 5.7	16.53%	B- / 7.9
2013	C-	309.17	13.12	C- / 4.0	-17.44%	B / 8.1
2012	A+	351.84	16.67	B+ / 8.7	15.67%	B / 8.7
2011	A	330.80	15.74	A / 9.3	25.00%	B / 8.8
2010	C+	322.68	13.49	C / 5.3	5.19%	C+ / 6.5

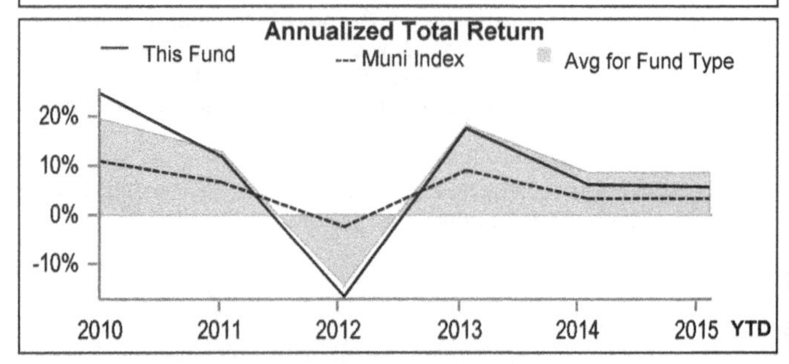

BlackRock MuniHoldings Quality (MUS) B Good

Fund Family: BlackRock Inc
Fund Type: Municipal - National
Inception Date: April 28, 1998

Major Rating Factors: Strong performance is the major factor driving the B (Good) TheStreet.com Investment Rating for BlackRock MuniHoldings Quality. The fund currently has a performance rating of B- (Good) based on an annualized return of 1.68% over the last three years and a total return of 9.73% year to date 2015. Factored into the performance evaluation is an expense ratio of 1.57% (above average).

The fund's risk rating is currently B- (Good). It carries a beta of 3.00, meaning it is expected to move 30.0% for every 10% move in the market. Volatility, as measured by both the semi-deviation and a drawdown factor, is considered low. As of December 31, 2015, BlackRock MuniHoldings Quality traded at a discount of 6.22% below its net asset value, which is worse than its one-year historical average discount of 9.18%.

Theodore R. Jaeckel, Jr. has been running the fund for 10 years and currently receives a manager quality ranking of 25 (0=worst, 99=best). If you desire only a moderate level of risk and strong performance, then this fund is an excellent option.

Data Date	Investment Rating	Net Assets ($Mil)	Price	Performance Rating/Pts	Total Return Y-T-D	Risk Rating/Pts
12-15	B	189.59	13.73	B- / 7.5	9.73%	B- / 7.2
2014	C+	190.80	13.32	C+ / 6.1	18.33%	B- / 7.3
2013	C-	199.24	11.86	C / 4.4	-18.90%	B- / 7.6
2012	A-	189.57	15.10	B+ / 8.6	16.30%	B / 8.3
2011	A	181.00	14.12	A / 9.4	27.11%	B / 8.5
2010	C	171.98	12.10	C / 4.5	1.24%	C+ / 6.5

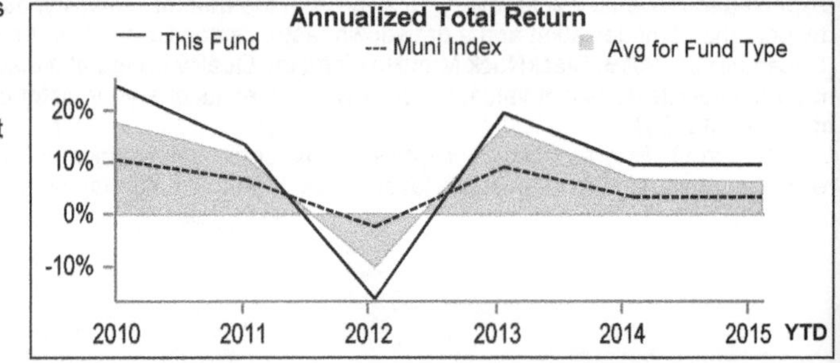

BlackRock MuniHoldings Quality II (MUE) C+ Fair

Fund Family: BlackRock Inc
Fund Type: Municipal - National
Inception Date: February 23, 1999

Major Rating Factors: Middle of the road best describes BlackRock MuniHoldings Quality II whose TheStreet.com Investment Rating is currently a C+ (Fair). The fund currently has a performance rating of C+ (Fair) based on an annualized return of 1.35% over the last three years and a total return of 6.85% year to date 2015. Factored into the performance evaluation is an expense ratio of 1.49% (average).

The fund's risk rating is currently B- (Good). It carries a beta of 2.38, meaning it is expected to move 23.8% for every 10% move in the market. Volatility, as measured by both the semi-deviation and a drawdown factor, is considered low. As of December 31, 2015, BlackRock MuniHoldings Quality II traded at a discount of 7.48% below its net asset value, which is worse than its one-year historical average discount of 8.52%.

Robert M. Shearer has been running the fund for 10 years and currently receives a manager quality ranking of 33 (0=worst, 99=best). If you desire an average level of risk, then this fund may be an option.

Data Date	Investment Rating	Net Assets ($Mil)	Price	Performance Rating/Pts	Total Return Y-T-D	Risk Rating/Pts
12-15	C+	325.91	13.61	C+ / 6.2	6.85%	B- / 7.4
2014	C+	331.50	13.48	C+ / 6.0	18.02%	B- / 7.6
2013	C	298.71	12.09	C / 4.5	-17.82%	B- / 7.7
2012	A	341.14	15.08	A- / 9.0	16.37%	B / 8.3
2011	A	313.70	14.30	A+ / 9.6	30.38%	B / 8.5
2010	C	303.67	11.96	C- / 4.0	-1.83%	C+ / 6.4

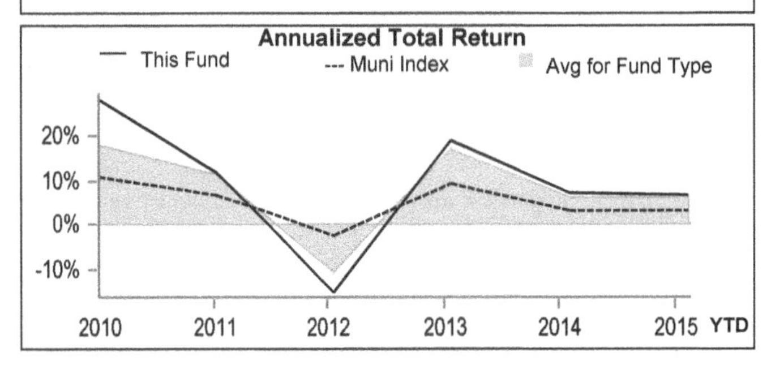

BlackRock MuniVest Fund (MVF) B- Good

Fund Family: BlackRock Inc
Fund Type: Municipal - National
Inception Date: September 22, 1988

Major Rating Factors: Strong performance is the major factor driving the B- (Good) TheStreet.com Investment Rating for BlackRock MuniVest Fund. The fund currently has a performance rating of B- (Good) based on an annualized return of 2.38% over the last three years and a total return of 9.63% year to date 2015. Factored into the performance evaluation is an expense ratio of 1.43% (average).

The fund's risk rating is currently B- (Good). It carries a beta of 2.42, meaning it is expected to move 24.2% for every 10% move in the market. Volatility, as measured by both the semi-deviation and a drawdown factor, is considered low. As of December 31, 2015, BlackRock MuniVest Fund traded at a premium of .79% above its net asset value, which is worse than its one-year historical average discount of 2.28%.

Theodore R. Jaeckel, Jr. has been running the fund for 10 years and currently receives a manager quality ranking of 41 (0=worst, 99=best). If you desire only a moderate level of risk and strong performance, then this fund is an excellent option.

Data Date	Investment Rating	Net Assets ($Mil)	Price	Performance Rating/Pts	Total Return Y-T-D	Risk Rating/Pts
12-15	B-	642.89	10.25	B- / 7.1	9.63%	B- / 7.1
2014	C+	657.40	9.91	C+ / 6.4	17.05%	B- / 7.7
2013	C-	584.72	8.91	C- / 4.2	-16.88%	B- / 7.9
2012	A+	679.21	11.03	A- / 9.2	19.23%	B / 8.8
2011	A+	626.10	10.44	A- / 9.2	21.24%	B / 8.9
2010	C+	625.20	9.46	C+ / 6.7	9.27%	C+ / 6.3

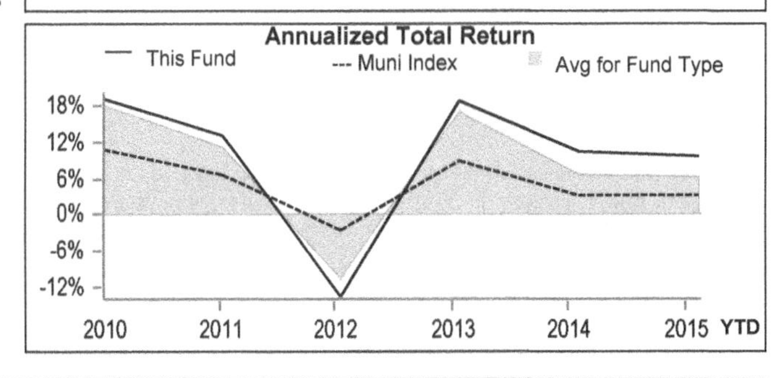

BlackRock MuniVest Fund II (MVT) B Good

Fund Family: BlackRock Inc
Fund Type: Municipal - National
Inception Date: March 19, 1993

Major Rating Factors: Strong performance is the major factor driving the B (Good) TheStreet.com Investment Rating for BlackRock MuniVest Fund II. The fund currently has a performance rating of B (Good) based on an annualized return of 3.35% over the last three years and a total return of 12.38% year to date 2015. Factored into the performance evaluation is an expense ratio of 1.50% (average).

The fund's risk rating is currently C+ (Fair). It carries a beta of 2.82, meaning it is expected to move 28.2% for every 10% move in the market. Volatility, as measured by both the semi-deviation and a drawdown factor, is considered low. As of December 31, 2015, BlackRock MuniVest Fund II traded at a premium of 2.50% above its net asset value, which is worse than its one-year historical average discount of 1.43%.

Theodore R. Jaeckel, Jr. has been running the fund for 10 years and currently receives a manager quality ranking of 35 (0=worst, 99=best). If you desire only a moderate level of risk and strong performance, then this fund is an excellent option.

Data Date	Investment Rating	Net Assets ($Mil)	Price	Performance Rating/Pts	Total Return Y-T-D	Risk Rating/Pts
12-15	B	336.32	16.41	B / 7.8	12.38%	C+ / 6.8
2014	C+	336.30	15.60	C+ / 6.4	18.68%	B- / 7.7
2013	C	349.00	13.92	C / 5.2	-17.10%	B- / 7.9
2012	A+	330.94	17.51	A- / 9.2	20.33%	B / 8.6
2011	A+	312.40	15.88	A+ / 9.8	28.61%	B / 8.6
2010	C+	295.47	14.00	C+ / 5.6	7.54%	C+ / 6.2

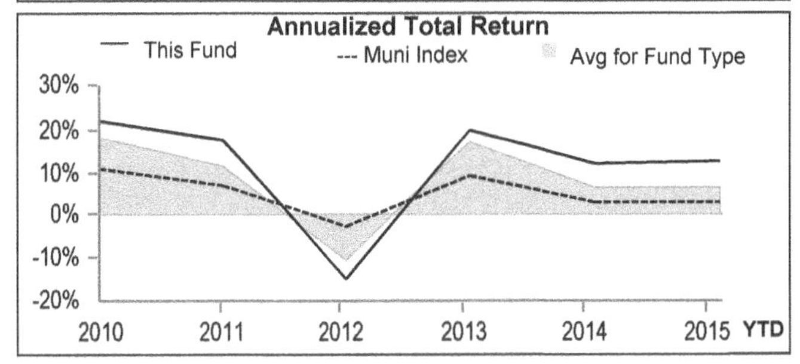

BlackRock MuniYield AZ Fund (MZA) B Good

Fund Family: BlackRock Inc
Fund Type: Municipal - Single State
Inception Date: October 22, 1993

Major Rating Factors: Strong performance is the major factor driving the B (Good) TheStreet.com Investment Rating for BlackRock MuniYield AZ Fund. The fund currently has a performance rating of B+ (Good) based on an annualized return of 7.49% over the last three years and a total return of 8.24% year to date 2015. Factored into the performance evaluation is an expense ratio of 1.63% (above average).

The fund's risk rating is currently C+ (Fair). It carries a beta of 2.08, meaning it is expected to move 20.8% for every 10% move in the market. Volatility, as measured by both the semi-deviation and a drawdown factor, is considered low. As of December 31, 2015, BlackRock MuniYield AZ Fund traded at a premium of 12.93% above its net asset value, which is better than its one-year historical average premium of 13.49%.

Michael A. Kalinoski has been running the fund for 23 years and currently receives a manager quality ranking of 81 (0=worst, 99=best). If you desire only a moderate level of risk and strong performance, then this fund is an excellent option.

Data Date	Investment Rating	Net Assets ($Mil)	Price	Perfor-mance Rating/Pts	Total Return Y-T-D	Risk Rating/Pts
12-15	B	67.71	16.86	B+ / 8.5	8.24%	C+ / 6.6
2014	B+	67.70	16.34	A / 9.5	31.56%	C+ / 6.4
2013	C+	62.17	12.91	C / 5.5	-13.16%	B / 8.2
2012	A	69.07	15.34	B+ / 8.6	17.05%	B / 8.7
2011	A+	64.90	14.12	A / 9.4	19.90%	B / 8.8
2010	C	62.62	12.62	C- / 3.9	8.80%	B- / 7.4

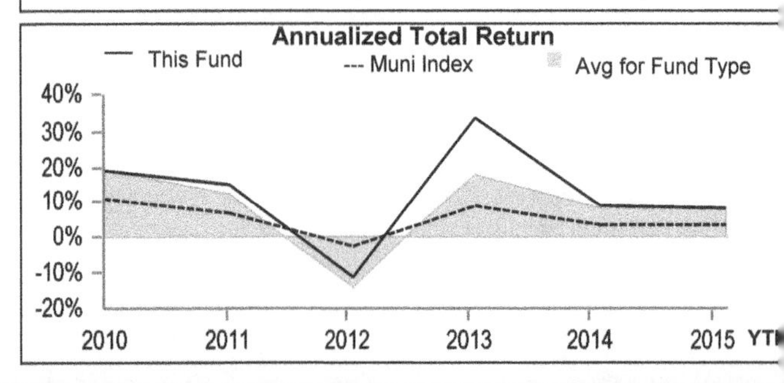

BlackRock MuniYield CA Fund (MYC) B- Good

Fund Family: BlackRock Inc
Fund Type: Municipal - Single State
Inception Date: February 21, 1992

Major Rating Factors: Strong performance is the major factor driving the B- (Good) TheStreet.com Investment Rating for BlackRock MuniYield CA Fund. The fund currently has a performance rating of B- (Good) based on an annualized return of 2.93% over the last three years and a total return of 8.74% year to date 2015. Factored into the performance evaluation is an expense ratio of 1.37% (average).

The fund's risk rating is currently B- (Good). It carries a beta of 2.54, meaning it is expected to move 25.4% for every 10% move in the market. Volatility, as measured by both the semi-deviation and a drawdown factor, is considered low. As of December 31, 2015, BlackRock MuniYield CA Fund traded at a discount of 4.12% below its net asset value, which is worse than its one-year historical average discount of 4.95%.

Walter O'Connor has been running the fund for 24 years and currently receives a manager quality ranking of 37 (0=worst, 99=best). If you desire only a moderate level of risk and strong performance, then this fund is an excellent option.

Data Date	Investment Rating	Net Assets ($Mil)	Price	Perfor-mance Rating/Pts	Total Return Y-T-D	Risk Rating/Pts
12-15	B-	348.85	15.82	B- / 7.1	8.74%	B- / 7.3
2014	B	354.70	15.45	B- / 7.0	18.68%	B- / 7.8
2013	C+	319.14	13.78	C / 5.4	-15.89%	B / 8.0
2012	A+	361.34	16.93	A / 9.4	18.07%	B / 8.7
2011	A+	327.80	15.08	A / 9.3	25.10%	B / 8.8
2010	C+	314.33	13.28	C / 5.4	9.82%	C+ / 6.2

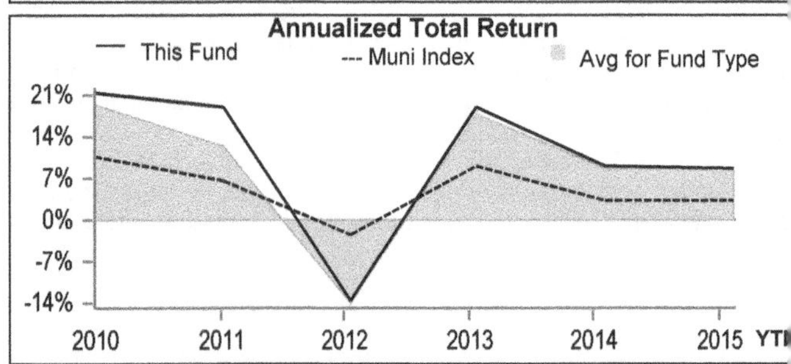

BlackRock MuniYield California Qly (MCA) B- Good

Fund Family: BlackRock Inc
Fund Type: Municipal - Single State
Inception Date: October 23, 1992

Major Rating Factors: Strong performance is the major factor driving the B- (Good) TheStreet.com Investment Rating for BlackRock MuniYield California Qly. The fund currently has a performance rating of B- (Good) based on an annualized return of 3.38% over the last three years and a total return of 8.49% year to date 2015. Factored into the performance evaluation is an expense ratio of 1.32% (average).

The fund's risk rating is currently B- (Good). It carries a beta of 2.02, meaning it is expected to move 20.2% for every 10% move in the market. Volatility, as measured by both the semi-deviation and a drawdown factor, is considered low. As of December 31, 2015, BlackRock MuniYield California Qly traded at a discount of 4.35% below its net asset value, which is worse than its one-year historical average discount of 6.33%.

Walter O'Connor has been running the fund for 24 years and currently receives a manager quality ranking of 50 (0=worst, 99=best). If you desire only a moderate level of risk and strong performance, then this fund is an excellent option.

Data Date	Investment Rating	Net Assets ($Mil)	Price	Perfor-mance Rating/Pts	Total Return Y-T-D	Risk Rating/Pts
12-15	B-	554.06	15.60	B- / 7.3	8.49%	B- / 7.2
2014	B	562.70	15.20	B- / 7.4	17.75%	B- / 7.8
2013	C+	510.02	13.64	C+ / 6.0	-13.69%	B / 8.0
2012	A+	570.56	16.43	A / 9.5	21.56%	B / 8.6
2011	A-	523.90	14.34	B+ / 8.9	23.38%	B / 8.7
2010	C	503.87	12.79	C / 4.6	8.05%	C+ / 6.1

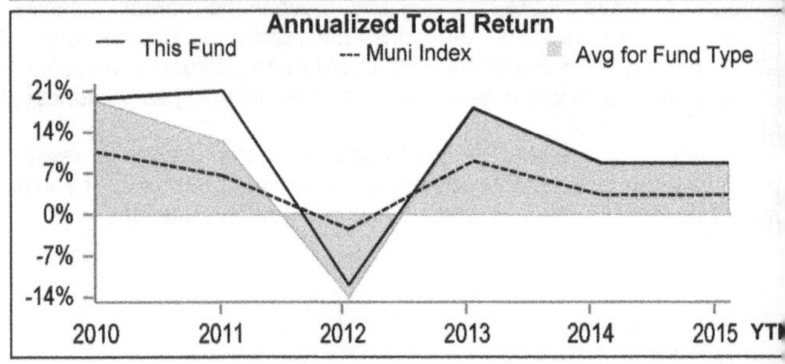

BlackRock MuniYield Fund (MYD) C+ Fair

Fund Family: BlackRock Inc
Fund Type: Municipal - National
Inception Date: November 21, 1991

Major Rating Factors: Middle of the road best describes BlackRock MuniYield Fund whose TheStreet.com Investment Rating is currently a C+ (Fair). The fund currently has a performance rating of C+ (Fair) based on an annualized return of 1.86% over the last three years and a total return of 7.36% year to date 2015. Factored into the performance evaluation is an expense ratio of 1.36% (average).

The fund's risk rating is currently C+ (Fair). It carries a beta of 2.60, meaning it is expected to move 26.0% for every 10% move in the market. Volatility, as measured by both the semi-deviation and a drawdown factor, is considered low. As of December 31, 2015, BlackRock MuniYield Fund traded at a discount of 3.13% below its net asset value, which is worse than its one-year historical average discount of 4.58%.

Theodore R. Jaeckel, Jr. has been running the fund for 10 years and currently receives a manager quality ranking of 32 (0=worst, 99=best). If you desire an average level of risk, then this fund may be an option.

Data Date	Investment Rating	Net Assets ($Mil)	Price	Performance Rating/Pts	Total Return Y-T-D	Risk Rating/Pts
12-15	C+	713.24	14.87	C+ / 6.5	7.36%	C+ / 6.7
2014	B-	712.70	14.74	B- / 7.4	21.81%	B- / 7.3
2013	C-	745.58	12.82	C- / 3.9	-19.30%	B- / 7.6
2012	A+	703.29	16.37	A / 9.4	21.19%	B / 8.5
2011	A-	660.60	14.79	B+ / 8.7	21.42%	B / 8.6
2010	C+	630.61	13.41	C / 4.7	11.94%	C+ / 6.8

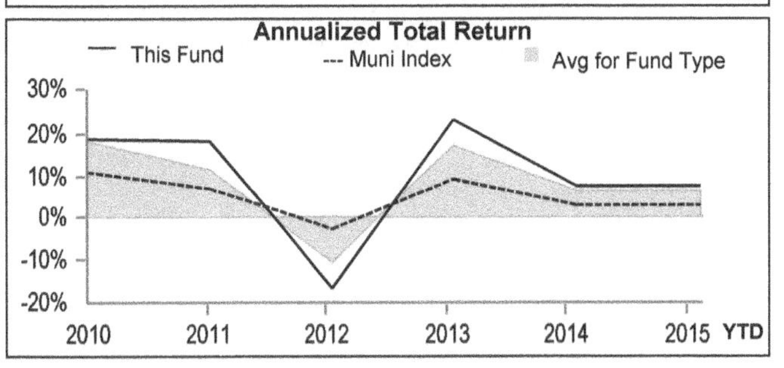

BlackRock MuniYield Inv Quality (MFT) C+ Fair

Fund Family: BlackRock Inc
Fund Type: Municipal - Single State
Inception Date: October 23, 1992

Major Rating Factors: Middle of the road best describes BlackRock MuniYield Inv Quality whose TheStreet.com Investment Rating is currently a C+ (Fair). The fund currently has a performance rating of C+ (Fair) based on an annualized return of 1.06% over the last three years and a total return of 8.39% year to date 2015. Factored into the performance evaluation is an expense ratio of 1.56% (average).

The fund's risk rating is currently B- (Good). It carries a beta of 2.52, meaning it is expected to move 25.2% for every 10% move in the market. Volatility, as measured by both the semi-deviation and a drawdown factor, is considered low. As of December 31, 2015, BlackRock MuniYield Inv Quality traded at a discount of 7.18% below its net asset value, which is worse than its one-year historical average discount of 9.50%.

Robert D. Sneeden has been running the fund for 14 years and currently receives a manager quality ranking of 29 (0=worst, 99=best). If you desire an average level of risk, then this fund may be an option.

Data Date	Investment Rating	Net Assets ($Mil)	Price	Performance Rating/Pts	Total Return Y-T-D	Risk Rating/Pts
12-15	C+	126.70	14.10	C+ / 6.2	8.39%	B- / 7.3
2014	C+	128.80	13.76	C+ / 6.4	18.32%	B- / 7.6
2013	C	115.29	12.23	C / 4.5	-19.99%	B- / 7.8
2012	A+	133.16	15.70	A- / 9.1	19.34%	B / 8.7
2011	A+	121.40	14.41	A / 9.4	27.33%	B / 8.8
2010	C-	117.34	12.31	C- / 4.1	2.49%	C / 5.4

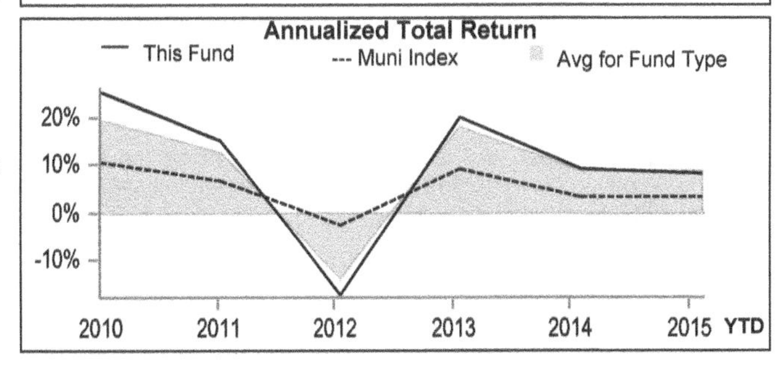

BlackRock MuniYield Invt Fund (MYF) C+ Fair

Fund Family: BlackRock Inc
Fund Type: Municipal - Single State
Inception Date: February 21, 1992

Major Rating Factors: Middle of the road best describes BlackRock MuniYield Invt Fund whose TheStreet.com Investment Rating is currently a C+ (Fair). The fund currently has a performance rating of C+ (Fair) based on an annualized return of 2.36% over the last three years and a total return of 8.05% year to date 2015. Factored into the performance evaluation is an expense ratio of 1.46% (average).

The fund's risk rating is currently B- (Good). It carries a beta of 2.55, meaning it is expected to move 25.5% for every 10% move in the market. Volatility, as measured by both the semi-deviation and a drawdown factor, is considered low. As of December 31, 2015, BlackRock MuniYield Invt Fund traded at a discount of .57% below its net asset value, which is worse than its one-year historical average discount of 3.22%.

Robert D. Sneeden has been running the fund for 14 years and currently receives a manager quality ranking of 36 (0=worst, 99=best). If you desire an average level of risk, then this fund may be an option.

Data Date	Investment Rating	Net Assets ($Mil)	Price	Performance Rating/Pts	Total Return Y-T-D	Risk Rating/Pts
12-15	C+	212.69	15.65	C+ / 6.9	8.05%	B- / 7.0
2014	B+	216.10	15.48	B / 7.8	21.12%	B- / 7.7
2013	C+	194.32	13.72	C+ / 5.8	-17.84%	B- / 7.9
2012	A+	221.78	16.87	A+ / 9.6	22.37%	B / 8.8
2011	A+	198.90	14.69	A+ / 9.7	27.99%	B / 8.8
2010	C+	193.27	12.98	C / 5.3	9.07%	C+ / 6.2

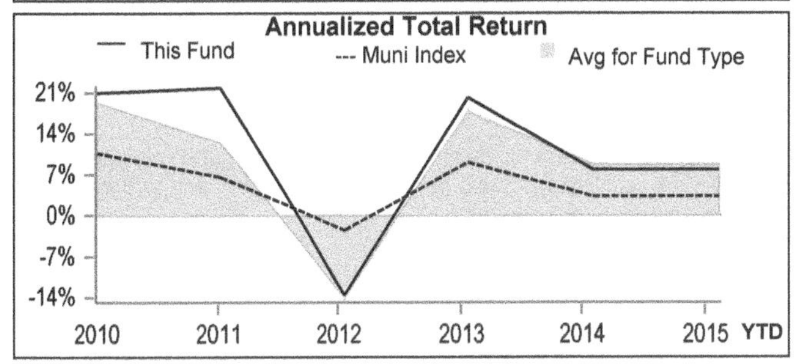

BlackRock MuniYield Michigan Qly (MIY) C+ Fair

Fund Family: BlackRock Inc
Fund Type: Municipal - Single State
Inception Date: October 23, 1992

Major Rating Factors: Middle of the road best describes BlackRock MuniYield Michigan Qly whose TheStreet.com Investment Rating is currently a C+ (Fair). The fund currently has a performance rating of C+ (Fair) based on an annualized return of 1.19% over the last three years and a total return of 6.67% year to date 2015. Factored into the performance evaluation is an expense ratio of 1.48% (average).

The fund's risk rating is currently B- (Good). It carries a beta of 2.58, meaning it is expected to move 25.8% for every 10% move in the market. Volatility, as measured by both the semi-deviation and a drawdown factor, is considered low. As of December 31, 2015, BlackRock MuniYield Michigan Qly traded at a discount of 11.42% below its net asset value, which is worse than its one-year historical average discount of 12.40%.

Theodore R. Jaeckel, Jr. has been running the fund for 10 years and currently receives a manager quality ranking of 29 (0=worst, 99=best). If you desire an average level of risk, then this fund may be an option.

Data Date	Investment Rating	Net Assets ($Mil)	Price	Performance Rating/Pts	Total Return Y-T-D	Risk Rating/Pts
12-15	C+	282.53	13.96	C+ / 6.2	6.67%	B- / 7.3
2014	C+	283.50	13.87	C+ / 5.6	16.10%	B- / 7.6
2013	C-	258.34	12.46	C- / 4.0	-16.87%	B- / 7.8
2012	A+	294.80	15.65	B+ / 8.9	16.13%	B / 8.6
2011	A+	279.40	15.50	A / 9.3	23.28%	B / 8.9
2010	C+	271.61	13.35	C / 5.3	9.67%	C+ / 6.2

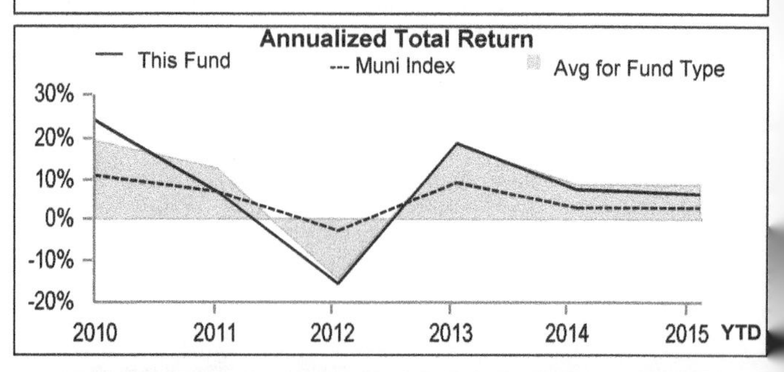

BlackRock MuniYield New York Qly (MYN) B- Good

Fund Family: BlackRock Inc
Fund Type: Municipal - Single State
Inception Date: February 21, 1992

Major Rating Factors: BlackRock MuniYield New York Qly receives a TheStreet.com Investment Rating of B- (Good). The fund currently has a performance rating of C+ (Fair) based on an annualized return of 1.67% over the last three years and a total return of 9.35% year to date 2015. Factored into the performance evaluation is an expense ratio of 1.44% (average).

The fund's risk rating is currently B- (Good). It carries a beta of 1.81, meaning it is expected to move 18.1% for every 10% move in the market. Volatility, as measured by both the semi-deviation and a drawdown factor, is considered low. As of December 31, 2015, BlackRock MuniYield New York Qly traded at a discount of 6.76% below its net asset value, which is worse than its one-year historical average discount of 7.30%.

Timothy T. Browse has been running the fund for 24 years and currently receives a manager quality ranking of 40 (0=worst, 99=best). If you desire an average level of risk, then this fund may be an option.

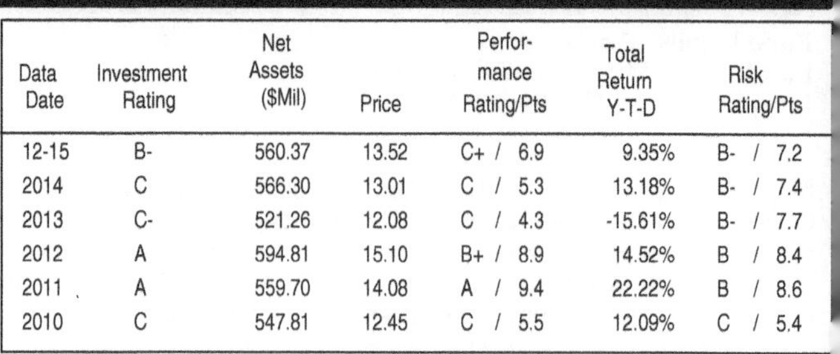

Data Date	Investment Rating	Net Assets ($Mil)	Price	Performance Rating/Pts	Total Return Y-T-D	Risk Rating/Pts
12-15	B-	560.37	13.52	C+ / 6.9	9.35%	B- / 7.2
2014	C	566.30	13.01	C / 5.3	13.18%	B- / 7.4
2013	C-	521.26	12.08	C / 4.3	-15.61%	B- / 7.7
2012	A	594.81	15.10	B+ / 8.9	14.52%	B / 8.4
2011	A	559.70	14.08	A / 9.4	22.22%	B / 8.6
2010	C	547.81	12.45	C / 5.5	12.09%	C / 5.4

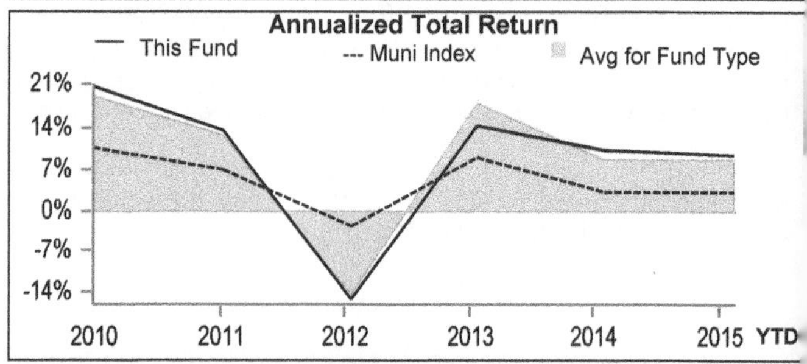

BlackRock MuniYield NJ Fund (MYJ) B Good

Fund Family: BlackRock Inc
Fund Type: Municipal - Single State
Inception Date: April 23, 1992

Major Rating Factors: Strong performance is the major factor driving the B (Good) TheStreet.com Investment Rating for BlackRock MuniYield NJ Fund. The fund currently has a performance rating of B- (Good) based on an annualized return of 2.84% over the last three years and a total return of 9.90% year to date 2015. Factored into the performance evaluation is an expense ratio of 1.50% (average).

The fund's risk rating is currently B- (Good). It carries a beta of 2.25, meaning it is expected to move 22.5% for every 10% move in the market. Volatility, as measured by both the semi-deviation and a drawdown factor, is considered low. As of December 31, 2015, BlackRock MuniYield NJ Fund traded at a discount of 4.98% below its net asset value, which is worse than its one-year historical average discount of 7.19%.

Robert M. Shearer currently receives a manager quality ranking of 41 (0=worst, 99=best). If you desire only a moderate level of risk and strong performance, then this fund is an excellent option.

Data Date	Investment Rating	Net Assets ($Mil)	Price	Performance Rating/Pts	Total Return Y-T-D	Risk Rating/Pts
12-15	B	228.63	15.47	B- / 7.3	9.90%	B- / 7.3
2014	C+	234.60	14.95	C+ / 6.2	15.98%	B- / 7.7
2013	C	213.10	13.66	C / 4.7	-14.68%	B- / 7.9
2012	A	240.76	16.60	B+ / 8.5	17.84%	B / 8.7
2011	A-	224.80	15.60	B+ / 8.6	20.13%	B / 8.8
2010	C	216.43	13.78	C- / 4.1	5.74%	C+ / 6.7

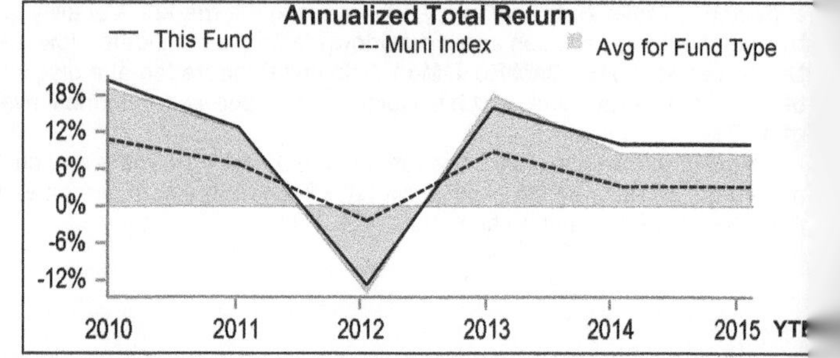

BlackRock MuniYield PA Qly (MPA) C+ Fair

Fund Family: BlackRock Inc
Fund Type: Municipal - Single State
Inception Date: October 23, 1992

Major Rating Factors: Middle of the road best describes BlackRock MuniYield PA Qly whose TheStreet.com Investment Rating is currently a C+ (Fair). The fund currently has a performance rating of C+ (Fair) based on an annualized return of 1.27% over the last three years and a total return of 7.66% year to date 2015. Factored into the performance evaluation is an expense ratio of 1.45% (average).

The fund's risk rating is currently B- (Good). It carries a beta of 2.10, meaning it is expected to move 21.0% for every 10% move in the market. Volatility, as measured by both the semi-deviation and a drawdown factor, is considered low. As of December 31, 2015, BlackRock MuniYield PA Qly traded at a discount of 9.69% below its net asset value, which is worse than its one-year historical average discount of 11.55%.

Theodore R. Jaeckel, Jr. has been running the fund for 10 years and currently receives a manager quality ranking of 34 (0=worst, 99=best). If you desire an average level of risk, then this fund may be an option.

Data Date	Investment Rating	Net Assets ($Mil)	Price	Performance Rating/Pts	Total Return Y-T-D	Risk Rating/Pts
12-15	C+	210.55	14.54	C+ / 6.4	7.66%	B- / 7.5
2014	C+	184.60	14.34	C+ / 5.7	18.23%	B- / 7.7
2013	C-	167.86	12.81	D+ / 2.9	-18.51%	B- / 7.9
2012	A	190.56	16.35	B+ / 8.4	9.29%	B / 8.7
2011	A+	180.10	15.79	A- / 9.2	23.44%	B / 8.9
2010	C	176.53	13.45	C- / 4.0	7.26%	C+ / 6.3

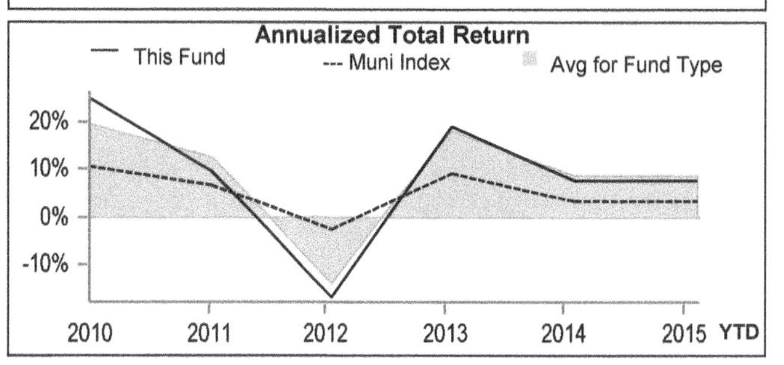

BlackRock MuniYield Quality Fund (MQY) C+ Fair

Fund Family: BlackRock Inc
Fund Type: Municipal - National
Inception Date: June 19, 1992

Major Rating Factors: Strong performance is the major factor driving the C+ (Fair) TheStreet.com Investment Rating for BlackRock MuniYield Quality Fund. The fund currently has a performance rating of B- (Good) based on an annualized return of 1.72% over the last three years and a total return of 9.13% year to date 2015. Factored into the performance evaluation is an expense ratio of 1.46% (average).

The fund's risk rating is currently C+ (Fair). It carries a beta of 2.31, meaning it is expected to move 23.1% for every 10% move in the market. Volatility, as measured by both the semi-deviation and a drawdown factor, is considered low. As of December 31, 2015, BlackRock MuniYield Quality Fund traded at a discount of 2.40% below its net asset value, which is worse than its one-year historical average discount of 4.05%.

Michael A. Kalinoski has been running the fund for 24 years and currently receives a manager quality ranking of 33 (0=worst, 99=best). If you desire only a moderate level of risk and strong performance, then this fund is an excellent option.

Data Date	Investment Rating	Net Assets ($Mil)	Price	Performance Rating/Pts	Total Return Y-T-D	Risk Rating/Pts
12-15	C+	494.48	15.83	B- / 7.1	9.13%	C+ / 6.7
2014	C+	498.10	15.34	C+ / 6.5	14.52%	B- / 7.3
2013	C+	516.00	14.06	C+ / 5.9	-16.28%	B- / 7.5
2012	A+	495.26	17.64	A / 9.4	20.98%	B / 8.4
2011	A-	470.20	15.82	A- / 9.1	25.97%	B / 8.5
2010	C+	445.16	13.72	C+ / 6.0	5.54%	C+ / 5.9

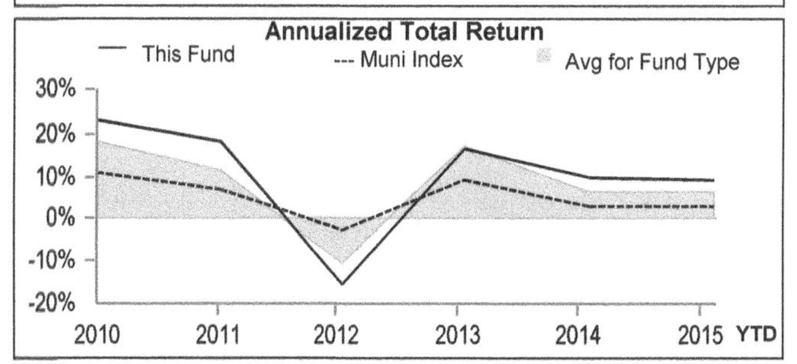

BlackRock MuniYield Quality Fund I (MQT) B- Good

Fund Family: BlackRock Inc
Fund Type: Municipal - National
Inception Date: August 21, 1992

Major Rating Factors: BlackRock MuniYield Quality Fund I receives a TheStreet.com Investment Rating of B- (Good). The fund currently has a performance rating of C+ (Fair) based on an annualized return of 2.65% over the last three years and a total return of 7.04% year to date 2015. Factored into the performance evaluation is an expense ratio of 1.47% (average).

The fund's risk rating is currently B- (Good). It carries a beta of 2.52, meaning it is expected to move 25.2% for every 10% move in the market. Volatility, as measured by both the semi-deviation and a drawdown factor, is considered low. As of December 31, 2015, BlackRock MuniYield Quality Fund I traded at a discount of 6.61% below its net asset value, which is worse than its one-year historical average discount of 7.52%.

Michael A. Kalinoski has been running the fund for 16 years and currently receives a manager quality ranking of 35 (0=worst, 99=best). If you desire an average level of risk, then this fund may be an option.

Data Date	Investment Rating	Net Assets ($Mil)	Price	Performance Rating/Pts	Total Return Y-T-D	Risk Rating/Pts
12-15	B-	319.85	13.28	C+ / 6.9	7.04%	B- / 7.5
2014	B-	321.30	13.19	C+ / 6.8	19.78%	B- / 7.6
2013	C+	331.17	11.68	C / 5.5	-15.84%	B- / 7.9
2012	A	317.28	14.44	B+ / 8.9	15.56%	B / 8.4
2011	A+	300.70	13.70	A+ / 9.7	31.84%	B / 8.6
2010	C	284.40	11.35	C- / 4.2	2.87%	C+ / 6.3

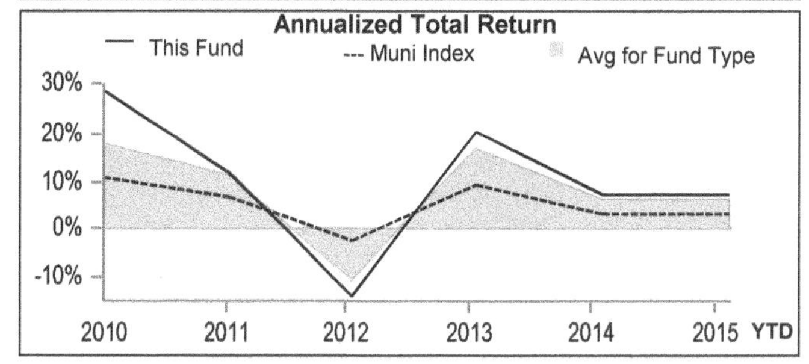

BlackRock MuniYield Quality III (MYI) B Good

Fund Family: BlackRock Inc
Fund Type: Municipal - National
Inception Date: March 20, 1992

Data Date	Investment Rating	Net Assets ($Mil)	Price	Performance Rating/Pts	Total Return Y-T-D	Risk Rating/Pts
12-15	B	1,003.62	14.73	B / 8.1	9.99%	C+ / 6.8
2014	C+	1,024.80	14.07	C+ / 6.7	16.92%	B- / 7.3
2013	C	925.81	12.66	C / 5.3	-15.14%	B- / 7.6
2012	A	1,036.02	15.30	A- / 9.0	16.08%	B / 8.4
2011	A	955.20	14.14	A / 9.5	23.99%	B / 8.6
2010	D+	920.23	12.47	C- / 3.4	8.16%	C / 5.5

Major Rating Factors: Strong performance is the major factor driving the B (Good) TheStreet.com Investment Rating for BlackRock MuniYield Quality III. The fund currently has a performance rating of B (Good) based on an annualized return of 3.40% over the last three years and a total return of 9.99% year to date 2015. Factored into the performance evaluation is an expense ratio of 1.39% (average).

The fund's risk rating is currently C+ (Fair). It carries a beta of 2.13, meaning it is expected to move 21.3% for every 10% move in the market. Volatility, as measured by both the semi-deviation and a drawdown factor, is considered low. As of December 31, 2015, BlackRock MuniYield Quality III traded at a discount of 1.80% below its net asset value, which is worse than its one-year historical average discount of 4.93%.

William R. Bock has been running the fund for 24 years and currently receives a manager quality ranking of 53 (0=worst, 99=best). If you desire only a moderate level of risk and strong performance, then this fund is an excellent option.

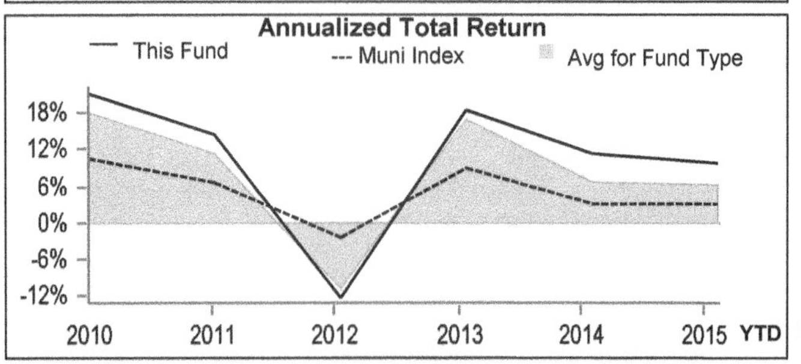

BlackRock New York Muni Inc Qly (BSE) C Fair

Fund Family: BlackRock Inc
Fund Type: Municipal - Single State
Inception Date: October 28, 2002

Data Date	Investment Rating	Net Assets ($Mil)	Price	Performance Rating/Pts	Total Return Y-T-D	Risk Rating/Pts
12-15	C	96.59	13.72	C / 5.5	9.12%	B- / 7.2
2014	C	97.10	13.26	C / 5.1	16.16%	B- / 7.4
2013	D+	84.26	12.07	D+ / 2.5	-23.04%	B- / 7.7
2012	A	100.87	16.11	B+ / 8.5	15.21%	B / 8.5
2011	B+	95.80	14.91	B+ / 8.4	21.63%	B / 8.7
2010	C-	96.62	13.05	D / 2.1	3.27%	B- / 7.1

Major Rating Factors: Middle of the road best describes BlackRock New York Muni Inc Qly whose TheStreet.com Investment Rating is currently a C (Fair). The fund currently has a performance rating of C (Fair) based on an annualized return of -0.80% over the last three years and a total return of 9.12% year to date 2015. Factored into the performance evaluation is an expense ratio of 1.70% (above average).

The fund's risk rating is currently B- (Good). It carries a beta of 2.35, meaning it is expected to move 23.5% for every 10% move in the market. Volatility, as measured by both the semi-deviation and a drawdown factor, is considered low. As of December 31, 2015, BlackRock New York Muni Inc Qly traded at a discount of 9.80% below its net asset value, which is worse than its one-year historical average discount of 11.30%.

Timothy T. Browse has been running the fund for 10 years and currently receives a manager quality ranking of 23 (0=worst, 99=best). If you desire an average level of risk, then this fund may be an option.

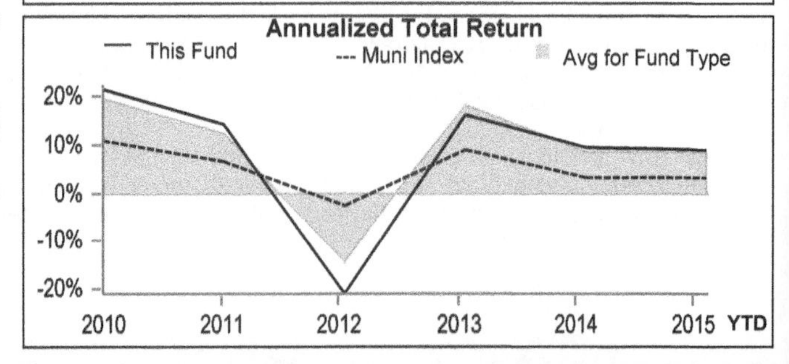

BlackRock NJ Muni Bond Trust (BLJ) C Fair

Fund Family: BlackRock Inc
Fund Type: Municipal - Single State
Inception Date: April 26, 2002

Data Date	Investment Rating	Net Assets ($Mil)	Price	Performance Rating/Pts	Total Return Y-T-D	Risk Rating/Pts
12-15	C	36.38	14.74	C / 5.3	4.70%	C+ / 6.6
2014	C	37.90	15.07	C+ / 6.2	19.75%	C+ / 6.6
2013	C-	32.84	13.31	C- / 4.1	-20.44%	C+ / 6.9
2012	B+	38.73	17.00	B+ / 8.6	17.89%	B- / 7.7
2011	A-	35.50	15.33	A / 9.3	25.18%	B / 8.0
2010	D+	35.28	13.38	D- / 1.3	-1.22%	C+ / 6.9

Major Rating Factors: Middle of the road best describes BlackRock NJ Muni Bond Trust whose TheStreet.com Investment Rating is currently a C (Fair). The fund currently has a performance rating of C (Fair) based on an annualized return of -0.45% over the last three years and a total return of 4.70% year to date 2015. Factored into the performance evaluation is an expense ratio of 1.98% (high).

The fund's risk rating is currently C+ (Fair). It carries a beta of 2.42, meaning it is expected to move 24.2% for every 10% move in the market. Volatility, as measured by both the semi-deviation and a drawdown factor, is considered low. As of December 31, 2015, BlackRock NJ Muni Bond Trust traded at a discount of 8.39% below its net asset value, which is better than its one-year historical average discount of 7.22%.

Theodore R. Jaeckel, Jr. has been running the fund for 10 years and currently receives a manager quality ranking of 25 (0=worst, 99=best). If you desire an average level of risk, then this fund may be an option.

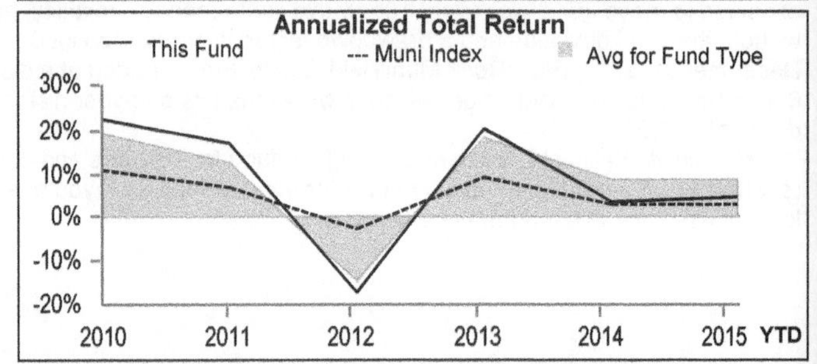

BlackRock NJ Municipal Income Trus (BNJ) C Fair

Fund Family: BlackRock Inc
Fund Type: Municipal - Single State
Inception Date: July 26, 2001

Major Rating Factors: Middle of the road best describes BlackRock NJ Municipal Income Trus whose TheStreet.com Investment Rating is currently a C (Fair). The fund currently has a performance rating of C+ (Fair) based on an annualized return of 1.14% over the last three years and a total return of 7.22% year to date 2015. Factored into the performance evaluation is an expense ratio of 1.79% (above average).

The fund's risk rating is currently C+ (Fair). It carries a beta of 2.87, meaning it is expected to move 28.7% for every 10% move in the market. Volatility, as measured by both the semi-deviation and a drawdown factor, is considered low. As of December 31, 2015, BlackRock NJ Municipal Income Trus traded at a discount of 3.80% below its net asset value, which is worse than its one-year historical average discount of 4.08%.

Theodore R. Jaeckel, Jr. has been running the fund for 10 years and currently receives a manager quality ranking of 24 (0=worst, 99=best). If you desire an average level of risk, then this fund may be an option.

Data Date	Investment Rating	Net Assets ($Mil)	Price	Perfor-mance Rating/Pts	Total Return Y-T-D	Risk Rating/Pts
12-15	C	119.17	15.19	C+ / 6.3	7.22%	C+ / 6.4
2014	C+	122.10	15.19	C+ / 6.9	22.90%	C+ / 6.9
2013	C-	109.95	13.10	C- / 3.8	-20.77%	B- / 7.2
2012	A	123.50	17.05	A- / 9.0	19.94%	B / 8.3
2011	B+	114.10	15.69	B+ / 8.8	28.15%	B / 8.4
2010	D+	109.26	13.43	D / 1.6	5.96%	C+ / 6.9

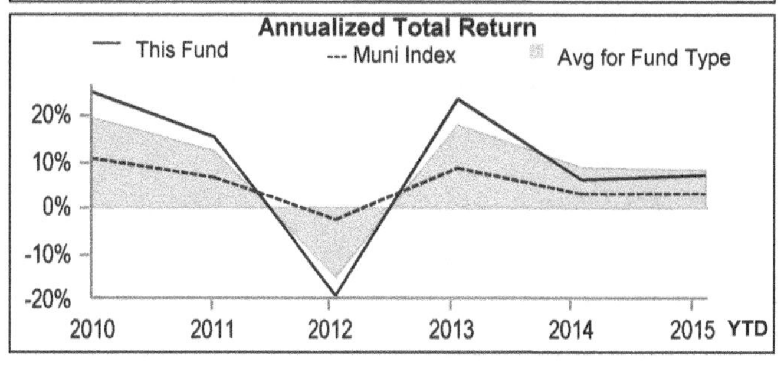

BlackRock NY Muni 2018 Income Trus (BLH) C Fair

Fund Family: BlackRock Inc
Fund Type: Municipal - Single State
Inception Date: October 25, 2001

Major Rating Factors: Middle of the road best describes BlackRock NY Muni 2018 Income Trus whose TheStreet.com Investment Rating is currently a C (Fair). The fund currently has a performance rating of C (Fair) based on an annualized return of -0.54% over the last three years and a total return of 2.03% year to date 2015. Factored into the performance evaluation is an expense ratio of 0.79% (very low).

The fund's risk rating is currently B (Good). It carries a beta of 0.63, meaning the fund's expected move will be 6.3% for every 10% move in the market. Volatility, as measured by both the semi-deviation and a drawdown factor, is considered low. As of December 31, 2015, BlackRock NY Muni 2018 Income Trus traded at a discount of .93% below its net asset value, which is worse than its one-year historical average discount of 1.45%.

F. Howard Downs has been running the fund for 10 years and currently receives a manager quality ranking of 54 (0=worst, 99=best). If you desire an average level of risk, then this fund may be an option.

Data Date	Investment Rating	Net Assets ($Mil)	Price	Perfor-mance Rating/Pts	Total Return Y-T-D	Risk Rating/Pts
12-15	C	55.28	14.94	C / 4.3	2.03%	B / 8.3
2014	C-	55.60	14.98	D+ / 2.7	-0.13%	B / 8.7
2013	C	56.92	15.23	C / 4.3	-3.41%	B / 8.9
2012	C	57.06	16.05	C- / 3.3	2.53%	B+ / 9.2
2011	B	56.80	16.71	C+ / 6.2	12.29%	B+ / 9.5
2010	B-	56.98	16.10	C+ / 6.3	1.84%	B- / 7.3

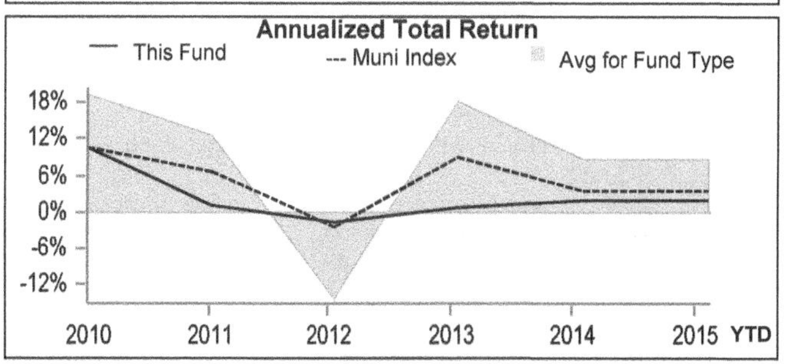

BlackRock NY Muni Bond Trust (BQH) C+ Fair

Fund Family: BlackRock Inc
Fund Type: Municipal - Single State
Inception Date: April 26, 2002

Major Rating Factors: Middle of the road best describes BlackRock NY Muni Bond Trust whose TheStreet.com Investment Rating is currently a C+ (Fair). The fund currently has a performance rating of C+ (Fair) based on an annualized return of 1.40% over the last three years and a total return of 9.93% year to date 2015. Factored into the performance evaluation is an expense ratio of 2.07% (high).

The fund's risk rating is currently C+ (Fair). It carries a beta of 3.07, meaning it is expected to move 30.7% for every 10% move in the market. Volatility, as measured by both the semi-deviation and a drawdown factor, is considered low. As of December 31, 2015, BlackRock NY Muni Bond Trust traded at a discount of 8.50% below its net asset value, which is worse than its one-year historical average discount of 11.05%.

Timothy T. Browse has been running the fund for 10 years and currently receives a manager quality ranking of 22 (0=worst, 99=best). If you desire an average level of risk, then this fund may be an option.

Data Date	Investment Rating	Net Assets ($Mil)	Price	Perfor-mance Rating/Pts	Total Return Y-T-D	Risk Rating/Pts
12-15	C+	44.11	14.85	C+ / 6.5	9.93%	C+ / 6.6
2014	C+	44.10	14.28	C+ / 6.3	20.09%	B- / 7.1
2013	D+	37.30	12.53	D+ / 2.4	-20.90%	B- / 7.3
2012	B+	46.16	16.57	B / 7.7	14.97%	B / 8.7
2011	B+	42.40	15.71	B+ / 8.4	17.00%	B / 8.7
2010	C-	43.41	14.01	D / 1.9	-2.55%	B- / 7.1

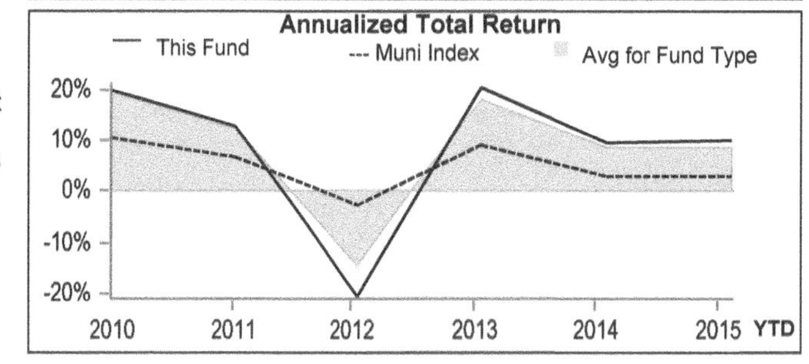

BlackRock NY Municipal Income Tr I (BFY) C+ Fair

Fund Family: BlackRock Inc
Fund Type: Municipal - Single State
Inception Date: July 25, 2002

Major Rating Factors: Strong performance is the major factor driving the C+ (Fair) TheStreet.com Investment Rating for BlackRock NY Municipal Income Tr I. The fund currently has a performance rating of B- (Good) based on an annualized return of 2.36% over the last three years and a total return of 9.12% year to date 2015. Factored into the performance evaluation is an expense ratio of 1.83% (above average).

The fund's risk rating is currently C+ (Fair). It carries a beta of 2.27, meaning it is expected to move 22.7% for every 10% move in the market. Volatility, as measured by both the semi-deviation and a drawdown factor, is considered low. As of December 31, 2015, BlackRock NY Municipal Income Tr I traded at a discount of 6.20% below its net asset value, which is worse than its one-year historical average discount of 7.33%.

Timothy T. Browse has been running the fund for 10 years and currently receives a manager quality ranking of 40 (0=worst, 99=best). If you desire only a moderate level of risk and strong performance, then this fund is an excellent option.

Data Date	Investment Rating	Net Assets ($Mil)	Price	Performance Rating/Pts	Total Return Y-T-D	Risk Rating/Pts
12-15	C+	77.85	14.98	B- / 7.1	9.12%	C+ / 6.8
2014	C+	78.10	14.67	C+ / 6.6	22.29%	B- / 7.1
2013	D+	66.77	12.65	D+ / 2.5	-18.91%	B- / 7.4
2012	B+	80.23	16.00	B- / 7.4	9.29%	B / 8.7
2011	A+	74.70	15.75	A+ / 9.6	22.45%	B+ / 9.1
2010	C	75.87	14.09	C / 4.9	5.74%	C+ / 5.8

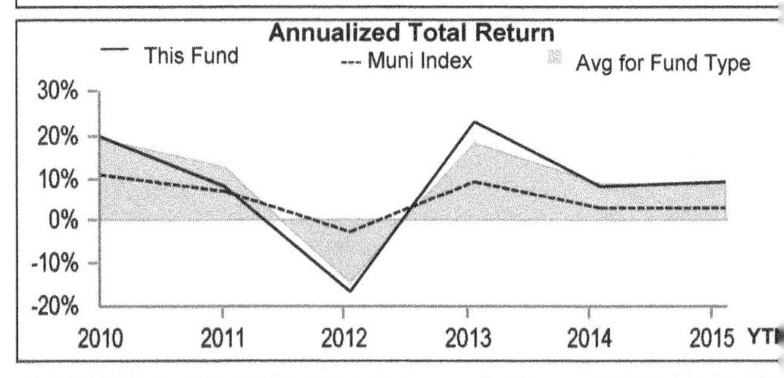

BlackRock NY Municipal Income Trus (BNY) B Good

Fund Family: BlackRock Inc
Fund Type: Municipal - Single State
Inception Date: July 26, 2001

Major Rating Factors: Strong performance is the major factor driving the B (Good) TheStreet.com Investment Rating for BlackRock NY Municipal Income Trus. The fund currently has a performance rating of B+ (Good) based on an annualized return of 3.08% over the last three years and a total return of 14.40% year to date 2015. Factored into the performance evaluation is an expense ratio of 1.73% (above average).

The fund's risk rating is currently C+ (Fair). It carries a beta of 2.40, meaning it is expected to move 24.0% for every 10% move in the market. Volatility, as measured by both the semi-deviation and a drawdown factor, is considered low. As of December 31, 2015, BlackRock NY Municipal Income Trus traded at a premium of 1.56% above its net asset value, which is worse than its one-year historical average discount of 3.12%.

Timothy T. Browse has been running the fund for 10 years and currently receives a manager quality ranking of 39 (0=worst, 99=best). If you desire only a moderate level of risk and strong performance, then this fund is an excellent option.

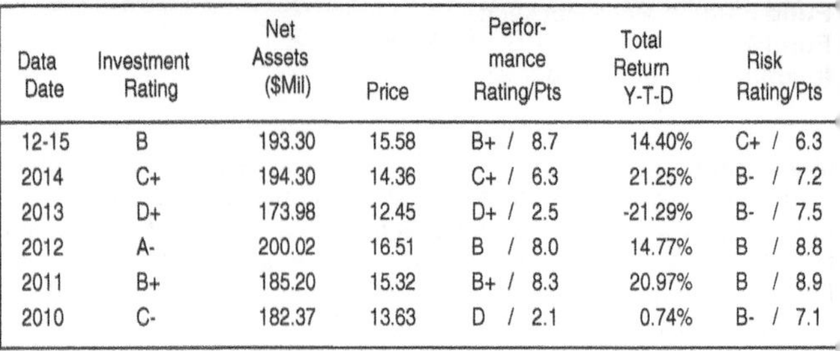

Data Date	Investment Rating	Net Assets ($Mil)	Price	Performance Rating/Pts	Total Return Y-T-D	Risk Rating/Pts
12-15	B	193.30	15.58	B+ / 8.7	14.40%	C+ / 6.3
2014	C+	194.30	14.36	C+ / 6.3	21.25%	B- / 7.2
2013	D+	173.98	12.45	D+ / 2.5	-21.29%	B- / 7.5
2012	A-	200.02	16.51	B / 8.0	14.77%	B / 8.8
2011	B+	185.20	15.32	B+ / 8.3	20.97%	B / 8.9
2010	C-	182.37	13.63	D / 2.1	0.74%	B- / 7.1

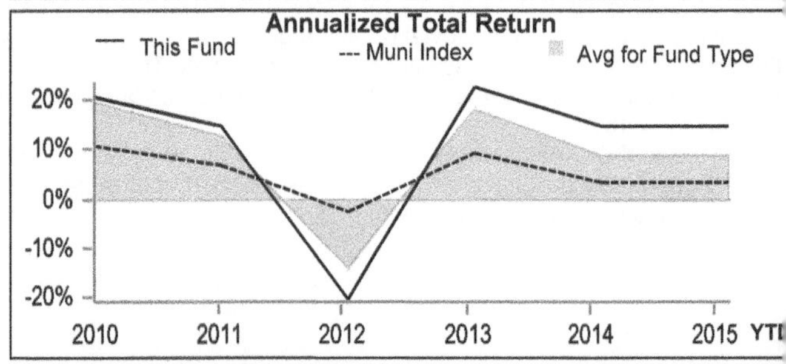

BlackRock Res & Commdty Strat Trus (BCX) D- Weak

Fund Family: BlackRock Inc
Fund Type: Income
Inception Date: March 30, 2011

Major Rating Factors:
Disappointing performance is the major factor driving the D- (Weak) TheStreet.com Investment Rating for BlackRock Res & Commdty Strat Trus. The fund currently has a performance rating of D- (Weak) based on an annualized return of -11.32% over the last three years and a total return of -19.98% year to date 2015. Factored into the performance evaluation is an expense ratio of 1.06% (low).

The fund's risk rating is currently C (Fair). It carries a beta of 0.88, meaning the fund's expected move will be 8.8% for every 10% move in the market. Volatility, as measured by both the semi-deviation and a drawdown factor, is considered average. As of December 31, 2015, BlackRock Res & Commdty Strat Trus traded at a discount of 14.61% below its net asset value, which is worse than its one-year historical average discount of 14.92%.

Christopher M. Accettella currently receives a manager quality ranking of 7 (0=worst, 99=best). This fund offers an average level of risk but investors looking for strong performance will be frustrated.

Data Date	Investment Rating	Net Assets ($Mil)	Price	Performance Rating/Pts	Total Return Y-T-D	Risk Rating/Pts
12-15	D-	582.22	7.13	D- / 1.5	-19.98%	C / 4.8
2014	D	610.40	9.76	D / 1.9	-8.22%	C+ / 6.0
2013	D	646.59	11.58	D+ / 2.4	-5.43%	C / 5.5
2012	D	783.79	12.82	D / 2.2	4.08%	C+ / 5.8

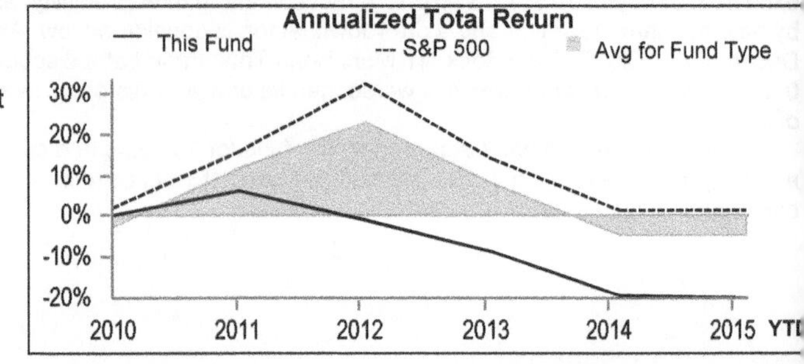

BlackRock Sci and Tech Trust (XBSTX) C Fair

Fund Family: BlackRock Fund Advisors
Fund Type: Global
Inception Date: October 30, 2014

Major Rating Factors: Strong performance is the major factor driving the C (Fair) TheStreet.com Investment Rating for BlackRock Sci and Tech Trust. The fund currently has a performance rating of B- (Good) based on an annualized return of 0.00% over the last three years and a total return of 4.87% year to date 2015.

The fund's risk rating is currently C (Fair). It carries a beta of 0.00, meaning the fund's expected move will be 0.0% for every 10% move in the market. Volatility, as measured by both the semi-deviation and a drawdown factor, is considered average. As of December 31, 2015, BlackRock Sci and Tech Trust traded at a discount of 12.18% below its net asset value, which is better than its one-year historical average discount of 10.92%.

If you desire an average level of risk and strong performance, then this fund is a good option.

Data Date	Investment Rating	Net Assets ($Mil)	Price	Performance Rating/Pts	Total Return Y-T-D	Risk Rating/Pts
12-15	C	0.00	17.31	B- / 7.5	4.87%	C / 5.1

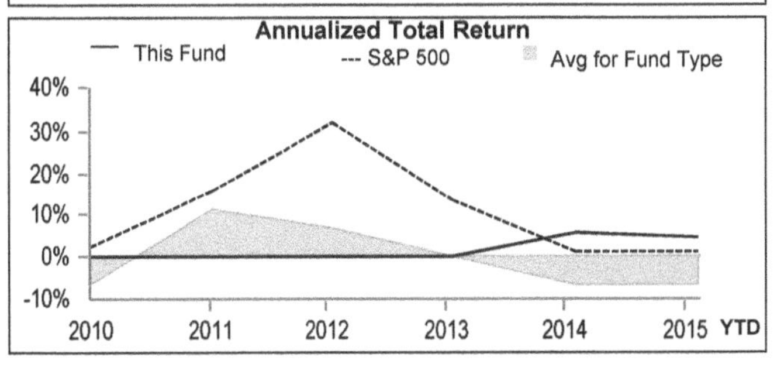

BlackRock Strategic Municipal Tr (BSD) C+ Fair

Fund Family: BlackRock Inc
Fund Type: Municipal - National
Inception Date: August 24, 1999

Major Rating Factors: Middle of the road best describes BlackRock Strategic Municipal Tr whose TheStreet.com Investment Rating is currently a C+ (Fair). The fund currently has a performance rating of C+ (Fair) based on an annualized return of 2.89% over the last three years and a total return of 5.06% year to date 2015. Factored into the performance evaluation is an expense ratio of 1.72% (above average).

The fund's risk rating is currently C+ (Fair). It carries a beta of 2.16, meaning it is expected to move 21.6% for every 10% move in the market. Volatility, as measured by both the semi-deviation and a drawdown factor, is considered low. As of December 31, 2015, BlackRock Strategic Municipal Tr traded at a discount of 6.29% below its net asset value, which is worse than its one-year historical average discount of 7.29%.

Theodore R. Jaeckel, Jr. has been running the fund for 10 years and currently receives a manager quality ranking of 46 (0=worst, 99=best). If you desire an average level of risk, then this fund may be an option.

Data Date	Investment Rating	Net Assets ($Mil)	Price	Performance Rating/Pts	Total Return Y-T-D	Risk Rating/Pts
12-15	C+	107.85	13.85	C+ / 6.7	5.06%	C+ / 6.9
2014	B	107.40	14.08	B / 7.9	23.03%	B- / 7.2
2013	C	111.60	12.13	C / 4.7	-15.45%	B- / 7.5
2012	A+	105.31	14.84	A- / 9.2	18.55%	B / 8.5
2011	A+	99.10	13.68	A / 9.5	21.93%	B / 8.8
2010	C-	94.74	12.32	C- / 3.0	10.86%	B- / 7.0

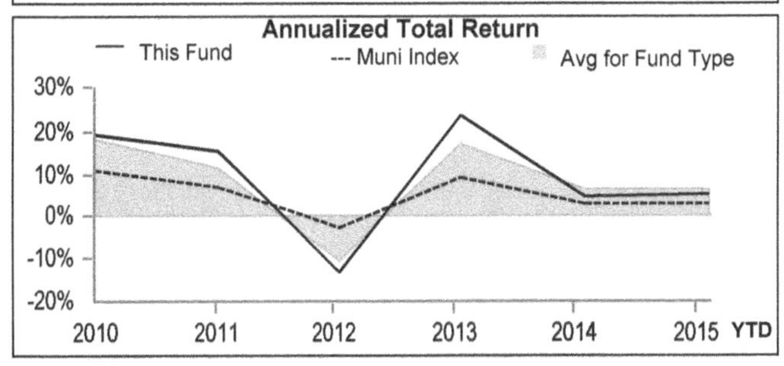

BlackRock Taxable Municipal Bond T (BBN) B Good

Fund Family: BlackRock Inc
Fund Type: Municipal - National
Inception Date: August 27, 2010

Major Rating Factors: Strong performance is the major factor driving the B (Good) TheStreet.com Investment Rating for BlackRock Taxable Municipal Bond T. The fund currently has a performance rating of B (Good) based on an annualized return of 5.33% over the last three years and a total return of 2.25% year to date 2015. Factored into the performance evaluation is an expense ratio of 1.18% (low).

The fund's risk rating is currently B- (Good). It carries a beta of 1.80, meaning it is expected to move 18.0% for every 10% move in the market. Volatility, as measured by both the semi-deviation and a drawdown factor, is considered low. As of December 31, 2015, BlackRock Taxable Municipal Bond T traded at a discount of 6.17% below its net asset value, which is worse than its one-year historical average discount of 8.05%.

Peter J. Hayes has been running the fund for 6 years and currently receives a manager quality ranking of 60 (0=worst, 99=best). If you desire only a moderate level of risk and strong performance, then this fund is an excellent option.

Data Date	Investment Rating	Net Assets ($Mil)	Price	Performance Rating/Pts	Total Return Y-T-D	Risk Rating/Pts
12-15	B	1,283.66	20.98	B / 7.9	2.25%	B- / 7.1
2014	A-	1,319.00	22.16	B+ / 8.8	25.92%	B- / 7.6
2013	C+	1,215.51	19.15	C+ / 6.6	-9.06%	B- / 7.8
2012	B	1,367.83	22.87	C+ / 6.9	13.97%	B / 8.5
2011	A+	1,260.90	21.35	A+ / 9.9	29.33%	B / 8.5

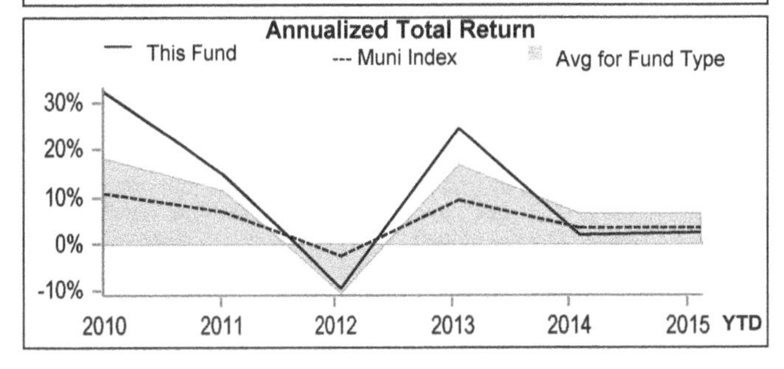

* Denotes ETF Fund

BlackRock Utility & Infrastructure (BUI) C Fair

Fund Family: BlackRock Fund Advisors
Fund Type: Global
Inception Date: November 25, 2011

Major Rating Factors: Middle of the road best describes BlackRock Utility & Infrastructure whose TheStreet.com Investment Rating is currently a C (Fair). The fund currently has a performance rating of C (Fair) based on an annualized return of 3.93% over the last three years and a total return of -11.81% year to date 2015. Factored into the performance evaluation is an expense ratio of 1.10% (low).

The fund's risk rating is currently B- (Good). It carries a beta of 0.69, meaning the fund's expected move will be 6.9% for every 10% move in the market. Volatility, as measured by both the semi-deviation and a drawdown factor, is considered low. As of December 31, 2015, BlackRock Utility & Infrastructure traded at a discount of 13.95% below its net asset value, which is better than its one-year historical average discount of 11.65%.

Kathleen M. Anderson has been running the fund for 5 years and currently receives a manager quality ranking of 77 (0=worst, 99=best). If you desire an average level of risk, then this fund may be an option.

Data Date	Investment Rating	Net Assets ($Mil)	Price	Perfor-mance Rating/Pts	Total Return Y-T-D	Risk Rating/Pts
12-15	C	378.76	16.78	C / 5.2	-11.81%	B- / 7.2
2014	B-	369.10	20.74	C+ / 6.4	25.41%	B / 8.4
2013	C	362.58	17.87	C- / 4.1	2.24%	B / 8.4
2012	D+	330.60	17.89	D- / 1.4	2.36%	B / 8.7

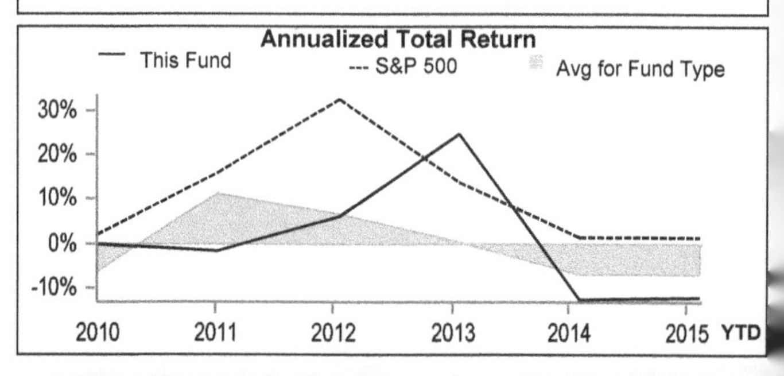

BlackRock VA Muni Bond Trust (BHV) B- Good

Fund Family: BlackRock Inc
Fund Type: Municipal - Single State
Inception Date: April 26, 2002

Major Rating Factors:
Exceptional performance is the major factor driving the B- (Good) TheStreet.com Investment Rating for BlackRock VA Muni Bond Trust. The fund currently has a performance rating of A+ (Excellent) based on an annualized return of 5.38% over the last three years and a total return of 29.42% year to date 2015. Factored into the performance evaluation is an expense ratio of 1.77% (above average).

The fund's risk rating is currently C (Fair). It carries a beta of 3.37, meaning it is expected to move 33.7% for every 10% move in the market. Volatility, as measured by both the semi-deviation and a drawdown factor, is considered average. As of December 31, 2015, BlackRock VA Muni Bond Trust traded at a premium of 22.52% above its net asset value, which is worse than its one-year historical average premium of 7.13%.

Theodore R. Jaeckel, Jr. has been running the fund for 10 years and currently receives a manager quality ranking of 33 (0=worst, 99=best). If you desire an average level of risk and strong performance, then this fund is a good option.

Data Date	Investment Rating	Net Assets ($Mil)	Price	Perfor-mance Rating/Pts	Total Return Y-T-D	Risk Rating/Pts
12-15	B-	25.34	19.75	A+ / 9.7	29.42%	C / 4.7
2014	D	25.40	16.30	C- / 3.1	16.55%	C / 4.3
2013	D	22.26	14.40	D / 1.9	-21.26%	C+ / 6.4
2012	C+	26.47	19.31	C+ / 6.4	7.26%	B- / 7.8
2011	B+	24.70	20.11	B+ / 8.3	28.04%	B / 8.2
2010	B-	25.14	17.66	C / 5.5	3.71%	B- / 7.3

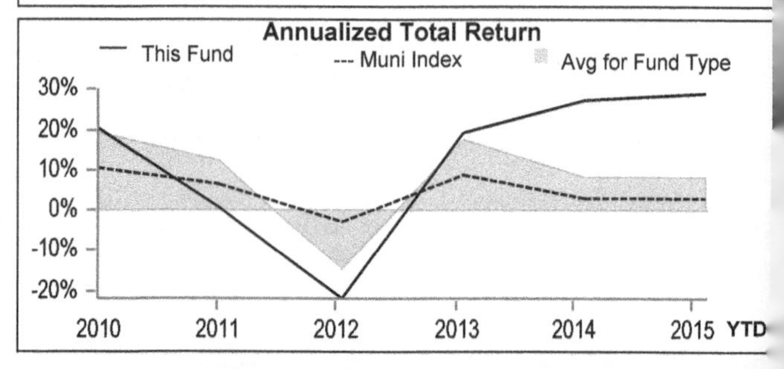

Blackstone / GSO Lng-Sht Credit In (BGX) C- Fair

Fund Family: GSO/Blackstone Debt Funds Managemen
Fund Type: Loan Participation
Inception Date: January 26, 2011

Major Rating Factors:
Disappointing performance is the major factor driving the C- (Fair) TheStreet.com Investment Rating for Blackstone / GSO Lng-Sht Credit In. The fund currently has a performance rating of D+ (Weak) based on an annualized return of -3.74% over the last three years and a total return of -6.01% year to date 2015. Factored into the performance evaluation is an expense ratio of 1.86% (above average).

The fund's risk rating is currently C+ (Fair). It carries a beta of 24.15, meaning it is expected to move 241.5% for every 10% move in the market. Volatility, as measured by both the semi-deviation and a drawdown factor, is considered low. As of December 31, 2015, Blackstone / GSO Lng-Sht Credit In traded at a discount of 12.24% below its net asset value, which is worse than its one-year historical average discount of 13.35%.

James M. Didden, Jr. has been running the fund for 5 years and currently receives a manager quality ranking of 44 (0=worst, 99=best). This fund offers only a moderate level of risk but investors looking for strong performance are still waiting.

Data Date	Investment Rating	Net Assets ($Mil)	Price	Perfor-mance Rating/Pts	Total Return Y-T-D	Risk Rating/Pts
12-15	C-	226.32	13.48	D+ / 2.8	-6.01%	C+ / 6.8
2014	C-	236.30	15.53	D+ / 2.9	-5.64%	B / 8.0
2013	C-	240.98	17.87	D+ / 2.6	-0.06%	B / 8.3
2012	B-	229.73	18.75	C+ / 6.5	16.94%	B / 8.3

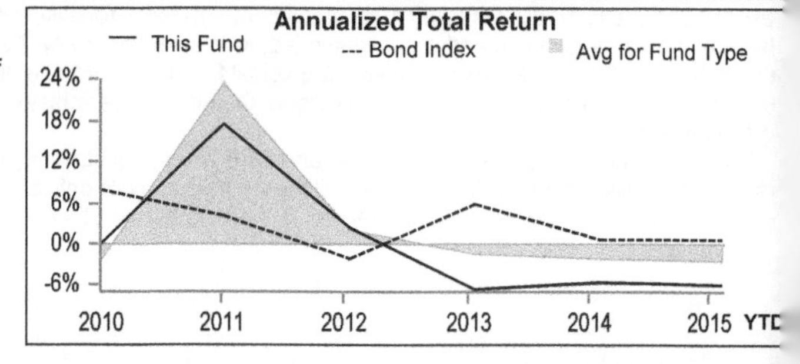

Blackstone / GSO Strategic Credit (BGB) D+ Weak

Fund Family: GSO/Blackstone Debt Funds Managemen
Fund Type: Corporate - High Yield
Inception Date: September 26, 2012

Major Rating Factors:
Disappointing performance is the major factor driving the D+ (Weak) TheStreet.com Investment Rating for Blackstone / GSO Strategic Credit. The fund currently has a performance rating of D+ (Weak) based on an annualized return of -4.05% over the last three years and a total return of -9.73% year to date 2015. Factored into the performance evaluation is an expense ratio of 2.32% (high).

The fund's risk rating is currently C+ (Fair). It carries a beta of 0.99, meaning that its performance tracks fairly well with that of the overall stock market. Volatility, as measured by both the semi-deviation and a drawdown factor, is considered low. As of December 31, 2015, Blackstone / GSO Strategic Credit traded at a discount of 12.04% below its net asset value, which is worse than its one-year historical average discount of 12.68%.

This fund has been team managed for 4 years and currently receives a manager quality ranking of 32 (0=worst, 99=best). This fund offers only a moderate level of risk but investors looking for strong performance are still waiting.

Data Date	Investment Rating	Net Assets ($Mil)	Price	Performance Rating/Pts	Total Return Y-T-D	Risk Rating/Pts
12-15	D+	803.03	13.37	D+ / 2.7	-9.73%	C+ / 6.6
2014	C-	836.00	16.48	D+ / 2.5	-0.47%	B- / 7.9
2013	C-	854.20	17.80	D+ / 2.8	-0.15%	B / 8.7

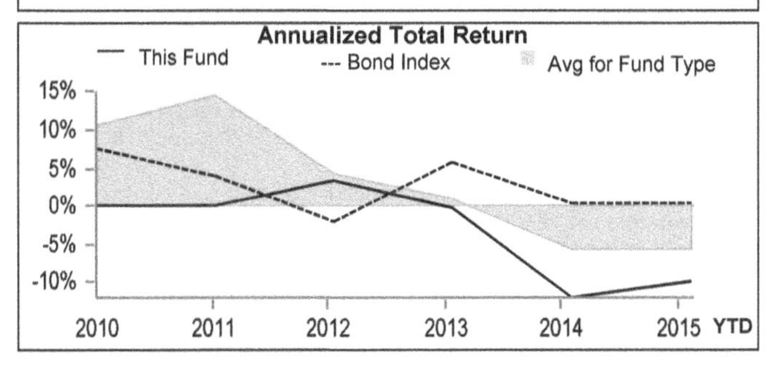

Blackstone/GSO Sr Floating Rate Tr (BSL) D+ Weak

Fund Family: GSO/Blackstone Debt Funds Managemen
Fund Type: Loan Participation
Inception Date: May 26, 2010

Major Rating Factors:
Disappointing performance is the major factor driving the D+ (Weak) TheStreet.com Investment Rating for Blackstone/GSO Sr Floating Rate Tr. The fund currently has a performance rating of D+ (Weak) based on an annualized return of -3.27% over the last three years and a total return of -5.58% year to date 2015. Factored into the performance evaluation is an expense ratio of 3.02% (high).

The fund's risk rating is currently C+ (Fair). Volatility, as measured by both the semi-deviation and a drawdown factor, is considered low. As of December 31, 2015, Blackstone/GSO Sr Floating Rate Tr traded at a discount of 6.90% below its net asset value, which is worse than its one-year historical average discount of 6.95%.

Debra Anderson currently receives a manager quality ranking of 53 (0=worst, 99=best). This fund offers only a moderate level of risk but investors looking for strong performance are still waiting.

Data Date	Investment Rating	Net Assets ($Mil)	Price	Performance Rating/Pts	Total Return Y-T-D	Risk Rating/Pts
12-15	D+	275.20	14.85	D+ / 2.9	-5.58%	C+ / 6.6
2014	C-	283.20	16.74	C- / 3.2	-4.24%	B- / 7.7
2013	C-	293.46	18.85	C- / 4.0	-0.83%	B / 8.1
2012	B+	285.30	20.33	B / 7.8	16.98%	B / 8.3
2011	C-	285.10	18.36	D+ / 2.4	1.87%	B / 8.2

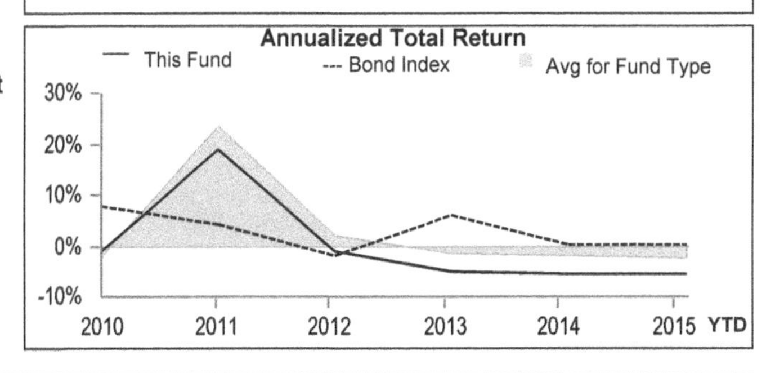

Boulder Growth&Income Fund (BIF) B- Good

Fund Family: Boulder Investment Advisors LLC
Fund Type: Growth and Income
Inception Date: December 7, 1972

Major Rating Factors: Boulder Growth&Income Fund receives a TheStreet.com Investment Rating of B- (Good). The fund currently has a performance rating of C+ (Fair) based on an annualized return of 9.41% over the last three years and a total return of -12.56% year to date 2015. Factored into the performance evaluation is an expense ratio of 1.72% (above average).

The fund's risk rating is currently B- (Good). It carries a beta of 0.98, meaning that its performance tracks fairly well with that of the overall stock market. Volatility, as measured by both the semi-deviation and a drawdown factor, is considered low. As of December 31, 2015, Boulder Growth&Income Fund traded at a discount of 20.29% below its net asset value, which is worse than its one-year historical average discount of 20.54%.

Brendon J. Fischer currently receives a manager quality ranking of 38 (0=worst, 99=best). If you desire an average level of risk, then this fund may be an option.

Data Date	Investment Rating	Net Assets ($Mil)	Price	Performance Rating/Pts	Total Return Y-T-D	Risk Rating/Pts
12-15	B-	288.63	7.74	C+ / 6.7	-12.56%	B- / 7.8
2014	A+	277.80	9.05	B+ / 8.9	17.83%	B / 8.9
2013	B	249.26	8.04	B- / 7.5	27.25%	B / 8.2
2012	C	186.67	6.33	C / 4.7	20.65%	B / 8.0
2011	C-	185.00	5.74	D+ / 2.7	-7.20%	B / 8.0
2010	D	169.15	6.23	D- / 1.1	8.35%	C / 5.3

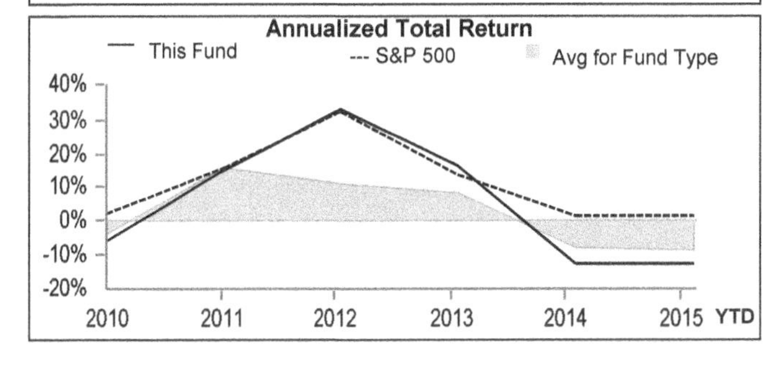

Brookfield Gl Lstd Infr Inc Fd (INF) D- Weak

Fund Family: Brookfield Investment Management In
Fund Type: Global
Inception Date: August 26, 2011

Major Rating Factors:
Disappointing performance is the major factor driving the D- (Weak) TheStreet.com Investment Rating for Brookfield Gl Lstd Infr Inc Fd. The fund currently has a performance rating of D- (Weak) based on an annualized return of -8.23% over the last three years and a total return of -37.95% year to date 2015. Factored into the performance evaluation is an expense ratio of 2.03% (high).

The fund's risk rating is currently C (Fair). It carries a beta of 1.15, meaning it is expected to move 11.5% for every 10% move in the market. Volatility, as measured by both the semi-deviation and a drawdown factor, is considered average. As of December 31, 2015, Brookfield Gl Lstd Infr Inc Fd traded at a discount of 17.25% below its net asset value, which is better than its one-year historical average discount of 12.85%.

This fund has been team managed for 5 years and currently receives a manager quality ranking of 12 (0=worst, 99=best). This fund offers an average level of risk but investors looking for strong performance will be frustrated.

Data Date	Investment Rating	Net Assets ($Mil)	Price	Performance Rating/Pts	Total Return Y-T-D	Risk Rating/Pts
12-15	D-	237.40	11.75	D- / 1.5	-37.95%	C / 4.5
2014	C+	275.40	20.89	C+ / 6.3	18.06%	B- / 7.6
2013	C-	165.88	19.77	C / 4.4	7.18%	B- / 7.3
2012	B	165.90	20.06	B / 7.7	19.21%	B- / 7.5

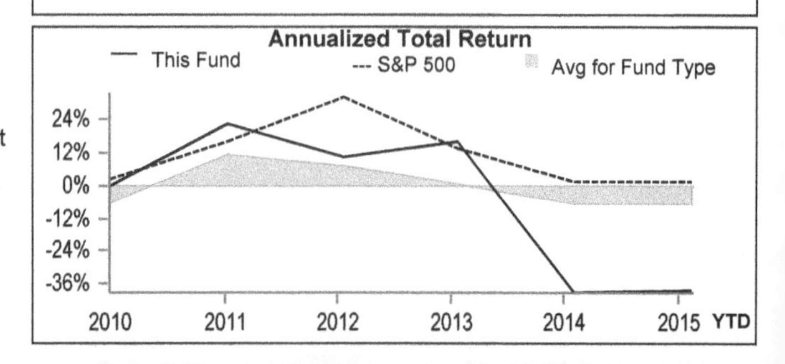

Brookfield High Income Fund (HHY) D+ Weak

Fund Family: Brookfield Investment Management In
Fund Type: Corporate - High Yield
Inception Date: July 27, 1998

Major Rating Factors:
Disappointing performance is the major factor driving the D+ (Weak) TheStreet.com Investment Rating for Brookfield High Income Fund. The fund currently has a performance rating of D+ (Weak) based on an annualized return of -3.62% over the last three years and a total return of -13.42% year to date 2015. Factored into the performance evaluation is an expense ratio of 1.92% (above average).

The fund's risk rating is currently C+ (Fair). It carries a beta of 1.44, meaning it is expected to move 14.4% for every 10% move in the market. Volatility, as measured by both the semi-deviation and a drawdown factor, is considered low. As of December 31, 2015, Brookfield High Income Fund traded at a discount of 10.42% below its net asset value, which is better than its one-year historical average discount of 10.14%.

Dana E. Erikson has been running the fund for 7 years and currently receives a manager quality ranking of 31 (0=worst, 99=best). This fund offers only a moderate level of risk but investors looking for strong performance are still waiting.

Data Date	Investment Rating	Net Assets ($Mil)	Price	Performance Rating/Pts	Total Return Y-T-D	Risk Rating/Pts
12-15	D+	210.98	6.88	D+ / 2.7	-13.42%	C+ / 6.6
2014	C	259.30	8.91	C- / 3.9	2.04%	B / 8.0
2013	B	69.46	9.70	C+ / 6.7	1.56%	B / 8.6
2012	A-	67.49	10.12	B / 8.0	13.30%	B / 8.8
2011	B+	65.00	9.79	B / 8.1	22.51%	B / 8.8
2010	B-	63.26	8.94	B / 7.9	25.40%	C / 4.8

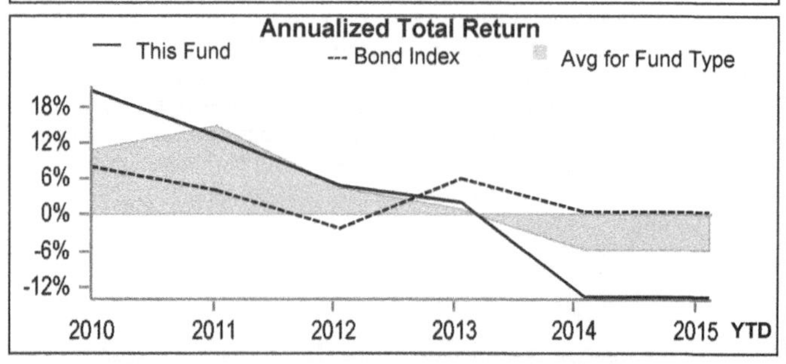

Brookfield Mortgage Opportunity In (BOI) C Fair

Fund Family: Brookfield Investment Management In
Fund Type: Mortgage
Inception Date: March 25, 2013

Major Rating Factors: Middle of the road best describes Brookfield Mortgage Opportunity In whose TheStreet.com Investment Rating is currently a C (Fair). The fund currently has a performance rating of C- (Fair) based on an annualized return of 0.00% over the last three years and a total return of -1.60% year to date 2015. Factored into the performance evaluation is an expense ratio of 2.32% (high).

The fund's risk rating is currently B (Good). It carries a beta of 0.00, meaning the fund's expected move will be 0.0% for every 10% move in the market. Volatility, as measured by both the semi-deviation and a drawdown factor, is considered low. As of December 31, 2015, Brookfield Mortgage Opportunity In traded at a discount of 13.54% below its net asset value, which is better than its one-year historical average discount of 13.41%.

Anthony Breaks currently receives a manager quality ranking of 52 (0=worst, 99=best). If you desire an average level of risk, then this fund may be an option.

Data Date	Investment Rating	Net Assets ($Mil)	Price	Performance Rating/Pts	Total Return Y-T-D	Risk Rating/Pts
12-15	C	412.56	14.75	C- / 4.2	-1.60%	B / 8.0
2014	C	432.40	16.44	C- / 3.9	6.89%	B / 8.8

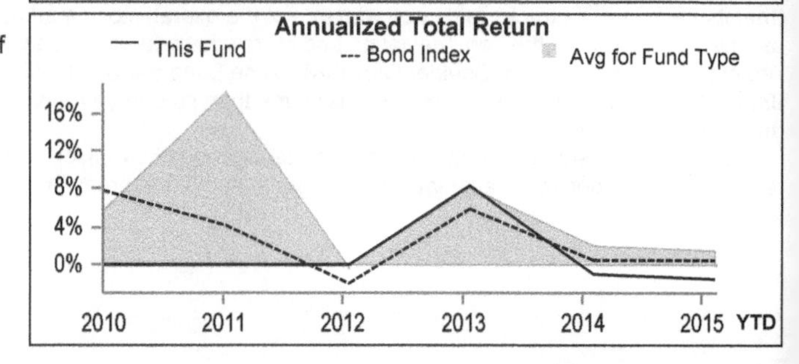

Brookfield Total Return (HTR) C Fair

Fund Family: Brookfield Investment Management In
Fund Type: Mortgage
Inception Date: July 28, 1989

Major Rating Factors: Middle of the road best describes Brookfield Total Return whose TheStreet.com Investment Rating is currently a C (Fair). The fund currently has a performance rating of C+ (Fair) based on an annualized return of 7.22% over the last three years and a total return of -0.33% year to date 2015. Factored into the performance evaluation is an expense ratio of 1.55% (average).

The fund's risk rating is currently C (Fair). It carries a beta of 2.04, meaning it is expected to move 20.4% for every 10% move in the market. Volatility, as measured by both the semi-deviation and a drawdown factor, is considered average. As of December 31, 2015, Brookfield Total Return traded at a price exactly equal to its net asset value, which is worse than its one-year historical average discount of 11.02%.

Michelle L. Russell-Dowe currently receives a manager quality ranking of 84 (0=worst, 99=best). If you desire an average level of risk, then this fund may be an option.

Data Date	Investment Rating	Net Assets ($Mil)	Price	Perfor-mance Rating/Pts	Total Return Y-T-D	Risk Rating/Pts
12-15	C	353.08	21.95	C+ / 6.8	-0.33%	C / 5.6
2014	C	377.70	24.32	C+ / 6.0	11.92%	C+ / 6.1
2013	C+	371.29	23.76	C+ / 6.8	10.51%	C+ / 6.6
2012	C	245.30	23.62	C+ / 5.6	16.15%	B- / 7.0
2011	B-	178.20	5.72	C+ / 6.3	13.02%	B / 8.1
2010	C+	168.91	5.68	C+ / 6.2	21.84%	C+ / 6.8

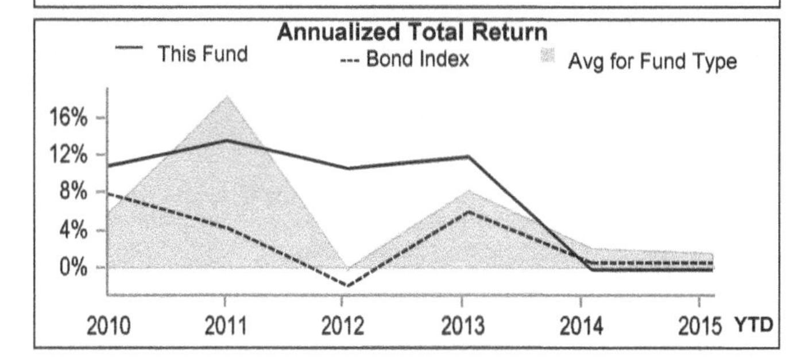

Calamos Convertible Opport&Income (CHI) C- Fair

Fund Family: Calamos Advisors LLC
Fund Type: Growth and Income
Inception Date: June 25, 2002

Major Rating Factors: Middle of the road best describes Calamos Convertible Opport&Income whose TheStreet.com Investment Rating is currently a C- (Fair). The fund currently has a performance rating of C- (Fair) based on an annualized return of 1.65% over the last three years and a total return of -15.59% year to date 2015. Factored into the performance evaluation is an expense ratio of 1.47% (average).

The fund's risk rating is currently B- (Good). It carries a beta of 0.78, meaning the fund's expected move will be 7.8% for every 10% move in the market. Volatility, as measured by both the semi-deviation and a drawdown factor, is considered low. As of December 31, 2015, Calamos Convertible Opport&Income traded at a discount of 9.17% below its net asset value, which is better than its one-year historical average discount of 5.34%.

John P. Calamos, Sr. has been running the fund for 14 years and currently receives a manager quality ranking of 20 (0=worst, 99=best). If you desire an average level of risk, then this fund may be an option.

Data Date	Investment Rating	Net Assets ($Mil)	Price	Perfor-mance Rating/Pts	Total Return Y-T-D	Risk Rating/Pts
12-15	C-	931.70	9.91	C- / 3.8	-15.59%	B- / 7.3
2014	B-	952.90	12.84	C+ / 5.9	5.40%	B / 8.8
2013	B	875.38	13.26	B- / 7.0	16.82%	B / 8.3
2012	C	827.34	11.94	C- / 4.0	15.95%	B / 8.2
2011	C+	860.64	11.26	C / 5.5	-0.59%	B / 8.2
2010	B-	733.71	13.18	B- / 7.4	17.29%	C / 5.0

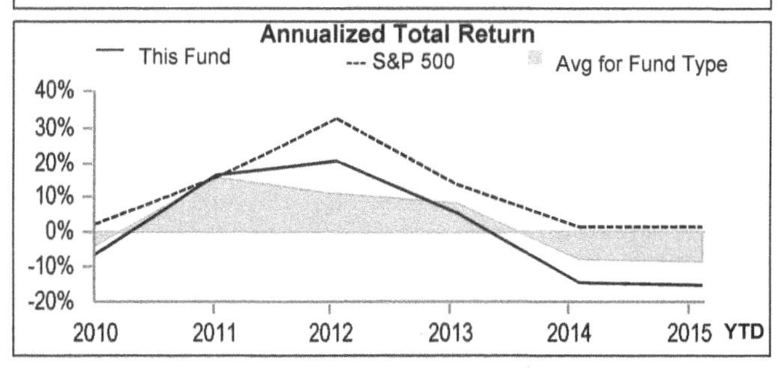

Calamos Convertible&High Income (CHY) C- Fair

Fund Family: Calamos Advisors LLC
Fund Type: Growth and Income
Inception Date: May 28, 2003

Major Rating Factors: Middle of the road best describes Calamos Convertible&High Income whose TheStreet.com Investment Rating is currently a C- (Fair). The fund currently has a performance rating of C- (Fair) based on an annualized return of 2.71% over the last three years and a total return of -16.66% year to date 2015. Factored into the performance evaluation is an expense ratio of 1.47% (average).

The fund's risk rating is currently B- (Good). It carries a beta of 0.96, meaning that its performance tracks fairly well with that of the overall stock market. Volatility, as measured by both the semi-deviation and a drawdown factor, is considered low. As of December 31, 2015, Calamos Convertible&High Income traded at a discount of 9.08% below its net asset value, which is better than its one-year historical average discount of 2.72%.

John P. Calamos, Sr. has been running the fund for 13 years and currently receives a manager quality ranking of 18 (0=worst, 99=best). If you desire an average level of risk, then this fund may be an option.

Data Date	Investment Rating	Net Assets ($Mil)	Price	Perfor-mance Rating/Pts	Total Return Y-T-D	Risk Rating/Pts
12-15	C-	1,029.90	10.51	C- / 3.9	-16.66%	B- / 7.1
2014	C+	1,061.50	13.83	C+ / 6.2	15.78%	B- / 7.1
2013	B-	981.09	12.93	C+ / 6.5	11.61%	B / 8.1
2012	C	917.54	12.15	C / 4.3	12.17%	B / 8.0
2011	B-	973.05	11.56	C+ / 6.6	5.34%	B / 8.0
2010	C+	896.19	12.66	B- / 7.3	19.18%	C / 5.0

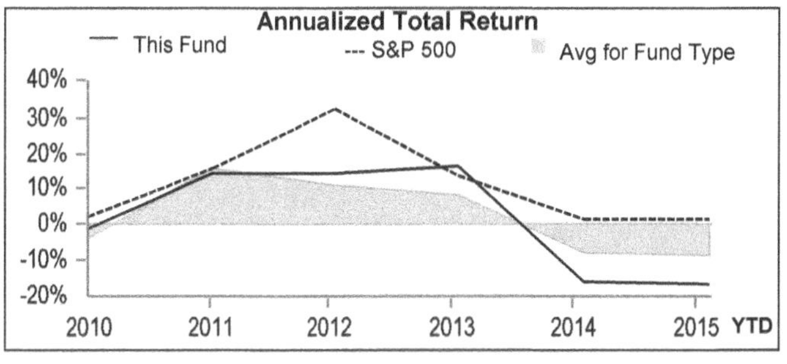

Calamos Global Dynamic Income Fd (CHW) — C — Fair

Fund Family: Calamos Advisors LLC
Fund Type: Global
Inception Date: June 26, 2007

Major Rating Factors: Middle of the road best describes Calamos Global Dynamic Income Fd whose TheStreet.com Investment Rating is currently a C (Fair). The fund currently has a performance rating of C (Fair) based on an annualized return of 2.96% over the last three years and a total return of -11.35% year to date 2015. Factored into the performance evaluation is an expense ratio of 1.79% (above average).

The fund's risk rating is currently C+ (Fair). It carries a beta of 0.98, meaning that its performance tracks fairly well with that of the overall stock market. Volatility, as measured by both the semi-deviation and a drawdown factor, is considered low. As of December 31, 2015, Calamos Global Dynamic Income Fd traded at a discount of 14.76% below its net asset value, which is better than its one-year historical average discount of 11.39%.

John P. Calamos, Sr. has been running the fund for 9 years and currently receives a manager quality ranking of 58 (0=worst, 99=best). If you desire an average level of risk, then this fund may be an option.

Data Date	Investment Rating	Net Assets ($Mil)	Price	Performance Rating/Pts	Total Return Y-T-D	Risk Rating/Pts
12-15	C	581.62	7.16	C / 4.6	-11.35%	C+ / 6.9
2014	B+	611.10	9.23	B- / 7.4	13.71%	B / 8.2
2013	C+	573.64	8.97	C+ / 6.8	11.50%	B- / 7.4
2012	C+	534.74	8.35	C+ / 6.0	26.76%	B- / 7.5
2011	C	620.56	7.30	C / 4.9	-3.57%	B- / 7.2
2010	D+	534.65	8.37	C- / 3.5	15.01%	C / 4.5

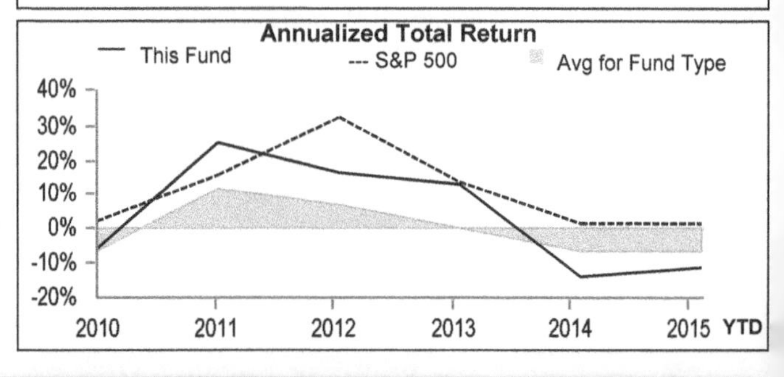

Calamos Global Total Return Fund (CGO) — C — Fair

Fund Family: Calamos Advisors LLC
Fund Type: Growth and Income
Inception Date: October 27, 2005

Major Rating Factors: Middle of the road best describes Calamos Global Total Return Fund whose TheStreet.com Investment Rating is currently a C (Fair). The fund currently has a performance rating of C (Fair) based on an annualized return of 1.88% over the last three years and a total return of -4.44% year to date 2015. Factored into the performance evaluation is an expense ratio of 1.92% (above average).

The fund's risk rating is currently B- (Good). It carries a beta of 1.09, meaning that its performance tracks fairly well with that of the overall stock market. Volatility, as measured by both the semi-deviation and a drawdown factor, is considered low. As of December 31, 2015, Calamos Global Total Return Fund traded at a discount of 9.58% below its net asset value, which is better than its one-year historical average discount of 5.97%.

John P. Calamos, Sr. has been running the fund for 11 years and currently receives a manager quality ranking of 13 (0=worst, 99=best). If you desire an average level of risk, then this fund may be an option.

Data Date	Investment Rating	Net Assets ($Mil)	Price	Performance Rating/Pts	Total Return Y-T-D	Risk Rating/Pts
12-15	C	120.28	11.42	C / 4.6	-4.44%	B- / 7.4
2014	C	126.10	13.22	C / 4.4	2.71%	B- / 7.9
2013	C	121.65	14.02	C+ / 5.6	8.38%	B- / 7.6
2012	C-	119.60	13.74	C- / 3.3	9.27%	B- / 7.6
2011	B-	131.71	13.64	C+ / 6.7	1.19%	B- / 7.8
2010	C-	117.48	14.60	C / 4.3	10.83%	C / 5.3

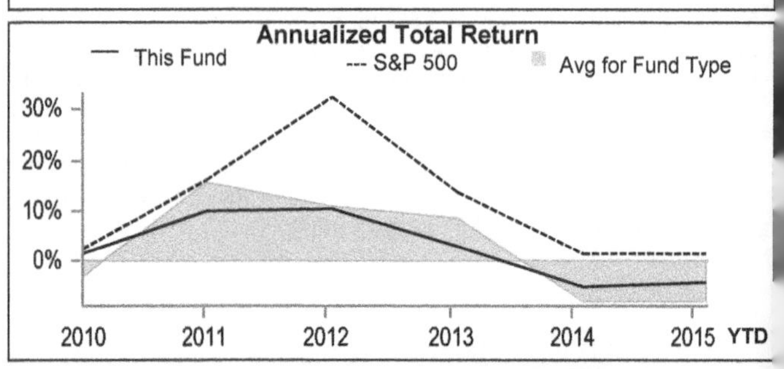

Calamos Strategic Total Return Fun (CSQ) — C+ — Fair

Fund Family: Calamos Advisors LLC
Fund Type: Growth and Income
Inception Date: March 26, 2004

Major Rating Factors: Middle of the road best describes Calamos Strategic Total Return Fun whose TheStreet.com Investment Rating is currently a C+ (Fair). The fund currently has a performance rating of C+ (Fair) based on an annualized return of 7.84% over the last three years and a total return of -4.78% year to date 2015. Factored into the performance evaluation is an expense ratio of 1.72% (above average).

The fund's risk rating is currently B- (Good). It carries a beta of 1.10, meaning it is expected to move 11.0% for every 10% move in the market. Volatility, as measured by both the semi-deviation and a drawdown factor, is considered low. As of December 31, 2015, Calamos Strategic Total Return Fun traded at a discount of 10.89% below its net asset value, which is better than its one-year historical average discount of 10.03%.

John P. Calamos, Sr. has been running the fund for 12 years and currently receives a manager quality ranking of 24 (0=worst, 99=best). If you desire an average level of risk, then this fund may be an option.

Data Date	Investment Rating	Net Assets ($Mil)	Price	Performance Rating/Pts	Total Return Y-T-D	Risk Rating/Pts
12-15	C+	1,932.22	9.90	C+ / 6.7	-4.78%	B- / 7.2
2014	A-	1,980.30	11.44	B / 7.8	14.62%	B / 8.2
2013	B-	1,724.91	10.89	B- / 7.4	15.16%	B- / 7.5
2012	C+	1,567.88	9.81	C+ / 6.9	28.40%	B- / 7.7
2011	C+	1,776.33	8.35	C+ / 5.8	-0.87%	B- / 7.5
2010	D	1,596.21	9.26	C- / 3.1	13.63%	C / 4.6

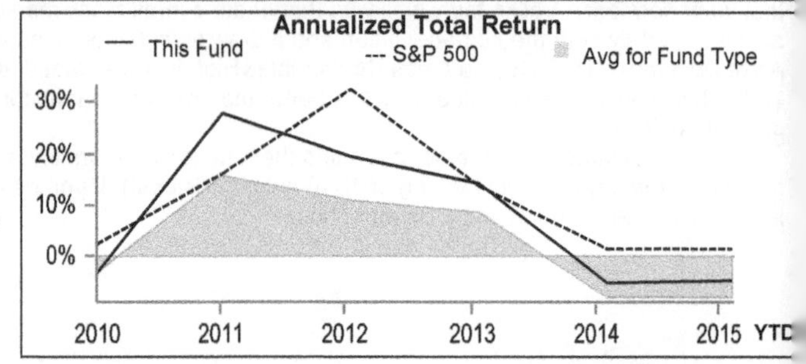

Canadian General Investments Ltd (T.CGI) C Fair

Fund Family: Morgan Meighen & Associates Limited
Fund Type: Foreign
Inception Date: N/A

Major Rating Factors: Strong performance is the major factor driving the C (Fair) TheStreet.com Investment Rating for Canadian General Investments Ltd. The fund currently has a performance rating of B- (Good) based on an annualized return of 10.17% over the last three years and a total return of -1.47% year to date 2015. Factored into the performance evaluation is an expense ratio of 3.57% (high).

The fund's risk rating is currently C (Fair). It carries a beta of 0.41, meaning the fund's expected move will be 4.1% for every 10% move in the market. Volatility, as measured by both the semi-deviation and a drawdown factor, is considered average. As of December 31, 2015, Canadian General Investments Ltd traded at a discount of 23.06% below its net asset value, which is worse than its one-year historical average discount of 26.85%.

Michael A. Smedley has been running the fund for 28 years and currently receives a manager quality ranking of 93 (0=worst, 99=best). If you desire an average level of risk and strong performance, then this fund is a good option.

Data Date	Investment Rating	Net Assets ($Mil)	Price	Performance Rating/Pts	Total Return Y-T-D	Risk Rating/Pts
12-15	C	288.01	18.75	B- / 7.4	-1.47%	C / 5.3
2014	B	575.60	20.05	C+ / 6.7	13.96%	B / 8.4
2013	C-	288.01	18.40	C+ / 5.7	20.65%	C / 5.0
2012	D	288.01	15.75	D+ / 2.8	4.07%	C / 4.9
2011	C	425.80	16.00	C+ / 6.8	-11.60%	C / 5.2
2010	D-	288.01	19.18	C- / 3.2	27.89%	D+ / 2.9

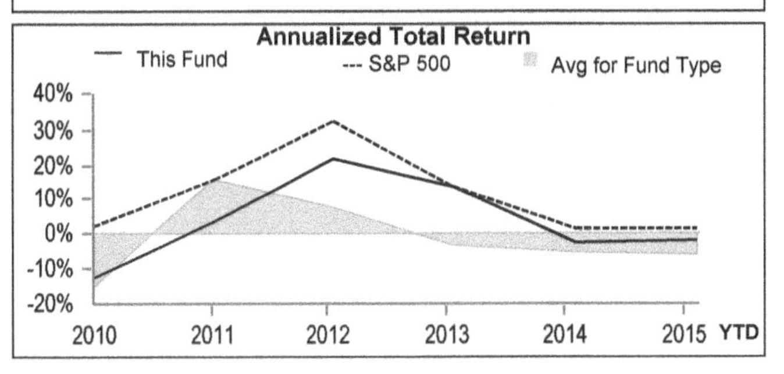

Canadian World Fund Limited (T.CWF) B Good

Fund Family: Morgan Meighen & Associates Limited
Fund Type: Global
Inception Date: February 25, 1994

Major Rating Factors: Strong performance is the major factor driving the B (Good) TheStreet.com Investment Rating for Canadian World Fund Limited. The fund currently has a performance rating of B+ (Good) based on an annualized return of 12.00% over the last three years and a total return of 19.81% year to date 2015. Factored into the performance evaluation is an expense ratio of 3.04% (high).

The fund's risk rating is currently C+ (Fair). It carries a beta of 0.47, meaning the fund's expected move will be 4.7% for every 10% move in the market. Volatility, as measured by both the semi-deviation and a drawdown factor, is considered low. As of December 31, 2015, Canadian World Fund Limited traded at a discount of 34.22% below its net asset value, which is worse than its one-year historical average discount of 34.56%.

Alex Sulzer currently receives a manager quality ranking of 95 (0=worst, 99=best). If you desire only a moderate level of risk and strong performance, then this fund is an excellent option.

Data Date	Investment Rating	Net Assets ($Mil)	Price	Performance Rating/Pts	Total Return Y-T-D	Risk Rating/Pts
12-15	B	20.47	4.96	B+ / 8.8	19.81%	C+ / 5.8
2014	C-	47.50	4.14	C- / 3.8	-1.66%	B- / 7.8
2013	D	20.47	4.21	C / 4.7	19.26%	C- / 4.1
2012	D-	20.47	3.45	D / 1.9	-0.85%	C / 4.4
2011	D+	35.50	3.56	C / 5.2	-13.08%	C / 4.9
2010	E	20.47	4.14	D- / 1.4	20.70%	D / 1.8

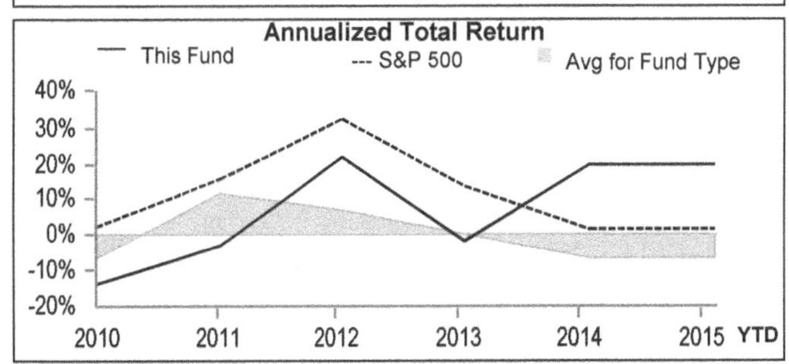

CBRE Clarion Global Real Estate In (IGR) C Fair

Fund Family: CBRE Clarion Securities LLC
Fund Type: Growth and Income
Inception Date: February 25, 2004

Major Rating Factors: Middle of the road best describes CBRE Clarion Global Real Estate In whose TheStreet.com Investment Rating is currently a C (Fair). The fund currently has a performance rating of C (Fair) based on an annualized return of 1.17% over the last three years and a total return of -9.29% year to date 2015. Factored into the performance evaluation is an expense ratio of 1.14% (low).

The fund's risk rating is currently B- (Good). It carries a beta of 0.68, meaning the fund's expected move will be 6.8% for every 10% move in the market. Volatility, as measured by both the semi-deviation and a drawdown factor, is considered low. As of December 31, 2015, CBRE Clarion Global Real Estate In traded at a discount of 15.49% below its net asset value, which is better than its one-year historical average discount of 14.67%.

T. Ritson Ferguson has been running the fund for 10 years and currently receives a manager quality ranking of 21 (0=worst, 99=best). If you desire an average level of risk, then this fund may be an option.

Data Date	Investment Rating	Net Assets ($Mil)	Price	Performance Rating/Pts	Total Return Y-T-D	Risk Rating/Pts
12-15	C	1,184.71	7.64	C / 4.4	-9.29%	B- / 7.1
2014	B	1,108.70	8.99	B / 7.7	20.92%	B- / 7.7
2013	C	1,105.00	7.92	C / 4.6	-6.02%	B- / 7.7
2012	B+	949.58	8.86	B+ / 8.6	36.06%	B- / 7.5
2011	C+	949.60	6.84	B / 7.6	-2.53%	C+ / 6.7
2010	D-	839.24	7.75	D / 1.7	31.18%	C- / 3.6

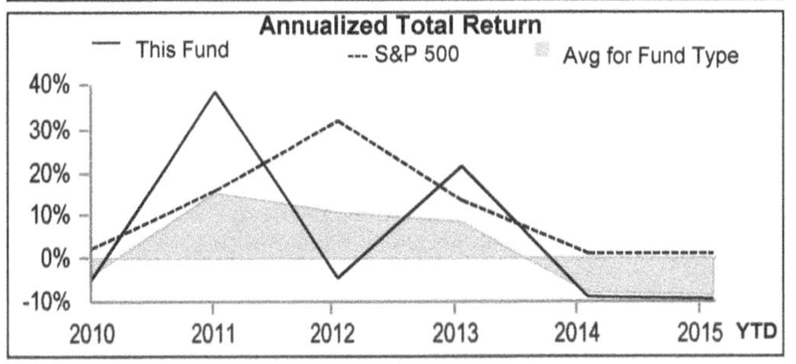

Center Coast MLP & Infrastructure (CEN) E+ Very Weak

Fund Family: Center Coast Capital Advisors LP
Fund Type: Energy/Natural Resources
Inception Date: September 26, 2013

Major Rating Factors:
Very poor performance is the major factor driving the E+ (Very Weak) TheStreet.com Investment Rating for Center Coast MLP & Infrastructure. The fund currently has a performance rating of E- (Very Weak) based on an annualized return of 0.00% over the last three years and a total return of -38.22% year to date 2015. Factored into the performance evaluation is an expense ratio of 2.26% (high).

The fund's risk rating is currently C- (Fair). It carries a beta of 0.00, meaning the fund's expected move will be 0.0% for every 10% move in the market. Volatility, as measured by both the semi-deviation and a drawdown factor, is considered average. As of December 31, 2015, Center Coast MLP & Infrastructure traded at a discount of 3.89% below its net asset value, which is worse than its one-year historical average discount of 4.58%.

This fund offers an average level of risk but investors looking for strong performance will be frustrated.

Data Date	Investment Rating	Net Assets ($Mil)	Price	Performance Rating/Pts	Total Return Y-T-D	Risk Rating/Pts
12-15	E+	297.93	10.12	E- / 0.1	-38.22%	C- / 3.8
2014	D-	322.50	17.76	D+ / 2.6	6.21%	C / 4.4

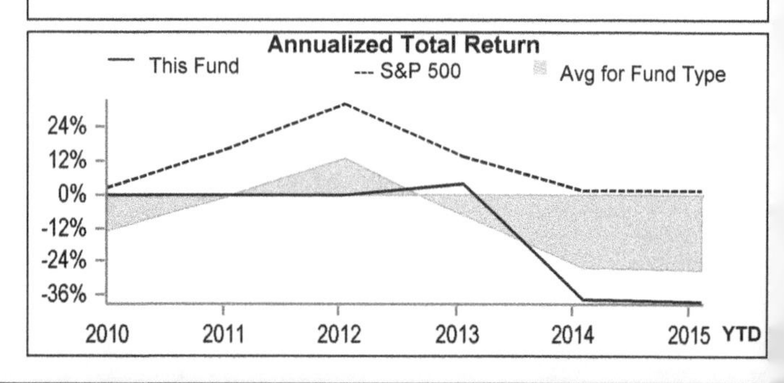

Central Europe Russia and Turkey (CEE) D- Weak

Fund Family: Deutsche Asset Mgmt International G
Fund Type: Foreign
Inception Date: March 6, 1990

Major Rating Factors:
Disappointing performance is the major factor driving the D- (Weak) TheStreet.com Investment Rating for Central Europe Russia and Turkey. The fund currently has a performance rating of D- (Weak) based on an annualized return of -17.36% over the last three years and a total return of -13.67% year to date 2015. Factored into the performance evaluation is an expense ratio of 1.31% (average).

The fund's risk rating is currently C (Fair). It carries a beta of 1.25, meaning it is expected to move 12.5% for every 10% move in the market. Volatility, as measured by both the semi-deviation and a drawdown factor, is considered average. As of December 31, 2015, Central Europe Russia and Turkey traded at a discount of 12.52% below its net asset value, which is better than its one-year historical average discount of 10.78%.

Sylwia Szczepek has been running the fund for 2 years and currently receives a manager quality ranking of 6 (0=worst, 99=best). This fund offers an average level of risk but investors looking for strong performance will be frustrated.

Data Date	Investment Rating	Net Assets ($Mil)	Price	Performance Rating/Pts	Total Return Y-T-D	Risk Rating/Pts
12-15	D-	257.37	16.63	D- / 1.1	-13.67%	C / 4.3
2014	D-	268.20	19.78	D- / 1.2	-31.11%	C / 5.0
2013	D-	448.13	30.55	D+ / 2.3	-6.06%	C / 5.4
2012	D+	505.93	33.92	C / 4.8	22.89%	C / 5.4
2011	C	416.00	28.55	B- / 7.0	-18.46%	C+ / 5.8
2010	D-	575.79	41.84	D / 2.1	27.56%	C- / 3.2

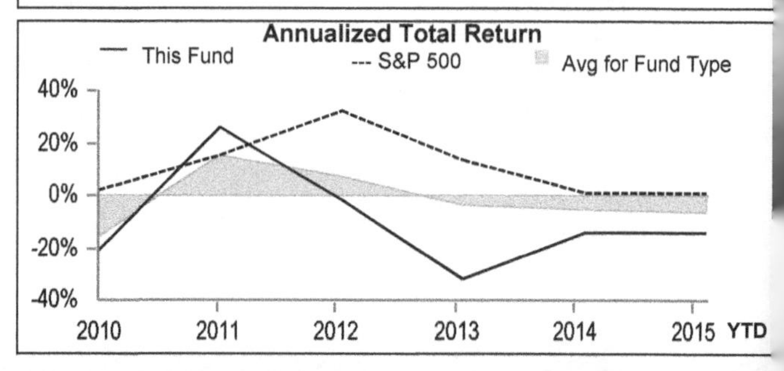

Central Fund of Canada (CEF) D- Weak

Fund Family: Central Group Alberta Ltd
Fund Type: Precious Metals
Inception Date: September 14, 1983

Major Rating Factors:
Very poor performance is the major factor driving the D- (Weak) TheStreet.com Investment Rating for Central Fund of Canada. The fund currently has a performance rating of E+ (Very Weak) based on an annualized return of -22.08% over the last three years and a total return of -14.31% year to date 2015. Factored into the performance evaluation is an expense ratio of 0.32% (very low).

The fund's risk rating is currently C- (Fair). It carries a beta of 1.30, meaning it is expected to move 13.0% for every 10% move in the market. Volatility, as measured by both the semi-deviation and a drawdown factor, is considered average. As of December 31, 2015, Central Fund of Canada traded at a discount of 11.28% below its net asset value, which is better than its one-year historical average discount of 8.56%.

Philip M. Spicer has been running the fund for 10 years and currently receives a manager quality ranking of 29 (0=worst, 99=best). This fund offers an average level of risk but investors looking for strong performance will be frustrated.

Data Date	Investment Rating	Net Assets ($Mil)	Price	Performance Rating/Pts	Total Return Y-T-D	Risk Rating/Pts
12-15	D-	3,237.86	9.99	E+ / 0.8	-14.31%	C- / 4.1
2014	E+	3,399.90	11.58	E+ / 0.9	-15.89%	C- / 4.2
2013	E+	4,409.95	13.25	E+ / 0.9	-34.86%	C / 4.9
2012	C-	5,620.88	21.03	C / 4.8	1.86%	B- / 7.0
2011	B-	4,902.00	19.61	B- / 7.2	4.55%	B- / 7.5
2010	A	2,382.34	20.73	A / 9.4	50.52%	C+ / 5.8

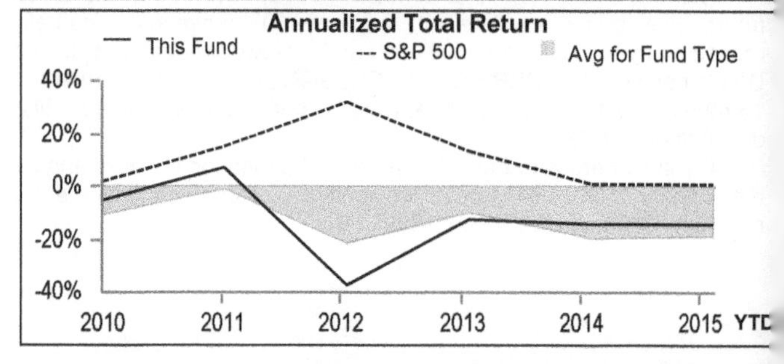

Central Gold-Trust (GTU) D Weak

Fund Family: Central Gold Trust
Fund Type: Precious Metals
Inception Date: September 22, 2006

Major Rating Factors:
Disappointing performance is the major factor driving the D (Weak) TheStreet.com Investment Rating for Central Gold-Trust. The fund currently has a performance rating of D- (Weak) based on an annualized return of -15.78% over the last three years and a total return of -7.33% year to date 2015. Factored into the performance evaluation is an expense ratio of 0.36% (very low).

The fund's risk rating is currently C+ (Fair). It carries a beta of 1.04, meaning that its performance tracks fairly well with that of the overall stock market. Volatility, as measured by both the semi-deviation and a drawdown factor, is considered low. As of December 31, 2015, Central Gold-Trust traded at a discount of 2.48% below its net asset value, which is worse than its one-year historical average discount of 4.90%.

This fund has been team managed for 13 years and currently receives a manager quality ranking of 56 (0=worst, 99=best). This fund offers only a moderate level of risk but investors looking for strong performance are still waiting.

Data Date	Investment Rating	Net Assets ($Mil)	Price	Perfor-mance Rating/Pts	Total Return Y-T-D	Risk Rating/Pts
12-15	D	855.28	37.70	D- / 1.3	-7.33%	C+ / 5.8
2014	D-	868.20	40.65	D- / 1.1	-6.36%	C / 5.4
2013	D-	1,189.57	41.51	D- / 1.2	-31.20%	C+ / 5.8
2012	C-	1,130.49	62.78	C- / 3.7	-0.57%	B- / 7.7
2011	B	1,130.50	59.17	B- / 7.3	20.25%	B / 8.0
2010	A+	451.92	54.35	B+ / 8.8	22.44%	B- / 7.5

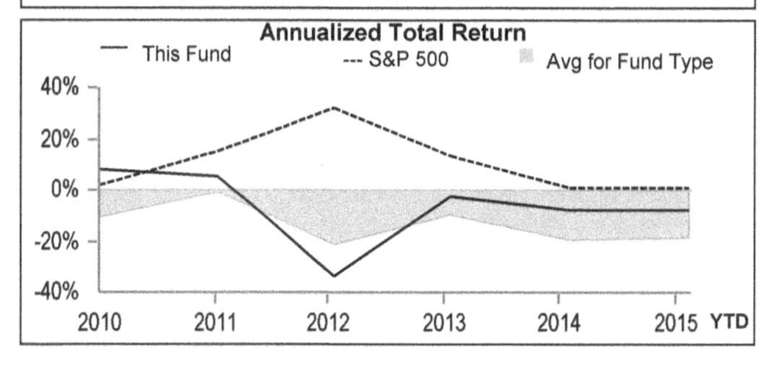

Central Securities (CET) B- Good

Fund Family: Central Securities Corporation
Fund Type: Growth
Inception Date: N/A

Major Rating Factors: Strong performance is the major factor driving the B- (Good) TheStreet.com Investment Rating for Central Securities. The fund currently has a performance rating of B- (Good) based on an annualized return of 9.79% over the last three years and a total return of -4.45% year to date 2015. Factored into the performance evaluation is an expense ratio of 0.67% (very low).

The fund's risk rating is currently B- (Good). It carries a beta of 0.81, meaning the fund's expected move will be 8.1% for every 10% move in the market. Volatility, as measured by both the semi-deviation and a drawdown factor, is considered low. As of December 31, 2015, Central Securities traded at a discount of 19.17% below its net asset value, which is better than its one-year historical average discount of 17.61%.

Wilmot H. Kidd, III has been running the fund for 43 years and currently receives a manager quality ranking of 51 (0=worst, 99=best). If you desire only a moderate level of risk and strong performance, then this fund is an excellent option.

Data Date	Investment Rating	Net Assets ($Mil)	Price	Perfor-mance Rating/Pts	Total Return Y-T-D	Risk Rating/Pts
12-15	B-	649.76	19.02	B- / 7.3	-4.45%	B- / 7.3
2014	B-	661.10	21.97	C+ / 6.1	9.48%	B / 8.1
2013	B-	569.47	21.72	B- / 7.1	26.51%	B- / 7.7
2012	C-	556.49	19.98	C- / 3.0	0.70%	B- / 7.8
2011	C	574.20	20.46	C / 5.2	-1.29%	B- / 7.8
2010	B+	499.95	21.97	B / 7.7	27.63%	C+ / 6.1

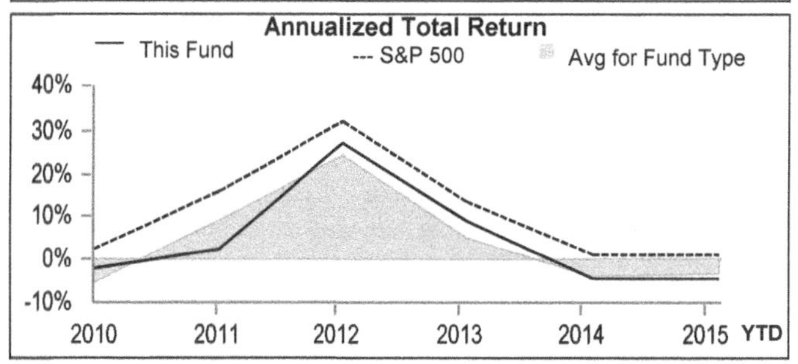

China Fund (CHN) C- Fair

Fund Family: RCM Asia Pacific Limited
Fund Type: Foreign
Inception Date: July 10, 1992

Major Rating Factors: Middle of the road best describes China Fund whose TheStreet.com Investment Rating is currently a C- (Fair). The fund currently has a performance rating of C (Fair) based on an annualized return of 2.80% over the last three years and a total return of -7.86% year to date 2015. Factored into the performance evaluation is an expense ratio of 1.31% (average).

The fund's risk rating is currently C (Fair). It carries a beta of 0.85, meaning the fund's expected move will be 8.5% for every 10% move in the market. Volatility, as measured by both the semi-deviation and a drawdown factor, is considered average. As of December 31, 2015, China Fund traded at a discount of 12.61% below its net asset value, which is worse than its one-year historical average discount of 13.08%.

Christina Chung has been running the fund for 4 years and currently receives a manager quality ranking of 59 (0=worst, 99=best). If you desire an average level of risk, then this fund may be an option.

Data Date	Investment Rating	Net Assets ($Mil)	Price	Perfor-mance Rating/Pts	Total Return Y-T-D	Risk Rating/Pts
12-15	C-	379.69	15.52	C / 4.6	-7.86%	C / 5.5
2014	C+	368.20	18.23	C+ / 6.3	6.71%	C+ / 6.9
2013	D	370.67	20.81	C- / 3.3	9.47%	C+ / 5.8
2012	D	660.44	21.41	C- / 3.6	19.44%	C+ / 5.9
2011	D	529.60	20.51	D / 2.1	-37.36%	C+ / 6.2
2010	C+	620.47	32.50	B / 8.2	23.60%	C- / 3.5

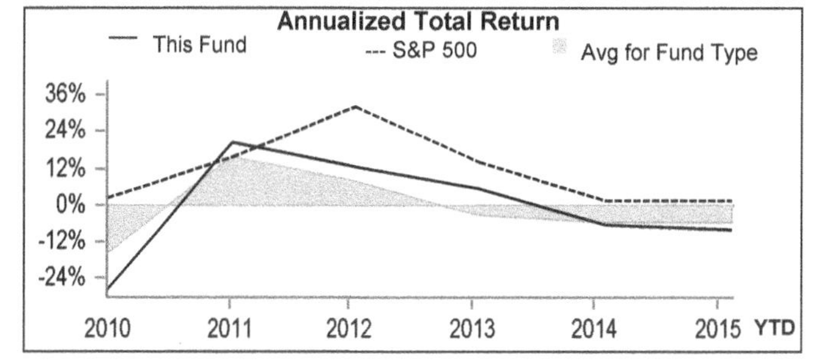

ClearBridge American Energy MLP In (CBA) E+ Very Weak

Fund Family: Legg Mason Partners Fund Advisor LL
Fund Type: Global
Inception Date: June 26, 2013

Major Rating Factors:
Very poor performance is the major factor driving the E+ (Very Weak) TheStreet.com Investment Rating for ClearBridge American Energy MLP In. The fund currently has a performance rating of E- (Very Weak) based on an annualized return of 0.00% over the last three years and a total return of -45.00% year to date 2015. Factored into the performance evaluation is an expense ratio of 2.65% (high).

The fund's risk rating is currently C- (Fair). It carries a beta of 0.00, meaning the fund's expected move will be 0.0% for every 10% move in the market. Volatility, as measured by both the semi-deviation and a drawdown factor, is considered average. As of December 31, 2015, ClearBridge American Energy MLP In traded at a discount of 9.50% below its net asset value, which is better than its one-year historical average discount of 7.77%.

This fund offers an average level of risk but investors looking for strong performance will be frustrated.

Data Date	Investment Rating	Net Assets ($Mil)	Price	Performance Rating/Pts	Total Return Y-T-D	Risk Rating/Pts
12-15	E+	1,096.00	8.19	E- / 0.1	-45.00%	C- / 3.9
2014	D	1,180.50	15.96	D- / 1.2	-3.55%	B- / 7.2

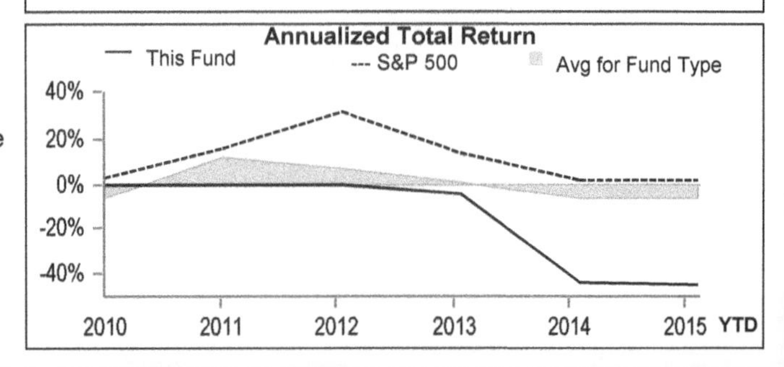

ClearBridge Energy MLP Fund Inc (CEM) D- Weak

Fund Family: Legg Mason Partners Fund Advisor LL
Fund Type: Energy/Natural Resources
Inception Date: June 25, 2010

Major Rating Factors:
Disappointing performance is the major factor driving the D- (Weak) TheStreet.com Investment Rating for ClearBridge Energy MLP Fund Inc. The fund currently has a performance rating of D- (Weak) based on an annualized return of -9.26% over the last three years and a total return of -40.79% year to date 2015. Factored into the performance evaluation is an expense ratio of 2.19% (high).

The fund's risk rating is currently C (Fair). It carries a beta of 0.95, meaning that its performance tracks fairly well with that of the overall stock market. Volatility, as measured by both the semi-deviation and a drawdown factor, is considered average. As of December 31, 2015, ClearBridge Energy MLP Fund Inc traded at a discount of 5.07% below its net asset value, which is better than its one-year historical average discount of 4.50%.

Christopher Eades currently receives a manager quality ranking of 35 (0=worst, 99=best). This fund offers an average level of risk but investors looking for strong performance will be frustrated.

Data Date	Investment Rating	Net Assets ($Mil)	Price	Performance Rating/Pts	Total Return Y-T-D	Risk Rating/Pts
12-15	D-	2,033.00	15.18	D- / 1.2	-40.79%	C / 4.4
2014	B-	2,150.60	27.60	C+ / 6.1	10.09%	B / 8.6
2013	B-	1,755.00	27.22	C+ / 6.8	14.52%	B / 8.1
2012	B-	1,363.00	23.03	C+ / 6.8	14.80%	B / 8.1
2011	C	1,441.10	22.44	C+ / 6.9	12.75%	C / 5.2

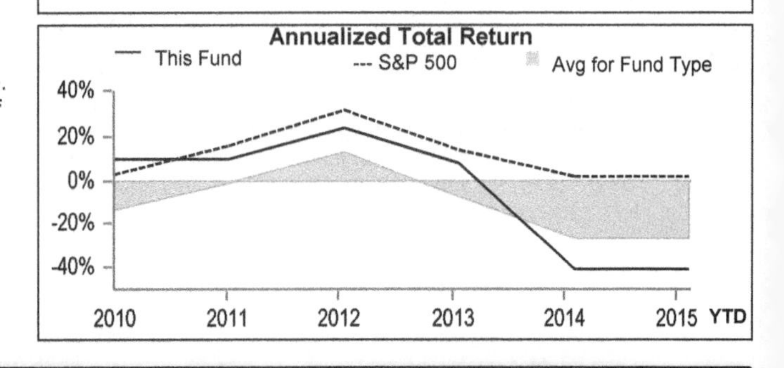

ClearBridge Energy MLP Oppty Fd In (EMO) D- Weak

Fund Family: Legg Mason Partners Fund Advisor LL
Fund Type: Energy/Natural Resources
Inception Date: June 10, 2011

Major Rating Factors:
Disappointing performance is the major factor driving the D- (Weak) TheStreet.com Investment Rating for ClearBridge Energy MLP Oppty Fd In. The fund currently has a performance rating of D- (Weak) based on an annualized return of -11.24% over the last three years and a total return of -41.79% year to date 2015. Factored into the performance evaluation is an expense ratio of 2.20% (high).

The fund's risk rating is currently C (Fair). It carries a beta of 0.90, meaning that its performance tracks fairly well with that of the overall stock market. Volatility, as measured by both the semi-deviation and a drawdown factor, is considered average. As of December 31, 2015, ClearBridge Energy MLP Oppty Fd In traded at a discount of 7.95% below its net asset value, which is worse than its one-year historical average discount of 9.21%.

Christopher Eades currently receives a manager quality ranking of 25 (0=worst, 99=best). This fund offers an average level of risk but investors looking for strong performance will be frustrated.

Data Date	Investment Rating	Net Assets ($Mil)	Price	Performance Rating/Pts	Total Return Y-T-D	Risk Rating/Pts
12-15	D-	798.00	12.74	D- / 1.1	-41.79%	C / 4.3
2014	B-	860.80	23.47	C+ / 6.0	9.52%	B / 8.6
2013	C	705.00	23.15	C / 5.0	8.51%	B / 8.1
2012	B-	568.00	20.70	B- / 7.1	15.96%	B / 8.0

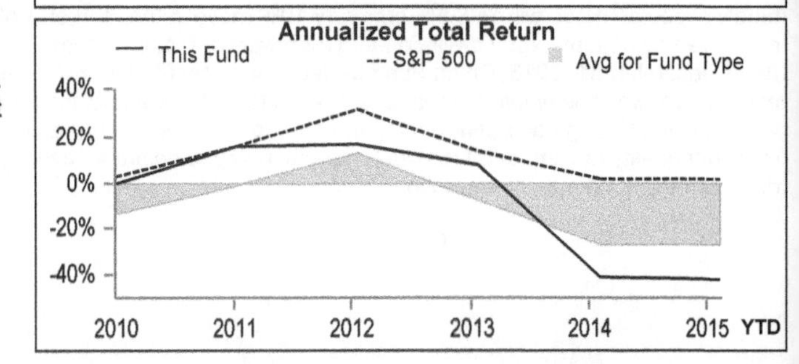

ClearBridge Engy MLP To Rtn Fd Inc (CTR) D- Weak

Fund Family: Legg Mason Partners Fund Advisor LL
Fund Type: Income
Inception Date: June 27, 2012

Major Rating Factors:
Disappointing performance is the major factor driving the D- (Weak) TheStreet.com Investment Rating for ClearBridge Engy MLP To Rtn Fd Inc. The fund currently has a performance rating of D- (Weak) based on an annualized return of -9.80% over the last three years and a total return of -38.57% year to date 2015. Factored into the performance evaluation is an expense ratio of 2.26% (high).

The fund's risk rating is currently C (Fair). It carries a beta of 1.25, meaning it is expected to move 12.5% for every 10% move in the market. Volatility, as measured by both the semi-deviation and a drawdown factor, is considered average. As of December 31, 2015, ClearBridge Engy MLP To Rtn Fd Inc traded at a discount of 8.75% below its net asset value, which is worse than its one-year historical average discount of 9.39%.

Christopher Eades currently receives a manager quality ranking of 6 (0=worst, 99=best). This fund offers an average level of risk but investors looking for strong performance will be frustrated.

Data Date	Investment Rating	Net Assets ($Mil)	Price	Performance Rating/Pts	Total Return Y-T-D	Risk Rating/Pts
12-15	D-	935.00	12.31	D- / 1.2	-38.57%	C / 4.6
2014	C-	1,003.60	21.39	D+ / 2.4	5.59%	B / 8.4
2013	C	852.00	22.05	C / 4.3	11.57%	B / 8.9

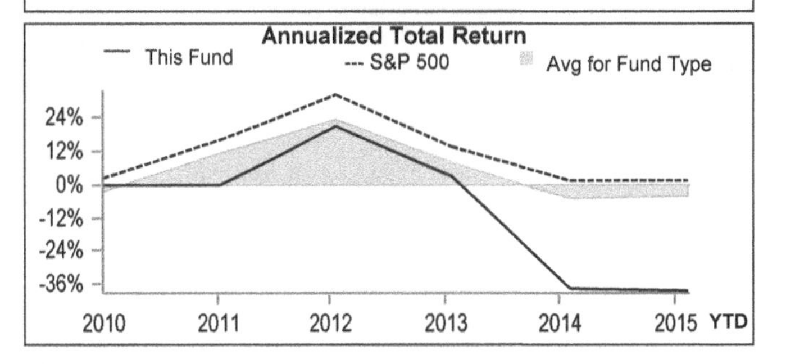

Clough Global Allocation Fund (GLV) B Good

Fund Family: Clough Capital Partners LP
Fund Type: Growth and Income
Inception Date: July 28, 2004

Major Rating Factors: Strong performance is the major factor driving the B (Good) TheStreet.com Investment Rating for Clough Global Allocation Fund. The fund currently has a performance rating of B- (Good) based on an annualized return of 8.61% over the last three years and a total return of 0.86% year to date 2015. Factored into the performance evaluation is an expense ratio of 3.25% (high).

The fund's risk rating is currently B- (Good). It carries a beta of 0.82, meaning the fund's expected move will be 8.2% for every 10% move in the market. Volatility, as measured by both the semi-deviation and a drawdown factor, is considered low. As of December 31, 2015, Clough Global Allocation Fund traded at a discount of 10.62% below its net asset value, which is worse than its one-year historical average discount of 13.45%.

Charles I. Clough, Jr. has been running the fund for 12 years and currently receives a manager quality ranking of 45 (0=worst, 99=best). If you desire only a moderate level of risk and strong performance, then this fund is an excellent option.

Data Date	Investment Rating	Net Assets ($Mil)	Price	Performance Rating/Pts	Total Return Y-T-D	Risk Rating/Pts
12-15	B	176.97	13.47	B- / 7.1	0.86%	B- / 7.6
2014	B	174.20	14.77	C+ / 6.7	6.75%	B / 8.6
2013	C+	181.31	15.38	C+ / 6.1	18.98%	B- / 7.6
2012	C-	170.12	13.70	C- / 3.8	19.25%	B- / 7.3
2011	C-	156.20	12.75	C- / 4.2	-12.19%	B- / 7.4
2010	D+	176.32	15.76	D+ / 2.9	10.41%	C / 5.5

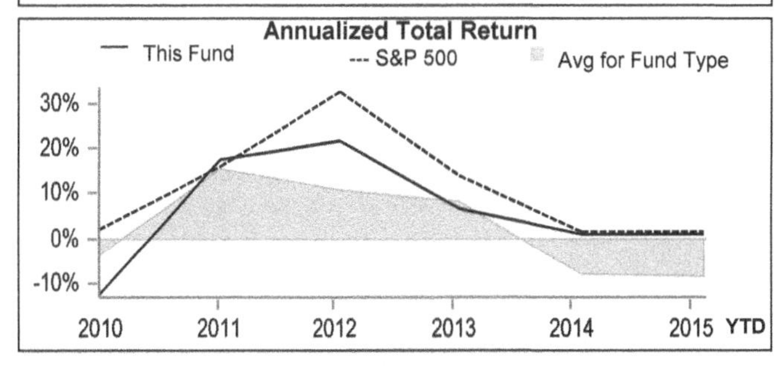

Clough Global Equity Fund (GLQ) C+ Fair

Fund Family: Clough Capital Partners LP
Fund Type: Global
Inception Date: April 26, 2005

Major Rating Factors: Middle of the road best describes Clough Global Equity Fund whose TheStreet.com Investment Rating is currently a C+ (Fair). The fund currently has a performance rating of C+ (Fair) based on an annualized return of 7.48% over the last three years and a total return of -5.41% year to date 2015. Factored into the performance evaluation is an expense ratio of 3.68% (high).

The fund's risk rating is currently B- (Good). It carries a beta of 0.74, meaning the fund's expected move will be 7.4% for every 10% move in the market. Volatility, as measured by both the semi-deviation and a drawdown factor, is considered low. As of December 31, 2015, Clough Global Equity Fund traded at a discount of 13.65% below its net asset value, which is better than its one-year historical average discount of 12.19%.

Charles I. Clough, Jr. has been running the fund for 11 years and currently receives a manager quality ranking of 88 (0=worst, 99=best). If you desire an average level of risk, then this fund may be an option.

Data Date	Investment Rating	Net Assets ($Mil)	Price	Performance Rating/Pts	Total Return Y-T-D	Risk Rating/Pts
12-15	C+	293.83	12.53	C+ / 6.1	-5.41%	B- / 7.2
2014	B	290.30	14.48	C+ / 6.9	3.71%	B / 8.5
2013	C+	296.71	15.71	C+ / 6.8	25.37%	B- / 7.5
2012	C	277.06	13.00	C / 4.8	22.30%	B- / 7.3
2011	C-	254.70	12.04	C / 4.4	-13.31%	B- / 7.4
2010	C-	409.63	15.12	C- / 4.1	15.67%	C / 5.0

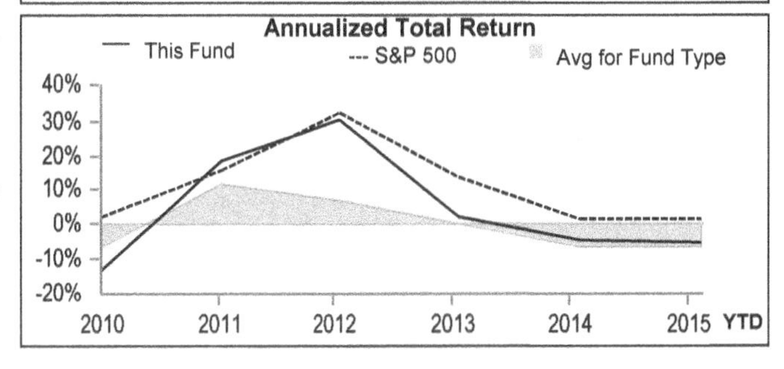

Clough Global Opportunities Fund (GLO) C Fair

Fund Family: Clough Capital Partners LP
Fund Type: Global
Inception Date: April 25, 2006

Major Rating Factors: Middle of the road best describes Clough Global Opportunities Fund whose TheStreet.com Investment Rating is currently a C (Fair). The fund currently has a performance rating of C (Fair) based on an annualized return of 5.16% over the last three years and a total return of -9.34% year to date 2015. Factored into the performance evaluation is an expense ratio of 3.86% (high).

The fund's risk rating is currently B- (Good). It carries a beta of 0.70, meaning the fund's expected move will be 7.0% for every 10% move in the market. Volatility, as measured by both the semi-deviation and a drawdown factor, is considered low. As of December 31, 2015, Clough Global Opportunities Fund traded at a discount of 16.01% below its net asset value, which is better than its one-year historical average discount of 13.68%.

Charles I. Clough, Jr. has been running the fund for 10 years and currently receives a manager quality ranking of 82 (0=worst, 99=best). If you desire an average level of risk, then this fund may be an option.

Data Date	Investment Rating	Net Assets ($Mil)	Price	Performance Rating/Pts	Total Return Y-T-D	Risk Rating/Pts
12-15	C	729.86	10.44	C / 5.4	-9.34%	B- / 7.2
2014	B+	719.50	12.82	B- / 7.5	10.62%	B / 8.5
2013	C+	757.45	13.07	C+ / 5.9	16.52%	B- / 7.5
2012	C	716.21	11.74	C / 4.9	24.12%	B- / 7.3
2011	C-	657.70	10.57	C- / 3.8	-14.32%	B- / 7.3
2010	D+	759.60	13.45	C- / 3.7	13.63%	C / 5.2

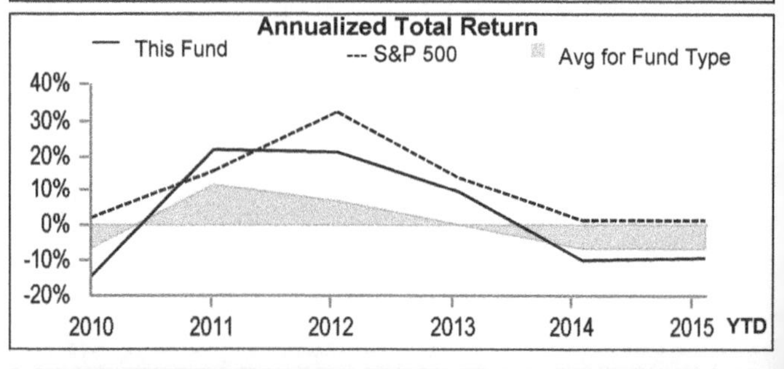

Cohen & Steers Closed-End Opp Fd (FOF) C Fair

Fund Family: Cohen & Steers Capital Management I
Fund Type: Global
Inception Date: November 24, 2006

Major Rating Factors: Middle of the road best describes Cohen & Steers Closed-End Opp Fd whose TheStreet.com Investment Rating is currently a C (Fair). The fund currently has a performance rating of C (Fair) based on an annualized return of 2.98% over the last three years and a total return of -9.01% year to date 2015. Factored into the performance evaluation is an expense ratio of 0.95% (low).

The fund's risk rating is currently B- (Good). It carries a beta of 0.50, meaning the fund's expected move will be 5.0% for every 10% move in the market. Volatility, as measured by both the semi-deviation and a drawdown factor, is considered low. As of December 31, 2015, Cohen & Steers Closed-End Opp Fd traded at a discount of 11.18% below its net asset value, which is better than its one-year historical average discount of 10.61%.

Douglas R. Bond currently receives a manager quality ranking of 78 (0=worst, 99=best). If you desire an average level of risk, then this fund may be an option.

Data Date	Investment Rating	Net Assets ($Mil)	Price	Performance Rating/Pts	Total Return Y-T-D	Risk Rating/Pts
12-15	C	392.40	10.96	C / 4.9	-9.01%	B- / 7.3
2014	B	382.70	13.16	C+ / 6.0	13.37%	B / 8.9
2013	C+	381.30	12.57	C / 5.0	5.82%	B / 8.5
2012	C	354.40	12.42	C / 4.6	14.30%	B / 8.4
2011	C+	389.10	11.97	C+ / 5.7	-1.23%	B / 8.3
2010	C	344.90	13.03	C / 5.0	16.13%	C+ / 6.0

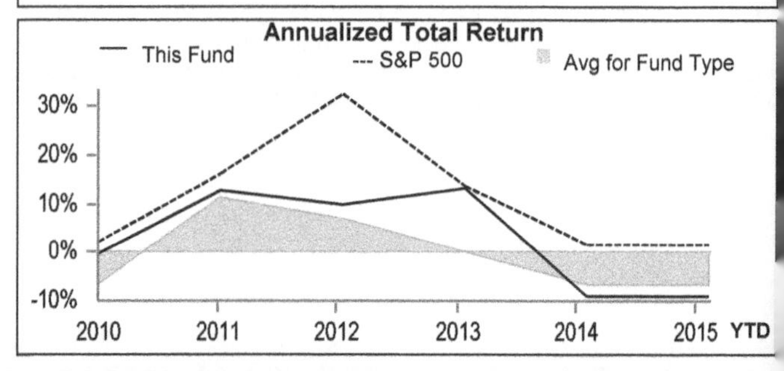

Cohen & Steers Global Inc Builder (INB) C+ Fair

Fund Family: Cohen & Steers Capital Management I
Fund Type: Global
Inception Date: July 27, 2007

Major Rating Factors: Middle of the road best describes Cohen & Steers Global Inc Builder whose TheStreet.com Investment Rating is currently a C+ (Fair). The fund currently has a performance rating of C+ (Fair) based on an annualized return of 6.61% over the last three years and a total return of -9.27% year to date 2015. Factored into the performance evaluation is an expense ratio of 1.72% (above average).

The fund's risk rating is currently B- (Good). It carries a beta of 0.73, meaning the fund's expected move will be 7.3% for every 10% move in the market. Volatility, as measured by both the semi-deviation and a drawdown factor, is considered low. As of December 31, 2015, Cohen & Steers Global Inc Builder traded at a discount of 8.33% below its net asset value, which is better than its one-year historical average discount of 3.99%.

Douglas R. Bond currently receives a manager quality ranking of 85 (0=worst, 99=best). If you desire an average level of risk, then this fund may be an option.

Data Date	Investment Rating	Net Assets ($Mil)	Price	Performance Rating/Pts	Total Return Y-T-D	Risk Rating/Pts
12-15	C+	269.10	9.46	C+ / 5.7	-9.27%	B- / 7.4
2014	B-	283.50	11.74	B / 7.6	15.26%	C+ / 6.9
2013	C+	260.90	11.34	B- / 7.0	17.38%	B- / 7.5
2012	C-	245.70	10.32	C / 4.5	23.61%	B- / 7.2
2011	C	276.10	9.30	C / 5.4	-5.61%	B- / 7.1
2010	D	224.60	11.21	C- / 3.1	10.13%	C / 4.4

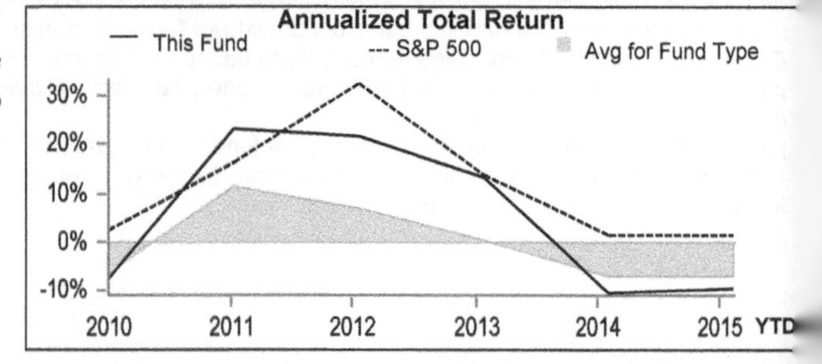

Cohen Steers Ltd Dur Pref and Inc (LDP) C+ Fair

Fund Family: Cohen & Steers Capital Management I
Fund Type: Global
Inception Date: July 27, 2012

Major Rating Factors: Middle of the road best describes Cohen Steers Ltd Dur Pref and Inc whose TheStreet.com Investment Rating is currently a C+ (Fair). The fund currently has a performance rating of C+ (Fair) based on an annualized return of 4.35% over the last three years and a total return of 6.02% year to date 2015. Factored into the performance evaluation is an expense ratio of 1.57% (above average).

The fund's risk rating is currently B- (Good). It carries a beta of 0.24, meaning the fund's expected move will be 2.4% for every 10% move in the market. Volatility, as measured by both the semi-deviation and a drawdown factor, is considered low. As of December 31, 2015, Cohen Steers Ltd Dur Pref and Inc traded at a discount of 10.88% below its net asset value, which is better than its one-year historical average discount of 9.29%.

Joseph M. Harvey currently receives a manager quality ranking of 91 (0=worst, 99=best). If you desire an average level of risk, then this fund may be an option.

Data Date	Investment Rating	Net Assets ($Mil)	Price	Performance Rating/Pts	Total Return Y-T-D	Risk Rating/Pts
12-15	C+	740.90	22.52	C+ / 6.1	6.02%	B- / 7.5
2014	C-	722.80	22.66	C- / 3.3	9.02%	B- / 7.8
2013	D+	711.80	22.62	D / 2.1	-3.21%	B / 8.2

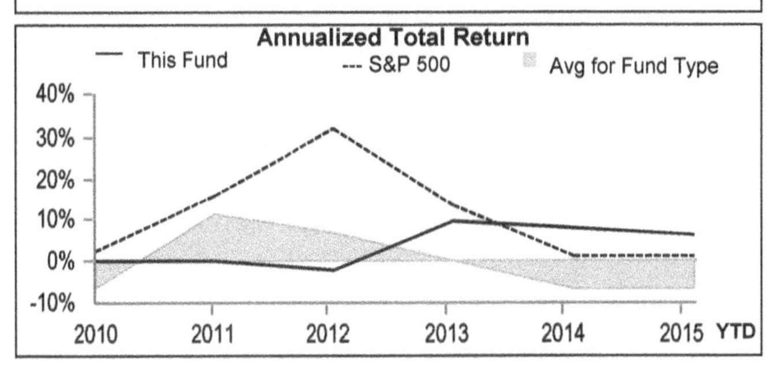

Cohen&Steers Infrastructure Fund (UTF) C+ Fair

Fund Family: Cohen & Steers Capital Management I
Fund Type: Utilities
Inception Date: March 26, 2004

Major Rating Factors: Middle of the road best describes Cohen&Steers Infrastructure Fund whose TheStreet.com Investment Rating is currently a C+ (Fair). The fund currently has a performance rating of C+ (Fair) based on an annualized return of 7.18% over the last three years and a total return of -9.74% year to date 2015. Factored into the performance evaluation is an expense ratio of 2.01% (high).

The fund's risk rating is currently B- (Good). It carries a beta of 0.66, meaning the fund's expected move will be 6.6% for every 10% move in the market. Volatility, as measured by both the semi-deviation and a drawdown factor, is considered low. As of December 31, 2015, Cohen&Steers Infrastructure Fund traded at a discount of 14.13% below its net asset value, which is worse than its one-year historical average discount of 14.42%.

Robert S. Becker has been running the fund for 12 years and currently receives a manager quality ranking of 66 (0=worst, 99=best). If you desire an average level of risk, then this fund may be an option.

Data Date	Investment Rating	Net Assets ($Mil)	Price	Performance Rating/Pts	Total Return Y-T-D	Risk Rating/Pts
12-15	C+	2,210.30	19.08	C+ / 6.1	-9.74%	B- / 7.0
2014	A-	2,007.70	22.72	B / 8.1	18.92%	B / 8.2
2013	B	1,769.37	20.60	B / 7.6	13.90%	B / 8.3
2012	B+	1,609.10	18.75	B / 8.0	26.40%	B / 8.3
2011	B-	1,593.10	15.80	B- / 7.0	8.14%	B- / 7.7
2010	D	1,314.10	16.42	D / 1.7	11.40%	C / 5.4

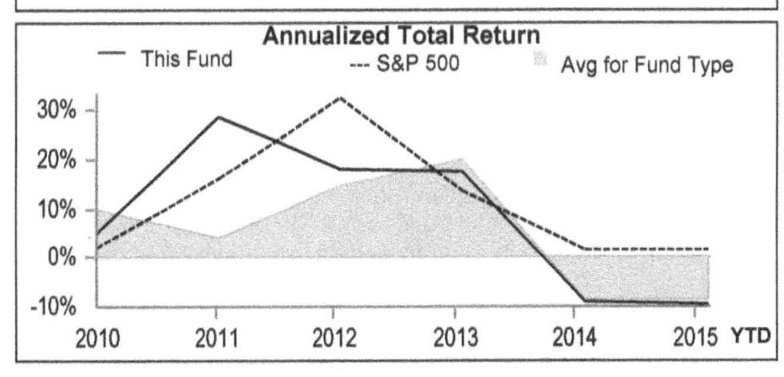

Cohen&Steers MLP Inc and Energy Op (MIE) D- Weak

Fund Family: Cohen & Steers Capital Management I
Fund Type: Income
Inception Date: March 26, 2013

Major Rating Factors:
Very poor performance is the major factor driving the D- (Weak) TheStreet.com Investment Rating for Cohen&Steers MLP Inc and Energy Op. The fund currently has a performance rating of E- (Very Weak) based on an annualized return of 0.00% over the last three years and a total return of -42.76% year to date 2015. Factored into the performance evaluation is an expense ratio of 2.26% (high).

The fund's risk rating is currently C (Fair). It carries a beta of 0.00, meaning the fund's expected move will be 0.0% for every 10% move in the market. Volatility, as measured by both the semi-deviation and a drawdown factor, is considered average. As of December 31, 2015, Cohen&Steers MLP Inc and Energy Op traded at a discount of 3.77% below its net asset value, which is worse than its one-year historical average discount of 10.11%.

This fund has been team managed for 3 years and currently receives a manager quality ranking of 1 (0=worst, 99=best). This fund offers an average level of risk but investors looking for strong performance will be frustrated.

Data Date	Investment Rating	Net Assets ($Mil)	Price	Performance Rating/Pts	Total Return Y-T-D	Risk Rating/Pts
12-15	D-	604.30	10.46	E- / 0.1	-42.76%	C / 4.7
2014	C-	634.50	19.62	C- / 4.0	14.82%	B- / 7.8

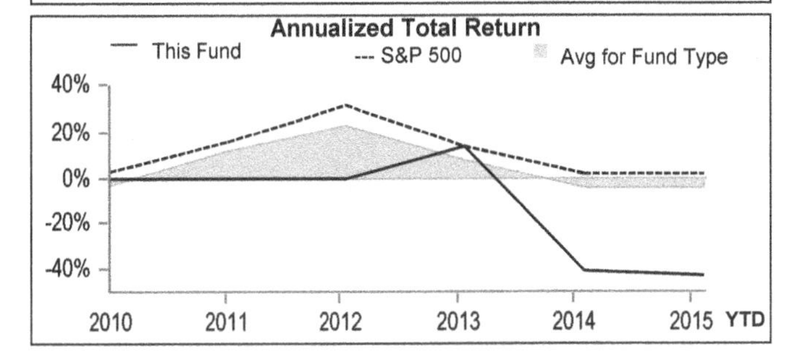

* Denotes ETF Fund

Cohen&Steers Quality Income Realty (RQI) B+ Good

Fund Family: Cohen & Steers Capital Management I
Fund Type: Growth and Income
Inception Date: February 25, 2002

Major Rating Factors:
Exceptional performance is the major factor driving the B+ (Good) TheStreet.com Investment Rating for Cohen&Steers Quality Income Realty. The fund currently has a performance rating of A- (Excellent) based on an annualized return of 13.33% over the last three years and a total return of 7.82% year to date 2015. Factored into the performance evaluation is an expense ratio of 1.89% (above average).

The fund's risk rating is currently C+ (Fair). It carries a beta of 0.32, meaning the fund's expected move will be 3.2% for every 10% move in the market. Volatility, as measured by both the semi-deviation and a drawdown factor, is considered low. As of December 31, 2015, Cohen&Steers Quality Income Realty traded at a discount of 9.21% below its net asset value, which is worse than its one-year historical average discount of 12.74%.

Joseph M. Harvey currently receives a manager quality ranking of 94 (0=worst, 99=best). If you desire only a moderate level of risk and strong performance, then this fund is an excellent option.

Data Date	Investment Rating	Net Assets ($Mil)	Price	Performance Rating/Pts	Total Return Y-T-D	Risk Rating/Pts
12-15	B+	1,484.80	12.22	A- / 9.1	7.82%	C+ / 6.8
2014	A+	1,154.10	12.19	A / 9.4	37.17%	B- / 7.6
2013	C	1,200.82	9.48	C / 5.4	-2.46%	B- / 7.2
2012	B+	1,191.30	10.16	A / 9.4	27.83%	B- / 7.0
2011	B-	1,051.80	8.47	A+ / 9.7	4.34%	C / 5.0
2010	D+	852.60	8.65	C / 5.4	53.21%	C- / 3.0

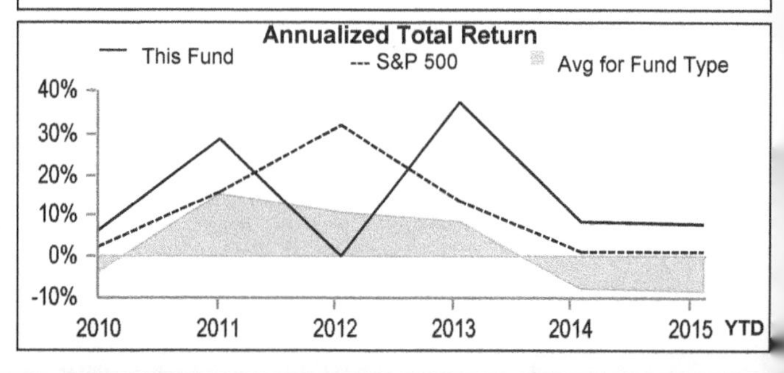

Cohen&Steers REIT& Preferred Incom (RNP) B+ Good

Fund Family: Cohen & Steers Capital Management I
Fund Type: Income
Inception Date: June 25, 2003

Major Rating Factors: Strong performance is the major factor driving the B+ (Good) TheStreet.com Investment Rating for Cohen&Steers REIT& Preferred Incom. The fund currently has a performance rating of B (Good) based on an annualized return of 9.68% over the last three years and a total return of 4.39% year to date 2015. Factored into the performance evaluation is an expense ratio of 1.71% (above average).

The fund's risk rating is currently B- (Good). It carries a beta of 0.42, meaning the fund's expected move will be 4.2% for every 10% move in the market. Volatility, as measured by both the semi-deviation and a drawdown factor, is considered low. As of December 31, 2015, Cohen&Steers REIT& Preferred Incom traded at a discount of 14.75% below its net asset value, which is worse than its one-year historical average discount of 15.25%.

Joseph M. Harvey has been running the fund for 13 years and currently receives a manager quality ranking of 88 (0=worst, 99=best). If you desire only a moderate level of risk and strong performance, then this fund is an excellent option.

Data Date	Investment Rating	Net Assets ($Mil)	Price	Performance Rating/Pts	Total Return Y-T-D	Risk Rating/Pts
12-15	B+	1,032.70	18.44	B / 8.1	4.39%	B- / 7.2
2014	A-	854.30	18.99	B+ / 8.7	29.19%	B- / 7.7
2013	C+	883.12	15.70	C+ / 6.0	-3.18%	B- / 7.3
2012	A-	737.70	16.99	A / 9.4	29.34%	B- / 7.5
2011	B	750.90	14.15	A+ / 9.9	12.24%	C+ / 6.2
2010	C+	632.80	14.29	B+ / 8.6	49.38%	C- / 3.6

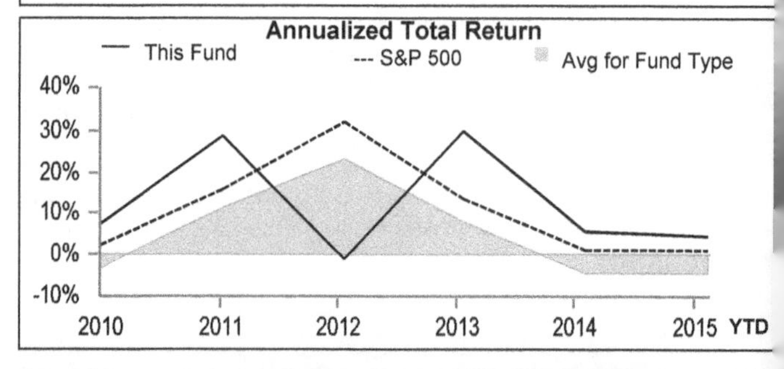

Cohen&Steers Sel Preferred & Incom (PSF) B- Good

Fund Family: Cohen & Steers Capital Management I
Fund Type: Income
Inception Date: November 24, 2010

Major Rating Factors: Strong performance is the major factor driving the B- (Good) TheStreet.com Investment Rating for Cohen&Steers Sel Preferred & Incom. The fund currently has a performance rating of B- (Good) based on an annualized return of 6.20% over the last three years and a total return of 5.03% year to date 2015. Factored into the performance evaluation is an expense ratio of 1.57% (above average).

The fund's risk rating is currently B- (Good). It carries a beta of 0.41, meaning the fund's expected move will be 4.1% for every 10% move in the market. Volatility, as measured by both the semi-deviation and a drawdown factor, is considered low. As of December 31, 2015, Cohen&Steers Sel Preferred & Incom traded at a discount of 6.88% below its net asset value, which is worse than its one-year historical average discount of 7.56%.

Joseph M. Harvey currently receives a manager quality ranking of 76 (0=worst, 99=best). If you desire only a moderate level of risk and strong performance, then this fund is an excellent option.

Data Date	Investment Rating	Net Assets ($Mil)	Price	Performance Rating/Pts	Total Return Y-T-D	Risk Rating/Pts
12-15	B-	325.60	24.90	B- / 7.1	5.03%	B- / 7.5
2014	B	314.20	25.70	B- / 7.1	16.75%	B / 8.2
2013	C+	325.74	24.69	C / 5.3	-2.98%	B / 8.3
2012	A+	271.40	26.76	A+ / 9.7	35.33%	B / 8.7
2011	D+	0.00	21.68	D / 1.6	-1.79%	B / 8.7

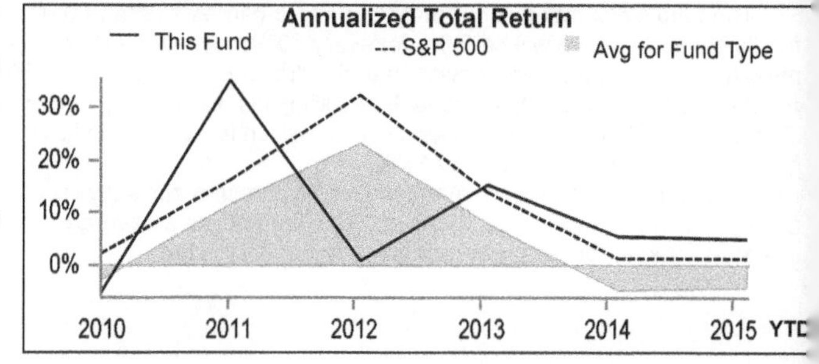

Cohen&Steers Total Return Realty (RFI) C Fair

Fund Family: Cohen & Steers Capital Management I
Fund Type: Growth and Income
Inception Date: September 17, 1993

Major Rating Factors: Middle of the road best describes Cohen&Steers Total Return Realty whose TheStreet.com Investment Rating is currently a C (Fair). The fund currently has a performance rating of C+ (Fair) based on an annualized return of 2.27% over the last three years and a total return of 3.19% year to date 2015. Factored into the performance evaluation is an expense ratio of 0.94% (low).

The fund's risk rating is currently B- (Good). It carries a beta of 0.42, meaning the fund's expected move will be 4.2% for every 10% move in the market. Volatility, as measured by both the semi-deviation and a drawdown factor, is considered low. As of December 31, 2015, Cohen&Steers Total Return Realty traded at a discount of 7.35% below its net asset value, which is worse than its one-year historical average discount of 8.45%.

Joseph M. Harvey currently receives a manager quality ranking of 51 (0=worst, 99=best). If you desire an average level of risk, then this fund may be an option.

Data Date	Investment Rating	Net Assets ($Mil)	Price	Performance Rating/Pts	Total Return Y-T-D	Risk Rating/Pts
12-15	C	369.80	12.60	C+ / 5.7	3.19%	B- / 7.1
2014	B	117.30	13.20	B / 7.6	19.77%	B- / 7.6
2013	D+	124.10	11.99	C- / 3.0	-14.03%	B- / 7.5
2012	A-	128.80	14.72	A / 9.5	30.01%	B- / 7.4
2011	C+	117.90	11.91	B / 7.6	-8.47%	C+ / 6.7
2010	B	107.40	14.88	A / 9.5	71.18%	C- / 3.4

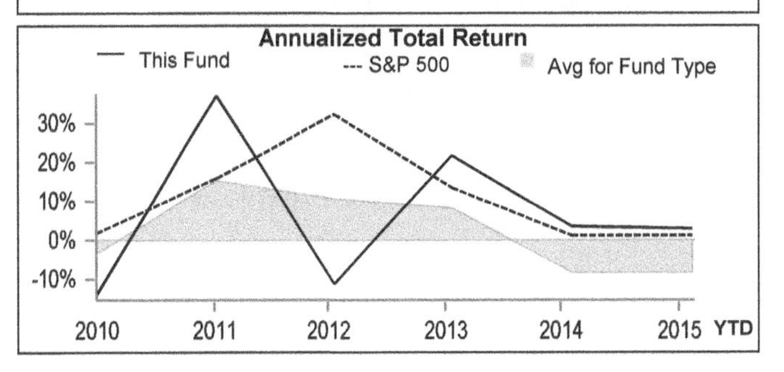

Columbia Seligman Prem Tech Gro (STK) A- Excellent

Fund Family: Columbia Management Inv Advisers LL
Fund Type: Growth
Inception Date: November 30, 2009

Major Rating Factors:
Exceptional performance is the major factor driving the A- (Excellent) TheStreet.com Investment Rating for Columbia Seligman Prem Tech Gro. The fund currently has a performance rating of A (Excellent) based on an annualized return of 18.87% over the last three years and a total return of 4.43% year to date 2015. Factored into the performance evaluation is an expense ratio of 1.17% (low).

The fund's risk rating is currently C+ (Fair). It carries a beta of 0.74, meaning the fund's expected move will be 7.4% for every 10% move in the market. Volatility, as measured by both the semi-deviation and a drawdown factor, is considered low. As of December 31, 2015, Columbia Seligman Prem Tech Gro traded at a premium of 3.70% above its net asset value, which is worse than its one-year historical average premium of 2.80%.

Ajay Diwan currently receives a manager quality ranking of 93 (0=worst, 99=best). If you desire only a moderate level of risk and strong performance, then this fund is an excellent option.

Data Date	Investment Rating	Net Assets ($Mil)	Price	Performance Rating/Pts	Total Return Y-T-D	Risk Rating/Pts
12-15	A-	271.30	17.93	A / 9.4	4.43%	C+ / 6.9
2014	B	267.80	18.93	A / 9.4	48.37%	C / 5.5
2013	D+	234.61	14.39	C- / 3.6	7.62%	B- / 7.0
2012	D	260.82	14.51	D / 1.6	3.36%	B- / 7.0
2011	D	260.80	15.66	D- / 1.4	-7.82%	B- / 7.7
2010	A	0.00	19.17	B / 7.9	6.01%	B / 8.0

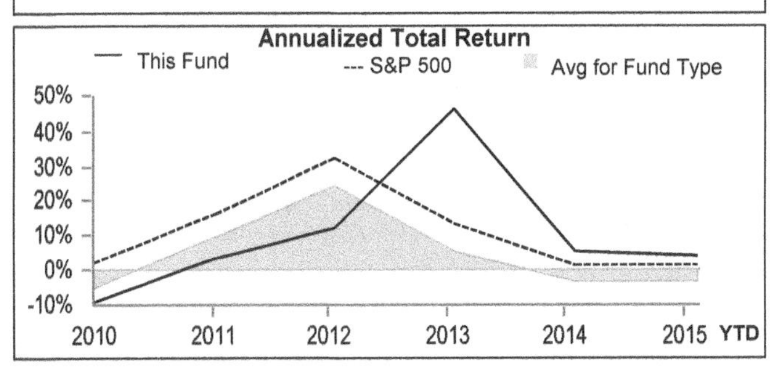

Cornerstone Strategic Value Fund (CLM) C Fair

Fund Family: Cornerstone Advisors Inc
Fund Type: Income
Inception Date: June 30, 1987

Major Rating Factors: Middle of the road best describes Cornerstone Strategic Value Fund whose TheStreet.com Investment Rating is currently a C (Fair). The fund currently has a performance rating of C (Fair) based on an annualized return of 4.26% over the last three years and a total return of -0.65% year to date 2015. Factored into the performance evaluation is an expense ratio of 1.33% (average).

The fund's risk rating is currently C+ (Fair). It carries a beta of 0.99, meaning that its performance tracks fairly well with that of the overall stock market. Volatility, as measured by both the semi-deviation and a drawdown factor, is considered low. As of December 31, 2015, Cornerstone Strategic Value Fund traded at a premium of 3.64% above its net asset value, which is better than its one-year historical average premium of 8.18%.

Ralph W. Bradshaw has been running the fund for 15 years and currently receives a manager quality ranking of 22 (0=worst, 99=best). If you desire an average level of risk, then this fund may be an option.

Data Date	Investment Rating	Net Assets ($Mil)	Price	Performance Rating/Pts	Total Return Y-T-D	Risk Rating/Pts
12-15	C	168.29	15.66	C / 5.5	-0.65%	C+ / 6.2
2014	C-	51.50	20.02	C / 4.9	-5.64%	C+ / 6.6
2013	C-	102.92	6.60	C+ / 6.1	24.08%	C+ / 5.6
2012	D-	87.14	6.00	D- / 1.3	18.31%	C / 4.9
2011	D-	64.27	6.60	D+ / 2.4	-11.01%	C / 5.5
2010	D-	57.45	8.84	E+ / 0.8	-10.20%	C / 4.3

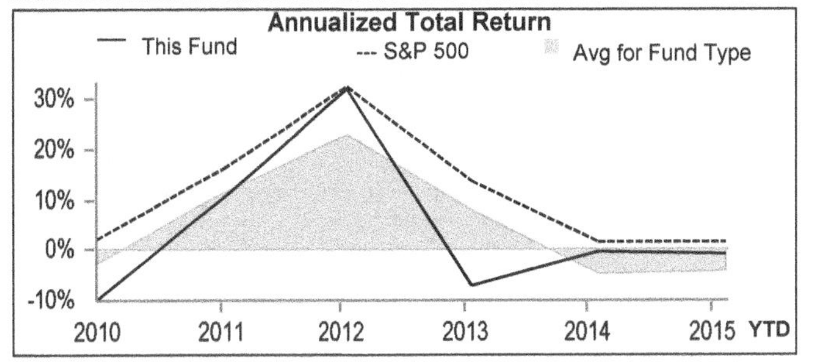

Cornerstone Total Return Fund (CRF) C+ Fair

Fund Family: Cornerstone Advisors Inc
Fund Type: Income
Inception Date: May 3, 1973

Major Rating Factors: Strong performance is the major factor driving the C+ (Fair) TheStreet.com Investment Rating for Cornerstone Total Return Fund. The fund currently has a performance rating of B- (Good) based on an annualized return of 9.95% over the last three years and a total return of 7.45% year to date 2015. Factored into the performance evaluation is an expense ratio of 1.44% (average).

The fund's risk rating is currently C+ (Fair). It carries a beta of 0.78, meaning the fund's expected move will be 7.8% for every 10% move in the market. Volatility, as measured by both the semi-deviation and a drawdown factor, is considered low. As of December 31, 2015, Cornerstone Total Return Fund traded at a premium of 12.23% above its net asset value, which is better than its one-year historical average premium of 19.83%.

Ralph W. Bradshaw currently receives a manager quality ranking of 74 (0=worst, 99=best). If you desire only a moderate level of risk and strong performance, then this fund is an excellent option.

Data Date	Investment Rating	Net Assets ($Mil)	Price	Performance Rating/Pts	Total Return Y-T-D	Risk Rating/Pts
12-15	C+	83.68	16.89	B- / 7.5	7.45%	C+ / 5.6
2014	C	88.00	5.00	C+ / 5.9	0.04%	C+ / 6.6
2013	C-	51.04	6.05	C+ / 6.1	27.06%	C+ / 5.6
2012	D-	35.92	5.36	D- / 1.1	13.65%	C / 5.0
2011	D-	25.91	5.97	D / 1.7	-12.04%	C / 5.0
2010	E+	17.08	7.88	E+ / 0.7	-9.94%	C- / 4.1

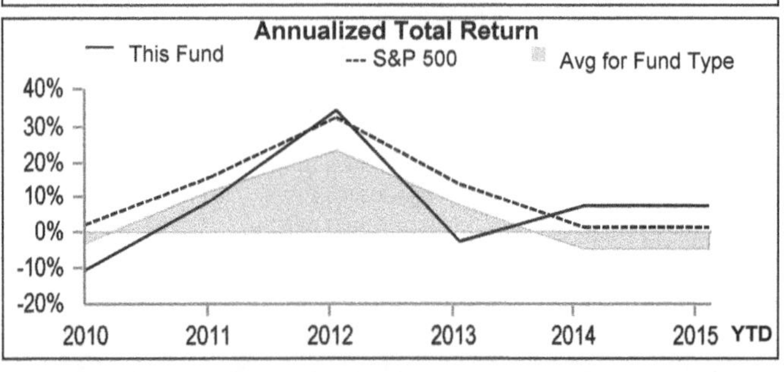

Credit Suisse Asset Mgmt Income (CIK) D+ Weak

Fund Family: Credit Suisse Asset Management LLC
Fund Type: Corporate - High Yield
Inception Date: April 8, 1987

Major Rating Factors:
Disappointing performance is the major factor driving the D+ (Weak) TheStreet.com Investment Rating for Credit Suisse Asset Mgmt Income. The fund currently has a performance rating of D+ (Weak) based on an annualized return of -4.41% over the last three years and a total return of -7.30% year to date 2015. Factored into the performance evaluation is an expense ratio of 0.71% (very low).

The fund's risk rating is currently C+ (Fair). It carries a beta of 1.26, meaning it is expected to move 12.6% for every 10% move in the market. Volatility, as measured by both the semi-deviation and a drawdown factor, is considered low. As of December 31, 2015, Credit Suisse Asset Mgmt Income traded at a discount of 13.40% below its net asset value, which is better than its one-year historical average discount of 13.33%.

Thomas J. Flannery currently receives a manager quality ranking of 25 (0=worst, 99=best). This fund offers only a moderate level of risk but investors looking for strong performance are still waiting.

Data Date	Investment Rating	Net Assets ($Mil)	Price	Performance Rating/Pts	Total Return Y-T-D	Risk Rating/Pts
12-15	D+	189.34	2.78	D+ / 2.8	-7.30%	C+ / 6.7
2014	C-	201.20	3.29	C- / 3.6	-0.08%	B- / 7.9
2013	C	197.17	3.56	C / 5.3	-5.10%	B- / 7.3
2012	B+	184.89	4.03	B- / 7.4	21.64%	B / 8.5
2011	B+	180.00	3.65	B / 7.8	14.55%	B / 8.4
2010	C+	176.38	3.56	B / 7.6	16.04%	C / 4.7

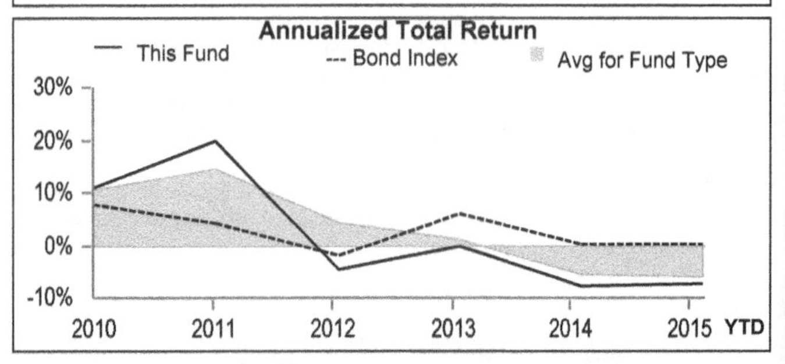

Credit Suisse High Yield Bond Fund (DHY) C- Fair

Fund Family: Credit Suisse Asset Management LLC
Fund Type: Corporate - High Yield
Inception Date: July 28, 1998

Major Rating Factors: Middle of the road best describes Credit Suisse High Yield Bond Fund whose TheStreet.com Investment Rating is currently a C- (Fair). The fund currently has a performance rating of C- (Fair) based on an annualized return of -1.23% over the last three years and a total return of -8.81% year to date 2015. Factored into the performance evaluation is an expense ratio of 1.82% (above average).

The fund's risk rating is currently B- (Good). It carries a beta of 1.71, meaning it is expected to move 17.1% for every 10% move in the market. Volatility, as measured by both the semi-deviation and a drawdown factor, is considered low. As of December 31, 2015, Credit Suisse High Yield Bond Fund traded at a discount of 5.39% below its net asset value, which is worse than its one-year historical average discount of 7.27%.

Thomas J. Flannery currently receives a manager quality ranking of 37 (0=worst, 99=best). If you desire an average level of risk, then this fund may be an option.

Data Date	Investment Rating	Net Assets ($Mil)	Price	Performance Rating/Pts	Total Return Y-T-D	Risk Rating/Pts
12-15	C-	302.74	2.28	C- / 3.5	-8.81%	B- / 7.0
2014	C	310.30	2.80	C / 4.5	-0.22%	B / 8.2
2013	C+	276.72	3.07	C+ / 6.8	5.90%	C+ / 6.8
2012	B-	212.12	3.20	C+ / 6.1	23.25%	B / 8.6
2011	B+	210.60	2.88	B+ / 8.8	10.26%	B / 8.0
2010	C-	165.31	2.89	C+ / 6.6	10.19%	C- / 3.1

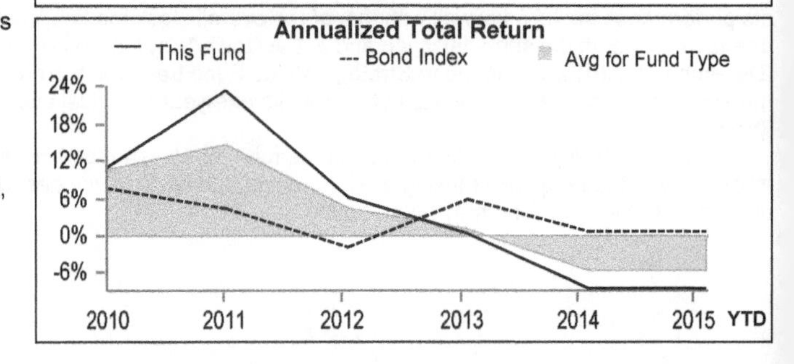

Cushing Energy Income (SRF) E- Very Weak

Fund Family: Cushing Asset Management LP
Fund Type: US Government/Agency
Inception Date: February 28, 2012

Major Rating Factors: Cushing Energy Income has adopted a very risky asset allocation strategy and currently receives an overall TheStreet.com Investment Rating of E- (Very Weak). The fund has a high level of volatility, as measured by both semi-deviation and drawdown factors. It carries a beta of -0.99, meaning the fund's expected move will be -9.9% for every 10% move in the market. As of December 31, 2015, Cushing Energy Income traded at a discount of 10.33% below its net asset value, which is better than its one-year historical average discount of 8.48%. Unfortunately, the high level of risk (D, Weak) failed to pay off as investors endured very poor performance.

The fund's performance rating is currently E- (Very Weak). It has registered an annualized return of -45.48% over the last three years and is down -75.37% year to date 2015. Factored into the performance evaluation is an expense ratio of 2.39% (high).

Jerry V. Swank currently receives a manager quality ranking of 1 (0=worst, 99=best). If you can tolerate very high levels of risk in the hope of improved future returns, holding this fund may be an option.

Data Date	Investment Rating	Net Assets ($Mil)	Price	Performance Rating/Pts	Total Return Y-T-D	Risk Rating/Pts
12-15	E-	150.71	8.42	E- / 0.1	-75.37%	D / 1.8
2014	E-	219.40	7.87	E- / 0	-46.66%	E+ / 0.6
2013	D	185.38	16.97	D- / 1.5	-6.08%	C+ / 6.8

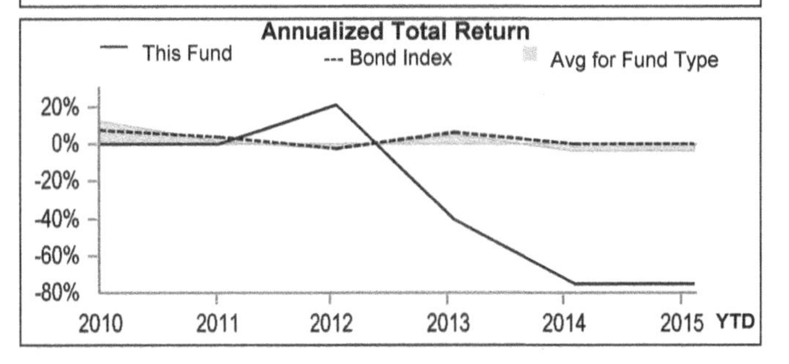

Cushing Renaissance (SZC) D Weak

Fund Family: Cushing Asset Management LP
Fund Type: Income
Inception Date: September 25, 2012

Major Rating Factors:
Disappointing performance is the major factor driving the D (Weak) TheStreet.com Investment Rating for Cushing Renaissance. The fund currently has a performance rating of D (Weak) based on an annualized return of -8.97% over the last three years and a total return of -27.13% year to date 2015. Factored into the performance evaluation is an expense ratio of 1.96% (above average).

The fund's risk rating is currently C (Fair). It carries a beta of 1.26, meaning it is expected to move 12.6% for every 10% move in the market. Volatility, as measured by both the semi-deviation and a drawdown factor, is considered average. As of December 31, 2015, Cushing Renaissance traded at a discount of 16.11% below its net asset value, which is better than its one-year historical average discount of 15.72%.

Jerry V. Swank has been running the fund for 4 years and currently receives a manager quality ranking of 6 (0=worst, 99=best). This fund offers an average level of risk but investors looking for strong performance will be frustrated.

Data Date	Investment Rating	Net Assets ($Mil)	Price	Performance Rating/Pts	Total Return Y-T-D	Risk Rating/Pts
12-15	D	156.09	14.27	D / 1.6	-27.13%	C / 5.1
2014	D	158.00	21.32	E+ / 0.6	-8.83%	C+ / 6.8
2013	B+	162.92	25.04	B / 7.6	12.57%	B / 8.7

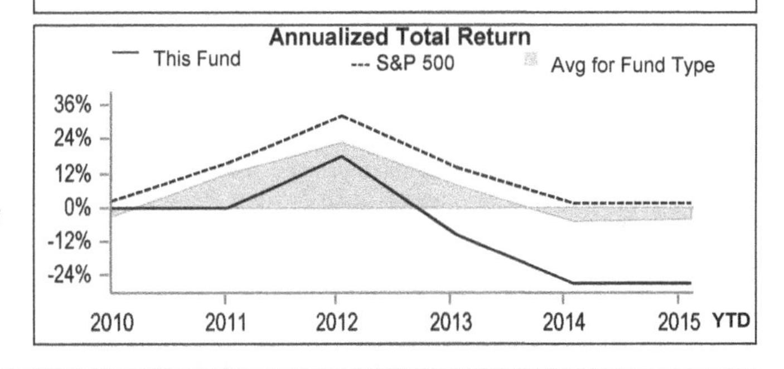

Cutwater Select Income (CSI) C+ Fair

Fund Family: Cutwater Asset Management Corp
Fund Type: Corporate - Investment Grade
Inception Date: September 29, 1971

Major Rating Factors: Middle of the road best describes Cutwater Select Income whose TheStreet.com Investment Rating is currently a C+ (Fair). The fund currently has a performance rating of C (Fair) based on an annualized return of 2.43% over the last three years and a total return of 0.21% year to date 2015. Factored into the performance evaluation is an expense ratio of 0.74% (very low).

The fund's risk rating is currently B- (Good). It carries a beta of 1.45, meaning it is expected to move 14.5% for every 10% move in the market. Volatility, as measured by both the semi-deviation and a drawdown factor, is considered low. As of December 31, 2015, Cutwater Select Income traded at a discount of 7.17% below its net asset value, which is worse than its one-year historical average discount of 7.59%.

Gautam Khanna has been running the fund for 11 years and currently receives a manager quality ranking of 75 (0=worst, 99=best). If you desire an average level of risk, then this fund may be an option.

Data Date	Investment Rating	Net Assets ($Mil)	Price	Performance Rating/Pts	Total Return Y-T-D	Risk Rating/Pts
12-15	C+	230.46	18.26	C / 5.3	0.21%	B- / 7.8
2014	C+	229.00	19.34	C / 4.9	12.64%	B / 8.3
2013	C+	230.61	18.31	C / 4.9	-4.11%	B / 8.6
2012	B-	218.32	19.65	C / 5.1	12.22%	B+ / 9.6
2010	B-	125.25	17.70	C+ / 6.6	15.48%	B- / 7.5

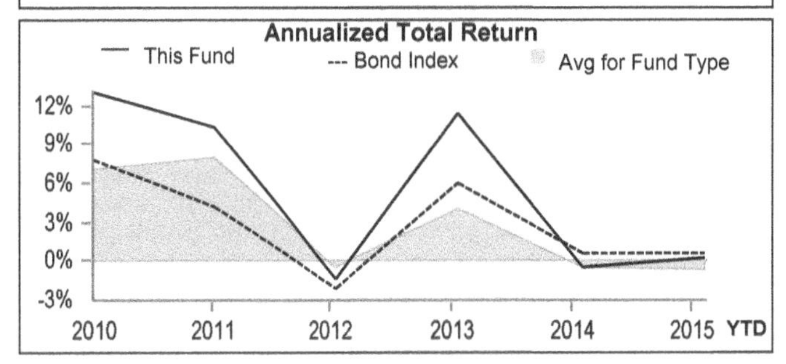

* Denotes ETF Fund

Delaware Enhanced Glb Div & Inc Fd (DEX) C- Fair

Fund Family: Delaware Management Company
Fund Type: Global
Inception Date: June 29, 2007

Major Rating Factors: Middle of the road best describes Delaware Enhanced Glb Div & Inc Fd whose TheStreet.com Investment Rating is currently a C- (Fair). The fund currently has a performance rating of C- (Fair) based on an annualized return of 0.05% over the last three years and a total return of -9.38% year to date 2015. Factored into the performance evaluation is an expense ratio of 1.88% (above average).

The fund's risk rating is currently B- (Good). It carries a beta of 0.94, meaning that its performance tracks fairly well with that of the overall stock market. Volatility, as measured by both the semi-deviation and a drawdown factor, is considered low. As of December 31, 2015, Delaware Enhanced Glb Div & Inc Fd traded at a discount of 16.07% below its net asset value, which is better than its one-year historical average discount of 14.22%.

Babak Zenouzi has been running the fund for 9 years and currently receives a manager quality ranking of 34 (0=worst, 99=best). If you desire an average level of risk, then this fund may be an option.

Data Date	Investment Rating	Net Assets ($Mil)	Price	Performance Rating/Pts	Total Return Y-T-D	Risk Rating/Pts
12-15	C-	209.28	9.35	C- / 3.7	-9.38%	B- / 7.1
2014	C	212.20	11.27	C / 4.6	0.32%	B / 8.1
2013	C+	206.31	12.22	C+ / 6.0	10.57%	B- / 7.5
2012	C-	176.47	11.60	C / 4.5	13.91%	C+ / 6.9
2011	B	180.90	10.77	B / 7.9	-3.78%	B- / 7.5
2010	C-	149.94	12.40	C+ / 6.8	16.55%	C- / 3.2

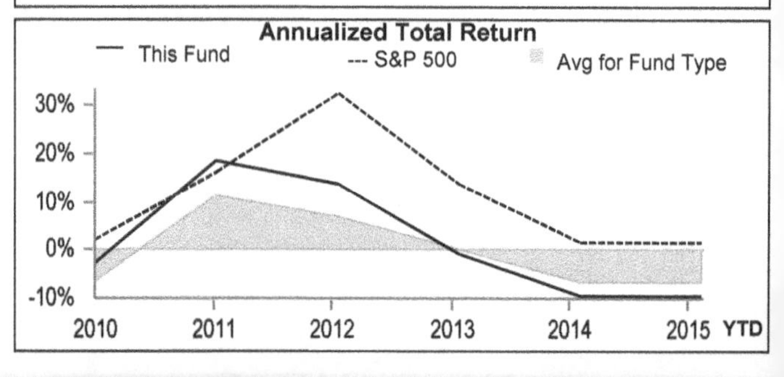

Delaware Inv CO Muni Inc (VCF) B Good

Fund Family: Delaware Management Company
Fund Type: Municipal - Single State
Inception Date: July 22, 1993

Major Rating Factors: Strong performance is the major factor driving the B (Good) TheStreet.com Investment Rating for Delaware Inv CO Muni Inc. The fund currently has a performance rating of B (Good) based on an annualized return of 2.75% over the last three years and a total return of 8.83% year to date 2015. Factored into the performance evaluation is an expense ratio of 1.43% (average).

The fund's risk rating is currently B- (Good). It carries a beta of 1.88, meaning it is expected to move 18.8% for every 10% move in the market. Volatility, as measured by both the semi-deviation and a drawdown factor, is considered low. As of December 31, 2015, Delaware Inv CO Muni Inc traded at a discount of 5.93% below its net asset value, which is worse than its one-year historical average discount of 7.74%.

Denise A. Franchetti has been running the fund for 12 years and currently receives a manager quality ranking of 53 (0=worst, 99=best). If you desire only a moderate level of risk and strong performance, then this fund is an excellent option.

Data Date	Investment Rating	Net Assets ($Mil)	Price	Performance Rating/Pts	Total Return Y-T-D	Risk Rating/Pts
12-15	B	75.23	14.59	B / 7.6	8.83%	B- / 7.6
2014	B	73.60	14.17	C+ / 6.8	19.38%	B / 8.0
2013	C-	74.35	12.38	C- / 3.2	-16.02%	B / 8.3
2012	B+	72.61	15.12	B- / 7.4	18.40%	B+ / 9.0
2011	C+	70.80	13.61	C+ / 5.6	12.17%	B / 8.7
2010	C-	67.65	12.86	D / 2.0	1.76%	B / 8.2

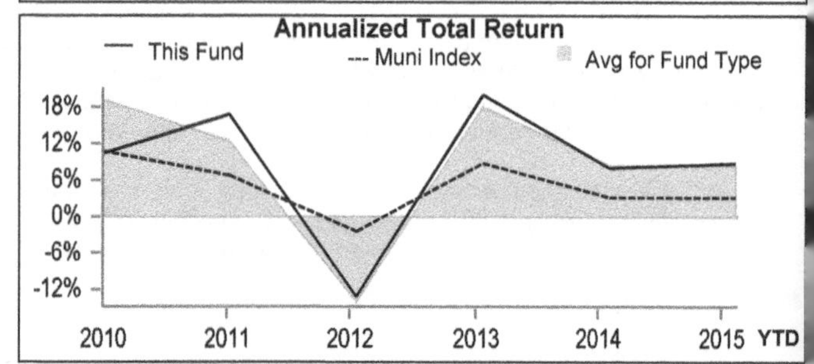

Delaware Inv Div & Inc (DDF) B- Good

Fund Family: Delaware Management Company
Fund Type: Growth and Income
Inception Date: March 18, 1993

Major Rating Factors: Strong performance is the major factor driving the B- (Good) TheStreet.com Investment Rating for Delaware Inv Div & Inc. The fund currently has a performance rating of B- (Good) based on an annualized return of 9.37% over the last three years and a total return of -4.53% year to date 2015. Factored into the performance evaluation is an expense ratio of 1.55% (average).

The fund's risk rating is currently B- (Good). It carries a beta of 1.02, meaning that its performance tracks fairly well with that of the overall stock market. Volatility, as measured by both the semi-deviation and a drawdown factor, is considered low. As of December 31, 2015, Delaware Inv Div & Inc traded at a discount of 11.27% below its net asset value, which is better than its one-year historical average discount of 10.74%.

Babak Zenouzi has been running the fund for 10 years and currently receives a manager quality ranking of 35 (0=worst, 99=best). If you desire only a moderate level of risk and strong performance, then this fund is an excellent option.

Data Date	Investment Rating	Net Assets ($Mil)	Price	Performance Rating/Pts	Total Return Y-T-D	Risk Rating/Pts
12-15	B-	99.89	8.82	B- / 7.0	-4.53%	B- / 7.4
2014	A	98.10	9.85	B / 7.6	12.62%	B+ / 9.0
2013	B	93.17	9.39	B / 7.7	21.41%	B / 8.1
2012	B-	76.09	7.92	B- / 7.3	23.98%	B- / 7.8
2011	B	74.50	7.07	B / 7.8	3.04%	B- / 7.8
2010	D+	67.11	7.79	C / 5.3	16.18%	C- / 3.4

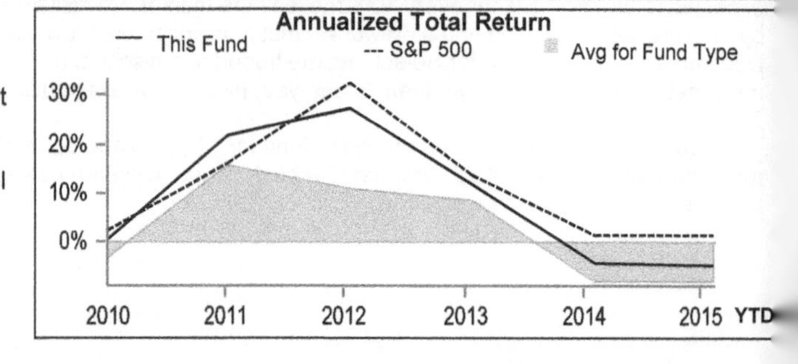

Delaware Inv MN Muni Inc Fund II (VMM) C Fair

Fund Family: Delaware Management Company
Fund Type: Municipal - Single State
Inception Date: February 19, 1993

Major Rating Factors: Middle of the road best describes Delaware Inv MN Muni Inc Fund II whose TheStreet.com Investment Rating is currently a C (Fair). The fund currently has a performance rating of C (Fair) based on an annualized return of -0.24% over the last three years and a total return of 4.45% year to date 2015. Factored into the performance evaluation is an expense ratio of 1.40% (average).

The fund's risk rating is currently B- (Good). It carries a beta of 1.93, meaning it is expected to move 19.3% for every 10% move in the market. Volatility, as measured by both the semi-deviation and a drawdown factor, is considered low. As of December 31, 2015, Delaware Inv MN Muni Inc Fund II traded at a discount of 10.66% below its net asset value, which is better than its one-year historical average discount of 9.29%.

Denise A. Franchetti has been running the fund for 13 years and currently receives a manager quality ranking of 30 (0=worst, 99=best). If you desire an average level of risk, then this fund may be an option.

Data Date	Investment Rating	Net Assets ($Mil)	Price	Performance Rating/Pts	Total Return Y-T-D	Risk Rating/Pts
12-15	C	172.28	13.33	C / 5.0	4.45%	B- / 7.6
2014	C+	170.80	13.37	C / 5.2	12.76%	B- / 7.9
2013	C-	175.63	12.31	C- / 3.8	-15.71%	B / 8.1
2012	A+	171.84	15.22	B+ / 8.5	18.67%	B+ / 9.4
2011	B	170.00	13.51	C+ / 6.7	13.83%	B+ / 9.3
2010	C+	161.72	12.62	C- / 3.9	7.83%	B / 8.3

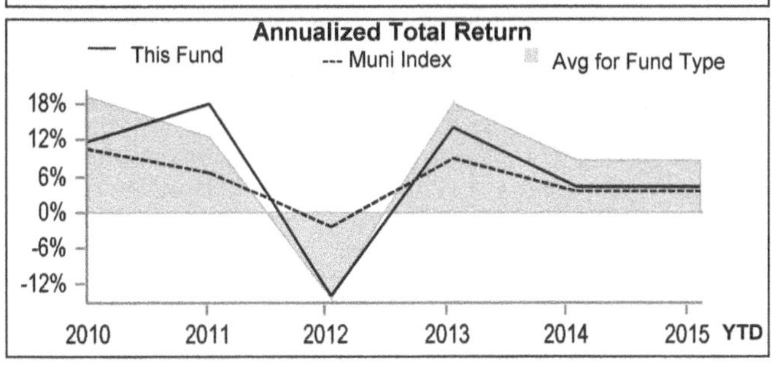

Delaware Inv Nat Muni Inc (VFL) C+ Fair

Fund Family: Delaware Management Company
Fund Type: Municipal - National
Inception Date: February 19, 1993

Major Rating Factors: Middle of the road best describes Delaware Inv Nat Muni Inc whose TheStreet.com Investment Rating is currently a C+ (Fair). The fund currently has a performance rating of C+ (Fair) based on an annualized return of 2.28% over the last three years and a total return of 6.07% year to date 2015. Factored into the performance evaluation is an expense ratio of 1.60% (above average).

The fund's risk rating is currently B- (Good). It carries a beta of 2.45, meaning it is expected to move 24.5% for every 10% move in the market. Volatility, as measured by both the semi-deviation and a drawdown factor, is considered low. As of December 31, 2015, Delaware Inv Nat Muni Inc traded at a discount of 12.58% below its net asset value, which is better than its one-year historical average discount of 12.27%.

Denise A. Franchetti has been running the fund for 13 years and currently receives a manager quality ranking of 35 (0=worst, 99=best). If you desire an average level of risk, then this fund may be an option.

Data Date	Investment Rating	Net Assets ($Mil)	Price	Performance Rating/Pts	Total Return Y-T-D	Risk Rating/Pts
12-15	C+	67.80	12.99	C+ / 6.3	6.07%	B- / 7.6
2014	B-	66.10	13.09	C+ / 6.7	17.64%	B- / 7.7
2013	C-	67.88	11.68	C- / 3.7	-13.67%	B / 8.0
2012	A-	63.49	14.03	B / 7.9	16.37%	B+ / 9.0
2011	B	61.90	12.91	B- / 7.2	13.08%	B / 8.9
2010	C-	31.65	12.09	C- / 3.7	2.62%	C+ / 6.1

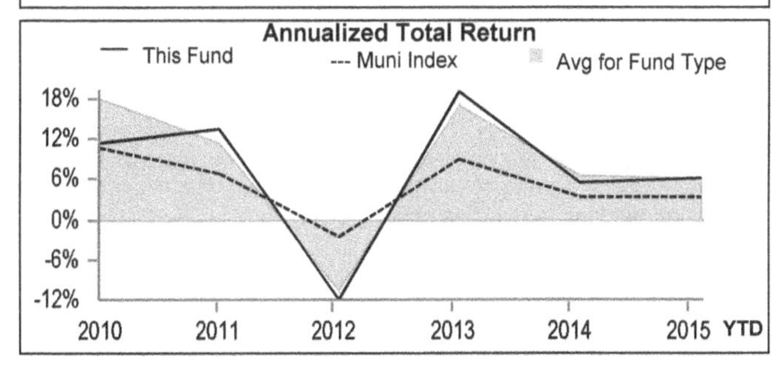

Deutsche Global High Income (LBF) C Fair

Fund Family: Deutsche Asset & Wealth Management
Fund Type: Global
Inception Date: July 24, 1992

Major Rating Factors: Middle of the road best describes Deutsche Global High Income whose TheStreet.com Investment Rating is currently a C (Fair). The fund currently has a performance rating of C (Fair) based on an annualized return of 0.84% over the last three years and a total return of 2.56% year to date 2015. Factored into the performance evaluation is an expense ratio of 2.29% (high).

The fund's risk rating is currently B- (Good). It carries a beta of 0.51, meaning the fund's expected move will be 5.1% for every 10% move in the market. Volatility, as measured by both the semi-deviation and a drawdown factor, is considered low. As of December 31, 2015, Deutsche Global High Income traded at a discount of 7.70% below its net asset value, which is worse than its one-year historical average discount of 8.95%.

Gary A. Russell has been running the fund for 10 years and currently receives a manager quality ranking of 87 (0=worst, 99=best). If you desire an average level of risk, then this fund may be an option.

Data Date	Investment Rating	Net Assets ($Mil)	Price	Performance Rating/Pts	Total Return Y-T-D	Risk Rating/Pts
12-15	C	61.00	7.55	C / 4.7	2.56%	B- / 7.4
2014	C	60.50	7.84	C / 4.4	4.27%	B / 8.3
2013	C	63.00	8.01	C / 5.1	-4.59%	B / 8.0
2012	B	63.00	8.78	B- / 7.5	26.80%	B- / 7.8
2011	C+	61.70	7.57	C+ / 6.6	5.62%	B- / 7.4
2010	C	84.00	7.80	C+ / 6.5	13.94%	C / 4.3

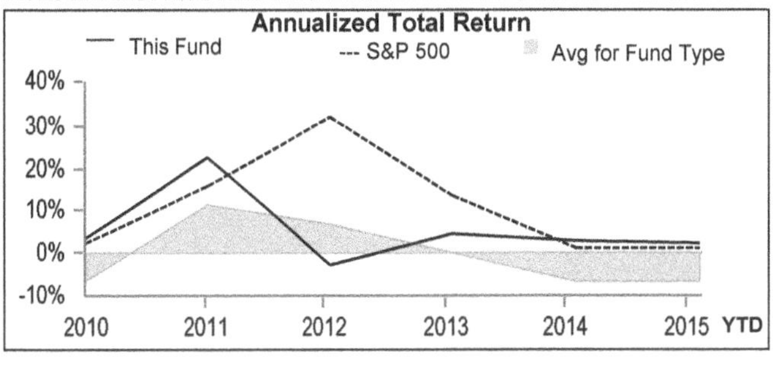

Deutsche High Income (KHI) C- Fair

Fund Family: Deutsche Asset & Wealth Management
Fund Type: Corporate - High Yield
Inception Date: April 21, 1988

Major Rating Factors: Middle of the road best describes Deutsche High Income whose TheStreet.com Investment Rating is currently a C- (Fair). The fund currently has a performance rating of C- (Fair) based on an annualized return of -1.13% over the last three years and a total return of -1.90% year to date 2015. Factored into the performance evaluation is an expense ratio of 1.57% (above average).

The fund's risk rating is currently B- (Good). It carries a beta of 1.31, meaning it is expected to move 13.1% for every 10% move in the market. Volatility, as measured by both the semi-deviation and a drawdown factor, is considered low. As of December 31, 2015, Deutsche High Income traded at a discount of 9.45% below its net asset value, which is worse than its one-year historical average discount of 10.52%.

Gary A. Russell has been running the fund for 18 years and currently receives a manager quality ranking of 45 (0=worst, 99=best). If you desire an average level of risk, then this fund may be an option.

Data Date	Investment Rating	Net Assets ($Mil)	Price	Perfor-mance Rating/Pts	Total Return Y-T-D	Risk Rating/Pts
12-15	C-	156.00	7.95	C- / 3.8	-1.90%	B- / 7.0
2014	C-	158.30	8.74	C- / 3.4	2.73%	B- / 7.9
2013	C	166.00	9.14	C / 5.0	-4.21%	B- / 7.9
2012	B-	154.00	10.20	C+ / 6.7	12.73%	B / 8.0
2011	B-	151.60	10.23	B+ / 8.6	16.45%	C+ / 6.5
2010	C+	146.00	9.39	B- / 7.5	21.08%	C- / 4.1

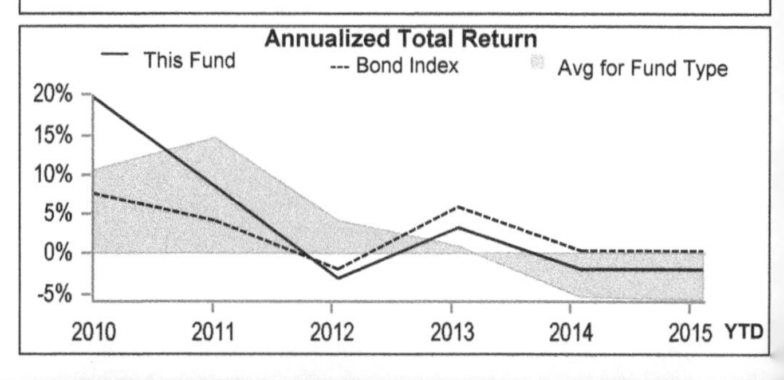

Deutsche High Income Opportunities (DHG) C Fair

Fund Family: Deutsche Asset & Wealth Management
Fund Type: Global
Inception Date: November 22, 2006

Major Rating Factors: Middle of the road best describes Deutsche High Income Opportunities whose TheStreet.com Investment Rating is currently a C (Fair). The fund currently has a performance rating of C (Fair) based on an annualized return of 1.39% over the last three years and a total return of 0.34% year to date 2015. Factored into the performance evaluation is an expense ratio of 2.04% (high).

The fund's risk rating is currently B- (Good). It carries a beta of 0.52, meaning the fund's expected move will be 5.2% for every 10% move in the market. Volatility, as measured by both the semi-deviation and a drawdown factor, is considered low. As of December 31, 2015, Deutsche High Income Opportunities traded at a discount of 8.42% below its net asset value, which is worse than its one-year historical average discount of 9.37%.

Gary A. Russell has been running the fund for 6 years and currently receives a manager quality ranking of 64 (0=worst, 99=best). If you desire an average level of risk, then this fund may be an option.

Data Date	Investment Rating	Net Assets ($Mil)	Price	Perfor-mance Rating/Pts	Total Return Y-T-D	Risk Rating/Pts
12-15	C	221.00	13.06	C / 4.7	0.34%	B- / 7.6
2014	C+	249.90	14.03	C / 4.7	4.29%	B / 8.4
2013	C+	260.00	14.40	C+ / 5.9	0.23%	B / 8.5
2012	C+	270.00	15.16	C+ / 6.8	20.46%	B- / 7.0
2011	B+	252.50	13.86	B / 8.1	9.18%	B / 8.3
2010	E	365.00	14.08	D- / 1.2	25.15%	D / 2.0

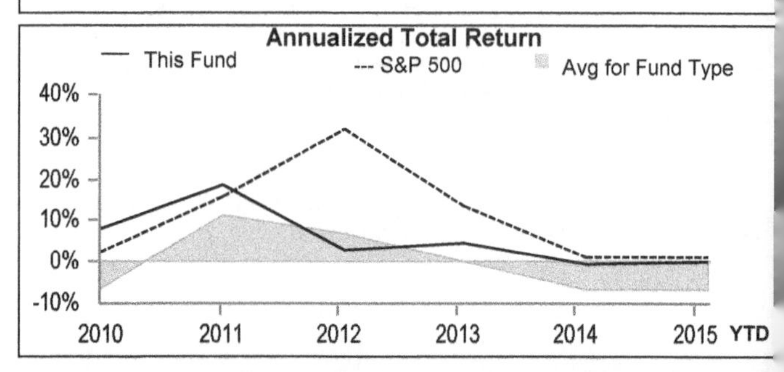

Deutsche Multi-Market Income (KMM) D+ Weak

Fund Family: Deutsche Asset & Wealth Management
Fund Type: Global
Inception Date: January 23, 1989

Major Rating Factors: Deutsche Multi-Market Income receives a TheStreet.com Investment Rating of D+ (Weak). The fund currently has a performance rating of C- (Fair) based on an annualized return of -3.22% over the last three years and a total return of -3.02% year to date 2015. Factored into the performance evaluation is an expense ratio of 1.52% (average).

The fund's risk rating is currently C+ (Fair). It carries a beta of 0.81, meaning the fund's expected move will be 8.1% for every 10% move in the market. Volatility, as measured by both the semi-deviation and a drawdown factor, is considered low. As of December 31, 2015, Deutsche Multi-Market Income traded at a discount of 11.78% below its net asset value, which is worse than its one-year historical average discount of 13.67%.

Gary A. Russell currently receives a manager quality ranking of 75 (0=worst, 99=best). If you desire an average level of risk, then this fund may be an option.

Data Date	Investment Rating	Net Assets ($Mil)	Price	Perfor-mance Rating/Pts	Total Return Y-T-D	Risk Rating/Pts
12-15	D+	238.00	7.64	C- / 3.3	-3.02%	C+ / 6.0
2014	D+	240.80	8.52	C- / 3.0	-1.76%	C+ / 6.9
2013	C-	251.00	9.39	C- / 4.2	-4.42%	C+ / 6.6
2012	C+	238.00	10.44	B- / 7.0	16.06%	B- / 7.2
2011	B	234.40	10.10	B+ / 8.6	11.07%	B- / 7.0
2010	B	218.10	9.91	B+ / 8.6	26.07%	C / 4.3

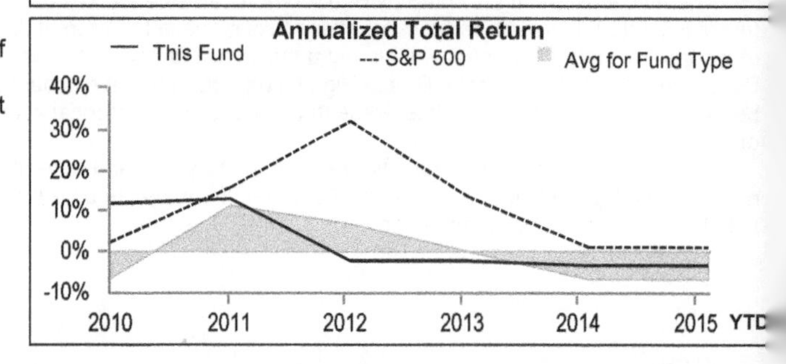

Deutsche Municipal Income (KTF) C+ Fair

Fund Family: Deutsche Asset & Wealth Management
Fund Type: Municipal - National
Inception Date: October 20, 1988

Major Rating Factors: Middle of the road best describes Deutsche Municipal Income whose TheStreet.com Investment Rating is currently a C+ (Fair). The fund currently has a performance rating of C+ (Fair) based on an annualized return of 2.36% over the last three years and a total return of 6.84% year to date 2015. Factored into the performance evaluation is an expense ratio of 1.45% (average).

The fund's risk rating is currently B- (Good). It carries a beta of 2.49, meaning it is expected to move 24.9% for every 10% move in the market. Volatility, as measured by both the semi-deviation and a drawdown factor, is considered low. As of December 31, 2015, Deutsche Municipal Income traded at a price exactly equal to its net asset value, which is worse than its one-year historical average discount of 2.11%.

Michael J. Generazo has been running the fund for 6 years and currently receives a manager quality ranking of 40 (0=worst, 99=best). If you desire an average level of risk, then this fund may be an option.

Data Date	Investment Rating	Net Assets ($Mil)	Price	Performance Rating/Pts	Total Return Y-T-D	Risk Rating/Pts
12-15	C+	544.00	13.48	C+ / 6.6	6.84%	B- / 7.2
2014	B-	542.20	13.37	C+ / 6.7	18.04%	B- / 7.9
2013	C+	549.00	11.99	C+ / 6.2	-15.39%	B / 8.1
2012	A+	536.00	14.39	A / 9.3	18.72%	B / 8.6
2011	A+	505.20	13.80	A+ / 9.8	31.48%	B / 8.8
2010	B+	465.33	11.42	B- / 7.0	3.85%	C+ / 6.5

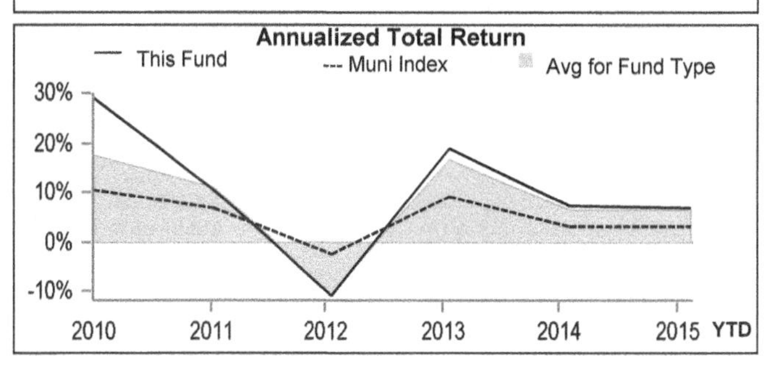

Deutsche Strategic Income (KST) C- Fair

Fund Family: Deutsche Asset & Wealth Management
Fund Type: Global
Inception Date: April 29, 1994

Major Rating Factors: Middle of the road best describes Deutsche Strategic Income whose TheStreet.com Investment Rating is currently a C- (Fair). The fund currently has a performance rating of C- (Fair) based on an annualized return of -2.83% over the last three years and a total return of -1.39% year to date 2015. Factored into the performance evaluation is an expense ratio of 1.83% (above average).

The fund's risk rating is currently C+ (Fair). It carries a beta of 0.83, meaning the fund's expected move will be 8.3% for every 10% move in the market. Volatility, as measured by both the semi-deviation and a drawdown factor, is considered low. As of December 31, 2015, Deutsche Strategic Income traded at a discount of 12.92% below its net asset value, which is worse than its one-year historical average discount of 14.14%.

Gary A. Russell currently receives a manager quality ranking of 78 (0=worst, 99=best). If you desire an average level of risk, then this fund may be an option.

Data Date	Investment Rating	Net Assets ($Mil)	Price	Performance Rating/Pts	Total Return Y-T-D	Risk Rating/Pts
12-15	C-	61.00	10.51	C- / 3.4	-1.39%	C+ / 6.4
2014	C-	62.70	11.56	C- / 3.2	-3.09%	B- / 7.4
2013	C+	67.00	12.99	C / 5.5	-4.07%	B / 8.3
2012	B-	63.00	14.26	B- / 7.0	19.74%	B- / 7.6
2011	B	62.40	13.35	B+ / 8.4	14.78%	B- / 7.4
2010	B-	60.13	12.68	B / 8.0	19.44%	C / 4.8

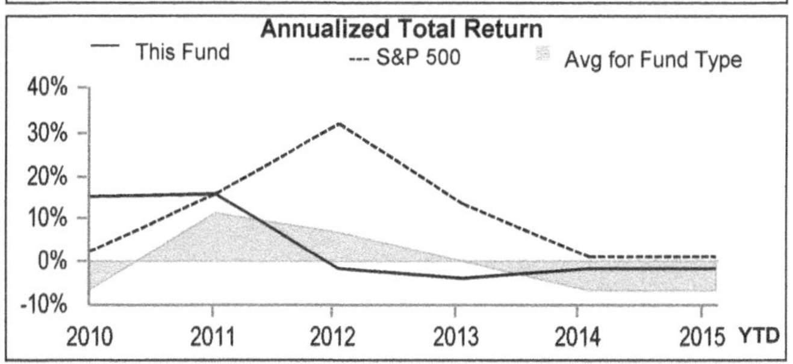

Deutsche Strategic Municipal Incom (KSM) C+ Fair

Fund Family: Deutsche Asset & Wealth Management
Fund Type: Municipal - National
Inception Date: March 22, 1989

Major Rating Factors: Middle of the road best describes Deutsche Strategic Municipal Incom whose TheStreet.com Investment Rating is currently a C+ (Fair). The fund currently has a performance rating of C+ (Fair) based on an annualized return of 2.11% over the last three years and a total return of 2.75% year to date 2015. Factored into the performance evaluation is an expense ratio of 1.73% (above average).

The fund's risk rating is currently C+ (Fair). It carries a beta of 2.79, meaning it is expected to move 27.9% for every 10% move in the market. Volatility, as measured by both the semi-deviation and a drawdown factor, is considered low. As of December 31, 2015, Deutsche Strategic Municipal Incom traded at a premium of 1.85% above its net asset value, which is better than its one-year historical average premium of 2.02%.

Rebecca L. Flinn has been running the fund for 17 years and currently receives a manager quality ranking of 31 (0=worst, 99=best). If you desire an average level of risk, then this fund may be an option.

Data Date	Investment Rating	Net Assets ($Mil)	Price	Performance Rating/Pts	Total Return Y-T-D	Risk Rating/Pts
12-15	C+	148.00	13.20	C+ / 6.1	2.75%	C+ / 6.9
2014	C+	147.80	13.70	C+ / 6.9	18.50%	C+ / 6.2
2013	C+	155.00	12.28	C+ / 6.0	-12.89%	B- / 7.9
2012	A-	150.00	14.55	B / 8.2	14.13%	B / 8.6
2011	A+	141.20	13.90	A+ / 9.9	29.77%	B / 8.9
2010	B+	138.00	12.28	B / 8.0	5.37%	C+ / 6.0

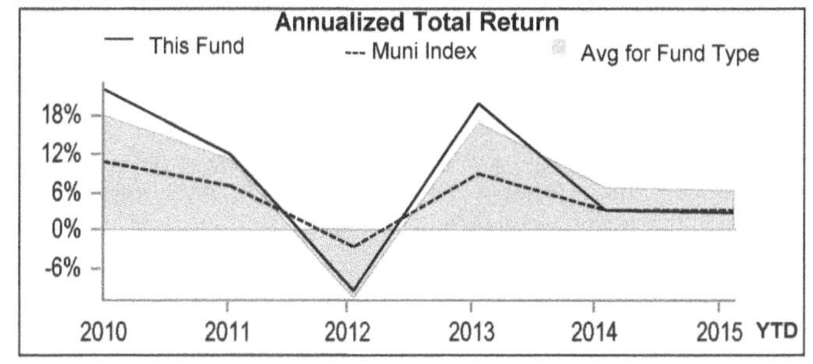

Diversified Real Asset Income Fund (XDRAX) D Weak

Fund Family: Nuveen Fund Advisors LLC
Fund Type: Global
Inception Date: September 8, 2014

Data Date	Investment Rating	Net Assets ($Mil)	Price	Performance Rating/Pts	Total Return Y-T-D	Risk Rating/Pts
12-15	D	409.56	15.51	D+ / 2.8	-1.67%	C / 4.9

Major Rating Factors:
Disappointing performance is the major factor driving the D (Weak) TheStreet.com Investment Rating for Diversified Real Asset Income Fund. The fund currently has a performance rating of D+ (Weak) based on an annualized return of 0.00% over the last three years and a total return of -1.67% year to date 2015. Factored into the performance evaluation is an expense ratio of 1.40% (average).

The fund's risk rating is currently C (Fair). It carries a beta of 0.00, meaning the fund's expected move will be 0.0% for every 10% move in the market. Volatility, as measured by both the semi-deviation and a drawdown factor, is considered average. As of December 31, 2015, Diversified Real Asset Income Fund traded at a discount of 13.45% below its net asset value, which is better than its one-year historical average discount of 11.13%.

Jon A. Loth currently receives a manager quality ranking of 56 (0=worst, 99=best). This fund offers an average level of risk but investors looking for strong performance will be frustrated.

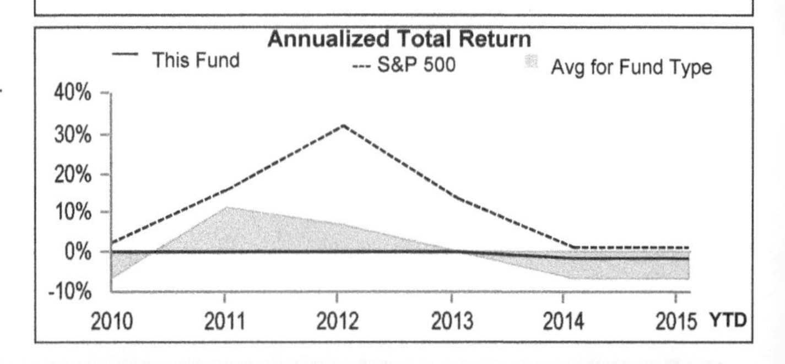

Dividend and Income Fund (DNI) C- Fair

Fund Family: Bexil Advisers LLC
Fund Type: Growth and Income
Inception Date: June 23, 1998

Data Date	Investment Rating	Net Assets ($Mil)	Price	Performance Rating/Pts	Total Return Y-T-D	Risk Rating/Pts
12-15	C-	144.28	11.01	C / 4.3	-16.31%	C+ / 6.1
2014	B	146.50	15.12	B- / 7.2	11.73%	B / 8.2
2013	C+	93.95	15.11	C+ / 6.5	22.21%	B- / 7.4
2012	D+	93.38	13.50	C- / 3.2	14.20%	B- / 7.2
2011	C-	73.32	3.41	C- / 3.8	-13.12%	B- / 7.0
2010	D	70.85	4.27	D+ / 2.7	25.35%	C- / 4.1

Major Rating Factors: Middle of the road best describes Dividend and Income Fund whose TheStreet.com Investment Rating is currently a C- (Fair). The fund currently has a performance rating of C (Fair) based on an annualized return of 3.45% over the last three years and a total return of -16.31% year to date 2015. Factored into the performance evaluation is an expense ratio of 1.55% (average).

The fund's risk rating is currently C+ (Fair). It carries a beta of 1.14, meaning it is expected to move 11.4% for every 10% move in the market. Volatility, as measured by both the semi-deviation and a drawdown factor, is considered low. As of December 31, 2015, Dividend and Income Fund traded at a discount of 16.02% below its net asset value, which is better than its one-year historical average discount of 12.82%.

John F. Ramirez has been running the fund for 5 years and currently receives a manager quality ranking of 15 (0=worst, 99=best). If you desire an average level of risk, then this fund may be an option.

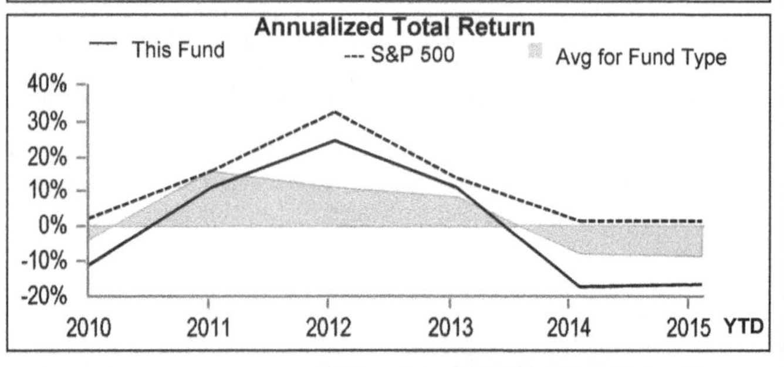

DNP Select Income Fund Inc (DNP) C Fair

Fund Family: Duff & Phelps Investment Mgmt Co
Fund Type: Utilities
Inception Date: January 28, 1987

Data Date	Investment Rating	Net Assets ($Mil)	Price	Performance Rating/Pts	Total Return Y-T-D	Risk Rating/Pts
12-15	C	2,820.58	8.96	C+ / 5.7	-6.23%	C+ / 6.9
2014	C	2,706.20	10.56	C+ / 6.0	20.65%	C+ / 6.5
2013	C+	2,219.46	9.42	C+ / 5.6	5.54%	B / 8.2
2012	C-	2,052.35	9.47	C- / 3.6	-3.42%	B / 8.1
2011	B+	2,014.00	10.92	B+ / 8.3	26.16%	B / 8.2
2010	C	1,703.40	9.14	C / 5.1	11.31%	C / 5.5

Major Rating Factors: Middle of the road best describes DNP Select Income Fund Inc whose TheStreet.com Investment Rating is currently a C (Fair). The fund currently has a performance rating of C+ (Fair) based on an annualized return of 5.46% over the last three years and a total return of -6.23% year to date 2015. Factored into the performance evaluation is an expense ratio of 1.60% (above average).

The fund's risk rating is currently C+ (Fair). It carries a beta of 0.42, meaning the fund's expected move will be 4.2% for every 10% move in the market. Volatility, as measured by both the semi-deviation and a drawdown factor, is considered low. As of December 31, 2015, DNP Select Income Fund Inc traded at a premium of 9.27% above its net asset value, which is better than its one-year historical average premium of 10.91%.

Geoffrey P. Dybas has been running the fund for 20 years and currently receives a manager quality ranking of 78 (0=worst, 99=best). If you desire an average level of risk, then this fund may be an option.

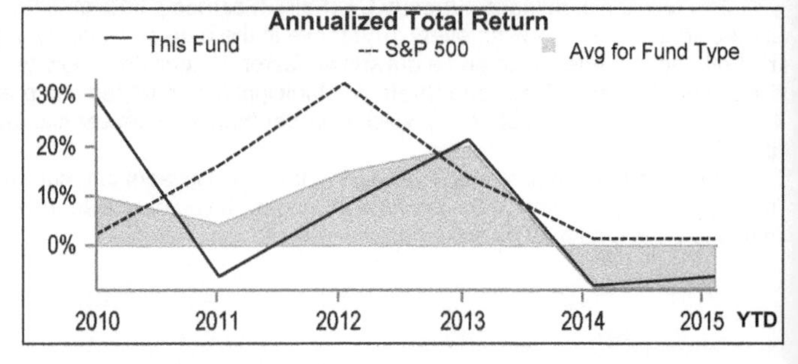

DoubleLine Income Solutions (DSL) D+ Weak

Fund Family: DoubleLine Capital LP
Fund Type: Corporate - High Yield
Inception Date: April 26, 2013

Data Date	Investment Rating	Net Assets ($Mil)	Price	Performance Rating/Pts	Total Return Y-T-D	Risk Rating/Pts
12-15	D+	2,006.69	16.22	D- / 1.4	-10.00%	B- / 7.1
2014	D+	2,348.70	19.90	D / 2.1	2.15%	B / 8.1

Major Rating Factors:
Disappointing performance is the major factor driving the D+ (Weak) TheStreet.com Investment Rating for DoubleLine Income Solutions. The fund currently has a performance rating of D- (Weak) based on an annualized return of 0.00% over the last three years and a total return of -10.00% year to date 2015. Factored into the performance evaluation is an expense ratio of 2.27% (high).

The fund's risk rating is currently B- (Good). It carries a beta of 0.00, meaning the fund's expected move will be 0.0% for every 10% move in the market. Volatility, as measured by both the semi-deviation and a drawdown factor, is considered low. As of December 31, 2015, DoubleLine Income Solutions traded at a discount of 10.34% below its net asset value, which is better than its one-year historical average discount of 10.04%.

Jeffrey E. Gundlach currently receives a manager quality ranking of 42 (0=worst, 99=best). This fund offers only a moderate level of risk but investors looking for strong performance are still waiting.

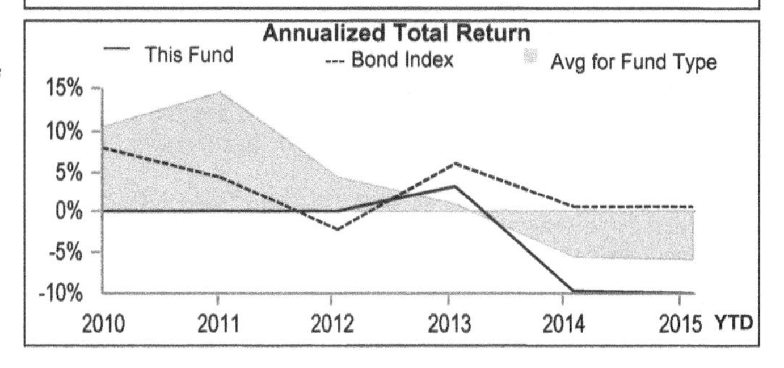

DoubleLine Opportunistic Credit Fd (DBL) B- Good

Fund Family: DoubleLine Capital LP
Fund Type: General - Investment Grade
Inception Date: January 27, 2012

Data Date	Investment Rating	Net Assets ($Mil)	Price	Performance Rating/Pts	Total Return Y-T-D	Risk Rating/Pts
12-15	B-	356.68	25.31	B / 8.0	14.11%	C+ / 6.4
2014	B	345.50	24.56	B+ / 8.9	19.72%	C+ / 6.3
2013	D+	338.66	22.32	D- / 1.4	-9.24%	B / 8.3

Major Rating Factors: Strong performance is the major factor driving the B- (Good) TheStreet.com Investment Rating for DoubleLine Opportunistic Credit Fd. The fund currently has a performance rating of B (Good) based on an annualized return of 7.55% over the last three years and a total return of 14.11% year to date 2015. Factored into the performance evaluation is an expense ratio of 1.65% (above average).

The fund's risk rating is currently C+ (Fair). It carries a beta of 2.27, meaning it is expected to move 22.7% for every 10% move in the market. Volatility, as measured by both the semi-deviation and a drawdown factor, is considered low. As of December 31, 2015, DoubleLine Opportunistic Credit Fd traded at a premium of 11.35% above its net asset value, which is worse than its one-year historical average premium of 3.60%.

Jeffrey E. Gundlach currently receives a manager quality ranking of 87 (0=worst, 99=best). If you desire only a moderate level of risk and strong performance, then this fund is an excellent option.

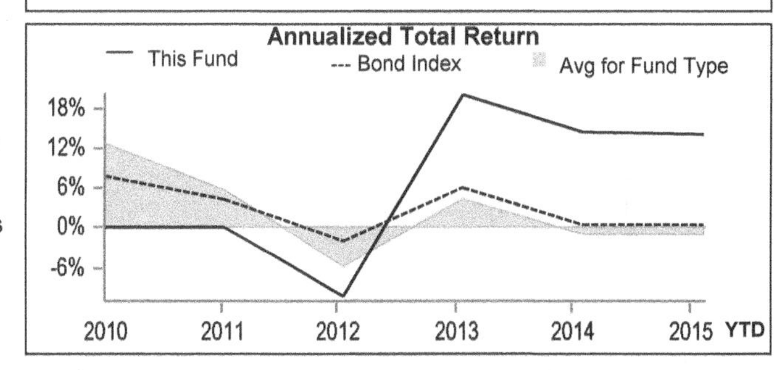

Dreyfus High Yield Strategies Fund (DHF) C- Fair

Fund Family: Dreyfus Corporation
Fund Type: Corporate - High Yield
Inception Date: April 29, 1998

Data Date	Investment Rating	Net Assets ($Mil)	Price	Performance Rating/Pts	Total Return Y-T-D	Risk Rating/Pts
12-15	C-	279.31	3.08	C- / 3.9	-5.96%	C+ / 6.4
2014	C-	404.90	3.61	C- / 3.0	-3.71%	B- / 7.4
2013	C	297.21	4.07	C+ / 5.8	8.02%	C+ / 6.4
2012	C-	281.90	4.12	C+ / 5.6	5.62%	C+ / 6.2
2011	B	384.10	4.43	A- / 9.1	12.01%	C+ / 6.3
2010	C+	291.96	4.43	B+ / 8.9	33.00%	C- / 3.0

Major Rating Factors: Middle of the road best describes Dreyfus High Yield Strategies Fund whose TheStreet.com Investment Rating is currently a C- (Fair). The fund currently has a performance rating of C- (Fair) based on an annualized return of -0.55% over the last three years and a total return of -5.96% year to date 2015. Factored into the performance evaluation is an expense ratio of 1.74% (above average).

The fund's risk rating is currently C+ (Fair). It carries a beta of 1.94, meaning it is expected to move 19.4% for every 10% move in the market. Volatility, as measured by both the semi-deviation and a drawdown factor, is considered low. As of December 31, 2015, Dreyfus High Yield Strategies Fund traded at a discount of 4.35% below its net asset value, which is worse than its one-year historical average discount of 7.90%.

Chris E. Barris currently receives a manager quality ranking of 43 (0=worst, 99=best). If you desire an average level of risk, then this fund may be an option.

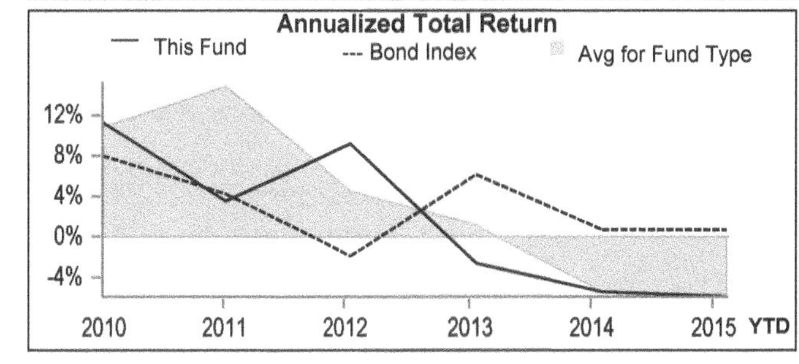

Dreyfus Municipal Bond Infra (DMB) A+ Excellent

Fund Family: Dreyfus Corporation
Fund Type: Municipal - National
Inception Date: April 26, 2013

Major Rating Factors:
Exceptional performance is the major factor driving the A+ (Excellent) TheStreet.com Investment Rating for Dreyfus Municipal Bond Infra. The fund currently has a performance rating of A (Excellent) based on an annualized return of 0.00% over the last three years and a total return of 8.15% year to date 2015. Factored into the performance evaluation is an expense ratio of 1.67% (above average).

The fund's risk rating is currently B- (Good). It carries a beta of 0.00, meaning the fund's expected move will be 0.0% for every 10% move in the market. Volatility, as measured by both the semi-deviation and a drawdown factor, is considered low. As of December 31, 2015, Dreyfus Municipal Bond Infra traded at a discount of 11.06% below its net asset value, which is better than its one-year historical average discount of 11.00%.

Daniel A. Rabasco currently receives a manager quality ranking of 43 (0=worst, 99=best). If you desire only a moderate level of risk and strong performance, then this fund is an excellent option.

Data Date	Investment Rating	Net Assets ($Mil)	Price	Performance Rating/Pts	Total Return Y-T-D	Risk Rating/Pts
12-15	A+	254.59	12.38	A / 9.5	8.15%	B- / 7.8
2014	A+	323.30	12.17	A+ / 9.7	23.56%	B / 8.7

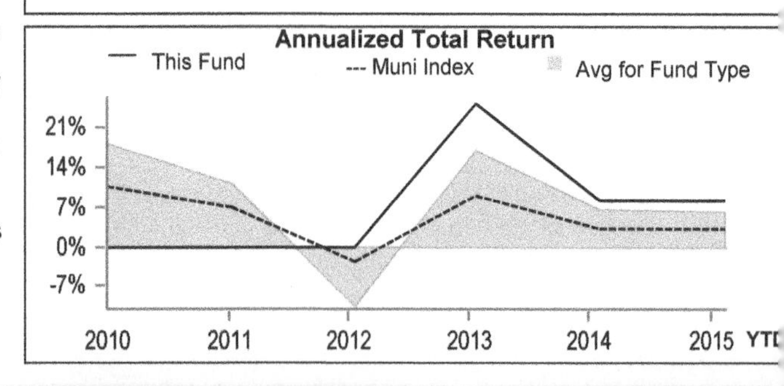

Dreyfus Municipal Income (DMF) C+ Fair

Fund Family: Dreyfus Corporation
Fund Type: Municipal - National
Inception Date: October 24, 1988

Major Rating Factors: Middle of the road best describes Dreyfus Municipal Income whose TheStreet.com Investment Rating is currently a C+ (Fair). The fund currently has a performance rating of C+ (Fair) based on an annualized return of 1.88% over the last three years and a total return of 4.94% year to date 2015. Factored into the performance evaluation is an expense ratio of 1.25% (average).

The fund's risk rating is currently B- (Good). It carries a beta of 2.92, meaning it is expected to move 29.2% for every 10% move in the market. Volatility, as measured by both the semi-deviation and a drawdown factor, is considered low. As of December 31, 2015, Dreyfus Municipal Income traded at a discount of 2.07% below its net asset value, which is worse than its one-year historical average discount of 2.25%.

Daniel A. Barton has been running the fund for 5 years and currently receives a manager quality ranking of 28 (0=worst, 99=best). If you desire an average level of risk, then this fund may be an option.

Data Date	Investment Rating	Net Assets ($Mil)	Price	Performance Rating/Pts	Total Return Y-T-D	Risk Rating/Pts
12-15	C+	197.73	9.44	C+ / 6.2	4.94%	B- / 7.2
2014	B-	250.60	9.62	B- / 7.1	20.75%	B- / 7.3
2013	C-	186.51	8.46	C / 4.6	-16.47%	B- / 7.6
2012	A-	204.08	10.43	B+ / 8.4	15.70%	B / 8.6
2011	A+	273.80	9.88	A+ / 9.6	26.18%	B / 8.8
2010	C+	199.20	8.93	C+ / 6.9	12.10%	C+ / 6.4

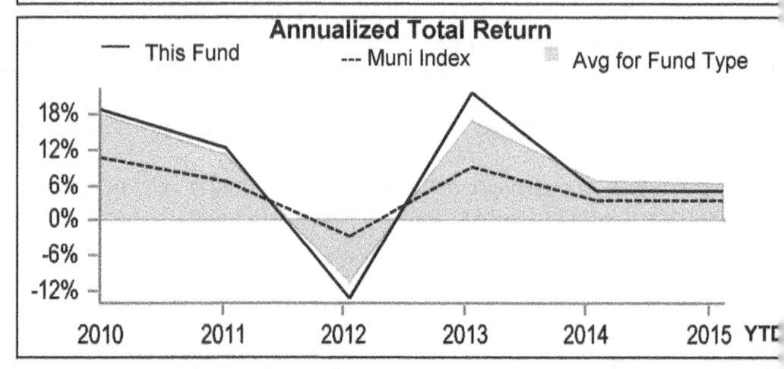

Dreyfus Strategic Muni Bond Fund (DSM) C+ Fair

Fund Family: Dreyfus Corporation
Fund Type: Municipal - National
Inception Date: November 22, 1989

Major Rating Factors: Middle of the road best describes Dreyfus Strategic Muni Bond Fund whose TheStreet.com Investment Rating is currently a C+ (Fair). The fund currently has a performance rating of C+ (Fair) based on an annualized return of 0.59% over the last three years and a total return of 7.25% year to date 2015. Factored into the performance evaluation is an expense ratio of 1.09% (low).

The fund's risk rating is currently B- (Good). It carries a beta of 2.60, meaning it is expected to move 26.0% for every 10% move in the market. Volatility, as measured by both the semi-deviation and a drawdown factor, is considered low. As of December 31, 2015, Dreyfus Strategic Muni Bond Fund traded at a discount of 6.60% below its net asset value, which is worse than its one-year historical average discount of 7.55%.

Stephen Buell currently receives a manager quality ranking of 26 (0=worst, 99=best). If you desire an average level of risk, then this fund may be an option.

Data Date	Investment Rating	Net Assets ($Mil)	Price	Performance Rating/Pts	Total Return Y-T-D	Risk Rating/Pts
12-15	C+	420.44	8.07	C+ / 5.8	7.25%	B- / 7.5
2014	C	513.40	7.96	C / 5.3	13.84%	B- / 7.6
2013	C	435.98	7.42	C / 4.8	-17.15%	B- / 7.8
2012	A+	430.99	9.36	A- / 9.0	18.76%	B / 8.7
2011	A+	545.10	8.69	A / 9.4	24.44%	B / 8.7
2010	C-	384.46	7.58	C- / 3.2	5.39%	C+ / 6.2

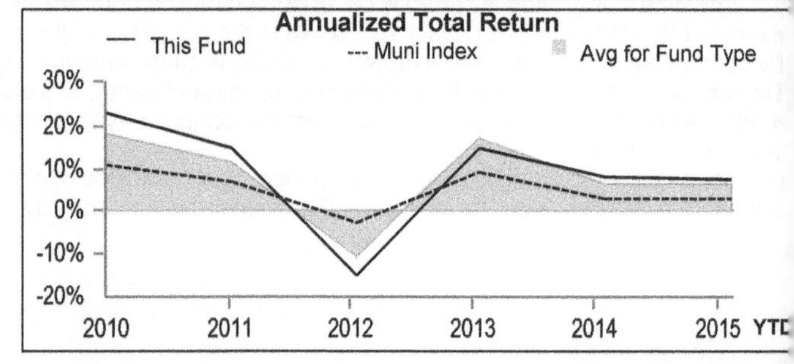

Dreyfus Strategic Municipals (LEO) C+ Fair

Fund Family: Dreyfus Corporation
Fund Type: Municipal - National
Inception Date: September 23, 1987

Major Rating Factors: Middle of the road best describes Dreyfus Strategic Municipals whose TheStreet.com Investment Rating is currently a C+ (Fair). The fund currently has a performance rating of C+ (Fair) based on an annualized return of 1.52% over the last three years and a total return of 10.98% year to date 2015. Factored into the performance evaluation is an expense ratio of 1.13% (low).

The fund's risk rating is currently B- (Good). It carries a beta of 2.52, meaning it is expected to move 25.2% for every 10% move in the market. Volatility, as measured by both the semi-deviation and a drawdown factor, is considered low. As of December 31, 2015, Dreyfus Strategic Municipals traded at a discount of 3.83% below its net asset value, which is worse than its one-year historical average discount of 6.49%.

Daniel A. Barton has been running the fund for 5 years and currently receives a manager quality ranking of 32 (0=worst, 99=best). If you desire an average level of risk, then this fund may be an option.

Data Date	Investment Rating	Net Assets ($Mil)	Price	Performance Rating/Pts	Total Return Y-T-D	Risk Rating/Pts
12-15	C+	541.09	8.54	C+ / 6.7	10.98%	B- / 7.3
2014	C	684.60	8.19	C / 5.3	14.00%	B- / 7.6
2013	C	499.31	7.60	C / 4.7	-17.29%	B- / 7.9
2012	A	541.93	9.55	B+ / 8.8	16.97%	B / 8.4
2011	A	738.90	8.89	A / 9.4	24.69%	B / 8.6
2010	C-	528.61	7.80	C- / 3.8	3.55%	C+ / 6.0

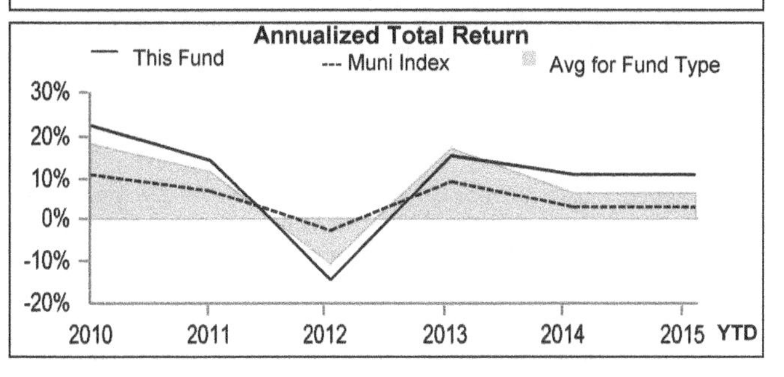

DTF Tax Free Income (DTF) C+ Fair

Fund Family: Duff & Phelps Investment Mgmt Co
Fund Type: Municipal - National
Inception Date: November 29, 1991

Major Rating Factors: Middle of the road best describes DTF Tax Free Income whose TheStreet.com Investment Rating is currently a C+ (Fair). The fund currently has a performance rating of C+ (Fair) based on an annualized return of 0.40% over the last three years and a total return of 4.43% year to date 2015. Factored into the performance evaluation is an expense ratio of 1.89% (above average).

The fund's risk rating is currently B- (Good). It carries a beta of 2.40, meaning it is expected to move 24.0% for every 10% move in the market. Volatility, as measured by both the semi-deviation and a drawdown factor, is considered low. As of December 31, 2015, DTF Tax Free Income traded at a discount of 8.31% below its net asset value, which is worse than its one-year historical average discount of 8.73%.

Warun Kumar currently receives a manager quality ranking of 28 (0=worst, 99=best). If you desire an average level of risk, then this fund may be an option.

Data Date	Investment Rating	Net Assets ($Mil)	Price	Performance Rating/Pts	Total Return Y-T-D	Risk Rating/Pts
12-15	C+	142.23	15.11	C+ / 5.7	4.43%	B- / 7.7
2014	C+	207.20	15.38	C / 5.5	15.14%	B- / 7.6
2013	C-	147.28	14.02	C- / 3.4	-15.61%	B- / 7.8
2012	B+	138.11	16.82	B / 7.6	11.16%	B / 8.7
2011	B+	131.89	16.06	B / 8.2	17.70%	B / 8.9
2010	C+	136.53	14.82	C+ / 6.3	7.59%	C+ / 6.8

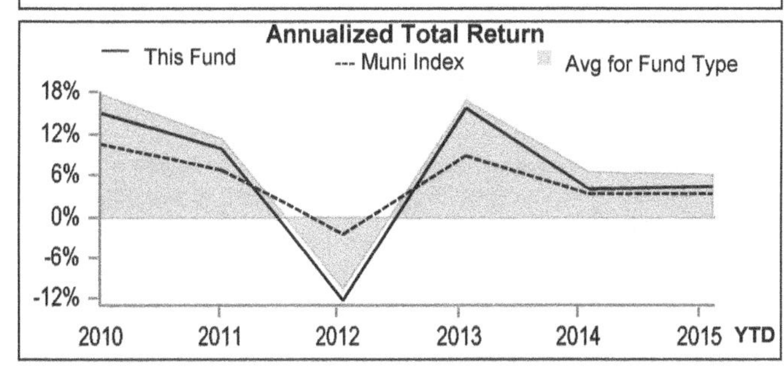

Duff & Phelps Global Utility Incom (DPG) D+ Weak

Fund Family: Duff & Phelps Investment Mgmt Co
Fund Type: Utilities
Inception Date: July 29, 2011

Major Rating Factors: Duff & Phelps Global Utility Incom receives a TheStreet.com Investment Rating of D+ (Weak). The fund currently has a performance rating of C- (Fair) based on an annualized return of 1.08% over the last three years and a total return of -25.14% year to date 2015. Factored into the performance evaluation is an expense ratio of 1.55% (average).

The fund's risk rating is currently C+ (Fair). It carries a beta of 0.55, meaning the fund's expected move will be 5.5% for every 10% move in the market. Volatility, as measured by both the semi-deviation and a drawdown factor, is considered low. As of December 31, 2015, Duff & Phelps Global Utility Incom traded at a discount of 14.61% below its net asset value, which is better than its one-year historical average discount of 13.96%.

Deborah A. Jansen currently receives a manager quality ranking of 38 (0=worst, 99=best). If you desire an average level of risk, then this fund may be an option.

Data Date	Investment Rating	Net Assets ($Mil)	Price	Performance Rating/Pts	Total Return Y-T-D	Risk Rating/Pts
12-15	D+	924.13	14.73	C- / 3.2	-25.14%	C+ / 6.2
2014	B+	911.20	21.64	B- / 7.1	22.92%	B / 8.4
2013	B-	828.82	19.08	C+ / 6.8	13.54%	B / 8.0
2012	D+	704.20	16.87	D / 1.9	4.66%	B- / 7.9

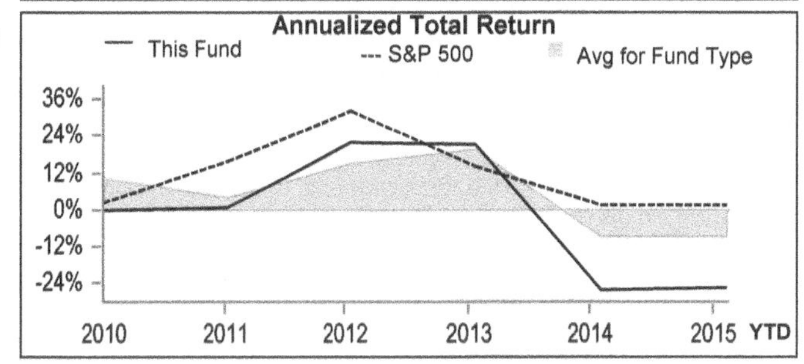

Duff & Phelps Select Energy MLP (DSE) E- Very Weak

Fund Family: Virtus Alternative Investment Advis
Fund Type: Energy/Natural Resources
Inception Date: June 25, 2014

Data Date	Investment Rating	Net Assets ($Mil)	Price	Performance Rating/Pts	Total Return Y-T-D	Risk Rating/Pts
12-15	E-	0.00	5.98	E- / 0	-53.71%	D / 1.7

Major Rating Factors: Duff & Phelps Select Energy MLP has adopted a very risky asset allocation strategy and currently receives an overall TheStreet.com Investment Rating of E- (Very Weak). The fund has a high level of volatility, as measured by both semi-deviation and drawdown factors. It carries a beta of 0.00, meaning the fund's expected move will be 0.0% for every 10% move in the market. As of December 31, 2015, Duff & Phelps Select Energy MLP traded at a discount of 8.42% below its net asset value, which is better than its one-year historical average discount of 2.23%. Unfortunately, the high level of risk (D, Weak) failed to pay off as investors endured very poor performance.

The fund's performance rating is currently E- (Very Weak). It has registered an annualized return of 0.00% over the last three years but is down -53.71% year to date 2015.

Charles J. Georgas has been running the fund for 2 years and currently receives a manager quality ranking of 2 (0=worst, 99=best). If you can tolerate very high levels of risk in the hope of improved future returns, holding this fund may be an option.

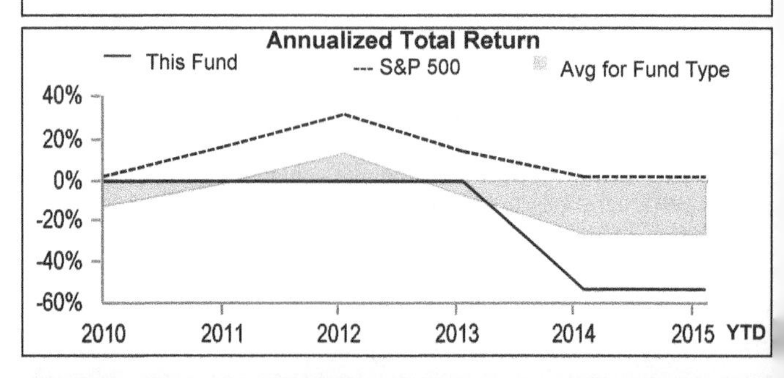

Duff & Phelps Utilities & Crp Bd T (DUC) C- Fair

Fund Family: Duff & Phelps Investment Mgmt Co
Fund Type: General - Investment Grade
Inception Date: January 22, 1993

Data Date	Investment Rating	Net Assets ($Mil)	Price	Performance Rating/Pts	Total Return Y-T-D	Risk Rating/Pts
12-15	C-	296.93	9.19	C- / 3.4	-0.12%	B- / 7.1
2014	C-	425.70	9.81	D+ / 2.9	5.00%	B- / 7.6
2013	C-	327.59	10.03	C- / 3.0	-12.75%	B / 8.1
2012	C-	324.21	12.26	C- / 3.3	9.35%	B / 8.7
2011	C+	319.92	12.04	C / 5.5	16.61%	B / 8.8
2010	B-	318.39	11.39	C+ / 5.9	-0.60%	B- / 7.3

Major Rating Factors: Middle of the road best describes Duff & Phelps Utilities & Crp Bd T whose TheStreet.com Investment Rating is currently a C- (Fair). The fund currently has a performance rating of C- (Fair) based on an annualized return of -2.95% over the last three years and a total return of -0.12% year to date 2015. Factored into the performance evaluation is an expense ratio of 1.48% (average).

The fund's risk rating is currently B- (Good). It carries a beta of 2.10, meaning it is expected to move 21.0% for every 10% move in the market. Volatility, as measured by both the semi-deviation and a drawdown factor, is considered low. As of December 31, 2015, Duff & Phelps Utilities & Crp Bd T traded at a discount of 8.56% below its net asset value, which is worse than its one-year historical average discount of 9.23%.

Daniel J. Petrisko has been running the fund for 20 years and currently receives a manager quality ranking of 28 (0=worst, 99=best). If you desire an average level of risk, then this fund may be an option.

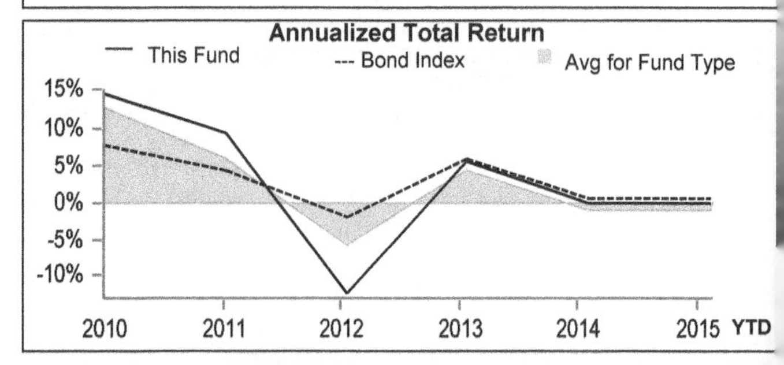

Eagle Capital Growth Fund (GRF) B+ Good

Fund Family: Sims Capital Management LLC
Fund Type: Growth
Inception Date: July 2, 1990

Data Date	Investment Rating	Net Assets ($Mil)	Price	Performance Rating/Pts	Total Return Y-T-D	Risk Rating/Pts
12-15	B+	27.16	7.59	B- / 7.5	-7.13%	B- / 7.8
2014	B+	27.60	8.70	C+ / 6.9	10.74%	B / 8.7
2013	A+	23.80	8.19	B+ / 8.9	29.70%	B / 8.7
2012	C+	23.68	7.10	C+ / 5.8	14.60%	B / 8.3
2011	B	22.20	7.00	B / 7.8	27.89%	B- / 7.7
2010	C-	21.00	6.62	C- / 3.3	9.34%	C+ / 6.3

Major Rating Factors: Strong performance is the major factor driving the B+ (Good) TheStreet.com Investment Rating for Eagle Capital Growth Fund. The fund currently has a performance rating of B- (Good) based on an annualized return of 10.08% over the last three years and a total return of -7.13% year to date 2015. Factored into the performance evaluation is an expense ratio of 1.40% (average).

The fund's risk rating is currently B- (Good). It carries a beta of 0.47, meaning the fund's expected move will be 4.7% for every 10% move in the market. Volatility, as measured by both the semi-deviation and a drawdown factor, is considered low. As of December 31, 2015, Eagle Capital Growth Fund traded at a discount of 10.92% below its net asset value, which is worse than its one-year historical average discount of 12.42%.

David C. Sims currently receives a manager quality ranking of 85 (0=worst, 99=best). If you desire only a moderate level of risk and strong performance, then this fund is an excellent option.

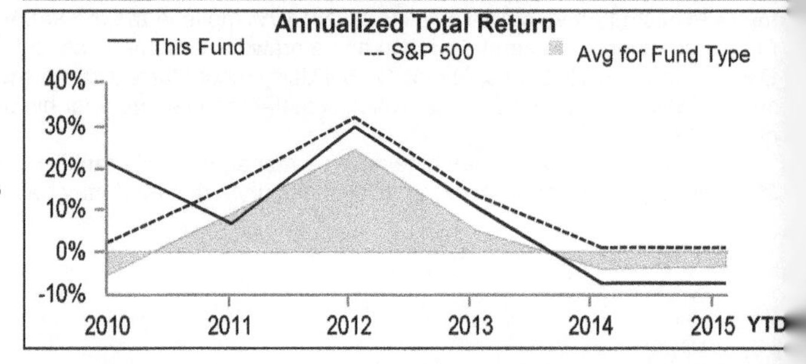

Eaton Vance CA Muni Bond (EVM) B+ Good

Fund Family: Eaton Vance Management
Fund Type: Municipal - Single State
Inception Date: August 27, 2002

Major Rating Factors: Strong performance is the major factor driving the B+ (Good) TheStreet.com Investment Rating for Eaton Vance CA Muni Bond. The fund currently has a performance rating of B (Good) based on an annualized return of 5.17% over the last three years and a total return of 9.82% year to date 2015. Factored into the performance evaluation is an expense ratio of 1.51% (average).

The fund's risk rating is currently B- (Good). It carries a beta of 2.29, meaning it is expected to move 22.9% for every 10% move in the market. Volatility, as measured by both the semi-deviation and a drawdown factor, is considered low. As of December 31, 2015, Eaton Vance CA Muni Bond traded at a discount of 6.03% below its net asset value, which is worse than its one-year historical average discount of 7.55%.

Craig R. Brandon has been running the fund for 2 years and currently receives a manager quality ranking of 57 (0=worst, 99=best). If you desire only a moderate level of risk and strong performance, then this fund is an excellent option.

Data Date	Investment Rating	Net Assets ($Mil)	Price	Performance Rating/Pts	Total Return Y-T-D	Risk Rating/Pts
12-15	B+	272.05	12.15	B / 8.2	9.82%	B- / 7.5
2014	C+	276.00	11.77	C+ / 6.2	21.61%	B- / 7.7
2013	C-	250.41	10.22	C- / 3.8	-12.54%	B- / 7.8
2012	C+	282.35	12.14	C / 5.5	5.29%	B / 8.1
2011	B+	257.20	12.82	B+ / 8.8	25.41%	B / 8.0
2010	D	273.91	11.25	D- / 1.5	5.61%	C+ / 6.2

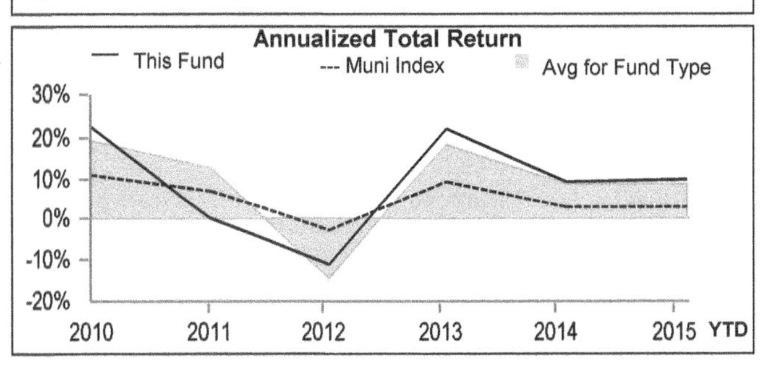

Eaton Vance CA Muni Bond II (EIA) C+ Fair

Fund Family: Eaton Vance Management
Fund Type: Municipal - Single State
Inception Date: November 25, 2002

Major Rating Factors: Middle of the road best describes Eaton Vance CA Muni Bond II whose TheStreet.com Investment Rating is currently a C+ (Fair). The fund currently has a performance rating of C+ (Fair) based on an annualized return of 1.09% over the last three years and a total return of 7.50% year to date 2015. Factored into the performance evaluation is an expense ratio of 1.38% (average).

The fund's risk rating is currently B- (Good). It carries a beta of 2.77, meaning it is expected to move 27.7% for every 10% move in the market. Volatility, as measured by both the semi-deviation and a drawdown factor, is considered low. As of December 31, 2015, Eaton Vance CA Muni Bond II traded at a discount of 4.90% below its net asset value, which is better than its one-year historical average discount of 3.81%.

Craig R. Brandon has been running the fund for 2 years and currently receives a manager quality ranking of 27 (0=worst, 99=best). If you desire an average level of risk, then this fund may be an option.

Data Date	Investment Rating	Net Assets ($Mil)	Price	Performance Rating/Pts	Total Return Y-T-D	Risk Rating/Pts
12-15	C+	50.91	12.81	C+ / 6.1	7.50%	B- / 7.0
2014	B-	51.60	12.60	B- / 7.4	25.78%	B- / 7.4
2013	C-	45.73	10.70	C- / 3.7	-23.72%	B- / 7.6
2012	A+	52.06	14.10	A+ / 9.6	27.57%	B / 8.2
2011	B+	46.50	12.77	B+ / 8.9	26.70%	B / 8.2
2010	D	48.53	11.00	D / 1.6	3.14%	C+ / 6.1

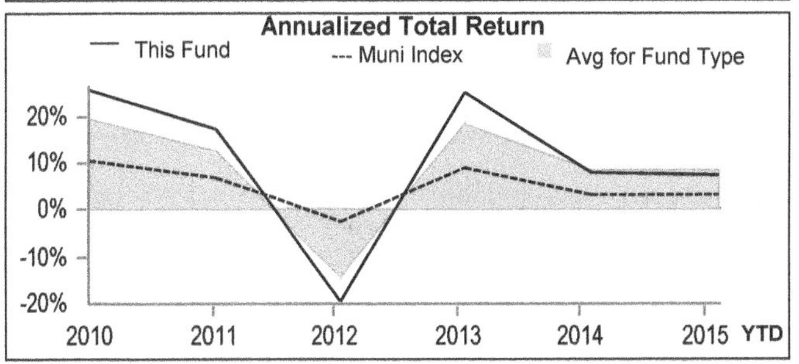

Eaton Vance CA Muni Inc Tr (CEV) B- Good

Fund Family: Eaton Vance Management
Fund Type: Municipal - Single State
Inception Date: January 26, 1999

Major Rating Factors: Strong performance is the major factor driving the B- (Good) TheStreet.com Investment Rating for Eaton Vance CA Muni Inc Tr. The fund currently has a performance rating of B- (Good) based on an annualized return of 3.25% over the last three years and a total return of 7.76% year to date 2015. Factored into the performance evaluation is an expense ratio of 1.69% (above average).

The fund's risk rating is currently B- (Good). It carries a beta of 2.69, meaning it is expected to move 26.9% for every 10% move in the market. Volatility, as measured by both the semi-deviation and a drawdown factor, is considered low. As of December 31, 2015, Eaton Vance CA Muni Inc Tr traded at a discount of 5.73% below its net asset value, which is worse than its one-year historical average discount of 6.72%.

Craig R. Brandon has been running the fund for 2 years and currently receives a manager quality ranking of 34 (0=worst, 99=best). If you desire only a moderate level of risk and strong performance, then this fund is an excellent option.

Data Date	Investment Rating	Net Assets ($Mil)	Price	Performance Rating/Pts	Total Return Y-T-D	Risk Rating/Pts
12-15	B-	102.13	13.33	B- / 7.1	7.76%	B- / 7.1
2014	B	101.20	13.08	B / 7.6	21.93%	B- / 7.7
2013	C	101.15	11.23	C / 5.1	-16.23%	B- / 7.9
2012	A-	100.33	14.27	B+ / 8.3	16.62%	B / 8.5
2011	A	93.00	13.06	A / 9.3	24.21%	B / 8.5
2010	D	93.25	11.67	D / 1.9	5.21%	C+ / 5.7

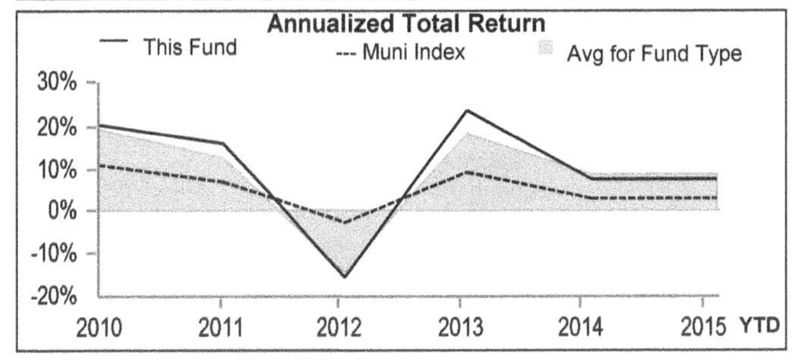

Eaton Vance Enhanced Eqty Inc (EOI) A Excellent

Fund Family: Eaton Vance Management
Fund Type: Income
Inception Date: October 29, 2004

Data Date	Investment Rating	Net Assets ($Mil)	Price	Performance Rating/Pts	Total Return Y-T-D	Risk Rating/Pts
12-15	A	525.00	13.42	A- / 9.2	5.57%	B- / 7.5
2014	A+	571.90	13.79	B / 8.2	15.75%	B / 8.8
2013	B-	524.59	13.00	B- / 7.3	26.63%	B- / 7.5
2012	D+	503.83	10.66	D+ / 2.8	18.28%	B- / 7.1
2011	D	476.70	10.18	D+ / 2.4	-10.22%	C+ / 6.8
2010	D	513.95	12.64	D / 2.1	-1.01%	C+ / 5.6

Major Rating Factors:
Exceptional performance is the major factor driving the A (Excellent) TheStreet.com Investment Rating for Eaton Vance Enhanced Eqty Inc. The fund currently has a performance rating of A- (Excellent) based on an annualized return of 15.55% over the last three years and a total return of 5.57% year to date 2015. Factored into the performance evaluation is an expense ratio of 1.11% (low).

The fund's risk rating is currently B- (Good). It carries a beta of 1.00, meaning that its performance tracks fairly well with that of the overall stock market. Volatility, as measured by both the semi-deviation and a drawdown factor, is considered low. As of December 31, 2015, Eaton Vance Enhanced Eqty Inc traded at a discount of 4.01% below its net asset value, which is worse than its one-year historical average discount of 8.76%.

Michael A. Allison has been running the fund for 8 years and currently receives a manager quality ranking of 78 (0=worst, 99=best). If you desire only a moderate level of risk and strong performance, then this fund is an excellent option.

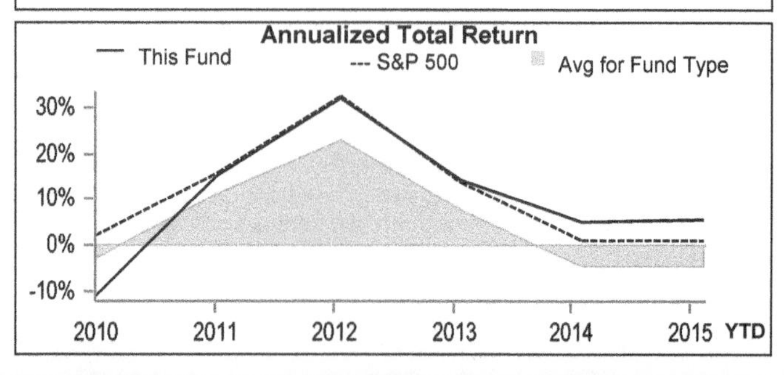

Eaton Vance Enhanced Eqty Inc II (EOS) A Excellent

Fund Family: Eaton Vance Management
Fund Type: Income
Inception Date: January 26, 2005

Data Date	Investment Rating	Net Assets ($Mil)	Price	Performance Rating/Pts	Total Return Y-T-D	Risk Rating/Pts
12-15	A	693.11	13.64	A / 9.3	6.44%	B- / 7.3
2014	A+	685.50	13.83	B+ / 8.5	16.68%	B / 8.5
2013	B-	572.04	12.99	B / 7.6	28.35%	B- / 7.0
2012	D	588.56	10.44	D+ / 2.7	14.39%	C+ / 6.8
2011	C-	569.60	10.21	C / 4.3	0.03%	C+ / 6.4
2010	D+	563.82	12.21	D / 2.2	-4.47%	C+ / 5.9

Major Rating Factors:
Exceptional performance is the major factor driving the A (Excellent) TheStreet.com Investment Rating for Eaton Vance Enhanced Eqty Inc II. The fund currently has a performance rating of A (Excellent) based on an annualized return of 16.82% over the last three years and a total return of 6.44% year to date 2015. Factored into the performance evaluation is an expense ratio of 1.11% (low).

The fund's risk rating is currently B- (Good). It carries a beta of 0.97, meaning that its performance tracks fairly well with that of the overall stock market. Volatility, as measured by both the semi-deviation and a drawdown factor, is considered low. As of December 31, 2015, Eaton Vance Enhanced Eqty Inc II traded at a discount of 5.34% below its net asset value, which is worse than its one-year historical average discount of 6.06%.

Michael A. Allison has been running the fund for 8 years and currently receives a manager quality ranking of 85 (0=worst, 99=best). If you desire only a moderate level of risk and strong performance, then this fund is an excellent option.

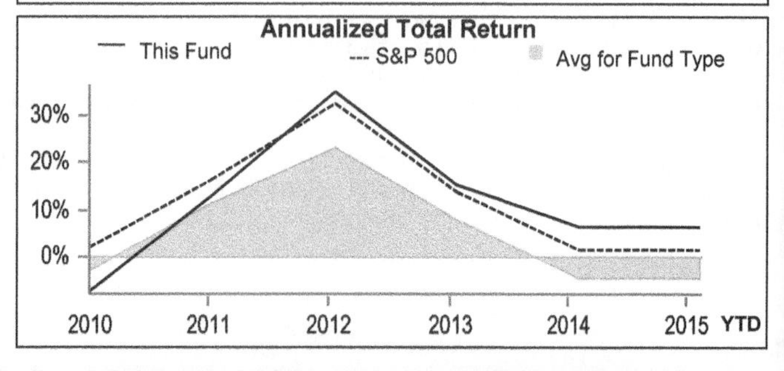

Eaton Vance Floating Rate Income T (EFT) C- Fair

Fund Family: Eaton Vance Management
Fund Type: Loan Participation
Inception Date: June 29, 2004

Data Date	Investment Rating	Net Assets ($Mil)	Price	Performance Rating/Pts	Total Return Y-T-D	Risk Rating/Pts
12-15	C-	623.44	12.64	D+ / 2.9	-2.48%	B- / 7.1
2014	C-	627.50	13.89	C- / 3.4	-3.25%	B / 8.0
2013	C-	646.84	15.27	C- / 3.5	-6.12%	B / 8.2
2012	B	582.01	17.04	B / 7.8	29.64%	B / 8.1
2011	B	564.10	14.23	B / 7.7	-4.38%	B / 8.2
2010	C+	556.61	16.00	B / 7.6	20.23%	C / 4.3

Major Rating Factors:
Disappointing performance is the major factor driving the C- (Fair) TheStreet.com Investment Rating for Eaton Vance Floating Rate Income T. The fund currently has a performance rating of D+ (Weak) based on an annualized return of -4.06% over the last three years and a total return of -2.48% year to date 2015. Factored into the performance evaluation is an expense ratio of 2.17% (high).

The fund's risk rating is currently B- (Good). It carries a beta of -22.32, meaning the fund's expected move will be -223.2% for every 10% move in the market. Volatility, as measured by both the semi-deviation and a drawdown factor, is considered low. As of December 31, 2015, Eaton Vance Floating Rate Income T traded at a discount of 9.65% below its net asset value, which is better than its one-year historical average discount of 8.97%.

Scott H. Page has been running the fund for 12 years and currently receives a manager quality ranking of 35 (0=worst, 99=best). This fund offers only a moderate level of risk but investors looking for strong performance are still waiting.

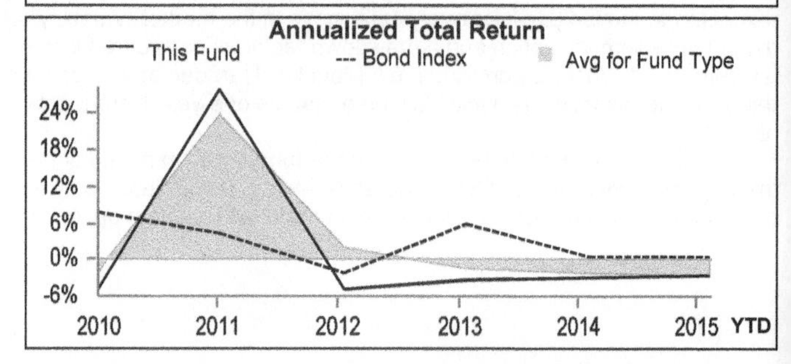

Eaton Vance Floating-Rate Inc Plus (EFF) C- Fair

Fund Family: Eaton Vance Management
Fund Type: Loan Participation
Inception Date: June 28, 2013

Major Rating Factors:
Disappointing performance is the major factor driving the C- (Fair) TheStreet.com Investment Rating for Eaton Vance Floating-Rate Inc Plus. The fund currently has a performance rating of D+ (Weak) based on an annualized return of 0.00% over the last three years and a total return of -5.98% year to date 2015. Factored into the performance evaluation is an expense ratio of 2.39% (high).

The fund's risk rating is currently B- (Good). It carries a beta of 0.00, meaning the fund's expected move will be 0.0% for every 10% move in the market. Volatility, as measured by both the semi-deviation and a drawdown factor, is considered low. As of December 31, 2015, Eaton Vance Floating-Rate Inc Plus traded at a discount of 10.39% below its net asset value, which is better than its one-year historical average discount of 10.32%.

Craig P. Russ has been running the fund for 3 years and currently receives a manager quality ranking of 25 (0=worst, 99=best). This fund offers only a moderate level of risk but investors looking for strong performance are still waiting.

Data Date	Investment Rating	Net Assets ($Mil)	Price	Performance Rating/Pts	Total Return Y-T-D	Risk Rating/Pts
12-15	C-	139.90	14.15	D+ / 2.3	-5.98%	B- / 7.5
2014	D+	144.90	16.13	D- / 1.5	-5.47%	B- / 7.8

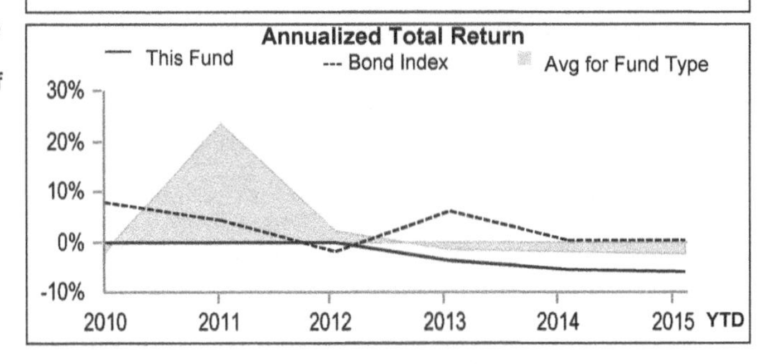

Eaton Vance Limited Duration Incom (EVV) C- Fair

Fund Family: Eaton Vance Management
Fund Type: General Bond
Inception Date: May 30, 2003

Major Rating Factors: Middle of the road best describes Eaton Vance Limited Duration Incom whose TheStreet.com Investment Rating is currently a C- (Fair). The fund currently has a performance rating of C- (Fair) based on an annualized return of -1.29% over the last three years and a total return of -0.90% year to date 2015. Factored into the performance evaluation is an expense ratio of 1.89% (above average).

The fund's risk rating is currently B- (Good). It carries a beta of 1.09, meaning that its performance tracks fairly well with that of the overall stock market. Volatility, as measured by both the semi-deviation and a drawdown factor, is considered low. As of December 31, 2015, Eaton Vance Limited Duration Incom traded at a discount of 11.27% below its net asset value, which is worse than its one-year historical average discount of 12.21%.

Payson F. Swaffield has been running the fund for 13 years and currently receives a manager quality ranking of 48 (0=worst, 99=best). If you desire an average level of risk, then this fund may be an option.

Data Date	Investment Rating	Net Assets ($Mil)	Price	Performance Rating/Pts	Total Return Y-T-D	Risk Rating/Pts
12-15	C-	1,881.99	12.76	C- / 3.8	-0.90%	B- / 7.0
2014	C-	1,895.30	14.12	C- / 3.6	-0.31%	B / 8.1
2013	C+	1,980.82	15.30	C / 4.9	-2.35%	B / 8.5
2012	C	1,941.50	16.66	C+ / 5.6	19.59%	B- / 7.7
2011	B-	1,899.70	15.23	B- / 7.1	6.14%	B- / 7.7
2010	C+	1,950.18	16.05	B / 7.6	16.59%	C / 4.4

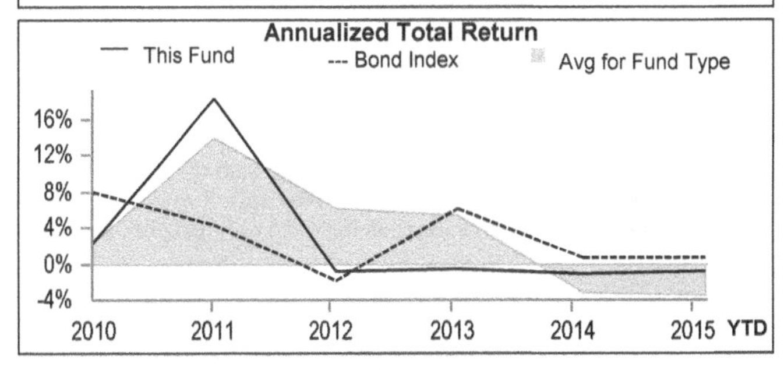

Eaton Vance MA Muni Bond (MAB) B- Good

Fund Family: Eaton Vance Management
Fund Type: Municipal - Single State
Inception Date: November 25, 2002

Major Rating Factors: Strong performance is the major factor driving the B- (Good) TheStreet.com Investment Rating for Eaton Vance MA Muni Bond. The fund currently has a performance rating of B- (Good) based on an annualized return of 2.47% over the last three years and a total return of 10.09% year to date 2015. Factored into the performance evaluation is an expense ratio of 1.49% (average).

The fund's risk rating is currently B- (Good). It carries a beta of 1.82, meaning it is expected to move 18.2% for every 10% move in the market. Volatility, as measured by both the semi-deviation and a drawdown factor, is considered low. As of December 31, 2015, Eaton Vance MA Muni Bond traded at a discount of 5.54% below its net asset value, which is worse than its one-year historical average discount of 6.32%.

Craig R. Brandon has been running the fund for 6 years and currently receives a manager quality ranking of 46 (0=worst, 99=best). If you desire only a moderate level of risk and strong performance, then this fund is an excellent option.

Data Date	Investment Rating	Net Assets ($Mil)	Price	Performance Rating/Pts	Total Return Y-T-D	Risk Rating/Pts
12-15	B-	26.69	14.83	B- / 7.3	10.09%	B- / 7.2
2014	C+	26.90	14.16	C+ / 6.0	21.96%	B- / 7.6
2013	C-	23.93	12.28	C- / 3.0	-20.13%	B- / 7.7
2012	B	28.14	15.90	B- / 7.3	14.35%	B / 8.4
2011	B-	25.60	14.36	C+ / 6.9	21.85%	B / 8.2
2010	C-	25.92	12.91	D / 1.8	-9.86%	B- / 7.3

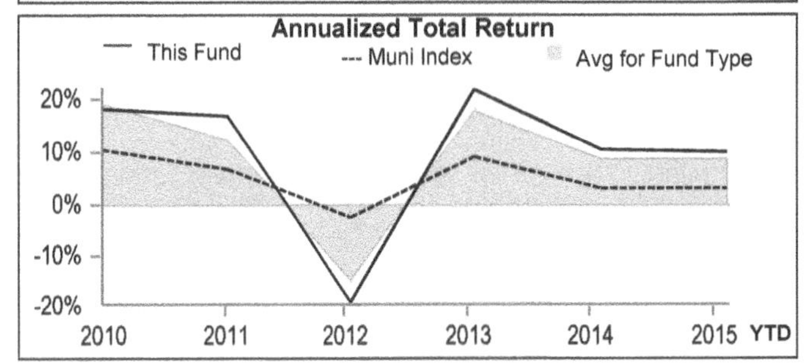

Eaton Vance MA Muni Inc Tr (MMV) B- Good

Fund Family: Eaton Vance Management
Fund Type: Municipal - Single State
Inception Date: January 26, 1999

Major Rating Factors: Strong performance is the major factor driving the B- (Good) TheStreet.com Investment Rating for Eaton Vance MA Muni Inc Tr. The fund currently has a performance rating of B- (Good) based on an annualized return of 1.60% over the last three years and a total return of 8.38% year to date 2015. Factored into the performance evaluation is an expense ratio of 1.73% (above average).

The fund's risk rating is currently B- (Good). It carries a beta of 2.17, meaning it is expected to move 21.7% for every 10% move in the market. Volatility, as measured by both the semi-deviation and a drawdown factor, is considered low. As of December 31, 2015, Eaton Vance MA Muni Inc Tr traded at a discount of 8.42% below its net asset value, which is worse than its one-year historical average discount of 9.66%.

Craig R. Brandon has been running the fund for 6 years and currently receives a manager quality ranking of 36 (0=worst, 99=best). If you desire only a moderate level of risk and strong performance, then this fund is an excellent option.

Data Date	Investment Rating	Net Assets ($Mil)	Price	Performance Rating/Pts	Total Return Y-T-D	Risk Rating/Pts
12-15	B-	41.53	14.03	B- / 7.0	8.38%	B- / 7.5
2014	C+	41.60	13.69	C / 5.5	16.77%	B- / 7.7
2013	D+	41.67	12.25	D+ / 2.6	-16.68%	B- / 7.9
2012	B-	42.00	15.26	C+ / 6.4	9.39%	B / 8.6
2011	A-	39.70	14.46	B+ / 8.7	18.40%	B / 8.7
2010	C+	39.13	13.50	C+ / 6.0	4.02%	C+ / 6.1

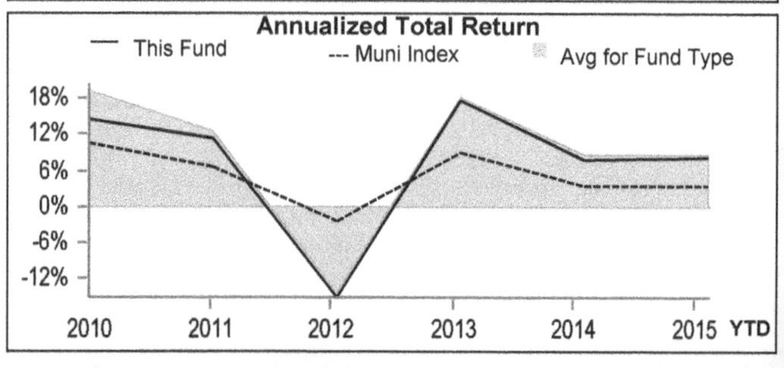

Eaton Vance MI Muni Bond (MIW) B+ Good

Fund Family: Eaton Vance Management
Fund Type: Municipal - Single State
Inception Date: November 25, 2002

Major Rating Factors: Strong performance is the major factor driving the B+ (Good) TheStreet.com Investment Rating for Eaton Vance MI Muni Bond. The fund currently has a performance rating of B (Good) based on an annualized return of 3.55% over the last three years and a total return of 10.26% year to date 2015. Factored into the performance evaluation is an expense ratio of 1.48% (average).

The fund's risk rating is currently B- (Good). It carries a beta of 2.51, meaning it is expected to move 25.1% for every 10% move in the market. Volatility, as measured by both the semi-deviation and a drawdown factor, is considered low. As of December 31, 2015, Eaton Vance MI Muni Bond traded at a discount of 10.59% below its net asset value, which is better than its one-year historical average discount of 9.41%.

Cynthia J. Clemson has been running the fund for 1 year and currently receives a manager quality ranking of 41 (0=worst, 99=best). If you desire only a moderate level of risk and strong performance, then this fund is an excellent option.

Data Date	Investment Rating	Net Assets ($Mil)	Price	Performance Rating/Pts	Total Return Y-T-D	Risk Rating/Pts
12-15	B+	22.41	13.85	B / 8.0	10.26%	B- / 7.2
2014	C	22.50	13.20	C / 5.2	21.25%	B- / 7.3
2013	C-	19.93	11.54	C- / 3.3	-17.63%	B- / 7.5
2012	C+	22.76	14.40	C / 5.4	7.93%	B / 8.4
2011	A+	21.60	14.76	A+ / 9.7	29.91%	B / 8.6
2010	D+	21.99	12.32	D+ / 2.3	-1.32%	C+ / 6.6

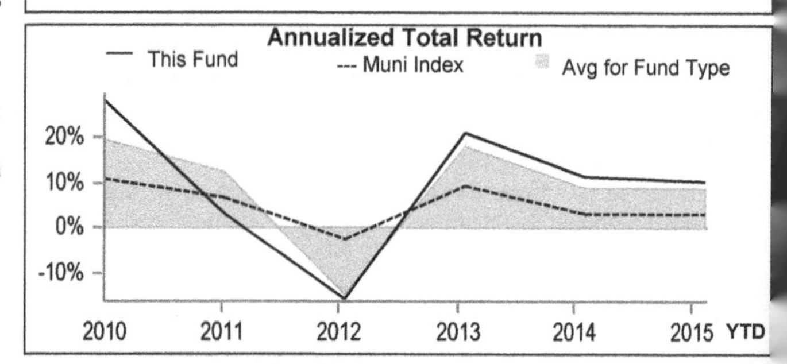

Eaton Vance MI Muni Inc Tr (EMI) B Good

Fund Family: Eaton Vance Management
Fund Type: Municipal - Single State
Inception Date: January 26, 1999

Major Rating Factors: Strong performance is the major factor driving the B (Good) TheStreet.com Investment Rating for Eaton Vance MI Muni Inc Tr. The fund currently has a performance rating of B- (Good) based on an annualized return of 3.09% over the last three years and a total return of 9.22% year to date 2015. Factored into the performance evaluation is an expense ratio of 1.87% (above average).

The fund's risk rating is currently B- (Good). It carries a beta of 2.27, meaning it is expected to move 22.7% for every 10% move in the market. Volatility, as measured by both the semi-deviation and a drawdown factor, is considered low. As of December 31, 2015, Eaton Vance MI Muni Inc Tr traded at a discount of 11.76% below its net asset value, which is worse than its one-year historical average discount of 13.37%.

Cynthia J. Clemson has been running the fund for 1 year and currently receives a manager quality ranking of 44 (0=worst, 99=best). If you desire only a moderate level of risk and strong performance, then this fund is an excellent option.

Data Date	Investment Rating	Net Assets ($Mil)	Price	Performance Rating/Pts	Total Return Y-T-D	Risk Rating/Pts
12-15	B	30.50	13.13	B- / 7.3	9.22%	B- / 7.4
2014	B-	30.60	12.71	C+ / 6.7	19.61%	B- / 7.7
2013	C-	30.50	11.09	C- / 4.1	-16.14%	B / 8.0
2012	A	30.72	13.80	B+ / 8.5	14.79%	B / 8.7
2011	A-	29.20	12.90	B+ / 8.8	20.19%	B / 8.7
2010	D+	28.49	11.43	D / 2.2	3.24%	C+ / 5.9

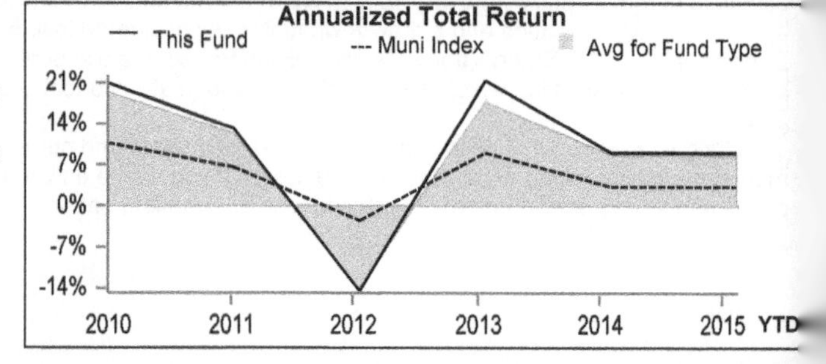

Eaton Vance Muni Bond Fund (EIM) B- Good

Fund Family: Eaton Vance Management
Fund Type: Municipal - National
Inception Date: August 27, 2002

Data Date	Investment Rating	Net Assets ($Mil)	Price	Performance Rating/Pts	Total Return Y-T-D	Risk Rating/Pts
12-15	B-	945.48	12.98	C+ / 6.7	7.21%	B- / 7.4
2014	B	950.50	12.83	B- / 7.3	20.62%	B- / 7.6
2013	C	837.45	11.30	C / 4.8	-17.05%	B- / 7.8
2012	B+	960.53	13.99	B / 7.9	17.80%	B / 8.3
2011	B+	866.50	12.68	B / 8.1	20.79%	B / 8.4
2010	D+	889.54	11.48	D- / 1.3	-0.42%	C+ / 6.8

Major Rating Factors: Eaton Vance Muni Bond Fund receives a TheStreet.com Investment Rating of B- (Good). The fund currently has a performance rating of C+ (Fair) based on an annualized return of 2.45% over the last three years and a total return of 7.21% year to date 2015. Factored into the performance evaluation is an expense ratio of 1.43% (average).

The fund's risk rating is currently B- (Good). It carries a beta of 2.80, meaning it is expected to move 28.0% for every 10% move in the market. Volatility, as measured by both the semi-deviation and a drawdown factor, is considered low. As of December 31, 2015, Eaton Vance Muni Bond Fund traded at a discount of 8.07% below its net asset value, which is worse than its one-year historical average discount of 9.52%.

Cynthia J. Clemson has been running the fund for 2 years and currently receives a manager quality ranking of 30 (0=worst, 99=best). If you desire an average level of risk, then this fund may be an option.

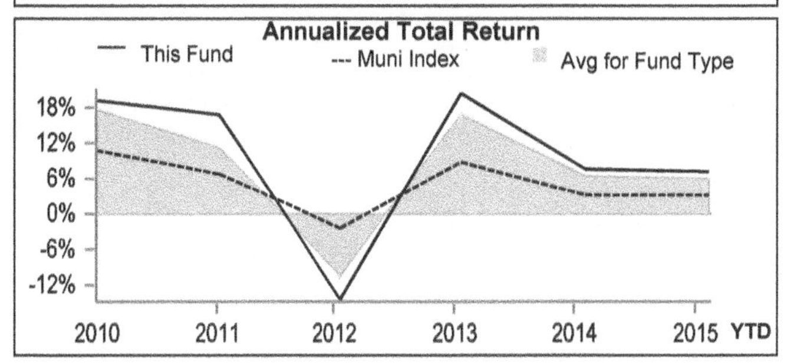

Eaton Vance Muni Bond II (EIV) B Good

Fund Family: Eaton Vance Management
Fund Type: Municipal - National
Inception Date: November 25, 2002

Data Date	Investment Rating	Net Assets ($Mil)	Price	Performance Rating/Pts	Total Return Y-T-D	Risk Rating/Pts
12-15	B	136.71	13.18	B / 7.9	9.78%	B- / 7.3
2014	C+	136.40	12.69	C+ / 6.0	22.34%	B- / 7.5
2013	C-	118.57	11.00	C- / 3.9	-16.40%	B- / 7.7
2012	C+	133.77	13.32	C / 5.4	2.62%	B / 8.6
2011	A+	121.50	13.87	A / 9.4	28.88%	B / 8.8
2010	D	126.81	12.00	D / 2.0	0.15%	C+ / 5.8

Major Rating Factors: Strong performance is the major factor driving the B (Good) TheStreet.com Investment Rating for Eaton Vance Muni Bond II. The fund currently has a performance rating of B (Good) based on an annualized return of 4.04% over the last three years and a total return of 9.78% year to date 2015. Factored into the performance evaluation is an expense ratio of 1.30% (average).

The fund's risk rating is currently B- (Good). It carries a beta of 2.54, meaning it is expected to move 25.4% for every 10% move in the market. Volatility, as measured by both the semi-deviation and a drawdown factor, is considered low. As of December 31, 2015, Eaton Vance Muni Bond II traded at a discount of 5.99% below its net asset value, which is worse than its one-year historical average discount of 8.03%.

Cynthia J. Clemson has been running the fund for 2 years and currently receives a manager quality ranking of 49 (0=worst, 99=best). If you desire only a moderate level of risk and strong performance, then this fund is an excellent option.

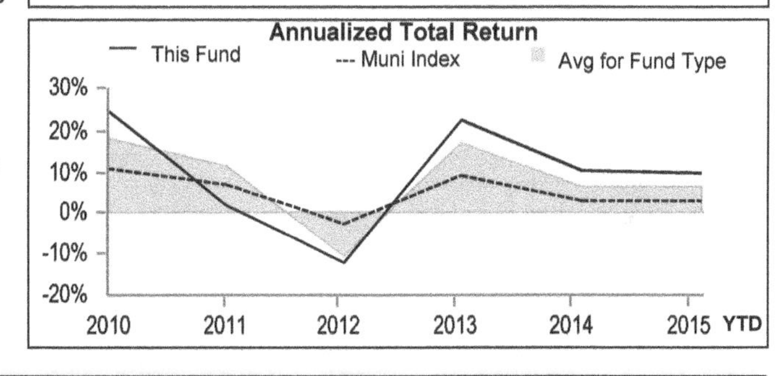

Eaton Vance Municipal Inc 2028 Ter (ETX) A+ Excellent

Fund Family: Eaton Vance Management
Fund Type: Municipal - National
Inception Date: March 26, 2013

Data Date	Investment Rating	Net Assets ($Mil)	Price	Performance Rating/Pts	Total Return Y-T-D	Risk Rating/Pts
12-15	A+	223.73	18.49	A+ / 9.7	10.24%	B- / 7.8
2014	A+	211.00	17.51	A+ / 9.6	23.62%	B- / 7.8

Major Rating Factors:
Exceptional performance is the major factor driving the A+ (Excellent) TheStreet.com Investment Rating for Eaton Vance Municipal Inc 2028 Ter. The fund currently has a performance rating of A+ (Excellent) based on an annualized return of 0.00% over the last three years and a total return of 10.24% year to date 2015. Factored into the performance evaluation is an expense ratio of 1.46% (average).

The fund's risk rating is currently B- (Good). It carries a beta of 0.00, meaning the fund's expected move will be 0.0% for every 10% move in the market. Volatility, as measured by both the semi-deviation and a drawdown factor, is considered low. As of December 31, 2015, Eaton Vance Municipal Inc 2028 Ter traded at a discount of 9.72% below its net asset value, which is worse than its one-year historical average discount of 11.09%.

Craig R. Brandon has been running the fund for 1 year and currently receives a manager quality ranking of 67 (0=worst, 99=best). If you desire only a moderate level of risk and strong performance, then this fund is an excellent option.

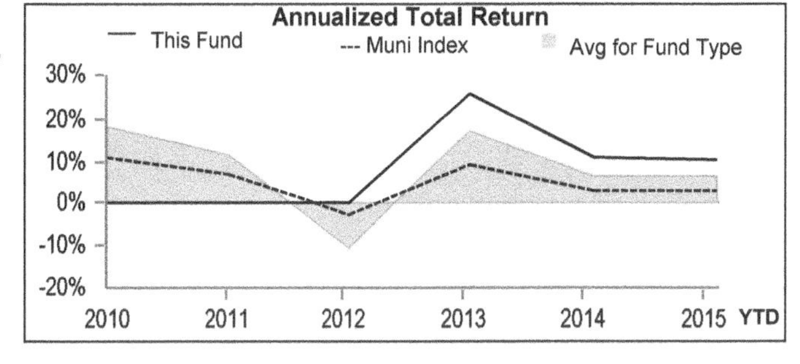

Eaton Vance Municipal Inc Tr (EVN) — B — Good

Fund Family: Eaton Vance Management
Fund Type: Municipal - National
Inception Date: January 26, 1999

Major Rating Factors: Strong performance is the major factor driving the B (Good) TheStreet.com Investment Rating for Eaton Vance Municipal Inc Tr. The fund currently has a performance rating of B+ (Good) based on an annualized return of 5.84% over the last three years and a total return of 9.79% year to date 2015. Factored into the performance evaluation is an expense ratio of 1.85% (above average).

The fund's risk rating is currently C+ (Fair). It carries a beta of 3.39, meaning it is expected to move 33.9% for every 10% move in the market. Volatility, as measured by both the semi-deviation and a drawdown factor, is considered low. As of December 31, 2015, Eaton Vance Municipal Inc Tr traded at a premium of 3.86% above its net asset value, which is worse than its one-year historical average premium of 1.70%.

Cynthia J. Clemson has been running the fund for 1 year and currently receives a manager quality ranking of 42 (0=worst, 99=best). If you desire only a moderate level of risk and strong performance, then this fund is an excellent option.

Data Date	Investment Rating	Net Assets ($Mil)	Price	Performance Rating/Pts	Total Return Y-T-D	Risk Rating/Pts
12-15	B	307.07	13.73	B+ / 8.8	9.79%	C+ / 6.4
2014	B	300.30	13.42	A / 9.3	34.88%	C+ / 5.9
2013	C-	286.44	10.51	C- / 4.0	-19.74%	B- / 7.6
2012	A+	276.76	13.77	A- / 9.1	20.45%	B / 8.5
2011	A-	252.60	12.75	A- / 9.2	23.20%	B / 8.5
2010	D	260.25	11.13	D / 1.6	4.67%	C / 5.2

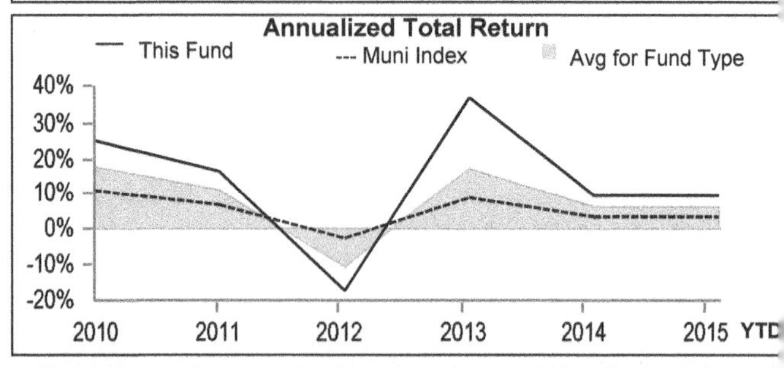

Eaton Vance National Municipal Opp (EOT) — B- — Good

Fund Family: Eaton Vance Management
Fund Type: Municipal - National
Inception Date: May 29, 2009

Major Rating Factors: Strong performance is the major factor driving the B- (Good) TheStreet.com Investment Rating for Eaton Vance National Municipal Opp. The fund currently has a performance rating of B- (Good) based on an annualized return of 3.10% over the last three years and a total return of 7.25% year to date 2015. Factored into the performance evaluation is an expense ratio of 0.86% (very low).

The fund's risk rating is currently B- (Good). It carries a beta of 2.04, meaning it is expected to move 20.4% for every 10% move in the market. Volatility, as measured by both the semi-deviation and a drawdown factor, is considered low. As of December 31, 2015, Eaton Vance National Municipal Opp traded at a discount of 5.76% below its net asset value, which is worse than its one-year historical average discount of 7.83%.

Dan Wasiolek has been running the fund for 7 years and currently receives a manager quality ranking of 49 (0=worst, 99=best). If you desire only a moderate level of risk and strong performance, then this fund is an excellent option.

Data Date	Investment Rating	Net Assets ($Mil)	Price	Performance Rating/Pts	Total Return Y-T-D	Risk Rating/Pts
12-15	B-	350.61	21.43	B- / 7.0	7.25%	B- / 7.3
2014	B-	343.00	21.00	B- / 7.0	18.49%	B- / 7.6
2013	C-	347.89	18.46	C- / 4.1	-14.17%	B- / 7.8
2012	B-	331.23	22.14	C+ / 6.8	14.04%	B / 8.3
2011	A-	318.80	20.90	A- / 9.1	17.27%	B / 8.4
2010	C-	324.33	19.09	D / 1.7	5.76%	B- / 7.9

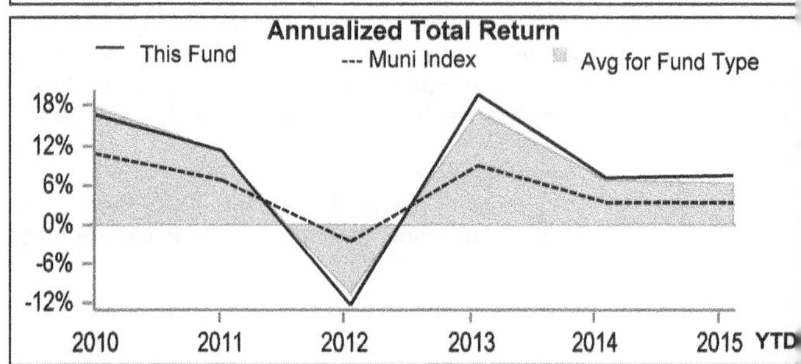

Eaton Vance NJ Muni Bond (EMJ) — C+ — Fair

Fund Family: Eaton Vance Management
Fund Type: Municipal - Single State
Inception Date: November 25, 2002

Major Rating Factors: Middle of the road best describes Eaton Vance NJ Muni Bond whose TheStreet.com Investment Rating is currently a C+ (Fair). The fund currently has a performance rating of C+ (Fair) based on an annualized return of -0.07% over the last three years and a total return of 15.01% year to date 2015. Factored into the performance evaluation is an expense ratio of 1.29% (average).

The fund's risk rating is currently C+ (Fair). It carries a beta of 2.08, meaning it is expected to move 20.8% for every 10% move in the market. Volatility, as measured by both the semi-deviation and a drawdown factor, is considered low. As of December 31, 2015, Eaton Vance NJ Muni Bond traded at a discount of 7.00% below its net asset value, which is worse than its one-year historical average discount of 7.28%.

Adam A. Weigold has been running the fund for 6 years and currently receives a manager quality ranking of 25 (0=worst, 99=best). If you desire an average level of risk, then this fund may be an option.

Data Date	Investment Rating	Net Assets ($Mil)	Price	Performance Rating/Pts	Total Return Y-T-D	Risk Rating/Pts
12-15	C+	36.71	13.81	C+ / 6.4	15.01%	C+ / 6.8
2014	C	37.80	12.72	C / 4.8	14.11%	B- / 7.5
2013	D+	34.22	11.66	D+ / 2.8	-23.85%	B- / 7.7
2012	B+	38.14	16.24	B / 8.1	20.89%	B / 8.3
2011	B	34.90	14.16	B / 7.7	18.79%	B / 8.3
2010	D+	37.22	12.61	D- / 1.5	-6.04%	C+ / 6.7

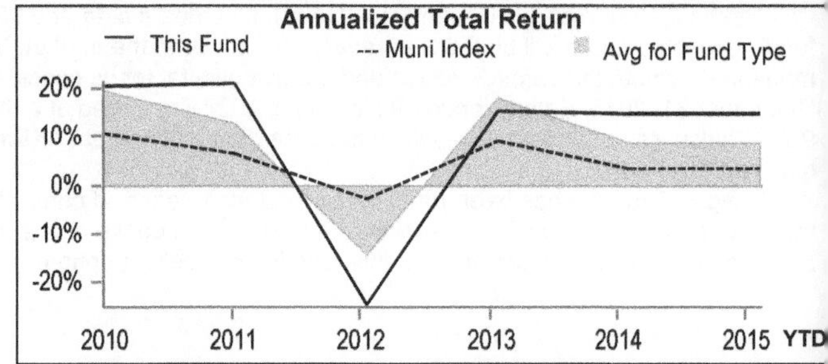

Eaton Vance NJ Muni Inc Tr (EVJ) C Fair

Fund Family: Eaton Vance Management
Fund Type: Municipal - Single State
Inception Date: January 26, 1999

Data Date	Investment Rating	Net Assets ($Mil)	Price	Performance Rating/Pts	Total Return Y-T-D	Risk Rating/Pts
12-15	C	65.62	12.69	C+ / 5.6	9.82%	B- / 7.2
2014	C-	66.00	12.28	C / 4.4	12.94%	B- / 7.4
2013	D+	66.43	11.58	D+ / 2.4	-22.06%	B- / 7.6
2012	B+	65.46	15.10	B / 7.6	17.70%	B / 8.4
2011	B+	62.10	13.95	B+ / 8.8	14.20%	B / 8.5
2010	C-	65.22	12.48	C- / 3.3	-2.98%	C+ / 5.8

Major Rating Factors: Middle of the road best describes Eaton Vance NJ Muni Inc Tr whose TheStreet.com Investment Rating is currently a C (Fair). The fund currently has a performance rating of C+ (Fair) based on an annualized return of -1.18% over the last three years and a total return of 9.82% year to date 2015. Factored into the performance evaluation is an expense ratio of 1.68% (above average).

The fund's risk rating is currently B- (Good). It carries a beta of 2.11, meaning it is expected to move 21.1% for every 10% move in the market. Volatility, as measured by both the semi-deviation and a drawdown factor, is considered low. As of December 31, 2015, Eaton Vance NJ Muni Inc Tr traded at a discount of 8.90% below its net asset value, which is worse than its one-year historical average discount of 11.09%.

Adam A. Weigold has been running the fund for 6 years and currently receives a manager quality ranking of 25 (0=worst, 99=best). If you desire an average level of risk, then this fund may be an option.

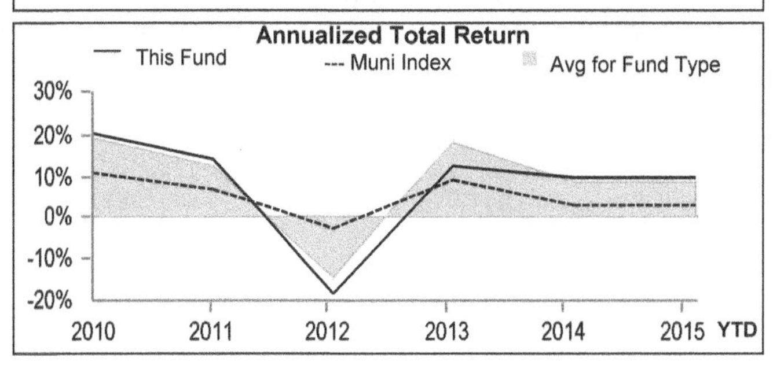

Eaton Vance NY Muni Bond (ENX) B Good

Fund Family: Eaton Vance Management
Fund Type: Municipal - Single State
Inception Date: August 27, 2002

Data Date	Investment Rating	Net Assets ($Mil)	Price	Performance Rating/Pts	Total Return Y-T-D	Risk Rating/Pts
12-15	B	218.28	13.13	B / 7.8	11.11%	B- / 7.3
2014	C	220.20	12.57	C+ / 5.6	17.51%	B- / 7.4
2013	C-	202.45	11.32	C- / 3.2	-16.70%	B- / 7.6
2012	C+	229.79	13.93	C / 5.2	10.82%	B / 8.3
2011	B+	212.70	13.97	B / 7.9	22.28%	B / 8.6
2010	D+	215.45	12.18	D- / 1.5	-5.41%	B- / 7.0

Major Rating Factors: Strong performance is the major factor driving the B (Good) TheStreet.com Investment Rating for Eaton Vance NY Muni Bond. The fund currently has a performance rating of B (Good) based on an annualized return of 2.65% over the last three years and a total return of 11.11% year to date 2015. Factored into the performance evaluation is an expense ratio of 1.57% (above average).

The fund's risk rating is currently B- (Good). It carries a beta of 2.15, meaning it is expected to move 21.5% for every 10% move in the market. Volatility, as measured by both the semi-deviation and a drawdown factor, is considered low. As of December 31, 2015, Eaton Vance NY Muni Bond traded at a discount of 7.14% below its net asset value, which is worse than its one-year historical average discount of 9.38%.

Craig R. Brandon has been running the fund for 11 years and currently receives a manager quality ranking of 42 (0=worst, 99=best). If you desire only a moderate level of risk and strong performance, then this fund is an excellent option.

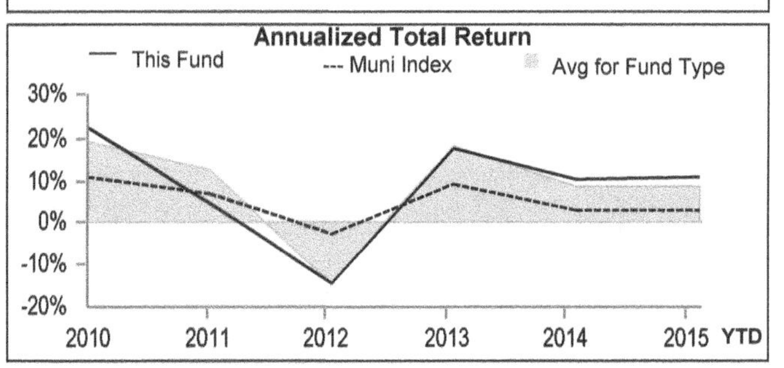

Eaton Vance NY Muni Bond II (NYH) B- Good

Fund Family: Eaton Vance Management
Fund Type: Municipal - Single State
Inception Date: November 25, 2002

Data Date	Investment Rating	Net Assets ($Mil)	Price	Performance Rating/Pts	Total Return Y-T-D	Risk Rating/Pts
12-15	B-	34.23	12.47	C+ / 6.8	9.21%	B- / 7.5
2014	C	34.60	12.05	C / 4.6	15.59%	B- / 7.7
2013	D+	31.78	11.04	D+ / 2.8	-16.88%	B- / 7.8
2012	B-	35.67	13.37	C+ / 6.3	7.30%	B / 8.4
2011	B+	33.50	13.69	B+ / 8.6	23.30%	B / 8.5
2010	D+	34.33	12.03	D / 1.9	-0.31%	C+ / 6.6

Major Rating Factors: Eaton Vance NY Muni Bond II receives a TheStreet.com Investment Rating of B- (Good). The fund currently has a performance rating of C+ (Fair) based on an annualized return of 1.68% over the last three years and a total return of 9.21% year to date 2015. Factored into the performance evaluation is an expense ratio of 1.53% (average).

The fund's risk rating is currently B- (Good). It carries a beta of 2.37, meaning it is expected to move 23.7% for every 10% move in the market. Volatility, as measured by both the semi-deviation and a drawdown factor, is considered low. As of December 31, 2015, Eaton Vance NY Muni Bond II traded at a discount of 9.31% below its net asset value, which is better than its one-year historical average discount of 8.74%.

Craig R. Brandon has been running the fund for 11 years and currently receives a manager quality ranking of 36 (0=worst, 99=best). If you desire an average level of risk, then this fund may be an option.

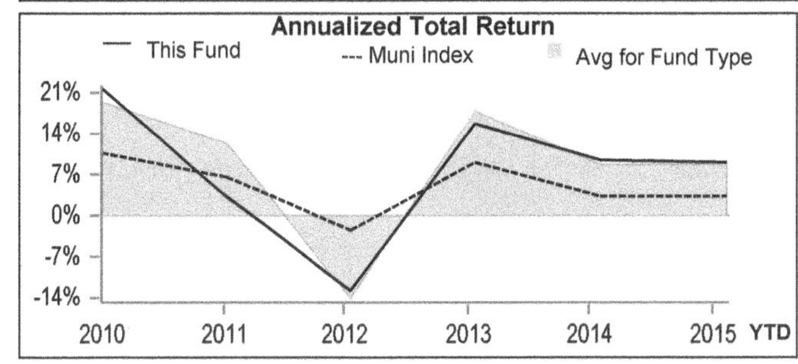

Eaton Vance NY Muni Inc Tr (EVY) B Good

Fund Family: Eaton Vance Management
Fund Type: Municipal - Single State
Inception Date: January 26, 1999

Major Rating Factors: Strong performance is the major factor driving the B (Good) TheStreet.com Investment Rating for Eaton Vance NY Muni Inc Tr. The fund currently has a performance rating of B- (Good) based on an annualized return of 1.80% over the last three years and a total return of 8.91% year to date 2015. Factored into the performance evaluation is an expense ratio of 1.75% (above average).

The fund's risk rating is currently B- (Good). It carries a beta of 2.05, meaning it is expected to move 20.5% for every 10% move in the market. Volatility, as measured by both the semi-deviation and a drawdown factor, is considered low. As of December 31, 2015, Eaton Vance NY Muni Inc Tr traded at a discount of 3.68% below its net asset value, which is worse than its one-year historical average discount of 6.32%.

Craig R. Brandon has been running the fund for 17 years and currently receives a manager quality ranking of 40 (0=worst, 99=best). If you desire only a moderate level of risk and strong performance, then this fund is an excellent option.

Data Date	Investment Rating	Net Assets ($Mil)	Price	Performance Rating/Pts	Total Return Y-T-D	Risk Rating/Pts
12-15	B	79.86	14.15	B- / 7.3	8.91%	B- / 7.3
2014	C+	79.90	13.84	C+ / 6.0	18.75%	B- / 7.7
2013	C	80.26	12.43	C / 4.9	-18.14%	B / 8.0
2012	A+	79.95	15.64	A- / 9.1	18.28%	B / 8.6
2011	A+	74.80	13.99	A+ / 9.6	23.59%	B / 8.6
2010	D+	74.31	12.46	D+ / 2.7	-0.23%	C / 5.2

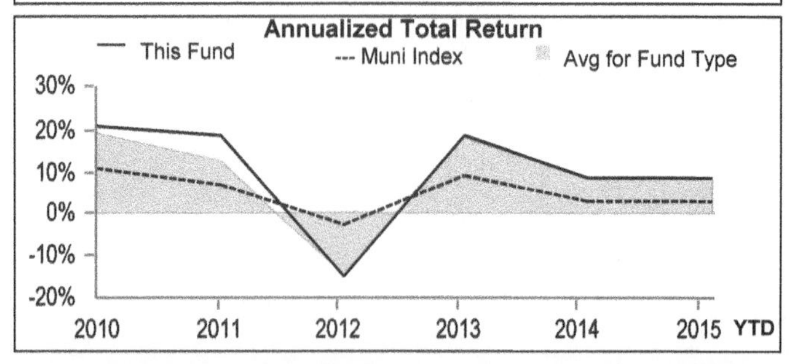

Eaton Vance OH Muni Bond (EIO) B+ Good

Fund Family: Eaton Vance Management
Fund Type: Municipal - Single State
Inception Date: November 25, 2002

Major Rating Factors: Strong performance is the major factor driving the B+ (Good) TheStreet.com Investment Rating for Eaton Vance OH Muni Bond. The fund currently has a performance rating of B+ (Good) based on an annualized return of 2.92% over the last three years and a total return of 12.64% year to date 2015. Factored into the performance evaluation is an expense ratio of 1.28% (average).

The fund's risk rating is currently B- (Good). It carries a beta of 3.21, meaning it is expected to move 32.1% for every 10% move in the market. Volatility, as measured by both the semi-deviation and a drawdown factor, is considered low. As of December 31, 2015, Eaton Vance OH Muni Bond traded at a discount of 6.55% below its net asset value, which is worse than its one-year historical average discount of 7.68%.

Cynthia J. Clemson has been running the fund for 1 year and currently receives a manager quality ranking of 26 (0=worst, 99=best). If you desire only a moderate level of risk and strong performance, then this fund is an excellent option.

Data Date	Investment Rating	Net Assets ($Mil)	Price	Performance Rating/Pts	Total Return Y-T-D	Risk Rating/Pts
12-15	B+	35.28	13.42	B+ / 8.5	12.64%	B- / 7.1
2014	C+	34.90	12.72	C+ / 6.0	20.88%	B- / 7.3
2013	D+	31.00	11.05	D+ / 2.8	-19.02%	B- / 7.5
2012	B-	34.99	14.08	C+ / 6.7	14.47%	B / 8.2
2011	B+	31.70	13.10	B / 8.1	22.43%	B / 8.3
2010	D+	32.73	11.51	D / 1.7	-0.56%	C+ / 6.4

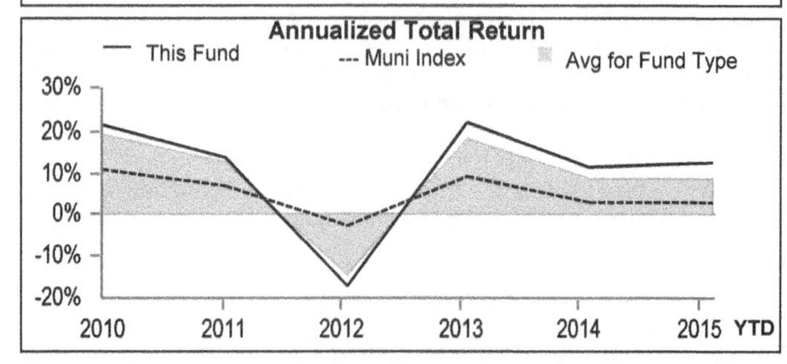

Eaton Vance OH Muni Inc Tr (EVO) C Fair

Fund Family: Eaton Vance Management
Fund Type: Municipal - Single State
Inception Date: January 26, 1999

Major Rating Factors: Middle of the road best describes Eaton Vance OH Muni Inc Tr whose TheStreet.com Investment Rating is currently a C (Fair). The fund currently has a performance rating of C (Fair) based on an annualized return of -1.28% over the last three years and a total return of 7.80% year to date 2015. Factored into the performance evaluation is an expense ratio of 1.70% (above average).

The fund's risk rating is currently B- (Good). It carries a beta of 2.65, meaning it is expected to move 26.5% for every 10% move in the market. Volatility, as measured by both the semi-deviation and a drawdown factor, is considered low. As of December 31, 2015, Eaton Vance OH Muni Inc Tr traded at a discount of 8.55% below its net asset value, which is worse than its one-year historical average discount of 10.01%.

Cynthia J. Clemson has been running the fund for 1 year and currently receives a manager quality ranking of 20 (0=worst, 99=best). If you desire an average level of risk, then this fund may be an option.

Data Date	Investment Rating	Net Assets ($Mil)	Price	Performance Rating/Pts	Total Return Y-T-D	Risk Rating/Pts
12-15	C	43.29	14.02	C / 5.2	7.80%	B- / 7.1
2014	C+	42.80	13.64	C+ / 6.0	17.12%	B- / 7.3
2013	C-	42.33	12.13	C- / 3.8	-24.25%	B- / 7.6
2012	A	42.42	16.45	A- / 9.0	21.03%	B / 8.2
2011	A-	39.70	13.85	A- / 9.2	21.11%	B / 8.3
2010	C-	39.19	12.50	C- / 4.0	-0.23%	C+ / 5.9

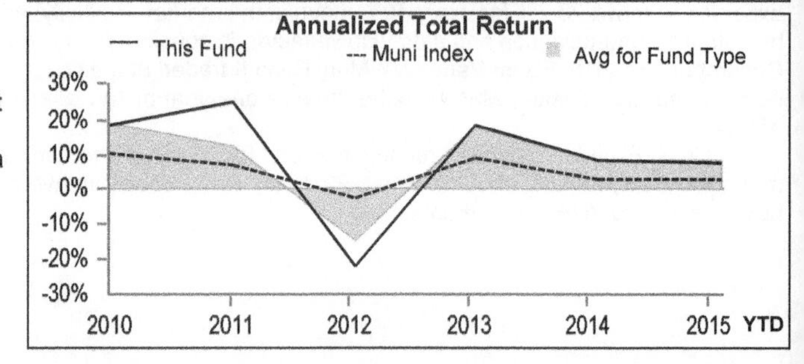

Eaton Vance PA Muni Bond (EIP) C+ Fair

Fund Family: Eaton Vance Management
Fund Type: Municipal - Single State
Inception Date: November 25, 2002

Major Rating Factors: Middle of the road best describes Eaton Vance PA Muni Bond whose TheStreet.com Investment Rating is currently a C+ (Fair). The fund currently has a performance rating of C+ (Fair) based on an annualized return of -0.17% over the last three years and a total return of 9.81% year to date 2015. Factored into the performance evaluation is an expense ratio of 1.33% (average).

The fund's risk rating is currently B- (Good). It carries a beta of 2.46, meaning it is expected to move 24.6% for every 10% move in the market. Volatility, as measured by both the semi-deviation and a drawdown factor, is considered low. As of December 31, 2015, Eaton Vance PA Muni Bond traded at a discount of 9.64% below its net asset value, which is worse than its one-year historical average discount of 10.37%.

Adam A. Weigold has been running the fund for 9 years and currently receives a manager quality ranking of 24 (0=worst, 99=best). If you desire an average level of risk, then this fund may be an option.

Data Date	Investment Rating	Net Assets ($Mil)	Price	Performance Rating/Pts	Total Return Y-T-D	Risk Rating/Pts
12-15	C+	41.69	13.22	C+ / 6.0	9.81%	B- / 7.0
2014	C	42.00	12.87	C+ / 5.6	18.54%	B- / 7.2
2013	C-	37.62	11.49	C- / 3.7	-23.09%	B- / 7.5
2012	B	42.79	15.40	B / 7.6	19.36%	B / 8.3
2011	B+	39.50	13.42	B+ / 8.7	25.04%	B / 8.1
2010	D+	40.26	11.73	D- / 1.5	-10.91%	C+ / 6.8

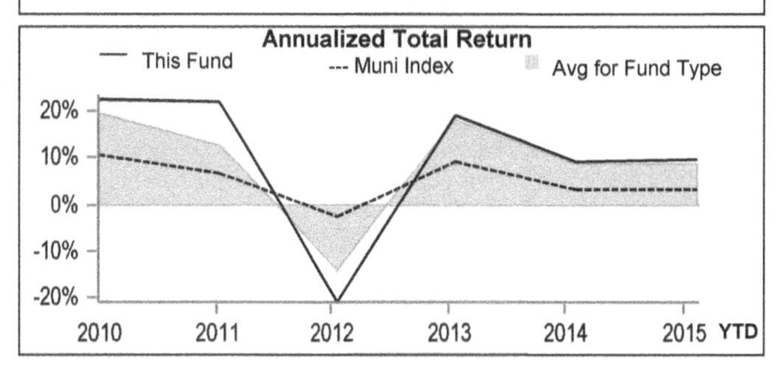

Eaton Vance PA Muni Inc Tr (EVP) C Fair

Fund Family: Eaton Vance Management
Fund Type: Municipal - Single State
Inception Date: January 26, 1999

Major Rating Factors: Middle of the road best describes Eaton Vance PA Muni Inc Tr whose TheStreet.com Investment Rating is currently a C (Fair). The fund currently has a performance rating of C (Fair) based on an annualized return of -0.11% over the last three years and a total return of 4.73% year to date 2015. Factored into the performance evaluation is an expense ratio of 1.83% (above average).

The fund's risk rating is currently B- (Good). It carries a beta of 2.24, meaning it is expected to move 22.4% for every 10% move in the market. Volatility, as measured by both the semi-deviation and a drawdown factor, is considered low. As of December 31, 2015, Eaton Vance PA Muni Inc Tr traded at a discount of 13.59% below its net asset value, which is better than its one-year historical average discount of 13.03%.

Adam A. Weigold has been running the fund for 9 years and currently receives a manager quality ranking of 24 (0=worst, 99=best). If you desire an average level of risk, then this fund may be an option.

Data Date	Investment Rating	Net Assets ($Mil)	Price	Performance Rating/Pts	Total Return Y-T-D	Risk Rating/Pts
12-15	C	37.53	12.08	C / 5.3	4.73%	B- / 7.2
2014	C	37.70	12.18	C / 5.2	15.80%	B- / 7.7
2013	D+	38.09	11.10	D+ / 2.7	-18.29%	B- / 7.9
2012	A-	38.40	14.46	B / 8.1	16.84%	B / 8.7
2011	A	36.80	13.46	A- / 9.2	17.87%	B / 8.6
2010	D+	37.74	12.30	C- / 3.1	-0.20%	C / 5.5

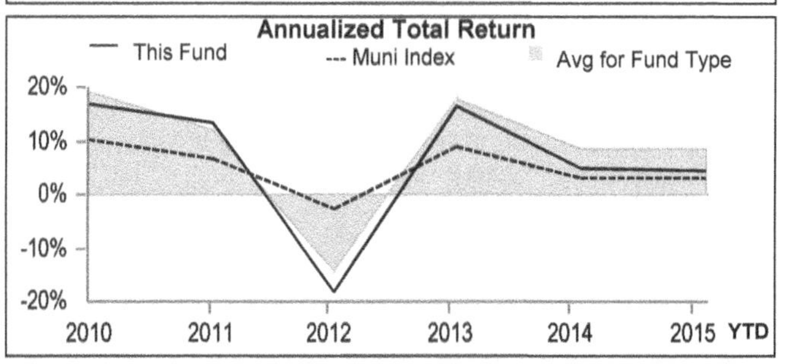

Eaton Vance Risk Mgd Div Eq Inc (ETJ) B Good

Fund Family: Eaton Vance Management
Fund Type: Income
Inception Date: July 31, 2007

Major Rating Factors: Strong performance is the major factor driving the B (Good) TheStreet.com Investment Rating for Eaton Vance Risk Mgd Div Eq Inc. The fund currently has a performance rating of B- (Good) based on an annualized return of 8.52% over the last three years and a total return of 4.23% year to date 2015. Factored into the performance evaluation is an expense ratio of 1.10% (low).

The fund's risk rating is currently B- (Good). It carries a beta of 0.60, meaning the fund's expected move will be 6.0% for every 10% move in the market. Volatility, as measured by both the semi-deviation and a drawdown factor, is considered low. As of December 31, 2015, Eaton Vance Risk Mgd Div Eq Inc traded at a discount of 8.88% below its net asset value, which is worse than its one-year historical average discount of 10.10%.

Michael A. Allison has been running the fund for 9 years and currently receives a manager quality ranking of 73 (0=worst, 99=best). If you desire only a moderate level of risk and strong performance, then this fund is an excellent option.

Data Date	Investment Rating	Net Assets ($Mil)	Price	Performance Rating/Pts	Total Return Y-T-D	Risk Rating/Pts
12-15	B	769.20	10.16	B- / 7.4	4.23%	B- / 7.5
2014	C+	787.30	10.66	C / 5.2	3.44%	B / 8.6
2013	C	839.70	11.27	C+ / 5.7	16.58%	B- / 7.5
2012	D	922.23	10.43	D- / 1.3	13.70%	C+ / 6.6
2011	D	922.20	10.45	D- / 1.5	-12.03%	C+ / 6.6
2010	C-	1,064.93	13.28	D / 2.1	-9.99%	B- / 7.9

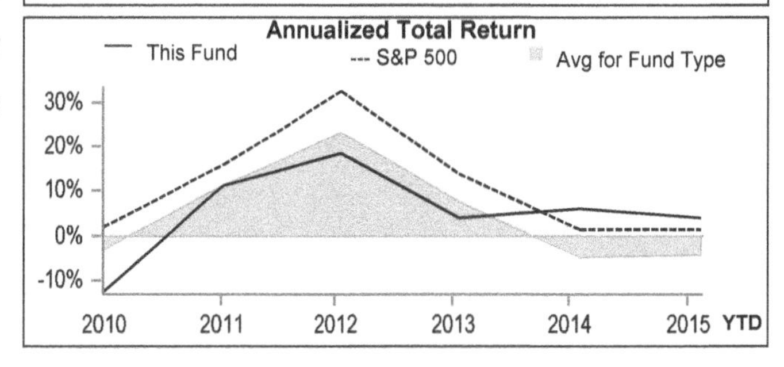

Eaton Vance Senior Floating Rate (EFR) C- Fair

Fund Family: Eaton Vance Management
Fund Type: Loan Participation
Inception Date: November 28, 2003

Major Rating Factors: Middle of the road best describes Eaton Vance Senior Floating Rate whose TheStreet.com Investment Rating is currently a C- (Fair). The fund currently has a performance rating of C- (Fair) based on an annualized return of -2.46% over the last three years and a total return of -2.38% year to date 2015. Factored into the performance evaluation is an expense ratio of 1.76% (above average).

The fund's risk rating is currently B- (Good). It carries a beta of -188.95, meaning the fund's expected move will be -1889.5% for every 10% move in the market. Volatility, as measured by both the semi-deviation and a drawdown factor, is considered low. As of December 31, 2015, Eaton Vance Senior Floating Rate traded at a discount of 8.68% below its net asset value, which is better than its one-year historical average discount of 7.72%.

Craig P. Russ has been running the fund for 13 years and currently receives a manager quality ranking of 26 (0=worst, 99=best). If you desire an average level of risk, then this fund may be an option.

Data Date	Investment Rating	Net Assets ($Mil)	Price	Performance Rating/Pts	Total Return Y-T-D	Risk Rating/Pts
12-15	C-	564.83	12.41	C- / 3.3	-2.38%	B- / 7.0
2014	C-	565.80	13.69	C- / 3.4	-2.77%	B / 8.0
2013	C-	577.30	15.06	C- / 3.4	-1.78%	B- / 7.6
2012	C	503.38	15.97	C+ / 5.7	20.69%	B- / 7.5
2011	B	496.40	14.38	B / 7.8	-5.18%	B- / 7.6
2010	C+	505.67	16.22	B / 7.9	19.54%	C- / 4.1

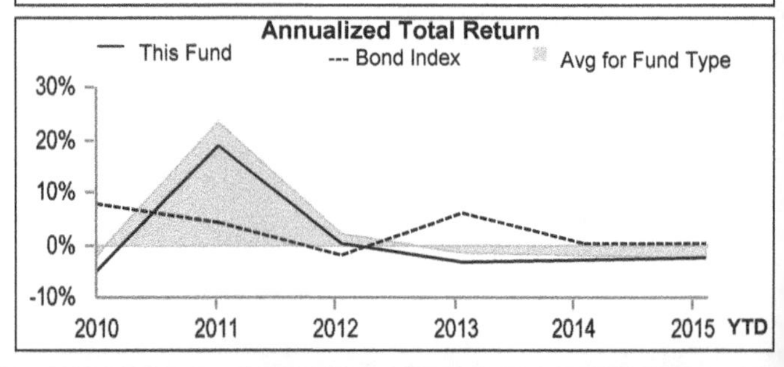

Eaton Vance Senior Income Trust (EVF) C- Fair

Fund Family: Eaton Vance Management
Fund Type: Loan Participation
Inception Date: October 27, 1998

Major Rating Factors: Middle of the road best describes Eaton Vance Senior Income Trust whose TheStreet.com Investment Rating is currently a C- (Fair). The fund currently has a performance rating of C- (Fair) based on an annualized return of -2.95% over the last three years and a total return of -0.78% year to date 2015. Factored into the performance evaluation is an expense ratio of 2.27% (high).

The fund's risk rating is currently B- (Good). Volatility, as measured by both the semi-deviation and a drawdown factor, is considered low. As of December 31, 2015, Eaton Vance Senior Income Trust traded at a discount of 9.56% below its net asset value, which is worse than its one-year historical average discount of 10.04%.

Scott H. Page has been running the fund for 18 years and currently receives a manager quality ranking of 75 (0=worst, 99=best). If you desire an average level of risk, then this fund may be an option.

Data Date	Investment Rating	Net Assets ($Mil)	Price	Performance Rating/Pts	Total Return Y-T-D	Risk Rating/Pts
12-15	C-	266.01	5.77	C- / 3.3	-0.78%	B- / 7.2
2014	C-	271.40	6.24	C- / 3.4	-5.43%	B / 8.2
2013	C	278.36	6.91	C / 4.3	-2.72%	B / 8.4
2012	B-	263.17	7.54	C+ / 6.6	26.89%	B / 8.4
2011	B	254.50	6.53	B / 7.8	-3.29%	B / 8.4
2010	C+	245.74	7.16	B- / 7.5	20.90%	C- / 4.1

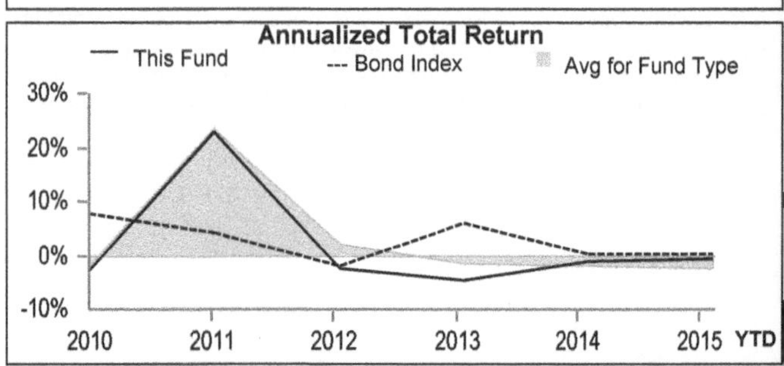

Eaton Vance Sh Dur Diversified Inc (EVG) C Fair

Fund Family: Eaton Vance Management
Fund Type: Global
Inception Date: February 23, 2005

Major Rating Factors: Middle of the road best describes Eaton Vance Sh Dur Diversified Inc whose TheStreet.com Investment Rating is currently a C (Fair). The fund currently has a performance rating of C- (Fair) based on an annualized return of -1.85% over the last three years and a total return of 1.46% year to date 2015. Factored into the performance evaluation is an expense ratio of 1.89% (above average).

The fund's risk rating is currently B- (Good). It carries a beta of 0.52, meaning the fund's expected move will be 5.2% for every 10% move in the market. Volatility, as measured by both the semi-deviation and a drawdown factor, is considered low. As of December 31, 2015, Eaton Vance Sh Dur Diversified Inc traded at a discount of 10.60% below its net asset value, which is worse than its one-year historical average discount of 12.11%.

Payson F. Swaffield has been running the fund for 11 years and currently receives a manager quality ranking of 74 (0=worst, 99=best). If you desire an average level of risk, then this fund may be an option.

Data Date	Investment Rating	Net Assets ($Mil)	Price	Performance Rating/Pts	Total Return Y-T-D	Risk Rating/Pts
12-15	C	306.21	13.41	C- / 3.9	1.46%	B- / 7.5
2014	C-	307.40	14.15	D+ / 2.9	-1.18%	B / 8.2
2013	C-	334.62	15.27	C- / 3.3	-6.55%	B / 8.7
2012	C	336.17	17.31	C- / 3.8	12.78%	B / 8.6
2011	C	330.80	16.20	C+ / 5.6	4.01%	B- / 7.6
2010	C+	347.81	16.88	C+ / 6.6	11.53%	C+ / 6.1

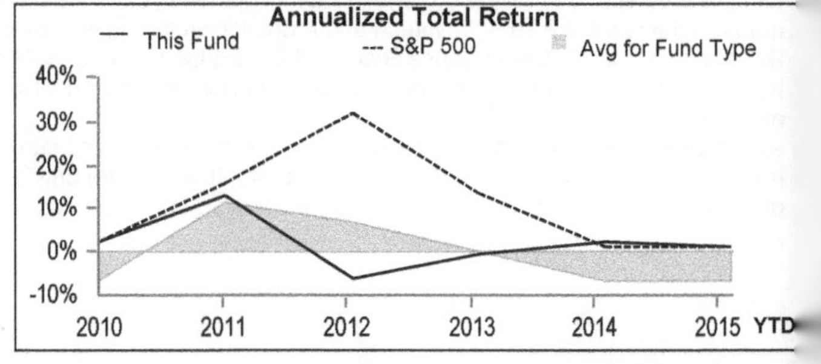

Eaton Vance Tax Adv Glob Div Inc (ETG) B+ Good

Fund Family: Eaton Vance Management
Fund Type: Global
Inception Date: January 30, 2004

Major Rating Factors: Strong performance is the major factor driving the B+ (Good) TheStreet.com Investment Rating for Eaton Vance Tax Adv Glob Div Inc. The fund currently has a performance rating of B (Good) based on an annualized return of 10.70% over the last three years and a total return of 3.41% year to date 2015. Factored into the performance evaluation is an expense ratio of 1.42% (average).

The fund's risk rating is currently B- (Good). It carries a beta of 1.05, meaning that its performance tracks fairly well with that of the overall stock market. Volatility, as measured by both the semi-deviation and a drawdown factor, is considered low. As of December 31, 2015, Eaton Vance Tax Adv Glob Div Inc traded at a discount of 8.87% below its net asset value, which is better than its one-year historical average discount of 7.29%.

John H. Croft has been running the fund for 6 years and currently receives a manager quality ranking of 91 (0=worst, 99=best). If you desire only a moderate level of risk and strong performance, then this fund is an excellent option.

Data Date	Investment Rating	Net Assets ($Mil)	Price	Performance Rating/Pts	Total Return Y-T-D	Risk Rating/Pts
12-15	B+	1,382.84	15.52	B / 7.9	3.41%	B- / 7.7
2014	B	1,384.30	16.17	C+ / 6.9	3.80%	B / 8.4
2013	B	1,263.03	16.94	B / 8.1	26.37%	B- / 7.5
2012	C+	1,097.14	13.58	C+ / 6.8	26.59%	B- / 7.5
2011	C-	1,064.30	12.22	C / 5.0	-1.28%	C+ / 6.7
2010	E+	1,117.10	14.11	D- / 1.2	11.75%	C- / 3.7

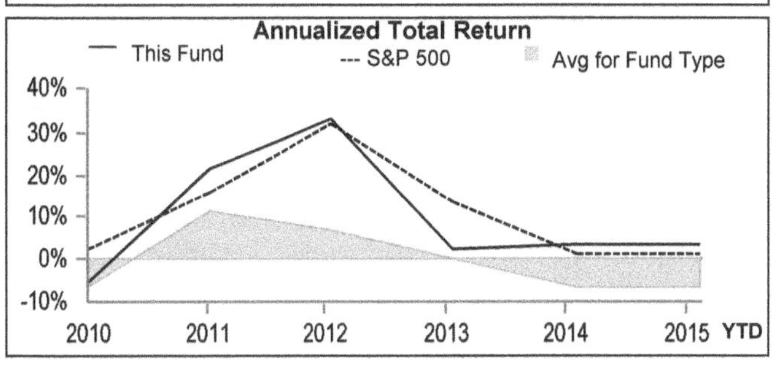

Eaton Vance Tax Adv Global Div Opp (ETO) B Good

Fund Family: Eaton Vance Management
Fund Type: Global
Inception Date: April 30, 2004

Major Rating Factors: Strong performance is the major factor driving the B (Good) TheStreet.com Investment Rating for Eaton Vance Tax Adv Global Div Opp. The fund currently has a performance rating of B (Good) based on an annualized return of 11.58% over the last three years and a total return of -2.24% year to date 2015. Factored into the performance evaluation is an expense ratio of 1.50% (average).

The fund's risk rating is currently B- (Good). It carries a beta of 0.87, meaning the fund's expected move will be 8.7% for every 10% move in the market. Volatility, as measured by both the semi-deviation and a drawdown factor, is considered low. As of December 31, 2015, Eaton Vance Tax Adv Global Div Opp traded at a discount of 7.26% below its net asset value, which is better than its one-year historical average discount of 3.51%.

John H. Croft has been running the fund for 6 years and currently receives a manager quality ranking of 93 (0=worst, 99=best). If you desire only a moderate level of risk and strong performance, then this fund is an excellent option.

Data Date	Investment Rating	Net Assets ($Mil)	Price	Performance Rating/Pts	Total Return Y-T-D	Risk Rating/Pts
12-15	B	379.68	21.32	B / 7.9	-2.24%	B- / 7.3
2014	A-	383.70	24.31	B / 8.1	10.28%	B / 8.3
2013	B-	361.98	24.50	B / 7.7	25.64%	B- / 7.1
2012	C+	303.82	20.09	C+ / 6.4	28.34%	B- / 7.2
2011	C-	291.70	17.00	C / 4.4	-9.56%	C+ / 6.8
2010	D-	319.53	20.52	D / 1.7	13.17%	C / 4.3

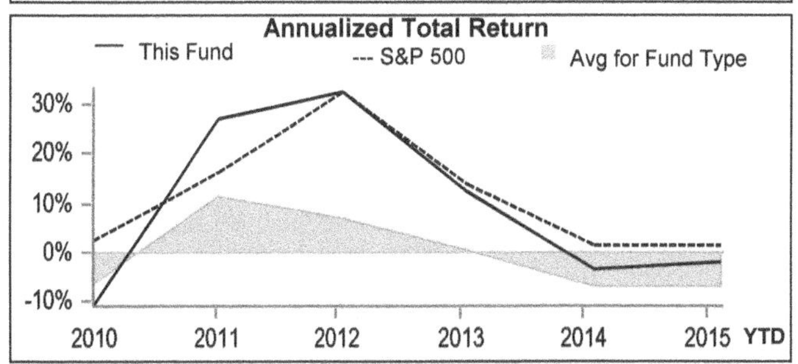

Eaton Vance Tax Advantage Div Inc (EVT) A- Excellent

Fund Family: Eaton Vance Management
Fund Type: Income
Inception Date: September 30, 2003

Major Rating Factors:
Strong performance is the major factor driving the A- (Excellent) TheStreet.com Investment Rating for Eaton Vance Tax Advantage Div Inc. The fund currently has a performance rating of B+ (Good) based on an annualized return of 11.54% over the last three years and a total return of 2.01% year to date 2015. Factored into the performance evaluation is an expense ratio of 1.35% (average).

The fund's risk rating is currently B- (Good). It carries a beta of 0.96, meaning that its performance tracks fairly well with that of the overall stock market. Volatility, as measured by both the semi-deviation and a drawdown factor, is considered low. As of December 31, 2015, Eaton Vance Tax Advantage Div Inc traded at a discount of 9.24% below its net asset value, which is worse than its one-year historical average discount of 9.81%.

John H. Croft has been running the fund for 6 years and currently receives a manager quality ranking of 56 (0=worst, 99=best). If you desire only a moderate level of risk and strong performance, then this fund is an excellent option.

Data Date	Investment Rating	Net Assets ($Mil)	Price	Performance Rating/Pts	Total Return Y-T-D	Risk Rating/Pts
12-15	A-	1,545.31	19.34	B+ / 8.3	2.01%	B- / 7.9
2014	A+	1,671.10	20.80	B+ / 8.4	18.44%	B / 8.9
2013	B-	1,420.00	19.02	B- / 7.1	16.24%	B- / 7.6
2012	C+	1,332.63	16.50	C+ / 6.0	24.30%	B- / 7.7
2011	C	1,223.00	14.60	C+ / 5.9	-1.90%	C+ / 6.7
2010	E+	1,161.72	16.55	D / 1.8	13.21%	D+ / 2.9

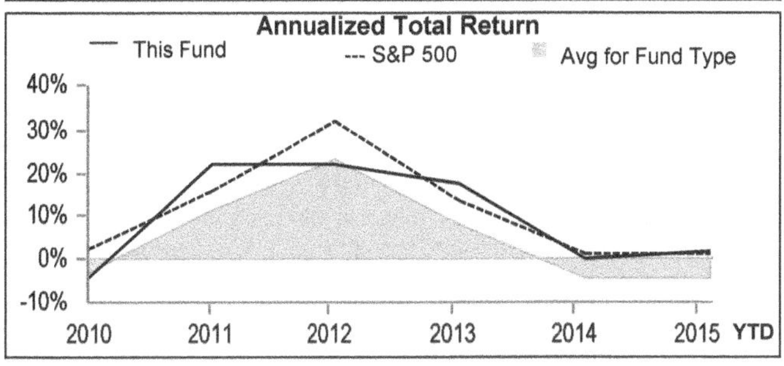

Eaton Vance Tax Mgd Buy Write Opp (ETV) A- Excellent

Fund Family: Eaton Vance Management
Fund Type: Income
Inception Date: June 27, 2005

Major Rating Factors:
Exceptional performance is the major factor driving the A- (Excellent) TheStreet.com Investment Rating for Eaton Vance Tax Mgd Buy Write Opp. The fund currently has a performance rating of A (Excellent) based on an annualized return of 16.13% over the last three years and a total return of 17.56% year to date 2015. Factored into the performance evaluation is an expense ratio of 1.09% (low).

The fund's risk rating is currently B- (Good). It carries a beta of 0.68, meaning the fund's expected move will be 6.8% for every 10% move in the market. Volatility, as measured by both the semi-deviation and a drawdown factor, is considered low. As of December 31, 2015, Eaton Vance Tax Mgd Buy Write Opp traded at a premium of 5.08% above its net asset value, which is worse than its one-year historical average premium of .07%.

Thomas Seto has been running the fund for 11 years and currently receives a manager quality ranking of 91 (0=worst, 99=best). If you desire only a moderate level of risk and strong performance, then this fund is an excellent option.

Data Date	Investment Rating	Net Assets ($Mil)	Price	Performance Rating/Pts	Total Return Y-T-D	Risk Rating/Pts
12-15	A-	945.20	15.30	A / 9.5	17.56%	B- / 7.0
2014	B+	951.50	14.06	B- / 7.0	11.42%	B / 8.5
2013	B-	876.15	14.01	B- / 7.3	18.07%	B- / 7.7
2012	C-	896.71	12.50	C- / 4.1	19.07%	B- / 7.2
2011	C	871.20	11.72	C+ / 5.6	1.41%	C+ / 6.9
2010	C	805.34	13.08	C / 4.4	-2.70%	C+ / 6.1

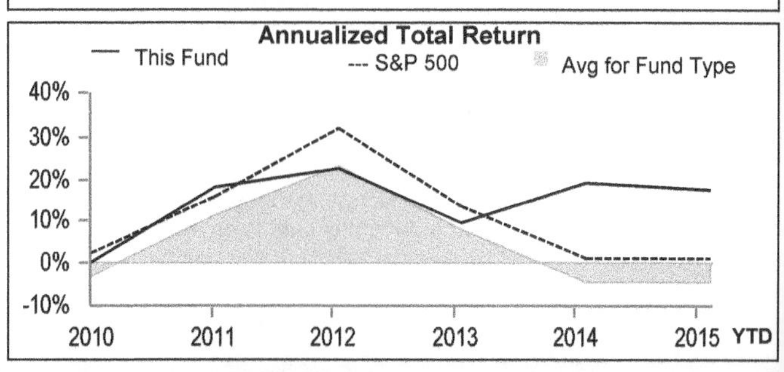

Eaton Vance Tax Mgd Div Eqty Inc (ETY) A Excellent

Fund Family: Eaton Vance Management
Fund Type: Income
Inception Date: November 30, 2006

Major Rating Factors:
Exceptional performance is the major factor driving the A (Excellent) TheStreet.com Investment Rating for Eaton Vance Tax Mgd Div Eqty Inc. The fund currently has a performance rating of A- (Excellent) based on an annualized return of 14.49% over the last three years and a total return of 9.21% year to date 2015. Factored into the performance evaluation is an expense ratio of 1.08% (low).

The fund's risk rating is currently B- (Good). It carries a beta of 1.00, meaning that its performance tracks fairly well with that of the overall stock market. Volatility, as measured by both the semi-deviation and a drawdown factor, is considered low. As of December 31, 2015, Eaton Vance Tax Mgd Div Eqty Inc traded at a discount of 5.56% below its net asset value, which is worse than its one-year historical average discount of 7.54%.

Michael A. Allison has been running the fund for 10 years and currently receives a manager quality ranking of 74 (0=worst, 99=best). If you desire only a moderate level of risk and strong performance, then this fund is an excellent option.

Data Date	Investment Rating	Net Assets ($Mil)	Price	Performance Rating/Pts	Total Return Y-T-D	Risk Rating/Pts
12-15	A	1,844.44	11.20	A- / 9.1	9.21%	B- / 7.7
2014	B+	1,836.50	11.17	B- / 7.5	13.06%	B / 8.5
2013	C+	1,725.71	10.92	C+ / 6.9	20.99%	B- / 7.3
2012	D+	1,651.55	9.37	C- / 3.2	20.65%	C+ / 6.5
2011	D	1,612.60	8.87	D+ / 2.8	-10.71%	C+ / 6.5
2010	D+	1,969.59	11.31	C- / 3.1	-1.22%	C+ / 5.8

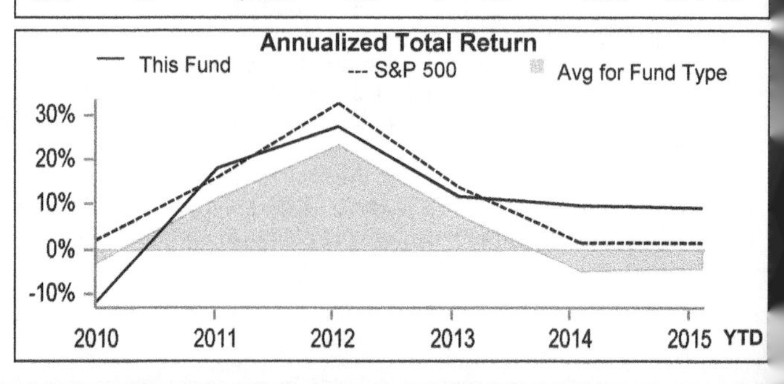

Eaton Vance Tax-Managed Buy-Write (ETB) A Excellent

Fund Family: Eaton Vance Management
Fund Type: Income
Inception Date: April 27, 2005

Major Rating Factors:
Exceptional performance is the major factor driving the A (Excellent) TheStreet.com Investment Rating for Eaton Vance Tax-Managed Buy-Write. The fund currently has a performance rating of A (Excellent) based on an annualized return of 13.64% over the last three years and a total return of 14.03% year to date 2015. Factored into the performance evaluation is an expense ratio of 1.13% (low).

The fund's risk rating is currently B- (Good). It carries a beta of 0.72, meaning the fund's expected move will be 7.2% for every 10% move in the market. Volatility, as measured by both the semi-deviation and a drawdown factor, is considered low. As of December 31, 2015, Eaton Vance Tax-Managed Buy-Write traded at a premium of 7.61% above its net asset value, which is worse than its one-year historical average premium of .12%.

Thomas Seto has been running the fund for 11 years and currently receives a manager quality ranking of 87 (0=worst, 99=best). If you desire only a moderate level of risk and strong performance, then this fund is an excellent option.

Data Date	Investment Rating	Net Assets ($Mil)	Price	Performance Rating/Pts	Total Return Y-T-D	Risk Rating/Pts
12-15	A	402.15	16.69	A / 9.3	14.03%	B- / 7.3
2014	B+	402.50	15.90	B- / 7.3	16.34%	B / 8.8
2013	C+	367.28	14.89	C+ / 6.4	10.69%	B / 8.1
2012	C-	371.29	14.03	C- / 3.9	22.80%	B- / 7.3
2011	C-	362.20	12.84	C / 5.0	-0.40%	C+ / 6.8
2010	C-	335.31	14.41	C / 4.5	-3.39%	C / 5.4

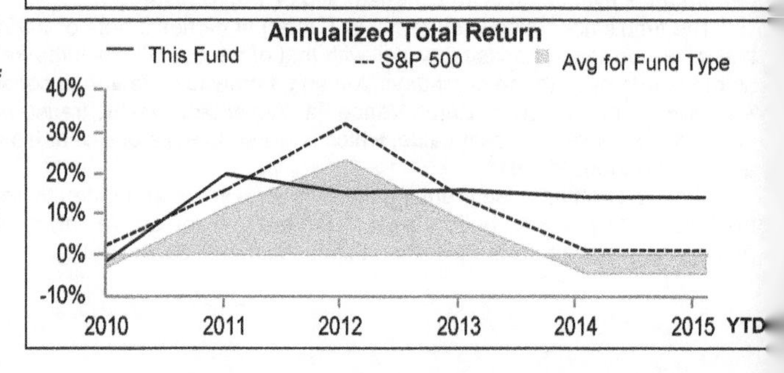

Eaton Vance Tax-Mgd Gbl Div Eq Inc (EXG) B Good

Fund Family: Eaton Vance Management
Fund Type: Global
Inception Date: February 27, 2007

Data Date	Investment Rating	Net Assets ($Mil)	Price	Performance Rating/Pts	Total Return Y-T-D	Risk Rating/Pts
12-15	B	3,198.33	8.85	B- / 7.5	3.03%	B- / 7.4
2014	B-	3,217.50	9.49	C+ / 6.5	5.44%	B / 8.1
2013	C+	3,207.57	10.00	C+ / 6.8	19.54%	B- / 7.0
2012	D+	3,122.46	8.81	C- / 3.6	22.42%	C+ / 6.5
2011	D+	3,023.50	8.25	C- / 3.3	-10.37%	C+ / 6.4
2010	D+	3,638.43	10.53	D+ / 2.5	-1.72%	C / 5.5

Major Rating Factors: Strong performance is the major factor driving the B (Good) TheStreet.com Investment Rating for Eaton Vance Tax-Mgd Gbl Div Eq Inc. The fund currently has a performance rating of B- (Good) based on an annualized return of 9.25% over the last three years and a total return of 3.03% year to date 2015. Factored into the performance evaluation is an expense ratio of 1.07% (low).

The fund's risk rating is currently B- (Good). It carries a beta of 0.94, meaning that its performance tracks fairly well with that of the overall stock market. Volatility, as measured by both the semi-deviation and a drawdown factor, is considered low. As of December 31, 2015, Eaton Vance Tax-Mgd Gbl Div Eq Inc traded at a discount of 8.86% below its net asset value, which is better than its one-year historical average discount of 6.90%.

Michael A. Allison has been running the fund for 9 years and currently receives a manager quality ranking of 89 (0=worst, 99=best). If you desire only a moderate level of risk and strong performance, then this fund is an excellent option.

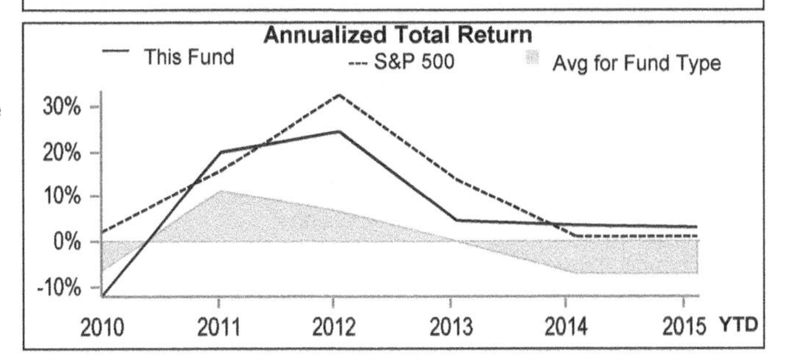

Eaton Vance Tx Adv Bd&Option Str (EXD) C- Fair

Fund Family: Eaton Vance Management
Fund Type: Municipal - National
Inception Date: June 29, 2010

Data Date	Investment Rating	Net Assets ($Mil)	Price	Performance Rating/Pts	Total Return Y-T-D	Risk Rating/Pts
12-15	C-	147.64	12.57	C- / 4.1	7.39%	C+ / 6.6
2014	D+	157.00	12.69	D+ / 2.6	-2.05%	B- / 7.0
2013	C-	193.07	14.20	C- / 3.1	-11.73%	B- / 7.9
2012	A	194.51	17.67	A- / 9.2	18.88%	B / 8.0
2011	C+	194.50	16.55	C / 5.3	7.69%	B / 8.0

Major Rating Factors: Middle of the road best describes Eaton Vance Tx Adv Bd&Option Str whose TheStreet.com Investment Rating is currently a C- (Fair). The fund currently has a performance rating of C- (Fair) based on an annualized return of -2.11% over the last three years and a total return of 7.39% year to date 2015. Factored into the performance evaluation is an expense ratio of 1.42% (average).

The fund's risk rating is currently C+ (Fair). It carries a beta of 1.95, meaning it is expected to move 19.5% for every 10% move in the market. Volatility, as measured by both the semi-deviation and a drawdown factor, is considered low. As of December 31, 2015, Eaton Vance Tx Adv Bd&Option Str traded at a discount of 12.22% below its net asset value, which is better than its one-year historical average discount of 11.60%.

James H. Evans has been running the fund for 6 years and currently receives a manager quality ranking of 22 (0=worst, 99=best). If you desire an average level of risk, then this fund may be an option.

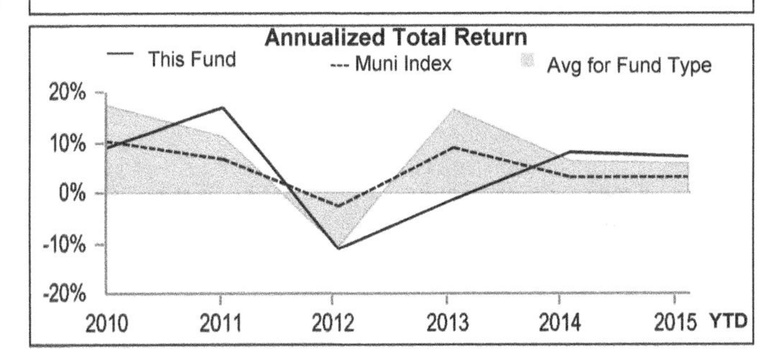

Eaton Vance Tx Mgd Glb Buy Wrt Opp (ETW) B+ Good

Fund Family: Eaton Vance Management
Fund Type: Global
Inception Date: September 27, 2005

Data Date	Investment Rating	Net Assets ($Mil)	Price	Performance Rating/Pts	Total Return Y-T-D	Risk Rating/Pts
12-15	B+	1,308.08	11.23	B+ / 8.3	11.13%	B- / 7.2
2014	C+	1,365.20	11.02	C / 5.4	1.28%	B / 8.2
2013	C+	1,317.27	12.10	B- / 7.0	18.59%	B- / 7.4
2012	D+	1,318.02	10.69	C- / 3.6	18.77%	C+ / 6.9
2011	C-	1,310.00	10.28	C / 4.4	-4.54%	C+ / 6.6
2010	D+	1,236.31	12.25	C- / 3.6	-0.83%	C / 5.3

Major Rating Factors: Strong performance is the major factor driving the B+ (Good) TheStreet.com Investment Rating for Eaton Vance Tx Mgd Glb Buy Wrt Opp. The fund currently has a performance rating of B+ (Good) based on an annualized return of 10.60% over the last three years and a total return of 11.13% year to date 2015. Factored into the performance evaluation is an expense ratio of 1.10% (low).

The fund's risk rating is currently B- (Good). It carries a beta of 0.84, meaning the fund's expected move will be 8.4% for every 10% move in the market. Volatility, as measured by both the semi-deviation and a drawdown factor, is considered low. As of December 31, 2015, Eaton Vance Tx Mgd Glb Buy Wrt Opp traded at a discount of 2.85% below its net asset value, which is worse than its one-year historical average discount of 4.37%.

Thomas Seto has been running the fund for 11 years and currently receives a manager quality ranking of 92 (0=worst, 99=best). If you desire only a moderate level of risk and strong performance, then this fund is an excellent option.

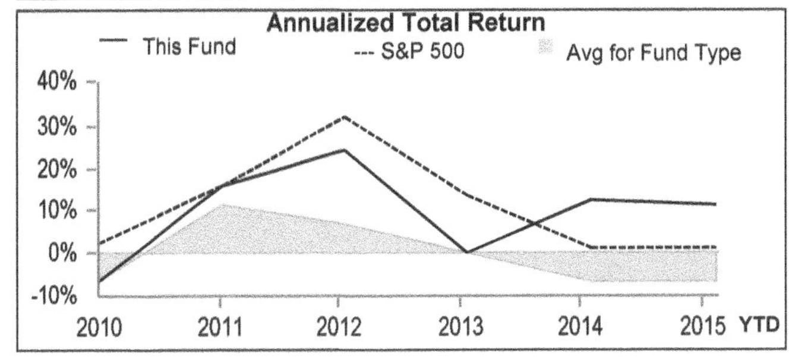

Ellsworth Growth and Income Fd Ltd (ECF) C+ Fair

Fund Family: Dinsmore Capital Management Co
Fund Type: Growth and Income
Inception Date: June 20, 1986

Major Rating Factors: Middle of the road best describes Ellsworth Growth and Income Fd Ltd whose TheStreet.com Investment Rating is currently a C+ (Fair). The fund currently has a performance rating of C+ (Fair) based on an annualized return of 7.93% over the last three years and a total return of -1.58% year to date 2015. Factored into the performance evaluation is an expense ratio of 1.10% (low).

The fund's risk rating is currently B- (Good). It carries a beta of 0.86, meaning the fund's expected move will be 8.6% for every 10% move in the market. Volatility, as measured by both the semi-deviation and a drawdown factor, is considered low. As of December 31, 2015, Ellsworth Growth and Income Fd Ltd traded at a discount of 15.67% below its net asset value, which is better than its one-year historical average discount of 15.39%.

Thomas H. Dinsmore has been running the fund for 30 years and currently receives a manager quality ranking of 38 (0=worst, 99=best). If you desire an average level of risk, then this fund may be an option.

Data Date	Investment Rating	Net Assets ($Mil)	Price	Performance Rating/Pts	Total Return Y-T-D	Risk Rating/Pts
12-15	C+	120.95	7.75	C+ / 6.6	-1.58%	B- / 7.0
2014	B	135.30	8.71	C+ / 6.6	13.78%	B / 8.2
2013	C+	128.81	8.19	C+ / 5.8	13.72%	B- / 7.7
2012	C-	114.15	7.14	C- / 3.5	10.10%	B- / 7.6
2011	C	104.60	6.60	C / 4.5	-4.46%	B / 8.3
2010	C	106.23	7.35	C / 5.1	16.86%	C+ / 6.1

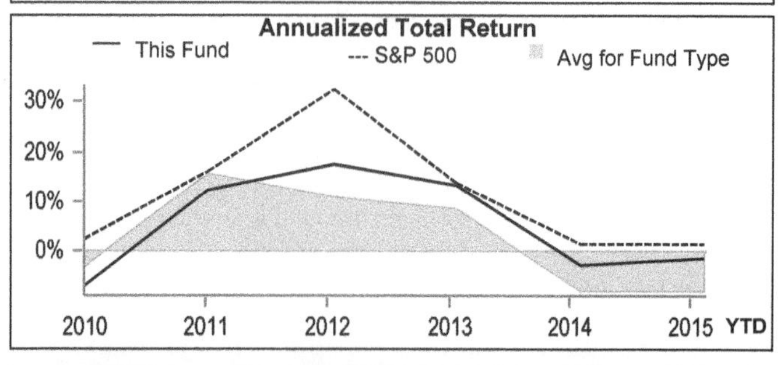

Federated Prem Intermediate Muni (FPT) B- Good

Fund Family: Federated Investors
Fund Type: Municipal - National
Inception Date: December 19, 2002

Major Rating Factors: Strong performance is the major factor driving the B- (Good) TheStreet.com Investment Rating for Federated Prem Intermediate Muni. The fund currently has a performance rating of B- (Good) based on an annualized return of 1.81% over the last three years and a total return of 11.01% year to date 2015. Factored into the performance evaluation is an expense ratio of 1.51% (average).

The fund's risk rating is currently B- (Good). It carries a beta of 1.79, meaning it is expected to move 17.9% for every 10% move in the market. Volatility, as measured by both the semi-deviation and a drawdown factor, is considered low. As of December 31, 2015, Federated Prem Intermediate Muni traded at a discount of 7.62% below its net asset value, which is worse than its one-year historical average discount of 9.76%.

Lee R. Cunningham, II has been running the fund for 14 years and currently receives a manager quality ranking of 45 (0=worst, 99=best). If you desire only a moderate level of risk and strong performance, then this fund is an excellent option.

Data Date	Investment Rating	Net Assets ($Mil)	Price	Performance Rating/Pts	Total Return Y-T-D	Risk Rating/Pts
12-15	B-	101.24	13.46	B- / 7.0	11.01%	B- / 7.5
2014	C	101.40	12.76	C / 4.4	9.84%	B- / 7.7
2013	C-	101.41	12.18	C- / 4.2	-13.46%	B- / 7.9
2012	B-	102.67	14.61	C+ / 6.1	11.95%	B / 8.6
2011	A-	100.30	13.78	B+ / 8.6	18.83%	B / 8.9
2010	C+	93.60	12.59	C / 5.1	-2.48%	C+ / 6.4

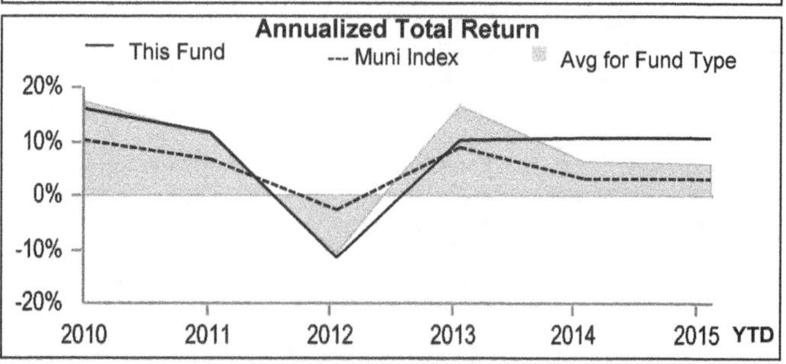

Federated Premier Muni Income (FMN) B Good

Fund Family: Federated Investors
Fund Type: Municipal - National
Inception Date: December 19, 2002

Major Rating Factors: Strong performance is the major factor driving the B (Good) TheStreet.com Investment Rating for Federated Premier Muni Income. The fund currently has a performance rating of B- (Good) based on an annualized return of 3.45% over the last three years and a total return of 8.90% year to date 2015. Factored into the performance evaluation is an expense ratio of 1.43% (average).

The fund's risk rating is currently B- (Good). It carries a beta of 2.11, meaning it is expected to move 21.1% for every 10% move in the market. Volatility, as measured by both the semi-deviation and a drawdown factor, is considered low. As of December 31, 2015, Federated Premier Muni Income traded at a discount of 3.31% below its net asset value, which is worse than its one-year historical average discount of 4.58%.

Lee R. Cunningham, II has been running the fund for 14 years and currently receives a manager quality ranking of 47 (0=worst, 99=best). If you desire only a moderate level of risk and strong performance, then this fund is an excellent option.

Data Date	Investment Rating	Net Assets ($Mil)	Price	Performance Rating/Pts	Total Return Y-T-D	Risk Rating/Pts
12-15	B	95.07	14.91	B- / 7.3	8.90%	B- / 7.4
2014	C+	94.70	14.51	C+ / 5.7	16.12%	B- / 7.6
2013	C	94.68	13.20	C / 5.4	-12.63%	B- / 7.8
2012	B	94.19	15.99	C+ / 6.9	14.56%	B / 8.5
2011	A	88.50	15.14	A / 9.5	21.41%	B / 8.4
2010	C	81.44	13.36	C / 5.2	-3.27%	C+ / 5.8

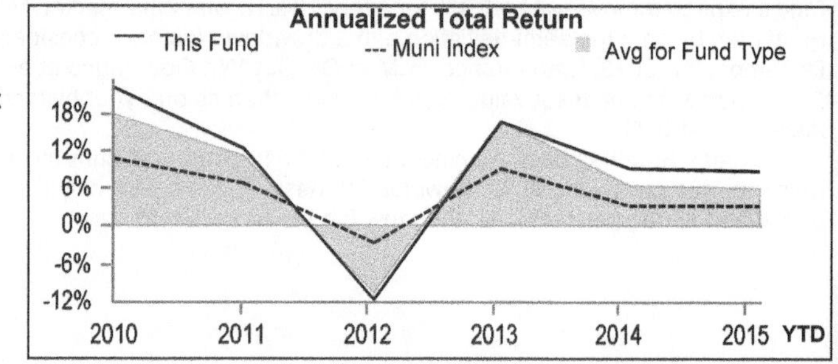

Fiduciary/Claymore MLP Opp (FMO) D- Weak

Fund Family: Guggenheim Funds Investment Advisor
Fund Type: Energy/Natural Resources
Inception Date: December 22, 2004

Major Rating Factors:
Disappointing performance is the major factor driving the D- (Weak) TheStreet.com Investment Rating for Fiduciary/Claymore MLP Opp. The fund currently has a performance rating of D- (Weak) based on an annualized return of -11.38% over the last three years and a total return of -46.51% year to date 2015. Factored into the performance evaluation is an expense ratio of 1.79% (above average).

The fund's risk rating is currently C (Fair). It carries a beta of 0.69, meaning the fund's expected move will be 6.9% for every 10% move in the market. Volatility, as measured by both the semi-deviation and a drawdown factor, is considered average. As of December 31, 2015, Fiduciary/Claymore MLP Opp traded at a discount of 10.05% below its net asset value, which is better than its one-year historical average discount of 2.10%.

James J. Cunnane, Jr. has been running the fund for 12 years and currently receives a manager quality ranking of 21 (0=worst, 99=best). This fund offers an average level of risk but investors looking for strong performance will be frustrated.

Data Date	Investment Rating	Net Assets ($Mil)	Price	Performance Rating/Pts	Total Return Y-T-D	Risk Rating/Pts
12-15	D-	891.63	12.98	D- / 1.0	-46.51%	C / 5.3
2014	C	955.30	26.12	C+ / 5.9	9.13%	C+ / 6.7
2013	B-	679.65	25.46	B- / 7.0	17.71%	B / 8.0
2012	C+	499.30	21.77	C+ / 6.2	13.92%	B- / 7.9
2011	B	523.10	21.47	B / 7.8	11.12%	B- / 7.8
2010	B-	282.09	21.59	B / 8.2	29.19%	C / 4.5

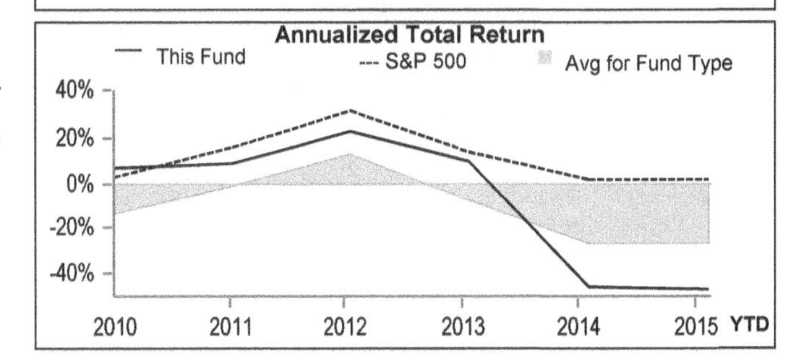

First Tr Senior Floating Rte Inc I (FCT) C- Fair

Fund Family: First Trust Advisors LP
Fund Type: Loan Participation
Inception Date: May 25, 2004

Major Rating Factors: Middle of the road best describes First Tr Senior Floating Rte Inc I whose TheStreet.com Investment Rating is currently a C- (Fair). The fund currently has a performance rating of C- (Fair) based on an annualized return of -1.67% over the last three years and a total return of 1.14% year to date 2015. Factored into the performance evaluation is an expense ratio of 1.69% (above average).

The fund's risk rating is currently B- (Good). It carries a beta of -195.68, meaning the fund's expected move will be -1956.8% for every 10% move in the market. Volatility, as measured by both the semi-deviation and a drawdown factor, is considered low. As of December 31, 2015, First Tr Senior Floating Rte Inc I traded at a discount of 8.86% below its net asset value, which is better than its one-year historical average discount of 8.60%.

Scott D. Fries currently receives a manager quality ranking of 32 (0=worst, 99=best). If you desire an average level of risk, then this fund may be an option.

Data Date	Investment Rating	Net Assets ($Mil)	Price	Performance Rating/Pts	Total Return Y-T-D	Risk Rating/Pts
12-15	C-	392.70	12.35	C- / 3.7	1.14%	B- / 7.3
2014	C-	390.90	13.01	C- / 3.4	-3.97%	B / 8.0
2013	C	400.83	14.50	C / 4.9	-2.50%	B / 8.2
2012	B	367.17	15.17	B- / 7.1	18.93%	B / 8.3
2011	B	357.00	13.19	B / 7.9	6.20%	B / 8.3
2010	C	353.11	13.97	C+ / 6.7	22.37%	C- / 3.9

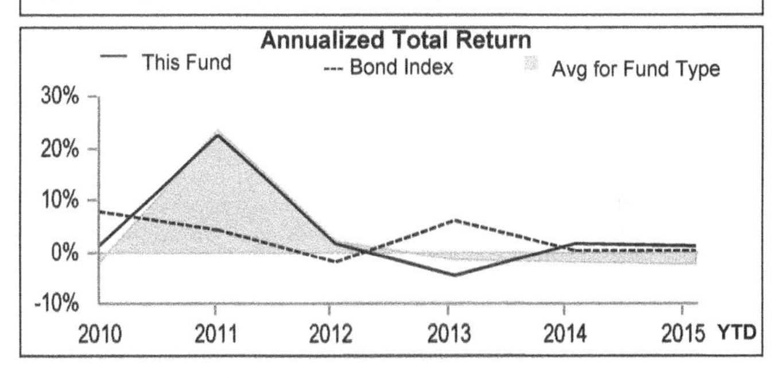

First Tr Specialty Finance &Fin Op (FGB) D+ Weak

Fund Family: First Trust Advisors LP
Fund Type: Financial Services
Inception Date: May 24, 2007

Major Rating Factors:
Disappointing performance is the major factor driving the D+ (Weak) TheStreet.com Investment Rating for First Tr Specialty Finance &Fin Op. The fund currently has a performance rating of D+ (Weak) based on an annualized return of -4.70% over the last three years and a total return of -20.47% year to date 2015. Factored into the performance evaluation is an expense ratio of 1.71% (above average).

The fund's risk rating is currently C+ (Fair). It carries a beta of 0.42, meaning the fund's expected move will be 4.2% for every 10% move in the market. Volatility, as measured by both the semi-deviation and a drawdown factor, is considered low. As of December 31, 2015, First Tr Specialty Finance &Fin Op traded at a discount of 8.24% below its net asset value, which is better than its one-year historical average discount of 2.37%.

David B. Miyazaki currently receives a manager quality ranking of 19 (0=worst, 99=best). This fund offers only a moderate level of risk but investors looking for strong performance are still waiting.

Data Date	Investment Rating	Net Assets ($Mil)	Price	Performance Rating/Pts	Total Return Y-T-D	Risk Rating/Pts
12-15	D+	110.40	5.57	D+ / 2.4	-20.47%	C+ / 6.5
2014	C+	109.40	7.86	C+ / 6.8	9.63%	C+ / 6.9
2013	C	117.96	7.86	C / 5.1	0.67%	B- / 7.6
2012	B+	101.81	7.80	A- / 9.1	36.89%	B- / 7.4
2010	C-	85.07	7.62	C+ / 5.7	39.34%	C- / 3.5

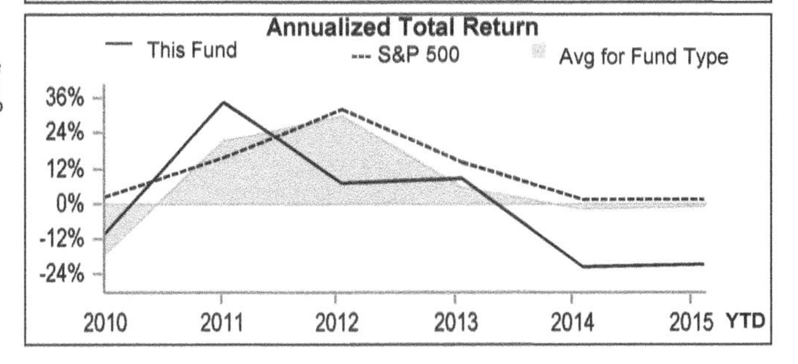

First Trust Dividend and Income (FAV) A- Excellent

Fund Family: First Trust Advisors LP
Fund Type: Global
Inception Date: September 20, 2007

Major Rating Factors:
Strong performance is the major factor driving the A- (Excellent) TheStreet.com Investment Rating for First Trust Dividend and Income. The fund currently has a performance rating of B+ (Good) based on an annualized return of 11.71% over the last three years and a total return of 0.44% year to date 2015. Factored into the performance evaluation is an expense ratio of 1.91% (above average).

The fund's risk rating is currently B- (Good). It carries a beta of 0.66, meaning the fund's expected move will be 6.6% for every 10% move in the market. Volatility, as measured by both the semi-deviation and a drawdown factor, is considered low. As of December 31, 2015, First Trust Dividend and Income traded at a discount of 7.24% below its net asset value, which is worse than its one-year historical average discount of 12.25%.

Bernard P. Schaffer currently receives a manager quality ranking of 94 (0=worst, 99=best). If you desire only a moderate level of risk and strong performance, then this fund is an excellent option.

Data Date	Investment Rating	Net Assets ($Mil)	Price	Performance Rating/Pts	Total Return Y-T-D	Risk Rating/Pts
12-15	A-	84.20	8.46	B+ / 8.4	0.44%	B- / 7.8
2014	B	84.10	9.26	C+ / 6.7	17.14%	B / 8.5
2013	C-	76.72	8.80	C- / 3.7	20.30%	B- / 7.1
2012	D-	70.36	7.55	E+ / 0.9	3.39%	C+ / 5.9
2011	D	77.40	8.38	D / 2.0	-18.13%	C+ / 6.0
2010	D	76.20	11.02	C- / 3.6	-0.73%	C- / 4.0

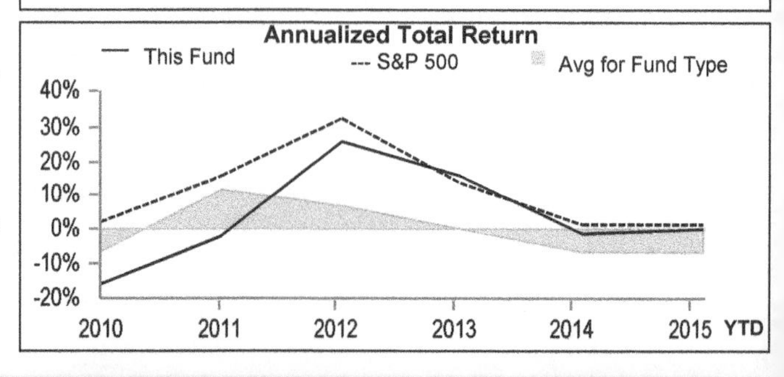

First Trust Energy Income and Gro (FEN) D Weak

Fund Family: First Trust Advisors LP
Fund Type: Energy/Natural Resources
Inception Date: June 24, 2004

Major Rating Factors:
Disappointing performance is the major factor driving the D (Weak) TheStreet.com Investment Rating for First Trust Energy Income and Gro. The fund currently has a performance rating of D (Weak) based on an annualized return of -3.85% over the last three years and a total return of -33.06% year to date 2015. Factored into the performance evaluation is an expense ratio of 2.04% (high).

The fund's risk rating is currently C+ (Fair). It carries a beta of 0.58, meaning the fund's expected move will be 5.8% for every 10% move in the market. Volatility, as measured by both the semi-deviation and a drawdown factor, is considered low. As of December 31, 2015, First Trust Energy Income and Gro traded at a discount of 2.34% below its net asset value, which is worse than its one-year historical average discount of 5.34%.

Eva Pao currently receives a manager quality ranking of 64 (0=worst, 99=best). This fund offers only a moderate level of risk but investors looking for strong performance are still waiting.

Data Date	Investment Rating	Net Assets ($Mil)	Price	Performance Rating/Pts	Total Return Y-T-D	Risk Rating/Pts
12-15	D	737.14	23.00	D / 2.0	-33.06%	C+ / 5.9
2014	A	752.90	36.50	B / 7.7	25.61%	B / 8.7
2013	B-	624.16	32.28	C+ / 6.3	4.51%	B / 8.5
2012	B+	385.33	30.65	B / 8.0	20.42%	B / 8.5
2011	B+	409.30	28.25	B+ / 8.8	14.71%	B / 8.3
2010	B+	136.52	26.88	B+ / 8.4	24.14%	C / 5.1

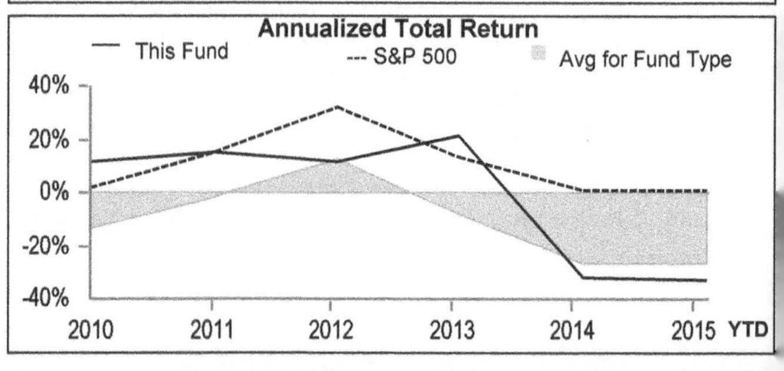

First Trust Energy Infrastructure (FIF) D Weak

Fund Family: First Trust Advisors LP
Fund Type: Energy/Natural Resources
Inception Date: September 27, 2011

Major Rating Factors:
Disappointing performance is the major factor driving the D (Weak) TheStreet.com Investment Rating for First Trust Energy Infrastructure. The fund currently has a performance rating of D+ (Weak) based on an annualized return of -2.22% over the last three years and a total return of -32.73% year to date 2015. Factored into the performance evaluation is an expense ratio of 1.80% (above average).

The fund's risk rating is currently C (Fair). It carries a beta of 0.74, meaning the fund's expected move will be 7.4% for every 10% move in the market. Volatility, as measured by both the semi-deviation and a drawdown factor, is considered average. As of December 31, 2015, First Trust Energy Infrastructure traded at a discount of 11.79% below its net asset value, which is better than its one-year historical average discount of 10.91%.

James J. Murchie currently receives a manager quality ranking of 81 (0=worst, 99=best). This fund offers an average level of risk but investors looking for strong performance will be frustrated.

Data Date	Investment Rating	Net Assets ($Mil)	Price	Performance Rating/Pts	Total Return Y-T-D	Risk Rating/Pts
12-15	D	455.85	14.59	D+ / 2.3	-32.73%	C / 5.1
2014	A	472.60	23.78	A- / 9.0	31.94%	B- / 7.7
2013	C-	418.68	20.83	D+ / 2.6	4.53%	B / 8.0
2012	A+	375.30	21.15	B+ / 8.5	18.49%	B+ / 9.2

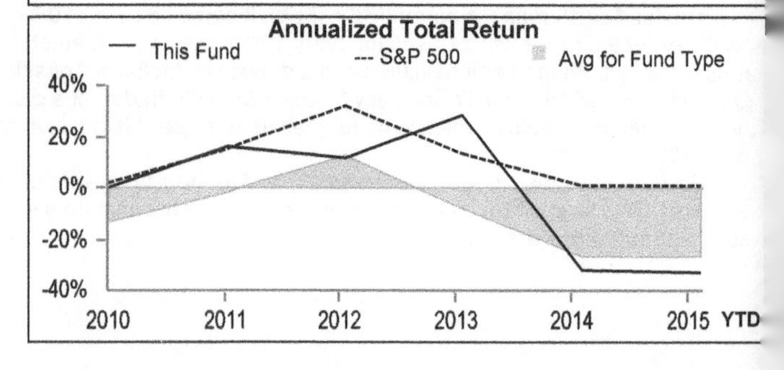

First Trust Enhanced Equity Income (FFA) B Good

Fund Family: First Trust Advisors LP
Fund Type: Income
Inception Date: August 27, 2004

Major Rating Factors: Strong performance is the major factor driving the B (Good) TheStreet.com Investment Rating for First Trust Enhanced Equity Income. The fund currently has a performance rating of B- (Good) based on an annualized return of 10.01% over the last three years and a total return of -1.19% year to date 2015. Factored into the performance evaluation is an expense ratio of 1.18% (low).

The fund's risk rating is currently B- (Good). It carries a beta of 0.96, meaning that its performance tracks fairly well with that of the overall stock market. Volatility, as measured by both the semi-deviation and a drawdown factor, is considered low. As of December 31, 2015, First Trust Enhanced Equity Income traded at a discount of 11.94% below its net asset value, which is better than its one-year historical average discount of 10.06%.

Douglas W. Kugler currently receives a manager quality ranking of 42 (0=worst, 99=best). If you desire only a moderate level of risk and strong performance, then this fund is an excellent option.

Data Date	Investment Rating	Net Assets ($Mil)	Price	Performance Rating/Pts	Total Return Y-T-D	Risk Rating/Pts
12-15	B	318.64	13.20	B- / 7.5	-1.19%	B- / 7.7
2014	A	316.90	14.34	B- / 7.5	15.99%	B+ / 9.1
2013	B-	265.01	13.32	C+ / 6.9	16.41%	B / 8.0
2012	C	262.11	11.84	C / 4.6	18.78%	B- / 7.8
2011	C	249.80	10.83	C / 5.2	-3.92%	B- / 7.8
2010	C+	225.65	12.64	C+ / 6.4	16.50%	C / 5.0

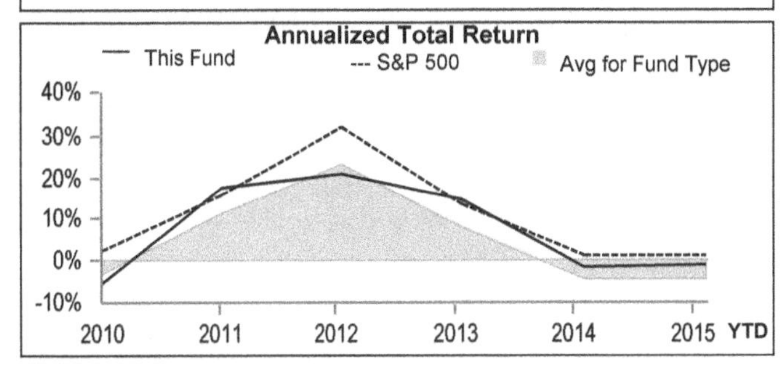

First Trust High Income Long/Short (FSD) C- Fair

Fund Family: First Trust Advisors LP
Fund Type: Global
Inception Date: September 27, 2010

Major Rating Factors: Middle of the road best describes First Trust High Income Long/Short whose TheStreet.com Investment Rating is currently a C- (Fair). The fund currently has a performance rating of C- (Fair) based on an annualized return of -1.88% over the last three years and a total return of -5.39% year to date 2015. Factored into the performance evaluation is an expense ratio of 1.75% (above average).

The fund's risk rating is currently B- (Good). It carries a beta of 0.55, meaning the fund's expected move will be 5.5% for every 10% move in the market. Volatility, as measured by both the semi-deviation and a drawdown factor, is considered low. As of December 31, 2015, First Trust High Income Long/Short traded at a discount of 14.20% below its net asset value, which is better than its one-year historical average discount of 14.10%.

Dan C. Roberts currently receives a manager quality ranking of 37 (0=worst, 99=best). If you desire an average level of risk, then this fund may be an option.

Data Date	Investment Rating	Net Assets ($Mil)	Price	Performance Rating/Pts	Total Return Y-T-D	Risk Rating/Pts
12-15	C-	701.96	14.08	C- / 3.4	-5.39%	B- / 7.0
2014	C	699.50	16.00	C / 4.5	0.15%	B / 8.2
2013	C	718.30	17.22	C / 4.6	-1.15%	B / 8.0
2012	B+	642.41	18.12	B+ / 8.7	26.83%	B- / 7.7
2011	D	613.70	15.27	D- / 1.4	-7.63%	B- / 7.7

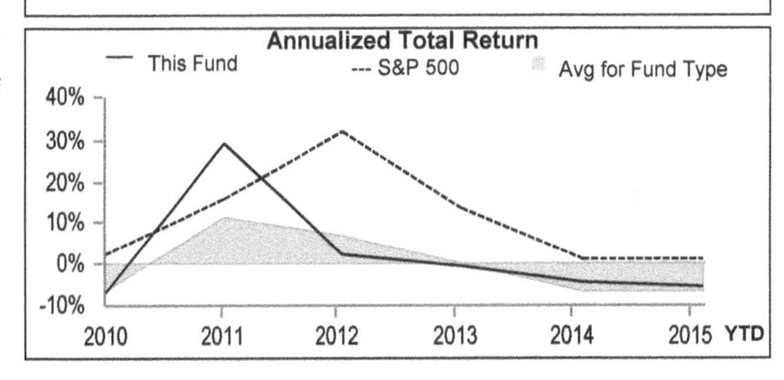

First Trust Inter Dur Pref & Inc (FPF) B- Good

Fund Family: First Trust Advisors LP
Fund Type: Income
Inception Date: May 23, 2013

Major Rating Factors: First Trust Inter Dur Pref & Inc receives a TheStreet.com Investment Rating of B- (Good). The fund currently has a performance rating of C+ (Fair) based on an annualized return of 0.00% over the last three years and a total return of 3.23% year to date 2015. Factored into the performance evaluation is an expense ratio of 1.69% (above average).

The fund's risk rating is currently B (Good). It carries a beta of 0.00, meaning the fund's expected move will be 0.0% for every 10% move in the market. Volatility, as measured by both the semi-deviation and a drawdown factor, is considered low. As of December 31, 2015, First Trust Inter Dur Pref & Inc traded at a discount of 9.41% below its net asset value, which is better than its one-year historical average discount of 8.13%.

Scott T. Fleming currently receives a manager quality ranking of 77 (0=worst, 99=best). If you desire an average level of risk, then this fund may be an option.

Data Date	Investment Rating	Net Assets ($Mil)	Price	Performance Rating/Pts	Total Return Y-T-D	Risk Rating/Pts
12-15	B-	1,482.49	21.27	C+ / 6.1	3.23%	B / 8.1
2014	A	1,478.80	22.71	B / 8.2	17.71%	B / 8.6

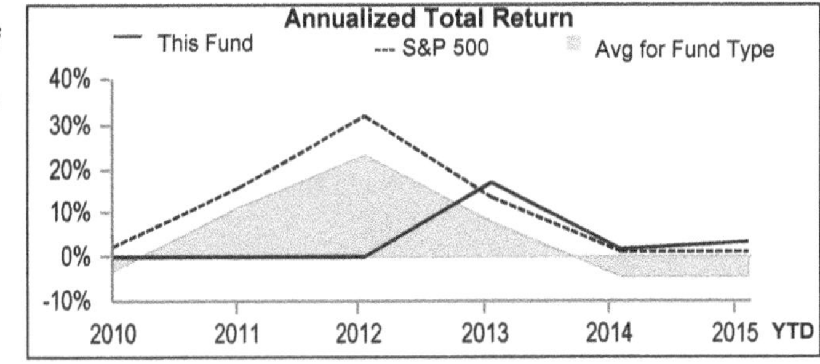

First Trust MLP and Energy Income (FEI) D Weak

Fund Family: First Trust Advisors LP
Fund Type: Income
Inception Date: November 27, 2012

Major Rating Factors:
Disappointing performance is the major factor driving the D (Weak) TheStreet.com Investment Rating for First Trust MLP and Energy Income. The fund currently has a performance rating of D- (Weak) based on an annualized return of -6.86% over the last three years and a total return of -33.70% year to date 2015. Factored into the performance evaluation is an expense ratio of 1.79% (above average).

The fund's risk rating is currently C+ (Fair). It carries a beta of 0.77, meaning the fund's expected move will be 7.7% for every 10% move in the market. Volatility, as measured by both the semi-deviation and a drawdown factor, is considered low. As of December 31, 2015, First Trust MLP and Energy Income traded at a discount of 8.19% below its net asset value, which is better than its one-year historical average discount of 7.59%.

Eva Pao currently receives a manager quality ranking of 9 (0=worst, 99=best). This fund offers only a moderate level of risk but investors looking for strong performance are still waiting.

Data Date	Investment Rating	Net Assets ($Mil)	Price	Performance Rating/Pts	Total Return Y-T-D	Risk Rating/Pts
12-15	D	1,057.32	13.22	D- / 1.5	-33.70%	C+ / 5.9
2014	B+	1,071.40	21.55	B- / 7.5	18.79%	B / 8.5
2013	C-	955.00	20.01	D+ / 2.6	2.49%	B / 8.8

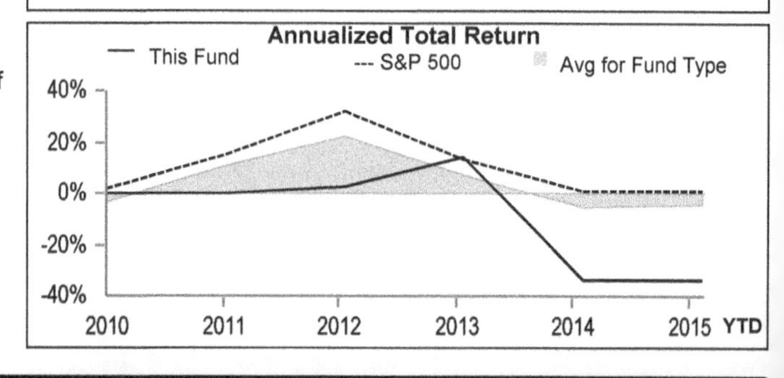

First Trust Mortgage Income Fund (FMY) C Fair

Fund Family: First Trust Advisors LP
Fund Type: Mortgage
Inception Date: May 25, 2005

Major Rating Factors: Middle of the road best describes First Trust Mortgage Income Fund whose TheStreet.com Investment Rating is currently a C (Fair). The fund currently has a performance rating of C (Fair) based on an annualized return of -0.95% over the last three years and a total return of 4.39% year to date 2015. Factored into the performance evaluation is an expense ratio of 1.78% (above average).

The fund's risk rating is currently B- (Good). It carries a beta of 1.74, meaning it is expected to move 17.4% for every 10% move in the market. Volatility, as measured by both the semi-deviation and a drawdown factor, is considered low. As of December 31, 2015, First Trust Mortgage Income Fund traded at a discount of 8.44% below its net asset value, which is worse than its one-year historical average discount of 10.75%.

Anthony Breaks currently receives a manager quality ranking of 43 (0=worst, 99=best). If you desire an average level of risk, then this fund may be an option.

Data Date	Investment Rating	Net Assets ($Mil)	Price	Performance Rating/Pts	Total Return Y-T-D	Risk Rating/Pts
12-15	C	71.71	14.54	C / 4.5	4.39%	B- / 7.1
2014	D+	72.80	14.86	D+ / 2.7	2.32%	C+ / 6.5
2013	D+	75.13	15.56	C- / 3.1	-8.97%	B- / 7.1
2012	C-	75.01	17.66	C- / 3.6	5.39%	B- / 7.2
2011	C	71.40	19.04	C+ / 5.9	11.04%	B- / 7.0
2010	B	82.10	19.40	B / 8.1	16.83%	C / 5.1

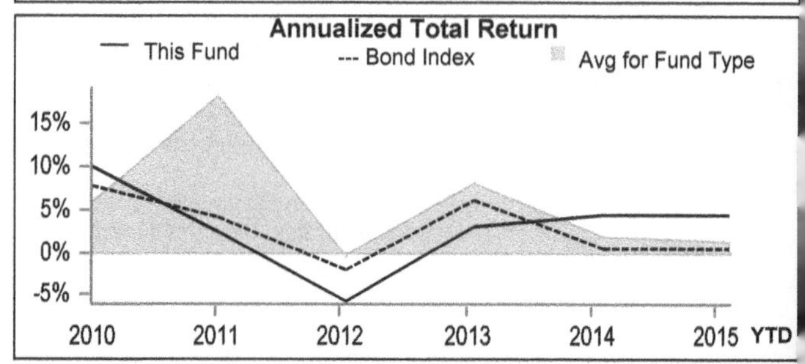

First Trust New Opptys MLP & Energ (FPL) D- Weak

Fund Family: First Trust Advisors LP
Fund Type: Energy/Natural Resources
Inception Date: March 26, 2014

Major Rating Factors:
Very poor performance is the major factor driving the D- (Weak) TheStreet.com Investment Rating for First Trust New Opptys MLP & Energ. The fund currently has a performance rating of E- (Very Weak) based on an annualized return of 0.00% over the last three years and a total return of -35.73% year to date 2015. Factored into the performance evaluation is an expense ratio of 1.94% (above average).

The fund's risk rating is currently C (Fair). It carries a beta of 0.00, meaning the fund's expected move will be 0.0% for every 10% move in the market. Volatility, as measured by both the semi-deviation and a drawdown factor, is considered average. As of December 31, 2015, First Trust New Opptys MLP & Energ traded at a discount of 7.47% below its net asset value, which is worse than its one-year historical average discount of 8.90%.

This fund offers an average level of risk but investors looking for strong performance will be frustrated.

Data Date	Investment Rating	Net Assets ($Mil)	Price	Performance Rating/Pts	Total Return Y-T-D	Risk Rating/Pts
12-15	D-	484.74	10.77	E- / 0.1	-35.73%	C / 5.1

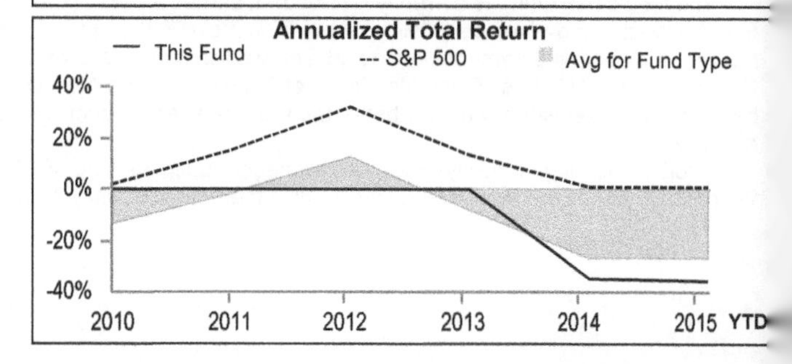

First Trust Strategic High Inc II (FHY) D+ Weak

Fund Family: First Trust Advisors LP
Fund Type: General Bond
Inception Date: March 28, 2006

Major Rating Factors:
Disappointing performance is the major factor driving the D+ (Weak) TheStreet.com Investment Rating for First Trust Strategic High Inc II. The fund currently has a performance rating of D+ (Weak) based on an annualized return of -4.70% over the last three years and a total return of -15.92% year to date 2015. Factored into the performance evaluation is an expense ratio of 2.34% (high).

The fund's risk rating is currently C+ (Fair). It carries a beta of 1.14, meaning it is expected to move 11.4% for every 10% move in the market. Volatility, as measured by both the semi-deviation and a drawdown factor, is considered low. As of December 31, 2015, First Trust Strategic High Inc II traded at a discount of 14.38% below its net asset value, which is better than its one-year historical average discount of 13.09%.

Anthony Breaks currently receives a manager quality ranking of 28 (0=worst, 99=best). This fund offers only a moderate level of risk but investors looking for strong performance are still waiting.

Data Date	Investment Rating	Net Assets ($Mil)	Price	Performance Rating/Pts	Total Return Y-T-D	Risk Rating/Pts
12-15	D+	140.74	11.13	D+ / 2.5	-15.92%	C+ / 6.5
2014	C	141.20	14.50	C / 4.3	0.52%	B- / 7.9
2013	C+	151.46	16.05	C+ / 6.9	1.15%	C+ / 6.7
2012	B	131.11	16.60	B- / 7.3	23.33%	B / 8.6
2011	C-	129.70	15.28	C / 4.7	19.09%	C+ / 5.9
2010	E+	48.16	4.68	E+ / 0.7	11.78%	C- / 4.1

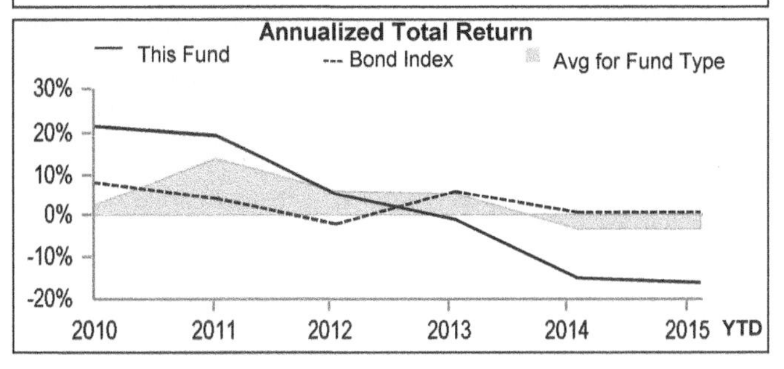

First Trust/Aberdeen Emerg Opp Fd (FEO) D Weak

Fund Family: First Trust Advisors LP
Fund Type: Global
Inception Date: August 28, 2006

Major Rating Factors:
Disappointing performance is the major factor driving the D (Weak) TheStreet.com Investment Rating for First Trust/Aberdeen Emerg Opp Fd. The fund currently has a performance rating of D (Weak) based on an annualized return of -10.04% over the last three years and a total return of -13.09% year to date 2015. Factored into the performance evaluation is an expense ratio of 1.71% (above average).

The fund's risk rating is currently C+ (Fair). It carries a beta of 0.95, meaning that its performance tracks fairly well with that of the overall stock market. Volatility, as measured by both the semi-deviation and a drawdown factor, is considered low. As of December 31, 2015, First Trust/Aberdeen Emerg Opp Fd traded at a discount of 14.86% below its net asset value, which is better than its one-year historical average discount of 13.48%.

Andrew P. S. Brown currently receives a manager quality ranking of 12 (0=worst, 99=best). This fund offers only a moderate level of risk but investors looking for strong performance are still waiting.

Data Date	Investment Rating	Net Assets ($Mil)	Price	Performance Rating/Pts	Total Return Y-T-D	Risk Rating/Pts
12-15	D	99.05	13.06	D / 1.9	-13.09%	C+ / 5.7
2014	D+	107.50	16.45	C- / 3.3	-0.01%	C+ / 6.8
2013	D+	126.09	18.07	D / 2.0	-16.67%	B- / 7.4
2012	B+	108.17	22.05	B+ / 8.6	34.77%	B- / 7.6
2011	B	108.20	17.82	B / 7.6	-10.59%	B- / 7.8
2010	B-	106.39	21.31	B+ / 8.4	26.55%	C- / 4.0

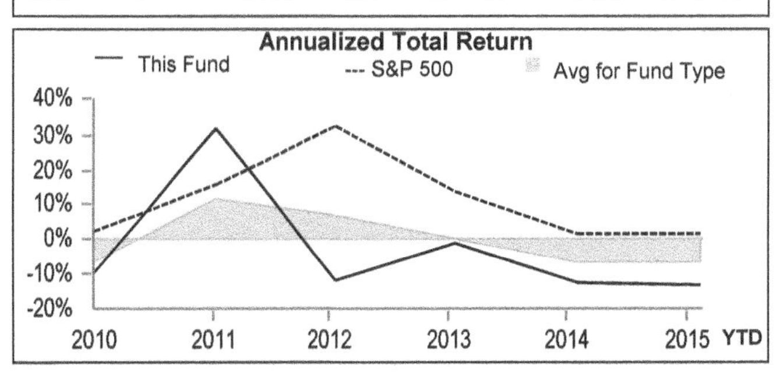

First Trust/Aberdeen Glob Opp Inc (FAM) D Weak

Fund Family: First Trust Advisors LP
Fund Type: Global
Inception Date: November 23, 2004

Major Rating Factors:
Disappointing performance is the major factor driving the D (Weak) TheStreet.com Investment Rating for First Trust/Aberdeen Glob Opp Inc. The fund currently has a performance rating of D+ (Weak) based on an annualized return of -8.93% over the last three years and a total return of -7.01% year to date 2015. Factored into the performance evaluation is an expense ratio of 2.16% (high).

The fund's risk rating is currently C+ (Fair). It carries a beta of 0.88, meaning the fund's expected move will be 8.8% for every 10% move in the market. Volatility, as measured by both the semi-deviation and a drawdown factor, is considered low. As of December 31, 2015, First Trust/Aberdeen Glob Opp Inc traded at a discount of 13.12% below its net asset value, which is worse than its one-year historical average discount of 14.64%.

Edwin F. Gutierrez currently receives a manager quality ranking of 30 (0=worst, 99=best). This fund offers only a moderate level of risk but investors looking for strong performance are still waiting.

Data Date	Investment Rating	Net Assets ($Mil)	Price	Performance Rating/Pts	Total Return Y-T-D	Risk Rating/Pts
12-15	D	239.81	10.13	D+ / 2.4	-7.01%	C+ / 5.8
2014	D+	258.30	12.04	D+ / 2.3	-4.68%	C+ / 6.7
2013	D+	319.57	14.05	D+ / 2.8	-15.14%	B- / 7.7
2012	B-	303.29	17.85	C+ / 6.4	23.80%	B / 8.2
2011	B+	294.50	15.76	B / 7.8	4.88%	B / 8.6
2010	B	290.78	17.36	B / 8.2	18.95%	C / 4.9

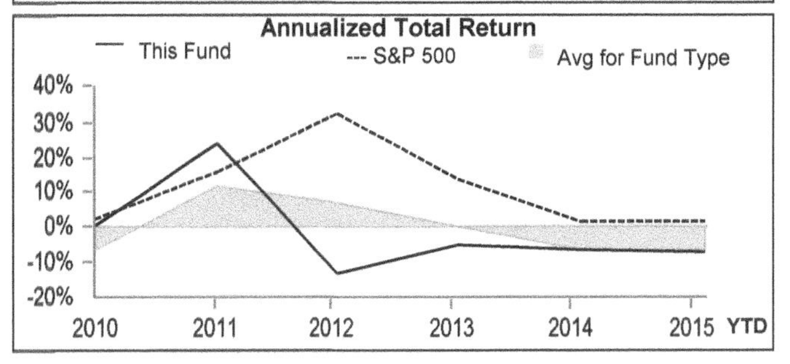

Flaherty & Crumrine Dyn Pfd and In (DFP) A Excellent

Fund Family: Flaherty & Crumrine Inc
Fund Type: Global
Inception Date: May 23, 2013

Major Rating Factors:
Strong performance is the major factor driving the A (Excellent) TheStreet.com Investment Rating for Flaherty & Crumrine Dyn Pfd and In. The fund currently has a performance rating of B+ (Good) based on an annualized return of 0.00% over the last three years and a total return of 9.75% year to date 2015. Factored into the performance evaluation is an expense ratio of 1.67% (above average).

The fund's risk rating is currently B- (Good). It carries a beta of 0.00, meaning the fund's expected move will be 0.0% for every 10% move in the market. Volatility, as measured by both the semi-deviation and a drawdown factor, is considered low. As of December 31, 2015, Flaherty & Crumrine Dyn Pfd and In traded at a discount of 5.37% below its net asset value, which is worse than its one-year historical average discount of 7.23%.

Bradford S. Stone currently receives a manager quality ranking of 96 (0=worst, 99=best). If you desire only a moderate level of risk and strong performance, then this fund is an excellent option.

Data Date	Investment Rating	Net Assets ($Mil)	Price	Performance Rating/Pts	Total Return Y-T-D	Risk Rating/Pts
12-15	A	475.16	22.90	B+ / 8.9	9.75%	B- / 7.8
2014	C-	469.30	22.25	C+ / 6.7	17.69%	C / 4.9

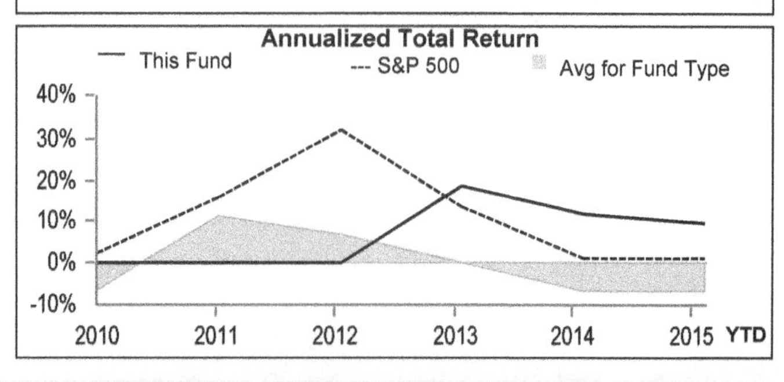

Flaherty & Crumrine Pref Sec Inc (FFC) B Good

Fund Family: Flaherty & Crumrine Inc
Fund Type: Income
Inception Date: January 28, 2003

Major Rating Factors: Strong performance is the major factor driving the B (Good) TheStreet.com Investment Rating for Flaherty & Crumrine Pref Sec Inc. The fund currently has a performance rating of B+ (Good) based on an annualized return of 9.81% over the last three years and a total return of 10.95% year to date 2015. Factored into the performance evaluation is an expense ratio of 1.39% (average).

The fund's risk rating is currently C+ (Fair). It carries a beta of 0.23, meaning the fund's expected move will be 2.3% for every 10% move in the market. Volatility, as measured by both the semi-deviation and a drawdown factor, is considered low. As of December 31, 2015, Flaherty & Crumrine Pref Sec Inc traded at a premium of 6.42% above its net asset value, which is worse than its one-year historical average premium of 2.33%.

Robert E. Chadwick has been running the fund for 13 years and currently receives a manager quality ranking of 91 (0=worst, 99=best). If you desire only a moderate level of risk and strong performance, then this fund is an excellent option.

Data Date	Investment Rating	Net Assets ($Mil)	Price	Performance Rating/Pts	Total Return Y-T-D	Risk Rating/Pts
12-15	B	864.64	20.05	B+ / 8.7	10.95%	C+ / 6.2
2014	B-	856.00	19.05	C+ / 6.5	16.77%	B- / 7.8
2013	B-	848.52	17.50	C+ / 6.7	-1.01%	B / 8.0
2012	A+	746.99	19.55	B+ / 8.9	25.83%	B / 8.9
2011	A-	699.40	17.46	A+ / 9.8	19.35%	B- / 7.6
2010	C	571.14	16.21	B+ / 8.3	27.69%	D+ / 2.5

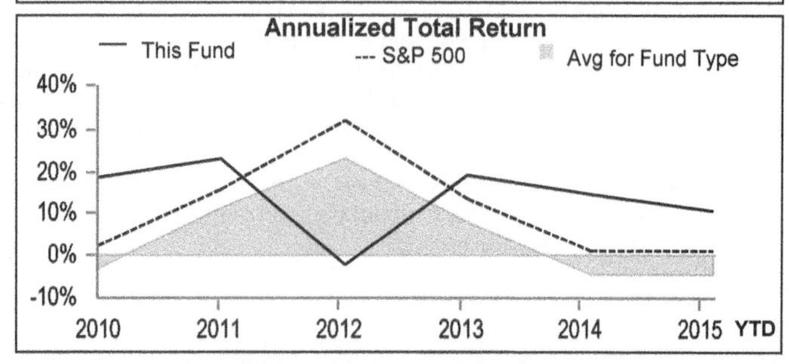

Flaherty & Crumrine Total Return (FLC) C+ Fair

Fund Family: Flaherty & Crumrine Inc
Fund Type: Income
Inception Date: August 29, 2003

Major Rating Factors: Middle of the road best describes Flaherty & Crumrine Total Return whose TheStreet.com Investment Rating is currently a C+ (Fair). The fund currently has a performance rating of C+ (Fair) based on an annualized return of 6.04% over the last three years and a total return of 3.89% year to date 2015. Factored into the performance evaluation is an expense ratio of 1.77% (above average).

The fund's risk rating is currently B- (Good). It carries a beta of 0.36, meaning the fund's expected move will be 3.6% for every 10% move in the market. Volatility, as measured by both the semi-deviation and a drawdown factor, is considered low. As of December 31, 2015, Flaherty & Crumrine Total Return traded at a discount of 4.91% below its net asset value, which is better than its one-year historical average discount of 4.10%.

Bradford S. Stone has been running the fund for 13 years and currently receives a manager quality ranking of 79 (0=worst, 99=best). If you desire an average level of risk, then this fund may be an option.

Data Date	Investment Rating	Net Assets ($Mil)	Price	Performance Rating/Pts	Total Return Y-T-D	Risk Rating/Pts
12-15	C+	208.86	19.17	C+ / 6.6	3.89%	B- / 7.3
2014	C+	206.90	19.78	C+ / 6.2	14.26%	B- / 7.9
2013	B-	205.96	18.57	C+ / 6.6	-0.85%	B / 8.1
2012	A+	182.40	20.14	B+ / 8.9	25.26%	B / 8.9
2011	A-	170.50	18.70	A+ / 9.8	19.66%	B- / 7.9
2010	C	140.59	17.26	B+ / 8.4	30.49%	D+ / 2.6

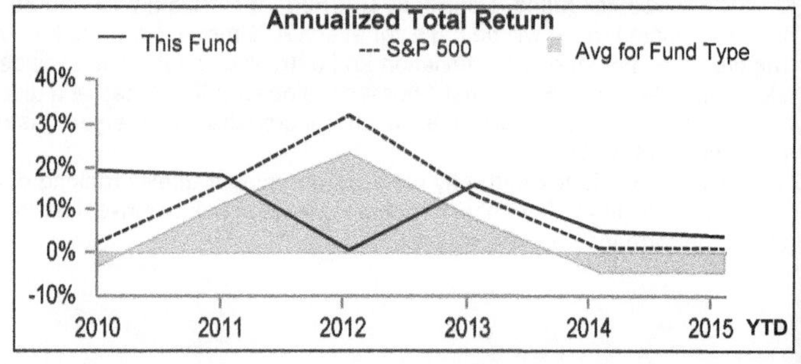

Flaherty&Crumrine Preferred Inc Op (PFO) C+ Fair

Fund Family: Flaherty & Crumrine Inc
Fund Type: Income
Inception Date: February 13, 1992

Major Rating Factors: Middle of the road best describes Flaherty&Crumrine Preferred Inc Op whose TheStreet.com Investment Rating is currently a C+ (Fair). The fund currently has a performance rating of C+ (Fair) based on an annualized return of 6.08% over the last three years and a total return of 0.01% year to date 2015. Factored into the performance evaluation is an expense ratio of 1.85% (above average).

The fund's risk rating is currently B- (Good). It carries a beta of 0.44, meaning the fund's expected move will be 4.4% for every 10% move in the market. Volatility, as measured by both the semi-deviation and a drawdown factor, is considered low. As of December 31, 2015, Flaherty&Crumrine Preferred Inc Op traded at a discount of 3.53% below its net asset value, which is better than its one-year historical average discount of .52%.

Bradford S. Stone currently receives a manager quality ranking of 72 (0=worst, 99=best). If you desire an average level of risk, then this fund may be an option.

Data Date	Investment Rating	Net Assets ($Mil)	Price	Performance Rating/Pts	Total Return Y-T-D	Risk Rating/Pts
12-15	C+	142.74	10.67	C+ / 6.5	0.01%	B- / 7.1
2014	C+	141.10	11.55	C+ / 6.6	22.00%	B- / 7.6
2013	C+	140.54	10.08	C+ / 6.2	-2.16%	B- / 7.9
2012	A-	124.39	11.22	B+ / 8.3	13.33%	B / 8.6
2011	A+	114.70	11.20	A+ / 9.8	27.96%	B / 8.9
2010	C+	95.02	9.48	B- / 7.0	25.08%	C / 4.3

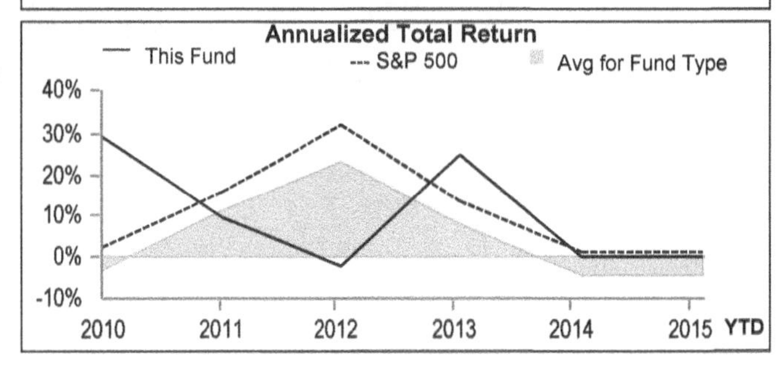

Flaherty&Crumrine Preferred Income (PFD) C+ Fair

Fund Family: Flaherty & Crumrine Inc
Fund Type: Income
Inception Date: January 31, 1991

Major Rating Factors: Middle of the road best describes Flaherty&Crumrine Preferred Income whose TheStreet.com Investment Rating is currently a C+ (Fair). The fund currently has a performance rating of C+ (Fair) based on an annualized return of 4.53% over the last three years and a total return of -0.84% year to date 2015. Factored into the performance evaluation is an expense ratio of 1.82% (above average).

The fund's risk rating is currently B- (Good). It carries a beta of 0.50, meaning the fund's expected move will be 5.0% for every 10% move in the market. Volatility, as measured by both the semi-deviation and a drawdown factor, is considered low. As of December 31, 2015, Flaherty&Crumrine Preferred Income traded at a discount of 2.71% below its net asset value, which is better than its one-year historical average premium of 2.51%.

Bradford S. Stone currently receives a manager quality ranking of 62 (0=worst, 99=best). If you desire an average level of risk, then this fund may be an option.

Data Date	Investment Rating	Net Assets ($Mil)	Price	Performance Rating/Pts	Total Return Y-T-D	Risk Rating/Pts
12-15	C+	153.69	12.92	C+ / 5.9	-0.84%	B- / 7.1
2014	C	152.00	14.08	C+ / 6.8	27.56%	C / 5.5
2013	C+	151.47	12.26	C+ / 5.7	-6.78%	B- / 7.7
2012	B+	135.17	13.63	B / 7.9	10.13%	B / 8.3
2011	B+	125.40	14.14	A / 9.5	33.70%	B- / 7.4
2010	C-	104.76	11.62	C+ / 6.8	21.26%	C- / 3.4

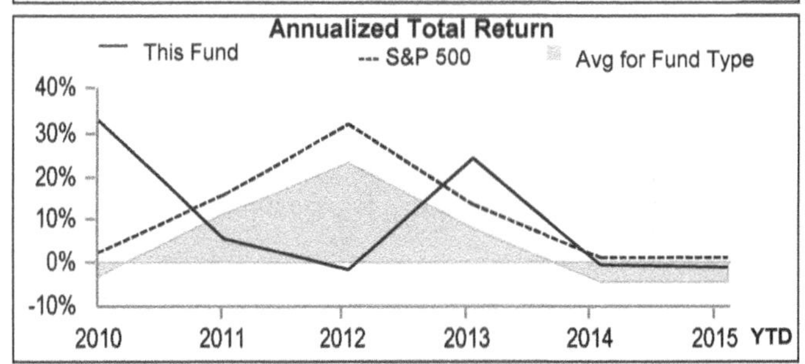

Fort Dearborn Inc. Secs. (FDI) C+ Fair

Fund Family: UBS Asset Mgmt (Americas) Inc
Fund Type: General - Investment Grade
Inception Date: December 15, 1972

Major Rating Factors: Middle of the road best describes Fort Dearborn Inc. Secs. whose TheStreet.com Investment Rating is currently a C+ (Fair). The fund currently has a performance rating of C+ (Fair) based on an annualized return of 1.44% over the last three years and a total return of 6.76% year to date 2015. Factored into the performance evaluation is an expense ratio of 0.75% (very low).

The fund's risk rating is currently B- (Good). It carries a beta of 1.65, meaning it is expected to move 16.5% for every 10% move in the market. Volatility, as measured by both the semi-deviation and a drawdown factor, is considered low. As of December 31, 2015, Fort Dearborn Inc. Secs. traded at a discount of 1.16% below its net asset value, which is worse than its one-year historical average discount of 7.82%.

Scott D. Wilkin currently receives a manager quality ranking of 57 (0=worst, 99=best). If you desire an average level of risk, then this fund may be an option.

Data Date	Investment Rating	Net Assets ($Mil)	Price	Performance Rating/Pts	Total Return Y-T-D	Risk Rating/Pts
12-15	C+	131.47	14.51	C+ / 5.6	6.76%	B- / 7.3
2014	C-	142.80	14.14	C- / 3.6	6.42%	B / 8.0
2013	C+	139.42	13.80	C+ / 5.8	-6.17%	B / 8.2
2012	B+	156.80	16.54	B- / 7.3	15.56%	B / 8.9
2011	B+	151.70	15.96	B- / 7.4	24.14%	B+ / 9.0
2010	B+	152.20	15.46	B / 7.6	17.35%	C+ / 6.4

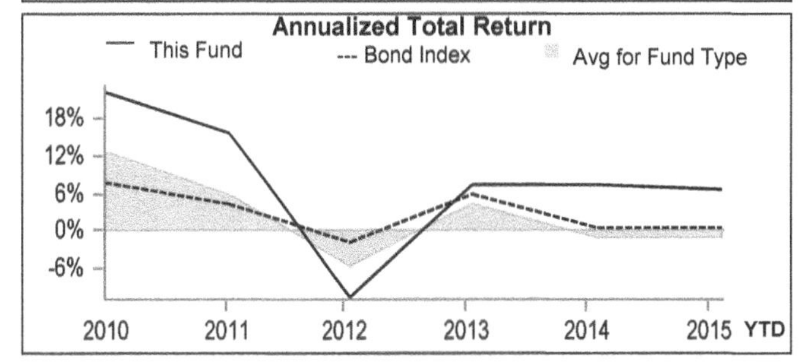

Foxby Corp (FXBY) C Fair

Fund Family: Midas Management Corporation
Fund Type: Income
Inception Date: October 26, 1999

Major Rating Factors: Middle of the road best describes Foxby Corp whose TheStreet.com Investment Rating is currently a C (Fair). The fund currently has a performance rating of C (Fair) based on an annualized return of 3.60% over the last three years and a total return of -13.90% year to date 2015. Factored into the performance evaluation is an expense ratio of 1.92% (above average).

The fund's risk rating is currently B- (Good). It carries a beta of 0.52, meaning the fund's expected move will be 5.2% for every 10% move in the market. Volatility, as measured by both the semi-deviation and a drawdown factor, is considered low. As of December 31, 2015, Foxby Corp traded at a discount of 34.84% below its net asset value, which is better than its one-year historical average discount of 31.90%.

Thomas B. Winmill has been running the fund for 11 years and currently receives a manager quality ranking of 43 (0=worst, 99=best). If you desire an average level of risk, then this fund may be an option.

Data Date	Investment Rating	Net Assets ($Mil)	Price	Performance Rating/Pts	Total Return Y-T-D	Risk Rating/Pts
12-15	C	7.00	1.59	C / 4.4	-13.90%	B- / 7.8
2014	B+	7.00	1.87	B- / 7.0	4.39%	B / 8.7
2013	A-	5.44	1.95	B+ / 8.5	25.05%	B / 8.3
2012	D+	5.31	1.45	D+ / 2.8	14.59%	B- / 7.4
2011	C+	4.70	1.24	B- / 7.1	8.70%	B- / 7.0
2010	E	3.71	1.10	E / 0.5	7.84%	D+ / 2.3

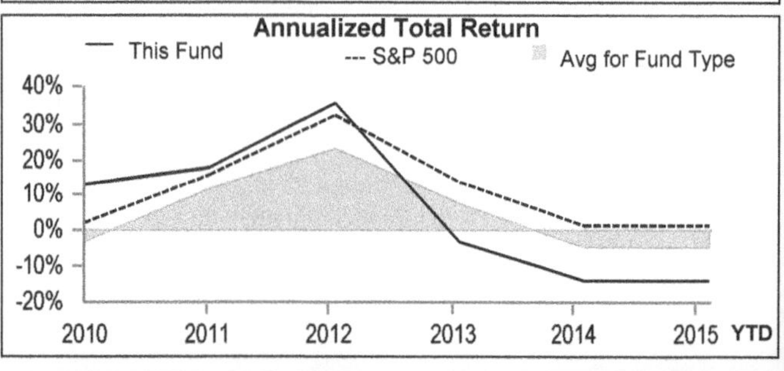

Franklin Limited Duration Income (FTF) C- Fair

Fund Family: Franklin Advisers Inc
Fund Type: General Bond
Inception Date: August 27, 2003

Major Rating Factors: Middle of the road best describes Franklin Limited Duration Income whose TheStreet.com Investment Rating is currently a C- (Fair). The fund currently has a performance rating of C- (Fair) based on an annualized return of -3.67% over the last three years and a total return of -5.58% year to date 2015. Factored into the performance evaluation is an expense ratio of 1.14% (low).

The fund's risk rating is currently B- (Good). It carries a beta of 0.70, meaning the fund's expected move will be 7.0% for every 10% move in the market. Volatility, as measured by both the semi-deviation and a drawdown factor, is considered low. As of December 31, 2015, Franklin Limited Duration Income traded at a discount of 13.41% below its net asset value, which is better than its one-year historical average discount of 13.32%.

Christopher J. Molumphy currently receives a manager quality ranking of 36 (0=worst, 99=best). If you desire an average level of risk, then this fund may be an option.

Data Date	Investment Rating	Net Assets ($Mil)	Price	Performance Rating/Pts	Total Return Y-T-D	Risk Rating/Pts
12-15	C-	372.08	10.72	C- / 3.0	-5.58%	B- / 7.5
2014	C-	385.70	12.19	C- / 3.6	-0.74%	B / 8.1
2013	C	383.63	12.99	C / 4.7	-5.47%	B / 8.4
2012	B-	370.10	14.37	C+ / 6.6	21.69%	B / 8.5
2011	B	357.50	13.14	B- / 7.2	6.70%	B / 8.6
2010	B-	360.80	13.10	B / 7.9	16.73%	C / 4.7

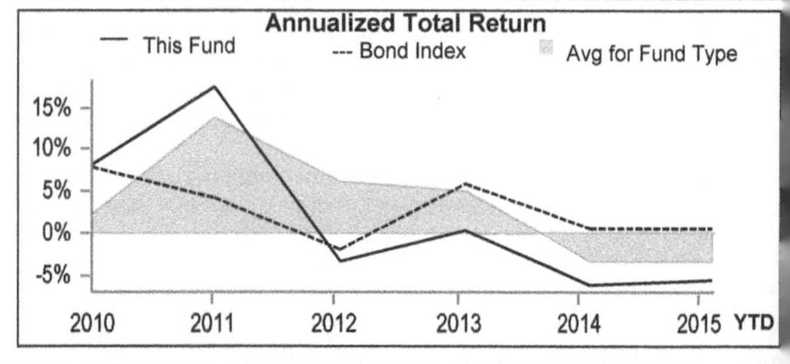

Franklin Universal Trust (FT) C- Fair

Fund Family: Franklin Advisers Inc
Fund Type: Growth and Income
Inception Date: September 23, 1988

Major Rating Factors: Middle of the road best describes Franklin Universal Trust whose TheStreet.com Investment Rating is currently a C- (Fair). The fund currently has a performance rating of C- (Fair) based on an annualized return of -0.94% over the last three years and a total return of -12.35% year to date 2015. Factored into the performance evaluation is an expense ratio of 1.97% (above average).

The fund's risk rating is currently C+ (Fair). It carries a beta of 0.64, meaning the fund's expected move will be 6.4% for every 10% move in the market. Volatility, as measured by both the semi-deviation and a drawdown factor, is considered low. As of December 31, 2015, Franklin Universal Trust traded at a discount of 14.09% below its net asset value, which is better than its one-year historical average discount of 12.60%.

Christopher J. Molumphy has been running the fund for 25 years and currently receives a manager quality ranking of 18 (0=worst, 99=best). If you desire an average level of risk, then this fund may be an option.

Data Date	Investment Rating	Net Assets ($Mil)	Price	Performance Rating/Pts	Total Return Y-T-D	Risk Rating/Pts
12-15	C-	178.75	5.73	C- / 3.3	-12.35%	C+ / 6.9
2014	C	209.70	7.10	C / 5.3	10.05%	B- / 7.4
2013	B-	191.22	6.94	C+ / 5.9	1.11%	B / 8.7
2012	C+	187.73	7.06	C+ / 6.3	18.11%	B- / 7.8
2011	B	179.20	6.69	B / 8.0	11.81%	B- / 7.3
2010	C	165.08	6.33	C+ / 6.7	17.60%	C- / 4.2

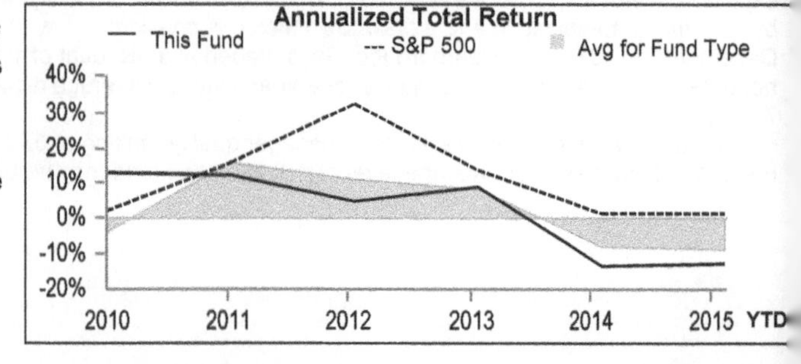

Gabelli Convertible&Income Sec Fun (GCV) C Fair

Fund Family: Gabelli Funds LLC
Fund Type: Growth and Income
Inception Date: July 3, 1989

Major Rating Factors: Middle of the road best describes Gabelli Convertible&Income Sec Fun whose TheStreet.com Investment Rating is currently a C (Fair). The fund currently has a performance rating of C (Fair) based on an annualized return of 4.30% over the last three years and a total return of -12.33% year to date 2015. Factored into the performance evaluation is an expense ratio of 1.62% (above average).

The fund's risk rating is currently B- (Good). It carries a beta of 0.69, meaning the fund's expected move will be 6.9% for every 10% move in the market. Volatility, as measured by both the semi-deviation and a drawdown factor, is considered low. As of December 31, 2015, Gabelli Convertible&Income Sec Fun traded at a discount of 9.81% below its net asset value, which is better than its one-year historical average discount of 3.30%.

Mario J. Gabelli has been running the fund for 27 years and currently receives a manager quality ranking of 30 (0=worst, 99=best). If you desire an average level of risk, then this fund may be an option.

Data Date	Investment Rating	Net Assets ($Mil)	Price	Performance Rating/Pts	Total Return Y-T-D	Risk Rating/Pts
12-15	C	85.08	4.78	C / 4.8	-12.33%	B- / 7.5
2014	B-	113.90	6.08	C+ / 6.7	8.34%	B- / 7.9
2013	C+	76.93	6.17	C+ / 6.5	21.85%	B- / 7.8
2012	C-	100.12	5.33	C- / 3.3	13.58%	B- / 7.5
2011	D+	98.20	5.11	D / 2.0	-6.57%	B- / 7.6
2010	C+	74.08	6.12	C / 5.2	15.79%	C+ / 6.3

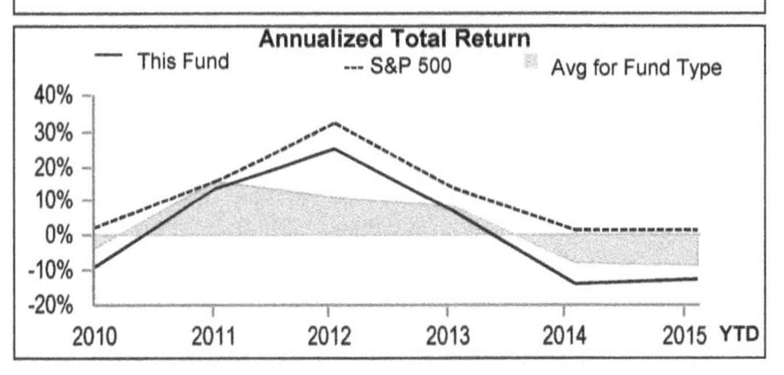

Gabelli Dividend & Income Trust (GDV) B Good

Fund Family: Gabelli Funds LLC
Fund Type: Income
Inception Date: November 24, 2003

Major Rating Factors: Strong performance is the major factor driving the B (Good) TheStreet.com Investment Rating for Gabelli Dividend & Income Trust. The fund currently has a performance rating of B- (Good) based on an annualized return of 10.72% over the last three years and a total return of -8.51% year to date 2015. Factored into the performance evaluation is an expense ratio of 1.36% (average).

The fund's risk rating is currently B- (Good). It carries a beta of 1.38, meaning it is expected to move 13.8% for every 10% move in the market. Volatility, as measured by both the semi-deviation and a drawdown factor, is considered low. As of December 31, 2015, Gabelli Dividend & Income Trust traded at a discount of 12.39% below its net asset value, which is better than its one-year historical average discount of 11.54%.

Kevin V. Dreyer currently receives a manager quality ranking of 21 (0=worst, 99=best). If you desire only a moderate level of risk and strong performance, then this fund is an excellent option.

Data Date	Investment Rating	Net Assets ($Mil)	Price	Performance Rating/Pts	Total Return Y-T-D	Risk Rating/Pts
12-15	B	1,951.03	18.46	B- / 7.2	-8.51%	B- / 7.5
2014	A+	2,474.30	21.66	B / 8.2	10.99%	B / 8.7
2013	A	1,538.80	22.17	B+ / 8.9	34.83%	B / 8.1
2012	C+	1,923.33	16.18	C+ / 6.6	16.51%	B / 8.0
2011	C+	1,888.80	15.42	B- / 7.0	5.72%	B- / 7.3
2010	C	1,168.13	15.36	C / 5.4	24.50%	C / 5.1

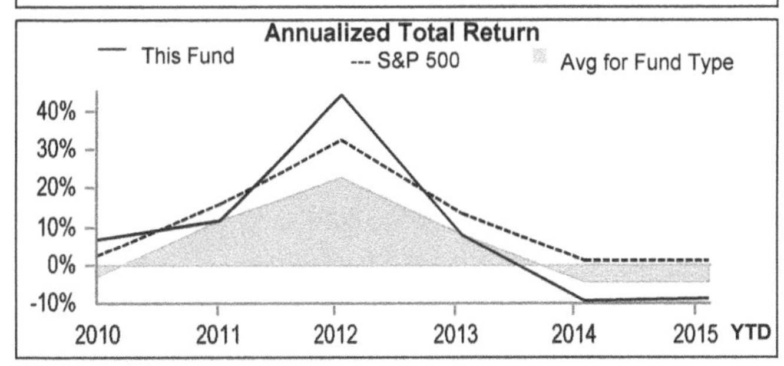

Gabelli Equity Trust (GAB) C Fair

Fund Family: Gabelli Funds LLC
Fund Type: Income
Inception Date: August 14, 1986

Major Rating Factors: Middle of the road best describes Gabelli Equity Trust whose TheStreet.com Investment Rating is currently a C (Fair). The fund currently has a performance rating of C+ (Fair) based on an annualized return of 8.16% over the last three years and a total return of -8.75% year to date 2015. Factored into the performance evaluation is an expense ratio of 1.33% (average).

The fund's risk rating is currently C+ (Fair). It carries a beta of 1.38, meaning it is expected to move 13.8% for every 10% move in the market. Volatility, as measured by both the semi-deviation and a drawdown factor, is considered low. As of December 31, 2015, Gabelli Equity Trust traded at a discount of 6.84% below its net asset value, which is better than its one-year historical average discount of 5.52%.

Mario J. Gabelli has been running the fund for 30 years and currently receives a manager quality ranking of 16 (0=worst, 99=best). If you desire an average level of risk, then this fund may be an option.

Data Date	Investment Rating	Net Assets ($Mil)	Price	Performance Rating/Pts	Total Return Y-T-D	Risk Rating/Pts
12-15	C	1,486.49	5.31	C+ / 6.3	-8.75%	C+ / 6.5
2014	B-	1,731.10	6.47	B- / 7.0	-7.38%	B- / 7.6
2013	A	1,527.85	7.75	A / 9.3	45.78%	B- / 7.7
2012	B	1,293.17	5.58	B / 8.1	26.90%	B- / 7.6
2011	C+	1,265.50	4.99	B- / 7.2	-0.65%	B- / 7.2
2010	C	822.41	5.67	C+ / 5.6	27.14%	C / 5.1

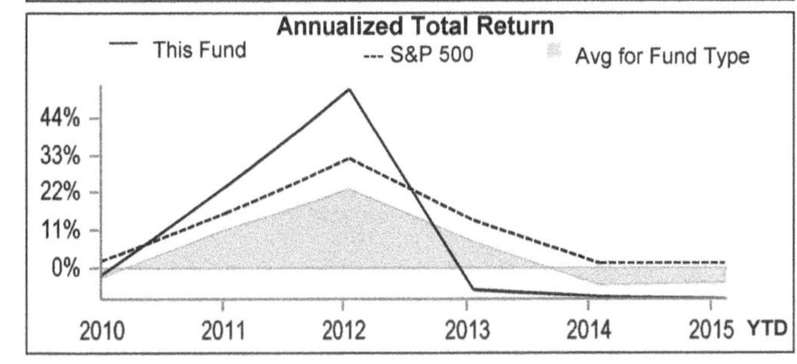

Gabelli Gl Sm & Mid Cap Value Tr (XGGZX) C- Fair

Fund Family: Gabelli Funds LLC
Fund Type: Global
Inception Date: June 23, 2014

Major Rating Factors: Middle of the road best describes Gabelli Gl Sm & Mid Cap Value Tr whose TheStreet.com Investment Rating is currently a C- (Fair). The fund currently has a performance rating of C (Fair) based on an annualized return of 0.00% over the last three years and a total return of 0.10% year to date 2015. Factored into the performance evaluation is an expense ratio of 1.58% (above average).

The fund's risk rating is currently C (Fair). It carries a beta of 0.00, meaning the fund's expected move will be 0.0% for every 10% move in the market. Volatility, as measured by both the semi-deviation and a drawdown factor, is considered average. As of December 31, 2015, Gabelli Gl Sm & Mid Cap Value Tr traded at a discount of 14.75% below its net asset value, which is better than its one-year historical average discount of 13.92%.

Mario J. Gabelli currently receives a manager quality ranking of 66 (0=worst, 99=best). If you desire an average level of risk, then this fund may be an option.

Data Date	Investment Rating	Net Assets ($Mil)	Price	Performance Rating/Pts	Total Return Y-T-D	Risk Rating/Pts
12-15	C-	97.86	10.40	C / 4.9	0.10%	C / 5.4

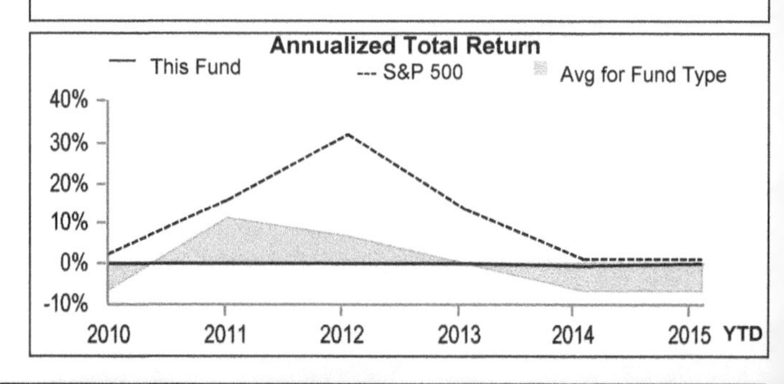

Gabelli Global Utility&Income Trus (GLU) C- Fair

Fund Family: Gabelli Funds LLC
Fund Type: Utilities
Inception Date: May 26, 2004

Major Rating Factors: Middle of the road best describes Gabelli Global Utility&Income Trus whose TheStreet.com Investment Rating is currently a C- (Fair). The fund currently has a performance rating of C- (Fair) based on an annualized return of 1.22% over the last three years and a total return of -8.17% year to date 2015. Factored into the performance evaluation is an expense ratio of 1.39% (average).

The fund's risk rating is currently C+ (Fair). It carries a beta of 0.56, meaning the fund's expected move will be 5.6% for every 10% move in the market. Volatility, as measured by both the semi-deviation and a drawdown factor, is considered low. As of December 31, 2015, Gabelli Global Utility&Income Trus traded at a discount of 15.07% below its net asset value, which is better than its one-year historical average discount of 14.40%.

Mario J. Gabelli has been running the fund for 12 years and currently receives a manager quality ranking of 34 (0=worst, 99=best). If you desire an average level of risk, then this fund may be an option.

Data Date	Investment Rating	Net Assets ($Mil)	Price	Performance Rating/Pts	Total Return Y-T-D	Risk Rating/Pts
12-15	C-	90.17	16.62	C- / 4.2	-8.17%	C+ / 6.7
2014	C	146.70	19.44	C / 4.5	5.29%	B- / 7.7
2013	C+	136.47	20.03	C+ / 6.1	7.80%	B / 8.0
2012	C	63.11	20.88	C- / 3.3	9.13%	B+ / 9.0
2011	C+	63.30	21.04	C+ / 6.4	12.54%	B- / 7.9
2010	C	55.20	20.46	C / 5.3	12.68%	C / 5.2

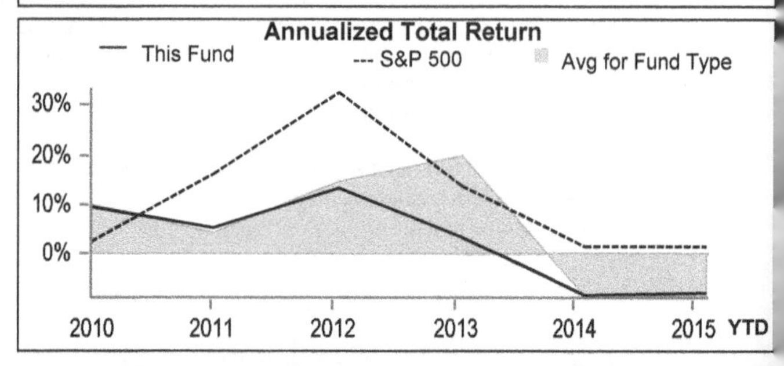

Gabelli Healthcare & WellnessRx Tr (GRX) A+ Excellent

Fund Family: Gabelli Funds LLC
Fund Type: Health
Inception Date: June 28, 2007

Major Rating Factors:
Exceptional performance is the major factor driving the A+ (Excellent) TheStreet.com Investment Rating for Gabelli Healthcare & WellnessRx Tr. The fund currently has a performance rating of A- (Excellent) based on an annualized return of 17.21% over the last three years and a total return of 3.05% year to date 2015. Factored into the performance evaluation is an expense ratio of 1.63% (above average).

The fund's risk rating is currently B- (Good). It carries a beta of 0.92, meaning that its performance tracks fairly well with that of the overall stock market. Volatility, as measured by both the semi-deviation and a drawdown factor, is considered low. As of December 31, 2015, Gabelli Healthcare & WellnessRx Tr traded at a discount of 13.06% below its net asset value, which is better than its one-year historical average discount of 12.32%.

Kevin V. Dreyer currently receives a manager quality ranking of 85 (0=worst, 99=best). If you desire only a moderate level of risk and strong performance, then this fund is an excellent option.

Data Date	Investment Rating	Net Assets ($Mil)	Price	Performance Rating/Pts	Total Return Y-T-D	Risk Rating/Pts
12-15	A+	234.60	10.25	A- / 9.2	3.05%	B- / 7.8
2014	A+	259.50	10.42	A / 9.4	9.50%	B / 8.7
2013	A+	156.26	10.38	A / 9.5	43.18%	B / 8.3
2012	A	95.58	8.62	B+ / 8.8	39.31%	B / 8.3
2011	C+	125.60	7.13	C / 5.4	8.17%	B / 8.3
2010	C+	63.00	7.10	C / 4.7	6.72%	B- / 7.3

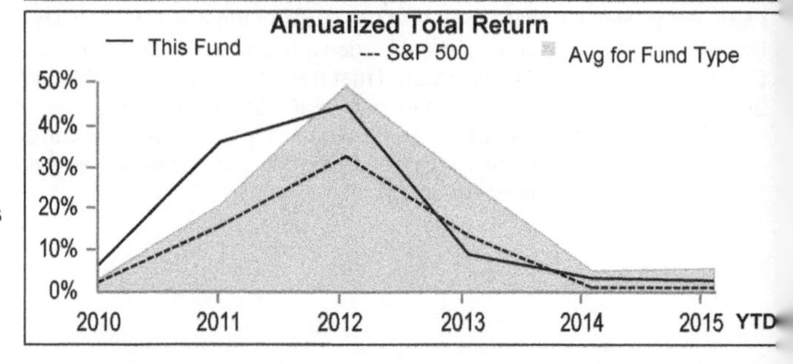

Gabelli Multimedia Trust (GGT) C Fair

Fund Family: Gabelli Funds LLC
Fund Type: Global
Inception Date: October 11, 1994

Major Rating Factors: Middle of the road best describes Gabelli Multimedia Trust whose TheStreet.com Investment Rating is currently a C (Fair). The fund currently has a performance rating of C+ (Fair) based on an annualized return of 8.89% over the last three years and a total return of -15.77% year to date 2015. Factored into the performance evaluation is an expense ratio of 1.50% (average).

The fund's risk rating is currently C+ (Fair). It carries a beta of 0.98, meaning that its performance tracks fairly well with that of the overall stock market. Volatility, as measured by both the semi-deviation and a drawdown factor, is considered low. As of December 31, 2015, Gabelli Multimedia Trust traded at a discount of 10.29% below its net asset value, which is better than its one-year historical average discount of 6.52%.

Mario J. Gabelli has been running the fund for 22 years and currently receives a manager quality ranking of 89 (0=worst, 99=best). If you desire an average level of risk, then this fund may be an option.

Data Date	Investment Rating	Net Assets ($Mil)	Price	Performance Rating/Pts	Total Return Y-T-D	Risk Rating/Pts
12-15	C	238.53	7.50	C+ / 6.1	-15.77%	C+ / 6.3
2014	B	286.00	10.01	A / 9.4	-2.41%	C+ / 5.7
2013	A-	200.42	12.41	A+ / 9.6	58.62%	B- / 7.0
2012	B+	135.20	7.85	A / 9.5	41.73%	C+ / 6.9
2011	C	170.00	6.23	C+ / 6.6	-6.91%	C+ / 6.6
2010	D-	106.39	8.21	C- / 3.0	34.34%	D+ / 2.7

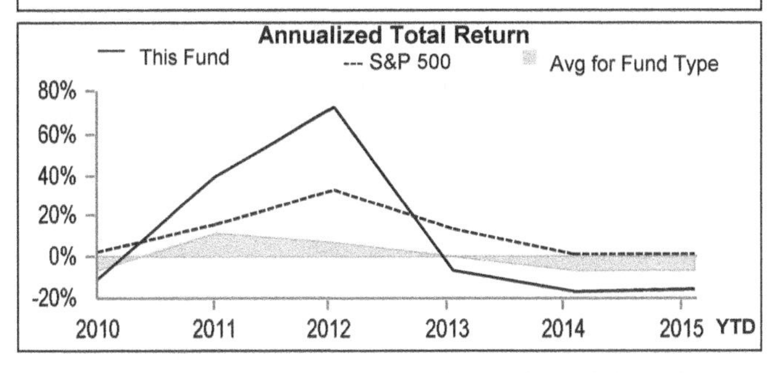

Gabelli Utility Trust (GUT) C Fair

Fund Family: Gabelli Funds LLC
Fund Type: Utilities
Inception Date: July 9, 1999

Major Rating Factors: Middle of the road best describes Gabelli Utility Trust whose TheStreet.com Investment Rating is currently a C (Fair). The fund currently has a performance rating of C+ (Fair) based on an annualized return of 5.84% over the last three years and a total return of -14.15% year to date 2015. Factored into the performance evaluation is an expense ratio of 1.59% (above average).

The fund's risk rating is currently C+ (Fair). It carries a beta of 0.65, meaning the fund's expected move will be 6.5% for every 10% move in the market. Volatility, as measured by both the semi-deviation and a drawdown factor, is considered low. As of December 31, 2015, Gabelli Utility Trust traded at a premium of 11.11% above its net asset value, which is better than its one-year historical average premium of 17.93%.

Mario J. Gabelli has been running the fund for 17 years and currently receives a manager quality ranking of 62 (0=worst, 99=best). If you desire an average level of risk, then this fund may be an option.

Data Date	Investment Rating	Net Assets ($Mil)	Price	Performance Rating/Pts	Total Return Y-T-D	Risk Rating/Pts
12-15	C	259.71	5.70	C+ / 5.7	-14.15%	C+ / 6.8
2014	C	310.20	7.32	C+ / 6.3	26.51%	C+ / 5.9
2013	C+	288.27	6.39	C+ / 6.3	9.16%	B- / 7.6
2012	D	230.78	6.16	D- / 1.2	-4.99%	C+ / 6.6
2011	C+	232.50	7.80	B / 8.1	34.81%	C+ / 6.2
2010	D	142.39	6.39	D- / 1.1	-20.15%	C+ / 6.1

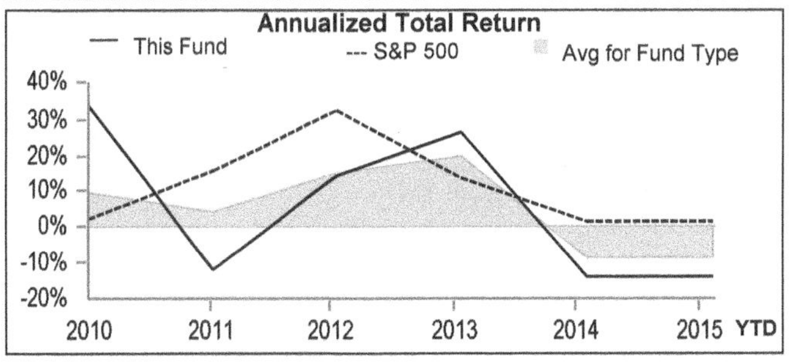

GAMCO Global Gold Nat ResandIncome (GGN) D- Weak

Fund Family: Gabelli Funds LLC
Fund Type: Precious Metals
Inception Date: March 29, 2005

Major Rating Factors:
Very poor performance is the major factor driving the D- (Weak) TheStreet.com Investment Rating for GAMCO Global Gold Nat ResandIncome. The fund currently has a performance rating of E+ (Very Weak) based on an annualized return of -19.14% over the last three years and a total return of -21.50% year to date 2015. Factored into the performance evaluation is an expense ratio of 1.24% (average).

The fund's risk rating is currently C (Fair). It carries a beta of 1.18, meaning it is expected to move 11.8% for every 10% move in the market. Volatility, as measured by both the semi-deviation and a drawdown factor, is considered average. As of December 31, 2015, GAMCO Global Gold Nat ResandIncome traded at a discount of 11.05% below its net asset value, which is better than its one-year historical average discount of 7.30%.

Barbara G. Marcin has been running the fund for 11 years and currently receives a manager quality ranking of 46 (0=worst, 99=best). This fund offers an average level of risk but investors looking for strong performance will be frustrated.

Data Date	Investment Rating	Net Assets ($Mil)	Price	Performance Rating/Pts	Total Return Y-T-D	Risk Rating/Pts
12-15	D-	828.03	4.75	E+ / 0.9	-21.50%	C / 4.5
2014	D-	1,283.80	7.00	E+ / 0.9	-14.51%	C / 4.6
2013	D-	1,137.38	9.02	E+ / 0.9	-20.67%	C / 5.2
2012	D	1,222.81	12.80	D / 2.1	-0.15%	C+ / 6.2
2011	D+	1,206.10	14.11	C- / 3.7	-9.65%	C+ / 5.9
2010	D	664.32	19.27	C / 4.9	32.00%	D / 2.2

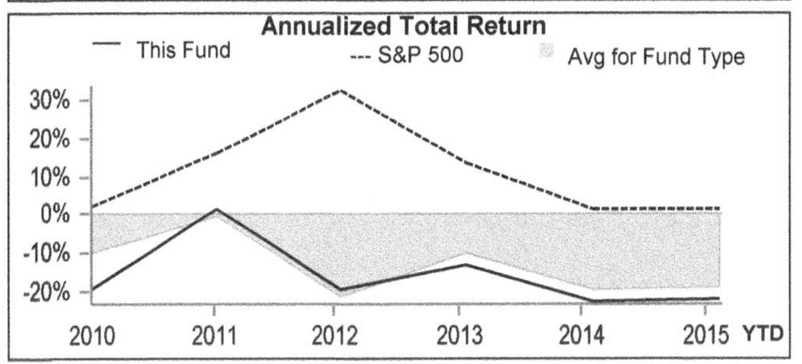

GAMCO Nat Res Gold & Income Trust (GNT) D- Weak

Fund Family: Gabelli Funds LLC
Fund Type: Energy/Natural Resources
Inception Date: January 31, 2011

Data Date	Investment Rating	Net Assets ($Mil)	Price	Performance Rating/Pts	Total Return Y-T-D	Risk Rating/Pts
12-15	D-	184.12	5.73	D- / 1.1	-19.50%	C- / 3.7
2014	D-	245.40	8.07	D- / 1.3	-11.36%	C / 4.5
2013	E+	230.42	10.02	E+ / 0.8	-17.30%	C / 4.7
2012	D	310.78	13.66	C- / 3.0	10.33%	C+ / 6.1

Major Rating Factors:
Disappointing performance is the major factor driving the D- (Weak) TheStreet.com Investment Rating for GAMCO Nat Res Gold & Income Trust. The fund currently has a performance rating of D- (Weak) based on an annualized return of -16.26% over the last three years and a total return of -19.50% year to date 2015. Factored into the performance evaluation is an expense ratio of 1.25% (average).

The fund's risk rating is currently C- (Fair). It carries a beta of 0.80, meaning the fund's expected move will be 8.0% for every 10% move in the market. Volatility, as measured by both the semi-deviation and a drawdown factor, is considered average. As of December 31, 2015, GAMCO Nat Res Gold & Income Trust traded at a discount of 11.44% below its net asset value, which is better than its one-year historical average discount of 11.05%.

Caesar M. P. Bryan currently receives a manager quality ranking of 12 (0=worst, 99=best). This fund offers an average level of risk but investors looking for strong performance will be frustrated.

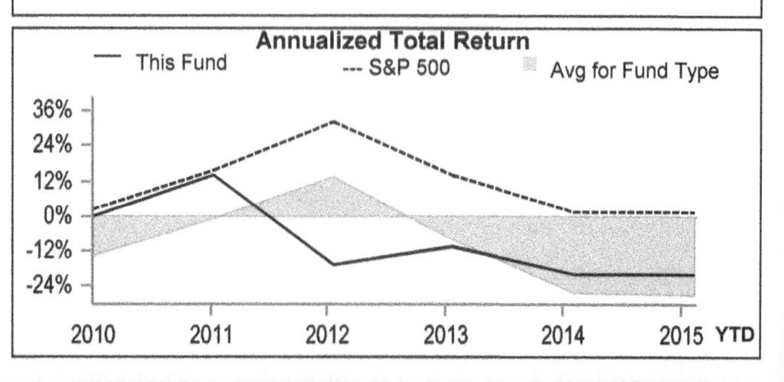

GDL Fund (GDL) C+ Fair

Fund Family: Gabelli Funds LLC
Fund Type: Global
Inception Date: January 26, 2007

Data Date	Investment Rating	Net Assets ($Mil)	Price	Performance Rating/Pts	Total Return Y-T-D	Risk Rating/Pts
12-15	C+	244.89	10.01	C+ / 6.0	4.38%	B / 8.0
2014	C	390.40	10.23	C- / 3.8	0.23%	B / 8.3
2013	C	278.97	11.02	C / 4.3	6.77%	B / 8.3
2012	D+	293.77	11.42	D+ / 2.3	7.24%	B / 8.1
2011	C-	438.10	11.80	D+ / 2.9	-2.01%	B / 8.1
2010	C+	315.08	13.37	C / 4.6	4.19%	C+ / 6.8

Major Rating Factors: Middle of the road best describes GDL Fund whose TheStreet.com Investment Rating is currently a C+ (Fair). The fund currently has a performance rating of C+ (Fair) based on an annualized return of 3.69% over the last three years and a total return of 4.38% year to date 2015. Factored into the performance evaluation is an expense ratio of 3.07% (high).

The fund's risk rating is currently B (Good). It carries a beta of 0.23, meaning the fund's expected move will be 2.3% for every 10% move in the market. Volatility, as measured by both the semi-deviation and a drawdown factor, is considered low. As of December 31, 2015, GDL Fund traded at a discount of 16.16% below its net asset value, which is worse than its one-year historical average discount of 16.18%.

Mario J. Gabelli has been running the fund for 9 years and currently receives a manager quality ranking of 83 (0=worst, 99=best). If you desire an average level of risk, then this fund may be an option.

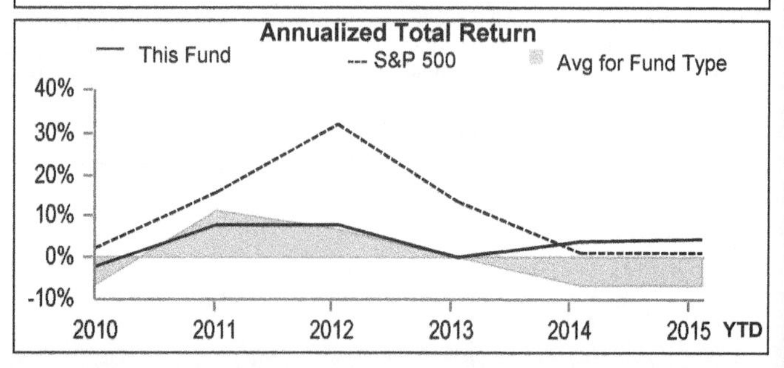

General American Investors (GAM) B Good

Fund Family: General American Investors Company
Fund Type: Growth
Inception Date: N/A

Data Date	Investment Rating	Net Assets ($Mil)	Price	Performance Rating/Pts	Total Return Y-T-D	Risk Rating/Pts
12-15	B	1,227.90	31.94	B- / 7.3	-4.32%	B- / 7.6
2014	A	1,424.30	35.00	B / 8.1	11.17%	B / 8.7
2013	B+	1.09	35.20	B / 8.0	26.85%	B- / 7.9
2012	C	915.45	27.82	C / 5.3	18.78%	B- / 7.6
2011	C	1,076.70	24.91	C / 4.9	-0.71%	B- / 7.6
2010	D+	864.32	26.82	D+ / 2.6	16.16%	C+ / 5.7

Major Rating Factors: Strong performance is the major factor driving the B (Good) TheStreet.com Investment Rating for General American Investors. The fund currently has a performance rating of B- (Good) based on an annualized return of 10.05% over the last three years and a total return of -4.32% year to date 2015. Factored into the performance evaluation is an expense ratio of 1.10% (low).

The fund's risk rating is currently B- (Good). It carries a beta of 1.09, meaning that its performance tracks fairly well with that of the overall stock market. Volatility, as measured by both the semi-deviation and a drawdown factor, is considered low. As of December 31, 2015, General American Investors traded at a discount of 15.32% below its net asset value, which is worse than its one-year historical average discount of 15.40%.

Jeffrey W. Priest currently receives a manager quality ranking of 34 (0=worst, 99=best). If you desire only a moderate level of risk and strong performance, then this fund is an excellent option.

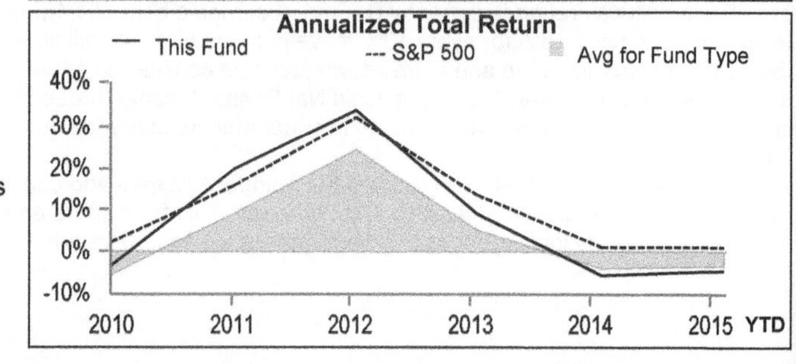

Global High Income Fund (GHI) D+ Weak

Fund Family: UBS Asset Mgmt (Americas) Inc
Fund Type: Emerging Market
Inception Date: September 30, 1993

Major Rating Factors: Global High Income Fund receives a TheStreet.com Investment Rating of D+ (Weak). The fund currently has a performance rating of C- (Fair) based on an annualized return of -6.19% over the last three years and a total return of 5.79% year to date 2015. Factored into the performance evaluation is an expense ratio of 1.31% (average).

The fund's risk rating is currently C+ (Fair). It carries a beta of 0.95, meaning that its performance tracks fairly well with that of the overall stock market. Volatility, as measured by both the semi-deviation and a drawdown factor, is considered low. As of December 31, 2015, Global High Income Fund traded at a discount of 3.52% below its net asset value, which is worse than its one-year historical average discount of 11.38%.

John C. Leonard currently receives a manager quality ranking of 53 (0=worst, 99=best). If you desire an average level of risk, then this fund may be an option.

Data Date	Investment Rating	Net Assets ($Mil)	Price	Performance Rating/Pts	Total Return Y-T-D	Risk Rating/Pts
12-15	D+	240.57	8.50	C- / 3.2	5.79%	C+ / 5.7
2014	D	239.40	8.82	D / 2.0	-4.28%	C+ / 6.3
2013	D	294.05	9.92	D / 2.0	-18.01%	C+ / 6.9
2012	C	280.80	12.92	C+ / 5.7	16.98%	B- / 7.4
2011	B-	270.80	12.08	B / 7.7	4.27%	B- / 7.4
2010	B	291.28	13.05	B- / 7.5	23.01%	C / 5.4

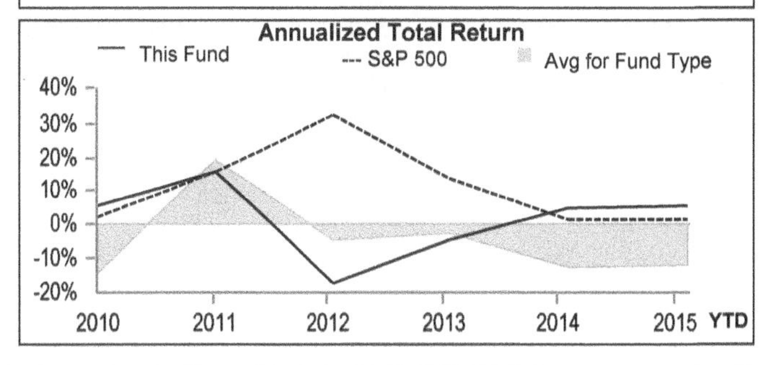

Goldman Sachs MLP and Energy Ren (XGERX) E- Very Weak

Fund Family: Goldman Sachs Asset Mgmt Internatio
Fund Type: Energy/Natural Resources
Inception Date: September 26, 2014

Major Rating Factors: Goldman Sachs MLP and Energy Ren has adopted a very risky asset allocation strategy and currently receives an overall TheStreet.com Investment Rating of E- (Very Weak). The fund has a high level of volatility, as measured by both semi-deviation and drawdown factors. It carries a beta of 0.00, meaning the fund's expected move will be 0.0% for every 10% move in the market. As of December 31, 2015, Goldman Sachs MLP and Energy Ren traded at a discount of 6.64% below its net asset value, which is better than its one-year historical average premium of 4.53%. Unfortunately, the high level of risk (D, Weak) failed to pay off as investors endured very poor performance.

The fund's performance rating is currently E- (Very Weak). It has registered an annualized return of 0.00% over the last three years but is down -57.97% year to date 2015.

If you can tolerate very high levels of risk in the hope of improved future returns, holding this fund may be an option.

Data Date	Investment Rating	Net Assets ($Mil)	Price	Performance Rating/Pts	Total Return Y-T-D	Risk Rating/Pts
12-15	E-	0.00	5.48	E- / 0	-57.97%	D / 1.8

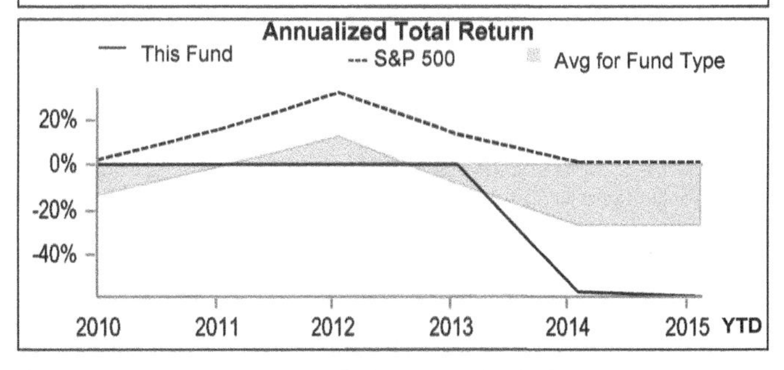

Goldman Sachs MLP Income Oppty (XGMZX) E Very Weak

Fund Family: Goldman Sachs Asset Mgmt Internatio
Fund Type: Energy/Natural Resources
Inception Date: November 26, 2013

Major Rating Factors: Goldman Sachs MLP Income Oppty has adopted a very risky asset allocation strategy and currently receives an overall TheStreet.com Investment Rating of E (Very Weak). The fund has a high level of volatility, as measured by both semi-deviation and drawdown factors. It carries a beta of 0.00, meaning the fund's expected move will be 0.0% for every 10% move in the market. As of December 31, 2015, Goldman Sachs MLP Income Oppty traded at a discount of 6.48% below its net asset value, which is better than its one-year historical average premium of .11%. Unfortunately, the high level of risk (D, Weak) failed to pay off as investors endured very poor performance.

The fund's performance rating is currently E- (Very Weak). It has registered an annualized return of 0.00% over the last three years but is down -49.36% year to date 2015. Factored into the performance evaluation is an expense ratio of 1.75% (above average).

Kyriacos A. Loupis has been running the fund for 3 years and currently receives a manager quality ranking of 3 (0=worst, 99=best). If you can tolerate very high levels of risk in the hope of improved future returns, holding this fund may be an option.

Data Date	Investment Rating	Net Assets ($Mil)	Price	Performance Rating/Pts	Total Return Y-T-D	Risk Rating/Pts
12-15	E	846.84	8.23	E- / 0	-49.36%	D / 1.9
2014	E+	971.90	17.44	E+ / 0.8	-6.84%	C- / 4.0

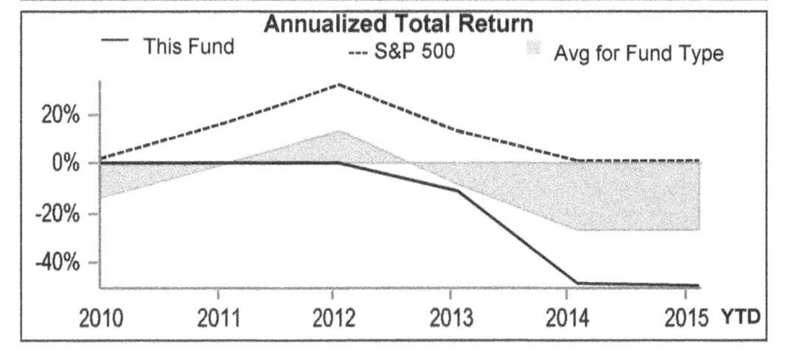

Guggenheim Build America Bd Mgd Du (GBAB) C+ Fair

Fund Family: Guggenheim Funds Investment Advisor
Fund Type: General - Investment Grade
Inception Date: October 28, 2010

Major Rating Factors: Middle of the road best describes Guggenheim Build America Bd Mgd Du whose TheStreet.com Investment Rating is currently a C+ (Fair). The fund currently has a performance rating of C+ (Fair) based on an annualized return of 4.99% over the last three years and a total return of 4.33% year to date 2015. Factored into the performance evaluation is an expense ratio of 1.32% (average).

The fund's risk rating is currently B- (Good). It carries a beta of 2.46, meaning it is expected to move 24.6% for every 10% move in the market. Volatility, as measured by both the semi-deviation and a drawdown factor, is considered low. As of December 31, 2015, Guggenheim Build America Bd Mgd Du traded at a discount of 5.40% below its net asset value, which is worse than its one-year historical average discount of 5.97%.

Anne Walsh currently receives a manager quality ranking of 80 (0=worst, 99=best). If you desire an average level of risk, then this fund may be an option.

Data Date	Investment Rating	Net Assets ($Mil)	Price	Performance Rating/Pts	Total Return Y-T-D	Risk Rating/Pts
12-15	C+	406.67	21.38	C+ / 6.4	4.33%	B- / 7.3
2014	C+	415.40	22.18	C+ / 6.1	20.22%	B- / 7.9
2013	C+	411.14	19.79	C / 5.5	-7.82%	B / 8.1
2012	C+	408.96	22.95	C / 5.0	15.44%	B+ / 9.2
2011	A	359.44	21.41	B+ / 8.5	25.64%	B+ / 9.3

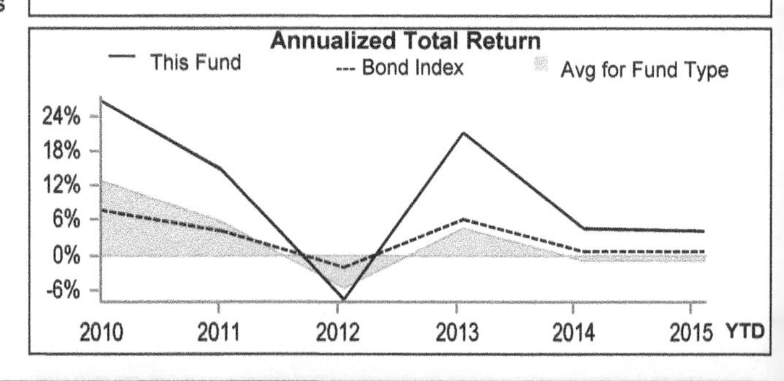

Guggenheim Credit Allocation (GGM) C- Fair

Fund Family: Guggenheim Funds Investment Advisor
Fund Type: General - Investment Grade
Inception Date: June 26, 2013

Major Rating Factors: Middle of the road best describes Guggenheim Credit Allocation whose TheStreet.com Investment Rating is currently a C- (Fair). The fund currently has a performance rating of C- (Fair) based on an annualized return of 0.00% over the last three years and a total return of -0.01% year to date 2015. Factored into the performance evaluation is an expense ratio of 2.04% (high).

The fund's risk rating is currently B- (Good). It carries a beta of 0.00, meaning the fund's expected move will be 0.0% for every 10% move in the market. Volatility, as measured by both the semi-deviation and a drawdown factor, is considered low. As of December 31, 2015, Guggenheim Credit Allocation traded at a discount of 2.45% below its net asset value, which is worse than its one-year historical average discount of 3.03%.

Byron S. Minerd currently receives a manager quality ranking of 60 (0=worst, 99=best). If you desire an average level of risk, then this fund may be an option.

Data Date	Investment Rating	Net Assets ($Mil)	Price	Performance Rating/Pts	Total Return Y-T-D	Risk Rating/Pts
12-15	C-	154.75	19.49	C- / 3.0	-0.01%	B- / 7.4
2014	D+	159.90	21.54	D / 2.1	4.09%	B / 8.0

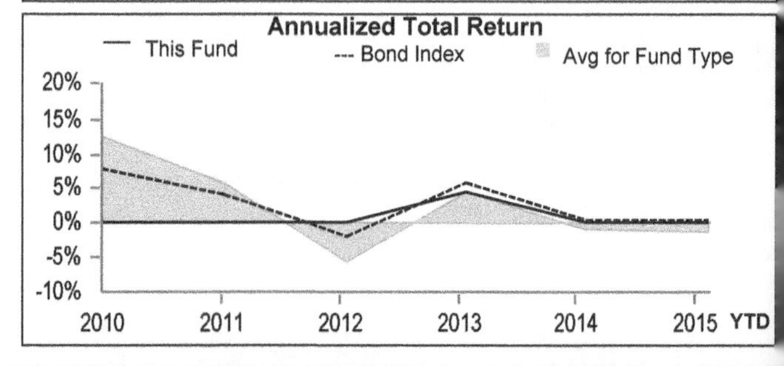

Guggenheim Enhanced Equity Income (GPM) B- Good

Fund Family: Guggenheim Funds Investment Advisor
Fund Type: Income
Inception Date: August 25, 2005

Major Rating Factors: Strong performance is the major factor driving the B- (Good) TheStreet.com Investment Rating for Guggenheim Enhanced Equity Income. The fund currently has a performance rating of B- (Good) based on an annualized return of 7.55% over the last three years and a total return of 1.41% year to date 2015. Factored into the performance evaluation is an expense ratio of 1.69% (above average).

The fund's risk rating is currently B- (Good). It carries a beta of 1.01, meaning that its performance tracks fairly well with that of the overall stock market. Volatility, as measured by both the semi-deviation and a drawdown factor, is considered low. As of December 31, 2015, Guggenheim Enhanced Equity Income traded at a discount of 8.24% below its net asset value, which is worse than its one-year historical average discount of 8.36%.

Byron S. Minerd currently receives a manager quality ranking of 29 (0=worst, 99=best). If you desire only a moderate level of risk and strong performance, then this fund is an excellent option.

Data Date	Investment Rating	Net Assets ($Mil)	Price	Performance Rating/Pts	Total Return Y-T-D	Risk Rating/Pts
12-15	B-	175.24	7.68	B- / 7.0	1.41%	B- / 7.1
2014	C+	178.50	8.64	C+ / 6.1	9.71%	B / 8.2
2013	C+	169.56	8.85	C+ / 6.3	13.13%	B- / 7.5
2012	C-	177.84	8.20	C / 4.5	17.20%	B- / 7.4
2011	C-	176.70	8.16	C- / 4.1	-2.36%	B- / 7.5
2010	D	154.55	9.33	C- / 3.8	22.63%	C- / 3.4

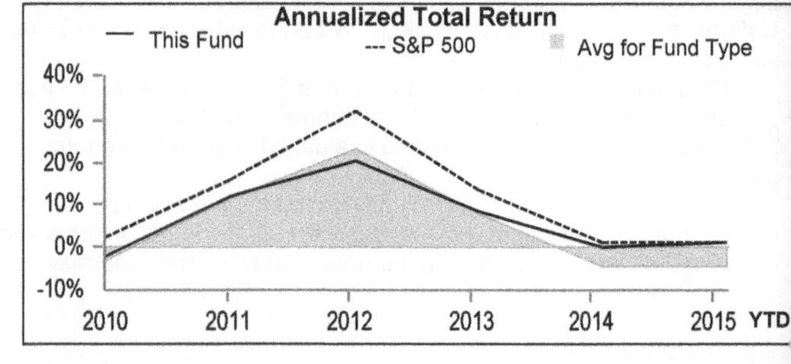

Guggenheim Enhanced Equity Strateg (GGE) C+ Fair

Fund Family: Guggenheim Funds Investment Advisor
Fund Type: Income
Inception Date: January 28, 2004

Major Rating Factors: Middle of the road best describes Guggenheim Enhanced Equity Strateg whose TheStreet.com Investment Rating is currently a C+ (Fair). The fund currently has a performance rating of C+ (Fair) based on an annualized return of 6.58% over the last three years and a total return of 0.56% year to date 2015. Factored into the performance evaluation is an expense ratio of 1.81% (above average).

The fund's risk rating is currently B- (Good). It carries a beta of 1.00, meaning that its performance tracks fairly well with that of the overall stock market. Volatility, as measured by both the semi-deviation and a drawdown factor, is considered low. As of December 31, 2015, Guggenheim Enhanced Equity Strateg traded at a discount of 10.83% below its net asset value, which is better than its one-year historical average discount of 9.97%.

Byron S. Minerd has been running the fund for 5 years and currently receives a manager quality ranking of 26 (0=worst, 99=best). If you desire an average level of risk, then this fund may be an option.

Data Date	Investment Rating	Net Assets ($Mil)	Price	Perfor-mance Rating/Pts	Total Return Y-T-D	Risk Rating/Pts
12-15	C+	97.78	15.81	C+ / 6.6	0.56%	B- / 7.3
2014	B-	98.80	17.73	C+ / 5.7	8.19%	B / 8.6
2013	B-	99.38	18.36	B- / 7.1	11.92%	B- / 7.8
2012	C+	90.33	16.66	C+ / 5.7	15.84%	B- / 7.7
2011	C+	93.70	16.03	B- / 7.3	14.58%	C+ / 6.1
2010	E	134.88	15.03	E / 0.3	-0.60%	C- / 3.0

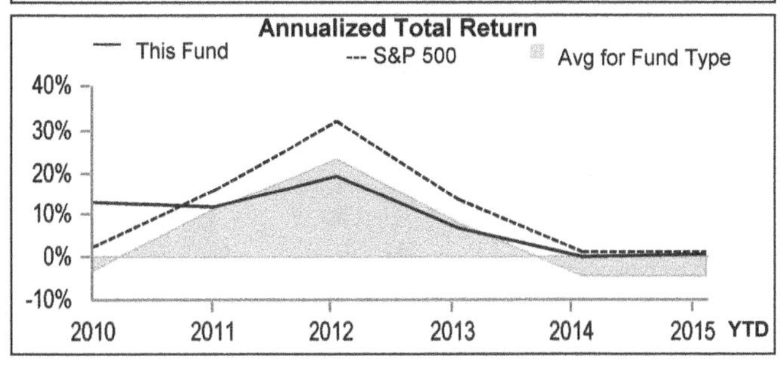

Guggenheim Equal Weight Enh Eq Inc (GEQ) C+ Fair

Fund Family: Guggenheim Funds Investment Advisor
Fund Type: Income
Inception Date: October 27, 2011

Major Rating Factors: Middle of the road best describes Guggenheim Equal Weight Enh Eq Inc whose TheStreet.com Investment Rating is currently a C+ (Fair). The fund currently has a performance rating of C+ (Fair) based on an annualized return of 6.37% over the last three years and a total return of -9.19% year to date 2015. Factored into the performance evaluation is an expense ratio of 1.71% (above average).

The fund's risk rating is currently B- (Good). It carries a beta of 0.83, meaning the fund's expected move will be 8.3% for every 10% move in the market. Volatility, as measured by both the semi-deviation and a drawdown factor, is considered low. As of December 31, 2015, Guggenheim Equal Weight Enh Eq Inc traded at a discount of 9.12% below its net asset value, which is better than its one-year historical average discount of 6.36%.

Farhan Sharaff has been running the fund for 5 years and currently receives a manager quality ranking of 36 (0=worst, 99=best). If you desire an average level of risk, then this fund may be an option.

Data Date	Investment Rating	Net Assets ($Mil)	Price	Perfor-mance Rating/Pts	Total Return Y-T-D	Risk Rating/Pts
12-15	C+	182.85	16.34	C+ / 6.0	-9.19%	B- / 7.4
2014	B+	185.10	20.42	B- / 7.0	18.58%	B / 8.6
2013	B+	167.22	18.89	B- / 7.5	12.43%	B / 8.6
2012	D+	168.00	17.73	D / 1.8	7.80%	B / 8.5

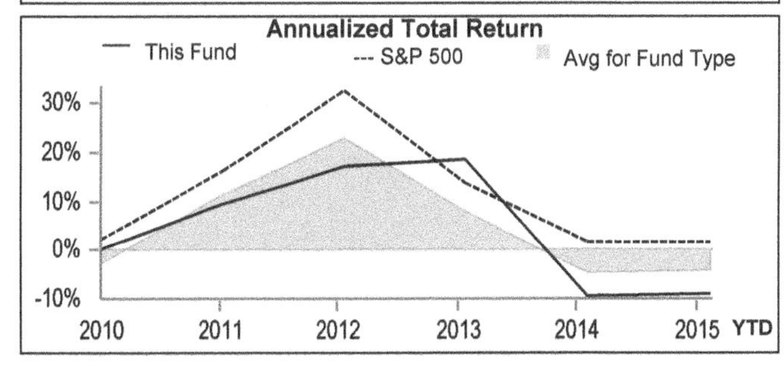

Guggenheim Strategic Opportunities (GOF) C- Fair

Fund Family: Guggenheim Funds Investment Advisor
Fund Type: Growth and Income
Inception Date: July 27, 2007

Major Rating Factors: Middle of the road best describes Guggenheim Strategic Opportunities whose TheStreet.com Investment Rating is currently a C- (Fair). The fund currently has a performance rating of C- (Fair) based on an annualized return of 1.87% over the last three years and a total return of -10.51% year to date 2015. Factored into the performance evaluation is an expense ratio of 2.16% (high).

The fund's risk rating is currently B- (Good). It carries a beta of 0.34, meaning the fund's expected move will be 3.4% for every 10% move in the market. Volatility, as measured by both the semi-deviation and a drawdown factor, is considered low. As of December 31, 2015, Guggenheim Strategic Opportunities traded at a discount of 4.59% below its net asset value, which is better than its one-year historical average premium of 3.44%.

Anne Walsh has been running the fund for 9 years and currently receives a manager quality ranking of 49 (0=worst, 99=best). If you desire an average level of risk, then this fund may be an option.

Data Date	Investment Rating	Net Assets ($Mil)	Price	Perfor-mance Rating/Pts	Total Return Y-T-D	Risk Rating/Pts
12-15	C-	342.99	16.83	C- / 3.9	-10.51%	B- / 7.1
2014	C	324.50	20.90	C+ / 5.7	9.03%	C+ / 6.9
2013	B-	286.47	21.39	C+ / 6.5	7.36%	B / 8.5
2012	A-	207.35	21.50	B+ / 8.3	21.67%	B / 8.5
2011	A	174.10	20.59	A / 9.5	12.45%	B / 8.5
2010	B-	161.78	19.93	B+ / 8.8	31.55%	C- / 4.0

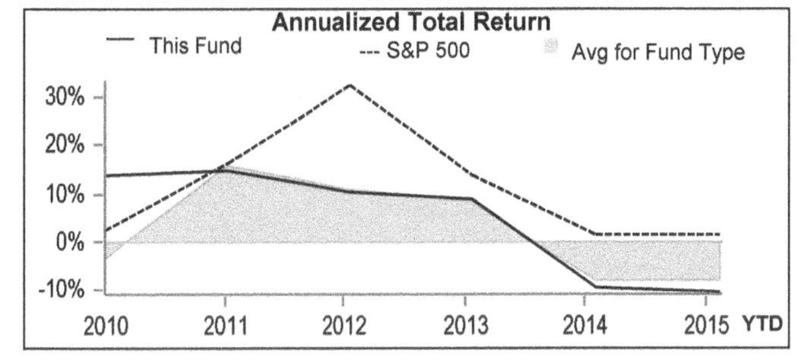

Herzfeld Caribbean Basin Fund (CUBA) D Weak

Fund Family: Thomas J Herzfeld Advisors Inc
Fund Type: Foreign
Inception Date: September 10, 1993

Major Rating Factors: Herzfeld Caribbean Basin Fund receives a TheStreet.com Investment Rating of D (Weak). The fund currently has a performance rating of C- (Fair) based on an annualized return of 1.85% over the last three years and a total return of -24.83% year to date 2015. Factored into the performance evaluation is an expense ratio of 2.97% (high).

The fund's risk rating is currently C (Fair). It carries a beta of 1.01, meaning that its performance tracks fairly well with that of the overall stock market. Volatility, as measured by both the semi-deviation and a drawdown factor, is considered average. As of December 31, 2015, Herzfeld Caribbean Basin Fund traded at a premium of 4.09% above its net asset value, which is better than its one-year historical average premium of 21.40%.

Thomas J. Herzfeld has been running the fund for 22 years and currently receives a manager quality ranking of 56 (0=worst, 99=best). If you desire an average level of risk, then this fund may be an option.

Data Date	Investment Rating	Net Assets ($Mil)	Price	Performance Rating/Pts	Total Return Y-T-D	Risk Rating/Pts
12-15	D	41.61	6.62	C- / 3.0	-24.83%	C / 4.9
2014	B+	32.70	8.89	B+ / 8.9	17.51%	C+ / 6.7
2013	B-	34.45	8.05	C+ / 6.7	14.49%	B / 8.2
2012	C+	29.33	7.64	C+ / 5.9	25.99%	B / 8.2
2011	C-	26.60	6.42	C- / 3.5	-9.43%	B / 8.0
2010	D+	22.71	7.17	C- / 3.4	11.68%	C / 5.4

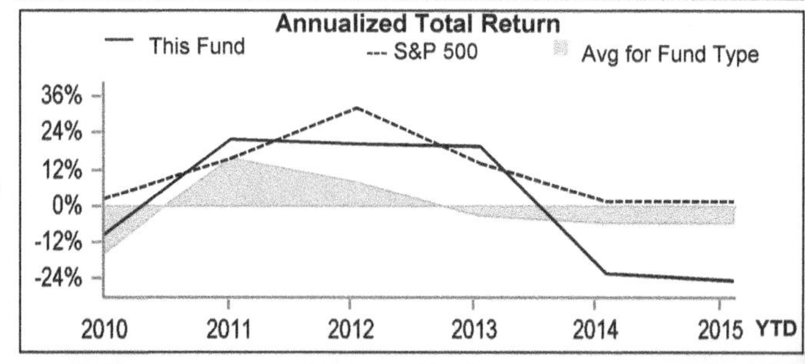

India Fund (IFN) C+ Fair

Fund Family: Aberdeen Asset Management Asia Ltd
Fund Type: Foreign
Inception Date: February 14, 1994

Major Rating Factors: Middle of the road best describes India Fund whose TheStreet.com Investment Rating is currently a C+ (Fair). The fund currently has a performance rating of C+ (Fair) based on an annualized return of 8.86% over the last three years and a total return of -6.64% year to date 2015. Factored into the performance evaluation is an expense ratio of 1.47% (average).

The fund's risk rating is currently C+ (Fair). It carries a beta of 0.83, meaning the fund's expected move will be 8.3% for every 10% move in the market. Volatility, as measured by both the semi-deviation and a drawdown factor, is considered low. As of December 31, 2015, India Fund traded at a discount of 12.37% below its net asset value, which is better than its one-year historical average discount of 9.82%.

Flavia Cheong currently receives a manager quality ranking of 89 (0=worst, 99=best). If you desire an average level of risk, then this fund may be an option.

Data Date	Investment Rating	Net Assets ($Mil)	Price	Performance Rating/Pts	Total Return Y-T-D	Risk Rating/Pts
12-15	C+	847.55	22.74	C+ / 6.5	-6.64%	C+ / 6.4
2014	B+	875.90	25.81	B+ / 8.9	40.31%	C+ / 6.7
2013	D-	852.61	20.00	D- / 1.3	-3.44%	C / 5.0
2012	E+	899.34	20.91	D- / 1.0	14.13%	C / 4.8
2011	D-	1,581.37	19.04	D / 1.6	-38.27%	C / 5.1
2010	E+	1,608.62	35.11	D / 1.8	14.63%	D+ / 2.7

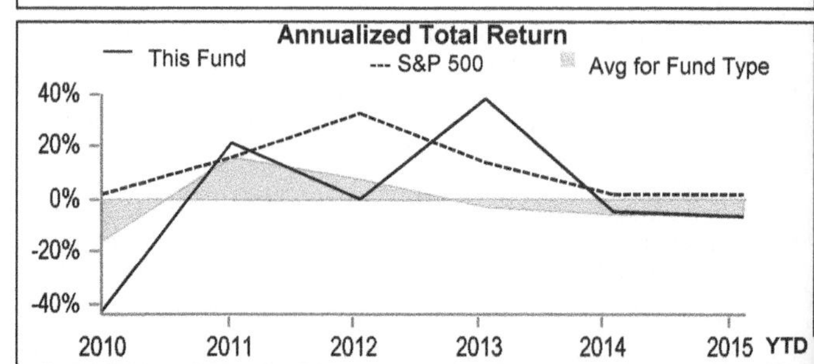

Invesco Adv Muni Inc II (VKI) B- Good

Fund Family: Invesco Advisers Inc
Fund Type: Municipal - National
Inception Date: August 27, 1993

Major Rating Factors: Invesco Adv Muni Inc II receives a TheStreet.com Investment Rating of B- (Good). The fund currently has a performance rating of C+ (Fair) based on an annualized return of 2.47% over the last three years and a total return of 8.51% year to date 2015. Factored into the performance evaluation is an expense ratio of 1.69% (above average).

The fund's risk rating is currently B- (Good). It carries a beta of 2.23, meaning it is expected to move 22.3% for every 10% move in the market. Volatility, as measured by both the semi-deviation and a drawdown factor, is considered low. As of December 31, 2015, Invesco Adv Muni Inc II traded at a discount of 6.73% below its net asset value, which is worse than its one-year historical average discount of 9.00%.

Robert J. Stryker has been running the fund for 11 years and currently receives a manager quality ranking of 39 (0=worst, 99=best). If you desire an average level of risk, then this fund may be an option.

Data Date	Investment Rating	Net Assets ($Mil)	Price	Performance Rating/Pts	Total Return Y-T-D	Risk Rating/Pts
12-15	B-	566.95	11.78	C+ / 6.9	8.51%	B- / 7.3
2014	C+	559.40	11.60	C+ / 6.3	17.67%	B- / 7.6
2013	C-	495.65	10.52	C- / 3.9	-16.31%	B- / 7.9
2012	A-	578.17	13.15	B / 8.2	14.35%	B / 8.7
2011	A+	544.80	12.46	A / 9.4	21.22%	B / 8.8
2010	C-	512.04	11.35	C- / 3.4	6.65%	C+ / 5.7

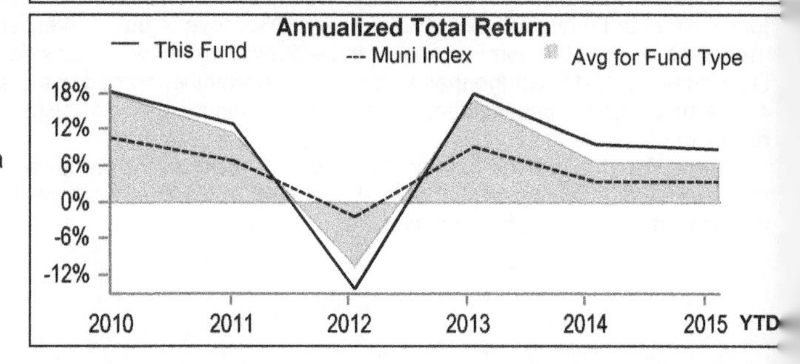

Invesco Bond (VBF) C Fair

Fund Family: Invesco Advisers Inc
Fund Type: General - Investment Grade
Inception Date: October 15, 1970

Major Rating Factors: Middle of the road best describes Invesco Bond whose TheStreet.com Investment Rating is currently a C (Fair). The fund currently has a performance rating of C (Fair) based on an annualized return of -0.28% over the last three years and a total return of 0.31% year to date 2015. Factored into the performance evaluation is an expense ratio of 0.55% (very low).

The fund's risk rating is currently B- (Good). It carries a beta of 2.12, meaning it is expected to move 21.2% for every 10% move in the market. Volatility, as measured by both the semi-deviation and a drawdown factor, is considered low. As of December 31, 2015, Invesco Bond traded at a discount of 7.09% below its net asset value, which is worse than its one-year historical average discount of 8.60%.

Chuck Burge has been running the fund for 6 years and currently receives a manager quality ranking of 43 (0=worst, 99=best). If you desire an average level of risk, then this fund may be an option.

Data Date	Investment Rating	Net Assets ($Mil)	Price	Performance Rating/Pts	Total Return Y-T-D	Risk Rating/Pts
12-15	C	233.15	17.57	C / 4.4	0.31%	B- / 7.3
2014	C	233.80	18.40	C / 4.5	11.60%	B- / 7.9
2013	C-	224.85	17.69	C- / 4.0	-11.70%	B / 8.1
2012	C	241.51	21.34	C- / 4.0	16.57%	B / 8.7
2011	C+	227.50	20.90	C / 5.0	14.65%	B / 8.7
2010	B-	223.60	18.64	C+ / 5.8	3.81%	B- / 7.0

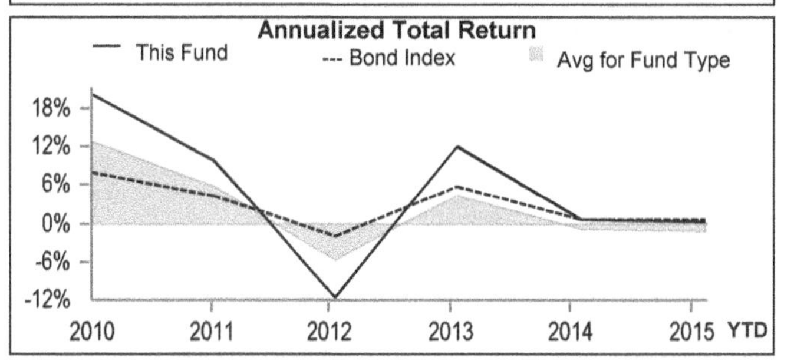

Invesco CA Value Municipal Income (VCV) B+ Good

Fund Family: Invesco Advisers Inc
Fund Type: Municipal - Single State
Inception Date: April 30, 1993

Major Rating Factors: Strong performance is the major factor driving the B+ (Good) TheStreet.com Investment Rating for Invesco CA Value Municipal Income. The fund currently has a performance rating of B (Good) based on an annualized return of 4.69% over the last three years and a total return of 9.38% year to date 2015. Factored into the performance evaluation is an expense ratio of 1.05% (low).

The fund's risk rating is currently B- (Good). It carries a beta of 2.10, meaning it is expected to move 21.0% for every 10% move in the market. Volatility, as measured by both the semi-deviation and a drawdown factor, is considered low. As of December 31, 2015, Invesco CA Value Municipal Income traded at a discount of 4.19% below its net asset value, which is worse than its one-year historical average discount of 5.82%.

Robert J. Stryker has been running the fund for 7 years and currently receives a manager quality ranking of 58 (0=worst, 99=best). If you desire only a moderate level of risk and strong performance, then this fund is an excellent option.

Data Date	Investment Rating	Net Assets ($Mil)	Price	Performance Rating/Pts	Total Return Y-T-D	Risk Rating/Pts
12-15	B+	662.09	13.25	B / 8.0	9.38%	B- / 7.3
2014	B	652.40	12.86	B- / 7.3	19.81%	B- / 7.7
2013	C+	562.02	11.40	C+ / 5.8	-12.98%	B / 8.0
2012	B+	652.46	13.74	B / 8.0	11.69%	B / 8.4
2011	A	278.00	12.87	A / 9.5	26.23%	B / 8.5
2010	D	259.74	11.28	D- / 1.2	1.81%	C+ / 6.5

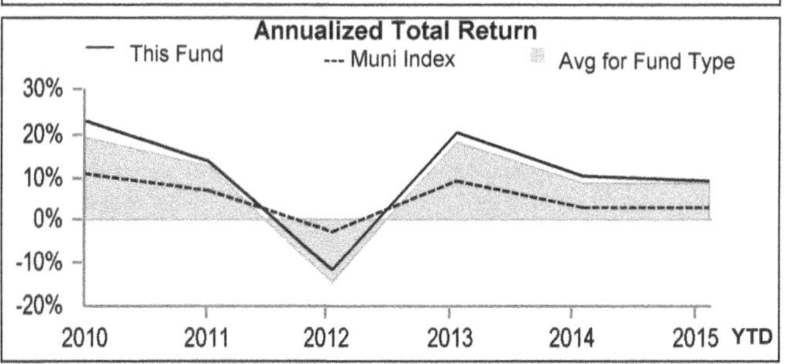

Invesco Dynamic Credit Opps (VTA) C Fair

Fund Family: Invesco Advisers Inc
Fund Type: Loan Participation
Inception Date: June 26, 2007

Major Rating Factors: Middle of the road best describes Invesco Dynamic Credit Opps whose TheStreet.com Investment Rating is currently a C (Fair). The fund currently has a performance rating of C- (Fair) based on an annualized return of 0.70% over the last three years and a total return of -3.76% year to date 2015. Factored into the performance evaluation is an expense ratio of 2.52% (high).

The fund's risk rating is currently B- (Good). Volatility, as measured by both the semi-deviation and a drawdown factor, is considered low. As of December 31, 2015, Invesco Dynamic Credit Opps traded at a discount of 12.88% below its net asset value, which is better than its one-year historical average discount of 12.07%.

Philip Yarrow has been running the fund for 9 years and currently receives a manager quality ranking of 85 (0=worst, 99=best). If you desire an average level of risk, then this fund may be an option.

Data Date	Investment Rating	Net Assets ($Mil)	Price	Performance Rating/Pts	Total Return Y-T-D	Risk Rating/Pts
12-15	C	983.80	10.55	C- / 4.2	-3.76%	B- / 7.6
2014	C+	1,136.50	11.85	C / 5.2	-0.35%	B / 8.8
2013	C+	983.20	12.90	C+ / 5.8	6.39%	B / 8.1
2012	C+	938.27	12.48	C+ / 5.7	27.92%	B / 8.0
2011	B-	877.50	10.57	C+ / 6.8	-5.86%	B- / 7.9
2010	C-	927.10	12.21	C / 5.4	12.20%	C / 4.5

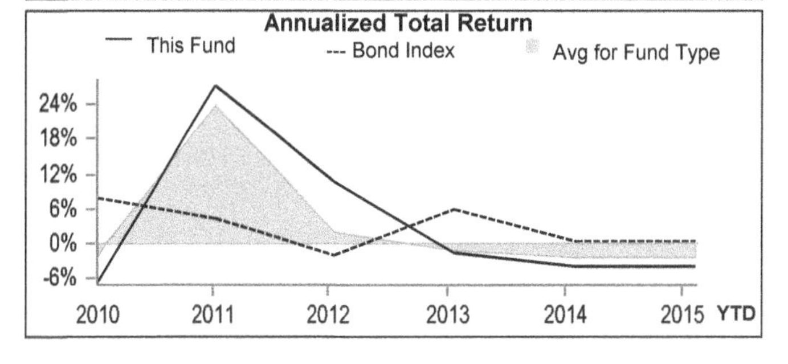

Invesco High Income Tr II (VLT) C- Fair

Fund Family: Invesco Advisers Inc
Fund Type: Corporate - High Yield
Inception Date: April 28, 1989

Major Rating Factors: Middle of the road best describes Invesco High Income Tr II whose TheStreet.com Investment Rating is currently a C- (Fair). The fund currently has a performance rating of C- (Fair) based on an annualized return of -2.35% over the last three years and a total return of -6.81% year to date 2015. Factored into the performance evaluation is an expense ratio of 1.49% (average).

The fund's risk rating is currently C+ (Fair). It carries a beta of 1.67, meaning it is expected to move 16.7% for every 10% move in the market. Volatility, as measured by both the semi-deviation and a drawdown factor, is considered low. As of December 31, 2015, Invesco High Income Tr II traded at a discount of 13.23% below its net asset value, which is better than its one-year historical average discount of 13.07%.

Darren S. Hughes currently receives a manager quality ranking of 36 (0=worst, 99=best). If you desire an average level of risk, then this fund may be an option.

Data Date	Investment Rating	Net Assets ($Mil)	Price	Performance Rating/Pts	Total Return Y-T-D	Risk Rating/Pts
12-15	C-	138.94	12.85	C- / 3.3	-6.81%	C+ / 6.9
2014	C	138.90	15.01	C- / 4.1	1.52%	B / 8.0
2013	C+	136.83	16.07	C+ / 5.6	-1.91%	B / 8.3
2012	B	136.19	17.25	B / 7.6	21.82%	B / 8.1
2011	B	57.40	15.50	B+ / 8.5	8.08%	B- / 7.7
2010	C-	58.00	16.02	C+ / 6.3	22.05%	C- / 3.2

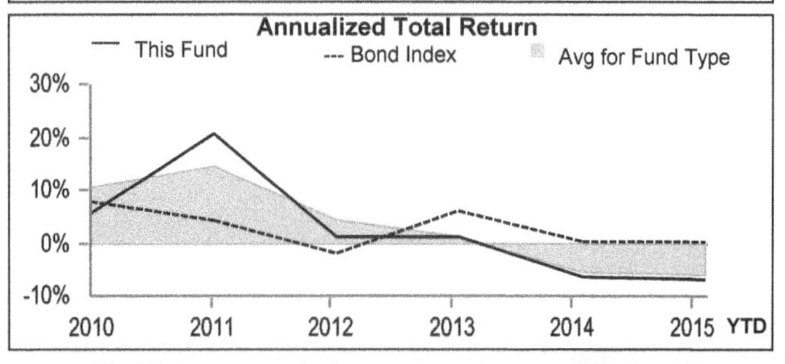

Invesco Municipal Income Opp Tr (OIA) B+ Good

Fund Family: Invesco Advisers Inc
Fund Type: Municipal - National
Inception Date: August 12, 1988

Major Rating Factors: Strong performance is the major factor driving the B+ (Good) TheStreet.com Investment Rating for Invesco Municipal Income Opp Tr. The fund currently has a performance rating of B+ (Good) based on an annualized return of 4.72% over the last three years and a total return of 11.18% year to date 2015. Factored into the performance evaluation is an expense ratio of 0.79% (very low).

The fund's risk rating is currently B- (Good). It carries a beta of 1.78, meaning it is expected to move 17.8% for every 10% move in the market. Volatility, as measured by both the semi-deviation and a drawdown factor, is considered low. As of December 31, 2015, Invesco Municipal Income Opp Tr traded at a discount of 4.46% below its net asset value, which is worse than its one-year historical average discount of 8.11%.

Mark Paris has been running the fund for 7 years and currently receives a manager quality ranking of 72 (0=worst, 99=best). If you desire only a moderate level of risk and strong performance, then this fund is an excellent option.

Data Date	Investment Rating	Net Assets ($Mil)	Price	Performance Rating/Pts	Total Return Y-T-D	Risk Rating/Pts
12-15	B+	359.60	7.29	B+ / 8.4	11.18%	B- / 7.2
2014	B-	400.50	6.98	B- / 7.2	18.00%	B- / 7.5
2013	C+	319.00	6.20	C / 5.5	-12.33%	B- / 7.9
2012	A	352.73	7.32	B+ / 8.9	19.81%	B / 8.5
2011	B+	135.00	6.66	B+ / 8.3	17.62%	B / 8.8
2010	C-	133.20	6.18	D / 2.2	6.65%	B- / 7.3

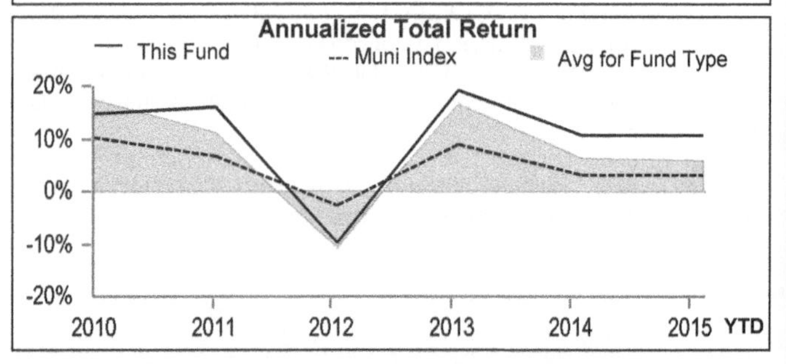

Invesco Municipal Opportunity (VMO) B- Good

Fund Family: Invesco Advisers Inc
Fund Type: Municipal - National
Inception Date: April 24, 1992

Major Rating Factors: Invesco Municipal Opportunity receives a TheStreet.com Investment Rating of B- (Good). The fund currently has a performance rating of C+ (Fair) based on an annualized return of 2.04% over the last three years and a total return of 9.77% year to date 2015. Factored into the performance evaluation is an expense ratio of 1.57% (above average).

The fund's risk rating is currently B- (Good). It carries a beta of 2.10, meaning it is expected to move 21.0% for every 10% move in the market. Volatility, as measured by both the semi-deviation and a drawdown factor, is considered low. As of December 31, 2015, Invesco Municipal Opportunity traded at a discount of 6.66% below its net asset value, which is worse than its one-year historical average discount of 9.16%.

Robert J. Stryker has been running the fund for 7 years and currently receives a manager quality ranking of 42 (0=worst, 99=best). If you desire an average level of risk, then this fund may be an option.

Data Date	Investment Rating	Net Assets ($Mil)	Price	Performance Rating/Pts	Total Return Y-T-D	Risk Rating/Pts
12-15	B-	960.24	13.17	C+ / 6.9	9.77%	B- / 7.3
2014	C+	944.40	12.86	C / 5.5	15.27%	B- / 7.5
2013	C-	835.35	11.71	C- / 4.0	-16.09%	B- / 7.8
2012	B+	492.56	14.59	B- / 7.4	12.98%	B / 8.7
2011	A+	462.60	14.48	A+ / 9.6	23.96%	B / 8.8
2010	C-	439.37	13.04	C- / 3.3	5.26%	C+ / 6.1

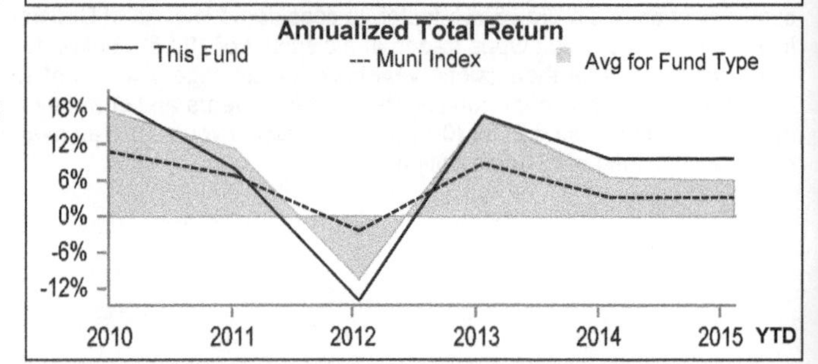

Invesco Municipal Trust (VKQ) C+ Fair

Fund Family: Invesco Advisers Inc
Fund Type: Municipal - National
Inception Date: September 20, 1991

Major Rating Factors: Middle of the road best describes Invesco Municipal Trust whose TheStreet.com Investment Rating is currently a C+ (Fair). The fund currently has a performance rating of C+ (Fair) based on an annualized return of 1.64% over the last three years and a total return of 7.94% year to date 2015. Factored into the performance evaluation is an expense ratio of 1.64% (above average).

The fund's risk rating is currently B- (Good). It carries a beta of 2.35, meaning it is expected to move 23.5% for every 10% move in the market. Volatility, as measured by both the semi-deviation and a drawdown factor, is considered low. As of December 31, 2015, Invesco Municipal Trust traded at a discount of 9.11% below its net asset value, which is worse than its one-year historical average discount of 10.42%.

Robert J. Stryker has been running the fund for 7 years and currently receives a manager quality ranking of 34 (0=worst, 99=best). If you desire an average level of risk, then this fund may be an option.

Data Date	Investment Rating	Net Assets ($Mil)	Price	Performance Rating/Pts	Total Return Y-T-D	Risk Rating/Pts
12-15	C+	783.00	12.77	C+ / 6.4	7.94%	B- / 7.3
2014	C+	772.90	12.66	C+ / 5.6	15.75%	B- / 7.5
2013	C-	685.53	11.59	C- / 4.0	-16.16%	B- / 7.7
2012	B	569.97	14.40	B- / 7.3	12.73%	B / 8.4
2011	A	535.40	13.99	A- / 9.2	22.74%	B / 8.5
2010	D+	505.46	12.49	D / 1.7	2.88%	C+ / 6.9

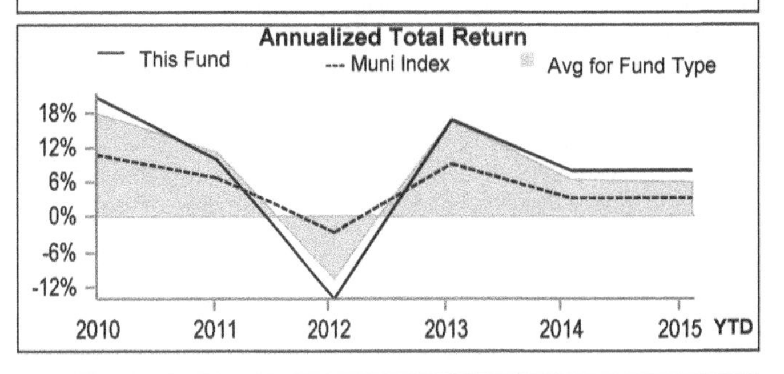

Invesco Pennsylvania Val Muni Inc (VPV) C Fair

Fund Family: Invesco Advisers Inc
Fund Type: Municipal - Single State
Inception Date: April 23, 1993

Major Rating Factors: Middle of the road best describes Invesco Pennsylvania Val Muni Inc whose TheStreet.com Investment Rating is currently a C (Fair). The fund currently has a performance rating of C (Fair) based on an annualized return of -0.47% over the last three years and a total return of -0.63% year to date 2015. Factored into the performance evaluation is an expense ratio of 1.61% (above average).

The fund's risk rating is currently B- (Good). It carries a beta of 2.17, meaning it is expected to move 21.7% for every 10% move in the market. Volatility, as measured by both the semi-deviation and a drawdown factor, is considered low. As of December 31, 2015, Invesco Pennsylvania Val Muni Inc traded at a discount of 11.40% below its net asset value, which is worse than its one-year historical average discount of 11.94%.

Julius D. Williams has been running the fund for 7 years and currently receives a manager quality ranking of 26 (0=worst, 99=best). If you desire an average level of risk, then this fund may be an option.

Data Date	Investment Rating	Net Assets ($Mil)	Price	Performance Rating/Pts	Total Return Y-T-D	Risk Rating/Pts
12-15	C	348.13	12.82	C / 4.9	-0.63%	B- / 7.6
2014	B-	345.70	13.89	B- / 7.4	20.56%	B- / 7.3
2013	C-	312.99	12.14	C / 4.7	-17.03%	B- / 7.5
2012	A+	367.39	15.30	A- / 9.0	18.95%	B / 8.5
2011	A+	343.00	14.22	A / 9.4	22.57%	B / 8.7
2010	C-	321.18	12.65	C- / 3.6	6.03%	C+ / 6.2

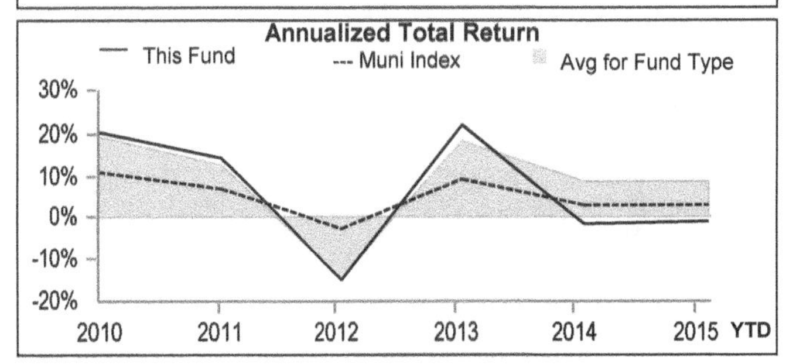

Invesco Quality Municipal Income T (IQI) B Good

Fund Family: Invesco Advisers Inc
Fund Type: Municipal - National
Inception Date: September 29, 1992

Major Rating Factors: Strong performance is the major factor driving the B (Good) TheStreet.com Investment Rating for Invesco Quality Municipal Income T. The fund currently has a performance rating of B- (Good) based on an annualized return of 2.95% over the last three years and a total return of 8.59% year to date 2015. Factored into the performance evaluation is an expense ratio of 1.07% (low).

The fund's risk rating is currently B- (Good). It carries a beta of 2.54, meaning it is expected to move 25.4% for every 10% move in the market. Volatility, as measured by both the semi-deviation and a drawdown factor, is considered low. As of December 31, 2015, Invesco Quality Municipal Income T traded at a discount of 8.90% below its net asset value, which is worse than its one-year historical average discount of 10.77%.

Robert J. Stryker has been running the fund for 7 years and currently receives a manager quality ranking of 38 (0=worst, 99=best). If you desire only a moderate level of risk and strong performance, then this fund is an excellent option.

Data Date	Investment Rating	Net Assets ($Mil)	Price	Performance Rating/Pts	Total Return Y-T-D	Risk Rating/Pts
12-15	B	738.29	12.69	B- / 7.2	8.59%	B- / 7.5
2014	C+	726.00	12.49	C+ / 6.1	19.01%	B- / 7.8
2013	C-	633.43	11.12	C- / 3.7	-15.64%	B / 8.0
2012	B	333.57	13.70	B- / 7.0	10.23%	B / 8.7
2011	A+	314.70	13.44	A / 9.5	24.02%	B / 8.8
2010	C	296.50	12.30	C / 4.9	9.06%	C+ / 6.0

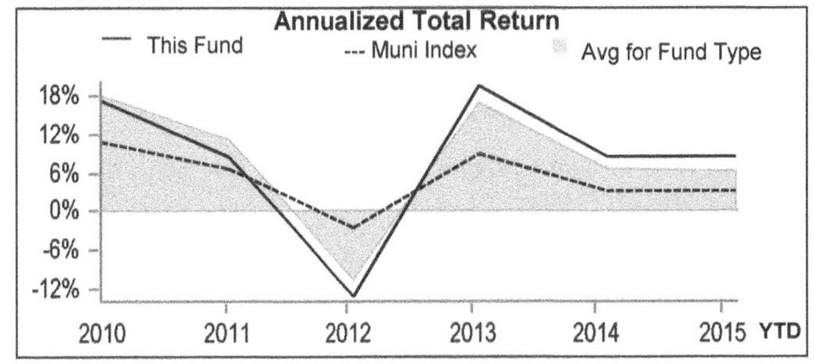

Invesco Senior Income Trust (VVR) C- Fair

Fund Family: Invesco Advisers Inc
Fund Type: Loan Participation
Inception Date: June 23, 1998

Major Rating Factors: Middle of the road best describes Invesco Senior Income Trust whose TheStreet.com Investment Rating is currently a C- (Fair). The fund currently has a performance rating of C- (Fair) based on an annualized return of -1.88% over the last three years and a total return of -4.51% year to date 2015. Factored into the performance evaluation is an expense ratio of 2.20% (high).

The fund's risk rating is currently B- (Good). It carries a beta of -2.67, meaning the fund's expected move will be -26.7% for every 10% move in the market. Volatility, as measured by both the semi-deviation and a drawdown factor, is considered low. As of December 31, 2015, Invesco Senior Income Trust traded at a discount of 10.02% below its net asset value, which is better than its one-year historical average discount of 9.16%.

Philip Yarrow has been running the fund for 9 years and currently receives a manager quality ranking of 56 (0=worst, 99=best). If you desire an average level of risk, then this fund may be an option.

Data Date	Investment Rating	Net Assets ($Mil)	Price	Performance Rating/Pts	Total Return Y-T-D	Risk Rating/Pts
12-15	C-	908.72	4.04	C- / 3.3	-4.51%	B- / 7.0
2014	C	945.40	4.56	C / 4.3	-3.70%	B / 8.1
2013	C+	934.13	5.04	C / 5.5	2.96%	B / 8.5
2012	B	898.69	5.18	B- / 7.5	28.71%	B / 8.3
2011	B	849.20	4.28	B / 7.6	-2.03%	B / 8.3
2010	D-	836.90	4.69	D / 2.2	18.70%	C- / 3.2

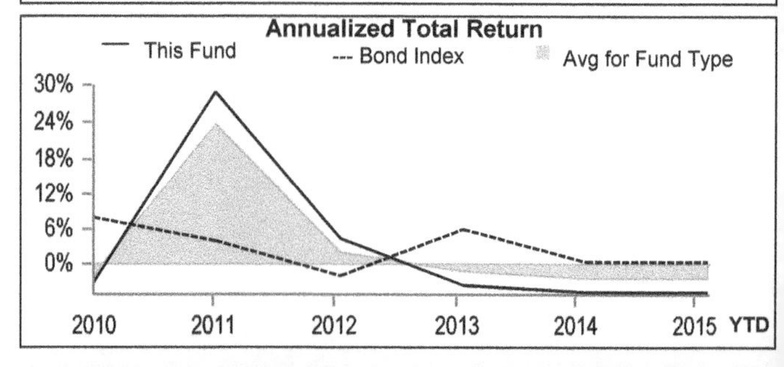

Invesco Tr Fr Inv Gr Mun (VGM) C+ Fair

Fund Family: Invesco Advisers Inc
Fund Type: Municipal - National
Inception Date: January 24, 1992

Major Rating Factors: Middle of the road best describes Invesco Tr Fr Inv Gr Mun whose TheStreet.com Investment Rating is currently a C+ (Fair). The fund currently has a performance rating of C+ (Fair) based on an annualized return of 1.40% over the last three years and a total return of 7.24% year to date 2015. Factored into the performance evaluation is an expense ratio of 1.64% (above average).

The fund's risk rating is currently B- (Good). It carries a beta of 2.04, meaning it is expected to move 20.4% for every 10% move in the market. Volatility, as measured by both the semi-deviation and a drawdown factor, is considered low. As of December 31, 2015, Invesco Tr Fr Inv Gr Mun traded at a discount of 8.38% below its net asset value, which is worse than its one-year historical average discount of 9.48%.

Robert J. Stryker has been running the fund for 7 years and currently receives a manager quality ranking of 38 (0=worst, 99=best). If you desire an average level of risk, then this fund may be an option.

Data Date	Investment Rating	Net Assets ($Mil)	Price	Performance Rating/Pts	Total Return Y-T-D	Risk Rating/Pts
12-15	C+	798.90	13.33	C+ / 6.2	7.24%	B- / 7.4
2014	C+	787.60	13.29	C+ / 5.8	15.80%	B- / 7.6
2013	C-	707.20	12.18	C- / 3.7	-16.50%	B- / 7.9
2012	B+	823.16	15.22	B / 7.9	13.01%	B / 8.8
2011	A+	775.90	14.98	A / 9.4	22.20%	B / 8.8
2010	C	733.60	13.35	C / 4.8	3.84%	C+ / 5.7

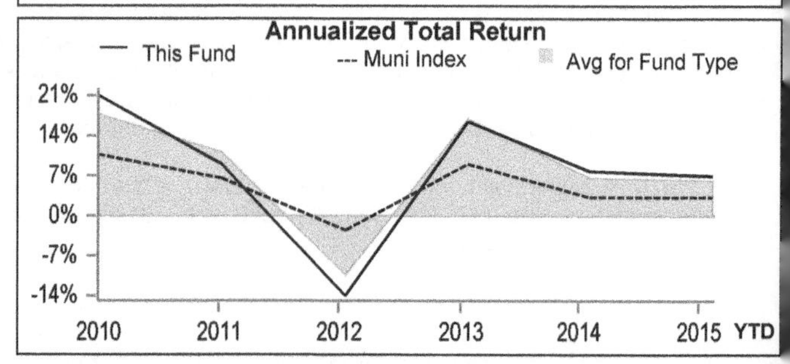

Invesco Tr Fr Inv NY Mun (VTN) B+ Good

Fund Family: Invesco Advisers Inc
Fund Type: Municipal - Single State
Inception Date: March 20, 1992

Major Rating Factors: Strong performance is the major factor driving the B+ (Good) TheStreet.com Investment Rating for Invesco Tr Fr Inv NY Mun. The fund currently has a performance rating of B (Good) based on an annualized return of 1.42% over the last three years and a total return of 13.73% year to date 2015. Factored into the performance evaluation is an expense ratio of 1.35% (average).

The fund's risk rating is currently B- (Good). It carries a beta of 2.28, meaning it is expected to move 22.8% for every 10% move in the market. Volatility, as measured by both the semi-deviation and a drawdown factor, is considered low. As of December 31, 2015, Invesco Tr Fr Inv NY Mun traded at a discount of 3.94% below its net asset value, which is worse than its one-year historical average discount of 8.46%.

Robert J. Stryker has been running the fund for 9 years and currently receives a manager quality ranking of 32 (0=worst, 99=best). If you desire only a moderate level of risk and strong performance, then this fund is an excellent option.

Data Date	Investment Rating	Net Assets ($Mil)	Price	Performance Rating/Pts	Total Return Y-T-D	Risk Rating/Pts
12-15	B+	296.26	14.61	B / 8.0	13.73%	B- / 7.4
2014	C	293.50	13.67	C / 4.6	8.87%	B- / 7.8
2013	C	263.96	13.09	C / 4.3	-15.87%	B / 8.1
2012	A	310.06	16.59	B+ / 8.7	17.09%	B / 8.8
2011	A+	228.00	15.25	A / 9.5	20.91%	B / 8.8
2010	C	212.05	13.63	C / 4.8	2.52%	C+ / 5.7

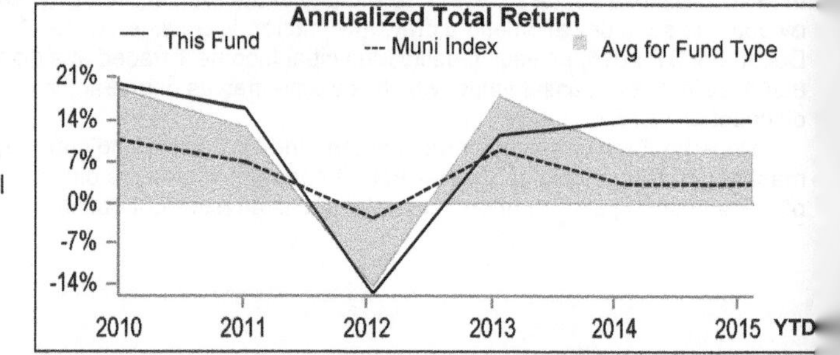

Invesco Value Municipal Income Tr (IIM) — B — Good

Fund Family: Invesco Advisers Inc
Fund Type: Municipal - National
Inception Date: February 19, 1993

Major Rating Factors: Strong performance is the major factor driving the B (Good) TheStreet.com Investment Rating for Invesco Value Municipal Income Tr. The fund currently has a performance rating of B (Good) based on an annualized return of 4.57% over the last three years and a total return of 5.27% year to date 2015. Factored into the performance evaluation is an expense ratio of 0.91% (low).

The fund's risk rating is currently B- (Good). It carries a beta of 2.69, meaning it is expected to move 26.9% for every 10% move in the market. Volatility, as measured by both the semi-deviation and a drawdown factor, is considered low. As of December 31, 2015, Invesco Value Municipal Income Tr traded at a discount of 1.93% below its net asset value, which is worse than its one-year historical average discount of 4.16%.

Robert J. Stryker has been running the fund for 7 years and currently receives a manager quality ranking of 40 (0=worst, 99=best). If you desire only a moderate level of risk and strong performance, then this fund is an excellent option.

Data Date	Investment Rating	Net Assets ($Mil)	Price	Performance Rating/Pts	Total Return Y-T-D	Risk Rating/Pts
12-15	B	779.33	16.25	B / 7.9	5.27%	B- / 7.3
2014	B+	768.30	16.39	B / 7.9	27.27%	B- / 7.8
2013	C	674.77	13.50	C / 5.1	-14.49%	B / 8.1
2012	B+	344.32	16.81	B / 7.7	4.89%	B / 8.5
2011	A+	325.00	16.05	A+ / 9.7	32.81%	B / 8.7
2010	C+	303.16	13.50	C / 4.7	2.39%	C+ / 6.6

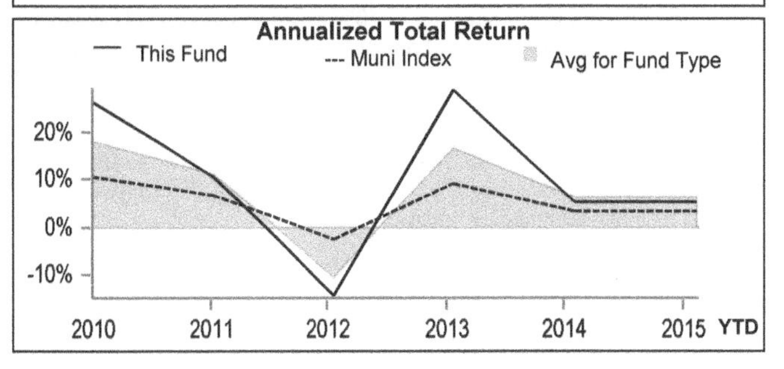

Ivy High Income Opportunities Fund (IVH) — D — Weak

Fund Family: Ivy Investment Management Company
Fund Type: Corporate - High Yield
Inception Date: May 29, 2013

Major Rating Factors:
Disappointing performance is the major factor driving the D (Weak) TheStreet.com Investment Rating for Ivy High Income Opportunities Fund. The fund currently has a performance rating of D- (Weak) based on an annualized return of 0.00% over the last three years and a total return of -12.95% year to date 2015. Factored into the performance evaluation is an expense ratio of 1.98% (high).

The fund's risk rating is currently C+ (Fair). It carries a beta of 0.00, meaning the fund's expected move will be 0.0% for every 10% move in the market. Volatility, as measured by both the semi-deviation and a drawdown factor, is considered low. As of December 31, 2015, Ivy High Income Opportunities Fund traded at a discount of 13.55% below its net asset value, which is better than its one-year historical average discount of 12.63%.

Chad Gunther has been running the fund for 2 years and currently receives a manager quality ranking of 41 (0=worst, 99=best). This fund offers only a moderate level of risk but investors looking for strong performance are still waiting.

Data Date	Investment Rating	Net Assets ($Mil)	Price	Performance Rating/Pts	Total Return Y-T-D	Risk Rating/Pts
12-15	D	258.00	12.38	D- / 1.4	-12.95%	C+ / 6.5
2014	D+	332.00	15.86	D / 1.8	-2.27%	B- / 7.9

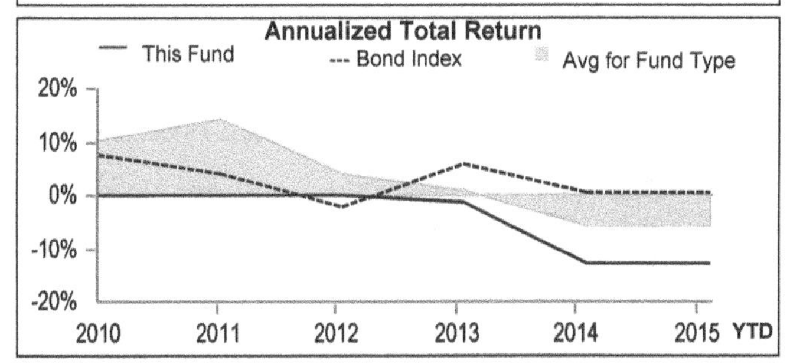

J Hancock Hedged Eqty & Inc Fd (HEQ) — C+ — Fair

Fund Family: John Hancock Advisers LLC
Fund Type: Growth and Income
Inception Date: May 26, 2011

Major Rating Factors: Middle of the road best describes J Hancock Hedged Eqty & Inc Fd whose TheStreet.com Investment Rating is currently a C+ (Fair). The fund currently has a performance rating of C+ (Fair) based on an annualized return of 5.83% over the last three years and a total return of -2.15% year to date 2015. Factored into the performance evaluation is an expense ratio of 1.17% (low).

The fund's risk rating is currently B- (Good). It carries a beta of 0.65, meaning the fund's expected move will be 6.5% for every 10% move in the market. Volatility, as measured by both the semi-deviation and a drawdown factor, is considered low. As of December 31, 2015, J Hancock Hedged Eqty & Inc Fd traded at a discount of 13.83% below its net asset value, which is better than its one-year historical average discount of 11.98%.

Gregg R. Thomas has been running the fund for 5 years and currently receives a manager quality ranking of 49 (0=worst, 99=best). If you desire an average level of risk, then this fund may be an option.

Data Date	Investment Rating	Net Assets ($Mil)	Price	Performance Rating/Pts	Total Return Y-T-D	Risk Rating/Pts
12-15	C+	248.46	14.46	C+ / 6.1	-2.15%	B- / 7.5
2014	C+	257.00	16.32	C / 5.5	5.74%	B / 8.4
2013	C+	255.00	17.07	C+ / 6.9	14.78%	B- / 7.7
2012	C	241.10	15.26	C / 4.7	13.90%	B- / 7.4

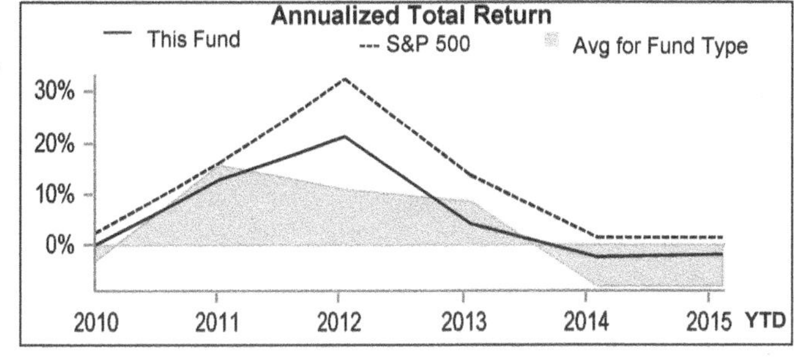

J Hancock Income Securities Tr (JHS) C Fair

Fund Family: John Hancock Advisers LLC
Fund Type: General - Investment Grade
Inception Date: February 14, 1973

Major Rating Factors: Middle of the road best describes J Hancock Income Securities Tr whose TheStreet.com Investment Rating is currently a C (Fair). The fund currently has a performance rating of C- (Fair) based on an annualized return of -0.73% over the last three years and a total return of -0.52% year to date 2015. Factored into the performance evaluation is an expense ratio of 1.43% (average).

The fund's risk rating is currently B- (Good). It carries a beta of 1.33, meaning it is expected to move 13.3% for every 10% move in the market. Volatility, as measured by both the semi-deviation and a drawdown factor, is considered low. As of December 31, 2015, J Hancock Income Securities Tr traded at a discount of 8.20% below its net asset value, which is worse than its one-year historical average discount of 9.36%.

Howard C. Greene has been running the fund for 10 years and currently receives a manager quality ranking of 51 (0=worst, 99=best). If you desire an average level of risk, then this fund may be an option.

Data Date	Investment Rating	Net Assets ($Mil)	Price	Performance Rating/Pts	Total Return Y-T-D	Risk Rating/Pts
12-15	C	176.00	13.43	C- / 3.9	-0.52%	B- / 7.4
2014	C	275.80	14.29	C / 4.3	4.74%	B / 8.0
2013	C+	190.00	14.30	C / 5.2	-6.63%	B / 8.2
2012	B-	170.00	16.34	C+ / 6.3	21.32%	B / 8.7
2011	B+	253.60	14.60	B- / 7.4	11.94%	B+ / 9.0
2010	B+	164.00	15.10	B+ / 8.3	21.62%	C+ / 5.6

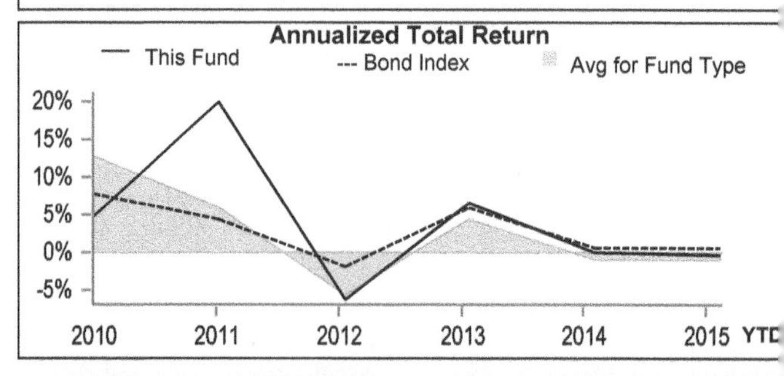

J Hancock Investors Trust (JHI) D+ Weak

Fund Family: John Hancock Advisers LLC
Fund Type: General - Investment Grade
Inception Date: January 29, 1971

Major Rating Factors:
Disappointing performance is the major factor driving the D+ (Weak) TheStreet.com Investment Rating for J Hancock Investors Trust. The fund currently has a performance rating of D+ (Weak) based on an annualized return of -7.21% over the last three years and a total return of -10.75% year to date 2015. Factored into the performance evaluation is an expense ratio of 1.53% (average).

The fund's risk rating is currently C+ (Fair). It carries a beta of 1.88, meaning it is expected to move 18.8% for every 10% move in the market. Volatility, as measured by both the semi-deviation and a drawdown factor, is considered low. As of December 31, 2015, J Hancock Investors Trust traded at a discount of 10.35% below its net asset value, which is better than its one-year historical average discount of 9.24%.

John F. Iles has been running the fund for 10 years and currently receives a manager quality ranking of 19 (0=worst, 99=best). This fund offers only a moderate level of risk but investors looking for strong performance are still waiting.

Data Date	Investment Rating	Net Assets ($Mil)	Price	Performance Rating/Pts	Total Return Y-T-D	Risk Rating/Pts
12-15	D+	151.00	14.38	D+ / 2.4	-10.75%	C+ / 6.2
2014	D+	258.00	17.70	D+ / 2.6	1.84%	B- / 7.0
2013	C-	180.00	18.60	C / 4.4	-12.01%	B- / 7.6
2012	B	164.00	22.57	C+ / 6.6	13.20%	B / 8.7
2011	B+	247.30	22.20	B+ / 8.9	22.22%	B- / 7.7
2010	B+	166.00	20.05	B / 8.1	21.55%	C+ / 5.9

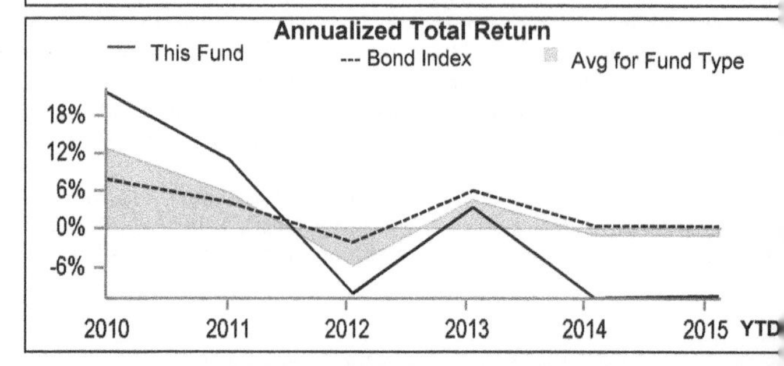

J Hancock Preferred Inc (HPI) C+ Fair

Fund Family: John Hancock Advisers LLC
Fund Type: Income
Inception Date: August 27, 2002

Major Rating Factors: Middle of the road best describes J Hancock Preferred Inc whose TheStreet.com Investment Rating is currently a C+ (Fair). The fund currently has a performance rating of C+ (Fair) based on an annualized return of 3.44% over the last three years and a total return of 5.07% year to date 2015. Factored into the performance evaluation is an expense ratio of 1.68% (above average).

The fund's risk rating is currently B- (Good). It carries a beta of 0.31, meaning the fund's expected move will be 3.1% for every 10% move in the market. Volatility, as measured by both the semi-deviation and a drawdown factor, is considered low. As of December 31, 2015, J Hancock Preferred Inc traded at a discount of 8.12% below its net asset value, which is better than its one-year historical average discount of 7.53%.

Mark T. Maloney has been running the fund for 14 years and currently receives a manager quality ranking of 72 (0=worst, 99=best). If you desire an average level of risk, then this fund may be an option.

Data Date	Investment Rating	Net Assets ($Mil)	Price	Performance Rating/Pts	Total Return Y-T-D	Risk Rating/Pts
12-15	C+	565.00	20.02	C+ / 6.1	5.07%	B- / 7.6
2014	C+	849.70	20.41	C+ / 5.7	23.27%	B- / 7.8
2013	C-	533.00	17.85	C- / 3.8	-15.20%	B / 8.0
2012	B+	572.00	21.91	B- / 7.4	13.73%	B / 8.9
2011	B-	786.50	21.48	B- / 7.5	26.47%	B- / 7.3
2010	B-	510.00	18.68	B- / 7.0	18.39%	C+ / 5.8

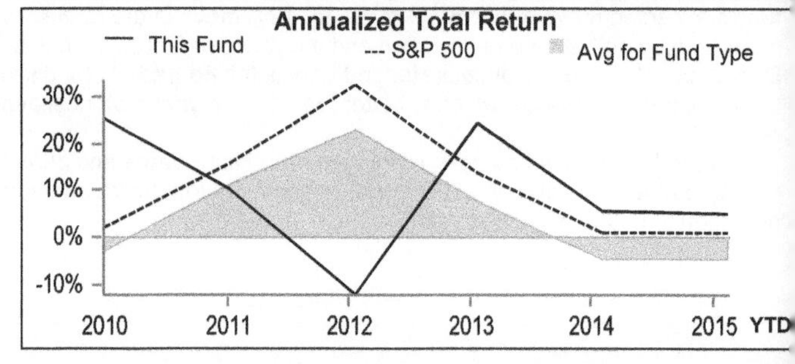

J Hancock Preferred Income II (HPF) C+ Fair

Fund Family: John Hancock Advisers LLC
Fund Type: Income
Inception Date: November 29, 2002

Major Rating Factors: Middle of the road best describes J Hancock Preferred Income II whose TheStreet.com Investment Rating is currently a C+ (Fair). The fund currently has a performance rating of C+ (Fair) based on an annualized return of 3.18% over the last three years and a total return of 3.43% year to date 2015. Factored into the performance evaluation is an expense ratio of 1.69% (above average).

The fund's risk rating is currently B- (Good). It carries a beta of 0.25, meaning the fund's expected move will be 2.5% for every 10% move in the market. Volatility, as measured by both the semi-deviation and a drawdown factor, is considered low. As of December 31, 2015, J Hancock Preferred Income II traded at a discount of 9.09% below its net asset value, which is better than its one-year historical average discount of 7.64%.

Mark T. Maloney has been running the fund for 14 years and currently receives a manager quality ranking of 76 (0=worst, 99=best). If you desire an average level of risk, then this fund may be an option.

Data Date	Investment Rating	Net Assets ($Mil)	Price	Performance Rating/Pts	Total Return Y-T-D	Risk Rating/Pts
12-15	C+	459.00	19.61	C+ / 5.9	3.43%	B- / 7.8
2014	C+	693.20	20.34	C+ / 5.9	22.57%	B / 8.0
2013	C-	434.00	17.90	C- / 4.0	-13.91%	B / 8.0
2012	B+	466.00	21.66	B- / 7.4	16.78%	B / 8.8
2011	B	644.00	20.87	B / 7.8	23.58%	B- / 7.9
2010	B	414.00	18.59	B- / 7.1	19.23%	C+ / 5.9

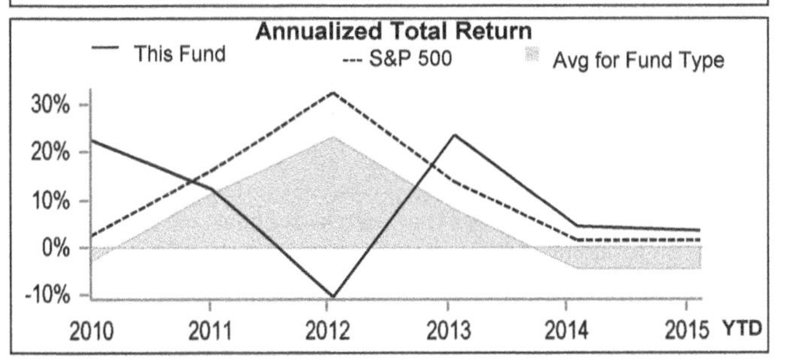

J Hancock Preferred Income III (HPS) B- Good

Fund Family: John Hancock Advisers LLC
Fund Type: Income
Inception Date: June 19, 2003

Major Rating Factors: J Hancock Preferred Income III receives a TheStreet.com Investment Rating of B- (Good). The fund currently has a performance rating of C+ (Fair) based on an annualized return of 5.03% over the last three years and a total return of 6.26% year to date 2015. Factored into the performance evaluation is an expense ratio of 1.67% (above average).

The fund's risk rating is currently B- (Good). It carries a beta of 0.27, meaning the fund's expected move will be 2.7% for every 10% move in the market. Volatility, as measured by both the semi-deviation and a drawdown factor, is considered low. As of December 31, 2015, J Hancock Preferred Income III traded at a discount of 6.64% below its net asset value, which is worse than its one-year historical average discount of 8.30%.

Mark T. Maloney has been running the fund for 13 years and currently receives a manager quality ranking of 82 (0=worst, 99=best). If you desire an average level of risk, then this fund may be an option.

Data Date	Investment Rating	Net Assets ($Mil)	Price	Performance Rating/Pts	Total Return Y-T-D	Risk Rating/Pts
12-15	B-	601.00	17.86	C+ / 6.8	6.26%	B- / 7.6
2014	B-	906.50	17.87	C+ / 6.4	22.80%	B / 8.0
2013	C	569.00	15.59	C / 4.3	-12.55%	B / 8.1
2012	B	598.00	18.75	C+ / 6.8	19.36%	B / 8.8
2011	B-	819.80	17.07	B- / 7.4	18.13%	B- / 7.6
2010	C-	530.00	15.99	C / 4.8	15.17%	C- / 4.2

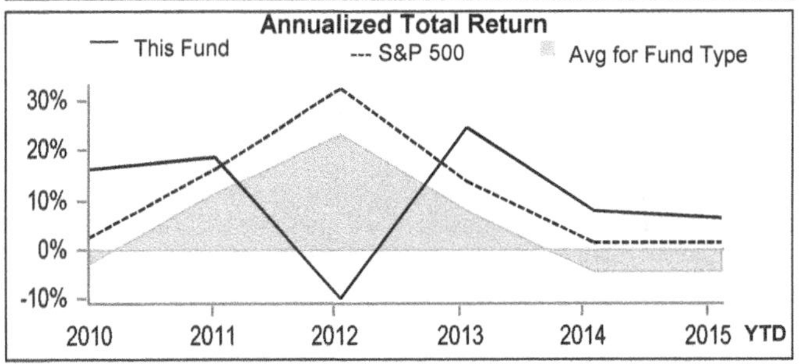

J Hancock Tax Adv Glb Shlr Yield (HTY) C+ Fair

Fund Family: John Hancock Advisers LLC
Fund Type: Global
Inception Date: September 26, 2007

Major Rating Factors: Strong performance is the major factor driving the C+ (Fair) TheStreet.com Investment Rating for J Hancock Tax Adv Glb Shlr Yield. The fund currently has a performance rating of B- (Good) based on an annualized return of 6.00% over the last three years and a total return of 3.90% year to date 2015. Factored into the performance evaluation is an expense ratio of 1.26% (average).

The fund's risk rating is currently C+ (Fair). It carries a beta of 0.55, meaning the fund's expected move will be 5.5% for every 10% move in the market. Volatility, as measured by both the semi-deviation and a drawdown factor, is considered low. As of December 31, 2015, J Hancock Tax Adv Glb Shlr Yield traded at a premium of 9.29% above its net asset value, which is worse than its one-year historical average premium of 2.69%.

Dennis M. Bein has been running the fund for 9 years and currently receives a manager quality ranking of 86 (0=worst, 99=best). If you desire only a moderate level of risk and strong performance, then this fund is an excellent option.

Data Date	Investment Rating	Net Assets ($Mil)	Price	Performance Rating/Pts	Total Return Y-T-D	Risk Rating/Pts
12-15	C+	106.00	10.23	B- / 7.1	3.90%	C+ / 6.1
2014	C-	117.60	11.22	C- / 4.0	2.00%	C+ / 6.2
2013	C+	120.00	12.46	C+ / 6.4	12.99%	B- / 7.7
2012	C-	115.00	11.84	C- / 4.1	11.56%	B- / 7.8
2011	B-	115.30	12.34	C+ / 6.7	7.22%	B / 8.0
2010	C+	115.00	12.73	C+ / 6.1	7.95%	C / 5.4

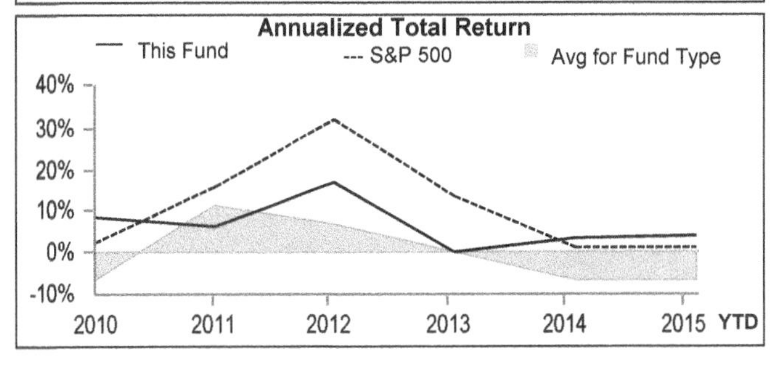

J Hancock Tax Advantage Div Income (HTD) A- Excellent

Fund Family: John Hancock Advisers LLC
Fund Type: Income
Inception Date: February 27, 2004

Data Date	Investment Rating	Net Assets ($Mil)	Price	Performance Rating/Pts	Total Return Y-T-D	Risk Rating/Pts
12-15	A-	836.00	20.57	B+ / 8.3	0.21%	B- / 7.9
2014	A+	1,273.90	22.27	B+ / 8.8	32.42%	B / 8.4
2013	B	854.00	18.22	C+ / 6.9	4.22%	B / 8.5
2012	B+	690.00	18.04	B / 7.6	12.77%	B / 8.8
2011	B	1,052.90	17.34	B+ / 8.8	25.30%	B- / 7.2
2010	B-	594.00	14.91	B- / 7.3	24.73%	C / 5.1

Major Rating Factors:
Strong performance is the major factor driving the A- (Excellent) TheStreet.com Investment Rating for J Hancock Tax Advantage Div Income. The fund currently has a performance rating of B+ (Good) based on an annualized return of 10.99% over the last three years and a total return of 0.21% year to date 2015. Factored into the performance evaluation is an expense ratio of 1.63% (above average).

The fund's risk rating is currently B- (Good). It carries a beta of 0.64, meaning the fund's expected move will be 6.4% for every 10% move in the market. Volatility, as measured by both the semi-deviation and a drawdown factor, is considered low. As of December 31, 2015, J Hancock Tax Advantage Div Income traded at a discount of 10.33% below its net asset value, which is worse than its one-year historical average discount of 10.35%.

Dennis M. Bein currently receives a manager quality ranking of 82 (0=worst, 99=best). If you desire only a moderate level of risk and strong performance, then this fund is an excellent option.

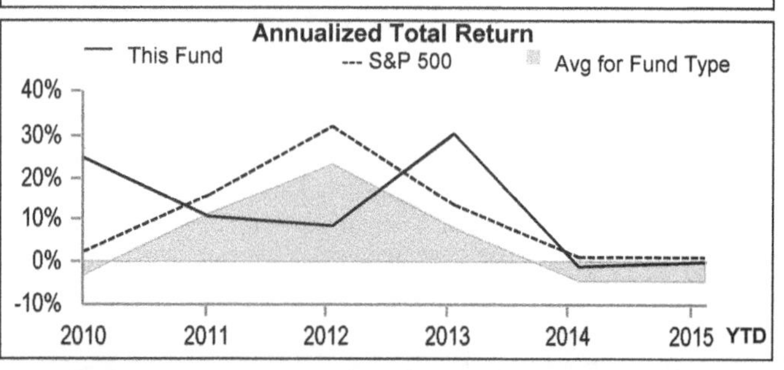

Japan Smaller Cap Fund Inc. (JOF) A+ Excellent

Fund Family: Nomura Asset Management USA Inc
Fund Type: Foreign
Inception Date: March 14, 1990

Data Date	Investment Rating	Net Assets ($Mil)	Price	Performance Rating/Pts	Total Return Y-T-D	Risk Rating/Pts
12-15	A+	311.09	10.23	A / 9.5	24.45%	B / 8.1
2014	C+	308.70	8.97	C / 4.6	0.58%	B / 8.4
2013	C-	266.33	9.17	C / 4.7	26.49%	B- / 7.4
2012	D	233.84	7.20	D- / 1.4	0.81%	B- / 7.3
2011	D	238.30	7.18	D / 1.7	-20.04%	B- / 7.5
2010	C+	179.38	8.97	C+ / 6.2	23.86%	C+ / 6.1

Major Rating Factors:
Exceptional performance is the major factor driving the A+ (Excellent) TheStreet.com Investment Rating for Japan Smaller Cap Fund Inc.. The fund currently has a performance rating of A (Excellent) based on an annualized return of 16.38% over the last three years and a total return of 24.45% year to date 2015. Factored into the performance evaluation is an expense ratio of 1.13% (low).

The fund's risk rating is currently B (Good). It carries a beta of 0.62, meaning the fund's expected move will be 6.2% for every 10% move in the market. Volatility, as measured by both the semi-deviation and a drawdown factor, is considered low. As of December 31, 2015, Japan Smaller Cap Fund Inc. traded at a discount of 12.04% below its net asset value, which is worse than its one-year historical average discount of 12.44%.

Investment Department currently receives a manager quality ranking of 97 (0=worst, 99=best). If you desire only a moderate level of risk and strong performance, then this fund is an excellent option.

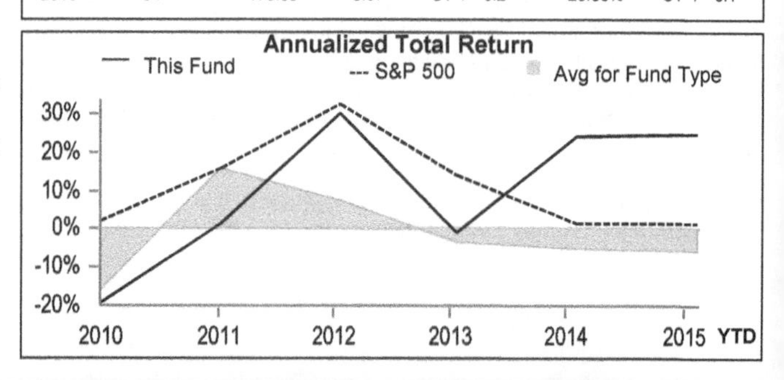

John Hancock Financial Opptys (BTO) A+ Excellent

Fund Family: John Hancock Advisers LLC
Fund Type: Financial Services
Inception Date: August 16, 1994

Data Date	Investment Rating	Net Assets ($Mil)	Price	Performance Rating/Pts	Total Return Y-T-D	Risk Rating/Pts
12-15	A+	482.00	28.03	A+ / 9.7	25.29%	B- / 7.3
2014	A+	553.30	23.56	B+ / 8.9	5.51%	B / 8.7
2013	B+	376.00	23.55	B+ / 8.7	34.59%	B- / 7.5
2012	B-	298.00	17.60	B / 8.2	32.66%	C+ / 6.9
2011	C-	300.00	13.70	C- / 3.8	-9.63%	B- / 7.2
2010	C	418.00	17.22	C / 4.7	29.28%	C+ / 6.0

Major Rating Factors:
Exceptional performance is the major factor driving the A+ (Excellent) TheStreet.com Investment Rating for John Hancock Financial Opptys. The fund currently has a performance rating of A+ (Excellent) based on an annualized return of 21.19% over the last three years and a total return of 25.29% year to date 2015. Factored into the performance evaluation is an expense ratio of 1.80% (above average).

The fund's risk rating is currently B- (Good). It carries a beta of 1.14, meaning it is expected to move 11.4% for every 10% move in the market. Volatility, as measured by both the semi-deviation and a drawdown factor, is considered low. As of December 31, 2015, John Hancock Financial Opptys traded at a premium of 7.11% above its net asset value, which is worse than its one-year historical average discount of 1.29%.

Susan A. Curry has been running the fund for 10 years and currently receives a manager quality ranking of 88 (0=worst, 99=best). If you desire only a moderate level of risk and strong performance, then this fund is an excellent option.

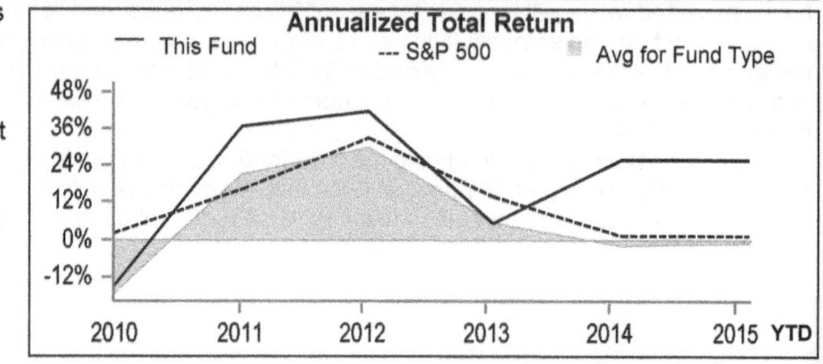

John Hancock Premium Dividend (PDT) B+ Good

Fund Family: John Hancock Advisers LLC
Fund Type: Income
Inception Date: December 14, 1989

Major Rating Factors: Strong performance is the major factor driving the B+ (Good) TheStreet.com Investment Rating for John Hancock Premium Dividend. The fund currently has a performance rating of B (Good) based on an annualized return of 8.82% over the last three years and a total return of 8.44% year to date 2015. Factored into the performance evaluation is an expense ratio of 1.85% (above average).

The fund's risk rating is currently B- (Good). It carries a beta of 0.60, meaning the fund's expected move will be 6.0% for every 10% move in the market. Volatility, as measured by both the semi-deviation and a drawdown factor, is considered low. As of December 31, 2015, John Hancock Premium Dividend traded at a discount of 8.36% below its net asset value, which is worse than its one-year historical average discount of 10.13%.

Mark T. Maloney has been running the fund for 11 years and currently receives a manager quality ranking of 71 (0=worst, 99=best). If you desire only a moderate level of risk and strong performance, then this fund is an excellent option.

Data Date	Investment Rating	Net Assets ($Mil)	Price	Performance Rating/Pts	Total Return Y-T-D	Risk Rating/Pts
12-15	B+	733.00	13.71	B / 8.1	8.44%	B- / 7.5
2014	B-	1,120.30	13.75	C+ / 6.8	26.96%	B- / 7.8
2013	C	778.00	11.60	C / 5.3	-6.56%	B- / 7.9
2012	B+	660.00	13.57	B- / 7.2	9.51%	B / 8.9
2011	B+	991.20	13.44	A- / 9.1	25.87%	B / 8.0
2010	B+	573.00	11.56	B+ / 8.5	25.73%	C / 5.3

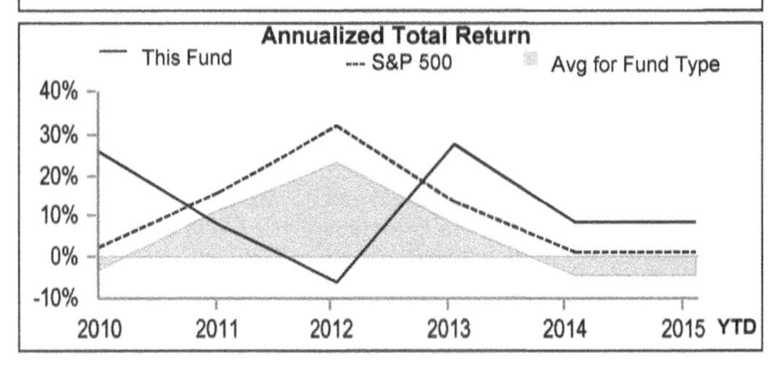

JPMorgan China Region (JFC) C Fair

Fund Family: JF International Management Inc
Fund Type: Foreign
Inception Date: July 16, 1992

Major Rating Factors: Middle of the road best describes JPMorgan China Region whose TheStreet.com Investment Rating is currently a C (Fair). The fund currently has a performance rating of C+ (Fair) based on an annualized return of 4.93% over the last three years and a total return of -3.83% year to date 2015. Factored into the performance evaluation is an expense ratio of 2.14% (high).

The fund's risk rating is currently C+ (Fair). It carries a beta of 0.93, meaning that its performance tracks fairly well with that of the overall stock market. Volatility, as measured by both the semi-deviation and a drawdown factor, is considered low. As of December 31, 2015, JPMorgan China Region traded at a discount of 12.41% below its net asset value, which is worse than its one-year historical average discount of 14.83%.

Howard H. Wang has been running the fund for 11 years and currently receives a manager quality ranking of 74 (0=worst, 99=best). If you desire an average level of risk, then this fund may be an option.

Data Date	Investment Rating	Net Assets ($Mil)	Price	Performance Rating/Pts	Total Return Y-T-D	Risk Rating/Pts
12-15	C	125.02	15.32	C+ / 5.8	-3.83%	C+ / 6.2
2014	B	111.20	16.91	B- / 7.1	11.78%	B / 8.4
2013	D+	97.38	15.16	D+ / 2.9	6.34%	C+ / 6.5
2012	D+	82.23	14.00	C- / 3.8	22.51%	C+ / 6.6
2011	D+	112.25	11.02	C- / 3.0	-27.64%	C+ / 6.7
2010	D	89.71	15.79	C / 4.9	14.73%	D+ / 2.3

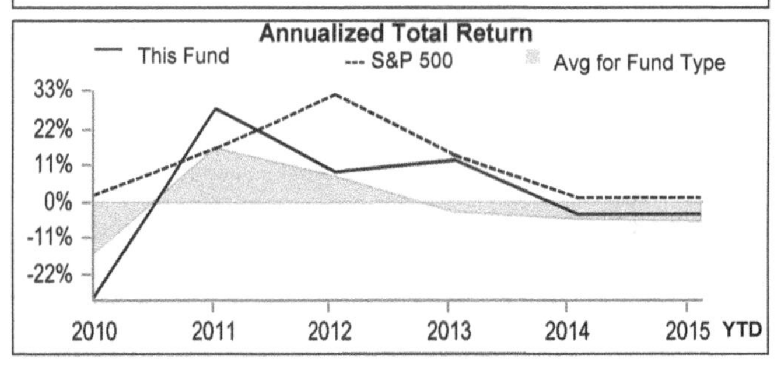

Kayne Anderson Energy Tot Ret (KYE) E+ Very Weak

Fund Family: KA Fund Advisors LLC
Fund Type: Energy/Natural Resources
Inception Date: June 28, 2005

Major Rating Factors:
Very poor performance is the major factor driving the E+ (Very Weak) TheStreet.com Investment Rating for Kayne Anderson Energy Tot Ret. The fund currently has a performance rating of E (Very Weak) based on an annualized return of -23.87% over the last three years and a total return of -66.00% year to date 2015. Factored into the performance evaluation is an expense ratio of 3.60% (high).

The fund's risk rating is currently C- (Fair). It carries a beta of 1.44, meaning it is expected to move 14.4% for every 10% move in the market. Volatility, as measured by both the semi-deviation and a drawdown factor, is considered average. As of December 31, 2015, Kayne Anderson Energy Tot Ret traded at a discount of 11.22% below its net asset value, which is better than its one-year historical average discount of 8.03%.

John C. Frey has been running the fund for 11 years and currently receives a manager quality ranking of 7 (0=worst, 99=best). This fund offers an average level of risk but investors looking for strong performance will be frustrated.

Data Date	Investment Rating	Net Assets ($Mil)	Price	Performance Rating/Pts	Total Return Y-T-D	Risk Rating/Pts
12-15	E+	1,050.35	8.47	E / 0.3	-66.00%	C- / 3.6
2014	C-	1,312.30	27.85	C / 4.9	8.54%	C+ / 6.2
2013	C-	1,026.36	27.35	C / 4.4	16.97%	B- / 7.3
2012	C-	883.97	24.59	C / 4.3	3.21%	B- / 7.2
2011	B	915.06	25.31	B+ / 8.9	-1.20%	B- / 7.3
2010	B-	677.68	29.11	B+ / 8.8	35.68%	C- / 3.6

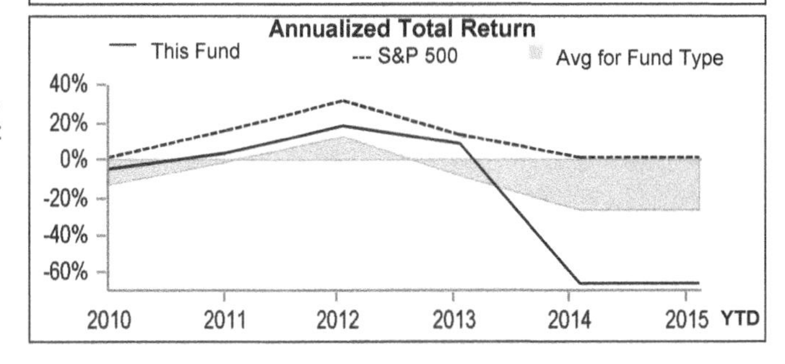

Kayne Anderson Engy Development Co (KED) D- Weak

Fund Family: KA Fund Advisors LLC
Fund Type: Energy/Natural Resources
Inception Date: September 21, 2006

Major Rating Factors:
Disappointing performance is the major factor driving the D- (Weak) TheStreet.com Investment Rating for Kayne Anderson Engy Development Co. The fund currently has a performance rating of D- (Weak) based on an annualized return of -5.77% over the last three years and a total return of -48.92% year to date 2015. Factored into the performance evaluation is an expense ratio of 3.40% (high).

The fund's risk rating is currently C (Fair). It carries a beta of 0.66, meaning the fund's expected move will be 6.6% for every 10% move in the market. Volatility, as measured by both the semi-deviation and a drawdown factor, is considered average. As of December 31, 2015, Kayne Anderson Engy Development Co traded at a discount of 25.09% below its net asset value, which is better than its one-year historical average discount of 4.98%.

Robert V. Sinnott currently receives a manager quality ranking of 45 (0=worst, 99=best). This fund offers an average level of risk but investors looking for strong performance will be frustrated.

Data Date	Investment Rating	Net Assets ($Mil)	Price	Performance Rating/Pts	Total Return Y-T-D	Risk Rating/Pts
12-15	D-	348.50	17.56	D- / 1.4	-48.92%	C / 4.5
2014	A+	297.30	35.74	A / 9.4	34.04%	B / 8.3
2013	D+	275.83	27.97	E+ / 0.9	-35.10%	B / 8.5
2012	A	238.03	0.00	A / 9.3	30.56%	B / 8.0
2011	B	211.04	0.00	A- / 9.1	24.03%	C+ / 6.2
2010	C-	168.54	18.01	B- / 7.4	33.91%	D+ / 2.8

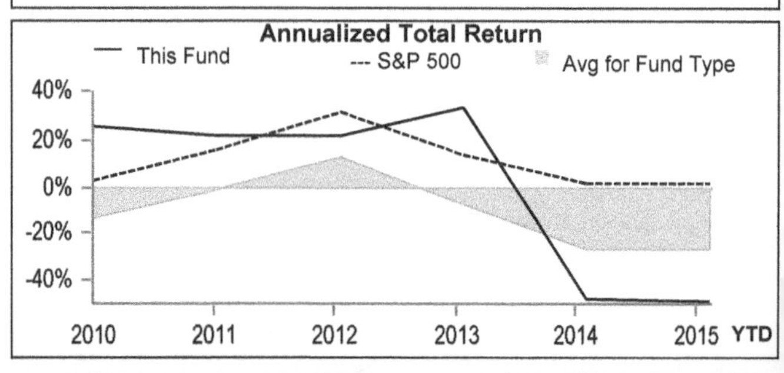

Kayne Anderson Midstream/Energy (KMF) E Very Weak

Fund Family: KA Fund Advisors LLC
Fund Type: Income
Inception Date: November 24, 2010

Major Rating Factors: Kayne Anderson Midstream/Energy has adopted a very risky asset allocation strategy and currently receives an overall TheStreet.com Investment Rating of E (Very Weak). The fund has a high level of volatility, as measured by both semi-deviation and drawdown factors. It carries a beta of 2.22, meaning it is expected to move 22.2% for every 10% move in the market. As of December 31, 2015, Kayne Anderson Midstream/Energy traded at a discount of 1.83% below its net asset value, which is worse than its one-year historical average discount of 7.82%. Unfortunately, the high level of risk (D, Weak) failed to pay off as investors endured very poor performance.

The fund's performance rating is currently E (Very Weak). It has registered an annualized return of -17.86% over the last three years and is down -57.65% year to date 2015. Factored into the performance evaluation is an expense ratio of 3.60% (high).

Robert V. Sinnott currently receives a manager quality ranking of 1 (0=worst, 99=best). If you can tolerate very high levels of risk in the hope of improved future returns, holding this fund may be an option.

Data Date	Investment Rating	Net Assets ($Mil)	Price	Performance Rating/Pts	Total Return Y-T-D	Risk Rating/Pts
12-15	E	854.26	12.37	E / 0.5	-57.65%	D / 2.1
2014	C+	1,027.30	34.03	C+ / 6.6	6.47%	B- / 7.3
2013	B+	737.04	34.37	B / 7.8	19.55%	B / 8.4
2012	A+	562.04	28.75	A+ / 9.6	30.41%	B / 8.5
2011	C-	0.00	24.60	C- / 3.1	1.09%	B / 8.5

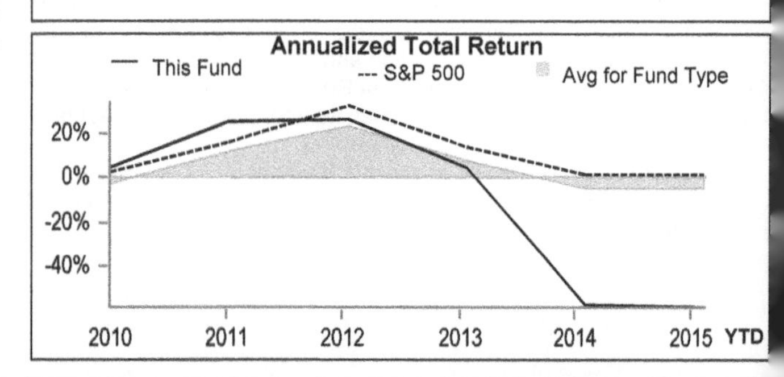

Kayne Anderson MLP Inv Co (KYN) D- Weak

Fund Family: KA Fund Advisors LLC
Fund Type: Energy/Natural Resources
Inception Date: September 27, 2004

Major Rating Factors:
Disappointing performance is the major factor driving the D- (Weak) TheStreet.com Investment Rating for Kayne Anderson MLP Inv Co. The fund currently has a performance rating of D- (Weak) based on an annualized return of -10.32% over the last three years and a total return of -50.61% year to date 2015. Factored into the performance evaluation is an expense ratio of 2.40% (high).

The fund's risk rating is currently C (Fair). It carries a beta of 0.68, meaning the fund's expected move will be 6.8% for every 10% move in the market. Volatility, as measured by both the semi-deviation and a drawdown factor, is considered average. As of December 31, 2015, Kayne Anderson MLP Inv Co traded at a discount of 2.43% below its net asset value, which is better than its one-year historical average premium of 6.99%.

John C. Frey has been running the fund for 12 years and currently receives a manager quality ranking of 20 (0=worst, 99=best). This fund offers an average level of risk but investors looking for strong performance will be frustrated.

Data Date	Investment Rating	Net Assets ($Mil)	Price	Performance Rating/Pts	Total Return Y-T-D	Risk Rating/Pts
12-15	D-	4,026.82	17.29	D- / 1.0	-50.61%	C / 4.5
2014	C+	4,511.20	38.18	C+ / 6.7	6.44%	B- / 7.1
2013	B+	3,071.98	39.85	B / 7.9	35.26%	B / 8.3
2012	B	2,029.60	29.47	B- / 7.3	12.10%	B / 8.2
2011	B+	1,825.89	30.37	B+ / 8.6	7.37%	B / 8.1
2010	B-	1,038.28	0.00	B+ / 8.8	35.72%	C- / 4.0

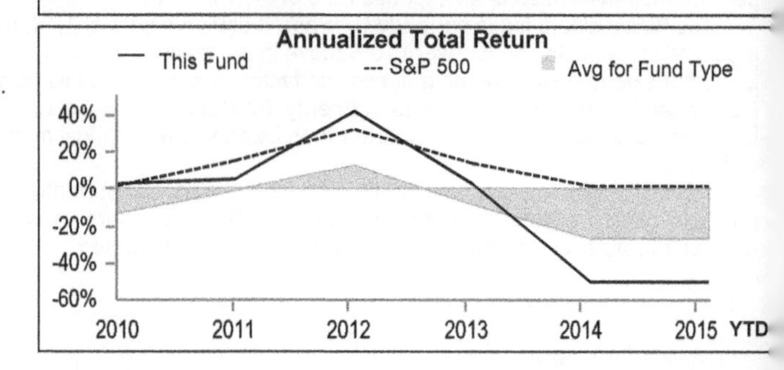

KKR Income Opportunities Fund (KIO) D+ Weak

Fund Family: KKR Asset Management LLC
Fund Type: General - Investment Grade
Inception Date: July 25, 2013

Data Date	Investment Rating	Net Assets ($Mil)	Price	Perfor-mance Rating/Pts	Total Return Y-T-D	Risk Rating/Pts
12-15	D+	289.47	13.86	D / 2.2	-5.82%	B- / 7.2
2014	D-	291.10	16.16	D / 1.7	-2.78%	C / 4.6

Major Rating Factors:
Disappointing performance is the major factor driving the D+ (Weak) TheStreet.com Investment Rating for KKR Income Opportunities Fund. The fund currently has a performance rating of D (Weak) based on an annualized return of 0.00% over the last three years and a total return of -5.82% year to date 2015. Factored into the performance evaluation is an expense ratio of 2.29% (high).

The fund's risk rating is currently B- (Good). It carries a beta of 0.00, meaning the fund's expected move will be 0.0% for every 10% move in the market. Volatility, as measured by both the semi-deviation and a drawdown factor, is considered low. As of December 31, 2015, KKR Income Opportunities Fund traded at a discount of 12.72% below its net asset value, which is better than its one-year historical average discount of 11.56%.

Erik A. Falk currently receives a manager quality ranking of 27 (0=worst, 99=best). This fund offers only a moderate level of risk but investors looking for strong performance are still waiting.

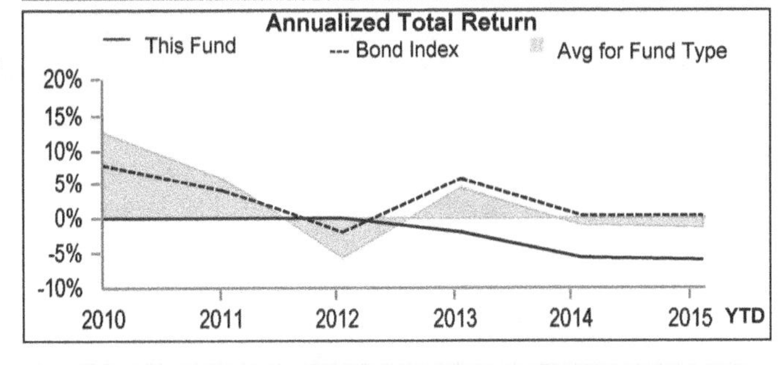

Korea Equity Fund (KEF) C- Fair

Fund Family: Nomura Asset Management USA Inc
Fund Type: Foreign
Inception Date: November 24, 1993

Data Date	Investment Rating	Net Assets ($Mil)	Price	Perfor-mance Rating/Pts	Total Return Y-T-D	Risk Rating/Pts
12-15	C-	87.45	6.97	C- / 3.1	-4.34%	C+ / 6.6
2014	D+	89.70	7.70	C- / 3.0	-3.72%	B- / 7.1
2013	D-	93.27	8.32	D / 1.9	-13.01%	C / 4.8
2012	C-	121.20	9.22	C+ / 5.9	12.17%	C / 5.4
2011	C+	103.50	9.08	B / 8.0	-2.48%	C+ / 5.8
2010	C-	109.46	12.23	C+ / 5.8	32.22%	C- / 4.0

Major Rating Factors: Middle of the road best describes Korea Equity Fund whose TheStreet.com Investment Rating is currently a C- (Fair). The fund currently has a performance rating of C- (Fair) based on an annualized return of -2.87% over the last three years and a total return of -4.34% year to date 2015. Factored into the performance evaluation is an expense ratio of 1.49% (average).

The fund's risk rating is currently C+ (Fair). It carries a beta of 0.66, meaning the fund's expected move will be 6.6% for every 10% move in the market. Volatility, as measured by both the semi-deviation and a drawdown factor, is considered low. As of December 31, 2015, Korea Equity Fund traded at a discount of 12.98% below its net asset value, which is better than its one-year historical average discount of 11.46%.

Shigeto Kasahara has been running the fund for 11 years and currently receives a manager quality ranking of 26 (0=worst, 99=best). If you desire an average level of risk, then this fund may be an option.

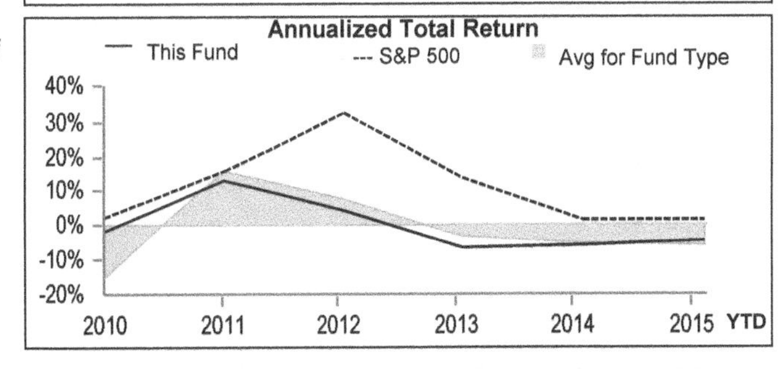

Korea Fund (KF) D+ Weak

Fund Family: Allianz Global Investors US LLC
Fund Type: Foreign
Inception Date: August 22, 1984

Data Date	Investment Rating	Net Assets ($Mil)	Price	Perfor-mance Rating/Pts	Total Return Y-T-D	Risk Rating/Pts
12-15	D+	329.46	31.85	D+ / 2.8	-2.36%	C+ / 6.3
2014	C-	380.20	37.52	D+ / 2.5	-6.29%	B- / 7.8
2013	D	334.83	41.26	D+ / 2.9	-4.35%	C+ / 6.2
2012	C-	387.63	41.26	C / 4.3	14.36%	C+ / 6.4
2011	D	549.09	35.75	C- / 3.0	-9.00%	C / 5.2
2010	D	393.37	44.11	C- / 3.1	24.08%	C- / 3.7

Major Rating Factors:
Disappointing performance is the major factor driving the D+ (Weak) TheStreet.com Investment Rating for Korea Fund. The fund currently has a performance rating of D+ (Weak) based on an annualized return of -4.69% over the last three years and a total return of -2.36% year to date 2015. Factored into the performance evaluation is an expense ratio of 1.13% (low).

The fund's risk rating is currently C+ (Fair). It carries a beta of 0.64, meaning the fund's expected move will be 6.4% for every 10% move in the market. Volatility, as measured by both the semi-deviation and a drawdown factor, is considered low. As of December 31, 2015, Korea Fund traded at a discount of 10.16% below its net asset value, which is better than its one-year historical average discount of 9.89%.

Raymond Chan currently receives a manager quality ranking of 21 (0=worst, 99=best). This fund offers only a moderate level of risk but investors looking for strong performance are still waiting.

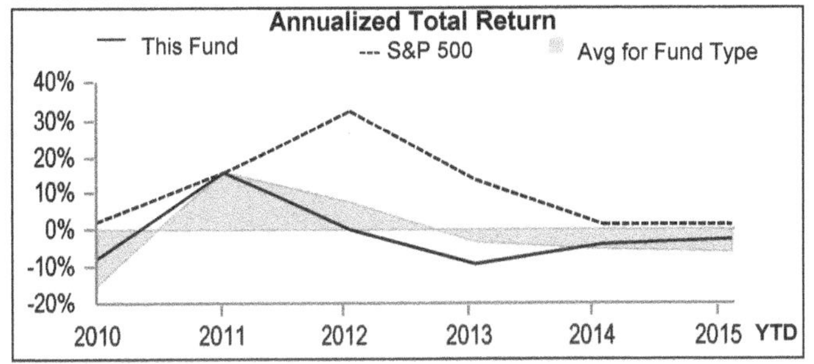

Latin American Discovery Fund (LDF) D- Weak

Fund Family: Morgan Stanley Investment Managemen
Fund Type: Foreign
Inception Date: June 23, 1992

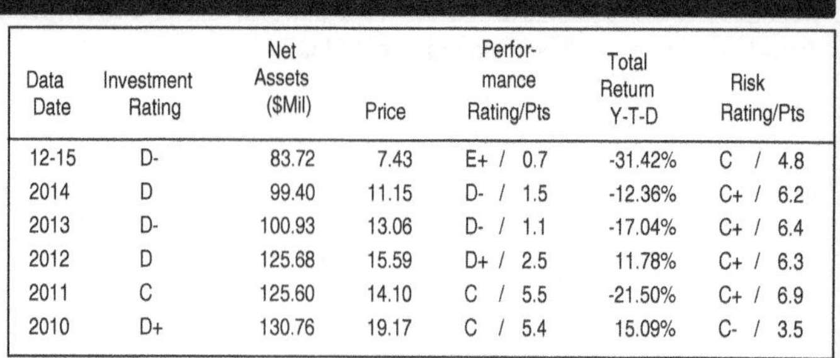

Data Date	Investment Rating	Net Assets ($Mil)	Price	Performance Rating/Pts	Total Return Y-T-D	Risk Rating/Pts
12-15	D-	83.72	7.43	E+ / 0.7	-31.42%	C / 4.8
2014	D	99.40	11.15	D- / 1.5	-12.36%	C+ / 6.2
2013	D-	100.93	13.06	D- / 1.1	-17.04%	C+ / 6.4
2012	D	125.68	15.59	D+ / 2.5	11.78%	C+ / 6.3
2011	C	125.60	14.10	C / 5.5	-21.50%	C+ / 6.9
2010	D+	130.76	19.17	C / 5.4	15.09%	C- / 3.5

Major Rating Factors:
Very poor performance is the major factor driving the D- (Weak) TheStreet.com Investment Rating for Latin American Discovery Fund. The fund currently has a performance rating of E+ (Very Weak) based on an annualized return of -21.36% over the last three years and a total return of -31.42% year to date 2015. Factored into the performance evaluation is an expense ratio of 1.40% (average).

The fund's risk rating is currently C (Fair). It carries a beta of 1.17, meaning it is expected to move 11.7% for every 10% move in the market. Volatility, as measured by both the semi-deviation and a drawdown factor, is considered average. As of December 31, 2015, Latin American Discovery Fund traded at a discount of 11.65% below its net asset value, which is better than its one-year historical average discount of 10.21%.

Cristina Piedrahita has been running the fund for 14 years and currently receives a manager quality ranking of 4 (0=worst, 99=best). This fund offers an average level of risk but investors looking for strong performance will be frustrated.

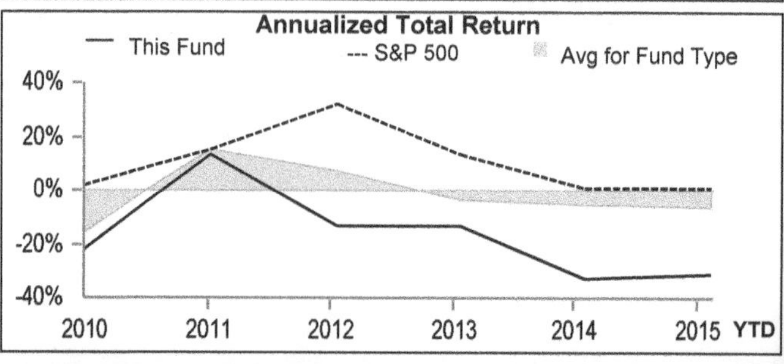

Lazard Global Total Return&Income (LGI) C- Fair

Fund Family: Lazard Asset Management LLC
Fund Type: Global
Inception Date: April 27, 2004

Data Date	Investment Rating	Net Assets ($Mil)	Price	Performance Rating/Pts	Total Return Y-T-D	Risk Rating/Pts
12-15	C-	171.19	13.08	C- / 3.9	-10.62%	C+ / 6.9
2014	C+	191.50	15.81	C / 5.5	-2.69%	B / 8.1
2013	B	174.11	17.62	B- / 7.2	18.51%	B / 8.0
2012	C	148.82	15.09	C+ / 5.6	24.78%	B- / 7.6
2011	C-	148.80	13.39	C- / 3.8	-4.19%	B- / 7.3
2010	D	139.30	15.06	D / 2.0	8.90%	C / 5.0

Major Rating Factors: Middle of the road best describes Lazard Global Total Return&Income whose TheStreet.com Investment Rating is currently a C- (Fair). The fund currently has a performance rating of C- (Fair) based on an annualized return of 0.95% over the last three years and a total return of -10.62% year to date 2015. Factored into the performance evaluation is an expense ratio of 1.51% (average).

The fund's risk rating is currently C+ (Fair). It carries a beta of 1.15, meaning it is expected to move 11.5% for every 10% move in the market. Volatility, as measured by both the semi-deviation and a drawdown factor, is considered low. As of December 31, 2015, Lazard Global Total Return&Income traded at a discount of 14.29% below its net asset value, which is better than its one-year historical average discount of 13.23%.

Andrew D. Lacey currently receives a manager quality ranking of 37 (0=worst, 99=best). If you desire an average level of risk, then this fund may be an option.

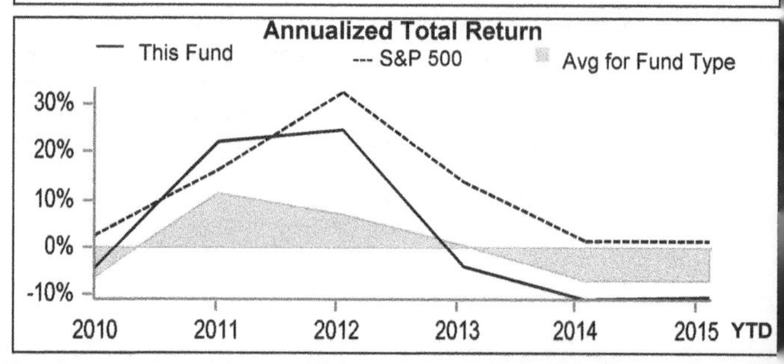

Lazard World Div&Inc Fd (LOR) D+ Weak

Fund Family: Lazard Asset Management LLC
Fund Type: Global
Inception Date: June 27, 2005

Data Date	Investment Rating	Net Assets ($Mil)	Price	Performance Rating/Pts	Total Return Y-T-D	Risk Rating/Pts
12-15	D+	97.12	9.11	D+ / 2.3	-24.41%	C+ / 6.2
2014	C+	112.60	13.10	C / 5.5	-5.70%	B- / 7.8
2013	B	96.72	14.49	B / 7.8	23.18%	B- / 7.6
2012	B	87.50	12.55	B / 8.1	30.82%	B- / 7.4
2011	C	84.30	10.86	C / 4.8	-7.88%	B- / 7.6
2010	C-	78.78	12.85	C- / 4.1	23.81%	C / 4.9

Major Rating Factors:
Disappointing performance is the major factor driving the D+ (Weak) TheStreet.com Investment Rating for Lazard World Div&Inc Fd. The fund currently has a performance rating of D+ (Weak) based on an annualized return of -4.27% over the last three years and a total return of -24.41% year to date 2015. Factored into the performance evaluation is an expense ratio of 1.75% (above average).

The fund's risk rating is currently C+ (Fair). It carries a beta of 1.25, meaning it is expected to move 12.5% for every 10% move in the market. Volatility, as measured by both the semi-deviation and a drawdown factor, is considered low. As of December 31, 2015, Lazard World Div&Inc Fd traded at a discount of 13.98% below its net asset value, which is better than its one-year historical average discount of 12.25%.

Andrew D. Lacey currently receives a manager quality ranking of 17 (0=worst, 99=best). This fund offers only a moderate level of risk but investors looking for strong performance are still waiting.

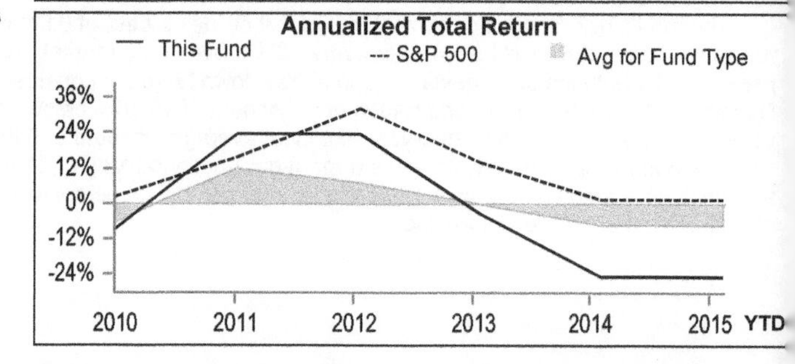

Legg Mason BW Global Income Opps (BWG) D Weak

Fund Family: Legg Mason Partners Fund Advisor LL
Fund Type: Global
Inception Date: March 28, 2012

Data Date	Investment Rating	Net Assets ($Mil)	Price	Performance Rating/Pts	Total Return Y-T-D	Risk Rating/Pts
12-15	D	420.10	11.58	D / 2.0	-20.92%	C / 5.1
2014	C-	414.60	16.71	C- / 4.2	8.80%	C+ / 6.9
2013	D	484.93	16.87	D / 1.9	-9.83%	B- / 7.2

Major Rating Factors:
Disappointing performance is the major factor driving the D (Weak) TheStreet.com Investment Rating for Legg Mason BW Global Income Opps. The fund currently has a performance rating of D (Weak) based on an annualized return of -8.29% over the last three years and a total return of -20.92% year to date 2015. Factored into the performance evaluation is an expense ratio of 1.74% (above average).

The fund's risk rating is currently C (Fair). It carries a beta of 1.17, meaning it is expected to move 11.7% for every 10% move in the market. Volatility, as measured by both the semi-deviation and a drawdown factor, is considered average. As of December 31, 2015, Legg Mason BW Global Income Opps traded at a discount of 15.47% below its net asset value, which is better than its one-year historical average discount of 14.87%.

This fund has been team managed for 4 years and currently receives a manager quality ranking of 41 (0=worst, 99=best). This fund offers an average level of risk but investors looking for strong performance will be frustrated.

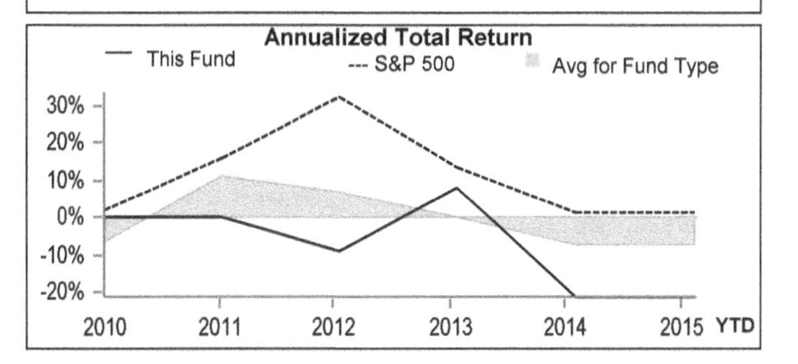

Liberty All-Star Equity Fund (USA) B+ Good

Fund Family: ALPS Advisors Inc
Fund Type: Income
Inception Date: October 24, 1986

Data Date	Investment Rating	Net Assets ($Mil)	Price	Performance Rating/Pts	Total Return Y-T-D	Risk Rating/Pts
12-15	B+	1,225.00	5.35	B / 7.7	-1.84%	B- / 7.6
2014	B+	1,186.90	5.98	B / 7.6	8.97%	B / 8.5
2013	B	1,099.00	5.97	B / 7.6	25.89%	B- / 7.6
2012	C	943.00	4.77	C / 5.2	17.40%	B- / 7.2
2011	C-	911.80	4.22	C / 4.9	-5.70%	B- / 7.0
2010	C-	840.00	4.93	C / 4.6	21.80%	C / 5.4

Major Rating Factors: Strong performance is the major factor driving the B+ (Good) TheStreet.com Investment Rating for Liberty All-Star Equity Fund. The fund currently has a performance rating of B (Good) based on an annualized return of 10.34% over the last three years and a total return of -1.84% year to date 2015. Factored into the performance evaluation is an expense ratio of 1.03% (low).

The fund's risk rating is currently B- (Good). It carries a beta of 1.17, meaning it is expected to move 11.7% for every 10% move in the market. Volatility, as measured by both the semi-deviation and a drawdown factor, is considered low. As of December 31, 2015, Liberty All-Star Equity Fund traded at a discount of 13.43% below its net asset value, which is worse than its one-year historical average discount of 13.80%.

Arnold C. Schneider, III has been running the fund for 14 years and currently receives a manager quality ranking of 29 (0=worst, 99=best). If you desire only a moderate level of risk and strong performance, then this fund is an excellent option.

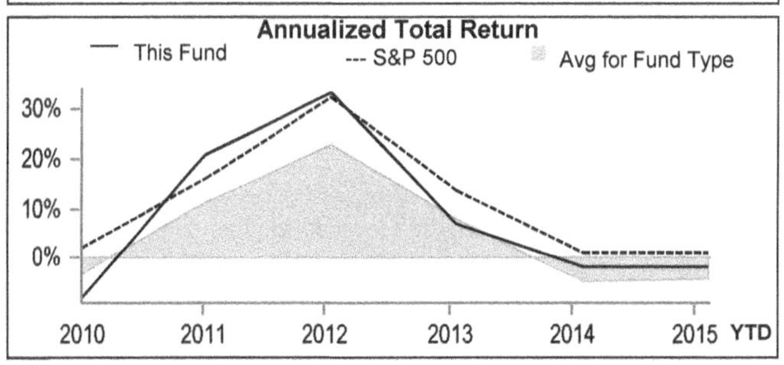

Liberty All-Star Growth Fund (ASG) B+ Good

Fund Family: ALPS Advisors Inc
Fund Type: Income
Inception Date: March 6, 1986

Data Date	Investment Rating	Net Assets ($Mil)	Price	Performance Rating/Pts	Total Return Y-T-D	Risk Rating/Pts
12-15	B+	138.00	4.58	A / 9.4	11.67%	C+ / 6.7
2014	B-	132.00	5.16	B- / 7.0	0.42%	B- / 7.6
2013	B	116.00	5.62	B+ / 8.9	38.00%	C+ / 6.9
2012	C	130.00	4.06	C+ / 6.2	15.70%	C+ / 6.2
2011	C	127.60	3.81	C+ / 6.3	-2.33%	C+ / 6.5
2010	C	113.00	4.25	C+ / 5.6	34.99%	C / 5.0

Major Rating Factors:
Exceptional performance is the major factor driving the B+ (Good) TheStreet.com Investment Rating for Liberty All-Star Growth Fund. The fund currently has a performance rating of A (Excellent) based on an annualized return of 15.51% over the last three years and a total return of 11.67% year to date 2015. Factored into the performance evaluation is an expense ratio of 1.34% (average).

The fund's risk rating is currently C+ (Fair). It carries a beta of 1.12, meaning it is expected to move 11.2% for every 10% move in the market. Volatility, as measured by both the semi-deviation and a drawdown factor, is considered low. As of December 31, 2015, Liberty All-Star Growth Fund traded at a discount of 8.22% below its net asset value, which is worse than its one-year historical average discount of 10.00%.

Matthew A. Weatherbie has been running the fund for 30 years and currently receives a manager quality ranking of 67 (0=worst, 99=best). If you desire only a moderate level of risk and strong performance, then this fund is an excellent option.

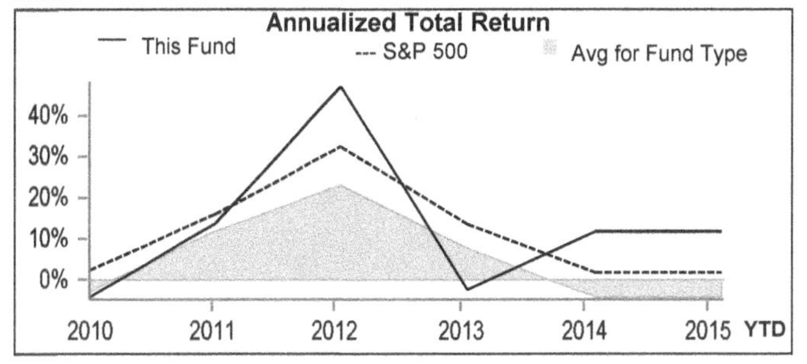

LMP Capital and Income Fund Inc (SCD) C- Fair

Fund Family: Legg Mason Partners Fund Advisor LL
Fund Type: Growth and Income
Inception Date: February 24, 2004

Major Rating Factors: Middle of the road best describes LMP Capital and Income Fund Inc whose TheStreet.com Investment Rating is currently a C- (Fair). The fund currently has a performance rating of C- (Fair) based on an annualized return of 2.36% over the last three years and a total return of -20.46% year to date 2015. Factored into the performance evaluation is an expense ratio of 1.44% (average).

The fund's risk rating is currently C+ (Fair). It carries a beta of 1.07, meaning that its performance tracks fairly well with that of the overall stock market. Volatility, as measured by both the semi-deviation and a drawdown factor, is considered low. As of December 31, 2015, LMP Capital and Income Fund Inc traded at a discount of 16.25% below its net asset value, which is better than its one-year historical average discount of 13.68%.

Timothy R. B. Daubenspeck has been running the fund for 5 years and currently receives a manager quality ranking of 16 (0=worst, 99=best). If you desire an average level of risk, then this fund may be an option.

Data Date	Investment Rating	Net Assets ($Mil)	Price	Performance Rating/Pts	Total Return Y-T-D	Risk Rating/Pts
12-15	C-	348.25	12.37	C- / 3.7	-20.46%	C+ / 6.7
2014	A-	334.70	16.76	B / 7.8	14.06%	B / 8.5
2013	B	299.72	15.80	B / 7.7	17.49%	B / 8.1
2012	B+	240.39	13.47	B+ / 8.4	24.25%	B / 8.0
2011	B-	268.30	12.36	C+ / 6.9	7.20%	B / 8.1
2010	C-	372.89	12.45	C- / 4.1	26.27%	C / 4.9

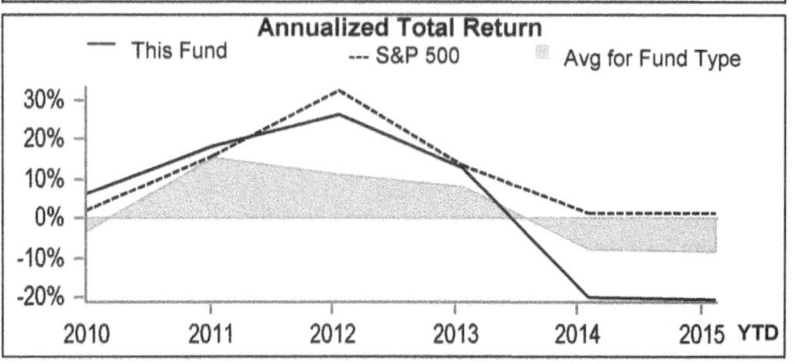

LMP Corporate Loan Fund Inc (TLI) C- Fair

Fund Family: Legg Mason Partners Fund Advisor LL
Fund Type: Loan Participation
Inception Date: November 19, 1998

Major Rating Factors: Middle of the road best describes LMP Corporate Loan Fund Inc whose TheStreet.com Investment Rating is currently a C- (Fair). The fund currently has a performance rating of C- (Fair) based on an annualized return of -2.23% over the last three years and a total return of -3.04% year to date 2015. Factored into the performance evaluation is an expense ratio of 1.88% (above average).

The fund's risk rating is currently B- (Good). It carries a beta of 0.01, meaning the fund's expected move will be 0.1% for every 10% move in the market. Volatility, as measured by both the semi-deviation and a drawdown factor, is considered low. As of December 31, 2015, LMP Corporate Loan Fund Inc traded at a discount of 10.34% below its net asset value, which is worse than its one-year historical average discount of 10.46%.

S. Kenneth Leech currently receives a manager quality ranking of 54 (0=worst, 99=best). If you desire an average level of risk, then this fund may be an option.

Data Date	Investment Rating	Net Assets ($Mil)	Price	Performance Rating/Pts	Total Return Y-T-D	Risk Rating/Pts
12-15	C-	117.00	9.88	C- / 3.3	-3.04%	B- / 7.1
2014	C-	125.50	11.03	C- / 3.8	-3.11%	B / 8.0
2013	C+	128.00	12.23	C / 5.4	-0.06%	B / 8.4
2012	B-	125.00	12.92	C+ / 6.4	20.40%	B / 8.4
2011	B+	120.00	11.11	B / 8.2	5.26%	B / 8.6
2010	C+	119.00	11.73	B- / 7.2	22.84%	C / 4.7

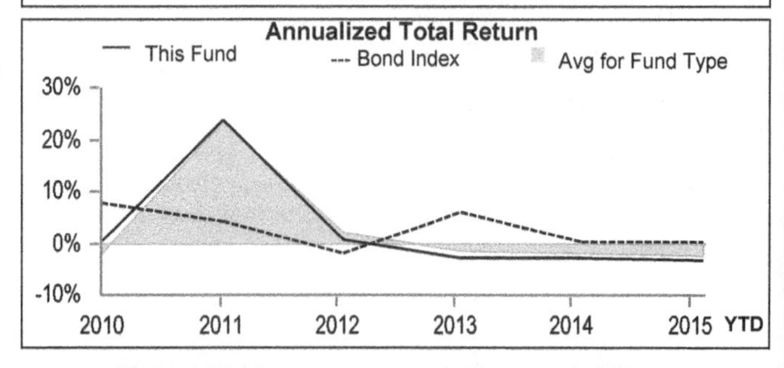

LMP Real Estate Income Fund Inc (RIT) B Good

Fund Family: Legg Mason Partners Fund Advisor LL
Fund Type: Growth and Income
Inception Date: July 31, 2002

Major Rating Factors: Strong performance is the major factor driving the B (Good) TheStreet.com Investment Rating for LMP Real Estate Income Fund Inc. The fund currently has a performance rating of B+ (Good) based on an annualized return of 10.81% over the last three years and a total return of 9.91% year to date 2015. Factored into the performance evaluation is an expense ratio of 1.48% (average).

The fund's risk rating is currently C+ (Fair). It carries a beta of 0.55, meaning the fund's expected move will be 5.5% for every 10% move in the market. Volatility, as measured by both the semi-deviation and a drawdown factor, is considered low. As of December 31, 2015, LMP Real Estate Income Fund Inc traded at a discount of 3.91% below its net asset value, which is worse than its one-year historical average discount of 9.16%.

John P. Baldi currently receives a manager quality ranking of 88 (0=worst, 99=best). If you desire only a moderate level of risk and strong performance, then this fund is an excellent option.

Data Date	Investment Rating	Net Assets ($Mil)	Price	Performance Rating/Pts	Total Return Y-T-D	Risk Rating/Pts
12-15	B	164.00	13.04	B+ / 8.6	9.91%	C+ / 6.4
2014	A-	145.90	12.55	A- / 9.2	32.72%	B- / 7.0
2013	C-	145.00	10.06	C- / 4.0	-6.78%	B- / 7.2
2012	B+	37.00	10.97	B+ / 8.8	30.01%	B- / 7.8
2011	B	122.30	9.25	A- / 9.0	-0.25%	C+ / 6.7
2010	C+	102.69	10.10	B / 8.1	35.86%	C- / 3.5

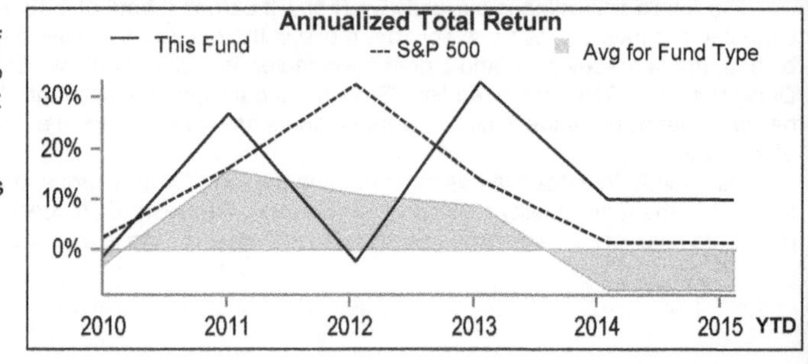

Macquarie Global Infr Total Return (MGU) C Fair

Fund Family: Macquarie Capital Investment Mgmt L
Fund Type: Global
Inception Date: August 26, 2005

Major Rating Factors: Middle of the road best describes Macquarie Global Infr Total Return whose TheStreet.com Investment Rating is currently a C (Fair). The fund currently has a performance rating of C (Fair) based on an annualized return of 4.90% over the last three years and a total return of -17.58% year to date 2015. Factored into the performance evaluation is an expense ratio of 2.20% (high).

The fund's risk rating is currently B- (Good). It carries a beta of 1.12, meaning it is expected to move 11.2% for every 10% move in the market. Volatility, as measured by both the semi-deviation and a drawdown factor, is considered low. As of December 31, 2015, Macquarie Global Infr Total Return traded at a discount of 16.37% below its net asset value, which is better than its one-year historical average discount of 14.10%.

Brad L. Frishberg has been running the fund for 4 years and currently receives a manager quality ranking of 69 (0=worst, 99=best). If you desire an average level of risk, then this fund may be an option.

Data Date	Investment Rating	Net Assets ($Mil)	Price	Performance Rating/Pts	Total Return Y-T-D	Risk Rating/Pts
12-15	C	356.36	19.05	C / 4.6	-17.58%	B- / 7.0
2014	A-	348.90	24.72	B / 7.9	19.92%	B / 8.4
2013	B	295.64	22.10	B- / 7.3	16.70%	B / 8.1
2012	C+	325.95	19.07	C+ / 6.6	22.67%	B- / 7.8
2011	C	330.80	16.99	C+ / 5.6	4.38%	B- / 7.3
2010	D-	280.77	17.28	D- / 1.2	15.34%	C / 5.0

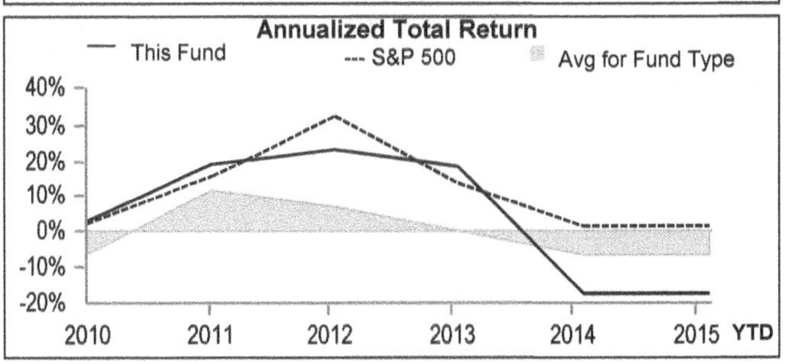

Macquarie/FTG Infr/ Util Div&Inc (MFD) D+ Weak

Fund Family: First Trust Advisors LP
Fund Type: Global
Inception Date: March 25, 2004

Major Rating Factors:
Disappointing performance is the major factor driving the D+ (Weak) TheStreet.com Investment Rating for Macquarie/FTG Infr/ Util Div&Inc. The fund currently has a performance rating of D+ (Weak) based on an annualized return of -1.18% over the last three years and a total return of -19.49% year to date 2015. Factored into the performance evaluation is an expense ratio of 1.95% (above average).

The fund's risk rating is currently C+ (Fair). It carries a beta of 0.97, meaning that its performance tracks fairly well with that of the overall stock market. Volatility, as measured by both the semi-deviation and a drawdown factor, is considered low. As of December 31, 2015, Macquarie/FTG Infr/ Util Div&Inc traded at a discount of 11.77% below its net asset value, which is better than its one-year historical average discount of 6.04%.

Brad L. Frishberg currently receives a manager quality ranking of 26 (0=worst, 99=best). This fund offers only a moderate level of risk but investors looking for strong performance are still waiting.

Data Date	Investment Rating	Net Assets ($Mil)	Price	Performance Rating/Pts	Total Return Y-T-D	Risk Rating/Pts
12-15	D+	150.67	11.62	D+ / 2.7	-19.49%	C+ / 6.8
2014	C+	154.60	15.91	C / 5.4	4.45%	B / 8.1
2013	B	139.12	16.74	B- / 7.4	14.97%	B / 8.1
2012	B-	122.83	15.25	C+ / 6.7	19.15%	B- / 7.9
2011	C+	130.30	14.21	C+ / 6.7	12.15%	B- / 7.2
2010	D-	117.04	14.48	D / 1.8	23.62%	C- / 3.6

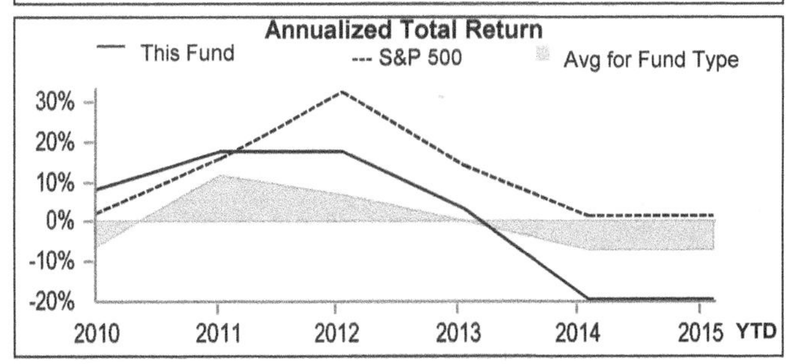

Madison Covered Call & Equity Stra (MCN) B- Good

Fund Family: Madison Asset Management LLC
Fund Type: Income
Inception Date: July 28, 2004

Major Rating Factors: Madison Covered Call & Equity Stra receives a TheStreet.com Investment Rating of B- (Good). The fund currently has a performance rating of C+ (Fair) based on an annualized return of 7.30% over the last three years and a total return of -0.61% year to date 2015. Factored into the performance evaluation is an expense ratio of 1.06% (low).

The fund's risk rating is currently B- (Good). It carries a beta of 0.79, meaning the fund's expected move will be 7.9% for every 10% move in the market. Volatility, as measured by both the semi-deviation and a drawdown factor, is considered low. As of December 31, 2015, Madison Covered Call & Equity Stra traded at a discount of 12.97% below its net asset value, which is better than its one-year historical average discount of 12.06%.

Frank E. Burgess currently receives a manager quality ranking of 41 (0=worst, 99=best). If you desire an average level of risk, then this fund may be an option.

Data Date	Investment Rating	Net Assets ($Mil)	Price	Performance Rating/Pts	Total Return Y-T-D	Risk Rating/Pts
12-15	B-	178.78	7.38	C+ / 6.7	-0.61%	B- / 7.6
2014	B-	180.40	8.14	C+ / 6.1	8.99%	B / 8.4
2013	C+	166.31	8.17	C / 5.5	13.89%	B- / 7.8
2012	D+	166.38	7.62	D+ / 2.9	12.61%	B- / 7.5
2011	C	167.00	7.47	C / 4.7	-8.56%	B- / 7.5
2010	C	185.39	9.05	C+ / 5.6	10.55%	C / 4.9

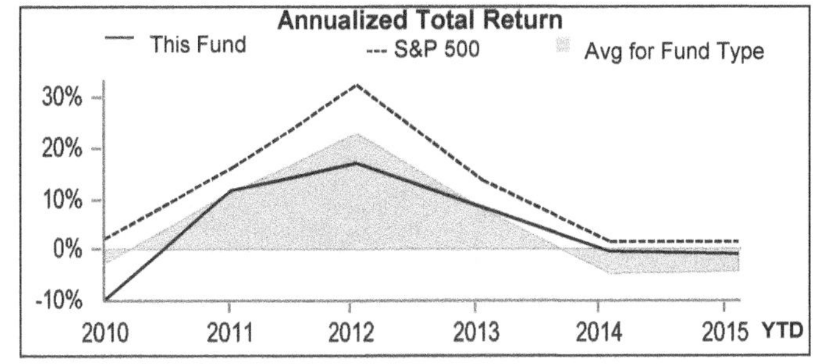

Madison Strategic Sector Premium (MSP) B- Good

Fund Family: Madison Asset Management LLC
Fund Type: Income
Inception Date: April 28, 2005

Major Rating Factors: Madison Strategic Sector Premium receives a TheStreet.com Investment Rating of B- (Good). The fund currently has a performance rating of C+ (Fair) based on an annualized return of 7.26% over the last three years and a total return of -0.52% year to date 2015. Factored into the performance evaluation is an expense ratio of 0.98% (low).

The fund's risk rating is currently B- (Good). It carries a beta of 0.63, meaning the fund's expected move will be 6.3% for every 10% move in the market. Volatility, as measured by both the semi-deviation and a drawdown factor, is considered low. As of December 31, 2015, Madison Strategic Sector Premium traded at a discount of 14.18% below its net asset value, which is better than its one-year historical average discount of 13.20%.

Frank E. Burgess has been running the fund for 11 years and currently receives a manager quality ranking of 59 (0=worst, 99=best). If you desire an average level of risk, then this fund may be an option.

Data Date	Investment Rating	Net Assets ($Mil)	Price	Performance Rating/Pts	Total Return Y-T-D	Risk Rating/Pts
12-15	B-	79.44	10.77	C+ / 6.6	-0.52%	B- / 7.8
2014	B-	80.60	11.87	C+ / 5.8	8.36%	B / 8.5
2013	C+	76.37	11.96	C+ / 5.8	14.56%	B- / 7.8
2012	C-	74.20	11.09	C- / 3.4	13.30%	B- / 7.9
2011	C+	73.20	10.64	C / 5.2	-6.77%	B- / 7.9
2010	C+	80.18	12.82	C+ / 6.3	14.04%	C / 5.4

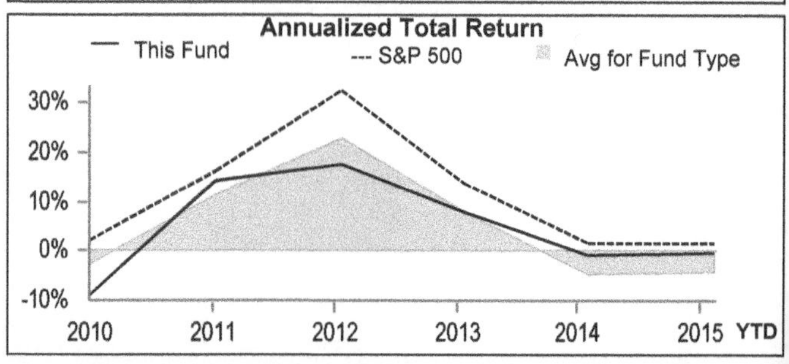

MainStay DefinedTerm Muncipal Opp (MMD) C+ Fair

Fund Family: New York Life Investment Management
Fund Type: General - Investment Grade
Inception Date: June 26, 2012

Major Rating Factors: Middle of the road best describes MainStay DefinedTerm Muncipal Opp whose TheStreet.com Investment Rating is currently a C+ (Fair). The fund currently has a performance rating of C+ (Fair) based on an annualized return of 4.09% over the last three years and a total return of 9.33% year to date 2015. Factored into the performance evaluation is an expense ratio of 1.56% (average).

The fund's risk rating is currently C+ (Fair). It carries a beta of 2.28, meaning it is expected to move 22.8% for every 10% move in the market. Volatility, as measured by both the semi-deviation and a drawdown factor, is considered low. As of December 31, 2015, MainStay DefinedTerm Muncipal Opp traded at a discount of 3.93% below its net asset value, which is worse than its one-year historical average discount of 5.62%.

David M. Dowden has been running the fund for 4 years and currently receives a manager quality ranking of 77 (0=worst, 99=best). If you desire an average level of risk, then this fund may be an option.

Data Date	Investment Rating	Net Assets ($Mil)	Price	Performance Rating/Pts	Total Return Y-T-D	Risk Rating/Pts
12-15	C+	524.40	18.83	C+ / 6.7	9.33%	C+ / 6.9
2014	B+	527.80	18.17	B+ / 8.3	18.98%	B- / 7.4
2013	D	550.77	15.77	D- / 1.0	-14.23%	B- / 7.5

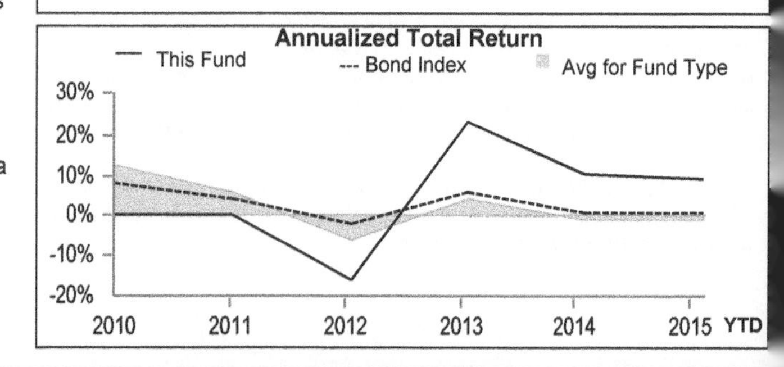

Managed Duration Investment Grd Mu (MZF) C+ Fair

Fund Family: Cutwater Investor Services Corp
Fund Type: Municipal - National
Inception Date: August 26, 2003

Major Rating Factors: Middle of the road best describes Managed Duration Investment Grd Mu whose TheStreet.com Investment Rating is currently a C+ (Fair). The fund currently has a performance rating of C+ (Fair) based on an annualized return of 1.62% over the last three years and a total return of 7.10% year to date 2015. Factored into the performance evaluation is an expense ratio of 1.35% (average).

The fund's risk rating is currently B- (Good). It carries a beta of 2.57, meaning it is expected to move 25.7% for every 10% move in the market. Volatility, as measured by both the semi-deviation and a drawdown factor, is considered low. As of December 31, 2015, Managed Duration Investment Grd Mu traded at a discount of 8.21% below its net asset value, which is worse than its one-year historical average discount of 10.39%.

Clifford D. Corso has been running the fund for 13 years and currently receives a manager quality ranking of 28 (0=worst, 99=best). If you desire an average level of risk, then this fund may be an option.

Data Date	Investment Rating	Net Assets ($Mil)	Price	Performance Rating/Pts	Total Return Y-T-D	Risk Rating/Pts
12-15	C+	101.10	13.76	C+ / 6.6	7.10%	B- / 7.3
2014	C	102.30	13.51	C / 5.2	15.05%	B- / 7.5
2013	C-	92.57	12.40	C- / 4.1	-15.22%	B- / 7.7
2012	B+	104.62	15.30	B / 8.1	13.41%	B / 8.5
2011	A+	98.90	14.90	A+ / 9.8	24.17%	B / 8.6
2010	C+	97.19	13.11	C+ / 6.9	6.65%	C+ / 6.1

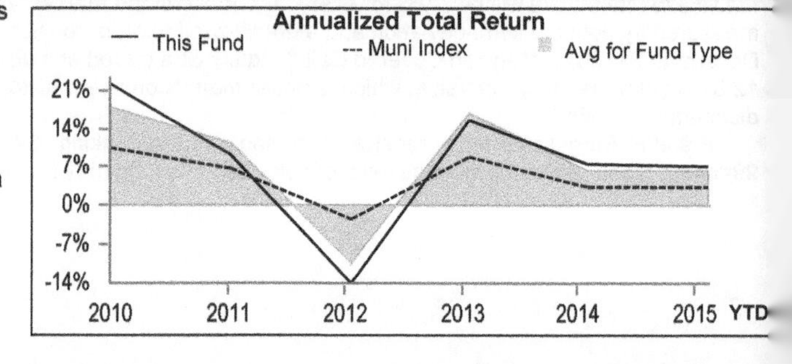

Managed High Yield Plus Fund (HYF) C Fair

Fund Family: UBS Asset Mgmt (Americas) Inc
Fund Type: Global
Inception Date: June 24, 1998

Major Rating Factors: Middle of the road best describes Managed High Yield Plus Fund whose TheStreet.com Investment Rating is currently a C (Fair). The fund currently has a performance rating of C+ (Fair) based on an annualized return of 2.00% over the last three years and a total return of 1.10% year to date 2015. Factored into the performance evaluation is an expense ratio of 1.46% (average).

The fund's risk rating is currently C+ (Fair). It carries a beta of 0.65, meaning the fund's expected move will be 6.5% for every 10% move in the market. Volatility, as measured by both the semi-deviation and a drawdown factor, is considered low. As of December 31, 2015, Managed High Yield Plus Fund traded at a discount of 4.86% below its net asset value, which is worse than its one-year historical average discount of 11.88%.

Matthew A. Iannucci has been running the fund for 7 years and currently receives a manager quality ranking of 90 (0=worst, 99=best). If you desire an average level of risk, then this fund may be an option.

Data Date	Investment Rating	Net Assets ($Mil)	Price	Perfor-mance Rating/Pts	Total Return Y-T-D	Risk Rating/Pts
12-15	C	135.49	1.76	C+ / 5.7	1.10%	C+ / 6.5
2014	C-	138.20	1.80	D+ / 2.8	-4.64%	B- / 7.5
2013	C	141.47	2.03	C+ / 5.6	4.28%	B- / 7.4
2012	C-	131.15	2.14	C- / 4.1	11.65%	B- / 7.3
2011	C+	126.90	2.13	B+ / 8.3	8.37%	C+ / 6.0
2010	D-	127.31	2.20	D+ / 2.7	23.34%	D+ / 2.3

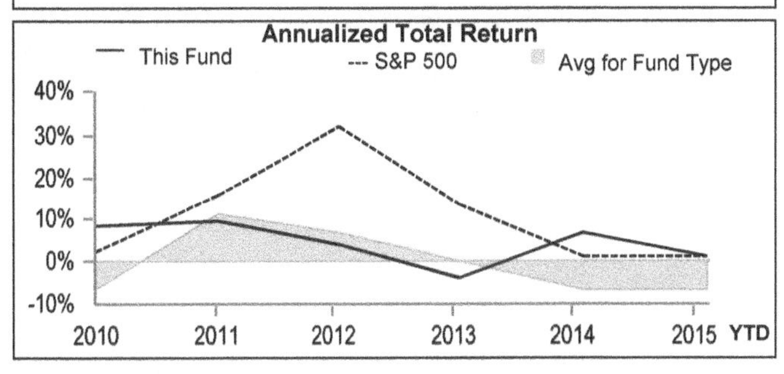

Mexico Equity & Income Fund (MXE) D+ Weak

Fund Family: Pichardo Asset Management SA de CV
Fund Type: Foreign
Inception Date: August 14, 1990

Major Rating Factors: Mexico Equity & Income Fund receives a TheStreet.com Investment Rating of D+ (Weak). The fund currently has a performance rating of C- (Fair) based on an annualized return of -0.67% over the last three years and a total return of -8.41% year to date 2015. Factored into the performance evaluation is an expense ratio of 1.76% (above average).

The fund's risk rating is currently C (Fair). It carries a beta of 0.85, meaning the fund's expected move will be 8.5% for every 10% move in the market. Volatility, as measured by both the semi-deviation and a drawdown factor, is considered average. As of December 31, 2015, Mexico Equity & Income Fund traded at a discount of 14.06% below its net asset value, which is better than its one-year historical average discount of 12.13%.

Maria-Eugenia Pichardo has been running the fund for 26 years and currently receives a manager quality ranking of 39 (0=worst, 99=best). If you desire an average level of risk, then this fund may be an option.

Data Date	Investment Rating	Net Assets ($Mil)	Price	Perfor-mance Rating/Pts	Total Return Y-T-D	Risk Rating/Pts
12-15	D+	102.45	10.76	C- / 3.5	-8.41%	C / 5.5
2014	C+	126.00	12.61	C+ / 6.6	-2.80%	B- / 7.0
2013	B-	109.34	14.88	B- / 7.1	11.45%	B- / 7.7
2012	A+	86.97	14.25	A+ / 9.7	54.56%	B / 8.0
2011	D+	89.18	9.95	C / 4.7	-14.42%	C+ / 5.7
2010	C-	74.61	11.33	B+ / 8.5	48.41%	D- / 1.5

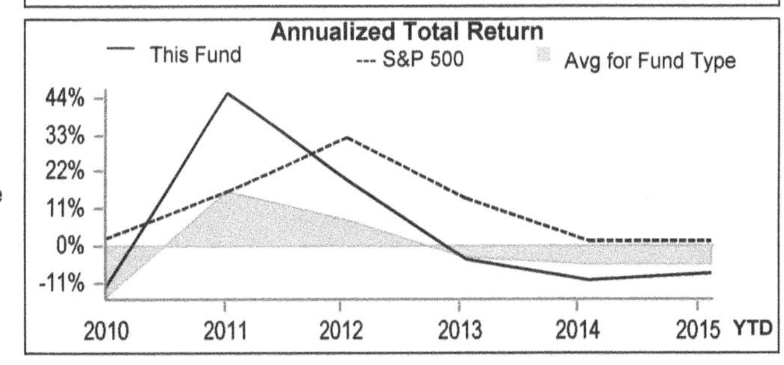

Mexico Fund (MXF) D Weak

Fund Family: Impulsora Del Fondo Mexico SA De CV
Fund Type: Foreign
Inception Date: June 3, 1981

Major Rating Factors:
Disappointing performance is the major factor driving the D (Weak) TheStreet.com Investment Rating for Mexico Fund. The fund currently has a performance rating of D (Weak) based on an annualized return of -9.82% over the last three years and a total return of -11.91% year to date 2015. Factored into the performance evaluation is an expense ratio of 1.57% (above average).

The fund's risk rating is currently C (Fair). It carries a beta of 0.94, meaning that its performance tracks fairly well with that of the overall stock market. Volatility, as measured by both the semi-deviation and a drawdown factor, is considered average. As of December 31, 2015, Mexico Fund traded at a discount of 11.92% below its net asset value, which is better than its one-year historical average discount of 6.51%.

Alberto Osorio Morales has been running the fund for 25 years and currently receives a manager quality ranking of 13 (0=worst, 99=best). This fund offers an average level of risk but investors looking for strong performance will be frustrated.

Data Date	Investment Rating	Net Assets ($Mil)	Price	Perfor-mance Rating/Pts	Total Return Y-T-D	Risk Rating/Pts
12-15	D	402.53	16.62	D / 1.8	-11.91%	C / 4.8
2014	D	411.10	20.80	C- / 3.1	-20.05%	C / 5.4
2013	C+	437.60	29.30	C+ / 6.4	4.49%	B- / 7.0
2012	A	339.05	29.02	A+ / 9.7	52.02%	B- / 7.5
2011	C+	318.50	21.85	C+ / 6.9	-12.80%	B- / 7.3
2010	B-	383.24	28.27	B+ / 8.7	42.37%	C- / 3.8

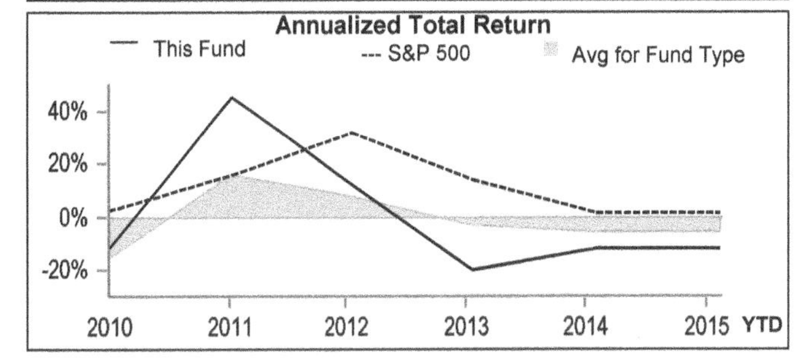

MFS CA Muni (CCA) A- Excellent

Fund Family: MFS Investment Management
Fund Type: Municipal - Single State
Inception Date: October 29, 1999

Major Rating Factors:
Exceptional performance is the major factor driving the A- (Excellent) TheStreet.com Investment Rating for MFS CA Muni. The fund currently has a performance rating of A- (Excellent) based on an annualized return of 4.50% over the last three years and a total return of 15.02% year to date 2015. Factored into the performance evaluation is an expense ratio of 2.38% (high).

The fund's risk rating is currently B- (Good). It carries a beta of 2.16, meaning it is expected to move 21.6% for every 10% move in the market. Volatility, as measured by both the semi-deviation and a drawdown factor, is considered low. As of December 31, 2015, MFS CA Muni traded at a discount of 7.21% below its net asset value, which is worse than its one-year historical average discount of 10.24%.

Geoffrey L. Schechter has been running the fund for 9 years and currently receives a manager quality ranking of 52 (0=worst, 99=best). If you desire only a moderate level of risk and strong performance, then this fund is an excellent option.

Data Date	Investment Rating	Net Assets ($Mil)	Price	Performance Rating/Pts	Total Return Y-T-D	Risk Rating/Pts
12-15	A-	34.97	11.84	A- / 9.0	15.02%	B- / 7.4
2014	C+	34.70	10.91	C+ / 5.8	14.19%	B- / 7.9
2013	C	34.84	9.99	C / 4.7	-12.80%	B / 8.0
2012	B	33.13	12.13	B- / 7.2	14.70%	B / 8.3
2011	B+	31.00	11.04	B+ / 8.7	19.03%	B / 8.3
2010	D	30.90	10.16	D / 1.6	-1.39%	C+ / 5.6

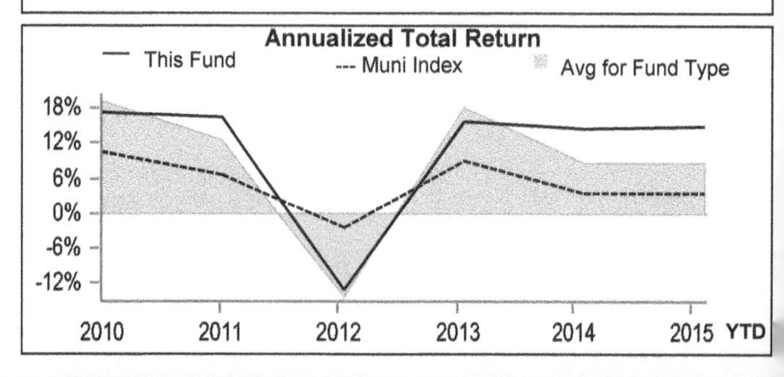

MFS Charter Income Trust (MCR) C- Fair

Fund Family: MFS Investment Management
Fund Type: General - Investment Grade
Inception Date: July 20, 1989

Major Rating Factors: Middle of the road best describes MFS Charter Income Trust whose TheStreet.com Investment Rating is currently a C- (Fair). The fund currently has a performance rating of C- (Fair) based on an annualized return of -2.60% over the last three years and a total return of -8.75% year to date 2015. Factored into the performance evaluation is an expense ratio of 0.87% (low).

The fund's risk rating is currently B- (Good). It carries a beta of 0.86, meaning the fund's expected move will be 8.6% for every 10% move in the market. Volatility, as measured by both the semi-deviation and a drawdown factor, is considered low. As of December 31, 2015, MFS Charter Income Trust traded at a discount of 15.05% below its net asset value, which is better than its one-year historical average discount of 12.44%.

Richard O. Hawkins has been running the fund for 12 years and currently receives a manager quality ranking of 42 (0=worst, 99=best). If you desire an average level of risk, then this fund may be an option.

Data Date	Investment Rating	Net Assets ($Mil)	Price	Performance Rating/Pts	Total Return Y-T-D	Risk Rating/Pts
12-15	C-	548.53	7.62	C- / 3.1	-8.75%	B- / 7.0
2014	C+	550.80	9.19	C / 5.2	9.32%	B / 8.4
2013	C	569.40	9.05	C / 4.5	-6.27%	B / 8.5
2012	B-	545.95	10.12	C+ / 5.9	20.27%	B / 8.8
2011	B-	535.80	9.15	C+ / 5.8	7.39%	B / 8.9
2010	A-	525.25	9.42	B / 7.6	11.32%	C+ / 6.6

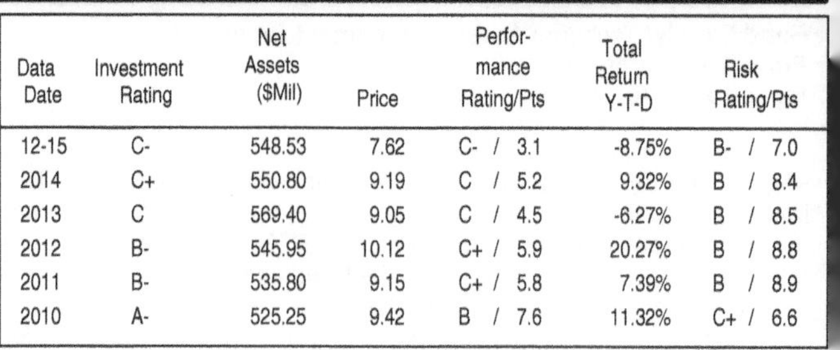

MFS Government Markets Income Trus (MGF) C Fair

Fund Family: MFS Investment Management
Fund Type: Global
Inception Date: May 28, 1987

Major Rating Factors: Middle of the road best describes MFS Government Markets Income Trus whose TheStreet.com Investment Rating is currently a C (Fair). The fund currently has a performance rating of C- (Fair) based on an annualized return of -0.97% over the last three years and a total return of -0.38% year to date 2015. Factored into the performance evaluation is an expense ratio of 0.75% (very low).

The fund's risk rating is currently B- (Good). It carries a beta of 0.58, meaning the fund's expected move will be 5.8% for every 10% move in the market. Volatility, as measured by both the semi-deviation and a drawdown factor, is considered low. As of December 31, 2015, MFS Government Markets Income Trus traded at a discount of 5.53% below its net asset value, which is worse than its one-year historical average discount of 6.33%.

Geoffrey L. Schechter currently receives a manager quality ranking of 78 (0=worst, 99=best). If you desire an average level of risk, then this fund may be an option.

Data Date	Investment Rating	Net Assets ($Mil)	Price	Performance Rating/Pts	Total Return Y-T-D	Risk Rating/Pts
12-15	C	197.83	5.30	C- / 4.0	-0.38%	B- / 7.5
2014	C-	197.40	5.67	C- / 3.2	5.79%	B / 8.0
2013	C-	212.66	5.73	D+ / 2.9	-9.12%	B / 8.3
2012	C-	226.95	6.85	D+ / 2.3	3.16%	B / 8.6
2011	C	228.00	6.96	C- / 3.8	11.26%	B / 8.4
2010	C+	232.78	6.80	C / 4.6	-1.88%	B- / 7.6

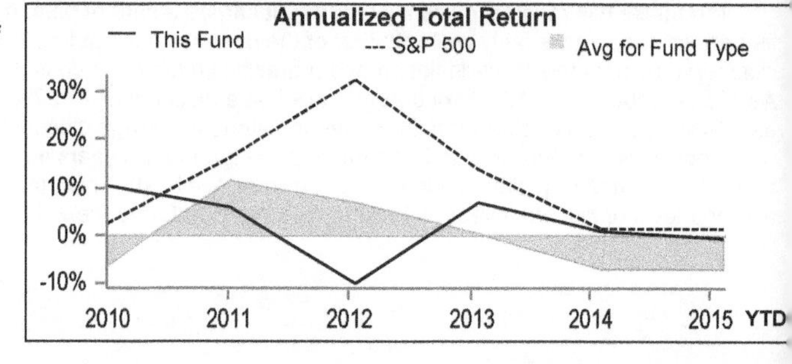

MFS High Inc Muni Tr (CXE) C+ Fair

Fund Family: MFS Investment Management
Fund Type: Municipal - High Yield
Inception Date: February 16, 1989

Major Rating Factors: Middle of the road best describes MFS High Inc Muni Tr whose TheStreet.com Investment Rating is currently a C+ (Fair). The fund currently has a performance rating of C+ (Fair) based on an annualized return of 1.75% over the last three years and a total return of 8.37% year to date 2015. Factored into the performance evaluation is an expense ratio of 2.19% (high).

The fund's risk rating is currently B- (Good). It carries a beta of 2.42, meaning it is expected to move 24.2% for every 10% move in the market. Volatility, as measured by both the semi-deviation and a drawdown factor, is considered low. As of December 31, 2015, MFS High Inc Muni Tr traded at a discount of 9.58% below its net asset value, which is worse than its one-year historical average discount of 11.07%.

Gary A. Lasman has been running the fund for 9 years and currently receives a manager quality ranking of 33 (0=worst, 99=best). If you desire an average level of risk, then this fund may be an option.

Data Date	Investment Rating	Net Assets ($Mil)	Price	Performance Rating/Pts	Total Return Y-T-D	Risk Rating/Pts
12-15	C+	169.93	4.91	C+ / 6.5	8.37%	B- / 7.2
2014	C+	169.20	4.88	C+ / 6.0	14.71%	B- / 7.4
2013	C-	172.65	4.47	C / 4.5	-14.38%	B- / 7.6
2012	B+	163.71	5.46	B / 8.1	13.57%	B / 8.6
2011	A+	152.20	5.35	A+ / 9.9	21.99%	B / 8.7
2010	D+	153.04	4.71	C- / 3.2	5.60%	C / 5.0

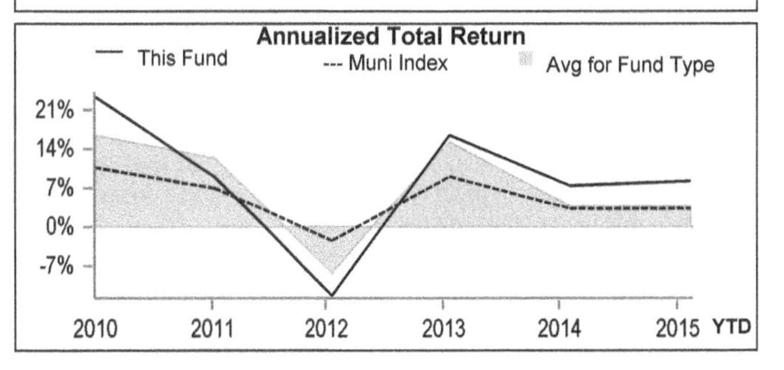

MFS High Yield Muni Trust (CMU) B- Good

Fund Family: MFS Investment Management
Fund Type: Municipal - High Yield
Inception Date: March 19, 1987

Major Rating Factors: MFS High Yield Muni Trust receives a TheStreet.com Investment Rating of B- (Good). The fund currently has a performance rating of C+ (Fair) based on an annualized return of 2.51% over the last three years and a total return of 8.49% year to date 2015. Factored into the performance evaluation is an expense ratio of 2.01% (high).

The fund's risk rating is currently B- (Good). It carries a beta of 2.86, meaning it is expected to move 28.6% for every 10% move in the market. Volatility, as measured by both the semi-deviation and a drawdown factor, is considered low. As of December 31, 2015, MFS High Yield Muni Trust traded at a discount of 7.39% below its net asset value, which is worse than its one-year historical average discount of 9.52%.

Gary A. Lasman has been running the fund for 9 years and currently receives a manager quality ranking of 31 (0=worst, 99=best). If you desire an average level of risk, then this fund may be an option.

Data Date	Investment Rating	Net Assets ($Mil)	Price	Performance Rating/Pts	Total Return Y-T-D	Risk Rating/Pts
12-15	B-	137.26	4.51	C+ / 6.9	8.49%	B- / 7.1
2014	C	136.70	4.39	C / 5.5	10.84%	B- / 7.3
2013	C	139.46	4.14	C+ / 5.6	-11.22%	B- / 7.7
2012	B+	132.05	4.86	B / 7.8	13.58%	B / 8.6
2011	A+	122.30	4.71	A+ / 9.8	21.29%	B / 8.8
2010	C-	122.46	4.32	C- / 3.7	5.92%	C+ / 5.7

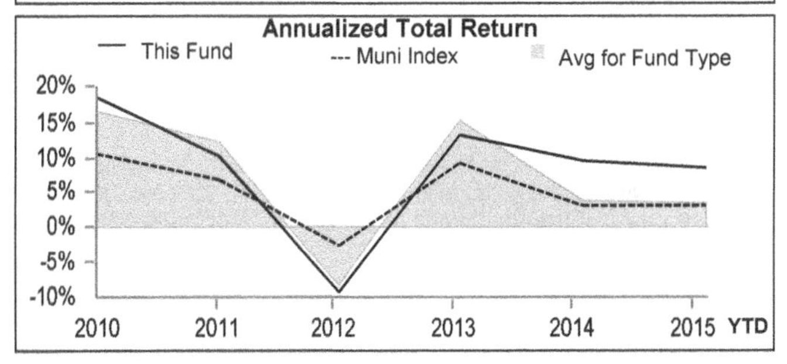

MFS Interm High Inc (CIF) C- Fair

Fund Family: MFS Investment Management
Fund Type: Corporate - High Yield
Inception Date: July 21, 1988

Major Rating Factors: Middle of the road best describes MFS Interm High Inc whose TheStreet.com Investment Rating is currently a C- (Fair). The fund currently has a performance rating of C- (Fair) based on an annualized return of -1.98% over the last three years and a total return of -3.29% year to date 2015. Factored into the performance evaluation is an expense ratio of 1.61% (above average).

The fund's risk rating is currently C+ (Fair). It carries a beta of 1.64, meaning it is expected to move 16.4% for every 10% move in the market. Volatility, as measured by both the semi-deviation and a drawdown factor, is considered low. As of December 31, 2015, MFS Interm High Inc traded at a discount of 10.42% below its net asset value, which is worse than its one-year historical average discount of 12.26%.

David P. Cole has been running the fund for 9 years and currently receives a manager quality ranking of 41 (0=worst, 99=best). If you desire an average level of risk, then this fund may be an option.

Data Date	Investment Rating	Net Assets ($Mil)	Price	Performance Rating/Pts	Total Return Y-T-D	Risk Rating/Pts
12-15	C-	65.10	2.32	C- / 3.4	-3.29%	C+ / 6.5
2014	C-	65.40	2.66	C- / 3.8	-0.90%	B / 8.0
2013	C+	66.99	2.89	C / 5.5	-1.37%	B / 8.3
2012	B	61.96	3.07	B- / 7.2	18.70%	B / 8.7
2011	B+	60.50	2.94	B+ / 8.7	7.70%	B- / 7.8
2010	C	58.49	2.95	B / 8.0	14.37%	C- / 3.0

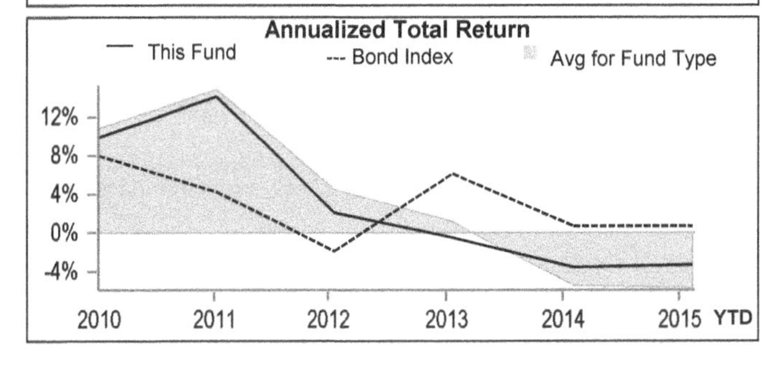

MFS Intermediate Income Trust (MIN) C- Fair

Fund Family: MFS Investment Management
Fund Type: Global
Inception Date: March 17, 1988

Major Rating Factors: Middle of the road best describes MFS Intermediate Income Trust whose TheStreet.com Investment Rating is currently a C- (Fair). The fund currently has a performance rating of C- (Fair) based on an annualized return of -2.58% over the last three years and a total return of 3.23% year to date 2015. Factored into the performance evaluation is an expense ratio of 0.65% (very low).

The fund's risk rating is currently C+ (Fair). It carries a beta of 0.61, meaning the fund's expected move will be 6.1% for every 10% move in the market. Volatility, as measured by both the semi-deviation and a drawdown factor, is considered low. As of December 31, 2015, MFS Intermediate Income Trust traded at a discount of 7.68% below its net asset value, which is worse than its one-year historical average discount of 9.25%.

James J. Calmas has been running the fund for 14 years and currently receives a manager quality ranking of 70 (0=worst, 99=best). If you desire an average level of risk, then this fund may be an option.

Data Date	Investment Rating	Net Assets ($Mil)	Price	Performance Rating/Pts	Total Return Y-T-D	Risk Rating/Pts
12-15	C-	641.94	4.57	C- / 3.8	3.23%	C+ / 6.6
2014	D+	644.50	4.78	D+ / 2.5	0.74%	B- / 7.2
2013	C-	717.14	5.18	D+ / 2.6	-12.91%	B / 8.2
2012	C-	745.54	6.44	D+ / 2.9	10.74%	B / 8.5
2011	C	735.30	6.30	C- / 4.1	8.52%	B / 8.7
2010	B-	792.81	6.31	C+ / 6.4	2.59%	B- / 7.6

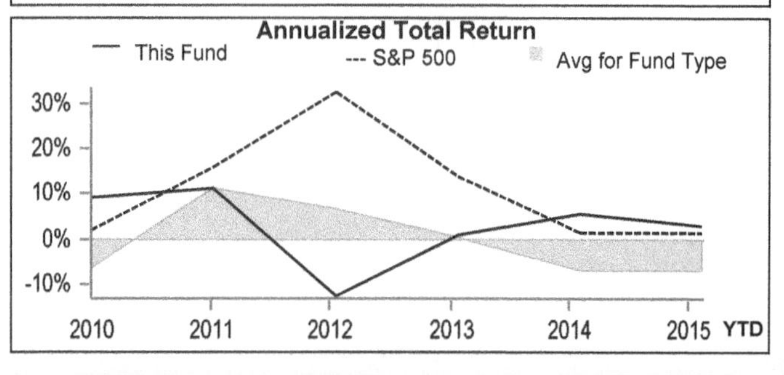

MFS Invst Gr Muni Tr (CXH) B Good

Fund Family: MFS Investment Management
Fund Type: Municipal - National
Inception Date: May 26, 1989

Major Rating Factors: Strong performance is the major factor driving the B (Good) TheStreet.com Investment Rating for MFS Invst Gr Muni Tr. The fund currently has a performance rating of B (Good) based on an annualized return of 3.02% over the last three years and a total return of 11.40% year to date 2015. Factored into the performance evaluation is an expense ratio of 1.74% (above average).

The fund's risk rating is currently B- (Good). It carries a beta of 1.85, meaning it is expected to move 18.5% for every 10% move in the market. Volatility, as measured by both the semi-deviation and a drawdown factor, is considered low. As of December 31, 2015, MFS Invst Gr Muni Tr traded at a discount of 6.93% below its net asset value, which is worse than its one-year historical average discount of 9.94%.

Geoffrey L. Schechter has been running the fund for 9 years and currently receives a manager quality ranking of 53 (0=worst, 99=best). If you desire only a moderate level of risk and strong performance, then this fund is an excellent option.

Data Date	Investment Rating	Net Assets ($Mil)	Price	Performance Rating/Pts	Total Return Y-T-D	Risk Rating/Pts
12-15	B	122.53	9.94	B / 7.8	11.40%	B- / 7.4
2014	C+	121.50	9.37	C+ / 5.8	14.71%	B- / 7.6
2013	C	122.60	8.62	C / 4.4	-14.80%	B- / 7.9
2012	B-	118.72	10.46	C+ / 6.2	12.75%	B / 8.6
2011	A	111.90	9.76	A- / 9.2	20.78%	B / 8.8
2010	C-	111.17	8.82	C- / 3.8	1.97%	C+ / 5.9

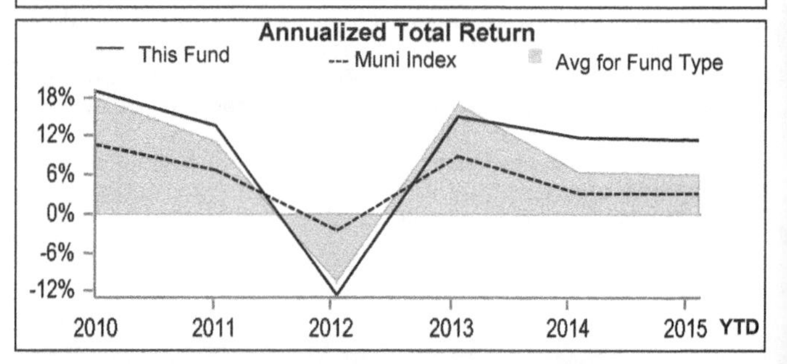

MFS Multimarket Income Trust (MMT) C- Fair

Fund Family: MFS Investment Management
Fund Type: General Bond
Inception Date: March 12, 1987

Major Rating Factors: Middle of the road best describes MFS Multimarket Income Trust whose TheStreet.com Investment Rating is currently a C- (Fair). The fund currently has a performance rating of C- (Fair) based on an annualized return of -1.13% over the last three years and a total return of -7.75% year to date 2015. Factored into the performance evaluation is an expense ratio of 0.98% (low).

The fund's risk rating is currently C+ (Fair). It carries a beta of 0.94, meaning that its performance tracks fairly well with that of the overall stock market. Volatility, as measured by both the semi-deviation and a drawdown factor, is considered low. As of December 31, 2015, MFS Multimarket Income Trust traded at a discount of 14.71% below its net asset value, which is better than its one-year historical average discount of 12.60%.

Richard O. Hawkins currently receives a manager quality ranking of 47 (0=worst, 99=best). If you desire an average level of risk, then this fund may be an option.

Data Date	Investment Rating	Net Assets ($Mil)	Price	Performance Rating/Pts	Total Return Y-T-D	Risk Rating/Pts
12-15	C-	570.45	5.51	C- / 3.4	-7.75%	C+ / 6.8
2014	C	566.70	6.50	C / 4.7	6.40%	B / 8.2
2013	C+	609.78	6.62	C / 5.1	-1.38%	B / 8.3
2012	C+	564.45	7.28	C / 4.9	16.09%	B / 8.5
2011	B	558.30	6.72	C+ / 6.6	7.63%	B+ / 9.0
2010	B+	563.16	6.90	B / 8.2	15.16%	C+ / 5.8

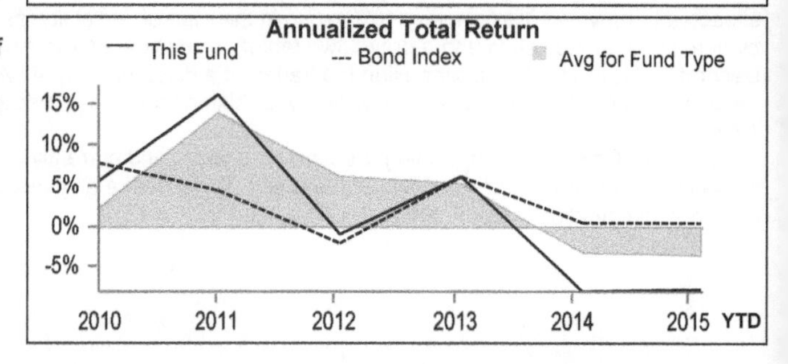

MFS Municipal Income Trust (MFM) C+ Fair

Fund Family: MFS Investment Management
Fund Type: Municipal - National
Inception Date: November 25, 1986

Data Date	Investment Rating	Net Assets ($Mil)	Price	Performance Rating/Pts	Total Return Y-T-D	Risk Rating/Pts
12-15	C+	302.37	6.80	C+ / 6.3	8.67%	B- / 7.2
2014	C+	300.10	6.64	C+ / 5.9	13.87%	B- / 7.4
2013	C-	309.67	6.25	C- / 3.9	-16.79%	B- / 7.7
2012	B+	271.03	7.62	B- / 7.5	14.98%	B / 8.6
2011	A+	274.80	7.11	A+ / 9.7	18.56%	B / 8.7
2010	C	273.60	6.41	C / 4.6	1.91%	C+ / 6.3

Major Rating Factors: Middle of the road best describes MFS Municipal Income Trust whose TheStreet.com Investment Rating is currently a C+ (Fair). The fund currently has a performance rating of C+ (Fair) based on an annualized return of 0.98% over the last three years and a total return of 8.67% year to date 2015. Factored into the performance evaluation is an expense ratio of 1.73% (above average).

The fund's risk rating is currently B- (Good). It carries a beta of 1.99, meaning it is expected to move 19.9% for every 10% move in the market. Volatility, as measured by both the semi-deviation and a drawdown factor, is considered low. As of December 31, 2015, MFS Municipal Income Trust traded at a discount of 8.36% below its net asset value, which is worse than its one-year historical average discount of 10.90%.

Geoffrey L. Schechter has been running the fund for 23 years and currently receives a manager quality ranking of 38 (0=worst, 99=best). If you desire an average level of risk, then this fund may be an option.

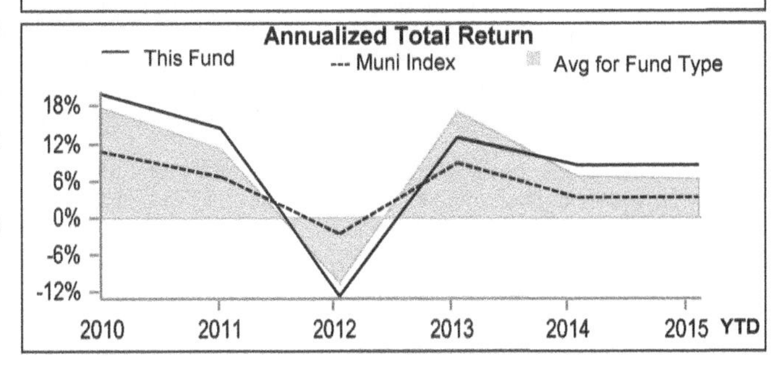

MFS Special Value Trust (MFV) D+ Weak

Fund Family: MFS Investment Management
Fund Type: Growth and Income
Inception Date: November 17, 1989

Data Date	Investment Rating	Net Assets ($Mil)	Price	Performance Rating/Pts	Total Return Y-T-D	Risk Rating/Pts
12-15	D+	47.90	5.31	C- / 3.5	-18.23%	C+ / 5.6
2014	C	47.70	7.27	C+ / 6.4	12.76%	C+ / 5.8
2013	C+	49.73	7.11	C+ / 5.8	10.30%	B- / 7.8
2012	C	46.44	6.91	C / 5.2	19.18%	B- / 7.8
2011	B	45.70	6.43	B- / 7.5	-3.58%	B- / 7.9
2010	C	49.44	7.38	C+ / 6.6	15.54%	C- / 3.8

Major Rating Factors: MFS Special Value Trust receives a TheStreet.com Investment Rating of D+ (Weak). The fund currently has a performance rating of C- (Fair) based on an annualized return of 0.38% over the last three years and a total return of -18.23% year to date 2015. Factored into the performance evaluation is an expense ratio of 1.35% (average).

The fund's risk rating is currently C+ (Fair). It carries a beta of 0.60, meaning the fund's expected move will be 6.0% for every 10% move in the market. Volatility, as measured by both the semi-deviation and a drawdown factor, is considered low. As of December 31, 2015, MFS Special Value Trust traded at a discount of 7.49% below its net asset value, which is better than its one-year historical average discount of 4.20%.

David P. Cole currently receives a manager quality ranking of 22 (0=worst, 99=best). If you desire an average level of risk, then this fund may be an option.

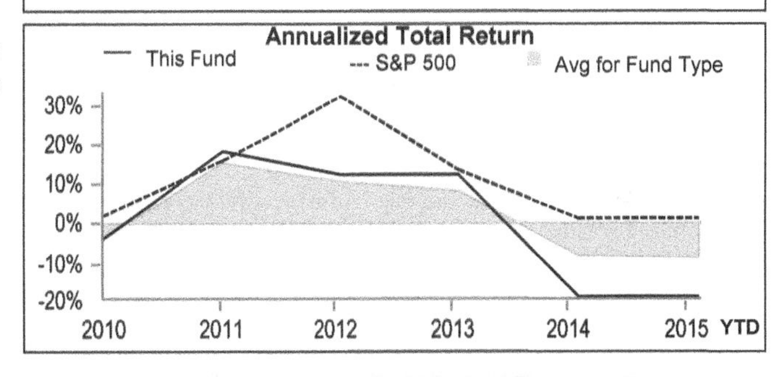

Miller/Howard High Income Equity (XHIEX) E+ Very Weak

Fund Family: Miller/Howard Investments Inc
Fund Type: Global
Inception Date: November 24, 2014

Data Date	Investment Rating	Net Assets ($Mil)	Price	Performance Rating/Pts	Total Return Y-T-D	Risk Rating/Pts
12-15	E+	0.00	11.46	E- / 0.2	-36.85%	C- / 3.4

Major Rating Factors:
Very poor performance is the major factor driving the E+ (Very Weak) TheStreet.com Investment Rating for Miller/Howard High Income Equity. The fund currently has a performance rating of E- (Very Weak) based on an annualized return of 0.00% over the last three years and a total return of -36.85% year to date 2015.

The fund's risk rating is currently C- (Fair). It carries a beta of 0.00, meaning the fund's expected move will be 0.0% for every 10% move in the market. Volatility, as measured by both the semi-deviation and a drawdown factor, is considered average. As of December 31, 2015, Miller/Howard High Income Equity traded at a discount of 11.09% below its net asset value, which is better than its one-year historical average discount of 4.87%.

Lowell G. Miller has been running the fund for 2 years and currently receives a manager quality ranking of 1 (0=worst, 99=best). This fund offers an average level of risk but investors looking for strong performance will be frustrated.

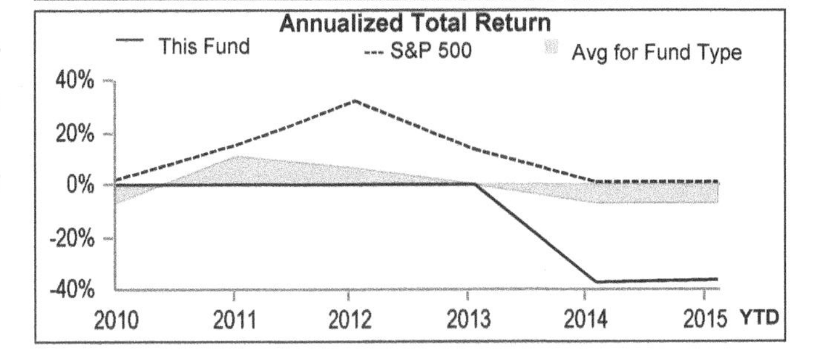

* Denotes ETF Fund

Morgan Stanley Asia Pacific Fund (APF) C- Fair

Fund Family: Morgan Stanley Investment Managemen
Fund Type: Foreign
Inception Date: July 25, 1994

Major Rating Factors: Middle of the road best describes Morgan Stanley Asia Pacific Fund whose TheStreet.com Investment Rating is currently a C- (Fair). The fund currently has a performance rating of C- (Fair) based on an annualized return of -0.32% over the last three years and a total return of -5.37% year to date 2015. Factored into the performance evaluation is an expense ratio of 1.32% (average).

The fund's risk rating is currently C+ (Fair). It carries a beta of 0.86, meaning the fund's expected move will be 8.6% for every 10% move in the market. Volatility, as measured by both the semi-deviation and a drawdown factor, is considered low. As of December 31, 2015, Morgan Stanley Asia Pacific Fund traded at a discount of 10.95% below its net asset value, which is worse than its one-year historical average discount of 11.64%.

Munib M. Madni has been running the fund for 4 years and currently receives a manager quality ranking of 37 (0=worst, 99=best). If you desire an average level of risk, then this fund may be an option.

Data Date	Investment Rating	Net Assets ($Mil)	Price	Perfor-mance Rating/Pts	Total Return Y-T-D	Risk Rating/Pts
12-15	C-	230.44	13.83	C- / 3.8	-5.37%	C+ / 6.7
2014	C	254.60	14.85	C- / 4.1	-2.40%	B / 8.0
2013	C-	316.88	16.56	C- / 3.7	8.09%	B- / 7.1
2012	D+	301.88	14.98	C- / 3.1	14.90%	B- / 7.1
2011	C-	306.30	13.10	C- / 3.6	-15.75%	C+ / 6.8
2010	C-	484.77	16.98	C / 5.5	17.90%	C- / 3.9

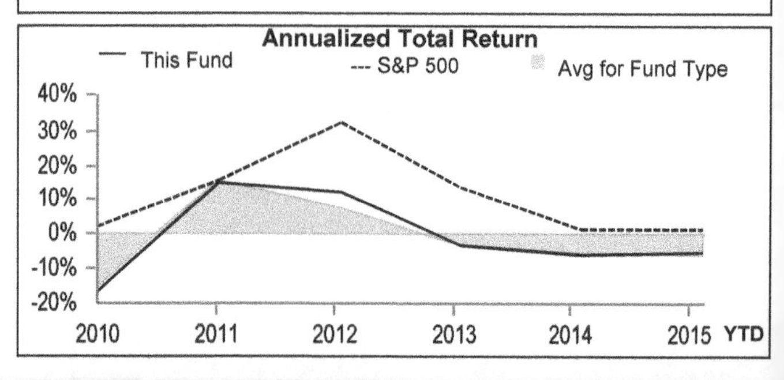

Morgan Stanley China A Share Fund (CAF) C Fair

Fund Family: Morgan Stanley Investment Managemen
Fund Type: Foreign
Inception Date: September 28, 2006

Major Rating Factors: Strong performance is the major factor driving the C (Fair) TheStreet.com Investment Rating for Morgan Stanley China A Share Fund. The fund currently has a performance rating of B (Good) based on an annualized return of 11.03% over the last three years and a total return of 2.43% year to date 2015. Factored into the performance evaluation is an expense ratio of 1.80% (above average).

The fund's risk rating is currently C (Fair). It carries a beta of 0.53, meaning the fund's expected move will be 5.3% for every 10% move in the market. Volatility, as measured by both the semi-deviation and a drawdown factor, is considered average. As of December 31, 2015, Morgan Stanley China A Share Fund traded at a discount of 15.17% below its net asset value, which is worse than its one-year historical average discount of 19.00%.

Gary Cheung currently receives a manager quality ranking of 94 (0=worst, 99=best). If you desire an average level of risk and strong performance, then this fund is a good option.

Data Date	Investment Rating	Net Assets ($Mil)	Price	Perfor-mance Rating/Pts	Total Return Y-T-D	Risk Rating/Pts
12-15	C	759.33	19.91	B / 8.1	2.43%	C / 4.5
2014	B+	565.60	30.37	A / 9.5	40.76%	C+ / 6.2
2013	D	458.33	23.81	D+ / 2.3	-6.02%	C+ / 5.6
2012	D	491.37	24.05	C- / 3.2	23.62%	C+ / 5.8
2011	D	493.20	19.35	D+ / 2.5	-27.23%	C / 5.3
2010	D	397.04	27.35	C- / 3.9	-0.73%	C- / 3.3

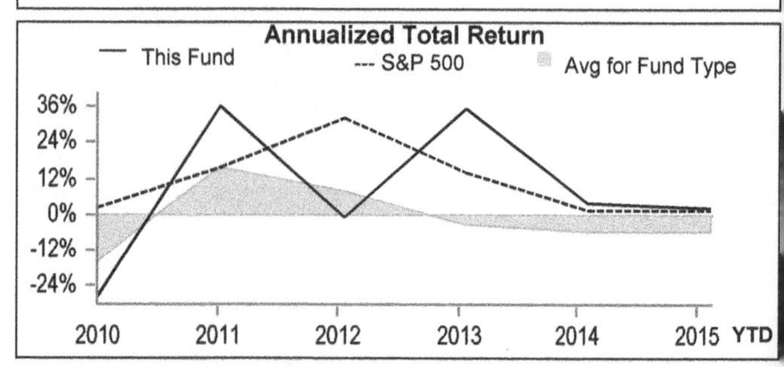

Morgan Stanley Emerging Markets (MSF) C- Fair

Fund Family: Morgan Stanley Investment Managemen
Fund Type: Emerging Market
Inception Date: October 25, 1991

Major Rating Factors:
Disappointing performance is the major factor driving the C- (Fair) TheStreet.com Investment Rating for Morgan Stanley Emerging Markets. The fund currently has a performance rating of D+ (Weak) based on an annualized return of -6.46% over the last three years and a total return of -10.20% year to date 2015. Factored into the performance evaluation is an expense ratio of 1.55% (average).

The fund's risk rating is currently B- (Good). It carries a beta of 0.90, meaning that its performance tracks fairly well with that of the overall stock market. Volatility, as measured by both the semi-deviation and a drawdown factor, is considered low. As of December 31, 2015, Morgan Stanley Emerging Markets traded at a discount of 10.08% below its net asset value, which is worse than its one-year historical average discount of 10.71%.

Ruchir Sharma has been running the fund for 25 years and currently receives a manager quality ranking of 69 (0=worst, 99=best). This fund offers only a moderate level of risk but investors looking for strong performance are still waiting.

Data Date	Investment Rating	Net Assets ($Mil)	Price	Perfor-mance Rating/Pts	Total Return Y-T-D	Risk Rating/Pts
12-15	C-	233.61	12.85	D+ / 2.4	-10.20%	B- / 7.2
2014	C-	250.00	14.55	C- / 3.3	-2.44%	B / 8.1
2013	D+	235.27	15.48	D / 2.1	-5.31%	B- / 7.5
2012	C-	262.63	15.50	C- / 3.9	19.93%	B- / 7.3
2011	C-	248.00	12.92	C / 4.5	-18.95%	B- / 7.5
2010	D	240.63	16.36	C / 4.5	17.74%	D+ / 2.7

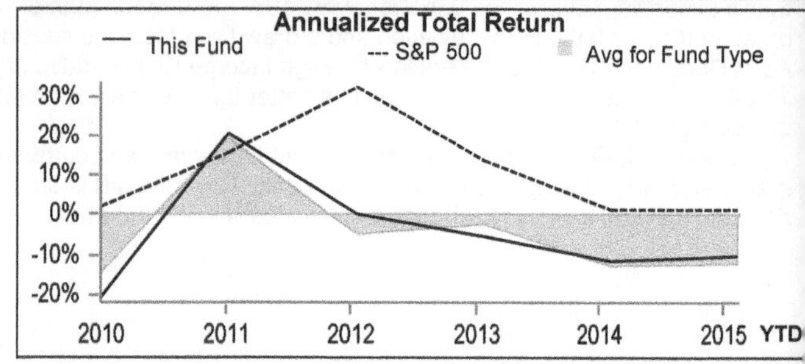

Morgan Stanley Emerging Mkts Debt (MSD) C- Fair

Fund Family: Morgan Stanley Investment Managemen
Fund Type: Emerging Market
Inception Date: July 16, 1993

Major Rating Factors: Middle of the road best describes Morgan Stanley Emerging Mkts Debt whose TheStreet.com Investment Rating is currently a C- (Fair). The fund currently has a performance rating of C- (Fair) based on an annualized return of -4.44% over the last three years and a total return of 1.15% year to date 2015. Factored into the performance evaluation is an expense ratio of 1.14% (low).

The fund's risk rating is currently C+ (Fair). It carries a beta of 0.71, meaning the fund's expected move will be 7.1% for every 10% move in the market. Volatility, as measured by both the semi-deviation and a drawdown factor, is considered low. As of December 31, 2015, Morgan Stanley Emerging Mkts Debt traded at a discount of 14.98% below its net asset value, which is worse than its one-year historical average discount of 15.71%.

Eric J. Baurmeister has been running the fund for 14 years and currently receives a manager quality ranking of 62 (0=worst, 99=best). If you desire an average level of risk, then this fund may be an option.

Data Date	Investment Rating	Net Assets ($Mil)	Price	Performance Rating/Pts	Total Return Y-T-D	Risk Rating/Pts
12-15	C-	242.97	8.57	C- / 3.2	1.15%	C+ / 6.4
2014	C-	256.30	9.09	C- / 3.1	-0.05%	B- / 7.3
2013	C-	309.65	9.54	C- / 3.3	-13.38%	B- / 7.6
2012	B-	286.47	11.95	C+ / 6.9	25.75%	B / 8.2
2011	B-	273.30	10.41	C+ / 6.8	4.57%	B / 8.1
2010	B-	267.21	10.48	B- / 7.5	13.75%	C / 5.1

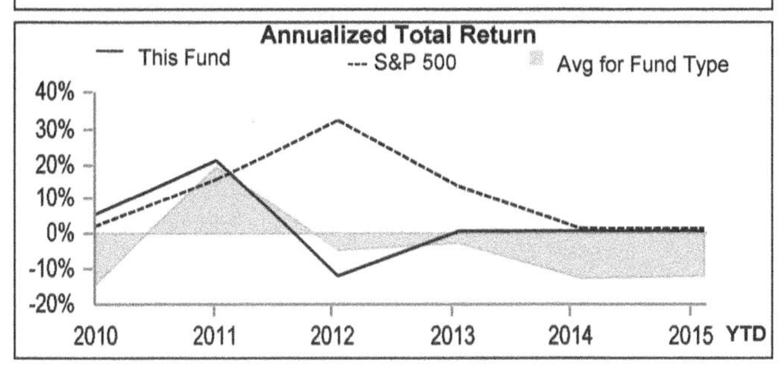

Morgan Stanley Emg Mkts Dom Debt (EDD) D- Weak

Fund Family: Morgan Stanley Investment Managemen
Fund Type: Emerging Market
Inception Date: April 24, 2007

Major Rating Factors:
Very poor performance is the major factor driving the D- (Weak) TheStreet.com Investment Rating for Morgan Stanley Emg Mkts Dom Debt. The fund currently has a performance rating of E+ (Very Weak) based on an annualized return of -19.03% over the last three years and a total return of -27.28% year to date 2015. Factored into the performance evaluation is an expense ratio of 2.20% (high).

The fund's risk rating is currently C (Fair). It carries a beta of 1.32, meaning it is expected to move 13.2% for every 10% move in the market. Volatility, as measured by both the semi-deviation and a drawdown factor, is considered average. As of December 31, 2015, Morgan Stanley Emg Mkts Dom Debt traded at a discount of 17.07% below its net asset value, which is better than its one-year historical average discount of 14.71%.

Eric J. Baurmeister has been running the fund for 9 years and currently receives a manager quality ranking of 12 (0=worst, 99=best). This fund offers an average level of risk but investors looking for strong performance will be frustrated.

Data Date	Investment Rating	Net Assets ($Mil)	Price	Performance Rating/Pts	Total Return Y-T-D	Risk Rating/Pts
12-15	D-	954.47	6.80	E+ / 0.9	-27.28%	C / 4.8
2014	D	950.80	10.56	D / 1.9	-12.11%	C+ / 6.1
2013	D+	1,172.02	13.02	D+ / 2.3	-15.47%	B- / 7.2
2012	C+	1,283.10	16.84	C+ / 6.6	19.69%	B- / 7.6
2011	C	1,153.50	14.15	C / 5.4	-2.29%	B- / 7.6
2010	B+	1,264.52	16.15	B / 7.6	27.14%	C+ / 5.8

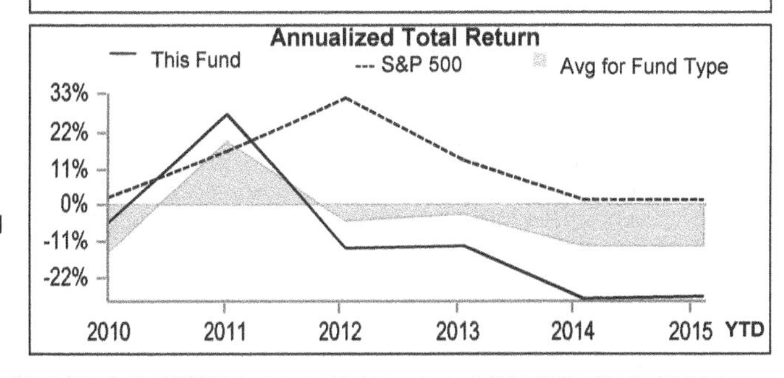

Morgan Stanley Income Sec (ICB) C+ Fair

Fund Family: Morgan Stanley Investment Advisors
Fund Type: General Bond
Inception Date: April 6, 1973

Major Rating Factors: Middle of the road best describes Morgan Stanley Income Sec whose TheStreet.com Investment Rating is currently a C+ (Fair). The fund currently has a performance rating of C (Fair) based on an annualized return of 1.45% over the last three years and a total return of -0.58% year to date 2015. Factored into the performance evaluation is an expense ratio of 0.72% (very low).

The fund's risk rating is currently B- (Good). It carries a beta of 1.71, meaning it is expected to move 17.1% for every 10% move in the market. Volatility, as measured by both the semi-deviation and a drawdown factor, is considered low. As of December 31, 2015, Morgan Stanley Income Sec traded at a discount of 7.51% below its net asset value, which is worse than its one-year historical average discount of 9.82%.

Joseph M. Mehlman has been running the fund for 8 years and currently receives a manager quality ranking of 60 (0=worst, 99=best). If you desire an average level of risk, then this fund may be an option.

Data Date	Investment Rating	Net Assets ($Mil)	Price	Performance Rating/Pts	Total Return Y-T-D	Risk Rating/Pts
12-15	C+	171.24	16.87	C / 5.1	-0.58%	B- / 7.9
2014	C	178.60	17.93	C / 4.4	10.74%	B / 8.6
2013	C	170.04	16.81	C- / 4.2	-5.25%	B / 8.6
2012	C	176.50	18.46	C- / 3.6	10.77%	B+ / 9.0
2011	B-	164.40	17.34	C / 5.4	10.99%	B+ / 9.1
2010	C+	165.95	16.83	C+ / 6.4	11.35%	C+ / 6.4

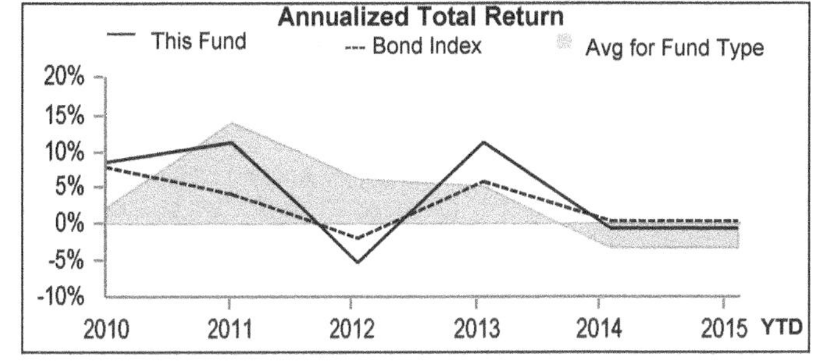

Morgan Stanley India Inv Fund (IIF) C+ Fair

Fund Family: Morgan Stanley Investment Managemen
Fund Type: Foreign
Inception Date: February 17, 1994

Major Rating Factors: Strong performance is the major factor driving the C+ (Fair) TheStreet.com Investment Rating for Morgan Stanley India Inv Fund. The fund currently has a performance rating of B- (Good) based on an annualized return of 10.87% over the last three years and a total return of -6.26% year to date 2015. Factored into the performance evaluation is an expense ratio of 1.44% (average).

The fund's risk rating is currently C+ (Fair). It carries a beta of 0.73, meaning the fund's expected move will be 7.3% for every 10% move in the market. Volatility, as measured by both the semi-deviation and a drawdown factor, is considered low. As of December 31, 2015, Morgan Stanley India Inv Fund traded at a discount of 12.38% below its net asset value, which is better than its one-year historical average discount of 11.37%.

Ruchir Sharma has been running the fund for 22 years and currently receives a manager quality ranking of 92 (0=worst, 99=best). If you desire only a moderate level of risk and strong performance, then this fund is an excellent option.

Data Date	Investment Rating	Net Assets ($Mil)	Price	Performance Rating/Pts	Total Return Y-T-D	Risk Rating/Pts
12-15	C+	449.99	25.47	B- / 7.1	-6.26%	C+ / 6.8
2014	A	419.70	26.88	A+ / 9.6	57.19%	B- / 7.1
2013	D-	329.05	17.48	D- / 1.3	-8.65%	C+ / 5.6
2012	D-	378.12	18.53	D / 1.9	22.96%	C / 5.2
2011	D-	350.00	14.01	D / 1.8	-39.92%	C / 5.3
2010	D-	553.10	25.65	C- / 3.2	24.45%	D / 2.2

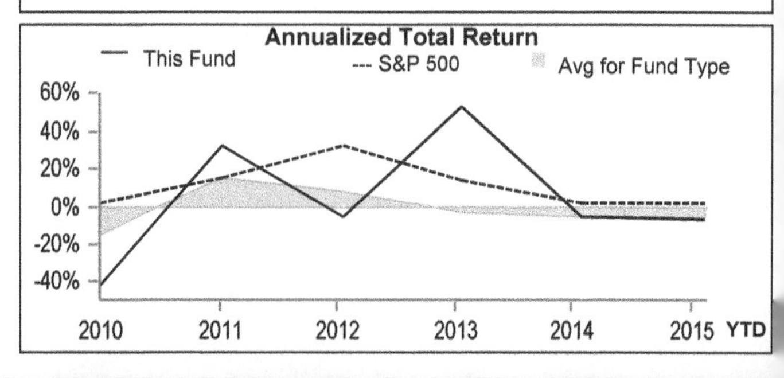

Neuberger Berman CA Inter Muni Fun (NBW) B+ Good

Fund Family: Neuberger Berman Management LLC
Fund Type: Municipal - Single State
Inception Date: September 24, 2002

Major Rating Factors: Strong performance is the major factor driving the B+ (Good) TheStreet.com Investment Rating for Neuberger Berman CA Inter Muni Fun. The fund currently has a performance rating of B (Good) based on an annualized return of 5.32% over the last three years and a total return of 4.34% year to date 2015. Factored into the performance evaluation is an expense ratio of 1.70% (above average).

The fund's risk rating is currently B- (Good). It carries a beta of 1.70, meaning it is expected to move 17.0% for every 10% move in the market. Volatility, as measured by both the semi-deviation and a drawdown factor, is considered low. As of December 31, 2015, Neuberger Berman CA Inter Muni Fun traded at a premium of 1.74% above its net asset value, which is worse than its one-year historical average discount of .75%.

James L. Iselin currently receives a manager quality ranking of 74 (0=worst, 99=best). If you desire only a moderate level of risk and strong performance, then this fund is an excellent option.

Data Date	Investment Rating	Net Assets ($Mil)	Price	Performance Rating/Pts	Total Return Y-T-D	Risk Rating/Pts
12-15	B+	85.90	15.75	B / 8.1	4.34%	B- / 7.4
2014	C+	84.90	16.00	B- / 7.5	21.14%	C+ / 6.6
2013	C	62.05	13.88	C / 4.6	-7.20%	B / 8.3
2012	B+	83.10	15.50	B- / 7.2	9.73%	B+ / 9.1
2011	A-	84.70	15.27	B / 8.2	13.93%	B+ / 9.2
2010	A-	59.54	14.34	B / 7.7	13.94%	C+ / 6.8

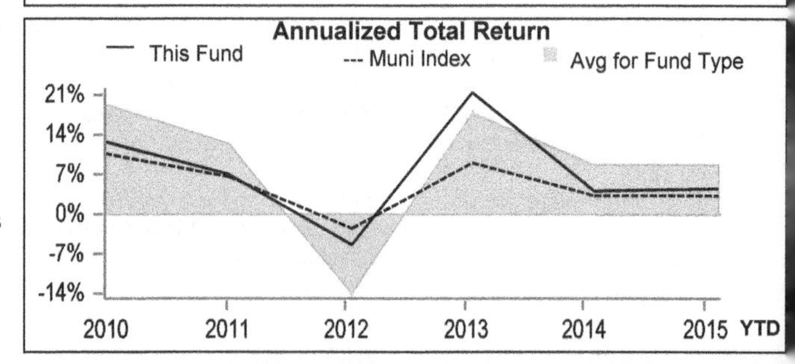

Neuberger Berman High Yield Strat (NHS) C- Fair

Fund Family: Neuberger Berman Management LLC
Fund Type: Corporate - High Yield
Inception Date: July 28, 2003

Major Rating Factors:
Disappointing performance is the major factor driving the C- (Fair) TheStreet.com Investment Rating for Neuberger Berman High Yield Strat. The fund currently has a performance rating of D+ (Weak) based on an annualized return of -3.20% over the last three years and a total return of -10.88% year to date 2015. Factored into the performance evaluation is an expense ratio of 1.89% (above average).

The fund's risk rating is currently C+ (Fair). It carries a beta of 1.78, meaning it is expected to move 17.8% for every 10% move in the market. Volatility, as measured by both the semi-deviation and a drawdown factor, is considered low. As of December 31, 2015, Neuberger Berman High Yield Strat traded at a discount of 13.17% below its net asset value, which is worse than its one-year historical average discount of 13.61%.

Ann H. Benjamin has been running the fund for 13 years and currently receives a manager quality ranking of 27 (0=worst, 99=best). This fund offers only a moderate level of risk but investors looking for strong performance are still waiting.

Data Date	Investment Rating	Net Assets ($Mil)	Price	Performance Rating/Pts	Total Return Y-T-D	Risk Rating/Pts
12-15	C-	281.72	10.09	D+ / 2.9	-10.88%	C+ / 6.8
2014	C-	279.10	12.30	C- / 3.5	0.20%	B- / 7.8
2013	C-	291.66	13.26	C / 5.4	1.75%	C+ / 6.5
2012	C-	253.17	13.90	C+ / 5.6	13.14%	C+ / 6.4
2011	B	249.40	13.65	A / 9.4	8.53%	C+ / 6.4
2010	B-	138.29	13.50	B+ / 8.6	24.86%	C- / 4.0

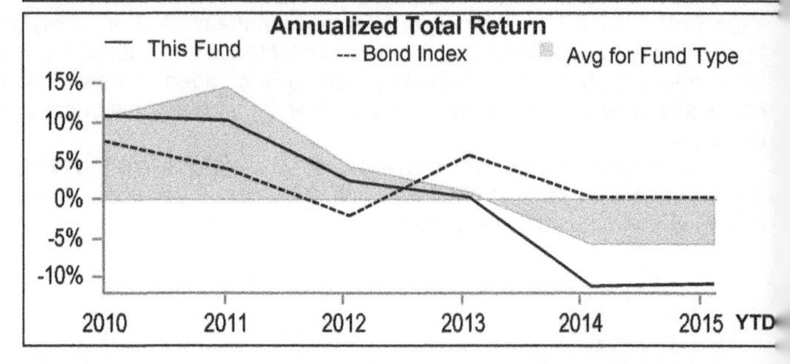

Neuberger Berman Intermediate Muni (NBH) B Good

Fund Family: Neuberger Berman Management LLC
Fund Type: Municipal - National
Inception Date: September 24, 2002

Major Rating Factors: Strong performance is the major factor driving the B (Good) TheStreet.com Investment Rating for Neuberger Berman Intermediate Muni. The fund currently has a performance rating of B- (Good) based on an annualized return of 3.71% over the last three years and a total return of 7.34% year to date 2015. Factored into the performance evaluation is an expense ratio of 1.41% (average).

The fund's risk rating is currently B- (Good). It carries a beta of 2.14, meaning it is expected to move 21.4% for every 10% move in the market. Volatility, as measured by both the semi-deviation and a drawdown factor, is considered low. As of December 31, 2015, Neuberger Berman Intermediate Muni traded at a discount of 1.63% below its net asset value, which is worse than its one-year historical average discount of 3.71%.

James L. Iselin currently receives a manager quality ranking of 52 (0=worst, 99=best). If you desire only a moderate level of risk and strong performance, then this fund is an excellent option.

Data Date	Investment Rating	Net Assets ($Mil)	Price	Performance Rating/Pts	Total Return Y-T-D	Risk Rating/Pts
12-15	B	302.30	15.72	B- / 7.2	7.34%	B- / 7.5
2014	B-	298.40	15.62	C+ / 6.6	15.01%	B / 8.1
2013	C+	66.89	14.04	C+ / 6.0	-9.03%	B / 8.3
2012	A+	277.50	16.18	B+ / 8.4	13.07%	B+ / 9.1
2011	A	283.20	15.90	B+ / 8.8	21.94%	B+ / 9.3
2010	B+	62.64	14.01	B- / 7.0	10.26%	B- / 7.1

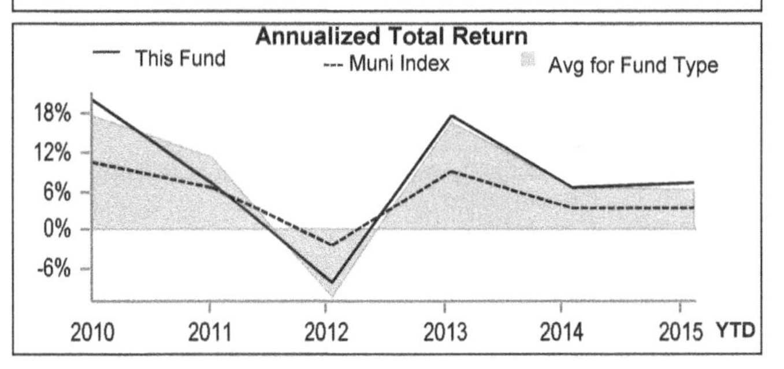

Neuberger Berman MLP Income (NML) E+ Very Weak

Fund Family: Neuberger Berman Management LLC
Fund Type: Global
Inception Date: March 26, 2013

Major Rating Factors:
Very poor performance is the major factor driving the E+ (Very Weak) TheStreet.com Investment Rating for Neuberger Berman MLP Income. The fund currently has a performance rating of E- (Very Weak) based on an annualized return of 0.00% over the last three years and a total return of -50.28% year to date 2015. Factored into the performance evaluation is an expense ratio of 1.77% (above average).

The fund's risk rating is currently C- (Fair). It carries a beta of 0.00, meaning the fund's expected move will be 0.0% for every 10% move in the market. Volatility, as measured by both the semi-deviation and a drawdown factor, is considered average. As of December 31, 2015, Neuberger Berman MLP Income traded at a discount of .49% below its net asset value, which is worse than its one-year historical average discount of 4.07%.

This fund offers an average level of risk but investors looking for strong performance will be frustrated.

Data Date	Investment Rating	Net Assets ($Mil)	Price	Performance Rating/Pts	Total Return Y-T-D	Risk Rating/Pts
12-15	E+	1.17	8.16	E- / 0	-50.28%	C- / 3.6
2014	D	1,126.70	17.60	D- / 1.1	-1.34%	B- / 7.3

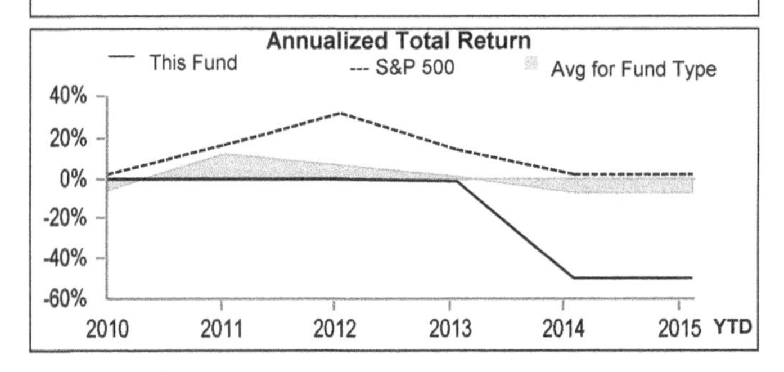

Neuberger Berman NY Int Muni (NBO) B- Good

Fund Family: Neuberger Berman Management LLC
Fund Type: Municipal - Single State
Inception Date: September 24, 2002

Major Rating Factors: Neuberger Berman NY Int Muni receives a TheStreet.com Investment Rating of B- (Good). The fund currently has a performance rating of C+ (Fair) based on an annualized return of 2.52% over the last three years and a total return of 8.37% year to date 2015. Factored into the performance evaluation is an expense ratio of 1.71% (above average).

The fund's risk rating is currently B- (Good). It carries a beta of 2.17, meaning it is expected to move 21.7% for every 10% move in the market. Volatility, as measured by both the semi-deviation and a drawdown factor, is considered low. As of December 31, 2015, Neuberger Berman NY Int Muni traded at a discount of 2.15% below its net asset value, which is worse than its one-year historical average discount of 2.71%.

James L. Iselin currently receives a manager quality ranking of 38 (0=worst, 99=best). If you desire an average level of risk, then this fund may be an option.

Data Date	Investment Rating	Net Assets ($Mil)	Price	Performance Rating/Pts	Total Return Y-T-D	Risk Rating/Pts
12-15	B-	73.70	14.10	C+ / 6.6	8.37%	B- / 7.4
2014	C	73.20	13.72	C / 4.6	9.20%	B- / 7.7
2013	C	64.36	13.23	C / 4.9	-8.65%	B- / 7.9
2012	B	73.10	15.21	B- / 7.3	9.79%	B / 8.6
2011	A	74.40	15.47	A- / 9.0	20.44%	B / 8.9
2010	C+	62.64	13.50	C+ / 5.7	8.09%	C+ / 6.7

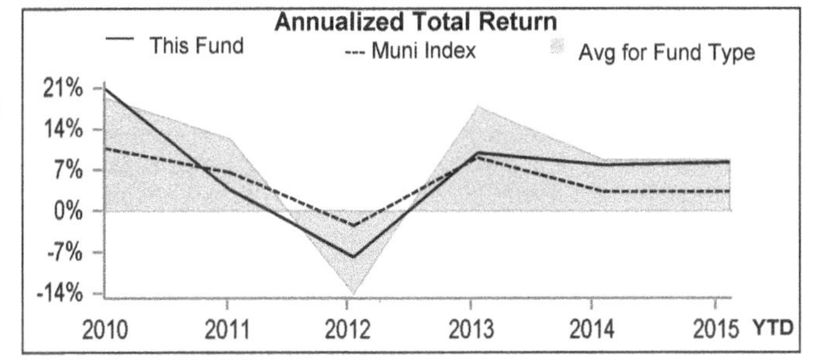

Neuberger Berman Real Est Secs Inc (NRO) B Good

Fund Family: Neuberger Berman Management LLC
Fund Type: Growth and Income
Inception Date: October 28, 2003

Major Rating Factors: Strong performance is the major factor driving the B (Good) TheStreet.com Investment Rating for Neuberger Berman Real Est Secs Inc. The fund currently has a performance rating of B- (Good) based on an annualized return of 7.94% over the last three years and a total return of 1.35% year to date 2015. Factored into the performance evaluation is an expense ratio of 2.09% (high).

The fund's risk rating is currently B- (Good). It carries a beta of 0.63, meaning the fund's expected move will be 6.3% for every 10% move in the market. Volatility, as measured by both the semi-deviation and a drawdown factor, is considered low. As of December 31, 2015, Neuberger Berman Real Est Secs Inc traded at a discount of 11.95% below its net asset value, which is worse than its one-year historical average discount of 15.34%.

Brian C. Jones currently receives a manager quality ranking of 64 (0=worst, 99=best). If you desire only a moderate level of risk and strong performance, then this fund is an excellent option.

Data Date	Investment Rating	Net Assets ($Mil)	Price	Performance Rating/Pts	Total Return Y-T-D	Risk Rating/Pts
12-15	B	340.40	5.01	B- / 7.5	1.35%	B- / 7.2
2014	A	318.60	5.29	B+ / 8.8	26.98%	B- / 7.7
2013	C	363.78	4.34	C / 5.1	-2.65%	B- / 7.8
2012	A-	257.20	4.59	B+ / 8.9	31.62%	B- / 7.9
2011	B-	245.60	3.75	B+ / 8.5	1.12%	C+ / 6.5
2010	E	260.60	3.99	D- / 1.5	40.04%	D / 2.1

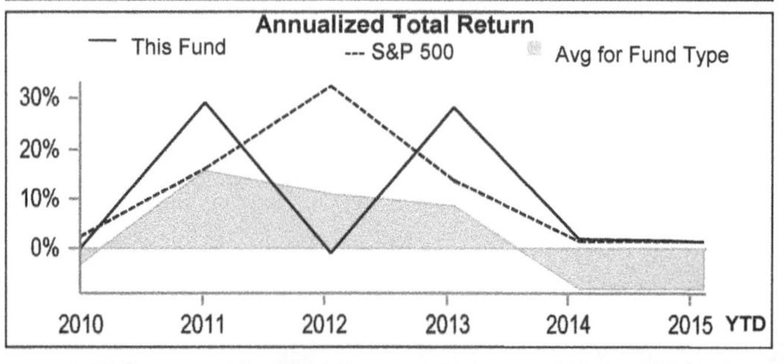

New America High Income Fund (HYB) C- Fair

Fund Family: T Rowe Price Associates Inc
Fund Type: Corporate - High Yield
Inception Date: February 26, 1988

Major Rating Factors: Middle of the road best describes New America High Income Fund whose TheStreet.com Investment Rating is currently a C- (Fair). The fund currently has a performance rating of C- (Fair) based on an annualized return of -1.92% over the last three years and a total return of -7.21% year to date 2015. Factored into the performance evaluation is an expense ratio of 1.54% (average).

The fund's risk rating is currently C+ (Fair). It carries a beta of 1.16, meaning it is expected to move 11.6% for every 10% move in the market. Volatility, as measured by both the semi-deviation and a drawdown factor, is considered low. As of December 31, 2015, New America High Income Fund traded at a discount of 13.35% below its net asset value, which is worse than its one-year historical average discount of 13.65%.

Brian C. Rogers currently receives a manager quality ranking of 39 (0=worst, 99=best). If you desire an average level of risk, then this fund may be an option.

Data Date	Investment Rating	Net Assets ($Mil)	Price	Performance Rating/Pts	Total Return Y-T-D	Risk Rating/Pts
12-15	C-	235.74	7.66	C- / 3.2	-7.21%	C+ / 6.7
2014	C-	255.40	8.94	C- / 3.8	1.08%	B- / 7.6
2013	C+	241.42	9.65	C+ / 5.7	-1.17%	B- / 7.9
2012	B	321.16	10.45	B / 7.7	22.82%	B / 8.2
2011	B	221.50	10.21	A- / 9.1	8.96%	C+ / 6.5
2010	B-	217.22	9.96	B+ / 8.6	22.09%	C- / 3.7

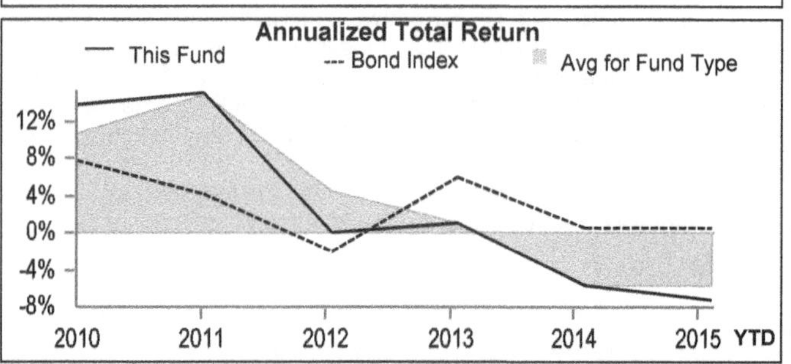

New Germany Fund (GF) B Good

Fund Family: Deutsche Asset Mgmt International G
Fund Type: Foreign
Inception Date: January 24, 1990

Major Rating Factors:
Exceptional performance is the major factor driving the B (Good) TheStreet.com Investment Rating for New Germany Fund. The fund currently has a performance rating of A (Excellent) based on an annualized return of 17.51% over the last three years and a total return of 14.57% year to date 2015. Factored into the performance evaluation is an expense ratio of 1.14% (low).

The fund's risk rating is currently C+ (Fair). It carries a beta of 0.92, meaning that its performance tracks fairly well with that of the overall stock market. Volatility, as measured by both the semi-deviation and a drawdown factor, is considered low. As of December 31, 2015, New Germany Fund traded at a discount of 9.20% below its net asset value, which is worse than its one-year historical average discount of 9.38%.

Rainer Vermehren currently receives a manager quality ranking of 96 (0=worst, 99=best). If you desire only a moderate level of risk and strong performance, then this fund is an excellent option.

Data Date	Investment Rating	Net Assets ($Mil)	Price	Performance Rating/Pts	Total Return Y-T-D	Risk Rating/Pts
12-15	B	228.41	14.70	A / 9.4	14.57%	C+ / 5.7
2014	B-	279.30	14.04	B+ / 8.8	-4.05%	C+ / 6.0
2013	B	314.66	19.93	A / 9.4	47.18%	C+ / 6.5
2012	B	262.51	15.58	B+ / 8.9	38.58%	C+ / 6.4
2011	C	241.50	12.24	C+ / 5.9	-13.03%	C+ / 6.5
2010	C-	271.35	15.72	C+ / 5.9	32.19%	C- / 3.9

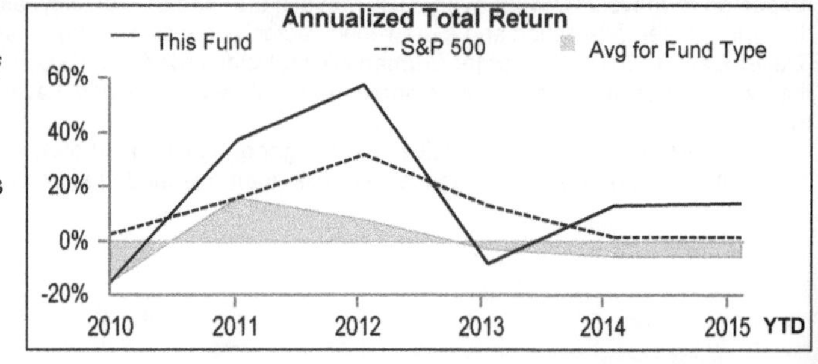

NexPoint Credit Strategies Fund (HCF) C- Fair

Fund Family: NexPoint Advisors LP
Fund Type: General Bond
Inception Date: June 26, 2006

Major Rating Factors: Middle of the road best describes NexPoint Credit Strategies Fund whose TheStreet.com Investment Rating is currently a C- (Fair). The fund currently has a performance rating of C+ (Fair) based on an annualized return of 14.02% over the last three years and a total return of -23.11% year to date 2015. Factored into the performance evaluation is an expense ratio of 2.48% (high).

The fund's risk rating is currently C- (Fair). It carries a beta of 1.01, meaning that its performance tracks fairly well with that of the overall stock market. Volatility, as measured by both the semi-deviation and a drawdown factor, is considered average. As of December 31, 2015, NexPoint Credit Strategies Fund traded at a discount of 13.65% below its net asset value, which is better than its one-year historical average discount of 13.07%.

Mark Okada currently receives a manager quality ranking of 96 (0=worst, 99=best). If you desire an average level of risk, then this fund may be an option.

Data Date	Investment Rating	Net Assets ($Mil)	Price	Performance Rating/Pts	Total Return Y-T-D	Risk Rating/Pts
12-15	C-	860.88	20.44	C+ / 6.7	-23.11%	C- / 3.2
2014	A+	800.70	11.23	A / 9.5	26.58%	B / 8.3
2013	A	545.58	9.42	A / 9.3	51.35%	B- / 7.7
2012	C-	443.05	6.64	C / 4.3	16.40%	B- / 7.6
2011	C-	445.10	6.18	C- / 3.7	-11.81%	B- / 7.5
2010	E+	458.76	7.58	D- / 1.3	30.86%	D+ / 2.8

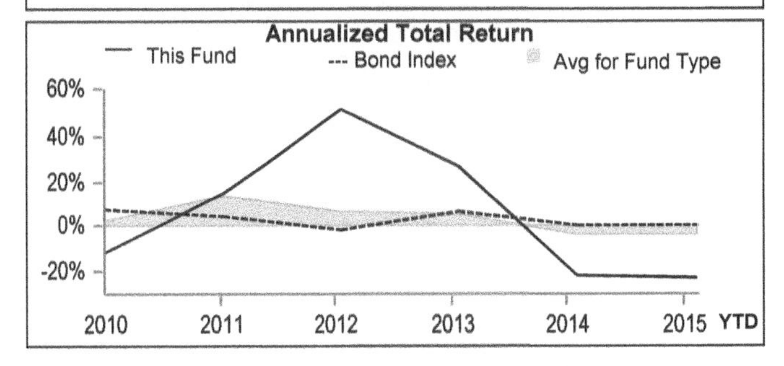

Nuveen All Cap Energy MLP Opps (JML) E- Very Weak

Fund Family: Nuveen Fund Advisors LLC
Fund Type: Energy/Natural Resources
Inception Date: March 27, 2014

Major Rating Factors: Nuveen All Cap Energy MLP Opps has adopted a very risky asset allocation strategy and currently receives an overall TheStreet.com Investment Rating of E- (Very Weak). The fund has a high level of volatility, as measured by both semi-deviation and drawdown factors. It carries a beta of 0.00, meaning the fund's expected move will be 0.0% for every 10% move in the market. As of December 31, 2015, Nuveen All Cap Energy MLP Opps traded at a discount of 7.07% below its net asset value, which is better than its one-year historical average discount of .77%. Unfortunately, the high level of risk (D, Weak) failed to pay off as investors endured very poor performance.

The fund's performance rating is currently E- (Very Weak). It has registered an annualized return of 0.00% over the last three years but is down -50.36% year to date 2015. Factored into the performance evaluation is an expense ratio of 1.77% (above average).

James J. Cunnane, Jr. has been running the fund for 2 years and currently receives a manager quality ranking of 2 (0=worst, 99=best). If you can tolerate very high levels of risk in the hope of improved future returns, holding this fund may be an option.

Data Date	Investment Rating	Net Assets ($Mil)	Price	Performance Rating/Pts	Total Return Y-T-D	Risk Rating/Pts
12-15	E-	236.28	6.97	E- / 0	-50.36%	D / 1.8

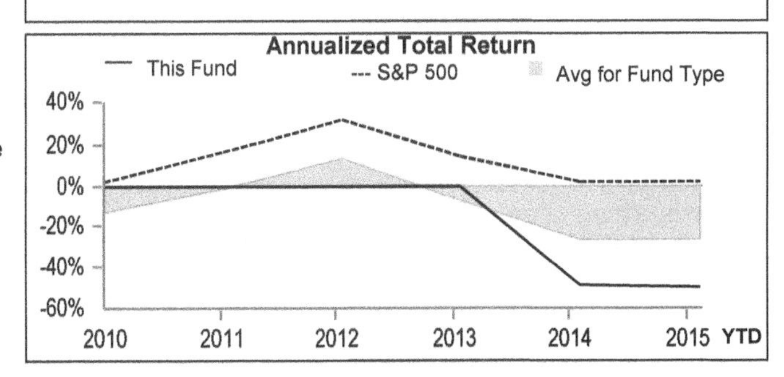

Nuveen AMT-Fr Muni Income (NEA) B- Good

Fund Family: Nuveen Fund Advisors LLC
Fund Type: Municipal - National
Inception Date: November 21, 2002

Major Rating Factors: Nuveen AMT-Fr Muni Income receives a TheStreet.com Investment Rating of B- (Good). The fund currently has a performance rating of C+ (Fair) based on an annualized return of 2.13% over the last three years and a total return of 6.15% year to date 2015. Factored into the performance evaluation is an expense ratio of 1.60% (above average).

The fund's risk rating is currently B- (Good). It carries a beta of 2.27, meaning it is expected to move 22.7% for every 10% move in the market. Volatility, as measured by both the semi-deviation and a drawdown factor, is considered low. As of December 31, 2015, Nuveen AMT-Fr Muni Income traded at a discount of 8.46% below its net asset value, which is worse than its one-year historical average discount of 10.32%.

Paul L. Brennan has been running the fund for 10 years and currently receives a manager quality ranking of 40 (0=worst, 99=best). If you desire an average level of risk, then this fund may be an option.

Data Date	Investment Rating	Net Assets ($Mil)	Price	Performance Rating/Pts	Total Return Y-T-D	Risk Rating/Pts
12-15	B-	1,193.11	13.85	C+ / 6.7	6.15%	B- / 7.5
2014	B-	1,180.80	13.82	C+ / 6.5	20.92%	B- / 7.8
2013	C-	2.16	12.04	D+ / 2.8	-17.06%	B / 8.0
2012	C+	326.91	14.84	C+ / 5.8	10.47%	B / 8.6
2011	B+	332.40	14.61	B / 7.8	18.56%	B / 8.7
2010	C-	320.59	13.39	D+ / 2.6	1.90%	B- / 7.7

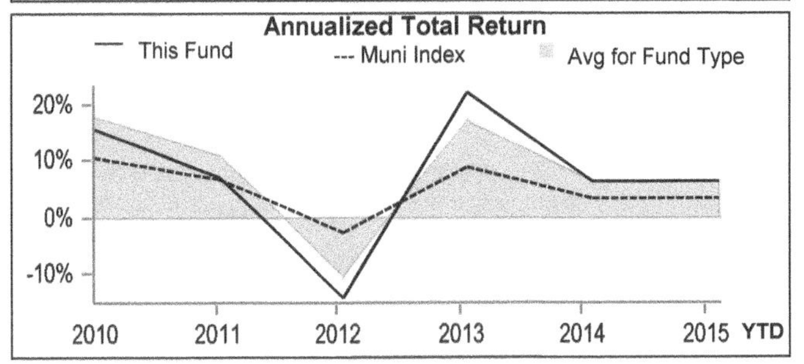

* Denotes ETF Fund

Nuveen AMT-Free Municipal Value (NUW) B- Good

Fund Family: Nuveen Fund Advisors LLC
Fund Type: Municipal - National
Inception Date: February 25, 2009

Data Date	Investment Rating	Net Assets ($Mil)	Price	Performance Rating/Pts	Total Return Y-T-D	Risk Rating/Pts
12-15	B-	226.86	17.86	B / 7.7	6.60%	C+ / 6.7
2014	C	225.30	17.46	B- / 7.1	19.39%	C+ / 5.7
2013	C	234.95	15.20	C / 4.4	-11.96%	B- / 7.8
2012	C+	212.87	17.63	C+ / 6.2	10.37%	B / 8.3
2011	A-	215.20	17.32	A- / 9.0	19.86%	B / 8.7
2010	C-	205.71	15.38	D- / 1.0	2.98%	B / 8.1

Major Rating Factors: Strong performance is the major factor driving the B- (Good) TheStreet.com Investment Rating for Nuveen AMT-Free Municipal Value. The fund currently has a performance rating of B (Good) based on an annualized return of 4.02% over the last three years and a total return of 6.60% year to date 2015. Factored into the performance evaluation is an expense ratio of 0.75% (very low).

The fund's risk rating is currently C+ (Fair). It carries a beta of 2.10, meaning it is expected to move 21.0% for every 10% move in the market. Volatility, as measured by both the semi-deviation and a drawdown factor, is considered low. As of December 31, 2015, Nuveen AMT-Free Municipal Value traded at a premium of 3.66% above its net asset value, which is worse than its one-year historical average discount of .88%.

Thomas C. Spalding has been running the fund for 7 years and currently receives a manager quality ranking of 57 (0=worst, 99=best). If you desire only a moderate level of risk and strong performance, then this fund is an excellent option.

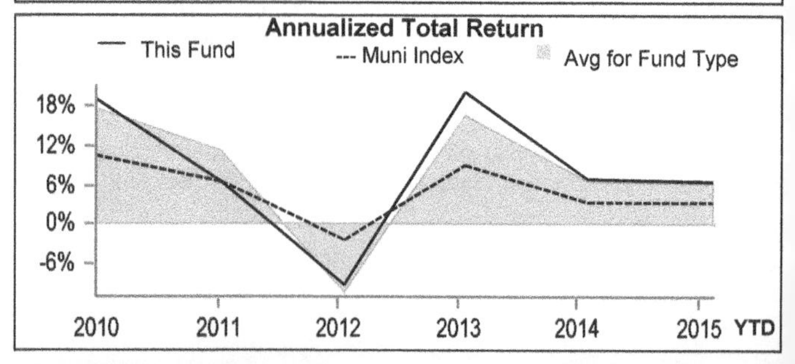

Nuveen AZ Prem Inc Muni (NAZ) B Good

Fund Family: Nuveen Fund Advisors LLC
Fund Type: Municipal - Single State
Inception Date: November 19, 1992

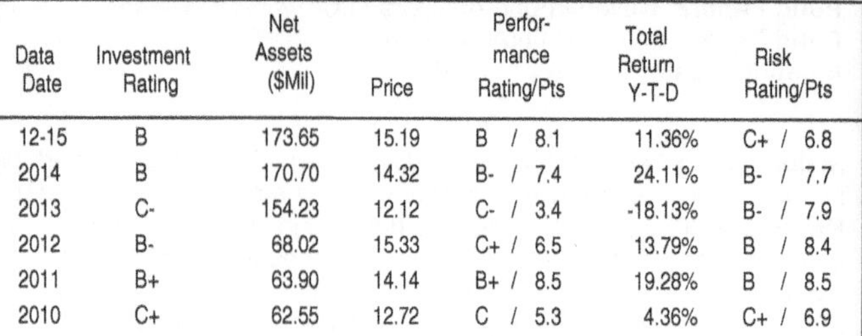

Data Date	Investment Rating	Net Assets ($Mil)	Price	Performance Rating/Pts	Total Return Y-T-D	Risk Rating/Pts
12-15	B	173.65	15.19	B / 8.1	11.36%	C+ / 6.8
2014	B	170.70	14.32	B- / 7.4	24.11%	B- / 7.7
2013	C-	154.23	12.12	C- / 3.4	-18.13%	B- / 7.9
2012	B-	68.02	15.33	C+ / 6.5	13.79%	B / 8.4
2011	B+	63.90	14.14	B+ / 8.5	19.28%	B / 8.5
2010	C+	62.55	12.72	C / 5.3	4.36%	C+ / 6.9

Major Rating Factors: Strong performance is the major factor driving the B (Good) TheStreet.com Investment Rating for Nuveen AZ Prem Inc Muni. The fund currently has a performance rating of B (Good) based on an annualized return of 4.40% over the last three years and a total return of 11.36% year to date 2015. Factored into the performance evaluation is an expense ratio of 1.56% (average).

The fund's risk rating is currently C+ (Fair). It carries a beta of 2.22, meaning it is expected to move 22.2% for every 10% move in the market. Volatility, as measured by both the semi-deviation and a drawdown factor, is considered low. As of December 31, 2015, Nuveen AZ Prem Inc Muni traded at a premium of 2.08% above its net asset value, which is worse than its one-year historical average discount of .49%.

Michael S. Hamilton has been running the fund for 5 years and currently receives a manager quality ranking of 54 (0=worst, 99=best). If you desire only a moderate level of risk and strong performance, then this fund is an excellent option.

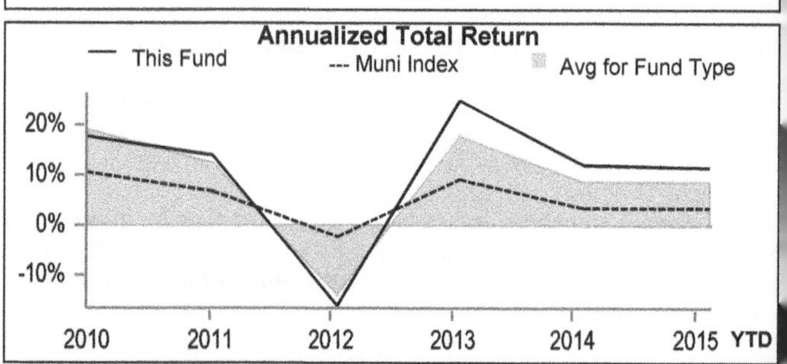

Nuveen Build America Bond Fund (NBB) B Good

Fund Family: Nuveen Fund Advisors LLC
Fund Type: Municipal - National
Inception Date: April 27, 2010

Data Date	Investment Rating	Net Assets ($Mil)	Price	Performance Rating/Pts	Total Return Y-T-D	Risk Rating/Pts
12-15	B	612.08	20.09	B- / 7.4	1.42%	B- / 7.5
2014	B+	593.90	21.18	B / 7.7	22.36%	B / 8.3
2013	C+	598.11	18.44	C+ / 5.7	-6.61%	B / 8.4
2012	B-	565.95	21.18	C+ / 5.9	10.44%	B / 8.8
2011	A+	556.80	20.53	A / 9.4	19.52%	B / 8.9

Major Rating Factors: Strong performance is the major factor driving the B (Good) TheStreet.com Investment Rating for Nuveen Build America Bond Fund. The fund currently has a performance rating of B- (Good) based on an annualized return of 5.04% over the last three years and a total return of 1.42% year to date 2015. Factored into the performance evaluation is an expense ratio of 1.07% (low).

The fund's risk rating is currently B- (Good). It carries a beta of 1.86, meaning it is expected to move 18.6% for every 10% move in the market. Volatility, as measured by both the semi-deviation and a drawdown factor, is considered low. As of December 31, 2015, Nuveen Build America Bond Fund traded at a discount of 6.12% below its net asset value, which is worse than its one-year historical average discount of 8.17%.

Craig M. Chambers currently receives a manager quality ranking of 61 (0=worst, 99=best). If you desire only a moderate level of risk and strong performance, then this fund is an excellent option.

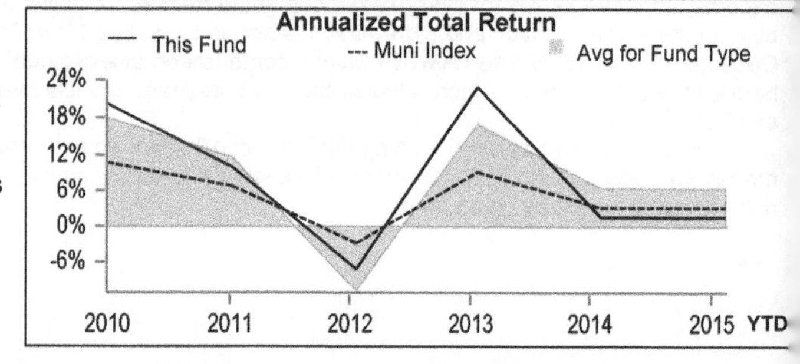

Nuveen Build America Bond Oppty Fd (NBD) C+ Fair

Fund Family: Nuveen Fund Advisors LLC
Fund Type: General - Investment Grade
Inception Date: November 24, 2010

Major Rating Factors: Middle of the road best describes Nuveen Build America Bond Oppty Fd whose TheStreet.com Investment Rating is currently a C+ (Fair). The fund currently has a performance rating of C+ (Fair) based on an annualized return of 4.06% over the last three years and a total return of -1.40% year to date 2015. Factored into the performance evaluation is an expense ratio of 1.02% (low).

The fund's risk rating is currently B- (Good). It carries a beta of 2.22, meaning it is expected to move 22.2% for every 10% move in the market. Volatility, as measured by both the semi-deviation and a drawdown factor, is considered low. As of December 31, 2015, Nuveen Build America Bond Oppty Fd traded at a discount of 7.18% below its net asset value, which is worse than its one-year historical average discount of 9.36%.

Daniel J. Close currently receives a manager quality ranking of 76 (0=worst, 99=best). If you desire an average level of risk, then this fund may be an option.

Data Date	Investment Rating	Net Assets ($Mil)	Price	Performance Rating/Pts	Total Return Y-T-D	Risk Rating/Pts
12-15	C+	172.32	20.29	C+ / 6.0	-1.40%	B- / 7.4
2014	C+	168.60	21.95	C+ / 5.8	19.51%	B / 8.1
2013	C+	172.33	19.43	C / 5.3	-4.36%	B / 8.3
2012	C-	162.58	21.66	D+ / 2.8	6.45%	B+ / 9.3
2011	A-	158.80	21.62	B / 8.0	23.86%	B+ / 9.3

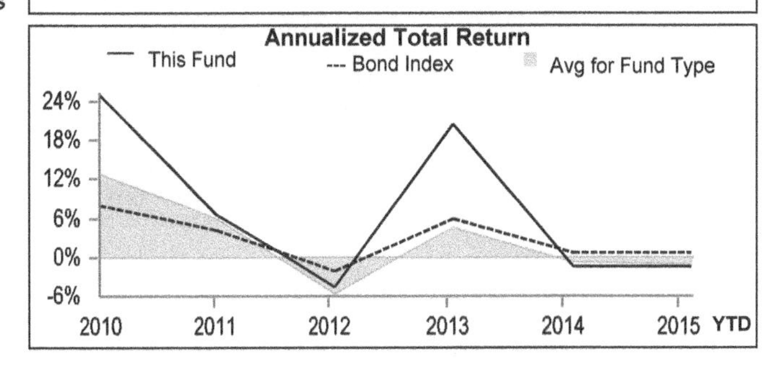

Nuveen CA AMT-Free Municipal Incom (NKX) A- Excellent

Fund Family: Nuveen Fund Advisors LLC
Fund Type: Municipal - Single State
Inception Date: November 21, 2002

Major Rating Factors:
Exceptional performance is the major factor driving the A- (Excellent) TheStreet.com Investment Rating for Nuveen CA AMT-Free Municipal Incom. The fund currently has a performance rating of A- (Excellent) based on an annualized return of 6.28% over the last three years and a total return of 11.47% year to date 2015. Factored into the performance evaluation is an expense ratio of 1.63% (above average).

The fund's risk rating is currently B- (Good). It carries a beta of 2.16, meaning it is expected to move 21.6% for every 10% move in the market. Volatility, as measured by both the semi-deviation and a drawdown factor, is considered low. As of December 31, 2015, Nuveen CA AMT-Free Municipal Incom traded at a discount of 4.42% below its net asset value, which is worse than its one-year historical average discount of 6.58%.

Scott R. Romans has been running the fund for 14 years and currently receives a manager quality ranking of 74 (0=worst, 99=best). If you desire only a moderate level of risk and strong performance, then this fund is an excellent option.

Data Date	Investment Rating	Net Assets ($Mil)	Price	Performance Rating/Pts	Total Return Y-T-D	Risk Rating/Pts
12-15	A-	760.79	15.36	A- / 9.0	11.47%	B- / 7.4
2014	B+	744.90	14.74	B+ / 8.4	27.40%	B- / 7.6
2013	C	553.65	12.17	C / 5.0	-14.72%	B- / 7.8
2012	B+	640.79	14.73	B / 7.9	12.09%	B / 8.4
2011	B+	84.50	14.60	B+ / 8.7	28.27%	B / 8.5
2010	C-	39.30	12.18	D / 1.7	2.01%	B- / 7.8

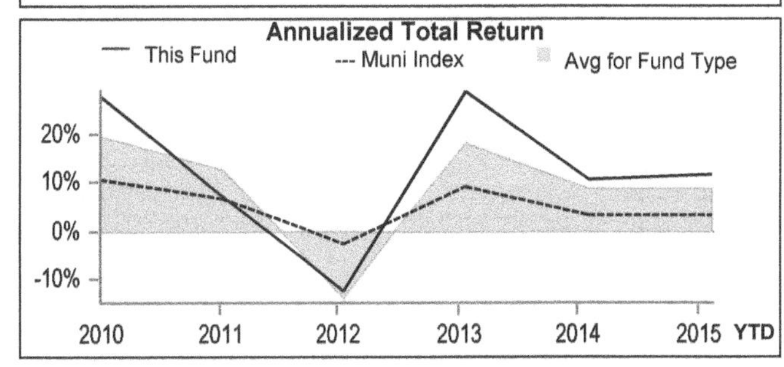

Nuveen CA Div Adv Muni (NAC) B Good

Fund Family: Nuveen Fund Advisors LLC
Fund Type: Municipal - Single State
Inception Date: May 25, 1999

Major Rating Factors: Strong performance is the major factor driving the B (Good) TheStreet.com Investment Rating for Nuveen CA Div Adv Muni. The fund currently has a performance rating of B (Good) based on an annualized return of 3.95% over the last three years and a total return of 9.35% year to date 2015. Factored into the performance evaluation is an expense ratio of 1.53% (average).

The fund's risk rating is currently B- (Good). It carries a beta of 2.49, meaning it is expected to move 24.9% for every 10% move in the market. Volatility, as measured by both the semi-deviation and a drawdown factor, is considered low. As of December 31, 2015, Nuveen CA Div Adv Muni traded at a discount of 3.07% below its net asset value, which is worse than its one-year historical average discount of 4.30%.

Scott R. Romans has been running the fund for 14 years and currently receives a manager quality ranking of 45 (0=worst, 99=best). If you desire only a moderate level of risk and strong performance, then this fund is an excellent option.

Data Date	Investment Rating	Net Assets ($Mil)	Price	Performance Rating/Pts	Total Return Y-T-D	Risk Rating/Pts
12-15	B	1,713.63	15.48	B / 7.6	9.35%	B- / 7.1
2014	A-	1,677.30	15.05	B+ / 8.8	25.10%	B- / 7.7
2013	C+	313.76	12.85	C+ / 5.6	-17.94%	B- / 7.9
2012	A+	364.25	16.10	A / 9.4	19.95%	B / 8.5
2011	A-	335.30	14.24	B+ / 8.8	25.77%	B / 8.5
2010	C-	325.79	12.31	D+ / 2.5	6.08%	C+ / 6.5

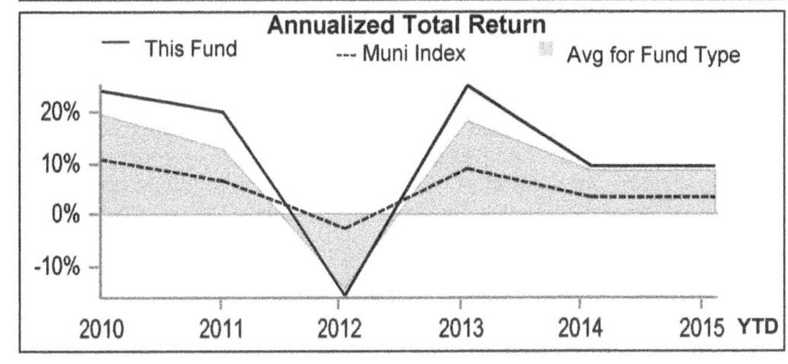

Nuveen CA Div Adv Muni 2 (NVX) B+ Good

Fund Family: Nuveen Fund Advisors LLC
Fund Type: Municipal - Single State
Inception Date: March 27, 2001

Major Rating Factors: Strong performance is the major factor driving the B+ (Good) TheStreet.com Investment Rating for Nuveen CA Div Adv Muni 2. The fund currently has a performance rating of B+ (Good) based on an annualized return of 4.42% over the last three years and a total return of 13.68% year to date 2015. Factored into the performance evaluation is an expense ratio of 1.50% (average).

The fund's risk rating is currently B- (Good). It carries a beta of 2.46, meaning it is expected to move 24.6% for every 10% move in the market. Volatility, as measured by both the semi-deviation and a drawdown factor, is considered low. As of December 31, 2015, Nuveen CA Div Adv Muni 2 traded at a discount of 4.01% below its net asset value, which is worse than its one-year historical average discount of 6.87%.

Scott R. Romans has been running the fund for 14 years and currently receives a manager quality ranking of 48 (0=worst, 99=best). If you desire only a moderate level of risk and strong performance, then this fund is an excellent option.

Data Date	Investment Rating	Net Assets ($Mil)	Price	Performance Rating/Pts	Total Return Y-T-D	Risk Rating/Pts
12-15	B+	233.44	15.31	B+ / 8.3	13.68%	B- / 7.1
2014	B-	229.20	14.34	C+ / 6.9	19.76%	B- / 7.6
2013	C	200.84	12.63	C / 4.4	-15.90%	B- / 7.9
2012	A-	236.02	15.61	B / 8.2	13.60%	B / 8.7
2011	A	219.70	14.75	B+ / 8.9	23.57%	B / 8.9
2010	C	213.69	13.10	C / 4.9	4.11%	C+ / 6.3

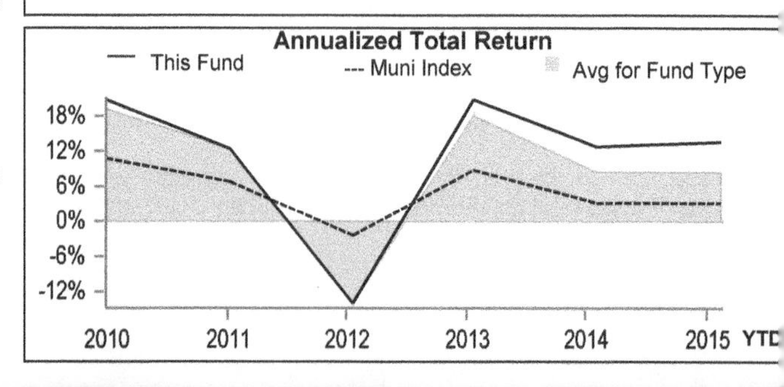

Nuveen CA Div Adv Muni 3 (NZH) B+ Good

Fund Family: Nuveen Fund Advisors LLC
Fund Type: Municipal - Single State
Inception Date: September 25, 2001

Major Rating Factors: Strong performance is the major factor driving the B+ (Good) TheStreet.com Investment Rating for Nuveen CA Div Adv Muni 3. The fund currently has a performance rating of B+ (Good) based on an annualized return of 4.97% over the last three years and a total return of 11.06% year to date 2015. Factored into the performance evaluation is an expense ratio of 1.56% (average).

The fund's risk rating is currently B- (Good). It carries a beta of 2.11, meaning it is expected to move 21.1% for every 10% move in the market. Volatility, as measured by both the semi-deviation and a drawdown factor, is considered low. As of December 31, 2015, Nuveen CA Div Adv Muni 3 traded at a discount of 4.52% below its net asset value, which is worse than its one-year historical average discount of 7.22%.

Scott R. Romans has been running the fund for 14 years and currently receives a manager quality ranking of 60 (0=worst, 99=best). If you desire only a moderate level of risk and strong performance, then this fund is an excellent option.

Data Date	Investment Rating	Net Assets ($Mil)	Price	Performance Rating/Pts	Total Return Y-T-D	Risk Rating/Pts
12-15	B+	354.96	14.15	B+ / 8.4	11.06%	B- / 7.3
2014	B+	347.90	13.53	B / 7.8	24.92%	B- / 7.8
2013	C	298.23	11.42	C / 4.4	-16.58%	B / 8.0
2012	A-	346.66	14.34	B / 8.0	13.52%	B / 8.7
2011	A-	322.20	13.51	B+ / 8.9	23.82%	B / 8.7
2010	D+	317.86	11.96	D / 2.2	3.36%	C+ / 6.1

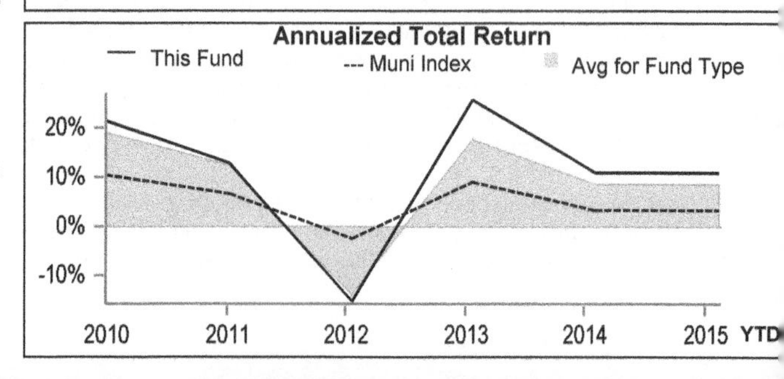

Nuveen CA Muni Value (NCA) A- Excellent

Fund Family: Nuveen Fund Advisors LLC
Fund Type: Municipal - Single State
Inception Date: October 7, 1987

Major Rating Factors:
Strong performance is the major factor driving the A- (Excellent) TheStreet.com Investment Rating for Nuveen CA Muni Value. The fund currently has a performance rating of B+ (Good) based on an annualized return of 6.64% over the last three years and a total return of 8.09% year to date 2015. Factored into the performance evaluation is an expense ratio of 0.64% (very low).

The fund's risk rating is currently B- (Good). It carries a beta of 1.29, meaning it is expected to move 12.9% for every 10% move in the market. Volatility, as measured by both the semi-deviation and a drawdown factor, is considered low. As of December 31, 2015, Nuveen CA Muni Value traded at a premium of 3.32% above its net asset value, which is worse than its one-year historical average premium of .83%.

Scott R. Romans has been running the fund for 14 years and currently receives a manager quality ranking of 85 (0=worst, 99=best). If you desire only a moderate level of risk and strong performance, then this fund is an excellent option.

Data Date	Investment Rating	Net Assets ($Mil)	Price	Performance Rating/Pts	Total Return Y-T-D	Risk Rating/Pts
12-15	A-	268.05	10.88	B+ / 8.8	8.09%	B- / 7.6
2014	A-	264.00	10.53	B- / 7.4	18.86%	B / 8.6
2013	B-	241.16	9.19	C+ / 6.2	-5.62%	B / 8.8
2012	B-	261.05	10.03	C+ / 5.9	14.63%	B / 8.8
2011	B	248.50	9.51	C+ / 6.5	17.41%	B / 8.9
2010	C	240.60	8.63	D+ / 2.6	-0.01%	B / 8.7

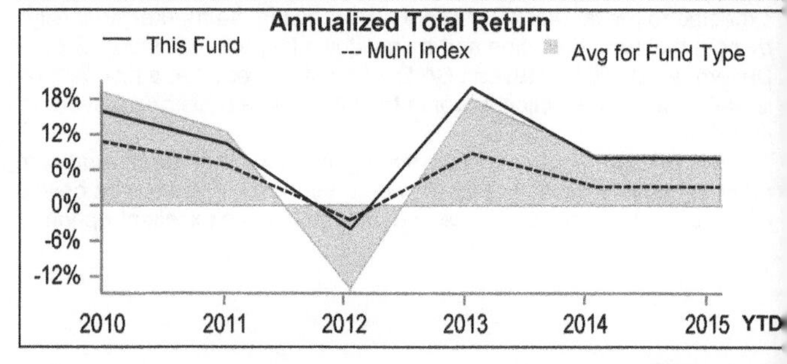

Nuveen CA Select Tax-Free Inc Port (NXC) B+ Good

Fund Family: Nuveen Fund Advisors LLC
Fund Type: Municipal - Single State
Inception Date: June 26, 1992

Major Rating Factors: Strong performance is the major factor driving the B+ (Good) TheStreet.com Investment Rating for Nuveen CA Select Tax-Free Inc Port. The fund currently has a performance rating of B (Good) based on an annualized return of 5.61% over the last three years and a total return of 5.96% year to date 2015. Factored into the performance evaluation is an expense ratio of 0.37% (very low).

The fund's risk rating is currently B- (Good). It carries a beta of 1.93, meaning it is expected to move 19.3% for every 10% move in the market. Volatility, as measured by both the semi-deviation and a drawdown factor, is considered low. As of December 31, 2015, Nuveen CA Select Tax-Free Inc Port traded at a premium of .84% above its net asset value, which is worse than its one-year historical average premium of .09%.

Scott R. Romans has been running the fund for 24 years and currently receives a manager quality ranking of 70 (0=worst, 99=best). If you desire only a moderate level of risk and strong performance, then this fund is an excellent option.

Data Date	Investment Rating	Net Assets ($Mil)	Price	Performance Rating/Pts	Total Return Y-T-D	Risk Rating/Pts
12-15	B+	97.42	15.63	B / 8.0	5.96%	B- / 7.6
2014	B-	96.60	15.44	B / 7.6	20.51%	C+ / 6.7
2013	C+	95.60	13.50	C / 5.5	-7.65%	B / 8.6
2012	A-	94.45	15.21	B / 7.9	15.53%	B+ / 9.0
2011	B	91.40	14.08	C+ / 6.8	15.27%	B+ / 9.0
2010	C	87.55	12.75	D+ / 2.7	4.93%	B / 8.5

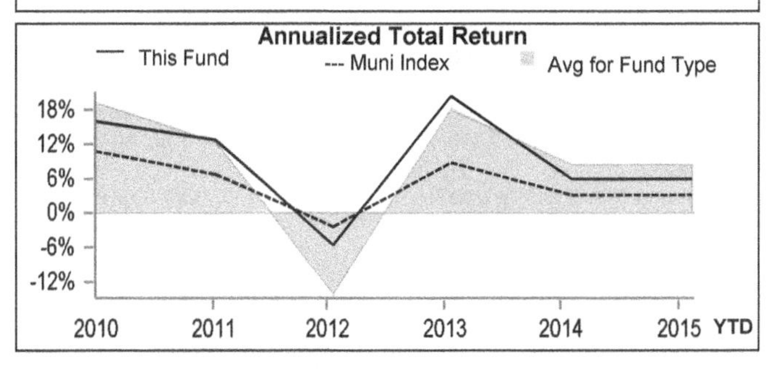

Nuveen California Municipal Value (NCB) B+ Good

Fund Family: Nuveen Fund Advisors LLC
Fund Type: Municipal - National
Inception Date: April 28, 2009

Major Rating Factors: Strong performance is the major factor driving the B+ (Good) TheStreet.com Investment Rating for Nuveen California Municipal Value. The fund currently has a performance rating of B+ (Good) based on an annualized return of 6.42% over the last three years and a total return of 8.26% year to date 2015. Factored into the performance evaluation is an expense ratio of 0.75% (very low).

The fund's risk rating is currently B- (Good). It carries a beta of 2.04, meaning it is expected to move 20.4% for every 10% move in the market. Volatility, as measured by both the semi-deviation and a drawdown factor, is considered low. As of December 31, 2015, Nuveen California Municipal Value traded at a discount of 1.10% below its net asset value, which is worse than its one-year historical average discount of 3.80%.

Scott R. Romans currently receives a manager quality ranking of 73 (0=worst, 99=best). If you desire only a moderate level of risk and strong performance, then this fund is an excellent option.

Data Date	Investment Rating	Net Assets ($Mil)	Price	Performance Rating/Pts	Total Return Y-T-D	Risk Rating/Pts
12-15	B+	57.53	17.02	B+ / 8.6	8.26%	B- / 7.3
2014	A-	57.50	16.71	B / 7.9	21.45%	B / 8.2
2013	C	52.07	14.57	C / 4.5	-8.47%	B / 8.4
2012	B	56.44	16.29	B- / 7.3	15.25%	B / 8.6
2011	B+	52.60	15.06	B / 7.6	11.36%	B / 8.6
2010	C-	51.66	14.40	D / 2.0	3.81%	B / 8.1

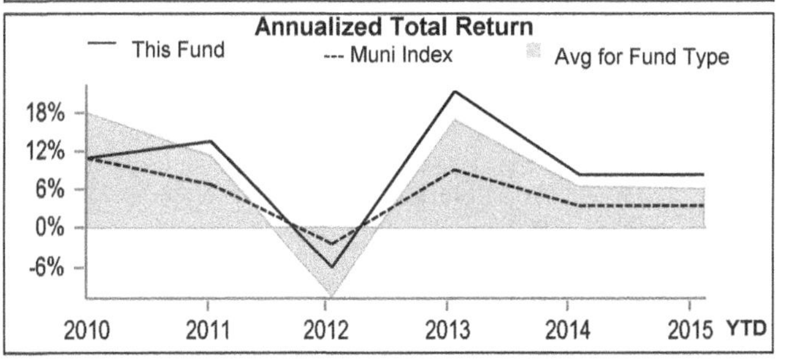

Nuveen Core Equity Alpha Fund (JCE) A- Excellent

Fund Family: Nuveen Fund Advisors LLC
Fund Type: Income
Inception Date: March 28, 2007

Major Rating Factors:
Exceptional performance is the major factor driving the A- (Excellent) TheStreet.com Investment Rating for Nuveen Core Equity Alpha Fund. The fund currently has a performance rating of A- (Excellent) based on an annualized return of 16.95% over the last three years and a total return of 0.43% year to date 2015. Factored into the performance evaluation is an expense ratio of 1.03% (low).

The fund's risk rating is currently B- (Good). It carries a beta of 0.97, meaning that its performance tracks fairly well with that of the overall stock market. Volatility, as measured by both the semi-deviation and a drawdown factor, is considered low. As of December 31, 2015, Nuveen Core Equity Alpha Fund traded at a discount of 4.42% below its net asset value, which is worse than its one-year historical average discount of 4.82%.

Adrian D. Banner currently receives a manager quality ranking of 85 (0=worst, 99=best). If you desire only a moderate level of risk and strong performance, then this fund is an excellent option.

Data Date	Investment Rating	Net Assets ($Mil)	Price	Performance Rating/Pts	Total Return Y-T-D	Risk Rating/Pts
12-15	A-	280.26	14.27	A- / 9.2	0.43%	B- / 7.2
2014	A+	289.80	17.47	A / 9.4	23.18%	B / 8.8
2013	A	259.54	16.98	B+ / 8.8	32.49%	B / 8.0
2012	C+	222.46	13.35	C+ / 5.9	17.19%	B- / 7.8
2011	C+	222.50	12.47	C+ / 6.4	4.73%	B- / 7.6
2010	C	211.37	13.12	C / 5.5	17.29%	C / 5.2

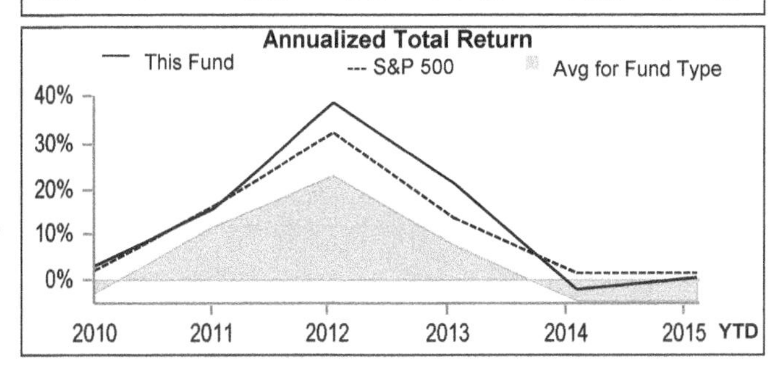

Nuveen Credit Strategies Income (JQC) — C- — Fair

Fund Family: Nuveen Fund Advisors LLC
Fund Type: Growth and Income
Inception Date: June 25, 2003

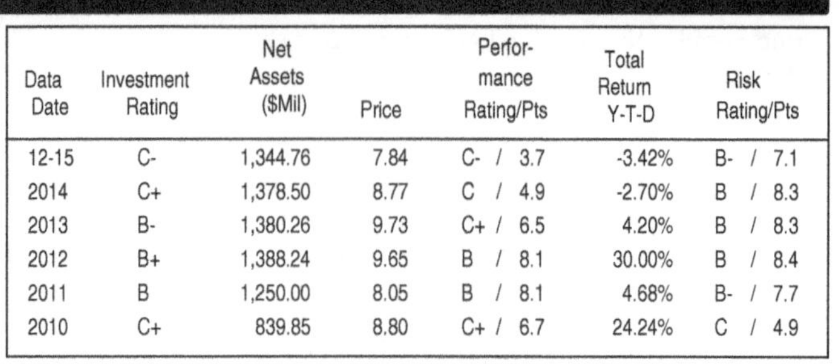

Data Date	Investment Rating	Net Assets ($Mil)	Price	Performance Rating/Pts	Total Return Y-T-D	Risk Rating/Pts
12-15	C-	1,344.76	7.84	C- / 3.7	-3.42%	B- / 7.1
2014	C+	1,378.50	8.77	C / 4.9	-2.70%	B / 8.3
2013	B-	1,380.26	9.73	C+ / 6.5	4.20%	B / 8.3
2012	B+	1,388.24	9.65	B / 8.1	30.00%	B / 8.4
2011	B	1,250.00	8.05	B / 8.1	4.68%	B- / 7.7
2010	C+	839.85	8.80	C+ / 6.7	24.24%	C / 4.9

Major Rating Factors: Middle of the road best describes Nuveen Credit Strategies Income whose TheStreet.com Investment Rating is currently a C- (Fair). The fund currently has a performance rating of C- (Fair) based on an annualized return of -0.97% over the last three years and a total return of -3.42% year to date 2015. Factored into the performance evaluation is an expense ratio of 1.95% (above average).

The fund's risk rating is currently B- (Good). It carries a beta of 0.43, meaning the fund's expected move will be 4.3% for every 10% move in the market. Volatility, as measured by both the semi-deviation and a drawdown factor, is considered low. As of December 31, 2015, Nuveen Credit Strategies Income traded at a discount of 12.21% below its net asset value, which is worse than its one-year historical average discount of 12.80%.

Gunther M. Stein has been running the fund for 13 years and currently receives a manager quality ranking of 25 (0=worst, 99=best). If you desire an average level of risk, then this fund may be an option.

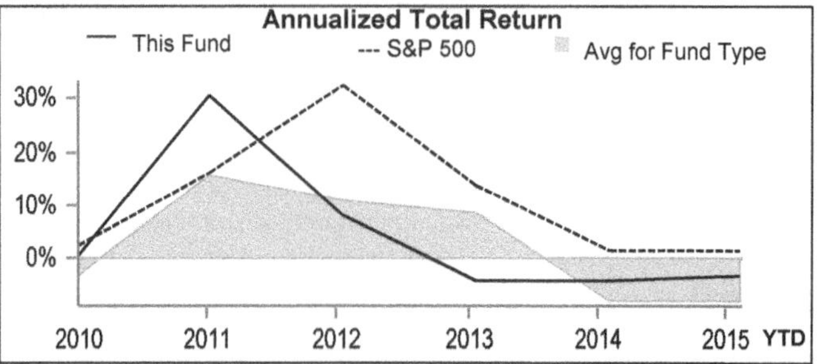

Nuveen CT Prem Inc Muni (NTC) — B- — Good

Fund Family: Nuveen Fund Advisors LLC
Fund Type: Municipal - Single State
Inception Date: May 20, 1993

Data Date	Investment Rating	Net Assets ($Mil)	Price	Performance Rating/Pts	Total Return Y-T-D	Risk Rating/Pts
12-15	B-	208.58	12.76	C+ / 6.2	6.73%	B- / 7.9
2014	C	210.80	12.54	C / 4.3	12.74%	B / 8.2
2013	C-	220.27	11.60	D+ / 2.4	-15.46%	B / 8.4
2012	C+	82.32	14.32	C / 4.3	8.43%	B+ / 9.1
2011	B+	79.80	14.06	B / 7.6	15.26%	B+ / 9.0
2010	C	78.11	13.05	C- / 3.3	0.42%	B- / 7.9

Major Rating Factors: Nuveen CT Prem Inc Muni receives a TheStreet.com Investment Rating of B- (Good). The fund currently has a performance rating of C+ (Fair) based on an annualized return of 0.79% over the last three years and a total return of 6.73% year to date 2015. Factored into the performance evaluation is an expense ratio of 1.68% (above average).

The fund's risk rating is currently B- (Good). It carries a beta of 1.84, meaning it is expected to move 18.4% for every 10% move in the market. Volatility, as measured by both the semi-deviation and a drawdown factor, is considered low. As of December 31, 2015, Nuveen CT Prem Inc Muni traded at a discount of 12.78% below its net asset value, which is worse than its one-year historical average discount of 13.12%.

Michael S. Hamilton currently receives a manager quality ranking of 35 (0=worst, 99=best). If you desire an average level of risk, then this fund may be an option.

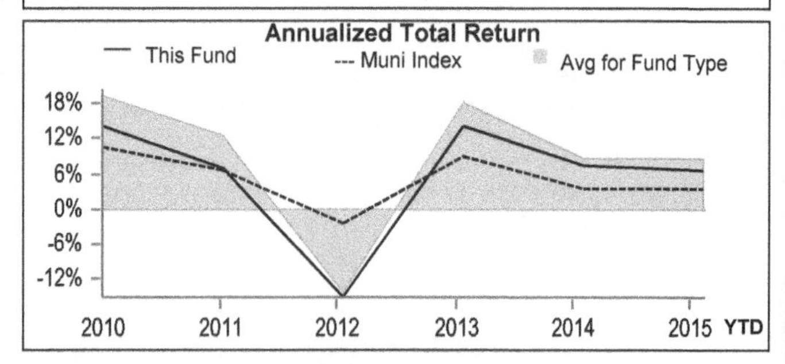

Nuveen Div Adv Muni (NAD) — B — Good

Fund Family: Nuveen Fund Advisors LLC
Fund Type: Municipal - National
Inception Date: May 25, 1999

Data Date	Investment Rating	Net Assets ($Mil)	Price	Performance Rating/Pts	Total Return Y-T-D	Risk Rating/Pts
12-15	B	614.45	14.55	B- / 7.2	7.74%	B- / 7.5
2014	B	608.40	14.33	B- / 7.0	18.60%	B- / 7.9
2013	C	639.65	12.59	C / 4.9	-14.71%	B / 8.2
2012	A-	565.36	15.48	B+ / 8.4	15.89%	B / 8.6
2011	A-	577.40	14.56	B+ / 8.7	21.63%	B / 8.7
2010	C-	561.83	12.90	C- / 3.7	1.95%	C+ / 6.5

Major Rating Factors: Strong performance is the major factor driving the B (Good) TheStreet.com Investment Rating for Nuveen Div Adv Muni. The fund currently has a performance rating of B- (Good) based on an annualized return of 2.98% over the last three years and a total return of 7.74% year to date 2015. Factored into the performance evaluation is an expense ratio of 1.73% (above average).

The fund's risk rating is currently B- (Good). It carries a beta of 2.19, meaning it is expected to move 21.9% for every 10% move in the market. Volatility, as measured by both the semi-deviation and a drawdown factor, is considered low. As of December 31, 2015, Nuveen Div Adv Muni traded at a discount of 7.09% below its net asset value, which is worse than its one-year historical average discount of 9.45%.

Thomas C. Spalding has been running the fund for 14 years and currently receives a manager quality ranking of 45 (0=worst, 99=best). If you desire only a moderate level of risk and strong performance, then this fund is an excellent option.

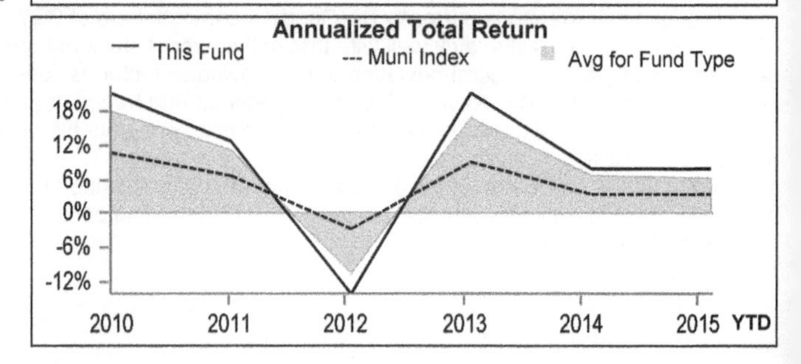

Nuveen Div Adv Muni 3 (NZF) B Good

Fund Family: Nuveen Fund Advisors LLC
Fund Type: Municipal - National
Inception Date: September 25, 2001

Major Rating Factors: Strong performance is the major factor driving the B (Good) TheStreet.com Investment Rating for Nuveen Div Adv Muni 3. The fund currently has a performance rating of B- (Good) based on an annualized return of 3.08% over the last three years and a total return of 9.61% year to date 2015. Factored into the performance evaluation is an expense ratio of 1.73% (above average).

The fund's risk rating is currently B- (Good). It carries a beta of 2.23, meaning it is expected to move 22.3% for every 10% move in the market. Volatility, as measured by both the semi-deviation and a drawdown factor, is considered low. As of December 31, 2015, Nuveen Div Adv Muni 3 traded at a discount of 10.42% below its net asset value, which is worse than its one-year historical average discount of 12.35%.

Paul L. Brennan has been running the fund for 10 years and currently receives a manager quality ranking of 41 (0=worst, 99=best). If you desire only a moderate level of risk and strong performance, then this fund is an excellent option.

Data Date	Investment Rating	Net Assets ($Mil)	Price	Performance Rating/Pts	Total Return Y-T-D	Risk Rating/Pts
12-15	B	574.72	14.36	B- / 7.4	9.61%	B- / 7.6
2014	C+	568.80	13.78	C+ / 5.9	17.01%	B- / 7.8
2013	C-	647.83	12.35	C- / 3.4	-15.09%	B / 8.0
2012	B	587.05	15.09	B- / 7.2	11.93%	B / 8.7
2011	B+	596.70	14.71	B+ / 8.3	18.02%	B / 8.8
2010	C	584.56	13.29	C- / 3.9	5.81%	C+ / 6.8

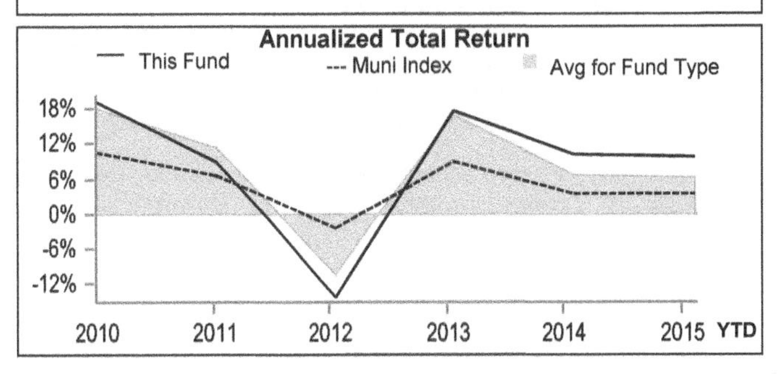

Nuveen Div Adv Muni Income (NVG) B Good

Fund Family: Nuveen Fund Advisors LLC
Fund Type: Municipal - National
Inception Date: March 25, 2002

Major Rating Factors: Strong performance is the major factor driving the B (Good) TheStreet.com Investment Rating for Nuveen Div Adv Muni Income. The fund currently has a performance rating of B- (Good) based on an annualized return of 2.96% over the last three years and a total return of 7.94% year to date 2015. Factored into the performance evaluation is an expense ratio of 1.75% (above average).

The fund's risk rating is currently B- (Good). It carries a beta of 2.37, meaning it is expected to move 23.7% for every 10% move in the market. Volatility, as measured by both the semi-deviation and a drawdown factor, is considered low. As of December 31, 2015, Nuveen Div Adv Muni Income traded at a discount of 11.38% below its net asset value, which is worse than its one-year historical average discount of 12.55%.

Paul L. Brennan has been running the fund for 10 years and currently receives a manager quality ranking of 38 (0=worst, 99=best). If you desire only a moderate level of risk and strong performance, then this fund is an excellent option.

Data Date	Investment Rating	Net Assets ($Mil)	Price	Performance Rating/Pts	Total Return Y-T-D	Risk Rating/Pts
12-15	B	433.09	14.48	B- / 7.0	7.94%	B- / 7.6
2014	C+	429.20	14.11	C+ / 6.0	18.24%	B- / 7.8
2013	C-	483.92	12.52	C- / 3.7	-14.86%	B / 8.1
2012	B	448.07	15.35	C+ / 6.9	10.96%	B+ / 9.0
2011	B+	454.20	15.05	B / 7.8	18.75%	B+ / 9.1
2010	C+	441.21	13.60	C / 4.9	0.77%	C+ / 6.9

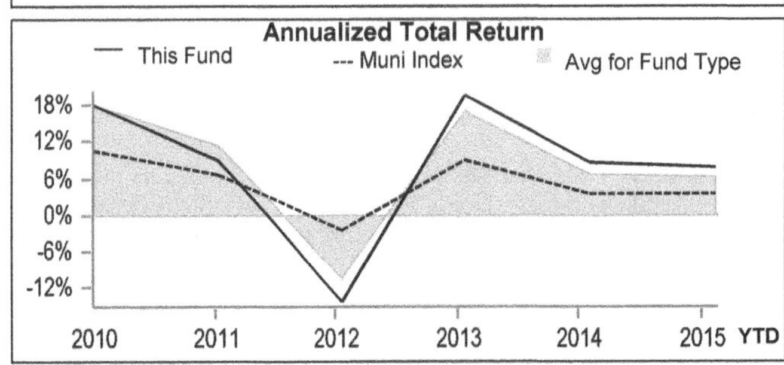

Nuveen Diversified Dividend&Income (JDD) C+ Fair

Fund Family: Nuveen Fund Advisors LLC
Fund Type: Growth and Income
Inception Date: September 30, 2003

Major Rating Factors: Middle of the road best describes Nuveen Diversified Dividend&Income whose TheStreet.com Investment Rating is currently a C+ (Fair). The fund currently has a performance rating of C+ (Fair) based on an annualized return of 5.91% over the last three years and a total return of 1.23% year to date 2015. Factored into the performance evaluation is an expense ratio of 1.84% (above average).

The fund's risk rating is currently C+ (Fair). It carries a beta of 0.85, meaning the fund's expected move will be 8.5% for every 10% move in the market. Volatility, as measured by both the semi-deviation and a drawdown factor, is considered low. As of December 31, 2015, Nuveen Diversified Dividend&Income traded at a discount of 13.57% below its net asset value, which is better than its one-year historical average discount of 12.83%.

Gunther M. Stein has been running the fund for 13 years and currently receives a manager quality ranking of 29 (0=worst, 99=best). If you desire an average level of risk, then this fund may be an option.

Data Date	Investment Rating	Net Assets ($Mil)	Price	Performance Rating/Pts	Total Return Y-T-D	Risk Rating/Pts
12-15	C+	270.33	10.83	C+ / 6.4	1.23%	C+ / 6.9
2014	C+	259.90	11.77	C+ / 6.4	14.84%	B- / 7.7
2013	C+	252.07	11.27	C+ / 5.8	2.19%	B- / 7.8
2012	B	239.89	11.60	B- / 7.4	24.13%	B / 8.0
2011	B	226.70	10.26	B+ / 8.4	6.97%	B- / 7.8
2010	C	222.57	10.89	C+ / 6.4	22.16%	C- / 4.0

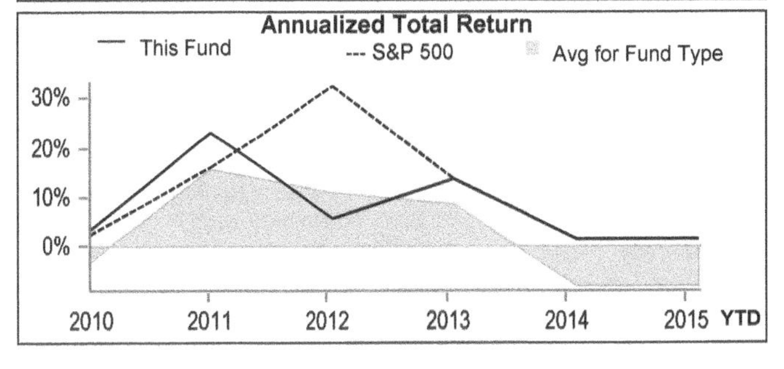

Nuveen Dividend Advantage Muni 2 (NXZ) B- Good

Fund Family: Nuveen Fund Advisors LLC
Fund Type: Municipal - National
Inception Date: March 27, 2001

Major Rating Factors: Nuveen Dividend Advantage Muni 2 receives a TheStreet.com Investment Rating of B- (Good). The fund currently has a performance rating of C+ (Fair) based on an annualized return of 2.49% over the last three years and a total return of 6.27% year to date 2015. Factored into the performance evaluation is an expense ratio of 1.60% (above average).

The fund's risk rating is currently B- (Good). It carries a beta of 2.30, meaning it is expected to move 23.0% for every 10% move in the market. Volatility, as measured by both the semi-deviation and a drawdown factor, is considered low. As of December 31, 2015, Nuveen Dividend Advantage Muni 2 traded at a discount of 11.50% below its net asset value, which is worse than its one-year historical average discount of 12.41%.

Thomas C. Spalding currently receives a manager quality ranking of 37 (0=worst, 99=best). If you desire an average level of risk, then this fund may be an option.

Data Date	Investment Rating	Net Assets ($Mil)	Price	Performance Rating/Pts	Total Return Y-T-D	Risk Rating/Pts
12-15	B-	466.29	14.16	C+ / 6.7	6.27%	B- / 7.7
2014	C+	461.00	14.11	C+ / 6.3	16.61%	B- / 7.9
2013	C	481.55	12.69	C / 4.5	-13.19%	B / 8.1
2012	B	427.09	15.22	C+ / 6.5	11.97%	B / 8.7
2011	B+	431.20	14.76	B / 8.1	21.82%	B / 8.7
2010	C-	436.38	13.30	D / 2.2	-1.17%	B- / 7.6

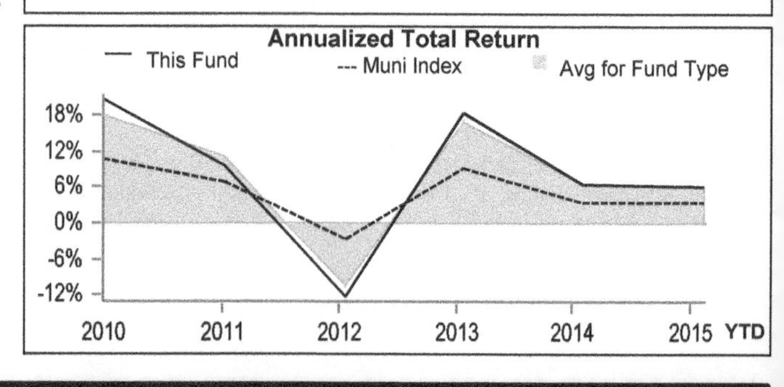

Nuveen Dow 30 Dynamic Overwrite (DPD) B+ Good

Fund Family: Nuveen Fund Advisors LLC
Fund Type: Income
Inception Date: May 6, 2005

Major Rating Factors: Strong performance is the major factor driving the B+ (Good) TheStreet.com Investment Rating for Nuveen Dow 30 Dynamic Overwrite. The fund currently has a performance rating of B- (Good) based on an annualized return of 9.36% over the last three years and a total return of -5.03% year to date 2015. Factored into the performance evaluation is an expense ratio of 1.12% (low).

The fund's risk rating is currently B (Good). It carries a beta of 0.87, meaning the fund's expected move will be 8.7% for every 10% move in the market. Volatility, as measured by both the semi-deviation and a drawdown factor, is considered low. As of December 31, 2015, Nuveen Dow 30 Dynamic Overwrite traded at a discount of 9.00% below its net asset value, which is worse than its one-year historical average discount of 9.58%.

James A. Colon has been running the fund for 5 years and currently receives a manager quality ranking of 46 (0=worst, 99=best). If you desire only a moderate level of risk and strong performance, then this fund is an excellent option.

Data Date	Investment Rating	Net Assets ($Mil)	Price	Performance Rating/Pts	Total Return Y-T-D	Risk Rating/Pts
12-15	B+	607.31	14.36	B- / 7.3	-5.03%	B / 8.1
2013	B	185.26	15.57	C+ / 6.9	21.90%	B / 8.3
2012	C-	173.87	13.25	C- / 3.0	11.62%	B / 8.2
2011	C-	171.00	13.12	C- / 3.6	-2.18%	B- / 7.5
2010	C	165.40	14.53	C+ / 5.6	7.76%	C / 5.3

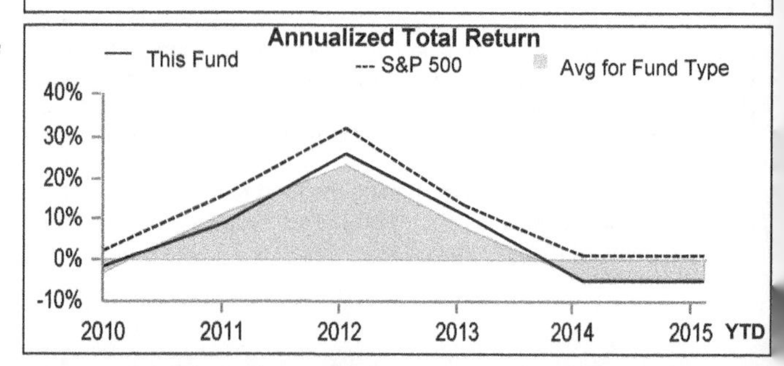

Nuveen Energy MLP Total Return Fun (JMF) D- Weak

Fund Family: Nuveen Fund Advisors LLC
Fund Type: Growth and Income
Inception Date: February 24, 2011

Major Rating Factors:
Disappointing performance is the major factor driving the D- (Weak) TheStreet.com Investment Rating for Nuveen Energy MLP Total Return Fun. The fund currently has a performance rating of D- (Weak) based on an annualized return of -9.78% over the last three years and a total return of -41.12% year to date 2015. Factored into the performance evaluation is an expense ratio of 1.84% (above average).

The fund's risk rating is currently C (Fair). It carries a beta of 1.20, meaning it is expected to move 12.0% for every 10% move in the market. Volatility, as measured by both the semi-deviation and a drawdown factor, is considered average. As of December 31, 2015, Nuveen Energy MLP Total Return Fun traded at a discount of 11.69% below its net asset value, which is better than its one-year historical average discount of 9.29%.

James J. Cunnane, Jr. currently receives a manager quality ranking of 6 (0=worst, 99=best). This fund offers an average level of risk but investors looking for strong performance will be frustrated.

Data Date	Investment Rating	Net Assets ($Mil)	Price	Performance Rating/Pts	Total Return Y-T-D	Risk Rating/Pts
12-15	D-	871.91	11.10	D- / 1.2	-41.12%	C / 4.7
2014	C+	938.40	20.32	C / 5.3	12.77%	B- / 7.9
2013	C-	774.14	19.55	C / 4.5	9.94%	B- / 7.3
2012	D+	409.91	17.70	C- / 3.4	10.00%	B- / 7.3

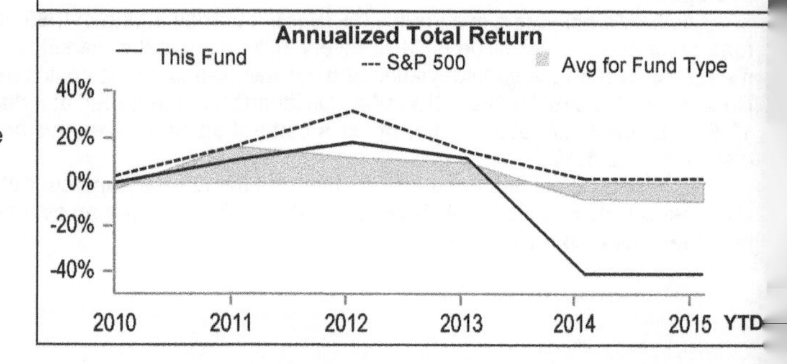

Nuveen EnhancedMunicipal Value (NEV) — C+ Fair

Fund Family: Nuveen Fund Advisors LLC
Fund Type: General - Investment Grade
Inception Date: September 25, 2009

Data Date	Investment Rating	Net Assets ($Mil)	Price	Perfor-mance Rating/Pts	Total Return Y-T-D	Risk Rating/Pts
12-15	C+	330.87	15.71	C+ / 6.6	10.19%	C+ / 6.6
2014	C+	328.10	15.21	C+ / 6.2	24.27%	B- / 7.6
2013	C-	334.39	12.96	C- / 4.0	-17.57%	B- / 7.8
2012	B-	269.05	16.10	C+ / 6.7	23.56%	B / 8.3
2011	B+	273.10	14.23	B+ / 8.3	24.07%	B / 8.2
2010	D+	240.98	12.71	E+ / 0.9	2.73%	B- / 7.6

Major Rating Factors: Middle of the road best describes Nuveen EnhancedMunicipal Value whose TheStreet.com Investment Rating is currently a C+ (Fair). The fund currently has a performance rating of C+ (Fair) based on an annualized return of 4.05% over the last three years and a total return of 10.19% year to date 2015. Factored into the performance evaluation is an expense ratio of 1.08% (low).

The fund's risk rating is currently C+ (Fair). It carries a beta of 2.87, meaning it is expected to move 28.7% for every 10% move in the market. Volatility, as measured by both the semi-deviation and a drawdown factor, is considered low. As of December 31, 2015, Nuveen EnhancedMunicipal Value traded at a premium of .58% above its net asset value, which is worse than its one-year historical average discount of 2.23%.

Steven M. Hlavin has been running the fund for 6 years and currently receives a manager quality ranking of 78 (0=worst, 99=best). If you desire an average level of risk, then this fund may be an option.

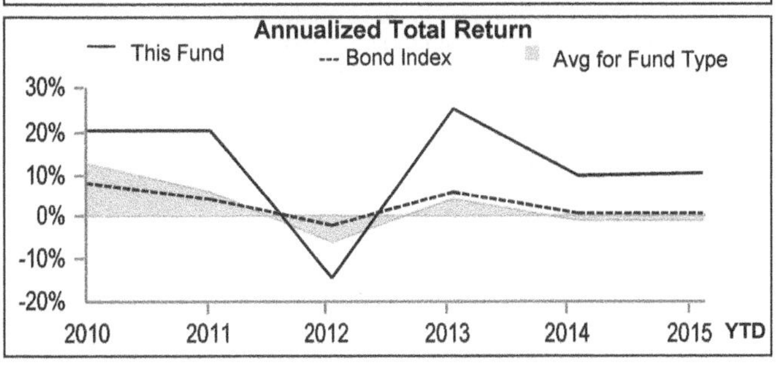

Nuveen Flexible Investment Income (JPW) — C- Fair

Fund Family: Nuveen Fund Advisors LLC
Fund Type: Income
Inception Date: June 25, 2013

Data Date	Investment Rating	Net Assets ($Mil)	Price	Perfor-mance Rating/Pts	Total Return Y-T-D	Risk Rating/Pts
12-15	C-	68.87	14.67	D+ / 2.9	-1.92%	B- / 7.0
2014	C-	73.95	16.38	C- / 3.7	10.85%	B / 8.0

Major Rating Factors:
Disappointing performance is the major factor driving the C- (Fair) TheStreet.com Investment Rating for Nuveen Flexible Investment Income. The fund currently has a performance rating of D+ (Weak) based on an annualized return of 0.00% over the last three years and a total return of -1.92% year to date 2015. Factored into the performance evaluation is an expense ratio of 1.82% (above average).

The fund's risk rating is currently B- (Good). It carries a beta of 0.00, meaning the fund's expected move will be 0.0% for every 10% move in the market. Volatility, as measured by both the semi-deviation and a drawdown factor, is considered low. As of December 31, 2015, Nuveen Flexible Investment Income traded at a discount of 14.61% below its net asset value, which is better than its one-year historical average discount of 11.46%.

Susi Budiman has been running the fund for 3 years and currently receives a manager quality ranking of 45 (0=worst, 99=best). This fund offers only a moderate level of risk but investors looking for strong performance are still waiting.

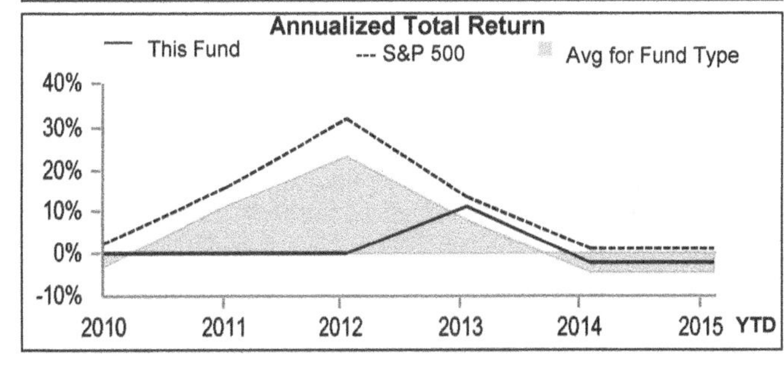

Nuveen Floating Rate Income Fund (JFR) — C Fair

Fund Family: Nuveen Fund Advisors LLC
Fund Type: Loan Participation
Inception Date: March 26, 2004

Data Date	Investment Rating	Net Assets ($Mil)	Price	Perfor-mance Rating/Pts	Total Return Y-T-D	Risk Rating/Pts
12-15	C	662.80	10.24	C / 4.4	-0.23%	B- / 7.2
2014	C	681.10	10.99	C- / 4.1	-1.77%	B / 8.3
2013	C+	691.31	11.92	C / 5.2	2.09%	B / 8.1
2012	C+	572.12	12.19	C+ / 6.5	22.55%	B / 8.0
2011	B	543.20	10.86	B / 7.6	-1.68%	B- / 7.9
2010	C+	542.46	11.81	B / 7.7	21.16%	C- / 3.7

Major Rating Factors: Middle of the road best describes Nuveen Floating Rate Income Fund whose TheStreet.com Investment Rating is currently a C (Fair). The fund currently has a performance rating of C (Fair) based on an annualized return of -0.01% over the last three years and a total return of -0.23% year to date 2015. Factored into the performance evaluation is an expense ratio of 2.29% (high).

The fund's risk rating is currently B- (Good). It carries a beta of -253.44, meaning the fund's expected move will be -2534.4% for every 10% move in the market. Volatility, as measured by both the semi-deviation and a drawdown factor, is considered low. As of December 31, 2015, Nuveen Floating Rate Income Fund traded at a discount of 5.71% below its net asset value, which is worse than its one-year historical average discount of 10.41%.

Gunther M. Stein currently receives a manager quality ranking of 31 (0=worst, 99=best). If you desire an average level of risk, then this fund may be an option.

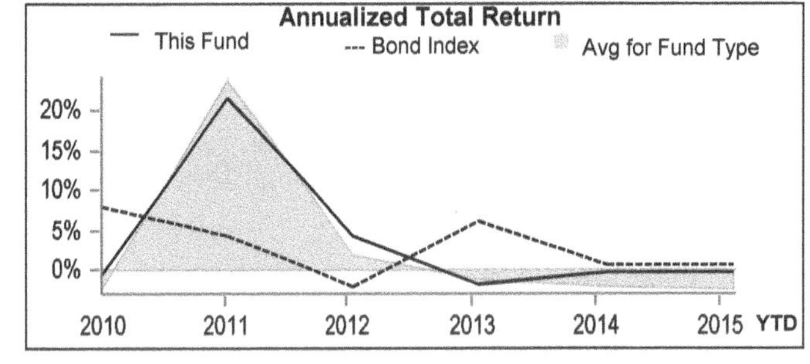

Nuveen Floating Rate Income Opp (JRO) C- Fair

Fund Family: Nuveen Fund Advisors LLC
Fund Type: Loan Participation
Inception Date: July 30, 2004

Major Rating Factors: Middle of the road best describes Nuveen Floating Rate Income Opp whose TheStreet.com Investment Rating is currently a C- (Fair). The fund currently has a performance rating of C- (Fair) based on an annualized return of -1.11% over the last three years and a total return of -6.83% year to date 2015. Factored into the performance evaluation is an expense ratio of 2.31% (high).

The fund's risk rating is currently B- (Good). It carries a beta of -62.23, meaning the fund's expected move will be -622.3% for every 10% move in the market. Volatility, as measured by both the semi-deviation and a drawdown factor, is considered low. As of December 31, 2015, Nuveen Floating Rate Income Opp traded at a discount of 9.34% below its net asset value, which is worse than its one-year historical average discount of 9.61%.

Gunther M. Stein has been running the fund for 9 years and currently receives a manager quality ranking of 50 (0=worst, 99=best). If you desire an average level of risk, then this fund may be an option.

Data Date	Investment Rating	Net Assets ($Mil)	Price	Performance Rating/Pts	Total Return Y-T-D	Risk Rating/Pts
12-15	C-	463.73	9.80	C- / 3.5	-6.83%	B- / 7.2
2014	C	478.30	11.27	C / 4.3	-0.94%	B / 8.3
2013	C	482.20	12.18	C / 5.0	4.59%	B / 8.1
2012	C+	369.94	12.25	C+ / 5.9	19.92%	B- / 7.9
2011	B+	340.90	11.04	B+ / 8.6	-4.23%	B- / 7.9
2010	C+	322.14	12.08	B / 7.9	19.90%	C- / 3.6

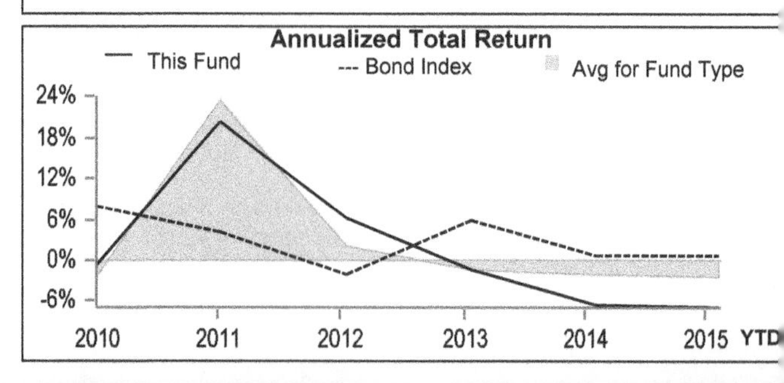

Nuveen GA Div Adv Muni Fund 2 (NKG) B Good

Fund Family: Nuveen Fund Advisors LLC
Fund Type: Municipal - Single State
Inception Date: September 25, 2002

Major Rating Factors: Strong performance is the major factor driving the B (Good) TheStreet.com Investment Rating for Nuveen GA Div Adv Muni Fund 2. The fund currently has a performance rating of B- (Good) based on an annualized return of 1.19% over the last three years and a total return of 12.46% year to date 2015. Factored into the performance evaluation is an expense ratio of 1.62% (above average).

The fund's risk rating is currently B- (Good). It carries a beta of 2.14, meaning it is expected to move 21.4% for every 10% move in the market. Volatility, as measured by both the semi-deviation and a drawdown factor, is considered low. As of December 31, 2015, Nuveen GA Div Adv Muni Fund 2 traded at a discount of 4.73% below its net asset value, which is worse than its one-year historical average discount of 7.95%.

Daniel J. Close has been running the fund for 9 years and currently receives a manager quality ranking of 31 (0=worst, 99=best). If you desire only a moderate level of risk and strong performance, then this fund is an excellent option.

Data Date	Investment Rating	Net Assets ($Mil)	Price	Performance Rating/Pts	Total Return Y-T-D	Risk Rating/Pts
12-15	B	147.44	13.50	B- / 7.3	12.46%	B- / 7.4
2014	C-	148.30	12.57	C- / 3.3	11.36%	B- / 7.9
2013	C-	153.83	11.73	D+ / 2.7	-17.51%	B / 8.1
2012	B-	67.04	14.85	C+ / 6.3	8.01%	B / 8.7
2011	A-	65.10	14.63	B+ / 8.6	22.34%	B / 8.8
2010	C	64.72	12.58	C- / 3.1	2.09%	B- / 7.4

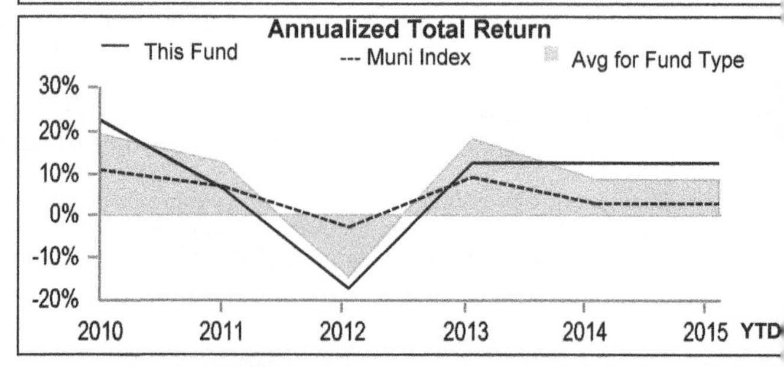

Nuveen Global Equity Income (JGV) D+ Weak

Fund Family: Nuveen Fund Advisors LLC
Fund Type: Global
Inception Date: July 25, 2006

Major Rating Factors: Nuveen Global Equity Income receives a TheStreet.com Investment Rating of D+ (Weak). The fund currently has a performance rating of C- (Fair) based on an annualized return of -2.75% over the last three years and a total return of -6.90% year to date 2015. Factored into the performance evaluation is an expense ratio of 1.11% (low).

The fund's risk rating is currently C+ (Fair). It carries a beta of 0.77, meaning the fund's expected move will be 7.7% for every 10% move in the market. Volatility, as measured by both the semi-deviation and a drawdown factor, is considered low. As of December 31, 2015, Nuveen Global Equity Income traded at a discount of 11.15% below its net asset value, which is worse than its one-year historical average discount of 13.27%.

Rod A. Parsley has been running the fund for 3 years and currently receives a manager quality ranking of 25 (0=worst, 99=best). If you desire an average level of risk, then this fund may be an option.

Data Date	Investment Rating	Net Assets ($Mil)	Price	Performance Rating/Pts	Total Return Y-T-D	Risk Rating/Pts
12-15	D+	277.74	10.92	C- / 3.3	-6.90%	C+ / 6.2
2014	D+	287.30	13.01	C- / 3.0	7.73%	C+ / 6.9
2013	D	268.18	13.17	D / 1.8	-6.58%	C+ / 6.5
2012	D	324.96	14.91	D / 2.0	0.36%	B- / 7.1
2011	C+	325.00	16.76	C+ / 5.8	-9.06%	B- / 7.7
2010	B+	351.82	20.30	B+ / 8.4	23.36%	C / 5.1

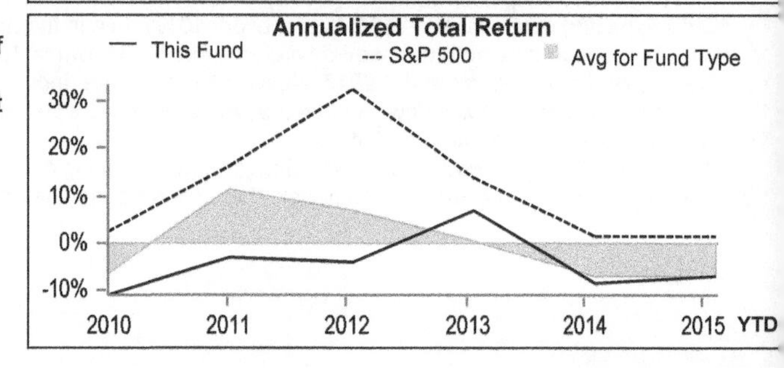

Nuveen Global High Income (XJGHX) D- Weak

Fund Family: Nuveen Fund Advisors LLC
Fund Type: Global
Inception Date: November 24, 2014

Data Date	Investment Rating	Net Assets ($Mil)	Price	Performance Rating/Pts	Total Return Y-T-D	Risk Rating/Pts
12-15	D-	0.00	13.74	D- / 1.3	-12.87%	C / 4.5

Major Rating Factors:
Disappointing performance is the major factor driving the D- (Weak) TheStreet.com Investment Rating for Nuveen Global High Income. The fund currently has a performance rating of D- (Weak) based on an annualized return of 0.00% over the last three years and a total return of -12.87% year to date 2015.

The fund's risk rating is currently C (Fair). It carries a beta of 0.00, meaning the fund's expected move will be 0.0% for every 10% move in the market. Volatility, as measured by both the semi-deviation and a drawdown factor, is considered average. As of December 31, 2015, Nuveen Global High Income traded at a discount of 14.34% below its net asset value, which is worse than its one-year historical average discount of 14.50%.

John T. Fruit has been running the fund for 2 years and currently receives a manager quality ranking of 13 (0=worst, 99=best). This fund offers an average level of risk but investors looking for strong performance will be frustrated.

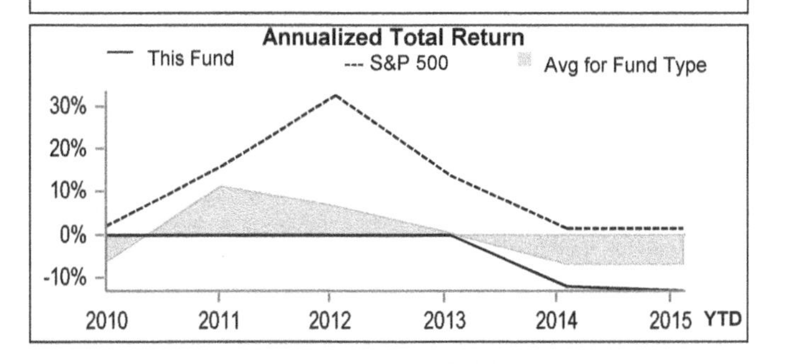

Nuveen Intermdt Dur Qlty Mun Term (NIQ) A Excellent

Fund Family: Nuveen Fund Advisors LLC
Fund Type: Municipal - National
Inception Date: February 7, 2013

Data Date	Investment Rating	Net Assets ($Mil)	Price	Performance Rating/Pts	Total Return Y-T-D	Risk Rating/Pts
12-15	A	179.34	12.88	A- / 9.2	6.37%	B- / 7.5
2014	B-	183.00	12.65	B / 7.6	13.83%	B- / 7.0

Major Rating Factors:
Exceptional performance is the major factor driving the A (Excellent) TheStreet.com Investment Rating for Nuveen Intermdt Dur Qlty Mun Term. The fund currently has a performance rating of A- (Excellent) based on an annualized return of 0.00% over the last three years and a total return of 6.37% year to date 2015. Factored into the performance evaluation is an expense ratio of 1.16% (low).

The fund's risk rating is currently B- (Good). It carries a beta of 0.00, meaning the fund's expected move will be 0.0% for every 10% move in the market. Volatility, as measured by both the semi-deviation and a drawdown factor, is considered low. As of December 31, 2015, Nuveen Intermdt Dur Qlty Mun Term traded at a discount of 7.93% below its net asset value, which is worse than its one-year historical average discount of 8.59%.

Daniel J. Close has been running the fund for 3 years and currently receives a manager quality ranking of 46 (0=worst, 99=best). If you desire only a moderate level of risk and strong performance, then this fund is an excellent option.

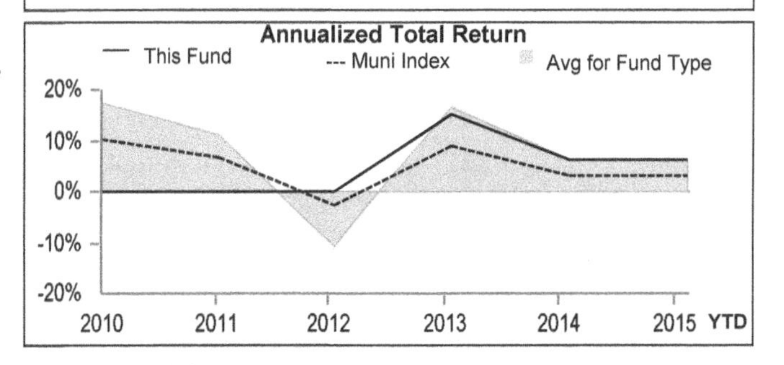

Nuveen Intermediate Dur Mun Term (NID) C Fair

Fund Family: Nuveen Fund Advisors LLC
Fund Type: Municipal - National
Inception Date: December 5, 2012

Data Date	Investment Rating	Net Assets ($Mil)	Price	Performance Rating/Pts	Total Return Y-T-D	Risk Rating/Pts
12-15	C	643.39	12.86	C+ / 5.7	7.85%	C+ / 6.9
2014	B+	647.40	12.50	B+ / 8.4	14.47%	B- / 7.2
2013	D	595.40	11.51	E+ / 0.8	-19.52%	B- / 7.3

Major Rating Factors: Middle of the road best describes Nuveen Intermediate Dur Mun Term whose TheStreet.com Investment Rating is currently a C (Fair). The fund currently has a performance rating of C+ (Fair) based on an annualized return of 0.01% over the last three years and a total return of 7.85% year to date 2015. Factored into the performance evaluation is an expense ratio of 1.23% (average).

The fund's risk rating is currently C+ (Fair). It carries a beta of 1.42, meaning it is expected to move 14.2% for every 10% move in the market. Volatility, as measured by both the semi-deviation and a drawdown factor, is considered low. As of December 31, 2015, Nuveen Intermediate Dur Mun Term traded at a discount of 6.68% below its net asset value, which is worse than its one-year historical average discount of 8.52%.

John V. Miller has been running the fund for 4 years and currently receives a manager quality ranking of 34 (0=worst, 99=best). If you desire an average level of risk, then this fund may be an option.

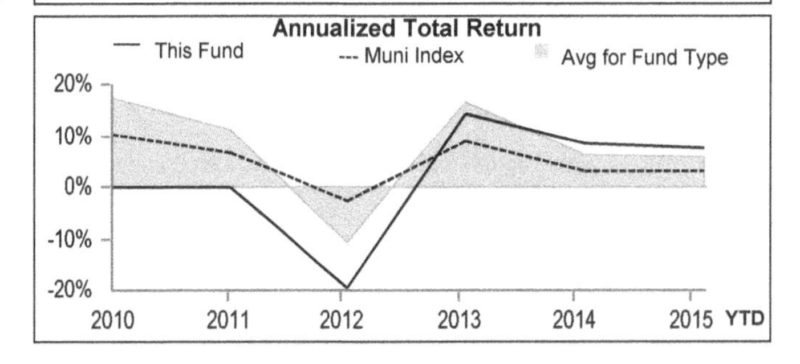

Nuveen Investment Quality Muni Fun (NQM) B Good

Fund Family: Nuveen Fund Advisors LLC
Fund Type: Municipal - National
Inception Date: June 21, 1990

Major Rating Factors: Strong performance is the major factor driving the B (Good) TheStreet.com Investment Rating for Nuveen Investment Quality Muni Fun. The fund currently has a performance rating of B- (Good) based on an annualized return of 3.71% over the last three years and a total return of 7.64% year to date 2015. Factored into the performance evaluation is an expense ratio of 1.67% (above average).

The fund's risk rating is currently B- (Good). It carries a beta of 2.31, meaning it is expected to move 23.1% for every 10% move in the market. Volatility, as measured by both the semi-deviation and a drawdown factor, is considered low. As of December 31, 2015, Nuveen Investment Quality Muni Fun traded at a discount of 4.76% below its net asset value, which is worse than its one-year historical average discount of 5.70%.

Christopher L. Drahn currently receives a manager quality ranking of 50 (0=worst, 99=best). If you desire only a moderate level of risk and strong performance, then this fund is an excellent option.

Data Date	Investment Rating	Net Assets ($Mil)	Price	Performance Rating/Pts	Total Return Y-T-D	Risk Rating/Pts
12-15	B	673.07	15.42	B- / 7.4	7.64%	B- / 7.4
2014	B-	575.40	15.23	B- / 7.0	19.49%	B- / 7.7
2013	C+	600.55	13.53	C / 5.4	-13.45%	B- / 7.9
2012	A	535.52	16.03	B+ / 8.6	13.94%	B / 8.6
2011	A	552.10	15.61	A- / 9.2	26.22%	B / 8.8
2010	C+	510.91	13.49	C / 4.3	7.98%	B- / 7.1

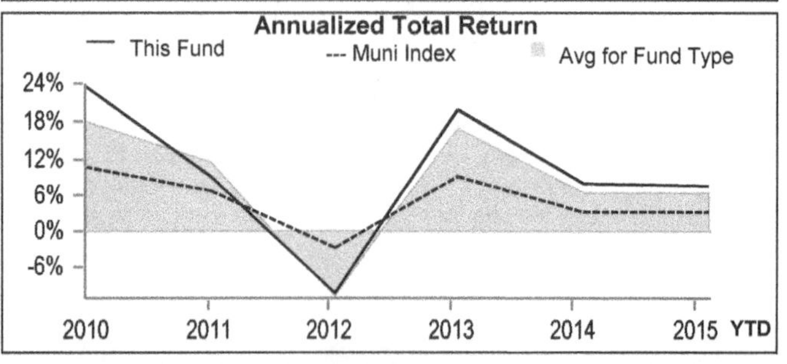

Nuveen MA Prem Inc Muni (NMT) C+ Fair

Fund Family: Nuveen Fund Advisors LLC
Fund Type: Municipal - Single State
Inception Date: March 18, 1993

Major Rating Factors: Middle of the road best describes Nuveen MA Prem Inc Muni whose TheStreet.com Investment Rating is currently a C+ (Fair). The fund currently has a performance rating of C+ (Fair) based on an annualized return of 1.43% over the last three years and a total return of 8.83% year to date 2015. Factored into the performance evaluation is an expense ratio of 1.96% (above average).

The fund's risk rating is currently B- (Good). It carries a beta of 1.38, meaning it is expected to move 13.8% for every 10% move in the market. Volatility, as measured by both the semi-deviation and a drawdown factor, is considered low. As of December 31, 2015, Nuveen MA Prem Inc Muni traded at a discount of 8.34% below its net asset value, which is worse than its one-year historical average discount of 9.42%.

Michael S. Hamilton has been running the fund for 5 years and currently receives a manager quality ranking of 52 (0=worst, 99=best). If you desire an average level of risk, then this fund may be an option.

Data Date	Investment Rating	Net Assets ($Mil)	Price	Performance Rating/Pts	Total Return Y-T-D	Risk Rating/Pts
12-15	C+	137.13	13.73	C+ / 6.4	8.83%	B- / 7.6
2014	C	138.00	13.24	C / 4.3	14.09%	B / 8.0
2013	D+	72.25	12.12	D+ / 2.4	-16.27%	B / 8.2
2012	C+	73.76	14.82	C / 4.9	9.86%	B / 8.7
2011	A-	71.10	14.61	B+ / 8.6	18.34%	B / 8.8
2010	C	69.03	13.35	C / 4.8	4.28%	C+ / 6.5

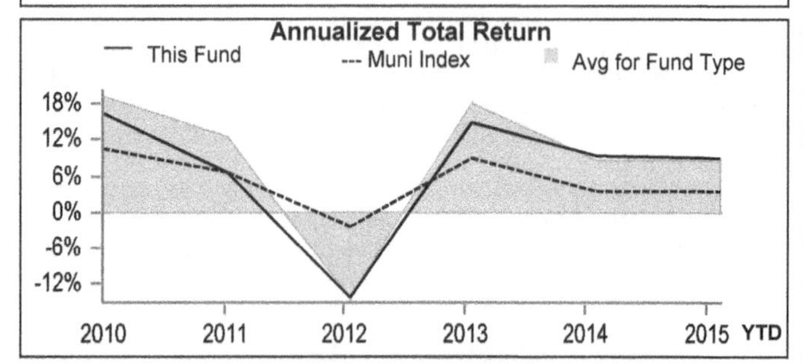

Nuveen MD Prem Inc Muni Fund (NMY) C Fair

Fund Family: Nuveen Fund Advisors LLC
Fund Type: Municipal - Single State
Inception Date: March 18, 1993

Major Rating Factors: Middle of the road best describes Nuveen MD Prem Inc Muni Fund whose TheStreet.com Investment Rating is currently a C (Fair). The fund currently has a performance rating of C (Fair) based on an annualized return of -1.64% over the last three years and a total return of 5.56% year to date 2015. Factored into the performance evaluation is an expense ratio of 1.55% (average).

The fund's risk rating is currently B- (Good). It carries a beta of 1.71, meaning it is expected to move 17.1% for every 10% move in the market. Volatility, as measured by both the semi-deviation and a drawdown factor, is considered low. As of December 31, 2015, Nuveen MD Prem Inc Muni Fund traded at a discount of 14.31% below its net asset value, which is worse than its one-year historical average discount of 14.73%.

Thomas C. Spalding has been running the fund for 5 years and currently receives a manager quality ranking of 26 (0=worst, 99=best). If you desire an average level of risk, then this fund may be an option.

Data Date	Investment Rating	Net Assets ($Mil)	Price	Performance Rating/Pts	Total Return Y-T-D	Risk Rating/Pts
12-15	C	344.30	12.69	C / 4.3	5.56%	B- / 7.6
2014	C-	349.00	12.65	D+ / 2.9	10.12%	B- / 7.8
2013	D+	375.16	11.92	D+ / 2.4	-18.29%	B / 8.0
2012	C+	167.21	15.20	C / 5.4	5.25%	B / 8.8
2011	A	160.60	14.93	A- / 9.0	21.69%	B / 8.9
2010	C+	157.24	13.45	C / 5.5	2.66%	C+ / 6.3

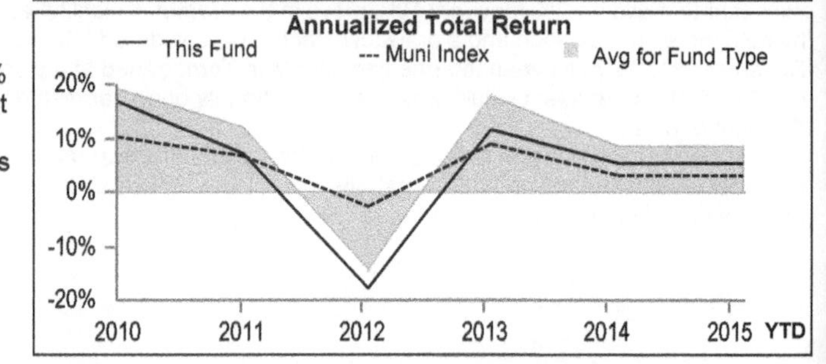

Nuveen MI Quality Inc Muni (NUM) C+ Fair

Fund Family: Nuveen Fund Advisors LLC
Fund Type: Municipal - Single State
Inception Date: October 24, 1991

Major Rating Factors: Middle of the road best describes Nuveen MI Quality Inc Muni whose TheStreet.com Investment Rating is currently a C+ (Fair). The fund currently has a performance rating of C+ (Fair) based on an annualized return of 1.11% over the last three years and a total return of 5.76% year to date 2015. Factored into the performance evaluation is an expense ratio of 1.57% (above average).

The fund's risk rating is currently B- (Good). It carries a beta of 2.28, meaning it is expected to move 22.8% for every 10% move in the market. Volatility, as measured by both the semi-deviation and a drawdown factor, is considered low. As of December 31, 2015, Nuveen MI Quality Inc Muni traded at a discount of 13.46% below its net asset value, which is worse than its one-year historical average discount of 13.60%.

Daniel J. Close has been running the fund for 9 years and currently receives a manager quality ranking of 32 (0=worst, 99=best). If you desire an average level of risk, then this fund may be an option.

Data Date	Investment Rating	Net Assets ($Mil)	Price	Performance Rating/Pts	Total Return Y-T-D	Risk Rating/Pts
12-15	C+	329.23	13.69	C+ / 5.9	5.76%	B- / 7.7
2014	C+	325.20	13.67	C / 5.2	14.63%	B- / 7.8
2013	C-	290.93	12.52	C- / 4.1	-15.04%	B / 8.1
2012	A-	187.26	15.31	B / 8.1	13.83%	B / 8.9
2011	A-	178.30	14.62	B+ / 8.5	19.36%	B+ / 9.1
2010	C	170.98	13.10	C / 4.8	9.07%	C+ / 6.5

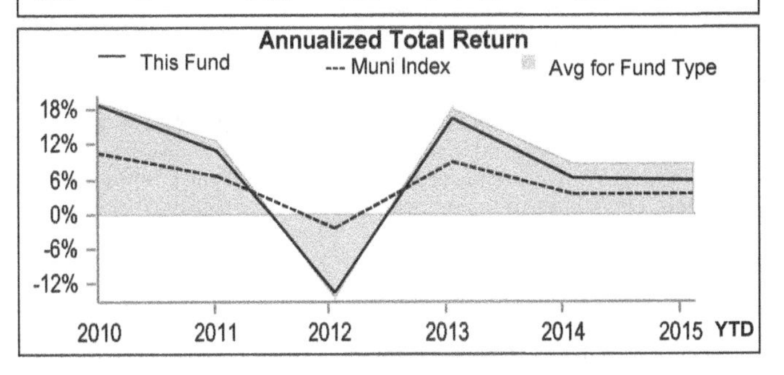

Nuveen Minnesota Municipal Income (MXA) C Fair

Fund Family: US Bancorp Asset Management Inc
Fund Type: Municipal - Single State
Inception Date: June 18, 1993

Major Rating Factors: Middle of the road best describes Nuveen Minnesota Municipal Income whose TheStreet.com Investment Rating is currently a C (Fair). The fund currently has a performance rating of C (Fair) based on an annualized return of -1.11% over the last three years and a total return of 6.23% year to date 2015. Factored into the performance evaluation is an expense ratio of 1.64% (above average).

The fund's risk rating is currently B- (Good). It carries a beta of 2.38, meaning it is expected to move 23.8% for every 10% move in the market. Volatility, as measured by both the semi-deviation and a drawdown factor, is considered low. As of December 31, 2015, Nuveen Minnesota Municipal Income traded at a discount of 6.47% below its net asset value, which is better than its one-year historical average discount of 5.02%.

Christopher L. Drahn currently receives a manager quality ranking of 23 (0=worst, 99=best). If you desire an average level of risk, then this fund may be an option.

Data Date	Investment Rating	Net Assets ($Mil)	Price	Performance Rating/Pts	Total Return Y-T-D	Risk Rating/Pts
12-15	C	64.00	14.60	C / 4.6	6.23%	B- / 7.6
2014	D+	64.90	14.36	D+ / 2.3	3.01%	B- / 7.6
2013	C	59.00	14.78	C / 5.2	-13.03%	B / 8.0
2012	B	67.00	17.17	C+ / 6.3	11.14%	B / 8.8
2011	A+	62.70	16.78	A+ / 9.7	26.97%	B+ / 9.0
2010	A-	63.00	14.36	B / 7.7	4.57%	C+ / 6.9

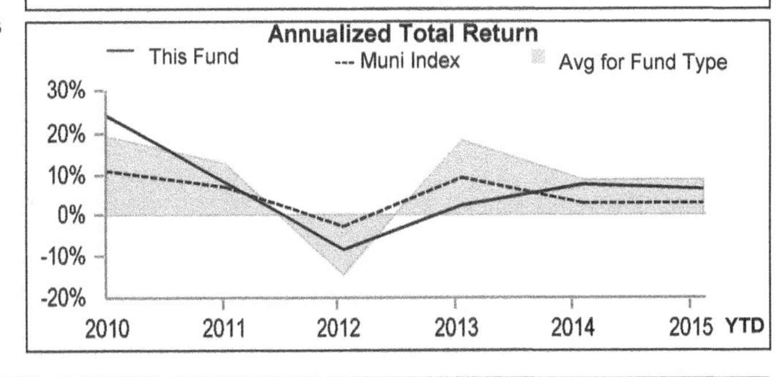

Nuveen MO Prem Inc Muni (NOM) C Fair

Fund Family: Nuveen Fund Advisors LLC
Fund Type: Municipal - Single State
Inception Date: May 20, 1993

Major Rating Factors: Middle of the road best describes Nuveen MO Prem Inc Muni whose TheStreet.com Investment Rating is currently a C (Fair). The fund currently has a performance rating of C+ (Fair) based on an annualized return of 0.20% over the last three years and a total return of 7.18% year to date 2015. Factored into the performance evaluation is an expense ratio of 2.80% (high).

The fund's risk rating is currently C+ (Fair). It carries a beta of 2.07, meaning it is expected to move 20.7% for every 10% move in the market. Volatility, as measured by both the semi-deviation and a drawdown factor, is considered low. As of December 31, 2015, Nuveen MO Prem Inc Muni traded at a premium of 8.69% above its net asset value, which is worse than its one-year historical average premium of 7.30%.

Christopher L. Drahn currently receives a manager quality ranking of 45 (0=worst, 99=best). If you desire an average level of risk, then this fund may be an option.

Data Date	Investment Rating	Net Assets ($Mil)	Price	Performance Rating/Pts	Total Return Y-T-D	Risk Rating/Pts
12-15	C	32.47	15.38	C+ / 5.8	7.18%	C+ / 6.7
2014	C-	33.00	15.00	C / 5.4	22.93%	C+ / 6.0
2013	D+	34.01	12.62	D / 1.9	-24.16%	B- / 7.6
2012	B	33.98	16.00	B- / 7.1	11.60%	B / 8.4
2011	A-	32.80	16.42	A- / 9.0	22.25%	B / 8.5
2010	C+	31.35	14.50	C / 5.0	-1.68%	C+ / 6.5

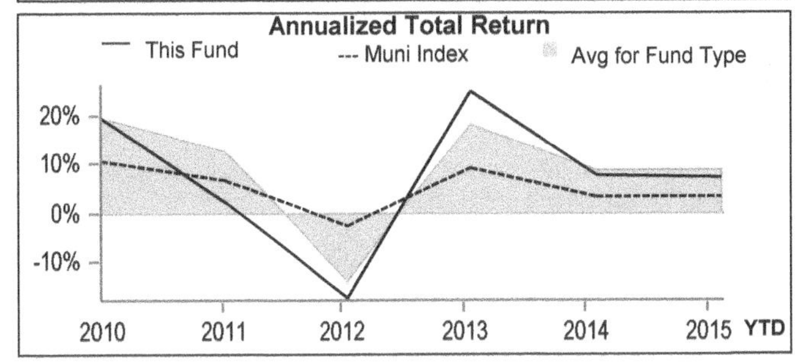

Nuveen Mortgage Opportunity Term (JLS) C Fair

Fund Family: Nuveen Fund Advisors LLC
Fund Type: Mortgage
Inception Date: November 25, 2009

Major Rating Factors: Middle of the road best describes Nuveen Mortgage Opportunity Term whose TheStreet.com Investment Rating is currently a C (Fair). The fund currently has a performance rating of C (Fair) based on an annualized return of 0.62% over the last three years and a total return of 4.91% year to date 2015. Factored into the performance evaluation is an expense ratio of 2.20% (high).

The fund's risk rating is currently B- (Good). It carries a beta of 1.69, meaning it is expected to move 16.9% for every 10% move in the market. Volatility, as measured by both the semi-deviation and a drawdown factor, is considered low. As of December 31, 2015, Nuveen Mortgage Opportunity Term traded at a discount of 9.49% below its net asset value, which is worse than its one-year historical average discount of 11.45%.

John V. Miller currently receives a manager quality ranking of 56 (0=worst, 99=best). If you desire an average level of risk, then this fund may be an option.

Data Date	Investment Rating	Net Assets ($Mil)	Price	Performance Rating/Pts	Total Return Y-T-D	Risk Rating/Pts
12-15	C	415.58	22.71	C / 5.4	4.91%	B- / 7.0
2014	C+	421.30	23.15	C+ / 5.8	4.64%	B- / 7.7
2013	C	417.22	23.14	C / 4.9	-7.12%	B- / 7.7
2012	B+	346.83	27.22	B+ / 8.3	39.78%	B / 8.2
2011	D+	346.80	20.35	D- / 1.4	-7.48%	B / 8.3
2010	A+	0.00	25.50	B / 8.2	10.44%	B / 8.7

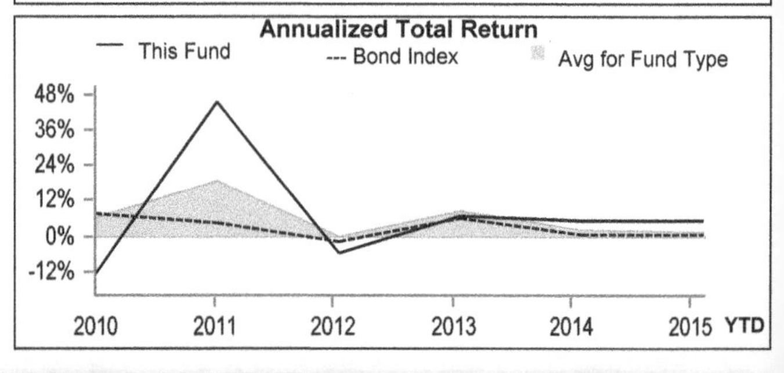

Nuveen Mortgage Opportunity Term 2 (JMT) C Fair

Fund Family: Nuveen Fund Advisors LLC
Fund Type: Mortgage
Inception Date: February 24, 2010

Major Rating Factors: Middle of the road best describes Nuveen Mortgage Opportunity Term 2 whose TheStreet.com Investment Rating is currently a C (Fair). The fund currently has a performance rating of C+ (Fair) based on an annualized return of 1.49% over the last three years and a total return of 4.69% year to date 2015. Factored into the performance evaluation is an expense ratio of 2.42% (high).

The fund's risk rating is currently C+ (Fair). It carries a beta of 1.41, meaning it is expected to move 14.1% for every 10% move in the market. Volatility, as measured by both the semi-deviation and a drawdown factor, is considered low. As of December 31, 2015, Nuveen Mortgage Opportunity Term 2 traded at a discount of 8.20% below its net asset value, which is worse than its one-year historical average discount of 11.09%.

John V. Miller currently receives a manager quality ranking of 66 (0=worst, 99=best). If you desire an average level of risk, then this fund may be an option.

Data Date	Investment Rating	Net Assets ($Mil)	Price	Performance Rating/Pts	Total Return Y-T-D	Risk Rating/Pts
12-15	C	123.78	22.29	C+ / 5.6	4.69%	C+ / 6.9
2014	B-	125.60	23.17	C+ / 6.6	8.81%	B- / 7.7
2013	C	130.86	22.97	C / 5.3	-6.75%	B- / 7.8
2012	A+	104.62	27.18	A+ / 9.8	41.29%	B / 8.3
2011	D+	104.60	20.40	D / 1.6	-5.19%	B / 8.3

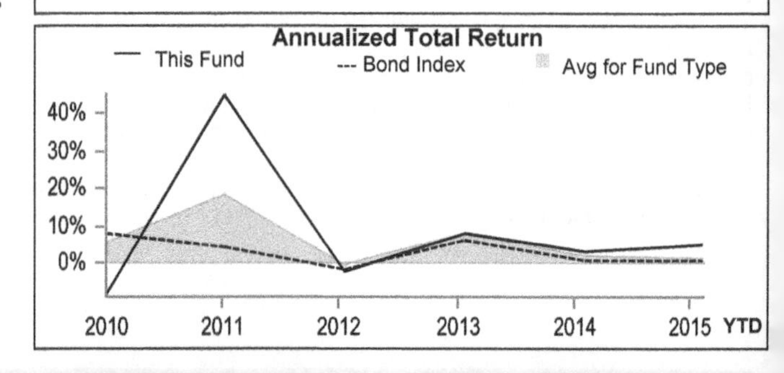

Nuveen Multi-Market Income (MRF) C Fair

Fund Family: US Bancorp Asset Management Inc
Fund Type: Mortgage
Inception Date: December 23, 1988

Major Rating Factors: Middle of the road best describes Nuveen Multi-Market Income whose TheStreet.com Investment Rating is currently a C (Fair). The fund currently has a performance rating of C (Fair) based on an annualized return of 0.00% over the last three years and a total return of -3.75% year to date 2015. Factored into the performance evaluation is an expense ratio of 1.26% (average).

The fund's risk rating is currently B- (Good). It carries a beta of 2.17, meaning it is expected to move 21.7% for every 10% move in the market. Volatility, as measured by both the semi-deviation and a drawdown factor, is considered low. As of December 31, 2015, Nuveen Multi-Market Income traded at a discount of 11.25% below its net asset value, which is worse than its one-year historical average discount of 12.06%.

Chris J. Neuharth currently receives a manager quality ranking of 40 (0=worst, 99=best). If you desire an average level of risk, then this fund may be an option.

Data Date	Investment Rating	Net Assets ($Mil)	Price	Performance Rating/Pts	Total Return Y-T-D	Risk Rating/Pts
12-15	C	79.50	7.10	C / 4.3	-3.75%	B- / 7.0
2014	C	81.30	7.67	C / 5.1	10.95%	B- / 7.4
2013	D+	79.00	7.33	D+ / 2.8	-8.77%	B- / 7.5
2012	C+	80.00	8.37	C+ / 6.6	21.42%	B- / 7.1
2011	C	77.80	7.69	C+ / 5.9	-3.29%	B- / 7.0
2010	B+	79.00	8.38	B / 7.8	22.25%	C+ / 5.7

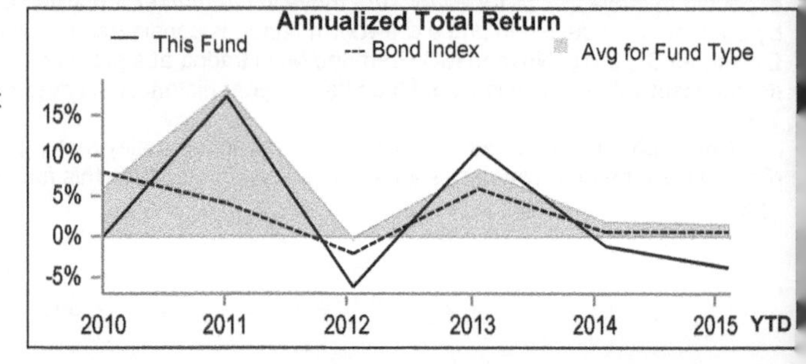

Nuveen Muni Advantage (NMA) C+ Fair

Fund Family: Nuveen Fund Advisors LLC
Fund Type: Municipal - National
Inception Date: December 28, 1989

Major Rating Factors: Middle of the road best describes Nuveen Muni Advantage whose TheStreet.com Investment Rating is currently a C+ (Fair). The fund currently has a performance rating of C+ (Fair) based on an annualized return of 1.82% over the last three years and a total return of 7.43% year to date 2015. Factored into the performance evaluation is an expense ratio of 1.71% (above average).

The fund's risk rating is currently B- (Good). It carries a beta of 2.35, meaning it is expected to move 23.5% for every 10% move in the market. Volatility, as measured by both the semi-deviation and a drawdown factor, is considered low. As of December 31, 2015, Nuveen Muni Advantage traded at a discount of 10.76% below its net asset value, which is worse than its one-year historical average discount of 12.09%.

Thomas C. Spalding has been running the fund for 14 years and currently receives a manager quality ranking of 33 (0=worst, 99=best). If you desire an average level of risk, then this fund may be an option.

Data Date	Investment Rating	Net Assets ($Mil)	Price	Performance Rating/Pts	Total Return Y-T-D	Risk Rating/Pts
12-15	C+	605.87	13.85	C+ / 6.4	7.43%	B- / 7.6
2014	C+	598.70	13.66	C+ / 6.3	18.47%	B- / 7.7
2013	C-	697.84	12.16	C- / 3.5	-17.13%	B- / 7.9
2012	B	626.62	15.21	B- / 7.5	14.21%	B / 8.4
2011	B+	634.30	14.68	B / 8.0	20.98%	B / 8.5
2010	C-	624.08	13.08	C- / 3.0	-1.70%	C+ / 6.5

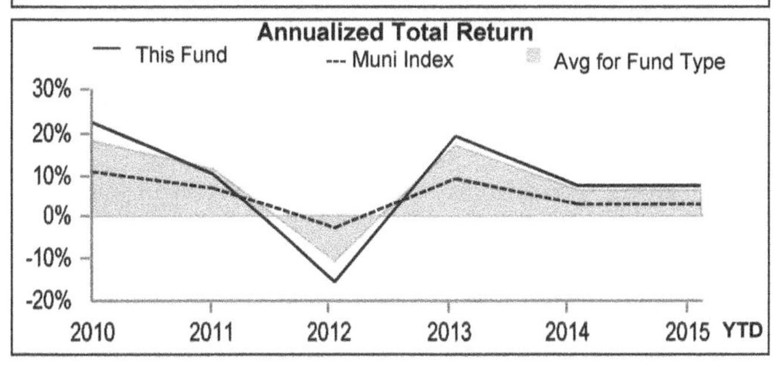

Nuveen Muni High Income Opport (NMZ) B+ Good

Fund Family: Nuveen Fund Advisors LLC
Fund Type: Municipal - High Yield
Inception Date: November 19, 2003

Major Rating Factors: Strong performance is the major factor driving the B+ (Good) TheStreet.com Investment Rating for Nuveen Muni High Income Opport. The fund currently has a performance rating of B+ (Good) based on an annualized return of 5.66% over the last three years and a total return of 9.86% year to date 2015. Factored into the performance evaluation is an expense ratio of 1.28% (average).

The fund's risk rating is currently C+ (Fair). It carries a beta of 1.95, meaning it is expected to move 19.5% for every 10% move in the market. Volatility, as measured by both the semi-deviation and a drawdown factor, is considered low. As of December 31, 2015, Nuveen Muni High Income Opport traded at a premium of .95% above its net asset value, which is worse than its one-year historical average discount of .93%.

John V. Miller has been running the fund for 13 years and currently receives a manager quality ranking of 69 (0=worst, 99=best). If you desire only a moderate level of risk and strong performance, then this fund is an excellent option.

Data Date	Investment Rating	Net Assets ($Mil)	Price	Performance Rating/Pts	Total Return Y-T-D	Risk Rating/Pts
12-15	B+	686.30	13.82	B+ / 8.8	9.86%	C+ / 6.9
2014	A-	680.70	13.40	B+ / 8.5	19.24%	B- / 7.7
2013	C+	432.14	12.00	C+ / 6.5	-10.34%	B- / 7.9
2012	A-	323.09	14.10	B+ / 8.6	21.21%	B / 8.1
2011	B+	330.90	12.11	B+ / 8.3	17.43%	B / 8.3
2010	D+	288.96	11.45	D- / 1.5	-1.31%	C+ / 6.9

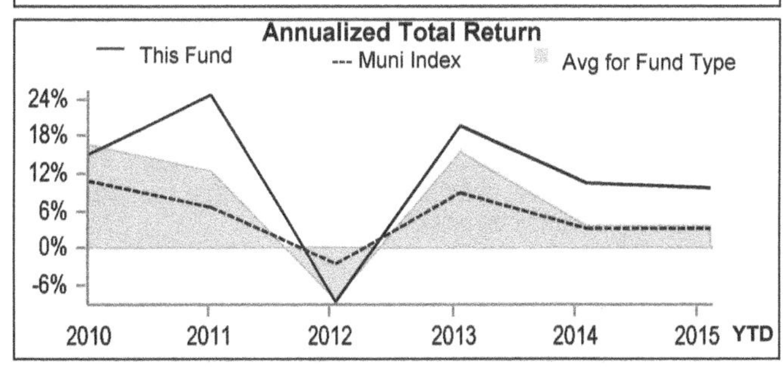

Nuveen Muni Income (NMI) B- Good

Fund Family: Nuveen Fund Advisors LLC
Fund Type: Municipal - National
Inception Date: April 20, 1988

Major Rating Factors: Strong performance is the major factor driving the B- (Good) TheStreet.com Investment Rating for Nuveen Muni Income. The fund currently has a performance rating of B (Good) based on an annualized return of 3.98% over the last three years and a total return of 5.65% year to date 2015. Factored into the performance evaluation is an expense ratio of 0.76% (very low).

The fund's risk rating is currently C+ (Fair). It carries a beta of 2.46, meaning it is expected to move 24.6% for every 10% move in the market. Volatility, as measured by both the semi-deviation and a drawdown factor, is considered low. As of December 31, 2015, Nuveen Muni Income traded at a premium of 3.72% above its net asset value, which is worse than its one-year historical average discount of .39%.

Christopher L. Drahn currently receives a manager quality ranking of 40 (0=worst, 99=best). If you desire only a moderate level of risk and strong performance, then this fund is an excellent option.

Data Date	Investment Rating	Net Assets ($Mil)	Price	Performance Rating/Pts	Total Return Y-T-D	Risk Rating/Pts
12-15	B-	95.46	11.98	B / 7.8	5.65%	C+ / 6.8
2014	C+	94.90	11.92	B / 7.8	23.08%	C+ / 6.3
2013	C-	97.21	10.13	C- / 4.0	-13.09%	B / 8.1
2012	B-	88.49	12.15	C+ / 6.2	12.26%	B / 8.7
2011	B+	90.20	11.53	B- / 7.4	18.87%	B / 8.9
2010	C+	84.88	10.30	C- / 3.9	-0.83%	B- / 7.9

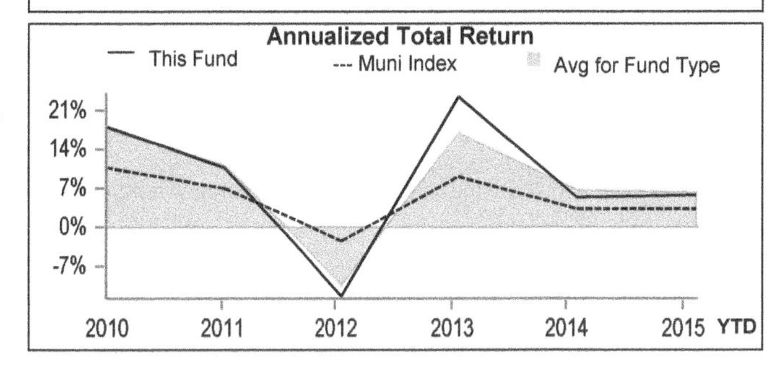

Nuveen Muni Market Opportunity (NMO) B Good

Fund Family: Nuveen Fund Advisors LLC
Fund Type: Municipal - National
Inception Date: March 22, 1990

Major Rating Factors: Strong performance is the major factor driving the B (Good) TheStreet.com Investment Rating for Nuveen Muni Market Opportunity. The fund currently has a performance rating of B- (Good) based on an annualized return of 2.92% over the last three years and a total return of 6.89% year to date 2015. Factored into the performance evaluation is an expense ratio of 1.76% (above average).

The fund's risk rating is currently B- (Good). It carries a beta of 2.14, meaning it is expected to move 21.4% for every 10% move in the market. Volatility, as measured by both the semi-deviation and a drawdown factor, is considered low. As of December 31, 2015, Nuveen Muni Market Opportunity traded at a discount of 10.74% below its net asset value, which is worse than its one-year historical average discount of 12.01%.

Thomas C. Spalding has been running the fund for 14 years and currently receives a manager quality ranking of 44 (0=worst, 99=best). If you desire only a moderate level of risk and strong performance, then this fund is an excellent option.

Data Date	Investment Rating	Net Assets ($Mil)	Price	Performance Rating/Pts	Total Return Y-T-D	Risk Rating/Pts
12-15	B	698.58	13.79	B- / 7.0	6.89%	B- / 7.7
2014	B	689.80	13.63	C+ / 6.9	20.29%	B / 8.0
2013	C-	707.78	12.00	C- / 3.6	-15.45%	B / 8.1
2012	B	622.82	14.66	B- / 7.3	13.65%	B / 8.5
2011	B+	636.00	13.84	B+ / 8.3	17.99%	B / 8.6
2010	C	636.76	12.87	C / 4.4	3.40%	C+ / 6.4

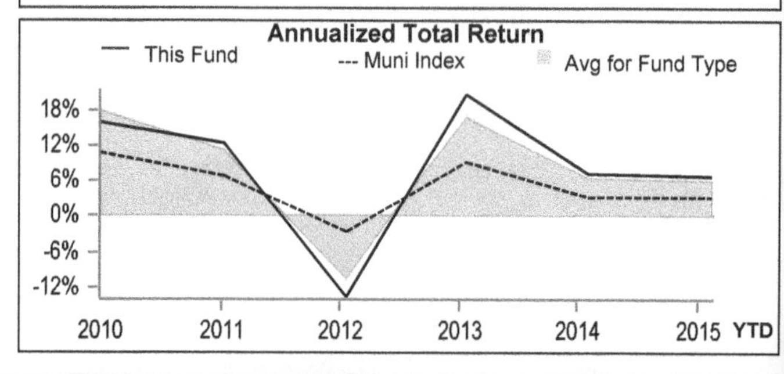

Nuveen Muni Opportunity (NIO) B- Good

Fund Family: Nuveen Fund Advisors LLC
Fund Type: Municipal - National
Inception Date: September 27, 1991

Major Rating Factors: Nuveen Muni Opportunity receives a TheStreet.com Investment Rating of B- (Good). The fund currently has a performance rating of C+ (Fair) based on an annualized return of 2.51% over the last three years and a total return of 3.92% year to date 2015. Factored into the performance evaluation is an expense ratio of 1.49% (average).

The fund's risk rating is currently B- (Good). It carries a beta of 1.78, meaning it is expected to move 17.8% for every 10% move in the market. Volatility, as measured by both the semi-deviation and a drawdown factor, is considered low. As of December 31, 2015, Nuveen Muni Opportunity traded at a discount of 9.25% below its net asset value, which is worse than its one-year historical average discount of 9.33%.

Paul L. Brennan has been running the fund for 10 years and currently receives a manager quality ranking of 53 (0=worst, 99=best). If you desire an average level of risk, then this fund may be an option.

Data Date	Investment Rating	Net Assets ($Mil)	Price	Performance Rating/Pts	Total Return Y-T-D	Risk Rating/Pts
12-15	B-	1,505.51	14.33	C+ / 6.4	3.92%	B- / 7.8
2014	B	1,493.80	14.67	C+ / 6.9	17.08%	B / 8.1
2013	C+	1,525.81	13.22	C+ / 5.6	-11.45%	B / 8.3
2012	B+	1,404.81	15.33	B / 7.8	12.26%	B / 8.8
2011	B+	1,435.40	14.92	B+ / 8.4	22.45%	B / 8.9
2010	C	1,358.84	13.04	C- / 4.0	3.04%	B- / 7.0

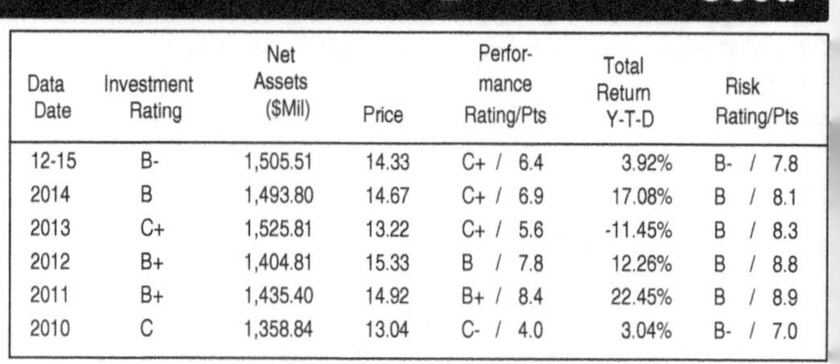

Nuveen Muni Value (NUV) B+ Good

Fund Family: Nuveen Fund Advisors LLC
Fund Type: Municipal - National
Inception Date: June 18, 1987

Major Rating Factors: Strong performance is the major factor driving the B+ (Good) TheStreet.com Investment Rating for Nuveen Muni Value. The fund currently has a performance rating of B (Good) based on an annualized return of 3.60% over the last three years and a total return of 9.84% year to date 2015. Factored into the performance evaluation is an expense ratio of 0.56% (very low).

The fund's risk rating is currently B- (Good). It carries a beta of 1.89, meaning it is expected to move 18.9% for every 10% move in the market. Volatility, as measured by both the semi-deviation and a drawdown factor, is considered low. As of December 31, 2015, Nuveen Muni Value traded at a discount of .97% below its net asset value, which is worse than its one-year historical average discount of 3.41%.

Thomas C. Spalding has been running the fund for 29 years and currently receives a manager quality ranking of 53 (0=worst, 99=best). If you desire only a moderate level of risk and strong performance, then this fund is an excellent option.

Data Date	Investment Rating	Net Assets ($Mil)	Price	Performance Rating/Pts	Total Return Y-T-D	Risk Rating/Pts
12-15	B+	2,099.10	10.18	B / 7.9	9.84%	B- / 7.7
2014	C+	2,083.40	9.65	C / 5.4	10.89%	B / 8.4
2013	C	2,138.47	9.04	C / 4.3	-8.72%	B / 8.6
2012	C+	1,915.23	10.25	C / 4.8	10.80%	B+ / 9.0
2011	B-	1,939.10	9.80	C / 5.4	13.64%	B+ / 9.0
2010	C+	1,872.03	9.19	C- / 3.7	-0.22%	B / 8.1

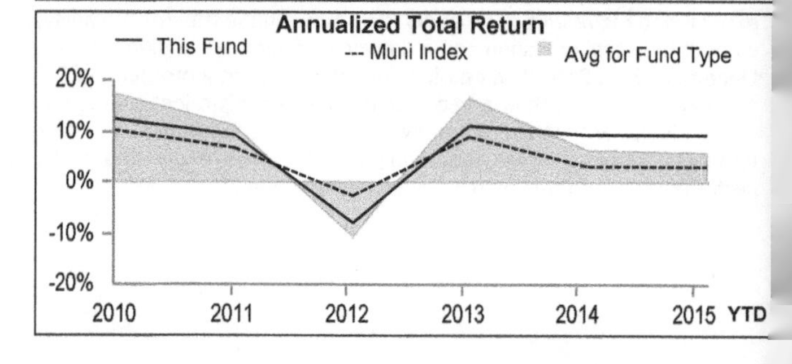

Nuveen Nasdaq 100 Dynamic Overwrit (QQQX) A Excellent

Fund Family: Nuveen Fund Advisors LLC
Fund Type: Income
Inception Date: January 30, 2007

Major Rating Factors:
Exceptional performance is the major factor driving the A (Excellent) TheStreet.com Investment Rating for Nuveen Nasdaq 100 Dynamic Overwrit. The fund currently has a performance rating of A (Excellent) based on an annualized return of 16.03% over the last three years and a total return of 9.21% year to date 2015. Factored into the performance evaluation is an expense ratio of 1.00% (low).

The fund's risk rating is currently B- (Good). It carries a beta of 1.07, meaning that its performance tracks fairly well with that of the overall stock market. Volatility, as measured by both the semi-deviation and a drawdown factor, is considered low. As of December 31, 2015, Nuveen Nasdaq 100 Dynamic Overwrit traded at a discount of 3.05% below its net asset value, which is worse than its one-year historical average discount of 6.18%.

James A. Colon has been running the fund for 5 years and currently receives a manager quality ranking of 72 (0=worst, 99=best). If you desire only a moderate level of risk and strong performance, then this fund is an excellent option.

Data Date	Investment Rating	Net Assets ($Mil)	Price	Performance Rating/Pts	Total Return Y-T-D	Risk Rating/Pts
12-15	A	726.28	19.37	A / 9.4	9.21%	B- / 7.2
2014	A+	361.10	19.25	A- / 9.0	20.47%	B / 8.3
2013	B	292.58	17.81	B / 8.0	21.38%	B- / 7.4
2012	C+	260.18	15.17	B- / 7.0	25.68%	B- / 7.0
2011	C+	260.20	12.97	B- / 7.3	3.19%	C+ / 6.9
2010	C-	259.73	14.10	C+ / 6.0	7.51%	C- / 4.0

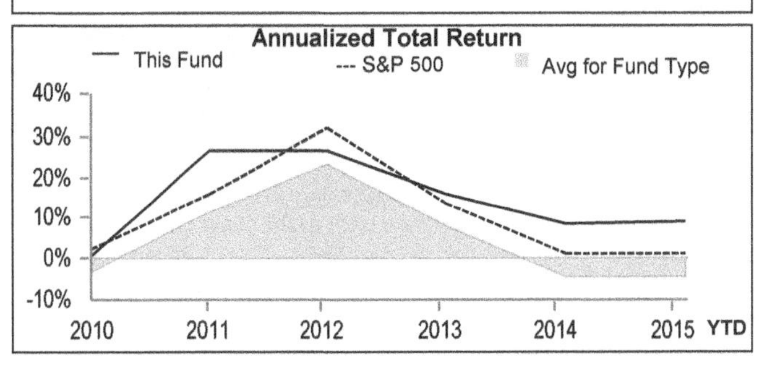

Nuveen NC Prem Inc Muni (NNC) C Fair

Fund Family: Nuveen Fund Advisors LLC
Fund Type: Municipal - Single State
Inception Date: May 20, 1993

Major Rating Factors: Middle of the road best describes Nuveen NC Prem Inc Muni whose TheStreet.com Investment Rating is currently a C (Fair). The fund currently has a performance rating of C (Fair) based on an annualized return of -0.98% over the last three years and a total return of 5.40% year to date 2015. Factored into the performance evaluation is an expense ratio of 1.54% (average).

The fund's risk rating is currently B- (Good). It carries a beta of 1.98, meaning it is expected to move 19.8% for every 10% move in the market. Volatility, as measured by both the semi-deviation and a drawdown factor, is considered low. As of December 31, 2015, Nuveen NC Prem Inc Muni traded at a discount of 14.04% below its net asset value, which is worse than its one-year historical average discount of 14.23%.

Daniel J. Close has been running the fund for 9 years and currently receives a manager quality ranking of 26 (0=worst, 99=best). If you desire an average level of risk, then this fund may be an option.

Data Date	Investment Rating	Net Assets ($Mil)	Price	Performance Rating/Pts	Total Return Y-T-D	Risk Rating/Pts
12-15	C	246.32	13.10	C / 4.8	5.40%	B- / 7.8
2014	C-	248.60	13.02	C- / 3.3	12.93%	B- / 7.9
2013	D+	248.60	11.96	D / 2.2	-18.42%	B / 8.1
2012	C	97.50	15.11	C / 4.4	5.46%	B / 8.8
2011	B+	95.10	15.25	B / 7.7	18.38%	B / 8.8
2010	C+	93.57	13.96	C+ / 6.3	2.69%	C+ / 6.9

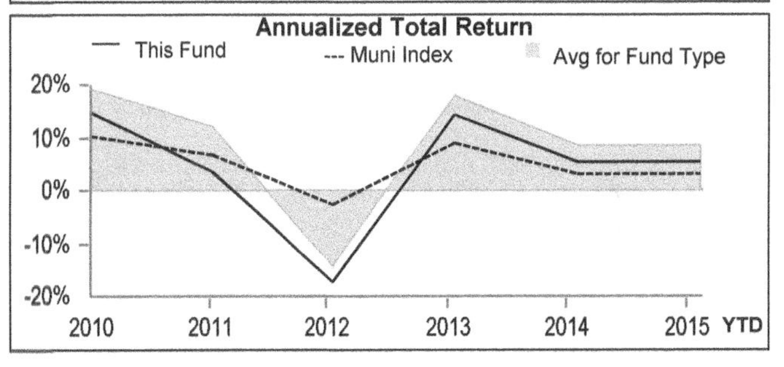

Nuveen New Jersey Municipal Value (NJV) C Fair

Fund Family: Nuveen Fund Advisors LLC
Fund Type: Municipal - National
Inception Date: April 28, 2009

Major Rating Factors: Middle of the road best describes Nuveen New Jersey Municipal Value whose TheStreet.com Investment Rating is currently a C (Fair). The fund currently has a performance rating of C (Fair) based on an annualized return of -0.85% over the last three years and a total return of 4.17% year to date 2015. Factored into the performance evaluation is an expense ratio of 0.87% (low).

The fund's risk rating is currently B- (Good). It carries a beta of 1.36, meaning it is expected to move 13.6% for every 10% move in the market. Volatility, as measured by both the semi-deviation and a drawdown factor, is considered low. As of December 31, 2015, Nuveen New Jersey Municipal Value traded at a discount of 10.22% below its net asset value, which is worse than its one-year historical average discount of 11.67%.

Paul L. Brennan currently receives a manager quality ranking of 34 (0=worst, 99=best). If you desire an average level of risk, then this fund may be an option.

Data Date	Investment Rating	Net Assets ($Mil)	Price	Performance Rating/Pts	Total Return Y-T-D	Risk Rating/Pts
12-15	C	25.43	14.49	C / 5.2	4.17%	B- / 7.4
2014	C+	25.70	14.63	C+ / 5.7	13.24%	B- / 7.8
2013	C-	26.57	13.62	C- / 3.2	-17.75%	B / 8.0
2012	A	25.96	17.14	B+ / 8.5	18.51%	B / 8.6
2011	B+	24.70	15.38	B+ / 8.3	14.95%	B / 8.7
2010	C+	24.72	14.87	C- / 3.7	5.49%	B / 8.5

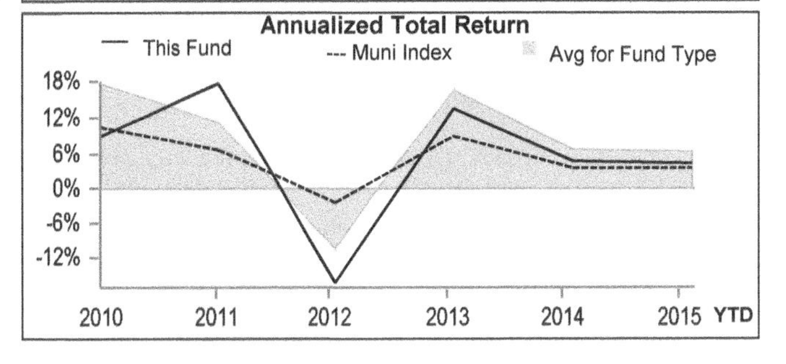

Nuveen New York Municipal Value 2 (NYV) C+ Fair

Fund Family: Nuveen Fund Advisors LLC
Fund Type: Municipal - National
Inception Date: April 28, 2009

Major Rating Factors: Middle of the road best describes Nuveen New York Municipal Value 2 whose TheStreet.com Investment Rating is currently a C+ (Fair). The fund currently has a performance rating of C+ (Fair) based on an annualized return of 2.48% over the last three years and a total return of 5.81% year to date 2015. Factored into the performance evaluation is an expense ratio of 0.75% (very low).

The fund's risk rating is currently B- (Good). It carries a beta of 1.53, meaning it is expected to move 15.3% for every 10% move in the market. Volatility, as measured by both the semi-deviation and a drawdown factor, is considered low. As of December 31, 2015, Nuveen New York Municipal Value 2 traded at a discount of 4.38% below its net asset value, which is worse than its one-year historical average discount of 6.66%.

Scott R. Romans currently receives a manager quality ranking of 58 (0=worst, 99=best). If you desire an average level of risk, then this fund may be an option.

Data Date	Investment Rating	Net Assets ($Mil)	Price	Performance Rating/Pts	Total Return Y-T-D	Risk Rating/Pts
12-15	C+	37.33	15.30	C+ / 6.4	5.81%	B- / 7.5
2014	C+	37.50	14.76	C+ / 5.8	13.83%	B / 8.2
2013	C-	35.63	13.56	C- / 3.4	-12.58%	B / 8.4
2012	B-	38.43	15.66	C+ / 6.0	15.41%	B / 8.7
2011	B	36.10	14.56	B- / 7.3	11.76%	B / 8.7
2010	C-	37.80	13.98	D- / 1.3	2.54%	B / 8.0

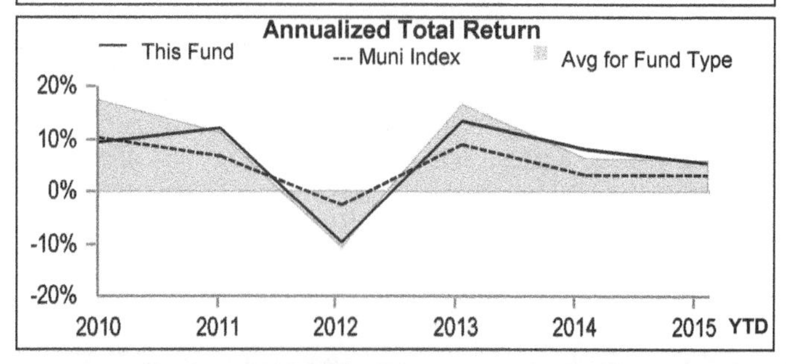

Nuveen NJ Div Adv Muni (NXJ) C+ Fair

Fund Family: Nuveen Fund Advisors LLC
Fund Type: Municipal - Single State
Inception Date: March 27, 2001

Major Rating Factors: Middle of the road best describes Nuveen NJ Div Adv Muni whose TheStreet.com Investment Rating is currently a C+ (Fair). The fund currently has a performance rating of C (Fair) based on an annualized return of -0.27% over the last three years and a total return of 5.92% year to date 2015. Factored into the performance evaluation is an expense ratio of 1.71% (above average).

The fund's risk rating is currently B- (Good). It carries a beta of 2.01, meaning it is expected to move 20.1% for every 10% move in the market. Volatility, as measured by both the semi-deviation and a drawdown factor, is considered low. As of December 31, 2015, Nuveen NJ Div Adv Muni traded at a discount of 13.96% below its net asset value, which is worse than its one-year historical average discount of 14.35%.

Paul L. Brennan has been running the fund for 5 years and currently receives a manager quality ranking of 29 (0=worst, 99=best). If you desire an average level of risk, then this fund may be an option.

Data Date	Investment Rating	Net Assets ($Mil)	Price	Performance Rating/Pts	Total Return Y-T-D	Risk Rating/Pts
12-15	C+	668.67	13.50	C / 5.5	5.92%	B- / 7.7
2014	C	101.70	13.47	C / 5.1	13.31%	B- / 7.7
2013	C-	105.89	12.48	C- / 3.5	-17.47%	B- / 7.9
2012	A-	100.58	15.34	B / 8.2	17.73%	B / 8.5
2011	B+	97.40	14.00	B+ / 8.6	18.03%	B / 8.7
2010	C	95.30	13.15	C / 5.0	9.08%	C+ / 6.3

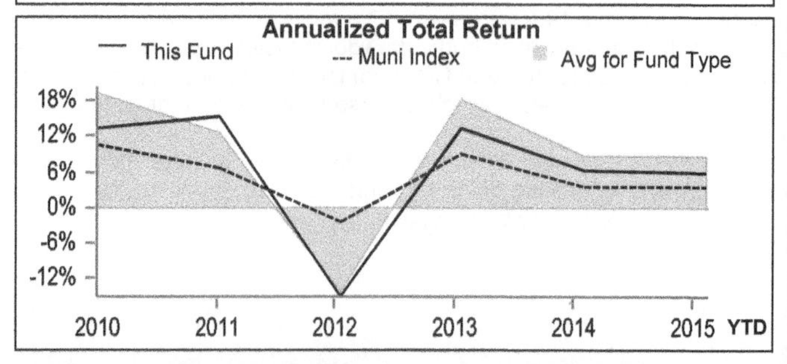

Nuveen NY AMT/Fr Muni Income (NRK) C+ Fair

Fund Family: Nuveen Fund Advisors LLC
Fund Type: Municipal - Single State
Inception Date: November 21, 2002

Major Rating Factors: Middle of the road best describes Nuveen NY AMT/Fr Muni Income whose TheStreet.com Investment Rating is currently a C+ (Fair). The fund currently has a performance rating of C+ (Fair) based on an annualized return of -0.03% over the last three years and a total return of 6.90% year to date 2015. Factored into the performance evaluation is an expense ratio of 1.43% (average).

The fund's risk rating is currently B- (Good). It carries a beta of 1.96, meaning it is expected to move 19.6% for every 10% move in the market. Volatility, as measured by both the semi-deviation and a drawdown factor, is considered low. As of December 31, 2015, Nuveen NY AMT/Fr Muni Income traded at a discount of 9.95% below its net asset value, which is worse than its one-year historical average discount of 10.67%.

Scott R. Romans currently receives a manager quality ranking of 30 (0=worst, 99=best). If you desire an average level of risk, then this fund may be an option.

Data Date	Investment Rating	Net Assets ($Mil)	Price	Performance Rating/Pts	Total Return Y-T-D	Risk Rating/Pts
12-15	C+	1,257.93	13.13	C+ / 5.6	6.90%	B- / 7.6
2014	C	1,260.50	12.90	C / 4.4	11.61%	B- / 7.9
2013	D+	1,189.20	12.28	D+ / 2.5	-16.76%	B / 8.1
2012	B	54.14	15.10	C+ / 6.8	12.63%	B+ / 9.0
2011	B+	52.90	14.13	B- / 7.3	13.37%	B+ / 9.0
2010	C+	53.87	13.17	C- / 3.6	2.25%	B / 8.0

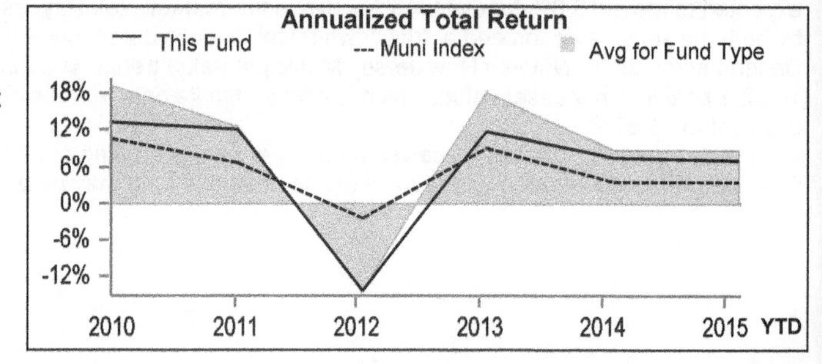

Nuveen NY Div Adv Muni (NAN) B Good

Fund Family: Nuveen Fund Advisors LLC
Fund Type: Municipal - Single State
Inception Date: May 25, 1999

Major Rating Factors: Strong performance is the major factor driving the B (Good) TheStreet.com Investment Rating for Nuveen NY Div Adv Muni. The fund currently has a performance rating of B- (Good) based on an annualized return of 2.00% over the last three years and a total return of 11.33% year to date 2015. Factored into the performance evaluation is an expense ratio of 1.70% (above average).

The fund's risk rating is currently B- (Good). It carries a beta of 1.80, meaning it is expected to move 18.0% for every 10% move in the market. Volatility, as measured by both the semi-deviation and a drawdown factor, is considered low. As of December 31, 2015, Nuveen NY Div Adv Muni traded at a discount of 7.96% below its net asset value, which is worse than its one-year historical average discount of 10.42%.

Scott R. Romans currently receives a manager quality ranking of 47 (0=worst, 99=best). If you desire only a moderate level of risk and strong performance, then this fund is an excellent option.

Data Date	Investment Rating	Net Assets ($Mil)	Price	Performance Rating/Pts	Total Return Y-T-D	Risk Rating/Pts
12-15	B	474.84	14.23	B- / 7.4	11.33%	B- / 7.6
2014	C	142.30	13.53	C / 5.1	12.57%	B- / 7.9
2013	C-	132.77	12.70	C- / 3.8	-15.32%	B / 8.1
2012	A-	149.42	15.29	B / 7.8	13.05%	B / 8.9
2011	A	140.50	14.24	B+ / 8.7	19.74%	B+ / 9.0
2010	C	140.53	12.90	C- / 3.6	5.84%	B- / 7.8

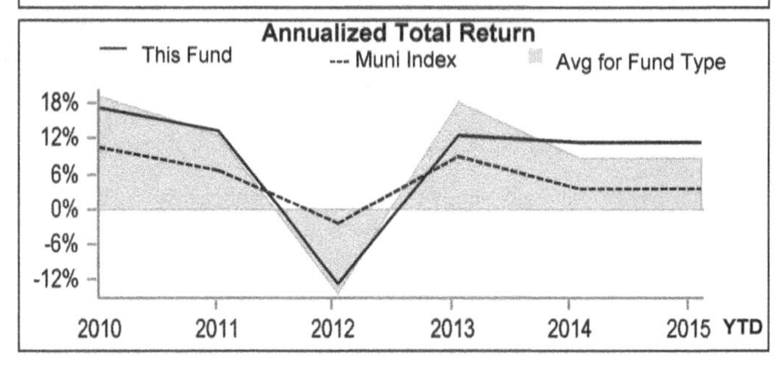

Nuveen NY Muni Value (NNY) B- Good

Fund Family: Nuveen Fund Advisors LLC
Fund Type: Municipal - Single State
Inception Date: October 7, 1987

Major Rating Factors: Nuveen NY Muni Value receives a TheStreet.com Investment Rating of B- (Good). The fund currently has a performance rating of C+ (Fair) based on an annualized return of 2.21% over the last three years and a total return of 6.70% year to date 2015. Factored into the performance evaluation is an expense ratio of 0.60% (very low).

The fund's risk rating is currently B- (Good). It carries a beta of 1.59, meaning it is expected to move 15.9% for every 10% move in the market. Volatility, as measured by both the semi-deviation and a drawdown factor, is considered low. As of December 31, 2015, Nuveen NY Muni Value traded at a discount of .59% below its net asset value, which is worse than its one-year historical average discount of 2.40%.

Scott R. Romans currently receives a manager quality ranking of 52 (0=worst, 99=best). If you desire an average level of risk, then this fund may be an option.

Data Date	Investment Rating	Net Assets ($Mil)	Price	Performance Rating/Pts	Total Return Y-T-D	Risk Rating/Pts
12-15	B-	152.14	10.04	C+ / 6.8	6.70%	B- / 7.7
2014	C+	153.10	9.79	C / 5.2	14.13%	B / 8.2
2013	C-	146.52	8.76	C- / 3.4	-12.32%	B / 8.4
2012	C+	157.98	10.30	C / 4.6	8.58%	B+ / 9.1
2011	B	151.80	9.92	C+ / 6.5	15.71%	B+ / 9.2
2010	B	152.03	9.08	C- / 4.2	0.46%	B / 8.8

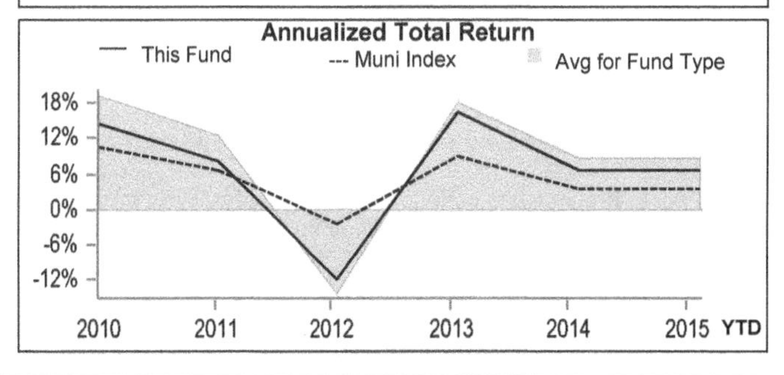

Nuveen NY Select Tax-Free Inc Port (NXN) C+ Fair

Fund Family: Nuveen Fund Advisors LLC
Fund Type: Municipal - Single State
Inception Date: June 19, 1992

Major Rating Factors: Middle of the road best describes Nuveen NY Select Tax-Free Inc Port whose TheStreet.com Investment Rating is currently a C+ (Fair). The fund currently has a performance rating of C (Fair) based on an annualized return of 0.20% over the last three years and a total return of 4.34% year to date 2015. Factored into the performance evaluation is an expense ratio of 0.43% (very low).

The fund's risk rating is currently B (Good). It carries a beta of 1.15, meaning it is expected to move 11.5% for every 10% move in the market. Volatility, as measured by both the semi-deviation and a drawdown factor, is considered low. As of December 31, 2015, Nuveen NY Select Tax-Free Inc Port traded at a discount of 5.12% below its net asset value, which is worse than its one-year historical average discount of 5.85%.

Scott R. Romans currently receives a manager quality ranking of 44 (0=worst, 99=best). If you desire an average level of risk, then this fund may be an option.

Data Date	Investment Rating	Net Assets ($Mil)	Price	Performance Rating/Pts	Total Return Y-T-D	Risk Rating/Pts
12-15	C+	56.99	13.70	C / 5.3	4.34%	B / 8.0
2014	C	56.50	13.65	C- / 4.2	7.47%	B / 8.2
2013	C	57.68	13.35	C / 4.6	-10.44%	B / 8.4
2012	B	57.17	15.27	C+ / 6.1	11.36%	B+ / 9.1
2011	B+	56.70	14.22	B- / 7.1	17.18%	B+ / 9.2
2010	B	55.01	13.09	C- / 4.0	1.30%	B / 8.9

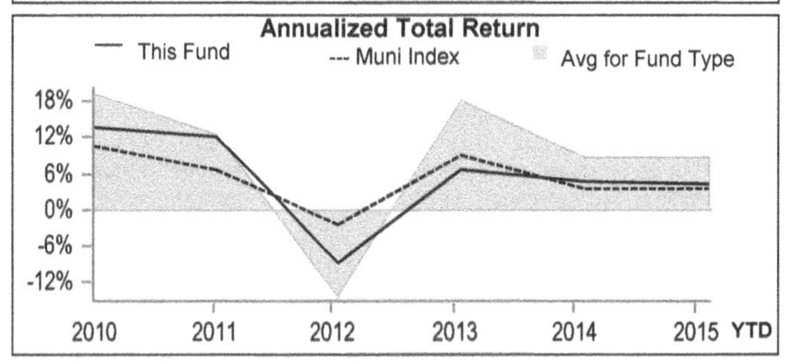

Nuveen OH Quality Inc Muni (NUO) — C — Fair

Fund Family: Nuveen Fund Advisors LLC
Fund Type: Municipal - Single State
Inception Date: October 11, 1991

Major Rating Factors: Middle of the road best describes Nuveen OH Quality Inc Muni whose TheStreet.com Investment Rating is currently a C (Fair). The fund currently has a performance rating of C (Fair) based on an annualized return of -1.97% over the last three years and a total return of 4.89% year to date 2015. Factored into the performance evaluation is an expense ratio of 1.62% (above average).

The fund's risk rating is currently B- (Good). It carries a beta of 2.01, meaning it is expected to move 20.1% for every 10% move in the market. Volatility, as measured by both the semi-deviation and a drawdown factor, is considered low. As of December 31, 2015, Nuveen OH Quality Inc Muni traded at a discount of 10.29% below its net asset value, which is worse than its one-year historical average discount of 11.65%.

Daniel J. Close currently receives a manager quality ranking of 21 (0=worst, 99=best). If you desire an average level of risk, then this fund may be an option.

Data Date	Investment Rating	Net Assets ($Mil)	Price	Performance Rating/Pts	Total Return Y-T-D	Risk Rating/Pts
12-15	C	315.14	15.26	C / 4.6	4.89%	B- / 7.4
2014	C	310.00	15.33	C / 5.0	15.06%	B- / 7.6
2013	C-	276.04	13.92	C- / 3.6	-22.23%	B- / 7.7
2012	A+	170.52	19.05	A / 9.3	23.39%	B / 8.8
2011	B+	162.30	16.70	B+ / 8.5	23.65%	B / 8.8
2010	C+	157.44	14.68	C / 5.1	-2.94%	C+ / 6.9

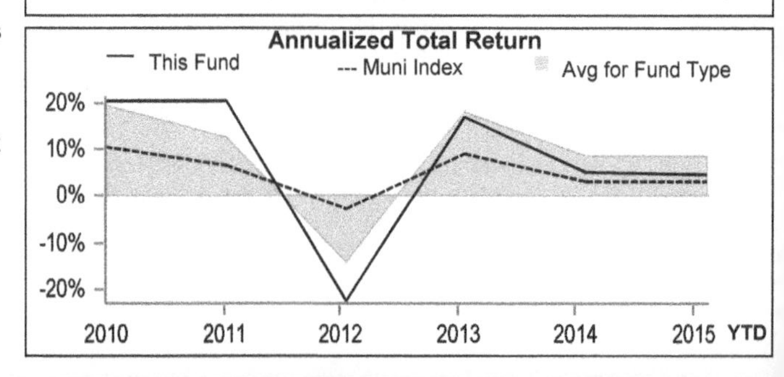

Nuveen PA Investment Quality Muni (NQP) — C+ — Fair

Fund Family: Nuveen Fund Advisors LLC
Fund Type: Municipal - Single State
Inception Date: February 21, 1991

Major Rating Factors: Middle of the road best describes Nuveen PA Investment Quality Muni whose TheStreet.com Investment Rating is currently a C+ (Fair). The fund currently has a performance rating of C+ (Fair) based on an annualized return of 0.34% over the last three years and a total return of 5.94% year to date 2015. Factored into the performance evaluation is an expense ratio of 1.60% (above average).

The fund's risk rating is currently B- (Good). It carries a beta of 2.15, meaning it is expected to move 21.5% for every 10% move in the market. Volatility, as measured by both the semi-deviation and a drawdown factor, is considered low. As of December 31, 2015, Nuveen PA Investment Quality Muni traded at a discount of 13.07% below its net asset value, which is worse than its one-year historical average discount of 13.49%.

Paul L. Brennan has been running the fund for 5 years and currently receives a manager quality ranking of 30 (0=worst, 99=best). If you desire an average level of risk, then this fund may be an option.

Data Date	Investment Rating	Net Assets ($Mil)	Price	Performance Rating/Pts	Total Return Y-T-D	Risk Rating/Pts
12-15	C+	592.54	13.70	C+ / 5.7	5.94%	B- / 7.6
2014	C	591.30	13.73	C / 5.2	16.32%	B- / 7.7
2013	C-	261.20	12.34	C- / 3.0	-18.09%	B / 8.0
2012	A	253.94	15.64	B / 8.2	11.78%	B / 8.9
2011	A	245.70	15.17	A- / 9.0	20.84%	B+ / 9.0
2010	C+	238.37	13.33	C / 5.3	7.97%	C+ / 6.3

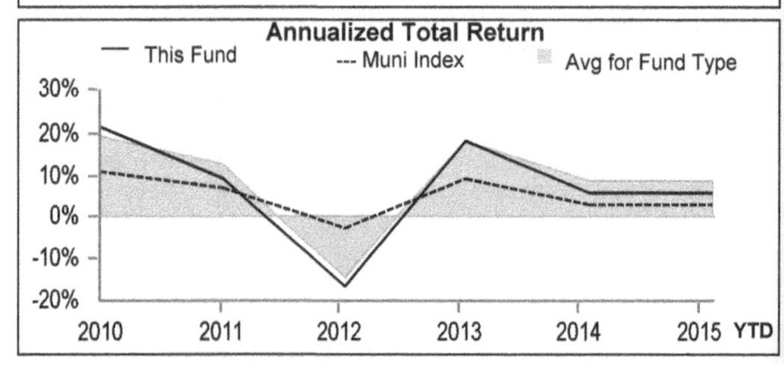

Nuveen Pennsylvania Municipal Valu (NPN) — C+ — Fair

Fund Family: Nuveen Fund Advisors LLC
Fund Type: Municipal - National
Inception Date: April 28, 2009

Major Rating Factors: Middle of the road best describes Nuveen Pennsylvania Municipal Valu whose TheStreet.com Investment Rating is currently a C+ (Fair). The fund currently has a performance rating of C+ (Fair) based on an annualized return of 1.91% over the last three years and a total return of 2.96% year to date 2015. Factored into the performance evaluation is an expense ratio of 0.85% (very low).

The fund's risk rating is currently B- (Good). It carries a beta of 1.37, meaning it is expected to move 13.7% for every 10% move in the market. Volatility, as measured by both the semi-deviation and a drawdown factor, is considered low. As of December 31, 2015, Nuveen Pennsylvania Municipal Valu traded at a discount of 8.24% below its net asset value, which is better than its one-year historical average discount of 7.30%.

Paul L. Brennan currently receives a manager quality ranking of 55 (0=worst, 99=best). If you desire an average level of risk, then this fund may be an option.

Data Date	Investment Rating	Net Assets ($Mil)	Price	Performance Rating/Pts	Total Return Y-T-D	Risk Rating/Pts
12-15	C+	19.95	15.03	C+ / 5.8	2.96%	B- / 7.7
2014	C+	19.80	15.08	C+ / 5.7	15.79%	B / 8.1
2013	C-	20.09	13.62	C- / 3.3	-12.04%	B / 8.4
2012	C+	19.95	15.75	C / 5.2	10.52%	B / 8.6
2011	B+	19.40	15.26	B / 7.6	12.82%	B / 8.8
2010	D+	18.81	14.20	E+ / 0.7	-3.16%	B / 8.2

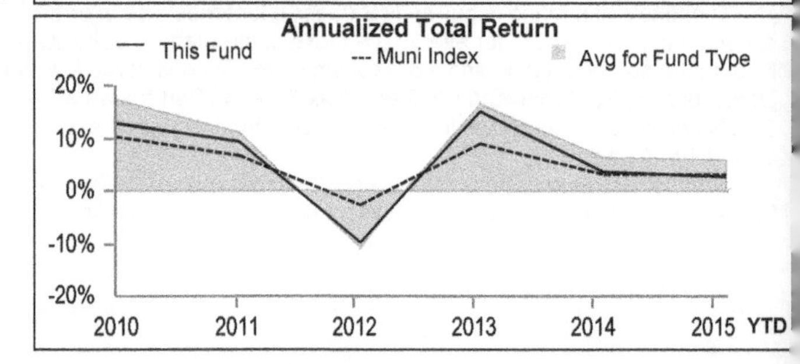

Nuveen Performance Plus Muni (NPP) B- Good

Fund Family: Nuveen Fund Advisors LLC
Fund Type: Municipal - National
Inception Date: June 22, 1989

Major Rating Factors: Nuveen Performance Plus Muni receives a TheStreet.com Investment Rating of B- (Good). The fund currently has a performance rating of C+ (Fair) based on an annualized return of 2.34% over the last three years and a total return of 7.38% year to date 2015. Factored into the performance evaluation is an expense ratio of 1.76% (above average).

The fund's risk rating is currently B- (Good). It carries a beta of 1.98, meaning it is expected to move 19.8% for every 10% move in the market. Volatility, as measured by both the semi-deviation and a drawdown factor, is considered low. As of December 31, 2015, Nuveen Performance Plus Muni traded at a discount of 8.33% below its net asset value, which is worse than its one-year historical average discount of 10.13%.

Thomas C. Spalding has been running the fund for 14 years and currently receives a manager quality ranking of 46 (0=worst, 99=best). If you desire an average level of risk, then this fund may be an option.

Data Date	Investment Rating	Net Assets ($Mil)	Price	Performance Rating/Pts	Total Return Y-T-D	Risk Rating/Pts
12-15	B-	979.55	14.96	C+ / 6.8	7.38%	B- / 7.5
2014	C+	969.60	14.75	C+ / 6.1	15.83%	B- / 7.7
2013	C	1,000.79	13.53	C / 5.3	-14.18%	B- / 7.9
2012	A	892.60	16.17	B+ / 8.4	14.39%	B / 8.7
2011	A-	918.30	15.28	B+ / 8.7	23.68%	B / 8.8
2010	C+	893.85	13.55	C+ / 5.6	3.45%	C+ / 6.8

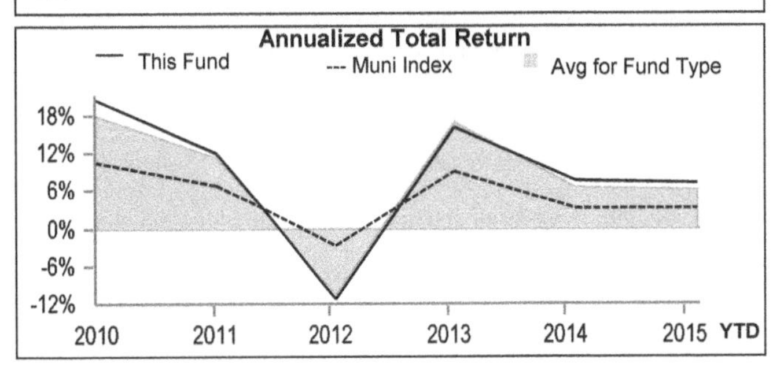

Nuveen Preferred and Income Term (JPI) B+ Good

Fund Family: Nuveen Fund Advisors LLC
Fund Type: Global
Inception Date: July 26, 2012

Major Rating Factors: Strong performance is the major factor driving the B+ (Good) TheStreet.com Investment Rating for Nuveen Preferred and Income Term. The fund currently has a performance rating of B (Good) based on an annualized return of 6.24% over the last three years and a total return of 10.60% year to date 2015. Factored into the performance evaluation is an expense ratio of 1.66% (above average).

The fund's risk rating is currently B- (Good). It carries a beta of 0.36, meaning the fund's expected move will be 3.6% for every 10% move in the market. Volatility, as measured by both the semi-deviation and a drawdown factor, is considered low. As of December 31, 2015, Nuveen Preferred and Income Term traded at a discount of 6.64% below its net asset value, which is worse than its one-year historical average discount of 7.78%.

Brenda A. Langenfeld currently receives a manager quality ranking of 94 (0=worst, 99=best). If you desire only a moderate level of risk and strong performance, then this fund is an excellent option.

Data Date	Investment Rating	Net Assets ($Mil)	Price	Performance Rating/Pts	Total Return Y-T-D	Risk Rating/Pts
12-15	B+	566.14	22.76	B / 7.6	10.60%	B- / 7.8
2014	C+	574.50	22.45	C / 4.6	9.39%	B / 8.4
2013	C-	570.30	22.07	D+ / 2.8	-1.38%	B / 8.7

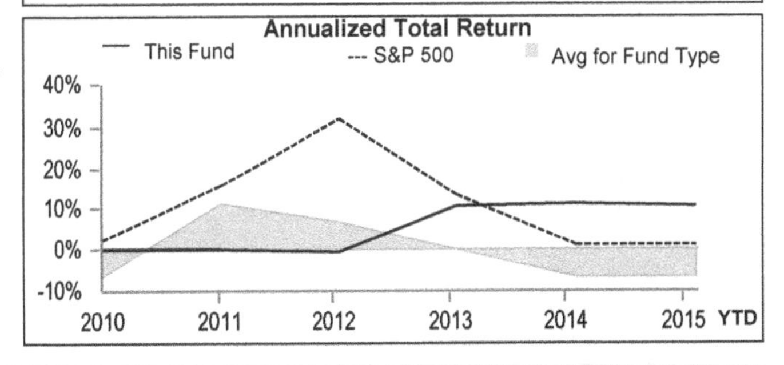

Nuveen Preferref Income Opps (JPC) B- Good

Fund Family: Nuveen Fund Advisors LLC
Fund Type: Growth and Income
Inception Date: March 26, 2003

Major Rating Factors: Nuveen Preferref Income Opps receives a TheStreet.com Investment Rating of B- (Good). The fund currently has a performance rating of C+ (Fair) based on an annualized return of 4.90% over the last three years and a total return of 5.69% year to date 2015. Factored into the performance evaluation is an expense ratio of 1.63% (above average).

The fund's risk rating is currently B- (Good). It carries a beta of 0.38, meaning the fund's expected move will be 3.8% for every 10% move in the market. Volatility, as measured by both the semi-deviation and a drawdown factor, is considered low. As of December 31, 2015, Nuveen Preferref Income Opps traded at a discount of 10.37% below its net asset value, which is better than its one-year historical average discount of 10.24%.

Douglas M. Baker currently receives a manager quality ranking of 73 (0=worst, 99=best). If you desire an average level of risk, then this fund may be an option.

Data Date	Investment Rating	Net Assets ($Mil)	Price	Performance Rating/Pts	Total Return Y-T-D	Risk Rating/Pts
12-15	B-	1,012.77	9.16	C+ / 6.5	5.69%	B- / 7.6
2014	B	1,028.30	9.56	B- / 7.2	16.43%	B / 8.2
2013	C+	995.46	8.87	C+ / 6.0	-4.90%	B / 8.1
2012	A-	914.51	9.71	B+ / 8.4	34.75%	B / 8.4
2011	B	840.50	8.01	B / 8.2	6.19%	B- / 7.7
2010	C	839.85	8.35	C+ / 6.2	21.28%	C / 4.6

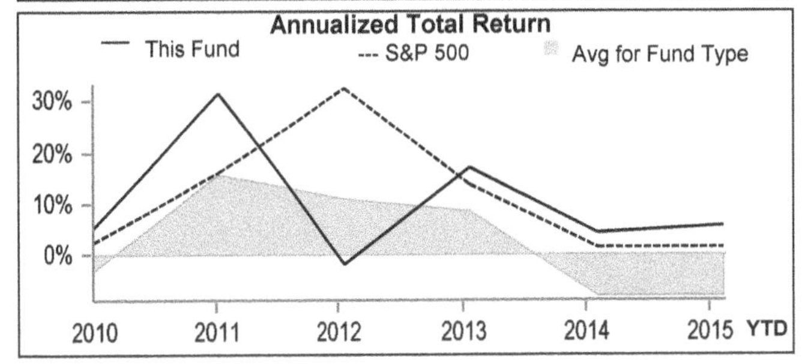

* Denotes ETF Fund

Nuveen Prem Inc Muni (NPI) B Good

Fund Family: Nuveen Fund Advisors LLC
Fund Type: Municipal - National
Inception Date: July 21, 1988

Major Rating Factors: Strong performance is the major factor driving the B (Good) TheStreet.com Investment Rating for Nuveen Prem Inc Muni. The fund currently has a performance rating of B- (Good) based on an annualized return of 3.08% over the last three years and a total return of 7.78% year to date 2015. Factored into the performance evaluation is an expense ratio of 1.58% (above average).

The fund's risk rating is currently B- (Good). It carries a beta of 2.30, meaning it is expected to move 23.0% for every 10% move in the market. Volatility, as measured by both the semi-deviation and a drawdown factor, is considered low. As of December 31, 2015, Nuveen Prem Inc Muni traded at a discount of 9.67% below its net asset value, which is worse than its one-year historical average discount of 11.52%.

Paul L. Brennan has been running the fund for 10 years and currently receives a manager quality ranking of 43 (0=worst, 99=best). If you desire only a moderate level of risk and strong performance, then this fund is an excellent option.

Data Date	Investment Rating	Net Assets ($Mil)	Price	Performance Rating/Pts	Total Return Y-T-D	Risk Rating/Pts
12-15	B	990.13	14.10	B- / 7.2	7.78%	B- / 7.6
2014	B-	974.20	13.86	C+ / 6.8	18.75%	B / 8.0
2013	C-	987.66	12.33	C- / 4.0	-14.62%	B / 8.2
2012	A-	900.46	14.97	B / 8.1	14.30%	B / 8.8
2011	B+	922.10	14.47	B / 8.1	18.56%	B / 8.9
2010	C	875.34	12.82	C- / 4.2	4.00%	C+ / 6.7

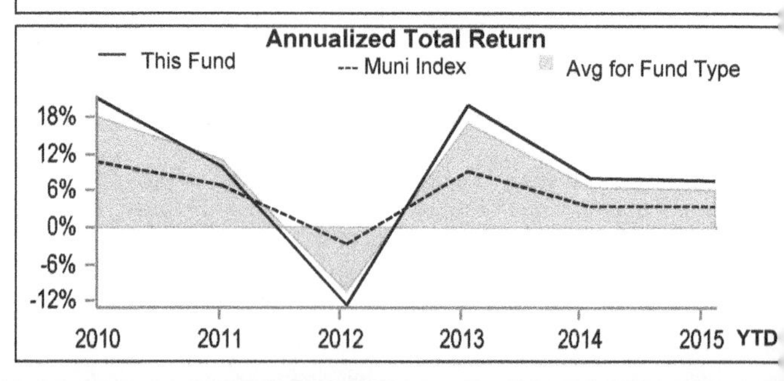

Nuveen Prem Inc Muni 4 (NPT) B Good

Fund Family: Nuveen Fund Advisors LLC
Fund Type: Municipal - National
Inception Date: February 19, 1993

Major Rating Factors: Strong performance is the major factor driving the B (Good) TheStreet.com Investment Rating for Nuveen Prem Inc Muni 4. The fund currently has a performance rating of B- (Good) based on an annualized return of 3.00% over the last three years and a total return of 6.41% year to date 2015. Factored into the performance evaluation is an expense ratio of 1.64% (above average).

The fund's risk rating is currently B- (Good). It carries a beta of 2.15, meaning it is expected to move 21.5% for every 10% move in the market. Volatility, as measured by both the semi-deviation and a drawdown factor, is considered low. As of December 31, 2015, Nuveen Prem Inc Muni 4 traded at a discount of 7.79% below its net asset value, which is worse than its one-year historical average discount of 8.30%.

Christopher L. Drahn currently receives a manager quality ranking of 48 (0=worst, 99=best). If you desire only a moderate level of risk and strong performance, then this fund is an excellent option.

Data Date	Investment Rating	Net Assets ($Mil)	Price	Performance Rating/Pts	Total Return Y-T-D	Risk Rating/Pts
12-15	B	625.13	13.38	B- / 7.2	6.41%	B- / 7.5
2014	B	615.40	13.26	B- / 7.1	18.14%	B- / 7.8
2013	C+	628.37	12.13	C / 5.4	-13.79%	B / 8.1
2012	A	565.53	14.11	B+ / 8.6	16.10%	B / 8.6
2011	A	579.30	13.44	A- / 9.2	23.85%	B / 8.7
2010	C+	543.81	11.97	C+ / 6.0	5.19%	C+ / 6.5

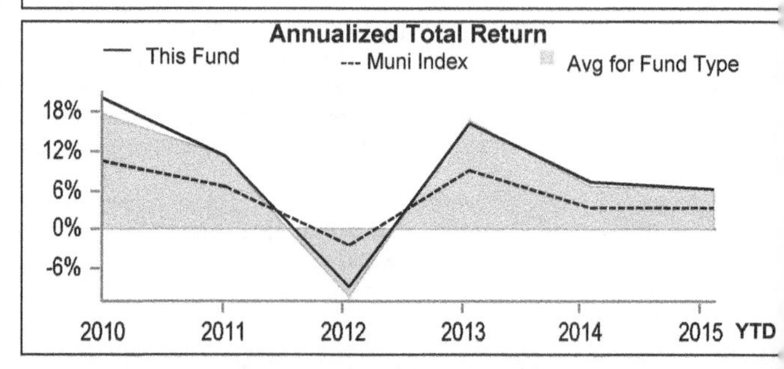

Nuveen Premier Muni Inc (NPF) C+ Fair

Fund Family: Nuveen Fund Advisors LLC
Fund Type: Municipal - National
Inception Date: December 18, 1991

Major Rating Factors: Middle of the road best describes Nuveen Premier Muni Inc whose TheStreet.com Investment Rating is currently a C+ (Fair). The fund currently has a performance rating of C+ (Fair) based on an annualized return of 1.95% over the last three years and a total return of 3.64% year to date 2015. Factored into the performance evaluation is an expense ratio of 1.66% (above average).

The fund's risk rating is currently B- (Good). It carries a beta of 2.37, meaning it is expected to move 23.7% for every 10% move in the market. Volatility, as measured by both the semi-deviation and a drawdown factor, is considered low. As of December 31, 2015, Nuveen Premier Muni Inc traded at a discount of 10.60% below its net asset value, which is worse than its one-year historical average discount of 11.20%.

Daniel J. Close currently receives a manager quality ranking of 35 (0=worst, 99=best). If you desire an average level of risk, then this fund may be an option.

Data Date	Investment Rating	Net Assets ($Mil)	Price	Performance Rating/Pts	Total Return Y-T-D	Risk Rating/Pts
12-15	C+	305.08	13.66	C+ / 6.2	3.64%	B- / 7.6
2014	B-	302.60	13.97	C+ / 6.6	18.35%	B- / 7.8
2013	C	311.28	12.37	C / 4.3	-13.86%	B / 8.1
2012	B+	287.47	14.92	B / 7.8	10.10%	B / 8.8
2011	A-	294.90	14.81	B+ / 8.9	22.46%	B / 8.8
2010	C+	275.67	13.05	C / 5.1	7.17%	C+ / 6.4

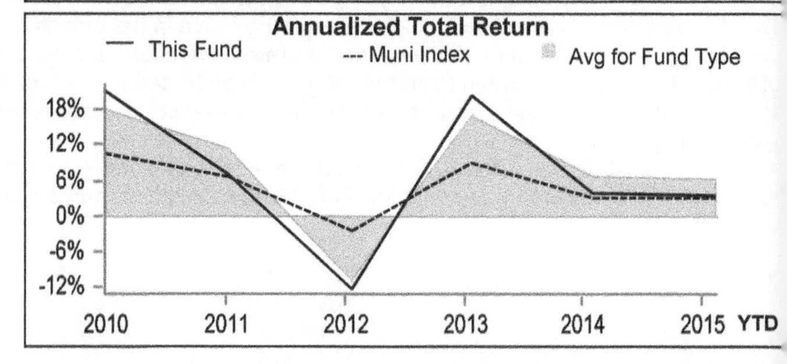

Nuveen Premium Income Muni 2 (NPM) B Good

Fund Family: Nuveen Fund Advisors LLC
Fund Type: Municipal - National
Inception Date: July 23, 1992

Major Rating Factors: Strong performance is the major factor driving the B (Good) TheStreet.com Investment Rating for Nuveen Premium Income Muni 2. The fund currently has a performance rating of B- (Good) based on an annualized return of 3.35% over the last three years and a total return of 8.28% year to date 2015. Factored into the performance evaluation is an expense ratio of 1.58% (above average).

The fund's risk rating is currently B- (Good). It carries a beta of 2.26, meaning it is expected to move 22.6% for every 10% move in the market. Volatility, as measured by both the semi-deviation and a drawdown factor, is considered low. As of December 31, 2015, Nuveen Premium Income Muni 2 traded at a discount of 7.60% below its net asset value, which is worse than its one-year historical average discount of 10.67%.

Paul L. Brennan has been running the fund for 19 years and currently receives a manager quality ranking of 46 (0=worst, 99=best). If you desire only a moderate level of risk and strong performance, then this fund is an excellent option.

Data Date	Investment Rating	Net Assets ($Mil)	Price	Performance Rating/Pts	Total Return Y-T-D	Risk Rating/Pts
12-15	B	1,106.46	14.46	B- / 7.5	8.28%	B- / 7.6
2014	B-	1,097.70	14.16	C+ / 6.7	18.90%	B / 8.0
2013	C	1,130.61	12.55	C- / 4.1	-14.55%	B / 8.2
2012	B+	1,039.72	15.20	B / 7.8	12.05%	B / 8.8
2011	A-	1,064.70	14.92	B+ / 8.5	20.97%	B+ / 9.0
2010	C	1,003.37	13.24	C- / 3.9	5.79%	C+ / 6.5

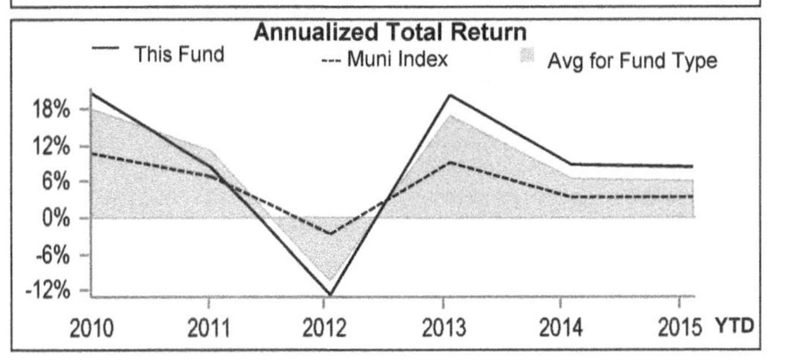

Nuveen Quality Inc Muni (NQU) B- Good

Fund Family: Nuveen Fund Advisors LLC
Fund Type: Municipal - National
Inception Date: June 19, 1991

Major Rating Factors: Nuveen Quality Inc Muni receives a TheStreet.com Investment Rating of B- (Good). The fund currently has a performance rating of C+ (Fair) based on an annualized return of 2.10% over the last three years and a total return of 7.64% year to date 2015. Factored into the performance evaluation is an expense ratio of 1.87% (above average).

The fund's risk rating is currently B- (Good). It carries a beta of 2.38, meaning it is expected to move 23.8% for every 10% move in the market. Volatility, as measured by both the semi-deviation and a drawdown factor, is considered low. As of December 31, 2015, Nuveen Quality Inc Muni traded at a discount of 10.76% below its net asset value, which is worse than its one-year historical average discount of 12.24%.

Thomas C. Spalding has been running the fund for 14 years and currently receives a manager quality ranking of 37 (0=worst, 99=best). If you desire an average level of risk, then this fund may be an option.

Data Date	Investment Rating	Net Assets ($Mil)	Price	Performance Rating/Pts	Total Return Y-T-D	Risk Rating/Pts
12-15	B-	768.05	14.18	C+ / 6.7	7.64%	B- / 7.4
2014	C+	757.80	13.97	C+ / 6.5	20.01%	B- / 7.6
2013	D+	883.99	12.25	D+ / 2.7	-17.67%	B- / 7.9
2012	B+	781.06	15.26	B / 7.7	13.68%	B / 8.7
2011	B+	800.60	14.60	B / 8.0	16.13%	B / 8.8
2010	C+	774.98	13.68	C / 4.8	7.08%	C+ / 6.6

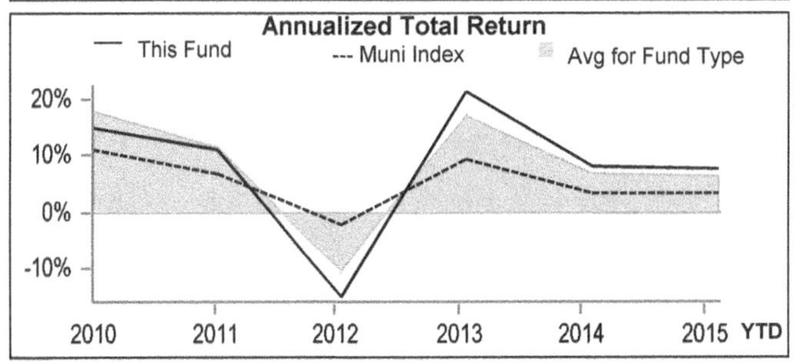

Nuveen Quality Municipal (NQI) C+ Fair

Fund Family: Nuveen Fund Advisors LLC
Fund Type: Municipal - National
Inception Date: December 19, 1990

Major Rating Factors: Middle of the road best describes Nuveen Quality Municipal whose TheStreet.com Investment Rating is currently a C+ (Fair). The fund currently has a performance rating of C+ (Fair) based on an annualized return of 1.27% over the last three years and a total return of 8.59% year to date 2015. Factored into the performance evaluation is an expense ratio of 1.54% (average).

The fund's risk rating is currently B- (Good). It carries a beta of 2.33, meaning it is expected to move 23.3% for every 10% move in the market. Volatility, as measured by both the semi-deviation and a drawdown factor, is considered low. As of December 31, 2015, Nuveen Quality Municipal traded at a discount of 10.73% below its net asset value, which is worse than its one-year historical average discount of 12.81%.

Douglas J. White currently receives a manager quality ranking of 31 (0=worst, 99=best). If you desire an average level of risk, then this fund may be an option.

Data Date	Investment Rating	Net Assets ($Mil)	Price	Performance Rating/Pts	Total Return Y-T-D	Risk Rating/Pts
12-15	C+	579.99	13.64	C+ / 6.3	8.59%	B- / 7.4
2014	C	574.90	13.18	C / 5.2	14.53%	B- / 7.7
2013	C-	595.36	12.08	C- / 3.9	-16.73%	B / 8.0
2012	B	544.50	14.97	C+ / 6.7	12.12%	B / 8.5
2011	B+	555.90	15.00	B+ / 8.5	24.29%	B / 8.7
2010	C-	521.22	12.55	D / 2.1	-1.89%	B- / 7.5

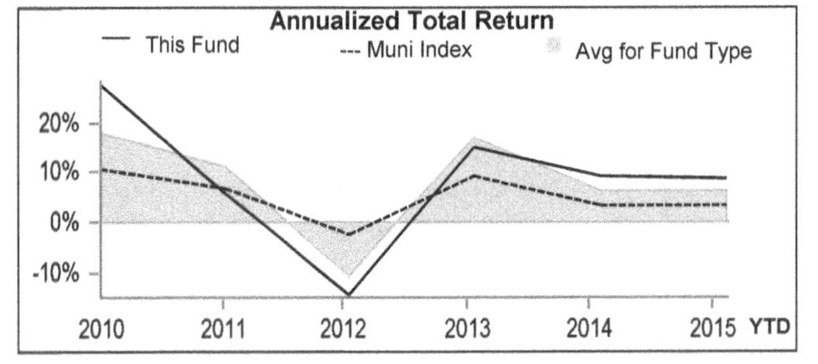

Nuveen Quality Preferred Income (JTP) B Good

Fund Family: Nuveen Fund Advisors LLC
Fund Type: Income
Inception Date: June 25, 2002

Major Rating Factors: Strong performance is the major factor driving the B (Good) TheStreet.com Investment Rating for Nuveen Quality Preferred Income. The fund currently has a performance rating of B- (Good) based on an annualized return of 6.01% over the last three years and a total return of 9.69% year to date 2015. Factored into the performance evaluation is an expense ratio of 1.69% (above average).

The fund's risk rating is currently B- (Good). It carries a beta of 0.27, meaning the fund's expected move will be 2.7% for every 10% move in the market. Volatility, as measured by both the semi-deviation and a drawdown factor, is considered low. As of December 31, 2015, Nuveen Quality Preferred Income traded at a discount of 8.10% below its net asset value, which is worse than its one-year historical average discount of 9.38%.

Lewis P. Jacoby, IV currently receives a manager quality ranking of 83 (0=worst, 99=best). If you desire only a moderate level of risk and strong performance, then this fund is an excellent option.

Data Date	Investment Rating	Net Assets ($Mil)	Price	Perfor-mance Rating/Pts	Total Return Y-T-D	Risk Rating/Pts
12-15	B	590.12	8.28	B- / 7.5	9.69%	B- / 7.4
2014	C+	598.90	8.06	C / 5.5	12.98%	B / 8.1
2013	C+	575.20	7.69	C+ / 5.6	-5.17%	B / 8.3
2012	B+	557.00	8.67	B- / 7.3	18.54%	B / 8.9
2011	C+	501.80	7.57	B- / 7.5	14.16%	C+ / 6.9
2010	D-	456.19	7.40	D+ / 2.3	21.90%	C- / 3.7

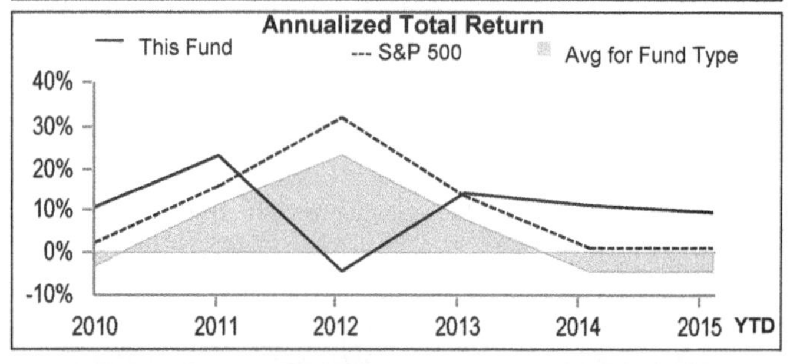

Nuveen Quality Preferred Income 2 (JPS) B Good

Fund Family: Nuveen Fund Advisors LLC
Fund Type: Income
Inception Date: September 23, 2002

Major Rating Factors: Strong performance is the major factor driving the B (Good) TheStreet.com Investment Rating for Nuveen Quality Preferred Income 2. The fund currently has a performance rating of B- (Good) based on an annualized return of 6.22% over the last three years and a total return of 9.85% year to date 2015. Factored into the performance evaluation is an expense ratio of 1.64% (above average).

The fund's risk rating is currently B- (Good). It carries a beta of 0.24, meaning the fund's expected move will be 2.4% for every 10% move in the market. Volatility, as measured by both the semi-deviation and a drawdown factor, is considered low. As of December 31, 2015, Nuveen Quality Preferred Income 2 traded at a discount of 5.10% below its net asset value, which is worse than its one-year historical average discount of 7.18%.

Lewis P. Jacoby, IV currently receives a manager quality ranking of 84 (0=worst, 99=best). If you desire only a moderate level of risk and strong performance, then this fund is an excellent option.

Data Date	Investment Rating	Net Assets ($Mil)	Price	Perfor-mance Rating/Pts	Total Return Y-T-D	Risk Rating/Pts
12-15	B	1,174.26	9.11	B- / 7.2	9.85%	B- / 7.4
2014	B-	1,192.10	8.90	C+ / 6.4	16.84%	B / 8.3
2013	C+	1,137.30	8.14	C / 5.5	-7.16%	B / 8.4
2012	B	1,097.39	9.46	B- / 7.2	24.95%	B / 8.6
2011	C+	979.60	7.83	B- / 7.3	10.84%	C+ / 6.6
2010	D-	922.35	7.90	D+ / 2.5	18.30%	C- / 3.7

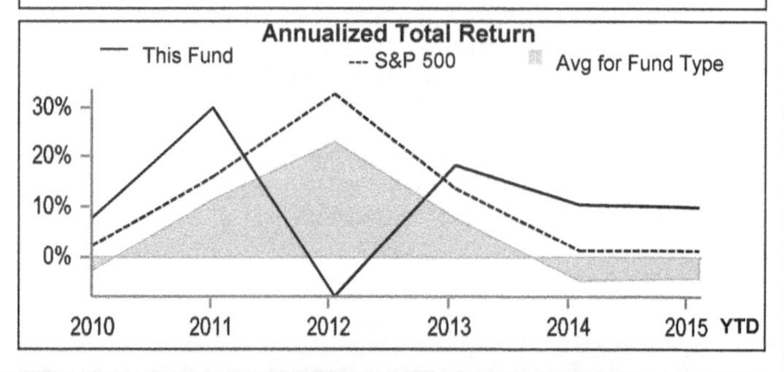

Nuveen Quality Preferred Income 3 (JHP) B Good

Fund Family: Nuveen Fund Advisors LLC
Fund Type: Income
Inception Date: December 18, 2002

Major Rating Factors: Strong performance is the major factor driving the B (Good) TheStreet.com Investment Rating for Nuveen Quality Preferred Income 3. The fund currently has a performance rating of B (Good) based on an annualized return of 6.00% over the last three years and a total return of 9.71% year to date 2015. Factored into the performance evaluation is an expense ratio of 1.74% (above average).

The fund's risk rating is currently B- (Good). It carries a beta of 0.38, meaning the fund's expected move will be 3.8% for every 10% move in the market. Volatility, as measured by both the semi-deviation and a drawdown factor, is considered low. As of December 31, 2015, Nuveen Quality Preferred Income 3 traded at a discount of 9.58% below its net asset value, which is worse than its one-year historical average discount of 11.11%.

Lewis P. Jacoby, IV currently receives a manager quality ranking of 76 (0=worst, 99=best). If you desire only a moderate level of risk and strong performance, then this fund is an excellent option.

Data Date	Investment Rating	Net Assets ($Mil)	Price	Perfor-mance Rating/Pts	Total Return Y-T-D	Risk Rating/Pts
12-15	B	225.69	8.49	B / 7.6	9.71%	B- / 7.6
2014	C+	227.40	8.33	C+ / 5.7	13.53%	B / 8.2
2013	C+	201.14	7.85	C / 5.2	-5.19%	B / 8.3
2012	B	208.73	8.89	B- / 7.2	20.64%	B / 8.5
2011	C+	186.50	7.84	B- / 7.4	10.01%	C+ / 6.8
2010	D	176.68	7.74	D+ / 2.8	20.63%	C- / 3.6

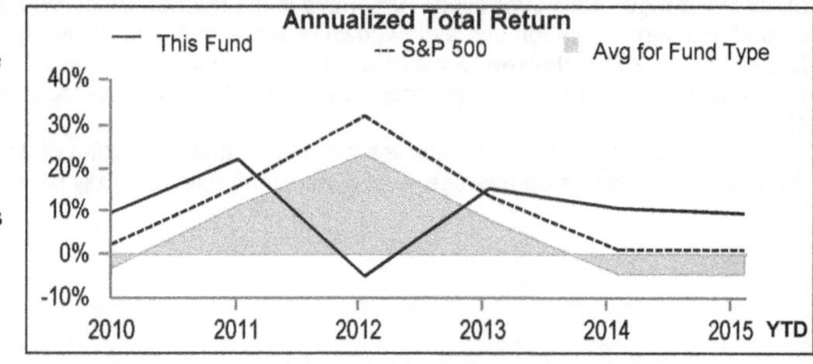

Nuveen Real Asset Income and Growt (JRI) C Fair

Fund Family: Nuveen Fund Advisors LLC
Fund Type: Global
Inception Date: April 25, 2012

Major Rating Factors: Middle of the road best describes Nuveen Real Asset Income and Growt whose TheStreet.com Investment Rating is currently a C (Fair). The fund currently has a performance rating of C+ (Fair) based on an annualized return of 6.70% over the last three years and a total return of -12.28% year to date 2015. Factored into the performance evaluation is an expense ratio of 1.91% (above average).

The fund's risk rating is currently C+ (Fair). It carries a beta of 0.98, meaning that its performance tracks fairly well with that of the overall stock market. Volatility, as measured by both the semi-deviation and a drawdown factor, is considered low. As of December 31, 2015, Nuveen Real Asset Income and Growt traded at a discount of 11.75% below its net asset value, which is better than its one-year historical average discount of 6.56%.

Jay L. Rosenberg currently receives a manager quality ranking of 80 (0=worst, 99=best). If you desire an average level of risk, then this fund may be an option.

Data Date	Investment Rating	Net Assets ($Mil)	Price	Performance Rating/Pts	Total Return Y-T-D	Risk Rating/Pts
12-15	C	194.04	15.24	C+ / 5.9	-12.28%	C+ / 6.4
2014	A	204.10	18.88	A- / 9.2	28.18%	B- / 7.6
2013	C+	203.52	16.75	C+ / 6.0	7.35%	B- / 7.8

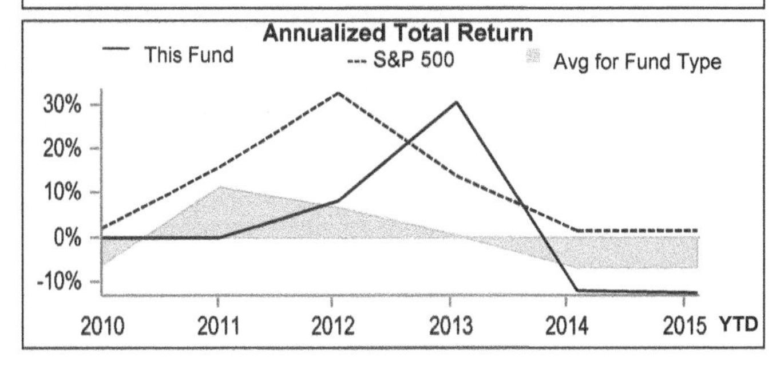

Nuveen Real Estate Inc Fund (JRS) C+ Fair

Fund Family: Nuveen Fund Advisors LLC
Fund Type: Growth and Income
Inception Date: November 15, 2001

Major Rating Factors: Strong performance is the major factor driving the C+ (Fair) TheStreet.com Investment Rating for Nuveen Real Estate Inc Fund. The fund currently has a performance rating of B- (Good) based on an annualized return of 7.41% over the last three years and a total return of -1.33% year to date 2015. Factored into the performance evaluation is an expense ratio of 1.75% (above average).

The fund's risk rating is currently C+ (Fair). It carries a beta of 0.70, meaning the fund's expected move will be 7.0% for every 10% move in the market. Volatility, as measured by both the semi-deviation and a drawdown factor, is considered low. As of December 31, 2015, Nuveen Real Estate Inc Fund traded at a discount of 9.31% below its net asset value, which is better than its one-year historical average discount of 6.79%.

Anthony R. Manno, Jr. currently receives a manager quality ranking of 61 (0=worst, 99=best). If you desire only a moderate level of risk and strong performance, then this fund is an excellent option.

Data Date	Investment Rating	Net Assets ($Mil)	Price	Performance Rating/Pts	Total Return Y-T-D	Risk Rating/Pts
12-15	C+	348.99	10.62	B- / 7.1	-1.33%	C+ / 6.8
2014	B-	315.40	11.50	B / 7.7	31.83%	C+ / 6.9
2013	D+	308.98	9.52	C- / 3.4	-6.92%	B- / 7.0
2012	B	305.65	10.48	B / 7.9	15.95%	B- / 7.4
2011	B	275.80	10.44	A+ / 9.6	10.94%	C+ / 6.4
2010	C-	230.33	10.11	B- / 7.3	37.66%	D+ / 2.3

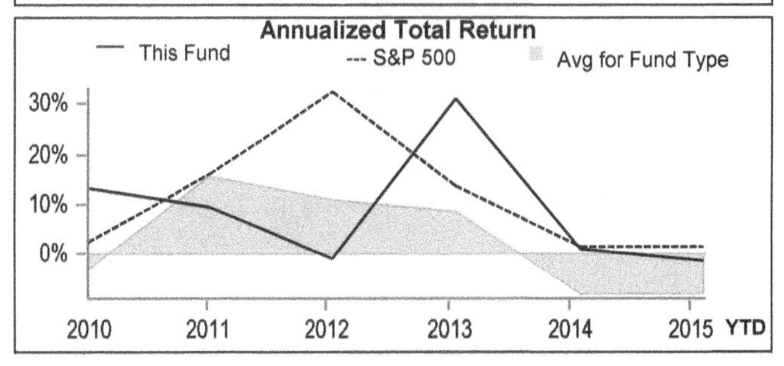

Nuveen S&P 500 Buy Write Income (JPZ) A+ Excellent

Fund Family: Nuveen Fund Advisors LLC
Fund Type: Income
Inception Date: October 26, 2004

Major Rating Factors:
Exceptional performance is the major factor driving the A+ (Excellent) TheStreet.com Investment Rating for Nuveen S&P 500 Buy Write Income. The fund currently has a performance rating of A- (Excellent) based on an annualized return of 11.85% over the last three years and a total return of 15.26% year to date 2015. Factored into the performance evaluation is an expense ratio of 1.02% (low).

The fund's risk rating is currently B- (Good). It carries a beta of 0.47, meaning the fund's expected move will be 4.7% for every 10% move in the market. Volatility, as measured by both the semi-deviation and a drawdown factor, is considered low. As of December 31, 2015, Nuveen S&P 500 Buy Write Income traded at a premium of .67% above its net asset value, which is worse than its one-year historical average discount of 5.89%.

Michael T. Buckius currently receives a manager quality ranking of 90 (0=worst, 99=best). If you desire only a moderate level of risk and strong performance, then this fund is an excellent option.

Data Date	Investment Rating	Net Assets ($Mil)	Price	Performance Rating/Pts	Total Return Y-T-D	Risk Rating/Pts
12-15	A+	1,413.55	13.43	A- / 9.2	15.26%	B- / 7.8
2014	B	529.40	12.59	C+ / 6.2	9.95%	B+ / 9.0
2013	C+	513.63	12.55	C+ / 6.0	10.42%	B / 8.4
2012	C-	508.42	11.83	C- / 4.0	18.79%	B- / 7.9
2011	C	496.10	11.18	C- / 4.2	-1.58%	B- / 7.8
2010	C-	502.49	12.76	C- / 4.2	8.13%	C / 5.4

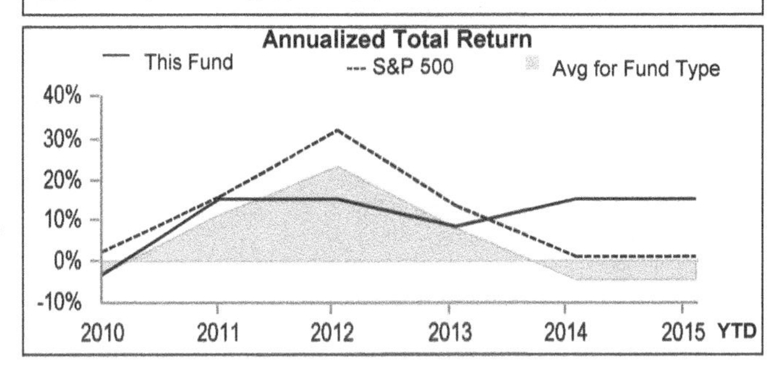

Nuveen S&P 500 Dynamic Overwrite (JPG) B+ Good

Fund Family: Nuveen Fund Advisors LLC
Fund Type: Income
Inception Date: November 22, 2005

Major Rating Factors: Strong performance is the major factor driving the B+ (Good) TheStreet.com Investment Rating for Nuveen S&P 500 Dynamic Overwrite. The fund currently has a performance rating of B- (Good) based on an annualized return of 8.32% over the last three years and a total return of 2.44% year to date 2015. Factored into the performance evaluation is an expense ratio of 0.96% (low).

The fund's risk rating is currently B (Good). It carries a beta of 0.62, meaning the fund's expected move will be 6.2% for every 10% move in the market. Volatility, as measured by both the semi-deviation and a drawdown factor, is considered low. As of December 31, 2015, Nuveen S&P 500 Dynamic Overwrite traded at a discount of 8.49% below its net asset value, which is worse than its one-year historical average discount of 9.15%.

David A. Friar has been running the fund for 2 years and currently receives a manager quality ranking of 70 (0=worst, 99=best). If you desire only a moderate level of risk and strong performance, then this fund is an excellent option.

Data Date	Investment Rating	Net Assets ($Mil)	Price	Perfor-mance Rating/Pts	Total Return Y-T-D	Risk Rating/Pts
12-15	B+	252.08	13.47	B- / 7.4	2.44%	B / 8.0
2014	B+	252.00	14.35	C+ / 6.9	10.11%	B+ / 9.1
2013	B-	240.69	14.12	C+ / 6.5	13.93%	B / 8.4
2012	C	231.98	12.93	C / 5.0	19.72%	B / 8.1
2011	C	225.70	12.07	C / 4.5	-2.06%	B / 8.0
2010	C	226.19	13.85	C+ / 6.0	14.90%	C / 5.3

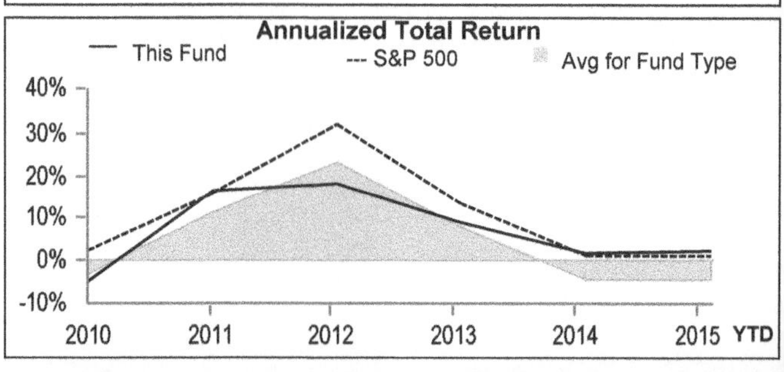

Nuveen Select Maturities Muni (NIM) B- Good

Fund Family: Nuveen Fund Advisors LLC
Fund Type: Municipal - National
Inception Date: September 18, 1992

Major Rating Factors: Nuveen Select Maturities Muni receives a TheStreet.com Investment Rating of B- (Good). The fund currently has a performance rating of C+ (Fair) based on an annualized return of 1.77% over the last three years and a total return of -0.20% year to date 2015. Factored into the performance evaluation is an expense ratio of 0.58% (very low).

The fund's risk rating is currently B (Good). It carries a beta of 1.33, meaning it is expected to move 13.3% for every 10% move in the market. Volatility, as measured by both the semi-deviation and a drawdown factor, is considered low. As of December 31, 2015, Nuveen Select Maturities Muni traded at a discount of 2.94% below its net asset value, which is better than its one-year historical average discount of 1.87%.

Paul L. Brennan currently receives a manager quality ranking of 57 (0=worst, 99=best). If you desire an average level of risk, then this fund may be an option.

Data Date	Investment Rating	Net Assets ($Mil)	Price	Perfor-mance Rating/Pts	Total Return Y-T-D	Risk Rating/Pts
12-15	B-	131.82	10.24	C+ / 5.6	-0.20%	B / 8.5
2014	C	131.30	10.66	C / 5.5	14.41%	C+ / 6.8
2013	C-	132.28	9.65	C- / 3.6	-7.09%	B / 8.5
2012	C-	129.87	10.39	D+ / 2.6	1.44%	B / 8.6
2011	C+	129.20	10.69	C / 5.4	13.30%	B / 8.9
2010	B-	126.83	9.97	C / 5.3	0.24%	B- / 7.8

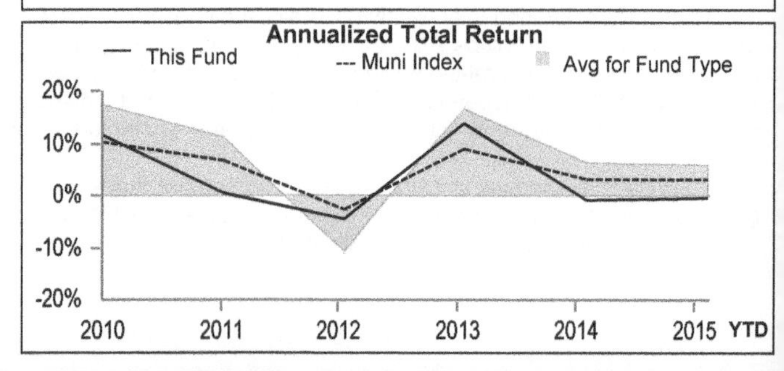

Nuveen Select Quality Muni (NQS) C+ Fair

Fund Family: Nuveen Fund Advisors LLC
Fund Type: Municipal - National
Inception Date: March 21, 1991

Major Rating Factors: Middle of the road best describes Nuveen Select Quality Muni whose TheStreet.com Investment Rating is currently a C+ (Fair). The fund currently has a performance rating of C+ (Fair) based on an annualized return of 0.86% over the last three years and a total return of 5.58% year to date 2015. Factored into the performance evaluation is an expense ratio of 1.67% (above average).

The fund's risk rating is currently B- (Good). It carries a beta of 2.06, meaning it is expected to move 20.6% for every 10% move in the market. Volatility, as measured by both the semi-deviation and a drawdown factor, is considered low. As of December 31, 2015, Nuveen Select Quality Muni traded at a discount of 10.96% below its net asset value, which is worse than its one-year historical average discount of 12.22%.

Thomas C. Spalding has been running the fund for 14 years and currently receives a manager quality ranking of 32 (0=worst, 99=best). If you desire an average level of risk, then this fund may be an option.

Data Date	Investment Rating	Net Assets ($Mil)	Price	Perfor-mance Rating/Pts	Total Return Y-T-D	Risk Rating/Pts
12-15	C+	552.10	14.05	C+ / 6.0	5.58%	B- / 7.5
2014	C+	548.30	13.96	C+ / 5.7	18.29%	B- / 7.7
2013	C-	566.17	12.40	C- / 3.3	-18.61%	B- / 7.9
2012	B+	491.45	15.83	B / 7.8	12.45%	B / 8.5
2011	A	501.20	15.47	A / 9.4	25.95%	B / 8.6
2010	C+	481.23	13.64	C / 5.0	4.67%	C+ / 6.3

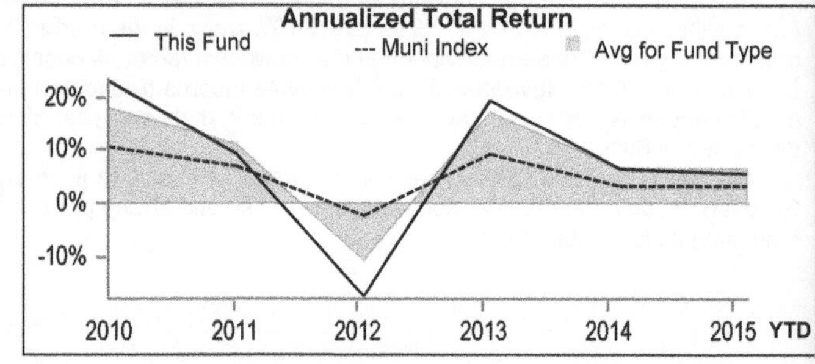

Nuveen Select T-F Inc Portf (NXP) C+ Fair

Fund Family: Nuveen Fund Advisors LLC
Fund Type: Municipal - National
Inception Date: March 19, 1992

Major Rating Factors: Middle of the road best describes Nuveen Select T-F Inc Portf whose TheStreet.com Investment Rating is currently a C+ (Fair). The fund currently has a performance rating of C+ (Fair) based on an annualized return of 1.68% over the last three years and a total return of 4.03% year to date 2015. Factored into the performance evaluation is an expense ratio of 0.32% (very low).

The fund's risk rating is currently B- (Good). It carries a beta of 1.79, meaning it is expected to move 17.9% for every 10% move in the market. Volatility, as measured by both the semi-deviation and a drawdown factor, is considered low. As of December 31, 2015, Nuveen Select T-F Inc Portf traded at a discount of 5.80% below its net asset value, which is worse than its one-year historical average discount of 7.01%.

Thomas C. Spalding has been running the fund for 17 years and currently receives a manager quality ranking of 45 (0=worst, 99=best). If you desire an average level of risk, then this fund may be an option.

Data Date	Investment Rating	Net Assets ($Mil)	Price	Performance Rating/Pts	Total Return Y-T-D	Risk Rating/Pts
12-15	C+	251.30	14.29	C+ / 6.1	4.03%	B- / 7.7
2014	C+	248.80	14.26	C+ / 5.9	15.69%	B / 8.0
2013	C-	249.13	12.89	C- / 3.2	-12.86%	B / 8.2
2012	C	240.69	14.93	C- / 4.0	8.74%	B / 8.7
2011	B-	234.20	14.65	C+ / 5.8	14.34%	B / 8.9
2010	C	233.87	13.54	D+ / 2.5	-3.80%	B / 8.5

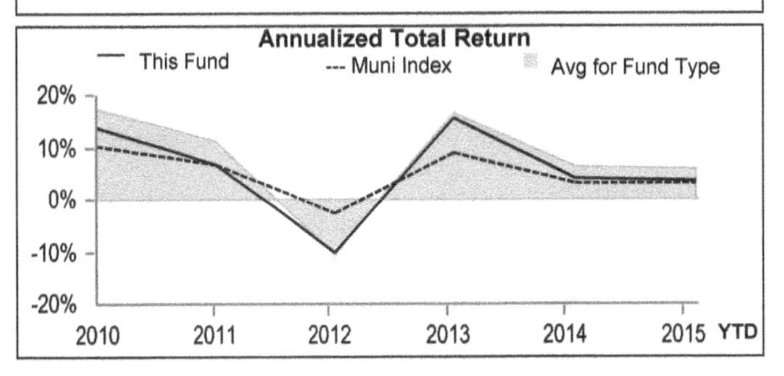

Nuveen Select T-F Inc Portf 2 (NXQ) B- Good

Fund Family: Nuveen Fund Advisors LLC
Fund Type: Municipal - National
Inception Date: May 21, 1992

Major Rating Factors: Nuveen Select T-F Inc Portf 2 receives a TheStreet.com Investment Rating of B- (Good). The fund currently has a performance rating of C+ (Fair) based on an annualized return of 2.49% over the last three years and a total return of 4.38% year to date 2015. Factored into the performance evaluation is an expense ratio of 0.37% (very low).

The fund's risk rating is currently B- (Good). It carries a beta of 2.08, meaning it is expected to move 20.8% for every 10% move in the market. Volatility, as measured by both the semi-deviation and a drawdown factor, is considered low. As of December 31, 2015, Nuveen Select T-F Inc Portf 2 traded at a discount of 6.75% below its net asset value, which is worse than its one-year historical average discount of 6.93%.

Thomas C. Spalding has been running the fund for 17 years and currently receives a manager quality ranking of 43 (0=worst, 99=best). If you desire an average level of risk, then this fund may be an option.

Data Date	Investment Rating	Net Assets ($Mil)	Price	Performance Rating/Pts	Total Return Y-T-D	Risk Rating/Pts
12-15	B-	259.38	13.68	C+ / 6.4	4.38%	B- / 7.9
2014	B-	254.70	13.60	C+ / 6.1	14.25%	B / 8.2
2013	C	254.69	12.36	C- / 3.9	-9.98%	B / 8.4
2012	C	245.78	14.09	C- / 3.5	11.52%	B / 8.7
2011	C	239.50	13.56	C- / 4.2	9.99%	B / 8.9
2010	C	239.10	12.73	C- / 3.0	-3.73%	B / 8.1

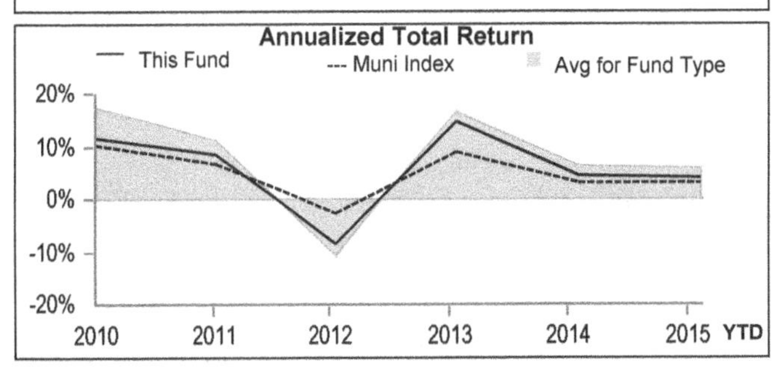

Nuveen Select Tax-Free Inc 3 (NXR) B Good

Fund Family: Nuveen Fund Advisors LLC
Fund Type: Municipal - National
Inception Date: July 24, 1992

Major Rating Factors: Nuveen Select Tax-Free Inc 3 receives a TheStreet.com Investment Rating of B (Good). The fund currently has a performance rating of C+ (Fair) based on an annualized return of 3.13% over the last three years and a total return of 5.81% year to date 2015. Factored into the performance evaluation is an expense ratio of 0.38% (very low).

The fund's risk rating is currently B- (Good). It carries a beta of 2.11, meaning it is expected to move 21.1% for every 10% move in the market. Volatility, as measured by both the semi-deviation and a drawdown factor, is considered low. As of December 31, 2015, Nuveen Select Tax-Free Inc 3 traded at a discount of 5.83% below its net asset value, which is worse than its one-year historical average discount of 6.69%.

Thomas C. Spalding has been running the fund for 17 years and currently receives a manager quality ranking of 47 (0=worst, 99=best). If you desire an average level of risk, then this fund may be an option.

Data Date	Investment Rating	Net Assets ($Mil)	Price	Performance Rating/Pts	Total Return Y-T-D	Risk Rating/Pts
12-15	B	200.15	14.54	C+ / 6.9	5.81%	B- / 7.7
2014	C+	196.30	14.24	C+ / 6.1	14.55%	B / 8.1
2013	C	194.92	12.88	C / 4.4	-9.87%	B / 8.3
2012	C	188.01	14.62	C- / 4.0	11.25%	B / 8.7
2011	C+	183.10	14.31	C / 4.7	13.95%	B / 8.9
2010	C+	182.78	13.10	C- / 3.0	-6.33%	B / 8.5

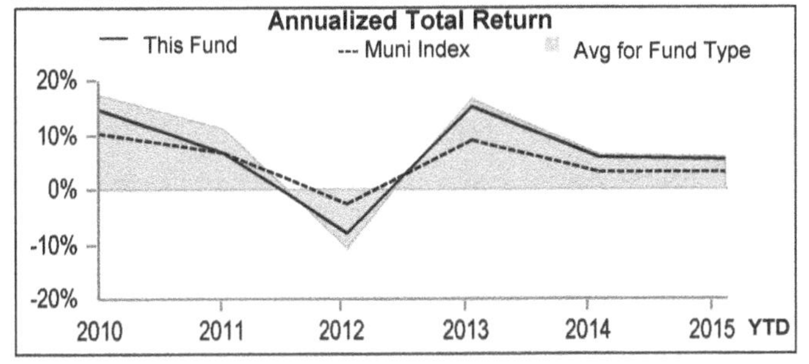

Nuveen Short Duration Credit Oppty (JSD) C- Fair

Fund Family: Nuveen Fund Advisors LLC
Fund Type: Growth and Income
Inception Date: May 25, 2011

Major Rating Factors: Middle of the road best describes Nuveen Short Duration Credit Oppty whose TheStreet.com Investment Rating is currently a C- (Fair). The fund currently has a performance rating of C- (Fair) based on an annualized return of -2.12% over the last three years and a total return of -4.72% year to date 2015. Factored into the performance evaluation is an expense ratio of 1.78% (above average).

The fund's risk rating is currently B- (Good). It carries a beta of 0.38, meaning the fund's expected move will be 3.8% for every 10% move in the market. Volatility, as measured by both the semi-deviation and a drawdown factor, is considered low. As of December 31, 2015, Nuveen Short Duration Credit Oppty traded at a discount of 11.57% below its net asset value, which is better than its one-year historical average discount of 11.52%.

Gunther M. Stein has been running the fund for 5 years and currently receives a manager quality ranking of 22 (0=worst, 99=best). If you desire an average level of risk, then this fund may be an option.

Data Date	Investment Rating	Net Assets ($Mil)	Price	Performance Rating/Pts	Total Return Y-T-D	Risk Rating/Pts
12-15	C-	188.03	14.83	C- / 3.3	-4.72%	B- / 7.0
2014	C-	193.40	16.65	C- / 3.8	-4.74%	B / 8.0
2013	C	201.03	18.84	C / 4.4	2.65%	B / 8.6
2012	A	195.17	19.95	B / 8.1	21.15%	B / 8.9

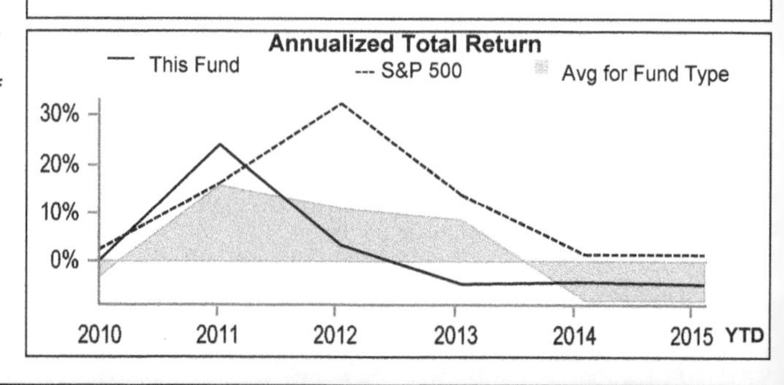

Nuveen Sr Inc (NSL) C- Fair

Fund Family: Nuveen Fund Advisors LLC
Fund Type: Loan Participation
Inception Date: October 26, 1999

Major Rating Factors: Middle of the road best describes Nuveen Sr Inc whose TheStreet.com Investment Rating is currently a C- (Fair). The fund currently has a performance rating of C- (Fair) based on an annualized return of -2.00% over the last three years and a total return of -7.08% year to date 2015. Factored into the performance evaluation is an expense ratio of 2.37% (high).

The fund's risk rating is currently B- (Good). It carries a beta of -154.05, meaning the fund's expected move will be -1540.5% for every 10% move in the market. Volatility, as measured by both the semi-deviation and a drawdown factor, is considered low. As of December 31, 2015, Nuveen Sr Inc traded at a discount of 10.82% below its net asset value, which is worse than its one-year historical average discount of 11.18%.

Gunther M. Stein has been running the fund for 17 years and currently receives a manager quality ranking of 31 (0=worst, 99=best). If you desire an average level of risk, then this fund may be an option.

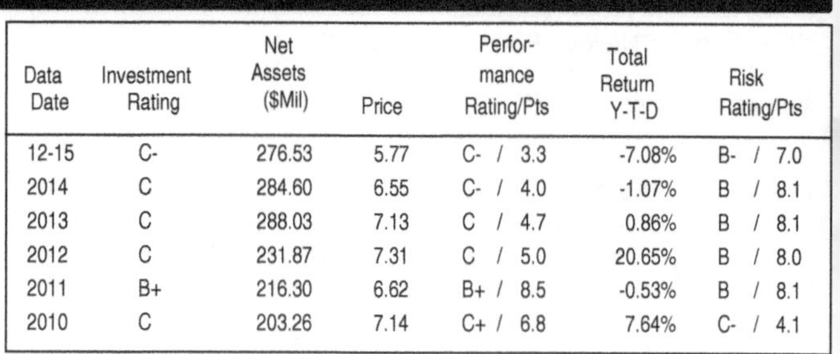

Data Date	Investment Rating	Net Assets ($Mil)	Price	Performance Rating/Pts	Total Return Y-T-D	Risk Rating/Pts
12-15	C-	276.53	5.77	C- / 3.3	-7.08%	B- / 7.0
2014	C	284.60	6.55	C- / 4.0	-1.07%	B / 8.1
2013	C	288.03	7.13	C / 4.7	0.86%	B / 8.1
2012	C	231.87	7.31	C / 5.0	20.65%	B / 8.0
2011	B+	216.30	6.62	B+ / 8.5	-0.53%	B / 8.1
2010	C	203.26	7.14	C+ / 6.8	7.64%	C- / 4.1

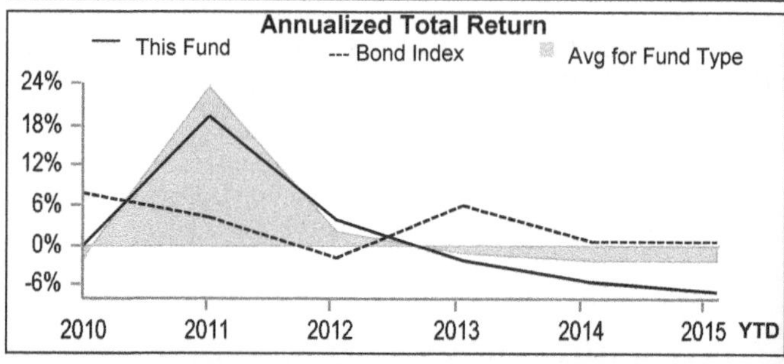

Nuveen Tax-Advant Tot Ret Strat Fd (JTA) B Good

Fund Family: Nuveen Fund Advisors LLC
Fund Type: Income
Inception Date: January 28, 2004

Major Rating Factors: Strong performance is the major factor driving the B (Good) TheStreet.com Investment Rating for Nuveen Tax-Advant Tot Ret Strat Fd. The fund currently has a performance rating of B- (Good) based on an annualized return of 9.77% over the last three years and a total return of -3.66% year to date 2015. Factored into the performance evaluation is an expense ratio of 1.85% (above average).

The fund's risk rating is currently B- (Good). It carries a beta of 1.17, meaning it is expected to move 11.7% for every 10% move in the market. Volatility, as measured by both the semi-deviation and a drawdown factor, is considered low. As of December 31, 2015, Nuveen Tax-Advant Tot Ret Strat Fd traded at a discount of 10.92% below its net asset value, which is better than its one-year historical average discount of 9.56%.

Gunther M. Stein has been running the fund for 12 years and currently receives a manager quality ranking of 30 (0=worst, 99=best). If you desire only a moderate level of risk and strong performance, then this fund is an excellent option.

Data Date	Investment Rating	Net Assets ($Mil)	Price	Performance Rating/Pts	Total Return Y-T-D	Risk Rating/Pts
12-15	B	199.26	11.67	B- / 7.2	-3.66%	B- / 7.6
2014	B	198.90	13.29	B- / 7.2	3.70%	B / 8.1
2013	B+	180.93	14.10	B+ / 8.6	33.09%	B- / 7.8
2012	C	155.52	10.51	C / 4.9	17.86%	B / 8.0
2011	C+	151.90	9.56	C+ / 5.7	-4.16%	B- / 7.6
2010	D-	161.40	11.24	D- / 1.1	14.72%	C / 4.3

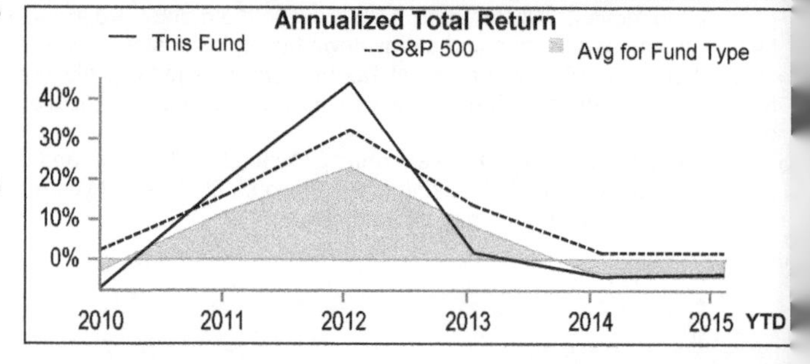

Nuveen Tax-Advantaged Dividend Grt (JTD) C+ Fair

Fund Family: Nuveen Fund Advisors LLC
Fund Type: Growth and Income
Inception Date: June 27, 2007

Major Rating Factors: Middle of the road best describes Nuveen Tax-Advantaged Dividend Grt whose TheStreet.com Investment Rating is currently a C+ (Fair). The fund currently has a performance rating of C+ (Fair) based on an annualized return of 5.43% over the last three years and a total return of -4.69% year to date 2015. Factored into the performance evaluation is an expense ratio of 1.95% (above average).

The fund's risk rating is currently B- (Good). It carries a beta of 0.93, meaning that its performance tracks fairly well with that of the overall stock market. Volatility, as measured by both the semi-deviation and a drawdown factor, is considered low. As of December 31, 2015, Nuveen Tax-Advantaged Dividend Grt traded at a discount of 11.23% below its net asset value, which is better than its one-year historical average discount of 9.62%.

James R. Boothe has been running the fund for 9 years and currently receives a manager quality ranking of 25 (0=worst, 99=best). If you desire an average level of risk, then this fund may be an option.

Data Date	Investment Rating	Net Assets ($Mil)	Price	Performance Rating/Pts	Total Return Y-T-D	Risk Rating/Pts
12-15	C+	250.66	13.91	C+ / 5.8	-4.69%	B- / 7.7
2014	A	248.40	16.15	B- / 7.5	12.85%	B+ / 9.1
2013	B	231.03	15.66	B- / 7.2	10.51%	B / 8.3
2012	A-	196.40	14.50	B+ / 8.7	28.18%	B / 8.3
2011	B-	196.40	12.29	B- / 7.2	5.81%	B- / 7.7
2010	C	189.01	13.01	C+ / 6.0	22.52%	C / 4.6

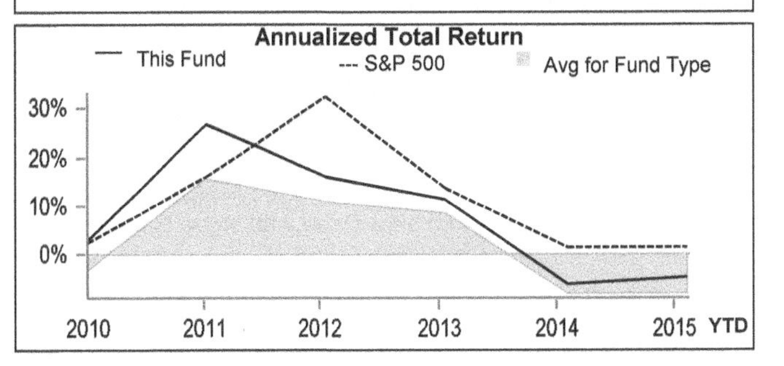

Nuveen TX Quality Inc Muni (NTX) C+ Fair

Fund Family: Nuveen Fund Advisors LLC
Fund Type: Municipal - Single State
Inception Date: October 17, 1991

Major Rating Factors: Middle of the road best describes Nuveen TX Quality Inc Muni whose TheStreet.com Investment Rating is currently a C+ (Fair). The fund currently has a performance rating of C+ (Fair) based on an annualized return of 0.90% over the last three years and a total return of 3.89% year to date 2015. Factored into the performance evaluation is an expense ratio of 2.33% (high).

The fund's risk rating is currently B- (Good). It carries a beta of 1.87, meaning it is expected to move 18.7% for every 10% move in the market. Volatility, as measured by both the semi-deviation and a drawdown factor, is considered low. As of December 31, 2015, Nuveen TX Quality Inc Muni traded at a discount of 8.03% below its net asset value, which is worse than its one-year historical average discount of 9.73%.

Daniel J. Close currently receives a manager quality ranking of 35 (0=worst, 99=best). If you desire an average level of risk, then this fund may be an option.

Data Date	Investment Rating	Net Assets ($Mil)	Price	Performance Rating/Pts	Total Return Y-T-D	Risk Rating/Pts
12-15	C+	157.64	14.43	C+ / 5.8	3.89%	B- / 7.8
2014	C	155.30	14.46	C / 4.4	17.35%	B- / 7.9
2013	D+	141.06	12.85	D / 2.1	-16.25%	B / 8.1
2012	C	151.86	15.84	C- / 3.9	3.75%	B+ / 9.0
2011	B+	143.60	16.34	B / 8.2	14.68%	B+ / 9.1
2010	B+	143.08	14.92	B- / 7.4	4.43%	C+ / 6.6

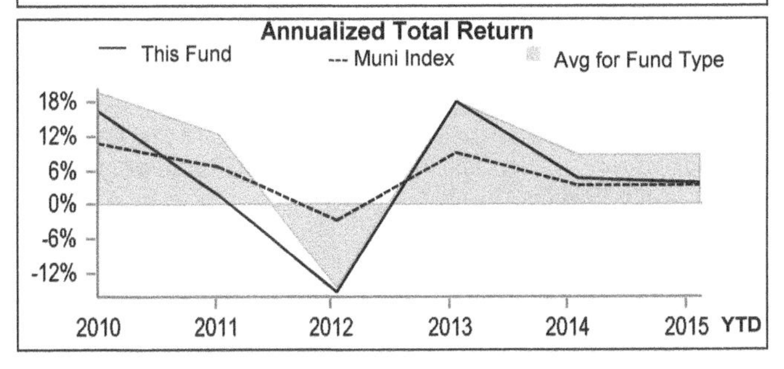

Nuveen VA Premium Income Municipal (NPV) C+ Fair

Fund Family: Nuveen Fund Advisors LLC
Fund Type: Municipal - Single State
Inception Date: March 18, 1993

Major Rating Factors: Middle of the road best describes Nuveen VA Premium Income Municipal whose TheStreet.com Investment Rating is currently a C+ (Fair). The fund currently has a performance rating of C+ (Fair) based on an annualized return of 0.08% over the last three years and a total return of 9.22% year to date 2015. Factored into the performance evaluation is an expense ratio of 1.67% (above average).

The fund's risk rating is currently B- (Good). It carries a beta of 2.12, meaning it is expected to move 21.2% for every 10% move in the market. Volatility, as measured by both the semi-deviation and a drawdown factor, is considered low. As of December 31, 2015, Nuveen VA Premium Income Municipal traded at a discount of 7.17% below its net asset value, which is worse than its one-year historical average discount of 7.27%.

Thomas C. Spalding currently receives a manager quality ranking of 27 (0=worst, 99=best). If you desire an average level of risk, then this fund may be an option.

Data Date	Investment Rating	Net Assets ($Mil)	Price	Performance Rating/Pts	Total Return Y-T-D	Risk Rating/Pts
12-15	C+	260.10	13.60	C+ / 5.9	9.22%	B- / 7.2
2014	C-	261.70	13.10	C- / 3.6	15.79%	B- / 7.4
2013	D+	275.87	11.82	D / 1.8	-20.85%	B- / 7.6
2012	C	141.10	15.55	C- / 4.2	4.95%	B / 8.5
2011	B	136.60	15.42	C+ / 6.7	12.58%	B / 8.6
2010	C+	132.30	14.70	C+ / 6.7	3.78%	C+ / 6.8

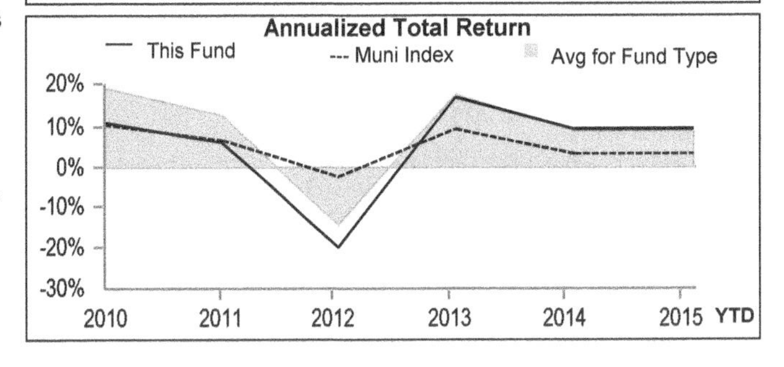

Pacholder High Yield Fund (PHF) — D+ Weak

Fund Family: JP Morgan Investment Management Inc
Fund Type: Corporate - High Yield
Inception Date: November 16, 1988

Data Date	Investment Rating	Net Assets ($Mil)	Price	Performance Rating/Pts	Total Return Y-T-D	Risk Rating/Pts
12-15	D+	106.36	6.07	D+ / 2.7	-9.85%	C+ / 6.3
2014	D+	114.00	7.35	D+ / 2.9	1.47%	B- / 7.3
2013	C	109,200.67	7.86	C / 5.0	-3.15%	B- / 7.7
2012	C+	106,346.02	8.87	B- / 7.0	13.51%	B- / 7.4
2011	A	101.90	8.95	A+ / 9.7	21.67%	B / 8.1
2010	C+	100.90	8.45	B / 8.2	21.63%	C- / 3.4

Major Rating Factors:
Disappointing performance is the major factor driving the D+ (Weak) TheStreet.com Investment Rating for Pacholder High Yield Fund. The fund currently has a performance rating of D+ (Weak) based on an annualized return of -3.95% over the last three years and a total return of -9.85% year to date 2015. Factored into the performance evaluation is an expense ratio of 2.04% (high).

The fund's risk rating is currently C+ (Fair). It carries a beta of 1.86, meaning it is expected to move 18.6% for every 10% move in the market. Volatility, as measured by both the semi-deviation and a drawdown factor, is considered low. As of December 31, 2015, Pacholder High Yield Fund traded at a discount of 13.04% below its net asset value, which is better than its one-year historical average discount of 12.78%.

James E. Gibson currently receives a manager quality ranking of 23 (0=worst, 99=best). This fund offers only a moderate level of risk but investors looking for strong performance are still waiting.

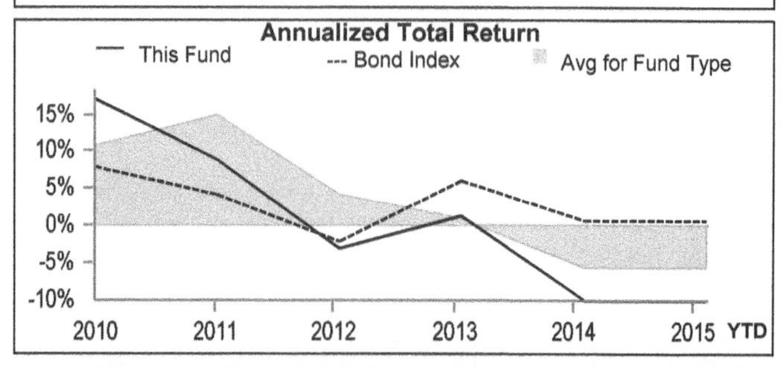

PCM Fund (PCM) — C- Fair

Fund Family: PIMCO
Fund Type: Mortgage
Inception Date: August 27, 1993

Data Date	Investment Rating	Net Assets ($Mil)	Price	Performance Rating/Pts	Total Return Y-T-D	Risk Rating/Pts
12-15	C-	123.63	9.24	C- / 4.0	-5.72%	C+ / 6.7
2014	C	128.00	10.65	C / 4.4	-0.60%	B- / 7.7
2013	B-	129.98	11.65	C+ / 6.9	5.60%	B / 8.2
2012	A+	117.80	12.02	A- / 9.0	24.67%	B / 8.8
2011	B+	113.02	10.77	B+ / 8.8	10.86%	B- / 7.8
2010	B-	88.29	10.80	B+ / 8.8	48.82%	C- / 4.0

Major Rating Factors: Middle of the road best describes PCM Fund whose TheStreet.com Investment Rating is currently a C- (Fair). The fund currently has a performance rating of C- (Fair) based on an annualized return of 0.33% over the last three years and a total return of -5.72% year to date 2015. Factored into the performance evaluation is an expense ratio of 1.89% (above average).

The fund's risk rating is currently C+ (Fair). It carries a beta of 2.34, meaning it is expected to move 23.4% for every 10% move in the market. Volatility, as measured by both the semi-deviation and a drawdown factor, is considered low. As of December 31, 2015, PCM Fund traded at a discount of 5.91% below its net asset value, which is better than its one-year historical average discount of 3.89%.

Daniel J. Ivascyn has been running the fund for 15 years and currently receives a manager quality ranking of 36 (0=worst, 99=best). If you desire an average level of risk, then this fund may be an option.

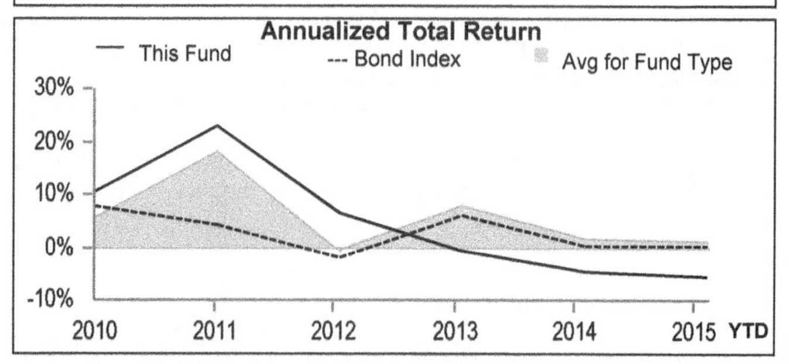

PIMCO CA Municipal Income Fund (PCQ) — B Good

Fund Family: PIMCO
Fund Type: Municipal - Single State
Inception Date: June 26, 2001

Data Date	Investment Rating	Net Assets ($Mil)	Price	Performance Rating/Pts	Total Return Y-T-D	Risk Rating/Pts
12-15	B	67.62	15.70	B+ / 8.3	7.48%	C+ / 6.7
2014	B+	263.20	15.65	A / 9.4	26.41%	C+ / 6.3
2013	B-	272.40	13.01	C+ / 6.6	-13.45%	B / 8.0
2012	A+	253.87	15.93	A+ / 9.6	24.29%	B / 8.3
2011	A-	236.00	13.44	A- / 9.1	24.16%	B / 8.3
2010	D+	234.79	12.40	D / 1.7	7.56%	C+ / 6.6

Major Rating Factors: Strong performance is the major factor driving the B (Good) TheStreet.com Investment Rating for PIMCO CA Municipal Income Fund. The fund currently has a performance rating of B+ (Good) based on an annualized return of 5.43% over the last three years and a total return of 7.48% year to date 2015. Factored into the performance evaluation is an expense ratio of 1.32% (average).

The fund's risk rating is currently C+ (Fair). It carries a beta of 2.40, meaning it is expected to move 24.0% for every 10% move in the market. Volatility, as measured by both the semi-deviation and a drawdown factor, is considered low. As of December 31, 2015, PIMCO CA Municipal Income Fund traded at a premium of 7.46% above its net asset value, which is worse than its one-year historical average premium of 6.46%.

Joseph P. Deane has been running the fund for 5 years and currently receives a manager quality ranking of 56 (0=worst, 99=best). If you desire only a moderate level of risk and strong performance, then this fund is an excellent option.

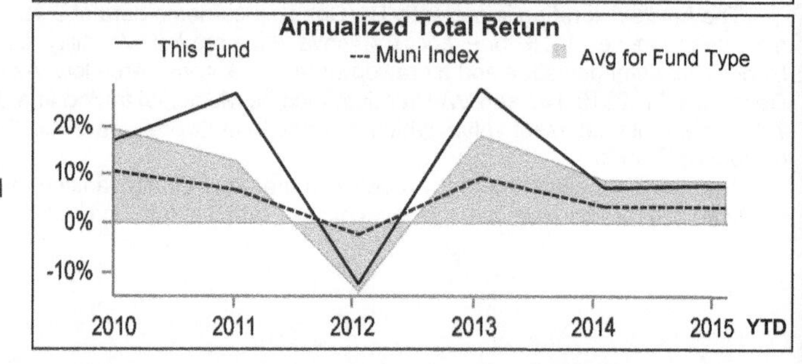

* Denotes ETF Fund

PIMCO CA Municipal Income Fund II (PCK) B+ Good

Fund Family: PIMCO
Fund Type: Municipal - Single State
Inception Date: June 25, 2002

Major Rating Factors: Strong performance is the major factor driving the B+ (Good) TheStreet.com Investment Rating for PIMCO CA Municipal Income Fund II. The fund currently has a performance rating of B+ (Good) based on an annualized return of 4.42% over the last three years and a total return of 13.01% year to date 2015. Factored into the performance evaluation is an expense ratio of 1.32% (average).

The fund's risk rating is currently B- (Good). It carries a beta of 1.97, meaning it is expected to move 19.7% for every 10% move in the market. Volatility, as measured by both the semi-deviation and a drawdown factor, is considered low. As of December 31, 2015, PIMCO CA Municipal Income Fund II traded at a premium of 11.06% above its net asset value, which is worse than its one-year historical average premium of 10.63%.

Joseph P. Deane has been running the fund for 5 years and currently receives a manager quality ranking of 62 (0=worst, 99=best). If you desire only a moderate level of risk and strong performance, then this fund is an excellent option.

Data Date	Investment Rating	Net Assets ($Mil)	Price	Performance Rating/Pts	Total Return Y-T-D	Risk Rating/Pts
12-15	B+	273.29	9.94	B+ / 8.6	13.01%	B- / 7.2
2014	C+	277.10	9.51	C+ / 6.8	11.47%	C+ / 6.5
2013	B-	282.18	9.00	C+ / 6.5	-9.72%	B / 8.3
2012	A+	272.57	10.59	A / 9.3	21.87%	B / 8.7
2011	B+	247.80	9.40	B+ / 8.3	20.49%	B / 8.6
2010	D-	252.82	8.77	D- / 1.0	10.09%	C- / 4.3

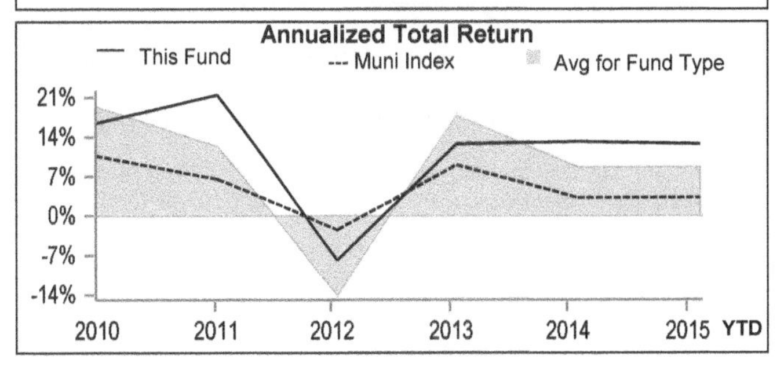

PIMCO CA Municipal Income Fund III (PZC) A- Excellent

Fund Family: PIMCO
Fund Type: Municipal - Single State
Inception Date: October 28, 2002

Major Rating Factors:
Exceptional performance is the major factor driving the A- (Excellent) TheStreet.com Investment Rating for PIMCO CA Municipal Income Fund III. The fund currently has a performance rating of A (Excellent) based on an annualized return of 8.42% over the last three years and a total return of 20.31% year to date 2015. Factored into the performance evaluation is an expense ratio of 1.30% (average).

The fund's risk rating is currently C+ (Fair). It carries a beta of 2.21, meaning it is expected to move 22.1% for every 10% move in the market. Volatility, as measured by both the semi-deviation and a drawdown factor, is considered low. As of December 31, 2015, PIMCO CA Municipal Income Fund III traded at a premium of 15.62% above its net asset value, which is worse than its one-year historical average premium of 8.13%.

Joseph P. Deane has been running the fund for 5 years and currently receives a manager quality ranking of 81 (0=worst, 99=best). If you desire only a moderate level of risk and strong performance, then this fund is an excellent option.

Data Date	Investment Rating	Net Assets ($Mil)	Price	Performance Rating/Pts	Total Return Y-T-D	Risk Rating/Pts
12-15	A-	223.03	11.92	A / 9.5	20.31%	C+ / 6.8
2014	B	221.40	10.71	B+ / 8.7	23.56%	C+ / 6.5
2013	C+	200.25	9.20	C+ / 5.9	-14.02%	B / 8.2
2012	A+	224.60	11.28	A- / 9.2	22.38%	B / 8.6
2011	A-	202.10	9.76	A- / 9.1	21.23%	B / 8.6
2010	D-	210.32	9.01	E+ / 0.9	7.20%	C / 4.9

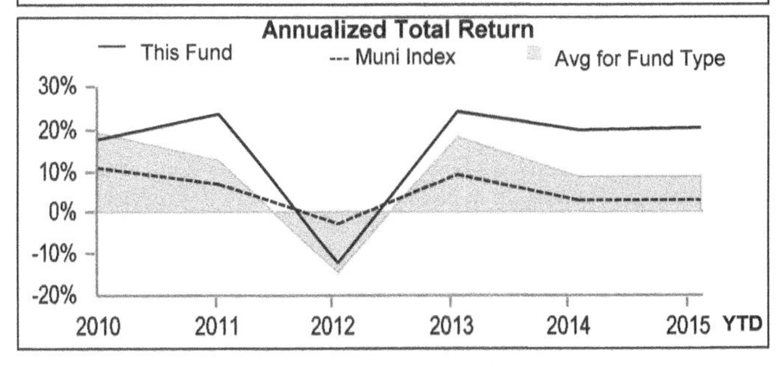

PIMCO Corporate and Income Oppty (PTY) C- Fair

Fund Family: PIMCO
Fund Type: Corporate - High Yield
Inception Date: December 23, 2002

Major Rating Factors: Middle of the road best describes PIMCO Corporate and Income Oppty whose TheStreet.com Investment Rating is currently a C- (Fair). The fund currently has a performance rating of C (Fair) based on an annualized return of 1.18% over the last three years and a total return of -8.78% year to date 2015. Factored into the performance evaluation is an expense ratio of 0.91% (low).

The fund's risk rating is currently C (Fair). It carries a beta of 1.39, meaning it is expected to move 13.9% for every 10% move in the market. Volatility, as measured by both the semi-deviation and a drawdown factor, is considered average. As of December 31, 2015, PIMCO Corporate and Income Oppty traded at a premium of 1.83% above its net asset value, which is better than its one-year historical average premium of 5.15%.

Alfred T. Murata currently receives a manager quality ranking of 62 (0=worst, 99=best). If you desire an average level of risk, then this fund may be an option.

Data Date	Investment Rating	Net Assets ($Mil)	Price	Performance Rating/Pts	Total Return Y-T-D	Risk Rating/Pts
12-15	C-	1,082.00	13.34	C / 4.3	-8.78%	C / 5.3
2014	D+	1,094.20	15.90	C / 4.8	-1.63%	C / 4.4
2013	B-	1,183.26	17.26	B / 7.6	7.66%	B- / 7.2
2012	A	1,046.09	19.41	A- / 9.2	30.62%	B- / 7.8
2011	C+	1,098.92	17.37	B / 7.9	10.90%	C+ / 6.4
2010	B	962.49	16.97	B+ / 8.7	28.50%	C / 4.3

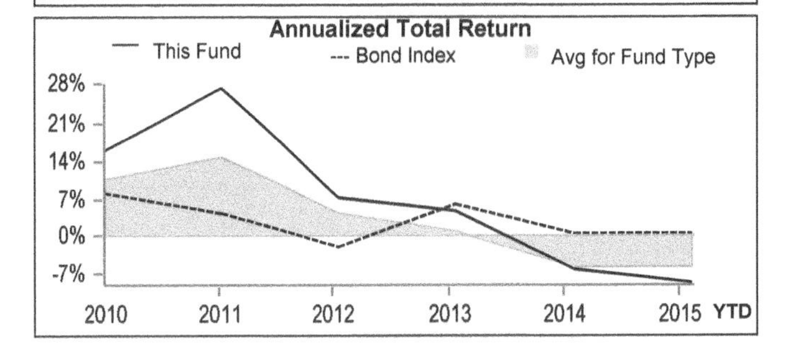

PIMCO Corporate and ncome Strategy (PCN) C- Fair

Fund Family: PIMCO
Fund Type: Corporate - High Yield
Inception Date: December 19, 2001

Major Rating Factors: Middle of the road best describes PIMCO Corporate and ncome Strategy whose TheStreet.com Investment Rating is currently a C- (Fair). The fund currently has a performance rating of C (Fair) based on an annualized return of 1.21% over the last three years and a total return of -4.21% year to date 2015. Factored into the performance evaluation is an expense ratio of 1.09% (low).

The fund's risk rating is currently C+ (Fair). It carries a beta of 1.21, meaning it is expected to move 12.1% for every 10% move in the market. Volatility, as measured by both the semi-deviation and a drawdown factor, is considered low. As of December 31, 2015, PIMCO Corporate and ncome Strategy traded at a discount of 4.35% below its net asset value, which is better than its one-year historical average discount of 2.05%.

Scott A. Mather currently receives a manager quality ranking of 68 (0=worst, 99=best). If you desire an average level of risk, then this fund may be an option.

Data Date	Investment Rating	Net Assets ($Mil)	Price	Performance Rating/Pts	Total Return Y-T-D	Risk Rating/Pts
12-15	C-	113.75	13.40	C / 4.6	-4.21%	C+ / 6.3
2014	D+	600.10	15.11	C / 4.7	3.00%	C / 5.1
2013	C+	623.52	15.80	C+ / 6.7	0.93%	B- / 7.6
2012	B+	515.04	17.65	B+ / 8.7	27.45%	B- / 7.9
2011	C+	589.03	15.95	B- / 7.4	11.42%	C+ / 6.1
2010	B	529.37	15.49	B+ / 8.5	22.06%	C / 4.8

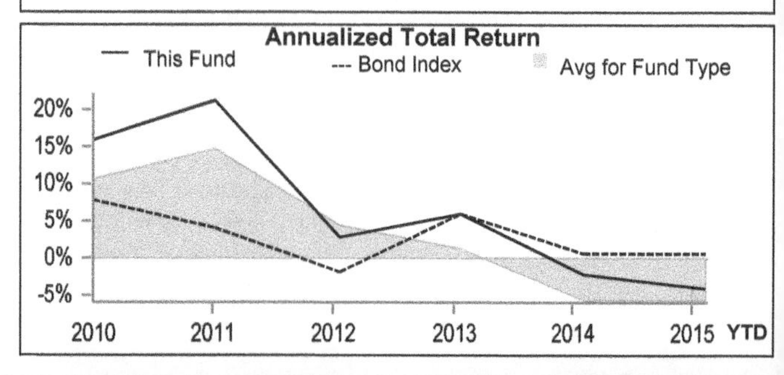

PIMCO Dynamic Credit Income (PCI) C- Fair

Fund Family: PIMCO
Fund Type: Global
Inception Date: January 31, 2013

Major Rating Factors: Middle of the road best describes PIMCO Dynamic Credit Income whose TheStreet.com Investment Rating is currently a C- (Fair). The fund currently has a performance rating of C- (Fair) based on an annualized return of 0.00% over the last three years and a total return of -2.57% year to date 2015. Factored into the performance evaluation is an expense ratio of 2.36% (high).

The fund's risk rating is currently B- (Good). It carries a beta of 0.00, meaning the fund's expected move will be 0.0% for every 10% move in the market. Volatility, as measured by both the semi-deviation and a drawdown factor, is considered low. As of December 31, 2015, PIMCO Dynamic Credit Income traded at a discount of 11.70% below its net asset value, which is worse than its one-year historical average discount of 11.99%.

Daniel J. Ivascyn has been running the fund for 3 years and currently receives a manager quality ranking of 63 (0=worst, 99=best). If you desire an average level of risk, then this fund may be an option.

Data Date	Investment Rating	Net Assets ($Mil)	Price	Performance Rating/Pts	Total Return Y-T-D	Risk Rating/Pts
12-15	C-	3,132.15	18.03	C- / 3.3	-2.57%	B- / 7.3
2014	D+	3,358.00	20.65	D / 1.6	-1.75%	B- / 7.6

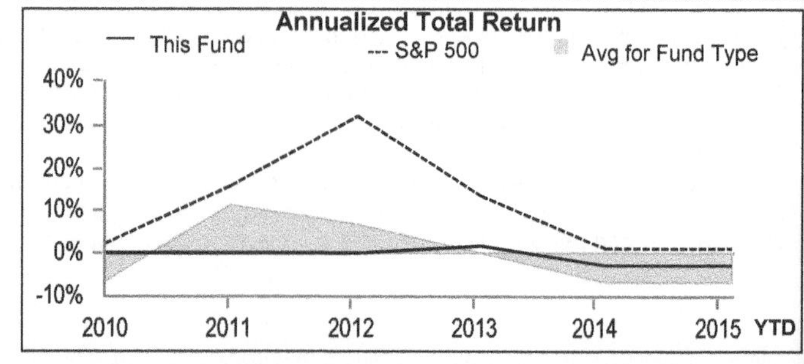

PIMCO Dynamic Income (PDI) B+ Good

Fund Family: PIMCO
Fund Type: Global
Inception Date: May 30, 2012

Major Rating Factors: Strong performance is the major factor driving the B+ (Good) TheStreet.com Investment Rating for PIMCO Dynamic Income. The fund currently has a performance rating of B+ (Good) based on an annualized return of 12.01% over the last three years and a total return of 7.30% year to date 2015. Factored into the performance evaluation is an expense ratio of 3.12% (high).

The fund's risk rating is currently C+ (Fair). It carries a beta of 0.79, meaning the fund's expected move will be 7.9% for every 10% move in the market. Volatility, as measured by both the semi-deviation and a drawdown factor, is considered low. As of December 31, 2015, PIMCO Dynamic Income traded at a premium of .70% above its net asset value, which is worse than its one-year historical average discount of 4.25%.

Daniel J. Ivascyn currently receives a manager quality ranking of 97 (0=worst, 99=best). If you desire only a moderate level of risk and strong performance, then this fund is an excellent option.

Data Date	Investment Rating	Net Assets ($Mil)	Price	Performance Rating/Pts	Total Return Y-T-D	Risk Rating/Pts
12-15	B+	1,397.99	27.36	B+ / 8.7	7.30%	C+ / 6.7
2014	C	1,527.10	30.74	C / 4.7	12.55%	B / 8.3
2013	B	1,393.10	29.13	C+ / 6.4	6.59%	B / 8.9

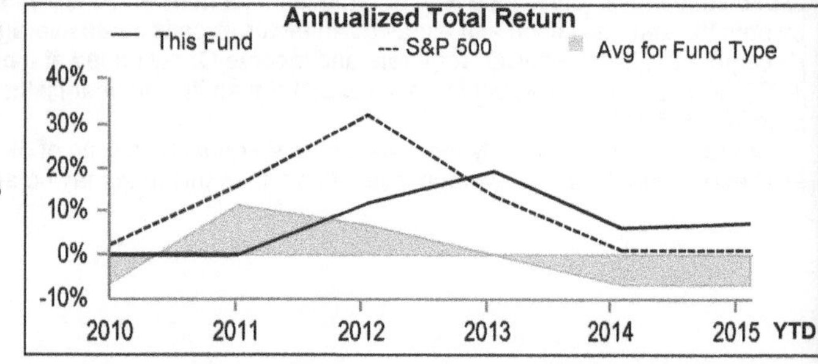

PIMCO Global StocksPLUS&Inc (PGP) C Fair

Fund Family: PIMCO
Fund Type: Global
Inception Date: May 26, 2005

Major Rating Factors: Strong performance is the major factor driving the C (Fair) TheStreet.com Investment Rating for PIMCO Global StocksPLUS&Inc. The fund currently has a performance rating of B (Good) based on an annualized return of 8.30% over the last three years and a total return of 4.57% year to date 2015. Factored into the performance evaluation is an expense ratio of 2.30% (high).

The fund's risk rating is currently C (Fair). It carries a beta of 1.41, meaning it is expected to move 14.1% for every 10% move in the market. Volatility, as measured by both the semi-deviation and a drawdown factor, is considered average. As of December 31, 2015, PIMCO Global StocksPLUS&Inc traded at a premium of 66.54% above its net asset value, which is worse than its one-year historical average premium of 54.44%.

Daniel J. Ivascyn has been running the fund for 11 years and currently receives a manager quality ranking of 87 (0=worst, 99=best). If you desire an average level of risk and strong performance, then this fund is a good option.

Data Date	Investment Rating	Net Assets ($Mil)	Price	Perfor-mance Rating/Pts	Total Return Y-T-D	Risk Rating/Pts
12-15	C	134.59	18.12	B / 8.1	4.57%	C / 4.3
2014	D	146.70	19.42	C- / 4.2	-7.88%	C- / 3.9
2013	C+	148.17	23.11	B- / 7.5	30.79%	C+ / 6.0
2012	C+	128.95	17.83	C+ / 6.6	16.99%	C+ / 6.8
2011	B	150.88	18.75	A / 9.3	-5.10%	C+ / 6.6
2010	C+	125.37	21.60	A- / 9.2	34.73%	D+ / 2.8

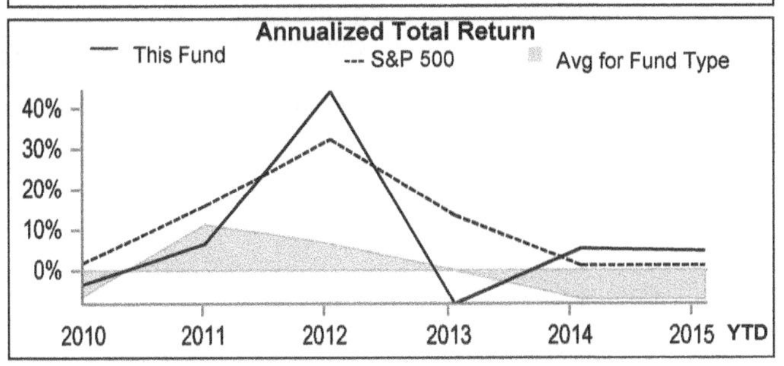

PIMCO High Income Fund (PHK) D+ Weak

Fund Family: PIMCO
Fund Type: Corporate - High Yield
Inception Date: April 24, 2003

Major Rating Factors: PIMCO High Income Fund receives a TheStreet.com Investment Rating of D+ (Weak). The fund currently has a performance rating of C- (Fair) based on an annualized return of 0.87% over the last three years and a total return of -17.99% year to date 2015. Factored into the performance evaluation is an expense ratio of 1.18% (low).

The fund's risk rating is currently C (Fair). It carries a beta of 2.95, meaning it is expected to move 29.5% for every 10% move in the market. Volatility, as measured by both the semi-deviation and a drawdown factor, is considered average. As of December 31, 2015, PIMCO High Income Fund traded at a premium of 21.01% above its net asset value, which is better than its one-year historical average premium of 38.41%.

Alfred T. Murata currently receives a manager quality ranking of 66 (0=worst, 99=best). If you desire an average level of risk, then this fund may be an option.

Data Date	Investment Rating	Net Assets ($Mil)	Price	Perfor-mance Rating/Pts	Total Return Y-T-D	Risk Rating/Pts
12-15	D+	949.88	8.18	C- / 3.7	-17.99%	C / 4.7
2014	D+	1,050.40	11.25	C / 4.9	6.65%	C / 5.1
2013	C+	1,063.86	11.65	C+ / 6.4	14.50%	C+ / 6.9
2012	C-	960.50	10.48	C / 5.1	7.74%	C+ / 6.8
2011	B	1,138.19	12.02	A+ / 9.6	8.69%	C+ / 6.3
2010	C	1,046.24	12.71	B+ / 8.7	32.67%	D / 2.1

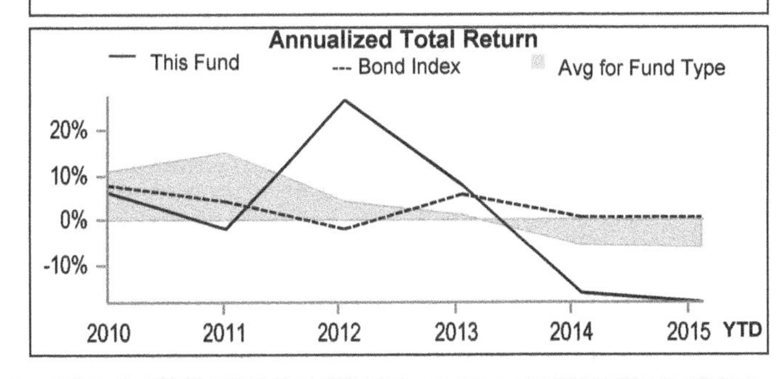

Pimco Income Opportunity Fund (PKO) C- Fair

Fund Family: PIMCO
Fund Type: Global
Inception Date: November 30, 2007

Major Rating Factors: Middle of the road best describes Pimco Income Opportunity Fund whose TheStreet.com Investment Rating is currently a C- (Fair). The fund currently has a performance rating of C- (Fair) based on an annualized return of 0.70% over the last three years and a total return of -5.70% year to date 2015. Factored into the performance evaluation is an expense ratio of 2.01% (high).

The fund's risk rating is currently C+ (Fair). It carries a beta of 0.70, meaning the fund's expected move will be 7.0% for every 10% move in the market. Volatility, as measured by both the semi-deviation and a drawdown factor, is considered low. As of December 31, 2015, Pimco Income Opportunity Fund traded at a discount of 6.66% below its net asset value, which is better than its one-year historical average discount of 4.18%.

Daniel J. Ivascyn has been running the fund for 9 years and currently receives a manager quality ranking of 88 (0=worst, 99=best). If you desire an average level of risk, then this fund may be an option.

Data Date	Investment Rating	Net Assets ($Mil)	Price	Perfor-mance Rating/Pts	Total Return Y-T-D	Risk Rating/Pts
12-15	C-	424.63	21.17	C- / 3.9	-5.70%	C+ / 5.8
2014	C-	425.20	25.05	C- / 4.2	-3.65%	C+ / 6.4
2013	B-	440.35	28.25	C+ / 6.9	2.77%	B / 8.1
2012	A	359.91	29.12	B+ / 8.9	28.12%	B / 8.4
2011	B	391.73	25.18	B- / 7.4	9.09%	B / 8.2
2010	A-	307.68	25.59	B / 7.9	24.64%	C+ / 6.6

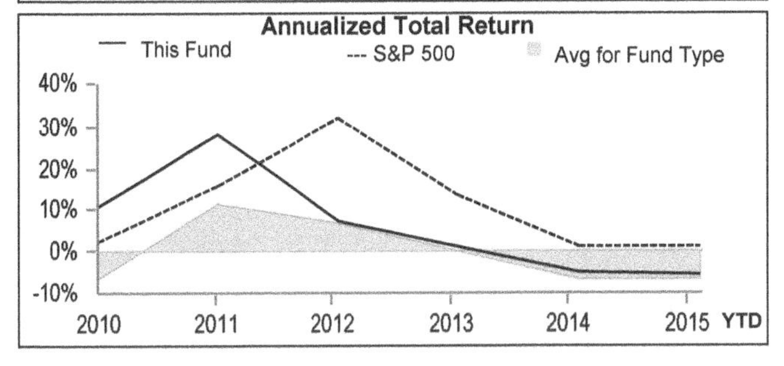

* Denotes ETF Fund

PIMCO Income Strategy Fund (PFL) C- Fair

Fund Family: PIMCO
Fund Type: Loan Participation
Inception Date: August 26, 2003

Major Rating Factors: Middle of the road best describes PIMCO Income Strategy Fund whose TheStreet.com Investment Rating is currently a C- (Fair). The fund currently has a performance rating of C- (Fair) based on an annualized return of -0.03% over the last three years and a total return of -9.14% year to date 2015. Factored into the performance evaluation is an expense ratio of 1.30% (average).

The fund's risk rating is currently C+ (Fair). It carries a beta of -106.50, meaning the fund's expected move will be -1065.0% for every 10% move in the market. Volatility, as measured by both the semi-deviation and a drawdown factor, is considered low. As of December 31, 2015, PIMCO Income Strategy Fund traded at a discount of 5.80% below its net asset value, which is better than its one-year historical average discount of 4.49%.

Alfred T. Murata currently receives a manager quality ranking of 53 (0=worst, 99=best). If you desire an average level of risk, then this fund may be an option.

Data Date	Investment Rating	Net Assets ($Mil)	Price	Performance Rating/Pts	Total Return Y-T-D	Risk Rating/Pts
12-15	C-	166.33	9.74	C- / 3.8	-9.14%	C+ / 6.7
2014	C	307.20	11.75	C+ / 6.6	11.39%	C / 5.5
2013	C+	294.02	11.31	C+ / 5.7	-3.40%	B- / 7.6
2012	B	283.29	12.74	B+ / 8.3	35.82%	B- / 7.6
2011	C-	282.69	10.40	C+ / 5.6	-1.69%	C+ / 5.7
2010	D	262.06	11.50	C- / 4.0	9.80%	D+ / 2.8

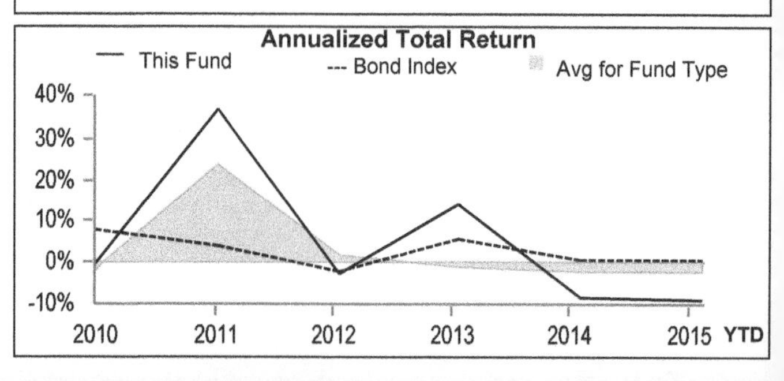

PIMCO Income Strategy Fund II (PFN) C Fair

Fund Family: PIMCO
Fund Type: Loan Participation
Inception Date: October 29, 2004

Major Rating Factors: Middle of the road best describes PIMCO Income Strategy Fund II whose TheStreet.com Investment Rating is currently a C (Fair). The fund currently has a performance rating of C (Fair) based on an annualized return of 1.58% over the last three years and a total return of -2.72% year to date 2015. Factored into the performance evaluation is an expense ratio of 1.16% (low).

The fund's risk rating is currently B- (Good). It carries a beta of -82.23, meaning the fund's expected move will be -822.3% for every 10% move in the market. Volatility, as measured by both the semi-deviation and a drawdown factor, is considered low. As of December 31, 2015, PIMCO Income Strategy Fund II traded at a discount of 5.29% below its net asset value, which is better than its one-year historical average discount of 4.87%.

Alfred T. Murata currently receives a manager quality ranking of 71 (0=worst, 99=best). If you desire an average level of risk, then this fund may be an option.

Data Date	Investment Rating	Net Assets ($Mil)	Price	Performance Rating/Pts	Total Return Y-T-D	Risk Rating/Pts
12-15	C	606.97	8.77	C / 4.7	-2.72%	B- / 7.1
2014	C+	641.40	9.81	C+ / 5.8	5.69%	B- / 7.6
2013	C+	605.84	9.95	C+ / 6.0	-1.88%	B- / 7.9
2012	B+	597.68	11.05	B+ / 8.5	36.21%	B / 8.1
2011	C	584.35	9.15	C+ / 6.3	0.62%	C+ / 6.6
2010	D-	537.34	9.90	D / 2.1	8.28%	C- / 3.5

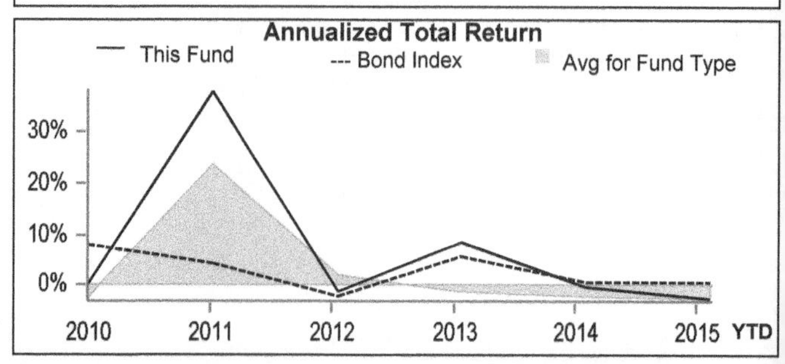

PIMCO Municipal Income Fund (PMF) B+ Good

Fund Family: PIMCO
Fund Type: Municipal - National
Inception Date: June 27, 2001

Major Rating Factors:
Exceptional performance is the major factor driving the B+ (Good) TheStreet.com Investment Rating for PIMCO Municipal Income Fund. The fund currently has a performance rating of A- (Excellent) based on an annualized return of 6.11% over the last three years and a total return of 15.69% year to date 2015. Factored into the performance evaluation is an expense ratio of 1.25% (average).

The fund's risk rating is currently C+ (Fair). It carries a beta of 3.92, meaning it is expected to move 39.2% for every 10% move in the market. Volatility, as measured by both the semi-deviation and a drawdown factor, is considered low. As of December 31, 2015, PIMCO Municipal Income Fund traded at a premium of 16.52% above its net asset value, which is worse than its one-year historical average premium of 12.42%.

Joseph P. Deane has been running the fund for 5 years and currently receives a manager quality ranking of 29 (0=worst, 99=best). If you desire only a moderate level of risk and strong performance, then this fund is an excellent option.

Data Date	Investment Rating	Net Assets ($Mil)	Price	Performance Rating/Pts	Total Return Y-T-D	Risk Rating/Pts
12-15	B+	69.05	15.45	A- / 9.0	15.69%	C+ / 6.3
2014	C	332.50	14.33	B- / 7.3	21.05%	C+ / 5.7
2013	C	348.16	12.23	C+ / 5.7	-15.15%	B- / 7.5
2012	A+	326.74	15.70	A- / 9.1	17.24%	B / 8.5
2011	A-	305.90	14.22	A- / 9.1	24.55%	B / 8.4
2010	D+	294.46	12.61	D+ / 2.8	9.70%	C+ / 5.6

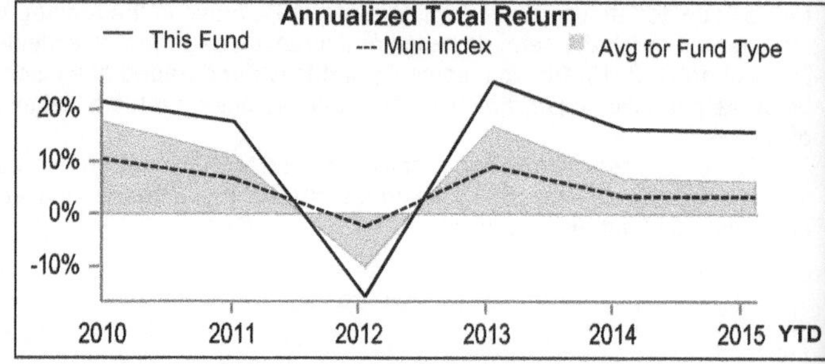

PIMCO Municipal Income Fund II (PML) B Good

Fund Family: PIMCO
Fund Type: Municipal - National
Inception Date: June 25, 2002

Major Rating Factors: Strong performance is the major factor driving the B (Good) TheStreet.com Investment Rating for PIMCO Municipal Income Fund II. The fund currently has a performance rating of B (Good) based on an annualized return of 4.19% over the last three years and a total return of 11.13% year to date 2015. Factored into the performance evaluation is an expense ratio of 1.16% (low).

The fund's risk rating is currently B- (Good). It carries a beta of 2.60, meaning it is expected to move 26.0% for every 10% move in the market. Volatility, as measured by both the semi-deviation and a drawdown factor, is considered low. As of December 31, 2015, PIMCO Municipal Income Fund II traded at a premium of .97% above its net asset value, which is worse than its one-year historical average discount of .54%.

Joseph P. Deane has been running the fund for 5 years and currently receives a manager quality ranking of 41 (0=worst, 99=best). If you desire only a moderate level of risk and strong performance, then this fund is an excellent option.

Data Date	Investment Rating	Net Assets ($Mil)	Price	Performance Rating/Pts	Total Return Y-T-D	Risk Rating/Pts
12-15	B	742.13	12.51	B / 7.9	11.13%	B- / 7.1
2014	B	740.70	11.88	B- / 7.2	17.98%	B- / 7.8
2013	C+	741.37	10.66	C+ / 6.2	-14.52%	B / 8.0
2012	A+	722.16	13.16	A- / 9.2	21.57%	B / 8.5
2011	A+	663.80	11.24	A+ / 9.7	25.80%	B / 8.6
2010	D	645.59	10.05	D- / 1.0	2.71%	C+ / 6.2

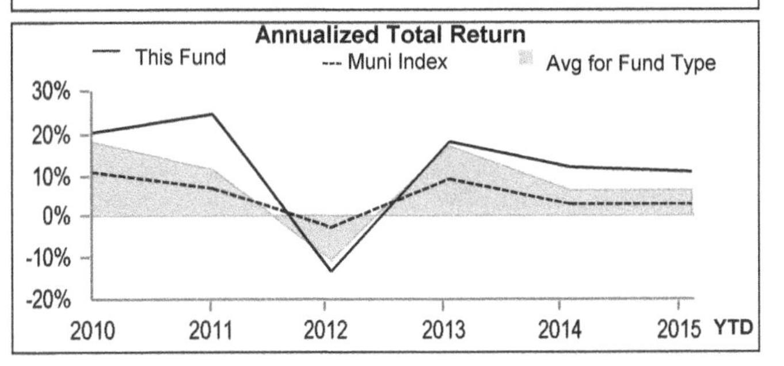

PIMCO Municipal Income Fund III (PMX) B+ Good

Fund Family: PIMCO
Fund Type: Municipal - National
Inception Date: October 28, 2002

Major Rating Factors: Strong performance is the major factor driving the B+ (Good) TheStreet.com Investment Rating for PIMCO Municipal Income Fund III. The fund currently has a performance rating of B+ (Good) based on an annualized return of 3.73% over the last three years and a total return of 11.27% year to date 2015. Factored into the performance evaluation is an expense ratio of 1.23% (average).

The fund's risk rating is currently B- (Good). It carries a beta of 2.58, meaning it is expected to move 25.8% for every 10% move in the market. Volatility, as measured by both the semi-deviation and a drawdown factor, is considered low. As of December 31, 2015, PIMCO Municipal Income Fund III traded at a premium of 3.41% above its net asset value, which is worse than its one-year historical average premium of 2.01%.

Joseph P. Deane has been running the fund for 5 years and currently receives a manager quality ranking of 43 (0=worst, 99=best). If you desire only a moderate level of risk and strong performance, then this fund is an excellent option.

Data Date	Investment Rating	Net Assets ($Mil)	Price	Performance Rating/Pts	Total Return Y-T-D	Risk Rating/Pts
12-15	B+	355.37	11.51	B+ / 8.4	11.27%	B- / 7.1
2014	C+	351.10	11.10	B- / 7.0	17.11%	C+ / 6.1
2013	C	311.23	10.00	C / 4.8	-14.27%	B- / 7.9
2012	A+	357.14	12.33	B+ / 8.9	18.28%	B / 8.8
2011	A+	321.10	11.05	A- / 9.2	17.89%	B / 8.9
2010	D-	330.84	10.44	D / 1.6	9.82%	C / 4.4

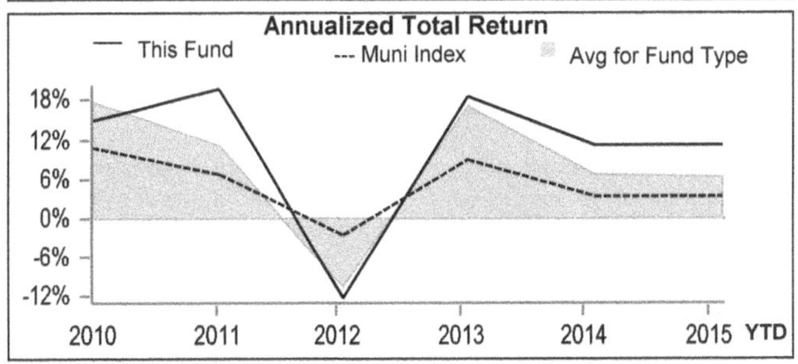

PIMCO NY Muni Income Fund (PNF) B+ Good

Fund Family: PIMCO
Fund Type: Municipal - Single State
Inception Date: June 27, 2001

Major Rating Factors: Strong performance is the major factor driving the B+ (Good) TheStreet.com Investment Rating for PIMCO NY Muni Income Fund. The fund currently has a performance rating of B (Good) based on an annualized return of 4.08% over the last three years and a total return of 10.02% year to date 2015. Factored into the performance evaluation is an expense ratio of 1.39% (average).

The fund's risk rating is currently B- (Good). It carries a beta of 2.79, meaning it is expected to move 27.9% for every 10% move in the market. Volatility, as measured by both the semi-deviation and a drawdown factor, is considered low. As of December 31, 2015, PIMCO NY Muni Income Fund traded at a discount of 1.65% below its net asset value, which is worse than its one-year historical average discount of 3.41%.

Joseph P. Deane has been running the fund for 5 years and currently receives a manager quality ranking of 38 (0=worst, 99=best). If you desire only a moderate level of risk and strong performance, then this fund is an excellent option.

Data Date	Investment Rating	Net Assets ($Mil)	Price	Performance Rating/Pts	Total Return Y-T-D	Risk Rating/Pts
12-15	B+	73.85	11.90	B / 8.0	10.02%	B- / 7.4
2014	C+	90.60	11.50	C+ / 6.2	18.63%	B- / 7.6
2013	C	92.51	10.14	C / 5.1	-13.39%	B- / 7.9
2012	A-	87.13	12.28	B+ / 8.3	15.24%	B / 8.6
2011	A	82.70	11.29	A / 9.4	21.03%	B / 8.7
2010	D+	81.07	10.21	D / 1.8	3.36%	C+ / 6.3

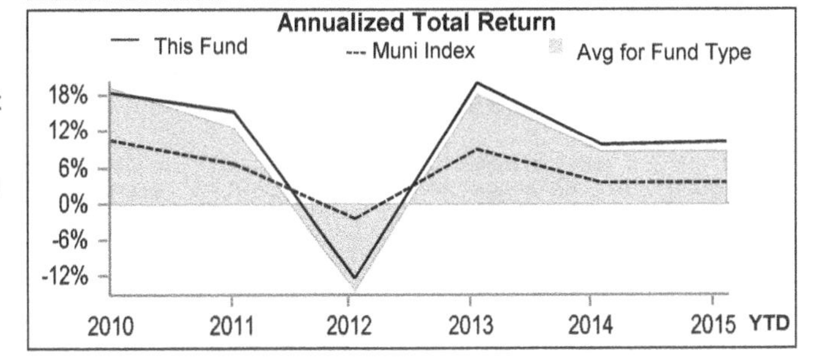

PIMCO NY Municipal Income Fund II (PNI) B Good

Fund Family: PIMCO
Fund Type: Municipal - Single State
Inception Date: June 25, 2002

Major Rating Factors: Strong performance is the major factor driving the B (Good) TheStreet.com Investment Rating for PIMCO NY Municipal Income Fund II. The fund currently has a performance rating of B (Good) based on an annualized return of 4.70% over the last three years and a total return of 8.71% year to date 2015. Factored into the performance evaluation is an expense ratio of 1.40% (average).

The fund's risk rating is currently C+ (Fair). It carries a beta of 2.74, meaning it is expected to move 27.4% for every 10% move in the market. Volatility, as measured by both the semi-deviation and a drawdown factor, is considered low. As of December 31, 2015, PIMCO NY Municipal Income Fund II traded at a premium of 8.24% above its net asset value, which is worse than its one-year historical average premium of 7.62%.

Joseph P. Deane has been running the fund for 5 years and currently receives a manager quality ranking of 47 (0=worst, 99=best). If you desire only a moderate level of risk and strong performance, then this fund is an excellent option.

Data Date	Investment Rating	Net Assets ($Mil)	Price	Performance Rating/Pts	Total Return Y-T-D	Risk Rating/Pts
12-15	B	124.42	12.35	B / 7.9	8.71%	C+ / 6.8
2014	B-	123.60	12.18	B+ / 8.7	26.10%	C+ / 5.9
2013	C-	123.69	10.23	C- / 4.0	-16.74%	B- / 7.8
2012	A+	123.67	12.78	B+ / 8.9	21.17%	B / 8.5
2011	B+	115.80	11.52	B+ / 8.7	19.78%	B / 8.6
2010	D	117.16	10.50	D- / 1.2	1.93%	C+ / 6.2

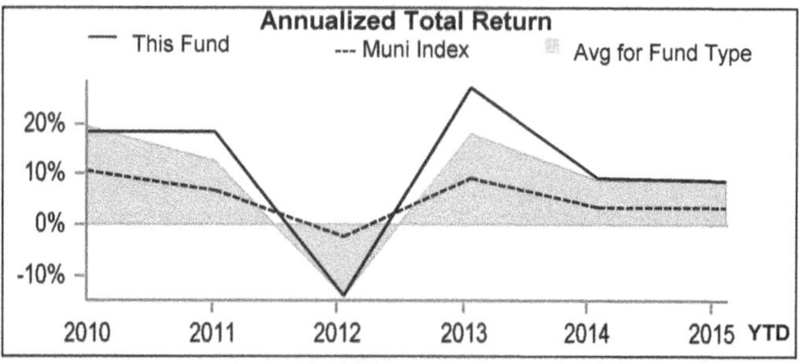

PIMCO NY Municipal Income Fund III (PYN) B+ Good

Fund Family: PIMCO
Fund Type: Municipal - Single State
Inception Date: October 28, 2002

Major Rating Factors: Strong performance is the major factor driving the B+ (Good) TheStreet.com Investment Rating for PIMCO NY Municipal Income Fund III. The fund currently has a performance rating of B+ (Good) based on an annualized return of 5.19% over the last three years and a total return of 11.21% year to date 2015. Factored into the performance evaluation is an expense ratio of 1.55% (average).

The fund's risk rating is currently B- (Good). It carries a beta of 1.76, meaning it is expected to move 17.6% for every 10% move in the market. Volatility, as measured by both the semi-deviation and a drawdown factor, is considered low. As of December 31, 2015, PIMCO NY Municipal Income Fund III traded at a premium of 7.54% above its net asset value, which is worse than its one-year historical average premium of 4.90%.

Joseph P. Deane has been running the fund for 5 years and currently receives a manager quality ranking of 69 (0=worst, 99=best). If you desire only a moderate level of risk and strong performance, then this fund is an excellent option.

Data Date	Investment Rating	Net Assets ($Mil)	Price	Performance Rating/Pts	Total Return Y-T-D	Risk Rating/Pts
12-15	B+	53.46	10.27	B+ / 8.5	11.21%	B- / 7.0
2014	C+	53.40	9.77	B- / 7.3	20.90%	C+ / 6.5
2013	C	48.01	8.65	C / 4.5	-14.76%	B / 8.3
2012	A	54.33	10.63	B+ / 8.3	16.44%	B / 8.7
2011	A-	50.10	9.47	B+ / 8.7	20.10%	B / 8.8
2010	D-	65.94	8.79	E+ / 0.9	5.63%	C / 4.4

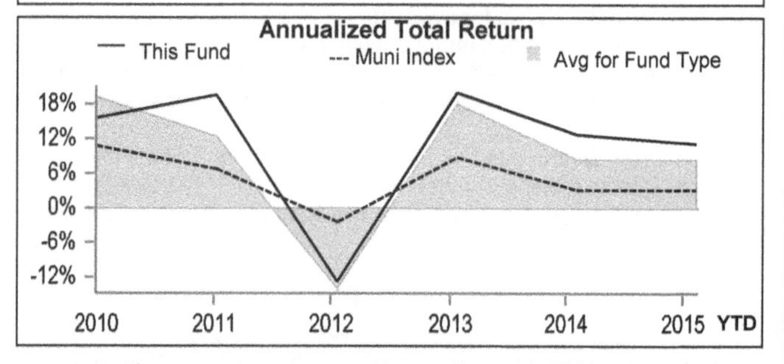

PIMCO Strategic Income (RCS) C Fair

Fund Family: PIMCO
Fund Type: Mortgage
Inception Date: February 17, 1994

Major Rating Factors: Middle of the road best describes PIMCO Strategic Income whose TheStreet.com Investment Rating is currently a C (Fair). The fund currently has a performance rating of C+ (Fair) based on an annualized return of 2.21% over the last three years and a total return of 4.72% year to date 2015. Factored into the performance evaluation is an expense ratio of 1.18% (low).

The fund's risk rating is currently C+ (Fair). It carries a beta of 2.75, meaning it is expected to move 27.5% for every 10% move in the market. Volatility, as measured by both the semi-deviation and a drawdown factor, is considered low. As of December 31, 2015, PIMCO Strategic Income traded at a premium of 11.46% above its net asset value, which is worse than its one-year historical average premium of 6.44%.

Daniel J. Ivascyn has been running the fund for 11 years and currently receives a manager quality ranking of 46 (0=worst, 99=best). If you desire an average level of risk, then this fund may be an option.

Data Date	Investment Rating	Net Assets ($Mil)	Price	Performance Rating/Pts	Total Return Y-T-D	Risk Rating/Pts
12-15	C	355.94	8.95	C+ / 5.9	4.72%	C+ / 6.0
2014	D	373.30	9.47	C- / 3.3	4.65%	C / 5.5
2013	C+	392.32	9.78	C / 5.5	-5.90%	B- / 7.9
2012	C+	376.75	11.35	C+ / 5.9	15.59%	B / 8.4
2011	B-	394.70	11.15	C+ / 6.8	19.36%	B- / 7.7
2010	A-	254.12	10.19	B- / 7.5	7.69%	B- / 7.0

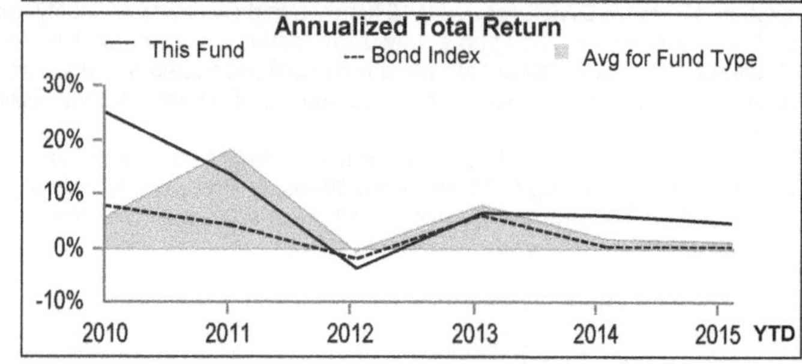

Pioneer Diversified High Income Tr (HNW) C- Fair

Fund Family: Pioneer Investment Management Inc
Fund Type: Global
Inception Date: May 24, 2007

Major Rating Factors: Middle of the road best describes Pioneer Diversified High Income Tr whose TheStreet.com Investment Rating is currently a C- (Fair). The fund currently has a performance rating of C- (Fair) based on an annualized return of -0.78% over the last three years and a total return of -8.46% year to date 2015. Factored into the performance evaluation is an expense ratio of 1.85% (above average).

The fund's risk rating is currently C+ (Fair). It carries a beta of 0.78, meaning the fund's expected move will be 7.8% for every 10% move in the market. Volatility, as measured by both the semi-deviation and a drawdown factor, is considered low. As of December 31, 2015, Pioneer Diversified High Income Tr traded at a discount of 8.81% below its net asset value, which is worse than its one-year historical average discount of 8.87%.

Andrew D. Feltus currently receives a manager quality ranking of 84 (0=worst, 99=best). If you desire an average level of risk, then this fund may be an option.

Data Date	Investment Rating	Net Assets ($Mil)	Price	Performance Rating/Pts	Total Return Y-T-D	Risk Rating/Pts
12-15	C-	153.28	14.59	C- / 3.6	-8.46%	C+ / 6.7
2014	C	162.90	17.75	C- / 4.1	-3.66%	B- / 7.8
2013	C+	171.65	20.53	C+ / 6.9	12.15%	C+ / 6.5
2012	C+	161.15	20.08	C+ / 6.9	18.33%	B- / 7.2
2011	B	154.70	19.27	B / 7.9	5.50%	B / 8.2
2010	B-	165.28	20.20	B+ / 8.3	25.55%	C / 4.4

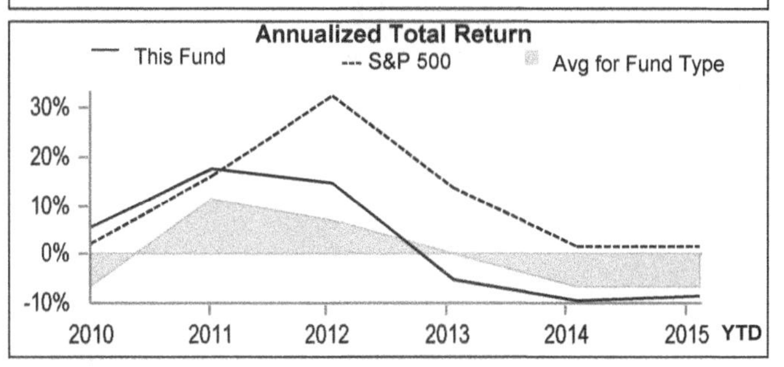

Pioneer Floating Rate Trust (PHD) C Fair

Fund Family: Pioneer Investment Management Inc
Fund Type: Loan Participation
Inception Date: December 28, 2004

Major Rating Factors: Middle of the road best describes Pioneer Floating Rate Trust whose TheStreet.com Investment Rating is currently a C (Fair). The fund currently has a performance rating of C- (Fair) based on an annualized return of -0.41% over the last three years and a total return of 1.31% year to date 2015. Factored into the performance evaluation is an expense ratio of 1.80% (above average).

The fund's risk rating is currently B- (Good). It carries a beta of -46.88, meaning the fund's expected move will be -468.8% for every 10% move in the market. Volatility, as measured by both the semi-deviation and a drawdown factor, is considered low. As of December 31, 2015, Pioneer Floating Rate Trust traded at a discount of 9.88% below its net asset value, which is worse than its one-year historical average discount of 10.40%.

Jonathan D. Sharkey currently receives a manager quality ranking of 58 (0=worst, 99=best). If you desire an average level of risk, then this fund may be an option.

Data Date	Investment Rating	Net Assets ($Mil)	Price	Performance Rating/Pts	Total Return Y-T-D	Risk Rating/Pts
12-15	C	317.24	10.85	C- / 4.1	1.31%	B- / 7.6
2014	C-	317.90	11.38	C- / 3.3	-5.64%	B / 8.1
2013	C+	307.14	12.72	C / 5.3	3.14%	B / 8.4
2012	C+	314.68	13.27	C+ / 5.8	18.29%	B / 8.1
2011	B+	483.40	12.47	B / 8.1	4.17%	B / 8.3
2010	C-	278.57	12.89	C+ / 6.5	20.27%	C- / 3.6

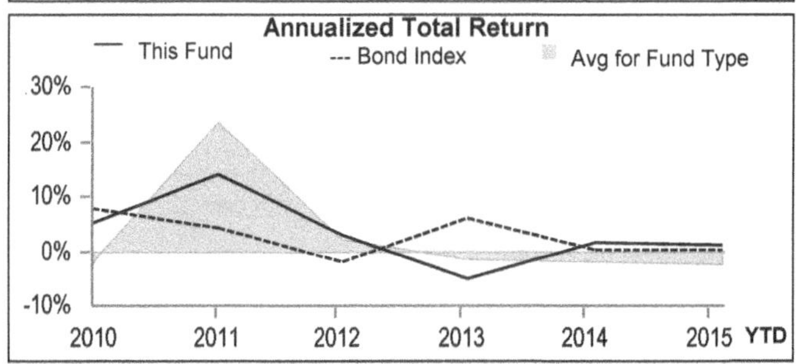

Pioneer High Income Trust (PHT) D- Weak

Fund Family: Pioneer Investment Management Inc
Fund Type: Global
Inception Date: April 25, 2002

Major Rating Factors:
Disappointing performance is the major factor driving the D- (Weak) TheStreet.com Investment Rating for Pioneer High Income Trust. The fund currently has a performance rating of D (Weak) based on an annualized return of -7.73% over the last three years and a total return of -38.01% year to date 2015. Factored into the performance evaluation is an expense ratio of 1.33% (average).

The fund's risk rating is currently C (Fair). It carries a beta of 1.11, meaning it is expected to move 11.1% for every 10% move in the market. Volatility, as measured by both the semi-deviation and a drawdown factor, is considered average. As of December 31, 2015, Pioneer High Income Trust traded at a premium of .85% above its net asset value, which is better than its one-year historical average premium of 6.31%.

Andrew D. Feltus currently receives a manager quality ranking of 55 (0=worst, 99=best). This fund offers an average level of risk but investors looking for strong performance will be frustrated.

Data Date	Investment Rating	Net Assets ($Mil)	Price	Performance Rating/Pts	Total Return Y-T-D	Risk Rating/Pts
12-15	D-	344.35	9.50	D / 1.7	-38.01%	C / 4.7
2014	C-	386.00	17.17	C / 5.5	10.53%	C+ / 6.3
2013	C+	404.50	17.00	B- / 7.3	13.32%	C+ / 6.8
2012	C	379.52	15.92	C+ / 5.7	4.77%	B- / 7.4
2011	A	356.20	17.33	A+ / 9.9	27.03%	B- / 7.9
2010	B-	367.09	15.49	B+ / 8.5	21.64%	C- / 3.9

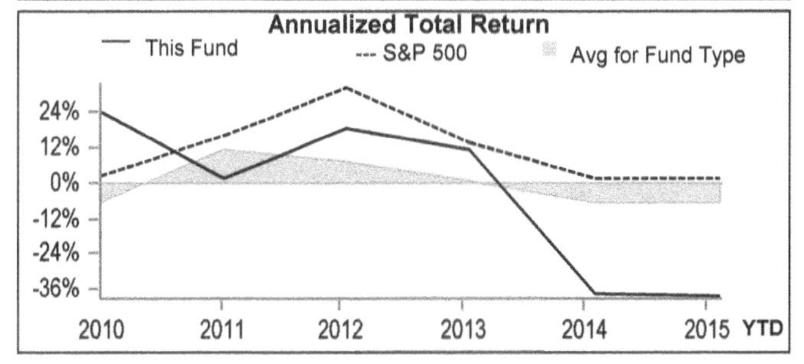

Pioneer Municipal High Income Adv (MAV) C Fair

Fund Family: Pioneer Investment Management Inc
Fund Type: Municipal - High Yield
Inception Date: October 20, 2003

Major Rating Factors: Middle of the road best describes Pioneer Municipal High Income Adv whose TheStreet.com Investment Rating is currently a C (Fair). The fund currently has a performance rating of C+ (Fair) based on an annualized return of 2.16% over the last three years and a total return of -3.89% year to date 2015. Factored into the performance evaluation is an expense ratio of 1.22% (average).

The fund's risk rating is currently C+ (Fair). It carries a beta of 2.75, meaning it is expected to move 27.5% for every 10% move in the market. Volatility, as measured by both the semi-deviation and a drawdown factor, is considered low. As of December 31, 2015, Pioneer Municipal High Income Adv traded at a premium of 7.06% above its net asset value, which is better than its one-year historical average premium of 11.24%.

David J. Eurkus currently receives a manager quality ranking of 29 (0=worst, 99=best). If you desire an average level of risk, then this fund may be an option.

Data Date	Investment Rating	Net Assets ($Mil)	Price	Perfor-mance Rating/Pts	Total Return Y-T-D	Risk Rating/Pts
12-15	C	300.33	13.35	C+ / 6.0	-3.89%	C+ / 6.8
2014	C+	296.60	14.97	B / 7.9	25.67%	C+ / 6.1
2013	C+	316.87	12.82	C+ / 6.5	-11.89%	B- / 7.8
2012	A+	299.64	15.47	A / 9.3	18.62%	B / 8.4
2011	A+	288.40	14.40	A+ / 9.9	31.17%	B / 8.3
2010	D+	281.55	12.42	C- / 3.5	6.42%	C / 4.8

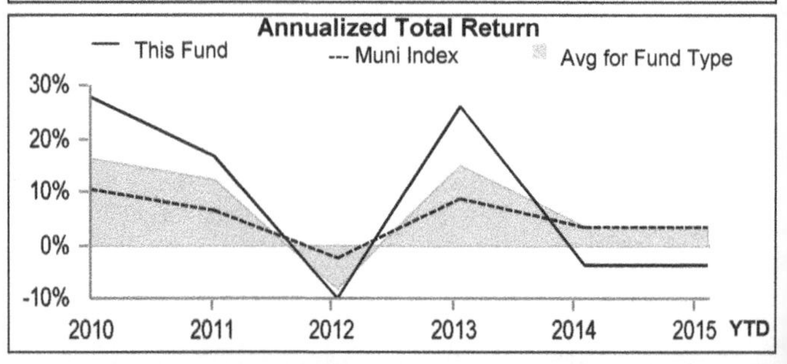

Pioneer Municipal High Income Trus (MHI) C Fair

Fund Family: Pioneer Investment Management Inc
Fund Type: Municipal - High Yield
Inception Date: July 17, 2003

Major Rating Factors: Middle of the road best describes Pioneer Municipal High Income Trus whose TheStreet.com Investment Rating is currently a C (Fair). The fund currently has a performance rating of C (Fair) based on an annualized return of 0.30% over the last three years and a total return of -0.47% year to date 2015. Factored into the performance evaluation is an expense ratio of 1.03% (low).

The fund's risk rating is currently C+ (Fair). It carries a beta of 2.52, meaning it is expected to move 25.2% for every 10% move in the market. Volatility, as measured by both the semi-deviation and a drawdown factor, is considered low. As of December 31, 2015, Pioneer Municipal High Income Trus traded at a discount of 2.39% below its net asset value, which is better than its one-year historical average discount of .17%.

David J. Eurkus currently receives a manager quality ranking of 25 (0=worst, 99=best). If you desire an average level of risk, then this fund may be an option.

Data Date	Investment Rating	Net Assets ($Mil)	Price	Perfor-mance Rating/Pts	Total Return Y-T-D	Risk Rating/Pts
12-15	C	302.72	13.06	C / 5.4	-0.47%	C+ / 6.9
2014	C-	305.80	14.06	C / 5.1	11.00%	C+ / 6.3
2013	C+	332.19	13.59	C+ / 6.3	-8.59%	B / 8.1
2012	A+	317.63	15.79	A / 9.3	20.52%	B / 8.4
2011	A+	304.60	14.87	A+ / 9.8	22.35%	B / 8.5
2010	C	308.46	13.42	C+ / 5.9	4.92%	C / 5.4

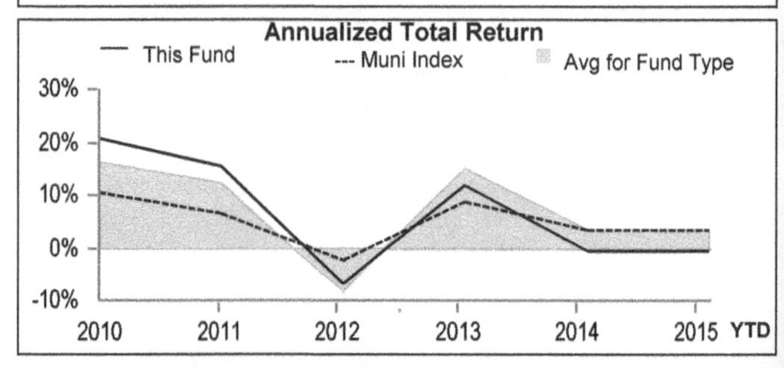

Principal Real Estate Income (PGZ) C- Fair

Fund Family: ALPS Advisors Inc
Fund Type: Growth and Income
Inception Date: June 25, 2013

Major Rating Factors: Middle of the road best describes Principal Real Estate Income whose TheStreet.com Investment Rating is currently a C- (Fair). The fund currently has a performance rating of C- (Fair) based on an annualized return of 0.00% over the last three years and a total return of -2.54% year to date 2015. Factored into the performance evaluation is an expense ratio of 2.59% (high).

The fund's risk rating is currently B- (Good). It carries a beta of 0.00, meaning the fund's expected move will be 0.0% for every 10% move in the market. Volatility, as measured by both the semi-deviation and a drawdown factor, is considered low. As of December 31, 2015, Principal Real Estate Income traded at a discount of 13.62% below its net asset value, which is better than its one-year historical average discount of 10.42%.

Keith Bokota has been running the fund for 3 years and currently receives a manager quality ranking of 49 (0=worst, 99=best). If you desire an average level of risk, then this fund may be an option.

Data Date	Investment Rating	Net Assets ($Mil)	Price	Perfor-mance Rating/Pts	Total Return Y-T-D	Risk Rating/Pts
12-15	C-	145.02	16.68	C- / 3.0	-2.54%	B- / 7.9
2014	B+	142.00	18.66	B- / 7.0	19.13%	B / 8.8

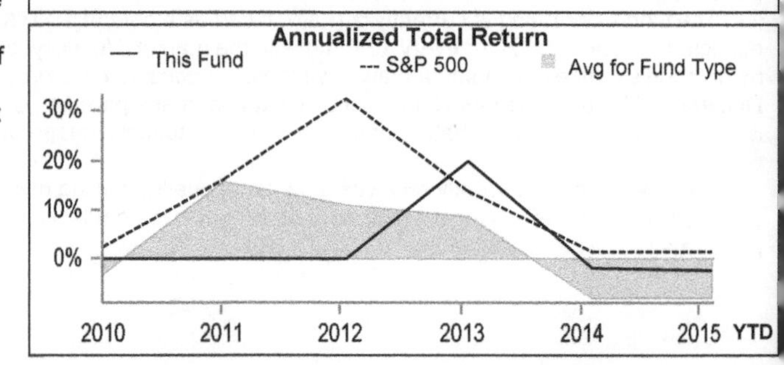

Prudential Glb Sht Dur Hi Yield In (GHY) C- Fair

Fund Family: Prudential Investments LLC
Fund Type: Global
Inception Date: December 26, 2012

Major Rating Factors: Middle of the road best describes Prudential Glb Sht Dur Hi Yield In whose TheStreet.com Investment Rating is currently a C- (Fair). The fund currently has a performance rating of C- (Fair) based on an annualized return of -1.67% over the last three years and a total return of -2.02% year to date 2015. Factored into the performance evaluation is an expense ratio of 1.61% (above average).

The fund's risk rating is currently C+ (Fair). It carries a beta of 0.97, meaning that its performance tracks fairly well with that of the overall stock market. Volatility, as measured by both the semi-deviation and a drawdown factor, is considered low. As of December 31, 2015, Prudential Glb Sht Dur Hi Yield In traded at a discount of 11.78% below its net asset value, which is better than its one-year historical average discount of 10.94%.

Paul E. Appleby currently receives a manager quality ranking of 83 (0=worst, 99=best). If you desire an average level of risk, then this fund may be an option.

Data Date	Investment Rating	Net Assets ($Mil)	Price	Performance Rating/Pts	Total Return Y-T-D	Risk Rating/Pts
12-15	C-	698.59	14.15	C- / 3.8	-2.02%	C+ / 6.9
2014	C-	735.40	15.92	D+ / 2.7	2.19%	B- / 7.7
2013	C-	765.48	17.35	D+ / 2.5	-5.50%	B / 8.4

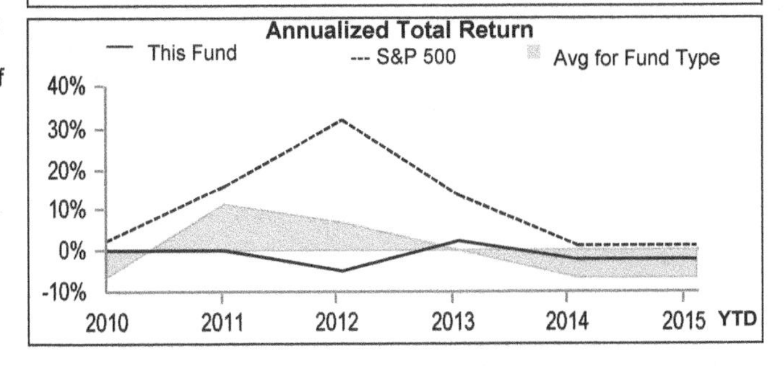

Prudential Sht Dur Hi Yield Fd Inc (ISD) C- Fair

Fund Family: Prudential Investments LLC
Fund Type: Corporate - High Yield
Inception Date: April 30, 2012

Major Rating Factors: Middle of the road best describes Prudential Sht Dur Hi Yield Fd Inc whose TheStreet.com Investment Rating is currently a C- (Fair). The fund currently has a performance rating of C- (Fair) based on an annualized return of -0.58% over the last three years and a total return of -2.07% year to date 2015. Factored into the performance evaluation is an expense ratio of 1.58% (above average).

The fund's risk rating is currently C+ (Fair). It carries a beta of 0.65, meaning the fund's expected move will be 6.5% for every 10% move in the market. Volatility, as measured by both the semi-deviation and a drawdown factor, is considered low. As of December 31, 2015, Prudential Sht Dur Hi Yield Fd Inc traded at a discount of 10.81% below its net asset value, which is worse than its one-year historical average discount of 11.16%.

Paul E. Appleby has been running the fund for 4 years and currently receives a manager quality ranking of 63 (0=worst, 99=best). If you desire an average level of risk, then this fund may be an option.

Data Date	Investment Rating	Net Assets ($Mil)	Price	Performance Rating/Pts	Total Return Y-T-D	Risk Rating/Pts
12-15	C-	593.17	14.60	C- / 4.1	-2.07%	C+ / 6.9
2014	C-	603.00	16.68	C- / 3.8	4.14%	B- / 7.7
2013	D+	637.70	17.39	D / 2.2	-2.90%	B / 8.3

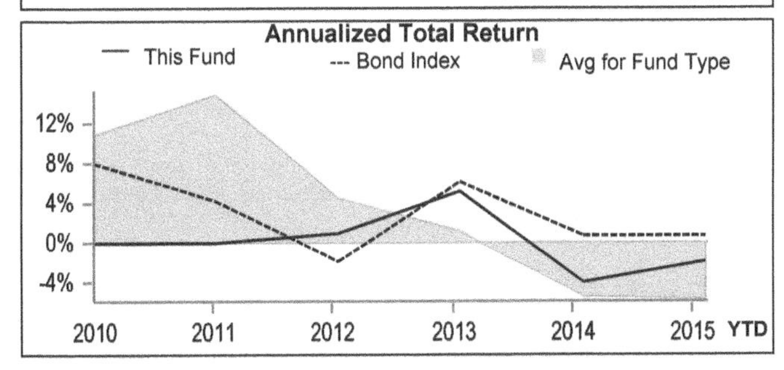

Putnam High Income Securities (PCF) C Fair

Fund Family: Putnam Investment Management LLC
Fund Type: General Bond
Inception Date: July 9, 1987

Major Rating Factors: Middle of the road best describes Putnam High Income Securities whose TheStreet.com Investment Rating is currently a C (Fair). The fund currently has a performance rating of C (Fair) based on an annualized return of 1.56% over the last three years and a total return of -5.20% year to date 2015. Factored into the performance evaluation is an expense ratio of 0.90% (low).

The fund's risk rating is currently B- (Good). It carries a beta of 0.88, meaning the fund's expected move will be 8.8% for every 10% move in the market. Volatility, as measured by both the semi-deviation and a drawdown factor, is considered low. As of December 31, 2015, Putnam High Income Securities traded at a discount of 11.29% below its net asset value, which is worse than its one-year historical average discount of 12.89%.

Eric N. Harthun currently receives a manager quality ranking of 75 (0=worst, 99=best). If you desire an average level of risk, then this fund may be an option.

Data Date	Investment Rating	Net Assets ($Mil)	Price	Performance Rating/Pts	Total Return Y-T-D	Risk Rating/Pts
12-15	C	127.03	7.31	C / 4.7	-5.20%	B- / 7.6
2014	C+	151.70	8.11	C- / 4.2	3.01%	B / 8.9
2013	C+	145.55	8.26	C / 5.3	7.54%	B / 8.0
2012	D+	141.00	7.95	C- / 3.5	11.05%	B- / 7.0
2011	C+	133.80	7.68	C+ / 6.4	1.26%	C+ / 6.9
2010	B	135.78	8.38	B / 8.0	24.09%	C / 5.0

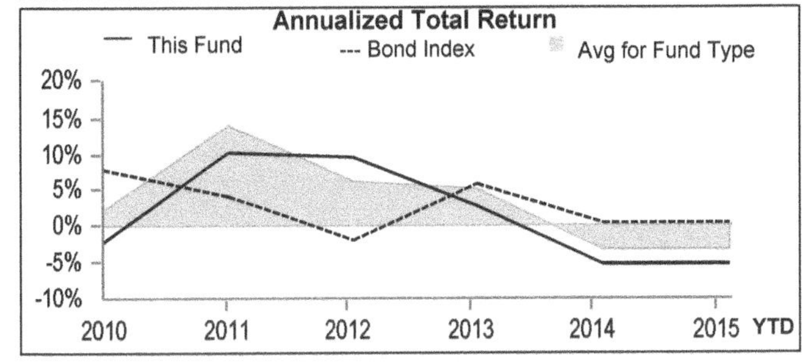

Putnam Managed Muni Inc Tr (PMM) B- Good

Fund Family: Putnam Investment Management LLC
Fund Type: Municipal - National
Inception Date: February 16, 1989

Major Rating Factors: Strong performance is the major factor driving the B- (Good) TheStreet.com Investment Rating for Putnam Managed Muni Inc Tr. The fund currently has a performance rating of B- (Good) based on an annualized return of 2.27% over the last three years and a total return of 8.40% year to date 2015. Factored into the performance evaluation is an expense ratio of 0.91% (low).

The fund's risk rating is currently B- (Good). It carries a beta of 2.03, meaning it is expected to move 20.3% for every 10% move in the market. Volatility, as measured by both the semi-deviation and a drawdown factor, is considered low. As of December 31, 2015, Putnam Managed Muni Inc Tr traded at a discount of 8.11% below its net asset value, which is worse than its one-year historical average discount of 9.68%.

Paul M. Drury has been running the fund for 27 years and currently receives a manager quality ranking of 44 (0=worst, 99=best). If you desire only a moderate level of risk and strong performance, then this fund is an excellent option.

Data Date	Investment Rating	Net Assets ($Mil)	Price	Performance Rating/Pts	Total Return Y-T-D	Risk Rating/Pts
12-15	B-	445.88	7.36	B- / 7.2	8.40%	B- / 7.3
2014	B-	446.00	7.25	C+ / 6.8	16.07%	B- / 7.7
2013	C	467.56	6.64	C / 4.6	-14.51%	B- / 7.9
2012	A	423.92	8.06	A- / 9.0	19.05%	B / 8.4
2011	A-	429.60	7.47	B+ / 8.9	17.77%	B / 8.6
2010	C+	422.05	6.91	C / 5.5	11.66%	C+ / 6.2

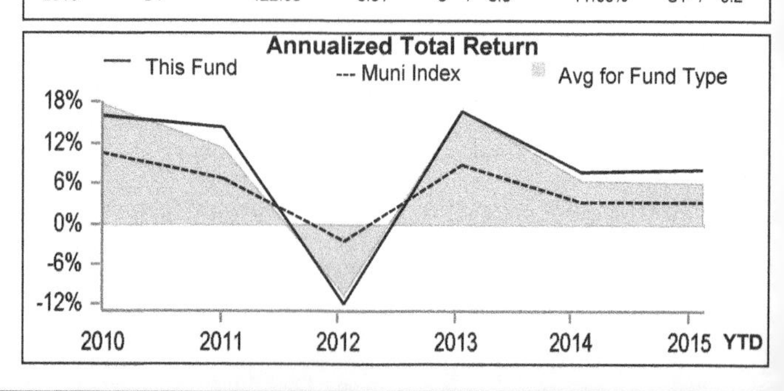

Putnam Master Intermediate Inc Tr (PIM) C+ Fair

Fund Family: Putnam Investment Management LLC
Fund Type: General Bond
Inception Date: April 11, 1988

Major Rating Factors: Middle of the road best describes Putnam Master Intermediate Inc Tr whose TheStreet.com Investment Rating is currently a C+ (Fair). The fund currently has a performance rating of C (Fair) based on an annualized return of 2.55% over the last three years and a total return of -0.99% year to date 2015. Factored into the performance evaluation is an expense ratio of 0.96% (low).

The fund's risk rating is currently B (Good). It carries a beta of 0.13, meaning the fund's expected move will be 1.3% for every 10% move in the market. Volatility, as measured by both the semi-deviation and a drawdown factor, is considered low. As of December 31, 2015, Putnam Master Intermediate Inc Tr traded at a discount of 8.82% below its net asset value, which is worse than its one-year historical average discount of 10.04%.

D. William Kohli has been running the fund for 22 years and currently receives a manager quality ranking of 83 (0=worst, 99=best). If you desire an average level of risk, then this fund may be an option.

Data Date	Investment Rating	Net Assets ($Mil)	Price	Performance Rating/Pts	Total Return Y-T-D	Risk Rating/Pts
12-15	C+	278.07	4.55	C / 5.4	-0.99%	B / 8.0
2014	C-	328.30	4.81	C- / 3.7	1.84%	C+ / 6.8
2013	D+	345.14	5.04	C- / 3.7	4.77%	C+ / 6.7
2012	D	356.30	5.06	D / 2.2	9.48%	C+ / 6.2
2011	C-	345.80	5.08	C / 4.7	-5.98%	C+ / 6.0
2010	C-	381.36	5.79	C / 5.3	6.52%	C / 4.5

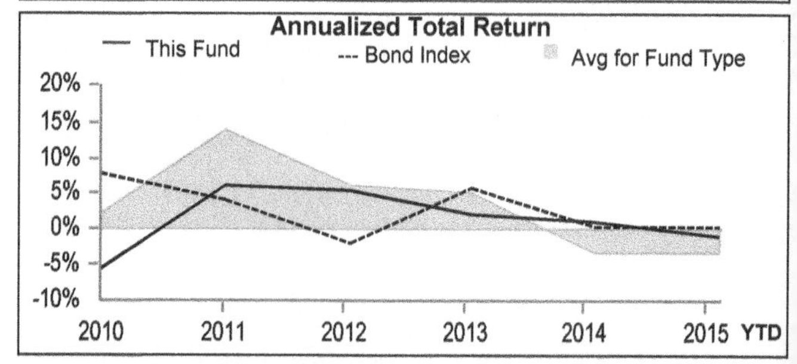

Putnam Muni Opp Tr (PMO) B Good

Fund Family: Putnam Investment Management LLC
Fund Type: Municipal - National
Inception Date: May 21, 1993

Major Rating Factors: Strong performance is the major factor driving the B (Good) TheStreet.com Investment Rating for Putnam Muni Opp Tr. The fund currently has a performance rating of B- (Good) based on an annualized return of 3.19% over the last three years and a total return of 8.39% year to date 2015. Factored into the performance evaluation is an expense ratio of 0.96% (low).

The fund's risk rating is currently B- (Good). It carries a beta of 2.03, meaning it is expected to move 20.3% for every 10% move in the market. Volatility, as measured by both the semi-deviation and a drawdown factor, is considered low. As of December 31, 2015, Putnam Muni Opp Tr traded at a discount of 8.49% below its net asset value, which is worse than its one-year historical average discount of 9.87%.

Susan A. McCormack has been running the fund for 17 years and currently receives a manager quality ranking of 50 (0=worst, 99=best). If you desire only a moderate level of risk and strong performance, then this fund is an excellent option.

Data Date	Investment Rating	Net Assets ($Mil)	Price	Performance Rating/Pts	Total Return Y-T-D	Risk Rating/Pts
12-15	B	522.10	12.28	B- / 7.1	8.39%	B- / 7.8
2014	B-	535.60	11.99	C+ / 6.7	17.92%	B / 8.0
2013	C	580.64	10.74	C / 4.7	-15.06%	B / 8.2
2012	A-	556.12	12.95	B / 8.2	14.76%	B / 8.7
2011	A	532.10	12.27	B+ / 8.9	22.59%	B / 8.8
2010	C+	514.09	10.87	C / 5.2	4.60%	C+ / 6.7

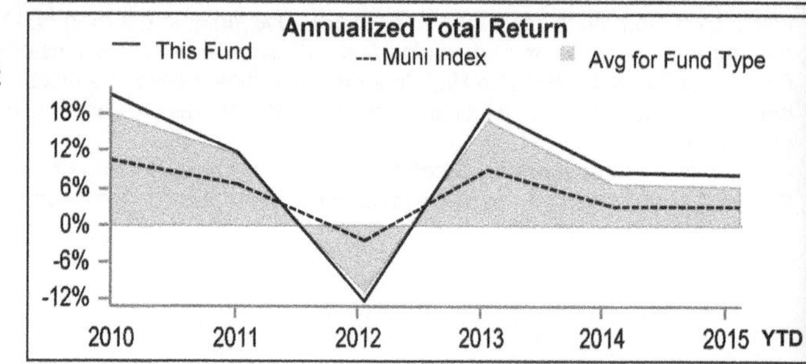

Putnam Premier Income Trust (PPT) C Fair

Fund Family: Putnam Investment Management LLC
Fund Type: General Bond
Inception Date: February 29, 1988

Data Date	Investment Rating	Net Assets ($Mil)	Price	Performance Rating/Pts	Total Return Y-T-D	Risk Rating/Pts
12-15	C	669.89	4.95	C / 5.5	-0.16%	C+ / 6.1
2014	C-	758.70	5.25	C- / 4.1	2.30%	B- / 7.0
2013	C-	825.43	5.44	C- / 4.0	5.93%	B- / 7.7
2012	D	818.08	5.46	D+ / 2.7	12.10%	C+ / 6.0
2011	C-	794.60	5.19	C / 5.5	-8.38%	C+ / 5.9
2010	C+	887.22	6.28	B- / 7.1	14.15%	C / 4.7

Major Rating Factors: Middle of the road best describes Putnam Premier Income Trust whose TheStreet.com Investment Rating is currently a C (Fair). The fund currently has a performance rating of C (Fair) based on an annualized return of 2.79% over the last three years and a total return of -0.16% year to date 2015. Factored into the performance evaluation is an expense ratio of 0.87% (low).

The fund's risk rating is currently C+ (Fair). It carries a beta of -0.04, meaning the fund's expected move will be -0.4% for every 10% move in the market. Volatility, as measured by both the semi-deviation and a drawdown factor, is considered low. As of December 31, 2015, Putnam Premier Income Trust traded at a discount of 9.84% below its net asset value, which is worse than its one-year historical average discount of 10.77%.

D. William Kohli has been running the fund for 22 years and currently receives a manager quality ranking of 84 (0=worst, 99=best). If you desire an average level of risk, then this fund may be an option.

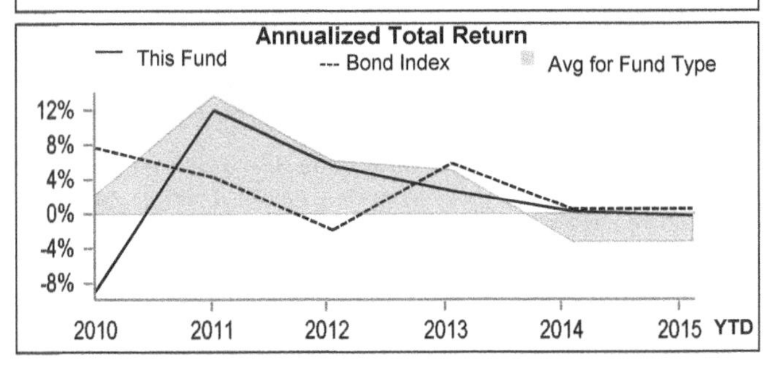

Reaves Utility Income Trust (UTG) C+ Fair

Fund Family: W H Reaves & Company Inc
Fund Type: Utilities
Inception Date: February 24, 2004

Data Date	Investment Rating	Net Assets ($Mil)	Price	Performance Rating/Pts	Total Return Y-T-D	Risk Rating/Pts
12-15	C+	949.09	25.97	C+ / 5.8	-15.60%	B- / 7.5
2014	A+	889.00	32.85	A / 9.3	40.34%	B / 8.3
2013	B-	809.73	25.09	C+ / 6.5	7.51%	B / 8.5
2012	C+	545.02	23.82	C+ / 5.8	3.95%	B / 8.7
2011	B+	557.60	26.01	A / 9.4	25.27%	B- / 7.5
2010	B-	438.31	22.35	B / 8.1	29.08%	C / 4.3

Major Rating Factors: Middle of the road best describes Reaves Utility Income Trust whose TheStreet.com Investment Rating is currently a C+ (Fair). The fund currently has a performance rating of C+ (Fair) based on an annualized return of 8.15% over the last three years and a total return of -15.60% year to date 2015. Factored into the performance evaluation is an expense ratio of 1.71% (above average).

The fund's risk rating is currently B- (Good). It carries a beta of 0.89, meaning the fund's expected move will be 8.9% for every 10% move in the market. Volatility, as measured by both the semi-deviation and a drawdown factor, is considered low. As of December 31, 2015, Reaves Utility Income Trust traded at a discount of 7.94% below its net asset value, which is better than its one-year historical average discount of 4.29%.

Ronald J. Sorenson has been running the fund for 12 years and currently receives a manager quality ranking of 54 (0=worst, 99=best). If you desire an average level of risk, then this fund may be an option.

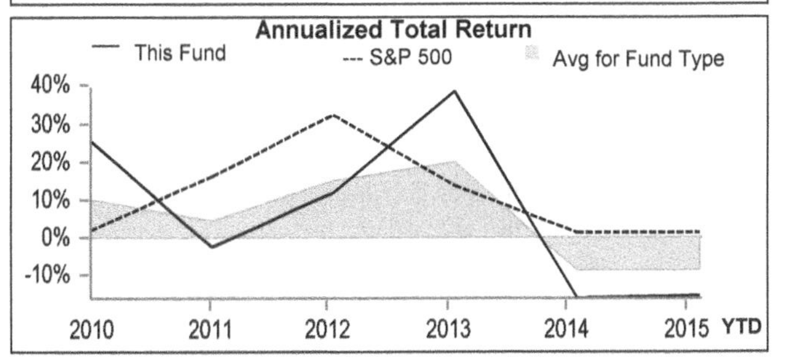

RENN Fund (RCG) D- Weak

Fund Family: RENN Capital Group Inc
Fund Type: Growth and Income
Inception Date: May 25, 1994

Data Date	Investment Rating	Net Assets ($Mil)	Price	Performance Rating/Pts	Total Return Y-T-D	Risk Rating/Pts
12-15	D-	9.86	0.90	D- / 1.0	-30.23%	C / 4.7
2014	D-	10.20	1.30	D- / 1.3	-5.80%	C / 5.3
2013	D-	11.27	1.45	D- / 1.1	-3.50%	C / 5.4
2012	E+	9.50	1.42	E / 0.5	-10.12%	C / 4.7
2011	D-	9.50	1.82	D- / 1.0	-7.89%	C / 5.1
2010	D-	18.17	1.96	E / 0.3	-24.62%	C / 4.7

Major Rating Factors:
Disappointing performance is the major factor driving the D- (Weak) TheStreet.com Investment Rating for RENN Fund. The fund currently has a performance rating of D- (Weak) based on an annualized return of -14.30% over the last three years and a total return of -30.23% year to date 2015. Factored into the performance evaluation is an expense ratio of 4.86% (high).

The fund's risk rating is currently C (Fair). It carries a beta of 0.04, meaning the fund's expected move will be 0.4% for every 10% move in the market. Volatility, as measured by both the semi-deviation and a drawdown factor, is considered average. As of December 31, 2015, RENN Fund traded at a discount of 41.56% below its net asset value, which is better than its one-year historical average discount of 39.44%.

Russell G. Cleveland has been running the fund for 22 years and currently receives a manager quality ranking of 11 (0=worst, 99=best). This fund offers an average level of risk but investors looking for strong performance will be frustrated.

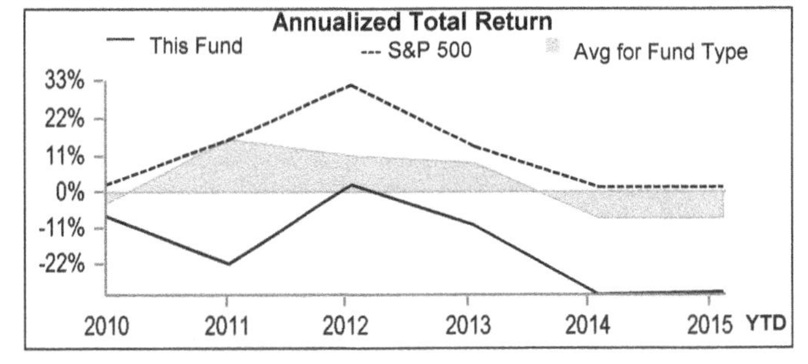

RMR Real Estate Income (RIF) B- Good

Fund Family: RMR Advisors Inc
Fund Type: Growth and Income
Inception Date: May 26, 2006

Major Rating Factors: Strong performance is the major factor driving the B- (Good) TheStreet.com Investment Rating for RMR Real Estate Income. The fund currently has a performance rating of B- (Good) based on an annualized return of 8.41% over the last three years and a total return of -2.26% year to date 2015. Factored into the performance evaluation is an expense ratio of 2.12% (high).

The fund's risk rating is currently C+ (Fair). It carries a beta of 0.61, meaning the fund's expected move will be 6.1% for every 10% move in the market. Volatility, as measured by both the semi-deviation and a drawdown factor, is considered low. As of December 31, 2015, RMR Real Estate Income traded at a discount of 18.06% below its net asset value, which is worse than its one-year historical average discount of 19.07%.

Craig Dunstan currently receives a manager quality ranking of 69 (0=worst, 99=best). If you desire only a moderate level of risk and strong performance, then this fund is an excellent option.

Data Date	Investment Rating	Net Assets ($Mil)	Price	Performance Rating/Pts	Total Return Y-T-D	Risk Rating/Pts
12-15	B-	192.62	19.28	B- / 7.4	-2.26%	C+ / 6.9
2014	A	170.60	20.82	A / 9.3	31.51%	B- / 7.5
2013	D	159.72	16.91	C- / 3.0	-2.28%	C / 5.2
2012	C+	153,778.87	18.21	B / 7.9	47.66%	C+ / 5.6
2011	D	54.80	14.02	D / 2.0	-21.00%	C+ / 6.7
2010	D-	72.61	18.37	E+ / 0.9	15.99%	C / 4.4

2010 D- 72.61 18.37 E+ / 0.9 15.99% C / 4.4

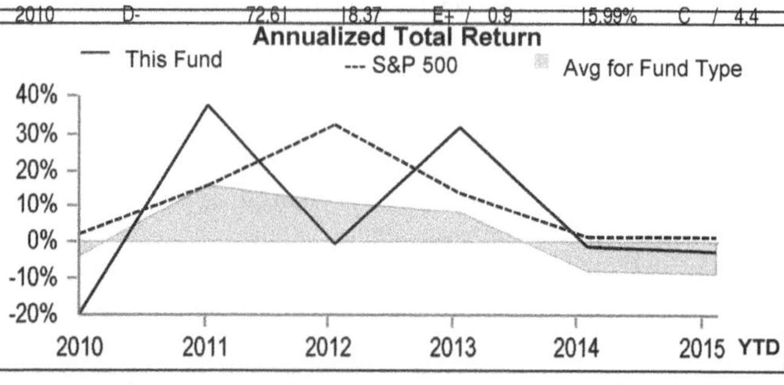

Royce Global Value Trust (RGT) C- Fair

Fund Family: Royce & Associates LLC
Fund Type: Global
Inception Date: October 18, 2013

Major Rating Factors:
Disappointing performance is the major factor driving the C- (Fair) TheStreet.com Investment Rating for Royce Global Value Trust. The fund currently has a performance rating of D+ (Weak) based on an annualized return of 0.00% over the last three years and a total return of -6.30% year to date 2015. Factored into the performance evaluation is an expense ratio of 1.49% (average).

The fund's risk rating is currently B- (Good). It carries a beta of 0.00, meaning the fund's expected move will be 0.0% for every 10% move in the market. Volatility, as measured by both the semi-deviation and a drawdown factor, is considered low. As of December 31, 2015, Royce Global Value Trust traded at a discount of 15.44% below its net asset value, which is better than its one-year historical average discount of 15.41%.

This fund offers only a moderate level of risk but investors looking for strong performance are still waiting.

Data Date	Investment Rating	Net Assets ($Mil)	Price	Performance Rating/Pts	Total Return Y-T-D	Risk Rating/Pts
12-15	C-	95.29	7.45	D+ / 2.6	-6.30%	B- / 7.1
2014	D-	100.70	8.04	D- / 1.1	-7.04%	C / 4.4

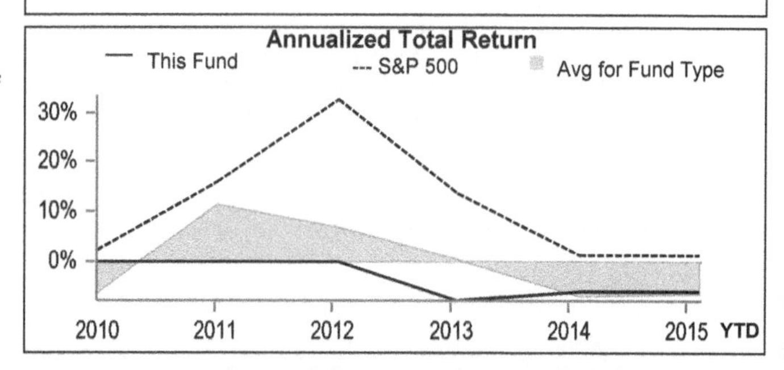

Royce Micro-Cap Trust (RMT) C Fair

Fund Family: Royce & Associates LLC
Fund Type: Growth
Inception Date: December 14, 1993

Major Rating Factors: Middle of the road best describes Royce Micro-Cap Trust whose TheStreet.com Investment Rating is currently a C (Fair). The fund currently has a performance rating of C+ (Fair) based on an annualized return of 8.40% over the last three years and a total return of -14.20% year to date 2015. Factored into the performance evaluation is an expense ratio of 1.18% (low).

The fund's risk rating is currently C+ (Fair). It carries a beta of 1.02, meaning that its performance tracks fairly well with that of the overall stock market. Volatility, as measured by both the semi-deviation and a drawdown factor, is considered low. As of December 31, 2015, Royce Micro-Cap Trust traded at a discount of 15.48% below its net asset value, which is better than its one-year historical average discount of 13.63%.

Charles M. Royce has been running the fund for 23 years and currently receives a manager quality ranking of 30 (0=worst, 99=best). If you desire an average level of risk, then this fund may be an option.

Data Date	Investment Rating	Net Assets ($Mil)	Price	Performance Rating/Pts	Total Return Y-T-D	Risk Rating/Pts
12-15	C	387.49	7.26	C+ / 6.1	-14.20%	C+ / 5.9
2014	B	431.20	10.08	B / 7.7	4.65%	B- / 7.5
2013	B+	356.63	12.61	A- / 9.0	40.88%	B- / 7.4
2012	C+	293.01	9.45	C+ / 6.7	18.30%	B- / 7.3
2011	C	339.30	8.77	C+ / 5.6	-4.85%	B- / 7.0
2010	C+	243.16	9.80	C+ / 6.8	34.06%	C / 5.1

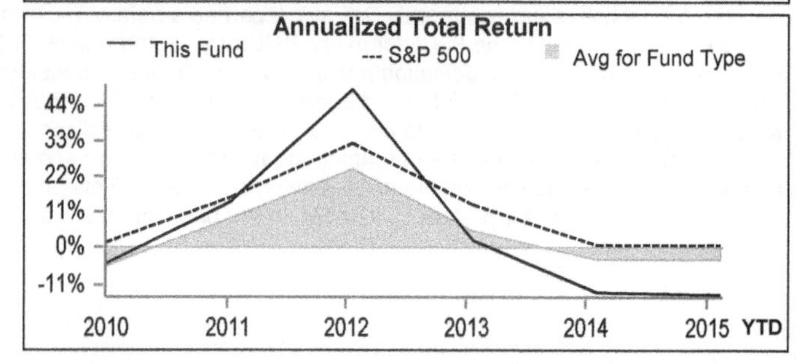

Royce Value Trust (RVT) C Fair

Fund Family: Royce & Associates LLC
Fund Type: Growth
Inception Date: November 19, 1986

Major Rating Factors: Middle of the road best describes Royce Value Trust whose TheStreet.com Investment Rating is currently a C (Fair). The fund currently has a performance rating of C+ (Fair) based on an annualized return of 6.11% over the last three years and a total return of -9.44% year to date 2015. Factored into the performance evaluation is an expense ratio of 0.61% (very low).

The fund's risk rating is currently B- (Good). It carries a beta of 1.01, meaning that its performance tracks fairly well with that of the overall stock market. Volatility, as measured by both the semi-deviation and a drawdown factor, is considered low. As of December 31, 2015, Royce Value Trust traded at a discount of 13.20% below its net asset value, which is worse than its one-year historical average discount of 13.34%.

Charles M. Royce has been running the fund for 30 years and currently receives a manager quality ranking of 23 (0=worst, 99=best). If you desire an average level of risk, then this fund may be an option.

Data Date	Investment Rating	Net Assets ($Mil)	Price	Performance Rating/Pts	Total Return Y-T-D	Risk Rating/Pts
12-15	C	1,231.96	11.77	C+ / 5.8	-9.44%	B- / 7.0
2014	B	1,296.40	14.33	C+ / 6.9	2.63%	B / 8.2
2013	C+	1,200.57	16.01	C+ / 6.3	18.67%	B- / 7.1
2012	C+	991.94	13.42	C+ / 6.9	16.88%	B- / 7.0
2011	C	1,186.90	12.27	C / 5.3	-8.23%	C+ / 6.9
2010	C+	849.78	14.54	C+ / 6.6	35.03%	C / 5.2

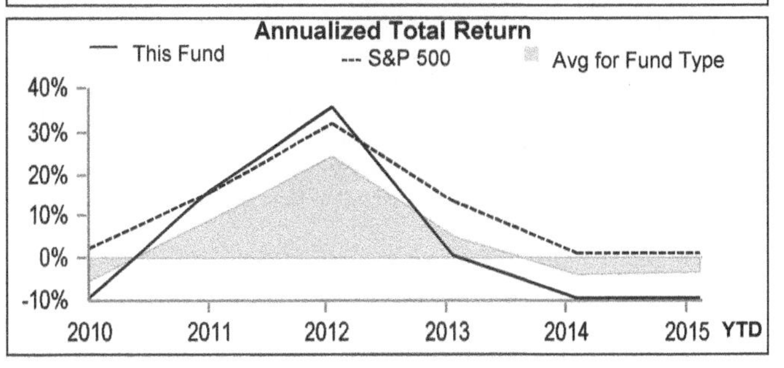

Salient Midstream and MLP Fund (SMM) E+ Very Weak

Fund Family: Salient Capital Advisors LLC
Fund Type: Income
Inception Date: May 29, 2012

Major Rating Factors:
Very poor performance is the major factor driving the E+ (Very Weak) TheStreet.com Investment Rating for Salient Midstream and MLP Fund. The fund currently has a performance rating of E+ (Very Weak) based on an annualized return of -14.79% over the last three years and a total return of -57.26% year to date 2015. Factored into the performance evaluation is an expense ratio of 2.44% (high).

The fund's risk rating is currently C- (Fair). It carries a beta of 1.70, meaning it is expected to move 17.0% for every 10% move in the market. Volatility, as measured by both the semi-deviation and a drawdown factor, is considered average. As of December 31, 2015, Salient Midstream and MLP Fund traded at a discount of 12.89% below its net asset value, which is better than its one-year historical average discount of 11.88%.

Frank T. Gardner, III currently receives a manager quality ranking of 2 (0=worst, 99=best). This fund offers an average level of risk but investors looking for strong performance will be frustrated.

Data Date	Investment Rating	Net Assets ($Mil)	Price	Performance Rating/Pts	Total Return Y-T-D	Risk Rating/Pts
12-15	E+	492.67	9.53	E+ / 0.6	-57.26%	C- / 3.4
2014	D	187.50	23.98	D- / 1.5	6.80%	B- / 7.0
2013	A+	217.64	23.73	A / 9.4	34.73%	B / 8.6

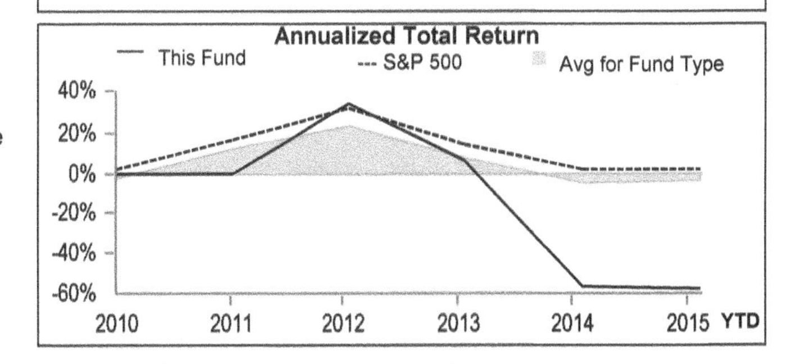

Self Storage Group (SELF) B- Good

Fund Family: CEF Advisers Inc
Fund Type: Global
Inception Date: August 30, 1983

Major Rating Factors: Self Storage Group receives a TheStreet.com Investment Rating of B- (Good). The fund currently has a performance rating of C+ (Fair) based on an annualized return of 6.32% over the last three years and a total return of 8.94% year to date 2015. Factored into the performance evaluation is an expense ratio of 3.71% (high).

The fund's risk rating is currently B- (Good). It carries a beta of -0.32, meaning the fund's expected move will be -3.2% for every 10% move in the market. Volatility, as measured by both the semi-deviation and a drawdown factor, is considered low. As of December 31, 2015, Self Storage Group traded at a discount of 34.21% below its net asset value, which is better than its one-year historical average discount of 31.75%.

Heidi Keating currently receives a manager quality ranking of 92 (0=worst, 99=best). If you desire an average level of risk, then this fund may be an option.

Data Date	Investment Rating	Net Assets ($Mil)	Price	Performance Rating/Pts	Total Return Y-T-D	Risk Rating/Pts
12-15	B-	38.10	3.75	C+ / 6.8	8.94%	B- / 7.3
2014	C	35.50	3.63	C / 5.5	6.81%	B- / 7.2
2013	D	35.16	3.59	E / 0.4	-48.23%	B / 8.0
2012	C	36.94	3.69	C / 4.5	16.70%	B / 8.0
2011	C	34.10	3.78	C / 4.8	-4.69%	B- / 7.8
2010	A-	31.19	4.17	B / 7.7	21.03%	B- / 7.0

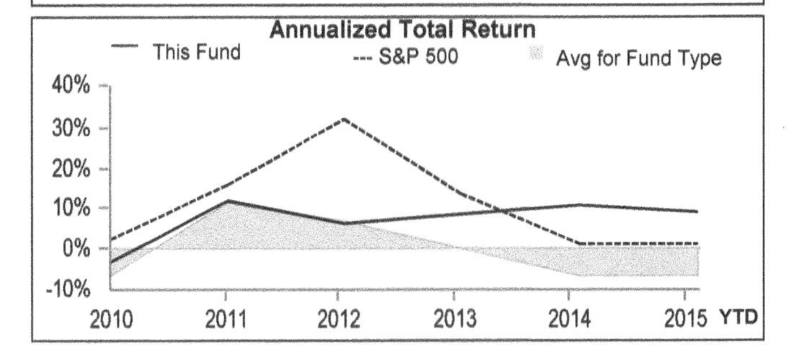

Source Capital (SOR) B+ Good

Fund Family: First Pacific Advisors LLC
Fund Type: Income
Inception Date: October 24, 1968

Data Date	Investment Rating	Net Assets ($Mil)	Price	Performance Rating/Pts	Total Return Y-T-D	Risk Rating/Pts
12-15	B+	696.24	66.26	B / 8.0	0.25%	B / 8.1
2014	A+	669.50	71.41	B+ / 8.6	12.64%	B / 8.5
2013	B-	567.71	67.10	B / 7.6	26.46%	B- / 7.3
2012	C+	472.48	52.22	B- / 7.2	19.78%	B- / 7.2
2011	C+	470.00	46.99	B- / 7.0	-5.80%	B- / 7.2
2010	B+	490.04	53.13	B / 7.8	30.34%	C+ / 5.8

Major Rating Factors: Strong performance is the major factor driving the B+ (Good) TheStreet.com Investment Rating for Source Capital. The fund currently has a performance rating of B (Good) based on an annualized return of 12.33% over the last three years and a total return of 0.25% year to date 2015. Factored into the performance evaluation is an expense ratio of 0.80% (very low).

The fund's risk rating is currently B (Good). It carries a beta of 0.98, meaning that its performance tracks fairly well with that of the overall stock market. Volatility, as measured by both the semi-deviation and a drawdown factor, is considered low. As of December 31, 2015, Source Capital traded at a discount of 9.32% below its net asset value, which is worse than its one-year historical average discount of 9.47%.

Eric S. Ende has been running the fund for 20 years and currently receives a manager quality ranking of 61 (0=worst, 99=best). If you desire only a moderate level of risk and strong performance, then this fund is an excellent option.

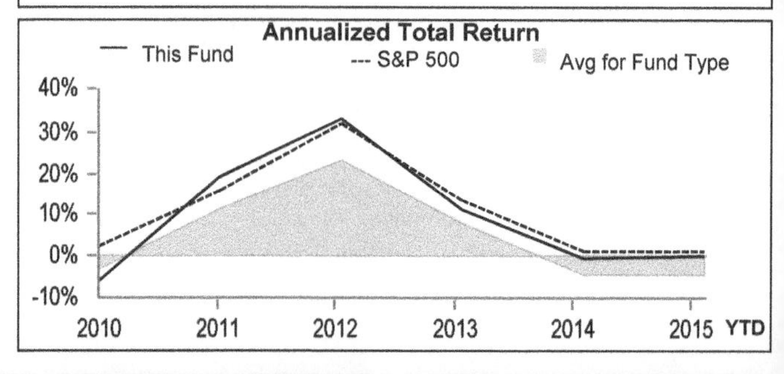

Special Opportunities Fund (SPE) C Fair

Fund Family: Bulldog Investors LLC
Fund Type: Municipal - National
Inception Date: May 28, 1993

Data Date	Investment Rating	Net Assets ($Mil)	Price	Performance Rating/Pts	Total Return Y-T-D	Risk Rating/Pts
12-15	C	172.20	13.22	C / 4.8	-15.20%	C+ / 6.7
2014	A-	182.60	15.37	B+ / 8.5	-1.37%	B- / 7.8
2013	A+	117.26	17.46	A+ / 9.6	35.81%	B+ / 9.0
2012	B	115.41	15.01	C+ / 6.3	11.86%	B+ / 9.1
2011	B	106.90	14.50	C+ / 6.9	2.86%	B+ / 9.1
2010	A	294.13	14.75	B / 8.1	4.90%	B- / 7.2

Major Rating Factors: Middle of the road best describes Special Opportunities Fund whose TheStreet.com Investment Rating is currently a C (Fair). The fund currently has a performance rating of C (Fair) based on an annualized return of 4.90% over the last three years and a total return of -15.20% year to date 2015. Factored into the performance evaluation is an expense ratio of 1.40% (average).

The fund's risk rating is currently C+ (Fair). It carries a beta of -0.36, meaning the fund's expected move will be -3.6% for every 10% move in the market. Volatility, as measured by both the semi-deviation and a drawdown factor, is considered low. As of December 31, 2015, Special Opportunities Fund traded at a discount of 12.51% below its net asset value, which is better than its one-year historical average discount of 11.55%.

Andrew Dakos currently receives a manager quality ranking of 95 (0=worst, 99=best). If you desire an average level of risk, then this fund may be an option.

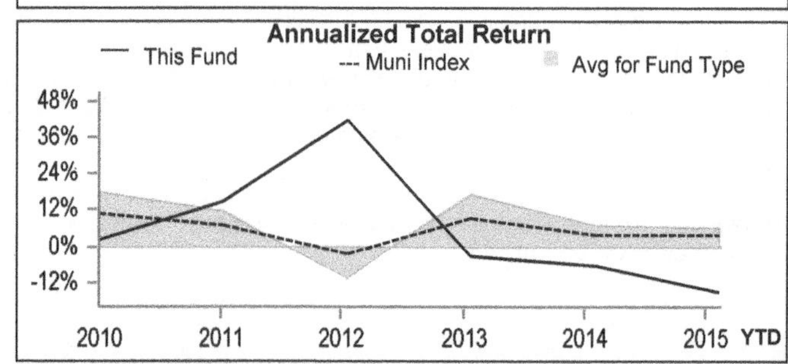

Sprott Focus Trust (FUND) C- Fair

Fund Family: Sprott Asset Management LP
Fund Type: Growth
Inception Date: March 2, 1988

Data Date	Investment Rating	Net Assets ($Mil)	Price	Performance Rating/Pts	Total Return Y-T-D	Risk Rating/Pts
12-15	C-	187.75	5.81	C- / 3.6	-13.34%	C+ / 6.9
2014	C	212.20	7.27	C / 4.7	1.25%	B / 8.2
2013	C+	165.93	7.63	C+ / 6.2	16.94%	B- / 7.2
2012	D+	148.84	6.60	C- / 3.2	11.86%	B- / 7.2
2011	C-	175.90	6.30	C / 4.3	-8.10%	B- / 7.2
2010	C-	141.50	7.57	C / 4.7	19.59%	C+ / 5.6

Major Rating Factors: Middle of the road best describes Sprott Focus Trust whose TheStreet.com Investment Rating is currently a C- (Fair). The fund currently has a performance rating of C- (Fair) based on an annualized return of 0.91% over the last three years and a total return of -13.34% year to date 2015. Factored into the performance evaluation is an expense ratio of 1.15% (low).

The fund's risk rating is currently C+ (Fair). It carries a beta of 0.90, meaning that its performance tracks fairly well with that of the overall stock market. Volatility, as measured by both the semi-deviation and a drawdown factor, is considered low. As of December 31, 2015, Sprott Focus Trust traded at a discount of 15.43% below its net asset value, which is better than its one-year historical average discount of 14.63%.

Whitney W. George has been running the fund for 14 years and currently receives a manager quality ranking of 17 (0=worst, 99=best). If you desire an average level of risk, then this fund may be an option.

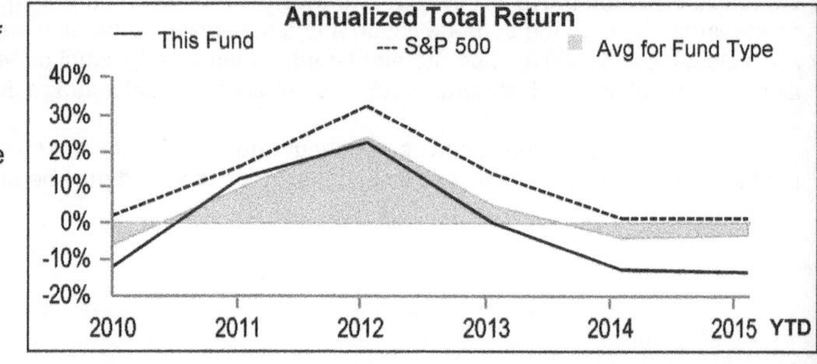

Stone Harbor Emg Markets Income (EDF) D- Weak

Fund Family: Stone Harbor Investment Partners LP
Fund Type: Emerging Market
Inception Date: December 22, 2010

Major Rating Factors:
Disappointing performance is the major factor driving the D- (Weak) TheStreet.com Investment Rating for Stone Harbor Emg Markets Income. The fund currently has a performance rating of D (Weak) based on an annualized return of -11.51% over the last three years and a total return of -9.79% year to date 2015. Factored into the performance evaluation is an expense ratio of 2.07% (high).

The fund's risk rating is currently C (Fair). It carries a beta of 1.02, meaning that its performance tracks fairly well with that of the overall stock market. Volatility, as measured by both the semi-deviation and a drawdown factor, is considered average. As of December 31, 2015, Stone Harbor Emg Markets Income traded at a discount of 10.81% below its net asset value, which is better than its one-year historical average discount of 7.63%.

Pablo Cisilino currently receives a manager quality ranking of 30 (0=worst, 99=best). This fund offers an average level of risk but investors looking for strong performance will be frustrated.

Data Date	Investment Rating	Net Assets ($Mil)	Price	Performance Rating/Pts	Total Return Y-T-D	Risk Rating/Pts
12-15	D-	0.29	12.05	D / 1.7	-9.79%	C / 4.7
2014	D	299.20	15.52	D / 2.0	-3.83%	C+ / 5.7
2013	D	359.58	18.31	D / 1.7	-20.08%	C+ / 6.9
2012	A-	335.27	24.76	B+ / 8.7	21.77%	B / 8.0
2011	D+	339.00	20.88	D / 1.6	-3.25%	B / 8.0

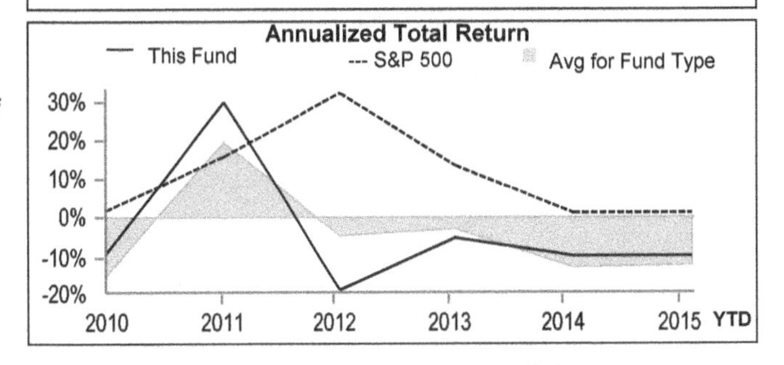

Stone Harbor Emg Markets Total Inc (EDI) D- Weak

Fund Family: Stone Harbor Investment Partners LP
Fund Type: Global
Inception Date: October 25, 2012

Major Rating Factors:
Disappointing performance is the major factor driving the D- (Weak) TheStreet.com Investment Rating for Stone Harbor Emg Markets Total Inc. The fund currently has a performance rating of D- (Weak) based on an annualized return of -14.61% over the last three years and a total return of -14.47% year to date 2015. Factored into the performance evaluation is an expense ratio of 2.13% (high).

The fund's risk rating is currently C (Fair). It carries a beta of 0.87, meaning the fund's expected move will be 8.7% for every 10% move in the market. Volatility, as measured by both the semi-deviation and a drawdown factor, is considered average. As of December 31, 2015, Stone Harbor Emg Markets Total Inc traded at a discount of 15.09% below its net asset value, which is better than its one-year historical average discount of 13.32%.

Pablo Cisilino currently receives a manager quality ranking of 16 (0=worst, 99=best). This fund offers an average level of risk but investors looking for strong performance will be frustrated.

Data Date	Investment Rating	Net Assets ($Mil)	Price	Performance Rating/Pts	Total Return Y-T-D	Risk Rating/Pts
12-15	D-	161.00	11.37	D- / 1.4	-14.47%	C / 4.6
2014	D-	186.10	15.25	E+ / 0.6	-12.26%	C / 5.3
2013	D	0.10	19.01	E+ / 0.8	-16.88%	C+ / 6.8

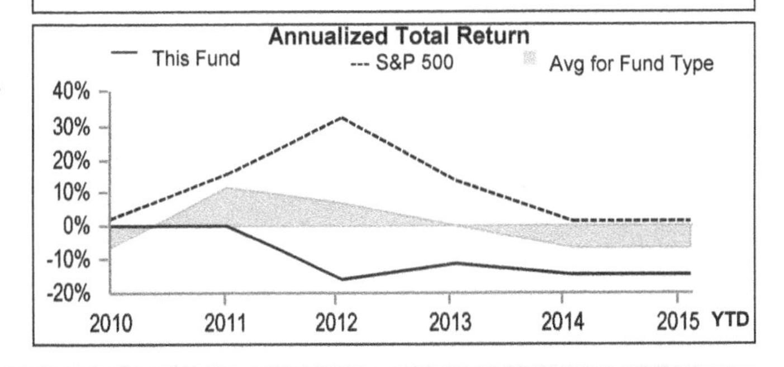

Strategic Global Income Fund (SGL) C Fair

Fund Family: UBS Asset Mgmt (Americas) Inc
Fund Type: Global
Inception Date: January 24, 1992

Major Rating Factors: Middle of the road best describes Strategic Global Income Fund whose TheStreet.com Investment Rating is currently a C (Fair). The fund currently has a performance rating of C (Fair) based on an annualized return of -0.94% over the last three years and a total return of 11.86% year to date 2015. Factored into the performance evaluation is an expense ratio of 1.16% (low).

The fund's risk rating is currently C+ (Fair). It carries a beta of 0.66, meaning the fund's expected move will be 6.6% for every 10% move in the market. Volatility, as measured by both the semi-deviation and a drawdown factor, is considered low. As of December 31, 2015, Strategic Global Income Fund traded at a discount of 3.84% below its net asset value, which is worse than its one-year historical average discount of 12.05%.

John E. Dugenske currently receives a manager quality ranking of 83 (0=worst, 99=best). If you desire an average level of risk, then this fund may be an option.

Data Date	Investment Rating	Net Assets ($Mil)	Price	Performance Rating/Pts	Total Return Y-T-D	Risk Rating/Pts
12-15	C	186.02	8.76	C / 5.5	11.86%	C+ / 6.9
2014	D+	189.20	8.48	D+ / 2.6	-0.57%	B- / 7.6
2013	D+	203.11	9.03	D+ / 2.6	-12.92%	B- / 7.6
2012	B-	203.46	10.97	B- / 7.1	17.39%	B- / 7.9
2011	B	204.10	10.17	B / 8.0	5.26%	B- / 7.9
2010	A-	209.28	11.00	A- / 9.0	28.41%	C+ / 6.0

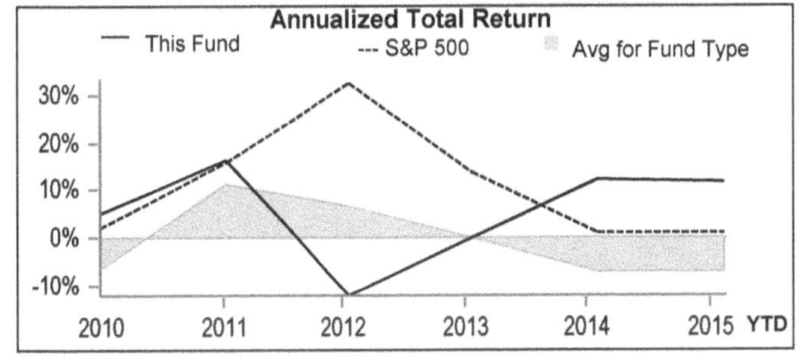

Swiss Helvetia Fund (SWZ) C+ Fair

Fund Family: Schroder Invst Mgmt North America I
Fund Type: Foreign
Inception Date: August 19, 1987

Major Rating Factors: Strong performance is the major factor driving the C+ (Fair) TheStreet.com Investment Rating for Swiss Helvetia Fund. The fund currently has a performance rating of B- (Good) based on an annualized return of 8.51% over the last three years and a total return of 0.88% year to date 2015. Factored into the performance evaluation is an expense ratio of 1.41% (average).

The fund's risk rating is currently C+ (Fair). It carries a beta of 0.73, meaning the fund's expected move will be 7.3% for every 10% move in the market. Volatility, as measured by both the semi-deviation and a drawdown factor, is considered low. As of December 31, 2015, Swiss Helvetia Fund traded at a discount of 14.36% below its net asset value, which is better than its one-year historical average discount of 13.74%.

Daniel Lenz currently receives a manager quality ranking of 89 (0=worst, 99=best). If you desire only a moderate level of risk and strong performance, then this fund is an excellent option.

Data Date	Investment Rating	Net Assets ($Mil)	Price	Performance Rating/Pts	Total Return Y-T-D	Risk Rating/Pts
12-15	C+	340.46	10.56	B- / 7.0	0.88%	C+ / 6.4
2014	C	411.90	11.14	C+ / 5.8	-1.36%	B- / 7.0
2013	C+	439.77	13.95	B- / 7.5	28.55%	C+ / 6.6
2012	C-	362.23	11.29	C / 5.0	16.97%	C+ / 6.5
2011	D	343.90	9.95	D / 2.1	-8.22%	C+ / 6.5
2010	C-	433.93	13.54	C- / 4.1	20.89%	C / 4.9

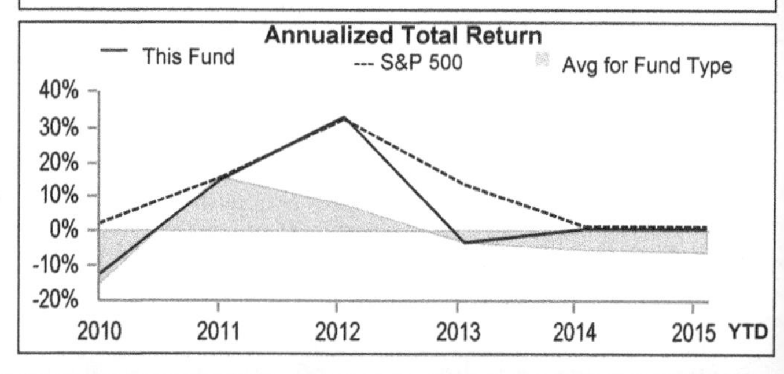

Taiwan Fund (TWN) C- Fair

Fund Family: JF International Management Inc
Fund Type: Foreign
Inception Date: December 16, 1986

Major Rating Factors: Middle of the road best describes Taiwan Fund whose TheStreet.com Investment Rating is currently a C- (Fair). The fund currently has a performance rating of C- (Fair) based on an annualized return of 1.09% over the last three years and a total return of -8.90% year to date 2015. Factored into the performance evaluation is an expense ratio of 1.86% (above average).

The fund's risk rating is currently C+ (Fair). It carries a beta of 0.70, meaning the fund's expected move will be 7.0% for every 10% move in the market. Volatility, as measured by both the semi-deviation and a drawdown factor, is considered low. As of December 31, 2015, Taiwan Fund traded at a discount of 12.60% below its net asset value, which is better than its one-year historical average discount of 10.40%.

Kok Hoi Wong has been running the fund for 5 years and currently receives a manager quality ranking of 49 (0=worst, 99=best). If you desire an average level of risk, then this fund may be an option.

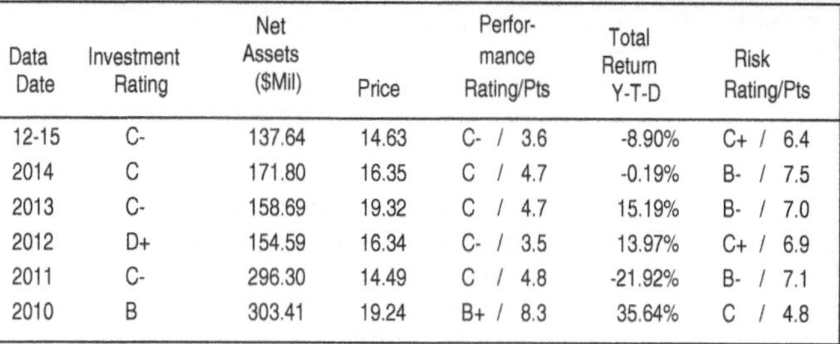

Data Date	Investment Rating	Net Assets ($Mil)	Price	Performance Rating/Pts	Total Return Y-T-D	Risk Rating/Pts
12-15	C-	137.64	14.63	C- / 3.6	-8.90%	C+ / 6.4
2014	C	171.80	16.35	C / 4.7	-0.19%	B- / 7.5
2013	C-	158.69	19.32	C / 4.7	15.19%	B- / 7.0
2012	D+	154.59	16.34	C- / 3.5	13.97%	C+ / 6.9
2011	C-	296.30	14.49	C / 4.8	-21.92%	B- / 7.1
2010	B	303.41	19.24	B+ / 8.3	35.64%	C / 4.8

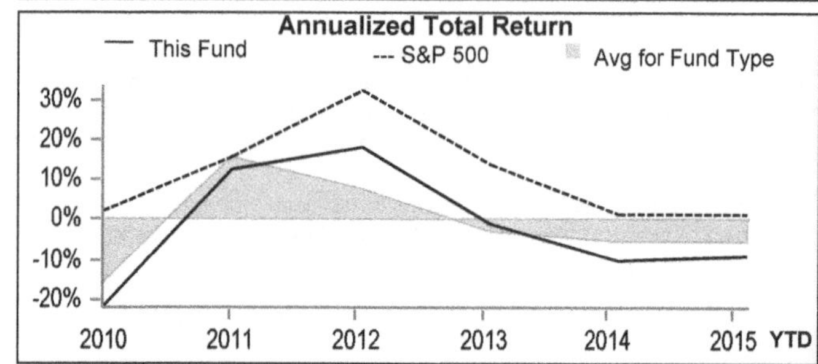

TCW Strategic Income Fund (TSI) C+ Fair

Fund Family: TCW Investment Management Company
Fund Type: Growth and Income
Inception Date: February 26, 1987

Major Rating Factors: Middle of the road best describes TCW Strategic Income Fund whose TheStreet.com Investment Rating is currently a C+ (Fair). The fund currently has a performance rating of C+ (Fair) based on an annualized return of 3.32% over the last three years and a total return of 1.06% year to date 2015. Factored into the performance evaluation is an expense ratio of 0.87% (low).

The fund's risk rating is currently B (Good). It carries a beta of 0.23, meaning the fund's expected move will be 2.3% for every 10% move in the market. Volatility, as measured by both the semi-deviation and a drawdown factor, is considered low. As of December 31, 2015, TCW Strategic Income Fund traded at a discount of 9.61% below its net asset value, which is worse than its one-year historical average discount of 10.40%.

Mitchell A. Flack currently receives a manager quality ranking of 78 (0=worst, 99=best). If you desire an average level of risk, then this fund may be an option.

Data Date	Investment Rating	Net Assets ($Mil)	Price	Performance Rating/Pts	Total Return Y-T-D	Risk Rating/Pts
12-15	C+	283.84	5.27	C+ / 5.7	1.06%	B / 8.1
2014	C+	283.50	5.39	C+ / 5.8	5.64%	B- / 7.7
2013	C+	271.86	5.34	C+ / 6.5	2.69%	B- / 7.5
2012	A	253.36	5.36	A- / 9.2	28.58%	B / 8.2
2011	B-	262.58	4.85	B- / 7.0	-4.09%	B- / 7.7
2010	B+	227.31	5.22	A- / 9.2	32.52%	C / 4.9

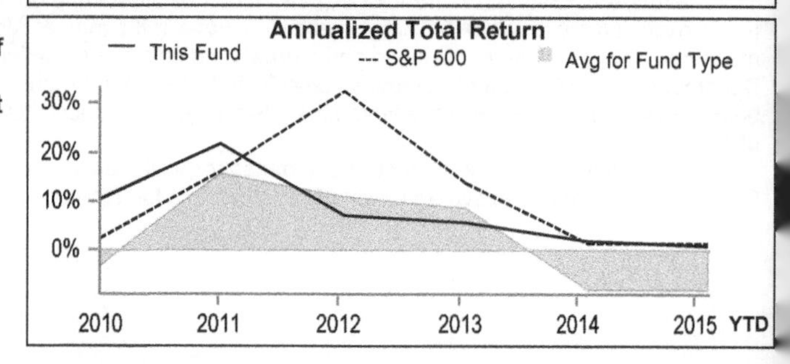

Tekla Healthcare Investors (HQH) B Good

Fund Family: Tekla Capital Management LLC
Fund Type: Health
Inception Date: April 23, 1987

Major Rating Factors:
Exceptional performance is the major factor driving the B (Good) TheStreet.com Investment Rating for Tekla Healthcare Investors. The fund currently has a performance rating of A+ (Excellent) based on an annualized return of 28.75% over the last three years and a total return of 4.01% year to date 2015. Factored into the performance evaluation is an expense ratio of 1.00% (low).

The fund's risk rating is currently C (Fair). It carries a beta of 1.48, meaning it is expected to move 14.8% for every 10% move in the market. Volatility, as measured by both the semi-deviation and a drawdown factor, is considered average. As of December 31, 2015, Tekla Healthcare Investors traded at a discount of 3.45% below its net asset value, which is better than its one-year historical average premium of 1.10%.

Daniel R. Omstead has been running the fund for 12 years and currently receives a manager quality ranking of 91 (0=worst, 99=best). If you desire an average level of risk and strong performance, then this fund is a good option.

Data Date	Investment Rating	Net Assets ($Mil)	Price	Performance Rating/Pts	Total Return Y-T-D	Risk Rating/Pts
12-15	B	1,104.00	29.66	A+ / 9.7	4.01%	C / 5.1
2014	A	1,053.20	31.49	A+ / 9.8	29.16%	C+ / 6.9
2013	B+	690.00	26.97	A+ / 9.7	56.98%	C+ / 6.5
2012	B	465.00	17.31	A / 9.3	36.56%	C+ / 6.3
2011	C+	404.80	14.11	C+ / 5.9	11.69%	B- / 7.4
2010	C+	365.00	13.37	C+ / 5.6	20.68%	C+ / 5.7

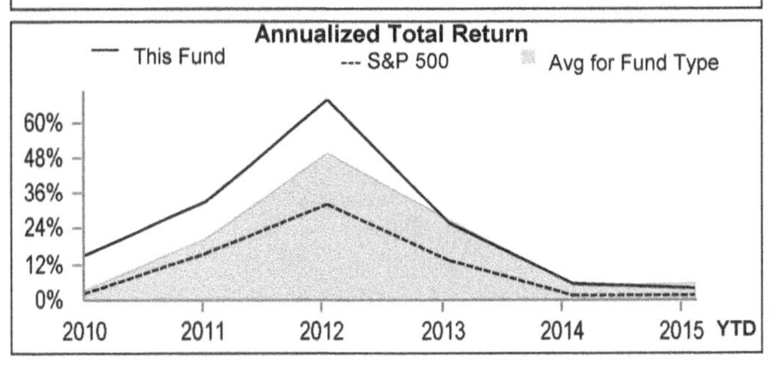

Tekla Healthcare Opportunities (THQ) C- Fair

Fund Family: Tekla Capital Management LLC
Fund Type: Global
Inception Date: July 31, 2014

Major Rating Factors:
Disappointing performance is the major factor driving the C- (Fair) TheStreet.com Investment Rating for Tekla Healthcare Opportunities. The fund currently has a performance rating of D+ (Weak) based on an annualized return of 0.00% over the last three years and a total return of -7.01% year to date 2015. Factored into the performance evaluation is an expense ratio of 1.60% (above average).

The fund's risk rating is currently B- (Good). It carries a beta of 0.00, meaning the fund's expected move will be 0.0% for every 10% move in the market. Volatility, as measured by both the semi-deviation and a drawdown factor, is considered low. As of December 31, 2015, Tekla Healthcare Opportunities traded at a discount of 10.77% below its net asset value, which is better than its one-year historical average discount of 9.13%.

Daniel R. Omstead currently receives a manager quality ranking of 31 (0=worst, 99=best). This fund offers only a moderate level of risk but investors looking for strong performance are still waiting.

Data Date	Investment Rating	Net Assets ($Mil)	Price	Performance Rating/Pts	Total Return Y-T-D	Risk Rating/Pts
12-15	C-	824.00	17.39	D+ / 2.7	-7.01%	B- / 7.3

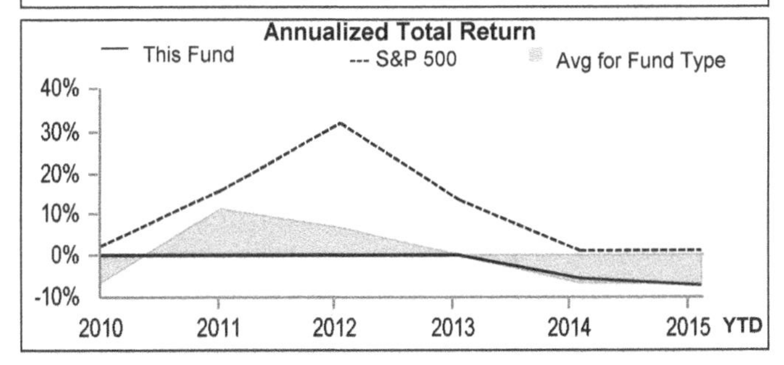

Tekla Life Sciences Investors (HQL) B- Good

Fund Family: Tekla Capital Management LLC
Fund Type: Health
Inception Date: May 8, 1992

Major Rating Factors:
Exceptional performance is the major factor driving the B- (Good) TheStreet.com Investment Rating for Tekla Life Sciences Investors. The fund currently has a performance rating of A+ (Excellent) based on an annualized return of 26.19% over the last three years and a total return of 5.44% year to date 2015. Factored into the performance evaluation is an expense ratio of 1.17% (low).

The fund's risk rating is currently C (Fair). It carries a beta of 1.47, meaning it is expected to move 14.7% for every 10% move in the market. Volatility, as measured by both the semi-deviation and a drawdown factor, is considered average. As of December 31, 2015, Tekla Life Sciences Investors traded at a discount of 2.23% below its net asset value, which is better than its one-year historical average premium of .33%.

Daniel R. Omstead has been running the fund for 24 years and currently receives a manager quality ranking of 88 (0=worst, 99=best). If you desire an average level of risk and strong performance, then this fund is a good option.

Data Date	Investment Rating	Net Assets ($Mil)	Price	Performance Rating/Pts	Total Return Y-T-D	Risk Rating/Pts
12-15	B-	463.00	23.64	A+ / 9.7	5.44%	C / 4.9
2014	B+	444.10	24.88	A+ / 9.7	32.77%	C+ / 6.3
2013	B	302.00	20.44	A+ / 9.6	42.78%	C+ / 6.3
2012	B	208.00	14.50	A / 9.5	37.86%	C+ / 6.2
2011	C+	178.80	11.47	B- / 7.3	18.67%	C+ / 6.1
2010	C	251.00	10.77	C+ / 5.9	21.84%	C / 4.5

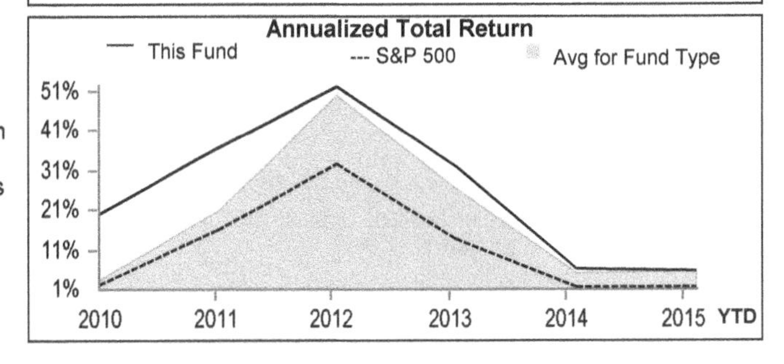

Templeton Dragon Fund (TDF) D+ Weak

Fund Family: Templeton Asset Management Ltd
Fund Type: Foreign
Inception Date: September 21, 1994

Data Date	Investment Rating	Net Assets ($Mil)	Price	Performance Rating/Pts	Total Return Y-T-D	Risk Rating/Pts
12-15	D+	925.02	17.81	C- / 3.2	-10.21%	C+ / 5.7
2014	C	1,003.90	24.04	C+ / 5.6	10.64%	B- / 7.4
2013	D+	1,174.23	25.88	D+ / 2.5	-6.36%	B- / 7.1
2012	C	1,089.56	28.44	C / 5.4	17.06%	B- / 7.3
2011	C+	1,054.50	25.45	C+ / 6.3	-10.93%	C+ / 6.9
2010	C+	1,092.71	30.74	B / 7.7	19.81%	C- / 4.2

Major Rating Factors: Templeton Dragon Fund receives a TheStreet.com Investment Rating of D+ (Weak). The fund currently has a performance rating of C- (Fair) based on an annualized return of -1.82% over the last three years and a total return of -10.21% year to date 2015. Factored into the performance evaluation is an expense ratio of 1.35% (average).

The fund's risk rating is currently C+ (Fair). It carries a beta of 0.71, meaning the fund's expected move will be 7.1% for every 10% move in the market. Volatility, as measured by both the semi-deviation and a drawdown factor, is considered low. As of December 31, 2015, Templeton Dragon Fund traded at a discount of 13.16% below its net asset value, which is better than its one-year historical average discount of 13.12%.

J. B. Mark Mobius has been running the fund for 22 years and currently receives a manager quality ranking of 77 (0=worst, 99=best). If you desire an average level of risk, then this fund may be an option.

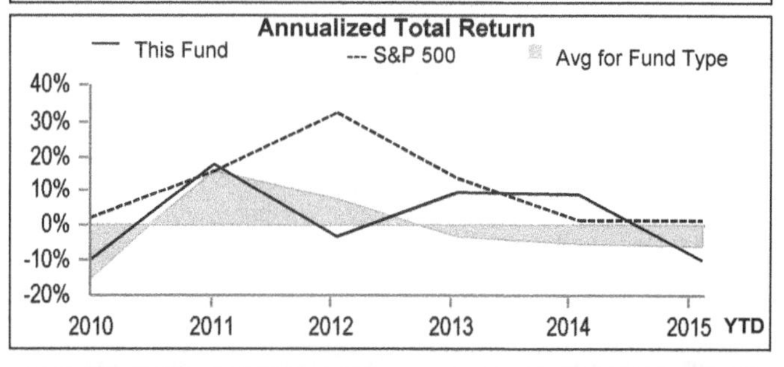

Templeton Emerging Markets Fd (EMF) D- Weak

Fund Family: Templeton Asset Management Ltd
Fund Type: Emerging Market
Inception Date: March 5, 1987

Data Date	Investment Rating	Net Assets ($Mil)	Price	Performance Rating/Pts	Total Return Y-T-D	Risk Rating/Pts
12-15	D-	240.29	9.97	D- / 1.2	-26.92%	C / 4.3
2014	D+	347.70	15.42	D+ / 2.5	-2.85%	C+ / 6.6
2013	D	342.42	17.50	D- / 1.5	-8.27%	C+ / 6.4
2012	D	348.00	20.00	D / 2.2	10.51%	C+ / 6.5
2011	C	343.20	17.86	C+ / 6.4	-21.96%	C+ / 6.7
2010	C	355.29	23.57	B / 7.7	20.71%	D+ / 2.7

Major Rating Factors:
Disappointing performance is the major factor driving the D- (Weak) TheStreet.com Investment Rating for Templeton Emerging Markets Fd. The fund currently has a performance rating of D- (Weak) based on an annualized return of -13.38% over the last three years and a total return of -26.92% year to date 2015. Factored into the performance evaluation is an expense ratio of 1.37% (average).

The fund's risk rating is currently C (Fair). It carries a beta of 1.20, meaning it is expected to move 12.0% for every 10% move in the market. Volatility, as measured by both the semi-deviation and a drawdown factor, is considered average. As of December 31, 2015, Templeton Emerging Markets Fd traded at a discount of 10.42% below its net asset value, which is worse than its one-year historical average discount of 10.85%.

J. B. Mark Mobius has been running the fund for 29 years and currently receives a manager quality ranking of 27 (0=worst, 99=best). This fund offers an average level of risk but investors looking for strong performance will be frustrated.

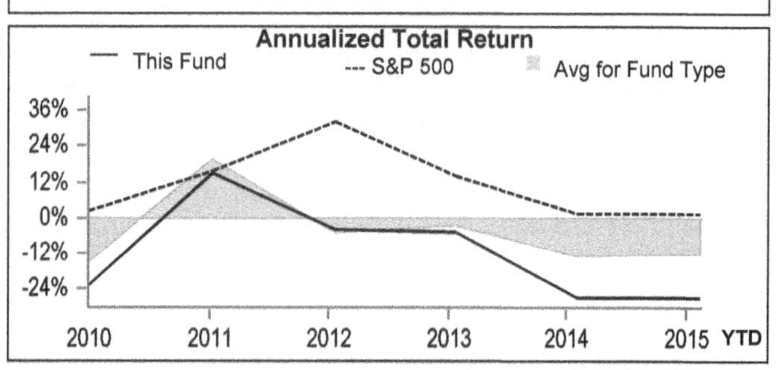

Templeton Emerging Markets Income (TEI) D Weak

Fund Family: Franklin Advisers Inc
Fund Type: Emerging Market
Inception Date: September 23, 1993

Data Date	Investment Rating	Net Assets ($Mil)	Price	Performance Rating/Pts	Total Return Y-T-D	Risk Rating/Pts
12-15	D	576.07	9.97	D+ / 2.3	-4.44%	C / 5.3
2014	D	669.00	11.34	D / 2.2	-8.97%	C+ / 6.1
2013	D+	699.41	13.65	C- / 3.1	-14.75%	B- / 7.0
2012	B-	759.02	17.31	B- / 7.4	22.22%	B- / 7.4
2011	B	714.20	15.57	B / 7.8	3.36%	B- / 7.9
2010	B	769.97	16.39	B+ / 8.6	21.06%	C / 4.3

Major Rating Factors:
Disappointing performance is the major factor driving the D (Weak) TheStreet.com Investment Rating for Templeton Emerging Markets Income. The fund currently has a performance rating of D+ (Weak) based on an annualized return of -9.64% over the last three years and a total return of -4.44% year to date 2015. Factored into the performance evaluation is an expense ratio of 1.09% (low).

The fund's risk rating is currently C (Fair). It carries a beta of 0.97, meaning that its performance tracks fairly well with that of the overall stock market. Volatility, as measured by both the semi-deviation and a drawdown factor, is considered average. As of December 31, 2015, Templeton Emerging Markets Income traded at a discount of 13.75% below its net asset value, which is better than its one-year historical average discount of 13.49%.

Michael Hasenstab currently receives a manager quality ranking of 30 (0=worst, 99=best). This fund offers an average level of risk but investors looking for strong performance will be frustrated.

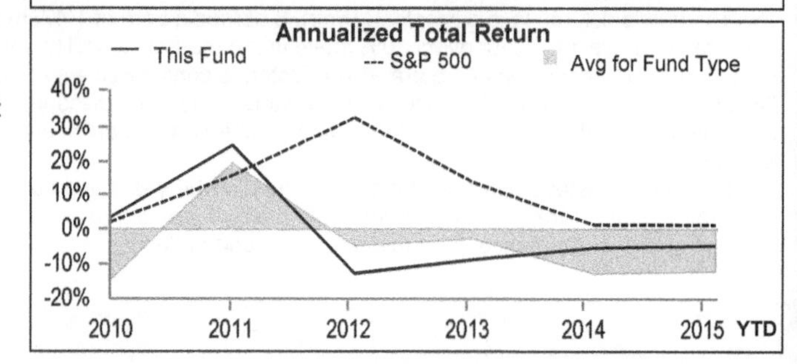

Templeton Global Income (GIM) D+ Weak

Fund Family: Franklin Advisers Inc
Fund Type: Global
Inception Date: March 17, 1988

Major Rating Factors:
Disappointing performance is the major factor driving the D+ (Weak) TheStreet.com Investment Rating for Templeton Global Income. The fund currently has a performance rating of D+ (Weak) based on an annualized return of -6.22% over the last three years and a total return of -8.97% year to date 2015. Factored into the performance evaluation is an expense ratio of 0.73% (very low).

The fund's risk rating is currently C+ (Fair). It carries a beta of 0.35, meaning the fund's expected move will be 3.5% for every 10% move in the market. Volatility, as measured by both the semi-deviation and a drawdown factor, is considered low. As of December 31, 2015, Templeton Global Income traded at a discount of 12.41% below its net asset value, which is better than its one-year historical average discount of 10.91%.

Michael Hasenstab has been running the fund for 28 years and currently receives a manager quality ranking of 33 (0=worst, 99=best). This fund offers only a moderate level of risk but investors looking for strong performance are still waiting.

Data Date	Investment Rating	Net Assets ($Mil)	Price	Performance Rating/Pts	Total Return Y-T-D	Risk Rating/Pts
12-15	D+	989.60	6.35	D+ / 2.6	-8.97%	C+ / 6.5
2014	D+	1,148.10	7.19	D+ / 2.6	-1.29%	B- / 7.2
2013	D+	1,124.61	7.95	D+ / 2.5	-9.49%	B- / 7.0
2012	C-	1,209.29	9.44	C- / 3.5	5.35%	B- / 7.7
2011	C	1,338.95	9.45	C / 5.1	0.28%	B- / 7.9
2010	A-	1,307.68	10.70	B+ / 8.5	19.09%	C+ / 6.3

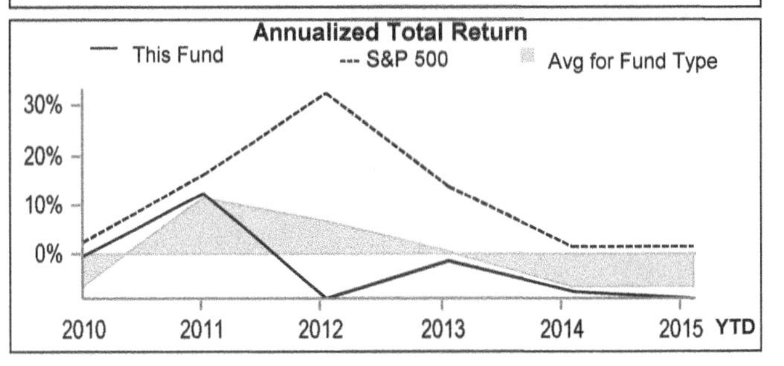

Thai Fund (TTF) D- Weak

Fund Family: Morgan Stanley Investment Managemen
Fund Type: Foreign
Inception Date: February 17, 1988

Major Rating Factors: Thai Fund has adopted a risky asset allocation strategy and currently receives an overall TheStreet.com Investment Rating of D- (Weak). The fund has an above average level of volatility, as measured by both semi-deviation and drawdown factors. It carries a beta of 0.81, meaning the fund's expected move will be 8.1% for every 10% move in the market. As of December 31, 2015, Thai Fund traded at a discount of 14.99% below its net asset value, which is better than its one-year historical average discount of 12.55%. Unfortunately, the high level of risk (D+, Weak) has only provided investors with average performance.

The fund's performance rating is currently C- (Fair). It has registered an annualized return of 0.86% over the last three years but is down -10.43% year to date 2015. Factored into the performance evaluation is an expense ratio of 1.01% (low).

Munib M. Madni has been running the fund for 8 years and currently receives a manager quality ranking of 46 (0=worst, 99=best). If you are comfortable owning a high risk investment, then this fund may be an option.

Data Date	Investment Rating	Net Assets ($Mil)	Price	Performance Rating/Pts	Total Return Y-T-D	Risk Rating/Pts
12-15	D-	160.73	6.86	C- / 3.5	-10.43%	D+ / 2.3
2014	C	176.20	11.79	A / 9.3	32.39%	C- / 3.0
2013	B+	343.54	18.15	A / 9.4	26.54%	C+ / 6.7
2012	A+	270.51	19.95	A+ / 9.8	69.21%	B- / 7.8
2011	B+	215.80	12.26	B+ / 8.4	0.38%	B- / 7.9
2010	B+	180.33	12.80	B+ / 8.7	49.50%	C / 5.0

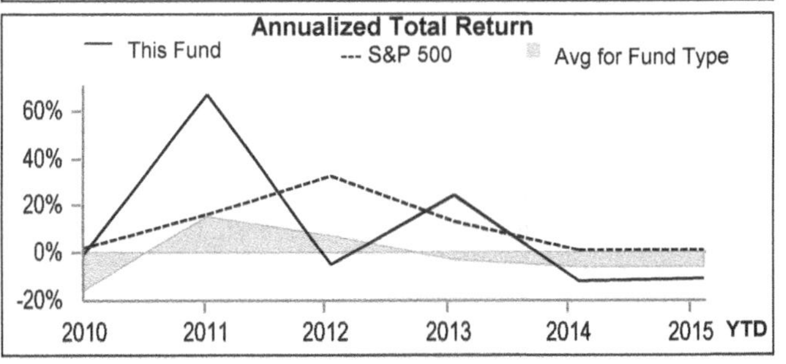

The Cushing MLP Total Return Fund (SRV) E+ Very Weak

Fund Family: Cushing Asset Management LP
Fund Type: Growth and Income
Inception Date: August 27, 2007

Major Rating Factors:
Very poor performance is the major factor driving the E+ (Very Weak) TheStreet.com Investment Rating for The Cushing MLP Total Return Fund. The fund currently has a performance rating of E (Very Weak) based on an annualized return of -28.40% over the last three years and a total return of -63.06% year to date 2015. Factored into the performance evaluation is an expense ratio of 2.93% (high).

The fund's risk rating is currently C- (Fair). It carries a beta of 1.80, meaning it is expected to move 18.0% for every 10% move in the market. Volatility, as measured by both the semi-deviation and a drawdown factor, is considered average. As of December 31, 2015, The Cushing MLP Total Return Fund traded at a discount of 11.31% below its net asset value, which is worse than its one-year historical average discount of 13.23%.

Jerry V. Swank has been running the fund for 9 years and currently receives a manager quality ranking of 1 (0=worst, 99=best). This fund offers an average level of risk but investors looking for strong performance will be frustrated.

Data Date	Investment Rating	Net Assets ($Mil)	Price	Performance Rating/Pts	Total Return Y-T-D	Risk Rating/Pts
12-15	E+	199.85	10.67	E / 0.3	-63.06%	C- / 3.8
2014	D-	235.30	5.90	D- / 1.4	-17.27%	C- / 4.1
2013	C-	240.27	8.02	C / 5.3	20.11%	C+ / 6.9
2012	D	216.30	7.17	D- / 1.4	-9.87%	C+ / 6.7
2011	B	258.40	8.90	B+ / 8.5	-4.55%	B- / 7.4
2010	D	64.51	10.52	C+ / 5.8	35.74%	D- / 1.2

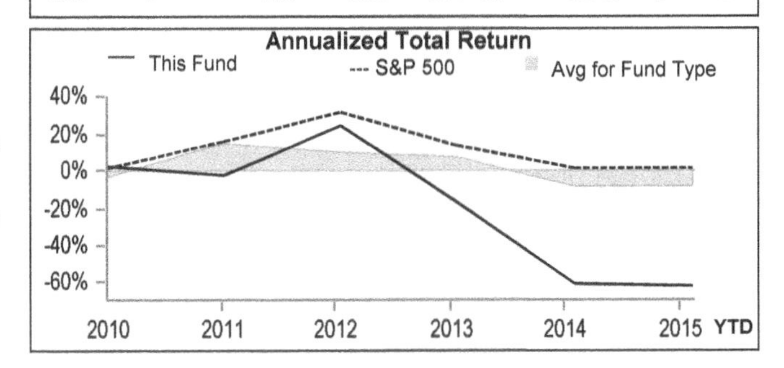

The European Equity Fund (EEA) C+ Fair

Fund Family: Deutsche Asset Mgmt International G
Fund Type: Foreign
Inception Date: July 18, 1986

Major Rating Factors: Middle of the road best describes The European Equity Fund whose TheStreet.com Investment Rating is currently a C+ (Fair). The fund currently has a performance rating of C+ (Fair) based on an annualized return of 5.02% over the last three years and a total return of -0.06% year to date 2015. Factored into the performance evaluation is an expense ratio of 1.59% (above average).

The fund's risk rating is currently B- (Good). It carries a beta of 0.85, meaning the fund's expected move will be 8.5% for every 10% move in the market. Volatility, as measured by both the semi-deviation and a drawdown factor, is considered low. As of December 31, 2015, The European Equity Fund traded at a discount of 10.24% below its net asset value, which is worse than its one-year historical average discount of 10.47%.

Gerd Kirsten has been running the fund for 7 years and currently receives a manager quality ranking of 76 (0=worst, 99=best). If you desire an average level of risk, then this fund may be an option.

Data Date	Investment Rating	Net Assets ($Mil)	Price	Perfor-mance Rating/Pts	Total Return Y-T-D	Risk Rating/Pts
12-15	C+	85.65	8.06	C+ / 6.0	-0.06%	B- / 7.7
2014	B-	85.80	8.23	C+ / 6.2	-3.59%	B / 8.1
2013	C	77.51	8.94	C+ / 6.6	20.23%	C+ / 6.5
2012	C	73.09	7.03	C+ / 5.8	34.49%	C+ / 6.4
2011	D	72.00	5.94	D / 1.9	-20.68%	C+ / 6.5
2010	E+	97.38	7.58	D- / 1.2	8.61%	D+ / 2.9

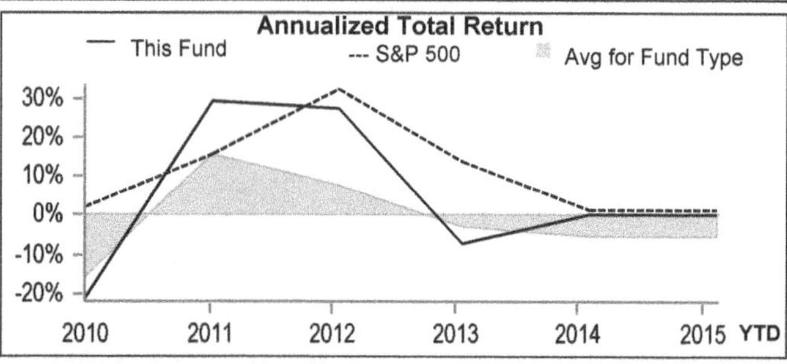

The New Ireland Fund (IRL) A+ Excellent

Fund Family: Kleinwort Benson Investors Intl Ltd
Fund Type: Foreign
Inception Date: March 30, 1990

Major Rating Factors:
Exceptional performance is the major factor driving the A+ (Excellent) TheStreet.com Investment Rating for The New Ireland Fund. The fund currently has a performance rating of A+ (Excellent) based on an annualized return of 25.10% over the last three years and a total return of 36.24% year to date 2015. Factored into the performance evaluation is an expense ratio of 1.68% (above average).

The fund's risk rating is currently B- (Good). It carries a beta of 0.48, meaning the fund's expected move will be 4.8% for every 10% move in the market. Volatility, as measured by both the semi-deviation and a drawdown factor, is considered low. As of December 31, 2015, The New Ireland Fund traded at a discount of 12.39% below its net asset value, which is worse than its one-year historical average discount of 14.28%.

Noel O'Halloran has been running the fund for 5 years and currently receives a manager quality ranking of 98 (0=worst, 99=best). If you desire only a moderate level of risk and strong performance, then this fund is an excellent option.

Data Date	Investment Rating	Net Assets ($Mil)	Price	Perfor-mance Rating/Pts	Total Return Y-T-D	Risk Rating/Pts
12-15	A+	71.36	13.93	A+ / 9.8	36.24%	B- / 7.9
2014	A+	73.70	12.62	B+ / 8.7	3.52%	B / 8.3
2013	A+	59.89	12.84	A / 9.3	38.39%	B / 8.0
2012	B-	54.07	9.10	B- / 7.5	35.49%	B- / 7.4
2011	D+	51.30	6.94	C- / 3.5	3.07%	C+ / 6.7
2010	E	58.57	6.86	E+ / 0.6	-2.52%	D+ / 2.5

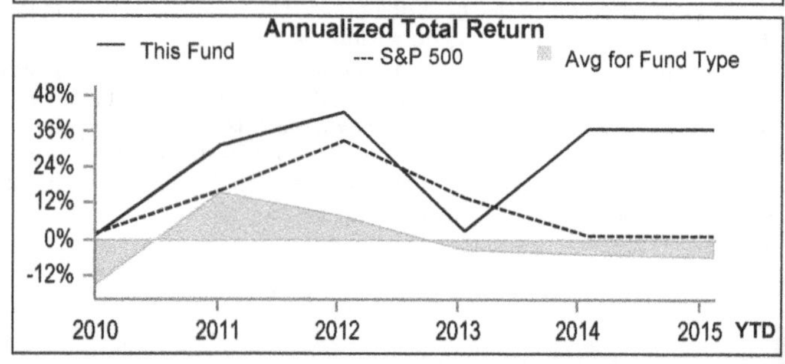

THL Credit Senior Loan (TSL) D+ Weak

Fund Family: Four Wood Capital Advisors LLC
Fund Type: Loan Participation
Inception Date: September 19, 2013

Major Rating Factors: THL Credit Senior Loan receives a TheStreet.com Investment Rating of D+ (Weak). The fund currently has a performance rating of C (Fair) based on an annualized return of 0.00% over the last three years and a total return of 0.58% year to date 2015. Factored into the performance evaluation is an expense ratio of 2.38% (high).

The fund's risk rating is currently C- (Fair). It carries a beta of 0.00, meaning the fund's expected move will be 0.0% for every 10% move in the market. Volatility, as measured by both the semi-deviation and a drawdown factor, is considered average. As of December 31, 2015, THL Credit Senior Loan traded at a discount of 8.16% below its net asset value, which is worse than its one-year historical average discount of 8.21%.

If you desire an average level of risk, then this fund may be an option.

Data Date	Investment Rating	Net Assets ($Mil)	Price	Perfor-mance Rating/Pts	Total Return Y-T-D	Risk Rating/Pts
12-15	D+	139.03	15.86	C / 5.3	0.58%	C- / 4.1
2014	E+	142.30	17.06	D+ / 2.4	0.13%	D / 2.0

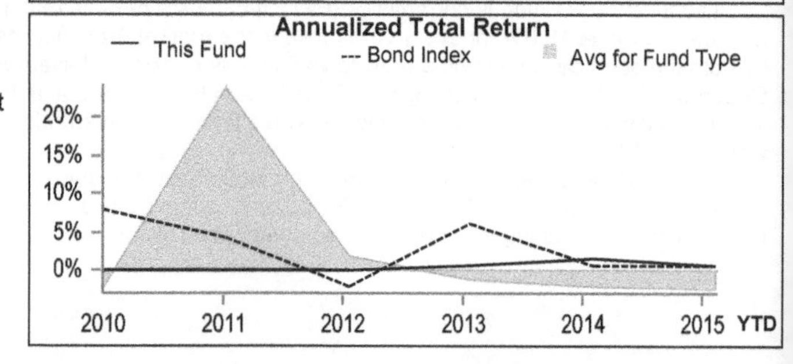

Tortoise Energy Independence Fund (NDP) D- Weak

Fund Family: Tortoise Capital Advisors LLC
Fund Type: Global
Inception Date: July 27, 2012

Major Rating Factors:
Disappointing performance is the major factor driving the D- (Weak) TheStreet.com Investment Rating for Tortoise Energy Independence Fund. The fund currently has a performance rating of D- (Weak) based on an annualized return of -13.85% over the last three years and a total return of -35.47% year to date 2015. Factored into the performance evaluation is an expense ratio of 1.38% (average).

The fund's risk rating is currently C- (Fair). It carries a beta of 1.41, meaning it is expected to move 14.1% for every 10% move in the market. Volatility, as measured by both the semi-deviation and a drawdown factor, is considered average. As of December 31, 2015, Tortoise Energy Independence Fund traded at a discount of 14.16% below its net asset value, which is better than its one-year historical average discount of 9.95%.

H. Kevin Birzer currently receives a manager quality ranking of 8 (0=worst, 99=best). This fund offers an average level of risk but investors looking for strong performance will be frustrated.

Data Date	Investment Rating	Net Assets ($Mil)	Price	Performance Rating/Pts	Total Return Y-T-D	Risk Rating/Pts
12-15	D-	330.46	11.28	D- / 1.0	-35.47%	C- / 4.0
2014	D-	402.10	18.95	E / 0.3	-18.08%	C+ / 6.0
2013	B+	357.59	25.10	B / 7.8	19.43%	B / 8.3

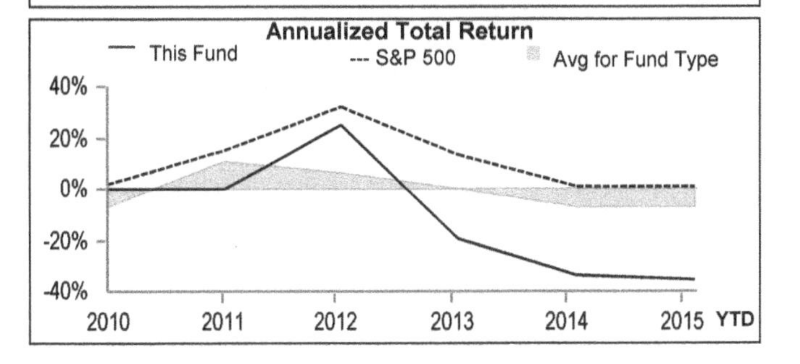

Tortoise Energy Infrastr Corp (TYG) D Weak

Fund Family: Tortoise Capital Advisors LLC
Fund Type: Energy/Natural Resources
Inception Date: February 27, 2004

Major Rating Factors:
Disappointing performance is the major factor driving the D (Weak) TheStreet.com Investment Rating for Tortoise Energy Infrastr Corp. The fund currently has a performance rating of D (Weak) based on an annualized return of -6.01% over the last three years and a total return of -33.14% year to date 2015. Factored into the performance evaluation is an expense ratio of 3.16% (high).

The fund's risk rating is currently C (Fair). It carries a beta of 0.82, meaning the fund's expected move will be 8.2% for every 10% move in the market. Volatility, as measured by both the semi-deviation and a drawdown factor, is considered average. As of December 31, 2015, Tortoise Energy Infrastr Corp traded at a discount of 3.37% below its net asset value, which is worse than its one-year historical average discount of 6.21%.

H. Kevin Birzer has been running the fund for 12 years and currently receives a manager quality ranking of 57 (0=worst, 99=best). This fund offers an average level of risk but investors looking for strong performance will be frustrated.

Data Date	Investment Rating	Net Assets ($Mil)	Price	Performance Rating/Pts	Total Return Y-T-D	Risk Rating/Pts
12-15	D	2,369.07	27.82	D / 1.8	-33.14%	C / 5.0
2014	C-	1,280.90	43.77	C- / 3.4	-5.62%	B- / 7.8
2013	B	1.17	47.67	B / 7.7	25.85%	B / 8.1
2012	C	907.10	0.00	C+ / 5.8	5.90%	C+ / 6.6
2011	A	990.20	39.99	A+ / 9.6	12.23%	B / 8.3
2010	B+	613.60	38.25	B+ / 8.8	32.04%	C / 5.0

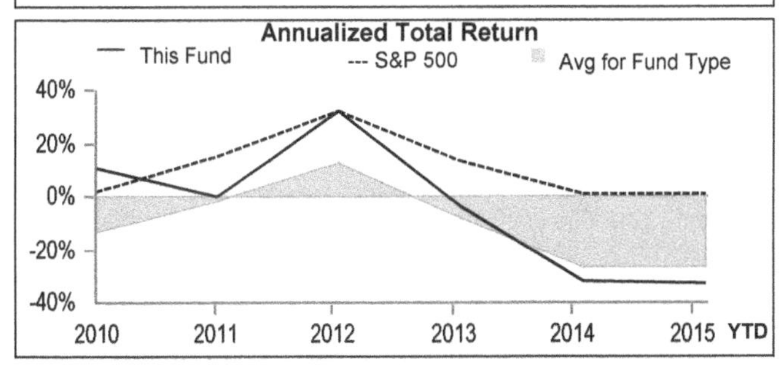

Tortoise MLP Fund Inc (NTG) D Weak

Fund Family: Tortoise Capital Advisors LLC
Fund Type: Growth
Inception Date: July 30, 2010

Major Rating Factors:
Disappointing performance is the major factor driving the D (Weak) TheStreet.com Investment Rating for Tortoise MLP Fund Inc. The fund currently has a performance rating of D (Weak) based on an annualized return of -5.82% over the last three years and a total return of -32.74% year to date 2015. Factored into the performance evaluation is an expense ratio of 2.51% (high).

The fund's risk rating is currently C+ (Fair). It carries a beta of 0.73, meaning the fund's expected move will be 7.3% for every 10% move in the market. Volatility, as measured by both the semi-deviation and a drawdown factor, is considered low. As of December 31, 2015, Tortoise MLP Fund Inc traded at a discount of 6.77% below its net asset value, which is worse than its one-year historical average discount of 9.98%.

H. Kevin Birzer currently receives a manager quality ranking of 11 (0=worst, 99=best). This fund offers only a moderate level of risk but investors looking for strong performance are still waiting.

Data Date	Investment Rating	Net Assets ($Mil)	Price	Performance Rating/Pts	Total Return Y-T-D	Risk Rating/Pts
12-15	D	1,401.93	17.34	D / 2.0	-32.74%	C+ / 5.6
2014	C+	1,308.40	27.92	C / 5.2	8.31%	B / 8.6
2013	C+	1.27	27.33	C+ / 6.3	14.57%	B / 8.2
2012	C-	1,085.82	0.00	C- / 3.0	6.14%	B- / 7.8
2011	B-	1,178.50	25.77	C+ / 5.9	12.48%	B / 8.5

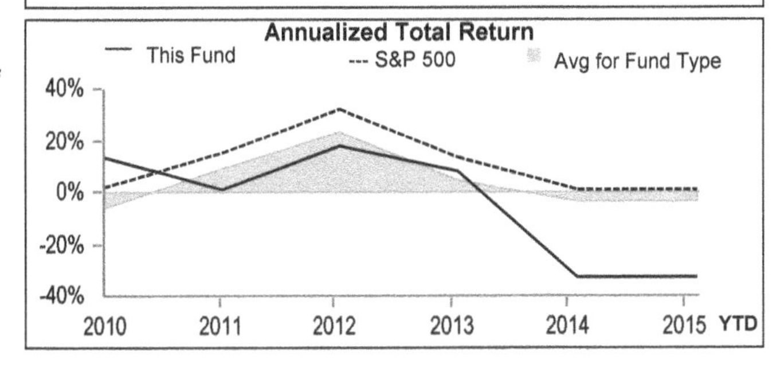

Tortoise Pipeline & Enrgy Fund Inc (TTP) E+ Very Weak

Fund Family: Tortoise Capital Advisors LLC
Fund Type: Energy/Natural Resources
Inception Date: October 27, 2011

Major Rating Factors:
Very poor performance is the major factor driving the E+ (Very Weak) TheStreet.com Investment Rating for Tortoise Pipeline & Enrgy Fund Inc. The fund currently has a performance rating of E+ (Very Weak) based on an annualized return of -12.38% over the last three years and a total return of -50.96% year to date 2015. Factored into the performance evaluation is an expense ratio of 2.11% (high).

The fund's risk rating is currently C- (Fair). It carries a beta of 1.12, meaning it is expected to move 11.2% for every 10% move in the market. Volatility, as measured by both the semi-deviation and a drawdown factor, is considered average. As of December 31, 2015, Tortoise Pipeline & Enrgy Fund Inc traded at a discount of 12.80% below its net asset value, which is better than its one-year historical average discount of 12.28%.

H. Kevin Birzer has been running the fund for 5 years and currently receives a manager quality ranking of 24 (0=worst, 99=best). This fund offers an average level of risk but investors looking for strong performance will be frustrated.

Data Date	Investment Rating	Net Assets ($Mil)	Price	Performance Rating/Pts	Total Return Y-T-D	Risk Rating/Pts
12-15	E+	350.98	14.51	E+ / 0.8	-50.96%	C- / 3.6
2014	B-	326.70	30.74	C+ / 6.4	13.70%	B / 8.1
2013	B+	286.17	28.45	B- / 7.3	19.13%	B / 8.9
2012	B	237.75	0.00	C+ / 6.8	13.89%	B / 8.6

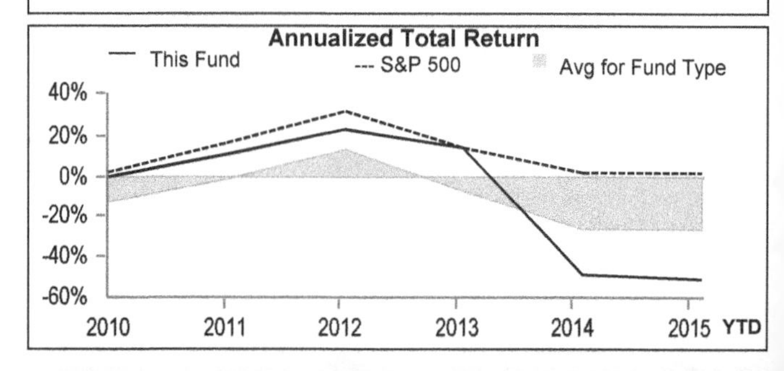

Tortoise Power and Energy Inf Fund (TPZ) D Weak

Fund Family: Tortoise Capital Advisors LLC
Fund Type: Energy/Natural Resources
Inception Date: July 29, 2009

Major Rating Factors:
Disappointing performance is the major factor driving the D (Weak) TheStreet.com Investment Rating for Tortoise Power and Energy Inf Fund. The fund currently has a performance rating of D (Weak) based on an annualized return of -6.94% over the last three years and a total return of -30.30% year to date 2015. Factored into the performance evaluation is an expense ratio of 1.50% (average).

The fund's risk rating is currently C (Fair). It carries a beta of 0.72, meaning the fund's expected move will be 7.2% for every 10% move in the market. Volatility, as measured by both the semi-deviation and a drawdown factor, is considered average. As of December 31, 2015, Tortoise Power and Energy Inf Fund traded at a discount of 13.37% below its net asset value, which is better than its one-year historical average discount of 10.52%.

H. Kevin Birzer currently receives a manager quality ranking of 43 (0=worst, 99=best). This fund offers an average level of risk but investors looking for strong performance will be frustrated.

Data Date	Investment Rating	Net Assets ($Mil)	Price	Performance Rating/Pts	Total Return Y-T-D	Risk Rating/Pts
12-15	D	216.05	16.78	D / 1.6	-30.30%	C / 5.2
2014	C+	197.60	25.76	C / 5.0	12.80%	B / 8.5
2013	C+	195.34	25.69	C+ / 5.6	3.56%	B / 8.6
2012	B	175.89	0.00	C+ / 6.8	9.55%	B / 8.3
2011	C+	182.50	24.99	C / 4.6	7.80%	B / 8.6
2010	A+	0.00	24.49	A / 9.4	29.38%	B / 8.3

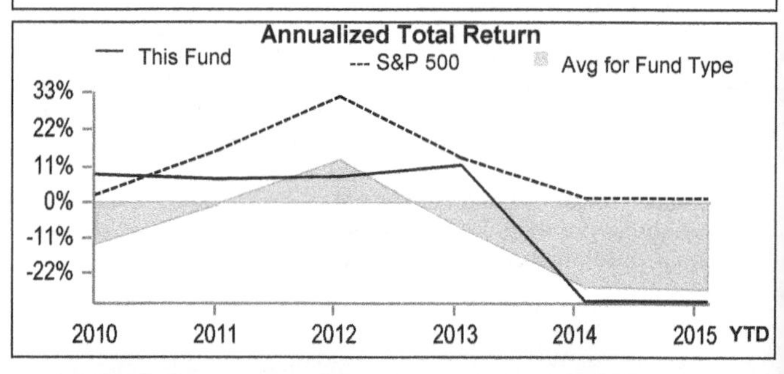

Tri-Continental Corporation (TY) B+ Good

Fund Family: Columbia Management Inv Advisers LL
Fund Type: Income
Inception Date: N/A

Major Rating Factors: Strong performance is the major factor driving the B+ (Good) TheStreet.com Investment Rating for Tri-Continental Corporation. The fund currently has a performance rating of B (Good) based on an annualized return of 10.60% over the last three years and a total return of -2.04% year to date 2015. Factored into the performance evaluation is an expense ratio of 0.49% (very low).

The fund's risk rating is currently B (Good). It carries a beta of 0.87, meaning the fund's expected move will be 8.7% for every 10% move in the market. Volatility, as measured by both the semi-deviation and a drawdown factor, is considered low. As of December 31, 2015, Tri-Continental Corporation traded at a discount of 14.77% below its net asset value, which is worse than its one-year historical average discount of 14.86%.

Brian M. Condon has been running the fund for 6 years and currently receives a manager quality ranking of 58 (0=worst, 99=best). If you desire only a moderate level of risk and strong performance, then this fund is an excellent option.

Data Date	Investment Rating	Net Assets ($Mil)	Price	Performance Rating/Pts	Total Return Y-T-D	Risk Rating/Pts
12-15	B+	1,511.29	20.02	B / 7.6	-2.04%	B / 8.2
2014	A	1,483.80	21.41	B / 7.7	11.98%	B+ / 9.1
2013	A-	1,183.29	19.98	B / 8.2	24.25%	B / 8.3
2012	B-	1,147.55	16.05	B- / 7.0	18.59%	B / 8.1
2011	C+	1,078.20	14.23	C+ / 6.0	6.99%	B / 8.0
2010	C-	946.34	13.76	D+ / 2.9	21.82%	C+ / 6.1

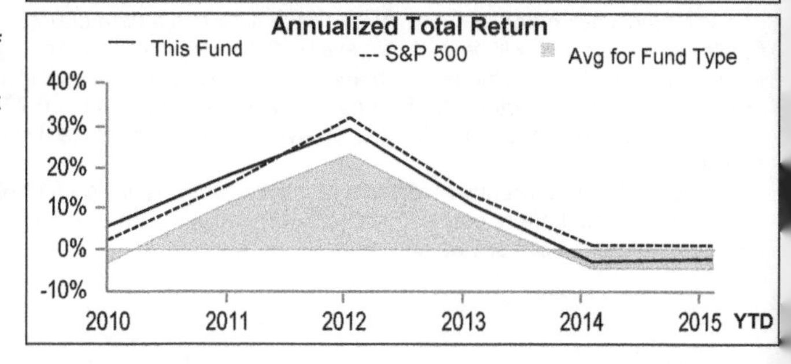

Turkish Investment Fund (TKF) E+ Very Weak

Fund Family: Morgan Stanley Investment Managemen
Fund Type: Foreign
Inception Date: December 5, 1989

Data Date	Investment Rating	Net Assets ($Mil)	Price	Performance Rating/Pts	Total Return Y-T-D	Risk Rating/Pts
12-15	E+	65.47	7.78	D- / 1.4	-26.92%	C- / 3.2
2014	C-	60.50	11.03	B- / 7.2	18.59%	C- / 4.2
2013	D+	104.24	14.67	C- / 4.2	2.47%	C+ / 6.0
2012	B-	112.74	16.64	B+ / 8.7	53.41%	C+ / 5.9
2011	C-	93.40	11.06	C / 5.1	-32.71%	C+ / 6.1
2010	D	97.73	16.50	C- / 3.0	24.92%	C- / 3.8

Major Rating Factors:
Disappointing performance is the major factor driving the E+ (Very Weak) TheStreet.com Investment Rating for Turkish Investment Fund. The fund currently has a performance rating of D- (Weak) based on an annualized return of -11.00% over the last three years and a total return of -26.92% year to date 2015. Factored into the performance evaluation is an expense ratio of 1.31% (average).

The fund's risk rating is currently C- (Fair). It carries a beta of 0.85, meaning the fund's expected move will be 8.5% for every 10% move in the market. Volatility, as measured by both the semi-deviation and a drawdown factor, is considered average. As of December 31, 2015, Turkish Investment Fund traded at a discount of 13.75% below its net asset value, which is better than its one-year historical average discount of 12.33%.

Paul C. Psaila has been running the fund for 19 years and currently receives a manager quality ranking of 11 (0=worst, 99=best). This fund offers an average level of risk but investors looking for strong performance will be frustrated.

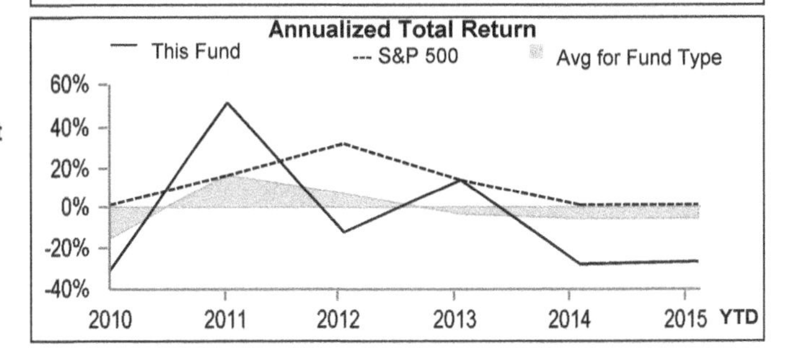

Virtus Global Multi-Sector Income (VGI) C- Fair

Fund Family: Virtus Investment Advisers Inc
Fund Type: Global
Inception Date: February 23, 2012

Data Date	Investment Rating	Net Assets ($Mil)	Price	Performance Rating/Pts	Total Return Y-T-D	Risk Rating/Pts
12-15	C-	204.22	14.13	C- / 4.2	0.40%	C+ / 6.9
2014	D+	217.00	15.85	D / 2.2	2.51%	B / 8.0
2013	D+	212.85	16.92	D / 1.9	-5.81%	B / 8.4

Major Rating Factors: Middle of the road best describes Virtus Global Multi-Sector Income whose TheStreet.com Investment Rating is currently a C- (Fair). The fund currently has a performance rating of C- (Fair) based on an annualized return of -0.06% over the last three years and a total return of 0.40% year to date 2015. Factored into the performance evaluation is an expense ratio of 2.13% (high).

The fund's risk rating is currently C+ (Fair). It carries a beta of 0.51, meaning the fund's expected move will be 5.1% for every 10% move in the market. Volatility, as measured by both the semi-deviation and a drawdown factor, is considered low. As of December 31, 2015, Virtus Global Multi-Sector Income traded at a discount of 13.31% below its net asset value, which is better than its one-year historical average discount of 11.69%.

David L. Albrycht currently receives a manager quality ranking of 84 (0=worst, 99=best). If you desire an average level of risk, then this fund may be an option.

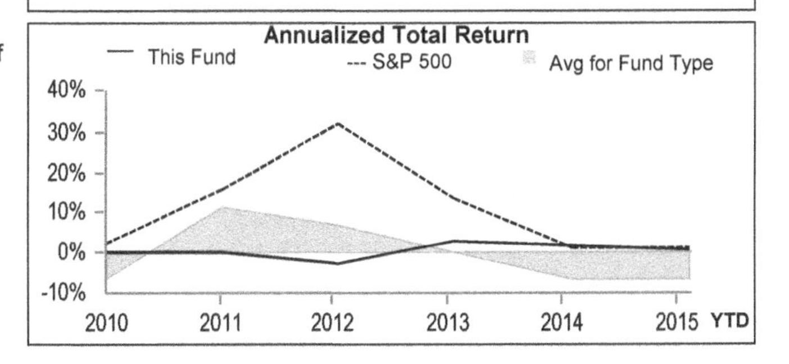

Virtus Total Return (DCA) C+ Fair

Fund Family: Virtus Investment Advisers Inc
Fund Type: Growth and Income
Inception Date: February 23, 2005

Data Date	Investment Rating	Net Assets ($Mil)	Price	Performance Rating/Pts	Total Return Y-T-D	Risk Rating/Pts
12-15	C+	139.63	3.81	C+ / 5.9	-6.71%	B- / 7.5
2014	B+	142.60	4.52	B- / 7.2	22.07%	B / 8.4
2013	B-	122.74	3.93	C+ / 6.3	7.21%	B / 8.3
2012	A+	115.01	3.87	A / 9.4	26.28%	B / 8.2
2011	C+	111.50	3.50	B+ / 8.4	5.01%	C / 5.5
2010	D-	39.18	3.45	D / 2.1	53.64%	C- / 3.2

Major Rating Factors: Middle of the road best describes Virtus Total Return whose TheStreet.com Investment Rating is currently a C+ (Fair). The fund currently has a performance rating of C+ (Fair) based on an annualized return of 6.48% over the last three years and a total return of -6.71% year to date 2015. Factored into the performance evaluation is an expense ratio of 1.93% (above average).

The fund's risk rating is currently B- (Good). It carries a beta of 0.95, meaning that its performance tracks fairly well with that of the overall stock market. Volatility, as measured by both the semi-deviation and a drawdown factor, is considered low. As of December 31, 2015, Virtus Total Return traded at a discount of 14.77% below its net asset value, which is better than its one-year historical average discount of 12.67%.

Connie M. Luecke currently receives a manager quality ranking of 25 (0=worst, 99=best). If you desire an average level of risk, then this fund may be an option.

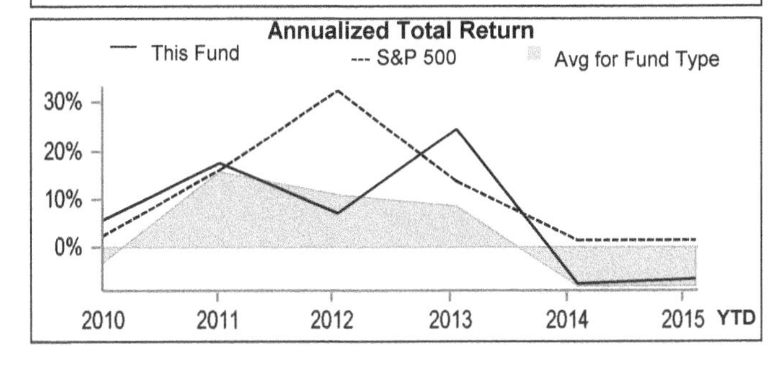

Voya Asia Pacific High Div Eq Inc (IAE) D Weak

Fund Family: Voya Investments LLC
Fund Type: Global
Inception Date: March 30, 2007

Major Rating Factors:
Disappointing performance is the major factor driving the D (Weak) TheStreet.com Investment Rating for Voya Asia Pacific High Div Eq Inc. The fund currently has a performance rating of D (Weak) based on an annualized return of -8.73% over the last three years and a total return of -11.49% year to date 2015. Factored into the performance evaluation is an expense ratio of 1.40% (average).

The fund's risk rating is currently C (Fair). It carries a beta of 0.92, meaning that its performance tracks fairly well with that of the overall stock market. Volatility, as measured by both the semi-deviation and a drawdown factor, is considered average. As of December 31, 2015, Voya Asia Pacific High Div Eq Inc traded at a discount of 11.73% below its net asset value, which is better than its one-year historical average discount of 10.73%.

Willem J.G. van Dommelen has been running the fund for 9 years and currently receives a manager quality ranking of 13 (0=worst, 99=best). This fund offers an average level of risk but investors looking for strong performance will be frustrated.

Data Date	Investment Rating	Net Assets ($Mil)	Price	Performance Rating/Pts	Total Return Y-T-D	Risk Rating/Pts
12-15	D	165.76	9.03	D / 2.1	-11.49%	C / 5.1
2014	D+	185.00	11.43	C- / 3.1	1.14%	C+ / 6.5
2013	D	171.74	12.74	D / 1.6	-14.98%	C+ / 6.2
2012	C-	207.42	15.72	C / 4.7	19.27%	C+ / 6.6
2011	C	179.00	14.19	C+ / 5.9	-18.10%	C+ / 6.7
2010	C-	208.61	19.65	C+ / 6.2	11.12%	C- / 3.5

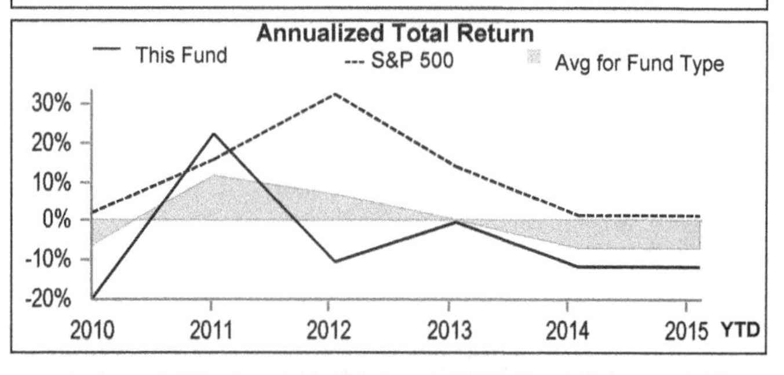

Voya Emerging Markets High Div Eqt (IHD) D- Weak

Fund Family: Voya Investments LLC
Fund Type: Emerging Market
Inception Date: April 26, 2011

Major Rating Factors:
Disappointing performance is the major factor driving the D- (Weak) TheStreet.com Investment Rating for Voya Emerging Markets High Div Eqt. The fund currently has a performance rating of D- (Weak) based on an annualized return of -12.70% over the last three years and a total return of -19.05% year to date 2015. Factored into the performance evaluation is an expense ratio of 1.42% (average).

The fund's risk rating is currently C (Fair). It carries a beta of 1.11, meaning it is expected to move 11.1% for every 10% move in the market. Volatility, as measured by both the semi-deviation and a drawdown factor, is considered average. As of December 31, 2015, Voya Emerging Markets High Div Eqt traded at a discount of 12.22% below its net asset value, which is better than its one-year historical average discount of 11.27%.

Manu Vandenbulck has been running the fund for 5 years and currently receives a manager quality ranking of 32 (0=worst, 99=best). This fund offers an average level of risk but investors looking for strong performance will be frustrated.

Data Date	Investment Rating	Net Assets ($Mil)	Price	Performance Rating/Pts	Total Return Y-T-D	Risk Rating/Pts
12-15	D-	226.15	7.40	D- / 1.4	-19.05%	C / 4.8
2014	D	247.50	10.36	D+ / 2.7	-2.16%	C+ / 6.1
2013	D-	243.16	11.75	E+ / 0.7	-15.42%	C+ / 5.7
2012	B	319.57	14.63	A+ / 9.6	23.70%	C+ / 6.1

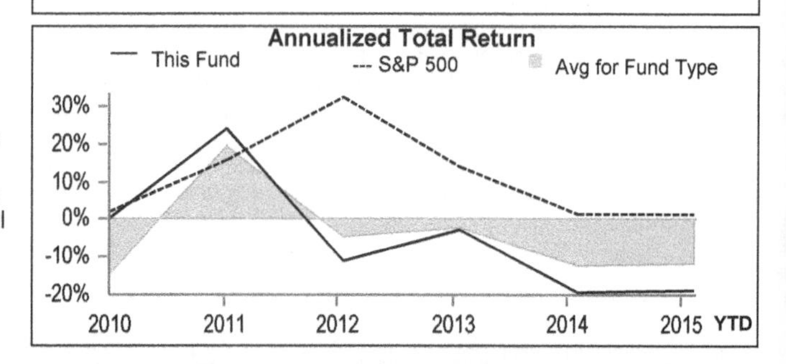

Voya Glbl Eqty Div & Prem Oppty (IGD) C Fair

Fund Family: Voya Investments LLC
Fund Type: Global
Inception Date: March 29, 2005

Major Rating Factors: Middle of the road best describes Voya Glbl Eqty Div & Prem Oppty whose TheStreet.com Investment Rating is currently a C (Fair). The fund currently has a performance rating of C (Fair) based on an annualized return of 2.80% over the last three years and a total return of -5.56% year to date 2015. Factored into the performance evaluation is an expense ratio of 1.20% (average).

The fund's risk rating is currently B- (Good). It carries a beta of 0.82, meaning the fund's expected move will be 8.2% for every 10% move in the market. Volatility, as measured by both the semi-deviation and a drawdown factor, is considered low. As of December 31, 2015, Voya Glbl Eqty Div & Prem Oppty traded at a discount of 13.04% below its net asset value, which is better than its one-year historical average discount of 10.79%.

Nicolas Simar has been running the fund for 11 years and currently receives a manager quality ranking of 61 (0=worst, 99=best). If you desire an average level of risk, then this fund may be an option.

Data Date	Investment Rating	Net Assets ($Mil)	Price	Performance Rating/Pts	Total Return Y-T-D	Risk Rating/Pts
12-15	C	908.60	7.00	C / 5.0	-5.56%	B- / 7.3
2014	C+	982.50	8.32	C / 4.8	4.53%	B / 8.3
2013	C	944.94	8.95	C / 4.7	9.88%	B- / 7.7
2012	D+	976.69	8.67	D+ / 2.6	16.04%	B- / 7.0
2011	D+	947.30	8.64	D+ / 2.9	-9.21%	C+ / 6.9
2010	D	1,117.91	10.85	D+ / 2.3	-0.57%	C / 5.5

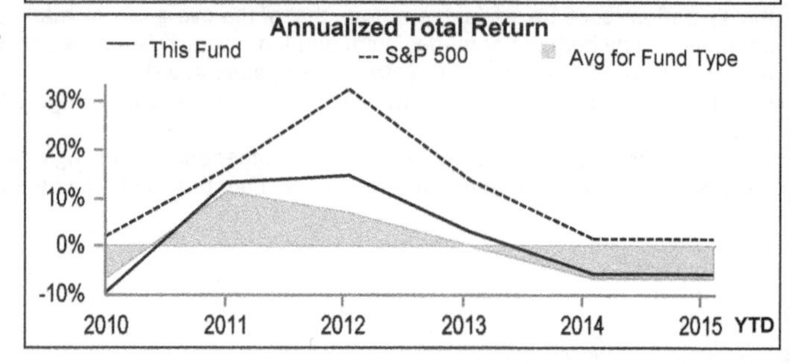

Voya Global Advantage and Prem Opp (IGA) C+ Fair

Fund Family: Voya Investments LLC
Fund Type: Global
Inception Date: October 26, 2005

Major Rating Factors: Middle of the road best describes Voya Global Advantage and Prem Opp whose TheStreet.com Investment Rating is currently a C+ (Fair). The fund currently has a performance rating of C+ (Fair) based on an annualized return of 6.21% over the last three years and a total return of 0.22% year to date 2015. Factored into the performance evaluation is an expense ratio of 0.97% (low).

The fund's risk rating is currently B- (Good). It carries a beta of 0.66, meaning the fund's expected move will be 6.6% for every 10% move in the market. Volatility, as measured by both the semi-deviation and a drawdown factor, is considered low. As of December 31, 2015, Voya Global Advantage and Prem Opp traded at a discount of 8.49% below its net asset value, which is better than its one-year historical average discount of 6.97%.

Pieter J. Schop has been running the fund for 4 years and currently receives a manager quality ranking of 85 (0=worst, 99=best). If you desire an average level of risk, then this fund may be an option.

Data Date	Investment Rating	Net Assets ($Mil)	Price	Performance Rating/Pts	Total Return Y-T-D	Risk Rating/Pts
12-15	C+	237.39	10.45	C+ / 6.1	0.22%	B- / 7.5
2014	C+	240.90	11.48	C+ / 6.0	9.37%	B / 8.2
2013	C	234.14	11.76	C / 4.6	9.12%	B- / 7.9
2012	C-	232.16	11.35	C- / 4.2	21.71%	B- / 7.4
2011	C-	218.20	10.71	C- / 3.3	-9.44%	B- / 7.2
2010	D+	242.43	13.55	C- / 3.5	7.04%	C / 5.1

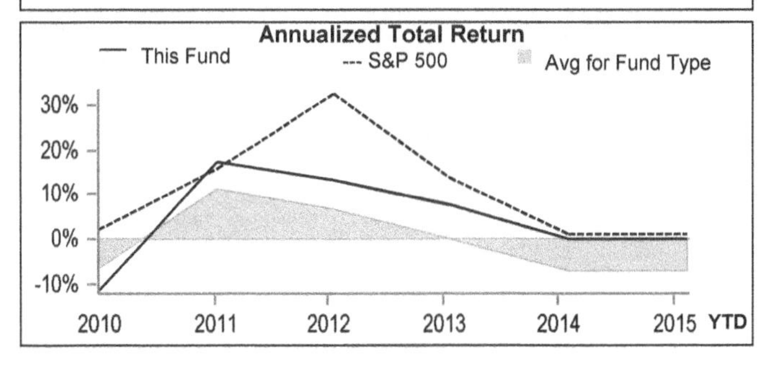

Voya Infrastructure Indus & Mtrls (IDE) C- Fair

Fund Family: Voya Investments LLC
Fund Type: Growth
Inception Date: January 26, 2010

Major Rating Factors: Middle of the road best describes Voya Infrastructure Indus & Mtrls whose TheStreet.com Investment Rating is currently a C- (Fair). The fund currently has a performance rating of C- (Fair) based on an annualized return of -0.70% over the last three years and a total return of -11.78% year to date 2015. Factored into the performance evaluation is an expense ratio of 1.19% (average).

The fund's risk rating is currently C+ (Fair). It carries a beta of 0.97, meaning that its performance tracks fairly well with that of the overall stock market. Volatility, as measured by both the semi-deviation and a drawdown factor, is considered low. As of December 31, 2015, Voya Infrastructure Indus & Mtrls traded at a discount of 14.03% below its net asset value, which is better than its one-year historical average discount of 12.05%.

Martin J. Jansen has been running the fund for 6 years and currently receives a manager quality ranking of 13 (0=worst, 99=best). If you desire an average level of risk, then this fund may be an option.

Data Date	Investment Rating	Net Assets ($Mil)	Price	Performance Rating/Pts	Total Return Y-T-D	Risk Rating/Pts
12-15	C-	340.41	12.26	C- / 3.5	-11.78%	C+ / 6.6
2014	C	364.80	15.66	C / 4.7	1.89%	B- / 7.9
2013	C-	350.32	17.12	C / 5.1	9.34%	C+ / 6.8
2012	C+	394.27	16.39	B / 7.7	16.34%	C+ / 6.6
2011	D-	354.20	15.39	D- / 1.1	-10.15%	C+ / 6.7

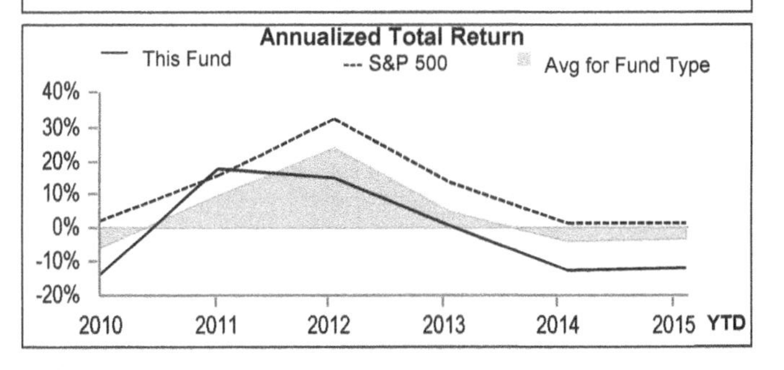

Voya International High Div Eq Inc (IID) D+ Weak

Fund Family: Voya Investments LLC
Fund Type: Global
Inception Date: September 26, 2007

Major Rating Factors:
Disappointing performance is the major factor driving the D+ (Weak) TheStreet.com Investment Rating for Voya International High Div Eq Inc. The fund currently has a performance rating of D+ (Weak) based on an annualized return of -4.59% over the last three years and a total return of -11.11% year to date 2015. Factored into the performance evaluation is an expense ratio of 1.25% (average).

The fund's risk rating is currently C+ (Fair). It carries a beta of 0.90, meaning that its performance tracks fairly well with that of the overall stock market. Volatility, as measured by both the semi-deviation and a drawdown factor, is considered low. As of December 31, 2015, Voya International High Div Eq Inc traded at a discount of 10.17% below its net asset value, which is better than its one-year historical average discount of 6.96%.

Martin J. Jansen has been running the fund for 9 years and currently receives a manager quality ranking of 19 (0=worst, 99=best). This fund offers only a moderate level of risk but investors looking for strong performance are still waiting.

Data Date	Investment Rating	Net Assets ($Mil)	Price	Performance Rating/Pts	Total Return Y-T-D	Risk Rating/Pts
12-15	D+	72.23	6.36	D+ / 2.6	-11.11%	C+ / 6.8
2014	C-	81.50	8.08	C- / 3.5	-3.01%	B- / 7.6
2013	C-	75.45	9.40	C- / 3.8	2.44%	B- / 7.3
2012	D+	82.21	9.64	C- / 3.7	20.14%	C+ / 6.9
2011	D+	73.80	8.86	C- / 3.6	-11.03%	C+ / 6.3
2010	D+	86.22	11.40	C / 4.4	6.43%	C / 4.4

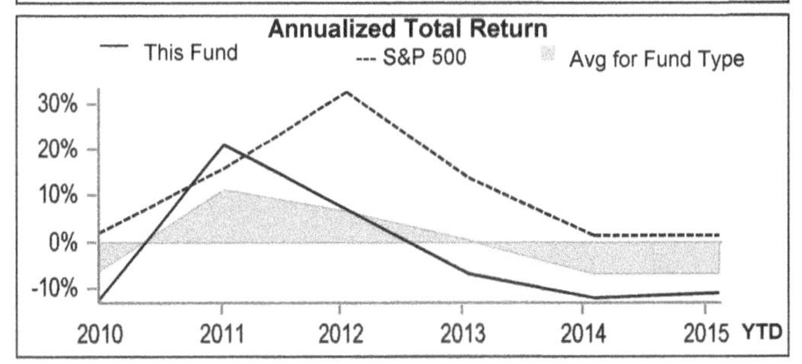

* Denotes ETF Fund

Voya Natural Resources Equity Inc (IRR) D Weak

Fund Family: Voya Investments LLC
Fund Type: Energy/Natural Resources
Inception Date: October 24, 2006

Data Date	Investment Rating	Net Assets ($Mil)	Price	Performance Rating/Pts	Total Return Y-T-D	Risk Rating/Pts
12-15	D	212.33	5.46	D- / 1.5	-25.34%	C / 5.4
2014	D+	278.40	8.29	D / 2.1	-5.89%	C+ / 6.9
2013	D	258.06	9.81	D / 2.0	1.57%	C+ / 6.9
2012	D	298.73	10.34	E+ / 0.9	2.58%	C+ / 6.8
2011	D+	289.10	11.40	D+ / 2.3	-14.36%	B- / 7.1
2010	C+	357.35	15.33	C / 5.0	-3.43%	B- / 7.2

Major Rating Factors:
Disappointing performance is the major factor driving the D (Weak) TheStreet.com Investment Rating for Voya Natural Resources Equity Inc. The fund currently has a performance rating of D- (Weak) based on an annualized return of -10.40% over the last three years and a total return of -25.34% year to date 2015. Factored into the performance evaluation is an expense ratio of 1.19% (average).

The fund's risk rating is currently C (Fair). It carries a beta of 0.81, meaning the fund's expected move will be 8.1% for every 10% move in the market. Volatility, as measured by both the semi-deviation and a drawdown factor, is considered average. As of December 31, 2015, Voya Natural Resources Equity Inc traded at a discount of 14.15% below its net asset value, which is better than its one-year historical average discount of 9.11%.

Jody I. Hrazanek has been running the fund for 10 years and currently receives a manager quality ranking of 23 (0=worst, 99=best). This fund offers an average level of risk but investors looking for strong performance will be frustrated.

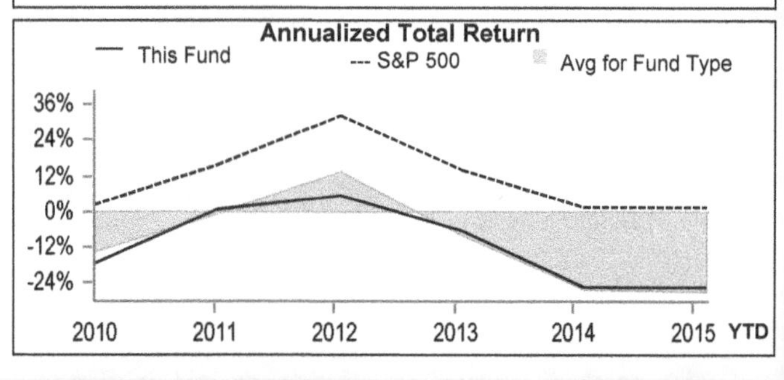

Voya Prime Rate Trust (PPR) C Fair

Fund Family: Voya Investments LLC
Fund Type: Loan Participation
Inception Date: May 2, 1988

Data Date	Investment Rating	Net Assets ($Mil)	Price	Performance Rating/Pts	Total Return Y-T-D	Risk Rating/Pts
12-15	C	876.41	5.06	C- / 4.2	1.51%	B- / 7.2
2014	C	879.20	5.31	C- / 4.2	-2.39%	B / 8.0
2013	C	887.05	5.82	C / 4.5	-1.95%	B / 8.1
2012	C+	851.28	6.21	C+ / 6.3	27.65%	B- / 8.0
2011	C+	822.30	5.10	C+ / 5.9	-3.65%	B- / 7.9
2010	C-	830.79	5.69	C+ / 5.8	14.73%	C / 4.4

Major Rating Factors: Middle of the road best describes Voya Prime Rate Trust whose TheStreet.com Investment Rating is currently a C (Fair). The fund currently has a performance rating of C- (Fair) based on an annualized return of -0.60% over the last three years and a total return of 1.51% year to date 2015. Factored into the performance evaluation is an expense ratio of 2.09% (high).

The fund's risk rating is currently B- (Good). It carries a beta of -115.16, meaning the fund's expected move will be -1151.6% for every 10% move in the market. Volatility, as measured by both the semi-deviation and a drawdown factor, is considered low. As of December 31, 2015, Voya Prime Rate Trust traded at a discount of 7.66% below its net asset value, which is worse than its one-year historical average discount of 9.02%.

Jeffrey Dutra currently receives a manager quality ranking of 47 (0=worst, 99=best). If you desire an average level of risk, then this fund may be an option.

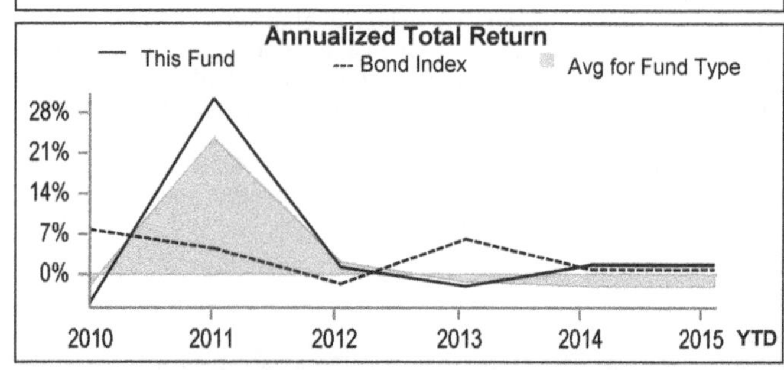

Wells Fargo Global Div Oppty (EOD) C- Fair

Fund Family: Wells Fargo Funds Management LLC
Fund Type: Global
Inception Date: March 28, 2007

Data Date	Investment Rating	Net Assets ($Mil)	Price	Performance Rating/Pts	Total Return Y-T-D	Risk Rating/Pts
12-15	C-	419.26	5.92	C- / 3.8	-11.39%	B- / 7.3
2014	C+	414.10	7.49	C / 5.1	13.73%	B / 8.2
2013	D+	412.92	7.25	C- / 3.2	3.43%	B- / 7.4
2012	D+	405.46	7.57	D+ / 2.3	13.62%	B- / 7.3
2011	D+	413.70	7.59	D+ / 2.4	-7.79%	B- / 7.3
2010	D-	561.05	9.55	D- / 1.1	2.46%	C / 5.2

Major Rating Factors: Middle of the road best describes Wells Fargo Global Div Oppty whose TheStreet.com Investment Rating is currently a C- (Fair). The fund currently has a performance rating of C- (Fair) based on an annualized return of 1.22% over the last three years and a total return of -11.39% year to date 2015. Factored into the performance evaluation is an expense ratio of 1.07% (low).

The fund's risk rating is currently B- (Good). It carries a beta of 0.66, meaning the fund's expected move will be 6.6% for every 10% move in the market. Volatility, as measured by both the semi-deviation and a drawdown factor, is considered low. As of December 31, 2015, Wells Fargo Global Div Oppty traded at a discount of 13.20% below its net asset value, which is better than its one-year historical average discount of 11.80%.

Kandarp Acharya has been running the fund for 3 years and currently receives a manager quality ranking of 55 (0=worst, 99=best). If you desire an average level of risk, then this fund may be an option.

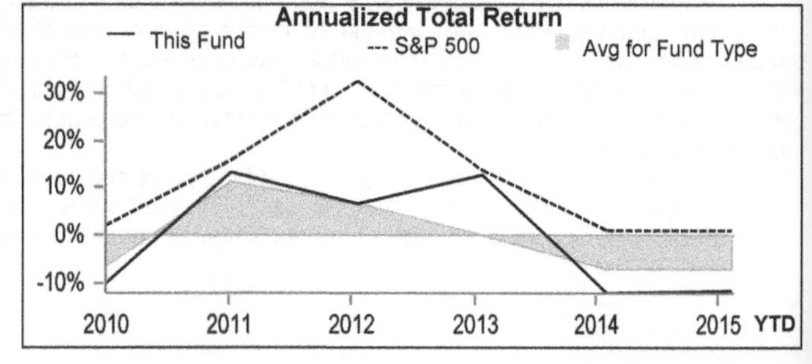

Wells Fargo Income Oppty (EAD) C- Fair

Fund Family: Wells Fargo Funds Management LLC
Fund Type: Corporate - High Yield
Inception Date: February 26, 2003

Major Rating Factors: Middle of the road best describes Wells Fargo Income Oppty whose TheStreet.com Investment Rating is currently a C- (Fair). The fund currently has a performance rating of C- (Fair) based on an annualized return of -1.62% over the last three years and a total return of -7.05% year to date 2015. Factored into the performance evaluation is an expense ratio of 0.96% (low).

The fund's risk rating is currently C+ (Fair). It carries a beta of 1.24, meaning it is expected to move 12.4% for every 10% move in the market. Volatility, as measured by both the semi-deviation and a drawdown factor, is considered low. As of December 31, 2015, Wells Fargo Income Oppty traded at a discount of 10.13% below its net asset value, which is worse than its one-year historical average discount of 10.83%.

Niklas Nordenfelt currently receives a manager quality ranking of 44 (0=worst, 99=best). If you desire an average level of risk, then this fund may be an option.

Data Date	Investment Rating	Net Assets ($Mil)	Price	Performance Rating/Pts	Total Return Y-T-D	Risk Rating/Pts
12-15	C-	692.17	7.45	C- / 3.4	-7.05%	C+ / 6.9
2014	C-	696.70	8.89	C- / 3.8	4.96%	B / 8.0
2013	C+	722.56	9.18	C / 5.5	-1.94%	B / 8.2
2012	C-	683.81	10.07	C / 4.6	11.48%	B- / 7.3
2011	B	667.50	10.18	A- / 9.0	16.45%	B- / 7.1
2010	C-	676.14	9.63	C+ / 6.5	12.95%	C- / 3.4

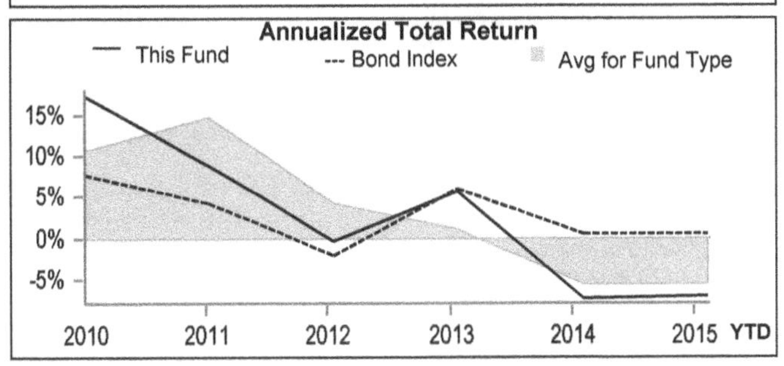

Wells Fargo Multi-Sector Inc (ERC) D+ Weak

Fund Family: Wells Fargo Funds Management LLC
Fund Type: Global
Inception Date: June 25, 2003

Major Rating Factors:
Disappointing performance is the major factor driving the D+ (Weak) TheStreet.com Investment Rating for Wells Fargo Multi-Sector Inc. The fund currently has a performance rating of D+ (Weak) based on an annualized return of -3.75% over the last three years and a total return of -9.69% year to date 2015. Factored into the performance evaluation is an expense ratio of 1.21% (average).

The fund's risk rating is currently C+ (Fair). It carries a beta of 0.92, meaning that its performance tracks fairly well with that of the overall stock market. Volatility, as measured by both the semi-deviation and a drawdown factor, is considered low. As of December 31, 2015, Wells Fargo Multi-Sector Inc traded at a discount of 14.24% below its net asset value, which is worse than its one-year historical average discount of 14.33%.

Christopher Y. Kauffman currently receives a manager quality ranking of 73 (0=worst, 99=best). This fund offers only a moderate level of risk but investors looking for strong performance are still waiting.

Data Date	Investment Rating	Net Assets ($Mil)	Price	Performance Rating/Pts	Total Return Y-T-D	Risk Rating/Pts
12-15	D+	677.00	11.32	D+ / 2.9	-9.69%	C+ / 6.5
2014	C	671.10	13.63	C- / 4.0	4.88%	B- / 7.9
2013	C	689.57	14.06	C- / 4.0	-6.66%	B / 8.2
2012	C+	715.37	16.17	C+ / 5.7	19.18%	B / 8.7
2011	B	668.70	14.78	B- / 7.0	5.38%	B / 8.6
2010	B-	677.42	15.32	B / 7.7	17.47%	C / 4.9

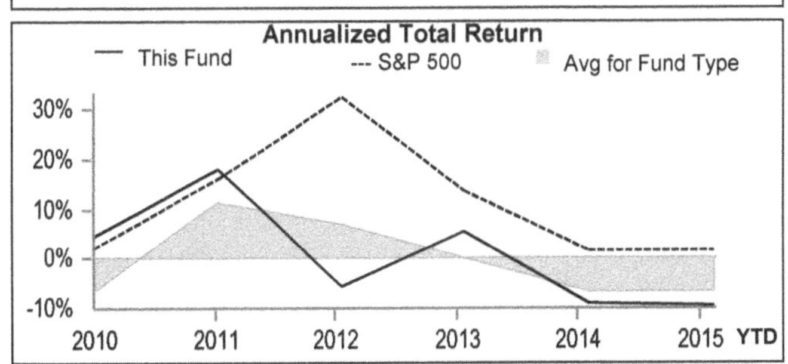

Wells Fargo Utilities&High Inc (ERH) C+ Fair

Fund Family: Wells Fargo Funds Management LLC
Fund Type: Utilities
Inception Date: April 28, 2004

Major Rating Factors: Middle of the road best describes Wells Fargo Utilities&High Inc whose TheStreet.com Investment Rating is currently a C+ (Fair). The fund currently has a performance rating of C+ (Fair) based on an annualized return of 6.97% over the last three years and a total return of -7.57% year to date 2015. Factored into the performance evaluation is an expense ratio of 1.19% (average).

The fund's risk rating is currently B- (Good). It carries a beta of 0.37, meaning the fund's expected move will be 3.7% for every 10% move in the market. Volatility, as measured by both the semi-deviation and a drawdown factor, is considered low. As of December 31, 2015, Wells Fargo Utilities&High Inc traded at a discount of 6.82% below its net asset value, which is worse than its one-year historical average discount of 7.15%.

Timothy P. O'Brien has been running the fund for 12 years and currently receives a manager quality ranking of 85 (0=worst, 99=best). If you desire an average level of risk, then this fund may be an option.

Data Date	Investment Rating	Net Assets ($Mil)	Price	Performance Rating/Pts	Total Return Y-T-D	Risk Rating/Pts
12-15	C+	114.85	11.20	C+ / 6.5	-7.57%	B- / 7.5
2014	B	122.50	12.80	C+ / 6.5	15.96%	B / 8.8
2013	C+	113.00	11.79	C+ / 5.8	11.83%	B / 8.4
2012	D	108.33	11.18	D- / 1.3	5.97%	C+ / 6.5
2011	D+	107.60	11.15	C- / 3.5	4.17%	C+ / 6.2
2010	D-	103.25	11.59	E+ / 0.6	-14.38%	C / 4.9

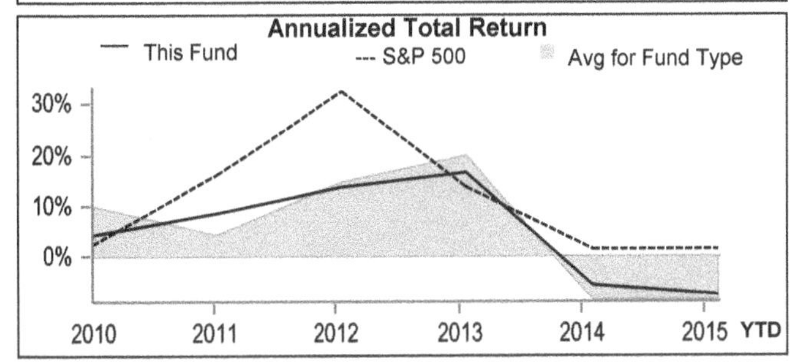

Western Asset Emerging Market Debt (ESD) D+ Weak

Fund Family: Legg Mason Partners Fund Advisor LL
Fund Type: Emerging Market
Inception Date: December 1, 2003

Data Date	Investment Rating	Net Assets ($Mil)	Price	Performance Rating/Pts	Total Return Y-T-D	Risk Rating/Pts
12-15	D+	559.16	13.73	D+ / 2.5	-4.18%	C+ / 5.8
2014	D+	597.00	15.76	D+ / 2.7	-0.03%	C+ / 6.8
2013	D+	610.25	17.20	C- / 3.2	-17.05%	B- / 7.2
2012	B+	653.87	21.80	B- / 7.5	24.80%	B / 8.6
2011	B	632.10	18.90	B / 7.9	11.46%	B- / 7.9
2010	B-	600.30	18.31	B- / 7.3	13.69%	C / 5.1

Major Rating Factors:
Disappointing performance is the major factor driving the D+ (Weak) TheStreet.com Investment Rating for Western Asset Emerging Market Debt. The fund currently has a performance rating of D+ (Weak) based on an annualized return of -7.58% over the last three years and a total return of -4.18% year to date 2015. Factored into the performance evaluation is an expense ratio of 1.25% (average).

The fund's risk rating is currently C+ (Fair). It carries a beta of 1.08, meaning that its performance tracks fairly well with that of the overall stock market. Volatility, as measured by both the semi-deviation and a drawdown factor, is considered low. As of December 31, 2015, Western Asset Emerging Market Debt traded at a discount of 16.13% below its net asset value, which is better than its one-year historical average discount of 14.65%.

S. Kenneth Leech has been running the fund for 3 years and currently receives a manager quality ranking of 47 (0=worst, 99=best). This fund offers only a moderate level of risk but investors looking for strong performance are still waiting.

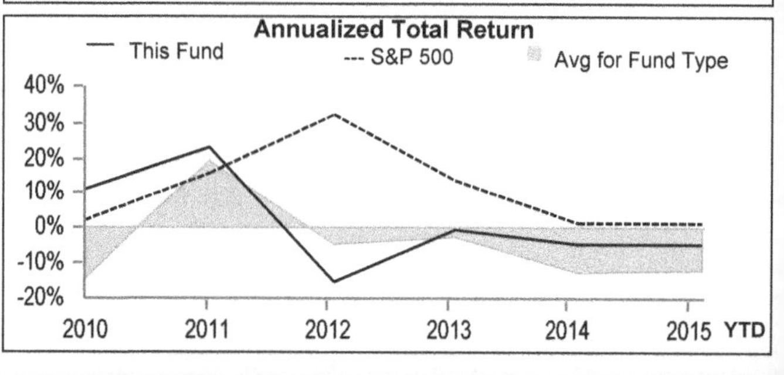

Western Asset Emerging Mkts Inc (EMD) D+ Weak

Fund Family: Legg Mason Partners Fund Advisor LL
Fund Type: Emerging Market
Inception Date: June 18, 1993

Data Date	Investment Rating	Net Assets ($Mil)	Price	Performance Rating/Pts	Total Return Y-T-D	Risk Rating/Pts
12-15	D+	374.86	9.73	D+ / 2.6	-1.62%	C+ / 5.6
2014	D	392.20	10.95	D+ / 2.5	0.22%	C+ / 6.2
2013	D+	429.25	11.84	D+ / 2.8	-19.14%	B- / 7.3
2012	C+	423.29	15.32	C+ / 6.1	22.25%	B / 8.1
2011	B	416.80	13.41	B / 7.9	11.89%	B / 8.0
2010	B	392.18	13.06	B- / 7.4	14.02%	C / 5.5

Major Rating Factors:
Disappointing performance is the major factor driving the D+ (Weak) TheStreet.com Investment Rating for Western Asset Emerging Mkts Inc. The fund currently has a performance rating of D+ (Weak) based on an annualized return of -7.22% over the last three years and a total return of -1.62% year to date 2015. Factored into the performance evaluation is an expense ratio of 1.33% (average).

The fund's risk rating is currently C+ (Fair). It carries a beta of 0.94, meaning that its performance tracks fairly well with that of the overall stock market. Volatility, as measured by both the semi-deviation and a drawdown factor, is considered low. As of December 31, 2015, Western Asset Emerging Mkts Inc traded at a discount of 16.62% below its net asset value, which is better than its one-year historical average discount of 15.74%.

S. Kenneth Leech has been running the fund for 3 years and currently receives a manager quality ranking of 48 (0=worst, 99=best). This fund offers only a moderate level of risk but investors looking for strong performance are still waiting.

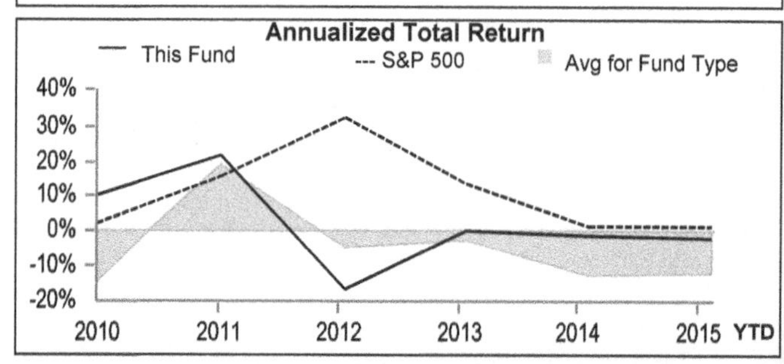

Western Asset Global Corp Def Oppt (GDO) C- Fair

Fund Family: Legg Mason Partners Fund Advisor LL
Fund Type: Global
Inception Date: November 23, 2009

Data Date	Investment Rating	Net Assets ($Mil)	Price	Performance Rating/Pts	Total Return Y-T-D	Risk Rating/Pts
12-15	C-	307.63	15.80	C- / 3.6	-5.86%	B- / 7.3
2014	C+	307.60	17.78	C / 4.6	6.40%	B / 8.5
2013	C+	322.96	18.07	C / 5.3	-5.39%	B / 8.6
2012	B-	291.50	20.75	C+ / 5.6	22.16%	B / 8.9
2011	C+	281.90	18.00	C / 4.8	10.69%	B / 8.5
2010	C-	0.00	17.93	D / 2.1	-2.44%	B- / 7.7

Major Rating Factors: Middle of the road best describes Western Asset Global Corp Def Oppt whose TheStreet.com Investment Rating is currently a C- (Fair). The fund currently has a performance rating of C- (Fair) based on an annualized return of -1.27% over the last three years and a total return of -5.86% year to date 2015. Factored into the performance evaluation is an expense ratio of 1.28% (average).

The fund's risk rating is currently B- (Good). It carries a beta of 0.55, meaning the fund's expected move will be 5.5% for every 10% move in the market. Volatility, as measured by both the semi-deviation and a drawdown factor, is considered low. As of December 31, 2015, Western Asset Global Corp Def Oppt traded at a discount of 12.03% below its net asset value, which is better than its one-year historical average discount of 11.38%.

Michael C. Buchanan currently receives a manager quality ranking of 74 (0=worst, 99=best). If you desire an average level of risk, then this fund may be an option.

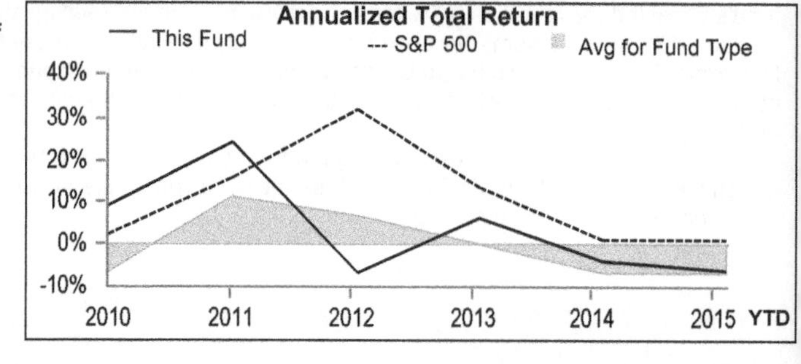

Western Asset Global High Income (EHI) D+ Weak

Fund Family: Legg Mason Partners Fund Advisor LL
Fund Type: Global
Inception Date: July 29, 2003

Data Date	Investment Rating	Net Assets ($Mil)	Price	Performance Rating/Pts	Total Return Y-T-D	Risk Rating/Pts
12-15	D+	382.74	8.72	D+ / 2.6	-11.48%	C+ / 6.3
2014	C-	404.40	11.10	C- / 3.5	-0.71%	B- / 7.8
2013	C+	425.79	12.24	C / 5.3	-3.65%	B / 8.3
2012	B-	395.09	13.78	B- / 7.2	19.75%	B- / 7.7
2011	B-	380.80	12.60	B / 8.2	7.03%	B- / 7.0
2010	B	369.75	12.88	B+ / 8.6	27.13%	C / 4.3

Major Rating Factors:
Disappointing performance is the major factor driving the D+ (Weak) TheStreet.com Investment Rating for Western Asset Global High Income. The fund currently has a performance rating of D+ (Weak) based on an annualized return of -5.22% over the last three years and a total return of -11.48% year to date 2015. Factored into the performance evaluation is an expense ratio of 1.48% (average).

The fund's risk rating is currently C+ (Fair). It carries a beta of 0.85, meaning the fund's expected move will be 8.5% for every 10% move in the market. Volatility, as measured by both the semi-deviation and a drawdown factor, is considered low. As of December 31, 2015, Western Asset Global High Income traded at a discount of 14.68% below its net asset value, which is better than its one-year historical average discount of 12.78%.

S. Kenneth Leech currently receives a manager quality ranking of 56 (0=worst, 99=best). This fund offers only a moderate level of risk but investors looking for strong performance are still waiting.

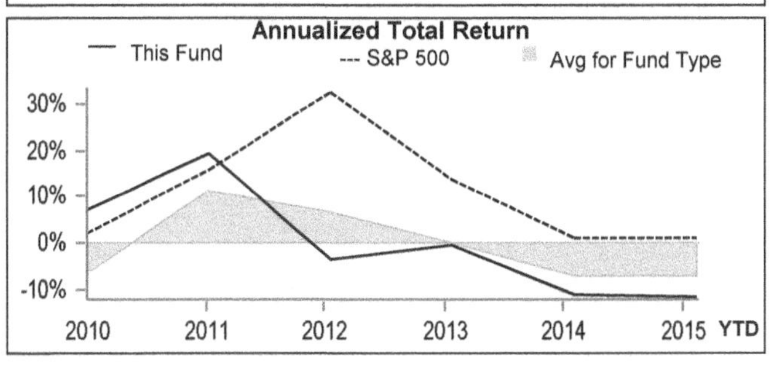

Western Asset Global Partners Inc (GDF) D Weak

Fund Family: Legg Mason Partners Fund Advisor LL
Fund Type: Global
Inception Date: October 21, 1993

Data Date	Investment Rating	Net Assets ($Mil)	Price	Performance Rating/Pts	Total Return Y-T-D	Risk Rating/Pts
12-15	D	156.75	7.73	D / 2.2	-12.30%	C+ / 6.0
2014	D+	179.50	9.80	D+ / 2.4	-0.82%	B- / 7.1
2013	C-	177.38	10.83	C- / 4.2	-8.41%	B- / 7.6
2012	C	188.08	12.65	C / 4.7	11.39%	B- / 7.5
2011	B+	172.30	13.12	A+ / 9.6	21.72%	B- / 7.1
2010	C+	178.84	11.87	B / 8.2	13.69%	C- / 4.1

Major Rating Factors:
Disappointing performance is the major factor driving the D (Weak) TheStreet.com Investment Rating for Western Asset Global Partners Inc. The fund currently has a performance rating of D (Weak) based on an annualized return of -7.76% over the last three years and a total return of -12.30% year to date 2015. Factored into the performance evaluation is an expense ratio of 1.65% (above average).

The fund's risk rating is currently C+ (Fair). It carries a beta of 0.94, meaning that its performance tracks fairly well with that of the overall stock market. Volatility, as measured by both the semi-deviation and a drawdown factor, is considered low. As of December 31, 2015, Western Asset Global Partners Inc traded at a discount of 16.43% below its net asset value, which is better than its one-year historical average discount of 13.74%.

Paul Shuttleworth currently receives a manager quality ranking of 40 (0=worst, 99=best). This fund offers only a moderate level of risk but investors looking for strong performance are still waiting.

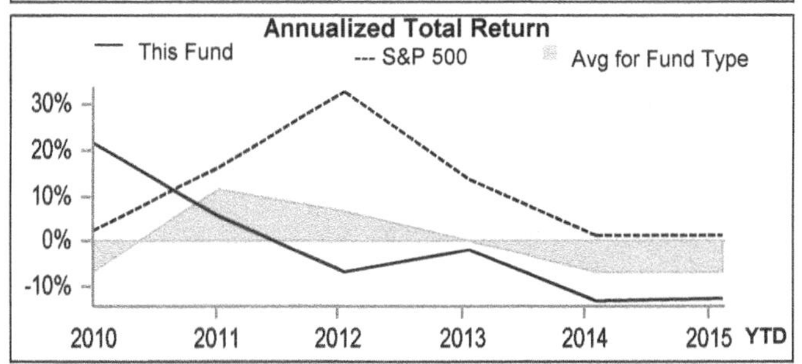

Western Asset High Inc Fd II (HIX) D+ Weak

Fund Family: Legg Mason Partners Fund Advisor LL
Fund Type: Global
Inception Date: May 22, 1998

Data Date	Investment Rating	Net Assets ($Mil)	Price	Performance Rating/Pts	Total Return Y-T-D	Risk Rating/Pts
12-15	D+	738.42	6.31	D+ / 2.5	-14.78%	C+ / 6.7
2014	C-	779.50	8.31	C- / 3.5	0.56%	B- / 7.8
2013	C+	822.40	9.02	C+ / 5.9	1.09%	B / 8.4
2012	C	756.45	9.66	C / 4.8	13.92%	B- / 7.9
2011	B	709.60	9.64	A / 9.3	16.22%	C+ / 6.6
2010	C+	751.12	9.37	B / 7.8	15.24%	C- / 3.9

Major Rating Factors:
Disappointing performance is the major factor driving the D+ (Weak) TheStreet.com Investment Rating for Western Asset High Inc Fd II. The fund currently has a performance rating of D+ (Weak) based on an annualized return of -4.99% over the last three years and a total return of -14.78% year to date 2015. Factored into the performance evaluation is an expense ratio of 1.45% (average).

The fund's risk rating is currently C+ (Fair). It carries a beta of 0.74, meaning the fund's expected move will be 7.4% for every 10% move in the market. Volatility, as measured by both the semi-deviation and a drawdown factor, is considered low. As of December 31, 2015, Western Asset High Inc Fd II traded at a discount of 9.08% below its net asset value, which is better than its one-year historical average discount of 7.81%.

S. Kenneth Leech currently receives a manager quality ranking of 58 (0=worst, 99=best). This fund offers only a moderate level of risk but investors looking for strong performance are still waiting.

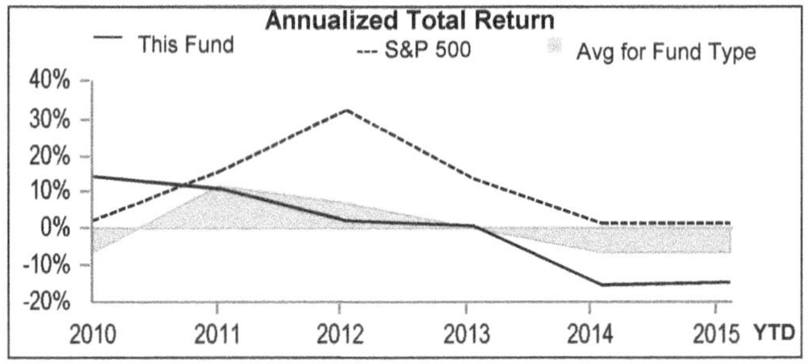

Western Asset High Income Opp Inc. (HIO) C- Fair

Fund Family: Legg Mason Partners Fund Advisor LL
Fund Type: Corporate - High Yield
Inception Date: October 21, 1993

Major Rating Factors: Middle of the road best describes Western Asset High Income Opp Inc. whose TheStreet.com Investment Rating is currently a C- (Fair). The fund currently has a performance rating of C- (Fair) based on an annualized return of -3.53% over the last three years and a total return of -5.49% year to date 2015. Factored into the performance evaluation is an expense ratio of 0.89% (low).

The fund's risk rating is currently C+ (Fair). It carries a beta of 1.13, meaning it is expected to move 11.3% for every 10% move in the market. Volatility, as measured by both the semi-deviation and a drawdown factor, is considered low. As of December 31, 2015, Western Asset High Income Opp Inc. traded at a discount of 9.28% below its net asset value, which is worse than its one-year historical average discount of 12.68%.

Michael C. Buchanan has been running the fund for 10 years and currently receives a manager quality ranking of 33 (0=worst, 99=best). If you desire an average level of risk, then this fund may be an option.

Data Date	Investment Rating	Net Assets ($Mil)	Price	Performance Rating/Pts	Total Return Y-T-D	Risk Rating/Pts
12-15	C-	457.00	4.69	C- / 3.1	-5.49%	C+ / 6.7
2014	C-	528.00	5.37	C- / 3.0	-3.58%	B- / 7.9
2013	C+	532.00	5.93	C / 5.4	-1.43%	B / 8.6
2012	C+	473.00	6.44	C+ / 5.7	17.36%	B- / 7.6
2011	B	443.00	6.17	B / 7.8	10.69%	B- / 7.4
2010	C	457.00	6.08	B / 7.6	12.07%	C- / 3.7

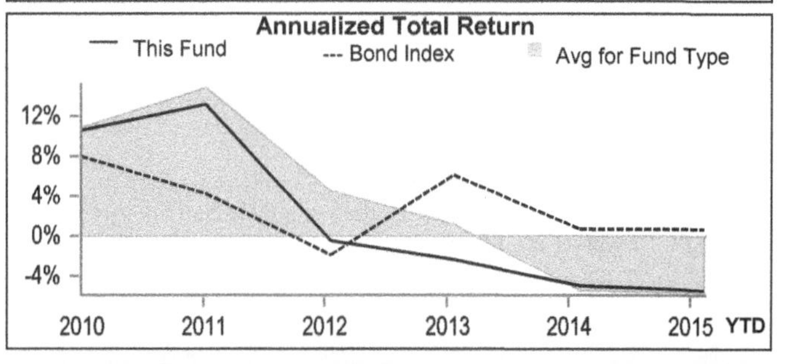

Western Asset High Yld Def Opp (HYI) C- Fair

Fund Family: Legg Mason Partners Fund Advisor LL
Fund Type: Corporate - High Yield
Inception Date: October 27, 2010

Major Rating Factors: Middle of the road best describes Western Asset High Yld Def Opp whose TheStreet.com Investment Rating is currently a C- (Fair). The fund currently has a performance rating of C- (Fair) based on an annualized return of -1.37% over the last three years and a total return of -2.30% year to date 2015. Factored into the performance evaluation is an expense ratio of 0.88% (low).

The fund's risk rating is currently C+ (Fair). It carries a beta of 1.27, meaning it is expected to move 12.7% for every 10% move in the market. Volatility, as measured by both the semi-deviation and a drawdown factor, is considered low. As of December 31, 2015, Western Asset High Yld Def Opp traded at a discount of 8.68% below its net asset value, which is worse than its one-year historical average discount of 11.98%.

Michael C. Buchanan has been running the fund for 6 years and currently receives a manager quality ranking of 46 (0=worst, 99=best). If you desire an average level of risk, then this fund may be an option.

Data Date	Investment Rating	Net Assets ($Mil)	Price	Performance Rating/Pts	Total Return Y-T-D	Risk Rating/Pts
12-15	C-	386.00	14.10	C- / 3.7	-2.30%	C+ / 6.8
2014	C-	429.00	15.77	C- / 3.7	-3.43%	B- / 7.9
2013	C+	433.00	17.71	C / 5.4	2.55%	B / 8.2
2012	C	417.00	18.33	C / 4.8	16.05%	B- / 7.9
2011	D+	384.80	16.56	D+ / 2.3	2.24%	B- / 7.8

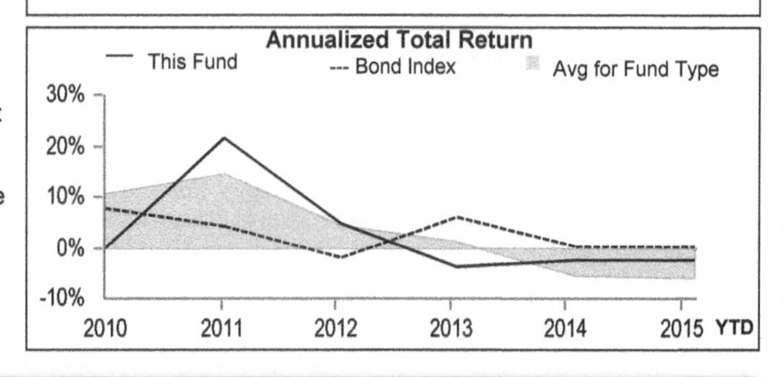

Western Asset Income Fund (PAI) C Fair

Fund Family: Western Asset Management Company
Fund Type: General - Investment Grade
Inception Date: March 15, 1973

Major Rating Factors: Middle of the road best describes Western Asset Income Fund whose TheStreet.com Investment Rating is currently a C (Fair). The fund currently has a performance rating of C (Fair) based on an annualized return of 0.28% over the last three years and a total return of 2.13% year to date 2015. Factored into the performance evaluation is an expense ratio of 0.71% (very low).

The fund's risk rating is currently B- (Good). It carries a beta of 1.79, meaning it is expected to move 17.9% for every 10% move in the market. Volatility, as measured by both the semi-deviation and a drawdown factor, is considered low. As of December 31, 2015, Western Asset Income Fund traded at a discount of 5.92% below its net asset value, which is worse than its one-year historical average discount of 8.03%.

Michael C. Buchanan has been running the fund for 6 years and currently receives a manager quality ranking of 54 (0=worst, 99=best). If you desire an average level of risk, then this fund may be an option.

Data Date	Investment Rating	Net Assets ($Mil)	Price	Performance Rating/Pts	Total Return Y-T-D	Risk Rating/Pts
12-15	C	140.44	13.02	C / 4.7	2.13%	B- / 7.5
2014	C	140.90	13.45	C- / 4.1	8.17%	B- / 7.8
2013	C	134.46	13.18	C / 4.4	-8.54%	B / 8.0
2012	C+	135.15	14.82	C / 4.4	17.35%	B+ / 9.0
2011	B-	129.90	13.81	C+ / 6.1	13.17%	B / 8.3
2010	C+	127.08	12.89	C+ / 6.3	12.19%	C+ / 6.4

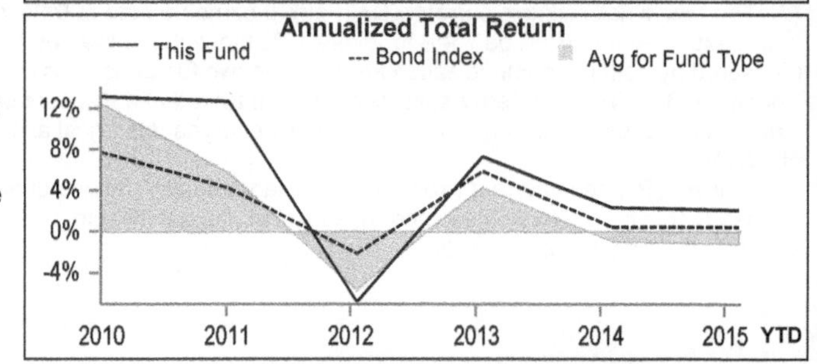

Western Asset Intermediate Muni (SBI) B+ Good

Fund Family: Legg Mason Partners Fund Advisor LL
Fund Type: Municipal - National
Inception Date: February 27, 1992

Major Rating Factors: Strong performance is the major factor driving the B+ (Good) TheStreet.com Investment Rating for Western Asset Intermediate Muni. The fund currently has a performance rating of B- (Good) based on an annualized return of 2.53% over the last three years and a total return of 11.02% year to date 2015. Factored into the performance evaluation is an expense ratio of 0.94% (low).

The fund's risk rating is currently B- (Good). It carries a beta of 1.36, meaning it is expected to move 13.6% for every 10% move in the market. Volatility, as measured by both the semi-deviation and a drawdown factor, is considered low. As of December 31, 2015, Western Asset Intermediate Muni traded at a discount of 2.95% below its net asset value, which is worse than its one-year historical average discount of 5.42%.

Dennis J. McNamara has been running the fund for 4 years and currently receives a manager quality ranking of 62 (0=worst, 99=best). If you desire only a moderate level of risk and strong performance, then this fund is an excellent option.

Data Date	Investment Rating	Net Assets ($Mil)	Price	Performance Rating/Pts	Total Return Y-T-D	Risk Rating/Pts
12-15	B+	0.15	10.21	B- / 7.4	11.02%	B- / 7.9
2014	C+	144.60	9.76	C+ / 5.7	12.11%	B / 8.3
2013	C	0.15	9.05	C- / 4.0	-12.42%	B / 8.5
2012	B+	145.00	10.58	B- / 7.5	14.89%	B+ / 9.1
2011	B	141.60	9.80	C+ / 6.8	11.08%	B+ / 9.2
2010	B-	137.00	9.43	C+ / 6.9	10.70%	B- / 7.2

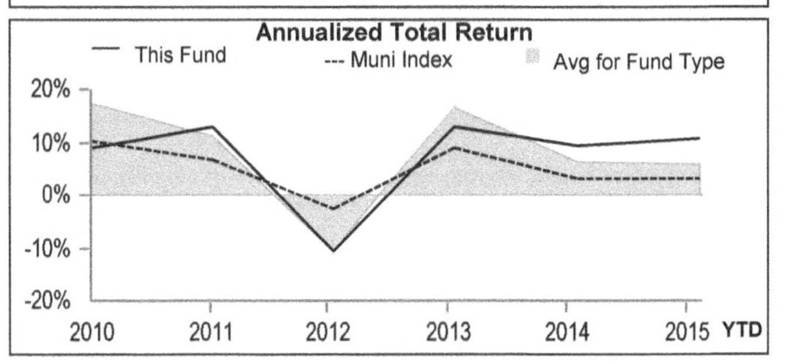

Western Asset Managed High Income (MHY) C- Fair

Fund Family: Legg Mason Partners Fund Advisor LL
Fund Type: Corporate - High Yield
Inception Date: March 18, 1993

Major Rating Factors: Middle of the road best describes Western Asset Managed High Income whose TheStreet.com Investment Rating is currently a C- (Fair). The fund currently has a performance rating of C- (Fair) based on an annualized return of -3.07% over the last three years and a total return of -4.42% year to date 2015. Factored into the performance evaluation is an expense ratio of 0.92% (low).

The fund's risk rating is currently C+ (Fair). It carries a beta of 1.05, meaning that its performance tracks fairly well with that of the overall stock market. Volatility, as measured by both the semi-deviation and a drawdown factor, is considered low. As of December 31, 2015, Western Asset Managed High Income traded at a discount of 9.42% below its net asset value, which is worse than its one-year historical average discount of 12.84%.

Paul Shuttleworth currently receives a manager quality ranking of 34 (0=worst, 99=best). If you desire an average level of risk, then this fund may be an option.

Data Date	Investment Rating	Net Assets ($Mil)	Price	Performance Rating/Pts	Total Return Y-T-D	Risk Rating/Pts
12-15	C-	277.00	4.52	C- / 3.2	-4.42%	C+ / 6.5
2014	C-	287.80	5.11	D+ / 2.8	-2.45%	B- / 7.7
2013	C	289.00	5.66	C / 4.4	-2.47%	B / 8.3
2012	C	283.00	6.17	C / 4.7	13.71%	B- / 7.6
2011	B-	267.50	6.04	B- / 7.2	7.68%	B / 8.0
2010	B	267.47	6.12	B / 7.9	16.81%	C / 5.1

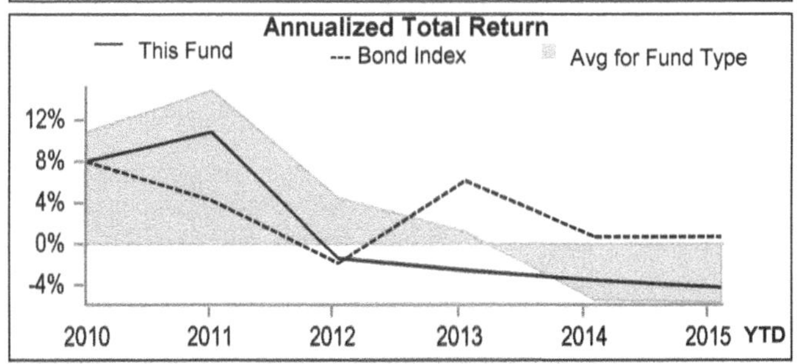

Western Asset Managed Municipals (MMU) B Good

Fund Family: Legg Mason Partners Fund Advisor LL
Fund Type: Municipal - National
Inception Date: June 18, 1992

Major Rating Factors: Strong performance is the major factor driving the B (Good) TheStreet.com Investment Rating for Western Asset Managed Municipals. The fund currently has a performance rating of B (Good) based on an annualized return of 3.70% over the last three years and a total return of 10.30% year to date 2015. Factored into the performance evaluation is an expense ratio of 0.99% (low).

The fund's risk rating is currently C+ (Fair). It carries a beta of 2.13, meaning it is expected to move 21.3% for every 10% move in the market. Volatility, as measured by both the semi-deviation and a drawdown factor, is considered low. As of December 31, 2015, Western Asset Managed Municipals traded at a discount of 1.12% below its net asset value, which is worse than its one-year historical average discount of 2.40%.

Joseph P. Deane has been running the fund for 24 years and currently receives a manager quality ranking of 57 (0=worst, 99=best). If you desire only a moderate level of risk and strong performance, then this fund is an excellent option.

Data Date	Investment Rating	Net Assets ($Mil)	Price	Performance Rating/Pts	Total Return Y-T-D	Risk Rating/Pts
12-15	B	616.79	14.18	B / 7.9	10.30%	C+ / 6.8
2014	B-	600.10	13.59	B- / 7.3	18.70%	B- / 7.4
2013	C	603.94	12.21	C / 5.0	-14.42%	B- / 7.6
2012	A+	594.96	14.37	B+ / 8.9	18.73%	B / 8.7
2011	A+	559.40	13.41	A- / 9.2	20.53%	B+ / 9.0
2010	B+	539.18	12.07	B- / 7.3	5.24%	C+ / 6.3

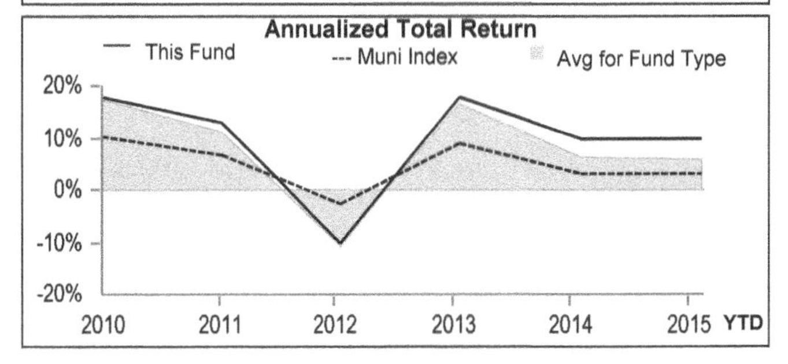

Western Asset Mtge Defined Oppty (DMO) B+ Good

Fund Family: Legg Mason Partners Fund Advisor LL
Fund Type: Mortgage
Inception Date: February 24, 2010

Major Rating Factors: Strong performance is the major factor driving the B+ (Good) TheStreet.com Investment Rating for Western Asset Mtge Defined Oppty. The fund currently has a performance rating of B+ (Good) based on an annualized return of 12.84% over the last three years and a total return of 13.42% year to date 2015. Factored into the performance evaluation is an expense ratio of 2.36% (high).

The fund's risk rating is currently C+ (Fair). It carries a beta of 1.08, meaning that its performance tracks fairly well with that of the overall stock market. Volatility, as measured by both the semi-deviation and a drawdown factor, is considered low. As of December 31, 2015, Western Asset Mtge Defined Oppty traded at a premium of 3.43% above its net asset value, which is worse than its one-year historical average discount of 1.51%.

S. Kenneth Leech currently receives a manager quality ranking of 95 (0=worst, 99=best). If you desire only a moderate level of risk and strong performance, then this fund is an excellent option.

Data Date	Investment Rating	Net Assets ($Mil)	Price	Perfor-mance Rating/Pts	Total Return Y-T-D	Risk Rating/Pts
12-15	B+	257.62	23.55	B+ / 8.9	13.42%	C+ / 6.7
2014	A	269.90	23.84	A- / 9.1	20.52%	B- / 7.8
2013	B-	249.37	23.18	B- / 7.1	5.98%	B- / 7.9
2012	A+	197.29	24.21	A+ / 9.8	46.13%	B / 8.5
2011	C-	197.30	19.61	D / 2.1	-0.65%	B / 8.7

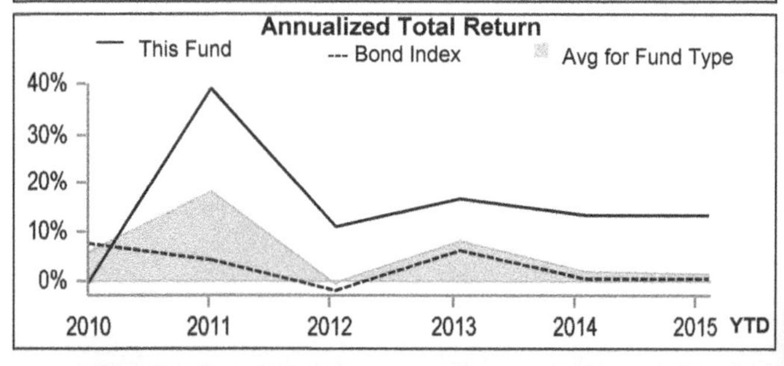

Western Asset Municipal Defined Op (MTT) B Good

Fund Family: Legg Mason Partners Fund Advisor LL
Fund Type: Municipal - National
Inception Date: March 27, 2009

Major Rating Factors: Strong performance is the major factor driving the B (Good) TheStreet.com Investment Rating for Western Asset Municipal Defined Op. The fund currently has a performance rating of B (Good) based on an annualized return of 5.01% over the last three years and a total return of 8.02% year to date 2015. Factored into the performance evaluation is an expense ratio of 0.70% (very low).

The fund's risk rating is currently C+ (Fair). It carries a beta of 1.38, meaning it is expected to move 13.8% for every 10% move in the market. Volatility, as measured by both the semi-deviation and a drawdown factor, is considered low. As of December 31, 2015, Western Asset Municipal Defined Op traded at a premium of 7.45% above its net asset value, which is worse than its one-year historical average premium of 3.22%.

Robert E. Amodeo has been running the fund for 7 years and currently receives a manager quality ranking of 80 (0=worst, 99=best). If you desire only a moderate level of risk and strong performance, then this fund is an excellent option.

Data Date	Investment Rating	Net Assets ($Mil)	Price	Perfor-mance Rating/Pts	Total Return Y-T-D	Risk Rating/Pts
12-15	B	276.49	24.24	B / 8.1	8.02%	C+ / 6.7
2014	C+	276.30	23.62	B- / 7.3	15.51%	C+ / 6.3
2013	C+	276.96	21.31	C+ / 5.8	-6.83%	B / 8.3
2012	B	272.25	23.06	B- / 7.0	14.02%	B / 8.7
2011	A-	260.30	22.06	B+ / 8.5	15.30%	B+ / 9.0
2010	C-	256.21	19.89	D- / 1.1	0.51%	B / 8.4

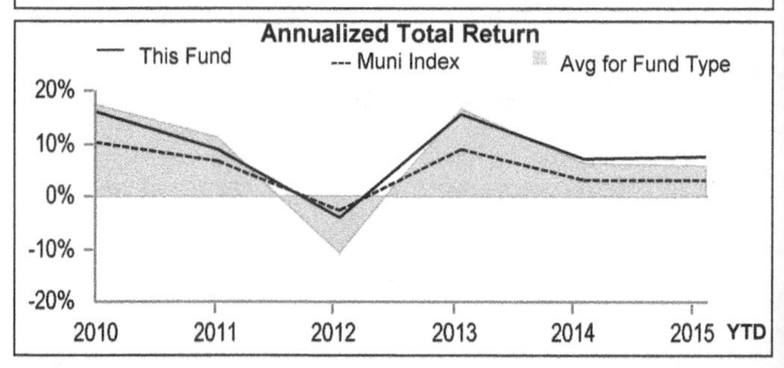

Western Asset Municipal High Inc (MHF) B Good

Fund Family: Legg Mason Partners Fund Advisor LL
Fund Type: Municipal - High Yield
Inception Date: November 17, 1988

Major Rating Factors: Strong performance is the major factor driving the B (Good) TheStreet.com Investment Rating for Western Asset Municipal High Inc. The fund currently has a performance rating of B- (Good) based on an annualized return of 3.00% over the last three years and a total return of 6.76% year to date 2015. Factored into the performance evaluation is an expense ratio of 0.71% (very low).

The fund's risk rating is currently B- (Good). It carries a beta of 1.66, meaning it is expected to move 16.6% for every 10% move in the market. Volatility, as measured by both the semi-deviation and a drawdown factor, is considered low. As of December 31, 2015, Western Asset Municipal High Inc traded at a discount of 2.50% below its net asset value, which is worse than its one-year historical average discount of 6.51%.

Ellen S. Cammer currently receives a manager quality ranking of 61 (0=worst, 99=best). If you desire only a moderate level of risk and strong performance, then this fund is an excellent option.

Data Date	Investment Rating	Net Assets ($Mil)	Price	Perfor-mance Rating/Pts	Total Return Y-T-D	Risk Rating/Pts
12-15	B	175.00	7.80	B- / 7.3	6.76%	B- / 7.4
2014	B-	174.70	7.70	C+ / 6.9	19.85%	B- / 7.6
2013	C-	177.00	6.73	C- / 3.3	-13.70%	B- / 7.8
2012	C+	164.00	7.92	C / 5.4	10.45%	B / 8.7
2011	B+	166.00	7.83	B- / 7.5	16.07%	B / 8.9
2010	C+	162.00	7.23	C / 4.9	3.19%	B- / 7.3

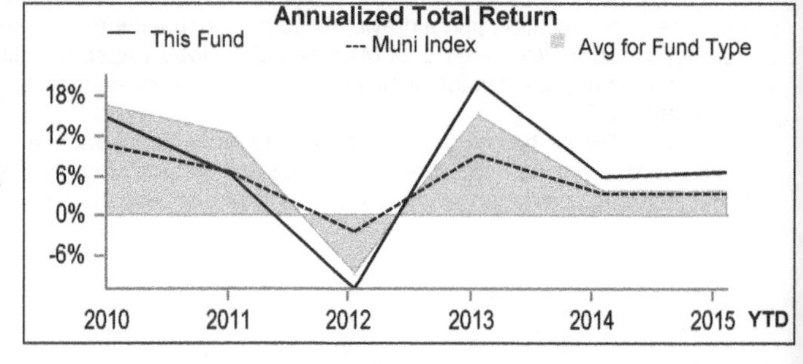

Western Asset Municipal Partners (MNP) B- Good

Fund Family: Legg Mason Partners Fund Advisor LL
Fund Type: Municipal - National
Inception Date: January 22, 1993

Major Rating Factors: Strong performance is the major factor driving the B- (Good) TheStreet.com Investment Rating for Western Asset Municipal Partners. The fund currently has a performance rating of B- (Good) based on an annualized return of 0.95% over the last three years and a total return of 11.23% year to date 2015. Factored into the performance evaluation is an expense ratio of 1.20% (average).

The fund's risk rating is currently B- (Good). It carries a beta of 2.41, meaning it is expected to move 24.1% for every 10% move in the market. Volatility, as measured by both the semi-deviation and a drawdown factor, is considered low. As of December 31, 2015, Western Asset Municipal Partners traded at a discount of 7.69% below its net asset value, which is worse than its one-year historical average discount of 8.72%.

Robert E. Amodeo currently receives a manager quality ranking of 30 (0=worst, 99=best). If you desire only a moderate level of risk and strong performance, then this fund is an excellent option.

Data Date	Investment Rating	Net Assets ($Mil)	Price	Performance Rating/Pts	Total Return Y-T-D	Risk Rating/Pts
12-15	B-	159.11	15.61	B- / 7.0	11.23%	B- / 7.5
2014	C+	158.60	14.83	C+ / 6.0	15.47%	B- / 7.6
2013	C	85.00	13.75	C / 4.8	-19.63%	B- / 7.9
2012	A+	159.77	17.22	A- / 9.2	19.70%	B / 8.7
2011	A+	152.10	15.36	A / 9.4	25.33%	B / 8.9
2010	C+	143.85	13.26	C+ / 5.7	5.45%	C+ / 6.6

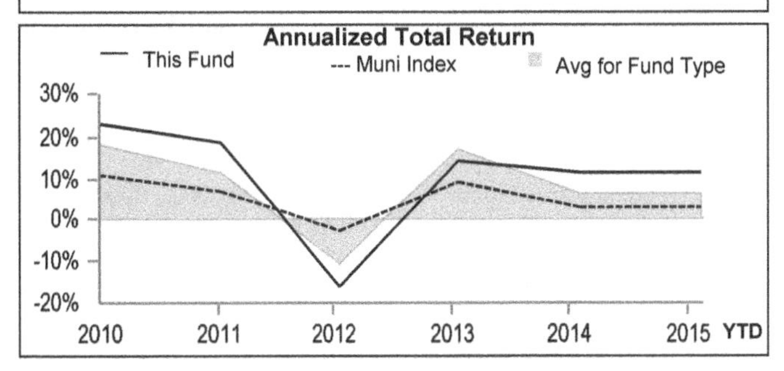

Western Asset Premier Bond Fund (WEA) C- Fair

Fund Family: Western Asset Management Company
Fund Type: General - Investment Grade
Inception Date: March 25, 2002

Major Rating Factors: Middle of the road best describes Western Asset Premier Bond Fund whose TheStreet.com Investment Rating is currently a C- (Fair). The fund currently has a performance rating of C- (Fair) based on an annualized return of -1.31% over the last three years and a total return of -4.12% year to date 2015. Factored into the performance evaluation is an expense ratio of 1.47% (average).

The fund's risk rating is currently C+ (Fair). It carries a beta of 3.02, meaning it is expected to move 30.2% for every 10% move in the market. Volatility, as measured by both the semi-deviation and a drawdown factor, is considered low. As of December 31, 2015, Western Asset Premier Bond Fund traded at a discount of 7.10% below its net asset value, which is better than its one-year historical average discount of 6.19%.

Michael C. Buchanan currently receives a manager quality ranking of 33 (0=worst, 99=best). If you desire an average level of risk, then this fund may be an option.

Data Date	Investment Rating	Net Assets ($Mil)	Price	Performance Rating/Pts	Total Return Y-T-D	Risk Rating/Pts
12-15	C-	176.39	12.16	C- / 3.6	-4.12%	C+ / 6.8
2014	C-	180.20	13.89	C- / 3.5	3.27%	B- / 7.0
2013	C	175.04	14.53	C+ / 5.7	-2.03%	B- / 7.5
2012	B-	163.49	15.54	C+ / 6.8	9.83%	B / 8.3
2011	B+	154.20	15.95	B+ / 8.8	22.43%	B- / 7.8
2010	B-	154.24	14.13	B / 7.7	17.57%	C / 4.9

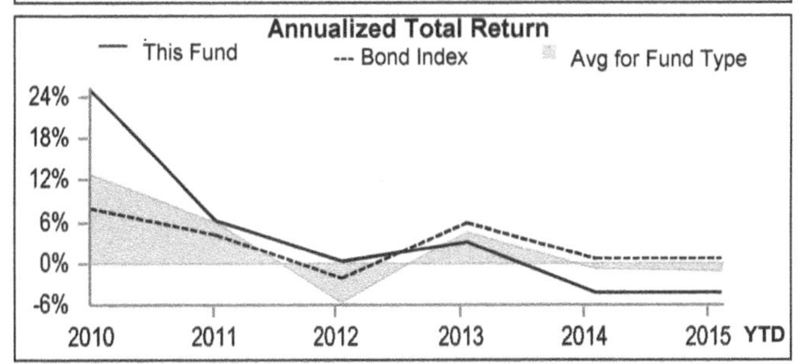

Western Asset Var Rt Strat Fd (GFY) C Fair

Fund Family: Legg Mason Partners Fund Advisor LL
Fund Type: Global
Inception Date: October 26, 2004

Major Rating Factors: Middle of the road best describes Western Asset Var Rt Strat Fd whose TheStreet.com Investment Rating is currently a C (Fair). The fund currently has a performance rating of C (Fair) based on an annualized return of 0.85% over the last three years and a total return of 0.65% year to date 2015. Factored into the performance evaluation is an expense ratio of 1.12% (low).

The fund's risk rating is currently B- (Good). It carries a beta of 0.16, meaning the fund's expected move will be 1.6% for every 10% move in the market. Volatility, as measured by both the semi-deviation and a drawdown factor, is considered low. As of December 31, 2015, Western Asset Var Rt Strat Fd traded at a discount of 8.76% below its net asset value, which is worse than its one-year historical average discount of 9.28%.

Dennis J. McNamara has been running the fund for 6 years and currently receives a manager quality ranking of 80 (0=worst, 99=best). If you desire an average level of risk, then this fund may be an option.

Data Date	Investment Rating	Net Assets ($Mil)	Price	Performance Rating/Pts	Total Return Y-T-D	Risk Rating/Pts
12-15	C	116.96	15.83	C / 4.9	0.65%	B- / 7.7
2014	C+	125.70	16.65	C / 4.9	1.11%	B / 8.7
2013	C+	124.76	17.52	C / 5.1	1.47%	B / 8.8
2012	B-	122.94	17.76	B- / 7.5	30.70%	B- / 7.5
2011	C	111.90	14.85	C- / 4.0	-5.40%	B / 8.3
2010	B+	113.54	16.99	B / 7.9	25.48%	C / 5.5

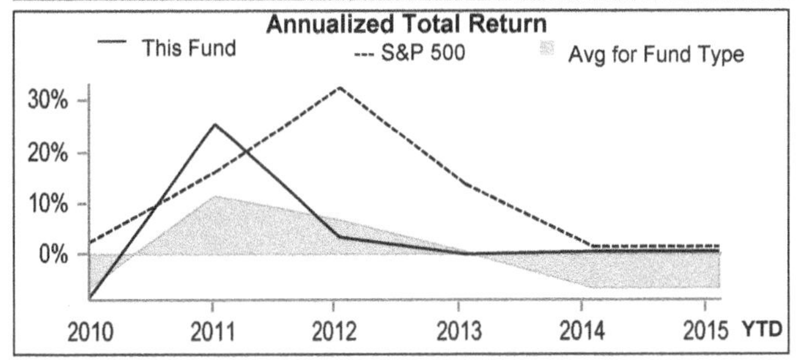

Western Asset Worldwide Inc Fd (SBW) D+ Weak

Fund Family: Legg Mason Partners Fund Advisor LL
Fund Type: Emerging Market
Inception Date: December 31, 1993

Major Rating Factors:
Disappointing performance is the major factor driving the D+ (Weak) TheStreet.com Investment Rating for Western Asset Worldwide Inc Fd. The fund currently has a performance rating of D+ (Weak) based on an annualized return of -5.80% over the last three years and a total return of -2.42% year to date 2015. Factored into the performance evaluation is an expense ratio of 1.38% (average).

The fund's risk rating is currently C+ (Fair). It carries a beta of 0.94, meaning that its performance tracks fairly well with that of the overall stock market. Volatility, as measured by both the semi-deviation and a drawdown factor, is considered low. As of December 31, 2015, Western Asset Worldwide Inc Fd traded at a discount of 14.94% below its net asset value, which is worse than its one-year historical average discount of 15.30%.

Chia-Liang Lian currently receives a manager quality ranking of 57 (0=worst, 99=best). This fund offers only a moderate level of risk but investors looking for strong performance are still waiting.

Data Date	Investment Rating	Net Assets ($Mil)	Price	Perfor-mance Rating/Pts	Total Return Y-T-D	Risk Rating/Pts
12-15	D+	171.19	10.08	D+ / 2.8	-2.42%	C+ / 6.1
2014	D+	182.40	11.41	D+ / 2.6	1.95%	B- / 7.0
2013	D+	186.33	12.18	C- / 3.0	-14.76%	B- / 7.5
2012	C+	200.54	15.12	C+ / 5.8	20.75%	B / 8.2
2011	B	194.10	13.78	B / 7.7	10.70%	B / 8.2
2010	B	184.25	13.30	B- / 7.2	11.85%	C+ / 5.7

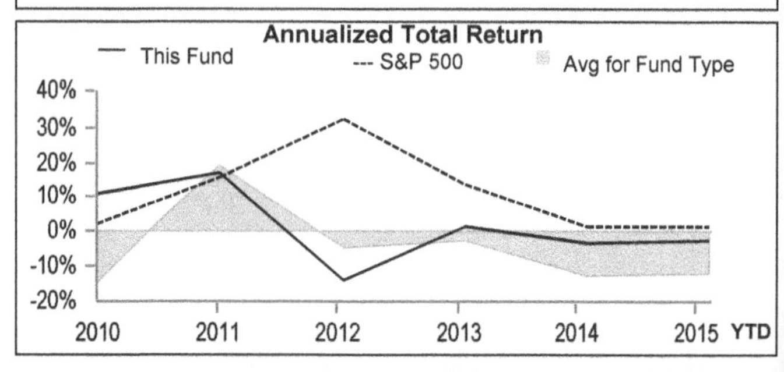

Western Asset/Claymore Inf-Link O& (WIW) C- Fair

Fund Family: Guggenheim Funds Investment Advisor
Fund Type: US Government/Agency
Inception Date: February 25, 2004

Major Rating Factors:
Disappointing performance is the major factor driving the C- (Fair) TheStreet.com Investment Rating for Western Asset/Claymore Inf-Link O&. The fund currently has a performance rating of D+ (Weak) based on an annualized return of -4.85% over the last three years and a total return of -6.72% year to date 2015. Factored into the performance evaluation is an expense ratio of 0.95% (low).

The fund's risk rating is currently B- (Good). It carries a beta of 0.39, meaning the fund's expected move will be 3.9% for every 10% move in the market. Volatility, as measured by both the semi-deviation and a drawdown factor, is considered low. As of December 31, 2015, Western Asset/Claymore Inf-Link O& traded at a discount of 15.38% below its net asset value, which is better than its one-year historical average discount of 14.20%.

Michael C. Buchanan currently receives a manager quality ranking of 26 (0=worst, 99=best). This fund offers only a moderate level of risk but investors looking for strong performance are still waiting.

Data Date	Investment Rating	Net Assets ($Mil)	Price	Perfor-mance Rating/Pts	Total Return Y-T-D	Risk Rating/Pts
12-15	C-	792.66	10.29	D+ / 2.7	-6.72%	B- / 7.4
2014	C-	820.40	11.30	D+ / 2.6	3.32%	B / 8.3
2013	C-	836.65	11.27	D+ / 2.3	-11.46%	B / 8.6
2012	C	896.97	13.20	D+ / 2.9	7.11%	B+ / 9.6
2011	C+	872.60	12.61	C / 4.5	7.67%	B+ / 9.6
2010	B-	813.12	12.51	C+ / 5.7	7.99%	B- / 7.0

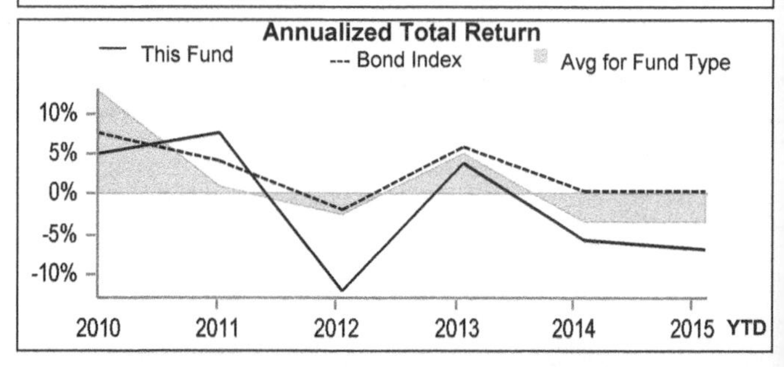

Western Asset/Claymore Inf-Link S& (WIA) C- Fair

Fund Family: Western Asset Management Company
Fund Type: US Government/Agency
Inception Date: September 26, 2003

Major Rating Factors:
Disappointing performance is the major factor driving the C- (Fair) TheStreet.com Investment Rating for Western Asset/Claymore Inf-Link S&. The fund currently has a performance rating of D+ (Weak) based on an annualized return of -3.87% over the last three years and a total return of -6.67% year to date 2015. Factored into the performance evaluation is an expense ratio of 0.89% (low).

The fund's risk rating is currently B- (Good). It carries a beta of 0.38, meaning the fund's expected move will be 3.8% for every 10% move in the market. Volatility, as measured by both the semi-deviation and a drawdown factor, is considered low. As of December 31, 2015, Western Asset/Claymore Inf-Link S& traded at a discount of 15.24% below its net asset value, which is better than its one-year historical average discount of 14.13%.

Chia-Liang Lian currently receives a manager quality ranking of 31 (0=worst, 99=best). This fund offers only a moderate level of risk but investors looking for strong performance are still waiting.

Data Date	Investment Rating	Net Assets ($Mil)	Price	Perfor-mance Rating/Pts	Total Return Y-T-D	Risk Rating/Pts
12-15	C-	385.13	10.57	D+ / 2.9	-6.67%	B- / 7.4
2014	C-	389.30	11.60	C- / 3.0	5.00%	B / 8.3
2013	C-	393.48	11.42	D / 2.2	-10.06%	B / 8.5
2012	C-	423.07	13.11	D+ / 2.5	6.30%	B+ / 9.5
2011	C+	412.20	12.64	C- / 3.8	4.28%	B+ / 9.6
2010	B-	384.76	12.83	C+ / 6.1	8.11%	B- / 7.1

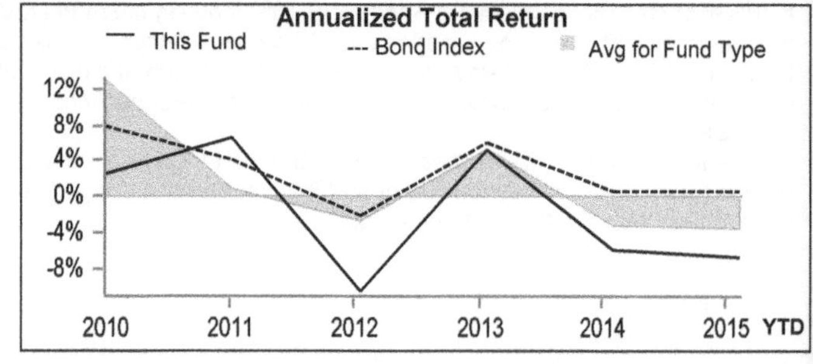

Western Asst Invst Grade Define Op (IGI) C Fair

Fund Family: Legg Mason Partners Fund Advisor LL
Fund Type: Corporate - Investment Grade
Inception Date: June 26, 2009

Data Date	Investment Rating	Net Assets ($Mil)	Price	Performance Rating/Pts	Total Return Y-T-D	Risk Rating/Pts
12-15	C	232.71	20.17	C / 5.0	2.91%	B- / 7.2
2014	C+	231.40	21.00	C / 5.0	13.49%	B / 8.0
2013	C	237.72	20.20	C- / 4.2	-10.01%	B / 8.2
2012	C+	230.29	23.05	C / 5.5	16.57%	B / 8.9
2011	B	224.30	21.93	C+ / 6.5	17.05%	B+ / 9.1
2010	C	217.59	20.04	D+ / 2.6	8.40%	B / 8.4

Major Rating Factors: Middle of the road best describes Western Asst Invst Grade Define Op whose TheStreet.com Investment Rating is currently a C (Fair). The fund currently has a performance rating of C (Fair) based on an annualized return of 1.14% over the last three years and a total return of 2.91% year to date 2015. Factored into the performance evaluation is an expense ratio of 0.80% (very low).

The fund's risk rating is currently B- (Good). It carries a beta of 1.21, meaning it is expected to move 12.1% for every 10% move in the market. Volatility, as measured by both the semi-deviation and a drawdown factor, is considered low. As of December 31, 2015, Western Asst Invst Grade Define Op traded at a premium of 1.46% above its net asset value, which is worse than its one-year historical average discount of .84%.

Michael C. Buchanan has been running the fund for 7 years and currently receives a manager quality ranking of 66 (0=worst, 99=best). If you desire an average level of risk, then this fund may be an option.

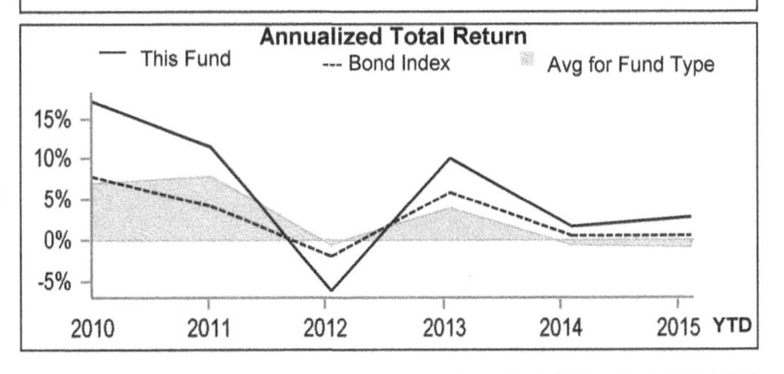

Zweig Fund (ZF) B- Good

Fund Family: Zweig Advisers LLC
Fund Type: Income
Inception Date: September 25, 1986

Data Date	Investment Rating	Net Assets ($Mil)	Price	Performance Rating/Pts	Total Return Y-T-D	Risk Rating/Pts
12-15	B-	359.15	13.14	C+ / 6.5	-8.92%	B- / 7.6
2014	B+	349.70	15.46	B- / 7.3	12.07%	B / 8.7
2013	B	319.25	14.86	B- / 7.4	23.71%	B- / 7.8
2012	C-	314.20	12.16	C- / 3.4	10.78%	B- / 7.6
2011	C-	310.00	2.90	C- / 4.0	-3.96%	B- / 7.6
2010	C-	353.05	3.35	C- / 3.5	13.02%	C+ / 6.5

Major Rating Factors: Zweig Fund receives a TheStreet.com Investment Rating of B- (Good). The fund currently has a performance rating of C+ (Fair) based on an annualized return of 8.67% over the last three years and a total return of -8.92% year to date 2015. Factored into the performance evaluation is an expense ratio of 1.26% (average).

The fund's risk rating is currently B- (Good). It carries a beta of 1.03, meaning that its performance tracks fairly well with that of the overall stock market. Volatility, as measured by both the semi-deviation and a drawdown factor, is considered low. As of December 31, 2015, Zweig Fund traded at a discount of 11.10% below its net asset value, which is worse than its one-year historical average discount of 12.45%.

David C. Dickerson has been running the fund for 13 years and currently receives a manager quality ranking of 33 (0=worst, 99=best). If you desire an average level of risk, then this fund may be an option.

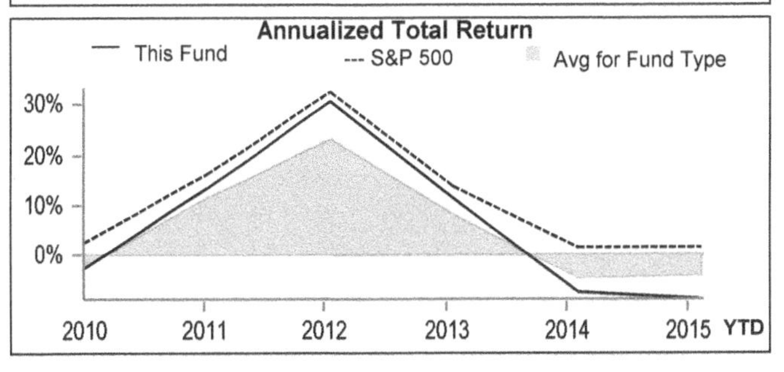

Zweig Total Return Fund (ZTR) B- Good

Fund Family: Zweig Advisers LLC
Fund Type: Growth and Income
Inception Date: September 22, 1988

Data Date	Investment Rating	Net Assets ($Mil)	Price	Performance Rating/Pts	Total Return Y-T-D	Risk Rating/Pts
12-15	B-	500.83	12.18	C+ / 6.8	-4.55%	B- / 7.5
2014	B+	498.40	14.01	C+ / 6.7	10.47%	B+ / 9.1
2013	B	492.69	13.94	C+ / 6.9	19.01%	B / 8.6
2012	D+	507.70	12.31	D+ / 2.6	11.71%	B / 8.1
2011	C-	513.80	3.03	C- / 3.1	-3.16%	B / 8.1
2010	C	473.22	3.56	C- / 3.5	1.07%	B- / 7.6

Major Rating Factors: Zweig Total Return Fund receives a TheStreet.com Investment Rating of B- (Good). The fund currently has a performance rating of C+ (Fair) based on an annualized return of 7.84% over the last three years and a total return of -4.55% year to date 2015. Factored into the performance evaluation is an expense ratio of 1.03% (low).

The fund's risk rating is currently B- (Good). It carries a beta of 0.74, meaning the fund's expected move will be 7.4% for every 10% move in the market. Volatility, as measured by both the semi-deviation and a drawdown factor, is considered low. As of December 31, 2015, Zweig Total Return Fund traded at a discount of 10.18% below its net asset value, which is worse than its one-year historical average discount of 12.21%.

David C. Dickerson has been running the fund for 13 years and currently receives a manager quality ranking of 49 (0=worst, 99=best). If you desire an average level of risk, then this fund may be an option.

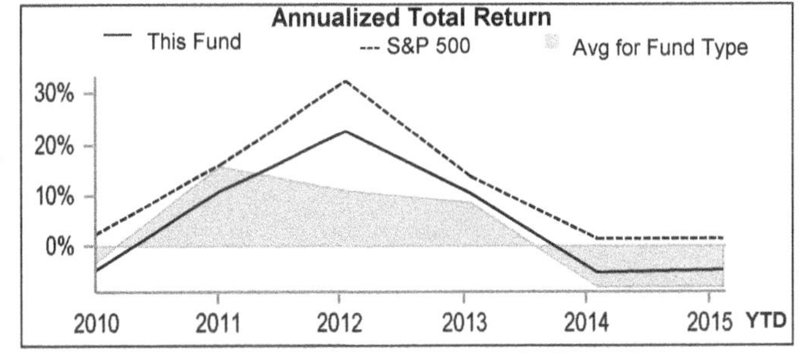

Section III

Top ETFs and Other Closed-End Funds

A compilation of those

Exchange-Traded Funds and Other

Closed-End Mutual Funds

receiving the highest TheStreet Investment Ratings.

Funds are listed in order by Overall Investment Rating.

Section III Contents

This section contains a summary analysis of each of the top ETFs and other closed-end mutual funds as determined by their overall TheStreet Investment Rating. You can use this section to identify those mutual funds that have achieved the best possible combination of total return on investment and reduced volatility over the past three years. Consult each fund's individual Performance Rating and Risk Rating to find the fund that best matches your investing style.

1. Fund Type

The mutual fund's peer category based on an analysis of its investment portfolio.

COH	Corporate – High Yield	HL	Health
COI	Corporate – Inv. Grade	IN	Income
EM	Emerging Market	LP	Loan Participation
EN	Energy/Natural Resources	MTG	Mortgage
FS	Financial Services	MUH	Municipal – High Yield
FO	Foreign	MUN	Municipal – National
GEI	General – Inv. Grade	MUS	Municipal – Single State
GEN	General Bond	PM	Precious Metals
GL	Global	USA	U.S. Gov. – Agency
GR	Growth	UT	Utilities
GI	Growth and Income		

A blank fund type means that the mutual fund has not yet been categorized.

2. Fund Name

The name of the mutual fund as stated in its prospectus, which can sometimes differ slightly from the name that the company uses for advertising. If you cannot find the particular mutual fund you are interested in, or if you have any doubts regarding the precise name, verify the information with your broker or on your account statement. Also, use the fund's ticker symbol for confirmation. (See column 3.)

3. Ticker Symbol

The unique alphabetic symbol used for identifying and trading a specific mutual fund. No two funds can have the same ticker symbol.

4. Overall Investment Rating

Our overall rating is measured on a scale from A to E based on each fund's risk-adjusted performance. Please see page 10 for specific descriptions of each letter grade. Also, refer to page 7 for information on how our ratings are derived. Most important, when using this rating, please be sure to consider the warnings beginning on page 11 regarding the ratings' limitations and the underlying assumptions.

5. Price

Closing price of the fund on the date shown.

6.	**Performance Rating/Points**	A letter grade rating based solely on the mutual fund's financial performance over the trailing three years, without any consideration for the amount of risk the fund poses. Like the overall Investment Rating, the Performance Rating is measured on a scale from A to E for ease of interpretation. The points score indicates where the Performance Rating falls on a scale of 0 to 10.
7.	**1-Year Total Return**	The total return the fund has provided investors over the preceeding 52 weeks. This total return figure is computed based on the fund's dividend distributions and share price appreciation/depreciation during the period, net of the expenses and fees it imposes on its shareholders.
8.	**1-Year Total Return Percentile**	The fund's percentile rank based on its one-year performance compared to that of all other closed-end funds in existence for at least one year. A score of 99 is the best possible, indicating that the fund outperformed 99% of the closed-end mutual funds. Zero is the worst possible percentile score.
9.	**3-Year Total Return**	The total annual return the fund has provided investors over the preceeding 156 weeks.
10.	**3-Year Total Return Percentile**	The fund's percentile rank based on its three-year performance compared to that of all other closed-end funds in existence for at least three years. A score of 99 is the best possible, indicating that the fund outperformed 99% of the closed-end mutual funds. Zero is the worst possible percentile score.
11.	**5-Year Total Return**	The total annual return the fund has provided investors over the preceeding 260 weeks.
12.	**5-Year Total Return Percentile**	The fund's percentile rank based on its five-year performance compared to that of all other closed-end funds in existence for at least five years. A score of 99 is the best possible, indicating that the fund outperformed 99% of the closed-end mutual funds. Zero is the worst possible percentile score.
13.	**Dividend Yield**	Most recent quarterly dividend to fund investors annualized, expressed as a percent of the fund's current share price. The dividend yield of a fund can have little correlation to the amount of dividends the fund has received from its underlying investments. Rather, dividend distributions are based on a fund's need to pass earnings from both dividends and gains on the sale of investments along to shareholders. Thus, these dividend distributions are included as a part of the fund's total return. Keep in mind that dividend income may be taxed at a different rate than capital gains depending on your income tax bracket.

14. Risk Rating/Points

A letter grade rating based solely on the mutual fund's risk as determined by its monthly performance volatility over the trailing three years. The risk rating does not take into consideration the overall financial performance the fund has achieved or the total return it has provided to its shareholders. Like the overall Investment Rating, the Risk Rating is measured on a scale from A to E for ease of interpretation. The points score indicates where the Risk Rating falls on a scale of 0 to 10.

15. Premium/ Discount

A comparison of the fund's price to its NAV as of the date indicated. The premium (+) or discount (-) indicates the percentage the shares are trading above or below the fund's NAV per share.

If the price is above the fund's NAV, the fund is said to be trading at a premium. If the price is lower than the fund's NAV, the fund is trading at a discount.

16. 1-Year Average Premium/ Discount

The average of the fund's premium/discount over the preceeding year.

It can be useful to compare the fund's current premium/discount to its one-year average. If the fund is currently trading at a premium/discount that is lower/higher than its one-year average, then there has been less demand for the fund in more recent times than over the past year. Conversely, if the fund is currently trading at a premium/discount that is higher/lower than its one-year average, this indicates that there has been greater demand for the fund in more recent times than over the past year.

99 Pct = Best
0 Pct = Worst

Fund Type	Fund Name	Ticker Symbol	Overall Investment Rating	Price As of 12/31/15	PERFORMANCE: Performance Rating/Pts	Annualized Total Return Through 12/31/15: 1Yr/Pct	3Yr/Pct	5Yr/Pct	Dividend Yield %	RISK: Risk Rating/Pts	VALUATION: Premium/Discount As of 12/31/15	1 Year Average
GR	*Guggenheim S&P 500 Eq WgCon St E	RHS	A+	116.02	A+ / 9.6	13.70 / 94	19.81 / 95	17.90 / 96	1.77	B- / 7.7	0.08	0.04
GR	*Guggenheim S&P 500 Eq Wght HC ET	RYH	A+	153.49	A+ / 9.6	7.93 / 85	24.52 / 97	20.15 / 98	0.56	B- / 7.5	-0.01	0.04
HL	*Health Care Select Sector SPDR	XLV	A+	72.03	A+ / 9.6	6.93 / 83	22.80 / 96	19.73 / 97	3.36	B / 8.1	-0.03	-0.01
HL	*iShares US Healthcare ETF	IYH	A+	150.01	A+ / 9.6	6.08 / 82	22.48 / 96	19.59 / 97	4.28	B / 8.1	-0.04	0.01
HL	*iShares US Medical Devices ETF	IHI	A+	122.48	A+ / 9.6	10.75 / 89	22.31 / 96	16.83 / 95	7.02	B- / 7.5	0.01	0.01
HL	*Vanguard HealthCare Index ETF	VHT	A+	132.88	A+ / 9.6	6.95 / 83	23.17 / 97	19.97 / 97	0.72	B- / 7.7	-0.02	0.02
HL	*iShares US Healthcare Providers	IHF	A+	124.35	A / 9.5	5.55 / 80	22.17 / 96	17.83 / 96	0.85	B / 8.2	-0.02	0.01
IN	*PowerShares Aerospace & Defense	PPA	A+	35.64	A / 9.5	4.24 / 77	19.67 / 95	14.73 / 90	2.97	B / 8.7	-0.06	-0.02
GR	*Consumer Discretionary Sel Sec S	XLY	A+	78.16	A / 9.4	11.18 / 90	18.85 / 94	17.52 / 95	3.33	B / 8.0	-0.05	N/A
GR	*Guggenheim S&P 500 Eq Wght Tech	RYT	A+	92.27	A / 9.4	2.90 / 74	18.67 / 94	12.00 / 78	1.69	B / 8.3	-0.06	0.01
HL	*iShares Global Healthcare	IXJ	A+	102.62	A / 9.4	7.57 / 84	18.92 / 94	17.33 / 95	0.60	B / 8.2	-0.30	0.04
IN	*iShares US Consumer Services ETF	IYC	A+	144.65	A / 9.4	7.18 / 84	18.65 / 94	17.64 / 95	2.10	B- / 7.7	-0.02	0.01
GR	*PowerShares Dynamic Large Cap Gr	PWB	A+	31.29	A / 9.4	7.97 / 85	17.87 / 93	14.77 / 90	0.81	B- / 7.5	0.03	0.01
IN	*PowerShares Dynamic Food & Bever	PBJ	A+	32.20	A / 9.3	7.18 / 84	17.75 / 93	13.71 / 87	2.09	B- / 7.7	0.03	-0.01
IN	*SP Insurance ETF	KIE	A+	69.50	A / 9.3	7.22 / 84	17.07 / 92	11.85 / 77	4.65	B / 8.1	0.00	N/A
GR	*Consumer Staples Select Sector S	XLP	A+	50.49	A- / 9.2	7.95 / 85	15.31 / 90	14.94 / 91	5.86	B / 8.3	0.00	N/A
GR	*Guggenheim S&P 500 Pure Growth	RPG	A+	80.70	A- / 9.2	2.25 / 72	17.47 / 93	13.80 / 87	1.05	B / 8.3	-0.06	0.02
GR	*iShares S&P 500 Growth	IVW	A+	115.80	A- / 9.2	5.93 / 81	16.16 / 92	13.77 / 87	3.46	B- / 7.8	0.00	N/A
GR	*SPDR S&P 500 Growth ETF	SPYG	A+	100.09	A- / 9.2	5.79 / 81	16.15 / 91	13.78 / 87	3.80	B / 8.4	-0.06	0.04
GR	*Technology Select Sector SPDR	XLK	A+	42.83	A- / 9.2	6.23 / 82	15.54 / 90	12.79 / 83	4.03	B / 8.6	-0.07	N/A
GR	*iShares US Technology ETF	IYW	A+	107.03	A- / 9.1	4.38 / 77	15.66 / 91	11.33 / 74	2.59	B- / 7.8	0.01	N/A
HL	*PowerShares DWA Healthcare Momen	PTH	A+	55.11	A- / 9.1	2.06 / 72	17.83 / 93	15.74 / 93	0.00	B- / 7.9	-0.07	0.03
IN	*PowerShares Dynamic Leisure&Ente	PEJ	A+	36.76	A- / 9.1	4.11 / 77	15.86 / 91	15.06 / 91	0.21	B / 8.5	-0.03	0.05
IN	*Vanguard Consumer Staples ETF	VDC	A+	129.07	A- / 9.1	6.49 / 82	15.19 / 90	14.88 / 91	1.39	B / 8.2	0.02	0.01
FO	*iShares MSCI Belgium Capped	EWK	A+	18.06	A- / 9.0	14.21 / 94	12.85 / 84	11.04 / 72	1.84	B / 8.7	-0.39	0.05
IN	*Guggenheim Russ Top 50 Mega Cap	XLG	A+	144.58	B+ / 8.9	4.42 / 78	13.38 / 85	12.21 / 80	1.89	B / 8.5	-0.03	0.02
GR	*iShares Core S&P 500 ETF	IVV	A+	204.87	B+ / 8.9	1.97 / 71	14.20 / 88	12.36 / 81	0.46	B / 8.6	-0.07	N/A
GL	*iShares Global Tech	IXN	A+	97.52	B+ / 8.9	4.87 / 79	14.00 / 88	10.67 / 69	2.29	B / 8.6	-0.34	-0.01
GR	*iShares Morningstar Large-Cp ETF	JKD	A+	119.07	B+ / 8.9	-0.37 / 58	14.86 / 90	13.39 / 86	2.29	B / 8.7	-0.07	N/A
FS	*SP Regional Banking ETF	KRE	A+	41.92	B+ / 8.9	6.67 / 82	14.50 / 89	12.31 / 81	4.43	B / 8.6	-0.05	-0.01
GR	*SPDR S&P 500 ETF	SPY	A+	203.87	B+ / 8.9	1.89 / 71	14.16 / 88	12.32 / 81	4.75	B / 8.6	-0.07	0.01
FO	*WisdomTree Europe Small Cap Div	DFE	A+	56.00	B+ / 8.9	11.27 / 90	13.77 / 87	10.13 / 66	1.23	B / 8.1	-0.52	0.12
FS	*Guggenheim S&P 500 Eq Wght Finl	RYF	A+	43.20	B+ / 8.8	-1.46 / 52	14.35 / 89	11.32 / 74	2.61	B / 8.9	-0.05	0.01
GR	*iShares Russell 1000 ETF	IWB	A+	113.31	B+ / 8.8	1.39 / 69	13.94 / 87	12.16 / 79	0.36	B / 8.8	-0.04	N/A
GR	*iShares S&P 100	OEF	A+	91.17	B+ / 8.8	3.11 / 74	13.62 / 86	12.14 / 79	4.27	B / 8.5	-0.03	N/A
FO	*WisdomTree Japan SmallCap Div Fd	DFJ	A+	56.56	B+ / 8.8	18.01 / 98	11.06 / 79	7.41 / 56	1.24	B / 8.5	-0.75	0.09
FS	*Financial Select Sector SPDR	XLF	A+	23.83	B+ / 8.7	-1.14 / 54	14.01 / 88	10.04 / 65	5.03	B / 8.8	-0.04	-0.01
GR	*Vanguard Large Cap ETF	VV	A+	93.50	B+ / 8.7	1.10 / 67	13.87 / 87	12.11 / 79	2.17	B / 8.4	-0.02	N/A
GI	*Vanguard Tot Stk Mkt Idx ETF	VTI	A+	104.30	B+ / 8.7	0.99 / 67	13.76 / 87	12.03 / 78	4.47	B / 8.7	-0.04	N/A
FS	*iShares US Financials ETF	IYF	A+	88.38	B+ / 8.6	0.05 / 60	13.68 / 86	10.55 / 68	4.58	B / 8.7	-0.03	N/A
GR	*Vanguard Mid Cap Value Index ETF	VOE	A+	85.95	B+ / 8.6	-1.85 / 51	14.30 / 89	12.10 / 79	1.88	B+ / 9.0	-0.05	0.01
IN	*Vanguard Value ETF	VTV	A+	81.52	B+ / 8.6	-0.30 / 58	13.37 / 85	11.54 / 75	5.77	B+ / 9.0	-0.05	N/A
GR	*Guggenheim S&P 500 Eq WgCon Dsc	RCD	A+	84.69	B+ / 8.5	-2.36 / 49	14.70 / 89	14.51 / 90	1.62	B / 8.7	-0.05	0.01
GR	*iShares Russell Mid Cap Growth	IWP	A+	91.92	B+ / 8.5	--	13.60 / 86	11.22 / 73	2.54	B / 8.6	-0.04	N/A
FS	*Vanguard Financials ETF	VFH	A+	48.45	B+ / 8.5	-0.59 / 57	13.20 / 85	10.08 / 66	3.03	B / 8.5	-0.02	0.02
GR	*First Trust Dow Jones Sel Micro	FDM	A+	32.90	B+ / 8.4	1.81 / 71	12.95 / 84	9.41 / 63	2.59	B / 8.5	-0.06	-0.01
IN	*Guggenheim S&P 500 Equal Wght	RSP	A+	76.64	B+ / 8.4	-2.62 / 48	13.42 / 86	11.77 / 77	1.76	B / 8.6	-0.07	-0.01
GR	*Industrial Select Sector SPDR	XLI	A+	53.01	B+ / 8.4	-3.60 / 44	13.10 / 85	10.92 / 71	4.81	B / 8.7	-0.04	-0.01
FS	*SP Bank ETF	KBE	A+	33.82	B+ / 8.4	3.82 / 76	12.53 / 83	7.18 / 55	4.13	B / 8.7	-0.09	N/A
GL	*iShares Global Consumer Staples	KXI	A+	93.03	B / 8.2	7.74 / 84	10.26 / 76	11.55 / 75	3.86	B / 8.8	-0.20	0.01

* Denotes ETF Fund, N/A denotes number is not available

Fund Type	Fund Name (99 Pct = Best, 0 Pct = Worst)	Ticker Symbol	Overall Investment Rating	Price As of 12/31/15	PERFORMANCE: Performance Rating/Pts	Annualized Total Return Through 12/31/15: 1Yr/Pct	3Yr/Pct	5Yr/Pct	Dividend Yield %	RISK: Risk Rating/Pts	VALUATION: Premium/Discount As of 12/31/15	1 Year Average
FO	The New Ireland Fund	IRL	A+	13.93	A+ / 9.8	36.24 / 99	25.10 / 97	21.61 / 98	1.17	B- / 7.9	-12.39	-14.28
MUN	Eaton Vance Municipal Inc 2028 Ter	ETX	A+	18.49	A+ / 9.7	10.24 / 96	--	--	4.59	B- / 7.8	-9.72	-11.09
FS	John Hancock Financial Opptys	BTO	A+	28.03	A+ / 9.7	25.29 / 99	21.19 / 96	16.40 / 94	5.28	B- / 7.3	7.11	-1.29
GEI	Babson Capital Corporate Investors	MCI	A+	17.25	A+ / 9.6	17.03 / 97	--	--	6.96	B- / 7.3	17.35	9.68
MUN	Dreyfus Municipal Bond Infra	DMB	A+	12.38	A / 9.5	8.15 / 92	--	--	6.06	B- / 7.8	-11.06	-11.00
FO	Japan Smaller Cap Fund Inc.	JOF	A+	10.23	A / 9.5	24.45 / 99	16.38 / 92	4.95 / 47	1.63	B / 8.1	-12.04	-12.44
HL	Gabelli Healthcare & WellnessRx Tr	GRX	A+	10.25	A- / 9.2	3.05 / 74	17.21 / 92	18.66 / 97	5.07	B- / 7.8	-13.06	-12.32
IN	Nuveen S&P 500 Buy Write Income	JPZ	A+	13.43	A- / 9.2	15.26 / 95	11.85 / 81	10.14 / 66	7.42	B- / 7.8	0.67	-5.89
IN	Nuveen Nasdaq 100 Dynamic Overwrit	QQQX	A	19.37	A / 9.4	9.21 / 87	16.03 / 91	14.83 / 91	7.23	B- / 7.2	-3.05	-6.18
IN	Eaton Vance Enhanced Eqty Inc II	EOS	A	13.64	A / 9.3	6.44 / 82	16.82 / 92	11.37 / 74	7.70	B- / 7.3	-5.34	-6.06
IN	Eaton Vance Tax-Managed Buy-Write	ETB	A	16.69	A / 9.3	14.03 / 94	13.64 / 86	12.03 / 78	7.77	B- / 7.3	7.61	0.12
IN	Eaton Vance Enhanced Eqty Inc	EOI	A	13.42	A- / 9.2	5.57 / 80	15.55 / 90	10.20 / 66	7.73	B- / 7.5	-4.01	-8.76
MUN	Nuveen Intermdt Dur Qlty Mun Term	NIQ	A	12.88	A- / 9.2	6.37 / 88	--	--	4.43	B- / 7.5	-7.93	-8.59
IN	Eaton Vance Tax Mgd Div Eqty Inc	ETY	A	11.20	A- / 9.1	9.21 / 87	14.49 / 89	9.92 / 65	9.03	B- / 7.7	-5.56	-7.54
GL	Flaherty & Crumrine Dyn Pfd and In	DFP	A	22.90	B+ / 8.9	9.75 / 88	--	--	8.38	B- / 7.8	-5.37	-7.23
GI	BlackRock Enhanced Capital and Inc	CII	A	14.14	B+ / 8.8	8.19 / 85	12.57 / 83	8.71 / 60	8.49	B- / 7.8	-6.42	-6.46
GEI	Babson Capital Participation Inv	MPV	A-	13.75	A+ / 9.6	12.54 / 92	--	--	7.86	C+ / 6.8	0.81	-5.61
IN	Eaton Vance Tax Mgd Buy Write Opp	ETV	A-	15.30	A / 9.5	17.56 / 97	16.13 / 91	13.45 / 86	8.69	B- / 7.0	5.08	0.07
MUS	PIMCO CA Municipal Income Fund III	PZC	A-	11.92	A / 9.5	20.31 / 99	8.42 / 84	13.94 / 98	6.04	C+ / 6.8	15.62	8.13
GR	Columbia Seligman Prem Tech Gro	STK	A-	17.93	A / 9.4	4.43 / 78	18.87 / 94	9.84 / 65	0.50	C+ / 6.9	3.70	2.80
IN	Nuveen Core Equity Alpha Fund	JCE	A-	14.27	A- / 9.2	0.43 / 63	16.95 / 92	14.46 / 89	8.49	B- / 7.2	-4.42	-4.82
FO	Aberdeen Japan Equity	JEQ	A-	7.70	A- / 9.1	17.25 / 97	12.60 / 83	6.55 / 53	0.63	B- / 7.4	-9.20	-11.47
MUS	MFS CA Muni	CCA	A-	11.84	A- / 9.0	15.02 / 99	4.50 / 67	9.48 / 90	5.17	B- / 7.4	-7.21	-10.24
MUS	Nuveen CA AMT-Free Municipal Incom	NKX	A-	15.36	A- / 9.0	11.47 / 97	6.28 / 74	11.45 / 95	6.09	B- / 7.4	-4.42	-6.58
MUS	Nuveen CA Muni Value	NCA	A-	10.88	B+ / 8.8	8.09 / 92	6.64 / 76	10.04 / 92	4.66	B- / 7.6	3.32	0.83
IN	Adams Diversified Equity	ADX	A-	12.83	B+ / 8.6	0.65 / 65	13.38 / 85	10.70 / 70	1.17	B- / 7.8	-14.69	-14.43
MUS	BlackRock Muni NY Interm Duration	MNE	A-	15.18	B+ / 8.6	13.89 / 98	3.37 / 62	8.75 / 86	4.55	B- / 7.5	-3.74	-8.82
GL	First Trust Dividend and Income	FAV	A-	8.46	B+ / 8.4	0.44 / 63	11.71 / 81	2.67 / 36	8.04	B- / 7.8	-7.24	-12.25
IN	Eaton Vance Tax Advantage Div Inc	EVT	A-	19.34	B+ / 8.3	2.01 / 72	11.54 / 80	10.90 / 71	8.25	B- / 7.9	-9.24	-9.81
IN	J Hancock Tax Advantage Div Income	HTD	A-	20.57	B+ / 8.3	0.21 / 62	10.99 / 78	14.08 / 88	7.06	B- / 7.9	-10.33	-10.35
IN	Liberty All-Star Growth Fund	ASG	B+	4.58	A / 9.4	11.67 / 91	15.51 / 90	11.69 / 76	37.12	C+ / 6.7	-8.22	-10.00
MUN	PIMCO Municipal Income Fund	PMF	B+	15.45	A- / 9.0	15.69 / 99	6.11 / 73	12.07 / 97	6.31	C+ / 6.3	16.52	12.42
MUN	BlackRock MuniAssets Fund	MUA	B+	14.27	B+ / 8.7	9.14 / 94	5.27 / 70	10.34 / 93	5.56	B- / 7.1	0.56	-2.12
MUS	BlackRock CA Municipal Income Trus	BFZ	B+	15.95	B+ / 8.6	12.49 / 98	3.78 / 63	11.52 / 96	5.43	C+ / 6.7	-0.25	-4.39
MUN	Invesco Municipal Income Opp Tr	OIA	B+	7.29	B+ / 8.4	11.18 / 97	4.72 / 68	10.17 / 92	5.40	B- / 7.2	-4.46	-8.11
MUS	Nuveen CA Div Adv Muni 3	NZH	B+	14.15	B+ / 8.4	11.06 / 97	4.97 / 69	10.42 / 93	6.16	B- / 7.3	-4.52	-7.22
MUS	Nuveen CA Div Adv Muni 2	NVX	B+	15.31	B+ / 8.3	13.68 / 98	4.42 / 66	10.16 / 92	5.73	B- / 7.1	-4.01	-6.87
IN	John Hancock Premium Dividend	PDT	B+	13.71	B / 8.1	8.44 / 86	8.82 / 72	12.42 / 82	7.88	B- / 7.5	-8.36	-10.13
MUS	Invesco CA Value Municipal Income	VCV	B+	13.25	B / 8.0	9.38 / 94	4.69 / 67	10.64 / 94	5.98	B- / 7.3	-4.19	-5.82
MUS	Invesco Tr Fr Inv NY Mun	VTN	B+	14.61	B / 8.0	13.73 / 98	1.42 / 49	8.20 / 83	5.82	B- / 7.4	-3.94	-8.46
MUS	Nuveen CA Select Tax-Free Inc Port	NXC	B+	15.63	B / 8.0	5.96 / 87	5.61 / 71	9.29 / 89	4.03	B- / 7.6	0.84	0.09
MUS	PIMCO NY Muni Income Fund	PNF	B+	11.90	B / 8.0	10.02 / 95	4.08 / 65	9.62 / 91	5.75	B- / 7.4	-1.65	-3.41
IN	Source Capital	SOR	B+	66.26	B / 8.0	0.25 / 62	12.33 / 82	10.30 / 67	8.75	B / 8.1	-9.32	-9.47
MUN	Nuveen Muni Value	NUV	B+	10.18	B / 7.9	9.84 / 95	3.60 / 63	6.95 / 69	3.83	B- / 7.7	-0.97	-3.41
MUN	BlackRock MuniEnhanced Fund	MEN	B+	11.85	B / 7.8	10.38 / 96	4.15 / 65	9.40 / 89	6.13	B- / 7.6	-3.81	-6.15
FO	Aberdeen Israel Fund	ISL	B+	17.26	B / 7.7	5.24 / 80	10.54 / 77	2.85 / 37	0.00	B / 8.1	-16.38	-14.31
IN	Liberty All-Star Equity Fund	USA	B+	5.35	B / 7.7	-1.84 / 51	10.34 / 76	8.83 / 60	9.72	B- / 7.6	-13.43	-13.80
IN	Tri-Continental Corporation	TY	B+	20.02	B / 7.6	-2.04 / 50	10.60 / 77	11.53 / 75	4.18	B / 8.2	-14.77	-14.86
GR	Eagle Capital Growth Fund	GRF	B+	7.59	B- / 7.5	-7.13 / 33	10.08 / 75	10.96 / 72	2.36	B- / 7.8	-10.92	-12.42
MUN	Western Asset Intermediate Muni	SBI	B+	10.21	B- / 7.4	11.02 / 96	2.53 / 57	6.99 / 70	4.70	B- / 7.9	-2.95	-5.42

* Denotes ETF Fund, N/A denotes number is not available

Section IV

Bottom ETFs and Other Closed-End Funds

A compilation of those

Exchange-Traded Funds and Other

Closed-End Mutual Funds

receiving the lowest TheStreet Investment Ratings.

Funds are listed in order by Overall Investment Rating.

Section IV Contents

This section contains a summary analysis of each of the bottom closed-end mutual funds as determined by their overall TheStreet.com Investment Rating. Typically, these funds have invested in securities that are currently out of favor, presenting a risky investment proposition. As such, these are the funds that you should generally avoid since they have historically underperformed most other mutual funds given the level of risk in their underlying investments.

1. Fund Type

The mutual fund's peer category based on an analysis of its investment portfolio.

COH	Corporate – High Yield	HL	Health
COI	Corporate – Inv. Grade	IN	Income
EM	Emerging Market	LP	Loan Participation
EN	Energy/Natural Resources	MTG	Mortgage
FS	Financial Services	MUH	Municipal – High Yield
FO	Foreign	MUN	Municipal – National
GEI	General – Inv. Grade	MUS	Municipal – Single State
GEN	General Bond	PM	Precious Metals
GL	Global	USA	U.S. Gov. – Agency
GR	Growth	UT	Utilities
GI	Growth and Income		

A blank fund type means that the mutual fund has not yet been categorized.

2. Fund Name

The name of the mutual fund as stated in its prospectus, which can sometimes differ slightly from the name that the company uses for advertising. If you cannot find the particular mutual fund you are interested in, or if you have any doubts regarding the precise name, verify the information with your broker or on your account statement. Also, use the fund's ticker symbol for confirmation. (See column 3.)

3. Ticker Symbol

The unique alphabetic symbol used for identifying and trading a specific mutual fund. No two funds can have the same ticker symbol.

4. Overall Investment Rating

Our overall rating is measured on a scale from A to E based on each fund's risk-adjusted performance. Please see page 10 for specific descriptions of each letter grade. Also, refer to page 7 for information on how our ratings are derived. Most important, when using this rating, please be sure to consider the warnings beginning on page 11 regarding the ratings' limitations and the underlying assumptions.

5.	**Price**	Closing price of the fund on the date shown.
6.	**Performance Rating/Points**	A letter grade rating based solely on the mutual fund's financial performance over the trailing three years, without any consideration for the amount of risk the fund poses. Like the overall Investment Rating, the Performance Rating is measured on a scale from A to E for ease of interpretation. The points score indicates where the Performance Rating falls on a scale of 0 to 10.
7.	**1-Year Total Return**	The total return the fund has provided investors over the preceeding 52 weeks. This total return figure is computed based on the fund's dividend distributions and share price appreciation/depreciation during the period, net of the expenses and fees it imposes on its shareholders.
8.	**1-Year Total Return Percentile**	The fund's percentile rank based on its one-year performance compared to that of all other closed-end funds in existence for at least one year. A score of 99 is the best possible, indicating that the fund outperformed 99% of the closed-end mutual funds. Zero is the worst possible percentile score.
9.	**3-Year Total Return**	The total annual return the fund has provided investors over the preceeding 156 weeks.
10.	**3-Year Total Return Percentile**	The fund's percentile rank based on its three-year performance compared to that of all other closed-end funds in existence for at least three years. A score of 99 is the best possible, indicating that the fund outperformed 99% of the closed-end mutual funds. Zero is the worst possible percentile score.
11.	**5-Year Total Return**	The total annual return the fund has provided investors over the preceeding 260 weeks.
12.	**5-Year Total Return Percentile**	The fund's percentile rank based on its five-year performance compared to that of all other closed-end funds in existence for at least five years. A score of 99 is the best possible, indicating that the fund outperformed 99% of the closed-end mutual funds. Zero is the worst possible percentile score.
13.	**Dividend Yield**	Most recent quarterly dividend to fund investors annualized, expressed as a percent of the fund's current share price. The dividend yield of a fund can have little correlation to the amount of dividends the fund has received from its underlying investments. Rather, dividend distributions are based on a fund's need to pass earnings from both dividends and gains on the sale of investments along to shareholders. Thus, these dividend distributions are included as a part of the fund's total return. Keep in mind that dividend income may be taxed at a different rate than capital gains depending on your income tax bracket.

14. Risk Rating/Points

A letter grade rating based solely on the mutual fund's risk as determined by its monthly performance volatility over the trailing three years. The risk rating does not take into consideration the overall financial performance the fund has achieved or the total return it has provided to its shareholders. Like the overall Investment Rating, the Risk Rating is measured on a scale from A to E for ease of interpretation. The points score indicates where the Risk Rating falls on a scale of 0 to 10.

15. Premium/ Discount

A comparison of the fund's price to its NAV as of the date indicated. The premium (+) or discount (-) indicates the percentage the shares are trading above or below the fund's NAV per share.

If the price is above the fund's NAV, the fund is said to be trading at a premium. If the price is lower than the fund's NAV, the fund is trading at a discount.

16. 1-Year Average Premium/ Discount

The average of the fund's premium/discount over the preceeding year.

It can be useful to compare the fund's current premium/discount to its one-year average. If the fund is currently trading at a premium/discount that is lower/higher than its one-year average, then there has been less demand for the fund in more recent times than over the past year. Conversely, if the fund is currently trading at a premium/discount that is higher/lower than its one-year average, this indicates that there has been greater demand for the fund in more recent times than over the past year.

99 Pct = Best
0 Pct = Worst

Fund Type	Fund Name	Ticker Symbol	Overall Investment Rating	Price As of 12/31/15	PERFORMANCE					RISK	VALUATION	
					Performance Rating/Pts	Annualized Total Return Through 12/31/15 1Yr/Pct	3Yr/Pct	5Yr/Pct	Dividend Yield %	Risk Rating/Pts	Premium/Discount As of 12/31/15	1 Year Average
IN	*C-Tracks ETN Citi Volatility Idx	CVOL	E-	0.43	E- / 0.0	-60.11 / 1	-73.97 / 0	-76.75 / 0	0.00	E- / 0.1	4.88	1.13
PM	*Direxion Daily Gold Mnrs Id Bull	NUGT	E-	24.26	E- / 0.0	-79.91 / 0	-83.17 / 0	-72.68 / 0	0.00	D / 1.8	-0.41	0.09
FO	*Direxion Daily Latin Amer Bull 3	LBJ	E-	12.00	E- / 0.0	-72.65 / 0	-58.11 / 1	-49.03 / 0	0.00	E- / 0.1	0.50	0.22
GR	*Direxion Daily Nat Gas Rel Bull	GASL	E-	6.14	E- / 0.0	-97.14 / 0	-82.35 / 0	-70.79 / 0	0.00	D / 1.8	-0.81	0.16
EN	*ProShares Ultra Bloomberg Crude	UCO	E-	12.54	E- / 0.0	-74.69 / 0	-56.35 / 1	-44.40 / 1	0.00	D / 1.8	-0.32	-0.17
EN	*ProShares Ultra Bloomberg Nat Ga	BOIL	E-	18.48	E- / 0.0	-71.16 / 1	-50.14 / 1	--	0.00	D / 1.8	-0.48	-0.05
FO	*ProShares Ultra MSCI Brazil Capp	UBR	E-	25.45	E- / 0.0	-68.36 / 1	-51.29 / 1	-43.04 / 1	0.00	D / 1.8	-2.75	0.07
GI	*ProShares Ultra VIX Sh-Tm Fut ET	UVXY	E-	28.35	E- / 0.0	-76.70 / 0	-79.00 / 0	--	0.00	E- / 0.1	0.93	0.36
GL	*VelocityShares 3x Long Crude ETN	UWTI	E-	3.95	E- / 0.0	-91.38 / 0	-76.34 / 0	--	0.00	D / 1.7	-1.00	-0.36
GL	*VelocityShares 3x Long Nat Gas E	UGAZ	E-	2.44	E- / 0.0	-88.07 / 0	-71.05 / 0	--	0.00	D / 1.8	-1.21	-0.02
GL	*VelocityShares 3x Long Silver ET	USLV	E-	9.81	E- / 0.0	-49.12 / 2	-66.28 / 0	--	0.00	E+ / 0.8	0.41	0.09
IN	*VelocityShares Daily 2x VIX S-T	TVIX	E-	6.27	E- / 0.0	-76.44 / 0	-79.26 / 0	-83.97 / 0	0.00	E+ / 0.6	1.79	1.80
IN	*Direxion Daily Semiconductor Bea	SOXS	E-	40.17	E- / 0.1	-25.17 / 10	-55.92 / 1	-48.55 / 1	0.00	D / 1.7	-0.10	-0.04
GR	*Direxion Daily Technology Bear 3	TECS	E-	31.10	E- / 0.1	-31.49 / 7	-43.75 / 1	-41.21 / 1	0.00	D- / 1.1	0.03	0.01
EN	*ProShares Ultra Silver	AGQ	E-	27.08	E- / 0.1	-29.52 / 8	-46.21 / 1	-37.05 / 2	0.00	E / 0.3	0.07	0.60
GR	*ProShares UltraPro Short QQQ	SQQQ	E-	18.72	E- / 0.1	-37.77 / 4	-50.09 / 1	-47.31 / 1	0.00	E+ / 0.6	0.11	-0.01
GL	*VelocityShares 3x Long Gold ETN	UGLD	E-	7.37	E- / 0.1	-35.12 / 6	-43.36 / 1	--	0.00	E+ / 0.9	0.00	0.21
IN	*VelocityShares Dly 2x VIX Med-T	TVIZ	E-	13.32	E- / 0.1	-38.59 / 4	-48.83 / 1	-55.60 / 0	0.00	D / 1.7	-2.06	-0.32
GL	*Direxion Emerging Markets Bull 3	EDC	E-	11.51	E- / 0.2	-47.92 / 2	-32.88 / 3	-29.57 / 3	0.00	D- / 1.0	0.00	0.02
FS	*Direxion Financial Bear 3x Share	FAZ	E-	41.18	E- / 0.2	-18.62 / 15	-42.30 / 1	-43.57 / 1	0.00	D- / 1.4	0.05	-0.05
EN	*iPath Bloomberg Ntrl Gas SI TR A	GAZ	E-	0.72	E- / 0.2	-64.18 / 1	-35.40 / 3	-38.43 / 2	0.00	E- / 0.1	33.33	7.13
IN	*IPath S&P 500 VIX Sm-Trm Futr ET	VXX	E-	20.10	E- / 0.2	-35.14 / 6	-43.29 / 1	-48.90 / 1	0.00	E+ / 0.6	0.75	0.22
EN	*iPath S&P GSCI Crude Oil TotRet	OIL	E-	6.23	E- / 0.2	-48.98 / 2	-34.48 / 3	-24.12 / 5	0.00	D- / 1.2	8.73	2.21
GI	*ProShares UltraPro Sht Finl Sel	FINZ	E-	20.08	E- / 0.2	-16.02 / 17	-41.46 / 1	--	0.00	D- / 1.5	7.04	0.26
GEI	*ProShares VIX Short-Term Futures	VIXY	E-	13.33	E- / 0.2	-35.32 / 5	-43.47 / 1	--	0.00	E- / 0.1	0.68	0.21
GL	*PureFunds ISE Jr Silver SCM/E ET	SILJ	E-	5.07	E- / 0.2	-38.70 / 4	-36.99 / 2	--	2.46	E+ / 0.6	0.40	0.71
EN	*United States Brent Oil Fund	BNO	E-	12.24	E- / 0.2	-44.41 / 2	-33.19 / 3	-17.03 / 7	0.00	E / 0.3	0.16	-0.12
GI	*VelocityShares VIX Short-Term ET	VIIX	E-	27.12	E- / 0.2	-35.14 / 6	-43.29 / 1	-48.92 / 1	0.00	E+ / 0.6	0.59	0.18
GR	*DB Agriculture Double Long ETN	DAG	E-	3.27	E / 0.3	-37.07 / 4	-33.49 / 3	-25.00 / 4	0.00	D- / 1.1	-0.30	8.00
GR	*Direxion S&P 500 Bear 3X Shares	SPXS	E-	16.92	E / 0.3	-18.14 / 15	-39.75 / 2	-39.73 / 1	0.00	D- / 1.4	0.06	N/A
EN	*ELEMENTS RIC Energy Total Return	RJN	E-	2.33	E / 0.3	-40.41 / 3	-29.18 / 4	-18.22 / 6	0.00	E+ / 0.9	0.00	0.02
EN	*iPath Bloomberg Energy SI TR A	JJE	E-	5.66	E / 0.3	-44.34 / 3	-30.74 / 4	-24.20 / 4	0.00	E- / 0.1	1.07	0.32
GR	*ProShares UltraPro Short S&P500	SPXU	E-	31.71	E / 0.3	-16.75 / 16	-38.84 / 2	-39.02 / 2	0.00	D / 1.6	0.16	0.01
GR	*DB Commodity Double Long ETN	DYY	E-	3.17	E / 0.4	-22.08 / 12	-30.41 / 4	-20.81 / 5	0.00	E- / 0.1	73.22	32.99
GR	*DB Crude Oil Long ETN	OLO	E-	4.63	E / 0.4	-43.16 / 3	-28.98 / 4	-19.36 / 6	0.00	E+ / 0.8	0.22	0.28
GR	*Direxion Daily Small Cap Bear 3x	TZA	E-	45.00	E / 0.4	-7.72 / 32	-38.57 / 2	-42.82 / 1	0.00	E+ / 0.9	0.45	0.01
IN	*iPath Pure Beta Crude Oil ETN	OLEM	E-	14.90	E / 0.4	-39.90 / 4	-27.39 / 5	--	0.00	D- / 1.1	-0.13	0.02
EN	*iPath Pure Beta Energy ETN	ONG	E-	15.45	E / 0.4	-40.85 / 3	-27.38 / 5	--	0.00	E- / 0.2	1.38	0.92
PM	*iShares MSCI Global Gold Miners	RING	E-	5.48	E / 0.4	-27.29 / 9	-33.25 / 3	--	1.58	E+ / 0.9	0.92	0.34
GR	*ProShares UltraPro Shrt Russell2	SRTY	E-	29.32	E / 0.4	-6.42 / 35	-37.67 / 2	-42.13 / 1	0.00	E+ / 0.8	0.38	0.08
PM	*DB Base Metals Double Long ETN	BDD	E-	4.10	E / 0.5	-43.40 / 3	-26.66 / 5	-25.75 / 4	0.00	D- / 1.0	0.24	0.64
GL	*Global X Gold Explorers ETF	GLDX	E-	16.43	E / 0.5	-12.92 / 20	-32.05 / 3	-32.25 / 2	11.70	D- / 1.3	0.49	-0.03
EN	*iPath Bloomberg Nkl SI TR A	JJN	E-	10.81	E / 0.5	-44.59 / 2	-23.93 / 6	-21.17 / 5	0.00	E+ / 0.6	1.22	0.50
IN	*IPath S&P 500 VIX Mid-Trm Futr E	VXZ	E-	11.14	E+ / 0.7	-14.50 / 18	-24.46 / 6	-29.52 / 3	0.00	E+ / 0.8	0.36	0.03
GI	*VelocityShares VIX Medium-Term E	VIIZ	E-	15.44	E+ / 0.7	-14.55 / 18	-24.51 / 6	-29.49 / 3	0.00	E+ / 0.7	0.32	-0.11
EN	*iPath Seasonal Natural Gas ETN	DCNG	E-	15.90	E+ / 0.8	-28.57 / 8	-18.65 / 9	--	0.00	D- / 1.0	0.38	0.42
GR	*UBS E Tracs CMCI Silver TR	USV	E-	18.71	E+ / 0.8	-11.62 / 23	-23.78 / 6	-14.48 / 9	0.00	E / 0.5	3.48	0.10
EM	*Direxion Daily India Bull 3X	INDL	E-	13.47	D- / 1.0	-36.19 / 5	-13.70 / 13	-21.70 / 5	0.00	E- / 0.2	0.67	0.01
GI	*Direxion Daily Russia Bear 3x	RUSS	E-	37.52	D- / 1.1	-65.78 / 1	-12.20 / 15	--	0.00	E- / 0.2	0.24	-0.04
FO	*Direxion Daily FTSE Ch Bull 3x E	YINN	E-	17.74	D- / 1.3	-50.58 / 1	-4.76 / 25	-17.54 / 6	0.00	E- / 0.2	0.06	0.02

* Denotes ETF Fund, N/A denotes number is not available

Fund Type	Fund Name (99 Pct = Best, 0 Pct = Worst)	Ticker Symbol	Overall Investment Rating	Price As of 12/31/15	PERFORMANCE: Performance Rating/Pts	Annualized Total Return Through 12/31/15: 1Yr/Pct	3Yr/Pct	5Yr/Pct	Dividend Yield %	RISK: Risk Rating/Pts	VALUATION: Premium/Discount As of 12/31/15	1 Year Average
EN	Duff & Phelps Select Energy MLP	DSE	E-	5.98	E- / 0.0	-53.71 / 1	--	--	21.07	D / 1.7	-8.42	-2.23
EN	Goldman Sachs MLP and Energy Ren	XGERX	E-	5.48	E- / 0.0	-57.97 / 1	--	--	24.45	D / 1.8	-6.64	4.53
EN	Nuveen All Cap Energy MLP Opps	JML	E-	6.97	E- / 0.0	-50.36 / 1	--	--	19.63	D / 1.8	-7.07	-0.77
USA	Cushing Energy Income	SRF	E-	8.42	E- / 0.1	-75.37 / 0	-45.48 / 1	--	17.38	D / 1.8	-10.33	-8.48
EN	Goldman Sachs MLP Income Oppty	XGMZX	E	8.23	E- / 0.0	-49.36 / 2	--	--	16.77	D / 1.9	-6.48	0.11
IN	Kayne Anderson Midstream/Energy	KMF	E	12.37	E / 0.5	-57.65 / 1	-17.86 / 10	-5.85 / 18	14.55	D / 2.1	-1.83	-7.82
GL	Neuberger Berman MLP Income	NML	E+	8.16	E- / 0.0	-50.28 / 2	--	--	15.44	C- / 3.6	-0.49	-4.07
EN	Center Coast MLP & Infrastructure	CEN	E+	10.12	E- / 0.1	-38.22 / 4	--	--	12.36	C- / 3.8	-3.89	-4.58
GL	ClearBridge American Energy MLP In	CBA	E+	8.19	E- / 0.1	-45.00 / 2	--	--	14.90	C- / 3.9	-9.50	-7.77
GL	Miller/Howard High Income Equity	XHIEX	E+	11.46	E- / 0.2	-36.85 / 5	--	--	12.15	C- / 3.4	-11.09	-4.87
EN	Kayne Anderson Energy Tot Ret	KYE	E+	8.47	E / 0.3	-66.00 / 1	-23.87 / 6	-15.16 / 8	15.58	C- / 3.6	-11.22	-8.03
GI	The Cushing MLP Total Return Fund	SRV	E+	10.67	E / 0.3	-63.06 / 1	-28.40 / 4	-17.14 / 6	9.28	C- / 3.8	-11.31	-13.23
PM	ASA Gold & Precious Metals Ltd	ASA	E+	7.17	E / 0.4	-30.86 / 7	-30.34 / 4	-24.08 / 5	0.56	C- / 3.7	-13.93	-10.75
IN	Salient Midstream and MLP Fund	SMM	E+	9.53	E+ / 0.6	-57.26 / 1	-14.79 / 12	--	15.49	C- / 3.4	-12.89	-11.88
FO	Aberdeen Latin America Equity Fund	LAQ	E+	15.25	E+ / 0.7	-29.29 / 8	-21.34 / 7	-12.07 / 12	2.06	C- / 3.7	-11.65	-10.42
EN	Tortoise Pipeline & Enrgy Fund Inc	TTP	E+	14.51	E+ / 0.8	-50.96 / 1	-12.38 / 14	--	12.41	C- / 3.6	-12.80	-12.28
FO	Aberdeen Chile Fund	CH	E+	5.58	E+ / 0.9	-16.07 / 17	-20.34 / 8	-12.84 / 11	10.75	C- / 3.7	-13.49	-10.36
FO	Turkish Investment Fund	TKF	E+	7.78	D- / 1.4	-26.92 / 9	-11.00 / 16	-5.89 / 18	1.92	C- / 3.2	-13.75	-12.33
IN	Cohen&Steers MLP Inc and Energy Op	MIE	D-	10.46	E- / 0.1	-42.76 / 3	--	--	9.46	C / 4.7	-3.77	-10.11
EN	First Trust New Opptys MLP & Energ	FPL	D-	10.77	E- / 0.1	-35.73 / 5	--	--	11.70	C / 5.1	-7.47	-8.90
FO	Latin American Discovery Fund	LDF	D-	7.43	E+ / 0.7	-31.42 / 7	-21.36 / 7	-15.30 / 8	0.44	C / 4.8	-11.65	-10.21
PM	Central Fund of Canada	CEF	D-	9.99	E+ / 0.8	-14.31 / 19	-22.08 / 7	-12.11 / 12	0.10	C- / 4.1	-11.28	-8.56
PM	GAMCO Global Gold Nat ResandIncome	GGN	D-	4.75	E+ / 0.9	-21.50 / 12	-19.14 / 9	-13.92 / 10	17.68	C / 4.5	-11.05	-7.30
EM	Morgan Stanley Emg Mkts Dom Debt	EDD	D-	6.80	E+ / 0.9	-27.28 / 9	-19.03 / 9	-8.34 / 15	11.76	C / 4.8	-17.07	-14.71
EN	Fiduciary/Claymore MLP Opp	FMO	D-	12.98	D- / 1.0	-46.51 / 2	-11.38 / 15	-3.04 / 22	13.28	C / 5.3	-10.05	-2.10
EN	Kayne Anderson MLP Inv Co	KYN	D-	17.29	D- / 1.0	-50.61 / 1	-10.32 / 17	-4.05 / 20	15.21	C / 4.5	-2.43	6.99
GI	RENN Fund	RCG	D-	0.90	D- / 1.0	-30.23 / 7	-14.30 / 13	-13.88 / 10	0.00	C / 4.7	-41.56	-39.44
GL	Tortoise Energy Independence Fund	NDP	D-	11.28	D- / 1.0	-35.47 / 5	-13.85 / 13	--	15.51	C- / 4.0	-14.16	-9.95
EM	Aberdeen Indonesia Fund	IF	D-	5.52	D- / 1.1	-32.92 / 6	-16.33 / 11	-6.38 / 17	0.01	C- / 3.8	-15.08	-12.13
FO	Central Europe Russia and Turkey	CEE	D-	16.63	D- / 1.1	-13.67 / 19	-17.36 / 10	-10.54 / 13	2.92	C / 4.3	-12.52	-10.78
EN	ClearBridge Energy MLP Oppty Fd In	EMO	D-	12.74	D- / 1.1	-41.79 / 3	-11.24 / 16	--	12.40	C / 4.3	-7.95	-9.21
EN	GAMCO Nat Res Gold & Income Trust	GNT	D-	5.73	D- / 1.1	-19.50 / 14	-16.26 / 11	--	14.66	C- / 3.7	-11.44	-11.05
EN	ClearBridge Energy MLP Fund Inc	CEM	D-	15.18	D- / 1.2	-40.79 / 3	-9.26 / 18	-0.98 / 25	11.59	C / 4.4	-5.07	-4.50
IN	ClearBridge Engy MLP To Rtn Fd Inc	CTR	D-	12.31	D- / 1.2	-38.57 / 4	-9.80 / 18	--	11.70	C / 4.6	-8.75	-9.39
GI	Nuveen Energy MLP Total Return Fun	JMF	D-	11.10	D- / 1.2	-41.12 / 3	-9.78 / 18	--	12.14	C / 4.7	-11.69	-9.29
EM	Templeton Emerging Markets Fd	EMF	D-	9.97	D- / 1.2	-26.92 / 9	-13.38 / 14	-10.28 / 13	3.13	C / 4.3	-10.42	-10.85
EN	BlackRock Energy & Resources	BGR	D-	12.53	D- / 1.3	-32.98 / 6	-9.61 / 18	-6.51 / 17	10.53	C / 5.1	-10.82	-3.29
GL	Nuveen Global High Income	XJGHX	D-	13.74	D- / 1.3	-12.87 / 20	--	--	11.53	C / 4.5	-14.34	-14.50
EN	Kayne Anderson Engy Development Co	KED	D-	17.56	D- / 1.4	-48.92 / 2	-5.77 / 24	5.38 / 49	9.05	C / 4.5	-25.09	-4.98
GL	Stone Harbor Emg Markets Total Inc	EDI	D-	11.37	D- / 1.4	-14.47 / 18	-14.61 / 12	--	15.95	C / 4.6	-15.09	-13.32
EM	Voya Emerging Markets High Div Eqt	IHD	D-	7.40	D- / 1.4	-19.05 / 14	-12.70 / 14	--	12.43	C / 4.8	-12.22	-11.27
IN	BlackRock Res & Commdty Strat Trus	BCX	D-	7.13	D- / 1.5	-19.98 / 13	-11.32 / 16	--	11.02	C / 4.8	-14.61	-14.92
GL	Brookfield Gl Lstd Infr Inc Fd	INF	D-	11.75	D- / 1.5	-37.95 / 4	-8.23 / 19	--	11.92	C / 4.5	-17.25	-12.85
GI	AllianzGI Convertible & Income II	NCZ	D-	5.05	D / 1.6	-37.87 / 4	-6.10 / 23	-1.72 / 23	13.66	C / 4.8	-9.01	2.03
GL	Pioneer High Income Trust	PHT	D-	9.50	D / 1.7	-38.01 / 4	-7.73 / 20	0.74 / 30	14.53	C / 4.7	0.85	6.31
EM	Stone Harbor Emg Markets Income	EDF	D-	12.05	D / 1.7	-9.79 / 26	-11.51 / 15	-3.66 / 21	17.93	C / 4.7	-10.81	-7.63
EM	Aberdeen Emerging Mkt Sm Co Opptys	ETF	D-	10.86	D / 2.0	-16.76 / 16	-8.37 / 19	-1.88 / 23	0.00	C- / 4.0	-14.22	-12.37
FO	Thai Fund	TTF	D-	6.86	C- / 3.5	-10.43 / 25	0.86 / 41	12.00 / 78	3.58	D+ / 2.3	-14.99	-12.55
FO	Mexico Fund	MXF	D	16.62	D / 1.8	-11.91 / 22	-9.82 / 18	-0.64 / 26	0.00	C / 4.8	-11.92	-6.51
FO	Aberdeen Singapore	SGF	D	8.56	D+ / 2.3	-17.48 / 16	-6.38 / 22	-4.01 / 20	23.25	C+ / 5.6	-14.49	-13.05

* Denotes ETF Fund, N/A denotes number is not available

Section V

Performance: Best and Worst ETFs and Other Closed-End Funds

A compilation of those

Exchange-Traded Funds and Other

Closed-End Mutual Funds

receiving the highest and lowest Performance Ratings.

Funds are listed in order by Performance Rating.

Section V Contents

This section contains a summary analysis of each of the top and bottom ETFs and other closed-end mutual funds as determined by their respective TheStreet Performance Ratings. Since the Performance Rating does not take into consideration the amount of risk a fund poses, the selection of funds presented here is based solely on each fund's financial performance over the past three years.

You can use this section to identify those funds that have historically given shareholders the highest returns on their investments. A word of caution though: past performance is not necessarily indicative of future results. While these funds have provided the highest returns, some of them may be currently overvalued and due for a correction.

1. Fund Type

The mutual fund's peer category based on an analysis of its investment portfolio.

COH	Corporate – High Yield	HL	Health
COI	Corporate – Inv. Grade	IN	Income
EM	Emerging Market	LP	Loan Participation
EN	Energy/Natural Resources	MTG	Mortgage
FS	Financial Services	MUH	Municipal – High Yield
FO	Foreign	MUN	Municipal – National
GEI	General – Inv. Grade	MUS	Municipal – Single State
GEN	General Bond	PM	Precious Metals
GL	Global	USA	U.S. Gov. – Agency
GR	Growth	UT	Utilities
GI	Growth and Income		

A blank fund type means that the mutual fund has not yet been categorized.

2. Fund Name

The name of the mutual fund as stated in its prospectus, which can sometimes differ slightly from the name that the company uses for advertising. If you cannot find the particular mutual fund you are interested in, or if you have any doubts regarding the precise name, verify the information with your broker or on your account statement. Also, use the fund's ticker symbol for confirmation. (See column 3.)

3. Ticker Symbol

The unique alphabetic symbol used for identifying and trading a specific mutual fund. No two funds can have the same ticker symbol.

4. Overall Investment Rating

Our overall rating is measured on a scale from A to E based on each fund's risk-adjusted performance. Please see page 10 for specific descriptions of each letter grade. Also, refer to page 7 for information on how our ratings are derived. Most important, when using this rating, please be sure to consider the warnings beginning on page 11 regarding the ratings' limitations and the underlying assumptions.

5. Price

Closing price of the fund on the date shown.

6. **Performance Rating/Points** — A letter grade rating based solely on the mutual fund's financial performance over the trailing three years, without any consideration for the amount of risk the fund poses. Like the overall Investment Rating, the Performance Rating is measured on a scale from A to E for ease of interpretation. The points score indicates where the Performance Rating falls on a scale of 0 to 10.

7. **1-Year Total Return** — The total return the fund has provided investors over the preceeding 52 weeks. This total return figure is computed based on the fund's dividend distributions and share price appreciation/depreciation during the period, net of the expenses and fees it imposes on its shareholders.

8. **1-Year Total Return Percentile** — The fund's percentile rank based on its one-year performance compared to that of all other closed-end funds in existence for at least one year. A score of 99 is the best possible, indicating that the fund outperformed 99% of the closed-end mutual funds. Zero is the worst possible percentile score.

9. **3-Year Total Return** — The total annual return the fund has provided investors over the preceeding 156 weeks.

10. **3-Year Total Return Percentile** — The fund's percentile rank based on its three-year performance compared to that of all other closed-end funds in existence for at least three years. A score of 99 is the best possible, indicating that the fund outperformed 99% of the closed-end mutual funds. Zero is the worst possible percentile score.

11. **5-Year Total Return** — The total annual return the fund has provided investors over the preceeding 260 weeks.

12. **5-Year Total Return Percentile** — The fund's percentile rank based on its five-year performance compared to that of all other closed-end funds in existence for at least five years. A score of 99 is the best possible, indicating that the fund outperformed 99% of the closed-end mutual funds. Zero is the worst possible percentile score.

13. **Dividend Yield** — Most recent quarterly dividend to fund investors annualized, expressed as a percent of the fund's current share price. The dividend yield of a fund can have little correlation to the amount of dividends the fund has received from its underlying investments. Rather, dividend distributions are based on a fund's need to pass earnings from both dividends and gains on the sale of investments along to shareholders. Thus, these dividend distributions are included as a part of the fund's total return.

    Keep in mind that dividend income may be taxed at a different rate than capital gains depending on your income tax bracket.

14. Risk Rating/Points

A letter grade rating based solely on the mutual fund's risk as determined by its monthly performance volatility over the trailing three years. The risk rating does not take into consideration the overall financial performance the fund has achieved or the total return it has provided to its shareholders. Like the overall Investment Rating, the Risk Rating is measured on a scale from A to E for ease of interpretation. The points score indicates where the Risk Rating falls on a scale of 0 to 10.

15. Premium/ Discount

A comparison of the fund's price to its NAV as of the date indicated. The premium (+) or discount (-) indicates the percentage the shares are trading above or below the fund's NAV per share.

If the price is above the fund's NAV, the fund is said to be trading at a premium. If the price is lower than the fund's NAV, the fund is trading at a discount.

16. 1-Year Average Premium/ Discount

The average of the fund's premium/discount over the preceeding year.

It can be useful to compare the fund's current premium/discount to its one-year average. If the fund is currently trading at a premium/discount that is lower/higher than its one-year average, then there has been less demand for the fund in more recent times than over the past year. Conversely, if the fund is currently trading at a premium/discount that is higher/lower than its one-year average, this indicates that there has been greater demand for the fund in more recent times than over the past year.

99 Pct = Best
0 Pct = Worst

Fund Type	Fund Name	Ticker Symbol	Overall Investment Rating	Price As of 12/31/15	PERFORMANCE: Performance Rating/Pts	Annualized Total Return Through 12/31/15: 1Yr/Pct	3Yr/Pct	5Yr/Pct	Dividend Yield %	RISK: Risk Rating/Pts	VALUATION: Premium/Discount As of 12/31/15	1 Year Average
IN	*ProShares UltraShort Bloomberg C	CMD	**A+**	140.41	**A+ / 9.9**	59.72 / 99	38.75 / 99	22.43 / 98	0.00	**B- / 7.3**	-1.05	-0.42
FO	*WisdomTree Japan Hedged Health C	DXJH	**A+**	34.70	**A+ / 9.9**	35.61 / 99	--	--	0.58	**B- / 7.9**	-1.00	N/A
EN	*United States Short Oil Fund	DNO	**B+**	81.43	**A+ / 9.9**	44.68 / 99	29.62 / 98	14.22 / 89	0.00	**C / 5.5**	0.23	0.12
GR	*DB Commodity Double Short ETN	DEE	**C+**	96.14	**A+ / 9.9**	59.04 / 99	49.77 / 99	20.47 / 98	0.00	**C- / 3.9**	-1.71	-0.44
PM	*DB Base Metals Double Short ETN	BOM	**C+**	25.40	**A+ / 9.9**	60.65 / 99	26.44 / 98	17.83 / 96	0.00	**C- / 3.4**	4.66	-0.19
GR	*DB Crude Oil Short ETN	SZO	**C+**	91.70	**A+ / 9.9**	50.63 / 99	29.87 / 98	15.26 / 92	0.00	**C- / 3.9**	-1.22	-0.51
GR	*DB Crude Oil Double Short ETN	DTO	**C+**	158.12	**A+ / 9.9**	92.54 / 99	54.95 / 99	23.30 / 99	0.00	**C- / 3.1**	-0.93	0.05
EN	*ProShares UltraShort Silver	ZSL	**C+**	64.55	**A+ / 9.9**	9.61 / 87	37.39 / 99	-10.45 / 13	0.00	**C- / 3.2**	-0.05	-0.62
GR	*ProShares Ultra QQQ	QLD	**C**	78.36	**A+ / 9.9**	15.22 / 95	40.03 / 99	29.80 / 99	0.12	**D / 2.1**	0.04	0.01
HL	*ProShares Ultra Health Care	RXL	**C**	65.98	**A+ / 9.9**	7.32 / 84	44.94 / 99	38.24 / 99	3.26	**D / 2.1**	-0.02	-0.01
EN	*ProShares UltraShort Bloomberg C	SCO	**C**	133.64	**A+ / 9.9**	67.26 / 99	50.45 / 99	20.05 / 97	0.00	**D+ / 2.8**	0.32	0.18
FO	*ProShares UltraShort MSCI Br Cap	BZQ	**C**	81.13	**A+ / 9.9**	85.40 / 99	38.82 / 99	21.19 / 98	0.00	**D+ / 2.3**	-0.37	-0.02
GR	*ProShares UltraPro QQQ	TQQQ	**C**	114.14	**A+ / 9.9**	17.94 / 97	60.47 / 99	41.79 / 99	0.00	**D+ / 2.9**	-0.03	0.01
GL	*VelocityShares 3x Inverse Silver	DSLV	**C**	71.69	**A+ / 9.9**	-0.26 / 58	38.29 / 99	--	0.00	**D / 1.9**	-0.31	-0.12
GR	*Direxion Daily Technology Bull 3	TECL	**C-**	36.43	**A+ / 9.9**	4.98 / 79	41.48 / 99	24.86 / 99	0.00	**D- / 1.0**	0.00	0.01
IN	*Direxion Daily Semiconductor Bul	SOXL	**C-**	26.77	**A+ / 9.9**	-20.58 / 13	53.39 / 99	14.25 / 89	0.00	**E- / 0.2**	0.07	0.01
HL	*ProShares Ultra Nasdaq Biotech	BIB	**C-**	71.49	**A+ / 9.9**	11.86 / 91	65.97 / 99	56.19 / 99	0.00	**E- / 0.2**	0.08	0.02
GR	*Direxion Daily Retail Bull 3X	RETL	**C-**	37.64	**A+ / 9.9**	47.33 / 99	62.27 / 99	55.49 / 99	0.00	**E- / 0.1**	0.29	0.14
HL	*Direxion Daily Healthcare Bull 3	CURE	**C-**	33.40	**A+ / 9.9**	6.24 / 82	67.86 / 99	--	0.00	**E- / 0.2**	0.03	0.01
GL	*VelocityShares 3x Inverse Crude	DWTI	**C-**	199.79	**A+ / 9.9**	59.26 / 99	62.92 / 99	--	0.00	**E+ / 0.9**	0.51	0.28
GEI	*WisdomTree Bloomberg US Dollar B	USDU	**A+**	27.36	**A+ / 9.8**	19.69 / 98	--	--	6.48	**B+ / 9.0**	-0.11	0.04
HL	*First Trust AMEX Biotechnology	FBT	**A**	113.02	**A+ / 9.8**	10.42 / 89	33.01 / 99	23.53 / 99	0.05	**C+ / 6.7**	-0.04	0.03
HL	*iShares Nasdaq Biotechnology	IBB	**B+**	338.33	**A+ / 9.8**	10.48 / 89	33.48 / 99	29.10 / 99	0.06	**C+ / 5.6**	-0.03	0.02
IN	*Market Vectors Biotech ETF	BBH	**B+**	126.95	**A+ / 9.8**	9.32 / 87	31.90 / 98	--	0.27	**C+ / 6.1**	0.10	0.01
HL	*PowerShares Dynamic Pharmaceutic	PJP	**B**	69.97	**A+ / 9.8**	14.64 / 95	30.56 / 98	28.09 / 99	0.87	**C / 5.2**	-0.01	N/A
IN	*ProShares Ultra Semiconductors	USD	**B-**	86.62	**A+ / 9.8**	-7.94 / 31	40.06 / 99	16.64 / 94	0.48	**C / 4.5**	0.52	-0.09
FO	*Market Vectors ChinaAMC SME-ChiN	CNXT	**B-**	41.29	**A+ / 9.8**	42.39 / 99	--	--	0.00	**C / 4.6**	-1.08	-0.45
IN	*ProShares Ultra Consumer Goods	UGE	**C+**	105.50	**A+ / 9.8**	11.83 / 91	28.20 / 98	25.68 / 99	0.61	**C- / 3.1**	1.12	-0.07
GR	*DB Agriculture Double Short ETN	AGA	**C+**	30.15	**A+ / 9.8**	23.65 / 99	28.69 / 98	10.27 / 67	0.00	**C- / 3.5**	-0.56	-0.14
IN	*ProShares Ultra Consumer Service	UCC	**C**	106.68	**A+ / 9.8**	9.62 / 87	37.33 / 99	34.11 / 99	0.15	**D+ / 2.9**	0.04	-0.04
GR	*ProShares Ultra Technology	ROM	**C**	78.74	**A+ / 9.8**	4.04 / 77	29.47 / 98	18.85 / 97	0.14	**D+ / 2.5**	0.61	-0.06
GR	*DB Commodity Short ETN	DDP	**C**	57.98	**A+ / 9.8**	30.96 / 99	23.75 / 97	11.42 / 75	0.00	**D+ / 2.9**	0.19	-0.99
GR	*Direxion S&P 500 Bull 3X Shares	SPXL	**C**	82.88	**A+ / 9.8**	-5.43 / 37	37.78 / 99	27.58 / 99	0.00	**D / 1.8**	-0.11	-0.04
IN	*ProShares UltraPro S&P500	UPRO	**C**	62.56	**A+ / 9.8**	-5.08 / 38	38.19 / 99	29.06 / 99	0.63	**D / 1.9**	-0.22	-0.03
GL	*VelocityShares 3x Inverse Gold E	DGLD	**C**	94.84	**A+ / 9.8**	23.84 / 99	30.74 / 98	--	0.00	**D+ / 2.9**	0.14	-0.21
HL	*SPDR S&P Biotech ETF	XBI	**C-**	70.20	**A+ / 9.8**	12.66 / 92	32.53 / 99	27.63 / 99	1.70	**E+ / 0.9**	0.00	-0.06
HL	*SPDR S&P Pharmaceuticals ETF	XPH	**C-**	51.20	**A+ / 9.8**	7.81 / 85	29.49 / 98	22.57 / 98	1.11	**D- / 1.5**	-0.02	0.01
FS	*Direxion Financial Bull 3x Share	FAS	**C-**	29.07	**A+ / 9.8**	-8.83 / 29	37.58 / 99	19.19 / 97	0.00	**D- / 1.0**	0.00	0.02
IN	*ProShares UltraShort Blmbrg Nat	KOLD	**C-**	139.66	**A+ / 9.8**	75.01 / 99	9.64 / 74	--	0.00	**E / 0.5**	0.04	0.05
GI	*ProShares UltraPro Finl Sel Sect	FINU	**C-**	80.27	**A+ / 9.8**	-8.19 / 30	37.28 / 99	--	0.62	**D- / 1.0**	2.52	0.12
GR	*PowerShares S&P SC Health Care	PSCH	**A**	71.87	**A+ / 9.7**	21.58 / 98	26.28 / 98	21.49 / 98	0.00	**C+ / 6.9**	0.11	0.05
EN	*ProShares UltraShort Gold	GLL	**A-**	115.83	**A+ / 9.7**	16.22 / 96	22.06 / 96	-0.66 / 26	0.00	**C+ / 6.7**	-0.04	-0.21
HL	*PowerShares Dynamic Biotech&Geno	PBE	**B+**	50.52	**A+ / 9.7**	1.40 / 69	29.56 / 98	19.01 / 97	1.83	**C / 5.5**	-0.08	-0.02
GR	*First Trust Dow Jones Internet I	FDN	**B+**	74.61	**A+ / 9.7**	21.81 / 98	22.75 / 96	16.23 / 93	0.00	**C+ / 6.1**	-0.03	0.01
FS	*ProShares Ultra S&P Regional Ban	KRU	**B**	98.88	**A+ / 9.7**	13.18 / 93	26.05 / 97	16.69 / 94	0.75	**C / 5.0**	2.45	-0.13
IN	*PowerShares NASDAQ Internet Port	PNQI	**B-**	80.23	**A+ / 9.7**	19.71 / 98	23.22 / 97	17.59 / 95	0.00	**C / 4.8**	0.14	-0.01
IN	*SPDR S&P Semiconductor ETF	XSD	**C+**	43.68	**A+ / 9.7**	10.31 / 89	23.86 / 97	9.35 / 62	1.34	**C- / 3.8**	-0.07	N/A
GR	*ProShares Ultra S&P500	SSO	**C+**	63.00	**A+ / 9.7**	-1.06 / 55	26.17 / 97	21.38 / 98	0.92	**C- / 3.3**	-0.05	-0.02
PM	*DB Gold Double Short ETN	DZZ	**C+**	8.87	**A+ / 9.7**	17.95 / 97	24.78 / 97	0.64 / 30	0.00	**C- / 3.2**	0.11	-0.07
GR	*ProShares UltraPro Dow30	UDOW	**C+**	64.54	**A+ / 9.7**	-8.48 / 30	30.37 / 98	26.18 / 99	0.21	**C- / 3.5**	-0.03	N/A

* Denotes ETF Fund, N/A denotes number is not available

99 Pct = Best
0 Pct = Worst

Fund Type	Fund Name	Ticker Symbol	Overall Investment Rating	Price As of 12/31/15	PERFORMANCE: Performance Rating/Pts	Annualized Total Return Through 12/31/15: 1Yr/Pct	3Yr/Pct	5Yr/Pct	Dividend Yield %	RISK: Risk Rating/Pts	VALUATION: Premium/Discount As of 12/31/15	1 Year Average
EN	*ProShares Ultra Bloomberg Crude	UCO	E-	12.54	E- / 0.0	-74.69 / 0	-56.35 / 1	-44.40 / 1	0.00	D / 1.8	-0.32	-0.17
FO	*Direxion Daily Latin Amer Bull 3	LBJ	E-	12.00	E- / 0.0	-72.65 / 0	-58.11 / 1	-49.03 / 0	0.00	E- / 0.1	0.50	0.22
FO	*ProShares Ultra MSCI Brazil Capp	UBR	E-	25.45	E- / 0.0	-68.36 / 1	-51.29 / 1	-43.04 / 1	0.00	D / 1.8	-2.75	0.07
GR	*Direxion Daily Nat Gas Rel Bull	GASL	E-	6.14	E- / 0.0	-97.14 / 0	-82.35 / 0	-70.79 / 0	0.00	D / 1.8	-0.81	0.16
PM	*Direxion Daily Gold Mnrs Id Bull	NUGT	E-	24.26	E- / 0.0	-79.91 / 0	-83.17 / 0	-72.68 / 0	0.00	D / 1.8	-0.41	0.09
IN	*C-Tracks ETN Citi Volatility Idx	CVOL	E-	0.43	E- / 0.0	-60.11 / 1	-73.97 / 0	-76.75 / 0	0.00	E- / 0.1	4.88	1.13
IN	*VelocityShares Daily 2x VIX S-T	TVIX	E-	6.27	E- / 0.0	-76.44 / 0	-79.26 / 0	-83.97 / 0	0.00	E+ / 0.6	1.79	1.80
GI	*ProShares Ultra VIX Sh-Tm Fut ET	UVXY	E-	28.35	E- / 0.0	-76.70 / 0	-79.00 / 0	--	0.00	E- / 0.1	0.93	0.36
EN	*ProShares Ultra Bloomberg Nat Ga	BOIL	E-	18.48	E- / 0.0	-71.16 / 1	-50.14 / 1	--	0.00	D / 1.8	-0.48	-0.05
GL	*VelocityShares 3x Long Silver ET	USLV	E-	9.81	E- / 0.0	-49.12 / 2	-66.28 / 0	--	0.00	E+ / 0.8	0.41	0.09
GL	*VelocityShares 3x Long Nat Gas E	UGAZ	E-	2.44	E- / 0.0	-88.07 / 0	-71.05 / 0	--	0.00	D / 1.8	-1.21	-0.02
GL	*VelocityShares 3x Long Crude ETN	UWTI	E-	3.95	E- / 0.0	-91.38 / 0	-76.34 / 0	--	0.00	D / 1.7	-1.00	-0.36
FO	*Direxion Brazil Bull 3X	BRZU	E-	11.63	E- / 0.0	-85.43 / 0	--	--	0.00	E- / 0.1	0.61	0.08
GR	*Direxion Jr Gold Miners Idx Bull	JNUG	E-	31.05	E- / 0.0	-77.20 / 0	--	--	0.00	D / 1.8	-0.26	0.19
FO	*Direxion Daily Russia Bull 3x	RUSL	E	11.17	E- / 0.0	-34.29 / 6	-63.71 / 0	--	0.00	D / 1.8	-0.27	0.05
EN	*ETFis InfraCap MLP	AMZA	E	11.15	E- / 0.0	-47.04 / 2	--	--	18.48	D+ / 2.8	0.00	0.25
EN	*ProShares Ultra Silver	AGQ	E-	27.08	E- / 0.1	-29.52 / 8	-46.21 / 1	-37.05 / 2	0.00	E / 0.3	0.07	0.60
GR	*Direxion Daily Technology Bear 3	TECS	E-	31.10	E- / 0.1	-31.49 / 7	-43.75 / 1	-41.21 / 1	0.00	D- / 1.1	0.03	0.01
GR	*ProShares UltraPro Short QQQ	SQQQ	E-	18.72	E- / 0.1	-37.77 / 4	-50.09 / 1	-47.31 / 1	0.00	E+ / 0.6	0.11	-0.01
IN	*Direxion Daily Semiconductor Bea	SOXS	E-	40.17	E- / 0.1	-25.17 / 10	-55.92 / 1	-48.55 / 1	0.00	D / 1.7	-0.10	-0.04
IN	*VelocityShares Dly 2x VIX Med-T	TVIZ	E-	13.32	E- / 0.1	-38.59 / 4	-48.83 / 1	-55.60 / 0	0.00	D / 1.7	-2.06	-0.32
GL	*VelocityShares 3x Long Gold ETN	UGLD	E-	7.37	E- / 0.1	-35.12 / 6	-43.36 / 1	--	0.00	E+ / 0.9	0.00	0.21
EN	*iPath S&P MLP ETN	IMLP	E-	18.35	E- / 0.1	-36.11 / 5	--	--	8.01	D- / 1.2	2.23	0.01
EN	*Barclays ETN + Select MLP ETN	ATMP	E-	18.61	E- / 0.1	-36.80 / 5	--	--	6.88	D- / 1.5	0.27	0.08
GEI	*iShares MSCI Colombia Capped	ICOL	E	10.57	E- / 0.1	-39.81 / 4	--	--	3.21	D / 1.8	0.28	0.94
HL	*ProShares UltraShort Nasdaq Biot	BIS	E	28.71	E- / 0.1	-36.47 / 5	-54.53 / 1	-50.68 / 0	0.00	D / 2.0	-0.14	N/A
GR	*UBS E-TRACS Mo Pay 2xLevd WF MLP	LMLP	E	12.67	E- / 0.1	-33.93 / 6	--	--	36.19	D+ / 2.7	-0.16	0.01
EN	*Global X Junior MLP ETF	MLPJ	E+	7.87	E- / 0.1	-39.37 / 4	--	--	13.72	C / 4.5	-0.38	-0.05
EN	*Yorkville High Income Infras MLP	YMLI	E+	12.62	E- / 0.1	-36.61 / 5	--	--	9.51	C- / 3.8	0.16	-0.04
EN	*ALPS Alerian Energy Infra ETF	ENFR	E+	17.44	E- / 0.1	-37.63 / 4	--	--	1.43	C- / 3.9	0.11	-0.10
EN	*Direxion Zacks MLP High Inc Shar	ZMLP	E+	17.39	E- / 0.1	-43.51 / 3	--	--	9.20	C- / 3.6	-0.34	0.13
EN	*Global X MLP & Energy Infra	MLPX	D-	11.61	E- / 0.1	-36.17 / 5	--	--	5.50	C+ / 5.7	-0.09	0.01
EN	*iPath S&P GSCI Crude Oil TotRet	OIL	E-	6.23	E- / 0.2	-48.98 / 2	-34.48 / 3	-24.12 / 5	0.00	D- / 1.2	8.73	2.21
EN	*iPath Bloomberg Ntrl Gas SI TR A	GAZ	E-	0.72	E- / 0.2	-64.18 / 1	-35.40 / 3	-38.43 / 2	0.00	E- / 0.1	33.33	7.13
FS	*Direxion Financial Bear 3x Share	FAZ	E-	41.18	E- / 0.2	-18.62 / 15	-42.30 / 1	-43.57 / 1	0.00	D- / 1.4	0.05	-0.05
GL	*Direxion Emerging Markets Bull 3	EDC	E-	11.51	E- / 0.2	-47.92 / 2	-32.88 / 3	-29.57 / 3	0.00	D- / 1.0	0.00	0.02
IN	*IPath S&P 500 VIX Sm-Trm Futr ET	VXX	E-	20.10	E- / 0.2	-35.14 / 6	-43.29 / 1	-48.90 / 1	0.00	E+ / 0.6	0.75	0.22
EN	*United States Brent Oil Fund	BNO	E-	12.24	E- / 0.2	-44.41 / 2	-33.19 / 3	-17.03 / 7	0.00	E / 0.3	0.16	-0.12
GI	*VelocityShares VIX Short-Term ET	VIIX	E-	27.12	E- / 0.2	-35.14 / 6	-43.29 / 1	-48.92 / 1	0.00	E+ / 0.6	0.59	0.18
GEI	*ProShares VIX Short-Term Futures	VIXY	E-	13.33	E- / 0.2	-35.32 / 5	-43.47 / 1	--	0.00	E- / 0.1	0.68	0.21
GI	*ProShares UltraPro Sht Finl Sel	FINZ	E-	20.08	E- / 0.2	-16.02 / 17	-41.46 / 1	--	0.00	D- / 1.5	7.04	0.26
GL	*PureFunds ISE Jr Silver SCM/E ET	SILJ	E-	5.07	E- / 0.2	-38.70 / 4	-36.99 / 2	--	2.46	E+ / 0.6	0.40	0.71
GR	*C-Tracks ETN MillerHoward MLP FI	MLPC	E-	15.46	E- / 0.2	-37.82 / 4	--	--	6.34	D- / 1.1	0.13	0.13
GR	*Direxion Jr Gold Miners Idx Bear	JDST	E-	29.74	E- / 0.2	-45.81 / 2	--	--	0.00	E- / 0.2	0.07	-0.18
IN	*ProShares UltraShort Semiconduct	SSG	E	39.50	E- / 0.2	-19.03 / 14	-41.22 / 2	-31.89 / 2	0.00	C- / 3.1	-4.96	0.03
IN	*First Trust ISE-Revere Natural G	FCG	E	4.46	E- / 0.2	-59.17 / 1	-34.11 / 3	-24.92 / 4	3.27	C- / 3.0	0.00	0.04
FO	*Market Vectors Brazil Small-Cap	BRF	E	10.38	E- / 0.2	-47.30 / 2	-35.60 / 2	-25.29 / 4	3.84	C- / 3.2	-0.57	0.37
GL	*Yorkville High Income MLP ETF	YMLP	E	4.68	E- / 0.2	-58.52 / 1	-29.51 / 4	--	25.21	C- / 3.0	-0.43	-0.01
EN	*Market Vectors Coal ETF	KOL	E+	6.25	E- / 0.2	-55.17 / 1	-36.11 / 2	-31.88 / 2	4.62	C / 4.5	-0.48	-0.35
FO	*iShares MSCI Brazil Small-Cap ET	EWZS	E+	6.88	E- / 0.2	-48.26 / 2	-35.49 / 2	-23.45 / 5	3.25	C- / 3.2	-2.55	0.35

* Denotes ETF Fund, N/A denotes number is not available

99 Pct = Best
0 Pct = Worst

Fund Type	Fund Name	Ticker Symbol	Overall Investment Rating	Price As of 12/31/15	PERFORMANCE: Performance Rating/Pts	Annualized Total Return Through 12/31/15: 1Yr/Pct	3Yr/Pct	5Yr/Pct	Dividend Yield %	RISK: Risk Rating/Pts	VALUATION: Premium/Discount As of 12/31/15	1 Year Average
FO	The New Ireland Fund	IRL	A+	13.93	A+ / 9.8	36.24 / 99	25.10 / 97	21.61 / 98	1.17	B- / 7.9	-12.39	-14.28
FS	John Hancock Financial Opptys	BTO	A+	28.03	A+ / 9.7	25.29 / 99	21.19 / 96	16.40 / 94	5.28	B- / 7.3	7.11	-1.29
MUN	Eaton Vance Municipal Inc 2028 Ter	ETX	A+	18.49	A+ / 9.7	10.24 / 96	--	--	4.59	B- / 7.8	-9.72	-11.09
HL	BlackRock Health Sciences Trust	BME	B+	39.35	A+ / 9.7	10.11 / 88	25.19 / 97	20.16 / 98	144.84	C+ / 6.2	8.79	3.01
HL	Tekla Healthcare Investors	HQH	B	29.66	A+ / 9.7	4.01 / 77	28.75 / 98	26.73 / 99	4.59	C / 5.1	-3.45	1.10
HL	Tekla Life Sciences Investors	HQL	B-	23.64	A+ / 9.7	5.44 / 80	26.19 / 97	27.27 / 99	7.36	C / 4.9	-2.23	0.33
MUS	BlackRock VA Muni Bond Trust	BHV	B-	19.75	A+ / 9.7	29.42 / 99	5.38 / 70	8.45 / 84	4.22	C / 4.7	22.52	7.13
GEI	Babson Capital Corporate Investors	MCI	A+	17.25	A+ / 9.6	17.03 / 97	--	--	6.96	B- / 7.3	17.35	9.68
GEI	Babson Capital Participation Inv	MPV	A-	13.75	A+ / 9.6	12.54 / 92	--	--	7.86	C+ / 6.8	0.81	-5.61
FO	Japan Smaller Cap Fund Inc.	JOF	A+	10.23	A / 9.5	24.45 / 99	16.38 / 92	4.95 / 47	1.63	B / 8.1	-12.04	-12.44
MUN	Dreyfus Municipal Bond Infra	DMB	A+	12.38	A / 9.5	8.15 / 92	--	--	6.06	B- / 7.8	-11.06	-11.00
MUS	PIMCO CA Municipal Income Fund III	PZC	A-	11.92	A / 9.5	20.31 / 99	8.42 / 84	13.94 / 98	6.04	C+ / 6.8	15.62	8.13
IN	Eaton Vance Tax Mgd Buy Write Opp	ETV	A-	15.30	A / 9.5	17.56 / 97	16.13 / 91	13.45 / 86	8.69	B- / 7.0	5.08	0.07
IN	Nuveen Nasdaq 100 Dynamic Overwrit	QQQX	A	19.37	A / 9.4	9.21 / 87	16.03 / 91	14.83 / 91	7.23	B- / 7.2	-3.05	-6.18
GR	Columbia Seligman Prem Tech Gro	STK	A-	17.93	A / 9.4	4.43 / 78	18.87 / 94	9.84 / 65	0.50	C+ / 6.9	3.70	2.80
IN	Liberty All-Star Growth Fund	ASG	B+	4.58	A / 9.4	11.67 / 91	15.51 / 90	11.69 / 76	37.12	C+ / 6.7	-8.22	-10.00
FO	New Germany Fund	GF	B	14.70	A / 9.4	14.57 / 94	17.51 / 93	13.76 / 87	0.54	C+ / 5.7	-9.20	-9.38
IN	Eaton Vance Enhanced Eqty Inc II	EOS	A	13.64	A / 9.3	6.44 / 82	16.82 / 92	11.37 / 74	7.70	B- / 7.3	-5.34	-6.06
IN	Eaton Vance Tax-Managed Buy-Write	ETB	A	16.69	A / 9.3	14.03 / 94	13.64 / 86	12.03 / 78	7.77	B- / 7.3	7.61	0.12
IN	Nuveen S&P 500 Buy Write Income	JPZ	A+	13.43	A- / 9.2	15.26 / 95	11.85 / 81	10.14 / 66	7.42	B- / 7.8	0.67	-5.89
HL	Gabelli Healthcare & WellnessRx Tr	GRX	A+	10.25	A- / 9.2	3.05 / 74	17.21 / 92	18.66 / 97	5.07	B- / 7.8	-13.06	-12.32
IN	Eaton Vance Enhanced Eqty Inc	EOI	A	13.42	A- / 9.2	5.57 / 80	15.55 / 90	10.20 / 66	7.73	B- / 7.5	-4.01	-8.76
MUN	Nuveen Intermdt Dur Qlty Mun Term	NIQ	A	12.88	A- / 9.2	6.37 / 88	--	--	4.43	B- / 7.5	-7.93	-8.59
IN	Nuveen Core Equity Alpha Fund	JCE	A-	14.27	A- / 9.2	0.43 / 63	16.95 / 92	14.46 / 89	8.49	B- / 7.2	-4.42	-4.82
IN	Eaton Vance Tax Mgd Div Eqty Inc	ETY	A	11.20	A- / 9.1	9.21 / 87	14.49 / 89	9.92 / 65	9.03	B- / 7.7	-5.56	-7.54
FO	Aberdeen Japan Equity	JEQ	A-	7.70	A- / 9.1	17.25 / 97	12.60 / 83	6.55 / 53	0.63	B- / 7.4	-9.20	-11.47
GI	Cohen&Steers Quality Income Realty	RQI	B+	12.22	A- / 9.1	7.82 / 85	13.33 / 85	14.70 / 90	3.93	C+ / 6.8	-9.21	-12.74
MUS	MFS CA Muni	CCA	A-	11.84	A- / 9.0	15.02 / 99	4.50 / 67	9.48 / 90	5.17	B- / 7.4	-7.21	-10.24
MUS	Nuveen CA AMT-Free Municipal Incom	NKX	A-	15.36	A- / 9.0	11.47 / 97	6.28 / 74	11.45 / 95	6.09	B- / 7.4	-4.42	-6.58
MUN	PIMCO Municipal Income Fund	PMF	B+	15.45	A- / 9.0	15.69 / 99	6.11 / 73	12.07 / 97	6.31	C+ / 6.3	16.52	12.42
GL	Flaherty & Crumrine Dyn Pfd and In	DFP	A	22.90	B+ / 8.9	9.75 / 88	--	--	8.38	B- / 7.8	-5.37	-7.23
MTG	Western Asset Mtge Defined Oppty	DMO	B+	23.55	B+ / 8.9	13.42 / 93	12.84 / 84	15.19 / 92	10.70	C+ / 6.7	3.43	-1.51
GI	BlackRock Enhanced Capital and Inc	CII	A	14.14	B+ / 8.8	8.19 / 85	12.57 / 83	8.71 / 60	8.49	B- / 7.8	-6.42	-6.46
MUS	Nuveen CA Muni Value	NCA	A-	10.88	B+ / 8.8	8.09 / 92	6.64 / 76	10.04 / 92	4.66	B- / 7.6	3.32	0.83
MUH	Nuveen Muni High Income Opport	NMZ	B+	13.82	B+ / 8.8	9.86 / 95	5.66 / 72	11.69 / 96	6.60	C+ / 6.9	0.95	-0.93
GL	Canadian World Fund Limited	T.CWF	B	4.96	B+ / 8.8	19.81 / 98	12.00 / 82	3.73 / 42	0.00	C+ / 5.8	-34.22	-34.56
MUN	Eaton Vance Municipal Inc Tr	EVN	B	13.73	B+ / 8.8	9.79 / 95	5.84 / 72	12.18 / 97	6.19	C+ / 6.4	3.86	1.70
MUN	BlackRock MuniAssets Fund	MUA	B+	14.27	B+ / 8.7	9.14 / 94	5.27 / 70	10.34 / 93	5.56	B- / 7.1	0.56	-2.12
GL	PIMCO Dynamic Income	PDI	B+	27.36	B+ / 8.7	7.30 / 84	12.01 / 82	--	76.97	C+ / 6.7	0.70	-4.25
MUS	BlackRock NY Municipal Income Trus	BNY	B	15.58	B+ / 8.7	14.40 / 98	3.08 / 60	9.18 / 88	5.31	C+ / 6.3	1.56	-3.12
IN	Flaherty & Crumrine Pref Sec Inc	FFC	B	20.05	B+ / 8.7	10.95 / 90	9.81 / 75	14.50 / 89	8.14	C+ / 6.2	6.42	2.33
IN	Adams Diversified Equity	ADX	A-	12.83	B+ / 8.6	0.65 / 65	13.38 / 85	10.70 / 70	1.17	B- / 7.8	-14.69	-14.43
MUS	BlackRock Muni NY Interm Duration	MNE	A-	15.18	B+ / 8.6	13.89 / 98	3.37 / 62	8.75 / 86	4.55	B- / 7.5	-3.74	-8.82
MUS	BlackRock CA Municipal Income Trus	BFZ	B+	15.95	B+ / 8.6	12.49 / 98	3.78 / 63	11.52 / 96	5.43	C+ / 6.7	-0.25	-4.39
MUS	PIMCO CA Municipal Income Fund II	PCK	B+	9.94	B+ / 8.6	13.01 / 98	4.42 / 66	11.00 / 95	6.49	B- / 7.2	11.06	10.63
MUN	Nuveen California Municipal Value	NCB	B+	17.02	B+ / 8.6	8.26 / 92	6.42 / 75	8.94 / 87	4.96	B- / 7.3	-1.10	-3.80
GI	LMP Real Estate Income Fund Inc	RIT	B	13.04	B+ / 8.6	9.91 / 88	10.81 / 78	12.29 / 80	5.52	C+ / 6.4	-3.91	-9.16
MUS	PIMCO NY Municipal Income Fund III	PYN	B+	10.27	B+ / 8.5	11.21 / 97	5.19 / 70	10.86 / 94	6.13	B- / 7.0	7.54	4.90
MUS	Eaton Vance OH Muni Bond	EIO	B+	13.42	B+ / 8.5	12.64 / 98	2.92 / 59	8.78 / 87	5.23	B- / 7.1	-6.55	-7.68
MUS	BlackRock MuniYield AZ Fund	MZA	B	16.86	B+ / 8.5	8.24 / 92	7.49 / 80	11.99 / 96	4.95	C+ / 6.6	12.93	13.49

* Denotes ETF Fund, N/A denotes number is not available

99 Pct = Best
0 Pct = Worst

Fund Type	Fund Name	Ticker Symbol	Overall Investment Rating	Price As of 12/31/15	PERFORMANCE: Performance Rating/Pts	Annualized Total Return Through 12/31/15: 1Yr/Pct	3Yr/Pct	5Yr/Pct	Dividend Yield %	RISK: Risk Rating/Pts	VALUATION: Premium/Discount As of 12/31/15	1 Year Average
EN	Nuveen All Cap Energy MLP Opps	JML	**E-**	6.97	**E- / 0.0**	-50.36 / 1	--	--	19.63	**D / 1.8**	-7.07	-0.77
EN	Duff & Phelps Select Energy MLP	DSE	**E-**	5.98	**E- / 0.0**	-53.71 / 1	--	--	21.07	**D / 1.7**	-8.42	-2.23
EN	Goldman Sachs MLP and Energy Ren	XGERX	**E-**	5.48	**E- / 0.0**	-57.97 / 1	--	--	24.45	**D / 1.8**	-6.64	4.53
EN	Goldman Sachs MLP Income Oppty	XGMZX	**E**	8.23	**E- / 0.0**	-49.36 / 2	--	--	16.77	**D / 1.9**	-6.48	0.11
GL	Neuberger Berman MLP Income	NML	**E+**	8.16	**E- / 0.0**	-50.28 / 2	--	--	15.44	**C- / 3.6**	-0.49	-4.07
USA	Cushing Energy Income	SRF	**E-**	8.42	**E- / 0.1**	-75.37 / 0	-45.48 / 1	--	17.38	**D / 1.8**	-10.33	-8.48
GL	ClearBridge American Energy MLP In	CBA	**E+**	8.19	**E- / 0.1**	-45.00 / 2	--	--	14.90	**C- / 3.9**	-9.50	-7.77
EN	Center Coast MLP & Infrastructure	CEN	**E+**	10.12	**E- / 0.1**	-38.22 / 4	--	--	12.36	**C- / 3.8**	-3.89	-4.58
IN	Cohen&Steers MLP Inc and Energy Op	MIE	**D-**	10.46	**E- / 0.1**	-42.76 / 3	--	--	9.46	**C / 4.7**	-3.77	-10.11
EN	First Trust New Opptys MLP & Energ	FPL	**D-**	10.77	**E- / 0.1**	-35.73 / 5	--	--	11.70	**C / 5.1**	-7.47	-8.90
GL	Miller/Howard High Income Equity	XHIEX	**E+**	11.46	**E- / 0.2**	-36.85 / 5	--	--	12.15	**C- / 3.4**	-11.09	-4.87
EN	Kayne Anderson Energy Tot Ret	KYE	**E+**	8.47	**E / 0.3**	-66.00 / 1	-23.87 / 6	-15.16 / 8	15.58	**C- / 3.6**	-11.22	-8.03
GI	The Cushing MLP Total Return Fund	SRV	**E+**	10.67	**E / 0.3**	-63.06 / 1	-28.40 / 4	-17.14 / 6	9.28	**C- / 3.8**	-11.31	-13.23
PM	ASA Gold & Precious Metals Ltd	ASA	**E+**	7.17	**E / 0.4**	-30.86 / 7	-30.34 / 4	-24.08 / 5	0.56	**C- / 3.7**	-13.93	-10.75
IN	Kayne Anderson Midstream/Energy	KMF	**E**	12.37	**E / 0.5**	-57.65 / 1	-17.86 / 10	-5.85 / 18	14.55	**D / 2.1**	-1.83	-7.82
IN	Salient Midstream and MLP Fund	SMM	**E+**	9.53	**E+ / 0.6**	-57.26 / 1	-14.79 / 12	--	15.49	**C- / 3.4**	-12.89	-11.88
FO	Aberdeen Latin America Equity Fund	LAQ	**E+**	15.25	**E+ / 0.7**	-29.29 / 8	-21.34 / 7	-12.07 / 12	2.06	**C- / 3.7**	-11.65	-10.42
FO	Latin American Discovery Fund	LDF	**D-**	7.43	**E+ / 0.7**	-31.42 / 7	-21.36 / 7	-15.30 / 8	0.44	**C / 4.8**	-11.65	-10.21
EN	Tortoise Pipeline & Enrgy Fund Inc	TTP	**E+**	14.51	**E+ / 0.8**	-50.96 / 1	-12.38 / 14	--	12.41	**C- / 3.6**	-12.80	-12.28
PM	Central Fund of Canada	CEF	**D-**	9.99	**E+ / 0.8**	-14.31 / 19	-22.08 / 7	-12.11 / 12	0.10	**C- / 4.1**	-11.28	-8.56
FO	Aberdeen Chile Fund	CH	**E+**	5.58	**E+ / 0.9**	-16.07 / 17	-20.34 / 8	-12.84 / 11	10.75	**C- / 3.7**	-13.49	-10.36
PM	GAMCO Global Gold Nat ResandIncome	GGN	**D-**	4.75	**E+ / 0.9**	-21.50 / 12	-19.14 / 9	-13.92 / 10	17.68	**C / 4.5**	-11.05	-7.30
EM	Morgan Stanley Emg Mkts Dom Debt	EDD	**D-**	6.80	**E+ / 0.9**	-27.28 / 9	-19.03 / 9	-8.34 / 15	11.76	**C / 4.8**	-17.07	-14.71
GI	RENN Fund	RCG	**D-**	0.90	**D- / 1.0**	-30.23 / 7	-14.30 / 13	-13.88 / 10	0.00	**C / 4.7**	-41.56	-39.44
EN	Kayne Anderson MLP Inv Co	KYN	**D-**	17.29	**D- / 1.0**	-50.61 / 1	-10.32 / 17	-4.05 / 20	15.21	**C / 4.5**	-2.43	6.99
EN	Fiduciary/Claymore MLP Opp	FMO	**D-**	12.98	**D- / 1.0**	-46.51 / 2	-11.38 / 15	-3.04 / 22	13.28	**C / 5.3**	-10.05	-2.10
GL	Tortoise Energy Independence Fund	NDP	**D-**	11.28	**D- / 1.0**	-35.47 / 5	-13.85 / 13	--	15.51	**C- / 4.0**	-14.16	-9.95
FO	Central Europe Russia and Turkey	CEE	**D-**	16.63	**D- / 1.1**	-13.67 / 19	-17.36 / 10	-10.54 / 13	2.92	**C / 4.3**	-12.52	-10.78
EM	Aberdeen Indonesia Fund	IF	**D-**	5.52	**D- / 1.1**	-32.92 / 6	-16.33 / 11	-6.38 / 17	0.01	**C- / 3.8**	-15.08	-12.13
EN	GAMCO Nat Res Gold & Income Trust	GNT	**D-**	5.73	**D- / 1.1**	-19.50 / 14	-16.26 / 11	--	14.66	**C- / 3.7**	-11.44	-11.05
EN	ClearBridge Energy MLP Oppty Fd In	EMO	**D-**	12.74	**D- / 1.1**	-41.79 / 3	-11.24 / 16	--	12.40	**C / 4.3**	-7.95	-9.21
EM	Templeton Emerging Markets Fd	EMF	**D-**	9.97	**D- / 1.2**	-26.92 / 9	-13.38 / 14	-10.28 / 13	3.13	**C / 4.3**	-10.42	-10.85
EN	ClearBridge Energy MLP Fund Inc	CEM	**D-**	15.18	**D- / 1.2**	-40.79 / 3	-9.26 / 18	-0.98 / 25	11.59	**C / 4.4**	-5.07	-4.50
GI	Nuveen Energy MLP Total Return Fun	JMF	**D-**	11.10	**D- / 1.2**	-41.12 / 3	-9.78 / 18	--	12.14	**C / 4.7**	-11.69	-9.29
IN	ClearBridge Engy MLP To Rtn Fd Inc	CTR	**D-**	12.31	**D- / 1.2**	-38.57 / 4	-9.80 / 18	--	11.70	**C / 4.6**	-8.75	-9.39
EN	BlackRock Energy & Resources	BGR	**D-**	12.53	**D- / 1.3**	-32.98 / 6	-9.61 / 18	-6.51 / 17	10.53	**C / 5.1**	-10.82	-3.29
GL	Nuveen Global High Income	XJGHX	**D-**	13.74	**D- / 1.3**	-12.87 / 20	--	--	11.53	**C / 4.5**	-14.34	-14.50
PM	Central Gold-Trust	GTU	**D**	37.70	**D- / 1.3**	-7.33 / 33	-15.78 / 11	-5.96 / 18	0.00	**C+ / 5.8**	-2.48	-4.90
FO	Turkish Investment Fund	TKF	**E+**	7.78	**D- / 1.4**	-26.92 / 9	-11.00 / 16	-5.89 / 18	1.92	**C- / 3.2**	-13.75	-12.33
EN	Kayne Anderson Engy Development Co	KED	**D-**	17.56	**D- / 1.4**	-48.92 / 2	-5.77 / 24	5.38 / 49	9.05	**C / 4.5**	-25.09	-4.98
EM	Voya Emerging Markets High Div Eqt	IHD	**D-**	7.40	**D- / 1.4**	-19.05 / 14	-12.70 / 14	--	12.43	**C / 4.8**	-12.22	-11.27
GL	Stone Harbor Emg Markets Total Inc	EDI	**D-**	11.37	**D- / 1.4**	-14.47 / 18	-14.61 / 12	--	15.95	**C / 4.6**	-15.09	-13.32
COH	Ivy High Income Opportunities Fund	IVH	**D**	12.38	**D- / 1.4**	-12.95 / 20	--	--	22.00	**C+ / 6.5**	-13.55	-12.63
COH	DoubleLine Income Solutions	DSL	**D+**	16.22	**D- / 1.4**	-10.00 / 25	--	--	17.53	**B- / 7.1**	-10.34	-10.04
IN	BlackRock Res & Commdty Strat Trus	BCX	**D-**	7.13	**D- / 1.5**	-19.98 / 13	-11.32 / 16	--	11.02	**C / 4.8**	-14.61	-14.92
GL	Brookfield Gl Lstd Infr Inc Fd	INF	**D-**	11.75	**D- / 1.5**	-37.95 / 4	-8.23 / 19	--	11.92	**C / 4.5**	-17.25	-12.85
EN	Voya Natural Resources Equity Inc	IRR	**D**	5.46	**D- / 1.5**	-25.34 / 10	-10.40 / 17	-8.87 / 15	14.80	**C / 5.4**	-14.15	-9.11
IN	First Trust MLP and Energy Income	FEI	**D**	13.22	**D- / 1.5**	-33.70 / 6	-6.86 / 22	--	10.74	**C+ / 5.9**	-8.19	-7.59
GI	AllianzGI Convertible & Income II	NCZ	**D-**	5.05	**D / 1.6**	-37.87 / 4	-6.10 / 23	-1.72 / 23	13.66	**C / 4.8**	-9.01	2.03
EN	Tortoise Power and Energy Inf Fund	TPZ	**D**	16.78	**D / 1.6**	-30.30 / 7	-6.94 / 21	-0.45 / 27	9.83	**C / 5.2**	-13.37	-10.52

* Denotes ETF Fund, N/A denotes number is not available

Section VI

Top-Rated ETFs and Other Closed-End Funds by Fund Type

A compilation of those

Exchange-Traded Funds and Other

Closed-End Funds

receiving the highest TheStreet Investment Rating

within each type of fund.

Funds are listed in order by Overall Investment Rating.

Section VI Contents

This section contains a summary analysis of the top rated ETFs and other closed-end mutual funds within each fund type. If you are looking for a particular type of mutual fund, these pages show those funds that have achieved the best combination of risk and financial performance over the past three years.

1. Fund Type The mutual fund's peer category based on an analysis of its investment portfolio.

COH	Corporate – High Yield	HL	Health
COI	Corporate – Inv. Grade	IN	Income
EM	Emerging Market	LP	Loan Participation
EN	Energy/Natural Resources	MTG	Mortgage
FS	Financial Services	MUH	Municipal – High Yield
FO	Foreign	MUN	Municipal – National
GEI	General – Inv. Grade	MUS	Municipal – Single State
GEN	General Bond	PM	Precious Metals
GL	Global	USA	U.S. Gov. – Agency
GR	Growth	UT	Utilities
GI	Growth and Income		

A blank fund type means that the mutual fund has not yet been categorized.

2. Fund Name The name of the mutual fund as stated in its prospectus, which can sometimes differ slightly from the name that the company uses for advertising. If you cannot find the particular mutual fund you are interested in, or if you have any doubts regarding the precise name, verify the information with your broker or on your account statement. Also, use the fund's ticker symbol for confirmation. (See column 3.)

3. Ticker Symbol The unique alphabetic symbol used for identifying and trading a specific mutual fund. No two funds can have the same ticker symbol.

4. Overall Investment Rating Our overall rating is measured on a scale from A to E based on each fund's risk-adjusted performance. Please see page 10 for specific descriptions of each letter grade. Also, refer to page 7 for information on how our ratings are derived. Most important, when using this rating, please be sure to consider the warnings beginning on page 11 regarding the ratings' limitations and the underlying assumptions.

5. Price Closing price of the fund on the date shown.

6. Performance Rating/Points
A letter grade rating based solely on the mutual fund's financial performance over the trailing three years, without any consideration for the amount of risk the fund poses. Like the overall Investment Rating, the Performance Rating is measured on a scale from A to E for ease of interpretation. The points score indicates where the Performance Rating falls on a scale of 0 to 10.

7. 1-Year Total Return
The total return the fund has provided investors over the preceeding 52 weeks. This total return figure is computed based on the fund's dividend distributions and share price appreciation/depreciation during the period, net of the expenses and fees it imposes on its shareholders.

8. 1-Year Total Return Percentile
The fund's percentile rank based on its one-year performance compared to that of all other closed-end funds in existence for at least one year. A score of 99 is the best possible, indicating that the fund outperformed 99% of the closed-end mutual funds. Zero is the worst possible percentile score.

9. 3-Year Total Return
The total annual return the fund has provided investors over the preceeding 156 weeks.

10. 3-Year Total Return Percentile
The fund's percentile rank based on its three-year performance compared to that of all other closed-end funds in existence for at least three years. A score of 99 is the best possible, indicating that the fund outperformed 99% of the closed-end mutual funds. Zero is the worst possible percentile score.

11. 5-Year Total Return
The total annual return the fund has provided investors over the preceeding 260 weeks.

12. 5-Year Total Return Percentile
The fund's percentile rank based on its five-year performance compared to that of all other closed-end funds in existence for at least five years. A score of 99 is the best possible, indicating that the fund outperformed 99% of the closed-end mutual funds. Zero is the worst possible percentile score.

13. Dividend Yield
Most recent quarterly dividend to fund investors annualized, expressed as a percent of the fund's current share price. The dividend yield of a fund can have little correlation to the amount of dividends the fund has received from its underlying investments. Rather, dividend distributions are based on a fund's need to pass earnings from both dividends and gains on the sale of investments along to shareholders. Thus, these dividend distributions are included as a part of the fund's total return.

Keep in mind that dividend income may be taxed at a different rate than capital gains depending on your income tax bracket.

14. Risk Rating/Points

A letter grade rating based solely on the mutual fund's risk as determined by its monthly performance volatility over the trailing three years. The risk rating does not take into consideration the overall financial performance the fund has achieved or the total return it has provided to its shareholders. Like the overall Investment Rating, the Risk Rating is measured on a scale from A to E for ease of interpretation. The points score indicates where the Risk Rating falls on a scale of 0 to 10.

15. Premium/ Discount

A comparison of the fund's price to its NAV as of the date indicated. The premium (+) or discount (-) indicates the percentage the shares are trading above or below the fund's NAV per share.

If the price is above the fund's NAV, the fund is said to be trading at a premium. If the price is lower than the fund's NAV, the fund is trading at a discount.

16. 1-Year Average Premium/ Discount

The average of the fund's premium/discount over the preceeding year.

It can be useful to compare the fund's current premium/discount to its one-year average. If the fund is currently trading at a premium/discount that is lower/higher than its one-year average, then there has been less demand for the fund in more recent times than over the past year. Conversely, if the fund is currently trading at a premium/discount that is higher/lower than its one-year average, this indicates that there has been greater demand for the fund in more recent times than over the past year.

Fund Type	Fund Name (99 Pct = Best, 0 Pct = Worst)	Ticker Symbol	Overall Investment Rating	Price As of 12/31/15	PERFORMANCE: Performance Rating/Pts	Annualized Total Return Through 12/31/15: 1Yr/Pct	3Yr/Pct	5Yr/Pct	Dividend Yield %	RISK: Risk Rating/Pts	VALUATION: Premium/Discount As of 12/31/15	1 Year Average
COH	*PowerShares S&P 500 Hi Div Low V	SPHD	**A**	33.34	**A- / 9.0**	4.86 / 79	13.96 / 88	--	3.58	**B- / 7.7**	0.06	-0.01
COH	*Guggenheim BltShs 2016 Hi Yld Co	BSJG	**B**	25.87	**C+ / 5.6**	2.56 / 73	3.15 / 54	--	2.82	**B+ / 9.5**	-0.04	-0.04
COH	*Guggenheim BltShs 2017 Hi Yld Co	BSJH	**B-**	24.96	**C / 5.1**	-0.55 / 57	2.13 / 49	--	3.99	**B+ / 9.2**	-0.04	0.16
COH	*PowerShares Fundamental High Yie	PHB	**C+**	17.44	**C- / 4.2**	-2.99 / 46	0.82 / 40	4.00 / 43	4.80	**B / 8.9**	-0.11	-0.04
COH	*Guggenheim BltShs 2018 Hi Yld Co	BSJI	**C+**	23.66	**C- / 4.1**	-4.16 / 42	1.19 / 43	--	5.33	**B / 8.8**	-0.38	0.18
COH	*SPDR Nuveen S&P Hi Yld Muni Bd E	HYMB	**C**	57.05	**C+ / 6.1**	3.74 / 76	4.14 / 58	--	4.50	**C+ / 6.7**	0.16	-0.33
COH	*ProShares CDS N Amer HY Credit	TYTE	**C**	39.05	**C- / 3.8**	-2.15 / 50	--	--	0.00	**B- / 7.6**	1.30	0.19
COH	*Guggenheim BltShs 2022 Hi Yld Co	BSJM	**C**	22.57	**D+ / 2.6**	-3.38 / 45	--	--	5.38	**B / 8.7**	-0.44	0.22
COH	PIMCO Corporate and ncome Strategy	PCN	**C-**	13.40	**C / 4.6**	-4.21 / 42	1.21 / 43	8.31 / 59	1.94	**C+ / 6.3**	-4.35	-2.05
COH	PIMCO Corporate and Income Oppty	PTY	**C-**	13.34	**C / 4.3**	-8.78 / 29	1.18 / 43	8.99 / 61	2.92	**C / 5.3**	1.83	5.15
COH	Prudential Sht Dur Hi Yield Fd Inc	ISD	**C-**	14.60	**C- / 4.1**	-2.07 / 50	-0.58 / 35	--	9.04	**C+ / 6.9**	-10.81	-11.16
COH	BlackRock Corporate High Yield	HYT	**C-**	9.78	**C- / 4.1**	-4.99 / 39	0.25 / 38	5.70 / 50	27.01	**B- / 7.1**	-9.78	-12.43
COH	BlackRock Debt Strategies Fund Inc	DSU	**C-**	3.37	**C- / 4.0**	-1.16 / 54	-0.61 / 35	5.43 / 49	7.12	**B- / 7.0**	-12.47	-13.59
COH	*iShares iBoxx $ Hi Yld Corp Bd E	HYG	**C-**	80.58	**C- / 4.0**	-4.93 / 39	0.59 / 39	4.00 / 43	11.57	**C+ / 6.8**	0.76	0.27
COH	Dreyfus High Yield Strategies Fund	DHF	**C-**	3.08	**C- / 3.9**	-5.96 / 36	-0.55 / 35	2.82 / 37	11.30	**C+ / 6.4**	-4.35	-7.90
COH	Deutsche High Income	KHI	**C-**	7.95	**C- / 3.8**	-1.90 / 51	-1.13 / 33	4.46 / 45	7.70	**B- / 7.0**	-9.45	-10.52
COH	Western Asset High Yld Def Opp	HYI	**C-**	14.10	**C- / 3.7**	-2.30 / 49	-1.37 / 32	3.10 / 38	9.36	**C+ / 6.8**	-8.68	-11.98
COH	*First Trust Tactical High Yield	HYLS	**C-**	46.97	**C- / 3.6**	0.06 / 61	--	--	5.88	**B- / 7.1**	0.04	0.10
COH	*SPDR Barclays High Yield Bond ET	JNK	**C-**	33.91	**C- / 3.6**	-6.91 / 34	-0.23 / 36	3.70 / 42	6.70	**C+ / 6.6**	0.47	0.25
COH	*SPDR Barclays Short Term HiYld B	SJNK	**C-**	25.69	**C- / 3.5**	-6.61 / 34	-0.42 / 36	--	5.94	**C+ / 6.8**	0.27	0.21
COH	Credit Suisse High Yield Bond Fund	DHY	**C-**	2.28	**C- / 3.5**	-8.81 / 29	-1.23 / 33	5.50 / 49	12.63	**B- / 7.0**	-5.39	-7.27
COH	MFS Interm High Inc	CIF	**C-**	2.32	**C- / 3.4**	-3.29 / 45	-1.98 / 31	3.82 / 42	11.28	**C+ / 6.5**	-10.42	-12.26
COH	Wells Fargo Income Oppty	EAD	**C-**	7.45	**C- / 3.4**	-7.05 / 33	-1.62 / 32	4.21 / 44	10.95	**C+ / 6.9**	-10.13	-10.83
COH	Invesco High Income Tr II	VLT	**C-**	12.85	**C- / 3.3**	-6.81 / 34	-2.35 / 30	4.08 / 43	9.67	**C+ / 6.9**	-13.23	-13.07
COH	Western Asset Managed High Income	MHY	**C-**	4.52	**C- / 3.2**	-4.42 / 41	-3.07 / 28	1.81 / 33	9.16	**C+ / 6.5**	-9.42	-12.84
COH	New America High Income Fund	HYB	**C-**	7.66	**C- / 3.2**	-7.21 / 33	-1.92 / 31	4.61 / 46	14.49	**C+ / 6.7**	-13.35	-13.65
COH	Western Asset High Income Opp Inc.	HIO	**C-**	4.69	**C- / 3.1**	-5.49 / 37	-3.53 / 28	2.71 / 37	9.08	**C+ / 6.7**	-9.28	-12.68
COH	*WisdomTree BofA ML HY Bd Zero Du	HYZD	**C-**	21.92	**C- / 3.0**	-1.05 / 55	--	--	4.65	**C+ / 6.8**	0.05	-0.35
COH	*ProShares Ultra High Yield	UJB	**C-**	47.78	**C- / 3.0**	-13.40 / 20	-1.20 / 33	--	4.85	**B- / 7.5**	-2.53	-0.35
COH	*iShares 0-5 Yr Hi Yld Corp Bd ET	SHYG	**C-**	44.53	**D+ / 2.9**	-3.02 / 46	--	--	9.78	**B- / 7.1**	0.45	0.36
COH	Neuberger Berman High Yield Strat	NHS	**C-**	10.09	**D+ / 2.9**	-10.88 / 24	-3.20 / 28	1.84 / 33	9.51	**C+ / 6.8**	-13.17	-13.61
COH	*Guggenheim BltShs 2021 Hi Yld Co	BSJL	**C-**	22.84	**D+ / 2.8**	-2.46 / 48	--	--	5.03	**B / 8.0**	0.00	0.23
COH	*Guggenheim BltShs 2019 Hi Yld Co	BSJJ	**C-**	22.73	**D+ / 2.4**	-4.80 / 40	--	--	5.23	**B / 8.6**	-0.26	0.20
COH	*iShares Interest Rate Hgd HY Bon	HYGH	**C-**	83.05	**D+ / 2.4**	-6.62 / 34	--	--	7.26	**B / 8.3**	-0.17	0.02
COH	*Market Vectors Trs Hdg Hi Yld Bd	THHY	**C-**	21.85	**D+ / 2.4**	-7.74 / 32	--	--	5.44	**B / 8.2**	-0.64	0.14
COH	*WisdomTree BofA ML HY Bd Neg Dur	HYND	**C-**	19.39	**D / 2.1**	-5.42 / 37	--	--	4.95	**B / 8.0**	-1.67	0.41
COH	*Guggenheim BltShs 2020 Hi Yld Co	BSJK	**C-**	22.52	**D / 2.1**	-6.03 / 36	--	--	5.98	**B / 8.5**	-0.27	0.25
COH	*ProShares Hi Yld-Int Rte Hdgd	HYHG	**C-**	62.57	**D / 1.7**	-9.65 / 26	--	--	6.00	**B- / 7.9**	-0.68	0.06
COH	PIMCO High Income Fund	PHK	**D+**	8.18	**C- / 3.7**	-17.99 / 15	0.87 / 41	3.38 / 40	15.18	**C / 4.7**	21.01	38.41
COH	Credit Suisse Asset Mgmt Income	CIK	**D+**	2.78	**D+ / 2.8**	-7.30 / 33	-4.41 / 26	3.75 / 42	9.50	**C+ / 6.7**	-13.40	-13.33
COH	Blackstone / GSO Strategic Credit	BGB	**D+**	13.37	**D+ / 2.7**	-9.73 / 26	-4.05 / 27	--	9.42	**C+ / 6.6**	-12.04	-12.68
COH	Pacholder High Yield Fund	PHF	**D+**	6.07	**D+ / 2.7**	-9.85 / 26	-3.95 / 27	2.95 / 38	9.88	**C+ / 6.3**	-13.04	-12.78
COH	Brookfield High Income Fund	HHY	**D+**	6.88	**D+ / 2.7**	-13.42 / 20	-3.62 / 27	4.74 / 46	13.08	**C+ / 6.6**	-10.42	-10.14
COH	Ares Dynamic Credit Allocation Fun	ARDC	**D+**	13.36	**D+ / 2.5**	-8.63 / 29	-5.73 / 24	--	10.51	**B- / 7.0**	-14.74	-13.78
COH	*Peritus High Yield ETF	HYLD	**D+**	32.64	**D / 2.2**	-14.14 / 19	-6.28 / 23	-1.12 / 25	12.84	**C+ / 6.5**	-1.33	-0.63
COH	DoubleLine Income Solutions	DSL	**D+**	16.22	**D- / 1.4**	-10.00 / 25	--	--	17.53	**B- / 7.1**	-10.34	-10.04
COH	Ivy High Income Opportunities Fund	IVH	**D**	12.38	**D- / 1.4**	-12.95 / 20	--	--	22.00	**C+ / 6.5**	-13.55	-12.63

* Denotes ETF Fund, N/A denotes number is not available

99 Pct = Best
0 Pct = Worst

Fund Type	Fund Name	Ticker Symbol	Overall Investment Rating	Price As of 12/31/15	PERFORMANCE: Performance Rating/Pts	Annualized Total Return Through 12/31/15: 1Yr/Pct	3Yr/Pct	5Yr/Pct	Dividend Yield %	RISK: Risk Rating/Pts	VALUATION: Premium/Discount As of 12/31/15	1 Year Average
COI	*iShares Aaa - A Rated Corporate	QLTA	B	50.52	C / 5.2	0.38 / 63	1.55 / 45	--	10.13	B+ / 9.4	-0.12	-0.09
COI	*Guggenheim BltShs 2016 Corp Bond	BSCG	B	22.08	C / 4.9	0.99 / 67	1.20 / 43	3.08 / 38	1.02	B+ / 9.9	-0.05	0.02
COI	*Guggenheim BltShs 2017 Corp Bond	BSCH	B	22.52	C / 4.9	0.81 / 66	1.26 / 43	3.72 / 42	1.49	B+ / 9.8	-0.09	0.14
COI	*Market Vectors Prfrd Secs ex Fin	PFXF	B-	19.15	C / 5.3	-2.86 / 47	3.20 / 54	--	10.15	B+ / 9.0	-0.62	-0.02
COI	*PIMCO Enhanced Sht Maturity Act	MINT	B-	100.61	C / 4.6	0.35 / 63	0.58 / 39	0.92 / 30	1.01	B+ / 9.7	-0.06	-0.03
COI	*Market Vectors Invest Grade FR E	FLTR	B-	24.67	C / 4.5	-0.45 / 58	0.57 / 39	--	0.80	B+ / 9.7	-0.24	-0.10
COI	*iShares iBonds Mar 2016 Corp ex-	IBCB	B-	99.35	C / 4.4	0.04 / 60	--	--	0.67	B+ / 9.9	-0.12	N/A
COI	*iShares Ultra Short-Term Bond	ICSH	B-	49.73	C / 4.3	0.26 / 62	--	--	2.01	B+ / 9.8	-0.14	-0.04
COI	*PIMCO Low Duration Active Exch T	LDUR	C+	99.67	C / 5.3	2.16 / 72	--	--	6.73	B / 8.0	0.34	0.04
COI	*Vanguard Intm-Term Corp Bd Idx E	VCIT	C+	84.10	C / 5.3	0.62 / 65	2.09 / 49	5.10 / 48	3.85	B- / 7.6	0.43	0.19
COI	*PIMCO Total Return Active Exch T	BOND	C+	104.22	C / 5.3	0.36 / 63	2.21 / 49	--	12.03	B- / 7.7	0.26	-0.03
COI	Cutwater Select Income	CSI	C+	18.26	C / 5.3	0.21 / 62	2.43 / 50	6.52 / 53	5.48	B- / 7.8	-7.17	-7.59
COI	*Guggenheim BltShs 2019 Corp Bond	BSCJ	C+	20.86	C / 5.2	1.46 / 70	1.77 / 47	--	2.12	B- / 7.8	0.14	0.27
COI	*Guggenheim BltShs 2020 Corp Bond	BSCK	C+	20.89	C / 5.2	1.39 / 69	2.14 / 49	--	3.00	B- / 7.7	0.24	0.29
COI	*Guggenheim BltShs 2018 Corp Bond	BSCI	C+	21.02	C / 5.1	1.40 / 69	1.61 / 46	--	1.81	B- / 7.9	0.29	0.26
COI	*Vanguard Short-Term Crp Bd Idx E	VCSH	C+	78.98	C / 5.1	1.36 / 69	1.59 / 46	2.58 / 36	2.54	B / 8.1	0.28	0.12
COI	*iShares 0-5 Yr Invest Grde Corp	SLQD	C+	50.24	C / 5.1	1.25 / 68	--	--	2.89	B / 8.1	0.58	0.32
COI	*PowerShares Fundmntl Inv Gr Corp	PFIG	C+	25.02	C / 5.1	0.91 / 66	1.53 / 45	--	2.70	B- / 7.8	0.32	0.11
COI	*iShares iBonds Mar 2023 Corporat	IBDD	C+	103.87	C / 5.1	0.48 / 64	--	--	5.52	B- / 7.7	1.94	0.93
COI	*iShares iBonds Mar 2018 Corporat	IBDB	C+	102.26	C / 5.0	1.38 / 69	--	--	2.53	B / 8.1	0.45	0.35
COI	*iShares CMBS ETF	CMBS	C+	50.66	C / 5.0	0.68 / 65	1.40 / 44	--	3.60	B- / 7.9	0.18	0.22
COI	*iShares Intrm Credit Bond ETF	CIU	C+	107.28	C / 5.0	0.45 / 63	1.47 / 45	3.34 / 40	5.27	B / 8.0	0.09	0.09
COI	*iShares iBoxx $ Inv Grade Cor B	LQD	C+	114.01	C / 5.0	-1.59 / 52	1.69 / 46	4.83 / 47	6.22	B / 8.3	0.00	0.07
COI	*SPDR Barclays Sht Trm Corp Bond	SCPB	C+	30.40	C / 4.9	0.87 / 66	1.05 / 42	1.65 / 32	1.52	B / 8.0	0.20	0.08
COI	*iShares iBonds Mar 2018 Corp ex-	IBCC	C+	98.99	C / 4.8	1.11 / 67	--	--	1.20	B / 8.0	0.94	0.66
COI	*PIMCO Investment Grade Crp Bond	CORP	C+	98.98	C / 4.8	-1.62 / 52	1.29 / 44	4.36 / 45	2.89	B / 8.9	-0.13	-0.02
COI	*iShares 1-3 Yr Credit Bd ETF	CSJ	C+	104.60	C / 4.7	0.68 / 65	0.81 / 40	1.39 / 31	2.67	B / 8.1	0.14	0.08
COI	*iShares Baa - Ba Rated Corp Bd E	QLTB	C+	48.63	C / 4.5	-4.22 / 42	1.39 / 44	--	12.16	B / 8.9	-0.45	0.22
COI	*First Trust Enhanced Short Matur	FTSM	C+	59.82	C / 4.4	0.22 / 62	--	--	0.80	B+ / 9.4	-0.07	-0.05
COI	*Fidelity Limited Term Bond ETF	FLTB	C+	49.69	C- / 4.2	0.71 / 65	--	--	1.59	B+ / 9.6	-0.06	0.21
COI	*Vident Core US Bond Strategy	VBND	C+	49.11	C- / 4.0	-0.26 / 58	--	--	2.90	B+ / 9.3	-0.02	N/A
COI	*ProShares Ultra Invest Grade Cor	IGU	C	57.38	C / 5.1	-2.07 / 50	1.86 / 48	--	2.34	C+ / 6.8	0.54	-0.37
COI	Western Asst Invst Grade Define Op	IGI	C	20.17	C / 5.0	2.91 / 74	1.14 / 42	6.51 / 53	5.95	B- / 7.2	1.46	-0.84
COI	*SPDR Barclays Iss Sco Corp Bond	CBND	C	30.99	C / 4.9	-1.58 / 52	1.59 / 46	--	3.18	B- / 7.6	0.42	0.39
COI	*iShares Core US Credit Bond	CRED	C	106.71	C / 4.9	-1.69 / 51	1.43 / 44	4.08 / 44	7.22	B- / 7.5	0.18	0.16
COI	*Vanguard Long-Term Corp Bd Idx E	VCLT	C	84.19	C / 4.9	-5.23 / 38	2.09 / 49	6.71 / 54	5.26	C+ / 6.8	0.65	0.20
COI	*iShares iBonds Mar 2023 Corp ex-	IBCE	C	94.80	C / 4.8	1.28 / 68	--	--	5.86	B- / 7.5	0.26	0.57
COI	*iShares iBonds Mar 2020 Corp ex-	IBCD	C	97.42	C / 4.6	0.88 / 66	--	--	4.12	B- / 7.9	0.44	0.49
COI	*iShares Floating Rate Bond ETF	FLOT	C	50.44	C / 4.5	0.44 / 63	0.38 / 39	--	1.17	B / 8.0	0.12	0.01
COI	*iShares iBonds Mar 2016 Corporat	IBDA	C	100.90	C / 4.5	0.35 / 63	--	--	0.32	B / 8.2	0.13	0.06
COI	*SPDR Barclays Invest Grade FlRt	FLRN	C	30.42	C / 4.4	0.47 / 64	0.34 / 38	--	0.73	B / 8.2	0.07	0.03
COI	*Guggenheim BltShs 2021 Corp Bond	BSCL	C	20.52	C- / 4.2	0.47 / 64	--	--	2.83	B- / 7.9	0.39	0.28
COI	*iShares iBonds Mar 2020 Corporat	IBDC	C	103.40	C- / 4.2	0.36 / 63	--	--	3.99	B / 8.0	0.52	0.59
COI	*WisdomTree Barclays US AB Zero D	AGZD	C	48.10	C- / 4.1	-0.79 / 56	--	--	1.75	B / 8.0	0.21	-0.16
COI	*Guggenheim BltShs 2022 Corp Bond	BSCM	C	20.29	C- / 4.0	0.01 / 60	--	--	3.05	B- / 7.8	0.25	0.18
COI	*PIMCO 0-5 Year Hi Yield Corp Bd	HYS	C	91.62	C- / 4.0	-5.22 / 38	0.70 / 40	--	4.92	B / 8.7	-0.43	-0.21
COI	*Guggenheim BltShs 2023 Corp Bond	BSCN	C	19.93	C- / 3.9	-0.62 / 57	--	--	4.37	B- / 7.8	0.35	0.47
COI	*Guggenheim BltShs 2024 Corp Bond	BSCO	C	19.77	C- / 3.8	-1.24 / 54	--	--	4.72	B / 8.4	0.00	0.24
COI	*WisdomTree Barclays US AB Neg Du	AGND	C	44.17	C- / 3.7	-0.31 / 58	--	--	1.90	B+ / 9.0	-0.23	-0.10
COI	*iShares Emerging Markets Corp B	CEMB	C	46.06	C- / 3.7	-1.65 / 52	-0.96 / 34	--	9.08	B / 8.5	-0.58	0.21
COI	*Fidelity Total Bond ETF	FBND	C	48.00	C- / 3.6	-1.16 / 54	--	--	3.90	B- / 7.7	0.69	0.24
COI	*ProShares Short Inv Grade Corp	IGS	C	28.34	C- / 3.1	-0.45 / 57	-4.20 / 26	--	0.00	B / 8.5	-0.14	0.21

* Denotes ETF Fund, N/A denotes number is not available

	99 Pct = Best 0 Pct = Worst				PERFORMANCE					RISK	VALUATION	
Fund Type	Fund Name	Ticker Symbol	Overall Investment Rating	Price As of 12/31/15	Performance Rating/Pts	Annualized Total Return Through 12/31/15 1Yr/Pct	3Yr/Pct	5Yr/Pct	Dividend Yield %	Risk Rating/ Pts	Premium/Discount As of 12/31/15	1 Year Average
EM	*ProShares Sh Trm USD Em Mkts Bd	EMSH	A	75.60	B- / 7.5	10.19 / 88	--	--	5.60	B+ / 9.1	-0.15	-0.46
EM	*iShares Core MSCI EAFE	IEFA	B-	54.38	C+ / 5.9	1.75 / 71	4.74 / 60	--	3.17	B / 8.2	-0.53	0.18
EM	*ProShares UltraShort MSCI Emg Mk	EEV	C+	23.85	B / 7.8	17.85 / 97	5.08 / 61	-5.83 / 18	0.00	C+ / 5.8	-0.13	-0.04
EM	*ProShares Short MSCI Emg Mkts	EUM	C+	29.46	C+ / 6.6	10.67 / 89	3.87 / 57	-0.96 / 25	0.00	C+ / 6.9	0.00	-0.03
EM	*Vanguard Total World Stock ETF	VT	C+	57.62	C+ / 6.5	-0.97 / 55	7.22 / 68	6.46 / 52	5.11	B- / 7.0	0.14	0.13
EM	*EMQQ The EM Intrt Ecom ETF	EMQQ	C	23.78	C+ / 6.6	2.94 / 74	--	--	0.08	C / 5.3	-0.17	0.27
EM	*Vanguard Em Mkt Govt Bd Idx ETF	VWOB	C	73.96	C / 4.6	1.61 / 70	--	--	5.92	B- / 7.4	0.37	0.46
EM	*iShares Core MSCI Total Intl Sto	IXUS	C	49.48	C / 4.3	-3.08 / 46	1.16 / 43	--	4.64	B / 8.0	-0.22	0.27
EM	*SPDR S&P Emerging Asia Pacific E	GMF	C	73.60	C- / 4.2	-5.63 / 37	1.25 / 43	0.56 / 29	13.21	B- / 7.6	-0.93	-0.18
EM	*Market Vectors Emg Mkts Hi Yld B	HYEM	C	22.12	C- / 4.0	2.84 / 74	-0.70 / 35	--	8.09	B / 8.1	-0.67	-0.57
EM	*WisdomTree EM Corporate Bond	EMCB	C	65.58	C- / 3.3	-3.66 / 44	-2.10 / 30	--	4.85	B / 8.1	-0.56	-0.70
EM	*PowerShares Emrg Mkt Sovereign D	PCY	C-	27.31	C / 4.5	2.67 / 73	-0.02 / 37	5.55 / 49	5.47	C+ / 6.7	0.00	-0.09
EM	*iShares India 50 ETF	INDY	C-	27.20	C / 4.4	-9.85 / 26	3.06 / 53	-1.16 / 25	0.69	C+ / 6.8	-0.95	0.08
EM	*iShares JPMorgan USD Emg Mkts B	EMB	C-	105.78	C / 4.3	1.54 / 70	-0.30 / 36	4.52 / 46	11.40	C+ / 6.3	0.32	0.40
EM	*iShares Emerging Markets HY Bd E	EMHY	C-	45.05	C- / 3.9	1.93 / 71	-1.21 / 33	--	16.21	C+ / 6.3	0.16	0.21
EM	*SPDR BofA Merrill Lynch Em Mkt C	EMCD	C-	26.99	C- / 3.9	-0.45 / 58	-0.58 / 35	--	4.93	C+ / 6.7	0.30	-0.48
EM	*iPath MSCI India Index ETN	INP	C-	63.91	C- / 3.9	-9.40 / 27	1.86 / 47	-2.71 / 22	0.00	C+ / 6.9	-1.04	0.20
EM	Morgan Stanley Emerging Mkts Debt	MSD	C-	8.57	C- / 3.2	1.15 / 68	-4.44 / 26	2.52 / 36	8.52	C+ / 6.4	-14.98	-15.71
EM	*Deutsche X-trackers MSCI Mx Hdg	DBMX	C-	20.22	C- / 3.2	-0.87 / 55	--	--	15.63	B- / 7.1	-0.98	0.16
EM	*iShares MSCI EM Asia ETF	EEMA	C-	50.40	C- / 3.0	-9.05 / 28	-2.50 / 29	--	6.74	B- / 7.4	-1.08	0.05
EM	*iShares MSCI Emerging Mkts Min V	EEMV	C-	48.66	D+ / 2.6	-10.15 / 25	-4.49 / 26	--	5.27	B- / 7.5	-0.39	0.19
EM	Morgan Stanley Emerging Markets	MSF	C-	12.85	D+ / 2.4	-10.20 / 25	-6.46 / 22	-4.09 / 20	0.21	B- / 7.2	-10.08	-10.71
EM	*SPDR S&P Emerging Markets ETF	GMM	C-	52.08	D+ / 2.3	-13.40 / 20	-6.22 / 23	-4.19 / 20	6.06	B- / 7.4	-0.71	-0.10
EM	*Deutsche X-trackers MSCI EM Hdg	DBEM	C-	18.28	D / 2.2	-13.09 / 20	-6.72 / 22	--	1.71	B- / 7.6	-0.87	0.02
EM	Global High Income Fund	GHI	D+	8.50	C- / 3.2	5.79 / 81	-6.19 / 23	-0.13 / 27	9.60	C+ / 5.7	-3.52	-11.38
EM	*iShares MSCI Emerging Mkts Sm-Ca	EEMS	D+	40.95	C- / 3.1	-5.04 / 39	-2.76 / 29	--	5.71	C+ / 5.7	0.29	0.34
EM	Western Asset Worldwide Inc Fd	SBW	D+	10.08	D+ / 2.8	-2.42 / 49	-5.80 / 23	1.97 / 34	17.26	C+ / 6.1	-14.94	-15.30
EM	Western Asset Emerging Mkts Inc	EMD	D+	9.73	D+ / 2.6	-1.62 / 52	-7.22 / 21	2.24 / 35	17.27	C+ / 5.6	-16.62	-15.74
EM	Western Asset Emerging Market Debt	ESD	D+	13.73	D+ / 2.5	-4.18 / 42	-7.58 / 20	1.92 / 33	18.35	C+ / 5.8	-16.13	-14.65
EM	*SPDR S&P International Div ETF	DWX	D+	33.36	D+ / 2.3	-14.92 / 18	-6.16 / 23	-3.33 / 22	12.77	B- / 7.0	-0.77	-0.10
EM	*iShares Core MSCI Emerging Marke	IEMG	D+	39.39	D / 2.2	-12.33 / 21	-7.04 / 21	--	5.55	B- / 7.1	-0.58	0.11
EM	*PowerShares DWA Emg Mkts Momentu	PIE	D+	14.95	D / 2.2	-13.21 / 20	-6.43 / 22	-3.18 / 22	1.92	C+ / 6.8	-1.19	-0.31
EM	*SPDR MSCI EM 50 ETF	EMFT	D+	37.25	D / 2.2	-15.28 / 17	-6.77 / 22	--	8.46	C+ / 6.5	-1.87	0.68
EM	*iShares MSCI Emerging Markets	EEM	D+	32.19	D / 2.1	-13.78 / 19	-8.12 / 20	-5.17 / 19	6.22	B- / 7.3	-0.83	-0.14
EM	*EGShares Emerging Markets Cons E	ECON	D+	21.26	D / 2.1	-13.80 / 19	-6.69 / 22	-0.64 / 26	1.10	B- / 7.1	-0.75	-0.09
EM	*Vanguard FTSE Emerging Markets E	VWO	D+	32.71	D / 2.1	-14.45 / 18	-7.56 / 20	-4.73 / 19	3.89	B- / 7.1	-0.46	-0.09
EM	*FlexShares MS EM Fact Tilt Idx	TLTE	D+	41.72	D / 2.0	-14.14 / 19	-7.96 / 20	--	2.00	B- / 7.2	-0.26	-0.07
EM	*WisdomTree Emg Mkts SmCap Div Fd	DGS	D+	35.06	D / 1.9	-15.55 / 17	-8.16 / 20	-5.17 / 19	0.96	C+ / 6.6	-1.41	-0.50
EM	*EGShares Emerging Markets Core E	EMCR	D+	16.20	D / 1.9	-19.52 / 14	-7.80 / 20	--	1.60	B- / 7.0	-1.28	0.20
EM	*PowerShares S&P EM Low Vol	EELV	D+	20.29	D / 1.8	-17.65 / 15	-8.81 / 19	--	2.19	C+ / 6.8	-1.31	-0.17
EM	*iShares Curr Hedged MSCI Em Mkts	HEEM	D	20.00	D+ / 2.4	-5.68 / 37	--	--	4.50	C+ / 5.7	0.25	0.19
EM	Templeton Emerging Markets Income	TEI	D	9.97	D+ / 2.3	-4.44 / 41	-9.64 / 18	-0.63 / 26	8.02	C / 5.3	-13.75	-13.49
EM	*BLDRS Emerging Market 50 ADR Ind	ADRE	D	29.07	D / 2.0	-15.25 / 17	-8.83 / 19	-6.97 / 17	3.13	C+ / 6.2	-0.21	-0.19
EM	*WisdomTree Emg Mkts Local Debt F	ELD	D	34.28	D / 1.9	-12.80 / 21	-9.81 / 18	-3.82 / 21	5.08	C+ / 5.9	0.00	-0.20
EM	*First Trust Emerg Mkt AlphaDEX	FEM	D	17.97	D / 1.7	-13.48 / 20	-10.25 / 17	--	0.63	C+ / 6.4	-0.72	-0.37
EM	*PowerShares Fundmntl Em Loc Dbt	PFEM	D	16.54	D / 1.6	-13.66 / 19	--	--	5.26	C+ / 5.6	1.10	-0.12
EM	*SPDR S&P Emerg Middle East&Afric	GAF	D	49.79	D / 1.6	-20.76 / 13	-9.19 / 18	-4.98 / 19	9.47	C+ / 6.4	-0.70	-0.85
EM	*PowerShares Emg Mkts Infrastruct	PXR	D	27.35	D- / 1.2	-22.40 / 12	-13.39 / 14	-11.08 / 12	0.97	C+ / 6.8	-0.73	-0.45
EM	*SPDR MSCI EM Beyond BRIC ETF	EMBB	D	46.20	D- / 1.0	-16.47 / 16	--	--	4.44	C+ / 6.7	-0.79	-0.25
EM	*WisdomTree Em Mkts Qual Div Gro	DGRE	D	19.36	E+ / 0.9	-16.47 / 16	--	--	5.06	C+ / 6.8	-1.53	0.23
EM	*iShares MSCI Emg Mkts Horizon ET	EMHZ	D	17.47	E+ / 0.8	-21.22 / 12	--	--	2.07	C+ / 6.9	-1.69	-0.62
EM	*WisdomTree Em Mkts Cons Gro	EMCG	D	19.33	E+ / 0.7	-19.63 / 14	--	--	1.60	C+ / 6.9	-0.15	-0.26

* Denotes ETF Fund, N/A denotes number is not available

	99 Pct = Best *0 Pct = Worst*				PERFORMANCE					RISK	VALUATION	
						Annualized Total Return Through 12/31/15					Premium/Discount	
Fund Type	Fund Name	Ticker Symbol	Overall Investment Rating	Price As of 12/31/15	Performance Rating/Pts	1Yr/Pct	3Yr/Pct	5Yr/Pct	Dividend Yield %	Risk Rating/Pts	As of 12/31/15	1 Year Average
EN	*First Trust ISE Glb Wind Energy	FAN	**A+**	11.36	**A / 9.5**	10.80 / 89	18.89 / 94	4.31 / 45	2.35	**B- / 7.9**	-0.09	-0.17
EN	*ProShares UltraShort Gold	GLL	**A-**	115.83	**A+ / 9.7**	16.22 / 96	22.06 / 96	-0.66 / 26	0.00	**C+ / 6.7**	-0.04	-0.21
EN	*United States Short Oil Fund	DNO	**B+**	81.43	**A+ / 9.9**	44.68 / 99	29.62 / 98	14.22 / 89	0.00	**C / 5.5**	0.23	0.12
EN	*PowerShares Global Clean Energy	PBD	**B+**	11.42	**B / 8.2**	-0.09 / 59	12.59 / 83	-2.58 / 23	1.94	**B- / 7.1**	-0.35	N/A
EN	*Market Vectors Global Alt Enrgy	GEX	**B**	54.81	**A- / 9.1**	1.42 / 69	17.30 / 92	-0.44 / 27	0.56	**C+ / 6.0**	0.44	0.06
EN	*Guggenheim S&P Global Water Idx	CGW	**B**	27.14	**C+ / 6.8**	-1.31 / 54	8.07 / 70	7.72 / 57	1.67	**B- / 7.8**	0.00	0.08
EN	*iShares Global Clean Energy ETF	ICLN	**B-**	9.84	**B / 8.2**	3.92 / 76	12.02 / 82	-6.15 / 17	3.10	**C+ / 6.1**	0.61	0.28
EN	*ProShares UltraShort Silver	ZSL	**C+**	64.55	**A+ / 9.9**	9.61 / 87	37.39 / 99	-10.45 / 13	0.00	**C- / 3.2**	-0.05	-0.62
EN	*Market Vectors Solar Energy ETF	KWT	**C+**	61.38	**B+ / 8.3**	-7.78 / 31	14.20 / 88	-16.20 / 7	0.97	**C / 5.2**	-0.42	-0.50
EN	*PowerShares Global Water Portfol	PIO	**C+**	20.93	**C+ / 5.8**	-7.15 / 33	6.38 / 66	2.86 / 37	1.67	**B- / 7.7**	-0.29	-0.21
EN	*ProShares UltraShort Bloomberg C	SCO	**C**	133.64	**A+ / 9.9**	67.26 / 99	50.45 / 99	20.05 / 97	0.00	**D+ / 2.8**	0.32	0.18
EN	*Guggenheim Solar ETF	TAN	**C**	30.64	**A / 9.3**	-8.39 / 30	20.70 / 95	-12.59 / 11	1.60	**C- / 3.5**	0.10	0.04
EN	*iPath Bloomberg Cocoa SI TR A	NIB	**C**	41.32	**B / 8.2**	7.60 / 84	11.05 / 79	0.52 / 29	0.00	**C- / 4.2**	-0.17	-0.14
EN	*PowerShares Wilder Clean Energy	PBW	**C**	4.74	**C+ / 5.7**	-8.54 / 30	5.00 / 61	-12.65 / 11	0.51	**C+ / 6.0**	-0.21	-0.10
EN	*iPath Cptl Glbl Carbon Tot Ret E	GRN	**C-**	10.21	**B / 7.7**	8.38 / 85	9.29 / 73	-16.78 / 7	0.00	**D / 2.0**	-0.97	0.66
EN	*ProShares UltraShort Oil & Gas	DUG	**D+**	71.87	**C+ / 6.2**	35.94 / 99	-2.86 / 29	-13.54 / 10	0.00	**C- / 3.4**	0.03	N/A
EN	*iShares MSCI ACWI Low Carbon Tar	CRBN	**D+**	93.03	**C / 5.3**	1.25 / 68	--	--	4.01	**C- / 3.4**	1.19	0.19
EN	*SPDR MSCI ACWI Low Carbon Target	LOWC	**D+**	70.36	**C- / 4.1**	-1.04 / 55	--	--	4.59	**C / 5.0**	-0.28	0.22
EN	*First Trust North Am Energy Infr	EMLP	**D+**	20.18	**D+ / 2.9**	-25.83 / 9	1.42 / 44	--	5.31	**C+ / 6.3**	0.00	0.03
EN	Adams Natural Resources	PEO	**D+**	17.74	**D+ / 2.5**	-19.75 / 14	-4.06 / 26	-1.51 / 24	1.69	**C+ / 5.9**	-14.46	-13.88
EN	*Energy Select Sector SPDR	XLE	**D+**	60.32	**D+ / 2.4**	-21.14 / 12	-4.03 / 27	-0.24 / 27	7.19	**C+ / 6.0**	0.00	N/A
EN	*Vanguard Energy ETF	VDE	**D+**	83.12	**D / 2.1**	-23.55 / 11	-5.61 / 24	-1.62 / 24	1.64	**C+ / 6.6**	-0.05	0.01
EN	*IQ Global Resources ETF	GRES	**D+**	20.84	**D / 1.6**	-19.66 / 14	-10.37 / 17	-6.06 / 18	2.70	**B- / 7.2**	-0.76	-0.26
EN	*iShares US Energy ETF	IYE	**D**	33.86	**D+ / 2.3**	-21.92 / 12	-4.86 / 25	-0.81 / 26	6.24	**C / 5.3**	0.03	-0.01
EN	First Trust Energy Infrastructure	FIF	**D**	14.59	**D+ / 2.3**	-32.73 / 7	-2.22 / 30	--	9.05	**C / 5.1**	-11.79	-10.91
EN	*Alps Alerian MLP ETF	AMLP	**D**	12.05	**D / 2.2**	-26.24 / 9	-3.87 / 27	0.72 / 30	9.93	**C / 4.7**	0.50	0.04
EN	*PowerShares Dynamic Enrg Exp & P	PXE	**D**	21.91	**D / 2.1**	-19.91 / 14	-5.71 / 24	1.02 / 30	3.90	**C / 4.6**	0.05	-0.06
EN	*iShares Global Energy	IXC	**D**	28.03	**D / 2.0**	-20.67 / 13	-7.52 / 21	-3.48 / 22	7.57	**C / 5.0**	0.04	0.06
EN	*iShares US Oil & Gas Exp & Pro E	IEO	**D**	52.95	**D / 2.0**	-24.70 / 10	-5.65 / 24	-2.65 / 23	3.80	**C / 4.7**	0.08	0.01
EN	First Trust Energy Income and Gro	FEN	**D**	23.00	**D / 2.0**	-33.06 / 6	-3.85 / 27	3.67 / 41	10.09	**C+ / 5.9**	-2.34	-5.34
EN	Tortoise Energy Infrastr Corp	TYG	**D**	27.82	**D / 1.8**	-33.14 / 6	-6.01 / 23	--	9.42	**C / 5.0**	-3.37	-6.21
EN	*iShares MSCI Global Engy Prod	FILL	**D**	16.34	**D / 1.7**	-20.51 / 13	-9.21 / 18	--	6.79	**C+ / 5.7**	-0.79	0.68
EN	*iShares North American Natural R	IGE	**D**	28.14	**D / 1.7**	-23.95 / 11	-8.31 / 19	-5.46 / 18	9.70	**C+ / 5.7**	0.00	-0.01
EN	*PowerShares WilderHill Progr Ene	PUW	**D**	19.46	**D / 1.6**	-25.08 / 10	-8.27 / 19	-5.82 / 18	1.21	**C+ / 6.1**	-0.10	-0.06
EN	Tortoise Power and Energy Inf Fund	TPZ	**D**	16.78	**D / 1.6**	-30.30 / 7	-6.94 / 21	-0.45 / 27	9.83	**C / 5.2**	-13.37	-10.52
EN	*Global X China Energy ETF	CHIE	**D**	10.10	**D- / 1.5**	-22.18 / 12	-10.74 / 16	-6.82 / 17	3.26	**C+ / 6.0**	-0.20	-0.22
EN	Voya Natural Resources Equity Inc	IRR	**D**	5.46	**D- / 1.5**	-25.34 / 10	-10.40 / 17	-8.87 / 15	14.80	**C / 5.4**	-14.15	-9.11
EN	*Guggenheim S&P 500 Eq Wght Engy	RYE	**D**	47.09	**D- / 1.5**	-28.92 / 8	-9.51 / 18	-4.27 / 20	2.54	**C / 5.2**	0.00	N/A
EN	*FlexShs Morningstar Gl Upstream	GUNR	**D**	22.25	**D- / 1.3**	-24.51 / 10	-12.34 / 15	--	4.50	**C+ / 6.0**	-0.58	0.06
EN	*First Trust Energy AlphaDEX	FXN	**D**	13.85	**D- / 1.2**	-32.89 / 6	-11.05 / 16	-7.05 / 17	1.98	**C / 5.5**	-0.14	-0.02
EN	*Direxion Energy Bear 3x Shares	ERY	**D-**	29.31	**C- / 3.7**	41.46 / 99	-11.55 / 15	-26.23 / 4	0.00	**D+ / 2.7**	-0.10	N/A
EN	*iPath Bloomberg Cotton SI TR A	BAL	**D-**	42.04	**C- / 3.1**	3.65 / 76	-4.98 / 25	-10.03 / 13	0.00	**C- / 3.3**	-0.02	0.03
EN	*Global X MLP ETF	MLPA	**D-**	10.39	**D / 1.8**	-30.78 / 7	-6.10 / 23	--	8.66	**C / 4.4**	0.29	N/A
EN	*PowerShares DWA Energy Momentum	PXI	**D-**	33.57	**D / 1.7**	-24.29 / 11	-7.75 / 20	-0.89 / 25	1.69	**C / 4.4**	0.12	-0.04
EN	*SPDR SP Intl Energy Sector ETF	IPW	**D-**	15.32	**D- / 1.4**	-21.17 / 12	-11.96 / 15	-7.42 / 16	10.81	**C / 4.7**	0.99	0.31
EN	*SPDR S&P Glbl Natural Resources	GNR	**D-**	32.10	**D- / 1.4**	-22.50 / 11	-12.09 / 15	-8.82 / 15	7.82	**C / 4.6**	0.06	0.09
EN	Kayne Anderson Engy Development Co	KED	**D-**	17.56	**D- / 1.4**	-48.92 / 2	-5.77 / 24	5.38 / 49	9.05	**C / 4.5**	-25.09	-4.98
EN	*iShares US Oil Equip & Svcs ETF	IEZ	**D-**	35.78	**D- / 1.3**	-26.87 / 9	-11.34 / 15	-7.15 / 16	4.06	**C / 4.7**	0.00	N/A
EN	BlackRock Energy & Resources	BGR	**D-**	12.53	**D- / 1.3**	-32.98 / 6	-9.61 / 18	-6.51 / 17	10.53	**C / 5.1**	-10.82	-3.29
EN	Fiduciary/Claymore MLP Opp	FMO	**D-**	12.98	**D- / 1.0**	-46.51 / 2	-11.38 / 15	-3.04 / 22	13.28	**C / 5.3**	-10.05	-2.10
EN	*WisdomTree Global Natural Resour	GNAT	**D-**	11.01	**E+ / 0.7**	-30.01 / 7	-20.69 / 8	-12.77 / 11	4.39	**C / 5.4**	-0.27	0.10
EN	*Fidelity MSCI Energy Index ETF	FENY	**D-**	17.09	**E+ / 0.6**	-22.86 / 11	--	--	5.38	**C+ / 5.6**	-0.06	0.02

* Denotes ETF Fund, N/A denotes number is not available

Fund Type	Fund Name (99 Pct = Best, 0 Pct = Worst)	Ticker Symbol	Overall Investment Rating	Price As of 12/31/15	PERFORMANCE: Performance Rating/Pts	Annualized Total Return Through 12/31/15: 1Yr/Pct	3Yr/Pct	5Yr/Pct	Dividend Yield %	RISK: Risk Rating/Pts	VALUATION: Premium/Discount As of 12/31/15	1 Year Average
FS	John Hancock Financial Opptys	BTO	**A+**	28.03	**A+ / 9.7**	25.29 / 99	21.19 / 96	16.40 / 94	5.28	**B- / 7.3**	7.11	-1.29
FS	*SP Regional Banking ETF	KRE	**A+**	41.92	**B+ / 8.9**	6.67 / 82	14.50 / 89	12.31 / 81	4.43	**B / 8.6**	-0.05	-0.01
FS	*Guggenheim S&P 500 Eq Wght Finl	RYF	**A+**	43.20	**B+ / 8.8**	-1.46 / 52	14.35 / 89	11.32 / 74	2.61	**B / 8.9**	-0.05	0.01
FS	*First Trust Financial AlphaDEX	FXO	**A+**	23.18	**B+ / 8.7**	1.30 / 69	13.99 / 88	11.42 / 75	2.68	**B / 8.9**	-0.04	0.01
FS	*Financial Select Sector SPDR	XLF	**A+**	23.83	**B+ / 8.7**	-1.14 / 54	14.01 / 88	10.04 / 65	5.03	**B / 8.8**	-0.04	-0.01
FS	*iShares US Financials ETF	IYF	**A+**	88.38	**B+ / 8.6**	0.05 / 60	13.68 / 86	10.55 / 68	4.58	**B / 8.7**	-0.03	N/A
FS	*Vanguard Financials ETF	VFH	**A+**	48.45	**B+ / 8.5**	-0.59 / 57	13.20 / 85	10.08 / 66	3.03	**B / 8.5**	-0.02	0.02
FS	*SP Bank ETF	KBE	**A+**	33.82	**B+ / 8.4**	3.82 / 76	12.53 / 83	7.18 / 55	4.13	**B / 8.7**	-0.09	N/A
FS	*iShares US Financial Services ET	IYG	**A**	89.98	**B+ / 8.8**	-0.15 / 59	14.75 / 89	10.36 / 67	3.36	**B- / 7.9**	0.01	0.02
FS	*iShares US Regional Banks ETF	IAT	**A**	34.96	**B+ / 8.5**	2.98 / 74	13.09 / 84	9.42 / 63	4.32	**B / 8.1**	0.00	0.01
FS	*iShares US Broker-Dealers ETF	IAI	**A-**	41.52	**A / 9.4**	-0.37 / 58	20.43 / 95	9.02 / 61	4.68	**B- / 7.0**	0.34	N/A
FS	*PowerShares DWA Financial Moment	PFI	**B+**	30.69	**B+ / 8.7**	1.37 / 69	13.51 / 86	11.62 / 76	1.80	**B- / 7.2**	0.26	-0.10
FS	*Oppenheimer Financials Sector Re	RWW	**B+**	48.09	**B+ / 8.5**	-3.31 / 45	13.83 / 87	9.13 / 61	1.38	**C+ / 6.8**	0.46	0.02
FS	*ProShares Ultra S&P Regional Ban	KRU	**B**	98.88	**A+ / 9.7**	13.18 / 93	26.05 / 97	16.69 / 94	0.75	**C / 5.0**	2.45	-0.13
FS	*PowerShares Financial Preferred	PGF	**B**	18.83	**B- / 7.5**	8.51 / 86	6.85 / 67	7.87 / 57	5.89	**B- / 7.7**	0.05	N/A
FS	*ProShares Ultra Financials	UYG	**C+**	71.00	**A+ / 9.6**	-4.45 / 41	25.43 / 97	16.49 / 94	1.36	**C- / 3.5**	-0.01	-0.02
FS	*SP Capital Markets ETF	KCE	**C+**	43.60	**C+ / 6.5**	-11.01 / 24	9.24 / 73	5.20 / 48	5.46	**C+ / 6.5**	0.65	-0.05
FS	*iShares Global Financials	IXG	**C+**	52.99	**C+ / 6.4**	-2.34 / 49	7.15 / 67	5.81 / 50	5.05	**B- / 7.1**	0.34	-0.03
FS	*SPDR SP Intl Finl Sector ETF	IPF	**C+**	19.82	**C+ / 6.0**	0.87 / 66	4.51 / 59	4.29 / 44	16.92	**C+ / 6.9**	2.53	0.25
FS	*Fidelity MSCI Financials Index E	FNCL	**C+**	28.30	**C / 5.1**	-0.19 / 59	--	--	3.48	**B- / 7.8**	0.00	0.03
FS	*AdvisorShares YieldPro	YPRO	**C+**	22.94	**C- / 3.7**	-1.99 / 50	--	--	3.31	**B+ / 9.1**	-0.22	-0.13
FS	*iShares MSCI Europ Financials ET	EUFN	**C**	20.30	**C / 5.0**	-4.00 / 42	3.33 / 54	2.38 / 35	3.21	**B- / 7.5**	-0.68	0.03
FS	*Direxion Financial Bull 3x Share	FAS	**C-**	29.07	**A+ / 9.8**	-8.83 / 29	37.58 / 99	19.19 / 97	0.00	**D- / 1.0**	0.00	0.02
FS	*Stock Split Index	TOFR	**C-**	15.01	**C- / 4.1**	1.13 / 68	--	--	1.33	**C+ / 6.9**	0.67	0.14
FS	*Global X China Financials ETF	CHIX	**C-**	13.69	**C- / 3.6**	-9.84 / 26	0.73 / 40	1.53 / 32	5.33	**C+ / 6.4**	-1.30	-0.32
FS	First Tr Specialty Finance &Fin Op	FGB	**D+**	5.57	**D+ / 2.4**	-20.47 / 13	-4.70 / 25	1.52 / 32	12.57	**C+ / 6.5**	-8.24	-2.37
FS	*ProShares Short Financials	SEF	**D**	16.87	**D- / 1.5**	-3.65 / 44	-14.84 / 12	-14.13 / 10	0.00	**C+ / 6.4**	-0.41	-0.01
FS	*ProShares UltraShort Financials	SKF	**D-**	45.87	**E+ / 0.6**	-8.42 / 30	-28.12 / 4	-28.40 / 3	0.00	**C / 4.4**	-0.20	N/A
FS	*Direxion Financial Bear 3x Share	FAZ	**E-**	41.18	**E- / 0.2**	-18.62 / 15	-42.30 / 1	-43.57 / 1	0.00	**D- / 1.4**	0.05	-0.05

* Denotes ETF Fund, N/A denotes number is not available

Fund Type	Fund Name (99 Pct = Best, 0 Pct = Worst)	Ticker Symbol	Overall Investment Rating	Price As of 12/31/15	PERFORMANCE: Performance Rating/Pts	PERFORMANCE: Annualized Total Return Through 12/31/15: 1Yr/Pct	3Yr/Pct	5Yr/Pct	Dividend Yield %	RISK: Risk Rating/Pts	VALUATION: Premium/Discount As of 12/31/15	1 Year Average
FO	*WisdomTree Japan Hedged Health C	DXJH	A+	34.70	A+ / 9.9	35.61 / 99	--	--	0.58	B- / 7.9	-1.00	N/A
FO	The New Ireland Fund	IRL	A+	13.93	A+ / 9.8	36.24 / 99	25.10 / 97	21.61 / 98	1.17	B- / 7.9	-12.39	-14.28
FO	*iShares MSCI Denmark Capped ETF	EDEN	A+	55.85	A+ / 9.6	19.14 / 98	21.52 / 96	--	0.07	B / 8.7	-0.98	-0.03
FO	Japan Smaller Cap Fund Inc.	JOF	A+	10.23	A / 9.5	24.45 / 99	16.38 / 92	4.95 / 47	1.63	B / 8.1	-12.04	-12.44
FO	*iShares MSCI Japan Minimum Vol E	JPMV	A+	57.00	A / 9.3	17.01 / 97	--	--	2.94	B / 8.8	-0.89	-0.03
FO	*ProShares UltraShort Yen	YCS	A+	87.89	A- / 9.2	-2.78 / 47	18.84 / 94	12.33 / 81	0.00	B / 8.7	-0.07	-0.01
FO	*iShares MSCI Belgium Capped	EWK	A+	18.06	A- / 9.0	14.21 / 94	12.85 / 84	11.04 / 72	1.84	B / 8.7	-0.39	0.05
FO	*WisdomTree Europe Small Cap Div	DFE	A+	56.00	B+ / 8.9	11.27 / 90	13.77 / 87	10.13 / 66	1.23	B / 8.1	-0.52	0.12
FO	*WisdomTree Japan SmallCap Div Fd	DFJ	A+	56.56	B+ / 8.8	18.01 / 98	11.06 / 79	7.41 / 56	1.24	B / 8.5	-0.75	0.09
FO	*iShares MSCI Japan Small Cap	SCJ	A+	58.45	B+ / 8.8	15.85 / 96	11.73 / 81	7.08 / 55	3.36	B / 8.6	-1.07	0.09
FO	*SPDR Russell/Nomura Small Cap Ja	JSC	A+	54.28	B+ / 8.5	16.01 / 96	10.32 / 76	6.49 / 53	3.04	B / 8.5	-0.80	-0.30
FO	*WisdomTree Japan Hedged SmallCap	DXJS	A+	34.02	B+ / 8.5	15.70 / 96	--	--	1.28	B / 8.6	-1.68	0.07
FO	*WisdomTree Japan Hedged Equity	DXJ	A	50.08	A- / 9.2	6.83 / 83	17.61 / 93	10.69 / 70	2.37	B- / 7.6	-1.42	N/A
FO	*Deutsche X-trackers MSCI Jp Hdg	DBJP	A	38.09	A- / 9.2	4.69 / 78	17.62 / 93	--	2.36	B- / 7.6	-1.32	0.05
FO	*Market Vectors Double Shrt Euro	DRR	A	59.70	B+ / 8.8	17.82 / 97	10.83 / 78	4.15 / 44	0.00	B / 8.0	-0.38	-0.08
FO	*iShares MSCI Germany Small-Cap	EWGS	A	41.35	B+ / 8.6	11.27 / 90	11.67 / 80	--	0.02	B / 8.1	-0.79	-0.02
FO	*ProShares UltraShort Euro	EUO	A	25.53	B+ / 8.4	16.31 / 96	9.72 / 74	3.28 / 39	0.00	B / 8.2	-0.04	N/A
FO	*WisdomTree Intl Hdgd Qual Div Gr	IHDG	A	26.43	B+ / 8.4	11.70 / 91	--	--	1.33	B / 8.4	-0.30	0.36
FO	*iShares MSCI UK Small-Cap ETF	EWUS	A	39.54	B+ / 8.4	11.54 / 91	11.63 / 80	--	6.17	B / 8.1	-0.38	-0.03
FO	*SPDR MSCI Japan Quality Mix ETF	QJPN	A	64.48	B+ / 8.4	11.23 / 90	--	--	3.16	B / 8.5	-1.23	-0.23
FO	*iShares MSCI Europe Small-Cap	IEUS	A	45.28	B / 7.9	12.01 / 92	9.91 / 75	6.63 / 53	3.65	B / 8.8	-0.79	0.51
FO	*iShares MSCI EAFE Small-Cap ETF	SCZ	A	49.95	B / 7.9	10.09 / 88	9.55 / 74	6.71 / 54	3.41	B / 8.8	-0.52	0.25
FO	*iShares MSCI EAFE Minimum Vol ET	EFAV	A	64.87	B / 7.8	9.53 / 87	9.10 / 73	--	4.13	B / 8.8	-0.45	0.17
FO	*iShares MSCI Ireland ETF	EIRL	A-	41.56	A+ / 9.6	22.97 / 98	20.77 / 95	18.28 / 96	2.44	C+ / 6.5	1.27	0.80
FO	Aberdeen Japan Equity	JEQ	A-	7.70	A- / 9.1	17.25 / 97	12.60 / 83	6.55 / 53	0.63	B- / 7.4	-9.20	-11.47
FO	*SPDR Russell/Nomura PRIME Japan	JPP	A-	46.16	B / 7.8	11.24 / 90	8.97 / 72	4.44 / 45	4.26	B / 8.3	-1.22	0.12
FO	*First Trust Japan AlphaDEX	FJP	A-	47.09	B / 7.7	5.25 / 80	10.21 / 76	--	0.67	B / 8.4	-0.19	0.04
FO	*Global X NASDAQ China Tech ETF	QQQC	B+	22.97	A / 9.3	9.60 / 87	16.66 / 92	6.68 / 53	0.63	C+ / 6.5	-0.09	-0.58
FO	*Guggenheim China Technology ETF	CQQQ	B+	36.01	A / 9.3	6.28 / 82	17.07 / 92	6.30 / 52	1.77	C+ / 6.3	-0.55	-0.33
FO	Aberdeen Israel Fund	ISL	B+	17.26	B / 7.7	5.24 / 80	10.54 / 77	2.85 / 37	0.00	B / 8.1	-16.38	-14.31
FO	*iShares MSCI Finland Capped ETF	EFNL	B+	32.61	B / 7.6	2.45 / 73	9.29 / 73	--	1.57	B / 8.0	-1.27	-0.10
FO	*Shares JPX-Nikkei 400	JPXN	B+	52.54	B- / 7.5	11.25 / 90	8.26 / 70	3.82 / 42	3.02	B / 8.3	-1.17	0.34
FO	*iShares MSCI Japan	EWJ	B+	12.12	B- / 7.5	9.76 / 88	8.68 / 71	3.71 / 42	2.89	B / 8.3	-1.30	-0.01
FO	*Deutsche X-trackers MSCI EAFE Hd	DBEF	B+	27.16	B- / 7.4	3.73 / 76	9.41 / 73	--	1.63	B / 8.1	-0.80	0.17
FO	*iShares MSCI Israel Capped	EIS	B+	49.19	B- / 7.2	9.63 / 88	7.80 / 69	-1.55 / 24	5.20	B / 8.3	-0.24	0.02
FO	New Germany Fund	GF	B	14.70	A / 9.4	14.57 / 94	17.51 / 93	13.76 / 87	0.54	C+ / 5.7	-9.20	-9.38
FO	*iShares MSCI NZ Capped ETF	ENZL	B	37.48	B / 7.9	0.69 / 65	8.01 / 70	11.29 / 74	7.40	B- / 7.1	-1.03	-0.11
FO	*WisdomTree Europe Hedged Equity	HEDJ	B	53.81	B- / 7.5	5.05 / 79	9.47 / 74	7.53 / 56	1.53	B- / 7.5	-0.81	0.13
FO	*Deutsche X-trackers MSCI Ger Hdg	DBGR	B	24.01	B- / 7.4	6.72 / 83	8.23 / 70	--	0.45	B- / 7.3	-1.40	0.09
FO	*PowerShares S&P Intl Dev High Qu	IDHQ	B	20.15	B- / 7.0	8.51 / 86	7.12 / 67	4.71 / 46	1.90	B- / 7.6	0.15	0.45
FO	*WisdomTree Intl Small Cap Divide	DLS	B	58.10	C+ / 6.9	7.26 / 84	7.22 / 67	6.77 / 54	2.43	B / 8.2	-0.50	0.14
FO	*PowerShares DWA Dev Mkt Momentum	PIZ	B	23.70	C+ / 6.8	-0.10 / 59	7.48 / 68	3.92 / 43	0.67	B / 8.0	-0.71	-0.13
FO	*iShares MSCI Netherlands	EWN	B	23.84	C+ / 6.6	2.59 / 73	7.23 / 68	5.85 / 51	2.42	B / 8.2	-0.46	0.02
FO	*iShares MSCI Switzerland Capped	EWL	B	31.04	C+ / 6.4	0.84 / 66	6.85 / 67	7.57 / 56	2.58	B / 8.3	-0.64	0.04
FO	*WisdomTree Intl MidCap Dividend	DIM	B	55.50	C+ / 6.3	2.73 / 73	6.16 / 65	5.28 / 49	2.10	B / 8.3	-0.63	0.23
FO	*iShares MSCI Europe Minimum Vol	EUMV	B	23.56	C+ / 6.1	5.30 / 80	--	--	2.39	B / 8.6	-0.63	0.19
FO	*Market Vectors ChinaAMC SME-ChiN	CNXT	B-	41.29	A+ / 9.8	42.39 / 99	--	--	0.00	C / 4.6	-1.08	-0.45
FO	*Deutsche X-trackers Hvst CSI500	ASHS	B-	41.46	A+ / 9.6	27.16 / 99	--	--	0.41	C / 4.7	-1.26	-0.14
FO	*KraneShares New China	KFYP	B-	63.40	A / 9.5	6.65 / 82	--	--	0.82	C / 4.9	8.75	-1.33
FO	*WisdomTree Germany Hedged Equity	DXGE	B-	26.62	C+ / 6.6	6.87 / 83	--	--	1.65	B- / 7.5	-1.52	0.09
FO	*iShares MSCI EAFE Growth ETF	EFG	B-	67.14	C+ / 6.3	4.36 / 77	5.67 / 63	4.52 / 45	1.57	B / 8.1	-0.59	0.09
FO	*PowerShares Intl BuyBack Achieve	IPKW	B-	26.01	C+ / 5.8	7.30 / 84	--	--	1.40	B / 8.4	-0.46	0.24

* Denotes ETF Fund, N/A denotes number is not available

	99 Pct = Best 0 Pct = Worst				PERFORMANCE					RISK	VALUATION	
						Annualized Total Return Through 12/31/15					Premium/Discount	
Fund Type	Fund Name	Ticker Symbol	Overall Investment Rating	Price As of 12/31/15	Performance Rating/Pts	1Yr/Pct	3Yr/Pct	5Yr/Pct	Dividend Yield %	Risk Rating/Pts	As of 12/31/15	1 Year Average
GEI	*WisdomTree Bloomberg US Dollar B	USDU	A+	27.36	A+ / 9.8	19.69 / 98	--	--	6.48	B+ / 9.0	-0.11	0.04
GEI	Babson Capital Corporate Investors	MCI	A+	17.25	A+ / 9.6	17.03 / 97	--	--	6.96	B- / 7.3	17.35	9.68
GEI	Babson Capital Participation Inv	MPV	A-	13.75	A+ / 9.6	12.54 / 92	--	--	7.86	C+ / 6.8	0.81	-5.61
GEI	DoubleLine Opportunistic Credit Fd	DBL	B-	25.31	B / 8.0	14.11 / 94	7.55 / 69	--	33.00	C+ / 6.4	11.35	3.60
GEI	*PowerShares Preferred Port	PGX	B-	14.95	B- / 7.3	7.53 / 84	6.65 / 66	7.72 / 57	5.79	B- / 7.3	0.27	0.10
GEI	*SPDR SSgA Ultra Short Term Bond	ULST	B-	39.90	C- / 4.2	0.14 / 61	--	--	0.45	B+ / 9.9	-0.05	0.01
GEI	*AdvisorShares Sage Core Rsvs ETF	HOLD	B-	98.90	C- / 4.2	0.10 / 61	--	--	0.59	B+ / 9.9	-0.12	0.03
GEI	MainStay DefinedTerm Muncipal Opp	MMD	C+	18.83	C+ / 6.7	9.33 / 87	4.09 / 58	--	6.25	C+ / 6.9	-3.93	-5.62
GEI	Nuveen EnhancedMunicipal Value	NEV	C+	15.71	C+ / 6.6	10.19 / 88	4.05 / 57	11.27 / 74	6.11	C+ / 6.6	0.58	-2.23
GEI	Guggenheim Build America Bd Mgd Du	GBAB	C+	21.38	C+ / 6.4	4.33 / 77	4.99 / 61	10.97 / 72	7.76	B- / 7.3	-5.40	-5.97
GEI	BlackRock Multi-Sector Income Trus	BIT	C+	15.81	C+ / 6.0	2.87 / 74	--	--	15.38	B- / 7.7	-13.27	-13.24
GEI	Nuveen Build America Bond Oppty Fd	NBD	C+	20.29	C+ / 6.0	-1.40 / 53	4.06 / 57	8.36 / 59	6.42	B- / 7.4	-7.18	-9.36
GEI	Fort Dearborn Inc. Secs.	FDI	C+	14.51	C+ / 5.6	6.76 / 83	1.44 / 45	8.23 / 59	4.48	B- / 7.3	-1.16	-7.82
GEI	*iShares Core US Aggregate Bond E	AGG	C+	108.01	C / 5.1	0.21 / 62	1.55 / 45	3.18 / 39	4.53	B- / 7.8	0.18	0.06
GEI	*Columbia Core Bond ETF	GMTB	C+	51.22	C / 5.0	0.55 / 64	1.41 / 44	--	2.09	B- / 7.8	1.55	0.12
GEI	*SPDR Barclays Int Term Crp Bond	ITR	C+	33.43	C / 5.0	0.17 / 61	1.58 / 46	3.67 / 41	2.75	B / 8.7	0.00	0.21
GEI	*Market Vectors FA Hi Yld Bd ETF	ANGL	C+	24.33	C / 4.9	-1.16 / 54	2.54 / 51	--	6.26	B / 8.6	-0.12	-0.05
GEI	*Vanguard Short-Term Bd Idx ETF	BSV	C+	79.57	C / 4.6	0.92 / 67	0.83 / 41	1.46 / 32	1.37	B / 8.2	0.10	0.06
GEI	*VelocityShares Dly Invs VIX M-T	ZIV	C	41.49	A- / 9.1	-1.03 / 55	17.62 / 93	24.36 / 99	0.00	C- / 3.7	-0.22	0.04
GEI	*Vanguard Intermediate Term Bond	BIV	C	83.06	C / 5.1	0.83 / 66	1.66 / 46	4.35 / 45	2.71	B- / 7.6	0.13	0.15
GEI	*iShares Core GNMA Bond ETF	GNMA	C	50.11	C / 5.0	0.75 / 65	1.27 / 44	--	1.85	B- / 7.8	0.16	0.12
GEI	*Vanguard Total Bond Market ETF	BND	C	80.76	C / 5.0	0.23 / 62	1.48 / 45	3.17 / 39	2.63	B- / 7.8	0.22	0.07
GEI	*Vanguard Long Term Bd Idx ETF	BLV	C	86.81	C / 5.0	-4.67 / 40	2.22 / 49	7.07 / 55	4.21	B- / 7.6	0.01	0.19
GEI	BlackRock Core Bond Trust	BHK	C	12.64	C / 4.8	2.01 / 71	0.58 / 39	7.49 / 56	6.74	B- / 7.4	-8.93	-9.98
GEI	*iShares Short Maturity Bond	NEAR	C	50.02	C / 4.8	0.84 / 66	--	--	1.28	B / 8.0	0.12	0.04
GEI	*iShares Intrm Govt/Crdt Bond ETF	GVI	C	109.61	C / 4.8	0.53 / 64	0.98 / 42	2.36 / 35	3.33	B- / 7.8	0.04	0.07
GEI	*SPDR Barclays LongTrm Corp Bond	LWC	C	37.58	C / 4.8	-5.87 / 36	1.86 / 47	6.49 / 53	4.68	C+ / 6.8	0.37	0.25
GEI	Western Asset Income Fund	PAI	C	13.02	C / 4.7	2.13 / 72	0.28 / 38	5.54 / 49	10.60	B- / 7.5	-5.92	-8.03
GEI	Invesco Bond	VBF	C	17.57	C / 4.4	0.31 / 62	-0.28 / 36	5.80 / 50	5.26	B- / 7.3	-7.09	-8.60
GEI	*SPDR Barclays 0-5 Year TIPS ETF	SIPE	C	19.35	C- / 4.2	0.18 / 61	--	--	0.00	B / 8.0	0.21	N/A
GEI	*SPDR Barclays 1-10 Year TIPS ETF	TIPX	C	19.18	C- / 4.1	-0.07 / 60	--	--	0.06	B- / 7.7	1.11	0.09
GEI	*Vanguard ST Inf Prot Sec Idx ETF	VTIP	C	48.35	C- / 4.0	0.04 / 60	-0.84 / 34	--	0.00	B- / 7.9	0.35	0.10
GEI	J Hancock Income Securities Tr	JHS	C	13.43	C- / 3.9	-0.52 / 57	-0.73 / 35	5.75 / 50	6.53	B- / 7.4	-8.20	-9.36
GEI	*Schwab US TIPS ETF	SCHP	C	53.13	C- / 3.5	-2.26 / 50	-2.08 / 31	2.36 / 35	0.28	B+ / 9.1	-0.04	0.05
GEI	*ProShares Investment Grd-Int Rte	IGHG	C-	73.21	C- / 3.7	-1.45 / 53	--	--	3.35	B- / 7.3	0.30	0.16
GEI	Western Asset Premier Bond Fund	WEA	C-	12.16	C- / 3.6	-4.12 / 42	-1.31 / 32	5.03 / 48	17.76	C+ / 6.8	-7.10	-6.19
GEI	*ProShares Short High Yield	SJB	C-	28.65	C- / 3.5	2.36 / 72	-3.55 / 28	--	0.00	B- / 7.7	0.00	-0.01
GEI	Duff & Phelps Utilities & Crp Bd T	DUC	C-	9.19	C- / 3.4	-0.12 / 59	-2.95 / 29	3.07 / 38	6.53	B- / 7.1	-8.56	-9.23
GEI	*ProShares Short 7-10 Year Treasu	TBX	C-	29.52	C- / 3.2	-2.91 / 47	-3.33 / 28	--	0.00	B- / 7.8	0.00	-0.06
GEI	*ProShares UltraShort 3-7 Yr Trea	TBZ	C-	28.54	C- / 3.1	-4.89 / 39	-3.78 / 27	--	0.00	C+ / 6.9	0.74	0.14
GEI	MFS Charter Income Trust	MCR	C-	7.62	C- / 3.1	-8.75 / 29	-2.60 / 29	3.33 / 39	9.75	B- / 7.0	-15.05	-12.44
GEI	Guggenheim Credit Allocation	GGM	C-	19.49	C- / 3.0	-0.01 / 60	--	--	11.16	B- / 7.4	-2.45	-3.03
GEI	*Market Vectors EM Aggregate Bd E	EMAG	C-	19.81	D+ / 2.7	-7.79 / 31	-4.96 / 25	--	4.97	B- / 7.7	-2.08	-0.57
GEI	Apollo Tactical Income Fund Inc	AIF	C-	13.89	D+ / 2.5	-4.55 / 40	--	--	22.16	B- / 7.2	-13.73	-13.26
GEI	*iShares iBonds Sep 2016 AMT-Fr M	IBME	D+	26.52	C / 4.6	0.11 / 61	0.63 / 40	2.47 / 35	0.67	C- / 3.9	-0.04	-0.08
GEI	J Hancock Investors Trust	JHI	D+	14.38	D+ / 2.4	-10.75 / 24	-7.21 / 21	2.22 / 34	10.39	C+ / 6.2	-10.35	-9.24
GEI	KKR Income Opportunities Fund	KIO	D+	13.86	D / 2.2	-5.82 / 36	--	--	10.82	B- / 7.2	-12.72	-11.56
GEI	*ProShares 30 Year TIPS TSY Sprea	RINF	D+	28.24	D / 2.0	-8.77 / 29	-10.23 / 17	--	1.63	B- / 7.1	-0.18	0.14
GEI	*Victory CEMP US Discovery Enh Vo	CSF	D+	34.55	D / 1.8	-7.42 / 32	--	--	1.46	C+ / 6.7	0.17	0.06
GEI	*iShares iBonds Sep 2017 AMT-Fr M	IBMF	D	27.35	C / 4.7	0.56 / 64	0.75 / 40	2.87 / 37	1.52	D / 2.2	0.07	0.09
GEI	*ProShares VIX Mid-Term Futures E	VIXM	E+	54.04	E+ / 0.7	-14.72 / 18	-24.76 / 5	--	0.00	D+ / 2.7	0.15	-0.10
GEI	*iShares MSCI Colombia Capped	ICOL	E	10.57	E- / 0.1	-39.81 / 4	--	--	3.21	D / 1.8	0.28	0.94

* Denotes ETF Fund, N/A denotes number is not available

Fund Type	Fund Name (99 Pct = Best, 0 Pct = Worst)	Ticker Symbol	Overall Investment Rating	Price As of 12/31/15	PERFORMANCE: Performance Rating/Pts	Annualized Total Return Through 12/31/15: 1Yr/Pct	3Yr/Pct	5Yr/Pct	Dividend Yield %	RISK: Risk Rating/Pts	VALUATION: Premium/Discount As of 12/31/15	1 Year Average
GEN	*First Trust Pref Sec and Inc	FPE	C+	18.95	C+ / 6.8	6.07 / 82	--	--	5.21	B- / 7.1	0.32	0.19
GEN	Putnam Master Intermediate Inc Tr	PIM	C+	4.55	C / 5.4	-0.99 / 55	2.55 / 51	1.57 / 32	6.86	B / 8.0	-8.82	-10.04
GEN	Morgan Stanley Income Sec	ICB	C+	16.87	C / 5.1	-0.58 / 57	1.45 / 45	5.07 / 48	3.20	B- / 7.9	-7.51	-9.82
GEN	*iShares Yield Optimized Bond ETF	BYLD	C+	24.01	C- / 3.5	-1.37 / 53	--	--	6.48	B+ / 9.4	-0.37	0.04
GEN	Putnam Premier Income Trust	PPT	C	4.95	C / 5.5	-0.16 / 59	2.79 / 52	1.94 / 33	6.30	C+ / 6.1	-9.84	-10.77
GEN	*Schwab US Aggregate Bond ETF	SCHZ	C	51.49	C / 5.1	0.08 / 61	1.54 / 45	--	1.98	B- / 7.7	0.16	0.09
GEN	Putnam High Income Securities	PCF	C	7.31	C / 4.7	-5.20 / 38	1.56 / 46	2.84 / 37	5.07	B- / 7.6	-11.29	-12.89
GEN	BlackRock Limited Duration Income	BLW	C	14.58	C / 4.6	0.62 / 65	0.04 / 37	5.72 / 50	12.16	B- / 7.4	-9.78	-11.24
GEN	*Newfleet Multi-Sector Income ETF	MINC	C	48.37	C / 4.5	0.96 / 67	--	--	3.34	B- / 7.8	0.04	0.03
GEN	*ALPS RiverFront Strategic Income	RIGS	C	24.19	C / 4.4	0.63 / 65	--	--	3.70	B- / 7.6	0.12	0.15
GEN	*PIMCO Dvsfd Inc Active Exch Trad	DI	C	45.83	C- / 3.6	-0.97 / 55	--	--	7.20	B / 8.7	-0.43	0.75
GEN	NexPoint Credit Strategies Fund	HCF	C-	20.44	C+ / 6.7	-23.11 / 11	14.02 / 88	8.52 / 59	15.26	C- / 3.2	-13.65	-13.07
GEN	Eaton Vance Limited Duration Incom	EVV	C-	12.76	C- / 3.8	-0.90 / 55	-1.29 / 32	3.77 / 42	9.56	B- / 7.0	-11.27	-12.21
GEN	MFS Multimarket Income Trust	MMT	C-	5.51	C- / 3.4	-7.75 / 32	-1.13 / 33	3.68 / 41	9.69	C+ / 6.8	-14.71	-12.60
GEN	Franklin Limited Duration Income	FTF	C-	10.72	C- / 3.0	-5.58 / 37	-3.67 / 27	2.92 / 38	6.94	B- / 7.5	-13.41	-13.32
GEN	First Trust Strategic High Inc II	FHY	D+	11.13	D+ / 2.5	-15.92 / 17	-4.70 / 25	4.90 / 47	11.86	C+ / 6.5	-14.38	-13.09

* Denotes ETF Fund, N/A denotes number is not available

Fund Type	Fund Name (99 Pct = Best, 0 Pct = Worst)	Ticker Symbol	Overall Investment Rating	Price As of 12/31/15	PERFORMANCE: Performance Rating/Pts	Annualized Total Return Through 12/31/15: 1Yr/Pct	3Yr/Pct	5Yr/Pct	Dividend Yield %	RISK: Risk Rating/Pts	VALUATION: Premium/Discount As of 12/31/15	1 Year Average
GL	*iShares Global Tech	IXN	A+	97.52	B+ / 8.9	4.87 / 79	14.00 / 88	10.67 / 69	2.29	B / 8.6	-0.34	-0.01
GL	*iShares Global Consumer Staples	KXI	A+	93.03	B / 8.2	7.74 / 84	10.26 / 76	11.55 / 75	3.86	B / 8.8	-0.20	0.01
GL	Flaherty & Crumrine Dyn Pfd and In	DFP	A	22.90	B+ / 8.9	9.75 / 88	--	--	8.38	B- / 7.8	-5.37	-7.23
GL	*iShares Global Consumer Discr	RXI	A	89.02	B+ / 8.9	6.74 / 83	13.94 / 88	12.51 / 82	1.93	B- / 7.8	-0.34	0.02
GL	*Global X Social Media Index ETF	SOCL	A-	19.87	A- / 9.0	9.54 / 87	13.91 / 87	--	0.01	B- / 7.3	-0.50	-0.14
GL	First Trust Dividend and Income	FAV	A-	8.46	B+ / 8.4	0.44 / 63	11.71 / 81	2.67 / 36	8.04	B- / 7.8	-7.24	-12.25
GL	*PowerShares Golden Dragon China	PGJ	B+	32.90	A+ / 9.6	17.00 / 96	19.56 / 95	5.31 / 49	0.18	C+ / 5.8	0.15	-0.14
GL	*First Trust ISE Cloud Computing	SKYY	B+	30.04	B+ / 8.9	5.66 / 80	13.84 / 87	--	0.18	B- / 7.2	0.20	0.09
GL	PIMCO Dynamic Income	PDI	B+	27.36	B+ / 8.7	7.30 / 84	12.01 / 82	--	76.97	C+ / 6.7	0.70	-4.25
GL	Eaton Vance Tx Mgd Glb Buy Wrt Opp	ETW	B+	11.23	B+ / 8.3	11.13 / 90	10.60 / 77	8.68 / 60	10.40	B- / 7.2	-2.85	-4.37
GL	*First Trust NASDAQ Smartphone In	FONE	B+	36.36	B+ / 8.3	-3.52 / 44	13.18 / 85	--	1.15	B- / 7.3	0.00	-0.05
GL	*Fidelity MSCI Cons Staples Idx E	FSTA	B+	30.28	B / 8.2	7.01 / 83	--	--	5.07	B- / 7.2	0.23	0.02
GL	*SPDR MSCI World Quality Mix ETF	QWLD	B+	60.16	B / 8.2	6.49 / 82	--	--	8.87	B- / 7.2	0.32	-0.22
GL	*SPDR SP Intl Telecom Sect ETF	IST	B+	25.08	B / 8.2	4.66 / 78	11.45 / 79	7.26 / 55	10.00	B- / 7.4	0.00	-0.11
GL	*Huntington EcoLogical Strategy E	HECO	B+	35.65	B / 8.2	1.93 / 71	11.47 / 79	--	0.09	B- / 7.0	0.48	-0.02
GL	*iShares Core High Dividend	HDV	B+	73.41	B / 8.0	0.60 / 65	10.93 / 78	--	7.80	B- / 7.9	0.00	N/A
GL	Eaton Vance Tax Adv Glob Div Inc	ETG	B+	15.52	B / 7.9	3.41 / 75	10.70 / 77	10.18 / 66	7.93	B- / 7.7	-8.87	-7.29
GL	*iShares MSCI ACW Minimum Vol	ACWV	B+	69.27	B / 7.8	4.44 / 78	9.88 / 75	--	4.90	B / 8.1	-0.01	0.12
GL	*Precidian Maxis Nikkei 225 Index	NKY	B+	18.48	B / 7.7	8.42 / 85	9.42 / 74	--	1.12	B / 8.4	-1.65	-0.10
GL	Nuveen Preferred and Income Term	JPI	B+	22.76	B / 7.6	10.60 / 89	6.24 / 65	--	0.15	B- / 7.8	-6.64	-7.78
GL	*iShares MSCI Kokusai ETF	TOK	B+	51.76	B- / 7.5	-0.02 / 60	9.73 / 74	8.48 / 59	5.69	B- / 7.7	0.00	0.12
GL	*SPDR SP Intl Con Disc Sect ETF	IPD	B+	36.80	B- / 7.0	2.27 / 72	8.37 / 71	7.04 / 55	4.36	B / 8.6	-0.92	-0.07
GL	*iShares Global Industrials	EXI	B+	67.62	B- / 7.0	-1.44 / 53	8.46 / 71	6.97 / 55	3.28	B / 8.5	-0.53	-0.12
GL	*IQ Global Agribusiness SmCp ETF	CROP	B+	27.85	C+ / 6.9	13.66 / 93	3.87 / 57	--	1.69	B / 8.6	-1.49	-0.29
GL	Canadian World Fund Limited	T.CWF	B	4.96	B+ / 8.8	19.81 / 98	12.00 / 82	3.73 / 42	0.00	C+ / 5.8	-34.22	-34.56
GL	Eaton Vance Tax Adv Global Div Opp	ETO	B	21.32	B / 7.9	-2.24 / 50	11.58 / 80	9.84 / 65	10.13	B- / 7.3	-7.26	-3.51
GL	*SPDR SP Intl Con Stap Sect ETF	IPS	B	41.47	B / 7.7	12.75 / 92	7.38 / 68	9.23 / 62	1.76	B- / 7.4	0.22	0.01
GL	Eaton Vance Tax-Mgd Gbl Div Eq Inc	EXG	B	8.85	B- / 7.5	3.03 / 74	9.25 / 73	7.10 / 55	11.02	B- / 7.4	-8.86	-6.90
GL	*First Trust NASDAQ Global Auto	CARZ	B	36.22	C+ / 6.9	-0.30 / 58	8.18 / 70	--	2.09	B- / 7.9	-0.58	0.01
GL	*iShares Global Telecom	IXP	B	57.85	C+ / 6.6	2.01 / 71	6.81 / 66	6.16 / 51	0.29	B / 8.0	-0.34	-0.08
GL	*iShares MSCI ACWI ETF	ACWI	B	55.82	C+ / 6.5	-0.82 / 56	7.18 / 67	6.29 / 52	0.19	B / 8.4	-0.25	N/A
GL	*iShares MSCI World	URTH	B-	69.60	B- / 7.4	0.43 / 63	9.41 / 73	--	4.30	C+ / 6.9	0.37	0.15
GL	*SPDR MSCI ACWI IMI ETF	ACIM	B-	61.50	B- / 7.4	-0.23 / 59	9.44 / 74	--	6.86	B- / 7.1	1.15	1.14
GL	Self Storage Group	SELF	B-	3.75	C+ / 6.8	8.94 / 86	6.32 / 65	6.43 / 52	6.93	B- / 7.3	-34.21	-31.75
GL	*SPDR SP Intl Tech Sector ETF	IPK	B-	31.20	C+ / 6.6	1.43 / 70	6.25 / 65	4.15 / 44	6.46	B- / 7.9	-0.89	-0.06
GL	*First Trust Long/Short Equity	FTLS	B-	32.73	C+ / 6.5	5.39 / 80	--	--	0.74	B- / 7.6	0.15	0.10
GL	*SPDR Global Dow ETF	DGT	B-	64.67	C+ / 6.3	-3.31 / 45	6.81 / 66	4.59 / 46	4.37	B / 8.3	-0.03	-0.05
GL	*Guggenheim Timber ETF	CUT	B-	23.57	C+ / 6.1	-0.71 / 56	5.83 / 64	4.32 / 45	1.52	B / 8.4	-0.51	-0.10
GL	*Global X FTSE Nordic Region ETF	GXF	B-	21.43	C+ / 6.0	0.12 / 61	5.73 / 63	4.91 / 47	2.95	B / 8.0	-0.56	-0.09
GL	*FlexShares Ready Access Var Inc	RAVI	B-	75.10	C / 4.6	0.15 / 61	0.59 / 39	--	0.64	B+ / 9.8	-0.08	-0.04
GL	*SPDR S&P International Mid Cap E	MDD	C+	29.79	B- / 7.2	8.62 / 86	7.46 / 68	5.21 / 48	4.19	C+ / 6.6	1.50	0.42
GL	*WCM/BNY Mellon Focused Gro ADR E	AADR	C+	38.53	B- / 7.1	5.72 / 81	7.39 / 68	5.88 / 51	0.05	C+ / 6.9	0.31	0.11
GL	*Fidelity MSCI Consmr Discr Idx E	FDIS	C+	30.68	C+ / 6.7	7.75 / 84	--	--	2.76	B- / 7.2	0.03	0.02
GL	AllianceBernstein Income Fund	ACG	C+	7.67	C+ / 6.5	9.42 / 87	4.35 / 58	7.45 / 56	14.24	B- / 7.3	-2.42	-7.03
GL	BlackRock Global Opportunities Eq	BOE	C+	12.76	C+ / 6.5	5.71 / 81	5.88 / 64	2.89 / 38	9.12	B- / 7.3	-10.46	-11.57
GL	Voya Global Advantage and Prem Opp	IGA	C+	10.45	C+ / 6.1	0.22 / 62	6.21 / 65	5.04 / 48	10.72	B- / 7.5	-8.49	-6.97
GL	GDL Fund	GDL	C+	10.01	C+ / 6.0	4.38 / 77	3.69 / 56	3.34 / 40	6.39	B / 8.0	-16.16	-16.18
GL	Alpine Total Dynamic Dividend Fund	AOD	C+	7.68	C+ / 5.9	-3.30 / 45	5.64 / 63	1.36 / 31	8.98	B- / 7.8	-16.61	-14.86
GL	*SPDR S&P WORLD EX-US ETF	GWL	C+	25.75	C+ / 5.6	0.37 / 63	3.60 / 55	3.20 / 39	5.42	B / 8.3	-0.43	0.15
GL	*SPDR SP Intl Industrial ETF	IPN	C+	27.75	C / 5.5	-0.85 / 56	3.45 / 55	2.18 / 34	6.20	B / 8.3	-0.86	-0.08
GL	*Market Vectors Uranium+Nuc Engy	NLR	C+	45.07	C / 5.4	-9.10 / 28	4.40 / 59	-5.29 / 19	3.30	B / 8.5	-0.40	-0.29
GL	*Global X SuperIncome Preferred E	SPFF	C+	13.15	C / 5.0	-3.90 / 43	2.32 / 50	--	6.57	B / 8.8	-0.30	0.03

* Denotes ETF Fund, N/A denotes number is not available

Fund Type	Fund Name (99 Pct = Best, 0 Pct = Worst)	Ticker Symbol	Overall Investment Rating	Price As of 12/31/15	PERFORMANCE: Performance Rating/Pts	Annualized Total Return Through 12/31/15: 1Yr/Pct	3Yr/Pct	5Yr/Pct	Dividend Yield %	RISK: Risk Rating/Pts	VALUATION: Premium/Discount As of 12/31/15	1 Year Average
GR	*Guggenheim S&P 500 Eq WgCon St E	RHS	**A+**	116.02	**A+ / 9.6**	13.70 / 94	19.81 / 95	17.90 / 96	1.77	**B- / 7.7**	0.08	0.04
GR	*Guggenheim S&P 500 Eq Wght HC ET	RYH	**A+**	153.49	**A+ / 9.6**	7.93 / 85	24.52 / 97	20.15 / 98	0.56	**B- / 7.5**	-0.01	0.04
GR	*Consumer Discretionary Sel Sec S	XLY	**A+**	78.16	**A / 9.4**	11.18 / 90	18.85 / 94	17.52 / 95	3.33	**B / 8.0**	-0.05	N/A
GR	*PowerShares Dynamic Large Cap Gr	PWB	**A+**	31.29	**A / 9.4**	7.97 / 85	17.87 / 93	14.77 / 90	0.81	**B- / 7.5**	0.03	0.01
GR	*Guggenheim S&P 500 Eq Wght Tech	RYT	**A+**	92.27	**A / 9.4**	2.90 / 74	18.67 / 94	12.00 / 78	1.69	**B / 8.3**	-0.06	0.01
GR	*iShares Russell Top 200 Growth	IWY	**A+**	53.54	**A / 9.3**	8.51 / 86	16.64 / 92	14.03 / 88	3.29	**B- / 7.6**	0.02	0.03
GR	*Consumer Staples Select Sector S	XLP	**A+**	50.49	**A- / 9.2**	7.95 / 85	15.31 / 90	14.94 / 91	5.86	**B / 8.3**	0.00	N/A
GR	*Technology Select Sector SPDR	XLK	**A+**	42.83	**A- / 9.2**	6.23 / 82	15.54 / 90	12.79 / 83	4.03	**B / 8.6**	-0.07	N/A
GR	*iShares S&P 500 Growth	IVW	**A+**	115.80	**A- / 9.2**	5.93 / 81	16.16 / 92	13.77 / 87	3.46	**B- / 7.8**	0.00	N/A
GR	*SPDR S&P 500 Growth ETF	SPYG	**A+**	100.09	**A- / 9.2**	5.79 / 81	16.15 / 91	13.78 / 87	3.80	**B / 8.4**	-0.06	0.04
GR	*First Trust Large Cap Gro AlphaD	FTC	**A+**	48.21	**A- / 9.2**	4.45 / 78	16.98 / 92	11.90 / 77	0.97	**B- / 7.9**	0.00	0.04
GR	*Guggenheim S&P 500 Pure Growth	RPG	**A+**	80.70	**A- / 9.2**	2.25 / 72	17.47 / 93	13.80 / 87	1.05	**B / 8.3**	-0.06	0.02
GR	*iShares US Technology ETF	IYW	**A+**	107.03	**A- / 9.1**	4.38 / 77	15.66 / 91	11.33 / 74	2.59	**B- / 7.8**	0.01	N/A
GR	*Vanguard Mega Cap Growth ETF	MGK	**A+**	83.04	**A- / 9.0**	3.91 / 76	15.03 / 90	13.27 / 85	1.68	**B / 8.3**	-0.04	0.02
GR	*iShares Core S&P 500 ETF	IVV	**A+**	204.87	**B+ / 8.9**	1.97 / 71	14.20 / 88	12.36 / 81	0.46	**B / 8.6**	-0.07	N/A
GR	*SPDR S&P 500 ETF	SPY	**A+**	203.87	**B+ / 8.9**	1.89 / 71	14.16 / 88	12.32 / 81	4.75	**B / 8.6**	-0.07	0.01
GR	*iShares Morningstar Large-Cp ETF	JKD	**A+**	119.07	**B+ / 8.9**	-0.37 / 58	14.86 / 90	13.39 / 86	2.29	**B / 8.7**	-0.07	N/A
GR	*iShares S&P 100	OEF	**A+**	91.17	**B+ / 8.8**	3.11 / 74	13.62 / 86	12.14 / 79	4.27	**B / 8.5**	-0.03	N/A
GR	*iShares Russell 1000 ETF	IWB	**A+**	113.31	**B+ / 8.8**	1.39 / 69	13.94 / 87	12.16 / 79	0.36	**B / 8.8**	-0.04	N/A
GR	*Vanguard Large Cap ETF	VV	**A+**	93.50	**B+ / 8.7**	1.10 / 67	13.87 / 87	12.11 / 79	2.17	**B / 8.4**	-0.02	N/A
GR	*Vanguard Mid Cap Value Index ETF	VOE	**A+**	85.95	**B+ / 8.6**	-1.85 / 51	14.30 / 89	12.10 / 79	1.88	**B+ / 9.0**	-0.05	0.01
GR	*Oppenheimer Large Cap Revenue	RWL	**A+**	39.44	**B+ / 8.6**	-1.93 / 51	14.15 / 88	12.31 / 81	2.32	**B / 8.7**	-0.03	0.01
GR	*iShares Russell Mid Cap Growth	IWP	**A+**	91.92	**B+ / 8.5**	--	13.60 / 86	11.22 / 73	2.54	**B / 8.6**	-0.04	N/A
GR	*Guggenheim S&P 500 Eq WgCon Dsc	RCD	**A+**	84.69	**B+ / 8.5**	-2.36 / 49	14.70 / 89	14.51 / 90	1.62	**B / 8.7**	-0.05	0.01
GR	*First Trust Dow Jones Sel Micro	FDM	**A+**	32.90	**B+ / 8.4**	1.81 / 71	12.95 / 84	9.41 / 63	2.59	**B / 8.5**	-0.06	-0.01
GR	*Industrial Select Sector SPDR	XLI	**A+**	53.01	**B+ / 8.4**	-3.60 / 44	13.10 / 85	10.92 / 71	4.81	**B / 8.7**	-0.04	-0.01
GR	*PowerShares S&P SC Health Care	PSCH	**A**	71.87	**A+ / 9.7**	21.58 / 98	26.28 / 98	21.49 / 98	0.00	**C+ / 6.9**	0.11	0.05
GR	*PowerShares KBW Prop & Casualty	KBWP	**A**	48.06	**A / 9.5**	16.26 / 96	19.06 / 94	16.59 / 94	2.73	**B- / 7.2**	0.63	0.04
GR	*PowerShares QQQ	QQQ	**A**	111.86	**A / 9.5**	9.50 / 87	20.21 / 95	16.24 / 93	0.92	**B- / 7.3**	-0.01	-0.01
GR	*PowerShares S&P SC Information T	PSCT	**A**	52.32	**A / 9.4**	5.74 / 81	18.25 / 94	12.54 / 82	0.15	**B- / 7.2**	0.10	0.02
GR	*Vanguard Info Tech Ind ETF	VGT	**A**	108.29	**A / 9.3**	5.32 / 80	16.74 / 92	12.63 / 83	0.74	**B- / 7.5**	0.02	0.01
GR	*First Trust NASDAQ-100 Equal Wei	QQEW	**A**	43.48	**A / 9.3**	2.37 / 72	18.22 / 94	13.34 / 86	0.83	**B- / 7.5**	0.00	0.01
GR	*First Trust NASDAQ-100-Technolog	QTEC	**A**	42.65	**A / 9.3**	-1.31 / 53	18.21 / 93	10.95 / 72	1.12	**B- / 7.3**	0.02	0.03
GR	*Vanguard S&P 500 G Indx ETF	VOOG	**A**	103.80	**A- / 9.2**	5.39 / 80	16.06 / 91	13.79 / 87	1.72	**B- / 7.6**	0.02	0.07
GR	*iShares Russell 1000 Growth ETF	IWF	**A**	99.48	**A- / 9.1**	6.01 / 81	15.76 / 91	13.18 / 85	3.08	**B- / 7.7**	-0.01	N/A
GR	*PowerShares Dynamic Software	PSJ	**A**	42.27	**A- / 9.0**	7.85 / 85	15.14 / 90	11.01 / 72	0.15	**B- / 7.6**	0.00	-0.03
GR	*Schwab US Large-Cap Growth ETF	SCHG	**A**	52.83	**A- / 9.0**	3.41 / 75	15.94 / 91	13.17 / 85	1.15	**B- / 7.5**	0.02	0.02
GR	*Vanguard Russell 1000 Index ETF	VONE	**A**	93.63	**B+ / 8.6**	0.75 / 65	13.75 / 87	12.00 / 78	2.29	**B / 8.0**	0.01	-0.01
GR	*WisdomTree MidCap Dividend Fund	DON	**A**	80.51	**B+ / 8.5**	-1.15 / 54	13.77 / 87	12.94 / 84	5.35	**B / 8.1**	-0.01	0.03
GR	*iShares Russell Mid Cap	IWR	**A**	160.18	**B+ / 8.3**	-2.08 / 50	13.00 / 84	11.25 / 73	4.39	**B / 8.6**	-0.06	-0.01
GR	*Vanguard Mid Cap Growth ETF	VOT	**A**	99.71	**B / 8.2**	-1.03 / 55	12.90 / 84	10.53 / 68	1.07	**B / 8.6**	-0.04	0.01
GR	*iShares Russell Mid Cap Value	IWS	**A**	68.66	**B / 7.9**	-4.39 / 41	12.20 / 82	11.08 / 73	5.83	**B / 8.7**	-0.06	N/A
GR	*PowerShares Russell Midcap Pure	PXMV	**A**	24.78	**B / 7.7**	-7.21 / 33	12.35 / 82	11.49 / 75	5.18	**B / 8.8**	-0.04	-0.02
GR	*Columbia Large Cap Growth ETF	RPX	**A-**	46.63	**A / 9.5**	10.30 / 89	18.56 / 94	14.10 / 88	0.23	**B- / 7.0**	0.93	0.07
GR	*PowerShares Russell Top 200 Pure	PXLG	**A-**	34.30	**A- / 9.1**	6.63 / 82	15.76 / 91	--	0.98	**B- / 7.2**	0.56	-0.04
GR	*Vanguard Russell 1000 Gro Idx ET	VONG	**A-**	102.00	**A- / 9.1**	5.58 / 80	15.67 / 91	13.05 / 85	1.74	**B- / 7.3**	0.03	N/A
GR	*Vanguard Growth ETF	VUG	**A-**	106.39	**A- / 9.0**	3.40 / 75	14.82 / 90	12.89 / 84	1.55	**B- / 7.5**	-0.01	0.01
GR	*Powershares S&P 500 Low Vol Port	SPLV	**A-**	38.57	**B+ / 8.9**	3.90 / 76	13.50 / 86	--	2.13	**B- / 7.5**	0.03	-0.04
GR	*iShares Core S&P Small-Cap ETF	IJR	**A-**	110.11	**B / 8.2**	-0.88 / 55	12.47 / 83	11.56 / 75	3.62	**B / 8.2**	-0.03	N/A
GR	*iShares S&P Mid Cap 400 Grow	IJK	**A-**	160.96	**B / 8.1**	2.15 / 72	12.03 / 82	10.92 / 71	2.90	**B / 8.3**	-0.04	N/A
GR	*Vanguard S&P SC 600 Indx ETF	VIOO	**A-**	99.15	**B / 8.0**	-1.47 / 52	12.12 / 82	11.26 / 73	1.26	**B / 8.5**	-0.10	0.03
GR	*Vanguard Div Appreciation ETF	VIG	**A-**	77.76	**B / 7.7**	-1.75 / 51	10.63 / 77	10.58 / 69	2.44	**B / 8.6**	-0.03	N/A

* Denotes ETF Fund, N/A denotes number is not available

	99 Pct = Best 0 Pct = Worst				PERFORMANCE					RISK	VALUATION	
						Annualized Total Return Through 12/31/15					Premium/Discount	
Fund Type	Fund Name	Ticker Symbol	Overall Investment Rating	Price As of 12/31/15	Performance Rating/Pts	1Yr/Pct	3Yr/Pct	5Yr/Pct	Dividend Yield %	Risk Rating/ Pts	As of 12/31/15	1 Year Average
GI	*ProShares UltraSht Australian Dl	CROC	A+	58.15	A- / 9.1	11.33 / 91	16.14 / 91	--	0.00	B- / 7.9	-0.67	-0.01
GI	*Vanguard Tot Stk Mkt Idx ETF	VTI	A+	104.30	B+ / 8.7	0.99 / 67	13.76 / 87	12.03 / 78	4.47	B / 8.7	-0.04	N/A
GI	*Schwab US Dividend Equity ETF	SCHD	A+	38.56	B+ / 8.5	-0.19 / 59	12.98 / 84	--	2.82	B / 8.8	-0.05	0.02
GI	BlackRock Enhanced Capital and Inc	CII	A	14.14	B+ / 8.8	8.19 / 85	12.57 / 83	8.71 / 60	8.49	B- / 7.8	-6.42	-6.46
GI	*WisdomTree LargeCap Dividend Fun	DLN	A	71.14	B / 8.1	-1.36 / 53	11.94 / 82	12.29 / 80	4.23	B / 8.7	-0.03	-0.01
GI	*Direxion All Cap Insider Sentime	KNOW	A-	71.15	A- / 9.2	3.83 / 76	16.98 / 92	--	0.33	B- / 7.2	0.32	0.06
GI	*First Trust Value Line Dividend	FVD	A-	23.88	B+ / 8.6	1.30 / 69	13.17 / 85	12.51 / 82	2.74	B- / 7.6	0.08	0.03
GI	Cohen&Steers Quality Income Realty	RQI	B+	12.22	A- / 9.1	7.82 / 85	13.33 / 85	14.70 / 90	3.93	C+ / 6.8	-9.21	-12.74
GI	*WisdomTree High Dividend	DHS	B+	59.09	B / 8.2	-0.84 / 56	11.73 / 81	12.82 / 84	4.64	B- / 7.6	0.07	0.01
GI	*First Trust Lrg Cap Core AlphaDE	FEX	B+	43.26	B / 8.0	-3.91 / 43	12.43 / 83	10.64 / 69	1.92	B / 8.0	0.00	0.02
GI	*iShares Core Aggressive Allocati	AOA	B+	44.84	C+ / 6.7	-0.96 / 55	7.96 / 70	7.73 / 57	2.56	B+ / 9.0	-0.04	0.06
GI	*ProShares Short Euro	EUFX	B+	43.74	C+ / 6.4	8.45 / 86	4.76 / 60	--	0.00	B / 8.8	-0.09	N/A
GI	LMP Real Estate Income Fund Inc	RIT	B	13.04	B+ / 8.6	9.91 / 88	10.81 / 78	12.29 / 80	5.52	C+ / 6.4	-3.91	-9.16
GI	*Guggenheim Wilshire US REIT ETF	WREI	B	45.82	B+ / 8.4	2.66 / 73	11.16 / 79	12.29 / 81	3.32	C+ / 6.5	0.31	-0.04
GI	*Schwab US REIT ETF	SCHH	B	39.64	B+ / 8.3	1.90 / 71	11.10 / 79	--	0.16	C+ / 6.3	0.05	0.03
GI	*iShares Europe Developed RE ETF	IFEU	B	37.59	B / 8.1	8.46 / 86	10.40 / 76	9.58 / 63	9.76	C+ / 6.8	0.70	0.23
GI	Neuberger Berman Real Est Secs Inc	NRO	B	5.01	B- / 7.5	1.35 / 69	7.94 / 70	10.82 / 70	7.19	B- / 7.2	-11.95	-15.34
GI	Clough Global Allocation Fund	GLV	B	13.47	B- / 7.1	0.86 / 66	8.61 / 71	5.86 / 51	10.69	B- / 7.6	-10.62	-13.45
GI	*Direxion S&P 500 Vol Response Sh	VSPY	B	54.60	C+ / 6.8	-6.95 / 33	9.33 / 73	--	1.42	B / 8.3	-0.05	0.04
GI	*Global X Guru Index ETF	GURU	B	23.22	C+ / 6.3	-10.89 / 24	9.02 / 72	--	0.47	B / 8.4	-0.04	-0.04
GI	*PowerShares Act US Real Estate	PSR	B-	72.75	B / 8.0	1.26 / 68	10.19 / 76	11.85 / 77	4.64	C+ / 6.5	0.44	0.03
GI	RMR Real Estate Income	RIF	B-	19.28	B- / 7.4	-2.26 / 50	8.41 / 71	7.39 / 56	6.85	C+ / 6.9	-18.06	-19.07
GI	*First Trust Total US Mkt AlphaDE	TUSA	B-	24.55	B- / 7.2	-5.05 / 38	10.18 / 75	5.05 / 48	1.27	B- / 7.1	0.86	0.04
GI	Delaware Inv Div & Inc	DDF	B-	8.82	B- / 7.0	-4.53 / 41	9.37 / 73	10.48 / 68	7.14	B- / 7.4	-11.27	-10.74
GI	Zweig Total Return Fund	ZTR	B-	12.18	C+ / 6.8	-4.55 / 40	7.84 / 69	6.44 / 52	3.05	B- / 7.5	-10.18	-12.21
GI	Boulder Growth&Income Fund	BIF	B-	7.74	C+ / 6.7	-12.56 / 21	9.41 / 73	7.78 / 57	1.22	B- / 7.8	-20.29	-20.54
GI	Bancroft Fund Ltd.	BCV	B-	18.20	C+ / 6.6	-0.21 / 59	7.90 / 69	5.79 / 50	5.08	B- / 7.7	-16.17	-15.18
GI	Nuveen Preferref Income Opps	JPC	B-	9.16	C+ / 6.5	5.69 / 80	4.90 / 61	10.73 / 70	8.78	B- / 7.6	-10.37	-10.24
GI	Nuveen Real Estate Inc Fund	JRS	C+	10.62	B- / 7.1	-1.33 / 53	7.41 / 68	9.75 / 64	9.04	C+ / 6.8	-9.31	-6.79
GI	*SPDR DJ Wilshire Glb Real Est ET	RWO	C+	46.80	C+ / 6.9	1.32 / 69	7.03 / 67	8.83 / 60	7.63	C+ / 6.8	0.02	0.09
GI	*SPDR Barclays Conv Sec ETF	CWB	C+	43.28	C+ / 6.9	-0.86 / 55	8.31 / 71	6.56 / 53	27.76	C+ / 6.7	0.28	0.07
GI	*EGShares India Consumer ETF	INCO	C+	32.11	C+ / 6.9	-1.95 / 51	9.08 / 72	--	0.00	C+ / 6.8	-1.08	0.19
GI	Calamos Strategic Total Return Fun	CSQ	C+	9.90	C+ / 6.7	-4.78 / 40	7.84 / 69	9.70 / 64	10.00	B- / 7.2	-10.89	-10.03
GI	Ellsworth Growth and Income Fd Ltd	ECF	C+	7.75	C+ / 6.6	-1.58 / 52	7.93 / 69	5.93 / 51	0.41	B- / 7.0	-15.67	-15.39
GI	Nuveen Diversified Dividend&Income	JDD	C+	10.83	C+ / 6.4	1.23 / 68	5.91 / 64	9.08 / 61	9.97	C+ / 6.9	-13.57	-12.83
GI	*iShares Global REIT ETF	REET	C+	25.25	C+ / 6.3	1.09 / 67	--	--	6.95	C+ / 6.6	0.96	0.51
GI	*iShares Core Growth Allocation	AOR	C+	38.88	C+ / 6.2	-1.02 / 55	6.31 / 65	6.56 / 53	0.13	B- / 7.5	0.18	0.04
GI	*Cohen & Steers Global Realty Maj	GRI	C+	42.53	C+ / 6.1	0.61 / 65	4.74 / 60	7.46 / 56	1.98	B- / 7.8	-0.35	0.14
GI	J Hancock Hedged Eqty & Inc Fd	HEQ	C+	14.46	C+ / 6.1	-2.15 / 50	5.83 / 64	--	10.40	B- / 7.5	-13.83	-11.98
GI	*FlexShares Global Quality RE Ind	GQRE	C+	56.85	C+ / 6.0	2.79 / 73	--	--	3.52	B- / 7.3	0.53	0.37
GI	*Arrow DWA Tactical	DWAT	C+	9.90	C+ / 6.0	0.05 / 61	--	--	0.00	B- / 7.0	0.20	-0.02
GI	Virtus Total Return	DCA	C+	3.81	C+ / 5.9	-6.71 / 34	6.48 / 66	8.82 / 60	10.50	B- / 7.5	-14.77	-12.67
GI	*IQ US Real Estate SmCp ETF	ROOF	C+	24.22	C+ / 5.9	-11.21 / 23	6.49 / 66	--	5.88	B / 8.1	-0.04	-0.01
GI	Nuveen Tax-Advantaged Dividend Grt	JTD	C+	13.91	C+ / 5.8	-4.69 / 40	5.43 / 62	9.75 / 64	9.29	B- / 7.7	-11.23	-9.62
GI	TCW Strategic Income Fund	TSI	C+	5.27	C+ / 5.7	1.06 / 67	3.32 / 54	8.88 / 60	3.64	B / 8.1	-9.61	-10.40
GI	*iShares Core Moderate Allocation	AOM	C+	34.05	C+ / 5.7	-1.18 / 54	4.14 / 58	4.78 / 46	0.17	B- / 7.7	0.03	0.06
GI	*SPDR SSgA Global Allocation ETF	GAL	C+	32.87	C+ / 5.7	-3.22 / 46	4.37 / 59	--	3.90	B- / 7.2	0.21	0.04
GI	*iShares Core Conservative Alloc	AOK	C+	31.64	C / 5.4	-1.07 / 54	2.98 / 53	4.09 / 44	4.05	B- / 7.6	0.16	0.01
GI	*Star Global Buy Write ETF	VEGA	C+	25.88	C / 4.8	-1.86 / 51	1.44 / 45	--	0.00	B+ / 9.1	-0.27	-0.10
GI	*WBI Tactical Income	WBII	C+	24.51	C- / 3.4	-0.78 / 56	--	--	4.00	B+ / 9.5	-0.08	0.06
GI	*First Trust FTSE EPRA/NAREIT Glb	FFR	C	42.68	C+ / 6.2	-0.65 / 56	5.23 / 62	7.20 / 55	1.18	C+ / 6.5	0.54	-0.16
GI	Cohen&Steers Total Return Realty	RFI	C	12.60	C+ / 5.7	3.19 / 75	2.27 / 50	6.82 / 54	1.07	B- / 7.1	-7.35	-8.45

* Denotes ETF Fund, N/A denotes number is not available

	99 Pct = Best *0 Pct = Worst*				PERFORMANCE					RISK	VALUATION	
						Annualized Total Return Through 12/31/15					Premium/Discount	
Fund Type	Fund Name	Ticker Symbol	**Overall Investment Rating**	Price As of 12/31/15	**Performance Rating/Pts**	1Yr/Pct	3Yr/Pct	5Yr/Pct	Dividend Yield %	**Risk Rating/Pts**	As of 12/31/15	1 Year Average
HL	*iShares US Medical Devices ETF	IHI	**A+**	122.48	**A+ / 9.6**	10.75 / 89	22.31 / 96	16.83 / 95	7.02	**B- / 7.5**	0.01	0.01
HL	*Vanguard HealthCare Index ETF	VHT	**A+**	132.88	**A+ / 9.6**	6.95 / 83	23.17 / 97	19.97 / 97	0.72	**B- / 7.7**	-0.02	0.02
HL	*Health Care Select Sector SPDR	XLV	**A+**	72.03	**A+ / 9.6**	6.93 / 83	22.80 / 96	19.73 / 97	3.36	**B / 8.1**	-0.03	-0.01
HL	*iShares US Healthcare ETF	IYH	**A+**	150.01	**A+ / 9.6**	6.08 / 82	22.48 / 96	19.59 / 97	4.28	**B / 8.1**	-0.04	0.01
HL	*iShares US Healthcare Providers	IHF	**A+**	124.35	**A / 9.5**	5.55 / 80	22.17 / 96	17.83 / 96	0.85	**B / 8.2**	-0.02	0.01
HL	*iShares Global Healthcare	IXJ	**A+**	102.62	**A / 9.4**	7.57 / 84	18.92 / 94	17.33 / 95	0.60	**B / 8.2**	-0.30	0.04
HL	Gabelli Healthcare & WellnessRx Tr	GRX	**A+**	10.25	**A- / 9.2**	3.05 / 74	17.21 / 92	18.66 / 97	5.07	**B- / 7.8**	-13.06	-12.32
HL	*PowerShares DWA Healthcare Momen	PTH	**A+**	55.11	**A- / 9.1**	2.06 / 72	17.83 / 93	15.74 / 93	0.00	**B- / 7.9**	-0.07	0.03
HL	*First Trust AMEX Biotechnology	FBT	**A**	113.02	**A+ / 9.8**	10.42 / 89	33.01 / 99	23.53 / 99	0.05	**C+ / 6.7**	-0.04	0.03
HL	*SPDR SP Intl Health Care ETF	IRY	**A**	50.37	**B+ / 8.9**	10.22 / 89	13.76 / 87	13.35 / 86	2.60	**B- / 7.9**	-0.40	0.01
HL	*iShares Nasdaq Biotechnology	IBB	**B+**	338.33	**A+ / 9.8**	10.48 / 89	33.48 / 99	29.10 / 99	0.06	**C+ / 5.6**	-0.03	0.02
HL	BlackRock Health Sciences Trust	BME	**B+**	39.35	**A+ / 9.7**	10.11 / 88	25.19 / 97	20.16 / 98	144.84	**C+ / 6.2**	8.79	3.01
HL	*PowerShares Dynamic Biotech&Geno	PBE	**B+**	50.52	**A+ / 9.7**	1.40 / 69	29.56 / 98	19.01 / 97	1.83	**C / 5.5**	-0.08	-0.02
HL	*First Trust Health Care AlphaDEX	FXH	**B+**	60.45	**A / 9.4**	-0.05 / 60	21.79 / 96	18.42 / 96	0.00	**C+ / 6.4**	0.03	0.02
HL	*PowerShares Dynamic Pharmaceutic	PJP	**B**	69.97	**A+ / 9.8**	14.64 / 95	30.56 / 98	28.09 / 99	0.87	**C / 5.2**	-0.01	N/A
HL	Tekla Healthcare Investors	HQH	**B**	29.66	**A+ / 9.7**	4.01 / 77	28.75 / 98	26.73 / 99	4.59	**C / 5.1**	-3.45	1.10
HL	Tekla Life Sciences Investors	HQL	**B-**	23.64	**A+ / 9.7**	5.44 / 80	26.19 / 97	27.27 / 99	7.36	**C / 4.9**	-2.23	0.33
HL	*iShares US Pharmaceuticals ETF	IHE	**B-**	161.69	**A+ / 9.6**	8.46 / 86	24.27 / 97	21.88 / 98	1.10	**C / 4.7**	0.13	0.01
HL	*Fidelity MSCI Health Care Index	FHLC	**C+**	34.53	**C+ / 6.4**	7.16 / 83	--	--	2.43	**C+ / 6.5**	0.09	0.03
HL	*ProShares Ultra Health Care	RXL	**C**	65.98	**A+ / 9.9**	7.32 / 84	44.94 / 99	38.24 / 99	3.26	**D / 2.1**	-0.02	-0.01
HL	*ProShares Ultra Nasdaq Biotech	BIB	**C-**	71.49	**A+ / 9.9**	11.86 / 91	65.97 / 99	56.19 / 99	0.00	**E- / 0.2**	0.08	0.02
HL	*Direxion Daily Healthcare Bull 3	CURE	**C-**	33.40	**A+ / 9.9**	6.24 / 82	67.86 / 99	--	0.00	**E- / 0.2**	0.03	0.01
HL	*SPDR S&P Biotech ETF	XBI	**C-**	70.20	**A+ / 9.8**	12.66 / 92	32.53 / 99	27.63 / 99	1.70	**E+ / 0.9**	0.00	-0.06
HL	*SPDR S&P Pharmaceuticals ETF	XPH	**C-**	51.20	**A+ / 9.8**	7.81 / 85	29.49 / 98	22.57 / 98	1.11	**D- / 1.5**	-0.02	0.01
HL	*SPDR S&P Health Care Equipment E	XHE	**C-**	44.57	**A+ / 9.7**	17.93 / 97	21.90 / 96	--	1.14	**D- / 1.4**	0.65	0.10
HL	*SPDR S&P Health Care Services ET	XHS	**C-**	57.38	**A / 9.5**	6.19 / 82	21.19 / 96	--	6.93	**D- / 1.5**	0.07	0.03
HL	*ETFis BioShares Biotech Products	BBP	**C-**	30.82	**B- / 7.5**	16.39 / 96	--	--	0.00	**D+ / 2.8**	0.13	0.06
HL	*ETFis BioShares Biotech Clinical	BBC	**D-**	29.05	**D+ / 2.8**	2.29 / 72	--	--	0.00	**D+ / 2.6**	0.07	-0.01
HL	*ProShares UltraShort Health Care	RXD	**E+**	47.39	**E / 0.3**	-21.23 / 12	-39.10 / 2	-36.37 / 2	0.00	**C- / 3.6**	-0.84	0.05
HL	*ProShares UltraShort Nasdaq Biot	BIS	**E**	28.71	**E- / 0.1**	-36.47 / 5	-54.53 / 1	-50.68 / 0	0.00	**D / 2.0**	-0.14	N/A

* Denotes ETF Fund, N/A denotes number is not available

99 Pct = Best
0 Pct = Worst

Fund Type	Fund Name	Ticker Symbol	Overall Investment Rating	Price As of 12/31/15	PERFORMANCE: Performance Rating/Pts	Annualized Total Return Through 12/31/15: 1Yr/Pct	3Yr/Pct	5Yr/Pct	Dividend Yield %	RISK: Risk Rating/Pts	VALUATION: Premium/Discount As of 12/31/15	1 Year Average
IN	*ProShares UltraShort Bloomberg C	CMD	A+	140.41	A+ / 9.9	59.72 / 99	38.75 / 99	22.43 / 98	0.00	B- / 7.3	-1.05	-0.42
IN	*Market Vectors Retail ETF	RTH	A+	77.72	A+ / 9.6	11.37 / 91	21.88 / 96	--	2.25	B / 8.1	0.01	0.02
IN	*PowerShares Aerospace & Defense	PPA	A+	35.64	A / 9.5	4.24 / 77	19.67 / 95	14.73 / 90	2.97	B / 8.7	-0.06	-0.02
IN	*iShares US Consumer Services ETF	IYC	A+	144.65	A / 9.4	7.18 / 84	18.65 / 94	17.64 / 95	2.10	B- / 7.7	-0.02	0.01
IN	*Market Vectors Semiconductor ETF	SMH	A+	53.28	A / 9.4	-0.16 / 59	18.91 / 94	--	2.14	B / 8.1	-0.15	0.01
IN	*SP Insurance ETF	KIE	A+	69.50	A / 9.3	7.22 / 84	17.07 / 92	11.85 / 77	4.65	B / 8.1	0.00	N/A
IN	*PowerShares Dynamic Food & Bever	PBJ	A+	32.20	A / 9.3	7.18 / 84	17.75 / 93	13.71 / 87	2.09	B- / 7.7	0.03	-0.01
IN	Nuveen S&P 500 Buy Write Income	JPZ	A+	13.43	A- / 9.2	15.26 / 95	11.85 / 81	10.14 / 66	7.42	B- / 7.8	0.67	-5.89
IN	*Vanguard Consumer Staples ETF	VDC	A+	129.07	A- / 9.1	6.49 / 82	15.19 / 90	14.88 / 91	1.39	B / 8.2	0.02	0.01
IN	*PowerShares Dynamic Leisure&Ente	PEJ	A+	36.76	A- / 9.1	4.11 / 77	15.86 / 91	15.06 / 91	0.21	B / 8.5	-0.03	0.05
IN	*iShares MSCI USA Minimum Vol ETF	USMV	A+	41.82	A- / 9.0	6.05 / 81	14.54 / 89	--	5.04	B / 8.4	0.00	0.02
IN	*Guggenheim Russ Top 50 Mega Cap	XLG	A+	144.58	B+ / 8.9	4.42 / 78	13.38 / 85	12.21 / 80	1.89	B / 8.5	-0.03	0.02
IN	*Vanguard 500 Index ETF	VOO	A+	186.93	B+ / 8.9	1.92 / 71	14.22 / 88	12.37 / 81	4.67	B / 8.6	-0.06	-0.01
IN	*TrimTabs Float Shrink ETF	TTFS	A+	54.09	B+ / 8.9	-1.31 / 54	15.98 / 91	--	0.77	B / 8.0	0.00	0.03
IN	*Vanguard High Dividend Yield ETF	VYM	A+	66.75	B+ / 8.7	1.21 / 68	13.34 / 85	13.09 / 85	7.18	B / 8.7	-0.03	0.01
IN	*Schwab US Broad Market ETF	SCHB	A+	49.04	B+ / 8.6	0.51 / 64	13.57 / 86	12.24 / 80	2.04	B / 8.5	-0.02	0.01
IN	*Vanguard Value ETF	VTV	A+	81.52	B+ / 8.6	-0.30 / 58	13.37 / 85	11.54 / 75	5.77	B+ / 9.0	-0.05	N/A
IN	*Guggenheim S&P 500 Equal Wght	RSP	A+	76.64	B+ / 8.4	-2.62 / 48	13.42 / 86	11.77 / 77	1.76	B / 8.6	-0.07	-0.01
IN	*First Trust Consumer Stap AlphaD	FXG	A	44.45	A / 9.5	6.91 / 83	21.12 / 95	17.82 / 96	1.35	B- / 7.3	0.05	0.02
IN	Nuveen Nasdaq 100 Dynamic Overwrit	QQQX	A	19.37	A / 9.4	9.21 / 87	16.03 / 91	14.83 / 91	7.23	B- / 7.2	-3.05	-6.18
IN	Eaton Vance Tax-Managed Buy-Write	ETB	A	16.69	A / 9.3	14.03 / 94	13.64 / 86	12.03 / 78	7.77	B- / 7.3	7.61	0.12
IN	Eaton Vance Enhanced Eqty Inc II	EOS	A	13.64	A / 9.3	6.44 / 82	16.82 / 92	11.37 / 74	7.70	B- / 7.3	-5.34	-6.06
IN	Eaton Vance Enhanced Eqty Inc	EOI	A	13.42	A- / 9.2	5.57 / 80	15.55 / 90	10.20 / 66	7.73	B- / 7.5	-4.01	-8.76
IN	Eaton Vance Tax Mgd Div Eqty Inc	ETY	A	11.20	A- / 9.1	9.21 / 87	14.49 / 89	9.92 / 65	9.03	B- / 7.7	-5.56	-7.54
IN	*iShares US Insurance ETF	IAK	A	51.15	A- / 9.1	4.82 / 79	16.08 / 91	11.95 / 78	3.98	B- / 7.4	0.10	-0.02
IN	*First Trust Capital Strength ETF	FTCS	A	38.20	A- / 9.1	1.99 / 71	15.73 / 91	12.45 / 82	1.50	B- / 7.5	0.21	0.03
IN	*iShares US Consumer Goods ETF	IYK	A	108.43	A- / 9.0	7.05 / 83	14.50 / 89	13.48 / 86	5.04	B- / 7.6	0.12	N/A
IN	*PowerShares High Yld Eq Div Ach	PEY	A	13.35	A- / 9.0	3.12 / 74	14.96 / 90	12.73 / 83	4.72	B- / 7.8	0.07	-0.01
IN	*Vanguard Mega Cap ETF	MGC	A	69.76	B+ / 8.8	1.57 / 70	13.89 / 87	12.25 / 80	2.45	B- / 7.9	-0.01	0.02
IN	*iShares MSCI KLD 400 Social ETF	DSI	A	75.71	B+ / 8.8	0.83 / 66	14.22 / 88	11.58 / 76	3.57	B- / 7.9	-0.01	0.05
IN	*Schwab US Large-Cap ETF	SCHX	A	48.57	B+ / 8.7	1.03 / 67	13.81 / 87	12.36 / 81	2.08	B / 8.0	0.00	0.02
IN	*iShares Russell 3000	IWV	A	120.31	B+ / 8.6	0.97 / 67	13.63 / 86	11.86 / 77	0.51	B- / 7.9	-0.01	N/A
IN	*PowerShares DWA Momentum	PDP	A	41.37	B+ / 8.5	1.56 / 70	13.39 / 85	12.16 / 80	0.25	B / 8.2	-0.07	N/A
IN	*Vanguard Mega Cap Value ETF	MGV	A	59.03	B+ / 8.5	-0.15 / 59	13.05 / 84	11.34 / 74	2.92	B / 8.1	0.02	0.03
IN	*First Trust Consumer Dis AlphaDE	FXD	A	34.10	B+ / 8.4	-3.08 / 46	14.30 / 89	12.51 / 82	0.92	B / 8.3	-0.03	0.02
IN	*iShares Select Dividend ETF	DVY	A	75.15	B+ / 8.3	-1.20 / 54	12.46 / 83	12.63 / 83	7.38	B / 8.3	-0.01	N/A
IN	*iShares S&P 500 Value	IVE	A	88.53	B / 8.0	-2.59 / 48	11.75 / 81	10.60 / 69	5.33	B / 8.7	-0.03	-0.01
IN	*Guggenheim S&P 500 Pure Value	RPV	A	49.20	B / 8.0	-8.26 / 30	13.58 / 86	13.00 / 84	2.13	B / 8.6	-0.08	-0.01
IN	*iShares Core US Value	IUSV	A	127.39	B / 7.9	-3.34 / 45	11.67 / 80	10.69 / 69	5.35	B / 8.7	-0.03	0.01
IN	*iShares Morningstar Large-Cp V E	JKF	A	81.76	B / 7.8	-1.00 / 55	10.42 / 76	9.34 / 62	6.36	B / 8.9	-0.04	-0.03
IN	*PowerShares DWA Cons Staples Mom	PSL	A-	56.79	A+ / 9.6	14.58 / 94	20.12 / 95	16.64 / 94	1.09	C+ / 6.9	0.04	0.02
IN	Eaton Vance Tax Mgd Buy Write Opp	ETV	A-	15.30	A / 9.5	17.56 / 97	16.13 / 91	13.45 / 86	8.69	B- / 7.0	5.08	0.07
IN	*iShares US Aerospace & Def ETF	ITA	A-	118.22	A / 9.5	4.54 / 78	20.29 / 95	15.80 / 93	1.52	B- / 7.0	0.05	0.01
IN	*Vanguard Consumer Discret ETF	VCR	A-	122.55	A / 9.3	7.19 / 84	17.54 / 93	16.52 / 94	0.77	B- / 7.2	0.01	0.02
IN	*Direxion NASDAQ-100 Eq Weighted	QQQE	A-	64.92	A / 9.3	2.61 / 73	18.55 / 94	--	0.11	B- / 7.1	0.03	0.01
IN	*SPDR S&P 1500 Momentum TILT ETF	MMTM	A-	90.07	A- / 9.2	6.02 / 81	15.42 / 90	--	3.99	B- / 7.3	2.15	0.22
IN	Nuveen Core Equity Alpha Fund	JCE	A-	14.27	A- / 9.2	0.43 / 63	16.95 / 92	14.46 / 89	8.49	B- / 7.2	-4.42	-4.82
IN	*SPDR S&P Dividend ETF	SDY	A-	73.57	A- / 9.0	3.22 / 75	14.00 / 88	12.90 / 84	6.11	B- / 7.4	0.03	-0.01
IN	*PowerShares S&P 500 High Quality	SPHQ	A-	23.13	A- / 9.0	1.80 / 71	15.06 / 90	13.82 / 87	3.92	B- / 7.4	0.04	N/A
IN	*PowerShares KBW Regional Banking	KBWR	A-	41.11	B+ / 8.9	6.66 / 82	14.44 / 89	--	2.99	B- / 7.4	0.00	-0.03
IN	Adams Diversified Equity	ADX	A-	12.83	B+ / 8.6	0.65 / 65	13.38 / 85	10.70 / 70	1.17	B- / 7.8	-14.69	-14.43
IN	*Vanguard Telecom Serv ETF	VOX	A-	83.91	B / 7.6	2.62 / 73	8.92 / 72	8.48 / 59	1.52	B / 8.8	-0.04	0.01

* Denotes ETF Fund, N/A denotes number is not available

	99 Pct = Best 0 Pct = Worst				PERFORMANCE					RISK	VALUATION	
						Annualized Total Return Through 12/31/15					Premium/Discount	
Fund Type	Fund Name	Ticker Symbol	Overall Investment Rating	Price As of 12/31/15	Performance Rating/Pts	1Yr/Pct	3Yr/Pct	5Yr/Pct	Dividend Yield %	Risk Rating/ Pts	As of 12/31/15	1 Year Average
LP	BlackRock Defined Opp Credit Trust	BHL	**C+**	13.02	**C+ / 6.0**	6.03 / 81	3.47 / 55	5.01 / 48	6.74	**B- / 7.5**	-1.51	-4.73
LP	*iShares Treasury Floatg Rate Bd	TFLO	**C+**	50.34	**C / 4.8**	0.69 / 65	--	--	1.27	**B / 8.1**	0.56	0.05
LP	*WisdomTree Bloomberg Float Rt Tr	USFR	**C+**	24.85	**C- / 4.1**	-0.12 / 59	--	--	0.00	**B+ / 9.8**	-0.44	-0.20
LP	*PowerShares Senior Loan	BKLN	**C+**	22.40	**C- / 4.0**	-2.89 / 47	0.37 / 39	--	4.42	**B+ / 9.0**	-0.13	-0.13
LP	*First Trust Senior Loan	FTSL	**C+**	46.87	**C- / 3.7**	0.17 / 61	--	--	4.10	**B+ / 9.4**	-0.17	0.15
LP	PIMCO Income Strategy Fund II	PFN	**C**	8.77	**C / 4.7**	-2.72 / 47	1.58 / 46	7.70 / 57	10.38	**B- / 7.1**	-5.29	-4.87
LP	BlackRock Floating Rate Inc Strat	FRA	**C**	12.90	**C / 4.6**	2.34 / 72	0.13 / 38	3.69 / 41	6.87	**B- / 7.6**	-9.54	-10.55
LP	Nuveen Floating Rate Income Fund	JFR	**C**	10.24	**C / 4.4**	-0.23 / 59	-0.01 / 37	3.95 / 43	7.03	**B- / 7.2**	-5.71	-10.41
LP	BlackRock Floating Rt Income	BGT	**C**	12.50	**C / 4.3**	2.39 / 73	-0.56 / 35	1.91 / 33	5.60	**B- / 7.5**	-9.22	-9.40
LP	*Highland/iBoxx Senior Loan ETF	SNLN	**C**	18.05	**C / 4.3**	-2.09 / 50	0.88 / 41	--	4.39	**B / 8.2**	0.00	-0.15
LP	Voya Prime Rate Trust	PPR	**C**	5.06	**C- / 4.2**	1.51 / 70	-0.60 / 35	3.94 / 43	6.28	**B- / 7.2**	-7.66	-9.02
LP	Invesco Dynamic Credit Opps	VTA	**C**	10.55	**C- / 4.2**	-3.76 / 43	0.70 / 40	4.16 / 44	8.53	**B- / 7.6**	-12.88	-12.07
LP	Pioneer Floating Rate Trust	PHD	**C**	10.85	**C- / 4.1**	1.31 / 69	-0.41 / 36	3.27 / 39	6.64	**B- / 7.6**	-9.88	-10.40
LP	*SPDR Blackstone/GSO Senior Loan	SRLN	**C**	46.13	**C- / 3.2**	-1.15 / 54	--	--	4.02	**B+ / 9.4**	-0.15	-0.02
LP	PIMCO Income Strategy Fund	PFL	**C-**	9.74	**C- / 3.8**	-9.14 / 28	-0.03 / 37	6.48 / 52	11.09	**C+ / 6.7**	-5.80	-4.49
LP	First Tr Senior Floating Rte Inc I	FCT	**C-**	12.35	**C- / 3.7**	1.14 / 68	-1.67 / 32	3.99 / 43	7.29	**B- / 7.3**	-8.86	-8.60
LP	Apollo Senior Floating Rate Fd Inc	AFT	**C-**	15.15	**C- / 3.6**	-2.63 / 48	-0.48 / 36	--	7.74	**B- / 7.2**	-10.51	-7.15
LP	Nuveen Floating Rate Income Opp	JRO	**C-**	9.80	**C- / 3.5**	-6.83 / 34	-1.11 / 33	2.37 / 35	0.40	**B- / 7.2**	-9.34	-9.61
LP	Eaton Vance Senior Income Trust	EVF	**C-**	5.77	**C- / 3.3**	-0.78 / 56	-2.95 / 29	1.96 / 33	7.89	**B- / 7.2**	-9.56	-10.04
LP	Eaton Vance Senior Floating Rate	EFR	**C-**	12.41	**C- / 3.3**	-2.38 / 49	-2.46 / 29	0.78 / 30	7.64	**B- / 7.0**	-8.68	-7.72
LP	LMP Corporate Loan Fund Inc	TLI	**C-**	9.88	**C- / 3.3**	-3.04 / 46	-2.23 / 30	3.51 / 40	8.81	**B- / 7.1**	-10.34	-10.46
LP	Invesco Senior Income Trust	VVR	**C-**	4.04	**C- / 3.3**	-4.51 / 41	-1.88 / 31	3.25 / 39	7.72	**B- / 7.0**	-10.02	-9.16
LP	Nuveen Sr Inc	NSL	**C-**	5.77	**C- / 3.3**	-7.08 / 33	-2.00 / 31	2.30 / 35	7.28	**B- / 7.0**	-10.82	-11.18
LP	Eaton Vance Floating Rate Income T	EFT	**C-**	12.64	**D+ / 2.9**	-2.48 / 48	-4.06 / 26	1.00 / 30	7.22	**B- / 7.1**	-9.65	-8.97
LP	Blackstone / GSO Lng-Sht Credit In	BGX	**C-**	13.48	**D+ / 2.8**	-6.01 / 36	-3.74 / 27	--	9.45	**C+ / 6.8**	-12.24	-13.35
LP	Eaton Vance Floating-Rate Inc Plus	EFF	**C-**	14.15	**D+ / 2.3**	-5.98 / 36	--	--	7.97	**B- / 7.5**	-10.39	-10.32
LP	THL Credit Senior Loan	TSL	**D+**	15.86	**C / 5.3**	0.58 / 64	--	--	16.65	**C- / 4.1**	-8.16	-8.21
LP	Blackstone/GSO Sr Floating Rate Tr	BSL	**D+**	14.85	**D+ / 2.9**	-5.58 / 37	-3.27 / 28	1.02 / 31	7.27	**C+ / 6.6**	-6.90	-6.95
LP	Avenue Income Credit Strategies	ACP	**D**	11.35	**D / 2.1**	-16.71 / 16	-6.04 / 23	--	12.69	**C+ / 5.8**	-11.33	-10.75

* Denotes ETF Fund, N/A denotes number is not available

Fund Type	Fund Name (99 Pct = Best, 0 Pct = Worst)	Ticker Symbol	Overall Investment Rating	Price As of 12/31/15	PERFORMANCE: Performance Rating/Pts	Annualized Total Return Through 12/31/15: 1Yr/Pct	3Yr/Pct	5Yr/Pct	Dividend Yield %	RISK: Risk Rating/Pts	VALUATION: Premium/Discount As of 12/31/15	1 Year Average
MTG	Western Asset Mtge Defined Oppty	DMO	**B+**	23.55	**B+ / 8.9**	13.42 / 93	12.84 / 84	15.19 / 92	10.70	**C+ / 6.7**	3.43	-1.51
MTG	*iShares MBS ETF	MBB	**B**	107.70	**C / 5.2**	1.33 / 69	1.82 / 47	2.69 / 36	7.89	**B+ / 9.4**	-0.06	0.03
MTG	BlackRock Income Trust	BKT	**C+**	6.38	**C+ / 5.6**	5.23 / 79	1.55 / 45	5.05 / 48	5.83	**B- / 7.6**	-8.07	-9.86
MTG	*SPDR Barclays Mortg Backed Bond	MBG	**C+**	26.82	**C / 5.3**	2.05 / 72	2.01 / 48	2.97 / 38	3.13	**B- / 7.9**	0.34	0.18
MTG	*FlexShs Dscpld Duration MBS Inde	MBSD	**C+**	24.73	**C / 5.3**	1.77 / 71	--	--	12.45	**B / 8.1**	0.82	0.27
MTG	*Vanguard Mort-Backed Secs Idx ET	VMBS	**C+**	52.72	**C / 5.3**	1.30 / 69	1.93 / 48	2.79 / 37	2.37	**B / 8.0**	0.08	0.07
MTG	Brookfield Total Return	HTR	**C**	21.95	**C+ / 6.8**	-0.33 / 58	7.22 / 67	9.49 / 63	10.39	**C / 5.6**	0.00	-11.02
MTG	PIMCO Strategic Income	RCS	**C**	8.95	**C+ / 5.9**	4.72 / 78	2.21 / 49	8.76 / 60	5.81	**C+ / 6.0**	11.46	6.44
MTG	Nuveen Mortgage Opportunity Term 2	JMT	**C**	22.29	**C+ / 5.6**	4.69 / 78	1.49 / 45	7.48 / 56	6.81	**C+ / 6.9**	-8.20	-11.09
MTG	Nuveen Mortgage Opportunity Term	JLS	**C**	22.71	**C / 5.4**	4.91 / 79	0.62 / 40	6.35 / 52	6.68	**B- / 7.0**	-9.49	-11.45
MTG	First Trust Mortgage Income Fund	FMY	**C**	14.54	**C / 4.5**	4.39 / 78	-0.95 / 34	2.85 / 37	6.43	**B- / 7.1**	-8.44	-10.75
MTG	Nuveen Multi-Market Income	MRF	**C**	7.10	**C / 4.3**	-3.75 / 43	--	3.33 / 40	6.76	**B- / 7.0**	-11.25	-12.06
MTG	Brookfield Mortgage Opportunity In	BOI	**C**	14.75	**C- / 4.2**	-1.60 / 52	--	--	10.34	**B / 8.0**	-13.54	-13.41
MTG	*First Trust Low Dur Mtge Oppty E	LMBS	**C-**	50.43	**C+ / 5.7**	2.83 / 74	--	--	6.07	**C- / 4.1**	0.42	0.20
MTG	PCM Fund	PCM	**C-**	9.24	**C- / 4.0**	-5.72 / 37	0.33 / 38	6.78 / 54	10.39	**C+ / 6.7**	-5.91	-3.89
MTG	*Market Vectors Mtge REIT Income	MORT	**D+**	19.53	**C- / 3.3**	-13.29 / 20	-0.22 / 36	--	10.24	**C / 4.9**	0.46	N/A

* Denotes ETF Fund, N/A denotes number is not available

Fund Type	Fund Name (99 Pct = Best, 0 Pct = Worst)	Ticker Symbol	Overall Investment Rating	Price As of 12/31/15	PERFORMANCE: Performance Rating/Pts	Annualized Total Return Through 12/31/15: 1Yr/Pct	3Yr/Pct	5Yr/Pct	Dividend Yield %	RISK: Risk Rating/Pts	VALUATION: Premium/Discount As of 12/31/15	1 Year Average
MUH	Nuveen Muni High Income Opport	NMZ	**B+**	13.82	**B+ / 8.8**	9.86 / 95	5.66 / 72	11.69 / 96	6.60	**C+ / 6.9**	0.95	-0.93
MUH	Western Asset Municipal High Inc	MHF	**B**	7.80	**B- / 7.3**	6.76 / 89	3.00 / 60	7.04 / 70	4.31	**B- / 7.4**	-2.50	-6.51
MUH	MFS High Yield Muni Trust	CMU	**B-**	4.51	**C+ / 6.9**	8.49 / 93	2.51 / 57	8.32 / 83	6.25	**B- / 7.1**	-7.39	-9.52
MUH	*PowerShares VRDO Tax-Free Weekly	PVI	**B-**	24.91	**C- / 4.2**	-0.18 / 59	-0.08 / 37	0.07 / 28	0.00	**B+ / 9.9**	-0.04	-0.02
MUH	MFS High Inc Muni Tr	CXE	**C+**	4.91	**C+ / 6.5**	8.37 / 93	1.75 / 52	8.02 / 81	6.11	**B- / 7.2**	-9.58	-11.07
MUH	*Market Vectors Hi-Yld Mun Idx ET	HYD	**C+**	30.88	**C+ / 6.5**	4.48 / 83	3.15 / 61	7.25 / 73	4.50	**C+ / 6.8**	0.32	-0.17
MUH	*Market Vectors Short HY Muni Ind	SHYD	**C+**	24.53	**C- / 3.9**	-0.57 / 57	--	--	3.13	**B+ / 9.5**	-1.72	-0.30
MUH	Pioneer Municipal High Income Adv	MAV	**C**	13.35	**C+ / 6.0**	-3.89 / 43	2.16 / 54	10.52 / 93	7.19	**C+ / 6.8**	7.06	11.24
MUH	Pioneer Municipal High Income Trus	MHI	**C**	13.06	**C / 5.4**	-0.47 / 57	0.30 / 39	7.80 / 78	6.43	**C+ / 6.9**	-2.39	-0.17

* Denotes ETF Fund, N/A denotes number is not available

Fund Type	Fund Name (99 Pct = Best, 0 Pct = Worst)	Ticker Symbol	Overall Investment Rating	Price As of 12/31/15	PERFORMANCE: Performance Rating/Pts	Annualized Total Return Through 12/31/15: 1Yr/Pct	3Yr/Pct	5Yr/Pct	Dividend Yield %	RISK: Risk Rating/Pts	VALUATION: Premium/Discount As of 12/31/15	1 Year Average
MUN	Eaton Vance Municipal Inc 2028 Ter	ETX	**A+**	18.49	**A+ / 9.7**	10.24 / 96	--	--	4.59	**B- / 7.8**	-9.72	-11.09
MUN	Dreyfus Municipal Bond Infra	DMB	**A+**	12.38	**A / 9.5**	8.15 / 92	--	--	6.06	**B- / 7.8**	-11.06	-11.00
MUN	Nuveen Intermdt Dur Qlty Mun Term	NIQ	**A**	12.88	**A- / 9.2**	6.37 / 88	--	--	4.43	**B- / 7.5**	-7.93	-8.59
MUN	PIMCO Municipal Income Fund	PMF	**B+**	15.45	**A- / 9.0**	15.69 / 99	6.11 / 73	12.07 / 97	6.31	**C+ / 6.3**	16.52	12.42
MUN	BlackRock MuniAssets Fund	MUA	**B+**	14.27	**B+ / 8.7**	9.14 / 94	5.27 / 70	10.34 / 93	5.56	**B- / 7.1**	0.56	-2.12
MUN	Nuveen California Municipal Value	NCB	**B+**	17.02	**B+ / 8.6**	8.26 / 92	6.42 / 75	8.94 / 87	4.96	**B- / 7.3**	-1.10	-3.80
MUN	PIMCO Municipal Income Fund III	PMX	**B+**	11.51	**B+ / 8.4**	11.27 / 97	3.73 / 63	9.61 / 91	6.50	**B- / 7.1**	3.41	2.01
MUN	Invesco Municipal Income Opp Tr	OIA	**B+**	7.29	**B+ / 8.4**	11.18 / 97	4.72 / 68	10.17 / 92	5.40	**B- / 7.2**	-4.46	-8.11
MUN	*Deutsche X-trackers Muni Inf Rev	RVNU	**B+**	26.29	**B+ / 8.3**	4.19 / 82	--	--	2.85	**B- / 7.6**	0.11	0.24
MUN	Nuveen Muni Value	NUV	**B+**	10.18	**B / 7.9**	9.84 / 95	3.60 / 63	6.95 / 69	3.83	**B- / 7.7**	-0.97	-3.41
MUN	BlackRock MuniEnhanced Fund	MEN	**B+**	11.85	**B / 7.8**	10.38 / 96	4.15 / 65	9.40 / 89	6.13	**B- / 7.6**	-3.81	-6.15
MUN	*First Trust Managed Municipal	FMB	**B+**	52.01	**B / 7.6**	4.50 / 83	--	--	2.65	**B / 8.1**	0.50	0.28
MUN	Western Asset Intermediate Muni	SBI	**B+**	10.21	**B- / 7.4**	11.02 / 96	2.53 / 57	6.99 / 70	4.70	**B- / 7.9**	-2.95	-5.42
MUN	*PowerShares NY AMT-Free Muni Bon	PZT	**B+**	24.31	**C+ / 6.5**	2.74 / 77	3.48 / 62	6.01 / 62	3.58	**B / 8.9**	-0.61	0.03
MUN	Eaton Vance Municipal Inc Tr	EVN	**B**	13.73	**B+ / 8.8**	9.79 / 95	5.84 / 72	12.18 / 97	6.19	**C+ / 6.4**	3.86	1.70
MUN	BlackRock MuniYield Quality III	MYI	**B**	14.73	**B / 8.1**	9.99 / 95	3.40 / 62	10.17 / 92	6.04	**C+ / 6.8**	-1.80	-4.93
MUN	Western Asset Municipal Defined Op	MTT	**B**	24.24	**B / 8.1**	8.02 / 92	5.01 / 69	8.72 / 86	2.04	**C+ / 6.7**	7.45	3.22
MUN	PIMCO Municipal Income Fund II	PML	**B**	12.51	**B / 7.9**	11.13 / 97	4.19 / 66	11.89 / 96	6.24	**B- / 7.1**	0.97	-0.54
MUN	Western Asset Managed Municipals	MMU	**B**	14.18	**B / 7.9**	10.30 / 96	3.70 / 63	9.75 / 91	5.50	**C+ / 6.8**	-1.12	-2.40
MUN	Eaton Vance Muni Bond II	EIV	**B**	13.18	**B / 7.9**	9.78 / 95	4.04 / 65	9.06 / 88	5.60	**B- / 7.3**	-5.99	-8.03
MUN	Invesco Value Municipal Income Tr	IIM	**B**	16.25	**B / 7.9**	5.27 / 85	4.57 / 67	10.24 / 93	5.17	**B- / 7.3**	-1.93	-4.16
MUN	BlackRock Taxable Municipal Bond T	BBN	**B**	20.98	**B / 7.9**	2.25 / 75	5.33 / 70	11.28 / 95	7.54	**B- / 7.1**	-6.17	-8.05
MUN	BlackRock MuniVest Fund II	MVT	**B**	16.41	**B / 7.8**	12.38 / 98	3.35 / 62	10.92 / 95	6.37	**C+ / 6.8**	2.50	-1.43
MUN	MFS Invst Gr Muni Tr	CXH	**B**	9.94	**B / 7.8**	11.40 / 97	3.02 / 60	8.76 / 86	5.13	**B- / 7.4**	-6.93	-9.94
MUN	BlackRock MuniHoldings Quality	MUS	**B**	13.73	**B- / 7.5**	9.73 / 95	1.68 / 51	9.38 / 89	5.90	**B- / 7.2**	-6.22	-9.18
MUN	Nuveen Premium Income Muni 2	NPM	**B**	14.46	**B- / 7.5**	8.28 / 92	3.35 / 62	8.57 / 85	5.98	**B- / 7.6**	-7.60	-10.67
MUN	Nuveen Div Adv Muni 3	NZF	**B**	14.36	**B- / 7.4**	9.61 / 95	3.08 / 60	7.83 / 79	5.77	**B- / 7.6**	-10.42	-12.35
MUN	Nuveen Investment Quality Muni Fun	NQM	**B**	15.42	**B- / 7.4**	7.64 / 91	3.71 / 63	9.75 / 91	6.03	**B- / 7.4**	-4.76	-5.70
MUN	Nuveen Build America Bond Fund	NBB	**B**	20.09	**B- / 7.4**	1.42 / 72	5.04 / 69	8.63 / 86	6.69	**B- / 7.5**	-6.12	-8.17
MUN	Federated Premier Muni Income	FMN	**B**	14.91	**B- / 7.3**	8.90 / 94	3.45 / 62	9.14 / 88	5.92	**B- / 7.4**	-3.31	-4.58
MUN	Invesco Quality Municipal Income T	IQI	**B**	12.69	**B- / 7.2**	8.59 / 93	2.95 / 59	8.27 / 83	6.00	**B- / 7.5**	-8.90	-10.77
MUN	Nuveen Prem Inc Muni	NPI	**B**	14.10	**B- / 7.2**	7.78 / 92	3.08 / 60	8.33 / 84	5.83	**B- / 7.6**	-9.67	-11.52
MUN	Nuveen Div Adv Muni	NAD	**B**	14.55	**B- / 7.2**	7.74 / 91	2.98 / 59	9.21 / 88	5.86	**B- / 7.5**	-7.09	-9.45
MUN	Neuberger Berman Intermediate Muni	NBH	**B**	15.72	**B- / 7.2**	7.34 / 90	3.71 / 63	8.73 / 86	5.73	**B- / 7.5**	-1.63	-3.71
MUN	Nuveen Prem Inc Muni 4	NPT	**B**	13.38	**B- / 7.2**	6.41 / 88	3.00 / 60	9.34 / 89	6.10	**B- / 7.5**	-7.79	-8.30
MUN	Putnam Muni Opp Tr	PMO	**B**	12.28	**B- / 7.1**	8.39 / 93	3.19 / 61	9.26 / 89	5.81	**B- / 7.8**	-8.49	-9.87
MUN	*PowerShares CA AMT-Free Muni Bon	PWZ	**B**	25.88	**B- / 7.1**	3.23 / 79	4.59 / 67	7.06 / 71	3.19	**B- / 7.8**	0.31	0.24
MUN	Nuveen Div Adv Muni Income	NVG	**B**	14.48	**B- / 7.0**	7.94 / 92	2.96 / 59	7.69 / 77	5.35	**B- / 7.6**	-11.38	-12.55
MUN	Nuveen Muni Market Opportunity	NMO	**B**	13.79	**B- / 7.0**	6.89 / 89	2.92 / 59	8.01 / 81	5.53	**B- / 7.7**	-10.74	-12.01
MUN	Nuveen Select Tax-Free Inc 3	NXR	**B**	14.54	**C+ / 6.9**	5.81 / 86	3.13 / 61	6.87 / 69	3.76	**B- / 7.7**	-5.83	-6.69
MUN	*SPDR Nuveen Barclays Bld Amr Bd	BABS	**B**	59.62	**C+ / 6.3**	-2.30 / 49	3.84 / 64	9.52 / 90	4.00	**B / 8.3**	-1.18	-1.15
MUN	*Market Vectors Short Muni Index	SMB	**B**	17.53	**C / 5.1**	1.10 / 71	0.81 / 43	1.95 / 38	1.16	**B+ / 9.6**	-0.06	-0.26
MUN	*PIMCO Short Term Muni Bd Act ETF	SMMU	**B**	50.27	**C / 4.9**	0.89 / 69	0.62 / 41	0.97 / 32	0.85	**B+ / 9.9**	-0.12	-0.09
MUN	Nuveen Muni Income	NMI	**B-**	11.98	**B / 7.8**	5.65 / 86	3.98 / 64	8.28 / 83	4.16	**C+ / 6.8**	3.72	-0.39
MUN	Nuveen AMT-Free Municipal Value	NUW	**B-**	17.86	**B / 7.7**	6.60 / 88	4.02 / 65	8.26 / 83	4.37	**C+ / 6.7**	3.66	-0.88
MUN	Putnam Managed Muni Inc Tr	PMM	**B-**	7.36	**B- / 7.2**	8.40 / 93	2.27 / 55	8.32 / 83	5.92	**B- / 7.3**	-8.11	-9.68
MUN	Western Asset Municipal Partners	MNP	**B-**	15.61	**B- / 7.0**	11.23 / 97	0.95 / 45	9.69 / 91	5.57	**B- / 7.5**	-7.69	-8.72
MUN	Federated Prem Intermediate Muni	FPT	**B-**	13.46	**B- / 7.0**	11.01 / 96	1.81 / 52	7.24 / 73	4.95	**B- / 7.5**	-7.62	-9.76
MUN	Nuveen Dividend Advantage Muni 2	NXZ	**B-**	14.16	**C+ / 6.7**	6.27 / 88	2.49 / 56	8.18 / 82	5.17	**B- / 7.7**	-11.50	-12.41
MUN	*SPDR Nuveen Barclays NY Muni Bd	INY	**B-**	23.77	**C+ / 6.7**	2.97 / 78	3.55 / 63	6.25 / 64	2.74	**B- / 7.7**	1.02	-0.28
MUN	Nuveen Select T-F Inc Portf 2	NXQ	**B-**	13.68	**C+ / 6.4**	4.38 / 83	2.49 / 56	6.08 / 62	3.90	**B- / 7.9**	-6.75	-6.93
MUN	BlackRock Muni 2020 Term Trust	BKK	**B-**	15.86	**C+ / 5.8**	0.62 / 67	2.05 / 53	6.26 / 64	3.39	**B / 8.7**	-1.86	-1.76

* Denotes ETF Fund, N/A denotes number is not available

Fund Type	Fund Name (99 Pct = Best, 0 Pct = Worst)	Ticker Symbol	Overall Investment Rating	Price As of 12/31/15	PERFORMANCE: Performance Rating/Pts	Annualized Total Return Through 12/31/15: 1Yr/Pct	3Yr/Pct	5Yr/Pct	Dividend Yield %	RISK: Risk Rating/Pts	VALUATION: Premium/Discount As of 12/31/15	1 Year Average
MUS	PIMCO CA Municipal Income Fund III	PZC	A-	11.92	A / 9.5	20.31 / 99	8.42 / 84	13.94 / 98	6.04	C+ / 6.8	15.62	8.13
MUS	MFS CA Muni	CCA	A-	11.84	A- / 9.0	15.02 / 99	4.50 / 67	9.48 / 90	5.17	B- / 7.4	-7.21	-10.24
MUS	Nuveen CA AMT-Free Municipal Incom	NKX	A-	15.36	A- / 9.0	11.47 / 97	6.28 / 74	11.45 / 95	6.09	B- / 7.4	-4.42	-6.58
MUS	Nuveen CA Muni Value	NCA	A-	10.88	B+ / 8.8	8.09 / 92	6.64 / 76	10.04 / 92	4.66	B- / 7.6	3.32	0.83
MUS	BlackRock Muni NY Interm Duration	MNE	A-	15.18	B+ / 8.6	13.89 / 98	3.37 / 62	8.75 / 86	4.55	B- / 7.5	-3.74	-8.82
MUS	PIMCO CA Municipal Income Fund II	PCK	B+	9.94	B+ / 8.6	13.01 / 98	4.42 / 66	11.00 / 95	6.49	B- / 7.2	11.06	10.63
MUS	BlackRock CA Municipal Income Trus	BFZ	B+	15.95	B+ / 8.6	12.49 / 98	3.78 / 63	11.52 / 96	5.43	C+ / 6.7	-0.25	-4.39
MUS	Eaton Vance OH Muni Bond	EIO	B+	13.42	B+ / 8.5	12.64 / 98	2.92 / 59	8.78 / 87	5.23	B- / 7.1	-6.55	-7.68
MUS	PIMCO NY Municipal Income Fund III	PYN	B+	10.27	B+ / 8.5	11.21 / 97	5.19 / 70	10.86 / 94	6.13	B- / 7.0	7.54	4.90
MUS	Nuveen CA Div Adv Muni 3	NZH	B+	14.15	B+ / 8.4	11.06 / 97	4.97 / 69	10.42 / 93	6.16	B- / 7.3	-4.52	-7.22
MUS	Nuveen CA Div Adv Muni 2	NVX	B+	15.31	B+ / 8.3	13.68 / 98	4.42 / 66	10.16 / 92	5.73	B- / 7.1	-4.01	-6.87
MUS	Eaton Vance CA Muni Bond	EVM	B+	12.15	B / 8.2	9.82 / 95	5.17 / 70	8.53 / 85	5.63	B- / 7.5	-6.03	-7.55
MUS	Neuberger Berman CA Inter Muni Fun	NBW	B+	15.75	B / 8.1	4.34 / 83	5.32 / 70	7.90 / 79	5.18	B- / 7.4	1.74	-0.75
MUS	Invesco Tr Fr Inv NY Mun	VTN	B+	14.61	B / 8.0	13.73 / 98	1.42 / 49	8.20 / 83	5.82	B- / 7.4	-3.94	-8.46
MUS	Eaton Vance MI Muni Bond	MIW	B+	13.85	B / 8.0	10.26 / 96	3.55 / 63	8.87 / 87	5.69	B- / 7.2	-10.59	-9.41
MUS	PIMCO NY Muni Income Fund	PNF	B+	11.90	B / 8.0	10.02 / 95	4.08 / 65	9.62 / 91	5.75	B- / 7.4	-1.65	-3.41
MUS	Invesco CA Value Municipal Income	VCV	B+	13.25	B / 8.0	9.38 / 94	4.69 / 67	10.64 / 94	5.98	B- / 7.3	-4.19	-5.82
MUS	Nuveen CA Select Tax-Free Inc Port	NXC	B+	15.63	B / 8.0	5.96 / 87	5.61 / 71	9.29 / 89	4.03	B- / 7.6	0.84	0.09
MUS	Alliance CA Municipal Income Fund	AKP	B+	14.09	B / 7.7	9.55 / 95	3.51 / 62	8.05 / 81	4.97	B- / 7.6	-8.68	-8.16
MUS	BlackRock NY Municipal Income Trus	BNY	B	15.58	B+ / 8.7	14.40 / 98	3.08 / 60	9.18 / 88	5.31	C+ / 6.3	1.56	-3.12
MUS	BlackRock MuniYield AZ Fund	MZA	B	16.86	B+ / 8.5	8.24 / 92	7.49 / 80	11.99 / 96	4.95	C+ / 6.6	12.93	13.49
MUS	PIMCO CA Municipal Income Fund	PCQ	B	15.70	B+ / 8.3	7.48 / 91	5.43 / 71	12.92 / 97	5.89	C+ / 6.7	7.46	6.46
MUS	Nuveen AZ Prem Inc Muni	NAZ	B	15.19	B / 8.1	11.36 / 97	4.40 / 66	9.69 / 91	5.25	C+ / 6.8	2.08	-0.49
MUS	PIMCO NY Municipal Income Fund II	PNI	B	12.35	B / 7.9	8.71 / 93	4.70 / 68	10.68 / 94	6.44	C+ / 6.8	8.24	7.62
MUS	Eaton Vance NY Muni Bond	ENX	B	13.13	B / 7.8	11.11 / 97	2.65 / 58	7.94 / 80	5.47	B- / 7.3	-7.14	-9.38
MUS	Nuveen CA Div Adv Muni	NAC	B	15.48	B / 7.6	9.35 / 94	3.95 / 64	11.82 / 96	6.38	B- / 7.1	-3.07	-4.30
MUS	Delaware Inv CO Muni Inc	VCF	B	14.59	B / 7.6	8.83 / 93	2.75 / 58	7.80 / 78	4.93	B- / 7.6	-5.93	-7.74
MUS	Nuveen NY Div Adv Muni	NAN	B	14.23	B- / 7.4	11.33 / 97	2.00 / 53	7.84 / 79	5.61	B- / 7.6	-7.96	-10.42
MUS	Nuveen GA Div Adv Muni Fund 2	NKG	B	13.50	B- / 7.3	12.46 / 98	1.19 / 47	6.48 / 65	4.76	B- / 7.4	-4.73	-7.95
MUS	BlackRock MuniYield NJ Fund	MYJ	B	15.47	B- / 7.3	9.90 / 95	2.84 / 59	8.92 / 87	6.39	B- / 7.3	-4.98	-7.19
MUS	Eaton Vance MI Muni Inc Tr	EMI	B	13.13	B- / 7.3	9.22 / 94	3.09 / 60	9.05 / 88	5.40	B- / 7.4	-11.76	-13.37
MUS	Eaton Vance NY Muni Inc Tr	EVY	B	14.15	B- / 7.3	8.91 / 94	1.80 / 52	9.51 / 90	5.66	B- / 7.3	-3.68	-6.32
MUS	BlackRock VA Muni Bond Trust	BHV	B-	19.75	A+ / 9.7	29.42 / 99	5.38 / 70	8.45 / 84	4.22	C / 4.7	22.52	7.13
MUS	BlackRock MuniHoldings New York QI	MHN	B-	14.56	B- / 7.5	9.35 / 94	1.82 / 52	8.04 / 81	5.58	B- / 7.0	-3.83	-6.21
MUS	BlackRock Municipal Income Invt Tr	BBF	B-	14.60	B- / 7.4	10.98 / 96	2.54 / 57	10.08 / 92	5.95	C+ / 6.7	-4.33	-9.16
MUS	Eaton Vance MA Muni Bond	MAB	B-	14.83	B- / 7.3	10.09 / 96	2.47 / 56	9.02 / 88	5.12	B- / 7.2	-5.54	-6.32
MUS	BlackRock MuniYield California Qly	MCA	B-	15.60	B- / 7.3	8.49 / 93	3.38 / 62	10.65 / 94	5.62	B- / 7.2	-4.35	-6.33
MUS	BlackRock MuniYield CA Fund	MYC	B-	15.82	B- / 7.1	8.74 / 93	2.93 / 59	10.51 / 93	5.63	B- / 7.3	-4.12	-4.95
MUS	Eaton Vance CA Muni Inc Tr	CEV	B-	13.33	B- / 7.1	7.76 / 91	3.25 / 61	10.32 / 93	5.29	B- / 7.1	-5.73	-6.72
MUS	Eaton Vance MA Muni Inc Tr	MMV	B-	14.03	B- / 7.0	8.38 / 93	1.60 / 51	6.53 / 66	4.89	B- / 7.5	-8.42	-9.66
MUS	BlackRock MuniYield New York Qly	MYN	B-	13.52	C+ / 6.9	9.35 / 94	1.67 / 51	8.21 / 83	5.60	B- / 7.2	-6.76	-7.30
MUS	Eaton Vance NY Muni Bond II	NYH	B-	12.47	C+ / 6.8	9.21 / 94	1.68 / 51	6.80 / 68	5.51	B- / 7.5	-9.31	-8.74
MUS	Nuveen NY Muni Value	NNY	B-	10.04	C+ / 6.8	6.70 / 89	2.21 / 54	6.31 / 64	3.88	B- / 7.7	-0.59	-2.40
MUS	Neuberger Berman NY Int Muni	NBO	B-	14.10	C+ / 6.6	8.37 / 93	2.52 / 57	6.68 / 67	4.85	B- / 7.4	-2.15	-2.71
MUS	*iShares California AMT Free Muni	CMF	B-	118.15	C+ / 6.6	2.98 / 78	3.78 / 64	6.65 / 66	4.22	B- / 7.8	0.23	0.24
MUS	*iShares New York AMT Free Muni B	NYF	B-	111.93	C+ / 6.3	3.19 / 79	2.91 / 59	5.29 / 58	4.58	B- / 7.8	0.21	0.16
MUS	Nuveen CT Prem Inc Muni	NTC	B-	12.76	C+ / 6.2	6.73 / 89	0.79 / 43	4.99 / 57	5.36	B- / 7.9	-12.78	-13.12
MUS	BlackRock FL Muni 2020 Term Tr	BFO	B-	14.94	C / 5.5	1.97 / 74	1.29 / 48	5.98 / 62	2.49	B / 8.9	-2.23	-2.68
MUS	BlackRock MuniYield Invt Fund	MYF	C+	15.65	C+ / 6.9	8.05 / 92	2.36 / 55	11.23 / 95	6.25	B- / 7.0	-0.57	-3.22
MUS	Nuveen MA Prem Inc Muni	NMT	C+	13.73	C+ / 6.4	8.83 / 93	1.43 / 49	6.12 / 63	4.85	B- / 7.6	-8.34	-9.42
MUS	BlackRock MuniYield PA Qly	MPA	C+	14.54	C+ / 6.4	7.66 / 91	1.27 / 48	7.57 / 76	5.90	B- / 7.5	-9.69	-11.55
MUS	BlackRock CA Muni 2018 Income Trus	BJZ	C+	15.04	C / 5.2	0.43 / 65	0.89 / 44	4.13 / 52	3.41	B / 8.6	-0.73	-1.22

* Denotes ETF Fund, N/A denotes number is not available

99 Pct = Best
0 Pct = Worst

Fund Type	Fund Name	Ticker Symbol	Overall Investment Rating	Price As of 12/31/15	PERFORMANCE: Performance Rating/Pts	Annualized Total Return Through 12/31/15: 1Yr/Pct	3Yr/Pct	5Yr/Pct	Dividend Yield %	RISK: Risk Rating/Pts	VALUATION: Premium/Discount As of 12/31/15	1 Year Average
PM	*DB Base Metals Double Short ETN	BOM	C+	25.40	A+ / 9.9	60.65 / 99	26.44 / 98	17.83 / 96	0.00	C- / 3.4	4.66	-0.19
PM	*DB Gold Double Short ETN	DZZ	C+	8.87	A+ / 9.7	17.95 / 97	24.78 / 97	0.64 / 30	0.00	C- / 3.2	0.11	-0.07
PM	*DB Gold Short ETN	DGZ	C+	17.10	B+ / 8.9	9.34 / 87	12.73 / 84	1.69 / 33	0.00	C- / 4.0	0.06	-0.05
PM	*DB Base Metals Short ETN	BOS	C	29.00	A / 9.5	26.51 / 99	12.61 / 83	9.03 / 61	0.00	C- / 3.0	-1.26	-0.93
PM	*IQ Hedge Market Neutral Tracker	QMN	C	24.93	C- / 4.2	-1.46 / 53	0.34 / 38	--	0.00	B- / 7.7	0.04	-0.04
PM	*ETFS Physical Swiss Gold Shares	SGOL	D	103.50	D- / 1.4	-11.02 / 24	-14.15 / 13	-5.34 / 18	0.00	C+ / 6.2	-0.14	0.12
PM	*iShares Gold Trust	IAU	D	10.23	D- / 1.4	-11.04 / 24	-14.05 / 13	-5.23 / 19	0.00	C+ / 6.3	-0.20	0.11
PM	*SPDR Gold Shares	GLD	D	101.46	D- / 1.4	-11.06 / 24	-14.17 / 13	-5.35 / 18	0.00	C+ / 6.2	-0.17	0.10
PM	Central Gold-Trust	GTU	D	37.70	D- / 1.3	-7.33 / 33	-15.78 / 11	-5.96 / 18	0.00	C+ / 5.8	-2.48	-4.90
PM	*PowerShares DB Gold Fund	DGL	D	34.66	D- / 1.3	-11.60 / 23	-15.15 / 12	-6.44 / 17	0.00	C+ / 6.2	-0.09	0.04
PM	*PowerShares DB Precious Metals F	DBP	D	32.22	D- / 1.1	-12.35 / 21	-17.11 / 10	-8.25 / 15	0.00	C+ / 5.7	-0.19	-0.01
PM	*UBS E-TRACS S&P 500 Gold Hedged	SPGH	D-	48.74	C- / 3.1	-9.95 / 26	-2.26 / 30	5.67 / 50	0.00	D+ / 2.7	1.33	0.36
PM	*ETFS Physical Palladium Shares	PALL	D-	54.17	D / 1.6	-29.85 / 7	-7.08 / 21	-6.20 / 17	0.00	C- / 3.7	2.65	0.26
PM	*ETFS Physical PM Basket Shares	GLTR	D-	52.29	D- / 1.1	-14.40 / 18	-17.18 / 10	-9.05 / 14	0.00	C- / 4.0	0.21	0.21
PM	GAMCO Global Gold Nat ResandIncome	GGN	D-	4.75	E+ / 0.9	-21.50 / 12	-19.14 / 9	-13.92 / 10	17.68	C / 4.5	-11.05	-7.30
PM	Central Fund of Canada	CEF	D-	9.99	E+ / 0.8	-14.31 / 19	-22.08 / 7	-12.11 / 12	0.10	C- / 4.1	-11.28	-8.56
PM	*Credit Suisse Gold Shs Covered C	GLDI	E+	10.26	D- / 1.1	-14.71 / 18	--	--	0.00	D+ / 2.9	-0.29	-0.02
PM	*ETFS Physical Platinum Shares	PPLT	E+	85.83	D- / 1.0	-26.37 / 9	-17.61 / 10	-13.10 / 11	0.00	C- / 3.4	2.03	0.33
PM	*ETFS Physical WM Basket Shares	WITE	E+	26.41	E+ / 0.9	-20.66 / 13	-19.56 / 8	-12.81 / 11	0.00	C- / 3.3	1.15	0.25
PM	*iShares Silver Trust	SLV	E+	13.19	E+ / 0.8	-12.71 / 21	-23.31 / 7	-14.04 / 10	0.00	D+ / 2.7	0.15	0.33
PM	*PowerShares DB Silver Fund	DBS	E+	21.87	E+ / 0.7	-13.93 / 19	-25.09 / 5	-15.49 / 8	0.00	C- / 4.1	-0.14	-0.04
PM	*Market Vectors Gold Miners ETF	GDX	E+	13.72	E / 0.4	-26.95 / 9	-32.31 / 3	-24.16 / 5	0.85	C- / 3.1	0.00	-0.01
PM	*PowerShares Glb Gold & Precious	PSAU	E+	11.75	E / 0.4	-27.45 / 8	-31.07 / 4	-23.54 / 5	0.51	C- / 4.0	-0.84	-0.12
PM	ASA Gold & Precious Metals Ltd	ASA	E+	7.17	E / 0.4	-30.86 / 7	-30.34 / 4	-24.08 / 5	0.56	C- / 3.7	-13.93	-10.75
PM	*Direxion Daily Gold Mnrs Id Bear	DUST	E	16.52	D+ / 2.3	-40.66 / 3	0.82 / 40	-3.88 / 21	0.00	E- / 0.1	1.60	-0.25
PM	*iPath Pure Beta S&P GW ETN	SBV	E	19.38	E+ / 0.6	-35.97 / 5	-22.55 / 7	--	0.00	D+ / 2.3	-0.62	-0.09
PM	*iShares MSCI Gl Met&MP	PICK	E	8.42	E+ / 0.6	-38.37 / 4	-24.11 / 6	--	9.02	D / 2.1	0.48	0.45
PM	*ProShares Ultra Gold	UGL	E	29.73	E / 0.5	-23.18 / 11	-29.12 / 4	-14.63 / 9	0.00	D+ / 2.3	0.00	0.20
PM	*DB Gold Double Long ETN	DGP	E	18.14	E / 0.5	-23.27 / 11	-29.09 / 4	-14.46 / 9	0.00	D- / 1.5	-0.22	0.10
PM	*ALPS Sprott Gold Miners ETF	SGDM	E	12.73	E / 0.5	-28.16 / 8	--	--	1.47	D+ / 2.4	0.08	0.01
PM	*Market Vectors Junior Gold Mnrs	GDXJ	E	19.21	E / 0.3	-22.49 / 11	-37.65 / 2	-31.67 / 2	0.72	D / 2.1	-0.05	0.05
PM	*Global X Silver Miners ETF	SIL	E	18.51	E / 0.3	-34.30 / 6	-34.91 / 3	-23.62 / 5	0.38	D+ / 2.8	-0.27	0.06
PM	*iShares MSCI Global Silver Miner	SLVP	E	5.62	E / 0.3	-36.28 / 5	-35.11 / 3	--	0.23	D / 1.8	0.00	0.50
PM	*Global X Copper Miners ETF	COPX	E	11.81	E / 0.3	-45.70 / 2	-32.70 / 3	-24.94 / 4	1.20	D+ / 2.4	0.00	0.28
PM	*DB Base Metals Double Long ETN	BDD	E-	4.10	E / 0.5	-43.40 / 3	-26.66 / 5	-25.75 / 4	0.00	D- / 1.0	0.24	0.64
PM	*iShares MSCI Global Gold Miners	RING	E-	5.48	E / 0.4	-27.29 / 9	-33.25 / 3	--	1.58	E+ / 0.9	0.92	0.34
PM	*Direxion Daily Gold Mnrs Id Bull	NUGT	E-	24.26	E- / 0.0	-79.91 / 0	-83.17 / 0	-72.68 / 0	0.00	D / 1.8	-0.41	0.09

* Denotes ETF Fund, N/A denotes number is not available

99 Pct = Best
0 Pct = Worst

Fund Type	Fund Name	Ticker Symbol	Overall Investment Rating	Price As of 12/31/15	PERFORMANCE: Performance Rating/Pts	Annualized Total Return Through 12/31/15: 1Yr/Pct	3Yr/Pct	5Yr/Pct	Dividend Yield %	RISK: Risk Rating/Pts	VALUATION: Premium/Discount As of 12/31/15	1 Year Average
USA	*PowerShares Build America Bond	BAB	B-	28.99	C+ / 5.7	-0.62 / 57	3.74 / 56	8.30 / 59	4.71	B / 8.7	-0.48	-0.33
USA	*iShares 10-20 Yr Treasury Bd ETF	TLH	B-	134.21	C / 5.4	0.60 / 65	2.50 / 51	6.18 / 51	4.08	B / 8.9	-0.12	0.05
USA	*iShares 7-10 Yr Treasury Bd ETF	IEF	B-	105.59	C / 5.1	1.01 / 67	1.63 / 46	4.51 / 45	3.41	B+ / 9.2	-0.09	0.03
USA	*iShares 1-3 Yr Treasury Bd ETF	SHY	B-	84.36	C / 4.4	0.33 / 62	0.37 / 38	0.56 / 29	1.12	B+ / 9.9	-0.05	0.02
USA	*PIMCO 1-3 Year US Treasury Idx E	TUZ	B-	50.66	C / 4.4	0.18 / 61	0.33 / 38	0.57 / 29	0.61	B+ / 9.9	-0.16	-0.01
USA	*SPDR Barclays LongTerm Treasury	TLO	C+	69.88	C+ / 5.6	-2.24 / 50	3.43 / 55	8.14 / 58	2.63	B / 8.4	-0.09	-0.01
USA	*iShares 20+ Yr Treasury Bd ETF	TLT	C+	120.58	C+ / 5.6	-2.84 / 47	3.51 / 55	8.78 / 60	4.63	B / 8.2	-0.12	0.04
USA	*ProShares Ultra 7-10 Year Treasu	UST	C+	56.13	C / 5.3	0.96 / 67	2.22 / 50	8.03 / 58	0.90	B / 8.4	-0.12	0.01
USA	*iShares Agency Bond ETF	AGZ	C+	113.15	C / 5.0	1.09 / 67	1.29 / 44	2.00 / 34	2.94	B / 8.0	0.33	0.11
USA	*SPDR Barclays Int Tr Treas ETF	ITE	C+	60.19	C / 4.9	1.54 / 70	1.03 / 42	2.19 / 34	1.26	B / 8.0	0.60	0.03
USA	*iShares 3-7 Yr Treasury Bd ETF	IEI	C+	122.61	C / 4.8	1.43 / 70	1.07 / 42	2.52 / 36	2.65	B / 8.8	-0.02	0.03
USA	*Schwab Intmdt-Term US Treasury E	SCHR	C+	53.60	C / 4.8	1.28 / 68	1.17 / 43	2.99 / 38	1.42	B / 8.0	0.09	0.02
USA	*iShares Core 1-5 Year USD Bond	ISTB	C+	99.27	C / 4.7	0.56 / 64	0.84 / 41	--	2.44	B / 8.2	0.31	0.29
USA	*Schwab Short-Term US Treas ETF	SCHO	C+	50.44	C / 4.5	0.38 / 63	0.42 / 39	0.59 / 29	0.68	B / 8.4	0.02	0.01
USA	*SPDR Barclays 1-3 Month T-Bill E	BIL	C+	45.68	C- / 4.2	-0.11 / 59	-0.10 / 37	-0.07 / 28	0.00	B / 8.9	0.00	N/A
USA	*FlexShs iB 3Y Tgt Dur TIPS Idx	TDTT	C+	24.18	C- / 3.7	-0.62 / 57	-1.33 / 32	--	0.00	B+ / 9.5	-0.29	0.01
USA	*FlexShs iB 5Y Tgt Dur TIPS Idx	TDTF	C+	24.32	C- / 3.6	-0.97 / 55	-1.78 / 32	--	0.21	B+ / 9.3	-0.08	0.07
USA	*Vanguard Extnd Durtn Trea Idx ET	EDV	C	113.20	C+ / 5.8	-6.52 / 35	4.71 / 60	13.01 / 84	3.60	C+ / 5.6	0.14	0.45
USA	*PIMCO 25+ Year Zero Coupon US Tr	ZROZ	C	109.31	C+ / 5.6	-8.14 / 31	4.48 / 59	13.48 / 86	2.55	B- / 7.2	-0.84	0.03
USA	*Vanguard Long-Term Govt Bd Idx E	VGLT	C	74.62	C / 5.5	-2.17 / 50	3.33 / 54	7.91 / 57	3.23	C+ / 6.7	0.13	0.10
USA	*ProShares Ultra 20+ Year Treasur	UBT	C	73.26	C / 5.5	-9.46 / 27	4.43 / 59	14.83 / 91	1.75	C+ / 6.6	-1.11	-0.02
USA	*PowerShares 1-30 Laddered Treasu	PLW	C	32.28	C / 5.3	-0.75 / 56	2.37 / 50	5.73 / 50	2.14	B- / 7.3	0.09	0.02
USA	*Vanguard Intm-Term Govt Bd Idx E	VGIT	C	64.44	C / 4.9	1.34 / 69	1.27 / 43	3.01 / 38	2.03	B- / 7.8	0.23	0.07
USA	*iShares Govt/Credit Bond ETF	GBF	C	111.70	C / 4.9	-0.24 / 59	1.25 / 43	3.29 / 39	4.70	B- / 7.8	0.21	0.19
USA	*iShares Core US Treasury Bond	GOVT	C	25.06	C / 4.8	0.22 / 62	1.10 / 42	--	1.22	B- / 7.7	0.04	0.06
USA	*SPDR Barclays Sht Trm Treasury E	SST	C	30.10	C / 4.6	0.83 / 66	0.62 / 40	--	0.99	B- / 7.8	0.10	0.02
USA	*Vanguard Short-Term Gvt Bd Idx E	VGSH	C	60.76	C / 4.5	0.46 / 64	0.46 / 39	0.61 / 30	1.11	B- / 7.9	0.05	0.03
USA	BlackRock Enhanced Government	EGF	C	13.65	C / 4.5	0.13 / 61	0.11 / 37	2.50 / 36	4.31	B- / 7.9	-4.48	-5.93
USA	*Franklin Short Duration US Govt	FTSD	C	98.27	C / 4.4	0.30 / 62	--	--	1.85	B / 8.0	0.27	0.03
USA	*iShares Short Treasury Bond ETF	SHV	C	110.22	C / 4.3	0.03 / 60	0.01 / 37	0.02 / 28	0.10	B / 8.2	0.03	0.02
USA	*iShares 0-5 Yr TIPS Bond ETF	STIP	C	98.92	C- / 3.9	-0.19 / 59	-1.00 / 33	0.56 / 29	0.00	B / 8.1	0.09	0.07
USA	*PIMCO 1-5 Year US TIPS Index ETF	STPZ	C	51.33	C- / 3.8	-0.45 / 57	-1.22 / 33	0.60 / 30	0.58	B- / 7.8	0.20	0.01
USA	*iShares TIPS Bond ETF	TIP	C	109.68	C- / 3.5	-2.38 / 49	-2.08 / 31	2.33 / 35	0.11	B+ / 9.0	-0.08	0.07
USA	*SPDR Barclays TIPS ETF	IPE	C	54.63	C- / 3.4	-3.18 / 46	-2.22 / 30	2.67 / 36	0.23	B / 8.8	-0.18	-0.01
USA	*PIMCO Broad US TIPS Index ETF	TIPZ	C	55.25	C- / 3.4	-3.22 / 45	-2.27 / 30	2.39 / 35	0.65	B / 8.8	-0.20	-0.01
USA	*iPath US Treas 10Yr Bull ETN	DTYL	C-	74.81	C / 5.2	1.64 / 70	2.13 / 49	9.71 / 64	0.00	C / 5.1	-0.53	0.06
USA	*Direxion Daily 20+ Yr Treas Bull	TMF	C-	74.23	C / 5.0	-16.30 / 16	3.75 / 56	18.46 / 96	0.00	C / 5.1	-1.17	-0.03
USA	Western Asset/Claymore Inf-Link S&	WIA	C-	10.57	D+ / 2.9	-6.67 / 34	-3.87 / 27	-0.31 / 27	3.33	B- / 7.4	-15.24	-14.13
USA	Western Asset/Claymore Inf-Link O&	WIW	C-	10.29	D+ / 2.7	-6.72 / 34	-4.85 / 25	-0.19 / 27	3.58	B- / 7.4	-15.38	-14.20
USA	*iPath US Treas Lng Bd Bull ETN	DLBL	D+	75.04	C / 5.5	0.42 / 63	2.99 / 53	10.16 / 66	0.00	C- / 3.3	1.19	0.07
USA	*iPath US Treas 2Yr Bull ETN	DTUL	D+	63.37	C / 5.4	5.06 / 79	2.90 / 52	4.49 / 45	0.00	C- / 4.0	1.51	-0.48
USA	*iPath ETN US Treasury 5Yr Bull E	DFVL	D+	64.42	C / 5.3	6.44 / 82	1.86 / 48	--	0.00	C- / 3.5	0.11	-0.07
USA	*Direxion Daily 7-10 Yr Trs Bull	TYD	D+	44.21	C / 5.2	-0.44 / 58	2.48 / 51	11.78 / 77	0.00	C- / 3.1	-1.18	-0.21
USA	*iPath US Treas Flattener ETN	FLAT	D+	60.04	C- / 4.0	-2.70 / 48	-0.86 / 34	5.25 / 49	0.00	C / 5.0	-0.43	-0.07
USA	*PIMCO 15 Plus Year US TIPS Idx E	LTPZ	D+	60.86	D+ / 2.9	-10.16 / 25	-3.52 / 28	4.47 / 45	0.34	C+ / 6.1	0.35	N/A
USA	*Direxion Daily 7-10 Yr Trs Bear	TYO	D+	16.66	D / 1.9	-10.04 / 25	-10.92 / 16	-18.34 / 6	0.00	C+ / 6.3	-0.30	0.01
USA	*DB 3x Long 25+ Year Treasury ETN	LBND	D	49.50	C / 5.4	-14.29 / 19	3.85 / 57	19.19 / 97	0.00	D+ / 2.7	-0.82	-0.34
USA	*iPath US Treas 2Yr Bear ETN	DTUS	D	33.17	D+ / 2.8	-8.37 / 30	-6.48 / 22	-7.65 / 16	0.00	C- / 4.0	-0.24	0.19
USA	*ProShares Short 20+ Year Treas	TBF	D	24.73	D+ / 2.7	-0.72 / 56	-6.29 / 23	-11.22 / 12	0.00	C / 5.3	0.04	-0.03
USA	*iPath US Treas Steepen ETN	STPP	D-	34.91	C- / 3.7	2.04 / 72	-1.21 / 33	-8.04 / 16	0.00	D+ / 2.8	0.55	-0.09
USA	*iPath ETN US Treasury 5Yr Bear E	DFVS	D-	31.91	D+ / 2.8	-8.96 / 28	-6.30 / 22	--	0.00	C- / 3.3	-0.44	0.04
USA	*iPath US Treas 10Yr Bear ETN	DTYS	D-	20.27	D+ / 2.3	-9.14 / 28	-9.98 / 17	-17.38 / 6	0.00	D+ / 2.9	-0.93	N/A

* Denotes ETF Fund, N/A denotes number is not available

	99 Pct = Best *0 Pct = Worst*				PERFORMANCE					RISK	VALUATION	
Fund Type	Fund Name	Ticker Symbol	Overall Investment Rating	Price As of 12/31/15	Performance Rating/Pts	Annualized Total Return Through 12/31/15 1Yr/Pct	3Yr/Pct	5Yr/Pct	Dividend Yield %	Risk Rating/Pts	Premium/Discount As of 12/31/15	1 Year Average
UT	*Guggenheim S&P 500 Eq Wght Util	RYU	A-	72.35	B / 7.8	-4.64 / 40	10.72 / 77	11.31 / 74	3.56	B / 8.4	-0.03	-0.01
UT	*First Trust Utilities AlphaDEX	FXU	A-	22.39	B- / 7.4	-6.88 / 34	10.36 / 76	9.18 / 61	4.53	B / 8.8	-0.04	-0.01
UT	*Utilities Select Sector SPDR	XLU	B+	43.28	B / 7.8	-4.40 / 41	10.92 / 78	10.86 / 71	8.23	B / 8.1	-0.02	-0.01
UT	*Vanguard Utilities Index ETF	VPU	B+	93.93	B / 7.7	-5.35 / 37	10.64 / 77	10.71 / 70	3.74	B- / 7.7	0.00	N/A
UT	*ProShares Ultra Utilities	UPW	B	92.00	A / 9.3	-13.27 / 20	19.65 / 95	19.01 / 97	2.39	C / 5.5	1.10	-0.04
UT	*PowerShares DWA Utilities Moment	PUI	B	22.41	B / 8.1	-2.76 / 47	11.05 / 79	10.34 / 67	4.80	B- / 7.1	0.72	-0.07
UT	*iShares US Utilities ETF	IDU	B	107.92	B / 8.0	-3.99 / 43	11.28 / 79	10.92 / 71	12.85	C+ / 6.8	0.05	N/A
UT	*iShares Global Utilities	JXI	B	44.02	C+ / 6.2	-5.78 / 36	6.33 / 65	4.10 / 44	6.03	B / 8.5	-0.47	-0.08
UT	Wells Fargo Utilities&High Inc	ERH	C+	11.20	C+ / 6.5	-7.57 / 32	6.97 / 67	6.88 / 54	8.04	B- / 7.5	-6.82	-7.15
UT	Cohen&Steers Infrastructure Fund	UTF	C+	19.08	C+ / 6.1	-9.74 / 26	7.18 / 67	11.19 / 73	8.39	B- / 7.0	-14.13	-14.42
UT	Reaves Utility Income Trust	UTG	C+	25.97	C+ / 5.8	-15.60 / 17	8.15 / 70	10.48 / 68	6.99	B- / 7.5	-7.94	-4.29
UT	*SPDR SP Intl Utils Sector ETF	IPU	C+	16.08	C / 4.9	-5.05 / 38	2.27 / 50	-0.57 / 26	5.39	B / 8.0	-0.86	-0.20
UT	DNP Select Income Fund Inc	DNP	C	8.96	C+ / 5.7	-6.23 / 35	5.46 / 63	7.31 / 55	8.71	C+ / 6.9	9.27	10.91
UT	Gabelli Utility Trust	GUT	C	5.70	C+ / 5.7	-14.15 / 19	5.84 / 64	7.80 / 57	10.53	C+ / 6.8	11.11	17.93
UT	*Fidelity MSCI Utilities Index ET	FUTY	C	27.89	C / 4.8	-4.13 / 42	--	--	7.26	C+ / 6.5	0.22	0.01
UT	*SPDR S&P Transportation ETF	XTN	C-	42.85	B+ / 8.3	-18.64 / 15	16.25 / 92	--	5.16	D- / 1.5	0.02	-0.03
UT	Gabelli Global Utility&Income Trus	GLU	C-	16.62	C- / 4.2	-8.17 / 31	1.22 / 43	4.59 / 46	7.22	C+ / 6.7	-15.07	-14.40
UT	*WisdomTree Global ex-US Utilitie	DBU	C-	15.25	D+ / 2.9	-12.32 / 21	-2.28 / 30	-0.63 / 26	2.66	B- / 7.8	-1.10	-0.20
UT	Duff & Phelps Global Utility Incom	DPG	D+	14.73	C- / 3.2	-25.14 / 10	1.08 / 42	--	9.50	C+ / 6.2	-14.61	-13.96
UT	*ProShares UltraShort Utilities	SDP	D-	47.72	E+ / 0.8	0.90 / 66	-24.56 / 6	-24.40 / 4	0.00	C / 4.4	-0.23	0.02

* Denotes ETF Fund, N/A denotes number is not available